境外资本市场重要法律文献译丛 ❷

美洲卷

美国证券交易委员会自身组织与通用规章

（中英文对照本）

Rules and Regulations for the Securities and Exchange Commission

（上 册）

中国证券监督管理委员会 组织编译

法律出版社
LAW PRESS · CHINA

《境外资本市场重要法律文献译丛》

编 委 会

《美国证券交易委员会自身组织与通用规章》

主　编：桂敏杰
副主编：黄红元　徐　明
编　委：卢文道　王升义　杨　懿　陈亦聪
谭　婧　武俊桥　张　媛　朱文超
王文心　徐　俊　陈建新

致　谢

上海证券交易所对本书的出版给予了大力支持！

译者说明

美国证券交易委员会(Securities and Exchange Commission, SEC)在该国金融监管体系中的重要性,无须赘述。《美国证券交易委员会规则与规章》(Rules and Regulations of the Securities and Exchange Commission,以下简称《SEC 规则与规章》)是 SEC 在证券领域基本法律基础上制定的一系列行政性规则,包含《美国证券交易委员会自身组织与通用规章》(以下简称《自身组织与通用规章》)、《有关 1933 年证券法的规章》、《有关 1934 年证券交易法的规章》、《有关 1939 年信托契约法的规章》、《有关 1940 年投资公司法的规章》、《有关 1940 年投资顾问法的规章》和《证券投资者保护公司规章》。

上述 7 项规章经公报后,被统一编入《美国联邦规章汇编》(Code of Federal Regulations, CFR)第十七编"商品和证券交易"下的第二章"证券交易委员会"。该章下又根据不同主题细分为部分(Parts)、子部分(Subparts)和节(Sections)。《SEC 规则与规章》是对证券基本法律的细化和完善,以落实法律基本原则和实现国会立法目的,是美国金融市场法律体系中非常重要的组成部分。

此次,我们选取《SEC 规则与规章》中的《自身组织与通用规章》进行翻译,英文文本摘自《联邦规章汇编》网上数据库,更新至 2011 年 2 月 7 日。顾名思义,《自身组织与通用规章》是关于 SEC 组织结构、行政程序方面的规则,包含了 CFR 第十七编第二章下第 200~205 部分、第 209~211 部分、第 228~229 部分等共 11 个。对其各主要内容简介如下:

(一)第 200 部分下有 A~N 等 14 个子部分,主要规定了 SEC 的组织架构、职能职责、运行计划,相关人员的行为准则和职业道德规范,SEC 对相关信息的采集、公开和保密职责,以及其他 SEC 的业务处理规则。此部分通过一般规定,为 SEC 搭建了基本组织框架、规范了组织人员的行为。

(二)第 201 部分下的 6 个子部分进一步对 SEC 的业务规则作出了详尽规定,包括一般规定、程序启动、听证与预听证、申诉与复议、临时命令与中止、没收与罚款处罚、行政裁决及其他非正式程序。另外,该部分还摘录有《司法公平法》中有关 SEC 行使司法权的相关规则。

(三)第 202 部分主要针对非正式程序和其他程序进行了分类规定,包括提交文件的相关程序、听证准备工作、执法行动、制定普适性规则程序,对小型企业合规指引和处罚政策，SEC对特殊主体的政策声明，SEC对公众公司会计监督委员会报告、预算及相关规则的监督程序等。

（四）第203部分专门对SEC调查中涉及的信息获取、处罚、正式调查、证人等进行了规定。

（五）SEC的债务催收程序规定在第204部分，其方式包括行政抵消、工资抵消、退税抵消、扣发工资等，该部分还规定了SEC其他催收服务和信贷局报告的内容。

（六）第205部分对代表发行人参与SEC程序并办理业务的律师，规定了一系列职业行为标准，同时明确了SEC对律师进行监督的职责和处罚规则。

（七）SEC就其《工作规则》规定的表格还制定了专门规则，即第209部分。该部分对表格的提供、信息披露等要求进行了详细说明。

（八）在第210部分，即《S-X管理办法》中，SEC就财务报表的格式和内容进行了规定，包括：会计师资格和报告、一般说明、合并和汇总财务报表、普适性规则、中期报表、备考信息、附表格式内容，并对一些特定主体的表格提出了特殊要求。

（九）第211部分就财务报告公告、公报、会计审计公告要求等进行了解释说明。

（十）本次翻译的最后一个文件，即《S-K管理办法》，是第229部分（第228部分为预留部分）。该部分对《1933年证券法》、《1934年证券交易法》和《1975年能源政策与保护法》中有关规定所要求提交的各类表格进行了具体说明。其内容涵盖业务、注册人证券、财务信息、管理层及特定证券持有人、注册说明书和招募说明书、附录、行业指引清单、并购重组交易（《M-A管理办法》）、资产支持证券（《AB管理办法》）以及从事特定活动注册人的披露事项等。

此外，为了规范明晰译文中的专业术语，译者还制作了统一的术语对照表。

SEC作为美国证券市场上的主要监管者，其设立的宗旨在于保护投资者利益，维护公平、有序、高效的市场，以及促进资本的形成。《自身组织与通用规章》的颁布实施正是从制度和组织运行上保障了上述目标的实现。对其进行全面翻译，一方面旨在将美国SEC的组织运行规则介绍给国内金融领域从业人员以及对该等问题感兴趣的人士；另一方面也是为我国证券市场的监管者提供有益借鉴，促进其更好地依法行政、维护证券市场秩序、保障证券市场有效运行、保护投资者利益。

北京大学法学院　郭　雳

总译校：

吴志攀，北京大学教授、博士研究生导师，中国法学会副会长，中国金融学会副会长、中国经济法学研究会会长，北京大学党委常委、常务副校长、法律总顾问，兼任北京大学亚太研究院院长、北京大学金融法研究中心主任，最高人民法院专家咨询员。北京大学法学博士，美国哈佛大学法学院访问学者，美国艾森豪威尔基金会学者。出版有《金融法概论》、《国际金融法》、《金融全球化与中国金融法》、《金融法的"四色定理"》、《美国金融机构监管》等十余部专著、译著和教材。

审校人员：

郭雳，北京大学法学院院聘教授、博士研究生导师，康奈尔大学客座教授，德国洪堡基金会学者，法学博士、经济学博士后，毕业于北京大学和哈佛大学，具有中国、美国纽约州执业律师资格。出版并发表《中国银行业创新与发展的法律思考》、《美国证券私募发行法律问题研究》、*Mergers and Acquisitions and Takeovers in China* 等中外文专著及论文若干，主编 *Peking University Journal of Legal Studies*。

刘庄，北京大学国际金融法博士研究生，美国芝加哥大学法学院硕士研究生，北京大学法学院学士、硕士。

翻译人员：

瞿乃明，法国巴黎高等翻译学校翻译学硕士、法国巴黎第九大学国际企业管理硕士、台湾大学经济学学士，北京优笔客翻译中心总经理。主要翻译作品有《欧盟金融工具市场指令》、《中国证监会2011年年报》、《美国商品交易法》、《欧盟金融监管改革法规汇编》和《多德—弗兰克华尔街改革与消费者保护法》等。

艾飞，北京大学法学院法学学士，2007年通过中国司法考试，北京优笔客翻译中心质量经理。主要翻译作品有《美国商品交易法》、《欧盟证券监管法规汇编》和《多德—弗兰克华尔街改革与消费者保护法》等。

王俊苏，复旦大学国际经济法学士、美国路易斯安那州立大学法学硕士，现任通用电气（中国）医疗集团高级法律顾问。

钱淳，北京语言大学文学学士，北京优笔客翻译中心专职译者。主要翻译作品有《多德—弗兰克华尔街改革与消费者保护法》等。

程宇凡，首都经贸大学法律学士，现任某美国律师事务所专职法律翻译。主要翻译作品有《欧盟金融监管改革法规汇编》、《欧盟另类投资基金管理人指令》和《多德—弗兰克华尔街改革与消费者保护法》等。

总　序

中国资本市场是适应我国经济体制改革和对外开放的形势要求逐步建立发展起来的。为了有效借鉴境外成熟市场的制度经验，中国资本市场从成立伊始，就特别注重按照“立足国情，为我所用”的原则，不断学习、消化和吸收境外成熟市场的运行规则和监管制度。目前，中国资本市场现行有效的法律、法规、规章、规范性文件共521件，加上大量的交易所和协会的自律规则，基本形成了我国资本市场的法律制度规范体系。这些制度规范构建起一整套与国际通行原则基本相符的法律框架、交易规则和监管体系，有效维护了市场秩序，保证了市场功能和作用的发挥，保护了投资者的合法权益。

经过20余年的改革发展，我国资本市场进入了创新发展的新阶段。立足于服务实体经济发展的大局需要，重点解决资本市场自身结构不平衡、服务实体经济能力不足、为居民提供投资理财产品相对匮乏等突出现实问题，资本市场现有的以股票公开发行并在交易所上市交易为主的境内市场体系，将逐步发展成为一个公募与私募并重、股票与债券平衡、场内与场外协调发展的资本市场体系。与此相适应，需要进一步发展壮大财富管理行业，立足于功能监管的制度定位，统一资产管理行为规则，放松行政管制，增强创新活力。实现这样的改革目标，需要我们更加重视学习境外成熟市场的制度经验，充分借鉴境外市场有关私募发行、债权融资、资产管理、期货及衍生品等方面的法律制度，在尊重市场规律的前提下，大胆进行制度和机制创新，确保我们的各项制度适应和满足市场改革的实际需要。

坚持对外开放是中国资本市场改革和发展的一贯方针。在经济全球化深入发展的时代背景下，适应我国经济结构调整和经济方式转变和“逐步实现人民币资本项目可兑换”的金融对外开放的总体要求，中国资本市场必须以更加积极的态度参与全球经济竞争，提高在全球范围内配置资源，服务实体经济发展的能力。不论是支持境内企业到境外发行融资，鼓励境内机构和个人到境外进行证券投资，还是畅通境外企业到境内发行融资渠道，平等保护境外机构和个人到境内进行证券投资，都需要在立足国情的前提下，实现制度衔接互通，消除制度壁垒。特别重要的是，市场竞争首先是制度规则的竞争，增强我国资本市场的国际竞争力，一方面要确保我国市场通过制度规则体现法治环境吸引力，另一方面还要增强我国在涉及资本市场对外开放的国际规则的制定中的话语权,增强我国在国际监管合作和跨境执法合作中的主动权。

同时,我们也注意到,2008 年国际金融危机发生后,境外资本市场对监管体制、机制做了较为重大的调整,提出了不少新的监管要求,出台了不少新的法律文件。例如,美国制定了具有金融综合监管性质的《多德—弗兰克法案》,英国则将原来集证券、银行、保险于一身的《2000 年金融服务与市场法》修改成《金融服务法》。对于境外相关法律制度的动态发展,需要及时掌握情况,借鉴有益经验,为进一步完善我国资本市场的基础性制度建设提供参考。

经过长期的努力,中国资本市场的制度借鉴和引进已经越过了概念化、碎片状的发展阶段,进入全面、系统、精细化的更高阶段。由于种种原因,对境外资本市场法律制度的介绍,无论是在法学界、法律界,还是在证券期货行业内,一直以来都存在及时性不够、系统性不足、权威性不强的情况。特别是翻译介绍的质量不高、精品不多,这在客观上影响了对境外经验的学习和借鉴。

为了适应资本市场学习借鉴境外制度经验的形势要求,中国证监会精选了境外资本市场国家和地区的重要法律文献,包括境外主要资本市场的重要法律、监管部门的监管规则、经典的司法判例、最新的资本市场立法成果以及相关法学理论权威著作等,组织翻译出版了这套《境外资本市场重要法律文献译丛》。译丛的翻译出版工作,在系统单位、部门和关心市场发展的专家学者的共同努力下,紧紧抓住保质量、出精品的关键环节,建立了“竞标择优确定翻译人员、知名专家评审保证翻译质量、适当报酬和学术声誉结合激励”的工作机制,落实“精选译题、精细翻译、精心审校、精致出版”的工作要求,是中国证监会打造国人了解国际资本市场法律制度权威平台的有益尝试。为此,愿以本文向参与丛书翻译、审校的国际金融、法律方面的专家和学者表示感谢,并与大家共勉,共同为建设起一个权利公平、机会公平、规则公平的资本市场而努力。

中国证监会

2013 年 2 月

序

法律只要是修改，就注定是渐进式的。中国的法律如此，美国也不例外。2008年金融危机后，美国的金融体系并没有质变性质的改革，但修改使法律变得更加精细和跟进现实。在美国以外的观察，也许不容易看到这一点，但进入美国市场，就可以明显察觉到了。奥巴马任内4年，美国虽然多发了美元，政府负债的数字增加了，公立大学的预算逐渐减少，学费慢慢增高，但美国国内市场物价基本没太上涨，相比中国的市场物价，许多商品甚至还要便宜。这似乎可以部分证明，法律修改已经取得了初步效果。

面对科技时代的金融危机，美国原有的法律一定是不足以应对的。不适应和反应迟缓，在高速传递信息的网络面前，几乎是必然的。这也是因为美国的金融法律体系庞大、金融全球化程度高。想要通过快速改革来解决如此前所未有的问题，确实有些艰难。同时，在美国金融监管背后的各种政治利益集团运行复杂，安全与预算、成本与就业、科技与政治，本国与世界等多重因素交织在一起相互作用，多元选择。当然，美国立法者所采取的行动，温和改良的制度改进，可以给中国的法律研究留出很丰富的思考空间。

我和同事们花费大量时间，校对了全部中文译稿。需要指出的是，翻译消除了语言上的障碍，却不能消除语言背后的制度差异，更没有消除支撑制度差异的经济、社会和文化条件的区别。比如，美国的这些金融立法卷帙浩繁，动辄上百页千页，已是家常便饭。这与我国简短精要的立法风格差异很大。更重要的是，这些浩瀚的立法仍并非美国金融法律的全部。作为普通法系国家，美国的金融法律还有一多半存在于法院的判决意见中。又如，美国常将在我们看来内容不同、目标各异的法条打包放到一个文件中，与受学者们推崇的层级分明、效力有序的立法模式迥异。再如，投资者保护是美国金融法律的首要目标，保障金融的效率、安全和秩序，是它的固有价值，而我们在金融监管的评价标准问题上，还有着自己的特色——比如，要发展“让人民满意”的金融行业，等等。这些差异，只是法律理念上的不同，还是根植于环境的差别？哪种法律制度选择将更有效？还是由于对历史和路径的依赖，人们并不能完全自由选择，而只能逐步改造呢？我想，这些差异和问题，都需要留待金融法律的研究者耐心地发掘和解释了。

翻阅此书的读者们，多数是我的同行，我们都关注中国的金融市场以及在背后提供有力支持的法律监管体系的发展。国内的金融家们不断进行产品创新,金融市场规模不断扩大,与此同时也带来了立法、监管、投资者和消费者保护等诸多方面的问题。对此,参考外国的法律,完善本国的法律,更需要我们自己不断努力实践和探索。

吴志攀

2013年1月

CONTENTS

目　　录

《联邦规章汇编》第十七编：商品和证券交易

CFR Title 17: Commodity and Securities Exchanges Part 200 Through Part 209

《联邦规章汇编》第十七编：商品和证券交易 第 200~209 部分

PART 200—ORGANIZATION; CONDUCT AND ETHICS; AND INFORMATION AND REQUESTS

Editorial Note: At 75 FR 47449, Aug. 6, 2010, the general authority citation for part 200 was revised; however, the amendment could not be incorporated due to inaccurate amendatory instruction.

Subpart A—Organization and Program Management

Authority: 15 U.S.C. 77o, 77s, 77sss, 78d, 78d–1, 78d–2, 78w, 78 *ll*(d), 78mm, 80a–37, 80b–11, and 7202, unless otherwise noted.

Sections 200.27 and 200.30–6 are also issued under 15 U.S.C. 77e, 77f, 77g, 77h, 77j, 77q, 77u, 78e, 78g, 78h, 78i, 78k, 78m, 78o, 78o–4, 78q, 78q–1, 78t–1, 78u, 77hhh, 77uuu, 80a–41, 80b–5, and 80b–9.

Section 200.30–1 is also issued under 15 U.S.C. 77f, 77g, 77h, 77j, 78c(b),78*l*, 78m, 78n, 78*o*(d).

Section 200.30–3 is also issued under 15 U.S.C. 78b, 78d, 78f, 78k–1, 78q, 78s, and 78eee.

Section 200.30–5 is also issued under 15 U.S.C. 77f, 77g, 77h, 77j, 78c(b), 78*l*, 78m, 78n, 78o(d), 80a–8, 80a–20, 80a–24, 80a–29, 80b–3, 80b–4.

Source: 27 FR 12712, Dec. 22, 1962, unless otherwise noted.

§200.1 General statement and statutory authority.

The Securities and Exchange Commission was created in 1934 under the Securities

第200部分——组织;行为准则和职业道德规范;信息及请求

编辑注:《联邦公报》第75卷第47449页(2010年8月6日)对第200部分的法律依据索引进行了修正;但是,因修正指令并不准确,无法将修正纳入此处。

第A子部分——组织和项目管理

法律依据:《美国法典》第十五编第77o节、第77s节、第77sss节、第78d节、第78d-1节、第78d-2节、第78w节、第78*ll*(d)节、第78mm节、第80a-37节、第80b-11节和第7202节,除非另有说明。

第200.27节和第200.30-6节同时见《美国法典》第十五编第77e节、第77f节、第77g节、第77h节、第77j节、第77q节、第77u节、第78e节、第78g节、第78h节、第78i节、第78k节、第78m节、第78o节、第78o-4节、第78q节、第78q-1节、第78t-1节、第78u节、第77hhh节、第77uuu节、第80a-41节、第80b-5节和第80b-9节。

第200.30-1节同时见《美国法典》第十五编第77f节、第77g节、第77h节、第77j节、第78c(b)节、第78*l*节、第78m节、第78n节、第78o(d)节。

第200.30-3节同时见《美国法典》第十五编第78b节、第78d节、第78f节、第78k-1节、第78q节、第78s节和第78eee节。

第200.30-5节同时见《美国法典》第十五编第77f节、第77g节、第77h节、第77j节、第78c(b)节、第78*l*节、第78m节、第78n节、第78o(d)节、第80a-8节、第80a-20节、第80a-24节、第80a-29节、第80b-3节、第80b-4节。

行政规则来源:《联邦公报》第27卷第12712页,1962年12月22日,除非另有说明。

第200.1节　综述及法定授权

证券交易委员会于1934年根据《证券交易法》成立,替代联邦贸易委员会负责实

Exchange Act. That Act transferred to the Commission the administration of the Securities Act of 1933, formerly administered by the Federal Trade Commission. Subsequent laws assigned to the Securities and Exchange Commission for administration are: Public Utility Holding Company Act of 1935, Trust Indenture Act of 1939, Investment Company Act of 1940, and Investment Advisers Act of 1940. In addition, under the Bankruptcy Code, the Commission is a statutory party in cases arising under chapters 9 and 11. Considered together, the laws administered by the Commission provided for the following.

(a) Public disclosure of pertinent facts concerning public offerings of securities and securities listed on national securities exchanges and certain securities traded in the over-the-counter markets.

(b) Enforcement of disclosure requirements in the soliciting of proxies for meetings of security holders by companies whose securities are registered pursuant to section 12 of the Securities Exchange Act of 1934, public utility holding companies, and their subsidiaries and investment companies.

(c) Regulation of the trading in securities on national securities exchanges and in the over-the-counter markets.

(d) Investigation of securities frauds, manipulations, and other violations, and the imposition and enforcement of legal sanctions therefor.

(e) Registration, and the regulation of certain activities, of brokers, dealers and investment advisers.

(f) Supervision of the activities of mutual funds and other investment companies.

(g) Administration of statutory standards governing protective and other provisions of trust indentures under which debt securities are sold to the public.

(h) Regulation of the purchase and sale of securities, utility properties, and other assets by registered public utility holding companies and their electric and gas utility subsidiaries; enforcement of statutory standards for public utility holding company system simplification and integration; and approval of their reorganization, mergers and consolidations.

(i) Protection of the interests of public investors involved in bankruptcy reorganization cases and in bankruptcy cases involving the adjustment of debts of a municipality.

(j) Administrative sanctions, injunctive remedies, civil money penalties and criminal prosecution. There are also private rights of action for investors injured by violations of the Acts.

(15 U.S.C. 78d-1, 78d-2; 11 U.S.C. 901, 1109(a))

[27 FR 12712, Dec. 22, 1962, as amended at 43 FR 13375, Mar. 30, 1978; 49 FR 12684, Mar. 30, 1984; 60 FR 14623, Mar. 20, 1995; 60 FR 32794, June 23, 1995]

施《1933年证券法》。之后陆续交由证券交易委员会负责实施的法律如下：《1935年公用事业控股公司法》、《1939年信托契约法》、《1940年投资公司法》及《1940年投资顾问法》。此外，根据《破产法典》，证券交易委员会属于第9章和第11章下案件的法定当事人。综合而言，证券交易委员会负责实施的法律涉及如下领域：

(a)与证券公开发行、在全国性证券交易所上市的证券以及在场外市场交易的某些证券相关之事实的公开披露；

(b)对于按《1934年证券交易法》第12条注册证券的公司、公用事业控股公司及其子公司和投资公司为举行证券持有人会议所进行的代理权征集，强制执行相关披露要求；

(c)全国性证券交易所及场外市场的证券交易监管；

(d)调查证券欺诈、操纵及其他违法违规行为，并处以和执行法律制裁；

(e)对经纪商、自营商和投资顾问进行注册并对其特定活动进行监管；

(f)监督共同基金及其他投资公司的活动；

(g)针对向公众出售债务证券的信托契约的保护性条款和其他条款，实施相关法定标准；

(h)监管注册公用事业控股公司及其电力和燃气子公司购买和出售证券、公用事业财产及其他资产的行为；就公用事业控股公司系统精简和整合执行法定标准；批准公用事业控股公司的重组、吸收合并与新设合并；

(i)在涉及市政债券调整的破产重组案件、破产案件中保护公共投资者的权益；

(j)行政制裁、禁令救济、民事罚金和刑事追诉。因他人违反上述法律的行为而受损的投资者还有权行使私人诉讼权利。

[《美国法典》第十五编第78d–1节、第78d–2节；《美国法典》第十一编第901节、第1109(a)节。]

[《联邦公报》第27卷第12712页，1962年12月22日，修正索引：《联邦公报》第43卷第13375页，1978年3月30日；《联邦公报》第49卷第12684页，1984年3月30日；《联邦公报》第60

§200.2 Statutory functions.

Following are brief descriptions of the Commission's functions under each of the statutes it administers:

(a) *Securities Act of 1933.* (1) Issuers of securities making public offerings for sale in interstate commerce or through the mails, directly or by others on their behalf, are required to file with the Commission registration statements containing financial and other pertinent data about the issuer and the offering. A similar requirement is provided with respect to such public offerings on behalf of a controlling person of the issuer. Unless a registration statement is in effect with respect to such securities, it is unlawful to sell the securities in interstate commerce or through the mails. (There are certain limited exemptions, such as government securities, non-public offerings, and intrastate offerings.) The effectiveness of a registration statement may be refused or suspended after a hearing if the statement contains material misstatements or omissions, thus barring sale of the securities until it is appropriately amended. Registration is not a finding by the Commission as to the accuracy of the facts disclosed; and it is unlawful so to represent. Moreover, registration of securities does not imply approval of the issue by the Commission or insure investors against loss in their purchase, but serves rather to provide information upon which investors may make an informed and realistic evaluation of the worth of the securities.

(2) Persons responsible for filing false information with the Commission subject themselves to the risk of fine or imprisonment or both; and the issuing company, its directors, officers, and the underwriters and dealers and others may be liable in damages to purchasers of registered securities if the disclosures in the registration statements and prospectus are materially defective. Also the statute contains antifraud provisions which apply generally to the sale of securities, whether or not registered.

(b) *Securities Exchange Act of 1934.* This Act requires the filing of registration applications and annual and other reports with national securities exchanges and the Commission, by companies whose securities are listed on the exchanges. Annual and other reports must be filed also by certain companies whose securities are traded on the over-the-counter markets. These must contain financial and other data prescribed by the Commission for the information of investors. Material misstatements or omissions are grounds for suspension or withdrawal of the security from exchange trading. This Act makes unlawful any solicitation of proxies, authorizations, or consents in contravention of Commission rules. These rules require disclosure of information about the subject of the solicitation to security holders. The Act requires disclosure of the holdings and the transactions by an officer, director, or beneficial owner of over 10 percent of any class of

卷第14623页,1995年3月20日;《联邦公报》第60卷第32794页,1995年6月23日。]

第200.2节　法定职能

证券交易委员会在其负责实施的各项法律下所行使的职能简述如下:

(a)《1933年证券法》。(1)证券发行人直接或通过代表间接地在跨州商业中或通过邮件公开发行出售证券的,有义务向证券交易委员会提交注册说明书,载明与发行人及发行相关的财务数据和其他有关数据。发行人的控制人通过代表公开发行证券的,也适用类似要求。除非相关证券的注册说明书已生效,否则在跨州商业中出售证券或通过邮件出售证券属于非法行为(不过,存在有限的豁免情形,如政府证券、非公开发行和州内发行)。如注册说明书存在重大不实陈述或疏漏,则证券交易委员会经听证后可拒绝注册说明书生效或暂停注册说明书的效力,进而禁止相关证券的销售,直至该注册说明书得以适当的修正。证券交易委员会对证券予以注册并不代表其认定所披露事实的准确性,如发行人对外声明证券交易委员会认定了所披露事实的准确性,该等声明将构成非法行为。此外,对证券的注册并不代表证券交易委员会批准证券的发行,亦不保证投资者购买证券不会产生损失,其作用在于提供信息,帮助投资者据此对证券价值作出知情而切合实际的评估。

(2)向证券交易委员会提交虚假信息的,相关责任人可被单处或并处罚金或监禁;且若注册说明书和招募说明书中的披露存在重大缺陷,发行公司及其董事、管理人员、承销商、自营商及其他人员可能有责任向注册证券购买人承担赔偿金义务。同时,《1933年证券法》还含有普遍适用于证券(包括注册证券和非注册证券)销售的反欺诈条款。

(b)《1934年证券交易法》。该法要求在全国性证券交易所上市的公司向该全国性证券交易所及证券交易委员会提交注册申请、年度报告和其他报告。证券在场外市场交易的某些公司也必须提交年度报告和其他报告。上述报告必须含有证券交易委员会规定的财务数据和其他数据,以为投资者提供相关信息。如果存在重大不实陈述或疏漏,证券可能停牌或退市。根据《1934年证券交易法》,所有违反证券交易委员会规则做出的代理权征集、授权或同意均属非法。证券交易委员会的规则要求,在向证券持有人进行代理权征集时应向其披露与代理权征集所涉主题相关之信息。《1934年证券交易法》要求,特定公司的管理人员、董事或持有任何类别股权证券10%以上份额的实益所有人,其持股和交易情况应予披露;同时还要求,持有注册公司任何类别股权证券5%以上份额的实益所有人,其身份应予披露。对于第三方或发行人提出的收购要约,该法为证券持有人提供了实体性和程序性保护。该法还规定,全国性证券交易所、

equity security of certain companies. It also requires disclosure of the beneficial owners of more than five percent of any class of equity securities of a registered company. It provides substantive and procedural protection to security holders in third-party and issuer tender offers. The Act also provides for the registration with, and regulation by, the Commission of national securities exchanges, brokers or dealers engaged in an over-the-counter securities business, and national associations of such brokers or dealers. It gives the Commission rulemaking power with respect to short sales, stabilizing, floor trading a ctivities of specialists and odd-lot dealers, and such matters as excessive trading by exchange members. The Act authorizes the Board of Governors of the Federal Reserve System to prescribe minimum margin requirements for listed securities.

(c) *Public Utility Holding Company Act of 1935.* This Act authorizes the Commission to regulate gas and electric public-utility holding companies under standards prescribed for the protection of the public interest and the interest of investors and consumers. The Act generally limits a public-utility holding company to a single integrated public-utility system, and requires simple corporate and capital structures. If not exempt, a public-utility holding company must register with the Commission. Generally, a registered holding company must obtain Commission approval before it can issue and sell securities, acquire utility securities or assets or any other interest in any business, or enter into transactions with its affiliates. It must also comply with extensive reporting and record-keeping requirements. Although largely free of these requirements, an exempt holding company remains subject to the geographic limitations of the Act. The Act permits the acquisition of interests in "exempt wholesale generators" and "foreign utility companies" unrelated to a system's utility operations.

(d) *Trust Indenture Act of 1939.* This Act safeguards the interests of purchasers of publicly-offered debt securities issued under trust indentures by requiring the inclusion of certain protective provisions in, and the exclusion of certain types of exculpatory clauses from, trust indentures. The Act also requires that an independent indenture trustee represent the debtors by proscribing certain relationships that could conflict with proper exercise of duties.

(e) *Investment Company Act of 1940.* This Act establishes a comprehensive regulatory framework for investment companies and subjects their activities to regulation under standards prescribed for the protection of investors. Among other things, the Act provides for the registration of investment companies with the Commission; requires them to disclose their financial condition and investment policies to their shareholders; prohibits them from substantially changing investment policies without shareholder approval; bars persons guilty of securities fraud from serving as officers or directors; prevents underwriters, investment bankers, or brokers from constituting more than a minority of the

从事证券场外交易业务的经纪商或自营商以及全国性经纪商或自营商协会,应向证券交易委员会注册并接受证券交易委员会的监管。该法亦授权证券交易委员会针对做市商和零股自营商的卖空活动、稳定活动、场内交易活动以及交易所会员过度交易等问题制定规则,授权联邦储备系统内的联邦储蓄委员会对上市证券的最低保证金作出规定。

(c)《1935年公用事业控股公司法》。该法授权证券交易委员会按照保护公共利益和投资者及消费者利益的标准对天然气和电力公用事业控股公司进行监管。一般情况下,该法规定,公用事业控股公司必须是一个单一、整合的公用事业系统,并要求其采用简单的公司和资本结构。除非取得豁免,否则公用事业控股公司必须在证券交易委员会注册。一般而言,注册公用事业控股公司在发行和出售证券,收购任何企业的公用事业证券、资产或任何其他权益之前,或与其关联方开展交易之前,必须获得证券交易委员会批准。注册公用事业控股公司还必须遵守广泛的报告和记录留存义务。获得豁免的控股公司虽然很大程度不必遵守上述要求,但仍然需要遵守《1935年公用事业控股公司》规定的地域限制。该法允许收购与某系统的公用事业运营无关联的"豁免批发发电商"和"外国公用事业公司"的权益。

(d)《1939年信托契约法》。对于在信托契约下公开发行的债权证券,该法要求信托契约中必须纳入特定保护条款,同时必须排除特定类型的豁免条款,以保护购买人的利益。该法要求代表债权人的契约信托人必须保持独立,因而对可能导致与适当履行职责相冲突的几类关系作出了禁止性规定。

(e)《1940年投资公司法》。该法设立了一个全面的投资公司监管框架,规定投资公司的活动必须遵守为保护投资者而设定的标准。该法还规定了如下等事项:投资公司须在证券交易委员会注册;投资公司必须向股东披露其财务状况和投资政策;禁止投资公司未经股东批准实质性地变更投资政策;禁止犯有证券欺诈罪的人士担任投资公司管理人员或董事;禁止承销商、投资银行或经纪商担任投资公司董事职位超过半数席数;管理层合同必须呈报股东批准;禁止投资公司未经证券交易委员会批准与其董事、管理人员或关联公司、关联人员交易;禁止投资公司发行优先证券,但在特定条款和条件下发行的除外。《1940年投资公司法》还对顾问费、证券出售/回购、换股收购

directors of an investment company; requires that management contracts be submitted to shareholders for their approval; prohibits transactions between investment companies and their directors, officers, or affiliated companies or persons, except when approved by the Commission; and prohibits investment companies from issuing senior securities except under specified terms and conditions. The Act also regulates advisory fees, sales and repurchases of securities, exchange offers, and other activities of investment companies. The Act authorizes the Commission to exempt any person or class of persons or securities from any provisions of, or rules under, the Act and to conduct any investigation it deems necessary to determine existing or potential violations of the Act. It also authorizes the Commission to prepare reports to security holders on the fairness of plans of reorganization, merger, or consolidation. The Commission may institute a court action to enjoin acts or practices of management involving, among other things, a breach of fiduciary duty and the consummation of plans of reorganization, merger, or consolidation that are grossly unfair to security holders.

(f) *Investment Advisers Act of 1940.* Persons who, for compensation, engage in the business of advising others with respect to their security transactions must register with the Commission. Their activities in the conduct of such business are subject to standards of the act which make unlawful those practices which constitute fraud or deceit and which require, among other things, disclosure of any interests they may have in transactions executed for clients. The Act grants to the Commission rule-making power with respect to fraudulent and other activities of investment advisers.

(g) *Chapter 11 of the Bankruptcy Code.* Chapter 11 of the Bankruptcy Code (11 U.S.C. 1101 *et seq.*) provides for Commission participation as a statutory party in reorganization cases. Under section 1109(a) of the Bankruptcy Code (11 U.S.C. 1109(a)), which also applies to Chapter 9 cases regarding municipalities, the Commission "may raise and may appear and be heard on any issue in the case."

(11 U.S.C. 901, 1109(a))

[27 FR 12712, Dec. 22, 1962, as amended at 49 FR 12684, Mar. 30, 1984; 60 FR 14624, Mar. 20, 1995]

General Organization

§200.10 The Commission.

The Commission is composed of five members, not more than three of whom may be members of the same political party. The members are appointed by the President, with the advice and consent of the Senate, for 5-year terms, one term ending each year. The Chairman is designated by the President pursuant to the provisions of section 3 of Reorganization Plan No. 10 of 1950(3 CFR, 1949-1953 Comp., p.1006). The Commission

要约和投资公司的其他活动进行了规制,授权证券交易委员会将任何主体或任何类型的主体或任何类别的证券豁免于该法任何条款或规定的适用,并授权证券交易委员会开展其认为必要的任何调查,以判定是否存在实际或潜在的违反该法的情形。《1940年投资公司法》授权证券交易委员会就重组、吸收合并或新设合并计划的公平性向证券持有人编制报告。证券交易委员会可以向法院提起诉讼,以禁止管理层从事涉及违反信托义务的行为或操作,或禁止管理层完成对证券持有人严重不公的重组、吸收合并或新设合并计划。

(f)《1940年投资顾问法》。向他人提供与证券交易相关的有偿建议的人士必须向证券交易委员会注册。投资顾问的顾问行为必须遵守《1940年投资顾问法》设定的标准。根据该法,构成欺诈、欺骗的做法均属非法,且投资顾问必须披露其在为客户开展的交易中具有的任何利益关联。该法授予证券交易委员会就投资顾问的欺诈性行为和其他行为制定规则的权力。

(g)《破产法典》第十一章。《破产法典》第十一章(《美国法典》第十一编第1101节及其后条文)规定,证券交易委员会应作为法定当事人参与重组案件。根据《破产法典》第1109(a)节[《美国法典》第十一编第1109(a)节],证券交易委员会"可以在案件中提出任何问题、就任何问题在法院出庭并获听审"。该条规定同样适用于第九章规定的与市政相关的案件。

[《美国法典》第十一编第901节、第1109(a)节。]

[《联邦公报》第27卷第12712页,1962年12月22日,修正索引:《联邦公报》第49卷第12684页,1984年3月30日;《联邦公报》第60卷第14624页,1995年3月20日。]

总体组织架构

第200.10节　证券交易委员会

证券交易委员会由5名委员组成,来自同一政党的委员不得超过3名。委员由总统任命,由参议院提出建议并批准。委员任期为5年,每年均有一名委员任期届满。证券交易委员会主席由总统根据《1950年第10号重组计划》第3条规定(《联邦规章汇编》第三编,1949~1953年版,第1006页)任命。证券交易委员会由员工协助工作,包括律师、会计师、工程师、金融证券分析师、调查人员、核查人员以及行政和文职职员。

is assisted by a staff, which includes lawyers, accountants, engineers, financial security analysts, investigators and examiners, as well as administrative and clerical employees.

§200.11 Headquarters Office—Regional Office Relationships.

(a)(1) Division and Office Heads in the Headquarters Office (100 F Street, NE., Washington, D.C. 20549) have Commission-wide responsibility to the Commission for the overall development, policy and technical guidance, and policy direction of the operating programs under their jurisdiction.

(2) Each Regional Director is responsible for the direction and supervision of his or her work force and for the execution of all programs in his or her office's region as shown in paragraph (b) of this section, in accordance with established policy, and reports, on enforcement matters, to the Deputy Director of the Division of Enforcement who is responsible for Regional Office enforcement matters and, on examination matters, to the Director of the Office of Compliance Inspections and Examinations. The Director of Regional Office Operations interacts with the Regional Directors and their staff on operational and administrative/management issues and serves as their representative in the Commission's Washington Headquarters in those areas.

(b) Regional Directors of the Commission.

Atlanta Regional Office: Alabama, Georgia, North Carolina, South Carolina, and Tennessee—Regional Director, 3475 Lenox Road, NE., Suite 1000, Atlanta, GA 30326-1232.

Boston Regional Office: Connecticut, Maine, Massachusetts, New Hampshire, Rhode Island, and Vermont—Regional Director, 33 Arch Street, 23rd Floor, Boston, MA 02110-1424.

Chicago Regional Office: Kentucky, Illinois, Indiana, Iowa, Michigan, Minnesota, Missouri, Ohio, and Wisconsin—Regional Director, 175 West Jackson Boulevard, Suite 900, Chicago, IL 60604-2908.

Denver Regional Office: Colorado, Kansas, Nebraska, New Mexico, North Dakota, South Dakota, and Wyoming—Regional Director, 1801 California Street, Suite 1500, Denver, CO 80202-2656.

Fort Worth Regional Office: Arkansas, Kansas (for certain purposes), Oklahoma, and Texas—Regional Director, Burnett Plaza, Suite 1900, 801 Cherry Street, Unit #18, Fort Worth, TX 76102-6882.

Los Angeles Regional Office: Arizona, Southern California (zip codes 93599 and below, except 93200-93299), Guam, Hawaii, and Nevada—Regional Director, 5670 Wilshire Boulevard, 11th Floor, Los Angeles, CA 90036-3648.

Miami Regional Office: Florida, Louisiana, Mississippi, Puerto Rico, and the Virgin

第200.11节 总部和地区办公室的关系

(a)(1)证券交易委员会总部（地址：华盛顿哥伦比亚特区东北分区100F大街，邮编：D.C.20549）各部门主任和办公室主任在其各自的管辖权范围内，就其负责的运营项目的总体发展、政策和技术指引及政策方向对证券交易委员会负责。

(2)各地区办公室主任负责按既定政策来指导、监督下属员工，执行本节第(b)款规定的其所辖地区内的所有项目，同时就执法工作向负责管理地区办公室执法工作的执法部副主任汇报工作，就核查事项向合规检查和核查办公室主任汇报工作。地区办公室运营部主任就运营和行政/管理问题与各地区办公室主任及其员工协调，并在上述事项中作为各地区办公室在证券交易委员会华盛顿哥伦比亚特区总部的代表。

(b)证券交易委员会的地区办公室主任。

亚特兰大地区办公室：阿拉巴马州、乔治亚州、北卡罗来纳州、南卡罗来纳州和田纳西州——地区办公室主任，乔治亚州亚特兰大市东北分区Lenox路3475号1000室，邮编：GA 30326-1232。

波士顿地区办公室：康涅狄格州、缅因州、马萨诸塞州、新罕布什尔州、罗德岛州和佛蒙特州——地区办公室主任，马萨诸塞州波士顿市Arch大街33号23楼，邮编：MA 02110-1424。

芝加哥地区办公室：肯塔基州、伊利诺伊州、印第安纳州、爱荷华州、密歇根州、明尼斯达州、密苏里州、俄亥俄州和威斯康星州——地区办公室主任，伊利诺伊州芝加哥西杰克逊大道175号900室，邮编：IL 60604-2908。

丹佛地区办公室：科罗拉多州、堪萨斯州、内布拉斯州、新墨西哥州、北达科他州、南达科他州和怀俄明州——地区办公室主任，科罗拉多州丹佛市加利福尼亚大街1801号1500室，邮编：CO 80202-2656。

沃斯堡地区办公室：阿肯色州、堪萨斯州（限于特定目的）、俄克拉荷马州和得克萨斯州——地区办公室主任，得克萨斯州沃斯堡市Cherry大街801号Burnett大厦1900室18单元，邮编：TX 76102-6882。

洛杉矶地区办公室：亚利桑那州、南加利福尼亚州（邮编为93599及以下编码，不包括93200-93299）、关岛、夏威夷和内华达州——地区办公室主任，加利福尼亚州洛杉矶市Wilshire大道5670号11层，邮编：CA 90036-3648。

迈阿密地区办公室：佛罗里达州、路易斯安那州、密西西比州、波多黎各州和维尔

Islands—Regional Director, 801 Brickell Avenue, Suite 1800, Miami, FL 33131-4901.

New York Regional Office: New York and New Jersey—Regional Director, 3 World Financial Center, Suite 400, New York, NY 10281-1022.

Philadelphia Regional Office: Delaware, District of Columbia, Maryland, Pennsylvania, Virginia, and West Virginia—Regional Director, 701 Market Street, Suite 2000, Philadelphia, PA 19106-1532.

Salt Lake City Regional Office: Utah—Regional Director, 15 W. South Temple Street, Suite 1800, Salt Lake City, UT 84101-1573.

San Francisco Regional Office: Alaska, Northern California (zip codes 93600 and up, plus 93200-93299), Idaho, Montana, Oregon, and Washington—Regional Director, 44 Montgomery Street, Suite 2600, San Francisco, CA 94104-4716.

(c) The geographic allocation set forth in paragraph (b) of this section determines where registered brokers, dealers, transfer agents, clearing agents, registered securities associations, investment advisers, and others as designated in this chapter must file reports required to be filed in regional offices.

[73 FR 32223, June 5, 2008]

§200.12 Functional Responsibilities.

This section sets forth the administrative and substantive responsibilities of the Division Directors, Office Heads, Regional Directors, and certain other Commission officers. All Commission officers and other staff members, except administrative law judges and the Inspector General, shall perform, in addition to the duties herein set forth, such additional duties as the chairman of the Commission may assign from time to time. These officers also serve as liaison with Government and other agencies concerning matters within their respective functional responsibilities.

[37 FR 23826, Nov. 9, 1972, as amended at 59 FR 5943, Feb. 9, 1994; 60 FR 14624, Mar. 20, 1995; 73 FR 32223, June 5, 2008]

§200.13 Executive Director.

(a) The Executive Director is responsible for developing and executing the overall management policies of the Commission for all its operating divisions and staff offices. The Executive Director also provides executive direction to, and exercises administrative control over, the Office of Administrative and Personnel Management, the Office of the Comptroller, the Office of Filings and Information Services, the Office of Freedom of Information and Privacy Act Operations, and the Office of Information Technology. In addition, the Executive Director implements the following statutes, regulations, and Executive orders, as well as those that the Chairman may designate:

京群岛——地区办公室主任,佛罗里达州迈阿密市Brickell大道801号1800室,邮编:FL 33131-4901。

纽约地区办公室:纽约州和新泽西州——地区办公室主任,纽约州纽约市世界金融中心3号400室,邮编:NY 10281-1022。

费城地区办公室:特拉华州、哥伦比亚特区、马里兰州、宾夕法尼亚州、弗吉尼亚州和西弗吉尼亚州——地区办公室主任,宾夕法尼亚州费城Market大街701号2000室,邮编:PA 19106-1532。

盐湖城地区办公室:犹他州——地区办公室主任,犹他州盐湖城South Temple西大街15号1800室,邮编:UT 84101-1573。

旧金山地区办公室:阿拉斯加州、加利福尼亚州北部(邮编为93600及以上编码,另包括93200-93299)、爱达荷州、蒙大拿州、俄勒冈州和华盛顿——地区办公室主任,加利福尼亚州旧金山Montgomery大街44号2600室,邮编:CA 94104-4716。

(c)注册经纪商、自营商、过户代理人、结算代理、注册证券协会、投资顾问和本章指定的其他主体必须按照本节第(b)款的地域区划规定向相应的办公室提交报告。

[《联邦公报》第73卷第32223页,2008年6月5日。]

第200.12节　职责

本节对部门主任、办公室主任、区域办公室主任及部分其他证券交易委员会管理人员的行政责任和实体责任作出规定。证券交易委员会的所有管理人员和其他员工(行政法官和监察长除外)在履行本节规定的职责同时,还应履行证券交易委员会主席随时向其委派的职责。该等管理人员应就其各自职能责任范围内的事项充当与政府和其他机构之间的联络人。

[《联邦公报》第37卷第23826页,1972年11月9日,修正索引:《联邦公报》第59卷第5943页,1994年2月9日;《联邦公报》第60卷第14624页,1995年3月20日;《联邦公报》第73卷第32223页,2008年6月5日。]

第200.13节　证券交易委员会执行主任

(a)证券交易委员会执行主任负责就证券交易委员会的所有运营部门和员工办公室制定和执行总体管理政策。证券交易委员会执行主任还负责为行政和人事管理办公室、审计办公室、档案和信息服务办公室、信息自由和隐私法管理办公室以及信息技术办公室提供执行指导和行政管理。此外,证券交易委员会执行主任应实施下述以及证券交易委员会主席指定的其他制定法、规章和行政命令:

(1) Paperwork Reduction Act of 1980 (44 U.S.C. 3501 *et seq.*).

(2) Small and Disadvantaged Business Utilization Program (15 U.S.C. 631 *et seq.*).

(3) Government Printing and Binding Regulations, U.S. Congress Joint Committee on Printing (1977).

(4) Occupational Safety and Health Programs for Federal Employees under Executive Order 12196 of February 26, 1980 (29 CFR 1960.1–1960.90).

(5) Federal Managers' Financial Integrity Act of 1982 (31 U.S.C. 3512).

(6) National Security Information under Executive Order 12356 of April 6, 1982.

(7) Government Performance and Results Act of 1993 (31 U.S.C. 1101 *et seq.*).

(8) Recommendations of the Report of the National Performance Review (September 1993).

(b) The Executive Director appoints personnel, reviews and approves policies and procedures, and assures appropriate resources to implement the programs set forth in paragraph (a) of this section, and authorizes and transmits reports required by them.

(c) The Executive Director also designates certifying officers for agency payments, prescribes procurement regulations, enters into contracts, designates contracting officers, and makes procurement determinations.

(d) As the Chief Operating Officer of the Commission, the Executive Director shall be responsible for:

(1) Implementing the goals of the President and the Chairman and the mission of the Commission;

(2) Providing overall organizational management to improve agency performance;

(3) Assisting the Chairman in promoting ongoing quality improvement, developing strategic plans, and measuring results;

(4) Directing ongoing reengineering of the Commission's administrative processes.

(e) Overseeing Commission–specific application of performance measu res, procurement reforms, personnel reductions, financial management improvements, telecommunications and information technology policies, and other government –wide systems reforms adopted as a result of the recommendations of the National Performance Review; and

(f) Reforming the Commission's management practices by incorporating the principles of the National Performance Review into day–to–day management.

[60 FR 14624, Mar. 20, 1995]

§200.13a The Secretary of the Commission.

(a) The Secretary of the Commission is responsible for the preparation of the daily and weekly agendas of Commission business; the orderly and expeditious flow of business at formal Commission meetings; the maintenance of the Official Minute record of all

(1)《1980年文书削减法》(《美国法典》第四十四编第3501节及其后条文)。
(2)《小型及弱势企业扶持计划》(《美国法典》第十五编第631节及其后条文)。
(3)美国国会印刷联合委员会《1977年政府印刷及装订管理办法》。

(4)《关于联邦雇员职业安全和健康计划的第12196号行政命令（1980年2月26日)》(《联邦规章汇编》第二十九编第1960.1~1960.90节)。
(5)《1982年联邦管理人员财务操守法》(《美国法典》第三十一编第3512节)。
(6)《关于国家安全信息的第12356号行政命令(1982年4月6日)》。
(7)《1993年政府绩效和成果法》(《美国法典》第三十一编第1101节及其后条文)。
(8)《国家绩效审查报告建议》(1993年9月)。

(b)证券交易委员会执行主任负责人员任命及政策和程序的审批,确保分配适当的资源以实施本节第(a)款所载计划,并授权编制和传发计划所需报告。

(c)证券交易委员会执行主任还负责指定负责核证证券交易委员会付款的核证官,同时负责制定采购规章、签订合同、指定订约官并作出采购决定。

(d)作为证券交易委员会的首席运营官,证券交易委员会执行主任应负责:

(1)执行总统和证券交易委员会主席确定的目标以及证券交易委员会的任务宗旨;

(2)开展总体的组织管理工作,提高证券交易委员会的工作绩效;
(3)协助证券交易委员会主席促进质量的持续提升、制订战略计划、考核工作成果;
(4)领导证券交易委员会行政流程的持续调整完善。
(e)针对基于《国家绩效评估》建议而采取的绩效措施、采购改革、人员裁减、财务管理改良、电信和信息技术政策及其他整个政府范围内的系统改革,监督其在证券交易委员会内部的具体实行;及

(f)将《国家绩效评估》的原则融入日常管理,改革证券交易委员会的管理实践。

[《联邦公报》第60卷第14624页,1995年3月20日。]

第200.13a节　证券交易委员会秘书

(a)证券交易委员会秘书负责如下事项:制定证券交易委员会每日和每周的日程表;确保证券交易委员会的正式会议有序、顺畅地开展;就证券交易委员会采取的所有行动维持官方记录;就证券交易委员会正式采取的行动发送相关文书。秘书负责保

actions of the Commission; and the service of all instruments of formal Commission action. He or she is custodian of the official seal of the Commission, and also has the responsibility for authenticating documents.

(b) The Secretary has been delegated responsibilities relating to the Commission's rules of practice, administrative proceedings under the Commission's statutes, and other responsibilities.

(c) In addition, he or she administers the Commission's Library.

[50 FR 12239, Mar. 28, 1985]

§200.13b Director of the Office of Public Affairs, Policy Evaluation, and Research.

The Director of the Office of Public Affairs, Policy Evaluation, and Research is the chief public information officer for the Commission, and oversees activities that communicate the Commission's actions to those interested in or affected by them. His or her responsibilities include liaison with the news media, dissemination of information to the news media and to the general public, supervision of internal and some external publications and of audio-visual presentations. Responsibilities of the Director, and of his or her staff, include special projects that may be deemed appropriate to communicate information on Commission actions.

[50 FR 12239, Mar. 28, 1985, as amended at 60 FR 14625, Mar. 20, 1995]

§200.14 Office of Administrative Law Judges.

(a) Under the Administrative Procedure Act (5 U.S.C. 551-559) and the federal securities laws, the Office of Administrative Law Judges conducts hearings in proceedings instituted by the Commission. The Administrative Law Judges are responsible for the fair and orderly conduct of the proceedings and have the authority to:

(1) Administer oaths and affirmations;

(2) Issue subpoenas;

(3) Rule on offers of proof;

(4) Examine witnesses;

(5) Regulate the course of a hearing;

(6) Hold pre-hearing conferences;

(7) Rule upon motions; and

(8) Unless waived by the parties, prepare an initial decision containing the conclusions as to the factual and legal issues presented, and issue an appropriate order.

(b) The Chief Administrative Law Judge performs the duties of an Administrative Law Judge under the Administrative Procedure Act and the duties delegated to him or her by the Commission that are compatible with those duties. The Chief Administrative Law

管证券交易委员会公章,并负责认证文件。

(b)授予秘书的职责包括与证券交易委员会的工作规则、与证券交易委员会依据其负责实施的制定法开展的行政处理程序相关的职责以及其他职责。

(c)此外,秘书还负责管理证券交易委员会的图书馆。

[《联邦公报》第50卷第12239页,1985年3月28日。]

第200.13b节　公共事务、政策评估和研究办公室主任

公共事务、政策评估和研究办公室主任是证券交易委员会的首席公共信息官,监督证券交易委员会向存在利害关系或受其行动影响的人士发布关于其行动的信息的活动,其职责包括与新闻媒体联系、向新闻媒体和一般公众传播信息、监督内部信息公布和某些外部信息公布以及视听介绍材料。公共事务、政策评估和研究主任及其下属员工的职责包括开展其认为适当的特殊项目,传达与证券交易委员会行动相关的信息。

[《联邦公报》第50卷第12239页,1985年3月28日,修正索引:《联邦公报》第60卷第14625页,1995年3月20日。]

第200.14节　行政法官办公室

(a)根据《行政程序法》(《美国法典》第五编第551~559节)以及联邦证券法,行政法官办公室负责在证券交易委员会发起的行政处理程序。[1]

(1)主持宣誓和证词声明程序;

(2)签发传票;

(3)对证据认定动议作出裁定;

(4)询问证人;

(5)管理听证程序;

(6)举行预听证会议;

(7)就动议作出裁定;及

(8)就提交听证的事实和法律问题作出初步决定并签发适当的命令,但当事人放弃的除外。

(b)首席行政法官根据《行政程序法》履行行政法官的职责以及证券交易委员会授予的与该等职责不相冲突的其他职责。首席行政法官除负责开展行政处理程序外,

1　为避免与administrative procedure(行政程序)混淆,administrative proceeding译为“行政处理程序”。——译者注

Judge is responsible for the orderly functioning of the Office of Administrative Law Judges apart from the conduct of administrative proceedings and acts as liaison between that Office and the Commission.

[60 FR 14625, Mar. 20, 1995]

§200.15 Office of International Affairs.

(a) The Office of International Affairs (OIA) is responsible for the negotiation and implementation of the Commission's bilateral and multilateral agreements and understandings with foreign financial regulatory authorities. OIA coordinates and participates in activities relating to the Commission's international cooperation programs and develops initiatives to enhance the Commission's ability to enforce the federal securities laws in matters with international elements.

(b) OIA assists in and facilitates the efforts of the Commission's other divisions and offices in responding to international issues and in developing legislative, rulemaking and other initiatives relating to international securities markets. OIA facilitates the development of and, where appropriate, provides advice and presents Commission positions relating to international initiatives of other U.S. Government departments and agencies affecting regulation of securities markets. OIA plans, coordinates and participates in Commission meetings with foreign financial regulatory authorities.

[58 FR 52418, Oct. 8, 1993]

§200.16 Executive Assistant to the Chairman.

The Executive Assistant to the Chairman assists the Chairman in consideration of legal, financial, and economic problems encountered in the administration of the Commission's statutes. He or she arranges for and conducts conferences with officials of the Commission, members of the staff, and/or representatives of the public on matters arising with regard to general programs or specific matters. Acting for the Chairman, he or she furnishes the initiative, executive direction, and authority for staff studies and reports bearing on the Commission's administration of the laws and its relations with the public, industry, and the Congress. The Executive Assistant is also responsible for assisting members of the Commission in the preparation of the opinions of the Commission, and to the Commission for the preparation of opinions and decisions on motions and certifications of questions and rulings by administrative law judges in the course of administrative proceedings under Rule 102(e) of the Commission's Rules of Practice (§201.102(e) of this chapter), and in other cases in which the Chairman or the General Counsel has determined that separation of functions requirements or other circumstances would make inappropriate the exercise of such functions by the General Counsel. In cases where, pursuant to a waiver by the parties of separation of function requirements, another Division or Office of the Commission's staff undertakes to prepare an opinion or decision,

还负责行政法官办公室工作的有序运作,并应充当行政法官办公室与证券交易委员会之间的联络人。

[《联邦公报》第60卷第14625页,1995年3月20日。]

第200.15节　国际事务办公室

(a)国际事务办公室(OIA)负责就证券交易委员会与国外金融监管机构之间的双边和多边协议和谅解开展磋商并予以实施。国际事务办公室负责协调、参与与证券交易委员会国际合作项目相关的活动,制定相关倡议以加强证券交易委员会在国际事务中执行联邦证券法的能力。

(b)国际事务办公室负责协助并促进证券交易委员会其他部门和办公室就国际问题作出响应、制定与国际证券市场相关的立法倡议、规则制定倡议和其他倡议。国际事务办公室负责协助对证券市场监管有影响的其他美国政府部门和机构制定国际倡议,并在适当时向证券交易委员会提供相关意见和建议。国际事务办公室负责规划、协调并参与证券交易委员会和国外金融监管机构之间举行的会议。

[《联邦公报》第58卷第52418页,1993年10月8日。]

第200.16节　主席执行助理

主席执行助理协助主席审议证券交易委员会实施制定法过程中遇到的法律、金融和经济问题。执行助理负责安排、开展与证券交易委员会官员、员工和/或公众代表就一般计划或具体事项开展的会议。执行助理作为主席的代表倡议工作人员就证券交易委员会法律实施工作及证券交易委员会与公众、行业和国会的关系开展研究和提供报告,并给予行政领导和授予权限。执行助理还负责协助证券交易委员会委员制定证券交易委员会的意见;在根据《证券交易委员会工作规则》的《102(e)规则》[本章第201.102(e)节]开展的行政处理程序中,主席执行助理应就行政法官制定的意见、对动议的裁定、对问题的认定及作出的裁决,向证券交易委员会负责;另外,如证券交易委员会主席或首席律师判定由于职能分离要求或其他情形令首席律师不宜行使上述职能,则执行助理亦应承担此等职能,对证券交易委员会负责。如当事人放弃职能分离要求,因而由证券交易委员会其他部门或办公室的员工承担制定意见或作出决定的职责,则由该部门或办公室而不由执行助理负责制定意见或作出决定,虽然执行助理可提供相关协助。对于证券交易委员会按《美国制定法汇编》第101卷第1254页(《美国法典》第十五编第78d-1节、第78d-2节)授权其裁决的事项或在其他情况下授权或交由其裁决的事项,执行助理亦负责行使上述审查职能。

such Division or Office rather than the Executive Assistant will prepare such opinion or decision, although the Executive Assistant may assist in such preparation. The Executive Assistant is further responsible for the exercise of such review functions with respect to adjudicatory matters as are delegated to him or her by the Commission pursuant to 101 Stat. 1254 (15 U.S.C. 78d-1, 78d-2) or as may be otherwise delegated or assigned to him or her.

[54 FR 18100, Apr. 27, 1989, as amended at 60 FR 32794, June 23, 1995]

§200.16a Inspector General.

(a) Under the Inspector General Act of 1978, as amended, (5 U.S.C. app.) the Inspector General performs independent and objective investigations and audits relating to the Commission's programs and operations. An investigation seeks to detect and prevent waste, fraud, and abuse in the Commission's programs and operations, such as violations of federal statutes or regulations by contractors and Commission employees or the Standards Of Ethical Conduct For Employees of the Executive Branch. An audit seeks to determine whether:

(1) Program goals and results identified in enabling legislation are achieved.

(2) Resources are efficiently and economically used and managed.

(3) Financial operations are properly conducted.

(4) Financial reports are fairly presented.

(5) Applicable laws and regulations are complied with.

(b) In cooperation with Commission management, the Inspector General generally promotes economy, efficiency, and the effectiveness of waste or fraud detection and prevention in the Commission's programs and operations. The Inspector General also keeps the Congress and the Chairman informed about problems and deficiencies in the Commission's programs and operations.

(c) The Inspector General reports to the Chairman, but is independent of all other Commission management. In addition, the Inspector General independently prepares semi-annual reports to the Congress.

(d) With respect to misconduct of Commission employees and contractors, the Inspector General, after consultation with the Ethics Counsel, where appropriate, serves as the Commission's liaison with other federal audit and investigative agencies, such as the Department of Justice and the Executive Council on Integrity and Efficiency.

(e) Subpoenas issued in the course of an audit or investigation conducted by the Office of the Inspector General shall be effected by any method prescribed by §201.232 (a) and (c) of this chapter.

[60 FR 14625, Mar. 20, 1995]

§200.17 Chief Management Analyst.

The Chief Management Analyst is responsible to the Executive Director for overseeing

[《联邦公报》第54卷第18100页,1989年4月27日,修正索引:《联邦公报》第60卷第32794页,1995年6月23日。]

第200.16a节　监察长

(a)根据《1978年监察长法》及其修正(《美国法典》第五编附件),监察长应就证券交易委员会的项目和运营进行独立和客观的调查和审计。调查旨在发现和阻止证券交易委员会项目和运营过程中的浪费、欺诈和滥用情形,如承包商和证监会员工违反联邦制定法或规章或《行政部门雇员职业道德行为标准》的情形。审计旨在确定:

(1)在赋权立法中确定的项目目标和结果是否得到实现;

(2)资源使用和管理是否有效、经济;

(3)财务运营是否适当;

(4)财务报告列报是否公允;

(5)适用法律和规章是否得到遵守。

(b)在与证券交易委员会管理层的合作中,监察长应广泛地提高对证券交易委员会项目和运营浪费或欺诈的发现和预防工作的经济性、有效性和效率。监察长还负责向国会和证券交易委员会主席报告证券交易委员会项目和运营出现的问题和缺陷。

(c)监察长向证券交易委员会主席报告工作,但其职能的行使独立于所有其他证券交易委员会管理层。此外,监察长负责独立制定向国会提交的半年报告。

(d)证券交易委员会雇员和承包方出现不当行为的,经与职业道德顾问磋商后,监察长可在适当情形下充当证券交易委员会与其他联邦审计和调查机构(如司法部和廉政效率执行委员会)的联络人。

(e)监察长办公室开展审计或调查过程中签发的传票应按本章第201.232(a)节和第201.232(c)节规定的方法执行。

[《联邦公报》第60卷第14625页,1995年3月20日。]

第200.17节　首席管理分析师

首席管理分析师向执行主任负责,监督开展与下述各项等相关的管理分析工作:

the performance of management analysis tasks which pertain, but are not limited, to:

(a) Agency work methods and procedures;

(b) Effective personnel and resource allocation and utilization;

(c) Organizational structures and delegations of authority;

(d) Management information systems and concepts; and

(e) The preparation of recurring special reports and analyses.

[60 FR 14625, Mar. 20, 1995]

§200.18 Director of Division of Corporation Finance.

The Director of the Division of Corporation Finance is responsible to the Commission for the administration of all matters (except those pertaining to investment companies registered under the Investment Company Act of 1940) relating to establishing and requiring adherence to standards of business and financial disclosure with respect to securities being offered for public sale pursuant to the registration requirements of the Securities Act of 1933 (15 U.S.C. 77a *et seq.*) or the exemptions therefrom; establishing and requiring adherence to standards of reporting and disclosure with respect to securities traded on national securities exchanges or required to be registered pursuant to section 12(g) of the Securities Exchange Act of 1934 (15 U.S.C. 78*l*(g)) and with respect to securities whose issuers are required to file reports pursuant to section 15(d) of that Act (15 U.S.C. 78 c(d)); establishing and requiring adherence to disclosure and procedural standards in the solicitation of proxies for the election of directors and other corporate actions; establishing and requiring adherence to standards of disclosure with respect to the filing of statements respecting beneficial ownership and transaction statements pursuant to sections 13 (d), (e), and (g) (15 U.S.C. 78m (d), 78m (e), and 78m (g)) of the Securities Exchange Act of 1934; administering the disclosure and substantive provisions of the Williams Act relating to tender offers; and ensuring adherence to enforcement of the standards set forth in the Trust Indenture Act of 1939(15 U.S.C. 77aaa *et seq.*) regarding indenture covering debt securities. Those duties shall include, with the exception of enforcement and related activities under the jurisdiction of the Division of Enforcement, the responsibility to the Commission for the administration of the disclosure requirements and other provisions of the Securities Act of 1933, the Securities Exchange Act of 1934, and the Trust Indenture Act of 1939, as listed below:

(a) All matters under the Securities Act of 1933 (15 U.S.C. 77a *et seq.*) including the examination and processing of material filed pursuant to the requirements of that Act (except such material filed by investment companies registered under the Investment Company Act of 1940), the interpretation of the provisions of the Securities Act of 1933, and the proposing to the Commission of rules under that Act.

(b) All matters, except those pertaining to investment companies registered under

(a)证券交易委员会的工作方法和程序;

(b)人员和资源分配和利用的有效性;

(c)组织结构和授权;

(d)管理信息系统和概念;及

(e)制作经常性的特殊报告和分析。

[《联邦公报》第60卷第14625页,1995年3月20日。]

第200.18节　公司融资部主任

公司融资部主任负责执行与下述各项相关的所有事项并就此向证券交易委员会负责(与依《1940年投资公司法》注册的投资公司相关的事项除外):针对依《1933年证券法》(《美国法典》第十五编第77a节及其后条文)的注册要求公开发行出售的证券,设定并执行相关业务和财务披露标准,或豁免对该等标准之遵守;针对在全国性证券交易所交易的证券及依《1934年证券交易法》第12(g)条[《美国法典》第十五编第78*l*(g)节]应注册的证券设定并执行报告和披露标准;针对发行人应按该法第15(d)节[《美国法典》第十五编第78 c(d)节]提交报告的证券设定并执行报告和披露标准;针对为选举董事或开展其他公司行动而进行的代理权征集设定并执行披露和程序性标准;针对依《1934年证券交易法》第13(d)节、第13(e)节和第13(g)节[《美国法典》第十五编第78m(d)节、第78m(e)节和第78m(g)节]提交的受益所有权说明书及交易说明书设定并执行披露标准;负责实施《威廉姆斯法》中与收购要约相关的披露条款和实体条款;以及确保《1939年信托契约法》(《美国法典》第十五编第77aaa节及其后条文)中关于债权证券契约的标准之执行得到遵守。在上述职责(执法部管辖权范围内的执法和相关活动除外)中,包括实施下文所列《1933年证券法》、《1934年证券交易法》以及《1939年信托契约法》的披露要求和其他条款并就此向证券交易委员会负责:

(a)《1933年证券法》(《美国法典》第十五编第77a节及其后条文)中的所有事项,包括核查和处理根据该法提交的材料(依《1940年投资公司法》注册的投资公司所提交的材料除外)、解释《1933年证券法》的条文并向证券交易委员会提出该法实施细则草案。

(b)《1934年证券交易法》(《美国法典》第十五编第78a节及其后条文)下产生的与

the Investment Company Act of 1940, arising under the Securities Exchange Act of 1934 (15 U.S.C. 78a *et seq.*) in connection with:

(1) The registration of securities pursuant to section 12 of the Act (15 U.S.C. 78 *l*), including the exemptive provisions of section 12(h) (15 U.S.C. 78*l*(h)).

(2) The examination and processing of periodic reports filed pursuant to sections 13 and 15(d) of the Act (15 U.S.C. 78m, 78o(d)).

(3) The examination and processing of proxy soliciting material filed pursuant to section 14(a) and information statements filed pursuant to section 14(c) of the Act (15 U.S.C. 78n(a), 78n(c)).

(4) The examination and processing of statements respecting beneficial ownership transaction statements and tender offer statements filed pursuant to sections 13(d), (e), and (g) and 14(d), (e), (f), and (g) of the Securities Exchange Act of 1934 (15 U.S.C. 78m(d), 78m(e), 78m(g), and 78n(d)), and the administration of the other protective standards of these provisions.

(5) The interpretation of the foregoing provisions of the Act, as well as Section 16 thereof (15 U.S.C. 78p), and proposing of rules under those portions of the Act to the Commission.

(c) All matters, except those pertaining to investment companies registered under the Investment Company Act of 1940, arising under the Trust Indenture Act of 1939 (15 U.S.C. 77aaa *et seq.*).

[41 FR 29374, July 16, 1976, as amended at 50 FR 12239, Mar. 28, 1985; 60 FR 14625, Mar. 20, 1995]

§200.19a Director of the Division of Trading and Markets.

The Director of the Division of Trading and Markets is responsible to the Commission for the administration and execution of the Commission's programs under the Securities Exchange Act of 1934 relating to the structure and operation of the securities markets and the prevention of manipulation in the securities markets. These responsibilities include oversight of the national market system, the national clearance and settlement system, and self–regulatory organizations, such as the national securities exchanges, registered securities associations, clearing agencies, the Municipal Securities Rulemaking Board, and the Securities Investor Protection Corporation. In addition, these responsibilities include administering the Commission's rules related to supervised investment bank holding companies and ultimate holding companies of brokers or dealers that compute deductions for market and credit risk pursuant to §240.15c3–1e of this chapter. This supervision includes the assessment of internal risk management controls and mathematical models used to calculate net capital and allowances for market, credit, and operational risks. Duties also include the registration and regulation of brokers, dealers, municipal securities

下述各项相关的所有事项(与依《1940年投资公司法》注册的投资公司相关的事项除外):

(1)依《1934年证券交易法》第12条(《美国法典》第十五编第78*l*节)进行的证券注册,包括依第12(h)条[《美国法典》第十五编第78*l*(h)节]豁免条款进行的证券注册;

(2)依该法第13条和第15(d)条[《美国法典》第十五编第78m节、第78o(d)节]提交的定期报告之审核和处理;

(3)依该法第14(a)条提交的代理权征集材料以及依该法第14(c)条[《美国法典》第十五编第78n(a)节、第78n(c)节]提交的信息说明书之审核和处理;

(4)依《1934年证券交易法》第13(d)节、第13(e)节和第13(g)条及第14(d)节、第14(e)节、第14(f)节和第14(g)条[《美国法典》第十五编第78m(d)节、第78m(e)节、第78m(g)节和第78n(d)节]提交的受益所有权交易说明书、收购要约说明书之审核和处理;并负责实施上述条款的其他保护性标准;

(5)对《1934年证券交易法》上述条文及该法第16条(《美国法典》第十五编第78p节)进行解释,向委员会提出上述条款的实施细则草案。

(c)《1939年信托契约法》(《美国法典》第十五编第77aaa节及其后条文)下产生的所有事项(与依《1940年投资公司法》注册的投资公司相关的除外)。

[《联邦公报》第41卷第29374页,1976年7月16日,修正索引:《联邦公报》第50卷第12239页,1985年3月28日;《联邦公报》第60卷第14625页,1995年3月20日。]

第200.19a节　交易和市场部主任

交易和市场部主任就《1934年证券交易法》项下与证券市场结构和运作及防止证券市场操纵行为相关的证券交易委员会项目之实施和执行向证券交易委员会负责。上述责任包括监督国内市场系统、国内清算、结算系统、自律组织(如全国性证券交易所、注册证券协会、结算机构、市政证券规则制定委员会和证券投资者保护公司)。此外,其承担的责任还包括负责实施证券交易委员会适用于以下实体的规则:依本章第240.15c3-1e节应按市场和信用风险计算资本金扣减额的受监督投资银行控股公司,以及经纪商或自营商的最终控股公司。履行上述监督职责时,应对内部风险管理控制以及用于计算净资本金及市场、信用和经营风险准备金的数学模型进行评估。此外,交易和市场部主任的职责还包括对经纪商、自营商、市政证券自营商、政府证券经纪商和自营商、过户代理人和证券信息处理机构的注册和监管。上述监管职能包括:审查自律组织的规则变更提案;就证券交易委员会规则之通过和修正提出建议;对解释、豁免和不行动请求进行答复;开展检查、核查和市场监督。此外,交易和市场部主任还应履行下述职责:

dealers, government securities brokers and dealers, transfer agents, and securities information processors. The functions involved in the regulation of such entities include reviewing proposed rule changes of self–regulatory organizations, recommending the adoption and amendment of Commission rules, responding to interpretive, exemptive, and no–action requests, and conducting inspections, examinations, and market surveillance. In addition, the Director shall have the duties specified below:

(a) Administration of all matters arising under the Securities Exchange Act of 1934 (15 U.S.C. 78a *et seq.*), except:

(1) The examination and processing of applications for registration of securities on national securities exchanges pursuant to section 12 of the Act (15 U.S.C. 78*l*).

(2) The examination and processing of periodic reports filed pursuant to sections 13 and 15(d) of the Act (15 U.S.C. 78m, 78o(d)).

(3) The examination and processing of proxy soliciting material pursuant to regulations adopted under section 14 of the Act (15 U.S.C. 78n).

(4) The examination and processing of ownership reports filed under section 16(a) of the Act (15 U.S.C. 78p(a)).

(5) The denial or suspension of registration of securities registered on national securities exchanges, pursuant to section 19(a)(2) (15 U.S.C. 78s(a)(2)) by reason of failure to comply with the reporting requirements of that Act.

(6) The enforcement and related activities under the jurisdiction of the Division of Enforcement.

[37 FR 16792, Aug. 19, 1972, as amended at 43 FR 13376, Mar. 30, 1978; 60 FR 14625, Mar. 20, 1995; 69 FR 34461, June 21, 2004; 73 FR 40152, July 11, 2008]

§200.19b Director of the Division of Enforcement.

The Director of the Division of Enforcement is responsible to the Commission for supervising and conducting all enforcement activities under the acts administered by the Commission. The Director recommends the institution of administrative and injunctive actions arising out of such enforcement activities and determines the sufficiency of evidence to support the allegations in any proposed complaint. The Director supervises the Regional Directors and, in collaboration with the General Counsel, reviews cases to be recommended to the Department of Justice for criminal prosecution. The Director grants or denies access to nonpublic information in the Commission's enforcement files under §240.24c–1 of this chapter; provided that access under that section shall be granted only with the concurrence of the head of the division or office responsible for the information or the files containing it.

[60 FR 14626, Mar. 20, 1995]

(a)执行《1934年证券交易法》(《美国法典》第十五编第78a节及其后条文)下产生的所有事项,但下述事项除外:

(1)根据该法第12条(《美国法典》第十五编第78*l*节)提出的全国性证券交易所注册申请之审核和处理;

(2)依该法第13条和第15(d)条[《美国法典》第十五编第78m节、第78o(d)节]提交的定期报告之审核和处理;

(3)依该法第14条(《美国法典》第十五编第78n节)项下规章进行的代理权征集材料之审核和处理;

(4)依该法第16(a)条[《美国法典》第十五编第78p(a)节]提交的所有权报告之审核和处理;

(5)基于申请人未遵守该法的报告要求而依第19(a)(2)条[《美国法典》第十五编第78s(a)(2)节]驳回或暂停证券在全国性证券交易所的注册;

(6)执法部管辖权范围内的执法活动和相关活动。

[《联邦公报》第37卷第16792页,1972年8月19日,修正索引:《联邦公报》第43卷第13376页,1978年3月30日;《联邦公报》第60卷第14625页,1995年3月20日;《联邦公报》第69卷第34461页,2004年6月21日;《联邦公报》第73卷第40152页,2008年7月11日。]

第200.19b节　执法部主任

执法部主任负责监督和开展证券交易委员会负责实施的所有法律的执法工作。执法部主任可以在执法活动过程中建议提起行政和禁令诉讼,并负责对支持指控的证据是否充分作出判定。执法部主任监督地区办公室主任;对于建议司法部进行刑事追诉的案件,应与首席律师共同合作进行审查。执法部主任可根据本章第240.24c-1节规定授予或拒不提供查询证券交易委员会执法文件中非公开信息的权限;但是,提供该节规定的非公开信息查询权的,应征得对上述信息或含有上述信息文档负责的部门或办公室主任的同意。

[《联邦公报》第60卷第14626页,1995年3月20日。]

§200.19c Director of the Office of Compliance Inspections and Examinations.

The Director of the Office of Compliance Inspections and Examinations(OCIE) is responsible for the compliance inspections and examinations relating to the regulation of exchanges, national securities associations, clearing agencies, securities information processors, the Municipal Securities Rulemaking Board, brokers and dealers, municipal securities dealers, transfer agents, investment companies, and investment advisers, under Sections 15C(d)(1) and 17(b) of the Securities Exchange Act of 1934 (15 U.S.C. 78o-5 (d)(1) and 78q(b)), Section 31(b) of the Investment Company Act of 1940 (15 U.S.C. 80a-30(b)), and Section 204 of the Investment Advisers Act of 1940 (15 U.S.C. 80b-4).

[60 FR 39644, Aug. 3, 1995]

§200.20b Director of Division of Investment Management.

The Director of the Division of Investment Management is responsible to the Commission for the administration of the Commission's responsibilities under the Investment Company Act of 1940 and the Investment Advisers Act of 1940, the administration and execution of the Public Utility Holding Company Act of 1935, and with respect to matters pertaining to investment companies registered under the Investment Company Act of 1940 and pooled investment funds or accounts, the administration of all matters relating to establishing and requiring adherence to standards of economic and financial reporting and the administration of fair disclosure and related matters under the Securities Act of 1933 and the Securities Exchange Act of 1934 and enforcement of the standards set forth in the Trust Indenture Act of 1939 regarding indentures covering debt securities, as listed in paragraphs(a) through(e) of this section. These duties shall include inspections arising in connection with such administration but shall exclude enforcement and related activities under the jurisdiction of the Division of Enforcement.

(a) The administration of all matters arising under the Investment Company Act of 1940 (15 U.S.C. 80a), except those arising under section 30(h) of the Act (15 U.S.C. 80a-29(h)).

(b) All matters arising under the Securities Act of 1933 (15 U.S.C. 77a *et seq.*) arising from or pertaining to material field pursuant to the requirements of that Act by investment companies registered under the Investment Company Act of 1940 (15 U.S.C. 80a-1 *et seq.*) and pooled investment funds or accounts.

(c) All matters arising under the Securities Exchange Act of 1934 (15 U.S.C. 78a *et seq.*), except the examination and processing of statements of beneficial ownership of securities and changes in such ownership filed under section 16(a) (15 U.S.C. 78p(a)) of such Act, pertaining to investment companies registered under the Investment Company Act of 1940 and pooled investment funds or accounts in connection with:

(1) The registration of securities pursuant to section 12 of the Act (15 U.S.C. 78*l*),

第200.19c节　合规检查和核查办公室主任

合规检查和核查办公室(OCIE)主任负责与下述活动相关的合规检查和审核:依《1934年证券交易法》第15C(d)(1)条和第17(b)条[《美国法典》第十五编第78o-5(d)(1)节和第78q(b)节]、《1940年投资公司法》第31(b)条[《美国法典》第十五编第80a-30(b)节]及《1940年投资顾问法》第204条(《美国法典》第十五编第80b-4节)对交易所、全国性证券协会、结算机构、证券信息处理机构、市政证券规则制定委员会、经纪商、自营商、市政证券交易商、过户代理人、投资公司和投资顾问进行的监管工作。

[《联邦公报》第60卷第39644页,1995年8月3日。]

第200.20b节　投资管理部主任

投资管理部主任就下述各项工作向证券交易委员会负责:证券交易委员会在《1940年投资公司法》和《1940年投资顾问法》中的责任;负责实施和执行《1935年公用事业控股公司法》;与依《1940年投资公司法》注册的投资公司和集合投资基金或账户相关的事项;与经济和财务报告标准之设定及执行相关的所有事项;《1933年证券法》、《1934年证券交易法》中的公平披露及相关事项,以及《1939年信托契约法》关于债务证券信托契约的标准之执行,详见本节第(a)款至第(e)款之规定。上述职责包括与上述实施活动相关的检查,但不包括执法部管辖权范围内的执法和相关活动。

(a)负责实施《1940年投资公司法》(《美国法典》第十五编第80a节)下产生的所有事项,但因该法第30(h)条[《美国法典》第十五编第80a-29(h)节]产生的事项除外;

(b)因《1933年证券法》(《美国法典》第十五编第77a节及其后条文)产生,并因依《1940年投资公司法》(《美国法典》第十五编第80a-1节及其后条文)注册的投资公司以及集合投资基金或账户根据《1933年证券法》(《美国法典》第十五编第77a节及其后条文)提交的材料引起或与之相关的所有事项。

(c)所有因《1934年证券交易法》(《美国法典》第十五编第78a节及其后条文)引起的事项,但依《1940年投资公司法》注册的投资公司以及集合投资基金或账户根据该法第16(a)条[《美国法典》第十五编第78p(a)节]提交且与以下各项相关的证券受益所有权说明书和所有权变更说明书的审核和处理除外:

(1)根据《1934年证券交易法》第12条(《美国法典》第十五编第78*l*节)进行的证券

including the exemptive provisions of section 12(h) (15 U.S.C. 78*l*(h)).

(2) The examination and processing of periodic reports filed pursuant to sections 13 and 15(d) of the Act (15 U.S.C. 78m, 78*o*(d)).

(3) The examination and processing of proxy soliciting material filed pursuant to section 14(a) and information material filed pursuant to section 14(c) of the Act (15 U.S.C. 78n(a), 78n(c)).

(d) All matters pertaining to investment companies registered under the Investment Company Act of 1940 and pooled investment funds or accounts arising under the Trust Indenture Act of 1939 (15 U.S.C. 77aaa *et seq.*).

(e) All matters arising under the Investment Advisers Act of 1940 (15 U.S.C. 80b–1 *et seq.*).

(f) The administration and execution of the Public Utility Holding Company Act of 1935 in connection with:

(1) The administration and processing of proxy solicitation material subject to §§240.14a–1—240.14a–14 of this chapter.

(2) The examination and processing of ownership reports filed under section 17(a) of the Act (15 U.S.C. 79q(a)).

[41 FR 29375, July 16, 1976, as amended at 50 FR 5064, Feb. 5, 1985; 60 FR 14626, Mar. 20, 1995; 67 FR 43535, July 8, 2002]

§200.20c Office of Filings and Information Services.

The Office of Filings and Information Services is responsible for the receipt and initial handling of all public documents filed at the Commission's headquarters office. The initial handling includes determining acceptability, extracting data for EDP input, calculating fees, conducting cursory and substantive examinations, assigning filings to branches and preparing deficiency correspondence. In addition, the Office is responsible for the custody and control of the Commission's official records; for the development of plans and implementation of the Commission's records management program; for authenticating all documents produced for administrative or judicial proceedings; for maintaining liaison with the National Archives and Records Service and other Government agencies with respect to the Commission's records and its records management program. The Office provides filer–support services relating to the Commission's EDGAR system and the receipt of fees and filings for all types of filers, regardless of filing media. The Office also manages the Commission's public reference facilities to facilitate public access to electronic filings and ensure that all information contained in public filings with the Commission is timely made available to investors.

(Sec. 4(b), 48 Stat. 885, sec. 1106(a), 63 Stat. 972, 15 U.S.C. 78d(b); secs. 1, 2,

注册，包括根据第12(h)条[《美国法典》第十五编第78*l*(h)节]豁免条款进行的证券注册；

(2)根据该法第13条和第15(d)条[《美国法典》第十五编第78m节、第78*o*(d)节]提交的定期报告之审核和处理；

(3)根据该法第14(a)条提交的代理权征集材料以及根据该法第14(c)条[《美国法典》第十五编第78n(a)节、第78n(c)节]提交的信息材料之审核和处理；

(d)与依《1940年投资公司法》注册的投资公司相关的所有事项，以及与《1939年信托契约法》(《美国法典》第十五编第77aaa节及其后条文)中的集合投资基金或账户相关的所有事项；

(e)《1940年投资顾问法》(《美国法典》第十五编第80b-1节及其后条文)下产生的所有事项；

(f)与下述各项相关的《1935年公用事业控股公司法》之实施和执行：

(1)在符合本章第240.14a-1~240.14a-14节的前提下对代理权征集材料的管理和处理；

(2)根据该法第17(a)条[《美国法典》第十五编第79q(a)节]提交的所有权报告之审核和处理。

[《联邦公报》第41卷第29375页，1976年7月16日，修正索引：《联邦公报》第50卷第5064页，1985年2月5日；《联邦公报》第60卷第14626页，1995年3月20日；《联邦公报》第67卷第43535页，2002年7月8日。]

第200.20c节　文件提交和信息服务办公室

文件提交和信息服务办公室负责接收申请人向证券交易委员会总部提交的公开文件并进行初步处理。初步处理包括确定文件是否可以接受、为EDP(电子数据处理)的输入进行数据提取、计算费用、进行表面和实质审核、将提交的文件转给相关分支机构并起草缺陷告知信件。此外，该办公室还负责：保管、控制证券交易委员会的官方记录；制订计划、实施证券交易委员会的记录管理项目；认证为行政或司法程序制作的所有文件；针对证券交易委员会的记录及记录管理计划，维持与国家档案和记录服务处及其他政府机构之间的联系。文件提交和信息服务办公室提供与证券交易委员会EDGAR系统相关的文件提交人支持服务；还负责接收各类文件提交人缴纳的费用和提交的材料(不论是通过何种媒介提交的)。该办公室也负责管理证券交易委员会的公共资料设施，以便公众访问电子文档，并确保及时向投资者提供向证券交易委员会提交的公开材料中的全部信息。

[《美国制定法汇编》第48卷第885页第4(b)条，《美国制定法汇编》第63卷第972页

76 Stat. 394, 395, 15 U.S.C. 78d-1, 78d-2; secs. 19, 48 Stat. 85, 908, 15 U.S.C. 77s; sec. 23(a), 48 Stat. 901, sec. 8, 49 Stat. 1379, 15 U.S.C. 78w(a); sec. 20, 49 Stat. 833, 15 U.S.C. 78t; sec. 319, 53 Stat. 1173, 15 U.S.C. 77sss; sec. 38, 54 Stat. 841, 15 U.S.C. 80a-37; sec. 211, 54 Stat. 855, sec. 14, 74 Stat. 888, 15 U.S.C. 80b-11; sec. 15B, 15 U.S.C. 78o-4(a); sec. 17A, 15 U.S.C. 78q-1(c)(2); 11 U.S.C. 901, 1109(a))

[43 FR 13376, Mar. 30, 1978, as amended at 49 FR 12685, Mar. 30, 1984; 60 FR 14626, Mar. 20, 1995]

§200.21 The General Counsel.

(a) The General Counsel is the chief legal officer of the Commission. He or she is responsible for the representation of the Commission in judicial proceedings in which it is involved as a party or as amicus curiae, for directing and supervising all civil litigation involving the Commission in the United States District Courts, except for law enforcement actions filed on behalf of the Commission, for directing and supervising the Commission's responsibilities under the Bankruptcy Code and all related litigation, and for representing the Commission in all cases in appellate courts. The General Counsel is responsible for the review of cases which the Division of Enforcement recommends be referred to the Department of Justice with a recommendation for criminal prosecution. In addition, he or she is responsible for advising the Commission at its request or at the request of any division director or office head, or on his or her own motion, with respect to interpretations involving questions of law; for the conduct of administrative proceedings relating to the disqualification of lawyers from practice before the Commission; for conducting preliminary investigations, as described in 17 CFR 202.5(a), into potential violations of 17 CFR 201.102(e) by attorneys; for the preparation of the Commission comments to the Congress on pending legislation; and for the drafting, in conjunction with appropriate divisions and offices, of legislative proposals to be sponsored by the Commission. The General Counsel is also responsible for the review and clearance of the form and content of articles, treatises, and prepared speeches and addresses by members of the staff relating to the Commission or to the statutes and rules administered by the Commission. He or she is responsible (with the Associate Executive Director of the Office of Administrative and Personnel Management) for administering the Commission's Ethics Program, and (with the Ethics Counsel) for interpreting subpart M of this part and 5 CFR part 2635. He or she serves as Counselor to the Commission and its staff with regard to

第1106(a)条,《美国法典》第十五编第78d(b)节;《美国制定法汇编》第76卷第394页、第395页第1条、第2条,《美国法典》第十五编第78d-1节、第78d-2节;《美国制定法汇编》第48卷第85页、第908页第19条,《美国法典》第十五编第77s节;《美国制定法汇编》第48卷第901页第23(a)条,《美国制定法汇编》第49卷第1379页第8条,《美国法典》第十五编第78w(a)节;《美国制定法汇编》第49卷第833页第20条,《美国法典》第十五编第78t节;《美国制定法汇编》第53卷第1173页第319条,《美国法典》第十五编第77sss节;《美国制定法汇编》第54卷第841页第38条,《美国法典》第十五编第80a-37节;《美国制定法汇编》第54卷第855页第211条,《美国制定法汇编》第74卷第888页第14条,《美国法典》第十五编第80b-11节;《美国法典》第十五编第78o-4(a)节第15B条;《美国法典》第十五编第78q-1(c)(2)节第17A条;《美国法典》第十一编第901节、第1109(a)节]

[《联邦公报》第43卷第13376页,1978年3月30日,修正索引:《联邦公报》第49卷第12685页,1984年3月30日;《联邦公报》第60卷第14626页,1995年3月20日。]

第200.21节　首席律师

(a)首席律师属于证券交易委员会的首席法务官,在证券交易委员会以当事人或法庭之友身份参与的司法程序中负责代表证券交易委员会;指导和监督在联邦地区法院中开展的涉及证券交易委员会的所有民事诉讼(代表证券交易委员会提起的执法诉讼除外);指导和监督证券交易委员会在《破产法典》项下承担的责任及所有相关诉讼;在所有上诉法院案件中代表证券交易委员会。首席律师负责审查执法部建议提交司法部进行刑事追诉的案件。此外,首席律师还负责:经证券交易委员会或证券交易委员会任何部门主任、办公室主任提出要求,或主动提出动议,向证券交易委员会提出建议,协助证券交易委员会对法律问题进行解释;开展关于取消律师出席证券交易委员会程序并办理业务的资格的行政处理程序;开展《联邦规章汇编》第十七编第202.5(a)节所述初步调查,以查明律师是否存在违反《联邦规章汇编》第十七编第201.102(e)节规定的情形;就审议中的立法向国会提交证券交易委员会的意见;与相关部门和办公室共同起草证券交易委员会的立法提案。首席律师还负责审查、许可与证券交易委员会或证券交易委员会实施的制定法和规则相关的文章、论文、演讲稿和发言稿的格式及内容,与行政和人事管理办公室的副执行主任共同负责执行证券交易委员会的职业道德项目,并与职业道德顾问共同解释本部分第M子部分以及《联邦规章汇编》第五编第2635部分的规定。首席律师应就职业道德和利益冲突问题担任证券交易委员会及其员工的顾问,并就该等事项充当证券交易委员会与行政和人事管理办公室、监察长办公室和司法部之间的联络人。首席律师还负责协调、审查各部门和办公室的解释权限。此外,首席律师还负责根据本章第200.30-14节授予的权限适当地处理根据《信息自由法》和《隐私法》提起的所有行政复议申请,并就因《信息自由法》、《隐私法》、《联邦报告法》、《联邦顾问委员会法》、公务员法律和规章以及适用于证券交易委员会采购、合同签署、税务和相关管理活动的制定法和规则引起的法律问题以及性质类似的普遍适用于政府机构的其他制定法和规章引起的法律问题,充当证券交易委员会的顾问。

ethical and conflicts of interest questions and acts as the Commission's liaison on such matters with the Office of Administrative and Personnel Management, the Office of the Inspector General and the Department of Justice. The General Counsel also is responsible for coordinating and reviewing the interpretive positions of the various divisions and offices. In addition, he or she is responsible for appropriate disposition of all Freedom of Information Act and Privacy Act appeals pursuant to the authority delegated in §200.30-14 of this chapter, and is the Commission's advisor with respect to legal problems arising under the Freedom of Information Act, the Privacy Act, the Federal Reports Act, the Federal Advisory Committee Act, the Civil Service laws and regulations, the statutes and rules applicable to the Commission's procurement, contracting, fiscal and related administrative activities, and other statutes and regulations of a similar nature applicable to a number of Government agencies.

(b) The General Counsel is also responsible for assisting members of the Commission in the preparation of the opinions of the Commission, and to the Commission for the preparation of opinions and decisions on motions and certifications of questions and rulings by administrative law judges in the course of administrative law proceedings, except (1) in cases where, pursuant to a waiver by the parties of separation of function requirements, another Division or Office of the Commission's staff undertakes to prepare an opinion or decision, in which cases the General Counsel may assist in such preparation, and (2) with respect to administrative proceedings against lawyers under Rule 102(e) of the Commission's Rules of Practice (§201.102(e) of this chapter) or other cases in which the Chairman or the General Counsel has determined that separation of function requirements or other circumstances would make inappropriate the exercise of such functions by the General Counsel. In the cases described in clause (2), the Executive Assistant to the Chairman exercises such functions. The General Counsel deals with general problems arising under the Administrative Procedure Act, including the revision or adoption of rules of practice. The General Counsel is also responsible for the exercise of such review functions with respect to adjudicatory matters as are delegated to him or her by the Commission pursuant to 101 Stat. 1254 (15 U.S.C. 78d-1, 78d-2) or as may be otherwise delegated or assigned to him or her.

(c) The General Counsel also is responsible to the Commission for the administration of the Government in the Sunshine Act for publicly certifying, pursuant to §200.406, that, in his or her opinion, particular Commission meetings may properly be closed to the public. In the absence of the General Counsel, the Solicitor to the Commission shall be deemed the General Counsel for purposes of §200.406. In the absence of the General Counsel and the Solicitor, the most senior Associate General Counsel available shall be deemed the General Counsel for purposes of §200.406. In the absence of the General

(b)首席律师还负责协助证券交易委员会委员制定证券交易委员会意见,并就行政法官在行政法处理程序中对动议的裁定、对问题的认定及作出的裁决对证券交易委员会负责,但下列情形除外:(1)当事人放弃职能分离要求,因而由证券交易委员会的其他部门或办公室的员工来承担该等制定意见或作出裁定的职责,不过首席律师在此种情况下亦可为上述工作人员提供相关协助;(2)根据《证券交易委员会工作规则》的《102(e)规则》[本章第201.102(e)节]下针对律师提起的行政处理程序;或证券交易委员会主席或首席律师判定由于职能分离要求或其他情形令首席律师不宜行使上述职能。在第(2)项所述情形下,应由主席执行助理行使上述职能。首席律师负责处理《行政程序法》下产生的一般性问题,包括工作规则的修正或通过。首席律师还应负责就证券交易委员会根据《美国制定法汇编》第101卷第1254页(《美国法典》第十五编第78d-1节、第78d-2节)授权其裁决的事项或在其他情况下授权或交由其裁决的事项行使上述审查职能。

(c)首席律师还将代表政府执行《阳光法》的以下工作:根据第200.406节公开认证,其任务,特定证券交易委员会会议可以适当地不向公众开放,并就此向证券交易委员会负责。就第200.406节而言,如首席律师无法履职,证券交易委员会的事务律师应被视为首席律师。就第200.406节而言,如首席律师和事务律师无法履职,在场的最高级的副首席律师应被视为首席律师。就第200.406节而言,如首席律师、事务律师和所有副首席律师均不在场,在场的最高级的助理首席律师应被视为首席律师。如首席律师、事务律师、所有副首席律师和所有助理首席律师均不在场,则应由首席律师指

Counsel, the Solicitor, and every Associate General Counsel, the most senior Assistant General Counsel available shall be deemed the General Counsel for purposes of §200.406. In the absence of the General Counsel, the Solicitor, every Associate General Counsel and every Assistant General Counsel, such attorneys as the General Counsel may designate (in such order of succession as the General Counsel directs) shall exercise the responsibilities imposed by §200.406.

[43 FR 13376, Mar. 30, 1978, as amended at 47 FR 26821, June 22, 1982; 47 FR 37077, Aug. 25, 1982; 49 FR 12685, Mar. 30, 1984; 49 FR 13866, Apr. 9, 1984; 50 FR 12240, Mar. 28, 1985; 54 FR 18100, Apr. 27, 1989; 54 FR 24331, June 7, 1989; 60 FR 14626, Mar. 20, 1995; 69 FR 13174, Mar. 19, 2004; 71 FR 27385, May 11, 2006]

§200.21a The Ethics Counsel.

(a) The Ethics Counsel within the Office of the General Counsel of the Commission shall oversee compliance with subpart M of this part and 5 CFR part 2635. When appropriate and subject to the authority of, and in consultation with, the Inspector General, the Ethics Counsel shall inquire into alleged violations of subparts C, F, and M of this part, and 5 CFR part 2635.

(b) Subject to the oversight of the General Counsel or his or her delegate, the Ethics Counsel shall:

(1) Receive and review allegations of misconduct by a Commission employee.

(2) Refer matters involving management questions to Division Directors, Office Heads, or Regional Directors, and matters involving alleged or apparent employee misconduct to the Office of the Inspector General, except for matters involving alleged professional misconduct ultimately referable to state professional boards or societies.

(3) Refer complaints that appear to involve a violation of Federal criminal statutes, and do not appear to be frivolous, to the Inspector General for referral to the Department of Justice under 28 U.S.C. 535.

(4) Act as liaison with the Office of the Inspector General on matters that the Ethics Counsel has referred to that Office, and with state or local authorities on matters that, on occasion, the Ethics Counsel may refer to them.

(5) Arrange for the review of proposed publications and prepared speeches under §200.735-4(e).

(6) Provide advice, counseling, interpretations, and opinions with respect to subparts C, F, and M of this part, and 5 CFR part 2635.

(7) Oversee investigations and refer findings of professional misconduct to state

定的律师(次序由首席律师确定)行使第200.406节规定的职责。

[《联邦公报》第43卷第13376页,1978年3月30日,修正索引:《联邦公报》第47卷第26821页,1982年6月22日;《联邦公报》第47卷第37077页,1982年8月25日;《联邦公报》第49卷第12685页,1984年3月30日;《联邦公报》第49卷第13866页,1984年4月9日;《联邦公报》第50卷第12240页,1985年3月28日;《联邦公报》第54卷第18100页,1989年4月27日;《联邦公报》第54卷第24331页,1989年6月7日;《联邦公报》第60卷第14626页,1995年3月20日;《联邦公报》第69卷第13174页,2004年3月19日;《联邦公报》第71卷第27385页,2006年5月11日。]

第200.21a节　职业道德顾问

(a)道德顾问隶属于证券交易委员会首席律师办公室,负责监督本部分第M子部分及《联邦规章汇编》第五编第2635部分的遵守。在适当情形下,经首席律师授权并与监察长磋商后,道德顾问应调查涉嫌违反本部分第C子部分、第F子部分和第M子部分及《联邦规章汇编》第五编第2635部分的情形。

(b)道德顾问应在首席律师或其授权人员的监督下:

(1)受理并审查关于证券交易委员会员工不当行为的指控;

(2)将涉及管理问题的事项移送部门主任、办公室主任或地区办公室主任;将被指控或表面的员工不当行为移送监察长办公室,但涉及职业不当行为指控且最终应移送州专业理事会或专业协会处理的事项除外;

(3)将初步判断涉及违反联邦刑事法且不属于情节轻微的指控提交监察长,由后者根据《美国法典》第二十八编第535节移送司法部处理;

(4)在其移送监察长办公室的事项中担任与该办公室的联络人,在其移送州或地方机构的事项中担任与该等机构的联络人;

(5)对于在第200.735-4(e)节下拟进行的信息发布和演讲稿,安排审查;

(6)就本部分第C子部分、第F子部分和第M子部分及《联邦规章汇编》第五编第2635部分提供咨询、建议、解释和意见;

(7)监督对职业不当行为的调查,并将调查认定结果移送州专业理事会或专业协

professional boards or societies.

(8) Draft rules and regulations as necessary to implement the Commission's Ethics Program.

[60 FR 14626, Mar. 20, 1995, as amended at 73 FR 32224, June 5, 2008]

§200.22 The Chief Accountant.

The Chief Accountant of the Commission is the principal adviser to the Commission on, and is responsible to the Commission for, all accounting and auditing matters arising in the administration of the federal securities laws. The Chief Accountant oversees the accounting profession's standard-setting and self-regulatory organizations, develops or supervises the development of accounting and auditing rules, regulations, opinions and policy, and interprets Commission accounting policy and positions. The Chief Accountant is responsible for recommending the institution of administrative and disciplinary proceedings relating to the disqualification of accountants to practice before the Commission. The Chief Accountant supervises the procedures to be followed in the Commission's enforcement activities involving accounting and auditing issues and helps resolve differences on accounting issues between registrants and the Commission staff.

[60 FR 14626, Mar. 20, 1995]

§200.23a Office of Economic Analysis.

The Office of Economic Analysis is responsible for providing an objective economic perspective to understand and evaluate the economic dimension of the Commission's regulatory oversight. It performs economic analyses of proposed rule changes, current or proposed policies, and capital market developments and offers advice on the basis of these analyses. The Office also assists the Commission's enforcement effort by applying economic analysis and statistical tools to issues raised in enforcement cases. It reviews certifications and initial and final regulatory flexibility analyses prepared by the operating divisions under the Regulatory Flexibility Act.

[60 FR 14627, Mar. 20, 1995]

§200.23b [Reserved]

§200.24 Office of the Comptroller.

This Office, under the direction of the Associate Executive Director of the Office of the Comptroller, is responsible to the Executive Director, Chairman and Commission for the internal financial management and programming functions of the Securities and Exchange Commission. These functions include: budgeting, accounting, payroll and adminstrative audit. The Associate Executive Director of the Office of the Comptroller, and his or her designees, serve as liaison to the Commission before the Office of Management and Budget and Congressional Appropriations Committees on appropriation

会处理;

(8)起草实施证券交易委员会道德项目所必要的规则与规章。

[《联邦公报》第60卷第14626页,1995年3月20日,修正索引:《联邦公报》第73卷第32224页,2008年6月5日。]

第200.22节 首席会计师

对于实施联邦证券法中产生的所有会计和审计问题,证券交易委员会的首席会计师是证券交易委员会的首席顾问,并就该等事项对证券交易委员会负责。首席会计师负责监督会计行业的标准设定、监督自律组织;制定或监督制定会计和审计规则、规章、意见和政策;并负责解释证券交易委员会的会计政策和立场。取消会计师与证券交易委员会办理业务资格的行政和处罚程序,由首席会计师建议发起。首席会计师监督证券交易委员会开展涉及会计审计事项的执法活动时所应遵守的程序,并协助解决注册人和证券交易委员会员工之间对会计问题产生的分歧。

[《联邦公报》第60卷第14626页,1995年3月20日。]

第200.23a节 经济分析办公室

经济分析办公室负责提供客观的经济观点,以利于理解和评估证券交易委员会监管工作的经济层面问题。该办公室对规则变更提案、当前政策或政策提案及资本市场发展动态进行经济分析,并基于上述分析提出建议。它还负责通过对执法中遇到的问题进行经济分析和统计工具分析,协助证券交易委员会开展执法工作。此外,《监管弹性法》下各运营部门作出的认证及进行的初步和最终监管弹性分析亦由该办公室进行审核。

[《联邦公报》第60卷第14627页,1995年3月20日。]

第200.23b节 [保留]

第200.24节 审计办公室

审计办公室由审计办公室副执行主任领导,就证券交易委员会的内部财务管理和项目规划职能向证券交易委员会执行主任、主席和证券交易委员会负责。这些职能具体包括:预算、会计、薪资单和行政审计。审计办公室的副执行主任及其指定人员,在拨款事项上充当证券交易委员会与行政管理和预算局以及国会拨款委员会之间的联络人,在财务和项目规划事项上充当证券交易委员会与财务部和总审计局的联络人。

matters, and the Treasury Department and the General Accounting Office on financial and progamming matters.

(11 U.S.C. 901, 1109(a))

[49 FR 12685, Mar. 30, 1984, as amended at 60 FR 14627, Mar. 20, 1995]

§200.24a Director of the Office of Consumer Affairs.

The Director of the Office of Consumer Affairs is responsible to the Chairman for the Commission's investor education and consumer protection program. The program includes, but is not limited to:

(a) Presenting seminars and instructional programs to educate investors about the securities markets and their rights as investors; preparing and distributing to the public materials describing the operations of the securities markets, prudent investor behavior, and the rights of investors in disputes they may have with individuals and entities regulated by the Commission; and increasing public knowledge of the functions of the Commission.

(b) Implementing and administering a nationwide system for resolving investor complaints against individuals and entities regulated by the Commission by processing complaints received from individual investors and assuring that regulated individual and entities process and respond to such complaints.

(c) Providing information to investors who inquire about individuals and entities regulated by the Commission, the operation of the securities markets, or the functions of the Commission.

(d) Advising the Commission and its staff about problems frequently encountered by investors and possible solutions to them.

(e) Transmitting to other offices and divisions of the Commission information provided by investors which concerns the responsibilities of these offices and divisions.

(f) Providing for greater consumer input in Commission rulemaking proceedings.

[60 FR 14627, Mar. 20, 1995]

§200.25 Office of Administrative and Personnel Management.

(a) The Office of Administrative and Personnel Management (OAPM) is responsible for providing a wide variety of programs for human resources, office services, and other administrative and management services for the Commission. The Associate Executive Director of the Office of Administrative and Personnel Management is responsible to the Executive Director and the Chairman of the Commission for developing and executing these programs.

(b) OAPM develops, implements, and evaluates the Commission's programs for human resources and personnel management, such as position management and pay

[《美国法典》第十一编第901节、第1109(a)节。]

[《联邦公报》第49卷第12685页,1984年3月30日,修正索引:《联邦公报》第60卷第14627页,1995年3月20日。]

第200.24a节　消费者事务办公室主任

消费者事务办公室主任就证券交易委员会的投资者教育和消费者保护项目向证券交易委员会主席负责。该项目包括但不限于:

(a)主办研讨会和培训项目,就证券市场及投资者权利向投资者提供教育;编制并向公众发送材料,介绍证券市场的运作、谨慎的投资者行为、投资者与受证券交易委员会监管的个人和实体产生争议时其可能享有的权利;向公众普及关于证券交易委员会职能的知识;

(b)实施并执行全国性的制度,受理个人投资者针对受证券交易委员会监管的个人和实体提起的投诉并确保该等受监管的个人和实体对此进行处理和答复,以解决该等投诉;

(c)向提出咨询的投资者提供关于受证券交易委员会监管的个人和实体的信息以及关于证券市场运作或证券交易委员会职能的信息;

(d)就投资者经常遇到的问题向证券交易委员会及其工作人员提供咨询,并就可能的解决方案提出建议;

(e)将投资者提供的与证券交易委员会其他办公室和部门职责相关的信息传递给该等办公室和部门;

(f)加强消费者在证监会规则制定程序中的作用。

[《联邦公报》第60卷第14627页,1995年3月20日。]

第200.25节　行政和人事管理办公室

(a)行政和人事管理办公室(OAPM)负责向证券交易委员会提供各类人力资源项目、办公服务和其他行政及管理服务;行政和人事管理办公室的副执行主任应就上述项目的开发和实施向证券交易委员会的执行主任和主席负责。

(b)该办公室负责开发、实施和评估证券交易委员会的人力资源和人力管理项目,如职位管理和工资管理;招聘、职位分派和人员配置;绩效管理和员工表扬;员工

administration; recruitment, placement, and staffing; performance management and employee recognition; employee training and career development; employee and labor relations; personnel management evaluation; employee benefits and counseling; and the processing and maintenance of employee records. OAPM administers the Ethics Program, and helps the Office of the Executive Director manage the Senior Executive Service Program. It reviews requests, recommendations, and justifications for certain awards, recruitment and relocation bonuses, retention allowances, special salary rates, and other personnel compensation or benefit determinations for sufficiency and compliance with law, regulations, and Commission policy. OAPM develops and executes programs for office services, such as telecommunications; procurement and contracting; property management; contract and lease administration; space acquisition and management; management of official vehicles; safety programs; emergency preparedness plans; physical security; mail receipt and distribution; and publications, printing, and desktop publishing.

(c) With respect to human resources management, the Associate Executive Director of the Office of Administrative and Personnel Management is the Commission's liaison with the Office of Personnel Management, other agencies, professional organizations, educational institutions, and private industry. He or she is also the Printing Liaison with the Joint Committee on Printing, and the Contract Officer.

[60 FR 14627, Mar. 20, 1995]

§200.26 [Reserved]

§200.26a Office of Information Technology.

The Office of Information Technology is responsible for the analysis, design programming, operation, and maintenance of all ADP systems; developing and implementing long-range ADP plans and programs; coordinating all ADP and systems analysis activities being considered or carried out by other divisions and offices, and furnishing such organizations with appropriate assistance and support; providing technical advice to the staff in connection with development of Commission rules and regulations having ADP implications; facilitating the Commission's surveillance of ADP in the securities industry; evaluating and recommending new information processing concepts and capabilities for application within the Commission; and, development of microcomputer and office automation capabilities and support within the Commission.

(15 U.S.C. 78d-1, 78d-2; 11 U.S.C. 901, 1109(a))

[43 FR 13377, Mar. 30, 1978, as amended at 49 FR 12685, Mar. 30, 1984; 60 FR 14627, Mar. 20, 1995]

§200.27 The Regional Directors.

Each Regional Director is responsible for executing the Commission's programs within his or her geographic region as set forth in §200.11(b), subject to review, on

培训和职业生涯发展;员工和劳动关系;人事管理评估;员工福利和咨询;员工记录处理和维护。行政和人事管理办公室负责执行职业道德项目,并协助证券交易委员会执行主任办公室管理高级管理人员服务项目。它负责审查某些奖励的申请、建议和授予的理由,招聘和安置费、留任津贴、特殊工资费率及其他关于人员报酬或福利的决定,以确认其是否充分以及是否符合法律、规章和证券交易委员会的政策。该办公室还负责制定和执行办公服务项目,如电信、采购和缔约、财产管理、合同和租约管理、空间购买和管理、公务车管理、安全项目、应急准备计划、物理安全、邮件接收和分发、出版、印刷和桌面出版。

(c)就人力资源管理而言,行政和人事管理办公室的副执行主任是证券交易委员会与人事管理局、其他政府机构、行业组织、教育机构和私有行业之间的联络人,还是印刷联合委员会的印刷联络人及合同官。

[《联邦公报》第60卷第14627页,1995年3月20日。]

第200.26节 [保留]

第200.26a节 信息技术办公室

信息技术办公室负责:所有ADP(自动数据处理)系统的分析、设计软件开发、运营和维护;开发和实施长期ADP计划和项目;协调其他部门和办公室正在审议或开展的所有ADP和系统分析活动,并为之提供适当协助和支持;就制定涉及ADP的证券交易委员会规则与规章向工作人员提供技术咨询;为证券交易委员会对证券业的ADP监督提供方便;评估新的信息处理理念和能力,并推荐其在证监会内部的应用;强化证券交易委员会内部的微机和办公室自动化能力与支持。

[《美国法典》第十五编第78d-1节、第78d-2节;《美国法典》第十一编第901节、第1109(a)节]

[《联邦公报》第43卷第13377页,1978年3月30日,修正索引:《联邦公报》第49卷第12685页,1984年3月30日;《联邦公报》第60卷第14627页,1995年3月20日。]

第200.27节 地区办公室主任

各地区办公室主任按第200.11(b)节规定,在其各自地理管辖区域内负责执行证券交易委员会项目;对于执法事项,地区办公室主任应接受负责地区执法事项的执法

enforcement matters, by the Deputy Director of the Division of Enforcement who is responsible for Regional Office enforcement matters and, on examination matters, by the Director of the Office of Compliance Inspections and Examinations, and subject to policy direction and review by the other Division Directors, the General Counsel, and the Chief Accountant. The Regional Directors' responsibilities include particularly the investigation of transactions in securities on national securities exchanges, in the over-the-counter market, and in distribution to the public; the examination of members of national securities exchanges and registered brokers and dealers, transfer agents, investment advisers and investment companies, including the examination of reports filed under §240.17a-5 of this chapter; the prosecution of injunctive actions in U.S. District Courts and administrative proceedings before Administrative Law Judges; the rendering of assistance to U.S. Attorneys in criminal cases; and the making of the Commission's facilities more readily available to the public in that area. In addition, the Regional Director of the New York Regional Office is responsible for the Commission's participation in cases under chapters 9 and 11 of the Bankruptcy Code in Connecticut, Maine, Massachusetts, New Hampshire, New Jersey, New York, Pennsylvania, Rhode Island, and Vermont; the Regional Director of the Atlanta Regional Office is responsible for such participation in Alabama, Delaware, District of Columbia, Florida, Georgia, Louisiana, Maryland, Mississippi, North Carolina, Puerto Rico, South Carolina, Tennessee, Virgin Islands, Virginia, and West Virginia; the Regional Director of the Chicago Regional Office is responsible for such participation in Arkansas, Colorado, Illinois, Indiana, Iowa, Kansas, Kentucky, Michigan, Minnesota, Missouri, Nebraska, New Mexico, North Dakota, Ohio, Oklahoma, South Dakota, Texas, Wisconsin, and Wyoming; and the Regional Director of the Los Angeles Regional Office is responsible for such participation in Alaska, Arizona, California, Guam, Hawaii, Idaho, Montana, Nevada, Oregon, Utah, and Washington.

[73 FR 32224, June 5, 2008]

§200.28 Issuance of instructions.

(a) Within the spheres of responsibilities heretofore set forth, Division and Office Heads, and all Regional Directors may issue such definitive instructions as may be necessary pursuant to this section.

(b) All existing procedures and authorizations not inconsistent with this section shall continue in effect until and unless modified by definitive instructions issued pursuant to this paragraph.

[27 FR 12712, Dec. 22, 1962, as amended at 73 FR 32224, June 5, 2008]

§200.29 Rules.

The individual operating divisions shall have the initial responsibility for proposing amendments to existing rules or new rules under the statutory provisions within the

部副主任的审查,对于核查事项,应接受合规检查和核查办公室主任的审查并且接受其他部门主任、首席律师和首席会计师的政策指导和审查。地区办公室主任的核心责任包括:对全国性证券交易所、场外市场上的证券及向公众分销的证券之交易开展调查;审核全国性证券交易所会员、注册经纪商和自营商、过户代理人、投资顾问和投资公司,包括审核按本章第240.17a-5节提交的报告;在联邦地区法院提起禁令诉讼,向行政法官提起行政处理程序;在刑事案件中向联邦检察官提供协助;使公众能更便利地在该领域获得证券交易委员会的服务。此外,纽约地区办公室主任负责代表证券交易委员会参与在康涅狄格州、缅因州、马萨诸塞州、新罕布什尔州、新泽西州、纽约州、宾夕法尼亚州、罗德岛州和佛蒙特州根据《破产法典》第九章和第十一章提起的案件;亚特兰大地区办公室主任负责参与在阿拉巴马州、特拉华州、哥伦比亚特区、佛罗里达州、佐治亚州、路易斯安那州、马里兰州、密西西比州、北卡罗来纳州、波多黎各州、南卡罗来纳州、田纳西州、维尔京群岛、弗吉尼亚州和西弗吉尼亚州提起的该类案件;芝加哥地区办公室主任负责参与在阿肯色州、科罗拉多州、伊利诺伊州、印第安那州、爱荷华州、堪萨斯州、肯塔基州、密歇根州、明尼斯达州、密苏里州、内布拉斯州、新墨西哥州、北达科他州、俄亥俄州、俄克拉荷马州、南达科他州、得克萨斯州、威斯康星州和怀俄明州提起的该类案件;洛杉矶地区办公室主任负责在阿拉斯加州、亚利桑那州、加利福尼亚州、关岛、夏威夷、爱达荷州、蒙大拿州、内华达州、俄勒冈州、犹他州和华盛顿提起的该类案件。

[《联邦公报》第73卷第32224页,2008年6月5日。]

第200.28节　指示的发布

(a)在前文所述的责任范围内,证券交易委员会各部门主任和办公室主任以及所有地区办公室主任可以根据本节规定签发必要的正式指示。

(b)所有不与本节规定冲突的现有程序和授权均应继续有效,直至且除非被根据本款签发的正式指示修改。

[《联邦公报》第27卷第12712页,1962年12月22日,修正索引:《联邦公报》第73卷第32224页,2008年6月5日。]

第200.29节　规则

对于依据各个部门管辖权范围内的制定法条文颁布的现有规则或新规则,各部

jurisdiction of the particular division. Where any such proposals presents a legal problem or is a matter of first impression, or involves a matter of enforcement policy or questions involving statutes other than those administered by the Commission, or may have an effect on prior judicial precedent or pending litigation, submission of the proposal should be made to the Office of the General Counsel for an expression of opinion prior to presentation of the matter to the Commission.

§200.30-1 Delegation of authority to Director of Division of Corporation Finance.

Pursuant to the provisions of Pub. L., No. 87-592, 76 Stat. 394 (15 U.S.C. 78d-1, 78d-2), the Securities and Exchange Commission hereby delegates, until the Commission orders otherwise, the following functions to the Director of the Division of Corporation Finance, to be performed by him or under his direction by such person or persons as may be designated from time to time by the Chairman of the Commission:

(a) With respect to registration of securities pursuant to the Securities Act of 1933 (15 U.S.C. 77a *et seq.*), and Regulation C thereunder (§230.400 *et seq.* of this chapter):

(1) To determine the effective dates of amendments to registration statements filed pursuant to section 8(c) of the Act (15 U.S.C. 77h(c)).

(2) To consent to the withdrawal of registration statements or amendments or exhibits thereto, pursuant to Rule 477 (§230.477 of this chapter), and to issue orders declaring registration statements abandoned, pursuant to Rule 479 (§230.479 of this chapter).

(3) To grant applications for confidential treatment of contract provisions pursuant to Rule 406 (§230.406 of this chapter) under the Act; to issue orders scheduling hearings on such applications and to deny any such application as to which the applicant waives his right to a hearing, provided such applicant is advised of his right to have such denial reviewed by the Commission.

(4) To accelerate the use or publication of any summary prospectus filed with the Commission pursuant to section 10(b) of the Act (15 U.S.C. 77j(b)) and Rule 431(g) (§230.431(g) of this chapter) thereunder.

(5) To take the following action pursuant to section 8(a) of the Act (15 U.S.C. 77h (a)):

(i) To determine registration statements to be effective within shorter periods of time than 20 days after the filing thereof;

(ii) To consent to the filing of amendments prior to the effective dates of registration statements as part thereof, or to determine that amendments filed prior to the effective dates of registration statements have been filed pursuant to orders of the Commission, so

门有提出修正提案的初始责任。如任一该等修正提案提出了法律问题或无先例可循的问题，或涉及执法政策事项，或涉及证券交易委员会负责实施的制定法之外的法律，或可能对司法先例或未决诉讼产生影响，则应在提交证券交易委员会之前先提交首席律师办公室要求其发表意见。

第200.30-1节　对公司融资部主任的委托授权

根据公法编号87-592《美国制定法汇编》第76卷第394页开始（《美国法典》第十五编第78d-1节、第78d-2节）的条文，证券交易委员会兹将下述职能委托公司融资部主任行使，或委托证券交易委员会主席随时指定的其他人员在公司融资部主任的领导下行使（直至证券交易委员会另行作出命令）：

（a）就根据《1933年证券法》（《美国法典》第十五编第77a节及其后条文）以及依其颁布的《C管理办法》（本章第230.400节及其后条文）进行的证券注册而言：

（1）确定根据该法第8（c）条［《美国法典》第十五编第77h（c）节］提交的注册说明书修正的生效日期；

（2）根据《477规则》（本章第230.477节）同意注册人撤回注册说明书或其修正、附录，并根据《479规则》（本章第230.479节）签发命令宣布注册说明书已被放弃；

（3）根据该法《406规则》（本章第230.406节）核准对合同条款进行保密处理的申请；签发命令安排对该等申请进行听证，并在申请人放弃听证权时驳回申请，但应向申请人告知其有权要求证券交易委员会对该等驳回决定进行复议；

（4）根据该法第10（b）条［《美国法典》第十五编第77j（b）节］以及依其颁布的《431（g）规则》［本章第230.431（g）节］提前使用或公布向证券交易委员会提交的任何简式招募说明书；

（5）根据该法第8（a）条［《美国法典》第十五编第77h（a）节］采取下述行动：

（i）在提交后不到20日的期间内判定注册说明书的有效性；

（ii）同意在注册人在注册说明书生效日之前提交作为注册说明书一部分的修正稿，或判定在生效日之前提交的修正稿系依据证券交易委员会命令发出，因此就该法第8（a）条［《美国法典》第十五编第77h（a）节］而言，应作为注册说明书的一部分予以处理；

as to be treated as parts of the registration statements for the purpose of section 8(a) of the Act (15 U.S.C. 77h(a));

(iii) To determine to be effective applications for qualification of trust indentures filed with registration statements.

(6) Pursuant to instructions as to financial statements contained in forms adopted under the Act:

(i) To permit the omission of one or more financial statements therein required or the filing in substitution therefor of appropriate statements of comparable character, or

(ii) To require the filing of other financial statements in addition to, or in substitution for, the statements therein required.

(7) Acting pursuant to section 4(3) of the Act (15 U.S.C. 77d(3)) or Rule 174 thereunder (§230.174 of this chapter), to reduce the 40-day period or the 90-day period with respect to transactions referred to in section 4(3)(b) of the Act (15 U.S.C. 77d(3)(B)).

(8) To act on applications to dispense with any written consents of an expert pursuant to Rule 437 (§230.437 of this chapter).

(9) To determine whether to object, pursuant to Rule 401(g)(1) (§230.401(g)(1) of this chapter), and to notify issuers, pursuant to Rule 401(g)(2) (§230.401(g)(2) of this chapter), of an objection to the use of an automatic shelf registration as defined in Rule 405 (§230.405 of this chapter) or any post-effective amendment thereto that becomes effective immediately pursuant to Rule 462 (§230.462 of this chapter).

(10) To authorize the granting or denial of applications, upon a showing of good cause, that it is not necessary under the circumstances that the issuer be considered an ineligible issuer as defined in Rule 405.

(b) With respect to the Securities Act of 1933 (15 U.S.C. 77a *et seq.*) and Regulation A thereunder (§230.251 *et seq.* of this chapter):

(1) to authorize the granting of applications under Rule 262 (§230.262 of this chapter) upon a showing of good cause that it is not necessary under the circumstances that an exemption under Regulation A be denied;

(2) to authorize the issuance of orders qualifying offering statements pursuant to Rule 252(g) (§230.252(g) of this chapter); and

(3) to issue orders declaring offering statements withdrawn or abandoned pursuant to Rule 259 (§230.259 of this chapter).

(c) With respect to the Securities Act of 1933 (15 U.S.C. 77a *et seq.*) and Regulation D thereunder (§230.501 *et seq.* of this chapter), to authorize the granting of applications under Rule 505(b)(2)(iii)(C), (§230.505(b)(2)(iii)(C) of this chapter) and under Rule 507(b) (§230.507(b) of this chapter) upon the showing of good cause

(iii)判定与注册说明书同时提交的信托契约资格申请是否有效。

(6)根据在该法下采用的表格中所包含的与财务报表相关的指示:

(i)允许不提交其中要求的一份或多份财务报表,或允许提交具有可比特征的适当报表作为替代;或

(ii)要求在该法要求提交的报表之外提交其他财务报表作为补充或替代。

(7)根据该法第4(3)条[《美国法典》第十五编第77d(3)节]或依其颁布的《174规则》(本章第230.174节),缩短该法第4(3)(b)条[《美国法典》第十五编第77d(3)(B)节]所述交易的40日或90日的期间。

(8)根据《437规则》(本章第230.437节)处理要求豁免专家书面同意的任何申请;

(9)根据《401(g)(1)规则》[本章第230.401(g)(1)节]判定是否拒绝使用《405规则》(本章第230.405节)定义的自动储架注册,或者是否拒绝使用在该自动储架注册生效后提交的任何修正稿[根据《462规则》(本章第230.462节),该等修正将立即生效];并根据《401(g)(2)规则》[本章第230.401(g)(2)节]向发行人发出相应通知;

(10)在发行人提出基于具体情形其不必被视为《405规则》定义的不适格发行人的申请时,基于充分理由同意核准或驳回该等申请。

(b)就《1933年证券法》(《美国法典》第十五编第77a节及其后条文)以及依其颁布的《A管理办法》(本章第230.251节及其后条文)而言:

(1)在申请人提出基于具体情形没有必要拒绝授予其在《A管理办法》中的豁免申请时并提出充分理由之时,根据《262规则》(本章第230.262节)同意核准该等申请;

(2)根据《252(g)规则》[本章第230.252(g)节]同意签发命令对发行说明书进行限制;及

(3)根据《259规则》(本章第230.259节)签发命令,宣布发行说明书已被撤回或放弃。

(c)就《1933年证券法》(《美国法典》第十五编第77a节及其后条文)以及依其颁布的《D管理办法》(本章第230.501节及其后条文)而言:在申请人提出充分理由,证明基于具体情形没有必要拒绝授予《D管理办法》中的豁免时,根据《505(b)(2)(iii)(C)规则》[本章第230.505(b)(2)(iii)(C)节]及《507(b)规则》[本章第230.507(b)节]同意

that it is not necessary under the circumstances that the exemption under Regulation D be denied.

(d) With respect to the Trust Indenture Act of 1939 (15 U.S.C. 77aaa *et seq.*):

(1) To determine to be effective prior to the 20th day after filing thereof applications for qualification of indentures filed on Form T-3 (§269.3 of this chapter) pursuant to section 307 of the Act (15 U.S.C. 77ggg), and Rule 7a-1 thereunder (§260.7a-1 of this chapter).

(2) To authorize the issuance of orders exempting certain securities from the Act under sections 304 (c) and (d) thereof (15 U.S.C. 77ddd (c) and 77ddd (d)) and §260.4c-1 and §260.4d-7 of this chapter.

(3) In cases in which opportunity for hearing is waived, to authorize the issuance of orders determining that a trusteeship under an indenture to be qualified and another indenture is not so likely to involve a material conflict of interest as to make it necessary to disqualify the trustee pursuant to section 310(b)(1)(ii) of the Act (15 U.S.C. 77jjj(b)(1)(ii)) and Rule 10b-2 thereunder (§260.10b-2 of this chapter).

(4) To authorize the issuance of orders exempting any person, registration statement, indenture, security or transaction, or any class or classes of persons, registration statements, indentures, securities, or transactions from the requirements of one or more provisions of the Act pursuant to section 304(d) of the Act (15 U.S.C. 77ddd(d)) and rule 4d-7 thereunder (17 CFR 260.4d-7 of this chapter).

(5) To determine to be effective prior to the 10th day after filing thereof an application for determining the eligibility under section 310(a) of the Act of a person designated as trustee for delayed offerings of debt securities under the Securities Act pursuant to section 305(b)(2) of the Act and rule 5b-1 [17 CFR 260.5b-1 of this chapter] thereunder.

(6) To authorize the issuance of an order permitting a foreign person to act as sole trustee under qualified indentures under section 310(a) of the Act (15 U.S.C. 77jjj(a)) and §260.10a-1 through §260.10a-5 of this chapter.

(7) To issue notices with respect to applications for, and authorize the issuance of orders granting, a stay of a trustee's duty to resign pursuant to section 310(b) of the Act and Rule 10b-4 [17 CFR 260.10b-4 of this chapter] thereunder.

(e) With respect to the Securities Exchange Act of 1934 (15 U.S.C. 78a *et seq.*):

(1) To determine to be effective applications for registration of securities on a national securities exchange prior to 30 days after receipt of a certification pursuant to section 12(d) of the Act (15 U.S.C. 78*l*(d));

(2) Pursuant to instructions as to financial statements contained in forms adopted under the Act:

核准申请。

（d）就《1939年信托契约法》（《美国法典》第十五编第77aaa节及其后条文）而言：

（1）对于按照该法第307条（《美国法典》第十五编第77ggg节）以及依其颁布的《7a-1规则》（本章第260.7a-1节）提出的《T-3表格》（本章第269.3节）信托契约资格申请，在其提交后20日内判定该申请是否有效。

（2）同意签发命令，根据该法第304（c）和第340（d）条[《美国法典》第十五编第77ddd（c）和77ddd（d）节]及本章第260.4c-1节和第260.4d-7节将特定证券豁免于该法规定的适用。

（3）在当事人放弃听证机会的情况下，同意签发命令判定信托契约中的信托关系合格，同时鉴于不存在其他很可能涉及重大利益冲突的信托契约，因此没有必要根据该法第310（b）（1）（ii）条[《美国法典》第十五编第77jjj（b）（1）（ii）节]以及依其颁布的《10b-2规则》（本章第260.10b-2节）判定其不具备信托受托人资格。

（4）根据该法第304（d）条（《美国法典》第十五编第77ddd（d）节）以及依其颁布的《4d-7规则》（《联邦规章汇编》第十七编本章第260.4d-7节），同意签发命令将任何人士、注册说明书、信托契约、证券、交易或任何类型的人士、注册说明书、信托契约、证券或交易豁免于该法一条或数条规定的适用。

（5）对该法第310（a）条中的依《证券法》被指定为迟延债务证券发行的信托受托人之主体的适格性认定申请，根据该法第305（b）（2）条以及依其颁布的《5b-1规则》（《联邦规章汇编》第十七编本章第260.5b-1节）在申请提交后10日内判定申请的有效性。

（6）根据该法第310(a)条[《美国法典》第十五编第77jjj(a)节]及本章第260.10a-1~260.10a-5节的规定，同意签发命令，允许外国主体担任合格信托契约的单一信托受托人。

（7）根据该法第310（b）条以及依其发布的《10b-4规则》（《联邦规章汇编》第十七编本章第260.10b-4节），就中止信托受托人履行辞职义务的申请发布公告，并同意签发命令核准该等中止申请。

（e）就《1934年证券交易法》（《美国法典》第十五编第78a节及其后条文）而言：

（1）根据该法第12（d）条[《美国法典》第十五编第78*l*（d）节]收到相关证明后30日内，判定在全国性证券交易的证券注册申请的有效性；

（2）根据该法采用的表格中与财务报表相关的指示：

(i) To extend the time for filing or to permit the commission of one or more financial statements therein required or the filing in substitution therefor of appropriate statements of comparable character.

(ii) To require the filing of other financial statements in addition to, or in substitution for, the statements therein required.

(3)(i) To grant and deny applications for confidential treatment filed pursuant to section 24(b) of the Act (15 U.S.C. 78x(b)) and Rule 24b-2 thereunder (§240.24b-2 of this chapter);

(ii) To revoke a grant of any such application for confidential treatment.

(4) To authorize the use of forms of proxies, proxy statements, or other soliciting material within periods of time less than that prescribed in §§240.14a-6, 240.14a-8(d), and 240.14a-11 of this chapter; to authorize the filing of information statements within periods of time less than that prescribed in §240.14c-5a of this chapter; and to authorize the filing of information under §240.14f-1 of this chapter within periods of time less than that prescribed therein.

(5) To grant or deny applications filed pursuant to section 12(g)(1) of the Act (15 U.S.C. 78*l*(g)(1)) for extensions of time within which to file registration statements pursuant to that section, provided the applicant is advised of his right to have any such denial reviewed by the Commission.

(6) To accelerate at the request of the issuer the effective date of registration statements filed pursuant to section 12(g) of the Act (15 U.S.C. 78*l*(g)).

(7) To issue notices of applications for exemptions and to grant exemptions under section 12(h) of the Act (15 U.S.C. 78*l*(h)).

(8) At the request of the issuer to accelerate the termination of registration of any class of equity securities as provided in section 12(g)(4) of the Act (15 U.S.C. 78*l*(g)(4)) or as provided in §240.12g-4(a) of this chapter.

(9) Upon receipt of a notification from the Secretary of the Treasury designating a security for exemption pursuant to section 3(a)(12), to issue public releases announcing such designation.

(10) To issue public releases listing those foreign issuers which appear to be current in submitting the information specified in Rule 12g3-2(b) (§240.12g3-2(b)).

(11) To grant exemptions from Rule 14d-10 (§240.14d-10 of this chapter) pursuant to Rule 14d-10(f) (§240.14d-10(f) of this chapter).

(12) To grant an exemption from §240.14b-2(b) or §240.14b-2(c), or both, of this chapter.

(13) To determine with respect to a tender or exchange offer otherwise eligible to be made pursuant to rule 13e-4(g) (§240.13e-4(g) of this chapter) or rule 14d-1(b)

(i)延长财务报表的提交期限,允许不提交[1]该法要求的一份或多份财务报表,或允许提交具有可比特征的适当报表作为替代。

(ii)要求在该法要求提交的报表之外提交其他财务报表作为补充或替代。

(3)(i)核准或驳回根据该法第24(b)条[《美国法典》第十五编第78x(b)节]以及依其颁布的《24b-2规则》(本章第240.24b-2节)提出的保密处理申请;

(ii)撤销任何对保密处理申请的核准。

(4)同意在不超过本章第240.14a-6节、第240.14a-8(d)节和第240.14a-11节规定的期间内使用代理委任书、代理委托说明书或其他代理权征集资料;同意在不超过本章第240.14c-5a条规定的期间内提交信息说明书;同意在不超过本章第240.14f-1节规定的期间内按照该节规定提交信息。

(5)核准或驳回根据该法第12(g)(1)条[《美国法典》第十五编第78*l*(g)(1)节]规定的注册说明书提交的延期申请,但驳回申请的,应向申请人告知其有权要求证券交易委员会进行复议。

(6)按照发行人提出的申请,使根据该法第12(g)条[《美国法典》第十五编第78*l*(g)节]提交的注册说明书提前生效。

(7)根据该法第12(h)条[《美国法典》第十五编第78*l*(h)节]发布关于豁免申请的公告并核准豁免。

(8)按照发行人提出的申请,按该法第12(g)(4)条[《美国法典》第十五编第78*l*(g)(4)节]或本章第240.12g-4(a)节规定提前终止任何类别的股权证券的注册。

(9)在收到财务部长根据第3(a)(12)条指定豁免证券的通知后,通过公告进行宣布。

(10)公开发布从表面判断正在呈报《12g3-2(b)规则》[第240.12g3-2(b)节]规定的信息的国外发行人列表。

(11)根据《14d-10(f)规则》[本章第240.14d-10(f)节]核准对《14d-10规则》(本章第240.14d-10节)的豁免。

(12)核准对本章第240.14b-2(b)节和/或第240.14b-2(c)节的豁免。

(13)在考虑到加拿大联邦、省或地区监管机构核准的任何豁免令的基础上,判定

1 原文拼写疑误,“commission”似应为“omission”,译文已按后者处理。——译者注

(§240.14d-1(b) of this chapter) whether, in light of any exemptive order granted by a Canadian federal, provincial or territorial regulatory authority, application of certain or all of the provisions of section 13(e)(1) and sections 14(d)(1) through 14(d)(7) of the Exchange Act, rule 13e-4, Regulation 14D (§§240.14d-1—240.14d-103 of this chapter) and Schedules TO and 14D-9 thereunder (§§240.14d-100 and 240.14d-101 of this chapter), and rule 14e-1 of Regulation 14E (§§240.14e-1—240.14f-1 of this chapter), to such offer is necessary or appropriate in the public interest.

(14) To administer the provisions of §240.24c-1 of this chapter; provided that access to nonpublic information as defined in such section shall be provided only with the concurrence of the head of the Commission division or office responsible for such information or the files containing such information.

(15) To administer the provisions of Section 24(d) of the Act (15 U.S.C. 78x(d)).

(16) To grant requests for exemptions from:

(i) Tender offer provisions of sections 13(e) and 14(d)(1) through 14(d)(7) of the Act (15 U.S.C. 78m(e) and 78n(d)(1) through 78n(d)(7)), Rule 13e-3 (§240.13e-3 of this chapter) and Rule 13e-4 (§240.13e-4 of this chapter), Regulation 14D(§§240.14d-1 through 240.14d-11 of this chapter) and Schedules 13E-3, TO, and 14D-9 (§§240.13e-100, 240.14d-100 and 240.14d-101 of this chapter) thereunder, pursuant to Sections 14(d)(5), 14(d)(8)(C) and 36(a) of the Act (15 U.S.C. 78n(d)(5), 78(d)(8)(C), and 78mm(a)); and

(ii) The tender offer provisions of Rules 14e-1, 14e-2 and 14e-5 of Regulation 14E (§§240.14e-1, 240.14e-2 and 240.14e-5 of this chapter) pursuant to section 36(a) of the Act (15 U.S.C. 78mm(a)).

(17) At the request of a foreign private issuer, pursuant to Rule 12h-6 (§240.12h-6 of this chapter), to accelerate the termination of the registration of a class of securities under section 12(g) of the Act (15 U.S.C. 78*l*(g)) or the duty to file reports under section 13(a) of the Act (15 U.S.C. 78m(a)) or section 15(d) of the Act (15 U.S.C. 78o(d)).

(18) To review and, either unconditionally or upon specified terms and conditions, grant or deny exemptions from the requirements of Rules 14a-3(b) and 14c-3(a) (§§240.14a-3(b) and 240.14c-3(a) of this chapter) under the Act pursuant to Section 36 of the Act, in cases where upon examination, the matter does not appear to the Director to present significant issues that have not been addressed previously or to raise questions of fact or policy indicating that the public interest or the interest of investors warrants that the Commission consider the matter, where an applicant demonstrates that it:

(i) Is required to hold a meeting of security holders as a result of an action taken by one or more of the applicant's security holders pursuant to state law;

出于公共利益的考虑,根据《13e-4(g)规则》[本章第240.13e-4(g)节]或《14d-1(b)规则》[本章第240.14d-1(b)节]本应有资格进行的股权收购要约或换股收购要约,是否有必要或适宜适用下述全部或部分规定:《证券交易法》第13(e)(1)条、第14(d)(1)条至第14(d)(7)条、依其颁布的《13e-4规则》、《14D管理办法》(本章第240.14d-1~240.14d-103条)、《附表TO》和《附表14D-9》(本章第240.14d-100节和第240.14d-101节)以及《14E管理办法》的《14e-1规则》(本章第240.14e-1~240.14f-1节)。

(14)负责实施本章第240.24c-1节的规定;但是提供该节定义之非公开信息查询权的,必须征得证券交易委员会内部对该等信息或包含该等信息的文件负责的部门或办公室的主任同意。

(15)负责实施该法第24(d)条[《美国法典》第十五编第78x(d)节]的规定。

(16)批准下述豁免申请:

(i)根据该法第14(d)(5)条、第14(d)(8)(C)条和第36(a)条[《美国法典》第十五编第78n(d)(5)节、第78(d)(8)(C)节和第78mm(a)节],豁免于该法第13(e)条、第14(d)(1)条至第14(d)(7)条[《美国法典》第十五编第78m(e)节及第78n(d)(1)~78n(d)(7)节]以及依其颁布的《13e-3管理办法》(本章第240.13e-3节)、《13e-4管理办法》(本章第240.13e-4条)、《14D管理办法》(本章第240.14d-1~240.14d-11节)及《附表13E-3》、《附表TO》和《附表14D-9》(本章第240.13e-100节、第240.14d-100节和第240.14d-101节)的股权收购要约规定的适用;

(ii)根据该法第36(a)条[《美国法典》第十五编第78mm(a)节]的规定,豁免于《14E管理办法》的《14e-1规则》、《14e-2规则》和《14e-5规则》的股权收购要约规定(本章第240.14e-1节、第240.14e-2节和第240.14e-5节)的适用。

(17)按照国外私人发行人的要求,根据《12h-6规则》(本章第240.12h-6节),提前终止依据该法第12(g)条[《美国法典》第十五编第78*l*(g)节]颁布的某类证券的注册,或提前结束该法第13(a)条[《美国法典》第十五编第78m(a)节]或第15(d)条[《美国法典》第十五编第78o(d)节]中的报告提交义务。

(18)根据该法第36条规定,审查豁免于该法《14a-3(b)规则》和《14c-3(a)规则》[本章第240.14a-3(b)节和第240.14c-3(a)节]的申请,并无条件或附加具体条款、条件地核准申请,或者驳回申请,前提是:公司融资部主任核查后认为,有关事项并不存在证券交易委员会之前未处理过的重大问题,亦未发现基于公共利益或投资者利益有必要提交证券交易委员会审议的事实问题或政策问题,且申请人应证明:

(i)由于申请人的一名或多名证券持有人根据州法律采取的行动,申请人有义务举行证券持有人会议;

(ii) Is unable to comply with the requirements of Rule 14a–3(b) or Rule 14c–3(a) under the Act for audited financial statements to be included in the annual report to security holders to be furnished to security holders in connection with the security holder meeting required to be held as a result of the security holder demand under state law;

(iii) Has made a good faith effort to furnish the audited financial statements before holding the security holder meeting;

(iv) Has made a determination that it has disclosed to security holders all available material information necessary for the security holders to make an informed voting decision in accordance with Regulation 14A or Regulation 14C (§§240.14a–1–240.14b–2 or §§240.14c–1–240.14c–101 of this chapter); and

(v) Absent a grant of exemptive relief, it would be forced to violate either state law or the rules and regulations administered by the Commission.

(f) Notwithstanding anything in the foregoing:

(1) Matters arising under the Investment Company Act of 1940 (15 U.S.C. 80a–1 *et seq.*), the Securities Act of 1933 (15 U.S.C. 77a *et seq.*), the Securities Exchange Act of 1934 (15 U.S.C. 78a *et seq.*) and the Trust Indenture Act of 1939 (15 U.S.C. 77aaa *et seq.*) pertaining to investment companies registered under the Investment Company Act of 1940 are not within the scope of the functions delegated to the Director of the Division of Corporation Finance, except those arising under section 30(f) of the Investment Company Act of 1940 (15 U.S.C. 80a–29(f));

(2) In any case in which the Director of the Division of Corporation Finance believes it appropriate, he may submit the matter to the Commission.

(g) With respect to the Securities Act of 1933 (15 U.S.C. 77a *et seq.*) and Rule 701 thereunder (§230.701 of this chapter), to authorize the granting of applications under Rule 703(b) (§230.703(b) of this chapter) upon a showing of good cause that it is not necessary under the circumstances that an exemption under Rule 701 be denied.

(h) With respect to the Securities Act of 1933 (15 U.S.C. 77a *et seq.*) and Rule 144A thereunder (§230.144A of this chapter), taking into account then–existing market practices, to designate any securities or classes of securities to be securities that will not be deemed "of the same class as securities listed on a national securities exchange or quoted in a U.S. automated inter–dealer quotation system" within the meaning of Rule 144A(d)(3)(i) (§230.144A(d)(3)(i) of this chapter).

(i) With respect to the Securities Act of 1933 (15 U.S.C. 77a *et seq.*) and Regulation S thereunder (§230.901 *et seq.* of this chapter), and in consultation with the Director of the Division of Trading and Markets, to designate any foreign securities exchange or non–exchange market as a "designated offshore securities market" within the meaning of Rule 902(a) (§230.902(a) of this chapter).

(ii)其无法遵守该法《14a-3(b)规则》或《14c-3(a)规则》:无法将已审计的财务报表纳入在证券持有人依州法律要求举行的证券持有人会议上向证券持有人提交的年报;

(iii)其已尽诚信努力在证券持有人会议举行之前提交经审计的财务报表;

(iv)其已作出如下判断:其已按《14A管理办法》或《14C管理办法》(本章第240.14a-1~240.14b-2节或第240.14c-1~240.14c-101节)向证券持有人披露所有可获得的且证券持有人作出知情表决所必需的所有重大信息;且

(v)如不核准豁免,其将被迫违反州法律或者违反由证券交易委员会负责实施的规则与规章。

(f)无论上文如何规定:

(1)因《1940年投资公司法》(《美国法典》第十五编第80a-1节及其后条文)、《1933年证券法》(《美国法典》第十五编第77a节及其后条文)、《1934年证券交易法》(《美国法典》第十五编第78a节及其后条文)及《1939年信托契约法》(《美国法典》第十五编第77aaa节及其后条文)引起的与依《1940年投资公司法》注册的投资公司相关的所有事项,均不在公司融资部主任的授权职能范围之内,但因《1940年投资公司法》第30(f)条[《美国法典》第十五编第80a-29(f)节]引起的除外;

(2)在任何情况下,如公司融资部主任认为适当,其均可以将相关事项提交证券交易委员会处理。

(g)就《1933年证券法》(《美国法典》第十五编第77a节及其后条文)以及依其颁布的《701规则》(本章第230.701节)而言,在申请人提出充分理由证明基于具体情形没有必要驳回《701规则》中的豁免时,同意核准根据《703(b)规则》[本章第230.703(b)节]提出的申请。

(h)就《1933年证券法》(《美国法典》第十五编第77a节及其后条文)以及依其颁布的《144A规则》(本章第230.144A节)而言,在考虑到当时市场实践的情况下,明确指定任何证券或任何类别的证券不视为《144A(d)(3)(i)规则》[本章第230.144A(d)(3)(i)节]所定义的"与在全国性证券交易所上市或通过交易商自动报价系统报价的证券同一类别的证券"。

(i)就《1933年证券法》(《美国法典》第十五编第77a节及其后条文)以及依其颁布的《S管理办法》(本章第230.901节及其后条文)而言,在咨询交易和市场部主任后,将任何国外证券交易所或非交易所市场指定为《902(a)规则》[本章第230.902(a)节]所定义的"指定海外证券市场"。

(j) With respect to the Securities Act of 1933 (15 U.S.C. 77a *et seq.*), the Securities Exchange Act of 1934 (15 U.S.C. 78a *et seq.*), the Trust Indenture Act of 1939 (15 U.S.C. 77aaa *et seq.*), and Regulation S–T thereunder (part 232 of this chapter), to grant or deny a request submitted pursuant to Rule 13(b) of Regulation S–T (§232.13(b) of this chapter) to adjust the filing date of an electronic filing.

(k) With respect to the Securities Act of 1933 (15 U.S.C. 77a *et seq.*), the Securities Exchange Act of 1934 (15 U.S.C. 78a *et seq* .), the Trust Indenture Act of 1939 (15 U.S.C. 77aaa *et seq* .), and Regulation S–T thereunder (part 232 of this chapter), to set the terms of, and grant or deny as appropriate, continuing hardship exemptions, pursuant to Rule 202 of Regulation S–T, (§232.202 of this chapter), from the electronic submission requirements of Regulation S–T (part 232 of this chapter).

[41 FR 29375, July 16, 1976]

Editorial Note: For Federal Register Citations affecting §200.30–1 see the List of CFR Sections Affected, which appears in the Finding Aids section of the printed volume and at www.fdsys.gov.

§200.30–3 Delegation of authority to Director of Division of Trading and Markets.

Pursuant to the provisions of Pub. L. 87–592, 76 Stat. 394, 15 U.S.C. 78d–1, 78d–2), the Securities and Exchange Commission hereby delegates, until the Commission orders otherwise, the following functions to the Director of the Division of Trading and Markets to be performed by him or under his direction by such person or persons as may be designated from time to time by the Chairman of the Commission:

(a) With respect to the Securities Exchange Act of 1934 (15 U.S.C. 78a *et seq.*):

(1) To approve the withdrawal or striking from listing and registration of securities registered on any national securities exchange pursuant to section 12(d) of the Act (15 U.S.C. 78*l*(d)) and Rules 12d2–1 and 12d2–2 thereunder (§§240.12d2–1 and 240.12d2–2 of this chapter);

(2) To extend unlisted trading privileges and to deny applications for unlisted trading privileges by national securities exchanges pursuant to section 12(f)(2) of the Act, 15 U.S.C. 78*l*(f)(2), and Rule 12f–1 thereunder, 17 CFR 240.12f–1, provided that any applicant exchange denied unlisted trading privileges is advised of its right to have such denial reviewed by the Commission.

(3) Pursuant to section 15(b) of the Act (15 U.S.C. 78*o*(b)):

(i) To authorize the issuance of orders granting registration of brokers or dealers within forty–five days of the filing of an application for registration as a broker or dealer (or within such longer period as to which the applicant consents);

(ii) To authorize the issuance of orders canceling registrations of brokers or dealers,

(j)就《1933年证券法》(《美国法典》第十五编第77a节及其后条文)、《1934年证券交易法》(《美国法典》第十五编第78a节及其后条文)、《1939年信托契约法》(《美国法典》第十五编第77aaa节及其后条文)以及依其颁布的《S-T管理办法》(本章第232部分)而言,核准或驳回根据《S-T管理办法》的《13(b)规则》[本章第232.13(b)节]提出的对电子文件提交日期进行调整的请求。

(k)就《1933年证券法》(《美国法典》第十五编第77a节及其后条文)、《1934年证券交易法》(《美国法典》第十五编第78a节及其后条文)、《1939年信托契约法》(《美国法典》第15编第77aaa节及其后条文)以及依其颁布的《S-T管理办法》(本章第232部分)而言,根据《S-T管理办法》的《202规则》(本章第232.202节),针对处于持续性困境之当事人提出的豁免适用《S-T管理办法》(本章第232部分)电子文件提交要求的申请,确定授予豁免的条款,并视情形核准或驳回豁免申请。

[《联邦公报》第41卷第29375页,1976年7月16日。]

编辑注:对第200.30-1节有影响的《联邦公报》索引,参见《受影响的联邦规章汇编条文列表》(见印刷版本的《检索协助》章节和www.fdsys.gov)。

第200.30-3节 对交易和市场部主任的委托授权

根据公法编号87-592,《美国制定法汇编》第76卷第394页(《美国法典》第十五编第78d-1节、第78d-2节),证券交易委员会兹将下述职能委托交易和市场部主任行使,或委托证券交易委员会主席随时指定的其他人员在交易和市场部主任的领导下行使(直至证券交易委员会另行作出命令):

(a)就《1934年证券交易法》(《美国法典》第十五编第78a节及其后条文)而言:

(1)根据该法第12(d)条[《美国法典》第十五编第78*l*(d)节]以及依其颁布的《12d2-1规则》和《12d2-2规则》(本章第240.12d2-1节和第240.12d2-2节)批准任何全国性证券交易所注册证券的申请退市、终止注册、强制退市或撤销注册;

(2)根据该法第12(f)(2)条[《美国法典》第十五编第78*l*(f)(2)节]以及依其颁布的《12f-1规则》(《联邦规章汇编》第十七编第240.12f-1节)核准非上市证券的交易权,或者驳回全国性证券交易所提起的非上市证券的交易权的申请,但应向任何申请被拒的交易所告知其有权要求证券交易委员会对驳回申请决定进行复议。

(3)根据该法第15(b)条[《美国法典》第十五编第78*o*(b)节]:

(i)同意签发命令,在经纪商或自营商注册申请提交后45日内(或申请人同意的其他更长的期间内)核准申请人注册为经纪商或自营商;

(ii)在经纪商、自营商或注册申请人不再存续或不再开展经纪商或自营商业务之

or pending applications for registration, if such brokers or dealers or applicants for registration are no longer in existence or have ceased to do business as brokers or dealers;

(4) Pursuant to Rule 19h-1 (§240.19h-1 of this chapter):

(i) To grant applications with respect to membership in, association with a member of, or participation in, a self-regulatory organization and for other relief as to persons who are subject to an applicable disqualification where such relationships or other relief have been approved or recommended by a self-regulatory organization;

(ii) To extend the time for Commission consideration of notices for admission to membership or participation in a self-regulatory organization or association with a member of persons subject to a statutory disqualification pursuant to paragraph (a)(7) of that rule.

(5) Pursuant to Rule 17a-5(1)(3) (§240.17a-5(1)(3) of this chapter), to consider applications, by brokers and dealers for exemptions from, and extension of time within which to file, reports required by Rule 17a-5 (§240.17a-5 of this chapter), and to grant, and to authorize the issuance of orders denying, such applications provided such applicant is advised of his right to have such denial reviewed by the Commission.

(6) Pursuant to Rules 14e-4(c), 14e-5(d), and 15c2-11(h) (§§240.14e-4(c), 240.14e-5(d), and 240.15c2-11(h) of this chapter), and Rules 101(d), 102(e), 104 (j), and 105(c) of Regulation M (§§242.101(d), 242.102(e), 242.104(j), and 242.105 (c) of this chapter), to grant requests for exemptions from Rules 14e-4, 14e-5, and 15c2-11 (§§240.14e-4, 240.14e-5, and 240.15c2-11 of this chapter), and Rules 101, 102, 104, and 105 of Regulation M (§§242.101, 242.102, 242.104, and 242.105 of this chapter).

(7) Pursuant to Rule 15c3-1 (§240.15c3-1 of this chapter):

(i) To approve lesser equity requirements in specialist or market maker accounts pursuant to Rule 15c3-1(a)(6)(iii)(E) (§240.15c3-1(a)(6)(iii)(E) of this chapter);

(ii) To grant exemptions from Rule 15c3-1 (§240.15c3-1 of this chapter) pursuant to Rule 15c3-1(b)(3) (§240.15c3-1(b)(3) of this chapter);

(iii) To grant temporary exemptions upon specified terms and conditions from the debt equity requirements of Rule 15c3-1(d)(§240.15c3-1(d) of this chapter);

(iv) To approve a change in election of the alternative capital requirement pursuant to Rule 15c3-1(f)(1)(i) and (ii) (§240.15c3-1(f)(1)(i) and (ii) of this chapter); and

(v) To review applications of OTC derivatives dealers filed pursuant to Appendix F of §240.15c3-1f of this chapter, and to grant or deny such applications in full or in part; and

时，同意签发命令注销该等经纪商、自营商的注册或暂缓申请人的注册；

（4）根据《19h–1规则》（本章第240.19h–1节）：

（i）在获得自律组织批准或推荐的前提下，核准不合格主体关于获得自律组织成员资格、充当自律组织成员的业务相关人[1]或参与自律组织的申请，以及向其授予其他救济；

（ii）根据该规则第（a）（7）款，延长证券交易委员会审议关于下述事项的通知的期限：不具备法定资格的主体获得自律组织成员资格、参与自律组织或充当自律组织成员的业务相关人。

（5）根据《17a–5（1）（3）规则》［本章第240.17a–5（1）（3）节］，审议经纪商和自营商提出的豁免于《17a–5规则》（本章第240.17a–5节）的报告要求及延长报告提交期限的申请，核准该等申请或同意签发命令驳回申请，但应告知申请人其有权要求证券交易委员会对驳回申请的决定进行复议。

（6）根据《14e–4（c）规则》、《14e–5（d）规则》和《15c2–11（h）规则》［本章第240.14e–4（c）节、第240.14e–5（d）节和第240.15c2–11（h）节］以及《M管理办法》的《101（d）规则》、《102（e）规则》、《104（j）规则》和《105（c）规则》［本章第242.101（d）节、第242.102（e）节、第242.104（j）节和第242.105（c）节］，核准关于下述规定的豁免请求：《14e–4规则》、《14e–5规则》和《15c2–11规则》（本章第240.14e–4节、第240.14e–5节和第240.15c2–11节）以及《M管理办法》的《101规则》、《102规则》、《104规则》和《105规则》（本章第242.101节、第242.102节、第242.104节和第242.105节）。

（7）根据《15c3–1规则》（本章第240.15c3–1节）：

（i）根据《15c3–1（a）（6）（iii）（E）规则》［本章第240.15c3–1（a）（6）（iii）（E）节］批准降低专业证券商账户或做市商账户的股本要求；

（ii）根据《15c3–1（b）（3）规则》［本章第240.15c3–1（b）（3）节］核准对《15c3–1规则》（本章第240.15c3–1节）的豁免；

（iii）基于特定条款和条件，核准对《15c3–1（d）规则》［本章第240.15c3–1（d）节］的债务权益要求的临时豁免；

（iv）根据《15c3–1（f）（1）（i）规则》和《15c3–1（f）（1）（ii）规则》［本章第240.15c3–1（f）（1）（i）和（ii）节］批准变更对替代性资本金要求的选择；

（v）审查根据本章第240.15c3–1f节《附件F》提交的场外交易衍生品自营商申请，并全面或部分核准或驳回该等申请；及

1 “association”不宜译为“关联”，避免与关联方（affiliated party）、关联交易（related transaction）的含义混淆，故“associated person”译为“业务相关人”，“association”译为“业务相关关系”。——译者注

(vi)(A) To review amendments to applications of brokers or dealers filed pursuant to §240.15c3-1e and §240.15c3-1g of this chapter and to approve such amendments, unconditionally or subject to specified terms and conditions;

(B) To grant extensions and exemptions from the notification requirements of §240.15c3-1g(e) of this chapter, unconditionally or subject to specified terms and conditions;

(C) To impose additional conditions, pursuant to §240.15c3-1e(e) of this chapter, on a broker or dealer that computes certain of its net capital deductions pursuant to §240.15c3-1e of this chapter or on an ultimate holding company of the broker or dealer that is not an ultimate holding company that has a principal regulator, as defined in §240.15c3-1(c)(13)(ii) of this chapter;

(D) To require that a broker or dealer or the ultimate holding company of the broker or dealer provide information to the Commission pursuant to §240.15c3-1e(a)(1)(viii)(G), §240.15c3-1e(a)(1)(ix)(C), §240.15c3-1e(a)(4), §240.15c3-1g(b)(1)(i)(H), and §240.15c3-1g(2)(i)(C) of this chapter; and

(E) To determine, pursuant to §240.15c3-1e(a)(10)(ii), that the notice that a broker or dealer must provide to the Commission pursuant to §240.15c3-1e(a)(10)(i) of this chapter will become effective for a shorter or longer period of time.

(8) Pursuant to Rule 17a-10(d) (§240.17a-10(d) of this chapter), to consider applications by broker-dealers for extensions of time in which to file reports required by Rule 17a-10(§240.17a-10 of this chapter), and to grant, and to authorize the issuance of orders denying, such applications provided such applicant is advised of his right to have such denial reviewed by the Commission. Any extension granted shall not be for more than 150 days after the close of the calendar year for which the report on Form X-17A-10 (§249.618 of this chapter) is made.

(9) Pursuant to Rule 10b-17(b)(2) (§240.10b-17(b)(2) of this chapter), to review applications of various issuers for exemption from the notice requirements of Rule 10b-17 (§240.10b-17 of this chapter) and to grant or deny such applications, with authority to issue orders granting and denying same, provided each applicant is advised of his right to have a denial reviewed by the Commission.

(10)(i) Pursuant to Rule 15c3-3 (§240.15c3-3 of this chapter) to find and designate as control locations for purposes of Rule 15c3-3(c)(7) (§240.15c3-3(c)(7) of this chapter) certain broker-dealer accounts which are adequate for the protection of customer securities.

(ii) Pursuant to section 36(a) of the Act (15 U.S.C. 78mm(a)) to review and, either unconditionally or on specified terms and conditions, grant or deny exemptions from the collateral requirements of paragraph (b)(3) of Rule 15c3-3 of the Act (§240.15c3-3

(vi)(A)审查经纪商或自营商对其根据本章第240.15c3-1e节和第240.15c3-1g节提出的申请所作之修正,并无条件或附具体条款、条件地批准该等修正;

(B)无条件或附具体条款、条件地核准本章第240.15c3-1g(e)节的通知要求的延期或豁免;

(C)根据本章第240.15c3-1e(e)节对以下对象施加额外条件要求:应按本章第240.15c3-1e条计算特定净资本金扣减额的经纪商或自营商,或者,不受主要监管者监管的经纪商或自营商的最终控股公司[如本章第240.15c3-1(c)(13)(ii)节所定义];

(D)要求经纪商或自营商或其最终控股公司根据本章第240.15c3-1e(a)(1)(viii)(G)节、第240.15c3-1e(a)(1)(ix)(C)节、第240.15c3-1e(a)(4)节、第240.15c3-1g(b)(1)(i)(H)节和第240.15c3-1g(2)(i)(C)节向证券交易委员会提交信息;且

(E)根据第240.15c3-1e(a)(10)(ii)节决定缩短或延长经纪商或自营商根据本章第240.15c3-1e(a)(10)(i)节必须提交的通知生效前的等待期间。

(8)根据《17a-10(d)规则》[本章第240.17a-10(d)节],审议经纪商和自营商提出的延长《17a-10规则》(本章第240.17a-10节)规定的报告提交期限的申请,核准该等申请或同意签发命令驳回申请,但应告知申请人其有权要求证券交易委员会对驳回申请决定进行复议。任何核准延期的时间不得超过《X-17A-10》(本章第249.618节)报告提交的日历年结束后150日。

(9)根据《10b-17(b)(2)规则》[本章第240.10b-17(b)(2)节],审查各发行人提交的关于《10b-17规则》(本章第240.10b-17节)中的通知要求的豁免申请,核准或驳回该等申请,并同意签发命令核准或驳回该等申请,但应向各申请人告知其有权要求证券交易委员会对驳回决定进行复议。

(10)(i)根据《15c3-3规则》(本章第240.15c3-3节)寻找并指定足以充分保护客户证券的某些经纪商和自营商账户《15c3-3(c)(7)规则》[本章第240.15c3-3(c)(7)节]作为控制点。

(ii)得出结论认为某类型担保品与证券交易委员会之前已经豁免的某一类型担保品的特点实质类似后,根据该法第36(a)条[《美国法典》第十五编第78mm(a)节],对于使该类型担保品豁免于该法《15c3-3规则》第(b)(3)款(本章第240.15c3-3节)之担

of this chapter) for a type of collateral after concluding that the characteristics of such collateral are substantially comparable to the characteristics of a type of collateral previously exempted by the Commission.

(iii) Pursuant to section 36(a) of the Act (15 U.S.C. 78mm(a)), to review and grant written applications for an exemption, unconditionally or subject to specified terms and conditions, for a broker or dealer to utilize a clearing agency registered with the Commission under section 17A of the Act (15 U.S.C. 78q-1) or a derivatives clearing organization registered with the Commodity Futures Trading Commission under section 5b of the Commodity Exchange Act (7 U.S.C. 7a-1) that does not meet the requirements of 17 CFR 240.15c3-3a, Note G.(b)(1)(i) through (iii).

(11) Upon written application or upon its own motion, either unconditionally or on specified terms and conditions, to grant or deny by order an exemption from the requirements of Regulation SHO (§242.200 of this chapter) under the Act pursuant to Section 36 of the Act (15 U.S.C. 78mm).

(12) Pursuant to section 19(b) of the Act, 15 U.S.C. 78s(b), and Rule 19b-4 (§240.19b-4) of this chapter, to publish notices of proposed rule changes filed by self-regulatory organizations and to approve such proposed rule changes, and to find good cause to approve a proposed rule change earlier than 30 days after the date of publication of such proposed rule change and to publish the reasons for such finding. Pursuant to section 19(b) of the Act, 15 U.S.C. 78s(b), and Rule 19b-4 (§240.19b-4) of this chapter, to disapprove a proposed rule change, provided that, with respect to a particular proposed rule change, if two (2) or more Commissioners object in writing to the Director within five (5) business days of being notified by the Director that the Division intends to exercise its authority to disapprove that particular proposed rule change, then the delegation of authority to approve or disapprove that proposal is withdrawn, and the Director shall either present a recommendation to the Commission or institute pursuant to delegated authority proceedings to determine whether the proposed rule change should be disapproved. In addition, pursuant to section 19(b)(10) of the Act, 15 U.S.C. 78s(b)(10), to notify a self-regulatory organization that a proposed rule change does not comply with the rules of the Commission relating to the required form of a proposed rule change, and to determine that a proposed rule change is unusually lengthy and complex or raises novel regulatory issues and to inform the self-regulatory organization of such determination.

(13) Pursuant to section 15B(a) of the Act [15 U.S.C. 78o-4(a)], to authorize the issuance of orders granting registration of municipal securities dealers within forty-five days of the filing of an application for registration as a municipal securities dealer (or within such longer period as to which the applicant consents).

保要求的申请进行审查，并无条件或附具体条款、条件地核准或驳回该等申请。

（iii）根据该法第36（a）条［《美国法典》第十五编第78mm（a）节］，审查经纪商或自营商提出的书面豁免申请，并无条件或附具体条款、条件地核准其使用不符合《联邦规章汇编》第十七编第240.15c3-3a节，注释G.（b）（1）（i）至（iii）要求的且根据该法第17A条（《美国法典》第十五编第78q-1节）向证券交易委员会注册的结算机构或根据《商品交易法》第5b条（《美国法典》第七编第7a-1节）向商品期货交易所注册的衍生品结算组织。

（11）根据该法第36条（《美国法典》第十五编第78mm节），应申请人的书面申请或主动提出动议，以命令形式无条件或附具体条款、条件地核准或驳回豁免于《SHO管理办法》（本章第242.200条）的要求的申请。

（12）根据该法第19（b）条［《美国法典》第十五编第78s（b）节］及本章《19b-4规则》（第240.19b-4节），就自律组织提交的规则变更提案发布公告，批准该等规则变更提案，并在公告发布后30日内认定并公布批准规则变更提案的充分理由。根据该法第19（b）条［《美国法典》第十五编第78s（b）节］及本章《19b-4规则》（第240.19b-4节），否决规则变更提案；但是，就任一具体的规则变更提案而言，若2名或2名以上的委员在交易和市场部主任发出拟行使否决权的公告后5个工作日内向主任提出书面反对意见，则主任应向证券交易委员会作出建议，或者根据被委托行使的权限发起程序以判定是否应否决该规则变更提案。此外，根据该法第19（b）（10）条［《美国法典》第十五编第78s（b）（10）节］，应通知自律组织规则变更提案不符合证券交易委员会相关的格式要求，或判定提案过分冗长、复杂或将引发新的监管问题并将该等判定结果通知自律组织。

（13）根据该法第15B（a）条［《美国法典》第十五编第78o-4（a）节］同意签发命令，在市政证券自营商注册申请提交后45日内（或申请人同意的其他更长的期间内）核准注册。

(14) Pursuant to section 17A(c)(2) of the Act (15 U.S.C. 78q-1(c)(2)), to authorize the issuance of orders accelerating registration of transfer agents for which the Commission is the appropriate regulatory agency before the expiration of thirty days following the dates on which applications for registration as a transfer agent are filed.

(15) Pursuant to Rule 10a-1(f) [§240.10a-1(f)] to grant requests for exemptions from Rule 10a-1.

(16) Pursuant to sections 17A(b)(1), 17A(b)(2) and 19(a) of the Act (15 U.S.C. 78q-1(b)(1), 78q-1(b)(2) and 78s(a)), to publish notice of the filing of applications for registration and for exemption from registration as a clearing agency.

(17) Pursuant to Rule 17f-2 (§240.17f-2 of this chapter).

(i) To disapprove a "Notice Pursuant to Rule 17f-2" pursuant to Rule 17f-2(e) (§240.17f-2(e) of this chapter).

(ii) To grant exemptions upon specified terms, conditions and periods, for classes of persons subject to Rule 17f-2 pursuant to Rule 17f-2(g) (§240.17f-2(g) of this chapter).

(iii) To approve amendments to plan of a registered national securities exchange or a national securities association submitted pursuant to Rule 17f-2(c) (§240.17f-2(c) of this chapter).

(18) Pursuant to Rule 17d-1 (§240.17d-1 of this chapter) to designate one self-regulatory organization responsible for the examination of brokers and dealers which are members of more than one such organization to insure compliance with applicable financial responsibility rules.

(19)(i) To grant and deny applications for confidential treatment filed pursuant to section 24(b) of the Act (15 U.S.C. 78x(b)) and Rule 24b-2 thereunder (240.24b-2 of this chapter);

(ii) To revoke a grant of confidential treatment for any such application.

(20) Pursuant to sections 8(c) and 15(c)(2) of the Act (15 U.S.C. 78h(c) and 78o(2)) and paragraphs (g) of Rules 8c-1 and 15c2-1 thereunder, to make findings that the agreements, safeguards, and provisions of registered clearing agencies are adequate for the protection of investors.

(21) Under section 17A(c)(4)(B) of the Act (15 U.S.C. 78q-1(c)(4)(B)), to set terms and conditions upon which transfer agents registered with the Commission may withdraw from registration as a transfer agent by filing a written notice of withdrawal.

(22) Under section 17A(c)(4)(B) of the Act (15 U.S.C. 78q-1(c)(4)(B)), to authorize the issuance of orders canceling registrations of transfer agents registered with the Commission or denying applications for registration as a transfer agent with the Commission, if such transfer agents are no longer in existence or are not engaged in

（14）对于证券交易委员会拥有相关监管权的过户代理人的注册申请，根据该法第17A（c）（2）条［《美国法典》第十五编第78q-1（c）（2）节］同意签发命令核准在申请提交后30日期限届满之前提前注册。

（15）根据《10a-1（f）规则》［第240.10a-1（f）节］，核准豁免适用《10a-1规则》的申请。

（16）根据该法第17A（b）（1）条、第17A（b）（2）条和第19（a）条［《美国法典》第十五编第78q-1（b）（1）节、第78q-1（b）（2）节和第78s（a）节］，就结算机构提交的注册申请及注册豁免申请发布公告。

（17）根据《17f-2规则》（本章第240.17f-2节）：

（i）根据《17f-2（e）规则》［本章第240.17f-2（e）节］否决《17f-2规则通知》。

（ii）根据《17f-2（g）规则》（本章第240.17f-2（g）节）核准受制于《17f-2规则》的类型的人士的豁免，并确定豁免的具体条款、条件和期限。

（iii）批准全国性注册证券交易所或全国性注册证券协会根据《17f-2（c）规则》［本章第240.17f-2（c）节］提出的计划的修正稿。

（18）根据《17d-1规则》（本章第240.17d-1节），指定一家自律组织负责对同时属于两家或两家以上自律组织的成员的经纪商和自营商进行核查，以确保其遵守适用的财务责任规则。

（19）（i）核准或驳回根据该法第24（b）条［《美国法典》第十五编第78x（b）节］以及依其颁布的《24b-2规则》（本章第240.24b-2节）提出的保密处理申请；

（ii）撤销对任何保密处理申请的核准。

（20）根据该法第8（c）条和第15（c）（2）条［《美国法典》第十五编第78h（c）节和第78o（2）节］以及依其颁布的《8c-1规则》和《15c2-1规则》第（g）款，认定注册结算机构的协议、保障和规定足以保护投资者。

（21）根据该法第17A（c）（4）（B）条［《美国法典》第十五编第78q-1（c）（4）（B）节］，针对在证券交易委员会注册的过户代理人的注册撤销（通过提交书面注册撤销通知来办理）设定条款、条件。

（22）根据该法第17A（c）（4）（B）条［《美国法典》第十五编第78q-1（c）（4）（B）节］，在过户代理人不再存续或不再从事过户代理人业务之时，同意签发命令，注销过户代理人在证券交易委员会的注册，或驳回申请人向证券交易委员会提出的过户代理人注册申请。

business as transfer agents.

(23) Pursuant to section 17(b) of the Act (15 U.S.C. 78q(b)), prior to any examination of a registered clearing agency, registered transfer agent, or registered municipal securities dealer whose appropriate regulatory agency is not the Commission, to notify and consult with the appropriate regulatory agency for such clearing agency, transfer agent, or municipal securities dealer.

(24) Pursuant to section 17(c)(3) of the Act, 15 U.S.C. 78q(c)(3), in regard to clearing agencies, transfer agents and municipal securities dealers for which the Commission is not the appropriate regulatory agency, (i) to notify the appropriate regulatory agency of any examination conducted by the Commission of any such clearing agency, transfer agent, or municipal securities dealer; (ii) to request from the appropriate regulatory agency a copy of the report of any examination of any such clearing agency, transfer agent, or municipal securities dealer conducted by such appropriate regulatory agency and any data supplied to it in connection with such examination; and (iii) to furnish to the appropriate regulatory agency on request a copy of the report of any examination of any such clearing agency, transfer agent, or municipal securities dealer conducted by the Commission and any data supplied to it in connection with such examination.

(25) Pursuant to Rule 17f–1 (§240.17f–1 of this chapter), to designate persons not subject to §240.17f–1 as reporting institutions upon specified terms, conditions, and time periods.

(26) [Reserved]

(27) To approve amendments to the joint industry plan governing consolidated transaction reporting declared effective by the Commission pursuant to Rule 601 (17 CFR 242.601) or its predecessors, Rule 11Aa3–1 and Rule 17a–15, and to grant exemptions from Rule 601 pursuant to Rule 601(f) (17 CFR 242.601(f)) to exchanges trading listed securities that are designated as national market system securities until such times as a Joint Reporting Plan for such securities is filed and approved by the Commission.

(28) To grant exemptions from Rule 602 (17 CFR 242.602), pursuant to Rule 602(d) (17 CFR 242.602(d)).

(29) To issue supplemental orders modifying the terms upon which self–regulatory organizations are authorized to act jointly in planning, developing, operating or regulating facilities of a national market system in accordance with the terms of amendments to plans which plans have been previously approved by the Commission under section 11A(a)(3)(B) of the Securities Exchange Act of 1934.

(30) Pursuant to section 17(a) of the Act, 15 U.S.C. 78q, to approve amendments to the plans which are consistent with the reporting structure of Rules 17a–5(a)(4) and

(23)根据该法第17(b)条[《美国法典》第十五编第78q(b)节],证券交易委员会希望对注册结算机构、注册过户代理人、注册市政证券自营商进行核查但本身并非其相应监管机构的,应先通知该等结算机构、过户代理人或市政证券自营商的相应监管机构并与之进行协商。

(24)根据该法第17(c)(3)条[《美国法典》第十五编第78q(c)(3)节],就证券交易委员会不拥有相应监管权的结算机构、过户代理人和市政证券自营商而言,(i)通知相应监管机构,证券交易委员会对任何该等结算机构、过户代理人和市政证券自营商的相应监管机构进行的任何核查;(ii)请求相应监管机构提供其对任何该等结算机构、过户代理人或市政证券自营商做过的任何核查的报告,请求相应监管机构提供其所获得的任何核查相关数据;及(iii)经相应的监管机构请求,向其提供证券交易委员会对任何该等结算机构、过户代理人和市政证券自营商作过的核查报告,及证券交易委员会所获得的任何相关的核查数据。

(25)根据《17f-1规则》(本章第240.17f-1节),将不受制于第240.17f-1节的主体指定为报告机构,并确定该等指定具体的条款、条件和期间。

(26)[保留]

(27)根据《601规则》(《联邦规章汇编》第十七编第242.601节)或其前身规则、《11Aa3-1规则》和《17a-15规则》,批准经证券交易委员会宣布有效的关于合并交易报告的联合行业计划的修正稿;并根据《601(f)规则》[《联邦规章汇编》第十七编第242.601(f)节],核准被指定为全国性市场系统证券的在交易所交易的上市证券豁免《601规则》的适用,豁免期直至该证券的《联合报告计划》向证券交易委员会提交并获批准为止。

(28)根据《602(d)规则》[《联邦规章汇编》第十七编第242.602(d)节],核准对《602规则》(《联邦规章汇编》第十七编第242.602节)的豁免。

(29)根据证券交易委员会已按《1934年证券交易法》第11A(a)(3)(B)条批准的计划的修正条款,签发补充命令,修改授权自律组织就全国性市场系统设施之规划、开发、运营或监管开展联合行动的条款。

(30)根据该法第17(a)条(《美国法典》第十五编第78q节),批准自律组织根据《17a-5(a)(4)规则》和《17a-10(b)规则》提交的符合《17a-5(a)(4)规则》和《17a-10(b)

17a–10(b) filed by self–regulatory organizations pursuant to Rules 17a–5(a)(4) and 17a–10(b).

(31) Pursuant to section 19(b)(2)(A) of the Act, 15 U.S.C. 78s(b)(2)(A), to extend for a period not exceeding 90 days from the date of publication of notice of the filing of a proposed rule change pursuant to section 19(b)(1) of the Act, 15 U.S.C. 78s(b)(1), the period during which the Commission must by order approve or disapprove the proposed rule change or institute proceedings to determine whether the proposed rule change should be disapproved and to determine whether such longer period is appropriate and publish the reasons for such determination.

(32) Under §240.10b–10(f) of this chapter, to grant exemptions from §240.10b–10 of this chapter.

(33) Pursuant to Rule 17a–6 (§240.17a–6 of this chapter) to approve record destruction plans and amendments thereto filed by a national securities exchange or a national securities association.

(34) Pursuant to Rule 17d–2 (§240.17d–2 of this chapter) to publish notice of plans and plan amendments filed pursuant to Rule 17d–2 and to approve such plans and plan amendments.

(35) [Reserved]

(36) To grant exemptions from Rule 603 (17 CFR 242.603), pursuant to Rule 603(d) (17 CFR 242.603(d)).

(37) Pursuant to Rule 600 (17 CFR 242.600), to publish notice of the filing of a designation plan with respect to national market system securities, or any proposed amendment thereto, and to approve such plan or amendment.

(38) To disclose:

(i) To the Comptroller of the Currency, the Board of Governors of the Federal Reserve System, the Federal Deposit Insurance Corporation, and the state banking authorities, information and documents deemed confidential regarding registered clearing agencies and registered transfer agents; and

(ii) To the Department of Treasury, information and documents deemed confidential regarding possible laundering of money through or by brokers or dealers, including compliance by brokers or dealers with the Currency and Foreign Transactions Reporting Act of 1970, as amended.

(39) Under §240.9b–1 of this chapter:

(i) To enable distribution of an options disclosure document or amendment to an options disclosure document to the public prior to the time required in the Rule or to lengthen the period before distribution can be made;

(ii) To require refiling of an amendment to an options disclosure document pursuant

规则》规定的报告结构的计划的修正稿。

(31)根据该法第19(b)(2)(A)条[《美国法典》第十五编第78s(b)(2)(A)节],延长证券交易委员会通过命令批准或否决规则变更提案的期限;或发起相关程序,以判定是否应否决该提案并判定延长的时间是否适当并公布相关理由。延长的时间自关于依该法第19(b)(1)条[《美国法典》第十五编第78s(b)(1)节]提交的规则变更提案的公告发布之日起不得超过90日。

(32)根据本章第240.10b–10(f)节,核准对本章第240.10b–10节的豁免。

(33)根据《17a–6规则》(本章第240.17a–6节)批准全国性证券交易所或全国性证券协会提交的记录销毁计划及其修正稿。

(34)根据《17d–2规则》(本章第240.17d–2节),就根据《17d–2规则》提交的计划和计划修正稿发布公告,并批准该等计划和计划修正稿。

(35)[保留]

(36)根据《603(d)规则》[《联邦规章汇编》第十七编第242.603(d)节],核准对《603规则》(《联邦规章汇编》第十七编第242.603节)的豁免。

(37)根据《600规则》(《联邦规章汇编》第十七编第242.600节),就全国性市场系统证券指定计划或其任何修正提案发布公告,并批准该等计划或修正稿。

(38)信息披露:

(i)向货币监理署、联邦储备系统的联邦储备委员会、联邦存款保险公司及州银行业监管机构披露视为保密的关于注册结算机构和注册过户代理人的信息和文件;及

(ii)向财政部披露与涉嫌由经纪商或自营商或通过经纪商或自营商开展的洗钱行为相关的视为保密的信息和文件,包括关于经纪商或自营商对《1970年货币和国外交易报告法》及其修正的遵守情况的信息和文件。

(39)根据本章第240.9b–1节:

(i)在该规则规定的时间之前或之后向公众发布期权披露文件或其修正;

(ii)要求根据本章第240.9b–1(b)(2)(i)节规定的程序重新提交期权披露文件的

to the procedure set forth in §240.9b–1(b)(2)(i) of this chapter.

(40) Pursuant to section 15B(b)(2)(B) of the Act, 15 U.S.C., 78o–4(b), to review and, where appropriate, approve the selection by the Municipal Securities Rulemaking Board ("Board") of public representatives to serve on the Board.

(41) Pursuant to Rule 6a–2(c) (§240.6a–2 of this chapter) to exempt registered national securities exchanges from the filing requirements imposed by Rule 6a–2 with respect to certain affiliates and subsidiaries of the exchange.

(42) Under 17 CFR 242.608(e), to grant or deny exemptions from 17 CFR 242.608, and pursuant to 17 CFR 242.608(b) to extend for a period not exceeding 180 days from the date of publication of notice of filing of a national market system plan or an amendment to an effective national market system plan the time for Commission consideration of the national market system plan or the amendment to an effective national market system plan and to determine whether such longer period is appropriate and publish the reasons for such determination.

(43) To grant or deny exemptions from Rule 17Ad–14 (§240.17Ad–14 of this chapter), pursuant to Rule 17Ad–14(d) (§240.17Ad–14(d) of this chapter). (Pub. L. 87–592, 76 Stat. 394, 15 U.S.C 78d–1, 78d–2).

(44) To review, publish notice of, and where appropriate, approve plans, and amendments to plans, submitted by self–regulatory organizations pursuant to Rule 19d–1 (c) under the Act (§240.19d–1(c)).

(45) To grant exemptions from Rule 3b–9 under the Act. (§240.3b–9(c) of this chapter).

(46) Pursuant to section 15(b)(9) of the Act, 15 U.S.C. 78*o*(b)(9) to review and, where appropriate, grant exemptions from the requirement of section 15(b)(8) of the Act, 15 U.S.C. 78*o*(b)(8).

(47) Pursuant to section 15(a)(2) of the Act, 15 U.S.C. 78*o*(a)(2), to review and, either unconditionally or on specified terms and conditions, grant exemptions from the broker–dealer registration requirements of section 15(a)(1) of the Act,15 U.S.C.78*o*(a)(1), to government securities brokers or government securities dealers that have registered with the Commissi on under section 15(a)(2) of the Act, 15 U.S.C. 78 *o* –5(a)(2), solely with respect to effecting any transactions in, or inducing or attempting to induce the purchase or sale of, any security principally backed by a guaranty of the United States.

(48) Pursuant to paragraph (d) of Rule 15c2–12 (17 CFR 15c2–12), to grant or deny exemptions, either unconditionally or on specified terms and conditions, from Rule 15c2–12.

(49) Pursuant to section 11A(b) of the Act (15 U.S.C. 78k–1(b)) and Rule 609

修正。

(40)根据该法第15B(b)(2)(B)条[《美国法典》第十五编第78o-4(b)节],审查并在适当情况下批准市政证券规则制定委员会(“委员会”)选任在委员会供职的公众代表;

(41)根据《6a-2(c)规则》(本章第240.6a-2节)对全国性注册证券交易所豁免以下要求:《6a-2规则》施加的与交易所某些关联方或子公司相关的信息提交要求。

(42)根据《联邦规章汇编》第十七编第242.608(e)节核准或驳回对《联邦规章汇编》第十七编第242.608节的豁免;根据《联邦规章汇编》第十七编第242.608(b)节延长证券交易委员会审议全国性市场系统计划或审议已生效的全国性市场计划的修正稿的期限,延长时间自关于该等计划或修正稿的提交的公告发布之日起不得超过180日;并判定延长的时间是否适当同时公布相关理由。

(43)根据《17Ad-14(d)规则》[(本章第240.17Ad-14(d)节]核准或驳回对《17Ad-14规则》(本章第240.17Ad-14节)的豁免。(公法编号87-592,《美国制定法汇编》第76卷第394页,《美国法典》第十五编第78d-1节、第78d-2节)。

(44)根据该法《19d-1(c)规则》[第240.19d-1(c)节]审查自律组织提交的计划及计划修正稿、就此发布公告并作出适当的批准。

(45)核准对该法《3b-9规则》[本章第240.3b-9(c)节]的豁免。

(46)根据该法第15(b)(9)条[《美国法典》第十五编第78*o*(b)(9)节]审查对该法第15(b)(8)条[《美国法典》第十五编第78*o*(b)(8)节]规定的豁免申请并作出适当核准。

(47)根据该法第15(a)(2)条[《美国法典》第十五编第78*o*(a)(2)节],审查并无条件或附具体条款、条件地向已根据该法第15(a)(2)条[《美国法典》第十五编第78*o*-5(a)(2)节]注册的政府证券经纪商或政府证券自营商核准对该法第15(a)(1)条[《美国法典》第十五编第78*o*(a)(1)节]的豁免,但豁免仅得限于主要由联邦政府担保支持的任何证券之交易实施,或诱导或试图诱导该等证券之购买和出售的行为。

(48)根据《15c2-12规则》(《联邦规章汇编》第十七编第15c2-12节)第(d)款,无条件或附具体条款、条件地核准或驳回对《15c2-12规则》的豁免。

(49)根据该法第11A(b)条[《美国法典》第十五编第78k-1(b)节]以及依其颁布的

thereunder (17 CFR 242.609), to publish notice of and, by order, grant under section 11A(b) of the Act and Rule 609 thereunder: Applications for registration as a securities information processor; and exemptions from that section and any rules or regulations promulgated thereunder, either conditionally or unconditionally.

(50) Pursuant to sections 17A(b) and 19(a) of the Act (15 U.S.C. 78q–1(b) and 78s(a)):

(i) To authorize the issuance of orders granting an extension to a temporary clearing agency registration, for up to two years or such longer period as the clearing agency consents.

(ii) To authorize the issuance of orders granting the withdrawal of an application to become a registered clearing agency, at any time prior to final determination of such application by the Commission, upon submission of a request for such withdrawal by applicant.

(51) Pursuant to paragraph (a)(4) of §240.9b–1 of this chapter, to authorize the issuance of orders designating securities as "standardized options".

(52) Pursuant to Rules 17h–1T and 17h–2T of the Act (§§240.17h–1T and 240.17h–2T of this chapter):

(i) To designate certain broker–dealers as Reporting Brokers or Dealers; *or and*

(ii) To grant or deny an exemption, conditionally or unconditionally, to a broker or dealer pursuant to section 17(h) of the Act.

(53) To administer the provisions of §240.24c–1 of this chapter; provided that access to nonpublic information as defined in such section shall be provided only with the concurrence of the head of the Commission division or office responsible for such information or the files containing such information.

(54) To administer the provisions of Section 24(d) of the Act (15 U.S.C. 78x(d)).

(55) Pursuant to §240.15c6–1 of this chapter, taking into account then existing market practices, to exempt contracts for the purchase or sale of any securities from the requirements of §240.15c6–1(a) of this chapter.

(56) Pursuant to §270.17Ad–16 of this chapter, to designate by order the appropriate qualified registered securities depository.

(57) Pursuant to section 19(b)(2) of the Act, 15 U.S.C. 78s(b)(2), and section 19(b)(3) of the Act, 15 U.S.C. 78s(b)(3), to institute proceedings to determine whether a proposed rule change of a self–regulatory organization should be disapproved and to provide to the self–regulatory organization notice of the grounds for disapproval under consideration. If the Commission has not taken action on a proposed rule change for which delegated authority has been withdrawn under paragraph (a)(12) of this section prior to the expiration of the applicable time period specified in section 19(b)(2) of the Act, 15 U.S.

《609规则》（《联邦规章汇编》第十七篇第242.609节），就以下各项发布公告并通过命令授予无条件或附条件的核准：根据该法第11A（b）条以及依其颁布的《609规则》提出的证券信息处理机构注册申请、要求豁免于该条规定以及依其颁发的所有规则或规章的申请。

（50）根据该法第17A（b）条和第19（a）条［《美国法典》第十五编第78q-1（b）节和第78s（a）节］：

（i）同意签发命令，核准将临时结算机构注册延长不超过2年的时间或结算机构同意的其他更长的时间。

（ii）申请人请求撤回结算机构注册申请的，在证券交易委员会尚未对之前提出的结算机构注册申请作出最终判定前的任何时候，同意签发命令核准该结算机构注册申请的撤回。

（51）根据本章第240.9b-1节第（a）（4）款，同意签发命令将证券指定为“标准化期权”。

（52）根据该法《17h-1T规则》和《17h-2T规则》（本章第240.17h-1T节和第240.17h-2T节）：

（i）将特定经纪自营商指定为报告经纪商或自营商；和/或

（ii）根据该法第17（h）条无条件或有条件地核准或驳回经纪商或自营商的豁免。

（53）实施本章第240.24c-1节的规定；但是，提供该节规定的非公开信息的查询权的，必须征得对上述信息或含有上述信息文档负责的部门或办公室的主任同意。

（54）负责实施该法第24（d）条［《美国法典》第十五编第78x（d）节］的规定。

（55）根据本章第240.15c6-1节，在考虑到现有市场实践的情况下，将任何证券的购销合同豁免于本章第240.15c6-1（a）节的要求。

（56）根据本章第270.17Ad-16条，通过命令指定适当、合格的注册证券存管机构。

（57）根据该法第19（b）（2）条［《美国法典》第十五编第78s（b）（2）节］及第19（b）（3）条［《美国法典》第十五编第78s（b）（3）节］，发起程序以判定是否应否决自律组织的规则变更提案，并将所考虑的否决理由通知自律组织。若证券交易委员会未就规则变更提案采取任何行动，而在该法第19（b）（2）节［《美国法典》第十五编第78s（b）（2）节］规定的适用期限届满之前相关授权已按本条第（a）（12）款撤销，则交易和市场部主任应根据授权发起程序，决定是否应否决规则变更提案。此外，还有权根据该法第19（b）（2）（B）条［《美国法典》第十五编第78s（b）（2）（B）节］，延长证券交易委员会通过命令批准或

C. 78s(b)(2), then the Director shall institute pursuant to delegated authority proceedings to determine whether the proposed rule change should be disapproved. In addition, pursuant to section 19(b)(2)(B) of the Act, 15 U.S.C. 78s(b)(2)(B), to extend for a period not exceeding 240 days from the date of publication of notice of the filing of a proposed rule change pursuant to Section 19(b)(1) of the Act, 15 U.S.C. 78s(b)(1), the period during which the Commission must issue an order approving or disapproving the proposed rule change and to determine whether such longer period is appropriate and publish the reasons for such determination.

(58) Pursuant to section 19(b)(3)(C) of the Act, 15 U.S.C. 78s(b)(3)(C), to temporarily suspend a change in the rules of a self-regulatory organization.

(59) Pursuant to paragraph (f)(6)(iii) of Rule 19b-4 (§240.19b-4 of this chapter), to reduce the period before which a proposed rule change can become operative, and to reduce the period between an SRO submission of a filing and a pre-filing notification.

(60) To grant exemptions from Rule 17a-23 (§240.17a-23 of this chapter), pursuant to Rule 17a-23(i) (§240.17a-23(i) of this chapter).

(61) To grant exemptions from Rule 604 (17 CFR 242.604), pursuant to Rule 604 (c) (17 CFR 242.604(c)).

(62) Pursuant to section 36 of the Act (15 U.S.C. 78mm) to review and, either unconditionally or on specified terms and conditions, grant or deny exemptions from section 11(d)(1) of the Act (15 U.S.C. 78k(d)(1)).

(63) Pursuant to §240.15a-1(b)(1) of this chapter, to issue orders identifying other permissible securities activities in which an OTC derivatives dealer may engage.

(64) Pursuant to §240.15a-1(b)(2) of this chapter, to issue orders determining that a class of fungible instruments that are standardized as to their material economic terms is within the scope of eligible OTC derivative instrument.

(65) Pursuant to §240.17a-12 of this chapter:

(i) To authorize the issuance of orders requiring OTC derivatives dealers to file, pursuant to §240.17a-12(a)(ii) of this chapter, monthly, or at such times as shall be specified, Part IIB of Form X-17A-5 (§249.617 of this chapter) and such other financial and operational information as shall be specified.

(ii) Pursuant to §240.17a-12(n) of this chapter, to consider applications by OTC derivatives dealers for exemptions from, and extensions of time within which to file, reports required by §240.17a-12 of this chapter, and to grant or deny such applications.

(66) To issue orders under Rules 15b3-1(c)(4), 15b6-1(e), 15Ba2-2(e)(4), 15Bc3-1(e), 15Ca2-1(c)(4), and 15Cc1-1(d) (17 CFR 240.15b3-1(c)(4), 240.15b6-1(e), 240.15Ba2-2(e)(4), 240.15Bc3-1(e), 240.15Ca2-1(c)(4), and

否决规则变更提案的期限,并判定延长的时间是否适当同时公布相关理由。延长时间自关于依该法第19(b)(1)条[《美国法典》第十五编第78s(b)(1)节]提交的规则变更提案的公告发布之日起不得超过240日。

(58)根据该法第19(b)(3)(C)条[《美国法典》第十五编第78s(b)(3)(C)节],临时暂停自律组织规则的变更。

(59)根据《19b-4规则》(本章第240.19b-4节)第(f)(6)(iii)款,缩短规则变更提案实施前的等待期,以及缩短自律组织提交申请通知和申请预通知之间的期间。

(60)根据《17a-23(i)规则》[本章第240.17a-23(i)节]核准对《17a-23规则》(本章第240.17a-23节)的豁免。

(61)根据《604(c)规则》[《联邦规章汇编》第十七编第242.604(c)节]核准对《604规则》(《联邦规章汇编》第17编第242.604节)的豁免。

(62)根据该法第36条(《美国法典》第十五编第78mm节)审查并无条件或附具体条款、条件地核准或驳回对该法第11(d)(1)条[《美国法典》第十五编第78k(d)(1)节]的豁免。

(63)根据本章第240.15a-1(b)(1)节,签发命令确定场外交易衍生品自营商可以从事的允许其开展的其他证券活动。

(64)根据本章第240.15a-1(b)(2)节,签发命令判定某类可替代金融工具根据其实质经济条款属于标准化金融工具,因此在适格场外交易衍生金融工具范围之内。

(65)根据本章第240.17a-12节:

(i)同意签发命令要求场外交易衍生品自营商根据本章第240.17a-12(a)(ii)节每月或按其他规定频率提交《X-17A-5表格》第IIB部分(本章第249.617节)及其他指定的财务和经营信息。

(ii)根据本章第240.17a-12(n)节,审查场外交易衍生品自营商提交的关于豁免本章第240.17a-12节的报告要求的申请和延长报告提交期限的申请,并核准或驳回该等申请。

(66)根据《15b3-1(c)(4)规则》、《15b6-1(e)规则》、《15Ba2-2(e)(4)规则》、《15Bc3-1(e)规则》、《15Ca2-1(c)(4)规则》和《15Cc1-1(d)规则》[《联邦规章汇编》第十七编第240.15b3-1(c)(4)节、第240.15b6-1(e)节、第240.15Ba2-2(e)(4)节、第

240.15Cc1-1(d)).

(67) Pursuant to Section 36(a) of the Act, 15 U.S.C. 78mm(a), to grant requests for exemptions from the tender offer provisions of Rule 14e-1 of Regulation 14E (§240.14e-1 of this chapter).

(68) Pursuant to Rule 605(b) (17 CFR 242.605(b)), to grant or deny exemptions, conditionally or unconditionally, from any provision or provisions of Rule 605 (17 CFR 242.605).

(69) Pursuant to Rule 606(c) (17 CFR 242.606(c)), to grant or deny exemptions, conditionally or unconditionally, from any provision or provisions of Rule 606 (17 CFR 242.606).

(70) Pursuant to Sections 15(a)(2) and 36 of the Act (15 U.S.C. 78o(a)(2) and 78mm), to review and, either unconditionally or on specified terms and conditions, to grant or deny exemptions to any bank, savings association, or savings bank from the broker-dealer registration requirements of Section 15(a)(1) of the Act (15 U.S.C. 78o (a)(1)) or any applicable provision of this Act (15 U.S.C. 78c *et seq.*) and the rules and regulations thereunder based solely on such bank's, savings association's, or savings bank's status as a broker or dealer.

(71) Pursuant to section 6(a) of the Act, 15 U.S.C. 78f(a), and Rule 6a-1 thereunder, 17 CFR 240.6a-1:

(i) To publish a notice of filing of an application for registration as a national securities exchange, or for exemption from registration based on limited volume;

(ii) To publish amendments to an application for registration as a national securities exchange, or for exemption from registration based on limited volume; and

(iii) To extend deadlines for submission of comments to an application for registration as a national securities exchange, or for exemption from registration based on limited volume; and amendments to an application for registration as a national securities exchange, or for exemption from registration based on limited volume.

(72) Pursuant to section 36 of the Act (15 U.S.C. 78mm) to review and, either unconditionally or on specified terms and conditions, grant, or deny exemptions from rule 17a-25 of the Act (§240.17a-25 of this chapter).

(73) Pursuant to Section 19(b)(7)(A) of the Act, 15 U.S.C. 78s(b)(7)(A), to publish notices of proposed rule changes filed by self-regulatory organizations relating to security futures products.

(74) Pursuant to Section 19(b)(7)(C) of the Act, 15 U.S.C. 78s(b)(7)(C), to abrogate a change in the rules of a self-regulatory organization relating to security futures products and require that it be refiled in accordance with Section 19(b)(1) of the Act, 15 U.S.C. 78s(b)(1).

240.15Bc3-1(e)节、第240.15Ca2-1(c)(4)节和第240.15Cc1-1(d)节]签发命令。

(67)根据该法第36(a)条[《美国法典》第十五编第78mm(a)节]核准对《14E管理办法》的《14e-1规则》(本章第240.14e-1节)的股权收购要约条款的豁免请求。

(68)根据《605(b)规则》[《联邦规章汇编》第十七编第242.605(b)节],有条件或无条件地核准或驳回对《605规则》(《联邦规章汇编》第十七编第242.605节)任何条款的豁免。

(69)根据《606(c)规则》[《联邦规章汇编》第十七编第242.606(c)节],有条件或无条件地核准或驳回对《606规则》(《联邦规章汇编》第十七编第242.606节)任何条款的豁免。

(70)根据该法第15(a)(2)条和第36条[《美国法典》第十五编第78o(a)(2)节、第78mm节],审核并无条件或附具体条款、条件地核准或驳回向任何银行、储蓄协会或储蓄银行授予对该法第15(a)(1)条[《美国法典》第十五编第78o(a)(1)节]或任何适用条款(《美国法典》第十五编第78c节及其后条文)以及依其颁布的任何规则与规章的豁免,作出核准或驳回的唯一基础应为该等银行、储蓄协会或储蓄银行作为经纪商或自营商开展业务的状态。

(71)根据该法第6(a)条[《美国法典》第十五编第78f(a)节]以及依其颁布的《6a-1规则》(《联邦规章汇编》第十七编第240.6a-1节):

(i)就全国性证券交易所注册申请或者以交易量有限为由提出的注册豁免申请发布公告;

(ii)就全国性证券交易所注册申请的修正稿或者以交易量有限为由提出的注册豁免申请的修正稿发布公告;

(iii)针对上述全国性证券交易所注册申请或者以交易量有限为由提出的注册豁免申请或者该等申请的修正稿,延长其意见征询期。

(72)根据该法第36条(《美国法典》第十五编第78mm节)审查并无条件或附具体条款、条件地核准或驳回对该法《17a-25规则》(本章第240.17a-25节)的豁免。

(73)根据该法第19(b)(7)(A)条[《美国法典》第十五编第78s(b)(7)(A)节],就自律组织提交的证券期货产品规则变更提案发布公告。

(74)根据该法第19(b)(7)(C)条[《美国法典》第十五编第78s(b)(7)(C)节],废除自律组织之证券期货产品规则变更,并要求按照该法第19(b)(1)条[《美国法典》第十五编第78s(b)(1)节]重新提交。

(75) Pursuant to Section 6(g)(3) of the Act, 15 U.S.C. 78f(g)(3), to publish acknowledgement of receipt of a notice of registration as a national securities exchange for the sole purpose of trading security futures products under Section 6(g) of the Act and Rule 6a-4 of the Act (17 CFR 240.6a-4).

(76) Pursuant to section 36 of the Act (15 U.S.C. 78mm) to review and grant or deny exemptions from the rule filing requirements of section 19(b) (15 U.S.C. 78s(b)) of the Act, in a case where a self-regulatory organization elects to incorporate by reference one or more rules of another self-regulatory organization, provided that the following specified terms and conditions are met:

(i) A self-regulatory organization electing to incorporate rules of another self-regulatory organization has requested to incorporate rules other than trading rules (e.g., the self-regulatory organization has requested to incorporate rules such as margin, suitability, arbitration);

(ii) A self-regulatory organization electing to incorporate rules of another self-regulatory organization has requested to incorporate by reference categories of rules (rather than to incorporate individual rules within a category); and

(iii) The incorporating self-regulatory organization has reasonable procedures in place to provide written notice to its members each time a change is proposed to the incorporated rules of another self-regulatory organization.

(77) To review amendments to a supervised investment bank holding company's Notice of Intention, and to approve such amendments pursuant to paragraph (d)(2)(ii) of Rule 17i-2 (17 CFR 240.17i-2(d)(2)(ii)) after reviewing the amended notice of intention to determine whether the amendment is necessary or appropriate in furtherance of the purposes of section 17 of the Act (15 U.S.C. 78q).

(78) To consider requests by supervised investment bank holding companies for exemptions from the requirement, and extensions of time within which, to file reports and notices required by Rule 17i-6 (17 CFR 240.17i-6), and to grant or deny such requests pursuant to paragraph (f) of that Rule (17 CFR 240.17i-6(f)).

(79) To consider requests by supervised investment bank holding companies for exemptions from the requirement, and extensions of time within which, to file notices required by Rule 17i-8 (17 CFR 240.17i-8), and to grant or deny such requests pursuant to paragraph (d) of that Rule (17 CFR 240.17i-8(d)).

(80) To calculate the amount of fees and assessments due from covered SROs based on the trade data that the covered SROs submit on Form R31 (17 CFR 249.11) and to issue Section 31 bills to covered SROs, in consultation with the Executive Director and the Chief Economist, pursuant to Rules 31 and 31T of this chapter (17 CFR 240.31 and 240.31T).

(75)根据该法第6(g)(3)条[《美国法典》第十五编第78f(g)(3)节],针对该法6(g)条及该法《6a-4规则》(《联邦规章汇编》第十七编第240.6a-4节)下仅为交易证券期货产品目的而注册全国性证券交易所之注册通知,发布收讫回执。

(76)根据该法第36条(《美国法典》第十五编第78mm节),自律组织选择通过引用其他自律组织的规则的方式来采用该等规则的,审查并核准或驳回对该法第19(b)条[《美国法典》第十五编第78s(b)节]的提交要求的豁免,前提是满足下述具体条款、条件:

(i)自律组织选择采用其他自律组织的规则,而所请求采用的规则为非交易性质的规则(如保证金、适当性和仲裁规则);

(ii)自律组织选择采用其他自律组织之规则,且以引用某类规则(而非仅引用属于某类规则范围内的个别规则)的方式来达到该目的;且

(iii)采用其他自律组织规则的自律组织本身制定有合理的程序,用以向其成员发送关于其他自律组织规则的变更提案的书面通知。

(77)审查受监督的银行控股公司的《意向通知》之修正稿,并在审查后判定该修正稿对于促进该法第17条(《美国法典》第十五编第78q节)之目的是否必要或适当,如得出肯定性结论的,可根据《17i-2规则》第(d)(2)(ii)款[《联邦规章汇编》第十七编第240.17i-2(d)(2)(ii)节]批准该等修正稿。

(78)审查受监督的银行控股公司提出的对《17i-6规则》(《联邦规章汇编》第十七编第240.17i-6节)的报告和通知要求的豁免请求及延长报告和通知提交期限的请求,并根据该规则第(f)款[《联邦规章汇编》第十七编第240.17i-6(f)节]核准或驳回该等请求。

(79)审查受监督的银行控股公司提出的对《17i-8规则》(《联邦规章汇编》第十七编第240.17i-8节)的通知要求的豁免请求及延长报告和通知提交期限的请求,并根据该规则第(d)款[《联邦规章汇编》第十七编第240.17i-8(d)节]核准或驳回该等请求。

(80)根据本章第《31规则》和《31T规则》(《联邦规章汇编》第十七编第240.31节和第240.31T节),在与证券交易委员会执行主任和首席经济师的协商之后,基于所涉自律组织按《R31表格》(《联邦规章汇编》第十七编第249.11节)提交的交易数据,计算自律组织应支付的费用和计征费用,并向所涉自律组织发出第31条规定的账单。

(81) To grant or deny exemptions from Rule 610 (17 CFR 242.610), pursuant to Rule 610(e) (17 CFR 242.610(e)).

(82) To grant or deny exemptions from Rule 611 (17 CFR 242.611), pursuant to Rule 611(d) (17 CFR 242.611(d)).

(83) To grant or deny exemptions from Rule 612 (17 CFR 242.612), pursuant to Rule 612(c) (17 CFR 242.612(c)).

(b) To designate officers empowered to administer oaths and affirmations, subpoena witnesses, compel their attendance, take evidence, and require the production of any books, papers, correspondence, memoranda, contracts, agreements, or other records in the course of investigations instituted by the Commission pursuant to section 21(b) of the Securities Exchange Act of 1934 (15 U.S.C. 78u(b)).

(c) In nonpublic investigatory proceedings within the responsibility of the Director or Deputy Director, to grant requests of persons to procure copies of the transcript of their testimony given pursuant to Rule 6 of the Commission's rules relating to investigations as in effect subsequent to November 16, 1972 (17 CFR 203.6).

(d) To notify the Securities Investor Protection Corporation (SIPC) of facts concerning the activities and the operational and financial condition of any registered broker or dealer which is or appears to be a member of SIPC and which is in or approaching financial difficulty within the meaning of section 5 of the Securities Investor Protection Act of 1970, as amended, 15 U.S.C. 78aaa *et seq.*

(e) To determine whether, and issue orders regarding, proposals for designation of a contract market for futures trading on an index or group of securities meet the eligibility criteria set forth under section 2(a)(1)(B)(ii) of the Commodity Exchange Act, 7 U.S.C. 2(a).

(f) With respect to the Securities Investor Protection Act of 1970, as amended, 15 U.S.C. 78aaa *et seq.* (SIPA):

(1) Pursuant to Section 3(a)(2)(B) of SIPA, to:

(i) Extend for a period not exceeding 90 days from the date of the filing of the determination by the Securities Investor Protection Corporation (SIPC) that a registered broker-dealer is not a SIPC member because it conducts its principal business outside the United States and its territories and possessions, the period during which the Commission must affirm, reverse or amend any determination by SIPC; and

(ii) Affirm such determination filed by SIPC.

(2) Pursuant to Section (3)(e)(1) of SIPA, to:

(i) Determine whether proposed bylaw changes filed by SIPC should not be disapproved or whether the proposed bylaw change is a matter of such significant public interest that public comment should be obtained, in which case the Division will notify SIPC of such finding and publish notice of the proposed bylaw change in accordance with

(81)根据《610(e)规则》[《联邦规章汇编》第十七编第242.610(e)节]核准或驳回对《610规则》(《联邦规章汇编》第十七编第242.610节)的豁免。

(82)根据《611(d)规则》[《联邦规章汇编》第十七编第242.611(d)节]核准或驳回对《611规则》(《联邦规章汇编》第十七编第242.611节)的豁免。

(83)根据《612(c)规则》[《联邦规章汇编》第十七编第242.612(c)节]核准或驳回对《612规则》(《联邦规章汇编》第十七编第242.612节)的豁免。

(b)指定被授权官员主持宣誓和证词声明程序、传唤证人程序、强制证人出席程序、取证程序,并要求在证券交易委员会根据《1934年证券交易法》第21(b)条[《美国法典》第十五编第78u(b)节]发起的调查程序中制作任何档案、文件、通信、备忘录、合同、协议或其他记录。

(c)在交易和市场部主任或副主任负责的非公开调查程序中,核准相关人员在根据1972年11月16日后生效的第6号证券交易委员会调查规则(《联邦规章汇编》第十七编第203.6节)提供证言后获得证词复本的请求。

(d)对于属于或从表面判断属于证券投资者保护公司(SIPC)成员且处于或濒临《1970年证券投资者保护法》及其修正第5条(《美国法典》第十五编第78aaa节及其后条文)定义的财务困境的任何注册经纪商或自营商,将其活动和经营财务状况事实通知证券投资者保护公司。

(e) 对于欲指定从事某一证券指数或某一组证券交易的期货合约市场的提议,判定该市场是否满足《商品交易法》第2(a)(1)(B)(ii)条[《美国法典》第七编第2(a)节]规定的适格性标准,并就此签发命令。

(f)就《1970年证券投资者保护法》(SIPA)及其修正而言(《美国法典》第十五编第78aaa节及其后条文):

(1)根据该法第3(a)(2)(B)条:

(i)在证券投资者保护公司(SIPC)提交意见判定注册经纪自营商在美国及其准州和属地之外开展主要业务因而不属于证券投资者保护公司成员后,延长证券交易委员会确认、推翻或修改证券投资者保护公司任何判定意见的期限,延长时间自证券投资者保护公司提交判定意见后不超过90日。

(ii)确认证券投资者保护公司提交的判定意见。

(2)根据该法第(3)(e)(1)条:

(i)判定是否应否决证券投资者保护公司提交的章程变更提案;或者,判定该等提案是否涉及重大公共利益因而应当征询公众意见,在该情形下,交易和市场部应将上述结论通知证券投资者保护公司并根据《1970年证券投资者保护法》第3(e)(2)条[1]发

1 原文的条款号“(3)”似与“3”混用,译文遵照原文执行。——译者注

Section 3(e)(2) of SIPA; and

(ii) Accelerate the effective date of proposed bylaw changes filed by SIPC.

(3) Pursuant to Section (3)(e)(2) of SIPA, to publish notice of proposed rule changes filed by SIPC.

(g) To consult on behalf of the Commission pursuant to section 18(t)(1) of the Federal Deposit Insurance Act (12 U.S.C. 1828(t)(1)) with respect to matters described in §200.19a.

(h) To consult on behalf of the Commission pursuant to sections 5318A(a)(4), 5318A(e)(2) and 5318(h)(2) of the Bank Secrecy Act (31 U.S.C. 5318A(a)(4), 5318A(e)(2) and 5318(h)(2)) with respect to matters described in §200.19a.

(i) To consult on behalf of the Commission pursuant to the Uniting and Strengthening America by Providing Appropriate Tools Required to Intercept and Obstruct Terrorism Act of 2001 (USA PATRIOT Act), as amended (Pub. L. 107–56 (2001), 115 Stat. 272) with respect to matters described in §200.19a.

(j) With respect to the Securities Act of 1933 (15 U.S.C. 77a *et seq.*), the Securities Exchange Act of 1934 (15 U.S.C. 78a *et seq.*), the Trust Indenture Act of 1939 (15 U.S.C. 77aaa *et seq.*), and Regulation S–T thereunder (part 232 of this chapter), to grant or deny a request submitted pursuant to Rule 13(b) of Regulation S–T (§232.13(b) of this chapter) to adjust the filing date of an electronic filing.

(k) With respect to the Securities Act of 1933 (15 U.S.C. 77a *et seq.*), the Securities Exchange Act of 1934 (15 U.S.C.) 78a *et seq.*), the Trust Indenture Act of 1939 (15 U.S.C. 77aaa *et seq.*), and Regulation S–T thereunder (part 232 of this chapter) to set the terms of, and grant or deny as appropriate, continuing hardship exemptions, pursuant to Rule 202 of Regulation S–T (§232.202 of this chapter), from the electronic submission requirements of Regulation S–T (part 232 of this chapter).

(l) Notwithstanding anything in the foregoing, in any case in which the Director of the Division of Market Regulation believes it appropriate, he may submit the matter to the Commission.

[37 FR 16795, Aug. 19, 1972]

Editorial Note: For Federal Register Citations affecting §200.30–3 see the List of CFR Sections Affected, which appears in the Finding Aids section of the printed volume and at www.fdsys.gov.

§200.30–4 Delegation of authority to Director of Division of Enforcement.

Pursuant to the provisions of Pub. L. No. 100–181, 101 Stat. 1254, 1255 (15 U.S.C. 78d–1, 78d–2), the Securities and Exchange Commission hereby delegates, until the Commission orders otherwise, the following functions to the Director of the Division of Enforcement to be performed by him or under his direction by such other person or

布章程变更提案公告;及

(ii)使证券投资者保护公司提交的章程变更提案提前生效。

(3)根据《1970年证券投资者保护法》第(3)(e)(2)条,就证券投资者保护公司提交的规则变更提案发布公告。

(g)根据《联邦存款保险法》第18(t)(1)条[(《美国法典》第十二编第1828(t)(1)节]代表证券交易委员会就第200.19a条所述事项进行磋商。

(h)根据《银行保密法》第5318A(a)(4)条、第5318A(e)(2)条和第5318(h)(2)条[《美国法典》第三十一编第5318A(a)(4)节、第5318A(e)(2)节和第5318(h)(2)节]代表证券交易委员会就第200.19a节所述事项进行磋商。

(i)根据《2001年使用适当手段阻止避免恐怖主义以团结并强化美国法》及其修正(《美国爱国者法》)[公法编号107-56(2001),《美国制定法汇编》第115卷第272页]代表证券交易委员会就第200.19a节所述事项进行磋商。

(j)就《1933年证券法》(《美国法典》第十五编第77a节及其后条文)、《1934年证券交易法》(《美国法典》 第十五编第78a节及其后条文)、《1939年信托契约法》(《美国法典》第十五编第77aaa节及其后条文)以及依其颁布的《S-T管理办法》(本章第232部分)而言,核准或驳回根据《S-T管理办法》的《13(b)规则》[本章第232.13(b)节]提出的对电子文件提交日期进行调整的请求。

(k)就《1933年证券法》(《美国法典》第十五编第77a节及其后条文)、《1934年证券交易法》(《美国法典》第十五编第78a节及其后条文)、《1939年信托契约法》(《美国法典》第十五编第77aaa节及其后条文)以及依其颁布的《S-T管理办法》(本章第232部分)而言,根据《S-T管理办法》的《202规则》(本章第232.202节),针对处于持续性困境之当事人提出的豁免适用《S-T管理办法》(本章第232部分)中的电子文件提交要求的申请,确定授予豁免的条款,并视适当情形核准或驳回豁免申请。

(l)无论上文如何规定,在任何情况下,如交易和市场部主任认为适当,其均可以将相关事项提交证券交易委员会处理。

[《联邦公报》第37卷第16795页,1972年8月19日。]

编辑注:对第200.30-3节有影响的《联邦公报》索引,参见《受影响的联邦规章汇编条文列表》(见印刷版本的《检索协助》章节和www.fdsys.gov)。

第200.30-4节　对执法部主任的委托授权

根据公法编号100-181,《美国制定法汇编》第101卷第1254页、第1255页的条文(《美国法典》第十五编第78d-1节、第78d-2节),证券交易委员会兹将下述职能委托执法部主任行使,或委托证券交易委员会主席随时指定的其他人员在执法部主任的领导下行使,直至证券交易委员会另行作出命令:

persons as may be designated from time to time by the Chairman of the Commission.

(a) (1) To designate officers empowered to administer oaths and affirmations, subpoena witnesses, compel their attendance, take evidence, and require the production of any books, papers, correspondence, memoranda, contracts, agreements, or other records in the course of investigations instituted by the Commission pursuant to section 19(c) of the Securities Act of 1933 (15 U.S.C. 77s(c)), section 21(b) of the Securities Exchange Act of 1934 (15 U.S.C. 78u(b)), section 42(b) of the Investment Company Act of 1940 (15 U.S.C. 80a–41(b)) and section 209(b) of the Investment Advisers Act of 1940 (15 U.S.C. 80b–9(b)).

(2) In nonpublic investigative proceedings, to grant requests of persons to procure copies of the transcript of their testimony under §203.6 of this chapter.

(3) To terminate and close all investigations authorized by the Commission pursuant to section 20 of the Securities Act of 1933 (15 U.S.C. 77t), section 21 of the Securities Exchange Act of 1934 (15 U.S.C. 78u), section 42 of the Investment Company Act of 1940 (15 U.S.C. 80a–41) and section 209 of the Investment Advisers Act of 1940 (15 U.S.C. 80b–9).

(4) To terminate the authority to administer oaths and affirmations, subpoena witnesses, compel their attendance, take evidence, and require the production of any books, papers, correspondence, memoranda, contracts, agreements, or other records in the course of investigations instituted by the Commission pursuant to section 19(c) of the Securities Act of 1933 (15 U.S.C. 77s(c)), section 21(b) of the Securities Exchange Act of 1934 (15 U.S.C. 78u(b)), section 42(b) of the Investment Company Act of 1940 (15 U.S.C. 80a–41(b)) and section 209(b) of the Investment Advisers Act of 1940 (15 U.S.C. 80b–9(b)).

(5) To grant or deny applications made pursuant to Rule 193 of the Commission's Rules of Practice, §201.193 of this chapter, provided, that, in the event of a denial, the applicant shall be notified that such a denial may be appealed to the Commission for review.

(6) To notify the Securities Investor Protection Corporation (SIPC) of facts concerning the activities and the operational and financial condition of any registered broker or dealer which is or appears to be a member of SIPC and which is in or approaching financial difficulty within the meaning of section 5 of the Securities Investor Protection Act of 1970, as amended, 15 U.S.C. 78aaa *et seq.*

(7) To administer the provisions of §240.24c–1 of this chapter; provided that access to nonpublic information as defined in such section shall be provided only with the concurrence of the head of the Commission division or office responsible for such information or the files containing such information.

(a)(1)指定被授权官员主持宣誓和证词声明程序、传唤证人程序、强制证人出席程序、取证程序,并要求在证券交易委员会根据《1933年证券法》第19(c)条[《美国法典》第十五编第77s(c)节]、《1934年证券交易法》第21(b)条[《美国法典》第十五编第78u(b)节]、《1940年投资公司法》第42(b)条[《美国法典》第十五编第80a-41(b)节]及《1940年投资顾问法》第209(b)条[《美国法典》第十五编第80b-9(b)节]发起的调查程序中制作任何档案、文件、通信、备忘录、合同、协议或其他记录。

(2)在非公开调查程序中,核准相关人士提出的获得根据本章第203.6节作出的证词之复本的请求。

(3)根据《1933年证券法》第20条(《美国法典》第十五编第77t节)、《1934年证券交易法》第21条(《美国法典》第十五编第78u节)、《1940年投资公司法》第42条(《美国法典》第十五编第80a-41节)及《1940年投资顾问法》第209条(《美国法典》第十五编第80b-9节)终止和结束证券交易委员会授权进行的所有调查程序。

(4)终止下述授权:主持宣誓和证词声明程序、传唤证人程序、强制证人出席程序、取证程序的权限,以及要求在证券交易委员会根据《1933年证券法》第19(c)条[《美国法典》第十五编第77s(c)节]、《1934年证券交易法》第21(b)条[《美国法典》第十五编第78u(b)节]、《1940年投资公司法》第42(b)条[《美国法典》第十五编第80a-41(b)节]及《1940年投资顾问法》第209(b)条[《美国法典》第十五编第80b-9(b)节]发起的调查程序中制作任何档案、文件、通信、备忘录、合同、协议或其他记录的权限。

(5)核准或驳回根据《证券交易委员会工作规则》的《193规则》(本章第201.193节)提交的申请,但是拒绝申请的,应向申请人告知其有权要求证券交易委员会进行复议。

(6)对于属于或从表面判断属于证券投资者保护公司(SIPC)成员且处于或濒临《1970年证券投资者保护法》及其修正第5条(《美国法典》第十五编第78aaa节及其后条文)定义的财务困境的注册经纪商或自营商,将其活动和经营财务状况事实通知证券投资者保护公司。

(7)负责实施本章第240.24c-1节的规定;但是,提供该条规定的非公开信息查询权的,必须征得对上述信息或含有上述信息的文档负责的部门或办公室的主任的同意。

(8) Pursuant to Rule 204-2(j)(3)(ii) (§275.204-2(j)(3)(ii) of this chapter) under the Investment Advisers Act of 1940 (15 U.S.C. 80b-1 *et seq.*), to make written demands upon non-resident investment advisers subject to the provisions of such rule to furnish to the Commission true, correct, complete and current copies of any or all books and records which such non-resident investment advisers are required to make, keep current or preserve pursuant to any provision of any rule or regulation of the Commission adopted under the Investment Advisers Act of 1940, or any part of such books and records which may be specified in any such demand.

(9) To administer the provisions of Section 24(d) of the Securities Exchange Act of 1934 (15 U.S.C. 78x(d)).

(10) To institute subpoena enforcement proceedings in federal court to seek an order compelling the production of documents or an individual's appearance for testimony pursuant to subpoenas issued pursuant to paragraph (a)(1) of this section in connection with investigations pursuant to section 19(c) of the Securities Act of 1933 (15 U.S.C. 77s (c)), section 21(b) of the Securities Exchange Act of 1934 (15 U.S.C. 78u(b)), section 42(b) of the Investment Company Act of 1940 (15 U.S.C. 80a-41(b)) and section 209 (b) of the Investment Advisers Act of 1940 (15 U.S.C. 80b-9(b)).

(11) To authorize staff to appear in federal bankruptcy court to preserve Commission claims in connection with investigations pursuant to section 19(c) of the Securities Act of 1933 (15 U.S.C. 77s(c)), section 21(b) of the Securities Exchange Act of 1934 (15 U.S. C. 78u(b)), section 42(b) of the Investment Company Act of 1940 (15 U.S.C. 80a-41 (b)) and section 209(b) of the Investment Advisers Act of 1940 (15 U.S.C. 80b-9(b)).

(12) Pursuant to Section 36 of the Securities Exchange Act of 1934 (15 U.S.C. 78mm) to review and, either unconditionally or on specified terms and conditions, grant, or deny exemptions from rule 17a-25 of the Act (§240.17a-25 of this chapter), provided that the Division of Trading and Markets is notified of any such granting or denial of an exemption.

(13) To order the making of private investigations pursuant to section 19(c) of the Securities Act of 1933 (15 U.S.C. 77s(c)), section 21(b) of the Securities Exchange Act of 1934 (15 U.S.C. 78u(b)), section 42(b) of the Investment Company Act of 1940 (15 U.S.C. 80a-41(b) and section 209(b) of the Investment Advisers Act of 1940 (15 U.S.C. 80b-9(b)).

(14) To submit witness immunity requests to the U.S. Attorney General for approval to seek an order compelling an individual to give testimony or provide other information pursuant to a subpoena that may be necessary to the public interest in connection with investigations and related enforcement actions pursuant to section 22(b) of the Securities Act of 1933 (15 U.S.C. 77v(b)), section 21(c) of the Securities Exchange Act of 1934

(8)根据《1940年投资顾问法》(《美国法典》第十五编第80b-1节及其后条文)的《204-2(j)(3)(ii)规则》[本章第275.204-2(j)(3)(ii)节],向受制于上述规则的非居民投资顾问发出书面要求,督促其向证券交易委员会提交根据证券交易委员会在《1940年投资顾问法》下通过的任何规则或规章之规定其应制作、更新或保存的任何及所有账簿和记录或者任何该等书面要求中指明的该等账簿和记录的任何部分之真实、准确、完整和最新的副本。

(9)负责实施《1934年证券交易法》第24(d)条[《美国法典》第十五编第78x(d)节]的规定。

(10)在根据《1933年证券法》第19(c)条[《美国法典》第十五编第77s(c)节]、《1934年证券交易法》第21(b)条[《美国法典》第十五编第78u(b)节]、《1940年投资公司法》第42(b)条[《美国法典》第十五编第80a-41(b)节]及《1940年投资顾问法》第209(b)条[《美国法典》第十五编第80b-9(b)节]发起的调查程序中,基于本节第(a)(1)款项下签发的传票,在联邦法院发起传票强制执行程序,提请法院签发强制要求提交文件或强制证人出席作证的命令。

(11)授权工作人员出席联邦破产法院庭审,在根据《1933年证券法》第19(c)条[《美国法典》第十五编第77s(c)节]、《1934年证券交易法》第21(b)条[《美国法典》第十五编第78u(b)节]、《1940年投资公司法》第42(b)条[《美国法典》第十五编第80a-41(b)节]及《1940年投资顾问法》第209(b)条[《美国法典》第十五编第80b-9(b)节]发起的调查程序中主张证券交易委员会的诉求。

(12)根据《1934年证券交易法》(《美国法典》第十五编第78mm节)第36条审核并无条件或附具体条款、条件地核准或驳回对该法的《17a-25规则》(本章第240.17a-25节)的豁免,但应将任何核准或驳回决定告知交易和市场部。

(13)根据《1933年证券法》第19(c)条[《美国法典》第十五编第77s(c)节]、《1934年证券交易法》第21(b)条[《美国法典》第十五编第78u(b)节]、《1940年投资公司法》第42(b)条[《美国法典》第十五编第80a-41(b)节]及《1940年投资顾问法》第209(b)条[《美国法典》第十五编第80b-9(b)节]命令提起私人调查。

(14)在根据《1933年证券法》第22(b)条[《美国法典》第十五编第77v(b)节]、《1934年证券交易法》第21(c)条[《美国法典》第十五编第78u(c)节]、《1940年投资公司法》第42(c)条[《美国法典》第十五编第80a-41(c)节]及《1940年投资顾问法》第209(c)条[《美国法典》第十五编第80b-9(c)节]提起的调查和相关执法活动中,向联邦总检察长提交证人豁免请求,提请其签发命令,强制相关个人根据为公共利益签发的传票提

(15 U.S.C. 78u(c)), section 42(c) of the Investment Company Act of 1940 (15 U.S.C. 80a–41(c)) and section 209(c) of the Investment Advisers Act of 1940 (15 U.S.C. 80b–9(c)).

(15) With respect to debts arising from actions to enforce the federal securities laws, to terminate collection activity or discharge debts, to accept offers to compromise debts when the principal amount of the debt is $5 million or less, to reject offers to compromise debts, and to accept or reject offers to enter into payment plans.

(b) Notwithstanding anything in the foregoing, in any case in which the Director of the Division of Enforcement believes it appropriate, he may submit the matter to the Commission.

[37 FR 16796, Aug. 19, 1972]

Editorial Note: For Federal Register Citations affecting §200.30–4, see the List of CFR Sections Affected, which appears in the Finding Aids section of the printed volume and at www.fdsys.gov.

§200.30–5 Delegation of authority to Director of Division of Investment Management.

Pursuant to the provisions of Pub. L. 87–592, 76 Stat. 394 (15 U.S.C. 78d–1, 78d–2), the Securities and Exchange Commission hereby delegates, until the Commission orders otherwise, the following functions to the Director of the Division of Investment Management, to be performed by him or under his direction by such person or persons as may be designated from time to time by the Chairman of the Commission:

(a) With respect to the Investment Company Act of 1940(15 U.S.C. 80a–1 *et seq.*):

(1) Except as otherwise provided in this section, to issue notices, under §270.0–5 of this chapter, with respect to applications for orders under the Act and the rules and regulations thereunder and, with respect to section 8(f) of the Act (15 U.S.C. 80a–8(f)), in cases where no application has been filed, where, upon examination, the matter does not appear to the Director to present significant issues that have not been previously settled by the Commission or to raise questions of fact or policy indicating that the public interest or the interest of investors warrants that the Commission consider the matter.

(2) Except as otherwise provided in this section, to authorize the issuance of orders where a notice, under §270.0–5 of this chapter, has been issued and no request for a hearing has been received from any interested person within the period specified in the notice and the Director believes that the matter presents no significant issues that have not been previously settled by the Commission and it does not appear to the Director to be necessary in the public interest or the interest of investors that the Commission consider the matter.

供证词或其他信息。

（15）就因执行联邦证券法的行动引起的债务而言，终止债务催收活动或解除债务，接受债务本金不高于500万美元的和解要约，拒绝债务和解要约，接受或拒绝付款计划要约。

（b）无论上文如何规定，在任何情况下，如执法部主任认为适当，其均可以将相关事项提交证券交易委员会处理。

[《联邦公报》第37卷第16796页，1972年8月19日。]

编辑注：对第200.30–4节有影响的《联邦公报》索引，参见《受影响的联邦规章汇编条文列表》（见印刷版本的《检索协助》章节和www.fdsys.gov）。

第200.30–5节　对投资管理部主任的委托授权

根据公法编号87–592，《美国制定法汇编》第76卷第394页（《美国法典》第十五编第78d–1节、第78d–2节），证券交易委员会兹将下述职能委托投资管理部主任行使，或委托证券交易委员会主席随时指定的其他人员在投资管理部主任的领导下行使（直至证券交易委员会另行作出命令）：

（a）就《1940年投资公司法》（《美国法典》第十五编第80a–1节及其后条文）而言：

（1）除本节另有规定的情形外：根据本章第270.0–5节针对在该法或其下规则与规章下提出的命令签发申请发布公告，或者，如未提出申请，则应针对该法第8（f）条[《美国法典》第十五编第80a–8（f）节]发布公告，前提是：投资管理部主任核查后认为，有关事项并不存在证券交易委员会之前未解决的重大问题，亦不涉及出于公共利益或投资者利益的考虑而有必要提交证券交易委员会审议的事实或政策问题。

（2）除本节另有规定的情形外：在已根据本章第270.0–5节发布公告且在公告规定的期间内未收到任何利害关系人听证请求的情况下同意签发命令，前提是：投资管理部主任认为，有关事项并不存在证券交易委员会之前未解决的重大问题，亦非出于公共利益或投资者利益的考虑而有必要提交证券交易委员会审议的事项。

(3) To permit the withdrawal of applications pursuant to the Act (15 U.S.C. 80a-1 *et seq.*)

(4) In connection with the mailing of reports to stockholders and the filing with the Commission of registration statements and of reports:

(i) To grant reasonable extensions of time, upon a showing of good cause and that it would not be contrary to the public interest or inconsistent with the protection of investors; and

(ii) To deny requests for extensions of time, provided the applicant is advised that he can request Commission review of any such denial.

(5) [Reserved]

(6) To authorize the issuance of orders granting confidential treatment pursuant to section 45(a) of the Act (15 U.S.C. 80a-44(a)) where applications for confidential treatment are made regarding matters of disclosure in registration statements filed pursuant to section 8 of the Act (15 U.S.C. 80a-8), or in reports filed pursuant to section 30 of the Act (15 U.S.C. 80a-29), but only when the Commission has previously by order granted confidential treatment to the same information.

(7) To issue notices, pursuant to Rule 0-5(a) (§270.0-5(a) of this chapter) with respect to applications for temporary and permanent orders under section 9(c) of the Investment Company Act of 1940 (15 U.S.C. 80a-9(c)), and to conditionally or unconditionally exempt persons, for a temporary period not exceeding 60 days, from section 9(a) of the Investment Company Act of 1940 (15 U.S.C. 80a-9(a)), if, on the basis of the facts then set forth in the application, it appears that:

(i)(A) The prohibitions of section 9(a), as applied to the applicant, may be unduly or disproportionately severe, or (B) the applicant's conduct has been such as not to make it against the public interest or the protection of investors to grant the temporary exemption; and

(ii) Granting the temporary exemption would protect the interests of the investment companies being served by the applicant by allowing time for the orderly consideration of the application for permanent relief or the orderly transition of the applicant's responsibilities to a successor, or both.

(8) To issue:

(i) Notices, pursuant to Rule 0-5(a) (§270.0-5(a) of this chapter), with respect to applications for permanent orders under section 9(c) of the Act [15 U.S.C. 80a-9(c)], and, orders, pursuant to paragraph (a)(2) of this section, that exempt conditionally or unconditionally persons from section 9(a) of the Act [15 U.S.C. 80a-9(a)], if, on the basis of the facts then set forth in the application, it appears that:

(A) The prohibitions of section 9(a) of the Act, as applied to the applicant, may be

(3)根据该法(《美国法典》第十五编第80a-1节及其后条文)允许撤回申请。

(4)就向股东寄送报告及向证券交易委员会提交注册说明书和报告而言:

(i)核准合理的延期请求,前提是申请人提供充分理由,且不会违反公共利益或与投资者保护产生冲突;且

(ii)驳回延期请求,但应告知申请人其有权请求证券交易委员会对任何该等驳回决定进行复议。

(5)[保留]

(6)根据该法第45(a)条[《美国法典》第十五编第80a-44(a)节]同意签发保密处理命令,但保密处理申请的对象应为根据该法第8条(《美国法典》第十五编第80a-8节)提交的注册说明书或根据该法第30条(《美国法典》第十五编第80a-29节)提交的报告中披露的事项,并且仅在证券交易委员会之前已对同样信息核准保密处理的情况下方得签发上述保密处理命令。

(7)根据《0-5(a)规则》[本章第270.0-5(a)节],就依据《1940年投资公司法》第9(c)条[《美国法典》第十五编第80a-9(c)节]提出的临时或永久命令签发申请发布公告,并有条件或无条件地在不超过60日的临时期间内豁免《1940年投资公司法》第9(a)条[《美国法典》第十五编第80a-9(a)节]规定对相关主体的适用,前提是根据申请中所载事实认定:

(i)(A)第9(a)条的禁止规定对申请人的具体适用可能显得异常或过分严厉;或(B)根据申请人的行为,授予临时豁免不会违反公共利益或与投资者保护相冲突;且

(ii)核准临时豁免可以为有序审议永久救济申请提供时间,和/或为申请人向继受人有序转移责任提供时间,从而保护申请人所服务的投资公司的利益。

(8)发布公告或命令:

(i)根据《0-5(a)规则》[本章第270.0-5(a)节],就该法第9(c)条[《美国法典》第十五编第80a-9(c)节]中的永久命令签发申请发布公告,并根据本节第(a)(2)款签发命令,有条件或无条件地豁免该法第9(a)条[《美国法典》第十五编第80a-9(a)节]规定对相关主体的适用,前提是,基于申请中所载事实判断:

(A)该法第9(a)条的禁止规定对申请人的具体适用可能显得异常或过分严厉;或

unduly or disproportionately severe, or the applicant's conduct has been such as not to make it against the public interest or the protection of investors to grant the exemption;

(B) The prohibitions arise under section 9(a)(3) of the Act solely because the applicant employs, or will employ, a person who is disqualified under section 9(a)(1) or (2) of the Act; and

(C) The employee does not and will not serve in any capacity directly related to providing investment advice to, or acting as depositor for, any registered investment company, or acting as principal underwriter for any registered open-end company, registered unit investment trust or registered face amount certificate company.

(ii) Temporary orders under section 9(c) of the Act [15 U.S.C. 80a-9(c)], exempting conditionally or unconditionally persons from section 9(a) of the Act [15 U.S.C. 80a-9(a)], if, on the basis of the application, it appears that:

(A) The prohibitions arise under section 9(a)(3) of the Act solely because the applicant employs a person who is disqualified under section 9(a)(1) or (2) of the Act; and

(B) Applicant meets the requirements of paragraphs (a)(8)(i)(A) and (C) of this section.

(b) With respect to matters pertaining to investment companies registered under the Investment Company Act of 1940 (15 U.S.C. 80a *et seq*.), pooled investment funds or accounts, and the general assets or separate accounts of insurance companies, all arising under the Securities Act of 1933 (15 U.S.C. 77a *et seq*.), the Securities Exchange Act of 1934 (15 U.S.C. 78a *et seq*.), and the Trust Indenture Act of 1939 (15 U.S.C. 77aaa *et seq*.), the same functions as are delegated to the Director of the Division of Corporation Finance in regard to companies other than such investment companies in paragraphs (a), (e), and (f) of §200.30-1.

(b-1) *With respect to the Securities Act of 1933.* (1) To issue notices with respect to applications for orders under section 3(a)(2) exempting from section 5 interests or participations issued in connection with stock bonus, pension, profit-sharing, or annuity plans covering employees some or all of whom are employees within the meaning of section 401(c)(1) of the Internal Revenue Code of 1954 where, upon examination, the matter does not appear to him to present issues not previously settled by the Commission or to raise questions of fact or policy indicating that the public interest or the interest of investors requires that a hearing be held.

(2) To authorize the issuance of orders where a notice has been issued and no request for a hearing has been received from any interested person within the period specified in the notice and the matter involved presents no issue that he believes has not been settled previously by the Commission and it does not appear to him to be necessary

根据申请人的行为,核准豁免不会违反公共利益或与投资者保护相冲突;

(B)该法第9(a)(3)条的禁止性规定之适用原因仅为申请人聘用或将聘用不符合该法第9(a)(1)或(2)条资格规定的主体;且

(C)所涉员工没有且不会担任直接涉及向任何注册投资公司提供投资顾问服务的任何职务,或担任其存管人,或担任注册开放式公司、注册单位投资信托或注册面额证券公司的主承销人。

(ii)根据该法第9(c)条[《美国法典》第十五编第80a-9(c)节]签发临时命令,有条件或无条件地豁免该法9(a)条[《美国法典》第十五编第80a-9(a)节]规定对相关主体的适用,前提是基于申请中所载事实判断:

(A)该法第9(a)(3)条的禁止性规定之适用原因仅为申请人聘用了不符合该法第9(a)(1)或(2)条资格规定的主体;且

(B)申请人符合本节第(a)(8)(i)(A)和(C)款的规定。

(b)就与根据《1940年投资公司法》(《美国法典》第十五编第80a节及其后条文)、集合投资基金或账户以及保险公司的总资产账户或独立账户相关的,且因《1933年证券法》(《美国法典》第十五编第77a节及其后条文)、《1934年证券交易法》(《美国法典》第十五编第78a节及其后条文)和《1939年信托契约法》(《美国法典》第十五编第77aaa节及其后条文)引起的事项而言,对第200.30-1节第(a)款、第(e)款和第(f)款规定的投资公司之外的公司行使与公司融资部主任相同的职能。

(b-1)就《1933年证券法》而言:(1)应针对在第3(a)(2)条下提出的将以下事项豁免第5条规定的适用的申请发布公告:涉及雇员的奖励配股、养老金、利润分享或年金计划的权益或参与权[其所覆盖的雇员应全部或部分为《1954年国内税收法典》第401(c)(1)条规定的雇员];前提是:投资管理部主任核查后认为,有关事项并不存在证券交易委员会之前未解决的重大问题,亦不涉及出于公共利益或投资者利益的考虑而有必要进行听证的事实或政策问题。

(2)应在已发布公告且在公告规定的期间内未收到任何利害关系人听证请求的情况下同意签发命令,前提是:投资管理部主任认为,有关事项并不存在证券交易委员会之前未解决的重大问题,亦非出于公共利益或投资者利益考虑而有必要举行听证会的事项。

in the public interest or the interest of investors that a hearing be held.

(b-2) With respect to post-effective amendments filed pursuant to §230.485(a) or §230.486(a) of this chapter:

(1) To suspend the operation of paragraph (a) of such sections and to issue written notices to registrants of such suspensions;

(2) To determine such amendments to be effective within shorter periods of time than the sixtieth day after the filing thereof.

(b-3) With respect to post-effective amendments filed pursuant to §230.485(b) or §230.486(b) of this chapter:

(1) To approve additional purposes for post-effective amendments which shall be eligible for immediate effectiveness pursuant to paragraph (b) of such sections.

(2) To suspend the operation of paragraph (b) of such sections and to issue written notices to registrants of such suspensions.

(b-4) With respect to registration statements filed pursuant to paragraph (a) of Rule 487 under the Act (17 CFR 230.487(a)):

(1) To suspend the operation of said paragraph (a) and to issue written notices to registrants of such suspensions.

(b-5) With respect to registration statements filed pursuant to paragraph (a) of rule 488 under the Act (17 CFR 230.488(a)):

(1) To suspend the operation of said paragraphs and to issue written notices to registrants of such suspensions;

(2) To determine such amendments to be effective within shorter periods of time than the thirtieth day after the filing thereof.

(c) With respect to the Securities Act of 1933 and Regulation E thereunder (§230.601 *et seq.* of this chapter):

(1) To authorize the offering of securities:

(i) Less than ten days subsequent to the filing with the Commission of a notification on Form 1-E (§239.200 of this chapter) pursuant to Rule 604(a) (§230.604(a) of this chapter);

(ii) Less than ten days subsequent to the filing of an amendment to a notification on Form 1-E (§239.200 of this chapter) pursuant to Rule 604(c) (§230.604(c) of this chapter).

(2) To authorize the use of a revised or amended offering circular less than ten days subsequent to the filing thereof pursuant to Rule 605(e) (§230.605(e) of this chapter).

(3) To authorize the use of communications specified in paragraphs (a), (b) and (c) of Rule 607 (§230.607 of this chapter), less than five days subsequent to the filing thereof.

（b-2）就根据本章第230.485（a）节或第230.486（a）节在生效后所提交的修正稿而言：

（1）暂停该节第（a）款的适用，并向注册人发送书面暂停通知；

（2）在提交后不到60日的期间内判定修正稿的有效性；

（b-3）就根据本章第230.485（b）节或第230.486（b）节在生效后提交的修正稿而言：

（1）对于生效后提交的根据该节第（b）款可以立即生效的修正稿，批准该修正稿附加的适用范围。

（2）暂停该节第（b）款的适用，并向注册人发送书面暂停通知；

（b-4）就根据该法《487》第（a）款[《联邦规章汇编》第十七编第230.487（a）节]提交的注册说明书而言：

（1）暂停该节第（a）款的适用，并向注册人发送书面暂停通知。

（b-5）就根据该法《488规则》第（a）款[《联邦规章汇编》第十七编第230.488（a）节]提交的注册说明书而言：

（1）暂停该款的适用，并向注册人发送书面暂停通知；

（2）在提交后不到30日的期间内判定修正稿的有效性。

（c）就《1933年证券法》以及依其颁布的《E管理办法》（本章第230.601节及其后条文）而言：

（1）在下述期间内核准证券发行：

（i）根据《604（a）规则》[本章第230.604（a）节]，在向证券交易委员会提交《1-E表格》（本章第239.200节）通知后不满10日的期间内；

（ii）根据《604（c）规则》[本章第230.604（c）节]，在向证券交易委员会提交对《1-E表格》（本章第239.200节）通知的修正稿后不满10日的期间内。

（2）根据《605（e）规则》[本章第230.605（e）节]，在提交修改或修正的发行通告后不满10日的期间内核准使用上述通告。

（3）在《607规则》（本章第230.607节）第（a）款、第（b）款和第（c）款规定的通信提交后不满5日的期间内核准使用该等通信。

(4) To permit the withdrawal of any notification, or any exhibit or other documents filed as a part thereof, pursuant to Rule 604(d) (§230.604(d) of this chapter).

(c–1) With respect to the Securities Exchange Act of 1934: (1) To grant and deny applications filed pursuant to section 24(b) of the Securities Exchange Act of 1934 (15 U.S.C. 78x(b)) and Rule 24b–2 thereunder (§240.24b–2 of this chapter) for confidential treatment of information filed pursuant to section 13(f) of that Act (15 U.S.C. 78m(f)) and Rule 13f–1 thereunder (§240.13f–1 of this chapter).

(2) To revoke a grant of confidential treatment for any such application.

(3) To administer the provisions of §240.24c–1 of this chapter; provided that access to nonpublic information as defined in such section shall be provided only with the concurrence of the head of the Commission division or office responsible for such information or the files containing such information.

(4) To administer the provisions of section 24(d) of the Act (15 U.S.C. 78x(d)).

(d) To issue certifications to investment companies that are principally engaged in the furnishing of capital to corporations that are principally engaged in the development or exploitation of inventions, technological improvements, new processes, or products not previously generally available, under Section 851(e) of the Internal Revenue Code of 1986 (26 U.S.C. 851(e)), where applications from the investment companies do not present issues that have not been previously settled by the Commission and do not require a hearing.

(e) With respect to the Investment Advisers Act of 1940 (15 U.S.C. 80b–1 to 80b–22):

(1) Pursuant to section 203(c) of the Act (15 U.S.C. 80b–3(c)): To authorize the issuance of orders granting registration of investment advisers within 45 days of the filing of an application for registration as an investment adviser (or within such longer period as to which the applicant consents).

(2) Pursuant to section 203(h) of the Act (15 U.S.C. 80b–3(h)), to authorize the issuance of orders canceling registration of investment advisers, or applications for registration, if such investment advisers or applicants for registration are no longer in existence, not engaged in business as investment advisers, or are prohibited from registering as investment advisers under Section 203A of the Act (15 U.S.C. 80b–3a).

(3) To issue notices, under §275.0–5 of this chapter, with respect to applications for orders under the Act and the rules and regulations thereunder where, upon examination, the matter does not appear to the Director to present significant issues that have not been previously settled by the Commission or to raise questions of fact or policy indicating that the public interest or the interest of investors warrants that theCommission consider the matter.

(4)根据《604(d)规则》[本章第230.604(d)节]允许撤回任何通知或作为其中一部分提交的附件或其他文件。

(c-1)就《1934年证券交易法》而言:(1)核准或驳回根据《1934年证券交易法》第24(b)条[《美国法典》第十五编第78x(b)节]以及依其颁布的《24b-2规则》(本章第240.24b-2节)提出的对根据该法第13(f)条[《美国法典》第十五编第78m(f)节]以及依其颁布的《13f-1规则》(本章第240.13f-1节)提交的信息进行保密处理的申请。

(2)撤销对上述任何保密处理申请的核准。

(3)负责实施本章第240.24c-1节的规定;但是提供该节定义之非公开信息查询权的,必须征得对该等信息或包含该等信息的文件负责的部门或办公室的主任同意。

(4)负责实施该法第24(d)条[《美国法典》第十五编第78x(d)节]的规定。

(d)根据《1986年国内税收法典》第851(e)条[《美国法典》第二十六编第851(e)节],向主要为下述公司提供资本的投资公司签发证明:主要从事于开发、利用发明、技术改良、新工艺或之前未广泛应用的产品业务的公司;前提是投资公司的申请并不存在证券交易委员会之前未解决的问题且不必举行听证。

(e)就《1940年投资顾问法》(《美国法典》第十五编第80b-1~80b-22节)而言:

(1)根据该法第203(c)条[《美国法典》第十五编第80b-3(c)节]:(i)同意签发命令,在投资顾问注册申请提交后45日内(或申请人同意的其他更长的期间内)核准注册;

(2)根据该法第203(h)条[《美国法典》第十五编第80b-3(h)节],在投资顾问或注册申请人不再存续、不再从事投资顾问业务或根据该法第203A条(《美国法典》第十五编第80b-3a节)被禁止注册为投资顾问之时,同意签发命令注销投资顾问的注册或撤销其注册申请。

(3)根据本章第275.0-5节,针对依据该法以及依其颁布的规则与规章提出的命令签发申请发布公告,前提是:投资管理部主任核查后认为,有关事项并不存在证券交易委员会之前未解决的重大问题,亦不涉及出于公共利益或投资者利益的考虑而有必要提交证券交易委员会审议的事实或政策问题。

(4) To authorize the issuance of orders where a notice, pursuant to §275.0–5 of this chapter, has been issued, no request for a hearing has been received from any interested person within the period specified in the notice, and the Director believes that the matter presents no significant issues that have not been previously settled by the Commission and it does not appear to the Director to be necessary in the public interest or the interest of investors that the Commission consider the matter.

(5) To permit the withdrawal of applications pursuant to the Act (15 U.S.C. 80b–1 *et seq.*).

(6) Pursuant to Rule 204–2(j)(3)(ii) (§275.204–2(j)(3)(ii) of this chapter), to make written demands upon non–resident investment advisers subject to the provisions of such rule to furnish to the Commission true, correct, complete and current copies of any or all books and records which such non–resident investment advisers are required to make, keep current or preserve pursuant to any provision of any rule or regulation of the Commission adopted under the Act, or any part of such books and records which may be specified in any such demand.

(7) Pursuant to section 203A(d) of the Act (15 U.S.C. 80b–3a(d)), to set the terms of, and grant or deny as appropriate, continuing hardship exemptions under §275.203–3 of this chapter.

(f) With respect to the Public Utility Holding Company Act of 1935 (15 U.S.C. 79 *et seq.*):

(1) To issue notices with respect to applications or declarations under the following sections of the Act:

(i) Section 2(a)(3), 15 U.S.C. 79(b)(a)(3).

(ii) Section 2(a)(4), 15 U.S.C. 79b(a)(4).

(iii) Section 2(a)(7), 15 U.S.C. 79b(a)(7).

(iv) Section 2(a)(8), 15 U.S.C. 79b(a)(8).

(v) Section 3(a), 15 U.S.C. 79c(a).

(vi) Section 3(b), 15 U.S.C. 79c(b).

(vii) Section 5(d), 15 U.S.C. 79e(d).

(viii) Section 6(b), 15 U.S.C. 79f(b).

(ix) Section 7, 15 U.S.C. 79g.

(x) Section 9(c)(3), 15 U.S.C. 79i(c)(3).

(xi) Section 10, 15 U.S.C. 79j.

(xii) Section 11(e), 15 U.S.C. 79k(e).

(xiii) Section 12(b), 15 U.S.C. 79l(b).

(xiv) Section 12(c), 15 U.S.C. 79l(c).

(xv) Section 12(d), 15 U.S.C. 79l(d).

(4) 在已根据本章第275.0-5节发布公告且在公告规定的期间内未收到任何利害关系人听证请求的情况下同意签发命令,前提是:投资管理部主任认为,有关事项并不存在证券交易委员会之前未解决的重大问题,亦非出于公共利益或投资者利益的考虑而有必要提交证券交易委员会审议的事项。

(5)根据该法(《美国法典》第十五编第80b-1节及其后条文)允许撤回申请。

(6)根据《204-2(j)(3)(ii)规则》[本章第275.204-2(j)(3)(ii)节],向受制于上述规则的非居民投资顾问发出书面要求,督促其根据证券交易委员会在该法下通过的规定向证券交易委员会提供其应制作、更新或保存的任何及所有账簿和记录以及书面要求中指明的该等账簿和记录的任何部分之真实、准确、完整和最新副本。

(7)根据该法第203A(d)条[《美国法典》第十五编第80b-3a(d)节],就本章第275.203-3节中的持续性困境豁免,确定授予该等豁免的条款,并视情形核准或驳回豁免申请。

(f)就《1935年公用事业控股公司法》(《美国法典》第十五编第79节及其后条文)而言:

(1)就依据该法以下各条提出的申请或声明发布公告:

(i)第2(a)(3)条[《美国法典》第十五编第79b(a)(3)节]。

(ii)第2(a)(4)条[《美国法典》第十五编第79b(a)(4)节]。

(iii)第2(a)(7)条[《美国法典》第十五编第79b(a)(7)节]。

(iv)第2(a)(8)条[《美国法典》第十五编第79b(a)(8)节]。

(v)第3(a)条[《美国法典》第十五编第79c(a)节]。

(vi)第3(b)条[《美国法典》第十五编第79c(b)节]。

(vii)第5(d)条[《美国法典》第十五编第79e(d)节]。

(viii)第6(b)条[《美国法典》第十五编第79f(b)节]。

(ix)第7条[《美国法典》第十五编第79g节]。

(x)第9(c)(3)条[《美国法典》第十五编第79i(c)(3)节]。

(xi)第10条[《美国法典》第十五编第79j节]。

(xii)第11(e)条[《美国法典》第十五编第79k(e)节]。

(xiii)第12(b)条[《美国法典》第十五编第79l(b)节]。

(xiv)第12(c)条[《美国法典》第十五编第79l(c)节]。

(xv)第12(d)条[《美国法典》第十五编第79l(d)节]。

(xvi) Section 12(e), 15 U.S.C. 79l(e).

(xvii) Section 12(f), 15 U.S.C. 79l(f).

(xviii) Section 12(g), 15 U.S.C. 79l(g).

(xix) Section 13(b), 15 U.S.C. 79m(b).

(xx) Section 13(c), 15 U.S.C. 79m(c).

(xxi) Section 13(d), 15 U.S.C. 79m(d).

(xxii) Section 13(e), 15 U.S.C. 79m(e).

(xxiii) Section 13(f), 15 U.S.C. 79m(f).

(xxiv) Section 32, 15 U.S.C. 79ff.

(xxv) Section 33, 15 U.S.C. 79gg.

(2) To authorize the issuance of orders where a notice has been issued and no request for a hearing has been received from any interested person within the period specified in the notice and the matter involved presents no issue that the director believes has not previously been settled by the Commission and it does not appear to the director to be necessary in the public interest or the interest of investors or consumers that a hearing be held; section 20(c) of the Act (15 U.S.C. 79t(c));

(3) To permit the withdrawal of applications or declarations filed pursuant to the Act (15 U.S.C. 79a *et seq.*);

(4) Upon a showing of good cause and that it would not be contrary to the public interest or inconsistent with the protection of investors or consumers, to grant reasonable extensions of time with respect to the time for the filing with the Commission of registration statements and of reports pursuant to section 20(a) of the Act (15 U.S.C. 79t(a)) and Rules 1(b), 1(c), 2, 24, and 29 (§§250.1(b), 250.1(c), 250.2, 250.4, and 250.29 of this chapter) thereunder;

(5) To permit the filing of preliminary registration statements pursuant to section 5(c) of the Act (15 U.S.C. 79e(c));

(6) To authorize the destruction of records pursuant to the provisions of General Instruction 1(f) (§257.1(f) of this chapter) to the appendix of the Uniform System of Accounts for Public Utility Holding Companies (§257.1 *et seq.* of this chapter) and pursuant to provisions of General Requirement 1(e) (§256a.0–1(e) of this chapter) of the Uniform System of Accounts for Mutual Service Companies and Subsidiary Service Companies (§256.00–1 *et seq.*, of this chapter);

(7) To authorize the discontinuance of reporting of information otherwise required to be reported under sections 5(b), 13(c), 13(e), 13(f), 14, and 20(a) of the Act (15 U.S.C. 79e(b), 79m(c), 79m(e), 79m(f), 79n, 79t(a));

(8) To grant extensions of time for filing registration statements and reports pursuant to sections 5(b), 13(c), 13(d), 13(f), 14, and 20(a) of the Act (15 U.S.C. 79e(b), 79m

(xvi)第12(e)条[《美国法典》第十五编第79l(e)节]。

(xvii)第12(f)条[《美国法典》第十五编第79l(f)节]。

(xviii)第12(g)条[《美国法典》第十五编第79l(g)节]。

(xix)第13(b)条[《美国法典》第十五编第79m(b)节]。

(xx)第13(c)条[《美国法典》第十五编第79m(c)节]。

(xxi)第13(d)条[《美国法典》第十五编第79m(d)节]。

(xxii)第13(e)条[《美国法典》第十五编第79m(e)节]。

(xxiii)第13(f)条[《美国法典》第十五编第79m(f)节]。

(xxiv)第32条[《美国法典》第十五编第79ff节]。

(xxv)第33条[《美国法典》第十五编第79gg节]。

(2)应在已发布公告且在公告规定的期间内未收到任何利害关系人听证请求的情况下同意签发命令,前提是:投资管理部主任核查后认为,有关事项并不存在证券交易委员会之前未解决的重大问题,亦非出于公共利益或投资者利益的考虑而有必要举行听证的事项;该法第20(c)条[《美国法典》第十五编第79t(c)节];

(3)允许撤回根据该法(《美国法典》第十五编第79a节及其后条文)提交的申请或声明。

(4)在申请人提供充分理由,且不违反公共利益或与投资者/消费者保护冲突的情况下,合理核准延长该法第20(a)条[《美国法典》第十五编第79t(a)节]以及依其颁布的《1(b)规则》、《1(c)规则》、《2规则》、《24规则》和《29规则》[本章第250.1(b)节、第250.1(c)节、第250.2节、第250.4节和第250.29节]规定的注册说明书和报告的提交期限。

(5)允许根据该法第5(c)条[《美国法典》第十五编第79e(c)节]提交初步注册说明书;

(6)根据《公用事业控股公司统一账户系统》(本章第257.1节及其后条文)附件的《总体指令1(f)》[本章第257.1(f)节]及《互助服务公司和从事服务业的子公司统一账户系统》(第256.00-1节及其后条文)的《总体要求1(e)》[本章第256a.0-1(e)节]的规定同意销毁记录;

(7)同意停止报告根据该法第5(b)条、第13(c)条、第13(e)条、第13(f)条、第14条和第20(a)条[《美国法典》第十五编第79e(b)节、第79m(c)节、第79m(e)节、第79m(f)节、第79n节、第79t(a)节]规定本应报告的信息;

(8)延长该法第5(b)条、第13(c)条、第13(d)条、第13(f)条、第14条和第20(a)条[《美国法典》第十五编第79e(b)节、和79m(c)节、第79m(d)节、第79m(f)节、第79n节、

(c), 79m(d), 79m(f), 79n, 79t(a)).

(g) To consult on behalf of the Commission pursuant to sections 5318A (a)(4), 5318A(e)(2) and 5318(h)(2) of the Bank Secrecy Act (31 U.S.C. 5318A(a)(4), 5318A(e)(2) and 5318(h)(2)) with respect to matters described in §200.20b.

(h) To consult on behalf of the Commission pursuant to the Uniting and Strengthening America by Providing Appropriate Tools Required to Intercept and Obstruct Terrorism Act of 2001 (USA PATRIOT Act), as amended (Pub. L. 107–56 (2001), 115 Stat. 272) with respect to matters described in §200.20b.

(i) Notwithstanding anything in the foregoing:

(1) The Director of the Division of Investment Management shall have the same authority with respect to the Securities Act of 1933 (15 U.S.C. 77a *et seq* .), §§230.251–230.263, and §§230.651–230.703(T) of this chapter as that delegated to each Regional Director in §200.30–6(b) and (c).

(2) In any case in which the Director of the Division of Investment Management believes it appropriate, he may submit the matter to the Commission.

(j) With respect to the Investment Company Act of 1940 (15 U.S.C. 80a *et seq.*), the Securities Act of 1933 (15 U.S.C. 77a *et seq.*), the Securities Exchange Act of 1934 (15 U.S.C. 78a *et seq.*), the Trust Indenture Act of 1939 (15 U.S.C. 77aaa *et seq.*), and Regulation S–T thereunder (part 232 of this chapter), to grant or deny a request submitted under Regulation S–T to adjust the filing date of an electronic filing.

(k) With respect to the Investment Company Act of 1940 (15 U.S.C. 80a *et seq.*) and rule 8b–25 thereunder (§270.8b–25), the Securities Act of 1933 (15 U.S.C. 77a *et seq.*), the Securities Exchange Act of 1934 (15 U.S.C. 78a *et seq.*), the Trust Indenture Act of 1939 (15 U.S.C. 77aaa *et seq.*), and Regulation S–T thereunder (part 232 of this chapter), to set the terms of, and grant or deny as appropriate, continuing hardship exemptions under rule 202 of Regulation S–T (§232.202 of this chapter) from the electronic submission requirements of Regulation S–T (part 232 of this chapter).

(l) With respect to the Public Utility Holding Company Act of 1935 (15 U.S.C. 79a *et seq.*) and Regulation S–T (part 232 of this chapter), to grant or deny a request to adjust the filing date of a filing submitted under Regulation S–T.

(m) With respect to the Public Utility Holding Company Act of 1935 (15 U.S.C. 79a *et seq.*) and Regulation S–T (part 232 of this chapter), to set the terms of, and grant or deny as appropriate, continuing hardship exemptions pursuant to rule 202 of Regulation S–T (§§232.202 of this chapter) from the electronic submission requirements of Regulation S–T (part 232 of this chapter).

[41 FR 29376, July 16, 1976]

Editorial Note: For Federal Register Citations affecting §200.30–5 see the List of

第79t(a)节]规定的注册说明书的提交期限。

(g)根据《银行保密法》第5318A(a)(4)条、第5318A(e)(2)条和第5318(h)(2)条[《美国法典》第三十一编第5318A(a)(4)节、第5318A(e)(2)节和第5318(h)(2)节]代表证券交易委员会就第200.20b条所述事项进行磋商。

(h)根据《2001年使用适当手段阻止避免恐怖主义以团结并强化美国法》(《美国爱国者法》)及其修正(公法编号107-56(2001),《美国制定法汇编》第115卷第272页)代表证券交易委员会就第200.20b条所述事项进行磋商。

(i)无论上文如何规定:

(1)就《1933年证券法》(《美国法典》第十五编第77a节及其后条文)及本章第230.251~230.263节和第230.651~230.703(T)节而言,投资管理部主任享有第200.30-6(b)节和第200.30-6(c)节授予各地区办公室主任的相同权限。

(2)在任何情况下,如投资管理部主任认为适当,其均可以将相关事项提交证券交易委员会处理。

(j)就《1940年投资公司法》(《美国法典》第十五编第80a节及其后条文)、《1933年证券法》(《美国法典》第十五编第77a节及其后条文)、《1934年证券交易法》(《美国法典》第十五编第78a节及其后条文)、《1939年信托契约法》(《美国法典》第十五编第77aaa节及其后条文)以及依其颁布的《S-T管理办法》(本章第232部分)而言,核准或驳回根据《S-T管理办法》提出的对电子文件提交日期进行调整的请求。

(k)就《1940年投资公司法》(《美国法典》第十五编第80a节及其后条文)以及依其颁布的《8b-25规则》(第270.8b-25节)、《1933年证券法》(《美国法典》第十五编第77a节及其后条文)、《1934年证券交易法》(《美国法典》第十五编第78a节及其后条文)、《1939年信托契约法》(《美国法典》第十五编第77aaa节及其后条文)以及依其颁布的《S-T管理办法》(本章第232部分)而言,在《S-T规章 》的《202规则》(本章第232.202节)下,针对处于持续性困境之当事人提出的豁免于《S-T管理办法》(本章第232部分)的电子文件提交要求的申请,确定授予豁免的条款,并视情形核准或驳回豁免申请。

(l)就《1935年公用事业控股公司法》(《美国法典》第十五编第79a节及其后条文)及《S-T管理办法》(本章第232部分)而言,核准或驳回调整《S-T管理办法》中的文件提交日期的请求。

(m)就《1935年公用事业控股公司法》(《美国法典》第十五编第79a节及其后条文)及《S-T管理办法》(本章第232部分)而言,确定授予《S-T管理办法》的《202规则》(本章第232.202节)的持续性困境豁免的条款,并核准或驳回基于持续性困境而提出的豁免《S-T管理办法》(本章第232部分)的电子提交要求的请求。

[《联邦公报》第41卷第29376页,1976年7月16日。]

编辑注:对第200.30-5节有影响的《联邦公报》索引,参见《受影响的联邦规章汇编

CFR Sections Affected, which appears in the Finding Aids section of the printed volume and at www.fdsys.gov.

§200.30–6 Delegation of authority to Regional Directors.

Pursuant to the provisions of Pub. L. 87–592, 76 Stat. 394, the Securities and Exchange Commission hereby delegates, until the Commission orders otherwise, the following functions to each Regional Director, to be performed by him or under his direction by such person or persons as may be designated from time to time by the Chairman of the Commission:

(a) With respect to the Securities Exchange Act of 1934, 15 U.S.C. 78 *et seq.*:

(1) Pursuant to section 15(b)(2)(C) of the Act (15 U.S.C. 78o(b)(2)(C)):

(i) To delay until the second six month period from registration with the Commission, the inspection of newly registered broker–dealers that have not commenced actual operations within six months of their registration with the Commission; and

(ii) To delay until the second six month period from registration with the Commission, the inspection of newly registered broker–dealers to determine whether they are in compliance with applicable provisions of the Act and rules thereunder, other than financial responsibility rules.

(2) Pursuant to Rule 0–4 (§240.0–4 of this chapter), to disclose to the Comptroller of the Currency, the Board of Governors of the Federal Reserve System and the Federal Deposit Insurance Corporation and to the state banking authorities, information and documents deemed confidential regarding registered clearing agencies and registered transfer agents; *Provided* That, in matters in which the Commission has entered a formal order of investigation, such disclosure shall be made only with the concurrence of the Director of the Division of Enforcement or his or her delegate, and the General Counsel or his or her delegate.

(b) With respect to the Investment Advisers Act of 1940, 15 U.S.C. 80b–1 *et seq.*: Pursuant to Rule 204–2(j)(3)(ii)(§275.204–2(j)(3)(ii) of this chapter), to make written demands upon non–resident investment advisers subject to the provisions of such rule to furnish to the Commission true, correct, complete and current copies of any or all books and records which such non–resident investment advisers are required to make, keep current or preserve pursuant to any provision of any rule or regulation of the Commission adopted under the Investment Advisers Act of 1940, or any part of such books and records which may be specified in any such demand.

(c) In nonpublic investigatory proceedings within the responsibility of the Regional Director, to grant requests of persons to procure copies of the transcript of their testimony given pursuant to Rule 6 of the Commission's rules relating to investigations as in effect subsequent to November 16, 1972 (17 CFR 203.6).

条文列表》(见印刷版本的《检索协助》章节和www.fdsys.gov)。

第200.30-6节　对地区办公室主任的委托授权

根据公法编号87-592,《美国制定法汇编》第76卷第394页,证券交易委员会兹将下述职能委托各地区办公室主任行使,或委托证券交易委员会主席随时指定的其他人员在地区办公室主任的领导下行使,直至证券交易委员会另行作出命令:

(a)就《1934年证券交易法》(《美国法典》第十五编第78节及其后条文)而言:

(1)根据该法第15(b)(2)(C)条[《美国法典》第十五编第78o(b)(2)(C)节]:

(i)对于新注册的经纪自营商,在注册后6个月内未开展实际经营的,将对其进行的检查工作推迟至注册后的第二个6个月期间;及

(ii)将检查新注册的经纪自营商是否遵守该法以及依其颁布的规则(经济责任规则除外)的工作推迟至注册后的第二个6个月期间。

(2)根据《0-4规则》(本章第240.0-4节),向货币监理署、联邦储备系统的联邦储备委员会、联邦存款保险公司和州银行业监管机构披露与注册结算机构和注册过户代理人相关的被视为机密的信息和文件;但是,对于证券交易委员会已发布正式调查令的事项,披露必须征得执法部主任或其授权代表以及首席律师或其授权代表的同意。

(b)就《1940年投资顾问法》(《美国法典》第十五编第80b-1节及其后条文)而言:根据《204-2(j)(3)(ii)规则》[本章第275.204-2(j)(3)(ii)节],向受上述规则约束的非居民投资顾问发出书面要求,督促其根据证券交易委员会在《1940年投资顾问法》下通过的规定向证券交易委员会提供其应制作、更新或保存的任何及所有账簿和记录以及书面要求中指明的该等账簿和记录的任何部分之真实、准确、完整和最新副本。

(c)在地区办公室主任或副主任负责的非公开调查程序中,核准相关人员在根据1972年11月16日后生效的第6号证券交易委员会调查规则(《联邦规章汇编》第十七编第203.6节)作出证词后获得证词复本的请求。

(d) To notify the Securities Investor Protection Corporation (SIPC) of facts concerning the activities and the operational and financial condition of any registered broker or dealer which is or appears to be a member of SIPC and which is in or approaching financial difficulty within the meaning of section 5 of the Securities Investor Protection Act of 1970, as amended, 15 U.S.C. 78aaa *et seq*.

(e) Notwithstanding anything in the foregoing, in any case in which the Regional Director believes it appropriate, he may submit the matter to the Commission.

(Secs. 6, 7, 8, 10, 19(a), 48 Stat. 78, 79, 81, 85; secs. 205, 209, 48 Stat. 906, 908; sec. 301, 54 Stat. 857; sec. 8, 68 Stat. 685; sec. 308(a)(2), 90 Stat. 57; secs. 3(b), 12, 13, 14, 15(d), 23(a), 48 Stat. 882, 892, 894, 895, 901; secs. 203(a), 1, 3, 8, 49 Stat. 704, 1375, 1377, 1379; sec. 202, 68 Stat. 686; secs. 4, 5, 6(d), 78 Stat. 569, 570–574; secs. 1, 2, 3, 82 Stat. 454, 455; secs. 28(c), 1, 2, 3, 4, 5, 84 Stat. 1435, 1497; sec. 105(b), 88 Stat. 1503; secs. 8, 9, 10, 89 Stat. 117, 118, 119; sec. 308(b), 90 Stat 57; sec. 18, 89 Stat. 155; secs. 202, 203, 204, 91 Stat. 1494, 1498–1500; sec. 20(a), 49 Stat. 833; sec. 319, 53 Stat. 1173; sec. 38, 54 Stat. 841; 15 U.S.C. 77f, 77g, 77h, 77j, 77s (a), 78c(b), 78 *l*, 78m, 78n, 78o(d), 78w(a), 79t(a), 77sss(a), 80a–37; secs. 3(b), 19(a), 48 Stat. 75, 85; sec. 209, 48 Stat. 908; c. 122, 59 Stat. 167; Pub. L. 91–565, 84 Stat. 1480; 15 U.S.C. 77c (b), 77s (a), 78d–1, 78n, 80a–37; secs. 2, 17 and 23 thereof (15 U.S.C. 78b, 78q and 78w))

[28 FR 2856, Mar. 22, 1963, as amended at 36 FR 7659, Apr. 23, 1971. Redesignated at 37 FR 16792, Aug. 19, 1972]

Editorial Note: For Federal Register Citations affecting §200.30–6 see the List of CFR Sections Affected, which appears in the Finding Aids section of the printed volume and at www.fdsys.gov.

§200.30–7 Delegation of authority to Secretary of the Commission.

Pursuant to the provisions of Pub. L. 87–592, 76 Stat. 394 (15 U.S.C. 78d–1), the Securities and Exchange Commission hereby delegates, until the Commission orders

(d)对于属于或从表面判断属于证券投资者保护公司(SIPC)成员且处于或濒临《1970年证券投资者保护法》及其修正第5条(《美国法典》第十五编第78aaa节及其后条文)定义的财务困境的任何注册经纪商或自营商,将其活动和经营财务状况事实通知证券投资者保护公司。

(e)无论上文如何规定,在任何情况下,如地区办公室主任认为适当,其均可以将相关事项提交证券交易委员会处理。

[《美国制定法汇编》第48卷第78页、第79页、第81页、第85页的第6条、第7条、第8条、第10条、第19(a)条;《美国制定法汇编》第48卷第906页、第908页的第205条、第209条;《美国制定法汇编》第54卷第857页第301条;《美国制定法汇编》第68卷第685页第8条;《美国制定法汇编》第90卷第57页第308(a)(2)条;《美国制定法汇编》第48卷第882页、第892页、第894页、第895页、第901页的第3(b)条、第12条、第13条、第14条、第15(d)条、第23(a)条;《美国制定法汇编》第49卷第704页、第1375页、第1377页、第1379页的第203(a)条、第1条、第3条、第8条;《美国制定法汇编》第68卷第686页第202条;《美国制定法汇编》第78卷第569页、第570~574页第4条、第5条、第6(d)条;《美国制定法汇编》第82卷第454页、第455页的第1条、第2条、第3条;《美国制定法汇编》第84卷第1435页、第1497页的第28(c)条、第1条、第2条、第3条、第4条、第5条;《美国制定法汇编》第88卷第1503页第105(b)条;《美国制定法汇编》第89卷第117页、第118页、第119页的第8条、第9条、第10条;《美国制定法汇编》第90卷第57页第308(b)条;《美国制定法汇编》第89卷第155页第18条;《美国制定法汇编》 第91卷第1494页、 第1498—1500页第202条、第203条、第204条;《美国制定法汇编》第49卷第833页第20(a)条;《美国制定法汇编》第53卷第1173页第319条;《美国制定法汇编》第54卷第841页第38条;《美国法典》第十五编第77f节、第77g节、第77h节、第77j节、第77s(a)节、第78c(b)节、第78 *l*节、第78m节、第78n节、第78o(d)节、第78w(a)节、第79t(a)节、第77sss(a)节、第80a-37节;《美国制定法汇编》第48卷第75条、第85页第3(b)条、第19(a)条;《美国制定法汇编》第48卷第908页第209条;《美国制定法汇编》第59卷第167页第122章;公法编号91-565,《美国制定法汇编》第84卷第1480页;《美国法典》第十五编第77c(b)节、第77s(a)节、第78d-1节、第78n节、第80a-37节;《美国法典》第十五编第78b节、第78q节和第78w节第2条、第17和第23条。]

[《联邦公报》第28卷第2856页,1963年3月22日,修正索引:《联邦公报》第36卷第7659页,1971年4月23日。重新公布索引:《联邦公报》第37卷第16792页,1972年8月19日。]

编辑注:对第200.30-6节有影响的《联邦公报》索引,参见《受影响的联邦规章汇编条文列表》(见印刷版本的《检索协助》章节和www.fdsys.gov)。

第200.30-7节　对证券交易委员会秘书的委托授权

根据公法编号87-592,《美国制定法汇编》第76卷第394页(《美国法典》第十五编第78d-1节),证券交易委员会兹将下述职能委托证券交易委员会秘书行使,或委托证

otherwise, the following functions to the Secretary of the Commission to be performed by him or under his direction by such person or persons as may be designated from time to time by the Chairman of the Commission:

(a) With respect to proceedings conducted pursuant to the Securities Act of 1933, 15 U.S.C. 77a *et seq.*, the Securities Exchange Act of 1934, 15 U.S.C. 78a *et seq.*, the Public Utility Holding Company Act of 1935, 15 U.S.C. 79a *et seq.*, the Trust Indenture Act of 1939, 15 U.S.C. 77aaa *et seq.*, the Investment Company Act of 1940, 15 U.S.C. 80a-1 *et seq.*, the Investment Advisers Act of 1940, 15 U.S.C. 80b-1 *et seq.*, the Securities Investor Protection Act of 1970, 15 U.S.C. 78aaa *et seq.*, the provisions of Rule 102(e) of the Commission's Rules of Practice, Section 201.102(e) of this chapter, and Title I of the Sarbanes-Oxley Act of 2002, 15 U.S.C. 7211-7219:

(1) To fix the time and place for hearings and oral arguments before the Commission pursuant to Rule 451 of the Commission's Rules of Practice, §201.451 of this chapter;

(2) In appropriate cases to extend and reallocate the time prescribed in Rule 451 (c) of the Commission's Rules of Practice, §201.451(c) of this chapter;

(3) To postpone or adjourn hearings or otherwise adjust the date for commencement of hearings before the Commission pursuant to Rule 161 of the Commission's Rules of Practice, §201.161 of this chapter, and to advance such hearings;

(4) To grant or deny extensions of time within which to file papers with the Commission under Rule 161 of the Commission's Rules of Practice, §201.161 of this chapter, or under part 201, subpart F of the Commission's Rules pertaining to Fair Fund and Disgorgement Plans, §§201.1100-201.1106;

(5) To permit the filing of briefs with the Commission exceeding 14,000 words in length, pursuant to Rule 450(c) of the Commission's Rule of Practice, §201.450(c) of this chapter, and to permit the filing of motions with the Commission in excess of 7,000 words pursuant to Rule 154(c) of the Commission's Rules of Practice, §201.154(c) of this chapter;

(6) To certify records of proceedings upon which are entered orders the subject of review in courts of appeals pursuant to section 9 of the Securities Act of 1933, 15 U.S.C. 77i, section 25 of the Securities Exchange Act of 1934, 15 U.S.C. 78y, section 24 of the Public Utility Holding Company Act of 1935, 15 U.S.C. 79x, section 322(a) of the Trust Indenture Act of 1939, 15 U.S.C. 77vvv(a), section 43 of the Investment Company Act of 1940, 15 U.S.C. 80a-42, section 213 of the Investment Advisers Act of 1940, 15 U.S.C. 80b-13, and Title I of the Sarbanes-Oxley Act of 2002, 15 U.S.C. 7211-7219;

(7) Except where the Commission otherwise directs, to issue findings and orders pursuant to offers of settlement which the Commission has determined should be accepted;

(8) To issue findings and orders taking the remedial action described in the order for proceedings where a respondent expressly consents to such action, fails to appear, or defaults

券交易委员会主席随时指定的其他人员在证券交易委员会秘书的领导下行使,直至证券交易委员会另行作出命令:

(a)就根据《1933年证券法》(《美国法典》第十五编第77a节及其后条文)、《1934年证券交易法》(《美国法典》第十五编第78a节及其后条文)、《1935年公用事业控股公司法》(《美国法典》第十五编第79a节及其后条文)、《1939年信托契约法》(《美国法典》第十五编第77aaa节及其后条文)、《1940年投资公司法》(《美国法典》第十五编第80a-1节及其后条文)、《1940年投资顾问法》(《美国法典》第十五编第80b-1节及其后条文)、《1970年证券投资者保护法》(《美国法典》第十五编第78aaa节及其后条文)、《证券交易委员会工作规则》的《102(e)规则》[本章第201.102(e)节]以及《2002年萨班斯—奥克斯利法》第一编(《美国法典》第十五编第7211~7219节)提起的程序而言:

(1)根据《证券交易委员会工作规则》的《451规则》(本章第201.451节)确定证券交易委员会听证及口头辩论的时间和地点;

(2)视适当情况延长和重新确定《证券交易委员会工作规则》的《451(c)规则》[本章第201.451(c)节]规定的期限;

(3)根据《证券交易委员会工作规则》的《161规则》(本章第201.161节)推迟或延期听证、以其他方式调整证券交易委员会开始听证的日期,以及提前举行听证;

(4)根据《证券交易委员会工作规则》的《161规则》(本章第201.161节)或《证券交易委员会公平基金和没收计划规则》第201部分第F子部分的规定(第201.1100~201.1106节)核准或驳回延长文件提交期限的申请;

(5)根据《证券交易委员会工作规则》的《450(c)规则》[本章第201.450(c)节]允许向证券交易委员会提交超过14000字的摘要,以及根据《证券交易委员会工作规则》的《154(c)规则》[本章第201.154(c)节]允许向证券交易委员会提交超过7000字的动议;

(6)根据《1933年证券法》第9条(《美国法典》第十五编第77i节)、《1934年证券交易法》第25条(《美国法典》第十五编第78y节)、《1935年公用事业控股公司法》第24条(《美国法典》第十五编第79x节)、《1939年信托契约法》第322(a)条[《美国法典》第十五编第77vvv(a)节]、《1940年投资公司法》第43条(《美国法典》第十五编第80a-42节)、《1940年投资顾问法》第213条(《美国法典》第十五编第80b-13节)以及《2002年萨班斯—奥克斯利法》(《美国法典》第十五编第7211~7219节)第一编,对接受上诉法院审查的命令所基的程序记录进行核证;

(7)除非证券交易委员会另有指令,根据证券交易委员会判定应接受的和解要约作出认定和签发命令;

(8)在相对人/被申请人明确表示同意,或未能出席或未按要求提交答辩状的程序中,作出认定,签发命令,采取程序命令中所载救济行动,并在相对人/被申请人提出充

in the filing of an answer required to be filed and to grant a request, based upon a showing of good cause, to vacate an order or default, so as to permit presentation of a defense;

(9) To designate officers of the Commission to serve notices of and orders for proceedings and decisions and orders in such proceedings, the service of which is required by Rules 141 and 150 of the Commission's Rules of Practice, §§201.141 and 201.150 of this chapter;

(10) To set the date for sanctions to take effect if an initial decision is not appealed and becomes final pursuant to Rule 360(d) or if an initial decision is affirmed pursuant to Rule 411;

(11) To publish pursuant to Rule 1103 of the Commission's Rules of Practice (§201.1103 of this chapter) notice for fair fund and disgorgement plans, and if no negative comments are received, to issue orders approving proposedfair fund plans and disgorgement plans pursuant to Rule 1104 of the Commission's Rules of Practice (§201.1104 of this chapter). As part of this plan approval, the requirement set forth in Rule 1105(c) (§201.1105(c) of this chapter) may be waived if the fair or disgorgement funds are held at the U.S. Department of the Treasury and will be disbursed by Treasury. Upon the motion of the staff for good cause shown, to approve the publication of proposed fair fund plans and disgorgement plans that omit plan elements required by Rule 1101 of the Commission's Rules of Practice (§201.1101 of this chapter);

(12) To issue orders instituting previously authorized administrative proceedings pursuant to sections 15(b)(4) or (6), 15B, 15C, or 17A of the Securities Exchange Act of 1934 (15 U.S.C. 78o(b)(4) or (6), 78o-4, 78o-5, or 78q-1), and section 203(e) or (f) of the Investment Advisers Act of 1940 (15 U.S.C. 80b-3(e) or (f)), based on the entry of an injunction or a criminal conviction, and to issue findings and orders in such cases where a respondent consents to a bar from association.

(b) To order the making of private investigations pursuant to section 21(a) of the Securities Exchange Act of 1934, on request of the Division of Corporation Finance or the Division of Enforcement, with respect to proxy contests subject to section 14 of that Act and regulation 14A thereunder, and tender offers filed pursuant to section 14(d) of the Act.

(c) To authenticate all Commission documents produced for administrative or judicial proceedings.

(d) Notwithstanding anything in the foregoing, in any case in which the Secretary of the Commission believes it appropriate he or she may submit the matter to the Commission.

[35 FR 17989, Nov. 24, 1970. Redesignated at 37 FR 16792, Aug. 19, 1972]

Editorial Note: For Federal Register Citations affecting §200.30-7, see the List of

分理由的情况下,核准撤销命令或缺席判决,以允许相对人/被申请人进行抗辩;

(9)指定证券交易委员会官员按《证券交易委员会工作规则》的《141规则》和《150规则》(本章第201.141节和第201.150节)的要求发送程序通知和命令以及在程序中作出的裁定和命令;

(10)根据《360(d)规则》就未提起上诉并已产生最终效力的初步决定,或根据《411规则》对得到确认的初步决定,来确定制裁生效日期;

(11)根据《证券交易委员会工作规则》的《1103规则》(本章第201.1103节)发布关于公平基金和没收计划的公告,且在未收到反对意见的情况下根据《证券交易委员会工作规则》的《1104规则》(本章第201.1104节)发布命令批准公平基金和没收计划提案。作为计划批准的一部分,如公平基金计划或没收计划由美国财政部所持有并拨款,《1105(c)规则》[本章第201.1105(c)节]的要求可免于执行。在其下属工作人员提出动议且理由充分的情况下,批准发布缺少《证券交易委员会工作规则》的《1101规则》(本章第201.1101节)规定要素的公平基金计划和没收计划提案;

(12)根据《1934年证券交易法》第15(b)(4)条或第15(6)条、第15B条、第15C条或第17A条[《美国法典》第十五编第78o(b)(4)节或第280(6)节、第78o-4节、第78o-5节或第78q-1节]及《1940年投资顾问法》第203(e)条或第23(f)条[《美国法典》第十五编第80b-3(e)节或第80b-3(f)节],基于发出的禁令或刑事判决来签发命令发动已获授权的行政处理程序,并在相对人同意处以禁止充当业务相关人的处罚的案件中作出认定并签发命令。

(b)根据《1934年证券交易法》第21(a)条,基于公司融资部或执法部的申请,就该法第14条以及依其颁布的《14A管理办法》中的代理权争议及根据该法第14(d)条提交的股权收购要约,签发私人调查命令。

(c)认证行政处理程序或司法程序中提交的所有证券交易委员会文件。

(d)无论上文如何规定,在任何情况下,如证券交易委员会秘书认为适当,其均可以将相关事项提交证券交易委员会处理。

[《联邦公报》第35卷第17989页,1970年11月24日。重新公布索引:《联邦公报》第37卷第16792页,1972年8月19日。]

编辑注:对第200.30-7节有影响的《联邦公报》索引,参见《受影响的联邦规章汇编

CFR Sections Affected, which appears in the Finding Aids section of the printed volume and at www.fdsys.gov.

§200.30-8 [Reserved]

§200.30-9 Delegation of authority to hearing officers.

Pursuant to the provisions of Section 4A of the Securities Exchange Act of 1934 (15 U.S.C. 78d-1), the Securities and Exchange Commission hereby delegates, until the Commission orders otherwise, to each Administrative Law Judge ("Judge") the authority:

(a) To make an initial decision in any proceeding at which the Judge presides in which a hearing is required to be conducted in conformity with the Administrative Procedure Act (5 U.S.C. 557) unless such initial decision is waived by all parties who appear at the hearing and the Commission does not subsequently order that an initial decision nevertheless be made by the Judge, and in any other proceeding in which the Commission directs the Judge to make such a decision; and

(b) To issue, upon entry pursuant to Rule 531 of the Commission's Rules of Practice, §201.531 of this chapter, of an initial decision on a permanent order, a separate order setting aside, limiting or suspending any temporary sanction, as that term is defined in Rule 101(a)(11) of the Commission's Rules of Practice, §201.101(a) of this chapter, then in effect in accordance with the terms of the initial decision.

[60 FR 32794, June 23, 1995]

§200.30-10 Delegation of authority to Chief Administrative Law Judge.

Pursuant to the provisions of Pub. L. 87-592, 76 Stat. 394 (15 U.S.C. 78d-1), the Securities and Exchange Commission hereby delegates, until the Commission orders otherwise, the following functions to the Chief Administrative Law Judge or to such administrative law judge or administrative law judges as may be designated by the Chief Administrative Law Judge in his absence, or as otherwise designated by the Chairman of the Commission in the absence of the Chief Administrative Law Judge:

(a) With respect to proceedings conducted before an administrative law judge, pursuant to the Securities Act of 1933, 15 U.S.C. 77a *et seq.*, the Securities Exchange Act of 1934, 15 U.S.C. 78a *et seq.*, the Trust Indenture Act of 1939, 15 U.S.C. 77aaa *et seq.*, the Investment Company Act of 1940, 15 U.S.C. 80a-1 *et seq.*, the Investment Advisers Act of 1940, 15 U.S.C. 80b-1 *et seq.*, the Securities Investor Protection Act of 1970, 15 U.S.C. 78aaa *et seq.*, and the provisions of Rule 102(e) of the Commission's Rules of Practice, §201.102(e) of this chapter:

(1) After a proceeding has been authorized, to fix the time and place for hearing pursuant to Rule 200 of the Commission's Rules of Practice, §201.200 of this chapter;

(2) To designate administrative law judges pursuant to Rule 110 of the Commission's Rules of Practice, §201.110 of this chapter;

条文列表》(见印刷版本的《检索协助》章节和www.fdsys.gov)。

第200.30-8节　[保留]

第200.30-9节　对听证官的委托授权

根据《1934年证券交易法》第4A条(《美国法典》第十五编第78d-1节)的规定,证券交易委员会兹委托各行政法官("法官")行使如下权限,直至证券交易委员会另行作出决定:

(a)在法官主持的应按《行政程序法》(《美国法典》第五编第557节)开展的听证程序中作出初步决定,除非出席听证的所有当事人均放弃要求法官作出初步决定,且证券交易委员会未在该等情况下仍然发出要求法官作出初步决定的后续命令;以及按证券交易委员会的指令在任何其他程序中作出决定;及

(b)基于按《证券交易委员会工作规则》的《531规则》(本章第201.531节)作出的关于永久性命令的初步决定,另行签发命令撤销、限制或暂停按初步决定的条款生效的任何临时制裁;"临时制裁"一词的定义见《证券交易委员会工作规则》的《101(a)(11)规则》[本章第201.101(a)节]。

[《联邦公报》第60卷第32794页,1995年6月23日。]

第200.30-10节　对首席行政法官的委托授权

证券交易委员会兹根据公法编号87-592,《美国制定法汇编》第76卷第394页的条文(《美国法典》第十五编第78d-1节),将下述权限委托首席行政法官行使,或在首席行政法官无法履职时由首席行政法官指定或证券交易委员会主席另行指定的其他一名或数名行政法官行使,直至证券交易委员会另行作出命令:

(a)就向行政法官提起的程序而言,根据《1933年证券法》(《美国法典》第十五编第77a节及其后条文)、《1934年证券交易法》(《美国法典》第十五编第78a节及其后条文)、《1939年信托契约法》(《美国法典》第十五编第77aaa节及其后条文)、《1940年投资公司法》(《美国法典》第十五编第80a-1节及其后条文)、《1940年投资顾问法》(《美国法典》第十五编第80b-1节及其后条文)、《1970年证券投资者保护法》(《美国法典》第十五编第78aaa节及其后条文)及《证券交易委员会工作规则》的《102(e)规则》[本章第201.102(e)节]:

(1)在程序获得批准后,根据《证券交易委员会工作规则》的《200规则》(本章第201.200节)确定听证时间和地点;

(2)根据《证券交易委员会工作规则》的《110规则》(本章第201.110节)指定行政法官;

(3) To postpone or adjourn hearings or otherwise adjust the date for commencement of hearings pursuant to Rule 161 of the Commission's Rules of Practice, §201.161 of this chapter, or to advance or cancel such hearings, if necessary;

(4) To grant extensions of time within which to file papers pursuant to Rule 161 of the Commission's Rules of Practice, §201.161 of this chapter;

(5) To permit the filing of briefs exceeding 14,000 words in length, pursuant to Rule 450(c) of the Commission's Rules of Practice, §201.450(c) of this chapter;

(6) In the event the designated presiding administrative law judge is unavailable to issue subpenas requiring the attendance and testimony of witnesses and subpenas requiring the production of documentary or other tangible evidence at any designated place of hearing upon request therefor by any party, pursuant to Rule 232 of the Commission's Rules of Practice,§201.232 of this chapter;

(7) Pursuant to sections 15(b)(1)(B), 15B(a)(2)(B), and 19(a)(1)(B) of the Securities Exchange Act of 1934 and section 203(c)(2)(B) of the Investment Advisers Act of 1940 to grant extensions of time for conclusion of proceedings instituted to determine whether applications for registration as a broker or dealer, municipal securities dealer, national securities exchange, registered securities association, or registered clearing agency, or as an investment adviser should be denied;

(8) To grant motions of staff counsel to discontinue administrative proceedings as to a particular respondent who has died or cannot be found, or because of a mistake in the identity of a respondent named in the order for proceedings.

(b) With respect to proceedings under the Equal Access to Justice Act, 5 U.S.C. 504, to make assignments as provided in §201.37(b) of this chapter, respecting applications made pursuant to that Act.

(c) Notwithstanding anything in the foregoing, in any case in which the Chief Administrative Law Judge believes it appropriate he or she may submit the matter to the Commission.

[37 FR 23827, Nov. 9, 1972, as amended at 41 FR 21183, May 24, 1976; 43 FR 13378, Mar. 30, 1978; 54 FR 53051, Dec. 27, 1989; 60 FR 32794, June 23, 1995; 69 FR 13174, Apr. 19, 2004; 70 FR 72569, Dec. 5, 2005; 71 FR 71037, Dec. 8, 2006]

§200.30-11 Delegation of authority to the Chief Accountant.

Pursuant to the provisions of Pub. L. 101-181, 101 Stat. 1254, 1255 (15 U.S.C. 78d-1, 78d-2), the Securities and Exchange Commission hereby delegates, until the Commission orders otherwise, the following functions to the Chief Accountant of the Commission, to be performed by him or her or under his or her direction by such person or persons as may be designated from time to time by the Chairman of the Commission:

(3)根据《证券交易委员会工作规则》的《161规则》(本章第201.161节)推迟或延期听证,或以其他方式调整听证开始的日期,以及在必要情况下提前举行或取消听证;

(4)根据《证券交易委员会工作规则》的《161规则》(本章第201.161节)核准延长文件提交期限;

(5)根据《证券交易委员会工作规则》的《450(c)规则》[本章第201.450(c)节]允许提交超过14000字的文件摘要;

(6)在指定的主审行政法官不能行使职能签发传票时,依据《证券交易委员会工作规则》的《232规则》(本章第201.232节)应任何当事人的申请,签发传票要求证人在指定的听证地点出席和作证或要求提交文件或其他实物证据;

(7)根据《1934年证券交易法》第15(b)(1)(B)条、第15B(a)(2)(B)条和第19(a)(1)(B)条以及《1940年投资顾问法》第203(c)(2)(B)条,核准延长以下程序审结期限:为判定是否应驳回经纪商、自营商、市政证券自营商、全国性证券交易所、注册证券协会或注册结算机构或投资顾问的注册申请而发起的程序;

(8)核准作为证券交易委员会员工的法律顾问基于特定相对人/被申请人死亡、失踪或程序命令所载之相对人/被申请人身份错误而提起的停止行政处理程序的动议。

(b)就《司法公平救济权法》(《美国法典》第5编第504节)中的程序而言,按本章第201.37(b)节的规定就根据该法提出的申请指定承办法官。

(c)无论上文如何规定,在任何情况下,如首席行政法官认为适当,其均可以将相关事项提交证券交易委员会处理。

[《联邦公报》第37卷第23827页,1972年11月9日,修正索引:《联邦公报》第41卷第21183页,1976年5月24日;《联邦公报》第43卷第13378页,1978年3月30日;《联邦公报》第54卷第53051页,1989年12月27日;《联邦公报》 第60卷第32794页,1995年6月23日;《联邦公报》第69卷第13174页,2004年4月19日;《联邦公报》第70卷第72569页,2005年12月5日;《联邦公报》第71卷第71037页,2006年12月8日。]

第200.30-11节　对首席会计师的委托授权

根据公法编号101-181,《美国制定法汇编》第101卷第1254页及1255页的条文(《美国法典》第十五编第78d-1节、第78d-2节),证券交易委员会兹将下述职能委托首席会计师行使,或委托证券交易委员会主席随时指定的其他人员在首席会计师的领导下行使,直至证券交易委员会另行作出命令:

(a) In connection with Commission review of inspection reports of the Public Company Accounting Oversight Board (PCAOB) under 15 U.S.C. 7214(h) and §202.140:

(1) To grant or deny review requests and notify the firm and the PCAOB as to whether the Commission will grant the review request under §202.140(d).

(2) To extend the time periods set forth in §202.140(e) within which the PCAOB, registered public accounting firm or an associated person may submit responsive information and documents in connection with a request for Commission review.

(3) To request additional information pursuant to §202.140 (e) relating to the PCAOB's assessments or determination under review from the PCAOB, the registered public accounting firm, or any associated person of the firm during the course of an interim review of an inspection report, and to grant the PCAOB, the firm or any associated person a period of up to seven calendar days to respond to any information obtained.

(4) To consider requests for review of inspection reports and, based on such review, to not object to all or part of the assessments or determination of the PCAOB and terminate the stay of publication, or to remand to the PCAOB with instructions that the stay of publication is permanent or that the PCAOB take such other actions as he or she deems necessary or appropriate with respect to publication, including, but not limited to, revising the final inspection report or determinations before publication, and to provide the written notice communicating the same to the PCAOB and the registered public accounting firm, consistent with §202.140.

(5) To determine that a timely review request by a firm will not operate as a stay of publication of those portions of the final inspection report or determinations described in §202.140(b) that are the subject of the firm's review request pursuant to §202.140(c)(5), as well as to determine that publication of the remainder of the final inspection report or criticisms or defects in the quality control systems would not be necessary or appropriate pursuant to §202.140(c)(5).

(6) To, in the event the Commission does grant a review request pursuant to §202.140, determine that the stay of publication shall not continue pursuant to §202.140(d).

(7) To, in the event that the review pursuant to §202.140 (e) has not been completed and a written notice has not been sent 75 calendar days after notification to the firm and the PCAOB that it is granting the request for an interim review, grant an extension of time under the authority set forth in §202.140(e).

(b)(1) Pursuant to section 107 of the Sarbanes-Oxley Act of 2002, 15 U.S.C. 7217, and section 19(b) of the Act, 15 U.S.C. 78s(b), and applicable rules of the Commission, to publish notices of proposed rule changes filed by the Public Company Accounting Oversight Board.

(2) Pursuant to section 107 of the Sarbanes-Oxley Act of 2002, 15 U.S.C. 7217, and section 19(b) of the Act, 15 U.S.C. 78s(b), and applicable rules of the Commission,

(a)关于在《美国法典》第十五编第7214(h)节和第202.140节下针对公众公司会计监督委员会(PCAOB)检查报告提起的证券交易委员会审查事宜:

(1)核准或驳回审查请求,并根据第202.140(d)节通知相关公司和公众公司会计监督委员会关于证券交易委员会是否核准审查请求的回复。

(2)延长第202.140(e)节规定的公众公司会计监督委员会、注册公共会计师事务所或业务相关人提交与证券交易委员会审查请求相关的答复信息和文件的期限。

(3)在对检查报告进行临时审查的过程中,根据第202.140(e)节要求公众公司会计监督委员会、注册公共会计师事务所或会计师事务所的任何业务相关人提交与审查中的公众公司会计监督委员会评估或判定结果相关的补充信息,并要求公众公司会计监督委员会、会计师事务所或任何业务相关人在不超过7个日历日的期间内针对其所获信息作出答复。

(4)对检查报告审查申请进行审议;基于审查结果,对公众公司会计监督委员会作出的评估或判定作出全部或部分不驳回的决定并撤销之前签发的报告公布中止令,或向公众公司会计监督委员会发回如下两类指示:所签发的报告公布中止令为永久性禁令,或者公众公司会计监督委员会应采取其认为必要或适当的与报告公布相关的其他行动,包括但不限于在公布最终的检查报告或判定结果之前对其进行修改;依据第202.140节的规定将上述指示以书面形式通知公众公司会计监督委员会或注册公共会计师事务所。

(5)判定即使会计师事务所及时提出审查请求,第202.140(b)节中所述的且根据第202.140(c)(5)节已由该会计师事务所提出审查请求的最终检查报告内容或判定结果也不应中止发布,并根据第202.140(c)(5)节判定,公布最终检查报告的其余部分或对质量控制系统的批评或其中存在的缺陷没必要或不适当。

(6)证券交易委员会如果根据第202.140节不核准审查请求,则根据第202.140(d)节判定公布中止令应停止生效。

(7)如果根据第202.140(e)节进行的审查尚未完成,且在向会计师事务所和公众公司会计监督委员会发出通知说明其将核准临时审查请求后75个日历日届满时,仍未发出书面通知,则根据第202.140(e)节的授权核准延长期间。

(b)(1)根据《2002年萨班斯—奥克斯利法》第107条(《美国法典》第十五编第7217节)、该法第19(b)条[《美国法典》第十五编第78s(b)节]以及证券交易委员会的相关规则,就公众公司会计监督委员会提交的规则变更提案发布公告。

(2)根据《2002年萨班斯—奥克斯利法》第107条(《美国法典》第十五编第7217节)、该法第19(b)条[《美国法典》第十五编第78s(b)节]以及证券交易委员会的相关规

to approve or disapprove a proposed rule change, and to find good cause to approve a proposed rule change earlier than 30 days after the date of publication of such proposed rule change and to publish the reasons for such finding. The Office of the Chief Accountant shall notify the Commission no less than five (5) business days before the Chief Accountant intends to exercise his or her authority to approve or disapprove a particular proposed rule change.

(3) Pursuant to section 107 of the Sarbanes-Oxley Act of 2002, 15 U.S.C. 7217, and section 19 (b)(2)(A) of the Act, 15 U.S.C. 78s (b)(2)(A), to extend for a period not exceeding 90 days from the date of publication of notice of the filing of a proposed rule change pursuant to section 19(b)(1) of the Act, 15 U.S.C. 78s(b)(1), the period during which the Commission must by order approve or disapprove the proposed rule change or institute proceedings to determine whether the proposed rule change should be disapproved and to determine whether such longer period is appropriate and publish the reasons for such determination.

(4) Pursuant to section 107 of the Sarbanes-Oxley Act of 2002, 15 U.S.C. 7217, section 19(b)(2) of the Act, 15 U.S.C. 78s(b)(2), and section 19(b)(3) of the Act, 15 U.S.C. 78s(b)(3), to institute proceedings to determine whether a proposed rule change of the Public Company Accounting Oversight Board should be disapproved and to provide to the Public Company Accounting Oversight Board notice of the grounds for disapproval under consideration. In addition, pursuant to section 107 of the Sarbanes-Oxley Act of 2002, 15 U.S.C. 7217, and section 19(b)(2)(B) of the Act, 15 U.S.C. 78s(b)(2)(B), to extend for a period not exceeding 240 days from the date of publication of notice of the filing of a proposed rule change pursuant to section 19(b)(1) of the Act, 15 U.S.C. 78s (b)(1), the period during which the Commission must issue an order approving or disapproving the proposed rule change and to determine whether such longer period is appropriate and publish the reasons for such determination.

(5) Pursuant to section 107 of the Sarbanes-Oxley Act of 2002, 15 U.S.C. 7217, and section 19(b)(3)(C) of the Act, 15 U.S.C. 78s(b)(3)(C), to temporarily suspend a rule of the Public Company Accounting Oversight Board.

(c) Notwithstanding anything in the foregoing, in any case in which the Chief Accountant believes it appropriate, he or she may submit the matter to the Commission.

[75 FR 47449, Aug. 6, 2010, as amended at 76 FR 2806, Jan. 18, 2011]

§200.30-12 [Reserved]

§200.30-13 Delegation of authority to Associate Executive Director of the Office of Financial Management.

Pursuant to the provisions of 15 U.S.C. 78d-1 and 78d-2, the Securities and Exchange

则,在就规则变更提案发布公告后30日内批准或否决规则变更提案;批准提案的,应在上述期间内找到支持该等决定的充分理由并公开发布作出上述认定的原因。首席会计师办公室拟就具体规则变更草案行使批准或否决权的,至少应提前5个工作日通知证券交易委员会。

(3)根据《2002年萨班斯—奥克斯利法》第107条(《美国法典》第十五编第7217节)、该法第19(b)(2)(A)条[《美国法典》第十五编第78s(b)(2)(A)节],延长不超过90日的期间{从针对根据该法第19(b)(1)条[《美国法典》第十五编第78s(b)(1)节]提交的规则变更草案发布公告之日起算},证券交易委员会必须在上述期间内发布命令批准或否决规则变更草案,或发起程序判定是否应否决该等草案并判定延长上述期间是否适当,并公布其作出该等判定所根据的原因。

(4)根据《2002年萨班斯—奥克斯利法》第107条(《美国法典》第十五编第7217节)、该法第19(b)(2)条[《美国法典》第十五编第78s(b)(2)节]、该法第19(b)(3)条[《美国法典》第十五编第78s(b)(3)节],发起程序判定是否应否决公众公司会计监督委员会的规则变更草案,并将所考虑的否决理由通知公众公司会计监督委员会。此外,根据《2002年萨班斯—奥克斯利法》第107条(《美国法典》第15编第7217节)、该法第19(b)(2)(B)条[《美国法典》第十五编第78s(b)(2)(B)节],延长不超过240日的期间(从根据该法第19(b)(1)条[《美国法典》第十五编第78s(b)(1)节]提交的规则变更草案发布公告之日起算),证券交易委员会必须在上述期间内发布命令批准或否决规则变更草案,并判定延长上述期间是否适当,并公布其作出该等判定所根据的原因。

(5)根据《2002年萨班斯—奥克斯利法》第107条(《美国法典》第十五编第7217节)、该法第19(b)(3)(C)条[《美国法典》第15编第78s(b)(3)(C)节],临时暂停公众公司会计监督委员会某一规则的适用。

(c)无论上文如何规定,在任何情况下,如首席会计师认为适当,其均可以将相关事项提交证券交易委员会处理。

[《联邦公报》第75卷第47449页,2010年8月6日,修正索引:《联邦公报》第76卷第2806页,2011年1月18日。]

第200.30-12节　[保留]

第200.30-13节　对财务管理办公室副执行主任的委托授权

根据《美国法典》第十五编第78d-1节和第78d-2节的规定,证券交易委员会兹将

Commission hereby delegates, until the Commission orders otherwise, the following functions to the Associate Executive Director of the Office of Financial Management, to be performed by him or her, or under his or her direction by such person or persons as may be designated from time to time by the Chairman of the Commission:

(a) The compromise and collection of federal claims as required by the Federal Claims Collection Act of 1966, as amended and recodified at 31 U.S.C. 3701–3720, in conformance with standards and procedures jointly promulgated by the Secretary of the Treasury and the Attorney General of the United States in 31 CFR Parts 900–904.

(b) The administration of filing fee account procedures and policies established in §202.3a of this chapter.

[68 FR 50954, Aug. 22, 2003]

§200.30–14 Delegation of authority to the General Counsel.

Pursuant to the provisions of Pub. L. 101–181, 101 Stat. 1254, 101 Stat. 1255, 15 U.S.C. 78d–1, 15 U.S.C. 78d–2, and 5 U.S.C. 552a(d)(2)(B)(ii), the Securities and Exchange Commission hereby delegates, until the Commission orders otherwise, the following functions to the General Counsel of the Commission, to be performed by him or her or under his or her direction by such person or persons as may be designated from time to time by the Chairman of the Commission:

(a) Grant waivers of imputed disqualification requested pursuant to 17 CFR 200.735–8(d).

(b) Determine whether the Commission will submit, after consultation with any Division or Office of the Commission designated by the Commission, and amicus curiae brief in private litigation on issues previously considered and designated by the Commission as appropriate for the exercise of delegated authority. A list of the issues designated by the Commission as subject to this delegated authority and, where determined by the Commission, the position to be taken on each such issue, may be obtained on request addressed to Securities and Exchange Commission, Washington, D.C. 20549.

(c) Determine the appropriate disposition of all Freedom of Information Act and confidential treatment appeals in accordance with §§200.80(d)(6), 200.80(e)(4), 200.83(e), 200.83(f), and 200.83(h).

(d) Determine the appropriate disposition of all Privacy Act appeals and related matters in accordance with §§200.304(a) and (c); 200.307(a) and (b); 200.308(a)(4)–(10); 200.308(b)(1)–(4); and 200.309(e)(1) and (2).

(e) File notices of appearance in bankruptcy reorganization cases under section 1109(a) of the Bankruptcy Code involving debtors, the securities of which are registered or required to be registered under section 12 of the Securities Exchange Act.

下述职能委托财务管理办公室副执行主任行使,或委托证券交易委员会主席随时指定的其他人员在财务管理办公室副执行主任的领导下行使(直至证券交易委员会另行作出命令):

(a)按照美国财政部长和联邦总检察长联合颁发的标准和程序,按《1966年联邦债权催收法》(修正及重新编纂后的索引为《美国法典》第三十一编第3701~3720节)的要求对联邦债权进行和解及催收。

(b)负责实施本章第202.3a节确定的文件提交费的会计程序和政策。

[《联邦公报》第68卷第50954页,2003年8月22日。]

第200.30-14节　对首席律师的委托授权

根据公法编号101-181,《美国制定法汇编》第101卷第1254页、《美国制定法汇编》第101卷第1255页的条文[《美国法典》第十五编第78d-1节、《美国法典》第十五编第78d-2节和《美国法典》第五编第552a(d)(2)(B)(ii)节],证券交易委员会兹将下述职能委托证券交易委员会首席律师行使,或委托证券交易委员会主席随时指定的其他人员在首席律师的领导下行使(直至证券交易委员会另行作出命令):

(a)核准根据《联邦规章汇编》第十七编第200.735-8(d)节提出的免予推定丧失资格的请求。

(b)在与证券交易委员会指定的任何下属司或办公室磋商后,判定证券交易委员会是否应在私人诉讼中就证券交易委员会之前审议和指定过的问题提交法庭之友书状,以适当行使授权;证券交易委员会指定的在上述权限范围之内的问题清单,以及证券交易委员会决定应就各问题采取的态度,可通过请求获得,请求应发送至华盛顿特区证券交易委员会,邮编:D.C.20549。

(c)按照第200.80(d)(6)节、第200.80(e)(4)节、第200.83(e)节、第200.83(f)节和第200.83(h)节决定对所有关于依《信息自由法》提出的行政复议申请和保密处理行政复议申请进行适当处置。

(d)决定按照第200.304(a)节和第200.304(c)节;第200.307(a)节和第200.307(b)节;第200.308(a)(4)~(10)节;第200.308(b)(1)~(4)节及第200.309(e)(1)~(2)节对所有《隐私法》中的行政复议申请及相关事项进行适当处置。

(e)对《破产法典》第1109(a)条下且所涉债权人的证券已根据或应根据《证券交易法》第12条进行注册的破产重组案件提交出庭通知。

(f) Approve non-expert, non-privileged, factual testimony by present or former staff members, and the production of non-privileged documents, when validly subpoenaed; and assert governmental privileges on behalf of the Commission in litigation where the Commission appears as a party or in response to third party subpoenas.

(g)(1) With respect to proceedings conducted pursuant to the Securities Act of 1933, 15 U.S.C. 77a *et seq.*, the Securities Exchange Act of 1934, 15 U.S.C. 78a *et seq.*, the Public Utility Holding Company Act of 1935, 15 U.S.C. 79a *et seq.*, the Trust Indenture Act of 1939, 15 U.S.C. 77aaa *et seq.*, the Investment Company Act of 1940, 15 U.S.C. 80a-1 *et seq.*, the Investment Advisers Act of 1940, 15 U.S.C. 80b-1 *et seq.*, the Securities Investor Protection Act of 1970, 15 U.S.C. 78aaa *et seq.*, the provisions of Rule 102(e) of the Commission Rules of Practice, §201.102(e) of this chapter, and Title I of the Sarbanes-Oxley Act of 2002, 15 U.S.C. 7211-7219:

(i) To consider an application for review of an interlocutory ruling which an administrative law judge has refused to certify, and to deny such application upon determining that the administrative law judge did not err in refusing to certify the matter.

(ii) To consider an interlocutory ruling which an administrative judge has certified, and to affirm such ruling upon determining that such action is appropriate.

(iii) To issue any order pursuant to an initial decision as to any person who has not filed a petition for review within the time provided, or has withdrawn his appeal, where the Commission has not on its own motion ordered that the initial decision be reviewed.

(iv) Except where the Commission otherwise directs, to issue findings and orders pursuant to offers of settlement which the Commission has determined should be accepted.

(v) To grant petitions for review of initial decisions by a hearing officer.

(vi) To grant motions of staff counsel to discontinue administrative proceedings as to a particular respondent who has died or cannot be found, or because of a mistake in the identity of a respondent named in the order for proceedings.

(vii) To request additional briefs or grant requests for the submission of late or additional briefs, or the acceptance of affidavits or other material for inclusion in the record or in support of motions or petitions addressed to the Commission.

(viii) To issue an order dismissing an application for review upon the request of the applicant that the application be withdrawn.

(ix) To issue an order dismissing an exemptive application upon the request of the applicant that the application be withdrawn.

(x) To determine motions to consolidate proceedings pending before the Commission.

(xi) To determine whether to permit or require that a record of proceedings be supplemented with additional evidence.

(xii) To issue an order setting the effective date of sanctions that were stayed

(f)批准在签发有效传票的情况下由现任或前任员工作出的非专家、非受保密特权约束的事实证词以及提交的非受保密特权约束的文件;并代表证券交易委员会在证券交易委员会作为当事人出庭或应第三方传票而出庭的诉讼中主张政府权利。

(g)(1)就根据《1933年证券法》(《美国法典》第十五编第77a节及其后条文)、《1934年证券交易法》(《美国法典》第十五编第78a节及其后条文)、《1935年公用事业控股公司法》(《美国法典》第十五编第79a节及其后条文)、《1939年信托契约法》(《美国法典》第十五编第77aaa节及其后条文)、《1940年投资公司法》(《美国法典》第十五编第80a-1节及其后条文)、《1940年投资顾问法》(《美国法典》第十五编第80b-1节及其后条文)、《1970年证券投资者保护法》(《美国法典》第十五编第78aaa节及其后条文)、《证券交易委员会工作规则》的《102(e)规则》[本章第201.102(e)节]以及《2002年萨班斯—奥克斯利法》第一编(《美国法典》第十五编第7211-7219节)提起的程序而言:

(i)行政法官拒绝认定中间裁定的,对复议申请进行审议;如判定行政法官之拒绝认定并无错误,则驳回该等申请。

(ii)对行政法官已认定的中间裁定进行审议;如判定该等行动适当,则对裁定予以确认。

(iii)任何人未在规定时间内对初步决定提出复议请求或已撤回复议请求的,则根据该裁定签发命令,前提是证券交易委员会未主动提出动议命令对初步决定进行复议。

(iv)除非证券交易委员会另有指令,根据证券交易委员会认为应接受的和解要约做出认定和签发命令。

(v)核准针对听证官的初步决定提出的复议请求。

(vi)核准作为证券交易委员会员工的法律顾问基于特定相对人/被申请人死亡、失踪或程序命令所载之相对人/被申请人身份错误而提起的停止行政处理程序的动议。

(vii)要求提交补充陈辩书,或核准提交最新或补充陈辩书的请求,或接受将宣誓书面证词或其他材料纳入记录或向证券交易委员会提交的支持动议或请求的材料之中。

(viii)在申请人提出撤回申请之时,签发命令撤销复议申请。

(ix)在申请人提出撤回申请之时,签发命令撤销豁免申请。

(x)就合并证券交易委员会未决程序的动议作出决定。

(xi)判定是否允许或要求对程序记录进行额外证据补充。

(xii)签发命令,在联邦法院发布确认证券交易委员会制裁命令的判决之时,确定

pending appeal to the federal courts, upon issuance of the mandate affirming the Commission's order imposing those sanctions.

(xiii) To issue a briefing schedule order pursuant to Rule 450 of the Commission's Rules of Practice, §201.450 of this chapter.

(xiv) To determine motions for expedited briefing schedules.

(xv) To issue an order raising, pursuant to the provisions of Rule 411(d) of the Commission's Rules of Practice, §201.411(d) of this chapter, any matter relating to whether any sanction, and if so what sanction, is in the public interest.

(2) With respect to proceedings conducted pursuant to the Securities Act of 1933 (15 U.S.C. 77a *et seq.*), the Securities Exchange Act of 1934 (15 U.S.C. 78a *et seq.*), the Investment Company Act of 1940 (15 U.S.C. 80a–1 *et seq.*), the Investment Advisers Act of 1940 (15 U.S.C. 80b–1 *et seq.*), the Securities Investor Protection Act of 1970 (15 U.S.C. 78aaa *et seq.*) and the provisions of Rule 102(e) of the Commission's Rules of Practice (§201.102(e) of this chapter), to issue findings and orders taking the remedial action described in the order for proceedings where the respondents expressly consent to such action, fail to appear or default in the filing of answers required to be filed; or to grant a request, based upon a showing of good cause, to vacate an order of default, so as to permit presentation of a defense.

(3) With respect to proceedings conducted pursuant to the Securities Exchange Act of 1934 (15 U.S.C. 78a *et seq.*), to issue an order dismissing an application for review of a denial by a self-regulatory organization of an application by a person subject to statutory disqualification to become associated with a member firm upon receipt of notice from the self-regulatory organization that the firm is no longer a member of the self-regulatory organization.

(4) With respect to proceedings conducted under sections 19(d), (e), and (f) of the Securities Exchange Act of 1934, 15 U.S.C. 78s(d), (e), and (f), and Title I of the Sarbanes–Oxley Act of 2002, 15 U.S.C. 7211–7219, to determine that an application for review under any of those sections has been abandoned, under the provisions of Rule 420 or 440 of the Commission's Rules of Practice, §201.420 or §201.440 of this chapter, or otherwise, and accordingly to issue an order dismissing the application.

(5) With respect to proceedings conducted pursuant to the Securities Exchange Act of 1934, 15 U.S.C. 78a *et seq.*, the Investment Company Act of 1940, 15 U.S.C. 80a–1 *et seq.*, the Investment Advisers Act of 1940, 15 U.S.C. 80b–1 *et seq.*, the provisions of Rule 102(e) of the Commission's Rules of Practice, §201.102(e) of this chapter, and Title I of the Sarbanes–Oxley Act of 2002, 15 U.S.C. 7211–7219, to determine applications to stay Commission orders pending appeal of those orders to the federal courts and to determine application to vacate such stays.

因向联邦法院上诉而暂缓实施的制裁的生效日期。

(xiii)根据《证券交易委员会工作规则》的《450规则》(本章第201.450节)签发陈辩书提交日程命令;

(xiv)对陈辩书提交日程加急动议作出决定。

(xv)根据《证券交易委员会工作规则》的《411(d)规则》[本章第201.411(d)节]签发命令,提起与下述各项相关的事项:处以制裁是否符合公共利益,如符合,何种制裁符合公共利益。

(2)就根据《1933年证券法》(《美国法典》第十五编第77a节及其后条文)、《1934年证券交易法》(《美国法典》第十五编第78a节及其后条文)、《1940年投资公司法》(《美国法典》第十五编第80a-1节及其后条文)、《1940年投资顾问法》(《美国法典》第十五编第80b-1节及其后条文)、《1970年证券投资者保护法》(《美国法典》第十五编第78aaa节及其后条文)、《证券交易委员会工作规则》的《102(e)规则》[本章第201.102(e)节]提起的程序而言,在相对人/被申请人明确表示同意,或未能出席或未按要求提交答辩状的程序中,作出认定,签发命令,采取程序命令中所载救济行动,并在相对人/被申请人提出充分理由的情况下,核准撤销命令或缺席判决,以允许相对人/被申请人进行抗辩。

(3)就根据《1934年证券交易法》(《美国法典》第十五编第78a节及其后条文)提起的程序而言,在收到自律组织发出的通知,说明所涉成员公司不再属于自律组织成员时,签发命令驳回不具备法定资格的主体针对自律组织拒绝其充当该成员公司的业务相关人的决定所提出的审查申请。

(4)就根据《1934年证券交易法》第19(d)条、第19(e)条和第19(f)条[《美国法典》第十五编第78s(d)节、第78s(e)节和第78s(f)节]以及《2002年萨班斯—奥克斯利法》第一编(《美国法典》第十五编第7211~7219节)提起的程序而言,根据《证券交易委员会工作规则》的《420规则》或《440规则》(本章第201.420节或第201.440节)或其他规则判定审查申请已被放弃,并基于此签发相应命令驳回申请。

(5)就根据《1934年证券交易法》(《美国法典》第十五编第78a节及其后条文)、《1940年投资公司法》(《美国法典》第十五编第80a-1节及其后条文)及《1940年投资顾问法》(《美国法典》第十五编第80b-1节及其后条文)、《证券交易委员会工作规则》的《102(e)规则》[本章第201.102(e)节]以及《2002年萨班斯—奥克斯利法》第一编(《美国法典》第十五编第7211~7219节)提起的程序而言,就基于向联邦法院上诉而提出的中止执行证券交易委员会命令的申请作出决定,以及就撤销该中止令的申请作出决定。

(6) With respect to review proceedings pursuant to Sections 19 (d), (e), and (f) of the Securities Exchange Act of 1934 (15 U.S.C. 78s(d), (e), and (f)), to determine applications for a stay of action taken by a self-regulatory organization pending Commission review of that action and to determine applications to vacate such stays.

(7) In connection with Commission review of actions taken by self-regulatory organizations pursuant to sections 19(d), (e), and (f) of the Securities Exchange Act of 1934, 15 U.S.C. 78s(d), (e), and (f), or by the Public Company Accounting Oversight Board pursuant to Title I of the Sarbanes-Oxley Act of 2002, 15 U.S.C. 7211-7219, to grant or deny requests for oral argument in accordance with the provisions of Rule 451 of the Commission's Rules of Practice, §201.451 of this chapter.

(8) In connection with Commission review of actions taken by the Public Company Accounting Oversight Board pursuant to Title I of the Sarbanes-Oxley Act of 2002, 15 U.S.C. 7211-7219, to determine whether to lift the automatic stay of a disciplinary sanction.

(h) Notwithstanding anything in paragraph(g) of this section, the functions described in paragraph (g) of this section are not delegated to the General Counsel with respect to proceedings in which the Chairman or the General Counsel determines that separation of functions requirements or other circumstances would make inappropriate the General Counsel's exercise of such delegated functions. With respect to such proceedings, such functions are delegated to the Executive Assistant to the Chairman pursuant to §200.30-16 of this chapter.

(i) Notwithstanding anything in paragraph (g) of this section, in any case described in paragraph(g) of this section in which the General Counsel believes it appropriate, he or she may submit the matter to the Commission.

(j) With respect to the Securities Exchange Act of 1934 (15 U.S.C. 78a *et seq.*):

(1) To administer the provisions of §240.24c-1 of this chapter; provided that access to nonpublic information as defined in such section shall be provided only with the concurrence of the head of the Commission division or office responsible for such information or the files containing such information.

(2) To administer the provisions of section 24(d) of the Act (15 U.S.C. 78x(d)).

(k) To refer matters and information concerning possible professional misconduct to state bar associations and other state professional boards or societies.

(l) File applications in district court under Section 21 (e) (1) of the Securities Exchange Act of 1934 (15 U.S.C. 78u(e)(1)) to obtain orders commanding persons to comply with Commission orders.

(m) (1) To designate officers empowered to administer oaths and affirmations, subpoena witnesses, compel their attendance, take evidence, and require the production of any books, papers, correspondence, memoranda, contracts, agreements, or other records in

(6)就根据《1934年证券交易法》第19(d)条、第19(e)条和第19(f)条[《美国法典》第十五编第78s(d)节、第78s(e)节和第78s(f)节]提起的复议程序而言,就基于证券交易委员会审查而提出的中止执行自律组织行动的申请作出决定,并就撤销该中止令的申请作出决定。

(7)就证券交易委员会根据《1934年证券交易法》第19(d)条、第19(e)条和第19(f)条[《美国法典》第十五编第78s(d)节、第78s(e)节和第78s(f)节]或公众公司会计监督委员会根据《2002年萨班斯—奥克斯利法》第一编(《美国法典》第十五编第7211~7219节)对自律组织采取的行动进行的审查而言,根据《证券交易委员会工作规则》的《451规则》(本章第201.451节)核准或驳回口头辩论请求。

(8)就证券交易委员会根据《2002年萨班斯—奥克斯利法》第一编(《美国法典》第十五编第7211~7219节)对公众公司会计监督委员会采取的行动进行的审查而言,决定是否撤销纪律处分的自动中止执行。

(h)无论本节第(g)款如何规定,如证券交易委员会主席或首席律师判定因职能分离要求或其他情形导致首席律师不宜行使上述职能,则首席律师不得在上述程序中被授权履行本节第(g)款所述职能。就上述程序而言,应由证券交易委员会主席的执行助理根据本章第200.30-16节行使相关职能。

(i)无论本节第(g)款如何规定,若首席律师认为适当,其均可以将本节第(g)款所述任何事项提交证券交易委员会处理。

(j)就《1934年证券交易法》(《美国法典》第十五编第78a节及其后条文)而言:

(1)负责实施本章第240.24c-1节的规定;但是提供该节定义之非公开信息查询权的,必须征得对该等信息或包含该等信息的文件负责的部门或办公室的主任同意。

(2)负责实施该法第24(d)条[《美国法典》第十五编第78x(d)节]的规定。

(k)将涉嫌涉及违反职业道德行为的事项和信息提交州律师协会或其他州行业理事会或协会。

(l)根据《1934年证券交易法》第21(e)(1)条[《美国法典》第十五编第78u(e)(1)节]向地区法院提出申请,要求法院签发命令向相关主体强制执行证券交易委员会的命令。

(m)(1)指定授权官员主持宣誓和证词声明程序、传唤证人程序、强制证人出席程序、取证程序,并要求在证券交易委员会根据《1934年证券交易法》第21条(《美国法典》第十五编第78u节)发起的调查程序{包括就律师涉嫌违反《证券交易委员会工作

the course of investigations instituted by the Commission pursuant to Section 21 of the Securities Exchange Act of 1934 (15 U.S.C. 78u) including for possible violations by attorneys of Rule 102(e) of the Commission Rules of Practice (17 CFR 201.102(e)).

(2) To terminate the authority of officers to administer oaths and affirmations, subpoena witnesses, compel their attendance, take evidence, and require the production of any books, papers, correspondence, memoranda, contracts, agreements, or other records in the course of investigations instituted by the Commission pursuant to Section 21 of the Securities Exchange Act of 1934 (15 U.S.C. 78u) including for possible violations by attorneys of Rule 102(e) of the Commission Rules of Practice (17 CFR 201.102(e)).

[47 FR 20288, May 12, 1982]

Editorial Note: For Federal Register Citations affecting §200.30-14, see the List of CFR Sections Affected, which appears in the Finding Aids section of the printed volume and at www.fdsys.gov.

§200.30-15 Delegation of authority to Executive Director.

Under Pub. L. 100-181, 101 Stat. 1254 (15 U.S.C. 78d-1, 78d-2), the Securities and Exchange Commission hereby delegates, until the Commission orders otherwise, the following functions to the Executive Director to be performed by him or her or under his or her direction by persons designated by the Chairman of the Commission: To identify and implement additional changes within the Commission that will promote the principles and standards of the National Performance Review and the strategic and quality management approaches described by the Federal Quality Institute's "Presidential Award for Quality" or its successor awards.

[60 FR 14630, Mar. 20, 1995]

§200.30-16 Delegation of authority to Executive Assistant to the Chairman.

Pursuant to the provisions of Pub. L. 101-181, 101 Stat. 1254, 101 Stat. 1255, 15 U.S.C. 78d-1, and 15 U.S.C. 78d-2, the Securities and Exchange Commission hereby delegates, until the Commission orders otherwise, the following functions to the Executive Assistant to the Chairman (or to such other person or persons designated pursuant to paragraph (c) of this section), to be performed by such Executive Assistant or under the Executive Assistant's direction by such person or persons as may be designated from time to time by the Chairman of the Commission (or by such other person or persons designated pursuant to paragraph (c) of this section):

(a) The functions otherwise delegated to the General Counsel under §200.30-14(g) of this chapter, with respect to any proceeding in which the Chairman or the General Counsel has determined, pursuant to §200.30-14(h) of this chapter, that separation of functions requirements or other circumstances would make inappropriate the General Counsel's exercise of such delegated functions.

规则》的《102(e)规则》[《联邦规章汇编》第十七编第201.102(e)节]而发起的程序}中制作任何档案、文件、通信、备忘录、合同、协议或其他记录。

(2)终止官员的下述授权:主持宣誓和证词声明程序、传唤证人程序、强制证人出席程序、取证程序的权限,以及要求在证券交易委员会根据《1934年证券交易法》第21条(《美国法典》第十五编第78u节)发起的调查程序{包括就律师涉嫌违反《证券交易委员会工作规则》的《102(e)规则》[《联邦规章汇编》第十七编第201.102(e)节]而发起的程序}中制作任何档案、文件、通信、备忘录、合同、协议或其他记录的权限。

[《联邦公报》第47卷第20288页,1982年5月12日。]

编辑注:对第200.30-14节有影响的《联邦公报》索引,参见《受影响的联邦规章汇编条文列表》(见印刷版本的《检索协助》章节和www.fdsys.gov)。

第200.30-15节　对执行主任的委托授权

根据公法编号100-181,《美国制定法汇编》第101卷第1254页的条文(《美国法典》第十五编第78d-1节、第78d-2节),证券交易委员会兹将下述职能委托执行主任行使,或委托证券交易委员会主席随时指定的其他人员在执行主任的领导下行使(直至证券交易委员会另行作出命令):

在证券交易委员会内部确定并实施进一步的变革,以促进国家绩效评估的原则和标准以及联邦质量协会的"总统质量奖"或其后继奖励中所述的战略和质量管理方法。

[《联邦公报》第60卷第14630页,1995年3月20日。]

第200.30-16节　对主席执行助理的委托授权

根据公法编号101-181,《美国制定法汇编》第101卷第1254页、《美国制定法汇编》第101卷第1255页的条文(《美国法典》第十五编第78d-1节和《美国法典》第十五编第78d-2节),证券交易委员会兹将下述职能委托主席执行助理[或根据本节第(c)款指定的其他一名或数名人员]行使,或委托证券交易委员会主席随时指定的其他人员[或根据本节第(c)款指定的其他人员]在执行主任的领导下行使(直至证券交易委员会另行作出命令):

(a)本章第200.30-14(g)节授权首席律师行使的职能,前提是证券交易委员会主席或首席律师根据本章第200.30-14(h)节基于职能分离要求或其他情形判定首席律师不宜在相关程序中行使上述职能。

(b) Notwithstanding anything in paragraph (a) of this section, in any proceeding described in paragraph (a) of this section in which the Executive Assistant believes it appropriate, the Executive Assistant may submit the matter to the Commission.

(c) Notwithstanding anything in this section, the functions otherwise delegated to the Executive Assistant respecting any proceeding in which the Chairman or the Executive Assistant determines that the Executive Assistant's exercise of such delegated functions would be inappropriate, are hereby delegated to such person or persons, not under the Executive Assistant's supervision, as may be designated by the Chairman.

[54 FR 18102, Apr. 27, 1989, as amended at 59 FR 39681, Aug. 4, 1994]

§200.30-17 Delegation of authority to Director of Office of International Affairs.

Pursuant to the provisions of Pub. L. 100-181, 101 Stat. 1254, 1255 (15 U.S.C. 78d-1, 78d-2), the Securities and Exchange Commission hereby delegates, until the Commission orders otherwise, the following functions to the Director of the Office of International Affairs to be performed by the Director or under the Director's direction by such other person or persons as may be designated from time to time by the Chairman of the Commission:

(a) To administer the provisions of §240.24c-1 of this chapter; provided that access to nonpublic information as defined in such section shall be provided only with the concurrence of the head of the Commission division or office responsible for such information or the files containing such information.

(b) To administer the provisions of section 24(d) of the Securities Exchange Act of 1934 (15 U.S.C. 78x(d)).

[58 FR 52419, Oct. 8, 1993]

§200.30-18 Delegation of authority to Director of the Office of Compliance Inspections and Examinations.

Pursuant to the provisions of Pub. L. 100-181, 101 Stat. 1254, 1255 (15 U.S.C. 78d-1, 78d-2), the Securities and Exchange Commission hereby delegates, until the Commission orders otherwise, the following authority to the Director of the Office of Compliance Inspections and Examinations (OCIE) to be performed by the Director or by such other person or persons as may be designated from time to time by the Chairman of the Commission:

(a) To administer the provisions of §240.24c-1 of this chapter; provided that access to nonpublic information as defined in such Section shall be provided only with the concurrence of the head of the Commission division or office responsible for such information or the files containing such information.

(b)无论本节第(a)款如何规定,若执行助理认为适当,其可以将本节第(a)款所述相关事项提交证券交易委员会处理。

(c)不论本节如何规定,若证券交易委员会主席或执行助理判定执行助理不宜在相关程序中行使上述职能,则应授权证券交易委员会主席指定的不受执行助理监督的其他人员行使上述职能。

[《联邦公报》第54卷第18102页,1989年4月27日,修正索引:《联邦公报》第59卷第39681页,1994年8月4日。]

第200.30-17节 对国际事务办公室主任的委托授权

根据公法编号100-181,《美国制定法汇编》第101卷第1254页、第1255页的条文(《美国法典》第十五编第78d-1节、第78d-2节),证券交易委员会兹将下述职能委托国际事务办公室主任行使或证券交易委员会主席随时指定的其他人员在国际事务办公室主任的领导下行使(直至证券交易委员会另行作出命令):

(a)负责实施本章第240.24c-1节的规定;但是提供该节定义之非公开信息查询权的,必须征得对该等信息或包含该等信息的文件负责的部门或办公室的主任同意。

(b)负责实施《1934年证券交易法》第24(d)条[《美国法典》第十五编第78x(d)节]的规定。

[《联邦公报》第58卷第52419页,1993年10月8日。]

第200.30-18节 对合规检查和核查办公室主任的委托授权

根据公法编号100-181,《美国制定法汇编》第101卷第1254页、第1255页的条文(《美国法典》第十五编第78d-1节、第78d-2节),证券交易委员会兹将下述职能委托合规检查和核查办公室(OCIE)主任行使或证券交易委员会主席随时指定的其他人员在合规检查和核查办公室主任的领导下行使(直至证券交易委员会另行作出命令):

(a)负责实施本章第240.24c-1节的规定;但是提供该节定义之非公开信息查询权的,必须征得对该等信息或包含该等信息的文件负责的部门或办公室的主任同意。

(b) Pursuant to the Securities Exchange Act of 1934 ("the Exchange Act") (15 U.S.C. 78a *et seq.*):

(1) To grant and deny applications for confidential treatment filed pursuant to Section 24(b) of the Exchange Act (15 U.S.C. 78x(b)) and Rule 24b-2 thereunder (§240.24b-2 of this chapter); and

(2) To revoke a grant of confidential treatment for any such application.

(c)(1) Pursuant to Section 17(b) of the Exchange Act (15 U.S.C. 78q(b)), prior to any examination of a registered clearing agency, registered transfer agent, or registered municipal securities dealer whose appropriate regulatory agency is not the Commission, to notify and consult with the appropriate regulatory agency for such clearing agency, transfer agent, or municipal securities dealer.

(2) Pursuant to section 17(b)(1)(B) of the Exchange Act (15 U.S.C. 78q(b)(1)(B)), prior to any examination of a broker or dealer registered pursuant to section 6(g) of the Exchange Act (15 U.S.C. 78f(g)) or a national securities association registered pursuant to section 15A(k) of the Exchange Act (15 U.S.C. 78o-3(k)), to notify and consult with the Commodity Futures Trading Commission regarding the feasibility and desirability of coordinating such examination with examinations conducted by the Commodity Futures Trading Commission in order to avoid unnecessary regulatory duplication or undue regulatory burdens.

(d) Pursuant to Section 17(c)(3) of the Exchange Act (15 U.S.C. 78q(c)(3)), in regard to clearing agencies, transfer agents and municipal securities dealers for which the Commission is not the appropriate regulatory agency:

(1) To notify the appropriate regulatory agency of any examination conducted by the Commission of any such clearing agency, transfer agent, or municipal securities dealer;

(2) To request from the appropriate regulatory agency a copy of the report of any examination of any such clearing agency, transfer agent, or municipal securities dealer conducted by such appropriate regulatory agency and any data supplied to it in connection with such examination; and

(3) To furnish to the appropriate regulatory agency on request a copy of the report of any examination of any such clearing agency, transfer agent, or municipal securities dealer conducted by the Commission and any data supplied to it in connection with such examination.

(e) To administer the provisions of Section 24(d) of the Exchange Act (15 U.S.C. 78x(d)).

(f) To notify the Securities Investor Protection Corporation ("SIPC") of facts concerning the activities and the operational and financial condition of any registered broker or dealer which is or appears to be a member of SIPC and which is in or

(b)根据《1934年证券交易法》(“《证券交易法》”)(《美国法典》第十五编第78a节及其后条文):

(1)核准或驳回根据该法第24(b)条[《美国法典》第十五编第78x(b)节]以及依其颁布的《24b-2规则》(本章第240.24b-2节)提出的保密处理申请;及

(2)撤销对上述任何保密处理申请的核准。

(c)(1)根据该《证券交易法》第17(b)条[《美国法典》第十五编第78q(b)节],在对证券交易委员会无相应监管权的注册结算机构、注册过户代理人、注册市政证券自营商进行任何检查之前,提前通知该等结算机构、过户代理人或市政证券自营商的相应监管机构并与之进行磋商。

(2)根据该《证券交易法》第17(b)(1)(B)条[《美国法典》第十五编第78q(b)(1)(B)节],在对根据该法第6(g)条[《美国法典》第十五编第78f(g)节]注册的经纪商或自营商以及根据该法第15A(k)条[《美国法典》第十五编第78o-3(k)节]注册的全国性证券协会进行检查之前,提前通知商品期货交易委员会,并就协调双方各自进行的检查工作的可行性和有益性进行磋商,以避免不必要的重复监管或产生不当的监管负担。

(d)根据《证券交易法》第17(c)(3)条[《美国法典》第十五编第78q(c)(3)节],对于相应监管机构并非证券交易委员会的结算机构、过户代理人和市政证券自营商而言:

(1)将证券交易委员会对任何该等结算机构、过户代理人和市政证券自营商开展的任何检查通知其相应监管机构;

(2)要求相应监管机构提供对任何该等结算机构、过户代理人和市政证券自营商开展的任何检查报告及获得的与检查相关的任何数据之复本;及

(3)经相应监管机构要求,将证券交易委员会对任何该等结算机构、过户代理人和市政证券自营商开展的任何检查报告及获得的与检查相关的任何数据之复本提供给相应监管机构;

(e)负责实施《证券交易法》第24(d)条[《美国法典》第十五编第78x(d)节]的规定。

(f)对于属于或从表面判断属于证券投资者保护公司(SIPC)成员且处于或濒临《1970年证券投资者保护法》及其修正第5条(《美国法典》第十五编第78aa节及其后条文)定义的财务困境的任何注册经纪商或自营商,将其活动和经营财务状况事实通知

approaching financial difficulty within the meaning of Section 5 of the Securities Investor Protection Act of 1970, as amended, 15 U.S.C. 78aa *et seq.*

(g) Pursuant to Section 15(b)(2)(C) of the Exchange Act (15 U.S.C. 78o(b)(2)(C)):

(1) To delay until the second six month period from registration with the Commission the inspection of newly registered broker-dealers that have not commenced actual operations within six months of their registration with the Commission; and

(2) To delay until the second six month period from registration with the Commission the inspection of newly registered broker-dealers to determine whether they are in compliance with applicable provisions of the Exchange Act and rules thereunder, other than financial responsibility rules.

(h) Pursuant to Section 36 of the Exchange Act (15 U.S.C. 78mm) to review and, either unconditionally or on specified terms and conditions, grant, or deny exemptions from rule 17a-25 of the Act (§240.17a-25 of this chapter), provided that the Division of Trading and Markets is notified of any such granting or denial of an exemption.

(i) With respect to the Investment Advisers Act of 1940 ("Advisers Act") (15 U.S.C. 80b-1 *et seq.*):

(1) Pursuant to Section 203(h) of the Advisers Act (15 U.S.C.80b-3(h)), to authorize the issuance of orders cancelling registration of investment advisers, or applications for registration, if such investment advisers or applicants for registration are no longer in existence or are not engaged in business as investment advisers; and

(2) Pursuant to Rule 204-2(j)(3)(ii) (§275.204-2(j)(3)(ii) of this chapter), to make written demands upon non-resident investment advisers subject to the provisions of such rule to furnish to the Commission true, correct, complete, and current copies of any or all books and records which such non-resident investment advisers are required to make, keep current, or preserve pursuant to any provision of any rule or regulation of the Commission adopted under the Advisers Act, or any part of such books and records which may be specified in any such demand.

(j) With respect to the Securities Exchange Act of 1934 (15 U.S.C. 78a *et seq.*):

(1) Under section 15(b) of the Act (15 U.S.C. 78o(b)):

(i) To authorize the issuance of orders granting registration of brokers or dealers within 45 days of the acceptance of an application for registration as a broker or dealer (or within such longer period as to which the applicant consents);

(ii) To grant registration of brokers or dealers sooner than 45 days after acceptance of an application for registration;

(iii) To authorize the issuance of orders canceling registrations of brokers or dealers, or pending applications for registration, if such brokers or dealers or applicants for

证券投资者保护公司。

(g)根据《证券交易法》第15(b)(2)(C)条[《美国法典》第十五编第78o(b)(2)(C)节]:

(1)对于新注册的经纪自营商,在注册后6个月内未开展实际经营的,将对其进行的检查工作推迟至注册后的第二个6个月期间;及

(2)将检查并判定新注册经纪自营商是否遵守《证券交易法》以及依其颁布的规则(财务责任规则除外)的工作推迟至注册后第二个6个月的期间。

(h)根据《证券交易法》(《美国法典》第十五编第78mm节)第36条审查并无条件或附具体条款、条件地核准或驳回对该法《17a-25规则》(本章第240.17a-25节)的豁免,但应将任何决定结果通知交易和市场部。

(i)就《1940年投资顾问法》(《顾问法》)(《美国法典》第十五编第80b-1节及其后条文)而言:

(1)根据《顾问法》第203(h)条[《美国法典》第十五编第80b-3(h)节],在投资顾问或注册申请人不再存续或不再从事投资顾问业务之时,同意签发命令注销投资顾问注册;及

(2)根据《204-2(j)(3)(ii)规则》[本章第275.204-2(j)(3)(ii)节],向受制于上述规则的非居民投资顾问发出书面要求,督促其根据证券交易委员会在《投资顾问法》下通过的规定向证券交易委员会提供其应制作、更新或保存的任何及所有账簿和记录或者任何该等书面要求中指明的该等账簿和记录的任何部分之真实、准确、完整和最新副本。

(j)就《1934年证券交易法》(《美国法典》第十五编第78a节及其后条文)而言:

(1)在该法第15(b)条[《美国法典》第十五编第78o(b)节]下:

(i)同意签发命令,在受理经纪商或自营商注册申请后45日内(或申请人同意的其他更长的期间内)核准申请人注册为经纪商或自营商;

(ii)在受理注册申请后45日内核准申请人注册为经纪商或自营商;

(iii)在经纪商、自营商或注册申请人不再存续或不再从事经纪商或自营商业务之时,同意签发命令注销该等经纪商、自营商的注册,或暂缓申请人的注册;

registration are no longer in existence or are not engaged in business as brokers or dealers; and

(iv) To determine whether notices of withdrawal from registration on Form BDW shall become effective sooner than the normal 60-day waiting period.

(2) Under section 15B(a) of the Act (15 U.S.C. 78o-4(a)):

(i) To authorize the issuance of orders granting registration of municipal securities dealers within 45 days of the filing of acceptable applications for registration as a municipal securities dealer (or within such longer period as to which the applicant consents); and

(ii) To grant registration of municipal securities dealers sooner than 45 days after receipt by the Commission of acceptable applications for registration.

(3) Under section 15B(c) of the Act (15 U.S.C. 78o-4(c)):

(i) To authorize the issuance of orders canceling registrations of municipal securities dealers, or pending applications for registration, if such municipal securities dealers or applicants for registration are no longer in existence or are not engaged in business as municipal securities dealers; and

(ii) To determine whether notices of withdrawal from registration on Form MSDW shall become effective sooner than the normal 60-day waiting period.

(4) Under section 15C(a) of the Act (15 U.S.C. 78o-5(a)):

(i) To authorize the issuance of orders granting registration of government securities brokers or government securities dealers for which the Commission is the appropriate regulatory agency within 45 days of the acceptance of an application for registration as a government securities broker or government securities dealer (or within such longer period as to which the applicant consents); and

(ii) To grant registration of government securities brokers or government securities dealers for which the Commission is the appropriate regulatory agency sooner than 45 days after acceptance of an application for registration.

(5) Under section 15C(c) of the Act (15 U.S.C. 78o-5(c)):

(i) To authorize the issuance of orders canceling registrations of government securities brokers or government securities dealers registered with the Commission, or pending applications for registration, if such government securities brokers or government securities dealers or applicants for registration are no longer in existence or are not engaged in business as government securities brokers or government securities dealers; and

(ii) To determine whether notices of withdrawal from registration on Form BDW shall become effective sooner than the normal 60-day waiting period.

(iv)判定撤销《BDW表格》注册的通知是否应在正常的60日等待期未届满时提前生效。

(2)在该法第15B(a)条[《美国法典》第十五编第78o-4(a)节]下:

(i)同意签发命令,在市政证券自营商提交合格注册申请后45日内(或申请人同意的其他更长的期间内)核准市政证券自营商注册;及

(ii)在证券交易委员会收到合格注册申请后45日内核准市政证券自营商注册;

(3)根据该法第15B(c)条[《美国法典》第十五编第78o-4(c)节]:

(i)在市政证券自营商或注册申请人不再存续或不再从事市政证券自营商业务之时,同意签发命令注销市政证券自营商的注册或暂缓申请人的注册;及

(ii)判定撤销《MSDW表格》注册的通知是否应在正常的60日等待期未届满时提前生效。

(4)在该法第15C(a)条[《美国法典》第十五编第78o-5(a)节]下:

(i)签发命令,在受理政府证券经纪商或政府证券自营商注册申请后45日之内(或申请人同意的其他更长的期间内)核准其注册为由证券交易委员会拥有相应监管权的政府证券经纪商或政府证券自营商;及

(ii)对于证券交易委员会拥有相应监管权的政府证券经纪商或政府证券自营商,在受理注册申请后45日内核准其注册。

(5)在该法第15C(c)条[《美国法典》第十五编第78o-5(c)节]下:

(i)在政府证券经纪商、政府证券自营商或注册申请人不再存续或不再从事政府证券经纪商或政府证券自营商业务之时,同意签发命令注销其向证券交易委员会进行的注册,或暂缓申请人的注册;及

(ii)判定《BDW表格》撤销注册通知是否应在正常的60日等待期未届满时提前生效。

(6) Under section 17A(c) of the Act (15 U.S.C. 78q-1(c)):

(i) To authorize the issuance of orders granting registration of transfer agents within 45 days of the filing of acceptable applications for registration as a transfer agent (or within such longer period as to which the applicant consents);

(ii) To grant registration of transfer agents sooner than 45 days after receipt by the Commission of acceptable applications for registration;

(iii) To authorize the issuance of orders canceling registrations of transfer agents, or pending applications for registration, if such transfer agents or applicants for registration are no longer in existence or are not engaged in business as transfer agents; and

(iv) To determine whether notices of withdrawal from registration on Form TA-W shall become effective sooner than the normal 60-day waiting period.

(k) With respect to the Investment Advisers Act of 1940 (15 U.S.C. 80b-1 *et seq*.):

(1) Under section 203(c) of the Act (15 U.S.C. 80b-3(c)):

(i) To authorize the issuance of orders granting registration of investment advisers within 45 days of the filing of acceptable applications for registration as an investment adviser (or within such longer period as to which the applicant consents); and

(ii) To grant registration of investment advisers sooner than 45 days after receipt by the Commission of acceptable applications for registration.

(2) Under section 203(h) of the Act (15 U.S.C. 80b-3(h)), to authorize the issuance of orders canceling registrations of investment advisers, or pending applications for registration, if such investment advisers or applicants for registration are no longer in existence or are not engaged in business as investment advisers.

(l) With respect to the Securities Investor Protection Act of 1970 (15 U.S.C. 78aaa *et seq.*):

(1) To cause a written notice to be sent by registered or certified mail, upon receipt of a copy of a notice sent by or on behalf of the Securities Investor Protection Corporation that a broker or dealer has failed to timely file any report or information or to pay when due all or any part of an assessment as required under section 10(a) of this Act, to such delinquent member advising such member that it is unlawful for him or her under the provisions of such section of the Act to engage in business as a broker-dealer while in violation of such requirements of the Act and requesting an explanation in writing within ten days stating what he or she intends to do in order to cure such delinquency;

(2) To authorize formerly delinquent brokers or dealers, upon receipt of written confirmation from or on behalf of the Securities Investor Protection Corporation that the delinquencies referred to in paragraph (c)(1) of this section have been cured, and upon having been advised by the appropriate regional office of this Commission and the Division of Enforcement and Division of Trading and Markets that there is no objection to

(6)在该法第17A(c)条[《美国法典》第十五编第78q-1(c)节]下:

(i)同意签发命令,在合格的过户代理人注册申请提交后45日内(或申请人同意的其他更长的期间内)核准注册为过户代理人;

(ii)在证券交易委员会收到合格注册申请后45日内核准过户代理人注册;

(iii)在过户代理人或注册申请人不再存续或不再开展过户代理人业务之时,同意签发命令注销该等过户代理人的注册,或暂缓申请人的注册;及

(iv)判定《TA-W表格》撤销注册通知是否应在正常的60日等待期未届满时提前生效。

(k)就《1940年投资顾问法》(《美国法典》第十五编第80b-1节及其后条文)而言:

(1)根据该法第203(c)条[《美国法典》第十五编第80b-3(c)节]:

(i)同意签发命令,在合格的投资顾问注册申请提交后45日内(或申请人同意的其他更长的期间内)核准注册;及

(ii)在证券交易委员会收到合格注册申请后45日内核准投资顾问注册。

(2)在该法第203(h)条[《美国法典》第十五编第80b-3(h)节]下,在投资顾问或注册申请人不再存续或不再从事投资顾问业务之时,同意签发命令注销投资顾问注册或暂缓申请人注册。

(l)就《1970年证券投资者保护法》(《美国法典》第十五编第78aaa节及其后条文)而言:

(1)在收到证券投资者保护公司或其代表发送的一份通知,说明某经纪商或自营商未按该法第10(a)条的要求及时提交任何报告或信息,或未能支付全部或部分计征费用之时,通过挂号信或带回执邮件向该违规会员发送一份书面通知,说明根据《1970年证券投资者保护法》上述条文,在违反该法的上述规定时,其经纪自营商业务将构成非法经营行为,并要求其在10日之内提供一份书面解释,说明其为补救违法违规行为而计划采取的行动;

(2)在收到证券投资者保护公司或其代表发出的书面确认,说明本节第(c)(1)款所述违法违规行为已得到补救,且证券交易委员会相应地区办公室、执法部和交易和市场部表示不反对准许上述成员恢复业务经营,且不存在有必要提交证券交易委员会直接审议的异常或全新情形之时,准许之前的违规经纪商或自营商恢复经营该法第10(a)条规定的注册经纪自营商业务。

such member being authorized to resume business, and upon there appearing to be no unusual or novel circumstances which would warrant direct consideration of the matter by this Commission, to resume business as registered broker-dealers as provided in section 10(a) of this Act.

(m) Notwithstanding anything in the foregoing, in any case in which the Director of the OCIE believes it appropriate, the Director may submit the matter to the Commission.

[60 FR 39644, Aug. 3, 1995, as amended at 66 FR 35842, July 9, 2001; 69 FR 41938, July 13, 2004; 73 FR 40152, July 11, 2008; 73 FR 69532, Nov. 19, 2008]

Subpart B—Disposition of Commission Business

Authority: 5 U.S.C. 552b; 15 U.S.C. 78d-1 and 78w.

Source: 42 FR 14692, Mar. 16, 1977, unless otherwise noted.

§200.40 Joint disposition of business by Commission meeting.

Any meeting of the Commission that is subject to the provisions of the Government in the Sunshine Act, 5 U.S.C. 552b, shall be held in accordance with subpart I of this part. The Commission's Secretary shall prepare and maintain a Minute Record reflecting the official action taken at such meetings.

[60 FR 17202, Apr. 5, 1995]

§200.41 Quorum of the Commission.

A quorum of the Commission shall consist of three members; provided, however, that if the number of Commissioners in office is less than three, a quorum shall consist of the number of members in office; and provided further that on any matter of business as to which the number of members in office, minus the number of members who either have disqualified themselves from consideration of such matter pursuant to §200.60 or are otherwise disqualified from such consideration, is two, two members shall constitute a quorum for purposes of such matter.

[60 FR 17202, Apr. 5, 1995]

§200.42 Disposition of business by seriatim Commission consideration.

(a) Whenever the Commission's Chairman, or the Commission member designated as duty officer pursuant to §200.43, is of the opinion that joint deliberation among the members of the Commission upon any matter is unnecessary in light of the nature of the matter, impracticable, or contrary to the requirements of agency business, but is of the view that such matter should be the subject of a vote of the Commission, such matter may

(m)无论上文如何规定,在任何情况下,如合规检查和核查办公室主任认为适当,其均可以将相关事项提交证券交易委员会处理。

[《联邦公报》第60卷第39644页,1995年8月3日,修正索引:《联邦公报》第66卷第35842页,2001年7月9日;《联邦公报》第69卷第41938页,2004年7月13日;《联邦公报》第73卷第40152页,2008年7月11日;《联邦公报》第73卷第69532页,2008年11月19日。]

第B子部分——证券交易委员会业务的处理

法律依据:《美国法典》第五编第552b节;《美国法典》第十五编第78d-1节和第78w节。

行政规则来源:《联邦公报》第42卷第14692页,1977年3月16日,除非另有说明。

第200.40节　证券交易委员会会议共同处理的事项

所有受制于《阳光法》(《美国法典》第五编第552b节)中关于政府的条款的证券交易委员会会议,均应按本部分第I子部分的规定举行。证券交易委员会秘书应制作并保存会议纪要,载明会议正式采取的行动。

[《联邦公报》第60卷第17202页,1995年4月5日。]

第200.41节　证券交易委员会的法定人数

证券交易委员会会议的法定人数应为3名委员,但是,若在职的证券交易委员会委员数少于3人,则法定人数应为在职成员的人数;此外,若对于任何议题,若在职委员的人数减去根据第200.60节或因其他原因而回避的委员人数为2名,则该两名委员即构成该议题的法定人数。

[《联邦公报》第60卷第17202页,1995年4月5日。]

第200.42节　证券交易委员会委员分别审议处理的事项

(a)无论何时,如证券交易委员会主席或根据第200.43节被指定为轮值官的证券交易委员会委员认为,根据具体事项的性质,证券交易委员会委员共同审议该事项没有必要、不可行或与证券交易委员会业务要求相冲突,但同时认为该事项应由证券交易委员会表决,则该事项应通过将相关资料发给所有证券交易委员会委员传阅的方式进行处理。参与传阅表决的各证券交易委员会委员均应将其投票选择结果报告给

be disposed of by circulation of any relevant materials concerning the matter among all Commission members. Each participating Commission member shall report his or her vote to the Secretary, who shall record it in the Minute Record of the Commission. Any matter circulated for disposition pursuant to this subsection shall not be considered final until each Commission member has reported his or her vote to the Secretary or has reported to the Secretary that the Commissioner does not intend to participate in the matter.

(b) Whenever any member of the Commission so requests, any matter circulated for disposition pursuant to §200.42(a) shall be withdrawn from circulation and scheduled instead for joint Commission deliberation.

[42 FR 14692, Mar. 16, 1977, as amended at 59 FR 53936, Oct. 27, 1994. Redesignated and amended at 60 FR 17202, Apr. 5, 1995]

§200.43 Disposition of business by exercise of authority delegated to individual Commissioner.

(a) *Delegation to duty officer.* (1) Pursuant to the provisions of Pub. L. No. 87–592, 76 Stat. 394, as amended by section 25 of Pub. L. 94–29, 89 Stat. 163, the Commission hereby delegates to an individual Commissioner, to be designated as the Commission's "duty officer" by the Chairman of the Commission (or by the Chairman's designee) from time to time, all of the functions of the Commission; *Provided, however,* That no such delegation shall authorize the duty officer (i) to exercise the function of rulemaking, as defined in the Administrative Procedure Act of 1946, as codified, 5 U.S.C. 551 *et seq.*, with reference to general rules as distinguished from rules of particular applicability; (ii) to make any rule, pursuant to section 19(c) of the Securities Exchange Act of 1934; or (iii) to preside at the taking of evidence as described in section 7(a) of the Administrative Procedure Act, 5 U.S.C. 556(b), except that the duty officer may preside at the taking of evidence with res pect to the issuance of a temporary cease-and-desist order as provided by Rule 511(c) of the Commission's Rules of Practice, §201.511(c) of this chapter.

(2) To the extent feasible, the designation of a duty officer shall rotate, under the administration of the Secretary, on a regular weekly basis among the members of the Commission other than the Chairman.

(b) *Exercise of duty officer authority.* (1) The authority delegated by this rule shall be exercised when, in the opinion of the duty officer, action is required to be taken which, by reason of its urgency, cannot practicably be scheduled for consideration at a Commission meeting. After consideration of a staff recommendation involving such a matter, the duty officer shall forthwith report his or her action thereon to the Secretary.

(2) The duty officer may, when in his or her opinion it would be proper and timely,

证券交易委员会秘书,由秘书在证券交易委员会会议纪要中予以记录。根据本子条传阅表决的任何事项,在全体证券交易委员会委员均已向证券交易委员会秘书报告其投票选择结果或宣布其放弃表决权之前,不得被视为已获得最终处理。

(b)无论何时,只要任何证券交易委员会委员提出要求,按第200.42(a)节提交传阅处理的任何事项即应立即撤销传阅程序并安排证券交易委员会会议共同审议。

[《联邦公报》第42卷第14692页,1977年3月16日,修正索引:《联邦公报》第59卷第53936页,1994年10月27日。重新公布和修正索引:《联邦公报》第60卷第17202页,1995年4月5日。]

第200.43节　委员个人根据授权处理事项

(a)对轮值官的委托授权。(1)根据公法编号87-592,《美国制定法汇编》第76卷第394页(包括公法编号94-29,《美国制定法汇编》第89卷第163页第25条开始对其进行的修正),证券交易委员会兹委托证券交易委员会主席(或主席指定的人员)随时指定为"轮值官"的个人委员行使证券交易委员会的所有职能;但是,在上述委托授权下,轮值官不得:(i)行使《1946年行政程序法》(法典索引:《美国法典》第五编第551节及其后条文)定义的规则制定权,即不得制定具有普遍适用性的规则(区别于特定适用性的规则);(ii)根据《1934年证券交易法》第19(c)条制定任何规则;或(iii)主持《行政程序法》第7(a)条[《美国法典》第五编第556(b)节]规定的取证程序,但是轮值官可主持与《证券交易委员会工作规则》的《511(c)规则》[本章第201.511(c)节]下签发临时制止令相关的取证程序。

(2)在可行范围内,轮值官应在秘书的安排下由所有证券交易委员会委员(主席除外)每周轮换。

(b)轮值官权限的行使。(1)本条规则授予的权限应在下述时机行使:轮值官认为需要采取行动,且由于情况紧急安排证券交易委员会会议审议不具有可行性。轮值官在审议证券交易委员会员工提出的与上述事项相关的建议后,应立即将其行动报告给证券交易委员会秘书。

(2)如轮值官认为适当且及时,其可以行使本节授予的权限,根据《1933年证券

exercise the authority delegated in this section to initiate by order a nonpublic formal investigative proceeding pursuant to section 19(b) of the Securities Act of 1933 (15 U.S.C. 77s(b)), section 21(b) of the Securities Exchange Act of 1934 (15 U.S.C. 78u(b)), section 18(c) of the Public Utility Holding Company Act of 1935 (15 U.S.C. 79r(c)), section 42(b) of the Investment Company Act of 1940 (15 U.S.C. 80a–41(b)), section 209(b) of the Investment Advisers Act of 1940 (15 U.S.C. 80b–9(b)), and part 203 (Rules Relating to Investigations) of this title (17 CFR part 203). After consideration of a staff recommendation for initiation by order of a nonpublic formal investigative proceeding, the duty officer shall forthwith report his or her action thereon to the Secretary.

(3) In any consideration of Commission business by a duty officer, the provisions of subpart I herein, §200.400 *et seq.*, shall not apply, whether or not the duty officer, in exercising his or her authority, consults with, or seeks the advice of, other members of the Commission individually.

(c) *Commission affirmation of duty officer action.* (1) Any action authorized by a duty officer pursuant to §200.43(a) shall be either(i) circulated to the members of the Commission for affirmation pursuant to §200.42; or (ii) scheduled for affirmation at a Commission meeting at the earliest practicable date consistent with the procedures in subpart I.

(2)(i) The Commission may, in its discretion, at any time review any unaffirmed action taken by a duty officer, either upon its own initiative or upon the petition of any person affected thereby. The vote of any one member of the Commission, including the duty officer, shall be sufficient to bring any such unaffirmed action taken by a duty officer before the Commission for review.

(ii) A person or party adversely affected by any unaffirmed action taken by a duty officer shall be entitled to seek review by the Commission of the duty officer's unaffirmed actions, but only in the event that the unaffirmed action by the duty officer (A) denies any request for action pursuant to sections 8(a) or 8(c) of the Securities Act of 1933, or the first sentence of section 12(d) of the Securities Exchange Act of 1934; (B) suspends trading in a security pursuant to section 12(k) of the Securities Exchange Act of 1934; or (C) is pursuant to any provision of the Securities Exchange Act of 1934 in a case of adjudication, as defined in section 551 of Title 5, U.S. Code, not required by that Act to be determined on the record after notice and opportunity for hearing (except to the extent there is involved a matter described in section 554(a) (1) through (6) of Title 5, United States Code).

(3) Affirmed or unaffirmed action taken by the duty officer shall be deemed to be, for all purposes, the action of the Commission unless and until the Commission directs

法》第19(b)条[《美国法典》第十五编第77s(b)节]、《1934年证券交易法》第21(b)条[《美国法典》第十五编第78u(b)节]、《1935年公用事业控股公司法》第18(c)条[《美国法典》第十五编第79r(c)节]、《1940年投资公司法》第42(b)条[《美国法典》第十五编第80a-41(b)节]、《1940年投资顾问法》第209(b)条[《美国法典》第十五编第80b-9(b)节]以及本编第203部分(《调查规则》)(《联邦规章汇编》第十七编第203部分),发布命令启动非公开正式调查程序。在审议证券交易委员会员工提出的发布命令启动非公开正式调查程序的建议后,轮值官应立即将其行动报告给证券交易委员会秘书。

(3)轮值官审议证券交易委员会事务的,此处第I子部分(第200.400节及其后条文)的规定不予适用,不论轮值官个人在行使授权时是否咨询了证券交易委员会其他委员的意见或是否与其进行过磋商。

(c)证券交易委员会对轮值官行动的确认。(1)轮值官根据第200.43(a)节授权采取的所有行动均应(i)依第200.42节由证券交易委员会全体委员传阅确认;或(ii)按照第I子部分规定的程序安排在最早可行之日由证券交易委员会会议确认。

(2)(i)证券交易委员会可以依其自由裁量权在任何时候主动决定或根据受影响的任何人的请求决定对轮值官所采取的但尚未获得确认的任何行动进行审查。经任何一名证券交易委员会委员(包括轮值官)投票,轮值官采取的但尚未获得确认的任何行动即应提交证券交易委员会审查。

(ii)任何主体或当事人如遭轮值官采取的但尚未获得确认的行动不利影响,均有权申请证券交易委员会审查上述行动,但前提必须是,轮值官所采取的但尚未获得确认的行动符合以下情况:(A)根据《1933年证券法》第8(a)条或第8(c)条或《1934年证券交易法》第12(d)条第一句,该行动拒绝了任何请求人提出的任何行动请求;(B)根据《1934年证券交易法》第12(K)条暂停了证券交易;或(C)该行动系根据《1934年证券交易法》的任何条款在行政裁决案件(如《美国法典》第五编第551节所定义)中采取的,且该法不要求经发布公告和提供听证机会后并基于书面记录才能作出该等裁决[但涉及《美国法典》第五编第554(a)(1)~(6)节所述事项的除外]。

(3)除非且直至证券交易委员会另有指示,否则轮值官采取的得到确认的或尚未得到确认的行动,均应被视为证券交易委员会的行动。《证券交易委员会工作规则》的

otherwise. Rules 430 and 431 of the Commission's Rules of Practice, §§201.430 and 201.431 of this chapter, shall not apply to duty officer action.

[42 FR 14692, Mar. 16, 1977, as amended at 59 FR 53936, Oct. 27, 1994. Redesignated and amended at 60 FR 17202, Apr. 5, 1995; 60 FR 32795, June 23, 1995; 69 FR 13175, Mar. 19, 2004]

Subpart C—Canons of Ethics

Authority: Secs. 19, 28, 48 Stat. 85, 901, as amended, sec. 20, 49 Stat. 833, sec. 319, 53 Stat. 1173, secs. 38, 211, 54 Stat. 841, 855; 15 U.S.C. 77s, 78w, 79t, 77sss, 80a–37, 80b–11.

Source: 25 FR 6725, July 15, 1960, unless otherwise noted.

§200.50 Authority.

The Canons of Ethics for Members of the Securities and Exchange Commission were approved by the Commission on July 22, 1958.

§200.51 Policy.

It is characteristic of the administrative process that the Members of the Commission and their place in public opinion are affected by the advice and conduct of the staff, particularly the professional and executive employees. It shall be the policy of the Commission to require that employees bear in mind the principles specified in the Canons.

§200.52 Copies of the Canons.

The Canons have been distributed to employees of the Commission. In addition, executive and professional employees are issued copies of the Canons upon entrance on duty.

§200.53 Preamble.

(a) Members of the Securities and Exchange Commission are entrusted by various enactments of the Congress with powers and duties of great social and economic significance to the American people. It is their task to regulate varied aspects of the American economy, within the limits prescribed by Congress, to insure that our private enterprise system serves the welfare of all citizens. Their success in this endeavor is a bulwark against possible abuses and injustice which, if left unchecked, might jeopardize the strength of our economic institutions.

(b) It is imperative that the members of this Commission continue to conduct

《430规则》和《431规则》（本章第201.430节和第201.431节）不适用于轮值官的行动。

[《联邦公报》第42卷第14692页，1977年3月16日，修正索引：《联邦公报》第59卷第53936页，1994年10月27日。重新公布和修正索引：《联邦公报》第60卷第17202页，1995年4月5日；《联邦公报》第60卷第32795页，1995年6月23日；《联邦公报》第69卷第13175页，2004年3月19日。]

第C子部分——职业道德守则

法律依据：《美国制定法汇编》第48卷第85页、第901页第19条、第28条、第48条及其修正，《美国制定法汇编》第49卷第833页第20条、第49条，《美国制定法汇编》第53卷第1173页第319条、第53条，《美国制定法汇编》第54卷第841页、第855页第38条、第211条、第54条；《美国法典》第十五编第77s节、第78w节、第79t节、第77sss节、第80a-37节、第80b-11节。

行政规则来源：《联邦公报》第25卷第6725页，1960年7月15日，除非另有说明。

第200.50节　效力

《证券交易委员会委员职业道德守则》由证券交易委员会于1958年7月22日批准。

第200.51节　政策

由于行政程序的特征，证券交易委员会委员及其在公众舆论中的地位会受到其工作人员（尤其是专业职员和高级管理人员）的建议和行动影响。根据证券交易委员会的政策，雇员应牢记《证券交易委员会委员职业道德守则》中规定的原则。

第200.52节　职业道德守则文本

《职业道德守则》已向证券交易委员会雇员分发。此外，高级管理人员和专业职员在上岗时均已收到《职业道德守则》文本。

第200.53节　序言

（a）国会各项立法向证券交易委员会的委员授予了对美国人民有重大社会和经济影响的权力和职责。各委员应在国会规定的范围内对美国经济的各个方面进行监管，确保美国的私人企业制度给全体公民带来福利。成功开展上述工作可起到制衡滥用和不公正现象的保护作用，防止美国经济制度受损。

（b）证券交易委员会委员必须持续保证其在官方和私人关系中的行为值得美国

themselves in their official and personal relationships in a manner which commands the respect and confidence of their fellow citizens. Members of this Commission shall continue to be mindful of, and strictly abide by, the standards of personal conduct set forth in its regulation regarding Conduct of Members and Employees and Former Members and Employees of the Commission, which is set forth in subpart M of this part 200, most of which has been in effect for many years, and which was originally codified in 1953.

(c) However, in addition to the continued observance of those principles of personal conduct, it is fitting and proper for the members of the Commission to restate and resubscribe to the standards of conduct applicable to its executive, legislative and judicial responsibilities.

[25 FR 6725, July 15, 1960, as amended at 31 FR 13533, Oct. 20, 1966]

§200.54 Constitutional obligations.

The members of this Commission have undertaken in their oaths of office to support the Federal Constitution. Insofar as the enactments of the Congress impose executive duties upon the members, they must faithfully execute the laws which they are charged with administering. Members shall also carefully guard against any infringement of the constitutional rights, privileges, or immunities of those who are subject to regulation by this Commission.

§200.55 Statutory obligations.

In administering the law, members of this Commission should vigorously enforce compliance with the law by all persons affected thereby. In the exercise of the rulemaking powers delegated this Commission by the Congress, members should always be concerned that the rulemaking power be confined to the proper limits of the law and be consistent with the statutory purposes expressed by the Congress. In the exercise of their judicial functions, members shall honestly, fairly and impartially determine the rights of all persons under the law.

§200.56 Personal conduct.

Appointment to the office of member of this Commission is a high honor and requires that the conduct of a member, not only in the performance of the duties of his office but also in his everyday life, should be beyond reproach.

§200.57 Relationships with other members.

Each member should recognize that his conscience and those of other members are distinct entities and that differing shades of opinion should be anticipated. The free expression of opinion is a safeguard against the domination of this Commission by less than a majority, and is a keystone of the commission type of administration. However, a member should never permit his personal opinion so to conflict with the opinion of

公民尊重和信任。证券交易委员会委员应持续牢记并严格遵守证券交易委员会关于《证券交易委员会现任及前任委员和雇员行为准则》中制定的个人行为准则(见本第200部分第M子部分),其中大多数准则已经适用多年,并于1953年首次编纂为制定法。

(c)但是,除持续遵守上述个人行为原则外,证券交易委员会委员还应当重申及重新确认适用于其行政、立法和司法职责的行为标准。

[《联邦公报》第25卷第6725页,1960年7月15日,修正索引:《联邦公报》第31卷第13533页,1966年10月20日。]

第200.54节　宪法义务

证券交易委员会委员在就职时宣誓忠于联邦宪法。只要国会立法要求委员承担行政义务,委员即必须忠实地执行被委托负责实施的法律。委员也应谨慎保护受证券交易委员会监管的人的宪法性权利、特权或豁免权,使之免受任何侵害。

第200.55节　法律义务

在实施法律的过程中,证券交易委员会委员应当积极执法,使所有相关主体遵守法律。在行使国会向证券交易委员会授予的规则制定权时,各委员应当始终注意不逾越法律赋予的适当权限,并遵守国会明确指定的立法宗旨。在行使司法职能之时,各委员应诚实、公平和公正地确定所有人依法享有的权利。

第200.56节　个人行为

担任证券交易委员会委员是一项极高的荣誉,因此委员应保证其履职行为及日常行为无可指摘。

第200.57节　与其他委员的关系

各委员均应认识到,自己与其他委员作为独立的个体存在,意见有所不同乃理所当然。自由表达意见的权利是防止少数人宰制证券交易委员会的保障机制,并且是证券交易委员会作为行政机构运作的基石。但是,委员在发表与其他委员相冲突的个人意见时不得导致在证券交易委员会内部形成敌意或不友好的氛围,且应尽最大努力使委员们在最终达成结论时团结一致。

another member as to develop animosity or unfriendliness in the Commission, and every effort should be made to promote solidarity of conclusion.

§200.58 Maintenance of independence.

This Commission has been established to administer laws enacted by the Congress. Its members are appointed by the President by and with the advice and consent of the Senate to serve terms as provided by law. However, under the law, this is an independent Agency, and in performing their duties, members should exhibit a spirit of firm independence and reject any effort by representatives of the executive or legislative branches of the government to affect their independent determination of any matter being considered by this Commission. A member should not be swayed by partisan demands, public clamor or considerations of personal popularity or notoriety; so also he should be above fear of unjust criticism by anyone.

§200.59 Relationship with persons subject to regulation.

In all matters before him, a member should administer the law without regard to any personality involved, and with regard only to the issues. Members should not become indebted in any way to persons who are or may become subject to their jurisdiction. No member should accept loans, presents or favors of undue value from persons who are regulated or who represent those who are regulated. In performing their judicial functions, members should avoid discussion of a matter with any person outside this Commission and its staff while that matter is pending. In the performance of his rule–making and administrative functions, a member has a duty to solicit the views of interested persons. Care must be taken by a member in his relationship with persons within or outside of the Commission to separate the judicial and the rule–making functions and to observe the liberties of discussion respectively appropriate. Insofar as it is consistent with the dignity of his official position, he should maintain contact with the persons outside the agency who may be affected by his rule–making functions, but he should not accept unreasonable or lavish hospitality in so doing.

§200.60 Qualification to participate in particular matters.

The question in a particular matter rests with that individual member. Each member should weigh carefully the question of his qualification with respect to any matter wherein he or any relatives or former business associates or clients are involved. He should disqualify himself in the event he obtained knowledge prior to becoming a member of the facts at issue before him in a quasi–judicial proceeding, or in other types of proceeding in any matter involving parties in whom he has any interest or relationship directly or indirectly. If an interested person suggests that a member should disqualify himself in a particular matter because of bias or prejudice, the member shall be the judge of his own qualification.

第200.58节　独立性的维持

证券交易委员会的设立目的是负责实施国会立法。证券交易委员会委员由总统任命,并由国会提名和批准,任期由法律规定。但是,根据法律,证券交易委员会是一个独立机构,在履职过程中,各委员应展现坚决独立的精神,对于证券交易委员会审议的事项,应拒绝政府行政或立法部门代表对其独立决定施加任何影响。委员不得受党派要求、公众意见或个人声誉或名望的考虑所左右,并不应惧怕任何人的不公正批评。

第200.59节　与被监管主体的关系

在处理所有事项时,委员在执法过程中不得考虑任何所涉主体的因素,应当就事论事。各委员不应对受其管辖或可能受其管辖的任何主体欠负任何债务或人情。任何委员均不得接受被监管主体或其代表提供的价值过高的贷款、礼物或恩惠。在履行司法职能的过程中,各委员应避免与证券交易委员会之外的任何人及其工作人员讨论任何未决事项。在履行规则制定权和行政职能的过程中,委员有义务征求利害关系人的意见。委员在与证券交易委员会内部或外部的主体的关系中,必须注意适当分离司法权和规则制定权,并遵守适当的言论自由权。只要不损及其职务尊严,委员应与可能受其规则制定权影响的机构外部主体保持联系,但在联系过程中不得接受不合理或过分的款待。

第200.60节　对特定事项的回避

特定事项的回避问题由委员个人处理。对于涉及自身或其亲属、之前的任何工作同事或客户的任何事项,各委员均应谨慎权衡其是否应予以回避。若其在准司法程序中或其他程序中,作为委员处理相关事实问题之前获知其与当事人存在任何直接或间接的利益关联或关系,应主动回避。若利益关系人以避免偏见或不公正为由建议委员回避特定事项时,是否回避由该委员自行决定。

§200.61 Impressions of influence.

A member should not, by his conduct, permit the impression to prevail that any person can improperly influence him, that any person unduly enjoys his favor or that he is affected in any way by the rank, position, prestige, or affluence of any person.

§200.62 Ex parte communications.

All proceedings required to be determined by the Commission on the record shall be determined by the members solely upon the record and the arguments of the parties or their counsel properly made in the regular course of such proceeding. A member shall at all times comply with the Commission's Code of Behavior governing ex parte communications between persons outside the Commission and decisional employees, §200.110 *et seq*.

[28 FR 4446, May 3, 1963]

§200.63 Commission opinions.

The opinions of the Commission should state the reasons for the action taken and contain a clear showing that no serious argument of counsel has been disregarded or overlooked. In such manner, a member shows a full understanding of the matter before him, avoids the suspicion of arbitrary conclusion, promotes confidence in his intellectual integrity and may contribute some useful precedent to the growth of the law. A member should be guided in his decisions by a deep regard for the integrity of the system of law which he administers. He should recall that he is not a repository of arbitrary power, but is acting on behalf of the public under the sanction of the law.

§200.64 Judicial review.

The Congress has provided for review by the courts of the decisions and orders by this Commission. Members should recognize that their obligation to preserve the sanctity of the laws administered by them requires that they pursue and prosecute, vigorously and diligently but at the same time fairly and impartially and with dignity, all matters which they or others take to the courts for judicial review.

§200.65 Legislative proposals.

Members must recognize that the changing conditions in a volatile economy may require that they bring to the attention of the Congress proposals to amend, modify or repeal the laws administered by them. They should urge the Congress, whenever necessary, to effect such amendment, modification or repeal of particular parts of the statutes which they administer. In any action a member's motivation should be the common weal and not the particular interests of any particular group.

§200.66 Investigations.

The power to investigate carries with it the power to defame and destroy. In determining to exercise their investigatory power, members should concern themselves

第200.61条　避免产生不正当影响的印象

委员不得通过其行为造成下述普遍印象:任何主体可能对委员施加不正当影响,或委员对任何主体有不正当的偏爱,或委员受到任何主体的地位、职务、威望或财富的影响。

第200.62节　单方交流

对于证券交易委员会应当基于书面记录作出判定的所有程序,委员仅得根据正当程序过程中的记录和双方或其律师的论证作出决定。对于证券交易委员会的外部主体与有决策权的雇员之间的单方交流,委员应始终遵守证券交易委员会相关的行为守则(第200.110节及其后条文)。

[《联邦公报》第28卷第4446页,1963年5月3日。]

第200.63节　证券交易委员会的意见

证券交易委员会的意见应说明所采取行动的理由,并清楚表明未遗漏或忽略律师的重要论证。委员应按上述方式表明其完全理解所处理的事项,避免武断作出结论的嫌疑,促进当事人对其智力完整性的信任,并可能为法律发展提供有用的先例。委员在作出决定时,应充分、总体考虑其所实施的法律制度。委员应秉承如下理念:其并非独裁权力的代言人,而是代表公众执行法律,并可能遭受法律制裁。

第200.64节　司法审查

国会规定证券交易委员会的决定和命令可被提交法院审查。委员应认识到,其有义务维持其所负责实施的法律的神圣和尊严,因此应积极、勤勉同时公平、公正和不失尊严地对其自身或其他人员提交法庭进行司法审查的所有事项进行追究和追诉。

第200.65节　立法提案

委员必须认识到,在快速变动的经济环境下,其可能需要向国会提交修正、修改或废止其所负责实施的法律的提案。委员应在必要之时敦促国会使其负责实施的立法的特定部分之修正、修改或废除生效。在任何行动中,委员的动机均应出于公益考虑,而不得仅代表某一特定团体的特殊利益。

第200.66节　调查

调查权可能会损害被调查主体的名誉甚至造成毁灭性的影响。在决定行使调查权之时,委员仅应关注已知事实及其合理推论。委员不得基于敌意、偏见或报复而提

only with the facts known to them and the reasonable inferences from those facts. A member should never suggest, vote for, or participate in an investigation aimed at a particular individual for reasons of animus, prejudice or vindictiveness. The requirements of the particular case alone should induce the exercise of the investigatory power, and no public pronouncement of the pendency of such an investigation should be made in the absence of reasonable evidence that the law has been violated and that the public welfare demand it.

§200.67 Power to adopt rules.

In exercising its rule-making power, this Commission performs a legislative function. The delegation of this power by the Congress imposes the obligation upon the members to adopt rules necessary to effectuate the stated policies of the statute in the interest of all of the people. Care should be taken to avoid the adoption of rules which seek to extend the power of the Commission beyond proper statutory limits. Its rules should never tend to stifle or discourage legitimate business enterprises or activities, nor should they be interpreted so as unduly and unnecessarily to burden those regulated with onerous obligations. On the other hand, the very statutory enactments evidence the need for regulation, and the necessary rules should be adopted or modifications made or rules should be repealed as changing requirements demand without fear or favor.

§200.68 Promptness.

Each member should promptly perform the duties with which he is charged by the statutes. The Commission should evaluate continuously its practices and procedures to assure that it promptly disposes of all matters affecting the rights of those regulated. This is particularly desirable in quasi-judicial proceedings. While avoiding arbitrary action in unreasonably or unjustly forcing matters to trial, members should endeavor to hold counsel to a proper appreciation of their duties to the public, their clients and others who are interested. Requests for continuances of matters should be determined in a manner consistent with this policy.

§200.69 Conduct toward parties and their counsel.

Members should be temperate, attentive, patient and impartial when hearing the arguments of parties or their counsel. Members should not condone unprofessional conduct by attorneys in their representation of parties. The Commission should continuously assure that its staff follows the same principles in their relationships with parties and counsel.

§200.70 Business promotions.

A member must not engage in any other business, employment or vocation while in office, nor may he ever use the power of his office or the influence of his name to promote the business interests of others.

议、同意或参与针对特定人员的调查。调查权仅得因所涉具体案件的需求而启动;且除非有合理证据表明存在违法情形且出于公共利益的需要,否则不得对进行中的调查程序发布公开宣告。

第200.67节　制定规则的权力

在行使规则制定权时,证券交易委员会行使的是立法职能。根据国会的上述授权,委员有义务为全体民众之利益制定并通过必要的规则有效落实制定法下的政策。委员应注意避免利用其制定规则的权限,试图让证券交易委员会的权限逾越适当的法定界限。证券交易委员会所制定的规则不得扼杀或阻止合法的商业企业或活动,在进行解释时亦不得向受规制方施加不适当和不必要的繁冗义务。另外,法律文件本身即足以证明制定规则的必要性,同时,委员应按照不断变化的需求不偏不倚地对规则进行必要的制定、修改或废止。

第200.68节　及时性

各委员均应及时履行其法定义务。证券交易委员会应持续评估其工作和程序,确保其及时处理对受规制方权利有影响的所有事项。在准司法程序中此点尤其重要。委员在避免通过武断行动,不合理或不公正地强行启动审判的同时,应尽力使律师正确对待其对公众、客户及其他利益相关人承担的义务。延期处理请求应以符合本政策的方式决定。

第200.69节　针对当事人及其律师的行动

委员在听取当事人及其律师的论证时应温和、专注、耐心和公正。委员不得放纵律师在代理当事人时的不职业行为。证券交易委员会应始终确保其员工在与当事人及其律师的关系中遵守上述原则。

第200.70节　业务促进

委员任职期间不得从事任何其他业务或接受任何其他雇佣或职务,亦不得利用其职权或以其名义施加任何影响力以促进其他人的业务利益。

§200.71 Fiduciary relationships.

A member should avoid service as a fiduciary if it would interfere or seem to interfere with the proper performance of his duties, or if the interests of those represented require investments in enterprises which are involved in questions to be determined by him. Such relationships would include trustees, executors, corporate directors, and the like.

§200.72 Supervision of internal organization.

Members and particularly the Chairman of the Commission should scrutinize continuously its internal organization in order to assure that such organization handles all matters before it efficiently and expeditiously, while recognizing that changing times bring changing emphasis in the administration of the laws.

Subpart D—Information and Requests

Authority: 5 U.S.C. 552, as amended, 15 U.S.C. 77f(d), 77s, 77ggg(a), 77sss, 78m (F)(3), 78w, 80a-37, 80a-44(a), 80a-44(b), 80b-10(a), and 80b-11.

Section 200.80 also issued under 5 U.S.C. 552b; 15 U.S.C. 78d-1, 78d-2; 78a *et seq.* ; 11 U.S.C. 901, 1109(a).

Section 200.80a also issued under 5 U.S.C. 552b.

Sections 200.80b and 200.80c also issued under 11 U.S.C. 901, 1109(a).

Section 200.82 also issued under 15 U.S.C. 78n.

Section 200.83 also issued under Exec. Order 12, 600, 3 CFR, 1987 Comp., p. 235.

§200.80 Commission records and information.

(a)(1) *Information published in the* Federal Register Except as provided in paragraph (b) of this section the following materials are published in the Federal Register for the guidance of the public:

(i) Description of the Commission's central and field organization and the established places at which, the employees from whom, and the methods whereby the public may obtain information, make submittals or requests, or obtain decisions;

(ii) Statements of the general course and method by which the Commission's functions are channeled and determined, including the nature and requirements of all formal and informal procedures available;

(iii) Rules of procedure, descriptions of forms available or the places at which forms may be obtained, and instructions as to the scope and contents of all papers, reports, or

第200.71节　受信义务关系

委员应避免下述受信义务服务:干扰或从表面判断将干扰其职务恰当履行的受信义务服务;受益人的利益涉及对某企业的投资,而该企业恰好是与委员所处理的问题相关的企业。上述受信义务关系包括信托、遗嘱执行人、公司董事及其他类似关系。

第200.72节　内部组织监督

委员,尤其是证券交易委员会主席应持续性地对内部组织进行仔细审查,以确保该组织能够有效、快捷地处理所有提交的事项,并应注意到法律实施的重点应随着时间而变化。

第D子部分——信息及请求

法律依据:《美国法典》第五编第552节及其修正,《美国法典》第十五编第77f(d)节、第77s节、第77ggg(a)节、第77sss节、第78m(F)(3)节、第78w节、第80a–37节、第80a–44(a)节、第80a–44(b)节、第80b–10(a)节和第80b–11节。

第200.80节同时见:《美国法典》第五编第552b节;《美国法典》第十五编第78d–1节、第78d–2节;第78a节及其后条文;《美国法典》第十一编第901节、第1109(a)节。

第200.80a节同时见《美国法典》第五编第552b节。

第200.80b节和第200.80c节同时见《美国法典》第十一编第901节、第1109(a)节。

第200.82节同时见《美国法典》第十五编第78n节。

第200.83节同时见第12600号行政命令,《联邦规章汇编》第三编,1987年版,第235页。

第200.80节　证券交易委员会的记录和信息

(a)(1)《联邦公报》中公布的信息;除本节第(b)款规定的情形外,下述信息将发布于《联邦公报》上,为公众提供指引:

(i)证券交易委员会的中央及地区组织以及公众可以获取信息、提交材料/请求或获取证券交易委员会作出的决定的常设地点、员工以及方式;

(ii)证券交易委员会职能分工和设定的一般过程和方法之声明,包括所有正式和非正式程序的性质和要求;

(iii)程序规则、可提供的表格以及可获得表格的地点;关于所有文件、报告或检查的范围和内容的说明;

examinations;

(iv) Substantive rules of general applicability adopted as authorized by law, and statements of general policy or interpretations of general applicability formulated and adopted by the Commission;

(v) Each amendment, revision, or repeal of the foregoing; and

(vi) The notice of Commission meetings described in §200.403, but only to the extent, and under the conditions, specified in §200.403.

(2) *Records available for public inspection and copying; documents published and indexed.* Except as provided in paragraph(b) of this section, the following materials are available for public inspection and copying from 10 a.m. to 3 p.m., E.T., at the public reference room located at 100 F Street, NE., Washington, D.C., and, except for indices, they are published weekly in a document entitled "SEC Docket" (see paragraph (e)(8)(ii) of this section):

(i) Final opinions of the Commission, including concurring and dissenting opinions, as well as orders made by the Commission in the adjudication of cases;

(ii) Statements of policy and interpretations which have been adopted by the Commission and are not published in the Federal Register;

(iii) Administrative staff manuals and instructions to staff that affect a member of the public;

(iv) A record of the final votes of each member of the Commission in every Commission proceeding concluded after July 1, 1967;

(v) Current indices (published quarterly or more frequently) providing identifying information to the public as to the materials made available pursuant to paragraphs (a)(2)(i), (ii), and (iii) of this section which have been issued, adopted or promulgated after July 1, 1967, and such other indices as the Commission may determine; and

(vi) Copies and a general index of all records which have been released to any person under the Freedom of Information Act and which, because of the nature of their subject matter, the Commission determines have become or are likely to become the subject matter of subsequent requests for substantially the same records.

(3) Records created on or after November 1, 1996, which are required to be available for public inspection and copying under paragraph (a)(2) of this section, shall be made available on the Internet.

(4) *Other records available upon request.* Except with respect to the records made available under paragraphs (a)(1) and (2) of this section, and subject to the provisions of paragraph (b) of this section, pertaining to nonpublic matters, the Commission, upon request for records which (i) reasonably describes such records and (ii) is made in accordance with the rules set forth in paragraphs (d) and (e) of this section, stating the

(iv)基于法律授权而通过的具有普遍适用性的实体规则,以及证券交易委员会制定和通过的具有普遍适用性的一般性政策或解释之声明;

(v)上述规则或解释的修正、修改或废止;及

(vi)第200.403节所述证券交易委员会通知,但仅以第200.403节规定的范围及条件为限。

(2)可供公众查阅和复制的记录;已发布和编制索引的文件。除本节第(b)款规定的情形外,下述材料可于东部标准时间上午10时下午3时在位于华盛顿哥伦比亚特区东北分区100F大街的公共资料室进行查阅和复制,且除索引外,下述材料均会每周在"证券交易委员会周志"上定期发布[见本节第(e)(8)(ii)款]。

(i)证券交易委员会的终局意见,包括赞同和不同意见以及证券交易委员会在行政裁决案件中作出的命令;

(ii)证券交易委员会已制定并通过但未在《联邦公报》上发布的政策和解释之声明;

(iii)行政人员手册以及向对公众有影响力的工作人员发布的指示;

(iv)在1967年7月1日后结束的所有证券交易委员会程序中各证券交易委员会委员的最终投票记录;

(v)1967年7月1日之后发布、通过或颁发的且根据本节第(a)(2)(i)款、第(a)(2)(ii)款和第(a)(2)(iii)款向公众开放的材料的当前索引,以便为公众提供相关识别信息(按季度发布或其他更高频率发布),以及证券交易委员会指定的其他索引;及

(vi)根据《信息自由法》已向任何人发布的记录的复本及一般索引,且证券交易委员会基于该记录所涉主题性质判断,后续已经有或可能有其他欲获得主题与之实质相同的记录的请求。

(3)在1996年11月1日或之后制作且根据本节第(a)(2)款应提供给公众查阅和复制的记录,应在互联网上公布。

(4)其他按请求提供的记录。除本节第(a)(1)款和第(a)(2)款下提供的记录外,在受制于本节第(b)款的前提下,如证券交易委员会收到符合下述条件的获取关于非公开事项的记录的请求,应及时向申请人提供该等记录,并说明相关时间、地点、费用(如有)和应遵守的程序:(i)请求中已合理说明请求获得的记录;且(ii)请求系按照本节第(d)款和第(e)款提出。存放于证券交易委员会主要办公场所的公共资料室的向公

time, place, fees (if any) and procedures to be followed, shall make the records promptly available to any person. A compilation of records generally available at the public reference room at the principal office of the Commission appears below as appendix A to this subpart (17 CFR 200.80a). Most of the records described in appendix A to this section are provided to the public pursuant to the Securities Act of 1933, 15 U.S.C. 77f (d), the Securities Exchange Act of 1934, 15 U.S.C. 78m(f)(3), the Public Utility Holding Company Act of 1935, 15 U.S.C. 79v(a), the Investment Company Act of 1940, 15 U.S.C. 80a-44(a)(b), and the Investment Advisers Act of 1940, 15 U.S.C. 80b-10 (a). Arrangements can be made through the Public Reference Branch as explained in paragraph (c) of this section for materials to be copied by the Commission's contract copying service at fees found in appendix E to this section.

(5) *Records available with identifying details deleted.* To the extent required to prevent a clearly unwarranted invasion of personal privacy, identifying details may be deleted from materials made public as set forth in paragraphs (a)(1), (2), and (3), of this section, e.g., apparently defamatory statements made about any person, information received by or given to the Commission in confidence, or any contents of personnel and medical and similar files. In addition, certain materials which are considered to be nonpublic, as described in paragraph (b) of this section may, as authorized by the Commission from time to time, be made available for public inspection and copying in an abridged or summary form or with identifying details deleted.

(b) *Nonpublic matters.* Certain records are nonpublic, but any reasonably segregable portion of a record shall be provided to any person requesting such record in accordance with paragraphs (d) and (e) of this section and after deletion of the portions which are considered nonpublic under paragraph (b) of this section. Except for such reasonably segregable portions of records, the Commission will generally not publish or make available to any person matters that are:

(1)(i) Specifically authorized under criteria established by an executive order to be kept secret in the interest of national defense or foreign policy, and (ii) are in fact properly classified pursuant to such executive order.

(2) Related solely to the internal personnel rules and practices of the Commission or any other agency, including, but not limited to:

(i) Operation rules, guidelines, and manuals of procedure for investigators, attorneys, accountants, and other employees other than those which establish legal requirements to which members of the public are expected to conform; or

(ii) Hiring, termination, promotion, discipline, compensation, or reward of any Commission employee or member, the existence, investigation, or disposition of a complaint against any Commission employee or member, the physical or mental condition

众开放的记录编纂见本子部分附件A(《联邦规章汇编》第十七编第200.80a节)。本节附件A所述大多数记录系根据如下法律向公众提供:《1933年证券法》[《美国法典》第十五编第77f(d)节]、《1934年证券交易法》[《美国法典》第十五编第78m(f)(3)节]、《1935年公用事业控股公司法》[《美国法典》第十五编第79v(a)节]、《1940年投资公司法》[《美国法典》第十五编第80a-44(a)(b)节]及《1940年投资顾问法》[《美国法典》第十五编第80b-10(a)节]。对于本节附件E中应由证券交易委员会通过有偿合同复印服务复印的材料,可如本节第(c)款所述通过公共资料科进行安排。

(5)删除识别信息后提供的记录。如需要防止明显不正当的对个人隐私的侵犯,本节第(a)(1)款、第(a)(1)(2)款和第(a)(1)(3)款中规定的公开材料中的识别信息可能会被删除,如针对任何人的具有明显诽谤性质的声明、证券交易委员会以保密状态收悉或提供的信息或任何人事档案、医疗档案及类似文件。此外,本节第(b)款所述某些被视为非公开的材料,经证券交易委员会随时授权,可以在删除识别信息的前提下,或以摘要或概要形式提供给公众查阅和复制。

(b)非公开事项。某些记录属于非公开记录,但记录中的任何可合理分割部分应按本节第(d)款和第(e)款在删除本节第(b)款中视为非公开的部分后提供给申请人。除上述可合理分割的部分外,证券交易委员会一般不会公布或向任何人提供下述信息:

(1)(i)行政命令特别准许为国防或外交目的而按相关标准保密的信息;及(ii)根据上述行政命令,在事实上已被适当定为保密信息的信息。

(2)仅与证券交易委员会或任何其他机构的内部人事规则和工作相关的信息,包括但不限于:

(i)调查人员、律师、会计师及其他员工的操作规则、指南和程序手册,但规定了公众应遵守的法定要求的除外;或

(ii)任何雇员或委员的聘用、解聘、晋升、处分、报酬和奖励;对任何证券交易委员会雇员或委员投诉的处理;任何证券交易委员会雇员或委员的身体或精神状况;纯内部事项的处理;易于侵犯证券交易委员会员工或委员隐私的事项或类似信息。

of any Commission employee or member, the handling of strictly internal matters, matters which would tend to infringe on the privacy of the staff or members of the Commission, or similar subjects.

(3) Specifically exempted from disclosure by statute (other than 5 U.S.C. 552): *Provided,* That such statute (i) requires that the matters be withheld from the public in such a manner as to leave no discretion on the issue, or (ii) establishes particular criteria for withholding or refers to particular types of matters to be withheld.

(4) Disclose trade secrets and commercial or financial information obtained from a person and privileged or confidential, including, but not limited to:

(i) Information contained in letters of comment in connection with registration statements, applications for registration or other material filed with the Commission, replies thereto, and related material which is deemed to have been submitted to the Commission in confidence or to be confidential at the instance of the registrant or person who has filed such material unless the contrary clearly appears; and

(ii) Information contained in any document submitted to or required to be filed with the Commission where the Commission has undertaken formally or informally to receive such submission or filing for its use or the use of specified persons only, such as preliminary proxy material filed pursuant to Rule 14a-6 under the Securities Exchange Act (17 CFR 240.14a-6) or preliminary information statements filed pursuant to Rule 14c-5 (17 CFR 240.14c-5) before definitive material has been filed with the Commission, reports filed pursuant to Rule 316(a) under the Securities Act (17 CFR 230.316(a)), agreements filed pursuant to Rule 15c3-1d (c)(6)(i) under the Securities Exchange Act (17 CFR 240.15c3-1d(c)(6)(i)), schedules filed pursuant to Part Ⅱ of Form X-17A-5 (17 CFR 249.617) in accordance with Rule 17a-5(b)(3) under the Securities Exchange Act (17 CFR 240.17a-5(b)(3)), statements filed pursuant to Rule 17a-5(k)(1) under the Securities Exchange Act (17 CFR 240.17a-5(k)(1)), and confidential reports filed pursuant to Rules 17a-10 and 17a-12 under the Securities Exchange Act (17 CFR 240.17a-10 and 240.17a-12); and

(iii) Information contained in reports, summaries, analyses, letters, or memoranda arising out of, in anticipation of or in connection with an examination or inspection of the books and records of any person or any other investigation.

(5) Interagency or intra-agency memoranda or letters, including generally records which reflect discussions between or consideration by members of the Commission or members of its staff, or both, of any action taken or proposed to be taken by the Commission or by any member of its staff, and specifically, reports, summaries, analyses, conclusions, or any other work product of members of the Commission or of attorneys, accountants, analysts, or other members of the Commission's staff, prepared in the course

(3)制定法(《美国法典》第五编第552节除外)明确豁免披露的信息;前提是该等法律:(i)要求该等信息向公众保密,且未留有任何自由裁量余地;或(ii)设定了保密标准,或列明了应保密的特定信息类型。

(4)将披露从任何主体处获得的受保密特权保护的或属于保密信息的商业秘密及商业或财务信息,包括但不限于:

(i)在向证券交易委员会提交的注册说明书、注册申请或其他材料的意见函及其回复中包含的信息,被视为在保密状态向证券交易委员会提交的相关材料或应注册人或材料提交人之请求而视为保密的相关材料(存在明确相反表示的除外)。

(ii)向证券交易委员会提交或按要求向证券交易委员会提交,且证券交易委员会已正式或非正式承诺仅将由其自身或仅特定主体使用的任何文件中包含的信息,例如:在提交最终材料之前,根据《证券交易法》的《14a-6规则》(《联邦规章汇编》第十七编第240.14a-6节)提交的初步代理权材料,或根据《14c-5规则》提交的初步信息说明书;根据《证券法》的《316(a)规则》[《联邦规章汇编》第十七编第230.316(a)节]提交的报告;根据《证券交易法》的《15c3-1d(c)(6)(i)规则》[《联邦规章汇编》第十七编第240.15c3-1d(c)(6)(i)节]提交的协议;根据《证券交易法》的《17a-5(b)(3)规则》[《联邦规章汇编》第十七编第240.17a-5(b)(3)节]按《X-17A-5表格》第Ⅱ部分(《联邦规章汇编》第十七编第249.617节)提交的数据表;根据《证券交易法》的《17a-5(k)(1)规则》[《联邦规章汇编》第十七编第240.17a-5(k)(1)节]提交的报表;以及根据《证券交易法》的《17a-10规则》和《17a-12规则》(《联邦规章汇编》第十七编第240.17a-10和240.17a-12节)提交的保密报告;及

(iii)因核查或检查任何人的账簿和记录、该等核查或检查的准备工作而产生的或与之相关的报告、摘要、信函、备忘录中包含的信息,或因任何其他调查、调查准备工作而产生的或与之相关的报告、摘要、信函、备忘录中包含的信息。

(5)机构内部或跨机构的备忘录或信函,一般包括关于证券交易委员会委员或其员工或两者就证券交易委员会、证券交易委员会任何委员或其员工采取或拟采取的任何行动而开展的讨论或审议的记录,特别是证券交易委员会委员,或作为证券交易委员会员工的律师、会计师、分析师或其他人员在检查业务受证券交易委员会监管的人的账簿或记录过程中,或在证券交易委员会或其代表开展的检查、调查或相关诉讼中做出的报告、摘要、分析、结论或任何其他工作成果,但按法律规定一般均将向证券

of an inspection of the books or records of any person whose affairs are regulated by the Commission, or prepared otherwise in the course of an examination or investigation or related litigation conducted by or on behalf of the Commission, except those which by law would routinely be made available to a party other than an agency in litigation with the Commission.

(6) Personnel and medical files and similar files the disclosure of which would constitute a clearly unwarranted invasion of personal privacy, including those concerning all employees of the Commission and those concerning persons subject to regulation by the Commission.

(7) Records or information compiled for law enforcement purposes to the extent that the production of such records or information:

(i) Could reasonably be expected to interfere with enforcement activities undertaken or likely to be undertaken by the Commission or the Department of Justice, or any United States Attorney, or any Federal, state, local, foreign governmental authority or foreign securities authority, any professional association, or any securities industry self-regulatory organization;

(ii) Would deprive a person of a right to a fair trial or an impartial adjudication;

(iii) Could reasonably be expected to constitute an unwarranted invasion of personal privacy;

(iv) Could reasonably be expected to disclose the identity of a confidential source including a state, local or foreign agency or authority or any private institution which furnished information on a confidential basis, and, in the case of a record or information compiled by a criminal law enforcement authority in the course of a criminal investigation, or by an agency conducting a lawful national security intelligence investigation, information furnished by a confidential source;

(v) Would disclose techniques or procedures or would disclose guidelines for law enforcement investigations or prosecutions if such disclosure could reasonably be expected to risk circumvention of the law; or

(vi) Could be reasonably expected to endanger the life or physical safety of any individual.

(8) Contained in, or related to, any examination, operating, or condition report prepared by, on behalf of, or for the use of, the Commission, any other Federal, state, local, or foreign governmental authority or foreign securities authority, or any securities industry self-regulatory organization, responsible for the regulation or supervision of financial institutions.

(9) Geological and geophysical information and data, including maps, concerning wells.

(c)(1) *Public reference facility.* In order to disseminate records, including those

交易委员会诉讼中机构相对方之外的当事人披露的除外。

(6)披露后将导致对个人隐私的明显不当侵权的人事档案、医疗档案以及类似文件,包括与证券交易委员会全体员工以及与受证券交易委员会监管的人相关的此类文件。

(7)为执法目的而编制的记录或信息,前提是提供该等记录或信息:

(i)据合理预期将干扰证券交易委员会、司法部、任何联邦检察官、任何联邦、州、地方、外国政府机构、外国证券机构、任何专业协会或任何证券行业自律组织采取或可能采取的执法活动;

(ii)将剥夺任何主体获得公平审判或公正判决的权利;

(iii)据合理预期将不合理地侵害个人隐私;

(iv)据合理预期将披露保密信息来源的身份,包括在保密基础上提供信息的州、地方或国外部门、机构或任何私人机构;就刑法执法机构在刑事调查中编制的或开展合法的全国性安全情报调查的机构编制的记录或信息而言,将披露由保密来源提供的信息;

(v)将披露执法调查或追诉的技术、程序或指引,且据合理预期该等披露将导致法律规避风险;或

(vi)据合理预期将危及任何个人的生命或人身安全。

(8)证券交易委员会、任何其他负责监管或监督金融机构的联邦、州、地方、外国政府机构、外国证券机构或任何证券行业自律组织或其代表制作或使用的任何检查、运营或状况报告中包含的信息或与之相关的信息。

(9)与水井相关的地质或地球物理信息和数据,包括地图。

(c)(1)公共资料设施。为了向公众提供记录(包括本节附件A中所列记录),证券

listed in appendix A to this section, the Commission has a specially staffed and equipped public reference room located at 100 F Street, NE., Washington, D.C. Copying machines, which are available to requestors on a self-service or contractor-operated basis, can be used to make immediate copies up to 81/2 by 11 inches in size of materials that are available for inspection in the Washington, D.C. Headquarters. Fees and levels of service are set out in the Commission's schedule of fees in appendix E to this section and in information available from the public reference room. The Commission accepts only written requests for copies of documents.

(i) The public reference room in Washington, D.C. has available for public inspection all of the publicly available records of the Commission as described in paragraph (a) of this section. Upon request, and only when suitable arrangements can be made with respect to the transportation, storage, and inspection of records, records may be sent to any other Commission office for inspection at that office, if the records are not needed by the Commission or the staff in connection with the performance of official duties. When the records are sent to another office at the request of a member of the public, the requestor shall be charged all costs incurred by the Commission in transporting the records.

(ii) All regional offices of the Commission have available for public examination the materials set forth in paragraph (a)(2) of this section and the *SEC Docket, SEC News Digest,* and other SEC publications. Blank forms as well as other general information about the operations of the Commission described in paragraph (a)(1) of this section may also be available at particular regional offices.

(iii) The addresses of the Commission's regional offices are:

Atlanta Regional Office—3475 Lenox Road, NE., Suite 1000, Atlanta, GA 30326-1232. Office hours—9 a.m. to 5:30 p.m. E.T.

Boston Regional Office—33 Arch Street, 23rd Floor, Boston, MA 02110-1424. Office hours—9 a.m. to 5:30 p.m. E.T.

Chicago Regional Office—175 West Jackson Boulevard, Suite 900, Chicago, IL 60604-2908. Office hours—8:45 a.m. to 5:15 p.m. C.T.

Denver Regional Office—1801 California Street, Suite 1500, Denver, CO 80202-2656. Office hours—8 a.m. to 4:30 p.m. M.T.

Fort Worth Regional Office—Burnett Plaza, Suite 1900, 801 Cherry Street, Unit #18, Fort Worth, TX 76102-6882. Office hours—8:30 a.m. to 5 p.m. C.T.

Los Angeles Regional Office—5670 Wilshire Boulevard, 11th Floor, Los Angeles, CA 90036-3648. Office hours—8:30 a.m. to 5 p.m. P.T.

Miami Regional Office—801 Brickell Avenue, Suite 1800, Miami, FL 33131-4901. Office hours—9 a.m. to 5:30 p.m. E.T.

New York Regional Office—3 World Financial Center, Suite 400, New York, NY

交易委员会在华盛顿哥伦比亚特区东北分区100F大街设立了公共资料室,并特别配备了相关人员和设备。请求人可通过自助服务或承包商服务使用复印机,以8.5×11英寸(21.59×27.94厘米)的规格即时复印华盛顿哥伦比亚特区总部公开提供以备查阅的资料。服务费用和级别见证券交易委员会在本节附件E费用表的规定,同时见公共资料室发布的相关信息。证券交易委员会仅接受书面文件复印请求。

(i)公众可在位于华盛顿哥伦比亚特区的公共资料室查阅本节第(a)款所述所有证券交易委员会公开记录。在其他证券交易委员会办公室提出申请,且已就记录运输、存储和查阅达成适当安排之时,可将不为证券交易委员会或其工作人员履行职务所需的记录发送至该等其他办公室的地点进行查阅。应某一公众之请求将记录发送至其他办公室之时,证券交易委员会运输记录的所有成本均应由请求人承担。

(ii)公众可在证券交易委员会的所有地区办公室查阅本节第(a)(2)款、《证券交易委员会新闻摘要》、《证券交易委员会周志》及其他证券交易委员会出版物中所载材料。各地区办公室也可提供空白表格及本节第(a)(1)款所述关于证券交易委员会运作的一般性信息。

(iii)证券交易委员会地区办公室的地址如下:

亚特兰大地区办公室——乔治亚州亚特兰大市东北分区Lenox路3475号1000室,邮编:GA 30326-1232。办公时间——东部标准时间上午9时至下午5时30分。

波士顿地区办公室——马萨诸塞州波士顿市Arch大街33号23楼,邮编:MA 02110-1424。办公时间——东部标准时间上午9时至下午5时30分。

芝加哥地区办公室——伊利诺伊州芝加哥西杰克逊大道175号900室,邮编:IL 60604-2908。办公时间——中部标准时间上午8时45分至下午5时15分。

丹佛地区办公室——科罗拉多州丹佛市加利福尼亚大街1801号1500室,邮编:CO 80202-2656。办公时间——山地标准时间上午8时至下午4时30分。

沃斯堡地区办公室——得克萨斯州沃斯堡市Cherry大街801号Burnett大厦1900室18单元,邮编:TX 76102-6882。办公时间——中部标准时间上午8时30分至下午5时。

洛杉矶地区办公室——加利福尼亚州洛杉矶市Wilshire大道5670号11层,邮编:CA 90036-3648。办公时间——太平洋标准时间上午8时30分至下午5时。

迈阿密地区办公室——佛罗里达州迈阿密市Brickell大道801号1800室,邮编:FL 33131-4901。办公时间——东部标准时间上午9时至下午5时30分。

纽约地区办公室——纽约州纽约市世界金融中心3号400室,邮编:NY 10281-

10281-1022. Office hours—9 a.m. to 5:30 p.m. E.T.

Philadelphia Regional Office—701 Market Street, Suite 2000, Philadelphia, PA 19106-1532. Office hours—9 a.m. to 5:30 p.m. E.T.

Salt Lake City Regional Office—15 W. South Temple Street, Suite 1800, Salt Lake City, UT 84101-1573. Office hours—8 a.m. to 4:30 p.m. M.T.

San Francisco Regional Office—44 Montgomery Street, Suite 2600, San Francisco, CA 94104-4716. Office hours—8:30 a.m. to 5 p.m. P.T.

(2) *Public reference inquiries.* Inquiries concerning the nature and extent of records available at the Commission's public reference room in Washington may be made in person or in writing. The addresses of all Commission Regional Offices are set forth at paragraph (c)(1) of this section. Written inquiries may be addressed to the Securities and Exchange Commission, Public Reference Branch, 100 F Street, NE., Washington, D.C. 20549.

(3) Electronic filings made through the Electronic Data Gathering, Analysis, and Retrieval system are publicly available through the Commission's Web site (*http://www.sec.gov*).

(d) *Requests for Commission records and copies thereof*— (1) *Time and place of requests for access to Commission records.* Requests for access to records available through the Commission's public reference facility may be made in person from 10 a.m. to 3 p.m., E.T., at this facility or by mail directed to the Public Reference Branch, Securities and Exchange Commission, Washington, D.C. 20549. In addition, access to agency records not available in the public reference facility may be requested pursuant to the Freedom of Information Act. Such requests must be in writing, should be clearly and prominently identified by a legend on the first page, such as "Freedom of Information Act Request", and should be addressed to the Freedom of Information Act Officer, SEC, 100 F Street, NE., Washington, D.C. 20549. The request may also be made by facsimile (202-772-9337) or by Internet (*foia/pa@sec.gov*).

(2) *Requests for copies of records.* Requests for copies of Commission records available through the Commission's public reference facility, including those listed in appendix A to this section, may be made directly to the facility either in person or by mail addressed to the Securities and Exchange Commission, Public Reference Branch, Washington, D.C. 20549. Levels of service and charges for copies are set out in the Commission's schedule of fees in appendix E to this section. Requests for copies of materials to which access has been granted pursuant to a Freedom of Information Act request will be processed pursuant to regulations found in this section in paragraphs (e)(9) and (e)(10) and at charges set out in appendix E to this section.

(3) *Description of requested records.* Each request for Commission records or copies

1022。办公时间——东部标准时间上午9时至下午5时30分。

费城地区办公室——宾夕法尼亚州费城Market大街701号2000室,邮编:PA 19106-1532。办公时间——东部标准时间上午9时至下午5时30分。

盐湖城地区办公室——犹他州盐湖城W. South Temple大街15号1800室,邮编:UT 84101-1573。办公时间——山地标准时间上午8时至下午4时30分。

旧金山地区办公室——加利福尼亚州旧金山Montgomery大街44号2600室,邮编:CA 94104-4716。办公时间——太平洋标准时间上午8时30分至下午5时。

(2)公共资料查询。公众可当面或以书面形式查询证券交易委员会华盛顿公共资料室所提供记录的性质和范围。各证券交易委员会地区办公室的地址见本节第(c)(1)款。书面查询应发送至证券交易委员会公共资料科,地址:华盛顿哥伦比亚特区东北分区100F大街,邮编:D.C.20549。

(3)通过电子数据收集、分析和检索系统(EDGAR)提交的电子文件公布于证券交易委员会网站上(http://www.sec.gov)。

(d)证券交易委员会记录及复本请求——(1)请求查阅证券交易委员会记录的时间和地点。通过证券交易委员会的公共资料设施请求查阅记录的,可于东部标准时间上午10时至下午3时提出当面请求,或向位于华盛顿哥伦比亚特区的证券交易委员会公共资料科发送邮件直接提出请求,邮编:D.C. 20549。此外,公共资料设施不提供的机构记录可根据《信息自由法》进行请求。此外,上述请求必须以书面形式作出,并在首页上的显著位置明确标明"《信息自由法》请求"等标志,并应发送至证券交易委员会信息自由法官员,地址:华盛顿哥伦比亚特区东北分区100F大街,邮编:D.C.20549。请求也可通过传真(202-772-9337)或互联网(foia/pa@sec.gov)提出。

(2)记录复本请求。复制证券交易委员会公共资料设施提供的证券交易委员会记录(包括本节《附件A》所列记录)的请求可当面或通过邮件提出,邮件应发送至华盛顿哥伦比亚特区的证券交易委员会公共资料科,邮编:D.C.20549。服务级别和复印费见证券交易委员会在本节附件E费用表中的规定。根据《信息自由法》请求复印相关资料的,应根据本节第(e)(9)款和第(e)(10)款的规定处理,并按本节附件E的规定收费。

(3)请求记录描述。所有查阅或复印证券交易委员会记录的请求均应合理描述所

thereof shall reasonably describe the records sought with sufficient specificity with respect to names, dates and subject matter to permit the records to be located among the records maintained by or for the Commission. A person who has requested Commission records or copies thereof will be promptly advised if the records cannot be located on the basis of the description given and that further identifying information must be provided before his request can be satisfied.

(4) *Normal availability.* Records maintained in the Commission's public reference facility or copies thereof will normally be made available in keeping with levels of service and fees set out in appendix E to this section. Records requested pursuant to the Freedom of Information Act will be made available as described in paragraphs (e)(9) and (e)(10) of this section.

(5) *Initial determination; multi-track processing, and denials* — (i) *Time within which to respond.* When a request complies with the procedures in this section for requesting records under the Freedom of Information Act, a response shall be sent within 20 business days from the date the Office of Freedom of Information and Privacy Act Operations receives the request, except as described in paragraphs (d)(5)(ii) and (d)(5)(iii) of this section. If that Office has identified the requested records, the response shall state that the records are being withheld, in whole or in part, under a specific exemption or are being released.

(ii) *Voluminous records.* The amount of separate and distinct records which are demanded in a single request or the amount of time or work (or both) involved may be such that the review of the records cannot be completed within 20 business days, as prescribed in paragraph (d)(5)(i) of this section. In such a case, the Office of Freedom of Information and Privacy Act Operations shall inform the requester of the approximate volume of the records and give him or her the option of limiting the scope of the request to qualify for 20-day processing or placing the request in the Commission's first-in, first-out (FIFO) system for reviewing voluminous records. In the latter case, the Office will inform the requester of the approximate time when the review will start. The FIFO system allows the Commission to serve all those requesting voluminous records on a first-come, first-served basis, such that all releasable records sought will be released at one time, unless the requester specifically requests that releasable records be released piecemeal as they are processed.

(iii) *Expedited processing.* The Office of Freedom of Information and Privacy Act Operations shall grant a request for expedited processing if the requester demonstrates a compelling need for the records. "Compelling need" means that a failure to obtain the requested records on an expedited basis could reasonably be expected to pose an imminent threat to an individual's life or physical safety or, if the requester is primarily

请求的记录，充分准确地说明名称、日期和主题，以便在证券交易委员会保存的记录中进行定位查找。如无法基于查阅或复印请求人的说明对记录进行定位查找的，请求人将及时获得通知，此时请求人必须提供进一步的识别信息，以便满足其请求。

(4)一般可提供性。证券交易委员会公共资料设施保存的记录或其复本一般均可按本节附件E所载服务级别和费用提供。根据《信息自由法》请求查阅或复印的记录按照本节第(e)(9)款和第(e)(10)款提供。

(5)初步决定：多轨道处理及拒绝披露——(i)响应时间。如请求符合本节中关于根据《信息自由法》请求查阅或复印的记录的程序，信息自由和隐私法管理办公室将于收到请求后20个工作日内进行答复，但本节第(d)(5)(ii)款和第(d)(5)(iii)款另有规定的除外。若该办公室已查找到所请求的记录，答复中应说明记录将基于特殊豁免而被全部或部分拒绝披露，或是将被提供给申请人。

(ii)大量记录。某些单份请求要求提供大量储存地点分散的不同记录，或需要花费大量时间或/和投入大量工作，以致无法按照本节第(d)(5)(i)款的规定在20个工作日内完成记录审阅工作。在该种情况下，信息自由和隐私法管理办公室应将需提供记录的大致数量告知请求人，由请求人选择将其请求范围限制在20天的处理量内，或者将请求输入证券交易委员会用于查找大量记录的“先到先得”(FIFO)系统。在后一种情况下，信息自由和隐私法管理办公室将告知请求人审阅工作开始的大致时间。FIFO系统将按照首先提交首先处理的原则处理所有包含大量记录的请求，以便证券交易委员会可以一次性地提供所有要求提供的可公开记录，但请求人特别请求在处理过程中逐一提供可提供的记录的除外。

(iii)加急处理。若请求人证明其存在紧迫需求，信息自由和隐私法管理办公室应核准加急处理请求。“紧迫需求”系指如无法迅速取得所申请的记录可合理预期某人的生命或人身安全将受到紧迫威胁；或若请求人主要从事信息传播活动，则指其必须紧急向公众公布实际或指称的联邦政府活动。请求人可通过提供一份经认证的、据其所知和所信属实和准确的声明以证明上述紧迫需求。信息自由和隐私法管理办公室

engaged in disseminating information, an urgency to inform the public of actual or alleged Federal government activity. A compelling need shall be demonstrated by a statement, certified to be true and correct to the best of the requester's knowledge and belief. The Office of Freedom of Information and Privacy Act Operations shall notify the requester of the decision to grant or deny the request for expedited treatment within ten business days of the date of the request. A request for records that has been granted expedited processing shall be processed as soon as practicable.

(iv) *Notice of denial.* Any notification of denial of any request for records shall state the name and title or position of the person responsible for the denial of the request, the reason for the decision, and the right of the requester to appeal to the General Counsel. The decision shall estimate the volume of records that are being withheld in their entirety, unless giving such an estimate would harm an interest protected by the applicable exemption. The amount of information redacted shall be indicated on the released portion of the record and, if technically feasible, at the place where the redaction is made.

(v) *Form of releasable records.* Releasable records shall be made available in any form or format requested if they are readily reproducible in that form or format.

(6) *Administrative review.* Any person who has received no response to a request within the period prescribed in paragraph (d)(5) of this section or within an extended period permitted under paragraph (d)(7) of this section, or whose request has been denied under paragraph (d)(5) of this section, may appeal the adverse decision or failure to respond to the General Counsel.

(i) The appeal shall be in writing, shall be clearly and prominently identified on the envelope or other cover and at the top of the first page by a legend such as "Freedom of Information Act Appeal," and shall identify the record in the form in which it was originally requested.

(ii) The appeal must be mailed to the Office of Freedom of Information and Privacy Act Operations, SEC, 100 F Street, NE., Washington, D.C. 20549, and a copy of it must be mailed to the General Counsel, Securities and Exchange Commission, 100 F Street, NE., Washington, D.C. 20549.

(iii) The appeal may include such facts and cite such legal or other authorities as the person submitting the appeal may consider appropriate.

(iv) The General Counsel shall have the authority to grant or deny all appeals, in whole or in part, and to release as an exercise of discretion records exempt from mandatory disclosure under 5 U.S.C. 552(b). In appropriate cases he or she may, in his or her sole and unfettered discretion, refer appeals to the Commission for determination.

(v) A determination with respect to any appeal shall be made within twenty days (excepting Saturdays, Sundays and legal public holidays) after the receipt of such appeal

应在上述请求之日后10个工作日内,将其是否核准加急处理请求的决定通知请求人。经核准的加急记录请求应尽快处理。

(iv)驳回通知。若某一记录请求被驳回,驳回通知中应注明作出驳回决定的负责人的姓名和职务、驳回原因,以及请求人向证券交易委员会首席律师提出复议申请的权利。决定中应对完全不予披露的记录数量作出预估,但进行该等预估可能损害受相关豁免所保护的利益的除外。应在提供的记录中注明经纂辑的信息数量,且在技术可行的情况下应在纂辑之处注明。

(v)可提供的记录的形式。如不必特别处理,即可将记录复制成请求中指定的任何形式和格式,并按照该等形式和格式提供可提供的记录。

(6)行政复议。若任何人在本节第(d)(5)款规定的期间内或在本节第(d)(7)款允许的延长期限内未收到答复,或若任何人的请求根据本节第(d)(5)款的规定被驳回,请求人可以就驳回决定或不答复行为向首席律师提出行政复议请求。

(i)行政复议请求应采用书面方式,在信封或其他封皮和首页以清晰和显著的方式注明"根据《信息自由法》提出的行政复议请求"字样,并应按照原请求的形式注明记录的识别信息。

(ii)行政复议请求须采用邮寄方式发送至证券交易委员会信息自由和隐私法管理办公室,地址:华盛顿哥伦比亚特区东北分区100F大街,邮编:D.C.20549,并抄送证券交易委员会首席律师,地址:华盛顿哥伦比亚特区东北分区100F大街,邮编:D.C. 20549。

(iii)行政复议请求中可包括行政复议申请人认为适当的事实和法律依据或其他依据。

(iv)首席律师有权部分或全部地核准或驳回任何行政复议请求,并依其自由裁量权决定提供豁免于《美国法典》第五编第552(b)节的强制性披露要求的记录。在适当的情况下,首席律师可独立不受约束地行使自由裁量权,自行决定将任何行政复议提交证券交易委员会裁定。

(v)关于任何行政复议的裁定应在收到相关行政复议书后20日内(不含周六、周日和法定公共假日)或在本节第(d)(7)款允许的延长期限内作出。

or within such extended period as may be permitted in accordance with paragraph (d)(7) of this section.

(vi) A denial of an appeal in whole or in part shall set forth the basis for the denial, and shall advise the requester that judicial review of the decision is available in accordance with 5 U.S.C. 552(a)(4).

(7) *Extension of time to consider requests and to consider administrative appeals.* In unusual circumstances, as specified in this paragraph, the time limits prescribed in either paragraphs (d)(5) or (6) of this section may be extended by written notice to the person making a request for a record or a copy, setting forth the unusual circumstances for such extension and the date on which a determination is expected to be dispatched. No such notice shall specify a date that would result in an extension for more than ten business days, except as provided in paragraph (d)(8) of this section. As used in this paragraph, "unusual circumstances" means, but only to the extent reasonably necessary to the proper processing of the particular request:

(i) The need to search for and collect the requested records from field facilities or other establishments that are separate from the office processing the request. (Many records of the Commission are stored in Federal Records Centers in accordance with law — including many of the documents which have been on file with the Commission for more than 2 years — and cannot be made available for several days after a request has been made. Other records may temporarily be located at a regional office of the Commission. Any person who has requested for personal examination a record stored at the Federal Records Center or temporarily located in a regional office of the Commission will be notified when and where the record will be made available to him. Any person who has ordered a copy of such record will be provided with a copy as soon as practicable). Some records have been disposed of in accordance with the Commission's Records Control Schedule (17 CFR 200.80(f)).

(ii) The need to search for, collect, and appropriately examine a voluminous amount of separate and distinct records which are demanded in a single request. (While every reasonable effort will be made fully to comply with each request as promptly as possible on a first-come, first-served basis, work done to search for, collect and appropriately examine records in response to a request for a large number of records will be contingent upon the availability of processing personnel in accordance with an equitable allocation of time to all members of the public who have requested or wish to request records.)

(iii) The need for consultation, which shall be conducted with all practicable speed, with another agency having a substantial interest in the determination of the request or among two or more components within the Commission having substantial subject-matter interest therein.

(vi)若某一行政复议被全部或部分驳回,驳回通知中应注明驳回依据,并告知请求人可依据《美国法典》第五编第552(a)(4)节对驳回决定提出司法审查请求。

(7)审议查询记录请求和行政复议请求的期限的延长。在本款明确规定的异常情况下,可通过向记录查询请求人或复本请求人发送书面通知的方式延长本节第(d)(5)款或第(d)(6)款规定的期限,书面通知中应列明造成延期的异常情况和预计发送裁定结果的日期。除本节第(d)(8)款规定的情形外,延长期限不得超过10个工作日。在本款中,"异常情况"系指仅限于恰当地处理具体请求所合理必要的情况:

(i)检索和收集请求查询的记录,需要到分散在负责处理请求的办公室之外的现场设施或其他机构进行操作(证券交易委员会的许多记录依法储存于联邦记录中心——包括许多已经在证券交易委员会存档时间超过两年的文件——这些记录很难在提出请求后的几天内提供。其他有些记录则可能临时储存于证券交易委员会的地区办公室。若请求人要求亲自查阅储存于联邦记录中心或临时储存于证券交易委员会地区办公室的记录,应通知请求人其可进行查阅的地点和时间。在合理可行的情况下,应尽快向已经订购上述记录复本的任何人提供该等复本)。某些记录已根据证券交易委员会的《记录控制计划》处置[《联邦规章汇编》第十七编第200.80(f)节]。

(ii)单独一份请求所涵盖的记录量大,且需要搜索、收集并适当查阅大量不同记录且记录储存地点分散(证券交易委员会应尽一切合理努力确保每一请求均能按照"先到先得"的原则得到及时处理,但是,为了完成一份包含大量记录的请求,检索、收集以及适当查阅记录的工作将取决于处理人员的可用时间,处理人员应根据请求或希望查询记录的公众人数公平分配其可用时间)。

(iii)需要和对请求的裁定拥有实质利害关系的其他政府机构展开磋商,或者,对请求的标的拥有实质利益的两个(含)以上的证券交易委员会内部机构之间需要磋商;上述磋商应以可行的速度尽快开展。

(8) *Inability to meet time limits.* If a request for records cannot be processed within the time prescribed under paragraph (d)(7) of this section, the Commission shall so notify and give the requester an opportunity to modify the request so that it may be processed within that time or to arrange an alternative time for processing the request or a modified request.

(i) *Records in use for another member of the public.* Any record being inspected by or copied for another member of the public will be made available as soon as practicable.

(ii) *Records in use by a member of the Commission or its staff.* Although every effort will be made to make a record in use by a member of the Commission or its staff available when requested, it may occasionally be necessary to delay making such a record available when doing so at the time the request is made would seriously interfere with the work of the Commission or its staff.

(iii) *Missing or lost records.* Any person who has requested a record or copy will be notified if the record sought cannot be found. If he so requests, he will be notified if it should subsequently be located.

(9) *Misdirected written requests.* The Commission cannot assure that a timely or satisfactory response will be given to written requests for inspection or copies of records that are directed to the Commission other than in the manner prescribed in paragraphs (d)(1) and (2) of this section. Any staff member who receives a written request for records should promptly forward the request to the Freedom of Information Act Officer. Misdirected requests for records will be considered to have been received for purposes of paragraph (d) of this section only when they have been actually received by the Freedom of Information Act Officer. The Commission will not entertain any appeal from an alleged denial or failure to comply with a misdirected request, unless it is clearly shown that the request was in fact received by the Freedom of Information Act Officer.

(e) *Fees for records services.* A current schedule of fees for record services, including locating, reviewing, and making records available, attestations and copying, appears in appendix E to this subpart D, 17 CFR 200.80e. Copies of the current schedule of fees may also be obtained upon request made in person, by telephone or by mail from the public reference room or at any regional office of the Commission.

(1) *Services provided without charge.* Generally, up to one-half hour of staff time devoted to searching for and reviewing Commission records will be provided without charge. Where a request for records pursuant to the Freedom of Information Act is determined not to serve a commercial purpose as defined in paragraph (e)(10)(ii) of this section, a total of two staff hours of search and review and one hundred pages of duplication as defined in paragraphs (e)(9)(i), (e)(9)(ii) and (e)(9)(iii) of this section, respectively, shall be made available without charge in the form most economical

(8)无法遵守时间限制的情形。若证券交易委员会无法在本节第(d)(7)款规定的时间内处理某一记录请求,应通知请求人并向请求人提供修改其请求的机会,以便能在规定的时间内得到处理,或另行安排时间处理请求或修改后的请求。

(i)其他公众正在使用的记录。如某一记录正在被其他公众查阅或复制,该记录将在可行的情况下尽快提供。

(ii)证券交易委员会委员或其员工正在使用的记录。对于证券交易委员会委员或其员工正在使用的记录,尽管证券交易委员会将尽力做到及时按请求提供,但在记录请求可能严重干扰证券交易委员会委员或其员工的工作的情况下,偶尔可能有必要延缓提供相关记录的时间。

(iii)丢失或遗失的记录。如无法找到请求人要求提供的某一记录或记录复本,请求人将获得相应通知。请求人如果要求之后找到相关记录时向其发送通知的,应遵照办理。

(9)误交书面请求。未按照本节第(d)(1)款和第(d)(2)款规定的方式向证券交易委员会提交书面的查阅记录请求的,证券交易委员会不能确保对该等书面请求作出及时或满意的答复。任何收到书面请求的证券交易委员会员工应及时将其转交信息自由法官员。如果出现请求被误交的情况,就本节第(d)款而言,仅在信息自由法官员实际收到书面请求时,请求才被视为已被证券交易委员会收悉;请求人如果指称证券交易委员会驳回了其被误交的请求或未能遵守被误交请求的相关规定,因而提起任何行政复议的,首席律师不予受理,除非请求人能明确证明信息自由法官员已确实收悉该请求。

(e)记录服务费。本法规第D子部分附件E(《联邦规章汇编》第十七编第200.80e节)中包含一份现行记录服务价目表,其中包括定位查找、审阅、提供记录以及证明和复制等服务。请求人可当面、通过电话或邮件向证券交易委员会公共资料室或证券交易委员会的任何地区办公室获取该现行服务价目表。

(1)无偿服务。一般而言,证券交易委员会员工为检索和审阅记录所花费时间在半小时以内的,将免予收费。若认定依据《信息自由法》提出的记录请求并非供本节第(e)(10)(ii)款中确定的商业目的所用,则证券交易委员会将以对政府最经济的方式,无偿提供本节第(e)(9)(i)款、第(e)(9)(ii)款和第(e)(9)(iii)款中所述的总计两个人工时的检索和查阅服务以及100页的复制服务。

for the government.

(2) *Services for which fees are charged.* For records available through the Commission's public reference facility, requestors may make arrangements for duplication in accordance with provisions of the Commission's dissemination contract. Copies of that contract, which contain tables of charges, may be inspected in the public reference room, 100 F Street, NE., Washington, D.C. A complete schedule of services offered by the contractor and fees charged for those services is available through the Commission's public reference facility. Fees for services provided in connection with requests made pursuant to the Freedom of Information Act shall be assessed as set out in appendix E to this section and in keeping with guidelines and procedures described in paragraphs (e)(9) and (e)(10) of this section.

(3) *Requests requiring large expenditures.* A request for Commission records may state that the requesting person is willing to pay fees up to a stated limit for services to be provided in locating, reviewing and making available requested records. In such circumstances, no work will be done that will result in fees beyond the stated limit without further written authorization. If no limit is initially stated by the person requesting records or copies, services in locating and making available the requested records will not be done so as to exceed fees of $28 (exclusive of applicable copying charges) without the express written authorization by the requesting person, and he will be so informed.

(4) *Waiver or reduction of fees.* (i) The Office of Freedom of Information and Privacy Act Operations may waive or reduce search, review, and duplication fees if:

(A) Disclosure of the requested records is in the public interest because it is likely to contribute significantly to public understanding of the operations or activities of the government; and

(B) Disclosure is not primarily in the commercial interest of the requester.

(ii) The Office of Freedom of Information and Privacy Act Operations will determine whether disclosure is likely to contribute significantly to public understanding of the operations or activities of the government based upon four factors:

(A) Whether the subject of the requested records concerns the operations and activities of the Federal government;

(B) Whether the requested records are meaningfully informative on those operations or activities so that their disclosure would likely contribute to increased public understanding of specific operations or activities of the government;

(C) Whether disclosure will contribute to the understanding of the public at large, rather than the understanding of the requester or a narrow segment of interested persons; and

(D) Whether disclosure would contribute significantly to public understanding of the

(2)有偿服务。对于通过证券交易委员会公共资料设施提供的记录,请求人可按照证券交易委员会传播合同中的规定进行复制。传播合同及其中包含的费用表可在位于华盛顿哥伦比亚特区东北分区100F大街的公共资料室查阅。请求人可通过证券交易委员会的公共资料设施查询承包商提供的复制服务项目完整清单及价目表。对于依据《信息自由法》提出的记录请求,相关服务费应按照本节附件E的规定以及本节第(e)(9)款和第(e)(10)款所述的指导原则和程序予以确定。

(3)涉及费用金额较高的请求。请求人可在向证券交易委员会提出的记录请求中说明其愿意为定位查找、审阅、提供请求的记录的服务支付的服务费上限。在此种情况下,未经请求人进一步书面同意,证券交易委员会不会作出可能造成服务费超过该等限额的工作。若请求人一开始未限定服务费上限,服务费金额超出28美元(不包括相关复印费)的定位查找和提供记录服务须经请求人明确书面同意后方可作出,且证券交易委员会应将此等情况告知请求人。

(4)费用减免。(i)在以下情况下,信息自由和隐私法管理办公室可减免检索、查阅和复制费:

(A)请求记录之披露符合公共利益,披露可能显著提升公众对政府运作或活动的理解。

(B)披露的主要作用并非促进请求人的商业利益。

(ii)信息自由和隐私法管理办公室将依据以下四个因素判定披露是否可能显著提升公众对政府运作或活动的理解:

(A)所请求的记录的内容是否涉及联邦政府的运作和活动;

(B)所请求的记录是否提供了关于联邦政府的运作和活动的有意义的信息,其披露是否可能有助于公众对政府具体运作或活动的理解;

(C)所请求的记录之披露是否将有助于一般公众,而不仅仅是请求人或狭义范围的利害关系人,对政府运作或活动的理解;和

(D)请求记录之披露是否会显著提升公众对政府运作或活动的理解程度。

governmental operations or activities.

(iii) The Office of Freedom of Information and Privacy Act Operations will determine whether disclosure of the requested records is not primarily in the commercial interest of the requester based upon two factors:

(A) Whether disclosure would further any commercial interests of the requester; and

(B) Whether the public interest in disclosure is greater than the requester's commercial interest.

(iv) If only a portion of the requested records satisfies both the requirements for a waiver or reduction of fees, a waiver or reduction of fees will be granted for only that portion.

(v) A request for a waiver or reduction of fees may be a part of a request for records. Such requests should address all the factors identified in paragraphs (e)(4)(ii) and (e)(4)(iii) of this section.

(vi) Denials of requests for a waiver or reduction of fees may be appealed to the General Counsel in accordance with the procedure set forth in paragraph (d)(6) of this section.

(5) *Records obtained from Federal Records Centers.* When, to fill a request for inspection or copying, records are required to be obtained from a Federal Records Center, fees, in addition to those provided on the Commission's current schedule of fees, will be charged to the extent authorized or required by rules or regulations promulgated by the National Archives and Records Administration.

(6) *Attestations.* In addition to any other fees or charges which may apply, a fee will be charged for records attestations as provided in the Commission's current schedule of fees. The seal of the Commission will be affixed to all attestations without additional charge.

(7) *Copying services.* Copies of records filed with or retained by the Commission, or portions thereof, will be provided subject to fees established by agreement between the Commission and a private contractor as set forth in the Commission's current schedule of fees and, where applicable, procedures and guidelines for Freedom of Information Act requests as set out in paragraphs (e)(9) and (e)(10) of this section.

(i) *Facsimile copies.* Requests for facsimile copies may be made either in person at the Commission's Washington, D.C. public reference room, or by mail addressed to the Securities and Exchange Commission, Public Reference Room, 100 F Street, NE., Washington, D.C. 20549. The contractor will send copies directly to the purchaser unless attestation is requested. Persons who request copies of documents through the public reference room will be billed by the contractor at regulated prices, and will be billed separately by the Commission for search, review and attestation charges, if any. Copies of documents requested directly from the contractor or from any other information service or

(iii)信息自由和隐私法管理办公室将依据以下两个因素判定披露所请求的记录的主要作用是否会促进请求人的商业利益:

(A)披露是否会促进请求人的任何商业利益;及
(B)披露产生的公共利益是否大于请求人的商业利益。

(iv)请求记录中如果仅有一部分符合上述两项费用减免要求,则将仅减免符合要求部分的费用。

(v)费用减免请求可在记录请求中载明。减免请求应论述本节第(e)(4)(ii)款和第(e)(4)(iii)款规定的所有因素。

(vi)费用减免请求被驳回的,可按照本节第(d)(6)款规定的程序向首席律师提出行政复议。

(5)从联邦记录中心获取的记录。记录查阅和复制请求涉及须从联邦记录中心获取的记录的,除证券交易委员会现行价目表中规定的服务费外,还将收取国家档案和记录管理局之规则与规章所准许或要求收取的费用。

(6)证明。除了其他可能收取的费用或收费外,证券交易委员会现行价目表还规定了记录证明服务费。证券交易委员会将在所有证明上将加盖公章,但盖章不另行收费。

(7)复制服务。证券交易委员会可向请求人提供证券交易委员会所存档或保留的记录或某份记录的部分内容,请求人应按照证券交易委员会和私营复制服务承包商约定的现行价目表支付费用,并遵守本节第(e)(9)款和第(e)(10)款所述的关于《信息自由法》请求的指导原则和程序(如适用)。

(i)传真复本。请求人可亲自前往证券交易委员会位于华盛顿州的公共资料室,或通过向证券交易委员会公共资料室发送信函(邮政地址:华盛顿哥伦比亚特区东北分区100F大街,邮编:D.C.20549)的方式申请获得传真复本。请求人如果并未要求提供证明服务,复制服务承包商将直接向购买人发送其所请求之复件。通过公共资料室请求获得复本的,复制服务承包商将按照规定价格向请求人收费,且证券交易委员会将另行收取检索、查看和证明服务费(若有)。直接请求复制服务承包商或任何其他信息服务公司或提供商提供的文件可以不按规定价格收费。本节未规定的或公共资料室张贴的现行价目表中未包含的特殊的复制服务种类(如传真),不由证券交易委员会提

vendor are not subject to regulated prices. Special classes of copying services, such as telecopies, not listed herein or in the current schedule of fees posted in the public reference room, are not provided or regulated by the Commission, but may be obtained from private vendors at market prices.

(ii) *Microfiche copies.* A contractor also makes available to the public microfiche copies of certain public documents on file with the Commission, at prices and on terms governed by its contract with the Commission. Microfiche services include subscription microfiche service on an annual basis. Microfiche subscription prices are regulated by the Commission whether requested through the public reference room or directly from the contractor. Certain other microfiche services are provided at prices that are regulated by the Commission only if ordered through the Commission's public reference room. The Commission will accept only subscription requests made in writing, although the contractor may elect to accept subscription requests by telephone. All microfiche subscription charges are payable directly to the contractor, whether placed through the Commission or not. Information concerning the types and cost of regulated microfiche services may be obtained by writing to the Commission at its public reference room located at 100 F Street, NE., Washington, D.C. 20549.

(iii) *Transcripts of public hearings.* Copies of the transcripts of recent public hearings may be obtained from the reporter subject to the fees established annually by contract between the Commission and the reporter. Copies of that contract, which contains tables of charges, may be inspected in the public reference room, 100 F Street, NE., Washington, D.C. and in each regional office. Copies of other public transcripts may be obtained, in the manner of other Commission records, subject to the charges referred to in paragraph (e)(7)(i) of this section.

(8) *Releases and publications.* (i) The Commission's decisions, reports, orders, rules and regulations are published initially in the form of releases and distributed.

(ii) The Commission publishes daily the *SEC News Digest,* which summarizes the releases published by the Commission each day, contains Commission announcements, and lists certain filings with the Commission. The Commission publishes weekly the *SEC Docket,* which prints the full text of every Commission release.

(iii) The Commission publishes an annual report to the Congress which sets forth the results of the Commission's operations during the past fiscal year under the various statutes committed to its charge. Copies may be obtained from the Superintendent of Documents, U.S. Government Printing Office, Washington, D.C. 20402.

(iv) The Commission also makes other information in the fields of securities and finance, including economic studies, available to the public through the issuance of releases on specific subject matters.

供或管理,但可按照市场价格从私营服务提供商处获得。

(ii)微缩胶片复本。复制服务承包商还可按照其与证券交易委员会之间的合同约定的价格和条件,向公众提供证券交易委员会档案中的某些公共文件的微缩胶片复本。微缩胶片服务包括按年度订阅微缩胶片的服务。无论是通过公共资料室提出的请求,还是直接向复制服务承包商提出的请求,微缩胶片的订购价格均受证券交易委员会管理。部分其他微缩胶片服务只有通过证券交易委员会公共资料室订购时,其订购价格才受证券交易委员会管理。复制服务承包商可选择接受以电话方式作出的订阅请求,但证券交易委员会仅接受书面订阅请求。无论订阅请求是否通过证券交易委员会作出,所有微缩胶片订阅费应直接支付给复制服务承包商。关于由证券交易委员会管理的微缩胶片服务的类型和费用的信息,可向证券交易委员会公共资料室致函垂询,邮政地址:华盛顿哥伦比亚特区东北分区100F大街,邮编:D.C.20549。

(iii)公开听证笔录。在按照证券交易委员会和笔录材料记录商之间的年度合同约定的费用付费的前提下,请求人可从笔录材料记录商处获得最新公开听证会的笔录复本。该合同中包括收费表,其内容可向公开资料室(地址:华盛顿哥伦比亚特区东北分区100F大街)和证券交易委员会的地区办公室查询。其他公开笔录在缴付了本节第(e)(7)(i)款所述费用后,可按照与证券交易委员会其他记录相同的方式获取。

(8)信息发布和公布。(i)证券交易委员会的决定、报告、命令、规则与规章首先采用信息发布的方式进行公布和传播。

(ii)证券交易委员会每日出版《证券交易委员会新闻摘要》,刊登证券交易委员会每日发布的信息(包括证券交易委员会公告)的摘要,并列出向证券交易委员会提交的某些申请。证券交易委员会每周出版《证券交易委员会周志》,全文刊载证券交易委员会的各项信息发布。

(iii)证券交易委员会发布向国会提交的年度报告,说明证券交易委员会负责实施的各项制定法在上一财务年度的实施结果。年度报告可向位于华盛顿哥伦比亚特区(邮编:D.C.20402)的美国政府印刷局文献管理办公室索取。

(iv)证券交易委员会还通过就具体主题进行信息发布的方式,向公众提供证券和金融领域的其他信息(包括经济研究)。

(v) A classification of the releases available from the Commission appears below as appendix B to this section. Other publications available from the Commission are set forth in appendix C to this section. Copies of rules, regulations, and miscellaneous publications set forth in appendix D to this section may be purchased from the Superintendent of Documents, U.S. Government Printing Office, Washington, D.C. 20402.

(9) *Fees for services required for processing Freedom of Information Act Requests.* In cases where records are requested pursuant to the Freedom of Information Act and according to procedures set forth in paragraph (d)(1) of this section, fees shall be charged as set out in the Commission's current schedule of fees, appendix E to this section, for services as described in the following:

(i) *Search.* The term "search" includes *all* time spent looking for material manually or by using electronic data processing equipment that is responsive to a request, as distinguished from "review" as defined at paragraph (e)(9)(ii) of this section. Searching for requested and specifically identified information, as described in paragraph (d)(1) of this section, includes the cost of staff time devoted to the search as indicated in appendix E to this section and direct costs for use of Commission electronic data processing equipment.

(ii) *Review.* The term "review" refers to the process of examining documents located in response to a request to determine whether any portion of any document is permitted to be withheld pursuant to provisions of the Freedom of Information Act. It also includes processing any documents for disclosure, e.g., doing all that is necessary to excise material from and otherwise prepare them for release.

(iii) *Duplication.* The term "duplication" refers to producing paper or microform copies of records. The Commission shall charge for duplication as established by agreement between the Commission and a private contractor. These charges are currently set out in appendix E to this section. Such charges shall be set so as not to exceed the direct cost that would be incurred by the Commission if it were to perform such services itself, as calculated to include the salary of operators, the cost of reproduction machinery, the cost of material and any other direct costs incurred by the Commission in copying materials responsive to a Freedom of Information Act request.

(iv) *Partial exemption from fee provisions.* No fees shall be charged for the first two hours of search time and the first one hundred pages of materials for requesters described in paragraphs (e)(10)(i) and (e)(10)(iii) of this section.

(v) *Minimum fee.* Fees will not be charged if the normal cost of collecting a fee would be equal to or greater than the fee itself.

(10) *Classification of Freedom of Information Act requesters for purposes of assessing fees.* Parties requesting records pursuant to the Freedom of Information Act will

(v)本节附件B列明了证券交易委员会可作出的信息发布的类型。证券交易委员会可作出的其他公告见本节附件C。本节附件D中规定的规则、规章和其他公告可向位于华盛顿哥伦比亚特区(邮编:D.C.20402)的美国政府印刷局文献管理办公室购买。

(9)处理《信息自由法》请求的服务费。根据《信息自由法》和本节第(d)(1)款规定的程序提出的记录请求,应按照本节附件E中证券交易委员会现行价目表的规定,就以下服务缴付费用:

(i)检索。"检索"一词包括:为根据某一请求,以手工方式或通过电子数据处理设备查询资料所花费的全部时间,其含义与本节第(e)(9)(ii)款所述的"审阅"一词不同。本节第(d)(1)款所述的对所请求的特定信息进行检索,其成本包括本节附件E规定的检索工作花费的人工时成本和使用证券交易委员会电子数据处理设备的直接成本。

(ii)审阅。"审阅"一词系指审阅依照请求查找到的文件,并根据《信息自由法》的规定判定任何文件的任何部分是否可保留不予提供的过程。审阅还包括为了披露文件而对该文件进行的处理,如材料删除和为公布而采取的其他必要准备工作。

(iii)复制。"复制"一词系指制作记录的纸质或微缩胶片形式的复本。证券交易委员会应按照其与私营复制服务承包商之间的协议约定收取复制工本费。这些费用目前规定于本节附件E之中,不应超过证券交易委员会如果自行提供复制服务所将发生的直接成本,计算直接成本时应包含操作人员的工资、复制设备的成本、材料成本和证券交易委员会根据《信息自由法》请求复制材料时发生的任何其他直接成本。

(iv)费用的部分免除。对于本节第(e)(10)(i)款和第(e)(10)(iii)款所述请求人,证券交易委员会对前两个小时的检索服务和前一百页以内的材料复制不应收取任何费用。

(v)最低费用。若收取某项费用的正常成本等于或超过费用本身的金额,则不收取该费用。

(10)针对不同类别信息自由法请求人适用的不同收费标准。依据《信息自由法》提出记录请求的各方将按照以下规定分类并缴纳本节附件E中规定的费用:

be classified and charged fees described in appendix E to this section as follows:

(i) The following types of requesters shall be charged for duplication of records as described in paragraph (e)(9)(iii) of this section as qualified in paragraph (e)(9)(iv) of this section: Educational institutions requesting information for purposes of scholarly research; non-commercial scientific institutions requesting information for purposes of scientific research; and representatives of the news media requesting information concerning current events or matters of current interest to the general public.

(ii) Commercial requesters, defined as parties other than those mentioned in paragraph (e)(10)(i) of this section who are requesting information to be used in any way which could reasonably be expected to result in corporate or personal financial gain or profit, shall be charged for search, review and duplication of records as described in paragraphs (e)(9)(i), (e)(9)(ii) and (e)(9)(iii), respectively, of this section.

(iii) All parties other than those described in paragraphs (e)(10)(i) and (e)(10)(ii) of this section requesting access to such records shall be charged for search and duplication of records as described in paragraphs (e)(9)(i) and (e)(9)(iii) of this section, respectively, as qualified in paragraph (e)(9)(iv) of this section.

(11) *Appeal of classification.* Classification under the provisions of paragraph (e)(10) of this section may be appealed to the General Counsel in accordance with the procedure set forth in paragraph (d)(6) of this section.

(12) *Aggregation of requests.* If the Freedom of Information Act Officer reasonably believes that a requester or group of requesters acting in concert is attempting to divide one request into a series of requests for the purpose of evading the assessment of fees, those requests may be aggregated and charges assessed accordingly.

(13) *Advance payment.* The Freedom of Information Act Officer may require advance payment of fees expected to be incurred in connection with a request, but only when the subject requester has failed to make timely payment in the past, or when the estimated processing costs exceed $250.00 and the requester has no previous payment records or has failed to make timely payment in the past. Processing in such cases shall be delayed until advance payment is received and statutory time limits will be appropriately extended.

(14) *Interest on unpaid bills.* On the 31st day following the date of a bill to a requester, the Commission may begin assessing interest on the unpaid amount at the rate prescribed in section 3717 of title 31 of the U.S. Code. Interest will accrue from the date of the bill.

[40 FR 8799, Mar. 3, 1975]

Editorial Note: For Federal Register Citations affecting §200.80, see the List of CFR Sections Affected, which appears in the Finding Aids section of the printed volume and at www.fdsys.gov.

(i)以下类型的请求人按本节第(e)(9)(iv)款规定应缴纳复制费的,应缴纳本节第(e)(9)(iii)款所述的记录复制的费用:为学术研究目的提出信息请求的教学机构;为科研目的提出信息请求的非商业科研机构;就涉及一般公众当前利益的当前事件或事项提出信息请求的新闻媒体代表。

(ii)商业请求人指除本节第(e)(10)(i)款所述类型之外的,可合理预期其将把请求的信息以任何方式用于获得公司或个人财务收益或利润的其他请求人。商业请求人应分别缴纳本节第(e)(9)(i)款、第(e)(9)(ii)款和第(e)(9)(iii)款所述的检索、审阅和复制费。

(iii)除本节第(e)(10)(i)款和第(e)(10)(ii)款所述之外的所有其他要求查询相关记录的请求人,按照本节第(e)(9)(iv)款的规定应缴纳复制费用的,将分别缴纳本节第(e)(9)(i)款和第(e)(9)(iii)款所述的记录检索和复制费。

(11)针对分类提起的行政复议请求。对于根据本节第(e)(10)款规定作出的分类,可按照本节第(d)(6)款规定的程序向首席律师提出行政复议请求。

(12)请求的合并。若信息自由法官员合理地认为一个请求人或行动一致的多个请求人出于逃避收费之目的,试图将一项请求分割为一系列的请求,证券交易委员会可将该等请求予以合并同时收取相应费用。

(13)预付款。信息自由法官员可要求请求人提前支付预期将发生的请求费用,前提是相关请求人有过不及时付款的不良历史;或处理费用预计将超过250美元且请求人的付款历史记录为空白或有不及时付款的不良历史。在该种情况下,证券交易委员会在收到预付款后才会对相关信息进行处理,且处理信息的法定期限将适当地顺延。

(14)未付账单的利息。自向请求人出具账单之日后第31日始,证券交易委员会可按照《美国法典》第三十一编第3717节规定的利率就未付金额征收利息。利息自账单出具之日起计算。

[《联邦公报》第40卷第8799页,1975年3月3日。]

编辑注:对第200.80节有影响的《联邦公报》索引,参见《受影响的联邦规章汇编条文列表》(见印刷版本的《检索协助》章节和www.fdsys.gov)。

§200.80a Appendix A—Documentary materials available to the public.

[See footnotes at end of table]

Description	Pursuant to section—
Securities Act of 1933	
Registration statement providing financial and other information concerning securities offered for public sale, filed under Regulation C (17 CFR 230.400 *et seq.*)	6
Prospectuses (selling circulars) in connection with registration statement	10
Periodic reports (annual, quarterly, and current) to keep reasonably current the information in registration statement	([1])
Requests for extension of time to file information, document, or report	([2])
Reports of sales of registered securities and use of proceeds thereunder by first time registrants	19(a), 20(a)
Report by issuers of securities quoted on NASDAQ Inter-Dealer Quotation System	([1])
Preliminary data (prospectus, circular letters, etc.) to oil offering (Regulation B) (17 CFR 230.300 *et seq.*)	3(b)
Offering sheets for oil or gas rights and royalties under Regulation B for exemption from registration provisions (17 CFR 230.300 *et seq.*)	3(b)
Notifications of exemption from registration filed under Regulation A, E, and F (17 CFR 230.251, 230.601, 230.651 *et seq*.)	3(b)
Offering circulars and written advertisements or other communications under Regulations A, E, and F (17 CFR 230.251, 230.601, 230.651 *et seq.*)	3(b)
Report of sales and use of proceeds (Regulations A and E) (17 CFR 230.251, 230.601 *et seq.*)	3(b)
Consent by non-resident to service of process (Regulation A) (17 CFR 230.251 *et seq.*)	3(b)
Application for relief from disability under Regulations A and F (17 CFR 230.651 *et seq.*)	3(b)
Notice of proposed resale of restricted securities and resale of securities by control persons (17 CFR 230.144)	4(1), 4(4)
Notice of proposed sale by non-controlling person of restricted securities of issuers which do not satisfy all of the conditions of Rule 144 (17 CFR 230.237)	3(b)
Notice of sale of securities by closely held issuers (issuers with 100 or less beneficial owners) other than investment companies, registered or required to be registered under the Investment Company Act of 1940 (17 CFR 230.240)	3(b)

第200.80a节 附件A——可向公众提供的文件资料

[参见表格下方脚注]

内容	依据条款
《1933 年证券法》	
根据《C 管理办法》提交的、包含与公开发售证券相关的财务信息和其他信息的注册说明书(《联邦规章汇编》第十七编第 230.400 节及其后条文)	6
与注册说明书相关的招募说明书(出售说明书)	10
为合理更新注册说明书中的信息而提供的定期报告(年度、季度和当期报告)	([1])
延长信息、文件或报告提交期限的请求	([2])
关于首次注册人的注册证券出售和募集资金使用情况的报告	19(a)、20(a)
在 NASDAQ 交易商报价系统报价的证券发行人提交的报告	([1])
石油证券发行前期资料(招募说明书、发行说明书等)(《B管理办法》)(《联邦规章汇编》第十七编第 230.300 节及其后条文)	3(b)
为取得对注册规定的豁免,根据《B管理办法》提供的石油或天然气矿权和使用费的发行条款清单(《联邦规章汇编》第十七编第 230.300 节及其后条文)	3(b)
根据《A管理办法》、《E管理办法》和《F管理办法》提交的注册豁免通知(《联邦规章汇编》第十七编第 230.251 节、第 230.601 节、第 230.651 节及其后条文)	3(b)
发行公告和书面广告或根据《A管理办法》、《E管理办法》和《F管理办法》做出的其他通信(《联邦规章汇编》第十七编第 230.251 节、第 230.601 节、第 230.651 节及其后条文)	3(b)
出售和募集资金使用报告(《A管理办法》和《E管理办法》)(《联邦规章汇编》第十七编第 230.251 节、第 230.601节及其后条文)	3(b)
非居民对送达程序作出的同意(《A管理办法》)(《联邦规章汇编》第十七编第 230.251 节及其后条文)	3(b)
根据《A管理办法》和《F 管理办法》提交的资格恢复申请(《联邦规章汇编》第十七编第 230.651 节及其后条文)	3(b)
关于限制性证券转售提议和控制人转售证券提议的公告(《联邦规章汇编》第十七编第 230.144 节)	4(1)、4(4)
关于非控制人出售不满足《144 规则》全部条件的发行人的限制性证券的意向的公告(《联邦规章汇编》第十七编第 230.237 节)	3(b)
已根据或应根据《1940 年投资公司法》注册的投资公司之外的封闭式发行人(实益所有人数目为 100 或以下)出售证券的公告(《联邦规章汇编》第十七编第 230.240 节)	3(b)

Description	Pursuant to section—
Securities Exchange Act of 1934	
Registration statement (securities listed on a national securities exchange)	12(b)
Registration statement (securities traded over – the – counter)	12(g)
Exemption from section 12(g), 13, 14, 15, or 16	12(h)
Information by a foreign issuer temporarily exempt from section 12(g)	12(g)(3)
Certification of exchange approving securities for listing and registration	12(d)
Periodic reports (annual, quarterly and current) to keep current the information in the above registration statements	13(a)
Request for extension of time to file information, document, or report	12(b)
Correspondence between the Commission and registrants that are delinquent in filing certain required reports	13(a), 15(d)
Report by issuers of securities quoted on NASDAQ Inter-Dealer Quotation System	15(d), 13(a)
Certificate of termination of Registration for a class of security	([3])
Notices of suspension of trading	12(d)
Application to withdraw or strike a security from listing and registration on a national securities exchange	12(d)
Notification by an exchange of the admission to trading of a substituted or additional class of security	12(a)
Definitive proxy soliciting materials filed under Regulation 14A (17 CFR 240. 14a – 1 *et seq.*)	14(a)
Distribution of information to security holders from whom proxies are not solicited filed under Regulation C (17 CFR 230. 400 *et seq.*)	14(c)
Acquisitions, tender offers and solicitations. (17 CFR 240. 14d – 1 *et seq.*)	13(d), 14(d)
Initial statement of beneficial ownership of equity securities by officers, directors and principal stockholders of issuers having listed equity securities; and changes in such ownership	16(a)
Application for permission to extend unlisted trading privileges, notification of changes, and notification of termination or suspension	12(f)
Application for registration as a broker and dealer, and amendments or supplements to such application	15(b)
Reports of financial condition of registered brokers and dealers	17

续表

内容	依据条款
《1934 年证券交易法》	
注册说明书(全国性证券交易所上市证券)	12(b)
注册说明书(场外交易证券)	12(g)
对第 12(g)条、第 13 条、第 14 条、第 15 条或第 16 条的豁免	12(h)
取得对第 12(g)条的临时豁免的外国发行人提供的信息	12(g)(3)
交易所批准证券上市和注册的证明	12(d)
为合理更新上述注册说明书中的信息而提供的定期报告(年度、季度和当期报告)	13(a)
延长信息、文件或报告提交期限的请求	12(b)
证券交易委员会和拖延提交某些规定报告的注册人之间的信函往来	13(a)、15(d)
在 NASDAQ 交易商报价系统报价的证券发行人提交的报告	15(d)、13(a)
某一类别证券的注册终止证明	([3])
停牌公告	12(d)
证券从全国性证券交易所退市或撤销注册的申请	12(d)
证券交易所关于准许某一替代性或补充类别证券交易的通知	12(a)
《14A 管理办法》(《联邦规章汇编》第十七编第 240. 14a-1 节及其后条文)中的最终代理权征集资料	14(a)
向代理权未被征集之证券持有人发布按《C管理办法》提交的信息(《联邦规章汇编》第十七编第 230. 400 节及其后条文)	14(c)
收购、收购要约和征集同意函(《联邦规章汇编》第十七编第 240. 14d-1 节及其后条文)	13(d)、14(d)
权益证券上市发行人的高级管理人员、董事和主要持股人关于权益证券受益所有权的初始声明以及该等所有权的变更	16(a)
要求授予非上市证券交易权的申请,变更通知和终止或暂停通知	12(f)
经纪商和自营商的注册申请及其修正或补充	15(b)
注册经纪商和自营商财务状况报告	17

Description	Pursuant to section —
Application for registration as a transfer agent and amendments to such application	17A(c)
Application for registration as a municipal securities dealer	15B(a)
Application for registration or exemption as a securities information processor	11A(b)
Application for registration or exemption as a clearing agency	17A(b)
Irrevocable appointment of agent for service of process, pleadings and other papers	23(a)
Notice by non-resident broker or dealer specifying address of place in United States where copies of books and records are located and undertaking to furnish to Commission, upon demand, copies of books and records he is required to maintain	17
Subordination agreements	15
Initial assessment and information form for registered brokers and dealers not members of a registered national securities association	15(b)(8)
Annual assessment and information form for registered brokers and dealers not members of a registered national securities association	15(b)(8)
Reports of market makers and other registered broker-dealers in securities traded on national securities exchanges	17(a)
Reports by registered brokers and dealers who are OTC Market in Makers in any OTC Margin Securities	17(a)
Proposed rule changes by all self-regulatory organizations	19(b)
Notice as to stated policies, practices and interpretations of self-regulatory organizations	19(b)
Application by an exchange for registration or exemption from registration as a national securities exchange	6(a)
Annual amendments and supplemental material filed to keep reasonably current the information contained in application for registration or exemption	6(e)
Record disposal plan of national securities exchanges	17
Application for listing securities on an exempted exchange	12(b)
Periodic reports to keep reasonably current the information contained in application for listing securities on exempted exchange	13
Certification of exempted exchange approving securities for listing	12(d)
Application for registration as a national securities association or affiliated securities association	15A

续表

内容	依据条款
过户代理人注册申请及其修正	17A(c)
市政证券自营商的注册申请	15B(a)
证券信息处理人的注册或豁免申请	11A(b)
结算机构的注册或豁免申请	17A(b)
对文书、答辩书和其他文件送达代理人作出的不可撤销的指定	23(a)
非居民经纪商和自营商作出的通知,说明在美国存放账簿和记录复本的地址并承诺按照证券交易委员会的要求提供其按规定应保存的账簿和记录复本	17
次级债权协议	15
不属于全国性注册证券协会会员的注册经纪商和自营商的初始评估和信息表	15(b)(8)
不属于全国性注册证券协会会员的注册经纪商和自营商的年度评估和信息表	15(b)(8)
在全国性证券交易所从事证券交易的做市商和其他注册经纪自营商的报告	17(a)
作为任何场外保证金证券做市商的注册经纪商和自营商提交的报告	17(a)
所有自律性组织提出的规则修改提案	19(b)
关于自律性组织的政策、操作或解释的通知	19(b)
证券交易所提交的全国性证券交易所注册申请或豁免注册申请	6(a)
为合理更新注册或豁免申请中的信息而提交的年度修正和补充材料	6(e)
全国性证券交易所的记录处置方案	17
在豁免交易所上市证券的申请	12(b)
为合理更新在豁免交易所上市证券的申请中的信息而提交的定期报告	13
豁免交易所批准证券上市的证明	12(d)
全国性证券协会或关联证券协会注册申请	15A

Description	Pursuant to section —
Annual supplement consolidated to keep reasonably current the information in the above application	15A
Report of changes in membership status of any of its members required of national securities exchanges and registered national securities associations	17, 19
Application by a national securities association or a broker or dealer for admission or continuance of a broker or dealer as member of a national securities association, notwithstanding a disqualification under section 15A(b)(4)	15A(b)(4)
Application for review of disciplinary action or denial of membership by registered securities association	15A(g)
Reports on stabilizing activities pertaining to a fixed price offering of securities registered or to be registered under the Securities Act of 1933, or offered or to be offered pursuant to an exemption under Regulation A (17 CFR 230.251 *et seq.*), or being or to be otherwise offered if aggregate offering price exceeds $500,000	17
Plans by exchanges authorizing payment of special commission in connection with a distribution of securities on exchanges	10
Suspensions of trading of securities otherwise than on a national securities exchange	15(c)(5)
Annual and supplemental reports of the Municipal Securities Rulemaking Board	17
Public Utility Holding Company Act of 1935	
Notification of registration and registration statement by public utility holding companies providing financial and other information concerning the issue and sale of securities	5(a), 5(b)
Annual reports by registered holding companies to keep reasonably current information in the registration statement	5(d)
Application for an order of the Commission declaring registrant has ceased to be a holding company	5(d)
Statement by a person employed or retained by a registered holding company or subsidiary thereof, of subject matter in respect of which retained or employed; and annual statement thereafter	12(i)
Application for exemption from provisions of the Act and applications for declaratory orders regarding status of company under Act by holding companies, subsidiaries, and other companies	2(a)(3), 2(a)(4), 2(a)(7)(B), 2(a)(8)(B), 3(a), (b)
Twelve-month statement by bank claiming exemption under the Act	3(a), (d)
Application for approval of mutual service company or declaration with respect to organization and conduct of business of subsidiary service company	13(b)

续表

内容	依据条款
为合理更新上述申请中的信息而提交的年度综合补充文件	15A
全国性证券交易所和全国性注册证券协会规定的任何成员状态变化报告	17、19
全国性证券协会或经纪商或自营商为不符合第15A(b)(4)条资格要求的经纪商或交易商提出的加入全国性证券协会或续延全国性证券协会会员资格的申请	15A(b)(4)
针对对注册证券协会成员作出的纪律处分或拒绝其加入协会的决定提出的复议申请	15A(g)
针对已根据或将根据《1933年证券法》注册的,或已根据或将根据《A管理办法》(《联邦规章汇编》第十七编第230.251节及其后条文)的豁免待遇发行的,或正在发行或将以其他方式发行的,且累计发行价格超过50万美元的证券,关于其定价发行的稳定活动报告	17
交易所批准就交易所分销证券支付专项佣金的计划	10
证券在全国性证券交易所以外的市场停牌	15(c)(5)
市政证券规则制定委员会的年度和补充报告	17
《1935年公用事业控股公司法》	
公用事业控股公司提供与证券发行和出售相关的财务信息和其他信息的注册通知和注册说明书	5(a)、5(b)
注册控股公司为合理更新注册说明书中的信息提供的年度报告	5(d)
请求证券交易委员会宣布注册人不再构成控股公司的申请	5(d)
注册控股公司或其子公司雇用或聘请的人员就雇用或聘请事宜作出的声明;以及其后每年作出的年度声明	12(i)
控股公司、子公司和其他公司提出的豁免适用《公用事业控股公司法》的申请和依据《公用事业控股公司法》对公司性质作出宣告令的申请	2(a)(3)、2(a)(4)、2(a)(7)(B)、2(a)(8)(B)、3(a)、(b)
依据《公用事业控股公司法》提出豁免请求的银行最近12个月的报表	3(a)、(d)
请求批准互助服务公司的申请或关于从事服务业的子公司业务组织和开展之声明	13(b)

Description	Pursuant to section —
Statement executed by financial institution authorizing representative to serve as officer or director of holding company or subsidiary, filed by representative	17(c)
Initial statement of beneficial ownership of securities filed by officers and directors of registered public utility holding companies, and changes in such ownership	17(a)
Annual reports by mutual and subsidiary service companies	13
Application by interested persons for approval of reorganization plans required in court proceedings for reorganization of registered holding companies and subsidiaries	11(f)
Application by or on behalf of persons requesting approval of payment of fees, expenses or remuneration for services rendered in connection with a proceeding in reorganization in a U. S. Court involving registered holding companies or subsidiaries	11(f)
Notices of intention regarding proposed sale of securities and other assets not requiring filing of application or declaration	11, 12(d), 12(f)
Statements in justification of fees and expenses proposed to be paid	6(b), 7, 9, 10, 12(d)
Reports to stockholders by registered holding company or subsidiary thereof and annual reports submitted by registered holding company or subsidiary thereof to a State commission covering operations not reported to Federal Power Commission	14, 15
Trust Indenture Act of 1939	
Statement of eligibility and qualification of corporations or individuals as trustees under qualified indenture under which debt security has been or is to be issued	305, 307
Application for qualification of indenture under which security (bonds, debentures, notes and similar debt securities) has been or is to be issued	307
Application for exemption from provisions of the Act in certain cases	304(c), (d)
Application re conflict of interest of trustees	310(b)(1)
Reports by indenture trustee to indenture security holders with respect to eligibility and qualification under section 310	313
Application relative to affiliations between trustees and underwriters	310(b)(3), 310(b)(6)
Investment Advisers Act of 1940	
Application for registration as investment adviser or to amend or supplement such an application	203(c), 204
Application for exemption and other relief	206A

续表

内容	依据条款
经金融机构签署的授权相关代表担任控股公司或子公司高级管理人员或董事的声明(由相关代表提供)	17(c)
注册公用事业控股公司的高级管理人员和董事提交的关于证券受益所有权的初始说明书以及该等所有权的变更	17(a)
互助服务公司和从事服务业的子公司的年度报告	13
利害关系人提出的批准注册控股公司和子公司重组的法院程序中所需的重组方案的申请	11(f)
请求人或请求人代表就在联邦法院进行的涉及注册控股公司或子公司重组程序中判定的服务费用、支出或酬金提出的付款批准申请	11(f)
关于不必经过申请或申报的证券或其他资产的出售意向公告	11、12(d)、12(f)
关于拟支付费用和支出的理由说明书	6(b)、7、9、10、12(d)
注册控股公司或其子公司向股东提交的报告以及注册控股公司或其子公司就不必向联邦电力委员会汇报的经营事项向州委员会提交的年度报告	14、15
《1939 年信托契约法》	
公司或个人在已发行或将发行债务证券的合格信托契约项下担任信托受托人的适格性和资格声明	305、307
对已发行或将发行证券(债券、信用债券、票据或类似债务证券)的信托契约的合格认定申请	307
在特定情况下豁免《信托契约法》规定的申请	304(c)、(d)
关于信托受托人利益冲突的申请	310(b)(1)
信托契约受托人根据第 310 条对信托契约证券持有人提交的关于适格性和资格的报告	313
关于信托受托人和承销商之间的关联的申请	310(b)(3)、310(b)(6)
《1940 年投资顾问法》	
投资顾问注册申请或对注册申请提出的修正或补充申请	203(c)、204
豁免和其他救济申请	206A

Description	Pursuant to section —
Irrevocable appointment of agent for service of process, pleadings and other papers	211(a)
Notice by non-resident investment adviser specifying address of place in United States where copies of books and records are located, or	204
Undertaking by non-resident investment adviser to furnish to Commission, upon demand, copies of any books or records he is required to maintain	204
Investment Company Act of 1940	
Notification of registration of investment company, and registration statement covering an offering of securities of investment company evidencing an interest in a portfolio of securities in which the investment company invests	8(a), 8(b)
Periodic reports (annual and quarterly) to keep reasonably current the information in above registration statement	30(a), 30(b)(1)
Periodic or interim reports to security holders of registered investment companies	30(b)(2)
Application for order of the Commission determining registrant has ceased to be an investment company	8(f)
Fidelity bond, resolution of board of directors, notice of cancellation or termination of bond for officers and employees of investment companies who have access to its securities or funds	17(g)
Waiver of indemnification of officers and directors of investment companies	17(h), 17(i)
Report of independent auditors examining records of investment companies	17(f)
Application by other than registrant for order of Commission declaring corporate name of registrant is misleading or deceptive	35(d)
Request by company for certificate to be issued to Secretary of Treasury	([4])
Proxy soliciting material	20(a)[5]
Initial statement of beneficial ownership of securities by officers, directors and other specified insiders of registered closed - end investment companies, and changes in such ownership	30(f)
Application for exemption from provisions of the Act and other relief	2(a)(9),3(b)(2),6(b),(c),(d),7(d),10(e),(f),11(a),(c),12(d)(1),(d)(2),14(a),15(a),16(a),17(a),(b),(d),(e),18(i),22(d),23(b)(5),(c)(3),24(d),26(a)(2)(C),28(c),35(d),and others.

续表

内容	依据条款
就文书、答辩书和其他文件送达代理人作出的不可撤销的指定	211(a)
非居民投资顾问发出的说明在美国存放账簿和记录复本的地址的通知	204
非居民投资顾问作出的一经证券交易委员会要求,即向证券交易委员会提供其按规定应保存的任何账簿或记录复本的承诺	204
《1940 年投资公司法》	
投资公司的注册通知,以及关于投资公司证券发行的注册说明书,以证明在投资公司投资的证券组合中的权益	8(a)、8(b)
为合理更新上述注册说明书中的信息提交的定期报告(年度与季度报告)	30(a)、30(b)(1)
向注册投资公司的证券持有人提交的定期或期中报告	30(b)(2)
请求证券交易委员会判定注册人不再构成投资公司的申请	8(f)
忠诚保险契约、董事会决议、向有权获得投资公司证券或资金的投资公司高级管理人员和职员发出的取消或终止契约的通知	17(g)
投资公司高级管理人员和董事放弃补偿金的声明	17(h)、17(i)
独立审计师的投资公司记录核证报告	17(f)
非注册人提出的请求证券交易委员会宣布注册人的公司名称具有误导性或欺骗性的申请	35(d)
公司向财政部长提出的签发证明请求	([4])
代理权征集材料	20(a)[5]
注册封闭式投资公司高级管理人员、董事和其他特定内幕人员提交的关于证券受益所有权的初始说明书以及该等所有权的变更	30(f)
豁免《1940 年投资公司法》规定的申请和其他救济申请	2(a)(9)、3(b)(2)、6(b)、(c)、(d)、7(d)、10(e)、(f)、11(a)、(c)、12(d)(1)、(d)(2)、14(a)、15(a)、16(a)、17(a)、(b)、(d)、(e)、18(i)、22(d)、23(b)(5)、(c)(3)、24(d)、26(a)(2)(C)、28(c)、35(d)及其他。

Description	Pursuant to section —
Statement of transactions—exemption from provisions of section 10(f)	10(f)
Application for an ineligible person to serve as officer, director, etc. of a registered investment company	9(b)
Request for advisory report of the Commission relating to the reorganization of registered investment company	25(b)
Report of repurchase of its own securities by a closed – end company	23(c)
Sales literature regarding securities of certain investment companies	24(b)
Statement of the Federal Savings and Loan Corporation relating to the exemption of certain issuers	6(a)(4)
Report submitted pursuant to an order of the Commission	
Documents and records resulting from derivative or representative law suits	33

Footnotes:

[1] Section 15(d)—Securities Exchange Act of 1934.

[2] Section 12(b)—Securities Exchange Act of 1934.

[3] Section 12(g)—Securities Exchange Act of 1934.

[4] Section 851(e)(1) of the Internal Revenue Code of 1954 is applicable.

[5] Regulation 14 under the Securities Exchange Act of 1934 is applicable (17 CFR 240.14a-1 *et seq.*).

Miscellaneous

Requests or petitions that a change in the Commission's rules, regulations or forms be made; comments on proposed rules, regulations or forms; issuance, amendment or repeal of rules, regulations or forms promulgated under the various Acts administered by the Commission.

Requests for no-action and interpretative letters and responses thereto.

Transcripts of proceedings in public hearings including testimony, exhibits received in evidence, intermediate decisions, oral arguments, motions, briefs, exceptions.

Commission findings, opinions, orders, rulings and notices issued for public release.

Final opinions of the Commission, including concurring and dissenting opinions, as well as orders made by the Commission in the adjudication of cases.

A record of the final votes of each member of the Commission in every Commission proceedings concluded after July 1, 1967.

Hearings and comments on proposed rules or statements of policy, etc., except where

续表

内容	依据条款
交易说明书——对第10(f)条规定的豁免	10(f)
请求由一名非适格人员担任注册投资公司高级管理人员、董事等职务的申请	9(b)
请求证券交易委员会提供关于注册投资公司重组的顾问报告	25(b)
封闭式公司回购其自身证券的报告	23(c)
关于特定投资公司证券的书面出售材料	24(b)
联邦储蓄贷款公司出具的关于特定发行人的豁免的说明书	6(a)(4)
根据证券交易委员会的命令呈报的报告	
股东派生或代表诉讼文件和记录	33

脚注:

1 《1934年证券交易法》第15(d)条。

2 《1934年证券交易法》第12(b)条。

3 《1934年证券交易法》第12(g)条。

4 适用《1954年国内税收法典》第851(e)(1)条。

5 适用《1934年证券交易法》中的《14管理办法》(《联邦规章汇编》第十七编第240.14a-1节及其后条文)。

其他

提议变更证券交易委员会规则、规章或表格的请求或动议;对规则、规章或表格草案提出的建议;证券交易委员会负责实施的各项法律项下颁发的规则、规章或表格之发布、修订或废止。

不行动请求及其解释函和答复。

公开听证笔录,包括证人证词、证物、调解决定、口头辩论、动议、陈辩书、异议。

公开发布的证券交易委员会作出的认定、意见、命令、裁决和公告。

证券交易委员会的最终意见,包括相同意见和不同意见,以及证券交易委员会在案件的判决中下达的命令。

在1967年7月1日之后终结的证券交易委员会程序中对证券交易委员会所有委员的最终表决作出的记录。

对规则或政策声明提案的听证和意见征询,意见提供人要求不公布其意见的情

the writer requests that his comments not be made public.

Periodic reports filed by the International Bank for Reconstruction and Development under Regulation BW—Rules 1 to 4, section 15(a) of the Bretton Woods Agreement Act (17 CFR part 285).

Periodic reports filed by the Inter-American Development Bank, pursuant to Regulation IA (17 CFR part 286) adopted pursuant to section 11 (a) of the Inter-American Bank Act.

Periodic reports filed by the Asian Development Bank, pursuant to Regulation AD (17 CFR part 287) adopted pursuant to section 11(a) of the Asian Development Bank Act.

Copies of papers filed in court, and papers and documents received from courts, are primarily for the use of the Commission attorneys and other members of the staff. These may not always be complete and accurate and may contain nonpublic staff notations. However, in appropriate situations, with the approval of the Office of the General Counsel, examination of such material may be made or copies obtained as a matter of courtesy.

Statements of policy and interpretations which have been adopted by the Commission and are not published in the Federal Register.

Administrative staff manuals and instructions to the staff that affect a member of the public.

Reports by the Commission to the Congress as a whole.

Notices of Commission meetings announced to the public as described in §200.403; announcements of Commission action to close a meeting, or any portion thereof, as described in §200.404(b) and §200.405(c); and certifications by the General Counsel, pursuant to §200.406, that a Commission meeting, or any portion thereof, may be closed to the public.

[41 FR 44696, Oct. 12, 1976, as amended at 42 FR 14693, Mar. 16, 1977]

§200.80b Appendix B — SEC releases.

Free mailing list distribution of releases has been discontinued by the Commission because of rising costs and staff limitations. However, the texts of all releases under the various Acts, the corporate reorganization releases, and the litigation releases are contained in the SEC Docket, which may be purchased through the Superintendent of Documents as described in §200.80c of this part. The Statistical series releases are contained in the *SEC Monthly Statistical Review*, which also can be obtained by purchase through the Superintendent of Documents.

[40 FR 1009, Jan. 6, 1975, as amended at 49 FR 12686, Mar. 30, 1984; 52 FR 24148, June 29, 1987; 52 FR 48193, Dec. 21, 1987]

况除外。

国际复兴开发银行根据《BW管理办法》——《布雷顿森林协定法》第15(a)条《1-4规则》(《联邦规章汇编》第十七编第285部分)提交的定期报告。

泛美开发银行根据《IA管理办法》(《联邦规章汇编》第十七编第286部分)提交的、根据《美洲银行法》第11(a)条通过的定期报告。

亚洲开发银行根据《AD管理办法》(《联邦规章汇编》第十七编第287部分)提交的、根据《亚洲开发银行法》第11(a)条通过的定期报告。

向法院提交的文书以及从法院收悉的文书和文件主要供证券交易委员会律师和其他员工使用。文书和文件可能存在不齐全和不准确的情形且可能包含非公开的员工注释。但是,在适当的情况下,经首席律师办公室批准,可以通融将该等材料开放查阅或提供其复本。

证券交易委员会已通过但未在《联邦公报》上公布的政策声明和解释。

对公众有影响的行政人员手册和员工须知。

证券交易委员会向国会提交的所有报告。

第200.403条所述的向公众发布的证券交易委员会会议公告;第200.404(b)条和第200.405(c)条所述的证券交易委员会决定不公开某一会议或会议部分内容的通告;首席律师根据第200.406条核定证券交易委员会的会议或会议的任何一部分可不对外公开的文件。

[《联邦公报》第41卷第44696页,1976年10月12日,修正索引:《联邦公报》第42卷第14693页,1977年3月16日。]

第200.80b节　附件B——证券交易委员会的信息发布

由于成本上涨和人力限制,证券交易委员会不再提供免费的邮件发布服务。但是,根据各项法律作出的所有信息发布、公司重组的信息发布以及诉讼信息发布均刊登在《证券交易委员会周志》内,《证券交易委员会周志》可如本部分第200.80c节所述向文献管理办公室购买。统计信息发布刊登在《证券交易委员会统计月刊》内,也可通过文献管理办公室购买。

[《联邦公报》第40卷第1009页,1975年1月6日,修正索引:《联邦公报》第49卷第12686页,1984年3月30日;《联邦公报》第52卷第24148页,1987年6月29日;《联邦公报》第52卷第48193页,1987年12月21日。]

§200.80c Appendix C—Rules and miscellaneous publications available from the Government Printing Office.

(a) The current rules of the Commission are not published by the Commission in pamphlet form. All SEC public rules and regulations, including its Rules of Practice, are contained in title 17 of the Code of Federal Regulations, which also is available for purchase from the Superintendent of Documents, Government Printing Office, Washington, D.C. 20402. New rules and rules changes, and other Commission releases, except statistical releases, also are published in the Federal Registers they are adopted.

(b) Copies of the following miscellaneous publications may be purchased from the Superintendent of Documents, Government Printing Office, Washington, D.C. 20402. Please address to him directly all inquiries, orders and payments concerning the following publications:

1. *Reports.*

SEC Annual Report to the Congress.

2. *Periodicals.*

Official Summary. A monthly summary of securities transactions and holdings reported under the provisions of the Securities Exchange Act of 1934, the Public Utility Holding Company Act of 1935, and the Investment Company Act of 1940 by officers, directors, and certain other persons.

SEC Monthly Statistical Review. A month publication containing data on round-lot and odd-lot share volume in stock exchanges, OTC volume in selected securities, block distributions, securities registrations and offerings, net change in corporate securities outstanding, working capital of U.S. corporations, assets of non-insured pension funds, Rule 144 filings and 8K reports.

Directory of Companies Filing Annual Reports with the Securities and Exchange Commission under the Securities Exchange Act of 1934. Published annually. Lists companies alphabetically and classified by industry groups according to the Standard Industrial Classification Manual of the Bureau of the Budget.

[40 FR 1010, Jan. 6, 1975, as amended at 49 FR 12686, Mar. 30, 1984; 52 FR 24148, June 29, 1987; 52 FR 48193, Dec. 21, 1987]

§200.80d Appendix D—Other publications available from the Commission.

(a) Limited amounts of the following materials among others are available free of charge upon request to the Commission's Publications Section, Public Reference Branch, 202-272-7460:

Work of the Securities and Exchange Commission.

Blank copies of all forms used under each of the Acts administered by the

第200.80c节　附件C——政府印刷局可提供的规则和其他出版物

(a)证券交易委员会不以手册形式出版其现行规则。所有证券交易委员会的公开规则与规章,包括其《工作规则》,均包含在《联邦规章汇编》第十七编中,可从位于华盛顿哥伦比亚特区(邮编:D.C.20402)的政府印刷局文献管理办公室购买。新规则与规章变更以及除统计数字以外的证券交易委员会信息发布也在《联邦公报》上公布。

(b)在位于华盛顿哥伦比亚特区(邮编:D.C.20402)的政府印刷局文献管理办公室还可购买以下其他出版物。请直接向文献管理办公室垂询、订购以下出版物并联系付款事宜:

1.报告。

证券交易委员会向国会提交的年度报告。

2.定期出版物。

《官方简报》。关于公司高级管理人员、董事和某些其他人员根据《1934年证券交易法》、《1935年公用事业控股公司法》和《1940年投资公司法》报告的证券交易和控股情况的月度简报。

《证券交易委员会统计月刊》。该出版物为月刊,其中包含证券交易所的整股和零股股份交易量、选定证券的场外交易量、大宗发售、证券注册和发行、发行在外的公司证券的净变化额、美国公司流动资金、无保险养老基金的资产、根据《144规则》提交的文件和8K报告。

《根据〈1934年证券交易法〉向证券交易委员会提交年度报告的公司名录》(年刊)。公司名单按字母顺序排列,并按照预算局《标准行业分类手册》按行业分类。

[《联邦公报》第40卷第1010页,1975年1月6日,修正索引:《联邦公报》第49卷第12686页,1984年3月30日;《联邦公报》第52卷第24148页,1987年6月29日;《联邦公报》第52卷第48193页,1987年12月21日。]

第200.80d节　附件D——证券交易委员会可提供的其他出版物

(a)证券交易委员会下属的出版处的公共资料科可在限定数量范围内免费提供包括以下资料在内的出版物,资料索取联系电话:202-272-7460。

证券交易委员会的工作说明。

证券交易委员会负责实施的每一项法律规定使用的所有空白表格。

Commission.

(b) Facsimile copies of other SEC publications which are out of print may be obtained through the Commission's Public Reference Section, at the cost of the copying service to be performed by the commercial copier employed to do the copying. Purchasers of copies will be billed by the copier. An example of the publications which are available in this way is the Litigation Actions and Proceedings Bulletin.

[52 FR 24148, June 29, 1987; 52 FR 48193, Dec. 21, 1987]

§200.80e Appendix E—Schedule of fees for records services.

Search and review services: Up to one half hour total—No fee. For each one half hour or fraction thereof of chargeable service—up to GS-11 employee performing service: $8.00; GS-12 or above employee performing service: $14.00.

Attestation with Commission seal: $4.00

Duplication services: The following duplication services are available. The stated time for delivery in each case begins to run only after receipt of the material by the contractor; if files cannot immediately be made available by the Commission, the time of shipment will be affected.

Regular service. Paper copies of original paper copies, or from microfiche accessible to the contractor, will be shipped within seven calendar days after the contractor receives the order and material at $0.24 per page, exclusive of any applicable shipment cost and sales taxes.

Other services. The Commission's dissemination contractor also provides a wide range of additional regulated dissemination services through the Commission's public reference room. Two offsite services also are provided at prices that are regulated: microfiche subscriptions and watch services. Information concerning the availability of all dissemination services may be obtained by writing to the Commission's public reference room located at 100 F Street, NE., Washington, D.C. 20549 or calling 202-551-8090. Copies made pursuant to requests submitted to the Commission's public reference room will be filled by the contractor and sent directly to the purchaser, unless attestation is requested. The contractor will bill the purchaser directly for the cost of copies plus postage or other delivery charges, and applicable taxes. Purchasers shall make full payment directly to the contractor for these services. Search, review or attestation charges will be billed separately by the Commission.

[52 FR 24148, June 29, 1987; 52 FR 48193, Dec. 21, 1987, as amended at 55 FR 41189, Oct. 10, 1990; 57 FR 48970, Oct. 29, 1992; 58 FR 64120, Dec. 6, 1993; 73 FR 32225, June 5, 2008]

(b)证券交易委员会下属的公共资料处还可提供已经绝版的证券交易委员会其他出版物的传真复本,但须向商业性复制服务提供商支付复制服务费。复制服务机构将向购买人收取费用。通过该种方式可获得的出版物包括《诉讼行动和程序公报》。

[《联邦公报》第52卷第24148页,1987年6月29日;《联邦公报》第52卷第48193页,1987年12月21日。]

第200.80e节　附件E——记录服务价目表

检索和审阅服务:半小时以内的检索和审阅服务不必支付任何费用。超出此范围之外每半小时或不足半小时的服务最高收费标准为:由GS-11雇员提供的服务按8美元收费,由GS-12(含)以上级别的雇员提供的服务按14美元收费。

加盖证券交易委员会公章的证明服务:4美元

复制服务:可提供的复制服务如下。对于每项服务而言,所告知的交付期限只有在承包商收到材料后方开始起算,若证券交易委员会未能立即提供文件,发件时间将受到影响。

常规服务:对于承包商可获得的纸质正本文件或微缩胶片的纸质复本,将在承包商收到指令和资料后7个日历日内发送,服务费为每页0.24美元(不含任何寄送成本和销售税)。

其他服务:证券交易委员会的传播服务承包商也通过证券交易委员会的公共资料室提供其他诸多传播服务,该等服务受证券交易委员会管理。另外,传播服务承包商还可提供微缩胶片订购和阅览两项异地服务,价格受证券交易委员会管理。申请人可通过书面方式(地址:华盛顿哥伦比亚特区东北分区100F大街,邮编:D.C.20549)或通过电话(电话号码:202-551-8090)向证券交易委员会公共资料室索取关于所有可提供的传播服务的信息。除非请求人要求提供证明服务,否则,根据证券交易委员会公共资料室收到的请求制作的复本将由传播服务承包商制作并直接发送给购买人。传播服务承包商将直接向购买人收取复制费用、邮费或其他投递费用以及适用的税费。购买人应直接向传播服务承包商支付全部上述服务费用。检索、审阅或证明费用将由证券交易委员会另行收取。

[《联邦公报》第52卷第24148页,1987年6月29日;《联邦公报》第52卷第48193页,1987年12月21日,修正索引:《联邦公报》第55卷第41189页,1990年10月10日;《联邦公报》第57卷第48970页,1992年10月29日;《联邦公报》 第58卷第64120页,1993年12月6日;《联邦公报》第73卷第32225页,2008年6月5日。]

§200.80f Appendix F—Records control schedule.

File No.	Type of filing	Retention period
Securities Act of 1933		
2 – 33	Registration statements and amendments thereto (Regulation C)	30 years.
2 – 33	Periodic reports (annual, quarterly, current, and proxy material)	30 years.
9 –	Notice of proposed resale of restricted securities and resale of securities by control persons (Form 144)	21 years.
15 –	Notice of sale of securities pursuant to Rule 242 (Form 242). (Obsolete)	6 years.
18 –	Applications for exemption from section 5 registration for interests or participations issued in connection with Keogh Plans (section 3 (a)(2))	10 years.
19 –	Notice of sale of securities pursuant to section 4(6) of the Securities Act of 1933 (Form 4(6)). (Obsolete)	6 years.
20 –	Offering sheets for oil or gas royalties—Regulation B (Schedules A, B, C)	15 years.
20 –	Reports of sale (accorded confidential treatment) (Form 1 – G)	7 years.
20 –	Reports after termination of offering (Form 3 – G)	7 years.
21 –	Notice of sale for offerings under Regulation D and section 4(6) (Form D)	6 years.
24 –	Notification of exemption from registration (Regulation A)	Until completion or termination of offering plus 10 years or order of the Commission permanently suspending exemption, whichever comes first.
29 –	Report of issuers of sale of securities deemed not to involve any public offering (Form 146). (Obsolete)	6 years.
92 –	Application for relief from disability (Regulation A)	Until when final action on appeal is taken plus 10 years.
94 –	Notification of exemption for assessment or assessable stock (Regulation F)	10 years.

第200.80f节　附件F——《记录控制计划》

文档编号	文件类型	保存期限
《1933年证券法》		
2-33	注册说明书及其修正(《C管理办法》)	30年
2-33	定期报告(年度报告、季度报告、当期报告和代理权材料)	30年
9-	关于限制性证券转售提议和控制人转售证券提议的公告(《144表格》)	21年
15-	关于根据《242规则》出售证券的公告(《242表格》)(已废止)	6年
18-	针对按照《基欧计划》发行的权益或参与份额提出的豁免第5条注册的申请[第3(a)(2)条]	10年
19-	关于根据《1933年证券法》第4(6)条出售证券的公告[《4(6)表格》](已废止)	6年
20-	石油或天然气使用费的发行条款清单——《B管理办法》(附表A、B、C)	15年
20-	出售报告(予以保密处理)(《1-G表格》)	7年
20-	发行终止后报告(《3-G表格》)	7年
21-	根据《D管理办法》和第4(6)条作出的发行出售公告(《D表格》)	6年
24-	注册豁免通知(《A管理办法》)	发行完成或终止后10年,或证券交易委员会发出正式中止豁免命令之日,以较早者为准
29-	发行人关于被视为不涉及任何公开发行的证券的出售报告(《146表格》)(已废止)	6年
92-	资格恢复申请(《A管理办法》)	对复议作出最终决定后10年
94-	关于股款追缴或可追缴股款的股票的豁免通知(《F管理办法》)	10年

File No.	Type of filing	Retention period
95 –	Notification of exemption for securities issued by a small business investment company (Regulation E)	Until completion or termination of offering plus 5 years or until order of Commission permanently suspending exemption, whichever comes first.
96 –	Application for relief from disability (Regulation F)	Until final action on appeal is taken plus 5 years.
98 –	Notice of proposed sale by non–controlling person of restricted securities of issuers which do not satisfy all of the conditions of Rule 144	6 years.
100 –	Notification of exemption pursuant to Rule 236	6 years.
Securities Exchange Act of 1934		
0 – 1	Registration statements (sections 12(b) and 12(g), exemptions thereunder)	30 years.
0 – 1	Periodic reports (annual, quarterly, current and proxy materials)	30 years.
3 –	Applications for continuance in membership and applications for review of disciplinary actions (self – regulatory organizations)	10 years.
4 – 281	Consolidated quotation system plan and amendments	For as long as plan remains approved plus 6 years.
4 – 208	Intermarket trading system plan and amendments	For as long as plan remains approved plus 6 years.
5 –	Acquisitions, tender offers and solicitations	20 years.
6 –	Reports of beneficial ownership of securities (Forms 3, 4, & 5)	6 years.
7 –	Applications for permission to extend unlisted trading privileges and related applications pursuant to Rule 12(f)	10 years.
8 –	Applications for registration as broker, dealer, municipal securities broker, or government securities broker or dealer and related reports	For as long as broker – dealer is registered with the Commission plus 50 years.

续表

文档编号	文件类型	保存期限
95 -	关于小型商业投资公司发行的证券的豁免通知(《E管理办法》)	发行完成或终止后5年,或证券交易委员会发出正式中止豁免命令之日,以较早者为准
96 -	资格恢复申请(《F管理办法》)	对复议作出最终决定后5年
98 -	关于非控制人出售不满足《144规则》全部条件的发行人的限制性证券的提议的公告	6年
100 -	《236规则》中的豁免通知	6年
《1934年证券交易法》		
0-1	注册说明书[第12(b)条和第12(g)条,该等条款中的豁免]	30年
0-1	定期报告(年度、季度和当期报告及代理权材料)	30年
3 -	会员资格续延申请和纪律处分复议申请(自律组织)	10年
4-281	合并报价系统计划及其修正	计划有效期加6年
4-208	市场间交易系统计划及其修正	计划有效期加6年
5 -	收购、收购要约和征集同意函	20年
6 -	证券受益所有权报告(《3、4和5表格》)	6年
7 -	要求延长未上市证券交易权的申请及按照《12(f)规则》提出的相关申请	10年
8 -	经纪商、自营商、市政证券经纪商或政府证券经纪商或自营商的注册申请及相关报告	经纪自营商在证券交易委员会的注册年限加50年

File No.	Type of filing	Retention period
8 -00 -2A	Annual audit report (fiscal or calendar year basis) (Form X - 17A-5). (Non - public) Supplemental report detailing Securities Investor Protection Corporation assessment payment or overpayments (Rule 17a -5). (Non - public)	For as long as broker-dealer is registered with the Commission plus 13 years.
8 -00 -2A -19	Reports of changes in membership of any of its members required of national securities exchanges and registered national securities associations (Form X - 17A - 19). (Public)	For as long as broker-dealer is registered with the Commission plus 6 years.
8 -00 -3X	Examination/inspection reports of brokers and dealers, investment companies and investment advisors	
	1. Exam reports:	
	a. Home Office	13 years.
	b. Regional Offices	13 years.
	2. Exam work papers	13 years.
8 -00 -9	Uniform application for securities and commodities industry representative and/or agent; certification for associated persons engaged in securities activities outside the jurisdiction of the United States; annual assessment form for registered brokers and dealers not members of a registered national securities association (Forms U -4, SECO 2 - F, SECO -4, 5)	For as long as broker-dealer is registered with the Commission plus 50 years.
8 -2A10	Annual report of revenue and expenses filed by exchange members, brokers and dealers (Form X-17A-10). (Obsolete)	10 years.
8 -2A12	Report by registered brokers and dealers who are over - the - counter market makers in any OTC margin securities (Form X - 17A - 12)	6 years.
8 -2A16 (1), -2A16(2)	Notification by qualified market makers at least five business days before such broker - dealers obtain third market maker exempt credit pursuant to Regulation U; and quarterly report by broker and dealer, who during a calendar quarter is or has been qualified as a third market maker (Forms X - 17A - 16(1); X - 17A - 16 (2)) (Obsolete)	6 years.
8 -2A17	Quarterly report filed by every broker - dealer block positioner who has filed a notice pursuant to paragraph (a) of Rule 17a - 17 (Form X - 17A - 17) (Obsolete)	6 years.
10 -	Applications by an exchange for registration as a national securities exchange	For as long as exchange is registered with the Commission plus 6 years.

续表

文档编号	文件类型	保存期限
8－00－2A	年度(会计年度或日历年)审计报告(《X－17A－5 表格》)。详细说明证券投资者保护公司计征款项的支付或超额支付的(非公开)补充报告(《17a－5 规则》)(非公开)	经纪自营商在证券交易委员会的注册年限加13年
8－00－2A－19	全国性证券交易所及全国性注册证券协会的任何会员资格变更报告(《X－17A－19 表格》)(公开)	经纪自营商在证券交易委员会的注册年限加6年
8－00－3X	经纪商和自营商、投资公司和投资顾问的核查/检查报告	
	1. 核查报告:	
	a. 证券交易委员会本部	13年
	b. 证券交易委员会地区办公室	13年
	2. 核查工作底稿	13年
8－00－9	证券和商品行业代表和/或代理的统一申请;在美国以外地区从事证券活动的业务相关人证明;不属于全国性注册证券协会会员的注册经纪商和自营商的年度评估表(《U－4 表格》、《SECO 2－F 表格》、《SECO－4、5 表格》)	经纪自营商在证券交易委员会的注册年限加50年
8－2A10	交易所会员、经纪商和自营商提交的收入和费用年报(《X－17A－10 表格》)(已废止)	10年
8－2A12	本身是场外保证金证券的场外做市商的任何注册经纪商和自营商的报告(《X－17A－12 表格》)	6年
8－2A16(1)、－2A16(2)	合格做市商在该等经纪自营商按照《U 管理办法》获得第三方做市商豁免信用前至少5个工作日发出的通知;以及在某一日历季度期间属于第三方做市商或获得第三方做市商资格的经纪商和自营商所作的季度报告(《X－17A－16(1)表格》;《X－17A－16(2)表格》)(已废止)	6年
8－2A17	已经按照《17a－17 规则》第(a)款提交通知的每一大宗头寸经纪自营商提交的季度报告(《X－17A－17 表格》)(已废止)	6年
10－	交易所提出的全国性证券交易所注册申请	交易所在证券交易委员会的注册年限加6年

File No.	Type of filing	Retention period
13 -	Applications for listing securities on an exempted exchange, periodic reports	10 years.
14 -	Annual reports of issuers having securities listed on an exempted exchange	10 years.
16 -	Application for registration as a national securities association or affiliated securities associations	For as long as association is registered with the Commission plus 6 years.
17 -	Reports on stabilizing activities (Form X - 17A - 1). (Obsolete)	6 years.
23 -	Applications for exemption pursuant to paragraph (g) of Rule 11Aa3 - 1	Until closed plus 6 years.
26 -	Plans by exchanges authorizing payment of special commission in connection with a distribution of securities on exchanges (Rule 10b - 2(d))	For as long as exchange is registered with the Commission plus 50 years.
27 -	Applications for exemption from section 13(f)	10 years.
28 -	Reports by institutional investment managers of information with respect to accounts over which they exercise discretion. (Form 13F)	4 years.
80 -	Annual and supplemental reports of Municipal Securities Rulemaking Board (Rule 17a - 21)	Indefinitely (contingent).
81 -	Exemptions from registration under section 12(g)	10 years.
82 -	Exemptions—American depositary receipts	10 years.
83 - 1	Periodic reports and related correspondence by the Inter - American Development Bank	3 years.
83 - 2	Periodic reports by the Asian Development Bank	3 years.
84 -	Application for registration as a transfer agent (non - bank) and amendments thereto	For as long as transfer agent is registered with the Commission plus 50 years.
85 -	Application for registration as a transfer agent (bank) and amendments thereto (Form TA - 1)	For as long as transfer agent is registered with the Commission plus 50 years.

续表

文档编号	文件类型	保存期限
13 -	证券在豁免交易所的挂牌申请,定期报告	10 年
14 -	豁免交易所挂牌证券的发行人的年度报告	10 年
16 -	全国性证券协会或关联证券协会的注册申请	协会在证券交易委员会的注册年限加 6 年
17 -	稳定活动报告(《X - 17A - 1 表格》)(已废止)	6 年
23 -	按照《11Aa3 - 1 规则》第(g)款提出的豁免申请	处理完毕后满 6 年
26 -	交易所批准就交易所分销证券支付专项佣金的计划(《10b - 2(d)规则》)	交易所在证券交易委员会的注册年限加 50 年
27 -	豁免于第 13(f)条规定的申请	10 年
28 -	机构投资管理人关于其拥有自由裁量权的账户的信息报告(《13F 表格》)	4 年
80 -	市政证券规则制定委员会的年报和补充报告(《17a - 21 规则》)	不定期(视具体情况而定)
81 -	第 12(g)条规定的注册豁免	10 年
82 -	豁免——美国存托凭证	10 年
83 - 1	泛美开发银行的定期报告及相关往来信函	3 年
83 - 2	亚洲开发银行的定期报告	3 年
84 -	过户代理人(非银行)注册申请及其修正	过户代理人在证券交易委员会的注册年限加 50 年
85 -	过户代理人(银行)注册申请及其修正(《TA - 1 表格》)	过户代理人在证券交易委员会的注册年限加 50 年

File No.	Type of filing	Retention period
86 –	Application for registration as a municipal securities dealer which is a bank or separately identifiable department or division of a bank (Form MSD)	For as long as municipal securities dealer is registered with the Commission plus 50 years.
87 –	Application for registration as a securities information processor and amendments thereto (Form SIP)	For as long as securities information processor is registered with the Commission plus 50 years.
88 –	Application for exemption as a securities information processor correspondence	For as long as securities information processor is registered with the Commission plus 50 years.
89 –	Waiver for foreign issuers furnished by American depositary receipts; waiver of information furnished by American depositary receipts regarding foreign issuers for Form F – 6; waiver of Rule 12g3-2(b) reporting requirements, annual reports to shareholders, F – 6 waiver, proxy	10 years.
89 –	Other waivers for foreign issuers furnished by American depositary receipts.	3 years.
128 – 8	Reports of disciplinary actions by stock exchanges (Rule 19d – 1)	6 years.
205 – 3c	Reports of disciplinary actions by NASD (Rule 19d – 1)	6 years.
500 –	Suspension of trading of securities other than on a national securities exchange	10 years.
600 –	Applications for registration as a (non – bank) clearing agency; amendments thereto	For as long as clearing agency is registered with the Commission plus 50 years.
600 – 9	Reports of disciplinary actions by clearing agencies (Rule 19d – 1)	6 years.
601 –	Applications for exemption from registration as a (non – bank) clearing agency	For as long as clearing agency has reporting requirements with the Commission plus 20 years.

续表

文档编号	文件类型	保存期限
86 -	银行、银行独立部门或机构提交的市政证券自营商注册申请(《MSD 表格》)	市政证券自营商在证券交易委员会的注册年限加 50 年
87 -	证券信息处理机构注册申请及其修正(《SIP 表格》)	证券信息处理机构在证券交易委员会的注册年限加 50 年
88 -	证券信息处理机构往来信函豁免申请	证券信息处理机构在证券交易委员会的注册年限加 50 年
89 -	美国存托凭证中提供的外国发行人豁免;美国存托凭证中为外国发行人提供的关于《F - 6 表格》的信息提交豁免;关于《12g3 - 2(b)规则》的报告要求的豁免、向股东呈交的年度报告、《F - 6 表格》豁免、代理委托书	10 年
89 -	美国存托凭证中为外国发行人提供的其他豁免	3 年
128 - 8	股票交易所纪律处分报告(《19d - 1 规则》)	6 年
205 - 3c	全国证券交易商协会纪律处分报告(《19d - 1 规则》)	6 年
500 -	证券在全国性证券交易所以外的市场停牌	10 年
600 -	(非银行)结算机构注册申请及其修正	结算机构在证券交易委员会的注册年限加 50 年
600 - 9	结算机构纪律处分报告(《19d - 1 规则》)	6 年
601 -	(非银行)结算机构豁免注册申请	按规定结算机构应向证券交易委员会提交报告的年限加 20 年

File No.	Type of filing	Retention period
SR	Proposed rule changes and notice as to stated policies and interpretations by self – regulatory organizations	For as long as self – regulatory organization is registered with the Commission plus 6 years.
XX	Reports for missing, lost or counterfeit securities (Form X – 17F – 1A)	Indefinitely.
Public Utility Holding Company Act of 1935		
12 –	Statements pursuant to section 12(i) by persons employed or retained by a registered holding company or subsidiary thereof (Forms U – 12(I) – A & B)	2 years.
30 –	Notification and registration by public utility holding companies, annual supplements	For as long as holding company has reporting requirements with the Commission plus 10 years.
31 –	Statement of exemption from the Act by Commission order	For as long as company relies on exemption plus 10 years.
32 –	Exemption of purchaser, assignee, etc. of leased facilities (Form U7D)	Until lease is terminated or cancelled plus 5 years.
33 – 1	Annual statement by banks holding public utility securities but claiming exemption under Rule 3	2 years.
34 –	Annual statement by banks holding public utility securities but claiming exemption under Rule 3 (Form U – 3A3 – 1)	2 years.
37 –	Applications and declarations for authorization of service companies (Form U – 13 – 1)	For as long as service company is part of a registered holding company plus 5 years.
38 –	Statement under Rule 70(a)(1) executed by financial authorizing representative to serve as officer/director of holding company, filed by representative	For as long as officer/director serves plus 3 years.
40 –	Certificates of notification by registered holding companies and subsidiaries of security issues exempted from section 6(a) by section 6(b) or exempt under Rule 47(b) and not the subject of an order of the Commission (Form U – 6B – 2)	3 years.

续表

文档编号	文件类型	保存期限
SR	自律组织规则变更提案及关于政策声明和解释的通知	自律组织机构在证券交易委员会的注册年限加6年
XX	关于丢失、遗失或伪造证券的报告(《X-17F-1A表格》)	不定期
《1935年公用事业控股公司法》		
12-	注册控股公司或其子公司雇用或聘请之人按照第12(i)条所作声明(《U-12(I)-A&B表格》)	2年
30-	公用事业控股公司的通知和注册,年度补充报告	按规定控股公司应向证券交易委员会提交报告的年限加10年
31-	关于证券交易委员会已发布命令批准豁免本法规定的声明	公司豁免期限加10年
32-	租赁设施的购买方、受让方等的豁免(《U7D表格》)	租赁终止或撤销后满5年
33-1	持有公用设施证券但主张《3规则》豁免的银行的年度报表	2年
34-	持有公用设施证券但主张《3规则》豁免的银行的年度报表(《U-3A3-1表格》)	2年
37-	服务公司资格申请表和声明(《U-13-1表格》)	服务公司作为注册控股公司一部分的期限加5年
38-	《70(a)(1)规则》项下金融机构签署[1]的授权相关代表担任控股公司高级管理人员或董事的声明(由相关代表提交)	高级管理人员/董事任期加3年
40-	注册控股公司和子公司关于证券发行根据第6(b)条而豁免适用第6(a)条的通知证明,或关于证券发行豁免适用《47(b)规则》且非证券交易委员会命令的主题事项的通知证明(《U-6B-2表格》)	3年

1 原文“financial”后似遗漏“institution”,已在译文中加入。——译者注

File No.	Type of filing	Retention period
49 –	Annual report by mutual and subsidiary service companies (Form U – 13 – 60)	For as long as service company is part of a registered holding company system plus 15 years.
50 –	Order granting or withdrawing exemptions from rules and related correspondence	Until close plus 3 years.
52 –	Application for approval or reorganization under section 11(f)	Until closed plus 3 years.
54 –	Divestment of securities, assets or control (section 11(e))	Until closed plus 3 years.
55 –	Application for approval of fees incurred in connection with plan under section 11(f)	Until closed plus 3 years.
59 –	Simplification of corporate structure, sections 11(b)(1) and (2)	Until closed plus 3 years.
62 –	Report by an affiliate service company or one engaged principally in the performance of services (Form U – 13E – 1)	For as long as service company is part of a registered holding company system plus 4 years.
68 –	Declaration with respect to solicitations regarding reorganizations of registered holding companies or subsidiaries subject to Rule 62 (Form U – R – 1)	10 years.
69 –	Annual statements by holding companies claiming exemption pursuant to Rule 2 (intrastate or predominantly operating companies (Form U – 3A – 2))	2 years.
70 –	Applications and declarations pursuant to sections 6(b), 7, 9, 9(c)(3), 10, 12(b), 12(c), 12(d), 12(f) and applicable rules thereunder (Form U – 1)	Until closed plus 3 years.
72 –	Report of communication with stockholders	2 years.
Trust Indenture Act of 1939		
22 –	Statements of eligibility and qualification of corporations or individuals as trustees under qualified indenture under which debt security has been or is to be issued and exemptions thereto	Until indenture is terminated or cancelled plus 30 years.
25 –	Applications relative to affiliations between trustees and underwriters (Rule 10b – 3)	Until applicable indenture is terminated or cancelled plus 33 years.

续表

文档编号	文件类型	保存期限
49 -	互助服务公司和子服务公司的年度报告(《U-13-60表格》)	服务公司作为注册控股公司系统一部分的期限加15年
50 -	核准或撤销规则豁免的命令和相关往来信函	处理完毕后满3年
52 -	第11(f)条规定的批准或重组申请	处理完毕后满3年
54 -	证券、资产或控制权的投资撤回[第11(e)条]	处理完毕后满3年
55 -	第11(f)条下计划费用的批准申请	处理完毕后满3年
59 -	公司结构精简,第11(b)(1)和(2)条	处理完毕后满3年
62 -	关联服务公司或主要从事服务业务的公司的报告(《U-13E-1表格》)	服务公司作为注册控股公司系统一部分的期限加4年
68 -	关于注册控股公司或子公司按照《62规则》重组同意征集函的声明(《U-R-1表格》)	10年
69 -	按照《2规则》主张豁免的控股公司的年度报表(《U-3A-2表格》)	2年
70 -	按照第6(b)条、第7条、第9条、第9(c)(3)条、第10条、第12(b)条、第12(c)条、第12(d)条、第12(f)条和适用规则提出的申请和声明(《U-1表格》)	处理完毕后满3年
72 -	股东通信报告	2年
《1939年信托契约法》		
22 -	公司或个人关于在已经或将要发行债务证券的合格信托契约下担任信托受托人的适格性和资格及其豁免的声明	信托契约终止或取消后满30年
25 -	关于信托受托人和承销商之间关联的申请(《10b-3规则》)	信托契约终止或取消后满33年

File No.	Type of filing	Retention period
93 –	Reports of indenture trustee to indenture security holders with respect to eligibility and qualification under Section 310	1 year.
Investment Advisers Act of 1940		
801 –	Application for registration as investment adviser and related correspondence	For as long as investment adviser is registered with the Commission plus 9 years.
803 –	Application for exemption from registered and other relief	For as long as investment adviser conducts business under an exemption plus 6 years.
Investment Company Act of 1940		
90 –	Notice of sales of securities by closed – end issuers (issuers with 100 or less beneficial owners) other than investment companies, registered or required to be registered	6 years.
811 –	Notifications and registration statements	For as long as registrant is registered with the Commission plus 30 years.
811 –	Periodic reports (annual, quarterly, semi – annual, proxy material)	10 years.
812 –	Applications for exemption and other relief	10 years.
812 –	Application by foreign management investment companies for order permitting registration	For as long as registrant has reporting requirement with the Commission plus 33 years.
813 –	Applications for exemption of an employee's security company (Section (b))	For as long as registrant has reporting requirement with the Commission plus 33 years.
814 –	Notice of intent to elect to be subject to sections 55 and 65	2 years from filing date.
814 –	Notification of withdrawal of election to be subject to sections 55 through 65	2 years from filing date.

续表

文档编号	文件类型	保存期限
93 -	信托契约受托人根据第310条向信托契约证券持有人提交的关于适格性和资格的报告	1年
《1940年投资顾问法》		
801 -	投资顾问注册申请及相关通信	投资顾问在证券交易委员会的注册年限加9年
803 -	注册豁免申请和其他救济申请	投资顾问开展豁免业务的期限加6年
《1940年投资公司法》		
90 -	已根据或应根据《1940年投资公司法》注册的投资公司之外的封闭式发行人(实益所有人数目为100或以下)出售证券的通知	6年
811 -	通知和注册说明书	注册人在证券交易委员会的注册年限加30年
811 -	定期报告(年度、季度、半年度报告或代理权资料)	10年
812 -	豁免申请和其他救济申请	10年
812 -	外国管理型投资公司的注册批准令申请	按规定注册人应向证券交易委员会提交报告的年限加33年
813 -	雇员的证券公司的豁免之申请[第(b)条]	注册人应向证券交易委员会提交报告的年限加33年
814 -	选择适用第55条和第65条的公告	提交日后2年
814 -	撤销选择适用第55条至第65条的通知	提交日后2年

File No.	Type of filing	Retention period
814 –	Notification of election to be subject to sections 55 through 65	30 years or for as long as a class of the issuer's equity securities is registered under the Securities Exchange Act of 1934 plus 10 years, whichever comes first.
816 –	Request for advisory report re reorganization of registered investment company (17 CFR 270.02), and related correspondence	6 years.
817 –	Report of repurchase of securities by closed – end investment company	6 years.
818 –	Sales literature regarding securities of certain investment companies	6 years.
819 –	Statement of the Federal Savings and Loan Corporation relating to the exemption of certain issuers	6 years.
820 –	Reports showing that companies have complied with requirements of the rule in purchasing new issues of securities from underwriters	6 years.
821 –	Reports by registered small business investment companies and affiliated banks, with respect to investments	10 years from date of such action(s).
Miscellaneous Files and Reports		
3 –	Disciplinary proceedings (broker–dealer and investment adviser)	25 years.
3 –	Administrative proceeding stop orders	For as long as registrant has reporting requirement with the Commission plus 30 years.
4 –	102(e) proceedings (previously 2(e) proceedings)(chaned to 3 –)	25 years.
4 –	Miscellaneous studies, general conferences, roundtable, etc., authorized by the Commission	25 years.
111 –	Federal government agencies miscellaneous correspondence	30 years.

续表

文档编号	文件类型	保存期限
814 -	选择适用第55~65条的通知	30年或发行人某一类别的权益证券根据《1934年证券法》注册的年限加10年,以较早者为准
816 -	关于注册投资公司重组的顾问报告请求(《联邦规章汇编》第十七编第270.02节)及相关往来信函	6年
817 -	封闭型投资公司回购证券报告	6年
818 -	特定投资公司的证券书面销售材料	6年
819 -	联邦储蓄及贷款保险公司[1]关于特定发行人的豁免声明	6年
820 -	表明公司从承销商处购买新发行证券时遵守了规则要求的报告	6年
821 -	注册小企业投资公司及关联银行关于投资的报告	报告之日起10年
其他文件与报告		
3 -	纪律处分程序(经纪自营商和投资顾问)	25年
3 -	行政处理程序停止令	按规定注册人应向证券交易委员会提交报告的年限加30年
4 -	102(e)程序[前2(e)程序](变更为3-程序)[2]	25年
4 -	证券交易委员会授权召开的其他研讨会、大会、圆桌会议等	25年
111 -	联邦政府机构其他往来信函	30年

1 原文"the Federal Savings and Loan Corporation"似遗漏"Insurance",应为"the Federal Savings and Loan Insurance Corporation",译文已按后者处理。——译者注

2 原文拼写似遗漏字母"g"(changed to),对译文无影响。——译者注

File No.	Type of filing	Retention period
119 –	Securities violation files (information regarding persons against whom actions were reported on charges of violating state or federal laws in the purchase and sale of securities)	Until date of last reported action plus 10 years.
122 – 2	Members of Congress (inquiries relating to various subjects)	1 year after expiration of term in office.
122 – 3	Correspondence and other materials between the various Senate Committees and the Commission	30 years.
122 – 4	Correspondence and other materials between the various House Committees and the Commission	30 years.
122 – 6	Correspondence and other materials between Congressional Commissions and Joint Committees and the Commission	30 years.
123 – 13	Correspondence relating to the development of a Canadian Extradition Treaty	30 years.
124 –	Stock exchanges (General Correspondence)	For as long as exchange is registered with the Commission.
124 – 1	Legislation and Laws: Drafts and comments concerning suggested amendments to the various Acts administered by the Commission	30 years.
124 – 6		
124 – 11		
124 – 20		
124 – 7, 124 – 7a	Subject files—Drafts, comments and correspondence concerning proposed legislation submitted by the Senate and the House to the Commission for comment	30 years.
124 – 7b	Drafts of bills not yet reported in Congress that are submitted to the Commission for comment	30 years.
132 – 3	General Correspondence—Active companies. Inquiries and complaints concerning companies registered under the various Acts administered by the Commission	10 years.
132 – 3	General Correspondence—Inactive companies (no longer required to file reports with the Commission). Inquiries and complaints concerning companies registered under the various Acts administered by the Commission	6 years.
132 – 3	General Correspondence—Miscellaneous. Requests for interpretation of rules and regulations under the Acts administered by the Commission	6 years.

续表

文档编号	文件类型	保存期限
119 -	证券违规文件(购买或销售证券中被指控违反州或联邦法律的主体的相关信息)	最后报告的行动之日后10年
122 - 2	国会议员(与各类主题相关的询问)	任期届满后1年
122 - 3	各参议院委员会与证券交易委员会之间的往来信函和其他资料	30年
122 - 4	各众议院委员会与证券交易委员会之间的往来信函和其他资料	30年
122 - 6	各国会委员会和联合委员会与证券交易委员会之间的往来信函和其他资料	30年
123 - 13	与制定《加拿大引渡条约》相关的往来信函	30年
124 -	股票交易所(一般往来信函)	交易所在证券交易委员会的注册年限
124 - 1	立法与法律:建议修正证券交易委员会负责实施的各项法律的草案和意见	30年
124 - 6		
124 - 11		
124 - 20		
124 - 7、124 - 7a	主题文件——由参议院和众议院递交给证券交易委员会征求其意见的立法草案、意见和往来信函	30年
124 - 7b	未向国会报告而递交给证券交易委员会征求其意见的立法草案	30年
132 - 3	一般往来信函——活跃公司。对根据证券交易委员会负责实施的各项法律注册的公司的询问和投诉	10年
132 - 3	一般往来信函——非活跃公司(不必再向证券交易委员会提交报告)。对根据证券交易委员会负责实施的各项法律注册的公司的询问和投诉	6年
132 - 3	一般往来信函——其他。要求证券交易委员会就其负责实施的规则与规章进行解释的请求	6年

File No.	Type of filing	Retention period
140 –	Drafts, internal memoranda, correspondence concerning rules and regulations under each of the Acts administered by the Commission	30 years.
206 – ,207 – to 215 – , 917 –	Reorganization proceedings under Chapters IX, X, XI of the Bankruptcy Act in which the Commission participates	30 years.
265 –	Advisory Committees established by the Commission (correspondence, questionnaires, reports)	30 years.
Confidential treatment materials	Periodic reports and other materials containing contracts, commercial and financial information, disclosure of which would impair the value thereof, submitted under confidential cover	10 years.
CHR	SEC Chairman's Subject Case Files	20 years.
CHR	SEC Chairman's Chronological Files for Period 1972 to Present	Chairman's tenure in office plus 3 years.
CHR	SEC Chairman's General Subject File	Chairman's tenure in office plus 3 years.
COMM	SEC Commissioners' Files (excluding Chairman), 1934 to Present	Commissioner's tenure in office plus 1 year.
ENF	Investigative Case Files—Closed	Until closed plus 25 years.
ENF	Investigative Case Files—Inactive	Until inactive plus 25 years.
LIT	Litigation files:	
	1. Briefs	25 years.
	2. File contents other than briefs	10 years.
S7	Issuance, amendment or rescission of rules under the various Acts—public comments and views, transcript of hearings, correspondence	30 years (permanent).
XX	Reports of internal inquiries:	
	1. Supporting documentation	Until date of final action plus 5 years, if no report is issued, or until date of final report plus 5 years.
	2. Final reports	5 years.

[60 FR 50091, Sept. 28, 1995]

续表

文档编号	文件类型	保存期限
140 –	关于证券交易委员会负责实施的法律下制定的规则与规章的草稿、内部备忘录与往来信函	30 年
206 –、207 – 至 215 –、917 –	证券交易委员会参与的《破产法》第 IX 章、第 X 章、第 XI 章中的重组程序	30 年
265 –	证券交易委员会设立的顾问委员会(往来信函、问卷、报告)	30 年
保密处理材料	通过保密方式提交的包含合同、商业和财务信息,以及如披露会损害其价值的定期报告和其他材料	10 年
CHR	证券交易委员会主席的主题案例文件	20 年
CHR	证券交易委员会主席的编年文件(1972 年至今)	主席任期加 3 年
CHR	证券交易委员会主席的一般主题文件	主席任期加 3 年
COMM	证券交易委员会委员(不包括主席)的文件(1934 年至今)	委员任期加 1 年
ENF	调查案件档案——已结案	结案后 25 年
ENF	调查案件档案——不活跃文件	成为不活跃文件后 25 年
LIT	诉讼文件:	
	1. 诉辩书	25 年
	2. 除诉辩书以外的文件内容	10 年
S7	各项法律的细则之发布、修正或废除——公众意见和观点、听证笔录、通信	30 年(永久)
XX	内部调查报告:	
	1. 支持文件	采取最终行动之日后 5 年(如未出具报告),或出具最终报告之日后 5 年
	2. 最终报告	5 年

[《联邦公报》第 60 卷第 50091 页,1995 年 9 月 28 日。]

§200.81 Publication of interpretative, no-action and certain exemption letters and other written communications.

(a) Except as provided in paragraphs (b) and (c) of this section, every letter or other written communication requesting the staff of the Commission to provide interpretative legal advice with respect to any statute administered by the Commission or any rule or regulation adopted thereunder; or requesting a statement that, on the basis of the facts stated in such letter or other communication, the staff would not recommend that the Commission take any enforcement action; or requesting an exemption, on the basis of the facts stated in such letter, from the provisions of the Securities Exchange Act of 1934 (15 U.S.C. 78a *et seq.*) or any rule or regulation thereunder, where the issuance of an order granting such exemption does not require public notice and an opportunity for hearing; together with any written response thereto, shall be made available for inspection and copying by any person as soon as practicable after the response has been sent or given to the person requesting it.

(b) Any person submitting such letter or other written communication may also submit therewith a request that it be accorded confidential treatment for a specified period of time, not exceeding 120 days from the date the response, together with a statement setting forth the considerations upon which the request for such treatment is based. If the staff determines that the request is reasonable and appropriate it will be granted and the letter or other communication will not be made available for public inspection or copying until the expiration of the specified period. If it appears to the staff that the request for confidential treatment should be denied, the staff shall so advise the person making the request and such person may withdraw the letter or other communication within 30 days thereafter. In such case, no response will be sent or given and the letter or other communication shall remain in the Commission's files but will not be made public. If such letter or other communication is not so withdrawn, it shall be deemed to be available for public inspection and copying together with any written response thereto.

Note: All letters or other written communications requesting interpretative advice, a no-action position, or an exemption shall indicate prominently, in a separate caption at the beginning of the request, each section of the Act and each rule to which the request relates. If more than one section or rule is involved, a separate copy of the request shall be submitted for each section or rule involved and an additional copy for the use of the staff of the Commission.

(c) This section shall not apply, however, to letters of comment or other communications relating to the accuracy or adequacy of any registration statement, report, proxy, or information statement or other document filed with the Commission, or relating to the extent to which such statement, report, or document complies with any applicable

第200.81节　解释函、无异议函、特定豁免函及其他书面通信的公布

(a)除本节第(b)款和第(c)款规定的情形外，请求证券交易委员会员工对证券交易委员会负责实施的制定法或在该制定法下通过的任何规则或规章提供解释性法律意见的每封信函或其他书面通信；或请求证券交易委员会员工说明不建议证券交易委员会采取任何执法行动的每封信函或其他书面通信(证券交易委员会员工应在该信函或书面通信中陈述其不建议采取执法行动所依据的事实)；或请求核准豁免适用《1934年证券交易法》(《美国法典》第十五编第78a节及其后条文)或其下任何规则或规章的每封信函或其他书面通信(该请求应基于信函中陈述的事实，且核准该等豁免的命令不必公告和提供听证机会即可签发)，其书面回复一经寄送或提供给请求人后，该等信函或其他通信及其回复即可供任何人查阅和复制。

(b)提交该等信函或其他书面通信的任何人也可以同时提交一份保密处理请求，要求核准在特定期限内对其提交的文件进行保密处理的请求，保密期不得超过收到回复之日起120日，同时应说明请求保密处理的原因。如果证券交易委员会员工判定该保密处理请求合理且适当，则应核准保密处理请求，在规定的保密期结束之前，该等信函或其他通信不会公开给公众查阅或复制。如果证券交易委员会员工认为应驳回保密处理请求，应将驳回决定通知请求人，请求人可在请求被拒后30日内撤回该等信函或通信。对于撤回的保密处理请求，证券交易委员会不会寄送或提供任何回复，且该等信函或通信应在证券交易委员会存档，但不应公之于众。如果该等信函或通信未被撤回，则该等信函或通信连同证券交易委员会对此作出的任何书面回复均将视为可供公众查阅和复制的资料。

注：所有请求提供解释性法律意见、请求说明证券交易委员会不采取行动的立场或请求豁免的信函或其他书面通信，应在请求书篇首显著位置单列标题注明该请求所涉之每一《证券法》条款和每一规则。如果涉及的条款或规则不止一个，应就所涉及的每一条款或每一规则分别提交请求书并另外提交一份复本供证券交易委员会员工使用。

(c)对于提交给证券交易委员会的任何注册说明书、报告、代理委托书或信息说明书或其他文件，本节不适用于与其准确度、充分性相关的意见函或其他通信，或者关于该等注册说明书、报告或文件对适用规定的符合程度的意见函或其他通信。此外，对于按照第240.24b-2节提交的与对证券交易委员会或任何交易所收到的公开披露提

requirement. Further, this section shall not apply to applications or other written communications filed pursuant to §240.24b–2 that relate to objections to public disclosure of information filed with the Commission or any exchange.

[35 FR 17779, Nov. 19, 1970, as amended at 53 FR 12413, Apr. 14, 1988; 53 FR 32605, Aug. 26, 1988]

§200.82 Public availability of materials filed pursuant to §240.14a–8(d) and related materials.

Materials filed with the Commission pursuant to Rule 14a–8(d) under the Securities Exchange Act of 1934 (17 CFR 240.14a–8(d)), written communications related thereto received from any person, and each related no–action letter or other written communication issued by the staff of the Commission, shall be made available to any person upon request for inspection or copying.

[37 FR 20558, Sept. 30, 1972]

§200.82a xxx

Link to an amendment published at 75 FR 56780, September 16, 2010.

The effective date of the above amendment was delayed until further notice at 75 FR 64641, October 20, 2010.

§200.83 Confidential treatment procedures under the Freedom of Information Act.

(a) *Purpose*. This section provides a procedure by which persons submitting information in any form to the Commission can request that the information not be disclosed pursuant to a request under the Freedom of Information Act, 5 U.S.C. 552. This section does not affect the Commission's right, authority, or obligation to disclose information in any other context. This section is procedural only and does not provide rights to any person or alter the rights of any person under the Freedom of Information Act or any other applicable statute or regulation.

(b) *Scope*. The provisions of this section shall apply only where no other statute or Commission rule provides procedures for requesting confidential treatment respecting particular categories of information (*see*, e.g., 17 CFR 240.24b–2) or where the Commission has not specified that an alternative procedure be utilized in connection with a particular study, report, investigation, or other matter. The provisions of this section shall not apply to any record which is contained in or is part of a personnel, medical or similar file relating to a Commission member or employee which would normally be exempt from disclosure pursuant to section 552(b)(6) of title 5, U.S. Code.

(c) *Written request for confidential treatment to be submitted with information.* (1) Any person who, either voluntarily or pursuant to any requirement of law, submits any information or causes or permits any information to be submitted to the Commission,

出的异议相关的申请或其他书面通信,亦不适用本节规定。

[《联邦公报》第35卷第17779页,1970年11月19日,修正索引:《联邦公报》第53卷第12413页,1988年4月14日;《联邦公报》第53卷第32605页,1988年8月26日。]

第200.82节　按照第240.14a-8(d)节提交的材料和相关材料的公开提供

按照依据《1934年证券交易法》[《联邦规章汇编》第十七编第240.14a-8(d)节]颁布的《14a-8(d)规则》向证券交易委员会提交的材料、从任何人处收到的与之相关的书面通信以及由证券交易委员会员工签发的每封相关不作为信函或其他书面通信均可提供给请求人查阅或复制。

[《联邦公报》第37卷第20558页,1972年9月30日。]

第200.82a节　xxx

链接至《联邦公报》第75卷第56780页发布的修正,2010年9月16日。

以上修正的生效日推迟至进一步公告发布之日,见《联邦公报》第75卷第64641页,2010年10月20日。

第200.83节　《信息自由法》规定的保密处理程序

(a)目的。本节规定了向证券交易委员会呈报任何形式信息的人可以在《信息自由法》(《美国法典》第五编第552节)下提出不披露请求的程序。本节不影响证券交易委员会在任何其他情境下披露信息的权利、权力和义务。本节仅为程序性规定,不为任何人创设权利,亦不改变任何人在《信息自由法》或任何其他适用制定法或规章下享有的权利。

(b)范围。本节规定仅适用于以下两种情况:其他制定法或证券交易委员会规则未针对请求以保密方式处理特定类别信息(如《联邦规章汇编》第十七编第240.24b-2节)的程序作出规定;证券交易委员会未明确规定对某一特别研究、报告、调查或其他事项采用替代程序。本节规定不适用于与某一证券交易委员会委员或雇员相关的人事、医疗或类似档案所包含的任何记录或作为该等档案一部分的记录,按照《美国法典》第五编第552(b)(6)节的规定这类记录通常可以豁免不予披露。

(c)连同信息一并呈报的保密处理请求书。(1)任何人如自愿或按任何法律要求向证券交易委员会呈报任何信息、促使或允许他人向证券交易委员会呈报信息,而该信息有权获得保密处理且不存在授予保密处理的其他特别程序,则该人可请求证券交

which information is entitled to confidential treatment and for which no other specific procedure exists for according confidential treatment, may request that the Commission afford confidential treatment under the Freedom of Information Act to such information for reasons of personal privacy or business confidentiality, or for any other reason permitted by Federal law, and should take all steps reasonably necessary to ensure, as nearly as practicable, that at the time the information is first received by the Commission (i) it is supplied segregated from information for which confidential treatment is not being requested, (ii) it is appropriately marked as confidential, and (iii) it is accompanied by a written request for confidential treatment which specifies the information as to which confidential treatment is requested.

(2) A person who submits a record to the Commission for which he or she seeks confidential treatment must clearly mark each page or segregable portion of each page with the words "Confidential Treatment Requested by [name]" and an identifying number and code, such as a Bates-stamped number. In his or her written confidential treatment request, the person must refer to the record by identifying number and code.

(3) In addition to giving a copy of any written request for confidential treatment to the Commission employee receiving the record in question, the person requesting confidential treatment must send a copy of the request (but not the record) by mail to the Office of Freedom of Information and Privacy Act Operations, SEC, 100 F Street, NE., Washington, D.C. 20549. The legend "FOIA Confidential Treatment Request" must clearly and prominently appear on the top of the first page of the written request, and the written request must contain the name, address, and telephone number of the person requesting confidential treatment. The person requesting confidential treatment is responsible for informing the Office of Freedom of Information and Privacy Act Operations promptly of any changes in address, telephone number, or representation.

(4) In some circumstances, such as when a person is testifying in the course of a Commission investigation or providing a record requested in the course of a Commission examination or inspection, it may be impracticable to submit a written request for confidential treatment at the time the record is first given to the Commission. In no circumstances can the need to comply with the requirements of this section justify or excuse any delay in submitting any record to the Commission. The person testifying or otherwise submitting the record must inform the Commission employee receiving it, at the time the record is submitted or as soon thereafter as possible, that he or she is requesting confidential treatment. The person must then submit a written confidential treatment request within 30 days from the date of the testimony or the submission of the record. Any confidential treatment request submitted under this paragraph must also comply with paragraph (c)(3) of this section.

易委员会出于个人隐私保护或商业保密性考虑,或出于联邦法律允许的任何其他原因之考虑,对信息授予《信息保护法》所规定的保密处理,并应采取所有合理必要措施尽量确保证券交易委员会首次收到该信息之时,该信息:(i)已经与未请求保密处理的信息相隔离;(ii)已适当地标记为保密信息;且(iii)附有一份保密处理请求书,该请求书应明确说明请求予以保密处理的信息。

(2)向证券交易委员会呈报记录并申请保密处理的人,须在每一页或在每一页的独立部分清晰标明“[姓名/名称]请求保密处理”字样和一个识别号码和编码,如贝茨编号。在其保密处理请求书中,请求人必须使用识别号码或编码指代保密记录。

(3)保密处理请求人应向证券交易委员会接收请求保密处理所涉记录的员工提交一份保密处理请求书,除此之外,还必须将一份请求(而非所涉记录本身)寄至信息自由和隐私法管理办公室,地址:美国证券交易委员会,华盛顿哥伦比亚特区东北分区100F大街,邮编:D.C.20549。请求人必须在请求书首页顶端清晰显著地标明“《信息自由和隐私法》保密处理请求”字样,且请求书必须包含保密处理请求人的姓名、地址和电话号码。保密处理请求人的地址、电话号码或代表人发生任何变更的,有责任及时通知信息自由和隐私法管理办公室。

(4)在某些情况下,如某人正在证券交易委员会调查程序中作证或正在按要求提供某一记录以供证券交易委员会核查或检查,在首次向证券交易委员会呈报记录之时即一并提交保密处理请求书可能不具备实际可行性。然而,在任何情况下均不得以本节规定作为拖延向证券交易委员会呈报任何记录的解释或借口。因作证或其他情况而呈报记录的人,须在呈报记录之时或呈报记录之后的最短时间内,通知证券交易委员会接收记录的员工其正在提交保密处理请求。该人应于作证或呈报记录之日起30日内提交一份保密处理请求书。根据本款呈报的任何保密处理请求还须符合本节第(c)(3)款的规定。

(5) Where confidential treatment is requested by the submitter on behalf of another person, the request must identify that person and provide the telephone number and address of that person or the person's responsible representative if the submitter would be unable to provide prompt substantiation of the request at the appropriate time.

(6) No determination on a request for confidential treatment will be made until the Office of Freedom of Information and Privacy Act Operations receives a request for disclosure of the record.

(7) A confidential treatment request will expire ten years from the date the Office of Freedom of Information and Privacy Act Operations receives it, unless that Office receives a renewal request before the confidential treatment request expires. The renewal request must be sent by mail to the Office of Freedom of Information and Privacy Act Operations, SEC, 100 F Street, NE., Washington, D.C. 20549, and must clearly identify the record for which confidential treatment is sought. A renewal request will likewise expire ten years from the date that Office receives it, unless that Office receives another timely renewal request which complies with the requirements of this paragraph.

(8) A confidential treatment request shall be nonpublic. If an action is filed in a Federal court, however, by either the Freedom of Information requester (under 5 U.S.C. 552(a)(4) and §200.80(d)(6)) or by the confidential treatment requester (under paragraph (e)(5) of this section), the confidential treatment request may become part of the court record.

(d) *Substantiation of request for confidential treatment.* (1) If it is determined that records which are the subject of a request for access under the Freedom of Information Act are also the subject of a request for confidential treatment under this rule and no other grounds appear to exist which would justify the withholding of the records [e.g., Freedom of Information Act Exemption 7(A), 5 U.S.C. 552(b)(7)(A)], the Commission's Freedom of Information Act Officer promptly shall so inform the person requesting confidential treatment or, in the case of a request made on behalf of a person other than the submitter, the person identified as able to provide substantiation, by telephone, facsimile or certified mail and require that substantiation of the request for confidential treatment be submitted in ten calendar days. Failure to submit a written substantiation within ten calendar days from the time of notification, or any extension thereof, may be deemed a waiver of the confidential treatment request and the confidential treatment requester's right to appeal an initial decision denying confidential treatment to the Commission's General Counsel as permitted by paragraph (e) of this section.

(2) Substantiation of a request for confidential treatment shall consist of a statement setting forth, to the extent appropriate or necessary for the determination of the request for confidential treatment, the following information regarding the request:

(5)代表他人呈报保密处理请求的,如果呈报人不能在适当时间迅速提供关于保密理由的说明,则须在请求书上注明被代表之人,并提供被代表之人或其负责人的电话号码和地址。

(6)信息自由和隐私法管理办公室收到相关记录的披露请求之前,不会对保密处理请求作出判定。

(7)保密处理请求的有效期为信息自由和隐私法管理办公室收到请求之日后10年,但该办公室在保密处理请求到期前收到续展请求的,该期限可以延长。续展请求须通过邮件寄送至信息自由和隐私法管理办公室,地址:美国证券交易委员会,华盛顿哥伦比亚特区东北分区100F大街,邮编:D.C.20549。续展请求必须明确指明请求予以保密处理的记录。续展请求也相应地于该管理办公室收到续展请求之日起10年后到期,但该办公室收到另一份及时提交的符合本款规定的续展请求的,该期限同样可以延长。

(8)保密处理请求不应公开。但是,如果[《美国法典》第五编第552(a)(4)节和第200.80(d)(6)节中的《信息自由法》请求人或本节第(e)(5)款中的保密处理请求人]在联邦法院提起诉讼的,保密信息请求可以纳入法院记录。

(d)保密理由。(1)如果根据《信息安全法》判定,《信息安全法》下被请求查询的记录同时也是本规则下被请求予以保密处理的记录,且从表面判断并不存在其他可以据不提供记录的理由[如《信息安全法》的7(A)豁免,《美国法典》第五编第552(b)(7)(A)节],则证券交易委员会的信息自由法官员应通过电话、传真或挂号信将上述情形及时通知保密处理请求人,如果请求由他人代为呈报,则应通知请求材料中注明的能提供保密理由的人,并要求其于10个日历日内提交关于保密理由的材料。未在通知后10个日历日内或任何续展期限内呈报书面证明材料的,可以被视为放弃保密处理请求,同时还可能被视为放弃本节第(e)款赋予保密处理请求人的复议申请权,即针对驳回保密处理请求的初步决定向证券交易委员会首席律师提起行政复议的权利。

(2)保密理由材料应包含一份说明,阐述对保密处理请求作出判定所需的与请求相关的如下适当及必要的信息:

(i) The reasons, concisely stated and referring to specific exemptive provisions of the Freedom of Information Act, why the information should be withheld from access under the Freedom of Information Act;

(ii) The applicability of any specific statutory or regulatory provisions which govern or may govern the treatment of the information;

(iii) The existence and applicability of any prior determinations by the Commission, other Federal agencies, or a court, concerning confidential treatment of the information;

(iv) The adverse consequences to a business enterprise, financial or otherwise, that would result from disclosure of confidential commercial or financial information, including any adverse effect on the business' competitive position;

(v) The measures taken by the business to protect the confidentiality of the commercial or financial information in question and of similar information, prior to, and after, its submission to the Commission;

(vi) The ease or difficulty of a competitor's obtaining or compiling the commercial or financial information;

(vii) Whether the commercial or financial information was voluntarily submitted to the Commission and, if so, whether and how disclosure of the information would tend to impede the availability of similar information to the Commission;

(viii) The extent, if any, to which portions of the substantiation of the request for confidential treatment should be afforded confidential treatment; and

(ix) Such additional facts and such legal and other authorities as the requesting person may consider appropriate.

(e) *Appeal from initial determination that confidential treatment is not warranted.* (1) In a preliminary decision, which shall be sent by mail or facsimile, or both, the Office of Freedom of Information and Privacy Act Operations will inform the confidential treatment requester whether it intends to grant confidentiality in whole or in part and give the requester ten calendar days from the date of the preliminary decision to submit supplemental arguments if the requester disagrees with the preliminary decision. A final decision, which shall also be sent by mail or facsimile, or both, no sooner than ten calendar days from the date of the preliminary decision, shall inform the Freedom of Information Act requester and the confidential treatment requester of his or her right to appeal an adverse decision to the Commission's General Counsel within ten calendar days from the date of the final decision. Records, which the Freedom of Information and Privacy Act Officer determines to be releasable, may be released to the Freedom of Information Act requester ten calendar days after the date of the final decision. However, if within those ten calendar days, the Freedom of Information and Privacy Act Officer receives an appeal from the confidential treatment requester, he or she shall inform the

(i)对于根据《信息安全法》信息不应开放给公众查阅的理由的简要说明,该说明应援引《信息安全法》特定豁免条款;

(ii)任何规制或可能规制信息处理的特定法律或规章条款的适用性;

(iii)证券交易委员会、其他联邦机构或法院之前已就该信息保密处理作出决定的事实及该决定的适用性;

(iv) 披露商业和财务保密信息是否会对金融企业或其他性质的企业带来不利后果,包括是否会对企业的竞争地位造成任何不利影响;

(v)企业向证券交易委员会提交该商业或财务信息以及类似信息之前和之后采取的对该信息的保密措施;

(vi)竞争对手获取或编纂该商业或财务信息的难易程度;

(vii)该商业或财务信息是否为自愿提交给证券交易委员会,如果是,披露该等信息是否以及将以何种方式阻碍证券交易委员会获得类似信息;

(viii)保密理由材料应给予保密处理的部分和范围(如有);及

(ix)请求人可能认为适当的其他事实、法律依据和其他依据。

(e)针对不授予保密处理的初步决定提起的行政复议申请。(1)在通过信函或传真或两者同时发出的初步决定中,信息自由和隐私法管理办公室将通知保密处理请求人其是否有意核准进行全部或部分保密处理,请求人不同意该初步决定的,可在初步决定作出之后10个日历日内呈报补充论证。最终决定至少应于初步决定作出后10个日历日后通过信函、传真或两者同时发出,并应告知信息自由法请求人和保密处理请求人,如决定对其不利,其有权于最终决定作出后10个日历日内向证券交易委员会首席律师申请行政复议。被信息自由和隐私法官员判定为可以发布的记录,可于最终裁定作出后10个日历日后向信息自由法请求人发布。但是,如果在上述10日的期间内信息自由和隐私法官员收到保密处理请求人的行政复议申请,信息自由和隐私法官员应告知信息自由法请求人行政复议未决期间不会发布记录。

Freedom of Information Act requester that an appeal is pending and that the records will not be released until the appeal is resolved.

(2) Any appeal of a denial of a request for confidential treatment shall be in writing, and shall be clearly and prominently identified on the envelope or other cover and at the top of the first page by the legend "FOIA Confidential Treatment Appeal." The appeal must be sent by mail to the Office of Freedom of Information and Privacy Act Operations, SEC, 100 F Street, NE., Washington, D.C. 20549, or by facsimile (202-772-9337). A copy of the appeal must be mailed to the General Counsel, Securities and Exchange Commission, 100 F Street, NE., Washington, D.C. 20549. The person requesting confidential treatment may supply additional substantiation of the request for confidential treatment in connection with the appeal to the General Counsel.

(3) The General Counsel shall have the authority to consider all appeals from decisions of the Freedom of Information Act Officer with respect to confidential treatment. All appeals taken under this section will be considered by the General Counsel as expeditiously as circumstances permit. Although other procedures may be employed, to the extent possible, the General Counsel will decide the matter on the basis of the affidavits and other documentary evidence submitted by the interested persons and such other information as is brought to the attention of the General Counsel. The General Counsel shall also have the authority to enter and vacate stays under the circumstances set forth in paragraph (e)(5) of this section. In appropriate cases the General Counsel may, in his or her sole and unfettered discretion, refer appeals and questions concerning stays under paragraph (e)(5) of this section to the Commission for decision.

(4) If it is determined that confidential treatment is not warranted with respect to all or any part of the information in question, the person requesting confidential treatment will be so informed by telephone, if possible, with a facsimile or certified mail letter directed to the person's last known address. Disclosure of the information under the Freedom of Information Act will occur ten calendar days after notice to the person requesting confidential treatment, subject to any stay entered pursuant to paragraph (e)(5) of this section.

(5) If within that ten calendar day period the General Counsel has been notified that the person requesting confidential treatment has commenced an action in a Federal court concerning the determination to make such information publicly available, the General Counsel will stay making the public disclosure of the information pending final judicial resolution of the matter. The General Counsel may vacate a stay under this section either on his or her own motion or at the request of a person seeking access to the information under the Freedom of Information Act. If the stay is vacated, the information will be released under the Freedom of Information Act ten calendar days after the person

(2)任何针对保密处理请求驳回决定提起的行政复议申请均应以书面形式作出,且应清晰显著地在信封或其他封面以及首页顶端标明“《信息自由法》保密处理行政复议申请”字样。行政复议申请须通过信函寄至信息自由和隐私法管理办公室,地址:美国证券交易委员会,华盛顿哥伦比亚特区东北分区100F大街,邮编:D.C.20549;或传真至(202-772-9337)。行政复议申请书应邮寄一份给证券交易委员会首席律师,地址:美国证券交易委员会,华盛顿哥伦比亚特区东北分区100F大街,邮编:D.C.20549。保密处理请求人可以向首席律师提供与行政复议申请相关的补充保密理由材料。

(3)首席律师有权审议针对请求人信息自由法官员的保密处理决定提出的所有行政复议申请。根据本节规定提起的行政复议申请应由首席律师在情况允许的最短时间内进行审议。虽然也可以采用其他程序,但是首席律师应尽可能地根据宣誓书面证词和利害关系人呈报的其他书证以及向首席律师提交的其他信息作出决定。在本节第(e)(5)款所述情形下,首席律师还有权签发或取消中止令。在适当情形下,首席律师可独立不受约束地行使自由裁量权,自行决定将与本节第(e)(5)款中的中止令相关的行政复议申请和问题提请证券交易委员会作出决定。

(4)如果证券交易委员会决定不核准对全部或任何部分所涉信息的保密处理请求,应通过电话通知保密处理请求人,如有可能,还应同时通过传真或挂号信将通知寄至所知的请求人最新地址。根据《信息自由法》进行的信息披露应于向保密处理请求人发出通知的10个日历日后进行,但已根据本节第(e)(5)款签发任何中止令的除外。

(5)如果在上述10个日历日的期间内,首席律师接到通知表明保密处理请求人已就公开提供信息的决定向联邦法院提起诉讼的,应在联邦法院作出最终司法判决之前中止信息的公开披露。首席律师可在本条规定下主动或根据依《信息自由法》要求查询信息之人的请求撤销中止令。除非法院另有命令,否则中止令被撤销的情况下,信息将根据《信息自由法》的规定发布,发布时间为以电话形式将信息发布行动告知保密处理请求人(如有可能,应同时通过传真或挂号信通知保密处理请求人)10个日历日后,传真或挂号信应发至所知的请求人最新地址。

requesting confidential treatment is notified of this action by telephone, if possible, with a facsimile or certified mail letter sent to the person's last known address, unless the court orders otherwise.

(f) *Initial determination that confidential treatment is warranted.* If it is determined by the Commission's Freedom of Information Act Officer that confidential treatment is warranted, the person submitting the information and the person requesting access to the information under the Freedom of Information Act will be so informed by mail. The person requesting access, pursuant to the Freedom of Information Act, will also be informed of the right to appeal the determination to the General Counsel. Any such appeal must be taken in accordance with the provisions of the Freedom of Information Act and Commission rules thereunder. *See* 17 CFR 200.80(d)(6).

(g) *Confidential treatment request and substantiation as nonpublic.* Any confidential treatment request and substantiation of it shall be nonpublic. If an action is filed in a Federal court, however, by either the Freedom of Information Act requester (under 5 U.S.C. 552(a)(4) and §200.80(d)(6)) or by the confidential treatment requester (under paragraph (e)(5) of this section), both request and substantiation may become part of the public court record.

(h) *Effect of no prior request for confidentiality.* (1) If access is requested under the Freedom of Information Act to information which is submitted to the Commission on or after October 20, 1980 with respect to which no request for confidential treatment has been made pursuant to either paragraph (c)(1) or (c)(5) of this section, it will be presumed that the submitter of the information has waived any interest in asserting an exemption from disclosure under the Freedom of Information Act for reasons of personal privacy or business confidentiality, or for other reasons.

(2) Notwithstanding paragraph (h)(1) of this section, in appropriate circumstances, any person who would be affected by the public disclosure of information under the Freedom of Information Act may be contacted by Commission personnel to determine whether the person desires to make a request for confidential treatment. Any request for confidential treatment that is asserted in response to such inquiry shall be made in accordance with provisions of this section.

(i) *Extensions of time limits.* Any time limit under this section may be extended in the discretion of the Commission, the Commission's General Counsel, or the Commission's Freedom of Information Act Officer for good cause shown.

(j) *Electronic filings.* Confidential treatment requests shall be submitted in paper format only, whether or not the person making the request is an electronic filer.

(k) In their discretion, the Commission, the Commission's General Counsel, and the Freedom of Information Act Officer may use alternative procedures for considering

(f)授予保密处理的初步决定。如果证券交易委员会的信息自由法官员决定授予保密处理,应将该决定邮递给信息呈报人以及依《信息自由法》请求查询该信息之人。另外,信息自由法官员还应通知依《信息自由法》请求查询该信息之人,其有权就该决定向首席律师提出行政复议申请。任何该等行政复议申请均须根据《信息自由法》的条款和依据该法颁布的证券交易委员会规则作出。见《联邦规章汇编》第十七编第200.80(d)(6)节。

(g)保密处理请求和理由不应公开。任何保密处理请求及保密理由材料均不应公开。但是,如果信息自由法请求人根据《美国法典》第五编第552(a)(4)节和第200.80(d)(6)节或保密处理请求人根据本节第(e)(5)款在联邦法院提起诉讼,保密信息请求及保密理由材料均可能纳入法院公开记录。

(h)未事先请求保密处理的后果。(1)1980年10月20日当日及此后呈报给证券交易委员会的信息,如果依《信息自由法》被提出查询请求,但未按本节第(c)(1)款或第(c)(5)款被提出保密处理请求,则应被推定为:信息呈报人已经放弃以个人隐私或商业保密或其他原因为由请求豁免《信息自由法》的信息披露的任何权利主张。

(2)无论本节第(h)(1)款如何规定,在适当情况下,证券交易委员会工作人员可以联系受《信息自由法》中的信息公开披露影响的任何人,以判定该人是否希望提出保密处理请求。收到此等询问后提出的任何保密处理请求,均应根据本节规定作出。

(i)时限的延长。在提出充分理由的情况下,证券交易委员会、证券交易委员会首席律师、证券交易委员会信息自由法官员依其自由裁量权自行决定延长本节规定的任何时限。

(j)电子文件提交。保密处理请求仅得以纸版形式呈报,无论请求人是否为电子文件提交人。

(k)证券交易委员会、证券交易委员会首席律师、证券交易委员会信息自由法官员可依其自由裁量权决定采用替代程序审议保密处理请求。

requests for confidential treatment.

[45 FR 62421, Sept. 19, 1980, as amended at 47 FR 20289, May 12, 1982; 58 FR 14659, Mar. 18, 1993; 65 FR 55184, 55185, Sept. 13, 2000; 73 FR 32225, June 5, 2008]

Subpart E [Reserved]

Subpart F—Code of Behavior Governing Ex Parte Communications Between Persons Outside the Commission and Decisional Employees

Authority: 15 U.S.C. 77s, 78w, 79t, 77sss, 80a-37, 80b-11, and 7202; and 5 U.S.C. 557.

§200.110 Purpose.

This code is adopted in conformity with section 4 of the Government in the Sunshine Act, Pub. L. 94-409, and is designed to insulate the administrative process from improper influence.

[42 FR 14690, Mar. 16, 1977]

§200.111 Prohibitions; application; definitions.

(a) *Prohibited communications*. In any agency proceeding which is subject to this subpart, except to the extent required for the disposition of ex parte matters as authorized by law:

(1) No interested person outside the agency shall make or knowingly cause to be made to any member of the Commission or decisional employee an ex parte communication relevant to the merits of the proceeding; and

(2) No member of the Commission or decisional employee shall make or knowingly cause to be made to any interested person outside the agency an ex parte communication relevant to the merits of the proceeding.

(b) *Proceedings to which prohibitions apply*. This subpart shall apply to all proceedings subject to 5 U.S.C. 557 (a), including suspension proceedings instituted pursuant to the provisions of Regulations A, B, E, and F of the Securities Act of 1933 (§230.251 *et seq.* of this chapter), all review proceedings instituted pursuant to section 19 (g) of the Securities Exchange Act of 1934, and all other proceedings where an

[《联邦公报》第45卷第62421页,1980年9月19日,修正索引:《联邦公报》第47卷第20289页,1982年5月12日;《联邦公报》第58卷第14659页,1993年3月18日;《联邦公报》第65卷第55184页、第55185页,2000年9月13日;《联邦公报》第73卷第32225页,2008年6月5日。]

第E子部分 [保　　留]

第F子部分——规制证券交易委员会外部主体和内部有决策权的雇员之间的单方交流的行为准则

法律依据:《美国法典》第十五编第77s节、第78w节、第79t节、第77sss节、第80a-37节、第80b-11节和第7202节;以及《美国法典》第五编第557节。

第200.110节　目的

本准则的通过符合《政府阳光法》第4条(公法编号94-409),目的是确保行政程序不受不当影响。

[《联邦公报》第42卷第14690页,1977年3月16日。]

第200.111节　禁止;申请;定义

(a)禁止交流。就受制于本子部分规定的任何证券交易委员会程序而言,除非法律准许且为处置单方事项所需:

(1)机构外的利害关系人不得向证券交易委员会的任何委员或有决策权的雇员就行政处理程序的实质内容进行或在知情情况下促使他人进行单方交流。

(2)证券交易委员会的任何委员或有决策权的雇员不得向机构外的任何利害关系人就行政处理程序的实质内容进行或在知情情况下促使他人进行单方交流。

(b)适用禁止单方交流规定的行政处理程序。本子部分规定适用于所有受制于《美国法典》第五编第557(a)节的程序,包括按照依据《1933年证券法》(本章第230.251节及其后条文)颁发的《A管理办法》、《B管理办法》、《E管理办法》和《F管理办法》的规定发起的暂停程序、依据《1934年证券交易法》第19(g)条发起的所有审查程序,以及根据证券交易委员会的制定法条款或规则下令召开取证听证且证券交易委员会须根据

evidentiary hearing has been ordered pursuant to a statutory provision or rule of the Commission and where the action of the Commission must be taken on the basis of an evidentiary record. In addition, this subpart shall apply to any other proceeding in which the Commission so orders.

(c) *Period during which prohibitions apply.* (1) The prohibitions in §200.111(a) shall begin to apply when the Commission issues an order for hearing; *Provided,*

(i) That in suspension proceedings pursuant to Regulations A, B, E and F of the Securities Act of 1933 (§230.251 *et seq.* of this chapter), these prohibitions shall commence when the Commission enters an order temporarily suspending the exemption; and

(ii) That in proceedings under section 19(d) of the Securities Exchange Act of 1934, 15 U.S.C. 78s(d), these prohibitions shall commence at the time that a copy of an application for review has been filed with the Commission and served on the self-regulatory organization.

(iii) That in proceedings under Title I of the Sarbanes-Oxley Act of 2002, 15 U.S.C. 7211-7219, these prohibitions shall commence at the time that a copy of an application for review has been filed with the Commission and served on the Public Company Accounting Oversight Board; and

(iv) In no case shall the prohibitions in §200.111(a) begin to apply later than the time at which a proceeding is noticed for hearing unless the person responsible for the communication has knowledge that it will be noticed, in which case the prohibitions shall apply beginning at the time of his or her acquisition of such knowledge.

(2) The prohibitions in §200.111(a) shall continue until the time to file a petition for rehearing from the final order of the Commission has expired. In the event a petition for rehearing is filed, these prohibitions shall cease if and when the petition for rehearing is denied.

(3) The Commission may, by specific order entered in a particular proceeding, determine that these prohibitions shall commence from some date earlier than the time specified in this paragraph (c) or shall continue until a date subsequent to the time specified herein.

(d) *Definitions.* As used in this subpart:

(1) *Ex parte communication* means an oral or written communication not on the public record with respect to which reasonable prior notice to all participants to the proceeding is not given, but it shall not include requests for status reports on any matter or proceeding. In addition, an ex parte communication shall not include:

(i) Any written communication of which copies are served by the communicator contemporaneously with the transmittal of the communication in accordance with

证据性记录方能采取行动的所有其他程序。另外,对于证券交易委员会特别发布命令,指定适用本子部分规定的所有其他行政处理程序,亦应适用本子部分规定。

(c)禁止单方交流规定的期限。(1)第200.111(a)节规定的禁止单方交流规定应于证券交易委员会签发听证令之时开始实施;但是:

(i)在按照依据《1933年证券法》颁发的《A管理办法》、《B管理办法》、《E管理办法》和《F管理办法》发起的暂停程序(本章的第230.251节及其后条文)中,应于证券交易委员会签发临时暂停豁免令之时开始禁止单方交流;且

(ii)在根据《1934年证券交易法》第19(d)条[《美国法典》第十五编第78s(d)节]发起的程序中,应于审查申请提交给证券交易委员会并送达自律机构之时开始禁止单方交流;

(iii)在根据《2002年萨班斯—奥克斯利法》第一编(《美国法典》第十五编第7211—7219节)发起的行政处理程序中,应于审查申请提交给证券交易委员会并送达美国公众公司会计监督委员会之时开始禁止单方交流;且

(iv)任何情况下,第200.111(a)节规定的禁止单方交流的实施时间不得晚于听证通知发出之时,但是负责交流之人如知晓将会发出听证通知,则自其获知之时即应被禁止进行单方交流。

(2)证券交易委员会签发最终命令后,在当事人提请再次举行听证的时限到期前将继续适用第200.111(a)节关于禁止单方交流的规定。当事人提请再次召开听证的请求被驳回的,则将停止禁止单方交流规定的适用。

(3)证券交易委员会可以在特定程序中签发明确命令,指明单方交流禁止规定应于本节第(c)款规定的时间之前的某一日期开始实施,或应持续生效直至本节第(c)款规定日期之后的某一日期。

(d)定义。以下词语在本子部分中的含义如下:

(1)“单方交流”系指没有纳入公开记录且没有合理提前通知所有程序参与人的口头或书面交流,但不应包括为获得任何事项或行政处理程序的现状报告所提出的请求。此外,单方交流不应包括:

(i)在根据《证券交易委员会工作规则》的《150规则》(本章第201.150节)传送任何通信的同时,向所有程序参与人(包括证券交易委员会的利害关系部门或办公室)抄

requirements of Rule 150 of the Commission's Rules of Practice, §201.150 of this chapter, upon all participants to the proceeding (including the interested Division or Office of the Commission); or

(ii) Any oral communication where 48 hours advance written notice is given to all participants to the proceeding (including the interested division of the Commission).

(2) *Participants to the proceeding* means all parties to the proceeding (including the interested Division or Office of the Commission) and any other persons who have been granted limited participation pursuant to the provisions of Rule 210(c) of the Commission's Rules of Practice, §201.210(c) of this chapter.

(3) *Decisional employee* means: (i) The administrative law judge assigned to the proceeding in question; and

(ii) All members of the staff of the Office of Opinions and Review; and

(iii) The legal and executive assistants to members of the Commission; and

(iv) Any employee of the Commission who has been specifically named by order of the administrative law judge or the Commission in the proceeding to assist thereafter in making or recommending a particular decision; and

(v) Any other employee of the Commission who is, or may reasonably be expected to be, involved in the decisional process of the proceeding.

[42 FR 14690, Mar. 16, 1977, as amended at 60 FR 32795, June 23, 1995; 69 FR 13175, Mar. 19, 2004]

§200.112 Duties of recipient; notice to participants.

(a) *Duties of recipient.* A member of the Commission or decisional employee who receives, or who make or knowingly causes to be made, a communication prohibited by this section, or who receives or makes a communication which he or she concludes should, in fairness, be brought to the attention of all participants to the proceeding, shall transmit to the Commission's Secretary, who shall place on the public record of the proceeding:

(1) All such written communications; and

(2) Memoranda stating the substance of all such oral communications; and

(3) All written responses, and memoranda stating the substance of all oral responses, to the materials described in paragraphs (a)(1) and (2) of this section.

(b) *Notice to participants.* The Secretary shall send copies of the communication to all participants to the proceeding with respect to which it was made, and shall notify the communicator of the provisions of this code prohibiting ex parte communications. If the communications are from persons other than participants to the proceedings or their agents, and the Secretary determines that it would be too burdensome to send copies of the communications to all participants because: (1) The communications are so

送的书面通信;或

(ii)提前48小时向所有程序参与人(包括证券交易委员会的利害关系部门或办公室)发送过书面通知的任何口头交流。

(2)“程序参与人”指程序的所有当事人(包括证券交易委员会的利害关系部门或办公室)和按照《证券交易委员会工作规则》的《210(c)规则》[本章第201.210(c)节]被授予有限参与权的任何其他人。

(3)“有决策权的雇员”系指:(i)为相关程序指定的行政法法官;和

(ii)意见与审查办公室的所有员工;和

(iii)证券交易委员会委员的法律助理和执行助理;和

(iv)行政法法官或证券交易委员会在程序中发布命令明确指定协助其作出具体决定或提供建议的任何证券交易委员会雇员;和

(v)程序决策过程中涉及的或据合理预期将涉及的任何其他证券交易委员会雇员。

[《联邦公报》第42卷第14690页,1977年3月16日,修正索引:《联邦公报》第60卷第32795页,1995年6月23日;《联邦公报》第69卷第13175页,2004年3月19日。]

第200.112节　接收方的责任;向程序参与人发出通知

(a)接收方的责任。证券交易委员会委员或有决策权的雇员如果收到本节禁止的交流信息,或作出或在知情情况下促使他人进行该等交流,或者,收到或发出其公平地认定应提请所有程序参与人注意的交流信息,应将该等信息转交证券交易委员会秘书。证券交易委员会秘书应将下述材料纳入程序的公开记录:

(1)所有上述书面交流信息;和

(2)说明上述口头交流内容的备忘录;和

(3)对本节第(a)(1)款和第(2)款所述材料作出的所有书面回复,和说明所有口头回复实质内容的备忘录。

(b)向程序参与人发出通知。证券交易委员会秘书应将交流信息发送给所涉程序的全体参与人,并应将本准则中关于禁止单方交流的条款告知交流信息发出人。程序参与人或其代理人以外的主体发出的交流信息,如证券交易委员会秘书判定由于:(1)交流信息篇幅过长,或(2)交流信息内容与程序争点的相关性较弱,或(3)程序参与人数量过多等原因,导致向所有程序参与人发送交流信息的工作过于繁重,则证券交易委员会秘书可以改而通知程序参与人其已收到该等交流信息、将其存档且程序

voluminous, or (2) the communications are of such borderline relevance to the issues of the proceedings, or (3) the participants to the proceeding are so numerous, the Secretary may, instead, notify the participants that the communications have been received, placed in the file, and are available for examination.

(c) *Post decisional communications.* Any Commission member or decisional employee who receives a communication which would be prohibited by this Code, but for the fact that it was received subsequent to the date when the prohibitions imposed hereby have ceased to apply, shall comply with the provisions of §200.112(a) with respect to such communication in the event that he or she is to act in a decisional capacity in the same proceeding pursuant to remand where he or she concludes, in fairness, that such communication should be brought to the attention of all participants to the proceeding.

[42 FR 14691 Mar. 16, 1977]

§200.113 Opportunity to respond; interception.

(a) *Opportunity to respond.* All participants to a proceeding may respond to any allegations or contentions contained in a prohibited ex parte communication placed in the public record in accordance with §200.112. Such responses shall be included in the public record.

(b) *Interception of communications.* All written communications addressed to the Commission respecting a proceeding will be deemed to be communications to the staff of the interested division and will be directed to that division by the Commission's mail room. A Commission member or decisional employee may instruct any of his assistants who are nondecisional employees to intercept any communication directed to him which might appear to violate this Code and authorize them either to transmit any such written communication to the staff of the interested division of the Commission, if it appears from the contents of the communication that the intent of the sender is consistent with such action, or to return the communication to the sender.

[28 FR 4447, May 3, 1963, as amended at 42 FR 14691, Mar. 16, 1977]

§200.114 Sanctions.

(a) *Discipline of persons practicing before the Commission.* The Commission may, to the extent not prohibited by law, censure, suspend, or revoke the privilege to practice before it of any person who makes, or solicits the making of, an unauthorized ex parte communication.

(b) *Adverse action on claim.* Upon receipt of a communication knowingly made or knowingly caused to be made by a party in violation of this subpart, the Commission, administrative law judge, or other employee presiding at the hearing may, to the extent consistent with the interests of justice and the policy of the underlying statutes, require

参与人可自行查阅该等交流信息。

(c)决策作出之后的交流。任何证券交易委员会委员或有决策权的雇员收到本应被本《准则》禁止的交流信息,但收到时本《准则》施加的禁止单方交流规定已停止实施的,该证券交易委员会委员或有决策权的雇员如果对被发回的同一程序有决策权且公平地得出该交流信息应提请所有程序参与人注意的结论,则其应遵守第200.112(a)节与该等交流信息相关的规定。

[《联邦公报》第42卷第14691页,1977年3月16日。]

第200.113节　答复机会;拦截

(a)答复机会。所有程序参与人均可就根据第200.112节纳入公开记录的任何被禁止的单方交流中的任何指控或论点作出答复。此等答复应纳入公开记录之中。

(b)交流拦截。向证券交易委员会发出的与某一程序相关的所有书面通信均应视为向利害关系部门员工发出的通信,应由证券交易委员会收发室分发给该部门。证券交易委员会委员或有决策权的雇员可以命令其任何助理(没有决策权的雇员)拦截分发给自己的其认为违反本《准则》的任何通信,并授权其助理将任何该等书面通信传发给证券交易委员会利害关系部门的雇员(若从通信的内容初步判断发送人的意图与此一致),或授权其助理将通信退回发信人。

[《联邦公报》第28卷第4447页,1963年5月3日,修正索引:《联邦公报》第42卷第14691页,1977年3月16日。]

第200.114节　罚则

(a)对在证券交易委员会办理业务的主体的纪律处罚。在证券交易委员会办理业务的任何主体,如果作出或怂恿他人作出未获授权的单方交流,证券交易委员会可以在法律不禁止的范围内予以谴责,或暂停或撤销其办理业务的资格。

(b)就权利主张采取的不利行动。一旦收到一方在知情情况下作出的或促使他人作出的违反本子部分规定的交流,证券交易委员会、行政法法官或主持听证的其他证券交易委员会雇员可以在符合司法利益和相关制定法立法目的的范围内,要求该方陈述其在程序中的权利主张或利益应予受理、不应驳回或被忽视的理由,或者不应因

the party to show cause why his claim or interest in the proceeding should not be dismissed, denied, disregarded, or otherwise adversely affected on account of such violation.

(c) *Discipline of Commission employees.* The Commission may censure, suspend, or dismiss any Commission employee who violates the prohibitions or requirements of this Code.

[28 FR 4447, May 3, 1963, as amended at 42 FR 14691, Mar. 16, 1977]

Subpart G—Plan of Organization and Operation Effective During Emergency Conditions

Authority: 15 U.S.C. 77s, 78d, 78d-1, 78w, 77sss, 80a-37, 80b-11; Reorganization Plan No. 10 of 1950 (15 U.S.C. 78d nt).

Source: 28 FR 6970, July 9, 1963, unless otherwise noted.

§200.200 Purpose.

This subpart describes the plan of organization and operation which will be observed by the Securities and Exchange Commission in discharging its duties and responsibilities in the event of emergency conditions as defined in the following section.

[28 FR 6970, July 9, 1963, as amended at 71 FR 33386, June 9, 2006; 71 FR 35730, June 21, 2006]

§200.201 General provisions.

(a) For purpose of this subpart, a person shall be considered unavailable or incapacitated in any situation and from any cause that prevents the person from assuming or performing on a timely basis his or her authorized duties, roles, or responsibilities of office, whether from a primary or alternate facility, or any other location.

(b) For purpose of this subpart, emergency conditions shall be deemed to commence upon the occurrence, or the imminent threat of the occurrence, of a natural or man-made disturbance, including, but not limited to, an armed attack against the United States, its territories or possessions, terrorist attack, civil disturbance, fire, pandemic, hurricane, or flood, that results in, or threatens imminently to result in, a substantial disruption of the organization or operations of the Commission. Such conditions shall be deemed to continue until the Commission shall, by notice or older, resume its normal organization and operations, whether at its headquarters in Washington, D.C. or elsewhere.

[71 FR 33386, June 9, 2006]

其违反本子部分规定而遭其他不利影响的理由。

(c)对证券交易委员会雇员的纪律处分。证券交易委员会任何雇员凡违反本《准则》的禁止性规定和命令性规定的,证券交易委员会可予以谴责,或处以停职、解聘等处分。

[《联邦公报》第28卷第4447页,1963年5月3日,修正索引:《联邦公报》第42卷第14691页,1977年3月16日。]

第G子部分——紧急情况下适用的组织和运行计划

法律依据:《美国法典》第十五编第77s节、第78d节、第78d-1节、第78w节、第77sss节、第80a-37节、第80b-11节;1950年《第10号重组计划》(《美国法典》第十五编第78d节注释)。

行政规则来源:《联邦公报》第28卷第6970页,1963年7月9日,除非另有说明。

第200.200节　目的

本子部分规定了证券交易委员会在下节规定的紧急情况下履行职务和责任时遵循的组织和运行计划。

[《联邦公报》第28卷第6970页,1963年7月9日,修正索引:《联邦公报》第71卷第33386页,2006年6月9日;《联邦公报》第71卷第35730页,2006年6月21日。]

第200.201节　一般规定

(a)就本子部分规定而言,如果某人由于任何情况或出于任何原因而无法在主要或备用办公场所或任何其他地点及时承担或履行其被赋予的职务、任务或责任,该人应视为无法履职或无行为能力。

(b)就本子部分规定而言,自然或人为动荡发生之时或发生自然或人为动荡的紧迫危险出现之时,即视为紧急情况开始之时,这些动荡情况包括但不限于美国及其准州或属地遭受的,对证券交易委员会的组织或运行造成实质性扰乱或有造成实质性扰乱的紧迫危险的武装攻击、恐怖袭击、内乱、火灾、瘟疫、龙卷风或洪水。证券交易委员会发布通知或命令恢复华盛顿哥伦比亚特区总部或其他地点的正常组织和运行之前,这些情况应视为持续存在。

[《联邦公报》第71卷第33386页,2006年6月9日。]

§200.202 Offices, and information and submittals.

(a) During emergency conditions, the location or headquarters of the Commission shall be as designated by the Chairman or his successor. The location of each Regional Office of the Commission, if different from the normal location, shall be as designated by the Chairman of the Commission or his successor, or in the absence of communications with him, by the Regional Director for the area or his acting successor.

(b) During emergency conditions, all formal or informal requests, filings, reports, or other submittals shall be submitted to the Commission as permitted in non-emergency conditions, unless the Chairman or his or her successor acting pursuant to §200.203 (c)(1) of this subpart specifies another means or location for submission of such requests, filings, reports, or other submittals, by a notice that is disseminated through a method (or combination of methods) that is reasonably designed to provide broad distribution of the information to the public.

[28 FR 6970, July 9, 1963, as amended at 59 FR 5944, Feb. 9, 1994; 71 FR 33387, June 9, 2006; 73 FR 32225, June 5, 2008]

§200.203 Organization, and delegations of authority.

(a) During emergency conditions, the respective functions and responsibilities of the Commissioners, the Chairman of the Commission, and the staff members shall be, to the extent possible, as set forth in Subpart A of this part (§200.1 *et seq.*).

(b) Action for and in the name of the Commission taken pursuant to this subpart by one or more Commissioners or by a successor as designated in this section shall mean and include the delegated authority to act for the unavailable or incapacitated Commissioners.

(c) Pursuant to the statutes governing the Commission, to Reorganization Plan No. 10 of 1950, and to Pub. L. 100-181, section 308(b), 101 Stat. 1249 (1987), the following automatic delegation of authority is made to provide continuity in the event of an emergency:

(1) In the event of the unavailability or incapacity of the Chairman of the Commission during emergency conditions, the authority of the Chairman to govern the affairs of the Commission and to act for the Commission, as provided for by law and by delegation from the Commission, will pass to the available person highest on the following list, until such time as the Chairman is no longer unavailable or incapacitated, or a successor Chairman has assumed office pursuant to Section 4 of the Securities Exchange Act of 1934 (15 U.S.C. 78d) and Reorganization Plan No. 10 of 1950 (15 FR 3175, 64 Stat. 1265):

(i) The Commissioners in order of seniority.

(ii) The General Counsel.

第200.202节　办公室、信息和文件呈报

(a)在紧急情况下,证券交易委员会的所在地或总部应由证券交易委员会主席或其继任者指定。证券交易委员会地区办公室的所在地如果与正常所在地不同,应由证券交易委员会主席或其继任者指定,无法联系到证券交易委员会主席时,由该地区的地区办公室主任或其代理继任者指定。

(b)在紧急情况下,所有正式或非正式请求、提交材料、报告或其他呈报文件应按非紧急情况下允许的方式提交给证券交易委员会,但证券交易委员会主席或其继任者依据本子部分第200.203(c)(1)条规定另行指明了提交方式或地点的除外。证券交易委员会主席另行指明提交方式和地点的,应采用通知的形式,通过一种或多种合理设计的可实现广泛传播的方法予以发布。

[《联邦公报》第28卷第6970页,1963年7月9日,修正索引:《联邦公报》第59卷第5944页,1994年2月9日;《联邦公报》第71卷第33387页,2006年6月9日;《联邦公报》第73卷第32225页,2008年6月5日。]

第200.203节　组织和委托授权

(a)在紧急情况下,证券交易委员会委员、主席以及员工应尽最大可能按本部分第A子部分(第200.1节及其后条文)的规定,履行其各自的职能和责任。

(b)一名或多名委员或者按本节指定的一名继任者依据本子部分规定代表证券交易委员会并以证券交易委员会名义采取行动,应具有并包括以下含义:该委员会或继任者根据委托授权代表无法履职或无行为能力的委员采取行动。

(c)根据规制证券交易委员会的制定法、《1950年第10号重组计划》和第100-181号公法第308(b)条,《美国制定法汇编》第101卷第1249页(1987)的规定,为保证紧急情况下工作的连续性,应适用如下自动授权规定:

(1)证券交易委员会主席在紧急情况下无法履职或无行为能力时,法律规定并由证券交易委员会授予证券交易委员会主席的管理证券交易委员会事务的权力和对外代表证券交易委员会行事的权力,将转移给如下名单中排名第一顺位的可工作之人,直至主席无法履职或无行为能力的情形结束或继任主席根据《1934年证券交易法》第4条(《美国法典》第十五编第78d节)和1950年《第10号重组计划》(《联邦公报》第15卷第3175页,《美国制定法汇编》第64卷第1265页)上任。

(i)资历最高的委员。

(ii)首席律师。

(iii) The Division Directors in the order designated by the Chairman in the most recent designation prior to the commencement of emergency conditions, or if no such designation has occurred, in order of seniority.

(iv) The Regional Directors in the order designated by the Chairman in the most recent designation prior to the commencement of emergency conditions, or if no such designation has occurred, in order of seniority.

(2) If and when a commissioner previously incapacitated or otherwise unavailable, again becomes available, he shall thereupon have all the powers and functions he would have had if he had not been incapacitated or otherwise unavailable.

(d) Actions taken for and in the name of the Commission as described above shall be effective immediately or as specified by the successor acting, but shall be subject to reconsideration by the Commissioners when the Commission has been reconstituted and is functioning.

(e) Except as may be determined otherwise by the Chairman or his successor, the duties of each head of a division or office of the Commission shall be discharged, in the event of the unavailability or incapacity of such person during emergency conditions, by the available staff member next in line of succession. The head of each division or office shall designate the line of succession within his division or office. If no such designation has been made or the designate is unavailable, such duties shall be assumed by the available subordinate officer or employee in the particular division or office who is highest in grade and in the event that there is more than one such person, in length of service with the Commission. A person who discharges or assumes the duties of the head of a division or office pursuant to this subsection is hereby delegated, throughout the period of the unavailability or incapacity of the head of the division or office during the emergency conditions, all of the functions that the Commission has delegated to the head of the division or office.

[28 FR 6970, July 9, 1963, as amended at 28 FR 7672, July 27, 1963; 28 FR 14493, Dec. 31, 1963; 54 FR 40862, Oct. 4, 1989; 59 FR 5945, Feb. 9, 1994; 71 FR 33387, June 9, 2006; 73 FR 32225, June 5, 2008]

§200.204 Personnel, fiscal, and service functions.

In the event of the unavailability or incapacity of the appropriate staff officer or his or her successor during emergency conditions, authority to effect temporary appointments of such additional officers and employees, to classify and allocate positions to their proper grades, to issue travel orders, and to effect emergency purchases of supplies, equipment and services shall be exercised by the respective Regional Directors, their deputies, or

(iii)部门主任,排序以紧急情况出现前主席最后一次指定的排序为准,如主席未对此作出指定,则按资历排序。

(iv)地区办公室主任,排序以紧急情况出现前主席最后一次指定的排序为准,如主席未对此作出指定,则按资历排序。

(2)如果之前无行为能力或出现其他无法履职情形的委员重新恢复履职能力,届时他将拥有原先的一切权力和职能,如同其未出现过无行为能力或无法履职的情形。

(d)上述代表证券交易委员会并以证券交易委员会名义采取的行动应立即生效,或根据采取行动的继任者规定的时间生效,但是证券交易委员会重新组建并恢复履行职能时,应由证券交易委员会委员对行动的生效时间进行复审。

(e)除非主席或其继任者作出相反决定,否则在紧急情况下如出现证券交易委员会部门或办公室负责人无法履职或无行为能力的情形,证券交易委员会每一部门或办公室负责人的职务应当由排名第一顺位的继任者履行。各部门或办公室负责人应指定其部门或办公室的继任顺序。如果未指定该等继任顺序或继任者无法履职,此等职务应由该部门或办公室内可以工作的下级管理人员或职员中级别最高者承担,如果符合条件的下级管理人员不止一名,则按在证券交易委员会工作时长的顺序继任。根据本子节履行某一部门或办公室负责人职务之人,在紧急情况下该部门或办公室负责人无法履职或无行为能力的整个期间,应履行或承担证券交易委员会委托该部门或办公室负责人行使的所有职能。

[《联邦公报》第28卷第6970页,1963年7月9日,修正索引:《联邦公报》第28卷第7672页,1963年7月27日;《联邦公报》第28卷第14493页,1963年12月31日;《联邦公报》第54卷第40862页,1989年10月4日;《联邦公报》第59卷第5945页,1994年2月9日;《联邦公报》第71卷第33387页,2006年6月9日;《联邦公报》第73卷第32225页,2008年6月5日。]

第200.204节　人事、财务和后勤职能

在紧急情况下,相关管理人员或其继任者无法履职或无行为能力时,其各自的地区办公室主任、地区办公室副主任及员工应按次序,为履行所涉职务的合法职责而行使以下权限:临时任命额外的管理人员或职员、按照合适的级别予以分级并分配工作岗位、签发出差命令、开展应急物资/设备/服务的采购。

staff in line of succession, as may be required for the discharge of the lawful duties of the respective offices.

[28 FR 6970, July 9, 1963, as amended at 59 FR 5945, Feb. 9, 1994; 71 FR 33387, June 9, 2006; 73 FR 32225, June 5, 2008]

§200.205 Effect upon existing Commission organization, delegations, and rules.

Except as otherwise provided herein, all outstanding Commission organizational statements, delegations of authority, orders, rules and regulations shall remain in force and effect during emergency conditions, subject to all lawful requirements and such changes as may be authorized by or in the name of the Chairman or the Commission.

[28 FR 6970, July 9, 1963, as amended at 71 FR 33387, June 9, 2006]

Subpart H—Regulations Pertaining to the Privacy of Individuals and Systems of Records Maintained by the Commission

Authority: 5 U.S.C. 552a(f), unless otherwise noted.

Section 200.312 is also issued under Pub. L. 93-579, sec. k, 5 U.S.C. 552a(k).

Section 200.313 is also issued under Pub. L. 93-579, sec. j, 5 U.S.C. 552a(j) and sec. k, 5 U.S.C. 552a(k).

Source: 40 FR 44068, Sept. 24, 1975, unless otherwise noted.

§200.301 Purpose and scope.

(a) The Privacy Act of 1974, Pub. L. 93-579, 88 Stat. 1896, is based, in part, on the finding by Congress that "in order to protect the privacy of individuals identified in information systems maintained by Federal agencies, it is necessary and proper for the Congress to regulate the collection, maintenance, use, and dissemination of information by such agencies." To achieve this objective the Act, among other things, provides, with some exceptions, that Federal agencies shall advise an individual upon request whether records maintained by the agency in a system of records pertain to the individual and shall grant the individual access to such records. The Act further provides that individuals may request amendments or corrections to records pertaining to them that are maintained by the agency, and that the agency shall either grant the requested amendments or set forth fully its reasons for refusing to do so.

[《联邦公报》第28卷第6970页,1963年7月9日,修正索引:《联邦公报》第59卷第5945页,1994年2月9日;《联邦公报》第71卷第33387页,2006年6月9日;《联邦公报》第73卷第32225页,2008年6月5日。]

第200.205节 对证券交易委员会现行组织、委托授权和规则的影响

除本节另有规定的情形外,否则所有现行有效的证券交易委员会的组织说明、委托授权、命令、规则与规章在紧急情况下均应保持有效,但如主席或证券交易委员会授权作出或以主席或证券交易委员会名义作出任何法律规定或变更的,则应受该等法律规定或变更的约束。

[《联邦公报》第28卷第6970页,1963年7月9日,修正索引:《联邦公报》第71卷第33387页,2006年6月9日。]

第H子部分——关于个人隐私和证券交易委员会维护的记录系统的规章

法律依据:《美国法典》第五编第552a(f)节,除非另有说明。

第200.312节同时见:第93-579号公法第k条,《美国法典》第五编第552a(k)节。

第200.313节同时见:第93-579号公法第j条,《美国法典》第五编第552a(j)节,和第93-579号公法第k条,《美国法典》第五编第552a(k)节。

行政规则来源:《联邦公报》第40卷第44068页,1975年9月24日,除非另有说明。

第200.301节 目的和范围

(a)《1974年隐私法》(公法编号93-579,《美国制定法汇编》第88卷第1896页)的部分立法规定乃基于国会的下列认定:"为保护出现在由联邦机构维护的信息系统中的个人隐私,国会应当且有必要监管此等机构收集、维护、使用和传播信息的行为。"为实现此目的,该法规定:除某些例外情况外,经任何个人提出请求,联邦机构均应告知在其记录系统中维护的记录是否与该个人有关,并赋予该个人查询该记录的权利。该法进一步规定,个人可以请求修正或改正政府机构维护的涉及自身的记录,而政府机构应根据其请求作出修正,拒绝修正的,应充分说明拒绝修正的理由。

(b) The Securities and Exchange Commission, pursuant to subsection (f) of the Privacy Act, adopts the following rules and procedures to implement the provisions of the Act summarized above, and other provisions of the Act. These rules and procedures are applicable to all requests for information, access or amendment to records pertaining to an individual that are contained in any system of records that is maintained by the Commission.

§200.302 Definitions.

The following definitions shall apply for purposes of this subpart:

(a) The terms *individual, maintain, record, system of records,* and *routine use* are defined for purposes of these rules as they are defined in 5 U.S.C. 552a(a)(2), (a)(3), (a)(4), (a)(5), and (a)(6).

(b) *Commission* means the Securities and Exchange Commission.

§200.303 Times, places and requirements for requests pertaining to individual records in a record system and for the identification of individuals making requests for access to the records pertaining to them.

(a) *Place to make request.* Any request by an individual to be advised whether any system of records maintained by the Commission and named by the individual contains a record pertaining to him or her, or any request by an individual for access to a record pertaining to him or her that is contained in a system of records maintained by the Commission, shall be submitted by mail to the Office of Freedom of Information and Privacy Act Operations, SEC, 100 F Street, NE., Washington, D.C. 20549, or by facsimile (202-772-9337). All requests will be required to be put in writing and signed by the individual making the request. In the case of requests for access that are made by mail, the envelope should be clearly marked "Privacy Act Request."

(1) *Information to be included in requests.* Each request by an individual concerning whether the Commission maintains in a system of records a record that pertains to him, or for access to any record pertaining to the individual that is maintained by the Commission in a system of records, shall include such information as will assist the Commission in identifying those records as to which the individual is seeking information or access. Where practicable, the individual should identify the system of records that is the subject of his request by reference to the Commission's notices of systems of records, which are published in the Federal Register, as required by section (e)(4) of the Privacy Act, 5 U.S.C. 552a(e)(4). Where a system of records is compiled on the basis of a specific identification scheme, the individual should include in his request the identification number or other identifier assigned to him. In the event the individual does not know the specific identifier assigned to him, he shall provide other information, including his full name, address, date of birth and subject matter of the record, to aid in processing his

(b)证券交易委员会按《隐私法》第(f)子条通过如下规则和程序,以实施上文简要总结的该法条款和该法的其他条款。这些规则和程序适用于所有对证券交易委员会维护的任何记录系统中个人记录的信息提供、记录查询或修正的请求。

第200.302节　定义

本子部分适用如下定义:

(a)就本子部分而言,"个人"、"维护"、"记录"、"记录系统"和"日常使用"等术语之含义,以《美国法典》第五编第552a(a)(2)节、第(a)(3)节、第(a)(4)节、第(a)(5)节和第(a)(6)节所给定义为准。

(b)"证券交易委员会"指美国证券交易委员会。

第200.303节　就记录系统中的个人记录提交请求的时间、地点和其他规定,以及就请求查询与其相关记录的个人提交身份识别请求的时间、地点和其他规定

(a)提交请求的地点。个人可提请委员会向其告知,委员会维护的该个人指定的任何记录系统是否包含与其自身有关的记录,或者个人也可在委员会维护的记录系统中提请查询与其自身相关的记录,该等请求应通过邮件呈报给委员会信息自由和隐私法管理办公室,地址:华盛顿哥伦比亚特区东北分区100F大街,邮编:D.C.20549;或传真至(202-772-9337)。所有请求均应以书面形式提交,由请求人签字。以邮件发出的信息查询请求,信封上应清晰标明"《隐私法》请求"字样。

(1)请求中应包括的信息。个人就证券交易委员会的记录系统中是否保存与其个人有关的记录提出询问请求,或就记录系统中由委员会保存的与其相关的任何记录提出查询请求时,应提供相关信息以协助委员会识别请求人寻找或查询的记录。如有可能,请求人应参照证券交易委员会信息系统通知{该等通知按《隐私法》第(e)(4)条[《美国法典》第五编第552a(e)(4)节]的规定公布在《联邦公报》上},指明其请求所涉之记录系统。记录系统如果以特定识别系统为基础汇编而成,请求人应在其请求中列明识别号码或向其分配的其他识别码。如果申请人不知道向其分配的识别码,则应提供其他信息,包括自己的全名、地址、出生日期、记录主题,以协助证券交易委员会对其请求进行处理。如果需要请求人提供补充信息方能处理请求的,应告知请求人。

request. If additional information is required before a request can be processed, the individual shall be so advised.

(2) *Verification of identity.* When the fact of the existence of a record is not required to be disclosed under the Freedom of Information Act, 5 U.S.C. 552, as amended, or when a record as to which access has been requested is not required to be disclosed under that Act, the individual seeking the information or requesting access to the record shall be required to verify his or her identity before access will be granted or information given. For this purpose, individuals shall appear at the Office of Freedom of Information and Privacy Act Operations, SEC, 100 F Street, NE., Washington, D.C. 20549, during normal business hours of 9 a.m. to 5:30 p.m. E.S.T., Monday through Friday, or at one of the Commission's Regional Offices. The addresses and business hours of those offices are listed below:

Atlanta Regional Office—3475 Lenox Road, NE., Suite 1000, Atlanta, GA 30326-1232. Office hours—9 a.m. to 5:30 p.m. E.T.

Boston Regional Office—33 Arch Street, 23rd Floor, Boston, MA 02110-1424. Office hours—9 a.m. to 5:30 p.m. E.T.

Chicago Regional Office—175 West Jackson Boulevard, Suite 900, Chicago, IL 60604-2908. Office hours—8:45 a.m. to 5:15 p.m. C.T.

Denver Regional Office—1801 California Street, Suite 1500, Denver, CO 80202-2656. Office hours—8 a.m. to 4:30 p.m. M.T.

Fort Worth Regional Office—Burnett Plaza, Suite 1900, 801 Cherry Street, Unit #18, Fort Worth, TX 76102-6882. Office hours—8:30 a.m. to 5 p.m. C.T.

Los Angeles Regional Office—5670 Wilshire Boulevard, 11th Floor, Los Angeles, CA 90036-3648. Office hours—8:30 a.m. to 5 p.m. P.T.

Miami Regional Office—801 Brickell Avenue, Suite 1800, Miami, FL 33131-4901. Office hours—9 a.m. to 5:30 p.m. E.T.

New York Regional Office—3 World Financial Center, Suite 400, New York, NY 10281-1022. Office hours—9 a.m. to 5:30 p.m. E.T.

Philadelphia Regional Office—701 Market Street, Suite 2000, Philadelphia, PA 19106-1532. Office hours—9 a.m. to 5:30 p.m. E.T.

Salt Lake City Regional Office—15 W. South Temple Street, Suite 1800, Salt Lake City, UT 84101-1573. Office hours—8 a.m. to 4:30 p.m. M.T.

San Francisco Regional Office—44 Montgomery Street, Suite 2600, San Francisco, CA 94104-4716. Office hours—8:30 a.m. to 5 p.m. P.T.

None of the Commission's offices is open on Saturday, Sunday or the following legal holidays: New Year's Day, Martin Luther King, Jr.'s Birthday, Presidents' Day, Memorial Day, Independence Day, Labor Day, Veterans' Day, Columbus Day, Thanksgiving Day,

(2)身份验证。如果《信息自由法》(《美国法典》第五编第552节)及其修正并未要求披露某记录存在的事实,或者,如果该法并未要求披露请求查询的记录,则在核准查询请求或提供信息之前应先验证请求询问信息或请求查询记录的个人的身份。为此目的,请求人应于周一至周五正常工作时间美国东部时间上午9时至下午5时30分之间亲自至委员会信息自由和隐私法管理办公室,地址:华盛顿哥伦比亚特区东北分区100F大街,邮编:D.C.20549;或亲自至证券交易委员会下属某一地区办公室,地区办公室地址和工作时间如下所列:

亚特兰大地区办公室——乔治亚州亚特兰大市东北分区Lenox路3475号1000室,邮编:GA 30326-1232。办公时间——东部标准时间上午9时至下午5时30分。

波士顿地区办公室——马萨诸塞州波士顿市Arch大街33号23楼,邮编:MA 02110-1424。办公时间——东部标准时间上午9时至下午5时30分。

芝加哥地区办公室——伊利诺伊州芝加哥西杰克逊大道175号900室,邮编:IL 60604-2908。办公时间——中部标准时间上午8时45分至下午5时15分。

丹佛地区办公室——科罗拉多州丹佛市加利福尼亚大街1801号1500室,邮编:CO 80202-2656。办公时间——山地标准时间上午8时至下午4时30分。

沃斯堡地区办公室——得克萨斯州沃斯堡市Cherry大街801号Burnett大厦1900室18单元,邮编:TX 76102-6882。办公时间——中部标准时间上午8时30分至下午5时。

洛杉矶地区办公室——加利福尼亚州洛杉矶市Wilshire大道5670号11层,邮编:CA 90036-3648。办公时间——太平洋标准时间上午8时30分至下午5时。

迈阿密地区办公室——佛罗里达州迈阿密市Brickell大道801号1800室,邮编:FL 33131-4901。办公时间——东部标准时间上午9时至下午5时30分。

纽约地区办公室——纽约州纽约市世界金融中心3号400室,邮编:NY 10281-1022。办公时间——东部标准时间上午9时至下午5时30分。

费城地区办公室——宾夕法尼亚州费城Market大街701号2000室,邮编:PA 19106-1532。办公时间——东部标准时间上午9时至下午5时30分。

盐湖城地区办公室——犹他州盐湖城W. South Temple大街15号1800室,邮编:UT 84101-1573。办公时间——山地标准时间上午8时至下午4时30分。

旧金山地区办公室——加利福尼亚州旧金山Montgomery大街44号2600室,邮编:CA 94104-4716。办公时间——太平洋标准时间上午8时30分至下午5时。

证券交易委员会办公室周六、周日和以下法定假日不工作:元旦、马丁·路德·金纪念日、总统日、阵亡将士纪念日、独立日、劳动节、退伍军人纪念日、哥伦布纪念日、感恩节和圣诞节。

and Christmas Day.

(3) *Methods for verifying identity—appearance in person.* An individual seeking information as to records pertaining to him or access to those records shall furnish documentation that may reasonably be relied on to establish the individual's identity. Such documentation might include a valid birth certificate, driver's license, employee or military identification card, or medicare card.

(4) *Method for verifying identity by mail.* Where an individual cannot appear at one of the Commission's Offices to verify his or her identity, he or she must submit, along with the request for information or access, a statement attesting to his or her identity. Where access is being sought, the statement shall include a representation that the requested records pertain to the individual and a statement that the individual is aware that knowingly and willfully requesting or obtaining records pertaining to an individual from the Commission under false pretenses is a criminal offense. This statement shall be a sworn statement, or in lieu of a sworn statement, an individual may submit an unsworn statement to the same effect if it is signed by him or her as true under penalty of perjury, dated, and in substantially the following form:

(i) If executed outside the United States: "I declare (or certify, verify, or state) under penalty of perjury under the laws of the United States of America that the foregoing is true and correct."

Executed on (date)____

(Signature) ________________________________

(ii) If executed within the United States, its territories, possessions, or commonwealths: "I declare (or certify, verify, or state) under penalty of perjury that the foregoing is true and correct."

Executed on (date)____

(Signature) ________________________________

(5) *Additional procedures for verifying identity.* When it appears appropriate, there may be made such other arrangements for the verification of identity as are reasonable under the circumstances and appear to be effective to prevent unauthorized disclosure of, or access to, individual records.

(b) *Acknowledgement of requests for information pertaining to individual records in a record system or for access to individual records.* (1) Except where an immediate acknowledgement is given for requests made in person, the receipt of a request for information pertaining to individual records in a record system will be acknowledged within 10 days after the receipt of such request. Requests will be processed as promptly as possible and a response to such requests will be given within 30 days (excluding Saturdays, Sundays, and legal holidays) unless, within the 30 day period and for cause

(3)身份验证方法——亲自到场。询问记录是否与本人有关的请求人或查询与其有关的记录的请求人,应提供可据以合理确定其个人身份的文件,包括有效的出生证明、驾照、工作证或军官证或医保卡。

(4)通过邮件验证身份。请求人若无法亲自到证券交易委员会任何一个办公室验证其身份时,必须在呈报询问请求或查询请求的同时,呈报一份身份证实声明。查询请求所附之身份证实声明应包括:请求查询的记录与其个人有关的声明,以及关于请求人了解在知情情况下故意以虚假身份向证券交易委员会请求查询或获得与某个人相关的记录属于刑事犯罪行为的声明。身份证实声明应为经宣誓的声明,或者,如果请求人本人签字确认声明的真实性,并表明其知晓作伪证会招致处罚、注明签字日期且基本符合如下格式的,亦可提交未经宣誓的声明:

(i)在美国以外的国家签署的身份证实声明:"本人声明(或证明、确认或陈述)上述内容真实准确,本人知晓根据美利坚合众国的法律作伪证会招致处罚。"

签署于(日期)____

(签字)________________________________

(ii)在美国、美国准州、属地或自治政区签署的身份证实声明:"本人声明(或证明、确认或陈述)上述内容真实准确,本人知晓作伪证会招致处罚。"

签署于(日期)____

(签字)________________________________

(5)额外身份验证程序。如有需要,可根据具体情况作出其他合理的身份验证安排,以有效防止个人记录被违规披露或查询。

(b)确认收悉有关记录系统中的记录是否与个人有关的询问请求或查询个人记录的请求的回执。(1)请求人亲自到场提交请求的可以当场向其提供回执,除此之外,收到在记录系统中的记录是否与个人有关的询问请求的,应在收到后10日内提供回执。该询问请求将尽快处理并在30日内(不包括周六、周日和法定假日)答复,除非在30日期间内说明理由并书面通知请求人对请求的答复需要更长时间。

shown, the individual making the request is notified in writing that a longer period is necessary.

(2) When an individual appears in person at the Office of Freedom of Information and Privacy Act Operations, SEC, 100 F Street, NE., Washington, D.C. 20549, or at one of its Regional Offices to request access to records pertaining to him, and such individual provides the required information and verification of identity, the Commission's staff, if practicable, will indicate at that time whether it is likely that the individual will be given access to the records and, if so, when and under what circumstances such access will be given. In the case of requests received by mail, whenever practicable, acknowledgement of the receipt of the request will be given within 10 days after receipt (excluding Saturdays, Sundays, and legal holidays). The acknowledgement will indicate, if practicable, whether or not access likely will be granted and, if so, when and under what circumstances.

[40 FR 44068, Sept. 24, 1975, as amended at 41 FR 44698, Oct. 12, 1976; 47 FR 26819, June 22, 1982; 52 FR 2677, Jan. 26, 1987; 54 FR 40862, Oct. 4, 1989; 54 FR 50307, Dec. 5, 1989; 59 FR 5945, Feb. 9, 1994; 59 FR 12543, Mar. 17, 1994; 65 FR 55185, 55186, Sept. 13, 2000; 73 FR 32225, June 5, 2008]

§200.304 Disclosure of requested records.

(a) *Initial review.* Requests by individuals for access to records pertaining to them will be referred to the Commission's Privacy Act Officer who initially will determine whether access will be granted, *Provided, however,* That a Director of a staff Division of the Commission or Office head, other than the General Counsel, whose zone of responsibility relates to the record requested (see 17 CFR 200.13 *et seq.*), may make a determination that access is not lawfully required to be granted and should not be granted, in which case he, and not the Privacy Act Officer, shall make the required notification to the individual making the request.

(b) *Grant of request for access.* (1) If it is determined that a request for access to records pertaining to an individual will be granted, the individual will be advised by mail that access will be given at the designated Office of the Commission or a copy of the requested record will be provided by mail if the individual shall so indicate. Where the individual requests that copies of the record be mailed to him or requests copies of a record upon reviewing it at a Commission Office, the individual shall pay the cost of making the requested copies, as set forth in §200.310 of this subpart.

(2) In granting access to an individual to a record pertaining to him, such steps shall be taken by the Commission's staff as are necessary to prevent the unauthorized disclosure at the same time of information pertaining to individuals other than the person

(2)本人亲自到信息自由和隐私法管理办公室(地址:美国证券交易委员会,华盛顿哥伦比亚特区东北分区100F大街,邮编:D.C.20549)或到证券交易委员会任一地区办公室请求查询与其有关的记录并且提供了所需信息和身份证件的,如有可能,证券交易委员会的员工应当场告知其查询请求是否可能获得核准。如给出肯定答复,还应告知核准请求的时间以及条件。对于通过邮件收到的请求,查询请求的回执应于收到之日起10日内(不包括周六、周日和法定假日)发出。如有可能,回执中应说明其查询请求是否可能获得核准,如给出肯定答复,则还应告知核准请求的时间以及条件。

[《联邦公报》第40卷第44068页,1975年9月24日,修正索引:《联邦公报》第41卷第44698页,1976年10月12日;《联邦公报》第47卷第26819页,1982年6月22日;《联邦公报》第52卷第2677页,1987年1月26日;《联邦公报》第54卷第40862页,1989年10月4日;《联邦公报》第54卷第50307页,1989年12月5日;《联邦公报》第59卷第5945页,1994年2月9日;《联邦公报》第59卷第12543页,1994年3月17日;《联邦公报》第65卷第55185页、第55186页,2000年9月13日;《联邦公报》第73卷第32225页,2008年6月5日。]

第200.304节　所请求记录的披露

(a)初步审查。个人查询与其有关的记录的请求将提交给证券交易委员会的隐私法官员,隐私法官员将初步判定是否核准查询请求。但是,被请求查询的记录如果属于除首席律师外的证券交易委员会内部某部门主任或办公室主任的责任范围(见《联邦规章汇编》第十七编第200.13节及其后条文),该部门主任或办公室主任可以判定法律并未要求核准该请求且该请求不应核准。在该种情况下,该部门主任或办公室主任,而非隐私法官员,应向请求人发出规定的通知。

(b)核准信息查询请求。(1)如果个人记录查询请求获得核准,应通过邮件通知请求人可在指定的证券交易委员会办公室查询该信息,或者如果请求人提出要求,应通过邮件向请求人提供请求查询的记录复本。个人请求为其邮递记录复本的或在证券交易委员会办公室查阅完毕后要求获得记录复本的,应按照本子部分第200.310节规定支付制作复本的费用。

(2)核准个人查询与其有关的记录时,证券交易委员会员工应采取必要措施,防止未经批准披露与请求人之外的其他人有关的信息或与请求人无关的其他信息。

making the request or of other information that does not pertain to the individual.

(c) *Denial of request for access.* If it is determined that access will not be granted, the individual making the request will be notified of that fact and given the reasons why access is being denied. The individual also will be advised (1) of his right to seek review by the General Counsel of the initial decision to deny access, in accordance with the procedures set forth in §200.308 of this subpart; and (2) of his right ultimately to obtain judicial review pursuant to 5 U.S.C. 552a(g)(1)(A) of a final denial of access by the General Counsel.

(d) *Time for acting on requests for access.* Access to a record pertaining to an individual normally will be granted or denied within 30 days (excluding Saturdays, Sundays and legal holidays) after the receipt of the request for access unless the individual making the request is notified in writing within the 30 day period that, for good cause shown, a longer time is required. In such cases, the individual making the request shall be informed in writing of the difficulties encountered and an indication shall be given as to when it is anticipated that access may be granted or denied.

(e) *Authorization to allow designated person to review and discuss records pertaining to another individual.* An individual who is granted access to records pertaining to him, and who appears at a Commission Office to review the records, may be accompanied by another person of his choosing. Where the records as to which access has been granted are not required to be disclosed under provisions of the Freedom of Information Act 5 U.S.C. 552, as amended, the individual requesting the records, before being granted access, shall execute a written statement, signed by him and the person accompanying him, which specifically authorizes the latter individual to review and discuss the records. If such authorization has not been given as described, the person who has accompanied the individual making the request will be excluded from any review or discussion of the records.

(f) *Exclusion for certain records.* Nothing contained in these rules shall allow an individual access to any information compiled in reasonable anticipation of a civil action or proceeding.

(5 U.S.C. 552a (f); sec. 19, Securities Act of 1933, 48 Stat. 85, as amended; sec. 23, Securities Exchange Act of 1934, 48 Stat. 901, as amended; sec. 20, Public Utility Holding Company Act of 1935, 49 Stat. 833; sec. 319, Trust Indenture Act of 1939, 53 Stat. 1173; sec. 38, Investment Company Act of 1940, 54 Stat. 841; sec. 211, Investment Advisers Act of 1940, 54 Stat. 855 (15 U.S.C. 77s, 78w, 79t, 77sss, 80a-37, 80b-11))

[40 FR 44068, Sept. 24, 1975, as amended at 49 FR 13866, Apr. 9, 1984]

(c)驳回查询记录请求。如果决定不予核准查询记录请求,应通知请求人请求被驳回事实及原因,并告知请求人:(1)请求人有权根据本子部分第200.308节规定的程序,提请首席律师对驳回查询记录请求的初步决定进行复议;并且(2)如果查询记录请求最终被首席律师驳回,请求人最后还有权按照《美国法典》第五编第552a(g)(1)(A)节提起司法审查。

(d)查询记录请求的答复时间。核准或驳回决定通常应在收到个人记录查询请求30日内(不包括周六、周日和法定假日)作出,除非在上述30日期限内书面通知请求人,说明出于充分理由的考虑,作出答复需要更长时间。在该种情况下,应将遇到的困难以书面形式通知请求人,并说明预期作出核准或驳回决定的时间。

(e)准许指定人员查看和讨论其他个人的记录。获准查询与其有关的记录的个人可以在其选择的其他人的陪同下至证券交易委员会办公室现场查阅记录。如果《信息自由法》(《美国法典》第五编第552节)及其修正的条款不要求披露获准查询的记录,则查询请求人在获得核准前应先签署一份书面说明,特别授权陪同人查阅和讨论记录,请求人本人及其选择的陪同人均应进行签字。如果未按上述要求作出授权,请求人的陪同人不得查看和讨论该等记录。

(f)某些记录的例外情况。本节任何规定均不允许任何个人查询因合理预期某项民事诉讼或程序将发生而编纂的任何信息。

[《美国法典》第五编第552a(f)节;《1933年证券法》第19条及其修正,《美国制定法汇编》第48卷第85页及其修正;《1934年证券交易法》第23条及其修正,《美国制定法汇编》第48卷第901页;《1935年公用事业控股公司法》第20条,《美国制定法汇编》第49卷第833页;《1939年信托契约法》第319条,《美国制定法汇编》第53卷第1173页;《1940年投资公司法》第38条,《美国制定法汇编》第54卷第841页;《1940年投资顾问法》第211条,《美国制定法汇编》第54卷第855页(《美国法典》第十五编第77s节、第78w节、第79t节、第77sss节、第80a-37节、第80b-11节)。]

[《联邦公报》第40卷第44068页,1975年9月24日,修正索引:《联邦公报》第49卷第13866页,1984年4月9日。]

§200.305 Special procedure: Medical records.

(a) *Statement of physician or mental health professional.* When an individual requests access to records pertaining to him that include medical and/or psychological information, the Commission, if it deems it necessary under the particular circumstances, may require the individual to submit with the request a signed statement by his physician or a mental health professional indicating that, in their opinion, disclosure of the requested records or information directly to the individual will not have an adverse effect on the individual.

(b) *Designation of physician or mental health professional to receive records.* If the Commission believes, in good faith, that disclosure of medical and/or psychological information directly to an individual could have an adverse effect on that individual, the individual may be asked to designate in writing a physician or mental health professional to whom he would like the records to be disclosed, and disclosure that otherwise would be made to the individual will instead be made to the designated physician or mental health professional.

§200.306 Requests for amendment or correction of records.

(a) *Place to make requests.* A written request by an individual to amend or correct records pertaining to him or her may be hand delivered during normal business hours to the SEC, Operations Center, Room 1418, 6432 General Green Way, Alexandria, VA 22312–2414, or be sent by mail to the Office of Information and Privacy Act Operations, SEC, Operations Center, 6432 General Green Way, Alexandria, VA 22312–2413, or by facsimile (703–914–1149).

(1) *Information to be included in requests.* Each request to amend or correct a Commission record shall reasonably describe the record sought to be amended or corrected. Such description should include, for example, relevant names, dates and subject matter to permit the record to be located among the records maintained by the Commission. An individual who has requested that a record pertaining to him be amended or corrected will be advised promptly if the record cannot be located on the basis of the description given and that further identifying information is necessary before his request can be processed. An initial evaluation of a request presented in person will be made immediately to ensure that the request is complete and to indicate what, if any, additional information will be required. Verification of the individual's identity as set forth in §200.303(a)(2), (3), (4) and (5) may also be required.

(2) *Basis for amendment or correction.* An individual requesting an amendment or correction to a record pertaining to him shall specify the substance of the amendment or correction and set forth facts and provide such materials that would support his contention that the record pertaining to him as maintained by the Commission is not accurate, timely or complete, or that the record is not necessary and relevant to accomplish a statutory

第200.305节　特殊程序:医疗记录

(a)医生或心理健康专家的声明。如个人请求查询与其有关的含有医疗和/或心理治疗信息的记录,而证券交易委员会根据具体情况认为有必要,可以要求请求人呈报一份由其医生或心理健康专家签字的声明,说明其认为向请求人直接披露该等记录或信息不会对请求人造成不利影响。

(b)指定医生或心理健康专家接收记录。如果证券交易委员会出于善意相信直接向某一个人披露医疗和/或心理治疗信息可能会对该人造成不利影响,可以要求该人书面指定一名医生或心理健康专家接收披露的记录,且其所请求之披露应转由其所指定的医生或心理健康专家接收。

第200.306节　修正或改正记录的请求

(a)提交请求的地点。个人修正或改正与其有关的记录的书面请求可于正常工作时间亲自递交至美国证券交易委员会运营中心,地址:亚历山德里亚General Green Way 6432号1418室,邮编:VA 22312-2414,或邮递至信息自由和隐私法管理办公室,地址:美国证券交易委员会运营中心,亚历山德里亚General Green Way 6432号,邮编:VA 22312-2413;或传真至(703-914-1149)。

(1)请求中应包括的信息。修正或改正证券交易委员会记录的每份请求均应对请求修正或改正的记录作出合理描述。描述信息应包括相关名称、日期和主题等信息,以帮助证券交易委员会在其所维护的记录中查找相关记录。如果无法根据所提供的描述查找到相关记录且在处理请求前有必要提供进一步的识别信息,应及时告知请求人此一事实。对于本人亲自到场提交的请求,应立即作出初步评估以确保所提交请求的完整性,并告知请求人需要提供的补充信息(如有)。请求人可能需要按照第200.303(a)(2)条、第200.303(a)(3)节、第200.303(a)(4)节和第200.303(a)(5)节的规定进行个人身份验证。

(2)修正或改正的理由。个人请求对与其有关的记录进行修正或改正的,应说明请求修正或改正的实质内容,并列明相关事实和提供相关材料证明证券交易委员会维护的与其有关之记录不准确、非最新或不完整,或证明记录并非为实现法律或总统行政命令授权的证券交易委员会的法定目的所必需,或证明记录与该等法定目的无关。

purpose of the Commission as authorized by law or by Executive Order of the President.

(b) *Acknowledgement of requests for amendment or correction.* Receipt of a request to amend or correct a record pertaining to an individual normally will be acknowledged in writing within 10 days after such request has been received. When a request to amend or correct is made in person, the individual making the request will be given a written acknowledgement when the request is presented. The acknowledgement will describe the request received and indicate when it is anticipated that action will be taken on the request. No acknowledgement will be sent when the request for amendment or correction will be reviewed, and an initial decision made, within 10 days from the date the request is received.

[40 FR 44068, Sept. 24, 1975, as amended at 47 FR 26819, June 22, 1982; 65 FR 55186, Sept. 13, 2000]

§200.307 Review of requests for amendment or correction.

(a) *Initial review.* As in the case of requests for access, requests by individuals for amendment or correction to records pertaining to them will be referred to the Commission's Privacy Act Officer for an initial determination, except that such requests may be considered by a Division Director or Office Head (other than the General Counsel) as set forth in §200.304(a) of this subpart.

(b) *Standards to be applied in reviewing requests.* In reviewing requests to amend or correct records, the Privacy Act Officer, or Division or Office head, will be guided by the criteria set forth in 5 U.S.C. 552a(e)(1), *i.e.* , that records maintained by the Commission shall contain only such information as is necessary and relevant to accomplish a statutory purpose of the Commission as required by statute or Executive Order of the President and that such information also be accurate, timely, and complete. These criteria will be applied whether the request is to add material to a record or to delete information from a record.

(c) *Time for acting on requests.* Initial review of a request by an individual to amend or correct a record pertaining to him shall be completed as promptly as is reasonably possible and normally within 30 days (excluding Saturdays, Sundays and legal holidays) from the date the request was received, unless unusual circumstances preclude completion of review within that time. If the anticipated completion date indicated in the acknowledgement cannot be met, the individual requesting the amendment will be advised in writing of the delay and the reasons therefor, and also advised when action is expected to be completed.

(d) *Grant of requests to amend or correct records.* If a request to amend or correct a record is granted in whole or in part, the Privacy Act Officer will: (1) Advise the individual making the request in writing of the extent to which it has been granted; (2) amend

(b)确认收悉修正或改正记录请求的回执。书面回执一般将于收到修正或改正个人记录的请求后10日内签发。本人亲自提交修正或改正记录请求的,证券交易委员会应在请求人提交请求之时提供书面回执。回执应对收到的请求作出描述并指明预计对该请求采取行动的时间。若修正或改正请求将在10日内完成审查并作出初步决定,则不需发出收讫回执。

[《联邦公报》第40卷第44068页,1975年9月24日,修正索引:《联邦公报》第47卷第26819页,1982年6月22日;《联邦公报》第65卷第55186页,2000年9月13日。]

第200.307节　修正或改正记录请求的审查

(a)初步审查。如同查询请求一样,个人记录的修正或改正请求将提交证券交易委员会隐私法官员作出初步判定,除非该请求根据本子部分第200.304(a)节可交由除法律顾问外的某一部门主任或办公室主任审议。

(b)审查请求的标准。审查修正或改正记录请求时,隐私法官员、部门主任或办公室主任应遵循《美国法典》第五编第552a(e)(1)节规定的标准,即证券交易委员会维持的记录所含信息应仅为实现法律或总统行政命令授权证券交易委员会的法定目的所必需且与之相关,且此等信息应保持准确、最新和完整。无论是对于在记录中增添资料的请求或从记录中删除信息的请求,均应适用上述标准。

(c)对请求采取行动的时间。证券交易委员会应在收到请求后30日内(不包括周六、周日和法定假日)尽合理可能及时地完成对修正或改正个人记录的请求的初步审查,出现异常情况不可能在该时限内完成初步审查的情况除外。如果无法按回执注明的日期完成初步审查,应延迟原因书面通知请求人,并告知预期完成初步审查的时间。

(d)核准记录修正改正请求。如果记录修正改正请求全部或部分获得核准,隐私法官员应:(1)书面告知请求人获得核准的范围;(2)对记录作出相应修正或改正;并且(3)所涉记录已根据《美国法典》第五编第552a(c)节作披露记录的,应告知该记录之

or correct the record accordingly; and (3) where an accounting of disclosures of the record has been kept pursuant to 5 U.S.C. 552a(c), advise all previous recipients of the record of the fact that the record has been amended or corrected and the substance of the amendment or correction.

(e) *Denial of requests to amend or correct records.* If an individual's request to amend or correct a record pertaining to him is denied in whole or in part, the Privacy Act Officer will:

(1) Promptly advise the individual making the request in writing of the extent to which the request has been denied;

(2) State the reasons for the denial of the request;

(3) Describe the procedures established by the Commission to obtain further review within the Commission of the request to amend or correct, including the name and address of the person to whom the appeal is to be addressed; and

(4) Inform the individual that the Privacy Act Officer will provide information and assistance to the individual in perfecting an appeal of the initial decision.

(5 U.S.C. 552a(f); sec. 19, Securities Act of 1933, 48 Stat. 85, as amended; sec. 23, Securities Exchange Act of 1934, 48 Stat. 901, as amended; sec. 20, Public Utility Holding Company Act of 1935, 49 Stat. 833; sec. 319, Trust Indenture Act of 1939, 53 Stat. 1173; sec. 38, Investment Company Act of 1940, 54 Stat. 841; sec. 211, Investment Advisers Act of 1940, 54 Stat. 855 (15 U.S.C. 77s, 78w, 79t, 77sss, 80a-37, 80b-11))

[40 FR 44068, Sept. 24, 1975, as amended at 49 FR 13866, Apr. 9, 1984]

§200.308 Appeal of initial adverse agency determination as to access or as to amendment or correction.

(a) *Administrative review.* Any person who has been notified pursuant to §200.304(c) that his request for access to records pertaining to him has been denied, or pursuant to Section 307(e) of this subpart that his request for amendment or correction has been denied in whole or in part, or who has received no response to a request for access or to amend within 30 days (excluding Saturdays, Sundays and legal holidays) after his request was received by the Office of Information and Privacy Act Operations (or within such extended period as may be permitted in accordance with §§200.304(d) and 200.307(c) of this subpart), may appeal the adverse determination or failure to respond to the General Counsel.

(1) The appeal shall be in writing and shall describe the record in issue and set forth the proposed amendment or correction and the reasons therefor.

前所有的通信接收人该记录已被修正或改正的事实以及修正或改正的实质内容。

(e)驳回记录修正改正请求。如果请求人提出的修正或改正其记录的请求被全部或部分驳回,隐私法官员应:

(1)及时书面告知请求人驳回范围;

(2)说明驳回请求的原因;

(3)说明证券交易委员会制定的请求人可据以提请证券交易委员会对记录修正改正请求进行复议的程序,包括负责受理请求人行政复议申请的主体名称和地址;并

(4)告知请求人,隐私法官员将为其提供信息与协助,帮助其完善针对证券交易委员会初步决定提交的行政复议申请文书。

[《美国法典》第五编552a(f)节;《1933年证券法》第19条及其修正,《美国制定法汇编》第48卷第85页;《1934年证券交易法》第23条及其修正,《美国制定法汇编》第48卷第901页;《1935年公用事业控股公司法》第20条,《美国制定法汇编》第49卷第833页;《1939年信托契约法》第319条,《美国制定法汇编》第53卷第1173页;《1940年投资公司法》第38条,《美国制定法汇编》第54卷第841页;《1940年投资顾问法》第211条,《美国制定法汇编》第54卷第855页(《美国法典》第十五编第77s节、第78w节、第79t节、第77sss节、第80a-37节、第80b-11节)。]

[《联邦公报》第40卷第44068页,1975年9月24日,修正索引:《联邦公报》第49卷第13866页,1984年4月9日。]

第200.308节　针对证券交易委员会不核准查询或不核准修正或改正记录请求的初步决定提出的行政复议申请

(a)行政复议。在下述任何情形下,任何请求人均可以就证券交易委员会对其作出的不利决定或不答复的行为向首席律师提起行政复议申请:按照第200.304(c)节请求人被通知其个人记录查询请求被驳回;按照本子部分第307(e)节请求人被通知其记录修正改正请求被全部或部分驳回;信息自由和隐私法管理办公室未在收到请求后30日内(不包括周六、周日和法定假日)[或在本子部分第200.304(d)节和第200.307(c)节允许的延长期内]对记录查询或修正请求作出答复。

(1)行政复议申请应以书面形式作出并应对所涉记录作出描述,说明拟进行修正或改正的内容及原因。

(2) The appeal shall be delivered or sent by mail to the Office of Information and Privacy Act Operations, SEC, Operations Center, 6432 General Green Way, Alexandria, VA 22312-2413, or by facsimile (703-914-1149).

(3) The applicant, if he wishes, may state such facts and cite such legal or other authorities as he may consider appropriate in support of his application.

(4) The General Counsel will make a determination with respect to any appeal within 30 days after the receipt of such appeal (excluding Saturdays, Sundays and legal holidays), unless for good cause shown, the General Counsel shall extend that period. If such an extension is made, the individual who is appealing shall be advised in writing of the extension, the reasons therefor, and the anticipated date when the appeal will be decided.

(5) In considering an appeal from a denial of a request to amend or correct a record, the General Counsel shall apply the same standards as set forth in §200.307(b).

(6) If the General Counsel shall conclude that access should be granted, he or she shall issue an order granting access and instructing the Privacy Act Officer to comply with §200.304(b).

(7) If the General Counsel shall conclude that the request to amend or correct the record should be granted in whole or in part, he or she shall issue an order granting the requested amendment or correction in whole or in part and instructing the Privacy Act Officer to comply with the requirements of §200.307(d) of this subpart, to the extent applicable.

(8) If the General Counsel affirms the initial decision denying access, he or she shall issue an order denying access and advising the individual seeking access of (i) The order; (ii) the reasons for denying access; and (iii) the individual's right to obtain judicial review of the decision pursuant to 5 U.S.C. 552a(g)(1)(B).

(9) If the General Counsel determines that the decision of the Privacy Act Officer denying a request to amend or correct a record should be upheld, he or she shall issue an order denying the request and the individual shall be advised of

(i) The order refusing to amend or correct the record and the reasons therefor;

(ii) His or her right to file a concise statement setting forth his or her disagreement with the General Counsel's decision not to amend or correct the record;

(iii) The procedures for filing such a statement of disagreement with the General Counsel;

(iv) The fact that any such statement of disagreement will be made available to anyone to whom the record is disclosed, together with, if the General Counsel deems it appropriate, a brief statement setting forth the General Counsel's reasons for refusing to amend or correct;

(2)行政复议申请应递交或邮寄至信息自由和隐私法管理办公室,地址:美国证券交易委员会运营中心,亚历山德里亚General Green Way 6432号,邮编:VA 22312-2413;或传真至(703-914-1149)。

(3)如果申请人愿意,可以说明其认为适当的事实,并引述其认为适当的法律依据或其他依据,借以支持其申请。

(4)首席律师应在收到任何行政复议申请后30日内(不包括周六、周日和法定假日)就行政复议申请作出判定,除非有充分理由表明首席律师应延长该期限。首席律师决定延长期限的,应书面告知行政复议申请人延长事宜、延长原因以及预计对行政复议申请作出裁定的日期。

(5)对于请求人针对驳回记录修正改正请求的决定提出的行政复议申请,首席律师应根据与第200.307(b)节相同的标准予以审议。

(6)首席律师得出结论,认为应核准查询记录请求的,应当签发命令,核准查询并指示隐私法官员遵照第200.304(b)节的规定。

(7)首席律师得出结论,认为应全部或部分核准记录修正改正请求的,应当签发命令,全部或部分核准修正改正请求,并指示隐私法官员在可适用的范围内遵照本子部分第200.307(d)节的规定。

(8)首席律师维持驳回查询记录请求的初步决定的,应签发驳回查询令并告知请求人:(i)该驳回令;(ii)驳回查询的原因;以及(iii)请求人有权按照《美国法典》第五编第552a(g)(1)(B)节提起司法审查。

(9)首席律师决定维持隐私法官员的驳回记录修正改正请求的决定的,首席律师应签发驳回请求令并告知请求人:

(i)驳回记录修正或改正请求的命令及其原因;

(ii)请求人有权提交一份简要声明,说明其不同意首席律师作出的不予修正或改正记录的决定;

(iii)提交针对首席律师决定的异议声明的程序;

(iv)任何获得记录披露的人均将被提供上述异议声明;此外,如果首席律师认为适当,还应在提供异议声明的同时,提供一份首席律师关于拒绝修正或改正记录的原因的简要说明;

(v) The fact that prior recipients of the record in issue will be provided with the statement of disagreement and the General Counsel's statement, if any, to the extent that an accounting of such disclosures has been maintained pursuant to 5 U.S.C. 552a(c); and

(vi) The individual's right to seek judicial review of the General Counsel's refusal to amend or correct, pursuant to 5 U.S.C. 552a(g)(1)(A).

(10) In appropriate cases the General Counsel may, in his or her sole and unfettered discretion, refer matters requiring administrative review of initial decisions to the Commission for determination and the issuance, where indicated, of orders.

(b) *Statement of disagreement.* As noted in paragraph (a)(9)(ii) of this section, an individual may file with the General Counsel a statement setting forth his disagreement with the General Counsel's denial of his request to amend or correct a record.

(1) Such statement of disagreement shall be delivered or sent by mail to the Office of Freedom of Information and Privacy Act Operations, SEC, Operations Center, 6432 General Green Way, Alexandria, VA 22312-2413, or by facsimile (703-914-1149), within 30 days after receipt by the individual of the General Counsel's order denying the amendment or correction. For good cause shown this period can be extended for a reasonable time.

(2) Such statement of disagreement shall concisely state the basis for the individual' s agreement. Generally a statement should be no more than two pages in length, except an individual may submit a slightly longer statement if it is necessary to set forth his disagreement effectively. Unduly lengthy or irrelevant materials will be returned to the individual by the General Counsel for appropriate revisions before they become a permanent part of the individual's record.

(3) The record about which a statement of disagreement has been filed will clearly note which part of the record is disputed and the General Counsel will provide copies of the statement of disagreement and, if the General Counsel deems it appropriate, provide a concise statement of his or her reasons for refusing to amend or correct the record, to persons or other agencies to whom the record has been or will be disclosed.

(4) In appropriate cases, the General Counsel may, in his or her sole and unfettered discretion, refer matters concerning statements of disagreement to the Commission for disposition.

(5 U.S.C. 552a(f); sec. 19, Securities Act of 1933, 48 Stat. 85, as amended; sec. 23, Securities Exchange Act of 1934, 48 Stat. 901, as amended; sec. 20, Public Utility Holding Company Act of 1935, 49 Stat. 833; sec. 319, Trust Indenture Act of 1939, 53 Stat. 1173; sec. 38, Investment Company Act of 1940, 54 Stat. 841; sec. 211, Investment Advisers Act of 1940, 54 Stat. 855 (15 U.S.C. 77s, 78w, 79t, 77sss, 80a-37, 80b-11))

(v)之前接收过相关记录的人将被提供请求人的异议声明和首席律师的说明(如有),但以已按照《美国法典》第五编第552a(c)节规定保存的披露记录为限。

(vi)请求人有权按照《美国法典》第五编第552a(g)(1)(A)节的规定,针对首席律师驳回记录修正改正请求的命令提起司法审查。

(10)在适当情况下,首席律师可独立不受约束地行使自由裁量权,自行决定将要求对初步决定进行行政复议的事项提交证券交易委员会作出判定和(如需要)签发命令。

(b)异议声明。如本节第(a)(9)(ii)款所述,个人可以向首席律师提交一份声明,说明其不同意首席律师作出的不予修正或改正记录的决定;

(1)该异议声明应于收到首席律师的驳回修正或改正的命令后30日内,递交或邮寄至美国证券交易委员会运营中心,地址:亚历山德里亚General Green Way 6432号,邮编:VA 22312-2413;或传真至(703-914-1149)。如果有充分理由,该期限可以合理延长。

(2)请求人应在异议声明中简要陈述异议[1]理由。该声明通常不应超过两页纸,不过,如果为了有效说明反对意见必须提交一份略长的说明书,请求人也可以呈报一份较长的说明书。材料篇幅过长或相关性薄弱的,首席律师将予以退回,要求请求人在该材料成为请求人的正式记录之前作出适当修改。

(3)与异议声明相关的记录,将清楚注明有争议的记录部分,且首席律师将向已获得记录或将获得记录的主体或其他机构提供异议声明的复本,同时,如果首席律师认为适当,还将向之提供一份关于首席律师拒绝修正或改正记录的理由的简要说明。

(4)在适当情况下,首席律师可独立不受约束地行使自由裁量权,自行决定将与异议声明有关的事项提交证券交易委员会处置。

[《美国法典》第五编第552a(f)节;《1933年证券法》第19条及其修正,《美国制定法汇编》第48卷第85页;《1934年证券交易法》第23条及其修正,《美国制定法汇编》第48卷第901页;《1935年公用事业控股公司法》第20条,《美国制定法汇编》第49卷第833页;《1939年信托契约法》第319条,《美国制定法汇编》第53卷第1173页;《1940年投资公司法》第38条,《美国制定法汇编》第54卷第841页;《1940年投资顾问法》第211条,《美国制定法汇编》第54卷第855页(《美国法典》第十五编第77s节、第78w节、第79t节、第77sss节、第80a-37节、第

1 原文"agreement"疑误,似应为"disagreement",译文已按后者处理。——译者注

[40 FR 44068, Sept. 24, 1975, as amended at 42 FR 40190, Aug. 9, 1977; 47 FR 26819, June 22, 1982; 49 FR 13866, Apr. 9, 1984; 65 FR 55186, Sept. 13, 2000]

§200.309 General provisions.

(a) *Extensions of time.* Pursuant to §§200.303(b), 200.304(d), 200.307(c) and 200.308(a)(4) of this subpart, the time within which a request for information, access or amendment by an individual with respect to records maintained by the Commission that pertain to him normally would be processed may be extended for good cause shown or because of unusual circumstances. As used in these rules, *good cause* and *unusual circumstances* shall include, but only to the extent reasonably necessary to the proper processing of a particular request:

(1) The need to search for and collect the requested records from field facilities or other establishments that are separate from the Office processing the request. Many records of the Commission are stored in Federal Records Centers in accordance with law — including many of the documents which have been on file with the Commission for more than 2 years — and cannot be made available promptly. Other records may temporarily be located at a Regional Office of the Commission. Any person who has requested for personal examination a record stored at the Federal Records Center or temporarily located in a Regional Office of the Commission will be notified when the record will be made available to him.

(2) The need to search for, collect, and appropriately examine a voluminous amount of separate and distinct records which may be demanded in a single request. While every reasonable effort will be made fully to comply with each request as promptly as possible on a first-come, first-served basis, work done to search for, collect and appropriately examine records in response to a request for a large number of records will be contingent upon the availability of processing personnel in accordance with an equitable allocation of time to all members of the public who have requested or wish to request records.

(3) The need for consultation, which shall be conducted with all practicable speed, with another agency having a substantial interest in the determination of the request, or among two or more components within the Commission having substantial subject-matter interest therein.

(b) *Effective date of action.* Whenever it is provided in this Subpart that an acknowledgement or response to a request will be given by specific times, deposit in the mails of such acknowledgement or response by that time, addressed to the person making the request, will be deemed full compliance.

80b-11节)。]

[《联邦公报》第40卷第44068页,1975年9月24日,修正索引:《联邦公报》第42卷第40190页,1977年8月9日;《联邦公报》第47卷第26819页,1982年6月22日;《联邦公报》第49卷第13866页,1984年4月9日;《联邦公报》第65卷第55186页,2000年9月13日。]

第200.309节　一般规定

(a)延期。按照本子部分第200.303(b)节、第200.304(d)节、第200.307(c)节和第200.308(a)(4)节的规定,个人针对证券交易委员会维护的与其有关的记录的询问请求、查询请求或修正请求处理所需的时间,通常可以出于充分理由或由于异常情况而延长。在本子部分中,"充分理由"和"异常情况"应包括以下各项,但仅以恰当地处理某一特殊请求合理所需为限:

(1)需从与处理请求的办公室互相独立的现场设施或其他机构检索并收集被请求的记录。证券交易委员会的许多记录依法储存在联邦记录中心——包括许多已经在证券交易委员会存储超过两年的文件——这些记录很难及时提供。其他记录可能临时储存在证券交易委员会的地区办公室。请求亲自查阅储存在联邦记录中心或临时储存于证券交易委员会地区办公室的记录的任何人,将获得关于可进行查阅的时间的通知。

(2)单独一份请求可能需要检索、收集并适当查阅大量不同且分散的记录。证券交易委员会应尽一切合理努力确保每一份请求都能按照"先到先得"的原则及时处理,但是,为了完成一份含有大量记录的请求,检索、收集以及适当查阅记录的工作将取决于处理人员的可用时间,而可用时间又应根据请求查阅或希望查阅记录的公众人数进行公平分配。

(3)证券交易委员会需要和对请求之判定有实质利益的其他政府机构展开协商,或者,两个(含)以上对请求的判定有实质利益的证券交易委员会内部机构彼此之间需要进行协商,协商应尽快进行。

(b)行动生效日。本子部分规定确认收悉请求的回执或对请求的答复应于某特定时限内提供或作出的,将此等回执或回复在规定日期之前投邮即视为完全符合时限规定。

(c) *Records in use by a member of the Commission or its staff.* Although every effort will be made to make a record in use by a member of the Commission or its staff available when requested, it may occasionally be necessary to delay making such a record available when doing so at the time the request is made would seriously interfere with the work of the Commission or its staff.

(d) *Missing or lost records.* Any person who has requested a record or a copy of a record pertaining to him will be notified if the record sought cannot be found. If he so requests, he will be notified if the record subsequently is found.

(e) *Oral requests; misdirected written requests* — (1) *Telephone and other oral requests.* Before responding to any request by an individual for information concerning whether records maintained by the Commission in a system of records pertain to him or to any request for access to records by an individual, such request must be in writing and signed by the individual making the request. The General Counsel will not entertain any appeal from an alleged denial or failure to comply with an oral request. Any person who has orally requested information or access to records pertaining to him that he believes to have been improperly denied to him should resubmit his request in appropriate written form in order to obtain proper consideration and, if need be, administrative review.

(2) *Misdirected written requests.* The Commission cannot assure that a timely or satisfactory response will be given to written requests for information, access or amendment by an individual with respect to records pertaining to him that are directed to the Commission other than in a manner prescribed in §§200.303(a), 200.306(a), 200.308(a)(2), and 200.310 of this subpart. Any staff member who receives a written request for information, access or amendment should promptly forward the request to the Privacy Act Officer. Misdirected requests for records will be considered to have been received by the Commission only when they have been actually received by the Privacy Act Officer in cases under §200.308(a)(2). The General Counsel will not entertain any appeal from an alleged denial or failure to comply with a misdirected request, unless it is clearly shown that the request was in fact received by the Privacy Act Officer.

[40 FR 44068, Sept. 24, 1975, as amended at 49 FR 13867, Apr. 9, 1984; 59 FR 5945, Feb. 9, 1994; 73 FR 32226, June 5, 2008]

§200.310 Fees.

(a) A request by an individual for copies of a record pertaining to him or her that is maintained by the Commission may be sent by mail to the Office of Freedom of Information and Privacy Act Operations, SEC, Operations Center, 6432 General Green Way, Alexandria, VA 22312-2413, or by facsimile (703-914-1149). There will be no charge assessed to the individual for the Commission's expense involved in searching for

(c)证券交易委员会委员或其员工正在使用的记录。虽然在请求人就证券交易委员会委员或其员工正在使用的记录提出请求时,证券交易委员会将在收到请求后尽一切努力向请求人提供该等记录,但如果在请求提出的当时立刻提供该等记录将严重干扰证券交易委员会或其员工的工作的,可能会有必要延迟该等记录的提供时间。

(d)缺失或遗失的记录。如果与请求相关的记录无法找到,应向查询或复制与自身相关的记录查询的任何请求人发出相应通知。请求人要求后续找到记录时向其发出通知的,应遵照执行。

(e)口头请求;误交书面请求——(1)电话及其他口头请求。在答复任何人提出的关于证券交易委员会维护的记录是否与其有关的询问请求之前,或答复任何记录查询请求之前,请求人必须以书面形式提交请求并在请求书上签字。请求人指称其口头请求被拒或未得到遵守而提起行政复议申请的,首席律师不予受理。如果任何人认为其口头提出的询问或查询请求被不当驳回,可以适当的书面格式重新呈报请求,以获得恰当的审议甚至行政复议(如需要)。

(2)误交书面请求,如果请求未按照本子部分第200.303(a)节、第200.306(a)节、第200.308(a)(2)节和第200.310节规定的方式送交证券交易委员会,证券交易委员会不能确保对与其个人记录有关的询问、查询或修改请求作出及时、满意的答复。收到询问、查询或修改请求书的任何证券交易委员会员工应及时转交隐私法官员。误交的记录请求只有按照第200.308(a)(2)节的规定被隐私法官员实际收悉之时,才视为已被证券交易委员会收悉。请求人误交请求,同时基于该等请求被拒或未得到遵守而提起任何行政复议申请的,首席律师不予受理,但能够明确证明隐私法官员实际已收悉请求的除外。

[《联邦公报》第40卷第44068页,1975年9月24日,修正索引:《联邦公报》第49卷第13867页,1984年4月9日;《联邦公报》第59卷第5945页,1994年2月9日;《联邦公报》第73卷第32226页,2008年6月5日。]

第200.310节 费用

(a)针对证券交易委员会维护的与其有关的记录提出的个人请求可以邮寄至信息自由和隐私法管理办公室,地址:美国证券交易委员会运营中心,亚历山德里亚General Green Way 6432号,邮编:VA 22312-2413;或传真至(703-914-1149)。证券交易委员会的检索或审阅工作不收费。证券交易委员会记录的复本将由一家商业复印商或证券交易委员会自己提供,并按照复印商与证券交易委员会之间的合同确定的价格

or reviewing the record. Copies of the Commission's records will be provided by a commercial copier or by the Commission at rates established by a contract between the copier and the Commission.

(b) *Waiver or reduction of fees.* Whenever the Privacy Act Officer determines that good cause exists to grant a request for reduction or waiver of fees for copying documents, he or she may reduce or waive any such fees.

(Pub. L. 87–592, 76 Stat. 394, 15 U.S.C. 78d–1, 78d–2; Pub. L. 93–502; 11 U.S.C. 901, 1109(a))

[42 FR 56727, Oct. 28, 1977, as amended at 47 FR 26819, June 22, 1982; 49 FR 12686, Mar. 30, 1984; 50 FR 50287, Dec. 10, 1985; 65 FR 55186, Sept. 13, 2000]

§200.311 Penalties.

Title 18 U.S.C. 1001 makes it a criminal offense, subject to a maximum fine of $10,000, or imprisonment for not more than 5 years or both, to knowingly and willingly make or cause to be made any false or fraudulent statements or representations in any matter within the jurisdiction of any agency of the United States. 5 U.S.C. 552a(i) makes it a misdemeanor punishable by a fine of not more than $5,000 for any person knowingly and willfully to request or obtain any record concerning an individual from the Commission under false pretenses. 5 U.S.C. 552a (i) (1) and (2) provide criminal penalties for certain violations of the Privacy Act by officers and employees of the Commission.

§200.312 Specific exemptions.

Pursuant to section (k) of the Privacy Act of 1974, the Chairman of the Securities and Exchange Commission, with the concurrence of the Commission, has deemed it necessary to promulgate the following exemptions to specified provisions of the Privacy Act:

(a) Pursuant to, and limited by 5 U.S.C. 552a(k)(2), the following systems of records maintained by the Commission shall be exempted from 5 U.S.C. 552a (c)(3), (d), (e)(1), (e)(4)(G), (H), and (I), and (f) and 17 CFR 200.303, 200.304, and 200.306, insofar as they contain investigatory materials compiled for law enforcement purposes:

(1) Enforcement Files;

(2) Office of General Counsel Working Files;

(3) Office of the Chief Accountant Working Files;

(4) Name-Relationship Index System;

(5) Rule 102(e) of the Commission's Rules of Practice—Appearing or Practicing before the Commission; and

收取费用。

(b)费用减免。若隐私法官员判定有充分理由可以核准减免任何文件复印费用请求,则请求人的复印费用可以减免。

[公法编号87-592,《美国制定法汇编》第76卷第394页,《美国法典》第十五编第78d-1节、第78d-2节;公法编号93-502;《美国法典》第十一编第901节、第1109(a)节。]

[《联邦公报》第42卷第56727页,1977年10月28日,修正索引:《联邦公报》第47卷第26819页,1982年6月22日;《联邦公报》第49卷第12686页,1984年3月30日;《联邦公报》第50卷第50287页,1985年12月10日;《联邦公报》第65卷第55186页,2000年9月13日。]

第200.311节　罚金

根据《美国法典》第十八编第1001节规定,就任何联邦政府机关管辖范围内的任何事项,在知情情况下故意作出或指使他人作出任何不实或欺骗性陈述或声明构成刑事犯罪,可单处或并处最高1万美元的罚金或5年以下有期徒刑。根据《美国法典》第五编第552a(i)节的规定,在知情情况下故意以虚假身份从证券交易委员会请求或获得任何与个人有关的记录构成轻罪,可以处以5000美元以下的罚金。《美国法典》第五编第552a(i)(1)节和第552a(i)(2)节规定证券交易委员会管理人员或职员某些违反《隐私法》的行为将构成刑事犯罪。

第200.312节　特定豁免

根据《1974年隐私法》第(K)条,美国证券交易委员会主席与证券交易委员会取得一致后,认为有必要颁发对《隐私法》具体条款的如下豁免:

(a)根据《美国法典》第五编第552a(k)(2)节并在遵守上述条款限制的前提下,证券交易委员会维持的如下记录系统,若包含为执法目的而编纂的调查材料,应豁免于《美国法典》第五编第552a(c)(3)节、第552a(d)节、第552a(e)(1)节、第552a(e)(4)(G)节、第552a(H)节、第552a(I)节和第552a(f)节,以及《联邦规章汇编》第十七编第200.303节、第200.304节和第200.306节的规定:

(1)执法档案;

(2)首席律师办公室工作档案;

(3)总会计师办公室工作档案;

(4)人名—关系索引系统;

(5)《证券交易委员会工作规则》的《102(e)规则》——出席证券交易委员会程序并办理有关业务;及

(6) Agency Correspondence Tracking System.

(b) Pursuant to 5 U.S.C. 552a(k)(5), the systems of records containing the Commission's (1) Office of Personnel Code of Conduct and Employee Performance Files and (2) Personnel Security Files shall be exempt from sections (c)(3), (d), (e)(1), (e)(4)(G), (H), and (I), and (f) of the Privacy Act, 5 U.S.C. 552a(c)(3), (d), (e)(1), (e)(4) (G), (H), and (I), and (f), and 17 CFR 200.303, 200.304, and 200.306 insofar as they contain investigatory material compiled to determine an individual's suitability, eligibility, and qualifications for Federal civilian employment or access to classified information, but only to the extent that the disclosure of such material would reveal the identity of a source who furnished information to the Government under an express promise that the identity of the source would be held in confidence, or, prior to September 27, 1975, under an implied promise that the identity of the source would be held in confidence.

(Pub. L. 93-579, Sec. k, 5 U.S.C. 552a(k))

[40 FR 44073, Sept. 24, 1975, as amended at 52 FR 2677, Jan. 26, 1987; 54 FR 24332, June 7, 1989; 54 FR 46373, Nov. 3, 1989; 60 FR 32795, June 23, 1995; 65 FR 55186, Sept. 13, 2000]

§200.313 Inspector General exemptions.

(a) Pursuant to section (j) of the Privacy Act of 1974, the Chairman of the Securities and Exchange Commission, with the concurrence of the Commission, has deemed it necessary to promulgate the following exemptions to specified provisions of the Privacy Act:

(1) Pursuant to, and limited by 5 U.S.C. 552a (j) (2), the system of records maintained by the Office of Inspector General of the Commission that contains the Investigative Files shall be exempted from the provisions of 5 U.S.C. 552a, except subsections (b), (c)(1) and (2), (e)(4)(A) through (F), (e)(6), (7), (9), (10), and (11), and (i), and 17 CFR 200.303, 200.304, 200.306, 200.307, 200.308, 200.309 and 200.310, insofar as the system contains information pertaining to criminal law enforcement investigations.

(2) [Reserved]

(b) Pursuant to section (k) of the Privacy Act of 1974, the Chairman of the Securities and Exchange Commission, with the concurrence of the Commission, has deemed it necessary to promulgate the following exemptions to specified provisions of the Privacy Act:

(1) Pursuant to, and limited by 5 U.S.C. 552a(k)(2), the system of records maintained by the Office of Inspector General of the Commission that contains the Investigative Files

(6)政府机构往来信函追踪系统。

(b)根据《美国法典》第五编第552a(k)(5)节,包含了证券交易委员会的(1)人员行为规范和雇员绩效办公室档案以及(2)人员安全档案的记录系统,如果含有用以判定个人是否适于从事联邦民事雇员工作或接触保密信息以及是否具有从事上述工作的适格性和资格的汇编调查材料,应豁免于《隐私法》第(c)(3)节、第(d)节、第(e)(1)节、第(e)(4)(G)节、第(H)节、第(I)节和第(f)节、《美国法典》第五编第552a(c)(3)节、第552a(d)节、第552a(e)(1)节、第552a(e)(4)(G)节、第552a(H)节、第552a(I)节和第552a(f)节以及《联邦规章汇编》第十七编第200.303节、第200.304节和第200.306节的规定。但是,豁免范围仅限于如下情况:材料披露后会揭露向政府提供信息的来源的身份,而该消息提供之时政府明确承诺对信息来源身份保密,或者,在1975年9月27日前政府曾暗示承诺对信息来源身份保密。

[第93-579号公法第k条,《美国法典》第五编第552a(k)节。]

[《联邦公报》第40卷第44073页,1975年9月24日,修正索引:《联邦公报》第52卷第2677页,1987年1月26日;《联邦公报》第54卷第24332页,1989年6月7日;《联邦公报》第54卷第46373页,1989年11月3日;《联邦公报》第60卷第32795页,1995年6月23日;《联邦公报》第65卷第55186页,2000年9月13日。]

第200.313节　监察长的豁免

(a)根据《1974年隐私法》第(j)条,证券交易委员会主席与证券交易委员会取得一致后,认为有必要颁发对《隐私法》具体条款的如下豁免:

(1)根据《美国法典》第五编第552a(j)(2)节并在遵守上述条款限制的前提下,证券交易委员会监察长办公室维护的含有调查档案的记录系统应豁免于《美国法典》第五编第552a节规定的条款,但是,若系统含有刑事执法调查信息,则不豁免适用第552a(b)子节、第552a(c)(1)子节、第552a(c)(2)子节、第552a(e)(4)(A)~(e)(4)(F)子节、第552a(e)(6)子节、第552a(e)(7)子节、第552a(e)(9)子节、第552a(e)(10)子节和第552a(e)(11)子节和第552a(i)子节,以及《联邦规章汇编》第十七编第200.303节、第200.304节、第200.306节、第200.307节、第200.308节、第200.309节和第200.310节的规定。

(2)[保留]

(b)根据《1974年隐私法》第(k)条,证券交易委员会主席与证券交易委员会取得一致后,认为有必要颁发对《隐私法》具体条款的如下豁免:

(1)根据《美国法典》第五编第552a(k)(2)节并在遵守上述条款限制的前提下,证券交易委员会监察长办公室维持的含有调查档案的记录系统,若包含为执法目的编

shall be exempted from 5 U.S.C. 552a(c)(3), (d), (e)(1), (e)(4) (G), (H), and (I), and (f) and 17 CFR 200.303, 200.304, and 200.306, insofar as it contains investigatory materials compiled for law enforcement purposes.

(2) [Reserved]

[55 FR 19872, May 14, 1990]

Subpart I—Regulations Pertaining to Public Observation of Commission Meetings

Authority: 5 U.S.C. 552b, unless otherwise noted. Section 200.410 also is issued under 29 U.S.C. 794.

Source: 42 FR 14693, Mar. 16, 1977, unless otherwise noted.

§200.400 Open meetings.

Except as otherwise provided in this subpart, meetings of the Commission shall be open to public observation.

§200.401 Definitions.

As used in this subpart:

(a) *Meeting* means the joint deliberations of at least the number of individual members of the Securities and Exchange Commission required to take action on behalf of the Commission where such deliberations determine or result in the joint conduct or disposition of official Commission business, but does not include deliberations required or permitted by §200.42 or §200.43 (respecting seriatim and duty officer disposition of Commission business, respectively), or by §§200.403, 200.404, or 200.405 (respecting whether particular Commission deliberations shall be open or closed and related matters).

(b) *Portion of a meeting* means the consideration during a meeting of a particular topic or item separately identified in the notice of Commission meetings described in §200.403.

(c) *Open,* when used in the context of a Commission meeting or a portion thereof, means that the public may attend and observe the deliberations of the Commission during such meeting or portion of a meeting, consistent with the provisions of §200.410 (respecting decorum at meetings and other related matters).

(d) *Closed,* when used in the context of a Commission meeting or a portion thereof, means that the public may not attend or observe the deliberations of the Commission during such meeting or portion of a meeting.

(e) *Announce,* and *make publicly available,* when used in the context of the

纂的调查材料,则应豁免适用《美国法典》第五编第552a(c)(3)节、第552a(d)节、第552a(e)(1)节、第552a(e)(4)(G)节、第552a(e)(4)(H)节和第552a(e)(4)(I)节和第552a(f)节,以及《联邦规章汇编》第十七编第200.303节、第200.304节和第200.306节的规定。

(2)[保留]

[《联邦公报》第55卷第19872页,1990年5月14日。]

第I子部分——关于允许公众作为观察员参与证券交易委员会会议的规定

法律依据:《美国法典》第五编第552b节,除非另有说明。第200.410节同时见《美国法典》第二十九编第794节。

行政规则来源:《联邦公报》第42卷第14693页,1977年3月16日,除非另有说明。

第200.400节　公开会议

除本子部分另有规定的情形外,否则证券交易委员会的会议应对公众开放,允许其到场观察。

第200.401节　定义

就本子部分而言:

(a)"会议"系指出席人数至少达到代表证券交易委员会采取行动所需证券交易委员会委员人数,并通过联合审议对证券交易委员会事务作出判定和采取联合行为或处置的会议,但不包括如下会议:第200.42节或第200.43节(内容分别为关于证券交易委员会分别审议处置证券交易委员会事务和由轮值官处置证券交易委员会事务的规定)要求或允许作出的审议,或根据第200.403节、第200.404节或第200.405节(内容为关于是否公开证券交易委员会的某些特别审议及其他相关事项的规定)作出的审议。

(b)"会议部分内容"系指在某会议中,针对第200.403节所述证券交易委员会会议通知中单列的某一具体议题或事项进行的审议。

(c)"公开",用于证券交易委员会的会议或会议部分内容之时,指公众可以在此等会议或会议部分内容中按照第200.410节(内容为会议礼仪及其他相关事项)的规定参加和观察证券交易委员会的审议。

(d)"不公开",用于证券交易委员会会议或会议部分内容之时,指公众无权在此等会议或会议部分内容中参加和观察证券交易委员会的审议。

(e)"公告"和"公开提供",在用于信息传播时指,除本子部分规定的任何具体公开

dissemination of information, mean, in addition to any specific method of publication described in this subpart, that a document containing the information in question will be posted for public inspection in, or adjacent to, the lobby of the Commission's headquarters offices, and will be available to the public through the Commission's Public Reference Section and the Commission's Office of Public Affairs, all in Washington, D.C..

(f) The term *likely to,* as used in §200.402, illustrating the circumstances under which Commission meetings may be closed, and the circumstances in which information may be deleted from the notice of Commission meetings, means that it is more probable than not that the discussion of Commission business, or publication of information, reasonably could encompass matters which the Commission is authorized, by the Government in the Sunshine Act, Pub. L. 94–409, as implemented by this subpart, to consider or discuss at a closed meeting (or a closed portion of a meeting).

(g) The term *financial institution,* as used in §200.402(a), authorizing the closure of certain Commission meetings, includes, but is not limited to, banks, savings and loan associations, credit unions, brokers and dealers in securities or commodities, exchanges dealing in securities or commodities, national securities associations, investment companies, investment advisers, securities industry self–regulatory organizations subject to 15 U.S.C. 78s, and institutional managers as defined in 15 U.S.C. 78m(f).

(h) The term *person* includes, but is not limited to, any corporation, partnership, company, association, joint stock corporation, business trust, unincorporated organization, government, political subdivision, agency, or instrumentality of a government.

[42 FR 14693, Mar. 16, 1977, as amended at 60 FR 17202, Apr. 5, 1995]

§200.402 Closed meetings.

(a) *Nonpublic matters.* Pursuant to the general or special procedures for closing Commission meetings, as set forth in §200.404 or §200.405, respectively, a meeting, or any portion thereof, shall be closed to public observation where the Commission determines that such meeting, or a portion thereof, is likely to:

(1) Disclose matters specifically authorized under criteria established by an executive order to be kept secret in the interests of national defense or foreign policy, and in fact properly classified pursuant to such executive order.

(2) Relate solely to the internal personnel rules and practices of the Commission or any other agency, including, but not limited to, discussion concerning:

(i) Operation rules, guidelines, and manuals of procedure for investigators, attorneys, accountants, and other employees, other than those rules, guidelines, and manuals which establish legal requirements to which members of the public are expected to conform; or

方式外,还应在证券交易委员会总部办公大楼大堂或相邻处张贴一份含有所涉信息的文件,以供公众查阅,并且通过证券交易委员会公共资料科和证券交易委员会的公共事务办公室向公众提供,这两个部门均位于华盛顿哥伦比亚特区。

(f)“可能”一词,就第200.402节而言,涉及证券交易委员会可以不向公众开放会议的情形以及信息可能从证券交易委员会会议通知中删除的情形时,指在一个理性人看来,证券交易委员会事务的讨论内容或公开的信息内容包含《阳光法》(公法编号94–409)(即本子部分贯彻的法律)授权证券交易委员会在非公开会议(或非公开的会议部分内容)中审议或讨论的事项的可能性更大。

(g)“金融机构”一词,就第200.402(a)节而言(该节准许证券交易委员会不向公众开放特定会议),包括但不限于《美国法典》第十五编第78s节规定的银行、储贷协会、信用社、证券或期货经纪商和自营商、证券或商品交易所、全国性证券协会、投资公司、投资顾问、证券行业自律组织,以及《美国法典》第十五编第78m(f)节所定义的机构投资管理人。[1]

(h)“人或主体”一词包括但不限于任何法人组织、合伙、公司、协会、合股公司、商业信托、非法人组织、政府、行政区域、政府机构或职能部门。

[《联邦公报》第42卷第14693页,1977年3月16日,修正索引:《联邦公报》第60卷第17202页,1995年4月5日。]

第200.402节　非公开会议

(a)非公开事项。证券交易委员会判定会议或会议部分内容可能涉及以下内容的,则根据第200.404节或第200.405节分别规定的不向公众开放会议的一般或特殊程序,该会议或该会议的任何一部分应不向公众观察开放:

(1)会议将披露如下事项:行政命令特别准许为国防或外交目的而按相关标准保密的事项;及根据上述行政命令,在事实上已被适当指定为保密信息的信息。

(2)会议仅与证券交易委员会或任何其他政府机构内部人事规则和操作有关,包括但不限于对以下事项的讨论:

(i)调查员、律师、会计师和其他雇员的操作规则、方针以及程序手册,但不包括制定期望公众遵守的法律要求的规则、方针和手册;或

1 原文“institutional managers”疑误,似应为“institutional investment managers”,译文已按后者处理。——译者注

(ii) Hiring, termination, promotion, discipline, compensation, or reward of any Commission employee or member, the existence, investigation, or disposition of a complaint against any Commission employee or member, the physical or mental condition of any Commission employee or member, the handling of strictly internal matters, which would tend to infringe on the privacy of the staff or members of the Commission, or similar subjects.

(3) Disclose matters specifically exempted from disclosure by statute (other than 5 U.S.C. 552): *Provided,* That such statute requires that the matters be withheld from the public in such a manner as to leave no discretion on the issue, or establishes particular criteria for withholding or refers to particular types of matters to be withheld.

(4) Disclose trade secrets and commercial or financial information obtained from a person and privileged or confidential, including, but not limited to:

(i) Information contained in letters of comment in connection with registration statements, applications for registration or other material filed with the Commission, replies thereto, and related material which is deemed to have been submitted to the Commission in confidence or to be confidential at the instance of the registrant or person who has filed such material unless the contrary clearly appears; and

(ii) Information contained in any document submitted to or required to be filed with the Commission where the Commission has undertaken formally or informally to receive such submission or filing for its use or the use of specified persons only, such as preliminary proxy material filed pursuant to Rule 14a-6 under the Securities Exchange Act (17 CFR 240.14a-6), reports filed pursuant to Rule 316(a) under the Securities Act (17 CFR 230.316 (a)), agreements filed pursuant to Rule 15c3-1 under the Securities Exchange Act, 17 CFR 240.15c3-1, schedules filed pursuant to Part I of Form X-17A-5 (17 CFR 249.617) in accordance with Rule 17a-5(b)(3) under the Securities Exchange Act (17 CFR 240.17a-5(b)(3)), statements filed pursuant to Rule 17a-5(k)(1) under the Securities Exchange Act (17 CFR 240.17a-5 (k)(1)), confidential reports filed pursuant to Rules 17a-9, 17a-10, 17a-12 and 17a-16 under the Securities Exchange Act (17 CFR 240.17a-9, 240.17a-10, 240.17a-12, and 240.17a-16), and any information filed with the Commission and confidential pursuant to section 45 of the Investment Company Act of 1940, 15 U.S.C. 80a-44, or Rule 45a-1 thereunder (17 CFR 270.45a-1); and

(iii) Information contained in reports, summaries, analyses, letters, of memoranda arising out of, in anticipation of, or in connection with, an examination or inspection of the books and records of any person or any other investigation.

(5) Involve accusing any person of a crime, or formally censuring any person, including, but not limited to, consideration of whether to:

(ii)易于导致证券交易委员会任何雇员或委员隐私受侵害的如下事项:证券交易委员会任何雇员或委员的聘用、解职、升职、纪律处分、薪酬或奖励;对证券交易委员会任何雇员或委员的投诉及与投诉相关的调查和处理;证券交易委员会雇员或委员的身体或精神状况;严格内部事务的处理;或者其他类似问题。

(3)会议将披露在制定法(不包括《美国法典》第五编第552节)明确豁免披露的事项,前提是,此等制定法以完全不留有任何自由裁量权的方式禁止向公众披露有关事项,或者,此等制定法确立了制定不向公众披露的具体标准或列举了不向公众披露的事项的具体类型。

(4)会议将披露从某人处获得的专属的或保密的商业机密和商业或财务信息,包括但不限于:

(i)与注册说明书、注册申请或提交给证券交易委员会的其他材料有关的征询意见函或回函中包含的信息,以及被视为在保密状态下向证券交易委员会呈报的相关材料,或经注册人、材料提交人的要求被视为保密的相关材料,除非存在明显相反的情况;及

(ii)呈报给证券委员会或规定应提交给证券交易委员会,且证券交易委员会已正式或非正式承诺接收以供其使用或仅供特定主体使用的任何文件中所包含的信息,如按照《证券交易法》的《14a-6规则》(《联邦规章汇编》第十七编第240.14a-6节)提交的初步代理权材料,按照《证券法》的《316(a)规则》[《联邦规章汇编》第十七编第230.316(a)节]提交的报告,按照《证券交易法》的《15c3-1规则》(《联邦规章汇编》第十七编第240.15c3-1节)提交的协议,在《证券交易法》的《17a-5(b)(3)规则》[《联邦规章汇编》第十七编第240.17a-5(b)(3)节]下按《X-17A表格》第I部分提交的计划,按照《证券交易法》的《17a-5(k)(1)规则》[《联邦规章汇编》第十七编第240.17a-5(k)(1)节]提交的说明书,按照《证券交易法》的《17a-9规则》、《17a-10规则》、《17a-12规则》和《17a-16规则》(《联邦规章汇编》第十七编第240.17a-9节、第240.17a-10节、第240.17a-12节和第240.17a-16节)提交的机密报告,以及向证券交易委员会提交的并且按照《1940年投资公司法》第45条(《美国法典》第十五编第80a-44节)或依其颁发的《45a-1规则》(《联邦规章汇编》第十七编第270.45a-1节)予以保密的任何信息;及

(iii)下列各项所含信息:由于对某人的账簿和记录的核查或检查或任何其他调查、因合理预期该等核查、检查或调查将发生而产生的报告、摘要、分析、信函、备忘录;以及与该等核查、检查或调查相关的报告、摘要、分析、信函、备忘录。

(5)涉及控诉任何人犯罪或对某人进行正式谴责的会议,包括但不限于对以下各项的审议:

(i) Institute, continue, or conclude administrative proceedings or any formal or informal investigation or inquiry, whether public or nonpublic, against or involving any person, alleging a violation of any provision of the federal securities laws, or the rules and regulations thereunder, or any other statute or rule a violation of which is punishable as a crime; or

(ii) Commence, participate in, or terminate judicial proceedings alleging a violation of any provision of the federal securities laws, or the rules and regulations thereunder, or any other statute or rule a violation of which is punishable as a crime; or

(iii) Issue a report or statement discussing the conduct of any person and the relationship of that conduct to possible violations of any provision of the federal securities laws, or the rules and regulations thereunder, or any other statute or rule a violation of which is punishable as a crime; or

(iv) Transmit, or disclose, with or without recommendation, any Commission memorandum, file, document, or record to the Department of Justice, a United States Attorney, any federal, state, local, or foreign governmental authority or foreign securities authority, any professional association, or any securities industry self-regulatory organization, in order that the recipient may consider the institution of proceedings against any person or the taking of any action that might involve accusing any person of a crime or formally censuring any person; or

(v) Seek from, act upon, or act jointly with respect to, any information, file, document, or record where such action could lead to accusing any person of a crime or formally censuring any person by any entity described in paragraph (a)(5)(iv) of this section.

(6) Disclose information of a personal nature, where disclosure would constitute a clearly unwarranted invasion of personal privacy.

(7)(i) Disclose investigatory records compiled for law enforcement purposes, or information which, if written, would be contained in such records, to the extent that the production of such records would:

(A) Interfere with enforcement activities undertaken, or likely to be undertaken, by the Commission or the Department of Justice, or any United States Attorney, or any Federal, State, local, or foreign governmental authority or foreign securities authority, any professional association, or any securities industry self-regulatory organization;

(B) Deprive a person of a right to a fair trial or an impartial adjudication;

(C) Constitute an unwarranted invasion of personal privacy;

(D) Disclose the identity of a confidential source and, in the case of a record compiled by a criminal law enforcement authority in the course of a criminal investigation, or by an agency conducting a lawful national security intelligence investigation,

(i)是否应发起、继续或结束针对任何人的任何公开或非公开的行政处理程序或正式或非正式的调查或盘问,或发起、继续或结束涉及任何人的该等行政处理程序、调查或盘问,指控违反联邦证券法任何规定的行为,或指控违反联邦证券法中的规则与规章的行为,或指控可处以刑事处罚的违反任何其他制定法或规则的行为;或

(ii)开始、参与或终止司法程序,指控违反任何联邦证券法规定的行为,违反联邦证券法项下规则与规章的行为或对任何其他可处以刑事处罚的违反制定法或规则的行为;或

(iii)签发一份报告或声明,讨论任何人的行为以及根据任何联邦证券法律或依其颁发的规则、规章或任何其他制定法或规定该行为是否构成可处以刑事处罚的违法违规行为;或

(iv)向美国司法部、联邦检察官、任何联邦、州、地方或外国政府机关或外国证券主管机构、任何专业协会或任何证券业自律组织传发或披露证券交易委员会的任何备忘录、文档、文件或记录(可附上或不附上建议),以便接收方考虑是否针对任何人发起行政处理程序、可能涉及犯罪指控的诉讼或采取可能涉及正式谴责的行动;或

(v)寻求任何信息、文档、文件或记录或基于该等信息、文件、文档或记录采取任何可能导致本节第(a)(5)(iv)款所述的任何实体针对任何人提起犯罪指控或进行正式谴责的行动或联合行动。

(6)明显构成对个人隐私无理侵犯的个人信息披露。

(7)(i)披露为执法目的编制的调查记录或该等档案中包含的书面信息,前提是提供该记录将造成以下结果:

(A)干扰证券交易委员会、司法部、任何联邦检察官、任何联邦、州、地方、外国政府机关、外国证券主管机构、任何专业协会或任何证券业自律组织采取或可能采取的执法行动;

(B)剥夺相关主体获得公平审判或公正裁决的权利;

(C)构成对个人隐私的无理侵犯;

(D)披露保密信息来源的身份;或者披露保密信息来源独家提供的保密信息(如果披露的信息是刑事执法机构在刑事调查过程中编制的记录或某机关在进行国家安全情报调查中编制的记录);

confidential information furnished only by the confidential source;

(E) Disclose investigative techniques and procedures; or

(F) Endanger the life or physical safety of law enforcement personnel.

(ii) The term *investigatory records* includes, but is not limited to, all documents, records, transcripts, evidentiary materials of any nature, correspondence, related memoranda, or work product concerning any examination, any investigation (whether formal or informal), or any related litigation, which pertains to, or may disclose, the possible violation by any person of any provision of any statute, rule, or regulation administered by the Commission, by any other Federal, State, local, or foreign governmental authority or foreign securities authority, by any professional association, or by any securities industry self-regulatory organization. The term *investigatory records* also includes all written communications from, or to, any person complaining or otherwise furnishing information respecting such possible violations, as well as all correspondence or memoranda in connection with such complaints or information.

(8) Disclose information contained in, or related to, any examination, operating, or condition report prepared by, on behalf of, or for the use of, the Commission, any other federal, state, local, or foreign governmental authority or foreign securities authority, or any securities industry self-regulatory organization, responsible for the regulation or supervision of financial institutions.

(9) Disclose information the premature disclosure of which would be likely to:

(i) (A) Lead to significant financial speculation in currencies, securities, or commodities, including, but not limited to, discussions concerning the proposed or continued suspension of trading in any security, or the possible investigation of, or institution of activity concerning, any person with respect to conduct involving or affecting publicly-traded securities, or

(B) Significantly endanger the stability of any financial institution; or

(ii) Significantly frustrate the implementation, or the proposed implementation, of any action by the Commission, any other federal, state, local or foreign governmental authority, any foreign securities authority, or any securities industry self-regulatory organization: *Provided, however*, That this paragraph (a)(9)(ii) shall not apply in any instance where the Commission has already disclosed to the public the precise content or nature of its proposed action, or where the Commission is expressly required by law to make such disclosure on its own initiative prior to taking final agency action on such proposal.

(10) Specifically concern the Commission's consideration of, or its actual: Issuance of a subpoena (whether by the Commission directly or by any Commission employee or member); participation in a civil action or proceeding, an action in a foreign court or

(E)披露调查技术和程序;或

(F)危及执法人员的生命或人身安全。

(ii)“调查记录”一词包括但不限于所有与下述行为相关或可能披露下述行为的文件、记录、笔录、各种性质的证物、书信往来、相关备忘录、检查工作成果、正式或非正式调查工作成果或任何相关诉讼工作成果:任何人涉嫌违反证券交易委员会或任何其他联邦、州、地方或外国政府机关或外国证券主管机构、任何专业协会或任何证券业自律组织负责实施的任何法律、规则或规章的行为。“调查记录”一词还包括与任何投诉上述违法违规行为或以其他方式提供信息的主体之间的往来通信,以及与该等投诉或信息有关的所有通信或备忘录。

(8)披露由证券交易委员会或负有金融机构监管责任的任何其他联邦、州、地方或外国政府机关、外国证券主管机构或任何证券业自律组织编制的或其代表编制的或为其使用而编制的任何检查、经营或现状报告中包含的信息或与之相关的信息。

(9)可能导致如下结果的过早披露信息的行为:

(i)(A)重大的货币、证券、商品投机,包括但不限于引发关于如下主题的讨论:任何证券停牌或继续停牌的可能性;对任何人涉及或影响公开交易证券的行为启动调查或行动的可能性;或

(B)严重危害任何金融机构的稳定;或

(ii)严重阻挠证券交易委员会、任何其他联邦、州、地方或外国政府机关、外国证券主管机构或任何证券业自律组织实施或拟实施的任何行动;但是,本第(a)(9)(ii)款不适用于任何以下情况:证券交易委员会已经向公众披露其拟采取的行动的详细内容或性质的情况,或法律明文规定证券交易委员会在采取上述拟议行动之前应主动进行披露的情况。

(10)会议具体涉及了证券交易委员会对以下事项的审议或实际行动:签发传票(不论是由证券交易委员会直接签发或由证券交易委员会任何员工或委员签发);参与民事诉讼或程序、在外国法院或国际法院提起的诉讼、仲裁;依照《美国法典》第五

international tribunal, or an arbitration; or initiation, conduct, or disposition of a particular case of formal adjudication pursuant to the procedures in 5 U.S.C. 554, or otherwise involving a determination on the record after opportunity for a hearing; including, but not limited to, matters involving:

(i) The institution, prosecution, adjudication, dismissal, settlement, or amendment of any administrative proceeding, whether public or nonpublic; or

(ii) The commencement, settlement, defense, or prosecution of any judicial proceeding to which the Commission, or any one or more of its members or employees, is or may become a party; or

(iii) The commencement, conduct, termination, status, or disposition of any inquiry, investigation, or proceedings to which the power to issue subpoenas is, or may become, attendant; or

(iv) The discharge of the Commission's responsibilities involving litigation under any statute concerning the subject of bankruptcy; or

(v) The participation by the Commission (or any employee or member thereof) in, or involvement with, any civil judicial proceeding or any administrative proceeding, whether as a party, as amicus curiae, or otherwise; or

(vi) The disposition of any application for a Commission order of any nature where the issuance of such an order would involve a determination on the record after opportunity for a hearing.

(b) *Interpretation of exemptions.* The examples set forth §200.402(a)(1) through (10) of particular matters which may be the subject of closed Commission deliberations are to be construed as illustrative, but not as exhaustive, of the scope of those exemptions.

(c) *Public interest determination.* Notwithstanding the provisions of §200.402(a) (concerning the closing of Commission meetings), but subject to the provisions of §200.409(a) (respecting the right of certain persons to petition for the closing of a Commission meeting), the Commission may conduct any meeting or portion of a meeting in public where the Commission determines, in its discretion, that the public interest renders it appropriate to open such a meeting.

(d) *Nonpublic matter in announcements.* The Commission may delete from the notice of Commission meetings described in §200.403, from the announcements concerning closed meetings described in §§200.404(b) and 200.405(c), and from the General Counsel's certification described in §200.406, any information or description the publication of which would be likely to disclose matters of the nature described in §200.402(a) (concerning the closing of Commission meetings).

(Pub. L. 94-409, 90 Stat. 1241)

[42 FR 14693, Mar. 16, 1977; 47 FR 37077, Aug. 25, 1982, as amended at 54 FR

编第554节规定的程序启动、开展或处置某个正式的行政裁决案件,或依据其他规定在给予听证机会后经书面审理作出决定;包括但不限于如下事项:

(i)任何公开或非公开行政处理程序的发起、追诉、裁决、撤销、和解或改判;或

(ii)证券交易委员会或证券交易委员会任何一名或多名委员或雇员作为或可能成为当事人的司法程序的发起、和解、辩护或追诉;或

(iii)有权或可能有权签发传票的任何盘问、调查或程序的开始、开展、终止、状态或处置;或

(iv)在根据破产领域的制定法提起的诉讼中履行证券交易委员会的责任;或

(v)证券交易委员会(或其任何雇员或委员)以当事人、法庭之友或其他身份参与或涉及的任何民事司法程序或任何行政处理程序;或

(vi)处置申请人向证券交易委员会提出的签发任何性质命令的申请,如果签发该等命令需要在给予听证机会后经书面审理作出判定。

(b)豁免解释。第200.402(a)(1)~200.402(a)(10)节列举的可能需要证券交易委员会进行封闭性审议的具体事项,属于豁免范围的举例性而非穷尽性列举。

(c)公共利益判定。无论第200.402(a)节(关于不公开证券交易委员会会议的规定)如何规定,在遵守第200.409(a)节(关于特定主体请求不公开举行证券交易委员会会议的权利的规定)的前提下,如证券交易委员会依其自由裁量权认定,出于公共利益应公开任何会议的全部或部分,证券交易委员会即可以公开该会议的全部或部分。

(d)通告中的非公开事项。证券交易委员会可以从第200.403节规定的证券交易委员会会议通知、第200.404(b)节和第200.405(c)节规定的非公开会议通告或第200.406节所述之首席律师认证函中,删除公布后可能导致披露第200.402(a)节(关于不公开证券交易委员会会议的规定)所述性质的事项的任何信息或描述。

[公法编号94-409,《美国制定法汇编》第90卷第1241页。]

[《联邦公报》第42卷第14693页,1977年3月16日;《联邦公报》第47卷第37077页,1982

24332, June 7, 1989]

§200.403 Notice of Commission meetings.

(a) *Content of notice.* (1) In the case of open meetings, or meetings closed pursuant to the procedures specified in §200.404, the Commission shall announce the items to be considered. For each such item, the announcement shall include:

(i) A brief description of the generic or precise subject matter to be discussed;

(ii) The date, place, and approximate time at which the Commission will consider the matter;

(iii) Whether the meeting, or the various portions thereof, shall be open or closed; and

(iv) The name and telephone number of the Commission official designated to respond to requests for information concerning the meeting at which the matter is to be considered.

(2) Every announcement of a Commission meeting described in this subsection, or any amended announcement described in paragraph (c), shall be transmitted to the Federal Register for publication.

(b) *Time of notice.* The announcement of Commission meetings referred to in paragraph (a) shall be made publicly available (and submitted immediately thereafter to the Federal Register for publication) at least one week prior to the consideration of any item listed therein, except where a majority of the members of the Commission determine, by a recorded vote, that Commission business requires earlier consideration of the matter. In the event of such a determination, the announcement shall be made publicly available (and submitted to the Federal Register) at the earliest practicable time.

(c) *Amendments to notice.* (1)(i) The time or place of a meeting may be changed following any public announcement that may be required by paragraph (a). In the event of such action, the Commission shall announce the change at the earliest practicable time.

(ii) The subject matter of a meeting, or the determination of the Commission to open or close a meeting (or a portion of a meeting), may be changed following any public announcement that may be required by paragraph (a), if (A) a majority of the entire membership of the Commission determines, by a recorded vote, that Commission business so requires and that no earlier announcement of the change was possible; and (B) the Commission publicly announces such change and the vote of each member upon such change at the earliest practicable time.

(2) Notwithstanding the provisions of this paragraph (c), matters which have been announced for Commission consideration may be deleted, or continued in whole or in part to the next scheduled Commission meeting, without notice.

年8月25日,修正索引:《联邦公报》第54卷第24332页,1989年6月7日。]

第200.403节 证券交易委员会会议公告

(a)公告内容。(1)对于公开会议或按第200.404节规定的程序举行的非公开会议,证券交易委员会应通告会议将审议的议题。对每一议题,通告应包含:

(i)对讨论的一般或具体议题的简要说明;

(ii)证券交易委员会审议该议题的日期、地点和大致时间;

(iii)会议或会议的各部分为公开或非公开;及

(iv)证券交易委员会指定对请求人要求获得会议议题相关信息的请求进行答复的官员的姓名和电话号码。

(2)本子节所述之所有证券交易委员会会议通告或第(c)款规定的任何修订后的会议通告均应刊登在《联邦公报》上。

(b)公告时间。第(a)款所述证券交易委员会会议通告至少应于对公告所列任何议题进行审议的一周之前向公众发布(并于发布后立即刊登在《联邦公报》上),除非证券交易委员会过半数委员通过记名投票判定证券交易委员会据其业务情况需要提前审议该议题。如果证券交易委员会作出该等判定,应于可行的最早时间向公众发布通告(并刊登在《联邦公报》上)。

(c)对公告的修订。(1)(i)会议召开的时间和地点可在根据第(a)款规定发布公开通告后进行变更。出现变更会议召开时间和地点的情况的,证券交易委员会应在可行的最早时间内就变更发布通告。

(ii)在下述情况下,会议议题、证券交易委员会公开或不公开会议(或会议部分内容)的决定,可以在根据第(a)款发布公开通告后进行变更:(A)证券交易委员会过半数委员通过记名投票判定证券交易委员会根据业务情况有必要进行变更,且无法在的更早时间发布通告;且(B)证券交易委员会在可行的最早时间就该变更以及每一委员的投票表决结果发布公开通告。

(2)无论第(c)款如何规定,证券交易委员会不必发出公告即可删除已经通告过的审议事项,或在下次证券交易委员会会议上继续讨论全部或部分已经通告过的审议事项。

(d) *Notice of meetings closed pursuant to special procedure.* In the case of meetings closed pursuant to the special procedures set forth in §200.405, the Commission shall make publicly available, in whole or in summary form,

(1) A brief description of the general subject matter considered or to be considered, and

(2) The date, place, and approximate time at which the Commission will, or did, consider the matter. The announcement described in this subsection shall be made publicly available at the earliest practicable time, and may be combined, in whole or in part, with the announcement described in paragraph (a).

Note: The Commission intends, to the extent convenient, to adhere to the following schedule in organizing its weekly agenda: Closed meetings to consider matters concerning the enforcement of the federal securities laws and the conduct of related investigations will generally be held on Tuesdays and on Thursday afternoons. An open meeting will generally be held each Thursday morning to consider matters of any appropriate nature. On Wednesdays, either open or closed meetings, or both, will generally be held according to the requirements of the Commission's agenda for the week in question. Normally, no meetings will be scheduled on Mondays, Fridays, Saturdays, Sundays, or legal holidays.

The foregoing tentative general schedule is set forth for the guidance of the public, but is not, in any event, binding upon the Commission. In every case, the scheduling of Commission meetings shall be determined by the demands of Commission business, consistent with the requirements of this subpart I. When feasible, the Commission will endeavor to announce the subject matter of all then-contemplated open meetings during a particular month at least one week prior to the commencement of that month.

When and if convenient after the conclusion of a closed Commission meeting, the Commission will endeavor to make publicly available a notice describing (subject to the provision in §200.402 (d) regarding nonpublic matter in announcements) the items considered at that meeting and any action taken thereon.

§200.404 General procedure for determination to close meeting.

(a) *Action to close meeting.* Action to close a meeting pursuant to §200.402(a) or (c) shall be taken only upon a vote of a majority of the entire membership of the Commission. A separate vote of the Commission members shall be taken with respect to each Commission meeting a portion or portions of which are proposed to be closed to the public pursuant to §200.402(a), or with respect to any information which is proposed to be withheld under §200.402(d); *Provided, however,* That a single vote may be taken with respect to a series of meetings, a portion or portions of which are proposed to be closed, or with respect to any information concerning such series of meetings, so long as each meeting in such series relates to the same matters and is scheduled to be held no more

（d）按照特别程序举行的不公开会议的公告。对于按照第200.405节规定的特别程序举行的不公开会议，证券交易委员会应以全文或摘要形式向公众公布如下信息：

（1）对证券交易委员会会议审议或即将审议的一般议题的简要说明；及

（2）证券交易委员会已经举行或将要举行的议题审议的日期、地点和大致时间。本子节规定的通告应在可行的最早时间向公众发布，并可与第（a）款规定的公告进行全文或部分合并。

注：证券交易委员会希望在方便之时按照如下日程组织周会：审议与联邦证券法执法和进行有关调查的非公开会议通常于周二和周四下午召开；审议性质适当的议题的公开会议通常于每周四上午召开；周三通常根据证券交易委员会当周的日程需要召开公开或非公开会议；周一、周五、周六、周日和法定假日通常不安排会议。

上述暂定通用日程仅用于为公众提供指引，任何情况下对证券交易委员会均无约束力。在任何情况下，证券交易委员会会议安排均应按照本第I子部分规定基于证券交易委员会业务需要确定。在可行之时，对于每月安排的所有公开会议，证券交易委员会应尽量于该月开始前至少一周通告审议的议题。

方便之时，证券交易委员会应于非公开会议结束后，尽量向公众发布一份公告［在不违反第200.402（d）节关于涉及非公开议题的通告的规定的前提下］，说明会议审议的事项以及决定采取的任何行动。

第200.404节　决定不公开举行会议的一般程序

（a）召开非公开会议的行动。只有经证券交易委员会全体委员过半数投票表决，才能按照第200.402（a）节或第200.402（c）节的规定召开非公开会议。对于拟按照第200.402（a）节不向公众公开某一部分或某几部分的证券交易委员会会议，以及拟按照第200.402（d）节保留的任何信息，证券交易委员会委员均应进行单独投票表决；但是，单次投票表决之效力也可及于一系列会议、拟不公开的会议的一部分或几部分内容，或与该系列会议相关的任何信息，只要该系列会议每次的议题相同，且所有后续会议均在首次会议召开后30日内召开。每名参与投票的证券交易委员会委员的投票均应记录在案，且不允许委托他人投票。

than thirty days after the initial meeting in such series. The vote of each Commission member participating in such vote shall be recorded and no proxies shall be allowed.

(b) *Announcement of action to close meeting.* Within one day of any vote pursuant to paragraph (a) of this section or §200.409 (a) (relating to review of Commission determinations to open a meeting), the Commission shall make publicly available:

(1) A written record reflecting the vote of each participating member of the Commission on the question; and

(2) In the case of a meeting or portion thereof to be closed to the public, a written explanation of the Commission's action closing the meeting or a portion thereof, together with a list describing generically or specifically the persons expected to attend the meeting and their affiliation; and

(3) For every closed meeting, the certification executed by the Commission's General Counsel as described in §200.406.

§200.405 Special procedure for determination to close meeting.

(a) *Finding.* Based, in part, on a review of several months of its meetings, as well as the legislative history of the Sunshine Act, the Commission finds that a majority of its meetings may properly be closed to the public pursuant to §200.402(a)(4), (8), (9)(i), or (10), or any combination thereof.

(b) *Action to close meeting.* The Commission may, by recorded vote of a majority of its members at the commencement of any meeting or portion thereof, determine to close any meeting or a portion thereof properly subject to being closed pursuant to §200.402(a)(4), (8), (9)(i), or (10), or any combination thereof. The procedure described in this rule may be utilized notwithstanding the fact that a meeting or portion thereof properly subject to being closed pursuant to §200.402(a)(4),(8),(9)(i), or(10), or any combination thereof, could also be closed pursuant to §200.402(a)(1),(2),(3),(5),(6),(7),or(9)(ii), or any combination thereof.

(c) *Announcement of action to close meeting.* In the case of a meeting or a portion of a meeting closed pursuant to this rule, as soon as practicable the Commission shall make publicly available:

(1) A written record reflecting the vote of each participating member of the Commission to close the meeting; and

(2) The certification described in §200.406, executed by the Commission's General Counsel.

§200.406 Certification by the General Counsel.

For every Commission meeting closed pursuant to §200.402(a)(1) through (10), the General Counsel of the Commission (or, in his or her absence, the attorney designated by General Counsel pursuant to §200.21) shall publicly certify that, in his or her opinion,

(b)召开非公开会议的通告。对于按照本节第(a)款或第200.409(a)节(关于证券交易委员会对公开举行会议的决定进行审查的规定)进行的任何投票表决,证券交易委员会应于投票表决后一天内向公众公布:

(1)一份反映每名参与表决的证券交易委员会委员就所涉事项投票的书面记录;及

(2)对于不向公众公开的会议或会议部分内容,向公众公布一份书面解释,说明证券交易委员会不公开该会议或会议部分内容的行动;同时,一份列明预期参与会议的人员类别或具体人员及该等人员所属单位的名单也应同时公开;及

(3)对每一非公开会议,均应根据第200.406节提供证券交易委员会首席律师签署的认证函。

第200.405节　决定不公开举行会议的特殊程序

(a)认定。根据对过去几个月会议的回顾,同时根据《阳光法》的立法史,证券交易委员会认定大多数会议均可按照第200.402(a)(4)节、第200.402(a)(8)节、第200.402(a)(9)(i)节或第200.402(a)(10)节的单项或多项规定恰当地不向公众公开。

(b)不公开会议的行动。证券交易委员会可以在任何会议或会议部分内容开始时以过半数委员记名投票的方式判定,按第200.402(a)(4)节、第200.402(a)(8)节、第200.402(a)(9)(i)节或第200.402(a)(10)节的单项或多项规定恰当地不公开任何会议或任何会议部分内容。如果,即使按第200.402(a)(4)节、第200.402(a)(8)节、第200.402(a)(9)(i)节或第200.402(a)(10)节的单项或多项规定不公开的会议或会议部分内容也可按第200.402(a)(1)节、第200.402(a)(2)节、第200.402(a)(3)节、第200.402(a)(5)节、第200.402(a)(6)节、第200.402(a)(7)节或第200.402(a)(9)(ii)节的单项或多项规定不予公开,仍然可以适用本规则规定的程序。

(c)召开非公开会议的行动的通告。如果某次会议或会议部分内容按照本条规则不予公开,证券交易委员会应尽快向公众公布:

(1)一份反映每位参与表决的证券交易委员会委员就所涉事项投票的书面记录;及

(2)第200.406节所述之证券交易委员会首席律师签署的认证函。

第200.406节　首席律师做出的认证

对于按照第200.402(a)(1)~(10)节不公开的每一证券交易委员会会议,应由证券交易委员会首席律师(如首席律师不在,则由首席律师按照第200.21节指定的律师)公开认证,说明其认为会议可以不向公众公开,且应说明各相关豁免条款。

the meeting may be closed to the public and shall state each relevant exemptive provision.

§200.407 Transcripts, minutes, and other documents concerning closed Commission meetings.

(a) *Record of closed meetings.* Except as provided in §200.407(b), the Commission's Secretary shall prepare a complete transcript or electronic recording adequate to record fully the proceedings of each closed meeting, or closed portion of a meeting.

(b) *Minutes of closed meetings.* In the case of a meeting, or portion of a meeting, closed to the public pursuant to §200.402(a)(8), (9)(i), or (10), the Secretary may, in his or her discretion or at the direction of the Commission, prepare either the transcript or recording described in §200.407(a), or a set of minutes. Such minutes shall fully and clearly describe all matters discussed and shall provide a full and accurate summary of any actions taken, and the reasons therefor, including a description of each of the views expressed on any item and the record of any rollcall vote (reflecting the vote of each participating Commission member on the question). All documents specifically considered by the Commission in connection with any action shall be identified in such minutes are maintained.

(c) *Retention of certificate and statement.* The Secretary shall retain a copy of every certification executed by the General Counsel pursuant to §200.406, together with a statement from the presiding officer of the meeting, or portion of a meeting to which the certification applies, setting forth the time and place of the meeting, and the persons present.

(d) *Minute Record.* Nothing herein shall affect the provisions of §§200.13a and 200.40 requiring the Secretary to prepare and maintain a Minute Record reflecting the official actions of the Commission.

§200.408 Public access to transcripts and minutes of closed Commission meetings; record retention.

(a) *Public access to record.* Within twenty days (excluding Saturdays, Sundays, and legal holidays) of the receipt by the Commission's Freedom of Information Act Officer of a written request, or within such extended period as may be agreeable to the person making the request, the Secretary shall make available for inspection by any person in the Commission's Public Reference Room, the transcript, electronic recording, or minutes (as required by §200.407(a) or (b)) of the discussion of any item on the agenda, except for such item or items as the Freedom of Information Act Officer determines to involve matters which may be withheld under §200.402 or otherwise. Copies of such transcript, or minutes, or a transcription of such recording disclosing the identity of each speaker, shall be furnished to any person at the actual cost of duplication, as set forth in §200.80e, and, if a transcript is prepared, the actual cost of such transcription.

第200.407节　与证券交易委员会非公开会议相关的会议笔录、纪要及其他文件

(a)非公开会议的记录。除第200.407(b)节规定的情形外,证券交易委员会秘书应制作一份完整会议笔录或电子记录,以记录每一非公开会议或会议非公开部分的完整过程。

(b)非公开会议的纪要。如果会议或会议部分内容按照第200.402(a)(8)节、第200.402(a)(9)(i)节或第200.402(a)(10)节的规定不向公众公开,证券交易委员会秘书依其自由裁量权可以自行或按证券交易委员会的指示制作第200.407(a)节所述之笔录或录音,或制作一套会议纪要。该等会议纪要应完整清晰说明审议的全部事项,并对所采取的所有行动、采取行动的原因提供完整准确的摘要,包括与会证券交易委员会委员就各议题表述的所有观点以及任何唱名投票记录(以反映每一与会委员的投票结果)。证券交易委员会审议的与所采取行动相关的全部文件均应在保存的会议纪要中注明。[1]

(c)认证函和说明书的保留。证券交易委员会秘书应保留由首席律师按照第200.406节签署的认证函的一份复本,同时应保留一份关于认证函所涉会议或会议的有关部分的说明书,列明会议时间、地点以及出席人名单,该说明书应由会议主持人或该部分会议之主持人出具。

(d)会议纪要记录。本节任何规定均不应影响第200.13a节和第200.40节要求证券交易委员会秘书长制作并维护反映证券交易委员会官方行动的会议纪要记录的规定。

第200.408节　公众获得证券交易委员会非公开会议笔录和纪要的渠道;记录保留

(a)公众获得记录的渠道。在证券交易委员会的信息自由法官员收到书面请求后20日内(不包括周六、周日和法定假日)或任何请求人可能同意的延长期限内,证券交易委员会秘书应按第200.407(a)节或第200.407(b)节的规定,在证券交易委员会公共资料室提供会议笔录、电子录音或会议纪要供公众查阅,但信息自由法官员判定涉及根据第200.402节或其他规定不应公开事项的记录除外。对于向任何人提供的披露每位发言人的身份的会议笔录或会议纪要,或根据会议录音整理的会议笔录,请求获得记录之人应按照第200.80e节的规定支付制作记录复本的实际费用,如果需要根据录音整理会议笔录,需要支付制作笔录的实际费用。

1　原文"All documents specifically considered by the Commission in connection with any action shall be identified in such minutes are maintained."语法疑误,"are maintained"之前似应有"that",对译文无影响。——译者注

(b) *Review of deletion from record.* Any person who has been notified that the Freedom of Information Act Officer has determined to withhold any transcript, recording, or minute, or portion thereof, which was the subject of a request for access pursuant to §200.402(a), or any person who has not received a response to his or her own request within the 20 days specified in §200.408(a), may appeal the adverse determination or failure to respond by applying for an order of the Commission determining and directing that the transcript, recording or minute, or deleted portion thereof, be made available. Such application shall be in writing and should be directed to the Secretary, Securities and Exchange Commission, Washington, D.C. 20549. The applicant shall state such facts and cite such legal or other authorities as the applicant may consider appropriate. The Commission shall make a determination with respect to any appeal pursuant to this subsection within 20 days (excepting Saturdays, Sundays and legal public holidays) after the receipt of such appeal, or within such extended period as may be agreeable to the person making the request. The Commission may determine to withhold any record that is exempt from disclosure pursuant to §200.402(a), although it may disclose a record, even if exempt, if, in its discretion, it determines it to be appropriate to do so.

(c) *Retention of record.* The Commission, by its Secretary, shall retain a complete verbatim copy of the transcript, or a complete copy of the minutes, or a complete electronic recording of each meeting, or portion of a meeting, closed to the public, for a period of at least two years after such meeting, or until one year after the conclusion of any Commission proceeding with respect to which the meeting or portion was held, whichever occurs later.

§200.409 Administrative appeals.

(a) *Review of determination to open meeting.* Following any announcement stating that the Commission intends to open a meeting or a portion thereof, any person whose interests may be directly and substantially affected by the disposition of the matter to be discussed at such meeting may make a request, directed to the Commission's Secretary, that the meeting, or relevant portion thereof, be closed pursuant to §200.402(a)(5), (6), or(7). The Secretary shall circulate such a request to the members of the Commission, along with a supporting statement provided by the requestor setting forth the requestor's interest in the matter and the reasons why the requestor believes that the meeting (or portion thereof) should be closed, and the Commission, upon the request of any one of its members, shall vote by recorded vote on whether to close such meeting or portion.

(b) *Review of determination to close meeting.* Following any announcement that the Commission intends to close a meeting or a portion thereof, any person may make written or telegraphic request, directed to the Commission's Secretary, that the meeting or a portion thereof be open. Such a request shall set forth the requestor's interest in the

(b)记录删除内容的审查。如果任何请求人被告知信息自由法官员已经根据第200.402(a)节判定,其请求获得的任何会议笔录、录音、会议纪要或其中的部分内容不应公开,或任何请求人未在第200.408(a)节规定的20日的期间内收到对其获得记录请求的答复,请求人可以就对其不利的判定或不答复行为提出复议申请,方法是申请证券交易委员会颁布命令,判定并指示信息自由法官员提供会议笔录、录音、会议纪要或其中的部分内容。申请应以书面形式作出,并交由证券交易委员会秘书处理,地址:华盛顿哥伦比亚特区证券交易委员会,邮编:D.C.20549。申请人应陈述相关事实并引用其认为适当的法律依据或其他依据。证券交易委员会应按照本子节规定,在收到任何复议申请后20日内(不包括周六、日和法定公共假日)或请求人同意的延长期内对复议申请作出判定。证券交易委员会可以按照第200.402(a)节的豁免披露规定决定不予公开记录,但如证券交易委员会依其自由裁量权判定确属适当,也可以决定公开按规定本应豁免披露的记录。

(c)记录的保留。证券交易委员会秘书应负责保留每次非公开会议或会议非公开部分的完整会议电子笔录,或完整会议纪要,或完整电子录音,保留时间不得短于会议后结束后两年,或证券交易委员会就上述会议或会议非公开部分开展的任何相关程序结束后一年(以较晚者为准)。

第200.409节　行政复议申请

(a)对公开举行会议的决定之审查。任何说明证券交易委员会有意公开某一会议或会议部分内容的通告发出后,其利益可能被即将在该等会议上讨论的事项之处置结果直接或严重影响的任何人均可提出请求,要求会议或相关会议部分内容按照第200.402(a)(5)节、第200.402(a)(6)节或第200.402(a)(7)节的规定不予公开,该等请求将交由证券交易委员会秘书处理。秘书长应将该请求与请求人提供的一份证明请求人在该事项上的利益以及请求人相信会议(或会议部分内容)不应公开的原因的说明书一并提交证券交易委员会委员传阅;任何一位委员提出请求之时,证券交易委员会均应就是否不公开举行该会议或会议部分举行记名投票。

(b)对不公开举行会议的决定之审查。任何说明证券交易委员会有意不公开某一会议或会议部分内容的通告发出后,任何人可以通过书面或电报形式提出请求公开该会议或该会议部分内容,该等请求将交由证券交易委员会秘书处理。该请求应说明请求人在该事项上的利益以及请求人相信会议(或会议部分内容)应予公开的原因。

matter and the reasons why the requestor believes that the meeting (or a portion thereof) should be open to the public. The Secretary shall circulate such a request and supporting statement to the members of the Commission, and the Commission, upon the request of any one of its members, shall vote whether to open such a meeting or a portion thereof.

§200.410 Miscellaneous.

(a) *Unauthorized activities; maintenance of decorum.* Nothing in this subpart shall authorize any member of the public to be heard at, or otherwise participate in, any Commission meeting, or to photograph or record by videotape or similar device any Commission meeting or portion thereof. The Commission may exclude any person from attendance at any meeting whenever necessary to preserve decorum, or where appropriate or necessary for health or safety reasons, or where necessary to terminate behavior unauthorized by this paragraph (a). Any person desiring to sound-record an open Commission meeting shall notify the Commission's Secretary of his intention to do so at least 48 hours in advance of the meeting in question. Any person desiring to photograph or videotape the Commission's proceedings may apply to the Secretary for permission to do so at least 48 hours in advance of the meeting in question. The Commission's determination to permit photography or videotaping at any meeting is confined to its exclusive discretion, and will be granted only if such activities will not result in undue disruption of Commission proceedings.

(b) *Suspension of open meeting.* Subject to the satisfaction of any procedural requirements which may be required by this subpart, nothing in this subpart shall preclude the Commission from directing that the room be cleared of spectators, temporarily or permanently, whenever it appears that the discussion during an open Commission meeting is likely to involve any matter described in §200.402(a) (respecting closed meetings).

(c) *Access to Commission documents.* Except as expressly provided, nothing in this subpart shall authorize any person to obtain access to any document not otherwise available to the public or not required to be disclosed pursuant to subpart D. Access to documents considered or mentioned at Commission meetings may only be obtained subject to the procedures set forth in, and the provisions of, subpart D.

(d) *Access to public meetings.* Any member of the public who plans to attend a public meeting of the Commission, and who requires an auxiliary aid such as a sign language interpreter, should contact the Commission's Selective Placement Coordinator, Office of Personnel at (202)272-7065 or TDD number (202)272-2552, prior to the meeting to make the necessary arrangements. The Selective Placement Coordinator will take all reasonable steps to accommodate requests made in advance of the scheduled meeting date.

秘书应将该请求与请求人提供的支持说明书一并提交证券交易委员会委员传阅；任何一位委员提出请求之时，证券交易委员会均应就是否公开该会议或该会议部分内容举行记名投票。

第200.410节　其他

（a）未授权的活动；维持会场秩序。本子部分的任何内容均不授权任何公众在证券交易委员会的任何会议上发言或以其他方式参与会议，或在证券交易委员会的任何会议或会议部分内容中拍照、使用录像机或类似设备进行录制。证券交易委员会可以出于保证会场秩序之必要目的，或保证健康或安全之恰当或必要目的，或停止本款禁止作出的行为之必要目的，谢绝任何人参与任何会议。任何希望在证券交易委员会会议上录音的人，应于会议召开前至少48小时前通知证券交易委员会秘书。任何希望在证券交易委员会会议上照相或摄像的人，可以于会议召开前至少48小时申请证券交易委员会秘书的批准。证券交易委员会对是否允许在任何会议上照相或摄像具有排他的自由裁量权，且照相或摄像申请只有在不对证券交易委员会会议造成不当干扰的情况下才会被核准。

（b）公开会议的暂停。在满足本子部分可能规定的任何程序性要求的前提下，只要在某次公开会议中讨论可能涉及第200.402（a）节（关于非公开会议）规定的任何事宜，本子部分任何规定均不应影响证券交易委员会命令听众临时或永久离开会场的权力。

（c）获取证券交易委员会文件的权利。除非另有明文规定，否则本子部分任何内容均不授权任何人获得不对公众公开的任何文件或者按照第D子部分不需要披露的文件。在证券交易委员会会议上审议或提及的文件只能按照第D子部分载明的程序和规定获得。

（d）参与公开会议的权利。任何有意参加证券交易委员会会议的公众如果需要手语翻译等辅助，应于会议开始前联系证券交易委员会人事办公室的展能就业协调员作出必要安排，电话号码：（202）272-7065或听障人士专线：（202）272-2552。展能就业协调员将采取所有合理步骤满足会议召开日期前提出的请求。

[42 FR 14693, Mar. 16, 1977, as amended at 44 FR 32366, June 6, 1979; 55 FR 10235, Mar. 20, 1990]

Subpart J—Classification and Declassification of National Security Information and Material

Authority: Sec. 19, Securities Act of 1933, as amended, 48 Stat. 84, 15 U.S.C. 77s. E.O. 12356, 47 FR 14874, Apr. 6, 1982. Information Security Oversight Office Directive No. 1 (47 FR 27836, June 25, 1982).

Source: 44 FR 65737, Nov. 15, 1979, unless otherwise noted.

§200.500 Purpose.

This part establishes general policies and procedures for the classification, declassification and safeguarding of national security information which is generated, processed and/or stored by the Commission, and supplements Executive Order 12356, April 6, 1982 (47 FR 14874), and Information Security Oversight Office Directive No. 1, June 25, 1982 (47 FR 27836).

[47 FR 47236, Oct. 25, 1982]

§200.501 Applicability.

This part applies to the handling of, and public access to, national security information and classified documents in the Commission's possession. Such documents no longer in the Commission's possession will be handled by the agency having possession, or in accordance with guidelines developed in consultation with the Archivist.

§200.502 Definition.

As used in this part: *Foreign government information* means either (a) information provided to the United States by a foreign government or governments, an international organization of governments, or any element thereof with the expectation, express or implied, that the information, the source of the information, or both, are to be held in confidence, or (b) information produced by the United States pursuant to or as a result of a joint arrangement with a foreign government or governments or an international organization of governments or any element thereof, requiring that the information, the arrangement, or both, are to be held in confidence.

[47 FR 47236, Oct. 25, 1982]

§200.503 Senior agency official.

The Executive Director of the Commission is designated the senior agency official responsible for conducting an oversight program to ensure effective implementation of

[《联邦公报》第42卷第14693页,1977年3月16日,修正索引:《联邦公报》第44卷第32366页,1979年6月6日;《联邦公报》第55卷第10235页,1990年3月20日。]

第J子部分——国家安全信息和材料的保密和解密

法律依据:《1933年证券法》第19条,修正索引:《美国制定法汇编》第48卷第84页,《美国法典》第十五编第77s.E.O.12356节,《联邦公报》第47卷第14874页,1982年4月6日。《信息安全监督办公室第1号指令》(《联邦公报》第47卷第27836页,1982年6月25日)

行政规则来源:1979年11月15日《联邦公报》第44卷65737页,除非另有说明。

第200.500节 目的

本部分制定了证券交易委员会生成、处理和/或存储的国家安全信息的保密、解密和保护的一般政策和程序,并构成对1982年4月6日《第12356号行政命令》(《联邦公报》第47卷第14874页)和1982年6月25日的《信息安全监督办公室第1号指令》(《联邦公报》第47卷第27836页)的补充。

[《联邦公报》第47卷第47236页,1982年10月25日。]

第200.501节 适用范围

本部分适用于证券交易委员会掌握的国家安全信息和保密文件的处理和公众查阅。该等文件不再由证券交易委员会掌握后,将由掌握该等文件的政府机构处理,或按照与美国国家档案馆馆长磋商制定的保密方针相应处理。

第200.502节 定义

就本部分而言,“外国政府信息”系指(a)由某外国政府或某几个外国政府、国际政府组织向美国政府提供的且明示或者暗示预期该信息和/或信息来源应予以保密的信息或其中的任何要素;或(b)美国政府根据或因为与某一外国政府或几个外国政府或某国际政府组织签订的联合安排而编制的信息或其中的任何要素,且该等安排要求对该信息和/或安排保密。

[《联邦公报》第47卷第47236页,1982年10月25日。]

第200.503节 证券交易委员会高级官员

证券交易委员会的执行主任被指定为负责执行监督计划,确保《第12356号行政命令》有效实施的证券交易委员会高级官员。与证券交易委员会信息安全计划有关的

Executive Order 12356. Any complaints or suggestions regarding the Commission's information security program should be directed to the Office of the Executive Director, Securities and Exchange Commission, Attn: Information Security Program, 100 F Street, NE., Washington, D.C. 20549.

(a) The Deputy Executive Director is the Senior Agency Official for purposes of the Paperwork Reduction Act of 1980. In this capacity, the Deputy Executive Director will carry out all responsibilities required by the Act (Pub. L. 96-511, 3506(b)), as well as serving as *Agency Clearance Officer* for purposes of the publication of notices in the Federal Register.

(b) [Reserved]

(11 U.S.C. 901, 1109(a))

[47 FR 47236, Oct. 25, 1982, as amended at 49 FR 12686, Mar. 30, 1984; 51 FR 5315, Feb. 13, 1986; 73 FR 32226, June 5, 2008]

§200.504 Oversight Committee.

An Oversight Committee is established, under the chairmanship of the Executive Director, with the following responsibilities:

(a) Establish a security education program to familiarize Commission and other personnel who have access to classified information with the provisions of Executive Order 12065, and encourage Commission personnel to challenge those classification decisions they believe to be improper.

(b) Establish controls to insure that classified information is used, processed, stored, reproduced, and transitted only under conditions that will provide adequate protection and prevent access by unauthorized persons.

(c) Establish procedures which require that a demonstrable need, under section 4-1 of Executive Order 12065, for access to classified information be established before administrative clearance procedures are initiated, as well as other appropriate procedures to prevent unnecessary access to classified information.

(d) Act on all suggestions and complaints concerning Commission administration of its information security program.

(e) Establish procedures within the Commission to insure the orderly and effective referral of requests for declassification of documents in the Commission's possession.

(f) Review on an annual basis all practices for safeguarding information and to eliminate those practices which are duplicative or unnecessary.

(g) Recommend to the Chairman of the Commission appropriate administrative action to correct abuse or violation of any provision of Executive Order 12356.

(h) Consider and decide other questions concerning classification and declassification

任何投诉或建议均应交由证券交易委员会执行主任办公室处理,注明:信息安全计划,地址为:华盛顿哥伦比亚特区东北分区100F大街,邮编:D.C.20549。

(a)副执行主任是负责《1980年文书削减法》实施工作的证券交易委员会高级官员,因此,将履行该法[公法编号96-511,3506(b)]规定的全部职责,并就《联邦公告》上公告的发布担任“机关发布审核官”。

(b)[保留]

[《美国法典》第十一编第901节、第1109(a)节。]

[《联邦公报》第47卷第47236页,1982年10月25日,修正索引:《联邦公报》第49卷第12686页,1984年3月30日;《联邦公报》第51卷第5315页,1986年2月13日;《联邦公报》第73卷第32226页,2008年6月5日。]

第200.504节 监督委员会

监督委员会由执行主任担任主席,委员会职责如下:

(a)制订安全教育计划,使证券交易委员会和其他可以获得保密信息的人员熟悉《第12065号行政命令》的规定,并鼓励证券交易委员会工作人员对其认为不适当的保密决定提出异议。

(b)制定控制措施确保在充分保护的条件下使用、处理、储存、复制或转移保密信息,防止未获授权的人士获得该等信息。

(c)制定相关程序,要求在启动行政发布程序前,按照《第12065号行政命令》第4-1条规定证明获得保密信息的必要性,并采取其他适当程序防止不必要的保密信息查询。

(d)处理与证券交易委员会对其信息安全计划的实施有关的任何建议或投诉。

(e)制定证券交易委员会内部程序,确保有序和有效地移交证券交易委员会掌握文件的解密请求。

(f)对保护信息安全的所有操作进行年度审查,并取消重复性或不必要的操作。

(g)建议证券交易委员会员主席采取适当的行政行动纠正滥用或任何违反《第12356号行政命令》任何条款的行为。

(h)审议任何提交其处理的有关保密和解密的问题并作出相应决定。

that may be brought before it.

(i) Develop special contingency plans for the protection of classified information used in or near hostile or potentially hostile areas.

(j) Promptly notify the Director of the Information Security Oversight Office whenever an officer or employee of the United States Government or its contractors, licensees or grantees knowingly, willfully or negligently (1) discloses to unauthorized persons information properly classified under Executive Order 12356 or predecessor orders or (2) classifies or continues the classification of information in violation of Executive Order 12356 or predecessor orders.

[44 FR 65737, Nov. 15, 1979, as amended at 47 FR 47236, Oct. 25, 1982; 51 FR 5315, Feb. 13, 1986]

§200.505 Original classification.

(a) No Commission Member or employee has the authority to classify any information on an original basis.

(b) If a Commission employee originates information that appears to require classification, the employee shall immediately notify the Secretary and protect the information accordingly.

(c) If the Executive Director believes the information warrants classification, it shall be sent to an agency with original classification authority over the subject matter, or to the information Security Oversight Office, for determination.

[44 FR 65737, Nov. 15, 1979, as amended at 51 FR 5315, Feb. 13, 1986]

§200.506 Derivative classification.

Any document that includes paraphrases, restatements, or summaries of, or incorporates in new form, information that is already classified shall be assigned the same level of classification as the source; if, however, the basic information appears to have been so changed that no classification, or a lower classification than originally assigned, should be used, the appropriate official of the originating agency or office of origin who has the authority to upgrade, downgrade or declassify the information must be consulted prior to assigning a different classification to the information.

[47 FR 47236, Oct. 25, 1982]

§200.507 Declassification dates on derivative documents.

(a) A document that derives its classification from information classified under Executive Order 12356 of predecessor orders shall be marked with the date or event assigned to that source information for its automatic declassification or for review of its continued need for classification.

(b) A derivative document that derives its classification from the approved use of the

(i)针对敌对地区、敌对地区周边或潜在敌对地区保密信息的使用制定特别应急保护方案。

(j)发现美国政府的任何管理人员、职员或承包商、被许可人或受让人在知情的情况下、故意或由于疏忽而作出下列行为的,应及时通知信息安全监督办公室主任:(1)向未获授权人士披露根据《第12356号行政命令》或其前身命令正式划为保密的信息,或(2)违反《第12356号行政命令》或其前身命令对信息进行保密或继续保密。

[《联邦公报》第44卷第65737页,1979年11月15日,修正索引:《联邦公报》第47卷第47236页,1982年10月25日;《联邦公报》第51卷第5315页,1986年2月13日。]

第200.505节　原始密级

(a)证券交易委员会的任何委员或雇员均没有对任何信息指定原始密级的权限。

(b)如果证券交易委员会员工创建了需要保密的信息,应立即通知秘书并对该信息采取相应的保护措施。

(c)如果执行主任相信信息应予保密,应将其送至对所涉事项具有指定原始密级权限的政府机构或信息安全监督办公室作出判定。

[《联邦公报》第44卷第65737页,1979年11月15日,修正索引:《联邦公报》第51卷第5315页,1986年2月13日。]

第200.506节　衍生密级

任何文件如果包括对保密信息的改写、重述、摘要,或以新的形式体现该保密信息的,应定为与源文件相同的密级;不过,如果基本信息经改变后,不应再被定为保密信息或应降低密级,则必须在为该信息指定不同的密级之前咨询原来指定密级的政府机关或作为文件源的办公室的对该信息具有提升密级、降低密级或解密的权限的相关官员。

[《联邦公报》第47卷第47236页,1982年10月25日。]

第200.507节　衍生文件的解密日期

(a)《第12356号行政命令》或其前身命令规定的保密信息中衍生出来的保密文件上应注明源信息的自动解密日期以及自动解密条件或者对继续保密必要性进行审查的日期或情形。

(b)获准按其他政府机构保密指南指定密级的衍生文件的解密日期,应为该保密

classification guide of another agency shall bear the declassification date required by the provisions of that classification guide.

[47 FR 47236, Oct. 25, 1982]

§200.508 Requests for mandatory review for declassification.

(a) Requests for mandatory review of a Commission document for declassification may be made by any United States citizen or permanent resident alien, including Commission employees, or a Federal agency, or a State or local government. The request shall be in writing and shall be sent to the Office of the Executive Director, Attn: Mandatory Review Request, Securities and Exchange Commission, 100 F Street, NE., Washington, D.C. 20549.

(b) The request shall describe the material sufficiently to enable the Commission to locate it. Requests with insufficient description of the material will be returned to the requester for further information.

(c) Within 5 days of receiving a request for declassification, the Commission shall acknowledge its receipt. If the document was derivatively classified by the Commission or originally classified by another agency, the request and the document shall be forwarded promptly to the agency with original classification authority together with the Commission's recommendation to withhold any of the information where appropriate. The requester shall be notified of the referral.

(d) If the request requires the provision of services by the Commission, fair and equitable fees may be charged under title 5 of the Independent Offices Appropriation Act, 65 Stat. 290, 31 U.S.C. 483a.

[44 FR 65737, Nov. 15, 1979, as amended at 47 FR 47237, Oct. 25, 1982; 51 FR 5315, Feb. 13, 1986; 73 FR 32226, June 5, 2008]

§200.509 Challenge to classification by Commission employees.

Commission employees who have reasonable cause to believe that information is classified unnecessarily, improperly, or for an inappropriate period of time, may challenge those classification decisions through mandatory review or other appropriate procedures as established by the Oversight Committee. Commission employees who challenge classification decisions may request that their identity not be disclosed.

§200.510 Access by historical researchers.

(a) Persons outside the executive branch performing historical research may have access to information over which the Commission has classification jurisdiction for the period requested (but not longer than 2 years unless renewed for an additional period of less than 2 years) if the Executive Director determines in writing that access to the information will be consistent with the interests of national security.

指南条款规定的解密日期。

[《联邦公报》第47卷第47236页,1982年10月25日。]

第200.508节　强制性解密审查请求

(a)任何美国公民或属于美国常住居民的外国人,包括证券交易委员会雇员、联邦政府机构或州政府或地方政府,均可以要求对证券交易委员会文件进行强制解密审查。请求应以书面形式作出,并寄送至执行主任办公室,注明:强制审查请求,地址:华盛顿哥伦比亚特区东北分区100F大街证券交易委员会,邮编:D.C.20549。

(b)请求应对所请求的材料进行充分描述,使证券交易委员会可以查找到该材料。未对所请求材料进行充分描述的请求将被退还给请求人,要求其提供补充信息。

(c)证券交易委员会应在收到解密请求后5日内进行收悉确认。对于证券交易委员会指定的衍生密级文件,或者另一个政府机关指定的原始密级文件,该文件和解密请求应及时转交给具备指定原始密级权限的政府机关,转交时还应附上证券交易委员会对其中任何信息进行保密的建议(如适当)。转交情况应通知请求人。

(d)如果请求中要求证券交易委员会提供服务,证券交易委员会可以按照《独立办公室拨款法》第五编(《美国制定法汇编》第65卷第290页,《美国法典》第三十一编第483a节)的规定收取公平合理的费用。

[《联邦公报》第44卷第65737页,1979年11月15日,修正索引:《联邦公报》第47卷第47237页,1982年10月25日;《联邦公报》第51卷第5315页,1986年2月13日;《联邦公报》第73卷第32226页,2008年6月5日。]

第200.509节　证券交易委员会雇员对密级提出异议

证券交易委员会雇员如果有合理理由相信对信息的保密不需要、不恰当或保密期限不适当,可以通过强制审查程序或监察委员会制定的其他适当程序对保密决定提出异议。对保密决定提出异议的证券交易委员会雇员可以要求对其个人身份进行保密。

第200.510节　历史研究人员的保密信息查询权

(a)行政部门外部人士出于历史研究需要,可以在请求的时限内(不得超过2年,除非获得延展,且延展期限亦不得超过2年)查询证券交易委员会有权指定密级的保密信息,条件是执行主任书面判定向其提供该信息查询权不违反国家安全利益。

(b) The person seeking access to classified information must agree in writing:

(1) To be subject to a national agency check;

(2) To protect the classified information in accordance with the provisions of Executive Order 12356; and

(3) Not to publish or otherwise reveal to unauthorized persons any classified information.

[44 FR 65737, Nov. 15, 1979, as amended at 47 FR 47237, Oct. 25, 1982; 51 FR 5315, Feb. 13, 1986]

§200.511 Access by former Presidential appointees.

(a) Former Commission Members appointed by the President may have access to classified information or documents over which the Commission has jurisdiction that they originated, reviewed, signed, or received while in public office, if the Executive Director determines in writing that access to the information will be consistent with the interest of nation security.

(b) The person seeking access to classified information must agree in writing:

(1) To be subject to a national agency check;

(2) To protect the classified information in accordance with the provisions of Executive Order 12356; and

(3) Not to publish or otherwise reveal to unauthorized persons any classified information.

[44 FR 65737, Nov. 15, 1979, as amended at 47 FR 47237, Oct. 25, 1982; 51 FR 5315, Feb. 13, 1986]

Subpart K—Regulations Pertaining to the Protection of the Environment

Authority: 15 U.S.C. 78w(a)(2).

Source: 44 FR 41177, July 16, 1979, unless otherwise noted.

§200.550 Purpose.

This subpart sets forth the procedures the Commission will follow to ensure compliance with the goals of the National Environmental Policy Act (*NEPA*) and with the procedures required by NEPA in the event that the Commission should take action subject to such procedural requirements.

§200.551 Applicability.

(a) Compliance with the procedures set forth in §§200.552 through 200.554 shall be

(b)请求查询保密信息之人必须书面同意:

(1)接受国家机关检查;

(2)根据《第12356号行政命令》的条款保护保密信息;并

(3)不发表或以其他方式向未获授权的人士泄露任何保密信息。

[《联邦公报》第44卷第65737页,1979年11月15日,修正索引:《联邦公报》第47卷第47237页,1982年10月25日;《联邦公报》第51卷第5315页,1986年2月13日。]

第200.511节　总统任命的前任委员的保密信息查询权

(a)由总统任命的证券交易委员会前任委员可以查询证券交易委员会有权指定密级的保密信息或文件,如果这些保密信息和文件是其在职期间创建、审阅、签字或收到的,条件是执行主任书面判定向其提供该等信息查询权不违反国家安全利益。

(b)请求查询保密信息之人必须书面同意:

(1)接受国家机关检查;

(2)根据《第12356号行政命令》的条款保护保密信息;并

(3)不发表或以其他方式向未获授权的人士泄露任何保密信息。

[《联邦公报》第44卷第65737页,1979年11月15日,修正索引:《联邦公报》第47卷第47237页,1982年10月25日;《联邦公报》第51卷第5315页,1986年2月13日。]

第K子部分——环境保护管理办法

法律依据:《美国法典》第十五编第78w(a)(2)节。

行政规则来源:1979年7月16日《联邦公报》第44卷第41177页,除非另有说明。

第200.550节　目的

本子部分规定了证券交易委员会为确保实现《国家环境保护政策法》(NEPA)的目标应遵守的程序,以及出现证券交易委员会应根据《国家环境保护政策法》程序要求采取行动时所遵循的程序。

第200.551节　适用范围

(a)证券交易委员会针对受制于《1935年公用事业控股公司法》第6(b)条和第7条

appropriate where Commission action taken with respect to security transactions subject to sections 6(b) and 7 of the Public Utility Holding Company Act of 1935 and acquisitions subject to sections 9 and 10 of that Act involves major Federal action significantly affecting the quality of the human environment.

(b) In addition to the foregoing, in the event of extraordinary circumstances in which a Commission action not specified in paragraph (a) of this section may involve major Federal action significantly affecting the quality of the human environment, the Commission shall follow the procedures set forth in §§200.552 through 200.554, unless doing so would be inconsistent with its statutory authority under the Federal securities laws.

§200.552 NEPA planning.

Where it is reasonably foreseeable by the Commission that it may be required to act on a matter specified in §200.551 and that matter is likely to involve major Federal action significantly affecting the quality of the human environment, the Commission shall:

(a) Advise the relevant persons as to information respecting the environment, if any, which may later be required to be submitted for Commission consideration should Commission action become necessary;

(b) Consult on any environmental factors involved with individuals, organizations, and state and local authorities interested in the planned action; and

(c) Begin implementing the procedures set forth in §§200.553 and 200.554 as soon as possible, *Provided,* That such procedures are not inconsistent with the Commission's authority under the Federal securities laws.

§200.553 Draft, final and supplemental impact statements.

If the Commission determines that the requirements of section 102(2)(C) of NEPA for preparation of an environmental impact statement are applicable in connection with a proposed Commission action, it shall prepare such statement generally in accordance with the procedures specified in 40 CFR parts 1500–1508, particularly part 1502 concerning impact statement preparation and content, §1505.1 concerning decision–making procedures, and §1501.6 concerning the function of cooperating agencies, to the extent that such procedures do not conflict with the Commission's statutory responsibilities and authority under the Federal securities laws.

§200.554 Public availability of information.

(a) Any environmental assessment or impact statement, and Commission responses pertaining to formal rulemaking proceedings or adjudicatory proceedings, shall be made part of the record in any such proceedings. In the case of formal adjudicatory proceedings, this shall be done in accordance with Rule 460 of the Commission's Rules of Practice, §201.460 of this chapter. In the case of formal rulemaking proceedings, this shall be done

的证券交易以及受制于《1935年公用事业控股公司法》第9条和第10条的收购采取的行动,如涉及显著影响人类生活环境质量的重大联邦行动,应符合第200.552~200.554节规定的程序(如适当)。

(b)除上述规定外,如果出现本节第(a)款未作规定的非常情况,且证券交易委员会采取的行动可能涉及影响人类生活环境质量的重大联邦行动,证券交易委员会应遵守第200.552~200.554节规定的程序,但与其在《联邦证券法》下享有的法定权限相冲突的除外。

第200.552节 《国家环境保护政策法》计划

如果证券交易委员会合理预测其可能需要就第200.551节规定的事项采取行动,且该事项可能涉及显著影响人类生活环境质量的重大联邦政府行动,证券交易委员会应:

(a)告知有关主体,此后在证券交易委员会有必要采取行动之时,可能需要将与环境有关的信息(如有)呈报证券交易委员会审议;

(b)与对计划行动的有利益关联的个人、组织、州和地方当局就所涉任何环境因素进行磋商;并

(c)尽快开始实施第200.553节和第200.554节规定的程序,前提是,该等程序与证券交易委员会在联邦证券法中的权限不相冲突。

第200.553节 环境影响报告的草案、终稿和补充

如果证券交易委员会认定根据《国家环境保护政策法》第102(2)(C)条的规定,应就证券交易委员会拟采取的行动编制一份环境影响报告,证券交易委员会总体上应根据《联邦规章汇编》第四十编第1500~1508部分规定的程序编制该报告——特别是第1502部分(环境影响报告的编制与内容)、第1505.1节(决策程序)、第1501.6节(协作政府机关的职能)制定的程序,前提是这些程序不能与证券交易委员会在联邦证券法中的法定职责和权限相冲突。

第200.554节 信息的公开提供

(a)任何环境评估或影响报告以及证券交易委员会对正式规则制定程序或审判程序有关的回复,均应纳入该等程序的记录之中。对于正式审判程序,应适用《证券交易委员会工作规则》的《460规则》(本章第201.460节)。如果是正式规则制定程序,则应适用证券交易委员会有关该等程序的规则。

in accordance with the Commission's rules respecting such proceedings.

(b) The location of publicly available environmental impact statements will be 100 F Street, NE., Washington, D.C. 20549.

(c) Interested persons may obtain information regarding and status reports on specific environmental impact statements and environmental assessments by contacting the division or office within the Commission which has responsibility for the particular proposed action.

[44 FR 41177, July 16, 1979, as amended at 47 FR 26819, June 22, 1982; 60 FR 32795, June 23, 1995; 73 FR 32226, June 5, 2008]

Subpart L—Enforcement of Nondiscrimination on the Basis of Handicap in Programs or Activities Conducted by the Securities and Exchange Commission

Authority: 29 U.S.C. 794.

Source: 53 FR 25885, July 8, 1988, unless otherwise noted.

§200.601 Purpose.

The purpose of this regulation is to effectuate section 119 of the Rehabilitation, Comprehensive Services, and Developmental Disabilities Amendments of 1978, which amended section 504 of the Rehabilitation Act of 1973 to prohibit discrimination on the basis of handicap in programs or activities conducted by Executive agencies or the United States Postal Service.

§200.602 Application.

This regulation (§§200.601–200.670) applies to all programs or activities conducted by the agency, except for programs or activities conducted outside the United States that do not involve individuals with handicaps in the United States.

§200.603 Definitions.

For purposes of this regulation, the term—

Assistant Attorney General means the Assistant Attorney General, Civil Rights Division, United States Department of Justice.

Auxiliary aids means services or devices that enable persons with impaired sensory, manual, or speaking skills to have an equal opportunity to participate in, and enjoy the

(b)公开提供环境影响报告的地址如下:华盛顿哥伦比亚特区东北分区100F大街,邮编:D.C.20549。

(c)任何人士,如有兴趣,均可联系证券交易委员会负责采取拟议行动的部门或办公室获得与具体环境影响报告相关的信息及其状态报告。

[《联邦公报》第44卷第41177页,1979年7月16日,修正索引:《联邦公报》第47卷第26819页,1982年6月22日;《联邦公报》第60卷第32795页,1995年6月23日;《联邦公报》第73卷第32226页,2008年6月5日。]

第L子部分——反残障歧视政策在证券交易委员会开展的项目或活动中的实施

法律依据:《美国法典》第二十九编第794节

行政规则来源:《联邦公报》第53卷第25885页,1988年7月8日,除非另有说明。

第200.601节　目的

本规章的目的是执行《1978年康复、全面服务和残疾修正案》第119条的规定——该规定修正了《1973年康复法》第504条,目的是在行政机构或美国邮政总局开展的项目或活动中杜绝歧视残障现象。

第200.602节　适用范围

本规章(第200.601~200.670节)适用于证券交易委员会开展的所有项目和活动,但不涉及美国境内残障人士的在美国境外开展的项目或活动除外。

第200.603节　定义

就本规章而言,下述词语之含义如下——

“司法部助理部长”系指主管美国司法部民权司的司法部助理部长。

“辅助服务或设备”系指帮助存在感官、运动或表达缺陷/障碍人士获得平等机会参与证券交易委员会开展的项目、活动并获得其利益的服务或设备。例如,对于视力

benefits of, programs or activities conducted by the agency. For example, auxiliary aids useful for persons with impaired vision include readers, Brailled materials, audio recordings, and other similar services and devices. Auxiliary aids useful for persons with impaired hearing include telephone handset amplifiers, telephones compatible with hearing aids, telecommunication devices for deaf persons (TDD's), interpreters, note takers, written materials, and other similar services and devices.

Complete complaint means a written statement that contains the complainant's name and address and describes the agency's alleged discriminatory action in sufficient detail to inform the agency of the nature and date of the alleged violation of section 504. It shall be signed by the complainant or by someone authorized to do so on his or her behalf. Complaints filed on behalf of classes or third parties shall describe or identify (by name, if possible) the alleged victims of discrimination.

Facility means all or any portion of buildings, structures, equipment, roads, walks, parking lots, rolling stock or other conveyances, or other real or personal property.

Historic preservation programs means programs conducted by the agency that have preservation of historic properties as a primary purpose.

Historic properties means those properties that are listed or eligible for listing in the National Register of Historic Places or properties designated as historic under a statute of the appropriate State or local government body.

Individual with handicaps means any person who has a physical or mental impairment that substantially limits one or more major life activities, has a record of such an impairment, or is regarded as having such an impairment.

As used in this definition, the phrase:

(1) *Physical or mental impairment* includes —

(i) Any physiological disorder or condition, cosmetic disfigurement, or anatomical loss affecting one or more of the following body systems: Neurological; musculoskeletal; special sense organs; respiratory, including speech organs; cardiovascular; reproductive; digestive; genitourinary; hemic and lymphatic; skin; and endocrine; or

(ii) Any mental or psychological disorder, such as mental retardation, organic brain syndrome, emotional or mental illness, and specific learning disabilities. The term *physical or mental impairment* includes, but is not limited to, such diseases and conditions as orthopedic, visual, speech, and hearing impairments, cerebral palsy, epilepsy, muscular dystrophy, multiple sclerosis, cancer, heart disease, diabetes, mental retardation, emotional illness, and drug addiction and alcoholism.

(2) *Major life activities* includes functions such as caring for one's self, performing manual tasks, walking, seeing, hearing, speaking, breathing, learning, and working.

(3) *Has a record of such an impairment* means has a history of, or has been

受损的人,辅助服务或设备包括放大阅读器、盲文材料、录音和其他类似服务、设备。对于听力受损的人,辅助服务或设备包括电话听筒扩音器、与助听设备兼容的电话、聋哑人通讯设备(TDD's)、手语译员、记录人员、书面材料及其他类似服务和设备。

"完整申诉书"系指符合下述条件的书面声明:注明申诉人姓名、地址并充分详细地说明其所指称的证券交易委员会歧视行为,并告知证券交易委员会其所指称的违反第504条的行为的性质和日期。申诉人或其授权代表应在申诉书上签名。集体申诉书或代表第三方提交的申诉书应说明或注明(如有可能,应逐一列出姓名)其所指称的歧视行为的受害人。

"设施"系指建筑物、构筑物、设备、道路、步道、停车场、车队或其他运输工具或其他不动产、动产之整体或任何部分。

"历史建筑保护项目"系指证券交易委员会开展的以保护历史建筑为主要目的之项目。

"历史建筑"系指《国家历史古迹名单》上列明的或有资格列于其上的建筑,或相应的国家或地方政府机构通过法律指定的历史建筑。

"残障人士"系指存在生理或精神残障且残障对其一种或多种主要日常生活活动造成了实质限制的任何人士,且该等人士应拥有残障记录或被视为存在残障。

在上述定义中:

(1)"生理或精神残障"包括——

(i)影响以下一个或多个身体系统的生理障碍/状况、体表缺陷或组织缺损:神经系统;肌肉骨骼系统;特殊感官;呼吸系统,包括语言器官;心血管系统;生殖系统;消化系统;泌尿系统;血液淋巴系统;皮肤和内分泌系统;或

(ii)任何精神或生理障碍,如智力迟钝、器质性脑综合症、情绪或心理疾病,以及特殊的学习障碍。"生理或精神障碍"包括但不限于外科、视力、语言和听力损伤、大脑性麻痹、癫痫、肌肉萎缩症、多发性硬化、癌症、心脏病、糖尿病、智力迟钝、情绪病、药物依赖和酒精成瘾等疾病和状态。

(2)"主要日常生活活动"包括生活自理、双手操作、步行、视听、语言表达、呼吸、学习和工作等。

(3)"拥有残障记录"系指有过对一种或多种主要日常生活活动造成实质限制的

misclassified as having, a mental or physical impairment that substantially limits one or more major life activities.

(4) *Is regarded as having an impairment* means —

(i) Has a physical or mental impairment that does not substantially limit major life activities but is treated by the agency as constituting such a limitation;

(ii) Has a physical or mental impairment that substantially limits major life activities only as a result of the attitudes of others toward such impairment; or

(iii) Has none of the impairments defined in paragraph (1) of this definition but is treated by the agency as having such an impairment.

Qualified individual with handicaps means —

(1) With respect to preschool, elementary, or secondary education services provided by the agency, an individual with handicaps who is a member of a class of persons otherwise entitled by statute, regulation, or agency policy to receive education services from the agency;

(2) With respect to any other agency program or activity under which a person is required to perform services or to achieve a level of accomplishment, an individual with handicaps who meets the essential eligibility requirements and who can achieve the purpose of the program or activity without modifications in the program or activity that the agency can demonstrate would result in a fundamental alteration in its nature;

(3) With respect to any other program or activity, an individual with handicaps who meets the essential eligibility requirements for participation in, or receipt of benefits from, that program or activity; and

(4) *Qualified handicapped person* as that term is defined for purposes of employment in 29 CFR 1613.702(f), which is made applicable to this regulation by §200.640.

Section 504 means section 504 of the Rehabilitation Act of 1973 (Pub. L. 93–112, 87 Stat. 394 (29 U.S.C. 794)), as amended by the Rehabilitation Act Amendments of 1974 (Pub. L. 93–516, 88 Stat. 1617); the Rehabilitation, Comprehensive Services, and Developmental Disabilities Amendments of 1978 (Pub. L. 95–602, 92 Stat. 2955); and the Rehabilitation Act Amendments of 1986 (Pub. L. 99–506, 100 Stat. 1810). As used in this regulation, section 504 applies only to programs or activities conducted by Executive agencies and not to federally assisted programs.

*Substantial impairment*means a significant loss of the integrity of finished materials, design quality, or special character resulting from a permanent alteration.

§§200.604–200.609 [Reserved]

§200.610 Self–evaluation.

(a) The agency shall, by September 6, 1989, evaluate its current policies and practices, and the effects thereof, that do not or may not meet the requirements of this

精神或生理障碍史或有过被误判为存在上述障碍的记录。

(4)“被视为存在障碍”指——

(i)其生理或精神障碍不对其主要日常生活活动造成实质限制,但被证券交易委员会视为构成上述限制;

(ii)其生理或精神障碍对其主要日常生活活动造成实质限制,但该等限制产生的唯一原因是其他人对该等障碍所持态度所致;或

(iii)不存在本定义第(1)款所定义的障碍,但被证券交易委员会视为存在上述障碍的情形。

“合格残障人士”——

(1)就证券交易委员会提供的学前、小学或中学教育服务而言,指根据法律、法规或机构政策有权获得机构教育服务的人群中的残障人士;

(2)就证券交易委员会任何其他项目或活动(指要求相关人员提供某些服务或达成一定水平成效的项目或活动)而言,指满足基本适格性要求、能够实现项目或活动宗旨的残障人士,并且该残障人士在实现项目或活动宗旨的同时不需要证券交易委员会对项目或活动作出导致项目性质发生根本变化的改动(如会导致项目性质发生根本变化,证券交易委员会须能对此提出证明);

(3)就任何其他项目或活动而言,指满足参与或获益于项目或活动的基本适格性要求的残障人士;且

(4)《联邦规章汇编》第二十九编第1613.702(f)节中针对雇佣目的作出的“合格残障人士”定义,依第200.640节规定也适用于本规章。

“第504条”指《1973年康复法》(公法编号93-112,《美国制定法汇编》第87卷第394页(《美国法典》第二十九编第794节)第504条,该法陆续受到下述法律修正:《1974年康复法修正案(公法编号93-516,《美国制定法汇编》第88卷第1617页);《1978年康复、全面服务和残疾修正案》(公法编号95-602,《美国制定法汇编》第92卷第2955页)及《1986年康复法修正案》(公法编号99-506,《美国制定法汇编》第100卷第1810页)。适用于本规章之时,第504条仅适用于联邦行政机构自身所开展的项目或活动,而不适用于联邦部门协助开展的项目。

“实质损伤” 指材料成品、设计质量的完整性所遭受的重大损伤,或发生永久性变化后出现的特殊性质。

第200.604~200.609节 [保留]

第200.610节 自我评估

(a)证券交易委员会须在1989年9月6日之前,对于其不满足或可能不满足本规章要求的当前政策和操作及其影响作出评估,如果需要,须对该等政策和操作进行必要

regulation and, to the extent modification of any such policies and practices is required, the agency shall proceed to make the necessary modifications.

(b) The agency shall provide an opportunity to interested persons, including individuals with handicaps or organizations representing individuals with handicaps, to participate in the self-evaluation process by submitting comments (both oral and written).

(c) The agency shall, for at least three years following completion of the self-evaluation, maintain on file and make available for public inspection:

(1) A description of areas examined and any problems identified; and

(2) A description of any modifications made.

§200.611 Notice.

The agency shall make available to employees, applicants, participants, beneficiaries, and other interested persons such information regarding the provisions of this regulation and its applicability to the programs or activities conducted by the agency, and make such information available to them in such manner as the head of the agency finds necessary to apprise such persons of the protections against discrimination assured them by section 504 and this regulation.

§§200.612–200.629 [Reserved]

§200.630 General prohibitions against discrimination.

(a) No qualified individual with handicaps shall, on the basis of handicap, be excluded from participation in, be denied the benefits of, or otherwise be subjected to discrimination under any program or activity conducted by the agency.

(b)(1) The agency, in providing any aid, benefit, or service, may not, directly or through contractual, licensing, or other arrangements, on the basis of handicap—

(i) Deny a qualified individual with handicaps the opportunity to participate in or benefit from the aid, benefit, or service;

(ii) Afford a qualified individual with handicaps an opportunity to participate in or benefit from the aid, benefit, or service that is not equal to that afforded others;

(iii) Provide a qualified individual with handicaps with an aid, benefit, or service that is not as effective in affording equal opportunity to obtain the same result, to gain the same benefit, or to reach the same level of achievement as that provided to others;

(iv) Provide different or separate aid, benefits, or services to individuals with handicaps or to any class of individuals with handicaps than is provided to others unless such action is necessary to provide qualified individuals with handicaps with aid, benefits, or services that are as effective as those provided to others;

(v) Deny a qualified individual with handicaps the opportunity to participate as a member of planning or advisory boards;

(vi) Otherwise limit a qualified individual with handicaps in the enjoyment of any

的整改。

(b)证券交易委员会应向利害关系人(包括残障人士或代表残障人士的组织)提供机会,使其能以提交口头或书面意见的方式参与上述自我评估程序。

(c)证券交易委员会至少应在自我评估完成后3年内将下述信息维持在案并开放给公众查阅:

(1)已审查领域和已发现任何问题的说明;及

(2)已采取的任何整改的说明。

第200.611节 通知

证券交易委员会应向雇员、申请人、参与人、受益人及其他利害关系人提供与本规章之条款相关的以及与适用于他们的证券交易委员会项目或活动相关的信息,通知方式由证券交易委员会负责人决定,必须能让上述人士知晓第504条及本规章授予他们的反歧视保护。

第200.612~200.629节 [保留]

第200.630节 一般性禁止歧视规定

(a)任何合格残障人士均不得因其残障而被拒绝参与或受益于证券交易委员会的任何项目或活动,或在该等项目或活动中遭受任何其他形式的歧视。

(b)(1)证券交易委员会在提供任何协助、福利或服务的过程中,不得以残障为由而直接或通过合约、许可或其他安排间接地——

(i)拒绝向合格残障人士授予参与或受益于该等协助、福利或服务的机会;

(ii)造成机会不均等,即向合格残障人士提供的参与或受益于该等协助、福利或服务的机会与提供给其他人士的机会不均等;

(iii)造成效能不均等,即向合格残障人士提供的协助、福利或服务的效能低于提供给其他人士的效能,导致机会不均等而无法取得相同的结果、利益或成果;

(iv)向残障人士或某一类别的残障人士提供的协助、福利或服务与提供给其他人士的不同或提供的完全是另外一套协助、福利或服务,除非该等行动是为了使提供给残障人士的协助、福利或服务与提供给其他人士的协助、福利或服务具有相同的效能所必要的;

(v)拒绝向合格残障人士提供以规划或顾问委员会委员身份参与项目或活动的机会;

(vi)以其他方式限制合格残障人士享受其他获得了协助、福利或服务的人士所享

right, privilege, advantage, or opportunity enjoyed by others receiving the aid, benefit, or service.

(2) The agency may not deny a qualified individual with handicaps the opportunity to participate in programs or activities that are not separate or different, despite the existence of permissibly separate or different programs or activities.

(3) The agency may not, directly or through contractual or other arrangements, utilize criteria or methods of administration the purpose or effect of which would—

(i) Subject qualified individuals with handicaps to discrimination on the basis of handicap; or

(ii) Defeat or substantially impair accomplishment of the objectives of a program or activity with respect to individuals with handicaps.

(4) The agency may not, in determining the site or location of a facility, make selections the purpose or effect of which would —

(i) Exclude individuals with handicaps from, deny them the benefits of, or otherwise subject them to discrimination under any program or activity conducted by the agency; or

(ii) Defeat or substantially impair the accomplishment of the objectives of a program or activity with respect to individuals with handicaps.

(5) The agency, in the selection of procurement contractors, may not use criteria that subject qualified individuals with handicaps to discrimination on the basis of handicap.

(6) The agency may not administer a licensing or certification program in a manner that subjects qualified individuals with handicaps to discrimination on the basis of handicap, nor may the agency establish requirements for the programs or activities of licensees or certified entities that subject qualified individuals with handicaps to discrimination on the basis of handicap. However, the programs or activities of entities that are licensed or certified by the agency are not, themselves, covered by this regulation.

(c) The exclusion of nonhandicapped persons from the benefits of a program limited by Federal statute or Executive order to individuals with handicaps or the exclusion of a specific class of individuals with handicaps from a program limited by Federal statute or Executive order to a different class of individuals with handicaps is not prohibited by this regulation.

(d) The agency shall administer programs and activities in the most integrated setting appropriate to the needs of qualified individuals with handicaps.

§§200.631–200.639 [Reserved]

§200.640 Employment.

No qualified individual with handicaps shall, on the basis of handicap, be subject to discrimination in employment under any program or activity conducted by the agency. The definitions, requirements, and procedures of section 501 of the Rehabilitation Act of 1973

有的任何权利、特权、利益或机会。

(2)尽管在获准的情况下为合格残障人士设置了不同的或属于另外一套的项目或活动，证券交易委员会亦不得拒绝合格残障人士参与该等项目或活动以外的其他常规项目或活动的机会。

(3)证券交易委员会不得直接或通过合同或其他安排间接地采取具有如下目的或将导致如下后果的标准或行政方法——

(i)使合格残障人士遭受残障歧视;或

(ii)挫败或实质损害项目或活动与残障人士相关的目标的实现。

(4)证券交易委员会在选择设施的场址或地点之时不得出于如下目的,亦不得作出将导致如下结果的选择——

(i)排除残障人士参与、受益于证券交易委员会开展的项目或活动,或以其他方式对之进行任何歧视;或

(ii)挫败或实质损害项目或活动与残障人士相关的目标的实现。

(5)证券交易委员会在选任采购承包商时使用的标准不得导致合格残障人士遭受任何残障歧视。

(6)证券交易委员会实施许可或认证项目的方式不得导致合格残障人士遭受残障歧视;证券交易委员会对被许可人或被认证实体的项目或活动所设置的要求,亦不得导致残障人士遭受残障歧视。但是,证券交易委员会许可或认证的实体的项目或活动本身并不受本规章规制。

(c)对于根据联邦制定法或行政命令的限制仅适用于残障人士的项目而言,将非残障人士排除在外并不违反本规章;同时,对于根据联邦制定法或行政命令的限制仅适用于某一类残障人士的项目而言,将其他类型的残障人士排除在外并不违反本规章。

(d)证券交易委员会实施项目和活动时,应根据合格残障人士的需求尽可能完整地考虑相关背景。

第200.631~200.639节　[保留]

第200.640节　雇佣

在证券交易委员会开展的任何项目或活动中,任何合格残障人士均不得因残障而受到雇佣歧视。《1973年康复法》第501条(《美国法典》第二十九编第791节)的定义、要求和程序(如平等就业机会委员会在《联邦规章汇编》第二十九编第1613部分中所

(29 U.S.C. 791), as established by the Equal Employment Opportunity Commission in 29 CFR part 1613, shall apply to employment in federally conducted programs or activities.

§§200.641–200.648V [Reserved]

§200.649 Program accessibility: Discrimination prohibited.

Except as otherwise provided in §200.650, no qualified individual with handicaps shall, because the agency's facilities are inaccessible to or unusable by individuals with handicaps, be denied the benefits of, be excluded from participation in, or otherwise be subjected to discrimination under any program or activity conducted by the agency.

§200.650 Program accessibility: Existing facilities.

(a) *General.* The agency shall operate each program or activity so that the program or activity, when viewed in its entirety, is readily accessible to and usable by individuals with handicaps. This paragraph does not —

(1) Necessarily require the agency to make each of its existing facilities accessible to and usable by individuals with handicaps;

(2) In the case of historic preservation programs, require the agency to take any action that would result in a substantial impairment of significant historic features of an historic property; or

(3) Require the agency to take any action that it can demonstrate would result in a fundamental alteration in the nature of a program or activity or in undue financial and administrative burdens. In those circumstances where agency personnel believe that the proposed action would fundamentally alter the program or activity or would result in undue financial and administrative burdens, the agency has the burden of proving that compliance with §200.650(a) would result in such alteration or burdens. The decision that compliance would result in such alteration or burdens must be made by the agency head or his or her designee after considering all agency resources available for use in the funding and operation of the conducted program or activity, and must be accompanied by a written statement of the reasons for reaching that conclusion. If an action would result in such an alteration or such burdens, the agency shall take any other action that would not result in such an alteration or such burdens but would nevertheless ensure that individuals with handicaps receive the benefits and services of the program or activity.

(b) *Methods* — (1) *General.* The agency may comply with the requirements of this section through such means as redesign of equipment, reassignment of services to accessible buildings, assignment of aides to beneficiaries, home visits, delivery of services at alternate accessible sites, alteration of existing facilities and construction of new facilities, use of accessible rolling stock, or any other methods that result in making its programs or activities readily accessible to and usable by individuals with handicaps. The agency is not required to make structural changes in existing facilities where other

规定的),应适用于联邦开展的项目或活动中的雇佣情形。

第200.641~200.648V节 [保留]

第200.649节 项目无障碍性:禁止歧视

除第200.650节另有规定的情形外,任何合格残障人士均不得因无法进入或使用证券交易委员会的设施而被拒绝参与、受益于证券交易委员会开展的任何项目或活动,或在该等项目或活动中遭受任何其他歧视。

第200.650节 项目无障碍性:现有设施

(a)一般规定。证券交易委员会开展的每一项目或活动均应整体上实现残障人士的无障碍使用。上述规定——

(1)并不必然要求证券交易委员会保证残障人士可进入并使用其全部的现有设施;

(2)就历史建筑保护项目而言,并不要求证券交易委员会采取将导致历史建筑之重大历史特征产生实质损害的任何行动;或

(3)不要求证券交易委员会采取任何其能够证明将导致项目或活动性质发生根本变化或产生过度财务和行政负担的行动。在上述情形下,若证券交易委员会的人员相信拟采取的行动将对项目或活动造成根本变化或导致过度财务和行政负担,则证券交易委员会负有证明遵守第200.650(a)节将导致发生上述变化或负担的举证责任。只有证券交易委员会负责人或其指定人员才可以裁定实现上述条款是否将导致上述变化或负担,且作出裁定时须考虑证券交易委员会在项目或活动的融资和运作中可以利用的所有资源,还须附上一份关于得出上述结论的原因的说明书。若某项行动将导致发生上述变化或负担,证券交易委员会应采取不致产生上述变化或负担但仍可最大限度地确保残障人士获得项目或活动的福利和服务的其他行动。

(b)方法——(1)一般规定。证券交易委员会可通过下述方式来实现本节的规定:重新设计设备、将服务地点迁移至无障碍建筑内、向受益人提供辅助、家庭访问、在替代性无障碍场址提供服务、变更现有设施、建设新设施、使用无障碍车辆或采取任何其他能保证残障人士无障碍使用项目或活动的方法。如通过其他方法即可有效地实现本节规定,证券交易委员会不必对现有设施作出结构性改造。证券交易委员会在改造现有建筑时应满足《1968年建筑障碍法》修正版(《美国法典》第四十二编第4151~4157节)及其任何实施规章的无障碍要求。在选择实施本节规定的方法时,证券交易

methods are effective in achieving compliance with this section. The agency, in making alterations to existing buildings, shall meet accessibility requirements to the extent compelled by the Architectural Barriers Act of 1968, as amended (42 U.S.C. 4151–4157), and any regulations implementing it. In choosing among available methods for meeting the requirements of this section, the agency shall give priority to those methods that offer programs and activities to qualified individuals with handicaps in the most integrated setting appropriate.

(2) *Historic preservation programs.* In meeting the requirements of §200.650(a) in historic preservation programs, the agency shall give priority to methods that provide physical access to individuals with handicaps. In cases where a physical alteration to an historic property is not required because of §200.650(a)(2) or (3), alternative methods of achieving program accessibility include —

(i) Using audio-visual materials and devices to depict those portions of an historic property that cannot otherwise be made accessible;

(ii) Assigning persons to guide individuals with handicaps into or through portions of historic properties that cannot otherwise be made accessible; or

(iii) Adopting other innovative methods.

(c) *Time period for compliance.* The agency shall comply with the obligations established under this section by November 7, 1988, except that where structural changes in facilities are undertaken, such changes shall be made by September 6, 1991, but in any event as expeditiously as possible.

(d) *Transition plan.* In the event that structural changes to facilities will be undertaken to achieve program accessibility, the agency shall develop, by March 6, 1989, a transition plan setting forth the steps necessary to complete such changes. The agency shall provide an opportunity to interested persons, including individuals with handicaps or organizations representing individuals with handicaps, to participate in the development of the transition plan by submitting comments (both oral and written). A copy of the transition plan shall be made available for public inspection. The plan shall, at a minimum —

(1) Identify physical obstacles in the agency's facilities that limit the accessibility of its programs or activities to individuals with handicaps;

(2) Describe in detail the methods that will be used to make the facilities accessible;

(3) Specify the schedule for taking the steps necessary to achieve compliance with this section and, if the time period of the transition plan is longer than one year, identify steps that will be taken during each year of the transition period; and

(4) Indicate the official responsible for implementation of the plan.

委员会应优先考虑可在最恰当完整的背景下向合格残障人士提供项目和活动的方法。

(2)历史建筑保护项目。为满足第200.650(a)节对历史建筑保护项目的要求,证券交易委员会应优先考虑为残障人士提供实体通道的方法。若根据第200.650(a)(2)节或第200.650(a)(3)节的规定不必对历史建筑作出实体改造,可采取的实现项目无障碍的替代方法包括——

(i)对于无法以其他方式进入的历史建筑的某些部分,以视听资料和设备来记录;

(ii)对于无法以其他方式进入和通过的历史建筑的某些部分,派遣相关人员来引导残障人士;或

(iii)采取其他创新的方法。

(c)合规期间。除已开展的设施结构改造应于1991年9月6日之前完成外,证券交易委员会应在1988年11月7日前完成本节设定的义务,但无论何时均应尽可能快地完成上述义务。

(d)过渡计划。如果为实现项目无障碍而需对设施进行结构改造,证券交易委员会应于1989年3月6日前制订一份过渡计划,载明完成上述改造所须采取的步骤。证券交易委员会应向利害关系人(包括残障人士或代表残障人士的组织)提供机会,使其能以提交口头或书面意见的方式参与制定该过渡计划。过渡计划应向公众开放。该计划至少应——

(1)识别证券交易委员会设施中有哪些物理障碍限制了残障人士对项目或活动的参与;

(2)详细说明其所采用的实现设施无障碍的方法;

(3)确定过渡时间表,按时间表采取必要措施达到本节规定,如过渡计划的期间长于1年,则应明确过渡期间内每年将采取的步骤;及

(4)指明负责实施计划的官员。

§200.651 Program accessibility: New construction and alterations.

Each building or part of a building that is constructed or altered by, on behalf of, or for the use of the agency shall be designed, constructed, or altered so as to be readily accessible to and usable by individuals with handicaps. The definitions, requirements, and standards of the Architectural Barriers Act (42 U.S.C. 4151–4157), as established in 41 CFR 101–19.600 to 101–19.607, apply to buildings covered by this section.

§§200.652–200.659 [Reserved]

§200.660 Communications.

(a) The agency shall take appropriate steps to ensure effective communication with applicants, participants, personnel of other Federal entities, and members of the public.

(1) The agency shall furnish appropriate auxiliary aids where necessary to afford an individual with handicaps an equal opportunity to participate in, and enjoy the benefits of, a program or activity conducted by the agency.

(i) In determining what type of auxiliary aid is necessary, the agency shall give primary consideration to the requests of the individual with handicaps.

(ii) The agency need not provide individually prescribed devices, readers for personal use or study, or other devices of a personal nature.

(2) Where the agency communicates with applicants and beneficiaries by telephone, telecommunication devices for deaf persons (TDD's) or equally effective telecommunication systems shall be used to communicate with persons with impaired hearing.

(b) The agency shall ensure that interested persons, including persons with impaired vision or hearing, can obtain information as to the existence and location of accessible services, activities, and facilities.

(c) The agency shall provide signage at a primary entrance to each of its inaccessible facilities, directing users to a location at which they can obtain information about accessible facilities. The international symbol for accessibility shall be used at each primary entrance of an accessible facility.

(d) This section does not require the agency to take any action that it can demonstrate would result in a fundamental alteration in the nature of a program or activity or in undue financial and administrative burdens. In those circumstances where agency personnel believe that the proposed action would fundamentally alter the program or activity or would result in undue financial and administrative burdens, the agency has the burden of proving that compliance with §200.660 would result in such alteration or burdens. The decision that compliance would result in such alteration or burdens must be made by the agency head or his or her designee after considering all agency resources available for use in the funding and operation of the conducted program or activity and must be accompanied by a written statement of the reasons for reaching that conclusion. If

第200.651节　项目无障碍性:新建筑和改造

证券交易委员会自身或他人代表证券交易委员会建设、改造或供证券交易委员会使用的每座建筑或其中的各部分,其设计、施工或改造应保证残障人士能够无障碍地进入及使用。《建筑障碍法》(《美国法典》第四十二编第4151~4157节)的定义、要求和标准(如《联邦规章汇编》第四十一编第101-19.600~101-19.607节所规定),应适用于本节中的建筑。

第200.652~200.659节　[保留]

第200.660节　沟通

(a)证券交易委员会应采取适当步骤,确保与申请人、参与人、其他联邦实体的人员以及公众进行有效沟通。

(1)必要时,证券交易委员会应提供适当的辅助服务或设备为残障人士提供参与、受益于证券交易委员会所开展的项目或活动的均等机会。

(i)在确定必不可少的辅助服务或设备类型时,证券交易委员会应首先考虑残障人士的请求。

(ii)证券交易委员会不必提供个人指定的设备、个人使用或研究用的放大阅读器或其他私人性质的设备。

(2)证券交易委员会通过电话与申请人和受益人沟通时,应使用听障人士专线(TDD's)或同等有效的系统与听力受损人士进行沟通。

(b)证券交易委员会应确保利害关系人,包括视力或听力受损的人士,可以获得关于无障碍服务、活动和设施的存在及地点的信息。

(c)证券交易委员会应在其未实现无障碍的所有设施主入口处设立标牌,向使用者指明可以在哪些地点获得无障碍设施。所有无障碍设施主入口处均应设置国际无障碍标识。

(d)本节规定并不要求证券交易委员会采取其能够证明将导致项目或活动性质发生根本变化或产生过度财务和行政负担的任何行动。在上述情形下,若证券交易委员会的人员相信拟采取的行动将对项目或活动造成根本变化或导致过度财务和行政负担,证券交易委员会负有证明遵守第200.660节将导致上述变化或负担的举证责任。只有证券交易委员会负责人或其指定人员才可以裁定实现上述条款是否将导致上述变化或负担,且作裁定时须考虑项目或活动的融资和运作中证券交易委员会可以利用的所有资源,还须附上一份关于得出上述结论的原因的说明书。若因遵守本条规定而采取某项行动将导致上述变化或负担,证券交易委员会应采取不致产生上述变化或负担(但仍可最大限度地确保残障人士获得项目或活动的福利和服务的任何其他行动。

an action required to comply with this section would result in such an alteration or such burdens, the agency shall take any other action that would not result in such an alteration or such burdens but would nevertheless ensure that, to the maximum extent possible, individuals with handicaps receive the benefits and services of the program or activity.

§§200.661–200.669 [Reserved]

§200.670 Compliance procedures.

(a) Except as provided in paragraph (b) of this section, this section applies to all allegations of discrimination on the basis of handicap in programs and activities conducted by the agency.

(b) The agency shall process complaints alleging violations of section 504 with respect to employment according to the procedures established by the Equal Employment Opportunity Commission in 29 CFR part 1613 pursuant to section 501 of the Rehabilitation Act of 1973 (29 U.S.C. 791).

(c) The Equal Employment Opportunity Manager shall be responsible for coordinating implementation of this section. Complaints may be sent to the EEO Manager, 100 F Street, NE., Washington, D.C. 20549.

(d) The agency shall accept and investigate all complete complaints for which it has jurisdiction. All complete complaints must be filed within 180 days of the alleged act of discrimination. The agency may extend this time period for good cause.

(e) If the agency receives a complaint over which it does not have jurisdiction, it shall promptly notify the complainant and shall make reasonable efforts to refer the complaint to the appropriate Government entity.

(f) The agency shall notify the Architectural and Transportation Barriers Compliance Board upon receipt of any complaint alleging that a building or facility that is subject to the Architectural Barriers Act of 1968, as amended (42 U.S.C. 4151–4157), is not readily accessible to and usable by individuals with handicaps.

(g) Within 180 days of the receipt of a complete complaint for which it has jurisdiction, the agency shall notify the complainant of the results of the investigation in a letter containing —

(1) Findings of fact and conclusions of law;

(2) A description of a remedy for each violation found; and

(3) A notice of the right to appeal.

(h) Appeals of the findings of fact and conclusions of law or remedies must be filed by the complainant within 90 days of receipt from the agency of the letter required by §200.670(g). The agency may extend this time for good cause.

(i) Timely appeals shall be accepted and processed by the head of the agency.

第200.661~200.669节 [保留]

第200.670节 合规程序

(a)除本节第(b)款规定的情形外,本节规定应适用于证券交易委员会开展的所有被指称存在残障歧视的项目和活动。

(b)证券交易委员会应按平等就业机会委员会根据《1973年康复法》第501条(《美国法典》第二十九编第791节)在《联邦规章汇编》第二十九编第1613部分中设立的程序,处理被指称违反第504条规定的雇佣情形的案件的申诉。

(c)平等就业机会主管应负责协调本节规定的实施。申诉书可发送至华盛顿哥伦比亚特区东北分区100F大街平等就业机会主管,邮编:D.C.20549。

(d)证券交易委员会应受理并调查其拥有管辖权的所有完整的申诉书。所有完整的申诉书均应在指称的歧视行为发生后180日内提交。存在正当理由的,证券交易委员会可延长上述期间。

(e)证券交易委员会收到其没有管辖权的申诉的,应及时通知申诉人,并尽合理努力将申诉书转交相应的政府实体。

(f)如果任何建筑应当遵守《1968年建筑障碍法》修正版(《美国法典》第四十二编第4151~4157节),但被指称没有实现无障碍化、无法供残障人士使用,则证券交易委员会应在收到任何相关申诉书后通知建筑与交通工具无障碍合规委员会。

(g)对于任何完整的申诉书,证券交易委员如拥有管辖权则应在收到申诉书后180日内向申诉人发送一份信函告知调查结果,该信函应包括如下信息:

(1)事实认定和法律结论;

(2)对认定的每一违法违规行为的救济之说明;及

(3)关于申请复议权的通知。

(h)申诉人请求对事实认定、法律结论或救济进行复议的,必须在收到证券交易委员会按第200.670(g)节发出的信函后90日内提出。存在正当理由的,证券交易委员会可延长上述期间。

(i)证券交易委员会负责人负责受理和处理及时提出的复议请求。

(j) The head of the agency shall notify the complainant of the results of the appeal within 60 days of the receipt of the request. If the head of the agency determines that additional information is needed from the complainant, he or she shall have 60 days from the date of receipt of the additional information to make his or her determination on the appeal.

(k) The time limits cited in paragraphs (g) and (j) of this section may be extended with the permission of the Assistant Attorney General.

(l) The agency may delegate its authority for conducting complaint investigations to other Federal agencies, except that the authority for making the final determination may not be delegated to another agency.

[53 FR 25882 and 25885, July 8, 1988, as amended at 53 FR 25882, July 8, 1988; 73 FR 32226, June 5, 2008]

§§200.671–200.699 [Reserved]

Subpart M—Regulation Concerning Conduct of Members and Employees and Former Members and Employees of the Commission

Authority: 15 U.S.C. 77s, 77sss, 78w, 80a–37, 80b–11; E.O. 11222, 3 CFR, 1964–1965 Comp., p. 36; 5 CFR 735.104; 5 CFR 2634; and 5 CFR 2635, unless otherwise noted.

Source: 45 FR 36064, May 29, 1980, unless otherwise noted.

§200.735–1 Purpose.

This subpart sets forth the standards of ethical conduct required of members, employees and special Government employees, and former members and employees of the Securities and Exchange Commission.

[75 FR 42276, July 20, 2010]

§200.735–2 Policy.

(a) The Securities and Exchange Commission has been entrusted by Congress with the protection of the public interest in a highly significant area of our national economy. In view of the effect which Commission action frequently has on the general public, it is important that members, employees and special Government employees maintain unusually high standards of honesty, integrity, impartiality and conduct. They must be constantly aware of the need to avoid situations which might result either in actual or apparent misconduct or conflicts of interest and to conduct themselves in their official relationships

(j)证券交易委员会负责人应在收到复议请求后60日内将结果通知申诉人。如果证券交易委员会负责人判定需要申诉人提交补充信息,证券交易委员会负责人可在收到补充信息后60日内就复议申请作出判定。

(k)经司法部助理部长允许,本节第(g)款和第(j)款规定的时限可以延长。

(l)证券交易委员会可以将开展申诉调查的权限委托其他联邦机构行使,但作出最终决定的权利不得转授。

[《联邦公报》第53卷第25882页和第25885页,1988年7月8日,修正索引:《联邦公报》第53卷第25882页,1988年7月8日;《联邦公报》第73卷第32226页,2008年6月5日。]

第200.671~200.699节 [保留]

第M子部分——证券交易委员会委员、雇员及前任委员、雇员的行为准则规章

法律依据:《美国法典》第十五编第77s节、第77sss节、第78w节、第80a-37节、第80b-11节;第11222号行政命令,《联邦规章汇编》第三编,1964~1965年版,第36页;《联邦规章汇编》第五编第735.104节;《联邦规章汇编》第五编第2634节;及《联邦规章汇编》第五编第2635节,另有说明的除外。

行政规则来源:《联邦公报》第45卷第36064页,1980年5月29日,另有说明的除外。

第200.735-1节 目的

本子部分规定了证券交易委员会的委员、雇员和特别政府雇员以及前任委员、雇员的行为道德标准。

[《联邦公报》第75卷第42276页,2010年7月20日。]

第200.735-2节 政策

(a)证券交易委员会受国会委托,在对本国国家经济具有重大意义的领域承担保护公共利益的责任。鉴于证券交易委员会的行动经常会对一般公众产生影响,证券交易委员会的委员、雇员和特别政府雇员有必要维持非同寻常的诚实、诚信、公正和行为高标准。他们必须始终意识到避免导致实际或表面不当行为或利益冲突的情形的必要性,并以值得公众尊重和信任的方式处理工作关系。

in a manner which commands the respect and confidence of their fellow citizens.

(b) For these reasons, members, employees, and special Government employees should at all times abide by the standards of ethical conduct for employees of the executive branch (codified in 5 CFR part 2635); the supplemental standards of ethical conduct for members and employees of the Securities and Exchange Commission (codified in 5 CFR part 4401); the standards of conduct set forth in this subpart; the Canons of ethics for members of the Securities and Exchange Commission (codified in subpart C of this part 200); and, in the case of a person practicing a profession as defined in 5 CFR 2636.305(b)(1), the applicable professional ethical standards.

[45 FR 36064, May 29, 1980, as amended at 75 FR 42276, July 20, 2010]

§200.735-3 General provisions.

(a) A member or employee shall comply with the requirements of 5 CFR part 2635, subpart A (General provisions) and in particular with the provisions of 5 CFR 2635.101 (Basic obligations of public service); 2635.103(Applicability to members of the uniformed services); and 2635.104 (Applicability to employees on detail).

(b) A member or employee of the Commission shall not:

(1) Engage, directly or indirectly, in any personal business transaction or private arrangement for personal profit the opportunity for which arises because of his or her official position or authority, or that is based upon confidential or nonpublic information which he or she gains by reason of such position or authority.

(2)(i) Divulge to any unauthorized person or release in advance of authorization for its release any nonpublic Commission document, or any information contained in any such document or any confidential information: (A) In contravention of the rules and regulations of the Commission promulgated under 5 U.S.C. 552, 552a and 552b; or (B) in circumstances where the Commission has determined to accord such information confidential treatment.

(ii) Except where the Commission or the General Counsel, pursuant to delegated authority, has previously granted approval or in relation to a Commission administrative proceeding or a judicial proceeding in which the Commission, or a present or former Commissioner, or present or former member of the staff, represented by Commission counsel, is a party, any officer, employee or former officer or employee who is served with a subpoena requiring the disclosure of confidential or non-public information or documents shall, unless the Commission or the General Counsel, pursuant to delegated authority, authorizes the disclosure of such information or documents, respectfully decline to disclose the information or produce the documents called for, basing his or her refusal on this paragraph.

(b)基于上述原因,委员、雇员和特别政府雇员应始终遵守:行政机关雇员的行为道德标准(编纂于《联邦规章汇编》第五编第2635部分);证券交易委员会委员和雇员的补充行为道德准则(编纂于《联邦规章汇编》第五编第4401部分);本子部分所载的行为准则;证券交易委员会委员的《职业道德守则》(编纂于本第200部分第C子部分);且对于《联邦规章汇编》第五编第2636.305(b)(1)节定义的在专业领域执业的人员,还应遵守相应的职业道德标准。

[《联邦公报》第45卷第36064页,1980年5月29日,修正索引:《联邦公报》第75卷第42276页,2010年7月20日。]

第200.735-3节　一般规定

(a)委员或雇员应遵守《联邦规章汇编》第五编第2635部分第A子部分(一般规定),特别是《联邦规章汇编》第五编第2635.101节(公共服务基本义务)、第2635.103节(统一服务对委员的适用)以及第2635.104节(对雇员的具体适用)的规定。

(b)证券交易委员会的委员或雇员不得:

(1)为牟取个人私利,而利用因其官方职务或职权产生的机会或利用因该等职务或职权获得的保密或非公开信息,直接或间接从事或作出任何个人业务交易或私人安排。

(2)(i)在以下情况下,向任何未获授权的人士披露或在获得发布批准前发布任何非公开的证券交易委员会文件或该等文件中包含的任何信息或任何保密信息:(A)违反证券交易委员会在《美国法典》第五编第552节、第552a节和第552b节下颁发的规则与规章;或(B)证券交易委员会已判定对该等信息进行保密处理。

(ii)其任何委员、雇员或前任委员、雇员收到传票要求其披露保密或非公开信息或文件的,该等官员、职员基于本款规定应恭敬地婉拒披露或提供其所要求的信息/文件;但是,证券交易委员会或首席律师已根据其权限事先予以批准的情况除外,或者涉及证券交易委员会的行政处理程序或者以证券交易委员会或其前任、现任委员或雇员(由证券交易委员会法律顾问代表)为当事人的司法程序除外。

(iii) Any member, employee or former member or employee who is served with such a subpoena not covered by the exceptions in paragraph (b)(7)(ii) of this section shall promptly advise the General Counsel of the service of such subpoena, the nature of the information or documents sought, and any circumstances which may bear upon the desirability in the public interest of making available such information or documents.[1] The Commission or the General Counsel, pursuant to delegated authority, shall authorize the disclosure of non-expert, non-privileged, factual staff testimony and the production of non-privileged documents when validly subpoenaed.

(c) A member or employee shall comply with the requirements of 5 CFR part 2635, subpart B (Gifts from outside sources).

(d) A member or employee shall comply with the requirements of 5 CFR part 2635, subpart C (Gifts between employees).

(e) A member or employee shall comply with the requirements of 5 CFR part 2635, subpart D (Conflicting financial requirements);

(f) A member or employee shall comply with the requirements of 5 CFR part 2635, subpart E (Impartiality).

(g) A member or employee shall comply with the requirements of 5 CFR part 2635, subpart G (Misuse of position).

(h) No member or employee shall accept host-paid travel or reimbursement except as in accordance with the requirements of the Supplemental standards of ethical conduct for members and employees of the Securities and Exchange Commission (codified at 5 CFR 4401.103 (Outside Employment and Activities)); 5 CFR part 2635, subpart H (Outside Activities); and 31 U.S.C. 353 and 41 CFR 304-1.1 (Acceptance of payment from a non-Federal source for travel expenses).

[45 FR 36064, May 29, 1980; 45 FR 40975, June 17, 1980, as amended at 50 FR 23287, June 3, 1985; 53 FR 17458, May 17, 1988; 54 FR 33500, Aug. 15, 1989; 73 FR 32226, June 5, 2008; 75 FR 42276, July 20, 2010]

§200.735-4 Outside employment and activities.

(a) Members and employees shall comply with the requirements of the Supplemental standards of ethical conduct for members and employees of the Securities and Exchange Commission (codified at 5 CFR 4401.103 (Outside employment and activities) and 5

1 Detailed prohibitions regarding disclosure or use of confidential or nonpublic information are set forth in Rule 122 (17 CFR 230.122) under the Securities Act of 1933; section 24(b) of the Securities Exchange Act of 1934 (15 U.S.C. 78x) and Rule 0-4 (17 CFR 240.0-4); and Rule 24(b)(2) (17 CFR 240.24b-2), thereunder; section 45(a)(1) of the Investment Company Act, and section 210(b) of the Investment Advisers Act of 1940 (15 U.S.C. 80b-10).

(iii)收到不能适用本节第(b)(7)(ii)款例外规定之传票的任何委员、雇员或前任委员、雇员，应及时将该传票送达之事实、传票要求提供的信息或文件之性质以及提供该等信息或文件时可能对公共利益造成影响的任何情况通知首席律师。[1]如传票有效，证券交易委员会或首席律师应根据其权限批准披露非专家的且非受保密特权保护的工作人员的事实证词、提供非受保密特权保护的文件。

(c)委员或雇员应遵守《联邦规章汇编》第五编第2635部分第B子部分(外部礼物)的规定。

(d)委员或雇员应遵守《联邦规章汇编》第五编第2635部分第C子部分(雇员互赠礼物)的规定。

(e)委员或雇员应遵守《联邦规章汇编》第五编第2635部分第D子部分(冲突性的财务要求)的规定。

(f)委员或雇员应遵守《联邦规章汇编》第五编第2635部分第E子部分(公正)的规定。

(g)委员或雇员应遵守《联邦规章汇编》第五编第2635部分第G子部分(职权滥用)的规定。

(h)任何委员或雇员均不得接受东道主支付的差旅或报销，但符合下述规定的除外：证券交易委员会委员和雇员补充行为道德准则[编纂于《联邦规章汇编》第五编第4401.103节(外部雇佣和活动)；《联邦规章汇编》第五编第2635部分第H子部分(外部活动]；和《美国法典》第三十一编第353节以及《联邦规章汇编》第41卷第304-1.1节(收受非联邦人士/实体支付的差旅费用)。

[《联邦公报》第45卷第36064页，1980年5月29日；《联邦公报》第45卷第40975页，1980年6月17日，修正索引：《联邦公报》第50卷第23287页，1985年6月3日；《联邦公报》第53卷第17458页，1988年5月17日；《联邦公报》第54卷第33500页，1989年8月15日；《联邦公报》第73卷第32226页，2008年6月5日；《联邦公报》第75卷第42276页，2010年7月20日。]

第200.735-4条　外部雇佣和活动

(a)委员和雇员应遵守证券交易委员会委员和雇员补充行为道德准则(编纂于《联邦规章汇编》第五编第4401.103节(外部雇佣和活动)以及《联邦规章汇编》第五编第2635部分第H子部分(外部活动)的规定。

1　关于禁止披露及使用保密或非公开信息的详细规定见：《1933年证券法》的《122规则》(《联邦规章汇编》第十七编第230.122节)；《1934年证券交易法》第24(b)条(《美国法典》第十五编第78x节)和《0—4规则》(《联邦规章汇编》第十七编第240.0-4节)；以及依其颁布的《24(b)(2)规则》(《联邦规章汇编》第十七编第240.24b-2节)；《投资公司法》第45(a)(1)条和《1940年投资顾问法》第210(b)条(《美国法典》第十五编第80b-10节)。

CFR part 2635, subpart H (Outside activities)).

(b) The Commission encourages employees to engage in teaching, lecturing, and writing activities with or without compensation.[1] In participating in such activities, employees should be guided by the following:

(1) No teaching, lecturing, or writing should be engaged in if prohibited by law, Executive order, Office of Personnel Management regulations, or the rules in this subpart.

(2) No teaching, lecturing, or writing should be engaged in (including for the purpose of the special preparation of a person or class of persons for an examination of the Office of Personnel Management or Board of Examiners for the Foreign Service) that depends on information filed with the Commission, or obtained by the Commission in an investigation or otherwise, or generated within the Commission which is nonpublic, unless the Commission gives formal approval for the use of such nonpublic information on the basis that the use thereof is in the public interest.[2]

(c) If otherwise permitted by 18 U.S.C. 203 and 205, the provisions of these rules or of 5 CFR 4401.103 do not preclude an employee from acting as agent or attorney:

(1) For any Commission employee who is sued or under investigation in connection with his or her official duties;

(2) For any Commission employee who is the subject of disciplinary, loyalty, or other personnel administrative proceedings in connection with those proceedings; or

(3) For any Commission employee who raises claims or against whom allegations of wrongdoing are made pursuant to the Commission's Equal Opportunity regulations, if such representation is not inconsistent with the faithful performance of the employee's duties.

(d)(1) As paragraph (b) of this section indicates, the Commission encourages employees to engage in teaching, lecturing and writing activities.[3] It is understood, however, that Commission employees in their teaching, writing and lecturing shall not:

(i) Use confidential or nonpublic information;

(ii) Make comments on pending litigation in which the Commission is participating as a party or *amicus curiae*; or

(iii) Make comments on rulemaking proceedings pending before the Commission which would adversely affect the operations of the Commission.

---

1 As to employees, while the receipt of honoraria is discouraged, that rule is not applicable to the receipt of compensation for teaching.

2 Since members of the Commission are covered by section 401(a) of Executive Order 11222, they are prohibited by Civil Service Regulations (5 CFR 735.203(c)) from receiving compensation or anything of monetary value for any consultation, lecture, discussion, writing, or appearance the subject matter of which is devoted substantially to the responsibilities, programs, or operations of their agencies, or which draws substantially on official data or ideas which have not become part of the body of public information.

3 This paragraph (d), requiring review of prepared speeches or writings relating to the Commission does not apply to teaching activities.

（b）证券交易委员会鼓励雇员从事有偿或无偿[1]的教学、演讲和写作活动。在参与上述活动时，雇员应遵循下述指引：

（1）不得从事被法律、行政命令、人事管理局规章或本子部分规定所禁止的教学、演讲或写作。

（2）不得利用当事人向证券交易委员会提交的信息、证券交易委员会在调查中或以其他方式获取的信息或证券交易委员会内部生成的非公开信息从事教学、演讲或写作活动（该等活动包括针对人事管理局或外事处考官委员会举办的考试为某人或某类人员提供辅导），但证券交易委员会认为使用上述信息符合公共利益并正式批准使用的情况除外。[2]

（c）若经《美国法典》第十八编第203节和第205节另行许可，本规则或《联邦规章汇编》第五编第4401.103节的规定并不禁止雇员担任下述人员的代理人或律师：

（1）因其公职被起诉或被调查的任何证券交易委员会雇员；

（2）被处以纪律处分、被施以忠诚度调查或被提起其他人事行政处理程序的任何证券交易委员会雇员；或

（3）根据证券交易委员会的机会均等规章提起权利主张或被指称存在渎职行为的任何证券交易委员会雇员，但是担任该等员工之代理人或律师不得与其忠诚履行职员自身职责相冲突。

（d）（1）如本条第（b）款所述，证券交易委员会鼓励雇员从事教学、演讲和写作活动。[3]但是，证券交易委员会雇员应理解，其教学、演讲和写作活动不得：

（i）使用保密或非公开信息；

（ii）就证券交易委员会作为当事人或法庭之友参与的未决诉讼作出评论；或

（iii）对证券交易委员会尚在进行中的规则制定程序作出将对证券交易委员会运作造成不利影响的评论。

1　尽管我们不鼓励雇员接受酬金，但该规则不适用于在有偿教学中接受报酬的行为。

2　由于证券交易委员会的委员受制于《第 11222 号行政命令》的第 401（a）条规定，因此，《公务员管理办法》［《联邦规章汇编》第五编第 735.203（c）节］禁止其在提供任何咨询、演讲、讨论、写作或出席之时收受任何报酬或具有金钱价值的任何物品，只要所涉之主题实质上与其所在机构的职责、项目或运作相关，或者大量引用未进入公共领域的官方数据或理念。

3　本第（d）款关于要求审查与证券交易委员会相关的演讲稿或书稿的规定不适用于教学活动。

(2) To assist employees in conforming to these requirements the following procedure for reviewing writings prior to publication, or prepared speeches prior to delivery, has been established:

(i) Employees must submit proposed publications or prepared speeches relating to the Commission, or the statutes or rules it administers, to the General Counsel for review. Employees will be notified as promptly as possible, with due regard to publication deadlines, but in any event within 30 days of receipt of the written document, whether such document conforms to the requirements of this Rule.

(ii)(A) A determination by the General Counsel that a proposed publication conforms to the requirements of the rule will not involve adoption of, or concurrence in, the views expressed. Therefore, such publication or speech shall include at an appropriate place or in a footnote or otherwise, the following disclaimer of responsibility:

The Securities and Exchange Commission disclaims responsibility for any private publication or statement of any SEC employee or Commissioner.

This [article, outline, speech, chapter] expresses the author's views and does not necessarily reflect those of the Commission, the [other] Commissioners, or [other] members of the staff.

(B) In appropriate cases, the above disclaimer may be modified by the General Counsel or the Commission to reflect the circumstances of an individual case. In addition, any publication or speech that reflects positions taken by the Commission shall set forth those positions accurately and, if it contains differences with Commission positions, it shall clearly state that such positions are those of the employee.

(e) With respect to host-paid travel, members and employees shall comply with the requirements of the Supplemental standards of ethical conduct for members and employees of the Securities and Exchange Commission (codified at 5 CFR 4401.103 (Outside employment and activities)); 5 CFR part 2635, subpart H (Outside Activities); and 31 U.S.C. 1353 and 41 CFR 304-1.1 (Acceptance of payment from a non-Federal source for travel expenses).

(f) (1) With respect to seeking or negotiating outside employment, members and employees shall comply with the requirements of the Supplemental standards of ethical conduct for members and employees of the Securities and Exchange Commission (codified at 5 CFR 4401.103 (Outside employment and activities)); 5 CFR part 2635, subpart F (Seeking other employment); 5 CFR part 2635, subpart H (Outside activities).

(2) Members and employees should be aware that 18 U.S.C. 208 (Acts affecting a personal interest) provides, among other things, that a member or employee is prohibited from participating personally and substantially in any particular matter in which, to his or her knowledge, the member or employee, his or her spouse, minor child, general partner,

(2)为协助雇员遵守上述要求,证券交易委员会制定了下述适用于书稿出版前和讲稿演讲前的审查程序:

(i)雇员必须将与证券交易委员会或其负责实施的制定法或规则相关的拟出版书稿或备好的讲稿呈报首席律师审查。首席律师将在适当考虑出版最后时限的情况下,尽快(但无论如何不得晚于收到书面文件后30日)通知雇员该等文件是否符合本规则的要求。

(ii)(A)首席律师判定拟出版书稿符合本规则要求的,并不表示其认同或附和书稿所表述的观点。因此,该等出版物或演讲稿应在适当的位置或脚注或其他位置注明下述免责声明:

证券交易委员会不就任何证券交易委员会雇员或委员的私人出版物或声明承担任何责任。

本[文章、大纲、演讲、章节]仅代表作者观点,不代表证券交易委员会及其委员或[其他]员工的观点。

(B)在适当情形下,首席律师或证券交易委员会可基于具体情况修改上述免责声明。此外,任何出版物或演讲中如反映了证券交易委员会的立场,均应予以准确说明,且若包含与上述立场不同的观点,应明确说明该等不同观点系员工自身之观点。

(e)对于东道主报销费用的差旅,委员或雇员应遵守下述规定:证券交易委员会委员和雇员补充行为道德准则[编纂于《联邦规章汇编》第五编第4401.103节(外部雇佣和活动)];《联邦规章汇编》第五编第2635部分第H子部分(外部活动);和《美国法典》第三十一编第1353页以及《联邦规章汇编》第四十一编第304-1.1节(收受非联邦人士/实体支付的差旅费用)。

(f)(1)寻求外部雇佣或就此开展磋商的,委员和雇员应遵守下述规定:证券交易委员会委员和雇员补充行为道德准则(编纂于《联邦规章汇编》第五编第4401.103节(外部雇佣和活动);第五编第2635部分第F子部分(寻求外部雇佣);第五编第2635部分第H子部分(外部活动)。

(2)委员和雇员应注意《美国法典》第十八编第208节(影响私人利益的行为)作出了如下规定:对于委员或雇员明知其自身、配偶、未成年子女、普通合伙人拥有经济利益的事项,或者对于委员或雇员以管理人员、董事、信托受托人、普通合伙人供职的组织拥有经济利益的事项,或对于正在与委员或雇员就潜在雇佣开展磋商或已就此达

organization of which the employee is an officer, director, trustee, general partner or employee, or any person or organization with whom he or she is negotiating or has any arrangement concerning prospective employment, has a financial interest. This provision does not apply if the employee has received a written determination by an authorized official that the financial interest is not so substantial as to be deemed likely to affect the integrity of the employee's government service.

(3) Members may follow the procedural provision contained in Part V, Section 503 of the Executive Order 11222.

(g) An employee who intends to accept or perform any outside or private employment or professional work shall obtain necessary authorization in advance of such acceptance or performance. A request for such authorization shall be submitted to the Division Director, Office Head or Regional Director concerned, together with all pertinent facts regarding the proposed employment, such as the name of the employer, the nature of the work to be performed, its estimated duration, and the fee or compensation to be received. Division Directors, Office Heads and Regional Directors have been delegated the authority to approve routine requests for outside employment. The approving official shall forward to the Director of Personnel a copy of each request showing the date of approval. Requests of a non-routine nature should be forwarded to the Director of Personnel.

(h) The Director of Personnel, or his designee, is authorized to approve or disapprove requests for outside or private employment under this rule, except as to those cases which, in his judgment, should be considered and decided by the Commission. An employee may appeal a disapproved request to the Commission. The written appeal, submitted through the Director of Personnel, shall give reasons why the proposed outside or private employment is consistent with this rule. The Director of Personnel may not approve proposed outside or private employment which is absolutely prohibited by these rules. The Commission may, in a particular case, approve such employment.

[45 FR 36064, May 29, 1980; 45 FR 40975, June 17, 1980; 48 FR 39216, Aug. 30, 1983; 50 FR 45603, Nov. 1, 1985; 73 FR 32226, June 5, 2008; 75 FR 42276, July 20, 2010]

§200.735-5 Securities transactions.

Securities transactions by members and employees must comply with the provisions of 5 CFR 4401.102 (Prohibited and restricted financial interests and transactions).

[75 FR 42277, July 20, 2010]

§200.735-6 Action in case of personal interest.

Members and employees shall comply with the requirements of 5 CFR part 2640

成安排的人员或组织拥有经济利益的事项,雇员或委员不得亲自或实际参与任何该等事项。如果授权官员以书面形式判定所涉经济利益不属于重大经济利益,不致影响雇员提供的政府服务的廉正,则不适用上述规定。

(3)委员可遵守《第11222号行政命令》第V部分第503条的程序性规定。

(g)雇员希望接受或履行任何外部/私人雇佣或专业工作的,应事先征得必要的批准。批准请求应呈报相关的部门主任、办公室主管或地区办公室主任,并提交相关事实,如雇主姓名/名称、工作性质、预计期间以及提供的费用或报酬。部门主任、办公室主任和地区办公室主任有权批准常规的外部雇佣请求。对于所有请求,批准官员均应向人事主任转交一份复本,复本上须载明批准日期。非常规性质的请求应转交给人事主任。

(h)人事主任或其指定人员有权根据本规则批准或拒绝外部或私人雇佣请求,但根据其判断应由证券交易委员会审议并裁定的除外。请求被拒绝的,雇员可以申请证券交易委员会复议。书面复议请求应呈报人事主任,说明拟议之外部或私人雇佣不违反本规则的原因。对于本规则绝对禁止的外部/私人雇佣,人事主任不得批准。但在特殊情况下,证券交易委员会可以批准上述雇佣。

[《联邦公报》第45卷第36064页,1980年5月29日;《联邦公报》第45卷第40975页,1980年6月17日;《联邦公报》第48卷第39216页,1983年8月30日;《联邦公报》第50卷第45603页,1985年11月1日;《联邦公报》第73卷第32226页,2008年6月5日;《联邦公报》第75卷第42276页,2010年7月20日。]

第200.735-5节　证券交易

委员和雇员进行的证券交易必须符合《联邦规章汇编》第五编第4401.102节(被禁止和受限制的经济利益和交易)的规定。

[《联邦公报》第75卷第42277页,2010年7月20日。]

第200.735-6节　涉及私人利益时应采取的行动

委员和雇员应遵守《联邦规章汇编》第五编第2640部分[关于《美国法典》第十八

(Interpretation, exemptions, and waiver guidance concerning 18 U.S.C. 208 (Acts affecting a personal interest)).

[75 FR 42277, July 20, 2010]

§200.735–7 Negotiation for employment.

Members and employees shall comply with the requirements of 18 U.S.C. 208 (Acts affecting a personal interest) and 5 CFR part 2635, subpart F (Seeking other employment). *See* §200.735–4(f)(2) of this subpart.

[75 FR 42277, July 20, 2010]

§200.735–8 Practice by former members and employees of the Commission.

(a) Members and employees and former members and employees shall comply with the requirements of 18 U.S.C. 207 and 5 CFR part 2641 (Post employment conflict of interest restrictions). Members and employees and former members and employees should be aware that, among other restrictions, 18 U.S.C. 207 generally prohibits a former member or employee from knowingly communicating to or appearing before a Federal agency with the intent to influence a particular matter involving specific parties in which that person personally and substantially participated while at the Commission.

(b)(1) Any former member or employee of the Commission who, within 2 years after ceasing to be such, is employed or retained as the representative of any person outside the Government in any matter in which it is contemplated that he or she will appear before the Commission, or communicate with the Commission or its employees, shall, within ten days of such retainer or employment, or of the time when appearance before, or communication with the Commission or its employees is first contemplated, file with the Secretary of the Commission a statement which includes:

(i) A description of the contemplated representation;

(ii) An affirmative representation that the former employee while on the Commission's staff had neither personal and substantial responsibility nor official responsibility for the matter which is the subject of the representation; and

(iii) The name of the Commission Division or Office in which the person had been employed.

(2) Employment of a recurrent character may be covered by a single comprehensive statement. Each such statement should include an appropriate caption indicating that it is filed pursuant to this section. The reporting requirements of this paragraph do not apply to

(i) Communications incidental to court appearances in litigation involving the Commission; and

(ii) Oral communications concerning ministerial or informational matters or requests for oral advice not otherwise prohibited by paragraph (a) of this section.

编第208节(影响私人利益的行为)的解释、豁免和免除指引]的规定。

[《联邦公报》第75卷第42277页,2010年7月20日。]

第200.735-7节 雇佣磋商

委员和雇员应遵守《美国法典》第十八编第208节(影响私人利益的行为)以及《联邦规章汇编》第五编第2635部分第F子部分(寻求其他雇佣)的规定。参见本子部分第200.735-4(f)(2)节。

[《联邦公报》第75卷第42277页,2010年7月20日。]

第200.735-8节 证券交易委员会前任委员和雇员的业务活动

(a)委员、雇员及前任委员、雇员应遵守《美国法典》第十八编第207节和《联邦规章汇编》第五编第2641部分(雇佣关系结束后的利益冲突限制)的规定。委员、雇员及前任委员、雇员应注意,《美国法典》第十八编第207节普遍禁止前任委员或雇员在知情的情况下与某联邦机构进行沟通或出席其程序,试图就其在证券交易委员会任职期间亲自实质参与过的并涉及具体当事人的特定事项施加影响。

(b)(1)证券交易委员会的任何前任委员或雇员停止担任上述职务后2年内,如果就任何事项受雇或受聘担任政府之外任何主体的代理,且预期其将出席证券交易委员会的程序或与证券交易委员会或其雇员进行沟通,则应于受聘或受雇后10日内或首次拟定与证券交易委员会进行上述沟通后10日内,向证券交易委员会秘书提交一份包含下述内容的声明:

(i)拟代理工作之说明;

(ii)关于该前任雇员在证券交易委员会任职期间对该代理事项不负有个人责任、实质责任或职务责任的肯定性声明;及

(iii)其曾受雇的证券交易委员会部门或办公室名称。

(2)重复发生的雇佣仅需提交一份综合性声明。每份声明均应包含一个适当的标题,说明其系按本节规定提交。本款的报告要求不适用于:

(i)在涉及证券交易委员会的诉讼中,与出庭相关的沟通;及

(ii)关于行政或信息事项的口头沟通,或本节第(a)款不禁止的口头咨询请求。

(c) As used in this section, the term *appear before the commission* means physical presence before the Commission or its employees in either a formal or informal setting or the conveyance of material in connection with a formal appearance or application to the Commission. As used in this section the term *communication with intent to influence* does not encompass communications which are not for the purpose of influencing the Commission or any of its employees or which, at the time of the filings, are reasonably believed not to involve any potential controversy. As used in this section, the term *representative* or *representative capacity* shall include not only the usual type of representation by an attorney, etc., but also representation of a corporation in the capacity of an officer, director or controlling stockholder thereof.

(d)(1) Partners or associates of any person disqualified from appearing or practicing before the Commission in a particular matter are also disqualified. Such partners or associates (the *firm*) may request a waiver of this prohibition from the Commission by writing a letter to the General Counsel of the commission setting forth the facts of the proposed representation and the individual's disqualification. In appropriate situations, a firm may request a generic waiver with respect to a number of different matters. Upon the advice of the Office of the General Counsel, the Commission, or the General Counsel exercising delegated authority, will advise the requestor of the Commission's response.

(2) Waivers ordinarily will be granted where the firm makes a satisfactory representation that it has adopted screening measures which will effectively isolate the individual lawyer disqualified from participating in the particular matter or matters and from sharing in any fees attributable to it. It will be considered significant for purposes of this determination that:

(i) The firm had a pre-existing securities law practice prior to the arrival of the disqualified attorney;

(ii) The matter was previously the subject of consideration by the firm or the client was already advised by the firm;

(iii) In cases where the matter or client became the subject of consideration by the firm subsequent to the firm's employment of the lawyer individually disqualified, that the matter was not brought to the firm because of the disqualified attorney.

(3) Notwithstanding the existence or non-existence of any of these factors, no waiver will be issued if the proposed representation would create a significant appearance of

(c)就本节而言,“出席证券交易委员会程序”一词系指在正式或非正式场合当面接触证券交易委员会或其雇员,或递交与正式出席程序或申请相关的材料。就本节而言,“以施加影响为目的进行沟通”不包括非为影响证券交易委员会或其任何雇员之目的而进行的沟通,以及在提交文件时,可合理相信不涉及潜在冲突的沟通。就本节规定而言,“代理或代理身份”一词不仅包括通常的律师代理,也包括以管理人员、董事或控股股东身份担任的公司代理。

(d)(1)任何主体如丧失了就特定事项出席证券交易委员会程序或办理业务的资格,则该主体之合伙人或同事亦无该等资格。上述合伙人或同事(合称事务所)可以向证券交易委员会首席律师发送一封信函,说明拟进行的代理工作,并说明上述个人不具备就所涉事项出席证券交易委员会程序或办理业务的资格之事实,请求证券交易委员会免除该等禁止规定的适用。在适当情况下,事务所可以请求对一系列不同的事项一般性地免除禁止规定的适用。征询首席律师办公室的意见后,证券交易委员会或首席律师可根据其授权将证券交易委员会的答复告知请求人。

(2)如果事务所能提供令人满意的声明,阐述其已采取隔离措施有效隔离不具备参与特定事项的资格的律师、不与该律师分享事务所收取的与该等事项相关的任何费用,则上述免除申请一般会得到核准。在作上述判定时,下述考量因素非常重要:

(i)在丧失资格的律师进入事务所之前,该事务所即已开展证券法业务;

(ii)事务所之前已承办了所涉事项,或者事务所之前已为所涉客户提供咨询服务;

(iii)如果,在聘用丧失资格的律师后,事务所才开始承办所涉事项或为所涉客户提供服务,则应阐明客户并非出于该丧失资格的律师的因素将该事项交由事务所承办。

(3)尽管存在或不存在上述任何因素,如果拟进行的代理工作将造成表面上显著

impropriety or would otherwise adversely affect the interests of the government.[1] All proceedings with respect to waivers shall be a matter of public record except to the extent that such public disclosure might violate attorney–client privilege or breach the attorney's obligation to preserve the confidences and secrets of this or her clients, reveal the existence of ongoing private investigations, interfere with law enforcement proceedings, or otherwise be inconsistent with the public interest.

(e) Persons in doubt as to the applicability of any portion of this section may apply for an advisory ruling of the Commission.[2]

[45 FR 36064, May 29, 1980, as amended at 50 FR 23669, June 5, 1985; 75 FR 42277, July 20, 2010]

§200.735–9 Indebtedness.

Members and employees shall comply with the requirements of 5 CFR 2635.809 (Just financial obligations).

[75 FR 42277, July 20, 2010]

§200.735–10 Miscellaneous statutory provisions.

Each member and employee is responsible for acquainting himself or herself with the statutory provisions listed in 5 CFR 2635.902 (Related statutes). A violation of any of these provisions is deemed a violation of this subpart M.

[75 FR 42277, July 20, 2010]

§200.735–11 Statement of employment and financial interests.

(a) Members and employees shall file financial disclosure reports in accordance with the requirements of 5 CFR part 2634 (Executive branch financial disclosure).

(b) Prior to the time of entry on duty, or upon designation to a position set forth in paragraph (c) of this section, such employee shall submit to the Director of Personnel a statement, on the official form made available for this purpose through the Office of Personnel, setting forth the following information:

(1) A list of the names of all corporations, companies, firms, or other business enterprises, partnerships, nonprofit organizations, and educational or other institutions with or in which the employee, his or her spouse, emancipated minor child or other member of his or her immediate household has —

(i) Any connection as an employee, officer, owner, director, member, trustee, partner, adviser or consultant; or

---

1 For example, no waiver will be granted if, during the course of representing a client who has an interest with respect to a matter before the Commission, a firm employs, or accepts as a partner, a member of the staff or of the Commission who at any time during the course of that representation had direct and substantial responsibility for the same matter, and whose departure would result in a significant adverse impact upon that matter at the Commission.

2 Attention of former members and employees is directed to Formal Opinion 342 of the Committee on Ethics of the American Bar Association, 62 A.B.A.J. 517 (1975) and to 18 U.S.C. 207.

不当的情况或将对政府利益造成其他不利影响,则不得核准免除。[1]所有与免除相关的程序均应进行公开记录,除非公开披露可能违反律师与客户之间的保密特权约定或违反律师保护其客户秘密或机密的义务、披露正在进行的私人调查、干扰执法程序或对公共利益造成其他损害。

(e)对于本节任何内容的适用性存在疑问的,可申请证券交易委员会进行咨询性裁决。[2]

[《联邦公报》第45卷第36064页,1980年5月29日,修正索引:《联邦公报》第50卷第23669页,1985年6月5日;《联邦公报》第75卷第42277页,2010年7月20日。]

第200.735-9节　负债

委员和雇员应遵守《联邦规章汇编》第五编第2635.809节(正当财务义务)的要求。

[《联邦公报》第75卷第42277页,2010年7月20日。]

第200.735-10节　其他制定法规定

所有委员和雇员均有义务熟知《联邦规章汇编》第五编第2635.902节(相关制定法)所列的法律条文。违反上述任何法律条文均将视为对本第M子部分的违反。

[《联邦公报》第75卷第42277页,2010年7月20日。]

第200.735-11节　雇佣和经济利益声明

(a)委员和雇员应按照《联邦规章汇编》第五编第2634部分(行政机构财务披露)的要求提交财务披露报告。

(b)在上岗之前或在被指定承担本节第(c)款规定的职务之时,该等雇员应按人事办公室为此制定的官方格式,向人事主任呈报一份声明,载明下述信息:

(1)任何雇员及其配偶、未独立生活的未成年子女或其他共同生活的直系亲属与之存在下列关联的任何法人、公司、事务所、其他商业企业、合伙、非营利组织、教育机构或其他机构之完整名单——

(i)职员、管理人员、所有人、董事、成员、信托受托人、合伙人、咨询人或顾问关系;

1　例如,如果在代理与证券交易委员会处理的事项有利害关系之客户的过程中,事务所聘用证券交易委员会员工或吸收其为合伙人,而该员工在代理期间的任何时候对同一事项承担直接或实体责任,且该员工离职将对证券交易委员会处理该事项造成重大不利影响,则不得核准免除。

2　前任委员和雇员应注意如下规定:美国律师协会职业道德委员会《第342号正式意见》[(《美国律师协会期刊》第62卷第517页(1975)]以及《美国法典》第十八编第207节。

(ii) Any continuing financial interest, through a pension or retirement plan, shared income, or other arrangement as a result of any current or prior employment or business or professional association.

(iii) Any financial interest through the ownership of stock, stock options, bonds, securities, or other arrangements including trusts.

(2) A list of the names of the employee's creditors and the creditors of his or her spouse, unemancipated minor child or other member of his or her immediate household, other than those creditors to whom any such person may be indebted by reason of a mortgage on property which he or she occupies as a personal residence, or to whom such person may be indebted for current and ordinary household and living expenses such as those incurred for household furnishings, vacations, an automobile, education, or the like.

(3) A list of the employee's interests and those of his or her spouse, unemancipated minor child, or other member of his or her immediate household in real property or rights in lands, other than property which he or she occupies as a personal residence.

(4) For the purpose of this section, *member of his or her immediate household* means a resident of the employee's household who is related to the employee by blood or marriage.

(5) In the instance where a spouse is not a *member of the employee's immediate household,* and the employee certifies he or she neither derives nor expects to derive any economic benefit from the holdings of the spouse, the Director of Personnel may waive the requirement of reporting the interests of such spouse.

(c) Statements of employment and financial interests filed pursuant to paragraph (a) of this section shall be sent to the Commission's Office of the General Counsel's Ethics Office in a sealed envelope marked "Confidential Employment and Financial Interests." They shall be maintained in a confidential file. Only those officials of the Commission whose participation is necessary for the carrying out of the purpose of this Conduct Regulation may have access to such statements and no information may be disclosed from them except as the Commission or the Office of Personnel Management may determine for good cause shown.

(d) In accordance with the requirements of the Ethics in Government Act of 1978, Pub. L. 95-521, the Commission's Office of the General Counsel's Ethics Office shall review the financial disclosure reports filed pursuant to that Act.

(e) The Commission's Office of the General Counsel's Ethics Office shall examine the statements of employment and financial interests filed pursuant to paragraph (a) of this section to determine whether conflicts of interest or apparent conflicts of interest on the part of employees exist. An employee shall be afforded the opportunity to explain

(ii)由于任何当前或之前的雇佣、业务关系或专业协会关系,通过养老金或退休计划、收益分享或通过其他安排享有任何持续性的经济利益;或

(iii)通过拥有股票、股票期权、债券、证券或其他安排(包括信托)而拥有任何经济利益。

(2)雇员及其配偶、未独立生活的未成年子女或其他共同生活的直系亲属的债权人名单,但上述人员因其个人居所抵押而对其发生负债的债权人,或欠负经常性或普通家居和生活费用(如家庭装修、度假、汽车、教育或类似费用)的债权人除外。

(3)雇员及其配偶、未独立生活的未成年子女或其他共同生活的直系亲属享有的不动产权益和土地权益列表,但个人居所除外。

(4)就本节而言,“共同生活的直系亲属”指与雇员共同生活的与雇员存在血缘或婚姻关系的个人。

(5)如配偶不属于本节所定义的“共同生活的直系亲属”,且雇员证明其不从配偶的财产获得任何经济利益并且也不预期获得该等经济利益,人事主任可免除上报该等配偶利益的要求。

(c)根据本节第(a)款提交的关于雇佣和经济利益的声明,应以密封信封发送至证券交易委员会下属的首席律师职业道德办公室,并注明“机密雇佣和经济利益信息”。上述声明应通过保密文件保存。只有有必要参与证券交易委员会的《行为准则管理办法》实施工作的官员才能接触该等声明,且除非证券交易委员会或人事管理局判定存在正当理由,否则该等官员不得披露声明中的任何信息。

(d)按照《1978年政府职业道德法》(公法编号95-521)的要求,证券交易委员会下属的首席律师职业道德办公室负责审查根据该法提交的财务披露报告。

(e)证券交易委员会下属的首席律师职业道德办公室负责审查根据本节第(a)款提交的雇佣和经济利益声明,判定雇员方面是否存在利益冲突或表面利益冲突。雇员应获得解释任何冲突或表面冲突的机会。如果人事主任或助理人事主任在咨询所涉雇员相关的上级主管后无法解决冲突或表面冲突,应通过按第200.735-15(a)节指定

any conflict or appearance of conflict. When the Director or Assistant Director of Personnel, in consultation with appropriate superiors of the employee involved, is unable to resolve a conflict or appearance of conflict, he or she shall report the matter to the Commission through the Counselor for the Commission designated under §200.735-15 (a).

(f) Except as otherwise provided in paragraph (a) of this section the statement of employment and financial interests and supplementary statements required of employees are in addition to, and not in substitution for, or in derogation of, any similar requirement imposed by law, order or regulation. The submission of a statement by an employee does not permit him or her or any other person to participate in a matter in which his or her or the other person's participation is prohibited by law, order or regulation.

(g) An employee has the right to ask for a review through the Commission's grievance procedure outlined in section 771, Part II, Manual of Administrative Regulations, of a complaint that his or her position has been improperly included under the provisions of this section as one requiring the submission of a statement of employment and financial interests.

[45 FR 36064, May 29, 1980; 45 FR 40975, June 17, 1980, as amended at 73 FR 32226, June 5, 2008; 75 FR 42278, July 20, 2010]

§200.735-12 Special Government employees.

(a) Special Government employee means a person defined in section 18 U.S.C. 202 as a *special Government employee*. All of the provisions of this Conduct Regulation are applicable to special Government employees, except that in specific appropriate cases the Commission may exempt such employees from, or modify the applicability of, any portion of any provision of the Conduct Regulation.

(b) In no event will the Commission waive a provision of the Conduct Regulation which would permit a special Government employee to:

(1) Use his or her Government employment for a purpose that is, or gives the appearance of being, motivated by the desire for private gain for himself or another person, particularly one with whom he or she has family, business, or financial ties.

(2) Use inside information obtained as a result of his or her Government employment for private gain for himself or herself or another person either by direct action on his or her part or by counsel, recommendation, or suggestion to another person, particularly one with whom he or she has family, business, or financial ties. For purposes of this paragraph, *inside information* means information obtained under Government authority which has not become part of the body of public information.

(3) Use his or her Government employment to coerce, or give the appearance of

的证券交易委员会顾问将该事项上报给证券交易委员会。

(f)除本节第(a)款另有规定的情形外,雇员提交雇佣和经济利益声明及补充声明的义务独立于法律、命令或规章的其他任何类似要求,不构成对该等要求的替代或减免。雇员呈报上述声明,并不表示其自身或他人已经获许参与法律、命令或规章所禁止参与的事项。

(g)雇员有权通过《行政规章手册》第Ⅱ部分第771条规定的证券交易委员会的员工申诉程序,主张其职务不应按本节规定被纳入须呈报雇佣和经济利益声明的职位之列,并可要求对此进行复议。

[《联邦公报》第45卷第36064页,1980年5月29日;《联邦公报》第45卷第40975页,1980年6月17日,修正索引:《联邦公报》第73卷第32226页,2008年6月5日;《联邦公报》第75卷第42278页,2010年7月20日。]

第200.735-12节　特别政府雇员

(a)"特别政府雇员"系指《美国法典》第十八编第202节定义的"特别政府雇员"。本《行为准则管理办法》的所有规定均适用于特别政府雇员,但在相关的具体情形下,证券交易委员会可以免除《行为准则管理办法》任何条款的任何部分对该等雇员的适用,或可以修改其适用范围。

(b)在任何情况下,如免除《行为准则管理办法》条款的适用将导致特别政府雇员有权从事下述行为,则证券交易委员会不得免除该等条款的适用:

(1)为其自身或他人(特别是与其有亲属、业务或经济关系的人)的私人利益所驱动之目的或从表面看来为此等私人利益所驱动之目的而利用其政府职务。

(2)为其自身或他人的私人利益,直接或向他人(特别是与其有亲属、业务或经济关系的人)提供咨询、推荐或建议,或使用因其政府职务获得的内幕信息。就本款而言,"内幕信息"系指依政府权限取得的未进入公共领域的信息。

(3)利用其政府职务,强迫或从表面上看强迫某人为自身或其他人(特别是与其

coercing, a person to provide financial benefit to himself or herself or another person, particularly one with whom he or she has family, business, or financial ties.

(4) Receive or solicit from a person having business with the Commission anything of value as a gift, gratuity, loan, entertainment, or favor for himself or herself or another person, particularly one with whom he or she has family, business or financial ties.

(c) Prior to entrance on duty, each special Government employee shall submit to the Director of Personnel a statement of employment and financial interests which contains such information as the Director of Personnel determines is relevant in the light of the duties the special Government employee is to perform and, if appropriate, the financial disclosure report as provided by title Ⅱ of the Ethics in Government Act of 1978, Pub. L. 95-521. It shall be kept current throughout the period of employment by the filing of supplementary statements in accordance with the requirements of §200.735-11(d). Statements shall be on the official form made available for this purpose through the Office of Personnel.

(d) The Commission may waive the requirement of paragraph (c) of this section in the case of a special Government employee who is not a *consultant* or an *expert*, as those terms are defined in chapter 304 of the Federal Personnel Manual (5 CFR 735.304), if the duties of the position are determined to be at a level of responsibility which does not require the submission of such statement to protect the integrity of the Commission.

§200.735-13 Disciplinary and other remedial action.

(a) Knowing participation in a violation of this subpart by persons not within the scope of the foregoing rules in this subpart shall likewise be deemed improper conduct and in contravention of Commission rules. Departure from any of the rules in this subpart by employees or special Government employees without specific approval may be cause for appropriate remedial and/or disciplinary action or, in the case of former members, employees, and special Government employees, for disqualification from appearing and practicing before the Commission, which may be in addition to any penalty prescribed by law.

(b) When there has been a departure from any of the rules of this subpart without specific approval or when a conflict of interest or an apparent conflict of interest on the part of an employee or special Government employee arises, the Director of Personnel may order immediate action to end such conflict or appearance of conflict of interest. Remedial action may include, but is not limited to (1) changes in assigned duties; (2) divestment by the employee or special Government employee of his conflicting interest; (3) disciplinary action; or (4) disqualification for a particular assignment. Remedial action, whether disciplinary or otherwise, shall be effected in accordance with any

有亲属、业务或经济关系的人)提供经济利益。

(4)为其自身或他人(特别是与其有亲属、业务或经济关系的人),收受任何与证券交易委员会存在业务关系的人提供的或向其索要任何礼品、赠品、贷款、招待、恩惠等有价物品。

(c)在上岗前,每一特别政府雇员均应向人事主任呈报一份雇佣和经济利益声明,在其中载明人事主任认定雇员承担该职责所需声明的信息,且如适当,还应呈报《1978年政府职业道德法》(公法编号95-521)第二编规定的财务披露报告。在整个雇佣期间内,雇员均应按照第200.735-11(d)节的要求提交补充声明进行更新。声明应按人事办公室为此制定的官方格式编制。

(d)如特别政府雇员不属于顾问或专家["顾问"或"专家"如《联邦人事手册》第304章(《联邦规章汇编》第五编第735.304节)所定义],且其职务所承担的责任未达到一定的水平,不必为保护证券交易委员会廉洁性之目的而提交上述声明,则证券交易委员会可以对其免除本节第(c)款的要求。

第200.735-13节 纪律处分和其他纠正行动

(a)本子部分前述规则覆盖范围之外的人在知情的情况下参与违反本子部分规定的行为,亦应视为违反证券交易委员会规则的不当行为。任何雇员或特别政府雇员未经特别批准擅自违反本上述任何规则,可能招致相关的纠正和/或纪律处分,前任委员、雇员和特别政府雇员除被处以法律规定的任何罚金外,还可能被取消出席证券交易委员会程序并办理业务的资格。

(b)对于未经特别批准擅自违反本子部分任何规则的情况,或雇员或特别政府雇员出现利益冲突或表面利益冲突的情况,人事主任可以命令立即采取行动结束上述利益冲突或表面利益冲突。纠正行动可包括但不限于:(1)变更职责分配;(2)雇员或特别政府雇员撤回存在利益冲突的投资;(3)纪律处分措施;或(4)取消其承担某特殊任务的资格。纠正行动,无论是纪律处分还是其他行动,均应按照适用法、行政命令和相关规章采取。人事主任可以将建议采取的任何行动提交证券交易委员会。对于人事主任命令采取的任何行动,雇员均可以要求证券交易委员会进行复议。复议期间,除非证券交易委员会另有指示,否则人事主任命令采取的行动将中止适用。

applicable laws, Executive Orders, and regulations. The Director of Personnel may refer any recommended action to the Commission. The employee may obtain review by the Commission of any action ordered to be taken by the Director of Personnel. During the period of review, unless otherwise directed by the Commission, the action ordered by the Director of Personnel is stayed.

(c) Former members or employees who violate the post-employment restriction provisions of 18 U.S.C. 207 (a), (b) or (c), which parallel the provisions of Rule 8(a), *supra,* will be subject to an administrative enforcement proceeding as set forth in Rule 102 (e) of the Commission's Rules of Practice, §201.102 (e) of this chapter, except that, when proceedings are brought to determine if violations of post-employment restrictions have occurred, denial of the privilege of appearing and practicing before the Commission will be based on a finding of violation of the provisions of Rule 8(a) and 18 U.S.C. 207 (a), (b) and (c). Procedures applicable to such administrative proceedings are to be found in the Commission's Rules of Practice, 17 CFR 201.100 *et seq.*

[45 FR 36064, May 29, 1980, as amended at 60 FR 32795, June 23, 1995]

§200.735-14 Employees on leave of absence.

The provisions of the rules in this subpart relative to employees of the Commission are applicable to employees on a leave with pay or a leave without pay status other than extended military service.

§200.735-15 Interpretive and advisory service.

(a) The General Counsel shall be designated *Counselor for the Commission* and shall serve as the Commission's delegate to the Office of Personnel Management on matters covered by the rules in this subpart. The General Counsel shall be responsible for coordinating the Commission's counseling services provided under this section and for assuring that counseling and interpretations on questions of conflicts of interest and other matters covered by the rules in this subpart are available to all members and employees.

(b) There shall be designated as Deputy Counselors the Commission's Office of the General Counsel's Ethics Office, the Regional Director of each regional office, and the person in charge of each branch office. The General Counsel or his or her designee shall provide guidance to the Deputy Counselors for the purpose of achieving uniform interpretations of this subpart.

(c) A member, employee, or former member or employee may obtain advice or guidance on the application of the rules in this subpart from any Deputy Counselor or the General Counsel. In addition, any former member or employee seeking advice or an

(c)违反《美国法典》第十八编第207(a)节、第207(b)节或第207(c)节关于雇佣关系终止后的限制规定以及《8(a)规则》(见上文)的前任委员或雇员,应适用《证券交易委员会工作规则》的《102(e)规则》[本章第201.102(e)节]规定的行政执法程序,但是,如果程序提起的目的是确定是否出现了违反适用于雇佣关系终止之后的限制规定的行为,则前任委员或雇员一旦被认定存在违反《8(a)规则》及《美国法典》第十八编第207(a)节、第207(b)节和第207(c)节的行为,其出席证券交易委员会程序并办理业务的特权将被取消。上述行政处理程序适用的程序见《证券交易委员会工作规则》(《联邦规章汇编》第十七编第201.100节及其后条文)。

[《联邦公报》第45卷第36064页,1980年5月29日,修正索引:《联邦公报》第60卷第32795页,1995年6月23日。]

第200.735-14节　休假期间的雇员

本子部分与证券交易委员会雇员相关的规则适用于处于带薪休假或无薪休假期间的雇员,但处于延长兵役期间的除外。

第200.735-15节　解释和顾问服务

(a)对于本子部分规则所涵盖的事项,首席律师应被指定为"证券交易委员会的顾问",并充当证券交易委员会在人事管理局的代表。首席律师应负责协调本节项下提供的证券交易委员会的顾问服务,并确保面向全体委员和雇员就本子部分项下规则所涵盖的利益冲突问题和其他事项提供顾问服务和解释。

(b)证券交易委员会下属的首席律师职业道德办公室、各地区办公室主任以及各分支办公室的主管人员应被指定为副顾问。首席律师或其指定人员应为实现对本子部分的统一解释之目的向副顾问提供指导。

(c)委员、雇员或前任委员、雇员可以就本子部分规则之适用获得任何副顾问或首席律师的建议或指引。此外,任何前任委员或雇员如果寻求与《政府职业道德法》相关的建议或解释,均应向首席律师提交该等请求。

interpretation relating to the Ethics in Government Act shall submit his or her request to the General Counsel.

(d) The General Counsel and Deputy Counselors will treat information they receive pursuant to requests for advice or guidance under this Rule on a confidential basis, except that information they receive indicating a possible past violation of any provision of this Conduct Regulation or of the law will be brought to the attention of appropriate persons.

(e) The Commission's Office of the General Counsel's Ethics Office shall furnish a copy of this Conduct Regulation (subpart M) to each member, employee and special Government employee immediately upon his or her entrance on duty and shall thereafter, annually, and at such other times as circumstances warrant, bring to the attention of each member, employee and special Government employee this Conduct Regulation (subpart M) and all revisions thereof.

(f) The Commission's Office of the General Counsel's Ethics Office shall notify each member, employee and special Government employee at the time of entrance on duty, and from time to time thereafter, of the availability of counseling services and of how and where these services are available.

[45 FR 36064, May 29, 1980, as amended at 73 FR 32227, June 5, 2008; 75 FR 42278, July 20, 2010]

§200.735-16 Delegation.

Any official responsibility assigned to a person in a particular position pursuant to this subpart may be delegated by such person to any other person.

§200.735-17 Administration of the conduct regulation.

Under the general direction of the General Counsel, the Designated Agency Ethics Official is responsible for the day-to-day administration of this conduct regulation except where otherwise provided.

[45 FR 36064, May 29, 1980, as amended at 75 FR 42278, July 20, 2010]

§200.735-18 Requests for waivers.

Unless a different procedure is specifically prescribed in a rule of this part, an employee may submit a request for a waiver, modification or postponement of a requirement included in this part to the Chairman. Such waiver, modification or postponement may be granted if it is determined by the Chairman that such waiver, modification of postponement would not adversely affect the interest of the Commission or the United States. Any such waiver, modification or postponement granted by the Chairman shall be made available to the public. The Chairman may submit any request made pursuant to this rule to the Commission for its consideration. Any Commission action on such request shall be made public only in the discretion of the Commission.

(d)首席律师和副顾问将对因请求人在本规则下请求获得顾问服务或指引而向其提交的信息进行保密处理,但所收到的信息如果表明可能存在违法本《行为准则管理办法》或法律的情形,该等信息将提交给相关人员。

(e)证券交易委员会下属的首席律师职业道德办公室应在每一委员、雇员和特别政府雇员上岗时立即向其提供一份《行为准则管理办法》(第M子部分),并在此后每年以及必要的具体情形下向其提供本《行为准则管理办法》(第M子部分)及其所有修改。

(f)证券交易委员会下属的首席律师职业道德办公室应在每一委员、雇员和特别政府雇员上岗时及上岗后的任何时间告知其可以获得的顾问服务以及获得的方式和地点。

[《联邦公报》第45卷第36064页,1980年5月29日,修正索引:《联邦公报》第73卷第32227页,2008年6月5日;《联邦公报》第75卷第42278页,2010年7月20日。]

第200.735-16节　委托授权

根据本子部分规定向特定职务的人员授予的任何职责可由其转授给任何其他人员。

第200.735-17节　行为准则规章的执行

根据首席律师的总体指示,除非另有规定,否则本《行为准则管理办法》的日常实施由指定机关职业道德官负责。

[《联邦公报》第45卷第36064页,1980年5月29日,修正索引:《联邦公报》第75卷第42278页,2010年7月20日。]

第200.735-18节　豁免请求

除非本子部分的规则特别规定了不同的程序,否则雇员可以向证券交易委员会主席呈报申请豁免、修改或延缓适用本部分规定的请求。如证券交易委员会主席判定,该等豁免、修改或延缓不会对证券交易委员会或美国的利益造成不利影响,可予以核准。证券交易委员会主席对任何豁免、修改或延缓请求的核准均应向公众公开。主席可将根据本规则提出的任何请求呈报给证券交易委员会审议。证券交易委员会依其自由裁量权可以自行决定是否对外公布针对该等请求采取的行动。本子部分中对普遍适用于行政机构的联邦法律、规章或行政命令的任何实施规定,不得依据本规定进行豁免。

Requirements included in this part which implement any provision of Federal law, regulation or Executive Order generally applicable to the Executive Branch shall not be waived under this provision.

Subpart N—Commission Information Collection Requirements Under the Paperwork Reduction Act: OMB Control Numbers

Authority: 44 U.S.C. 3506; 44 U.S.C. 3507.

Source: 67 FR 14634, Mar. 27, 2002, unless otherwise noted.

§200.800 OMB control numbers assigned pursuant to the Paperwork Reduction Act.

(a) *Purpose*: This subpart collects and displays the control numbers assigned to information collection requirements of the Commission by the Office of Management and Budget pursuant to the Paperwork Reduction Act of 1980, 44 U.S.C. 3500 *et seq.* This subpart displays current OMB control numbers for those information collection requirements of the Commission that are rules and regulations and codified in 17 CFR either in full text or incorporated by reference with the approval of the Director of the Office of the Federal Register.

(b) *Display.*

Information collection requirement	17 CFR part or section where identified and described	Current OMB control No.
Regulation S – X	Part 210	3235 – 0009
Regulation S – B	Part 228	3235 – 0417
Regulation S – K	Part 229	3235 – 0071
Rule 154	230. 154	3235 – 0495
Rule 155	230. 155	3235 – 0549
Rule 236	230. 236	3235 – 0095
Rule 237	230. 237	3235 – 0528
Regulation A	230. 251 thru 230. 263	3235 – 0286
Regulation C	230. 400 thru 230. 494	3235 – 0074
Rule 425	230. 425	3235 – 0521

第N子部分——证券交易委员会在《文书削减法》中的信息采集要求:行政管理和预算局控制编号

法律依据:《美国法典》第四十四编第3506节;《美国法典》第四十四编第3507节。

行政规则来源:《联邦公报》第67卷第14634页,2002年3月27日,除非另有说明。

第200.800节　根据《1980年文书削减法》指定的行政管理和预算局控制编号

(a)目的:本子部分收编并列出行政管理和预算局根据《1980年文书削减法》(《美国法典》第四十四编第3500节及其后条文)为各种信息采集要求指定的控制编号。对于属于证券交易委员会规则与规章性质的信息采集要求,本子部分列出了当前的行政管理和预算局控制编号(见下文),该等规则与规章经联邦公报办公室主任批准,已全文编纂于或者通过引述的方式纳入《联邦规章汇编》第十七编中。

(b)列表。

信息采集要求	《联邦规章汇编》第十七编中对信息采集要求进行列举和说明的相关章节	当前美国行政管理和预算局控制编号
《S－X 管理办法》	第 210 部分	3235－0009
《S－B 管理办法》	第 228 部分	3235－0417
《S－K 管理办法》	第 229 部分	3235－0071
《154 规则》	230. 154	3235－0495
《155 规则》	230. 155	3235－0549
《236 规则》	230. 236	3235－0095
《237 规则》	230. 237	3235－0528
《A 管理办法》	230. 251 至 230. 263	3235－0286
《C 管理办法》	230. 400 至 230. 494	3235－0074
《425 规则》	230. 425	3235－0521

Information collection requirement	17 CFR part or section where identified and described	Current OMB control No.
Rule 477	230.477	3235 – 0550
Rule 489	230.489	3235 – 0411
Rule 498	230.498	3235 – 0488
Regulation D	230.501 thru 230.506	3235 – 0076
Regulation E	230.601 thru 230.610a	3235 – 0232
Rule 604	230.604	3235 – 0232
Rule 605	230.605	3235 – 0232
Rule 609	230.609	3235 – 0233
Rule 701	230.701	3235 – 0522
Regulation S	230.901 thru 230.905	3235 – 0357
Regulation S – T	Part 232	3235 – 0424
Form SB – 1	239.9	3235 – 0423
Form SB – 2	239.10	3235 – 0418
Form S – 1	239.11	3235 – 0065
Form S – 2	239.12	3235 – 0072
Form S – 3	239.13	3235 – 0073
Form N – 2	239.14	3235 – 0026
Form N – 1A	239.15A	3235 – 0307
Form S – 6	239.16	3235 – 0184
Form S – 8	239.16b	3235 – 0066
Form N – 3	239.17a	3235 – 0316
Form N – 4	239.17b	3235 – 0318
Form S – 11	239.18	3235 – 0067
Form N – 14	239.23	3235 – 0336
Form N – 5	239.24	3235 – 0169
Form S – 4	239.25	3235 – 0324
Form F – 1	239.31	3235 – 0258
Form F – 2	239.32	3235 – 0257

续表

信息采集要求	《联邦规章汇编》第十七编中对信息采集要求进行列举和说明的相关章节	当前美国行政管理和预算局控制编号
《477 规则》	230.477	3235－0550
《489 规则》	230.489	3235－0411
《498 规则》	230.498	3235－0488
《D 管理办法》	230.501 至 230.506	3235－0076
《E 管理办法》	230.601 至 230.610a	3235－0232
《604 规则》	230.604	3235－0232
《605 规则》	230.605	3235－0232
《609 规则》	230.609	3235－0233
《701 规则》	230.701	3235－0522
《S 管理办法》	230.901 至 230.905	3235－0357
《S－T 管理办法》	第 232 部分	3235－0424
《SB－1 表格》	239.9	3235－0423
《SB－2 表格》	239.10	3235－0418
《S－1 表格》	239.11	3235－0065
《S－2 表格》	239.12	3235－0072
《S－3 表格》	239.13	3235－0073
《N－2 表格》	239.14	3235－0026
《N－1A 表格》	239.15A	3235－0307
《S－6 表格》	239.16	3235－0184
《S－8 表格》	239.16b	3235－0066
《N－3 表格》	239.17a	3235－0316
《N－4 表格》	239.17b	3235－0318
《S－11 表格》	239.18	3235－0067
《N－14 表格》	239.23	3235－0336
《N－5 表格》	239.24	3235－0169
《S－4 表格》	239.25	3235－0324
《F－1 表格》	239.31	3235－0258
《F－2 表格》	239.32	3235－0257

Information collection requirement	17 CFR part or section where identified and described	Current OMB control No.
Form F – 3	239. 33	3235 – 0256
Form F – 4	239. 34	3235 – 0325
Form F – 6	239. 36	3235 – 0292
Form F – 7	239. 37	3235 – 0383
Form F – 8	239. 38	3235 – 0378
Form F – 9	239. 39	3235 – 0377
Form F – 10	239. 40	3235 – 0380
Form F – 80	239. 41	3235 – 0404
Form F – X	239. 42	3235 – 0379
Form F – N	239. 43	3235 – 0411
Form ET	239. 62	3235 – 0329
Form ID	239. 63	3235 – 0328
Form SE	239. 64	3235 – 0327
Form TH	239. 65	3235 – 0425
Form 1 – A	239. 90	3235 – 0286
Form 2 – A	239. 91	3235 – 0286
Form 144	239. 144	3235 – 0101
Form 1 – E	239. 200	3235 – 0232
Form CB	239. 800	3235 – 0518
Rule 6a – 1	240. 6a – 1	3235 – 0017
Rule 6a – 3	240. 6a – 3	3235 – 0021
Rule 6a – 4	240. 6a – 4	3235 – 0554
Rule 6h – 1	240. 6h – 1	3235 – 0555
Rule 8c – 1	240. 8c – 1	3235 – 0514
Rule 9b – 1	240. 9b – 1	3235 – 0480
Rule 10a – 1	240. 10a – 1	3235 – 0475
Rule 10b – 10	240. 10b – 10	3235 – 0444
Rule 10b – 17	240. 10b – 17	3235 – 0476

续表

信息采集要求	《联邦规章汇编》 第十七编中对信息采集要求 进行列举和说明的相关章节	当前美国行政管理 和预算局控制编号
《F－3 表格》	239.33	3235－0256
《F－4 表格》	239.34	3235－0325
《F－6 表格》	239.36	3235－0292
《F－7 表格》	239.37	3235－0383
《F－8 表格》	239.38	3235－0378
《F－9 表格》	239.39	3235－0377
《F－10 表格》	239.40	3235－0380
《F－80 表格》	239.41	3235－0404
《F－X 表格》	239.42	3235－0379
《F－N 表格》	239.43	3235－0411
《ET 表格》	239.62	3235－0329
《ID 表格》	239.63	3235－0328
《SE 表格》	239.64	3235－0327
《TH 表格》	239.65	3235－0425
《1－A 表格》	239.90	3235－0286
《2－A 表格》	239.91	3235－0286
《144 表格》	239.144	3235－0101
《1－E 表格》	239.200	3235－0232
《CB 表格》	239.800	3235－0518
《6a－1 规则》	240.6a－1	3235－0017
《6a－3 规则》	240.6a－3	3235－0021
《6a－4 规则》	240.6a－4	3235－0554
《6h－1 规则》	240.6h－1	3235－0555
《8c－1 规则》	240.8c－1	3235－0514
《9b－1 规则》	240.9b－1	3235－0480
《10a－1 规则》	240.10a－1	3235－0475
《10b－10 规则》	240.10b－10	3235－0444
《10b－17 规则》	240.10b－17	3235－0476

Information collection requirement	17 CFR part or section where identified and described	Current OMB control No.
Rule 10b – 18	240. 10b – 18	3235 – 0474
Rule 10A – 1	240. 10A – 1	3235 – 0468
Rule 11a1 – 1(T)	240. 11a1 – 1(T)	3235 – 0478
Rule 12a – 5	240. 12a – 5	3235 – 0079
Regulation 12B	240. 12b – 1 thru 240. 12b – 36	3235 – 0062
Rule 12d1 – 3	240. 12d1 – 3	3235 – 0109
Rule 12d2 – 1	240. 12d2 – 1	3235 – 0081
Rule 12d2 – 2	240. 12d2 – 2	3235 – 0080
Rule 12f – 1	240. 12f – 1	3235 – 0128
Rule 13a – 16	240. 13a – 16	3235 – 0116
Regulation 13D/G	240. 13d – 1 thru 240. 13d – 7	3235 – 0145
Schedule 13D	240. 13d – 101	3235 – 0145
Schedule 13G	240. 13d – 102	3235 – 0145
Rule 13e – 1	240. 13e – 1	3235 – 0305
Rule 13e – 3	240. 13e – 3	3235 – 0007
Schedule 13E – 3	240. 13e – 100	3235 – 0007
Schedule 13e – 4F	240. 13e – 101	3235 – 0375
Regulation 14A	240. 14a – 1 thru 240. 14a – 12	3235 – 0059
Schedule 14A	240. 14a – 101	3235 – 0059
Regulation 14C	240. 14c – 1	3235 – 0057
Schedule 14C	240. 14c – 101	3235 – 0057
Regulation 14D	240. 14d – 1 thru 240. 14d – 9	3235 – 0102
Schedule TO	240. 14d – 100	3235 – 0515
Schedule 14D – 1	240. 14d – 101	3235 – 0102
Schedule 14D – 9	240. 14d – 101	3235 – 0102
Schedule 14D – 1F	240. 14d – 102	3235 – 0376
Schedule 14D – 9F	240. 14d – 103	3235 – 0382
Regulation 14E	240. 14e – 1 thru 240. 14e – 2	3235 – 0102

续表

信息采集要求	《联邦规章汇编》第十七编中对信息采集要求进行列举和说明的相关章节	当前美国行政管理和预算局控制编号
《10b－18 规则》	240. 10b－18	3235－0474
《10A－1 规则》	240. 10A－1	3235－0468
《11a1－1(T)规则》	240. 11a1－1(T)	3235－0478
《12a－5 规则》	240. 12a－5	3235－0079
《12B 管理办法》	240. 12b－1 至 240. 12b－36	3235－0062
《12d1－3 规则》	240. 12d1－3	3235－0109
《12d2－1 规则》	240. 12d2－1	3235－0081
《12d2－2 规则》	240. 12d2－2	3235－0080
《12f－1 规则》	240. 12f－1	3235－0128
《13a－16 规则》	240. 13a－16	3235－0116
《13D/G 管理办法》	240. 13d－1 至 240. 13d－7	3235－0145
《附表 13D》	240. 13d－101	3235－0145
《附表 13G》	240. 13d－102	3235－0145
《13e－1 规则》	240. 13e－1	3235－0305
《13e－3 规则》	240. 13e－3	3235－0007
《附表 13E－3》	240. 13e－100	3235－0007
《附表 13e－4F》	240. 13e－101	3235－0375
《14A 管理办法》	240. 14a－1 至 240. 14a－12	3235－0059
《附表 14A》	240. 14a－101	3235－0059
《14C 管理办法》	240. 14c－1	3235－0057
《附表 14C》	240. 14c－101	3235－0057
《14D 管理办法》	240. 14d－1 至 240. 14d－9	3235－0102
《附表 TO》	240. 14d－100	3235－0515
《附表 14D－1》	240. 14d－101	3235－0102
《附表 14D－9》	240. 14d－101	3235－0102
《附表 14D－1F》	240. 14d－102	3235－0376
《附表 14D－9F》	240. 14d－103	3235－0382
《14E 管理办法》	240. 14e－1 至 240. 14e－2	3235－0102

Information collection requirement	17 CFR part or section where identified and described	Current OMB control No.
Rule 14f-1	240.14f-1	3235-0108
Rule 15a-4	240.15a-4	3235-0010
Rule 15a-6	240.15a-6	3235-0371
Rule 15b1-1	240.15b1-1	3235-0012
Rule 15b6-1(a)	240.15b6-1(a)	3235-0018
Rule 15c1-5	240.15c1-5	3235-0471
Rule 15c1-6	240.15c1-6	3235-0472
Rule 15c1-7	240.15c1-7	3235-0134
Rule 15c2-1	240.15c2-1	3235-0485
Rule 15c2-5	240.15c2-5	3235-0198
Rule 15c2-7	240.15c2-7	3235-0479
Rule 15c2-8	240.15c2-8	3235-0481
Rule 15c2-11	240.15c2-11	3235-0202
Rule 15c2-12	240.15c2-12	3235-0372
Rule 15c3-1	240.15c3-1	3235-0200
Rule 15c3-1(c)(13)	240.15c3-1(c)(13)	3235-0499
Appendix F to Rule 15c3-1	240.15c3-1f	3235-0496
Rule 15c3-3	240.15c3-3	3235-0078
Rule 15c3-4	240.15c3-4	3235-0497
Rule 15d-16	240.15d-16	3235-0116
Rule 15g-2	240.15g-2	3235-0434
Rule 15g-3	240.15g-3	3235-0392
Rule 15g-4	240.15g-4	3235-0393
Rule 15g-5	240.15g-5	3235-0394
Rule 15g-6	240.15g-6	3235-0395
Rule 15g-9	240.15g-9	3235-0385
Rule 15Aj-1	240.15Aj-1	3235-0044
Rule 15Ba2-1	240.15Ba2-1	3235-0083

续表

信息采集要求	《联邦规章汇编》第十七编中对信息采集要求进行列举和说明的相关章节	当前美国行政管理和预算局控制编号
《14f－1 规则》	240.14f－1	3235－0108
《15a－4 规则》	240.15a－4	3235－0010
《15a－6 规则》	240.15a－6	3235－0371
《15b1－1 规则》	240.15b1－1	3235－0012
《15b6－1(a)规则》	240.15b6－1(a)	3235－0018
《15c1－5 规则》	240.15c1－5	3235－0471
《15c1－6 规则》	240.15c1－6	3235－0472
《15c1－7 规则》	240.15c1－7	3235－0134
《15c2－1 规则》	240.15c2－1	3235－0485
《15c2－5 规则》	240.15c2－5	3235－0198
《15c2－7 规则》	240.15c2－7	3235－0479
《15c2－8 规则》	240.15c2－8	3235－0481
《15c2－11 规则》	240.15c2－11	3235－0202
《15c2－12 规则》	240.15c2－12	3235－0372
《15c3－1 规则》	240.15c3－1	3235－0200
《15c3－1(c)(13)规则》	240.15c3－1(c)(13)	3235－0499
《15c3－1 规则》的附件 F	240.15c3－1f	3235－0496
《15c3－3 规则》	240.15c3－3	3235－0078
《15c3－4 规则》	240.15c3－4	3235－0497
《15d－16 规则》	240.15d－16	3235－0116
《15g－2 规则》	240.15g－2	3235－0434
《15g－3 规则》	240.15g－3	3235－0392
《15g－4 规则》	240.15g－4	3235－0393
《15g－5 规则》	240.15g－5	3235－0394
《15g－6 规则》	240.15g－6	3235－0395
《15g－9 规则》	240.15g－9	3235－0385
《15Aj－1 规则》	240.15Aj－1	3235－0044
《15Ba2－1 规则》	240.15Ba2－1	3235－0083

Information collection requirement	17 CFR part or section where identified and described	Current OMB control No.
Rule 15Ba2 – 5	240. 15Ba2 – 5	3235 – 0088
Rule 15Bc3 – 1	240. 15Bc3 – 1	3235 – 0087
Rule 17a – 1	240. 17a – 1	3235 – 0208
Rule 17a – 2	240. 17a – 2	3235 – 0201
Rule 17a – 3	240. 17a – 3	3235 – 0033
Rule 17a – 3(a)(16)	240. 17a – 3(a)(16)	3235 – 0508
Rule 17a – 4	240. 17a – 4	3235 – 0279
Rule 17a – 4(b)(10)	240. 17a – 4(b)(10)	3235 – 0506
Rule 17a – 5	240. 17a – 5	3235 – 0123
Rule 17a – 5(c)	240. 17a – 5(c)	3235 – 0199
Rule 17a – 6	240. 17a – 6	3235 – 0489
Rule 17a – 7	240. 17a – 7	3235 – 0131
Rule 17a – 8	240. 17a – 8	3235 – 0092
Rule 17a – 9T	240. 17a – 9T	3235 – 0524
Rule 17a – 10	240. 17a – 10	3235 – 0122
Rule 17a – 11	240. 17a – 11	3235 – 0085
Rule 17a – 12	240. 17a – 12	3235 – 0498
Rule 17a – 13	240. 17a – 13	3235 – 0035
Rule 17a – 19	240. 17a – 19	3235 – 0133
Rule 17a – 22	240. 17a – 22	3235 – 0196
Rule 17a – 25	240. 17a – 25	3235 – 0540
Rule 17f – 1(b)	240. 17f – 1(b)	3235 – 0032
Rule 17f – 1(c)	240. 17f – 1(c)	3235 – 0037
Rule 17f – 1(g)	240. 17f – 1(g)	3235 – 0290
Rule 17f – 2(a)	240. 17f – 2(a)	3235 – 0034
Rule 17f – 2(c)	240. 17f – 2(c)	3235 – 0029
Rule 17f – 2(d)	240. 17f – 2(d)	3235 – 0028
Rule 17f – 2(e)	240. 17f – 2(e)	3235 – 0031

续表

信息采集要求	《联邦规章汇编》第十七编中对信息采集要求进行列举和说明的相关章节	当前美国行政管理和预算局控制编号
《15Ba2-5 规则》	240.15Ba2-5	3235-0088
《15Bc3-1 规则》	240.15Bc3-1	3235-0087
《17a-1 规则》	240.17a-1	3235-0208
《17a-2 规则》	240.17a-2	3235-0201
《17a-3 规则》	240.17a-3	3235-0033
《17a-3(a)(16)规则》	240.17a-3(a)(16)	3235-0508
《17a-4 规则》	240.17a-4	3235-0279
《17a-4(b)(10)规则》	240.17a-4(b)(10)	3235-0506
《17a-5 规则》	240.17a-5	3235-0123
《17a-5(c)规则》	240.17a-5(c)	3235-0199
《17a-6 规则》	240.17a-6	3235-0489
《17a-7 规则》	240.17a-7	3235-0131
《17a-8 规则》	240.17a-8	3235-0092
《17a-9T 规则》	240.17a-9T	3235-0524
《17a-10 规则》	240.17a-10	3235-0122
《17a-11 规则》	240.17a-11	3235-0085
《17a-12 规则》	240.17a-12	3235-0498
《17a-13 规则》	240.17a-13	3235-0035
《17a-19 规则》	240.17a-19	3235-0133
《17a-22 规则》	240.17a-22	3235-0196
《17a-25 规则》	240.17a-25	3235-0540
《17f-1(b)规则》	240.17f-1(b)	3235-0032
《17f-1(c)规则》	240.17f-1(c)	3235-0037
《17f-1(g)规则》	240.17f-1(g)	3235-0290
《17f-2(a)规则》	240.17f-2(a)	3235-0034
《17f-2(c)规则》	240.17f-2(c)	3235-0029
《17f-2(d)规则》	240.17f-2(d)	3235-0028
《17f-2(e)规则》	240.17f-2(e)	3235-0031

Information collection requirement	17 CFR part or section where identified and described	Current OMB control No.
Rule 17f – 5	240. 17f – 5	3235 – 0269
Rule 17h – 1T	240. 17h – 1T	3235 – 0410
Rule 17h – 2T	240. 17h – 2T	3235 – 0410
Rule 17Ab2 – 1	240. 17Ab2 – 1(a)	3235 – 0195
Rule 17Ac2 – 1	240. 17Ac2 – 1	3235 – 0084
Rule 17Ad – 2(c), (d), and (h)	240. 17Ad – 2(c), (d) and (h)	3235 – 0130
Rule 17Ad – 3(b)	240. 17Ad – 3(b)	3235 – 0473
Rule 17Ad – 4(b) and (c)	240. 17Ad – 4(b) and (c)	3235 – 0341
Rule 17Ad – 6	240. 17Ad – 6	3235 – 0291
Rule 17Ad – 7	240. 17Ad – 7	3235 – 0291
Rule 17Ad – 10	240. 17Ad – 10	3235 – 0273
Rule 17Ad – 11	240. 17Ad – 11	3235 – 0274
Rule 17Ad – 13	240. 17Ad – 13	3235 – 0275
Rule 17Ad – 15	240. 17Ad – 15	3235 – 0409
Rule 17Ad – 16	240. 17Ad – 16	3235 – 0413
Rule 17Ad – 17	240. 17Ad – 17	3235 – 0469
Rule 19b – 1	240. 19b – 1	3235 – 0354
Rule 19b – 4	240. 19b – 4	3235 – 0045
Rule 19b – 4(e)	240. 19b – 4(e)	3235 – 0504
Rule 19b – 5	240. 19b – 5	3235 – 0507
Rule 19b – 7	240. 19b – 7	3235 – 0553
Rule 19d – 1	240. 19d – 1(b) thru 240. 19d – 1(i)	3235 – 0206
Rule 19d – 2	240. 19d – 2	3235 – 0205
Rule 19d – 3	240. 19d – 3	3235 – 0204
Rule 19h – 1	240. 19h – 1(a),(c)thru(e),and (g)	3235 – 0259
Rule 24b – 1	240. 24b – 1	3235 – 0194
Rule 101	242. 101	3235 – 0464
Rule 102	242. 102	3235 – 0467

续表

信息采集要求	《联邦规章汇编》第十七编中对信息采集要求进行列举和说明的相关章节	当前美国行政管理和预算局控制编号
《17f－5 规则》	240. 17f－5	3235－0269
《17h－1T 规则》	240. 17h－1T	3235－0410
《17h－2T 规则》	240. 17h－2T	3235－0410
《17Ab2－1 规则》	240. 17Ab2－1(a)	3235－0195
《17Ac2－1 规则》	240. 17Ac2－1	3235－0084
《17Ad2－2(c)、(d)和(h)规则》	240. 17Ad－2(c),(d)和(h)	3235－0130
《17Ad－3(b)规则》	240. 17Ad－3(b)	3235－0473
《17Ad－4(b)和(c)规则》	240. 17Ad－4(b)和(c)	3235－0341
《17Ad－6 规则》	240. 17Ad－6	3235－0291
《17Ad－7 规则》	240. 17Ad－7	3235－0291
《17Ad－10 规则》	240. 17Ad－10	3235－0273
《17Ad－11 规则》	240. 17Ad－11	3235－0274
《17Ad－13 规则》	240. 17Ad－13	3235－0275
《17Ad－15 规则》	240. 17Ad－15	3235－0409
《17Ad－16 规则》	240. 17Ad－16	3235－0413
《17Ad－17 规则》	240. 17Ad－17	3235－0469
《19b－1 规则》	240. 19b－1	3235－0354
《19b－4 规则》	240. 19b－4	3235－0045
《19b－4(e)规则》	240. 19b－4(e)	3235－0504
《19b－5 规则》	240. 19b－5	3235－0507
《19b－7 规则》	240. 19b－7	3235－0553
《19d－1 规则》	240. 19d－1(b)至 240. 19d－1(i)	3235－0206
《19d－2 规则》	240. 19d－2	3235－0205
《19d－3 规则》	240. 19d－3	3235－0204
《19h－1 规则》	240. 19h－1(a),(c)至(e)和(g)	3235－0259
《24b－1 规则》	240. 24b－1	3235－0194
《101 规则》	242. 101	3235－0464
《102 规则》	242. 102	3235－0467

Information collection requirement	17 CFR part or section where identified and described	Current OMB control No.
Rule 103	242. 103	3235 – 0466
Rule 104	242. 104	3235 – 0465
Rule 301	242. 301	3235 – 0509
Rule 302	242. 302	3235 – 0510
Rule 303	242. 303	3235 – 0505
Rule 604	242. 604	3235 – 0462
Rule 605	242. 605	3235 – 0542
Rule 606	242. 606	3235 – 0541
Rule 607	242. 607	3235 – 0435
Rule 608	242. 608	3235 – 0500
Rule 609	242. 609	3235 – 0043
Rule 611	242. 611	3235 – 0600
Regulation S – P	Part 248	3235 – 0537
Form 1	249. 1	3235 – 0017
Form 1 – N	249. 10	3235 – 0554
Form 25	249. 25	3235 – 0080
Form 26	249. 26	3235 – 0079
Form 3	249. 103	3235 – 0104
Form 4	249. 104	3235 – 0287
Form 5	249. 105	3235 – 0362
Form 8 – A	249. 208a	3235 – 0056
Form 10	249. 210	3235 – 0064
Form 10 – SB	249. 210b	3235 – 0419
Form 18	249. 218	3235 – 0121
Form 20 – F	249. 220f	3235 – 0288
Form 40 – F	249. 240f	3235 – 0381
Form 6 – K	249. 306	3235 – 0116
Form 8 – K	249. 308	3235 – 0060

续表

信息采集要求	《联邦规章汇编》第十七编中对信息采集要求进行列举和说明的相关章节	当前美国行政管理和预算局控制编号
《103 规则》	242.103	3235－0466
《104 规则》	242.104	3235－0465
《301 规则》	242.301	3235－0509
《302 规则》	242.302	3235－0510
《303 规则》	242.303	3235－0505
《604 规则》	242.604	3235－0462
《605 规则》	242.605	3235－0542
《606 规则》	242.606	3235－0541
《607 规则》	242.607	3235－0435
《608 规则》	242.608	3235－0500
《609 规则》	242.609	3235－0043
《611 规则》	242.611	3235－0600
《S－P 管理办法》	第 248 部分	3235－0537
《1 表格》	249.1	3235－0017
《1－N 表格》	249.10	3235－0554
《25 表格》	249.25	3235－0080
《26 表格》	249.26	3235－0079
《3 表格》	249.103	3235－0104
《4 表格》	249.104	3235－0287
《5 表格》	249.105	3235－0362
《8－A 表格》	249.208a	3235－0056
《10 表格》	249.210	3235－0064
《10－SB 表格》	249.210b	3235－0419
《18 表格》	249.218	3235－0121
《20－F 表格》	249.220f	3235－0288
《40－F 表格》	249.240f	3235－0381
《6－K 表格》	249.306	3235－0116
《8－K 表格》	249.308	3235－0060

Information collection requirement	17 CFR part or section where identified and described	Current OMB control No.
Form 10 – Q	249. 308a	3235 – 0070
Form 10 – QSB	249. 308b	3235 – 0416
Form 10 – K	249. 310	3235 – 0063
Form 10 – KSB	249. 310b	3235 – 0420
Form 11 – K	249. 311	3235 – 0082
Form 18 – K	249. 318	3235 – 0120
Form 12B – 25	249. 322	3235 – 0058
Form 15	249. 323	3235 – 0167
Form 13F	249. 325	3235 – 0006
Form SE	249. 444	3235 – 0327
Form ET	249. 445	3235 – 0329
Form ID	249. 446	3235 – 0328
Form DF	249. 448	3235 – 0482
Form BD	249. 501	3235 – 0012
Form BDW	249. 501a	3235 – 0018
Form BD – N	249. 501b	3235 – 0556
Form X – 17A – 5	249. 617	3235 – 0123
Form X – 17A – 19	249. 635	3235 – 0133
Form ATS	249. 637	3235 – 0509
Form ATS – R	249. 638	3235 – 0509
Form X – 15AJ – 1	249. 802	3235 – 0044
Form X – 15AJ – 2	249. 803	3235 – 0044
Form 19b – 4	249. 819	3235 – 0045
Form 19b – 4(e)	249. 820	3235 – 0504
Form Pilot	249. 821	3235 – 0507
Form SIP	249. 1001	3235 – 0043
Form MSD	249. 1100	3235 – 0083
Form MSDW	249. 1110	3235 – 0087

续表

信息采集要求	《联邦规章汇编》第十七编中对信息采集要求进行列举和说明的相关章节	当前美国行政管理和预算局控制编号
《10 - Q 表格》	249.308a	3235 - 0070
《10 - QSB 表格》	249.308b	3235 - 0416
《10 - K 表格》	249.310	3235 - 0063
《10 - KSB 表格》	249.310b	3235 - 0420
《11 - K 表格》	249.311	3235 - 0082
《18 - K 表格》	249.318	3235 - 0120
《12B - 25 表格》	249.322	3235 - 0058
《15 表格》	249.323	3235 - 0167
《13F 表格》	249.325	3235 - 0006
《SE 表格》	249.444	3235 - 0327
《ET 表格》	249.445	3235 - 0329
《ID 表格》	249.446	3235 - 0328
《DF 表格》	249.448	3235 - 0482
《BD 表格》	249.501	3235 - 0012
《BDW 表格》	249.501a	3235 - 0018
《BD - N 表格》	249.501b	3235 - 0556
《X - 17A - 5 表格》	249.617	3235 - 0123
《X - 17A - 19 表格》	249.635	3235 - 0133
《ATS 表格》	249.637	3235 - 0509
《ATS - R 表格》	249.638	3235 - 0509
《X - 15AJ - 1 表格》	249.802	3235 - 0044
《X - 15AJ - 2 表格》	249.803	3235 - 0044
《19b - 4 表格》	249.819	3235 - 0045
《19b - 4(e)表格》	249.820	3235 - 0504
《试点表格》	249.821	3235 - 0507
《SIP 表格》	249.1001	3235 - 0043
《MSD 表格》	249.1100	3235 - 0083
《MSDW 表格》	249.1110	3235 - 0087

Information collection requirement	17 CFR part or section where identified and described	Current OMB control No.
Form X - 17F - 1A	249. 1200	3235 - 0037
Form TA - 1	249b. 100	3235 - 0084
Form TA - W	249b. 101	3235 - 0151
Form TA - 2	249b. 102	3235 - 0337
Form CA - 1	249b. 200	3235 - 0195
Rule 1(a)	250. 1(a)	3235 - 0170
Rule 1(b)	250. 1(b)	3235 - 0170
Rule 1(c)	250. 1(c)	3235 - 0164
Rule 2	250. 2	3235 - 0161
Rule 3	250. 3	3235 - 0160
Rule 7	250. 7	3235 - 0165
Rule 7(d)	250. 7(d)	3235 - 0165
Rule 20(b)	250. 20(b)	3235 - 0125
Rule 20(c)	250. 20(c)	3235 - 0125
Rule 20(d)	250. 20(d)	3235 - 0163
Rule 23	250. 23	3235 - 0125
Rule 24	250. 24	3235 - 0126
Rule 26	250. 26	3235 - 0183
Rule 29	250. 29	3235 - 0149
Rule 44	250. 44	3235 - 0147
Rule 45	250. 45	3235 - 0154
Rule 47(b)	250. 47(b)	3235 - 0163
Rule 52	250. 52	3235 - 0369
Form 53	250. 53	3235 - 0426
Rule 54	250. 54	3235 - 0427
Rule 57(a)	250. 57(a)	3235 - 0428
Rule 57(b)	250. 57(b)	3235 - 0429
Rule 58	250. 58	3235 - 0457

续表

信息采集要求	《联邦规章汇编》第十七编中对信息采集要求进行列举和说明的相关章节	当前美国行政管理和预算局控制编号
《X－17F－1A 表格》	249.1200	3235－0037
《TA－1 表格》	249b.100	3235－0084
《TA－W 表格》	249b.101	3235－0151
《TA－2 表格》	249b.102	3235－0337
《CA－1 表格》	249b.200	3235－0195
《1(a)规则》	250.1(a)	3235－0170
《1(b)规则》	250.1(b)	3235－0170
《1(c)规则》	250.1(c)	3235－0164
《2 规则》	250.2	3235－0161
《3 规则》	250.3	3235－0160
《7 规则》	250.7	3235－0165
《7(d)规则》	250.7(d)	3235－0165
《20(b)规则》	250.20(b)	3235－0125
《20(c)规则》	250.20(c)	3235－0125
《20(d)规则》	250.20(d)	3235－0163
《23 规则》	250.23	3235－0125
《24 规则》	250.24	3235－0126
《26 规则》	250.26	3235－0183
《29 规则》	250.29	3235－0149
《44 规则》	250.44	3235－0147
《45 规则》	250.45	3235－0154
《47(b)规则》	250.47(b)	3235－0163
《52 规则》	250.52	3235－0369
《53 表格》	250.53	3235－0426
《54 规则》	250.54	3235－0427
《57(a)规则》	250.57(a)	3235－0428
《57(b)规则》	250.57(b)	3235－0429
《58 规则》	250.58	3235－0457

Information collection requirement	17 CFR part or section where identified and described	Current OMB control No.
Rule 62	250. 62	3235 – 0152
Rule 71(a)	250. 71(a)	3235 – 0173
Rule 72	250. 72	3235 – 0149
Rule 83	250. 83	3235 – 0181
Rule 87	250. 87	3235 – 0552
Rule 88	250. 88	3235 – 0182
Rule 93	250. 93	3235 – 0153
Rule 94	250. 94	3235 – 0153
Rule 95	250. 95	3235 – 0162
Rule 100(a)	250. 100(a)	3235 – 0125
Uniform System of Accounts for Mutual Service Companies and Subsidiary Service Companies, Public Utility Holding Company Act of 1935	Part 256	3235 – 0153
Preservation and Destruction of Records of Registered Public Utility Holding Companies and of Mutual and Subsidiary Service Companies	Part 257	3235 – 0306
Form U5A	259. 5a	3235 – 0170
Form U5B	259. 5b	3235 – 0170
Form U5S	259. 5s	3235 – 0164
Form U – 1	259. 101	3235 – 0125
Form U – 13 – 1	259. 113	3235 – 0182
Form U – 6B – 2	259. 206	3235 – 0163
Form U – 57	259. 207	3235 – 0428
Form U – 9C – 3	259. 208	3235 – 0457
Form U – 12(I) – A	259. 212a	3235 – 0173
Form U – 12(I) – B	259. 212b	3235 – 0173
Form U – 13E – 1	259. 213	3235 – 0162
Form U – R – 1	259. 221	3235 – 0152
Form U – 13 – 60	259. 313	3235 – 0153

续表

信息采集要求	《联邦规章汇编》第十七编中对信息采集要求进行列举和说明的相关章节	当前美国行政管理和预算局控制编号
《62 规则》	250.62	3235-0152
《71(a)规则》	250.71(a)	3235-0173
《72 规则》	250.72	3235-0149
《83 规则》	250.83	3235-0181
《87 规则》	250.87	3235-0552
《88 规则》	250.88	3235-0182
《93 规则》	250.93	3235-0153
《94 规则》	250.94	3235-0153
《95 规则》	250.95	3235-0162
《100(a)规则》	250.100(a)	3235-0125
互助服务公司和从事服务业的子公司统一账户系统,《1935 年公用事业控股公司法》	第 256 部分	3235-0153
注册公用事业控股公司的记录和互助服务公司与从事服务业的子公司的记录的保留与销毁	第 257 部分	3235-0306
《U5A 表格》	259.5a	3235-0170
《U5B 表格》	259.5b	3235-0170
《U5S 表格》	259.5s	3235-0164
《U-1 表格》	259.101	3235-0125
《U-13-1 表格》	259.113	3235-0182
《U-6B-2 表格》	259.206	3235-0163
《U-57 表格》	259.207	3235-0428
《U-9C-3 表格》	259.208	3235-0457
《U-12I-A 表格》	259.212a	3235-0173
《U-12I-B 表格》	259.212b	3235-0173
《U-13E-1 表格》	259.213	3235-0162
《U-R-1 表格》	259.221	3235-0152
《U-13-60 表格》	259.313	3235-0153

Information collection requirement	17 CFR part or section where identified and described	Current OMB control No.
Form U-3A-2	259.402	3235-0161
Form U-3A3-1	259.403	3235-0160
Form U-7D	259.404	3235-0165
Form U-33-S	259.405	3235-0429
Form ET	259.601	3235-0329
Form ID	259.602	3235-0328
Form SE	259.603	3235-0327
Rule 7a-15 thru 7a-37	260.7a-15 thru 260.7a-37	3235-0132
Form T-1	269.1	3235-0110
Form T-2	269.2	3235-0111
Form T-3	269.3	3235-0105
Form T-4	269.4	3235-0107
Form ET	269.6	3235-0329
Form ID	269.7	3235-0328
Form SE	269.8	3235-0327
Form T-6	269.9	3235-0391
Rule 0-1	270.0-1	3235-0531
Rule 2a-7	270.2a-7	3235-0268
Rule 2a19-1	270.2a19-1	3235-0332
Rule 3a-4	270.3a-4	3235-0459
Rule 6c-7	270.6c-7	3235-0276
Rule 6e-2	270.6e-2	3235-0177
Rule 7d-1	270.7d-1	3235-0311
Rule 7d-2	270.7d-2	3235-0527
Section 8(b) of the Investment Company Act of 1940	270.8b-1 thru 270.8b-32	3235-0176
Rule 10f-3	270.10f-3	3235-0226
Rule 11a-2	270.11a-2	3235-0272
Rule 11a-3	270.11a-3	3235-0358
Rule 12b-1	270.12b-1	3235-0212
Rule 17a-7	270.17a-7	3235-0214
Rule 17a-8	270.17a-8	3235-0235
Rule 17e-1	270.17e-1	3235-0217
Rule 17f-1	270.17f-1	3235-0222

续表

信息采集要求	《联邦规章汇编》第十七编中对信息采集要求进行列举和说明的相关章节	当前美国行政管理和预算局控制编号
《U－3A－2 表格》	259.402	3235－0161
《U－3A3－1 表格》	259.403	3235－0160
《U－7D 表格》	259.404	3235－0165
《U－33－S 表格》	259.405	3235－0429
《ET 表格》	259.601	3235－0329
《ID 表格》	259.602	3235－0328
《SE 表格》	259.603	3235－0327
《7a－15 规则》至《7a－37 规则》	260.7a－15 至 260.7a－37	3235－0132
《T－1 表格》	269.1	3235－0110
《T－2 表格》	269.2	3235－0111
《T－3 表格》	269.3	3235－0105
《T－4 表格》	269.4	3235－0107
《ET 表格》	269.6	3235－0329
《ID 表格》	269.7	3235－0328
《SE 表格》	269.8	3235－0327
《T－6 表格》	269.9	3235－0391
《0－1 规则》	270.0－1	3235－0531
《2a－7 规则》	270.2a－7	3235－0268
《2a19－1 规则》	270.2a19－1	3235－0332
《3a－4 规则》	270.3a－4	3235－0459
《6c－7 规则》	270.6c－7	3235－0276
《6e－2 规则》	270.6e－2	3235－0177
《7d－1 规则》	270.7d－1	3235－0311
《7d－2 规则》	270.7d－2	3235－0527
《1940 年投资公司法》第 8(b)条	270.8b－1 至 270.8b－32	3235－0176
《10f－3 规则》	270.10f－3	3235－0226
《11a－2 规则》	270.11a－2	3235－0272
《11a－3 规则》	270.11a－3	3235－0358
《12b－1 规则》	270.12b－1	3235－0212
《17a－7 规则》	270.17a－7	3235－0214
《17a－8 规则》	270.17a－8	3235－0235
《17e－1 规则》	270.17e－1	3235－0217
《17f－1 规则》	270.17f－1	3235－0222

Information collection requirement	17 CFR part or section where identified and described	Current OMB control No.
Rule 17f-2	270.17f-2	3235-0223
Rule 17f-4	270.17f-4	3235-0225
Rule 17f-6	270.17f-6	3235-0447
Rule 17f-7	270.17f-7	3235-0529
Rule 17g-1(g)	270.17g-1(g)	3235-0213
Rule 17j-1	270.17j-1	3235-0224
Rule 18f-1	270.18f-1	3235-0211
Rule 18f-3	270.18f-3	3235-0441
Rule 19a-1	270.19a-1	3235-0216
Rule 20a-1	270.20a-1	3235-0158
Rule 22d-1	270.22d-1	3235-0310
Rule 23c-1	270.23c-1	3235-0260
Rule 23c-3	270.23c-3	3235-0422
Rule 27e-1	270.27e-1	3235-0545
Rule 30b2-1	270.30b2-1	3235-0220
Rule 30d-2	270.30d-2	3235-0494
Rule 30e-1	270.30e-1	3235-0025
Rule 31a-1	270.31a-1	3235-0178
Rule 31a-2	270.31a-2	3235-0179
Rule 32a-4	270.32a-4	3235-0530
Rule 34b-1	270.34b-1	3235-0346
Rule 35d-1	270.35d-1	3235-0548
Form N-5	274.5	3235-0169
Form N-8A	274.10	3235-0175
Form N-2	274.11a-1	3235-0026
Form N-3	274.11b	3235-0316
Form N-4	274.11c	3235-0318
Form N-8B-2	274.12	3235-0186
Form N-6F	274.15	3235-0238
Form 24F-2	274.24	3235-0456
Form N-18F-1	274.51	3235-0211
Form N-54A	274.53	3235-0237
Form N-54C	274.54	3235-0236
Form N-SAR	274.101	3235-0330

续表

信息采集要求	《联邦规章汇编》第十七编中对信息采集要求进行列举和说明的相关章节	当前美国行政管理和预算局控制编号
《7f-2 规则》	270.17f-2	3235-0223
《17f-4 规则》	270.17f-4	3235-0225
《17f-6 规则》	270.17f-6	3235-0447
《17f-7 规则》	270.17f-7	3235-0529
《17g-1(g)规则》	270.17g-1(g)	3235-0213
《7j-1 规则》	270.17j-1	3235-0224
《18f-1 规则》	270.18f-1	3235-0211
《18f-3 规则》	270.18f-3	3235-0441
《19a-1 规则》	270.19a-1	3235-0216
《20a-1 规则》	270.20a-1	3235-0158
《22d-1 规则》	270.22d-1	3235-0310
《23c-1 规则》	270.23c-1	3235-0260
《23c-3 规则》	270.23c-3	3235-0422
《27e-1 规则》	270.27e-1	3235-0545
《30b2-1 规则》	270.30b2-1	3235-0220
《30d-2 规则》	270.30d-2	3235-0494
《30e-1 规则》	270.30e-1	3235-0025
《31a-1 规则》	270.31a-1	3235-0178
《31a-2 规则》	270.31a-2	3235-0179
《32a-4 规则》	270.32a-4	3235-0530
《34b-1 规则》	270.34b-1	3235-0346
《35d-1 规则》	270.35d-1	3235-0548
《N-5 表格》	274.5	3235-0169
《N-8A 表格》	274.10	3235-0175
《N-2 表格》	274.11a-1	3235-0026
《N-3 表格》	274.11b	3235-0316
《N-4 表格》	274.11c	3235-0318
《N-8B-2 表格》	274.12	3235-0186
《N-6F 表格》	274.15	3235-0238
《24F-2 表格》	274.24	3235-0456
《N-18F-1 表格》	274.51	3235-0211
《N-54A 表格》	274.53	3235-0237
《N-54C 表格》	274.54	3235-0236
《N-SAR 表格》	274.101	3235-0330

Information collection requirement	17 CFR part or section where identified and described	Current OMB control No.
Form N – 27E – 1	274. 127e – 1	3235 – 0545
Form N – 27F – 1	274. 127f – 1	3235 – 0546
Form N – 17D – 1	274. 200	3235 – 0229
Form N – 23C – 1	274. 201	3235 – 0230
Form N – 8F	274. 218	3235 – 0157
Form N – 17F – 1	274. 219	3235 – 0359
Form N – 17F – 2	274. 220	3235 – 0360
Form N – 23c – 3	274. 221	3235 – 0422
Form ET	274. 401	3235 – 0329
Form ID	274. 402	3235 – 0328
Form SE	274. 403	3235 – 0327
Rule 0 – 2	275. 0 – 2	3235 – 0240
Rule 203 – 3	275. 203 – 3	3235 – 0538
Rule 204 – 2	275. 204 – 2	3235 – 0278
Rule 204 – 3	275. 204 – 3	3235 – 0047
Rule 206(3) – 2	275. 206(3) – 2	3235 – 0243
Rule 206(4) – 2	275. 206(4) – 2	3235 – 0241
Rule 206(4) – 3	275. 206(4) – 3	3235 – 0242
Rule 206(4) – 4	275. 206(4) – 4	3235 – 0345
Form ADV	279. 1	3235 – 0049
Schedule I to Form ADV	279. 1	3235 – 0490
Form ADV – W	279. 2	3235 – 0313
Form ADV – H	379. 3	3235 – 0538
Form 4 – R	279. 4	3235 – 0240
Form 5 – R	279. 5	3235 – 0240
Form 6 – R	279. 6	3235 – 0240
Form 7 – R	279. 7	3235 – 0240
Form ADV – E	279. 8	3235 – 0361

[67 FR 14634, Mar. 27, 2002, as amended at 70 FR 37611, June 29, 2005]

续表

信息采集要求	《联邦规章汇编》第十七编中对信息采集要求进行列举和说明的相关章节	当前美国行政管理和预算局控制编号
《N－27E－1 表格》	274.127e－1	3235－0545
《N－27F－1 表格》	274.127f－1	3235－0546
《N－17D－1 表格》	274.200	3235－0229
《N－23C－1 表格》	274.201	3235－0230
《N－8F 表格》	274.218	3235－0157
《N－17F－1 表格》	274.219	3235－0359
《N－17F－2 表格》	274.220	3235－0360
《N－23c－3 表格》	274.221	3235－0422
《ET 表格》	274.401	3235－0329
《ID 表格》	274.402	3235－0328
《SE 表格》	274.403	3235－0327
《0－2 规则》	275.0－2	3235－0240
《203－3 规则》	275.203－3	3235－0538
《204－2 规则》	275.204－2	3235－0278
《204－3 规则》	275.204－3	3235－0047
《206(3)－2 规则》	275.206(3)－2	3235－0243
《206(4)－2 规则》	275.206(4)－2	3235－0241
《206(4)－3 规则》	275.206(4)－3	3235－0242
《206(4)－4 规则》	275.206(4)－4	3235－0345
《ADV 表格》	279.1	3235－0049
《ADV 表格》附表 I	279.1	3235－0490
《ADV－W 表格》	279.2	3235－0313
《ADV－H 表格》	379.3	3235－0538
《4－R 表格》	279.4	3235－0240
《5－R 表格》	279.5	3235－0240
《6－R 表格》	279.6	3235－0240
《7－R 表格》	279.7	3235－0240
《ADV－E 表格》	279.8	3235－0361

[《联邦公报》第 67 卷第 14634 页,2002 年 3 月 27 日,修正索引:《联邦公报》第 70 卷第 37611 页,2005 年 6 月 29 日。]

PART 201—RULES OF PRACTICE

Authority: 15 U.S.C. 77s, 77sss, 78w, 78x, 80a-37, and 80b-11; 5 U.S.C. 504(c)(1).

Sections 201.700 to 201.702 are also issued under sec. 916, Pub. L. 111-203, 124 Stat. 1376.

Source: 47 FR 610, Jan. 6, 1982, unless otherwise noted.

Subpart A—[Reserved]

Subpart B—Regulations Pertaining to the Equal Access to Justice Act

§201.31 Purpose of these rules.

The Equal Access to Justice Act, 5 U.S.C. 504 (called *the Act* in this subpart B), provides for the award of attorney fees and other expenses to eligible individuals and entities who are parties to certain administrative proceedings (called *adversary adjudications*)before the Commission. An eligible party may receive an award when it prevails over the Commission, unless the Commission's position was substantially justified or special circumstances make an award unjust. The rules in this subpart describe the parties eligible for awards and the proceedings that are covered. They also explain how to apply for awards, and the procedures and standards that the Commission will use in ruling on those applications.

[54 FR 53051, Dec. 27, 1989]

§201.32 When the Act applies.

The Act applies to adversary adjudications described in §201.33 pending or commenced before the Commission on or after August 5, 1985. It also applies to any

第201部分——工 作 规 则

法律依据:《美国法典》第十五编第77s节、第77sss节、第78w节、第78x节、第80a-37节和第80b-11节;《美国法典》第五编第504(c)(1)节。

第201.700~201.702节同时见:第111~203号公法,《美国制定法汇编》第124卷第1376页,第916条。

法律渊源:《联邦公报》第47卷第610页,1982年1月6日,除非另有说明。

第A子部分——[保 留]

第B子部分——与《司法公平法》相关的规章

第201.31节 目的

《司法公平法》(《美国法典》第五编第504节)(第B子部分中下称该法)规定,作为证券交易委员会特定行政处理程序("对抗式裁决程序")的当事人的个人及实体,如符合相关资格条件,可以获判律师费和其他费用。如果合格当事人胜诉、证券交易委员会败诉,该等当事人可以获判上述费用,但证券交易委员会的立场具有实质正当性,或基于具体情形判给上述费用将造成不公的除外。本子部分规则说明了有资格获判上述费用的当事人及适用该等规则的程序,同时说明了申请费用判决的程序以及证券交易委员会在就该等申请作出裁定时适用的程序和标准。

[《联邦公报》第54卷第53051页,1989年12月27日。]

第201.32节 该法适用的时间效力

该法适用于第201.33节所述在1985年8月5日及其后启动的或在上述日期尚未审结的对抗式裁决程序,以及在1984年10月1日及其后启动并在1985年8月5日之前获得

adversary adjudication commenced on or after October 1, 1984, and finally disposed of before August 5, 1985, provided that an application for fees and expenses, as described in these rules, has been filed with the Commission within 30 days after August 5, 1985. Proceedings which have been substantially concluded are not deemed pending under these rules although officially pending for purposes such as concluding remedial actions found in Commission orders or private undertakings.

[54 FR 53051, Dec. 27, 1989]

§201.33 Proceedings covered.

(a) The Act applies to adversary adjudications conducted by the Commission. These are on the record adjudications under 5 U.S.C. 554 in which the position of an Office or Division of the Commission as a party, not including*amicus* participation, is presented by an attorney or other representative who enters an appearance and participates in the proceeding. *See* appendix, 17 CFR 201.60.

(b) The fact that the Commission has not identified a type of proceeding as an adversary adjudication shall not preclude the filing of an application by a party who believes the proceeding is covered by the Act; whether the proceeding is covered will then be an issue for resolution in proceedings on the application.

(c)If a proceeding includes both matters covered by the Act and matters specifically excluded from coverage, any award made will include only fees and expenses related to covered issues.

[47 FR 610, Jan. 6, 1982, as amended at 54 FR 53051, Dec. 27, 1989]

§201.34 Eligibility of applicants.

(a) To be eligible for an award of attorney fees and other expenses under the Act, the applicant must be a party to the adversary adjudication for which it seeks it seeks an award. The term*party* is defined in 5 U.S.C. 551(3). The applicant must show that it meets all conditions of eligibility set out in this subpart.

(b) The types of eligible applicants are as follows:

(1) An individual with a net worth of not more than $2 million;

(2) The sole owner of an unincorporated business who has a net worth of not more than $7 million, including both personal and business interests, and not more than 500 employees;

(3) A charitable or other tax-exempt organization described in section 501(c)(3)of the Internal Revenue Code (26 U.S.C. 501(c)(3))with not more than 500 employees;

(4) A cooperative association as defined in section 15(a)of the Agricultural Marketing Act (12 U.S.C. 1141j(a)) with more than 500 employees; and

(5) Any other partnership, corporation, association, unit of local government, or public or private organization with a new worth of not more than $7 million and not more

最终处理的对抗式裁决程序。在后一种情况下,本规则所述律师费和费用申请已在1985年8月5日之后30日内向证券交易委员会提出。就本规则而言,已经实质审结的程序不视为尚未审结的程序,即使严格而言,证券交易委员会发布的命令或当事人达成的私下承诺中仍未作出终局救济。

[《联邦公报》第54卷第53051页,1989年12月27日。]

第201.33节　受该法规制的程序

(a)该法适用于证券交易委员会开展的对抗式裁决程序。该等程序属于《美国法典》第五编第554节规定的应记录在案的裁决程序,且证券交易委员会的一个办公室或部门作为当事人(不包括作为法庭之友参与的情况),通过律师或其他代理出席并参与程序。参见附件:《联邦规章汇编》第十七编第201.60节。

(b)证券交易委员会未将某一类型的程序指明为对抗式裁决程序,但当事人相信该程序应受该法规制的,不影响当事人就此提出申请;该程序是否应受该法规制的问题应在就该申请启动的相关程序中作出决定。

(c)如果某一程序同时涉及受该法规制的事项以及被明确排除在该法规制范围之外的事项,费用判决仅应涉及与受规制事项相关的律师费和费用。

[《联邦公报》第47卷第610页,1982年1月6日,修正索引:《联邦公报》第54卷第53051页,1989年12月27日。]

第201.34节　申请人资格

(a)如欲根据该法申请判决律师费和其他费用,申请人必须属于引发该等费用的对抗式裁决程序的当事人。"当事人"一词的定义以《美国法典》第五编第551(3)节为准。申请人必须证明其满足本子部分所载的全部资格条件。

(b)合格申请人包括如下类型:

(1)净值不超过200万美元的个人;

(2)净值(包括个人和企业权益)不超过700万美元且雇员不超过500人的非法人企业的个体独资所有人;

(3)《国内税收法典》第501(c)(3)条[《美国法典》第二十六编第501(c)(3)节]所述的雇员不超过500人的慈善组织或其他免税组织;

(4)《农业营销法》第15(a)条[《美国法典》第十二编第1141j(a)节]定义的雇员不超过500人的合作协会;以及

(5)任何其他净值不超过700万美元且雇员不超过500人的合伙、公司、协会、地方政府单位或公共/私人组织。

than 500 employees.

(c) For the purpose of eligibility, the net worth and number of employees of an applicant shall be determined as of the date the proceeding was initiated.

(d) An applicant who owns an unincorporated business will be considered as an*individual* rather than a *sole owner of an unincorporated business* if the issues on which the applicant prevails are related primarily to personal interests rather than to business interests.

(e) The employees of an applicant include all persons who regularly perform services for remuneration for the applicant, under the applicant's direction and control. Part–time employees shall be included on a proportional basis.

(f) The net worth and number of employees of the applicant and all of its affiliates shall be aggregated to determine eligibility. Any individual, corporation or other entity that directly or indirectly controls or owns a majority of the voting shares or other interest of the applicant, or any corporation or entity of which the applicant directly or indirectly owns or controls a majority of the voting shares or other interest, will be considered an affiliate for purposes of this subpart, unless the administrative law judge determines that such treatment would be unjust and contrary to the purposes of the Act in light of the actual relationship between the affiliated entities. In addition, the administrative law judge may determine that financial relationships of the applicant other than those described in this paragraph constitute special circumstances that would make an award unjust.

(g) An applicant that participates in a proceeding primarily on behalf of one or more other persons or entities that would be ineligible is not itself eligible for an award.

[47 FR 610, Jan. 6, 1982, as amended at 54 FR 53051, Dec. 27, 1989]

§201.35 Standards for awards.

(a) A prevailing applicant may receive an award for fees and expenses incurred in connection with a proceeding or in a significant and discrete substantive portion of the proceeding, unless the position of the Office or Division over which the applicant has prevailed was substantially justified. The position of the Office or Division includes, in addition to the position taken by the Office or Division in the adversary adjudication, the action or failure to act by the Office or Division upon which the adversary adjudication is based. The burden of proof that an award should not be made to an eligible prevailing applicant is on counsel for an Office or Division of the Commission, which must show that its position was reasonable in law and fact.

(b) An award will be reduced or denied if the applicant has unduly or unreasonably protracted the proceeding or if special circumstances make the award sought unjust.

[47 FR 610, Jan. 6, 1982, as amended at 54 FR 53051, Dec. 27, 1989]

(c)在判断申请人是否符合资格时,相关净值和雇员数应以程序启动之日的数字为准。

(d)申请人尽管拥有非法人企业,但其胜诉的事项主要与其个人利益而非企业利益相关的,应视为"个人"而非"非法人企业的个体独资所有人"。

(e)申请人的雇员包括接受申请人指示和控制,为取得报酬而常规性地为申请人提供服务的所有人员。兼职雇员应基于工作时间按比例计入雇员人数。

(f)在判断申请人是否符合资格时,申请人及其关联方的净值和雇员数量应予以加总。就本子部分而言,直接或间接控制、拥有申请人多数表决权股份或其他权益的任何个人、公司或其他实体,以及其多数表决权股份或其他权益被申请人直接或间接控制或拥有的任何个人、公司或其他实体,均应视为关联方,但行政法官基于关联方之间的实际关系判定上述处理将造成不公并与该法之宗旨相冲突的除外。此外,行政法官可以判定本款所述之外的申请人的财务关系构成将导致判给费用不公的特殊情形。

(g)如果申请人主要作为一个或多个不合格人士或实体的代表参与对抗式裁决程序,其本身亦无资格申请判决律师费和其他费用。

[《联邦公报》第47卷第610页,1982年1月6日,修正索引:《联邦公报》第54卷第53051页,1989年12月27日。]

第201.35节 费用判给标准

(a)胜诉申请人可以获判全部程序或程序的核心、独立的实质部分所产生的律师费和费用,但败诉的证券交易委员会办公室或部门的立场具有实质正当性的除外。证券交易委员会办公室或部门的立场,除证券交易委员会办公室或部门在对抗式裁决程序中的立场外,还包括引发该等对抗式裁决程序的证券交易委员会办公室或部门的作为或不作为。证明不应向合格胜诉申请人判给费用的举证责任由证券交易委员会办公室或部门的律师承担,该律师必须证明证券交易委员会办公室或部门的立场具有法律和事实上的合理性。

(b)如果申请人不正当或不合理地拖延程序,或存在特殊情形使满足其费用申请将造成不公,费用判给应予以降低或驳回。

[《联邦公报》第47卷第610页,1982年1月6日,修正索引:《联邦公报》第54卷第53051页,1989年12月27日。]

§201.36 Allowable fees and expenses.

(a) Subject to the limitation of paragraph(b), awards will be based on rates customarily charged, in the locale of the hearing, by persons engaged in the business of acting as attorneys, agents and expert witnesses, even if the services were made available without charge or at a reduced rate to the applicant.

(b) No award of the fee of an attorney or agent under these rules may exceed $75.00 per hour. No award to compensate an expert witness may exceed the reasonable rate at which the Commission pays witnesses with similar expertise. However, an award may also include the reasonable expenses of the attorney, agent or witness as a separate item, if the attorney, agent or witness ordinarily charges clients separately for such expenses.

(c) In determining the reasonableness of the fee sought for an attorney, agent or expert witness, the administrative law judge shall consider the following:

(1) If the attorney, agent or witness is in private practice, his or her customary fee for similar services, or, if an employee of the applicant the fully allocated cost of the services;

(2) The prevailing rate for similar services in the community in which the attorney, agent or witness ordinarily performs services;

(3) The time actually spent in the representation of the applicant;

(4) The time reasonably spent in light of the difficulty or complexity of the issues in the proceeding; and

(5) Such other factors as may bear on the value of the services provided.

(d) The reasonable cost of any study, analysis, engineering report, test, project or similar matter prepared on behalf of a party may be awarded, to the extent that the charge for the service does not exceed the prevailing rate for similar services, and the study or other matter was necessary for preparation of the applicant's case.

[47 FR 610, Jan. 6, 1982, as amended at 54 FR 53051, Dec. 27, 1989]

§201.37 Delegations of authority.

(a) The Commission may by order delegate authority to take final action on matters pertaining to the Equal Access to Justice Act in particular cases.

(b) Unless the Commission shall order otherwise, applications for awards of fees and expenses made pursuant to this subject shall be assigned by the Chief Administrative Law Judge to an administrative law judge for determination.

[54 FR 53051, Dec. 27, 1989]

§201.41 Contents of application.

(a) An application for an award of fees and expenses under the Act shall identify the applicant, the proceeding for which an award is sought and contain the information required in this subpart. The application shall show that the applicant has prevailed and specify the position(s) of the opposing Office or Division in the proceeding that the applicant

第201.36节　可以判给的律师费和费用

(a)在不违反第(b)款限制的前提下,即使申请人可以免费或以优惠价格获得相关服务,费用判决仍应按听证所在地从事律师、代理和专家证人业务的主体通常收取的费率确定。

(b)根据本规则判决的律师费或代理费不得超过75美元每小时。判决的专家证人报酬不得超过证券交易委员会向类似专家证人支付的合理费率。但是,判决也可包括律师、代理或证人单项收取的合理费用,前提是该等费用通常都由律师、代理或证人单项收取。

(c)在判断申请人申请判决的律师、代理或专家证人费是否合理之时,行政法官应考虑如下因素:

(1)律师、代理或证人是否私人执业;律师、代理或证人为类似服务通常收取的费用,或该等服务的完全分摊成本(如律师、代理或证人属于申请人的雇员);

(2)相关业界就类似服务收取的现行费率;

(3)为申请人提供代理实际花费的时间;

(4)考虑到诉讼问题的疑难性或复杂性而确定的合理花费时间;及

(5)可能影响所提供服务的价值的其他因素。

(d)代表当事人开展或制作的研究、分析、工程报告、测试、项目或类似事项的合理成本可以判给,但以该等服务收费不超过类似服务的现行费率且该等服务应以准备申请人的案件所必要为限。

[《联邦公报》第47卷第610页,1982年1月6日,修正索引:《联邦公报》第54卷第53051页,1989年12月27日。]

第201.37节　委托授权

(a)证券交易委员会可以发布命令,转授在具体案件中就与《司法公平法》相关的事项采取最终行动的权限。

(b)除非证券交易委员会另行发布命令,否则根据本子部分提出的律师费和其他费用判决申请应由首席行政法官指派给一名行政法官作出决定。

[《联邦公报》第54卷第53051页,1989年12月27日。]

第201.41节　申请内容

(a)根据该法申请判给律师费和费用的,应在申请中注明申请人、产生该等费用的行政裁决程序,并载明本子部分中要求提供的信息。申请人应在申请中证明其已经胜诉,并说明作为相对方的证券交易委员会办公室或部门的立场,且申请人认为该等立场不存在实质正当性。除非申请人为个人,否则申请中还应说明申请人雇员的数目并

alleges was not substantially justified. Unless the applicant is an individual, the application shall also state the number of employees of the applicant and describe briefly the type and purpose of its organization or business.

(b) The application shall also include a statement that the applicant's net worth does not exceed $2 million (if an individual)or $7 million (for all other applicants, including their affiliates). However, an applicant may omit this statement if:

(1) It attaches a copy of a ruling by the Internal Revenue Service that it qualifies as an organization described in section 501(c)(3) of the Internal Revenue Code (26 U.S.C. 501(c)(3)) or, in the case of a tax-exempt organization not required to obtain a ruling from the Internal Revenue Service on its exempt status, a statement that describes the basis for the applicant's belief that it qualifies under such section; or

(2) It states that it is a cooperative association as defined in section 15(a) of the Agricultural Marketing Act (12 U.S.C. 1141j(a)).

(c) The application shall state the amount of fees and expenses for which an award is sought.

(d) The application may also include any other matters that the applicant wishes the Commission to consider in determining whether and in what amount an award should be made.

(e) The application shall be signed by the applicant or an authorized officer or attorney of the applicant. It shall also contain or be accompanied by a written verification under oath or under penalty of perjury that the information provided in the application is true and correct.

[47 FR 610, Jan. 6, 1982, as amended at 54 FR 53051, Dec. 27, 1989]

§201.42 Net worth exhibit.

(a) Each applicant, except a qualified tax- exempt organization or cooperative association, must provide with its application a detailed exhibit showing the net worth of the applicant and any affiliates (as defined in §201.34(f) of this part) when the proceeding was initiated. The exhibit may be in any form convenient to the applicant that provides full disclosure of the applicant's and its affiliates' assets and liabilities and is sufficient to determine whether the applicant qualifies under the standards in this subpart. The administrative law judge or the Commission may require an applicant to file additional information to determine its eligibility for an award.

(b) Ordinarily, the net worth exhibit will be included in the public record of the proceeding. However, an applicant that objects to public disclosure of information in any portion of the exhibit and believes there are legal grounds for withholding it from disclosure may submit that exhibit in accordance with 17 CFR 201.190.

[47 FR 610, Jan. 6, 1982, as amended at 60 FR 32795, June 23, 1995]

简要说明其组织或业务的类型和宗旨。

(b)个人申请人应在申请中声明其净值不超过200万美元;其他申请人应声明其净值不超过700万美元(计算净值时应包括其关联方)。但是,如满足下列条件,申请人可免予作出上述声明:

(1)申请人已附上一份美国国家税务局作出的认定其属于《国内税收法典》第501(c)(3)条[《美国法典》第二十六编第501(c)(3)节]规定的组织的裁定;或如申请人系不需获得美国国家税务局就其豁免状态作出裁定的免税组织,申请人应附上一份说明书,说明其认为其符合上述条款规定的依据;或

(2)申请人声明其为《农业营销法》第15(a)条[《美国法典》第十二编第1141j(a)节]定义的合作协会。

(c)申请中应说明申请判给的律师费和费用。

(d)申请中还可包括申请人希望证券交易委员会在决定是否判给以及决定判给额度时应考虑的任何其他事项。

(e)申请应由申请人或申请人的获得授权的管理人员或律师签署。申请还应包括或附上一份经宣誓或承担伪证责任的书面文件,确认申请中所载信息的真实性和准确性。

[《联邦公报》第47卷第610页,1982年1月6日,修正索引:《联邦公报》第54卷第53051页,1989年12月27日。]

第201.42节　净值附录

(a)每一申请人(合格免税组织或合作协会除外)进行申请时均须提供详细的附录,说明程序启动之时申请人及任何关联方[定义见本部分第201.34(f)节]的净值。附录可采用申请人认为方便的任何形式,但应完整披露申请人及其关联方的资产、债务,并应足以确定申请人是否满足本子部分规定的标准。行政法官或证券交易委员会可以要求申请人提交补充信息,以确定其是否有资格获得费用判给。

(b)一般而言,净值附录将纳入程序公开记录之中。但是,申请人反对公开披露附录中任何部分的信息,并相信存在免予披露的法律依据的,可以按照《联邦规章汇编》第十七编第201.190节提交该附录。

[《联邦公报》第47卷第610页,1982年1月6日,修正索引:《联邦公报》第60卷第32795页,1995年6月23日。]

§201.43 Documentation of fees and expenses.

The application shall be accompanied by full documentation of the fees and expenses, including the cost of any study, analysis, engineering report, test, project or similar matter, for which an award is sought. A separate itemized statement shall be submitted for each professional firm or individual whose services are covered by the application, showing the hours spent in connection with the proceeding by each individual, a description of the specific services performed, the rate at which each fee has been computed, any expenses for which reimbursement is sought, the total amount claimed, and the total amount paid or payable by the applicant or by any other person or entity for the services provided. The applicant may be required to provide vouchers, receipts, or other substantiation for any fees or expenses claimed.

§201.44 When an application may be filed.

(a) An application may be filed whenever the applicant has prevailed in the proceeding or in a significant and discrete substantive portion of the proceeding, but in no case later than 30 days after the Commission's final disposition of the proceeding.

(b) For purposes of this rule, final disposition means the date on which a decision or order disposing of the merits of the proceeding or any other complete resolution of the proceeding, such as a settlement or voluntary dismissal, becomes final and unappealable, both within the Commission and to the courts.

(c) If review or reconsideration is sought or taken of a decision as to which an applicant believes it has prevailed, proceedings for the award of fees shall be stayed pending final disposition of the underlying controversy.

[47 FR 610, Jan. 6, 1982, as amended at 54 FR 53052, Dec. 27, 1989]

§201.51 Filing and service of documents.

Any application for an award or other document related to an application shall be filed and served in the same manner as other papers in proceedings under the Commission's Rules of Practice. In addition, a copy of each application for fees and expenses shall be served on the General Counsel of the Commission.

§201.52 Answer to application.

(a) Within 30 days after service of an application, counsel representing the Office or Division of the Commission may file an answer to the application. Unless the Office or Division of the Commission counsel requests an extension of time for filing or files a statement of intent to negotiate under paragraph (b) of this section, failure to file an answer within the 30-day period may be treated as a consent to the award requested.

(b) If counsel for the Office or Division of the Commission and the applicant believe that the issues in the fee application can be settled, they may jointly file a statement of their intent to negotiate a settlement. The filing of this statement shall extend the time for

第201.43节 律师费和费用的证明文件

申请应附上证明申请人请求判给的律师费和费用的完整文件,包括研究、分析、工程报告、测试、项目或类似事项的成本。申请人应按申请所涵盖的每一事务所或个人提交明细声明,说明每一个人花费的与程序相关的工作时数,说明已履行的具体服务、计算使用的费率、请求补偿的费用、主张的总金额以及申请人或任何其他人或实体就所提供服务实付或应付的金额。申请人可能需要就所主张的任何律师费或费用提交凭证、收据或任何其他证据。

第201.44节 申请提交时间

(a)只要申请人在程序或程序的核心、独立的实质部分中胜诉,申请人即可随时提交申请,但无论何时,申请时间不得迟于证券交易委员会就该程序作出最终处理后30日。

(b)就本规则而言,最终处理指就程序的实质内容作出处理的决定或命令的效力得到最终确定,或程序获得其他全面解决(如和解或撤诉)并且效力得到最终确定,且不可再向证券交易委员会和法院提出申诉或提请司法审查之日。

(c)如果申请人相信其已胜诉的裁定被提请司法审查或复审,则在该争议获得最终处理之前,费用判给程序应予中止。

[《联邦公报》第47卷第610页,1982年1月6日,修正索引:《联邦公报》第54卷第53052页,1989年12月27日。]

第201.51节 文件的提交和送达

费用判决申请或与申请相关的其他文件应像其他程序文件一样按照《证券交易委员会工作规则》规定的方式提交和送达。此外,每份律师费和费用判决申请均应抄送证券交易委员会的首席律师。

第201.52节 申请答辩

(a)证券交易委员会办公室或部门的代理律师可在申请送达后30日内提交申请答辩。除非证券交易委员会办公室或部门的代理律师请求延长提交期限,或者提交一份声明表明其有意按照本节第(b)款开展谈判,否则,逾期提交答辩可被视为同意申请人的费用判决请求。

(b)证券交易委员会办公室或部门的代理律师和申请人相信费用申请事项可以和解的,双方可共同提交一份和解谈判意向声明。上述声明提交后,答辩提交期限将另行延长30日;证券交易委员会律师和申请人此后再提出请求的,上述期限可以进一

filing an answer for an additional 30 days, and further extensions may be granted upon request by agency counsel and the applicant.

(c) The answer shall explain any objections to the award requested and identify the facts relied on in support of that position. If the answer is based on any alleged facts not already in the record of the proceeding, it shall include supporting affidavits or a request for further proceedings under §201.55.

§201.53 Reply.

Within 15 days after service of an answer, the applicant may file a reply. If the reply is based on any alleged facts not already in the record of the proceeding, the applicant shall include with the reply either supporting affidavits or a request for further proceedings under §201.55.

§201.54 Settlement.

The applicant and counsel for the Office or Division of the Commission may agree on a proposed settlement of the award before final action on the application, either in connection with a settlement of the underlying proceeding or after the underlying proceeding has been concluded, in accordance with the Commission's standard settlement procedure. See 17 CFR 201.240. If a prevailing party and counsel for the Office or Division of the Commission agree on a proposed settlement of an award before an application has been filed, the application shall be filed with the proposed settlement. If a proposed settlement provides that each side shall bear its own expenses, and the settlement is accepted, no application may be filed.

[54 FR 53052, Dec. 27, 1989, as amended at 60 FR 32795, June 23, 1995]

§201.55 Further proceedings.

(a) Ordinarily, the determination of an award will be made on the basis of the written record. However, on request of either the applicant or counsel for the Office or Division of the Commission, or on his or her own initiative, the administrative law judge may order further proceedings, such as an informal conference, oral argument, additional written submissions or, as to issues other than substantial justification (such as the applicant's eligibility or substantiation of fees and expenses)an evidentiary hearing. The administrative law judge may order all proceedings that are otherwise available under §201.221 and §201.222(a). Such further proceedings shall be held only when necessary for full and fair resolution of the issues arising from the application, and shall be conducted as promptly as possible. Whether or not the Commission's position was substantially justified shall be determined on the basis of the administrative record, as a whole, which is made in the adversary adjudication for which fees and other expenses are sought.

(b) A request for further proceedings under this section shall specifically identify

步延长。

(c)证券交易委员会办公室或部门的代理律师应在答辩中说明其对费用判决申请的异议,并指明支持其立场的事实。答辩所基于的事实主张属于程序记录之外的事实的,答辩书还应附上宣誓书作为支持,或根据第201.55节提出启动进一步程序的请求。

第201.53节　答复

申请人可在答辩送达后15日内提交答复。如果答复所基于的事实属于程序记录之外的事实,申请人还应提交支持性的宣誓证词,或根据第201.55节提出启动进一步程序的请求。

第201.54节　和解

申请人和证券交易委员会办公室或部门的律师可按照证券交易委员会的标准和解程序,在证券交易委员会就申请采取最终行动之前就费用承担和解方案达成一致,和解包括就引发该等费用的行政裁决程序达成和解以及在该等程序审结之后进行的和解。参见《联邦规章汇编》第十七编第201.240节。胜诉方和证券交易委员会办公室或部门的律师在申请提交之前已就费用承担和解方案达成约定的,和解方案应与申请共同提交。如果和解方案规定各方应自行承担费用,且和解已被接受,当事人不得再提出申请。

[《联邦公报》第54卷第53052页,1989年12月27日,修正索引:《联邦公报》第60卷第32795页,1995年6月23日。]

第201.55节　进一步程序

(a)一般而言,费用判决将基于书面记录作出。但是,行政法官可自行决定,或按申请人或证券交易委员会办公室或部门的律师的请求,命令启动进一步程序,如非正式会议、口头辩论、提交补充书面材料;对于申请人资格或律师费和费用证明等实体证明事项之外的事项而言,还可以启动举证听证程序。行政法官可以命令启动第201.221节和第201.222(a)节规定的其他程序。启动该等其他程序必须以完整、公平地裁决因申请引起的所有事项所必要为限,且应尽可能及时地开展。证券交易委员会的立场是否具有实质正当性,应基于产生所涉律师费和费用的对抗性裁决程序的整体行政记录判定。

(b)根据本节请求启动进一步程序的,应在请求中具体指明所寻求获得的信息或

the information sought or the disputed issues and shall explain why the additional proceedings are necessary to resolve the issues.

[47 FR 610, Jan. 6, 1982, as amended at 54 FR 53052, Dec. 27, 1989; 70 FR 72569, Dec. 5, 2005]

§201.56 Decision.

The administrative law judge shall issue an initial decision on the application promptly after completion of proceedings on the application. The decision shall include written findings and conclusions on the applicant's eligibility and status as a prevailing party, and an explanation of the reasons for any difference between the amount requested and the amount awarded. The decision shall also include, if at issue, findings on whether the Commission's position was substantially justified, whether the applicant unduly protracted the proceedings, or whether special circumstances make an award unjust.

§201.57 Commission review.

In accordance with the procedures set forth in 17 CFR 201.410 and 201.411, either the applicant or counsel for the Office or Division of the Commission may seek review of the initial decision on the fee application, or the Commission may decide to review the decision on its own initiative. If neither the applicant nor counsel for the Division or Office of the Commission seeks review and the Commission does not take review on its own initiative, the initial decision on the application shall become a final decision of the Commission 30 days after it is issued. Whether to review a decision is a matter within the discretion of the Commission. If review is taken, the Commission will issue a final decision on the application or remand the application to the administrative law judge for further proceedings.

[47 FR 610, Jan. 6, 1982, as amended at 60 FR 32795, June 23, 1995]

§201.58 Judicial review.

Judicial review of final Commission decisions on awards may be sought as provided in 5 U.S.C. 504(c)(2).

§201.59 Payment of award.

An applicant seeking payment of an award shall submit to the Comptroller of the Commission a copy of the Commission's final decision granting the award, accompanied by a sworn statement that the applicant will not seek review of the decision in the United States courts. The Commission will pay the amount awarded to the applicant as authorized by law, unless judicial review of the award has been sought by the applicant.

[54 FR 53052, Dec. 27, 1989]

§201.60 [Reserved]

争议事项,并说明为何有必要启动该等进一步程序解决该等事项。

[《联邦公报》第47卷第610页,1982年1月6日,修正索引:《联邦公报》第54卷第53052页,1989年12月27日;《联邦公报》第70卷第72569页,2005年12月5日。]

第201.56节　决定

行政法官应于申请程序审结后及时签发一份初步决定。决定中应阐述关于申请人胜诉方资格和地位的书面认定和结论,同时,如请求金额与实际判决金额之间存在差异,应说明相关原因。例如,双方对证券交易委员会的立场是否具有实质正当性、申请人是否不正当地拖延了程序以及是否存在使费用判决丧失正当性等问题存在争议,该决定还应对此作出认定。

第201.57节　证券交易委员会复议

按照《联邦规章汇编》第十七编第201.410节和第201.411节规定的程序,申请人或证券交易委员会办公室或部门的律师均可以提请证券交易委员会对初步决定进行复议,证券交易委员会亦可以主动提起复议。如果申请人或证券交易委员会办公室或部门的律师均未提请复议,证券交易委员会亦未主动提起复议,初步决定将于签发届满30日后成为证券交易委员会的最终决定。是否对决定进行复议属于证券交易委员会的自由裁量事项。如进行复议,证券交易委员会将就该申请签发一份最终决定,或将该申请发回行政法官启动进一步程序。

[《联邦公报》第47卷第610页,1982年1月6日,修正索引:《联邦公报》第60卷第32795页,1995年6月23日。]

第201.58节　司法审查

证券交易委员会就费用判决作出的最终决定,可按照《美国法典》第五编第504(c)(2)节提请司法审查。

第201.59节　获判费用的支付

申请人请求支付获判费用的,应向证券交易委员会审计长提交证券交易委员会核准费用判决的最终决定,并附上一份宣誓声明,表明其不会提请联邦法院对上述最终决定进行审查。证券交易委员会将按照法律授权,向申请人支付判决金额,但申请人提请司法审查的除外。

[《联邦公报》第54卷第53052页,1989年12月27日。]

第201.60节　[保留]

Subpart C [Reserved]

Subpart D—Rules of Practice

Authority: 15 U.S.C. 77f, 77g, 77h, 77h-1, 77j, 77s, 77u, 78c (b), 78d-1, 78d-2, 78*l*, 78m, 78n, 78*o* (d), 78*o*-3, 78s, 78u-2, 78u-3, 78v, 78w, 79c, 79s, 79t, 79z-5a, 77sss, 77ttt, 80a-8, 80a-9, 80a-37, 80a-38, 80a-39, 80a-40, 80a-41, 80a-44, 80b-3, 80b-9, 80b-11, 80b-12, 7202, 7215, and 7217.

Source: 60 FR 32796, June 23, 1995, unless otherwise noted.

General Rules

§201.100 Scope of the rules of practice.

(a) Unless provided otherwise, these Rules of Practice govern proceedings before the Commission under the statutes that it administers.

(b) These rules do not apply to:

(1) Investigations, except where made specifically applicable by the Rules Relating to Investigations, part 203 of this chapter; or

(2) Actions taken by the duty officer pursuant to delegated authority under 17 CFR 200.43.

(3) Initiation of proceedings for SRO proposed rule changes under 17 CFR 201.700-701, except where made specifically applicable therein.

(c) The Commission, upon its determination that to do so would serve the interests of justice and not result in prejudice to the parties to the proceeding, may by order direct, in a particular proceeding, that an alternative procedure shall apply or that compliance with an otherwise applicable rule is unnecessary.

[60 FR 32796, June 23, 1995; 60 FR 46499, Sept. 7, 1995, as amended at 69 FR 13175, Mar. 19, 2004; 76 FR 4070, Jan. 24, 2011]

§201.101 Definitions.

(a) For purposes of these Rules of Practice, unless explicitly stated to the contrary:

(1) *Commission* means the United States Securities and Exchange Commission, or a

第C子部分 [保 留]

第D子部分——工作规则

法律依据:《美国法典》第十五编第77f节、第77g节、第77h节、第77h-1节、第77j节、第77s节、第77u节、第78c(b)节、第78d-1节、第78d-2节、第78l节、第78m节、第78n节、第78o(d)节、第78o-3节、第78s节、第78u-2节、第78u-3节、第78v节、第78w节、第79c节、第79s节、第79t节、第79z-5a节、第77sss节、第77ttt节、第80a-8节、第80a-9节、第80a-37节、第80a-38节、第80a-39节、第80a-40节、第80a-41节、第80a-44节、第80b-3节、第80b-9节、第80b-11节、第80b-12节、第7202节、第7215节和第7217节。

行政规则来源:《联邦公报》第60卷第32796页,1995年6月23日,除非另有说明。

一般规定

第201.100节 《工作规则》的适用范围

(a)除非另有规定,证券交易委员会根据其负责实施的制定法所主持的程序受《工作规则》规制。

(b)该等规则不适用于:

(1)调查,但《调查规则》(本章第203部分)特别规定应适用《工作规则》的除外;或

(2)轮值官根据《联邦规章汇编》第十七编第200.43节的委托授权采取的行动;

(3)根据《联邦规章汇编》第十七编第201.700~701节就自律组织规则变更提案启动相关程序的行为,但上述规章特别规定应适用《工作规则》的除外。

(c)如证券交易委员会判定有助于实现公正且不会损害程序当事人利益,证券交易委员会可以在具体程序中发布命令,指示适用替代性程序或指示免予适用某一规则。

[《联邦公报》第60卷第32796页,1995年6月23日;《联邦公报》第60卷第46499页,1995年9月7日,修正索引:《联邦公报》第69卷第13175页,2004年3月19日;《联邦公报》第76卷第4070页,2011年1月24日。]

第201.101节 定义

(a)就《工作规则》而言,除非存在相反的明文规定:

(1)"证券交易委员会"一词系指美国证券交易委员会,或达到法定人数的证券交

panel of Commissioners constituting a quorum of the Commission, or a single Commissioner acting as duty officer pursuant to 17 CFR 200.43;

(2) *Counsel* means any attorney representing a party or any other person representing a party pursuant to §201.102(b);

(3) *Disciplinary proceeding* means an action pursuant to §201.102(e);

(4) *Enforcement proceeding* means an action, initiated by an order instituting proceedings, held for the purpose of determining whether or not a person is about to violate, has violated, has caused a violation of, or has aided or abetted a violation of any statute or rule administered by the Commission, or whether to impose a sanction as defined in Section 551(10) of the Administrative Procedure Act, 5 U.S.C. 551(10);

(5) *Hearing officer* means an administrative law judge, a panel of Commissioners constituting less than a quorum of the Commission, an individual Commissioner, or any other person duly authorized to preside at a hearing;

(6) *Interested division* means a division or an office assigned primary responsibility by the Commission to participate in a particular proceeding;

(7) *Order instituting proceedings* means an order issued by the Commission commencing a proceeding or an order issued by the Commission to hold a hearing;

(8) *Party* means the interested division, any person named as a respondent in an order instituting proceedings, any applicant named in the caption of any order, persons entitled to notice in a stop order proceeding as set forth in §201.200(a)(2) or any person seeking Commission review of a decision;

(9) *Proceeding* means any agency process initiated:

(i) By an order instituting proceedings; or

(ii) By the filing, pursuant to §201.410, of a petition for review of an initial decision by a hearing officer; or

(iii) By the filing, pursuant to §201.420, of an application for review of a self-regulatory organization determination; or

(iv) By the filing, pursuant to §201.430, of a notice of intention to file a petition for review of a determination made pursuant to delegated authority; or

(v) By the filing, pursuant to §201.440, of an application for review of a determination by the Public Company Accounting Oversight Board; or

(vi) By the filing, pursuant to §242.601 of this chapter, of an application for review of an action or failure to act in connection with the implementation or operation of any effective transaction reporting plan; or

(vii) By the filing, pursuant to §242.608 of this chapter, of an application for review of an action taken or failure to act in connection with the implementation or operation of any effective national market system plan; or

易委员会委员组成的工作小组,或根据《联邦规章汇编》第十七编第200.43节担任轮值官的单个委员;

(2)"律师"一词系指一方当事人的代理律师,或根据第201.102(b)节担任一方当事人代理人的任何其他人;

(3)"纪律处分程序"一词系指根据第201.102(e)节采取的行动;

(4)"执法程序"一词系指通过程序发起令启动的程序,目的是判定某一人是否即将或已经违反证券交易委员会负责实施的任何制定法或规则,或存在促成、协助、教唆他人违反该等制定法或规则的行为,或判定是否应处以《行政程序法》第551(10)条[《美国法典》第五编第551(10)节]规定的制裁;

(5)"听证官"一词系指行政法官、证券交易委员会委员组成的低于法定人数的工作小组、单个委员或经正式授权主持听证的任何其他人;

(6)"利害关系部门"一词系指证券交易委员会指派的参与具体程序的主要负责部门或办公室;

(7)"程序发起令"一词系指证券交易委员会签发的启动某一程序的命令,或证券交易委员会签发的举行听证的命令;

(8)"当事人"一词系指利害关系部门、程序发起令中指明的任何行政相对人或被申请人、[1] 命令标题中指明的任何申请人、第201.200(a)(2)节规定的停止令程序中有权获得通知的人或提请证券交易委员会对某项决定进行复议的任何人;

(9)"程序"一词系指通过下述方式启动的证券交易委员会程序:

(i)程序发起令;或

(ii)根据第201.410节针对听证官的初步决定提出复议请求;或

(iii)根据第201.420节针对自律组织的决定提出复议申请;或

(iv)根据第201.430节提交意在对依据委托授权所作决定请求复议的通知;或

(v)根据第201.440节针对公众公司会计监督委员会的决定提出复议申请;或

(vi)根据本章第242.601节针对与有效交易报告计划之实施或运作相关的作为或不作为提出复议申请;或

(vii)根据本章第242.608节针对与有效全国市场系统计划之实施或运作相关的作为或不作为提出复议申请;或

1 "Respondent"按我国的通行用语,在行政处罚程序中,使用的是"行政相对人",在争议处理程序中,使用的是"被申请人",难以找到一个统一的、完全对应的词,故分列处理。——译者注

(viii) By the filing, pursuant to Section 11A(b)(5) of the Securities Exchange Act of 1934, of an application for review of a determination of a registered securities information processor;

(10) *Secretary* means the Secretary of the Commission;

(11) *Temporary sanction* means a temporary cease–and–desist order or a temporary suspension of the registration of a broker, dealer, municipal securities dealer, government securities broker, government securities dealer, or transfer agent pending final determination whether the registration shall be revoked; and

(12) *Board* means the Public Company Accounting Oversight Board.

(b) [Reserved]

[60 FR 32796, June 23, 1995, as amended at 69 FR 13175, Mar. 19, 2004; 70 FR 37617, June 29, 2005]

§201.102 Appearance and practice before the Commission.

A person shall not be represented before the Commission or a hearing officer except as stated in paragraphs (a) and (b) of this section or as otherwise permitted by the Commission or a hearing officer.

(a) *Representing oneself.* In any proceeding, an individual may appear on his or her own behalf.

(b) *Representing others.* In any proceeding, a person may be represented by an attorney at law admitted to practice before the Supreme Court of the United States or the highest court of any State (as defined in Section 3 (a)(16) of the Exchange Act, 15 U.S.C. 78c(a)(16)); a member of a partnership may represent the partnership; a bona fide officer of a corporation, trust or association may represent the corporation, trust or association; and an officer or employee of a state commission or of a department or political subdivision of a state may represent the state commission or the department or political subdivision of the state.

(c) *Former Commission employees.* Former employees of the Commission must comply with the restrictions on practice contained in the Commission's Conduct Regulation, Subpart M, 17 CFR 200.735.

(d) *Designation of address for service; notice of appearance; power of attorney; withdrawal* — (1)*Representing oneself.* When an individual first makes any filing or otherwise appears on his or her own behalf before the Commission or a hearing officer in a proceeding as defined in §201.101(a), he or she shall file with the Commission, or otherwise state on the record, and keep current, an address at which any notice or other written communication required to be served upon him or her or furnished to him or her may be sent and a telephone number where he or she may be reached during business hours.

(viii)根据《1934年证券交易法》第11A(b)(5)条,针对注册证券信息处理机构的决定提出复议申请;

(10)"秘书"一词系指证券交易委员会秘书;

(11)"临时制裁"一词系指临时制止令,以及在作出是否撤销注册资格的最后决定前暂停经纪商、自营商、市政证券自营商、政府证券经纪商、政府证券自营商以及过户代理人的注册;且

(12)"委员会"一词系指公众公司会计监督委员会。

(b)[保留]

[《联邦公报》第60卷第32796页,1995年6月23日,修正索引:《联邦公报》第69卷第13175页,2004年3月19日;《联邦公报》第70卷第37617页,2005年6月29日。]

第201.102节　出席证券交易委员会程序并办理业务

除本节第(a)款和第(b)款规定的情形或经证券交易委员会或听证官允许外,当事不得由他人代理出席证券交易委员会程序或听证官主持的程序。

(a)代表本人出席。在任何程序中,个人均可代表本人出席证券交易委员会程序。

(b)代理他人出席。在任何程序中,均可采用如下形式的代理:某人可由具备办理与联邦最高法院或各州最高法院相关的业务资格的律师[定义见《证券交易法》第3(a)(16)条,《美国法典》第十五编第78c(a)(16)节]代理;合伙可由其合伙人代理;公司、信托、协会可由其善意的管理人员代理;州委员会、部门或州行政区域可由其官员或职员代理。

(c)证券交易委员会前任雇员。证券交易委员会前任雇员必须遵守《证券交易委员会行为准则管理办法》(第M子部分,《联邦规章汇编》第十七编第200.735节)规定的各项行为限制。

(d)送达地址的指定;出席通知;代理委托书;退出代理——(1)代理本人出席。某人在第201.101(a)节规定的各种证券交易委员会程序或听证官主持的程序中第一次提交文件或以其他方式代表本人出席上述程序之时,应向证券交易委员会提交或在记录中载明并及时更新地址和本人的电话号码,以便接收应该或可能向其送达、提供或发送的通知或其他书面通信并且在工作时间内可以联系到其本人。

(2) *Representing others.* When a person first makes any filing or otherwise appears in a representative capacity before the Commission or a hearing officer in a proceeding as defined in §201.101(a), that person shall file with the Commission, and keep current, a written notice stating the name of the proceeding; the representative's name, business address and telephone number; and the name and address of the person or persons represented.

(3) *Power of attorney.* Any individual appearing or practicing before the Commission in a representative capacity may be required to file a power of attorney with the Commission showing his or her authority to act in such capacity.

(4) *Withdrawal.* Any person seeking to withdraw his or her appearance in a representative capacity shall file a notice of withdrawal with the Commission or the hearing officer. The notice shall state the name, address, and telephone number of the withdrawing representative; the name, address, and telephone number of the person for whom the appearance was made; and the effective date of the withdrawal. If the person seeking to withdraw knows the name, address, and telephone number of the new representative, or knows that the person for whom the appearance was made intends to represent him–or herself, that information shall be included in the notice. The notice must be served on the parties in accordance with §201.150. The notice shall be filed at least five days before the proposed effective date of the withdrawal.

(e) *Suspension and disbarment* — (1) *Generally.* The Commission may censure a person or deny, temporarily or permanently, the privilege of appearing or practicing before it in any way to any person who is found by the Commission after notice and opportunity for hearing in the matter:

(i) Not to possess the requisite qualifications to represent others; or

(ii) To be lacking in character or integrity or to have engaged in unethical or improper professional conduct; or

(iii) To have willfully violated, or willfully aided and abetted the violation of any provision of the Federal securities laws or the rules and regulations thereunder;

(iv) With respect to persons licensed to practice as accountants, "improper professional conduct" under §201.102(e)(1)(ii) means:

(A) Intentional or knowing conduct, including reckless conduct, that results in a violation of applicable professional standards; or

(B) Either of the following two types of negligent conduct:

(1) A single instance of highly unreasonable conduct that results in a violation of applicable professional standards in circumstances in which an accountant knows, or should know, that heightened scrutiny is warranted.

(2) Repeated instances of unreasonable conduct, each resulting in a violation of

(2)代理他人出席。某人在第201.101(a)节规定的各种证券交易委员会程序或听证官主持的程序中第一次代理他人提交文件或以其他方式代理他人出席上述程序之时,应向证券交易委员会提供一份书面通知,载明并及时更新程序名称、代理人姓名、工作地址和电话号码以及被代理人的姓名和地址。

(3)代理委托书。任何以代理身份出席证券交易委员会的程序或办理业务的个人均可能需要向证券交易委员会提供代理委托书,证明其有权担任代理。

(4)退出代理。希望退出以代理身份出席证券交易委员会程序的任何人,应向证券交易委员会或听证官发送一份退出通知。通知中应载明:退出代理人的姓名、地址和电话号码;被代理人的姓名、地址和电话号码;以及退出的生效日期。退出代理人知悉新代理人的姓名、地址和电话号码,或知悉被代理人拟自行代理的,亦应在通知中予以说明。通知必须按第201.150节之规定送达各方当事人,提交时间不得迟于拟定的退出生效日前5日。

(e)暂停和永久取消资格——(1)一般规定。证券交易委员会在发送通知并提供听证机会后认定任何人存在下述情形的,可予以谴责,或暂停或永久性地取消其出席证券交易委员会程序或办理业务的资格:

(i)不具备代理他人的必要资格;或

(ii)人格或诚信缺失,或曾从事不道德或不当职业行为;或

(iii)故意违反或故意协助、教唆他人违反联邦证券法或依其颁发的规则与规章的任何规定;

(iv)就获得会计师执业许可的人而言,第201.102(e)(1)(ii)节中的"不当职业行为"指:

(A)在故意或明知(包括疏忽大意)的主观状态下从事相关行为,导致违反相关职业准则的;或

(B)下述两类过失行为之一:

(1)会计师在明知或应知应从严审查的情况下仍然出现了单次高度不合理行为,导致违反相关职业准则的;

(2)重复性地从事违反相关职业准则的不合理行为,表明其缺乏在证券交易委员

applicable professional standards, that indicate a lack of competence to practice before the Commission.

(2) *Certain professionals and convicted persons.* Any attorney who has been suspended or disbarred by a court of the United States or of any State; or any person whose license to practice as an accountant, engineer, or other professional or expert has been revoked or suspended in any State; or any person who has been convicted of a felony or a misdemeanor involving moral turpitude shall be forthwith suspended from appearing or practicing before the Commission. A disbarment, suspension, revocation or conviction within the meaning of this section shall be deemed to have occurred when the disbarring, suspending, revoking or convicting agency or tribunal enters its judgment or order, including a judgment or order on a plea of nolo contendere, regardless of whether an appeal of such judgment or order is pending or could be taken.

(3) *Temporary suspensions.* An order of temporary suspension shall become effective upon service on the respondent. No order of temporary suspension shall be entered by the Commission pursuant to paragraph (e)(3)(i) of this section more than 90 days after the date on which the final judgment or order entered in a judicial or administrative proceeding described in paragraph (e)(3)(i)(A) or (e)(3)(i)(B) of this section has become effective, whether upon completion of review or appeal procedures or because further review or appeal procedures are no longer available.

(i) The Commission, with due regard to the public interest and without preliminary hearing, may, by order, temporarily suspend from appearing or practicing before it any attorney, accountant, engineer, or other professional or expert who has been by name:

(A) Permanently enjoined by any court of competent jurisdiction, by reason of his or her misconduct in an action brought by the Commission, from violating or aiding and abetting the violation of any provision of the Federal securities laws or of the rules and regulations thereunder; or

(B) Found by any court of competent jurisdiction in an action brought by the Commission to which he or she is a party or found by the Commission in any administrative proceeding to which he or she is a party to have violated (unless the violation was found not to have been willful)or aided and abetted the violation of any provision of the Federal securities laws or of the rules and regulations thereunder.

(ii) Any person temporarily suspended from appearing and practicing before the Commission in accordance with paragraph (e)(3)(i) of this section may, within 30 days after service upon him or her of the order of temporary suspension, petition the Commission to lift the temporary suspension. If no petition has been received by the Commission within 30 days after service of the order, the suspension shall become permanent.

会办理业务的能力的。

(2)特定专业人士和已定罪的人。被联邦法院或任何州法院暂停或永久取消执业资格的人,或其会计师、工程师或其他专业人士或专家的执业资格在任何州被暂停或永久性地取消的任何人,或被判决犯有重罪或涉及反公德行为的轻罪的任何人,均应立即被暂停出席证券交易委员会程序并办理业务的资格。就本节而言,永久取消、暂停、撤销资格或定罪的发生时间应被视为相关机构或法庭作出永久取消、暂停、撤销资格或定罪判决或命令的时间,包括当事人作出不辩护也不认罪的答辩时相关机构或法庭作出的判决或命令,而不论该等判决或命令是否仍然可能被申请复议、上诉或该等复议、上诉是否仍然处于未决状态。

(3)暂停资格。暂停资格令自送达相对人之时生效。本节第(e)(3)(i)(A)款或第(e)(3)(i)(B)款所述的司法程序或行政处理程序中作出的最终判决或命令因复议或上诉程序终结或无法再提起进一步复议或上诉程序而生效后满90日的,证券交易委员会不得再依据本节第(e)(3)(i)款作出暂停资格令。

(i)证券交易委员会在适当顾及公共利益的情况下,可以不举行预听证,直接发布命令暂停任何律师、会计师、工程师或其他专业人士或专家出席证券交易委员会程序或办理业务的资格,前提是该等专业人士或专家:

(A)因其在证券交易委员会提起的诉讼中的不当行为,被任何有管辖权的法院签发永久性禁令,不得违反或协助、教唆他人违反任何联邦证券法律或依其颁发的规则与规章;或

(B)在其作为当事人参与的证券交易委员会提起的诉讼中,被任何有管辖权的法院认定,或在其作为当事人参与的任何行政处理程序中被证券交易委员会认定违反了或曾协助、教唆他人违反任何联邦证券法律或依其颁发的规则与规章(但被认定为非故意违反的除外)。

(ii)按照本节第(e)(3)(i)款被暂停出席证券交易委员会程序并办理业务资格的任何人,均可以在暂停资格令送达后30日内请求证券交易委员会撤销暂停资格令。证券交易委员未在命令送达后30日内收到撤销请求书的,暂停资格令将长期有效。

(iii) Within 30 days after the filing of a petition in accordance with paragraph (e)(3)(ii) of this section, the Commission shall either lift the temporary suspension, or set the matter down for hearing at a time and place designated by the Commission, or both, and, after opportunity for hearing, may censure the petitioner or disqualify the petitioner from appearing or practicing before the Commission for a period of time or permanently. In every case in which the temporary suspension has not been lifted, every hearing held and other action taken pursuant to this paragraph (e)(3) shall be expedited in accordance with §201.500. If the hearing is held before a hearing officer, the time limits set forth in §201.540 will govern review of the hearing officer's initial decision.

(iv) In any hearing held on a petition filed in accordance with paragraph (e)(3)(ii) of this section, the staff of the Commission shall show either that the petitioner has been enjoined as described in paragraph (e)(3)(i)(A)of this section or that the petitioner has been found to have committed or aided and abetted violations as described in paragraph (e)(3)(i)(B) of this section and that showing, without more, may be the basis for censure or disqualification. Once that showing has been made, the burden shall be upon the petitioner to show cause why he or she should not be censured or temporarily or permanently disqualified from appearing and practicing before the Commission. In any such hearing, the petitioner may not contest any finding made against him or her or fact admitted by him or her in the judicial or administrative proceeding upon which the proceeding under this paragraph (e)(3) is predicated. A person who has consented to the entry of a permanent injunction as described in paragraph (e)(3)(i)(A) of this section without admitting the facts set forth in the complaint shall be presumed for all purposes under this paragraph (e)(3) to have been enjoined by reason of the misconduct alleged in the complaint.

(4) *Filing of prior orders.* Any person appearing or practicing before the Commission who has been the subject of an order, judgment, decree, or finding as set forth in paragraph (e)(3) of this section shall promptly file with the Secretary a copy thereof (together with any related opinion or statement of the agency or tribunal involved). Failure to file any such paper, order, judgment, decree or finding shall not impair the operation of any other provision of this section.

(5) *Reinstatement.* (i) An application for reinstatement of a person permanently suspended or disqualified under paragraph (e)(1) or (e)(3) of this section may be made at any time, and the applicant may, in the Commission's discretion, be afforded a hearing; however, the suspension or disqualification shall continue unless and until the applicant has been reinstated by the Commission for good cause shown.

(ii) Any person suspended under paragraph (e)(2) of this section shall be reinstated by the Commission, upon appropriate application, if all the grounds for

（iii）在请求人按照本节第（e）（3）（ii）款规定提交请求书后30日内，证券交易委员会应选择撤销暂停资格令，或在证券交易委员会指定的时间和地点安排对该事项进行听证，或同时采取以上两项措施；在提供听证机会之后，证券交易委员会可以对请求人予以谴责，或在特定时间段内暂停或永久性地取消其出席证券交易委员会程序或在证券交易委员会办理业务的资格。无论何时，在暂停资格令尚未被撤销的情况下，根据本第（e）（3）款举行的所有听证和采取的所有行动均应按照第201.500节的规定加快开展。听证由听证官主持的，第201.540节规定的时限应适用于对听证官初步决定的复议。

（iv）基于按照本节第（e）（3）（ii）款提交的请求书而举行听证的，证券交易委员会的工作人员应证明请求人已如本节第（e）（3）（i）（A）款所述被证券交易委员会签发了禁令，不得从事相关行为；或者证明请求人已被认定从事了或协助、教唆他人从事本节第（e）（3）（i）（B）款所述违法违规行为并且证券交易委员会工作人员作出的该等证明足以作为谴责请求人或取消请求人资格的基础。证券交易委员会工作人员完成上述证明的，请求人应承担举证责任，出具其不应被处以谴责或被临时或永久取消出席证券交易委员会程序或办理业务的资格的理由。在引发本节第（e）（3）款所述的司法程序或行政处理程序中针对请求人作出的任何认定或请求人承认的任何事实，请求人不得再在上述听证中提出异议。就本节第（e）（3）款而言，同意证券交易委员会作出本节第（e）（3）（i）（A）款所述的永久禁令，但不承认申诉书中所载事实的人，应被推定为已因申诉书中主张的不当行为而在所有方面均被禁止从事相关行为。

（4）提交之前收到的命令。出席证券交易委员会程序或与证券交易委员会办理业务的任何人，如曾被作出本节第（e）（3）款所述的任何命令、判决、判令或认定，应及时向证券交易委员会秘书提交一份复本（如相关机构或法庭做出相关意见或声明的，亦应一并提交）。未能按上述规定提交该等文件、命令、判决、判令或认定，不影响本节任何其他规定之适用。

（5）恢复资格。（i）对于根据本节第（e）（1）款或第（e）（3）款被正式暂停或永久性地取消资格的人，在任何时间均可提出恢复资格的申请，且经证券交易委员会自行裁量，申请人可获得听证机会；但是，除非且直至证券交易委员会已基于充分理由恢复申请人的资格，否则暂停或取消资格不得停止适用。

（ii）申请人提出适当申请，且定罪已被推翻，或暂停、永久取消、撤销资格令已被终止，导致适用本节第（e）（2）款规定的所有理由之后均不复存在的，证券交易委员会

application of the provisions of that paragraph are subsequently removed by a reversal of the conviction or termination of the suspension, disbarment, or revocation. An application for reinstatement on any other grounds by any person suspended under paragraph (e)(2) of this section may be filed at any time and the applicant shall be accorded an opportunity for a hearing in the matter; however, such suspension shall continue unless and until the applicant has been reinstated by order of the Commission for good cause shown.

(6) *Other proceedings not precluded.* A proceeding brought under paragraph (e)(1), (e)(2) or (e)(3) of this section shall not preclude another proceeding brought under these same paragraphs.

(7) *Public hearings.* All hearings held under this paragraph (e) shall be public unless otherwise ordered by the Commission on its own motion or after considering the motion of a party.

(f) *Practice defined.* For the purposes of these Rules of Practice, practicing before the Commission shall include, but shall not be limited to:

(1) Transacting any business with the Commission; and

(2) The preparation of any statement, opinion or other paper by any attorney, accountant, engineer or other professional or expert, filed with the Commission in any registration statement, notification, application, report or other document with the consent of such attorney, accountant, engineer or other professional or expert.

[60 FR 32796, June 23, 1995, as amended at 63 FR 57122, Oct. 26, 1998; 69 FR 13176, Mar. 19, 2004; 70 FR 72569, Dec. 5, 2005]

§201.103 Construction of rules.

(a) The Rules of Practice shall be construed and administered to secure the just, speedy, and inexpensive determination of every proceeding.

(b) In any particular proceeding, to the extent that there is a conflict between these rules and a procedural requirement contained in any statute, or any rule or form adopted thereunder, the latter shall control.

(c) For purposes of these rules:

(1) Any term in the singular includes the plural, and any term in the plural includes the singular, if such use would be appropriate;

(2) Any use of a masculine, feminine, or neuter gender encompasses such other genders as would be appropriate; and

(3) Unless the context requires otherwise, counsel for a party may take any action required or permitted to be taken by such party.

§201.104 Business hours.

The Headquarters office of the Commission, at 100 F Street, NE., Washington, D.C.

应恢复根据本节第(e)(2)款被暂停资格的人的资格。根据本节第(e)(2)款被暂停资格的任何人可在任何时间基于任何其他理由提出恢复资格的申请,且申请人应获得就该事项进行听证的机会;但是,除非且直至证券交易委员会已基于充分理由恢复申请人的资格,否则暂停资格不得停止适用。

(6)不妨碍其他程序。根据本节第(e)(1)款、第(e)(2)款或第(e)(3)款提起的程序,不妨碍依据上述条款提起其他程序。

(7)公开听证。根据本第(e)款举行的所有听证均应公开举行,但证券交易委员会主动另行发布命令或审议一方当事人的动议后另行发布命令的除外。

(f)办理业务之定义。就《工作规则》而言,在证券交易委员会办理业务应包括但不限于:

(1)与证券交易委员会交涉任何业务;且

(2)任何律师、会计师、工程师或其他专业人士或专家准备任何声明、意见或其他文件,且该等声明、意见或文件经其同意被纳入向证券交易委员会提交的注册申请书、通知、申请、报告或其他文件之中。

[《联邦公报》第60卷第32796页,1995年6月23日,修正索引:《联邦公报》第63卷第57122页,1998年10月26日;《联邦公报》第69卷第13176页,2004年3月19日;《联邦公报》第70卷第72569页,2005年12月5日。]

第201.103节 规则解释

(a)解释和执行《工作规则》时应确保公平、快速和低成本地对所有程序作出决定。

(b)在任何具体程序中,本《工作规则》与任何制定法或依其制定的规则或表格中的程序性要求相冲突的,以后者为准。

(c)就《工作规则》而言:

(1)如不致产生不当结果,任何单数词语均应包括复数含义,反之亦然;

(2)如不致产生不当结果,任何阳性、阴性或中性代词均应包括其他性别;且

(3)除非与上下文冲突,否则一方的律师可以采取该方所应采取的或可以采取的所有行动。

第201.104节 工作时间

证券交易委员会总部(地址:华盛顿哥伦比亚特区东北分区100F大街,邮编:D.C.

20549, is open each day, except Saturdays, Sundays, and Federal legal holidays, from 9 a.m. to 5:30 p.m., Eastern Standard Time or Eastern Daylight Saving Time, whichever is currently in effect in Washington, D.C. Federal legal holidays consist of New Year's Day; Birthday of Martin Luther King, Jr.; Presidents Day; Memorial Day; Independence Day; Labor Day; Columbus Day; Veterans Day; Thanksgiving Day; Christmas Day; and any other day appointed as a holiday in Washington, D.C. by the President or the Congress of the United States.

[60 FR 32796, June 23, 1995, as amended at 70 FR 72569, Dec. 5, 2005]

§201.110 Presiding officer.

All proceedings shall be presided over by the Commission or, if the Commission so orders, by a hearing officer. When the Commission designates that the hearing officer shall be an administrative law judge, the Chief Administrative Law Judge shall select, pursuant to 17 CFR 200.30–10, the administrative law judge to preside.

§201.111 Hearing officer: Authority.

The hearing officer shall have the authority to do all things necessary and appropriate to discharge his or her duties. No provision of these Rules of Practice shall be construed to limit the powers of the hearing officer provided by the Administrative Procedure Act, 5 U.S.C. 556, 557. The powers of the hearing officer include, but are not limited to, the following:

(a) Administering oaths and affirmations;

(b) Issuing subpoenas authorized by law and revoking, quashing, or modifying any such subpoena;

(c) Receiving relevant evidence and ruling upon the admission of evidence and offers of proof;

(d) Regulating the course of a proceeding and the conduct of the parties and their counsel;

(e) Holding prehearing and other conferences as set forth in §201.221 and requiring the attendance at any such conference of at least one representative of each party who has authority to negotiate concerning the resolution of issues in controversy;

(f) Recusing himself or herself upon motion made by a party or upon his or her own motion;

(g) Ordering, in his or her discretion, in a proceeding involving more than one respondent, that the interested division indicate, on the record, at least one day prior to the presentation of any evidence, each respondent against whom that evidence will be offered;

(h) Subject to any limitations set forth elsewhere in these Rules of Practice,

20549)的开放时间为每日上午9时至下午5时30分(东部标准时间或东部夏令时,以华盛顿哥伦比亚特区届时有效适用的时间标准为准),周六、周日及联邦法定节假日除外。联邦法定节假日包括元旦、马丁·路德·金诞辰、总统日、阵亡将士纪念日、独立日、劳动节、哥伦布纪念日、退伍军人节、感恩节、圣诞节以及美国总统或国会指定的华盛顿哥伦比亚特区的任何其他节假日。

[《联邦公报》第60卷第32796页,1995年6月23日,修正索引:《联邦公报》第70卷第72569页,2005年12月5日。]

第201.110节　听证主持人

所有程序均应由证券交易委员会或证券交易委员会通过命令指定的听证官主持。证券交易委员会指定听证官应当由行政法官担任的,首席行政法官应根据《联邦规章汇编》第十七编第200.30–10节选定主持听证的行政法官。

第201.111节　听证官:权限

听证官有权为履行职务而采取所有必要且适当的行动。本《工作规则》的任何内容均不得被解释为限制《行政程序法》(《美国法典》第五编第556节、第557节)规定的听证官的权力。听证官的权力包括但不限于:

(a)执行宣誓和证词声明程序;

(b)依据法律授权签发及撤销、修改传票或宣布传票无效;

(c)接收相关证据,并就证据的可采性和证据认定动议作出裁定;

(d)规范程序进程和当事人及其律师的行为;

(e)举行第201.221节规定的预听证会议和其他会议,并要求各方至少一名有权谈判争议解决事宜的代表出席该等会议;

(f)主动申请回避或应一方当事人的动议进行回避;

(g)在涉及一个以上相对人的程序中,命令利害关系部门至少在提交证据前一日,在记录上列明证据所针对的每名相对人;

(h)在不违反本《工作规则》其他条款规定的任何限制的前提下,审议所有程序性

considering and ruling upon all procedural and other motions, including a motion to correct a manifest error of fact in the initial decision. A motion to correct is properly filed under this Rule only if the basis for the motion is a patent misstatement of fact in the initial decision. Any motion to correct must be filed within ten days of the initial decision. A brief in opposition may be filed within five days of a motion to correct. The hearing officer shall have 20 days from the date of filing of any brief in opposition filed to rule on a motion to correct;

(i) Preparing an initial decision as provided in §201.360;

(j) Upon notice to all parties, reopening any hearing prior to the filing of an initial decision therein, or, if no initial decision is to be filed, prior to the time fixed for the filing of final briefs with the Commission; and

(k) Informing the parties as to the availability of one or more alternative means of dispute resolution, and encouraging the use of such methods.

[60 FR 32796, June 23, 1995, as amended at 69 FR 13176, Mar. 19, 2004; 70 FR 72569, Dec. 5, 2005]

§201.112 Hearing officer: Disqualification and withdrawal.

(a) *Notice of disqualification.* At any time a hearing officer believes himself or herself to be disqualified from considering a matter, the hearing officer shall issue a notice stating that he or she is withdrawing from the matter and setting forth the reasons therefor.

(b) *Motion for withdrawal.* Any party who has a reasonable, good faith basis to believe that a hearing officer has a personal bias, or is otherwise disqualified from hearing a case, may make a motion to the hearing officer that the hearing officer withdraw. The motion shall be accompanied by an affidavit setting forth in detail the facts alleged to constitute grounds for disqualification. If the hearing officer finds himself or herself not disqualified, he or she shall so rule and shall continue to preside over the proceeding.

§201.120 Ex parte communications.

(a) Except to the extent required for the disposition of *exparte* matters as authorized by law, the person presiding over an evidentiary hearing may not:

(1) Consult a person or party on a fact in issue, unless on notice and opportunity for all parties to participate; or

(2) Be responsible to or subject to the supervision or direction of an employee or agent engaged in the performance of investigative or prosecuting functions for the Commission.

(b) The Commission's code of behavior regarding*ex parte* communications between persons outside the Commission and decisional employees, 17 CFR 200.110 through 200.114, governs other prohibited communications during a proceeding conducted under the Rules of Practice.

动议及其他动议并作出裁定,包括请求改正初步决定中的明显事实错误的动议。根据本规则提起改正任何错误动议的,初步决定中应存在明显事实错误陈述,且动议必须在初步决定作出后10日内提交。改正动议提出后5日内,另一方可提交反驳陈辩书。任何反驳陈辩书提交后,听证官均应20日内就该动议作出裁定;

(i)按第201.360节制定初步决定;

(j)在向所有当事人发出通知的情况下,在向证券交易委员会提交初步决定之前(如不必提交初步决定,则在指定的向证券交易委员会提交最终决定摘要的时间之前)进行重新听证;及

(k)告知当事人可以采取一种或多种替代性争议解决方式,并鼓励当事人采取该等方式。

[《联邦公报》第60卷第32796页,1995年6月23日,修正索引:《联邦公报》第69卷第13176页,2004年3月19日;《联邦公报》第70卷第72569页,2005年12月5日。]

第201.112节　听证官:主动回避和申请回避

(a)主动回避通知。听证官在任何时候相信其应回避某一事项的审议的,应签发一份通知声明其将进行回避并说明原因。

(b)回避动议。任何一方合理、善意相信听证官存在个人偏见或因其他原因而应回避对某案的听证的,可以向听证官提出要求其回避的动议。动议应附上一份宣誓证词,详细说明其指称构成回避情形的事实。听证官认定其不存在回避情形的,应作出裁定并继续主持程序。

第201.120节　单方交流

(a)除了依据法律授权处理单方面事务之外,主持举证听证的程序的主审人不得:

(1)就争议事实咨询某人或一方当事人,除非已向所有当事人发送通知并为之提供参与机会;或

(2)监督、领导履行证券交易委员会调查或追诉职能的雇员或代理人或接受其监督、领导。

(b)根据《工作规则》开展的程序中其他被禁止的交流,应适用证券交易委员会关于外部主体与内部有决策权的雇员之间的单方交流的行为准则(《联邦规章汇编》第十七编第200.110~200.114节)。

§201.121 Separation of functions.

Any Commission officer, employee or agent engaged in the performance of investigative or prosecutorial functions for the Commission in a proceeding as defined in §201.101(a) may not, in that proceeding or one that is factually related, participate or advise in the decision, or in Commission review of the decision pursuant to Section 557 of the Administrative Procedure Act, 5 U.S.C. 557, except as a witness or counsel in the proceeding.

§201.140 Commission orders and decisions: Signature and availability.

(a) *Signature required.* All orders and decisions of the Commission shall be signed by the Secretary or any other person duly authorized by the Commission.

(b) *Availability for inspection.* Each order and decision shall be available for inspection by the public from the date of entry, unless the order or decision is nonpublic. A nonpublic order or decision shall be available for inspection by any person entitled to inspect it from the date of entry.

(c) *Date of entry of orders.* The date of entry of a Commission order shall be the date the order is signed. Such date shall be reflected in the caption of the order, or if there is no caption, in the order itself.

§201.141 Orders and decisions: Service of orders instituting proceedings and other orders and decisions.

(a) *Service of an order instituting proceedings*— (1) *By whom made.* The Secretary, or another duly authorized officer of the Commission, shall serve a copy of an order instituting proceedings on each person named in the order as a party. The Secretary may direct an interested division to assist in making service.

(2) *How made.* (i) *To individuals.* Notice of a proceeding shall be made to an individual by delivering a copy of the order instituting proceedings to the individual or to an agent authorized by appointment or by law to receive such notice. *Delivery* means — handing a copy of the order to the individual; or leaving a copy at the individual's office with a clerk or other person in charge thereof; or leaving a copy at the individual's dwelling house or usual place of abode with some person of suitable age and discretion then residing therein; or sending a copy of the order addressed to the individual by U.S. Postal Service certified, registered or Express Mail and obtaining a confirmation of receipt; or giving confirmed telegraphic notice.

(ii) *To corporations or entities.* Notice of a proceeding shall be made to a person other than a natural person by delivering a copy of the order instituting proceedings to an officer, managing or general agent, or any other agent authorized by appointment or law to receive such notice, by any method specified in paragraph (a)(2)(i) of this section, or, in the case of an issuer of a class of securities registered with the Commission, by sending

第201.121节　职权分离

第201.101(a)节所定义的代表证券交易委员会从事调查或追诉职能的任何证券交易委员会官员、职员或代理人,在同一程序或与之存在事实关联的程序中,不得参与决定或为决定提供建议,亦不得参与根据《行政程序法》第557条(《美国法典》第五编第557节)对决定进行的复议或为之提供建议,但作为证人或律师参与程序的除外。

第201.140节　证券交易委员会命令和决定:签名和提供

(a)签名要求。证券交易委员会的所有命令和决定均应由证券交易委员会秘书或证券交易委员会的任何其他获得正式授权的人签署。

(b)开放查阅。每一命令和决定,除非属于非公开命令和决定,均应自作出之日起开放给公众查阅。非公开命令和决定应自作出之日起开放给任何有权查阅的人查阅。

(c)命令作出日期。证券交易委员会命令签署之日即为其作出之日。上述日期应于命令标题之中注明,如无标题,应于命令正文中注明。

第201.141节　命令和决定:程序发起令和其他命令、决定的送达

(a)程序发起令的送达——(1)由作出命令的人送达。证券交易委员会秘书或其他获得正式授权的人应向程序发起令中列明的所有当事人发送命令。证券交易委员会秘书可以指示利害关系部门协助送达。

(2)送达方式。(i)向个人送达。向个人发送程序通知的,应向该个人或委任书指定的或法律授权的负责接收通知的代理人发送程序发起令。"送达"系指——向个人当面交付命令;在有文员或其他负责人在场的情况下将命令留置于该个人的办公室;在有年龄适当和具备辨识力的同住人员在场的情况下,将命令留置于该个人的住所或常住居所;通过美国邮政总局的带回执邮件、挂号邮件或快件寄送给该个人,并应取得收讫确认;或通过确认的电报通知进行送达。

(ii)向公司或实体送达。向非自然人发送程序通知的,应按照本节第(a)(2)(i)款规定的任何方式向委任书指定的或法律授权的负责接收通知的管理人员、管理代理人、一般代理人或任何其他代理人发送程序发起令;如被送达人发行的某一类证券已在证券交易委员会获得注册,可按其向证券交易委员会提交的最新文件所载地址,通过美国邮政总局的带回执邮件、挂号邮件或快件进行送达,并应取得送达确认。

a copy of the order addressed to the most recent address shown on the entity's most recent filing with the Commission by U.S. Postal Service certified, registered, or Express Mail and obtaining a confirmation of attempted delivery.

(iii) *Upon persons registered with the Commission.* In addition to any other method of service specified in paragraph (a)(2) of this section, notice may be made to a person currently registered with the Commission as a broker, dealer, municipal securities dealer, government securities broker, government securities dealer, investment adviser, investment company or transfer agent by sending a copy of the order addressed to the most recent business address shown on the person's registration form by U.S. Postal Service certified, registered or Express Mail and obtaining a confirmation of attempted delivery.

(iv) *Upon persons in a foreign country.* Notice of a proceeding to a person in a foreign country may be made by any method specified in paragraph (a)(2) of this section, or by any other method reasonably calculated to give notice, provided that the method of service used is not prohibited by the law of the foreign country.

(v) *In stop order proceedings.* Notwithstanding any other provision of paragraph (a)(2) of this section, in proceedings pursuant to Sections 8 or 10 of the Securities Act of 1933, 15 U.S.C. 77h or 77j, or Sections 305 or 307 of the Trust Indenture Act of 1939, 15 U.S.C. 77eee or 77ggg, notice of the institution of proceedings shall be made by personal service or confirmed telegraphic notice, or a waiver obtain pursuant to paragraph (a)(4) of this section.

(vi) *To persons registered with self-regulatory organizations.* Notice of a proceeding shall be made to a person registered with a self-regulatory organization by any method specified in paragraph (a)(2)(i) of this section, or by sending a copy of the order addressed to the most recent address for the person shown in the Central Registration Depository by U.S. Postal Service certified, registered, or Express Mail and obtaining a confirmation of attempted delivery.

(3) *Record of service.* The Secretary shall maintain a record of service on parties (in hard copy or computerized format), identifying the party given notice, the method of service, the date of service, the address to which service was made, and the person who made service. If service is made in person, the certificate of service shall state, if available, the name of the individual to whom the order was given. If service is made by U.S. Postal Service certified or Express Mail, the Secretary shall maintain the confirmation of receipt or of attempted delivery. If service is made to an agent authorized by appointment to receive service, the certificate of service shall be accompanied by evidence of the appointment.

(4) *Waiver of service.* In lieu of service as set forth in paragraph (a)(2) of this section, the party may be provided a copy of the order instituting proceedings by first

(iii)向证券交易委员会注册主体送达。除本节第(a)(2)款所述任何其他送达方式外,对于已在证券交易委员会注册的经纪商、自营商、市政证券自营商、政府证券经纪商、政府证券自营商、投资顾问、投资公司或过户代理人,可按该主体注册表格中所载最新办公地址,通过美国邮政总局的带回执邮件、挂号邮件或快件进行送达,并应取得送达确认。

(iv)向境外主体送达。向境外主体发送的程序通知,可按本节第(a)(2)款规定的任何方式或任何其他合理的通知送达方式发送,前提是所使用的送达方式不得为外国法律所禁止。

(v)停止令程序中的送达。无论本节第(a)(2)款是否存在任何其他相反规定,在根据《1933年证券法》第8条或第10条(《美国法典》第十五编第77h节或第77j节)或《1939年信托契约法》第305条或第307条(《美国法典》第十五编第77eee节或第77ggg节)发起的程序中,程序发起通知应通过专人送达或确认的电报通知进行送达,或根据本条第(a)(4)款取得豁免。

(vi)向自律组织注册主体送达。对已在自律组织注册的主体发送的程序通知,可按本节第(a)(2)(i)款规定的任何方式送达,或按该主体在中央注册存管系统登记的最新地址,通过美国邮政总局的带回执邮件、挂号邮件或快件进行送达,并应取得送达确认。

(3)送达记录。证券交易委员会秘书应保存向各方当事人进行送达的记录(记录保存形式包括纸质或电子形式),注明通知的被送达人、送达方式、送达日期、送达地址以及送达人。当面送达通知的,送达证明中应说明命令被送达人的姓名(如可获得)。通过美国邮政总局的带回执邮件或快件送达的,证券交易委员会秘书应保存收讫确认或送达确认。向委任书授权的收信代理人送达的,送达证明应附上委任书证明。

(4)送达豁免。作为本节第(a)(2)款规定的送达的替代,如已取得当事人的送达豁免并载入记录,可通过普通邮件或其他可靠方式向当事人送达该程序发起令。

class mail or other reliable means if a waiver of service is obtained from the party and placed in the record.

(b) *Service of orders or decisions other than an order instituting proceedings.* Written orders or decisions issued by the Commission or by a hearing officer shall be served promptly on each party pursuant to any method of service authorized under paragraph (a) of this section or §201.150(c)(1)-(3). Such orders or decisions may also be served by facsimile transmission if the party to be served has agreed to accept such service in a writing, signed by the party, and has provided the Commission with information concerning the facsimile machine telephone number and hours of facsimile machine operation. Service of orders or decisions by the Commission, including those entered pursuant to delegated authority, shall be made by the Secretary or, as authorized by the Secretary, by a member of an interested division. Service of orders or decisions issued by a hearing officer shall be made by the Secretary or the hearing officer.

[60 FR 32796, June 23, 1995, as amended at 69 FR 13176, Mar. 19, 2004; 70 FR 72569, Dec. 5, 2005]

§201.150 Service of papers by parties.

(a) *When required.* In every proceeding as defined in §201.101(a), each paper, including each notice of appearance, written motion, brief, or other written communication, shall be served upon each party in the proceeding in accordance with the provisions of this section; provided, however, that absent an order to the contrary, no service shall be required for motions which may be heard *ex parte*.

(b) *Upon a person represented by counsel.* Whenever service is required to be made upon a person represented by counsel who has filed a notice of appearance pursuant to §201.102, service shall be made pursuant to paragraph (c) of this section upon counsel, unless service upon the person represented is ordered by the Commission or the hearing officer.

(c) *How made.* Service shall be made by delivering a copy of the filing. *Delivery* means:

(1) Personal service — handing a copy to the person required to be served; or leaving a copy at the person's office with a clerk or other person in charge thereof, or, if there is no one in charge, leaving it in a conspicuous place therein; or, if the office is closed or the person to be served has no office, leaving it at the person's dwelling house or usual place of abode with some person of suitable age and discretion then residing therein;

(2) Mailing the papers through the U.S. Postal Service by first class, registered, or certified mail or Express Mail delivery addressed to the person;

(b)程序发起令之外的命令或决定的送达。证券交易委员会或听证官签发的书面命令或决定应按照本节第(a)款或第201.150(c)(1)~(3)节准许的任何送达方式及时向各方送达。如果被送达人签署书面文件表示同意,并已向证券交易委员会提供传真号码和传真机运行时间的信息,上述命令或决定也可通过传真送达。证券交易委员会作出的命令或决定,包括根据委托授权作出的命令和决定,应由证券交易委员会秘书或秘书委托授权的利害关系部门的成员送达。听证官签发的命令或决定,应由证券交易委员会秘书或听证官送达。

[《联邦公报》第60卷第32796页,1995年6月23日,修正索引:《联邦公报》第69卷第13176页,2004年3月19日;《联邦公报》第70卷第72569页,2005年12月5日。]

第201.150节　向当事人送达文件[1]

(a)需要送达的情形。在第201.101(a)节定义的所有程序中,每一文件,包括出席通知、书面动议、诉辩书或其他书面文件,均应按照本节规定向程序各方当事人送达;但是,如无相反命令,对于可以单方听证的动议,不必进行送达。

(b)向有律师代理的人进行送达。对于已按照第201.102节提交出席通知的有律师代理的人,应按照本节第(c)款之规定向律师进行送达,但证券交易委员会或听证官命令向被代理人送达的除外。

(c)送达方式。送达应通过交付相关的提交文件进行。"送达"系指:

(1)当面送达——将文件当面交付被送达人;在有文员或其他负责人在场的情况下将文件留置于该个人的办公室,如没有负责人在场,将文件留置于办公室的显著位置;如办公室已关闭或被送达人没有办公室,在有年龄适当和具备辨识力的同住人员在场的情况下,将文件留置于该个人的住所或常住居所;

(2)通过美国邮政总局的普通邮件、挂号邮件、带回执邮件或快件将文件寄送给该个人;

1　原文"Service of papers by parties"中的"by",按下文内容应为"to",即"向当事人送达的文件",译文已按后者处理。——译者注

(3) Sending the papers through a commercial courier service or express delivery service; or

(4) Transmitting the papers by facsimile transmission where the following conditions are met:

(i) The persons so serving each other have provided the Commission and the parties with notice of the facsimile machine telephone number to be used and the hours of facsimile machine operation;

(ii) The transmission is made at such a time that it is received during the Commission's business hours as defined in §201.104; and

(iii) The sender of the transmission previously has not been served in accordance with §201.150 with a written notice from the recipient of the transmission declining service by facsimile transmission.

(d) *When service is complete.* Personal service, service by U.S. Postal Service Express Mail or service by a commercial courier or express delivery service is complete upon delivery. Service by mail is complete upon mailing. Service by facsimile is complete upon confirmation of transmission by delivery of a manually signed receipt.

[60 FR 32796, June 23, 1995, as amended at 69 FR 13176, Mar. 19, 2004]

§201.151 Filing of papers with the Commission: Procedure.

(a) *When to file.* All papers required to be served by a party upon any person shall be filed contemporaneously with the Commission. Papers required to be filed with the Commission must be received within the time limit, if any, for such filing. Filing with the Commission may be made by facsimile transmission if the party also contemporaneously transmits to the Commission a non-facsimile original with a manual signature. However, any person filing with the Commission by facsimile transmission will be responsible for assuring that the Commission receives a complete and legible filing within the time limit set for such filing.

(b) *Where to file.* Filing of papers with the Commission shall be made by filing them with the Secretary. When a proceeding is assigned to a hearing officer, a person making a filing with the Secretary shall promptly provide to the hearing officer a copy of any such filing, provided, however, that the hearing officer may direct or permit filings to be made with him or her, in which event the hearing officer shall note thereon the filing date and promptly provide the Secretary with either the original or a copy of any such filings.

(c) *To whom to direct the filing.* Unless otherwise provided, where the Commission has assigned a case to a hearing officer, all motions, objections, applications or other filings made during a proceeding prior to the filing of an initial decision therein, or, if no initial decision is to be filed, prior to the time fixed for the filing of briefs with the

(3)通过商业速递服务或快递服务发送文件;或

(4)通过传真传送文件,但以满足下述条件为前提:

(i)以此等方式向彼此进行送达的人已向证券交易委员会及各当事人提供传真号码和传真机运行时间的信息;

(ii)传送时间应保证证券交易委员会在第201.104节定义的工作时间内收到文件;且

(iii)通过传真发送文件的一方未曾收到接收方按照第201.150节发送的拒绝传真送达的书面通知。

(d)送达完成时间。通过当面送达、美国邮政总局快件、商业速递或快递服务进行送达的,于交付之时视为完成送达。通过邮件进行送达的,于邮件寄抵之时视为完成送达。通过传真进行送达的,于交付手签回执确认传真送达之时视为完成。

[《联邦公报》第60卷第32796页,1995年6月23日,修正索引:《联邦公报》第69卷第13176页,2004年3月19日。]

第201.151节　向证券交易委员会提交文件:程序

(a)提交时间。一方当事人应向任何人送达的文件,均应同时向证券交易委员会提交。应向证券交易委员会提交的文件,必须保证证券交易委员会在提交时限内(如有)收悉。当事人亦可通过传真方式向证券交易委员会提交文件,但必须同时提交一份手签非传真原件。但是,通过传真发送向证券交易委员会提交文件的任何人,均应负责确保证券交易委员会在提交时限内收到完整、可清晰辨认的提交文件。

(b)提交地点。向证券交易委员会提交的文件应提交至证券交易委员会秘书。对于已指派听证官主持的程序,向证券交易委员会秘书提交文件的人应及时向听证官提交一份复本,但是听证官可以指示或允许仅向其本人进行文件提交,此时,听证官应注明提交日期,并及时向证券交易委员会秘书提供任何该等文件的原件或复本。

(c)提交文件之分发对象。除非另有规定,证券交易委员会已指派听证官处理某一案件的,在提交案件的初步决定之前(如不必提交初步决定,则在指定的向证券交易委员会提交最终决定摘要的时间之前),程序中的所有动议、反对、申请或其他文件均

Commission, shall be directed to and decided by the hearing officer.

(d) *Certificate of service.* Papers filed with the Commission or a hearing officer shall be accompanied by a certificate stating the name of the person or persons served, the date of service, the method of service and the mailing address or facsimile telephone number to which service was made, if not made in person. If the method of service to any party is different from the method of service to any other party or the method for filing with the Commission, the certificate shall state why a different means of service was used.

[60 FR 32796, June 23, 1995, as amended at 69 FR 13176, Mar. 19, 2004]

§201.152 Filing of papers: Form.

(a) *Specifications.* Papers filed in connection with any proceeding as defined in §201.101(a) shall:

(1) Be on one grade of unglazed white paper measuring 81/2×11 inches, except that, to the extent that the reduction of larger documents would render them illegible, such documents may be filed on larger paper;

(2) Be typewritten or printed in 12-point or larger typeface or otherwise reproduced by a process that produces permanent and plainly legible copies;

(3) Include at the head of the paper, or on a title page, the name of the Commission, the title of the proceeding, the names of the parties, the subject of the particular paper or pleading, and the file number assigned to the proceeding;

(4) Be paginated with left hand margins at least 1 inch wide, and other margins of at least 1 inch;

(5) Be double-spaced, with single-spaced footnotes and single-spaced indented quotations; and

(6) Be stapled, clipped or otherwise fastened in the upper left corner.

(b) *Signature required.* All papers must be dated and signed as provided in §201.153.

(c) *Suitability for recordkeeping.* Documents which, in the opinion of the Commission, are not suitable for computer scanning or microfilming may be rejected.

(d) *Number of copies.* An original and three copies of all papers shall be filed, unless filing is made by facsimile in accordance with §201.151. If filing is made by facsimile, the filer shall also transmit to the Office of the Secretary one non-facsimile original with a manual signature, contemporaneously with the facsimile transmission. The non-facsimile original must be accompanied by a statement of the date on which, and the facsimile number to which, the party made transmission of the facsimile filing.

(e) *Form of briefs.* All briefs containing more than 10 pages shall include a table of contents, an alphabetized table of cases, a table of statutes, and a table of other authorities

应分发给听证官,并由听证官裁决。

(d)送达证明。向证券交易委员会或听证官提交的文件应附上一份证明,说明被送达人姓名/名称、送达日期、送达方式、邮寄地址或接收送达的传真号码(如未使用当面送达方式)。如果向任何当事人进行送达的方式不同于向任何其他当事人送达的方式或向证券交易委员会提交文件的方式,证明中应说明采用不同送达方式的原因。

[《联邦公报》第60卷第32796页,1995年6月23日,修正索引:《联邦公报》第69卷第13176页,2004年3月19日。]

第201.152节　文件提交:格式

(a)规格。与第201.101(a)节定义的任何程序相关的提交文件均应:

(1)采用8.5×11英寸(21.59×27.94厘米)的一级无光白纸,但是,如文件规格大于此,且缩小规格将导致文字难以辨认的,可采用大规格纸张提交文件;

(2)采用12磅或以上的字体进行打字或印刷,或通过其他复制程序形成永久性和清晰、易辨认的复本;

(3)在文件抬头或标题页中注明证券交易委员会名称、程序名称、当事人名称、具体文件或诉辩状的主题以及为程序分配的文件编号;

(4)左边距及其他边距均不得低于1英寸(2.54厘米);

(5)采用双倍行距,脚注采用单倍行距,引文采用首行缩进、单倍行距;且

(6)在左上角装订、别住或以其他方式固定。

(b)签字要求。所有文件均应按第201.153节的规定注明日期并签字。

(c)适于记录保存。证券交易委员会认为不适于电脑扫描或微缩胶片处理的文件,可予以拒绝。

(d)文本数量。所有文件均应提供一份原件和三份复本,但按第201.151节的规定通过传真提交文件的除外。通过传真提交文件的,文件提交人还应同时向证券交易委员会秘书办公室提交一份手签非传真原件,并附上一份声明,说明通过传真提交文件的日期以及接收传真的传真号。

(e)陈辩书格式。所有10页以上的陈辩书均应包含目录表、按字母顺序排列的案例索引表、制定法表及其他依据索引表,并说明引用上述案例、制定法和其他依据的

cited, with references to the pages of the brief wherein they are cited.

(f) *Scandalous or impertinent matter.* Any scandalous or impertinent matter contained in any brief or pleading or in connection with any oral presentation in a proceeding may be stricken on order of the Commission or the hearing officer.

[60 FR 32796, June 23, 1995, as amended at 69 FR 13176, Mar. 19, 2004; 70 FR 72569, Dec. 5, 2005]

§201.153 Filing of papers: Signature requirement and effect.

(a) *General requirements.* Following the issuance of an order instituting proceedings, every filing of a party represented by counsel shall be signed by at least one counsel of record in his or her name and shall state that counsel's business address and telephone number. A party who acts as his or her own counsel shall sign his or her individual name and state his or her address and telephone number on every filing.

(b) *Effect of signature.* (1) The signature of a counsel or party shall constitute a certification that:

(i) the person signing the filing has read the filing;

(ii) to the best of his or her knowledge, information, and belief, formed after reasonable inquiry, the filing is well grounded in fact and is warranted by existing law or a good faith argument for the extension, modification, or reversal of existing law; and

(iii) the filing is not made for any improper purpose, such as to harass or to cause unnecessary delay or needless increase in the cost of adjudication.

(2) If a filing is not signed, the hearing officer or the Commission shall strike the filing, unless it is signed promptly after the omission is called to the attention of the person making the filing.

§201.154 Motions.

(a) *Generally.* Unless made during a hearing or conference, a motion shall be in writing, shall state with particularity the grounds therefor, shall set forth the relief or order sought, and shall be accompanied by a written brief of the points and authorities relied upon. All written motions shall be served in accordance with §201.150, be filed in accordance with §201.151, meet the requirements of §201.152, and be signed in accordance with §201.153. The Commission or the hearing officer may order that an oral motion be submitted in writing. Unless otherwise ordered by the Commission or the hearing officer, if a motion is properly made to the Commission concerning a proceeding to which a hearing officer is assigned, the proceeding before the hearing officer shall continue pending the determination of the motion by the Commission. No oral argument shall be heard on any motion unless the Commission or the hearing officer otherwise directs.

(b) *Opposing and reply briefs.* Except as provided in §201.401, briefs in opposition

页码。

(f)诽谤性或无关事项。任何陈辩书或诉辩状中出现与程序口头陈述相关的任何诽谤性或无关事项的,证券交易委员会或听证官可发布命令予以删除。

[《联邦公报》第60卷第32796页,1995年6月23日,修正索引:《联邦公报》第69卷第13176页,2004年3月19日;《联邦公报》第70卷第72569页,2005年12月5日。]

第201.153节　文件提交:签字要求及效力

(a)一般要求。程序发起令签发之后,有律师代理的当事人所提交的每份文件均应至少由一名正式代理律师以自身名义签署,并说明律师的办公地址和电话号码。自行代理的当事人,应在每份提交文件上签署其本人姓名并注明其地址和电话号码。

(b)签字效力。(1)律师或当事人的签字应构成如下事项的证明:

(i)提交文件的签字人已阅读提交文件;

(ii)根据签字人具有的知识、信息及进行合理询问后形成的信念,提交文件存在有力的事实根据,为现行法律所支持,或存在延伸、修改或推翻现行法律的善意根据;及

(iii)提交文件非出于任何不当目的,如干扰裁决、对裁决造成不必要的拖延或不必要地增加裁决成本。

(2)提交文件未签字的,听证官或证券交易委员会应予以驳回,但文件提交人在被告知上述疏漏后及时补签的除外。

第201.154节　动议

(a)一般规定。除听证或会议中提出的动议外,所有动议均应采用书面形式,说明其作出理由、所寻求的救济或命令,并附上其理由和依据的书面陈辩书。所有书面动议均应按第201.150节的规定送达,按第201.151节的规定提交,遵守第201.152节的要求并按第201.153节的规定签字。对于口头动议,证券交易委员会或听证官可以命令以书面形式提交。除非证券交易委员会或听证官另有命令,否则,如果在已指派听证官的程序中向证券交易委员会提出恰当的动议,听证官在证券交易委员会对任何动议做出裁定之前应继续主持程序。除非证券交易委员会或听证官另有指示,否则不得就任何动议听取口头辩论。

(b)反对和答复陈辩书。除第201.401节规定的情形外,针对动议提出的反对陈辩

to a motion shall be filed within five days after service of the motion. Reply briefs shall be filed within three days after service of the opposition.

(c) *Length limitation.* No motion (together with the brief in support of the motion), brief in opposition to the motion, or reply brief shall exceed 7,000 words, exclusive of any table of contents or table of authorities. The word limit shall not apply to any addendum that consists solely of copies of applicable cases, pertinent legislative provisions or rules, or relevant exhibits. Requests for leave to file motions and briefs in excess of 7,000 words are disfavored. A motion or brief, together with any accompanying brief, that does not exceed 15 pages in length, exclusive of pages containing the table of contents, table of authorities, and any addendum that consists solely of copies of applicable cases, pertinent legislative provisions, or rules and exhibits, but inclusive of pleadings incorporated by reference, is presumptively considered to contain no more than 7,000 words. Any motion or brief that exceeds these page limits must include a certificate by the attorney, or an unrepresented party, stating that the document complies with the length limitation set forth in this paragraph and stating the number of words in the document. The person preparing the certificate may rely on the word count of a word–processing program to prepare the document.

[60 FR 32796, June 23, 1995, as amended at 69 FR 13177, Mar. 19, 2004; 70 FR 72569, Dec. 5, 2005]

§201.155 Default; motion to set aside default.

(a) A party to a proceeding may be deemed to be in default and the Commission or the hearing officer may determine the proceeding against that party upon consideration of the record, including the order instituting proceedings, the allegations of which may be deemed to be true, if that party fails:

(1) To appear, in person or through a representative, at a hearing or conference of which that party has been notified;

(2) To answer, to respond to a dispositive motion within the time provided, or otherwise to defend the proceeding; or

(3) To cure a deficient filing within the time specified by the commission or the hearing officer pursuant to §201.180(b).

(b) A motion to set aside a default shall be made within a reasonable time, state the reasons for the failure to appear or defend, and specify the nature of the proposed defense in the proceeding. In order to prevent injustice and on such conditions as may be appropriate, the hearing officer, at any time prior to the filing of the initial decision, or the Commission, at any time, may for good cause shown set aside a default.

§201.160 Time computation.

(a) *Computation.* In computing any period of time prescribed in or allowed by these

书应于动议送达后5日内提交。答复陈辩书应于反对陈辩书送达后3日内提交。

(c)篇幅限制。任何动议(包括支持动议的陈辩书)、反对陈辩书或答复陈辩书均不得超过7000字(不包括目录和法律依据索引表)。完全由适用案例、相关立法条文或规则或相关证据构成的任何附录,不受此字数限制。证券交易委员会不鼓励提交超过7000字的动议和陈辩书的请求。动议、陈辩书以及附随的陈辩书如篇幅不超过15页,将被推定和视为不超过7000字,上述页数不包括目录、法律依据索引表以及完全由适用案例、相关立法条文或规则或相关证据构成的附录的页数,但包括通过引用而纳入的诉辩状。超出上述页数限制的任何动议或陈辩书必须附上一份律师证明或当事人本人(如其没有代理律师)出具的证明,说明该文件符合本款规定的篇幅限制,并注明该文件的字数。编制上述证明的人可以采信编制该文件的文字处理程序的字数统计结果。

[《联邦公报》第60卷第32796页,1995年6月23日,修正索引:《联邦公报》第69卷第13177页,2004年3月19日;《联邦公报》第70卷第72569页,2005年12月5日。]

第201.155节　缺席决定;撤销缺席决定之动议

(a)如果程序一方当事人出现下述情形,该当事人可被视为缺席,证券交易委员会或听证官可在审议记录(包括程序发起令)后对该当事人作出不利决定:

(1)当事人在已获得通知的情况下,未能亲自或委派代理人出席听证或会议;

(2)当事人未能在规定时间内针对处置性动议作出答辩、回复或进行其他形式的抗辩;或

(3)当事人未能在证券交易委员会或听证官依据第201.180(b)节规定的时间内对有缺陷的提交文件进行补正。

(b)撤销缺席决定的动议应在合理时间内作出,并说明未能到场或未进行抗辩的原因以及拟进行的抗辩之性质。为防止不公正现象的产生,缺席决定可由听证官在提交初步决定之前的任何时间基于适当条件撤销,或由证券交易委员会在任何时间基于正当理由撤销。

第201.160节　时间计算

(a)计算。在计算《工作规则》或证券交易委员会命令中规定或允许的任何期限之

Rules of Practice or by order of the Commission, the day of the act, event, or default from which the designated period of time begins to run shall not be included. The last day of the period so computed shall be included unless it is a Saturday, Sunday, or Federal legal holiday (as defined in §201.104), in which event the period runs until the end of the next day that is not a Saturday, Sunday, or Federal legal holiday. Intermediate Saturdays, Sundays, and Federal legal holidays shall be excluded from the computation when the period of time prescribed or allowed is seven days or less, not including any additional time allowed for service by mail in paragraph (b) of this section. If on the day a filing is to be made, weather or other conditions have caused the Secretary's office or other designated filing location to close, the filing deadline shall be extended to the end of the next day that is neither a Saturday, a Sunday, nor a Federal legal holiday.

(b) *Additional time for service by mail.* If service is made by mail, three days shall be added to the prescribed period for response unless an order of the Commission or the hearing officer specifies a date certain for filing. In the event that an order of the Commission or the hearing officer specifies a date certain for filing, no time shall be added for service by mail.

[60 FR 32796, June 23, 1995, as amended at 69 FR 13177, Mar. 19, 2004]

§201.161 Extensions of time, postponements and adjournments.

(a) *Availability.* Except as otherwise provided by law, the Commission, at any time, or the hearing officer, at any time prior to the filing of his or her initial decision or, if no initial decision is to be filed, at any time prior to the closing of the record, may, for good cause shown, extend or shorten any time limits prescribed by these Rules of Practice for the filing of any papers and may, consistent with paragraphs (b) and (c) of this section, postpone or adjourn any hearing.

(b) *Considerations in determining whether to extend time limits or grant postponements, adjournments and extensions.* (1) In considering all motions or requests pursuant to paragraph (a) or (b) of this section, the Commission or the hearing officer should adhere to a policy of strongly disfavoring such requests, except in circumstances where the requesting party makes a strong showing that the denial of the request or motion would substantially prejudice their case. In determining whether to grant any requests, the Commission or hearing officer shall consider, in addition to any other relevant factors:

(i) The length of the proceeding to date;

(ii) The number of postponements, adjournments or extensions already granted;

(iii) The stage of the proceedings at the time of the request;

(iv) The impact of the request on the hearing officer's ability to complete the

时,指定期限起算的行为、事件发生之日或缺席发生之日不应计算在内,但按上述方式计算的期限的最后之日应包括在内,除非该日为周六、周日或联邦法定节假日(定义见第201.104节)。如最后一日为周六、周日或联邦法定节假日,相关期限应截至下一个非周六、非周日、非联邦法定节假日之日结束之时。如规定或允许的期限[不包括本节第(b)款允许的邮寄送达的任何延长期限]不长于7日,期限中间出现的周六、周日或联邦法定节假日不计算在内。如文件提交日的天气或其他状况导致证券交易委员会秘书办公室或其他指定提交地点关闭的,文件提交最后期限应延长至下一个非周六、非周日、非联邦法定节假日之日结束之时。

(b)邮寄送达的延长期限。通过邮寄送达的,规定的答复期限应延长3日,但证券交易委员会或听证官发布命令指定了具体提交日期的除外。证券交易委员会或听证官发布命令指定具体提交日期的,不得延长邮寄送达的期限。

[《联邦公报》第60卷第32796页,1995年6月23日,修正索引:《联邦公报》第69卷第13177页,2004年3月19日。]

第201.161节　时限延长、推迟和延期

(a)适用情形。除法律另有规定的情形外,证券交易委员会可以在任何时间,听证官亦可以在提交其初步决定之前(如不必提交初步决定,则于记录封档之前)的任何时间,基于正当理由,延长或缩短《工作规则》就文件提交规定的任何时限,并可以按照本节第(b)款和第(c)款的规定,推迟或延期任何听证。

(b)判定是否延长期限及是否核准推迟、延期和延长申请时限的考量因素。(1)在根据本节第(a)款或第(b)款审议所有动议或请求之时,证券交易委员会或听证官应遵守强烈不鼓励该等请求的政策,除非请求方有力地证明拒绝其请求或动议将对案件造成实质偏见。在判定是否核准该等请求之时,除任何其他相关因素之外,证券交易委员会还应考虑如下因素:

(i)截至当日程序已经持续的时间;
(ii)已经核准的推迟、延期或时限延长的天数;
(iii)请求提出之时程序所处的阶段;
(iv)该等请求对听证官在证券交易委员会规定的时限内终结程序的能力造成的

proceeding in the time specified by the Commission; and

(v) Any other such matters as justice may require.

(2) To the extent that the Commission has chosen a timeline under which the hearing would occur beyond the statutory 60-day deadline, this policy of strongly disfavoring requests for postponement will not apply to a request by a respondent to postpone commencement of a cease and desist proceeding hearing beyond the statutory 60-day period.

(c)(1) *Time limit.* Postponements, adjournments or extensions of time for filing papers shall not exceed 21 days unless the Commission or the hearing officer states on the record or sets forth in a written order the reasons why a longer period of time is necessary.

(2) *Stay pending Commission consideration of offers of settlement.* (i) If the Commission staff and one or more respondents in the proceeding file a joint motion notifying the hearing officer that they have agreed in principle to a settlement on all major terms, then the hearing officer shall stay the proceeding as to the settling respondent(s), or in the discretion of the hearing officer as to all respondents, pending completion of Commission consideration of the settlement offer. Any such stay will be contingent upon:

(A) The settling respondent(s) submitting to the Commission staff, within fifteen business days of the stay, a signed offer of settlement in conformance with §201.240; and

(B) Within twenty business days of receipt of the signed offer, the staff submitting the settlement offer and accompanying recommendation to the Commission for consideration.

(ii) If the parties fail to meet either of these deadlines or if the Commission rejects the offer of settlement, the hearing officer must be promptly notified and, upon notification of the hearing officer, the stay shall lapse and the proceeding will continue. In the circumstance where:

(A) A hearing officer has granted a stay because the parties have "agreed in principle to a settlement;"

(B) The agreement in principle does not materialize into a signed settlement offer within 15 business days of the stay; and

(C) The stay lapses, the hearing officer will not be required to grant another stay related to the settlement process until both parties have notified the hearing officer in writing that a signed settlement offer has been prepared, received by the Commission's staff, and will be submitted to the Commission.

(iii) The granting of any stay pursuant to this paragraph (c) shall not affect any deadline set pursuant to §201.360.

[60 FR 32796, June 23, 1995, as amended at 68 FR 35788, June 17, 2003]

影响;及

(v)为实现公正需要考量的任何其他事项。

(2)如果在证券交易委员会选择的时间框架下,听证时间将超出法定的60日期限,被申诉人请求将制止令程序听证开始时间推迟至该60日法定期限之后的请求,不适用本强烈不鼓励延期请求的政策。

(c)(1)时限。文件提交时间的推迟、延期或延长不得超过21日,但证券交易委员会或听证官在记录中载明或在书面命令中说明有必要核准更长的期限并说明相关原因的除外。

(2)证券交易委员会审议和解要约期间的程序中止。(i)证券交易委员会工作人员及程序的一个或多个相对人联合提交动议,通知听证官其已经就所有重大和解条款达成原则一致的,听证官应在证券交易委员会完成对和解要约的审议之前,中止程序对进行和解的相对人的适用;听证官亦可依其自由裁量决定中止程序对所有相对人的适用。上述程序中止之适用以满足如下条件为前提:

(A)进行和解的相对人在程序中止后15个工作日内向证券交易委员会工作人员呈报一份符合第201.240节规定的已签署的和解要约;且

(B)证券交易委员会工作人员在收到已签署要约后20个工作日内将和解要约和相关建议呈报给证券交易委员会审议。

(ii)如果当事人未能满足上述任一期限要求,或证券交易委员会驳回该和解要约,须及时通知听证官,听证官获得通知之时,中止令即应失效,程序应继续开展。出现下述情形时:

(A)基于当事人已"原则上同意和解",听证官已签发中止令;

(B)双方达成的原则一致未能在程序中止后15个工作日内形成已签署的和解要约;且

(C)中止已失效,则听证官不必再次授予与和解程序相关的中止令,直至当事人双方书面通知听证官已准备已签署的和解要约,且证券交易委员会工作人员已收悉上述要约并将呈报给证券交易委员会。

(iii)根据本第(c)款授予的任何中止令不影响第201.360节的任何期限规定。

[《联邦公报》第60卷第32796页,1995年6月23日,修正索引:《联邦公报》第68卷第35788页,2003年6月17日。]

§201.180 Sanctions.

(a) *Contemptuous conduct* — (1) *Subject to exclusion or suspension.* Contemptuous conduct by any person before the Commission or a hearing officer during any proceeding, including any conference, shall be grounds for the Commission or the hearing officer to:

(i) Exclude that person from such hearing or conference, or any portion thereof; and/or

(ii) Summarily suspend that person from representing others in the proceeding in which such conduct occurred for the duration, or any portion, of the proceeding.

(2) *Review procedure.* A person excluded from a hearing or conference, or a counsel summarily suspended from practice for the duration or any portion of a proceeding, may seek review of the exclusion or suspension by filing with the Commission, within three days of the exclusion or suspension order, a motion to vacate the order. The Commission shall consider such motion on an expedited basis as provided in §201.500.

(3) *Adjournment.* Upon motion by a party represented by counsel subject to an order of exclusion or suspension, an adjournment shall be granted to allow the retention of new counsel. In determining the length of an adjournment, the Commission or hearing officer shall consider, in addition to the factors set forth in §201.161, the availability of co-counsel for the party or of other members of a suspended counsel's firm.

(b) *Deficient filings; leave to cure deficiencies.* The Commission or the hearing officer may reject, in whole or in part, any filing that fails to comply with any requirements of these Rules of Practice or of any order issued in the proceeding in which the filing was made. Any such filings shall not be part of the record. The Commission or the hearing officer may direct a party to cure any deficiencies and to resubmit the filing within a fixed time period.

(c) *Failure to make required filing or to cure deficient filing.* The Commission or the hearing officer may enter a default pursuant to §201.155, dismiss the case, decide the particular matter at issue against that person, or prohibit the introduction of evidence or exclude testimony concerning that matter if a person fails:

(1) To make a filing required under these Rules of Practice; or

(2) To cure a deficient filing within the time specified by the Commission or the hearing officer pursuant to paragraph (b) of this section.

§201.190 Confidential treatment of information in certain filings.

(a) *Application.* An application for confidential treatment pursuant to the provisions of Clause 30 of Schedule A of the Securities Act of 1933, 15 U.S.C. 77aa(30), and Rule 406 thereunder, 17 CFR 230.406; Section 24(b)(2) of the Securities Exchange Act of 1934, 15 U.S.C. 78x(b)(2), and Rule 24b-2 thereunder, 17 CFR 240.24b-2; Section 22 (b)of the Public Utility Holding Company Act of 1935, 15 U.S.C. 79v(b), and Rule 104 thereunder, 17 CFR 250.104; Section 45(a) of the Investment Company Act of 1940, 15

第201.180节 罚则

(a)藐视行为——(1)驱逐程序或暂停代理资格。任何人在任何程序(包括会议)中出现对证券交易委员会或听证官的藐视行为的,证券交易委员会或听证官可以据此:

(i)将其驱逐出听证或会议或其中的任何部分程序;及/或

(ii)立即暂停其在出现藐视行为的程序中或其任何部分程序中代理他人的资格。

(2)复议程序。被驱逐出听证或会议的人,或被立即暂停在程序或任何部分程序中办理代理业务资格的律师,可以在驱逐或暂停资格令发布后3日内向证券交易委员会申请复议,提交撤销命令的动议。证券交易委员会应按照第201.500节的规定及时审议该动议。

(3)休庭。律师被驱逐或暂停代理资格的,经其代理的当事人提出动议,应核准休庭,以便当事人重新聘请律师。在确定休庭时间时,除第201.161节规定的因素外,证券交易委员会或听证官还应考虑当事人是否可以获得协理律师的服务,或是否可以获得被暂停代理资格的律师所在事务所的其他律师的服务。

(b)文件缺陷;补正缺陷许可。对于不符合《工作规则》要求或相关程序中发布的任何命令的文件,证券交易委员会或听证官可予以全部或部分驳回。任何被驳回的文件不得载入记录。证券交易委员会或听证官可以指示一方当事人在指定期限内补正所有缺陷并重新提交文件。

(c)不提交规定文件或不补正文件缺陷的情形。在下述情形下,证券交易委员会或听证官可以根据第201.155节作出缺席裁决、驳回案件、就具体事项针对相关主体作出不利决定或禁止就相关事项提供证据或排除相关证词:

(1)相关主体未能按照《工作规则》提交文件;或

(2)相关主体未能在证券交易委员会或听证官根据本节第(b)款规定的时间内补正缺陷。

第201.190节 对特定提交文件所含信息的保密处理

(a)申请。根据以下规定提出的保密处理申请应向证券交易委员会秘书长提交:《1933年证券法》附表A第30项[《美国法典》第十五编第77aa(30)节]以及依其颁发的《406规则》[《联邦规章汇编》第十七编第230.406节;《1934年证券交易法》第24(b)(2)条《美国法典》第十五编第78x(b)(2)节]以及依其颁发的《24b-2规则》(《联邦规章汇编》第十七编第240.24b-2节);《1935年公用事业控股公司法》第22(b)条[《美国法典》第十五编第79v(b)节]以及依其颁发的《104规则》(《联邦规章汇编》第十七编第250.104

U.S.C. 80a–44(a), and Rule 45a–1 thereunder, 17 CFR 270.45a–1; or Section 210(a)of the Investment Advisers Act of 1940, 15 U.S.C. 80b–10(a), shall be filed with the Secretary. The application shall be accompanied by a sealed copy of the materials as to which confidential treatment is sought.

(b) *Procedure for supplying additional information.* The applicant may be required to furnish in writing additional information with respect to the grounds for objection to public disclosure. Failure to supply the information so requested within 14 days from the date of receipt by the applicant of a notice of the information required shall be deemed a waiver of the objection to public disclosure of that portion of the information to which the additional information relates, unless the Commission or the hearing officer shall otherwise order for good cause shown at or before the expiration of such 14–day period.

(c) *Confidentiality of materials pending final decision.* Pending the determination of the application for confidential treatment, transcripts, non–final orders including an initial decision, if any, and other materials in connection with the application shall be placed under seal; shall be for the confidential use only of the hearing officer, the Commission, the applicant, and any other parties and counsel; and shall be made available to the public only in accordance with orders of the Commission.

(d) *Public availability of orders.* Any final order of the Commission denying or sustaining an application for confidential treatment shall be made public. Any prior findings or opinions relating to an application for confidential treatment under this section shall be made public at such time as the material as to which confidentiality was requested is made public.

§201.191 Adjudications not required to be determined on the record after notice and opportunity for hearing.

(a) *Scope of the rule.* This rule applies to every case of adjudication, as defined in 5 U.S.C. 551, pursuant to any statute which the Commission administers, where adjudication is not required to be determined on the record after notice and opportunity for hearing and which the Commission has not chosen to determine on the record after notice and opportunity for hearing.

(b) *Procedure.* In every case of adjudication under paragraph (a) of this section, the Commission shall give prompt notice of any adverse action or final disposition to any person who has requested the Commission to make (or not to make) any such adjudication, and furnish to any such person a written statement of reasons therefor. Additional procedures may be specified in rules relating to specific types of such adjudications. Where any such rule provides for the publication of a Commission order, notice of the action or disposition shall be deemed to be given by such publication.

(c) *Contents of the record.* If the Commission provides notice and opportunity for the

节);《1940年投资公司法》第45(a)条[《美国法典》第十五编第80a-44(a)节]以及依其颁发的《45a-1规则》(《联邦规章汇编》第十七编第270.45a-1节);或《1940年投资顾问法》第210(a)条[《美国法典》第十五编第80b-10(a)节]。申请应附上申请人寻求保密处理的材料的密封复本。

(b)提供补充信息的程序。申请人可能被要求提供书面补充信息,以说明反对公开披露的理由。申请人未在收到要求提供信息的通知后14日内按要求提供信息的,将被视为放弃反对公开披露相关部分的信息,但证券交易委员会或听证官在上述14日的期限届满之时或之前基于正当理由另行发布命令的除外。

(c)最终决定作出之前材料的保密性。在就保密处理申请作出决定之前,所有笔录、非终局命令,包括初步决定(如有)以及与申请相关的其他材料均应进行密封,仅得供听证官、证券交易委员会、申请人以及任何其他当事人和律师保密使用,且只有证券交易委员会发布命令时始得向公众提供。

(d)命令的公开。证券交易委员会发布的驳回或支持保密处理申请的所有终局命令均应公开。之前作出的与本节中的保密处理申请相关的任何认定或意见的公开时间应为被申请保密的材料公开之时。

第201.191节 不必给予通知和听证机会并且记录在案的裁决程序

(a)规则适用范围。对于所有行政裁决案件(定义见《美国法典》第五编第551节),如证券交易委员会根据其负责实施的制定法不必给予通知和听证机会,也不必将裁决记录在案,且证券交易委员会未选择给予当事人通知和听证机会并将裁决记录在案的,适用本规则。

(b)程序步骤。对于本节第(a)款中的所有裁决,证券交易委员会均应将所有相关的不利行动或最终处理结果及时通知请求证券交易委员会作出(或不作出)裁决的任何人,并提供一份关于该等行动或处理的理由的书面说明。根据适用于具体类型的裁决程序的规则,证券交易委员会可能还需要履行其他程序步骤。如该等规则要求公布证券交易委员会的命令,关于行动或处理的通知的发出时间应视为命令公布之时。

(c)记录内容。证券交易委员会向当事人或其他利害关系人(视情况而定)发出通

submission of written comments by parties to the adjudication or, as the case may be, by other interested persons, written comments received on or before the closing date for comments, unless accorded confidential treatment pursuant to statute or rule of the Commission, become a part of the record of the adjudication. The Commission, in its discretion, may accept and include in the record written comments filed with the Commission after the closing date.

§201.192 Rulemaking: Issuance, amendment and repeal of rules of general application.

(a) *By petition.* Any person desiring the issuance, amendment or repeal of a rule of general application may file a petition therefor with the Secretary. Such petition shall include a statement setting forth the text or the substance of any proposed rule or amendment desired or specifying the rule the repeal of which is desired, and stating the nature of his or her interest and his or her reasons for seeking the issuance, amendment or repeal of the rule. The Secretary shall acknowledge, in writing, receipt of the petition and refer it to the appropriate division or office for consideration and recommendation. Such recommendations shall be transmitted with the petition to the Commission for such action as the Commission deems appropriate. The Secretary shall notify the petitioner of the action taken by the Commission.

(b) *Notice of proposed issuance, amendment or repeal of rules.* Except where the Commission finds that notice and public procedure are impracticable, unnecessary, or contrary to the public interest, whenever the Commission proposes to issue, amend, or repeal any rule or regulation of general application other than an interpretive rule; general statement of policy; or rule of agency organization, procedure, or practice; or any matter relating to agency management or personnel or to public property, loans, grants, benefits, or contracts, there shall first be published in the Federal Register a notice of the proposed action. Such notice shall include:

(1) A statement of the time, place, and nature of the rulemaking proceeding, with particular reference to the manner in which interested persons shall be afforded the opportunity to participate in such proceeding;

(2) Reference to the authority under which the rule is proposed; and

(3) The terms or substance of the proposed rule or a description of the subjects and issues involved.

§201.193 Applications by barred individuals for consent to associate.

Preliminary note

This rule governs applications to the Commission by certain persons, barred by Commission order from association with brokers, dealers, municipal securities dealers,

知并向其提供提交书面意见的机会的,在提交书面意见期届满之日或之前收到的书面意见应纳入裁决案件的记录,但已根据制定法或证券交易委员会规则予以保密处理的除外。证券交易委员会可依其自由裁量权决定接受提交书面意见期届满之后提交的书面意见并将其纳入裁决案件的记录。

第201.192节　规则制定:普适性规则的发布、修正和废止

(a)请求。任何希望发布、修正或废止某一普适性规则的人均可向证券交易委员会秘书提交请求书。请求书中应纳入一份声明,载明规则或修正草案的文本或内容,或指明希望废止的规则,并说明其具有的利害关系之性质以及寻求发布、修正或废止该规则的原因。证券交易委员会秘书收到请求书后应进行书面确认,并将之转交适当的部门或办公室审议和提出建议。部门或办公室的建议应与请求一并发送给证券交易委员会,以便证券交易委员会采取其认为适当的行动。证券交易委员会应将其采取的行动通知请求人。

(b)关于拟发布、修正或废止规则的通知。除非证券交易委员会认定公告和公开程序不切实际、没有必要或与公共利益相冲突,无论何时,如证券交易委员会拟发布、修正或废止任何下述规则之时,应首先在《联邦公报》上发布关于拟采取的行动的公告:任何普适性规则或规章(解释性规则除外);关于政策的一般性说明;证券交易委员会组织、程序或工作规则;与证券交易委员会管理、人事或与公共财产、贷款、补助、福利或合同相关的任何事项。上述公告应包含如下内容:

(1)关于规则制定程序的时间、地点和性质的声明,特别是应指明利害关系人被提供参与该等程序的机会的方式;

(2)指明规则提案的依据;及

(3)规则提案的条款或内容,或关于所涉主题和问题的说明。

第201.193节　受禁人申请业务相关许可

初步说明

被证券交易委员会发布命令禁止充当经纪商、自营商、市政证券自营商、政府证券经纪商、政府证券自营商、投资顾问、投资公司、过户代理人的业务相关人的特定主

government securities brokers, government securities dealers, investment advisers, investment companies or transfer agents, for consent to become so associated. Applications made pursuant to this section must show that the proposed association would be consistent with the public interest. In addition to the information specifically required by the rule, applications should be supplemented, where appropriate, by written statements of individuals (other than the applicant) who are competent to attest to the applicant's character, employment performance, and other relevant information. Intentional misstatements or omissions of fact may constitute criminal violations of 18 U.S.C. 1001 *et seq.* and other provisions of law.

The nature of the supervision that an applicant will receive or exercise as an associated person with a registered entity is an important matter bearing upon the public interest. In meeting the burden of showing that the proposed association is consistent with the public interest, the application and supporting documentation must demonstrate that the proposed supervision, procedures, or terms and conditions of employment are reasonably designed to prevent a recurrence of the conduct that led to imposition of the bar. As an associated person, the applicant will be limited to association in a specified capacity with a particular registered entity and may also be subject to specific terms and conditions.

Normally, the applicant's burden of demonstrating that the proposed association is consistent with the public interest will be difficult to meet where the applicant is to be supervised by, or is to supervise, another barred individual. In addition, where an applicant wishes to become the sole proprietor of a registered entity and thus is seeking Commission consent notwithstanding an absence of supervision, the applicant's burden will be difficult to meet.

In addition to the factors set forth in paragraph (d) of this section, the Commission will consider the nature of the findings that resulted in the bar when making its determination as to whether the proposed association is consistent with the public interest. In this regard, attention is directed to Rule 5(e) of the Commission's Rules on Informal and Other Procedures, 17 CFR 202.5(e). Among other things, Rule 5(e) sets forth the Commission's policy "not to permit a * * * respondent [in an administrative proceeding] to consent to * * * [an] order that imposes a sanction while denying the allegations in the * * * order for proceedings." Consistent with the rationale underlying that policy, and in order to avoid the appearance that an application made pursuant to this section was granted on the basis of such denial, the Commission will not consider any application that attempts to reargue or collaterally attack the findings that resulted in the Commission's bar order.

(a) *Scope of rule.* Applications for Commission consent to associate, or to change the

体,向证券交易委员会申请充当该等业务相关人的,适用本规则。根据本节提出的申请必须证明其申请的业务相关关系符合公共利益。除本规则明确要求提供的信息外,在适当之时,还应由申请人之外的有鉴证能力的个人提供书面声明对申请人的品行、雇佣工作绩效和其他相关信息做出证明,作为申请的补充。故意对事实进行虚假陈述或故意遗漏事实的,可能构成《美国法典》第十八编第1001节及其后条文以及其他法律规定中的犯罪行为。

申请人作为注册实体的业务相关人接受或行使的监督之性质,属于对公共利益有影响的重大事项。为满足应由其承担的论证责任,以证明所申请的业务相关关系符合公共利益,申请书和支持文件必须证明拟采取的监督、程序或雇佣条款和条件设计合理,足以防范再次出现引发取消资格情况的行为。作为业务相关人,申请人限于以特定的身份与特定的注册实体发生业务相关关系,并且同时受制于具体的条款和条件。

通常,如申请人需要受另一受禁人监督或需要监督另一受禁人,则申请人将难以完成证明所申请的业务相关关系符合公共利益的论证责任。此外,如申请人希望成为注册实体的个体独资所有人,因此在不存在监督的情形下寻求证券交易委员会的同意,此种情况下申请人也难以完成论证责任。

除本节第(d)款规定的因素外,证券交易委员会在判定所申请的业务相关关系是否符合公共利益之时,还将考虑引发禁令的事实认定之性质。此时,证券交易委员会应考虑《证券交易委员会关于非正式程序和其他程序的规则》的《5(e)规则》[《联邦规章汇编》第十七编第202.5(e)节]。《5(e)规则》规定了证券交易委员会的如下政策:“不允许……相对人[在行政处理程序中]在同意对其处以制裁的……命令的同时,否认……程序命令中指控的事实。”按照该政策的精神,为避免导致证券交易委员会被误认为因否认该等事实而核准依据本节提出的申请,证券交易委员会不会考虑任何试图对引发证券交易委员会禁令的事实认定进行重新辩论或间接攻击的申请。

(a)规则适用范围。证券交易委员会发布命令禁止个人与注册实体发生业务相关

terms and conditions of association, with a registered broker, dealer, municipal securities dealer, government securities broker, government securities dealer, investment adviser, investment company or transfer agent may be made pursuant to this section where a Commission order bars the individual from association with a registered entity and:

(1) Such barred individual seeks to become associated with an entity that is not a member of a self-regulatory organization; or

(2) The order contains a proviso that application may be made to the Commission after a specified period of time.

(b) *Form of application.* Each application shall be supported by an affidavit, manually signed by the applicant, that addresses the factors set forth in paragraph (d) of this section. One original and three copies of the application shall be filed pursuant to §§201.151, 201.152 and 201.153. Each application shall include as exhibits:

(1) A copy of the Commission order imposing the bar;

(2) An undertaking by the applicant to notify immediately the Commission in writing if any information submitted in support of the application becomes materially false or misleading while the application is pending;

(3) The following forms, as appropriate:

(i) A copy of a completed Form U-4, where the applicant's proposed association is with a broker-dealer or municipal securities dealer;

(ii) A copy of a completed Form MSD-4, where the applicant's proposed association is with a bank municipal securities dealer;

(iii) The information required by Form ADV, 17 CFR 279.1, with respect to the applicant, where the applicant's proposed association is with an investment adviser;

(iv) The information required by Form TA-1, 17 CFR 249b.100, with respect to the applicant, where the applicant's proposed association is with a transfer agent; and

(4) A written statement by the proposed employer that describes:

(i) The terms and conditions of employment and supervision to be exercised over such applicant and, where applicable, by such applicant;

(ii) The qualifications, experience, and disciplinary records of the proposed supervisor(s) of the applicant;

(iii) The compliance and disciplinary history, during the two years preceding the filing of the application, of the office in which the applicant will be employed; and

(iv) The names of any other associated persons in the same office who have previously been barred by the Commission, and whether they are to be supervised by the applicant.

(c) *Required showing.* The applicant shall make a showing satisfactory to the Commission that the proposed association would be consistent with the public interest.

关系,且满足下述条件之时,受禁人可按照本节规定向证券交易委员会申请许可其与注册经纪商、自营商、市政证券自营商、政府证券经纪商、政府证券自营商、投资顾问、投资公司或过户代理人发生业务相关关系,或申请变更业务相关条款和条件:

(1)受禁人寻求与自律组织成员之外的实体发生业务相关关系;或

(2)命令中的但书条款规定在特定期限届满后可向证券交易委员会提出申请。

(b)申请格式。每份申请均应附上申请人手签的宣誓书面证词,说明本节第(d)款中规定的各项要素。申请书应按照第201.151节、第201.152节和第201.153节提交一份正本和三份复本。每份申请书均应包含如下附录:

(1)证券交易委员会的禁令复本;

(2)申请人作出的在呈报的支持信息在申请待决期间出现重大失实或重大误导性之时立即通知证券交易委员会的承诺;

(3)下述表格(视具体情况而定):

(i)一份完整填写的《U-4表格》(如申请人申请与经纪自营商或市政证券自营商发生业务相关关系);

(ii)一份完整填写的《MSD-4表格》(如申请人申请与银行市政证券自营商发生业务相关关系);

(iii)《ADV表格》(《联邦规章汇编》第十七编第279.1节)要求提供的申请人信息(如申请人申请与投资顾问发生业务相关关系);

(iv)《TA-1表格》(《联邦规章汇编》第十七编第249b.100节)要求提供的申请人信息(如申请人申请与过户代理人发生业务相关关系);及

(4)拟聘用申请人的雇主签发的一份关于如下事项的书面说明:

(i)雇佣条款和条件,以及申请人将接受或进行的(如适用)监督;

(ii)负责监督申请人的监督人选的资质、经验和纪律处分记录;

(iii)拟聘用申请人的办公室在申请提交前两年的合规和纪律处分记录;及

(iv)同一办公室的之前曾被证券交易委员会发布禁令的任何其他业务相关人的姓名,以及他们是否将接受申请人监督。

(c)证明要求。申请人应作出令证券交易委员会满意的证明,证明所申请的业务相关关系符合公共利益。

(d) *Factors to be addressed.* The affidavit required by paragraph (b) of this section shall address each of the following:

(1) The time period since the imposition of the bar;

(2) Any restitution or similar action taken by the applicant to recompense any person injured by the misconduct that resulted in the bar;

(3) The applicant's compliance with the order imposing the bar;

(4) The applicant's employment during the period subsequent to imposition of the bar;

(5) The capacity or position in which the applicant proposes to be associated;

(6) The manner and extent of supervision to be exercised over such applicant and, where applicable, by such applicant;

(7) Any relevant courses, seminars, examinations or other actions completed by the applicant subsequent to imposition of the bar to prepare for his or her return to the securities business; and

(8) Any other information material to the application.

(e) *Notification to applicant and written statement.* In the event an adverse recommendation is proposed by the staff with respect to an application made pursuant to this section, the applicant shall be so advised and provided with a written statement of the reasons for such recommendation. The applicant shall then have 30 days to submit a written statement in response.

(f) *Concurrent applications.* The Commission will not consider any application submitted pursuant to this section if any other application for consent to associate concerning the same applicant is pending before any self-regulatory organization.

Initiation of Proceedings and Prehearing Rules

§201.200 Initiation of proceedings.

(a) *Order instituting proceedings: Notice and opportunity for hearing* — (1) *Generally.* Whenever an order instituting proceedings is issued by the Commission, appropriate notice thereof shall be given to each party to the proceeding by the Secretary or another duly designated officer of the Commission. Each party shall be given notice of any hearing within a time reasonable in light of the circumstances, in advance of the hearing; provided, however, no prior notice need be given to a respondent if the Commission has authorized the Division of Enforcement to seek a temporary sanction *ex parte*.

(2) *Stop order proceedings: Additional persons entitled to notice.* Any notice of a proceeding relating to the issuance of a stop order suspending the effectiveness of a registration statement pursuant to Section 8(d)of the Securities Act of 1933, 15 U.S.C. 77h(d), shall be sent to or served on the issuer; or, in the case of a foreign government or

(d)应说明的要素。本节第(b)款要求提供的宣誓书面证词应说明如下要素：

(1)禁令作出后已经历的时间；

(2)申请人对其引发禁令的不当行为所伤害的任何人采取的任何恢复原状或类似的补偿行动；

(3)申请人对禁令的遵守情况；

(4)申请人在禁令发出后的期间内的雇佣情况；

(5)申请人希望充当的业务相关人的身份或职位；

(6)申请人将接受或进行的(如适用)监督的方式和程度；

(7)申请人在禁令作出后为重操证券业务而完成的任何相关课程、研讨会、考试或类似行动；及

(8)对申请有重大意义的任何其他信息。

(e)向申请人发出的通知以及书面声明。证券交易委员会工作人员对根据本条提出的申请提出反对意见的，应通知申请人，并向其提供一份关于反对意见原因的书面说明。申请人应在此后30日的期限内提出书面声明进行答复。

(f)重复申请。如任何自律组织同一时间正在审议同一申请人呈报的业务相关许可申请，证券交易委员会不会受理该申请人根据本节呈报的任何申请。

程序的启动和预听证规则

第201.200节　程序的启动

(a)程序发起令：通知和听证机会——(1)一般规定。证券交易委员会发布程序发起令之时，证券交易委员会秘书或证券交易委员会正式指定的其他官员应向程序各方当事人发送适当通知。各方当事人均应在听证前的合理时间获得通知，具体时间应根据具体情况确定；但是，证券交易委员会已批准执法部寻求单方面临时制裁的除外。

(2)停止令程序：有权获得通知的其他人。根据《1933年证券法》第8(d)条[《美国法典》第十五编第77h(d)节]签发停止令，暂停注册说明书效力的，相关程序的通知应发送或送达给发行人；如发行人为外国政府或行政区域，则应发送或送达给承销人；如发行人为外国主体或准州主体，则应发送或送达至注册说明书中指定的美国正式

political subdivision thereof, sent to or served on the underwriter; or, in the case of a foreign or territorial person, sent to or served on its duly authorized representative in the United States named in the registration statement, properly directed in the case of telegraphic notice to the address given in such statement. In addition, if such proceeding is commenced within 90 days after the registration statement has become effective, notice of the proceeding shall be given to the agent for service named on the facing sheet of the registration statement and to each other person designated on the facing sheet of the registration statement as a person to whom copies of communications to such agent are to be sent.

(b) *Content of order.* The order instituting proceedings shall:

(1) State the nature of any hearing;

(2) State the legal authority and jurisdiction under which the hearing is to be held;

(3) Contain a short and plain statement of the matters of fact and law to be considered and determined, unless the order directs an answer pursuant to §201.220 in which case the order shall set forth the factual and legal basis alleged therefor in such detail as will permit a specific response thereto; and

(4) State the nature of any relief or action sought or taken.

(c) *Time and place of hearing.* The time and place for any hearing shall be fixed with due regard for the public interest and the convenience and necessity of the parties, other participants, or their representatives.

(d) *Amendment to order instituting proceedings*—(1) *By the Commission.* Upon motion by a party, the Commission may, at any time, amend an order instituting proceedings to include new matters of fact or law.

(2) *By the hearing officer.* Upon motion by a party, the hearing officer may, at any time prior to the filing of an initial decision or, if no initial decision is to be filed, prior to the time fixed for the filing of final briefs with the Commission, amend an order instituting proceedings to include new matters of fact or law that are within the scope of the original order instituting proceedings.

(e) *Publication of notice of public hearings.* Unless otherwise ordered by the Commission, notice of any public hearing shall be given general circulation by release to the public, by publication in the *SEC News Digest* and, where directed, by publication in the Federal Register.

§201.201 Consolidation and severance of proceedings.

(a) *Consolidation.* By order of the Commission or a hearing officer, proceedings involving a common question of law or fact may be consolidated for hearing of any or all the matters at issue in such proceedings. The Commission or the hearing officer may make such orders concerning the conduct of such proceedings as it deems appropriate to avoid

授权代表,对于电报通知,应按注册说明书中所载地址恰当地发送。此外,上述程序在注册说明书生效后90日内开始的,则程序通知应发送给注册说明书封面中指定的送达代理人以及其他每位应抄送的人。

(b)命令内容。程序发起令应:

(1)说明听证之性质;

(2)说明所举行听证的法律依据和管辖权限;

(3)简洁、明了地说明应予以审议和判定的事实和法律问题,除非命令根据第201.220节指令当事人进行答辩,此时命令应详细载明所主张的事实和法律基础,详细程度应足以使当事人进行具体答复;及

(4)说明所寻求或采取的任何救济或行动之性质。

(c)听证时间和地点。确定听证时间和地点时,应适当顾及公共利益以及当事人、其他参与人或其代理人的方便和需求。

(d)程序发起令之修正——(1)证券交易委员会进行的修正。一方当事人提起动议的,证券交易委员会可以在任何时间修正程序发起令,以纳入新的事实或法律问题。

(2)听证官进行的修正。一方当事人提起动议的,听证官可以在向证券交易委员会提交初步决定之前的任何时间(如不必提交初步决定,则在指定的向证券交易委员会提交最终决定摘要的时间之前)修正程序发起令,纳入原程序发起令范围之内的新的事实或法律问题。

(e)公开听证通知的发布。除非证券交易委员会另有命令,否则任何公开听证通知都应在《证券交易委员会新闻摘要》上向一般公众发布,如有明确指示,则应在《联邦公报》上发布。

第201.201节　程序合并和分离

(a)程序合并。经证券交易委员会或听证官发布命令,在涉及共同法律或事实问题的程序中,争论事项可以合并听证。证券交易委员会或听证官可以就程序开展发布其认为适当的命令,以避免不必要的成本或拖延。程序合并不得损及《工作规则》中的任何权利,且不得影响任一方当事人在程序未合并之时本应享有的提起问题的权利。本

unnecessary cost or delay. Consolidation shall not prejudice any rights under these Rules of Practice and shall not affect the right of any party to raise issues that could have been raised if consolidation had not occurred. For purposes of this section, no distinction is made between joinder and consolidation of proceedings.

(b) *Severance.* By order of the Commission, any proceeding may be severed with respect to one or more parties. Any motion to sever must be made solely to the Commission and must include a representation that a settlement offer is pending before the Commission or otherwise show good cause.

[60 FR 32796, June 23, 1995, as amended at 69 FR 13177, Mar. 19, 2004; 70 FR 72570, Dec. 5, 2005]

§201.202 Specification of procedures by parties in certain proceedings.

(a) *Motion to specify procedures.* In any proceeding other than an enforcement or disciplinary proceeding, a proceeding to review a determination by a self-regulatory organization pursuant to §§201.420 and 201.421, or a proceeding to review a determination of the Board pursuant to §§201.440 and 201.441, a party may, at any time up to 20 days prior to the start of a hearing, make a motion to specify the procedures necessary or appropriate for the proceeding with particular reference to:

(1) Whether there should be an initial decision by a hearing officer;

(2) Whether any interested division of the Commission may assist in the preparation of the Commission's decision; and

(3) Whether there should be a 30-day waiting period between the issuance of the Commission's order and the date it is to become effective.

(b) *Objections; effect of failure to object.* Any other party may object to the procedures so specified, and such party may specify such additional procedures as it considers necessary or appropriate. In the absence of such objection or such specification of additional procedures, such other party may be deemed to have waived objection to the specified procedures.

(c) *Approval required.* Any proposal pursuant to paragraph (a) of this section, even if not objected to by any party, shall be subject to the written approval of the hearing officer.

(d) *Procedure upon agreement to waive an initial decision.* If an initial decision is waived pursuant to paragraph (a) of this section, the hearing officer shall notify the Secretary and, unless the Commission directs otherwise within 14 days, no initial decision shall be issued.

[60 FR 32796, June 23, 1995, as amended at 69 FR 13177, Mar. 19, 2004]

节规定在适用于追加当事人程序和合并程序时不作区分。

(b)程序分离。经证券交易委员会发布命令,任何程序都可以按照一方或多方当事人进行分离。任何分离程序的动议仅得向证券交易委员会提出,且必须包含一份声明,说明证券交易委员会正在审议和解要约或说明存在其他充分理由。

[《联邦公报》第60卷第32796页,1995年6月23日,修正索引:《联邦公报》第69卷第13177页,2004年3月19日;《联邦公报》第70卷第72570页,2005年12月5日。]

第201.202节　特定程序当事人对程序步骤的确定

(a)确定程序步骤的动议。除执法程序、纪律处分程序、根据第201.420节和第201.421节审查自律组织决定的程序,或根据第201.440节和第201.441节审议董事会决定的程序之外,在任何程序中,任一方当事人均可以在听证前20日的任何时间提出动议,要求确定程序中的必要或适当步骤,特别是:

(1)听证官是否应作出初步决定;

(2)证券交易委员会的任何利害关系部门是否可以协助证券交易委员会作出决定;及

(3)证券交易委员会发布命令之后,是否应在命令生效之前设定30日的等待期。

(b)反对;未提出反对的后果。任何其他当事人均可以就按上述规定确定的程序步骤提出反对,且提出反对的当事人可以提出其认为必要或适当的其他程序步骤。当事人未提出反对或未提出其他程序步骤的,可被视为已放弃其对程序步骤提出反对的权利。

(c)批准要求。根据本节第(a)款提出的任何提议,即使所有当事人均未提出反对,仍需取得听证官书面批准。

(d)书面同意放弃初步决定时适用的程序。根据本节第(a)款放弃要求听证官作出初步决定的,听证官应通知证券交易委员会秘书,且除非证券交易委员会在14日内另行作出指示,听证官不得签发初步决定。

[《联邦公报》第60卷第32796页,1995年6月23日,修正索引:《联邦公报》第69卷第13177页,2004年3月19日。]

§201.210 Parties, limited participants and amici curiae.

(a) *Parties in an enforcement or disciplinary proceeding, a proceeding to review a self-regulatory organization determination, or a proceeding to review a Board determination*—(1) *Generally*. No person shall be granted leave to become a party or a non-party participant on a limited basis in an enforcement or disciplinary proceeding, a proceeding to review a determination by a self-regulatory organization pursuant to §§201.420 and 201.421, or a proceeding to review a determination by the Board pursuant to §§201.440 and 201.441, except as authorized by paragraph (c) of this section.

(2) *Disgorgement proceedings*. In an enforcement proceeding, a person may state his or her views with respect to a proposed plan of disgorgement or file a proof of claim pursuant to §201.1103.

(b) *Intervention as a party*—(1) *Generally*. In any proceeding, other than an enforcement proceeding, a disciplinary proceeding, a proceeding to review a self- regulatory determination, or a proceeding to review a Board determination, any person may seek leave to intervene as a party by filing a motion setting forth the person's interest in the proceeding. No person, however, shall be admitted as a party to a proceeding by intervention unless it is determined that leave to participate pursuant to paragraph (c) of this section would be inadequate for the protection of the person's interests.

(i) In a proceeding under the Public Utility Holding Company Act of 1935, any representative of interested consumers or security holders, or any other person whose participation in the proceeding may be in the public interest or for the protection of investors or consumers, may be admitted as a party upon the filing of a written motion setting forth the person's interest in the proceeding.

(ii) In a proceeding under the Investment Company Act of 1940, any representative of interested security holders, or any other person whose participation in the proceeding may be in the public interest or for the protection of investors, may be admitted as a party upon the filing of a written motion setting forth the person's interest in the proceeding.

(2) *Intervention as of right*. (i) In proceedings under the Public Utility Holding Company Act of 1935, any interested representative, agency, authority or instrumentality of the United States or any interested State, State commission, municipality or other political subdivision of a state shall be admitted as a party to any proceeding upon the filing of a written motion requesting leave to be admitted.

(ii) In proceedings under the Investment Company Act of 1940, any interested State or State agency shall be admitted as a party to any proceeding upon the filing of a written motion requesting leave to be admitted.

(c) *Leave to participate on a limited basis*. In any proceeding, other than an enforcement proceeding, a disciplinary proceeding, a proceeding to review a self-regulatory

第201.210节　当事人、有限参与人和法庭之友

(a)执法程序、纪律处分程序、审查自律组织决定的程序、审查董事会决定的程序的当事人——(1)一般规定。除非按本节第(c)款获得批准,任何人均不得获准作为当事人参与或作为非当事人有限制地参与执法程序、纪律处分程序、根据第201.420节和第201.421节审查自律组织决定的程序,或根据第201.440节和第201.441节审查董事会决定的程序。

(2)没收程序。在执法程序中,相关主体可以说明其关于没收计划提案的意见或根据第201.1103节提交支持其主张的证明。

(b)追加当事人——(1)一般规定。除执法程序、纪律处分程序、审查自律组织决定的程序、审议董事会决定的程序外,在任何程序中,任何人均可以提交动议,说明其对程序所具有的利害关系,申请追加为当事人。但是,除非已判定根据本节第(c)款允许相关人参与程序并无法保护该人的权益,不得批准追加当事人。

(i)在根据《1935年公用事业控股公司法》提起的程序中,具有利害关系的消费者或证券持有人的任何代表,或出于公共利益、保护投资者或消费者目的而参与程序的任何其他人,在提交书面动议说明对程序具有的利害关系后,可获准追加为当事人。

(ii)在根据《1940年投资公司法》提起的程序中,证券持有人的任何代表,或出于公共利益、保护投资者或消费者目的而参与程序的任何其他人,在提交书面动议说明对程序具有的利害关系后,可获准追加为当事人。

(2)当然追加。(i)在根据《1935年公用事业控股公司法》提起的程序中,联邦或任何具有利害关系的州、州委员会、州下属的市或其他政治辖区的任何具有利害关系的代表、机构、部门或职能部门,在提交书面动议请求追加为当事人后,均应被追加为当事人。

(ii)在根据《1940年投资公司法》提起的程序中,任何具有利害关系的州或州政府机构在提交书面动议请求追加为当事人后,均应被追加为当事人。

(c)作为有限当事人参与程序的许可。除执法程序、纪律处分程序、审查自律组织的决定的程序、审议董事会决定的程序外,在任何程序中,对于影响其利益的任何事

determination, or a proceeding to review a Board determination, any person may seek leave to participate on a limited basis as a non–party participant as to any matter affecting the person's interests:

(1) *Procedure.* Motions for leave to participate shall be in writing, shall set forth the nature and extent of the movant's interest in the proceeding, and, except where good cause for late filing is shown, shall be filed not later than 20 days prior to the date fixed for the commencement of the hearing. Leave to participate pursuant to this paragraph (c) may include such rights of a party as the hearing officer may deem appropriate. Persons granted leave to participate shall be served in accordance with §201.150; provided, however, that a party to the proceeding may move that the extent of notice of filings or other papers to be provided to persons granted leave to participate be limited, or may move that the persons granted leave to participate bear the cost of being provided copies of any or all filings or other papers. Persons granted leave to participate shall be bound, except as may be otherwise determined by the hearing officer, by any stipulation between the parties to the proceeding with respect to procedure, including submission of evidence, substitution of exhibits, corrections of the record, the time within which briefs or exceptions may be filed or proposed findings and conclusions may be submitted, the filing of initial decisions, the procedure to be followed in the preparation of decisions and the effective date of the Commission's order in the case. Where the filing of briefs or exceptions or the submission of proposed findings and conclusions are waived by the parties to the proceedings, a person granted leave to participate pursuant to this paragraph (c) shall not be permitted to file a brief or exceptions or submit proposed findings and conclusions except by leave of the Commission or of the hearing officer.

(2) *Certain persons entitled to leave to participate.* The hearing officer is directed to grant leave to participate under this paragraph (c) to any person to whom it is proposed to issue any security in exchange for one or more bona fide outstanding securities, claims or property interests, or partly in such exchange and partly for cash, where the Commission is authorized to approve the terms and conditions of such issuance and exchange after a hearing upon the fairness of such terms and conditions.

(3) *Leave to participate in certain Commission proceedings by a representative of the United States Department of Justice, a United States Attorney's Office, or a criminal prosecutorial authority of any State or any other political subdivision of a State.* The Commission or the hearing officer may grant leave to participate on a limited basis to an authorized representative of the United States Department of Justice, an authorized representative of a United States Attorney, or an authorized representative of any criminal prosecutorial authority of any State or any other political subdivision of a State for the purpose of requesting a stay during the pendency of a criminal investigation or

项,任何人均可以请求获准作为有限当事人参与程序:

(1)程序步骤。请求参与程序的动议应采用书面形式,说明动议人对程序具有的利益之性质和程度;且除非提出了推迟提交的充分理由,动议提出时间不得晚于指定的听证开始日前20日。根据本第(c)款授予的参与核准可包括授予听证官认为适当的当事人权利。对于获准参与程序的人,应按照第201.150节的规定对之进行送达;但是,程序当事人可提出动议,要求限制向获准参与程序的人提供关于文书或其他提交文件的通知,或要求获准参与程序的人承担提供文书或其他文件复本的成本。除非听证官另有决定,获准参与程序的人应受程序当事人之间关于程序步骤的协议约束,包括关于如下事项的协议:证据提交、证物替换、记录改正、陈辩书或反对意见的提交时间、认定建议和结论建议的呈报时间、初步决定的提交、作出决定的程序以及证券交易委员会在案件中作出的命令的生效日期。程序当事人放弃提交陈辩书、反对意见、认定建议或结论建议的,根据本第(c)款获准参与程序的人不得提交陈辩书、反对意见、认定建议或结论建议,但证券交易委员会或听证官准许其提交的除外。

(2)有权获准参与程序的特定人。任何人收到以真实发行在外的证券、债权或财产权益作为对价(或以上述各者与现金的结合作为对价)发行证券之提议的,听证官应按照本第(c)款核准该等人参与程序,此时,证券交易委员会有权在对发行及对价的条款和条件的公平性进行听证后,批准该等条款和条件。

(3)批准联邦司法部、联邦检察长办公室或任何州或州下属行政区域的刑事追诉机构的代表参与证券交易委员会程序。证券交易委员会或听证官可以批准联邦司法部、联邦检察长办公室或任何州或州下属行政区域的刑事追诉机构的代表作为有限当事人参与证券交易委员会程序,但参与的目的仅限于对正在进行的证券交易委员会执法或纪律处分程序中的同一或类似事实问题进行刑事调查或追诉期间提出程序中止申请。在上述代表证明程序中止符合公共利益或有助于保护投资者之后,应批准中止动议。根据本第(c)(3)款核准的中止期间和条件以证券交易委员会或听证官认为适当者为准。

prosecution arising out of the same or similar facts that are at issue in the pending Commission enforcement or disciplinary proceeding. Upon a showing that such a stay is in the public interest or for the protection of investors, the motion for stay shall be favored. A stay granted under this paragraph (c)(3) may be granted for such a period and upon such conditions as the Commission or the hearing officer deems appropriate.

(d) *Amicus participation*— (1) *Availability*. An amicus brief may be filed only if:

(i) A motion for leave to file the brief has been granted;

(ii) The brief is accompanied by written consent of all parties;

(iii) The brief is filed at the request of the Commission or the hearing officer; or

(iv) The brief is presented by the United States or an officer or agency thereof, or by a State, Territory or Commonwealth.

(2) *Procedure*. An amicus brief may be filed conditionally with the motion for leave. The motion for leave shall identify the interest of the movant and shall state the reasons why a brief of an amicus curiae is desirable. Except as all parties otherwise consent, any amicus curiae shall file its brief within the time allowed the party whose position the amicus will support, unless the Commission or hearing officer, for cause shown, grants leave for a later filing. In the event that a later filing is allowed, the order granting leave to file shall specify when an opposing party may reply to the brief. A motion of an amicus curiae to participate in oral argument will be granted only for extraordinary reasons.

(e) *Permission to state views*. Any person may make a motion seeking leave to file a memorandum or make an oral statement of his or her views. Any such communication may be included in the record; provided, however, that unless offered and admitted as evidence of the truth of the statements therein made, any assertions of fact submitted pursuant to the provisions of this paragraph (e) will be considered only to the extent that the statements therein made are otherwise supported by the record.

(f) *Modification of participation provisions*. The Commission or the hearing officer may, by order, modify the provisions of this section which would otherwise be applicable, and may impose such terms and conditions on the participation of any person in any proceeding as it may deem necessary or appropriate in the public interest.

[60 FR 32796, June 23, 1995, as amended at 63 FR 63405, Nov. 13, 1998; 69 FR 13177, Mar. 19, 2004; 70 FR 72570, Dec. 5, 2005]

§201.220 Answer to allegations.

(a) *When required*. In its order instituting proceedings, the Commission may require any party to file an answer to each of the allegations contained therein. Even if not so ordered, any party in any proceeding may elect to file an answer. Any other person granted leave by the Commission or the hearing officer to participate on a limited basis in

(d)作为法庭之友参与程序——(1)适用条件。提交法庭之友书状必须满足下述条件:

(i)提交书状的动议已获得核准;

(ii)书状附有所有当事人的书面同意;

(iii)书状系按证券交易委员会或听证官之请求而提交;或

(iv)书状由联邦、联邦官员、联邦机构或州、准州或自由邦提交。

(2)程序步骤。提交法庭之友书状必须以请求获准参与程序的动议为前提。请求获准参与程序的动议应说明动议人具有的利益,并说明需要法庭之友书状的原因。除非所有当事人另行同意,任何法庭之友均应按其支持的当事人适用的时间期限提交书状,但证券交易委员会或听证官基于法庭之友提出的理由批准延迟提交期限的除外。批准延迟提交书状的,批准令中应说明对方当事人可以对书状进行答复的时间。除非存在特别原因,一般不会批准法庭之友提出的参与口头辩论的动议。

(e)陈述观点的许可。任何人均可以提出动议,请求获准就其观点提交备忘录或进行口头说明。该等文件交流均应纳入记录之内;但是,除非作为证明声明真实性的证据提交并获得采纳,根据本第(e)款提交的事实主张只有在获得记录支持之时才会被考虑。

(f)程序参与规定之修改。证券交易委员会或听证官可以发布命令修改本应适用的本节规定,并可以基于公共利益,对参与任何程序的任何人施加其认为必要或适当的条款或条件。

[《联邦公报》第60卷第32796页,1995年6月23日,修正索引:《联邦公报》第63卷第63405页,1998年11月13日;《联邦公报》第69卷第13177页,2004年3月19日;《联邦公报》第70卷第72570页,2005年12月5日。]

第201.220节　对指控的答辩

(a)要求提交答辩的时间。证券交易委员会可以在程序发起令中要求任何一方当事人就发起令中的每一项指控提交答辩。即使证券交易委员会未作出上述命令,程序的任何当事人亦可以选择提交答辩。经证券交易委员会或听证官按照第201.210(c)节批准作为有限当事人参与程序的任何其他人均可能被要求提交答辩。

such proceedings pursuant to §201.210(c) may be required to file an answer.

(b) *When to file*. Except where a different period is provided by rule or by order, a party required to file an answer as provided in paragraph (a) of this section shall do so within 20 days after service upon the party of the order instituting proceedings. Persons granted leave to participate on a limited basis in the proceeding pursuant to §201.210(c) may file an answer within a reasonable time, as determined by the Commission or the hearing officer. If the order instituting proceedings is amended, the Commission or the hearing officer may require that an amended answer be filed and, if such an answer is required, shall specify a date for the filing thereof.

(c) *Contents; effect of failure to deny*. Unless otherwise directed by the hearing officer or the Commission, an answer shall specifically admit, deny, or state that the party does not have, and is unable to obtain, sufficient information to admit or deny each allegation in the order instituting proceedings. When a party intends in good faith to deny only a part of an allegation, the party shall specify so much of it as is true and shall deny only the remainder. A statement of a lack of information shall have the effect of a denial. A defense of res judicata, statute of limitations or any other matter constituting an affirmative defense shall be asserted in the answer. Any allegation not denied shall be deemed admitted.

(d) *Motion for more definite statement*. A party may file with an answer a motion for a more definite statement of specified matters of fact or law to be considered or determined. Such motion shall state the respects in which, and the reasons why, each such matter of fact or law should be required to be made more definite. If the motion is granted, the order granting such motion shall set the periods for filing such a statement and any answer thereto.

(e) *Amendments*. A party may amend its answer at any time by written consent of each adverse party or with leave of the Commission or the hearing officer. Leave shall be freely granted when justice so requires.

(f) *Failure to file answer: default*. If a party respondent fails to file an answer required by this section within the time provided, such person may be deemed in default pursuant to §201.155(a). A party may make a motion to set aside a default pursuant to §201.155(b).

§201.221 Prehearing conference.

(a) *Purposes of conference*. The purposes of a prehearing conference include, but are not limited to:

(1) Expediting the disposition of the proceeding;

(2) Establishing early and continuing control of the proceeding by the hearing officer; and

(b)提交时间。除非相关规则或命令中规定了其他期限,按照本节第(a)款被要求提交答辩的当事人应在程序发起令向其送达后20日内进行答辩。按照第201.210(c)节获准作为有限当事人参与程序的人可以在证券交易委员会或听证官确定的合理期限内提交答辩。程序发起令被修正的,证券交易委员会或听证官可要求提交修正答辩,此时应相应指定提交修正答辩的日期。

(c)内容;未进行否认的后果。除非听证官或证券交易委员会另有指示,答辩中应对程序发起令中的各项指控一一进行明确承认、否认或说明当事人当前不拥有且无法获得充分的信息以承认或否认该等指控。如一方当事人善意地否认某一指控的一部分,应说明其认为真实的部分,并仅得否认其余部分。当事人声明指控信息缺失的,其效力与否认指控一致。基于已作出最终判决、时限规定或构成积极抗辩的其他事项进行的抗辩应在答辩中提出。当事人未否认指控的,即视为已作出承认。

(d)请求作出更确切的声明的动议。提交答辩的当事人可同时提出动议,要求对将审议或判定的具体事实或法律问题作出更确切的声明。动议中应说明该等事实或法律问题应予以确切化的方面以及原因。动议获得批准的,批准令中应指明提交声明及相应答辩的期限。

(e)修正。经每名对方当事人书面同意或证券交易委员会或听证官核准,任一方当事人均可以在任何时间修正其答辩。证券交易委员会或听证官可出于实现公正的目的,自由核准修正。

(f)未能提交答辩:缺席。如相对当事人未能在规定时间内按本节规定提交答辩,该等当事人将被视为构成第201.155(a)节规定的缺席。当事人可以根据第201.155(b)节提出撤销缺席决定的动议。

第201.221节 预备庭会议

(a)会议目的。预备庭会议之目的包括但不限于:

(1)加快程序处理;

(2)确立听证官对程序的及早和持续控制;及

(3) Improving the quality of the hearing through more thorough preparation.

(b) *Procedure.* On his or her own motion or at the request of a party, the hearing officer may, in his or her discretion, direct counsel or any party to meet for an initial, final or other prehearing conference. Such conferences may be held with or without the hearing officer present as the hearing officer deems appropriate. Where such a conference is held outside the presence of the hearing officer, the hearing officer shall be advised promptly by the parties of any agreements reached. Such conferences also may be held with one or more persons participating by telephone or other remote means.

(c) *Subjects to be discussed.* At a prehearing conference consideration may be given and action taken with respect to any and all of the following:

(1) Simplification and clarification of the issues;

(2) Exchange of witness and exhibit lists and copies of exhibits;

(3) Stipulations, admissions of fact, and stipulations concerning the contents, authenticity, or admissibility into evidence of documents;

(4) Matters of which official notice may be taken;

(5) The schedule for exchanging prehearing motions or briefs, if any;

(6) The method of service for papers other than Commission orders;

(7) Summary disposition of any or all issues;

(8) Settlement of any or all issues;

(9) Determination of hearing dates;

(10) Amendments to the order instituting proceedings or answers thereto;

(11) Production of documents as set forth in §201.230, and prehearing production of documents in response to subpoenas ducestecum as set forth in §201.232;

(12) Specification of procedures as set forth in §201.202; and

(13) Such other matters as may aid in the orderly and expeditious disposition of the proceeding.

(d) *Required prehearing conference.* Except where the emergency nature of a proceeding would make a prehearing conference clearly inappropriate, at least one prehearing conference should be held.

(e) *Prehearing orders.* At or following the conclusion of any conference held pursuant to this section, the hearing officer shall enter a ruling or order which recites the agreements reached and any procedural determinations made by the hearing officer.

(f) *Failure to appear: default.* Any person who is named in an order instituting proceedings as a person against whom findings may be made or sanctions imposed and who fails to appear, in person or through a representative, at a prehearing conference of which he or she has been duly notified may be deemed in default pursuant to §201.155(a). A party may make a motion to set aside a default pursuant to §201.155(b).

(3)通过更详尽的准备提高听证质量。

(b)程序步骤。听证官可以主动或应当事人的请求,依其自由裁量权指示律师或任何当事人为举行初步、最终或其他预备庭会议进行会面。听证官可视适当情形决定出席或不出席会议。听证官未出席会议的,当事人应及时将达成的任何协议告知听证官。与会人士也可通过电话或其他远程方式参与会议。

(c)讨论主题。在预备庭会议上,可审议下述任何或全部事项并采取相应行动:

(1)问题的简化和澄清;

(2)交换证人和证物列表及证物复件;

(3)诉讼协议、对事实的承认、关于文件证据内容、真实性和可采纳性的约定;

(4)可进行正式认知的事项;

(5)交换预备庭动议或陈辩书(如有)的时间表;

(6)证券交易委员会命令之外的文书的送达方式;

(7)任何或所有问题的简易处理;

(8)任何或所有问题的和解;

(9)听证日期的确定;

(10)对程序发起令或答辩的修正;

(11)按照第201.230节提交文件,以及按照第201.232节规定的文件传票提供预备庭文件;

(12)按照第201.202节确定程序步骤;及

(13)有助于有序、快速处理程序的其他事项。

(d)预备庭会议举行要求。除非程序的紧急性导致明显不宜举行预备庭会议,至少应举行一次预备庭会议。

(e)预备庭命令。根据本节举行的任何会议结束之时或之后,听证官应作出裁定或命令,说明所达成的协议以及听证官作出的任何程序性决定。

(f)未能出席:缺席。程序发起令中指明的可能被作出事实认定或处以制裁的任何人,如已获得正式通知,但未能亲自或委派代理出席预备庭会议,将根据第201.155(a)节被视为缺席。当事人可以根据第201.155(b)节提出撤销缺席决定的动议。

[60 FR 32796, June 23, 1995, as amended at 63 FR 63405, Nov. 13, 1998]

§201.222 Prehearing submissions.

(a) *Submissions generally.* The hearing officer, on his or her own motion, or at the request of a party or other participant, may order any party, including the interested division, to furnish such information as deemed appropriate, including any or all of the following:

(1) An outline or narrative summary of its case or defense;

(2) The legal theories upon which it will rely;

(3) Copies and a list of documents that it intends to introduce at the hearing; and

(4) A list of witnesses who will testify on its behalf, including the witnesses' names, occupations, addresses and a brief summary of their expected testimony.

(b) *Expert witnesses.* Each party who intends to call an expert witness shall submit, in addition to the information required by paragraph (a)(4) of this section, a statement of the expert's qualifications, a listing of other proceedings in which the expert has given expert testimony, and a list of publications authored or co-authored by the expert.

§ 201. 230 Enforcement and disciplinary proceedings: Availability of documents for inspection and copying.

For purposes of this section, the term *documents* shall include writings, drawings, graphs, charts, photographs, recordings and other data compilations, including data stored by computer, from which information can be obtained.

(a) *Documents to be available for inspection and copying.* (1) Unless otherwise provided by this section, or by order of the Commission or the hearing officer, the Division of Enforcement shall make available for inspection and copying by any party documents obtained by the Division prior to the institution of proceedings, in connection with the investigation leading to the Division's recommendation to institute proceedings. Such documents shall include:

(i) Each subpoena issued;

(ii) Every other written request to persons not employed by the Commission to provide documents or to be interviewed;

(iii) The documents turned over in response to any such subpoenas or other written requests;

(iv) All transcripts and transcript exhibits;

(v) Any other documents obtained from persons not employed by the Commission; and

(vi) Any final examination or inspection reports prepared by the Office of Compliance Inspections and Examinations, the Division of Market Regulation, or the

[《联邦公报》第60卷第32796页,1995年6月23日,修正索引:《联邦公报》第63卷第63405页,1998年11月13日。]

第201.222节　预备庭程序中的文件呈交

(a)一般文件呈交。听证官可以主动或应一方当事人或其他参与人的请求,命令任何当事人(包括利害关系部门)提交其认为适当的信息,包括下述任何或所有信息:

(1)其主张或抗辩的概要或文字摘要;

(2)其依据的法律理论;

(3)拟在听证上出示的文件复本和列表;及

(4)将为其作证的证人名单,包括证人姓名、职务、地址和预期将提供的证言的简短摘要。

(b)专家证人。除本节第(a)(4)款要求提供的信息外,希望传唤专家证人的各当事人均应呈报一份关于专家证人资质的声明、该专家曾提供专家证言的其他程序之列表,以及该专家著写或合著的出版物列表。

第201.230节　执法和纪律处分程序:文件的查阅和复制

就本节而言,“文件 ”一词应包括可以提供信息的文章、图纸、图形、图表、照片、记录和其他数据编纂,包括电脑存储数据。

(a)开放查阅和复制的文件。(1)除非本节或证券交易委员会或听证官作出的命令中另有规定,执法部在作出调查后建议发起程序的,应在程序发起之前,将其获取的与调查相关的文件开放给各方当事人查阅和复制。该等文件应包括:

(i)已签发的每一份传票;

(ii)向证券交易委员会雇员之外的人发出的要求提交文件或要求当面访谈的书面请求;

(iii)作为该等传票或其他书面请求之答复而提交的文件;

(iv)所有笔录和笔录证据;

(v)从证券交易委员会雇员之外的人获取的任何其他文件;及

(vi)合规检查和核查办公室、市场监管部、投资管理部编制的任何最终核查或检查报告,前提是执法部希望将任何该等报告纳为证据或利用任何该等报告唤起证人

Division of Investment Management, if the Division of Enforcement intends either to introduce any such report into evidence or to use any such report to refresh the recollection of any witness.

(2) Nothing in this paragraph (a) shall limit the right of the Division to make available any other document, or shall limit the right of a respondent to seek access to or production pursuant to subpoena of any other document, or shall limit the authority of the hearing officer to order the production of any document pursuant to subpoena.

(b) *Documents that may be withheld.* (1) The Division of Enforcement may withhold a document if:

(i) The document is privileged;

(ii) The document is an internal memorandum, note or writing prepared by a Commission employee, other than an examination or inspection report as specified in paragraph (a)(1)(vi) of this section, or is otherwise attorney work product and will not be offered in evidence;

(iii) The document would disclose the identity of a confidential source; or

(iv) The hearing officer grants leave to withhold a document or category of documents as not relevant to the subject matter of the proceeding or otherwise, for good cause shown.

(2) Nothing in this paragraph (b) authorizes the Division of Enforcement in connection with an enforcement or disciplinary proceeding to withhold, contrary to the doctrine of*Brady v. Maryland*, 373 U.S. 83, 87 (1963), documents that contain material exculpatory evidence.

(c) *Withheld document list.* The hearing officer may require the Division of Enforcement to submit for review a list of documents or categories of documents withheld pursuant to paragraphs (b)(1)(i) through (b)(1)(iv) of this section or to submit any document withheld, and may determine whether any such document should be made available for inspection and copying. When similar documents are withheld pursuant to paragraphs (b)(1)(i) through (b)(1)(iv) of this section, those documents may be identified by category instead of by individual document. The hearing officer retains discretion to determine when an identification by category is insufficient.

(d) *Timing of inspection and copying.* Unless otherwise ordered by the Commission or the hearing officer, the Division of Enforcement shall commence making documents available to a respondent for inspection and copying pursuant to this section no later than 7 days after service of the order instituting proceedings. In a proceeding in which a temporary cease-and-desist order is sought pursuant to §201.510 or a temporary suspension of registration is sought pursuant to §201.520, documents shall be made available no later than the day after service of the decision as to whether to issue a temporary cease-and-desist order or temporary suspension order.

的记忆。

(2)本第(a)款的任何内容均不得限制执法部开放任何其他文件的权利,亦不得限制相对人根据传票寻求查阅或提供任何其他文件的权利,亦不得限制听证官根据传票发布命令要求提供任何文件的权限。

(b)可以保留的文件。(1)在下述情况下,执法部可以保留文件而不予提供:

(i)文件受保密特权约束;

(ii)文件属于证券交易委员会雇员制作的内部备忘录、记录或文件[本节第(a)(1)(vi)款所述核查或检查报告除外]或属于不会作为证据提交的律师工作成果;

(iii)文件将披露保密来源信息;或

(iv)听证官基于文件与程序标的无关或其他充分理由核准保留某一文件或某一类型的文件。

(2)本第(b)款的任何内容均不授权执法部在执法或纪律处分程序中违反“布雷迪诉马里兰”一案中确立的原则[《美国判例汇编》第373卷第83页、第87页(1963)]保留包含重大无罪抗辩证据的文件。

(c)保留文件列表。听证官可以要求执法部呈报根据本节第(b)(1)(i)款至第(b)(1)(iv)款规定保留的文件或文件类型之列表,或呈报保留的任何文件,并可以判定任何该等文件是否应开放查阅和复制。根据本节第(b)(1)(i)款至第(b)(1)(iv)款规定保留类似文件之时,该等文件应按类别而非按件进行标识。听证官保留判定按类标识是否充分的自由裁量权。

(d)查阅和复制时间。除非证券交易委员会或听证官另有命令,执法部应在程序发起令送达后7日内根据本节规定向相对人开放文件查阅和复制。在根据第201.510节寻求临时制止令的程序中,或根据第201.520节寻求暂停注册的程序中,文件开放查阅和复制之日不得迟于是否签发临时制止令或暂停令的决定送达之日。

(e) *Place of inspection and copying.* Documents subject to inspection and copying pursuant to this section shall be made available to the respondent for inspection and copying at the Commission office where they are ordinarily maintained, or at such other place as the parties, in writing, may agree. A respondent shall not be given custody of the documents or leave to remove the documents from the Commission's offices pursuant to the requirements of this section other than by written agreement of the Division of Enforcement. Such agreement shall specify the documents subject to the agreement, the date they shall be returned and such other terms or conditions as are appropriate to provide for the safekeeping of the documents.

(f) *Copying costs and procedures.* The respondent may obtain a photocopy of any documents made available for inspection. The respondent shall be responsible for the cost of photocopying. Unless otherwise ordered, charges for copies made by the Division of Enforcement at the request of the respondent will be at the rate charged pursuant to the fee schedule at 17 CFR 200.80e for copies. The respondent shall be given access to the documents at the Commission's offices or such other place as the parties may agree during normal business hours for copying of documents at the respondent's expense.

(g) *Issuance of investigatory subpoenas after institution of proceedings.* The Division of Enforcement shall promptly inform the hearing officer and each party if investigatory subpoenas are issued under the same investigation file number or pursuant to the same order directing private investigation ("formal order")under which the investigation leading to the institution of proceedings was conducted. The hearing officer shall order such steps as necessary and appropriate to assure that the issuance of investigatory subpoenas after the institution of proceedings is not for the purpose of obtaining evidence relevant to the proceedings and that any relevant documents that may be obtained through the use of investigatory subpoenas in a continuing investigation are made available to each respondent for inspection and copying on a timely basis.

(h) *Failure to make documents available—harmless error.* In the event that a document required to be made available to a respondent pursuant to this section is not made available by the Division of Enforcement, no rehearing or redecision of a proceeding already heard or decided shall be required, unless the respondent shall establish that the failure to make the document available was not harmless error.

[60 FR 32796, June 23, 1995; 60 FR 46499, Sept. 7, 1995, as amended at 68 FR 35789, June 17, 2003; 69 FR 13177, Mar. 19, 2004]

§201.231 Enforcement and disciplinary proceedings: Production of witness statements.

(a) *Availability.* Any respondent in an enforcement or disciplinary proceeding may

(e)查阅和复制地点。根据本节开放查阅和复制的文件应在通常的保存地点(即证券交易委员会的办公室),或当事人书面约定的其他地点开放给相对人查阅和复制。除非执法部书面同意,不得根据本节规定将文件交予文件相对人保存或获准将文件带离证券交易委员会办公室。执法部作出书面同意的,应具体说明书面同意所适用的文件、返还日期以及其他适当的文件保存条款和条件。

(f)复制成本和程序。对于开放查阅的所有文件,相对人均可进行影印,影印成本由相对人承担。除非另有命令,执法部按照相对人的请求进行复制的费用应按《联邦规章汇编》第十七编第200.80e节规定的费用表收取。相对人应在正常工作时间内在证券交易委员会办公室或诉讼协议约定的其他地点复制文件,复制成本由相对人承担。

(g)程序发起之后签发调查传票。执法部在进行调查后导致程序发起,之后又按照同一调查文件编号或根据同一非公开调查指示令("正式命令")签发调查传票的,应及时告知听证官和各方当事人。听证官应命令采取必要和适当的步骤,确保程序发起之后签发调查传票的目的不是获取与程序相关的证据,且在持续性调查中通过调查传票获取的相关文件可及时提供给相对人查阅和复制。

(h)未能开放文件——无害错误。执法部未根据本节规定向相对人开放相关文件的,不必对已经听证或裁决的程序进行重新听证或重新裁决,除非相对人证明执法部未开放相关文件不属于无害错误。

[《联邦公报》第60卷第32796页,1995年6月23日;《联邦公报》第60卷第46499页,1995年9月7日,修正索引:《联邦公报》第68卷第35789页,2003年6月17日;《联邦公报》第69卷第13177页,2004年3月19日。]

第201.231节　执法和纪律处分程序:证人声明的提供

(a)证人声明的提供。执法或纪律处分程序中的任何相对人可提出动议,要求执法

move that the Division of Enforcement produce for inspection and copying any statement of any person called or to be called as a witness by the Division of Enforcement that pertains, or is expected to pertain, to his or her direct testimony and that would be required to be produced pursuant to the Jencks Act, 18 U.S.C. 3500. For purposes of this section, *statement* shall have the meaning set forth in 18 U.S.C. 3500(e). Such production shall be made at a time and place fixed by the hearing officer and shall be made available to any party, provided, however, that the production shall be made under conditions intended to preserve the items to be inspected or copied.

(b) *Failure to produce—harmless error.* In the event that a statement required to be made available for inspection and copying by a respondent is not turned over by the Division of Enforcement, no rehearing or redecision of a proceeding already heard or decided shall be required unless the respondent establishes that the failure to turn over the statement was not harmless error.

[60 FR 32796, June 23, 1995, as amended at 69 FR 13177, Mar. 19, 2004]

§201.232 Subpoenas.

(a) *Availability; procedure.* In connection with any hearing ordered by the Commission, a party may request the issuance of subpoenas requiring the attendance and testimony of witnesses at the designated time and place of hearing, and subpoenas requiring the production of documentary or other tangible evidence returnable at any designated time or place. Unless made on the record at a hearing, requests for issuance of a subpoena shall be made in writing and served on each party pursuant to §201.150. A person whose request for a subpoena has been denied or modified may not request that any other person issue the subpoena.

(1) *Unavailability of hearing officer.* In the event that the hearing officer assigned to a proceeding is unavailable, the party seeking issuance of the subpoena may seek its issuance from the first available of the following persons: The Chief Administrative Law Judge, the law judge most senior in service as a law judge, the duty officer, any other member of the Commission, or any other person designated by the Commission to issue subpoenas. Requests for issuance of a subpoena made to the Commission, or any member thereof, must be submitted to the Secretary, not to an individual Commissioner.

(2) *Signing may be delegated.* A hearing officer may authorize issuance of a subpoena, and may delegate the manual signing of the subpoena to any other person authorized to issue subpoenas.

(b) *Standards for issuance.* Where it appears to the person asked to issue the subpoena that the subpoena sought may be unreasonable, oppressive, excessive in scope, or unduly burdensome, he or she may, in his or her discretion, as a condition precedent to

部提供证人的声明或将作为证人被传唤的任何人的声明以供查阅和复制,前提是该等声明与其直接证词相关或预期将与其直接证词相关,且将按照《简克斯法》(《美国法典》第十八编第3500节)被要求提供。就本节而言,“声明”一词的含义以《美国法典》第十八编第3500(e)节的规定为准。提供上述声明的时间和地点由听证官确定,且应向所有当事人提供,但是必须满足为保护查阅或复制对象而确定的条件。

(b)未能提供——无害错误。执法部未根据本条规定向相对人提供声明供其查阅或复制的,不必对已经听证或裁决的程序进行重新听证或重新裁决,除非相对人证明执法部未提供该等声明不属于无害错误。

[《联邦公报》第60卷第32796页,1995年6月23日,修正索引:《联邦公报》第69卷第13177页,2004年3月19日。]

第201.232节　传票

(a)适用范围;程序步骤。在证券交易命令举委员会行的所有听证中,一方当事人可以请求签发传票,要求证人在指定的时间和地点出席听证并提供证言,以及请求签发传票,要求在任何指定时间或地点提供可归还的文件证据以及其他实物证据。除非已在听证中记录在案,签发传票请求应采用书面形式,并根据第201.150节向各方当事人送达。签发传票请求被驳回或修改的,请求人不得请求任何其他人签发传票。

(1)听证官无法履职情形。如被指派审理程序的听证官无法履职,签发传票请求人可按次序向下述人提出请求:首席行政法官、担任行政法官资历最久的法官、轮值官、任何其他证券交易委员会委员、证券交易委员会指定的签发传票的任何其他人。向证券交易委员会或其任何委员提出的签发传票请求必须向证券交易委员会秘书而非任何个人委员提出。

(2)签字委托授权。听证官可批准签发传票,并将手签传票的权限委托任何其他获准签发传票的人行使。

(b)签发标准。被请求签发传票的人认为传票不合理、具有压迫性、范围过大或设定义务过重的,可依其自由裁量权设定签发传票的先决条件,要求请求人证明所寻求的证言或其他证据的一般关联性并说明其合理范围。如被请求签发传票的人在综合

the issuance of the subpoena, require the person seeking the subpoena to show the general relevance and reasonable scope of the testimony or other evidence sought. If after consideration of all the circumstances, the person requested to issue the subpoena determines that the subpoena or any of its terms is unreasonable, oppressive, excessive in scope, or unduly burdensome, he or she may refuse to issue the subpoena, or issue it only upon such conditions as fairness requires. In making the foregoing determination, the person issuing the subpoena may inquire of the other participants whether they will stipulate to the facts sought to be proved.

(c) *Service.* Service shall be made pursuant to the provisions of §201.150 (b) through (d). The provisions of this paragraph (c) shall apply to the issuance of subpoenas for purposes of investigations, as required by 17 CFR 203.8, as well as hearings.

(d) *Tender of fees required.* When a subpoena compelling the attendance of a person at a hearing or deposition is issued at the instance of anyone other than an officer or agency of the United States, service is valid only if the subpoena is accompanied by a tender to the subpoenaed person of the fees for one day's attendance and mileage specified by paragraph (f) of this section.

(e) *Application to quash or modify.* (1) Any person to whom a subpoena is directed, or who is an owner, creator or the subject of the documents that are to be produced pursuant to a subpoena, or any party may, prior to the time specified therein for compliance, but in no event more than 15 days after the date of service of such subpoena, request that the subpoena be quashed or modified. Such request shall be made by application filed with the Secretary and served on all parties pursuant to §201.150. The party on whose behalf the subpoena was issued may, within five days of service of the application, file an opposition to the application. If a hearing officer has been assigned to the proceeding, the application to quash shall be directed to that hearing officer for consideration, even if the subpoena was issued by another person.

(2) *Standards governing application to quash or modify.* If compliance with the subpoena would be unreasonable, oppressive or unduly burdensome, the hearing officer or the Commission shall quash or modify the subpoena, or may order return of the subpoena only upon specified conditions. These conditions may include but are not limited to a requirement that the party on whose behalf the subpoena was issued shall make reasonable compensation to the person to whom the subpoena was addressed for the cost of copying or transporting evidence to the place for return of the subpoena.

(f) *Witness fees and mileage.* Witnesses summoned before the Commission shall be paid the same fees and mileage that are paid to witnesses in the courts of the United States, and witnesses whose depositions are taken and the persons taking the same shall severally be entitled to the same fees as are paid for like services in the courts of the

考虑所有情形后,判定传票或传票的任何条款不合理、具有压迫性、范围大或设定义务过重,其可以拒绝签发传票,或仅在符合公平条件的情况下签发传票。在作出上述判定之时,签发传票的人可询问其他参与人是否愿意通过约定的方式对待证明事实达成一致。

(c)送达。送达将按照第201.150(b)~201.150(d)节的规定进行。本第(c)款的规定适用于为调查目的进行的传票签发(如《联邦规章汇编》第十七编第203.8节所规定)以及为听证目的进行的传票签发。

(d)规定费用的支付。针对联邦官员或机关之外的任何人签发传票,强制要求其出席听证或提供场外证言的,只有在按本节第(f)款规定向传票送达对象提供一天的出席费和交通补贴的情况下,传票方得有效。

(e)撤销或修改申请。(1)传票送达对象,或按照传票应提供的文件的所有人、创建人或主体,或任何当事人,均可以在指定的履行传票规定的期限届满之前(但无论何时不得迟于传票送达后15日),请求撤销或修改传票。撤销或修改申请应向证券交易委员会秘书提交,并按照第201.150节的规定向所有当事人送达。传票签发请求人可以在撤销或修改申请送达后5日内提交反对意见。如已为程序指派听证官,即使传票系由听证官以外的人签发,撤销申请亦应交由听证官审议。

(2)关于撤销或修改申请的标准。如履行传票要求不合理、具有压迫性或义务过重,听证官或证券交易委员会应撤销或修改传票,或命令只有在满足具体条件时才需返还传票。上述具体条件可能包括但不限于传票签发请求人向传票送达对象合理补偿复制证据的成本或将证据运至返还传票地的交通成本。

(f)证人费和交通补贴。传唤至证券交易委员会作证的证人,应按照美国联邦法院证人的标准支付证人费和交通补贴,进行场外作证的证人以及进行取证的人均应按照在美国联邦法院提供类似服务的人的标准支付费用。证人费和交通补贴应由请求其作证的当事人支付。

United States. Witness fees and mileage shall be paid by the party at whose instance the witnesses appear.

[60 FR 32796, June 23, 1995, as amended at 69 FR 13177, Mar. 19, 2004]

§201.233 Depositions upon oral examination.

(a) *Procedure.* Any party desiring to take the testimony of a witness by deposition shall make a written motion setting forth the reasons why such deposition should be taken including the specific reasons why the party believes the witness will be unable to attend or testify at the hearing; the name and address of the prospective witness; the matters concerning which the prospective witness is expected to be questioned; and the proposed time and place for the taking of the deposition.

(b) *Required finding when ordering a deposition.* In the discretion of the Commission or the hearing officer, an order for a deposition may be issued upon a finding that the prospective witness will likely give testimony material to the proceeding; that it is likely the prospective witness, who is then within the United States, will be unable to attend or testify at the hearing because of age, sickness, infirmity, imprisonment, other disability, or absence from the United States, unless it appears that the absence of the witness was procured by the party requesting the deposition; and that the taking of a deposition will serve the interests of justice.

(c) *Contents of order.* An order for deposition shall designate by name a deposition officer. The designated officer may be the hearing officer or any other person authorized to administer oaths by the laws of the United States or of the place where the deposition is to be held. An order for deposition also shall state:

(1) The name of the witness whose deposition is to be taken;

(2) The scope of the testimony to be taken;

(3) The time and place of the deposition;

(4) The manner of recording, preserving and filing the deposition; and

(5) The number of copies, if any, of the deposition and exhibits to be filed upon completion of the deposition.

(d) *Procedure at depositions.* A witness whose testimony is taken by deposition shall be sworn or shall affirm before any questions are put to him or her. Examination and cross-examination of deponents may proceed as permitted at a hearing. The witness being deposed may have counsel present during the deposition.

(e) *Objections to questions or evidence.* Objections to questions or evidence shall be in short form, stating the grounds of objection relied upon. Objections to questions or evidence shall be noted by the deposition officer upon the deposition, but a deposition officer other than the hearing officer shall not have the power to decide on the

[《联邦公报》第60卷第32796页,1995年6月23日,修正索引:《联邦公报》第69卷第13177页,2004年3月19日。]

第201.233节　通过口头询问提取场外证言

(a)程序步骤。当事人希望通过场外证言的方式提取证人证言的,应提出一份书面动议,说明如下事项:提取场外证言的原因;当事人认为证人无法出席听证会并现场作证的具体原因;潜在证人的姓名和地址;潜在证人预期将被询问的事项;拟议的提取场外证言的时间和地点。

(b)命令提取场外证言时需作出的认定。只有在作出如下认定之后,证券交易委员会或听证官依其自由裁量权方可要求签发提取场外证言令:潜在证人很可能会提供对程序具有重大意义的证言;潜在证人当时位于美国境内,且因年老、疾病、虚弱、监禁、残疾或离开美国等原因而无法出席听证程序并作证,但从表面判断证人离开美国系因请求提取证言的当事人导致的除外;最后,提取场外证言符合公正目的。

(c)命令内容。提取场外证言的命令应明确指明场外证言提取官姓名。场外证言提取官可以是听证官、美国联邦法律或提取证言地的法律授权主持宣誓程序的任何其他人。提取场外证言的命令应说明:

(1)被提取证言的证人姓名;
(2)提取证言的范围;
(3)提取证言的时间和地点;
(4)记录、保存和提交证言的方式;及
(5)证言提取完成之后提交的证言和证物的数量(如有)。

(d)场外证言提取程序。提取场外证言之时,证人应在被询问之前进行宣誓或确认。提取场外证言之时,可像听证程序一样对证人进行询问和交叉询问。证人在提取场外证言的过程中,可有律师在场。

(e)对问题或证据的反对。对问题或证据的反对应尽量简洁,说明反对的理由。场外证言提取官应记录对问题或证据提出的反对,但除听证官之外,场外证言提取官无权就证据的证明力、重大性或相关性作出决定。未向场外证言提取官对问题或证据提出反对的,不构成弃权,但当场提出反对将导致反对理由被排除或消除的除外。

competency, materiality or relevance of evidence. Failure to object to questions or evidence before the deposition officer shall not be deemed a waiver unless the ground of the objection is one that might have been obviated or removed if presented at that time.

(f) *Filing of depositions.* The questions propounded and all answers or objections shall be recorded or transcribed verbatim, and a transcript prepared by the deposition officer, or under his or her direction. The transcript shall be subscribed by the witness and certified by the deposition officer. The original deposition and exhibits shall be filed with the Secretary. A copy of the deposition shall be available to the deponent and each party for purchase at prescribed rates.

(g) *Payment.* The cost of the transcript shall be paid by the party requesting the deposition.

[60 FR 32796, June 23, 1995, as amended at 69 FR 13178, Mar. 19, 2004]

§201.234 Depositions upon written questions.

(a) *Availability.* Depositions may be taken and submitted on written questions upon motion of any party. The motion shall include the information specified in §201.233(a). A decision on the motion shall be governed by the provisions of §201.233(b).

(b) *Procedure.* Written questions shall be filed with the motion. Within 10 days after service of the motion and written questions, any party may file objections to such written questions and any party may file cross-questions. When a deposition is taken pursuant to this section no persons other than the witness, counsel to the witness, the deposition officer, and, if the deposition officer does not act as reporter, a reporter, shall be present at the examination of the witness. No party shall be present or represented unless otherwise permitted by order. The deposition officer shall propound the questions and cross-questions to the witness in the order submitted.

(c) *Additional requirements.* The order for deposition, filing of the deposition, form of the deposition and use of the deposition in the record shall be governed by paragraphs (c) through (g) of §201.233, except that no cross-examination shall be made.

§201.235 Introducing prior sworn statements of witnesses into the record.

(a) At a hearing, any person wishing to introduce a prior, sworn statement of a witness, not a party, otherwise admissible in the proceeding, may make a motion setting forth the reasons therefor. If only part of a statement is offered in evidence, the hearing officer may require that all relevant portions of the statement be introduced. If all of a statement is offered in evidence, the hearing officer may require that portions not relevant to the proceeding be excluded. A motion to introduce a prior sworn statement may be granted if:

(1) The witness is dead;

(f)场外证言的提交。提出的问题以及所有回答和反对均应逐字进行记录或笔录,笔录应由场外证言提取官制作或按场外证言提取官的指示制作。笔录应由证人签署,并由场外证言提取官认证。场外证言和证据正本应向证券交易委员会秘书提交。证人及各当事人均可按规定费率购买证言复本。

(g)付款。笔录成本由请求提取场外证言的当事人支付。

[《联邦公报》第60卷第32796页,1995年6月23日,修正索引:《联邦公报》第69卷第13178页,2004年3月19日。]

第201.234节　通过书面问题提取场外证言

(a)适用范围。任一方当事人提出动议的,可以通过书面问题的方式提取和呈报场外证言。动议应包括第201.233(a)节规定的信息。对动议的决定应适用第201.233(b)节的规定。

(b)程序步骤。书面问题应与动议共同提交。动议和书面问题送达后10日内,任一方当事人均可以对书面问题提交反对意见,且任一方当事人均可以提出交叉问题。根据本节提取场外证言的,在询问证人之时,除证人、证人律师、场外证言提取官以及笔录材料记录人(如不由场外证言提取官负责记录)之外,任何其他人均不得在场。除非命令另行许可,任一方当事人均不得亲自或委派代理在场。场外证言提取官应按所呈报的顺序向证人提出问题和交叉问题。

(c)补充要求。除了不得进行交叉询问之外,场外证言提取令、场外证言的提交、场外证言的形式以及将场外证言纳入记录均应适用第201.233(c)~(g)节的规定。

第201.235节　将过往的宣誓证人声明纳入记录

(a)在听证中,任何人希望纳入非当事人的证人之前做出的在程序中本可采纳的宣誓声明的,均可以提出动议,说明相关原因。申请人仅请求将一部分声明作为证据提供的,听证官可以要求纳入声明的所有相关部分。申请人请求将声明整体作为证据提供的,听证官可以要求排除与程序无关的部分。在下述情况下,可核准纳入过往的宣誓声明的动议:

(1)证人死亡;

(2) The witness is out of the United States, unless it appears that the absence of the witness was procured by the party offering the prior sworn statement;

(3) The witness is unable to attend or testify because of age, sickness, infirmity, imprisonment or other disability;

(4) The party offering the prior sworn statement has been unable to procure the attendance of the witness by subpoena; or

(5) In the discretion of the Commission or the hearing officer, it would be desirable, in the interests of justice, to allow the prior sworn statement to be used. In making this determination, due regard shall be given to the presumption that witnesses will testify orally in an open hearing. If the parties have stipulated to accept a prior sworn statement in lieu of live testimony, consideration shall also be given to the convenience of the parties in avoiding unnecessary expense.

(b) [Reserved]

§201.240 Settlement.

(a) *Availability.* Any person who is notified that a proceeding may or will be instituted against him or her, or any party to a proceeding already instituted, may, at any time, propose in writing an offer of settlement.

(b) *Procedure.* An offer of settlement shall state that it is made pursuant to this section; shall recite or incorporate as a part of the offer the provisions of paragraphs (c)(4) and (5) of this section; shall be signed by the person making the offer, not by counsel; and shall be submitted to the interested division.

(c) *Consideration of offers of settlement.* (1) Offers of settlement shall be considered by the interested division when time, the nature of the proceedings, and the public interest permit.

(2) Where a hearing officer is assigned to a proceeding, the interested division and the party submitting the offer may request that the hearing officer express his or her views regarding the appropriateness of the offer of settlement. A request for the hearing officer to express his or her views on an offer of settlement or otherwise to participate in a settlement conference constitutes a waiver by the persons making the request of any right to claim bias or prejudgment by the hearing officer based on the views expressed.

(3) The interested division shall present the offer of settlement to the Commission with its recommendation, except that, if the division's recommendation is unfavorable, the offer shall not be presented to the Commission unless the person making the offer so requests.

(4) By submitting an offer of settlement, the person making the offer waives, subject to acceptance of the offer:

(i) All hearings pursuant to the statutory provisions under which the proceeding is to

(2)证人不在美国境内,但从表面判断,证人不在美国境内的事实系由请求提供过往的宣誓声明的一方所导致的除外;

(3)证人因年老、疾病、虚弱、监禁或残疾原因而无法出席或作证;

(4)请求提供过往的宣誓声明的当事人无法通过传票使证人出席;或

(5)证券交易委员会或听证官依其自由裁量权判定,出于公正目的,宜应允许使用过往的宣誓声明。在作出上述判定之时,应适当考虑证人将在公开听证中进行口头作证的推定。如当事人已达成约定同意接受过往的宣誓声明以替代现场作证的,也应考虑当事人的便利,从而避免不必要的费用。

(b)[保留]

第201.240节 和解

(a)适用情形。任何人在被通知可能或将要针对其提起程序之后均可以提出书面和解要约,同时,已经发起的程序中的任何当事人均可以在任何时间提出书面和解要约。

(b)程序步骤。和解要约应声明其系按本节规定作出;应引用本节第(c)(4)款和第(c)(5)款的规定或将之作为要约的一部分;应由做出要约的人而非律师签署;并应呈报给利害关系部门。

(c)对和解要约的审议。(1)如时间、程序性质及公共利益许可,和解要约应由利害关系部门审议。

(2)如已为程序指定听证官的,利害关系部门和呈报和解要约的当事人可以请求听证官就和解要约的适当性发表意见。请求听证官就和解要约发表意见或以其他方式参与和解会议,即表明请求人已放弃基于听证官的意见主张听证官存在偏见或预判的权利。

(3)利害关系部门应向证券交易委员会提交和解要约及建议,但是利害关系部门作出反对建议的,不得向证券交易委员会提交,但要约人明确请求向证券交易委员会提交的除外。

(4)提出和解要约,即表明要约人放弃对如下事项享有的权利(但以要约被接受为前提):

(i)按发起程序所依据的制定法条文开展任何听证;

be or has been instituted;

(ii) The filing of proposed findings of fact and conclusions of law;

(iii) Proceedings before, and an initial decision by, a hearing officer;

(iv) All post-hearing procedures; and

(v) Judicial review by any court.

(5) By submitting an offer of settlement the person further waives:

(i) Such provisions of the Rules of Practice or other requirements of law as may be construed to prevent any member of the Commission's staff from participating in the preparation of, or advising the Commission as to, any order, opinion, finding of fact, or conclusion of law to be entered pursuant to the offer; and

(ii) Any right to claim bias or prejudgment by the Commission based on the consideration of or discussions concerning settlement of all or any part of the proceeding.

(6) If the Commission rejects the offer of settlement, the person making the offer shall be notified of the Commission's action and the offer of settlement shall be deemed withdrawn. The rejected offer shall not constitute a part of the record in any proceeding against the person making the offer, provided, however, that rejection of an offer of settlement does not affect the continued validity of waivers pursuant to paragraph (c)(5) of this section with respect to any discussions concerning the rejected offer of settlement.

(7) Final acceptance of any offer of settlement will occur only upon the issuance of findings and an order by the Commission.

§201.250 Motion for summary disposition.

(a) After a respondent's answer has been filed and, in an enforcement or a disciplinary proceeding, documents have been made available to that respondent for inspection and copying pursuant to §201.230, the respondent, or the interested division may make a motion for summary disposition of any or all allegations of the order instituting proceedings with respect to that respondent. If the interested division has not completed presentation of its case in chief, a motion for summary disposition shall be made only with leave of the hearing officer. The facts of the pleadings of the party against whom the motion is made shall be taken as true, except as modified by stipulations or admissions made by that party, by uncontested affidavits, or by facts officially noted pursuant to §201.323.

(b) The hearing officer shall promptly grant or deny the motion for summary disposition or shall defer decision on the motion. The hearing officer may grant the motion for summary disposition if there is no genuine issue with regard to any material fact and the party making the motion is entitled to a summary disposition as a matter of law. If it appears that a party, for good cause shown, cannot present by affidavit prior to hearing facts essential to justify opposition to the motion, the hearing officer shall deny or defer

(ii)提交事实认定和法律结论建议;

(iii)请求听证官主持程序并作出初步决定;

(iv)开展所有听证后程序;及

(v)请求法院进行司法审查。

(5)提出和解要约的,还表明和解要约人进一步:

(i)免除可能作出如下解释的《工作规则》条款或其他法律规定的适用:阻止证券交易委员会工作人员参与制作根据要约应制作的任何命令、意见、认定或结论或就此向证券交易委员会提供建议;以及

(ii)放弃基于对全部或任何部分程序的和解的审议或讨论主张证券交易委员会存在偏见或预判的任何权利。

(6)如果证券交易委员会驳回和解要约,要约人应获得相应通知,且和解要约应视为已经撤回。在针对要约人提起的任何程序中,被驳回的要约均不得构成程序记录的一部分,但是就对被驳回的和解要约的讨论而言,驳回和解要约并不影响本节第(c)(5)款规定的弃权的持续效力。

(7)任何和解要约的最终接受时间应为证券交易委员会发布事实认定和命令之时。

第201.250节　简易处理程序动议

(a)在相对人已经提交答辩,且就执法和纪律处分程序而言,相关文件已根据第201.230节开放给相对人查阅和复制之后,相对人或利害关系部门可提出动议,请求就程序发起令中关于相对人的任何或全部主张进行简易处理。如果利害关系部门自身尚未完成其案件陈词,提出简易处理程序动议必须经听证官许可。动议所针对的当事人的诉辩状所载事实应视为真实,但可基于如下原因修改:双方约定、动议针对方承认、双方无异议的宣誓证词或根据第201.323节已进行正式认知的事实。

(b)听证官应及时核准或驳回简易处理动议,或推迟就动议作出决定。如并不存在任何真正的重大事实争议,且动议方依据法律有权获得简易处理,听证官可以核准简易处理动议。如从表面判断,一方当事人存在充分理由,无法通过宣誓证词在听证前提出基本性的事实,证明反对动议的正当性,听证官应驳回动议或推迟对动议作出决定。听证官决定驳回提交简易处理动议申请的,当事人不得提起中间上诉。

the motion. A hearing officer's decision to deny leave to file a motion for summary disposition is not subject to interlocutory appeal.

(c) The motion for summary disposition, together with any supporting memorandum of points and authorities (exclusive of any declarations, affidavits, or attachments), shall not exceed 9,800 words. Requests for leave to file motions and accompanying documents in excess of 9,800 words are disfavored. A motion that does not, together with any accompanying memorandum of points and authorities, exceed 35 pages in length, inclusive of pleadings incorporated by reference (but excluding any declarations, affidavits, or attachments)is presumptively considered to contain no more than 9,800 words. Any motion that exceeds these page limits must include a certificate by the attorney, or an unrepresented party, stating that the brief complies with the length limitation set forth in this paragraph and stating the number of words in the motion. The person preparing the certificate may rely on the word count of a word-processing program to prepare the document.

[60 FR 32796, June 23, 1995, as amended at 70 FR 72570, Dec. 5, 2005]

Rules Regarding Hearings

§201.300 Hearings.

Hearings for the purpose of taking evidence shall be held only upon order of the Commission. All hearings shall be conducted in a fair, impartial, expeditious and orderly manner.

§201.301 Hearings to be public.

All hearings, except hearings on applications for confidential treatment filed pursuant to §201.190, hearings held to consider a motion for a protective order pursuant to §201.322, and hearings on *ex parte* application for a temporary cease-and-desist order, shall be public unless otherwise ordered by the Commission on its own motion or the motion of a party. No hearing shall be nonpublic where all respondents request that the hearing be made public.

§201.302 Record of hearings.

(a) *Recordation.* Unless ordered otherwise by the hearing officer or the Commission, all hearings shall be recorded and a written transcript thereof shall be prepared.

(b) *Availability of a transcript.* Transcripts of public hearings shall be available for purchase at prescribed rates. Transcripts of nonpublic proceedings, and transcripts subject to a protective order pursuant to §201.322, shall be available for purchase only by parties; provided, however, that any person compelled to submit data or evidence in a hearing may purchase a copy of his or her own testimony.

(c)简易处理动议以及任何附随的要点和依据备忘录(不包括任何声明、宣誓证词或附件)不得超过9800字。不鼓励提交超过9800字的动议和陈辩书。动议与附随要点和依据备忘录总长度不超过35页的(包括通过引用而纳入的诉辩状,但不包括任何声明、宣誓证词或附件),推定为不超过9800字。超出上述页数限制的任何动议必须附上一份律师证明或当事人本人(如其没有代理律师)出具的证明,说明该文件符合本款规定的篇幅限制,并注明该文件的字数。制作上述证明的人可以采信用于编制该文件的文字处理程序的字数统计结果。

[《联邦公报》第60卷第32796页,1995年6月23日,修正索引:《联邦公报》第70卷第72570页,2005年12月5日。]

听证规则

第201.300节　听证

为取证而举行听证的,必须由证券交易委员会发布命令。所有听证均应公平、公正、快速和有序开展。

第201.301节　听证的公开举行

除关于根据第201.190节提交的保密处理申请的听证、为审议根据第201.322节提出的保护令动议而举行的听证、就单方临时制止令申请举行的听证外,所有听证均应公开举行,但证券交易委员会主动或应一方当事人的动议而另行作出命令的除外。所有相对人均请求公开举行听证的,必须公开举行听证。

第201.302节　听证记录

(a)记录。除非听证官或证券交易委员会另行作出命令,所有听证均应进行记录,并制作书面笔录。

(b)笔录的提供。公开听证笔录应可以按照规定费率购买。非公开程序的笔录,以及根据第201.322节受保护令约束的笔录,仅得提供给当事人购买;但是,在听证中被强制呈报数据或证据的任何人均可购买一份其自身作出的证言。

(c) *Transcript correction.* Prior to the filing of post-hearing briefs or proposed findings and conclusions, or within such earlier time as directed by the Commission or the hearing officer, a party or witness may make a motion to correct the transcript. Proposed corrections of the transcript may be submitted to the hearing officer by stipulation pursuant to §201.324, or by motion. Upon notice to all parties to the proceeding, the hearing officer may, by order, specify corrections to the transcript.

§201.310 Failure to appear at hearings: Default.

Any person named in an order instituting proceedings as a person against whom findings may be made or sanctions imposed who fails to appear at a hearing of which he or she has been duly notified may be deemed to be in default pursuant to §201.155(a). A party may make a motion to set aside a default pursuant to §201.155(b).

§201.320 Evidence: Admissibility.

The Commission or the hearing officer may receive relevant evidence and shall exclude all evidence that is irrelevant, immaterial or unduly repetitious.

§201.321 Evidence: Objections and offers of proof.

(a) *Objections.* Objections to the admission or exclusion of evidence must be made on the record and shall be in short form, stating the grounds relied upon. Exceptions to any ruling thereon by the hearing officer need not be noted at the time of the ruling. Such exceptions will be deemed waived on appeal to the Commission, however, unless raised:

(1) Pursuant to interlocutory review in accordance with §201.400;

(2) In a proposed finding or conclusion filed pursuant to §201.340; or

(3) In a petition for Commission review of an initial decision filed in accordance with §201.410.

(b) *Offers of proof.* Whenever evidence is excluded from the record, the party offering such evidence may make an offer of proof, which shall be included in the record. Excluded material shall be retained pursuant to §201.350(b).

§201.322 Evidence: Confidential information, protective orders.

(a) *Procedure.* In any proceeding as defined in §201.101(a), a party, any person who is the owner, subject or creator of a document subject to subpoena or which may be introduced as evidence, or any witness who testifies at a hearing may file a motion requesting a protective order to limit from disclosure to other parties or to the public documents or testimony that contain confidential information. The motion should include a general summary or extract of the documents without revealing confidential details. If the movant seeks a protective order against disclosure to other parties as well as the public, copies of the documents shall not be served on other parties. Unless the documents are unavailable, the movant shall file for *in camera* inspection a sealed copy of the documents as to which the order is sought.

(c)笔录改正。在听证后提交陈辩书或认定建议和结论建议之前,或在证券交易委员会或听证官指示的更早的时间内,任何一方当事人或证人均可提出改正笔录的动议。当事人根据第201.324节达成约定或提出动议的,可向听证官呈报改正笔录的提议。向所有程序当事人发出通知后,听证官可以发布命令具体指明对笔录的改正。

第201.310节　未能出席听证:缺席

程序发起令中指明的将被作出事实认定或处以制裁的任何人,如已获得正式通知,但未能出席听证的,将根据第201.155(a)节被视为缺席。当事人可以根据第201.155(b)节提出撤销缺席决定的动议。

第201.320节　证据:可采性

证券交易委员会或听证官可以接收相关证据,并应排除所有不相关、不具重大意义或不必要的重复的证据。

第201.321节　证据:反对和证据认定动议

(a)反对。对证据采纳或排除的反对必须记录在案,形式应尽量简洁并说明所依据的基础。对听证官裁定的异议不必在作出裁定之时予以记录。该等异议将于向证券交易委员会提出上诉之时视为被放弃,但是下述异议除外:

(1)按照第201.400节依据中间复议提起的异议;

(2)在根据第201.340节提交的认定建议或结论建议中提出的异议;或

(3)在按照第201.410节向证券交易委员会提交的针对初步决定的复议请求书中提出的异议。

(b)证据认定动议。证据被排除在记录之外的,提供证据的当事人可以提出证据认定动议,该动议应纳入记录之内。被排除的材料应按照第201.350(b)节的规定保留。

第201.322节　证据:保密信息、保护令

(a)程序步骤。在第201.101(a)节定义的任何程序中,一方当事人,或传票要求提供的文件或可能作为证据提供的文件的所有人、主体或创建人,或在听证上作证的任何证人,均可以提交请求发布保护令的动议,限制向其他当事人或公众披露包含保密信息的文件或证言。动议应在不泄露保密信息的基础上对文件进行一般性的摘要或摘录。动议人寻求避免其他向当事人及公众披露的保护令的,不应向其他当事人送达文件复本。动议人应就其寻求保护的文件提供一份密封件,以供秘密查阅,但无法提供文件的除外。

(b) *Basis for issuance.* Documents and testimony introduced in a public hearing are presumed to be public. A motion for a protective order shall be granted only upon a finding that the harm resulting from disclosure would outweigh the benefits of disclosure.

(c) *Requests for additional information supporting confidentiality.* A movant under paragraph (a) of this section may be required to furnish in writing additional information with respect to the grounds for confidentiality. Failure to supply the information so requested within five days from the date of receipt by the movant of a notice of the information required shall be deemed a waiver of the objection to public disclosure of that portion of the documents to which the additional information relates, unless the Commission or the hearing officer shall otherwise order for good cause shown at or before the expiration of such five-day period.

(d) *Confidentiality of documents pending decision.* Pending a determination of a motion under this section, the documents as to which confidential treatment is sought and any other documents that would reveal the confidential information in those documents shall be maintained under seal and shall be disclosed only in accordance with orders of the Commission or the hearing officer. Any order issued in connection with a motion under this section shall be public unless the order would disclose information as to which a protective order has been granted, in which case that portion of the order that would reveal the protected information shall be nonpublic.

§201.323 Evidence: Official notice.

Official notice may be taken of any material fact which might be judicially noticed by a district court of the United States, any matter in the public official records of the Commission, or any matter which is peculiarly within the knowledge of the Commission as an expert body. If official notice is requested or taken of a material fact not appearing in the evidence in the record, the parties, upon timely request, shall be afforded an opportunity to establish the contrary.

§201.324 Evidence: Stipulations.

The parties may, by stipulation, at any stage of the proceeding agree upon any pertinent facts in the proceeding. A stipulation may be received in evidence and, when received, shall be binding on the parties to the stipulation.

§201.325 Evidence: Presentation under oath or affirmation.

A witness at a hearing for the purpose of taking evidence shall testify under oath or affirmation.

§201.326 Evidence: Presentation, rebuttal and cross-examination.

In any proceeding in which a hearing is required to be conducted on the record after opportunity for hearing in accord with 5 U.S.C. 556(a), a party is entitled to present its case or defense by oral or documentary evidence, to submit rebuttal evidence, and to

(b)签发基础。在公开听证中提出的文件和证词均推定为具有公开性。只有认定披露导致的损害将超出披露带来的利益之时,才能核准保护令动议。

(c)要求提供关于保密理由的补充信息。本节第(a)款规定的动议人可能被要求提供关于保密理由的书面补充信息。动议人未能在收到关于所需信息的通知后5日内按要求提供信息的,将被视为已放弃反对公开披露与补充信息相关的文件部分,但证券交易委员会或听证官在上述5日的期限届满之前或之后基于充分理由而另行作出命令的除外。

(d)待决期间文件的保密性。在根据本节对动议作出决定之前,寻求保密处理的文件以及任何将披露该等文件中的保密信息的其他文件均应密封保存,仅得按照证券交易委员会或听证官的命令进行披露。已发布的与本节项下动议相关的所有命令均应公开,但公开命令将导致已核准签发保护令的信息被披露的除外,此时将导致受保护信息被披露的命令部分应不予公开。

第201.323节　证据:正式认知

对于联邦地区法院可能进行司法认知的任何重大事实、证券交易委员会公开正式记录中的任何事项或证券交易委员会作为专业机构的知识范围之内的任何事项,均可进行正式认知。请求对于记录在案的证据之外的重大事实进行正式认知或实际对此进行正式认知的,当事人在及时提出请求的情况下,应获得证明不应进行正式认知的机会。

第201.324节　证据:当事人协议

当事人可以在程序的任何阶段,通过协议的形式就程序中的任何相关事实达成一致。当事人协议可作为证据接收,且一旦接收,即对约定双方有约束力。

第201.325节　证据:在宣誓或证词声明程序下进行的陈述

在为取证而进行的听证中,证人应当按照宣誓或证词声明程序作证。

第201.326节　证据:提交、反驳和交叉询问

在按照《美国法典》第五编第556(a)节应提供听证机会并记录在案的任何程序中,任一方当事人均有权通过口头或文件证据提交其主张或抗辩、呈报反证,以及证券交易委员会或听证官依其自由裁量权决定的开展完整、真实地披露事实所需的交叉询

conduct such cross-examination as, in the discretion of the Commission or the hearing officer, may be required for a full and true disclosure of the facts. The scope and form of evidence, rebuttal evidence, if any, and cross-examination, if any, in any other proceeding shall be determined by the Commission or the hearing officer in each proceeding.

§201.340 Proposed findings, conclusions and supporting briefs.

(a) *Opportunity to file.* Before an initial decision is issued, each party shall have an opportunity, reasonable in light of all the circumstances, to file in writing proposed findings and conclusions together with, or as a part of, its brief.

(b) *Procedure.* Proposed findings of fact must be supported by citations to specific portions of the record. If successive filings are directed, the proposed findings and conclusions of the party assigned to file first shall be set forth in serially numbered paragraphs, and any counter statement of proposed findings and conclusions must, in addition to any other matter, indicate those paragraphs of the proposals already filed as to which there is no dispute. A reply brief may be filed by the party assigned to file first, or, where simultaneous filings are directed, reply briefs may be filed by each party, within the period prescribed therefor by the hearing officer. No further briefs may be filed except with leave of the hearing officer.

(c) *Time for filing.* In any proceeding in which an initial decision is to be issued:

(1) At the end of each hearing, the hearing officer shall, by order, after consultation with the parties, prescribe the period within which proposed findings and conclusions and supporting briefs are to be filed. The party or parties directed to file first shall make its or their initial filing within 30 days of the end of the hearing unless the hearing officer, for good cause shown, permits a different period and sets forth in the order the reasons why the different period is necessary.

(2) The total period within which all such proposed findings and conclusions and supporting briefs and any counter statements of proposed findings and conclusions and reply briefs are to be filed shall be no longer than 90 days after the close of the hearing unless the hearing officer, for good cause shown, permits a different period and sets forth in an order the reasons why the different period is necessary.

§ 201.350 Record in proceedings before hearing officer; retention of documents; copies.

(a) *Contents of the record.* The record shall consist of:

(1) The order instituting proceedings, each notice of hearing and any amendments;

(2) Each application, motion, submission or other paper, and any amendments, motions, objections, and exceptions to or regarding them;

(3) Each stipulation, transcript of testimony and document or other item admitted into evidence;

问。在任何其他程序中证据、反证(如有)以及交叉询问(如有)的范围和形式均应由证券交易委员会或听证官在每一具体程序中作出决定。

第201.340节　认定建议、结论建议和支持性陈辩书

(a)提交机会。在发布初步决定之前,各当事人均应拥有合理机会(机会的合理性应综合考虑所有情形判断)提交书面认定建议、结论建议,该等建议可与陈辩书共同提交或作为陈辩书的一部分提交。

(b)程序步骤。事实认定建议必须引用具体记录内容作为支持。按指示依次提交建议的,被指定首先提交建议的当事人的认定建议和结论建议需对每个段落进行流水编号,对方当事人关于认定建议和结论的建议的声明,必须指明已提交的建议中不存在争议的段落。被指定首先提交的当事人(在按指示依次提交提议的情形下)或各当事人(在按指示同时提交提议的情形下),均可以在听证官规定的期限内提交答复陈辩书。除此之外,除非经听证官批准,不得提交其他陈辩书。

(c)提交时间。在需要发布初步决定的任何程序中:

(1)每次听证结束之时,听证官应在咨询各方当事人之后,通过命令指定提交认定建议和结论建议以及支持性陈辩书的期限。被指定首先提交的当事人应在听证结束后30日内进行初次提交,但听证官基于当事人提出的充分理由,批准其他提交期限并在命令中说明设定该等其他期限的必要性的原因的除外。

(2)所有上述认定建议和结论建议以及支持性陈辩书、对方关于认定建议和结论建议的声明以及答复陈辩书的提交期限加总不得超过听证结束后90日,但听证官基于当事人提出的充分理由,允许适用其他期限并在命令中说明设定该等其他期限的必要性的原因的除外。

第201.350节　听证官主持的程序之记录;文件保留;复本

(a)记录内容。记录应包含如下内容:

(1)程序发起令、所有听证通知及其所有修正;

(2)所有申请、动议、呈报文件或其他文件以及关于上述各者的修正、动议、反对和异议;

(3)所有约定、证言笔录以及被采纳为证据的文件和其他项目;

(4) Each written communication accepted by the hearing officer pursuant to §201.210;

(5) With respect to a request to disqualify a hearing officer or to allow the hearing officer's withdrawal under §201.112, each affidavit or transcript of testimony taken and the decision made in connection with the request;

(6) All motions, briefs and other papers filed on interlocutory appeal;

(7) All proposed findings and conclusions;

(8) Each written order issued by the hearing officer or Commission; and

(9) Any other document or item accepted into the record by the hearing officer.

(b) *Retention of documents not admitted.* Any document offered into evidence but excluded shall not be considered a part of the record. The Secretary shall retain any such document until the later of the date upon which a Commission order ending the proceeding becomes final, or the conclusion of any judicial review of the Commission's order.

(c) *Substitution of copies.* A true copy of a document may be substituted for any document in the record or any document retained pursuant to paragraph (b) of this section.

[60 FR 32796, June 23, 1995, as amended at 69 FR 13178, Mar. 19, 2004]

§201.351 Transmittal of documents to Secretary; record index; certification.

(a) *Transmittal from hearing officer to Secretary of partial record index.* The hearing officer may, at any time, transmit to the Secretary motions, exhibits or any other original documents filed with or accepted into evidence by the hearing officer, together with a list of such documents.

(b) *Preparation, certification of record index.* Promptly after the close of the hearing, the hearing officer shall transmit to the Secretary an index of the originals of any motions, exhibits or any other documents filed with or accepted into evidence by the hearing officer that have not been previously transmitted to the Secretary, and the Secretary shall prepare a record index. Prior to issuance of an initial decision, or if no initial decision is to be prepared, within 30 days of the close of the hearing, the Secretary shall transmit the record index to the hearing officer and serve a copy of the record index on each party. Any person may file proposed corrections to the record index with the hearing officer within 15 days of service of the record index. The hearing officer shall, by order, direct whether any corrections to the record index shall be made. The Secretary shall make such corrections, if any, and issue a revised record index. If an initial decision is to be issued, the initial decision shall include a certification that the record consists of the items set forth in the record index or revised record index issued by the Secretary.

(4)听证官根据第201.210节接受的每份书面通信;

(5)就第201.112节下当事人要求或听证官主动请求回避的情形而言,所有宣誓证词、提取的证言笔录以及就请求作出的决定;

(6)在中间上诉中提交的所有动议、陈辩书和其他文件;
(7)所有认定建议和结论建议;
(8)听证官或证券交易委员会发布的所有书面命令;及
(9)听证官纳入记录的任何其他文件或项目。

(b)未采纳文件的保留。作为证据提出但被排除的任何文件不得视为记录的一部分。证券交易委员会秘书应负责保留任何该等文件,直至证券交易委员会的程序终止令取得最终效力之日,或对证券交易委员会的命令进行的司法审查结束之日(以较迟者为准)。

(c)文件的替代。任何已纳入记录的文件或根据本节第(b)款保留的任何文件均可用于替代文件的真实复本。

[《联邦公报》第60卷第32796页,1995年6月23日,修正索引:《联邦公报》第69卷第13178页,2004年3月19日。]

第201.351条　向证券交易委员会秘书传送文件;记录索引;认证

(a)听证官向证券交易委员会秘书传送部分记录索引。听证官可以在任何时间向证券交易委员会秘书传送向听证官提交的或听证官采纳为证据的动议、证物或任何其他原始文件,并附上该等文件的列表。

(b)记录索引的制作和认证。听证结束之后,听证官应及时向证券交易委员会秘书传送一份关于下述各项的索引:向听证官提交或听证官作为证据接收的,但之前未向证券交易委员会秘书传送的所有动议、证物或任何其他文件的原件。证券交易委员会秘书应制作一份记录索引。在签发初步决定之前,或听证结束后30日内(如不必制作初步决定),证券交易委员会秘书应将记录索引传送给听证官,并向各当事人送达一份复本。任何人均可在记录索引送达后15日内向听证官提交改正记录索引的提议。听证官应发布命令指示是否应对记录索引进行任何改正。任何改正均应由证券交易委员会秘书作出,且秘书应签发一份修改后的记录索引。需要签发初步决定的,初步决定中应包含一份认证,证明记录中已包含证券交易委员会秘书签发的记录索引或修改后的记录索引中载明的各个项目。

(c) *Final transmittal of record items to the Secretary.* After the close of the hearing, the hearing officer shall transmit to the Secretary originals of any motions, exhibits or any other documents filed with, or accepted into evidence by, the hearing officer, or any other portions of the record that have not already been transmitted to the Secretary. Prior to service of the initial decision by the Secretary, or if no initial decision is to be issued, within 60 days of the close of the hearing, the Secretary shall inform the hearing officer if any portions of the record are not in the Secretary's custody.

[60 FR 32796, June 23, 1995, as amended at 69 FR 13178, Mar. 19, 2004]

§201.360 Initial decision of hearing officer.

(a)(1) *When required.* Unless the Commission directs otherwise, the hearing officer shall prepare an initial decision in any proceeding in which the Commission directs a hearing officer to preside at a hearing, provided, however, that an initial decision may be waived by the parties with the consent of the hearing officer pursuant to §201.202.

(2) *Time period for filing initial decision.* In the order instituting proceedings, the Commission will specify a time period in which the hearing officer's initial decision must be filed with the Secretary. In the Commission's discretion, after consideration of the nature, complexity, and urgency of the subject matter, and with due regard for the public interest and the protection of investors, this time period will be either 120, 210 or 300 days from the date of service of the order. Under the 300–day timeline, the hearing officer shall issue an order providing that there shall be approximately 4 months from the order instituting the proceeding to the hearing, approximately 2 months for the parties to obtain the transcript and submit briefs, and approximately 4 months after briefing for the hearing officer to issue an initial decision. Under the 210–day timeline, the hearing officer shall issue an order providing that there shall be approximately 21/2 months from the order instituting the proceeding to the hearing, approximately 2 months for the parties to review the transcript and submit briefs, and approximately 21/2 months after briefing for the hearing officer to issue an initial decision. Under the 120–day timeline, the hearing officer shall issue an order providing that there shall be approximately 1 month from the order instituting the proceeding to the hearing, approximately 2 months for the parties to review the transcript and submit briefs, and approximately 1 month after briefing for the hearing officer to issue an initial decision. These deadlines confer no substantive rights on respondents. If a stay is granted pursuant to §201.210(c)(3), the time period specified in the order instituting proceedings in which the hearing officer's initial decision must be filed with the Secretary, as well as any other time limits established in orders issued by the hearing officer in the proceeding, shall be automatically tolled during the period while the stay is in effect.

（c）最终向证券交易委员会秘书进行的记录传送。听证结束之后，听证官应向证券交易委员会传送下述各项的原件：向听证官提交或听证官作为证据接收的，但之前未向证券交易委员会秘书传送的所有动议、证物、任何其他文件或任何其他部分的记录。在证券交易委员会秘书送达初步决定之前，或听证结束后60日内（如不必签发初步决定），证券交易委员会秘书应告知听证官是否存在不由证券交易委员会秘书保管的任何记录部分。

[《联邦公报》第60卷第32796页，1995年6月23日，修正索引：《联邦公报》第69卷第13178页，2004年3月19日。]

第201.360节　听证官的初步决定

（a）（1）需要作出初步决定的时间。除非证券交易委员会另有指示，对于证券交易委员会指示听证官主持的所有程序，听证官均应制作一份初步决定，但是，经听证官同意，双方可以根据第201.202节放弃要求听证官作出初步决定。

（2）提交初步决定的期限。在程序发起令中，证券交易委员会将指定听证官必须向证券交易委员会秘书提交初步决定的期限。证券交易委员会在考虑标的之性质、复杂程度和紧急性后，并在适当顾及公共利益和投资者保护的情况下，可依其自由裁量权将期限定为程序发起令送达后120日、210日或300日。在300日的期限下，听证官应签发一份命令，规定从程序发起令签发到听证的时间应为4个月左右；当事人获得笔录和提交陈辩书的时间应为2个月左右；提交陈辩书至听证官签发初步决定的时间应为4个月左右。在210日的期限内，听证官应签发一份命令，规定从程序发起令签发到听证的时间应为两个半月左右；当事人获得笔录和提交陈辩书的时间应为2个月左右；提交陈辩书至听证官签发初步决定的时间应为两个半月左右。在120日的期限下，听证官应签发一份命令，规定从程序发起令签发到听证的时间应为1个月左右；当事人获得笔录和提交陈辩书的时间应为2个月左右；提交陈辩书至听证官签发初步决定的时间应为1个月左右。相对人不因上述最后期限享有任何实体权利。根据第201.210（c）（3）节核准中止的，程序发起令中规定的听证官必须向证券交易委员会提交初步决定的期限以及听证官在程序中发布命令确立的其他时限，均应按中止令的有效期自动延展。

(3) *Motion for extension.* In the event that the hearing officer presiding over the proceeding determines that it will not be possible to issue the initial decision within the specified period of time, the hearing officer should consult with the Chief Administrative Law Judge. Following such consultation, the Chief Administrative Law Judge may determine, in his or her discretion, to submit a motion to the Commission requesting an extension of the time period for filing the initial decision. This motion must be filed no later than 30 days prior to the expiration of the time specified in the order for issuance of an initial decision. The motion will be served upon all parties in the proceeding, who may file with the Commission statements in support of or in opposition to the motion. If the Commission determines that additional time is necessary or appropriate in the public interest, the Commission shall issue an order extending the time period for filing the initial decision.

(b) *Content.* An initial decision shall include: Findings and conclusions, and the reasons or basis therefor, as to all the material issues of fact, law or discretion presented on the record and the appropriate order, sanction, relief, or denial thereof. The initial decision shall also state the time period, not to exceed 21 days after service of the decision, except for good cause shown, within which a petition for review of the initial decision may be filed. The reasons for any extension of time shall be stated in the initial decision. The initial decision shall also include a statement that, as provided in paragraph (d) of this section:

(1) The Commission will enter an order of finality as to each party unless a party or an aggrieved person entitled to review timely files a petition for review of the initial decision or a motion to correct a manifest error of fact in the initial decision with the hearing officer, or the Commission determines on its own initiative to review the initial decision; and

(2) If a party or an aggrieved person entitled to review timely files a petition for review or a motion to correct a manifest error of fact in the initial decision with the hearing officer, or if the Commission takes action to review as to a party or an aggrieved person entitled to review, the initial decision shall not become final as to that party or person.

(c) *Filing, service and publication.* The hearing officer shall file the initial decision with the Secretary. The Secretary shall promptly serve the initial decision upon the parties and shall promptly publish notice of the filing thereof in the *SEC News Digest.* Thereafter, the Secretary shall publish the initial decision in the *SEC Docket* ; provided, however, that in nonpublic proceedings no notice shall be published unless the Commission otherwise directs.

(d) *Finality.* (1) If a party or an aggrieved person entitled to review timely files a

(3)延期动议。主持程序的听证官判定无法在规定的期限内签发初步决定的,应与首席行政法官协商。协商之后,首席行政法官可自行裁量决定向证券交易委员会呈报一份动议,请求延长提交初步决定的期限。动议至迟必须于初步决定签发令规定的期限届满前30日提交。动议将向全体程序当事人送达,当事人可向证券交易委员会提交支持或反对动议的声明。证券交易委员会判定出于公共利益考虑,有必要或宜应给予额外时间的,应签发一份命令,延长提交初步决定的期限。

(b)内容。初步决定应包括:关于记录中提出的所有重大事实、法律或自由裁量问题的认定和结论及其理由或依据,以及作出的适当命令、制裁、救济或否决。初步决定还应说明可请求对初步决定进行复议的期限,除非当事人提出充分理由,该等期限不得超过决定送达后21日。决定延长上述期限的,延期原因应在初步决定中说明。初步决定还应按本节第(d)款的规定,纳入关于如下事项的声明:

(1)证券交易委员会应向每一当事人作出一份终局命令,但一方当事人或有权提请复议的利益受侵害人及时向听证官提交对初步决定进行复议的请求,或提交改正初步决定中明显事实错误的动议,或证券交易委员会主动决定对初步决定进行复议的除外;以及

(2)如果一方当事人或有权提请复议的利益受侵害人及时向听证官提交对初步决定进行复议的请求,或提交改正初步决定中明显事实错误的动议,或证券交易委员会针对一方当事人或有权提请复议的利益受侵害人主动提起复议,则对于该当事人或利益受侵害人而言,初步决定不具有终局效力。

(c)提交、送达和公布。听证官应向证券交易委员会秘书提交初步决定。证券交易委员会秘书应及时向各当事人送达初步决定,并应及时就初步决定的提交在《证券交易委员会新闻摘要》上发布通知。此后,证券交易委员会秘书应在《证券交易委员会周志》上发布初步决定;但是,对于非公开程序,除非证券交易委员会另有指示,否则不得发布通知。

(d)终局效力。(1)如果一方当事人或有权提请复议的利益受侵害人及时向听证

petition for review or a motion to correct a manifest error of fact in the initial decision, or if the Commission on its own initiative orders review of a decision with respect to a party or a person aggrieved who would be entitled to review, the initial decision shall not become final as to that party or person.

(2) If a party or aggrieved person entitled to review fails to file timely a petition for review or a motion to correct a manifest error of fact in the initial decision, and if the Commission does not order review of a decision on its own initiative, the Commission will issue an order that the decision has become final as to that party. The decision becomes final upon issuance of the order. The order of finality shall state the date on which sanctions, if any, take effect. Notice of the order shall be published in the *SEC Docket* and on the SEC Web site.

[60 FR 32796, June 23, 1995, as amended at 68 FR 35789, June 17, 2003; 69 FR 13178, Mar. 19, 2004]

Appeal to the Commission and Commission Review

§201.400 Interlocutory review.

(a) *Availability.* The Commission may, at any time, on its own motion, direct that any matter be submitted to it for review. Petitions by parties for interlocutory review are disfavored, and the Commission ordinarily will grant a petition to review a hearing officer ruling prior to its consideration of an initial decision only in extraordinary circumstances. The Commission may decline to consider a ruling certified by a hearing officer pursuant to paragraph (c) of this section or the petition of a party who has been denied certification if it determines that interlocutory review is not warranted or appropriate under the circumstances. This section is the exclusive remedy for review of a hearing officer's ruling prior to Commission consideration of the entire proceeding and is the sole mechanism for appeal of actions delegated pursuant to §§200.30-9 and 200.30-10 of this chapter.

(b) *Expedited consideration.* Interlocutory review of a hearing officer's ruling shall be expedited in every way, consistent with the Commission's other responsibilities.

(c) *Certification process.* A ruling submitted to the Commission for interlocutory review must be certified in writing by the hearing officer and shall specify the material relevant to the ruling involved. The hearing officer shall not certify a ruling unless:

(1) His or her ruling would compel testimony of Commission members, officers or employees or the production of documentary evidence in their custody; or

(2) Upon application by a party, within five days of the hearing officer's ruling, the hearing officer is of the opinion that:

(i) The ruling involves a controlling question of law as to which there is substantial ground for difference of opinion; and

官提交对初步决定进行复议的请求,或提交改正初步决定中明显事实错误的动议,或证券交易委员会主动命令对针对一方当事人或有权提请复议的利益受侵害人作出的决定进行复议,则对于该当事人或利益受侵害人而言,初步决定不具有终局效力。

(2)如果一方当事人或有权提请复议的利益受侵害人未及时提交复议请求或提交改正初步决定中明显事实错误的动议,且证券交易委员会未主动命令对决定进行复议,则证券交易委员会将签发一份命令,说明决定已对该当事人产生终局效力。上述命令签发之时,决定即取得终局效力。终局命令应说明制裁(如有)的生效日期。关于上述命令的通知应于《证券交易委员会周志》和证券交易委员会网站上发布。

[《联邦公报》第60卷第32796页,1995年6月23日,修正索引:《联邦公报》第68卷第35789页,2003年6月17日;《联邦公报》第69卷第13178页,2004年3月19日。]

向证券交易委员会提出的复议以及证券交易委员会开展的复议

第201.400节　中间复议

(a)适用情形。证券交易委员会可以在任何时间主动指令将任何事项提交其复议。不鼓励当事人提交中间复议请求书;一般而言,只有在特殊情况下,证券交易委员会才会在其审议初步决定之前,核准对听证官的裁定进行复议。对于听证官已根据本节第(c)款进行认证的裁定,或被拒绝认证的当事人提出的请求,如证券交易委员会根据具体情形判定不应或不宜进行中间复议,证券交易委员会可以拒绝进行审议。对于证券交易委员会审议整体程序之前对听证官裁定进行的复议,本节规定构成唯一救济,同时也是对本章第200.30-9节和第200.30-10节所委托授权的行动的唯一复议机制。

(b)加快审议。对听证官裁定的中间复议应在不与证券交易委员会其他职责冲突的情况下,尽可能快速地进行。

(c)认证程序。呈报证券交易委员会进行中间复议的裁定必须由听证官进行书面认证,并注明与裁定相关的材料。听证官不得对裁定进行认证,除非:

(1)其裁定将强制要求证券交易委员会委员、管理人员或职员提供证言或提供其所保管的文件证据;或

(2)一方当事人在听证官作出裁定后5日内提出申请,且听证官认为:

(i)裁定涉及关键性的法律问题,且存在提出异议的实体基础;及

(ii) An immediate review of the order may materially advance the completion of the proceeding.

(d) *Proceedings not stayed.* The filing of an application for review or the grant of review shall not stay proceedings before the hearing officer unless he or she, or the Commission, shall so order. The Commission will not consider the motion for a stay unless the motion shall have first been made to the hearing officer.

[60 FR 32796, June 23, 1995, as amended at 69 FR 13178, Mar. 19, 2004]

§201.401 Consideration of stays.

(a) *Procedure.* A request for a stay shall be made by written motion, filed pursuant to §201.154, and served on all parties pursuant to §201.150. The motion shall state the reasons for the relief requested and the facts relied upon, and, if the facts are subject to dispute, the motion shall be supported by affidavits or other sworn statements or copies thereof. Portions of the record relevant to the relief sought, if available to the movant, shall be filed with the motion. The Commission may issue a stay based on such motion or on its own motion.

(b) *Scope of relief.* The Commission may grant a stay in whole or in part, and may condition relief under this section upon such terms, or upon the implementation of such procedures, as it deems appropriate.

(c) *Stay of a Commission order.* A motion for a stay of a Commission order may be made by any person aggrieved thereby who would be entitled to review in a federal court of appeals. A motion seeking to stay the effectiveness of a Commission order pending judicial review may be made to the Commission at any time during which the Commission retains jurisdiction over the proceeding.

(d) *Stay of an action by a self-regulatory organization*—(1) *Availability.* A motion for a stay of an action by a self-regulatory organization for which the Commission is the appropriate regulatory agency, for which action review may be sought pursuant to §201.420, may be made by any person aggrieved thereby at the time an application for review is filed in accordance with §201.420 or thereafter.

(2) *Summary entry.* A stay may be entered summarily, without notice and opportunity for hearing.

(3) *Expedited consideration.* Where the action complained of has already taken effect and the motion for stay is filed within 10 days of the effectiveness of the action, or where the action complained of, will, by its terms, take effect within five days of the filing of the motion for stay, the consideration of and decision on the motion for a stay shall be expedited in every way, consistent with the Commission's other responsibilities. Where consideration will be expedited, persons opposing the motion for a stay may file a

(ii)立即对裁定进行复议可以实质性地推动程序的完成。

(d)程序不中止。提交复议申请或核准复议的,听证官主持的程序不因此而中止,但听证官或证券交易委员会命令予以中止的除外。除非已先行向听证官提出中止动议,否则证券交易委员会不受理中止动议。

[《联邦公报》第60卷第32796页,1995年6月23日,修正索引:《联邦公报》第69卷第13178页,2004年3月19日。]

第201.401节 对中止的审议

(a)程序步骤。程序中止请求应通过书面动议作出,根据第201.154节提交,并按照第201.150节的规定向各当事人送达。动议应说明寻求救济的原因、所依赖的事实基础,且如事实存在争议,还应附上宣誓证词或其他宣誓声明或其复本作为支持文件。对于与所寻求救济相关的记录内容,应与动议共同提交,但以动议人可以获得该等内容为前提。证券交易委员会可以基于该等动议签发或主动签发中止令。

(b)救济范围。证券交易委员会可以核准对程序进行全部或部分中止,并可以就本节中的救济设定其认为适当的条件、条款或实施其认为适当的程序步骤。

(c)证券交易委员会命令的中止执行。权益受到证券交易委员会命令侵害,且有权向联邦上诉法院提请审查的任何主体,均可以提出中止证券交易委员会命令的动议。在证券交易委员会保有对程序的管辖权的期间,任何时间均可以司法审查尚未结束为由提出请求中止执行证券交易委员会命令的动议。

(d)自律组织行动的中止执行——(1)适用情形。对于可以根据第201.420节寻求复议的自律组织的行动,且证券交易委员会属于该等自律组织的相应监管机构的,权益受该等行动侵害的任何人均可以在按照第201.420节提交复议申请之时或之后提出中止自律组织行动的动议。

(2)简易裁决。中止令可通过简易程序作出,不必发送通知和提供听证机会。

(3)加快审议。如被提起申诉的行动已经生效且中止动议在行动生效后10日内提起,或被提起申诉的行动按其条款将在中止动议提起后5日内生效,对中止动议的审议和决定应在不违反证券交易委员会其他职责的情况下加速开展。进行加快审议时,反对中止动议的人可以在动议送达后2日内提交反对声明,但委员会通过书面命令另行指定其他期限的除外。

statement in opposition within two days of service of the motion unless the Commission, by written order, shall specify a different period.

(e) *Lifting of stay of action by the Public Company Accounting Oversight Board*—(1) *Availability.* Any person aggrieved by a stay of action by the Board entered in accordance with 15 U.S.C. 7215(e) for which review has been sought pursuant to §201.440 or which the Commission has taken up on its motion pursuant to §201.441 may make a motion to lift the stay. The Commission may, at any time, on its own motion determine whether to lift the automatic stay.

(2) *Summary action.* The Commission may lift a stay summarily, without notice and opportunity for hearing.

(3) *Expedited consideration.* The Commission may expedite consideration of a motion to lift a stay of Board action, consistent with the Commission's other responsibilities. Where consideration is expedited, persons opposing the lifting of the stay may file a statement in opposition within two days of service of the motion requesting lifting of the stay unless the Commission, by written order, shall specify a different period.

[60 FR 32796, June 23, 1995, as amended at 69 FR 13178, Mar. 19, 2004]

§201.410 Appeal of initial decisions by hearing officers.

(a) *Petition for review; when available.* In any proceeding in which an initial decision is made by a hearing officer, any party, and any other person who would have been entitled to judicial review of the decision entered therein if the Commission itself had made the decision, may file a petition for review of the decision with the Commission.

(b) *Procedure.* The petition for review of an initial decision shall be filed with the Commission within such time after service of the initial decision as prescribed by the hearing officer pursuant to §201.360(b) unless a party has filed a motion to correct an initial decision with the hearing officer. If such correction has been sought, a party shall have 21 days from the date of the hearing officer's order resolving the motion to correct to file a petition for review. The petition shall set forth the specific findings and conclusions of the initial decision as to which exception is taken, together with supporting reasons for each exception. Supporting reasons may be stated in summary form. Any exception to an initial decision not stated in the petition for review, or in a previously filed proposed finding made pursuant to §201.340 may, at the discretion of the Commission, be deemed to have been waived by the petitioner. In the event a petition for review is filed, any other party to the proceeding may file a cross-petition for review within the original time allowed for seeking review or within ten days from the date that the petition for review was filed, whichever is later.

(c) *Financial disclosure statement requirement.* Any person who files a petition for

(e)取消公众公司会计监督委员会行动的中止执行——(1)适用范围。公众公司会计监督委员会的行动根据《美国法典》第十五编第7215(e)节被中止执行,且已根据第201.440节被提起复议,或证券交易委员会根据第201.441节主动提起复议的,权益受中止令侵害的任何人均可以提出取消中止的动议。证券交易委员会可以在任何时间主动判定是否取消自动中止。

(2)简易行动。证券交易委员会可以通过简易程序取消中止执行,而不必发出通知和提供听证机会。

(3)加快审议。证券交易委员会可以在不与证券交易委员会其他职责相冲突的情况下,加速对取消中止执行公众公司会计监督委员会行动的动议进行审查。进行加快审查时,反对取消中止的人可以在取消中止的动议送达后2日内提交反对声明,但委员会通过书面命令另行指定其他期限的除外。

[《联邦公报》第60卷第32796页,1995年6月23日,修正索引:《联邦公报》第69卷第13178页,2004年3月19日。]

第201.410节　对听证官初步决定的复议

(a)复议请求;适用时间。听证官在任何程序中作出初步决定的,任何当事人及如该等决定系由证券交易委员会作出时有权提请司法审查的任何其他人,均可以针对该等初步决定向证券交易委员会提出复议请求。

(b)程序步骤。针对初步决定的复议请求应在听证官根据第201.360(b)节规定的初步决定送达后的期间内向证券交易委员会提出,但一方当事人向听证官提出改正初步决定的错误的动议的除外。当事人提请改正初步决定的,当事人可在听证官就动议发布命令后21日内提交复议请求书。请求书中应载明请求人存在异议的初步决定的具体认定和结论,以及支持每个异议的理由。支持理由可简要说明。对于未在复议请求书中提出的异议,或未在之前根据第201.340节提交的认定建议中提出的异议,证券交易委员会可依其自由裁量权视为请求人已放弃该等异议。如已提交复议请求书,程序的任何其他当事人均可以在原来的允许提出复议的期限或复议申请提交后10日内(以较迟者为准)提出交叉复议请求。

(c)财务披露报表要求。任何人针对初步决定提交复议请求书,主张其无力支付没

review of an initial decision that asserts that person's inability to pay either disgorgement, interest or a penalty shall file with the opening brief a sworn financial disclosure statement containing the information specified in §201.630(b).

(d) [Reserved]

(e) *Prerequisite to judicial review.* Pursuant to Section 704 of the Administrative Procedure Act, 5 U.S.C. 704, a petition to the Commission for review of an initial decision is a prerequisite to the seeking of judicial review of a final order entered pursuant to such decision.

[60 FR 32796, June 23, 1995, as amended at 69 FR 13179, Mar. 19, 2004]

§201.411 Commission consideration of initial decisions by hearing officers.

(a) *Scope of review.* The Commission may affirm, reverse, modify, set aside or remand for further proceedings, in whole or in part, an initial decision by a hearing officer and may make any findings or conclusions that in its judgment are proper and on the basis of the record.

(b) *Standards for granting review pursuant to a petition for review* — (1) *Mandatory review.* After a petition for review has been filed, the Commission shall review any initial decision that:

(i) Denies any request for action pursuant to Section 8(a) or Section 8(c) of the Securities Act of 1933, 15 U.S.C. 77h(a), (c), or the first sentence of Section 12(d) of the Exchange Act, 15 U.S.C. 78*l* (d);

(ii) Suspends trading in a security pursuant to Section 12(k) of the Exchange Act, 15 U.S.C. 78l(k); or

(iii) Is in a case of adjudication (as defined in 5 U.S.C. 551) not required to be determined on the record after notice and opportunity for hearing (except to the extent there is involved a matter described in 5 U.S.C. 554(a)(1) through (6)).

(2) *Discretionary review.* The Commission may decline to review any other decision. In determining whether to grant review, the Commission shall consider whether the petition for review makes a reasonable showing that:

(i) A prejudicial error was committed in the conduct of the proceeding; or

(ii) The decision embodies:

(A) A finding or conclusion of material fact that is clearly erroneous; or

(B) A conclusion of law that is erroneous; or

(C) An exercise of discretion or decision of law or policy that is important and that the Commission should review.

(c) *Commission review other than pursuant to a petition for review.* The Commission may, on its own initiative, order review of any initial decision, or any portion of any initial

收款项、利息或罚款的,应在提交开案陈辩书的同时提交一份经宣誓的财务披露报表,载明第201.630(b)节规定的信息。

(d)[保留]

(e)司法审查的先决条件。根据《行政程序法》第704条(《美国法典》第五编第704节),向证券交易委员会提交针对初步决定的复议请求书,是提请对根据该决定作出的最终命令进行司法审查的先决条件。

[《联邦公报》第60卷第32796页,1995年6月23日,修正索引:《联邦公报》第69卷第13179页,2004年3月19日。]

第201.411节　证券交易委员会对听证官初步决定的审议

(a)复议范围。对于听证官作出的初步决定,证券交易委员会可予以全部或部分确认、推翻、修改、撤销或发回进一步审理,并可以基于记录,根据其判断作出其认为适当的任何认定或结论。

(b)根据复议请求核准复议的标准——(1)强制性复议。下述初步决定被提出复议请求的,证券交易委员会应进行复议:

(i)根据《1933年证券法》第8(a)条、第8(c)条[《美国法典》第十五编第77h(a)节、第77h(c)节]或《证券交易法》第12(d)条第一句规定[《美国法典》第十五编第78 l(d)节]驳回任何行动申请的初步决定;

(ii)根据《证券交易法》第12(k)条[《美国法典》第十五编第78 l(k)节]暂停证券交易的初步决定;或

(iii)不必给予通知和听证机会并记录在案的所有行政裁决案件(定义见《美国法典》第五编第551节)中作出的初步决定,但涉及《美国法典》第五编第554(a)(1)~554(a)(6)节所述事项的除外。

(2)全权决定是否受理复议。证券交易委员会可以拒绝对任何其他决定进行复议。在判定是否核准复议时,证券交易委员会应考虑复议请求是否合理证明了如下事项:

(i)程序开展中存在偏见性错误;或

(ii)该决定:

(A)关于关键事实的认定或结论存在明显错误;或

(B)关于法律的结论存在明显错误;或

(C)对自由裁量权的行使或对法律或政策作出的决定十分重大,需要证券交易委员会进行复议。

(c)证券交易委员会非基于复议请求开展的复议。在根据第210.410(b)节指定的复议请求提交期限结束后21日内,证券交易委员会可以主动命令对任何初步决定或

decision, within 21 days after the end of the period established for filing a petition for review pursuant to §210.410(b). A party who does not intend to file a petition for review, and who desires the Commission's determination whether to order review on its own initiative to be made in a shorter time, may make a motion for an expedited decision, accompanied by a written statement that the party waives its right to file a petition for review. The vote of one member of the Commission, conveyed to the Secretary, shall be sufficient to bring a matter before the Commission for review.

(d) *Limitations on matters reviewed.* Review by the Commission of an initial decision shall be limited to the issues specified in the petition for review or the issues, if any, specified in the briefing schedule order issued pursuant to §201.450(a). On notice to all parties, however, the Commission may, at any time prior to issuance of its decision, raise and determine any other matters that it deems material, with opportunity for oral or written argument thereon by the parties.

(e) *Summary affirmance.* (1) At any time within 21 days after the filing of a petition for review pursuant to §201.410(b), any party may file a motion in accordance with §201.154 asking that the Commission summarily affirm an initial decision. Any party may file an opposition and reply to such motion in accordance with §201.154. Pending determination of the motion for summary affirmance, the Commission, in its discretion, may delay issuance of a briefing schedule order pursuant to §201.450.

(2) Upon consideration of the motion and any opposition or upon its own initiative, the Commission may summarily affirm an initial decision. The Commission may grant summary affirmance if it finds that no issue raised in the initial decision warrants consideration by the Commission of further oral or written argument. The Commission will decline to grant summary affirmance upon a reasonable showing that a prejudicial error was committed in the conduct of the proceeding or that the decision embodies an exercise of discretion or decision of law or policy that is important and that the Commission should review.

(f) *Failure to obtain a majority.* In the event a majority of participating Commissioners do not agree to a disposition on the merits, the initial decision shall be of no effect, and an order will be issued in accordance with this result.

[60 FR 32796, June 23, 1995, as amended at 69 FR 13179, Mar. 19, 2004; 70 FR 72570, Dec. 5, 2005]

§201.420 Appeal of determinations by self-regulatory organizations.

(a) *Application for review; when available.* An application for review by the Commission may be filed by any person who is aggrieved by a self-regulatory organization determination as to which a notice is required to be filed with the Commission pursuant to Section 19(d)(1) of the Exchange Act, 15 U.S.C. 78s(d)(1). Such determinations include any:

其任何部分进行复议。无意提交复议请求以及希望证券交易委员会在更短期限内决定是否主动发布命令进行复议的一方当事人,可提出动议,请求证券交易委员会加快作出决定,并附上其放弃提交复议请求的书面声明。一名证券交易委员会委员投票,并传达给证券交易委员会秘书的,即应将相关事项提交证券交易委员会复议。

(d)复议事项的限制。证券交易委员会对初步决定的复议应当限于复议请求书中指定的事项,或根据第201.450(a)节签发的陈辩书提交日程命令中指定的事项(如有)。但是,向所有当事人发出通知并向当事人提供口头或书面辩论机会后,证券交易委员会可以在签发决定前的任何时间,提起其认为具有重大性质的事项并作出决定。

(e)简易确认。(1)在根据第201.410(b)节提交复议请求后21日的任何时间内,任一方当事人均可以依据第201.154节提交动议,要求证券交易委员会对初步决定进行简易确认。任一方当事人均可以依据第201.154节就该等动议提交反对和答复。在对简易确认动议作出最终决定之前,证券交易委员会可依其自由裁量权推迟根据第201.450节签发陈辩书提交日程命令。

(2)证券交易委员会可以主动,或在审议动议和对动议的任何反对意见后,对初步决定进行简易确认。如证券交易委员会认定初步决定中提出的问题不必证券交易委员会审议,亦不必进行进一步的口头或书面辩论,证券交易委员会可以对初步决定进行简易确认。如能合理表明程序开展中存在偏见性错误,或决定中行使的自由裁量权或对法律或政策作出的决定性质重大,需要证券交易委员会进行复议,证券交易委员会将拒绝批准简易确认。

(f)未能取得过半数同意。实质问题的处理若未取得参与复议的过半数证券交易委员会委员同意,初步决定应归于无效,证券交易委员会应按上述结果签发一份命令。

[《联邦公报》第60卷第32796页,1995年6月23日,修正索引:《联邦公报》第69卷第13179页,2004年3月19日;《联邦公报》第70卷第72570页,2005年12月5日。]

第201.420节　对自律组织决定的复议

(a)复议申请;适用时间。自律组织的决定,如根据《证券交易法》第19(d)(1)条[《美国法典》第十五编第78s(d)(1)节]应通知证券交易委员会,则权益受该等决定侵害的任何人均可以向证券交易委员会提出复议申请。该等决定包括:

(1) Final disciplinary sanction;

(2) Denial or conditioning of membership or participation;

(3) Prohibition or limitation in respect to access to services offered by that self-regulatory organization or a member thereof; or

(4) Bar from association.

(b) *Procedure.* As required by section 19(d)(1) of the Securities Exchange Act of 1934, 15 U.S.C. 78s(d)(1), an applicant must file an application for review with the Commission within 30 days after the notice of the determination is filed with the Commission and received by the aggrieved person applying for review. The Commission will not extend this 30-day period, absent a showing of extraordinary circumstances. This section is the exclusive remedy for seeking an extension of the 30-day period.

(c) *Application.* The application shall be filed with the Commission pursuant to §201.151. The applicant shall serve the application on the self-regulatory organization. The application shall identify the determination complained of and set forth in summary form a brief statement of the alleged errors in the determination and supporting reasons therefor. The application shall state an address where the applicant can be served. The application should not exceed two pages in length. If the applicant will be represented by a representative, the application shall be accompanied by the notice of appearance required by §201.102(d).

(d) *Determination not stayed.* Filing an application for review with the Commission pursuant to paragraph (b) of this section shall not operate as a stay of the complained of determination made by the self-regulatory organization unless the Commission otherwise orders either pursuant to a motion filed in accordance with §201.401 or on its own motion.

(e) *Certification of the record; service of the index.* Fourteen days after receipt of an application for review or a Commission order for review, the self-regulatory organization shall certify and file with the Commission one copy of the record upon which the action complained of was taken, and shall file with the Commission three copies of an index to such record, and shall serve upon each party one copy of the index.

[60 FR 32796, June 23, 1995, as amended at 69 FR 13179, Mar. 19, 2004]

§201.421 Commission consideration of determinations by self-regulatory organizations.

(a) *Commission review other than pursuant to a petition for review.* The Commission may, on its own initiative, order review of any determination by a self-regulatory organization that could be subject to an application for review pursuant to §201.420 (a) within 40 days after notice thereof was filed with the Commission pursuant to Section 19 (d)(1) of the Exchange Act, 15 U.S.C. 78s(d)(1).

(1)最终纪律处分决定;

(2)拒绝批准或限制成员资格或参与资格的决定;

(3)禁止或限制获取自律组织或其成员提供的服务的决定;或

(4)禁止发生业务相关关系的决定。

(b)程序步骤。如《1934年证券交易法》第19(d)(1)条[《美国法典》第十五编第78s(d)(1)节]所规定,申请人必须在关于决定的通知向证券交易委员会提交并被权益受侵害而申请复议的人收悉后30日内向证券交易委员会提交复议申请。如申请人不能证明存在特殊情形,证券交易委员会不会延长上述30日的期限。申请人要求延长上述30日期限的,本节规定是其享有的排他性救济。

(c)申请。申请应根据第201.151节向证券交易委员会提交。申请人应将申请送达自律组织。申请中应指明被提起复议的自律组织决定,并简要说明申请人声称决定中存在的错误及支持其主张的理由。申请中应说明申请人接收文书送达的地址。申请不得超过两页。申请人由代理人代理的,应按第201.102(d)节的规定附上出席通知。

(d)不中止决定执行。根据本节第(b)款向证券交易委员会提交复议申请的,被提起复议的自律组织决定不中止执行,但证券交易委员会主动或根据按照第201.401节提交的动议另行作出命令的除外。

(e)记录认证;索引的送达。自律组织应在收到复议申请或证券交易委员会的复议命令后14日内,对被提起复议的行动的记录进行认证,并向证券交易委员会提交一份复本,同时向证券交易委员会提交三份以及向每一方当事人提交一份记录索引。

[《联邦公报》第60卷第32796页,1995年6月23日,修正索引:《联邦公报》第69卷第13179页,2004年3月19日。]

第201.421节 证券交易委员会对自律组织决定的审议

(a)证券交易委员会非根据复议请求进行的复议。对于可能根据第201.420(a)节被提起复议申请的自律组织决定,证券交易委员会可以在关于任何该等决定的通知按照《证券交易法》第19(d)(1)条[《美国法典》第十五编第78s(d)(1)节]向证券交易委员会提交后40日内,主动命令对之进行复议。

(b) *Supplemental briefing.* The Commission may at any time prior to issuance of its decision raise or consider any matter that it deems material, whether or not raised by the parties. Notice to the parties and an opportunity for supplemental briefing with respect to issues not briefed by the parties shall be given where the Commission believes that such briefing would significantly aid the decisional process.

§201.430 Appeal of actions made pursuant to delegated authority.

(a) *Scope of rule.* Any person aggrieved by an action made by authority delegated in §§200.30-1 through 200.30-8 or §§200.30-11 through 200.30-18 of this chapter may seek review of the action pursuant to paragraph (b) of this section.

(b) *Procedure*—(1) *Notice of intention to petition for review.* A party to an action made pursuant to delegated authority, or a person aggrieved by such action, may seek Commission review of the action by filing a written notice of intention to petition for review within five days after actual notice of the action to that party or aggrieved person, or 15 days after publication of the notice of action in the Federal Register,or 5 days after service of notice of the action on that party or aggrieved person pursuant to §201.141(b), whichever is the earliest.

(2) *Petition for review.* Within 5 days after the filing of a notice of intention to petition for review pursuant to paragraph (b)(1) of this section, the person seeking review shall file a petition for review containing a clear and concise statement of the issues to be reviewed and the reasons why review is appropriate. The petition shall include exceptions to any findings of fact or conclusions of law made, together with supporting reasons for such exceptions based on appropriate citations to such record as may exist. These reasons may be stated in summary form.

(c) *Prerequisite to judicial review.* Pursuant to Section 704 of the Administrative Procedure Act, 5 U.S.C. 704, a petition to the Commission for review of an action made by authority delegated in §§200.30-1 through 200.30-18 of this chapter is a prerequisite to the seeking of judicial review of a final order entered pursuant to such an action. Pursuant to 15 U.S.C. 7214(h)(2), any decision by the Commission pursuant to 200.30-11 shall not be reviewable under 15 U.S.C. 78y and shall not be deemed "final agency action" for purposes of 5 U.S.C. 704.

[60 FR 32796, June 23, 1995; 60 FR 46500, Sept. 7, 1995, as amended at 69 FR 13179, Mar. 19, 2004; 70 FR 72570, Dec. 5, 2005; 75 FR 47449, Aug. 6, 2010]

§201.431 Commission consideration of actions made pursuant to delegated authority.

(a) *Scope of review.* The Commission may affirm, reverse, modify, set aside or remand for further proceedings, in whole or in part, any action made pursuant to authority

(b)补充陈辩书。证券交易委员会可以在签发决定前任何时间提出或审议其认为具有重大性质的任何事项,而不论当事人是否提出了该等事项。对于当事人未在陈辩书中提出的问题,如证券交易委员会认为将有力地推动决策程序的开展,应向各当事人发送通知并为之提供提交补充陈辩书的机会。

第201.430节 对委托授权行动的复议

(a)规则适用范围。对于根据本章第200.30-1~200.30-8节或第200.30-11~200.30-18节的委托授权采取的行动,权益受侵害的任何人均可以根据本条第(b)款提请复议。

(b)程序步骤——(1)复议请求意向通知。对于根据委托授权采取的行动,当事人或权益受该等行动侵害的人可以在实际知悉该等行动后5日内,或该等通知在《联邦公报》上发布后15日内,或在根据第201.141(b)节向该当事人或利益受侵害人送达通知后5日内(以最早者为准),提交复议请求意向通知,提请证券交易委员会进行复议。

(2)复议请求书。根据本节第(b)(1)款提交复议请求的意向通知后5日内,复议提请人应提交一份复议请求书,清晰、简要地说明需要复议的问题以及证明复议正当性的理由。请求书应包括对任何认定、结论的异议,以及支持该等异议的理由,并适当引用可能存在的记录。支持异议的理由简单说明即可。

(c)司法审查的先决条件。根据《行政程序法》第704条(《美国法典》第五编第704节),针对根据本章第200.30-1~200.30-18节的委托授权采取的行动向证券交易委员会提出复议请求书,是提请对根据该等行动作出的最终命令进行司法审查的先决条件。根据《美国法典》第十五编第7214(h)(2)节,证券交易委员会根据第200.30-11节作出的任何行动不得根据《美国法典》第十五编第78y节进行复议,且不得视为《美国法典》第五编第704节规定的"最终机构行动"。

[《联邦公报》第60卷第32796页,1995年6月23日;《联邦公报》第60卷第46500页,1995年9月7日,修正索引:《联邦公报》第69卷第13179页,2004年3月19日;《联邦公报》第70卷第72570页,2005年12月5日;《联邦公报》第75卷第47449页,2010年8月6日。]

第201.431节 证券交易委员会对委托授权行动的审议

(a)复议范围。对于根据本章第200.30-1~200.30-18节的委托授权采取的任何行动,证券交易委员会可予以全部或部分确认、推翻、修改、撤销或发回启动进一步

delegated in §§200.30–1 through 200.30–18 of this chapter.

(b) *Standards for granting review pursuant to a petition for review*—(1)*Mandatory review.* After a petition for review has been filed, the Commission shall review any action that it would be required to review pursuant to §201.411(b)(1) if the action was made as the initial decision of a hearing officer.

(2) *Discretionary review.* The Commission may decline to review any other action. In determining whether to grant review, the Commission shall consider the factors set forth in §201.411(b)(2).

(c) *Commission review other than pursuant to a petition for review.* The Commission may, on its own initiative, order review of any action made pursuant to delegated authority at any time, provided, however, that where there are one or more parties to the matter, such review shall not be ordered more than ten days after the action. The vote of one member of the Commission, conveyed to the Secretary, shall be sufficient to bring a matter before the Commission for review.

(d) *Required items in an order for review.* In an order granting a petition for review or directing review on the Commission's own initiative, the Commission shall set forth the time within which any party or other person may file a statement in support of or in opposition to the action made by delegated authority and shall state whether a stay shall be granted, if none is in effect, or shall be continued, if in effect pursuant to paragraph (e) of this section.

(e) *Automatic stay of delegated action.* An action made pursuant to delegated authority shall have immediate effect and be deemed the action of the Commission. Upon filing with the Commission of a notice of intention to petition for review, or upon notice to the Secretary of the vote of a Commissioner that a matter be reviewed, an action made pursuant to delegated authority shall be stayed until the Commission orders otherwise, provided, however, there shall be no automatic stay of an action:

(1) To grant a stay of action by the Commission or a self–regulatory organization as authorized by 17 CFR 200.30–14(g)(5)–(6); or

(2) To commence a subpoena enforcement proceeding as authorized by 17 CFR 200.30–4(a)(10).

(f) *Effectiveness of stay or of Commission decision to modify or reverse a delegated action.* As against any person who shall have acted in reliance upon any action at a delegated level, any stay or any modification or reversal by the Commission of such action shall be effective only from the time such person receives actual notice of such stay, modification or reversal.

[60 FR 32796, June 23, 1995; 60 FR 46500, Sept. 7, 1995]

程序。

（b）根据复议请求核准复议的标准——（1）强制性复议。假设被提请复议的行动是听证官作出的初步决定，且根据第201.411（b）（1）节必须进行复议的，则经提起复议请求后，证券交易委员会应对该等行动进行复议。

（2）全权决定是否受理复议。证券交易委员会可以拒绝对任何其他行动进行复议。在判定是否核准复议时，证券交易委员会应考虑第201.411（b）（2）节中规定的因素。

（c）证券交易委员会非基于复议请求开展的复议。证券交易委员会可以在任何时间主动命令对任何委托授权行动进行复议，但是相关事项存在一个或多个当事人的，主动复议命令不得在行动采取10日之后作出。一名证券交易委员会委员投票，并传达给证券交易委员会秘书的，即应将相关事项提交证券交易委员会复议。

（d）复议命令的必要要素。在复议请求的核准命令或证券交易委员会主动指示进行复议的命令中，证券交易委员会应载明任何当事人或其他人可以提交支持或反对委托授权行动的声明的期限，并说明是否应核准中止委托授权行动（如中止尚未生效）或继续中止委托授权行动［如中止已根据本节第（e）款生效］。

（e）委托授权行动的自动中止。委托授权行动应立即生效，并视为证券交易委员会的行动。在向证券交易委员会提交复议请求意向通知后，或向证券交易委员会秘书通知证券交易委员会委员已投票要求对某一事项进行复议后，委托授权行动应予以中止，直至证券交易委员会另行作出命令；但是，下述行动不适用自动中止：

（1）按照《联邦规章汇编》第十七编第200.30-14（g）（5）~（6）节的委托授权，核准中止证券交易委员会或自律组织行动的行动；或

（2）按照《联邦规章汇编》第十七编第200.30-14（a）（10）节的委托授权，启动传票执行程序的行动。

（f）证券交易委员会中止、修改或推翻委托授权行动的决定的效力。对于依赖委托授权行动行事的任何人，证券交易委员会任何中止、修改或推翻该等行动的决定，仅在该等人实际知悉证券交易委员会的中止、修改或推翻决定后才生效。

［《联邦公报》第60卷第32796页，1995年6月23日；《联邦公报》第60卷第46500页，1995年9月7日。］

§201.440 Appeal of determinations by the Public Company Accounting Oversight Board.

(a) *Application for review; when available.* Any person who is aggrieved by a determination of the Board with respect to any final disciplinary sanction, including disapproval of a completed application for registration of a public accounting firm, may file an application for review.

(b) *Procedure.* An aggrieved person may file an application for review with the Commission pursuant to §201.151 within 30 days after the notice filed by the Board of its determination with the Commission pursuant to §240.19d-4 of this chapter is received by the aggrieved person applying for review. The applicant shall serve the application on the Board at the same time. The application shall identify the determination complained of, set forth in summary form a brief statement of alleged errors in the determination and supporting reasons therefor, and state an address where the applicant can be served. The notice of appearance required by §201.102(d) shall accompany the application.

(c) *Stay of determination.* Filing an application for review with the Commission pursuant to paragraph (b) of this section operates as a stay of the Board's determination unless the Commission otherwise orders either pursuant to a motion filed in accordance with §201.401(e) or upon its own motion.

(d) *Certification of the record; service of the index.* Within fourteen days after receipt of an application for review, the Board shall certify and file with the Commission one copy of the record upon which it took the complained-of action. The Board shall file with the Commission three copies of an index of such record, and shall serve one copy of the index on each party.

[69 FR 13179, Mar. 19, 2004]

§201.441 Commission consideration of Board determinations.

(a) *Commission review other than pursuant to an application for review.* The Commission may, on its own initiative, order review of any final disciplinary sanction, including disapproval of a completed application for registration of a public accounting firm, imposed by the Board that could be subject to an application for review pursuant to §201.440(a) within 40 days after the Board filed notice thereof pursuant to §240.19d-4 of this chapter.

(b) *Supplemental briefing.* The Commission may at any time prior to the issuance of its decision raise or consider any matter that it deems material, whether or not raised by the parties. The Commission will give notice to the parties and an opportunity for supplemental briefing with respect to issues not briefed by the parties where the Commission believes that such briefing could significantly aid the decisional process.

[69 FR 13179, Mar. 19, 2004]

第201.440节　对公众公司会计监督委员会的决定的复议

(a)复议申请;适用时间。对于公众公司会计监督委员会的纪律处分决定(包括驳回完整的公众会计事务所注册申请的决定),权益受到侵害的任何人均可以提交复议申请。

(b)程序步骤。公众公司会计监督委员会根据本章第240.19d-4节向证券交易委员会提交关于决定的通知后,权益受到侵害的人均可以在收到该等通知后30日内,根据第201.151节向证券交易委员会提交复议申请。申请人应通知将申请送达公众公司会计监督委员会。申请应指明被提请复议的决定,简要说明其声称决定中所存在的错误、支持其主张的理由,并注明其可以接收文书送达的地址。申请还应按第201.102(d)节的规定附上出席通知。

(c)决定的中止执行。根据本节第(b)款向证券交易委员会提交复议申请的,公众公司会计监督委员会的决定即应中止适用,但证券交易委员会主动,或根据按照第201.401(e)条提交的动议另行作出决定的除外。

(d)记录认证;索引的送达。公众公司会计监督委员会应在收到复议申请后14日内,对被提请复议的行动所依据的记录进行认证,并向证券交易委员会提交一份复本,同时向证券交易委员会提交三份以及向每一方当事人提交一份记录索引。

[《联邦公报》第69卷第13179页,2004年3月19日。]

第201.441节　证券交易委员会对公众公司会计监督委员会决定的审议

(a)证券交易委员会非根据复议申请进行的复议。对于可能根据第201.440(a)节被提起复议申请的公众公司会计监督委员会的任何纪律处分决定(包括驳回完整的公众会计事务所注册申请的决定),证券交易委员会可以在公众公司会计监督委员会按照本章第240.19d-4节提交关于该等决定的通知后40日内,主动命令对之进行复议。

(b)补充陈辩书。证券交易委员会可以在签发决定前的任何时间提出或审议其认为具有重大性质的任何事项,而不论当事人是否提出了该等事项。对于当事人未在陈辩书中提出的问题,如证券交易委员会认为将有力推动决策程序的开展,应向各当事人发送通知并为之提供提交补充陈辩书的机会。

[《联邦公报》第69卷第13179页,2004年3月19日。]

§201.450 Briefs filed with the Commission.

(a) *Briefing schedule order.* Other than review ordered pursuant to §201.431, if review of a determination is mandated by statute, rule, or judicial order or the Commission determines to grant review as a matter of discretion, the Commission shall issue a briefing schedule order directing the party or parties to file opening briefs and specifying particular issues, if any, as to which briefing should be limited or directed. Unless otherwise provided, opening briefs shall be filed within 30 days of the date of the briefing schedule order. Opposition briefs shall be filed within 30 days after the date opening briefs are due. Reply briefs shall be filed within 14 days after the date opposition briefs are due. No briefs in addition to those specified in the briefing schedule order may be filed except with leave of the Commission. The briefing schedule order shall be issued:

(1) At the time the Commission orders review on its own initiative pursuant to §§201.411 or 201.421, or orders interlocutory review on its own motion pursuant to §201.400(a); or

(2) Within 21 days, or such longer time as provided by the Commission, after:

(i) The last day permitted for filing a petition for review pursuant to §201.410(b) or a brief in opposition to a petition for review pursuant to §201.410(d);

(ii) Receipt by the Commission of an index to the record of a determination of a self-regulatory organization filed pursuant to §201.420(d);

(iii) Receipt by the Commission of an index to the record of a determination by the Board filed pursuant to §201.440(d);

(iv) Receipt by the Commission of the mandate of a court of appeals with respect to a judicial remand; or

(v) Certification of a ruling for interlocutory review pursuant to §201.400(c).

(b) *Contents of briefs.* Briefs shall be confined to the particular matters at issue. Each exception to the findings or conclusions being reviewed shall be stated succinctly. Exceptions shall be supported by citation to the relevant portions of the record, including references to the specific pages relied upon, and by concise argument including citation of such statutes, decisions and other authorities as may be relevant. If the exception relates to the admission or exclusion of evidence, the substance of the evidence admitted or excluded shall be set forth in the brief, in an appendix thereto, or by citation to the record. Reply briefs shall be confined to matters in opposition briefs of other parties.

(c) *Length limitation.* Except with leave of the Commission, opening and opposition briefs shall not exceed 14,000 words and reply briefs shall not exceed 7,000 words, exclusive of pages containing the table of contents, table of authorities, and any addendum that consists solely of copies of applicable cases, pertinent legislative provisions or rules, and exhibits. The number of words shall include pleadings incorporated by reference.

第201.450节　向证券交易委员会提交的陈辩书

(a)陈辩书提交日程命令。除根据第201.431节命令进行的复议外,如制定法、相关规则或司法命令强制要求复议,或证券交易委员会行使自由裁量权核准复议,证券交易委员会应签发一份陈辩书提交日程命令,指令一方或各方当事人提交开案陈辩书,并说明关于陈辩书的范围或方向的具体事项(如有)。除非另有规定,开案陈辩书应在陈辩书提交日程命令签发日后30日内提交。反对陈辩书应在开案陈辩书提交期限到期后30日内提交。答复陈辩书应在反对陈辩书提交期限到期后14日内提交。非经证券交易委员会许可,不得在陈辩书提交日程命令中指定范围之外提交陈辩书。陈辩书提交日程命令应在下述时间签发:

(1)证券交易委员会根据第201.411节或第201.421节主动命令进行复议的时间,或根据第201.400(a)节主动命令进行中间复议的时间;或

(2)下述日期之后21日内或证券交易委员会规定的更长的期限内:

(i)第201.410(b)节允许的提交复议请求书期限的最后一日,或第201.410(d)节允许的就复议请求提交反对陈辩书的期限的最后一日;

(ii)证券交易委员会收到自律组织根据第201.420(d)节提交的决定记录索引之日;

(iii)证券交易委员会收到公众公司会计监督委员会根据第201.440(d)节提交的决定记录索引之日;

(iv)证券交易委员会收到上诉法院发回启动进一步程序的司法命令之日;或

(v)根据第201.400(c)节对被提起中间复议的裁定进行认证之日。

(b)陈辩书内容。陈辩书内容应以具体争议事项为限。对被提起复议的认定或结论的所有异议均应予以简洁说明,并通过引用相关记录部分(包括具体页数)予以支持,并进行简单的论证,包括引用相关制定法、决定和其他依据。异议涉及证据采纳或排除的,被采纳或排除的证据的内容应通过附件或记录引用的方式在陈辩书中说明。答复陈辩书的内容应以其他当事人的反对陈辩书中所涉及的事项为限。

(c)篇幅限制。非经证券交易委员会许可,开案陈辩书和反对陈辩书均不得超过1.4万字,答复陈辩书不得超过7000字,计算上述字数时不包括目录、索引表、完全由适用案例、相关立法条文或规则、证据构成的任何附录。上述字数包括通过引用而纳入的诉辩状。不鼓励提交超过上述限制的陈辩书的动议。

Motions to file briefs in excess of these limitations are disfavored.

(d) *Certificate of compliance.* An opening or opposition brief that does not exceed 30 pages in length, exclusive of pages containing the table of contents, table of authorities, and any addendum that consists solely of copies of applicable cases, pertinent legislative provisions, or rules and exhibits, but inclusive of pleadings incorporated by reference, is presumptively considered to contain no more than 14,000 words. A reply brief that does not exceed 15 pages in length, exclusive of pages containing the table of contents, table of authorities, and any addendum that consists solely of copies of applicable cases, pertinent legislative provisions, or rules and exhibits, but inclusive of pleadings incorporated by reference, is presumptively considered to contain no more than 7,000 words. Any brief that exceeds these page limits must include a certificate by the party's representative, or an unrepresented party, stating that the brief complies with the length limitation set forth in §201.450(c)and stating the number of words in the brief. The person preparing the certificate may rely on the word count of the word-processing system used to prepare the brief.

[60 FR 32796, June 23, 1995, as amended at 68 FR 35789, June 17, 2003; 69 FR 13180, Mar. 19, 2004]

§201.451 Oral argument before the Commission.

(a) *Availability.* The Commission, on its own motion or the motion of a party or any other aggrieved person entitled to Commission review, may order oral argument with respect to any matter. Motions for oral argument with respect to whether to affirm all or part of an initial decision by a hearing officer shall be granted unless exceptional circumstances make oral argument impractical or inadvisable. The Commission will consider appeals, motions and other matters properly before it on the basis of the papers filed by the parties without oral argument unless the Commission determines that the presentation of facts and legal arguments in the briefs and record and the decisional process would be significantly aided by oral argument.

(b) *Procedure.* Requests for oral argument shall be made by separate motion accompanying the initial brief on the merits. The Commission shall issue an order as to whether oral argument is to be heard, and if so, the time and place therefor. If oral argument is granted, the time fixed for oral argument shall be changed only by written order of the Commission, for good cause shown. The order shall state at whose request the change is made and the reasons for any such changes. No visual aids may be used at oral argument unless copies have been provided to the Commission and all parties at least 5 business days before the argument is to be held.

(c) *Time allowed.* Unless the Commission orders otherwise, not more than one half-hour per side will be allowed for oral argument. The Commission may, in its discretion,

(d)合规认证。开案陈辩书或反对陈辩书如不超过30页,将被推定和视为不超过1.4万字,上述页数不包括目录、索引表以及完全由适用案例、相关立法条文或规则、证据构成的任何附录的页数,但包括通过引用而纳入的诉辩状。答复陈辩书如不超过15页,将被推定和视为不超过7000字,同样,上述页数不包括目录、索引表以及完全由适用案例、相关立法条文或规则、证据构成的任何附录的页数,但包括通过引用而纳入的诉辩状。超出上述页数限制的任何陈辩书必须附上一份律师证明或当事人本人(如其没有代理律师)出具的证明,说明该文件符合第201.450(c)节规定的篇幅限制,并注明该文件的字数。制作上述证明的人可以采信编制该文件的字处理程序的字数统计结果。

[《联邦公报》第60卷第32796页,1995年6月23日,修正索引:《联邦公报》第68卷第35789页,2003年6月17日;《联邦公报》第69卷第13180页,2004年3月19日。]

第201.451节　证券交易委员会主持的口头辩论

(a)适用情形。证券交易委员会可以主动,或应一方当事人或权益受侵害且有权提请证券交易委员会进行复议的任何其他人之动议,命令就任何事项开展口头辩论。当事人或其他人提出动议,要求针对是否应对听证官的初步决定进行全部或部分确认进行口头辩论的,应予核准,但存在特殊情形,导致不便或不宜进行口头辩论的除外。对于以适当形式向证券交易委员会提交的上诉、动议和其他事项,证券交易委员会将基于当事人提交的文件进行审议,而不必进行口头辩论,但证券交易委员会判定口头辩论将对陈辩书和记录中的事实陈述、法律辩论以及作出决定的程序提供重大帮助的除外。

(b)程序步骤。口头辩论申请应通过单独的动议提出,附于关于实质问题的初步陈辩书之后。证券交易委员会应签发一份关于是否听取口头辩论的命令,如决定听取口头辩论,还应规定辩论的时间和地点。口头辩论被核准的,只有证券交易委员会基于充分理由发布书面命令,才能更改已确定的口头辩论时间。命令中应说明申请更改人的身份以及申请更改的原因。除非至少在辩论举行前5日已向证券交易委员会及全体当事人发送相关复本,否则在口头辩论中不得使用任何视觉辅助材料。

(c)允许的辩论时间。除非证券交易委员会另有命令,每一方的口头辩论时间不应超过一个半小时。证券交易委员会可依其自由裁量权判定数人具有共同利益,且在分

determine that several persons have a common interest, and that the interests represented will be considered a single side for purposes of allotting time for oral argument. Time will be divided equally among persons on a single side, provided, however, that by mutual agreement they may reallocate their time among themselves. A request for additional time must be made by motion filed reasonably in advance of the date fixed for argument.

(d) *Participation of Commissioners.* A member of the Commission who was not present at the oral argument may participate in the decision of the proceeding, provided that the member has reviewed the transcript of such argument prior to such participation. The decision shall state whether the required review was made.

[60 FR 32796, June 23, 1995, as amended at 69 FR 13180, Mar. 19, 2004]

§201.452 Additional evidence.

Upon its own motion or the motion of a party, the Commission may allow the submission of additional evidence. A party may file a motion for leave to adduce additional evidence at any time prior to issuance of a decision by the Commission. Such motion shall show with particularity that such additional evidence is material and that there were reasonable grounds for failure to adduce such evidence previously. The Commission may accept or hear additional evidence, may remand the proceeding to a self-regulatory organization, or may remand or refer the proceeding to a hearing officer for the taking of additional evidence, as appropriate.

§201.460 Record before the Commission.

The Commission shall determine each matter on the basis of the record.

(a) *Contents of the record.* (1) In proceedings for final decision before the Commission other than those reviewing a determination by a self-regulatory organization, the record shall consist of:

(i) All items part of the record below in accordance with §201.350;

(ii) Any petitions for review, cross-petitions or oppositions; and

(iii) All briefs, motions, submissions and other papers filed on appeal or review.

(2) In a proceeding for final decision before the Commission reviewing a determination by a self-regulatory organization, the record shall consist of:

(i) The record certified pursuant to §201.420(d) by the self-regulatory organization;

(ii) Any application for review; and

(iii) Any submissions, moving papers, and briefs filed on appeal or review.

(3) In a proceeding for final decision before the Commission reviewing a determination of the Board, the record shall consist of:

(i) The record certified pursuant to §201.440(d) by the Board;

(ii) Any application for review; and

配口头辩论时间时,其所代表的利益将被视为一方。对于同属一方的人,口头辩论时间将平均分配,但是,该等人也可通过相互约定在其内部重新分配辩论时间。延长时间的申请必须在指定的辩论日之前的合理时间通过动议提出。

(d)证券交易委员会委员的参与。未出席口头辩论的证券交易委员会委员可以参与对程序作出决定,前提是该委员在参与决定之前已经查阅口头辩论笔录。决定中应说明委员是否已按上述规定查阅笔录。

[《联邦公报》第60卷第32796页,1995年6月23日,修正索引:《联邦公报》第69卷第13180页,2004年3月19日。]

第201.452节　补充证据

证券交易委员会可以主动或应一方当事人的动议,允许提交补充证据。一方当事人可以在证券交易委员会发布决定之前的任何时间提交动议要求引入补充证据。动议应详细说明补充证据具有重大性质,且之前未举证存在合理理由。证券交易委员会可以接受补充证据或就此开展听证,或视适当情形将程序发回自律组织审理,或发回或提交听证官审理以决定证据的采纳。

第201.460节　证券交易委员会的记录

证券交易委员会应基于记录对每一事项进行判定。

(a)记录内容。(1)对于证券交易委员会作出最终决定的程序(对自律组织决定进行复议的程序除外),记录应包含如下内容:

(i)第201.350节规定应予记录的项目;

(ii)任何复议请求、交叉请求或反对;及

(iii)在复议请求或复议过程中提交的所有陈辩书、动议、呈报材料及其他文件。

(2)对于证券交易委员会对自律组织决定进行复议,并作出最终决定的程序,记录应包含如下内容:

(i)自律组织根据第201.420(d)节进行认证的记录;

(ii)任何复议申请;及

(iii)在复议请求或复议过程中提交的呈报材料、动议文件和陈辩书。

(3)对于证券交易委员会对公众公司会计监督委员会的决定进行复议,并作出最终决定的程序,记录应包含如下内容:

(i)公众公司会计监督委员会根据第201.440(d)节进行认证的记录;

(ii)任何复议申请;及

(iii) Any submissions, moving papers, and briefs filed on appeal or review.

(b) *Transmittal of record to Commission.* Within 14 days after the last date set for filing briefs or such later date as the Commission directs, the Secretary shall transmit the record to the Commission.

(c) *Review of documents not admitted.* Any document offered in evidence but excluded by the hearing officer or the Commission and any document marked for identification but not offered as an exhibit shall not be considered a part of the record before the Commission on appeal but shall be transmitted to the Commission by the Secretary if so requested by the Commission. In the event that the Commission does not request the document, the Secretary shall retain the document not admitted into the record until the later of:

(1) The date upon which the Commission's order becomes final, or

(2) The conclusion of any judicial review of that order.

[60 FR 32796, June 23, 1995, as amended at 69 FR 13180, Mar. 19, 2004]

§201.470 Reconsideration.

(a) *Scope of rule.* A party or any person aggrieved by a determination in a proceeding may file a motion for reconsideration of a final order issued by the Commission.

(b) *Procedure.* A motion for reconsideration shall be filed within 10 days after service of the order complained of, or within such time as the Commission may prescribe upon motion for extension of time filed by the person seeking reconsideration, if the motion is made within the foregoing 10-day period. The motion for reconsideration shall briefly and specifically state the matters of record alleged to have been erroneously decided, the grounds relied upon, and the relief sought. A motion for reconsideration shall conform to the requirements, including the limitation on the numbers of words, provided in §201.154. No response to a motion for reconsideration shall be filed unless requested by the Commission. Any response so requested shall comply with §201.154.

[60 FR 32796, June 23, 1995, as amended at 69 FR 13180, Mar. 19, 2004; 70 FR 72570, Dec. 5, 2005]

§201.490 Receipt of petitions for judicial review pursuant to 28 U.S.C. 2112(a)(1).

The Commission officer and office designated pursuant to 28 U.S.C. 2112(a)(1) to receive copies of petitions for review of Commission orders from the persons instituting review in a court of appeals, are the Secretary and the Office of the Secretary at the Commission's Headquarters. Ten copies of each petition shall be submitted. Each copy shall state on its face that it is being submitted to the Commission pursuant to 28 U.S.C. 2112 by the person or persons who filed the petition in the court of appeals.

(iii)在复议请求或复议过程中提交的所有呈报材料、动议文件和陈辩书。

(b)向证券交易委员会传送记录。证券交易委员会秘书应在指定的陈辩书提交期限的最后一日后14日内,或证券交易委员会指定的其他较晚日期,将记录传送给证券交易委员会。

(c)未采纳文件的审查。作为证据提交但被听证官或证券交易委员会排除的任何文件,以及已进行证物登记,但未作为证物提供的任何文件,在复议中均不得视为证券交易委员会审查的记录的一部分,但如证券交易委员会提出要求,证券交易委员会秘书应将之传送给证券交易委员会。如果证券交易委员会未要求提供文件,证券交易委员会秘书应保留未被纳入记录的文件,直至下述日期(以较晚者为准):

(1)证券交易委员会的命令获得最终效力之日;或

(2)对该命令进行的司法审查结束之日。

[《联邦公报》第60卷第32796页,1995年6月23日,修正索引:《联邦公报》第69卷第13180页,2004年3月19日。]

第201.470节　复审

(a)规则适用范围。程序的当事人或权益受程序决定侵害的任何人均可以提出动议,要求对证券交易委员会作出的最终命令进行复审。

(b)程序步骤。复审动议应于被提请审议的命令送达后10日内提交,如申请人在上述10日的期限内提出延期动议的,证券交易委员会亦可规定其他期限。复审动议应简明、具体地说明申请人声称被作出错误决定的记录事项,申请人主张所基于的基础以及所寻求的救济。复审动议应符合第201.154节规定的要求,包括对字数的限制。除非证券交易委员会提出要求,不得对复审动议提交答复。按证券交易委员会要求提交任何答复的,应遵守第201.154节的规定。

[《联邦公报》第60卷第32796页,1995年6月23日,修正索引:《联邦公报》第69卷第13180页,2004年3月19日;《联邦公报》第70卷第72570页,2005年12月5日。]

第201.490节　根据《美国法典》第二十八编第2112(a)(1)节接收司法审查请求书复本

在上诉法院提请对证券交易委员会命令进行审查的,根据《美国法典》第二十八编第2112(a)(1)节被指定为接收请求书复本的证券交易委员会官员和办公室为位于证券交易委员会总部的证券交易委员会秘书长和秘书长办公室。每份请求书应提交10份复本。每份复本均应在封面说明该文件系根据《美国法典》第二十八编第2112节由在上诉法院提请复议的人向证券交易委员会呈报。

Rules Relating to Temporary Orders and Suspensions

§201.500 Expedited consideration of proceedings.

Consistent with the Commission's or the hearing officer's other responsibilities, every hearing shall be held and every decision shall be rendered at the earliest possible time in connection with:

(a) An application for a temporary sanction, as defined in §201.101 (a), or a proceeding to determine whether a temporary sanction should be made permanent;

(b) A motion or application to review an order suspending temporarily the effectiveness of an exemption from registration pursuant to Regulations A, B, E or F under the Securities Act, §§230.258, 230.336, 230.610 or 230.656 of this chapter; or,

(c) A motion to or petition to review an order suspending temporarily the privilege of appearing before the Commission under §201.102(e)(3), or a sanction under §201.180(a)(1).

§201.510 Temporary cease-and-desist orders: Application process.

(a) *Procedure.* A request for entry of a temporary cease-and-desist order shall be made by application filed by the Division of Enforcement. The application shall set forth the statutory provision or rule that each respondent is alleged to have violated; the temporary relief sought against each respondent, including whether the respondent would be required to take action to prevent the dissipation or conversion of assets; and whether the relief is sought *exparte*.

(b) *Accompanying documents.* The application shall be accompanied by a declaration of facts signed by a person with knowledge of the facts contained therein, a memorandum of points and authorities, a proposed order imposing the temporary relief sought, and, unless relief is sought *exparte*, a proposed notice of hearing and order to show cause whether the temporary relief should be imposed. If a proceeding for a permanent cease-and-desist order has not already been commenced, a proposed order instituting proceedings to determine whether a permanent cease-and-desist order should be imposed shall also be filed with the application.

(c) *With whom filed.* The application shall be filed with the Secretary or, if the Secretary is unavailable, with the duty officer. In no event shall an application be filed with an administrative law judge.

(d) *Record of proceedings.* Hearings, including *exparte* presentations made by the Division of Enforcement pursuant to §201.513, shall be recorded or transcribed pursuant to §201.302.

与临时命令和暂停相关的规则

第201.500节　程序的加快审议

在不违反证券交易委员会或听证官的其他职责的情况下，对于与下述各项相关的每次听证均应在最早时间举行，并在最早时间作出决定：

(a)临时制裁[定义见第201.101(a)节]申请，或判定是否应将临时制裁转为正式制裁的程序；

(b)对依《证券法》颁发的《A管理办法》、《B管理办法》、《E管理办法》或《F管理办法》(本章第230.258节、第230.336节、第230.610节或第230.656节)中的暂停注册豁免效力的命令进行复议的动议或申请；或

(c)对第201.102(e)(3)节中的暂停出席证券交易委员会程序的特权的命令或对第201.180(a)(1)节中的制裁进行复议的动议或请求。

第201.510节　临时制止令：申请程序

(a)程序步骤。执法部可提交申请，请求作出临时制止令。申请应载明声称遭各相对人违反的制定法条文或规则；针对各相对人寻求的临时救济，包括是否要求相对人采取行动防止资产流失或转移，以及所寻求的救济是否为单方面救济。

(b)附随文件。申请应附上由知情人签署的事实声明、要点和依据备忘录、给予所寻求的临时救济的命令建议，以及(除非所寻求的救济为单方面救济)一份听证通知建议和一份提出是否应给予临时救济的理由的命令的建议。正式制止令程序尚未开始的，还应随申请附上一份发起程序以判定是否应签发正式制止令的命令的建议。

(c)提交对象。申请应向证券交易委员会秘书长提交，如证券交易委员会秘书无法履职，应向轮值官提交。无论何时均不得向行政法官提交申请。

(d)程序记录。听证，包括执法部根据第201.513节所作的单方面声明，应按照第201.302节的规定进行记录或笔录。

§201.511 Temporary cease-and-desist orders: Notice; procedures for hearing.

(a) *Notice: how given.* Notice of an application for a temporary cease-and-desist order shall be made by serving a notice of hearing and order to show cause pursuant to §201.141(b) or, where timely service of a notice of hearing pursuant to §201.141(b) is not practicable, by any other means reasonably calculated to give actual notice that a hearing will be held, including telephonic notification of the general subject matter, time, and place of the hearing. If an application is made *ex parte*, pursuant to §201.513, no notice to a respondent need be given prior to the Commission's consideration of the application.

(b) *Hearing before the Commission.* Except as provided in paragraph (d) of this section, hearings on an application for a temporary cease-and-desist order shall be held before the Commission.

(c) *Presiding officer: designation.* The Chairman shall preside or designate a Commissioner to preside at the hearing. If the Chairman is absent or unavailable at the time of hearing and no other Commissioner has been designated to preside, the duty officer on the day the hearing begins shall preside or designate another Commissioner to preside.

(d) *Procedure at hearing.* (1) The presiding officer shall have all those powers of a hearing officer set forth in §201.111 and shall rule on the admissibility of evidence and other procedural matters, including, but not limited to whether oral testimony will be heard; the time allowed each party for the submission of evidence or argument; and whether post-hearing submission of briefs, proposed findings of fact and conclusions of law will be permitted and if so, the procedures for submission; provided, however, that the person presiding may consult with other Commissioners participating in the hearing on these or any other question of procedure.

(2) Each Commissioner present at the hearing shall be afforded a reasonable opportunity to ask questions of witnesses, if any, or of counsel.

(3) A party or witness may participate by telephone. Alternative means of remote access, including a video link, shall be permitted in the Commission's discretion. Factors the Commission may consider in determining whether to permit alternative means of remote access include, but are not limited to, whether allowing an alternative means of access will delay the hearing, whether the alternative means is reliable, and whether the party proposing its use has made arrangements to pay for its cost.

(4) After a hearing has begun, the Commission may, on its own motion, or the motion of a party, assign a hearing officer to preside at the taking of oral testimony or other evidence and to certify the record of such testimony or other evidence to the Commission within a fixed period of time. No recommended or initial decision shall be made by such a hearing officer.

第201.511节　临时制止令:通知;听证程序

(a)通知:发送方式。发送关于临时制止令申请的通知的,应根据第201.141(b)节送达一份听证通知和一份提供理由的命令,如无法根据第201.141(b)节及时送达听证通知,可通过任何其他合理方式发送举行听证的实际通知,包括以电话方式通知听证的一般事项、时间和地点。如申请系根据第201.513节提出的单方面申请,在证券交易委员会审议申请之前,不必向相对人发送通知。

(b)证券交易委员会举行听证。除本节第(d)款规定的情形外,对临时制止令申请的听证应由证券交易委员会举行。

(c)听证主持人:指定。证券交易委员会主席应主持或指定一名委员主持听证。听证之时证券交易委员会主席缺席或无法履职,且其未指定任何其他委员主持听证的,听证开始当天的轮值官应主持或指定其他一名委员主持听证。

(d)听证的程序步骤。(1)听证主持人应拥有第201.111节规定的所有听证官的权力,并应对证据可采性及其他程序事项作出裁定,该等程序性事项包括但不限于是否听取口头证言、每一方提交证据或辩论的时间、是否允许在听证结束之后提交陈辩书、认定建议和结论建议,以及提交的程序步骤(如允许提交);但是,听证主持人可以就上述或任何其他程序问题咨询其他参与听证的证券交易委员会委员。

(2)出席听证的每一证券交易委员会委员均应获得合理机会,对证人(如有)或律师提问。

(3)当事人或证人可通过电话参与程序。证券交易委员会可自行裁量决定允许采用替代性的远程接入方式,包括视频连接。在判定是否允许使用替代性远程接入方式的过程中,证券交易委员会可考虑的因素包括但不限于:使用该等方式是否将对听证造成拖延;该等方式是否可靠;以及建议使用该等方式的当事人是否已就成本支付作出安排。

(4)听证开始之后,证券交易委员会可以主动或应一方当事人的动议,委任一名听证官主持提取证言或其他证据的程序,以及在指定的期限内对该等证言或其他证据为证券交易委员会提供认证。上述听证官不得提出任何建议或作出初步决定。

§201.512 Temporary cease–and–desist orders: Issuance after notice and opportunity for hearing.

(a) *Basis for issuance.* A temporary cease–and–desist order shall be issued only if the Commission determines that the alleged violation or threatened violation specified in an order instituting proceedings whether to enter a permanent cease–and–desist order pursuant to Securities Act Section 8A(a), 15 U.S.C. 77h–1(a), Exchange Act Section 21C(a), 15 U.S.C. 78u–3(a), Investment Company Act Section 9(f)(1), 15 U.S.C. 80a–9(f)(1), or Investment Advisers Act Section 203(k)(1), 15 U.S.C. 80b–3(k)(1), or the continuation thereof, is likely to result in significant dissipation or conversion of assets, significant harm to investors, or substantial harm to the public interest, including, but not limited to, losses to the Securities Investor Protection Corporation, prior to the completion of proceedings on the permanent cease–and–desist order.

(b) *Content, scope and form of order.* Every temporary cease–and–desist order granted shall:

(1) Describe the basis for its issuance, including the alleged or threatened violations and the harm that is likely to result without the issuance of an order;

(2) Describe in reasonable detail, and not by reference to the order instituting proceedings or any other document, the act or acts the respondent is to take or refrain from taking; and

(3) Be indorsed with the date and hour of issuance.

(c) *Effective upon service.* A temporary cease–and–desist order is effective upon service upon the respondent.

(d) *Service: how made.* Service of a temporary cease–and–desist order shall be made pursuant to §201.141 (a). The person who serves the order shall promptly file a declaration of service identifying the person served, the method of service, the date of service, the address to which service was made and the person who made service; provided, however, failure to file such a declaration shall have no effect on the validity of the service.

(e) *Commission review.* At any time after the respondent has been served with a temporary cease–and–desist order, the respondent may apply to the Commission to have the order set aside, limited or suspended. The application shall set forth with specificity the facts that support the request.

§201.513 Temporary cease–and–desist orders: Issuance without prior notice and opportunity for hearing.

In addition to the requirements for issuance of a temporary cease–and–desist order set forth in §201.512, the following requirements shall apply if a temporary cease–and–desist order is to be entered without prior notice and opportunity for hearing:

第201.512节　临时制止令:在通知和提供听证机会之后签发命令

(a)签发基础。根据《证券法》第8A(a)条[《美国法典》第十五编第77h-1(a)节]、《证券交易法》第21C(a)条[《美国法典》第十五编第78u-3(a)节]、《投资公司法》第9(f)(1)条[《美国法典》第十五编第80a-9(f)(1)节]或《投资顾问法》第203(k)(1)条[《美国法典》第十五编第80b-3(k)(1)节]或其后续规定发布程序发起令,以判定是否应作出正式制止令的,只有在证券交易委员会判定在正式制止令程序结束之前,程序发起令中指明和声称的违法违规行为或潜在违法违规行为可能导致重大资产流失或转移,对投资者造成重大损害,或对公共利益造成实质损害,包括但不限于给证券投资者保护公司造成损失的,才能签发临时制止令。

(b)命令的内容、范围和形式。每一份核准签发的临时制止令均应:

(1)说明签发基础,包括所声称的违法违规行为或潜在违法违规行为,以及如不签发命令可能造成的损害;

(2)合理详细地说明相对人应采取或不应采取的行为,而不引用程序发起令或任何其他文件;及

(3)注明签发日期和时间。

(c)送达之时生效。临时制止令于送达相对人之时生效。

(d)送达:方式。临时制止令应按照第201.141(a)节的规定送达。命令送达人应及时提交一份送达声明,说明送达对象的身份、送达方式、送达日期、送达地址以及送达人;但是,未提交上述声明的,送达效力不受影响。

(e)证券交易委员会的复议。相对人可以在收到临时制止令后的任何时间申请证券交易委员会撤销、限制或暂停执行临时制止令。申请应具体说明支持其请求的事实。

第201.513节　临时制止令:在不经事先通知和未提供听证机会的情况下签发命令

除第201.512节规定的关于临时制止令签发的要求外,如在不经事先通知和未提供听证机会的情况下作出临时制止令,还应适用如下规定:

(a) *Basis for issuance without prior notice and opportunity for hearing.* A temporary cease-and-desist order may be issued without notice and opportunity for hearing only if the Commission determines, from specific facts in the record of the proceeding, that notice and hearing prior to entry of an order would be impracticable or contrary to the public interest.

(b) *Content of the order.* An *exparte* temporary cease-and-desist order shall state specifically why notice and hearing would have been impracticable or contrary to the public interest.

(c) *Hearing before the Commission.* If a respondent has been served with a temporary cease-and-desist order entered without a prior Commission hearing, the respondent may apply to the Commission to have the order set aside, limited, or suspended, and if the application is made within 10 days after the date on which the order was served, may request a hearing on such application. The Commission shall hold a hearing and render a decision on the respondent's application at the earliest possible time. The hearing shall begin within 2 days of the filing of the application unless the applicant consents to a longer period or the Commission, by order, for good cause shown, sets a later date. The Commission shall render a decision on the application within five calendar days of its filing, provided, however, that the Commission, by order, for good cause shown, may extend the time within which a decision may be rendered for a single period of 5 calendar days, or such longer time as consented to by the applicant. If the Commission does not render its decision within 10 days of the respondent's application or such longer time as consented to by the applicant, the temporary order shall be suspended until a decision is rendered.

(d) *Presiding officer, procedure at hearing.* Procedures with respect to the selection of a presiding officer and the conduct of the hearing shall be in accordance with §201.511.

§201.514 Temporary cease-and-desist orders: Judicial review; duration.

(a) *Availability of judicial review.* Judicial review of a temporary cease-and-desist order shall be available as provided in Section 8A(d)(2) of the Securities Act, 15 U.S.C. 77h-1(d)(2), Section 21C(d)(2) of the Exchange Act, 15 U.S.C. 78u-3(d)(2), Section 9(f)(4)(B) of the Investment Company Act, 15 U.S.C. 80a-9(f)(4)(B), or Section 203(k)(4)(B) of the Investment Advisers Act, 15 U.S.C. 80b-3(k)(4)(B).

(b) *Duration.* Unless set aside, limited, or suspended, either by order of the Commission, a court of competent jurisdiction, or a hearing officer acting pursuant to §201.531, or by operation of §201.513, a temporary cease-and-desist order shall remain effective and enforceable until the earlier of:

(1) The completion of the proceedings whether a permanent order shall be entered; or

(a)不经事先通知和不提供听证机会签发命令的基础。只有证券交易委员会基于程序记录中的具体事实,判定在作出命令之前给予通知和进行听证不可行或有违公共利益,才可以在不经事先通知和未提供听证机会的情况下签发临时制止令。

(b)命令内容。单方临时制止令应具体说明进行事先通知和听证不可行或有违公共利益的理由。

(c)证券交易委员会举行听证。相对人收到证券交易委员会在未举行事先听证的情况下作出的临时制止令的,可以申请证券交易委员会撤销、限制或暂停执行临时制止令;申请在命令送达后10日内作出的,相对人还可请求就申请举行听证。证券交易委员会应在尽可能早的时间举行听证,并就相对人的申请作出决定。听证应于申请提交后2日内开始,除非申请人同意在更长的期限内举行,或证券交易委员会基于充分理由发布命令指定了较晚的日期。证券交易委员会应在申请提交后5个日历日内对申请作出决定,但是,证券交易委员会可以基于充分理由发布命令将作出决定的期限一次性延长5个日历日或申请人同意的更长的期限。证券交易委员会未能在相对人提交申请后10日内或申请人同意的更长的期限内作出决定的,临时命令应在作出决定之前暂停执行。

(d)听证主持人、听证程序步骤。听证主持人选任和听证开展的程序步骤应遵守第201.511节的规定。

第201.514节　临时制止令:司法审查;期限

(a)司法审查的适用情形。临时制止令可按照《证券法》第8A(d)(2)条[《美国法典》第十五编第77h-1(d)(2)节]、《证券交易法》第21C(d)(2)条[《美国法典》第十五编第78u-3(d)(2)节]、《投资公司法》第9(f)(4)(B)条[《美国法典》第十五编第80a-9(f)(4)(B)节]或《投资顾问法》第203(k)(4)(B)条[《美国法典》第十五编第80b-3(k)(4)(B)节]的规定进行司法审查。

(b)期限。除非证券交易委员会、有管辖权的法院或根据第201.531节行事的听证官发布命令撤销、限制或暂停临时制止令,或因第201.513节之适用而导致临时制止令被撤销、限制或暂停,临时制止令应保持效力和可执行力,直至下述日期(以较早者为准):

(1)关于是否应作出正式命令的程序完结之日;或

(2) 180 days, or such longer time as consented to by the respondent, after issuance of a briefing schedule order pursuant to §201.540(b), if an initial decision whether a permanent order should be entered is appealed.

§201.520 Suspension of registration of brokers, dealers, or other Exchange Act-registered entities: Application.

(a) *Procedure.* A request for suspension of a registered broker, dealer, municipal securities dealer, government securities broker, government securities dealer, or transfer agent pending a final determination whether the registration shall be revoked shall be made by application filed by the Division of Enforcement. The application shall set forth the statutory provision or rule that each respondent is alleged to have violated and the temporary suspension sought as to each respondent.

(b) *Accompanying documents.* The application shall be accompanied by a declaration of facts signed by a person with knowledge of the facts contained therein, a memorandum of points and authorities, a proposed order imposing the temporary suspension of registration sought, and a proposed notice of hearing and order to show cause whether the temporary suspension of registration should be imposed. If a proceeding to determine whether to revoke the registration permanently has not already been commenced, a proposed order instituting proceedings to determine whether a permanent sanction should be imposed shall also be filed with the application.

(c) *With whom filed.* The application shall be filed with the Secretary or, if the Secretary is unavailable, with the duty officer. In no event shall an application be filed with an administrative law judge.

(d) *Record of hearings.* All hearings shall be recorded or transcribed pursuant to §201.302.

§201.521 Suspension of registration of brokers, dealers, or other Exchange Act-registered entities: Notice and opportunity for hearing on application.

(a) *How given.* Notice of an application to suspend a registration pursuant to §201.520 shall be made by serving a notice of hearing and order to show cause pursuant to §201.141(b) or, where timely service of a notice of hearing pursuant to §201.141(b) is not practicable, by any other means reasonably calculated to give actual notice that a hearing will be held, including telephonic notification of the general subject matter, time, and place of the hearing.

(b) *Hearing: before whom held.* Except as provided in paragraph (d) of this section, hearings on an application to suspend a registration pursuant to §201.520 shall be held before the Commission.

(c) *Presiding officer: designation.* The Chairman shall preside or designate a Commissioner to preside at the hearing. If the Chairman is absent or unavailable at the

(2)根据第201.540(b)条签发陈辩书提交日程命令后180日或其他更长的期限(如关于是否应作出正式命令的初步决定被提起复议)。

第201.520节　暂停经纪商、自营商或其他依据《证券交易法》注册的实体的注册资格:申请

(a)程序步骤。在作出是否撤销注册的最终决定之前,请求暂停注册经纪商、自营商、市政证券自营商、政府证券经纪商、政府证券自营商或过户代理人注册资格的,应由执法部提交申请。申请应载明执法部声称各相对人已违反的法定条款或规则,以及所寻求的暂停各相对人注册资格的命令。

(b)附随文件。申请应附上由知情人签署的事实声明、要点和依据备忘录,说明所寻求的暂停注册令,并附上一份听证通知建议和一份要求提供是否应暂停注册的理由的命令的建议。决定是否正式撤销注册的程序尚未开始的,还应随申请附上一份发起程序以判定是否应处以正式制裁的命令的建议。

(c)提交对象。申请应向证券交易委员会秘书提交,如证券交易委员会秘书无法履职,应向轮值官提交。无论何时均不得向行政法官提交申请。

(d)听证记录。所有听证均应按照第201.302节的规定进行记录或笔录。

第201.521节　暂停经纪商、自营商或其他依据《证券交易法》注册的实体的注册资格:关于申请的通知及听证机会

(a)作出方式。根据第201.520节发送关于暂停注册申请的通知的,应根据第201.141(b)节送达一份听证通知和一份要求提供理由的命令,如无法根据第201.141(b)节及时送达听证通知,可通过任何其他合理方式发送举行听证的实际通知,包括以电话方式通知听证的一般事项、时间和地点。

(b)听证:举行主体。除本节第(d)款规定的情形外,根据第201.520节就暂停注册申请开展的听证应由证券交易委员会举行。

(c)听证主持人:指定。证券交易委员会主席应主持或指定一名委员主持听证。听证之时证券交易委员会主席缺席或无法履职,且其未指定任何其他委员主持听证的,

time of hearing and no other Commissioner has been designated to preside, the duty officer on the day the hearing begins shall preside or designate another Commissioner to preside.

(d) *Procedure at hearing.* (1) The presiding officer shall have all those powers of a hearing officer set forth in §201.111 and shall rule on the admissibility of evidence and other procedural matters, including, but not limited to whether oral testimony will be heard; the time allowed each party for the submission of evidence or argument; and whether post-hearing submission of briefs, proposed findings of fact and conclusions of law will be permitted and if so, the procedures for submission; provided, however, that the person presiding may consult with other Commissioners participating in the hearing on these or any other question of procedure.

(2) Each Commissioner present at the hearing shall be afforded a reasonable opportunity to ask questions of witnesses, if any, or counsel.

(3) A party or witness may participate by telephone. Alternative means of remote access, including a video link, shall be permitted in the Commission's discretion. Factors the Commission may consider in determining whether to permit alternative means of remote access include, but are not limited to, whether allowing an alternative means of access will delay the hearing, whether the alternative means is reliable, and whether the party proposing its use has made arrangements to pay for its cost.

(4) After a hearing has begun, the Commission may, on its own motion or the motion of a party, assign a hearing officer to preside at the taking of oral testimony or other evidence and to certify the record of such testimony or other evidence to the Commission within a fixed period of time. No recommended or initial decision shall be made.

§201.522 Suspension of registration of brokers, dealers, or other Exchange Act-registered entities: Issuance and review of order.

(a) *Basis for issuance.* An order suspending a registration, pending final determination as to whether the registration shall be revoked shall be issued only if the Commission finds that the suspension is necessary or appropriate in the public interest or for the protection of investors.

(b) *Content, scope and form of order.* Each order suspending a registration shall:

(1) Describe the basis for its issuance, including the alleged or threatened violations and the harm that is likely to result without the issuance of an order;

(2) Describe in reasonable detail, and not by reference to the order instituting proceedings or any other document, the act or acts the respondent is to take or refrain from taking; and

(3) Be indorsed with the date and hour of issuance.

(c) *Effective upon service.* An order suspending a registration is effective upon

听证开始当天的轮值官应主持或指定其他一名委员主持听证。

(d)听证的程序步骤。(1)听证主持人应拥有第201.111节规定的所有听证官的权力,并应对证据可采性及其他程序事项作出裁定,该等程序性事项包括但不限于是否听取口头证言、每一方提交证据或辩论的时间、是否允许在听证结束之后提交陈辩书、认定建议和结论建议,以及如允许提交,提交的程序步骤;但是,听证主持人可以就上述或任何其他程序问题咨询其他参与听证的证券交易委员会委员。

(2)出席听证的每一证券交易委员会委员均应获得合理机会,对证人(如有)或律师提问。

(3)当事人或证人可通过电话参与程序。证券交易委员会可自行裁量决定允许采用替代性的远程接入方式,包括视频连接。在判定是否允许使用替代性远程接入方式的过程中,证券交易委员会可考虑的因素包括但不限于:使用该等方式是否将对听证造成拖延;该等方式是否可靠;以及建议使用该等方式的当事人是否已就成本支付作出安排。

(4)听证开始之后,证券交易委员会可以主动或应一方当事人的动议,委任一名听证官主持提取证言或其他证据的程序,以及在指定的期限内对该等证言或其他证据为证券交易委员会提供认证。上述听证官不得提出任何建议或作出初步决定。

第201.522节　暂停经纪商、自营商或其他依据《证券交易法》注册的实体的注册资格:命令的签发和复议

(a)签发基础。只有证券交易委员会在作出是否撤销注册的最终决定之前,判定出于公共利益或保护投资者之目的而有必要或适宜暂停资格,才能签发暂停注册的命令。

(b)命令的内容、范围和形式。每一份暂停注册令均应:

(1)说明签发基础,包括所声称的违法违规行为或潜在违法违规行为,以及如不签发命令可能造成的损害;

(2)合理详细地说明相对人应采取或不应采取的行为,而不引用程序发起令或任何其他文件;及

(3)注明签发日期和时间。

(c)送达即生效。暂停注册令于送达相对人之时生效。

service upon the respondent.

(d) *Service: how made.* Service of an order suspending a registration shall be made pursuant to §201.141(a). The person who serves the order shall promptly file a declaration of service identifying the person served, the method of service, the date of service, the address to which service was made and the person who made service; provided, however, failure to file such a declaration shall have no effect on the validity of the service.

(e) *Commission review.* At any time after the respondent has been served with an order suspending a registration, the respondent may apply to the Commission or the hearing officer to have the order set aside, limited, or suspended. The application shall set forth with specificity the facts that support the request.

§201.523 [Reserved]

§201.524 Suspension of registrations: Duration.

Unless set aside, limited or suspended by order of the Commission, a court of competent jurisdiction, or a hearing officer acting pursuant to §201.531, an order suspending a registration shall remain effective and enforceable until the earlier of:

(a) The completion of the proceedings whether the registration shall be permanently revoked; or

(b) 180 days, or such longer time as consented to by the respondent, after issuance of a briefing schedule order pursuant to §201.540(b), if an initial decision whether the registration shall be permanently revoked is appealed.

§201.530 Initial decision on permanent order: Timing for submitting proposed findings and preparation of decision.

Unless otherwise ordered by the Commission or hearing officer, if a temporary cease-and-desist order or suspension of registration order is in effect, the following time limits shall apply to preparation of an initial decision as to whether such order should be made permanent:

(a) Proposed findings and conclusions and briefs in support thereof shall be filed 30 days after the close of the hearing;

(b) The record in the proceedings shall be served by the Secretary upon the hearing officer 3 days after the date for the filing of the last brief called for by the hearing officer; and

(c) The initial decision shall be filed with the Secretary at the earliest possible time, but in no event more than 30 days after service of the record, unless the hearing officer, by order, shall extend the time for good cause shown for a period not to exceed 30 days.

§201.531 Initial decision on permanent order: Effect on temporary order.

(a) *Specification of permanent sanction.* If, at the time an initial decision is issued, a

(d)送达:方式。暂停注册令应按照第201.141(a)节的规定送达。命令送达人应及时提交一份送达声明,说明送达对象的身份、送达方式、送达日期、送达地址以及送达人;但是,未提交上述声明的,送达效力不受影响。

(e)证券交易委员会的复议。相对人可以在收到暂停注册令后的任何时间申请证券交易委员会撤销、限制或暂停执行暂停注册令。申请应具体说明支持其请求的事实。

第201.523节 [保留]

第201.524节 暂停注册:期限

除非证券交易委员会、有管辖权的法院或根据第201.531节行事的听证官发布命令撤销、限制或暂停执行暂停注册令,暂停注册令应保持效力和执行状态,直至下述日期(以较早者为准):

(a)关于是否应正式撤销注册资格的程序完结之日;或

(b)根据第201.540(b)节签发陈辩书提交日程命令后180日或其他更长的期限届满之时(如关于是否应正式撤销注册资格的初步决定被提起复议)。

第201.530节 关于正式命令的初步决定:提交认定建议和制定决定的时间

除非证券交易委员会或听证官另有命令,若临时制止令或暂停注册的临时命令生效,则在制定关于该等命令是否应予以正式化的初步决定时,应适用如下时间限制:

(a)认定建议和结论建议以及支持该等建议的陈辩书应于听证结束后30日内提交;

(b)证券交易委员会秘书应于听证官要求提交最后一份陈辩书之日后3日向听证官送达程序记录;且

(c)初步决定应在尽可能早的时间向证券交易委员会秘书提交,但无论何时不得迟于记录送达后30日,但听证官有权基于充分理由,发布命令在上述期限的基础上延长不超过30日的期限。

第201.531节 关于正式命令的初步决定:对临时命令效力的影响

(a)正式制裁的格式。如初步决定签发之时,临时制裁已针对任何相对人生效,初

temporary sanction is in effect as to any respondent, the initial decision shall specify:

(1) Which terms or conditions of a temporary cease–and–desist order, if any, shall become permanent; and

(2) Whether a temporary suspension of a respondent's registration, if any, shall be made a permanent revocation of registration.

(b) *Modification of temporary order.* If any temporary sanction shall not become permanent under the terms of the initial decision, the hearing officer shall issue a separate order setting aside, limiting or suspending the temporary sanction then in effect in accordance with the terms of the initial decision. The hearing officer shall decline to suspend a term or condition of a temporary cease–and–desist order if it is found that the continued effectiveness of such term or condition is necessary to effectuate any term of the relief ordered in the initial decision, including the payment of disgorgement, interest or penalties. An order modifying temporary sanctions shall be effective 14 days after service. Within one week of service of the order modifying temporary sanctions any party may seek a stay or modification of the order from the Commission pursuant to §201.401.

§201.540 Appeal and Commission review of initial decision making a temporary order permanent.

(a) *Petition for review.* Any person who seeks Commission review of an initial decision as to whether a temporary sanction shall be made permanent shall file a petition for review pursuant to §201.410, provided, however, that the petition must be filed within 10 days after service of the initial decision.

(b) *Review procedure.* If the Commission determines to grant or order review, it shall issue a briefing schedule order pursuant to §201.450. Unless otherwise ordered by the Commission, opening briefs shall be filed within 21 days of the order granting or ordering review, and opposition briefs shall be filed within 14 days after opening briefs are filed. Reply briefs shall be filed within 7 days after opposition briefs are filed. Oral argument, if granted by the Commission, shall be held within 90 days of the issuance of the briefing schedule order.

§201.550 Summary suspensions pursuant to Exchange Act Section 12(k)(1)(A).

(a) *Petition for termination of suspension.* Any person adversely affected by a suspension pursuant to Section 12(k)(1)(A) of the Exchange Act, 15 U.S.C. 78*l* (k)(1)(A), who desires to show that such suspension is not necessary in the public interest or for the protection of investors may file a sworn petition with the Secretary, requesting that the suspension be terminated. The petition shall set forth the reasons why the petitioner believes that the suspension of trading should not continue and state with particularity the facts upon which the petitioner relies.

步决定应说明:

(1)临时制止令的哪些条款和条件(如有)应予以正式化;及

(2)相对人注册资格的临时暂停(如有)是否应更改为正式的撤销注册。

(b)临时命令的修改。如根据初步决定的规定,任何临时制裁不应予以正式化,听证官应按照初步决定的规定,另行签发一份命令撤销、限制或暂停执行当时生效的临时制裁。如果听证官认定为使初步决定中命令采取的救济生效(包括支付没收款项、利息或罚款),有必要使临时制止令的某一条款或条件继续生效,听证官应拒绝暂停执行该等条款或条件。修改临时制裁的命令应于送达14日后生效。任一方当事人均可以在修改临时制裁的命令送达后一周内根据第201.401节提请证券交易委员会中止或修改该命令。

第201.540节　针对使临时命令正式化的初步决定提起的复议和证券交易委员会的复议

(a)复议请求。是否应使临时制裁正式化的初步决定作出后,提请证券交易委员会对该等初步决定进行复议的任何人均应按照第201.410节的规定并在初步决定送达后10日内提交复议请求书。

(b)复议程序。如果证券交易委员会核准或命令进行复议,应根据第201.450节签发一份陈辩书提交日程命令。除非证券交易委员会另有命令,开案陈辩书应于核准或命令进行复议的命令签发后21日内提交,反对陈辩书应于开案陈辩书提交后14日内提交。答复陈辩书应于反对陈辩书提交后7日内提交。证券交易委员会核准进行口头辩论的,应于陈辩书提交日常命令签发后90日内举行。

第201.550节　根据《证券交易法》第12(k)(1)(A)条进行的简易暂停

(a)终止暂停请求。根据《证券交易法》第12(k)(1)(A)条[《美国法典》第十五编第78 l(k)(1)(A)节]进行暂停的,任何利益受侵害人如希望证明该等暂停并非为维护公共利益或对投资者进行保护所必要,可以向证券交易委员会秘书提交一份宣誓请求书,要求终止暂停。请求书应说明请求人认为不应继续暂停交易的原因,并具体说明请求人所基于的事实。

(b) *Commission consideration of a petition.* The Commission, in its discretion, may schedule a hearing on the matter, request additional written submissions, or decide the matter on the facts presented in the petition and any other relevant facts known to the Commission. If the petitioner fails to cooperate with, obstructs, or refuses to permit the making of an examination by the Commission, such conduct shall be grounds to deny the petition.

Rules Regarding Disgorgement and Penalty Payments

§201.600 Interest on sums disgorged.

(a) *Interest required.* Prejudgment interest shall be due on any sum required to be paid pursuant to an order of disgorgement. The disgorgement order shall specify each violation that forms the basis for the disgorgement ordered; the date which, for purposes of calculating disgorgement, each such violation was deemed to have occurred; the amount to be disgorged for each such violation; and the total sum to be disgorged. Prejudgment interest shall be due from the first day of the month following each such violation through the last day of the month preceding the month in which payment of disgorgement is made. The order shall state the amount of prejudgment interest owed as of the date of the disgorgement order and that interest shall continue to accrue on all funds owed until they are paid.

(b) *Rate of interest.* Interest on the sum to be disgorged shall be computed at the underpayment rate of interest established under Section 6621(a)(2) of the Internal Revenue Code, 26 U.S.C. 6621(a)(2), and shall be compounded quarterly. The Commission or the hearing officer may, by order, specify a lower rate of prejudgment interest as to any funds which the respondent has placed in an escrow or otherwise guaranteed for payment of disgorgement upon a final determination of the respondent's liability. Escrow and other guarantee arrangements must be approved by the Commission or the hearing officer prior to entry of the disgorgement order.

§201.601 Prompt payment of disgorgement, interest and penalties.

(a) *Timing of payments.* Unless otherwise provided, funds due pursuant to an order by the Commission requiring the payment of disgorgement, interest, or penalties shall be paid no later than 21 days after service of the order, and funds due pursuant to an order by a hearing officer shall be paid in accordance with the order of finality issued pursuant to §201.360(d)(2).

(b) *Stays.* A stay of any order requiring the payment of disgorgement, interest or penalties may be sought at any time pursuant to §201.401.

(c) *Method of making payment.* Payment shall be made by United States postal money order, wire transfer, certified check, bank cashier's check, or bank money order

(b)证券交易委员会对请求的审议。证券交易委员会可依其自由裁量权安排就事项开展听证,要求提交补充书面材料,或基于请求书中提出的事实和证券交易委员会已知的任何其他相关事实作出决定。请求人未能提供合作,或阻碍、或拒绝允许证券交易委员会开展审查的,证券交易委员会有权基于该等行为拒绝请求。

关于没收款项和罚款支付的规则

第201.600节　没收款项的利息

(a)应付利息。对于根据没收令应予支付的款项,应计算判决前利息。没收令应具体说明:构成没收依据的每次违法违规行为;在计算没收款项时,各次违法违规行为视为发生之日;应就每次违法违规行为没收的款项;应没收的总款项。判决前利息的起算期间为违法违规行为后一月的首日直至没收款项支付前一月的最后一日。命令中应说明自没收令签发之日起的应付判决前利息金额,且在所有欠付款项支付之前,利息应持续计算。

(b)利率。没收款项利息应按《国内税收法典》第6621(a)(2)条[《美国法典》第二十六编第6621(a)(2)节]的短付利率计算,并按季度计算复利。证券交易委员会或听证官可以发布命令,在对相对人的责任作出最终判定时,对于相对人已存入托管账户的或以其他方式进行担保的用于支付没收款项的基金指定相对较低的判决前利率。托管或其他担保安排必须由证券交易委员会或听证官在作出没收令之前批准。

第201.601节　及时支付没收款项、利息和罚款

(a)支付时间。除非另有规定,证券交易委员会命令支付没收款项、利息或罚款的,应付金额应于命令送达后21日内支付;听证官命令支付的,应付金额应按照根据第201.360(d)(2)节签发的最终命令支付。

(b)中止。任何时候均可根据第201.401节寻求没收款项、利息或罚款的中止支付令。

(c)支付方式。付款应通过美国邮政汇票、电汇、认证支票、银行本票、银行汇票支付,以证券交易委员会为收款人。款项应邮寄或交付至证券交易委员会指定的办公

made payable to the Securities and Exchange Commission. The payment shall be mailed or delivered to the office designated by this Commission. Payment shall be accompanied by a letter that identifies the name and number of the case and the name of the respondent making payment. A copy of the letter and the instrument of payment shall be sent to counsel for the Division of Enforcement.

[60 FR 32796, June 23, 1995, as amended at 69 FR 13180, Mar. 19, 2004; 70 FR 72570, Dec. 5, 2005]

§§201.610–201.614 [Reserved]

§201.620 [Reserved]

§201.630 Inability to pay disgorgement, interest or penalties.

(a) *Generally.* In any proceeding in which an order requiring payment of disgorgement, interest or penalties may be entered, a respondent may present evidence of an inability to pay disgorgement, interest or a penalty. The Commission may, in its discretion, or the hearing officer may, in his or her discretion, consider evidence concerning ability to pay in determining whether disgorgement, interest or a penalty is in the public interest.

(b) *Financial disclosure statement.* Any respondent who asserts an inability to pay disgorgement, interest or penalties may be required to file a sworn financial disclosure statement and to keep the statement current. The financial statement shall show the respondent's assets, liabilities, income or other funds received and expenses or other payments, from the date of the first violation alleged against that respondent in the order instituting proceedings, or such later date as specified by the Commission or a hearing officer, to the date of the order requiring the disclosure statement to be filed. By order, the Commission or the hearing officer may prescribe the use of the Disclosure of Assets and Financial Information Form (*see* Form D-A at §209.1 of this chapter)or any other form, may specify other time periods for which disclosure is required, and may require such other information as deemed necessary to evaluate a claim of inability to pay.

(c) *Confidentiality.* Any respondent submitting financial information pursuant to this section or §201.410(c) may make a motion, pursuant to §201.322, for the issuance of a protective order against disclosure of the information submitted to the public or to any parties other than the Division of Enforcement. Prior to a ruling on the motion, no party receiving information as to which a motion for a protective order has been made may transfer or convey the information to any other person without the prior permission of the Commission or the hearing officer.

(d) *Service required.* Notwithstanding any provision of §201.322, a copy of the financial disclosure statement shall be served on the Division of Enforcement.

(e) *Failure to file required financial information: sanction.* Any respondent who, after

室,附上一封信函,说明案件名称、编号以及付款相对人的姓名,并向执法部律师抄送一份信函和付款文书复本。

[《联邦公报》第60卷第32796页,1995年6月23日,修正索引:《联邦公报》第69卷第13180页,2004年3月19日;《联邦公报》第70卷第72570页,2005年12月5日。]

第201.610~201.614节 [保留]

第201.620节 [保留]

第201.630节 无力支付没收款项、利息或罚款的情形

(a)一般规定。在可能发布命令,要求支付没收款项、利息或罚款的任何程序中,相对人均可以提交证据,证明其无力支付没收款项、利息或罚款。证券交易委员会或听证官在判定支付没收款项、利息或罚款是否符合公共利益之时,可依其自由裁量权审议关于支付能力的证据。

(b)财务披露报表。主张无力支付没收款项、利息或罚款的任何相对人可能被要求提交宣誓财务披露报表,并对报表进行更新。财务报表应说明自程序发起令中指称的首次违法违规行为之日,直至要求提交披露报表的命令发布之日期间相对人的资产、负债、收益或其他实收资金、费用和其他付款。证券交易委员会或听证官可以发布命令,规定资产和财务信息披露表(参见本章第209.1节的《D-A表格》)或任何其他表格的使用,并可以规定其他披露期间,要求相对人在该等期间内提供其认为对无力支付主张进行评估所必要的其他信息。

(c)保密。根据第201.410(c)节呈报财务信息的任何相对人均可以按照第201.322节提交动议,要求签发保护令,避免向公众以及执法部之外的任何当事人披露所呈报的信息。如已提出保护令动议,在就动议作出决定之前,未经证券交易委员会或听证官事先许可,接受信息的任何当事人均不得将信息转让或传递给任何其他人。

(d)规定送达。无论第201.322节如何规定,仍应向执法部送达一份财务披露报表。

(e)未能按规定提交财务信息:制裁。如果相对人在提出无力支付没收款项、利息

making a claim of inability to pay either disgorgement, interest or a penalty, fails to file a financial disclosure statement when such a filing has been ordered or is required by rule may, in the discretion of the Commission or the hearing officer, be deemed to have waived the claim of inability to pay. No sanction pursuant to §§201.155 or 201.180 shall be imposed for a failure to file such a statement.

§201.700 Initiation of proceedings for SRO proposed rule changes.

(a) *Rules of Practice.* For purposes of these Rules of Practice contained at 17 CFR 201.700 through 201.701, the following Rules of Practice apply:

(1) Rule 103, 17 CFR 201.103 (Construction of Rules);

(2) Rule 104, 17 CFR 201.104 (Business Hours); and

(3) Rule 160, 17 CFR 201.160 (Time Computation).

(b) *Institution of proceedings; notice and opportunity to submit written views*—(1) *Generally.* If the Commission determines to initiate proceedings to determine whether a self-regulatory organization's proposed rule change should be disapproved, it shall provide notice thereof to the self-regulatory organization that filed the proposed rule change, as well as all interested parties and the public, by publication in the Federal Register of the grounds for disapproval under consideration.

(i) *Prior to notice.* If the Commission determines to institute proceedings prior to initial publication by the Commission of the notice of the self-regulatory organization's proposed rule change in the Federal Register,then the Commission shall publish notice of the proposed rule change simultaneously with a brief summary of the grounds for disapproval under consideration.

(ii) *Subsequent to notice.* If the Commission determines to institute proceedings subsequent to initial publication by the Commission of the notice of the self-regulatory organization's proposed rule change in the Federal Register, then the Commission shall publish separately in the Federal Register a brief summary of the grounds for disapproval under consideration.

(iii) *Service of an order instituting proceedings.* In addition to publication in the Federal Register of the grounds for disapproval under consideration, the Secretary, or another duly authorized officer of the Commission, shall serve a copy of the grounds for disapproval under consideration to the self-regulatory organization that filed the proposed rule change by serving notice to the person listed as the contact person on the cover page of the Form 19b-4 filing. Notice shall be made by delivering a copy of the order to such contact person either by any method specified in 17 CFR 201.141(a) or by electronic means including e-mail.

(2) *Notice of the grounds for disapproval under consideration.* The grounds for disapproval under consideration shall include a brief statement of the matters of fact and

或罚款的主张后,未能按命令或裁定提交财务披露报表,证券交易委员会或听证官可依其自由裁量权视为相对人已放弃无力支付主张。未能提交报表的,不得按照第201.155节或第201.180节处以制裁。

第201.700节　就自律组织规则变更提案发起的程序

(a)工作规则。就《联邦规章汇编》第十七编第201.700~201.701节所包含的《工作规则》而言,应适用如下规则:

(1)《103规则》,《联邦规章汇编》第十七编第201.103节(规则的解释);

(2)《104规则》,《联邦规章汇编》第十七编第201.104节(工作时间);及

(3)《160规则》,《联邦规章汇编》第十七编第201.160节(时间的计算)。

(b)发起程序;通知和提交书面意见的机会——(1)一般规定。证券交易委员会决定发起程序,以判定是否应否决自律组织的规则变更草案的,应就此向提交规则变更草案的自律组织、所有利害关系方以及公众发送通知,通知方式为在《联邦公报》上发布正在审议的否决理由。

(i)通知之前发起程序。证券交易委员会决定在《联邦公报》上就自律组织的规则变更草案初次发布通知之前发起程序的,应在就规则变更草案发布通知同时就审议中的否决理由发布一份简单摘要。

(ii)通知之后发起程序。证券交易委员会决定在《联邦公报》上就自律组织的规则变更草案初次发布通知之后发起程序的,应另行在《联邦公报》上就审议中的否决理由发布一份简单摘要。

(iii)程序发起令的送达。除在《联邦公报》上发布审议中的否决理由外,证券交易委员会秘书长或证券交易委员会的其他正式授权官员,应向提交规则变更草案的自律组织送达一份审议中的否决理由的复本,送达方式为向《19b-4表格》封面所列联系人发送通知。向联系人发送通知的方式为按照《联邦规章汇编》第十七编第201.141(a)节规定的任何方式或通过电子方式(包括电邮)向该等联系人送达命令复本。

(2)关于审议中的否决理由的通知。审议中的否决理由应包括一份关于证券交易委员会发起程序所依据的事实和法律问题的简短声明,包括证券交易委员会可能存

law on which the Commission instituted the proceedings, including the areas in which the Commission may have questions or may need to solicit additional information on the proposed rule change. The Commission may consider during the course of the proceedings additional matters of fact and law beyond what was set forth in its notice of the grounds for disapproval under consideration.

(3) *Demonstration of consistency with the Exchange Act.* The burden to demonstrate that a proposed rule change is consistent with the Exchange Act and the rules and regulations issued thereunder that are applicable to the self-regulatory organization is on the self-regulatory organization that proposed the rule change. As reflected in the General Instructions to Form 19b-4, the Form is designed to elicit information necessary for the public to provide meaningful comment on the proposed rule change and for the Commission to determine whether the proposed rule change is consistent with the requirements of the Exchange Act and the rules and regulations thereunder applicable to the self-regulatory organization. The self-regulatory organization must provide all information elicited by the Form, including the exhibits, and must present the information in a clear and comprehensible manner. In particular, the self-regulatory organization must explain why the proposed rule change is consistent with the requirements of the Exchange Act and the rules and regulations thereunder applicable to the self-regulatory organization. A mere assertion that the proposed rule change is consistent with those requirements, or that another self-regulatory organization has a similar rule in place, is not sufficient. Instead, the description of the proposed rule change, its purpose and operation, its effect, and a legal analysis of its consistency with applicable requirements must all be sufficiently detailed and specific to support an affirmative Commission finding. Any failure of the self-regulatory organization to provide the information elicited by Form 19b-4 may result in the Commission not having a sufficient basis to make an affirmative finding that a proposed rule change is consistent with the Exchange Act and the rules and regulations issued thereunder that are applicable to the self-regulatory organization.

(c) *Conduct of hearings*—(1) *Initial comment period in writing.* Unless otherwise specified by the Commission in its notice of grounds for disapproval under consideration, all interested persons will be given an opportunity to submit written data, views, and arguments concerning the proposed rule change under consideration and whether the Commission should approve or disapprove the proposed rule change. The self-regulatory organization that submitted the proposed rule change may file a written statement in support of its proposed rule change demonstrating, in specific detail, how such proposed rule change is consistent with the requirements of the Exchange Act and the rules and regulations thereunder applicable to the self-regulatory organization, including a response to each of the grounds for disapproval under consideration. Such statement may include

在问题的领域,或需要获取关于规则变更草案的补充信息的领域。证券交易委员会可以在程序过程中,在通知范围之外审议其他事实和法律问题。

(3)证明符合《证券交易法》。证明规则变更草案符合《证券交易法》以及依其颁发的适用于自律组织的规则与规章的举证责任,由提出规则变更草案的自律组织承担。如《19b-4表格》的一般说明中所述,该表格的设计目的是征集必要信息,以便公众就规则变更草案提出有意义的意见,同时使证券交易委员会能够判定规则变更草案是否符合《证券交易法》以及依其颁发的适用于自律组织的规则与规章。自律组织必须清楚、全面地提供表格(包括附录)要求提供的所有信息。特别是,自律组织必须解释为什么规则变更草案符合《证券交易法》以及依其颁发的适用于自律组织的规则与规章。单纯地主张规则变更草案符合上述规定,或其他自律组织制定有类似规则,不足以完成上述举证责任。相反,对规则变更草案及其宗旨、适用、效力的说明,以及对其符合适用规定的法律分析,都必须详细、具体,足以支持证券交易委员会作出肯定性的认定。自律组织未能提供《19b-4表格》要求提供的所有信息的,可能导致证券交易委员会没有充分的依据作出肯定性结论,认定规则变更草案符合《证券交易法》以及依其颁发的适用于自律组织的规则与规章。

(c)听证的开展——(1)初始书面评论期。除非证券交易委员会在关于审议中的否决理由的通知中另有规定,所有利害相关人均应获得机会就审议中的规则变更草案以及证券交易委员会是否应批准该草案呈报书面数据、观点和辩论意见。呈报规则变更草案的自律组织可以提交书面声明(包括对审议中的否决理由一一作出回复),支持其规则变更草案,详细证明为什么规则变更草案符合《证券交易法》以及依其颁发的适用于自律组织的规则与规章。该等声明可包括自律组织的具体声明或承诺。证券交易委员会将在审议中的否决理由摘要中指定初始评论期的期间。

specific representations or undertakings by the self-regulatory organization. The Commission will specify in the summary of the grounds for disapproval under consideration the length of the initial comment period.

(2) *Oral.* The Commission, in its sole discretion, may determine whether any issues relevant to approval or disapproval would be facilitated by the opportunity for an oral presentation of views.

(3) *Rebuttal.* At the end of the initial comment period, the self-regulatory organization that filed the proposed rule change will be given an opportunity to respond to any comments received. The self-regulatory organization may voluntarily file, or the Commission may request a self-regulatory organization to file, a response to a comment received regarding any aspect of the proposed rule change under consideration to assist the Commission in determining whether the proposed rule change should be disapproved. The Commission will specify in the summary of the grounds for disapproval under consideration the length of the rebuttal period.

(4) *Non-response.* Any failure by the self-regulatory organization to provide a complete response, within the applicable time period specified, to a comment letter received or to the Commission's grounds for disapproval under consideration may result in the Commission not having a sufficient basis to make an affirmative finding that a proposed rule change is consistent with the Exchange Act and the rules and regulations issued thereunder that are applicable to the self-regulatory organization.

(d) *Record before the Commission* — (1) *Filing of papers with the Commission.* Filing of papers with the Commission shall be made by filing them with the Secretary, including through electronic means. In its notice setting forth the grounds for disapproval under consideration for a proposed rule change, the Commission shall inform interested parties of the methods by which they may submit written comments and arguments for or against Commission approval.

(2) *Public availability of materials received.* During the conduct of the proceedings, the Commission generally will make available publicly all written comments it receives without change. In its notice setting forth the grounds for disapproval under consideration for a proposed rule change, the Commission shall inform interested parties of the methods by which they may view all written communications relating to the proposed rule change between the Commission and any person, other than those that may be withheld from the public in accordance with the provisions of 5 U.S.C. 552.

(3) *Record before the Commission.* The Commission shall determine each matter on the basis of the record. The record shall consist of the proposed rule change filed on Form 19b-4 by the self-regulatory organization, including all attachments and exhibits thereto, and all written materials received from any interested parties on the proposed rule change,

(2)口头陈述。提供口头陈述观点的机会是否将有助于解决与批准或否决相关的任何问题完全由证券交易委员会自行裁量判断。

(3)反驳。初始评论期结束之时,提交规则变更草案的自律组织将获得机会,对收到的任何评论进行答复。自律组织可以主动,证券交易委员会也可以要求自律组织就收到的关于审议中的规则变更草案的任何方面的意见提交答复,以协助证券交易委员会决定是否应否决规则变更草案。证券交易委员会将在审议中的否决理由摘要中指定提交反驳意见的期间。

(4)不答复。自律组织未在指定期间内,就收到的意见函或证券交易委员会审议中的否决理由作出完整答复的,可能导致证券交易委员会没有充分的依据作出肯定性结论,认定规则变更草案符合《证券交易法》以及依其颁发的适用于自律组织的规则与规章。

(d)证券交易委员会的记录——(1)向证券交易委员会提交文件。向证券交易委员会提交的文件应向证券交易委员会秘书提交,包括以电子方式提交。在就审议中的否决规则变更草案的理由发布的通知中,证券交易委员会应向利害关系人告知其可以呈报支持或反对证券交易委员会批准该草案的书面意见或辩论的方式。

(2)所收材料的公开。在程序开展过程中,证券交易委员会一般会按原貌公开其收到的所有书面意见。在就审议中的否决规则变更草案的理由发布的通知中,证券交易委员会应向利害关系人告知其查阅证券交易委员会与任何人之间关于规则变更草案的书面通信往来的方式,但根据《美国法典》第五编第552节可以拒不向公众披露的除外。

(3)证券交易委员会的记录。证券交易委员会应基于记录对各事项作出判定。记录应由以下各项构成:自律组织按《19b-4表格》提交的规则变更草案(包括所有附件和附录);通过证券交易委员会在第(1)款规定的方式从任何利害关系方(包括提交规则变更草案的自律组织)收到的关于规则变更草案的所有书面材料;以及反映证券交

including the self-regulatory organization that filed the proposed rule change, through the means identified by the Commission as provided in paragraph (1), as well as any written materials that reflect communications between the Commission and any interested parties.

(e) *Amended notice not required.* The Commission is not required to amend its notice of grounds for disapproval under consideration in order to consider, during the course of the proceedings, additional matters of fact and law beyond what was set forth in the notice of the grounds for disapproval under consideration.

[76 FR 4070, Jan. 24, 2011]

§201.701 Issuance of order.

At any time following conclusion of the rebuttal period specified in 17 CFR 201.700(b)(4), the Commission may issue an order approving or disapproving the self-regulatory organization's proposed rule change together with a written statement of the reasons therefor.

[76 FR 4070, Jan. 24, 2011]

Informal Procedures and Supplementary Information Concerning Adjudicatory Proceedings

§201.900 Informal Procedures and Supplementary Information Concerning Adjudicatory Proceedings.

(a) *Guidelines for the timely completion of proceedings.* (1) Timely resolution of adjudicatory proceedings is one factor in assessing the effectiveness of the adjudicatory program in protecting investors, promoting public confidence in the securities markets and assuring respondents a fair hearing. Establishment of guidelines for the timely completion of key phases of contested administrative proceedings provides a standard for both the Commission and the public to gauge the Commission's adjudicatory program on this criterion. The Commission has directed that, to the extent possible:

(i) A decision by the Commission on review of an interlocutory matter should be completed within 45 days of the date set for filing the final brief on the matter submitted for review.

(ii) A decision by the Commission on a motion to stay a decision that has already taken effect or that will take effect within five days of the filing of the motion, should be issued within 5 days of the date set for filing of the opposition to the motion for a stay. If the decision complained of has not taken effect, the Commission's decision should be issued within 45 days of the date set for filing of the opposition to the motion for a stay.

(iii) Ordinarily, a decision by the Commission with respect to an appeal from the initial decision of a hearing officer, a review of a determination by a self-regulatory organization, or a remand of a prior Commission decision by a court of appeals should be

易委员会与任何利害关系方之间的通信往来的所有书面材料。

(e)不必修正通知。证券交易委员会在程序进程中超出关于审议中的否决理由的通知所规定的范围,审议其他事实和法律问题的,不必对通知进行修正。

[《联邦公报》第76卷第4070页,2011年1月24日。]

第201.701节　命令的签发

证券交易委员会可以在《联邦规章汇编》第十七编第201.700(b)(4)节规定的反驳期间结束后的任何时间,签发命令批准或否决自律组织的规则变更草案,并附上一份关于其决定理由的书面声明。

[《联邦公报》第76卷第4070页,2011年1月24日。]

非正式程序以及关于行政裁决程序的补充信息

第201.900节　非正式程序以及关于行政裁决程序的补充信息

(a)及时结束程序指引。(1)及时结束行政裁决程序,是评估保护投资者、促进公众对证券市场的信任以及确保为相对人提供公平听证的行政裁决项目效率的一个因素。制定指引,以及时完成对抗性行政处理程序的关键阶段,为证券交易委员会和公众提供了一个评估证券交易委员会行政裁决项目的标准。证券交易委员会已指示在可能的限度内:

(i)证券交易委员会对中间事项的审议,应于指定的就复议事项提交最终陈辩书之日后45日内完成。

(ii)申请人提出动议要求中止已经生效或将在动议提交后5日内生效的决定的,证券交易委员会应在指定的针对中止动议提交反对意见的日期后5日内签发关于中止动议的决定。如果被提起动议的决定尚未生效,证券交易委员会应在指定的针对中止动议提交反对意见的日期后45日内签发关于中止动议的决定。

(iii)一般而言,对于针对听证官初步决定提起的复议,针对自律组织决定进行的复议,证券交易委员会作出的决定应在复议请求书或复议申请书提交后7个月内或法庭命令备案后7个月内签发;上诉法院将之前的证券交易委员会决定发回启动进一步

issued within seven months from the date the petition for review, application for review, or mandate of the court is filed, unless the Commission determines that the matter presents unusual complicating circumstances, in which case a decision by the Commission on the matter may be issued within 11 months from the date the petition for review, application for review, or mandate of the court is filed. The Commission retains discretion to take additional time to dispose of an appeal from the initial decision of a hearing officer, a review of a determination by a self-regulatory organization, or a remand of a prior Commission decision by a court of appeals when the Commission determines that extraordinary facts and circumstances of the matter so require. The deadlines in §201.900 confer no substantive rights on the parties.

(2) The guidelines in this paragraph (a) do not create a requirement that each portion of a proceeding or the entire proceeding be completed within the periods described. Among other reasons, a proceeding at either the hearing stage or on review by the Commission may require additional time because it is unusually complex or because the record is exceptionally long. In addition, fairness is enhanced if the Commission's deliberative process is not constrained by an inflexible schedule. In some proceedings, deliberation may be delayed by the need to consider more urgent matters, to permit the preparation of dissenting opinions, or for other good cause. The guidelines will be used by the Commission as one of several criteria in monitoring and evaluating its adjudicatory program. The guidelines will be examined periodically, and, if necessary, readjusted in light of changes in the pending caseload and the available level of staff resources.

(b) *Reports to the Commission on pending cases.* The administrative law judges, the Secretary and the General Counsel have each been delegated authority to issue certain orders or adjudicate certain proceedings. *See* 17 CFR 200.30-1 *et seq.* Proceedings are also assigned to the General Counsel for the preparation of a proposed order or opinion which will then be recommended to the Commission for consideration. In order to improve accountability by and to the Commission for management of the docket, the Commission has directed that confidential status reports with respect to all filed adjudicatory proceedings shall be made periodically to the Commission. These reports will be made through the Secretary, with a minimum frequency established by the Commission. In connection with these periodic reports, if a proceeding pending before the Commission has not been concluded within 30 days of the guidelines established in paragraph (a) of this section, the General Counsel shall specifically apprise the Commission of that fact, and shall describe the procedural posture of the case, project an estimated date for conclusion of the proceeding, and provide such other information as is necessary to enable the Commission to determine whether additional steps are necessary to reach a fair and timely resolution of the matter.

程序的,应在法院命令备案后7个月内签发,但证券交易委员会判定存在非同寻常的复杂情形的除外,此时证券交易委员会应在复议请求书或复议申请书提交之日或法院命令备案后11个月内签发。证券交易委员会判定存在特殊事实或情况的,可依其自由裁量权决定延长处置期间。各方当事人不得依据第201.900节规定的最终期限而享有任何实体权利。

(2)本节第(a)款规定的指引并不要求程序的每一部分或整个程序均在规定的期限内完成。听证阶段或证券交易委员会复议阶段中的程序需要延长时间的理由包括但不限于案件特别复杂或记录非常冗长。此外,如果证券交易委员会的审议程序不受固定日程约束,也有助于实现公平。在某些程序中,如需要审议更紧急的事项,或需要制定不同意见,或存在其他充分理由,审议程序也可以延长。证券交易委员会将使用上述指引作为监控和评估行政裁决工作的标准之一。指引定期进行审查,如有必要,将基于案件数量和可用工作人员数量的变化进行重新调整。

(b)就待决案件向证券交易委员会提交报告。行政法官、证券交易委员会秘书和首席律师均有权签发特定命令或对特定程序作出行政裁决。参见《联邦规章汇编》第十七编第200.30-1节及其后条文。某些程序也由首席律师负责制定命令或意见建议,再提交证券交易委员会审议。为了改进证券交易委员会对案件名册管理的可问责性,证券交易委员会已发布指示要求定期就所有已立案的行政裁决程序向证券交易委员会提交保密报告。报告应通过证券交易委员会秘书提交,报告提交的最低频率由证券交易委员会确定。就定期报告而言,如果证券交易委员会审理的程序未在本节第(a)款确定的指引结束后30日内审结,首席律师应将该事实特别提请证券交易委员会注意,说明案件的程序迟延,提出预期的程序审结日期,并提供其他必要信息,使证券交易委员会能够判定是否有必要采取其他步骤,对该事项作出公平和及时的解决。

(c) *Publication of information concerning the pending case docket.* Ongoing disclosure of information about the adjudication program caseload increases awareness of the importance of the program, facilitates oversight of the program and promotes confidence in the efficiency and fairness of the program by investors, securities industry participants, self-regulatory organizations and other members of the public. The Commission has directed the Secretary to publish in the *SEC Docket* in the first and seventh months of each fiscal year summary statistical information about the status of pending adjudicatory proceedings and changes in the Commission's caseload over the prior 6 months. The report will include the number of cases pending before the administrative law judges and the Commission at the beginning and end of the six-month period. The report will also show increases in the caseload arising from new cases being instituted, appealed or remanded to the Commission and decreases in the caseload arising from the disposition of proceedings by issuance of initial decisions, issuance of final decisions issued on appeal of initial decisions, other dispositions of appeals of initial decisions, final decisions on review of self-regulatory organization determinations, other dispositions on review of self-regulatory organization determinations, and decisions with respect to stays or interlocutory motions. For each category of decision, the report shall also show the median age of the cases at the time of the decision and the number of cases decided within the guidelines for the timely completion of adjudicatory proceedings.

[60 FR 32796, June 23, 1995, as amended at 68 FR 35789, June 17, 2003; 70 FR 72570, Dec. 5, 2005]

Subpart E—Adjustment of Civil Monetary Penalties

Authority: 28 U.S.C. 2461 note.

Source: 61 FR 57774, Nov. 8, 1996, unless otherwise noted.

§201.1001 Adjustment of civil monetary penalties—1996.

As required by the Debt Collection Improvement Act of 1996, the maximum amounts of all civil monetary penalties under the Securities Act of 1933, the Securities Exchange Act of 1934, the Investment Company Act of 1940, and the Investment Advisers Act of 1940 are adjusted for inflation in accordance with Table I to this subpart. The adjustments set forth in Table I apply to violations occurring after December 9, 1996 and before February 2, 2001.

[66 FR 8762, Feb. 2, 2001]

(c)未决案件名册信息的公布。对未审结的行政裁决项目进行持续信息披露,可以提升对行政裁决项目重要性的意识,促进对项目的监督,并增强投资者、证券行业参与人、自律组织和其他公众成员对项目效率和公平性的信心。证券交易委员会已指示证券交易委员会秘书在每一会计年度的第一个月和第七个月在《证券交易委员会周志》上发布过去6个月未决程序状态的统计信息摘要以及证券交易委员会未决案件量的变动。该报告将包括在6个月期间的期初及期末之时行政法官和证券交易委员会仍未审结的案件。报告还会说明因提起新案件、案件复议或发回启动进一步程序等而导致的未决案件数量的上升,以及通过签发初步决定、在初步决定被提起复议申请后签发最终决定或进行其他处置、对自律组织决定的复议申请签发最终决定及其他处置以及就中止或中间动议作出决定而导致的未决案件数量的下降。就每类决定而言,报告还应说明作出决定之时案件的平均案龄,以及按照及时审结行政裁决程序指引确立的期限作出裁决的案件数量。

[《联邦公报》第60卷第32796页,1995年6月23日,修正索引:《联邦公报》第68卷第35789页,2003年6月17日;《联邦公报》第70卷第72570页,2005年12月5日。]

第E子部分——民事罚款调整

法律依据:《美国法典》第二十八编第2461节注。

行政规则来源:《联邦公报》第61卷第57774页,1996年11月8日,除非另有说明。

第201.1001节　民事罚款调整——1996

按照《1996年债务催收改进法》的规定,《1933年证券法》、《1934年证券交易法》、《1940年投资公司法》和《1940年投资顾问法》中的所有民事罚款最高限额均按照本子部分表I进行通胀调整。表I规定的调整适用于1996年12月9日之后、2001年2月2日之前发生的违法违规行为。

[《联邦公报》第66卷第8762页,2001年2月2日。]

Table Ⅰ to Subpart E of Part 201—Civil Monetary Penalty Inflation Adjustments

U. S. Code citation	Civil monetary penalty description	Year penalty amount was last set by law	Original statutory maximum penalty amount	Adjusted maximum penalty amount
SECURITIES AND EXCHANGE COMMISSION:				
15 USC 77t(d)	FOR NATURAL PERSON	1990	$5,000	$5,500
	FOR ANY OTHER PERSON	1990	50,000	55,000
	FOR NATURAL PERSON/FRAUD	1990	50,000	55,000
	FOR ANY OTHER PERSON/FRAUD	1990	250,000	275,000
	FOR NATURAL PERSON/SUBSTANTIAL LOSSES OR RISK OF LOSSES TO OTHERS	1990	100,000	110,000
	FOR ANY OTHER PERSON/SUBSTANTIAL LOSSES OR RISK OF LOSSES TO OTHERS	1990	500,000	550,000
15 USC 78ff(b)	EXCHANGE ACT/FAILURE TO FILE INFORMATION DOCUMENTS, REPORTS	1936	100	110
15 USC 78ff(c)(1)(B)	FOREIGN CORRUPT PRACTICES—ANY ISSUER	1988	10,000	11,000
15 USC 78ff(c)(2)(C)	FOREIGN CORRUPT PRACTICES—ANY AGENT OR STOCKHOLDER ACTING ON BEHALF OF ISSUER	1988	10,000	11,000
15 USC 78u-1(a)(3)	INSIDER TRADING—CONTROLLING PERSONS	1988	1,000,000	1,100,000
15 USC 78u-2	FOR NATURAL PERSON	1990	5,000	5,500
	FOR ANY OTHER PERSON	1990	50,000	55,000

第201部分第E子部分表Ⅰ——民事罚款通胀调整

《美国法典》索引	民事罚款说明	法律上次规定罚款额度的年份	原法定最高罚款限额(美元)	调整后的最高罚款限额(美元)
证券交易委员会:				
《美国法典》第十五编第77t(d)节	适用于自然人	1990	5000	5500
	适用于任何其他主体	1990	50,000	55,000
	适用于自然人/欺诈	1990	50,000	55,000
	适用于任何其他主体/欺诈	1990	250,000	275,000
	适用于自然人/给他人造成重大损失或损失风险	1990	100,000	110,000
	适用于任何其他主体/给他人造成重大损失或损失风险	1990	500,000	550,000
《美国法典》第十五编第78ff(b)节	《证券交易法》/未提交信息文件、报告	1936	100	110
《美国法典》第十五编第78ff(c)(1)(B)节	反海外腐败行为——所有发行人	1988	10,000	11,000
《美国法典》第十五编第78ff(c)(2)(C)节	反海外腐败行为——所有代表发行人行事的代理人或股东	1988	10,000	11,000
《美国法典》第十五编第78u－1(a)(3)节	内幕交易——控制人	1988	1,000,000	1,100,000
《美国法典》第十五编第78u－2节	适用于自然人	1990	5000	5500
	适用于任何其他主体	1990	50,000	55,000

U. S. Code citation	Civil monetary penalty description	Year penalty amount was last set by law	Original statutory maximum penalty amount	Adjusted maximum penalty amount
	FOR NATURAL PERSON/FRAUD	1990	50,000	55,000
	FOR ANY OTHER PERSON/FRAUD	1990	250,000	275,000
	FOR NATURAL PERSON/SUBSTANTIAL LOSSES TO OTHERS/GAINS TO SELF	1990	100,000	110,000
	FOR ANY OTHER PERSONS/SUBSTANTIAL LOSSES TO OTHERS/GAIN TO SELF	1990	500,000	550,000
15 USC 78u(d)(3)	FOR NATURAL PERSON	1990	5,000	5,500
	FOR ANY OTHER PERSON	1990	50,000	55,000
	FOR NATURAL PERSON/FRAUD	1990	50,000	55,000
	FOR ANY OTHER PERSON/FRAUD	1990	250,000	275,000
	FOR NATURAL PERSON/SUBSTANTIAL LOSSES OR RISK OF LOSSES TO OTHERS	1990	100,000	110,000
	FOR ANY OTHER PERSON/SUBSTANTIAL LOSSES OR RISK OF LOSSES TO OTHERS	1990	500,000	550,000
15 USC 80a-9(d)	FOR NATURAL PERSON	1990	5,000	5,500
	FOR ANY OTHER PERSON	1990	50,000	55,000
	FOR NATURAL PERSON/FRAUD	1990	50,000	55,000
	FOR ANY OTHER PERSON/FRAUD	1990	250,000	275,000

续表

《美国法典》索引	民事罚款说明	法律上次规定罚款额度的年份	原法定最高罚款限额(美元)	调整后的最高罚款限额(美元)
	适用于自然人/欺诈	1990	50,000	55,000
	适用于任何其他主体/欺诈	1990	250,000	275,000
	适用于自然人/给他人造成重大损失/自己获利	1990	100,000	110,000
	适用于任何其他主体/给他人造成重大损失/自己获利	1990	500,000	550,000
《美国法典》第十五编第78u(d)(3)节	适用于自然人	1990	5000	5500
	适用于任何其他主体	1990	50,000	55,000
	适用于自然人/欺诈	1990	50,000	55,000
	适用于任何其他主体/欺诈	1990	250,000	275,000
	适用于自然人/给他人造成重大损失或损失风险	1990	100,000	110,000
	适用于任何其他主体/给他人造成重大损失或损失风险	1990	500,000	550,000
《美国法典》第十五编第80a-9(d)节	适用于自然人	1990	5000	5500
	适用于任何其他主体	1990	50,000	55,000
	适用于自然人/欺诈	1990	50,000	55,000
	适用于任何其他主体/欺诈	1990	250,000	275,000

U. S. Code citation	Civil monetary penalty description	Year penalty amount was last set by law	Original statutory maximum penalty amount	Adjusted maximum penalty amount
	FOR NATURAL PERSON/SUBSTANTIAL LOSSES TO OTHERS/GAINS TO SELF	1990	100,000	110,000
	FOR ANY OTHER PERSON/SUBSTANTIAL LOSSES TO OTHER/GAINS TO SELF	1990	500,000	550,000
15 USC 80a-41(e)	FOR NATURAL PERSON	1990	5,000	5,500
	FOR ANY OTHER PERSON	1990	50,000	55,000
	FOR NATURAL PERSON/FRAUD	1990	50,000	55,000
	FOR ANY OTHER PERSON/FRAUD	1990	250,000	275,000
	FOR NATURAL PERSON/SUBSTANTIAL LOSSES OR RISK OF LOSSES TO OTHERS	1990	100,000	110,000
	FOR ANY OTHER PERSON/SUBSTANTIAL LOSSES OR RISK OF LOSSES TO OTHERS	1990	500,000	550,000
15 USC 80b-3(i)	FOR NATURAL PERSON	1990	5,000	5,500
	FOR ANY OTHER PERSON	1990	50,000	55,000
	FOR NATURAL PERSON/FRAUD	1990	50,000	55,000
	FOR ANY OTHER PERSON/FRAUD	1990	250,000	275,000
	FOR NATURAL PERSON/SUBSTANTIAL LOSSES TO OTHERS/GAIN TO SELF	1990	100,000	110,000

续表

《美国法典》索引	民事罚款说明	法律上次规定罚款额度的年份	原法定最高罚款限额(美元)	调整后的最高罚款限额(美元)
	适用于自然人/给他人造成重大损失/自己获利	1990	100,000	110,000
	适用于任何其他主体/给他人造成重大损失/自己获利	1990	500,000	550,000
《美国法典》第十五编第80a-41(e)节	适用于自然人	1990	5000	5500
	适用于任何其他主体	1990	50,000	55,000
	适用于自然人/欺诈	1990	50,000	55,000
	适用于任何其他主体/欺诈	1990	250,000	275,000
	适用于自然人/给他人造成重大损失或损失风险	1990	100,000	110,000
	适用于其他主体/给他人造成重大损失或损失风险	1990	500,000	550,000
《美国法典》第十五编第80b-3(i)节	适用于自然人	1990	5000	5500
	适用于任何其他主体	1990	50,000	55,000
	适用于自然人/欺诈	1990	50,000	55,000
	适用于任何其他主体/欺诈	1990	250,000	275,000
	适用于自然人/给他人造成重大损失/自己获利	1990	100,000	110,000

U. S. Code citation	Civil monetary penalty description	Year penalty amount was last set by law	Original statutory maximum penalty amount	Adjusted maximum penalty amount
	FOR ANY OTHER PERSON/ SUBSTANTIAL LOSSES TO OTHERS/GAIN TO SELF	1990	500,000	550,000
15 USC 80b-9(e)	FOR NATURAL PERSON	1990	5000	5500
	FOR ANY OTHER PERSON	1990	50,000	55,000
	FOR NATURAL PERSON/FRAUD	1990	50,000	55,000
	FOR ANY OTHER PERSON/FRAUD	1990	250,000	275,000
	FOR NATURAL PERSON/SUBSTANTIAL LOSSES OR RISK OF LOSSES TO OTHERS	1990	100,000	110,000
	FOR ANY OTHER PERSON/ SUBSTANTIAL LOSSES OR RISK OF LOSSES TO OTHERS	1990	500,000	550,000

§201.1002 Adjustment of civil monetary penalties—2001.

As required by the Debt Collection Improvement Act of 1996, the maximum amounts of all civil monetary penalties under the Securities Act of 1933, the Securities Exchange Act of 1934, the Investment Company Act of 1940, and the Investment Advisers Act of 1940 are adjusted for inflation in accordance with Table Ⅱ to this subpart. The adjustments set forth in Table Ⅱ apply to violations occurring after February 2, 2001.

[66 FR 8762, Feb. 2, 2001]

续表

《美国法典》索引	民事罚款说明	法律上次规定罚款额度的年份	原法定最高罚款限额(美元)	调整后的最高罚款限额(美元)
	适用于任何其他主体/给他人造成重大损失/自己获利	1990	500,000	550,000
《美国法典》第十五编第80b－9(e)节	**适用于自然人**	1990	5000	5500
	适用于任何其他主体	1990	50,000	55,000
	适用于自然人/欺诈	1990	50,000	55,000
	适用于任何其他主体/欺诈	1990	250,000	275,000
	适用于自然人/给他人造成重大损失或损失风险	1990	100,000	110,000
	适用于任何其他主体/给他人造成重大损失或损失风险	1990	500,000	550,000

第201.1002节　民事罚款调整——2001

按照《1996年债务催收改进法》的规定,《1933年证券法》、《1934年证券交易法》、《1940年投资公司法》和《1940年投资顾问法》中的所有民事罚款最高限额均按照本子部分表I进行通胀调整。表Ⅱ规定的调整适用于2001年2月2日之后发生的违法违规行为。

[《联邦公报》第66卷第8762页,2001年2月2日。]

Table Ⅱ to Subpart E of Part 201—Civil Monetary Penalty Inflation Adjustments

U. S. Code citation	Civil monetary penalty description	Year penalty amount was last adjusted	Maximum penalty amount pursuant to 1996 adjustment	Adjusted maximum penalty amount
Securities and Exchange Commission:				
15 USC 77t(d)	For natural person	1996	$5,500	$6,500
	For any other person	1996	55,000	60,000
	For natural person/fraud	1996	55,000	60,000
	For any other person/fraud	1996	275,000	300,000
	For natural person/substantial losses or risk of losses to others	1996	110,000	120,000
	For any other person/substantial losses or risk of losses to others	1996	550,000	600,000
15 USC 78ff(b)	Exchange Act/failure to file information documents, reports	1996	110	110
15 USC 78ff(c)(1)(B)	Foreign Corrupt Practices—any issuer	1996	11,000	11,000
15 USC 78ff(c)(2)(C)	Foreign Corrupt Practices—any agent or stockholder acting on behalf of issuer	1996	11,000	11,000
15 USC 78u-1(a)(3)	Insider Trading—controlling person	1996	1,100,000	1,200,000
15 USC 78u-2	For natural person	1996	5,500	6,500
	For any other person	1996	55,000	60,000
	For natural person/fraud	1996	55,000	60,000

第201部分第E子部分表Ⅱ——民事罚款通胀调整

《美国法典》索引	民事罚款说明	法律上次规定罚款额度的年份	1996年调整后的最高罚款限额(美元)	调整后的最高罚款限额(美元)
证券交易委员会:				
《美国法典》第十五编第77t(d)节	适用于自然人	1996	5500	6500
	适用于任何其他主体	1996	55,000	60,000
	适用于自然人/欺诈	1996	55,000	60,000
	适用于任何其他主体/欺诈	1996	275,000	300,000
	适用于自然人/给他人造成重大损失或损失风险	1996	110,000	120,000
	适用于任何其他主体/给他人造成重大损失或损失风险	1996	550,000	600,000
《美国法典》第十五编第78ff(b)节	《证券交易法》/未提交信息文件、报告	1996	110	110
《美国法典》第十五编第78ff(c)(1)(B)节	反海外腐败行为——所有发行人	1996	11,000	11,000
《美国法典》第十五编第78ff(c)(2)(C)节	反海外腐败行为——所有代表发行人行事的代理人或股东	1996	11,000	11,000
《美国法典》第十五编第78u-1(a)(3)节	内幕交易——控制人	1996	1,100,000	1,200,000
《美国法典》第十五编第78u-2节	适用于自然人	1996	5500	6500
	适用于任何其他主体	1996	55,000	60,000
	适用于自然人/欺诈	1996	55,000	60,000

U. S. Code citation	Civil monetary penalty description	Year penalty amount was last adjusted	Maximum penalty amount pursuant to 1996 adjustment	Adjusted maximum penalty amount
	For any other person/fraud	1996	275,000	300,000
	For natural person/substantial losses to others/gains to self	1996	110,000	120,000
	For any other person/substantial losses to others/gain to self	1996	550,000	600,000
15 USC 78u(d)(3)	For natural person	1996	5,500	6,500
	For any other person	1996	55,000	60,000
	For natural person/fraud	1996	55,000	60,000
	For any other person/fraud	1996	275,000	300,000
	For natural person/substantial losses or risk of losses to others	1996	110,000	120,000
	For any other person/substantial losses or risk of losses to others	1996	550,000	600,000
15 USC 80a-9(d)	For natural person	1996	5,500	6,500
	For any other person	1996	55,000	60,000
	For natural person/fraud	1996	55,000	60,000
	For any other person/fraud	1996	275,000	300,000
	For natural person/substantial losses to others/gains to self	1996	110,000	120,000
	For any other person/substantial losses to others/gain to self	1996	550,000	600,000

续表

《美国法典》索引	民事罚款说明	法律上次规定罚款额度的年份	1996 年调整后的最高罚款限额(美元)	调整后的最高罚款限额(美元)
	适用于任何其他主体/欺诈	1996	275,000	300,000
	适用于自然人/给他人造成重大损失/自己获利	1996	110,000	120,000
	适用于任何其他主体/给他人造成重大损失/自己获利	1996	550,000	600,000
《美国法典》第十五编第 78u(d)(3)节	适用于自然人	1996	5500	6500
	适用于任何其他主体	1996	55,000	60,000
	适用于自然人/欺诈	1996	55,000	60,000
	适用于任何其他主体/欺诈	1996	275,000	300,000
	适用于自然人/给他人造成重大损失或损失风险	1996	110,000	120,000
	适用于任何其他主体/给他人造成重大损失或损失风险	1996	550,000	600,000
《美国法典》第十五编第 80a－9(d)节	适用于自然人	1996	5500	6500
	适用于任何其他主体	1996	55,000	60,000
	适用于自然人/欺诈	1996	55,000	60,000
	适用于任何其他主体/欺诈	1996	275,000	300,000
	适用于自然人/给他人造成重大损失/自己获利	1996	110,000	120,000
	适用于任何其他主体/给他人造成重大损失/自己获利	1996	550,000	600,000

U. S. Code citation	Civil monetary penalty description	Year penalty amount was last adjusted	Maximum penalty amount pursuant to 1996 adjustment	Adjusted maximum penalty amount
15 USC 80a-41(e)	For natural person	1996	5,500	6,500
	For any other person	1996	55,000	60,000
	For natural person/fraud	1996	55,000	60,000
	For any other person/fraud	1996	275,000	300,000
	For natural person/substantial losses or risk of losses to others	1996	110,000	120,000
	For any other person/substantial losses or risk of losses to others	1996	550,000	600,000
15 USC 80b-3(i)	For natural person	1996	5,500	6,500
	For any other person	1996	55,000	60,000
	For natural person/fraud	1996	55,000	60,000
	For any other person/fraud	1996	275,000	300,000
	For natural person/substantial losses to others/gains to self	1996	110,000	120,000
	For any other person/substantial losses to others/gain to self	1996	550,000	600,000
15 USC 80b-9(e)	For natural person	1996	5,500	6,500
	For any other person	1996	55,000	60,000
	For natural person/fraud	1996	55,000	60,000

续表

《美国法典》索引	民事罚款说明	法律上次规定罚款额度的年份	1996 年调整后的最高罚款限额（美元）	调整后的最高罚款限额（美元）
《美国法典》第十五编第 80a－41(e)节	适用于自然人	1996	5500	6500
	适用于任何其他主体	1996	55,000	60,000
	适用于自然人/欺诈	1996	55,000	60,000
	适用于任何其他主体/欺诈	1996	275,000	300,000
	适用于自然人/给他人造成重大损失或损失风险	1996	110,000	120,000
	适用于任何其他主体/给他人造成重大损失或损失风险	1996	550,000	600,000
《美国法典》第十五编第 80b－3(i)节	适用于自然人	1996	5500	6500
	适用于任何其他主体	1996	55,000	60,000
	适用于自然人/欺诈	1996	55,000	60,000
	适用于任何其他主体/欺诈	1996	275,000	300,000
	适用于自然人/给他人造成重大损失/自己获利	1996	110,000	120,000
	适用于任何其他主体/给他人造成重大损失/自己获利	1996	550,000	600,000
《美国法典》第十五编第 80b－9(e)节	适用于自然人	1996	5500	6500
	适用于任何其他主体	1996	55,000	60,000
	适用于自然人/欺诈	1996	55,000	60,000

U. S. Code citation	Civil monetary penalty description	Year penalty amount was last adjusted	Maximum penalty amount pursuant to 1996 adjustment	Adjusted maximum penalty amount
	For any other person/fraud	1996	275,000	300,000
	For natural person/substantial losses or risk of losses to others	1996	110,000	120,000
	For any other person/substantial losses or risk of losses to others	1996	550,000	600,000

[66 FR 8762, Feb. 2, 2001]

§201.1003 Adjustment of civil monetary penalties—2005.

As required by the Debt Collection Improvement Act of 1996, the maximum amounts of all civil monetary penalties under the Securities Act of 1933, the Securities Exchange Act of 1934, the Investment Company Act of 1940, the Investment Advisers Act of 1940, and certain penalties under the Sarbanes-Oxley Act of 2002 are adjusted for inflation in accordance with Table Ⅲ to this subpart. The adjustments set forth in Table Ⅲ apply to violations occurring after February 14, 2005.

[70 FR 7607, Feb. 14, 2005]

续表

《美国法典》索引	民事罚款说明	法律上次规定罚款额度的年份	1996年调整后的最高罚款限额（美元）	调整后的最高罚款限额（美元）
	适用于任何其他主体/欺诈	1996	275,000	300,000
	适用于自然人/给他人造成重大损失或损失风险	1996	110,000	120,000
	适用于任何其他主体/给他人造成重大损失或损失风险	1996	550,000	600,000

[《联邦公报》第66卷第8762页，2001年2月2日。]

第201.1003节　民事罚款调整——2005

按照《1996年债务催收改进法》的规定，《1933年证券法》、《1934年证券交易法》、《1940年投资公司法》和《1940年投资顾问法》中的所有民事罚款以及《2002年萨班斯—奥克斯利法》中的某些民事罚款的最高限额均按照本子部分表Ⅲ进行通胀调整。表Ⅲ规定的调整适用于2005年2月14日之后发生的违法违规行为。

[《联邦公报》第70卷第7607页，2005年2月14日。]

Table Ⅲ to Subpart E of Part 201—Civil Monetary Penalty Inflation Adjustments

U. S. Code citation	Civil monetary penalty description	Year penalty amount was last adjusted	Maximum penalty amount pursuant to last adjustment	Adjusted maximum penalty amount
Securities and Exchange Commission				
15 U. S. C. 77t(d)	For natural person	2001	$6,500	$6,500
	For any other person	2001	60,000	65,000
	For natural person/fraud	2001	60,000	65,000
	For any other person/fraud	2001	300,000	325,000
	For natural person/substantial losses or risk of losses to others	2001	120,000	130,000
	For any other person/substantial losses or risk of losses to others	2001	600,000	650,000
15 U. S. C. 78ff(b)	Exchange Act/failure to file information documents, reports	1996	110	110
15 U. S. C. 78ff(c)(1)(B)	Foreign Corrupt Practices—any issuer	1996	11,000	11,000
15 U. S. C. 78ff(c)(2)(C)	Foreign Corrupt Practices—any agent or stockholder acting on behalf of issuer	1996	11,000	11,000
15 U. S. C. 78u-1(a)(3)	Insider Trading—controlling person	2001	1,200,000	1,275,000
15 U. S. C. 78u-2	For natural person	2001	6,500	6,500
	For any other person	2001	60,000	65,000
	For natural person/fraud	2001	60,000	65,000

第201部分第E子部分表Ⅲ——民事罚款通胀调整

《美国法典》索引	民事罚款说明	法律上次规定罚款额度的年份	上次调整后的最高罚款限额(美元)	调整后的最高罚款限额(美元)
证券交易委员会				
《美国法典》第十五编第77t(d)节	适用于自然人	2001	6500	6500
	适用于任何其他主体	2001	60,000	65,000
	适用于自然人/欺诈	2001	60,000	65,000
	适用于任何其他主体/欺诈	2001	300,000	325,000
	适用于自然人/给他人造成重大损失或损失风险	2001	120,000	130,000
	适用于任何其他主体/给他人造成重大损失或损失风险	2001	600,000	650,000
《美国法典》第十五编第78ff(b)节	《证券交易法》/未提交信息文件、报告	1996	110	110
《美国法典》第十五编第78ff(c)(1)(B)节	反海外腐败行为——所有发行人	1996	11,000	11,000
《美国法典》第十五编第78ff(c)(2)(C)节	反海外腐败行为——所有代表发行人行事的代理人或股东	1996	11,000	11,000
《美国法典》第十五编第78u-1(a)(3)节	内幕交易——控制人	2001	1,200,000	1,275,000
《美国法典》第十五编第78u-2节	适用于自然人	2001	6500	6500
	适用于任何其他主体	2001	60,000	65,000
	适用于自然人/欺诈	2001	60,000	65,000

U. S. Code citation	Civil monetary penalty description	Year penalty amount was last adjusted	Maximum penalty amount pursuant to last adjustment	Adjusted maximum penalty amount
	For any other person/fraud	2001	300,000	325,000
	For natural person/substantial losses to others/gains to self	2001	120,000	130,000
	For any other person/substantial losses to others/gain to self	2001	600,000	650,000
15 U. S. C. 78u(d)(3)	For natural person	2001	6,500	6,500
	For any other person	2001	60,000	65,000
	For natural person/fraud	2001	60,000	65,000
	For any other person/fraud	2001	300,000	325,000
	For natural person/substantial losses or risk of losses to others	2001	120,000	130,000
	For any other person/substantial losses or risk of losses to others	2001	600,000	650,000
15 U. S. C. 80a-9(d)	For natural person	2001	6,500	6,500
	For any other person	2001	60,000	65,000
	For natural person/fraud	2001	60,000	65,000
	For any other person/fraud	2001	300,000	325,000
	For natural person/substantial losses to others/gains to self	2001	120,000	130,000
	For any other person/substantial losses to others/gain to self	2001	600,000	650,000

续表

《美国法典》索引	民事罚款说明	法律上次规定罚款额度的年份	上次调整后的最高罚款限额（美元）	调整后的最高罚款限额（美元）
	适用于任何其他主体/欺诈	2001	300,000	325,000
	适用于自然人/给他人造成重大损失/自己获利	2001	120,000	130,000
	适用于任何其他主体/给他人造成重大损失/自己获利	2001	600,000	650,000
《美国法典》第十五编第78u(d)(3)节	适用于自然人	2001	6500	6500
	适用于任何其他主体	2001	60,000	65,000
	适用于自然人/欺诈	2001	60,000	65,000
	适用于任何其他主体/欺诈	2001	300,000	325,000
	适用于自然人/给他人造成重大损失或损失风险	2001	120,000	130,000
	适用于任何其他主体/给他人造成重大损失或损失风险	2001	600,000	650,000
《美国法典》第十五编第80a-9(d)节	适用于自然人	2001	6500	6500
	适用于任何其他主体	2001	60,000	65,000
	适用于自然人/欺诈	2001	60,000	65,000
	适用于任何其他主体/欺诈	2001	300,000	325,000
	适用于自然人/给他人造成重大损失/自己获利	2001	120,000	130,000
	适用于任何其他主体/给他人造成重大损失/自己获利	2001	600,000	650,000

U. S. Code citation	Civil monetary penalty description	Year penalty amount was last adjusted	Maximum penalty amount pursuant to last adjustment	Adjusted maximum penalty amount
15 U. S. C. 80a-41(e)	For natural person	2001	6,500	6,500
	For any other person	2001	60,000	65,000
	For natural person/fraud	2001	60,000	65,000
	For any other person/fraud	2001	300,000	325,000
	For natural person/substantial losses or risk of losses to others	2001	120,000	130,000
	For any other person/substantial losses or risk of losses to others	2001	600,000	650,000
15 U. S. C. 80b-3(i)	For natural person	2001	6,500	6,500
	For any other person	2001	60,000	65,000
	For natural person/fraud	2001	60,000	65,000
	For any other person/fraud	2001	300,000	325,000
	For natural person/substantial losses to others/gains to self	2001	120,000	130,000
	For any other person/substantial losses to others /gain to self	2001	600,000	650,000
15 U. S. C. 80b-9(e)	For natural person	2001	6,500	6,500
	For any other person	2001	60,000	65,000
	For natural person/fraud	2001	60,000	65,000

续表

《美国法典》索引	民事罚款说明	法律上次规定罚款额度的年份	上次调整后的最高罚款限额(美元)	调整后的最高罚款限额(美元)
《美国法典》第十五编第 80a - 41(e)节	适用于自然人	2001	6500	6500
	适用于任何其他主体	2001	60,000	65,000
	适用于自然人/欺诈	2001	60,000	65,000
	适用于任何其他主体/欺诈	2001	300,000	325,000
	适用于自然人/给他人造成重大损失或损失风险	2001	120,000	130,000
	适用于任何其他主体/给他人造成重大损失或损失风险	2001	600,000	650,000
《美国法典》第十五编第 80b - 3(i)节	适用于自然人	2001	6500	6500
	适用于任何其他主体	2001	60,000	65,000
	适用于自然人/欺诈	2001	60,000	65,000
	适用于任何其他主体/欺诈	2001	300,000	325,000
	适用于自然人/给他人造成重大损失/自己获利	2001	120,000	130,000
	适用于任何其他主体/给他人造成重大损失/自己获利	2001	600,000	650,000
《美国法典》第十五编第 80b - 9(e)节	适用于自然人	2001	6500	6500
	适用于任何其他主体	2001	60,000	65,000
	适用于自然人/欺诈	2001	60,000	65,000

U. S. Code citation	Civil monetary penalty description	Year penalty amount was last adjusted	Maximum penalty amount pursuant to last adjustment	Adjusted maximum penalty amount
	For any other person/fraud	2001	300,000	325,000
	For natural person/substantial losses or risk of losses to others	2001	120,000	130,000
	For any other person/substantial losses or risk of losses to others	2001	600,000	650,000
15 U. S. C. 7215 (c)(4)(D)(i)	For natural person	2002	100,000	110,000
	For any other person	2002	2,000,000	2,100,000
15 U. S. C. 7215 (c)(4)(D)(ii)	For natural person	2002	750,000	800,000
	For any other person	2002	15,000,000	15,825,000

[70 FR 7607, Feb. 14, 2005]

§201.1004 Adjustment of civil monetary penalties—2009.

As required by the Debt Collection Improvement Act of 1996, the maximum amounts of all civil monetary penalties under the Securities Act of 1933, the Securities Exchange Act of 1934, the Investment Company Act of 1940, the Investment Advisers Act of 1940, and certain penalties under the Sarbanes-Oxley Act of 2002 are adjusted for inflation in accordance with Table Ⅳ to this subpart. The adjustments set forth in Table Ⅳ apply to violations occurring after March 3, 2009.

[74 FR 9160, Mar. 3, 2009]

续表

《美国法典》索引	民事罚款说明	法律上次规定罚款额度的年份	上次调整后的最高罚款限额（美元）	调整后的最高罚款限额（美元）
	适用于任何其他主体/欺诈	2001	300,000	325,000
	适用于自然人/给他人造成重大损失或损失风险	2001	120,000	130,000
	适用于任何其他主体/给他人造成重大损失或损失风险	2001	600,000	650,000
《美国法典》第十五编第7215(c)(4)(D)(i)节	适用于自然人	2002	100,000	110,000
	适用于任何其他主体	2002	2,000,000	2,100,000
《美国法典》第十五编第7215(c)(4)(D)(ii)节	适用于自然人	2002	750,000	800,000
	适用于任何其他主体	2002	15,000,000	15,825,000

[《联邦公报》第70卷第7607页，2005年2月14日。]

第201.1004节　民事罚款调整——2009

按照《1996年债务催收改进法》的规定，《1933年证券法》、《1934年证券交易法》、《1940年投资公司法》和《1940年投资顾问法》中的所有民事罚款以及《2002年萨班斯—奥克斯利法》中的某些民事罚款的最高限额均按照本子部分表Ⅳ进行通胀调整。表Ⅳ规定的调整适用于2009年3月3日之后发生的违法违规行为。

[《联邦公报》第74卷第9160页，2009年3月3日。]

Table Ⅳ to Subpart E of Part 201—Civil Monetary Penalty Inflation Adjustments

Table Ⅳ to Subpart E	Civil monetary penalty inflation adjustments	Year penalty amount was last adjusted	Maximum penalty amount pursuant to last adjustment	Adjusted maximum penalty amount
U.S. Code citation	Civil monetary penalty description			
Securities and Exchange Commission:				
15 U.S.C. 77t(d)	For natural person	2001	$6,500	$7,500
	For any other person	2005	65,000	75,000
	For natural person/fraud	2005	65,000	75,000
	For any other person/fraud	2005	325,000	375,000
	For natural person/substantial losses or risk of losses to others	2005	130,000	150,000
	For any other person/substantial losses or risk of losses to others	2005	650,000	725,000
15 U.S.C. 78ff(b)	Exchange Act/failure to file information documents, reports	1996	110	110
15 U.S.C. 78ff(c)(1)(B)	Foreign Corrupt Practices—any issuer	1996	11,000	16,000
15 U.S.C. 78ff(c)(2)(C)	Foreign Corrupt Practices—any agent or stockholder acting on behalf of issuer	1996	11,000	16,000
15 U.S.C. 78u-1(a)(3)	Insider Trading—controlling person	2005	1,275,000	1,425,000
15 U.S.C. 78u-2	For natural person	2001	6,500	7,500
	For any other person	2005	65,000	75,000
	For natural person/fraud	2005	65,000	75,000
	For any other person/fraud	2005	325,000	375,000

第201部分第E子部分表Ⅳ——民事罚款通胀调整

第E子部分表Ⅳ	民事罚款通胀调整	法律上次规定罚款额度的年份	上次调整后的最高罚款限额(美元)	调整后的最高罚款限额(美元)
《美国法典》索引	民事罚款说明			
证券交易委员会:				
《美国法典》第十五编第77t(d)节	适用于自然人	2001	6500	7500
	适用于任何其他主体	2005	65,000	75,000
	适用于自然人/欺诈	2005	65,000	75,000
	适用于任何其他主体/欺诈	2005	325,000	375,000
	适用于自然人/给他人造成重大损失或损失风险	2005	130,000	150,000
	适用于任何其他主体/给他人造成重大损失或损失风险	2005	650,000	725,000
《美国法典》第十五编第78ff(b)节	《证券交易法》/未提交信息文件、报告	1996	110	110
《美国法典》第十五编第78ff(c)(1)(B)节	反海外腐败行为——所有发行人	1996	11,000	16,000
《美国法典》第十五编第78ff(c)(2)(C)节	反海外腐败行为——所有代表发行人行事的代理人或股东	1996	11,000	16,000
《美国法典》第十五编第78u-1(a)(3)节	内幕交易——控制人	2005	1,275,000	1,425,000
《美国法典》第十五编第78u-2节	适用于自然人	2001	6500	7500
	适用于任何其他主体	2005	65,000	75,000
	适用于自然人/欺诈	2005	65,000	75,000
	适用于任何其他主体/欺诈	2005	325,000	375,000

Table Ⅳ to Subpart E	Civil monetary penalty inflation adjustments	Year penalty amount was last adjusted	Maximum penalty amount pursuant to last adjustment	Adjusted maximum penalty amount
U. S. Code citation	Civil monetary penalty description			
	For natural person/substantial losses to others/gains to self	2005	130,000	150,000
	For any other person/substantial losses to others/gain to self	2005	650,000	725,000
15 U. S. C. 78u(d)(3)	For natural person	2001	6,500	7,500
	For any other person	2005	65,000	75,000
	For natural person/fraud	2005	65,000	75,000
	For any other person/fraud	2005	325,000	375,000
	For natural person/substantial losses or risk of losses to others	2005	130,000	150,000
	For any other person/substantial losses or risk of losses to others	2005	650,000	725,000
15 U. S. C. 80a-9(d)	For natural person	2001	6,500	7,500
	For any other person	2005	65,000	75,000
	For natural person/fraud	2005	65,000	75,000
	For any other person/fraud	2005	325,000	375,000
	For natural person/substantial losses to others/gains to self	2005	130,000	150,000
	For any other person/substantial losses to others/gain to self	2005	650,000	725,000
15 U. S. C. 80a-41(e)	For natural person	2001	6,500	7,500

续表

第E子部分表Ⅳ	民事罚款通胀调整	法律上次规定罚款额度的年份	上次调整后的最高罚款限额(美元)	调整后的最高罚款限额(美元)
《美国法典》索引	民事罚款说明			
	适用于自然人/给他人造成重大损失/自己获利	2005	130,000	150,000
	适用于任何其他主体/给他人造成重大损失/自己获利	2005	650,000	725,000
《美国法典》第十五编第78u(d)(3)节	适用于自然人	2001	6500	7500
	适用于任何其他主体	2005	65,000	75,000
	适用于自然人/欺诈	2005	65,000	75,000
	适用于任何其他主体/欺诈	2005	325,000	375,000
	适用于自然人/给他人造成重大损失或损失风险	2005	130,000	150,000
	适用于任何其他主体/给他人造成重大损失或损失风险	2005	650,000	725,000
《美国法典》第十五编第80a－9(d)节	适用于自然人	2001	6500	7500
	适用于任何其他主体	2005	65,000	75,000
	适用于自然人/欺诈	2005	65,000	75,000
	适用于任何其他主体/欺诈	2005	325,000	375,000
	适用于自然人/给他人造成重大损失/自己获利	2005	130,000	150,000
	适用于任何其他主体/给他人造成重大损失/自己获利	2005	650,000	725,000
《美国法典》第十五编第80a－41(e)节	适用于自然人	2001	6500	7500

Table Ⅳ to Subpart E	Civil monetary penalty inflation adjustments	Year penalty amount was last adjusted	Maximum penalty amount pursuant to last adjustment	Adjusted maximum penalty amount
U. S. Code citation	Civil monetary penalty description			
	For any other person	2005	65,000	75,000
	For natural person/fraud	2005	65,000	75,000
	For any other person/fraud	2005	325,000	375,000
	For natural person/substantial losses or risk of losses to others	2005	130,000	150,000
	For any other person/substantial losses or risk of losses to others	2005	650,000	725,000
15 U. S. C. 80b-3(i)	For natural person	2001	6,500	7,500
	For any other person	2005	65,000	75,000
	For natural person/fraud	2005	65,000	75,000
	For any other person/fraud	2005	325,000	375,000
	For natural person/substantial losses to others/gains to self	2005	130,000	150,000
	For any other person/substantial losses to others/gain to self	2005	650,000	725,000
15 U. S. C. 80b-9(e)	For natural person	2001	6,500	7,500
	For any other person	2005	65,000	75,000
	For natural person/fraud	2005	65,000	75,000
	For any other person/fraud	2005	325,000	375,000
	For natural person/substantial losses or risk of losses to others	2005	130,000	150,000

续表

第E子部分表Ⅳ	民事罚款通胀调整	法律上次规定罚款额度的年份	上次调整后的最高罚款限额(美元)	调整后的最高罚款限额(美元)
《美国法典》索引	民事罚款说明			
	适用于任何其他主体	2005	65,000	75,000
	适用于自然人/欺诈	2005	65,000	75,000
	适用于任何其他主体/欺诈	2005	325,000	375,000
	适用于自然人/给他人造成重大损失或损失风险	2005	130,000	150,000
	适用于任何其他主体/给他人造成重大损失或损失风险	2005	650,000	725,000
《美国法典》第十五编第80b-3(i)节	适用于自然人	2001	6500	7500
	适用于任何其他主体	2005	65,000	75,000
	适用于自然人/欺诈	2005	65,000	75,000
	适用于任何其他主体/欺诈	2005	325,000	375,000
	适用于自然人/给他人造成重大损失/自己获利	2005	130,000	150,000
	适用于任何其他主体/给他人造成重大损失/自己获利	2005	650,000	725,000
《美国法典》第十五编第80b-9(e)节	适用于自然人	2001	6500	7500
	适用于任何其他主体	2005	65,000	75,000
	适用于自然人/欺诈	2005	65,000	75,000
	适用于任何其他主体/欺诈	2005	325,000	375,000
	适用于自然人/给他人造成重大损失或损失风险	2005	130,000	150,000

Table Ⅳ to Subpart E	Civil monetary penalty inflation adjustments	Year penalty amount was last adjusted	Maximum penalty amount pursuant to last adjustment	Adjusted maximum penalty amount
U. S. Code citation	Civil monetary penalty description			
	For any other person/substantial losses or risk of losses to others	2005	650,000	725,000
15 U. S. C. 7215 (c)(4)(D)(i)	For natural person	2005	110,000	120,000
	For any other person	2005	2,100,000	2,375,000
15 U. S. C. 7215 (c)(4)(D)(ii)	For natural person	2005	800,000	900,000
	For any other person	2005	15,825,000	17,800,000

[74 FR 9160, Mar. 3, 2009]

Subpart F—Fair Fund and Disgorgement Plans

Authority: 15 U.S.C. 77h–1, 77s, 77u, 78c(b), 78d–1, 78d–2, 78u–2, 78u–3, 78v, 78w, 80a–9, 80a–37, 80a–39, 80a–40, 80b–3, 80b–11, 80b–12, and 7246.

Source: 69 FR 13180, Mar. 19, 2004, unless otherwise noted.

§201.1100 Creation of Fair Fund.

In any agency process initiated by an order instituting proceedings in which the Commission or the hearing officer issues an order requiring the payment of disgorgement by a respondent and also assessing a civil money penalty against that respondent, the Commission or the hearing officer may order that the amount of disgorgement and of the civil penalty, together with any funds received pursuant to 15 U.S.C. 7246(b), be used to create a fund for the benefit of investors who were harmed by the violation.

[70 FR 72570, Dec. 5, 2005]

续表

第E子部分表Ⅳ	民事罚款通胀调整	法律上次规定罚款额度的年份	上次调整后的最高罚款限额（美元）	调整后的最高罚款限额（美元）
《美国法典》索引	民事罚款说明			
	适用于任何其他主体/给他人造成重大损失或损失风险	2005	650,000	725,000
《美国法典》第十五编第7215(c)(4)(D)(i)节	适用于自然人	2005	110,000	120,000
	适用于任何其他主体	2005	2,100,000	2,375,000
《美国法典》第十五编第7215(c)(4)(D)(ii)节	适用于自然人	2005	800,000	900,000
	适用于任何其他主体	2005	15,825,000	17,800,000

[《联邦公报》第74卷第9160页，2009年3月3日。]

第F子部分——公平基金和没收计划

法律依据：《美国法典》第十五编第77h-1节、第77s节、第77u节、第78c(b)节、第78d-1节、第78d-2节、第78u-2节、第78u-3节、第78v节、第78w节、第80a-9节、第80a-37节、第80a-39节、第80a-40节、第80b-3节、第80b-11节、第80b-12节和第7246节。

行政规则来源：《联邦公报》第69卷第13180页，2004年3月19日，除非另有说明。

第201.1100节　公平基金的创立

通过程序发起令发起的任何证券交易委员会程序中，如证券交易委员会或听证官签发命令要求相对人支付没收款项和民事罚款的，证券交易委员会或听证官可以命令将没收款项、民事罚款以及根据《美国法典》第十五编第7246(b)节收取的所有资金用于创立基金，以维护受违法违规行为侵害的投资者的利益。

[《联邦公报》第70卷第72570页，2005年12月5日。]

§201.1101 Submission of plan of distribution; contents of plan.

(a) *Submission.* The Commission or the hearing officer may, at any time, order any party to submit a plan for the administration and distribution of funds in a Fair Fund or disgorgement fund. Unless ordered otherwise, the Division of Enforcement shall submit a proposed plan no later than 60 days after the respondent has turned over the funds or other assets pursuant to the Commission's order imposing disgorgement and, if applicable, a civil money penalty and any appeals of the Commission's order have been waived or completed, or appeal is no longer available.

(b) *Contents of plan.* Unless otherwise ordered, a plan for the administration of a Fair Fund or a disgorgement fund shall include the following elements:

(1) Procedures for the receipt of additional funds, including the specification of any account where funds will be held, the instruments in which the funds may be invested; and, in the case of a Fair Fund, the receipt of any funds pursuant to 15 U.S.C. 7246(b), if applicable;

(2) Specification of categories of persons potentially eligible to receive proceeds from the fund;

(3) Procedures for providing notice to such persons of the existence of the fund and their potential eligibility to receive proceeds of the fund;

(4) Procedures for making and approving claims, procedures for handling disputed claims, and a cut-off date for the making of claims;

(5) A proposed date for the termination of the fund, including provision for the disposition of any funds not otherwise distributed;

(6) Procedures for the administration of the fund, including selection, compensation, and, as necessary, indemnification of a fund administrator to oversee the fund, process claims, prepare accountings, file tax returns, and, subject to the approval of the Commission, make distributions from the fund to investors who were harmed by the violation; and

(7) Such other provisions as the Commission or the hearing officer may require.

§201.1102 Provisions for payment.

(a) *Payment to registry of the court or court-appointed receiver.* Subject to such conditions as the Commission or the hearing officer shall deem appropriate, a plan for the administration of a Fair Fund or a disgorgement fund may provide for payment of funds into a court registry or to a court-appointed receiver in any case pending in federal or state court against a respondent or any other person based upon a complaint alleging violations arising from the same or substantially similar facts as those alleged in the Commission's order instituting proceedings.

(b) *Payment to the United States Treasury under certain circumstances.* When, in

第201.1101节　分配计划的呈报;计划内容

(a)呈报。证券交易委员会或听证官可以在任何时间命令任何当事人呈报公平基金或没收基金的资金管理和分配计划。除非另有命令,如相对人已按照证券交易委员会的没收令和支付民事罚款令(如适用)上缴款项或其他资产,且针对证券交易委员会命令的任何复议申请已被放弃、结束或相对人已无权申请复议,执法部至迟应在此后60日内呈报计划提案。

(b)计划内容。除非另有命令,公平基金或没收基金的管理计划应包括如下要素:

(1)接收其他资金的程序,包括说明持有资金的账户、可以作为资金投资对象的工具;对于公平基金而言,还应包括按照《美国法典》第十五编第7246(b)节规定接收任何资金的程序(如适用);

(2)说明具有获得基金收益的潜在资格的主体类型;

(3)向该等主体发出通知说明基金的存在及其具有获得基金收益的潜在资格的程序;

(4)提出和批准权利主张的程序、处理争议主张的程序以及提出主张的截止日;

(5)提议的基金终止日,包括关于任何未分配资金的处置的规定;

(6)基金管理程序,包括基金管理人的选任、报酬以及(如有必要)赔偿,基金管理人负责监督基金、处理权利主张、编制会计报表、提交纳税申报单以及在获取证券交易委员会批准的前提下,通过基金向受违法违规行为侵害的投资者进行分配;及

(7)证券交易委员会或听证官要求说明的任何其他规定。

第201.1102节　付款规定

(a)向法院登记处或法院指定的收款人付款。在遵守证券交易委员会或听证官认为适当的条件的前提下,公平基金或没收基金管理计划可以规定,基于与证券交易委员会的程序发起令中所声称的同一事实或实质类似的违法违规事实,而在联邦法院或州法院向相对人或任何其他人提起的案件中,应向法院登记处或法院指定的收款人支付资金。

(b)在特定情形下向美国财政部付款。如证券交易委员会或听证官认为,考虑到

the opinion of the Commission or the hearing officer, the cost of administering a plan of disgorgement relative to the value of the available disgorgement funds and the number of potential claimants would not justify distribution of the disgorgement funds to injured investors, the plan may provide that the disgorgement funds and any civil penalty shall be paid directly to the general fund of the United States Treasury.

§201.1103 Notice of proposed plan and opportunity for comment by non-parties.

Notice of a proposed plan of disgorgement or a proposed Fair Fund plan shall be published in the *SEC Docket,* on the SEC website, and in such other publications as the Commission or the hearing officer may require. The notice shall specify how copies of the proposed plan may be obtained and shall state that persons desiring to comment on the proposed plan may submit their views, in writing, to the Commission.

§201.1104 Order approving, modifying, or disapproving proposed plan.

At any time after 30 days following publication of notice of a proposed plan of disgorgement or of a proposed Fair Fund plan, the Commission shall, by order, approve, approve with modifications, or disapprove the proposed plan. In the discretion of the Commission, a proposed plan that is substantially modified prior to adoption may be republished for an additional comment period pursuant to §201.1103. The order approving or disapproving the plan should be entered within 30 days after the end of the final period allowed for comments on the proposed plan unless the Commission or the hearing officer, by written order, allows a longer period for good cause shown.

§201.1105 Administration of plan.

(a) *Appointment and removal of administrator.* The Commission or the hearing officer shall have discretion to appoint any person, including a Commission employee, as administrator of a plan of disgorgement or a Fair Fund plan and to delegate to that person responsibility for administering the plan. An administrator may be removed at any time by order of the Commission or hearing officer.

(b) *Assistance by respondent.* A respondent may be required or permitted to administer or assist in administering a plan of disgorgement subject to such terms and conditions as the Commission or the hearing officer deems appropriate to ensure the proper distribution of the funds.

(c) *Administrator to post bond.* If the administrator is not a Commission employee, the administrator shall be required to obtain a bond in the manner prescribed in 11 U.S.C. 322, in an amount to be approved by the Commission. The cost of the bond may be paid for as a cost of administration. The Commission may waive posting of a bond for good cause shown.

(d) *Administrator's fees.* If the administrator is a Commission employee, no fee shall

没收资金的价值以及潜在的权利主张人的数量,没收计划的执行成本过高,不宜于向受损害的投资者分配没收资金,该计划可以规定,没收资金和任何民事罚款应直接缴入美国财政部的一般基金。

第201.1103节 关于计划提案的通知以及非当事人提供意见的机会

关于没收计划提案或公平基金计划提案的通知应在《证券交易委员会周志》、证券交易委员会网站以及证券交易委员会或听证官可能要求的其他出版物上发布。通知应具体说明如何获取计划提案,并说明希望就计划提案发表意见的人可以向证券交易委员会提交书面意见。

第201.1104节 批准、修改或否决计划提案的命令

关于没收计划提案或公平基金计划提案的通知发布后30日内,证券交易委员会应发布命令,批准、附带修改地批准或否决计划提案。证券交易委员会可依其自由裁量权决定,作出重大修改的计划提案应在通过前根据第201.1103节重新发布,并规定补充意见征询期。批准或否决计划的命令应在最终的意见征询期结束后30日内作出,但证券交易委员会或听证官基于充分理由,通过书面允许延长期间的除外。

第201.1105节 计划执行

(a)管理人的任免。证券交易委员会或听证官可自行决定任命任何人(包括证券交易委员会的雇员)担任没收计划或公平基金计划的管理人,并委托其履行执行计划的职责。证券交易委员会或听证官可以在任何时间免除管理人的职务。

(b)相对人的协助。相对人可能被要求或被允许执行或协助执行没收计划,但应遵守证券交易委员会或听证官认为适当的为确保资金适当分配而确立的条款和条件。

(c)应缴纳保证金的管理人。如果计划管理人不属于证券交易委员会雇员,管理人应按《美国法典》第十一编第322节规定的方式提供保证金,金额由证券交易委员会批准。保证金的成本可以作为管理成本支付。管理人提出充分理由的,证券交易委员会可以免除缴纳保证金的责任。

(d)管理人费用。如果计划管理人属于证券交易委员会雇员,不应就计划管理服

be paid to the administrator for his or her services. If the administrator is not a Commission employee, the administrator may file an application for fees for completed services, and upon approval by the Commission or a hearing officer, may be paid a reasonable fee for those services. Any objections thereto shall be filed within 21 days of service of the application on the parties.

(e) *Source of funds.* Unless otherwise ordered, fees and other expenses of administering the plan shall be paid first from the interest earned on the funds, and if the interest is not sufficient, then from the corpus.

(f) *Accountings.* During the first 10 days of each calendar quarter, or as otherwise directed by the Commission or the hearing officer, the administrator shall file an accounting of all monies earned or received and all monies spent in connection with the administration of the plan of disgorgement. A final accounting shall be submitted for approval of the Commission or hearing officer prior to discharge of the administrator and cancellation of the administrator's bond, if any.

(g) *Amendment.* A plan may be amended upon motion by any party or by the plan administrator or upon the Commission's or the hearing officer's own motion.

§201.1106 Right to challenge.

Other than in connection with the opportunity to submit comments as provided in §201.1103, no person shall be granted leave to intervene or to participate or otherwise to appear in any agency proceeding or otherwise to challenge an order of disgorgement or creation of a Fair Fund; or an order approving, approving with modifications, or disapproving a plan of disgorgement or a Fair Fund plan; or any determination relating to a plan based solely upon that person's eligibility or potential eligibility to participate in a fund or based upon any private right of action such person may have against any person who is also a respondent in the proceeding.

务向其支付任何费用。如果不属于证券交易委员会雇员,管理人可以就已完成的服务提交费用申请,经证券交易委员会或听证官批准,可以就服务获得合理费用支付。任何反对意见均应于向当事人送达费用申请后21日内提交。

(e)资金来源。除非另有命令,管理人费用和计划管理的其他支出首先应从资金利息中支付,如利息不足,再从本金中支付。

(f)会计。在每个季度的最初10日内或证券交易委员会或听证官指定的其他期间内,计划管理人应就赚取或收到的所有款项以及与没收计划执行相关的所有支出款项提交一份会计说明。最终的会计说明应在计划管理人免职或其保证金(如有)被撤销之前呈报证券交易委员会或听证官批准。

(g)修正。证券交易委员会或听证官可经任何一方当事人或计划管理人的动议,或经其主动决定对计划进行修正。

第201.1106节　异议权

除了按第201.1103节的规定拥有提交意见的机会外,任何人均不得仅仅基于其有参与基金的资格或潜在资格,或基于其对程序任何其他相对方拥有的任何私人诉讼权利而获准干涉、参与或以其他方式出席证券交易委员会的任何程序,或以其他方式对没收令、创立公平基金的命令、与计划相关的任何决定提出异议。

PART 202—INFORMAL AND OTHER PROCEDURES

Authority: 15 U.S.C. 77s, 77t, 78d–1, 78u, 78w, 78ll(d), 79r, 79t, 77sss, 77uuu, 80a–37, 80a–41, 80b–9, 80b–11, and 7201 *et seq*., unless otherwise noted.

Section 202.5 is also issued under sec. 20, 48 Stat. 86, sec. 21, 48 Stat. 899, sec. 18, 49 Stat. 831, sec. 321, 53 Stat. 1174, sec. 1, 76 Stat. 394, 15 U.S.C. 77t, 77uuu, 78d–1, 78u, 80a–4l, and 80b–9.

Section 202.9 is also issued under sec. 223, 110 Stat. 859 (Mar. 29, 1996).

Source: 25 FR 6736, July 15, 1960, unless otherwise noted.

§202.1 General.

(a) The statutes administered by the Commission provide generally (1) for the filing with it of certain statements, such as registration statements, periodic and ownership reports, and proxy solicitation material, and for the filing of certain plans of reorganization, applications and declarations seeking Commission approvals; (2) for Commission determination through formal procedures of matters initiated by private parties or by the Commission; (3) for the investigation and examination of persons and records where necessary to carry out the purposes of the statutes and for enforcement of statutory provisions; and (4) for the adoption of rules and regulations where necessary to effectuate the purposes of the statutes.

(b) In addition to the Commission's rules of practice set forth in part 201 of this chapter, the Commission has promulgated rules and regulations pursuant to the several statutes it administers (parts 230, 240, 250, 260, 270 and 275 of this chapter). These parts contain substantive provisions and include as well numerous provisions detailing the procedure for meeting specific standards embodied in the statutes. The Commission's rules and regulations under each of the statutes are available in pamphlet form upon request to the Superintendent of Documents, U.S. Government Printing Office, Washington, D.C. 20402.

(c) The statutes and the published rules, regulations and forms thereunder prescribe the course and method of formal procedures to be followed in Commission proceedings.

第202部分——非正式程序和其他程序

法律依据：《美国法典》第十五编第77s节、第77t节、第78d-1节、第78u节、第78w节、第78ll(d)节、第79r节、第79t节、第77sss节、第77uuu节、第80a-37节、第80a-41节、第80b-9节、第80b-11节和第7201节及其后条文，除非另有说明。

第202.5节同时见：《美国制定法汇编》第48卷第86页第20条、《美国制定法汇编》第48卷第899页第21条、《美国制定法汇编》第49卷第831页第18条、《美国制定法汇编》第53卷第1174页第321条、《美国制定法汇编》第76卷第394页第1条、《美国法典》第十五编第77t节、第77uuu节、第78d-1节、第78u节、第80a-4l节和第80b-9节。

第202.9节同时见：《美国制定法汇编》第110卷第859页第223条(1996年3月29日)。

行政规则来源：《联邦公报》第25卷第6736页，1960年7月15日，除非另有说明。

第202.1节　一般规定

(a)总体而言，证券交易委员会负责实施的制定法涉及以下方面的内容：(1)向证券交易委员会提交特定声明，如注册说明书、定期报告、所有权报告及代理权征集材料，以及提交需获得证券交易委员会批准的特定重组方案、申请和声明；(2)证券交易委员会通过正式程序对私人当事方提出或证券交易委员会主动提出的事宜作出决定；(3)为实现制定法的目的执行法律条款，调查和检查必要的主体和记录；以及(4)为实现制定法的目的制定必要的规则与规章。

(b)除本章第201部分规定的《证券交易委员会工作规则》外，证券交易委员会还依照其负责实施的制定法颁发了若干规则与规章(本章第230部分、第240部分、第250部分、第260部分、第270部分和第275部分)。这些章节中不仅有实体规定，同时还包含大量程序性规定，对执行制定法规定的具体标准的程序作出了详细说明。证券交易委员会依据各项制定法通过的规则与规章均印刷成册，可向位于华盛顿哥伦比亚特区(邮编：D.C.20402)的美国政府印刷局文献管理办公室索取。

(c)制定法和根据制定法颁布的规则、规章和表格对证券交易委员会正式程序中应遵循的步骤和方法作出了规定。在可行的情况下，还可通过某些非正式程序对此作

These are supplemented where feasible by certain informal procedures designed to aid the public and facilitate the execution of the Commission's functions. There follows a brief description of procedures generally followed by the Commission which have not been formalized in rules.

(d) The informal procedures of the Commission are largely concerned with the rendering of advice and assistance by the Commission's staff to members of the public dealing with the Commission. While opinions expressed by members of the staff do not constitute an official expression of the Commission's views, they represent the views of persons who are continuously working with the provisions of the statute involved. And any statement by the director, associate director, assistant director, chief accountant, chief counsel, or chief financial analyst of a division can be relied upon as representing the views of that division. In certain instances an informal statement of the views of the Commission may be obtained. The staff, upon request or on its own motion, will generally present questions to the Commission which involve matters of substantial importance and where the issues are novel or highly complex, although the granting of a request for an informal statement by the Commission is entirely within its discretion.

§202.2 Pre-filing assistance and interpretative advice.

The staff of the Commission renders interpretative and advisory assistance to members of the general public, prospective registrants, applicants and declarants. For example, persons having a question regarding the availability of an exemption may secure informal administrative interpretations of the applicable statute or rule as they relate to the particular facts and circumstances presented. Similarly, persons contemplating filings with the Commission may receive advice of a general nature as to the preparation thereof, including information as to the forms to be used and the scope of the items contained in the forms. Inquiries may be directed to an appropriate officer of the Commission's staff. In addition, informal discussions with members of the staff may be arranged whenever feasible, at the Commission's central office or, except in connection with matters under the Public Utility Holding Company Act of 1935 and certain matters under the Investment Company Act of 1940, at one of its regional offices.

[25 FR 6736, July 15, 1960, as amended at 59 FR 5945, Feb. 9, 1994; 73 FR 32227, June 5, 2008]

§202.3 Processing of filings.

(a) Registration statements, proxy statements, letters of notification, periodic reports, applications for qualification of indentures, and similar documents filed with the Commission under the Securities Act of 1933 and the Trust Indenture Act of 1939, and certain filings under the Securities Exchange Act of 1934 and the Public Utility Holding Company Act of 1935 are routed to the Division of Corporation Finance, which passes

出补充,非正式程序的目的在于为公众提供帮助并促进证券交易委员会顺利实施职能。下文将对证券交易委员会通常遵循的,但并未在规则中作出正式规定的程序作出扼要的说明。

(d)证券交易委员会的非正式程序主要涉及证券交易委员会工作人员对公众提供的建议和协助。证券交易委员会工作人员的意见并不构成证券交易委员会的官方意见,只代表长期从事与具体制定法相关工作的工作人员的个人看法。某一部门的主任、副主任、助理主任、首席会计师、首席律师或首席财务分析师作出的任何声明则可被信赖为代表了该部门的意见。在特定情况下,相关主体可以获得关于证券交易委员会意见的非正式声明。在一般情况下,对于涉及特别重要事项的问题或全新、高度复杂的问题,证券交易委员会的工作人员将应公众要求或主动提交证券交易委员会,但是否核准就某一问题作出非正式声明完全由证券交易委员会自行决定。

第202.2节　提交文件前的协助和解释性建议

证券交易委员会的工作人员向一般公众、潜在注册人、申请人和申报人提供解释性和建议性协助。例如,如相关主体对于是否可以获得豁免存在疑问,证券交易委员会工作人员可根据该等人员说明的具体事实和情况提供关于适用制定法或规则的非正式行政解释。同样,有意向证券交易委员会提交文件的主体可获得关于文件准备工作的一般性建议,如应采用的表格、表格内容的范围等。咨询问题可转交给证券交易委员会工作人员的相关上级管理人员。此外,在可行的情况下,还可在证券交易委员会的总部办公室,或某一地区办公室(与《1935年公用事业控股公司法》规定的事宜和《1940年投资公司法》规定的部分事宜相关的情况除外),安排与证券交易委员会工作人员举行非正式会谈。

[《联邦公报》第25卷第6736页,1960年7月15日,修正索引:《联邦公报》第59卷第5945页,1994年2月9日;《联邦公报》第73卷第32227页,2008年6月5日。]

第202.3节　提交文件的处理

(a)根据《1933年证券法》和《1939年信托契约法》向证券交易委员会提交的注册说明书、征集投票权报告、通知函、定期报告、信托契约资格申请和类似文件,以及根据《1934年证券交易法》和《1935年公用事业控股公司法》提交的部分文件均交由公司融资部处理,由公司融资部对披露的充分性进行初步审查并对应采取的初步行动提出建议。若初步判断提交文件的披露不充分,如遗漏了重大性信息或违反公认会计原则

initially on the adequacy of disclosure and recommends the initial action to be taken. If the filing appears to afford inadequate disclosure, as for example through omission of material information or through violation of accepted accounting principles and practices, the usual practice is to bring the deficiency to the attention of the person who filed the document by letter from the Assistant Director assigned supervision over the particular filing, and to afford a reasonable opportunity to discuss the matter and make the necessary corrections. This informal procedure is not generally employed when the deficiencies appear to stem from careless disregard of the statutes and rules or a deliberate attempt to conceal or mislead or where the Commission deems formal proceedings necessary in the public interest. If an electronic filing is not prepared in accordance with the requirements of the current EDGAR Filer Manual, the filing may be suspended and the filer so notified. Reasonable opportunity will be afforded the filer to make the necessary corrections or resubmit the filing as needed. Where it appears that the filing affords adequate disclosure, acceleration of its effectiveness when appropriate normally will be granted. A similar procedure is followed with respect to filings under the Investment Company Act of 1940 and certain filings relating to investment companies under the Securities Act of 1933, the Securities Exchange Act of 1934, and the Trust Indenture Act of 1939, which are routed to the Division of Investment Management, and filings under the Public Utility Holding Company Act of 1935 which are also routed to the Division of Investment Management. A similar procedure is also followed in the Commission's Regional Offices with respect to registration statements on Forms SB-1 and SB-2 (17 CFR 239.9 and 239.10)and related filings under the Trust Indenture Act of 1939.

(b)(1) Applications for registration as brokers, dealers, investment advisers,municipal securities dealers and transfer agents are submitted to the Office of Filings and Information Services where they are examined to determine whether all necessary information has been supplied and whether all required financial statements and other documents have been furnished in proper form. Defective applications may be returned with a request for correction or held until corrected before being accepted as a filing. The files of the Commission and other sources of information are considered to determine whether any person connected with the applicant appears to have engaged in activities which would warrant commencement of proceedings on the question of denial of registration. The staff confers with applicants and makes suggestions in appropriate cases for amendments and supplemental information. Where it appears appropriate in the public interest and where a basis therefore exists, denial proceedings may be instituted. Within 45 days of the date of the filing of a broker-dealer, investment adviser or municipal securities dealer application (or within such longer period as to which the applicant consents), the Commission shall by order grant registration or institute proceedings to determine whether

和做法,通常的做法是由被指派负责监督具体文件提交工作的助理主任向文件提交人发出信函,告知其存在的缺陷,并为之提供合理的机会就相关事宜进行讨论和作出必要的改正。在一般情况下,若存在的缺陷系因随意漠视制定法和规则或故意试图隐瞒相关信息或误导证券交易委员会而造成的,或若证券交易委员会认为出于公共利益考虑有必要采用正式程序,则不适用上述非正式程序。若以电子方式提交的文件不符合现行《EDGAR提交人手册》中规定的要求,可中止文件提交并向提交人发出通知。提交人应获得作出必要改正或在必要时重新提交文件的机会。若初步判断提交的文件已作出充分披露,一般会在适当的情况下核准该等文件提前生效。根据《1940年投资公司法》提交的文件,根据《1933年证券法》、《1934年证券交易法》和《1939年信托契约法》提交并交由投资管理部处理的涉及投资公司的部份文件,以及根据《1935年公用事业控股公司法》提交并同样交由投资管理部处理的文件均遵循类似程序。对于采用《SB-1表格》和《SB-2表格》(《联邦规章汇编》第十七编第239.9节和第239.10节)提交的注册说明书和根据《1939年信托契约法》提交的相关文件,证券交易委员会地区办公室也适用类似程序。

(b)(1)经纪商、自营商、投资顾问、市政证券自营商和过户代理人的注册申请应呈报给文件提交和信息服务办公室,由文件提交和信息服务办公室审查确定申请人是否已提供了所有必要信息以及是否已按适当格式提供了所有规定的财务报表和其他文件。存在缺陷的申请可予以退回并要求申请人作出补正;或者不予退回,但在收到补正后才视为受理。在判断与申请人相关的任何主体是否从事了相关行为,从而有必要启动驳回注册的程序之时,应考虑证券交易委员会的文件和其他信息来源。证券交易委员会的工作人员应与申请人进行讨论,并在适当的情况下就文件修正和补充提供建议。在从表面判断符合公共利益和拥有相关依据的情况下,可启动驳回程序。在经纪自营商、投资顾问或市政证券自营商提交申请后45日内(或在申请人同意的更长的期间内),证券交易委员会应发布命令核准注册或者启动程序以判定是否应驳回注册。过户代理人的注册申请在证券交易委员会收到申请后30日内(或证券交易委员会可能指定的更短的期间内)生效。文件提交和信息服务办公室还负责对根据《1934年证券交易法》、《1935年公用事业控股公司法》和《1940年投资公司法》提交的证券受益所有权说明书以及该等所有权的变更进行处理和实质检查,同时负责核查根据本章第230.144节提交的报告。

registration should be denied. An application for registration as a transfer agent shall become effective within 30 days after receipt of the application (or within such shorter period as the Commission may determine). The Office of Filings and Information Services is also responsible for the processing and substantive examination of statements of beneficial ownership of securities and changes in such ownership filed under the Securities Exchange Act of 1934, the Public Utility Holding Company Act of 1935, and the Investment Company Act of 1940, and for the examination of reports filed pursuant to §230.144 of this chapter.

(2) Applications for registration as national securities exchanges, or exemption from registration as exchanges by reason of such exchanges' limited volume of transactions filed with the Commission are routed to the Division of Market Regulation, which examines these applications to determine whether all necessary information has been supplied and whether all required financial statements and other documents have been furnished in proper form. Defective applications may be returned with a request for correction or held until corrected before being accepted as a filing. The files of the Commission and other sources of information are considered to determine whether any person connected with the applicant appears to have engaged in activities which would warrant commencement of proceedings on the question of denial of registration. The staff confers with applicants and makes suggestions in appropriate cases for amendments and supplemental information. Where it appears appropriate in the public interest and where a basis therefore exists, denial proceedings may be instituted. Within 90 days of the date of publication of a notice of the filing of an application for registration as a national securities exchange, or exemption from registration by reason of such exchanges' limited volume of transactions (or within such longer period as to which the applicant consents), the Commission shall by order grant registration, or institute proceedings to determine whether registration should be denied as provided in §240.19 (a) (1) of this chapter.

(3) Notice forms for registration as national securities exchanges pursuant to Section 6(g)(1) of the Securities Exchange Act of 1934 (15 U.S.C. 78f(g)(1)) filed with the Commission are routed to the Division of Market Regulation, which examines these notices to determine whether all necessary information has been supplied and whether all other required documents have been furnished in proper form. Defective notices may be returned with a request for correction or held until corrected before being accepted as a filing.

[41 FR 44699, Oct. 12, 1976, as amended at 44 FR 21567, Apr. 10, 1979; 49 FR 12686, Mar. 30, 1984; 57 FR 18216, Apr. 29, 1992; 58 FR 15004, Mar. 18, 1993; 59 FR 5945, Feb. 9, 1994; 63 FR 70916, Dec. 22, 1998; 64 FR 19451, April 21, 1999; 66 FR 43741, Aug. 20, 2001]

(2)向证券交易委员会提交的注册全国性证券交易所的申请,或基于交易所成交量有限而提出的注册豁免申请将交由市场监管部处理,由市场监管部审查确定申请人是否已经提供了所有必要信息或是否已按适当格式提供了所有规定的财务报表和其他文件。存在缺陷的申请可予以退回并要求申请人作出补正;或者不予退回,但在收到补正后才视为受理。在判断与申请人相关的任何主体是否从事了相关行为,从而有必要启动驳回注册的程序之时,应考虑证券交易委员会的文件和其他信息来源。证券交易委员会的工作人员应与申请人进行讨论,并在适当的情况下就文件修正和补充提供建议。在从表面判断符合公共利益和拥有相关依据的情况下,可启动驳回程序。在就全国性证券交易所注册申请的提交,或基于交易所成交量有限而提出的注册豁免申请之提交发布通知后90日内,证券交易委员会应发布命令核准注册,或者按照本章第240.19(a)(1)节的规定启动程序以判定是否应驳回注册。

(3)根据《1934年证券交易法》第6(g)(1)条[《美国法典》第十五编第78f(g)(1)节]向证券交易委员会提交的全国性证券交易所的注册通知表将交由市场监管部处理,由市场监管部核查确定申请人是否已经提供了所有必要信息或是否已按适当格式提供了所有规定的财务报表和其他文件。存在缺陷的申请可予以退回并要求申请人作出补正;或者不予退回,但在收到补正后才视为受理。

[《联邦公报》第41卷第44699页,1976年10月12日,修正索引:《联邦公报》第44卷第21567页,1979年4月10日;《联邦公报》第49卷第12686页,1984年3月30日;《联邦公报》第57卷第18216页,1992年4月29日,《联邦公报》 第58卷第15004页,1993年3月18日;《联邦公报》第59卷第5945页,1994年2月9日;《联邦公报》第63卷第70916页,1998年12月22日;

§202.3a Instructions for filing fees.

(a) *General instructions for remittance of filing fees.* Payment of filing fees specified by the following sections shall be made according to the directions listed in this section: §230.111 of this chapter, §240.0–9 of this chapter, and §270.0–8 of this chapter. All such fees are to be paid through the U.S. Treasury designated lockbox depository and may be paid by wire transfer, certified check, bank cashier's check, United States postal money order, or bank money order pursuant to the specific instructions set forth in paragraph (b) of this section. Personal checks will not be accepted for payment of fees. To ensure proper posting, all filers must include their Commission–assigned Central Index Key (CIK) number (also known as the Commission–assigned registrant or payor account number) on fee payments. If a third party submits a fee payment, the fee payment must specify the account number to which the fee is to be applied.

(b) *Instructions for payment of filing fees.* Except as provided in paragraph (c) of this section, these instructions provide direction for remitting fees specified in paragraph (a) of this section. You may contact the Fee Account Services Branch in the Office of Financial Management at (202)551–8989 for additional information if you have questions.

(1) *Instructions for payment of fees by wire transfer (FEDWIRE).* U.S. Bank, N.A. in St. Louis, Missouri is the U.S. Treasury designated lockbox depository and financial agent for Commission filing fee payments. The hours of operation at U.S. Bank are 8:30 a.m. to 6 p.m. Eastern time for wire transfers. Any bank or wire transfer service may initiate wire transfers of filing fee payments through the FEDWIRE system to U.S. Bank. A filing entity does not need to establish an account at U.S. Bank in order to remit filing fee payments.

(i) To ensure proper credit and prompt filing acceptance, in all wire transfers of filing fees to the Commission, you must include:

(A) The Commission's account number at U.S. Bank (152307768324); and

(B) The payor's CIK number.

(ii) You may refer to the examples found on the Commission's Web site at *http://www.sec.gov* for the proper format.

(2) *Instructions for payment of fees by check or money order.* To remit a filing fee payment by check (certified or bank cashier's check) or money order (United States postal or bank money order), you must make it payable to the Securities and Exchange Commission, omitting the name or title of any official of the Commission. On the front of the check or money order, you must include the Commission's account number (152307768324) and CIK number of the account to which the fee is to be applied. U.S.

《联邦公报》第64卷第19451页,1999年4月21日;《联邦公报》第66卷第43741页,2001年8月20日。]

第202.3a节　文件提交费说明

(a)关于文件提交费汇付的一般说明。本章第230.111节、第240.0-9节和第270.0-8节具体规定的文件提交费应根据本节的指示支付。所有上述费用均应通过美国财政部指定的锁箱存款机构支付,也可以按照本节第(b)款的具体说明,通过电汇、保付支票、银行本票、美国邮政汇票或银行汇票支付。证券交易委员会不接受通过私人支票支付文件提交费。为了确保正确记账,所有注册人必须在付款时使用证券交易委员会向其分配的中央索引键值(CIK)号码(即证券交易委员会分配的注册人或付款人账号)。第三方付费的,必须注明该费用对应的账号。

(b)文件提交费支付说明。除本节第(c)款规定的情形外,本条第(a)款具体规定的文件提交费之汇付应按本说明的指示进行。如有任何问题,请联系财务管理办公室的费用会计服务部门获取更多信息,电话号码:(202)551-8989。

(1)关于通过电汇(联储电汇网络系统)支付文件提交费的说明。对于证券交易委员会的文件提交费而言,位于密苏里州圣路易斯市的全美银行是美国财政部指定的锁箱存款机构和财务代理人。全美银行电汇业务的营业时间为美国东部时间上午8时30分至下午6时。任何银行或电汇服务机构均可通过联储电汇网络系统(FEDWIRE)向全美银行汇付文件提交费。提交文件的实体不必为汇付文件提交费在全美银行开立账户。

(i)为了确保正确入账和及时受理文件提交,您应在向证券交易委员会支付文件提交费的电汇单上填写:

(A)证券交易委员会在全美银行的账号(152307768324);及

(B)付款人的CIK号码。

(ii)您可以参考证券交易委员会网站(http://www.sec.gov)上的正确格式样本。

(2)使用支票或汇票付款说明。使用支票(保付支票或银行本票)或汇票(美国邮政汇票或银行汇票)支付文件提交费的,应在收款人一栏填写美国证券交易委员会,而不填写任何证券交易委员会官员的姓名或职务。在支票或汇票正面,必须填写证券交易委员会的账号(152307768324)和文件提交费对应的CIK账户号码。全美银行不接受个人当面缴付的文件提交费。您必须按如下地址将支票或汇票寄送至全美银行:

Bank does not accept walk-in deliveries by individuals. You must mail checks or money orders to the following U.S. Bank addresses:

(i) Remittances through the U.S. Postal Service must be sent to the following address: Securities and Exchange Commission, P.O. Box 979081, St. Louis, MO 63197-9000.

(ii) The following address can be used for remittances through other common carriers: U.S. Bank, Government Lockbox 979081, 1005 Convention Plaza, SL-MO-C2-GL, St. Louis, MO 63101.

Note to paragraph (b). Wire transfers are not instantaneous. The time required to process a wire transfer through the FEDWIRE system, from origination to receipt by U.S. Bank, varies substantially. Specified filings, such as registration statements pursuant to section 6(b) of the Securities Act of 1933 that provide for the registration of securities and mandate the receipt of the appropriate fee payment upon filing, and transactional filings pursuant to the Securities Exchange Act of 1934, such as many proxy statements involving extraordinary business transactions, will not be accepted if sufficient funds have not been received by the Commission at the time of filing. You should obtain from your bank or wire transfer service the reference number of the wire transfer. Having this number can greatly facilitate tracing the funds if any problems occur. If a wire transfer of filing fees does not contain the required information in the proper format, the Commission may not be able to identify the payor and the acceptance of filings may be delayed. To ensure proper credit, you must provide all required information to the sending bank or wire transfer service. Commission data must be inserted in the proper fields. The most critical data are the Commission's account number at U.S. Bank and the Commission-assigned account number identified as the CIK number.

(c) *Special instructions for §§230.462(b) and 230.110(d) of this chapter.* Notwithstanding paragraphs (a) and (b) of this section, for registration statements filed pursuant to §§230.462(b) and §230.110(d) of this chapter, payment of filing fees for the purposes of this section may be made by:

(1) The registrant or its agent instructing its bank or a wire transfer service to transmit to the Commission the applicable filing fee by a wire transfer of such amount from the issuer's account or its agent's account to the U.S. Treasury designated lockbox depository as soon as practicable, but no later than the close of the next business day following the filing of the registration statement; and

(2) The registrant submitting with the registration statement at the time of filing a certification that:

(i) The registrant or its agent has so instructed its bank or a wire transfer service;

(ii) The registrant or its agent will not revoke such instructions; and

(i)通过美国邮政汇款的,必须寄往如下地址:证券交易委员会,密苏里州圣路易斯市979081号邮政信箱,邮政编码:MO 63197-9000。

(ii)通过其他普通快递公司汇款的,可以寄往如下地址:全美银行,979081号政府锁箱,密苏里州圣路易斯市1005号会展中心SL-MO-C2-GL,邮政编码:MO 63101。

关于第(b)款的注释:电汇并非实时到帐。联储电汇网络系统处理电汇(从电汇发出到实际到账)所需时间差别很大。对于特定提交文件,如按照《1933年证券法》第6(b)条(该条对证券注册作出了规定,并要求在提交文件的同时必须收到适当的费用)提交的注册说明书,以及按照《1934年证券交易法》提交的交易性文件(如多数涉及特殊业务交易的征集投票权报告),证券交易委员会如果在文件提交时未收到足额资金,将不予受理。您应该要求您的银行或电汇服务机构提供电汇编号。电汇出现任何问题之时,电汇编号可以为您追踪资金提供关键线索。如果文件提交费的电汇单上未以正确格式填写所需信息,证券交易委员会可能无法识别付款人的身份,且文件的受理可能会因此延误。为了确保正确入账,您必须向汇款银行或电汇服务机构提供所需的全部信息。证券交易委员会数据必须填入正确的区域。最关键的数据是证券交易委员会在全美银行的账号和证券交易委员会分配的CIK账户识别号码。

(c)关于本章第230.462(b)节和第230.110(d)节的特殊说明。无论本节第(a)款和第(b)款如何规定,就本节而言,根据本章第230.462(b)节和第230.110(d)节提交的注册说明书、文件提交费应按如下规定支付:

(1) 注册人或其代理人应指示其银行或电汇服务机构向证券交易委员会支付相关文件提交费,从发行人的账户或其代理人的账户中尽快将文件提交费电汇至美国财政部指定的锁箱存款机构,时间不得晚于提交注册说明书的下一个营业日停止营业的时间;且

(2)注册人在呈报注册说明书的同时应提交一份证明,证明:

(i)注册人或其代理人已经指示其银行或电汇服务机构汇款;

(ii)注册人或其代理人不会撤销汇款指令;且

(iii) The registrant or its agent has sufficient funds in such account to cover the amount of such filing fee.

Note to paragraph (c). Such instructions may be sent on the date of filing the registration statement after the close of business of such bank or wire transfer service, provided that the registrant undertakes in the certification sent to the Commission with the registration statement that it will confirm receipt of such instructions by the bank or wire transfer service during regular business hours on the following business day.

(d) *Filing fee accounts.* A filing fee account is maintained for each filer who submits a filing requiring a fee on the Commission's EDGAR system or who submits funds to the U.S. Treasury designated depository in anticipation of paying a filing fee. Account statements are regularly prepared and provided to account holders. Account holders must maintain a current account address with the Commission to ensure timely access to these statements.

Note to paragraph (d). The deposit of money into a filing fee account does not constitute payment of a filing fee. Payment of the filing fee occurs at the time the filing is made, commensurate with the drawing down of the balance of the fee account.

(e) *Return of funds from inactive accounts.* Funds held in any filing fee account in which there has not been a deposit, withdrawal or other adjustment for more than 180 calendar days will be returned to the account holder, and account statements will not be sent again until a deposit, withdrawal or other adjustment is made with respect to the account. Filers must maintain a current account address to assure the timely return of funds. It may not be possible to return funds from inactive accounts if the Commission is unable to identify a current account address of an account holder after making reasonable efforts to do so.

Note to paragraph (e). A company must update its account and other addresses using the EDGAR Web site. This method ensures data integrity and the timeliest update. Simply changing an address in the text of the cover page of a filing made on the EDGAR system will not be sufficient to update the Commission's account address records.

[73 FR 6013, Feb. 1, 2008]

§202.4 Facilitating administrative hearings.

(a) Applications, declarations, and other requests involving formal Commission action after opportunity for hearing are scrutinized by the appropriate division for conformance with applicable statutory standards and Commission rules and generally the filing party is advised of deficiencies. Prior to passing upon applications and declarations the Commission receives the views of all interested persons at public hearings whenever appropriate; hence, any applicant or declarant seeking Commission approval of proposed transactions by a particular time should file his application or declaration in time to allow

(iii)注册人或其代理人上述账户内的资金足以支付文件提交费。

关于第(c)款的注释:汇款指令可以于提交注册说明书当日在银行或电汇服务机构结束营业后发出,条件是注册人在与注册说明书同时递交给证券交易委员会的证明中确认其将在下一个营业日的正常营业时间确认银行或电汇服务机构已经收到了汇款指令。

(d)文件提交费账户。对于每名通过证券交易委员会的EDGAR系统提交资料时需要付费的注册人,或为支付文件提交费之目的向美国财政部指定的存款机构注入资金的文件提交人,证券交易委员会均会维持一个文件提交费账户,并定期为账户持有人制作并提供对账单。账户持有人必须在证券交易委员会维持一个经常账户地址,以确保能及时收到对账单。

关于第(d)款的注释:向文件提交费账户中存款并不构成文件提交费的支付。文件提交费的支付应于文件提交之时进行,并从文件提交费账户余额中扣除相应金额。

(e)静止账户资金退还。任何文件提交费账户,如超过180个日历日未发生任何存款、提款或其他调整,账户中持有的资金应退还给账户持有人,且在该账户再次发生存款、提款或其他调整前不会再为该账户持有人寄送对账单。文件提交人必须维持一个经常账户地址,以确保能及时收到退还资金。如果证券交易委员会在尽合理努力后仍无法确定账户持有人的经常账户地址,静止账户中的资金可能无法退还给持有人。

关于第(e)款的注释:公司必须使用EDGAR网站更新其账户地址和其他地址。本方法可以确保数据的完整和及时更新。仅在通过EDGAR系统提交的文件的封面上更改地址的,证券交易委员会的账户地址记录并不会因此得到更新。

[《联邦公报》第73卷第6013页,2008年2月1日。]

第202.4节　为使行政听证顺利举行而开展的准备工作

(a)需要证券交易委员会在听证之后采取正式行动的申请、声明和其他请求,将由适当部门进行监督,以确保符合适用制定法标准和证券交易委员会的规则,并确保一般情况下文件提交方均将获得关于文件缺陷的通知。在核准申请和声明前,证券交易委员会应在公开听证(如恰当)上听取所有利害关系人的意见;因此,所有希望证券交易委员会在特定时间之前批准拟议事项的注册人或声明人均应及时提交申请或声明,以便该等意见获得陈述和考虑。

for the presentation and consideration of such views.

(b) After the staff has had an opportunity to study an application or declaration, interested persons may informally discuss the problems therein raised to the extent that time and the nature of the case permit (e.g., consideration is usually given to whether the proceeding is contested and if so to the nature of the contest). In such event, the staff will, to the extent feasible, advise as to the nature of the issues raised by the filing, the necessity for any amendments to the documents filed, the type of evidence it believes should be presented at the hearing and, in some instances, the nature, form, and contents of documents to be submitted as formal exhibits. The staff will, in addition, generally advise as to Commission policy in past cases which dealt with the same subject matter as the filing under consideration.

(c) During the course of the hearings, the staff is generally available for informal discussions to reconcile bona fide divergent views not only between itself and other persons interested in the proceedings, but among all interested persons; and, when circumstances permit, an attempt is made to narrow, if possible, the issues to be considered at the formal hearing.

(d) In some instances the Commission in the order accompanying its findings and opinion reserves jurisdiction over certain matters relating to the proceeding, such as payment of fees and expenses, accounting entries, terms and conditions relating to securities to be issued, and other matters. In such cases, upon receipt of satisfactory information and data the Commission considers whether further hearing is required before releasing jurisdiction.

§202.5 Enforcement activities.

(a) Where, from complaints received from members of the public, communications from Federal or State agencies, examination of filings made with the Commission, or otherwise, it appears that there may be violation of the acts administered by the Commission or the rules or regulations thereunder, a preliminary investigation is generally made. In such preliminary investigation no process is issued or testimony compelled. The Commission may, in its discretion, make such formal investigations and authorize the use of process as it deems necessary to determine whether any person has violated, is violating, or is about to violate any provision of the federal securities laws or the rules of a self–regulatory organization of which the person is a member or participant. Unless otherwise ordered by the Commission, the investigation or examination is non–public and the reports thereon are for staff and Commission use only.

(b) After investigation or otherwise the Commission may in its discretion take one or more of the following actions: Institution of administrative proceedings looking to the imposition of remedial sanctions, initiation of injunctive proceedings in the courts, and, in

(b)在证券交易委员会工作人员获得机会对申请或声明开展研究后,利害关系人可以在时间和案件性质许可的范围内就其中的问题展开非正式讨论(如通常会考虑程序是否存在争议,如存在争议,争议的性质如何)。在该种情况下,工作人员应在可行的范围内就如下问题提出建议:提交的文件所提出的问题之性质、对已提交文件作出任何修正的必要性、其认为应在听证中提交的证据类型;在某些情况下,还应就应作为正式证物呈交的文件之性质、格式和内容提出建议。此外,工作人员还应就在与当前审议文件标的相同的既往案例中,证券交易委员会所采用的政策提供一般性建议。

(c)在听证过程中,一般可有工作人员参与非正式讨论,以协调其本人与其他程序利害关系人之间的善意意见分歧,以及各利害关系人自身之间的意见分歧;情况允许时,还应尽可能努力缩小正式听证中审议事项的范围。

(d)在某些情况下,证券交易委员会在其公布认定结果和意见的同时还应发布命令,通过该等命令保留其在费用和开支支付、会计分录、与即将发行的证券相关的条款和条件以及其他事项上的管辖权。在该种情况下,证券交易委员会将在收到令其满意的信息和数据后,考虑是否需要在行使管辖权以前召开进一步听证。

第202.5节　执法活动

(a)证券交易委员会收到公众投诉、来自联邦或州政府机构的通信以及在检查向证券交易委员会提交的文件的过程中或通过其他方式,初步判断可能存在违反证券交易委员会负责实施的法律、规则和规章的情况的,通常会展开初步调查。在初步调查过程中,不会签发传票或强制要求作证。证券交易委员会可依其自由裁量权决定开展其认为必要的正式调查并允许使用其认为必要的传票以判定任何人是否已经、正在或即将违反联邦证券法的任何条款或自律组织的规章(如果该人是自律组织的会员或参与者)。除非证券交易委员会另有命令,否则调查或检查不应向公众公开,且调查报告或核查报告仅得供证券交易委员会及其工作人员使用。

(b)在开展调查或采取其他行动后,证券交易委员会可依其自由裁量权决定采取如下一个或多个行动:启动行政处理程序以实施救济性制裁、在法院启动禁令程序以及将故意违法违规行为提交司法部进行刑事追诉。在某些情况下,证券交易委员会还

the case of a willful violation, reference of the matter to the Department of Justice for criminal prosecution. The Commission may also, on some occasions, refer the matter to, or grant requests for access to its files made by, domestic and foreign governmental authorities or foreign securities authorities, self-regulatory organizations such as stock exchanges or the National Association of Securities Dealers, Inc., and other persons or entities.

(c) Persons who become involved in preliminary or formal investigations may, on their own initiative, submit a written statement to the Commission setting forth their interests and position in regard to the subject matter of the investigation. Upon request, the staff, in its discretion, may advise such persons of the general nature of the investigation, including the indicated violations as they pertain to them, and the amount of time that may be available for preparing and submitting a statement prior to the presentation of a staff recommendation to the Commission for the commencement of an administrative or injunction proceeding. Submissions by interested persons should be forwarded to the appropriate Division Director or Regional Director with a copy to the staff members conducting the investigation and should be clearly referenced to the specific investigation to which they relate. In the event a recommendation for the commencement of an enforcement proceeding is presented by the staff, any submissions by interested persons will be forwarded to the Commission in conjunction with the staff memorandum.

(d) In instances where the staff has concluded its investigation of a particular matter and has determined that it will not recommend the commencement of an enforcement proceeding against a person, the staff, in its discretion, may advise the party that its formal investigation has been terminated. Such advice if given must in no way be construed as indicating that the party has been exonerated or that no action may ultimately result from the staff's investigation of the particular matter.

(e) The Commission has adopted the policy that in any civil lawsuit brought by it or in any administrative proceeding of an accusatory nature pending before it, it is important to avoid creating, or permitting to be created, an impression that a decree is being entered or a sanction imposed, when the conduct alleged did not, in fact, occur. Accordingly, it hereby announces its policy not to permit a defendant or respondent to consent to a judgment or order that imposes a sanction while denying the allegations in the complaint or order for proceedings. In this regard, the Commission believes that a refusal to admit the allegations is equivalent to a denial, unless the defendant or respondent states that he neither admits nor denies the allegations.

(f) In the course of the Commission's investigations, civil lawsuits, and administrative proceedings, the staff, with appropriate authorization, may discuss with persons involved

可以将事项移交本国或外国政府机构或外国证券监管机构、自律组织(如证券交易所或全国证券交易商协会公司)以及其他个人或实体,或核准该等机构、个人或实体访问其文件的请求。

(c)初步调查或正式调查所涉之主体可以主动向证券交易委员会呈报一份书面说明,阐述其在调查事项中的利益和立场。上述主体提出请求之时,向证券交易委员会工作人员可依其自由裁量权决定就调查的一般性质向其提供建议,包括向其告知所指控的违法违规行为以及在证券交易委员会工作人员建议证券交易委员会启动行政处理程序或禁令程序之前,该等主体拥有的可以编制和呈报声明的时间。利害关系人提交的声明应转交相关的部门主任或地区主任,并抄送开展调查的证券交易委员会工作人员,并明确注明与之相关的具体调查。如果证券交易委员会工作人员建议启动执法程序,利害关系人的所有声明均应与工作人员备忘录共同转交证券交易委员会。

(d)证券交易委员会工作人员结束对某具体事项的调查,并决定不建议针对被调查人启动执法程序的,证券交易委员会工作人员可依其自由裁量权决定通知当事人正式调查已经结束。证券交易委员会工作人员发出上述通知的,不得解释为被调查人已经被认定无罪,或被解释为工作人员对该事项的调查最终不会导致造成对被调查人采取任何行动。

(e)证券交易委员会制定有如下政策:在其提起的任何民事诉讼中或由其主持的任何究责性质的行政处理程序中,非常重要的一点是,如被指控的行为事实上并未发生,应避免实际造成或放任造成已经签发判令或处以制裁的印象。因此,证券交易委员会特此宣布如下政策:不允许被告或相对人在同意对其处以制裁的判决或命令的同时,否认申诉书或程序命令中的指控。有鉴于此,证券交易委员会认为拒绝承认指控即等同于否认指控,除非被告或相对人明确说明其既不承认也不否认指控。

(f)在证券交易委员会开展调查、民事诉讼和行政处理程序的过程中,具有恰当授权的工作人员可以与相关主体讨论以同意、和解或其他方式处理该事项。但是,根据

the disposition of such matters by consent, by settlement, or in some other manner. It is the policy of the Commission, however, that the disposition of any such matter may not, expressly or impliedly, extend to any criminal charges that have been, or may be, brought against any such person or any recommendation with respect thereto. Accordingly, any person involved in an enforcement matter before the Commission who consents, or agrees to consent, to any judgment or order does so solely for the purpose of resolving the claims against him in that investigative, civil, or administrative matter and not for the purpose of resolving any criminal charges that have been, or might be, brought against him. This policy reflects the fact that neither the Commission nor its staff has the authority or responsibility for instituting, conducting, settling, or otherwise disposing of criminal proceedings. That authority and responsibility are vested in the Attorney General and representatives of the Department of Justice.

[25 FR 6736, July 15, 1960, as amended at 37 FR 23829, Nov. 9, 1972; 37 FR 25224, Nov. 29, 1972; 44 FR 50835, Aug. 30, 1979; 46 FR 47532, Sept. 29, 1981; 47 FR 26822, June 22, 1982; 54 FR 24332, June 7, 1989; 59 FR 5945, Feb. 9, 1994; 73 FR 32227, June 5, 2008]

§202.6 Adoption, revision, and rescission of rules and regulations of general application.

(a) The procedure followed by the Commission in connection with the adoption, revision, and rescission of rules of general application necessarily varies in accordance with the nature of the rule, the extent of public interest therein, and the necessity for speed in its adoption. Rules relating to Commission organization, procedure and management, for example, are generally adopted by the Commission without affording public discussion thereof. On the other hand, in the adoption of substantive rules materially affecting an industry or a segment of the public, such as accounting rules, every feasible effort is made in advance of adoption to receive the views of persons to be affected. In such cases, proposals for the adoption, revision, or rescission of rules are initiated either by the Commission or by members of the public, and to the extent practicable, the practices set forth in paragraph (b) of this section are observed.

(b) After preliminary consideration by the Commission a draft of the proposed rule is published in the Federal Registerand mailed to interested persons (e.g., other interested regulatory bodies, principal registrants or persons to be affected, stock exchanges, professional societies and leading authorities on the subject concerned and other persons requesting such draft) for comments. Unless accorded confidential treatment pursuant to statute or rule of the Commission, written comments filed with the Commission on or

证券交易委员会的政策,对任何此等事项的处理的效力不能明示或暗示地及于已经或可能对任何该等主体作出的任何刑事指控或指控建议。因此,证券交易委员会执法过程中所涉主体同意或约定同意任何判决或命令的,其效力仅适用于解决该调查、民事诉讼或行政处理程序中对其提起的权利主张,而不适用于已经或可能对其提起的任何刑事诉讼。本政策反映了证券交易委员会及其工作人员没有启动、开展、和解或以其他方式处理刑事诉讼的权限或责任。上述权限和责任由总检察长和司法部代表行使。

[《联邦公报》第25卷第6736页,1960年7月15日,修正索引:《联邦公报》第37卷第23829页,1972年11月9日;《联邦公报》第37卷第25224页,1972年11月29日;《联邦公报》第44卷第50835页,1979年8月30日;《联邦公报》第46卷第47532页,1981年9月29日;《联邦公报》第47卷第26822页,1982年6月22日;《联邦公报》第54卷第24332页,1989年6月7日;《联邦公报》第59卷第5945页,1994年2月9日;《联邦公报》第73卷第32227页,2008年6月5日。]

第202.6节 普适性规则与规章的通过、修订和撤销

(a)证券交易委员会在通过、修订和撤销普适性规则与规章时适用的程序不可避免地存在差异,其中考虑的因素包括规则的性质、所涉公共利益的范围以及快速通过该等规则与规章的必要性。例如,与证券交易委员会的组织结构、程序与管理相关的规则,一般由证券交易委员会通过,不必公开讨论。另一方面,在通过会计规则等会对行业或部分公众产生实质影响的重大规则时,应在通过前尽一切可行努力征求可能受该规则影响的主体的意见。在该种情况下,通过、修订或撤销规则的提案可由证券交易委员会或公众提出,并在可行范围内,遵守本节第(b)款规定的做法。

(b)证券交易委员会进行初步审议后,应将规则草案在《联邦公报》上发布并寄送给利害关系人(如其他利害关系监管机构、主注册人、受影响人、证券交易所、专业协会和该事项相关领导机构以及请求获得该草案的其他主体)征求意见。除非已根据制定法或证券交易委员会规则予以保密处理,否则在意见征询截止日期前向证券交易委员会提交的书面意见将纳入关于规则草案的公共记录。证券交易委员会可依其自由裁量权决定接受在截止日期后收到的书面意见并将之纳入公共记录。

before the closing date for comments become a part of the public record upon the proposed rule. The Commission, in its discretion, may accept and include in the public record written comments received by the Commission after the closing date.

(c) Following analysis of comments received, the rule may be adopted in the form published or in a revised form in the light of such comments. In some cases, a revised draft is prepared and published and, where appropriate, an oral hearing may be held before final action upon the proposal. Any interested person may appear at the hearing and/or may submit written comment for consideration in accordance with the Commission's notice of the rulemaking procedure to be followed. The rule in the form in which it is adopted by the Commission is publicly released and is published in the Federal Register.

(Sec. 19(a), 48 Stat. 908; sec. 23(a), 48 Stat. 901; sec. 20(a), 49 Stat. 833; sec. 319(a), 53 Stat. 1173; sec. 38(a), 54 Stat. 841; sec. 211(a), 54 Stat. 855; 15 U.S.C. 77s(a), 78w(a), 78t(a), 77sss(a), 80a–37(a), 80b–11(a))

[25 FR 6736, July 15, 1960, as amended at 44 FR 35208, June 19, 1979]

§202.7 Submittals.

(a) All required statements, reports, applications, etc. must be filed with the principal office of the Commission unless otherwise specified in the Commission's rules, schedules and forms. Reports by exchange members, brokers and dealers required by § 240.17a–5 of this chapter under the Securities Exchange Act of 1934 must be filed with the appropriate regional office as provided in §230.255(a) of this chapter under the Securities Act of 1933, and with the principal office of the Commission and the appropriate regional office as provided under §240.17a–5(a) *et seq.* of this chapter under the Securities Exchange Act of 1934.

(b) *Electronic filings.* All documents required to be filed in electronic format with the Commission pursuant to the federal securities laws or the rules and regulations thereunder shall be filed at the principal office in Washington, D.C. via EDGAR by delivery to the Commission of a magnetic tape or diskette, or by direct transmission.

[41 FR 44699, Oct. 12, 1976, as amended at 58 FR 14659, Mar. 18, 1993; 59 FR 5945, Feb. 9, 1994; 73 FR 32227, June 5, 2008]

§202.8 Small entity compliance guides.

The following small entity compliance guides are available to the public from the Commission's Publications Room and regional offices:

(a) *Q & A: Small Business and the SEC.*

(c)证券交易委员会在对收到的意见进行分析后,可按之前公布的草案通过规章或基于意见对草案作出修订后再通过规章。在某些情况下,可以编制并公布修订后的草案,并在最终通过草案前举行口头听证(如恰当)。任何利害关系人均可根据证券交易委员会关于规则制定程序的通知出席听证和/或呈交书面意见供证券交易委员会审议。证券交易委员会最终通过的规则会公开发布并在《联邦公报》上公布。

[《美国制定法汇编》第48卷第908页第19(a)条;《美国制定法汇编》第48卷第901页第23(a)条;《美国制定法汇编》第49卷第833页第20(a)条;《美国制定法汇编》第53卷第1173页第319(a)条;《美国制定法汇编》第54卷第841页第38(a)条;《美国制定法汇编》第54卷第855页第211(a)条;《美国法典》第十五编第77s(a)节、第78w(a)节、第78t(a)节、第77sss(a)节、第80a-37(a)节、第80b-11(a)节。]

[《联邦公报》第25卷第6736页,1960年7月15日,修正索引:《联邦公报》第44卷第35208页,1979年6月19日。]

第202.7节　呈报文件

(a)除非证券交易委员会的规则、附表或表格中另有规定,所有按要求提交的说明书、报告、申请均须提交至证券交易委员会的主要办公场所。交易所会员、经纪商和自营商在《1934年证券交易法》——本章第240.17a-5节项下提交的报告,必须向《1933年证券法》[本章第230.255(a)节]规定的适当的地区办公室和《1934年证券交易法》[本章第240.17a-5(a)节及其后条文]规定的证券交易委员会的主要办公场所提交。

(b)电子文件提交。所有按照联邦证券法或依据联邦证券法颁发的规则和规章的要求以电子格式提交的文件,均应通过EDGAR系统向证券交易委员会递送磁带或磁盘或通过直接传输的方式提交至证券交易所位于华盛顿哥伦比亚特区的主要办公场所。

[《联邦公报》第41卷第44699页,1976年10月12日,修正索引:《联邦公报》第58卷第14659页,1993年3月18日;《联邦公报》第59卷第5945页,1994年2月9日;《联邦公报》第73卷第32227页,2008年6月5日。]

第202.8节　小型企业合规指引

证券交易委员会的出版室和地区办公室公开提供下述小型企业合规指引:

(a)常见问题:小型企业和证券交易委员会。

(b) *The Work of the SEC.* [1]

(c) *Broker-Dealer Registration Package.*

(d) *Investment Adviser Registration Package.*

(e) *Investment Company Registration Package.*

(f) *Examination Information for Broker-Dealers, Transfer Agents, Investment Advisers and Investment Companies.*

[62 FR 4105, Jan. 28, 1997]

§202.9 Small entity enforcement penalty reduction policy.

The Commission's policy with respect to whether to reduce or assess civil money penalties against a small entity is:

(a) The Commission will consider on a case-by-case basis whether to reduce or not assess civil money penalties against a small entity. In determining whether to reduce or not assess penalties against a specific small entity, the following considerations will apply:

(1) Except as provided in paragraph (a)(3) of this section, penalty reduction will not be available for any small entity if:

(i) The small entity was subject previously to an enforcement action;

(ii) Any of the small entity's violations involved willful or criminal conduct; or

(iii) The small entity did not make a good faith effort to comply with the law.

(2) In considering whether the Commission will reduce or refrain from assessing a civil money penalty, the Commission may consider:

(i) The egregiousness of the violations;

(ii) The isolated or repeated nature of the violations;

(iii) The violator's state of mind when committing the violations;

(iv) The violator's history (if any) of legal or regulatory violations;

(v) The extent to which the violator cooperated during the investigation;

(vi) Whether the violator has engaged in subsequent remedial efforts to mitigate the effects of the violation and to prevent future violations;

(vii) The degree to which a penalty will deter the violator or others from committing future violations; and

(viii) Any other relevant fact.

(3) The Commission also may consider whether to reduce or not assess a civil money penalty against a small entity, including a small entity otherwise excluded from this policy under paragraphs (a)(1)(i)-(iii) of this section, if the small entity can demonstrate to the Commission's satisfaction that it is financially unable to pay the penalty, immediately or over a reasonable period of time, in whole or in part.

---

1 These items are also available on the Securities and Exchange Commission Web site on the Internet, http://www.sec.gov.

(b)证券交易委员会的工作。[1]

(c)经纪自营商注册文件包。

(d)投资顾问注册文件包。

(e)投资公司注册文件包。

(f)经纪自营商、过户代理人、投资顾问和投资公司检查信息。

[《联邦公报》第62卷第4105页,1997年1月28日。]

第202.9节　减免执法过程中对小型企业的罚款的政策

证券交易委员会关于是否减免[2]小型企业民事罚款的政策如下:

(a)证券交易委员会应在一事一议的基础上,考虑是否减免小型企业的民事罚款。在判定是否减免小型企业的民事罚款时,应考虑如下事项:

(1)除本节第(a)(3)款规定的情形外,在下述情形下,不得减免罚款:

(i)小型企业曾被启动执法行动;

(ii)小型企业的任何违法违规行为出于蓄意或涉及刑事犯罪;或

(iii)小型企业未尽善意努力遵守法律。

(2)在考虑是否减免民事罚款时,证券交易委员会可以考虑如下因素:

(i)违法违规行为的严重程度;

(ii)违法违规行为的性质是一次性行为或重复性行为;

(iii)违法违规者在做出违法违规行为时的主观状态;

(iv)违法违规者过去违法或违规的历史记录(如有);

(v)违法违规者在调查期间的合作程度;

(vi)违法违规者是否努力进行了后续补救,以减轻违法违规行为的影响并预防未来违法违规行为的发生;

(vii)罚款对违法违规者或其他人未来作出违法违规行为的威慑程度;及

(viii)任何其他相关事实。

(3)如果小型企业能以令证券交易委员会满意的方式,证明其没有立即或在合理期限内支付全部或部分罚款的财务能力,证券交易委员会也可考虑减免小型企业的民事罚款,包括本节第(a)(1)(i)款至第(a)(1)(iii)款规定的被本政策排除在外的小型企业。

1　可通过证券交易委员会网站:http://www.sec.gov。

2　原文为“assess”,据上下文似应为“not assess”,参见下文第(a)款,译文已按后者处理。——译者注

(4) For purposes of this policy, an entity qualifies as "small" if it is a small business or small organization as defined by Commission rules adopted for the purpose of compliance with the Regulatory Flexibility Act.[1] An entity not included in these definitions will be considered "small" for purposes of this policy if it meets the total asset amount that applies to issuers as set forth in §230.157a of this chapter.[2]

(b) This policy does not create a right or remedy for any person. This policy shall not apply to any remedy that may be sought by the Commission other than civil money penalties, whether or not such other remedy may be characterized as penal or remedial.

[62 FR 16079, Apr. 4, 1997]

§202.10 Policy statement of the Securities and Exchange Commission concerning subpoenas to members of the news media.

Freedom of the press is of vital importance to the mission of the Securities and Exchange Commission. Effective journalism complements the Commission's efforts to ensure that investors receive the full and fair disclosure that the law requires, and that they deserve. Diligent reporting is an essential means of bringing securities law violations to light and ultimately helps to deter illegal conduct. In this *Policy Statement the Commission sets forth guidelines for the agency's professional staff* to ensure that vigorous enforcement of the federal securities laws is conducted completely consistently with the principles of the First Amendment's guarantee of freedom of the press, and specifically to avoid the issuance of subpoenas to members of the media that might impair the news gathering and reporting functions. These guidelines shall be adhered to by all members of the staff in all cases:

(a) In determining whether to issue a subpoena to a member of the news media, the approach in every case must be to strike the proper balance between the public's interest in the free dissemination of ideas and information and the public's interest in effective enforcement of the federal securities laws.

(b) When the staff investigating a matter determines that a member of the news

---

1 Pursuant to the Reg. Flex. Act, 5 U.S.C. § 601(3), the Commission has adopted appropriate definitions of "small business" for purposes of the Reg. Flex. Act. See 17 CFR 270.0-10, 275.0-7, 240.0-10, 230.157, 250.110, and 260.0-7. The Commission recently proposed amendments to certain of these definitions. Definitions of "Small Business" or "Small Organization" Under the Investment Company Act of 1940, the Investment Advisers Act of 1940, the Securities Exchange Act of 1934, and the Securities Act of 1933, Securities Act Rel. No. 7383, 62 FR 4106 (Jan. 28, 1997). The Commission extended the comment period for the proposed amendments to April 30, 1997, 62 FR 13356 (Mar. 20, 1997). Based on an analysis of the language and legislative history of the Reg. Flex. Act, Congress does not appear to have intended that Act to apply to natural persons (as opposed to individual proprietorships) or to foreign entities. The Commission understands that staff at the Small Business Administration have taken the same position.

2 At present, this threshold is $5 million. Thus, non-regulated entities, such as general partnerships, privately held corporations or professional service organizations, with assets of $5 million or less may qualify for penalty-reduction.

(4)就本政策而言,“小型企业”系指证券交易委员会为执行《监管弹性法》而通过的规则中定义的小型企业或组织。[1]未包括在上述定义中的企业,如果满足本章第230.157a节规定的适用于发行人的总资产数额标准,也应作为“小型企业”考虑。[2]

(b)本政策并不为任何人创设权利或救济。证券交易委员会寻求民事罚款以外的任何刑罚或救济的,不适用本政策。

[《联邦公报》第62卷第16079页,1997年4月4日。]

第202.10节　关于证券交易委员会向新闻媒体工作人员签发传票的政策声明

出版自由对于证券交易委员会实现其使命具有至关重要的作用。有效的新闻传播可以作为证券交易委员会工作的补充,确保投资者依法获得其应该获得的完整和公平的信息披露。勤勉的报道是曝光该等违法违规行为的基本手段,最终也将有助于威慑非法行为的发生。本政策声明规定了证券交易委员会对其专业工作人员的指引,以确保在完全符合《宪法第一修正案》保证出版自由的原则的情况下有效开展联邦证券法的执法行动,特别是应确保避免向新闻媒体工作人员签发的传票影响新闻采集和报道工作。无论何时,证券交易委员会的全体工作人员均应遵守如下指引:

(a)在每次判定是否应向新闻媒体工作人员签发传票时,都必须保证自由发表意见和传播信息所带来的公众利益以及有效执行联邦证券法所带来的公众利益获得适当平衡。

(b)负责调查某一事项的工作人员判定某新闻媒体工作人员可能掌握与调查相

1　按照《监管弹性法》[《美国法典》第五编第601(3)节]的规定,证券交易委员会已经为实施《监管弹性法》之目的对“小型企业”作出了适当定义。参见《联邦规章汇编》第十七编第270.0-10节、第275.0-7节、第240.0-10节、第230.157节、第250.110节和第260.0-7节。证券交易委员会近期针对下述部分定义提出了修正案:《1940年投资公司法》、《1940年投资顾问法》、《1934年证券交易法》和《1933年证券法》中的“小型企业”或“小型组织”的定义[第7383号《证券法公告》,《联邦公报》第62卷第4106页(1997年1月28日)]。证券交易委员会将修正草案的意见征询期延长到了1997年4月30日[《联邦公报》第62卷第13356页(1997年3月20日)]。基于对《联邦监管弹性法》的语言和立法历史的分析,国会似乎无意将该法适用于自然人(与个体企业相对)或外国企业。证券交易委员会了解,小企业管理署工作人员的立场与此相同。

2　目前,这一门槛设定为500万美元。因此,不受监管的企业,如资产为500万美元或不足500万美元的普通合伙、私有公司或专业服务机构均符合减免罚款资格。

media may have information relevant to the investigation, the staff should:

(1) Determine whether the information might be obtainable from alternative non-media sources.

(2) Make all reasonable efforts to obtain that information from those alternative sources. Whether all reasonable efforts have been made will depend on the particular circumstances of the investigation, including whether there is an immediate need to preserve assets or protect investors from an ongoing fraud.

(3) Determine whether the information is essential to successful completion of the investigation.

(c) If the information cannot reasonably be obtained from alternative sources and the information is essential to the investigation, then the staff, after seeking approval from the responsible Regional Director, District Administrator, or Associate Director, should contact legal counsel for the member of the news media. Staff should contact a member of the news media directly only if the member is not represented by legal counsel. The purpose of this contact is to explore whether the member may have information essential to the investigation, and to determine the interests of the media with respect to the information. If the nature of the investigation permits, the staff should make clear what its needs are as well as its willingness to respond to particular problems of the media. The staff should consult with the Commission's Office of Public Affairs, as appropriate.

(d) The staff should negotiate with news media members or their counsel, consistently with this Policy Statement, to obtain the essential information through informal channels, avoiding the issuance of a subpoena, if the responsible Regional Director, District Administrator, or Associate Director determines that such negotiations would not substantially impair the integrity of the investigation. Depending on the circumstances of the investigation, informal channels may include voluntary production, informal interviews, or written summaries.

(e) If negotiations are not successful in achieving a resolution that accommodates the Commission's interest in the information and the media's interests without issuing a subpoena, the staff investigating the matter should then consider whether to seek the issuance of a subpoena for the information. The following principles should guide the determination of whether a subpoena to a member of the news media should be issued:

(1) There should be reasonable grounds to believe that the information sought is essential to successful completion of the investigation. The subpoena should not be used to obtain peripheral or nonessential information.

(2) The staff should have exhausted all reasonable alternative means of obtaining the information from non-media sources. Whether all reasonable efforts have been made to obtain the information from alternative sources will depend on the particular circumstances of the

关的信息时,该工作人员应:

(1)判定该信息是否可以通过媒体之外的其他来源获得。

(2)尽一切合理努力从其他来源获得该信息。是否已经尽一切合理努力须基于调查的具体情况判断,包括是否存在保护资产或保护投资者免受正在进行的欺诈损害的现实需要。

(3)判定该信息是否对成功完成调查不可或缺。

(c)如果信息不能从其他来源合理获得且信息对调查不可或缺,则工作人员在获得负责的地区主任、区域主管或副主任批准后,应联系新闻媒体工作人员的法律顾问。只有在新闻媒体工作人员没有聘请法律顾问的情况下,才可以直接联系该新闻媒体工作人员。联系的目的是确定该人是否掌握对调查不可或缺的信息,并判定媒体对该信息具有的利益。如果调查性质允许,证券交易委员会工作人员应明确指明其所需信息,并说明其愿意答复媒体提出的具体问题。在适当情况下,证券交易委员会工作人员应咨询证券交易委员会公共事务办公室的意见。

(d)工作人员应在遵守本政策声明的情况下与新闻媒体工作人员或其律师谈判,通过非正式渠道获取上述不可或缺的信息,避免签发传票;条件是负责的地区主任、区域主管或副主任判定此等协商不会对调查的公正性造成实质影响。基于调查情况的不同,非正式渠道可包括自愿提供信息、非正式询问或书面摘要。

(e)如果无法通过谈判成功达成解决方案,因而无法在不签发传票的情况下协调证券交易委员会获取信息的利益以及新闻媒体的利益,负责调查该事项的工作人员应考虑是否通过签发传票来获取信息。在判定是否应向新闻媒体工作人员签发传票时,应遵循如下原则:

(1)证券交易委员会应有合理理由相信获取该信息对成功完成调查不可或缺。传票不得用于获取次要的或非不可或缺的信息。

(2)证券交易委员会工作人员在试图从媒体之外的来源获得该信息时,应已穷尽所有合理替代方法。是否已尽一切合理努力从其他来源获取信息应基于具体调查情况判定,包括是否存在保护资产或保护投资者免受正在进行中的欺诈损害的现实

investigation, including whether there is an immediate need to preserve assets or protect investors from an ongoing fraud.

(f) If there are reasonable grounds to believe the information sought is essential to the investigation, all reasonable alternative means of obtaining it have been exhausted, and all efforts at negotiation have failed, then the staff investigating the matter shall seek authorization for the subpoena from the Director of the Division of Enforcement. No subpoena shall be issued unless the Director, in consultation with the General Counsel, has authorized its issuance.

(g) In the event the Director of the Division of Enforcement, after consultation with the General Counsel, authorizes the issuance of a subpoena, notice shall immediately be provided to the Chairman of the Commission.

(h) Counsel (or the member of the news media, if not represented by counsel) shall be given reasonable and timely notice of the determination of the Director of the Division of Enforcement to authorize the subpoena and the Director's intention to issue it.

(i) Subpoenas should be negotiated with counsel for the member of the news media to narrowly tailor the request for only essential information. In negotiations with counsel, the staff should attempt to accommodate the interests of the Commission in the information with the interests of the media.

(j) Subpoenas should, wherever possible, be directed at material information regarding a limited subject matter, should cover a reasonably limited period of time, and should avoid requiring production of a large volume of unpublished material. They should give reasonable and timely notice of their demand for documents.

(k) In the absence of special circumstances, subpoenas to members of the news media should be limited to the verification of published information and to surrounding circumstances relating to the accuracy of published information.

(l) Because the intent of this policy statement is to protect freedom of the press, news gathering functions, and news media sources, this policy statement does not apply to demands for purely commercial or financial information unrelated to the news gathering function.

(m) Failure to follow this policy may constitute grounds for appropriate disciplinary action. The principles set forth in this statement are not intended to create or recognize any legally enforceable rights in any person.

[71 FR 20340, Apr. 20, 2006]

§202.12 Policy statement concerning cooperation by individuals in its investigations and related enforcement actions.

Cooperation by individuals and entities in the Commission's investigations and related enforcement actions can contribute significantly to the success of the agency's

需要。

(f)如果证券交易委员会有合理理由相信获取该信息对调查不可或缺,并已经穷尽获取该信息的所有合理替代方法,且一切谈判努力均告失败,负责调查该事项的工作人员应提请执法部主任核准签发传票。在执法部主任咨询首席律师的意见并核准签发传票前,不得签发传票。

(g)执法部主任在咨询首席律师的意见后核准签发传票的,应立即通知证券交易委员会主席。

(h)关于执法部批准签发传票的决定以及执法部主任签发传票意图的通知应合理、及时通知新闻媒体工作人员的律师或其本人(如果新闻媒体工作人员未聘请律师)。

(i)签发传票时,应与新闻媒体工作人员的律师谈判,以将传票要求提供的信息限制在不可或缺的范围内。在与律师谈判时,证券交易委员会工作人员应尽量协调证券交易委员会和媒体对该信息具有的利益。

(j)如有可能,传票应关乎被调查事项的实质信息,提供一个合理限期,并避免要求提供大量未出版材料。证券交易委员会工作人员应就其文件需求作出合理和及时的通知。

(k)如果没有特殊情况,向新闻媒体工作人员签发的传票应仅限于验证已出版的信息和与该等信息真实性相关的情况。

(l)由于本政策声明的意图是保护出版自由、新闻采集工作和新闻媒体来源,本政策声明不适用于要求提供与新闻采集无关的纯粹商业或财务信息的情况。

(m)未遵守本政策的,可处以适当的纪律处分。本政策声明中规定的原则并不旨在为任何人创设任何可依法强制执行的权利,亦不构成对该等权利的承认。

[《联邦公报》第71卷第20340页,2006年4月20日。]

第202.12节 关于个人配合调查和相关执法行动的政策声明

个人和机构的合作对于委员会成功开展调查和相关执法行动意义重大。借由个人和机构的合作,证券交易委员会能够更好地发现违反联邦证券法的行为,同时也能

mission. Cooperation can enhance the Commission's ability to detect violations of the federal securities laws, increase the effectiveness and efficiency of the Commission's investigations, and provide important evidence for the Commission's enforcement actions. There is a wide spectrum of tools available to the Commission and its staff for facilitating and rewarding cooperation by individuals, ranging from taking no enforcement action to pursuing reduced charges and sanctions in connection with enforcement actions. As with any cooperation program, there exists some tension between the objectives of holding individuals fully accountable for their misconduct and providing incentives for individuals to cooperate with law enforcement authorities. This policy statement sets forth the analytical framework employed by the Commission and its staff for resolving this tension in a manner that ensures that potential cooperation arrangements maximize the Commission's law enforcement interests. Although the evaluation of cooperation requires a case-by-case analysis of the specific circumstances presented, as described in greater detail below, the Commission's general approach is to determine whether, how much, and in what manner to credit cooperation by individuals by evaluating four considerations: the assistance provided by the cooperating individual in the Commission's investigation or related enforcement actions ("Investigation"); the importance of the underlying matter in which the individual cooperated; the societal interest in ensuring that the cooperating individual is held accountable for his or her misconduct; and the appropriateness of cooperation credit based upon the profile of the cooperating individual. In the end, the goal of the Commission's analysis is to protect the investing public by determining whether the public interest in facilitating and rewarding an individual's cooperation in order to advance the Commission's law enforcement interests justifies the credit awarded to the individual for his or her cooperation.

(a) *Assistance provided by the individual.* The Commission assesses the assistance provided by the cooperating individual in the Investigation by considering, among other things:

(1) The value of the individual's cooperation to the Investigation including, but not limited to:

(i) Whether the individual's cooperation resulted in substantial assistance to the Investigation;

(ii) The timeliness of the individual's cooperation, including whether the individual was first to report the misconduct to the Commission or to offer his or her cooperation in the Investigation, and whether the cooperation was provided before he or she had any knowledge of a pending investigation or related action;

(iii) Whether the Investigation was initiated based on information or other cooperation provided by the individual;

提高证券交易委员会调查工作的效率和成效,并为证券交易委员会的执法行动提供重要证据。证券交易委员会及其工作人员用于促进和奖励个人提供合作的工具十分广泛,包括完全撤销执法行动以及减轻指控和制裁。与任何其他鼓励合作的项目一样,证券交易委员会也处于某种程度的两难境地:一方面,证券交易委员会的目标是要完全追究个人不当行为的责任;另一方面,也要提供激励措施鼓励个人与执法机关合作。本政策声明解释了证券交易委员会及其工作人员在解决上述矛盾,确保合作安排计划最大限度符合证券交易委员会执法利益时使用的分析框架。虽然对合作进行评估时必须针对具体情况进行具体分析(详见下文),但是,证券交易委员会一般采取的做法是通过评估以下四个因素来判定是否应为个人合作提供奖励以及奖励额度和奖励方式:合作人为证券交易委员会调查或相关执法行动(下称调查)提供的协助;合作人提供合作的事项的重要性;追究合作人不当行为责任所牵涉的社会利益;以及,考虑到合作人的身份,向其授予奖励是否合适。总而言之,证券交易委员会进行上述分析的目的是判定为了促进证券交易委员会的执法而为合作人提供鼓励和奖赏是否构成授予奖励的充分理由,并最终实现保护公众投资者的目标。

(a)个人提供的协助。证券交易委员会评估合作人为调查提供的协助时考虑的因素包括但不限于:

(1)合作对调查工作的价值,包括但不限于:

(i)合作是否为调查工作提供了实质协助;

(ii)合作是否及时,包括此人是否为第一个向证券交易委员会报告不当行为或者为调查工作提供合作的人以及合作发生在其获悉调查或相关执法行动已经启动之前或之后;

(iii)调查工作是否基于该个人提供的信息或其他合作行为而启动;

(iv) The quality of cooperation provided by the individual, including whether the cooperation was truthful, complete, and reliable; and

(v) The time and resources conserved as a result of the individual's cooperation in the Investigation.

(2) The nature of the individual's cooperation in the Investigation including, but not limited to:

(i) Whether the individual's cooperation was voluntary or required by the terms of an agreement with another law enforcement or regulatory organization;

(ii) The types of assistance the individual provided to the Commission;

(iii) Whether the individual provided non-privileged information, which information was not requested by the staff or otherwise might not have been discovered;

(iv) Whether the individual encouraged or authorized others to assist the staff who might not have otherwise participated in the Investigation; and

(v) Any unique circumstances in which the individual provided the cooperation.

(b) *Importance of the underlying matter.* The Commission assesses the importance of the Investigation in which the individual cooperated by considering, among other things:

(1) The character of the Investigation including, but not limited to:

(i) Whether the subject matter of the Investigation is a Commission priority;

(ii) The type of securities violations;

(iii) The age and duration of the misconduct;

(iv) The number of violations; and

(v) The isolated or repetitive nature of the violations.

(2) The dangers to investors or others presented by the underlying violations involved in the Investigation including, but not limited to:

(i) The amount of harm or potential harm caused by the underlying violations;

(ii) The type of harm resulting from or threatened by the underlying violations; and

(iii) The number of individuals or entities harmed.[1]

(c) *Interest in holding the individual accountable.* The Commission assesses the societal interest in holding the cooperating individual fully accountable for his or her misconduct by considering, among other things:

(1) The severity of the individual's misconduct assessed by the nature of the violations and in the context of the individual's knowledge, education, training, experience, and position of responsibility at the time the violations occurred;

(2) The culpability of the individual, including, but not limited to, whether the

1 Cooperation in Investigations that involve priority matters or serious, ongoing, or widespread violations will be viewed most favorably.

(iv)合作的质量,包括合作行为是否真实、完整和可靠;及

(v)由于该个人对调查的合作而节省的时间和资源。

(2)合作的性质,包括但不限于:

(i)合作行为是出于自愿,或是出于执行与另一个执法机构或监管机构签订的协议条款;

(ii)向证券交易委员会提供的协助的类型;

(iii)是否提供了不受保密特权保护、证券交易委员会工作人员此前并未要求提供且如该个人不提供可能无法发现的信息;

(iv)该个人是否鼓励或同意本来可能不会参与调查的其他人员协助证券交易委员会工作人员开展工作;及

(v)个人提供合作的任何特殊情况。

(b)所涉事件的重要性。证券交易委员会评估该个人合作所涉调查的重要性时考虑的因素包括但不限于:

(1)调查的性质,包括但不限于:

(i)调查内容是否为证券交易委员会的工作重点;

(ii)证券违法违规行为的类型;

(iii)不当行为发生后已经经过的时间和不当行为的持续时间;

(iv)违法违规行为的数目;及

(v)违法违规行为是一次性行为或重复性行为。

(2)被调查的违法违规行为对投资者或他人造成的危害,包括但不限于:

(i)违法违规行为造成的损害或潜在损害的数额;

(ii)违法违规行为造成的或可能造成的损害的类型;及

(iii)受损害的个人或实体的数量。[1]

(c)追究个人责任的社会意义。证券交易委员会在评估追究合作人的责任所具有的社会意义时考虑的因素包括但不限于:

(1)个人不当行为的严重性,考量因素包括违法违规行为的性质以及违法违规行为发生时个人所具有的知识、教育水平、培训水平、经历和所承担的职责等;

(2)个人的可责性,包括但不限于是否明知故犯,包括一般意义上的明知故犯的

1 为调查提供的合作涉及重点或严重事项或正在进行、大规模的违法违规行为的,将被视为具有重大价值。

individual acted with scienter, both generally and in relation to others who participated in the misconduct;

(3) The degree to which the individual tolerated illegal activity including, but not limited to, whether he or she took steps to prevent the violations from occurring or continuing, such as notifying the Commission or other appropriate law enforcement agency of the misconduct or, in the case of a violation involving a business organization, by notifying members of management not involved in the misconduct, the board of directors or the equivalent body not involved in the misconduct, or the auditors of such business organization of the misconduct;

(4) The efforts undertaken by the individual to remediate the harm caused by the violations including, but not limited to, whether he or she paid or agreed to pay disgorgement to injured investors and other victims or assisted these victims and the authorities in the recovery of the fruits and instrumentalities of the violations; and

(5) The sanctions imposed on the individual by other federal or state authorities and industry organizations for the violations involved in the Investigation.

(d) *Profile of the individual.* The Commission assesses whether, how much, and in what manner it is in the public interest to award credit for cooperation, in part, based upon the cooperating individual's personal and professional profile by considering, among other things:

(1) The individual's history of lawfulness, including complying with securities laws or regulations;

(2) The degree to which the individual has demonstrated an acceptance of responsibility for his or her past misconduct; and

(3) The degree to which the individual will have an opportunity to commit future violations of the federal securities laws in light of his or her occupation — including, but not limited to, whether he or she serves as: A licensed individual, such as an attorney or accountant; an associated person of a regulated entity, such as a broker or dealer; a fiduciary for other individuals or entities regarding financial matters; an officer or director of public companies; or a member of senior management — together with any existing or proposed safeguards based upon the individual's particular circumstances.

Note to §202.12: Before the Commission evaluates an individual's cooperation, it analyzes the unique facts and circumstances of the case. The above principles are not listed in order of importance nor are they intended to be all–inclusive or to require a specific determination in any particular case. Furthermore, depending upon the facts and circumstances of each case, some of the principles may not be applicable or may deserve greater weight than others. Finally, neither this statement, nor the principles set forth herein creates or recognizes any legally enforceable rights for any person.

程度,以及与其他共同参与不当行为的人相比所具有的明知故犯的程度;

(3)个人放任非法活动的程度,包括但不限于,是否采取了相关行动阻止违法违规行为的发生或持续,如是否已将不当行为通知证券交易委员会或其他负责处理不当行为的相关执法机构,或者(如果违法违规行为涉及商业组织)是否通知了该商业组织的未参与不当行为的管理人员、董事会或与董事会相当的机构或审计人员。

(4)个人为弥补其违法违规行为造成的伤害而采取的行动,包括但不限于,是否已实际或同意向受损害投资者或其他受害人支付非法所得,或者是否为受害人或有关主管部门追回非法所得提供了协助;及

(5)其他联邦主管部门或州主管部门和行业组织已就调查所涉违法违规行为处以的制裁。

(d)该人的个人情况。证券交易委员会在评估对合作进行奖励是否符合公共利益以及在多大程度上和以何种方式促进了公共利益时,合作人的个人情况和职业情况是考虑因素之一,包括:

(1)该个人的守法历史,包括遵守证券法律或规章的历史;

(2)该个人表现出来的对其过往不当行为导致的责任的承担程度;及

(3)该人再次触犯联邦证券法律的几率,评估时应考虑其担任的职务——包括但不限于其是否担任:凭证执业人士,如律师或会计师;受监管实体(如经纪商或自营商)的业务相关人;其他个人或实体的受信义务人;公众公司的管理人员或董事;高级管理层成员——同时应针对该人的具体情况考虑任何现有或提议的防范保障措施。

关于第202.12节的注释:证券交易委员会将在评估个人的合作行为之前,分析案件的具体事实和情况。以上原则并非按重要性先后排列,也未穷尽列举证券交易委员会应考虑的所有因素,同时也不要求证券交易委员会在具体案件中对以上所有原则作出具体判断。此外,根据具体案件的事实和情况不同,以上某些原则可能并不适用,而某些原则可能需要重点考虑。最后,本声明以及声明中罗列的原则并不为任何人创设任何可依法强制执行的权利,亦不构成对该等权利的承认。

[75 FR 3123, Jan. 19, 2010]

Subpart A—Public Company Accounting Oversight Board (Regulation P)

§202.140 Interim Commission review of PCAOB inspection reports.

(a) *Definitions.*

(1) *Board* or *PCAOB* means the Public Company Accounting Oversight Board.

(2) *Registered public accounting firm* or *Firm* shall have the meaning set forth in 15 U.S.C. 7201(a)(12).

(3) *Associated person* means a person associated with the registered public accounting firm as defined in 15 U.S.C. 7201(a)(9).

(b) *Reviewable matters.* A registered public accounting firm may request interim Commission review of an assessment or determination by the PCAOB contained in an inspection report prepared under 15 U.S.C. 7214 and relating to that firm, if the firm:

(1) Has provided the PCAOB with a response, pursuant to the rules of the PCAOB, to the substance of particular items in a draft inspection report and disagrees with the assessments relating to those items contained in any final inspection report prepared by the PCAOB following such response;

(2) Disagrees with an assessment contained in any final inspection report that was not contained in the draft inspection report provided to the firm under 15 U.S.C. 7214(f) or the rules of the PCAOB; or

(3) Disagrees with the determination of the PCAOB that criticisms or defects in the quality control systems of the firm that were identified in an inspection report, but not disclosed to the public, have not been addressed to the satisfaction of the PCAOB within 12 months after the date of that inspection report.

(c) *Procedures for requesting interim Commission review.* (1) A request for interim Commission review with respect to matters described in paragraph (b) of this section must be submitted to the Commission's Office of the Secretary within 30 calendar days of the following:

(i) The date the firm is provided a copy of the final inspection report described in paragraph (b)(1) or (b)(2) of this section; or

(ii) The date the firm receives notice of the PCAOB's determination described in paragraph (b)(3) of this section.

(2) The PCAOB shall not make publicly available the final inspection report or

[《联邦公报》第75卷第3123页,2010年1月19日。]

第A子部分——公众公司会计监督委员会(P规章)

第202.140节　证券交易委员会对公众公司会计监督委员会检查报告的中期审查

(a)定义

(1)“委员会 ”或“PCAOB”系指公众公司会计监督委员会。

(2)“注册公共会计师事务所 ”或“事务所 ”的定义见《美国法典》第十五编第7201(a)(12)节。

(3)“业务相关人 ”系指注册公共会计师事务所的业务相关人[如《美国法典》第十五编第7201(a)(9)节所定义]。

(b)可审查事项。注册公共会计师事务所可以提请证券交易委员会对公众公司会计监督委员会根据《美国法典》第十五编第7214节在检查报告中作出的有关该事务所的评估或判定进行审查,前提是该事务所:

(1)已经按照公众公司会计监督委员会的规则针对检查报告草案具体事项的内容向公众公司会计监督委员会作出答复,并且该事务所不同意公众公司会计监督委员会在收到答复之后编制的最终检查报告中对上述事项的评估;

(2)对任何最终检查报告内包含的,但在公众公司会计监督委员会按照《美国法典》第十五编第7214(f)节或其规则向该事务所提供的检查报告草案中并未提及的评估持有异议;或

(3)不同意公众公司会计监督委员会的如下认定:公众公司会计监督委员会对该事务所的质量控制系统所作的批评或者指出的缺陷(此类批评或缺陷体现在检查报告中,但并未向公众公布)并没有在上述检查报告作出后12个月内作出令公众公司会计监督委员会满意的调整。

(c)申请证券交易委员会进行中期审查的程序。(1)提请证券交易委员会对本节第(b)款所述事项进行中期审查的申请必须在以下日期后30个日历日之内向证券交易委员会秘书办公室提出:

(i)事务所收到本节第(b)(1)款或第(b)(2)款所述最终检查报告之日;或

(ii)事务所收到本节第(b)(3)款所述关于公众公司会计监督委员会认定的通知之日。

(2)在事务所可以提请证券交易委员会进行中期审查的30日的期限内,公众公司

criticisms or defects in the quality control systems of the firm subject to a determination described in paragraph (b) of this section, as applicable, during the 30-day period during which the firm may request interim Commission review, unless the firm consents in writing to earlier publication of the report.

(3) A request for interim Commission review ("request" or "submission")must be marked "Request for Interim Commission Review With Respect to PCAOB Inspection Report." The request must focus on the specific matters for which relief is requested and succinctly address the issues raised by the PCAOB. The request, to the extent possible, should include, for example:

(i) A copy of the particular inspection report that is the subject of the request;

(ii) The specific assessments or determinations that are the subject of the request;

(iii) The alleged errors or deficiencies in the PCAOB's assessments or determination and the reasons for the firm's position;

(iv) If the matter is being reviewed under paragraph (b)(3) of this section, any actions taken by the registered public accounting firm to address criticisms or defects identified in the inspection report; and

(v) Any supporting documentation relevant to the review.

(4) The firm must provide a copy of its review request to the PCAOB simultaneously with its submission to the Commission.

(5) A timely review request by a firm will operate as a stay of publication of those portions of the final inspection report or criticisms or defects in the quality control systems of the firm subject to a determination described in paragraph (b) of this section, as applicable, that are the subject of the firm's review request, unless the Commission otherwise determines in its own discretion. Upon expiration of the 30-day period during which the firm may request interim Commission review, the PCAOB shall make publicly available the remainder of the final inspection report or criticisms or defects in the quality control systems of the firm that were indentified in an inspection report, as applicable, that are not the subject of the firm's review request, unless the Commission otherwise determines that such a result would not be necessary or appropriate.

(6) If the firm fails to make a timely review request, pursuant to Section 104(g)(2) of the Act, the PCAOB shall make publicly available the final inspection report or criticisms or defects in the quality control systems of the firm that were indentified in an inspection report, as applicable.

(d) *Procedures for granting or denying the review request.* Within 30 calendar days of a timely review request, the Commission will notify the firm and the PCAOB as to whether the Commission will exercise its discretion to grant the request for an interim review. If the Commission does not grant the review request, the stay of publication is

会计监督委员会不得公布最终检查报告,也不得公布需要按照本节第(b)款进行认定的有关该事务所质量控制体系的批评或缺陷信息,但该事务所书面同意提前公布报告的除外。

(3)提请证券交易委员会进行中期审查的申请(下称申请或申请文件)必须标注为"提请证券交易委员会就公众公司会计监督委员会检查报告进行中期审查"。申请的重点应当是事务所申请救济的具体事项,并简要说明公众公司会计监督委员会提出的问题。如有可能,申请应尽可能包括:

(i)申请针对的具体检查报告;

(ii)申请针对的具体评估或判定;

(iii)事务所指称公众公司会计监督委员会的评估或判定中存在的错误或缺陷,以及支持其立场的理由;

(iv)如果该事项正在按照本节第(b)(3)款进行审查,那么还应包括注册公共会计师事务所针对该检查报告提出的批评或缺陷采取的任何行动;及

(v)与审查相关的任何支持文件。

(4)在向证券交易委员会提出审查申请的同时,事务所必须同时将申请抄送向公众公司会计监督委员会。

(5)事务所及时提出审查申请的,申请所针对的最终报告中需要按照本节第(b)款作出认定的内容以及关于该所质量控制体系的批评意见或缺陷信息应暂缓公布,但证券交易委员会行使自由裁量权另行作出决定的除外。事务所可以提请证券交易委员会进行中期审查的30日的期限届满之后,公众公司会计监督委员会应公布申请所针对的最终检查报告中需要按照本节第(b)款作出认定的内容以及关于该所质量控制体系的批评意见或缺陷信息,但证券交易委员会判定不必或不宜进行公布的除外。

(6)事务所未及时提出审查申请的,则根据本法第104(g)(2)节,公众公司会计监督委员会应公布最终检查报告或检查报告中指出的关于该所质量控制体系的批评意见或缺陷信息。

(d)核准或驳回审查申请的程序。事务所及时提出审查报告申请后30个日历日内,证券交易委员会应通知事务所和公众公司会计监督委员会,说明其是否将行使自由裁量权核准申请。证券交易委员会不核准申请的,证券交易委员会向事务所和公众公司会计监督委员会发出不核准通知之时,报告或信息暂缓公布的效力即应终止。证

terminated upon notification to the firm and the PCAOB. If the Commission does grant the review request, the stay of publication shall continue unless the Commission determines otherwise in its own discretion, or unless the firm consents in writing to the PCAOB, with a copy to the Commission, to earlier publication.

(e) *Procedures where a review request has been granted.* (1) Where the Commission has notified the firm and the PCAOB that it is granting the request for an interim review, the PCAOB may submit responsive information and documents with the Commission within 15 calendar days of receipt of such notice. The PCAOB must provide a copy of such information and documents simultaneously to the firm.

(2) During the course of the interim review, the Commission may request additional information relating to the PCAOB's assessments or determination under review, and provide a period of up to seven calendar days to respond to such request, from the PCAOB, the firm, and any associated person of the firm. The Commission may grant the firm or the PCAOB a period of up to seven calendar days to respond to any information obtained pursuant to this paragraph. The firm or the PCAOB, as applicable, shall provide simultaneously to the other party all information provided as a result of a request for additional information or responses thereto. The firm with which any associated person from whom information is requested shall provide simultaneously to the PCAOB all information provided as a result of a request for additional information or responses thereto. If the firm (including any associated person) or the PCAOB fails to respond timely to a request from the Commission, such failure may serve as the basis for the Commission to conclude its review and make a determination adverse to the non-responsive party.

(3) The Commission, based on the information submitted by the firm, the PCAOB and any associated persons, shall consider whether the PCAOB's assessments or determination are arbitrary and capricious, or otherwise not consistent with the purposes of the Act.

(4) At the conclusion of its review, the Commission shall inform the firm and the PCAOB in writing that the Commission:

(i) Does not object to all or part of the assessments or determination of the PCAOB and the stay of publication is terminated; or

(ii) Remands to the PCAOB with instructions that the stay of publication is permanent or that the PCAOB take such other actions as the Commission deems necessary or appropriate with respect to publication, including, but not limited to, revising the final inspection report or determinations before publication.

(5) The review pursuant to this section shall be completed and a written notice pursuant to this section shall be sent no more than 75 calendar days after notification to the firm and the PCAOB that the Commission is granting the request for an interim

券交易委员会核准申请的,报告或信息应继续暂缓公布,但证券交易委员会行使自由裁量权另行作出判定,或者,事务所以书面形式向公众公司会计监督委员会表示同意提前公布,并抄送证券交易委员会的除外。

(e)审查申请核准之后适用的程序。(1)证券交易委员会通知事务所和公众公司会计监督委员会其将核准中期审查申请的,公众公司会计监督委员会应当在收到通知后15个日历日之内向证券交易委员会提供相关答复信息和文件,并同时抄送事务所。

(2)在中期审查过程中,证券交易委员会可以要求提供与正在接受审查的公众公司会计监督委员会的评估或判定相关的补充信息,并允许公众公司会计监督委员会、事务所和事务所的任何业务相关人在不超过7个日历日的期间内对此作出答复。对于根据本款获取的任何信息,证券交易委员会均可以允许事务所或公众公司会计监督委员会在不超过7个日历日的期间内作出答复。事务所或公众公司会计监督委员会根据证券交易委员会的要求或在答复中向证券交易委员会提供补充信息的,应同时抄送对方。被要求提供信息的任何业务相关人根据证券交易委员会的要求提供补充信息或者在答复中提供信息的,该等主体所在的事务所也应同时抄送公众公司会计监督委员会。如果事务所(包括任何业务相关人)或公众公司会计监督委员会未能及时对证券交易委员会的要求作出答复,证券交易委员会可以就此结束审查,并作出对不答复方不利的判定。

(3)证券交易委员会应根据事务所、公众公司会计监督委员会和任何业务相关人提供的信息,考虑公众公司会计监督委员会的评估或判定是否恣意专断或违反该法宗旨的情形。

(4)审查结束之后,证券交易委员会应书面通知事务所和公众公司会计监督委员会:

(i)证券交易委员会并不反对公众公司会计监督委员会所作的部分或全部评估或判定,暂缓公布的效力应予终止;或

(ii)证券交易委员会把案件发回公众公司会计监督委员会,同时指示相关报告或信息应永不公布,或者要求公众公司会计监督委员会就公布采取证券交易委员会认为必要或适当的其他措施,包括但不限于,在公布前修改最终检查报告或认定。

(5)证券交易委员会向事务所和公众公司会计监督委员会发出核准中期审查通知后,应在75个日历日之内根据本节完成审查并按本节规定发出书面通知,但证券交易委员会基于充分理由延长上述期间的除外。

review, unless the Commission extends the period for good cause.

(f) *Treatment of review.* (1) Time periods in this section shall be computed as provided in the Commission's Rules of Practice, 17 CFR 201.160.

(2) Unless otherwise determined by the Commission, the decision to grant or deny a review request and the conclusions of the Commission's review shall be non–public, and the information or documents submitted, created, or obtained by the Commission or its staff in the course of the review shall be deemed non–public. Nothing in this rule shall be construed to impair or limit the ability of any party to request confidential treatment under the Freedom of Information Act, 15 U.S.C. 7215(b)(5), or any other applicable law.

(3) Pursuant to 15 U.S.C. 7214(h)(2), any decision of the Commission as a result of an interim review with respect to a PCAOB inspection report, including whether a request for review is granted or denied, shall not be reviewable under 15 U.S.C. 78y and shall not be deemed to be "final agency action" for purposes of 5 U.S.C. 704.

(4) Any action taken by the Commissionrelates solely to the publication of the relevant inspection report and does not affect the ability of the Commission or PCAOB to take appropriate action.

(g) *Designation of address; Representation.* (1) When a registered public accounting firm first submits a request for interim Commission review, or an associated person first submits information related to a request, the firm or associated person shall submit to the Commission, and keep current, an address at which any notice or other written communication furnished to the firm or associated person may be sent, a contact name and telephone number where the firm or associated person may be reached during business hours and, if represented, the representative's name, business address, and telephone number.

(2) If the firm, PCAOB, or associated person will be represented by a representative, the initial submission of that person shall be accompanied by the notice of appearance required by §201.102 (d). The other provisions of §201.102 with respect to representation before the Commission shall apply.

[75 FR 47449, Aug. 6, 2010]

§202.170 Initiation of disapproval proceedings for PCAOB proposed rules.

Initiation of disapproval proceedings for proposed rules of the Public Company Accounting Oversight Board as defined by section 107 of the Sarbanes–Oxley Act of 2002 are subject to the provisions of §§201.700 and 201.701 of this chapter as fully as if it were a*registered securities association*, except that:

(a) *Demonstration of consistency with the Sarbanes–Oxley Act of 2002.* For purposes of proposed rules of the Public Company Accounting Oversight Board, apply this paragraph in lieu of paragraph (b)(3) of §201.700 of this chapter. The burden to

(f)审查的处理。(1)本节规定的时间期限按《证券交易委员会工作规则》(《联邦规章汇编》第十七编第201.160节)计算。

(2)除非证券交易委员会另行决定,否则核准或驳回审查申请的决定以及证券交易委员会的审查结论均不得公开,证券交易委员会或其工作人员在审查过程中呈报、创造或获取的信息或文件也应视为非公开信息或文件。本规则不得解释为影响或限制任何一方按照《信息自由法》[《美国法典》第十五编第7215(b)(5)节]或任何其他适用法律请求获得保密待遇的能力。

(3)根据《美国法典》第十五编第7214(h)(2)节,证券交易委员会在对公众公司会计监督委员会检查报告进行中期审查后所作的任何决定,包括核准或驳回审查申请的决定,均不得按照《美国法典》第十五编第78(y)节进行复议,也不得视为《美国法典》第五编第704节中的"最终机构行动"。

(4)证券交易委员会采取的任何行动均仅针对相关检查报告的公布,不影响证券交易委员会或公众公司会计监督委员会采取适当行动的能力。

(g)指定地址;代理。(1)注册公共会计师事务所首次向证券交易委员会提交中期审查申请时;或者,业务相关人首次按要求提交信息之时,事务所或业务相关人应向证券交易委员会提供一份地址并随时进行更新,以便证券交易委员会向其递送通知或其他书面通信,同时应提供可以在营业时间联系到该事务所或业务相关人的联系人姓名和电话号码,另外,如果存在代理,还应提供代理人的姓名、营业地址和电话号码。

(2)如果事务所、公众公司会计监督委员会或业务相关人由其他人代理,那么代理人在首次提交信息时应附上第201.102(d)节规定的出席通知,同时也应适用第201.102节中关于代理他人出席证券交易委员会程序并办理业务的其他规定。

[《联邦公报》第75卷第47449页,2010年8月6日]

第202.170节　发起否决公众公司会计监督委员会规则草案的程序

按照《2002年萨班斯—奥克斯利法》第107条规定发起否决公众公司会计监督委员会规则草案的程序,应完全遵守本章第201.700节和第201.701节的规定,如同该委员会属于"注册证券协会",但是:

(a)必须证明规则草案符合《2002年萨班斯—奥克斯利法》的规定。对于公众公司会计监督委员会的规则草案,应适用本款,而非本章第201.700节第(b)(3)款的规定。公众会计公司监督委员会应承担举证责任,证明规则草案符合《2002年萨班斯—奥克

demonstrate that a proposed rule is consistent with the requirements of title I of the Sarbanes–Oxley Act of 2002, and the rules and regulations issued thereunder, or as necessary or appropriate in the public interest or for the protection of investors, is on the Public Company Accounting Oversight Board. In its filing the Public Company Accounting Oversight Board must explain in a clear and comprehensible manner why the proposed rule change is consistent with the requirements of title I of the Sarbanes–Oxley Act of 2002 and the rules and regulations thereunder, or as necessary or appropriate in the public interest or for the protection of investors. A mere assertion that the proposed rule change is consistent with those requirements is not sufficient. Instead, the description of the proposed rule, its purpose and operation, its effect, and a legal analysis of its consistency with applicable requirements must all be sufficiently detailed and specific to support an affirmative Commission finding. Any failure by the Public Company Accounting Oversight Board in its proposed rule filing with the Commission may result in the Commission not having a sufficient basis to make an affirmative finding that a proposed rule change is consistent with the title I of the Sarbanes–Oxley Act of 2002, and the rules and regulations issued thereunder, or as necessary or appropriate in the public interest or for the protection of investors.

(b) For each reference to "the Exchange Act and the rules and regulations thereunder applicable to the self–regulatory organization" apply "title I of the Sarbanes–Oxley Act of 2002, and the rules and regulations issued thereunder applicable to such organization, or as necessary or appropriate in the public interest or for the protection of investors."

[76 FR 4072, Jan. 24, 2011]

§202.190 Public Company Accounting Oversight Board budget approval process.

(a) *Purpose*. These procedures are established in connection with consideration and approval of the budget and the accounting support fee for the Public Company Accounting Oversight Board (PCAOB). Actions attributed to the PCAOB in this section shall be performed as authorized by the Sarbanes–Oxley Act of 2002 and the PCAOB's bylaws.

(b) *Definitions*. For the purposes of this section, the following definitions shall apply:

(1) *Budget category* means a grouping of similar expenditures within the PCAOB's budget. Budget categories shall include, among others: personnel, training, recruiting and relocation expenses, information technology, consulting and professional fees, travel, administrative expenses, lease costs and related expenses, and capital improvements of facilities.

(2) *Budget justification* means the justification for each annual budget, prepared in concise and specific terms, covering all of the PCAOB's programs and activities, and

斯利法》第一编以及依其颁发的规则与规章的要求，或证明该等草案对于保护公共利益或保护投资者是必要或适当的。在提交草案时，公众公司会计监督委员会必须清晰、全面地论证规则变更提案符合《2002年萨班斯—奥克斯利法》第一编以及依其颁发的规则与规章的要求，或论证该等提案对于保护公共利益或保护投资者是必要或适当的。单纯主张规则变更提案符合该等要求并不表示举证责任已得到满足。相反，对规则草案的内容及其宗旨、适用和效力的说明，以及对规则草案是否符合相关规定进行的法律分析，必须充分详细、具体，足以供证券交易委员会作出肯定性的认定。公众公司会计监督委员会在向证券交易委员会提交规则草案时不符合上述规定的，可能导致证券交易委员会没有充分的依据认定规则变更提案符合《2002年萨班斯—奥克斯利法》第一编以及依其颁发的规则与规章的要求，或认定该等草案对于保护公共利益或保护投资者是必要或适当的。

(b)每次提及"《证券交易法》以及依其颁发的适用于自律组织的规则与规章"时，均应替以"《2002年萨班斯—奥克斯利法》第一编以及依其颁发的适用于该等自律组织的规则与规章，或对于保护公共利益或保护投资者所必要或适当的规则与规章"。

[《联邦公报》第76卷第4072页，2011年1月24日。]

第202.190节　公众公司会计监督委员会的预算批准程序

(a)目的。本程序适用于公众公司会计监督委员会(PCAOB)预算和会计支持费的审议和批准。本节所述的公众公司会计监督委员会行动应按照《2002年萨班斯—奥克斯利法》和公众公司会计监督委员会内部章程的授权进行。

(b)定义。就本节规定而言，应适用如下定义：

(1)"预算科目"系指公众公司会计监督委员会预算内类似开支的分类。预算科目包括但不限于：人事、培训、招聘和安置费用；信息技术、咨询和专业费用；差旅、行政费用；租赁成本和相关费用以及设施的改良性资本支出等。

(2)"预算论证"系指每年度预算的论证理由，论证理由应简明、具体，涵盖公众公司会计监督委员会所有项目和活动，包括但不限于证券交易委员会可能要求的如下

including, among other things as may be requested by the Commission:

(i) A performance budget for the budget year;

(ii) An analysis of the PCAOB's budget, including a tabular presentation that identifies the budgetary resources required for each program area (with a breakout of resources by budget category); a description of the budgetary resources identified in the budget in the context of the PCAOB's programs and activities; and an explanation of the analysis used to determine the resources needed to accomplish each program and strategic goal that demonstrates that reasonable opportunities for making more efficient and effective use of resources have been explored;

(iii) A description of the relationship between the results or outcomes the PCAOB expects to achieve (as discussed in the PCAOB's strategic plan)and the resources requested in the budget;

(iv) Assumptions underlying the calculation of the working capital reserve as permitted in paragraph (d)(3) of this section and assumptions underlying PCAOB estimates, including work years, program outputs, base compensation levels and proposed compensation increases, and costs of inputs such as materials or contract costs;

(v) A discussion of any models used to develop PCAOB estimates;

(vi) Detailed funding levels for education, training, and travel of the PCAOB workforce;

(vii) Information sufficient for the Commission to assess current and proposed capital projects and information technology projects; and

(viii) A statement that the PCAOB has considered relative costs and benefits in formulating the programs, projects and activities described in the budget.

(3) *Budget year* means the PCAOB fiscal year that is the subject of the budget prepared and submitted by the PCAOB to the Commission for approval.

(4) *Current year* means the PCAOB fiscal year that precedes the budget year, and is the year in which the PCAOB prepares the budget.

(5) *Performance budget* means a budget that presents what the PCAOB proposes to accomplish in the budget year and what resources these proposals will require, and that serves as the primary basis for the justification of the budget submitted to the Commission for approval. The performance budget includes:

(i) A description of what the PCAOB plans to accomplish, organized by strategic goal;

(ii) Background on what the PCAOB has accomplished, organized by strategic goal;

(iii) Analyses of the strategies the PCAOB uses to influence strategic outcomes, including whether those strategies could be improved and, if so, how they could be improved;

内容:

(i)预算年度的绩效预算;

(ii)公众公司会计监督委员会的预算分析,包括以表格形式列明每个计划领域所需预算资源(在每一预算科目下对资源进行细分);基于公众公司会计监督委员会的各个计划和活动说明预算表中所需的预算资源;说明用以确定完成各个项目和战略目标所需资源的分析方法,证明已经尝试一切合理方法实现对资源的更具成效和效率的使用。

(iii)说明公众公司会计监督委员会预期获得的结果或成效(详见公众公司会计监督委员会战略计划)与预算请求配给的资源之间的关系;

(iv)计算本节第(d)(3)款允许的运营资本准备时所依据的假设,以及公众公司会计监督委员会测算所依据的假设,包括工作年限、计划产出、基本薪酬水平和拟议加薪和投入成本(如材料或合约成本);

(v)公众公司会计监督委员会开展测算时使用的模型之介绍;

(vi)公众公司会计监督委员会职工教育、培训和差旅的具体资金投入水平;

(vii)证券交易委员会评估当前和拟议资本项目和信息技术项目所需的充分信息;及

(viii)关于公众公司会计监督委员会在制定预算所述计划、项目和活动时已考虑相对成本和效益的声明。

(3)“预算年度”系指公众公司会计监督委员会编制并呈报证券交易委员会批准的预算所针对的会计年度。

(4)“本年度”系指预算年度的前一会计年度,即公众公司会计监督委员会编制预算的年度。

(5)“绩效预算”系指说明如下内容的预算:公众公司会计监督委员会计划在该预算年度实现的目标和所需资源,以及提交证券交易委员会审批的主要论证理由。绩效预算包括以下内容:

(i)说明公众公司会计监督委员会计划实现的目标(按战略目标分类);

(ii)公众公司会计监督委员会已实现目标的背景信息(按战略目标分类);

(iii)分析公众公司会计监督委员会用以影响战略结果的战略,包括这些战略是否可以改善以及,如果可以改善的话,应如何改善;

(iv) Analyses of the programs that contribute to each goal and their relative roles and effectiveness;

(v) Performance targets for the budget year and the current year and how the PCAOB expects to achieve those targets, as well as actual performance levels achieved in the year immediately preceding the current year;

(vi) The budgetary resources the PCAOB is requesting to achieve those targets;

(vii) Descriptions of the operations, processes, staff skills, information and other technologies, human resources, capital assets, and other resources to be used in achieving the PCAOB's performance goals; and

(viii) Descriptions of the programs, policies, and management, regulatory, and other initiatives and approaches to be used in achieving the PCAOB's performance goals.

(6) *Preliminary budget* means the draft budget submitted for initial consideration by the Commission, which shall be a complete or substantially complete budget for the budget year, and which is accompanied by a budget justification.

(7) *Program area* means the array of the budgeted amounts and other budget-related data according to the major purpose served, such as registration, inspection, standard-setting, enforcement, and administration.

(8) *Receipts* means collections that result from issuers' payments of accounting support fees; public accounting firms' payment of registration fees and fees associated with annual reports; interest income; and other sources of revenue.

(9) *Strategic plan* means the PCAOB's overarching plan for accomplishing its strategic goals, including forecasts for the current and four following years; estimates of the effect that reasonably foreseeable changes impacting the auditing profession and securities markets could have on program levels; and a discussion of the impact that program levels and changes in methods of program delivery, including advances in technology, could have on program operations and administration.

(10) *Supplemental budget* means a budget or amendment thereto submitted to the Commission for approval subsequent to Commission approval of the budget for the budget year, when:

(i) There is a need for additional funds in a program area;

(ii) Resources are to be applied in a manner not fairly implied in the Commission-approved budget and budget justification, such as when programs are created to perform functions that are not, or to perform functions in a way that is not, fairly implied from the Commission-approved budget and budget justification; or

(iii) Programs described in the Commission-approved budget and budget justification are to be eliminated.

(c) *Timetable*. The timetable for preparation and submission of the annual budget is as follows:

（iv）分析促进各目标实现的计划以及这些计划的相对作用和成效；

（v）预算年度和本年度的绩效目标和公众公司会计监督委员会预期如何实现这些目标，以及本年度前一年度的实际绩效水平；

（vi）公众公司会计监督委员会为实现该等目标而请求配给的预算资源；

（vii）说明实现公众公司会计监督委员会绩效目标所必要的经营、流程、工作人员技能、信息和其他技术、人力资源、资本资产和其他资源；及

（viii）说明实现公众公司会计监督委员会绩效目标所必要的计划、政策以及管理/监管计划和其他行动、方法。

（6）“初步预算”系指提交证券交易委员会进行初步审议的预算草案，预算草案应为预算年度的完整预算或基本完整的预算，同时应附上预算论证。

（7）“计划领域”系指根据其主要业务作用（如注册、检查、标准设定、执法和行政）而列明的预算金额和与预算相关的其他数据。

（8）“收款”系指通过以下各项来源收到的款项：发行人支付的会计支持费、公共会计师事务所支付的注册费和与年报相关的费用、利息收入以及其他收入来源。

（9）“战略计划”系指公众公司会计监督委员会为实现其战略目标而制定的宏观计划，包括对本年度和随后4年所作的预测；对可合理预见的、影响审计行业和证券市场的变化对项目带来的影响的测算；以及关于计划水平和计划交付方法的变动（包括技术进步）可能对计划运作和管理带来的影响的讨论。

（10）“补充预算”系指证券交易委员会批准预算年度的预算后，在下述情况下提交给证券交易委员会审批的预算或修正：

（i）某个计划领域需要追加资金；

（ii）需要以证券交易委员会批准的预算和预算论证中未合理暗示的方式使用资源，如需要创建计划来实现证券交易委员会审批的预算和预算论证中未合理暗示的功能；或需要以证券交易委员会审批的预算和预算论证未合理暗示的方式来实现功能；或

（iii）证券交易委员会已批准的预算和预算论证中所述计划被取消。

（c）时间表。编制和提交年度预算的时间表如下：

Date	Event
On or before March 15	PCAOB provides a narrative of its program issues and outlook for the budget year.
On or before April 30	Commission provides economic assumptions and general budgetary guidance to the PCAOB.
On or before July 31	PCAOB submits preliminary budget and budget justification for Commission review.
August–October	Consultation between Commission and PCAOB; Commission staff conducts review of PCAOB preliminary budget, budget justification and related information.
On or before October 31	Commission passback of budget to the PCAOB with proposed revisions.
On or before November 30	PCAOB adopts budget and submits it, along with the budget justification, to the Commission.
On or before December 23	Commission votes on the PCAOB budget.

(d) *Contents of budget.* (1) To facilitate Commission review and approval, each budget (including each preliminary budget and budget submitted for Commission approval) shall:

(i) Be accompanied by a budget justification.

(ii) Include information for the budget year, the current year, and the year immediately preceding the current year, regarding actual or projected spending by program area, receipts, debt, and employment levels.

(iii) Be consistent with, or explain any deviations from, the economic assumptions and budgetary guidance provided by the Commission.

(iv) Include statements of PCAOB programs, initiatives and strategies for the budget year.

(v) Earmark each amount for a specific budget category within a program area.

(vi) Include planned beginning–of–year and end–of–year headcounts for each program area.

(2) Each budget submitted for Commission approval shall be consistent with the preliminary budget and any revisions proposed by the Commission when the budget was passed from the Commission back to the PCAOB or explain any changes from the preliminary budget and/or such proposed revisions.

(3) In addition to amounts needed to fund disbursements during the budget year, a budget may reflect receipts in amounts needed to fund expected disbursements during a period not to exceed the first five months of the fiscal year immediately following the

日期	事件
3月15日或之前	公众公司会计监督委员会提供关于计划内容的文字说明,并对预算年度进行展望。
4月30日或之前	证券交易委员会向公众公司会计监督委员会提供经济情况假设和总体预算指引。
7月31日或之前	公众公司会计监督委员会将初步预算和预算论证提交证券交易委员会审查。
8~10月	证券交易委员会与公众公司会计监督委员会之间进行磋商;证券交易委员会工作人员对公众公司会计监督委员会的初步预算、预算论证和相关信息进行审查。
10月31日或之前	证券交易委员会将预算反馈给公众公司会计监督委员会并提供修改意见。
11月30日或之前	公众公司会计监督委员会通过预算,并将预算和预算论证提交证券交易委员会。
12月23日或之前	证券交易委员会对公众公司会计监督委员会的预算进行表决。

(d)预算内容。(1)为协助证券交易委员会开展审查和批准工作,每份预算(包括所有初步预算和提交证券交易委员会审批的预算)均应:

(i)附上预算论证。

(ii)包括该预算年度、本年度和本年度前一年度与计划领域的实际和预期支出、收款、债务和雇佣水平的信息。

(iii)符合证券交易委员会提供的经济假设和预算指引,如有任何出入,应提供解释。

(iv)包括公众公司会计监督委员会关于该预算年度的项目、计划和战略的声明。

(v)在计划领域内针对各具体预算类别分配专项预算。

(vi)说明每个计划领域年初和年底的预计人员编制。

(2)提交给证券交易委员会审批的每份预算均应与初步预算和证券交易委员会将预算反馈给公众公司会计监督委员会时提出的任何修改意见保持一致,如有出入,应提供解释。

(3)除了为预算年度的开支提供资金之外,预算还可以反映预算年度后一会计年度内不超过前5个月的期间的预期支出所需资金(营运资本准备),但是后者的拨付必须按照证券交易委员会批准的后一年度的预算或者补充预算的规定进行。

budget year (theworking capital reserve), provided such amounts shall be disbursed only as specified in the following year's budget or in a supplemental budget approved by the Commission.

(4) In approving the budget the Commission may not change the amounts earmarked for programs, program areas, or activities, or any other aspects of the budget; provided, that if the budget is conditionally rather than finally approved, then the Commission may transmit to the Board such proposed changes as are consistent with the preliminary budget and any revisions previously proposed by the Commission when it passed the budget back to the PCAOB. No proposed reduction or increase may be greater than that included in the preliminary budget and any revisions previously proposed by the Commission when it passed the budget back to the PCAOB.

(5) In the event the budget is conditionally approved by the Commission, the PCAOB shall have the opportunity to consider the changes proposed by the Commission and to vote again for final approval of the budget as amended. If this iterative process has not resolved differences between the Commission and the PCAOB by December 23, then the terms of the most recent conditional approval shall become final, and the budget shall be deemed finally approved.

(e) *Limitation on spending.* (1) The PCAOB shall not spend in a budget year more than the amount specified in the Commission-approved PCAOB budget for that year, regardless of the source of the funds, unless such expenses have been approved by the Commission through a supplemental budget request.

(2) Funds may be disbursed by the PCAOB only in accordance with the Commission approved budget,*provided however*, during the budget year the PCAOB may transfer amounts totaling not more than $1,000,000 into or out of each program area without prior Commission approval. Further, the PCAOB shall not:

(i) Apply its resources in a manner not fairly implied in the Commission-approved budget and budget justification, such as to create programs to perform functions that are not, or to perform functions in a way that is not, fairly implied from the Commission-approved budget and budget justification; or

(ii) Eliminate programs described in the Commission-approved budget and budget justification.

(3) In the event that the Commission has not approved a budget for a PCAOB fiscal year before the beginning of that fiscal year, the PCAOB may spend funds from the reserve and continue to incur obligations as if the PCAOB budget or supplemental budget most recently approved by the Commission were continuing in effect for that fiscal year.

(f) *Supplemental budget.* (1) The PCAOB may submit to the Commission a request for approval of a supplemental budget subsequent to Commission approval of the budget

(4)审批预算之时,证券交易委员会不得修改针对计划、计划领域或者活动或预算的任何其他方面的专项拨款。但是,如果证券交易委员会并未最终批准预算而仅仅是有条件地批准预算,证券交易委员会可以在不违反初步预算和证券交易委员会此前将预算反馈给公众公司会计监督委员会时提出的任何修改意见的前提下,将改动建议通知公众公司会计监督委员会。建议的增减额不得大于初步预算中包含的额度或者证券交易委员会此前将预算反馈给公众公司会计监督委员会时提出的任何修改意见中建议的额度。

(5)证券交易委员会有条件地批准预算的,应向公众公司会计监督委员会提供机会考虑证券交易委员会提出的改动意见,并再次就修正后的预算进行表决和批准。如果证券交易委员会和公众公司会计监督委员会之间的分歧未能在12月23日之前通过上述反复性程序获得解决,则最后一次有条件批准的预算将成为最终预算,而该预算也将视为已获得证券交易委员会最终批准。

(e)开支限制。(1)无论资金来源为何,公众公司会计监督委员会在某一预算年度的开支不得超过证券交易委员会批准的公众公司会计监督委员会在该年度的预算,但超额开支已经通过补充预算请求获得证券交易委员会批准的除外。

(2)公众公司会计监督委员会支出资金时必须遵守证券交易委员会批准的预算,但是,在预算年度内,公众公司会计监督委员会可以在未获证券交易委员会批准的情况下对每个计划领域转入或转出不超过100万美元的资金。此外,公众公司会计监督委员会不得:

(i)以证券交易委员会批准的预算和预算论证中未合理暗示的方式使用资源,如创建项目来实现证券交易委员会审批的预算和预算论证中未合理暗示的功能,或以证券交易委员会审批的预算和预算论证未合理暗示的方式来实现功能;或

(ii)取消证券交易委员会批准的预算和预算论证中所述的项目。

(3)如果证券交易委员会在某会计年度开始之前尚未批准公众公司会计监督委员会该会计年度的预算,则公众公司会计监督委员会可从准备金中支取资金并继续产生债务,此时,证券交易委员会最近一次批准的公众公司会计监督委员会预算或补充预算视同在新的会计年度继续有效。

(f)补充预算。(1)证券交易委员会批准某一预算年度的预算后,公众公司会计监督委员会可以提请证券交易委员会批准补充预算,以超出或违反本节第(e)(1)款和第

for the budget year in order to spend any amounts in excess of, or contrary to, the limitations described in paragraphs (e)(1) and (e)(2) of this section.

(2) To facilitate Commission review and approval, a supplemental budget shall include:

(i) Detailed information regarding the impact of the supplemental budget on each affected program area, including costs by cost category, project or activity;

(ii) A statement regarding how the supplemental budget facilitates the strategic and policy goals of the PCAOB;

(iii) Information indicating why the amount was not included in the budget for the current year, including a description of any subsequent and unforeseen events or circumstances necessitating the supplemental budget request;

(iv) Information indicating why the request should not or cannot be postponed until the next regular annual budget process; and

(v) The proposed source for the funds, including any offsets to be made elsewhere in the PCAOB's programs and activities.

(g) *Maintenance of records; reports.* (1) The PCAOB shall maintain, and make available to the Commission or Commission staff upon request, a strategic plan and records in reasonable detail that support each preliminary budget, budget, budget justification, supplemental budget and other report or communication in compliance with this section, including past and projected receipts, outlays, obligations, and employment levels.

(2) The PCAOB is required to maintain and, within 30 business days after the end of each fiscal quarter, to furnish to the Commission a report of its spending and staffing levels for the quarter just ended, comparing those levels to the levels in the Commission approved budget.

(h) *Publication of budget.* (1) Following submission of the PCAOB-approved budget to the Commission, such budget and budget justification, subject to any applicable exemption under the Freedom of Information Act, shall be made available to the public. Neither the Commission nor the PCAOB shall publish a preliminary budget, budget, budget justification, or any underlying materials in connection therewith, until such time as the budget is approved by the PCAOB and submitted to the Commission for its approval.

(2) Supplemental budgets shall be made public, following approval by the PCAOB and submission to the Commission, in the same manner as described in paragraph (h)(1) of this section.

(3) The Commission-approved budget shall be made available to the public at the time of such approval.

(e)(2)款规定的限制支出资金。

(2)为协助证券交易委员会的审批工作,补充预算应包括:

(i)关于补充预算对每个受影响计划领域的影响的详细信息,包括按照成本类别、项目或活动细分的成本;

(ii)关于补充预算将以何种方式促进公众公司会计监督委员会实现战略或政策目标的声明;

(iii)说明该资金没有纳入本年度预算的原因,包括描述预算批准后发生的任何不可预见的,使公众公司会计监督委员会必须作出补充预算申请的事件或情况;

(iv)说明申请不应或不能推迟至下次常规年度预算审批时处理的原因;及

(v)资金来源提议,包括通过任何冲抵公众公司会计监督委员会其他计划或活动的支出的做法获得资金来源。

(g)记录维护;报告。(1)公众公司会计监督委员会应维护一份合理详细的战略计划和记录,按照本节规定为所有初步预算、预算、预算论证、补充预算和其他报告或通信文件提供支持,包括过往和预期的收款、支出、义务和雇佣水平。上述战略计划和记录应按要求提供给证券交易委员会或证券交易委员会的工作人员。

(2)公众公司会计监督委员会必须就刚结束的季度维护一份支出和雇佣水平报告,与证券交易委员会批准的预算水平进行比较,并于每个财政季度结束后30个营业日之内,将该报告提供给证券交易委员会。

(h)预算公布。(1)在将公众公司会计监督委员会批准的预算提交给证券交易委员会后,该预算和预算论证应向公众公布,但已根据《信息自由法案》获得任何相关豁免的除外。在预算获得公众公司会计监督委员会批准并提交证券交易委员会批准之前,证券交易委员会和公众公司会计监督委员会均不得公布初步预算、预算、预算论证或任何相关材料。

(2)补充预算应按本节第(h)(1)款规定的方式,在获得公众公司会计监督委员会批准并提交证券交易委员会之后公布。

(3)证券交易委员会批准的预算应在批准之时向公众公布。

(i) *Waivers of rule provisions.* The Commission, in its discretion, may waive compliance with any provision of this §202.11.

[71 FR 42001, July 24, 2006. Redesignated at 75 FR 47451, Aug. 6, 2010]

(i)豁免规则的适用。证券交易委员会可依其自由裁量权豁免对本第202.11节任何规定的遵守义务。

[《联邦公报》第71卷第42001页,2006年7月24日;重新公布索引:《联邦公报》第75卷第47451页,2010年8月6日。]

PART 203—RULES RELATING TO INVESTIGATIONS

Authority: 15 U.S.C. 77s, 77sss, 78w, 80a-37, and 80b-11, unless otherwise noted.

Source: 29 FR 3620, Mar. 21, 1964, unless otherwise noted.

Subpart A—In General

§203.1 Application of the rules of this part.

The rules of this part apply only to investigations conducted by the Commission. They do not apply to adjudicative or rulemaking proceedings.

§203.2 Information obtained in investigations and examinations.

Information or documents obtained by the Commission in the course of any investigation or examination, unless made a matter of public record, shall be deemed non-public, but the Commission approves the practice whereby officials of the Divisions of Enforcement, Corporation Finance, Market Regulation and Investment Management and the Office of International Affairs at the level of Assistant Director or higher, and officials in Regional Offices at the level of Assistant Regional Director or higher, may engage in and may authorize members of the Commission's staff to engage in discussions with persons identified in §240.24c-1(b) of this chapter concerning information obtained in individual investigations or examinations, including formal investigations conducted pursuant to Commission order.

[58 FR 52419, Oct. 8, 1993, as amended at 59 FR 5945, Feb. 9, 1994; 73 FR 32227, June 5, 2008]

§203.3 Suspension and disbarment.

The provisions of §201.102(e) of this chapter (Rule 102(e) of the Commission's rules of practice) are hereby made specifically applicable to all investigations.

[29 FR 3620, Mar. 21, 1964, as amended at 60 FR 32823, June 23, 1995]

第203部分——调 查 规 则

法律依据:《美国法典》第十五编第77s节、第77sss节、第78w节、第80a-37节和第80b-11节,除非另有说明。

行政规则来源:《联邦公报》第29卷第3620页,1964年3月21日,除非另有说明。

第A子部分——通　　则

第203.1节　本部分规则的适用范围

本部分规则仅适用于证券交易委员会开展的调查,不适用于行政裁决程序或规则制定程序。

第203.2节　调查和询问中获取的信息

证券交易委员会在任何调查或询问过程中获取的信息或文件,除非已纳入公开记录,否则均应视为非公开信息或文件,但是根据证券交易委员会批准的惯例,执法部、公司融资部、市场监管部和投资管理部和国际事务办公室的副主任或以上级别官员,以及地区办公室副地区主任或以上级别官员可以参与和授权证券交易委员会工作人员与本章第240.24c-1(b)节指明之人共同讨论具体调查或询问(包括依照证券交易委员会命令进行的正式调查)中获取的信息。

[《联邦公报》第58卷第52419页,1993年10月8日,修正索引:《联邦公报》第59卷第5945页,1994年2月9日;《联邦公报》第73卷第32227页,2008年6月5日。]

第203.3节　暂停和永久取消资格

兹特别规定,本章第201.102(e)节规定[《证券交易委员会工作规则》的《102(e)规则》]适用于所有调查。

[《联邦公报》第29卷第3620页,1964年3月21日,修正索引:《联邦公报》第60卷第32823页,1995年6月23日。]

Subpart B—Formal Investigative Proceedings

§203.4 Applicability of §§203.4 through 203.8.

(a) Sections 203.4 through 203.8 shall be applicable to a witness who is sworn in a proceeding pursuant to a Commission order for investigation or examination, such proceeding being hereinafter referred to as a *formal investigative proceeding*.

(b) Formal investigative proceedings may be held before the Commission, before one or more of its members, or before any officer designated by it for the purpose of taking testimony of witnesses and received other evidence. The term *officer conducting the investigation* shall mean any of the foregoing.

§203.5 Non–public formal investigative proceedings.

Unless otherwise ordered by the Commission, all formal investigative proceedings shall be non–public.

§203.6 Transcripts.

Transcripts, if any, of formal investigative proceedings shall be recorded solely by the official reporter, or by any other person or means designated by the officer conducting the investigation. A person who has submitted documentary evidence or testimony in a formal investigative proceeding shall be entitled, upon written request, to procure a copy of his documentary evidence or a transcript of his testimony on payment of the appropriate fees: *Provided, however,* That in a nonpublic formal investigative proceeding the Commission may for good cause deny such request. In any event, any witness, upon proper identification, shall have the right to inspect the official transcript of the witness' own testimony.

(15 U.S.C. 78d–1)

[37 FR 25166, Nov. 28, 1972]

§203.7 Rights of witnesses.

(a) Any person who is compelled or requested to furnish documentary evidence or testimony at a formal investigative proceeding shall, upon request, be shown the Commission's order of investigation. Copies of formal orders of investigation shall not be furnished, for their retention, to such persons requesting the same except with the express approval of officials in the Regional Offices at the level of Assistant Regional Director or higher, or officials in the Division or Divisions conducting or supervising the investigation at the level of Assistant Director or higher. Such approval shall not be given unless the person granting such approval, in his or her discretion, is satisfied that there exist reasons consistent both with the protection of privacy of persons involved in the investigation and with the unimpeded conduct of the investigation.

第B子部分——正式调查程序

第203.4节　第203.4~203.8节的适用范围

(a)第203.4~203.8节适用于在依照证券交易委员会命令开展的调查或询问程序(下称正式调查程序)中宣誓作证的证人。

(b)正式调查程序可由证券交易委员会、证券交易委员会的一名或多名委员或被指定提取证人证言和接收其他证据的任何官员主持。"调查官员"即指上述任何一者。

第203.5节　非公开正式调查程序

除非证券交易委员会另有命令,所有正式调查程序应非公开进行。

第203.6节　笔录

正式调查程序的笔录(如有)应完全由官方笔录材料记录人,或通过调查官员指定的任何其他个人或手段进行记录。在正式调查程序中提交书证或证言之人有权在提出书面请求后,支付适当费用购买其书证或证言笔录的副本;但是,对于非公开正式调查程序,证券交易委员会存在充分理由的,可拒绝购买书证或证言笔录副本的请求。在任何情况下,任何证人经适当确认身份后,均有权查阅其本人证言的官方笔录。

(《美国法典》第十五编第78d-1节。)

[《联邦公报》第37卷第25166页,1972年11月28日。]

第203.7节　证人的权利

(a)在正式调查程序中强制任何主体提供或要求任何主体提供书证或证言之时,应按该等主体的要求向其出示证券交易委员会的调查令。除非已获得地区办公室副地区主任或以上级别的官员,或负责开展调查或监督调查的部门副主任或以上级别的官员明确批准,正式调查令不得交由请求出示调查令的个人保留。除非批准人依其自由裁量权认定批准该等请求不会侵犯调查所涉主体的隐私保护,且不会阻碍调查的顺利进行,否则不得批准该等请求。

(b) Any person compelled to appear, or who appears by request or permission of the Commission, in person at a formal investigative proceeding may be accompanied, represented and advised by counsel, as defined in §201.101(a) of this chapter (Rule 101(a) of the Commission's rules of practice): *Provided,* however, That all witnesses shall be sequestered, and unless permitted in the discretion of the officer conducting the investigation no witness or the counsel accompanying any such witness shall be permitted to be present during the examination of any other witness called in such proceeding.

(c) The right to be accompanied, represented and advised by counsel shall mean the right of a person testifying to have an attorney present with him during any formal investigative proceeding and to have this attorney (1) advise such person before, during and after the conclusion of such examination, (2) question such person briefly at the conclusion of the examination to clarify any of the answers such person has given, and (3) make summary notes during such examination solely for the use of such person.

(d) Unless otherwise ordered by the Commission, in any public formal investigative proceeding, if the record shall contain implications of wrongdoing by any person, such person shall have the right to appear on the record; and in addition to the rights afforded other witnesses hereby, he shall have a reasonable opportunity of cross-examination and production of rebuttal testimony or documentary evidence. *Reasonable* shall mean permitting persons as full an opportunity to assert their position as may be granted consistent with administrative efficiency and with avoidance of undue delay. The determination of reasonableness in each instance shall be made in the discretion of the officer conducting the investigation.

(e) The officer conducting the investigation may report to the Commission any instances where any witness or counsel has been guilty of dilatory, obstructionist or contumacious conduct during the course of an investigation or any other instance of violation of these rules. The Commission will thereupon take such further action as the circumstances may warrant, including suspension or disbarment of counsel from further appearance or practice before it, in accordance with §201.102(e) of this chapter (Rule 102(e) of the Commission's rules of practice), or exclusion from further participation in the particular investigation.

[29 FR 3620, Mar. 21, 1964, as amended at 52 FR 12148, Apr. 15, 1987; 59 FR 5945, Feb. 9, 1994; 60 FR 32823, June 23, 1995; 73 FR 32227, June 5, 2008]

§203.8 Service of subpoenas.

Service of subpoenas issued in formal investigative proceedings shall be effected in the manner prescribed by Rule 232 (c) of the Commission's Rules of Practice, §201.232(c) of this chapter.

[29 FR 3620, Mar. 21, 1964, as amended at 60 FR 32823, June 23, 1995]

(b)被证券交易委员会强制、要求或许可出席正式调查程序的任何主体,可以由律师[定义见本章第201.101(a)节——《证券交易委员会工作规则》的《101(a)规则》]陪同、代理和提供法律意见;但是,所有证人均应相互隔离,且除非调查官员依其自由裁量权予以许可,否则在对程序中传唤的其他证人进行询问时,不得准许任何证人或陪同证人的律师在场。

(c)由律师陪同、代理或提供法律意见的权利指证人有权在律师的陪同下出席任何正式调查程序,且该律师有权:(1)在询问之前、之中或之后为证人提供法律意见,(2)在询问结束时简要地向证人发问,以澄清证人作出的任何回答,以及(3)在询问过程中作简要笔记,专门供证人使用。

(d)除非证券交易委员会另有命令,否则在任何公开正式调查程序中,如果记录内容暗示任何人从事了不当行为,该人有权发表意见,并将其意见纳入记录之中;且除本部分规定向其他证人授予的权利外,该人应获得合理机会进行交叉询问并有权提供反驳证言或书证。"合理"系指在符合行政效率原则和避免不当拖延的前提下,为相关主体提供主张其立场的充分机会。在任何情况下,对合理性的认定均应由调查官员依其自由裁量权自行作出。

(e)任何证人或律师在调查过程中犯有拖延、妨碍程序开展或不服从行为或出现任何其他违反本部分规则的情况,调查官员可以报告证券交易委员会。证券交易委员会将在收到报告后依据具体情形采取进一步行动,包括依据本章第201.102(e)节[《证券交易委员会工作规则》的《102(e)规则》]暂停律师出席证券交易委员会程序或办理业务的资格或予以永久取消资格,或禁止其继续参与具体调查。

[《联邦公报》第29卷第3620页,1964年3月21日,修正索引:《联邦公报》第52卷第12148页,1987年4月15日;《联邦公报》第59卷第5945页,1994年2月9日;《联邦公报》第60卷第32823页,1995年6月23日;《联邦公报》第73卷第32227页,2008年6月5日。]

第203.8节　传票送达

正式调查程序发出的传票应按《证券交易委员会工作规则》的《232(c)规则》和本章第201.232(c)节规定的方式送达。

[《联邦公报》第29卷第3620页,1964年3月21日,修正索引:《联邦公报》第60卷第32823页,1995年6月23日。]

PART 204—RULES RELATING TO DEBT COLLECTION

Subpart A—Administrative Offset

Authority: 31 U.S.C. 3716, 31 CFR 901.3.

Source: 58 FR 64370, Dec. 7, 1993, unless otherwise noted.

§204.1 Applicability and scope.

(a) The procedures authorized for administrative offset are contained in Section 10 of the Debt Collection Act (codified at 31 U.S.C. 3716). The Act requires that notice procedures be observed by the agency. The debtor is also afforded an opportunity to inspect and copy government records pertaining to the claim, enter into an agreement for repayment, and to a review of the claim (if requested). Like salary offset, agencies may cooperate with one another in order to effectuate recovery of the claim.

(b) The provisions of this subpart apply to the collection of debts owed to the United States arising from transactions with the Securities and Exchange Commission (Commission). These regulations are consistent with the Debt Collection Act and the Federal Claims Collection Standards on administrative offset issued jointly by the Department of Justice and the Department of the Treasury (31 CFR 901.3).

[58 FR 64370, Dec. 7, 1993, as amended at 66 FR 54130, Oct. 26, 2001]

§204.2 Definitions.

(a) *Administrative offset* as defined in 31 U.S.C. 3701(a)(1) means withholding funds payable by the United States (including funds payable by the United States on behalf of a State government) to, or held by the United States for, a person to satisfy a claim.

(b) *Person* includes a natural person or persons, profit or nonprofit corporation,

第204部分——债务催收规则

第A子部分——行 政 抵 消

法律依据:《美国法典》第三十一编第3716节,《联邦规章汇编》第三十一编第901.3节。

行政规则来源:《联邦公报》第58卷第64370页,1993年12月7日,除非另有说明。

第204.1节 适用性和范围

(a)授权进行行政抵消的程序规定于《债务催收法》第10条(编纂于《美国法典》第三十一编第3716节)。该法要求政府机构遵守通知程序,并给予债务人查阅并复制与债权相关的政府记录、签订还款协议和提请审查债权的机会。与工资抵消一样,政府机构可以为完成债权催收之目的与其他政府机构合作。

(b)本子部分规定适用于债务人因与证券交易委员会办理业务而欠负联邦政府的债务之催收,与司法部和财政部联合签发的《债务催收法》和《联邦债权催收标准》中关于行政抵消的规定一致(《联邦规章汇编》第三十一编第901.3节)。

[《联邦公报》第58卷第64370页,1993年12月7日,修正索引:《联邦公报》第66卷第54130页,2001年10月26日。]

第204.2节 定义

(a)“行政抵消”按《美国法典》第三十一编第3701(a)(1)节的定义,系指为收回债权之目的,扣留联邦政府(包括联邦政府代表州政府)应向债务人支付的款项,或联邦政府代表债务人持有的款项。

(b)“人或主体”包括一个或多个自然人、营利性或非营利性公司、合伙、协会、信

partnership, association, trust, estate, consortium, or other entity which is capable of owing a debt to the United States Government except that agencies of the United States, or of any State or local government shall be excluded.

[58 FR 64370, Dec. 7, 1993, as amended at 66 FR 54130, Oct. 26, 2001]

§204.3 General.

(a) The Chairperson (or designee) may initiate administrative offset with regard to debts owed by a person to another agency of the United States Government, upon receipt of a request from the head of another agency or his or her designee, and a certification that the debt exists and that the person has been afforded the necessary due process rights.

(b) The Chairperson (or designee) may notify the Department of the Treasury of delinquent debts for purposes of administrative offset, and may request another agency which holds funds payable to a Commission debtor to offset that debt against the funds held; the Commission will provide certification that:

(1) The debt is past due and legally enforceable; and

(2) The person has been afforded the necessary due process rights.

(c) No collection by administrative offset shall be made on any debt that has been outstanding for more than 10 years unless facts material to the Government's right to collect the debt were not known, and reasonably could not have been known, by the official or officials responsible for discovering the debt. This limitation does not apply to debts reduced to judgment.

(d) Administrative offset under this subpart may not be initiated against:

(1) A debt in which administrative offset of the type of debt involved is explicitly provided for or prohibited by another statute;

(2) Debts owed by other agencies of the United States or by any State or local Government; or

(3) Debts arising under the Internal Revenue Code of 1954; the Social Security Act; or the tariff laws of the United States.

(e) The procedures for administrative offset in this subpart do not apply to the offset of Federal salaries under 5 U.S.C. 5514 or Federal tax refunds under 31 U.S.C. 3720A and 31 CFR 285.2.

[58 FR 64370, Dec. 7, 1993, as amended at 66 FR 54130, Oct. 26, 2001]

§204.4 Demand for payment—notice.

(a) Before offset is made, a written notice will be sent to the debtor. This notice will include:

托、财产、联合体或有能力欠联邦政府债务的其他实体，但联邦政府机构或任何州或地方政府除外。

［《联邦公报》第58卷第64370页，1993年12月7日，修正索引：《联邦公报》第66卷第54130页，2001年10月26日。］

第204.3节　一般规定

（a）证券交易委员会主席（或其指定人员）在收到其他联邦政府机关负责人或其指定人员的请求和一份关于债务存在并且已经给予相关主体必要的正当程序权的证明后，可以就该主体欠负该联邦政府机构的债务启动行政抵消。

（b）证券交易委员会主席（或其指定人员）可以为行政抵消之目的，将拖欠债务通知财政部，并请求其他应向证券交易委员会债务人支付款项的政府机构通过该等应付款项抵消债务人的债务；证券交易委员会应提供关于如下事项的证明：

（1）债务已经过期且可以依法强制执行；且

（2）已经给予该人必要的正当程序权。

（c）债龄已达10年以上的债务，不得通过行政抵消的方式催收，但负责发现债务的一名或多名官员不知道且无法合理获知确立政府催收债务权所需的基本事实的除外。该限制不适用于已经判决的债务。

（d）不得针对如下债务启动本子部分中的行政抵消：

（1）行政抵消所涉债务类型为其他制定法明文规定或禁止的债务；

（2）其他联邦政府机构或任何州或地方政府欠负的债务；或

（3）《1954年国内税收法典》、《社会保障法》或美国关税法下产生的债务。

（e）本子部分规定的行政抵消程序不适用于《美国法典》第五编第5514节或《美国法典》第三十一编第3720A节和《联邦规章汇编》第三十一编第285.2节中的联邦工资抵消。

［《联邦公报》第58卷第64370页，1993年12月7日，修正索引：《联邦公报》第66卷第54130页，2001年10月26日。］

第204.4节　款项催付——通知

（a）进行抵消前，应向债务人发送一份书面通知。通知中应包括如下信息：

(1) The type and amount of the debt;

(2) The date when payment is due (not less than thirty days from the date of mailing or hand delivery of the notice);

(3) The agency's intention to collect the debt by administrative offset, including asking the assistance of other Federal agencies to help in the offset whenever possible, if the debtor has not made payment by the payment due date or has not made an arrangement for payment by the payment due date;

(4) The right of the debtor to inspect and copy the Commission's records related to the claim;

(5) The right of the debtor to request a review of the determination of indebtedness and, in the circumstances described in §204.7, to request an oral hearing from the Commission's designee; and

(6) The right of the debtor to enter into a written agreement with the agency to repay the debt in some other way.

(b) Claims for payment of travel advances and employee training expenses require notification prior to administrative offset as described in this section. Because no oral hearing is required, notice of the right to a hearing need not be included in the notification.

[58 FR 64370, Dec. 7, 1993, as amended at 66 FR 54130, Oct. 26, 2001]

§204.5 Debtor's failure to respond.

If the debtor fails to respond to the notice described in §204.4(a) by the proposed effective date specified in the notice, the Commission may take further action under this section or under the Federal Claims Collection Standards (31 CFR 901.3). The commission may collect by administrative offset if the debtor:

(a) Has not made payment by the payment due date;

(b) Has not requested a review of the claim within the agency as set out in §204.6; or

(c) Has not made an arrangement for payment by the payment due date.

[58 FR 64370, Dec. 7, 1993, as amended at 66 FR 54130, Oct. 26, 2001]

§204.6 Agency review.

(a) To the extent that a debt owed has not been established by judicial or administrative order, a debtor may request a hearing concerning the existence or amount of the debt or the terms of repayment. With respect to debts established by a judicial or administrative order, a debtor may request a hearing concerning the payment or other discharge of the debt. A request to review a disputed debt must be submitted to the Commission official who provided notification within 30 calendar days of the receipt of the

(1)债务的类型和金额;

(2)款项的到期应付日(不早于该通知寄送或当面递交后30日);

(3)如果债务人未在付款到期日前付款或作出付款安排,证券交易委员会将试图通过行政抵消催收债务,包括在可能之时请求其他联邦机构为行政抵消提供协助;

(4)债务人有权查阅和复制证券交易委员会与债权相关的记录;

(5)债务人有权请求对债务认定进行审查,且在第204.7节规定的情形下,有权请求证券交易委员会指定人员举行口头听证;及

(6)债务人有权与政府机构签订书面协议,以其他方式偿还债务。

(b)与预支差旅费和雇员培训费用相关的债权需要在本节规定的行政抵消之前发出通知。由于该等债权不必举行口头听证,通知中不必向债务人告知听证权。

[《联邦公报》第58卷第64370页,1993年12月7日,修正索引:《联邦公报》第66卷第54130页,2001年10月26日。]

第204.5节　债务人未进行答复的情形

债务人未能在第204.4(a)节规定的通知中具体指定的生效日前作出答复的,证券交易委员会可以依据本节或《联邦债权催收法》(《联邦规章汇编》第三十一编第901.3节)采取进一步行动。在下述情形下,证券交易委员会可以通过行政抵消的方式催收债务:

(a)债务人未在到期日前支付到期应付款项;

(b)债务人未按照第204.6节规定提请证券交易委员会对债权进行审查;或

(c)债务人未在到期日前作出付款安排。

[《联邦公报》第58卷第64370页,1993年12月7日,修正索引:《联邦公报》第66卷第54130页,2001年10月26日。]

第204.6节　证券交易委员会的审查

(a)如债务人所欠债务尚未通过司法或行政命令予以确认,债务人可以请求就债务的存在、金额或还款条件举行听证。就已通过司法或行政命令确认的债务而言,债务人可以请求就还款或其他债务清偿方式举行听证。针对争议债务提出的审查请求必须在收到第204.4(c)节规定的书面通知后30个日历日内呈报给发出通知的证券交易委员会官员。

written notice described in §204.4(c).

(b) The Commission will provide a copy of the record to the debtor and advise him/her to furnish available evidence to support his or her position. Upon receipt of the evidence, the written record of indebtedness will be reviewed and the debtor will be informed of the results of that review.

(c) Pending the resolution of a dispute by the debtor, transactions in any of the debtor's accounts maintained by the Commission may be temporarily suspended. Depending on the type of transaction, the suspension could preclude its payment, removal, or transfer, as well as prevent the payment of interest or discount due thereon. Should the dispute be resolved in the debtor's favor, the suspension will be immediately lifted.

(d) During the review period, interest, penalties, and administrative costs will continue to accrue.

[58 FR 64370, Dec. 7, 1993, as amended at 66 FR 54131, Oct. 26, 2001]

§204.7 Hearing.

(a) A debtor will be provided a reasonable opportunity for an oral hearing by the Commission's designee when:

(1)(i) By statute, consideration must be given to a request to waive the indebtedness;

(ii) The debtor requests waiver of the indebtedness; and

(iii) The waiver determination rests on an issue of credibility or veracity; or

(2) The debtor requests reconsideration and the Commission's designee determines that the question of indebtedness cannot be resolved by reviewing the documentary evidence.

(b) In cases where an oral hearing is provided to the debtor, the Commission's designee will conduct the hearing, and provide the debtor with a written decision 30 days after the hearing.

[58 FR 64370, Dec. 7, 1993, as amended at 66 FR 54131, Oct. 26, 2001]

§204.8 Written agreement for repayment.

If the debtor requests a repayment agreement in place of offset, the Commission has discretion to determine whether to accept a repayment agreement in place of offset. If the debt is delinquent and the debtor has not disputed its existence or amount, the Commission will not accept a repayment agreement in place of offset unless the debtor is able to establish that offset would cause undue financial hardship or be unjust. No repayment arrangement will be considered unless the debtor submits a financial statement, executed under penalty of perjury, reflecting the debtor's assets, liabilities, income, and expenses. The financial statement must be submitted within ten business days of the

(b)证券交易委员会将向债务人提供一份记录,并建议债务人提供可获得的证据以支持其立场。在收到证据后,证券交易委员会应对书面债务记录进行审查,并将审查结果告知债务人。

(c)在债务人所提起争议的待决期间,证券交易委员会维持的任何债务人账户均可能被临时暂停交易。基于交易类型的不同,暂停可能影响其支付、注销或转账,还可能阻止账户应付利息或贴现的支付。如果证券交易委员会对争议作出有利于债务人的裁决,暂停应立即取消。

(d)在审查期间,利息、罚款和行政费用应继续计算。

[《联邦公报》第58卷第64370页,1993年12月7日,修正索引:《联邦公报》第66卷第54131页,2001年10月26日。]

第204.7节　听证

(a)在下述情况下,证券交易委员会应向债务人提供口头听证的合理机会:

(1)(i)根据制定法,必须对债务免除请求进行审议;

(ii)债务人请求免除债务;且

(iii)是否作出免除债务的决定取决于债务人的信用或诚信问题;或

(2)债务人要求复审,且证券交易委员会的指定人员判定债务问题不能通过审查书证的方式作出决定。

(b)在向债务人提供口头听证的情况下,证券交易委员会的指定人员应主持听证,并在听证后30日内向债务人提供一份书面决定。

[《联邦公报》第58卷第64370页,1993年12月7日,修正索引:《联邦公报》第66卷第54131页,2001年10月26日。]

第204.8节　书面还款协议

债务人请求签订还款协议替代行政抵消的,证券交易委员会可依其自由裁量权决定是否接受债务人的提议。如果债务已过期且债务人未对债务的存在或金额提出异议,证券交易委员会不会接受以还款协议替代行政抵消的提议,但债务人可以证明抵消将给其造成过度的经济困难或证明抵消不公正的除外。除非债务人提交一份财务报表,说明债务人的资产、负债、收益和支出,并签字表明其确知作伪证会招致处罚,否则证券交易委员会不会考虑任何还款安排。财务报表必须于证券交易委员会提出要求后10个营业日内提交。双方签订分期还款协议的,证券交易委员会可以要求债务人提供判决无异议说明或赔偿保证书,并提供担保。无论本节如何规定,对债权的

Commission's request for the statement. At the Commission's option, a confess-judgment note or bond of indemnity with surety may be required for installment agreements. Notwithstanding the provisions of this section, any reduction or compromise of a claim will be governed by the Debt Collection Act, 31 U.S.C. 3711–3720E, and the Federal Claims Collection Standards, 31 CFR 900.1–904.4.

[58 FR 64370, Dec. 7, 1993, as amended at 66 FR 54131, Oct. 26, 2001]

§204.9 Administrative offset procedures.

(a) If the debtor does not exercise the right to request a review within the time specified in §204.4, or if as a result of the review, it is determined that the debt is due and no written agreement is executed, then administrative offset shall be ordered in accordance with this subpart without further notice.

(b) *Travel advance.* The Commission will deduct outstanding advances provided to Commission travelers from other amounts owed the traveler by the agency whenever possible and practicable. Monies owed by an employee for outstanding travel advances that cannot be deducted from other travel amounts due that employee will be collected through salary offset as described in subpart B of this part.

(c) *Requests for offset to the Department of the Treasury or other Federal agencies.* The Chairperson (or his or her designee) may notify the Department of the Treasury of delinquent debts for purposes of administrative offset, and may request that a debt owed to the Commission be administratively offset against funds due and payable to a debtor by another Federal agency. In requesting administrative offset, the Commission, as creditor, will certify in writing to the Federal agency holding funds of the debtor that:

(1) The debtor owes the past due and legally enforceable debt; and

(2) The debtor has been afforded the necessary due process rights.

(d) *Requests for offset from other Federal agencies.* Any Federal agency may request that funds due and payable to its debtor by the Commission be administratively offset in order to collect a debt owed to such Federal agency by the debtor. The Commission shall initiate the requested offset only upon:

(1) Receipt of written certification from the crecitor agency that:

(i) The debtor owes the past due and legally enforceable debt; and

(ii) The debtor has been afforded the necessary due process rights.

(2) A determination by the Commission that collection by offset against funds payable by the Commission would be in the best interest of the United States as determined by the facts and circumstances of the particular case, and that such offset would not otherwise be contrary to law.

[58 FR 64370, Dec. 7, 1993, as amended at 66 FR 54131, Oct. 26, 2001]

任何减免或和解均应受《债务催收法》(《美国法典》第三十一编第3711-3720E节)以及《联邦行政抵消债权催收标准》(《联邦规章汇编》第三十一编第900.1-904.4节)管辖。

[《联邦公报》第58卷第64370页,1993年12月7日,修正索引:《联邦公报》第66卷第54131页,2001年10月26日。]

第204.9节　行政抵消程序

(a)如果债务人未在第204.4节具体规定的时间内请求对债务进行审查,或如果根据审查结果,债务被认定已经到期且双方未签订书面协议,证券交易委员会应根据本子部分规定签发行政抵消令,而不必另行发出通知。

(b)预支差旅费。只要有可能并且实际可行,证券交易委员会应从其欠负出差人的其他金额中,扣除向证券交易委员会出差人提供的预付款的余额。预支差旅费余额无法从其他应向雇员支付的差旅费款项中扣除的,应按照本部分第B子部分规定通过工资抵消的方式催收。

(c)请求财政部或其他联邦政府机构抵消债务。证券交易委员会主席(或其指定人员)可以为行政抵消之目的,将过期债务通知财政部,并可以请求通过其他联邦政府部门向债务人欠负的到期应付款项抵消债务人欠负证券交易委员会的债务。在请求行政抵消时,证券交易委员会作为债权人,应向扣留债务人款项的联邦政府机构作出关于如下事项的书面保证:

(1)债务人所欠债务过期且可以依法强制执行;且

(2)已经给予债务人必要的正当程序权。

(d)其他联邦政府机构请求证券交易委员会抵消债务。任何联邦政府机构均可以请求证券交易委员会,通过债务人欠负证券交易委员会的到期应付款项对债务人欠负该等联邦政府机构的债务进行行政抵消,以催收该等债务。证券交易委员会启动其他联邦政府部门请求的抵消的,必须满足以下条件:

(1)证券交易委员会已收到该等其他政府机构债权人关于如下事项的书面证明:

(i)债务人所欠债务过期且可以依法强制执行;且

(ii)已经给予债务人必要的正当程序权。

(2)证券交易委员会根据具体事实和情形判定,通过债务人欠负证券交易委员会的到期应付款项对债务进行抵消和催收符合联邦的最佳利益,且该等抵消不违反法律。

[《联邦公报》第58卷第64370页,1993年12月7日,修正索引:《联邦公报》第66卷第

§204.10 [Reserved]

§204.11 Jeopardy procedure.

The Commission may effect an administrative offset against a payment to be made to the debtor prior to the completion of the procedures required by §204.4(a) if failure to take the offset would substantially jeopardize the Commission's ability to collect the debt, and the time available before the payment is to be made does not reasonably permit the completion of those procedures. Such prior offset shall be promptly followed by the completion of those procedures. Amounts recovered by offset but later found not to be owed to the Commission shall be promptly refunded. This section applies only to administrative offset pursuant to 31 CFR 901.3(c), and does not apply when debts are referred to the Department of the Treasury for mandatory centralized administrative offset under 31 CFR 901.3(b)(1).

[58 FR 64370, Dec. 7, 1993, as amended at 66 FR 54131, Oct. 26, 2001]

§§204.12–204.29 [Reserved]

Subpart B—Salary Offset

Authority: 5 U.S.C. 5514, 5 CFR 550.1104.

Source: 58 FR 38520, July 19, 1993, unless otherwise noted.

§204.30 Purpose and scope.

(a) This regulation provides procedures for the collection by administrative offset against a federal employee's current pay account without his/her consent under 5 U.S.C. 5514 to satisfy certain debts owed to the Commission. This regulation does not apply when the employee consents to recovery from his/her current pay account.

(b) This regulation does not preclude an employee from requesting a waiver or questioning the amount or validity of a debt by submitting a claim to the General Accounting Office in accordance with procedures prescribed by the General Accounting Office.

(c) This Salary Offset plan is for internal use and Government-wide claims collections. 5 CFR 550.1104 (a). This regulation implements 5 U.S.C. 5514; 5 CFR part 550, subpart K.

§204.31 Excluded debts or claims.

This regulation does not apply to:

54131页,2001年10月26日。]

第204.10节 [保留]

第204.11节 紧急程序

如果不进行抵消将对证券交易委员会催收债务的能力造成重大损害,且付款前所剩余的时间无法合理完成第204.4(a)节规定的程序,证券交易委员会可以在完成该等程序之前,提前对应向债务人支付的款项实施行政抵消。证券交易委员会进行提前抵消的,应在抵消后及时补充完成该等程序。如果发现通过抵消催收的债务金额并非欠负证券交易委员会的债务,应及时归还。本节仅适用于依照《联邦规章汇编》第三十一编第901.3(c)节进行的行政抵消,不适用于依照《联邦规章汇编》第三十一编第901.3(b)(1)节移交财政部进行强制集中行政抵消的债务。

[《联邦公报》第58卷第64370页,1993年12月7日,修正索引:《联邦公报》第66卷第54131页,2001年10月26日。]

第204.12~204.29节 [保留]

第B子部分——工 资 抵 消

法律依据:《美国法典》第五编第5514节,《联邦规章汇编》第五编第550.1104节。

行政规则来源:《联邦公报》第58卷第38520页,1993年7月19日,除非另有说明。

第204.30节 目的和范围

(a)本规章规定了在未取得债务人在《美国法典》第五编第5514节下作出的同意,通过行政抵消从联邦雇员的当前工资账户中扣款以催收其欠负证券交易委员会的特定债务的程序。债务人同意通过其当前工资账户偿还债务的,不适用本规章。

(b)本规章不影响雇员根据美国审计总署规定的程序向美国审计总署提出主张,请求免除债务或对债务金额或有效期提出异议的权利。

(c)本工资抵消规章仅限于证券交易委员会内部使用,并仅适用于政府范围内的债权催收。《联邦规章汇编》第五编第550.1104(a)节。本规章属于《美国法典》第五编第5514节、《联邦规章汇编》第五编第550部分第K子部分的实施规章。

第204.31节 不适用本部分规定的债务或债权

本规章不适用于:

(a) Debts or claims arising under the Internal Revenue Code of 1954 as amended (26 U.S.C. 1), or the tariff laws of the United States.

(b) Any case where collection of a debt by salary offset is explicitly provided for or prohibited by another statute, such as travel advances in 5 U.S.C. 5705 and employee training expenses in 5 U.S.C. 4108.

[58 FR 38520, July 19, 1993, as amended at 66 FR 54131, Oct. 26, 2001]

§204.32 Definitions.

The following definitions apply to this regulation:

Chairman means the Chairman of the Securities and Exchange Commission.

Commission means the Securities and Exchange Commission.

Creditor agency means the agency to which the debt is owed.

Debt means an amount owed to the United States from sources which include but are not necessarily limited to, erroneous payments made to employees such as overpayment of benefits, salary or other allowances; loans when insured or guaranteed by the United States; and other amounts due the United States from fees, leases, rents, royalties, services, sales of real or personal property, overpayment, penalties, damages, interest, fines and forfeitures (except those arising under the Uniform Code of Military Justice) and all other similar sources.

Disposable pay means the amount that remains from an employee's federal pay after required deductions for federal, state and local income taxes; Social Security taxes, including Medicare taxes; federal retirement programs; premiums for life and health insurance benefits; and such other deductions that are required by law to be withheld. (See 5 CFR 581.105(b) through (f) for items required by law to be withheld, and therefore excluded from disposable pay for the purposes of this regulation.)

Employee means a current employee of the Securities and Exchange Commission, or other agency, including an active duty member or reservist in the U.S. Armed Forces or a former employee (or former active duty member or Reservist in the Armed Forces) with a current pay account.

FCCS means the Federal Claims Collection Standards jointly published by the Justice Department and the Department of the Treasury at 31 CFR parts 900–904.

Hearing official means an individual responsible for conducting any hearing with respect to the existence or amount of a debt claimed, and who renders a decision on the basis of such hearing. A hearing official may not be under the Chairman's supervision or control, except that nothing in this regulation shall be construed to prohibit the appointment of an administrative law judge.

Pay means basic pay, special pay, incentive pay, retired pay, retainer pay, or in the

(a)《1954年国内税收法典》(修正版)(《美国法典》第二十六编第1节)下或美国关税法下产生的债务或债权。

(b)任何其他制定法已就通过工资抵消催收债务作出明文规定或禁止的情况,例如《美国法典》第五编第5705节规定的预支差旅费和《美国法典》第五编第4108节规定的雇员培训费用。

[《联邦公报》第58卷第38520页,1993年7月19日,修正索引:《联邦公报》第66卷第54131页,2001年10月26日。]

第204.32节　定义

就本规章而言,应适用如下定义:

"主席"系指证券交易委员会主席。

"证券交易委员会"系指美国证券交易委员会。

"政府机构债权人"系指作为债务债权人的政府机构。

"债务"系指欠负联邦政府的款项,款项来源包括但不限于:由于错误向雇员超额支付的福利、工资或其他津贴;联邦政府提供保险或担保的贷款;以及因费用、租约、租金、使用费、服务、不动产或个人财产出售、超额付款、罚款、损害赔偿金、利息、罚金和没收款项(《军事审判统一法典》下引起的除外)和所有其他类似来源而应向联邦政府支付的款项。

"可支配工资"系指从雇员联邦工资中扣除如下各项之后的余额:所有联邦、州和地方所得税、社会保险税(包括医疗保险税)、联邦退休金计划缴款、人寿保险费和健康保险福利以及法律要求预扣的其他扣款额[依法应予以预扣,因此不包括在本规章规定的可支配工资范围内的项目,请参见《联邦规章汇编》第五编第581.105(b)—581.105(f)节]。

"雇员"系指证券交易委员会或其他政府机构的具有当前工资账户的现任雇员或前任雇员,包括美国武装部队的现役或预备役成员(或美国武装部队前现役或预备役成员)。

"《联邦债权催收标准》"系指司法部和财政部在《联邦规章汇编》第三十一编第900~904部分中联合颁布的《联邦债权催收标准》。

"听证官"系指负责就所主张债务的存在或金额开展任何听证并基于该等听证作出决定的个人。听证官可以不在主席的监督或控制下行事,但本规章的任何规定不得解释为禁止任命行政法官担任听证官。

"工资"系指基本工资、特殊工资、激励工资、退休工资、预聘金;对于无权获得基

case of an individual not entitled to basic pay, other authorized pay.

Program official means, for the purpose of implementing this offset regulation, the Comptroller or designee.

Salary offset means an administrative offset to collect a debt under 5 U.S.C. 5514 by deduction(s), at one or more officially established pay intervals, from the current pay account of an employee, without his or her consent.

Waiver means the cancellation, remission, forgiveness, or non-recovery of a debt allegedly owed by an employee to an agency as permitted or required by 5 U.S.C. 5584, 10 U.S.C. 2774, 32 U.S.C. 716, 5 U.S.C. 8346(b), or any other law.

[58 FR 38520, July 19, 1993, as amended at 66 FR 54131, Oct. 26, 2001]

§204.33 Pre-offset notice.

A program official must provide an employee with written notice at least 30 calendar days prior to offseting his/her salary. A program official need not notify an employee of: any adjustment to pay arising out of an employee's election of coverage or a change in coverage under a Federal benefits program requiring periodic deductions from pay, if the amount to be recovered was accumulated over four pay periods or less; a routine intra-agency adjustment of pay that is made to correct an overpayment of pay attributable to clerical or administrative errors or delays in processing pay documents, if the overpayment occurred within the four pay periods preceding the adjustment and, at the time of such adjustment, or as soon thereafter as practical, the individual is provided written notice of the nature and the amount of the adjustment and point of contact for contesting such adjustment; or any adjustment to collect a debt amounting to $50 or less, if, at the time of such adjustment, or as soon thereafter as practical, the individual is provided written notice of the nature and the amount of the adjustment and a point of contact for contesting such adjustment. When required, the written notice must include the following:

(a) The nature, origin and amount of the indebtedness determined by the Commission to be due;

(b) The intention of the Commission to collect the debt through deductions from the employee's current disposable pay account;

(c) The frequency and amount of the intended deductions (stated as a fixed dollar amount or as a percentage of pay, not to exceed 15 percent of disposable pay) and the intention to continue the deductions until the debt is paid in full or otherwise resolved;

(d) An explanation of the Commission's policy concerning interest, penalties, and administrative costs, including a statement that such assessments must be made unless excused in accordance with the FCCS;

(e) The employee's right to inspect and copy Commission records relating to the debt

本工资的个人而言则指其他获批支付款项。

“计划官”就本抵消规章之实施而言,系指总审计长或其指定人员。

“工资抵消”系指未经雇员同意,在正式确定的一个或多个付薪周期从雇员当前工资账户中扣除工资以催收《美国法典》第五编第5514节下债务的行政抵消。

“免除”系指《美国法典》第五编第5584节、《美国法典》第十编第2774节、《美国法典》第三十二编第716节、《美国法典》第五编第8346(b)节或其他任何法律许可或要求的对雇员欠负政府机构债务的取消、减少、免除或免予催收。

[《联邦公报》第58卷第38520页,1993年7月19日,修正索引:《联邦公报》第66卷第54131页,2001年10月26日。]

第204.33节　抵消预通知

计划官必须至少在抵消雇员工资30个日历日前,向雇员提供书面通知。对于下述事项,计划官不必通知雇员:在需要从工资中定期扣款的联邦福利计划中,因雇员选择的福利覆盖范围或该等范围之变更而导致的对支付金额的任何调整,条件是催收金额累计不超过4个付薪周期;政府机构内部为更正由于文书或行政错误或工资文件处理延误造成的超额支付工资进行的例行调整,条件是超额支付工资发生在调整前4个付薪周期内,且在调整之时或执行调整后应及时向个人提供书面通知,说明调整性质、金额以及对调整存有异议时可以联系的联系人;或额度不超过50美元的债务,条件是应在调整之时或执行调整后应及时向个人提供书面通知,说明调整性质、金额以及对调整存有异议时可以联系的联系人。如有必要,书面通知应包含如下内容:

(a)证券交易委员会认定的到期应付债务的性质、原因和金额;

(b)证券交易委员会有意通过从雇员当前可支配工资账户中扣除工资催收债务;

(c)拟议工资扣除的频率和金额(以固定金额表示或以工资的百分数表示,不得超过可支配工资的15%),以及说明证券交易委员会将在债务全额支付或得到其他方式的解决前持续扣除工资;

(d)对证券交易委员会的利息、罚款和行政费用政策的说明,包括除非获得《联邦债权催收标准》豁免,必须计征该等利息、罚款和行政费用的声明;

(e)雇员有权查阅和复制证券交易委员会与债务相关的记录(如果该等记录复本

(if copies of such records are not attached), or if the employee or his or her representative cannot personally inspect the records, the right to request and receive a copy of such records. The Commission will respond to a request for inspection and/or copying as soon as practicable;

(f) The opportunity, under terms agreeable to the Commission, to enter into a written agreement to establish a schedule for repayment in lieu of offset. The agreement must be in writing, signed by both the employee and the Commission, and documented in the Commission's files (31 CFR 901.3(b));

(g) The employee's right to a hearing conducted by an official arranged by the Commission if a petition is filed as prescribed by §204.35, Petition for pre–offset hearing. Such hearing official will be either an administrative law judge or at the chief administrative law judge's discretion, another hearing official who is also not under the control of the head of the agency;

(h) The method and time period for petitioning for a hearing, including a statement that the timely filing of a petition for hearing will stay the commencement of collection proceedings;

(i) If a hearing is requested, the hearing official will issue a final decision, based on information presented to the hearing official, at the earliest practicable date, but no later than 60 days after the petition for the hearing is filed unless the employee requests and the hearing official, for good cause or in the interests of justice, deems it necessary to extend that time period (5 CFR 550.1104(d)(10));

(j) That any knowingly false or frivolous statements, representations, or evidence may subject the employee to:

(1) Disciplinary procedures appropriate under 5 U.S.C. chapter 75, 5 CFR part 752, or any other applicable statutes or regulations;

(2) Penalties under the False Claims Act, 31 U.S.C. 3729–3731, or any other applicable statutory authority; and/or

(3) Criminal penalties under 18 U.S.C. 286, 287, 1001, and 1002, or any other applicable statutory authority.

(k) Any other rights and remedies available to the employee under statutes or regulations governing the program for which the collection is being made;

(l) The employee's right to a prompt refund if amounts paid or deducted by salary offset are later waived or found not owed to the United States, unless otherwise provided by law or contract; and

(m) The specific address to which all correspondence shall be directed regarding the debt.

[58 FR 38520, July 19, 1993, as amended at 66 FR 54131, Oct. 26, 2001]

未附于通知之后),或如果雇员或其代表不能亲自查阅记录,雇员有权请求发送并有权接收该等记录的复本。证券交易委员会应在可行的最短时间内答复查阅和/或复制请求;

(f)雇员有机会在证券交易委员会同意的期限内签署一份书面协议,确定替代债务抵消的还款计划。协议必须采用书面形式,由雇员和证券交易委员会共同签署,并归入证券交易委员会的档案[《联邦规章汇编》第三十一编第901.3(b)节];

(g)按照第204.35节“抵消预听证请求”规定的程序提出请求的雇员,有权要求证券交易委员会安排官员举行听证。该等听证官应由行政法官担任,首席行政法官也可自行决定指定另一名不受证券交易委员会负责人控制的听证官;

(h)提交听证请求的方法和时间,同时应说明如及时提交听证请求书,催收程序将暂缓启动;

(i)收到听证请求后,听证官应基于向听证官呈报的信息在可行的最早日期(但无论何时不得晚于收到听证请求后60日内)签发最终决定,但是如果雇员提出请求且听证官有充分理由或出于公平利益之考虑认为有必要的,该期限可以延长[《联邦规章汇编》第五编第550.1104(d)(10)节];

(j)任何蓄意提供的虚假或无关紧要的声明、陈述或证据均可能导致雇员遭受:

(1)《美国法典》第五编第七十五章、《联邦规章汇编》第五编第752部分或任何其他适用制定法或规章规定的适当的纪律处分程序;

(2)《反欺骗政府法》(《美国法典》第三十一编第3729~3731节)或任何其他适用制定法规定的罚款;和/或

(3)《美国法典》第十八编第286节、第287节、第1001节、第1002节或任何其他适用制定法规定的刑事处罚。

(k)雇员在适用于催收计划的制定法或规章下可以获得的任何其他权利或救济;

(l)如果雇员通过工资抵消清偿或部分偿付的债务后来被免除或被发现并不属于欠负美国政府的债务,雇员有权迅速获得退款,但法律或合同另有规定的除外;及

(m)与债务有关的所有通信的具体邮寄地址。

[《联邦公报》第58卷第38520页,1993年7月19日,修正索引:《联邦公报》第66卷第

§204.34 Employee response.

(a) *Introduction.* An employee must respond to a pre-offset notice, if at all, within 15 calendar days following receipt, in one or more of the ways discussed in §204.34, Employee response, and §204.35, Petition for pre-offset hearing. Where applicable, the employee bears the burdens of proof and persuasion.

(b) Responses must be submitted in writing to the program official who signed the pre-offset notice. A timely response will stay the commencement of collection by salary offset, at least until the issuance of a written decision. (See §204.37, Extensions of time). Failure to submit a timely response will be treated as an admission of indebtedness, and will result in salary offset in accordance with the terms specified in the pre-offset notice.

(c) A response filed after expiration of the 15 day period may be accepted if the employee can show that the delay was due to circumstances beyond his or her control or failure to receive notice of the time limit (unless otherwise aware of it).

(d) *Voluntary repayment agreement.* An employee may request to enter into a voluntary written agreement for repayment of the debt in lieu of offset. It is within the discretion of the program official whether to enter into such an agreement, and if so, upon what terms. Voluntary deductions may exceed 15 percent of the employee's disposable pay. If an agreement is reached, the agreement must be in writing, and must be signed by both the employee and the program official. A signed copy must be sent to the Comptroller's office. The program official shall notify the employee in writing of its decision not to accept the proposed voluntary repayment schedule before making any deductions from the employee's salary.

(e) *Waiver.* Any request for waiver of the debt must be accompanied by evidence that the waiver is authorized by law.

(f) *Reconsideration.* An employee may request reconsideration of the existence or amount of the debt or the offset schedule as reflected in the pre-offset notice. The request must be accompanied by a detailed narrative and supporting documentation as to why the offset decision is erroneous and/or why the offset schedule imposes an undue hardship.

§204.35 Petition for pre-offset hearing.

(a) The employee may petition for a pre-offset hearing. The petition must state with specificity why the employee believes the agency's determination is in error. To the extent that a debt has not been established by judicial or administrative order, a debtor may request a pre-offset hearing concerning the existence or amount of the debt or the terms of repayment. With respect to debts established by a judicial or administrative order, a debtor may request a pre-offset hearing concerning the payment or other discharge

54131页,2001年10月26日。]

第204.34节　雇员答复

(a)概述。雇员必须在收到抵消预通知后15个日历日内,以第204.34节("雇员答复")和第204.35节("抵消预听证请求")中所述的一种或多种方式对抵消预通知作出答复。如适用,雇员应承担举证责任和说服责任。

(b)答复必须以书面形式呈报给签发抵消预通知的计划官。雇员及时呈报答复的,通过工资抵消催收债务的程序将暂缓启动,至少应推迟至书面决定签发之日(参见第204.37条"延期")。雇员未及时提交答复的,将被视为已承认债务,工资抵消将于抵消预通知具体规定的日期启动。

(c)如果雇员能够证明答复延误是由超出其控制的情况或者由于未收到时限通知(但雇员已另行获知该等时限的除外)造成的,证券交易委员会也可接受雇员于15日期限到期后提交的答复。

(d)自愿还款协议。雇员可以请求签订一份通过自愿偿还债务替代债务抵消的书面协议。计划官对于是否签订该等协议具有自由裁量权,如果计划官同意签订,应确定具体条款。自愿扣款可以超过雇员的可支配工资的15%。双方达成协议的,必须采用书面形式,且必须由雇员和计划官共同签署。签字协议必须递送一份至总审计长办公室。计划官决定扣除雇员工资的,应在任何扣款之前书面通知雇员其不接受自愿还款计划提议的决定。

(e)免除。任何免除债务的请求均必须附上免除债务已获得法律授权的证据。

(f)复审。雇员可以提请对抵消预通知中所列债务的存在或金额或抵消计划进行复审。提出请求的同时,必须提交一份详细的说明性支持文件,说明抵消决定存在错误和/或抵消计划会给债务人造成过度困难的原因。

第204.35节　抵消预听证请求

(a)雇员可以请求举行抵消预听证。雇员须在请求书中说明其认为政府机构的判定存在错误的具体原因。对于未经司法或行政命令确认的债务,债务人可以提请就债务的存在、金额或还款条件举行抵消预听证。对于司法或行政命令已经确认的债务,债务人可以提请就债务的偿还或其他清偿方式举行抵消预听证。

of the debt.

(b) The petition must fully identify and explain, with reasonable specificity, all the facts, evidence and witnesses, if any, that the employee believes support his or her position. The petition must be signed by the employee.

[58 FR 38520, July 19, 1993, as amended at 66 FR 54131, Oct. 26, 2001]

§204.36 Granting of a pre-offset hearing.

(a) If the employee timely requests a pre-offset hearing or the timeliness is waived, the program official must:

(1) arrange for a hearing official. If the hearing official is an administrative law judge, he or she shall be designated by the Chief Administrative Law Judge as set forth in 17 CFR 200.310(a)(2); and

(2) provide the hearing official with a copy of all records on which the determination of the debt and any involuntary repayment schedule are based.

(b) The hearing official shall notify the employee by personal service, by first class, registered or certified mail, or by a reliable commercial courier or overnight delivery service whether the employee is entitled to an oral or "paper" (*i.e.*, a review on the written record)hearing. (See 31 CFR 901.3(e).)Within 20 calendar days of receipt of this notice the employee shall provide the hearing official with a full description of all relevant facts, documentary evidence, and witnesses which the employee believes support his or her position. The hearing official may extend the time for the employee to respond to the notice for good cause shown.

(c) If an oral hearing is scheduled, the hearing official shall notify the program official and the employee in writing of the date, time and location of the hearing. The place for the hearing shall be fixed by the hearing official with due regard for the public interest and the convenience and necessity of the parties, the participants, or their representatives.

(d) If the employee is entitled to an oral hearing, but requests to have the hearing based only on the written submissions, the employee must notify the hearing official and the program official at least 3 calendar days before the date of the oral hearing. The hearing official may waive the 3-day requirement for good cause.

(e) Failure of the employee to appear at the oral hearing may result in dismissal of the petition and affirmation of the program official's decision.

[58 FR 38520, July 19, 1993, as amended at 66 FR 54131, Oct. 26, 2001]

§204.37 Extensions of time.

The hearing official may for good cause or in the interests of justice postpone the

(b)雇员须在请求书中完整说明并合理、详细地解释其认为可以支持其立场的所有具体事实、证据和证人(如有)。请求书必须由雇员签字。

[《联邦公报》第58卷第38520页,1993年7月19日,修正索引:《联邦公报》第66卷第54131页,2001年10月26日。]

第204.36节　抵消预听证申请的核准

(a)如果雇员及时请求举行抵消预听证或虽然未在时限内提出申请,但已获得时限豁免,计划官必须:

(1)安排一名听证官。如果听证官由行政法官担任,应按照《联邦规章汇编》第十七编第200.310(a)(2)节的规定,由首席行政法官指定;且

(2)向听证官提供关于债务和任何非自愿还款计划的决定所基的全部记录之复本。

(b)在对雇员是否有权获得口头或"书面"听证(即基于书面记录审查举行的听证)作出决定后,听证官应通过专人送达、普通邮件、挂号邮件或带回执邮件或可靠的商业快递或隔夜送达服务通知该雇员[参见《联邦规章汇编》第三十一编第901.3(e)节]在收到通知后20个日历日内,雇员应向听证官提供一份完整说明,说明其认为可以支持其立场的所有事实、书证和证人。存在充分理由的,听证官可延长雇员答复通知的时间。

(c)安排进行口头听证的,听证官应将听证日期、时间和地点书面通知计划官和雇员。听证地点应由听证官适当考虑公共利益和各当事人、参与人或其代表的方便程度和必要需求确定。

(d)雇员有权要求举行口头听证,但仅提请举行书面听证的,必须至少在口头听证举行日期前3个日历日,通知听证官和计划官。存在充分理由的,听证官可免除该3日的时限要求。

(e)雇员未出席口头听证可能造成听证请求被撤销并构成对计划官决定的确认。

[《联邦公报》第58卷第38520页,1993年7月19日,修正索引:《联邦公报》第66卷第54131页,2001年10月26日。]

第204.37节　延期

听证官可以基于正当理由或出于公平利益之考虑,推迟听证开始的时间,将已举

commencement of the hearing, adjourn a convened hearing for a reasonable period of time or extend or shorten any other time limits prescribed under this section. This extension is not intended to abridge the 30 day initial notice or extend the 60 day decision requirement other than as provided for in 5 CFR 550.1104(d)(10).

§204.38 Pre-offset hearing.

(a) The hearing official shall determine the form and content of hearings granted under this section, pursuant to 31 CFR 901.3(e). All oral hearings shall be on the record. Except as otherwise ordered by the hearing official, hearings shall be recorded or transcribed verbatim by shorthand, mechanical means, electronic sound recording, or any other method, subject to the discretion and approval of the hearing official, and a transcript thereof shall be made.

(b) Oral hearings are informal in nature. The Commission, represented by an attorney from the Office of General Counsel, and accompanied by a program official and the employee, and/or the employee's representative, orally shall explain their respective positions using relevant documentation. The employee may testify on his or her own behalf, subject to cross examination. Other witnesses may be called to testify where the hearing official determines the testimony to be relevant and not redundant. The Federal Rules of Evidence serve as a guideline, but are not controlling. The employee bears the burdens of proof and persuasion.

(c) The hearing official shall:

(1) Conduct a fair and impartial hearing;

(2) Preside over the course of the hearing, maintain decorum and avoid delay in the disposition of the hearing; and

(3) Issue a decision in accordance with §204.39, Written decision, on the basis of the oral hearing and the written record.

(d) Oral hearings are normally open to the public. However, the hearing official may close all or any portion of the hearing at either the request of either party or upon the hearing official's initiative when doing so is in the best interest[s] of the employee or the public.

(e) Oral hearings may be conducted by conference call at the request of the employee or at the discretion of the hearing official.

(f) *Pre-offset "paper" hearing.* If a hearing is to be held only upon written submissions, the hearing official shall issue a decision based solely upon the written record.

[58 FR 38520, July 19, 1993, as amended at 66 FR 54132, Oct. 26, 2001]

§204.39 Written decision.

(a) *If pre-offset hearing is held.* Within 60 days of the filing of the employee's petition

行的听证顺延至其他合理时间举行,或延长或缩短本节规定的任何其他时间限制。设置本节延期规则的意图并非是要缩短30日首次通知期限或延长《联邦规章汇编》第五编第550.1104(d)(10)节规定的情形之外的60日决定期限。

第204.38节 抵消预听证

(a)对于根据本节核准的听证,听证官应依照《联邦规章汇编》第三十一编第901.3(e)节确定听证的形式和内容。所有口头听证均应记录在案。除非听证官另有命令,否则听证应通过速记、机械方式、电子录音或听证官依其自由裁量权决定并批准的任何其他方法逐字记录或誊写,并保留记录笔录。

(b)口头听证属于非正式听证。证券交易委员会由来自首席律师办公室的一名律师代表,在一名计划官和雇员和/或雇员代表的陪同下,利用相关文件对其各自的立场进行口头说明。雇员可以为其本人作证,但应接受交叉询问。听证官判定证人证词具有相关性且并非多余的,还可以传唤其他证人作证。《联邦证据规则》作为指导方针,而非规范性文件使用。雇员应承担举证责任和说服责任。

(c)听证官应:

(1)公平和公正地开展听证;

(2)主持听证过程、维持听证秩序并避免听证处置的拖延;且

(3)基于口头听证和书面记录根据第204.39节("书面决定")签发决定。

(d)口头听证一般对公众公开。但是,如果符合雇员或公众的最佳利益,听证官可以应一方当事人的请求或者主动决定不对公众公开听证的全部或部分程序。

(e)雇员提出请求或听证官依其自由裁量权决定的,听证可以通过电话会议的方式举行。

(f)抵消前的"书面"预听证。如果仅基于书面材料举行听证,听证官应完全基于书面记录签发决定。

[《联邦公报》第58卷第38520页,1993年7月19日,修正索引:《联邦公报》第66卷第54132页,2001年10月26日。]

第204.39节 书面决定

(a)召开抵消预听证的情况。雇员提交抵消预听证请求后60日内,听证官应签发一

for a pre–offset hearing, the hearing official will issue a written decision setting forth the basis of his/her findings in accordance with 5 CFR 550.1104(g)(3).

(b) If the employee challenges the pre–offset notice under §204.34, Employee response and/or §204.35, Petition for pre–offset hearing, without requesting a hearing or a hearing is denied, the program official must notify the employee of his/her final determination in writing before offset can begin. The agency's execution of a voluntary repayment agreement satisfies this requirement.

§204.40 Deductions.

(a) When deductions may begin:

(1) If a pre–offset hearing is held, deductions shall be made in accordance with the hearing official's decision.

(2) If parties execute a voluntary repayment agreement, deductions shall be made in accordance with the terms of that agreement.

(3) If the employee requests a waiver or reconsideration or the program official refuses to accept a proposed alternate repayment schedule, deductions shall be made in accordance with the program official's written decision.

(4) If the employee consents to the terms and conditions set forth in the Commission's Pre–offset Notice or fails to respond in timely fashion to the Pre–offset Notice, or waives his/her right to a hearing without otherwise challenging the terms of the Pre–offset Notice, deductions shall be made in accordance with the terms and conditions set forth therein.

(b) *Retired or separated employees.* If the employee retires, resigns, or is terminated before the debt is fully repaid, the remaining indebtedness will be offset pursuant to 31 U.S.C. 3716 and the FCCS.

(1) To the extent possible, the remaining indebtedness will be liquidated from any final payment due the former employee as of the date of separation (e.g., final salary payment, lump–sum leave, etc.). See §204.40d(3), Offset deductions from final salary and/or lump–sum leave payment.

(2) Thereafter, the remaining indebtedness will be recovered from later payments of any kind due the former employee from the United States. See the FCCS.

(c) *Method of collection and source of deduction.* The method of collecting debts under these regulations shall be by salary offset. Deductions will be made from the employee's current disposable pay account except as provided for in §204.34b, Employee response.

(d) *Amount and duration of deductions.* Debts must be collected in one lump sum where possible. If the employee demonstrates financial hardship to the Commission's satisfaction or the amount of the debt exceeds 15 percent of the indebted employee's

份书面决定,根据《联邦规章汇编》第五编第550.1104(g)(3)节说明其作出认定的基础。

(b)如果雇员对第204.34节("雇员答复")和/或第204.35节("抵消预听证请求")中的抵消预通知提出异议,但未提出听证请求或听证请求被拒绝,计划官必须在抵消开始前,将最终决定书面通知雇员。证券交易委员会签署自愿还款协议的,即视为已履行本款规定的要求。

第204.40节　扣款

(a)扣款时间应遵循如下规定:

(1)召开抵消预听证的,扣款应在听证官决定的时间作出。

(2)各方签订自愿还款协议的,扣款应根据协议条款作出。

(3)雇员请求豁免或复审的,或计划官拒绝接受雇员提出的替代还款计划的,扣款应根据计划官书面决定作出。

(4)雇员同意证券交易委员会签发的抵消预通知的条款和条件,或未按时回复抵消预通知,或放弃其听证权利且未对抵消预通知的条款提出其他异议的,扣款应根据抵消预通知规定的条款和条件作出。

(b)退休或离职雇员。如果雇员在债务尚未清偿前退休、辞职或终止任职,债务余额应依照《美国法典》第三十一编第3716节和《联邦债权催收标准》的规定抵消。

(1)在可能的范围内,债务余额应从前任雇员离职之日应向其支付的任何最终款项(如最终工资、一次性离职补偿金等)中支付清偿。参见第204.40d(3)节("通过扣除最终工资和/或一次性离职补偿金进行的抵消")。

(2)此后,债务余额应通过联邦应向前任雇员支付的任何类型的款项收回。参见《联邦债权催收标准》。

(c)催收方法和扣款来源。在本规章下催收债务的方法应为工资抵消。扣款通过雇员当前可支配工资账户进行,但第204.34b节("雇员答复")中规定的情形除外。

(d)扣款金额和期限。如有可能,债务须一次性催收。如果雇员出示证券交易委员会认可的经济困难证明,或债务金额超过雇员当前可支配工资的15%,债务可以在该雇员的劳动关系有效期内分笔催收,但催收期限不得超过该雇员劳动关系的预期有

current disposable pay, collection must be made in installments over a period not greater than the anticipated period of active employment, except as provided in Section 34b, Employee Response.

(1) Installment deductions will be made over the shortest period possible. The size and frequency of installment deductions will bear a reasonable relation to the size of the debt and the employee's ability to pay.

(2) The amount deducted for any period will not exceed 15 percent of the disposable pay from which the deduction is made, unless the employee has agreed in writing to the deduction of a greater amount. Installment payment of less than $100 per pay period will be accepted only in the most unusual circumstances.

(3) Offset deductions from final salary and/or lump-sum leave payment. Such an offset deduction may exceed 15 percent of an employee's final salary and/or lump-sum leave payment pursuant to 31 U.S.C. 3716, 64 CG 907.

(e) Interest, penalties and administrative costs on debts under this part will be assessed and/or waived according to the provisions of 31 CFR 901.9.

[58 FR 38520, July 19, 1993, as amended at 66 FR 54132, Oct. 26, 2001]

§204.41 Non-waiver of rights.

An employee's involuntary payment of all or any portion of a debt being collected under 5 U.S.C. 5514 shall not be construed as a waiver of any rights that the employee may have under 5 U.S.C. 5514 or any other provision of contract or law, unless there are statutory or contractual provisions to the contrary.

§204.42 Refunds.

(a) The Commission will refund promptly to the appropriate individual amounts offset under this regulation when:

(1) A debt is waived or otherwise found not owing the United States (unless expressly prohibited by statute or regulation); or

(2) The Commission is directed by an administrative or judicial order to refund amounts deducted from the employee's current pay.

(b) Refunds do not bear interest unless required or permitted by law or contract.

§204.43 Coordinating offset with another federal agency.

(a) *Responsibility of the Commission as the Creditor Agency.* When possible, salary offset through the centralized administrative offset procedures in 5 CFR 550.1108 shall be attempted before applying the procedures in this section. If centralized administrative offset is not possible, the Commission shall request recovery from the current paying agency. Upon completion of the procedures established in these regulations and pursuant to 5 U.S.C. 5514, 5 CFR 550.1109 the Commission must:

效期,但第204.34b节("雇员答复")中规定的情形除外。

(1)分笔扣款应尽可能在最短的时间内作出。分笔扣款的规模和频率应与债务的规模和雇员的支付能力形成合理比例。

(2)任何一期扣款金额均不得超过扣款账户中可支配工资的15%,但员工已经书面同意扣除更高金额的除外。每期金额低于100美元的分期付款仅在最特殊的情况下才会被接受。

(3)通过扣除最终工资和/或一次性离职补偿金进行的抵消。根据《美国法典》第三十一编第3716节(64 CG 907),通过该种扣款方式进行的抵消可以超过雇员最终工资和/或一次性离职补偿金的15%。

(e)本部分下债务的利息、罚款和行政费用应按照《联邦规章汇编》第三十一编第901.9节的规定计征和/或免除。

[《联邦公报》第58卷第38520页,1993年7月19日,修正索引:《联邦公报》第66卷第54132页,2001年10月26日。]

第204.41节 不弃权

对于按照《美国法典》第五编第5514节规定催收的全部或部分债务,雇员进行的非自愿支付不得解释为其已放弃在《美国法典》第五编第5514节下或任何其他合同或法律中的任何权利,但成文法或合同条款中存在相反规定的除外。

第204.42节 退款

(a)在下述情形下,证券交易委员会应及时向相关个人退还在本规章下抵消的金额:

(1)债务已经被免除或该债务被认定为不属于欠负联邦政府的债务(但制定法或规章明文禁止的除外);或

(2)证券交易委员会收到要求退还从雇员现有工资中扣除的金额的行政命令或者司法命令。

(b)退款不计利息,但法律或合同另有要求或许可的除外。

第204.43节 与其他联邦机构协调抵消

(a)证券交易委员会作为政府机构债权人的责任。如有可能,通过《联邦规章汇编》第五编第550.1108节规定的集中行政抵消程序进行的工资抵消,应在适用本节程序前进行。无法进行集中行政抵消的,证券交易委员会应请求通过当前付薪机构催收债务。在本规章规定的程序完成之后,证券交易委员会应根据《美国法典》第五编第5514节、《联邦规章汇编》第五编第550.1109节的规定:

(1) Certify, in writing, that the employee owes the debt, the amount and basis of the debt, the date on which payment(s) is due, the date the Government's right to collect the debt first accrued and that the Commission's regulations implementing 5 U.S.C. 5514 have been approved by OPM.

(2) If the collection must be made in installments, the Commission also must advise the paying agency of the amount or percentage of disposable pay to be collected in each installment, and if the Commission wishes, the number and the commencing date of the installments (if a date other than the next officially established pay period is required).

(3) Advise the paying agency of the actions taken pursuant to 5 U.S.C. 5514(b) and give the date(s) the action(s) was taken (unless the employee has consented to the salary offset in writing or signed a statement acknowledging receipt of the required procedures and the written consent or statement is forwarded to the paying agency).

(4) Except as otherwise provided in this paragraph (a)(4), the Commission must submit a debt claim containing the information specified in paragraphs (a)(1) through (3) of this section and an installment agreement (or other instruction on the payment schedule), if applicable, to the employee's paying agency.

(5) If the employee is in the process of separating, the Commission must submit its debt claim to the employee's paying agency for collection as provided in 5 CFR 550.1104 (l). Pursuant to 5 CFR 1101, the paying agency must certify the total amount of its collection and notify the creditor agency and employee. If the paying agency is aware that the employee is entitled to payments from the Civil Service Retirement and Disability Fund, or other similar payments, it must provide written notification to the agency responsible for making such payments that the debtor owes a debt (including the amount) and that the paying agency has fully complied with the provisions of this section. The Commission must submit a properly certified claim to the agency responsible for making such payments before the collection can be made.

(6) If the employee is already separated and all payments due from his or her former paying agency have been paid, the Commission may request, unless otherwise prohibited, that money due and payable to the employee from the Civil Service Retirement and Disability Fund (5 CFR 831.1801) or other similar funds, be administratively offset to collect the debt (See 31 U.S.C. 3716 and the FCCS).

(7) When an employee transfers to another paying agency, the Commission shall not repeat the due process procedures described in 5 U.S.C. 5514 and subpart B of this part to resume the collection. The Commission must review the debt upon receiving the former paying agency's notice of the employee's transfer to make sure the collection is resumed by the new paying agency. The Commission must submit a properly certified claim to the new paying agency before collection can be resumed.

(1)书面证明雇员欠负债务之事实、债务金额和原因、应付款项到期日、联邦政府债务催收权的产生日期以及证券交易委员会为实施《美国法典》第五编第5514节而发布的规章已经获得美国人事管理局批准。

(2)如果催收必须分笔进行,证券交易委员会还必须就催收的每笔欠款金额、占雇员可支配工资的比例向付薪机构提出建议;如证券交易委员会愿意,还可就还款期数和开始还款的日期(如果所要求的还款日期并非正式确认的下一个付薪周期)提出建议。

(3)告知付薪机构证券交易委员会已经依据《美国法典》第五编第5514(b)节采取的行动并提供采取行动的日期(除非雇员已经书面同意工资抵消或已签署一份声明确认证券交易委员会已向其提供规定的程序权,并已将书面同意书或说明书转交给付薪机构)。

(4)除本第(a)(4)款另有规定的情形外,证券交易委员会必须向付薪机构呈报一份债务主张,债务主张中应包含本节第(a)(1)款至第(a)(3)款列明的信息和分期付款协议或就付款计划作出的其他说明(如适用)。

(5)如果雇员正处于离职过程中,证券交易委员会必须按照《联邦规章汇编》第五编第550.1104(l)节规定向雇员的付薪机构呈报催收债务的权利主张。根据《联邦规章汇编》第五编第1101部分,付薪机构须认证其催收款项的总金额并通知政府机构债权人和雇员。如果该雇员的付薪机构发现雇员有权获得公务员退休和残疾基金的付款或其他类似付款,必须向负责支付该等款项的政府机构提供书面通知,说明债务人负有债务的事实(包括债务金额),且付薪机构已经完全遵守本节规定。证券交易委员会在催收债务前,必须向负责支付该等款项的政府机构呈报一份经适当认证的债权证明。

(6)如果雇员已经离职,且其付薪机构已经向其付清所有应付款项,则除非另有禁止,否则证券交易委员会可以请求从公务员退休和残疾基金(《联邦规章汇编》第五编第831.1801节)或其他类似基金应向雇员支付的到期款项中进行行政抵消以催收债务(参见《美国法典》第三十一编第3716节和《联邦债权催收标准》)。

(7)被证券交易委员会催收欠款的雇员换岗到另一个付薪机构工作时,证券交易委员会不应重新启动《美国法典》第五编第5514节和本部分第B子部分规定的正当程序催收欠款。证券交易委员会在收到向该雇员支付工资的政府机构关于该雇员换岗的通知后,必须对债务进行审查并确保新的付薪机构继续催收欠款。证券交易委员会在继续催收欠款前,必须向新付薪机构呈报一份经适当认证的债权主张。

(b) *Responsibility of the Commission as the paying agency*—(1) *Complete claim.* When the Commission receives a properly certified claim from a creditor agency, deductions should be scheduled to begin at the next officially established pay interval. The Commission must notify the employee in writing that the Commission has received a certified debt claim from the creditor agency (including the amount) and the date salary offset will begin and the amount of such deductions.

(2) *Incomplete claim.* When the Commission receives an incomplete certification of debt from a creditor agency, the Commission must return the debt claim with notice that procedures under 5 U.S.C. 5514 and subpart B of this part must be provided and a properly certified debt claim received before action will be taken to collect from the employee's current pay account.

(3) *Review.* The Commission is not authorized to review the merits of the creditor agency's determination with respect to the amount or validity of the debt certified by the creditor agency.

(4) *Employees who transfer from one paying agency to another.* If, after the creditor agency has submitted the debt claim to the Commission and before the Commission collects the debt in full, the employee transfers to another agency, the Commission must certify the total amount collected on the debt. One copy of the certification must be furnished to the employee and one copy to the creditor agency along with notice of the employee's transfer.

(c) *Responsibility of the Program Official.* (1) The Program Official shall coordinate debt collections and shall, as appropriate:

(i) Arrange for a hearing upon proper petition by a federal employee; and

(ii) Prescribe, upon consultation with the General Counsel, such practices and procedures as may be necessary to carry out the intent of this regulation.

(2) The Program Official shall be responsible for:

(i) Ensuring that each certification of debt sent to a paying agency is consistent with the pre-offset notice (§204.33, Pre-offset notice).

(ii) Obtaining hearing officials from other agencies pursuant to §204.36, Granting of a pre-offset hearing.

(iii) Ensuring that hearings are properly scheduled.

[58 FR 38520, July 19, 1993, as amended at 66 FR 54132, Oct. 26, 2001]

§204.44 Interest, penalties, and administrative costs.

Charges may be assessed for interest, penalties, and administrative costs in accordance with the Federal Claims Collection Standards, 31 CFR 901.9.

[58 FR 38520, July 19, 1993, as amended at 66 FR 54132, Oct. 26, 2001]

(b)证券交易委员会作为付薪机构的责任——(1)完整的债权主张。证券交易委员会从政府机构债权人处收到经适当认证的债权证明时，应在正式确认的下一个付薪周期进行扣款。证券交易委员会须书面通知雇员证券交易委员会已经从政府机构债权人处收到一份经认证的债权主张(包括金额),并通知雇员工资抵消开始的日期和扣款金额。

(2)不完整的债权主张。证券交易委员会从政府机构债权人处收到的债权证明不完整时,证券交易委员会必须退回债权主张,通知政府机构债权人必须提供《美国法典》第五编第 5514 节和本部分第 B 子部分规定的程序,且证券交易委员会必须在收到经适当认证的债权主张后才能采取行动,通过雇员的当前工资账户催收债务。

(3)审查。证券交易委员会无权对政府机构债权人就其所认证债务的金额或有效性所作判定进行实质审查。

(4)从一个付薪机构换岗到另一个付薪机构的雇员。如果政府机构债权人已经向证券交易委员会呈报债权主张,且在证券交易委员会全额催收债务之前,雇员换岗到另一机构,证券交易委员会必须对已经催收的债务总额进行认证,并向雇员和政府机构债权人各提供一份上述证明,同时向政府机构债权人提供该雇员的换岗通知。

(c)计划官的职责。(1)计划官应协调债务催收,且应适时:

(i)在收到联邦雇员提交的适当请求后安排听证;并

(ii)在咨询首席律师的意见后视具体情况规定相关做法和程序,以实现本规章的目的。

(2)计划官应负责:

(i)确保向付薪机构递送的每份债务证明的内容均与抵消预通知(第 204.33 节“抵消预通知”)一致。

(ii)依照第 204.36 节(“抵消预听证请求的核准”)的规定,请求其他政府机构指定听证官。

(iii)确保听证得到妥善安排。

[《联邦公报》第58卷第38520页,1993年7月19日,修正索引:《联邦公报》第66卷第54132页,2001年10月26日。]

第204.44节　利息、罚款和行政成本

利息、罚款和行政成本可以根据《联邦债权催收标准》(《联邦规章汇编》第三十一编第901.9节)的规定计征。

[《联邦公报》第58卷第38520页,1993年7月19日,修正索引:《联邦公报》第66卷第

Subpart C—Tax Refund Offset

Authority: 31 U.S.C. 3720A, 31 CFR 285.2(c).

Source: 58 FR 64372, Dec. 7, 1993, unless otherwise noted.

§204.50 Purpose.

This subpart establishes procedures for the Commission's referral of past-due legally enforceable debts to the Department of the Treasury's Financial Management Service (FMS) for offset against the income tax refunds of the debtor.

[66 FR 54132, Oct. 26, 2001]

§204.51 [Reserved]

§204.52 Notification of intent to collect.

(a) *Notification before tax refund offset.* Reduction of an income tax refund will be made only after the Commission makes a determination that an amount is owed and past-due and gives or makes a reasonable attempt to give the debtor 60 days written notice of the intent to collect by tax refund offset.

(b) *Contents of notice.* The Commission's notice of intent to collect by tax refund offset (Notice of Intent) will state:

(1) The amount of the debt;

(2) That unless the debt is repaid within 60 days from the date of the Commission's Notice of Intent, the Commission intends to collect the debt by requesting a reduction of any amounts payable to the debtor as a Federal income tax refund by an amount equal to the amount of the debt and all accumulated interest and other charges;

(3) A mailing address for forwarding any written correspondence and a contact name and a telephone number for any questions; and

(4) That the debtor may present evidence to the Commission that all or part of the debt is not past due or legally enforceable by:

(i) Sending a written request for a review of the evidence to the address provided in the notice;

(ii) Stating in the request the amount disputed and the reasons why the debtor believes that the debt is not past due or is not legally enforceable; and

(iii) Including in the request any documents that the debtor wishes to be considered or stating that the additional information will be submitted within the remainder of the 60-day period.

54132页,2001年10月26日。]

第C子部分——退 税 抵 消

法律依据:《美国法典》第三十一编第3720A节;《联邦规章汇编》第三十一编第285.2(c)节。

行政规则来源:《联邦公报》第58卷第64372页,1993年12月7日,除非另有说明。

第204.50节　目的

本子部分规定了证券交易委员会向财政部金融管理服务局(FMS)移送过期可依法强制执行的债权,通过债务人的所得税退税抵消债务的程序。

[《联邦公报》第66卷第54132页,2001年10月26日]

第204.51节　[保留]

第204.52节　催收意向通知

(a)退税抵消预通知。通过扣减所得税退税抵消债务人债务时,证券交易委员会应判定债务人欠有债务、债务过期,并已提前60日给予或已通过合理努力提前60日给予债务人书面通知,告知证券交易委员会有意通过退税抵消的方式催收债务。

(b)通知内容。证券交易委员会在说明其有意通过退税抵消的方式催收债务的通知(意向通知)中应说明:

(1)债务金额;

(2)除非债务人在证券交易委员会发出催收意向通知后的60日内偿还债务,否则证券交易委员会将试图请求从应向债务人支付的任何联邦所得税退税中扣减债务人所欠债务金额以及所有累计利息和其他费用;

(3)债务人递交任何书面通信的邮寄地址和回答债务人问题的联系人姓名和电话;及

(4)债务人可以通过下述方式向证券交易委员会出示证据,证明债务的全部或者部分并未过期或不能依法强制执行:

(i)按通知中提供的地址递送一份审核证据的书面请求;

(ii)在请求中说明争议金额和债务人认为债务并未过期或不能依法强制执行的理由;并

(iii)在请求中纳入债务人希望被考虑的任何文件,或说明将于60日期限内的剩余时间提交补充信息。

(c) To the extent that a debt owed has not been established by judicial or administrative order, a debtor may dispute the existence or amount of the debt or the terms of repayment. With respect to debts established by a judicial or administrative order, Commission review will be limited to issues concerning the payment or other discharge of the debt.

[58 FR 64372, Dec. 7, 1993, as amended at 66 FR 54132, Oct. 26, 2001; 66 FR 56383, Nov. 7, 2001]

§204.53 [Reserved]

§204.54 Commission action as a result of consideration of evidence submitted in response to the notice of intent.

(a) *Consideration of evidence.* If, as a result of the Notice of Intent, the Commission receives notice that the debtor will submit additional evidence or receives additional evidence from the debtor within the prescribed time period, tax refund offset will be stayed until the Commission can:

(1) Consider the evidence presented by the debtor; and

(2) Determine whether or not all or a portion of the debt is still past due and legally enforceable; and

(3) Notify the debtor of its determination.

(b) *Commission action on the debt.* (1) The Commission will notify the debtor of its intent to refer the debt to the IRS for offset against the debtor's Federal income tax refund if it sustains its decision that the debt is past-due and legally enforceable. The Commission will also notify the debtor whether the amount of the debt remains the same or is modified; and

(2) The Commission will not refer the debt to the IRS for offset against the debtor's Federal income tax refund if it reverses its decision that the debt is past due and legally enforceable.

[58 FR 64372, Dec. 7, 1993, as amended at 66 FR 54132, Oct. 26, 2001]

§204.55 Change in notification to Financial Management Service.

After the Commission sends FMS notification of an individual's liability for a debt, the Commission will promptly notify FMS of any change in the notification, if the Commission:

(a) Determines that an error has been made with respect to the information contained in the notification;

(b) Receives a payment or credits a payment to the account of the debtor named in the notification that reduces the amount of the debt referred to FMS for offset; or

(c) If the debt amount is otherwise incorrect, except that the amount of a debt

(c)如所欠债务尚未获得司法或行政命令确认,债务人可以就债务的存在、金额或者还款条款提出异议。对于司法或行政命令已经确认的债务,证券交易委员会的审查应仅限于与还款或其他债务清偿方式相关的事项。

[《联邦公报》第58卷第64372页,1993年12月7日,修正索引:《联邦公报》第66卷第54132页,2001年10月26日;《联邦公报》第66卷第56383页,2001年11月7日。]

第204.53节　[保留]

第204.54节　证券交易委员会审查债务人在对催收意向通知的答复中提交的证据后采取的行动

(a)证据的审查。如果在发出催收意向通知之后,证券交易委员会在规定的时限内收到债务人将呈报补充证据的通知或收到债务人呈报的补充证据,退税抵消应暂时中止,直至证券交易委员会可以:

(1)审查债务人呈报的证据;并

(2)认定债务是否仍然全部或部分过期并可依法强制执行;并

(3)将其认定结果通知债务人。

(b)证券交易委员会对债务采取的行动。(1)如果证券交易委员会维持决定,认为债务过期并可依法强制执行,应通知债务人其有意将债务移交至美国国税局,通过债务人的所得税退税抵消债务。证券交易委员会还应通知债务人债务金额是否将保持不变或已作出修改;并

(2)证券交易委员会推翻其认为债务过期并可依法强制执行的决定的,不会将债务移交至美国国税局通过债务人所得税退税抵消债务。

[《联邦公报》第58卷第64372页,1993年12月7日,修正索引:《联邦公报》第66卷第54132页,2001年10月26日。]

第204.55节　向金融管理服务局递送的通知之变更

对于向金融管理服务局递送的个人负债通知发生的任何变更,证券交易委员会应及时通知金融管理服务局,条件是证券交易委员会:

(a)判定通知中包含的信息有误;

(b)通知中指明的债务人账款收到相应还款,或有款项被记入贷方,从而减少了移交至金融管理服务局抵消的金额;或

(c)债务金额存在其他错误,但是除非证券交易委员会已经遵守本子部分的正当

referred to FMS will not be increased unless the Commission has complied with the due process requirements of this subpart and the Federal Claims Collection Standards as to the amount of the increase.

[66 FR 54132, Oct. 26, 2001]

§204.56 Administrative charges.

To the extent permitted by law, all administrative charges incurred in connection with the referral of the debts for tax refund offset will be assessed on the debt and thus increase the amount of the offset.

[66 FR 54132, Oct. 26, 2001]

§§204.57–204.59 [Reserved]

Subpart D—Administrative Wage Garnishment

Authority: 31 U.S.C. 3720D, 31 CFR 285.11(f).

Source: 66 FR 54132, Oct. 26, 2001, unless otherwise noted.

§204.60 Purpose.

This subpart provides procedures for the Commission to collect money from a debtor's disposable pay by means of administrative wage garnishment to satisfy a delinquent nontax debt owed to the United States.

§204.61 Scope.

(a) The receipt of payments pursuant to this subpart does not preclude the Commission from pursuing other debt collection remedies, including the offset of Federal payments to satisfy a delinquent nontax debt owed to the United States. The Commission may pursue such debt collection remedies separately or in conjunction with administrative wage garnishment.

(b) This subpart does not apply to the collection of delinquent nontax debt owed to the United States from the wages of Federal employees from their Federal employment. Federal pay is subject to the Federal salary offset procedures set forth in 5 U.S.C. 5514 and other applicable laws.

§204.62 Definitions.

The following definitions apply to this subpart:

Debt or *delinquent nontax debt* means any money, funds or property that has been determined to be owed to the Commission by an individual that has not been paid by the date specified in the demand or order for payment, or applicable agreement. For purposes of this subpart, the terms "debt" and "claim" are synonymous.

程序要求和《联邦债权催收标准》关于提高债务金额的规定,否则不能提高移交至金融管理服务局进行抵消的债务金额。

[《联邦公报》第66卷第54132页,2001年10月26日。]

第204.56节　行政费用

在法律许可的范围内,移交债务进行退税抵消产生的所有行政费用均应计入债务,从而提高抵消金额。

[《联邦公报》第66卷第54132页,2001年10月26日。]

第204.57~204.59节　[保留]

第D子部分——行政扣发工资

法律依据:《美国法典》第三十一编第3720D节,《联邦规章汇编》第三十一编第285.11(f)节。

行政规则来源:《联邦公报》第66卷第54132页,2001年10月26日,除非另有说明。

第204.60节　目的

本子部分规定了证券交易委员会以行政扣发工资的方式,通过债务人可支配工资催收债务人欠负联邦政府的过期非税债务的程序。

第204.61节　范围

(a)依照本子部分规定扣发债务人工资并不影响证券交易委员会寻求其他债务催收救济,包括通过联邦工资抵消债务人欠负联邦政府的过期非税债务。证券交易委员会可以单独寻求该行政扣发工资救济,也可将之与其他救济相结合。

(b)本子部分不适用于通过联邦雇员的工资催收其欠负联邦政府的过期非税债务。联邦工资受《美国法典》第五编第5514节和其他适用法律规定的联邦工资抵消程序规制。

第204.62节　定义

就本子部分而言,应适用如下定义:

"债务或过期非税债务"系指个人被判定欠负证券交易委员会,且未在催付通知或命令或适用协议指定的日期前支付的任何金钱、资金或财产。就本子部分而言,"债务"和"债权主张"为同义词。

Disposable pay means that part of the debtor's compensation (including, but not limited to, salary, bonuses, commissions, and vacation pay) from an employer remaining after the deduction of health insurance premiums and any amounts required by law to be withheld. For purposes of this subpart, "amounts required by law to be withheld" include amounts for deductions such as social security taxes and withholding taxes, but do not include any amount withheld pursuant to a court order.

Employer means a person or entity that employs the services of others and that pays their wages or salaries. The term employer includes, but is not limited to, State and local Governments, but does not include an agency of the Federal Government.

Garnishment means the process of withholding amounts from an employee's disposable pay and the paying of those amounts to a creditor in satisfaction of a withholding order.

Withholding order means any order for withholding or garnishment of pay issued by an agency, or judicial or administrative body. For purposes of this subpart, the terms "wage garnishment order" and "garnishment order" have the same meaning as "withholding order."

§204.63 Notice.

(a) At least 30 days before the initiation of garnishment proceedings, the Commission will mail, by first class mail to the debtor's last known address, a written notice informing the debtor of:

(1) The nature and amount of the debt;

(2) The Commission's intention to initiate proceedings to collect the debt through deductions from pay until the debt and all accumulated interest, penalties and administrative costs are paid in full; and

(3) An explanation of the debtor's rights, including those set forth in paragraph (b) of this section, and the time frame within which the debtor may exercise these rights.

(b) The debtor will be afforded the opportunity:

(1) To inspect and copy records related to the debt;

(2) To enter into a written repayment agreement with the Commission, under terms agreeable to the Commission; and

(3) To the extent that a debt owed has not been established by judicial or administrative order, to request a hearing concerning the existence or amount of the debt or the terms of the debt's repayment schedule. With respect to debts established by a judicial or administrative order, a debtor may request a hearing concerning the payment or other discharge of the debt. The debtor is not entitled to a hearing concerning the terms of the proposed repayment schedule if these terms have been established by written agreement under paragraph (b)(2) of this section.

(c) The notice required by this section may be included with the Commission's

“可支配工资”系指债务人的薪酬(包括但不限于工资、奖金、佣金和假期工资)扣除医疗保险费和任何法定预扣额后的余额。就本子部分而言,“法定预扣额”包括社保税和预扣税等,但不包括依照法院命令预扣的任何金额。

“雇主”系指雇佣他人服务并支付工资或薪水的个人或实体。“雇主”一词包括但不限于州政府和地方政府,但不包括联邦政府机关。

“扣发”系指从雇员的可支配工资中扣除金额,并执行预扣令将该金额支付给债权人的程序。

“预扣令”系指政府机构或司法、行政机构签发的任何预扣或扣发工资的命令。就本子部分而言,“工资扣发令”、“扣发令”与“预扣令”是同义词。

第204.63节　通知

(a)证券交易委员会至少应在扣发程序启动前30日,按照已知的债务人的最新地址通过普通邮件邮寄一份书面通知,通知债务人:

(1)债务的性质和金额;

(2)证券交易委员会有意启动程序,通过扣除工资的方式催收债务,直至债务和所有累计利息、罚款和行政费用全额缴清为止;及

(3)债务人享有的权利,包括本节第(b)款规定的权利和债务人可以行使这些权利的时间表。

(b)债务人应获得机会:

(1)查阅并复制与债务有关的记录;

(2)按照证券交易委员会同意的条款,与证券交易委员会签订书面还款协议;且

(3)如果债务尚未获得司法或行政命令确认,债务人可以提请就债务的存在、金额或还款计划的条件举行听证。对于司法或行政命令已经确认的债务,债务人可以提请就还款或其他债务清偿方式举行听证。如果已经按本节第(b)(2)款签订书面协议对还款条件提议进行确认,则债务人无权请求就还款计划条件提议举行听证。

(c)本节规定的通知可以纳入本部分第A子部分规定的证券交易委员会催款函中。

demand letter required by subpart A of this part.

(d) The Commission will keep a copy of the certificate of service indicating the date of mailing of the notice.

§204.64 Hearing.

(a) *Request for hearing.* The Commission will order a hearing, which at the Commission's option may be oral or written, if the debtor submits a written request for a hearing concerning, for debts not previously established by judicial or administrative order, the existence or amount of the debt or the terms of the repayment schedule (for repayment schedules established other than by written agreement under §204.63(b)(2)), or for debts established by judicial or administrative order, the payment or other discharge of the debt.

(b) *Type of hearing or review.* (1) For purposes of this subpart, whenever the Commission is required to afford a debtor a hearing, the Commission will provide the debtor with a reasonable opportunity for an oral hearing when the Commission determined that the issues in dispute cannot be resolved by review of the documentary evidence, for example, when the validity of the claim turns on the issue of credibility or veracity.

(2) If the Commission determines that an oral hearing is appropriate, the time and location of the hearing shall be established by the Commission. An oral hearing may, at the debtor's option, be conducted either in-person or by telephone conference. All travel expenses incurred by the debtor in connection with an in-person hearing will be borne by the debtor. All telephonic charges incurred during the hearing will be the responsibility of the agency.

(3) In those cases when an oral hearing is not required by this section, the Commission will nevertheless accord the debtor a "paper hearing", that is, the Commission will decide the issues in dispute based upon a review of the written record.

(c) *Effect of timely request.* Subject to paragraph (l) of this section, if the debtor's written request is received by the Commission on or before the 15th business day following the mailing of the notice of the Commission's intent to seek garnishment, the Commission will not issue a withholding order until the debtor has been provided the requested hearing, and a decision in accordance with paragraphs (i) and (j) of this section has been rendered.

(d) *Failure to timely request a hearing.* If the debtor's written request is received by the agency after the 15th business day following the mailing of the notice of the Commission's intent to seek garnishment, the Commission shall provide a hearing to the debtor. However, the Commission will not delay issuance of a withholding order unless the Commission determines that the delay in filing the request was caused by factors over which the debtor had no control, or the Commission receives information that the

(d)证券交易委员会应保留一份送达证明,送达证明上应标明通知邮寄日期。

第204.64节 听证

(a)听证申请。如果:对于此前未经司法或行政命令确认的债务,债务人提交书面申请,要求就债务的存在、金额或还款计划[已根据第 204.63(b)(2)节签订书面协议确认的还款计划除外]的条款举行听证;或者对于已经获得司法或行政命令确认的债务,债务人提交书面申请,要求就还款或其他债务清偿方式举行听证,则证券交易委员会应命令举行听证,听证的形式(口头或书面)由证券交易委员会自行决定。

(b)听证或审查类型。(1)就本子部分而言,证券交易委员会有义务向债务人提供听证之时,如证券交易委员会判定争议事项不能通过审查书证解决(如债权主张的效力取决于债务人信用或诚信问题时),应向债务人提供获得口头听证的合理机会。

(2)如果证券交易委员会判定宜应举行口头听证,应指定听证的时间和地点。债务人可以选择当面出席或通过电话会议的方式参与口头听证。债务人当面出席发生的所有差旅费用由债务人承担。听证中发生的所有通话费由政府机构承担。

(3)在本节不要求举行口头听证的情况下,证券交易委员会仍将向债务人提供"书面听证"机会,即证券交易委员会将在审查书面记录的基础上对争议事项作出决定。

(c)及时提交听证申请的效力。在不违反本节第(l)款的前提下,如果证券交易委员会在向债务人寄送扣发意向通知后第 15 个工作日当天或之前收到债务人的书面申请,则证券交易委员会在为债务人提供所申请的听证,并根据本节第(i)款和第(j)款作出决定之前,不会签发预扣令。

(d)未及时提交听证申请的情形。如果证券交易委员会在向债务人寄送扣发意向通知后第 15 个工作日之后收到债务人的书面申请,证券交易委员会仍应向债务人提供听证。但是,除非证券交易委员会判定延误提交听证申请是由超出债务人控制的情况造成的,或者证券交易委员会获得相关信息,并据以判断应该推迟签发或取消预扣令,否则证券交易委员会不会推迟预扣令的签发。

Commission believes justifies a delay or cancellation of the withholding order.

(e) *Hearing official.* All hearings shall be presided over by the Commission, or if the Commission so orders, by a hearing official. When the Commission designates that the hearing official shall be an administrative law judge, the Chief Administrative Law Judge shall select, pursuant to 17 CFR 200.30–10, the administrative law judge to preside.

(f) *Procedure.* After the debtor requests a hearing, the hearing official shall notify the debtor of:

(1) The date and time of a telephonic hearing;

(2) The date, time, and location of an in–person oral hearing; or

(3) The deadline for the submission of evidence for a written hearing.

(g) *Burden of proof.* (1) The Commission will have the burden of going forward to prove the existence or amount of the debt.

(2) Thereafter, if the debtor disputes the existence or amount of the debt, the debtor must prove by a preponderance of the evidence that no debt exists or that the amount of the debt is incorrect. In addition, the debtor may present evidence that the terms of the repayment schedule are unlawful, would cause a financial hardship to the debtor, or that collection of the debt may not be pursued due to operation of law.

(h) *Record.* The hearing official will maintain a record of any hearing provided under this section. A hearing is not required to be a formal evidentiary–type hearing, however, witnesses who testify in oral hearings will do so under oath or affirmation.

(i) *Date of decision.* The hearing official shall issue a written opinion stating his or her decision, as soon as practicable, but not later than sixty (60) days after the date on which the request for such hearing was received by the Commission. If the Commission is unable to provide the debtor with a hearing and a decision is not rendered within sixty (60) days after the receipt of the request for such hearing:

(1) A withholding order will not be issued until the hearing is held and a decision rendered; or

(2) If a withholding order had previously been issued to the debtor's employer, the withholding order will be suspended beginning on the 61st day after the receipt of the hearing request and continuing until a hearing is held and a decision is rendered.

(j) *Content of decision.* The written decision shall include:

(1) A summary of the facts presented;

(2) The findings, analysis and conclusions; and

(3) The terms of any repayment schedules, if applicable.

(k) *Finality of agency action.* Unless the Commission on its own initiative orders review of a decision by a hearing official pursuant to 17 CFR 201.431(c), a decision by a hearing official shall become the final decision of the Commission for the purpose of

(e)听证官。所有听证均应由证券交易委员会主持,或按照证券交易委员会的命令由听证官主持。证券交易委员会指定听证官应由行政法官担任的,首席行政法官应依照《联邦规章汇编》第十七编第200.30-10节的规定选任主持听证的行政法官。

(f)程序步骤。债务人申请举行听证后,听证官应通知债务人:

(1)电话听证的日期和时间;
(2)当面口头听证的日期、时间和地点;或
(3)口头听证中提交证据的截止日期。
(g)举证责任。(1)证券交易委员会有责任证明债务的存在或该债务的金额。

(2)证券交易委员会履行证明责任之后,如果债务人对债务的存在或金额存在争议,债务人必须通过优势证据证明债务不存在或者债务金额不正确。此外,债务人还可以出示证据证明还款计划的条款不合法、会给债务人造成经济困难或者由于法律实施原因证券交易委员会无权催收债务。

(h)记录。听证官应保存本节下所有听证的记录。听证不必是正式的举证听证,不过,在口头听证中作证的证人应按照宣誓或证词声明程序进行作证。

(i)裁决日期。听证官应在可行的最短时间内(但不得晚于证券交易委员会收到听证申请之日后60日)签发书面裁决意见。如果证券交易委员会不能向债务人提供听证或不能在证券交易委员会收到听证申请后60日内作出裁决,则:

(1)在举行听证并作出裁决前不得签发预扣令;或

(2)如果此前曾向债务人的雇主签发预扣令,则预扣令应于证券交易委员会收到听证申请后第61日暂停执行,直至听证举行并作出裁决之日。

(j)裁决内容。书面裁决应包括:
(1)陈述事实的摘要;
(2)认定、分析和结论;及
(3)任何还款计划(如有)的条款。
(k)最终机构行动。除非证券交易委员会依照《联邦规章汇编》第十七编第201.431(c)节主动发起对听证官裁决的复议程序,否则就《行政程序法》中的司法审查而言,听证官的裁决应视为证券交易委员会的最终决定。

judicial review under the Administrative Procedure Act.

(l) *Failure to appear.* In the absence of good cause shown, a debtor who fails to appear at a scheduled hearing will be deemed as not having timely filed a request for a hearing.

§204.65 Wage garnishment order.

(a) Unless the Commission receives information that the Commission believes justifies a delay or cancellation of the withholding order, the Commission will send, by first class mail, a withholding order to the debtor's employer within 30 days after the debtor fails to make a timely request for a hearing (*i.e.* , within 15 business days after the mailing of the notice of the Commission's intent to seek garnishment) or, if a timely request for a hearing is made by the debtor, within 30 days after a decision to issue a withholding order becomes final.

(b) The withholding order sent to the employer will be in the form prescribed by the Secretary of the Treasury, on the Commission's letterhead, and signed by the Chairperson or his or her delegatee. The order will contain the information necessary for the employer to comply with the withholding order. This information includes the debtor's name, address, and social security number, as well as instructions for withholding and information as to where payments should be sent.

(c) The Commission will keep a copy of the certificate of service indicating the date of mailing of the order.

(d) *Certification by employer.* Along with the withholding order, the Commission will send to the employer a certification in a form prescribed by the Secretary of the Treasury. The employer shall complete and return the certification to the Commission within the time frame prescribed in the instructions to the form. The certification will address matters such as information about the debtor's employment status and disposable pay available for withholding.

(e) *A mounts withheld.* (1) After receipt of the garnishment order issued under this section, the employer shall deduct from all disposable pay paid to the applicable debtor during each pay period the amount of garnishment described in paragraph (e)(2) of this section.

(2) Subject to the provisions of paragraphs (e)(3) and (e)(4) of this section, the amount of garnishment shall be the lesser of:

(i) The amount indicated on the garnishment order up to 15% of the debtor's disposable pay; or

(ii) The amount set forth in 15 U.S.C. 1673(a)(2) (Restriction on Garnishment). The amount set forth at U.S.C. 1673(a)(2) is the amount by which the debtor's disposable pay exceeds an amount equivalent to thirty times the minimum wage *See* 29 CFR 870.10.

(l)缺席情形。债务人没有出席按计划召开的听证,且没有充分理由的,应视为未按时提交听证请求。

第204.65节 工资扣发令

(a)除非证券交易委员会收到相关信息,并据以判定应该推迟签发或取消预扣令,否则如果债务人未及时提交听证请求(即债务人收到证券交易委员会邮寄的扣发工资意向通知后15个工作日内),证券交易委员会应在30日内通过普通邮件向债务人的雇主寄送预扣令;如果债务人已及时提交听证请求,证券交易委员会应在签发预扣令的决定取得终局效力后30日内通过普通邮件向债务人的雇主寄送预扣令。

(b)寄送给雇主的预扣令应采用财政部长规定的格式,使用证券交易委员会的信头纸,并由证券交易委员会主席或其指定人员签署。命令应包含雇主执行预扣令所必要的信息,包括债务人的姓名、地址、社保号码、预扣指令和款项应支付至何处的信息。

(c)证券交易委员会应保留送达证明,送达证明上应标明通知寄达日期。

(d)雇主出具的证明。证券交易委员会应随预扣令向雇主寄送一份证明,证明的格式由财政部长规定。雇主应按填写证明中规定的期限,将填写好的证明交回证券交易委员会。证明应说明债务人的劳动关系状态和可供预扣的可支配工资等事项。

(e)预扣金额。(1)在收到本节下签发的预扣令后,雇主应从相关债务人每一付薪周期的所有可支配工资中扣除本节第(e)(2)款中规定的扣发金额。

(2)在不违反本节第(e)(3)款和第(e)(4)款规定的前提下,扣发金额应为下述二者中的较低者:

(i)预扣令中列明的金额(不超过债务人可支配工资的 15%);或

(ii)《美国法典》第十五编第 1673(a)(2)节("扣发限制")规定的金额。《美国法典》第十五编第1673(a)(2)节规定的限制金额为债务人可支配工资超过最低工资的30倍的部分(参见《联邦规章汇编》第二十九编第870.10节)。

(3) When a debtor's pay is subject to withholding orders with priority, the following shall apply:

(i) Unless otherwise provided by Federal law, withholding orders issued under this section shall be paid in the amounts set forth under paragraph (e)(2) of this section and shall have priority over other withholding orders which are served later in time. However, withholding orders for family support shall have priority over withholding orders issued under this section.

(ii) If amounts are being withheld from a debtor's pay pursuant to a withholding order served on an employer before a withholding order issued pursuant to this section, or if a withholding order for family support is served on an employer at any time, the amounts withheld pursuant to the withholding order issued under this section shall be the lesser of:

(A) The amount calculated under paragraph (e)(2) of this section; or

(B) An amount equal to 25% of the debtor's disposable pay less the amount(s) withheld under the withholding order(s) with priority.

(iii) If a debtor owes more than one debt to the Commission, the Commission may issue multiple withholding orders. The total amount garnished from the debtor's pay for such orders will not exceed the amount set forth in paragraph (e)(2) of this section.

(4) An amount greater than that set forth in paragraphs (e)(2) and (e)(3) of this section may be withheld upon the written consent of the debtor.

(5) The employer shall promptly pay to the Commission all amounts withheld in accordance with the withholding order issued pursuant to this section.

(6) An employer shall not be required to vary its normal pay and disbursement cycles in order to comply with the withholding order.

(7) Any assignment or allotment by the employee of the employee's earnings shall be void to the extent it interferes with or prohibits execution of the withholding order under this section, except for any assignment or allotment made pursuant to a family support judgment or order.

(8) The employer shall withhold the appropriate amount from the debtor's wages for each pay period until the employer receives notification from the Commission to discontinue wage withholding. The garnishment order shall indicate a reasonable period of time within which the employer is required to commence wage withholding.

(f) *Exclusions from garnishment.* The Commission will not garnish the wages of a debtor it knows has been involuntarily separated from employment until the debtor has been reemployed continuously for at least 12 months. The debtor has the burden of informing the Commission of the circumstances surrounding an involuntary separation from employment.

(g) *Financial hardship.* (1) A debtor whose wages are subject to a wage withholding

(3)债务人工资被签发不同优先级别的预扣令之时,应适用如下规则:

(i)除非联邦法律另有规定,否则应按照本节第(e)(2)款规定的金额执行本节下签发的预扣令,且本节中的预扣令应优先于送达时间较晚的其他预扣令。但是,为赡养家人目的签发的预扣令应优先于本节下签发的预扣令。

(ii)如果在依照本节签发预扣令前,雇主已经在按送达雇主的其他预扣令扣除债务人工资,或者雇主在任何时候收到为赡养家人目的签发的预扣令,则按照本条下签发的预扣令扣除的金额应为下述两者中的较低者:

(A)根据本节第(e)(2)款计算出的金额;或

(B)债务人可支配工资的金额执行了具有优先权的一项或多项预扣令后的余额的25%。

(iii)如果债务人欠负证券交易委员会的债务超过一笔,证券交易委员会可以签发多项预扣令。为执行该等预扣令从债务人工资中扣发的总金额不得超过本节第(e)(2)款规定的金额。

(4)经债务人书面同意,预扣金额可以超过本节第(e)(2)款和第(e)(3)款规定的金额。

(5)雇主应及时向证券交易委员会支付按照本节下签发的预扣令预扣的全部金额。

(6)雇主不必为执行预扣令改变其正常的工资和付薪周期。

(7)雇员对其收入的任何转让或分配如干涉或禁止本节下预扣令的执行,该等转让或分配应为无效,但按照赡养家判决或命令作出的转让或分配除外。

(8)雇主应在每个付薪周期从债务人工资中预扣适当金额,直至收到证券交易委员会停止预扣工资的通知为止。扣发令应说明雇主应开始预扣工资的合理期间。

(f)例外情形。证券交易委员会明知债务人已经非自愿离职的,在债务人重新就职且连续雇佣期间满12个月之前,证券交易委员会不得扣发债务人工资。债务人有责任将与其非自愿离职相关的情形通知证券交易委员会。

(g)经济困难。(1)债务人的工资被发布本节中的预扣令,且发生残疾、离婚、重大

order under this section, may, at any time, request a review by the Commission of the amount garnished, based on materially changed circumstances such as disability, divorce, or catastrophic illness which result in financial hardship.

(2) A debtor requesting a review under this section shall submit the basis for claiming that the current amount of garnishment results in a financial hardship to the debtor, along with supporting documentation.

(3) If a financial hardship is found, the Commission will downwardly adjust, by an amount and for a period of time agreeable to the Commission, the amount garnished to reflect the debtor's financial condition. The Commission will notify the employer of any adjustments to the amounts to be withheld.

(h) *Ending garnishment.* (1) Once the Commission has fully recovered the amounts owed by the debtor, including interest, penalties, and administrative costs consistent with the Federal Claims Collection Standards (31 CFR 901.9), the Commission will send the debtor's employer notification to discontinue wage withholding.

(2) At least annually, the Commission will review its debtors' accounts to ensure that garnishment has been terminated for accounts that have been paid in full.

(i) *Actions prohibited by the employer.* The Debt Collection Act prohibits an employer from discharging, refusing to employ, or taking disciplinary action against the debtor due to the issuance of a withholding order under this section (31 U.S.C. 3720D (e)).

(j) *Refunds.* (1) If a hearing official determines that a debt is not legally due and owing to the United States, the Commission shall promptly refund any amount collected by means of administrative wage garnishment.

(2) Unless required by Federal law or contract, refunds under this section shall not bear interest.

(k) *Right of action.* The Commission may sue any employer for any amount that the employer fails to withhold from wages owed and payable to an employee in accordance with this section. However, a suit will not be filed before the termination of the collection action involving a particular debtor, unless earlier filing is necessary to avoid expiration of any applicable statute of limitations. For purposes of this section, "termination of the collection action" occurs when the agency has terminated collection action in accordance with the Federal Claims Collection Standards (31 CFR 903.1–903.5) or other applicable standards. In any event, termination of the collection action will have been deemed to occur if the Commission has not received any payments to satisfy the debt from the particular debtor whose wages were subject to garnishment, in whole or in part, for a period of one (1) year.

疾病等造成债务人经济困难的重大情形变更的,债务人可以在任何时候基于此等情形请求证券交易委员会对扣发金额进行审查。

(2)根据本节提请审查的债务人主张现有扣发金额造成其经济困难的,应呈报主张的理由并附上支持文件。

(3)证券交易委员会认定债务人存在经济困难的,应基于债务人的财务状况,在证券交易委员会同意的期间内,按照证券交易委员会同意的金额下调扣发金额。证券交易委员会对预扣金额进行任何调整的,均应通知雇主。

(h)终止扣发。(1)在全额收回债务人所欠债务[包括按照《联邦债权催收标准》(《联邦规章汇编》第三十一编第 901.9 节)计征的利息、罚款和行政成本]后,证券交易委员会应向债务人的雇主寄送停止扣发工资通知。

(2)证券交易委员会至少应每年审核一次债务人的账款,以确保在债务人已经全额支付账款的情况下终止工资扣发。

(i)禁止雇主采取的行动。《债务催收法》禁止雇主基于本节下签发的预扣令解聘、拒绝雇佣债务人或对债务人处以纪律处分[《美国法典》第三十一编第 3720D(e)节]。

(j)退款。(1)如果听证官判定债务并非欠负联邦政府的合法到期应付款项,证券交易委员会应及时退还通过行政扣发工资催收的任何款项。

(2)除非联邦法律或合同另有规定,否则本节中的退款不计利息。

(k)诉讼权。如果任何雇主未根据本节规定预扣应向雇员支付的工资,证券交易委员会可以起诉雇主。但是,在对具体债务人的催收行动终止前,不应针对雇主提起案件,但为了避免任何适用时效过期有必要提前提起诉讼的除外。就本节而言,“催收行动终止”系指政府机构已根据《联邦债权催收标准》(《联邦规章汇编》第三十一编第903.1–903.5节)或其他适用标准终止催收行动。在任何情况下,如果证券交易委员会未从工资被扣发的具体债务人处收到任何付款以偿还全部或部分债务的时间超过1年,催收行动应视为已经终止。

Subpart E—Miscellaneous: Credit Bureau Reporting, Collection Services

Authority: 31 U.S.C. 3701, 3711, 3718.

Source: 58 FR 64373, Dec. 7, 1993, unless otherwise noted.

§204.75 Collection services.

Section 13 of the Debt Collection Act (31 U.S.C. 3718) authorizes agencies to enter into contracts for collection services to recover debts owed the United States. The Act requires that certain provisions be contained in such contracts, including:

(a) The agency retains the authority to resolve a dispute, including the authority to terminate a collection action or refer the matter to the Attorney General for civil remedies; and

(b) The contractor is subject to the Privacy Act of 1974, as it applies to private contractors, as well as subject to State and Federal laws governing debt collection practices.

§204.76 Use of credit bureau or consumer reporting agencies.

(a) The Commission may report delinquent debts to consumer reporting agencies (See 31 U.S.C. 3701(a)(3), 3711). Sixty days prior to release of information to a consumer reporting agency, the debtor shall be notified, in writing, of the intent to disclose the existence of the debt to a consumer reporting agency. Such notice of intent may be a separate correspondence or included in correspondence demanding direct payment. The notice shall be in conformance with 31 U.S.C. 3711(e) and the Federal Claims Collection Standards. The Commission shall provide, in this notice, the debtor with:

(1) An opportunity to inspect and copy agency records pertaining to the debt;

(2) An opportunity for an administrative review of the legal enforceability or past due status of the debt;

(3) An opportunity to enter into a repayment agreement on terms satisfactory to the Commission to prevent the Commission from reporting the debt as overdue to consumer reporting agencies, and provide deadlines and method for requesting this relief;

(4) An explanation of the rate of interest that will accrue on the debt, that all costs incurred to collect the debt will be charged to the debtor, the authority for assessing these costs, and the manner in which the Commission will calculate the amount of these cost;

(5) An explanation that the Commission will report the debt to the consumer reporting agencies to the detriment of the debtor's credit rating; and

第E子部分——其他:信贷局报告、催收服务

法律依据:《美国法典》第三十一编第3701节、第3711节、第3718节。

行政规则来源:《联邦公报》第58卷第64373页,1993年12月7日,除非另有说明。

第204.75节　催收服务

《债务催收法》第13条(《美国法典》第三十一编第3718节)授权政府机构签订催收服务合同,以催收欠负联邦政府的债务。根据该法,该等合同中应包含特定条款,包括:

(a)政府机构保留解决争议的权限,包括终止催收行动的权限和将事项移交给总检察长寻求民事救济的权限;及

(b)催收服务承包商应遵守《1974年隐私法》中关于私人承包商的规定;并应遵守管辖债务催收做法的州法律和联邦法律的限制。

第204.76节　与信贷局或消费者征信机构的合作

(a)证券交易委员会可以向消费者征信机构报告过期债务[参见《美国法典》第三十一编第3701(a)(3)节和第3711节]。证券交易委员会应在向消费者征信机构发布消息60日前,以书面形式通知债务人其有意向消费者征信机构披露债务的存在。该意向通知可以是一封独立信函,也可以纳入要求直接付款的通信之中。通知应符合《美国法典》第三十一编第3711(e)节和《联邦债权催收标准》的规定。证券交易委员会应在通知中:

(1)为债务人提供查阅和复制证券交易委员会与债务相关记录的机会;

(2)为债务人提供就债务是否可依法强制执行或是否处于过期状态提请行政复议的机会;

(3)为债务人提供按照证券交易委员会同意的条款签署一份还款协议,以阻止证券交易委员会向消费者征信机构报告过期债务的机会,并应向债务人说明本救济的截止日期和方法;

(4)对债务将适用的利率作出说明,并说明催收债务发生的所有费用均应由债务人支付以及证券交易委员会计征此等费用的权限和计算费用具体金额的方式;

(5)说明证券交易委员会向消费者征信机构报告债务将损害债务人信用评级;及

(6) A description of the collection actions that the agency may take in the future if those presently proposed actions do not result in repayment of the loan obligation, including the filing of a lawsuit against the borrower by the agency and assignment of the debt for collection by offset against Federal income tax refunds or the filing of a lawsuit against the debtor by the Federal Government.

(b) The information that may be disclosed to the consumer reporting agency is limited to:

(1) The debtor's name, address, social security number or taxpayer identification number, and any other information necessary to establish the identity of the individual;

(2) The amount, status, and history of the claim; and

(3) The Commission program or activity under which the claim arose.

[58 FR 64373, Dec. 7, 1993, as amended at 66 FR 54135, Oct. 26, 2001]

§204.77 Referrals to collection agencies.

(a) The Commission has authority to contract for collection services to recover delinquent debts in accordance with 31 U.S.C. 3718(a) and the Federal Claims Collection Standards (31 CFR 901.5).

(b) The Commission will use private collection agencies where it determines that their use is in the best interest of the Government. Where the Commission determines that there is a need to contract for collection services, the contract will provide that:

(1) The authority to resolve disputes, compromise claims, suspend or terminate collection action, or refer the matter to the Department of Justice for litigation or to take any other action under this part will be retained by the Commission;

(2) Contractors are subject to the Privacy Act of 1974, as amended, to the extent specified in 5 U.S.C. 552a(m) and to applicable Federal and State laws and regulations pertaining to debt collection practices, such as the Fair Debt Collection Practices Act, 15 U.S.C. 1692;

(3) The contractor is required to strictly account for all amounts collected;

(4) The contractor must agree that uncollectible accounts shall be returned with appropriate documentation to enable Commission to determine whether to pursue collection through litigation or to terminate collection; and

(5) The contractor must agree to provide any data in its files requested by the Commission upon returning the account to the Commission for subsequent referral to the Department of Justice for litigation.

[58 FR 64373, Dec. 7, 1993, as amended at 66 FR 54135, Oct. 26, 2001]

(6)说明如果采取当前拟议的行动后,债务人仍未归还贷款,证券交易委员会可能采取的催收行动,包括证券交易委员会直接针对借款人提起诉讼、通过联邦所得税退税进行抵消的方式催收债务或交由联邦政府针对债务人提起诉讼。

(b)可以向消费者征信机构披露的信息限于:

(1)债务人的姓名、地址、社保号码或纳税人识别号码和任何其他可以确认个人身份的必要信息;

(2)债权主张的金额、状态和历史;及

(3)引发证券交易委员会债权的计划或活动。

[《联邦公报》第58卷第64373页,1993年12月7日,修正索引:《联邦公报》第66卷第54135页,2001年10月26日。]

第204.77节　移交催收机构

(a)证券交易委员会有权根据《美国法典》第三十一编第3718(a)节和《联邦债权催收标准》(《联邦规章汇编》第三十一编第901.5节)分包过期债务催收服务。

(b)证券交易委员会判定使用私人催收机构符合政府的最大利益的,可以使用私人催收机构。证券交易委员会判定需要分包催收服务的,分包合同应规定:

(1)证券交易委员会将保留解决争议、债权和解、暂停或终止催收行动、将事项移交司法部提起诉讼或采取本部分下任何行动的权限;

(2)在《美国法典》第五编第552a(m)节具体规定的范围内,催收服务承包商应遵守《1974年隐私法》及其修正,以及关于债务催收做法的适用联邦法律法规或州法律法规,如《公平债务催收作业法》(《美国法典》第十五编第1692节);

(3)催收服务承包商有义务严格说明所有催收金额;

(4)催收服务承包商必须同意,对于无法催收的账款,承包商应返回适当文件,以便证券交易委员会判定是否寻求通过诉讼手段进行催收或终止催收;及

(5)催收服务承包商必须同意,在将账款返回证券交易委员会时,将按证券交易委员会的请求提供任何文件数据,以便证券交易委员会在此后移交司法部提起诉讼。

[《联邦公报》第58卷第64373页,1993年12月7日,修正索引:《联邦公报》第66卷第54135页,2001年10月26日。]

PART 205—STANDARDS OF PROFESSIONAL CONDUCT FOR ATTORNEYS APPEARING AND PRACTICING BEFORE THE COMMISSION IN THE REPRESENTATION OF AN ISSUER

Authority: 15 U.S.C. 77s, 78d-3, 78w, 80a-37, 80a-38, 80b-11, 7202, 7245, and 7262.

Source: 68 FR 6320, Feb. 6, 2003, unless otherwise noted.

§205.1 Purpose and scope.

This part sets forth minimum standards of professional conduct for attorneys appearing and practicing before the Commission in the representation of an issuer. These standards supplement applicable standards of any jurisdiction where an attorney is admitted or practices and are not intended to limit the ability of any jurisdiction to impose additional obligations on an attorney not inconsistent with the application of this part. Where the standards of a state or other United States jurisdiction where an attorney is admitted or practices conflict with this part, this part shall govern.

§205.2 Definitions.

For purposes of this part, the following definitions apply:

(a) *Appearing and practicing* before the Commission:

(1) Means:

(i) Transacting any business with the Commission, including communications in any form;

(ii) Representing an issuer in a Commission administrative proceeding or in connection with any Commission investigation, inquiry, information request, or subpoena;

(iii) Providing advice in respect of the United States securities laws or the Commission's rules or regulations thereunder regarding any document that the attorney has notice will be filed with or submitted to, or incorporated into any document that will be filed with or submitted to, the Commission, including the provision of such advice in the context of preparing, or participating in the preparation of, any such document; or

(iv) Advising an issuer as to whether information or a statement, opinion, or other writing is required under the United States securities laws or the Commission's rules or regulations thereunder to be filed with or submitted to, or incorporated into any document

第205部分——代表发行人出席证券交易委员会程序并办理业务的律师的职业行为标准

法律依据:《美国法典》第十五编第77s节、第78d-3节、第78w节、第80a-37节、第80a-38节、第80b-11节、第7202节、第7245节和第7262节。

行政规则来源:《联邦公报》第68卷第6320页,2003年2月6日,除非另有说明。

第205.1节 目的和范围

本部分规定了代表发行人出席证券交易委员会程序并办理业务的律师的最低职业行为标准。本部分规定的标准构成律师获得执业资格所在地或者实际执业所在地的任何司法辖区的适用标准之补充。本部分规定无意限制任何司法辖区对律师施加与本部分规定不相冲突的补充义务。各州标准或律师获得执业资格所在地或实际执业所在地的其他美国司法辖区的标准与本部分规定相冲突的,以本部分规定为准。

第205.2节 定义

就本部分而言,应适用如下定义:

(a)“出席证券交易委员会程序并办理业务”:

(1)系指:

(i)与证券交易委员会办理任何业务,包括进行任何形式的沟通;

(ii)在证券交易委员会的行政处理程序或证券交易委员会的任何调查、询问、信息请求或传票送达程序中为发行人提供代理;

(iii)针对据律师所知应向证券交易委员会提交或呈报的任何文件(或将被纳入该等文件的文件),提供与美国证券法或证券交易委员会依美国证券法制定的规则或规章有关的咨询,包括在编制或参与编制任何上述文件的过程中提供咨询;或

(iv)针对美国证券法或证券交易委员会依美国证券法制定的规则或规章是否要求发行人向证券交易委员会提交或呈报相关信息、声明、意见或其他书面文件,或者是否要求将相关信息、声明、意见或其他书面文件纳入应向证券交易委员会提交或呈报的任

that will be filed with or submitted to, the Commission; but

(2) Does not include an attorney who:

(i) Conducts the activities in paragraphs (a)(1)(i) through (a)(1)(iv) of this section other than in the context of providing legal services to an issuer with whom the attorney has an attorney–client relationship; or

(ii) Is a non–appearing foreign attorney.

(b) *Appropriate response* means a response to an attorney regarding reported evidence of a material violation as a result of which the attorney reasonably believes:

(1) That no material violation, as defined in paragraph (i) of this section, has occurred, is ongoing, or is about to occur;

(2) That the issuer has, as necessary, adopted appropriate remedial measures, including appropriate steps or sanctions to stop any material violations that are ongoing, to prevent any material violation that has yet to occur, and to remedy or otherwise appropriately address any material violation that has already occurred and to minimize the likelihood of its recurrence; or

(3) That the issuer, with the consent of the issuer's board of directors, a committee thereof to whom a report could be made pursuant to §205.3(b)(3), or a qualified legal compliance committee, has retained or directed an attorney to review the reported evidence of a material violation and either:

(i) Has substantially implemented any remedial recommendations made by such attorney after a reasonable investigation and evaluation of the reported evidence; or

(ii) Has been advised that such attorney may, consistent with his or her professional obligations, assert a colorable defense on behalf of the issuer (or the issuer's officer, director, employee, or agent, as the case may be) in any investigation or judicial or administrative proceeding relating to the reported evidence of a material violation.

(c) *Attorney* means any person who is admitted, licensed, or otherwise qualified to practice law in any jurisdiction, domestic or foreign, or who holds himself or herself out as admitted, licensed, or otherwise qualified to practice law.

(d) *Breach of fiduciary duty* refers to any breach of fiduciary or similar duty to the issuer recognized under an applicable Federal or State statute or at common law, including but not limited to misfeasance, nonfeasance, abdication of duty, abuse of trust, and approval of unlawful transactions.

(e) *Evidence of a material violation* means credible evidence, based upon which it would be unreasonable, under the circumstances, for a prudent and competent attorney not to conclude that it is reasonably likely that a material violation has occurred, is ongoing, or is about to occur.

(f) *Foreign government issuer* means a foreign issuer as defined in 17 CFR 230.405

何文件,为发行人提供相关咨询;但是

(2)该定义不适用于如下律师:

(i)不是在接受发行人的委托为其提供法律服务的情况下从事本节第(a)(1)(i)款至第(a)(1)(iv)款的活动的律师;或

(ii)无出席证券交易委员会程序资格的外国律师。

(b)“适当答复”系指发行人在收到关于实质违法违规行为的证据之后向律师所作的答复,且律师根据该答复合理相信:

(1)并无任何本节第(i)款定义的实质违法违规行为已经发生、正在进行或即将发生;

(2)发行人已经采取必要和适当的补救措施,包括采取适当步骤或制裁以制止正在进行中的任何实质违法违规行为,阻止尚未发生的任何实质违法违规行为,补救或以其他方式适当处理已经发生的任何实质违法违规行为,并将实质违法违规行为再次发生的几率减到最低限度;或

(3)发行人已获得其董事会、按照第 205.3(b)(3)节可以接受报告的董事会下属委员会或合格的法律合规委员会同意,聘用或指示一名律师审查所报告的关于实质违法违规行为的证据,且:

(i)发行人在对所报告证据进行合理调查和评估后,基本贯彻了上述律师建议的所有补救措施;或

(ii)上述律师已经向发行人提供意见,表明其可以在不违反职业义务的前提下作为发行人(或发行人的管理人员、董事、职员或代理人,视具体情况而定)的代理,在与所报告的实质违法违规证据有关的任何调查、司法程序或行政处理程序中提供合理辩护。

(c)“律师”系指在任何本国或外国司法辖区获得执业资格、取得执照或以其他方式取得法律执业资格的人,或以该等身份自居的人。

(d)“违反受信义务”系指违反任何适用联邦制定法、州制定法或普通法下认定的律师对发行人承担的受信义务或类似义务,包括但不限于违法、渎职、失职、滥用信任以及批准非法交易。

(e)“实质违法违规证据”系指如被提交给审慎胜任的律师,则合理情况下该律师不可能不认定某一实质违法违规行为已经发生、正在进行或即将发生的可靠证据。

(f)“外国政府发行人”系指《联邦规章汇编》第十七编第230.405节定义的有资格根

eligible to register securities on Schedule B of the Securities Act of 1933 (15 U.S.C. 77a *et seq.*, Schedule B).

(g) *In the representation of an issuer* means providing legal services as an attorney for an issuer, regardless of whether the attorney is employed or retained by the issuer.

(h) *Issuer* means an issuer (as defined in section 3 of the Securities Exchange Act of 1934 (15 U.S.C. 78c)), the securities of which are registered under section 12 of that Act (15 U.S.C. 78l), or that is required to file reports under section 15(d) of that Act (15 U.S.C. 78o(d)), or that files or has filed a registration statement that has not yet become effective under the Securities Act of 1933 (15 U.S.C. 77a *et seq.*), and that it has not withdrawn, but does not include a foreign government issuer. For purposes of paragraphs (a) and (g) of this section, the term "issuer" includes any person controlled by an issuer, where an attorney provides legal services to such person on behalf of, or at the behest, or for the benefit of the issuer, regardless of whether the attorney is employed or retained by the issuer.

(i) *Material violation* means a material violation of an applicable United States federal or state securities law, a material breach of fiduciary duty arising under United States federal or state law, or a similar material violation of any United States federal or state law.

(j) *Non-appearing foreign attorney* means an attorney:

(1) Who is admitted to practice law in a jurisdiction outside the United States;

(2) Who does not hold himself or herself out as practicing, and does not give legal advice regarding, United States federal or state securities or other laws (except as provided in paragraph (j)(3)(ii) of this section); and

(3) Who:

(i) Conducts activities that would constitute appearing and practicing before the Commission only incidentally to, and in the ordinary course of, the practice of law in a jurisdiction outside the United States; or

(ii) Is appearing and practicing before the Commission only in consultation with counsel, other than a non-appearing foreign attorney, admitted or licensed to practice in a state or other United States jurisdiction.

(k) *Qualified legal compliance committee* means a committee of an issuer (which also may be an audit or other committee of the issuer) that:

(1) Consists of at least one member of the issuer's audit committee (or, if the issuer has no audit committee, one member from an equivalent committee of independent directors) and two or more members of the issuer's board of directors who are not employed, directly or indirectly, by the issuer and who are not, in the case of a registered investment company, "interested persons" as defined in section 2 (a) (19) of the

据《1933年证券法》附表B(《美国法典》第十五编第77a节及其后条文,附表B)注册证券的外国发行人。

(g)"作为发行人的代理"系指以律师身份为发行人提供法律服务,无论律师是否受雇或受聘于发行人。

(h)"发行人"系指根据《1934 年证券交易法》第 12 条(《美国法典》第十五编第 78l 节)注册证券的发行人[定义见《1934 年证券交易法》第 3 条(《美国法典》第十五编第 78c 节)],或按照《1934 年证券交易法》第 15(d)条[《美国法典》第十五编第 78o(d)节]的规定负有报告义务的发行人,或提交或已经提交注册说明书,但根据《1933 年美国证券法》(《美国法典》第十五编第 77a 节及其后条文)该等注册说明书尚未生效且未予撤回的发行人,不包括外国政府发行人。就本节第(a)款和第(g)款而言,如果律师代表发行人、应发行人的请求或为发行人的利益向受发行人控制的人提供法律服务,则"发行人"一词包括受发行人控制的任何人,而无论律师是否受雇或受聘于发行人。

(i)"实质违规"系指对适用的美国联邦证券法或州证券法的实质违反,对联邦法律或州法律中的受信义务的实质违反,或对任何美国联邦法律或州法律的类似实质违反。

(j)"无出席程序资格的外国律师"系指符合以下条件的律师:

(1)在美国以外司法辖区获得法律执业资格;

(2)不以美国联邦证券法或州证券法或其他法律领域的执业律师身份自居,且不就该等法律提供法律咨询[本节第(j)(3)(ii)款规定的情形除外];

(3)并且:

(i)在美国以外司法辖区执业的正常工作中附带性地从事构成出席证券交易委员会程序并办理相关业务的活动;或

(ii)仅在与无出席程序资格的外国律师以外的律师(并且该等律师获得美国某个州或美国其他司法辖区的执业资格)磋商后才出席证券交易委员会程序并办理相关业务。

(k)"合格的法律合规委员会"系指符合下述条件的发行人委员会(也可为发行人的审计委员会或其他委员会):

(1)至少包含发行人审计委员会的一名委员(如果发行人没有审计委员会,则应至少包含同等的独立董事委员会的一位委员),同时至少包含发行人董事会中非发行人直接或间接雇佣的两名(含)以上董事,且对于注册投资公司而言,该等董事不得构成《1940 年投资公司法》第 2(a)(19)条[《美国法典》第十五编第80a-2(a)(19)节]定义的"利害关系人";

Investment Company Act of 1940 (15 U.S.C. 80a-2(a)(19));

(2) Has adopted written procedures for the confidential receipt, retention, and consideration of any report of evidence of a material violation under §205.3;

(3) Has been duly established by the issuer's board of directors, with the authority and responsibility:

(i) To inform the issuer's chief legal officer and chief executive officer (or the equivalents thereof) of any report of evidence of a material violation (except in the circumstances described in §205.3(b)(4));

(ii) To determine whether an investigation is necessary regarding any report of evidence of a material violation by the issuer, its officers, directors, employees or agents and, if it determines an investigation is necessary or appropriate, to:

(A) Notify the audit committee or the full board of directors;

(B) Initiate an investigation, which may be conducted either by the chief legal officer (or the equivalent thereof) or by outside attorneys; and

(C) Retain such additional expert personnel as the committee deems necessary; and

(iii) At the conclusion of any such investigation, to:

(A) Recommend, by majority vote, that the issuer implement an appropriate response to evidence of a material violation; and

(B) Inform the chief legal officer and the chief executive officer (or the equivalents thereof) and the board of directors of the results of any such investigation under this section and the appropriate remedial measures to be adopted; and

(4) Has the authority and responsibility, acting by majority vote, to take all other appropriate action, including the authority to notify the Commission in the event that the issuer fails in any material respect to implement an appropriate response that the qualified legal compliance committee has recommended the issuer to take.

(l) *Reasonable* or *reasonably* denotes, with respect to the actions of an attorney, conduct that would not be unreasonable for a prudent and competent attorney.

(m) *Reasonably believes* means that an attorney believes the matter in question and that the circumstances are such that the belief is not unreasonable.

(n) *Report* means to make known to directly, either in person, by telephone, by e-mail, electronically, or in writing.

§205.3 Issuer as client.

(a) *Representing an issuer.* An attorney appearing and practicing before the Commission in the representation of an issuer owes his or her professional and ethical duties to the issuer as an organization. That the attorney may work with and advise the issuer's officers, directors, or employees in the course of representing the issuer does not make such individuals the attorney's clients.

(2)已经就在保密状态下接收、保留并审查第205.3节中的任何关于实质违法违规证据的报告制定书面程序;

(3)已经由发行人的董事会正式设立,并具有如下权限和职责:

(i)将任何实质违法违规证据报告通知发行人的首席法务官和首席执行官(或同级别高管)[第205.3(b)(4)节所述的情形除外];

(ii)判定是否有必要就任何关于发行人及其管理人员、董事、职员或代理人的实质违法违规证据的报告开展必要调查,且如果判定调查确属必要或适当的,具有如下权限和职责:

(A)通知审计委员会或全体董事会;

(B)发起调查,调查可由首席法务官(或同级别高管)或外部律师开展;且

(C)聘用委员会认为有必要聘用的其他专业人士;且

(iii)在上述任何调查结束之时:

(A)通过多数表决建议发行人对实质违法违规证据作出适当答复;并

(B)将依据本节开展的任何调查的结果以及需要采取的补救措施通知首席法务官和首席执行官(或同级别高管)和董事会;并

(4)拥有通过多数表决采取所有其他恰当行动的权限和责任,包括在发行人在任何重大方面未能贯彻合格的法律合规委员会建议的适当答复的情况下,有向证券交易委员会发出通知的权限和责任。

(l)"合理的或合理地",就律师采取的行动而言,系指审慎胜任的律师认为合理的行为。

(m)"合理相信"系指律师根据具体情形合理相信相关事项。

(n)"报告"系指当面或通过电话、电子邮件、电子或书面方式直接告知。

第205.3节　律师的委托人为发行人而非发行人的高管、董事或职员

(a)作为发行人的代理。作为发行人的代理出席证券交易委员会的程序并办理业务的律师,对组织意义上的发行人承担职业和道德责任。律师在代理发行人的过程中与发行人的高管、董事或职员合作或提供法律意见,并不表示发行人的管理人员、董事或职员构成律师的委托人。

(b) *Duty to report evidence of a material violation.* (1) If an attorney, appearing and practicing before the Commission in the representation of an issuer, becomes aware of evidence of a material violation by the issuer or by any officer, director, employee, or agent of the issuer, the attorney shall report such evidence to the issuer's chief legal officer (or the equivalent thereof) or to both the issuer's chief legal officer and its chief executive officer (or the equivalents thereof) forthwith. By communicating such information to the issuer's officers or directors, an attorney does not reveal client confidences or secrets or privileged or otherwise protected information related to the attorney's representation of an issuer.

(2) The chief legal officer (or the equivalent thereof) shall cause such inquiry into the evidence of a material violation as he or she reasonably believes is appropriate to determine whether the material violation described in the report has occurred, is ongoing, or is about to occur. If the chief legal officer (or the equivalent thereof) determines no material violation has occurred, is ongoing, or is about to occur, he or she shall notify the reporting attorney and advise the reporting attorney of the basis for such determination. Unless the chief legal officer (or the equivalent thereof) reasonably believes that no material violation has occurred, is ongoing, or is about to occur, he or she shall take all reasonable steps to cause the issuer to adopt an appropriate response, and shall advise the reporting attorney thereof. In lieu of causing an inquiry under this paragraph (b), a chief legal officer (or the equivalent thereof) may refer a report of evidence of a material violation to a qualified legal compliance committee under paragraph (c)(2) of this section if the issuer has duly established a qualified legal compliance committee prior to the report of evidence of a material violation.

(3) Unless an attorney who has made a report under paragraph (b)(1) of this section reasonably believes that the chief legal officer or the chief executive officer of the issuer (or the equivalent thereof) has provided an appropriate response within a reasonable time, the attorney shall report the evidence of a material violation to:

(i) The audit committee of the issuer's board of directors;

(ii) Another committee of the issuer's board of directors consisting solely of directors who are not employed, directly or indirectly, by the issuer and are not, in the case of a registered investment company, "interested persons" as defined in section 2(a)(19) of the Investment Company Act of 1940 (15 U.S.C. 80a-2(a)(19))(if the issuer's board of directors has no audit committee); or

(iii) The issuer's board of directors (if the issuer's board of directors has no committee consisting solely of directors who are not employed, directly or indirectly, by the issuer and are not, in the case of a registered investment company, "interested persons" as defined in section 2 (a)(19) of the Investment Company Act of 1940 (15

(b)报告实质违法违规证据的责任。(1)律师在作为发行人的代理出席证券交易委员会程序并办理业务的过程中,发现发行人或发行人的任何管理人员、董事、职员或发行人的代理人的实质违法违规证据的,应立即报告发行人的首席法务官(或同级别高管)或同时报告发行人的首席法务官和首席执行官(或同级别高管)。律师将该等信息通知发行人的高管或董事时,不应披露委托人的机密、秘密或与代理相关的受委托特权保护的信息或其他受保护信息。

(2)首席法务官(或同级别高管)应指示对实质违法违规证据进行其合理认为适当的调查,以判定报告所述的实质违规是否已经发生、正在进行或即将发生。如果首席法务官(或同级别高管)判定没有任何实质违法违规行为已经发生、正在进行或即将发生,应通知报告实质违法违规证据的律师并向该律师提供作出该等判定的依据。除非首席法务官(或同级别高管)合理相信没有任何实质违法违规行为已经发生、正在进行或即将发生,否则应采取合理步骤促使发行人作出适当答复,并通知报告实质违法违规证据的律师。除依据本第(b)款指示调查证据外,如果发行人已经在律师作出报告前按本节第(c)(2)款规定正式设立合格的法律合规委员会,首席法务官(或同级别高管)可以将实质违法违规证据报告转交该委员会。

(3)除非根据本节第(b)(1)款报告实质违法违规证据的律师合理相信发行人的首席法务官或首席执行官(或同级别高管)已经在合理时间内作出适当答复,否则该律师应将实质违法违规证据报告给:

(i)发行人董事会下属的审计委员会;

(ii)若发行人董事会未下设审计委员会,则为发行人董事会下属的另一个完全由不受发行人直接或间接雇佣的董事组成的委员会,对于注册投资公司而言,该等董事还不得构成《1940年美国投资公司法》第2(a)(19)条[《美国法典》第十五编第80a-2(a)(19)节]定义的“利害关系人”;或

(iii)发行人的董事会{如果发行人的董事会没有设立符合下述条件的下属委员会:完全由非发行人直接或间接雇佣的董事组成,且对于注册投资公司而言,该等董事不得构成《1940年美国投资公司法》第2(a)(19)条[《美国法典》第十五编第80a-2(a)(19)节]定义的“利害关系人”}。

U.S.C. 80a-2(a)(19))).

(4) If an attorney reasonably believes that it would be futile to report evidence of a material violation to the issuer's chief legal officer and chief executive officer (or the equivalents thereof)under paragraph (b)(1) of this section, the attorney may report such evidence as provided under paragraph (b)(3) of this section.

(5) An attorney retained or directed by an issuer to investigate evidence of a material violation reported under paragraph (b)(1), (b)(3), or (b)(4) of this section shall be deemed to be appearing and practicing before the Commission. Directing or retaining an attorney to investigate reported evidence of a material violation does not relieve an officer or director of the issuer to whom such evidence has been reported under paragraph (b)(1), (b)(3), or (b)(4) of this section from a duty to respond to the reporting attorney.

(6) An attorney shall not have any obligation to report evidence of a material violation under this paragraph (b) if:

(i) The attorney was retained or directed by the issuer's chief legal officer (or the equivalent thereof) to investigate such evidence of a material violation and:

(A) The attorney reports the results of such investigation to the chief legal officer (or the equivalent thereof); and

(B) Except where the attorney and the chief legal officer (or the equivalent thereof) each reasonably believes that no material violation has occurred, is ongoing, or is about to occur, the chief legal officer (or the equivalent thereof) reports the results of the investigation to the issuer's board of directors, a committee thereof to whom a report could be made pursuant to paragraph (b)(3) of this section, or a qualified legal compliance committee; or

(ii) The attorney was retained or directed by the chief legal officer (or the equivalent thereof) to assert, consistent with his or her professional obligations, a colorable defense on behalf of the issuer (or the issuer's officer, director, employee, or agent, as the case may be) in any investigation or judicial or administrative proceeding relating to such evidence of a material violation, and the chief legal officer (or the equivalent thereof) provides reasonable and timely reports on the progress and outcome of such proceeding to the issuer's board of directors, a committee thereof to whom a report could be made pursuant to paragraph (b)(3) of this section, or a qualified legal compliance committee.

(7) An attorney shall not have any obligation to report evidence of a material violation under this paragraph (b) if such attorney was retained or directed by a qualified legal compliance committee:

(i) To investigate such evidence of a material violation; or

(ii) To assert, consistent with his or her professional obligations, a colorable defense

(4)如果律师合理相信将实质违法违规证据报告给本节第(b)(1)款中的发行人首席法务官或首席执行官(或同级别高管)没有意义,律师可以按照本条第(b)(3)款规定进行报告。

(5)律师接受发行人的聘用或指示调查本条第(b)(1)款、第(b)(3)款或依据第(b)(4)款报告的实质违法违规证据的行为应视为出席证券交易委员会程序并办理业务的行为。发行人指示或聘用律师调查报告的实质违法违规证据的,并不免除收到依据本节第(b)(1)款、第(b)(3)款或第(b)(4)款报告的证据的发行人高管或董事对报告律师作出答复的责任。

(6)在下述情形下,律师不承担依据本第(b)款对实质违法违规证据进行报告的义务:

(i)律师系按照发行人首席法务官(或同级别高管)的聘用或指示调查实质违法违规证据,且:

(A)该律师已将调查结果报告给首席法务官(或同级别高管);且

(B)除律师和首席法务官(或同级别高管)均合理相信并无任何实质违法违规行为已经发生、正在进行或即将发生以外,首席法务官(或同级别高管)已将调查结果报告给发行人的董事会、依照本节第(b)(3)款可以接受报告的董事会下属委员会或合格的法律合规委员会;或

(ii)律师系按照发行人首席法务官(或同级别高管)的聘用或指示,在不违反其职业义务的情况下,在与该等实质违法违规证据有关的任何调查、司法或行政处理程序中代表发行人(或发行人的管理人员、董事、职员或代理人,视具体情况而定)提供合理辩护,且首席法务官(或同级别高管)合理且及时地将关于该等程序的进展和结果的报告提供给发行人的董事会、依照本节第(b)(3)款可以接受报告的、董事会下属委员会或合格的法律合规委员会。

(7)在下述情形下,律师不承担按照本节第(b)款报告实质违法违规证据的任何义务:

(i)律师系按照合格的法律合规委员会的聘用或指示调查该等实质违法违规证据;或

(ii)律师系按照合格的法律合规委员会的聘用或指示,在与该等实质违法违规证

on behalf of the issuer (or the issuer's officer, director, employee, or agent, as the case may be) in any investigation or judicial or administrative proceeding relating to such evidence of a material violation.

(8) An attorney who receives what he or she reasonably believes is an appropriate and timely response to a report he or she has made pursuant to paragraph (b)(1), (b)(3), or (b)(4) of this section need do nothing more under this section with respect to his or her report.

(9) An attorney who does not reasonably believe that the issuer has made an appropriate response within a reasonable time to the report or reports made pursuant to paragraph (b)(1), (b)(3), or (b)(4) of this section shall explain his or her reasons therefor to the chief legal officer (or the equivalent thereof), the chief executive officer (or the equivalent thereof), and directors to whom the attorney reported the evidence of a material violation pursuant to paragraph (b)(1), (b)(3), or (b)(4) of this section.

(10) An attorney formerly employed or retained by an issuer who has reported evidence of a material violation under this part and reasonably believes that he or she has been discharged for so doing may notify the issuer's board of directors or any committee thereof that he or she believes that he or she has been discharged for reporting evidence of a material violation under this section.

(c) *Alternative reporting procedures for attorneys retained or employed by an issuer that has established a qualified legal compliance committee.* (1) If an attorney, appearing and practicing before the Commission in the representation of an issuer, becomes aware of evidence of a material violation by the issuer or by any officer, director, employee, or agent of the issuer, the attorney may, as an alternative to the reporting requirements of paragraph (b) of this section, report such evidence to a qualified legal compliance committee, if the issuer has previously formed such a committee. An attorney who reports evidence of a material violation to such a qualified legal compliance committee has satisfied his or her obligation to report such evidence and is not required to assess the issuer's response to the reported evidence of a material violation.

(2) A chief legal officer (or the equivalent thereof) may refer a report of evidence of a material violation to a previously established qualified legal compliance committee in lieu of causing an inquiry to be conducted under paragraph (b)(2) of this section. The chief legal officer (or the equivalent thereof) shall inform the reporting attorney that the report has been referred to a qualified legal compliance committee. Thereafter, pursuant to the requirements under §205.2(k), the qualified legal compliance committee shall be responsible for responding to the evidence of a material violation reported to it under this paragraph (c).

(d) *Issuer confidences.* (1) Any report under this section (or the contemporaneous

据有关的任何调查、司法或行政处理程序中,在不违反其职业义务的情况下代表发行人(或发行人的管理人员、董事、职员、代理人,视具体情况而定)提供合理辩护。

(8)律师依照本节第(b)(1)款、第(b)(3)款或第(b)(4)款作出报告,并收到其合理相信为恰当和及时的答复的,不必在本条项下就其报告采取任何进一步行动。

(9)律师依照本节第(b)(1)款、第(b)(3)款或第(b)(4)款作出报告,但据其合理相信,发行人并未在合理时间内作出恰当答复的,应向依照本节第(b)(1)款、第(b)(3)款或第(b)(4)款收到实质违法违规证据报告的首席法务官(或同级别高管)、首席执行官(或同级别高管)以及董事说明其作出如是判断的原因。

(10)曾经受雇于或受聘于发行人的律师,如果合理相信其系由于按照本部分规定报告实质违法违规证据被解职的,可以将该情形通知发行人的董事会或其任何下属委员会。

(c)已设立合格的法律合规委员会的发行人聘用或雇佣的律师的替代报告程序。(1)作为本节第(b)款规定的报告程序之替代,律师在作为发行人的代理出席证券交易委员会程序并办理业务的过程中,发现发行人或发行人的任何管理人员、董事、职员或代理人的实质违法违规证据的,可以将该等证据报告给发行人的合格的法律合规委员会,条件是发行人此前已经设立该等委员会。律师将实质违法违规证据报告给合格的法律合规委员会即已完成其报告证据的义务,不必进一步对发行人针对该实质违规的答复进行评估。

(2)首席法务官(或同级别高管)可以将实质违法违规证据报告转交给已设立的合格的法律合规委员会,而不必按照本节第(b)(2)款开展调查。首席法务官(或同级别高管)应通知报告律师,报告已转交合格的法律合规委员会。因此,根据第205.2(k)节的规定,合格的法律合规委员会应负责就依据本节第(c)款向其提交的实质违法违规证据报告作出答复。

(d)发行人的保密信息。(1)在涉及本部分合规问题的任何调查、程序或诉讼中,

record thereof) or any response thereto (or the contemporaneous record thereof) may be used by an attorney in connection with any investigation, proceeding, or litigation in which the attorney's compliance with this part is in issue.

(2) An attorney appearing and practicing before the Commission in the representation of an issuer may reveal to the Commission, without the issuer's consent, confidential information related to the representation to the extent the attorney reasonably believes necessary:

(i) To prevent the issuer from committing a material violation that is likely to cause substantial injury to the financial interest or property of the issuer or investors;

(ii) To prevent the issuer, in a Commission investigation or administrative proceeding from committing perjury, proscribed in 18 U.S.C. 1621; suborning perjury, proscribed in 18 U.S.C. 1622; or committing any act proscribed in 18 U.S.C. 1001 that is likely to perpetrate a fraud upon the Commission; or

(iii) To rectify the consequences of a material violation by the issuer that caused, or may cause, substantial injury to the financial interest or property of the issuer or investors in the furtherance of which the attorney's services were used.

§205.4 Responsibilities of supervisory attorneys.

(a) An attorney supervising or directing another attorney who is appearing and practicing before the Commission in the representation of an issuer is a supervisory attorney. An issuer's chief legal officer (or the equivalent thereof) is a supervisory attorney under this section.

(b) A supervisory attorney shall make reasonable efforts to ensure that a subordinate attorney, as defined in §205.5(a), that he or she supervises or directs conforms to this part. To the extent a subordinate attorney appears and practices before the Commission in the representation of an issuer, that subordinate attorney's supervisory attorneys also appear and practice before the Commission.

(c) A supervisory attorney is responsible for complying with the reporting requirements in §205.3 when a subordinate attorney has reported to the supervisory attorney evidence of a material violation.

(d) A supervisory attorney who has received a report of evidence of a material violation from a subordinate attorney under §205.3 may report such evidence to the issuer's qualified legal compliance committee if the issuer has duly formed such a committee.

§205.5 Responsibilities of a subordinate attorney.

(a) An attorney who appears and practices before the Commission in the representation of an issuer on a matter under the supervision or direction of another attorney (other than under the direct supervision or direction of the issuer's chief legal

律师均可以使用本节中的任何报告(或报告的同期记录)或对报告的任何答复(或答复的同期纪录)。

(2)作为发行人的代理出席证券交易委员会的程序并办理业务的律师可以出于下述目的,在其合理相信的必要范围内向证券交易委员会披露与代理有关的保密信息,而不必征得发行人的同意:

(i)阻止发行人从事可能对发行人或投资人的经济利益或财产造成重大损害的实质违法违规行为;

(ii)阻止发行人在证券交易委员会调查或行政处理程序中从事《美国法典》第十八编第1621节规定的伪证行为;阻止发行人从事《美国法典》第十八编第1622节规定的唆使他人作伪证的行为;阻止发行人从事《美国法典》第十八编第1001节规定的可能构成对证券交易委员会的欺诈的任何行为;或

(iii)补救发行人实质违规引起或可能引起的对律师服务的对象——发行人或投资者——的经济利益或财产的重大损害。

第205.4节　监督律师的责任

(a)监督律师,系指监督或指导其他作为发行人的代理出席证券交易委员会程序并办理业务的律师。本节中的监督律师指发行人的首席法务官(或同级别高管)。

(b)监督律师应采用合理努力确保其监督或指导的下属律师[定义见第205.5(a)节]遵守本部分规定。下属律师作为发行人的代理出席证券交易委员会程序并办理业务的,监督律师也视为出席证券交易委员会程序并办理业务。

(c)下属律师向监督律师报告实质违法违规证据的,监督律师有义务遵守第205.3节的报告要求。

(d)监督律师收到下属律师依据第205.3节提供的实质违法违规证据报告后,可以将该等证据报告给发行人的合格的法律合规委员会,条件是发行人已经正式组建该等委员会。

第205.5节　下属律师的责任

(a)下属律师指在其他律师监督或指导下[不包括在发行人的首席法务官(或同级别高管)的直接监督或指导下]作为发行人的代理出席证券交易委员会程序并办理业务的律师。

officer (or the equivalent thereof)) is a subordinate attorney.

(b) A subordinate attorney shall comply with this part notwithstanding that the subordinate attorney acted at the direction of or under the supervision of another person.

(c) A subordinate attorney complies with §205.3 if the subordinate attorney reports to his or her supervising attorney under §205.3(b) evidence of a material violation of which the subordinate attorney has become aware in appearing and practicing before the Commission.

(d) A subordinate attorney may take the steps permitted or required by §205.3(b) or (c) if the subordinate attorney reasonably believes that a supervisory attorney to whom he or she has reported evidence of a material violation under §205.3(b) has failed to comply with §205.3.

§205.6 Sanctions and discipline.

(a) A violation of this part by any attorney appearing and practicing before the Commission in the representation of an issuer shall subject such attorney to the civil penalties and remedies for a violation of the federal securities laws available to the Commission in an action brought by the Commission thereunder.

(b) An attorney appearing and practicing before the Commission who violates any provision of this part is subject to the disciplinary authority of the Commission, regardless of whether the attorney may also be subject to discipline for the same conduct in a jurisdiction where the attorney is admitted or practices. An administrative disciplinary proceeding initiated by the Commission for violation of this part may result in an attorney being censured, or being temporarily or permanently denied the privilege of appearing or practicing before the Commission.

(c) An attorney who complies in good faith with the provisions of this part shall not be subject to discipline or otherwise liable under inconsistent standards imposed by any state or other United States jurisdiction where the attorney is admitted or practices.

(d) An attorney practicing outside the United States shall not be required to comply with the requirements of this part to the extent that such compliance is prohibited by applicable foreign law.

§205.7 No private right of action.

(a) Nothing in this part is intended to, or does, create a private right of action against any attorney, law firm, or issuer based upon compliance or noncompliance with its provisions.

(b) Authority to enforce compliance with this part is vested exclusively in the Commission.

(b)下属律师尽管在他人指导或监督下行事,仍应遵守本部分规定。

(c)下属律师将其在出席证券交易委员会程序并办理业务过程中知悉的实质违法违规证据报告给第205.3(b)节中的监督律师的,即视为已遵守第205.3节的规定。

(d)如果下属律师合理相信收到其根据第205.3(b)节提出的实质违法违规证据报告的监督律师未遵守第205.3节的规定,下属律师可以采取第205.3(b)节或第205.3(c)节许可或要求的行动。

第205.6节　罚则和纪律处分

(a)任何作为发行人的代理出席证券交易委员会程序并办理业务的律师违反本部分规定的,证券交易委员会可以依据联邦证券法提起诉讼,并依据该等法律请求对该律师处以民事罚款和寻求其他救济。

(b)出席证券交易委员会程序并办理业务的律师违反本部分任何规定的,证券交易委员会有权予以纪律处分,无论该律师获得执业资格所在地或实际执业所在地的司法辖区是否可能基于同一行为对该律师进行纪律处分。律师违反本部分规定的,证券交易委员会可以发起行政纪律处罚程序,对律师予以谴责或临时或永久性地取消其出席证券交易委员会程序并办理业务的权利。

(c)善意遵守本部分规定的律师不得因为其获得执业资格所在地或实际执业所在地的任何州或其他美国司法辖区施加的与本部分规定有冲突的标准而受到纪律处分或承担其他责任。

(d)如相关外国法律禁止适用本部分规定,则在美国之外执业的律师不必遵守本部分规定。

第205.7节　无私人诉讼权利

(a)本部分任何规定均不旨在,且事实上也不创设基于任何律师、律师事务所或发行人符合或不符合本部分规定而对之提起私人诉讼的权利。

(b)证券交易委员会享有执行本部分规定的排他性权利。

PART 209—FORMS PRESCRIBED UNDER THE COMMISSION'S RULES OF PRACTICE

Authority: 15 U.S.C. 77h–1, 77u, 78u–2, 78u–3, 78v, 78w, 80a–9, 80a–37, 80a–38, 80a–39, 80a–40, 80a–41, 80a–44, 80b–3, 80b–9, 80b–11, and 80b–12, unless otherwise noted.

Source: 60 FR 32823, June 23, 1995, unless otherwise noted.

§209.0–1 Availability of forms.

(a) This part identifies and describes the forms for use under the Securities and Exchange Commission's Rules of Practice, part 201 of this chapter.

(b) Any person may obtain a copy of any form prescribed for use in this part by written request to the Securities and Exchange Commission, 100 F Street, NE., Washington, D.C. 20549. Any person may inspect the forms at this address and at the Commission's regional offices. (See §200.11 of this chapter for the addresses of the SEC regional offices.)

[60 FR 32823, June 23, 1995, as amended at 73 FR 32227, June 5, 2008]

§209.1 Form D–A: Disclosure of assets and financial information.

(a) Rules 410 and 630 of the Rules of Practice (17 CFR 201.410 and 201.630) provide that under certain circumstances a respondent who asserts or intends to assert an inability to pay disgorgement, interest or penalties may be required to disclose certain financial information. Unless otherwise ordered, this form may be used by individuals required to supply such information.

(b) The respondent filing Form D–A is required promptly to notify the Commission of any material change in the answer to any question on this form.

(c) Form D–A may not be withheld from the interested division. A respondent making financial information disclosures on this form after the institution of proceedings may make a motion, pursuant to Rule 322 of the Commission's Rules of Practice (17 CFR 201.322), for the issuance of a protective order to limit disclosure to the public or parties other than the interested division of the information submitted on Form D–A. A request

第209部分——《证券交易委员会工作规则》规定的表格

法律依据:《美国法典》第十五编第77h-1节、第77u节、第78u-2节、第78u-3节、第78v节、第78w节、第80a-9节、第80a-37节、第80a-38节、第80a-39节、第80a-40节、第80a-41节、第80a-44节、第80b-3节、第80b-9节、第80b-11节和第80b-12节,除非另有说明。

行政规则来源:《联邦公报》第60卷第32823页,1995年6月23日,除非另有说明。

第209.0-1节　表格的提供

(a)本部分指明并描述了《证券交易委员会工作规则》(本章第201部分)中使用的表格。

(b)任何人均可向证券交易委员会提交书面请求(地址:华盛顿哥伦比亚特区东北分区100F大街,邮编:D.C.20549)获取本部分规定的任何表格,并在上述地址以及证券交易委员会的地区办公室查阅该等表格(证券交易委员会地区办公室的地址见本章第200.11节)。

[《联邦公报》第60卷第32823页,1995年6月23日,修正索引:《联邦公报》第73卷第32227页,2008年6月5日。]

第209.1节　《D-A表格》:资产和财务信息披露

(a)《工作规则》(《联邦规章汇编》第十七编第201.410节和第201.630节)的《410规则》和《630规则》规定,在特定情况下,对于主张或拟主张其无力支付没收款项、利息或罚款的相对人,可以要求其披露特定财务信息。除非另有命令,否则被要求提供此等信息的个人可以使用本表格提供该等信息。

(b)对本表格任何问题的回答发生任何实质变更的,提交《D-A表格》的相对人有义务及时通知证券交易委员会。

(c)《D-A表格》不得对利害关系部门保密。在程序发起后通过本表格披露财务信息的相对人可依据《证券交易委员会工作规则》的《322规则》(《联邦规章汇编》第十七编第201.322节)提出动议,要求签发保护令,限制向公众或除利害关系部门以外的相关方披露《D-A表格》中提交的信息。请求人可利用请求签发保护令的机会说明保密理由,但是提出保护令动议并不保证证券交易委员会将会对披露作出限制。

for a protective order allows the requester an opportunity to justify the need for confidentiality. The making of a motion for a protective order, however, does not guarantee that disclosure will be limited.

(d) No party receiving information for which a motion for a protective order has been made may transfer or convey the information to any other person prior to a ruling on the motion without the prior permission of the Commission or a hearing officer.

(e) A person making financial information disclosures on Form D-A prior to the institution of proceedings, in connection with an offer of settlement or otherwise, may request confidential treatment of the information pursuant to the Freedom of Information Act. *See* the Commission's Freedom of Information Act ("FOIA") regulations, 17 CFR 200.83. A request for confidential treatment allows the requester an opportunity to substantiate the need for confidentiality. No determination as to the validity of any request for confidential treatment will be made until a request for disclosure of the information under FOIA is received.

(d)如相对人已就相关信息提起保护令动议,则未经证券交易委员会或听证官事先许可,收到该等信息的任何利害关系方均不得在关于保护令动议的裁定作出之前,将该等信息转移或移交给任何其他人。

(e)发起程序前为达成和解要约或其他目的通过《D-A表格》披露财务信息的人,可以依据《信息自由法》请求对信息进行保密处理。参见证券交易委员会依据《信息自由法》(FOIA)发布的规章(《联邦规章汇编》第十七编第200.83节)。请求人可利用提出保密处理请求的机会证明保密的必要性。证券交易委员会在收到依据《信息自由法》提交的信息披露请求前,不对任何保密处理请求作出决定。

Glossary 词汇表

Administrative offset	行政抵消
Administrative Procedure Act	《行政程序法》
Administrative wage garnishment	行政扣发工资
Adversary adjudications	对抗式裁决程序
Advisers Act	《投资顾问法》
Affidavits	宣誓证词
Agency Clearance Officer	机关发布审核官
Aggrieved person	利益受侵害人
Agricultural Marketing Act	《农业营销法》
American depositary receipt	美国存托凭证
Amicus Curiae	法庭之友
Architectural and Transportation Barriers Compliance Board	建筑与交通工具无障碍合规委员会
Architectural Barriers Act of 1968	《1968 年建筑障碍法》
Asian Development Bank	亚洲开发银行
Asian Development Bank Act	《亚洲开发银行法》
Assessable stock	可追缴股款的股票
Associated Person	业务相关人
Attorney General	总检察长
Automated Inter-Dealer Quotation System	交易商自动报价系统
Automatic shelf registration	自动储架注册
Bank Secrecy Act	《银行保密法》
Bankruptcy Act	《破产法》
Bankruptcy Code	《破产法典》
Beneficial owner	受益所有人
Board of Examiners for the Foreign Service	外事处考官委员会
Bretton Woods Agreement Act	《布雷顿森林协定法》
Broker	经纪商
Broker-Dealer	经纪自营商

续表

Canadian Extradition Treaty	《加拿大引渡条约》
Canons of Ethics	职业道德守则
Cease-and-Desist Orders	制止令
Central Registration Depository	中央注册存管系统
CFR	《联邦规章汇编》
Chief Management Analyst	首席管理分析师
Chief Public Information Officer	首席公共信息官
Civil Service Regulations	《公务员管理办法》
Clearing agency	结算机构
Closing market price	收盘市价
Commission's Rules of Practice	《证券交易委员会工作规则》
Commission's Rules on Informal and Other Procedures	《证券交易委员会关于非正式程序和其他程序的规则》
Committee on Ethics of the American Bar Association	美国律师协会职业道德委员会
Commodity Exchanges Act	《商品交易法》
Comptroller of the Currency; OCC	货币监理署
Conduct of Members and Employees and Former Members and Employees of the Commission	《证券交易委员会委员、雇员及前任委员、雇员的行为准则》
Congress Joint Committee on Printing	国会印刷联合委员会
Congressional Appropriations Committees	国会拨款委员会
Consolidated quotation system	合并报价系统
Consumer Reporting Agencies	消费者征信机构
Credit Bureau	信贷局
Currency and Foreign Transactions Reporting Act of 1970	《1970 年货币和国外交易报告法》
Dealer	自营商
Debt Collection Improvement Act of 1996	《1996 年债务催收改进法》
Declassification	解密
Department of Justice	司法部
Deputy Director of the Division Of Enforcement	执法部副主任
Designated Agency Ethics Official	指定机关职业道德官

续表

Director of Division of Corporation Finance	公司融资部主任
Director of Regional Office Operations	地区办公室运营部主任
Director of the Office of Public Affairs, Policy Evaluation, and Research	公共事务、政策评估和研究办公室主任
Disgorgement	没收
Division of Corporation Finance	公司融资部
Division of Enforcement	执法部
Documentary Evidence	书证
Duty Officer	轮值官
EDGAR Filer Manual	《EDGAR 提交人手册》
Equal Access to Justice Act	《司法公平法》
Ethics in Government Act of 1978	《1978 年政府职业道德法》
Evidentiary Hearing	举证听证
Ex Parte Communications	单方交流
Executive Assistant to the Chairman	主席执行助理
Executive Council on Integrity and Efficiency	廉政效率执行委员会
Fair Debt Collection Practices Act	《公平债务催收作业法》
Fair Fund and Disgorgement Plans	公平基金和没收计划
Fair value	公允价值
False Claims Act	《反欺骗政府法》
Federal Advisory Committee Act	《联邦顾问委员会法》
Federal Claims Collection Act of 1966	《1966 年联邦债权催收法》
Federal Deposit Insurance Act	《联邦存款保险法》
Federal Managers' Financial Integrity Act of 1982	《1982 年联邦管理人员财务操守法》
Federal Power Commission	联邦电力委员会
Federal Quality Institute	联邦质量协会
Federal Records Centers	联邦记录中心
Federal Register	《联邦公报》
Federal Reports Act	《联邦报告法》
Federal Reserve Board; Board of Governors of the Federal Reserve System	联邦储备委员会
Federal Reserve System	联邦储备系统

续表

Fiduciary duty	受信义务
Financial disclosure statement	财务披露报表
Financial Management Service	金融管理服务局
Freedom of Information Act	《信息自由法》
Freedom of Information and Privacy Act	《信息自由和隐私法》
General Accounting Office; GAO	美国审计总署
General Counsel	首席律师
Government in the Sunshine Act	《政府阳光法》
Government Performance and Results Act of 1993	《1993 年政府绩效和成果法》
Government securities	政府证券
Hearing Officer	听证官
Indenture	信托契约
Information Security Oversight Office	信息安全监督办公室
Inspector General	监察长
Inspector General Act of 1978	《1978 年监察长法》
Inter-American Bank Act	《美洲银行法》
Inter-American Development Bank	泛美开发银行
Interested Division	利害关系部门
Interested Person	利害关系人
Interim Review	中期审查
Interlocutory Appeal	中间上诉
Interlocutory Review	中间复议
Interlocutory ruling	中间裁定
Intermarket trading system plan	市场间交易系统计划
Internal Revenue Code of 1954	《1954 年国内税收法典》
Investment Company Act of 1940	《1940 年投资公司法》
Jencks Act	《简克斯法》
Joint Reporting Plan	《联合报告计划》
Keogh Plans	《基欧计划》
Litigation Actions and Proceedings Bulletin	《诉讼行动和程序公报》
Manual of Administrative Regulations	《行政规章手册》

续表

Market capitalizations	市值
Market maker	做市商
Municipal Securities Rulemaking Board；MSRB	市政证券规则制定委员会
National Archives and Records Administration	国家档案和记录管理局
National Archives and Records Service	国家档案和记录服务处
National Environmental Policy Act	《国家环境保护政策法》
National Register of Historic Places	《国家历史古迹名单》
National Securities Associations	全国性证券协会
National Securities Exchange	全国性证券交易所
Offers of proof	证据认定动议
Office of Administrative and Personnel Management	行政和人事管理办公室
Office of Administrative Law Judges	行政法官办公室
Office of Compliance Inspections and Examinations	合规检查和核查办公室
Office of Filings and Information Services	文件提交和信息服务办公室
Office of Freedom of Information and Privacy Act Operations	信息自由和隐私法管理办公室
Office of Information Technology	信息技术办公室
Office of Inspector General	监察长办公室
Office of International Affairs	国际事务办公室
Office of Management and Budget	行政管理和预算局
Office of Public Affairs	公共事务办公室
Office of the Comptroller	审计办公室
Office of the General Counsel's Ethics Office	首席律师职业道德办公室
Offices Appropriation Act	《独立办公室拨款法》
Opening brief	开案陈辩书
Opposition brief	反对陈辩书
Orders Instituting Proceedings	程序发起令
Original classification	原始密级
OTC derivatives	场外交易衍生品
Over-the-counter markets	场外市场
Paperwork Reduction Act of 1980	《1980 年文书削减法》

续表

Pooled investment funds or accounts	集合投资基金或账户
Power of attorney	代理委托书
Prehearing conference	预备庭会议
Pre-offset hearing	抵消预听证
Prior judicial precedent	司法先例
Privacy Act of 1974	《1974 年隐私法》
Private right of action	私人诉讼权利
Prospectus	招募说明书
Proxy statement	征集投票权报告
Public Company Accounting Oversight Board	公众公司会计监督委员会
Public Utility Holding Company Act of 1935	《1935 年公用事业控股公司法》
Quorum	法定人数
Rebuttal evidence	反证
Records Control Schedule	《记录控制计划》
Regional Office	地区办公室
Registration statements	注册说明书
Regulatory Flexibility Act	《监管弹性法》
Rehabilitation Act of 1973	《1973 年康复法》
Rehabilitation, Comprehensive Services, and Developmental Disabilities Amendments of 1978	《1978 年康复、全面服务和残疾修正案》
Reply brief	答复陈辩书
Sarbanes-Oxley Act of 2002	《2002 年萨班斯—奥克斯利法》
Savings association	储蓄协会
SEC Docket	《证券交易委员会周志》
Sec Monthly Statistical Review	《证券交易委员会统计月刊》
SEC News Digest	《证券交易委员会新闻摘要》
Secretary of the Treasury	财政部长
Securities Act of 1933	《1933 年证券法》
Securities and Exchange Commission; SEC	证券交易委员会
Securities Exchange Act of 1934	《1934 年证券交易法》
Securities Information Processor	证券信息处理机构

续表

Securities Investor Protection Corporation	证券投资者保护公司
Securities Investors Protection Act of 1970	《1970 年证券投资者保护法》
Self-Regulatory Organization	自律组织
Small and Disadvantaged Business Utilization Program	《小型及弱势企业扶持计划》
Small Entity Compliance Guides	小型企业合规指引
Social Security Act	《社会保障法》
Standard Industrial Classification Manual	《标准行业分类手册》
Standards of Ethical Conduct for Employees of the Executive Branch	《行政机关雇员的行为道德标准》
Sworn statements of witnesses	宣誓证人声明
Temporary sanction ex parte	单方面临时制裁
Tender offer	股权收购要约
Territory	准州
Trading privileges	交易权
Transfer agent	过户代理人
Trust Indenture Act of 1939	《1939 年信托契约法》
U. S. Government Printing Office	美国政府印刷局
U. S. Treasury	美国财政部
U. S. C.	《美国法典》
Uniform Code of Military Justice	《军事审判统一法典》
Uniting and Strengthening America by Providing Appropriate Tools Required to Intercept and Obstruct Terrorism Act of 2001	《2001 年使用适当手段阻止避免恐怖主义以团结并强化美国法》
USA Patriot Act	《美国爱国者法》
Williams Act	《威廉姆斯法》

图书在版编目(CIP)数据

美国证券交易委员会自身组织与通用规章:全2册/中国证券监督管理委员会组织编译.—北京:法律出版社,2013.2
(境外资本市场重要法律文献译丛)
ISBN 978-7-5118-4542-9

Ⅰ.①美… Ⅱ.①中… Ⅲ.①证券法—研究—美国
Ⅳ.①D971.222.8

中国版本图书馆CIP数据核字(2013)第018423号

责任编辑/王津京　　**装帧设计**/贾丹丹

出版/法律出版社　　**编辑统筹**/财税出版分社
总发行/中国法律图书有限公司　　**经销**/新华书店
印刷/北京中科印刷有限公司　　**责任印制**/吕亚莉

开本/787毫米×1092毫米　1/16　　**印张**/49.75　**字数**/980千
版本/2013年4月第1版　　**印次**/2013年4月第1次印刷

法律出版社/北京市丰台区莲花池西里7号(100073)
电子邮件/info@lawpress.com.cn　　**销售热线**/010-63939792/9779
网址/www.lawpress.com.cn　　**咨询电话**/010-63939796

中国法律图书有限公司/北京市丰台区莲花池西里7号(100073)
全国各地中法图分、子公司电话:
第一法律书店/010-63939781/9782　**西安分公司**/029-85388843　**重庆公司**/023-65382816/2908
上海公司/021-62071010/1636　**北京分公司**/010-62534456　**深圳公司**/0755-83072995

书号:ISBN 978-7-5118-4542-9　　**定价(上、下册)**:560.00元

(如有缺页或倒装,中国法律图书有限公司负责退换)

境外资本市场重要法律文献译丛 ❷

美洲卷

美国证券交易委员会自身组织与通用规章

（中英文对照本）

Rules and Regulations for the Securities and Exchange Commission

（下 册）

中国证券监督管理委员会　组织编译

法律出版社
LAW PRESS · CHINA

CONTENTS

目　　录

1　原文目录此处没有“Part 211”的标题级，但正文中有。为统一体例，在此处加上。——译者注

CFR Title 17: Commodity and Securities Exchanges Part 210 Through Part 229

《联邦规章汇编》第十七编:商品和证券交易 第210~229部分

PART 210 — FORM AND CONTENT OF AND REQUIREMENTS FOR FINANCIAL STATEMENTS, SECURITIES ACT OF 1933, SECURITIES EXCHANGE ACT OF 1934, PUBLIC UTILITY HOLDING COMPANY ACT OF 1935, INVESTMENT COMPANY ACT OF 1940, INVESTMENT ADVISERS ACT OF 1940, AND ENERGY POLICY AND CONSERVATION ACT OF 1975

Authority: 15 U.S.C. 77f, 77g, 77h, 77j, 77s, 77z–2, 77z–3, 77aa(25), 77aa(26), 77nn (25), 77nn(26), 78c, 78j–1, 78l,78m, 78n, 78o(d), 78q, 78u–5, 78w, 78ll,78mm, 80a–8, 80a–20, 80a–29, 80a–30, 80a–31, 80a–37 (a), 80b–3, 80b–11, 7202 and 7262, unless otherwise noted.

ATTENTION ELECTRONIC FILERS

THIS REGULATION SHOULD BE READ IN CONJUNCTION WITH REGULATION S–T (PART 232 OF THIS CHAPTER), WHICH GOVERNS THE PREPARATION AND SUBMISSION OF DOCUMENTS IN ELECTRONIC FORMAT. MANY PROVISIONS RELATING TO THE PREPARATION AND SUBMISSION OF DOCUMENTS IN PAPER FORMAT CONTAINED IN THIS REGULATION ARE SUPERSEDED BY THE PROVISIONS OF REGULATION S–T FOR DOCUMENTS REQUIRED TO BE FILED IN ELECTRONIC FORMAT.

第210部分——财务报表的格式、内容及要求,《1933年证券法》、《1934年证券交易法》、《1935年公用事业控股公司法》、《1940年投资公司法》、《1940年投资顾问法》及《1975年能源政策与保护法》

法律依据:《美国法典》第十五编第77f节、第77g节、第77h节、第77j节、第77s节、第77z-2节、第77z-3节、第77aa(25)节、第77aa(26)节、第77nn(25)节、第77nn(26)节、第78c节、第78j-1节、第78*l*节、第78m节、第78n节、第78o(d)节、第78q节、第78u-5节、第78w节、第78*ll*节、第78mm节、第80a-8节、第80a-20节、第80a-29节、第80a-30节、第80a-31节、第80a-37(a)节、第80b-3节、第80b-11节、第7202节和第7262节,除非另有说明。

以电子形式提交文件的人请注意

在阅读本《管理办法》时,应参阅规范电子文件编制和列报的《S-T管理办法》(本章第232部分)。对于应以电子格式提交的文件,本《管理办法》中关于纸质文件编制和列报的规定均应替以《S-T管理办法》中的相应规定。

Application of Regulation S-X (17 CFR Part 210)

§210.1-01 Application of Regulation S-X (17 CFR part 210).

(a) This part (together with the Financial Reporting Releases (part 211 of this chapter)) sets forth the form and content of and requirements for financial statements required to be filed as a part of:

(1) Registration statements under the Securities Act of 1933 (part 239 of this chapter), except as otherwise specifically provided in the forms which are to be used for registration under this Act;

(2) Registration statements under section 12 (subpart C of part 249 of this chapter), annual or other reports under sections 13 and 15(d) (subparts D and E of part 249 of this chapter), and proxy and information statements under section 14 of the Securities Exchange Act of 1934 except as otherwise specifically provided in the forms which are to be used for registration and reporting under these sections of this Act;

(3) Registration statements and annual reports filed under the Public Utility Holding Company Act of 1935 (part 259 of this chapter) by public utility holding companies registered under such Act; and

(4) Registration statements and shareholder reports under the Investment Company Act of 1940 (part 274 of this chapter), except as otherwise specifically provided in the forms which are to be used for registration under this Act.

(b) The term *financial statements* as used in this part shall be deemed to include all notes to the statements and all related schedules.

(c) In addition to filings pursuant to the Federal securities laws, §210.4-10 applies to the preparation of accounts by persons engaged, in whole or in part, in the production of crude oil or natural gas in the United States pursuant to section 503 of the Energy Policy and Conservation Act of 1975 (42 U.S.C. 6383) (*EPCA*) and section 1(c) of the Energy Supply and Environmental Coordination Act of 1974 (15 U.S.C. 796), as amended by section 505 of EPCA.

[37 FR 14593, July 21, 1972, as amended at 43 FR 40712, Sept. 12, 1978; 45 FR 63680, 63687, Sept. 25, 1980; 46 FR 36124, July 14, 1981; 50 FR 25214, June 18, 1985]

§210.1-02 Definitions of terms used in Regulation S-X (17 CFR part 210).

Unless the context otherwise requires, terms defined in the general rules and regulations or in the instructions to the applicable form, when used in Regulation S-X (this part 210), shall have the respective meanings given in such instructions or rules. In addition, the following terms shall have the meanings indicated in this section unless the

《S-X管理办法》的适用范围(《联邦规章汇编》第十七编第210部分)

第210.1-01节 《S-X管理办法》的适用范围(《联邦规章汇编》第十七编第210部分)

(a)本部分[以及《财务报告公告》(本章第211部分)]规定了在提交下列文件时,应纳入的财务报表之格式、内容和要求:

(1)《1933年证券法》(本章第239部分)规定的注册说明书,但根据该法办理注册时,所使用的表格另有特别规定的,以该等特别规定为准;

(2)《1934年证券交易法》第12条(本章第249部分第C子部分)规定的注册说明书、第13条和第15(d)条(本章第249部分第D子部分和第E子部分)规定的年度报告或其他报告,及第14条规定的征集投票权报告和信息说明书,但根据该法上述条款办理注册和提交报告时,所使用的表格另有特别规定的,以该等特别规定为准;

(3)依《1935年公用事业控股公司法》(本章第259部分)注册的公用事业控股公司按该法提交的注册说明书和年度报告;及

(4)《1940年投资公司法》(本章第274部分)规定的注册说明书和股东报告,但根据该法办理注册时,所使用的表格另有特别规定的,以该等特别规定为准。

(b)就本部分而言,"财务报表"一词应视为涵盖报表所有附注和所有相关附表。

(c)除适用于根据联邦证券法律提交的文件之外,第210.4-10节还适用于如下报表:在美国完全从事或兼营原油或天然气生产的主体按照《1975年能源政策与保护法》(英文简称EPCA)第503条(《美国法典》第四十二编第6383节)和《1974年能源供应和环境协调法》第1条第(c)款(《美国法典》第十五编第796节)(以经《1975年能源政策与保护法》第505条修正后的版本为准)编制的报表。

[《联邦公报》第37卷第14593页,1972年7月21日,修正索引:《联邦公报》第43卷第40712页,1978年9月12日;《联邦公报》第45卷第63680、63687页,1980年9月25日;《联邦公报》第46卷第36124页,1981年7月14日;《联邦公报》第50卷第25214页,1985年6月18日。]

第210.1-02节 《S-X管理办法》(《联邦规章汇编》第十七编第210部分)使用的术语定义

除非上下文另有所指,在一般规则和规章中或在相关表格说明中已定义的词语,适用于本《S-X管理办法》(本第210部分)时,其含义以该等规则、规章或说明的定义为准。此外,除非上下文另有所指,否则下列词语之含义应以本节规定为准。

context otherwise requires.

(a)(1) *Accountant's report.* The term *accountant's report,* when used in regard to financial statements, means a document in which an independent public or certified public accountant indicates the scope of the audit (or examination) which he has made and sets forth his opinion regarding the financial statements taken as a whole, or an assertion to the effect that an overall opinion cannot be expressed. When an overall opinion cannot be expressed, the reasons therefor shall be stated.

(2) *Attestation report on internal control over financial reporting.* The term *attestation report on internal control over financial reporting* means a report in which a registered public accounting firm expresses an opinion, either unqualified or adverse, as to whether the registrant maintained, in all material respects, effective internal control over financial reporting (as defined in §240.13a–15(f) or 240.15d–15(f) of this chapter), except in the rare circumstance of a scope limitation that cannot be overcome by the registrant or the registered public accounting firm which would result in the accounting firm disclaiming an opinion.

(3) *Attestation report on assessment of compliance with servicing criteria for asset-backed securities.* The term *attestation report on assessment of compliance with servicing criteria for asset-backed securities* means a report in which a registered public accounting firm, as required by §240.13a–18(c) or 240.15d–18(c) of this chapter, expresses an opinion, or states that an opinion cannot be expressed, concerning an asserting party's assessment of compliance with servicing criteria, as required by §240.13a–18(b) or 240.15d–18(b) of this chapter, in accordance with standards on attestation engagements. When an overall opinion cannot be expressed, the registered public accounting firm must state why it is unable to express such an opinion.

(4) *Definitions of terms related to internal control over financial reporting.*

Material weakness means a deficiency, or a combination of deficiencies, in internal control over financial reporting (as defined in §240.13a–15(f) or 240.15d–15(f) of this chapter) such that there is a reasonable possibility that a material misstatement of the registrant's annual or interim financial statements will not be prevented or detected on a timely basis.

Significant deficiency means a deficiency, or a combination of deficiencies, in internal control over financial reporting that is less severe than a material weakness, yet important enough to merit attention by those responsible for oversight of the registrant's financial reporting.

(b) *Affiliate.* An *affiliate* of, or a person *affiliated* with, a specific person is a person that directly, or indirectly through one or more intermediaries, controls, or is controlled by, or is under common control with, the person specified.

(c) *Amount.* The term *amount,* when used in regard to securities, means the principal

(a)(1)会计师报告。用于财务报表时,“会计师报告”系指独立的公共会计师或注册会计师针对财务报表出具的文件,以说明其对财务报表的审计(或核验)范围,并发表对财务报表的整体意见,或声明其无法就财务报表出具整体意见。如果无法出具整体意见,应在报告中阐明原因。

(2)财务报告内部控制鉴证报告。“财务报告内部控制鉴证报告”系指注册公共会计师事务所出具的报告,该报告应针对注册人是否在财务报告所有实质方面均维持了有效的内部控制[定义见本章第240.13a-15(f)节或第240.15d-15(f)节]出具无保留意见或否定意见,但出现注册人或注册公共会计师事务所无法克服审计范围限制的少数情形,导致会计师事务所放弃出具意见的除外。

(3)对资产支持证券服务标准合规性评价的鉴证报告。“对资产支持证券服务标准合规性评价的鉴证报告”系指注册公共会计师事务所出具的报告,在该等报告中,针对审计客户提供的关于资产支持证券对第240.13a-18(b)节或第240.15d-18(b)节规定的服务标准的合规性的评价,事务所按本章第240.13a-18(c)节或第240.15d-18(c)节规定以及鉴证工作标准出具意见,或作出无法出具意见的声明。如果无法出具整体意见,注册公共会计师事务所必须说明理由。

(4)与财务报告内部控制有关的术语定义。

“实质缺陷”系指财务报告内部控制[定义见本章第240.13a-15(f)节或第240.15d-15(f)节]存在的单项缺陷或多项累积缺陷,且根据合理预期,该等缺陷可能导致无法避免注册人年度或中期财务报表出现重大错报,或导致无法及时发现该等错报。

“重大缺陷”系指财务报告内部控制存在的单项缺陷或多项累积缺陷,其严重程度低于实质缺陷,但足以引起注册人财务报告监督负责人的注意。

(b)控制性关联方。某主体的“控制性关联方”或与其“存在控制性关联的”主体系指直接或通过一名或数名中间方间接控制该主体、为其所控制或与之受同一控制的主体。

(c)金额(数量)。针对证券使用时,“金额”(数量)一词就债务凭证而言,系指债务

amount if relating to evidences of indebtedness, the number of shares if relating to shares, and the number of units if relating to any other kind of security.

(d) *Audit (or examination)*. The term *audit* (or *examination*), when used in regard to financial statements, means an examination of the financial statements by an independent accountant in accordance with generally accepted auditing standards, as may be modified or supplemented by the Commission, for the purpose of expressing an opinion thereon.

(e) *Bank holding company.* The term *bank holding company* means a person which is engaged, either directly or indirectly, primarily in the business of owning securities of one or more banks for the purpose, and with the effect, of exercising control.

(f) *Certified.* The term *certified,* when used in regard to financial statements, means examined and reported upon with an opinion expressed by an independent public or certified public accountant.

(g) *Control.* The term *control* (including the terms *controlling, controlled by and under common control with*) means the possession, direct or indirect, of the power to direct or cause the direction of the management and policies of a person, whether through the ownership of voting shares, by contract, or otherwise.

(h) *Development stage company.*A company shall be considered to be in the development stage if it is devoting substantially all of its efforts to establishing a new business and either of the following conditions exists: (1) Planned principal operations have not commenced. (2) Planned principal operations have commenced, but there has been no significant revenue therefrom.

(i) *Equity security.*The term *equity security* means any stock or similar security; or any security convertible, with or without consideration, into such a security, or carrying any warrant or right to subscribe to or purchase such a security; or any such warrant or right.

(j) *Fifty-percent-owned person.*The term *50-percent-owned person,* in relation to a specified person, means a person approximately 50 percent of whose outstanding voting shares is owned by the specified person either directly, or indirectly through one or more intermediaries.

(k) *Fiscal year.*The term *fiscal year* means the annual accounting period or, if no closing date has been adopted, the calendar year ending on December 31.

(l) *Foreign business.*A business that is majority owned by persons who are not citizens or residents of the United States and is not organized under the laws of the United States or any state thereof, and either:

(1) More than 50 percent of its assets are located outside the United States; or

(2) The majority of itsexecutive officers and directors are not United States citizens or residents.

凭证的本金数额,就股份而言,系指股数,就其他种类的证券而言,系指任何该等其他证券的单位数目。

(d)审计(或核验)。针对财务报表使用时,"审计"(或核验)一词系指独立会计师为对财务报表出具意见而按照公认审计标准(证券交易委员会对此进行修改或补充的,以该等修改补充版为准)对财务报表实施的核验。

(e)银行控股公司。"银行控股公司"一词系指以直接或间接持有一家或数家银行的证券为主营业务,并以控制该等银行为目的并实际取得其控制的主体。

(f)已核证。针对财务报表使用时,"已核证"一词系指财务报表已由独立公共会计师或注册会计师核验、出具报告并发表审计意见。

(g)控制。"控制"一词(包括"被控制"和"受同一控制"等词)系指通过拥有表决股、合同或其他方式直接或间接获得主导或通过他人主导某主体经营和政策的权力。

(h)发展阶段公司。如果某个公司将绝大部分精力用于建立新业务,并且满足以下任一条件,该公司即应视为处于发展阶段:(1)计划的主营业务尚未启动;(2)计划的主营业务已启动,但仍未产生大额收入。

(i)股权证券。"股权证券"一词系指任何股票或类似证券;可在支付或不支付对价的情形下转换成任何股票或类似证券的证券;附带购买上述证券的任何权证或认购权的证券;或任何该等权证或认购权本身。

(j)50%股权被控主体。某一特定主体的"50%股权被控主体"系指约50%发行在外的表决股被该特定主体直接持有,或通过一名或数名中间方间接持有的另一主体。

(k)会计年度。"会计年度"一词系指年度会计期间;在未确定结账日的情形下,系指结束于12月31日的日历年。

(l)外国企业。"外国企业"一词系指既非由美国公民或居民拥有多数所有权,也非按美国联邦或任何州法律成立,并且符合下列条件之一的企业:

(1)50%以上资产位于美国境外;或者

(2)过半数高级管理人员和董事不属于美国公民或居民。

(m) *Insurance holding company.* The term *insurance holding company* means a person which is engaged, either directly or indirectly, primarily in the business of owning securities of one or more insurance companies for the purpose, and with the effect, of exercising control.

(n) *Majority-owned subsidiary.* The term *majority-owned subsidiary* means a subsidiary more than 50 percent of whose outstanding voting shares is owned by its parent and/or the parent's other majority-owned subsidiaries.

(o) *Material.* The term *material,* when used to qualify a requirement for the furnishing of information as to any subject, limits the information required to those matters about which an average prudent investor ought reasonably to be informed.

(p) *Parent.* A *parent* of a specified person is an affiliate controlling such person directly, or indirectly through one or more intermediaries.

(q) *Person.* The term *person* means an individual, a corporation, a partnership, an association, a joint-stock company, a business trust, or an unincorporated organization.

(r) *Principal holder of equity securities.* The term *principal holder of equity securities,* used in respect of a registrant or other person named in a particular statement or report, means a holder of record or a known beneficial owner of more than 10 percent of any class of equity securities of the registrant or other person, respectively, as of the date of the related balance sheet filed.

(s) *Promoter.* The term *promoter* includes:

(1) Any person who, acting alone or in conjunction with one or more other persons, directly or indirectly takes initiative in founding and organizing the business or enterprise of an issuer;

(2) Any person who, in connection with the founding and organizing of the business or enterprise of an issuer, directly or indirectly receives in consideration of services or property, or both services and property, 10 percent or more of any class of securities of the issuer or 10 percent or more of the proceeds from the sale of any class of securities. However, a person who receives such securities or proceeds either solely as underwriting commissions or solely in consideration of property shall not be deemed a promoter within the meaning of this paragraph if such person does not otherwise take part in founding and organizing the enterprise.

(t) *Registrant.*The term *registrant* means the issuer of the securities for which an application, a registration statement, or a report is filed.

(u) *Related parties.* The term *related parties* is used as that term is defined in the Glossary to Statement of Financial Accounting Standards No.57, "Related Party Disclosures."

(v) *Share.* The term *share* means a share of stock in a corporation or unit of interest

(m)保险控股公司。“保险控股公司”一词系指以直接或间接拥有一家或数家保险公司的证券为主营业务,并以控制该等公司为目的并实际取得其控制的主体。

(n)控股子公司。“控股子公司”一词系指50%以上发行在外的表决股由其母公司持有和/或由母公司的其他控股子公司持有的子公司。

(o)重大。在要求针对任何主题提供“重大”信息之时,“重大”信息系指普通的审慎投资者应合理获知的事项。

(p)母公司。某主体的“母公司”系指直接控制该主体或通过一个或数个中间方间接控制该主体的控制性关联方。

(q)人或主体。“人或主体”系指个人、法人、合伙、协会、股份公司、商业信托或非法人组织。

(r)主要股权证券持有人。就注册人或具体说明书或报告中的其他具名主体而言,“主要股权证券持有人”一词系指截至相关资产负债表提交日,持有该等注册人或其他主体任一类股权证券10%以上的登记持有人或显名受益所有人。

(s)创始人。“创始人”一词涵盖下列主体:

(1)单独或与其他一个或多个主体合作,主动地直接或间接创立和组建发行人的业务或企业的任何主体;

(2)在创立和组建发行人的业务或企业的活动中,就其提供的服务和/或财产直接或间接收取如下对价的任何主体:发行人任何类型证券的10%(含)以上,或任一类证券出售募集资金的10%(含)以上。但是,如果某主体收取的上述证券或募集资金完全属于承销佣金,或完全属于其提供的财产的对价,且该主体并未以其他方式参与企业的创立和组建,则不应视为本款意义上的创始人。

(t)注册人。“注册人”一词系指提交申请、注册说明书或报告的证券发行人。

(u)关联方。“关联方”一词的含义以《财务会计准则公告第57号——关联方披露》的词汇表所给定义为准。

(v)股份。“股份”一词系指公司的股份或非公司形式的主体的权益单位。

in an unincorporated person.

(w) *Significant subsidiary.* The term *significant subsidiary* means a subsidiary, including its subsidiaries, which meets any of the following conditions:

(1) The registrant's and its other subsidiaries' investments in and advances to the subsidiary exceed 10 percent of the total assets of the registrant and its subsidiaries consolidated as of the end of the most recently completed fiscal year (for a proposed combination between entities under common control, this condition is also met when the number of common shares exchanged or to be exchanged by the registrant exceeds 10 percent of its total common shares outstanding at the date the combination is initiated); or

(2) The registrant's and its other subsidiaries' proportionate share of the total assets (after intercompany eliminations) of the subsidiary exceeds 10 percent of the total assets of the registrants and its subsidiaries consolidated as of the end of the most recently completed fiscal year; or

(3) The registrant's and its other subsidiaries' equity in the income from continuing operations before income taxes, extraordinary items and cumulative effect of a change in accounting principle of the subsidiary exclusive of amounts attributable to any noncontrolling interests exceeds 10 percent of such income of the registrant and its subsidiaries consolidated for the most recently completed fiscal year.

Note to paragraph (w): A registrant that files its financial statements in accordance with or provides a reconciliation to U.S. Generally Accepted Accounting Principles shall make the prescribed tests using amounts determined under U.S. Generally Accepted Accounting Principles.A foreign private issuer that files its financial statements in accordance with IFRS as issued by the IASB shall make the prescribed tests using amounts determined under IFRS as issued by the IASB.

Computational note: For purposes of making the prescribed income test the following guidance should be applied:

1. When a loss exclusive of amounts attributable to any noncontrolling interests has been incurred by either the parent and its subsidiaries consolidated or the tested subsidiary, but not both, the equity in the income or loss of the tested subsidiary exclusive of amounts attributable to any noncontrolling interests should be excluded from such income of the registrant and its subsidiaries consolidated for purposes of the computation.

2. If income of the registrant and its subsidiaries consolidated exclusive of amounts attributable to any noncontrolling interests for the most recent fiscal year is at least 10 percent lower than the average of the income for the last five fiscal years, such average income should be submitted for purposes of the computation. Any loss years should be omitted for purposes of computing average income.

3. Where the test involves combined entities, as in the case of determining whether

(w)重要子公司。“重要子公司”一词系指符合以下任一条件的子公司(包括该等子公司的符合以下任一条件的子公司):

(1)注册人以及注册人其他子公司向该子公司提供投资和垫款,金额超过截至最近结束的一个会计年度年末注册人及其并表子公司资产总额的10%(对计划合并的受同一控制的数个实体而言,注册人在合并中已经或将要交换的普通股股数超过合并发起日其发行在外的普通股总数10%的,亦视为符合本条件);或者

(2)注册人以及注册人其他子公司在该子公司总资产中按比例持有之份额(该份额应为进行公司间抵消后的份额)超过截至最近结束的一个会计年度年末注册人及其并表子公司资产总额10%;或者

(3)在最近结束的一个会计年度,注册人以及注册人其他子公司在该子公司持续经营收益(指扣除非经常项目和会计原则变更累积影响数之前的所得税税前收益,但不包括归属于任何非控制权益的收益)中拥有的权益,超过注册人及其并表子公司该会计年度的持续经营收益总额10%。

关于第(w)款的注释:按照《美国公认会计原则》提交财务报表或按照该原则对财务报表进行账目调整的注册人,应当采用根据该等原则确定的数额进行测试,以判断是否符合本款规定的标准。按照国际会计准则委员会(IASB)发布的《国际财务报告准则》(IFRS)提交财务报表的外国私募发行人,应当采用根据该准则确定的数额进行测试,以判断是否符合本款规定的标准。

计算说明:进行规定的收益测试时,应适用下列指导原则:

1.如果母公司及其并表子公司发生任何不归属于任何非控制权益的损失,或者被测试子公司发生任何不归属于非控制权益的损失(不包括母公司及其并表子公司连同被测试的子公司同时发生该等损失的情况),则母公司及其并表子公司在被测试子公司的损益中所占份额(不包括归属于任何非控制权益的损益),在计算注册人及其并表子公司的收益时应予扣除。

2.如果注册人及其并表子公司最近一个会计年度的收益(不含归属于任何非控制权益的收益)比过去5个会计年度的收益平均值低10%(含)以上,计算收益时应采用过去5个会计年度的收益平均值。计算收益平均值时应忽略任何亏损年度。

3.在确定是否应提交摘要财务数据时,所作测试如果涉及汇总实体,则报告损失

summarized financial data should be presented, entities reporting losses shall not be aggregated with entities reporting income.

(x) *Subsidiary.* A *subsidiary* of a specified person is an affiliate controlled by such person directly, or indirectly through one or more intermediaries.

(y) *Totally held subsidiary.* The term *totally held subsidiary* means a subsidiary (1) substantially all of whose outstanding equity securities are owned by its parent and/or the parent's other totally held subsidiaries, and (2) which is not indebted to any person other than its parent and/or the parent's other totally held subsidiaries, in an amount which is material in relation to the particular subsidiary, excepting indebtedness incurred in the ordinary course of business which is not overdue and which matures within 1 year from the date of its creation, whether evidenced by securities or not. Indebtedness of a subsidiary which is secured by its parent by guarantee, pledge, assignment, or otherwise is to be excluded for purposes of paragraph (x)(2) of this section.

(z) *Voting shares.* The term *voting shares* means the sum of all rights, other than as affected by events of default, to vote for election of directors and/or the sum of all interests in an unincorporated person.

(aa) *Wholly owned subsidiary.* The term *wholly owned subsidiary* means a subsidiary substantially all of whose outstanding voting shares are owned by its parent and/or the parent's other wholly owned subsidiaries.

(bb) *Summarized financial information.* (1) Except as provided in paragraph (aa) (2), *summarized financial information* referred to in this regulation shall mean the presentation of summarized information as to the assets, liabilities and results of operations of the entity for which the information is required. Summarized financial information shall include the following disclosures:

(i) Current assets, noncurrent assets, current liabilities, noncurrent liabilities, and, when applicable, redeemable preferred stocks (see §210.5-02.27) and noncontrolling interests (for specialized industries in which classified balance sheets are normally not presented, information shall be provided as to the nature and amount of the majority components of assets and liabilities);

(ii) Net sales or gross revenues, gross profit (or, alternatively, costs and expenses applicable to net sales or gross revenues), income or loss from continuing operations before extraordinary items and cumulative effect of a change in accounting principle, net income or loss, and net income or loss attributable to the entity (for specialized industries, other information may be substituted for sales and related costs and expenses if necessary for a more meaningful presentation); and

(2) Summarized financial information for unconsolidated subsidiaries and 50 percent or less owned persons referred to in and required by §210.10-01(b) for interim periods shall

的实体收益不应与报告盈利的实体加总计算。

（x）子公司。某主体的“子公司”系指该主体直接控制或通过一个或数个中间方间接控制的控制性关联方。

（y）完全控股子公司。“完全控股子公司”一词系指符合下述两项条件的子公司：（1）其绝大部分发行在外的股权证券由其母公司和/或母公司的其他完全控股子公司持有，且（2）除其母公司和/或母公司的其他完全控股子公司外，不对任何其他主体负有对该子公司而言金额重大的负债（包括以证券作为凭证和不以证券作为凭证的负债，但不含正常业务运作中产生的期限短于一年且尚未逾期的负债）。就本节第（x）款第（2）项而言，子公司的负债不包括其母公司通过保证、质押、让与或其他方式担保的负债。

（z）表决股。“表决股”一词系指选举董事的全部表决权（不包括受到违约事件影响的权利）和/或非公司形式的主体的全部权益之和。

（aa）全资子公司。“全资子公司”一词系指其绝大部分发行在外的表决股均由其母公司和/或母公司的其他全资子公司拥有的子公司。

（bb）摘要财务信息。（1）除第（aa）（2）款规定的情形外，本《管理办法》所述“摘要财务信息”系指按规定应提供该等信息的实体所提交的关于其资产、负债和经营成果的摘要信息。摘要财务信息包括下列披露项目：

（i）流动资产、非流动资产、流动负债、非流动负债以及（如适用）可回赎优先股（参见第210.5-02.27节）和非控制权益（对于一般情况下不提交分类资产负债表的特殊行业，应提供大部分资产和负债要素的性质和金额）；

（ii）净销售额或毛收入、毛利润（或者与净销售额或毛收入相关的成本和费用）、持续经营损益（指扣除非经常项目和会计原则变更累积影响数之前的损益）、净损益，以及归属于该实体的净损益（为使列报的信息更有意义，对于特殊行业而言，必要时可以其他信息替代销售额及相关成本和费用）；及

（2）第210.10-01（b）节所述和要求提供的非并表子公司以及50%或以下股权被控主体的中期摘要财务信息应包括本节第（aa）（1）（ii）款规定的信息。

include the information required by paragraph (aa)(1)(ii) of this section.

[37 FR 14593, July 21, 1972]

Editorial Note: For Federal Registercitations affecting §210.1–02, see the List of CFR Sections Affected, which appears in the Finding Aids section of the printed volume and at www.fdsys.gov.

Qualifications and Reports of Accountants

Source: Sections 210.2–01 through 210.2–05 appear at 37 FR 14594, July 21, 1972, unless otherwise noted.

§210.2–01 Qualifications of accountants.

Preliminary Note to §210.2–01

1. Section 210.2–01 is designed to ensure that auditors are qualified and independent of their audit clients both in fact and in appearance. Accordingly, the rule sets forth restrictions on financial, employment, and business relationships between an accountant and an audit client and restrictions on an accountant providing certain non–audit services to an audit client.

2. Section 210.2–01(b) sets forth the general standard of auditor independence. Paragraphs (c)(1) to (c)(5) reflect the application of the general standard to particular circumstances. The rule does not purport to, and the Commission could not, consider all circumstances that raise independence concerns, and these are subject to the general standard in §210.2–01(b). In considering this standard, the Commission looks in the first instance to whether a relationship or the provision of a service: creates a mutual or conflicting interest between the accountant and the audit client; places the accountant in the position of auditing his or her own work; results in the accountant acting as management or an employee of the audit client; or places the accountant in a position of being an advocate for the audit client.

3. These factors are general guidance only and their application may depend on particular facts and circumstances. For that reason, §210.2–01 provides that, in determining whether an accountant is independent, the Commission will consider all relevant facts and circumstances. For the same reason, registrants and accountants are encouraged to consult with the Commission's Office of the Chief Accountant before entering into relationships, including relationships involving the provision of services, that are not explicitly described in the rule.

(a) The Commission will not recognize any person as a certified public accountant who is not duly registered and in good standing as such under the laws of the place of his residence or principal office. The Commission will not recognize any person as a public accountant who is not in good standing and entitled to practice as such under the laws of

[《联邦公报》第37卷第14593页,1972年7月21日。]

编者按:对第210.1-02节有影响的《联邦公报》索引,参见《受影响的联邦规章汇编条文列表》(见印刷版本的《检索协助》章节和www.fdsys.gov)。

会计师资格和报告

行政规则来源:《联邦公报》第37卷第14594页,(1972年7月21日)第210.2-01~210.2-05节,除非另有说明。

第210.2-01节　会计师资格

关于第210.2-01节的文前说明

1.第210.2-01节旨在确保审计师具有相应资质,并且在表面上和事实上均独立于审计客户。因此,该规则对会计师和审计客户之间的财务、雇佣和业务关系设定了相关限制,并对向审计客户提供特定非审计服务的会计师设定了相关限制。

2.第210.2-01(b)节规定了审计师独立性的一般标准。第(c)(1)款至第(c)(5)款规定了一般标准在具体情形下的适用。该规则无意一一列举,且证券交易委员会也无法全盘考虑引发独立性问题的所有情形,具体情形发生时应以第210.2-01(b)节规定的一般标准为准。根据此项标准判断审计师独立性时,证券交易委员会将首先考虑双方的关系以及审计师的服务是否会造成如下后果:在会计师和审计客户之间形成共同利益或造成利益冲突;导致会计师对其自身所作工作进行自我审计;导致会计师成为审计客户的管理人员或职员;或导致会计师成为审计客户的权益维护者。

3.上述因素仅具有一般指引性,适用时应以具体事实和情形为准。因此,第210.2-01节规定,在判断某名会计师是否具有独立性时,证券交易委员会应当考虑所有相关事实和情形。出于同一理由,证券交易委员会鼓励注册人和会计师在确立本规则未明确规定的业务关系(包括服务提供关系)之前,首先征询证券交易委员会首席会计师办公室的意见。

(a)证券交易委员会认可注册会计师的必要条件是:会计师已按其居住地或主要办公场所所在地法律合法注册且有效存续。证券交易委员会认可公共会计师的必要条件是:会计师有效存续且根据其居住地或主要办公场所所在地法律有权以公共会计师身份执业。

the place of his residence or principal office.

(b) The Commission will not recognize an accountant as independent, with respect to an audit client, if the accountant is not, or a reasonable investor with knowledge of all relevant facts and circumstances would conclude that the accountant is not, capable of exercising objective and impartial judgment on all issues encompassed within the accountant's engagement. In determining whether an accountant is independent, the Commission will consider all relevant circumstances, including all relationships between the accountant and the audit client, and not just those relating to reports filed with the Commission.

(c) This paragraph sets forth a non-exclusive specification of circumstances inconsistent with paragraph (b) of this section.

(1) *Financial relationships.* An accountant is not independent if, at any point during the audit and professional engagement period, the accountant has a direct financial interest or a material indirect financial interest in the accountant's audit client, such as:

(i) *Investments in audit clients.* An accountant is not independent when:

(A) The accounting firm, any covered person in the firm, or any of his or her immediate family members, has any direct investment in an audit client, such as stocks, bonds, notes, options, or other securities. The term *direct investment* includes an investment in an audit client through an intermediary if:

(1) The accounting firm, covered person, or immediate family member, alone or together with other persons, supervises or participates in the intermediary's investment decisions or has control over the intermediary; or

(2) The intermediary is not a diversified management investment company, as defined by section 5 (b)(1) of the Investment Company Act of 1940, 15 U.S.C. 80a-5 (b)(1), and has an investment in the audit client that amounts to 20% or more of the value of the intermediary's total investments.

(B) Any partner, principal, shareholder, or professional employee of the accounting firm, any of his or her immediate family members, any close family member of a covered person in the firm, or any group of the above persons has filed a Schedule 13D or 13G (17 CFR 240.13d-101 or 240.13d-102) with the Commission indicating beneficial ownership of more than five percent of an audit client's equity securities or controls an audit client, or a close family member of a partner, principal, or shareholder of the accounting firm controls an audit client.

(C) The accounting firm, any covered person in the firm, or any of his or her immediate family members, serves as voting trustee of a trust, or executor of an estate, containing the securities of an audit client, unless the accounting firm, covered person in the firm, or immediate family member has no authority to make investment decisions for

（b）证券交易委员会认可会计师对审计客户具有独立性的必要条件是：会计师有能力（或者了解所有相关事实和情形的理性投资者会认为会计师有能力）对委托的审计业务涉及的所有事项作出客观、公允判断。在判断会计师的独立性时，证券交易委员会将考虑所有相关情形，包括会计师与审计客户之间存在的所有关系，而不仅限于与提交给证券交易委员会的报告有关的关系。

（c）本款列明了与本节第（b）款不符的某些具体情形，但本款的列举不具穷尽性。

（1）财务关系：在审计期以及专业委托期内的任何时点，会计师对其审计客户拥有直接财务利益或重大间接财务利益的，即不具备独立性，如

（i）拥有对审计客户的投资。下列情形下会计师不具独立性：

（A）会计师事务所、所内任何所涉人员或其任何直系亲属，拥有对审计客户的直接投资，例如股票、债券、票据、期权或其他证券。在下列情形下，“直接投资”涵盖通过中间方对审计客户进行的投资：

（1）会计师事务所、所内所涉人员或其直系亲属单独或与其他主体共同监督或参与中间方的投资决策，或对中间方拥有控制权；或者

（2）中间方不属于《1940年投资公司法》第5（b）（1）条［《美国法典》第十五编第80a-5（b）（1）节］所定义的分散管理型投资公司，并且对审计客户的投资达到或超过中间方投资总额的20%。

（B）会计师事务所任何合伙人、负责人、股东、专业职员或其任何直系亲属、所内任何所涉人员的任何近亲属，或者上述任何人员组成的团体，向证券交易委员会提交了《附表13D》或《附表13G》（《联邦规章汇编》第十七编第240.13d-101节或第240.13d-102节），说明其对审计客户的股权证券拥有5%以上的受益所有权，或对审计客户拥有控制权；或者会计师事务所合伙人、负责人或股东的近亲属对审计客户拥有控制权。

（C）会计师事务所、所内任何所涉人员或其任何直系亲属担任某信托的有表决权受托人，或某一财产的执行人，而该信托或财产含有审计客户的证券；但是会计师事务所、所内所涉人员或其直系亲属无权就信托或财产作出投资决定的除外。

the trust or estate.

(D) The accounting firm, any covered person in the firm, any of his or her immediate family members, or any group of the above persons has any material indirect investment in an audit client. For purposes of this paragraph, the term *material indirect investment* does not include ownership by any covered person in the firm, any of his or her immediate family members, or any group of the above persons of 5% or less of the outstanding shares of a diversified management investment company, as defined by section 5(b)(1) of the Investment Company Act of 1940, 15 U.S.C. 80a–5(b)(1), that invests in an audit client.

(E) The accounting firm, any covered person in the firm, or any of his or her immediate family members:

(1) Has any direct or material indirect investment in an entity where:

(*i*) An audit client has an investment in that entity that is material to the audit client and has the ability to exercise significant influence over that entity; or

(*ii*) The entity has an investment in an audit client that is material to that entity and has the ability to exercise significant influence over that audit client;

(2) Has any material investment in an entity over which an audit client has the ability to exercise significant influence; or

(3) Has the ability to exercise significant influence over an entity that has the ability to exercise significant influence over an audit client.

(ii) *Other financial interests in audit client.* An accountant is not independent when the accounting firm, any covered person in the firm, or any of his or her immediate family members has:

(A) *Loans/debtor–creditor relationship.* Any loan (including any margin loan) to or from an audit client, or an audit client's officers, directors, or record or beneficial owners of more than ten percent of the audit client's equity securities, except for the following loans obtained from a financial institution under its normal lending procedures, terms, and requirements:

(1) Automobile loans and leases collateralized by the automobile;

(2) Loans fully collateralized by the cash surrender value of an insurance policy;

(3) Loans fully collateralized by cash deposits at the same financial institution; and

(4) A mortgage loan collateralized by the borrower's primary residence provided the loan was not obtained while the covered person in the firm was a covered person.

(B) *Savings and checking accounts.* Any savings, checking, or similar account at a bank, savings and loan, or similar institution that is an audit client, if the account has a balance that exceeds the amount insured by the Federal Deposit Insurance Corporation or any similar insurer, except that an accounting firm account may have an uninsured

（D）会计师事务所、所内任何所涉人员或其任何直系亲属，或者上述人组成的任何团体拥有对审计客户的任何重大间接投资。如某一家分散管理型投资公司｛定义见《1940年投资公司法》第5（b）（1）条［《美国法典》第十五编第80a-5（b）（1）节］｝对审计客户进行投资，而所内任何所涉人员或其任何直系亲属或者上述人组成的任何团体仅拥有该等分散管理型投资公司不超过5%发行在外股份的所有权，则该等股份不构成本款所述的“重大间接投资”。

（E）会计师事务所、所内任何所涉人员或其任何直系亲属：

（1）拥有对任一实体的任何直接投资或重大间接投资，并且：

（i）审计客户也拥有对该实体的投资并能对该实体施加重大影响，且该等投资对于审计客户而言构成重大投资；或者

（ii）该实体拥有对审计客户的投资并能对审计客户施加重大影响，且该等投资对于该实体而言构成重大投资；

（2）拥有对某实体的任何重大投资，而审计客户能对该实体施加重大影响；或者

（3）能对某实体施加重大影响，而该实体能对审计客户施加重大影响。

（ii）在审计客户中拥有其他财务利益。下列情形下会计师不具独立性：会计师事务所、所内任何所涉人员或其任何直系亲属拥有：

（A）贷款/债权债务关系。向审计客户或审计客户的管理人员、董事或拥有审计客户10%以上股权证券的登记或受益所有权人提供的任何贷款（包括任何保证金贷款），或获得该等人员提供的贷款（包括保证金贷款），但金融机构按照正常贷款程序、条款和要求发放的下列贷款除外：

（1）以汽车担保的汽车贷款和租赁；

（2）以保险单退保现金价值全额担保的贷款；

（3）以同一金融机构的现金存款全额担保的贷款；及

（4）以借款人主要居所担保的抵押贷款，前提是该项贷款并非所内所涉人员在身为所涉人员期间获得的贷款。

（B）储蓄和活期存款账户。在审计客户（指身份为银行、储蓄和贷款机构或类似机构的客户）处开立任何储蓄、活期存款账户或类似账户，且账户余额超过了联邦存款保险公司或任何类似保险公司承保的金额（但如果该银行、储蓄和贷款机构或类似机构陷入财务困境的几率很小，会计师事务所的账户可以有超过投保范围的余额）。

balance provided that the likelihood of the bank, savings and loan, or similar institution experiencing financial difficulties is remote.

(C) *Broker–dealer accounts.* Brokerage or similar accounts maintained with a broker–dealer that is an audit client, if:

(1) Any such account includes any asset other than cash or securities (within the meaning of "security" provided in the Securities Investor Protection Act of 1970 ("SIPA") (15 U.S.C. 78aaa *et seq.*));

(2) The value of assets in the accounts exceeds the amount that is subject to a Securities Investor Protection Corporation advance, for those accounts, under Section 9 of SIPA (15 U.S.C. 78fff–3); or

(3) With respect to non–U.S. accounts not subject to SIPA protection, the value of assets in the accounts exceeds the amount insured or protected by a program similar to SIPA.

(D) *Futures commission merchant accounts.* Any futures, commodity, or similar account maintained with a futures commission merchant that is an audit client.

(E) *Credit cards.* Any aggregate outstanding credit card balance owed to a lender that is an audit client that is not reduced to $10,000 or less on a current basis taking into consideration the payment due date and any available grace period.

(F) *Insurance products.* Any individual policy issued by an insurer that is an audit client unless:

(1) The policy was obtained at a time when the covered person in the firm was not a covered person in the firm; and

(2) The likelihood of the insurer becoming insolvent is remote.

(G) *Investment companies.* Any financial interest in an entity that is part of an investment company complex that includes an audit client.

(iii) *Exceptions.* Notwithstanding paragraphs (c)(1)(i) and (c)(1)(ii) of this section, an accountant will not be deemed not independent if:

(A) *Inheritance and gift.* Any person acquires an unsolicited financial interest, such as through an unsolicited gift or inheritance, that would cause an accountant to be not independent under paragraph (c) (1) (i) or (c) (1) (ii) of this section, and the financial interest is disposed of as soon as practicable, but no later than 30 days after the person has knowledge of and the right to dispose of the financial interest.

(B) *New audit engagement.* Any person has a financial interest that would cause an accountant to be not independent under paragraph (c)(1)(i) or (c)(1)(ii) of this section, and

(1) The accountant did not audit the client's financial statements for the immediately preceding fiscal year; and

(C)经纪自营商账户。在审计客户(指身份为经纪自营商的客户)处开立经纪账户或类似账户,并且:

(1)任一该等账户中存在现金或证券以外的任何资产("证券"一词的含义以《1970年证券投资者保护法》[《美国法典》第十五编第78aaa节及其后条文)(英文简称SIPA)的定义为准];

(2)账户中的资产价值超过了按照《1970年证券投资者保护法》第9条(《美国法典》第十五编第78fff-3节)规定,证券投资者保护公司对该等账户提供的预先偿付限额;或者

(3)对于不受《1970年证券投资者保护法》保护的非美国账户,账户资产价值超过与《1970年证券投资者保护法》的机制类似的机制所承保或保护的金额。

(D)期货代理商账户。在审计客户(指身份为期货代理商的客户)处开立的任何期货、商品或类似账户。

(E)信用卡。向审计客户(指身份为贷款人的客户)欠付的信用卡当前累计未偿余额未控制在1万美元或以下,该等未偿余额系指考虑付款到期日和任何可获得的宽限期之后所确定的金额。

(F)保险产品。拥有审计客户(指身份为保险公司的客户)出具的任何个人保险单,除非:

(1)获得保险单之时,所内所涉人员并不具有所涉人员身份;且

(2)保险公司出现资不抵债情形的几率微乎其微;

(G)投资公司。在与审计客户同属某一投资公司集团的实体中拥有任何财务利益。

(iii)例外情形。无论本节第(c)(1)(i)款和第(c)(1)(ii)款如何规定,下列情形下会计师不视为丧失独立性:

(A)继承和赠与。任何主体被动获得(如未经主动请求被赠与或继承)根据本节第(c)(1)(i)款和第(c)(1)(ii)款规定将使会计师丧失独立性的财务利益,但该主体以尽可能快的速度在不晚于获知该财务利益并有权处置该利益后30日内进行了处置。

(B)新的审计委托。任何主体虽然拥有根据本节第(c)(1)(i)款和第(c)(1)(ii)款规定将使会计师丧失独立性的财务利益,但是:

(1)会计师并未承接客户上一会计年度的财务报表审计工作;且

(2) The accountant is independent under paragraph (c)(1)(i) and (c)(1)(ii) of this section before the earlier of:

(*i*) Signing an initial engagement letter or other agreement to provide audit, review, or attest services to the audit client; or

(*ii*) Commencing any audit, review, or attest procedures (including planning the audit of the client's financial statements).

(C) *Employee compensation and benefit plans.* An immediate family member of a person who is a covered person in the firm only by virtue of paragraphs (f)(11)(iii) or (f)(11)(iv) of this section has a financial interest that would cause an accountant to be not independent under paragraph (c)(1)(i) or (c)(1)(ii) of this section, and the acquisition of the financial interest was an unavoidable consequence of participation in his or her employer's employee compensation or benefits program, provided that the financial interest, other than unexercised employee stock options, is disposed of as soon as practicable, but no later than 30 days after the person has the right to dispose of the financial interest.

(iv) *Audit clients' financial relationships.* An accountant is not independent when:

(A) *Investments by the audit client in the accounting firm.* An audit client has, or has agreed to acquire, any direct investment in the accounting firm, such as stocks, bonds, notes, options, or other securities, or the audit client's officers or directors are record or beneficial owners of more than 5% of the equity securities of the accounting firm.

(B) *Underwriting.* An accounting firm engages an audit client to act as an underwriter, broker-dealer, market-maker, promoter, or analyst with respect to securities issued by the accounting firm.

(2) *Employment relationships.* An accountant is not independent if, at any point during the audit and professional engagement period, the accountant has an employment relationship with an audit client, such as:

(i) *Employment at audit client of accountant.* A current partner, principal, shareholder, or professional employee of the accounting firm is employed by the audit client or serves as a member of the board of directors or similar management or governing body of the audit client.

(ii) *Employment at audit client of certain relatives of accountant.* A close family member of a covered person in the firm is in an accounting role or financial reporting oversight role at an audit client, or was in such a role during any period covered by an audit for which the covered person in the firm is a covered person.

(iii) *Employment at audit client of former employee of accounting firm.* (A) A former partner, principal, shareholder, or professional employee of an accounting firm is in an accounting role or financial reporting oversight role at an audit client, unless the

(2)在下述事件发生之前(以较早发生者为准),会计师根据本节第(c)(1)(i)款和第(c)(1)(ii)款的规定具备独立性:

(i)为向客户提供审计、审查或鉴证服务而与审计客户签订首份委托书或其他协议;或者

(ii)启动任何审计、审查或鉴证程序(包括制定客户财务报表的审计计划)。

(C)员工薪酬和福利计划。仅因本节第(f)(11)(iii)款或第(f)(11)(iv)款的规定而被认定为所内所涉人员的主体,其直系亲属拥有根据本节第(c)(1)(i)款或第(c)(1)(ii)款规定将使会计师丧失独立性的财务利益,但该等财务利益是该主体参与雇主的员工薪酬或福利计划必然获得的利益,并且该主体以尽可能快的速度在其有权处置该利益后30日内进行了处置(未行使的员工股票期权除外)。

(iv)审计客户的财务关系。下列情形下会计师不具独立性:

(A)审计客户拥有对会计师事务所的投资。审计客户拥有,或者已同意购买对会计师事务所的任何直接投资(如股票、债券、票据、期权或其他证券投资),或者审计客户的管理人员或董事是会计师事务所5%以上股权证券的登记或受益所有人。

(B)承销。会计师事务所为其发行的证券委托审计客户担任承销商、经纪自营商、做市商、发起人或分析师。

(2)雇佣关系。在审计期以及专业委托期内的任何时点,会计师与审计客户有如下雇佣关系的,即不具备独立性:

(i)会计师被审计客户雇佣。会计师事务所现任合伙人、负责人、股东或专业职员被审计客户雇佣或担任审计客户的董事会或类似治理机构的成员。

(ii)会计师特定亲属被审计客户雇佣。所内所涉人员的近亲属担任审计客户的会计职务或财务报告监督职务,或者所内所涉人员在身为所涉人员的任何审计期内曾担任该等职务。

(iii)会计师事务所前员工被审计客户雇佣。(A)会计师事务所前合伙人、负责人、股东或专业职员担任审计客户的会计职务或财务报告监督职务,但以下情形除外:

individual:

(1) Does not influence the accounting firm's operations or financial policies;

(2) Has no capital balances in the accounting firm; and

(3) Has no financial arrangement with the accounting firm other than one providing for regular payment of a fixed dollar amount (which is not dependent on the revenues, profits, or earnings of the accounting firm):

(*i*) Pursuant to a fully funded retirement plan, rabbi trust, or, in jurisdictions in which a rabbi trust does not exist, a similar vehicle; or

(*ii*) In the case of a former professional employee who was not a partner, principal, or shareholder of the accounting firm and who has been disassociated from the accounting firm for more than five years, that is immaterial to the former professional employee; and

(B) A former partner, principal, shareholder, or professional employee of an accounting firm is in a financial reporting oversight role at an issuer (as defined in section 10A(f) of the Securities Exchange Act of 1934 (15 U.S.C. 78j-1(f)), except an issuer that is an investment company registered under section 8 of the Investment Company Act of 1940 (15 U.S.C. 80a-8), unless the individual:

(1) Employed by the issuer was not a member of the audit engagement team of the issuer during the one year period preceding the date that audit procedures commenced for the fiscal period that included the date of initial employment of the audit engagement team member by the issuer;

(2) For purposes of paragraph (c)(2)(iii)(B)(1) of this section, the following individuals are not considered to be members of the audit engagement team:

(*i*) Persons, other than the lead partner and the concurring partner, who provided ten or fewer hours of audit, review, or attest services during the period covered by paragraph (c)(2)(iii)(B)(1) of this section;

(*ii*) Individuals employed by the issuer as a result of a business combination between an issuer that is an audit client and the employing entity, provided employment was not in contemplation of the business combination and the audit committee of the successor issuer is aware of the prior employment relationship; and

(*iii*) Individuals that are employed by the issuer due to an emergency or other unusual situation provided that the audit committee determines that the relationship is in the interest of investors;

(3) For purposes of paragraph (c)(2)(iii)(B)(1) of this section, audit procedures are deemed to have commenced for a fiscal period the day following the filing of the issuer's periodic annual report with the Commission covering the previous fiscal period; or

(C) A former partner, principal, shareholder, or professional employee of an

(1)该等前员工对会计师事务所的经营或财务政策不具影响力;

(2)该等前员工在会计师事务所中未保留持有任何资本;且

(3)与会计师事务所之间不存在任何财务安排,但下述定额定期付款安排(即金额与会计师事务所收入、利润或盈利无关的安排)除外:

(i)拥有充分资金来源的退休计划、拉比信托,或者(在不存在拉比信托的司法辖区内)类似拉比信托的载体作出的财务安排;或者

(ii)对于在事务所任职期间未担任过会计师事务所合伙人、负责人或股东并且与会计师事务所解除业务关系已届满5年的前专业职员而言,对该等职员而言属于非重大性质的财务安排;及

(B)会计师事务所前合伙人、负责人、股东或专业职员担任发行人{定义见《1934年证券交易法》第10A(f)条[《美国法典》第十五编第78j-1(f)节)],发行人属于依《1940年投资公司法》第8条(《美国法典》第十五编第80a-8节)注册的投资公司的除外}的财务报告监督职务,但下列情形除外:

(1)该等受雇于发行人的个人在下述期间内不属于发行人审计委托团队成员:该等个人成为发行人审计委托团队成员之日所在会计期间的审计程序启动前一年的期间;

(2)就本节第(c)(2)(iii)(B)(1)款而言,下列个人不视为审计委托团队成员:

(i)在本节第(c)(2)(iii)(B)(1)款所述期间内提供的审计、审查或鉴证服务不多于10小时的人(审计项目主查合伙人和复核合伙人除外);

(ii)由于发行人(即审计客户)和雇佣单位进行业务合并而成为发行人雇员的个人,前提是此人并非为业务合并之目的而被雇佣,且作为存续实体的发行人的审计委员会知悉该等之前存在的雇佣关系;及

(iii)在紧急或其他非常情况下被发行人雇佣的个人,前提是审计委员会判定该等雇佣关系符合投资者利益;

(3)就本节第(c)(2)(iii)(B)(1)款而言,在发行人向证券交易委员会提交上一会计期间的定期年度报告的次日,针对该会计期间开展的审计程序即视为启动;或者

(C)会计师事务所前合伙人、负责人、股东或专业职员担任依据《1940年投资公司

accounting firm is in a financial reporting oversight role with respect to an investment company registered under section 8 of the Investment Company Act of 1940 (15 U.S.C. 80a-8), if:

(1) The former partner, principal, shareholder, or professional employee of an accounting firm is employed in a financial reporting oversight role related to the operations and financial reporting of the registered investment company at an entity in the investment company complex, as defined in (f)(14) of this section, that includes the registered investment company; and

(2) The former partner, principal, shareholder, or professional employee of an accounting firm employed by the registered investment company or any entity in the investment company complex was a member of the audit engagement team of the registered investment company or any other registered investment company in the investment company complex during the one year period preceding the date that audit procedures commenced that included the date of initial employment of the audit engagement team member by the registered investment company or any entity in the investment company complex.

(3) For purposes of paragraph (c)(2)(iii)(C)(2) of this section, the following individuals are not considered to be members of the audit engagement team:

(*i*) Persons, other than the lead partner and concurring partner, who provided ten or fewer hours of audit, review or attest services during the period covered by paragraph (c)(2)(iii)(C)(2) of this section;

(*ii*) Individuals employed by the registered investment company or any entity in the investment company complex as a result of a business combination between a registered investment company or any entity in the investment company complex that is an audit client and the employing entity, provided employment was not in contemplation of the business combination and the audit committee of the registered investment company is aware of the prior employment relationship; and

(*iii*) Individuals that are employed by the registered investment company or any entity in the investment company complex due to an emergency or other unusual situation provided that the audit committee determines that the relationship is in the interest of investors.

(4) For purposes of paragraph (c)(2)(iii)(C)(2) of this section, audit procedures are deemed to have commenced the day following the filing of the registered investment company's periodic annual report with the Commission.

(iv) *Employment at accounting firm of former employee of audit client.* A former officer, director, or employee of an audit client becomes a partner, principal, shareholder, or professional employee of the accounting firm, unless the individual does not participate

法》第8条(《美国法典》第十五编第80a-8节)注册的投资公司的财务报告监督职务,前提是:

(1)会计师事务所前合伙人、负责人、股东或专业职员系由上述注册投资公司所属投资公司集团[定义见本节第(f)(14)款]的下属实体所雇佣,担任与注册投资公司的业务和财务报告有关的财务报告监督职务;且

(2)注册投资公司或投资公司集团下属任何实体雇佣的会计师事务所前合伙人、负责人、股东或专业职员,在该等审计程序启动前一年期间(该一年期应包含注册投资公司或投资公司集团下属任何实体委托审计委托团队的首日),属于该注册投资公司或投资公司集团下属其他注册投资公司的审计委托团队成员。

(3)就本节第(c)(2)(iii)(C)(2)款而言,以下个人不视为审计委托团队成员:

(i)在本节第(c)(2)(iii)(C)(2)款所述期间内提供的审计、审查或鉴证服务不多于10小时的人(审计项目主查合伙人和复核合伙人除外);

(ii)由于注册投资公司/投资公司集团下属任何实体(即审计客户)与雇佣单位业务合并而成为该等投资公司/投资公司集团下属任何实体员工的人,前提是此人并非为业务合并之目的而被雇佣且注册投资公司的审计委员会知悉该等之前存在的雇佣关系;及

(iii)在紧急或其他非常情况下被注册投资公司/投资公司集团下属任何实体雇佣的个人,前提是审计委员会认定该等雇佣关系符合投资者利益;

(4)就本节第(c)(2)(iii)(C)(2)款而言,在注册投资公司向证券交易委员会提交定期年度报告的次日,审计程序即视为启动。

(iv)会计师事务所雇佣审计客户前员工。审计客户前管理人员、董事或职员成为会计师事务所合伙人、负责人、股东或专业职员,但以下情形除外:该等个人在会计师事务所内,并不参与审计其受雇于审计客户期间或作为业务相关人在审计客户任职

in, and is not in a position to influence, the audit of the financial statements of the audit client covering any period during which he or she was employed by or associated with that audit client.

(3) *Business relationships.* An accountant is not independent if, at any point during the audit and professional engagement period, the accounting firm or any covered person in the firm has any direct or material indirect business relationship with an audit client, or with persons associated with the audit client in a decision-making capacity, such as an audit client's officers, directors, or substantial stockholders. The relationships described in this paragraph do not include a relationship in which the accounting firm or covered person in the firm provides professional services to an audit client or is a consumer in the ordinary course of business.

(4) *Non-audit services.* An accountant is not independent if, at any point during the audit and professional engagement period, the accountant provides the following non-audit services to an audit client:

(i) *Bookkeeping or other services related to the accounting records or financial statements of the audit client.* Any service, unless it is reasonable to conclude that the results of these services will not be subject to audit procedures during an audit of the audit client's financial statements, including:

(A) Maintaining or preparing the audit client's accounting records;

(B) Preparing the audit client's financial statements that are filed with the Commission or that form the basis of financial statements filed with the Commission; or

(C) Preparing or originating source data underlying the audit client's financial statements.

(ii) *Financial information systems design and implementation.* Any service, unless it is reasonable to conclude that the results of these services will not be subject to audit procedures during an audit of the audit client's financial statements, including:

(A) Directly or indirectly operating, or supervising the operation of, the audit client's information system or managing the audit client's local area network; or

(B) Designing or implementing a hardware or software system that aggregates source data underlying the financial statements or generates information that is significant to the audit client's financial statements or other financial information systems taken as a whole.

(iii) *Appraisal or valuation services, fairness opinions, or contribution-in-kind reports.* Any appraisal service, valuation service, or any service involving a fairness opinion or contribution-in-kind report for an audit client, unless it is reasonable to conclude that the results of these services will not be subject to audit procedures during an audit of the audit client's financial statements.

(iv) *Actuarial services.* Any actuarially-oriented advisory service involving the

期间内的财务报表,也无法对该等审计产生影响。

(3)业务关系。在审计和专业委托期内的任何时点,会计师事务所或所内任何所涉人员与审计客户或其决策人员(如管理人员、董事或大股东)存在任何直接或重大间接业务关系的,会计师即不具备独立性。本款所述关系不包括会计师事务所或所内所涉人员在正常业务运作中向审计客户提供专业服务或作为审计客户的消费者所产生的关系。

(4)非审计服务。在审计和专业委托期内的任何时点,会计师向审计客户提供下列非审计服务的,即不具备独立性:

(i)与审计客户的会计记录或财务报表相关的簿记服务或其他服务。除非在对客户财务报表进行审计的过程中,可合理判定服务成果不属于审计程序的涵盖范围,否则,任何该等服务均包括:

(A)维护或编制审计客户的会计记录;

(B)编制审计客户提交给证券交易委员会的财务报表或构成此类财务报表依据的财务报表;或者

(C)编制或创建审计客户财务报表的基础原始数据。

(ii)财务信息系统设计和实施。除非在对客户财务报表进行审计的过程中,可合理判定服务成果不属于审计程序的涵盖范围,否则,任何该等服务均包括:

(A)直接或间接运行审计客户信息系统或监督该等系统的运行,或者管理审计客户的局域网;或者

(B)设计或实施用于整合财务报表基础原始数据或生成审计客户财务报表重要信息的一套硬件或软件系统,或数套其他财务信息系统共同构成的一整套财务系统。

(iii)评估或估值服务、公允意见书或实物出资报告。除非在对客户财务报表进行审计的过程中,可合理判定服务成果不属于审计程序的涵盖范围,否则,该等服务指为审计客户提供的任何评估服务、任何估值服务或涉及公允意见书或实物出资报告的任何服务。

(iv)精算服务。除非在对客户财务报表进行审计的过程中,可合理判定服务成果

determination of amounts recorded in the financial statements and related accounts for the audit client other than assisting a client in understanding the methods, models, assumptions, and inputs used in computing an amount, unless it is reasonable to conclude that the results of these services will not be subject to audit procedures during an audit of the audit client's financial statements.

(v) *Internal audit outsourcing services.* Any internal audit service that has been outsourced by the audit client that relates to the audit client's internal accounting controls, financial systems, or financial statements, for an audit client unless it is reasonable to conclude that the results of these services will not be subject to audit procedures during an audit of the audit client's financial statements.

(vi) *Management functions.* Acting, temporarily or permanently, as a director, officer, or employee of an audit client, or performing any decision-making, supervisory, or ongoing monitoring function for the audit client.

(vii) *Human resources.* (A) Searching for or seeking out prospective candidates for managerial, executive, or director positions;

(B) Engaging in psychological testing, or other formal testing or evaluation programs;

(C) Undertaking reference checks of prospective candidates for an executive or director position;

(D) Acting as a negotiator on the audit client's behalf, such as determining position, status or title, compensation, fringe benefits, or other conditions of employment; or

(E) Recommending, or advising the audit client to hire, a specific candidate for a specific job (except that an accounting firm may, upon request by the audit client, interview candidates and advise the audit client on the candidate's competence for financial accounting, administrative, or control positions).

(viii) *Broker-dealer, investment adviser, or investment banking services.* Acting as a broker-dealer (registered or unregistered), promoter, or underwriter, on behalf of an audit client, making investment decisions on behalf of the audit client or otherwise having discretionary authority over an audit client's investments, executing a transaction to buy or sell an audit client's investment, or having custody of assets of the audit client, such as taking temporary possession of securities purchased by the audit client.

(ix) *Legal services.* Providing any service to an audit client that, under circumstances in which the service is provided, could be provided only by someone licensed, admitted, or otherwise qualified to practice law in the jurisdiction in which the service is provided.

(x) *Expert services unrelated to the audit.* Providing an expert opinion or other expert service for an audit client, or an audit client's legal representative, for the purpose of advocating an audit client's interests in litigation or in a regulatory or administrative proceeding or investigation. In any litigation or regulatory or administrative proceeding or

不属于审计程序的涵盖范围,否则,该等服务系指:为确定审计客户财务报表数额和相关账目数额而进行的以精算主导的咨询服务,但不包括帮助客户理解数额计算方法、模型、假设和输入值的任何服务。

(v)内部审计外包服务。除非在对客户财务报表进行审计的过程中,可合理判定服务成果不属于审计程序的涵盖范围,否则,该等服务指:审计客户外包的,与其内部会计控制措施、财务系统或财务报表有关的任何内部审计服务。

(vi)管理职能。临时或正式担任审计客户的董事、管理人员或职员,或者为审计客户履行任何决策、监督或持续监控职能。

(vii)人力资源。(A)为管理、管理人员或董事职位搜寻或定位潜在候选人;

(B)从事心理测试或开展其他正式测试或评估项目;

(C)对管理人员或董事职位潜在候选人进行背景调查;

(D)代表审计客户进行谈判,如为确定职位、身份或职称、薪酬待遇、附加福利或其他雇佣条件而代表其进行谈判;或者

(E)推荐或建议审计客户聘用特定候选人担任特定职位(但会计师事务所应审计客户的要求,为财务会计、行政或管理职位面试候选人或就该等候选人的胜任性向审计客户提供建议的情形除外)。

(viii)经纪自营商、投资顾问或投资银行服务。代表审计客户以经纪自营商(不论是否已注册)、发起人或承销商的身份行事;代表审计客户作出投资决策或以其他方式对审计客户的投资行使全权代理权;执行审计客户投资的买卖交易或存管审计客户的资产(如临时占有审计客户购买的证券)。

(ix)法律服务。于某司法辖区内向审计客户提供根据服务所涉的具体情形,仅有获得该司法辖区法律执业许可、核准或其他资格的人才可提供的任何服务。

(x)与审计无关的专家服务。为在诉讼、监管程序、行政处理程序或调查中维护审计客户权益之目的,向审计客户或其法定代表人提供专家意见或其他专家服务。在任何诉讼、监管程序、行政处理程序或调查中,如果会计师对其为审计客户提供服务期间开展的工作作出事实陈述(包括提供证词),或对其在此期间采取的立场或得出的

investigation, an accountant's independence shall not be deemed to be impaired if the accountant provides factual accounts, including in testimony, of work performed or explains the positions taken or conclusions reached during the performance of any service provided by the accountant for the audit client.

(5) *Contingent fees.* An accountant is not independent if, at any point during the audit and professional engagement period, the accountant provides any service or product to an audit client for a contingent fee or a commission, or receives a contingent fee or commission from an audit client.

(6) *Partner rotation.* (i) Except as provided in paragraph (c)(6)(ii) of this section, an accountant is not independent of an audit client when:

(A) Any audit partner as defined in paragraph (f)(7)(ii) of this section performs:

(1) The services of a lead partner, as defined in paragraph (f)(7)(ii)(A) of this section, or concurring partner, as defined in paragraph (f)(7)(ii)(B) of this section, for more than five consecutive years; or

(2) One or more of the services defined in paragraphs (f)(7)(ii)(C) and (D) of this section for more than seven consecutive years;

(B) Any audit partner:

(1) Within the five consecutive year period following the performance of services for the maximum period permitted under paragraph (c)(6)(i)(A)(1) of this section, performs for that audit client the services of a lead partner, as defined in paragraph (f)(7)(ii)(A) of this section, or concurring partner, as defined in paragraph (f)(7)(ii)(B) of this section, or a combination of those services; or

(2) Within the two consecutive year period following the performance of services for the maximum period permitted under paragraph (c)(6)(i)(A)(2) of this section, performs one or more of the services defined in paragraph (f)(7)(ii) of this section.

(ii) Any accounting firm with less than five audit clients that are issuers (as defined in section 10A(f) of the Securities Exchange Act of 1934 (15 U.S.C. 78j-1(f))) and less than ten partners shall be exempt from paragraph (c)(6)(i) of this section *provided* the Public Company Accounting Oversight Board conducts a review at least once every three years of each of the audit client engagements that would result in a lack of auditor independence under this paragraph.

(iii) For purposes of paragraph (c)(6)(i) of this section, an audit client that is an investment company registered under section 8 of the Investment Company Act of 1940 (15 U.S.C. 80a-8), does not include an affiliate of the audit client that is an entity in the same investment company complex, as defined in paragraph (f)(14) of this section, except for another registered investment company in the same investment company complex. For purposes of calculating consecutive years of service under paragraph (c)(6)

结论作出解释,其独立性不视为受损。

(5)风险收费。在审计和专业委托期内的任何时点,会计师为获取收取风险收费或佣金而向审计客户提供服务,或者从审计客户处收到风险收费或佣金的,即不具备独立性。

(6)合伙人轮换。(i)除本节第(c)(6)(ii)款规定的情形外,下列情形下会计师应视为对审计客户不具独立性:

(A)会计师属于本节第(f)(7)(ii)款定义的审计合伙人,且:

(1)连续5年以上担任本节第(f)(7)(ii)(A)款定义的审计项目主查合伙人或本节第(f)(7)(ii)(B)款定义的复核合伙人;或者

(2)连续7年以上提供本节第(f)(7)(ii)(C)款和第(f)(7)(ii)(D)款定义的一项或多项服务;

(B)会计师为审计合伙人,且:

(1)在本节第(c)(6)(i)(A)(1)款允许的最长服务期过后,又在连续5年期间内作为审计项目主查合伙人[定义见本节第(f)(7)(ii)(A)款]和/或复核合伙人[定义见本节第(f)(7)(ii)(B)款]为同一审计客户提供服务;或者

(2)在本节第(c)(6)(i)(A)(2)款允许的最长服务期过后,又在连续2年期间内提供本节第(f)(7)(ii)款所定义的一项或多项服务。

(ii)会计师事务所具有发行人身份的审计客户少于5名("发行人"定义见《1934年证券交易法》第10A(f)条[《美国法典》第十五编第78j-1(f)节)]、合伙人少于10人的,应豁免于本节第(c)(6)(i)款的规定,前提是对于审计客户委托会计师进行的,使其在本款下丧失独立性的每项服务,美国公众公司会计监督委员会至少应每3年进行一次审查。

(iii)在本节第(c)(6)(i)款中,具有依《1940年投资公司法》第8条(《美国法典》第十五编第80a-8节)注册的投资公司身份的审计客户,不包括同一投资公司集团[定义见本节第(f)(14)款]下属的且属于该审计客户控制性关联方的另一实体,但该实体本身也是注册投资公司的除外。对于依本节第(c)(6)(i)款提供给投资公司集团下属各投资公司的服务而言,计算连续服务期时,如果各注册投资公司会计年度终结时间各不相同,则连续12个月的审计周期计为一个连续年度。

(i) of this section with respect to investment companies in an investment company complex, audits of registered investment companies with different fiscal year-ends that are performed in a continuous 12-month period count as a single consecutive year.

(7) *Audit committee administration of the engagement.* An accountant is not independent of an issuer (as defined in section 10A(f) of the Securities Exchange Act of 1934 (15 U.S.C. 78j-1(f))), other than an issuer that is an Asset-Backed Issuer as defined in §229.1101 of this chapter, or an investment company registered under section 8 of the Investment Company Act of 1940 (15 U.S.C. 80a-8), other than a unit investment trust as defined by section 4(2) of the Investment Company Act of 1940 (15 U.S.C. 80a-4(2)), unless:

(i) In accordance with Section 10A(i) of the Securities Exchange Act of 1934 (15 U.S.C. 78j-1(i)) either:

(A) Before the accountant is engaged by the issuer or its subsidiaries, or the registered investment company or its subsidiaries, to render audit or non-audit services, the engagement is approved by the issuer's or registered investment company's audit committee; or

(B) The engagement to render the service is entered into pursuant to pre-approval policies and procedures established by the audit committee of the issuer or registered investment company, *provided* the policies and procedures are detailed as to the particular service and the audit committee is informed of each service and such policies and procedures do not include delegation of the audit committees responsibilities under the Securities Exchange Act of 1934 to management; or

(C) With respect to the provision of services other than audit, review or attest services the pre-approval requirement is waived if:

(1) The aggregate amount of all such services provided constitutes no more than five percent of the total amount of revenues paid by the audit client to its accountant during the fiscal year in which the services are provided;

(2) Such services were not recognized by the issuer or registered investment company at the time of the engagement to be non-audit services; and

(3) Such services are promptly brought to the attention of the audit committee of the issuer or registered investment company and approved prior to the completion of the audit by the audit committee or by one or more members of the audit committee who are members of the board of directors to whom authority to grant such approvals has been delegated by the audit committee.

(ii) A registered investment company's audit committee also must pre-approve its accountant's engagements for non-audit services with the registered investment company's investment adviser (not including a sub-adviser whose role is primarily portfolio management

(7)审计委员会对审计委托的管理。会计师满足下列条件始得视为独立于发行人{定义见《1934年证券交易法》第10A(f)节[《美国法典》第十五编第78j-1(f)节)],但本项所指发行人不包括本章第229.1101条所定义的资产支持证券发行人,也不包括依《1940年投资公司法》第8条(《美国法典》第十五编第80a-8节)注册的投资公司(《1940年投资公司法》第4(2)条[《美国法典》第十五编第80a-4(2)节]定义的单位投资信托除外}:

(i)根据《1934年证券交易法》第10A(i)条[《美国法典》第十五编第78j-1(i)节]:

(A)在发行人或其子公司或者注册投资公司或其子公司委托会计师提供审计服务或非审计服务前,委托已获发行人/注册投资公司审计委员会批准;或者

(B)审计服务委托系遵循发行人/注册投资公司审计委员会制定的事先批准政策和程序达成,并满足以下前提:该等政策和程序针对该等特定服务作出了详细规定,并且每项服务均已告知审计委员会,此外,该等政策和程序的任何规定均不允许将《1934年证券交易法》所述的审计委员会职责转授给管理层;或者

(C)会计师提供审计、审查或鉴证以外的服务不必事先获得批准,条件是:

(1)该等服务费用总额不超过该会计年度内会计师从审计客户处获得的总收入的5%;

(2)该等服务在委托之时并未被发行人/注册投资公司认定为非审计服务;且

(3)该等服务已被及时告知发行人/注册投资公司的审计委员会,且在审计完成前已由审计委员会或审计委员会一名或数名委员批准(该等委员应为董事会成员且已获得审计委员会转授权,有权作出该等批准)。

(ii)同时,注册投资公司的会计师欲将非审计服务委托给下列主体的,也须事先获得注册投资公司审计委员会批准:注册投资公司的投资顾问(不包括主要从事投资组合管理并且从其他投资顾问处承接分包服务或受其他投资顾问监督的二级顾问);

and is sub–contracted or overseen by another investment adviser) and any entity controlling, controlled by, or under common control with the investment adviser that provides ongoing services to the registered investment company in accordance with paragraph (c)(7)(i) of this section, if the engagement relates directly to the operations and financial reporting of the registered investment company, except that with respect to the waiver of the pre-approval requirement under paragraph (c)(7)(i)(C) of this section, the aggregate amount of all services provided constitutes no more than five percent of the total amount of revenues paid to the registered investment company's accountant by the registered investment company, its investment adviser and any entity controlling, controlled by, or under common control with the investment adviser that provides ongoing services to the registered investment company during the fiscal year in which the services are provided that would have to be pre-approved by the registered investment company's audit committee pursuant to this section.

(8) *Compensation.* An accountant is not independent of an audit client if, at any point during the audit and professional engagement period, any audit partner earns or receives compensation based on the audit partner procuring engagements with that audit client to provide any products or services other than audit, review or attest services. Any accounting firm with fewer than ten partners and fewer than five audit clients that are issuers (as defined in section 10A(f) of the Securities Exchange Act of 1934 (15 U.S.C. 78j–1(f))) shall be exempt from the requirement stated in the previous sentence.

(d) *Quality controls.* An accounting firm's independence will not be impaired solely because a covered person in the firm is not independent of an audit client provided:

(1) The covered person did not know of the circumstances giving rise to the lack of independence;

(2) The covered person's lack of independence was corrected as promptly as possible under the relevant circumstances after the covered person or accounting firm became aware of it; and

(3) The accounting firm has a quality control system in place that provides reasonable assurance, taking into account the size and nature of the accounting firm's practice, that the accounting firm and its employees do not lack independence, and that covers at least all employees and associated entities of the accounting firm participating in the engagement, including employees and associated entities located outside of the United States.

(4) For an accounting firm that annually provides audit, review, or attest services to more than 500 companies with a class of securities registered with the Commission under section 12 of the Securities Exchange Act of 1934 (15 U.S.C. 78*l*), a quality control system will not provide such reasonable assurance unless it has at least the following

以及,控制投资顾问、受投资顾问控制或与投资顾问受同一控制并按本节第(c)(7)(i)款向注册投资公司提供持续服务的任何实体。除本节第(c)(7)(i)(C)款规定的免予事先批准的情形外,将上述非审计服务委托给上两类主体的前提是,该等服务之性质属于与注册投资公司的经营和财务报告直接相关的非审计服务。上述免予事先批准的情形指:在某会计年度内提供的按本节规定本应事先获得注册投资公司审计委员会批准的全部服务,其费用总额不超过该会计年度会计师从注册投资公司、注册投资公司之投资顾问和向注册投资公司提供持续服务的任何实体(该等实体指控制投资顾问、受投资顾问控制或与投资顾问受同一控制的实体)处获得的收入总额的5%;

(8)报酬。如果在审计期以及专业委托期内的任何时点,审计合伙人因其与审计客户之间达成的产品或服务委托安排(审计、审查或鉴证服务除外)而赚取或收到报酬,则相关会计师应视为对审计客户不具独立性。会计师事务所的合伙人少于10人,具有发行人身份的审计客户少于5名的{“发行人”定义见《1934年证券交易法》第10A(f)条[《美国法典》第十五编第78j-1(f)节]},不必遵循上句规定。

(d)质量控制。会计师事务所的独立性不会仅因所内所涉人员对审计客户不具独立性而受损,前提是:

(1)所涉人员对导致其缺乏独立性的情形并不知情;

(2)所涉人员或会计师事务所获知所涉人员在相关情形下不具独立性后,及时作出了纠正;且

(3)会计师事务所具备一套质量控制体系,能根据事务所的业务规模和性质合理保证事务所及其员工不致缺乏独立性,并且该体系的实施应至少涵盖参与该业务委托的事务所全体员工和联营实体,包括美国境外员工和联营实体。

(4)如果每年接受会计师事务所的审计、审查或鉴证服务的客户中超过500家公司依《1934年证券交易法》第12条(《美国法典》第十五编第78*l*节)在证券交易委员会注册了某一类证券,则要提供上述合理保证,该会计师事务所的质量控制体系至少须做到:

features:

(i) Written independence policies and procedures;

(ii) With respect to partners and managerial employees, an automated system to identify their investments in securities that might impair the accountant's independence;

(iii) With respect to all professionals, a system that provides timely information about entities from which the accountant is required to maintain independence;

(iv) An annual or on-going firm-wide training program about auditor independence;

(v) An annual internal inspection and testing program to monitor adherence to independence requirements;

(vi) Notification to all accounting firm members, officers, directors, and employees of the name and title of the member of senior management responsible for compliance with auditor independence requirements;

(vii) Written policies and procedures requiring all partners and covered persons to report promptly to the accounting firm when they are engaged in employment negotiations with an audit client, and requiring the firm to remove immediately any such professional from that audit client's engagement and to review promptly all work the professional performed related to that audit client's engagement; and

(viii) A disciplinary mechanism to ensure compliance with this section.

(e)(1) *Transition and grandfathering.* Provided the following relationships did not impair the accountant's independence under pre-existing requirements of the Commission, the Independence Standards, Board, or the accounting profession in the United States, the existence of the relationship on May 6, 2003 will not be deemed to impair an accountant's independence:

(i) Employment relationships that commenced at the issuer prior to May 6, 2003 as described in paragraph (c)(2)(iii)(B) of this section.

(ii) Compensation earned or received, as described in paragraph (c)(8) of this section during the fiscal year of the accounting firm that includes the effective date of this section.

(iii) Until May 6, 2004, the provision of services described in paragraph (c)(4) of this section provided those services are pursuant to contracts in existence on May 6, 2003.

(iv) The provision of services by the accountant under contracts in existence on May 6, 2003 that have not been pre-approved by the audit committee as described in paragraph (c)(7) of this section.

(v) Until the first day of the issuer's fiscal year beginning after May 6, 2003 by a "lead" partner and other audit partner (other than the "concurring" partner) providing services in excess of those permitted under paragraph (c)(6) of this section. An accountant's independence will not be deemed to be impaired until the first day of the

(i)具备书面独立性政策和程序;

(ii)具备一套证券投资自动识别系统,以识别合伙人和承担管理工作的雇员作出的可能有损会计师独立性的证券投资;

(iii)具备一套信息提供系统,及时向所内全体专业职员提供会计师应与之保持独立的实体的信息;

(iv)制订有针对审计师独立性的年度或日常全员培训计划;

(v)制订有监督独立性要求合规性的年度内部检查和测试计划;

(vi)向会计师事务所全体成员、管理人员、董事和职员发出通知,告知负责审计师独立性要求合规工作的高级管理人员姓名和职务;

(vii)制定有一套书面政策和程序,要求所有合伙人和所涉人员一旦与审计客户进行雇佣谈判,即应及时向会计师事务所报告,并要求事务所在此情形下立即取消任何该等专业职员参与该审计客户委托业务的资格,并对该等专业职员已完成的与该审计客户委托业务相关的工作进行及时审查;且

(viii)具备确保本节规定得到遵守的纪律处分制度。

(e)(1)过渡和不溯及既往。2003年5月6日业已存在的下列关系不视为有损会计师独立性,前提是根据证券交易委员会、独立标准委员会或美国会计行业的既有规定,该等关系无损于会计师的独立性:

(i)本节第(c)(2)(iii)(B)款所述,始于2003年5月6日之前的与发行人的雇佣关系。

(ii)本节生效日所在会计年度,会计师事务赚取或收到的本节第(c)(8)款所述报酬。

(iii)2004年5月6日之前提供的本节第(c)(4)款所述服务,前提是该等服务系根据2003年5月6日之前业已签订的合同提供。

(iv)会计师在未按本节第(c)(7)款规定事先获得审计委员会批准的情形下根据2003年5月6日之前业已签订的合同提供的服务。

(v)对于起始日晚于2003年5月6日的发行人会计年度而言,“主查”合伙人和其他审计合伙人(不包括“复核”合伙人)在该等会计年度起始日之前所提供的超出本节第(c)(6)款允许范围的服务。对于起始日晚于2004年5月6日的发行人会计年度而言,在该等会计年度起始日之前,会计师的独立性不因复核合伙人提供了超出本节第(c)(6)

issuer's fiscal year beginning after May 6, 2004 by a "concurring" partner providing services in excess of those permitted under paragraph (c)(6) of this section. For the purposes of calculating periods of service under paragraph (c)(6) of this section:

(A) For the "lead" and "concurring" partner, the period of service includes time served as the "lead" or "concurring" partner prior to May 6, 2003; and

(B) For audit partners other than the "lead" partner or "concurring" partner, and for audit partners in foreign firms, the period of service does not include time served on the audit engagement team prior to the first day of issuer's fiscal year beginning on or after May 6, 2003.

(2) *Settling financial arrangements with former professionals.* To the extent not required by pre-existing requirements of the Commission, the Independence Standards Board, or the accounting profession in the United States, the requirement in paragraph (c)(2)(iii) of this section to settle financial arrangements with former professionals applies to situations that arise after the effective date of this section.

(f) *Definitions of terms.* For purposes of this section:

(1) *Accountant,* as used in paragraphs (b) through (e) of this section, means a registered public accounting firm, certified public accountant or public accountant performing services in connection with an engagement for which independence is required. References to the accountant include any accounting firm with which the certified public accountant or public accountant is affiliated.

(2) *Accounting firm* means an organization (whether it is a sole proprietorship, incorporated association, partnership, corporation, limited liability company, limited liability partnership, or other legal entity) that is engaged in the practice of public accounting and furnishes reports or other documents filed with the Commission or otherwise prepared under the securities laws, and all of the organization's departments, divisions, parents, subsidiaries, and associated entities, including those located outside of the United States. Accounting firm also includes the organization's pension, retirement, investment, or similar plans.

(3)(i) *Accounting role* means a role in which a person is in a position to or does exercise more than minimal influence over the contents of the accounting records or anyone who prepares them.

(ii) *Financial reporting oversight role* means a role in which a person is in a position to or does exercise influence over the contents of the financial statements or anyone who prepares them, such as when the person is a member of the board of directors or similar management or governing body, chief executive officer, president, chief financial officer, chief operating officer, general counsel, chief accounting officer, controller, director of internal audit, director of financial reporting, treasurer, or any equivalent position.

款允许范围的服务而视为受损。计算本节第(c)(6)款规定的服务期时:

(A)对于“主查合伙人”和“复核合伙人”,服务期包括2003年5月6日之前以“主查合伙人”或“复核合伙人”身份提供服务的时间;及

(B)对于“主查合伙人”和“复核合伙人”之外的审计合伙人和外国事务所审计合伙人,服务期不包括对于起始日为2003年5月6日当日或晚于2003年5月6日的发行人会计年度,该等合伙人在该等会计年度起始日之前在审计委托团队内服务的时间。

(2)与前专业职员之间的财务安排的结算。本节第(c)(2)(iii)款关于与前专业职员之间的财务安排的结算规定适用于在本节生效日后出现的情形,但证券交易委员会、独立标准委员会或美国会计行业的既有规定作出了相关要求的,以该等要求为准。

(f)术语定义。就本节而言:

(1)用于本节第(b)款至第(e)款之时,“会计师”系指根据业务委托提供服务且须具备独立性的注册公共会计师事务所、注册公共会计师或公共会计师。提及“会计师”一词时包括与注册公共会计师或公共会计师存在控制性关联的任何会计师事务所。

(2)“会计师事务所”系指从事下列活动的组织(包括个体企业、公司形式的协会、合伙、公司、有限责任公司、有限责任合伙或其他法律实体):公共会计业务;提供需向证券交易委员会提交的报告或其他文件,或提供根据证券法律编制的其他报告或文件。“会计师事务所”一词涵盖其所有部门、单位、母公司、子公司和联营实体(包括美国境外实体),并且还包括其养老金计划、退休计划、投资计划或类似计划。

(3)(i)“会计职务”系指如下职务:任何人承担该职务即有能力对会计记录内容或编制会计记录的工作人员施加影响,或事实上施加了该等影响,且其影响程度超出最低限度的影响力。

(ii)“财务报告监督职务”系指如下职务:任何人承担该职务即有能力对财务报表内容或编制财务报表的工作人员施加影响,或事实上施加了该等影响,且其影响程度超出最低限度的影响力,如董事会成员或类似的管理或治理机构成员、首席执行官、总裁、首席财务官、首席运营官、首席律师、首席会计官、审计主任、内部审计总监、财务报告总监、司库或担任任何同等职位的人。

(4) *Affiliate of the audit client* means:

(i) An entity that has control over the audit client, or over which the audit client has control, or which is under common control with the audit client, including the audit client's parents and subsidiaries;

(ii) An entity over which the audit client has significant influence, unless the entity is not material to the audit client;

(iii) An entity that has significant influence over the audit client, unless the audit client is not material to the entity; and

(iv) Each entity in the investment company complex when the audit client is an entity that is part of an investment company complex.

(5) *Audit and professional engagement period*includes both:

(i) The period covered by any financial statements being audited or reviewed (the "audit period"); and

(ii) The period of the engagement to audit or review the audit client's financial statements or to prepare a report filed with the Commission (the "professional engagement period"):

(A) The professional engagement period begins when the accountant either signs an initial engagement letter (or other agreement to review or audit a client's financial statements) or begins audit, review, or attest procedures, whichever is earlier; and

(B) The professional engagement period ends when the audit client or the accountant notifies the Commission that the client is no longer that accountant's audit client.

(iii) For audits of the financial statements of foreign private issuers, the "audit and professional engagement period" does not include periods ended prior to the first day of the last fiscal year before the foreign private issuer first filed, or was required to file, a registration statement or report with the Commission, provided there has been full compliance with home country independence standards in all prior periods covered by any registration statement or report filed with the Commission.

(6) *Audit client* means the entity whose financial statements or other information is being audited, reviewed, or attested and any affiliates of the audit client, other than, for purposes of paragraph (c)(1)(i) of this section, entities that are affiliates of the audit client only by virtue of paragraph (f)(4)(ii) or (f)(4)(iii) of this section.

(7)(i) *Audit engagement team* means all partners, principals, shareholders and professional employees participating in an audit, review, or attestation engagement of an audit client, including audit partners and all persons who consult with others on the audit engagement team during the audit, review, or attestation engagement regarding technical or industry-specific issues, transactions, or events.

(4)“审计客户的控制性关联方”系指:

(i)对审计客户拥有控制权的实体,或者审计客户对其拥有控制权的实体,或者与审计客户受同一控制的实体,包括审计客户的母公司和子公司;

(ii)审计客户对其拥有重要影响力的实体,但该实体本身对审计客户不具重大意义的除外;

(iii)对审计客户拥有重要影响力的实体,但审计客户对该实体不具重大意义的除外;及

(iv)审计客户所属投资公司集团下属每一实体。

(5)“审计和专业委托期”同时包括:

(i)被审计或审查的任何财务报表覆盖的期间(“审计期”);及

(ii)审计客户委托会计师审计或审查其财务报表,或委托会计师编制向证券交易委员会提交的报告的期间(“专业委托期”):

(A)专业委托期始于会计师签署首份委托书(或者关于客户财务报表审查或审计的其他协议)之时,或审计、审查或鉴证程序启动之时(以较早发生者为准);且

(B)审计客户或会计师通知证券交易委员会该审计客户不再属于会计师的审计客户时,专业委托期即告结束。

(iii)对于对外国私募发行人的财务报表进行的审计而言,“审计和专业委托期”不包括在下述日期之前结束的审计和专业委托期:外国私募发行人实际或按规定应向证券交易委员会提交注册说明书或报告之日前最后一个会计年度的起始日。适用前述定义的前提是,在向证券交易委员会提交的任何注册说明书或报告所覆盖的此前所有期间内,外国私募发行人均完全遵守了其母国的独立性标准。

(6)“审计客户”系指其财务报表或其他信息正在接受审计、审查或鉴证的实体,以及该审计客户的任何控制性关联方,但是对于本节第(c)(1)(i)款而言,审计客户不包括仅因本节第(f)(4)(ii)款或第(f)(4)(iii)款的规定被视为审计客户控制性关联方的实体。

(7)(i)“审计委托团队”系指参与审计客户委托的审计、审查或鉴证服务的所有合伙人、负责人、股东和专业职员,包括审计合伙人,也包括在审计、审查或鉴证委托期间就技术或行业特定问题、交易或事件向审计委托团队其他成员提供咨询的所有人员。

(ii) *Audit partner* means a partner or persons in an equivalent position, other than a partner who consults with others on the audit engagement team during the audit, review, or attestation engagement regarding technical or industry-specific issues, transactions, or events, who is a member of the audit engagement team who has responsibility for decision-making on significant auditing, accounting, and reporting matters that affect the financial statements, or who maintains regular contact with management and the audit committee and includes the following:

(A) The lead or coordinating audit partner having primary responsibility for the audit or review (the "lead partner");

(B) The partner performing a second level of review to provide additional assurance that the financial statements subject to the audit or review are in conformity with generally accepted accounting principles and the audit or review and any associated report are in accordance with generally accepted auditing standards and rules promulgated by the Commission or the Public Company Accounting Oversight Board (the "concurring or reviewing partner");

(C) Other audit engagement team partners who provide more than ten hours of audit, review, or attest services in connection with the annual or interim consolidated financial statements of the issuer or an investment company registered under section 8 of the Investment Company Act of 1940 (15 U.S.C. 80a-8); and

(D) Other audit engagement team partners who serve as the "lead partner" in connection with any audit or review related to the annual or interim financial statements of a subsidiary of the issuer whose assets or revenues constitute 20% or more of the assets or revenues of the issuer's respective consolidated assets or revenues.

(8) *Chain of command* means all persons who:

(i) Supervise or have direct management responsibility for the audit, including at all successively senior levels through the accounting firm's chief executive;

(ii) Evaluate the performance or recommend the compensation of the audit engagement partner; or

(iii) Provide quality control or other oversight of the audit.

(9) *Close family members* means a person's spouse, spousal equivalent, parent, dependent, nondependent child, and sibling.

(10) *Contingent fee* means, except as stated in the next sentence, any fee established for the sale of a product or the performance of any service pursuant to an arrangement in which no fee will be charged unless a specified finding or result is attained, or in which the amount of the fee is otherwise dependent upon the finding or result of such product or service. Solely for the purposes of this section, a fee is not a "contingent fee" if it is fixed by courts or other public authorities, or, in tax matters, if

(ii)“审计合伙人”系指属于审计委托团队成员的合伙人或担任同等职位的人,审计合伙人对影响财务报表的重大审计、会计和报告问题负有决策责任,或者负责与管理层和审计委员会保持定期联络,但不包括在审计、审查或鉴证委托期间专门就技术或行业特定问题、交易或事件向审计委托团队其他成员提供咨询的合伙人。审计合伙人包括:

(A)对审计或审查负有主要责任的主查审计合伙人或协理审计合伙人(“主查合伙人”);

(B)负责进行第二轮审查的合伙人:第二轮审查的目的是进一步确保所审计或审查的财务报表符合公认会计原则、所作审计或审查和任何相关报告均符合公认审计准则以及美国证券交易委员会或美国公众公司会计监督委员会颁发的规则(“复核或复审合伙人”);

(C)符合下列条件的审计委托团队的其他合伙人:为发行人或根据《1940年投资公司法》第8条(《美国法典》第十五编第80a-8节)注册的投资公司的年度或中期合并财务报表提供了超过10小时的审计、审查或鉴证服务;及

(D)符合以下条件的审计委托团队的其他合伙人:在对发行人下属的资产或收入达到或超过其并表资产或收入20%的子公司的年度或中期财务报表进行的任何审计或审查中,担任“主查合伙人”。

(8)“指挥链”系指:

(i)负责对审计进行监督或对审计负有直接管理职责的全部人员,包括自会计师事务所首席执行官以下所有级别的高级管理人员;

(ii)负责对审计委托业务合伙人绩效进行评估,或就其薪酬提出建议的全部人员;或者

(iii)对审计进行质量控制或行使其他监察职责的全部人员。

(9)“近亲属”系指某人的配偶、事实配偶、父母、受抚养人、不受其抚养的子女及其兄弟姊妹。

(10)“风险代理收费”,除下一句话规定的情形外,系指按照一定安排确定的任何产品销售或服务提供费,根据该安排,除非获得特定认定或结果,否则不收取任何费用;或者费用的金额将通过该等产品或服务的认定或结果确定。仅就本节而言:法院或其他公共机构确定的费用不属于风险代理收费,在税务事宜中基于司法程序结果或政府机构认定所确定的费用也不属于风险代理收费。风险代理收费可能因提供服务的复杂程度等因素而变化。

determined based on the results of judicial proceedings or the findings of governmental agencies. Fees may vary depending, for example, on the complexity of services rendered.

(11) *Covered persons in the firm* means the following partners, principals, shareholders, and employees of an accounting firm:

(i) The "audit engagement team";

(ii) The "chain of command";

(iii) Any other partner, principal, shareholder, or managerial employee of the accounting firm who has provided ten or more hours of non-audit services to the audit client for the period beginning on the date such services are provided and ending on the date the accounting firm signs the report on the financial statements for the fiscal year during which those services are provided, or who expects to provide ten or more hours of non-audit services to the audit client on a recurring basis; and

(iv) Any other partner, principal, or shareholder from an "office" of the accounting firm in which the lead audit engagement partner primarily practices in connection with the audit.

(12) *Group* means two or more persons who act together for the purposes of acquiring, holding, voting, or disposing of securities of a registrant.

(13) *Immediate family members* means a person's spouse, spousal equivalent, and dependents.

(14) *Investment company complex.* (i) "Investment company complex" includes:

(A) An investment company and its investment adviser or sponsor;

(B) Any entity controlled by or controlling an investment adviser or sponsor in paragraph (f)(14)(i)(A) of this section, or any entity under common control with an investment adviser or sponsor in paragraph (f)(14)(i)(A) of this section if the entity:

(1) Is an investment adviser or sponsor; or

(2) Is engaged in the business of providing administrative, custodian, underwriting, or transfer agent services to any investment company, investment adviser, or sponsor; and

(C) Any investment company or entity that would be an investment company but for the exclusions provided by section 3(c) of the Investment Company Act of 1940 (15 U.S.C. 80a-3 (c)) that has an investment adviser or sponsor included in this definition by either paragraph (f)(14)(i)(A) or (f)(14)(i)(B) of this section.

(ii) An investment adviser, for purposes of this definition, does not include a sub-adviser whose role is primarily portfolio management and is subcontracted with or overseen by another investment adviser.

(iii) Sponsor, for purposes of this definition, is an entity that establishes a unit investment trust.

(15) *Office* means a distinct sub-group within an accounting firm, whether distinguished

(11)“所内所涉人员”系指会计师事务所的下列合伙人、负责人、股东和职员:

(i)“审计委托团队”;

(ii)“指挥链”;

(iii)自非审计服务提供之日起,直至会计师事务所针对非审计服务所处会计年度的财务报表出具并签署相关报告之日,向审计客户提供了10小时(含)以上非审计服务的会计师事务所的任何其他合伙人、负责人、股东或管理人员;或者向审计客户提供经常性非审计服务预计将达10小时(含)以上的其他合伙人、负责人、股东或管理人员;以及

(iv)作为审计委托业务的主查合伙人开展审计工作的主要所在地的“办事处”的任何其他合伙人、负责人或股东。

(12)“团体”系指为了购买、持有、处置某注册人的证券或基于该等证券行使表决权而共同行动的两个(含)以上的主体。

(13)“直系亲属”系指某人的配偶、事实配偶以及受抚养人。

(14)“投资公司集团”。(i)“投资公司集团”包括:

(A)投资公司及其投资顾问或发起人;

(B)控制本节第(f)(14)(i)(A)款所述投资顾问或发起人、受其控制或与之受同一控制的任何实体,前提是该实体:

(1)本身是投资顾问或发起人;或者

(2)为投资公司、投资顾问或发起人提供行政管理、存管、承销或过户代理人服务;及

(C)拥有按照本节第(f)(14)(i)(A)款或第(f)(14)(i)(B)款规定属于投资公司集团的投资顾问或发起人,且若非因适用《1940年投资公司法》第3(c)条[《美国法典》第十五编第80a-3(c)节]的除外规定,将被认定为投资公司的任何投资公司或实体。

(ii)就本定义而言,投资顾问不包括主要从事投资组合管理并且从其他投资顾问处承接分包服务或受其他投资顾问监督的二级顾问。

(iii)就本定义而言,发起人指设立单位投资信托的实体。

(15)“办事处”系指会计师事务所内部从地域或从业务层面单独划出的二级

along geographic or practice lines.

(16) *Rabbi trust* means an irrevocable trust whose assets are not accessible to the accounting firm until all benefit obligations have been met, but are subject to the claims of creditors in bankruptcy or insolvency.

(17) *Audit committee* means a committee (or equivalent body) as defined in section 3(a)(58) of the Securities Exchange Act of 1934 (15 U.S.C. 78c(a)(58)).

[37 FR 14594, July 21, 1972, as amended at 48 FR 9521, Mar. 7, 1983; 65 FR 76082, Dec. 5, 2000; 68 FR 6044, Feb. 5, 2003; 70 FR 1593, Jan. 7, 2005]

§210.2-02 Accountants' reports and attestation reports.

(a) *Technical requirements for accountants' reports.* The accountant's report:

(1) Shall be dated;

(2) Shall be signed manually;

(3) Shall indicate the city and State where issued; and

(4) Shall identify without detailed enumeration the financial statements covered by the report.

(b) *Representations as to the audit included in accountants' reports.* The accountant's report:

(1) Shall state whether the audit was made in accordance with generally accepted auditing standards; and

(2) Shall designate any auditing procedures deemed necessary by the accountant under the circumstances of the particular case, which have been omitted, and the reasons for their omission. Nothing in this rule shall be construed to imply authority for the omission of any procedure which independent accountants would ordinarily employ in the course of an audit made for the purpose of expressing the opinions required by paragraph (c) of this section.

(c) *Opinions to be expressed in accountants' reports.* The accountant's report shall state clearly:

(1) The opinion of the accountant in respect of the financial statements covered by the report and the accounting principles and practices reflected therein; and

(2) the opinion of the accountant as to the consistency of the application of the accounting principles, or as to any changes in such principles which have a material effect on the financial statements.

(d) *Exceptions identified in accountants' reports.* Any matters to which the accountant takes exception shall be clearly identified, the exception thereto specifically and clearly stated, and, to the extent practicable, the effect of each such exception on the related financial statements given. (See section 101 of the Codification of Financial

团体。

(16)“拉比信托”系指其福利义务全部清偿之前会计师事务所无法获得其资产的不可撤销的信托,但在破产或资不抵债的情形下该等信托的资产应首先用于满足债权人的债权主张。

(17)“审计委员会”系指《1934年证券交易法》第3(a)(58)条[《美国法典》第十五编第78c(a)(58)节]定义的委员会(或同等机构)。

[《联邦公报》第37卷第14594页,1972年7月21日,修正索引:《联邦公报》第48卷第9521页,1983年3月7日;《联邦公报》第65卷第76082页,2000年12月5日;《联邦公报》第68卷第6044页,2003年2月5日;《联邦公报》第70卷第1593页,2005年1月7日。]

第210.2-02节　会计师报告和鉴证报告

(a)会计师报告的技术性要求。会计师报告:

(1)应注明日期;

(2)应由相关人员亲笔签名;

(3)应注明出具报告的城市和州名;及

(4)应注明报告所涵盖的财务报表,但不必详细列举。

(b)会计师报告应包含的审计声明。会计师报告:

(1)应说明审计之实施是否遵循公认审计标准;且

(2)应指明会计师认为根据审计的具体情况有必要实施,但实际并未实施的任何审计程序,以及未实施的理由。本项规则不得被解释为暗示会计师有权不实施独立会计师为出具本节第(c)款规定的意见所开展的审计工作中通常会实施的程序。

(c)会计师报告应出具的意见。会计师报告应明确说明:

(1)会计师对报告涵盖的财务报表的意见以及财务报表遵循的会计原则和惯例;及

(2)会计师对会计原则适用一致性的意见;或者,关于对财务报表有重大影响的任何原则变动的意见;

(d)会计师报告中提出的异议。会计师提出异议的任何事项均应清楚说明,所提出的异议亦应具体、清楚地说明,在可行范围内,每项异议对相关财务报表的影响亦应予说明(见证券交易委员会的《财务报告政策汇编》第101条)。

Reporting Policies.)

(e) Paragraph (e) of this section applies only to registrants that are providing financial statements in a filing for a period with respect to which Arthur Andersen LLP or a foreign affiliate of Arthur Andersen LLP ("Andersen") issued an accountants' report. Notwithstanding any other Commission rule or regulation, a registrant that cannot obtain an accountants' report that meets the technical requirements of paragraph (a) of this section after reasonable efforts may include in the document a copy of the latest signed and dated accountants' report issued by Andersen for such period in satisfaction of that requirement, if prominent disclosure that the report is a copy of the previously issued Andersen accountants' report and that the report has not been reissued by Andersen is set forth on such copy.

(f) *Attestation report on internal control over financial reporting.* (1) Every registered public accounting firm that issues or prepares an accountant's report for a registrant, other than a registrant that is neither an accelerated filer nor a large accelerated filer (as defined in §240.12b-2 of this chapter) or an investment company registered under section 8 of the Investment Company Act of 1940 (15 U.S.C. 80a-8), that is included in an annual report required by section 13(a) or 15(d) of the Securities Exchange Act of 1934 (15 U.S.C. 78a *et seq.*) containing an assessment by management of the effectiveness of the registrant's internal control over financial reporting must include an attestation report on internal control over financial reporting.

(2) If an attestation report on internal control over financial reporting is included in an annual report required by section 13(a) or 15(d) of the Securities Exchange Act of 1934 (15 U.S.C. 78a*et seq.*), it shall clearly state the opinion of the accountant, either unqualified or adverse, as to whether the registrant maintained, in all material respects, effective internal control over financial reporting, except in the rare circumstance of a scope limitation that cannot be overcome by the registrant or the registered public accounting firm which would result in the accounting firm disclaiming an opinion. The attestation report on internal control over financial reporting shall be dated, signed manually, identify the period covered by the report and indicate that the accountant has audited the effectiveness of internal control over financial reporting. The attestation report on internal control over financial reporting may be separate from the accountant's report.

(g) *Attestation report on assessment of compliance with servicing criteria for asset-backed securities.* The attestation report on assessment of compliance with servicing criteria for asset-backed securities, as required by §240.13a-18(c) or 240.15d-18(c) of this chapter, shall be dated, signed manually, identify the period covered by the report and clearly state the opinion of the registered public accounting firm as to whether the asserting party's assessment of compliance with the servicing criteria is fairly stated in all

(e)本节第(e)款仅适用于符合下列条件的注册人:注册人提交的某一期间的财务报表的会计师报告,是由安达信会计师事务所或其外国控制性关联方(下称安达信)出具的。无论证券交易委员会的任何其他规则或规章是否存在任何相反规定,如果注册人尽合理努力后仍无法获得满足本节第(a)款技术性要求的会计师报告,则可在其提交的文件中附上安达信就该等期间出具并签署的最近一期会计师报告,以满足上述要求,但应在该报告显著位置注明该报告系安达信会计师之前出具的报告,且安达信并未重新出具该等报告。

(f)财务报告内部控制鉴证报告。(1)注册公共会计师事务所按照《1934年证券交易法》第13(a)条或第15(d)条[《美国法典》第十五编第78(a)节及其后条文]的要求,为注册人出具或编制年度报告中的会计师报告之时,如其中含有管理层对注册人财务报告内部控制有效性的评价,则该等会计师报告必须含有财务报告内部控制鉴证报告。前述注册人指如下注册人——既非加速报告人或大型加速报告人(定义见本章第240.12b-2节),也非根据《1940年投资公司法》第8条(《美国法典》第十五编第80a-8节)注册的投资公司的注册人。

(2)如果《1934年证券交易法》第13(a)条或第15(d)条[《美国法典》第十五编第78(a)节及其后条文]规定,年度报告中应包含财务报告内部控制鉴证报告,该鉴证报告应明确说明会计师针对注册人是否在所有重大方面均就财务报告维持了有效内部控制出具的无保留意见或否定意见,但是出现注册人或注册公共会计师事务所无法克服审计范围限制,从而导致会计师事务所放弃出具意见的少数情形时除外。财务报告内部控制鉴证报告应注明日期,由相关人员亲笔签名,指明报告覆盖期间并说明会计师已对财务报告内部控制的有效性进行了审计。财务报告内部控制鉴证报告可以与会计师报告分开出具。

(g)对资产支持证券服务标准合规性评价的鉴证报告。本章第240.13a-18(c)节或第240.15d-18(c)节规定的对资产支持证券服务标准合规性评价的鉴证报告应注明日期,由相关人员亲笔签名,指明报告覆盖期间并明确说明注册公共会计师事务所关于如下事项的意见:审计客户提供的对该等证券服务标准合规性评价是否在所有重要方面均不失公允;如公共会计师事务所无法出具整体意见,公共会计师事务所应作出相关声明,并说明原因。

material respects, or must include an opinion to the effect that an overall opinion cannot be expressed. If an overall opinion cannot be expressed, explain why.

[37 FR 14594, July 21, 1972, as amended at 41 FR 35479, Aug. 23, 1976; 45 FR 63668, Sept. 25, 1980; 50 FR 25215, June 18, 1985; 67 FR 13533, Mar. 22, 2002; 68 FR 36660, June 18, 2003; 70 FR 1593, Jan. 7, 2005; 72 FR 35321, June 27, 2007; 75 FR 57387, Sept. 21, 2010]

§210.2-03 Examination of financial statements by foreign government auditors.

Notwithstanding any requirements as to examination by independent accountants, the financial statements of any foreign governmental agency may be examined by the regular and customary auditing staff of the respective government if public financial statements of such governmental agency are customarily examined by such auditing staff.

§210.2-04 Examination of financial statements of persons other than the registrant.

If a registrant is required to file financial statements of any other person, such statements need not be examined if examination of such statements would not be required if such person were itself a registrant.

§210.2-05 Examination of financial statements by more than one accountant.

If, with respect to the examination of the financial statements, part of the examination is made by an independent accountant other than the principal accountant and the principal accountant elects to place reliance on the work of the other accountant and makes reference to that effect in his report, the separate report of the other accountant shall be filed. However, notwithstanding the provisions of this section, reports of other accountants which may otherwise be required in filings need not be presented in annual reports to security holders furnished pursuant to the proxy and information statement rules under the Securities Exchange Act of 1934 [§§240.14a-3 and 240.14c-3].

[46 FR 40872, Aug. 13, 1981]

§210.2-06 Retention of audit and review records.

(a) For a period of seven years after an accountant concludes an audit or review of an issuer's financial statements to which section 10A(a) of the Securities Exchange Act of 1934 (15 U.S.C. 78j-1(a)) applies, or of the financial statements of any investment company registered under section 8 of the Investment Company Act of 1940 (15 U.S.C. 80a-8), the accountant shall retain records relevant to the audit or review, including workpapers and other documents that form the basis of the audit or review, and memoranda,

[《联邦公报》第37卷第14594页,1972年7月21日,修正索引:《联邦公报》第41卷第35479页,1976年8月23日;《联邦公报》第45卷第63668页,1980年9月25日;《联邦公报》第50卷第25215页,1985年6月18日;《联邦公报》第67卷第13533页,2002年3月22日;《联邦公报》第68卷第36660页,2003年6月18日;《联邦公报》第70卷第1593页,2005年1月7日;《联邦公报》第72卷第35321页,2007年6月27日;《联邦公报》第75卷第57387页,2010年9月21日。]

第210.2-03节 外国政府审计师对财务报表的核验

不论是否存在任何要求由独立会计师进行核验的规定,任何外国政府机构的公开财务报表可依照惯例,由其内部一贯负责审查该等财务报表的审计人员进行核验。

第210.2-04节 对注册人以外的主体的财务报表的核验

注册人如果按规定应提交任何其他主体的财务报表,而该等主体假使自行以注册人身份提交财务报表,将不必交由会计师进行核验,则该等主体的财务报表不必进行核验。

第210.2-05节 两名或两名以上会计师对财务报表进行的核验

如果主查会计师并未亲自执行财务报表所有核验工作,即部分工作系由其他独立会计师完成,而主查会计师选择采信其他会计师的工作并在报告中作出了相应声明,则该等其他会计师出具的报告应单独提交。但是,无论本节如何规定,按《1934年证券交易法》[第240.14a-3节和第240.14c-3节]中的征集投票权报告和信息说明书规则向证券持有人提交的年度报告,不必包含其他规定要求提交的其他会计师出具的报告。

[《联邦公报》第46卷第40872页,1981年8月13日。]

第210.2-06节 审计和审查记录的留存

(a)会计师在审计或审查完适用《1934年证券交易法》第10A(a)条[《美国法典》第十五编第78j-1(a)节]的发行人财务报表,或者审计或审查完根据《1940年投资公司法》第8条(《美国法典》第十五编第80a-8节)注册的任何投资公司财务报表后,与审计或审查相关的记录应留存7年,该等记录包括:作为审计或审查依据的工作底稿和其他文件,以及符合下列条件的备忘录、通信、通讯、其他文件和记录(包括电子记录),该等记录应满足如下条件:

correspondence, communications, other documents, and records (including electronic records), which:

(1) Are created, sent or received in connection with the audit or review, and

(2) Contain conclusions, opinions, analyses, or financial data related to the audit or review.

(b) For the purposes of paragraph (a) of this section, *workpapers* means documentation of auditing or review procedures applied, evidence obtained, and conclusions reached by the accountant in the audit or review engagement, as required by standards established or adopted by the Commission or by the Public Company Accounting Oversight Board.

(c) Memoranda, correspondence, communications, other documents, and records (including electronic records) described in paragraph (a) of this section shall be retained whether they support the auditor's final conclusions regarding the audit or review, or contain information or data, relating to a significant matter, that is inconsistent with the auditor's final conclusions regarding that matter or the audit or review. Significance of a matter shall be determined based on an objective analysis of the facts and circumstances. Such documents and records include, but are not limited to, those documenting a consultation on or resolution of differences in professional judgment.

(d) For the purposes of paragraph (a) of this section, the term *issuer* means an issuer as defined in section 10A(f) of the Securities Exchange Act of 1934 (15 U.S.C. 78j-1 (f)).

[68 FR 4872, Jan. 30, 2003]

§210.2-07 Communication with audit committees.

(a) Each registered public accounting firm that performs for an audit client that is an issuer (as defined in section 10A(f) of the Securities Exchange Act of 1934 (15 U.S.C. 78j-1 (f))), other than an issuer that is an Asset-Backed Issuer as defined in §229.1101 of this chapter, or an investment company registered under section 8 of the Investment Company Act of 1940 (15 U.S.C. 80a-8), other than a unit investment trust as defined by section 4(2) of the Investment Company Act of 1940 (15 U.S.C. 80a-4(2)), any audit required under the securities laws shall report, prior to the filing of such audit report with the Commission (or in the case of a registered investment company, annually, and if the annual communication is not within 90 days prior to the filing, provide an update, in the 90 day period prior to the filing, of any changes to the previously reported information), to the audit committee of the issuer or registered investment company:

(1) All critical accounting policies and practices to be used;

(2) All alternative treatments within Generally Accepted Accounting Principles for policies and practices related to material items that have been discussed with management

(1)其创建、发送或接收与审计或审查相关,并且

(2)含有与审计或审查相关的结论、意见、分析或财务数据。

(b)就本节第(a)款而言,“工作底稿”系指:在审计或审查委托业务中,会计师按照美国证券交易委员会或美国公众公司会计监督委员会规定或采纳的标准实施的审计或审查程序、获得的证据、得出的结论所形成的相关文字资料。

(c)本节第(a)款所述备忘录、通信、通讯、其他文件和记录(包括电子记录),无论其能够支持审计师的最终审计或审查结论,还是含有与审计师的重大问题结论或最终审计或审查结论不一致的信息或数据,均应予以留存。某个问题是否属于“重大问题”应当基于对事实和情形的客观分析确定。上述文件和记录包括但不限于与咨询或解决专业判断分歧相关的书面记录。

(d)就本节第(a)款而言,“发行人”一词指《1934年证券交易法》第10A(f)条[《美国法典》第十五编第78j-1(f)节]定义的发行人。

[《联邦公报》第68卷第4872页,2003年1月30日。]

第210.2-07节 与审计委员会的沟通

(a)注册公共会计师事务所按照证券法要求为审计客户提供审计服务,且审计客户属于《1934年证券交易法》第10A(f)条[《美国法典》第十五编第78j-1(f)节]定义的发行人(不包括本章第229.1101节所定义的资产支持证券发行人)或根据《1940年投资公司法》第8条(《美国法典》第十五编第80a-8节)注册的投资公司(不包括《1940年投资公司法》第4(2)条[《美国法典》第十五编第80a-4(2)节]定义的单位投资信托)的,会计师事务所应在审计报告提交给证券交易委员会之前向发行人或注册投资公司的审计委员会报告如下事项(对注册投资公司而言,应每年进行该等报告,如果该等年度报告日早于审计报告提交日90日,还应提供一份更新材料,说明之前报告的信息所发生的任何变动):

(1)审计报告遵循的所有关键会计政策和惯例;

(2)对于和发行人或注册投资公司管理层讨论过的重大会计科目政策和惯例,在公认会计原则允许范围内所有可能的替代性处理方法;包括:

of the issuer or registered investment company, including:

(i) Ramifications of the use of such alternative disclosures and treatments; and

(ii) The treatment preferred by the registered public accounting firm;

(3) Other material written communications between the registered public accounting firm and the management of the issuer or registered investment company, such as any management letter or schedule of unadjusted differences;

(4) If the audit client is an investment company, all non-audit services provided to any entity in an investment company complex, as defined in §210.2-01(f)(14), that were not pre-approved by the registered investment company's audit committee pursuant to §210.2-01(c)(7).

(b) [Reserved]

[68 FR 6048, Feb. 5, 2003, as amended at 70 FR 1593, Jan. 7, 2005]

General Instructions as to Financial Statements

Source: Sections 210.3-01 through 210.3-16 appear at 45 FR 63687, Sept. 25, 1980, unless otherwise noted.

Note: These instructions specify the balance sheets and statements of income and cash flows to be included in disclosure documents prepared in accordance with Regulation S-X. Other portions of Regulation S-X govern the examination, form and content of such financial statements, including the basis of consolidation and the schedules to be filed. The financial statements described below shall be audited unless otherwise indicated.

For filings under the Securities Act of 1933, attention is directed to §230.411(b) regarding incorporation by reference to financial statements and to section 10(a)(3) of the Act regarding information required in the prospectus.

For filings under the Securities Exchange Act of 1934, attention is directed to §240.12b-23 regarding incorporation by reference and §240.12b-36 regarding use of financial statements filed under other acts.

[45 FR 63687, Sept. 25, 1980, as amended at 57 FR 45292, Oct. 1, 1992]

§210.3-01 Consolidated balance sheets.

(a) There shall be filed, for the registrant and its subsidiaries consolidated, audited balance sheets as of the end of each of the two most recent fiscal years. If the registrant has been in existence for less than one fiscal year, there shall be filed an audited balance sheet as of a date within 135 days of the date of filing the registration statement.

(b) If the filing, other than a filing on Form 10-K or Form 10, is made within 45

(i)采用该等替代性披露和处理方法的后果;以及

(ii)注册公共会计师事务所首选的处理方法;

(3)注册公共会计师事务所与发行人或注册投资公司管理层之间的其他重大书面通信,如任何管理建议书或未调整差异明细表等;

(4)向第210.2-01(f)(14)节所定义的投资公司集团下属任何实体提供的且未按第210.2-01(c)(7)节规定事先获得注册投资公司审计委员会批准的所有非审计服务(如果审计客户属于投资公司)。

(b)[保留]

[《联邦公报》第68卷第6048页,2003年2月5日,修正索引:《联邦公报》第70卷第1593页,2005年1月7日。]

关于财务报表的一般说明

行政规则来源:《联邦公报》第45卷第63687页(1980年9月25日)第210.3-01~210.3-16节,除非另有说明。

注:本说明详细规定了按《S-X管理办法》编制的披露文件应包含的资产负债表、损益表和现金流量表。财务报表的核验、形式和内容,包括财务报表合并的依据以及应提交的附表,受《S-X管理办法》其他部分的规定管辖。除非另有说明,下文所述财务报表应为经审计的财务报表。

对于根据《1933年证券法》提交的文件,请注意第230.411(b)节(关于以援引方式在财务报表中纳入相关信息的规定)以及该法第10(a)(3)条(关于招募说明书中应包含的信息的规定)。

对于根据《1934年证券交易法》提交的文件,请注意第240.12b-23节(关于以援引方式纳入相关信息的规定)以及第240.12b-36节(关于使用根据其他法律提交的财务报表的规定)。

[《联邦公报》第45卷第63687页,1980年9月25日,修正索引:《联邦公报》第57卷第45292页,1992年10月1日。]

第210.3-01节 合并资产负债表

(a)注册人应提交其自身及并表子公司最近两个会计年度每一年截至年末的经审计的资产负债表。注册人存续期不足一个会计年度的,应提交截止日位于注册说明书提交日后135日内的经审计的资产负债表。

(b)如果财务报告(不包括《10-K表格》或《10表格》)在注册人会计年度结束后45

days after the end of the registrant's fiscal year and audited financial statements for the most recent fiscal year are not available, the balance sheets may be as of the end of the two preceding fiscal years and the filing shall include an additional balance sheet as of an interim date at least as current as the end of the registrant's third fiscal quarter of the most recently completed fiscal year.

(c) The instruction in paragraph (b) of this section is also applicable to filings, other than on Form 10-K or Form 10, made after 45 days but within the number of days of the end of the registrant's fiscal year specified in paragraph (i) of this section: *Provided,* that the following conditions are met:

(1) The registrant files annual, quarterly and other reports pursuant to section 13 or 15(d) of the Securities Exchange Act of 1934 and all reports due have been filed;

(2) For the most recent fiscal year for which audited financial statements are not yet available the registrant reasonably and in good faith expects to report income attributable to the registrant, after taxes but before extraordinary items and cumulative effect of a change in accounting principle; and

(3) For at least one of the two fiscal years immediately preceding the most recent fiscal year the registrant reported income attributable to the registrant, after taxes but before extraordinary items and cumulative effect of a change in accounting principle.

(d) For filings made after 45 days but within the number of days of the end of the registrant's fiscal year specified in paragraph (i) of this section where the conditions set forth in paragraph (c) of this section are not met, the filing must include the audited balance sheets required by paragraph (a) of this section.

(e) For filings made after the number of days specified in paragraph (i)(2) of this section, the filing shall also include a balance sheet as of an interim date within the following number of days of the date of filing:

(1) 130 days for large accelerated filers and accelerated filers (as defined in §240.12b-2 of this chapter); and

(2) 135 days for all other registrants.

(f) Any interim balance sheet provided in accordance with the requirements of this section may be unaudited and need not be presented in greater detail than is required by §210.10-01. Notwithstanding the requirements of this section, the most recent interim balance sheet included in a filing shall be at least as current as the most recent balance sheet filed with the Commission on Form 10-Q.

(g) For filings by registered management investment companies, the requirements of §210.3-18 shall apply in lieu of the requirements of this section.

(h) Any foreign private issuer, other than a registered management investment company or an employee plan, may file the financial statements required by Item 8.A of

日内提交,并且注册人无法提供最近一个会计年度的经审计的财务报表,则注册人可提供分别截至前两个会计年度年末的资产负债表,并在提交的文件中增加一份中期资产负债表,其截止日期不得早于注册人最近结束的一个会计年度的第三季度末。

(c)本节第(b)款的说明也适用于在注册人会计年度结束后45日之后但在本节第(i)款规定的期限内提交的文件(不包括《10-K表格》或《10表格》),但以满足下列条件为前提:

(1)注册人依据《1934年证券交易法》第13条或第15(d)条提交年度报告、季度报告和其他报告并且已提交所有应提交的报告;

(2)对于尚无法提供经审计的财务报表的最近一个会计年度,注册人合理并善意预期该会计年度的财务报表将报告可归属于注册人的收益(收益指扣除非经常项目和会计原则变更累积影响数之前的税后收益);且

(3)在最近一个会计年度前的两个会计年度中的至少一个会计年度,注册人报告了可归属于注册人的收益(收益指扣除非经常项目和会计原则变更累积影响数之前的税后收益)。

(d)对于在注册人会计年度结束后45日之后,但在本节第(i)款规定的期限内提交的文件,如果注册人不满足本节第(c)款规定的条件,则注册人提交的文件必须包括本节第(a)款规定的经审计的资产负债表。

(e)在本节第(i)(2)款规定的期限后提交的文件应包含一份中期资产负债表,其截止日期应在下述期间内:

(1)对于大型加速报告人和加速报告人(定义见本章第240.12b-2节)而言,文件提交日后130日内;

(2)对于所有其他注册人而言,文件提交日后135日内。

(f)根据本节规定提交的任何中期财务报表不必经过审计,且其详细程度不必超过第210.10-01节的规定。无论本节如何规定,提交文件所含的最近一期中期资产负债表的截止日期不得早于按《10-Q表格》提交给证券交易委员会的最近一期资产负债表。

(g)对于注册管理型投资公司提交的文件,第210.3-18节的规定应取代本节规定适用。

(h)任何外国私募发行人(不包括注册管理型投资公司或员工计划)可提交《20-F表格》第8.A条(本章第249.220节)规定的财务报表,作为本规则规定的财务报表之替代。

Form 20-F (§249.220 of this chapter) in lieu of the financial statements specified in this rule.

(i)(1) For purposes of paragraphs (c) and (d) of this section, the number of days shall be:

(i) 60 days(75 days for fiscal years ending before December 15, 2006) for large accelerated filers (as defined in §240.12b-2 of this chapter);

(ii) 75 days for accelerated filers (as defined in §240.12b-2 of this chapter); and

(iii) 90 days for all other registrants.

(2) For purposes of paragraph (e) of this section, the number of days shall be:

(i) 129 days subsequent to the end of the registrant's most recent fiscal year for large accelerated filers and accelerated filers (as defined in §240.12b-2 of this chapter); and

(ii) 134 days subsequent to the end of the registrant's most recent fiscal year for all other registrants.

[45 FR 63687, Sept. 25, 1980, as amended at 46 FR 12491, Feb. 17, 1981; 46 FR 36124, July 14, 1981; 50 FR 49531, Dec. 3, 1985; 56 FR 30053, July 1, 1991; 64 FR 53908, Oct. 5, 1999; 67 FR 58503, Sept. 16, 2002; 68 FR 17880, Apr. 14, 2003; 69 FR 68235, Nov. 23, 2004; 70 FR 76640, Dec. 27, 2005; 73 FR 952, Jan. 4, 2008; 74 FR 18614, Apr. 23, 2009]

§210.3-02 Consolidated statements of income and changes in financial positions.

(a) There shall be filed, for the registrant and its subsidiaries consolidated and for its predecessors, audited statements of income and cash flows for each of the three fiscal years preceding the date of the most recent audited balance sheet being filed or such shorter period as the registrant (including predecessors) has been in existence.

(b) In addition, for any interim period between the latest audited balance sheet and the date of the most recent interim balance sheet being filed, and for the corresponding period of the preceding fiscal year, statements of income and cash flows shall be provided. Such interim financial statements may be unaudited and need not be presented in greater detail than is required by §210.10-01.

(c) For filings by registered management investment companies, the requirements of §210.3-18 shall apply in lieu of the requirements of this section.

(d) Any foreign private issuer, other than a registered management investment company or an employee plan, may file the financial statements required by Item 8.A of Form 20-F (§249.220 of this chapter) in lieu of the financial statements specified in this

(i)(1)本节第(c)款和第(d)款提及的期限如下:

(i)对于大型加速报告人(定义见本章第240.12b-2节)而言,为会计年度结束后60日(会计年度在2006年12月15日之前结束的,为75日);

(ii)对于加速报告人(定义见本章第240.12b-2节)而言,为会计年度结束后75日;及

(iii)对于所有其他注册人而言,为会计年度结束后90日。

(2)本节第(e)款提及的期限如下:

(i)对于大型加速报告人和加速报告人(定义见本章第240.12b-2节)而言,为注册人最近一个会计年度结束后129日;及

(ii)对于所有其他注册人而言,为注册人最近一个会计年度结束后134日。

[《联邦公报》第45卷第63687页,1980年9月25日,修正索引:《联邦公报》第46卷第12491页,1981年2月17日;《联邦公报》第46卷第36124页,1981年7月14日;《联邦公报》第50卷第49531页,1985年12月3日;《联邦公报》第56卷第30053页,1991年7月1日;《联邦公报》第64卷第53908页,1999年10月5日;《联邦公报》第67卷第58503页,2002年9月16日;《联邦公报》第68卷第17880页,2003年4月14日;《联邦公报》第69卷第68235页,2004年11月23日;《联邦公报》第70卷第76640页,2005年12月27日;《联邦公报》第73卷第952页,2008年1月4日;《联邦公报》第74卷第18614页,2009年4月23日。]

第210.3-02节　合并损益表和财务状况变化表

(a)对于注册人提交最近一期经审计的资产负债表之日前3个会计年度的每一会计年度,注册人均应提交其自身、其并表子公司及其前身公司的经审计的年度损益表和现金流量表;注册人存续期不足3个会计年度的,则应提交其自身(包括其前身公司)存续期内的经审计的年度损益表和现金流量表。

(b)此外,对于从最近一期经审计的资产负债表日,至最近一期中期资产负债表提交日止的任一中期报告期,以及上一会计年度的同一期间,注册人均应提交损益表和现金流量表。该等中期财务报表不必经过审计,且详细程度不必超过第210.10-01节的规定。

(c)对于注册管理型投资公司提交的文件,第210.3-18节的规定应取代本节规定适用。

(d)任何外国私募发行人(不包括注册管理型投资公司或员工计划)可提交《20-F表格》第8.A条(本章第249.220节)规定的财务报表,作为本规则规定的财务报表之替代。

rule.

[45 FR 63687, Sept. 25, 1980, as amended at 46 FR 12491, Feb. 17, 1981; 46 FR 36125, July 14, 1981; 50 FR 49531, Dec. 3, 1985; 56 FR 30053, July 1, 1991; 57 FR 45292, Oct. 1, 1992; 64 FR 53908, Oct. 5, 1999]

§210.3–03 Instructions to income statement requirements.

(a) The statements required shall be prepared in compliance with the applicable requirements of this regulation.

(b) If the registrant is engaged primarily (1) in the generation, transmission or distribution of electricity, the manufacture, mixing, transmission or distribution of gas, the supplying or distribution of water, or the furnishing of telephone or telegraph service; or (2) in holding securities of companies engaged in such businesses, it may at its option include statements of income and cash flows (which may be unaudited) for the twelve–month period ending on the date of the most recent balance sheet being filed, in lieu of the statements of income and cash flows for the interim periods specified.

(c) If a period or periods reported on include operations of a business prior to the date of acquisition, or for other reasons differ from reports previously issued for any period, the statements shall be reconciled as to sales or revenues and net income in the statement or in a note thereto with the amounts previously reported: *Provided, however,* That such reconciliations need not be made (1) if they have been made in filings with the Commission in prior years or (2) the financial statements which are being retroactively adjusted have not previously been filed with the Commission or otherwise made public.

(d) Any unaudited interim financial statements furnished shall reflect all adjustments which are, in the opinion of management, necessary to a fair statement of the results for the interim periods presented. A statement to that effect shall be included. Such adjustments shall include, for example, appropriate estimated provisions for bonus and profit sharing arrangements normally determined or settled at year–end. If all such adjustments are of a normal recurring nature, a statement to that effect shall be made; otherwise, there shall be furnished information describing in appropriate detail the nature and amount of any adjustments other than normal recurring adjustments entering into the determination of the results shown.

(e) Disclosures regarding segments required by generally accepted accounting principles shall be provided for each year for which an audited statement of income is provided. To the extent that the segment information presented pursuant to this instruction complies with the provisions of Item 101 of Regulation S–K, the disclosures may be combined by cross referencing to or from the financial statements.

[《联邦公报》第45卷第63687页,1980年9月25日,修正索引:《联邦公报》第46卷第12491页、1981年2月17日;《联邦公报》第46卷第36125页,1981年7月14日;《联邦公报》第50卷第49531页,1985年12月3日;《联邦公报》第56卷第30053页,1991年7月1日;《联邦公报》第57卷第45292页,1992年10月1日;《联邦公报》第64卷第53908页,1999年10月5日。]

第210.3-03节 关于损益表要求的说明

(a)损益表应按本《管理办法》相关规定编制。

(b)对于(1)主要从事发电、输电或配电,天然气生产、混合、传输或配送,自来水供应或配送,或者提供电话或电报服务的注册人;或者(2)以持有从事上述业务的公司的证券为主营业务的注册人,可选择提供覆盖最近一期资产负债表提交日后12个月期间的损益表和现金流量表(可不经审计),作为规定的中期损益表和现金流量表之替代。

(c)如果一个或数个报告期涉及收购日之前的业务经营,或者由于其他原因与以前针对任何报告期出具的报告存在差异,则报表或附注中的销售额、收入以及净收益应当按照以前报告的金额进行调整:但是,下列情形不必进行调整:(1)往年提交给证券交易委员会的文件已作过调整;或者(2)正在进行追溯调整的财务报表以前并未向证券交易委员会提交过,亦未以其他方式公开过。

(d)注册人提供的任何未审计中期财务报表均应作出管理层认为必要的一切调整,以公允反映相应的中期成果,并应在上述财务报表中作出相应声明。举例而言,该等调整应当包括通常在年末决定或结算的适当的预估奖金拨备和利润分享安排。如果所有调整均属正常的经常性调整,应作出相应声明;否则,对于确定报告结果时所作的正常经常性调整之外的任何调整,均应提供适当、详细的信息,说明调整的性质和金额。

(e)对于注册人提供了经审计的损益表的每一年度,注册人还应按照公认会计原则要求,提供行业细分披露信息。如果按照本节说明提交的行业细分信息符合《S-K管理办法》第101条规定,在披露时,可结合交叉引用财务报表的方式。

[45 FR 63687, Sept. 25, 1980. Redesignated at 47 FR 29836, July 9, 1982, and amended at 50 FR 25215, June 18, 1985; 50 FR 49532, Dec. 3, 1985; 57 FR 45292, Oct. 1, 1992; 64 FR 1734, Jan 12, 1999]

§210.3–04 Changes in stockholders' equity and noncontrolling interests.

An analysis of the changes in each caption of stockholders' equity and noncontrolling interests presented in the balance sheets shall be given in a note or separate statement. This analysis shall be presented in the form of a reconciliation of the beginning balance to the ending balance for each period for which an income statement is required to be filed with all significant reconciling items described by appropriate captions with contributions from and distribution to owners shown separately. Also, state–separately the adjustments to the balance at the beginning of the earliest period presented for items which were retroactively applied to periods prior to that period. With respect to any dividends, state the amount per share and in the aggregate for each class of shares. Provide a separate schedule in the notes to the financial statements that shows the effects of any changes in the registrant's ownership interest in a subsidiary on the equity attributable to the registrant.

[74 FR 18614, Apr. 23, 2009]

§210.3–05 Financial statements of businesses acquired or to be acquired.

(a) *Financial statements required.* (1) Financial statements prepared and audited in accordance with this regulation should be furnished for the periods specified in paragraph (b) below if any of the following conditions exist:

(i) A business combination has occurred or is probable (for purposes of this section, this encompasses the acquisition of an interest in a business accounted for by the equity method); or

(ii) Consummation of a combination between entities under common control is probable.

(2) For purposes of determining whether the provisions of this rule apply, the determination of whether a *business* has been acquired should be made in accordance with the guidance set forth in §210.11–01(d).

(3) Acquisitions of a group of related businesses that are probable or that have occurred subsequent to the latest fiscal year–end for which audited financial statements of the registrant have been filed shall be treated under this section as if they are a single business combination. The required financial statements of related businesses may be presented on a combined basis for any periods they are under common control or management. For purposes of this section, businesses shall be deemed to be related if:

(i) They are under common control or management;

[《联邦公报》第45卷第63687页,1980年9月25日,重新发布索引:《联邦公报》第47卷第29836页,1982年7月9日,修正索引:《联邦公报》第50卷第25215页,1985年6月18日;《联邦公报》第50卷第49532页,1985年12月3日;《联邦公报》第57卷第45292页,1992年10月1日;《联邦公报》第64卷第1734页,1999年1月12日。]

第210.3-04节　股东权益和非控制权益的变动

注册人应当通过资产负债表附注或一份单独的报表,对资产负债表的股东权益和非控制权益变动的每一科目进行分析。进行此项分析时,对于注册人按规定应提交损益表的每一报告期,注册人均应根据期末余额调整期初余额,所有重大调整项目均应冠以适当的会计科目,并分栏单列所有者的出资以及向所有者进行的分配。此外,涉及对之前的期间进行追溯调整的项目,应单列对首次列报该等项目的报告期的期初余额作出的调整。对于任何股息,均应说明每股股息金额以及每类股份的股息总额。在财务报表附注中,应提供一份单独的附表,注明注册人在任一子公司中的所有者权益变动对归属于注册人的权益的影响数。

[《联邦公报》第74卷第18614页,2009年4月23日。]

第210.3-05节　已收购企业或目标收购企业的财务报表

(a)要求提供的财务报表。(1)存在下列任何一项条件的,即应就下文第(b)款规定的各个报告期提供根据本《管理办法》编制和审计的财务报表:

(i)已经或者可能发生业务合并(就本节而言,所谓"合并"包括按权益法核算的业务权益收购);或者

(ii)可能完成和受同一控制的实体的合并。

(2)判断是否应适用本节规定时,应当按照第210.11-01(d)节列明的指导方针确定某一企业是否已被收购。

(3)就本节而言,注册人提交的经审计的财务报表覆盖的最近一个会计年度结束后,可能或已经作出的对一组关联企业的收购,应按一宗业务合并处理。关联企业在受同一控制或管理的期间,可以采用汇总报表的形式提供规定的财务报表。就本节而言,在下列情形下,不同的企业之间应视为存在关联关系:

(i)该等企业受同一控制或管理;

(ii) The acquisition of one business is conditional on the acquisition of each other business; or

(iii) Each acquisition is conditioned on a single common event.

(4) This rule shall not apply to a business which is totally held by the registrant prior to consummation of the transaction.

(b) *Periods to be presented.* (1) If securities are being registered to be offered to the security holders of the business to be acquired, the financial statements specified in §§210.3-01 and 210.3-02 shall be furnished for the business to be acquired, except as provided otherwise for filings on Form N-14, S-4 or F-4 (§§239.23, 239.25 or 239.34 of this chapter). The financial statements covering fiscal years shall be audited except as provided in Item 14 of Schedule 14A (§240.14a-101 of this chapter) with respect to certain proxy statements or in registration statements filed on Forms N-14, S-4 or F-4 (§§239.23, 239.25 or 239.34 of this chapter).

(2) In all cases not specified in paragraph (b)(1) of this section, financial statements of the business acquired or to be acquired shall be filed for the periods specified in this paragraph (b)(2) or such shorter period as the business has been in existence. The periods for which such financial statements are to be filed shall be determined using the conditions specified in the definition of significant subsidiary in §210.1-02(w) as follows:

(i) If none of the conditions exceeds 20 percent, financial statements are not required. However, if the aggregate impact of the individually insignificant businesses acquired since the date of the most recent audited balance sheet filed for the registrant exceeds 50%, financial statements covering at least the substantial majority of the businesses acquired shall be furnished. Such financial statements shall be for at least the most recent fiscal year and any interim periods specified in §§210.3-01 and 210.3-02.

(ii) If any of the conditions exceeds 20 percent, but none exceed 40 percent, financial statements shall be furnished for at least the most recent fiscal year and any interim periods specified in §§210.3-01 and 210.3-02.

(iii) If any of the conditions exceeds 40 percent, but none exceed 50 percent, financial statements shall be furnished for at least the two most recent fiscal years and any interim periods specified in §§210.3-01 and 210.3-02.

(iv) If any of the conditions exceed 50 percent, the full financial statements specified in §§210.3-01 and 210.3-02 shall be furnished. However, financial statements for the earliest of the three fiscal years required may be omitted if net revenues reported by the acquired business in its most recent fiscal year are less than $50 million.

(3) The determination shall be made by comparing the most recent annual financial statements of each such business, or group of related businesses on a combined basis, to

(ii)对其中一家企业的收购,以收购其他每家企业为条件;或者

(iii)对每家企业的收购均以同一事件之发生为条件。

(4)本节规定不适用于在收购交易完成前已由注册人完全控股的企业。

(b)应提交财务报表的报告期。(1)如果证券注册之目的是向目标收购企业的证券持有人进行发售,则应按第210.3-01节和第210.3-02节的规定提交该目标收购企业的财务报表,但是对于按《N-14表格》、《S-4表格》或《F-4表格》(本章第239.23节、第239.25节或第239.34节)提交的文件,如存在另行规定的,以该等规定为准。各会计年度的财务报表均应为经审计的财务报表,但《附表14A》第14条(本章第240.14a-101节)对某些征集投票权报告另有规定的,以及按《N-14表格》、《S-4表格》或《F-4表格》(本章第239.23节、第239.25节或第239.34节)提交的征集投票权报告另有规定的除外。

(2)对于本节第(b)(1)款未予明确规定的情形,注册人均应提交已收购企业或目标收购企业在本第(b)(2)款规定的各个报告期的财务报表或者该等企业存续期的财务报表[如企业存续期短于本第(b)(2)款规定的期间]。在确定应提交该等财务报表的报告期时,应根据第210.1-02(w)节关于"重要子公司"的定义中的条件并按下述标准作出判定:

(i)如果已收购企业或目标收购企业未超过任何一项条件的20%,不必提交财务报表。但是,如果注册人在最近一期经审计的资产负债表提交日后收购的各非重要企业的合计影响超过50%,则至少应提交涵盖绝大部分已收购企业的财务报表。该等财务报表至少应覆盖最近一个会计年度以及第210.3-01节和第210.3-02节规定的任何中期报告期。

(ii)如果已收购企业或目标收购企业超过任何一项条件的20%,但是没有超过任何一项条件的40%,则至少应提交最近一个会计年度以及第210.3-01节和第210.3-02节规定的任何中期报告期的财务报表。

(iii)如果已收购企业或目标收购企业超过任何一项条件的40%,但是没有超过任何一项条件的50%,则至少应提交最近两个会计年度以及第210.3-01节和第210.3-02节规定的任何中期报告期的财务报表。

(iv)如果已收购企业或目标收购企业超过任何一项条件的50%,则应提交第210.3-01节和第210.3-02节规定的完整财务报表。但是,如果已收购企业在最近一个会计年度报告的净收入少于5000万美元,可不提供3个会计年度中最早一年的财务报表。

(3)确定应提交财务报表的报告期时,应将每一已收购企业或目标收购企业最近一个年度各自的财务报表或一组关联企业的汇总报表,与注册人在收购当日或之

the registrant's most recent annual consolidated financial statements filed at or prior to the date of acquisition. However, if the registrant made a significant acquisition subsequent to the latest fiscal year-end and filed a report on Form 8-K (§249.308 of this chapter) which included audited financial statements of such acquired business for the periods required by this section and the pro forma financial information required by §210.11, such determination may be made by using pro forma amounts for the latest fiscal year in the report on Form 8-K (§249.308 of this chapter) rather than by using the historical amounts of the registrant. The tests may not be made by "annualizing" data.

(4) Financial statements required for the periods specified in paragraph (b)(2) of this section may be omitted to the extent specified as follows:

(i) Registration statements not subject to the provisions of §230.419 of this chapter (Regulation C) and proxy statements need not include separate financial statements of the acquired or to be acquired business if it does not exceed any of the conditions of significance in the definition of significant subsidiary in §210.1-02 at the 50 percent level, and either:

(A) The consummation of the acquisition has not yet occurred; or

(B) The date of the final prospectus or prospectus supplement relating to an offering as filed with the Commission pursuant to §230.424(b) of this chapter, or mailing date in the case of a proxy statement, is no more than 74 days after consummation of the business combination, and the financial statements have not previously been filed by the registrant.

(ii) An issuer, other than a foreign private issuer required to file reports on Form 6-K, that omits from its initial registration statement financial statements of a recently consummated business combination pursuant to paragraph (b)(4)(i) of this section shall furnish those financial statements and any pro forma information specified by Article 11 of this chapter under cover of Form 8-K (§249.308 of this chapter) no later than 75 days after consummation of the acquisition.

(iii) Separate financial statements of the acquired business need not be presented once the operating results of the acquired business have been reflected in the audited consolidated financial statements of the registrant for a complete fiscal year unless such financial statements have not been previously filed or unless the acquired business is of such significance to the registrant that omission of such financial statements would materially impair an investor's ability to understand the historical financial results of the registrant. For example, if, at the date of acquisition, the acquired business met at least one of the conditions in the definition of significant subsidiary in §210.1-02 at the 80 percent level, the income statements of the acquired business should normally continue to be furnished for such periods prior to the purchase as may be necessary when added to the time for which audited income statements after the purchase are filed to cover the

前提交的最近一个年度的注册人合并财务报表进行比较。但是，如果注册人在最近一个会计年度结束后进行重大收购，并按《8-k表格》（本章第249.308节）提交了一份报告，在报告中提供了该等已收购企业在本节规定报告期内的经审计的财务报表以及第210.11节所要求的备考财务信息，则在确定应提交财务报表的报告期时，可使用按照《8-k表格》（本章第249.308节）提交的最近一个会计年度的报告的备考数额替代注册人的历史数据。在进行测试，以判断是否符合上述标准时，不得采用“年化”数据。

（4）在下文规定的情形之下，不必提交本节第（b）（2）款规定的各个报告期的财务报表：

（i）不受本章第230.419节（《C管理办法》）规定管辖的注册说明书以及征集投票权报告，不必包含已收购企业或目标收购企业的单独财务报表，只要该企业不超过第210.1-02节关于重要子公司的定义中任何一项重大条件的50%，并且满足以下任一条件：

（A）收购尚未完成；或者

（B）按照本章第230.424（b）节提交给证券交易委员会的与发售相关的最终招股说明书或补充招股说明书的日期，或者征集投票权报告的邮递日，均不晚于业务合并完成后第74日，并且注册人之前未提交过财务报表。

（ii）按照本节第（b）（4）（i）款规定，未在初始注册说明书中就最近完成的业务合并提交财务报表的发行人（应按《6-k表格》提交报告的外国私募发行人除外），应当在收购完成后75日内，按照《8-k表格》（本章第249.308节）提交该等财务报表以及本章第11条规定的任何备考信息。

（iii）如果注册人某一完整会计年度的经审计的合并财务报表已经反映了已收购企业的经营成果，注册人不必提交已收购企业的单独财务报表，但之前未提交过该等财务报表，或者已收购企业对于注册人意义重大，以至于不提交该等财务报表将严重影响投资者了解注册人历史财务成果的能力的除外。例如，如果在收购日已收购企业至少符合第210.1-02节关于重要子公司的定义中一项条件的80%，则注册人通常应就收购前必要的报告期继续提交已收购企业的损益表，所谓“必要的报告期”与收购后提交的经审计的损益表所覆盖的期间累计之后，应足以覆盖第210.3-02节规定的报告期。

equivalent of the period specified in §210.3-02.

(iv) A separate audited balance sheet of the acquired business is not required when the registrant's most recent audited balance sheet required by §210.3-01 is for a date after the date the acquisition was consummated.

(c) *Financial statements of foreign business.* If the business acquired or to be acquired is a foreign business, financial statements of the business meeting the requirements of Item 17 of Form 20-F (§249.220f of this chapter) will satisfy this section.

[47 FR 29836, July 9, 1982, as amended at 50 FR 49532, Dec. 3, 1985; 51 FR 42056, Nov. 20, 1986; 59 FR 65636, Dec. 20, 1994; 61 FR 54514, Oct. 18, 1996; 73 FR 952, Jan. 4, 2008; 74 FR 18614, Apr. 23, 2009]

§210.3-06 Financial statements covering a period of nine to twelve months.

Except with respect to registered investment companies, the filing of financial statements covering a period of 9 to 12 months shall be deemed to satisfy a requirement for filing financial statements for a period of 1 year where:

(a) The issuer has changed its fiscal year;

(b) The issuer has made a significant business acquisition for which financial statements are required under §210.3-05 of this chapter and the financial statements covering the interim period pertain to the business being acquired; or

(c) The Commission so permits pursuant to §210.3-13 of this chapter.

Where there is a requirement for filing financial statements for a time period exceeding one year but not exceeding three consecutive years (with not more than 12 months included in any period reported upon), the filing of financial statements covering a period of nine to 12 months shall satisfy a filing requirement of financial statements for one year of that time period only if the conditions described in either paragraph (a), (b), or (c) of this section exist and financial statements are filed that cover the full fiscal year or years for all other years in the time period.

[54 FR 10315, Mar. 13, 1989]

§§210.3-07-210.3-08 [Reserved]

§210.3-09 Separate financial statements of subsidiaries not consolidated and 50 percent or less owned persons.

(a) If any of the conditions set forth in §210.1-02(w), substituting 20 percent for 10 percent in the tests used therein to determine a significant subsidiary, are met for a majority-owned subsidiary not consolidated by the registrant or by a subsidiary of the

(iv)如果注册人按照第210.3-01节规定提交的最近一期经审计的资产负债表截止日期晚于收购完成日期,则注册人不必单独提交已收购企业的经审计的资产负债表。

(c)外国企业的财务报表。如果已收购企业或目标收购企业为外国企业,则该企业的财务报表满足《20-F表格》第17条(本章第249.220f节)要求的,即视为符合本节要求。

[《联邦公报》第47卷第29836页,1982年7月9日,修正索引:《联邦公报》第50卷第49532页,1985年12月3日;《联邦公报》第51卷第42056页,1986年11月20日;《联邦公报》第59卷第65636页,1994年12月20日;《联邦公报》第61卷第54514页,1996年10月18日;《联邦公报》第73卷第952页,2008年1月4日;《联邦公报》第74卷第18614页,2009年4月23日。]

第210.3-06节　9~12个月期间的财务报表

除注册投资公司外,在下列条件下,提交9~12个月期间的财务报表即视为已满足提交一年期财务报表的要求:

(a)发行人对会计年度起止日期作出了调整;

(b)发行人完成了按本章第210.3-05节规定应提交财务报表的重大企业收购,且其所提交的覆盖中期报告期的财务报表与被收购企业有关;或者

(c)证券交易委员会按本章第210.3-13节的规定允许发行人提交9~12个月期间的报表。

如果按规定,注册人应就一个以上报告期提交财务报表,且累计总报告期超过一年但不超过连续3年,且任一报告期均不超过12个月,则当且仅当存在本节第(a)款、第(b)款或第(c)款规定的条件,并且发行人已就总报告期内所有其他一个或数个完整会计年度提交财务报表的前提下,对于总报告期内的非完整会计年度,注册人只需提交9~12个月期间的财务报表,即视同满足提交一年期财务报表的要求。

[联邦公报》第54卷第10315页,1989年3月13日。]

第210.3-07~210.3-08节　[保留]

第210.3-09节　非并表子公司和50%或以下股权被控主体的单独财务报表

(a)如果注册人或注册人某一子公司下属的非并表控股子公司符合第210.1-02(w)节规定的任何一项条件(但应将认定重要子公司的10%的测试标准替换为20%),即应单独提交该等子公司的财务报表。同样,如果50%或以下股权被注册人或注册人某一

registrant, separate financial statements of such subsidiary shall be filed. Similarly, if either the first or third condition set forth in §210.1–02(w), substituting 20 percent for 10 percent, is met by a 50 percent or less owned person accounted for by the equity method either by the registrant or a subsidiary of the registrant, separate financial statements of such 50 percent or less owned person shall be filed.

(b) Insofar as practicable, the separate financial statements required by this section shall be as of the same dates and for the same periods as the audited consolidated financial statements required by §§210.3–01 and 3–02. However, these separate financial statements are required to be audited only for those fiscal years in which either the first or third condition set forth in §210.1–02(w), substituting 20 percent for 10 percent, is met. For purposes of a filing on Form 10–K (§249.310 of this chapter):

(1) If the registrant is an accelerated filer (as defined in §240.12b–2 of this chapter) but the 50 percent or less owned person is not an accelerated filer, the required financial statements may be filed as an amendment to the report within 90 days, or within six months if the 50 percent or less owned person is a foreign business, after the end of the registrant's fiscal year.

(2) If the fiscal year of any 50 percent or less owned person ends within the *registrant's number of filing days* before the date of the filing, or if the fiscal year ends after the date of the filing, the required financial statements may be filed as an amendment to the report within the *subsidiary's number of filing days*, or within six months if the 50 percent or less owned person is a foreign business, after the end of such subsidiary's or person's fiscal year.

(3) The term*registrant's number of filing days* means:

(i) 60 days (75 days for fiscal years ending before December 15, 2006) if the registrant is a large accelerated filer;

(ii) 75 days if the registrant is an accelerated filer; and

(iii) 90 days for all other registrants.

(4) The term*subsidiary's number of filing days* means:

(i) 60 days (75 days for fiscal years ending before December 15, 2006) if the 50 percent or less owned person is a large accelerated filer;

(ii) 75 days if the 50 percent or less owned person is an accelerated filer; and

(iii) 90 days for all other 50 percent or less owned persons.

(c) Notwithstanding the requirements for separate financial statements in paragraph (a) of this section, where financial statements of two or more majority–owned subsidiaries not consolidated are required, combined or consolidated statements of such subsidiaries may be filed subject to principles of inclusion and exclusion which clearly exhibit the financial position, cash flows and results of operations of the combined or consolidated

子公司控制的主体(按权益法核算)符合第210.1-02(w)节规定的第1项或第3项条件(但应将10%的测试标准替换为20%),即应单独提交该等主体的财务报表。

(b)在可行范围内,本条要求单独提交的财务报表的截止日期和覆盖期间应与第210.3-01节和第210.3-02节规定的经审计的合并财务报表保持一致。但是,只有对于存在第210.1-02(w)节规定的第1项或第3项条件的会计年度(但应将10%的测试标准替换为20%),才需要提交经审计的单独财务报表。在提交《10-K表格》(本章第249.310节)时:

(1)如果注册人属于加速报告人(定义见本章第240.12b-2节),但是50%或以下股权被控主体不属于加速报告人,则按要求应提交的财务报表可以作为报告的修正,在注册人会计年度结束后90日内提交,或者在注册人会计年度结束后6个月内提交(如果50%或以下股权被控主体是外国企业)。

(2)50%或以下股权被控主体的会计年度截止日期处于注册人文件提交日前的"注册人文件提交期"内,或者迟于文件提交日的,则按要求应提交的财务报表可以作为报告的修正,在该等子公司或主体的会计年度结束后的"子公司文件提交期"内提交,如果50%或以下股权被控主体是外国企业,则可在该等子公司或主体会计年度结束后6个月内提交。

(3)"注册人文件提交期"一词具体所指如下:

(i)对于属于大型加速报告人的注册人而言,为60日(会计年度在2006年12月15日之前结束的,为75日);

(ii)对于属于加速报告人的注册人而言,为75日;及

(iii)对于所有其他注册人而言,为90日。

(4)"子公司的文件提交期"一词具体所指如下:

(i)对于属于大型加速报告人的50%或以下股权被控主体而言,为60日(会计年度在2006年12月15日之前结束的,为75日);

(ii)对于属于加速报告人的50%或以下股权被控主体而言,为75日;及

(iii)对于所有其他50%或以下股权被控主体而言,为90日。

(c)无论本节第(a)款对单独财务报表如何规定,注册人如果有义务提交两个或两个以上非并表控股子公司的财务报表,则在符合下述原则的前提下,注册人可以提交该等子公司的汇总或合并报表:纳入或排除任何子公司时能够确保汇总或合并报表明确反映汇总或合并集团的财务状况、现金流量和经营成果。同样,注册人如果有义务提交两个(含)以上50%或以下股权被控主体的财务报表,则在符合与上文所述相同

group. Similarly, where financial statements of two or more 50 percent or less owned persons are required, combined or consolidated statements of such persons may be filed subject to the same principles of inclusion or exclusion referred to above.

(d) If the 50 percent or less owned person is a foreign business, financial statements of the business meeting the requirements of Item 17 of Form 20-F (§249.220f of this chapter) will satisfy this section.

[46 FR 56179, Nov. 16, 1981, as amended at 47 FR 29837, July 9, 1982; 57 FR 45292, Oct. 1, 1992; 59 FR 65636, Dec. 20, 1994; 67 FR 58504, Sept. 16, 2002; 69 FR 68235, Nov. 23, 2004; 70 FR 76640, Dec. 27, 2005]

§210.3-10 Financial statements of guarantors and issuers of guaranteed securities registered or being registered.

(a)(1) *General rule.* Every issuer of a registered security that is guaranteed and every guarantor of a registered security must file the financial statements required for a registrant by Regulation S-X.

(2) *Operation of this rule.* Paragraphs (b), (c), (d), (e) and (f) of this section are exceptions to the general rule of paragraph (a)(1) of this section. Only one of these paragraphs can apply to a single issuer or guarantor. Paragraph (g) of this section is a special rule for recently acquired issuers or guarantors that overrides each of these exceptions for a specific issuer or guarantor. Paragraph (h) of this section defines the following terms used in this section: 100% owned, full and unconditional, annual report, quarterly report, no independent assets or operations, minor, finance subsidiary and operating subsidiary. Paragraph (i) of this section states the requirements for preparing the condensed consolidating financial information required by paragraphs (c), (d), (e) and (f) of this section.

Note to paragraph (a)(2). Where paragraphs (b), (c), (d), (e) and (f) of this section specify the filing of financial statements of the parent company, the financial statements of an entity that is not an issuer or guarantor of the registered security cannot be substituted for those of the parent company.

(3) *Foreign private issuers.* Where any provision of this section requires compliance with §§210.3-01 and 3-02, a foreign private issuer may comply by providing financial statements for the periods specified by Item 8.A of Form 20-F (§249.220f of this chapter).

(b) *Finance subsidiary issuer of securities guaranteed by its parent company.* When a finance subsidiary issues securities and its parent company guarantees those securities, the registration statement, parent company annual report, or parent company quarterly

的纳入或排除原则的前提下,也可以提交汇总或合并报表。

(d)如果50%或以下股权被控主体属于外国企业,该企业财务报表满足《20-F表格》第17条(本章第249.220节)规定的,即将视为符合本节规定。

[《联邦公报》第46卷第56179页,1981年11月16日,修正索引:《联邦公报》第47卷第29837页,1982年7月9日;《联邦公报》第57卷第45292页,1992年10月1日;《联邦公报》第59卷第65636页,1994年12月20日;《联邦公报》第67卷第58504页,2002年9月16日;《联邦公报》第69卷第68235页,2004年11月23日;《联邦公报》第70卷第76640页,2005年12月27日。]

第210.3-10节　担保人的财务报表以及已经注册或正在申请注册的担保证券的发行人的财务报表

(a)(1)一般规定。每一注册担保证券的发行人以及每一注册证券的担保人均须提交《S-X管理办法》要求注册人提交的财务报表。

(2)本规则的实施。本节第(b)款、第(c)款、第(d)款、第(e)款和第(f)款属于本节第(a)(1)款"一般规定"的例外规定。一名发行人或担保人只能适用其中一项例外规定。本节第(g)款是针对最近被收购的发行人或担保人作出的特殊规定,该款效力凌驾于上述各项例外规定之上。本节第(h)款对本条使用的下列术语进行了定义:全资、完全和无条件、年度报告、季度报告、无独立资产或经营、次要的、财务子公司和运营子公司。本节第(i)款说明了第(c)款、第(d)款、第(e)款和第(f)款规定的简要并表财务信息的编写要求。

关于第(a)(2)款的注释。本节第(b)款、第(c)款、第(d)款、第(e)款和第(f)款要求提交母公司财务报表之时,不得以注册证券发行人或担保人之外的实体的财务报表替代母公司的财务报表。

(3)外国私募发行人。如本节规定发行人应遵守第210.3-01节和第210.3-02节的要求,外国私募发行人可通过提供《20-F表格》第8.A条(本章第249.220f节)规定期间的财务报表满足此项要求。

(b)财务子公司发行由母公司担保的证券。财务子公司发行证券时,母公司为该等证券提供担保的,注册说明书、母公司年度报告或母公司季度报告中不必包含发行人的财务报表,前提是:

report need not include financial statements of the issuer if:

(1) The issuer is 100% owned by the parent company guarantor;

(2) The guarantee is full and unconditional;

(3) No other subsidiary of the parent company guarantees the securities; and

(4) The parent company's financial statements are filed for the periods specified by §§210.3-01 and 210.3-02 and include a footnote stating that the issuer is a 100%-owned finance subsidiary of the parent company and the parent company has fully and unconditionally guaranteed the securities. The footnote also must include the narrative disclosures specified in paragraphs (i)(9) and (i)(10) of this section.

Note to paragraph (b). Paragraph (b) is available if a subsidiary issuer satisfies the requirements of this paragraph but for the fact that, instead of the parent company guaranteeing the security, the subsidiary issuer co-issued the security, jointly and severally, with the parent company. In this situation, the narrative information required by paragraph (b)(4) must be modified accordingly.

(c) *Operating subsidiary issuer of securities guaranteed by its parent company.* When an operating subsidiary issues securities and its parent company guarantees those securities, the registration statement, parent company annual report, or parent company quarterly report need not include financial statements of the issuer if:

(1) The issuer is 100% owned by the parent company guarantor;

(2) The guarantee is full and unconditional;

(3) No other subsidiary of the parent company guarantees the securities; and

(4) The parent company's financial statements are filed for the periods specified by §§210.3-01 and 210.3-02 and include, in a footnote, condensed consolidating financial information for the same periods with a separate column for:

(i) The parent company;

(ii) The subsidiary issuer;

(iii) Any other subsidiaries of the parent company on a combined basis;

(iv) Consolidating adjustments; and

(v) The total consolidated amounts.

Notes to paragraph (c). 1. Instead of the condensed consolidating financial information required by paragraph (c)(4), the parent company's financial statements may include a footnote stating, if true, that the parent company has no independent assets or operations, the guarantee is full and unconditional, and any subsidiaries of the parent company other than the subsidiary issuer are minor. The footnote also must include the narrative disclosures specified in paragraphs (i)(9) and (i)(10) of this section.

2. If the alternative disclosure permitted by Note 1 to this paragraph is not

(1)发行人系担保人(即发行人的母公司)的全资子公司;

(2)担保属于完全和无条件担保;

(3)母公司的任何其他子公司均未对证券提供担保;且

(4)母公司就第210.3-01节和第210.3-02节规定的报告期提交了财务报表,在报表的脚注中声明发行人属于母公司的全资财务子公司且母公司已为该子公司发行之证券提供完全和无条件担保。该脚注还须包括本节第(i)(9)款和第(i)(10)款规定的文字披露。

关于第(b)款的注释。如果以发行人身份行事的子公司满足本款其他规定,但是母公司并不担任证券担保人,而是与子公司共同发行证券并对其承担连带责任,则应适用第(b)款的规定。在此种情况下,第(b)(4)款要求提供的文字信息须相应修改。

(c)运营子公司发行由母公司担保的证券。运营子公司发行证券时,母公司为该等证券提供担保的,注册说明书、母公司年度报告或母公司季度报告不必包含发行人的财务报表,前提是:

(1)发行人系担保人(即发行人的母公司)的全资子公司;

(2)担保属于完全和无条件担保;

(3)母公司的任何其他子公司均未对证券提供担保;且

(4)母公司就第210.3-01节和第210.3-02节规定的报告期提交了财务报表,并在报表的脚注中提供了同期简要并表财务信息,并单设栏目,分别说明了下列各项信息:

(i)母公司;

(ii)以发行人身份行事的子公司;

(iii)母公司的任何其他子公司(汇总信息);

(iv)并表调整;及

(v)并表总额。

关于第(c)款的注释。1. 如以下情况属实,可在母公司财务报表中纳入一个脚注,作出相应声明,以之替代第(c)(4)款要求提供的简要并表财务信息:母公司无独立资产或经营,担保属于完全和无条件担保,并且除以发行人身份行事的子公司外,母公司任何其他子公司都属于次要子公司。该脚注还须包括本节第(i)(9)款和第(i)(10)款规定的文字披露。

2.如果母公司的其他子公司均属于次要子公司,但由于母公司拥有独立资产或经

applicable because the parent company has independent assets or operations, the condensed consolidating financial information described in paragraph (c)(4) may omit the column for "any other subsidiaries of the parent company on a combined basis" if those other subsidiaries are minor.

3. Paragraph (c) is available if a subsidiary issuer satisfies the requirements of this paragraph but for the fact that, instead of the parent company guaranteeing the security, the subsidiary issuer co-issued the security, jointly and severally, with the parent company. In this situation, the narrative information required by paragraph (i)(8) of this section must be modified accordingly.

(d) *Subsidiary issuer of securities guaranteed by its parent company and one or more other subsidiaries of that parent company.* When a subsidiary issues securities and both its parent company and one or more other subsidiaries of that parent company guarantee those securities, the registration statement, parent company annual report, or parent company quarterly report need not include financial statements of the issuer or any subsidiary guarantor if:

(1) The issuer and all subsidiary guarantors are 100% owned by the parent company guarantor;

(2) The guarantees are full and unconditional;

(3) The guarantees are joint and several; and

(4) The parent company's financial statements are filed for the periods specified by §§210.3-01 and 210.3-02 and include, in a footnote, condensed consolidating financial information for the same periods with a separate column for:

(i) The parent company;

(ii) The subsidiary issuer;

(iii) The guarantor subsidiaries of the parent company on a combined basis;

(iv) Any other subsidiaries of the parent company on a combined basis;

(v) Consolidating adjustments; and

(vi) The total consolidated amounts.

Notes to paragraph (d). 1. Paragraph (d) applies in the same manner whether the issuer is a finance subsidiary or an operating subsidiary.

2. The condensed consolidating financial information described in paragraph (d)(4) may omit the column for "any other subsidiaries of the parent company on a combined basis" if those other subsidiaries are minor.

3. Paragraph (d) is available if a subsidiary issuer satisfies the requirements of this paragraph but for the fact that, instead of the parent company guaranteeing the security, the subsidiary issuer co-issued the security, jointly and severally, with the parent company. In this situation, the narrative information required by paragraph (i)(8) of this section

营,致使本款注释1所允许的替代性披露不适用,则第(c)(4)款规定的简要并表财务信息可以不设“母公司的任何其他子公司(汇总信息)”栏目。

3.如果以发行人身份行事的子公司满足本款其他规定,但是母公司并不担任证券担保人,而是与子公司共同发行证券并承担连带责任,则应适用第(c)款规定。在此种情况下,本节第(i)(8)款要求提供的文字信息须相应修改。

(d)子公司发行由母公司及其一个或数个其他子公司担保的证券。子公司发行证券时,母公司及其一个或数个其他子公司为该等证券提供担保的,注册说明书、母公司年度报告或母公司季度报告不必包含发行人或任何担任担保人的子公司的财务报表,前提是:

(1)发行人以及所有担任担保人的子公司均系担保人(即发行人的母公司)的全资子公司;

(2)担保属于完全和无条件担保;

(3)各担保人承担连带担保责任;且

(4)母公司就第210.3-01节和第210.3-02节规定的报告期提交了财务报表,并在报表的脚注中提供了同期简要并表财务信息,并单设栏目,分别说明了下列各项信息:

(i)母公司;

(ii)以发行人身份行事的子公司;

(iii)母公司下属的担任担保人的子公司(汇总信息);

(iv)母公司的任何其他子公司(汇总信息)

(v)并表调整;及

(vi)并表总额。

关于第(d)款的注释。1. 无论以发行人身份行事的子公司属于财务子公司还是运营子公司,第(d)款规定均以相同方式适用。

2.如母公司的其他子公司均属于次要子公司,第(d)(4)款规定的简要并表财务信息可以不设“母公司其他子公司(汇总信息)”栏目。

3.如果以发行人身份行事的子公司满足本款其他规定,但是母公司并不担任证券担保人,而是与以发行人身份行事的子公司共同发行证券并承担连带责任,则应适用第(d)款规定。在此种情况下,本节第(i)(8)款要求提供的文字信息须相应修改。

must be modified accordingly.

4. If all of the requirements in paragraph (d) are satisfied except that the guarantee of a subsidiary is not joint and several with, as applicable, the parent company's guarantee or the guarantees of the parent company and the other subsidiaries, then each subsidiary guarantor whose guarantee is not joint and several need not include separate financial statements, but the condensed consolidating financial information should include a separate column for each guarantor whose guarantee is not joint and several.

5. Instead of the condensed consolidating financial information required by paragraph (d)(4), the parent company's financial statements may include a footnote stating, if true, that the parent company has no independent assets or operations, the subsidiary issuer is a 100% owned finance subsidiary of the parent company, the parent company has guaranteed the securities, all of the parent company's subsidiaries other than the subsidiary issuer have guaranteed the securities, all of the guarantees are full and unconditional, and all of the guarantees are joint and several. The footnote also must include the narrative disclosures specified in paragraphs (i)(9) and (i)(10) of this section.

(e) *Single subsidiary guarantor of securities issued by the parent company of that subsidiary.* When a parent company issues securities and one of its subsidiaries guarantees those securities, the registration statement, parent company annual report, or parent company quarterly report need not include financial statements of the subsidiary guarantor if:

(1) The subsidiary guarantor is 100% owned by the parent company issuer;

(2) The guarantee is full and unconditional;

(3) No other subsidiary of that parent guarantees the securities; and

(4) The parent company's financial statements are filed for the periods specified by §§210.3-01 and 210.3-02 and include, in a footnote, condensed consolidating financial information for the same periods with a separate column for:

(i) The parent company;

(ii) The subsidiary guarantor;

(iii) Any other subsidiaries of the parent company on a combined basis;

(iv) Consolidating adjustments; and

(v) The total consolidated amounts.

Notes to paragraph (e). 1. Paragraph (e) applies in the same manner whether the guarantor is a finance subsidiary or an operating subsidiary.

2. Instead of the condensed consolidating financial information required by paragraph (e)(4), the parent company's financial statements may include a footnote stating, if true, that the parent company has no independent assets or operations, the guarantee is full and

4.如果符合第(d)款的所有规定,但是某个子公司不与母公司或母公司及其他子公司(视具体情况而定)承担连带担保责任,则担任担保人但是不承担连带担保责任的每一子公司均不必提供单独财务报表,但是简要并表财务信息中应对每一该等子公司单设相应栏目。

5.如以下情况属实,可在母公司财务报表中纳入一个脚注,作出相应声明,以之替代第(d)(4)款要求提供的简要并表财务信息:母公司无独立资产或经营,以发行人身份行事的子公司属于母公司的全资财务子公司,母公司为证券提供了担保,除以发行人身份行事的子公司之外的所有其他子公司也都为证券提供了担保,担保属于完全和无条件担保,并且所有担保均为连带担保。该脚注还须包括本节第(i)(9)款和第(i)(10)款规定的文字披露。

(e)母公司发行由单独一家子公司担保的证券。母公司发行证券时,某一家子公司为该等证券提供担保的,注册说明书、母公司年度报告或母公司季度报告不必包含担任担保人的子公司的财务报表,前提是:

(1)担任担保人的子公司系发行人(即其母公司)的全资子公司;

(2)担保属于完全和无条件担保;

(3)母公司的任何其他子公司均未对证券提供担保;且

(4)母公司就第210.3-01节和第210.3-02节规定的报告期提交了财务报表,并在报表的脚注中提供了同期简要并表财务信息,并单设栏目,分别说明了下列各项信息:

(i)母公司;

(ii)担任担保人的子公司;

(iii)母公司的任何其他子公司(汇总信息);

(iv)并表调整;及

(v)并表总额。

关于第(e)款的注释。1. 无论担任担保人的子公司是财务子公司还是运营子公司,第(e)款均应以相同方式适用。

2.如以下情况属实,可在母公司财务报表中纳入一个脚注,作出相应声明,以之替代第(e)(4)款要求提供的简要并表财务信息:母公司无独立资产或经营,担保属于完全和无条件担保,并且除担任担保人的子公司外,母公司任何其他子公司都属于次要

unconditional, and any subsidiaries of the parent company other than the subsidiary guarantor are minor. The footnote also must include the narrative disclosures specified in paragraphs (i)(9) and (i)(10) of this section.

3. If the alternative disclosure permitted by Note 2 to this paragraph is not applicable because the parent company has independent assets or operations, the condensed consolidating financial information described in paragraph (e)(4) may omit the column for "any other subsidiaries of the parent company on a combined basis" if those other subsidiaries are minor.

4. If, instead of guaranteeing the subject security, a subsidiary co-issues the security jointly and severally with its parent company, this paragraph (e) does not apply. Instead, the appropriate financial information requirement would depend on whether the subsidiary is a finance subsidiary or an operating subsidiary. If the subsidiary is a finance subsidiary, paragraph (b) applies. If the subsidiary is an operating company, paragraph (c) applies.

(f) *Multiple subsidiary guarantors of securities issued by the parent company of those subsidiaries.* When a parent company issues securities and more than one of its subsidiaries guarantee those securities, the registration statement, parent company annual report, or parent company quarterly report need not include financial statements of the subsidiary guarantors if:

(1) Each of the subsidiary guarantors is 100% owned by the parent company issuer;

(2) The guarantees are full and unconditional;

(3) The guarantees are joint and several; and

(4) The parent company's financial statements are filed for the periods specified by §§210.3-01 and 210.3-02 and include, in a footnote, condensed consolidating financial information for the same periods with a separate column for:

(i) The parent company;

(ii) The subsidiary guarantors on a combined basis;

(iii) Any other subsidiaries of the parent company on a combined basis;

(iv) Consolidating adjustments; and

(v) The total consolidated amounts.

Notes to paragraph (f) 1. Instead of the condensed consolidating financial information required by paragraph (f)(4), the parent company's financial statements may include a footnote stating, if true, that the parent company has no independent assets or operations, the guarantees are full and unconditional and joint and several, and any subsidiaries of the parent company other than the subsidiary guarantors are minor. The footnote also must include the narrative disclosures specified in paragraphs (i) (9) and (i) (10) of this section.

2. If the alternative disclosure permitted by Note 1 to this paragraph is not

子公司。该脚注还须包括本节第(i)(9)款和第(i)(10)款规定的文字披露。

3.如果母公司的其他子公司均属于次要子公司,但由于母公司拥有独立资产或经营,致使本款注释2所允许的替代性披露不适用,则第(e)(4)款规定的简要并表财务信息可以不设"母公司的任何其他子公司(汇总信息)"栏目。

4.如果子公司并不担任标的证券的担保人,而是与母公司共同发行证券并承担连带责任,则不适用本第(e)款的规定。在此种情形下,将根据子公司属于财务子公司还是运营子公司来确定适当的财务信息要求。如果子公司属于财务子公司,应适用第(b)款的规定;如果子公司属于运营子公司,则适用第(c)款的规定。

(f)母公司发行由多家子公司共同担保的证券。母公司发行证券时,超过一家子公司为该等证券提供担保的,注册说明书、母公司年度报告或母公司季度报告不必包含担任担保人的各子公司的财务报表,前提是:

(1)每家担任担保人的子公司均属于发行人(即其母公司)的全资子公司;

(2)担保属于完全和无条件担保;

(3)各担保人承担连带担保责任;且

(4)母公司就第210.3-01节和第210.3-02节规定的报告期提交了财务报表,并在报表的脚注中提供了同期简要并表财务信息,并单设栏目,分别说明了下列各项信息:

(i)母公司;

(ii)担任担保人的各子公司(汇总信息);

(iii)母公司的任何其他子公司(汇总信息);

(iv)并表调整;及

(v)并表总额。

关于第(f)款的注释。如以下情况属实,可在母公司财务报表中纳入一个脚注,作出相应声明,以之替代第(f)(4)款要求提供的简要并表财务信息:母公司无独立资产或经营,各项均担保属于完全、无条件和连带担保,并且除担任担保人的各子公司外,母公司任何其他子公司都属于次要子公司。该脚注还须包括本节第(i)(9)款和第(i)(10)款规定的文字披露。

2.如果母公司的其他子公司均属于次要子公司,但由于母公司拥有独立资产或经

applicable because the parent company has independent assets or operations, the condensed consolidating financial information described in paragraph (f)(4) may omit the column for "any other subsidiaries of the parent company on a combined basis" if those other subsidiaries are minor.

3. If any of the subsidiary guarantees is not joint and several with the guarantees of the other subsidiaries, then each subsidiary guarantor whose guarantee is not joint and several need not include separate financial statements, but the condensed consolidating financial information must include a separate column for each subsidiary guarantor whose guarantee is not joint and several.

(g) *Recently acquired subsidiary issuers or subsidiary guarantors.* (1) The Securities Act registration statement of the parent company must include the financial statements specified in paragraph (g) (2) of this section for any subsidiary that otherwise meets the conditions in paragraph (c), (d), (e) or (f) of this section for omission of separate financial statements if:

(i) The subsidiary has not been included in the audited consolidated results of the parent company for at least nine months of the most recent fiscal year; and

(ii) The net book value or purchase price, whichever is greater, of the subsidiary is 20% or more of the principal amount of the securities being registered.

(2) Financial statements required.

(i) Audited financial statements for a subsidiary described in paragraph (g)(1) of this section must be filed for the subsidiary's most recent fiscal year preceding the acquisition. In addition, unaudited financial statements must be filed for any interim periods specified in §§210.3-01 and 210.3-02.

(ii) The financial statements must conform to the requirements of Regulation S-X (§§210.1-01 through 12-29), except that supporting schedules need not be filed. If the subsidiary is a foreign business, financial statements of the subsidiary meeting the requirements of Item 17 of Form 20-F (§249.220f) will satisfy this item.

(3) Instructions to paragraph (g).

(i) The significance test of paragraph (g)(1)(ii) of this section should be computed using net book value of the subsidiary as of the most recent fiscal year end preceding the acquisition.

(ii) Information required by this paragraph (g) is not required to be included in an annual report or quarterly report.

(iii) Acquisitions of a group of subsidiary issuers or subsidiary guarantors that are related prior to their acquisition shall be aggregated for purposes of applying the 20% test in paragraph (g)(1)(ii) of this section. Subsidiaries shall be deemed to be related prior to their acquisition if:

营,致使本款注释1所允许的替代性披露不适用,则第(f)(4)款规定的简要并表财务信息可以不设“母公司的任何其他子公司(汇总信息)”栏目。

3.如果任何担任担保人的子公司不与其他子公司承担连带担保责任,则担任担保人但是不承担连带担保责任的该等子公司均不必提供单独的财务报表,但是简要并表财务信息中应对每一该等子公司单设相应栏目。

(g)由最近收购的子公司担任发行人或担保人的情形。(1)在下列情形下,《证券法》中的母公司注册说明书仍须包含本节第(g)(2)款规定的任何子公司财务报表,即使该等子公司符合本节第(c)款、第(d)款、第(e)款或第(f)款关于不提供单独财务报表的要求:

(i)子公司未被纳入母公司最近一个会计年度至少9个月的经审计的并表成果中;且

(ii)子公司的账面净值或购买价格(以较高者为准)达到或超过正在申请注册的证券本金金额的20%。

(2)要求提供的财务报表。

(i)对于本节第(g)(1)款所述子公司,应提交其在收购前最近一个会计年度的经审计的财务报表,另外还须按照第210.3-01节和第210.3-02节的规定提交未审计的任何中期财务报表。

(ii)财务报表须符合《S-X管理办法》(第210.1-01~210.12-29节)的要求,但是不必提交相关附表。如果子公司属于外国企业,子公司的财务报表符合《20-F表格》第17条(第249.220f节)要求的,即视为满足本项规定。

(3)关于第(g)款的说明。

(i)进行本节第(g)(1)(ii)款规定的重大性测试时,应采用子公司截至收购前最近一个会计年度年末的账面净值进行计算。

(ii)年度报告或季度报告不必包含本第(g)款要求提供的信息。

(iii)如果收购涉及以发行人或担保人身份行事的一组子公司,且该等子公司在收购前即存在关联关系,则进行本节第(g)(1)(ii)款规定的20%比例的测试时,应对所有该等子公司进行加总计算。在下列情形下,子公司之间应视为在收购前即存在关联关系:

(A) They are under common control or management;

(B) The acquisition of one subsidiary is conditioned on the acquisition of each subsidiary; or

(C) The acquisition of each subsidiary is conditioned on a single common event.

(h) *Definitions*. For the purposes of this section:

(1) A subsidiary is "100% owned" if all of its outstanding voting shares are owned, either directly or indirectly, by its parent company. A subsidiary not in corporate form is 100% owned if the sum of all interests are owned, either directly or indirectly, by its parent company other than:

(i) Securities that are guaranteed by its parent and, if applicable, other 100%-owned subsidiaries of its parent; and

(ii) Securities that guarantee securities issued by its parent and, if applicable, other 100%-owned subsidiaries of its parent.

(2) A guarantee is "full and unconditional," if, when an issuer of a guaranteed security has failed to make a scheduled payment, the guarantor is obligated to make the scheduled payment immediately and, if it doesn't, any holder of the guaranteed security may immediately bring suit directly against the guarantor for payment of all amounts due and payable.

(3) *Annual report* refers to an annual report on Form 10-K or Form 20-F (§249.310 or 249.220f of this chapter).

(4) *Quarterly report* refers to a quarterly report on Form 10-Q (§249.308a of this chapter).

(5) A parent company has no independent assets or operations if each of its total assets, revenues, income from continuing operations before income taxes, and cash flows from operating activities (excluding amounts related to its investment in its consolidated subsidiaries) is less than 3% of the corresponding consolidated amount.

(6) A subsidiary is minor if each of its total assets, stockholders' equity, revenues, income from continuing operations before income taxes, and cash flows from operating activities is less than 3% of the parent company's corresponding consolidated amount.

Note to paragraph (h)(6). When considering a group of subsidiaries, the definition applies to each subsidiary in that group individually and to all subsidiaries in that group in the aggregate.

(7) A subsidiary is a finance subsidiary if it has no assets, operations, revenues or cash flows other than those related to the issuance, administration and repayment of the security being registered and any other securities guaranteed by its parent company.

(8) A subsidiary is an operating subsidiary if it is not a finance subsidiary.

(i) Instructions for preparation of condensed consolidating financial information

(A)该等公司受同一控制或管理;

(B)对其中一家子公司的收购,以收购其他每家子公司为条件;或者

(C)对每家子公司的收购均以同一事件之发生为条件。

(h)定义。就本节而言:

(1)如果某一子公司所有发行在外的表决股均由其母公司直接或间接拥有,则该子公司属于其母公司的"全资"子公司。对于以非公司形式存在的子公司,如其全部权益均由其母公司直接或间接拥有,亦可认定为母公司的"全资"子公司,但上述权益不包括下列权益:

(i)由母公司以及(如适用)母公司其他全资子公司担保的证券;及

(ii)为其母公司以及(如适用)母公司其他全资子公司发行的证券提供担保的证券。

(2)担保满足下列条件的,即属于"完全和无条件担保":担保证券的发行人未能按期履行付款义务时,担保人有义务立即代为清偿;担保人不偿付的,任何担保证券的持有人可以立即直接起诉担保人,要求其全额支付到期应付款项。

(3)"年度报告"系指按照《10-K表格》或《20-F表格》(本章第249.310节或第249.220f节)提交的年度报告。

(4)"季度报告"系指按照《10-Q表格》(本章第249.308a节)提交的季度报告。

(5)母公司满足下列条件的,即可认定为"无独立资产或经营":母公司的总资产、收入、税前持续经营收益以及经营活动现金流量(不包括与其对并表子公司投资相关的数额)均低于相应并表数额的3%。

(6)子公司满足下列条件的,即可认定为"次要子公司":子公司的总资产、股东权益、收入、税前持续经营收益以及经营活动现金流量均低于母公司相应并表数额的3%。

关于第(h)(6)款的注释。在考虑一组子公司是否属于"次要子公司"时,应将上述定义适用于其中的每一子公司,同时对该组子公司的相应数额进行加总,并判断加总后的数额是否符合"次要子公司"的定义。

(7)满足下列条件的子公司属于财务子公司:除与正在申请注册的证券以及母公司担保的任何其他证券之发行、管理和偿付有关的资产、经营、收入或现金流之外,子公司无任何其他资产、经营、收入或现金流。

(8)财务子公司之外的其他子公司均属于运营子公司。

(i)关于本节第(c)款、第(d)款、第(e)款和第(f)款要求提供的简要并表财务信息

required by paragraphs (c), (d), (e) and (f) of this section.

(1) Follow the general guidance in §210.10–01 for the form and content for condensed financial statements and present the financial information in sufficient detail to allow investors to determine the assets, results of operations and cash flows of each of the consolidating groups;

(2) The financial information should be audited for the same periods that the parent company financial statements are required to be audited;

(3) The parent company column should present investments in all subsidiaries based upon their proportionate share of the subsidiary's net assets;

(4) The parent company's basis shall be "pushed down" to the applicable subsidiary columns to the extent that push down would be required or permitted in separate financial statements of the subsidiary;

(5) All subsidiary issuer or subsidiary guarantor columns should present the following investments in subsidiaries under the equity method:

(i) Non–guarantor subsidiaries;

(ii) Subsidiary issuers or subsidiary guarantors that are not 100% owned or whose guarantee is not full and unconditional;

(iii) Subsidiary guarantors whose guarantee is not joint and several with the guarantees of the other subsidiaries; and

(iv) Subsidiary guarantors with differences in domestic or foreign laws that affect the enforceability of the guarantees;

(6) Provide a separate column for each subsidiary issuer or subsidiary guarantor that is not 100% owned, whose guarantee is not full and unconditional, or whose guarantee is not joint and several with the guarantees of other subsidiaries. Inclusion of a separate column does not relieve that issuer or guarantor from the requirement to file separate financial statements under paragraph (a) of this section. However, paragraphs (b) through (f) of this section will provide this relief if the particular paragraph is satisfied except that the guarantee is not joint and several;

(7) Provide separate columns for each guarantor by legal jurisdiction if differences in domestic or foreign laws affect the enforceability of the guarantees;

(8) Include the following disclosure, if true:

(i) Each subsidiary issuer or subsidiary guarantor is 100% owned by the parent company;

(ii) All guarantees are full and unconditional; and

(iii) Where there is more than one guarantor, all guarantees are joint and several;

(9) Disclose any significant restrictions on the ability of the parent company or any guarantor to obtain funds from its subsidiaries by dividend or loan;

的编写说明。

(1)应遵循第210.10-01节中关于简要财务报表格式及内容的一般指导方针,所提供的财务信息应充分详细,使投资者足以了解每组并表子公司的资产、经营成果以及现金流状况;

(2)对于按规定应提交经审计的母公司财务报表的报告期,针对相同报告期提交的简要并表财务信息也应经过审计;

(3)母公司一栏应填写对所有子公司的投资额(按母公司在所涉子公司净资产中所持比例计算);

(4)如果子公司的单独财务报表要求或允许根据母公司的基数“往下分拆”,则应将母公司基数“往下分拆”至相应子公司栏目中。

(5)应在关于以发行人或担保人身份行事的子公司的所有栏目中,填写按权益法核算的对下列子公司的投资:

(i)未担任担保人的子公司;

(ii)以发行人或担保人身份行事的非全资子公司,或者其提供的担保不属于完全和无条件担保的子公司;

(iii)担任担保人但是不与其他子公司承担连带担保责任的子公司;及

(iv)因国内法或外国法的差异,导致其所提供的担保的可强制执行性受到影响的子公司。

(6)对于以发行人或担保人身份行事的每一下述子公司,均应单设栏目:非全资子公司;提供的担保不属于完全和无条件担保的子公司;不与其他子公司承担连带担保责任的子公司。为上述子公司单设栏目并不能豁免该发行人或担保人根据本节第(a)款提交单独财务报表的义务。但是,如果发行人或担保人符合本节第(b)款至第(f)款任一款规定的条件,可以获得豁免,不必提交单独财务报表,但担保不属于连带担保的除外;

(7)如果由于适用于担保人的国内法或外国法存在的差异,导致其提供的担保的可强制执行性受到影响,应按司法辖区对每一担保人单设相应栏目;

(8)如存在以下真实情况,应予以披露:

(i)每一以发行人或担保人身份行事的子公司均属于母公司的全资子公司;

(ii)所有担保均属于完全和无条件担保;

(iii)存在超过一名担保人的,所有担保人均承担连带责任;

(9)母公司或任何担保人通过股息或贷款形式从其子公司获得资金的能力如受到任何重大限制,应予披露:

(10) Provide the disclosures prescribed by §210.4-08(e)(3) with respect to the subsidiary issuers and subsidiary guarantors;

(11) The disclosure:

(i) May not omit any financial and narrative information about each guarantor if the information would be material for investors to evaluate the sufficiency of the guarantee;

(ii) Shall include sufficient information so as to make the financial information presented not misleading; and

(iii) Need not repeat information that would substantially duplicate disclosure elsewhere in the parent company's consolidated financial statements; and

(12) Where the parent company's consolidated financial statements are prepared on a comprehensive basis other than U.S. Generally Accepted Accounting Principles or International Financial Reporting Standards as issued by the International Accounting Standards Board, reconcile the information in each column to U.S. Generally Accepted Accounting Principles to the extent necessary to allow investors to evaluate the sufficiency of the guarantees. The reconciliation may be limited to the information specified by Item 17 of Form 20-F (§249.220f of this chapter). The reconciling information need not duplicate information included elsewhere in the reconciliation of the consolidated financial statements.

[65 FR 51707, Aug. 24, 2000, as amended at 73 FR 952, Jan. 4, 2008; 73 FR 1009, Jan. 4, 2008; 74 FR 18615, Apr. 23, 2009]

§210.3-11 Financial statements of an inactive registrant.

If a registrant is an inactive entity as defined below, the financial statements required by this regulation for purposes of reports pursuant to the Securities Exchange Act of 1934 may be unaudited. An inactive entity is one meeting all of the following conditions:

(a) Gross receipts from all sources for the fiscal year are not in excess of $100,000;

(b) The registrant has not purchased or sold any of its own stock, granted options therefor, or levied assessments upon outstanding stock;

(c) Expenditures for all purposes for the fiscal year are not in excess of $100,000;

(d) No material change in the business has occurred during the fiscal year, including any bankruptcy, reorganization, readjustment or succession or any material acquisition or disposition of plants, mines, mining equipment, mine rights or leases; and

(e) No exchange upon which the shares are listed, or governmental authority having jurisdiction, requires the furnishing to it or the publication of audited financial statements.

§210.3-12 Age of financial statements at effective date of registration statement or at mailing date of proxy statement.

(a) If the financial statements in a filing are as of a date the number of days

(10)按照第210.4-08(e)(3)节的规定,披露与以发行人和担保人身份行事的子公司相关的信息;

(11)披露信息中:

(i)不得省略对于投资者评估担保充分性具有重大意义的任一担保人的财务和文字信息;

(ii)应包含充分信息,避免财务信息产生误导性;及

(iii)不必重复与母公司合并财务报表中已提供的信息基本一致的信息;

(12)如母公司合并财务报表的编制依据是《美国公认会计原则》或国际会计准则委员会发布的《国际财务报告准则》以外的综合标准,应在必要范围内按照《美国公认会计原则》调整每一栏目的信息,以便投资者评估担保的充分性。调整可限定在《20-F表格》第17条(本章第249.220f节)规定的信息范围内。涉及调整的信息,与已提交过的合并财务报表调整相关的信息重复的,不必再重复披露。

[《联邦公报》第65卷第51707页,2000年8月24日,修正索引:《联邦公报》第73卷第952页,2008年1月4日;《联邦公报》第73卷第1009页,2008年1月4日;《联邦公报》第74卷第18615页,2009年4月23日。]

第210.3-11节　不活跃注册人的财务报表

如果注册人属于下文定义的不活跃实体,则本《管理办法》根据《1934年证券交易法》要求为报告目的提交的财务报表可以是未审计的财务报表。不活跃实体系指满足下列全部条件的实体:

(a)该会计年度所有来源的毛收入不超过10万美元;

(b)注册人未曾买入或卖出自身的任何股票,亦未曾就自身股票授予期权,或就发行在外的股票要求增缴股本;

(c)该会计年度所有费用总额不超过10万美元;

(d)在本会计年度内业务未发生重大变化,包括任何破产、重组、重整、继受或涉及工厂、矿区、采矿设备、采矿权或租赁的任何重大收购或处置;及

(e)注册人股票上市的证券交易所或对注册人有管辖权的政府机构,未要求注册人向其提供或公布经审计的财务报表。

第210.3-12节　截至注册说明书生效日或征集投票权报告邮递日财务报表的表龄

(a)如果注册人提交注册说明书时,其中所含财务报表的截止日期早于注册说明

specified in paragraph (g) of this section or more before the date the filing is expected to become effective, or proposed mailing date in the case of a proxy statement, the financial statements shall be updated, except as specified in the following paragraphs, with a balance sheet as of an interim date within the number of days specified in paragraph (g) of this section and with statements of income and cash flows for the interim period between the end of the most recent fiscal year and the date of the interim balance sheet provided and for the corresponding period of the preceding fiscal year. Such interim financial statements may be unaudited and need not be presented in greater detail than is required by §210.10–01. Notwithstanding the above requirements, the most recent interim financial statements shall be at least as current as the most recent financial statements filed with the Commission on Form 10–Q.

(b) Where the anticipated effective date of a filing, or in the case of a proxy statement the proposed mailing date, falls within the number of days subsequent to the end of the fiscal year specified in paragraph (g) of this section, the filing need not include financial statements more current than as of the end of the third fiscal quarter of the most recently completed fiscal year unless the audited financial statements for such fiscal year are available or unless the anticipated effective date or proposed mailing date falls after 45 days subsequent to the end of the fiscal year and the registrant does not meet the conditions prescribed under paragraph (c) of §210.3–01. If the anticipated effective date or proposed mailing date falls after 45 days subsequent to the end of the fiscal year and the registrant does not meet the conditions prescribed under paragraph (c) of §210.3–01, the filing must include audited financial statements for the most recently completed fiscal year.

(c) Where a filing is made near the end of a fiscal year and audited financial statements for that fiscal year are not included in the filing, the filing shall be updated with such audited financial statements if they become available prior to the anticipated effective date, or proposed mailing date in the case of a proxy statement.

(d) The age of the registrant's most recent audited financial statements included in a registration statement filed under the Securities Act of 1933 or filed on Form 10 (17 CFR 249.210) under the Securities Exchange Act of 1934 shall not be more than one year and 45 days old at the date the registration statement becomes effective if the registration statement relates to the security of an issuer that was not subject, immediately before the time of filing the registration statement, to the reporting requirements of section 13 or 15(d) of the Securities Exchange Act of 1934.

(e) For filings by registered management investment companies, the requirements of §210.3–18 shall apply in lieu of the requirements of this section.

(f) Any foreign private issuer may file financial statements whose age is specified in

书预期生效日(提交征集投票权报告的,其中所含财务报表早于计划邮递日),且两者相距天数(下称表龄)不短于本节第(g)款规定的期限,则除下列各款规定的情形外,应对财务报表进行更新、提交一份中期资产负债表[其截止日期应在本节第(g)款规定的期限内],并提供从最近一个会计年度年末起至所提交的中期资产负债表日止的期间以及上一会计年度同期的损益表和现金流量表。上述中期财务报表可以不经审计,其详细程度亦不必超出第210.10-01节的要求。无论上文如何规定,最近一期中期财务报表的截止日期不得早于按《10-Q表格》向证券交易委员会所提交的最近一期财务报表的截止日期。

(b)如果提交的注册说明书的预期生效日(提交征集投票权报告的,为计划邮递日)处于本节第(g)款规定的期限内,则所含财务报表的截止日期不必晚于最近结束的一个会计年度的第三个财务季度末,但该会计年度的经审计的财务报表已经可以提供,或者,预期生效日或计划邮递日晚于该会计年度结束后第45日并且注册人不符合第210.3-01节(c)款规定的条件的除外。如果预期生效日或计划邮递日晚于该会计年度结束后第45日,并且注册人不符合第210.3-01节(c)款规定的条件,则提交的文件须包括最近结束的一个会计年度经审计的财务报表。

(c)注册说明书提交日临近某一会计年度年末而该会计年度经审计的财务报表未包含在注册说明书中的,如果在预期生效日(提交征集投票权报告的,为计划邮递日)前可以提供经审计的财务报表,则应提交该等报表,以便更新之前提交的文件。

(d)如果在紧接注册说明书提交之前,注册说明书所涉证券之发行人不受《1934年证券交易法》第13条或第15(d)条的报告要求约束,则根据《1933年证券法》或者根据《1934年证券交易法》以《10表格》(《美国法典》第十七编第249.210条)形式提交的注册说明书所含的注册人最近一期经审计的财务报表的表龄不应超过1年零45日。

(e)对于注册管理型投资公司提交的文件,第210.3-18节的规定应取代本节规定适用。

(f)任何外国私募发行人可按《20-F表格》第8.A条(本章第249.220f节)规定的表龄

Item 8.A of Form 20–F (§249.220f of this chapter). Financial statements of a foreign business which are furnished pursuant to §§210.3–05 or 210.3–09 because it is an acquired business or a 50 percent or less owned person may be of the age specified in Item 8.A of Form 20–F.

(g)(1) For purposes of paragraph (a) of this section, the number of days shall be:

(i) 130 days for large accelerated filers and accelerated filers (as defined in §240.12b–2 of this chapter); and

(ii) 135 days for all other registrants.

(2) For purposes of paragraph (b) of this section, the number of days shall be:

(i) 60 days (75 days for fiscal years ending before December 15, 2006) for large accelerated filers (as defined in §240.12b–2 of this chapter);

(ii) 75 days for accelerated filers (as defined in §240.12b–2 of this chapter); and

(iii) 90 days for all other registrants.

[45 FR 62687, Sept. 25, 1980]

Editorial Note: ForFederal Registercitations affecting §210.3–12, see the List of CFR Sections Affected, which appears in the Finding Aids section of the printed volume and at www.fdsys.gov.

§210.3–13 Filing of other financial statements in certain cases.

The Commission may, upon the informal written request of the registrant, and where consistent with the protection of investors, permit the omission of one or more of the financial statements herein required or the filing in substitution therefor of appropriate statements of comparable character. The Commission may also by informal written notice require the filing of other financial statements in addition to, or in substitution for, the statements herein required in any case where such statements are necessary or appropriate for an adequate presentation of the financial condition of any person whose financial statements are required, or whose statements are otherwise necessary for the protection of investors.

§210.3–14 Special instructions for real estate operations to be acquired.

(a) If, during the period for which income statements are required, the registrant has acquired one or more properties which in the aggregate are significant, or since the date of the latest balance sheet required has acquired or proposes to acquire one or more properties which in the aggregate are significant, the following shall be furnished with respect to such properties:

(1) Audited income statements (not including earnings per unit) for the three most recent fiscal years, which shall exclude items not comparable to the proposed future operations of the property such as mortgage interest, leasehold rental, depreciation, corporate expenses and Federal and state income taxes: *Provided, however,* That such

提交财务报表。外国公司如属于已收购企业或50%或以下股权被控主体,因此按照第210.3-05节或第210.3-09节规定提交财务报表的,可按《20-F表格》第8.A条规定的表龄提交文件。

(g)(1)本节第(a)款提及的期限如下:

(i)对于大型加速报告人和加速报告人(定义见本章第240.12b-2节)而言,为会计年度结束后130日;及

(ii)对于所有其他注册人而言,为会计年度结束后13日。

(2)本节第(b)款提及的期限如下:

(i)对于大型加速报告人(定义见本章第240.12b-2节)而言,为会计年度结束后60日(会计年度在2006年12月15日前结束的,为75日);

(ii)对于加速报告人(定义见本章第240.12b-2节)而言,为会计年度结束后75日;及

(iii)对于所有其他注册人而言,为会计年度结束后90日。

[《联邦公报》第45卷第62687页,1980年9月25日。]

编辑注:对第210.3-12节有影响的《联邦公报》索引,参见《受影响的联邦规章汇编条文列表》(见印刷版本的《检索协助》章节和www.fdsys.gov)。

第210.3-13节　特定情形下其他财务报表的提交

注册人提出非正式书面请求的,证券交易委员会可以在符合投资者保护原则的前提下,允许任何主体不提交本《管理办法》规定的一份或多份财务报表,或允许其提交性质相当的其他适当报表作为替代。证券交易委员会也可以通过非正式书面通知,要求注册人在本《管理办法》规定的财务报表之外提交其他财务报表,或提交替代性的财务报表,只要该等报表对于充分说明财务报表提供义务人的财务状况确属必要或适当,或者对投资者保护确属必要。

第210.3-14节　关于房地产业务收购的特殊说明

(a)如果在按规定应提交损益表的报告期内,注册人购置了金额较高的一处物业或合计金额较高的多处物业,或者自最近一期资产负债表日起购置了或计划购置金额较高的一处物业或合计金额较高的多处物业,注册人应当就该等物业提供如下文件:

(1)最近3个会计年度的经审计的损益表(不含证券单位盈利),表中应剔除与该等物业未来拟议经营性质不同的项目(如抵押权益、租赁收入、折旧、公司总部费用以及联邦和州所得税):但是,如满足下列条件,则仅需提供最近一个会计年度的经审计的财务报表:

audited statements need be presented for only the most recent fiscal year if:

(i) The property is not acquired from a related party;

(ii) Material factors considered by the registrant in assessing the property are described with specificity in the filing with regard to the property, including sources of revenue (including, but not limited to, competition in the rental market, comparative rents, occupancy rates) and expense (including, but not limited to, utility rates, ad valorem tax rates, maintenance expenses, capital improvements anticipated); and

(iii) The registrant indicates in the appropriate filing that, after reasonable inquiry, the registrant is not aware of any material factors relating to that specific property other than those discussed in response to paragraph (a)(1)(ii) of this section that would cause the reported financial information not to be necessarily indicative of future operating results.

Note: The discussion of material factors considered should be combined with that required by Item 15 of Form S-11.

(2) If the property is to be operated by the registrant, there shall be furnished a statement showing the estimated taxable operating results of the registrant based on the most recent twelve month period including such adjustments as can be factually supported. If the property is to be acquired subject to a net lease the estimated taxable operating results shall be based on the rent to be paid for the first year of the lease. In either case, the estimated amount of cash to be made available by operations shall be shown. There shall be stated in an introductory paragraph the principal assumptions which have been made in preparing the statements of estimated taxable operating results and cash to be made available by operations.

(3) If appropriate under the circumstances, there shall be given in tablular form for a limited number of years the estimated cash distribution per unit showing the portion thereof reportable as taxable income and the portion representing a return of capital together with an explanation of annual variations, if any. If taxable net income per unit will become greater than the cash available for distribution per unit, that fact and approximate year of occurrence shall be stated, if significant.

(b) Information required by this section is not required to be included in a filing on Form 10-K.

[45 FR 63687, Sept. 25, 1980, as amended at 47 FR 25122, June 10, 1982; 73 FR 953, Jan. 4, 2008]

§210.3-15 Special provisions as to real estate investment trusts.

(a)(1) The income statement prepared pursuant to §210.5-03 shall include the following additional captions between those required by §210.5-03.15 and 16: (i) Income or loss before gain or loss on sale of properties, extraordinary items and cumulative effects

(i)物业并非购自关联方;

(ii)注册人在对物业估值时所考虑的任何重大因素已在就物业提供的有关文件中作出详细说明,包括收入来源(包括但不限于租赁市场的竞争状况、比较租金、租用率)和费用(包括但不限于公用事业费、从价税率、维护费用、预计的资本资产改造费用);及

(iii)注册人在适当的提交文件中表明,经过合理调查,除了根据本节第(a)(1)(ii)款的规定已进行讨论的因素外,注册人未发现与该特定物业有关的、可能导致所报告的财务信息不能充分反映未来经营成果的重大因素。

注:关于重大考量因素的讨论应与《S-11表格》第15条的要求相结合。

(2)如果物业将由注册人亲自经营,则应基于注册人最近12个月的经营成果提供一份预期应税经营成果报表,包括能提出事实依据的调整。如果所收购物业处于净租赁状态,则预期应税经营成果应根据租赁首年的应付租金确定。在上述任何一种情形下,均应列示预期经营将产生的现金数额。在编制预期应税经营成果报表和经营将产生的现金数额报表的过程中,所做基本假设应当在导言部分予以阐述。

(3)如情况适当,还应以表格形式提供一定年数内,每幢物业的预计平均现金分配额,分列应作为应税收益报告的部分和应作为资本回报报告的部分,并附上每年增减额(如有)的说明。如果预期每幢物业的平均应税净收益高于每幢物业的平均现金分配额,且两者差额较大,应说明该事实以及该事实预期发生的大致年份。

(b)按照《10-K表格》提交的文件不必包括本节要求提供的信息。

[《联邦公报》第45卷第63687页,1980年9月25日,修正索引:《联邦公报》第47卷第25122页,1982年6月10日;《联邦公报》第73卷第953页,2008年1月4日。]

第210.3-15节　关于房地产投资信托的特别规定

(a)(1)按照第210.5-03节编制的损益表应列报以下科目,替代第210.5-03.15节和第210.5-03.16节规定的科目:(i)扣除物业出售收益或损失、非经常项目和会计原则变更累积影响数之前的损益,以及(ii)扣除适用所得税之后的物业出售收益或损失。

of accounting changes, and (ii) gain or loss on sale of properties, less applicable income tax.

(2) The balance sheet required by §210.5–02 shall set forth in lieu of the captions required by §210.5–02.31(a)(3): (i) The balance of undistributed income from other than gain or loss on sale of properties and (ii) accumulated undistributed net realized gain or loss on sale of properties. The information specified in §2103–04 shall be modified similarly.

(b) The trust's status as a *real estate investment trust* under applicable provisions of the Internal Revenue Code as amended shall be stated in a note referred to in the appropriate statements. Such note shall also indicate briefly the principal present assumptions on which the trust has relied in making or not making provisons for Federal income taxes.

(c) The tax status of distributions per unit shall be stated (e.g., ordinary income, capital gain, return of capital).

[45 FR 63687, Sept. 25, 1980, as amended at 50 FR 49532, Dec. 3, 1985]

§210.3–16 Financial statements of affiliates whose securities collateralize an issue registered or being registered.

(a) For each of the registrant's affiliates whose securities constitute a substantial portion of the collateral for any class of securities registered or being registered, there shall be filed the financial statements that would be required if the affiliate were a registrant and required to file financial statements. However, financial statements need not be filed pursuant to this section for any person whose statements are otherwise separately included in the filing on an individual basis or on a basis consolidated with its subsidiaries.

(b) For the purposes of this section, securities of a person shall be deemed to constitute a substantial portion of collateral if the aggregate principal amount, par value, or book value of the securities as carried by the registrant, or the market value of such securities, whichever is the greatest, equals 20 percent or more of the principal amount of the secured class of securities.

[65 FR 51710, Aug. 24, 2000]

§210.3–17 Financial statements of natural persons.

(a) In lieu of the financial statements otherwise required, a natural person may file an unaudited balance sheet as of a date within 90 days of date of filing and unaudited statements of income for each of the three most recent fiscal years.

(b) Financial statements conforming with the instructions as to financial statements of subsidiaries not consolidated and 50 percent or less owned persons under §210.3–09

(2)第210.5-02节要求提供的资产负债表应列报以下科目,替代第210.5-02.31(a)(3)节规定的科目:(i)来源于物业出售收益或损失之外的未分配盈利余额,和(ii)物业出售实现净收益或损失的累计未分配金额。第210.3-04节规定的信息亦应相应修改。

(b)应在适当报表提及的附注中注明:根据《国内税收法典》及其修正的有关规定,该信托之性质属于“房地产投资信托”。该附注还应简要说明该信托作出计提或不计提联邦所得税拨备的决定时所采信的基本当前假设。

(c)每信托单位分配的税务状况均应予说明(如普通所得、资本利得、资本回报)。

[《联邦公报》第45卷第63687页,1980年9月25日,修正索引:《联邦公报》第50卷第49532页,1985年12月3日。]

第210.3-16节 通过自身证券为已注册或正在申请注册的发行提供担保的控制性关联公司的财务报表

(a)注册人的控制性关联公司的证券如构成已注册或正在申请注册的任一类证券之担保品的重要组成部分,则注册人应提交每一该等控制性关联公司的财务报表,提交范围为该等关联公司假使自行以注册人身份行事时有义务提交的财务报表。但是,如果任何主体的财务报表已依据其他规定单独纳入或通过与其子公司的财务报表合并纳入提交文件,则不必按本节规定重复提交。

(b)就本节而言,如果注册人持有的证券累计本金数额、票面价值、账面价值或市场价值(以最高者为准),大于或等于被担保的类别的证券本金数额20%,则该人的证券将视为构成担保品的重要组成部分。

[《联邦公报》第65卷第51710页,2000年8月24日。]

第210.3-17节 自然人的财务报表

(a)与其他主体不同,自然人可以提交截止日期位于财务报表提交日前90日内的未审计的资产负债表,同时,对于最近3个会计年度中的每一年,均可以提交未审计的损益表。

(b)对于下列每一实体,自然人均应提交单独的财务报表,且财务报表应符合第210.3-09(a)节关于非并表子公司和50%或以下股权被控主体的财务报表说明:(1)自

(a) shall be separately presented for: (1) Each business owned as a sole proprietor, (2) each partnership, business trust, unincorporated association, or similar business organization of which the person holds a controlling interest and (3) each corporation of which the person, directly or indirectly, owns securities representing more than 50 percent of the voting power.

(c) Separate financial statements may be omitted, however, for each corporation, business trust, unincorporated association, or similar business organization if the person's total investment in such entity does not exceed 5 percent of his total assets *and* the person's total income from such entity does not exceed 5 percent of his gross income; *Provided,* that the person's aggregate investment in and income from all such omitted entities shall not exceed 15 percent of his total assets and gross income, respectively.

[46 FR 12491, Feb. 17, 1981, as amended at 50 FR 25215, June 18, 1985]

§210.3-18 Special provisions as to registered management investment companies and companies required to be registered as management investment companies.

(a) For filings by registered management investment companies, the following financial statements shall be filed:

(1) An audited balance sheet or statement of assets and liabilities as of the end of the most recent fiscal year.

(2) An audited statement of operations for the most recent fiscal year conforming to the requirements of §210.6-07.

(3) An audited statement of cash flows for the most recent fiscal year if necessary to comply with generally accepted accounting principles. (Further references in this rule to the requirement for such statement are likewise applicable only to the extent that they are consistent with the requirements of generally accepted accounting principles.)

(4) Audited statements of changes in net assets conforming to the requirements of §210.6-09 for the two most recent fiscal years.

(b) If the filing is made within 60 days after the end of the registrant's fiscal year and audited financial statements for the most recent fiscal year are not available, the balance sheet or statement of assets and liabilities may be as of the end of the preceding fiscal year and the filing shall include an additional balance sheet or statement of assets and liabilities as of an interim date within 245 days of the date of filing. In addition, the statements of operations and cash flows (if required by generally accepted accounting principles) shall be provided for the preceding fiscal year and the statement of changes in net assets shall be provided for the two preceding fiscal years and each of the statements shall be provided for the interim period between the end of the preceding fiscal year and the date

然人作为个体独资所有者拥有的每家企业;(2)自然人拥有控制权益的每一合伙、商业信托、非公司形式的协会或类似商业组织;以及(3)自然人直接或间接持有代表50%以上表决权的证券的公司。

(c)但是,就每一公司、商业信托、非公司形式的协会或类似商业组织而言,如果自然人在该等实体的总投资不超过该自然人总资产的5%,并且,自然人来源于该等实体的总收入不超过该自然人毛收入的5%,则可以不提交单独财务报表;前提是,该自然人对所有免于提交单独报表的实体的总投资以及由此获得的收入,均不超过该自然人总资产和毛收入的15%。

[《联邦公报》第46卷第12491页,1981年2月17日,修正索引:《联邦公报》第50卷第25215页,1985年6月18日。]

第210.3-18节　关于注册管理型投资公司和按规定应作为管理型投资公司注册的公司之特别规定

(a)注册管理型投资公司应提交如下财务报表:

(1)截至最近一个会计年度年末的经审计的资产负债表;

(2)符合第210.6-07节要求的最近一个会计年度的经审计的经营报表。

(3)如有必要,还应提交最近一个会计年度的经审计的现金流量表,以满足公认会计原则的要求(类似地,本规则对报表的其他规定,其适用以符合公认会计原则为前提)。

(4)符合第210.6-09节要求的最近2个会计年度的经审计的净资产变动表。

(b)如果注册人在其会计年度结束后60日内提交财务报表,并且尚无法提供其最近一个会计年度的经审计的财务报表,则可采用截至上一会计年度年末的资产负债表,并在提交的文件中另行纳入一份中期资产负债表,其截止日期应不得早于提交日前245日。此外,还应提供上一会计年度的经营报表和现金流量表(如公认会计原则要求提供)、上两个会计年度的净资产变动表;对于从上一会计年度年末起至所提交的最近一期资产负债表日止的中期报告期,每一种报表均应提供相应的中期报表。上一会计年度的同期财务报表则不必提供。

of the most recent balance sheet or statement of assets and liabilities being filed. Financial statements for the corresponding period of the preceding fiscal year need not be provided.

(c) If the most current balance sheet or statement of assets and liabilities in a filing is as of a date 245 days or more prior to the date the filing is expected to become effective, the financial statements shall be updated with a balance sheet or statement of assets and liabilities as of an interim date within 245 days. In addition, the statements of operations, cash flows, and changes in net assets shall be provided for the interim period between the end of the most recent fiscal year for which a balance sheet or statement of assets and liabilities is presented and the date of the most recent interim balance sheet or statement of assets and liabilities filed.

(d) Interim financial statements provided in accordance with these requirements may be unaudited but shall be presented in the same detail as required by §§210.6-01 to 210.6-10. When unaudited financial statements are presented in a registration statement, they shall include the statement required by §210.3-03(d).

(Secs. 7 and 19a of the Securities Act, 15 U.S.C. 77g, 77s(a), 77aa(25)(26); secs. 12, 13, 14, 15(d), and 23(a) of the Securities Exchange Act of 1934, 15 U.S.C. 78*l*, 78m, 78n, 78o(d), 78w(a), secs. 5(b), 10(a), 14, 20(a) of the Public Utility Holding Company Act, 15 U.S.C. 79e(a), 79n, 79t(a); secs. 8, 20, 30, 31(c), 38(a) of the Investment Company Act of 1940, 15 U.S.C. 80a-8, 80a-20, 80a-29, 80a-30(c), 80a-37(a))

[46 FR 36125, July 14, 1981; 46 FR 46795, Sept. 22, 1981, as amended at 47 FR 29837, July 9, 1982; 47 FR 56838, Dec. 21, 1982; 57 FR 45292, Oct. 1, 1992]

§210.3-19 [Reserved]

§210.3-20 Currency for financial statements of foreign private issuers.

(a) A foreign private issuer, as defined in §230.405 of this chapter, shall state amounts in its primary financial statements in the currency which it deems appropriate.

(b) The currency in which amounts in the financial statements are stated shall be disclosed prominently on the face of the financial statements. If dividends on publicly-held equity securities will be declared in a currency other than the reporting currency, a note to the financial statements shall identify that currency. If there are material exchange restrictions or controls relating to the issuer's reporting currency, the currency of the issuer's domicile, or the currency in which the issuer will pay dividends, prominent disclosure of this fact shall be made in the financial statements. If the reporting currency is not the U.S. dollar, dollar-equivalent financial statements or convenience translations shall not be presented, except a translation may be presented of the most recent fiscal

(c)如果注册人提交的最近一期资产负债表的截止日期比提交文件的预期生效日早245日(含)以上,应当提供截止日期不早于预期生效日245日的中期资产负债表,以便对财务报表作出更新。此外,对于从所提交的资产负债表覆盖的最近一个会计年度年末起,至最近一期中期资产负债表日止的中期报告期,还应提供中期经营报表、现金流量表和净资产变动表。

(d)根据上述要求提供的中期财务报表可以不经审计,但其详细程度应达到第210.6-01~210.6-10节的要求。如果在注册说明书中提供未审计的财务报表,则注册说明书还应包括第210.3-03(d)节要求提供的报表。

[《证券法》第7条和第19a条,《美国法典》第十五编第77g节、第77s(a)节、第77aa(25)节和第77aa(26)节;《1934年证券交易法》)第12条、第13条、第14条、第15(d)条和第23(a)条,《美国法典》第十五编第78l节、第78m节、第78n节、第78o(d)节、第78w(a)节;《公用事业控股公司法》第5(b)条、第10(a)条、第14条和第20(a)条,《美国法典》第十五编第79e(a)节、第79(n)节、第79t(a)节;《1940年投资公司法》第8条、第20条、第30条、第31(c)条、第38(a)条,《美国法典》第十五编第80a-8节、第80a-20节、第80-a29节、第80a-30(c)节、第80a-37(a)节。]

[《联邦公报》第46卷第36125页,1981年7月14日;《联邦公报》第46卷第46795页,1981年9月22日,修正索引:《联邦公报》第47卷第29837页,1982年7月9日;《联邦公报》第47卷第56838页,1982年12月21日;《联邦公报》第57卷第45292页,1992年10月1日。]

第210.3-19节　[保留]

第210.3-20节　外国私募发行人财务报表的货币单位

(a)本章第230.405节所定义的外国私募发行人应采用其认为合适的币种作为其主要财务报表的货币单位。

(b)财务报表中采用的货币单位应在财务报表扉页的显著位置披露。如果公众持有的股权证券将以报表币种以外的币种宣布股息,财务报表的附注中应予注明。如果发行人报表采用的货币、发行人住所地的货币或发行人支付股息的货币存在重大的外汇限制或管制,应在财务报表的显著位置披露该等限制或管制。如果报表货币单位不是美元,不应提交以等值美元表示的或经简易折算的财务报表,但是,对于最近一个会计年度的报表及任何期后中期报表,可提交经折算的报表,折算采用的汇率以最近一期资产负债表日的汇率为准,但如该等汇率与可行的最近一日的汇率存在重大差异的,则应采用可行的最近一日的汇率。

year and any subsequent interim period presented using the exchange rate as of the most recent balance sheet included in the filing, except that a rate as of the most recent practicable date shall be used if materially different.

(c) If the financial statements of a foreign private issuer are stated in a currency of a country that has experienced cumulative inflationary effects exceeding a total of 100 percent over the most recent three year period, and have not been recast or otherwise supplemented to include information on a historical cost/constant currency or current cost basis prescribed or permitted by appropriate authoritative standards, the issuer shall present supplementary information to quantify the effects of changing prices upon its financial position and results of operations.

(d) Notwithstanding the currency selected for reporting purposes, the issuer shall measure separately its own transactions, and those of each of its material operations (e.g., branches, divisions, subsidiaries, joint ventures, and similar entities) that is included in the issuer's consolidated financial statements and not located in a hyperinflationary environment, using the particular currency of the primary economic environment in which the issuer or the operation conducts its business. Assets and liabilities so determined shall be translated into the reporting currency at the exchange rate at the balance sheet date; all revenues, expenses, gains, and losses shall be translated at the exchange rate existing at the time of the transaction or, if appropriate, a weighted average of the exchange rates during the period; and all translation effects of exchange rate changes shall be included as a separate component ("cumulative translation adjustment") of shareholder's equity. For purposes of this paragraph, the currency of an operation's primary economic environment is normally the currency in which cash is primarily generated and expended; a hyperinflationary environment is one that has cumulative inflation of approximately 100% or more over the most recent three year period. Departures from the methodology presented in this paragraph shall be quantified pursuant to Item 17(c)(2) of Form 20-F (§249.220f of this chapter).

(e) The issuer shall state its primary financial statements in the same currency for all periods for which financial information is presented. If the financial statements are stated in a currency that is different from that used in financial statements previously filed with the Commission, the issuer shall recast its financial statements as if the newly adopted currency had been used since at least the earliest period presented in the filing. The decision to change and the reason for the change in the reporting currency shall be disclosed in a note to the financial statements in the period in which the change occurs.

[59 FR 65631, Dec. 20, 1994, as amended at 64 FR 53908, Oct. 5, 1999]

(c)如果外国私募发行人的财务报表以某个国家的货币列报,而最近3年内该货币累计通货膨胀率超过100%,并且发行人没有重新计算其财务报表,也未以其他方式进行补充,因而未按照适当的权威标准,提供该等标准规定的或允许的历史成本/恒定货币或现行成本信息,则发行人应提交补充信息,对价格变动对其财务状况和经营成果产生的影响进行量化。

(d)不论选择何种货币作为报表的货币单位,发行人均应分别计量其自身的交易,以及发行人合并财务报表所涵盖的不处于恶性通货膨胀环境的每一重大运营单位(如各分公司、部门、子公司、合营公司和类似实体)的交易,使用的货币应为发行人或该运营单位业务所在的主要经济环境的特定货币。按上述规定计算得出的资产和负债应按资产负债表日的汇率折算成报表货币;所有收入、费用、收益和损失均应按照交易当时的汇率(或者,如果适当,按该期间的加权平均汇率)折算;且汇率变化对折算造成的所有影响均应作为股东权益中一项单独要素列入(“累计折算调整”)。就本款而言,某一运营单位的主要经济环境的货币通常为该环境内产生现金和支出现金时采用的主要货币;恶性通货膨胀环境是指最近3年内累计通货膨胀率基本达到或超过100%的环境。采用的方法与本款规定不同的,应按《20-F表格》第17(c)(2)条(本章第249.220f节)的规定进行量化。

(e)对于发行人提供财务信息的所有报告期,发行人的主要财务报表应统一使用同一货币单位。如果财务报表的货币单位与此前向证券交易委员会提交的财务报表的货币单位不同,发行人应重新编制其财务报表,且重新编制之后,应达到如下效果:如同其之前提交的所有财务报表至少从最早一期报告期开始,即已采用新货币单位。变更报表货币的决定及变更的理由应在变更发生期间的财务报表的附注中披露。

[《联邦公报》第59卷第65631页,1994年12月20日,修正索引:《联邦公报》第64卷第53908页,1999年10月5日。]

Consolidated and Combined Financial Statements

§210.3A–01 Application of §210.3A–01 to §210.3A–05.

Sections 210.3A–01 to 210.3A–05 shall govern the presentation of consolidated and combined financial statements.

[44 FR 19386, Apr. 3, 1979. Redesignated at 45 FR 63687, Sept. 25, 1980, and amended at 50 FR 25215, June 18, 1985]

§210.3A–02 Consolidated financial statements of the registrant and its subsidiaries.

In deciding upon consolidation policy, the registrant must consider what financial presentation is most meaningful in the circumstances and should follow in the consolidated financial statements principles of inclusion or exclusion which will clearly exhibit the financial position and results of operations of the registrant. There is a presumption that consolidated statements are more meaningful than separate statements and that they are usually necessary for a fair presentation when one entity directly or indirectly has a controlling financial interest in another entity. Other particular facts and circumstances may require combined financial statements, an equity method of accounting, or valuation allowances in order to achieve a fair presentation. In any case, the disclosures required by §210.3A–03 should clearly explain the accounting policies followed by the registrant in this area, including the circumstances involved in any departure from the normal practice of consolidating majority owned subsidiaries and not consolidating entities that are less than majority owned. Among the factors that the registrant should consider in determining the most meaningful presentation are the following:

(a) *Majority ownership:* Generally, registrants shall consolidate entities that are majority owned and shall not consolidate entities that are not majority owned. The determination of *majority ownership* requires a careful analysis of the facts and circumstances of a particular relationship among entities. In rare situations, consolidation of a majority owned subsidiary may not result in a fair presentation, because the registrant, in substance, does not have a controlling financial interest (for example, when the subsidiary is in legal reorganization or in bankruptcy). In other situations, consolidation of an entity, notwithstanding the lack of technical majority ownership, is necessary to present fairly the financial position and results of operations of the registrant, because of the existence of a parent–subsidiary relationship by means other than record ownership of voting stock.

(b) *Different fiscal periods:* Generally, registrants shall not consolidate any entity whose financial statements are as of a date or for periods substantially different from those of the registrant. Rather, the earnings or losses of such entities should be reflected in the registrant's financial statements on the equity method of accounting.

合并和汇总财务报表

第210.3A-01节　第210.3A-01~210.3A-05节的适用范围

合并和汇总财务报表的列报应遵循第210.3A-01~210.3A-05节的规定。

[《联邦公报》第44卷第19386页,1979年4月3日,重新公布索引:《联邦公报》第45卷第63687页,1980年9月25日,修正索引:《联邦公报》第50卷第25215页,1985年6月18日。]

第210.3A-02节　注册人及其子公司的合并财务报表

在确定并表政策时,注册人须考虑在具体情形下采取何种财务列报方式最有意义,并且在确定其所提交的合并财务报表应纳入或排除的子公司时,应遵循一定的原则,即合并报表应能够明确反映注册人的财务状况和经营成果。编制合并财务报表系基于如下假设:合并报表较单独报表更有意义,并且通常只有合并报表才能公允反映一个实体直接或间接拥有另一实体控制性经济权益的情形。在其他特定事实和情形下,则可能需要采用汇总财务报表、权益核算法或估价备抵才能公允地反映所涉权益。在任何情形下,第210.3A-03节要求作出的披露均应清晰地说明注册人在该领域所遵循的会计政策,包括偏离一般惯例——控股子公司纳入并表范围、非控股实体不纳入并表范围——的情况。注册人在确定最有意义的列报方式时应考虑的因素包括:

(a)控股所有权:一般而言,注册人应将其控股实体纳入并表范围,非控股实体则不纳入并表范围。在判断是否拥有"控股所有权"之时,应根据所涉实体之间具体关系的事实和情形进行仔细分析。在少数情形下,合并控股子公司的财务报表未必能实现公允列报,因为注册人可能实际上并不持有控制性经济权益(如子公司处于合法的重组或破产程序之下的情形)。在另一些情形下,尽管从技术上来讲,两者并不存在控股关系,但是,由于表决股登记所有权以外的原因形成了母子公司关系,则将另一个实体纳入并表范围,对于公允反映注册人的财务状况和经营成果而言仍属必要。

(b)会计期间不同的情形:一般而言,注册人不应将财务报表日或报告期与其迥异的任何实体纳入并表范围。该等些实体的盈利或亏损应通过权益核算法在注册人的财务报表中反映。但是:

However:

(1) A difference in fiscal periods does not of itself justify the exclusion of an entity from consolidation. It ordinarily is feasible for such entity to prepare, for consolidation purposes, statements for a period which corresponds with or closely approaches the fiscal year of the registrant. Where the difference is not more than 93 days, it is usually acceptable to use, for consolidation purposes, such entity's statements for its fiscal period. Such difference, when it exists, should be disclosed as follows: the closing date of the entity should be expressly indicated, and the necessity for the use of different closing dates should be briefly explained. Furthermore, recognition should be given by disclosure or otherwise to the effect of intervening events which materially affect the financial position or results of operations.

(2) Notwithstanding the 93-day provision specified in paragraph (b)(1) of this section, in connection with the retroactive combination of financial statements of entities following a combination between entities under common control, the financial statements of the constituents may be combined even if their respective fiscal periods do not end within 93 days, except that the financial statements for the latest fiscal year shall be recast to dates which do not differ by more than 93 days, if practicable. Disclosure shall be made of the periods combined and of the sales or revenues, net income before extraordinary items and net income of any interim periods excluded from or included more than once in results of operations as a result of such recasting.

(c) *Bank Holding Company Act:* Registrants shall not consolidate any subsidiary or group of subsidiaries of a registrant subject to the Bank Holding Company Act of 1956 as amended as to which (1) a decision requiring divestiture has been made; or (2) there is substantial likelihood that divestiture will be necessary in order to comply with provisions of the Bank Holding Company Act.

(d) *Foreign subsidiaries*: Due consideration shall be given to the propriety of consolidating with domestic corporations foreign subsidiaries which are operated under political, economic or currency restrictions. If consolidated, disclosure should be made as to the effect, insofar as this can reasonably be determined, of foreign exchange restrictions upon the consolidated financial position and operating results of the registrant and its subsidiaries.

[51 FR 17330, May 12, 1986, as amended at 74 FR 18615, Apr. 23, 2009]

§210.3A -03 Statement as to principles of consolidation or combination followed.

(a) A brief description of the principles followed in consolidating or combining the separate financial statements, including the principles followed in determining the inclusion

(1)会计期间的差异本身并不足以构成将某个实体排除在并表范围之外的理由。对该实体而言,为了并表目的而编制与注册人的会计年度相符的或相近的期间的财务报表一般是可行的。如果差异不超过93日,通常可以接受在并表时采用该等实体按自身会计期间编制的报表。存在上述差异时,应按如下规定进行披露:应明确说明实体的结账日,同时简要说明使用不同结账日的必要性。此外,对财务状况或经营成果造成重大影响的干预事件亦应披露,或通过其他方式予以说明。

(2)尽管有本节第(b)(1)款所述93日差异的规定,受同一控制的不同实体进行并表后,追溯汇总其财务报表时,即使各自的会计期间结束日相差超过93日,各实体的财务报表依然可以汇总,但是,在可行的情形下,各实体最后一会计年度的财务报表应重新编制,使其截止日期相差不超过93日。下列事项应予披露:汇总报告期、销售额或收入、未扣除非经常项目的净收益、由于重新编制财务报表导致被排除在经营成果之外或重复计入经营成果的任何中期报告期的净收益。

(c)《银行控股公司法》:注册人不应对受《1956年银行控股公司法》(修正版)管辖的下列任一子公司或任一组子公司进行财务报表合并:(1)已被作出剥离决定的子公司;或(2)为了符合《银行控股公司法》的规定极有可能需要剥离的子公司。

(d)外国子公司:对于经营活动受政治、经济或外汇限制的外国子公司财务报表是否适宜与国内公司的财务报表进行合并,应慎重考虑。合并财务报表的,只要可以合理确定外汇管制将对注册人及其子公司并表财务状况和经营成果产生的影响,即应披露该等影响。

[《联邦公报》第51卷第17330页,1986年5月12日,修正索引:《联邦公报》第74卷第18615页,2009年4月23日。]

第210.3A-03节 关于应遵循的合并或汇总原则的说明

(a)对于在合并或汇总各单独财务报表过程中所遵循的原则,应在相应财务报表的附注中简要说明,包括决定纳入或排除下列公司时所遵循的原则:(1)合并或汇总

or exclusion of (1) subsidiaries in consolidated or combined financial statements; and (2) companies in consolidated or combined financial statements, shall be stated in the notes to the respective financial statements.

(b) As to each consolidated financial statement and as to each combined financial statement, if there has been a change in the persons included or excluded in the corresponding statement for the preceding fiscal period filed with the Commission which has a material effect on the financial statements, the persons included and the persons excluded shall be disclosed. If there have been any changes in the respective fiscal periods of the persons included made during the periods of the report which have a material effect on the financial statements, indicate clearly such changes and the manner of treatment.

[37 FR 14597, July 21, 1972. Redesignated at 45 FR 63687, Sept. 25, 1980, and 46 FR 56179, Nov. 16, 1981]

§210.3A-04 Intercompany items and transactions.

In general, there shall be eliminated intercompany items and transactions between persons included in the (a) consolidated financial statements being filed and, as appropriate, (b) unrealized intercompany profits and losses on transactions between persons for which financial statements are being filed and persons the investment in which is presented in such statements by the equity method. If such eliminations are not made, a statement of the reasons and the methods of treatment shall be made.

[37 FR 14597, July 21, 1972. Redesignated at 46 FR 56179, Nov. 16, 1981]

§210.3A-05 Special requirements as to public utility holding companies.

There shall be shown in the consolidated balance sheet of a public utility holding company the difference between the amount at which the parent's investment is carried and the underlying book equity of subsidiaries as at the respective dates of acquisition.

[37 FR 14597, July 21, 1972. Redesignated at 45 FR 63687, Sept. 25, 1980, and 46 FR 56179, Nov. 16, 1981]

Rules of General Application

Source: Sections 210.4-01 through 210.4-10 appear at 45 FR 63669, Sept. 25, 1980, unless otherwise noted.

§210.4-01 Form, order, and terminology.

(a) Financial statements should be filed in such form and order, and should use such generally accepted terminology, as will best indicate their significance and character in the light of the provisions applicable thereto. The information required with respect to any statement shall be furnished as a minimum requirement to which shall be added such

财务报表中的子公司;以及(2)合并或汇总财务报表中的公司。

(b)对每份合并财务报表和每份汇总财务报表而言,如果和上一会计期间向证券交易委员会提交的相应报表相比,纳入或不纳入合并和汇总财务报表范围的主体发生了变化,且该变化对财务报表具有重大影响,则应对纳入或不纳入的主体进行披露。如果报告期内被纳入合并和汇总财务报表范围的主体各自的会计期间发生了对财务报表有重大影响的任何变化,应清楚说明该等变化以及相应的处理方式。

[《联邦公报》第37卷第14597页,1972年7月21日,重新公布索引:《联邦公报》第45卷第63687页,1980年9月25日;《联邦公报》第46卷第56179页,1981年11月16日。]

第210.3A-04节　公司间项目及交易

一般而言,(a)在提交合并财务报表之时,被纳入该等财务报表的不同主体之间的公司间项目和交易应相互抵消,此外,在适当情形下,(b)在提交财务报表之时,该等财务报表的会计主体和该等财务报表中按权益法核算的被投资主体,两者之间交易的未实现公司间损益应相互抵消。如未进行该等抵消,应说明相关原因以及相应的处理方式。

[《联邦公报》第37卷第14597页,1972年7月21日,重新公布索引:《联邦公报》第46卷第56179页,1981年11月16日。]

第210.3A-05节　关于公用事业控股公司的特别规定

在公用事业控股公司的合并资产负债表中应列示,在各个相应收购日,母公司投资的账面值与相对应的子公司权益账面值之间的差额。

[《联邦公报》第37卷第14597页,1972年7月21日,重新公布索引:《联邦公报》第45卷第63687页,1980年9月25日,以及《联邦公报》第46卷第56179页,1981年11月16日。]

一般性规则

行政规则来源:第210.4-01~210.4-10节刊载《联邦公报》第45卷第63669页,1980年9月25日,除非另有说明。

第210.4-01节　格式、顺序和术语

(a)注册人提交的财务报表所采用的格式、顺序及公认术语,应为根据相关规定的标准能够完美地体现其重要性和特征的格式、顺序及公认术语。报表的信息提供要求均为最低要求,必要时应根据报表编制时所处具体情形进一步补充重大信息,以确保按要求提供的报表不具误导性。

further material information as is necessary to make the required statements, in the light of the circumstances under which they are made, not misleading.

(1) Financial statements filed with the Commission which are not prepared in accordance with generally accepted accounting principles will be presumed to be misleading or inaccurate, despite footnote or other disclosures, unless the Commission has otherwise provided. This article and other articles of Regulation S-X provide clarification of certain disclosures which must be included in any event, in financial statements filed with the Commission.

(2) In all filings of foreign private issuers (see §230.405 of this chapter), except as stated otherwise in the applicable form, the financial statements may be prepared according to a comprehensive set of accounting principles, other than those generally accepted in the United States or International Financial Reporting Standards as issued by the International Accounting Standards Board, if a reconciliation to U.S. Generally Accepted Accounting Principles and the provisions of Regulation S-X of the type specified in Item 18 of Form 20-F (§249.220f of this chapter) is also filed as part of the financial statements. Alternatively, the financial statements may be prepared according to U.S. Generally Accepted Accounting Principles or International Financial Reporting Standards as issued by the International Accounting Standards Board.

(3)(i) Notwithstanding the effective dates set forth in Statement of Financial Accounting Standards No. 123 (revised 2004), *Share-Based Payment* ("Statement No. 123R"), financial statements shall be prepared in accordance with Statement No. 123R beginning with:

(A) The first interim or annual reporting period of the registrant's first fiscal year beginning on or after June 15, 2005, provided the registrant does not file as a smaller reporting company; and

(B) The first interim or annual reporting period of the registrant's first fiscal year beginning on or after December 15, 2005, provided the registrant files as a smaller reporting company.

(ii) For periods prior to the effective dates set forth in this paragraph, both Statement No. 123R and Statement of Financial Accounting Standards No. 123, *Accounting for Stock-Based Compensation* (October 1995), shall be considered to be generally accepted accounting principles.

(b) All money amounts required to be shown in financial statements may be expressed in whole dollars or multiples thereof, as appropriate:*Provided,* That, when stated in other than whole dollars, an indication to that effect is inserted immediately beneath the caption of the statement or schedule, at the top of the money columns, or at an appropriate point in narrative material.

(1)向证券交易委员会提交的财务报表,不论是否提供了任何相关脚注或进行了任何其他披露,只要不是根据公认会计原则编制的,即视为具有误导性或不准确,但证券交易委员会另有规定的除外。本条及《S-X管理办法》的其他条款进一步明确规定了在任何情形下在向证券交易委员会提交的财务报表中均须披露的事项。

(2)对于外国私募发行人提交的所有财务报表(见本章第230.405节),除非相关表格另有相反规定,否则,财务报表可以按照美国公认会计原则或国际会计准则委员会颁布的国际会计报告准则以外的一套综合会计原则编制,前提是,在提交该等财务报表时,一并提交根据美国公认会计原则和《S-X管理办法》作出的《20-F表格》第18条(本章第249.220f节)所述类型的调整。但是,外国私募发行人也可以选择按照美国公认会计原则或根据国际会计准则委员会颁布的国际会计报告准则编制财务报表。

(3)(i)尽管有《财务会计准则公告第123号》(2004年修订版)、"股票薪酬"("《第123R号公告》")对生效日的规定,财务报表仍应按照《第123R号公告》编制,起始报告期应为:

(A)始于2005年6月15日或之后的注册人首个会计年度的首个中期报告期或年度报告期,前提是注册人并非以小型报告公司的身份提交财务报表;及

(B)始于2005年12月15日或之后的注册人首个会计年度的首个中期报告期或年度报告期,前提是注册人并非以小型报告公司的身份提交财务报表。

(ii)对在本款规定的生效日之前的报告期而言,《第123R号公告》和《财务会计准则公告第123号》[《股份薪酬的会计处理》(1995年10月)]均应视为公认会计原则。

(b)按规定应在财务报表中列明的所有货币金额均可视情形用美元整数或其整数倍数表示,但是,如果货币金额不是用美元整数表示的,应在紧接着报表或附表的标题下方、金额栏的最上方或叙述性文字的适当位置对此加以标注。

(c) Negative amounts (red figures) shall be shown in a manner which clearly distinguishes the negative attribute. When determining methods of display, consideration should be given to the limitations of reproduction and microfilming processes.

[45 FR 63669, Sept. 25, 1980, as amended at 47 FR 54767, Dec. 6, 1982; 70 FR 20719, Apr. 21, 2005; 73 FR 953, Jan. 4, 2008; 73 FR 1009, Jan. 4, 2008]

§210.4–02 Items not material.

If the amount which would otherwise be required to be shown with respect to any item is not material, it need not be separately set forth. The combination of insignificant amounts is permitted.

§210.4–03 Inapplicable captions and omission of unrequired or inapplicable financial statements.

(a) No caption should be shown in any financial statement as to which the items and conditions are not present.

(b) Financial statements not required or inapplicable because the required matter is not present need not be filed.

(c) The reasons for the omission of any required financial statements shall be indicated.

§210.4–04 Omission of substantially identical notes.

If a note covering substantially the same subject matter is required with respect to two or more financial statements relating to the same or affiliated persons, for which separate sets of notes are presented, the required information may be shown in a note to only one of such statements: *Provided,* That a clear and specific reference thereto is made in each of the other statements with respect to which the note is required.

§§210.4–05–210.4–06 [Reserved]

§210.4–07 Discount on shares.

Discount on shares, or any unamortized balance thereof, shall be shown separately as a deduction from the applicable account(s) as circumstances require.

§210.4–08 General notes to financial statements.

If applicable to the person for which the financial statements are filed, the following shall be set forth on the face of the appropriate statement or in appropriately captioned notes. The information shall be provided for each statement required to be filed, except that the information required by paragraphs (b), (c), (d), (e) and (f) shall be provided as of the most recent audited balance sheet being filed and for paragraph (j) as specified therein. When specific statements are presented separately, the pertinent notes shall accompany such statements unless cross–referencing is appropriate.

(a) *Principles of consolidation or combination.* With regard to consolidated or combined

(c)负数(赤字)应以能显著表明其负数特性的方式显示。在确定显示方式时，应考虑复印和缩印时将遇到的限制。

[《联邦公报》第45卷第63669页，1980年9月25日，修正索引：《联邦公报》第47卷第54767页，1982年12月6日；《联邦公报》第70卷第20719页，2005年4月21日；《联邦公报》第73卷第953页，2008年1月4日；《联邦公报》第73卷第1009页，2008年1月4日。]

第210.4–02节　非重大项目

任何与非重大项目相关的金额均不必单列。允许对非重大金额进行合并。

第210.4–03节　不适用项目及不要求提供或不适用的财务报表

(a)会计科目下不存在任何相关项目和条件的，财务报表不应列示该等科目。

(b)不必提交由于规定事项不存在从而无义务提交的或不适用的财务报表。

(c)未提供规定的财务报表的，均应说明原因。

第210.4–04节　不必提供实质相同的附注

如果同一主体或控制性关联主体的两份(含)以上财务报表附注(指单列的附注)涵盖主题实质相同，则要求提供的信息可以只在一份报表的附注中体现：前提是，需要提供该等附注的其他每份报表均须提供清晰、具体的索引。

第210.4–05~210.4–06节　[保留]

第210.4–07节　股票贴水

根据情况需要，股票贴水或其任何未摊销余额均应作为相应报表的扣除项予以单列。

第210.4–08节　一般财务报表附注

下列信息如适用于编制财务报表的会计主体，应在相应的报表正文或冠以适当科目名称的附注中列出。信息提供的目的是编制按规定应提交的报表，但是按照第(b)款、第(c)款、第(d)款、第(e)款和第(f)款规定提供的信息应为截至最近一期经审计的资产负债表日的最新信息，第(j)款规定的信息应按该款规定提供。单独编制的具体报表应附有相应附注，但可以进行适当的交叉引用的除外。

(a)合并或汇总原则。关于合并或汇总财务报表，参见第210.3A–01~210.3A–08节

financial statements, refer to §§210.3A-01 to 3A-08 for requirements for supplemental information in notes to the financial statements.

(b) *Assets subject to lien.* Assets mortgaged, pledged, or otherwise subject to lien, and the approximate amounts thereof, shall be designated and the obligations collateralized briefly identified.

(c) *Defaults.* The facts and amounts concerning any default in principal, interest, sinking fund, or redemption provisions with respect to any issue of securities or credit agreements, or any breach of covenant of a related indenture or agreement, which default or breach existed at the date of the most recent balance sheet being filed and which has not been subsequently cured, shall be stated in the notes to the financial statements. If a default or breach exists but acceleration of the obligation has been waived for a stated period of time beyond the date of the most recent balance sheet being filed, state the amount of the obligation and the period of the waiver.

(d) *Preferred shares.* (1) Aggregate preferences on involuntary liquidation, if other than par or stated value, shall be shown parenthetically in the equity section of the balance sheet.

(2) Disclosure shall be made of any restriction upon retained earnings that arises from the fact that upon involuntary liquidation the aggregate preferences of the preferred shares exceeds the par or stated value of such shares.

(e) *Restrictions which limit the payment of dividends by the registrant.* (1) Describe the most significant restrictions, other than as reported under paragraph (d) of this section, on the payment of dividends by the registrant, indicating their sources, their pertinent provisions, and the amount of retained earnings or net income restricted or free of restrictions.

(2) Disclose the amount of consolidated retained earnings which represents undistributed earnings of 50 percent or less owned persons accounted for by the equity method.

(3) The disclosures in paragraphs (e)(3)(i) and (ii) in this section shall be provided when the restricted net assets of consolidated and unconsolidated subsidiaries and the parent's equity in the undistributed earnings of 50 percent or less owned persons accounted for by the equity method together exceed 25 percent of consolidated net assets as of the end of the most recently completed fiscal year. For purposes of this test, restricted net assets of subsidiaries shall mean that amount of the registrant's proportionate share of net assets (after intercompany eliminations) reflected in the balance sheets of its consolidated and unconsolidated subsidiaries as of the end of the most recent fiscal year which may not be transferred to the parent company in the form of loans, advances or cash dividends by the subsidiaries without the consent of a third party (*i.e.* ,

关于要求在财务报表附注中提供的补充信息的规定。

(b)设有留置权的资产。应指明设有抵押、质押或留置权的资产及其大致金额,同时简要列明受担保的债务。

(c)违约。对于违反任何证券发行或信贷协议的本金、利息、偿债基金或回赎条款的任何违约事实和金额,或者任何违反相关信托契约或协议中的约定的情形,如果违约在提交的最近一期资产负债表日即已存在且发生后未予补救,应当在财务报表附注中说明。如果存在不履约或违约情形,但守约方放弃要求违约方提前履约,且豁免期超过了所提交的最近一期资产负债表日,则须注明债务金额和豁免的期限。

(d)优先股。(1)强制清算时优先受偿股份的合计金额如果不以票面价值或设定价值显示,则应在资产负债表的权益栏中以括号注明。

(2)强制清算时优先股的优先受偿金额合计超出优先股票面价值或设定价值,对留存盈利造成任何限制的,均应披露。

(e)注册人的股息支付限制。(1)说明注册人股息支付受到的最大限制[本节第(d)款项下报告的限制除外],注明限制的来源、相关规定以及受限或不受限的留存盈利或净收益的金额。

(2)披露并表留存盈利的金额,该金额应代表以权益法核算的50%或以下股权被控主体的未分配盈利。

(3)并表子公司和非并表子公司的受限净资产加上母公司在按权益法核算的50%或以下股权被控主体未分配盈利中所享有的权益之和,超过最近结束的一个会计年度年末并表净资产25%的,应按照本节第(e)(3)(i)款和第(e)(3)(ii)款的规定进行披露。在进行测试,以判断是否符合上述标准时,子公司的受限净资产指并表子公司和非并表子公司最近一个会计年度年末的资产负债表所反映的,注册人在子公司净资产中按比例持有的数额(该数额应为抵消公司间交易之后的数额),该金额未经第三方(即贷款人、监管机构、外国政府等)同意,不得以贷款、垫款或现金股息形式从子公司转移至母公司。在进行上述测试时,并非所有关于资产可转移性的限制均将视为限制,只有由第三方对子公司资金转移至其实体外的能力施加的特定限制才视为上文规定的限制。例如,子公司提供其某些资产作为自身债务担保的,并不构成本节规则

lender, regulatory agency, foreign government, etc.). Not all limitations on transferability of assets are considered to be restrictions for purposes of this test, which considers only specific third party restrictions on the ability of subsidiaries to transfer funds outside of the entity. For example, the presence of subsidiary debt which is secured by certain of the subsidiary's assets does not constitute a restriction under this rule. However, if there are any loan provisions prohibiting dividend payments, loans or advances to the parent by a subsidiary, these are considered restrictions for purposes of computing restricted net assets. When a loan agreement requires that a subsidiary maintain certain working capital, net tangible asset, or net asset levels, or where formal compensating arrangements exist, there is considered to be a restriction under the rule because the lender's intent is normally to preclude the transfer by dividend or otherwise of funds to the parent company. Similarly, a provision which requires that a subsidiary reinvest all of its earnings is a restriction, since this precludes loans, advances or dividends in the amount of such undistributed earnings by the entity. Where restrictions on the amount of funds which may be loaned or advanced differ from the amount restricted as to transfer in the form of cash dividends, the amount least restrictive to the subsidiary shall be used. Redeemable preferred stocks (§210.5-02.27) and noncontrolling interests shall be deducted in computing net assets for purposes of this test.

(i) Describe the nature of any restrictions on the ability of consolidated subsidiaries and unconsolidated subsidiaries to transfer funds to the registrant in the form of cash dividends, loans or advances (*i.e.*, borrowing arrangements, regulatory restraints, foreign government, etc.).

(ii) Disclose separately the amounts of such restricted net assets for unconsolidated subsidiaries and consolidated subsidiaries as of the end of the most recently completed fiscal year.

(f) *Significant changes in bonds, mortgages and similar debt.* Any significant changes in the authorized or issued amounts of bonds, mortgages and similar debt since the date of the latest balance sheet being filed for a particular person or group shall be stated.

(g) *Summarized financial information of subsidiaries not consolidated and 50 percent or less owned persons.* (1) The summarized information as to assets, liabilities and results of operations as detailed in §210.1-02(bb) shall be presented in notes to the financial statements on an individual or group basis for:

(i) Subsidiaries not consolidated; or

(ii) For 50 percent or less owned persons accounted for by the equity method by the registrant or by a subsidiary of the registrant, if the criteria in §210.1-02 (w) for a significant subsidiary are met:

(A) Individually by any subsidiary not consolidated or any 50% or less owned

中的限制。但是,如果任何贷款条款禁止子公司向母公司支付股息、提供贷款或垫款,该等条款将在受限净资产的计算中视为限制。某一贷款协议要求子公司维持一定的流动资金、净有形资产或净资产水平,或者存在正式的补偿安排时,该等规定将视为本节规则中的限制,因为贷款人的意图通常是通过上述规定限制子公司将资金通过股息或其他方式转移给母公司。同样,要求子公司将其所有盈利用于再投资的规定也是一种限制,因为这排除了该实体将未分配盈利用于提供贷款、垫款或支付股息的可能性。贷款或垫款金额上限和可以以现金股息形式转移的资金的金额上限存在差异时,应采用对子公司限制较低的金额。在进行本测试时,计算净资产时应扣除可回赎优先股(见第210.5-02.27节)及非控制权益。

(i)并表和非并表子公司通过现金股息、贷款或垫款向注册人转移资金的能力受到限制(即借款安排、监管限制、外国政府等)的,应对任何限制的性质进行说明。

(ii)单独披露并表和非并表子公司最近结束的一个会计年度年末的受限净资产金额。

(f)债券、抵押及类似债务的重大变化。某特定主体或集团在所提交的最近一期资产负债表日后,其授权发行或实际发行的债券、抵押和类似债务的金额发生重大变化的,应予说明。

(g)非并表子公司和50%或以下股权被控主体的摘要财务信息。(1)对于下列公司,应在财务报表附注中单独或集中列报第210.1-02(bb)节详细规定的资产、负债和经营成果的简要信息:

(i)非并表子公司;或

(ii)注册人或注册人的子公司持股50%或以下的主体(按权益法核算),前提是下列主体按下述相关条件满足第210.1-02(w)节规定的重要子公司标准:

(A)任一非并表子公司或任一50%或以下股权被控主体满足该等标准;或

person; or

(B) On an aggregated basis by any combination of such subsidiaries and persons.

(2) Summarized financial information shall be presented insofar as is practicable as of the same dates and for the same periods as the audited consolidated financial statements provided and shall include the disclosures prescribed by §210.1-02(bb). Summarized information of subsidiaries not consolidated shall not be combined for disclosure purposes with the summarized information of 50 percent or less owned persons.

(h) *Income tax expense.* (1) Disclosure shall be made in the income statement or a note thereto, of (i) the components of income (loss) before income tax expense (benefit) as either domestic or foreign; (ii) the components of income tax expense, including (A) taxes currently payable and (B) the net tax effects, as applicable, of timing differences (indicate separately the amount of the estimated tax effect of each of the various types of timing differences, such as depreciation, warranty costs, etc., where the amount of each such tax effect exceeds five percent of the amount computed by multiplying the income before tax by the applicable statutory Federal income tax rate; other differences may be combined.)

Note: Amounts applicable to United States Federal income taxes, to foreign income taxes and the other income taxes shall be stated separately for each major component. Amounts applicable to foreign income (loss) and amounts applicable to foreign or other income taxes which are less than five percent of the total of income before taxes or the component of tax expense, respectively, need not be separately disclosed. For purposes of this rule, foreign income (loss) is defined as income (loss) generated from a registrant's foreign operations, *i.e.*, operations that are *located outside* of the registrant's home country.

(2) Provide a reconciliation between the amount of reported total income tax expense (benefit) and the amount computed by multiplying the income (loss) before tax by the applicable statutory Federal income tax rate, showing the estimated dollar amount of each of the underlying causes for the difference. If no individual reconciling item amounts to more than five percent of the amount computed by multiplying the income before tax by the applicable statutory Federal income tax rate, and the total difference to be reconciled is less than five percent of such computed amount, no reconciliation need be provided unless it would be significant in appraising the trend of earnings. Reconciling items that are individually less than five percent of the computed amount may be aggregated in the reconciliation. The reconciliation may be presented in percentages rather than in dollar amounts. Where the reporting person is a foreign entity, the income tax rate in that person's country of domicile should normally be used in making the above computation, but different rates should not be used for subsidiaries or other segments of a reporting

(B)上述子公司和主体的任意组合经合并计算之后,满足该等标准。

(2)在可行范围内,简要财务信息的日期和报告期均应与提供的经审计的财务报表相同,并应包括第210.1-02(bb)节规定的披露事项。在披露之时,非并表子公司的简要信息不应与50%或以下股权被控主体的简要信息合并。

(h)所得税费用。(1)应在损益表或其附注中披露:(i)扣除所得税费用(利益)前的损益构成要素,包括国内和国外损益构成;(ii)所得税费用的构成要素,包括(A)当前应付税款,和(B)如适用,时间差异的净纳税影响(当任一类型的时间差异——如折旧、保修成本等——的预期纳税影响数超过税前收益乘以适用法定联邦所得税率得出的金额的5%时,须单独注明该等预期纳税影响数;其他差异则可以合并)。

注:适用联邦所得税、外国所得税和其他所得税的金额,其每一主要组成要素均应单列。可计入国外损益的金额以及适用外国所得税或其他所得税的金额,如低于税前收益总额或税款支出要素的5%,则在披露时不必单列。就本规则而言,"国外损益"系指注册人在外国的业务(即位于注册人母国境外的业务)产生的损益。

(2)所报告的总所得税费用(利益),与税前损益乘以适用法定联邦所得税率的乘积两者之间存在差异的,应进行调整,列明造成差异的每一相关原因的估算金额。如果每一单个调整项目均不超过税前损益乘以适用法定联邦所得税率的乘积的5%,并且需调整之总差额低于上述计算结果的5%,则不必进行调整,但调整对盈利趋势评估具有重大影响的除外。单项小于5%的调整项可以累计进行调整。调整可以用百分比而非金额表示。如果报告人为外国实体,通常应使用该实体住所地国内所得税率进行上述计算,但报告人的子公司或其他部门不应使用不同的税率。如果报告人采用的是美国联邦公司所得税率以外的税率,应披露采用的税率及使用理由。

entity. When the rate used by a reporting person is other than the United States Federal corporate income tax rate, the rate used and the basis for using such rate shall be disclosed.

(3) Paragraphs (h)(1) and (2) of this section shall be applied in the following manner to financial statements which reflect the adoption of Statement of Financial Accounting Standards 109, Accounting for Income Taxes.

(i) The disclosures required by paragraph (h)(1)(ii) of this section and by the parenthetical instruction at the end of paragraph (h)(1) of this section and by the introductory sentence of paragraph (h)(2) of this section shall not apply.

(ii) The instructional note between paragraphs (h)(1) and(2) of this section and the balance of the requirements of paragraphs (h)(1) and (2) of this section shall continue to apply.

(i) *Warrants or rights outstanding.* Information with respect to warrants or rights outstanding at the date of the related balance sheet shall be set forth as follows:

(1) Title of issue of securities called for by warrants or rights.

(2) Aggregate amount of securities called for by warrants or rights outstanding.

(3) Date from which warrants or rights are exercisable.

(4) Price at which warrant or right is exercisable.

(j) [Reserved]

(k) *Related party transactions which affect the financial statements.* (1) Related party transactions should be identified and the amounts stated on the face of the balance sheet, income statement, or statement of cash flows.

(2) In cases where separate financial statements are presented for the registrant, certain investees, or subsidiaries, separate disclosure shall be made in such statements of the amounts in the related consolidated financial statements which are (i) eliminated and (ii) not eliminated. Also, any intercompany profits or losses resulting from transactions with related parties and not eliminated and the effects thereof shall be disclosed.

(l) [Reserved]

(m) *Repurchase and reverse repurchase agreements* —(1) *Repurchase agreements (assets sold under agreements to repurchase).* (i) If, as of the most recent balance sheet date, the carrying amount (or market value, if higher than the carrying amount or if there is no carrying amount) of the securities or other assets sold under agreements to repurchase (*repurchase agreements*) exceeds 10% of total assets, disclose separately in the balance sheet the aggregate amount of liabilities incurred pursuant to repurchase agreements including accrued interest payable thereon.

(ii)(A) If, as of the most recent balance sheet date, the carrying amount (or market value, if higher than the carrying amount) of securities or other assets sold under

(3)本节第(h)(1)款和第(h)(2)款应以下列方式适用于财务报表,以反映《财务会计准则公告第109号——所得税会计》的适用。

(i)本节第(h)(1)(ii)款、本节第(h)(1)款款末的括号内的说明以及本节第(h)(2)款引导句所要求的披露不应适用。

(ii)本节第(h)(1)款和第(h)(2)款之间的指示性说明以及本节第(h)(1)款和第(h)(2)款的其他要求应继续适用。

(i)发行在外的认股权证或权利。对于在相关的资产负债表日发行在外的认股权证,应载明如下信息:

(1)认股权证或权利对应的发行证券的名称。

(2)认股权证或权利对应的发行在外的证券之累计金额。

(3)认股权证或权利可行权的起始日期。

(4)认股权证或权利的行权价格。

(j)[保留]

(k)影响财务报表的关联交易。(1)关联交易及交易金额应于资产负债表、损益表和现金流量表的正文注明。

(2)如果注册人、某些被投资者或子公司编制了单独财务报表,在该等报表中应单独披露相关的合并财务报表中(i)已进行抵消的金额;和(ii)未进行抵消的金额。此外,由于关联交易导致的、未进行抵消的任何公司间损益及其影响数亦应披露。

(l)[保留]

(m)回购和逆回购协议——(1)回购协议(根据回购协议出售的资产)。(i)如果根据回购协议("回购协议")出售的证券或其他资产在最近一期资产负债表日的账面金额(或市场价值,如市场价值高于账面金额或不存在账面金额)超过总资产的10%,应在资产负债表中单独披露由于回购协议产生的累计债务金额,包括应计应付利息金额。

(ii)(A)如果根据回购协议出售的证券或其他资产[本节第(m)(1)(ii)(B)款规定的证券或资产除外]在最近一期资产负债表日的账面金额(或市场价值,如市场价值

repurchase agreements, other than securities or assets specified in paragraph (m)(1)(ii)(B) of this section, exceeds 10% of total assets, disclose in an appropriately captioned footnote containing a tabular presentation, segregated as to type of such securities or assets sold under agreements to repurchase (e.g., U.S. Treasury obligations, U.S. Government agency obligations and loans), the following information as of the balance sheet date for each such agreement or group of agreements (other than agreements involving securities or assets specified in paragraph (m)(1)(ii)(B) of this section) maturing (1) overnight; (2) term up to 30 days; (3) term of 30 to 90 days; (4) term over 90 days and (5) demand:

(*i*) The carrying amount and market value of the assets sold under agreement to repurchase, including accrued interest plus any cash or other assets on deposit under the repurchase agreements; and

(*ii*) The repurchase liability associated with such transaction or group of transactions and the interest rate(s) thereon.

(B) For purposes of paragraph (m)(1)(ii)(A) of this section only, do not include securities or other assets for which unrealized changes in market value are reported in current income or which have been obtained under reverse repurchase agreements.

(iii) If, as of the most recent balance sheet date, the amount at risk under repurchase agreements with any individual counterparty or group of related counterparties exceeds 10% of stockholders' equity (or in the case of investment companies, net asset value), disclose the name of each such counterparty or group of related counterparties, the amount at risk with each, and the weighted average maturity of the repurchase agreements with each. The amount at risk under repurchase agreements is defined as the excess of carrying amount (or market value, if higher than the carrying amount or if there is no carrying amount) of the securities or other assets sold under agreement to repurchase, including accrued interest plus any cash or other assets on deposit to secure the repurchase obligation, over the amount of the repurchase liability (adjusted for accrued interest). (Cash deposits in connection with repurchase agreements shall not be reported as unrestricted cash pursuant to rule 5-02.1.)

(2) *Reverse repurchase agreements* (*assets purchased under agreements to resell*). (i) If, as of the most recent balance sheet date, the aggregate carrying amount of *reverse repurchase agreements* (securities or other assets purchased under agreements to resell) exceeds 10% of total assets: (A) Disclose separately such amount in the balance sheet; and (B) disclose in an appropriately captioned footnote: (1) The registrant's policy with regard to taking possession of securities or other assets purchased under agreements to resell; and (2) whether or not there are any provisions to ensure that the market value of the underlying assets remains sufficient to protect the registrant in the event of default by

高于账面金额)超过总资产的10%,应按照回购协议项下出售的证券的类型(如美国国库券、美国政府机构债务和贷款),针对到期日为(1)隔夜;(2)期限不超过30日;(3)期限在30~90日之间;(4)期限超过90日,和(5)即期的每一份或每一组协议[涉及本节第(m)(1)(ii)(B)款规定的证券或资产的协议除外],在适当的栏目标题下通过表式脚注披露截至资产负债表日的下列信息:

(*i*)根据回购协议出售的资产的账面金额和市场价值,包括应计利息加上回购协议项下已缴存的任何现金或其他资产;和

(*ii*)与该等交易或系列交易相关的回购义务和适用利率。

(B)仅就本节第(m)(1)(ii)(A)款而言,披露范围不包括已报告的作为当期收益一部分的未实现市场价值变化或者根据逆回购协议获得的证券或其他资产。

(iii)如果在最近一期资产负债表日,与任何单个对手方或一组关联对手方之间签订的回购协议中的风险金额超过股票持有人权益的10%(或超过投资公司资产净值的10%),应披露每一对手方或每组对手方的名称、与每一对手方或每组对手方相关的风险金额以及与每一对手方或每组对手方签订的回购协议的加权平均期限。回购协议的风险金额指在回购协议项下出售的证券或其他资产的账面金额(或市场价值,如市场价值高于账面金额或不存在账面金额),加上应计利息以及为了担保回购义务所缴存的现金或其他资产的总和,超出回购债务的金额(最终数额应根据应计利息进行调整)(担保回购协议项下的现金存款不得根据《5-02.1规则》作为非受限现金报告)。

(2)逆回购协议(根据转售协议购入的资产)。(i)如果在最近一期资产负债表日,"逆回购协议"的账面金额合计(在转售协议项下购入的证券或其他资产)超过总资产的10%,则应:(A)在资产负债表中单独披露上述金额;并(B)在适当栏目标题下的脚注中披露下列事项:(1)注册人关于占有在转售协议项下购入的证券或其他资产的政策;以及(2)是否存在任何条款可确保相关资产将留存足够的市场价值,以便在对手方违约时保护注册人,如果有,则应披露该等条款的性质。

the counterparty and if so, the nature of those provisions.

(ii) If, as of the most recent balance sheet date, the amount at risk under reverse repurchase agreements with any individual counterparty or group of related counterparties exceeds 10% of stockholders' equity (or in the case of investment companies, net asset value), disclose the name of each such counterparty or group of related counterparties, the amount at risk with each, and the weighted average maturity of the reverse repurchase agreements with each. The amount at risk under reverse repurchase agreements is defined as the excess of the carrying amount of the reverse repurchase agreements over the market value of assets delivered pursuant to the agreements by the counterparty to the registrant (or to a third party agent that has affirmatively agreed to act on behalf of the registrant) and not returned to the counterparty, exept in exchange for their approximate market value in a separate transaction.

(n) *Accounting policies for certain derivative instruments.* Disclosures regarding accounting policies shall include descriptions of the accounting policies used for derivative financial instruments and derivative commodity instruments and the methods of applying those policies that materially affect the determination of financial position, cash flows, or results of operation. This description shall include, to the extent material, each of the following items:

(1) A discussion of each method used to account for derivative financial instruments and derivative commodity instruments;

(2) The types of derivative financial instruments and derivative commodity instruments accounted for under each method;

(3) The criteria required to be met for each accounting method used, including a discussion of the criteria required to be met for hedge or deferral accounting and accrual or settlement accounting (e.g., whether and how risk reduction, correlation, designation, and effectiveness tests are applied);

(4) The accounting method used if the criteria specified in paragraph (n)(3) of this section are not met;

(5) The method used to account for terminations of derivatives designated as hedges or derivatives used to affect directly or indirectly the terms, fair values, or cash flows of a designated item;

(6) The method used to account for derivatives when the designated item matures, is sold, is extinguished, or is terminated. In addition, the method used to account for derivatives designated to an anticipated transaction, when the anticipated transaction is no longer likely to occur; and

(7) Where and when derivative financial instruments and derivative commodity instruments, and their related gains and losses, are reported in the statements of financial

(ii)如果在最近一期资产负债表日,与任何单个对手方或多个关联对手方签订的逆回购协议中的风险金额超过股票持有人权益的10%(或超过投资公司资产净值的10%),应披露每一对手方或每组对手方的名称、与每一对手方或每组对手方相关的风险金额以及与每一对手方或每组对手方签订的逆回购协议加权平均期限。逆回购协议中的风险金额指逆回购协议账面金额超出对手方按照协议交付给注册人(或已确认同意代表注册人行事的第三方代理人)且尚未获得返还的资产市场价值的部分,但该等资产不包括在另一交易中按照与接近市价的价格交易的资产。

(n)某些衍生工具的会计政策。对会计政策进行披露时,应说明适用于衍生金融工具和衍生商品工具的会计政策,以及对确定财务状况、现金流量或经营成果有重大影响的会计政策的应用方法。如以下各项内容具有重大性,亦应包含在上述说明之中:

(1)关于每一种衍生金融工具和衍生商品工具的会计方法的讨论;

(2)每一种会计方法所对应的衍生金融工具和衍生商品工具的类型;

(3)使用的每一种会计方法所需达到的标准,包括关于套期保值(下称套期)或递延会计法以及权责发生制或结算制核算方法所需达到的标准的讨论(如是否以及如何降低风险、建立相关性、进行指定和开展有效性测试);

(4)未达到本节第(n)(3)款规定的标准时采用的会计方法;

(5)下列衍生品终止时的核算方法:被指定为套期工具的衍生品,或被用于直接或间接影响被套期项目之期限、公允价值或现金流的衍生品;

(6)当被指定为套期工具的衍生品到期、出售、清偿或终止时的核算方法。此外,当预期交易不再可能发生时,为预期交易指定的衍生品的核算方法;及

(7)在何种情形下以及何时,衍生金融工具和衍生商品工具以及相关的收益与损失应当在财务状况表、现金流量表和经营成果报表中进行报告。

position, cash flows, and results of operations.

Instructions to paragraph (n): 1. For purposes of this paragraph (n), derivative financial instruments and derivative commodity instruments (collectively referred to as "derivatives") are defined as follows:

(i) *Derivative financial instruments* have the same meaning as defined by generally accepted accounting principles (see e.g., Financial Accounting Standards Board ("FASB"), *Statement of Financial Accounting Standards No. 119, "Disclosure about Derivative Financial Instruments and Fair Value of Financial Instruments,"* ("FAS 119") paragraphs 5-7, (October 1994)), and include futures, forwards, swaps, options, and other financial instruments with similar characteristics.

(ii) *Derivative commodity instruments* include, to the extent such instruments are not derivative financial instruments, commodity futures, commodity forwards, commodity swaps, commodity options, and other commodity instruments with similar characteristics that are permitted by contract or business custom to be settled in cash or with another financial instrument. For purposes of this paragraph, settlement in cash includes settlement in cash of the net change in value of the derivative commodity instrument (e.g., net cash settlement based on changes in the price of the underlying commodity).

2. For purposes of paragraphs (n)(2), (n)(3), (n)(4), and (n)(7), the required disclosures should address separately derivatives entered into for trading purposes and derivatives entered into for purposes other than trading. For purposes of this paragraph, *trading purposes* has the same meaning as defined by generally accepted accounting principles (see, e.g., FAS 119, paragraph 9a (October 1994)).

3. For purposes of paragraph (n)(6), *anticipated transactions* means transactions (other than transactions involving existing assets or liabilities or transactions necessitated by existing firm commitments) an enterprise expects, but is not obligated, to carry out in the normal course of business (see, e.g., FASB, *Statement of Financial Accounting Standards No. 80, "Accounting for Futures Contracts,"* paragraph 9, (August 1984)).

4. Registrants should provide disclosures required under paragraph (n) in filings with the Commission that include financial statements of fiscal periods ending after June 15, 1997.

[45 FR 63669, Sept. 25, 1980, as amended at 46 FR 56179, Nov. 16, 1981; 50 FR 25215, June 18, 1985; 50 FR 49532, Dec. 3, 1985; 51 FR 3770, Jan. 30, 1986; 57 FR 45293, Oct. 1, 1992; 59 FR 65636, Dec. 20, 1994; 62 FR 6063, Feb. 10, 1997; 74 FR 18615, Apr. 23, 2009]

关于第(n)款的说明:1. 就本第(n)款而言,衍生金融工具和衍生商品工具(合称“衍生品”)定义如下:

(i)“衍生金融工具”一词的含义以公认会计原则之定义为准[如请参见财务会计准则委员会(FASB)发布的《财务会计准则公告第119号——“关于衍生金融工具和金融工具公允价值的披露”》(FAS 119)第5款至第7款(1994年10月)]。“衍生金融工具”包括期货、远期、互换、期权和具有类似特性的其他金融工具。

(ii)“衍生商品工具”包括不属于衍生金融工具的商品期货、商品远期、商品互换、商品期权,以及根据合同或商业习惯的约定允许以现金或另一种金融工具结算的具有类似特性的其他商品工具。就本款而言,现金结算包括以现金结算衍生商品工具价值的净变动值(如基于基础商品价格变化的净现金结算)。

2.就第(n)(2)款、第(n)(3)款、第(n)(4)款和第(n)(7)款而言,应区分以下两类披露:为交易目的达成的衍生品交易以及为非交易目的达成的衍生品交易。就本款而言,“交易目的”之定义以公认会计原则的定义为准[如请参见《财务会计准则公告第119号》第9a款(1994年10月)]。

3.就第(n)(6)款而言,“预期交易”一词系指一家企业预期但没有义务在正常业务运作中开展的交易(涉及既有资产或负债的交易除外,履行既有的确定承诺所必须开展的交易亦除外)[如请参见财务会计准则委员会发布的《财务会计准则公告第80号——“期货合约的会计”》第9款(1984年8月)]。

4.注册人在向证券交易委员会提交财务报告时应按第(n)款的规定进行披露,包括针对截至1997年6月15日之后的会计期间提交财务报表。

[《联邦公报》第45卷第63669页,1980年9月25日,修正索引:《联邦公报》第46卷第56179页,1981年11月16日;《联邦公报》第50卷第25215页,1985年6月18日;《联邦公报》第50卷第49532页,1985年12月3日;《联邦公报》第51卷第3770页,1986年1月30日;《联邦公报》第57卷第45293页,1992年10月1日;《联邦公报》第59卷第65636页,1994年12月20日;《联邦公报》第62卷第6063页,1997年2月10日;《联邦公报》第74卷第18615页,2009年4月23日。]

§210.4-09 [Reserved]

§210.4-10 Financial accounting and reporting for oil and gas producing activities pursuant to the Federal securities laws and the Energy Policy and Conservation Act of 1975.

This section prescribes financial accounting and reporting standards for registrants with the Commission engaged in oil and gas producing activities in filings under the Federal securities laws and for the preparation of accounts by persons engaged, in whole or in part, in the production of crude oil or natural gas in the United States, pursuant to section 503 of the Energy Policy and Conservation Act of 1975 (42 U.S.C. 6383) (*EPCA*) and section 11(c) of the Energy Supply and Environmental Coordination Act of 1974 (15 U.S.C. 796)(*ESECA*), as amended by section 505 of EPCA. The application of this section to those oil and gas producing operations of companies regulated for ratemaking purposes on an individual-company-cost-of-service basis may, however, give appropriate recognition to differences arising because of the effect of the ratemaking process.

Exemption. Any person exempted by the Department of Energy from any record-keeping or reporting requirements pursuant to section 11(c) of ESECA, as amended, is similarly exempted from the related provisions of this section in the preparation of accounts pursuant to EPCA. This exemption does not affect the applicability of this section to filings pursuant to the Federal securities laws.

Definitions

(a) *Definitions.* The following definitions apply to the terms listed below as they are used in this section:

(1) *Acquisition of properties.* Costs incurred to purchase, lease or otherwise acquire a property, including costs of lease bonuses and options to purchase or lease properties, the portion of costs applicable to minerals when land including mineral rights is purchased in fee, brokers' fees, recording fees, legal costs, and other costs incurred in acquiring properties.

(2) *Analogous reservoir.* Analogous reservoirs, as used in resources assessments, have similar rock and fluid properties, reservoir conditions (depth, temperature, and pressure) and drive mechanisms, but are typically at a more advanced stage of development than the reservoir of interest and thus may provide concepts to assist in the interpretation of more limited data and estimation of recovery. When used to support proved reserves, an "analogous reservoir" refers to a reservoir that shares the following characteristics with the reservoir of interest:

(i) Same geological formation (but not necessarily in pressure communication with the reservoir of interest);

第210.4-09节 [保留]

第210.4-10节 联邦证券法和《1975年能源政策与保护法》关于油气生产活动的财务会计及报告规定

本节规定的财务会计及报告的标准之适用对象为根据联邦证券法向证券交易委员会注册登记从事油气生产活动之注册人,以及在美国境内完全从事或兼营原油或天然气生产,并根据《1975年能源政策与保护法》(《美国法典》第四十二编第6383节,EPCA)第503条及《1974年能源供应与环境协调法》(《美国法典》第十五编第796节,ESECA)第11(c)条(以《1975年能源政策与保护法》第505条修正后的版本为准)编制账目的主体。但是,对于定价受监管的公司的油气生产经营业务,本节规定应基于"各公司的服务成本"适用,在适用过程中应适当考虑并认可因上述定价程序所产生的差异。

豁免。经能源部豁免,不受《1974年能源供应与环境协调法》第11(c)条(以修正后的版本为准)规定的任何档案保存或报告义务约束的任何主体,同样也不受本节关于根据《1975年能源政策与保护法》编制账目的相关规定约束,但对于根据联邦证券法进行的文件提交,上述豁免并不影响本节的适用。

定义

(a)定义:就本节而言,下述术语之定义如下:

(1)矿区权益取得成本。"矿区权益取得成本"系指因购买、租赁或通过其他方式取得矿区而产生的成本,包括租赁补助费及矿区购买或承租选择权的成本、购买附带采矿权的可自由继承的土地时属于矿物部分的成本、经纪费、档案费、法律成本及因取得矿区而产生的其他成本。

(2)相似油气藏。"相似油气藏"一词用于资源评估时,系指具有类似的岩石及流体特性、储层条件(深度、温度及压力)与驱动机理,且与评估中的油气藏相比通常处于更高的开发阶段,因而有助于对有限的数据作出解释和对预估采收率作出说明。用于为探明储量的评估提供支持时,"相似油气藏"指与评估中的油气藏一样,具有下列相同特性的油气藏:

(i)相同的地质构造(但不必与评估中的油气藏之间有压力连通);

(ii) Same environment of deposition;

(iii) Similar geological structure; and

(iv) Same drive mechanism.

Instruction to paragraph (a)(2): Reservoir properties must, in the aggregate, be no more favorable in the analog than in the reservoir of interest.

(3) *Bitumen*. Bitumen, sometimes referred to as natural bitumen, is petroleum in a solid or semi–solid state in natural deposits with a viscosity greater than 10,000 centipoise measured at original temperature in the deposit and atmospheric pressure, on a gas free basis. In its natural state it usually contains sulfur, metals, and other non–hydrocarbons.

(4) *Condensate*. Condensate is a mixture of hydrocarbons that exists in the gaseous phase at original reservoir temperature and pressure, but that, when produced, is in the liquid phase at surface pressure and temperature.

(5) *Deterministic estimate*. The method of estimating reserves or resources is called deterministic when a single value for each parameter (from the geoscience, engineering, or economic data) in the reserves calculation is used in the reserves estimation procedure.

(6) *Developed oil and gas reserves*. Developed oil and gas reserves are reserves of any category that can be expected to be recovered:

(i) Through existing wells with existing equipment and operating methods or in which the cost of the required equipment is relatively minor compared to the cost of a new well; and

(ii) Through installed extraction equipment and infrastructure operational at the time of the reserves estimate if the extraction is by means not involving a well.

(7) *Development costs*. Costs incurred to obtain access to proved reserves and to provide facilities for extracting, treating, gathering and storing the oil and gas. More specifically, development costs, including depreciation and applicable operating costs of support equipment and facilities and other costs of development activities, are costs incurred to:

(i) Gain access to and prepare well locations for drilling, including surveying well locations for the purpose of determining specific development drilling sites, clearing ground, draining, road building, and relocating public roads, gas lines, and power lines, to the extent necessary in developing the proved reserves.

(ii) Drill and equip development wells, development–type stratigraphic test wells, and service wells, including the costs of platforms and of well equipment such as casing, tubing, pumping equipment, and the wellhead assembly.

(iii) Acquire, construct, and install production facilities such as lease flow lines, separators, treaters, heaters, manifolds, measuring devices, and production storage tanks, natural gas cycling and processing plants, and central utility and waste disposal systems.

(ii)相同的沉积环境;

(iii)相同的地质结构;和

(iv)相同的驱动机理。

关于第(a)(2)款的说明:相似油气藏的特性总体上不得优于评估中的油气藏。

(3)沥青。"沥青"或称"天然沥青",是一种固态或半固态的石油天然沉积物,在原始温度和常压下,不含气的天然沥青质黏度超过1万厘泊。在自然状态下,沥青通常含有硫、金属及其他非烃物质。

(4)凝析油。"凝析油"是一种碳氢化合物的混合物,在油气藏原始温度及压力下以气相状态存在,但生产出来后,在表面压力与温度下呈液相。

(5)确定性估算。在油气藏估算的程序中,如每一个参数(无论是源自地质科学数据、工程数据或经济数据)均只取一个单独的数值,则该等评估油气藏或资源的方法称为"确定性估算"。

(6)已开发油气储量。"已开发油气储量"系指预计可通过下列任何一种方式采收的储量:

(i)通过现有设备及操作方法开采现有油井的方式;或者,所需设备的成本与开凿新油井的成本相比很低的方式;和

(ii)通过进行储量估算时已安装的萃取设备以及已投入运营的基础设施进行开采(前提是萃取过程并不涉及油井)的方式。

(7)开发成本。"开发成本"系指为取得探明储量并提供萃取、加工、采集与储存油气的设施所产生之成本。更确切而言,开发成本(包括支持设备与设施的折旧及相关营运成本、开发活动的其他成本)涵盖下列活动产生的成本:

(i)取得必要的进入开发油井位置的权利、准备钻井位置,包括为确定具体的开发钻井井位而对油井位置进行勘测,以及进行地面清理、排水、修筑道路,以及迁移公共道路、天然气管线与电线,但均以开发探明储量所必要为限;

(ii)开钻开发井、开发型地层试井及辅助井并提供设备,包括平台及油井设备成本(如套管、油管、抽油设备及井口装备成本);

(iii)获取、建造及安装生产设施,如出油管线、分离器、处理器、加热炉、多支管、测量装置,以及生产储存槽、天然气循环与处理厂以和中央公共设施与垃圾处理系统;及

(iv) Provide improved recovery systems.

(8) *Development project.* A development project is the means by which petroleum resources are brought to the status of economically producible. As examples, the development of a single reservoir or field, an incremental development in a producing field, or the integrated development of a group of several fields and associated facilities with a common ownership may constitute a development project.

(9) *Development well.* A well drilled within the proved area of an oil or gas reservoir to the depth of a stratigraphic horizon known to be productive.

(10) *Economically producible.* The term economically producible, as it relates to a resource, means a resource which generates revenue that exceeds, or is reasonably expected to exceed, the costs of the operation. The value of the products that generate revenue shall be determined at the terminal point of oil and gas producing activities as defined in paragraph (a)(16) of this section.

(11) *Estimated ultimate recovery (EUR).* Estimated ultimate recovery is the sum of reserves remaining as of a given date and cumulative production as of that date.

(12) *Exploration costs.* Costs incurred in identifying areas that may warrant examination and in examining specific areas that are considered to have prospects of containing oil and gas reserves, including costs of drilling exploratory wells and exploratory-type stratigraphic test wells. Exploration costs may be incurred both before acquiring the related property (sometimes referred to in part as prospecting costs) and after acquiring the property. Principal types of exploration costs, which include depreciation and applicable operating costs of support equipment and facilities and other costs of exploration activities, are:

(i) Costs of topographical, geographical and geophysical studies, rights of access to properties to conduct those studies, and salaries and other expenses of geologists, geophysical crews, and others conducting those studies. Collectively, these are sometimes referred to as geological and geophysical or *G&G* costs.

(ii) Costs of carrying and retaining undeveloped properties, such as delay rentals, ad valorem taxes on properties, legal costs for title defense, and the maintenance of land and lease records.

(iii) Dry hole contributions and bottom hole contributions.

(iv) Costs of drilling and equipping exploratory wells.

(v) Costs of drilling exploratory-type stratigraphic test wells.

(13) *Exploratory well.* An exploratory well is a well drilled to find a new field or to find a new reservoir in a field previously found to be productive of oil or gas in another reservoir. Generally, an exploratory well is any well that is not a development well, an extension well, a service well, or a stratigraphic test well as those items are defined in this

(iv)提供改良的采收系统。

(8)开发项目。“开发项目”系指使石油资源具有经济可采性的手段。例如,单一油气藏或油田的开发、已投产油田的增量开发,或共同所有的多处油田与配套设施的整体开发,均可构成一个开发项目。

(9)开发井。“开发井”系指在探明确有油矿或天然气藏的区域内,深及已知具有可采性的地层的井。

(10)具有经济可采性。“具有经济可采性”一词用于修饰资源时,系指资源产生的收入超过或合理预期将超过运营成本。创收产品的价值应根据石油与天然气生产活动终端点[定义见本节第(a)(16)款]产出的价值确定。

(11)预估最终采收量(EUR)。“预估最终采收量”系指截至某一特定日期的剩余储量及累计产量的合计数量。

(12)勘探成本。“勘探成本”系指为识别有调查价值的区域以及调查被认为可能含有油矿及天然气矿藏的特定区域所产生的成本,包括开钻勘探井及勘探型地层试井的成本。勘探成本可能发生在取得相关矿区之前(其中一部分有时可能称为勘察成本),也可能发生在取得相关矿区之后。勘探成本(包括支持设备与设施的折旧、相关运营成本及勘探活动的其他成本)主要类型如下:

(i)地形、地理与地球物理研究成本;为开展上述研究而取得所需矿区使用权的成本;以及地质学家、地球物理研究人员和其他开展上述研究的人员的薪资及相关费用。上述成本和费用有时统称为地质及地球科研成本。

(ii)持有并保留未开发矿区的成本,如延缓开发租金、矿区从价税、为维护所有权而产生的法律成本,以及土地与租赁档案的维护费用。

(iii)干井成本分摊及井底成本分摊。

(iv)开钻勘探井及提供相关设备的成本。

(v)开钻勘探型地层试井的成本。

(13)勘探井。“勘探井”系指为了在已发现存在可开采石油或天然气的油气藏的油田中发现新油田或油气藏而开钻的井。一般而言,本节定义的开发井、探边井、辅助井或地层试井之外的任何井,均属于勘探井。

section.

(14) *Extension well.* An extension well is a well drilled to extend the limits of a known reservoir.

(15) *Field.* An area consisting of a single reservoir or multiple reservoirs all grouped on or related to the same individual geological structural feature and/or stratigraphic condition. There may be two or more reservoirs in a field that are separated vertically by intervening impervious, strata, or laterally by local geologic barriers, or by both. Reservoirs that are associated by being in overlapping or adjacent fields may be treated as a single or common operational field. The geological terms *structural feature* and *stratigraphic condition* are intended to identify localized geological features as opposed to the broader terms of basins, trends, provinces, plays, areas-of-interest, etc.

(16) *Oil and gas producing activities.*(i) Oil and gas producing activities include:

(A) The search for crude oil, including condensate and natural gas liquids, or natural gas ("oil and gas") in their natural states and original locations;

(B) The acquisition of property rights or properties for the purpose of further exploration or for the purpose of removing the oil or gas from such properties;

(C) The construction, drilling, and production activities necessary to retrieve oil and gas from their natural reservoirs, including the acquisition, construction, installation, and maintenance of field gathering and storage systems, such as:

(1) Lifting the oil and gas to the surface; and

(2) Gathering, treating, and field processing (as in the case of processing gas to extract liquid hydrocarbons); and

(D) Extraction of saleable hydrocarbons, in the solid, liquid, or gaseous state, from oil sands, shale, coalbeds, or other nonrenewable natural resources which are intended to be upgraded into synthetic oil or gas, and activities undertaken with a view to such extraction.

Instruction 1 to paragraph (a)(16)(i): The oil and gas production function shall be regarded as ending at a "terminal point", which is the outlet valve on the lease or field storage tank. If unusual physical or operational circumstances exist, it may be appropriate to regard the terminal point for the production function as:

a. The first point at which oil, gas, or gas liquids, natural or synthetic, are delivered to a main pipeline, a common carrier, a refinery, or a marine terminal; and

b. In the case of natural resources that are intended to be upgraded into synthetic oil or gas, if those natural resources are delivered to a purchaser prior to upgrading, the first point at which the natural resources are delivered to a main pipeline, a common carrier, a refinery, a marine terminal, or a facility which upgrades such natural resources into synthetic oil or gas.

(14)探边井。“探边井”系指为进一步查明已知油气藏边界而开钻的井。

(15)油田。“油田”系指包含一个或多个具有或涉及同一地质结构特性和/或地层条件的油气藏的区域。一块油田中可能有两个(含)以上的油气藏,该等油气藏因彼此之间在垂直方向存在油气无法渗透之岩层,和/或在水平方向存在局部地质屏障,而相互隔离。因重叠或邻近油田而相连的油气藏,可视为单一油田或共同经营的油田。局部的地质特征应以“构造特征”及“地层条件”等地质学名词等加以限定,不使用“盆地”、“走向”、“区域”、“间隙”、“评估中的地区”等宽泛性词语。

(16)石油与天然气生产活动。(i)石油与天然气生产活动包括:

(A)寻找原油,包括凝析油与天然气液,或处于自然状态和原始位置的天然气(下称石油与天然气);

(B)为进一步勘探或开采矿区所产石油或天然气而购买矿区权或矿区;

(C)从天然油气藏收采石油与天然气所必要的建筑、钻井及生产活动,包括油田采集与储存系统的购买、建筑、安装以及维护,如

(1)将石油与天然气提取至地表;及

(2)采集、加工与现场处理(如为萃取液烃而对天然气进行的处理);及

(D)从油砂、泥岩、煤层或其他拟被升级为合成石油或天然气的不可再生天然资源中萃取固态、液态或气态适销烃,以及为进行此等萃取而从事的活动。

关于第(a)(16)(i)款的说明1:石油与天然气生产流程应止于“终端点”,即矿场租地或油田储存槽的出口阀。如物理环境或操作环境存在异常,生产流程终端点亦可视为:

a.石油、天然气或天然气液体(天然或合成状态)运送至干线、公共运油商、炼油厂或海上油库的首个交接点;和

b.就拟被升级为合成石油或天然气的天然资源而言,如该等天然资源在升级之前即向买方交付,则为天然资源运送至干线、公共运油商、炼油厂、海上油库或负责将该等天然资源升级为合成石油或天然气的设施的首个交接点。

Instruction 2 to paragraph (a)(16)(i): For purposes of this paragraph (a)(16), the term *saleable hydrocarbons* means hydrocarbons that are saleable in the state in which the hydrocarbons are delivered.

(ii) Oil and gas producing activities do not include:

(A) Transporting, refining, or marketing oil and gas;

(B) Processing of produced oil, gas or natural resources that can be upgraded into synthetic oil or gas by a registrant that does not have the legal right to produce or a revenue interest in such production;

(C) Activities relating to the production of natural resources other than oil, gas, or natural resources from which synthetic oil and gas can be extracted; or

(D) Production of geothermal steam.

(17) *Possible reserves.* Possible reserves are those additional reserves that are less certain to be recovered than probable reserves.

(i) When deterministic methods are used, the total quantities ultimately recovered from a project have a low probability of exceeding proved plus probable plus possible reserves. When probabilistic methods are used, there should be at least a 10% probability that the total quantities ultimately recovered will equal or exceed the proved plus probable plus possible reserves estimates.

(ii) Possible reserves may be assigned to areas of a reservoir adjacent to probable reserves where data control and interpretations of available data are progressively less certain. Frequently, this will be in areas where geoscience and engineering data are unable to define clearly the area and vertical limits of commercial production from the reservoir by a defined project.

(iii) Possible reserves also include incremental quantities associated with a greater percentage recovery of the hydrocarbons in place than the recovery quantities assumed for probable reserves.

(iv) The proved plus probable and proved plus probable plus possible reserves estimates must be based on reasonable alternative technical and commercial interpretations within the reservoir or subject project that are clearly documented, including comparisons to results in successful similar projects.

(v) Possible reserves may be assigned where geoscience and engineering data identify directly adjacent portions of a reservoir within the same accumulation that may be separated from proved areas by faults with displacement less than formation thickness or other geological discontinuities and that have not been penetrated by a wellbore, and the registrant believes that such adjacent portions are in communication with the known (proved) reservoir. Possible reserves may be assigned to areas that are structurally higher or lower than the proved area if these areas are in communication with the proved

关于第(a)(16)(i)款的说明2:就本第(a)(16)款而言,"适销烃"一词系指能够以交付状态销售的烃。

(ii)石油与天然气生产活动不包括:

(A)石油与天然气的运输、提炼或营销;

(B)不拥有合法生产权或对生产不拥有收入权的注册人,将采出的石油、天然气或天然资源升级为合成石油或天然气的活动;

(C)除石油、天然气或可萃取合成石油及天然气的天然资源之外的其他天然资源的相关生产活动;或

(D)地热蒸汽的生产。

(17)可能储量。"可能储量"指采收可能性低于概算储量的其他储量。

(i)使用确定分析法时,指某项目最终采收总量超过探明储量、概算储量与可能储量之和的可能性较低。使用概率分析法时,指最终采收总量等于或超过探明储量、概算储量与可能储量之和的预估值的几率至少应有10%。

(ii)可能储量可以分配至邻近概算储量,且数据可控性与可得数据解读确定性较低的油气藏区域。通常这种区域,是无法通过地球科学与工程数据清楚界定具体项目之油气藏商业开采面积和垂直边界的区域。

(iii)可能储量还包括超出概算储量的采收量的、随着烃采收百分比的增加而新增的储量。

(iv)探明储量加上概算储量的预估值,以及探明储量加上概算储量再加可能储量的预估值,必须基于对油气藏或标的项目的合理替代性技术与商业性的解读确定(该等解读必须有清晰的文件支持),包括与成功的类似项目的结果进行比较。

(v)可能储量可分配至通过地球科学与工程数据识别的直接与同一累积层中某一油气藏相连的部分,该等部分可能因为断层位移小于地层厚度或其他地质间断面而与探明区域分离,未有钻井孔穿透其间,但注册人相信该等相连部分与已知(探明)油气藏连通。可能储量也可分配至结构上比探明区域更高或更低的区域,前提是该等区域与探明油气藏连通。

reservoir.

(vi) Pursuant to paragraph (a)(22)(iii) of this section, where direct observation has defined a highest known oil (HKO) elevation and the potential exists for an associated gas cap, proved oil reserves should be assigned in the structurally higher portions of the reservoir above the HKO only if the higher contact can be established with reasonable certainty through reliable technology. Portions of the reservoir that do not meet this reasonable certainty criterion may be assigned as probable and possible oil or gas based on reservoir fluid properties and pressure gradient interpretations.

(18) *Probable reserves*. Probable reserves are those additional reserves that are less certain to be recovered than proved reserves but which, together with proved reserves, are as likely as not to be recovered.

(i) When deterministic methods are used, it is as likely as not that actual remaining quantities recovered will exceed the sum of estimated proved plus probable reserves. When probabilistic methods are used, there should be at least a 50% probability that the actual quantities recovered will equal or exceed the proved plus probable reserves estimates.

(ii) Probable reserves may be assigned to areas of a reservoir adjacent to proved reserves where data control or interpretations of available data are less certain, even if the interpreted reservoir continuity of structure or productivity does not meet the reasonable certainty criterion. Probable reserves may be assigned to areas that are structurally higher than the proved area if these areas are in communication with the proved reservoir.

(iii) Probable reserves estimates also include potential incremental quantities associated with a greater percentage recovery of the hydrocarbons in place than assumed for proved reserves.

(iv) See also guidelines in paragraphs (a)(17)(iv) and (a)(17)(vi) of this section.

(19) *Probabilistic estimate*. The method of estimation of reserves or resources is called probabilistic when the full range of values that could reasonably occur for each unknown parameter (from the geoscience and engineering data) is used to generate a full range of possible outcomes and their associated probabilities of occurrence.

(20) *Production costs*. (i) Costs incurred to operate and maintain wells and related equipment and facilities, including depreciation and applicable operating costs of support equipment and facilities and other costs of operating and maintaining those wells and related equipment and facilities. They become part of the cost of oil and gas produced. Examples of production costs (sometimes called lifting costs) are:

(A) Costs of labor to operate the wells and related equipment and facilities.

(B) Repairs and maintenance.

(C) Materials, supplies, and fuel consumed and supplies utilized in operating the

(vi)根据本节第(a)(22)(iii)款的规定,如通过直接观察确定了最高已知石油(HKO)海拔,并且可能存在相关气顶,则仅当能通过可靠技术能合理确定更高的接触面时,探明石油储量才能分配至结构上高于最高已知石油海拔的油气藏部分。油气藏达不到上述合理确定性标准的部分,可根据油气藏液体特性及压力梯度的解读分配至石油或天然气概算储量或可能储量。

(18)概算储量。“概算储量”系指采收的确定性低于探明储量,但不能采收的可能性与探明储量相同的额外储量。

(i)使用确定分析法时,系指实际剩余开采量很可能超过探明储量加上概算储量的预估合计值。使用概率分析法时,指实际开采量等于或超过探明储量加上可能储量之和的预估值的几率至少应有50%。

(ii)即使解读出的油气藏结构或生产率的连续性不符合合理确定性标准,概算储量也可分配至邻近探明储量,且数据可控性与可得数据解读确定性较低的油气藏区域。概算储量可分配至结构上高于探明区域并与探明油气藏连通的区域。

(iii)概算储量预估值还包括超出预设的探明储量、随着烃开采百分比的增加而新增的储量。

(iv)同时请参考本节第(a)(17)(iv)款与第(a)(17)(vi)款规定的指引。

(19)概率预估。“概率预估”方法,系指对于每一未知参数(无论是地球科学还是工程数据),均使用可能合理发生的最小数值和最大数值,以计算可能发生的最小结果和最大结果以及相关的发生几率。

(20)生产成本。(i)油井与相关设备设施的运营和维护成本,包括:支持设备和设施的折旧和适用的运营成本,以及上述油井与相关设备设施的其他运营和维护成本。上述成本均构成石油与天然气生产成本的一部分。生产成本(有时称为采油成本)包括但不限于:

(A)运营油井与相关设备设施的劳力成本;

(B)维修和维护成本;

(C)原材料、物资及运营油井与相关设备设施时所使用的燃料消耗以及物资

wells and related equipment and facilities.

(D) Property taxes and insurance applicable to proved properties and wells and related equipment and facilities.

(E) Severance taxes.

(ii) Some support equipment or facilities may serve two or more oil and gas producing activities and may also serve transportation, refining, and marketing activities. To the extent that the support equipment and facilities are used in oil and gas producing activities, their depreciation and applicable operating costs become exploration, development or production costs, as appropriate. Depreciation, depletion, and amortization of capitalized acquisition, exploration, and development costs are not production costs but also become part of the cost of oil and gas produced along with production (lifting) costs identified above.

(21) *Proved area.* The part of a property to which proved reserves have been specifically attributed.

(22) *Proved oil and gas reserves.* Proved oil and gas reserves are those quantities of oil and gas, which, by analysis of geoscience and engineering data, can be estimated with reasonable certainty to be economically producible — from a given date forward, from known reservoirs, and under existing economic conditions, operating methods, and government regulations — prior to the time at which contracts providing the right to operate expire, unless evidence indicates that renewal is reasonably certain, regardless of whether deterministic or probabilistic methods are used for the estimation. The project to extract the hydrocarbons must have commenced or the operator must be reasonably certain that it will commence the project within a reasonable time.

(i) The area of the reservoir considered as proved includes:

(A) The area identified by drilling and limited by fluid contacts, if any, and

(B) Adjacent undrilled portions of the reservoir that can, with reasonable certainty, be judged to be continuous with it and to contain economically producible oil or gas on the basis of available geoscience and engineering data.

(ii) In the absence of data on fluid contacts, proved quantities in a reservoir are limited by the lowest known hydrocarbons (LKH) as seen in a well penetration unless geoscience, engineering, or performance data and reliable technology establishes a lower contact with reasonable certainty.

(iii) Where direct observation from well penetrations has defined a highest known oil (HKO) elevation and the potential exists for an associated gas cap, proved oil reserves may be assigned in the structurally higher portions of the reservoir only if geoscience, engineering, or performance data and reliable technology establish the higher contact with reasonable certainty.

成本;

(D)适用于探明矿区、探明油井及其相关设备设施的房地产税与保险成本;及

(E)开采税。

(ii)部分支持设备或设施可能用于两项(含)以上的石油与天然气生产活动,并可能同时用于运输、炼油与营销活动。支持设备与设施用于石油与天然气生产活动的,其折旧与相关运营成本即应构成勘探、开发或生产成本(视具体情况而定)。资本化的收购、勘探与开发成本之折旧、折损与摊销不属于生产成本,但也与上述生产(采油)成本共同构成所产石油与天然气成本的一部分。

(21)探明区域。"探明区域"系指矿区中已具体分配了探明储量的部分。

(22)探明石油与天然气储量。"探明石油与天然气储量"系指经地球科学与工程数据分析,从某一特定日期开始,到提供经营权的合同到期之前(除非证据显示续约具有合理确定性),根据合理确定的预估具有经济可采性的已知油气藏所含石油与天然气数量(须将现有经济条件、经营方法及政府法规考虑进去),而不论预估时使用的是确定分析法或概率分析法。烃萃取项目必须已经启动,或经营商必须合理确信该项目将于合理期限内启动。

(i)视为探明油气藏的区域包括:

(A)通过钻井识别的区域,区域边界以流体接触面(如有)为准,和

(B)根据可获得的地球科学与工程数据,可合理确定地判断具有连续性且包含具有经济可采性的石油或天然气的油气藏附近尚未开钻的部分。

(ii)如缺乏流体接触面数据,在计算油气藏的探明数量时,应以油井钻探所显示的最低已知烃量(LKH)为限,除非地球科学、工程或性能数据与可靠技术能合理地确定存在更低的接触面。

(iii)如通过直接观察油井钻探已可确定最高已知石油海拔,并且可能存在相关气顶,则仅当地球科学、工程或性能数据和可靠技术能合理地确定更低的接触面之时,探明石油储量才能分配至结构上更高的油气藏部分。

(iv) Reserves which can be produced economically through application of improved recovery techniques (including, but not limited to, fluid injection) are included in the proved classification when:

(A) Successful testing by a pilot project in an area of the reservoir with properties no more favorable than in the reservoir as a whole, the operation of an installed program in the reservoir or an analogous reservoir, or other evidence using reliable technology establishes the reasonable certainty of the engineering analysis on which the project or program was based; and

(B) The project has been approved for development by all necessary parties and entities, including governmental entities.

(v) Existing economic conditions include prices and costs at which economic producibility from a reservoir is to be determined. The price shall be the average price during the 12-month period prior to the ending date of the period covered by the report, determined as an unweighted arithmetic average of the first-day-of-the-month price for each month within such period, unless prices are defined by contractual arrangements, excluding escalations based upon future conditions.

(23) *Proved properties.* Properties with proved reserves.

(24) *Reasonable certainty.* If deterministic methods are used, reasonable certainty means a high degree of confidence that the quantities will be recovered. If probabilistic methods are used, there should be at least a 90% probability that the quantities actually recovered will equal or exceed the estimate. A high degree of confidence exists if the quantity is much more likely to be achieved than not, and, as changes due to increased availability of geoscience (geological, geophysical, and geochemical), engineering, and economic data are made to estimated ultimate recovery (EUR) with time, reasonably certain EUR is much more likely to increase or remain constant than to decrease.

(25) *Reliable technology.* Reliable technology is a grouping of one or more technologies (including computational methods) that has been field tested and has been demonstrated to provide reasonably certain results with consistency and repeatability in the formation being evaluated or in an analogous formation.

(26) *Reserves.* Reserves are estimated remaining quantities of oil and gas and related substances anticipated to be economically producible, as of a given date, by application of development projects to known accumulations. In addition, there must exist, or there must be a reasonable expectation that there will exist, the legal right to produce or a revenue interest in the production, installed means of delivering oil and gas or related substances to market, and all permits and financing required to implement the project.

Note to paragraph (a)(26): Reserves should not be assigned to adjacent reservoirs isolated by major, potentially sealing, faults until those reservoirs are penetrated and

(iv)在下列情形下,通过改良开采技术(包括但不限于流体注入)即可具有经济可采性的储量可划定为探明储量:

(A)通过试验项目,在油气藏的部分区域进行了成功测试,且测试结果显示该区域特性不比整个油气藏更为优越;或者,油气藏或相似油气藏已安装项目的经营结果或其他借助可靠技术获得的证据表明,作为项目依据的工程分析具有合理确定性;且

(B)项目开发已获得所有必要的合作方与实体(包括政府实体)批准。

(v)现有经济条件包括用以确定油气藏是否具有经济可采性时适用的价格与成本。除非价格系通过合同安排确定,并排除了基于未来状况而进行的价格调整,价格应为报告所覆盖期间截止之日前12个月期间的平均价格,按该期间每月第一天价格的不加权算术平均值计算。

(23)探明矿区。“探明矿区”系指拥有探明储量的矿区。

(24)合理确定性。如使用确定分析法,“合理确定性”系指对将被开采的矿藏数量具有高度信心。如使用概率分析法,则指实际开采量等于或超过预估值的几率至少应达90%。在下列情形下,可认定为具有高度信心:实现开采数量的可能性远超过无法实现该数量的可能性,且由于在进展过程中,可获得的地球科学数据(地质、地球物理与地球化学数据)、工程数据与经济数据不断增加,而对预估最终开采量进行调整时,可合理确定地认为预估最终开采量增加或保持不变的可能性远高于其降低的可能性。

(25)可靠技术。“可靠技术”系指一项或一项以上的技术(包括运算方法)所构成的一组技术,且该等技术已经进行过实地测试,被证明可合理确定地针对评估地层或相似地层提供一致、可重复的结果。

(26)储量。“储量”系指截至特定日期,在已知累积层开发项目实施过程中预期具有经济可采性的石油、天然气以及相关物质的预估剩余量。此外,在确定储量时,还必须存在或合理预期将存在如下条件:生产所需之法律权利和生产收益权;将石油、天然气或相关物质运送至市场的已安装设施;以及实施该项目所需的一切许可与融资。

关于第(a)(26)款的注释:储量不得分配至被可能封闭的大型断层所隔绝的邻近油气藏,除非该等油气藏已被钻穿并评估为具有经济可采性。储量不得分配至一个被

evaluated as economically producible. Reserves should not be assigned to areas that are clearly separated from a known accumulation by a non–productive reservoir (*i.e.*, absence of reservoir, structurally low reservoir, or negative test results). Such areas may contain prospective resources (*i.e.*, potentially recoverable resources from undiscovered accumulations).

(27) *Reservoir.* A porous and permeable underground formation containing a natural accumulation of producible oil and/or gas that is confined by impermeable rock or water barriers and is individual and separate from other reservoirs.

(28) *Resources.* Resources are quantities of oil and gas estimated to exist in naturally occurring accumulations. A portion of the resources may be estimated to be recoverable, and another portion may be considered to be unrecoverable. Resources include both discovered and undiscovered accumulations.

(29) *Service well.* A well drilled or completed for the purpose of supporting production in an existing field. Specific purposes of service wells include gas injection, water injection, steam injection, air injection, salt–water disposal, water supply for injection, observation, or injection for in–situ combustion.

(30) *Stratigraphic test well.* A stratigraphic test well is a drilling effort, geologically directed, to obtain information pertaining to a specific geologic condition. Such wells customarily are drilled without the intent of being completed for hydrocarbon production. The classification also includes tests identified as core tests and all types of expendable holes related to hydrocarbon exploration. Stratigraphic tests are classified as "exploratory type" if not drilled in a known area or "development type" if drilled in a known area.

(31) *Undeveloped oil and gas reserves.* Undeveloped oil and gas reserves are reserves of any category that are expected to be recovered from new wells on undrilled acreage, or from existing wells where a relatively major expenditure is required for recompletion.

(i) Reserves on undrilled acreage shall be limited to those directly offsetting development spacing areas that are reasonably certain of production when drilled, unless evidence using reliable technology exists that establishes reasonable certainty of economic producibility at greater distances.

(ii) Undrilled locations can be classified as having undeveloped reserves only if a development plan has been adopted indicating that they are scheduled to be drilled within five years, unless the specific circumstances, justify a longer time.

(iii) Under no circumstances shall estimates for undeveloped reserves be attributable to any acreage for which an application of fluid injection or other improved recovery technique is contemplated, unless such techniques have been proved effective by actual projects in the same reservoir or an analogous reservoir, as defined in paragraph (a)(2) of this section, or by other evidence using reliable technology establishing reasonable

不具可采性的油气藏(即缺乏油气藏、结构较低的油气藏或测试结果为否定性的油气藏)所明显隔离的已知累积层区域。该等区域可能包含潜在资源(即未发现的累积层中有开采潜力的资源)。

(27)油气藏。“油气藏”系指包含具可采性的石油和/或天然气天然累积层的多孔且可渗透的地层,其边界由不可渗透的岩石或水层界定,因此具有独立性,并区别于其他油气藏。

(28)资源。“资源”系指存在于天然累积层中的石油与天然气预估数量。资源中的一部分可以被预估为可开采资源,另一部分则可视为不可开采资源。资源包括已发现与未发现的累积层。

(29)辅助井。“辅助井”系指为支持既有油田生产之目的而开钻或完成的油井。辅助井的具体目的包括注气、注水、注气、注空气、盐水处置、注水供水、观察或火烧驱油所需注入。

(30)地层试井。“地层试井”系指为获取特定地质状况的相关信息而开钻的地质井。地层试井通常不以开钻完成后生产烃为目的。其分类包括岩心测试井及所有与烃勘探相关的一次性井眼。地层测试如非在已知区域进行则归类为“勘探型”,如在已知区域进行则归类为“开发型”。

(31)未开发石油与天然气储量。“未开发石油与天然气储量”系指预期可通过未开钻区域内的新井开采的任何一类储量,或预期可通过需要相对大额的资金才能重新完井的现有油井开采的任何一类储量。

(i)未开钻区域的储量应以可合理确定一经开钻即具可采性的地区的储量为限,且该等地区的储量应与开发间隔区的储量直接抵消。但是,基于可靠技术所获证据而合理确定地证明在距离更远的地区存在经济可采性的情形除外。

(ii)未开钻地点只有在下述情形下才可被划定为拥有未开发储量:开发计划已经通过,且根据该计划,该等地点将于5年内开钻,但在特定状况下有必要延后开钻时间的除外。

(iii)在任何情形下,均不得因考虑应用流体注入或其他改良开采技术而建立任何相关区域的未开发储量预估值,除非此等技术已由同一油气藏或相似油气藏[定义见本节第(a)(2)款]的实际项目或其他基于可靠技术所获证据而合理确定地证明为有效技术。

certainty.

(32) *Unproved properties.* Properties with no proved reserves.

Successful Efforts Method

(b) A reporting entity that follows the successful efforts method shall comply with the accounting and financial reporting disclosure requirements of Statement of Financial Accounting Standards No. 19, as amended.

Full Cost Method

(c) *Application of the full cost method of accounting.* A reporting entity that follows the full cost method shall apply that method to all of its operations and to the operations of its subsidiaries, as follows:

(1) *Determination of cost centers.* Cost centers shall be established on a country-by-country basis.

(2) *Costs to be capitalized.* All costs associated with property acquisition, exploration, and development activities (as defined in paragraph (a) of this section) shall be capitalized within the appropriate cost center. Any internal costs that are capitalized shall be limited to those costs that can be directly identified with acquisition, exploration, and development activities undertaken by the reporting entity for its own account, and shall not include any costs related to production, general corporate overhead, or similar activities.

(3) *Amortization of capitalized costs.* Capitalized costs within a cost center shall be amortized on the unit-of-production basis using proved oil and gas reserves, as follows:

(i) Costs to be amortized shall include (A) all capitalized costs, less accumulated amortization, other than the cost of properties described in paragraph (ii) below; (B) the estimated future expenditures (based on current costs) to be incurred in developing proved reserves; and (C) estimated dismantlement and abandonment costs, net of estimated salvage values.

(ii) The cost of investments in unproved properties and major development projects may be excluded from capitalized costs to be amortized, subject to the following:

(A) All costs directly associated with the acquisition and evaluation of unproved properties may be excluded from the amortization computation until it is determined whether or not proved reserves can be assigned to the properties, subject to the following conditions:

(1) Until such a determination is made, the properties shall be assessed at least annually to ascertain whether impairment has occurred. Unevaluated properties whose costs are individually significant shall be assessed individually. Where it is not practicable to individually assess the amount of impairment of properties for which costs are not individually significant, such properties may be grouped for purposes of assessing

(32)未探明矿区。“探明矿区”指不具有探明储量的矿区。

成功成本法

(b)采用成功成本法的报告实体,应遵守《财务会计准则公告第19号》(修正版)中关于会计与财务报告披露的要求。

完全成本法

(c)会计完全成本法的适用。采用完全成本法的报告实体,其所有运营及其子公司的运营,均应依下列规定适用完全成本法:

(1)成本中心的确定。成本中心应根据各国的具体情况确定。

(2)应予资本化的成本。与矿区购买、勘探与开发活动相关的所有成本[定义见本节第(a)款],应在适当的成本中心内予以资本化处理。任何资本化的内部成本应限于报告实体自行负担、可直接归入收购、勘探与开发活动的成本,不得包括与生产、公司一般性管理费用或类似活动相关的任何成本。

(3)资本化成本的摊销。每个成本中心的资本化成本均应根据探明石油与天然气储量摊销至每单位产量,具体规定如下:

(i)应摊销的成本包括:(A)全部资本化成本扣除摊销总额后的金额[摊销总额不包括下文第(ii)款所述矿区成本];(B)开发探明储量所产生的预估未来开支(预估应基于现行成本确定);和(C)预估拆卸与废弃成本(指扣除预估残值后的净值)。

(ii)未探明矿区与大型开发项目的投资成本可排除在应摊销的资本化成本之外,但应遵守如下规定:

(A)在计算摊销时,可排除与购买及评估未探明矿区直接相关的所有成本,直至已确定探明储量是否可分配至该矿区,前提是:

(1)在得出上述确定结论之前,矿区至少应每年进行一次评估,以查明是否发生了减值。单块未评估矿区,如其成本具有重大性,应单独进行评估。单块而言成本不具重大性的矿区,如单独评估其减值金额并不可行,则在评估减值时可将该等矿区予以组合。预估减值时,可将基于历史经验及其他数据的因素(如矿区的主要租赁条款、未探明矿区的平均持有期间及地理地形数据),适用于一组单块而言不具有重大性的矿

impairment. Impairment may be estimated by applying factors based on historical experience and other data such as primary lease terms of the properties, average holding periods of unproved properties, and geographic and geologic data to groupings of individually insignificant properties and projects. The amount of impairment assessed under either of these methods shall be added to the costs to be amortized.

(2) The costs of drilling exploratory dry holes shall be included in the amortization base immediately upon determination that the well is dry.

(3) If geological and geophysical costs cannot be directly associated with specific unevaluated properties, they shall be included in the amortization base as incurred. Upon complete evaluation of a property, the total remaining excluded cost (net of any impairment) shall be included in the full cost amortization base.

(B) Certain costs may be excluded from amortization when incurred in connection with major development projects expected to entail significant costs to ascertain the quantities of proved reserves attributable to the properties under development (e.g., the installation of an offshore drilling platform from which development wells are to be drilled, the installation of improved recovery programs, and similar major projects undertaken in the expectation of significant additions to proved reserves). The amounts which may be excluded are applicable portions of (1) the costs that relate to the major development project and have not previously been included in the amortization base, and (2) the estimated future expenditures associated with the development project. The excluded portion of any common costs associated with the development project should be based, as is most appropriate in the circumstances, on a comparison of either (*i*) existing proved reserves to total proved reserves expected to be established upon completion of the project, or (*ii*) the number of wells to which proved reserves have been assigned and total number of wells expected to be drilled. Such costs may be excluded from costs to be amortized until the earlier determination of whether additional reserves are proved or impairment occurs.

(C) Excluded costs and the proved reserves related to such costs shall be transferred into the amortization base on an ongoing (well-by-well or property-by-property) basis as the project is evaluated and proved reserves established or impairment determined. Once proved reserves are established, there is no further justification for continued exclusion from the full cost amortization base even if other factors prevent immediate production or marketing.

(iii) Amortization shall be computed on the basis of physical units, with oil and gas converted to a common unit of measure on the basis of their approximate relative energy content, unless economic circumstances (related to the effects of regulated prices) indicate that use of units of revenue is a more appropriate basis of computing amortization. In the

区与项目。以上述任何一种方法进行评估的减值金额,应加计于应予摊销的成本之中。

(2)开钻勘探干井的成本,应在确认该井为干井后立即计入摊销基数之中。

(3)如地质及地球科研成本无法直接与具体未估价矿区相关,则应按实际发生的金额计入摊销基数之中。在完成矿区估价时,剩余的除外成本(指扣除任何减值之后的净值)应全部计入完全成本摊销基数之中。

(B)对于大型开发项目,如果要查明可归属于开发中矿区的探明储量,可能需要花费大量成本(如需要安装开钻开发井的海上钻油平台、安装改良开采项目以及由于预期探明储量将大幅新增而需启动类似大型项目),则可将特定成本排除在摊销之外。可排除的金额为以下各项的相关部分:(1)与大型开发项目相关且之前未计入摊销基数的成本,及(2)与开发项目相关的预估未来支出。与开发项目有关的任何共同成本中被排除的部分应基于以下任何一项比较结果确定(根据具体情形确定最恰当的比较项):(*i*)现有探明储量与项目完成时可望确定的总体探明储量之比较,或(*ii*)已分配至探明储量的井数与可望开钻的井数之比较。在确认附加储量是否为探明储量之前或减值发生之前(以较早者为准),该等成本可排除在应摊销成本之外。

(C)一旦项目完成估价、探明储量得到确定或减值得到确定,除外成本及与该等成本相关的探明储量即应持续转入每口井或每块矿区的摊销基数。一旦探明储量得到确定,即使存在其他因素导致无法立即生产或营销,亦不应再继续从完全成本摊销基数中排除除外成本。

(iii)摊销应按物理单位计算,根据石油与天然气大致的相对能量含量转换为通用的度量单位,除非根据经济情势(指管制价格带来的影响),更适于按收入单位进行摊销计算。在后一种情形下,应基于当期生产毛收入与未来毛收入的比较结果进行摊销,其中当期毛收入应扣除矿区使用费付款与净利润分配,未来毛收入为来自探明石

latter case, amortization shall be computed on the basis of current gross revenues (excluding royalty payments and net profits disbursements) from production in relation to future gross revenues, based on current prices (including consideration of changes in existing prices provided only by contractual arrangements), from estimated production of proved oil and gas reserves. The effect of a significant price increase during the year on estimated future gross revenues shall be reflected in the amortization provision only for the period after the price increase occurs.

(iv) In some cases it may be more appropriate to depreciate natural gas cycling and processing plants by a method other than the unit-of-production method.

(v) Amortization computations shall be made on a consolidated basis, including investees accounted for on a proportionate consolidation basis. Investees accounted for on the equity method shall be treated separately.

(4) *Limitation on capitalized costs.* (i) For each cost center, capitalized costs, less accumulated amortization and related deferred income taxes, shall not exceed an amount (the cost center ceiling) equal to the sum of:

(A) The present value of estimated future net revenues computed by applying current prices of oil and gas reserves (with consideration of price changes only to the extent provided by contractual arrangements) to estimated future production of proved oil and gas reserves as of the date of the latest balance sheet presented, less estimated future expenditures (based on current costs) to be incurred in developing and producing the proved reserves computed using a discount factor of ten percent and assuming continuation of existing economic conditions; plus

(B) the cost of properties not being amortized pursuant to paragraph (i)(3)(ii) of this section; plus

(C) the lower of cost or estimated fair value of unproven properties included in the costs being amortized; less

(D) income tax effects related to differences between the book and tax basis of the properties referred to in paragraphs (i)(4)(i)(B) and (C) of this section.

(ii) If unamortized costs capitalized within a cost center, less related deferred income taxes, exceed the cost center ceiling, the excess shall be charged to expense and separately disclosed during the period in which the excess occurs. Amounts thus required to be written off shall not be reinstated for any subsequent increase in the cost center ceiling.

(5) *Production costs.* All costs relating to production activities, including workover costs incurred solely to maintain or increase levels of production from an existing completion interval, shall be charged to expense as incurred.

(6) *Other transactions.* The provisions of paragraph (h) of this section, "Mineral property

油与天然气储量的预估生产量带来的收入，按照现行价格计算（但完全通过合约规定的现有价格变动，应予考虑）。当年重大价格上涨对预估未来总收入的影响应反映于摊销拨备中，但仅以价格上涨发生之后的期间为限。

(iv)在某些情形下，对天然气循环与处理厂进行折旧时，可能更适合采用产量单位法以外的方法。

(v)摊销应在并表的基础上进行计算，并表对象包括按比例并表法核算的投资对象。按权益法核算的投资对象应单独处理。

(4)资本化成本的限制。(i)对每一个成本中心而言，资本化成本扣除累积摊销与相关递延所得税之后的金额，不得超过下列各项之和（成本中心上限）：

(A)预估未来净收入的现值。其计算方式为，将截至最近的资产负债表日的探明石油与天然气储量的预估未来产量乘以现行价格（仅考虑合约规定的价格变化），减去开发及生产探明储量所产生的预估未来开支（未来开支应基于现行成本计算，折扣系数为10%，并假设现有经济条件将持续存在）；加上

(B)根据本节第(i)(3)(ii)款规定不必摊销的矿区成本；加上

(C)成本或包括在摊销成本中的未探明矿区预估公允价值（以较低者为准）；减去

(D)与本节第(i)(4)(i)(B)款和第(i)(4)(i)(C)款所述之矿区账面值和计税基础之差额相关的所得税影响数。

(ii)如果成本中心的未摊销资本化成本在扣除相关递延所得税之后，超过了成本中心上限，超出部分应记入费用借方，并在发生超出情形的期间单独披露。因此，需要减记的金额，不得因为期后发生任何成本中心上限提高的情况而转回。

(5)生产成本。与生产活动相关的所有成本（包括完全因维持或增加现有完井层段的产量而产生的修井成本），应按实际发生金额记入费用借方。

(6)其他交易。本节第(h)款——“矿地产转让与相关交易（如遵循成功成本

conveyances and related transactions if the successful efforts method of accounting is followed," shall apply also to those reporting entities following the full cost method except as follows:

(i) *Sales and abandonments of oil and gas properties.* Sales of oil and gas properties, whether or not being amortized currently, shall be accounted for as adjustments of capitalized costs, with no gain or loss recognized, unless such adjustments would significantly alter the relationship between capitalized costs and proved reserves of oil and gas attributable to a cost center. For instance, a significant alteration would not ordinarily be expected to occur for sales involving less than 25 percent of the reserve quantities of a given cost center. If gain or loss is recognized on such a sale, total capitalization costs within the cost center shall be allocated between the reserves sold and reserves retained on the same basis used to compute amortization, unless there are substantial economic differences between the properties sold and those retained, in which case capitalized costs shall be allocated on the basis of the relative fair values of the properties. Abandonments of oil and gas properties shall be accounted for as adjustments of capitalized costs; that is, the cost of abandoned properties shall be charged to the full cost center and amortized (subject to the limitation on capitalized costs in paragraph (b) of this section).

(ii) *Purchases of reserves.* Purchases of oil and gas reserves in place ordinarily shall be accounted for as additional capitalized costs within the applicable cost center; however, significant purchases of production payments or properties with lives substantially shorter than the composite productive life of the cost center shall be accounted for separately.

(iii) *Partnerships, joint ventures and drilling arrangements.* (A) Except as provided in paragraph (i)(6)(i) of this section, all consideration received from sales or transfers of properties in connection with partnerships, joint venture operations, or various other forms of drilling arrangements involving oil and gas exploration and development activities (e.g., carried interest, turnkey wells, management fees, etc.) shall be credited to the full cost account, except to the extent of amounts that represent reimbursement of organization, offering, general and administrative expenses, etc., that are identifiable with the transaction, if such amounts are currently incurred and charged to expense.

(B) Where a registrant organizes and manages a limited partnership involved only in the purchase of proved developed properties and subsequent distribution of income from such properties, management fee income may be recognized provided the properties involved do not require aggregate development expenditures in connection with production of existing proved reserves in excess of 10% of the partnership's recorded cost of such properties. Any income not recognized as a result of this limitation would be credited to the full cost account and recognized through a lower amortization provision as reserves are produced.

法)”——亦应适用于遵循成功成本法的报告实体,但下列情形除外:

(i)石油与天然气矿区的出售与废弃。石油与天然气矿区的出售所得(不论当前是否正在摊销),在不确认收益或损失的情况下,应计入资本化成本调整项,但该等调整将大幅改变资本化成本与可分配至成本中心的探明油气储量之间的关系的除外。例如,低于某成本中心储量25%的出售,一般可预期其并不会导致大幅变化。如该等出售确认产生收益或损失,成本中心内全部的资本化成本即应按照与摊销相同的计算基础,分摊到出售的储量与保留的储量之下,除非出售的矿区与保留的矿区之间存在实质经济差异(在此种情形下,资本化成本以矿区的相对公允价值为基础进行分摊)。石油与天然气矿区的废弃应计入资本化成本调整项,即废弃矿区的成本应记入完全成本中心借方并予以摊销[但应遵守本节第(b)款规定的资本化成本限制]。

(ii)购买储量。购买已有的石油与天然气储量通常应在适用的成本中心内计为追加资本化成本;但是,花费大额资金购买以生产收入支付租金的租约,或花费大额资金购买矿区,但相关租约或矿区的期限或寿命远低于成本中心综合生产寿命的,应予以独立核算。

(iii)合伙、合营与钻井安排。(A)除本节第(i)(6)(i)款规定的情形外,所有与石油与天然气勘探及开发活动的合伙、合营经营或其他各种形式的钻井安排相关的、因矿区出售或转让所收取的对价(如干股、全承包井、管理费等),均应记入完全成本账目贷方,但属于组织、要约、一般费用及行政费用等报销项目的金额除外,前提是该等金额为当期发生且已记入费用借方。

(B)如注册人组建并管理一家有限合伙,且该合伙仅涉及已开发探明矿区之购买及之后对该等矿区所得之分配,管理费所得可予以确认,前提是相关矿区并不要求与现有探明储量生产相关的总开发支出超过合伙关于该等矿区的记录成本的10%。因上述限制而未确认的任何所得均应记入完全成本账目贷方并在储量实际产出时,通过较低的摊销拨备予以确认。

(iv) *Other services.* No income shall be recognized in connection with contractual services performed (e.g. drilling, well service, or equipment supply services, etc.) in connection with properties in which the registrant or an affiliate (as defined in §210.1–02(b)) holds an ownership or other economic interest, except as follows:

(A) Where the registrant acquires an interest in the properties in connection with the service contract, income may be recognized to the extent the cash consideration received exceeds the related contract costs plus the registrant's share of costs incurred and estimated to be incurred in connection with the properties. Ownership interests acquired within one year of the date of such a contract are considered to be acquired in connection with the service for purposes of applying this rule. The amount of any guarantees or similar arrangements undertaken as part of this contract should be considered as part of the costs related to the properties for purposes of applying this rule.

(B) Where the registrant acquired an interest in the properties at least one year before the date of the service contract through transactions unrelated to the service contract, and that interest is unaffected by the service contract, income from such contract may be recognized subject to the general provisions for elimination of inter-company profit under generally accepted accounting principles.

(C) Notwithstanding the provisions of paragraphs (i)(6)(iv)(A) and (B) of this section, no income may be recognized for contractual services performed on behalf of investors in oil and gas producing activities managed by the registrant or an affiliate. Furthermore, no income may be recognized for contractual services to the extent that the consideration received for such services represents an interest in the underlying property.

(D) Any income not recognized as a result of these rules would be credited to the full cost account and recognized through a lower amortization provision as reserves are produced.

(7) *Disclosures.* Reporting entities that follow the full cost method of accounting shall disclose all of the information required by paragraph (k) of this section, with each cost center considered as a separate geographic area, except that reasonable groupings may be made of cost centers that are not significant in the aggregate. In addition:

(i) For each cost center for each year that an income statement is required, disclose the total amount of amortization expense (per equivalent physical unit of production if amortization is computed on the basis of physical units or per dollar of gross revenue from production if amortization is computed on the basis of gross revenue).

(ii) State separately on the face of the balance sheet the aggregate of the capitalized costs of unproved properties and major development projects that are excluded, in accordance with paragraph (i)(3) of this section, from the capitalized costs being amortized. Provide a description in the notes to the financial statements of the current

(iv)其他服务。对于注册人或控制性关联方[定义见第210.1-02(b)节]拥有所有权或其他经济权益的矿区,与相关合同服务(如钻井、油井服务或设备供应服务等)有关的所得不得予以确认,但下列情形除外:

(A)注册人收购与服务合同相关之矿区权益时,确认的收益应以所获现金对价超出下述金额的部分为限:相关合同成本与注册人所应承担的矿区产生或预期产生的成本份额之和。就本规则之适用而言,在该等合同日期后一年内收购的所有者权益,应视为与该等合同服务相关。就本规则之适用而言,在该合同内作出的任何保证或类似安排的金额,均应视为构成矿区相关成本的一部分。

(B)如注册人至少在服务合同日期一年之前,通过与该服务合同无关的交易取得矿区权益,且该权益不受服务合同影响,则来自该合同的所得可根据公认会计原则,按照公司间利润抵消的一般规定予以确认。

(C)无论本节第(i)(6)(iv)(A)款与第(i)(6)(iv)(B)款如何规定,对于在注册人或控制性关联方管理的石油与天然气生产活动中代表投资者开展的合同服务,所获金额不得确认为所得。此外,如合同服务的对价为相关矿区的权益,亦不得确认为所得。

(D)根据上述规则未予确认的所有所得,均应记入完全成本贷方,并在储量实际产出时,通过较低的摊销拨备予以确认。

(7)披露。采用会计完全成本法的报告实体,应披露本节第(k)款规定的所有信息,每个成本中心均视为单独的地理区域,但对于合计金额达不到重大水平的成本中心,可以进行合理分组。此外:

(i)就每个成本中心而言,对于应提交损益表的每一年,均应披露摊销费用的总金额(如摊销按物理单位进行计算,则以相同的产量物理单位计;如摊销按毛收入进行计算,则以美元毛收入计)。

(ii)应在资产负债表的正文单独列示,根据本节第(i)(3)款的规定排除在摊销资本化成本以外的未探明矿区和大型开发计划的资本化成本总额。在财务报表的附注中提供相关大型矿区或项目现状的说明,包括预期将成本纳入摊销计算的时间。提交一份按成本分类的表格,说明:(A)截至最近一个会计年度被排除的总成本;及(B)在下

status of the significant properties or projects involved, including the anticipated timing of the inclusion of the costs in the amortization computation. Present a table that shows, by category of cost, (A) the total costs excluded as of the most recent fiscal year; and (B) the amounts of such excluded costs, incurred (1) in each of the three most recent fiscal years and (2) in the aggregate for any earlier fiscal years in which the costs were incurred. Categories of cost to be disclosed include acquisition costs, exploration costs, development costs in the case of significant development projects and capitalized interest.

(8) For purposes of this paragraph (c), the term "current price" shall mean the average price during the 12-month period prior to the ending date of the period covered by the report, determined as an unweighted arithmetic average of the first-day-of-the-month price for each month within such period, unless prices are defined by contractual arrangements, excluding escalations based upon future conditions.

Income Taxes

(d) *Income taxes.* Comprehensive interperiod income tax allocation by a method which complies with generally accepted accounting principles shall be followed for intangible drilling and development costs and other costs incurred that enter into the determination of taxable income and pretax accounting income in different periods.

[43 FR 60405, Dec. 27, 1978, as amended at 43 FR 60417, Dec. 27, 1978; 44 FR 57036, 57038, Oct. 9, 1979; 45 FR 27749, Apr. 24, 1980. Redesignated and amended at 45 FR 63669, Sept. 25, 1980; 47 FR 57913, Dec. 29, 1982; 48 FR 44200, Sept. 28, 1983; 49 FR 18473, May 1, 1984; 57 FR 45293, Oct. 1, 1992; 61 FR 30401, June 14, 1996; 74 FR 2190, Jan. 14, 2009]

Commercial and Industrial Companies

§210.5-01 Application of §§210.5-01 to 210.5-04.

Sections 210.5-01 to 210.5-04 shall be applicable to financial statements filed for all persons except—

(a) Registered investment companies (see §§210.6-01 to 210.6-10).

(b) Employee stock purchase, savings and similar plans (see §§210.6A-01 to 210.6A-05).

(c) Insurance companies (see §§210.7-01 to 210.7-05).

(d) Bank holding companies and banks (see §§210.9-01 to 210.9-07).

(e) Brokers and dealers when filing Form X-17A-5 [249.617] (see §§240.17a-5 and 240.17a-10 under the Securities Exchange Act of 1934).

[50 FR 49533, Dec. 3, 1985]

述期间被排除的上述成本之金额:(1)最近3个会计年度内每年排除的金额;及(2)产生上述成本的所有之前会计年度内被排除的总金额。应披露的成本类别包括收购成本、勘探成本、大型开发项目的开发成本及资本化利息。

(8)就本第(c)款而言,除非价格系通过合同安排确定,并排除了基于未来状况而进行的价格调整,"现行价格"一词系指报告所覆盖期间截止之日前12个月期间的平均价格,按该期间每月第一天价格的不加权算术平均值计算。

所得税

(d)所得税。对于钻井与开发的无形成本,以及用于确定不同会计期间的应税所得与税前会计所得的成本,其所得税应以符合公认会计原则的方法进行全面跨期分摊。

[《联邦公报》第43卷第60405页,1978年12月27日,修正索引:《联邦公报》第43卷第60417页,1978年12月27日;《联邦公报》第44卷第57036页和第57038页,1979年10月9日;《联邦公报》第45卷第27749页,1980年4月24日。重新公布及修正索引:《联邦公报》第45卷第63669页,1980年9月25日;《联邦公报》第47卷第57913页,1982年12月29日;《联邦公报》第48卷第44200页,1983年9月28日;《联邦公报》第49卷第18473页,1984年5月1日;《联邦公报》第57卷第45293页,1992年10月1日;《联邦公报》第61卷第30401页,1996年6月14日;《联邦公报》第74卷第2190页,2009年1月14日。]

商业与工业公司

第210.5-01节 第210.5-01~210.5-04节的适用范围

第210.5-01~210.5-04节规定适用于所有主体提交的财务报表,但下列主体除外:

(a)注册投资公司(见第210.6-01~210.6-10节)。

(b)员工购股、储蓄和类似计划(见第210.6A-01~210.6A-05节)。

(c)保险公司(见第210.7-01~210.7-05节)。

(d)银行控股公司与银行(见第210.9-01~210.9-07节)。

(e)提交《X-17A-5表格》[《联邦规章汇编》第十七编第249.617节]的经纪商和自营商(见《1934年证券交易法》第240.17a-5节与第240.17a-10节)。

[《联邦公报》第50卷第49533页,1985年12月3日。]

§210.5–02 Balance sheets.

The purpose of this rule is to indicate the various line items and certain additional disclosures which, if applicable, and except as otherwise permitted by the Commission, should appear on the face of the balance sheets or related notes filed for the persons to whom this article pertains (see §210.4–01(a)).

Assets and Other Debits

Current Assets, when appropriate

1. *Cash and cash items.* Separate disclosure shall be made of the cash and cash items which are restricted as to withdrawal or usage. The provisions of any restrictions shall be described in a note to the financial statements. Restrictions may include legally restricted deposits held as compensating balances against short–term borrowing arrangements, contracts entered into with others, or company statements of intention with regard to particular deposits; however, time deposits and short–term certificates of deposit are not generally included in legally restricted deposits. In cases where compensating balance arrangements exist but are not agreements which legally restrict the use of cash amounts shown on the balance sheet, describe in the notes to the financial statements these arrangements and the amount involved, if determinable, for the most recent audited balance sheet required and for any subsequent unaudited balance sheet required in the notes to the financial statements. Compensating balances that are maintained under an agreement to assure future credit availability shall be disclosed in the notes to the financial statements along with the amount and terms of such agreement.

2. *Marketable securities.* The accounting and disclosure requirements for current marketable equity securities are specified by generally accepted accounting principles. With respect to all other current marketable securities, state, parenthetically or otherwise, the basis of determining the aggregate amount shown in the balance sheet, along with the alternatives of the aggregate cost or the aggregate market value at the balance sheet date.

3. *Accounts and notes receivable.* (a) State separately amounts receivable from (1) customers (trade); (2) related parties (see §210.4–08(k)); (3) underwriters, promoters, and employees (other than related parties) which arose in other than the ordinary course of business; and (4) others.

(b) If the aggregate amount of notes receivable exceeds 10 percent of the aggregate amount of receivables, the above information shall be set forth separately, in the balance sheet or in a note thereto, for accounts receivable and notes receivable.

(c) If receivables include amounts due under long–term contracts (see §210.5–02.6(d)), state separately in the balance sheet or in a note to the financial statements the following amounts:

第210.5-02节　资产负债表

本规则旨在说明适用本节规则的会计主体的资产负债表的正文或相关附注所应列示的行项目和特定补充披露内容(如适用),证券交易委员会另行允许不予披露的除外[见第210.4-01(a)节]。

资产与其他债务

流动资产(如适当)

(见第210.4-05节)

1.现金与现金项目。支取或使用受限的现金与现金项目,均应单独披露。限制性条款应通过财务报表附注予以说明,任何该等限制性条款均可包括:在短期借款安排中,作为补偿性余额持有的法定限制性存款;与他人订立的合同;或针对具体存款作出的公司意图声明;但是,一般而言,法定限制性存款并不包括定期存款与短期存单。如果存在补偿性余额安排,但该等安排并不属于以法定方式限制资产负债表现金的使用之协议,注册人应于财务报表附注中,针对最近一期经审计的资产负债表和任何未审计的期后资产负债表,注明与之相关的上述安排和所涉金额(如可确定)。如果为了确保未来可以获得信贷而签订任何协议,则在该等协议项下维持的补偿性余额以及该等协议的金额和条件均应于财务报表附注中披露。

2.有价证券。流动有价股权证券的会计要求和披露要求根据公认会计原则确定。就所有其他流动有价证券而言,应通过括号注释或其他方式说明确定资产负债表所列总金额时采用的基础,以及截至资产负债表日的总成本或总市值。

3.应收账款与应收票据。(a)单独列示以下应收项目:(1)客户(贸易)应收项目;(2)关联方[见第210.4-08(k)节]应收项目;(3)非正常业务运作中产生的承销商、创始人与员工(关联方除外)应收项目;及(4)其他应收项目。

(b)如应收票据总金额超过应收项目总金额的10%,应于资产负债表或其附注中,分别针对应收账款与应收票据提供上述信息。

(c)如应收账款包括长期合同下的到期金额[见第210.5-02.6(d)节],应于资产负债表或财务报表附注中单独列示如下金额:

(1) Balances billed but not paid by customers under retainage provisions in contracts.

(2) Amounts representing the recognized sales value of performance and such amounts that had not been billed and were not billable to customers at the date of the balance sheet. Include a general description of the prerequisites for billing.

(3) Billed or unbilled amounts representing claims or other similar items subject to uncertainty concerning their determination or ultimate realization. Include a description of the nature and status of the principal items comprising such amount.

(4) With respect to (1) through (3) above, also state the amounts included in each item which are expected to be collected after one year. Also state, by year, if practicable, when the amounts of retainage (see (1) above) are expected to be collected.

4. *Allowances for doubtful accounts and notes receivable.* The amount is to be set forth separately in the balance sheet or in a note thereto.

5. *Unearned income.*

6. *Inventories.* (a) State separately in the balance sheet or in a note thereto, if practicable, the amounts of major classes of inventory such as: (1) Finished goods; (2) inventoried costs relating to long-term contracts or programs (see (d) below and §210.4-05); (3) work in process (see §210.4-05); (4) raw materials; and (5) supplies. If the method of calculating a LIFO inventory does not allow for the practical determination of amounts assigned to major classes of inventory, the amounts of those classes may be stated under cost flow assumptions other that LIFO with the excess of such total amount over the agggregate LIFO amount shown as a deduction to arrive at the amount of the LIFO inventory.

(b) The basis of determining the amounts shall be stated.

If *cost* is used to determine any portion of the inventory amounts, the description of this method shall include the nature of the cost elements included in inventory. Elements of *cost* include, among other items, retained costs representing the excess of manufacturing or production costs over the amounts charged to cost of sales or delivered or in-process units, initial tooling or other deferred startup costs, or general and administrative costs.

The method by which amounts are removed from inventory (e.g., *average cost, first-in, first-out, last-in, first-out, estimated average cost per unit*) shall be described. If the estimated average cost per unit is used as a basis to determine amounts removed from inventory under a total program or similar basis of accounting, the principal assumptions (including, where meaningful, the aggregate number of units expected to be delivered under the program, the number of units delivered to date and the number of units on order) shall be disclosed.

If any general and administrative costs are charged to inventory, state in a note to the

(1)根据合同中的保留金条款已开具账单但客户尚未支付之余额。

(2)合同服务已确认的销售值金额,以及截至资产负债表日尚未且无法向客户开具账单的该等金额。此外,应对开具账单的基础条件进行一般性说明。

(3)已开具账单或尚未开具账单的下列项目的金额:索赔,或者,其金额尚未确定或最终是否能实现尚不明确的其他类似项目。此外,应对构成该等金额的主要项目之性质与状态进行说明。

(4)就上文第(1)项至第(3)项的规定而言,还应说明一年之后,每一项目预期将收回的金额。同时也应按年份说明(如可行)保留金的预期收回时间[见上文第(1)项的规定]。

4.可疑应收账款与可疑应收票据备抵。相关金额应于资产负债表或其附注中单列。

5.消极所得。

6.库存。(a)在资产负债表或其附注中单独列示主要类型库存的金额(如可行),包括但不限于:(1)成品;(2)与长期合同或计划相关的库存成本[见下文第(d)项与第210.4-05节];(3)在制品(见第210.4-05节);(4)原材料;与(5)物资。如果采用后进先出法,计算某一库存的价格,无法确定分配至主要类型库存的金额,则该等主要类型库存金额可不采用后进先出库存法,而采用成本流假设(而非后进先出法)列报,由此计算的主要类型库存的总额超出以后进先出法计算出的总金额的部分应作为扣除项列示,扣除后所得金额即为后进先出库存金额。

(b)确定相关金额的基础应予以说明。

如果使用"成本"法确定库存金额的任何一部分,对该方法进行描述时应说明库存中所含成本要素的性质。"成本"要素包括但不限于保留成本[保留成本指:制造或生产成本超出记入销售成本或已交货产品成本(按单位计算)或在制产品成本(按单位计算)借方的部分]、初始工装成本或其他递延启动成本,以及一般费用及行政费用。

应说明减计库存金额的方法(如"平均成本法"、"先进先出法"、"后进先出法"、"估算单位平均成本法")。如以估算单位平均成本法作为某一完整计划下减计库存金额的基础,或以其作为类似的核算基础,则应披露主要的假设(如有必要,应包括计划下预计交付产品的合计单位数量、至今已交付的单位数量和已下单单位数量)。

如果任何一般费用及行政费用记入库存借方,则应于财务报表附注中说明每一

financial statements the aggregate amount of the general and administrative costs incurred in each period and the actual or estimated amount remaining in inventory at the date of each balance sheet.

(c) If the LIFO inventory method is used, the excess of replacement or current cost over stated LIFO value shall, if material, be stated parenthetically or in a note to the financial statements.

(d) For purposes of §§210.5–02.3 and 210.5–02.6, long–term contracts or programs include (1) all contracts or programs for which gross profits are recognized on a percentage–of–completion method of accounting or any variant thereof (e.g., delivered unit, cost to cost, physical completion), and (2) any contracts or programs accounted for on a completed contract basis of accounting where, in either case, the contracts or programs have associated with them material amounts of inventories or unbilled receivables and where such contracts or programs have been or are expected to be performed over a period of more than twelve months. Contracts or programs of shorter duration may also be included, if deemed appropriate.

For all long–term contracts or programs, the following information, if applicable, shall be stated in a note to the financial statements:

(i) The aggregate amount of manufacturing or production costs and any related deferred costs (e.g., initial tooling costs) which exceeds the aggregate estimated cost of all in–process and delivered units on the basis of the estimated average cost of all units expected to be produced under long–term contracts and programs not yet complete, as well as that portion of such amount which would not be absorbed in cost of sales based on existing firm orders at the latest balance sheet date. In addition, if practicable, disclose the amount of deferred costs by type of cost (e.g., initial tooling, deferred production, etc.).

(ii) The aggregate amount representing claims or other similar items subject to uncertainty concerning their determination or ultimate realization, and include a description of the nature and status of the principal items comprising such aggregate amount.

(iii) The amount of progress payments netted against inventory at the date of the balance sheet.

7. *Prepaid expenses.*

8. *Other current assets.* State separately, in the balance sheet or in a note thereto, any amounts in excess of five percent of total current assets.

9. *Total current assets, when appropriate.*

10. *Securities of related parties* (See §210.4–08(k).).

11. *Indebtedness of related parties — not current* (See §210.4–08(k).).

报告期发生的一般费用及行政费用总金额,以及截至每一资产负债表日的实际或预估剩余库存量。

(c)如使用后进先出库存法,重置成本或现行成本大幅超出所述后进先出价值时,超出部分应通过括号注释或在财务报表附注中加以说明。

(d)就第210.5-02.3节和第210.5-02.6节而言,长期合同或计划包括:(1)确认毛利时以完工百分比法或任何类似方法(如已交付单位法、成本比例法、实际完成比例法)作为核算基础的所有合约或计划;和(2)以履行完毕合同法为核算基础的任何合同或计划,且在以上两种情形下,该等合同或计划均应有大额库存量或大额未开具账单的应收账款,同时该等合同或计划履行的时间或预期履行时间超过12个月。但在适当情况下,也可包括期限较短的合同或计划。

应于财务报表附注中说明所有长期合同或计划的如下信息(如适用):

(i)制造或生产成本以及任何相关递延成本(如初始工装成本)超出所有在制单位数量产品及已交付单位数量产品的预估总成本的总金额(预估总成本以尚未履行完毕的长期合同及计划下预期将生产的所有单位数量产品的预估平均成本为基础进行计算),以及该等金额中不会被销售成本所吸纳的部分(以截至最近一期资产负债表日的现有确定订单为基础进行计算)。此外,如可行,应按成本类型披露递延成本金额(如初始工装成本、递延生产成本等)。

(ii)索赔总金额,或者,其金额尚未确定或最终是否能实现尚不明确的类似项目的总金额。此外,应对构成该等金额的主要项目之性质和状态进行说明。

(iii)截至资产负债表日,进度款扣除库存之后的金额。

7.预付费用。

8.其他流动资产。在资产负债表或其附注中单独列示所有超过总流动资产5%的金额。

9.总流动资产(如适当)。

10.关联方证券[见第210.4-08(k)节]。

11.关联方债务——非流动债务[见第210.4-08(k)节]。

12. *Other investments.* The accounting and disclosure requirements for non-current marketable equity securities are specified by generally accepted accounting principles. With respect to other security investments and any other investment, state, parenthetically or otherwise, the basis of determining the aggregate amounts shown in the balance sheet, along with the alternate of the aggregate cost or aggregate market value at the balance sheet date.

13. *Property, plant and equipment.*

(a) State the basis of determining the amounts.

(b) Tangible and intangible utility plant of a public utility company shall be segregated so as to show separately the original cost, plant acquisition adjustments, and plant adjustments, as required by the system of accounts prescribed by the applicable regulatory authorities. This rule shall not be applicable in respect to companies which are not required to make such a classification.

14. *Accumulated depreciation, depletion, and amortization of property, plant and equipment.* The amount is to be set forth separately in the balance sheet or in a note thereto.

15. *Intangible assets.* State separately each class of such assets which is in excess of five percent of the total assets, along with the basis of determining the respective amounts. Any significant addition or deletion shall be explained in a note.

16. *Accumulated depreciation and amortization of intangible assets.* The amount is to be set forth separately in the balance sheet or in a note thereto.

17. *Other assets.* State separately, in the balance sheet or in a note thereto, any other item not properly classed in one of the preceding asset captions which is in excess of five percent to total assets. Any significant addition or deletion should be explained in a note. With respect to any significant deferred charge, state the policy for deferral and amortization.

18. *Total assets.*

Liabilities and Stockholders' Equity

Current Liabilities, When Appropriate (See §210.4-05)

19. *Accounts and notes payable.* (a) State separately amounts payable to (1) banks for borrowings; (2) factors or other financial institutions for borrowings; (3) holders of commercial paper; (4) trade creditors; (5) related parties (see §210.4-08(k)); (6) underwriters, promoters, and employees (other than related parties); and (7) others. Amounts applicable to (1), (2) and (3) may be stated separately in the balance sheet or in a note thereto.

(b) The amount and terms (including commitment fees and the conditions under which lines may be withdrawn) of unused lines of credit for short-term financing shall be

12.其他投资。非流动有价股权证券的会计要求和披露要求根据公认会计原则确定。就其他证券投资和所有其他投资而言,应通过括号注释或其他方式说明计算资产负债表所列总金额的基础,以及截至资产负债表日的总成本或总市值。

13.财产、厂房和设备。

(a)说明相关金额的计算基础。

(b)公用事业公司的有形和无形公用设施应予分离,以根据相关监管部门规定的会计系统要求,单列各自的原始成本、厂房购买调整和厂房调整。不必进行此等分类的公司则不适用本规则。

14.累计折旧、折损以及财产、厂房和设备的摊销。相关金额应于资产负债表或其附注中单列。

15.无形资产。超过总资产5%的每类无形资产,以及每一金额的计算基础均应单独列示。金额的所有重大增减亦均应通过附注进行解释。

16.累计折旧和有形资产的摊销。折旧和摊销金额应于资产负债表或其附注中单独列出。

17.其他资产。应于资产负债表或其附注中,单独列出未能适当归入以上资产科目且金额超过总资产5%的所有其他项目。金额的所有重大增减均应通过附注进行解释。任何重大递延费用均应说明递延和摊销政策。

18.总资产。

负债和股东权益

流动负债(如适当)(见第210.4-05节)

19.应付账款和应付票据。(a)单独列示应向以下各方支付的金额:(1)借款银行;(2)借款代理人或其他金融机构;(3)商业票据持有人;(4)贸易债权人;(5)关联方[见第210.4-08(k)节];(6)承销商、创始人与员工(关联方除外);和(7)其他。第(1)项、第(2)项和第(3)项的金额可于资产负债表或其附注中单独列示。

(b)如果短期融资信用的未用额度显著偏高,应通过财务报表附注披露未用额度的金额和条件(包括贷款承诺费及取消信用额度的条件)。截至资产负债表提交日的

disclosed, if significant, in the notes to the financial statements. The weighted average interest rate on short term borrowings outstanding as of the date of each balance sheet presented shall be furnished in a note. The amount of these lines of credit which support a commercial paper borrowing arrangement or similar arrangements shall be separately identified.

20. *Other current liabilities.* State separately, in the balance sheet or in a note thereto, any item in excess of 5 percent of total current liabilities. Such items may include, but are not limited to, accrued payrolls, accrued interest, taxes, indicating the current portion of deferred income taxes, and the current portion of long-term debt. Remaining items may be shown in one amount.

21. *Total current liabilities, when appropriate.*

Long-Term Debt

22. *Bonds, mortgages and other long-term debt, including capitalized leases.* (a) State separately, in the balance sheet or in a note thereto, each issue or type of obligation and such information as will indicate (see §210.4-06):

(1) The general character of each type of debt including the rate of interest; (2) the date of maturity, or, if maturing serially, a brief indication of the serial maturities, such as "maturing serially from 1980 to 1990"; (3) if the payment of principal or interest is contingent, an appropriate indication of such contingency; (4) a brief indication of priority; and (5) if convertible, the basis. For amounts owed to related parties, see §210.4-08(k).

(b) The amount and terms (including commitment fees and the conditions under which commitments may be withdrawn) of unused commitments for long-term financing arrangements that would be disclosed under this rule if used shall be disclosed in the notes to the financial statements if significant.

23. *Indebtedness to related parties — noncurrent.* Include under this caption indebtedness to related parties as required under §210.4-08(k).

24. *Other liabilities.* State separately, in the balance sheet or in a note thereto, any item not properly classified in one of the preceding liability captions which is in excess of 5 percent of total liabilities.

25. *Commitments and contingent liabilities.*

26. *Deferred credits.* State separately in the balance sheet amounts for (a) deferred income taxes, (b) deferred tax credits,and (c) material items of deferred income.

Redeemable Preferred Stocks

27. Preferred stocks subject to mandatory redemption requirements or whose redemption is outside the control of the issuer. (a) Include under this caption amounts applicable to any class of stock which has any of the following characteristics: (1) it is redeemable at a

未偿短期贷款余额加权平均利率，亦应在附注中说明。为商业票据借款安排或类似安排提供支持的信用额度，应分别注明金额。

20.其他流动负债。应于资产负债表或其附注中单独列示金额超过流动负债总额5%的所有项目，此等项目应包括但不限于应付工资、应计利息、税款，并说明递延所得税的流动部分和长期债务的流动部分。其余项目可以通过一个单独的总金额予以反映。

21.总流动负债(如适当)。

长期债务

22.债券、抵押及其他长期债务，包括资本化租赁。(a)于资产负债表或其附注中，单独列示每次债务发行或每种债务类别，并说明以下相关信息(见第210.4-06节)：

(1)每类债务的一般特性(包括利率)；(2)到期日(如分次到期，则简要说明相关信息，如"于1980年至1990年期间分次到期")；(3)如本金或利息支付属于或有项目，应适当注明其或有性质；(4)简单注明优先级别；和(5)如属于可转换债务，则须注明转换基础。至于向关联方欠负的金额，见第210.4-08(k)节。

(b)根据本规定一经使用则须披露的长期融资安排，如未用信用额度显著偏高，应通过财务报表附注披露未用额度的金额和条件(包括承诺费及取消信用额度的条件)。

23.欠负关联方的债务——非流动债务。应按照第210.4-08(k)节的规定，将欠负关联方的债务计入本科目下。

24.其他负债。应于资产负债表或其附注中，单列所有未能适当归入以上负债项目且金额超过总负债5%的任何项目。

25.承诺和或有负债。

26.递延贷项。应于资产负债表中单列如下金额：(a)递延所得税；(b)递延税收抵免；和(c)重大递延所得项目。

可回赎优先股

27.可强制回赎的优先股或回赎与否不由发行人控制的优先股。(a)具有任何下列性质的任何类别股票金额均应计入本科目：(1)将于一个或数个固定日期或可确定的日期，以固定价格或可确定的价格回赎的股票，不论是通过偿债基金回赎还是通过其

fixed or determinable price on a fixed or determinable date or dates, whether by operation of a sinking fund or otherwise; (2) it is redeemable at the option of the holder; or (3) it has conditions for redemption which are not solely within the control of the issuer, such as stocks which must be redeemed out of future earnings. Amounts attributable to preferred stock which is not redeemable or is redeemable solely at the option of the issuer shall be included under §210.5-02.28 unless it meets one or more of the above criteria.

(b) State on the face of the balance sheet the title of each issue, the carrying amount, and redemption amount. (If there is more than one issue, these amounts may be aggregated on the face of the balance sheet and details concerning each issue may be presented in the note required by paragraph (c) below.) Show also the dollar amount of any shares subscribed but unissued, and show the deduction of subscriptions receivable therefrom. If the carrying value is different from the redemption amount, describe the accounting treatment for such difference in the note required by paragraph (c) below. Also state in this note or on the face of the balance sheet, for each issue, the number of shares authorized and the number of shares issued or outstanding, as appropriate (See §210.4-07).

(c) State in a separate note captioned "Redeemable Preferred Stocks" (1) a general description of each issue, including its redemption features (e.g. sinking fund, at option of holders, out of future earnings) and the rights, if any, of holders in the event of default, including the effect, if any, on junior securities in the event a required dividend, sinking fund, or other redemption payment(s) is not made; (2) the combined aggregate amount of redemption requirements for all issues each year for the five years following the date of the latest balance sheet; and (3) the changes in each issue for each period for which an income statement is required to be filed (See also §210.4-08(d).).

(d) Securities reported under this caption are not to be included under a general heading "stockholders' equity" or combined in a total with items described in captions 29, 30 or 31 which follow.

Non-Redeemable Preferred Stocks

28. *Preferred stocks which are not redeemable or are redeemable solely at the option of the issuer.* State on the face of the balance sheet, or if more than one issue is outstanding state in a note, the title of each issue and the dollar amount thereof. Show also the dollar amount of any shares subscribed but unissued, and show the deduction of subscriptions receivable therefrom. State on the face of the balance sheet or in a note, for each issue, the number of shares authorized and the number of shares issued or outstanding, as appropriate (see §210.4-07). Show in a note or separate statement the changes in each class of preferred shares reported under this caption for each period for

他方式回赎;(2)是否回赎取决于持有人的选择的股票;或(3)回赎条件并不完全由发行人控制的股票,如股票只能通过未来盈利回赎的情形。归属于不可回赎或只能由发行人选择回赎的优先股的金额,除非符合以上一项或多项标准,否则均应按照第210.5-02.28节计入资产负债表。

(b)在资产负债表正文说明每次发行的名称、账面金额和回赎金额[如发行次数为一次以上,则可于资产负债表正文对各次发行金额进行合计汇总,每次发行的详细信息均可依下文第(c)款规定通过附注列示]。同时,应列明已认购但尚未发行的任何股票的金额,并列明相关应收认购股款的扣除额。如果账面价值与回赎金额存在差异,请依照下文第(c)款规定在附注中说明此等差异的会计处理方法。同时,还应于该附注或资产负债表正文中注明每次发行的授权股数,并视适当情况说明已发行股数或仍发行在外的股数(见第210.4-07节)。

(c)单设名为"可回赎优先股"附注,并在其中说明:(1)对每次发行的一般性说明,包括其回赎特点(如通过偿债基金回赎、持有人行使选择权进行回赎、通过未来盈利回赎)以及发生违约时持有人的权利(如有),包括未按要求支付股息、偿债基金或其他回赎款时对次级证券的影响(如有);(2)最近一期资产负债表日后5年内,每年度所有发行的回赎要求的合并总金额;和(3)按规定应提交损益表的每个报告期内每次发行的变动[见第210.4-08(d)节]。

(d)在本科目下报告的证券,并不计入一般性科目"股东权益"下,也不并入下文第29项、第30科目或第31科目的总额之内。

不可回赎优先股

28.不可回赎或只能由发行人选择回赎的优先股。应于资产负债表正文(如发行次数为一次以上,则应通过附注)说明每次发行的名称及相关金额。同时,应列明已认购但尚未发行的任何股票的金额,并列明相关应收认购股款的扣除额。应于资产负债表正文或附注中注明每次发行的授权股数,并视适当情况说明已发行股数或仍发行在外的股数(见第210.4-07节)。在本科目中报告的每类优先股于应提交损益表的报告期内发生的变动,应通过附注或另外一份报表予以列明[见第210.4-08(d)节]。

which an income statement is required to be filed (See also §210.4–08(d).).

Common Stocks

29. *Common stocks.* For each class of common shares state, on the face of the balance sheet, the number of shares issued or outstanding, as appropriate (see §210.4–07), and the dollar amount thereof. If convertible, this fact should be indicated on the face of the balance sheet. For each class of common shares state, on the face of the balance sheet or in a note, the title of the issue, the number of shares authorized, and, if convertible, the basis of conversion (see also §210.4–08(d)). Show also the dollar amount of any common shares subscribed but unissued, and show the deduction of subscriptions receivable therefrom. Show in a note or statement the changes in each class of common shares for each period for which an income statement is required to be filed.

Other Stockholders' Equity

30. *Other stockholders' equity.* (a) Separate captions shall be shown for (1) additional paid–in capital, (2) other additional capital, and (3) retained earnings (i) appropriated and (ii) unappropriated (See §210.4–08(e).). Additional paid–in capital and other additional capital may be combined with the stock caption to which it applies, if appropriate.

(b) For a period of at least 10 years subsequent to the effective date of a quasi–reorganization, any description of retained earnings shall indicate the point in time from which the new retained earnings dates and for a period of at least three years shall indicate, on the face of the balance sheet, the total amount of the deficit eliminated.

Noncontrolling Interests

31. *Noncontrolling interests in consolidated subsidiaries.* State separately in a note the amounts represented by preferred stock and the applicable dividend requirements if the preferred stock is material in relation to the consolidated equity.

32. *Total liabilities and equity.*

[45 FR 63671, Sept. 25, 1980, as amended at 46 FR 43412, Aug. 28, 1981; 47 FR 29837, July 9, 1982; 50 FR 25215, June 18, 1985; 50 FR 49533, Dec. 3, 1985; 59 FR 65636, Dec. 20, 1994; 74 FR 18615, Apr. 23, 2009]

§210.5–03 Income statements.

(a) The purpose of this rule is to indicate the various line items which, if applicable, and except as otherwise permitted by the Commission, should appear on the face of the income statements filed for the persons to whom this article pertains (see §210.4–01(a)).

(b) If income is derived from more than one of the subcaptions described under §210.5–03.1, each class which is not more than 10 percent of the sum of the items may

普通股

29.普通股。应视适当情况于资产负债表正文说明每类普通股的已发行股数或发行在外的股数(见第210.4-07节)及相关金额。如股票属于可转换股票,应于资产负债表正文注明。应于资产负债表的正文或附注中注明每类普通股的授权股数,如股票属于可转换股票,应说明其转换基础[同时参见第210.4-08(d)节]。同时,还应列明所有已认购但尚未发行的任何普通股的金额,并列明相关应收认购股款的扣除额。每类普通股于应提交损益表的报告期内发生的变动,应通过附注或另外一份报表予以列明。

其他股东权益

30.其他股东权益。(a)按单独的科目列明:(1)资本溢价;(2)其他追加资本;及(3)(i)拨定留存盈利,和(ii)未拨定留存盈利[见第210.4-08(e)节]。资本溢价和其他追加资本可视情况并入相关的股票科目。

(b)在准重组生效日之后至少10年的期间内,有关留存盈余的任何说明均应注明新留存盈余开始的时点,且至少应于准重组生效日后3年期间内,在资产负债表的正文注明抵消赤字的总金额。

非控制权益

31.并表子公司的非控制权益。如优先股在并表权益中占重大比例,应于附注中单独列示优先股代表的金额以及相关的股息规定。

32.负债和权益总额

[《联邦公报》第45卷第63671页,1980年9月25日,修正索引:《联邦公报》第46卷第43412页,1981年8月28日;《联邦公报》第47卷第29837页,1982年7月9日;《联邦公报》第50卷第25215页,1985年6月18日;《联邦公报》第50卷第49533页,1985年12月3日;《联邦公报》第59卷第65636页,1994年12月20日;《联邦公报》第74卷第18615页;2009年4月23日。]

第210.5-03节　损益表

(a)本规则旨在说明适用本节规则的会计主体的损益表正文所应列示的行项目(如适用),证券交易委员会另行允许不予披露的除外[见第210.4-01(a)节]。

(b)如所得来自第210.5-03.1节所述一个以上的子科目,则金额不超过各所得项目金额总和10%的每类所得均可与另一类所得归并。项目按上述规定归并的,第

be combined with another class. If these items are combined, related costs and expenses as described under §210.5–03.2 shall be combined in the same manner.

1. *Net sales and gross revenues.* State separately:

(a) Net sales of tangible products (gross sales less discounts, returns and allowances); (b) operating revenues of public utilities or others; (c) income from rentals; (d) revenues from services; and (e) other revenues. Amounts earned from transactions with related parties shall be disclosed as required under §210.4–08(k). A public utility company using a uniform system of accounts or a form for annual report prescribed by federal or state authorities, or a similar system or report, shall follow the general segregation of operating revenues and operating expenses reported under §210.5–03.2 prescribed by such system or report. If the total of sales and revenues reported under this caption includes excise taxes in an amount equal to 1 percent or more of such total, the amount of such excise taxes shall be shown on the face of the statement parenthetically or othewise.

2. *Costs and expenses applicable to sales and revenues.*

State separately the amount of (a) cost of tangible goods sold, (b) operating expenses of public utilities or others, (c) expenses applicable to rental income, (d) cost of services, and (e) expenses applicable to other revenues. Merchandising organizations, both wholesale and retail, may include occupancy and buying costs under caption 2(a). Amounts of costs and expenses incurred from transactions with related parties shall be disclosed as required under §210.4–08(k).

3. *Other operating costs and expenses.* State separately any material amounts not included under caption 2 above.

4. *Selling, general and administrative expenses.*

5. *Provision for doubtful accounts and notes.*

6. *Other general expenses.* Include items not normally included in caption 4 above. State separately any material item.

7. *Non–operating income.*

State separately in the income statement or in a note thereto amounts earned from (a) dividends, (b) interest on securities, (c) profits on securities (net of losses), and (d) miscellaneous other income. Amounts earned from transactions in securities of related parties shall be disclosed as required under §210.4–08 (k). Material amounts included under miscellaneous other income shall be separately stated in the income statement or in a note thereto, indicating clearly the nature of the transactions out of which the items arose.

8. *Interest and amortization of debt discount and expense.*

210.5-03.2节所述的相关成本与费用应以同样方式归并。

1.净销售额和毛收入。分别列示:

(a)有形产品净销售额(销售毛收入减去折扣、退货和折让);(b)公用事业营业收入或其他收入;(c)租金收益;(d)服务收入;及(e)其他收入。因关联交易赚取的金额应根据第210.4-08(k)节的要求进行披露。使用统一的会计系统,或依照联邦或各州主管机构规定的年度报告格式,或使用类似系统或报告的公用事业公司,应根据该等系统或报告的规定,对根据第210.5-03.2节报告的营业收入与营业费用适用一般分离的原则。如本科目下报告的销售总额和收入总额包括金额大于等于该总额1%的消费税,则消费税金额应在报表正文中通过括号注释或以其他方式说明。

2.与销售额与收入相关的成本与费用。

分别列示下列金额:(a)有形商品销货成本;(b)公用事业营业费用或其他费用;(c)与租金收益相关的费用;(d)服务成本;和(e)与其他收入相关的费用。销售组织(包括批发和零售组织)可将场地使用费与采购成本计入第2(a)科目。关联交易产生的成本和费用应依照第210.4-08(k)节的要求披露。

3.其他营业成本与费用。请单独列示所有不包括在上文第二科目中的重大金额。

4.销售费用、一般费用及行政费用。

5.呆账备抵。

6.其他一般费用。包括通常不列入上文第4科目中的项目。任何重大项目均应单独列示。

7.营业外收入。

于损益表或其附注中单独列示因下列项目赚取的金额:(a)股息;(b)证券利息;(c)证券利润(指扣除损失之后的净利润);和(d)其他杂项所得。交易关联方的证券所赚取的金额应根据第210.4-08(k)节规定披露。包括在其他杂项所得项下的重大金额应于损益表或其附注中单独列示,并明确注明与该项目相关的交易之性质。

8.利息以及债务折扣和费用的摊销。

9. *Non-operating expenses.*

State separately in the income statement or in a note thereto amounts of (a) losses on securities (net of profits) and (b) miscellaneous income deductions. Material amounts included under miscellaneous income deductions shall be separately stated in the income statement or in a note thereto, indicating clearly the nature of the transactions out of which the items arose.

10. *Income or loss before income tax expense and appropriate items below.*

11. *Income tax expense.* Include under this caption only taxes based on income (see §210.4–08(h)).

12. *Equity in earnings of unconsolidated subsidiaries and 50 percent or less owned persons.* State, parenthetically or in a note, the amount of dividends received from such persons. If justified by the circumstances, this item may be presented in a different position and a different manner (see §210.4–01(a)).

13. *Income or loss from continuing operations.*

14. *Discontinued operations.*

15. *Income or loss before extraordinary items and cumulative effects of changes in accounting principles.*

16. *Extraordinary items, less applicable tax.*

17. *Cumulative effects of changes in accounting principles.*

18. *Net income or loss.*

19. *Net income attributable to the noncontrolling interest.*

20. *Net income attributable to the controlling interest.*

21. *Earnings per share data.*

[45 FR 63671, Sept. 25, 1980, as amended at 45 FR 76977, Nov. 21, 1980; 50 FR 25215, June 18, 1985; 74 FR 18615, Apr. 23, 2009]

§210.5–04 What schedules are to be filed.

(a) Except as expressly provided otherwise in the applicable form:

(1) The schedules specified below in this Section as Schedules Ⅱ and Ⅲ shall be filed as of the date of the most recent audited balanced sheet for each person or group.

(2) Schedule Ⅱ shall be filed for each period for which an audited income statement is required to be filed for each person or group.

(3) Schedules Ⅰ and Ⅳ shall be filed as of the date and for periods specified in the schedule.

(b) When information is required in schedules for both the registrant and the registrant and its subsidiaries consolidated it may be presented in the form of a single schedule: *Provided,* That items pertaining to the registrant are separately shown and that

9.营业外费用。

于损益表或其附注中单独列示下列项目的金额:(a)证券损失(指扣除利润之后的净损失);和(b)杂项所得扣除项。计入杂项所得扣除项的重大金额应于损益表或其附注中单独列示,并明确注明与该项目相关的交易性质。

10.扣除所得税费用和下列适当项目之前的损益。

11.所得税费用。本科目仅包括基于所得之税收[见第210.4-08(h)节]。

12.在非并表子公司及50%或以下股权被控主体的盈利中享有的权益。应通过括号注释或附注说明从该等主体处收到的股息金额。如无不当,此项目可在损益表的不同部分以不同方式列报[见第210.4-01(a)节]。

13.持续经营损益。

14.已终止经营的业务。

15.扣除非经常项目和会计原则变更累积影响数之前的损益。

16.非经常项目,减去适用税款。

17.会计原则变更累积影响数。

18.净损益。

19.归属于非控制权益的净收益。

20.归属于控制权益的净收益。

21.每股盈利数据。

[《联邦公报》第45卷第63671页,1980年9月25日,修正索引:《联邦公报》第45卷第76977页,1980年11月21日;《联邦公报》第50卷第25215页,1985年6月18日;《联邦公报》第74卷第18615页,2009年4月23日。]

第210.5-04节　应提交的附表

(a)除非申请表另有明确规定:

(1)本节下文所述附表Ⅱ和附表Ⅲ,其截止日期以各主体或集团最近一期经审计的资产负债表日为准。

(2)本节下文所述附表Ⅱ,其报告期以按规定应提交各主体或集团经审计的损益表的报告期为准。

(3)附表Ⅰ和附表Ⅳ,其截止日期和报告期以相应附表所述日期为准。

(b)注册人的附表及注册人和其子公司的合并附表中均要求提供的信息,可以通过单一附表统一列报;但是,与注册人有关的项目应单列,且该单一附表应对各项事实进行适当的摘要性列报。如果任何附表(包括其附注)要求提供的信息可以在相关

such single schedule affords a properly summarized presentation of the facts. If the information required by any schedule (including the notes thereto) may be shown in the related financial statement or in a note thereto without making such statement unclear or confusing, that procedure may be followed and the schedule omitted.

(c) The schedules shall be examined by the independent accountant if the related financial statements are so examined.

Schedule I — Condensed financial information of registrant. The schedule prescribed by §210.12-04 shall be filed when the restricted net assets (§210.4-08(e)(3)) of consolidated subsidiaries exceed 25 percent of consolidated net assets as of the end of the most recently completed fiscal year. For purposes of the above test, restricted net assets of consolidated subsidiaries shall mean that amount of the registrant's proportionate share of net assets of consolidated subsidiaries (after intercompany eliminations) which as of the end of the most recent fiscal year may not be transferred to the parent company by subsidiaries in the form of loans, advances or cash dividends without the consent of a third party (*i.e.*, lender, regulatory agency, foreign government, etc.). Where restrictions on the amount of funds which may be loaned or advanced differ from the amount restricted as to transfer in the form of cash dividends, the amount least restrictive to the subsidiary shall be used. Redeemable preferred stocks (§210.5-02.27) and noncontrolling interests shall be deducted in computing net assets for purposes of this test.

*Schedule Ⅱ — Valuation and qualifying accounts.*The schedule prescribed by §210.12-09 shall be filed in support of valuation and qualifying accounts included in each balance sheet but not included in Schedule Ⅵ (See §210.4-02.).

*Schedule Ⅲ — Real estate and accumulated depreciation.*The schedule prescribed by §210.12-28 shall be filed for real estate (and the related accumulated depreciation) held by persons a substantial portion of whose business is that of acquiring and holding for investment real estate or interests in real estate, or interests in other persons a substantial portion of whose business is that of acquiring and holding real estate or interests in real estate for investment. Real estate used in the business shall be excluded from the schedule.

*Schedule IV — Mortgage loans on real estate.*The schedule prescribed by §210.12-29 shall be filed by persons specified under Schedule Ⅺ for investments in mortgage loans on real estate.

*Schedule V — Supplemental Information Concerning Property-casualty Insurance Operations.*The schedule prescribed by §210.12-18 shall be filed when a registrant, its subsidiaries or 50%-or-less-owned equity basis investees, have liabilities for property-casualty ("P/C") insurance claims. The required information shall be presented as of the same dates and for the same periods for which the information is reflected in the audited

财务报表或其附注中体现并且该等做法不会导致该报表不清楚或造成混淆,则可以将该等信息纳入该财务报表或其附注中,不必另行提交附表。

(c)如相关财务报表经独立会计师核验,附表亦应由独立会计师核验。

附表I——注册人的简明财务信息。并表子公司的受限净资产[见第210.4-08(e)(3)节]超过截至最近结束的一个会计年度年末其被纳入合并报表的净资产的25%时,应提交第210.12-04节规定的附表。在进行测试以判断是否符合上述标准时,并表子公司的受限净资产指截至最近一个会计年度年末,该子公司未经第三方(即贷款人、监管机构、外国政府等)同意,不得以贷款、垫款或现金股息的形式向母公司转移的,注册人按比例在并表子公司净资产占有的数额(该数额应为进行公司间抵消后的数额)。如受限贷款或垫款金额与受限制不得以现金股息形式转移的金额存在差异,应采用对子公司限制较低的金额。本测试中,计算净资产时应扣除可回赎优先股(第210.5-02.27节)及非控制权益。

附表Ⅱ——估值和合格账户。按第210.12-09节规定提交的附表应当用于支持纳入所有资产负债表、但未纳入附表Ⅵ的估值和合格账户(见第210.4-02节)。

附表Ⅲ——房地产和累计折旧。对于房地产持有者,如其业务的一个重大组成部分是为投资目的购买或持有房地产或房地产权益,或购买或持有以购买或持有投资性房地产或房地产权益为重大业务组成部分的其他主体的权益,则应提交第210.12-28节规定的附表。为营业目的使用的房地产应排除于本附表之外。

附表IV——房地产抵押贷款。附表XI规定的主体应就房地产抵押贷款投资提交第210.12-29节规定的附表。

附表V——关于财险业务的补充信息。注册人、其子公司或50%或以下股权被控的投资对象因财产意外险索赔而承担债务的,应提交第210.12-18节规定的附表,其截止日期和报告期应与第210.3-01节和第210.3-02节要求提供的经审计的合并财务报表中所体现的信息保持一致。如果截至会计年度年初,注册人及其并表子公司、非并表子公司和50%或以下股权被控的投资对象的未付财产意外险赔款金额和赔款调整

consolidated financial statements required by §§210.3-01 and 3-02. The schedule may be omitted if reserves for unpaid P/C claims and claims adjustment expenses of the registrant and its consolidated subsidiaries, its unconsolidated subsidiaries and its 50%-or-less-owned equity basis investees did not, in the aggregate, exceed one-half of common stockholders' equity of the registrant and its consolidated subsidiaries as of the beginning of the fiscal year. For purposes of this test only the proportionate share of the registrant and its other subsidiaries in the reserves for unpaid claims and claim adjustment expenses of 50%-or-less-owned equity basis investees taken in the aggregate after intercompany eliminations shall be taken into account.

[45 FR 63671, Sept. 25, 1980, as amended at 46 FR 48137, Oct. 1, 1981; 46 FR 56180, Nov. 16, 1981; 49 FR 47598, Dec. 6, 1984; 50 FR 25215, June 18, 1985; 59 FR 65636, Dec. 20, 1994; 74 FR 18615, Apr. 23, 2009]

Registered Investment Companies

Source: Sections 210.6-01 through 210.6-10 appear at 47 FR 56838, Dec. 21, 1982, unless otherwise noted.

§210.6-01 Application of §§210.6-01 to 210.6-10.

Sections 210.6-01 to 210.6-10 shall be applicable to financial statements filed for registered investment companies.

§210.6-02 Definition of certain terms.

The following terms shall have the meaning indicated in this rule unless the context otherwise requires. (Also see §210.1-02 of this part.)

(a) *Affiliate.* The term *affiliate* means an *affiliated person* as defined in section 2(a)(3) of the Investment Company Act of 1940 unless otherwise indicated. The term *control* has the meaning in section 2(a)(9) of that Act.

(b) *Value.* As used in §§210.6-01 to 210.6-10, the term *value* shall have the meaning given in section 2(a)(41)(B) of the Investment Company Act of 1940.

(c) *Balance sheets; statements of net assets.* As used in §§210.6-01 to 210.6-10, the term *balance sheets* shall include statements of assets and liabilities as well as statements of net assets unless the context clearly indicates the contrary.

(d) *Qualified assets.* (1) For companies issuing face-amount certificates subsequent to December 31, 1940 under the provisions of section 28 of the Investment Company Act of 1940, the term *qualified assets* means qualified investments as that term is defined in section 28(b) of the Act. A statement to that effect shall be made in the balance sheet.

费用准备金总计不超过注册人及其并表子公司于会计年度年初的普通股股东权益的一半,则可以不提交此附表。在进行测试,以判断是否符合上述标准之时,仅得考虑进行公司间抵消后,在注册人50%或以下股权被控的投资对象的未付赔款金额和赔款调整费用准备金中,注册人及其他子公司按比例持有的总份额。

[《联邦公报》第45卷第63671页,1980年9月25日,修正索引:《联邦公报》第46卷第48137页,1981年10月1日;《联邦公报》第46卷第56180页,1981年11月16日;《联邦公报》第49卷第47598页,1984年12月6日;《联邦公报》第50卷第25215页,1985年6月18日;《联邦公报》第59卷第65636页,1994年12月20日;《联邦公报》第74卷第18615页,2009年4月23日。]

注册投资公司

行政规则来源:第210.6-01~210.6-10节,见《联邦公报》第47卷第56838页,1982年12月21日,除非另有说明。

第210.6-01节　第210.6-01~210.6-10节的适用范围

第210.6-01~210.6-10节适用于针对注册投资公司提交的财务报表。

第210.6-02节　部分术语定义

除非上下文另有所指,下列术语之含义应以本规则的规定为准(同时参见本部分第210.1-02节)。

(a)控制性关联方。"控制性关联方"一词系指《1940年投资公司法》第2(a)(3)条定义的"控制性关联人",除非另有说明。"控制"一词的定义以该法第2(a)(9)条为准。

(b)价值。就第210.6-01~210.6-10节而言,"价值"一词的定义以《1940年投资公司法》第2(a)(41)(B)条为准。

(c)资产负债表;净资产报表。就第210.6-01~210.6-10节而言,"资产负债表"一词包括资产负债表以及净资产报表,除非上下文明确另有所指。

(d)合格资产。(1)对于在1940年12月31日之后根据《1940年投资公司法》第28条规定发行面额证券的公司,"合格资产"一词系指该法第28(b)条定义的合格投资。资产负债表中应对此予以说明。

(2) For other companies, the term *qualified assets* means cash and investments which such companies do maintain or are required, by applicable governing legal instruments, to maintain in respect of outstanding face-amount certificates.

(3) Loans to certificate holders may be included as qualified assets in an amount not in excess of certificate reserves carried on the books of account in respect of each individual certificate upon which the loans were made.

§210.6-03 Special rules of general application to registered investment companies.

The financial statements filed for persons to which §§210.6-01 to 210.6-10 are applicable shall be prepared in accordance with the following special rules in addition to the general rules in §§210.1-01 to 210.4-10 (Articles 1, 2, 3, and 4). Where the requirements of a special rule differ from those prescribed in a general rule, the requirements of the special rule shall be met.

(a) *Content of financial statements.* The financial statements shall be prepared in accordance with the requirements of this part (Regulation S-X) notwithstanding any provision of the articles of incorporation, trust indenture or other governing legal instruments specifying certain accounting procedures inconsistent with those required in §§210.6-01 to 210.6-10.

(b) *Audited financial statements.* Where, under Article 3 of this part, financial statements are required to be audited, the independent accountant shall have been selected and ratified in accordance with section 32 of the Investment Company Act of 1940.

(c) *Consolidated and combined statements.* (1) Consolidated and combined statements filed for registered investment companies shall be prepared in accordance with §§210.3A-01 to 210.3A-05 (Article 3A) except that (i) statements of the registrant may be consolidated only with the statements of subsidiaries which are investment companies; (ii) a consolidated statement of the registrant and any of its investment company subsidiaries shall not be filed unless accompanied by a consolidating statement which sets forth the individual statements of each significant subsidiary included in the consolidated statement: *Provided, however,* That a consolidating statement need not be filed if all included subsidiaries are totally held; and (iii) consolidated or combined statements filed for subsidiaries not consolidated with the registrant shall not include any investment companies unless accompanied by consolidating or combining statements which set forth the individual statements of each included investment company which is a significant subsidiary.

(2) If consolidating or combining statements are filed, the amounts included under each caption in which financial data pertaining to affiliates is required to be furnished

（2）对于其他公司而言，“合格资产”一词系指此等公司就发行在外的面额证券实际维持的或根据适用的规范性法律文件应当维持的现金与投资。

（3）向证券持有人提供的贷款，如其金额不超过账面上记载的为该笔贷款所涉每一份证券提供的准备金，可计入合格资产。

第210.6-03节　普遍适用于注册投资公司的特别规则

适用第210.6-01~210.6-10节规定的会计主体的财务报表，其编制除应遵循第210.1-01~210.4-10节（第1节、第2节、第3节、第4节）中的一般规则外，还应遵循下列特别规则。特别规则的规定与一般规则不一致的，以特别规则为准。

（a）财务报表的内容。无论章程、信托契约或其他规范性法律文件是否规定了与第210.6-01~210.6-10节不一致的特定会计程序，财务报表均应根据本部分的规定（《S-X管理办法》）进行编制。

（b）经审计的财务报表。如根据本部分第3条规定，财务报表必须进行审计，注册人应已根据《1940年投资公司法》第32条规定选任并批准独立会计师。

（c）合并与汇总报表。（1）注册人应根据第210.3A-01~210.3A-05节（第3A条）的规定编制并提交注册投资公司的合并与汇总报表，但是：（i）注册人的报表仅能与具有投资公司身份的子公司的报表合并；（ii）除非注册人附上一份财务报表合并说明书，载明纳入合并报表的每家重要子公司的单独报表，否则注册人不得提交与任何一家投资公司子公司的合并报表；但是，如果所有纳入合并报表的子公司均为注册人的全资子公司，则不必提交财务报表合并说明书；且（iii）除非注册人附上一份财务报表合并或汇总说明书，载明纳入合并或汇总报表的属于重要子公司的每家投资公司的单独报表，否则注册人在为其非并表子公司提交的合并或汇总报表中，不得纳入任何投资公司。

（2）如果注册人提交了财务报表合并或汇总说明书，则对于应提供控制性关联方财务数据的每一科目，均应进行细分，以便分别显示：（i）财务报表合并过程中已抵消

shall be subdivided to show separately the amounts: (i) Eliminated in consolidation; and (ii) not eliminated in consolidation.

(d) *Valuation of assets.* The balance sheets of registered investment companies, other than issuers of face-amount certificates, shall reflect all investments at value, with the aggregate cost of each category of investment reported under §§210.6-04.1, 6-04.2 and 6-04.3 and of the total investments reported under §210.6-04.4 or §210.6-05.1 shown parenthetically. State in a note the methods used in determining value of investments. As required by section 28(b) of the Investment Company Act of 1940, *qualified* assets of face-amount certificate companies shall be valued in accordance with certain provisions of the Code of the District of Columbia. For guidance as to valuation of securities, see §§404.03 to 404.05 of the Codification of Financial Reporting Policies.

(e) *Qualified assets.* State in a note the nature of any investments and other assets maintained or required to be maintained, by applicable legal instruments, in respect of outstanding face-amount certificates. If the nature of the qualifying assets and amount thereof are not subject to the provisions of section 28 of the Investment Company Act of 1940, a statement to that effect shall be made.

(f) *Restricted securities.* State in a note unless disclosed elsewhere the following information as to investment securities which cannot be offered for public sale without first being registered under the Securities Act of 1933 (restricted securities):

(1) The policy of the person with regard to acquisition of restricted securities.

(2) The policy of the person with regard to valuation of restricted securities. Specific comments shall be given as to the valuation of an investment in one or more issues of securities of a company or group of affiliated companies if any part of such investment is restricted and the aggregate value of the investment in all issues of such company or affiliated group exceeds five percent of the value of total assets. (As used in this paragraph, the term *affiliated* shall have the meaning given in §210.6-02(a) of this part.)

(3) A description of the person's rights with regard to demanding registration of any restricted securities held at the date of the latest balance sheet.

(g) *Income recognition.* Dividends shall be included in income on the ex-dividend date; interest shall be accured on a daily basis. Dividends declared on short positions existing on the record date shall be recorded on the ex-dividend date and included as an expense of the period.

(h) *Federal income taxes.* The company's status as a *regulated investment company* as defined in subtitle A, chapter 1, subchapter M of the Internal Revenue Code, as amended, shall be stated in a note referred to in the appropriate statements. Such note shall also indicate briefly the principal assumptions on which the company relied in making or not making provisions for income taxes. However, a company which retains

的金额；和(ii)财务报表合并过程中未抵消的金额。

(d)资产估值。注册投资公司（面额证券发行人除外）的资产负债表应反映所有投资价值，并通过括号注释列明根据第210.6-04.1节、第210.6-04.2节和第210.6-04.3节报告的每类投资的合计成本，以及根据第210.6-04.4节或第210.6-05.1节报告的总投资成本。确定投资价值的方法应通过附注予以说明。按照《1940年投资公司法》第28(b)条的规定，面额证券公司的"合格资产"应根据《哥伦比亚特区法典》中的特定条款进行估值。证券估值的指导原则，参见《财务报告政策汇编》第404.03条至第404.05条。

(e)合格资产。在附注中说明就发行在外的面额证券实际维持的或根据适用的法律文件应当维持的任何投资和其他资产的性质。如合格资产的性质及其金额不受《1940年投资公司法》第28条限制，应予声明。

(f)受限证券。除非已于他处披露，对于《1993年证券法》规定未经注册不得公开发行的投资性证券（受限证券），应通过附注说明下列信息：

(1)该主体关于购买受限证券的政策。

(2)该主体关于受限证券估值的政策。如该主体对一家公司或控制性关联公司集团的一次或多次证券发行进行投资，且投资的任何部分属于受限证券，同时该主体对该公司或控制性关联公司集团所有发行的投资总价值超过其总资产价值的5%的，应针对投资的估值明确说明相关意见[就本款而言，"控制性关联"一词的含义以本部分第210.6-02(a)节的定义为准]。

(3)关于该主体要求对截至最近一期资产负债表日所持有的任何受限证券进行注册的权利之说明。

(g)所得确认。除息日当天的股息应包括在所得之内；利息应按日累计。就登记日的既有空头持仓宣布的股息，应在除息日予以记录，并列入该期间的费用。

(h)联邦所得税。公司属于《国内税收法典》（修正版）第A子编第一章第M子章定义的"受监管投资公司"的，应在适当报表中通过附注予以说明。该附注还应简单注明该公司计提或不计提所得税拨备时所基于的主要假设。但是，留存已实现资本利得并根据《国内税收法典》第852(b)(3)(D)条规定将该等利得指定为股东分配金额的公司，应于其课税年度的最后一天（不得提前），计提该年度上述未分配但已实现的资本利

realized capital gains and designates such gains as a distribution to shareholders in accordance with section 852(b)(3)(D) of the Internal Revenue Code shall, on the last day of its taxable year (and not earlier), make provision for taxes on such undistributed capital gains realized during such year.

(i) *Issuance and repurchase by a registered investment company of its own securities.* Disclose for each class of the company's securities:

(1) The number of shares, units, or principal amount of bonds sold during the period of report, the amount received therefor, and, in the case of shares sold by closed-end management investment companies, the difference, if any, between the amount received and the net asset value or preference in involuntary liquidation (whichever is appropriate) of securities of the same class prior to such sale; and

(2) The number of shares, units, or principal amount of bonds repurchased during the period of report and the cost thereof. Closed-end management investment companies shall furnish the following additional information as to securities repurchased during the period of report:

(i) As to bonds and preferred shares, the aggregate difference between cost and the face amount or preference in involuntary liquidation and, if applicable net assets taken at value as of the date of repurchase were less than such face amount or preference, the aggregate difference between cost and such net asset value;

(ii) As to common shares, the weighted average discount per share, expressed as a percentage, between cost of repurchase and the net asset value applicable to such shares at the date of repurchases.

The information required by paragraphs (h)(i)(2)(i) and (ii) of this section may be based on reasonable estimates if it is impracticable to determine the exact amounts involved.

(j) *Series companies.* (1) The information required by this part shall, in the case of a person which in essence is comprised of more than one separate investment company, be given as if each class or series of such investment company were a separate investment company; this shall not prevent the inclusion, at the option of such person, of information applicable to other classes or series of such person on a comparative basis, except as to footnotes which need not be comparative.

(2) If the particular class or series for which information is provided may be affected by other classes or series of such investment company, such as by the offset of realized gains in one series with realized losses in another, or through contingent liabilities, such situation shall be disclosed.

(k) *Certificate reserves.* (1) For companies issuing face-amount certificates subsequent to December 31, 1940 under the provisions of section 28 of the Investment

得税款拨备。

(i)注册投资公司对自身证券的发行与回购。对于公司每类证券,均应披露如下信息:

(1)在报告期间出售的股数、任何其他证券单位数目或债券本金金额,以及因该等出售收到的金额;封闭型管理型投资公司出售股份的,还应披露因出售收到的金额与出售之前同类别证券的资产净值或该等证券在强制清算中享有的优先分配价值(视具体情况而定)之间的差额(如有);和

(2)在报告期间回购的股数、任何其他证券单位数目或债券本金金额,以及因此支出的成本。封闭型管理型投资公司还应针对报告期内回购的证券,提供下列额外信息:

(i)对于债券和优先股而言,应提供成本与该等债券和优先股的面额或在强制清算中享有的优先分配价值之间的合计差额;如截至回购日债券和优先股的资产净值低于上述面额或优先分配价值,则应提供成本与该等资产净值之间的合计差额。

(ii)对于普通股而言,应按照回购成本与截至回购日与该等股份相对应的资产净值之间的差额,提供每股加权平均贴现(以百分比表示)。

对于本节第(h)(i)(2)(i)款和第(h)(i)(2)(ii)款要求提供的信息,如果要得出所涉金额确切数字不可行,可以进行合理估算。

(j)系列公司。(1)如某主体实质上为一个以上的独立投资公司所组成,则在按本部分规定提供信息时,可将每类或每一系列的投资公司视为一家独立的投资公司;但这并不妨碍上述主体为比较之目的,自行选择提供其他类别或系列的信息(但不必进行比较的脚注除外)。

(2)如果已提供信息的某一类别或某一系列投资公司可能受其他类别或系列投资公司影响,如通过某系列公司的已实现损失或或有负债对另一系列公司的已实现收益进行抵消,则应披露该等情形。

(k)证券准备金。(1)于1940年12月31日之后根据《1940年投资公司法》第28条规定发行面额证券的公司,其资产负债表应反映发行在外证券的准备金,准备金应按该

Company Act of 1940, balance sheets shall reflect reserves for outstanding certificates computed in accordance with the provisions of section 28(a) of the Act.

(2) For other companies, balance sheets shall reflect reserves for outstanding certificates determined as follows:

(i) For certificates of the installment type, such amount which, together with the lesser of future payments by certificate holders as and when accumulated at a rate not to exceed 31/2per centum per annum (or such other rate as may be appropriate under the circumstances of a particular case) compounded annually, shall provide the minimum maturity or face amount of the certificate when due.

(ii) For certificates of the fully -paid type, such amount which, as and when accumulated at a rate not to exceed 31/2per centum per annum (or such other rate as may be appropriate under the circumstances of a particular case) compounded annually, shall provide the amount or amounts payable when due.

(iii) Such amount or accrual therefor, as shall have been credited to the account of any certificate holder in the form of any credit, or any dividend, or any interest in addition to the minimum maturity or face amount specified in the certificate, plus any accumulations on any amount so credited or accrued at rates required under the terms of the certificate.

(iv) An amount equal to all advance payments made by certificate holders, plus any accumulations thereon at rates required under the terms of the certificate.

(v) Amounts for other appropriate contingency reserves, for death and disability benefits or for reinstatement rights on any certificate providing for such benefits or rights.

(l) *Inapplicable captions.* Attention is directed to the provisions of §§210.4-02 and 210.4-03 which permit the omission of separate captions in financial statements as to which the items and conditions are not present, or the amounts involved not significant. However, amounts involving directors, officers, and affiliates shall nevertheless be separately set forth except as otherwise specifically permitted under a particular caption.

§210.6-04 Balance sheets.

This rule is applicable to balance sheets filed by registered investment companies except for persons who substitute a statement of net assets in accordance with the requirements specified in §210.6-05, and issuers of face-amount certificates which are subject to the special provisions of §210.6-06 of this part. Balance sheets filed under this rule shall comply with the following provisions:

Assets

1. *Investments in securities of unaffiliated issuers.*

2. *Investments in and advances to affiliates.* State separately investments in and advances to: (a) Controlled companies and (b) other affiliates.

法第28(a)条规定计算。

(2)对于其他公司,资产负债表应反映发行在外证券的准备金,其金额依下列规定确定:

(i)分期偿还型证券:准备金金额加上持有人未来各期付款中金额较低者之和,在按不超过年复利3%的利率(或在特殊情形下,按其他适当的利率)计算时,应足以为证券的最低到期额或到期时的证券面额提供准备。

(ii)完全偿还型证券:准备金金额在按不超过年复利3%的利率(或照特殊情形下,按其他适当的利率)计算时,应足以为证券的最低到期额或到期时的证券面额提供准备。

(iii)如下金额之和:证券的最低到期额或证券载明的面额,加上任何以信用、股息或利息形式记入任何面额证券持有人账户贷方的金额或相关应计额,再加上该等贷记金额或应计额根据面额证券条款规定的利率累计的任何金额。

(iv)如下金额之和:相当于证券持有人支付的所有垫款的金额,加上根据证券条款规定的利率累计的金额。

(v)其他适当应急准备金、死亡或伤残抚恤金,或为附带死亡或伤残抚恤金的任何证券的复效权提供准备的金额。

(l)不适用科目。请注意,根据第210.4–02节和第210.4–03节的规定,对于不存在相关项目和条件的个别会计科目,或所涉金额较小的会计科目,可免予在财务报表中单设该等科目。但是,涉及董事、管理人员及控制性关联方的金额应单独列出,但具体会计科目允许不予单独列出的除外。

第210.6–04节　资产负债表

本规则适用于注册投资公司提交的资产负债表,但不适用于根据第210.6–05节的规定不提交资产负债表,而提交净资产报表的主体,亦不适用于发行受制于本部分第210.6–06节特别规定的面额证券的发行人。根据本规则提交的资产负债表应符合如下规定:

资产

1.对非控制性关联发行人证券的投资。

2.对控制性关联方的投资和垫款。单独列示对下列对象的投资和垫款:(a)受控公司;和(b)其他控制性关联方。

3. *Investments—other than securities.* State separately each major category.

4. *Total investments.*

5. *Cash.* Include under this caption cash on hand and demand deposits. Provide in a note to the financial statements the information required under §210.5-02.1 regarding restrictions and compensating balances.

6. *Receivables.* (a) State separately amounts receivable from (1) sales of investments; (2) subscriptions to capital shares; (3) dividends and interest; (4) directors and officers; and (5) others.

(b) If the aggregate amount of notes receivable exceeds 10 percent of the aggregate amount of receivables, the above information shall be set forth separately, in the balance sheet or in a note thereto, for accounts receivable and notes receivable.

7. *Deposits for securities sold short and open option contracts.* State separately amounts held by others in connection with: (a) Short sales and (b) open option contracts.

8. *Other assets.* State separately (a) prepaid and deferred expenses; (b) pension and other special funds; (c) organization expenses; and (d) any other significant item not properly classified in another asset caption.

9. *Total assets.*

Liabilities

10. *Accounts payable and accrued liabilities.* State separately amounts payable for: (a) Securities sold short; (b) open option contracts written; (c) other purchases of securities; (d) capital shares reedeemed; (e) dividends or other distributions on capital shares; and (f) others. State separately the amount of any other liabilities which are material. Securities sold short and open option contracts written shall be stated at value.

11. *Deposits for securities loaned.* State the value of securities loaned and indicate the nature of the collateral received as security for the loan, including the amount of any cash received.

12. *Other liabilities.* State separately (a) amounts payable for investment advisory, management and service fees; and (b) the total amount payable to: (1) Officers and directors; (2) controlled companies; and (3) other affiliates, excluding any amounts owing to noncontrolled affiliates which arose in the ordinary course of business and which are subject to usual trade terms.

13. *Notes payable, bonds and similar debt.* (a) State separately amounts payable to: (1) Banks or other financial institutions for borrowings; (2) controlled companies; (3) other affiliates; and (4) others, showing for each category amounts payable within one year and amounts payable after one year.

(b) Provide in a note the information required under §210.5-02.19(b) regarding unused lines of credit for short-term financing and §210.5-02.22(b) regarding unused

3.投资——证券投资除外。说明各主要投资类型。

4.总投资。

5.现金。此科目包括库存现金与活期存款。在财务报表附注中，根据第210.5-02.1节的要求提供关于限制与补偿性余额的信息。

6.应收项目。(a)单独列示下列来源的应收项目：(1)投资出售；(2)股本认购；(3)股息和利息；(4)董事与管理人员；和(5)其他。

(b)如应收票据总金额超过应收项目总金额的10%，应于资产负债表或其附注中，分别针对应收账款与应收票据提供上述信息。

7.卖空证券和开放式期权合约的保证金。单独列示其他人持有的与下列各项相关的金额：(a)卖空，以及(b)开放式期权合约。

8.其他资产。单独列示：(a)预付和递延费用；(b)养老基金和其他特别基金；(c)组织费用；和(d)无法适当归入其他资产科目的任何其他重大项目。

9.总资产。

负债

10.应付账款和应计负债。单独列示下列各项的应付金额：(a)卖空证券；(b)卖出的期权合约中的未平仓合约；(c)其他证券购买；(d)回赎股本；(e)股息或其他的股本分配；和(f)其他。单独列示任何其他重大负债之金额。卖空证券和卖出的期权合约中的未平仓合约应列示其价值。

11.贷出证券的保证金。说明贷出证券的价值，并注明为担保贷出证券而收到的担保品之性质，包括任何实收现金的金额。

12.其他负债。单独列示：(a)投资顾问、管理和服务费的应付金额；和(b)应向下列对象支付的总金额：(1)管理人员与董事；(2)受控公司；和(3)其他控制性关联方，但在正常业务运作中产生的且适用通常贸易条款的欠负非受控的控制性关联方的任何金额除外。

13.应付票据、债券和类似债务。(a)单独列示应向下列对象支付的金额：(1)银行或其他借贷金融机构；(2)受控公司；(3)其他控制性关联方；和(4)其他；列出一年内每类应付金额及一年之后的应付金额。

(b)第210.5-02.19(b)节要求提供的关于短期融资未用信用额度的信息，及第210.5-02.22(b)节要求提供的关于长期融资安排未用承诺的信息，应通过附注的形式

commitments for long-term financing arrangements.

14. *Total liabilities.*

15. *Commitments and contingent liabilities.*

Net Assets

16. *Units of capital.* (a) Disclose the title of each class of capital shares or other capital units, the number authorized, the number outstanding, and the dollar amount thereof.

(b) Unit investment trusts, including those which are issuers of periodic payment plan certificates, also shall state in a note to the financial statements: (1) The total cost to the investors of each class of units or shares; (2) the adjustment for market depreciation or appreciation; (3) other deductions from the total cost to the investors for fees, loads and other charges, including an explanation of such deductions; and (4) the net amount applicable to the investors.

17. *Accumulated undistributed income (loss).* Disclose:

(a) The accumulated undistributed investment income-net;

(b) accumulated undistributed net realized gains (losses) on investment transactions, and (c) net unrealized appreciation (depeciation) in value of investments at the balance sheet date.

18. *Other elements of capital.* Disclose any other elements of capital or residual interests appropriate to the capital structure of the reporting entity.

19. *Net assets applicable to outstanding units of capital.* State the net asset value per share.

§210.6-05 Statements of net assets.

In lieu of the balance sheet otherwise required by §210.6-04 of this part, persons may substitute a statement of net assets if at least 95 percent of the amount of the person's total assets are represented by investments in securities of unaffiliated issuers. If presented in such instances, a statement of net assets shall consist of the following:

Statements of Net Assets

1. A schedule of investments in securities of unaffiliated issuers as prescribed in §210.12-12.

2. The excess (or deficiency) of other assets over (under) total liabilities stated in one amount, except that any amounts due from or to officers, directors, controlled persons, or other affiliates, excluding any amounts owing to noncontrolled affiliates which arose in the ordinary course of business and which are subject to usual trade terms, shall be stated separately.

3. Disclosure shall be provided in the notes to the financial statements for any item required under §§210.6-04.10 to 210.6-04.13.

予以提供。

14.总负债。

15.承诺和或有负债。

净资产

16.资本单位。(a)披露每类股本或其他资本单位的名称、授权数量、发行在外数量及其金额。

(b)单位投资信托(包括定期定额投资计划凭证的发行人)还应于财务报表附注中说明:(1)每类单位或股份的投资者总成本;(2)市场价值增减调整;(3)从投资者总成本中扣除的费用、认购费和其他收费,包括对该等扣除的解释;和(4)投资者的净投资金额。

17.累计未分配损益。应披露:

(a)累计未分配投资收入净额;

(b)投资交易已实现净收益(损失)的累计未分配金额;和(c)截至资产负债表日,投资未实现的净增值(贬值)。

18.其他资本要素。披露任何其他资本要素或与报告实体资本结构相称的剩余权益。

19.发行在外资本单位对应的净资产。说明每股资产净值。

第210.6-05节　资产净值表

如某主体总资产金额至少有95%用于投资非控制性关联发行人的证券,则该主体可以提交资产净值表,作为本部分第210.6-04节所要求提供的资产负债表之替代。在该等情况下,资产净值表应包含如下信息:

资产净值表

1.第210.12-12节规定的非控制性关联发行人证券投资附表。

2.以一个数字统一说明其他资产超过(或低于)总负债的部分,但应向管理人员、董事、受控主体或其他控制性关联方收取或支付的任何金额均应单独列示(但在正常业务运作中产生的且适用通常贸易条款的欠负非受控的控制性关联方的任何金额除外)。

3.第210.6-04.10~210.6-04.13节要求提供的任何项目信息,均应通过财务报表附注披露。

4. The balance of the amounts captioned as *net assets*. The number of outstanding shares and net asset value per share shall be shown parenthetically.

5. The information required by (i) §210.6–04.16, (ii) §210.6–04.17 and (iii) §210.6–04.18 shall be furnished in a note to the financial statements.

§210.6–06 Special provisions applicable to the balance sheets of issuers of face–amount certificates.

Balance sheets filed by issuers of face–amount certificates shall comply with the following provisions:

Assets

1. *Investments.* State separately each major category: such as, real estate owned, first mortgage loans on real estate, other mortgage loans on real estate, investments in securities of unaffiliated issuers, and investments in and advances to affiliates.

2. *Cash.* Include under this caption cash on hand and demand deposits. Provide in a note to the financial statements the information required under §210.5–02.1 regarding restrictions and compensating balances.

3. *Receivables.* (a) State separately amounts receivable from (1) sales of investments; (2) dividends and interest; (3) directors and officers; and (4) others.

(b) If the aggregate amount of notes receivable exceeds 10 percent of the aggregate amount of receivables, the above information shall be set forth separately, in the balance sheet or in a note thereto, for accounts receivable and notes receivable.

4. *Total qualified assets.* State in a note to the financial statements the amount of qualified assets on deposit classified as to general categories of assets and as to general types of depositories, such as banks and states, together with a statement as to the purpose of the deposits.

5. *Other assets.* State separately: (a) Investments in securities of unaffiliated issuers not included in qualifying assets in item 1 above; (b) investments in and advances to affiliates not included in qualifying assets in item 1 above; and (c) any other significant item not properly classified in another asset caption.

6. *Total assets.*

Liabilities

7. *Certificate reserves.* Issuers of face–amount certificates shall state separately reserves for: (a) Certificates of the installment type; (b) certificates of the fully–paid type; (c) advance payments; (d) additional amounts accrued for or credited to the account of certificate holders in the form of any credit, dividend, or interest in addition to the minimum amount specified in the certificate; and (e) other certificate reserves. State in an appropriate manner the basis used in determining the reserves, including the rates of interest of accumulation.

4.“净资产”项目余额。应通过括号注释说明发行在外的股数与每股资产净值。

5.(i)第210.6-04.16节、(i)第210.6-04.17节和(iii)第210.6-04.18节要求提供的信息，应通过财务报表附注提供。

第210.6-06节　适用于面额证券发行人资产负债表的特别规定

面额证券发行人所提交的资产负债表应符合如下规定：

资产

1.投资。单独列示每一主要类别的投资：如自有房地产、房地产第一顺位抵押贷款、房地产其他抵押贷款、对非控制性关联发行人证券的投资，以及对控制性关联方的投资与垫款。

2.现金。包括库存现金和活期存款。在财务报表附注中，根据第210.5-02.1节的要求提供关于限制与补偿性余额的信息。

3.应收项目。(a)单独列示下列来源的应收项目：(1)投资出售；(2)股息和利息；(3)董事与管理人员；和(4)其他。

(b)如应收票据总金额超过应收项目总金额的10%，应于资产负债表或其附注中，分别针对应收账款与应收票据提供上述信息。

4.合格资产总额。将合格资产存量依照一般资产类型和一般存管人类型（如银行和国家）予以分类，并根据分类在财务报表附注中说明相应的合格资产存量金额，同时应说明保有该等资产存量之目的。

5.其他资产。单独列示：(a)不包括在上文第1项合格资产内的，对非控制性关联发行人证券的投资；(b)不包括在上文第1项合格资产内的，对控制性关联方的投资和垫款；和(c)无法适当归入其他资产项目的任何其他重大科目。

6.总资产。

负债

7.证券准备金。面额证券发行人应单独列示就下列各项提供的准备金：(a)分期偿还型证券；(b)完全偿还型证券；(c)垫款；(d)除面额证券列明的最小金额外，以信用、股息或利息形式记入证券持有人账户贷方的任何其他金额或相关应计项目；和(e)其他面额证券准备金。适当说明确定该准备金的计算基础，包括用于计算利息的利率。

8. *Notes payable, bonds and similar debt.* (a) State separately amounts payable to: (1) Banks or other financial institutions for borrowings; (2) controlled companies; (3) other affiliates; and (4) others, showing for each category amounts payable within one year and amounts payable after one year.

(b) Provide in a note the information required under §210.5-02.19 (b) regarding unused lines of credit for short-term financing and §210.5-02.22 (b) regarding unused commitments for long-term financing arrangements.

9. *Accounts payable and accrued liabilities.* State separately (a) amounts payable for investment advisory, management and service fees; and (b) the total amount payable to: (1) Officers and directors; (2) controlled companies; and (3) other affiliates, excluding any amounts owing to noncontrolled affiliates which arose in the ordinary course of business and which are subject to usual trade terms. State separately the amount of any other liabilities which are material.

10. *Total liabilities.*

11. *Commitments and contingent liabilities.*

Stockholders' Equity

12. *Capital shares.* Disclose the title of each class of capital shares or other capital units, the number authorized, the number outstanding and the dollar amount thereof. Show also the dollar amount of any capital shares subscribed but unissued, and show the deduction for subscriptions receivable therefrom.

13. *Other elements of capital.* (a) Disclose any other elements of capital or residual interests appropriate to the capital structure of the reporting entity.

(b) A summary of each account under this caption setting forth the information prescribed in §210.3-04 shall be given in a note or separate statement for each period in which a statement of operations is presented.

14. *Total liabilities and stockholders' equity.*

§210.6-07 Statements of operations.

Statements of operations filed by registered investment companies, other than issuers of face-amount certificates subject to the special provisions of §210.6-08 of this part, shall comply with the following provisions:

Statements of Operations

1. *Investment income.* State separately income from: (a) dividends; (b) interest on securities; and (c) other income. If income from investments in or indebtedness of affiliates is included hereunder, such income shall be segregated under an appropriate caption subdivided to show separately income from: (1) Controlled companies; and (2) other affiliates. If non-cash dividends are included in income, the bases of recognition and measurement used in respect to such amounts shall be disclosed. Any other category of

8.应付票据、债券和类似债务。(a)单独列示应向下列对象支付的金额:(1)银行或其他借贷金融机构;(2)受控公司;(3)其他控制性关联方;和(4)其他;列出一年内及一年之后每类应付金额。

(b)第210.5-02.19(b)节要求提供的关于短期融资未用信用额度的信息,及第210.5-02.22(b)节要求提供的关于长期融资安排未用承诺的信息,应通过附注的形式予以提供。

9.应付账款和应计负债。单独列示:(a)投资顾问、管理和服务费的应付金额;和(b)应向下列对象支付的总金额:(1)管理人员与董事;(2)受控公司;和(3)其他控制性关联方,但在正常业务运作中产生的且适用通常贸易条款的欠负非受控的控制性关联方的任何金额除外。单独列示所有其他重大负债。

10.总负债。

11.承诺和或有负债。

股东权益

12.股本。披露每类股本或其他资本单位的名称、授权数量、发行在外数量及其金额。同时标明已经认购但并未发行的任何股票金额,并标明相关应收认购股款的扣除额。

13.其他资本要素。(a)披露任何其他资本要素或与报告实体资本结构相称的剩余权益。

(b)应通过附注或另一份报表,针对每期经营报表所对应的报告期,就本科目每一账目进行摘要,提供第210.3-04节规定的信息。

14.总负债和股东权益。

第210.6-07节　经营报表

除发行受制于本部分第210.6-08节特别规定的面额证券的发行人之外,注册投资公司所提交的经营报表应符合如下规定:

经营报表

1.投资收入。单独列示来源于以下各项的收益:(a)股息;(b)证券利息;和(c)其他收益。来源于对控制性关联方的投资或控制性关联方负债的收益,只要计入投资收益的,均应通过适当科目进行细分,以便单独列示来源于以下主体的收益:(1)受控公司;和(2)其他控制性关联方。非现金股息被计入收益之中的,应披露与此等金额相关的确认和计量基础。超过本科目所列总金额5%的所有其他类型收益,均应单独列示。

income which exceeds five percent of the total shown under this caption shall be stated separately.

2. *Expenses.* (a) State separately the total amount of investment advisory, management and service fees, and expenses in connection with research, selection, supervision, and custody of investments. Amounts of expenses incurred from transactions with affiliated persons shall be disclosed together with the identity of and related amount applicable to each such person accounting for five percent or more of the total expenses shown under this caption together with a description of the nature of the affiliation. Expenses incurred within the person's own organization in connection with research, selection and supervision of investments shall be stated separately. Reductions or reimbursements of management or service fees shall be shown as a negative amount or as a reduction of total expenses shown under this caption.

(b) State separately any other expense item the amount of which exeeds five percent of the total expenses shown under this caption.

(c) A note to the financial statements shall include information concerning management and service fees, the rate of fee, and the base and method of computation. State separately the amount and a description of any fee reductions or reimbursements representing: (1) Expense limitation agreements or commitments; and (2) offsets received from broker–dealers showing separately for each amount received or due from (i) unaffiliated persons; and (ii) affiliated persons. If no management or service fees were incurred for a period, state the reason therefor.

(d) If any expenses were paid otherwise than in cash, state the details in a note.

(e) State in a note to the financial statements the amount of brokerage commissions (including dealer markups) paid to affiliated broker–dealers in connection with purchase and sale of investment securities. Open–end management companies shall state in a note the net amounts of sales charges deducted from the proceeds of sale of capital shares which were retained by any affiliated principal underwriter or other affiliated broker–dealer.

(f) State separately all amounts paid in accordance with a plan adopted under rule 12b–1 of the Investment Company Act of 1940 [17 CFR 270.12b–1]. Reimbursement to the fund of expenses incurred under such plan (12b–1 expense reimbursement) shall be shown as a negative amount and deducted from current 12b–1 expenses. If 12b–1 expense reimbursements exceed current 12b–1 costs, such excess shall be shown as a negative amount used in the calculation of total expenses under this caption.

(g)(1) *Brokerage/Service Arrangements.* If a broker–dealer or an affiliate of the broker–dealer has, in connection with directing the person's brokerage transactions to the broker–dealer, provided, agreed to provide, paid for, or agreed to pay for, in whole or in

2.费用。(a)单独列示投资顾问、管理和服务费,以及与投资的研究、选择、监督和存管相关的费用。应披露与控制性关联主体交易所产生的费用金额;同时,对于占本科目下总费用5%(含)以上的每一控制性关联主体,均应披露其身份信息和相关金额,并说明控制性关联关系的性质。在注册人组织内部发生的,与投资的研究、选择和监督相关的费用,应单独列示。管理或服务费的扣减或退还应作为本科目总费用的负数金额或扣减金额列出。

(b)单独列示金额超过本科目总费用5%的任何其他费用项目。

(c)财务报表的附注应包含与管理和服务费、费率以及计算基础和方法相关的信息。单独列示并说明下列各项费用扣减或退还:(1)费用限制协议或承诺;和(2)从经纪自营商处收到的可抵消金额,分别列示从下述主体收到的或下述主体应付的每一笔金额:(i)非控制性关联主体;和(ii)控制性关联主体。如某报告期并未产生任何管理或服务费,应说明相关原因。

(d)对于以现金以外的方式支付的任何费用,应在附注中说明详细信息。

(e)通过财务报表附注说明向控制性关联经纪自营商支付的,与投资证券买卖相关的经纪佣金(包括经纪商加成)。开放式管理公司应在附注中说明,任何控制性关联主承销商或其他控制性关联经纪自营商留存的从股本出售募集资金中扣减的销售费用净额。

(f)对于根据《1940年投资公司法》的《12b-1规则》[《联邦规章汇编》第十七编第270.12b-1节]通过的计划支付的所有金额,均应单独列示。该等计划产生的费用之退还(12b-1退还费用),应列为负数金额,并自现行12b-1费用中扣除。如12b-1退还费用超过现行12b-1成本,计算本科目的总费用时,应将超出部分列为负数金额。

(g)(1)经纪/服务安排。如注册人将经纪交易交给经纪自营商办理,而经纪自营商或经纪自营商的控制性关联方对注册人提供了或同意提供全部或部分服务,或就该等服务支付了或同意支付费用{《1934年证券交易法》第28(e)条[《美国法典》第十五

part, services provided to the person (other than brokerage and research services as those terms are used in section 28(e) of the Securities Exchange Act of 1934 [15 U.S.C. 78bb (e)]), include in the expense items set forth under this caption the amount that would have been incurred by the person for the services had it paid for the services directly in an arms-length transaction.

(2) *Expense Offset Arrangements.* If the person has entered into an agreement with any other person pursuant to which such other person reduces, or pays a third party which reduces, by a specified or reasonably ascertainable amount, its fees for services provided to the person in exchange for use of the person's assets, include in the expense items set forth under this caption the amount of fees that would have been incurred by the person if the person had not entered into the agreement.

(3) *Financial Statement Presentation.* Show the total amount by which expenses are increased pursuant to paragraphs (1) and (2) of this paragraph 2(g) as a corresponding reduction in total expenses under this caption. In a note to the financial statements, state separately the total amounts by which expenses are increased pursuant to paragraphs (1) and (2) of this paragraph 2(g), and list each category of expense that is increased by an amount equal to at least 5 percent of total expenses. If applicable, the note should state that the person could have employed the assets used by another person to produce income if it had not entered into an arrangement described in paragraph 2(g)(2) of this section.

3. *Interest and amortization of debt discount and expense.* Provide in the body of the statements or in the footnotes, the average dollar amount of borrowings and the average interest rate.

4. *Investment income before income tax expense.*

5. *Income tax expense.* Include under this caption only taxes based on income.

6. *Investment income-net.*

7. *Realized and unrealized gain(loss) on investments-net.* (a) State separately the net realized gain or loss on transactions in: (1) Investment securities of unaffiliated issuers, (2) investment securities of affiliated issuers, and (3) investments other than securities.

(b) Distributions of realized gains by other investment companies shall be shown separately under this caption.

(c) State separately: (1) The gain or loss from expiration or closing of option contracts written, (2) the gain or loss on closed short positions in securities, and (3) other realized gain or loss. Disclose in a note to the financial statements the number and associated dollar amounts as to option contracts written: (i) At the beginning of the period; (ii) during the period; (iii) expired during the period; (iv) closed during the period; (v) exercised during the period; (vi) balance at end of the period.

编第78bb(e)节]所述经纪和研究服务除外}，则计入本科目费用项目的金额以注册人通过公平交易获取该等服务时将直接支付的金额为准。

(2)费用抵消安排。如注册人与任何其他主体订有协议，而根据该协议，任何该其他主体为使用注册人之资产将从其向注册人收取的服务费中冲减双方约定的或可合理确定的金额；或者，该其他主体将相关款项付给第三方，而该第三方从其向注册人收取的服务费中冲减双方约定的或可合理确定的金额的，则计入本科目费用项目的金额应以注册人假使未签订该协议将产生的费用金额为准。

(3)财务报表列报。依据本第2(g)款第(1)段与第(2)段的规定增加的费用总金额，应作为本科目总费用的相应扣减金额列报。在财务报表的附注中，单独列示依据本第2(g)款第(1)段与第(2)段的规定增加的费用总金额，并列出增加幅度大于或等于总费用5%的每类费用。如适用，应在附注中说明假使未签署本节第2(g)(2)款所述安排，注册人完全可利用其他主体使用的资产来产生所得。

3.利息以及债务折扣和费用的摊销。在报表正文或脚注中，提供借款平均金额和平均利率。

4.扣除所得税费用之前的投资收入。

5.所得税费用。本科目仅包含基于所得之税收。

6.投资收入净额。

7.投资已实现和未实现净收益(损失)。(a)单独列示下列交易的已实现净收益(损失)：(1)非控制性关联发行人的投资证券，(2)控制性关联发行人的投资证券，和(3)证券以外的投资。

(b)其他投资公司已实现收益的分配，应在本科目中单独列报。

(c)单独列示下列项目：(1)卖出的期权合约中未平仓的合约到期或了结产生的收益或损失；(2)证券空头持仓了结产生的收益或损失；和(3)其他已实现收益或损失。通过财务报表附注披露所卖出的期权合约如下数量和金额：(i)期初数量和金额；(ii)报告期内的数量和金额；(iii)报告期内到期的数量和金额；(iv)报告期内了结的数量和金额；(v)报告期内行权的数量和金额；(vi)期末数量和金额余额。

(d) State separately the amount of the net increase or decrease during the period in the unrealized appreciation or depreciation in the value of investment securities and other investments held at the end of the period.

(e) State separately any: (1) Federal income taxes and (2) other income taxes applicable to realized and unrealized gain(loss) on investments, distinguishing taxes payable currently from deferred income taxes.

8. *Net gain(loss) on investments.*

9. *Net increase(decrease) in net assets resulting from operations.*

[47 FR 56838, Dec. 21, 1982, as amended at 52 FR 23172, June 18, 1987; 59 FR 65636, Dec. 20, 1994; 60 FR 38923, July 28, 1995]

§210.6-08 Special provisions applicable to the statements of operations of issuers of face-amount certificates.

Statements of operations filed by issuers of face-amount certificates shall comply with the following provisions:

Statements of Operations

1. *Investment income.*State separately income from: (a) Interest on mortgages; (b) interest on securities; (c) dividends; (d) rental income; and (e) other investment income. If income from investments in or indebtedness of affiliates is included hereunder, such income shall be segregated under an appropriate caption subdivided to show separately income from: (1) Controlled companies; and (2) other affiliates. If non-cash dividends are included in income, the bases of recognition and measurement used in respect to such amounts shall be disclosed. Any other category of income which exceeds five percent of the total shown under this caption shall be stated separately.

2. *Investment expenses.* (a) State separately the total amount of investment advisory, management and service fees, and expenses in connection with research, selection, supervision, and custody of investments. Amounts of expenses incurred from transactions with affiliated persons shall be disclosed together with the identity of and related amount applicable to each such person accounting for five percent or more of the total expenses shown under this caption together with a description of the nature of the affiliation. Expenses incurred within the person's own organization in connection with research, selection and supervision of investments shall be stated separately. Reductions or reimbursements of management or service fees shall be shown as a negative amount or as a reduction of total expenses shown under this caption.

(b) State separately any other expense item the amount of which exceeds five percent of the total expenses shown under this caption.

(c) A note to the financial statements shall include information concerning

(d)单独列示期末持有的投资证券和其他投资的未实现增值或贬值在期间内的净增减额。

(e)单独列示以下所得税(如有):(1)联邦所得税;和(2)针对已实现和未实现投资收益(损失)征收的其他所得税(区分当期应付税款与递延所得税)。

8.投资收益(损失)净额。

9.经营导致的净资产净增减额。

[《联邦公报》第47卷第56838页,1982年12月21日,修正索引:《联邦公报》第52卷第23172页,1987年6月18日;《联邦公报》第59卷第65636页,1994年12月20日;《联邦公报》第60卷第38923页,1995年7月28日。]

第210.6-08节　适用于面额证券发行人经营报表的特别规定

面额证券发行人提交的经营报表应符合如下规定:

经营报表

1.投资收入。单独列示下列来源的收益:(a)抵押利息;(b)证券利息;(c)股息;(d)租金收益;和(e)其他投资收入。源于对控制性关联方的投资或控制性关联方负债的收益,只要纳入本报表,均应通过适当科目进行细分,以便单独列示来源于以下主体的收益:(1)受控公司;和(2)其他控制性关联方。非现金股息被计入收益之中的,应披露与此等金额相关的确认与计量基础。超过本科目所列总金额5%的任何其他类型收益应单独列示。

2.投资费用。(a)单独列示投资顾问、管理和服务费,以及与投资的研究、选择、监督和存管相关的费用。应披露与控制性关联主体交易所产生的费用金额;同时,对于占本科目总费用5%(含)以上的每一控制性关联主体,均应披露其身份信息和相关金额,并说明控制性关联关系的性质。在注册人组织内部发生的,与投资研究、选择和监督相关的费用,应单独列示。管理或服务费的扣减或退还应作为本科目总费用的负数金额或扣减金额列出。

(b)单独列示金额超过本科目总费用5%的任何其他费用项目。

(c)财务报表的附注应包含与管理和服务费、费率以及计算基础和方法相关的信

management and service fees, the rate of fee, and the base and method of computation. State separately the amount and a description of any fee reductions or reimbursements representing: (1) Expense limitation agreements or commitments; and (2) offsets received from broker-dealers showing separately for each amount received or due from: (i) Unaffiliated persons; and (ii) affiliated persons. If no management or service fees were incurred for a period, state the reason therefor.

(d) If any expenses were paid otherwise than in cash, state the details in a note.

(e) State in a note to the financial statements the amount of brokerage commissions (including dealer markups) paid to affiliated broker-dealers in connection with purchase and sale of investment securities.

3. *Interest and amortization of debt discount and expense.*

4. *Provision for certificate reserves.* State separately any provision for additional credits, or dividends, or interests, in addition to the minimum maturity or face amount specified in the certificates.State also in an appropriate manner reserve recoveries from surrenders or other causes.

5. *Investment income before income tax expense.*

6. *Income tax expense.* Include under this caption only taxes based on income.

7. *Investment income-net.*

8. *Realized gain(loss) on investments-net.*

(a) State separately the net realized gain or loss on transactions in: (1) Investment securities of unaffiliated issuers, (2) investment securities of affiliated issuers, and (3) other investments.

(b) Distributions of capital gains by other investment companies shall be shown separately under this caption.

(c) State separately any: (1) Federal income taxes and (2) other income taxes applicable to realized gain(loss) on investments, distinguishing taxes payable currently from deferred income taxes.

9. *Net income or loss.*

§210.6-09 Statements of changes in net assets.

Statements of changes in net assets filed for persons to whom this article is applicable shall comply with the following provisions:

Statements of Changes in Net Assests

1. *Operations.* State separately: (a) Investment income-net as shown by §210.6-07.6; (b) realized gain (loss) on investments-net of any Federal or other income taxes applicable to such amounts; (c) increase (decrease) in unrealized appreciation or depreciation-net of any Federal or other income taxes applicable to such amounts; and (d) net increase (decrease) in net assets resulting from operations as shown by §210.6-07.9.

息。单独列示并说明下列各项费用扣减或退还:(1)费用限制协议或承诺;和(2)从经纪自营商处收到的可抵消的金额,分别列示从下述主体收到的或下述主体应付的每一笔金额:(i)非控制性关联主体;和(ii)控制性关联主体。如某报告期并未产生任何管理或服务费,应说明相关原因。

(d)对于以现金以外的方式支付的任何费用,均应在附注中说明详细信息。

(e)通过财务报表附注说明向控制性关联经纪自营商支付的,与投资证券买卖相关的经纪佣金(包括经纪商加成)。

3.利息以及债务折扣和费用的摊销。

4.证券准备金的拨备。单独列示面额证券任何规定之最短期限或最小面额以外追加的信用、股息、或利息之拨备。同时以适当方式说明因解约或其他原因所造成的准备金回收。

5.扣除所得税费用之前的投资收入。

6.所得税费用。本科目仅包含基于所得之税收。

7.投资收入净额。

8.投资的已实现净收益(损失)。

(a)单独列示下列各项交易的已实现净收益(损失):(1)非控制性关联发行人的投资证券;(2)控制性关联发行人的投资证券;和(3)其他投资。

(b)其他投资公司已实现资本利得的分配,应在本科目中单独列示。

(c)单独列示以下所得税(如有):(1)联邦所得税;和(2)已实现投资收益(损失)的其他所得税(区分当期应付税款与递延所得税)。

9.净损益。

第210.6-09节　净资产变动表

适用本节规定的会计主体的净资产变动表应符合如下规定:

净资产变动表

1.运营。单独列示:(a)第210.6-07.6节反映的投资收入净额;(b)已实现投资净收益(损失)(不含针对该等金额征收的任何联邦所得税或其他所得税);(c)未实现增值或贬值的净增减额(不含针对该等金额的任何联邦所得税或其他所得税);和(d)第210.6-07.9节反映的运营所产生的净资产净增减额。

2. *Net equalization charges and credits*. State the net amount of accrued undivided earnings separately identified in the price of capital shares issued and repurchased.

3. *Distributions to shareholders*. State separately distributions to shareholders from: (a) Investment income–net; (b) realized gain from investment transactions–net; and (c) other sources.

4. *Capital share transactions*. (a) State the increase or decrease in net assets derived from the net change in the number of outstanding shares or units.

(b) Disclose in the body of the statements or in the notes, for each class of the person's shares, the number and value of shares issued in reinvestment of dividends as well as the number of dollar amounts received for shares sold and paid for shares redeemed.

5. *Total increase (decrease)*.

6. *Net assets at the beginning of the period.*

7. *Net assets at the end of the period.* Disclose parenthetically the balance of undistributed net investment income included in net assets at the end of the period.

§210.6–10 What schedules are to be filed.

(a) When information is required in schedules for both the person and its subsidiaries consolidated, it may be presented in the form of a single schedule, provided that items pertaining to the registrant are separately shown and that such single schedule affords a properly summarized presentation of the facts. If the information required by any schedule (including the notes thereto) is shown in the related financial statement or in a note thereto without making such statement unclear or confusing, that procedure may be followed and the schedule omitted.

(b) The schedules shall be examined by an independent accountant if the related financial statements are so examined.

(c) *Management investment companies*. (1) Except as otherwise provided in the applicable form, the schedules specified in this paragraph shall be filed for management investment companies as of the dates of the most recent audited balance sheet and any subsequent unaudited statement being filed for each person or group.

Schedule I—Investments in securities of unaffiliated issuers. The schedule prescribed by §210.12–12 shall be filed in support of caption 1 of each balance sheet.

Schedule II—Investments—other than securities. The schedule prescribed by §210.12–13 shall be filed in support of caption 3 of each balance sheet. This schedule may be omitted if the investments, other than securities, at both the beginning and end of the period amount to less than one percent of the value of total investments (§210.6–04.4).

Schedule III—Investments in and advances to affiliates. The schedule prescribed by

2.税负平衡费用和抵税净额。列出在股本发行和回购价格中可单独辨认的应计净滚存盈利。

3.股东分配。单独列示向股东分配的如下收益:(a)投资收入净额;(b)投资交易已实现净收益;和(d)其他来源产生的收益。

4.股本交易。(a)列出发行在外股数或任何其他证券单位数量净变动值导致的净资产增减额。

(b)在报表正文或附注中,针对该主体拥有的每类股份,披露因股息再投资而发行的股数与价值,以及因出售股份而收到的金额和回赎股份时支付的金额。

5.增减总额。

6.期初净资产。

7.期末净资产。通过括号注释披露该期间结束时,计入净资产的未分配投资净收入的余额。

第210.6-10节 应提交的附表

(a)上述主体的附表及上述主体和其子公司的合并附表二者均要求提供的信息,可以通过单一附表统一列报;但是,与该主体有关的项目应单列,且该单一附表应对各项事实进行适当的摘要性列报。如果任何附表(包括其附注)要求提供的信息可以在相关的财务报表或其附注中体现并且该等做法不会导致该报表不清楚或造成混淆,则可以将该等信息纳入该财务报表或其附注中,不必另行提交附表。

(b)如相关财务报表经独立会计师核验,附表亦应由独立会计师核验。

(c)管理型投资公司。(1)除非相关表格另有规定,对于管理型投资公司,应提交本款所述附表,报表的截止日期应为各主体或集团最近一期经审计的资产负债表日以及任何未审计期后报表日。

附表Ⅰ——对非控制性关联发行人证券的投资。应按照第210.12-12节规定提交附表,作为每份资产负债表第1科目的支持文件。

附表Ⅱ——投资——证券以外的投资。应按照第210.12-13节的规定提交附表,作为每份资产负债表第3科目的支持文件。如果在期初和期末,投资金额(证券投资除外)均低于总投资价值的1%,则可免于提供此附表(第210.6-04.4节)。

附表Ⅲ——对控制性关联方的投资与垫款。应按照第210.12-14节的规定提交附

§210.12–14 shall be filed in support of caption 2 of each balance sheet.

Schedule Ⅳ—Investments—securities sold short. The schedule prescribed by §210.12–12A shall be filed in support of caption 10(a) of each balance sheet.

Schedule Ⅴ—Open option contracts written. The schedule prescribed by §210.12–12B shall be filed in support of caption 10(b) of each balance sheet.

(2) When permitted by the applicable form, the schedule specified in this paragraph may be filed for management investment companies as of the dates of the most recent audited balance sheet and any subsequent unaudited statement being filed for each person or group.

Schedule Ⅵ—Summary schedule of investments in securities of unaffiliated issuers. The schedule prescribed by §210.12–12C may be filed in support of caption 1 of each balance sheet.

(d) *Unit investment trusts*. Except as otherwise provided in the applicable form:

(1) Schedules Ⅰ and Ⅱ, specified below in this section, shall be filed for unit investment trusts as of the dates of the most recent audited balance sheet and any subsequent unaudited statement being filed for each person or group.

(2) Schedule Ⅲ, specified below in this section, shall be filed for unit investment trusts for each period for which a statement of operations is required to be filed for each person or group.

Schedule Ⅰ—Investment in securities. The schedule prescribed by §210.12–12 shall be filed in support of caption 1 of each balance sheet (§210.6–04).

Schedule Ⅱ—Allocation of trust assets to series of trust shares. If the trust assets are specifically allocated to different series of trust shares, and if such allocation is not shown in the balance sheet in columnar form or by the filing of separate statements for each series of trust shares, a schedule shall be filed showing the amount of trust assets, indicated by each balance sheet filed, which is applicable to each series of trust shares.

Schedule Ⅲ—Allocation of trust income and distributable funds to series of trust shares. If the trust income and distributable funds are specifically allocated to different series of trust shares and if such allocation is not shown in the statement of operations in columnar form or by the filing of separate statements for each series of trust shares, a schedule shall be submitted showing the amount of income and distributable funds, indicated by each statement of operations filed, which is applicable to each series of trust shares.

(e) *Face-amount certificate investment companies*. Except as otherwise provided in the applicable form:

(1) Schedules Ⅰ, Ⅴ and Ⅹ, specified below, shall be filed for face-amount certificate investment companies as of the dates of the most recent audited balance sheet and any

表,作为每份资产负债表第2科目的支持文件。

附表Ⅳ——投资—卖空证券。应按照第210.12-12A节的规定提交附表,作为每份资产负债表第10(a)科目的支持文件。

附表Ⅴ——卖出的期权合约中未平仓的合约。应按照第210.12-12B节的规定提交附表,作为每份资产负债表第10(b)科目的支持文件。

(2)如相关表格允许,对于管理型投资公司,可提交本款所述附表,报表的截止日期应为所提交的各主体或集团最近一期经审计的资产负债表日以及任何未审计期后报表日。

附表Ⅵ——非控制性关联发行人证券投资摘要附表。可按照第210.12-12C节的规定提交附表,作为每份资产负债表第1科目的支持文件。

(d)单位投资信托。除非相关表格另有规定:

(1)对于单位投资信托,应提交本节下文所述附表I和附表II,其截止日期应为已提交的各主体或集团最近一期经审计的资产负债表日以及任何未审计期后报表日。

(2)应就单位投资信托提交本节下文所述附表Ⅲ,报告期以按规定应提交的各主体或集团经审计的经营报表的报告期为准。

附表Ⅰ——证券投资。应按照第210.12-12节的规定提交附表,作为每份资产负债表第1科目(第210.6-04节)的支持文件。

附表Ⅱ——信托资产在各系列信托股份之间的分配。如信托资产被明确分配至不同系列的信托股份,且如果该等分配并未在资产负债表中以分栏格式显示,亦未针对每一系列的信托股份提交单独报表,则应提交一份附表,按照提交的每份资产负债表所示金额,列明分配至每一系列信托股份的信托资产金额。

附表Ⅲ——信托收益及可分配资金在各系列信托股份之间的分配。如信托收益与可分配资金被明确分配至不同系列的信托股份,且如果该等分配并未以分栏格式在资产负债表中予以反映,亦未针对每一系列的信托股份提交单独报表,则应提交一份附表,按照提交的每份资产负债表所示金额,列明分配至每一系列的信托股份收益与可分配资金金额。

(e)面额证券投资公司。除非相关表格另有规定:

(1)面额证券投资公司应提交下文所述附表I、附表V和附表X,其截止日期应为所提交的各主体或集团最近一期经审计的资产负债表日以及任何未审计期后报表日。

subsequent unaudited statement being filed for each person or group.

(2) All other schedules specified below in this section shall be filed for face-amount certificate investment companies for each period for which a statement of operations is filed, except as indicated for Schedules Ⅲ and Ⅳ.

*Schedule I—Investment in securities of unaffiliated issuers.*The schedule prescribed by §210.12-21 shall be filed in support of caption 1 and, if applicable, caption 5(a) of each balance sheet. Separate schedules shall be furnished in support of each caption, if applicable.

*Schedule Ⅱ—Investments in and advances to affiliates and income thereon.*The schedule prescribed by §210.12-22 shall be filed in support of captions 1 and 5(b) of each balance sheet and caption 1 of each statement of operations. Separate schedules shall be furnished in support of each caption, if applicable.

*Schedule Ⅲ—Mortgage loans on real estate and interest earned on mortgages.*The schedule prescribed by §210.12-23 shall be filed in support of captions 1 and 5(c) of each balance sheet and caption 1 of each statement of operations, except that only the information required by column G and note 8 of the schedule need be furnished in support of statements of operations for years for which related balance sheets are not required.

*Schedule Ⅳ—Real estate owned and rental income.*The schedule prescribed by §210.12-24 shall be filed in support of captions 1 and 5(a) of each balance sheet and caption 1 of each statement of operations for rental income included therein, except that only the information required by columns H, I and J, and item "Rent from properties sold during the period" and note 4 of the schedule need be furnished in support of statements of operations for years for which related balance sheets are not required.

*Schedule Ⅴ—Qualified assets on deposit.*The schedule prescribed by §210.12-27 shall be filed in support of the information required by caption 4 of §210.6-06 as to total amount of qualified assets on deposit.

*Schedule Ⅵ—Certificate reserves.*The schedule prescribed by §210.12-26 shall be filed in support of caption 7 of each balance sheet.

*Schedule Ⅶ—Valuation and qualifying accounts.*The schedule prescribed by §210.12-09 shall be filed in support of all other reserves included in the balance sheet.

[47 FR 56838, Dec. 21, 1982, as amended at 59 FR 65636, Dec. 20, 1994; 69 FR 11262, Mar. 9, 2004]

Employee Stock Purchase, Savings and Similar Plans

§210.6A-01 Application of §§210.6A-01 to 210.6A-05.

(a) Sections 210.6A-01 to 210.6A-05 shall be applicable to financial statements

(2)除非附表Ⅲ与附表Ⅳ另有说明,应就面额证券投资公司提交本节下文所述的所有其他附表,附表涵盖的期间以已提交经营报表的报告期为准。

附表Ⅰ——对非控制性关联发行人证券的投资。应按照第210.12-21节的规定提交附表,作为每份资产负债表第1科目及第5(a)科目(如适用)的支持文件。如适当,应单独提供相关附表,作为每一科目的支持文件。

附表Ⅱ——对控制性关联方的投资、垫款以及相关收益。应按照第210.12-22节的规定提交附表,作为每份资产负债表第1科目、第5(b)科目以及每份经营报表第1科目的支持文件。如适当,应单独提供相关附表,作为每一科目的支持文件。

附表Ⅲ——房地产的抵押贷款及抵押利息收入。应按照第210.12-23节的规定提交附表,作为每份资产负债表第1科目、第5(c)科目以及每份经营报表第1科目的支持文件,但是,对于不必提交相关资产负债表的年份,仅需提供附表G栏与附注8要求提供的信息,以之作为经营报表的支持文件。

附表Ⅳ——自有房地产及租金收益。应按照第210.12-24节的规定提交附表,作为每份资产负债表第1科目、第5(a)科目以及每份经营报表第1科目所载租金收益的支持文件,但是,对于不必提交相关资产负债表的年份,仅需提供附表H栏、I栏、J栏、"报告期内售出物业的租金"项目以及附注4所要求提供的信息,以作为经营报表的支持文件。

附表Ⅴ——合格存管资产。应按照第210.12-27节的规定提交附表,作为第210.6-06节下第4项所要求提供的关于合格存管资产总金额的信息的支持文件。

附表Ⅵ——证券准备金。应按照第210.12-26节的规定提交附表,作为每份资产负债表第7科目的支持文件。

附表Ⅶ——估值与合格账户。应按照第210.12-09节的规定提交附表,作为资产负债表中所包括的所有其他准备金的支持文件。

[《联邦公报》第47卷第56838页,1982年12月21日,修正索引:《联邦公报》第59卷第65636页,1994年12月20日;《联邦公报》第69卷第11262页,2004年3月9日。]

员工购股、储蓄计划及类似计划

第210.6A-01节　第210.6A-01~210.6A-05节的适用范围

(a)第210.6A-01~210.6A-05节规定适用于针对员工购股、储蓄计划及类似计划提

filed for employee stock purchase, savings and similar plans.

(b) [Reserved]

[47 FR 56843, Dec. 21, 1982]

§210.6A-02 Special rules applicable to employee stock purchase, savings and similar plans.

The financial statements filed for persons to which this article is applicable shall be prepared in accordance with the following special rules in addition to the general rules in §§210.1-01 to 210.4-10. Where the requirements of a special rule differ from those prescribed in a general rule, the requirements of the special rule shall be met.

(a) *Investment programs.* If the participating employees have an option as to the manner in which their deposits and contributions may be invested, a description of each investment program shall be given in a footnote or otherwise. The number of employees under each investment program shall be stated.

(b) *Net asset value per unit.* Where appropriate, the number of units and the net asset value per unit shall be given by footnote or otherwise.

(c) *Federal income taxes.* (1) If the plan is not subject to Federal income taxes, a note shall so state indicating briefly the principal assumptions on which the plan relied in not making provision for such taxes.

(2) State the Federal income tax status of the employee with respect to the plan.

(d) *V aluation of assets.* The statement of financial condition shall reflect all investments at value, showing cost parenthetically. For purposes of this rule, the term *value* shall mean (1) market value for those securities having readily available market quotations and (2) fair value as determined in good faith by the trustee (s) for the plan (or by the person or persons who exercise similar responsibilities) with respect to other securities and assets.

[47 FR 56843, Dec. 21, 1982]

§210.6A-03 Statements of financial condition.

Statements of financial condition filed under this rule shall comply with the following provisions:

Plan Assets

1. *Investments in securities of participating employers.* State separately each class of securities of the participating employer or employers.

2. *Investments in securities of unaffiliated issuers.*

(a) *United States Government bonds and other obligations.* Include only direct obligations of the United States Government.

(b) *Other securities.* State separately (1) marketable securities and (2) other securities.

交的财务报表。

(b)[保留]

[《联邦公报》第47卷第56843页,1982年12月21日。]

第210.6A-02节　适用于员工购股、储蓄计划及类似计划的特别规则

适用本节规则的会计主体的财务报表，其编制除应遵守第210.1-01~210.4-10节所载一般规则外,还应遵守下列特别规则。特别规则的规定与一般规则不一致的,以特别规则为准。

(a)投资计划。如果参与员工购股、储蓄计划及类似计划(下称员工计划)的员工可选择对其缴款及供款进行投资的方式,应通过脚注或其他方式对每项投资计划作出说明;同时,应说明参与每项投资计划的员工人数。

(b)单位资产净值。在适当情况下,应通过脚注或其他方式说明投资单位的数量及每单位的资产净值。

(c)联邦所得税。(1)如投资计划不必缴纳联邦所得税,应通过脚注予以说明,并简要注明投资计划不拨备该等税款所基于的主要假设。

(2)说明投资计划相关员工的联邦所得税纳税状态。

(d)资产估值。财务状况表应按投资的价值列明所有投资,并通过括号注释标明投资成本。就本规则而言,“价值”一词:(1)对于随时可获得市场报价的证券,指其市场价值;和(2)对于其他证券和资产,指员工计划的信托受托人(或行使类似职责的一个或一个以上主体)善意确定的公允价值。

[《联邦公报》第47卷第56843页,1982年12月21日。]

第210.6A-03节　财务状况表

根据本规则提交的财务状况表应符合如下规定:

员工计划资产

1.对参与员工计划的雇主所发行的证券的投资。分别列示参与员工计划的雇主的每类证券。

2.对非控制性关联发行人的证券的投资。

(a)美国政府公债及其他债务。仅包括美国政府的直接债务。

(b)其他证券。分别列示:(1)有价证券;和(2)其他证券。

3. *Investments. Other than securities.* State separately each major class.

4. *Dividends and interest receivable.*

5. *Cash.*

6. *Other assets.* State separately (a) total of amounts due from participating employers or any of their directors, officers and principal holders of equity securities; (b) total of amounts due from trustees or managers of the plan; and (c) any other significant amounts.

Liabilities and Plan Equity

7. *Liabilities.* State separately (a) total of amounts payable to participating employers; (b) total of amounts payable to participating employees; and (c) any other significant amounts.

8. *Reserves and other credits.* State separately each significant item and describe each such item by using an appropriate caption or by a footnote referred to in the caption.

9. *Plan equity at close of period.*

[27 FR 7870, Aug. 9, 1962. Redesignated at 47 FR 56843, Dec. 21, 1982]

§210.6A–04 Statements of income and changes in plan equity.

Statements of income and changes in plan equity filed under this rule shall comply with the following provisions:

1. *Net investment income.*

(a) *Income.* State separately income from (1) cash dividends; (2) interest, and (3) other sources. Income from investments in or indebtedness of participating employers shall be segregated under the appropriate subcaption.

(b) *Expenses.*State separately any significant amounts.

(c) *Net investment income.*

2. *Realized gain or loss on investments.* (a) State separately the net of gains or losses arising from transactions in (1) investments in securities of the participating employer or employers; (2) other investments in securities; and (3) other investments.

(b) State in a footnote or otherwise for each category of investment in paragraph (a) above the aggregate cost, the aggregate proceeds and the net gain or loss. State the principle followed in determining the cost of securities sold, e.g.,*average cost* or *first–in, first–out.*

3. *Unrealized appreciation or depreciation of investments.* (a) State the amount of increase or decrease in unrealized appreciation or depreciation of investments during the period.

(b) State in a footnote or otherwise the amount of unrealized appreciation or depreciation of investments at the beginning of the period of report, at the end of the period of report, and the increase or decrease during the period.

3.投资——证券投资除外。分别列示每一主要类别的投资。

4.应收股息和利息。

5.现金。

6.其他资产。分别列示:(a)应向参与员工计划的雇主或其任何董事、管理人员及主要股权证券持有人收取的总金额;(b)应向参与员工计划的信托受托人或管理人收取的总金额;和(c)任何其他重大金额。

负债及员工计划权益

7.负债。分别列示:(a)应向参与员工计划的雇主支付的总金额;(b)应向参与员工计划的员工支付的总金额;和(c)任何其他重大金额。

8.准备金与其他信用。单独列示每一重大项目,并通过适当科目或科目中引述的脚注对该等项目一一进行说明。

9.期末员工计划权益。

[《联邦公报》第27卷第7870页,1962年8月9日,重新公布索引:《联邦公报》第47卷第56843页,1982年12月21日。]

第210.6A-04节　损益表及员工计划权益变动表

根据本规则提交的损益表及员工计划权益变动表应符合如下规定:

1.投资净收入。

(a)收益。单独列示以下来源的收益:(1)现金股息;(2)利息;和(3)其他来源。源于对参与员工计划的雇主的投资或该等雇主的负债的收益,应分列于适当的子科目之下。

(b)费用。单独列示任何重大费用金额。

(c)投资净收入。

2.已实现投资收益或损失。(a)单独列示因下列交易而产生的收益或损失之净额:(1)对参与员工计划的一个或多个雇主的证券进行投资;(2)其他证券投资;和(3)其他投资。

(b)通过脚注或其他方式说明上述(a)款中每类投资的合计成本、合计收入及净收益或损失。说明确定售出证券的成本时所遵循的原则,如“平均成本法”或“先进先出法”。

3.投资的未实现增值或贬值。(a)说明该期间内投资未实现增值或贬值的增减额。

(b)通过脚注或其他方式说明,报告期间期初和期末的投资未实现增值或贬值的金额,以及该期间内的增减金额。

4. *Contributions and deposits.* (a) State separately: (1) total of amounts deposited by participating employees, and (2) total of amounts contributed by the participating employer or employers.

(b) If employees of more than one employer participate in the plan, state in tabular form in a footnote or otherwise the amount contributed by each employer and the deposits of the employees of each such employer.

5. *Withdrawals, lapses and forfeitures.* State separately: (a) balances of employees' accounts withdrawn, lapsed or forfeited during the period; (b) amounts disbursed in settlement of such accounts; and (c) disposition of balances remaining after settlement specified in (b).

6. *Plan equity at beginning of period.*

7. *Plan equity at end of period.*

[27 FR 7870, Aug. 9, 1962. Redesignated at 47 FR 56843, Dec. 21, 1982]

§210.6A-05 What schedules are to be filed.

(a) Schedule I, specified below, shall be filed as of the most recent audited statement of financial condition and any subsequent unaudited statement of financial condition being filed. Schedule Ⅱ shall be filed as of the date of each statement of financial condition being filed. Schedule Ⅲ shall be filed for each period for which a statement of income and changes in plan equity is filed. All schedules shall be audited if the related statements are audited.

Schedule I—Investments. A schedule substantially in form prescribed by §210.12-12 shall be filed in support of captions 1, 2 and 3 of each statement of financial condition unless substantially all of the information is given in the statement of financial condition by footnote or otherwise.

Schedule II—Allocation of plan assets and liabilities to investment program. If the plan provides for separate investment programs with separate funds, and if the allocation of assets and liabilities to the several funds is not shown in the statement of financial condition in columnar form or by the submission of separate statements for each fund, a schedule shall be submitted showing the allocation of each caption of each statement of financial condition filed to the applicable fund.

Schedule III—Allocation of plan income and changes in plan equity to investment programs. If the plan provides for separate investment programs with separate funds, and if the allocation of income and changes in plan equity to the several funds is not shown in the statement of income and changes in plan equity in columnar form or by the submission of separate statements for each fund, a schedule shall be submitted showing

4.供款及缴款。(a)分别列示:(1)参与员工计划的员工的缴款总额;和(2)参与员工计划的雇主的供款总额。

(b)如参与员工计划的员工曾受雇于一个以上的雇主,应通过脚注或其他方式,以表格形式说明每一雇主的供款金额及每一雇主的员工的缴款金额。

5.支取、失效和没收。分别列示:(a)期间内发生过支取、已失效或被没收的员工账户的余额;(b)该等账户的结算费用金额;和(c)完成(b)项所述结算后所剩余额的处置。

6.期初员工计划权益。

7.期末员工计划权益。

[《联邦公报》第27卷第7870页,1962年8月9日,重新公布索引:《联邦公报》第47卷第56843页,1982年12月21日。]

第210.6A-05节　应提交的附表

(a)下文所述附表Ⅰ,其截止日期应为提交的最近一期经审计的财务状况表日及任何未审计期后财务状况表日。附表Ⅱ,其截止日期应为提交的每期财务状况表日。附表Ⅲ,其报告期以所提交的每一期损益表和员工计划权益变动表的报告期为准。如相关报表已经过审计,则所有附表亦应进行审计。

附表Ⅰ——投资。应大体按照第210.12-12节规定的格式提交一份附表,作为每份财务状况表第1科目、第2科目及第3科目的支持文件,但财务状况表中几乎所有信息均已通过脚注或其他方式提供的除外。

附表Ⅱ——员工计划资产及负债在各投资项目之间的分摊。如员工计划下设立了不同的投资项目,且不同投资项目使用的基金各不相同,同时资产和负债在该等不同的基金之间的分摊并未分栏反映于财务状况表中,亦未就各基金提交单独报表,则应提交一份附表,列示所提交的每份财务状况表的每一科目对相关基金的分摊。

附表Ⅲ——员工计划所得及员工计划权益变动在各投资项目之间的分摊。如员工计划下设立了不同的投资项目,且不同投资项目使用的基金各不相同,且所得和员工计划权益的变动在各基金之间的分摊并未分栏反映于财务状况表中,亦未就各基金提交单独报表,则应提交一份附表,列示所提交的每份财务状况表的每一科目对相关基金的分摊。

the allocation of each caption of each statement of income and changes in plan equity filed to the applicable fund.

(b) [Reserved]

[45 FR 63676, Sept. 25, 1980. Redesignated at 47 FR 56843, Dec. 21, 1982, and amended at 50 FR 25215, June 18, 1985]

Insurance Companies

Source: Sections 210.7–01 through 210.7–05 appears at 46 FR 54335, Nov. 2, 1981, unless otherwise noted.

§210.7–01 Application of §§210.7–01 to 210.7–05.

This article shall be applicable to financial statements filed for insurance companies.

§210.7–02 General requirement.

(a) The requirements of the general rules in §§210.1–01 to 210.4–10 (Articles 1, 2, 3, 3A and 4) shall be applicable except where they differ from requirements of §§210.7–01 to 210.7–05.

(b) Financial statements filed for mutual life insurance companies and wholly owned stock insurance company subsidiaries of mutual life insurance companies may be prepared in accordance with statutory accounting requirements. Financial statements prepared in accordance with statutory accounting requirements may be condensed as appropriate, but the amounts to be reported for net gain from operations (or net income or loss) and total capital and surplus (or surplus as regards policyholders) shall be the same as those reported on the corresponding Annual Statement.

§210.7–03 Balance sheets.

(a) The purpose of this rule is to indicate the various items which, if applicable, and except as otherwise permitted by the Commission, should appear on the face of the balance sheets and in the notes thereto filed for persons to whom this article pertains. (See §210.4–01(a).)

Assets

1. *Investments—other than investments in related parties.*

(a) *Fixed maturities.*

(b) *Equity securities.*

(c) *Mortgage loans on real estate.*

(d) *Investment real estate.*

(e) *Policy loans.*

(f) *Other long–term investments.*

(g) *Short–term investments.*

(b)[保留]

[《联邦公报》第45卷第63676页,1980年9月25日,重新公布索引:《联邦公报》第47卷第56843页,1982年12月21日,修正索引:《联邦公报》第50卷第25215页,1985年6月18日。]

保险公司

行政规则来源:第210.7-01~210.7-05节,见《联邦公报》第46卷第54335页,1981年11月2日,除非另有说明。

第210.7-01节　第210.7-01~210.7-05节的适用范围

本条款适用于保险公司的财务报表。

第210.7-02节　一般要求

(a)除非与第210.7-01~210.7-05节的规定冲突,否则第210.1-01~210.4-10节中的一般规则(第1条、第2条、第3条、第3A条及第4条)均应适用。

(b)互助人寿保险公司及其全资保险子公司的财务报表,应根据法定会计要求进行编制。根据法定会计要求编制的财务报表可以采用适当的简要报表形式,但报告的净营业收益(或净损益)以及总资本与盈余(或投保人相关盈余),应与相应年度报表的报告内容保持一致。

第210.7-03节　资产负债表

(a)本规则旨在说明适用本条规则的会计主体的资产负债表正文或相关附注所应列示的行项目(如适用),证券交易委员会另行允许不予披露的除外(见第210.4-01(a)节)。

资产

1.投资——对关联方的投资之外的投资。

(a)固定期限投资。

(b)股权证券。

(c)房地产抵押贷款。

(d)投资性房地产。

(e)保单贷款。

(f)其他长期投资。

(g)短期投资。

(h) *Total investments.*

Notes: (1) State parenthetically or otherwise in the balance sheet (a) the basis of determining the amounts shown in the balance sheet and (b) as to fixed maturities and equity securities either aggregate cost or aggregate value at the balance sheet date, whichever is the alternate amount of the carrying value in the balance sheet. Consideration shall be given to the discussion of "Valuation of Securities" in §404.03 of the Codification of Financial Reporting Policies.

(2) Include under fixed maturities: bonds, notes, marketable certificates of deposit with maturities beyond one year, and redeemable preferred stocks. Include under equity securities: common stocks and nonredeemable preferred stocks.

(3) State separately in the balance sheet or in a note thereto the amount of accumulated depreciation and amortization deducted from investment real estate. Subcaption (d) shall not include real estate acquired in settling title claims, mortgage guaranty claims, and similar insurance claims. Real estate acquired in settling claims shall be included in caption 10, "Other Assets," or shown separately, if material.

(4) Include under subcaption (g) investments maturing within one year, such as commercial paper maturing within one year, marketable certificates of deposit maturing within one year, savings accounts, time deposits and other cash accounts and cash equivalents earning interest. State in a note any amounts subject to withdrawal or usage restrictions (See §210.5-02.1.).

(5) State separately in a note the amount of any class of investments included in subcaption (f) if such amount exceeds ten percent of stockholders' equity.

(6) State in a note the name of any person in which the total amount invested in the person and its affiliates, included in the above subcaptions, exceeds ten percent of total stockholders' equity. For this disclosure, include in the amount invested in a person and its affiliates the aggregate of indebtedness and stocks issued by such person and its affiliates that is included in the several subcaptions above, and the amount of any real estate included in subcaption (d) that was purchased or acquired from such person and its affiliates. Indicate the amount included in each subcaption. An investment in bonds and notes of the United States Government or of a United States Government agency or authority which exceeds ten percent of total stockholders' equity need not be reported.

(7) State in a note the amount of investments included under each subcaption (a), (c), (d) and (f) which have been non-income producing for the twelve months preceding the balance sheet date.

2. *Cash.* Cash on hand or on deposit that is restricted as to withdrawal or usage shall be disclosed separately on the balance sheet. The provisions of any restrictions shall be described in a note to the financial statements. Restrictions may include legally restricted

(h)总投资。

注:(1)在资产负债表中通过括号注释或其他方式说明:(a)确定资产负债表中所列金额的计算基础;和(b)固定期限投资及股权证券截至资产负债表日的总成本或总价值,具体取何者以资产负债表账面所载金额为准。应考虑《财务报告政策汇编》第404.03条中有关“证券估值”的讨论。

(2)下列各项计入固定期限投资:债券、票据、期限超过一年的可转让存款凭证以及可回赎优先股。下列各项计入股权证券:普通股以及不可回赎优先股。

(3)在资产负债表或其附注中单独列示自投资性房地产中扣除的累计折旧和摊销。第(d)子科目不包括从产权索赔、抵押保证索赔及类似保险索赔和解中取得的房地产。索赔和解中取得的房地产应计入第10科目“其他资产”,如金额重大则应单独列示。

(4)第(g)子科目包括一年内到期的投资,如一年内到期的商业票据、一年内到期的可转让存款凭证、存款账户、定期存款及其他现金账户以及有利息所得的现金等价物。在附注中说明存在支取或使用限制的任何金额(见第210.5-02.1节)。

(5)如果第(f)子科目中任何类别的投资金额超过股东权益的10%,应在附注中单独列示。

(6)对于计入上述子科目的对任何主体及其控制性关联方的投资,如投资总金额超过全部股东权益总额10%的,应在附注中列出该主体名称。披露该等信息时,对该主体及其控制性关联方的投资金额中应包括计入上述各子科目的该主体及其控制性关联方发行的债券及股票总金额,以及计入第(d)子科目的向该主体及其控制性关联方购买或取得的任何房地产金额。注明计入每一子科目的金额。对美国政府或美国政府机构或部门的债券或票据的投资,即使超过股东权益总额的10%,亦不必报告。

(7)在附注中说明已计入第(a)子科目、第(c)子科目、第(d)子科目及第(f)子科目,且在资产负债表日之前12个月期间并未产生收益的投资金额。

2.现金。支取或使用受限的库存现金或存款现金,均应于资产负债表中单独披露。限制性条款应通过资产负债表附注予以说明,任何该等限制性条款可包括:在短期借款安排中,作为补偿性余额持有的法定限制性存款;与他人订立的合同;或针对具体

deposits held as compensating balances against short–term borrowing arrangements, contracts entered into with others, or company statements of intention with regard to particular deposits. In cases where compensating balance arrangements exist but are not agreements which legally restrict the use of cash amounts shown on the balance sheet, describe in the notes to the financial statements these arrangements and the amount involved, if determinable, for the most recent audited balance sheet required. Compensating balances that are maintained under an agreement to assure future credit availability shall be disclosed in the notes to the financial statements along with the amount and terms of the agreement.

3. *Securities and indebtedness of related parties.* State separately (a) investments in related parties and (b) indebtedness from such related parties (See §210.4–08(k).).

4. *Accrued investment income.*

5. *Accounts and notes receivable.* Include under this caption (a) amounts receivable from agents and insureds, (b) uncollected premiums and (c) other receivables. State separately in the balance sheet or in a note thereto any category of other receivable which is in excess of five percent of total assets. State separately in the balance sheet or in a note thereto the amount of allowance for doubtful accounts that was deducted.

6. *Reinsurance recoverable on paid losses.*

7. *Deferred policy acquisition costs.*

8. *Property and equipment.* (a) State the basis of determining the amounts.

(b) State separately in the balance sheet or in a note thereto the amount of accumulated depreciation and amortization of property and equipment.

9. *Title plant.*

10. *Other assets.* State separately in the balance sheet or in a note thereto any other asset the amount of which exceeds five percent of total assets.

11. *Assets held in separate accounts.* Include under this caption the aggregate amount of assets used to fund liabilities related to variable annuities, pension funds and similar activities. The aggregate liability shall be included under caption 18. Describe in a note to the financial statements the general nature of the activities being reported on in the separate accounts.

12. *Total assets.*

Liabilities and Stockholders' Equity

13. *Policy liabilities and accruals.* (a) State separately in the balance sheet the amounts of (1) future policy benefits and losses, claims and loss expenses, (2) unearned preminums and (3) other policy claims and benefits payable.

(b) State in a note to the financial statements the basis of assumptions (interest rates, mortality, withdrawals) for future policy benefits and claims and settlements which

存款作出的公司意图声明。如果存在补偿性余额安排,但该等安排并不属于以法定方式限制资产负债表现金的使用之协议,注册人应于财务报表附注中,针对最近一期经审计的资产负债表和任何未审计的期后资产负债表,注明与之相关的上述安排和所涉金额(如可确定)。如果为了确保未来可以获得信贷而签订任何协议,则在该等协议项下维持的补偿性余额以及该等协议的金额与条件均应于财务报表附注中披露。

3.关联方的证券与债务。分别列示:(a)对关联方的投资;和(b)该关联方所欠负债[见第210.4-08(k)节]。

4.应计投资收入。

5.应收账款与应收票据。本科目包括:(a)代理人与被保险人所欠应收账款;(b)未收保费;和(c)其他应收账款。应在资产负债表或其附注中单独列示超过总资产5%的其他任何类别的应收账款。应在资产负债表或相关附注中单独列示已扣除的呆账备抵金额。

6.已付赔款的再保摊回。

7.递延保单取得成本。

8.财产与设备。(a)说明确定金额的基础。

(b)于资产负债表或其附注中单独列示财产与设备的累计折旧和摊销。

9.自有产权工厂。

10.其他资产。在资产负债表或其附注中单独列示金额超过总资产5%的任何其他资产。

11.独立账户中持有的资产。下列各项计入本科目:为与可变年金、退休金和类似活动相关的负债提供资金的资产总额。总负债应计入第18科目。在财务报表附注中说明独立账户中报告的活动的一般性质。

12.总资产。

负债及股东权益

13.保单负债及应计项目。(a)于资产负债表中单独列示下列金额:(1)未来保单利益和损失、索赔及损失费用;(2)预收保费;和(3)其他保单索赔及应付利益。

(b)在财务报表附注中,说明确定未来保单利益、索赔及理赔(按现有价值计算)的假设基础(利率、死亡率、退保)。

are stated at present value.

(c) Information shall be given in a note concerning the general nature of reinsurance transactions, including a description of the significant types of reinsurance agreements executed. The information provided shall include (1) the nature of the contingent liability in connection with insurance ceded and (2) the nature and effect of material nonrecurring reinsurance transactions.

14. *Other policyholders' funds.* (a) Include amounts of supplementary contracts without life contingencies, policyholders' dividend accumulations, undistributed earnings on participating business, dividends to policyholders and retrospective return premiums (not included elsewhere) and any similar items. State separately in the balance sheet or in a note thereto any item the amount of which is in excess of five percent of total liabilities.

(b) State in a note to the financial statements the relative significance of participating insurance expressed as percentages of (1) insurance in force and (2) premium income; and the method by which earnings and dividends allocable to such insurance is determined.

15. *Other liabilities.* (a) Include under this caption such items as accrued payrolls, accrued interest and taxes. State separately in the balance sheet or in a note thereto any item included in other liabilities the amount of which exceeds five percent of total liabilities.

(b) State separately in the balance sheet or in a note thereto the amount of (1) income taxes payable and (2) deferred income taxes. Disclose separately the amount of deferred income taxes applicable to unrealized appreciation of equity securities.

16. *Notes payable, bonds, mortgages and similar obligations, including capitalized leases.* (a) State separately in the balance sheet the amounts of (1) short-term debt and (2) long-term debt including capitalized leases.

(b) The disclosure required by §210.5-02.19(b) shall be given if the aggregate of short-term borrowings from banks, factors and other financial institutions and commercial paper issued exceeds five percent of total liabilities.

(c) The disclosure requirements of §210.5-02.22 shall be followed for long-term debt.

17. *Indebtedness to related parties* (See §210.4-0.8(k).).

18. *Liabilities related to separate accounts.*

19. *Commitments and contingent liabilities.*

Redeemable Preferred Stocks

20. *Preferred stocks subject to mandatory redemption requirements or whose redemption is outside the control of the issuer.* The classification and disclosure requirements of §210.5-02.27 shall be followed.

Nonredeemable Preferred Stocks

(c)在附注中提供关于再保险交易一般性质的信息,包括说明已签订的再保险协议的主要类型。所提供的信息应包括:(1)与分出保险相关的或有负债之性质;和(2)重大非经常性再保交易的性质和影响。

14.其他投保人的资金。(a)包括无寿险精算的补充合同金额、投保人红利累计金额、分红业务的未分配盈利金额、投保人红利与追溯性退回保费(前提是未计入其他项目)和任何类似项目。在资产负债表或其附注中单独列示金额超过总负债5%的任何项目。

(b)在财务报表附注中,说明分红保险占下列数据的百分比,以说明其相对重要性:(1)处于有效期之内的保险;和(2)保费收入。并说明确定应向该等保险分摊的盈利与红利的方法。

15.其他负债。(a)此科目包括应计工资、应计利息与税款。在资产负债表或其附注中单独列示金额超过总负债5%的任何其他负债。

(b)在资产负债表或其附注中单独列示下列金额:(1)应付所得税;和(2)递延所得税。单独披露股权证券未实现增值适用的递延所得税金额。

16.应付票据、债券、抵押及类似债务,包括资本化租赁。(a)在资产负债表中单独列示下列金额:(1)短期债务;和(2)包括资本化租赁在内的长期债务。

(b)如银行、代理人和其他金融机构提供的短期贷款以及所发行商业票据的总额超过总负债的5%,应根据第210.5-02.19(b)节的要求进行披露。

(c)长期债务应根据第210.5-02.22节的要求进行披露。

17.向关联方欠负的债务[见第210.4-0.8(k)节]。

18.独立账户的负债[见第11科目]。

19.承诺和或有负债。

可回赎优先股

20.受制于遵守强制回赎要求或回赎不由发行人控制的优先股。应遵守第210.5-02.27节的分类与披露要求。

不可回赎的优先股

21. *Preferred stocks which are not redeemable or are redeemable solely at the option of the issuer.* The classification and disclosure requirements of §210.5–02.28 shall be followed.

Common Stocks

22. *Common stocks.* The classification and disclosure requirements of §210.5–02.29 shall be followed.

Other Stockholders' Equity

23. *Other stockholders' equity.* (a) Separate captions shall be shown for (1) additional paid–in capital, (2) other additional capital, (3) unrealized appreciation or depreciation of equity securities less applicable deferred income taxes, (4) retained earnings (i) appropriated and (ii) unappropriated (See §210.4–08 (e).). Additional paid–in capital and other additional capital may be combined with the stock caption to which they apply, if appropriate.

(b) The classification and disclosure requirements of §210.5–02.30(b) shall be followed for dating and effect of a quasi–reorganization.

(c) State in a note the following information separately for (1) life insurance legal entities, and (2) property and liability insurance legal entities: the amount of statutory stockholders' equity as of the date of each balance sheet presented and the amount of statutory net income or loss for each period for which an income statement is presented.

Noncontrolling Interests

24. *Noncontrolling interests in consolidated subsidiaries.* The disclosure requirements of §210.5–02.31 shall be followed.

25. *Total liabilities and equity.*

[46 FR 54335, Nov. 2, 1981, as amended at 50 FR 25215, June 18, 1985; 74 FR 18615, Apr. 23, 2009]

§210.7–04 Income statements.

The purpose of this rule is to indicate the various items which, if applicable, should appear on the face of the income statements and in the notes thereto filed for persons to whom this article pertains (See §210.4–01(a).).

Revenues

1. *Premiums.* Include premiums from reinsurance assumed and deduct premiums on reinsurance ceded. Where applicable, the amounts included in this caption should represent premiums earned.

2. *Net investment income.* State in a note to the financial statements, in tabular form, the amounts of (a) investment income from each category of investments listed in the subcaptions of §210.7–03.1 that exceeds five percent of total investment income, (b) total investment income, (c) applicable expenses, and (d) net investment income.

3. *Realized investment gains and losses.* Disclose the following amounts:

21.不可回赎或只能由发行人选择回赎的优先股。应遵守第210.5-02.28节的分类与披露要求。

普通股

22.普通股。应遵守第210.5-02.29节的分类与披露要求。

其他股东权益

23.其他股东权益。(a)应通过不同科目反映:(1)资本溢价;(2)其他追加资本;(3)扣除适用的递延所得税之后的股权证券未实现增值或贬值;(4)(i)已拨定留存盈利和(ii)未拨定留存盈利[见第210.4-08(e)节]。在适当情况下,资本溢价及其他追加资本可与适用的股票科目归并。

(b)准重组的日期与生效,应遵守第210.5-02.30(b)节的分类与披露要求。

(c)在附注中分别列示(1)寿险法律实体,和(2)财产和责任险法律实体的下列信息:截至所提交的每期资产负债表日的法定股东权益,以及提交的每期损益表所对应的报告期的法定净损益。

非控制权益

24.并表子公司的非控制权益。应遵守第210.5-02.31节的分类与披露要求。

25.总负债及权益。

[《联邦公报》第46卷第54335页,1981年11月2日,修正索引:《联邦公报》第50卷第25215页,1985年6月18日;《联邦公报》第74卷第18615页,2009年4月23日。]

第210.7-04节　损益表

本规则之目的,是说明适用本节规则的会计主体的资产负债表正文或附注中应列明的各个项目[见第210.4-01(a)节]。

收入

1.保费。在保费中计入分入再保保费,扣除分出再保保费。在适用情况下,计入本科目的金额应代表满期保费。

2.投资净收入。在财务报表附注中以表格形式列示下列金额:(a)第210.7-03.1节所列子科目中,超过投资总收入5%的每一投资类别的投资收入;(b)投资总收入;(c)适用费用;和(d)投资净收入。

3.已实现投资收益(损失)。须披露下列金额:

(a) Net realized investment gains and losses, which shall be shown separately regardless of size.

(b) Indicate in a footnote the registrant's policy with respect to whether investment income and realized gains and losses allocable to policyholders and separate accounts are included in the investment income and realized gain and loss amounts reported in the income statement. If the income statement includes investment income and realized gains and losses allocable to policyholders and separate accounts, indicate the amounts of such allocable investment income and realized gains and losses and the manner in which the insurance enterprise's obligation with respect to allocation of such investment income and realized gains and losses is otherwise accounted for in the financial statements.

(c) The method followed in determining the cost of investments sold (e.g., "average cost," "first-in, first-out," or "identified certificate") shall be disclosed.

(d) For each period for which an income statement is filed, include in a note an analysis of realized and unrealized investment gains and losses on fixed maturities and equity securities. For each period, state separately for fixed maturities [see §210.7-03.1(a)] and for equity securities [see §210.7-03.1(b)] the following amounts:

(1) Realized investment gains and losses, and

(2) The change during the period in the difference between value and cost.

The change in the difference between value and cost shall be given for both categories of investments even though they may be shown on the related balance sheet on a basis other than value.

4. *Other income.* Include all revenues not included in captions 1 and 2 above. State separately in the statement any amounts in excess of five percent of total revenue, and disclose the nature of the transactions from which the items arose.

Benefits, Losses and Expenses

5. *Benefits, claims, losses and settlement expenses.*

6. *Policyholders' share of earnings on participating policies, dividends and similar items.* (See §210.7-03.14(b).)

7. *Underwriting, acquisition and insurance expenses.* State separately in the income statement or in a note thereto (a) the amount included in this caption representing deferred policy acquisition costs amortized to income during the period, and (b) the amount of other operating expenses. State separately in the income statement any material amount included in all other operating expenses.

8. *Income or loss before income tax expense and appropriate items below.*

9. *Income tax expense.* Include under this caption only taxes based on income. (See §210.4-08(g).)

10. *Equity in earnings of unconsolidated subsidiaries and 50% or less owned*

(a)已实现投资净收益(损失),不论金额大小均应单列。

(b)应在脚注中注明,根据注册人的政策,应向投保人及独立账户分摊的投资收入和已实现收益(损失),是否包括在损益表中的投资收入与已实现收益(损失)金额中。如果损益表包括应向投保人及独立账户分摊的投资收入和已实现收益(损失),则应注明该等应分摊的投资收入及已实现收益(损失)的金额,还应注明对于保险公司分摊此等投资收入与已实现收益(损失)的义务,财务报表中具体采用的会计方法。

(c)应披露确定出售投资的成本时所遵循的方法(如“平均成本法”、“先进先出法”或“识别凭证法”)。

(d)应在附注中对每次提交的损益表所对应的报告期内,固定期限证券与股权证券已实现和未实现的投资收益(损失)进行分析。针对每个报告期,均应就固定期限证券[见第210.7-03.1(a)节]与股权证券[见第210.7-03.1(b)节]分别列示下列金额:

(1)已实现投资收益(损失),和

(2)该期间内价值与成本差额的变动。

尽管相关资产负债表完全可以不按价值反映上述两类证券的投资收益(损失),但应提供其价值与成本差额的变动。

4.其他收益。所有未计入第1科目和第2科目的收入均应计入其他收益。在报表中单独列示超过总收入5%的任何金额,并披露产生该项目的交易的性质。

利益、损失及费用

5.保险利益、索赔、损失及理赔费用。

6.投保人分得的分红保单收益、红利及类似项目[见第210.7-03.14(b)条]。

7.承保、保单取得及保险费用。在损益表或其附注中单独列示:(a)报告期内摊销至所得项下的递延保单取得成本计入本科目的金额;和(b)其他营业费用金额。在损益表中单独列示计入所有其他营业费用的重大金额。

8.扣除所得税费用及下列适当项目之前的损益。

9.所得税费用。本项目仅包括基于所得之税收[见第210.4-08(g)节]。

10.在非并表子公司及50%或以下股权被控主体的盈利中享有的权益。通过括号

persons. State, parenthetically or in a note, the amount of dividends received from such persons. If justified by the circumstances, this item may be presented in a different position and a different manner. (See §210.4-01(a).)

11. *Income or loss from continuing operations.*

12. *Discontinued operations.*

13. *Income or loss before extraordinary items and cumulative effects of changes in accounting principles.*

14. *Extraordinary items, less applicable tax.*

15. *Cumulative effects of changes in accounting principles.*

16. *Net income or loss.*

17. *Net income attributable to the noncontrolling interest.*

18. *Net income attributable to the controlling interest.*

19. *Earnings per share data.*

[46 FR 54335, Nov. 2, 1981, as amended at 57 FR 45293, Oct. 1, 1992; 74 FR 18615, Apr. 23, 2009]

§210.7-05 What schedules are to be filed.

(a) Except as expressly provided otherwise in the applicable form:

(1) The schedule specified below in this section as Schedules I shall be as of the date of the most recent audited balance sheet for each person or group.

(2) The schedules specified below in this section as Schedule IV and V shall be filed for each period for which an audited income statement is required to be filed for each person or group.

(3) Schedules Ⅱ, Ⅲ and Ⅴ shall be filed as of the date and for periods specified in the schedule.

(b) When information is required in schedules for both the registrant and the registrant and its subsidiaries consolidated it may be presented in the form of a single schedule:*Provided,* That items pertaining to the registrant are shown separately and that such single schedule affords a properly summarized presentation of the facts. If the information required by any schedule (including the notes thereto) may be shown in the related financial statement or in a note thereto without making such statement unclear or confusing, that procedure may be followed and the schedule omitted.

(c) The schedules shall be examined by the independent accountant.

*Schedule I—Summary of investments—other than investments in related parties.*The schedule prescribed by §210.12-15 shall be filed in support of caption 1 of the most recent audited balance sheet.

*Schedule II—Condensed financial information of registrant.*The schedule prescribed by §210.12-04 shall be filed when the restricted net assets (§210.4.08(e)(3)) of

注释或附注说明从该等主体处收到的股息金额。如情况允许,此项目可在不同位置以不同方式列报[见第210.4-01(a)节]。

11.持续经营损益。
12.已终止经营的业务。
13.扣除非经常项目和会计原则变更累积影响数之前的损益。

14.非经常项目,减去适用税款。
15.会计原则变更累积影响数。
16.净损益。
17.归属于非控制权益的净收益。
18.归属于控制权益的净收益。
19.每股盈利数据。

[《联邦公报》第46卷第54335页,1981年11月2日,修正索引:《联邦公报》第57卷第45293页,1992年10月1日;《联邦公报》第74卷第18615页,2009年4月23日]

第210.7-05节　应提交的附表

(a)除非相关表格另有明确规定:

(1)本节下文所述附表I,其截止日期应为各主体或集团的最近一期经审计的资产负债表日。

(2)本节下文所述附表IV和附表V,报告期以按规定应提交的各主体或集团经审计的损益表的报告期为准。

(3)附表Ⅱ、附表Ⅲ和附表Ⅴ应按相应附表所述截止日期和报告期提交。

(b)注册人的附表及注册人和其子公司的合并附表中均要求提供的信息,可以通过单一附表统一列报;但是,与注册人有关的项目应单列,且该单一附表应对各项事实进行适当的摘要性列报。如果任何附表(包括其附注)要求提供的信息可以在相关的财务报表或其附注中体现并且该等做法不会导致该报表不清楚或造成混淆,则可以将该等信息纳入该财务报表或其附注中,不必另行提交附表。

(c)附表应由独立会计师核验。

附表I——投资摘要——对关联方的投资之外的投资。应提交第210.12-15节规定的附表,作为最近一期经审计的资产负债表第1科目的支持文件。

附表II——注册人的简要财务信息。并表子公司的受限净资产[见第210.4.08(e)(3)节]超过截至最近结束的一个会计年度年末其被纳入合并报表的净资产25%之时,

consolidated subsidiaries exceed 25 percent of consolidated net assets as of the end of the most recently completed fiscal year. For purposes of the above test, restricted net assets of consolidated subsidiaries shall mean that amount of the registrant's proportionate share of net assets of consolidated subsidiaries (after intercompany eliminations) which as of the end of the most recent fiscal year may not be transferred to the parent company by subsidiaries in the form of loans, advances or cash dividends without the consent of a third party (*i.e.* , lender, regulatory agency, foreign government, etc.). Where restrictions on the amount of funds which may be loaned or advanced differ from the amount restricted as to transfer in the form of cash dividends, the amount least restrictive to the subsidiary shall be used. Redeemable preferred stocks (§210.7-03.20) and noncontrolling interests shall be deducted in computing net assets for purposes of this test.

*Schedule Ⅲ—Supplementary insurance information.*The schedule prescribed by §210.12-16 shall be filed giving segment detail in support of various balance sheet and income statement captions. The required balance sheet information shall be presented as of the date of each audited balance sheet filed, and the income statement information shall be presented for each period for which an audited income statement is required to be filed, for each person or group.

*Schedule Ⅳ—Reinsurance.*The schedule prescribed by §210.12-17 shall be filed for reinsurance ceded and assumed.

*Schedule Ⅴ—Valuation and qualifying accounts.*The schedule prescribed by §210.12-09 shall be filed in support of valuation and qualifying accounts included in the balance sheet (see §210.4-02).

Schedule Ⅵ—Supplemental Information Concerning Property-Casualty Insurance Operations. The information required by §210.12-18 shall be presented as of the same dates and for the same periods for which the information is reflected in the audited consolidated financial statements required by §§210.3-01 and 3-02. The schedule may be omitted if reserves for unpaid property-casualty claims and claim adjustment expenses of the registrant and its consolidated subsidiaries, its unconsolidated subsidiaries and its 50%-or-less-owned equity basis investees did not in the aggregate, exceed one-half of common stockholders' equity of the registrant and its consolidated subsidiaries as of the beginning of the fiscal year. For purposes of this test, only the proportionate share of the registrant and its other subsidiaries in the reserves for unpaid claims and claim adjustment expenses of 50%-or-less-owned equity investees taken in the aggregate after intercompany eliminations shall be taken into account. Article 12—Form and Content of Schedules (17 CFR 210).

[46 FR 54335, Nov. 2, 1981, as amended at 47 FR 29837, July 9, 1982; 49 FR 47598, Dec. 6, 1984; 59 FR 65637, Dec. 20, 1994; 74 FR 18615, Apr. 23, 2009]

应提交第210.12-04节规定的附表。在进行测试,以判断是否符合上述标准之时,并表子公司的受限净资产系指截至最近一个会计年度年末,该子公司未经第三方(即贷款人、监管机构、外国政府等)同意,不得以贷款、垫款或现金股息的形式向母公司转移的,注册人按比例在并表子公司净资产中所占的数额(该数额应为进行公司间抵消后的数额)。贷款或垫款金额上限和可以以现金股息形式转移的资金的金额上限存在差异时,应采用对子公司限制较低的金额。在进行本测试时,计算净资产时应扣除可回赎优先股(见第210.7-03.20节)及非控制权益。

附表Ⅲ——补充保险信息。应提交第210.12-16节规定的附表以提供相关节段信息,作为各项资产负债表和损益表的支持文件。各主体或集团应按所提交的每一经审计的资产负债表日列报应提交的资产负债表相关信息,并按应提交经审计的损益表的每一报告期列报损益表相关信息。

附表Ⅳ——再保险。应提交第210.12-17节规定的附表,提供与分出和分入再保险相关的信息。

附表Ⅴ——估值和合格账户。应提交第210.12-09节规定的附表,作为资产负债表的估值和合格账户(见第210.4-02节)的支持文件。

附表Ⅵ——关于财产意外险经营的补充信息。第210.12-18节要求提供的信息,其截止日期与覆盖的期间应与第210.3-01节和第210.3-02节要求提供的经审计的合并财务报表中所体现的信息保持一致。如果截至会计年度年初,注册人及其并表子公司、非并表子公司和50%或以下股权被控的投资对象的财产意外险未付赔款金额和赔款费用调整准备金总计不超过注册人及其并表子公司的普通股股东权益的一半,则可以不提交此附表。在进行测试,以判断是否符合上述标准之时,应仅考虑在进行公司间抵消后,在注册人拥有50%或以下股权的投资对象的未付赔款金额和赔款费用准备金中,注册人及其他子公司按比例持有的总份额。第12条——附表的格式和内容(《联邦规章汇编》第十七编第210节)。

[《联邦公报》第46卷第54335页,1981年11月2日,修正索引:《联邦公报》第47卷第29837页,1982年7月9日;《联邦公报》第49卷第47598页,1984年12月6日;《联邦公报》第59卷第65637页,1994年12月20日;《联邦公报》第74卷第18615页,2009年4月23日。]

Article 8 Financial Statements of Smaller Reporting Companies

Source: 73 FR 953, Jan. 4, 2008, unless otherwise noted.

§210.8–01 Preliminary Notes to Article 8.

Sections 210.8–01 to 210.8–08 shall be applicable to financial statements filed for smaller reporting companies. These sections are not applicable to financial statements prepared for the purposes of Item 17 or Item 18 of Form 20–F.

Note 1 to §210.8: Financial statements of a smaller reporting company, as defined by §229.10(f)(1) of this chapter, its predecessors or any businesses to which the smaller reporting company is a successor shall be prepared in accordance with generally accepted accounting principles in the United States.

Note 2 to §210.8: Smaller reporting companies electing to prepare their financial statements with the form and content required in this article need not apply the other form and content requirements in Regulation S–X with the exception of the following:

a. The report and qualifications of the independent accountant shall comply with the requirements of Article 2 of this part;

b. The description of accounting policies shall comply with Article 4–08(n) of this part; and

c. Smaller reporting companies engaged in oil and gas producing activities shall follow the financial accounting and reporting standards specified in Article 4–10 of this part with respect to such activities.

To the extent that Article 11–01 of this part (Pro Forma Presentation Requirements) offers enhanced guidelines for the preparation, presentation and disclosure of pro forma financial information, smaller reporting companies may wish to consider these items.

Note 3 to §210.8: Financial statements for a subsidiary of a smaller reporting company that issues securities guaranteed by the smaller reporting company or guarantees securities issued by the smaller reporting company must be presented as required by §210.3–10, except that the periods presented are those required by §210.8–02.

Note 4 to §210.8: Financial statements for a smaller reporting company's affiliates whose securities constitute a substantial portion of the collateral for any class of securities registered or being registered must be presented as required by §210.3–16, except that the periods presented are those required by §210.8–02.

Note 5 to §210.8: The Commission, where consistent with the protection of investors, may permit the omission of one or more of the financial statements or the substitution of appropriate statements of comparable character. The Commission by informal written notice may require the filing of other financial statements where necessary or appropriate.

第210.8节　小型报告公司财务报表

行政规则来源:《联邦公报》第73卷第953页,2008年1月4日,除非另有说明。

第210.8-01节　关于第210.8节的文前说明

第210.8-01~210.8-08节应适用于小型报告公司的财务报表,但不适用于为《20-F表格》第17条或第18条之目的编制的财务报表。

第210.8节附注1:本章第229.10(f)(1)节定义的小型报告公司及其前身或任何继受企业的财务报表,应根据美国公认会计原则编制。

第210.8节附注2:选择以本条规定的格式和内容编制财务报表的小型报告公司,不必适用《S-X管理办法》中的其他格式和内容要求,但是:

a.独立会计师的报告和资质应符合本部分第2条的要求;

b.对会计政策的说明应符合本部分第4-08(n)条的要求;且

c.从事石油与天然气生产活动的小型报告公司应遵循本部分第4-10条关于该等活动的财务会计和报告准则的规定。

如本部分第11-01条(备考信息列报要求)就备考财务信息的编制、列报和披露提供了要求更高的指引,小型报告公司可考虑适用该等条目。

第210.8节附注3:小型报告公司的子公司发行证券并由小型报告公司提供担保的,或者子公司为小型报告公司发行的证券提供担保的,该等子公司的财务报表须按照第210.3-10节的要求列报,但列报期间应为第210.8-02节规定的报告期。

第210.8节附注4:小型报告公司的控制性关联方以其自身证券为已注册或正在申请注册的任何类别证券提供担保,且其自身证券构成担保品的重大部分的,该等控制性关联方的财务报表须按照第210.3-16节的要求列报,但列报期间应为第210.8-02节规定的期间。

第210.8节附注5:在符合投资者保护原则的前提下,证券交易委员会可允许免予提交一份或多份财务报表,或允许提交具有可比性质的适当报表作为替代。证券交易委员会可以在必要或适当时,发出非正式的书面通知,要求提交其他财务报表。

Note 6 to §210.8: Section 210.4–01(a)(3) shall apply to the preparation of financial statements of smaller reporting companies.

§210.8–02 Annual financial statements.

Smaller reporting companies shall file an audited balance sheet as of the end of each of the most recent two fiscal years, or as of a date within 135 days if the issuer has existed for a period of less than one fiscal year, and audited statements of income, cash flows and changes in stockholders' equity for each of the two fiscal years preceding the date of the most recent audited balance sheet (or such shorter period as the registrant has been in business).

§210.8–03 Interim financial statements.

Interim financial statements may be unaudited; however, before filing, interim financial statements included in quarterly reports on Form 10–Q(§249.308(a) of this chapter) must be reviewed by an independent public accountant using professional standards and procedures for conducting such reviews, as established by generally accepted auditing standards, as may be modified or supplemented by the Commission. If, in any filing, the issuer states that interim financial statements have been reviewed by an independent public accountant, a report of the accountant on the review must be filed with the interim financial statements. Interim financial statements shall include a balance sheet as of the end of the issuer's most recent fiscal quarter, a balance sheet as of the end of the preceding fiscal year, and income statements and statements of cash flows for the interim period up to the date of such balance sheet and the comparable period of the preceding fiscal year.

(a) *Condensed format.* Interim financial statements may be condensed as follows:

(1) Balance sheets should include separate captions for each balance sheet component presented in the annual financial statements that represents 10% or more of total assets. Cash and retained earnings should be presented regardless of relative significance to total assets. Registrants that present a classified balance sheet in their annual financial statements should present totals for current assets and current liabilities.

(2) Income statements should include net sales or gross revenue, each cost and expense category presented in the annual financial statements that exceeds 20% of sales or gross revenues, provision for income taxes, discontinued operations, extraordinary items and cumulative effects of changes in accounting principles or practices. (Financial institutions should substitute net interest income for sales for purposes of determining items to be disclosed.) Dividends per share should be presented.

(3) Cash flow statements should include cash flows from operating, investing and financing activities as well as cash at the beginning and end of each period and the

第210.8节附注6:第210.4-01(a)(3)节应适用于小型报告公司财务报表的编制。

第210.8-02节 年度财务报表

小型报告公司应提交分别截至最近2个会计年度年末的经审计的资产负债表(如发行人的存续期间不足一个会计年度,则应提交截至此前135日期间内某一天的经审计的资产负债表),以及最近一期经审计的资产负债表日之前2个会计年度的经审计的损益表、现金流量表和股东权益变动表(如注册人开展业务的期间不足2个会计年度,则为注册人开展业务的期间的相应报表)。

第210.8-03节 中期财务报表

中期财务报表可以不经审计,但对于按《10-Q表格》[本章第249.308(a)节]提交的季度报告中所含中期财务报表,应在提交之前由独立公共会计师按照根据公认审计准则(包括证券交易委员会作出的修改或补充)确定的专业审查标准和程序进行审查。如发行人在提交财务报表之时,说明中期财务报表已经经过独立公共会计师审查,则必须在提交该中期财务报表的同时提交会计师审查报告。中期财务报表应包括截至发行人最近一个财务季度季末的资产负债表、截至上一会计年度年末的资产负债表,以及截至该资产负债表日的中期报告期以及上一会计年度同期的损益表和现金流量表。

(a)简要格式。中期财务报表可以按如下规定进行简化:

(1)对于年度财务报表中列报的、占总资产10%(含)以上的每一资产负债表组成部分,资产负债表均应单列科目。所有现金和留存盈利均应进行列报,无论其相对总资产而言是否具有重大性。注册人在年度财务报表中列报分类资产负债表的,应列报流动资产和流动负债的总额。

(2)损益表应包括净销售额或毛收入、在年度财务报表中列报的超过销售额或毛收入20%的各类成本和费用、所得税拨备、已终止经营的业务、非经常项目和会计原则或惯例变动的累积影响数(在判断应披露的项目之时,金融机构应以净利息收入替代销售额)。同时,应列报每股股息。

(3)现金流量表应包括经营、投资和融资活动产生的现金流量、各个报告期的期初和期末现金,以及期初和期末现金的增减额。

increase or decrease in such balance.

(4) Additional line items may be presented to facilitate the usefulness of the interim financial statements, including their comparability with annual financial statements.

(b) *Disclosure required and additional instructions as to content*—(1) *Footnotes.* Footnote and other disclosures should be provided as needed for fair presentation and to ensure that the financial statements are not misleading.

(2) *Material subsequent events and contingencies.* Disclosure must be provided of material subsequent events and material contingencies notwithstanding disclosure in the annual financial statements.

(3) *Significant equity investees.*Sales, gross profit, net income (loss) from continuing operations, net income, and net income attributable to the investee must be disclosed for equity investees that constitute 20 percent or more of a registrant's consolidated assets, equity or income from continuing operations attributable to the registrant.

(4) *Significant dispositions and business combinations.* If a significant disposition or business combination has occurred during the most recent interim period and the transaction required the filing of a Form 8-K (§249.308 of this chapter), pro forma data must be presented that reflects revenue, income from continuing operations, net income, net income attributable to the registrant and income per share for the current interim period and the corresponding interim period of the preceding fiscal year as though the transaction occurred at the beginning of the periods.

(5) *Material accounting changes.* Disclosure must be provided of the date and reasons for any material accounting change. The registrant's independent accountant must provide a letter in the first Form 10-Q (§249.308a of this chapter) filed after the change indicating whether or not the change is to a preferable method. Disclosure must be provided of any retroactive change to prior period financial statements, including the effect of any such change on income and income per share.

(6) *Development stage companies.* A registrant in the development stage must provide cumulative financial information from inception.

Instruction 1 to §210.8-03: Where Article 8 is applicable to a Form 10-Q and the interim period is more than one quarter, income statements must also be provided for the most recent interim quarter and the comparable quarter of the preceding fiscal year.

Instruction 2 to §210.8-03: Interim financial statements must include all adjustments that, in the opinion of management, are necessary in order to make the financial statements not misleading. An affirmative statement that the financial statements have been so adjusted must be included with the interim financial statements.

[73 FR 953, Jan. 4, 2008, as amended at 74 FR 18615, Apr. 23, 2009]

(4)为了提高中期财务报表的实用性,也可列报其他行项目(包括该报表与年度财务报表的比较信息)。

(b)披露要求和关于内容的其他说明——(1)脚注。为了满足公允列报的要求,并确保财务报表不具有误导性,应提供脚注和其他披露。

(2)重大期后事件和重大或有事项。即使在年度财务报表中进行了披露,仍需披露重大期后事件和重大或有事项。

(3)权益投资的重大投资对象。销售额、毛利润、持续经营净收益(损失)、净收益以及归属于投资对象的净收益,在归属于注册人的并表资产、权益或持续经营收益中的占比达20%(含)以上的,必须按权益投资的投资对象进行披露。

(4)重大处置和业务合并。如在最近一期的中期报告期发生了重大处置或业务合并,且该交易必须提交《8-k表格》(本章第249.308节)进行备案,则必须列报备考数据,以反映假使此项交易发生在当前中期报告期期初,当前中期报告期和上一会计年度同期的中期报告期将实现的收入、持续经营收益、净收益、归属于注册人的净收益以及每股盈利。

(5)重大会计变更。发生任何重大会计变更的,其日期和原因均须进行披露。注册人的独立会计师必须在此项变更发生后按《10-Q表格》(本章第249.308a节)首次提交财务报表时提供一份信函,说明变更之后的方法是否更为可取。对前期财务报表的任何追溯变更亦须披露,包括任何该等变更对收益和每股盈利的影响数。

(6)发展阶段的公司。处于发展阶段的注册人须提供自创立时起的累计财务信息。

关于第210.8-03节的说明1:如第210.8节适用《10-Q表格》,且中期报告期达一个季度以上,还须提供最近一个中期季度和上一会计年度同一季度的损益表。

关于第210.8-03节的说明2:中期财务报表须包括管理层认为必要的所有调整,使财务报表不致产生误导性。已经对财务报表进行上述调整的,中期财务报表中须进行相应的肯定性陈述。

[《联邦公报》第73卷第953页,2008年1月4日,修正索引:《联邦公报》第74卷第18615页,2009年4月23日。]

§210.8–04 Financial statements of businesses acquired or to be acquired.

(a) If a business combination has occurred or is probable, financial statements of the business acquired or to be acquired shall be furnished for the periods specified in paragraph (c) of this section:

(1) This encompasses the purchase of an interest in a business accounted for by the equity method.

(2) Acquisitions of a group of related businesses that are probable or that have occurred subsequent to the latest fiscal year end for which audited financial statements of the issuer have been filed shall be treated as if they are a single business combination for purposes of this section. The required financial statements of related businesses may be presented on a combined basis for any periods they are under common control or management. A group of businesses is deemed to be related if:

(i) They are under common control or management;

(ii) The acquisition of one business is conditioned on the acquisition of each other business; or

(iii) Each acquisition is conditioned on a single common event.

(3) Annual financial statements required by this rule shall be audited. The form and content of the financial statements shall be in accordance with §§210.8–02 and 8–03.

(b) The periods for which financial statements are to be presented are determined by comparison of the most recent annual financial statements of the business acquired or to be acquired and the smaller reporting company's most recent annual financial statements filed at or before the date of acquisition to evaluate each of the following conditions:

(1) Compare the smaller reporting company's investments in and advances to the acquiree to the total consolidated assets of the smaller reporting company as of the end of the most recently completed fiscal year.

(2) Compare the smaller reporting company's proportionate share of the total assets (after intercompany eliminations) of the acquiree to the total consolidated assets of the smaller reporting company as of the end of the most recently completed fiscal year.

(3) Compare the smaller reporting company's equity in the income from continuing operations before income taxes, extraordinary items and cumulative effect of a change in accounting principles of the acquiree exclusive of amounts attributable to any noncontrolling interests to such consolidated income of the smaller reporting company for the most recently completed fiscal year.

Computational note to §210.8–04(b): For purposes of making the prescribed income test the following guidance should be applied: If income of the smaller reporting company and its subsidiaries consolidated exclusive of amounts attributable to any noncontrolling interests for the most recent fiscal year is at least 10 percent lower than the average of the

第210.8-04节　已收购企业或目标收购企业的财务报表

(a)如果已经或可能发生业务合并,应提交已收购企业或目标收购企业在本节第(c)款所述期间内的财务报表:

(1)上述业务合并包括购买按权益法核算的企业权益。

(2)就本节而言,注册人在其提交的经审计的财务报表覆盖的最近一个会计年度结束后,可能或已经作出的对一组关联企业的收购,应按一宗业务合并处理。关联企业在受同一控制或管理的期间,可以采用汇总报表的形式提供规定的财务报表。在下列情形下,不同企业之间应视为存在关联关系:

(i)该等企业受同一控制或管理;

(ii)对其中一家企业的收购,以收购其他每家企业为条件;或者

(iii)对每家企业的收购均以同一事件之发生为条件。

(3)本规则要求提供的年度财务报表应经过审计。财务报表的格式与内容应符合第210.8-02节和第210.8-03节的规定。

(b)在确定应提交财务报表的报告期时,应将已收购企业或目标收购企业最近一个年度的财务报表,与该小型报告公司在收购当日或之前提交的最近一个年度的财务报表进行比较,在进行该等比较时,应对以下各项条件进行评估:

(1)将小型报告公司对被收购方的投资和垫款与该小型报告公司截至最近结束的一个会计年度的并表总资产相比较。

(2)将小型报告公司在被收购方总资产中按比例持有之数额(该数额应为进行公司间抵消后的数额)与该小型报告公司截至最近结束的一个会计年度的并表总资产相比较;

(3)将小型报告公司在扣除所得税、非经常项目及会计原则变更累积影响数之前的被收购方持续经营收益中的权益(不含归属于任何非控制权益的金额)与该小型报告公司在最近结束的一个会计年度的并表收益相比较。

关于第210.8-04(b)节的计算说明:在进行规定的收益测试时,应适用下列指导原则:如果小型报告公司及其并表子公司在最近一个会计年度的收益(不含归属于任何非控制权益的收益)比过去5个会计年度的收益平均值低10%(含)以上,计算收益时应使用该等收益平均值。计算平均收益时应忽略任何亏损年度。

income for the last five fiscal years, such average income should be substituted for purposes of the computation. Any loss years should be omitted for purposes of computing average income.

(c)(1) If none of the conditions specified in paragraph (b) of this section exceeds 20%, financial statements are not required. If any of the conditions exceed 20%, but none exceeds 40%, financial statements shall be furnished for the most recent fiscal year and any interim periods specified in §210.8-03. If any of the conditions exceed 40%, financial statements shall be furnished for the two most recent fiscal years and any interim periods specified in §210.8-03.

(2) The separate audited balance sheet of the acquired business is not required when the smaller reporting company's most recent audited balance sheet filed is for a date after the acquisition was consummated.

(3) If the aggregate impact of individually insignificant businesses acquired since the date of the most recent audited balance sheet filed for the registrant exceeds 50%, financial statements covering at least the substantial majority of the businesses acquired shall be furnished. Such financial statements shall be for the most recent fiscal year and any interim periods specified in §210.8-03.

(4) Registration statements not subject to the provisions of §230.419 of this chapter (Regulation C) and proxy statements need not include separate financial statements of the acquired or to be acquired business if it does not meet or exceed any of the conditions specified in paragraph (b) of this section at the 50 percent level, and either:

(i) The consummation of the acquisition has not yet occurred; or

(ii) The effective date of the registration statement, or mailing date in the case of a proxy statement, is no more than 74 days after consummation of the business combination, and the financial statements have not been filed previously by the registrant.

(5) An issuer that omits from its initial registration statement financial statements of a recently consummated business combination pursuant to paragraph (c)(4) of this section shall furnish those financial statements and any pro forma information specified by §210.8-05 under cover of Form 8-K (§249.308 of this chapter) no later than 75 days after consummation of the acquisition.

(d) If the smaller reporting company made a significant business acquisition after the latest fiscal year end and filed a report on Form 8-K, which included audited financial statements of such acquired business for the periods required by paragraph (c) of this section and the pro forma financial information required by §210.8-05, the determination of significance may be made by using pro forma amounts for the latest fiscal year in the report on Form 8-K rather than by using the historical amounts of the registrant. The tests may not be made by "annualizing" data.

(c)(1)如果已收购企业或目标收购企业未超过本节第(b)款规定的任何一项条件的20%,不必提交财务报表。如果任何一项条件在20%~40%之间,应提交最近一个会计年度以及第210.8-03节规定的任何中期报告期的财务报表。如果任何一项条件超过40%,应提交最近两个会计年度以及第210.8-03节规定的任何中期报告期的财务报表。

(2) 如果小型报告公司提交的最近一期经审计的资产负债表日迟于收购完成之日,则不必提交单独的已收购企业的经审计的资产负债表。

(3)如果在注册人最近一期经审计的资产负债表提交日后收购的各个非重要企业的合计影响数超过50%,则至少应提供涵盖绝大部分已收购企业的财务报表。该等财务报表应至少覆盖最近一个会计年度以及第210.8-03节规定的任何中期报告期。

(4)如果已收购企业或目标收购企业未达到或超过本节第(b)款所规定的任何条件的50%,并且符合下列任一条件,则征集投票权报告不受本章第230.419节(《C管理办法》)规定约束,并且注册说明书不必包含已收购企业或目标收购企业的单独财务报表:

(i)收购尚未完成,或

(ii)注册说明书的生效日或征集投票权报告的邮递日不迟于业务合并完成后第74天,且注册人此前未提交财务报表。

(5)如果发行人在初始注册说明书中没有根据本节第(c)(4)款提交关于最近完成的业务合并的财务报表,则该发行人最迟应在收购完成后75日内提交该等财务报表,并通过《8-K表格》(本章第249.308节)提交第210.8-05节规定的任何备考财务信息。

(d)如果小型报告公司在最近会计年度结束后进行了一笔重大企业收购,并通过《8-K表格》提交了一份报告[包括该等已收购企业在本节第(c)款规定的期间的经审计的财务报表以及第210.8-05节规定的备考财务信息],则在判断收购的重要程度时,可以使用按照《8-K表格》提交的最近一个会计年度的报告的备考数额替代注册人的历史数额。在进行测试,以判断是否符合上述标准时,不得采用"年化"数据。

(e) If the business acquired or to be acquired is a foreign business, financial statements of the business meeting the requirements of Item 17 of Form 20-F (§249.220f of this chapter) will satisfy this section.

[73 FR 953, Jan. 4, 2008, as amended at 74 FR 18616, Apr. 23, 2009]

§210.8-05 Pro forma financial information.

(a) Pro forma information showing the effects of the acquisition shall be furnished if financial statements of a business acquired or to be acquired are presented.

(b) Pro forma statements should be condensed, in columnar form showing pro forma adjustments and results, and should include the following:

(1) If the transaction was consummated during the most recent fiscal year or subsequent interim period, pro forma statements of income reflecting the combined operations of the entities for the latest fiscal year and interim period, if any; or

(2) If consummation of the transaction has occurred or is probable after the date of the most recent balance sheet required by §210.8-02 or §210.8-03, a pro forma balance sheet giving effect to the combination as of the date of the most recent balance sheet. For a purchase, pro forma statements of income reflecting the combined operations of the entities for the latest fiscal year and interim period, if any, are required.

§210.8-06 Real estate operations acquired or to be acquired.

If, during the period for which income statements are required, the smaller reporting company has acquired one or more properties that in the aggregate are significant, or since the date of the latest balance sheet required by §210.8-02 or §210.8-03, has acquired or proposes to acquire one or more properties that in the aggregate are significant, the following shall be furnished with respect to such properties:

(a) Audited income statements (not including earnings per unit) for the two most recent years, which shall exclude items not comparable to the proposed future operations of the property such as mortgage interest, leasehold rental, depreciation, corporate expenses and federal and state income taxes;*Provided, however,* that such audited statements need be presented for only the most recent fiscal year if:

(1) The property is not acquired from a related party;

(2) Material factors considered by the smaller reporting company in assessing the property are described with specificity in the registration statement with regard to the property, including source of revenue (including, but not limited to, competition in the rental market, comparative rents, occupancy rates) and expenses (including but not limited to, utilities,*ad valorem* tax rates, maintenance expenses, and capital improvements anticipated); and

(3) The smaller reporting company indicates that, after reasonable inquiry, it is not

(e)如果已收购企业或目标收购企业系外国企业,则该企业的财务报表满足《20-F表格》(本章第249.220f节)第17条要求的,视为符合本节要求。

[《联邦公报》第73卷第953页,2008年1月4日,修正索引:《联邦公报》第74卷第18616页,2009年4月23日。]

第210.8-05节 备考财务信息

(a)如果已收购企业或目标收购企业的财务报表已经提交,则应提供显示收购影响数的备考财务信息。

(b)备考报表应简明扼要,分栏显示备考调整与结果,并包含下列信息:

(1)如果交易的完成时间位于最近一个会计年度之内,或位于其后的中期报告期之内,则应纳入一份备考报表,以反映各实体在最近一个会计年度及该中期报告期的合并经营(如有);或

(2)如果交易的完成时间迟于或可能迟于第210.8-02节或第210.8-03节要求提交的最近一期资产负债表日,则应纳入一份备考资产负债表,反映该合并在最近一期资产负债表日后的影响。就收购而言,应提交一份备考报表,以反映各实体在最近一个会计年度及中期报告期的合并经营(如有)。

第210.8-06节 已收购或目标收购房地产经营业务

如果在按规定应提交损益表的报告期内,小型报告公司购置了金额较高的一处物业或合计金额较高的多处物业,或者自第210.8-02节或第210.8-03节要求提交的最近一期资产负债表日起购置了或计划购置金额较高的一处物业或合计金额较高的多处物业,小型报告公司应当就该等物业提供如下文件:

(a)最近两个会计年度的经审计的损益表(不含单位盈利),表中应剔除与该等物业未来拟议经营性质不同的项目(如抵押权益、租赁收入、折旧、公司总部费用以及联邦和州所得税):但是,如满足下列条件,则仅需提供最近一个会计年度的经审计的财务报表:

(1)物业并非购自关联方;

(2)小型报告公司在对物业估值时所考虑的重大因素已在关于该物业的注册说明书中作出详细说明,包括收入来源(包括但不限于租赁市场的竞争状况、比较租金、租用率)和费用(包括但不限于公用事业费、从价税率、维护费用和预计的资本改造费用);及

(3)小型报告公司表明,经过合理调查,除了根据本节第(a)(2)款的规定已进行讨

aware of any material factors relating to the specific property other than those discussed in response to paragraph (a)(2) of this section that would cause the reported financial information not to be necessarily indicative of future operating results.

(b) If the property will be operated by the smaller reporting company, a statement shall be furnished showing the estimated taxable operating results of the smaller reporting company based on the most recent twelve-month period, including such adjustments as can be factually supported. If the property will be acquired subject to a net lease, the estimated taxable operating results shall be based on the rent to be paid for the first year of the lease. In either case, the estimated amount of cash to be made available by operations shall be shown. Disclosure must be provided of the principal assumptions that have been made in preparing the statements of estimated taxable operating results and cash to be made available by operations.

(c) If appropriate under the circumstances, a table should be provided that shows, for a limited number of years, the estimated cash distribution per unit, indicating the portion reportable as taxable income and the portion representing a return of capital with an explanation of annual variations, if any. If taxable net income per unit will be greater than the cash available for distribution per unit, that fact and the approximate year of occurrence shall be stated, if significant.

§210.8-07 Limited partnerships.

(a) Smaller reporting companies that are limited partnerships must provide the balance sheets of the general partners as described in paragraphs (b) through (d) of this section.

(b) Where a general partner is a corporation, the audited balance sheet of the corporation as of the end of its most recently completed fiscal year must be filed. Receivables, other than trade receivables, from affiliates of the general partner should be deducted from shareholders' equity of the general partner. Where an affiliate has committed itself to increase or maintain the general partner's capital, the audited balance sheet of such affiliate must also be presented.

(c) Where a general partner is a partnership, there shall be filed an audited balance sheet of such partnership as of the end of its most recently completed fiscal year.

(d) Where the general partner is a natural person, there shall be filed, as supplemental information, a balance sheet of such natural person as of a recent date. Such balance sheet need not be audited. The assets and liabilities should be carried at estimated fair market value, with provisions for estimated income taxes on unrealized gains. The net worth of such general partner(s), based on such balance sheet(s), singly or in the aggregate, shall be disclosed in the registration statement.

论的因素外，其未发现与该特定物业有关的、可能导致所报告的财务信息不能充分反映未来经营成果的任何重大因素。

(b)如果物业将由小型报告公司亲自经营，则应基于小型报告公司最近12个月的经营成果提供一份预期应税经营成果报表，包括能提出事实依据的调整。如果所收购物业处于净租赁状态，则预期应税经营成果应根据租赁首年的应付租金确定。在上述任何一种情形下，均应列示预期经营将产生的现金数额。在编制关于预期应税经营成果报表和经营将产生的现金数额报表的过程中，所作基本假设应予披露。

(c)如情况适当，还应以表格形式提供一定年数的每幢物业现金分配估算，分列可作为应税收益报告的部分和代表投资回报的部分，并附上每年增减额（如有）的说明。如果预期每幢物业平均应税净收益高于每幢物业的平均分配现金额，且两者差额较大，应说明该事实以及该事实预期发生的大致年份。

第210.8-07节　有限合伙

(a)如果小型报告公司属于有限合伙，则该公司必须按本节第(b)~(d)款的规定提供普通合伙人的资产负债表。

(b)如果普通合伙人系公司，则必须提交该公司截至最近结束的一个会计年度的经审计的资产负债表。该普通合伙人的控制性关联方所欠应收账款（不含贸易应收账款）应从该普通合伙人的股东权益中扣除。如果某控制性关联方承诺增加或保持普通合伙人的资本，则必须提供该控制性关联方的经审计的资产负债表。

(c)如果普通合伙人系合伙，则应提交该合伙截至最近结束的一个会计年度年末的经审计的资产负债表。

(d)如果普通合伙人系自然人，则应提交该自然人截至某最近日期的资产负债表作为补充资料。该资产负债表不必是经审计的报表。资产与负债应按估算公允市价入账，并为未实现收益的预计所得税计提拨备。该等普通合伙人的净值应基于上述资产负债表在注册说明书中单独或一并披露。

§210.8–08 Age of financial statements.

At the date of filing, financial statements included in filings other than filings on Form 10–K must be not less current than the financial statements that would be required in Forms 10–K and 10–Q if such reports were required to be filed. If required financial statements are as of a date 135 days or more before the date a registration statement becomes effective or proxy material is expected to be mailed, the financial statements shall be updated to include financial statements for an interim period ending within 135 days of the effective or expected mailing date. Interim financial statements must be prepared and presented in accordance with paragraph (b) of this section.

(a) When the anticipated effective or mailing date falls within 45 days after the end of the fiscal year, the filing may include financial statements only as current as of the end of the third fiscal quarter;*Provided, however,* that if the audited financial statements for the recently completed fiscal year are available or become available before effectiveness or mailing, they must be included in the filing; and

(b) If the effective date or anticipated mailing date falls after 45 days but within 90 days of the end of the smaller reporting company's fiscal year, the smaller reporting company is not required to provide the audited financial statements for such year end provided that the following conditions are met:

(1) If the smaller reporting company is a reporting company, all reports due must have been filed;

(2) For the most recent fiscal year for which audited financial statements are not yet available, the smaller reporting company reasonably and in good faith expects to report income from continuing operations attributable to the registrant before taxes; and

(3) For at least one of the two fiscal years immediately preceding the most recent fiscal year the smaller reporting company reported income from continuing operations attributable to the registrant before taxes.

[73 FR 953, Jan. 4, 2008, as amended at 74 FR 18616, Apr. 23, 2009]

Bank Holding Companies

Source: Sections 210.9–01 through 210.9–07 appear at 48 FR 11107, Mar. 16, 1983, unless otherwise noted.

§210.9–01 Application of §§210.9–01 to 210.9–07

This article is applicable to consolidated financial statements filed for bank holding companies and to any financial statements of banks that are included in filings with the Commission.

第210.8-08节　财务报表表龄

在提交日,如果在《10-K表格》要求提交的范围之外还应提交其他财务报表,则该等财务报表日截止日期不得早于《10-K表格》及《10-Q表格》要求提交的财务报表。如果按规定应提交的财务报表的截止日期比注册说明书生效日或征集投票权报告预期邮递日至少早135日,应提交一份中期财务报表(其截止日期应在生效日或预期邮递日后135日期间内),对财务报表进行更新。中期财务报表的编制及列报必须符合本节第(b)款的规定。

(a)如果预期生效日或邮递日在该会计年度结束后45日内,所提交的财务报表的截止日期最早可以在第三财务季度季末;但是,如果在上述生效日或邮递日之前,已经存在或可以提供最近结束的一个会计年度的经审计的财务报表,则必须提交该财务报表;且

(b) 如果生效日或预期邮递日在小型报告公司会计年度结束后45~90日之间,该小型报告公司不必提供截止于该年度年末的经审计的财务报表,前提是须符合以下条件:

(1)如果该小型报告公司属于报告公司,且必须已经提交所有到期应提交的报告;

(2)对于尚无法提供经审计的财务报表的最近一个会计年度,小型报告公司合理并善意预期该会计年度报告将显示有可归属于注册人的税前持续经营收益;及

(3)在最近一个会计年度前的两个会计年度中的至少一个会计年度,小型报告公司的报告显示有可归属于注册人的税前持续经营收益。

[《联邦公报》第73卷第953页,2008年1月4日,修正索引:《联邦公报》第74卷第18616页,2009年4月23日。]

银行控股公司

行政规则来源:第210.9-01~210.9-07节,见《联邦公报》第48卷第11107页,1983年3月16日,除非另有说明。

第210.9-01节　第210.9-01~210.9-07节的适用范围

本条适用于银行控股公司的合并财务报表,并适用于向证券交易委员会提交的材料中包含的任何银行财务报表。

§210.9-02 General requirement.

The requirements of the general rules in §§210.1 to 210.4 (Articles 1, 2, 3, 3A and 4) should be complied with where applicable.

§210.9-03 Balance sheets.

The purpose of this rule is to indicate the various items which, if applicable, should appear on the face of the balance sheets or in the notes thereto.

Assets

1. *Cash and due from banks.* The amounts in this caption should include all noninterest bearing deposits with other banks.

(a) Any withdrawal and usage restrictions (including requirements of the Federal Reserve to maintain certain average reserve balances) or compensating balance requirements should be disclosed (see §210.5-02-1).

2. Interest-bearing deposits in other banks.

3. *Federal funds sold and securities purchased under resale agreements of similar arrangements.* These amounts should be presented gross and not netted against Federal funds purchased and securities sold under agreement to repurchase as reported in Caption 13.

4. *Trading account assets.* Include securities or any other investments held for trading purposes only.

5. Other short-term investments.

6. *Investment securities* Include securities held for investment only. Disclose the aggregate book value of investment securities; show on the balance sheet the aggregate market value at the balance sheet date. The aggregate amounts should include securities pledged, loaned or sold under repurchase agreements and similar arrangements; borrowed securities and securities purchased under resale agreements or similar arrangements should be excluded.

(a) Disclose in a note the carrying value and market value of securities of (1) the U.S. Treasury and other U.S. Government agencies and corporations; (2) states of the U.S. and political subdivisions; and (3) other securities.

7. *Loans.* Disclose separately (1) total loans, (2) the related allowance for losses and (3) unearned income.

(a) Disclose on the balance sheet or in a note the amount of total loans in each of the following categories:

(1) Commercial, financial and agricultural

(2) Real estate—construction

(3) Real estate—mortgage

(4) Installment loans to individuals

第210.9-02节　一般要求

如适用,应遵守第210.1~210.4节(第1条、第2条、第3条、第3A条和第4条)中一般规则的要求。

第210.9-03节　资产负债表

本节规则旨在说明资产负债表正文或相关附注所应列示的行项目(如适用)。

资产

1.现金及银行存款。计入本科目的金额应包括存入其他银行的所有无息存款。

(a)所有支取及使用限制(包括联邦储备系统规定的维持一定水平的平均准备金余额的要求)或补偿性余额要求(见第210.5-02-1节)均应披露。

2.存入其他银行的有息存款。

3.按照类似安排或转售协议出售的联邦基金和购买的证券。上述金额应列报总额,不应与第13科目下报告的在回购协议下购买的联邦基金和出售的证券进行净额结算。

4.交易账户资产。包括仅为交易目的持有的证券或任何其他投资。

5.其他短期投资。

6.“投资证券”包括仅为投资目的持有的证券。应披露投资证券的合计账面价值;应在资产负债表上显示截至资产负债表日的合计市值。合计金额应包括在回购协议和类似安排下质押、贷出或出售的证券;借入证券和根据转售协议或类似安排购买的证券除外。

(a)在附注中披露以下证券的账面价值和市值:(1)美国财政部和其他美国政府机关和公司发行的证券;(2)美国各州和行政区域发行的证券;以及(3)其他证券。

7.贷款。分别披露(1)总贷款;(2)损失备抵;以及(3)消极所得。

(a)在资产负债表或附注中披露以下每类贷款总额:

(1)商业、金融和农业贷款

(2)房地产——建筑

(3)房地产——抵押

(4)个人分期贷款

(5) Lease financing

(6) Foreign

(7) Other (State separately any other loan category regardless of relative size if necessary to reflect any unusual risk concentration).

(b) A series of categories other than those specified in (a) above may be used to present details of loans if considered a more appropriate presentation.

(c) The amount of foreign loans must be presented if the disclosures provided by §210.9–05 are required.

(d) For each period for which an income statement is required, furnish in a note a statement of changes in the allowance for loan losses showing the balances at beginning and end of the period provision charged to income, recoveries of amounts charged off and losses charged to the allowance.

(e)(1)(i) As of each balance sheet date, disclose in a note the aggregate dollar amount of loans (exclusive of loans to any such persons which in the aggregate do not exceed $60,000 during the latest year) made by the registrant or any of its subsidiaries to directors,executive officers, or principal holders of equity securities (§210.1–02) of the registrant or any of its significant subsidiaries (§210.1–02), or to any associate of such persons. For the latest fiscal year, an analysis of activity with respect to such aggregate loans to related parties should be provided. The analysis should include the aggregate amount at the beginning of the period, new loans, repayments, and other changes. (Other changes, if significant, should be explained.)

(ii) This disclosure need not be furnished when the aggregate amount of such loans at the balance sheet date (or with respect to the latest fiscal year, the maximum amount outstanding during the period) does not exceed 5 percent of stockholders equity at the balance sheet date.

(2) If a significant portion of the aggregate amount of loans outstanding at the end of the fiscal year disclosed pursuant to (e)(1)(i) above relates to loans which are disclosed as nonaccrual, past due, restructured or potential problems (see Item III.C. 1. or 2. of Industry Guide 3, Statistical Disclosure by Bank Holding Companies), so state and disclose the aggregate amounts of such loans along with such other information necessary to an understanding of the effects of the transactions on the financial statements.

(3) Notwithstanding the aggregate disclosure called for by (e)(1) above, if any loans were not made in the ordinary course of business during any period for which an income statement is required to be filed, provide an appropriate description of each such loan (see §210.4–08(L)(3)).

(4) Definition of terms. For purposes of this rule, the following definitions shall apply:

(5)租赁融资

(6)国外贷款

(7)其他(如为反映任何异常风险集中情况所必要,应单独列示所有其他贷款类别,无论其相对规模如何)。

(b)如认为使用上文(a)款规定的贷款类别之外的贷款类别可以更恰当地进行列报,则可以使用该等其他贷款类别来说明贷款的细节。

(c)如果按规定必须按第210.9-05节的要求进行信息披露,则必须列报国外贷款的金额。

(d)对于按规定应提交损益表的每一报告期,均应在附注中提供一份贷款损失备抵变动表,说明期初余额和期末余额、记入收益借方的拨备、核销的收回款项以及记入备抵借方的损失。

(e)(1)(i)应在附注中披露截至每期资产负债表日,注册人或其任何子公司向该注册人或其任何重要子公司(见第210.1-02节)的董事、高级管理人员或主要股权证券持有人(见第210.1-02节)或上述主体的任何业务相关人提供的贷款的合计金额(在最近一年内向上述任何主体提供的合计不超过6万美元的贷款除外)。就最近一个会计年度而言,应针对向关联方提供的与上述贷款总额相关的活动进行分析,分析应包括该期间的合计期初金额、新增贷款额、还款金额以及其他变动额(如果发生其他重大变动,应予解释)。

(ii)截至资产负债表日,如果上述贷款合计金额(就最近一个会计年度而言,指该期间内尚未偿还的最高金额)不超过截至上述日期的股东权益的5%,则不必进行相应信息披露。

(2)如果按上文第(e)(1)(i)款披露的截至会计年度年末尚未偿还的贷款合计金额的重大部分是作为不再计息贷款、过期贷款、债务重组或潜在问题而披露的贷款(见《银行控股公司数据披露——行业指引之三》的第III.C.1项或第III.C.2项),应说明并披露该等贷款的合计金额,并提供对于理解该交易对财务报表的影响不可或缺的其他信息。

(3)尽管上文第(e)(1)款要求披露贷款合计金额,但是,在按要求必须提交损益表的期间内,如果任何贷款并非在正常业务中发放的,则应针对该等每一项贷款作出适当说明[见第210.4-08(L)(3)节]。

(4)术语定义。就本规则而言,应适用如下定义:

Associate means (i) a corporation, venture or organization of which such person is a general partner or is, directly or indirectly, the beneficial owner of 10 percent or more of any class of equity securities; (ii) any trust or other estate in which such person has a substantial beneficial interest or for which such person serves as trustee or in a similar capacity and (iii) any member of the immediate family of any of the foregoing persons.

executive officers means the president, any vice president in charge of a principal business unit, division or function (such as loans, investments, operations, administration or finance), and any other officer or person who performs similar policymaking functions.

Immediate Family means such person's spouse; parents; children; siblings; mothers and fathers-in-law; sons and daughters-in-law; and brothers and sisters-in-law.

Ordinary course of business means those loans which were made on substantially the same terms, including interest rate and collateral, as those prevailing at the same time for comparable transactions with unrelated persons and did not involve more than the normal risk of collectibility or present other unfavorable features.

8. *Premises and equipment.*

9. *Due from customers on acceptances.*Include amounts receivable from customers on unmatured drafts and bills of exchange that have been accepted by a bank subsidiary or by other banks for the account of a subsidiary and that are outstanding—that is, not held by a subsidiary bank, on the reporting date.(If held by a bank subsidiary, they should be reported as "loans" under §210.9-03.7.)

10. *Other assets.* Disclose separately on the balance sheet or in a note thereto any of the following assets or any other asset the amount of which exceeds thirty percent of stockholders equity. The remaining assets may be shown as one amount.

(1) Excess of cost over tangible and identifiable intangible assets acquired (net of amortization).

(2) Other intangible assets (net of amortization).

(3) Investments in and indebtness of affiliates and other persons.

(4) Other real estates.

(a) Disclose in a note the basis at which other real estate is carried. An reduction to fair market value from the carrying value of the related loan at the time of acquisition shall be accounted for as a loan loss. Any allowance for losses on other real estate which has been established subsequent to acquisition should be deducted from other real estate. For each period for which an income statement is required, disclosures should be made in a note as to the changes in the allowances, including balance at beginning and end of period, provision charged to income, and losses charged to the allowance.

11. Total assets.

Liabilities and Stockholders' Equity

某主体的“业务相关人”系指(i)该主体担任普通合伙人的公司、企业或组织,或作为受益所有者直接或间接持有其任何类别股权证券的10%(含)以上的公司、企业或组织;(ii)该主体拥有实际受益权或担任其信托人或类似身份的任何信托或其他财产;以及(iii)该主体的任何直系亲属。

“高级管理人员”系指总裁;负责某个主要业务单位、部门或职能(如贷款、投资、运营、行政或财务)的任何副总裁;以及履行类似政策制定职能的任何其他管理人员或人士。

某人的“直系亲属”系指该人的配偶、父母、子女、兄弟姐妹、配偶的父母、子女的配偶以及兄弟姐妹的配偶。

“正常业务运作”系指贷款条件(包括利率和担保品)基本和同时期与非关联人进行的可比交易的现行条款相同,且收款风险在正常范围内,也不存在其他不利条件的贷款。

8.场地和设备。

9.承兑后应向客户收取的账款。包括银行子公司或代表子公司的其他银行已承兑但尚未支付未到期票据和汇票时,应向客户收取的账款——换言之,在报告当天,并非由子公司银行持有的账款(如果由银行子公司持有,则应按照第210.9-03.7节作为“贷款”进行报告)。

10.其他资产。在资产负债表或其附注中分别披露以下任一资产以及超过股东权益30%的任何其他资产。任何其余资产可以通过一个总数显示。

(1)成本超过有形资产和可辨认无形资产的部分(扣除摊销)。

(2)其他无形资产(扣除摊销)。

(3)对控制性关联方和其他主体的投资,以及控制性关联方和其他主体欠负的债务。

(4)其他房地产。

(a)在附注中披露其他房地产账面金额的计算基础。如果将取得房地产之时相关贷款的账面价值降至公允市场价值进行计算,该差价应计为贷款损失。任何其他房地产在取得之后产生的损失备抵,应从其他房地产项下扣除。对于按规定应提交损益表的每个报告期,均应在附注中提供一份贷款损失备抵变动表,说明期初余额和期末余额、记入收益借方的拨备以及记入备抵借方的损失。

11.总资产。

负债和股东权益

Liabilities

12. *Deposits.* Disclose separately the amounts of noninterest bearing deposits and interest bearing deposits.

(a) The amount of noninterest bearing deposits and interest bearing deposits in foreign banking offices must be presented if the disclosure provided by §210.0–05 are required.

13. *Short–term borrowing.* Disclosure separately on the balance sheet or in a note, amounts payable for (1) Federal funds purchased and securities sold under agreements to repurchase; (2) commercial paper; and (3) other short–term borrowings.

(a) Disclose any unused lines of credit for short–term financing: (§210.5–02.19(b)).

14. *Bank acceptances outstanding.* Disclose the aggregate of unmatured drafts and bills of exchange accepted by a bank subsidiary, or by some other bank as its agent, less the amount of such acceptances acquired by the bank subsidiary through discount or purchase.

15. *Other liabilities.* Disclose separately on the balance sheet or in a note any of the following liabilities or any other items which are individually in excess of thirty percent of stockholders' equity (except that amounts in excess of 5 percent of stockholders' equity should be disclosed with respect to item (4)). The remaining items may be shown as one amount.

(1) Income taxes payable.

(2) Deferred income taxes.

(3) Indebtedness to affiliates and other persons the investments in which are accounted for by the equity method.

(4) Indebtedness to directors, executive officers, and principal holders of equity securities of the registrant or any of its significant subsidiaries (the guidance in §210.9–03.7(e) shall be used to identify related parties for purposes of this disclosure).

(5) Accounts payable and accrued expenses.

16. *Long–term debt.* Disclose in a note the information required by §210.5–02.22.

17. *Commitments and contingent liabilities.*

Redeemable Preferred Stocks

18. *Preferred stocks subject to mandatory redemption requirements or whose redemption is outside the control of the issuer.* See §210.5–02.27.

Non–redeemable Preferred Stocks

19. *Preferred stocks which are not redeemable or are redeemable solely at the option of the issuer.* See §210.5–02.28.

Common Stocks

20. *Common stocks.* See §210.5–02.29.

负债

12.存款。分别披露无息存款和有息存款金额。

(a)如果按规定必须根据第210.0-05节进行信息披露,则必须列示存入外国银行办事处的无息存款和有息存款金额。

13.短期借款。应在资产负债表或附注中分别披露以下应付金额:(1)按照回购协议购买的联邦基金和出售的证券;(2)商业票据;以及(3)其他短期借款。

(a)披露所有短期融资的未用信用额度[见第210.5-02.19(b)节]。

14.未支付的银行承兑额。应披露银行子公司或作为银行子公司代理人的其他银行承兑的未到期票据和汇票总额,但该总额应减去该银行子公司通过折扣或购买获得的承兑金额。

15.其他负债。在资产负债表或附注中分别披露以下所有负债或单项金额超过股东权益30%的任何其他负债[但是,就第(4)项而言,上述标准应定为超过股东权益5%的其他负债]。其余项目可以通过一个总数显示。

(1)应缴所得税;

(2)递延所得税;

(3)向控制性关联方欠负的债务,以及向使用权益法核算投资的其他主体欠负的债务;

(4)向注册人或其任何重要子公司的董事、高级管理人员和主要股权证券持有人欠负的债务[就本披露要求而言,应使用第210.9-03.7(e)节规定的指引来识别关联方]。

(5)应付账款和应计费用。

16.长期债务。在附注中披露第210.5-02.22节规定的信息。

17.承诺和或有负债。

可回赎优先股

18.可强制回赎的优先股或回赎与否不由发行人控制的优先股。见第210.5-02.27节。

不可回赎优先股

19.不可回赎的优先股,或者回赎与否完全取决于发行人的优先股。见第210.5-02.28节。

普通股

20.普通股。见第210.5-02.29节。

Other Stockholders' Equity

21. *Other stockholders' equity. See §210.5–02.30.*

Noncontrolling Interests

22. *Noncontrolling interests in consolidated subsidiaries.* The disclosure requirements of §210.5–02.31 shall be followed.

23. *Total liabilities and equity.*

[48 FR 11107, Mar. 16, 1983, as amended at 48 FR 37612, Aug. 19, 1983; 50 FR 25215, June 18, 1985; 74 FR 18616, Apr. 23, 2009]

§210.9–04 Income statements.

The purpose of this rule is to indicate the various items which, if applicable, should appear on the face of the income statement or in the notes thereto.

1. *Interest and fees on loans.* Include commitment and origination fees, late charges and current amortization of premium and accretion of discount on loans which are related to or are an adjustment of the loan interest rate.

2. *Interest and dividends on investment securities.*Disclosure separately (1) taxable interest income,(2) nontaxable interest income, and (3) dividends.

3. *Trading account interest.*

4. *Other interest income.*

5. *Total interest income (total of lines 1 through 4).*

6. *Interest on deposits.*

7. *Interest on short–term borrowings.*

8. *Interest on long–term debt.*

9. *Total interest expense (total of lines 6 through 8).*

10. *Net interest income (line 5 minus line 9).*

11. *Provision for loan losses.*

12. *Net interest income after provision for loan losses.*

13. *Other income.* Disclose separately any of the following amounts, or any other item of other income, which exceed one percent of the aggregate of total interest income and other income. The remaining amounts may be shown as one amount, except for investment securities gains or losses which shall be shown separately regardless of size.

(a) Commissions and fees and fiduciary activities.

(b) Commissions, broker's fees and markups on securities underwriting and other securities activities.

(c) Insurance commissions, fees and premiums.

(d) Fees for other customer services.

(e) Profit or loss on transactions in securities in dealer trading account.

其他股东权益

21.其他股东权益。见第210.5-02.30节。

非控制权益

22.对并表子公司拥有的非控制权益。应遵守第210.5-02.31节的披露要求。

23.债务和股权总额。

[《联邦公报》第48卷第11107页,1983年3月16日,修正索引:《联邦公报》第48卷第37612页,1983年8月19日;《联邦公报》第50卷第25215页,1985年6月18日;《联邦公报》第74卷第18616页,2009年4月23日。]

第210.9-04节　损益表

本节规则旨在说明损益表正文或相关附注所应列示的行项目(如适用)。

1.贷款利息和费用。包括贷款承诺和发起费、滞纳金以及贷款的当期溢价摊销和贴现增值,上述溢价摊销和贴现增值系针对贷款利率而言,或指贷款利率的调整。

2.投资证券的利息和股息。分别披露:(1)应税利息收益;(2)非应税利息收益;以及(3)股息。

3.交易账户利息。

4.其他利息收益。

5.总利息收益(第1行至第4行之和)。

6.存款利息。

7.短期借款利息。

8.长期债务利息。

9.总利息费用(第6行至第8行之和)。

10.净利息收益(第5行减去第9行之差)。

11.贷款损失拨备。

12.减去贷款损失拨备后的净利息收益。

13.其他收益。分别披露以下所有项目的金额,或超过总利息收益和其他收益合计总额1%的所有其他收益项目。其余数额可以通过一个总数显示,但是,投资证券的收益或损失不论金额大小,均应单独披露。

(a)佣金、费用和受信义务活动。

(b)证券承销和其他证券活动的佣金、经纪人费用和加成。

(c)保险佣金、费用和保费。

(d)其他客户服务费。

(e)自营商交易账户进行的证券交易的利润或损失。

(f) Equity in earnings of unconsolidated subsidiaries and 50 percent or less owned persons.

(g) Gains or losses on disposition of equity in securities of subsidiaries or 50 percent or less owned persons.

(h) Investment securities gains or losses. The method followed in determining the cost of investments sold (e.g., "average cost," "first –in, first –out," or "identified certificate) and related income taxes shall be disclosed.

14. *Other expenses.* Disclose separately any of the following amounts, or any other item of other expense, which exceed one percent of the aggregate of total interest income and other income. The remaining amounts may be shown as one amount.

(a) Salaries and employee benefits.

(b) Net occupancy expense of premises.

(c) Goodwill amortization.

(d) Net cost of operation of other real estate (including provisions for real estate losses, rental income and gains and losses on sales of real estate).

15. *Income or loss before income tax expense.*

16. *Income tax expense*. The information required by §210.4–08(h) should be disclosed.

17. *Income or loss before extraordinary items and cumulative effects of changes in accounting principles.*

18. *Extraordinary items, less applicable tax.*

19. *Cumulative effects of changes in accounting principles.*

20. *Net income or loss.*

21. *Net income attributable to the noncontrolling interest.*

22. *Net income attributable to the controlling interest.*

23. *Earnings per share data.*

[48 FR 11107, Mar. 16, 1983, as amended at 50 FR 25215, June 18, 1985; 74 FR 18616, Apr. 23, 2009]

§210.9–05 Foreign activities.

(a) *General requirement.* Separate disclosure concerning foreign activities shall be made for each period in which either (1) assets; or (2) revenue; or (3) income (loss) before income tax expense; or (4) net income (loss), each as associated with foreign activities, exceeded ten percent of the corresponding amount in the related financial statements.

(b) *Disclosures.* (1) Disclose total identifiable assets (net of valuation allowances) associated with foreign activities.

(2) For each period for which an income statement is filed, state the amount of

(f)在非并表子公司以及50%或以下股权被控主体的盈利中所占权益。

(g)对子公司或50%或以下股权被控主体的证券权益进行处置产生的收益或损失。

(h)投资证券的收益或损失。应披露确定出售投资的成本的方式(如“平均成本法”、“先进先出法”或“识别凭证法”等方式)以及相关所得税的计算方式。

14.其他费用。分别披露以下所有项目的金额,以及超过总利息收入和其他收入合计总额1%的所有其他费用项目。其余数额可以通过一个总数显示。

(a)薪资和员工福利。
(b)净场地占用费。
(c)商誉摊销。
(d)其他房地产的净运营成本(包括房地产损失备抵、租赁收益和房地产出售的收益和损失)。
15.扣除所得税费用前的损益。
16.所得税费用。应按照第210.4-08(h)节的要求披露相关信息。

17.在扣除非经常项目和会计原则变更累积影响数之前的收益或损失。

18.非经常项目,减去适用税款。
19.会计原则变更累积影响数。
20.净收益或损失。
21.归属于非控制权益的净收益。
22.归属于控制权益的净收益。
23.每股盈利数据。
[《联邦公报》第48卷第11107页,1983年3月16日,修正索引:《联邦公报》第50卷第25215页,1985年6月18日;《联邦公报》第74卷第18616页,2009年4月23日。]

第210.9-05节　国外活动

(a)一般要求。任一报告期内出现与国外活动相关的下述项目:(1)资产;(2)收入;(3)扣除所得税费用前的收益(损失);或(4)净收益(损失),且金额超过相关财务报表内相应金额的10%的,均应针对相关的国外活动进行单独披露。

(b)披露。(1)披露与国外活动相关的可辨认总资产(扣除估价备抵)。

(2)对于已提交损益表的每个报告期,均应说明与国外活动相关的收入、税前收

revenue, income(loss) before taxes, and net income(loss) associated with foreign activities. Disclose significant estimates and assumptions(including those related to the cost of capital) used in allocating revenue and expenses to foreign activities; describe the nature and effects of any changes in such estimates and assumptions which have a significant impact on interperiod comparability.

(3) The information in paragraph (b)(1) and (2) of this section shall be presented separately for each significant geographic area and in the aggregate for all other geographic areas not deemed significant.

(c) *Definitions*. (1) *Foreign activities* include loans and other revenues producing assets and transactions in which the debtor or customer, whether an affiliated or unaffiliated person, is domiciled outside the United States.

(2) The term*revenue* includes the total of the amount reported at §§210.9–04.5 and 210.9–04.13.

(3) A*significant geographic area* is one in which assets or revenue or income before income tax or net income exceed 10 percent of the comparable amount as reported in the financial statements.

§210.9–06 Condensed financial information of registrant.

The information prescribed by §210.12–04 shall be presented in a note to the financial statements when the restricted net assets (§210.4–08(e)(3)) of consolidated subsidiaries exceed 25 percent of consolidated net assets as of the end of the most recently completed fiscal year. The investment in and indebtedness of and to bank subsidiaries shall be stated separately in the condensed balance sheet from amounts for other subsidiaries; the amount of cash dividends paid to the registrant for each of the last three years by bank subsidiaries shall be stated separately in the condensed income statement from amounts for other subsidiaries. For purposes of the above test, restricted net assets of consolidated subsidiaries shall mean that amount of the registrant's proportionate share of net assets of consolidated subsidiaries (after intercompany eliminations) which as of the end of the most recent fiscal year may not be transferred to the parent company by subsidiaries in the form of loans, advances or cash dividends without the consent of a third party (*i.e.*, lender, regulatory agency, foreign government, etc.). Where restrictions on the amount of funds which may be loaned or advanced differ from the amount restricted as to transfer in the form of cash dividends, the amount least restrictive to the subsidiary shall be used. Redeemable preferred stocks (§210.5–02.27) and noncontrolling interests shall be deducted in computing net assets for purposes of this test.

[48 FR 11107, Mar. 16, 1983, as amended at 74 FR 18616, Apr. 23, 2009]

益（损失）以及净收益（损失）。将收入和费用分配至国外活动项下时所采用的重大估计和假设（包括与资本成本相关的估计和假设）亦应进行披露；如果该估计和假设对不同报告期之间的可比性存在重要影响，应说明任何该估计和假设所发生的变更的性质和影响。

（3）对于每一重要地理区域，均应单独列示本节第（b）（1）款和第（b）（2）款所述信息，对于其他非重要地理区域，通过一个总数进行整体说明。

（c）定义。（1）“国外活动”包括债务人或客户（无论是否属于控制性关联人）的住所位于美国境外的相关贷款和其他创收资产和交易。

（2）“收入”一词系指按照第210.9-04.5节和第210.9-04.13节报告的总金额。

（3）“重要地理区域”系指资产、收入或所得税税前收益或净收益超过财务报表中相应金额10%地理区域。

第210.9-06节　注册人的简要财务信息

如果截至最近结束的一个会计年度年末，并表子公司的受限净资产［见第210.4-08（e）（3）节］超过并表净资产的25%，应在财务报表的附注中说明第210.12-04节规定的信息。对银行子公司的投资、向银行子公司欠负的债务以及银行子公司欠负的债务，应在简要资产负债表中，区分于其他子公司，单独列示；对于过去3年中每一年银行子公司向注册人支付的现金股息金额，均应在简要资产负债表中，区分于其他子公司，单独列示。在进行测试，以判断是否符合上述25%的标准时，并表子公司的受限净资产指截至最近一个会计年度年末，该子公司未经第三方（即贷款人、监管机构、外国政府等）同意，不得以贷款、垫款或现金股息的形式向母公司转移的，注册人按比例在并表子公司净资产中所占的数额（该数额应为进行公司间抵消后的数额）。如受限贷款或垫款金额与受限制不得以现金股息形式转移的金额存在差异，应采用对子公司限制较低的金额。本测试中，计算净资产时应扣除可回赎优先股（第210.5-02.27节）及非控制权益。

［《联邦公报》第48卷第11107页，1983年3月16日，修正索引：《联邦公报》第74卷第18616页，2009年4月23日。］

§210.9–07 [Reserved]

Interim Financial Statements

§210.10–01 Interim financial statements.

(a) *Condensed statements.* Interim financial statements shall follow the general form and content of presentation prescribed by the other sections of this Regulation with the following exceptions:

(1) Interim financial statements required by this rule need only be provided as to the registrant and its subsidiaries consolidated and may be unaudited. Separate statements of other entities which may otherwise be required by this regulation may be omitted.

(2) Interim balance sheets shall include only major captions (*i.e.*, numbered captions) prescribed by the applicable sections of this Regulation with the exception of inventories. Data as to raw materials, work in process and finished goods inventories shall be included either on the face of the balance sheet or in the notes to the financial statements, if applicable. Where any major balance sheet caption is less than 10% of total assets, and the amount in the caption has not increased or decreased by more than 25% since the end of the preceding fiscal year, the caption may be combined with others.

(3) Interim statements of income shall also include major captions prescribed by the applicable sections of this Regulation. When any major income statement caption is less than 15% of average net income for the most recent three fiscal years and the amount in the caption has not increased or decreased by more than 20% as compared to the corresponding interim period of the preceding fiscal year, the caption may be combined with others. In calculating average net income, loss years should be excluded. If losses were incurred in each of the most recent three years, the average loss shall be used for purposes of this test. Notwithstanding these tests, §210.4–02 applies and de minimis amounts therefore need not be shown separately, except that registrants reporting under §210.9 shall show investment securities gains or losses separately regardless of size.

(4) The statement of cash flows may be abbreviated starting with a single figure of net cash flows from operating activities and showing cash changes from investing and financing activities individually only when they exceed 10% of the average of net cash flows from operating activities for the most recent three years. Notwithstanding this test, §210.4–02 applies and*de minimis* amounts therefore need not be shown separately.

(5) The interim financial information shall include disclosures either on the face of the financial statements or in accompanying footnotes sufficient so as to make the interim information presented not misleading. Registrants may presume that users of the interim financial information have read or have access to the audited financial statements for the

第210.9-07节 ［保留］

中期财务报表

第210.10-01节 中期财务报表

（a）简要报表。中期财务报表应遵循本《管理办法》其他各条对列报格式和内容的一般规定，同时应适用如下例外规定：

（1）本规则要求提供的中期财务报表可以只针对注册人及其并表子公司提供，中期财务报表可以未经审计。本《管理办法》另行要求提供的其他实体的单独报表可免予提供。

（2）中期资产负债表仅应包括本《管理办法》适用条款规定的主要科目（即带有编号的科目），但库存例外。原材料、在制品、成品库存等数据应在资产负债表的正文或财务报表的附注（如适用）中载明。如果资产负债表任何主要科目下的金额少于总资产的10%，且该科目下的金额自上一会计年度年末以来增减幅度不超过25%，则该科目可以与其他科目归并。

（3）中期损益表也应包括本《管理办法》相关条款规定的主要科目。如果损益表内任何主要科目的金额小于最近3个会计年度平均净收益的15%，且该科目下的金额与上一会计年度同期的中期报告期数额相比增减幅度不超过20%，则该科目可以与其他科目归并。计算平均净收益之时，应将亏损年度排除。如果最近3年每一年都发生亏损，则在进行测试，以判断是否符合上述标准时，应使用平均亏损数值。尽管有上述测试标准，仍应适用第210.4-02节的规定，因此，金额较低，不具重大性的科目，不必单列，但是按照第210.9节的要求进行报告的注册人一律应单独列示投资证券的收益或损失（无论收益或损失金额大小）。

（4）现金流量表可以精简，甚至可以使用一个单一数值显示经营活动产生的净现金流，只有当投资及融资活动产生的现金水平波动超过最近3年经营活动产生的平均净现金流水平的10%之时，才需单列该现金水平的变动值。尽管有上述测试标准，仍应适用第210.4-02节的规定，因此，金额较低，不具重大性的，不必单列。

（5）中期财务信息应在财务报表的正文或相应附注中进行充分披露，以避免中期信息产生误导性。注册人可以假定，中期财务信息的使用者已经阅读或可以获得上一会计年度的经审计的财务报表，而且，可以以此为基础来判断为实现公允列报而补充披露的信息是否充分（但涉及重大或有事项的情形除外）。相应地，如果通过脚注进行

preceding fiscal year and that the adequacy of additional disclosure needed for a fair presentation, except in regard to material contingencies, may be determined in that context. Accordingly, footnote disclosure which would substantially duplicate the disclosure contained in the most recent annual report to security holders or latest audited financial statements, such as a statement of significant accounting policies and practices, details of accounts which have not changed significantly in amount or composition since the end of the most recently completed fiscal year, and detailed disclosures prescribed by Rule 4-08 of this Regulation, may be omitted. However, disclosure shall be provided where events subsequent to the end of the most recent fiscal year have occurred which have a material impact on the registrant. Disclosures should encompass for example, significant changes since the end of the most recently completed fiscal year in such items as: accounting principles and practices; estimates inherent in the preparation of financial statements; status of long-term contracts; capitalization including significant new borrowings or modification of existing financing arrangements; and the reporting entity resulting from business combinations or dispositions. Notwithstanding the above, where material contingencies exist, disclosure of such matters shall be provided even though a significant change since year end may not have occurred.

(6) Detailed schedules otherwise required by this Regulation may be omitted for purposes of preparing interim financial statements.

(7) In addition to the financial statements required by paragraphs (a)(2), (3) and (4) of this section, registrants in the development stage shall provide the cumulative financial statements (condensed to the same degree as allowed in this paragraph) and disclosures required by Statement of Financial Accounting Standards No. 7, "Accounting and Reporting by Development Stage Enterprises" to the date of the latest balance sheet presented.

(b) *Other instructions as to content.* The following additional instructions shall be applicable for purposes of preparing interim financial statements:

(1) Summarized income statement information shall be given separately as to each subsidiary not consolidated or 50 percent or less owned persons or as to each group of such subsidiaries or fifty percent or less owned persons for which separate individual or group statements would otherwise be required for annual periods. Such summarized information, however, need not be furnished for any such unconsolidated subsidiary or person which would not be required pursuant to Rule 13a-13 or 15d-13 to file quarterly financial information with the Commission if it were a registrant.

(2) If appropriate, the income statement shall show earnings per share and dividends declared per share applicable to common stock. The basis of the earnings per share computation shall be stated together with the number of shares used in the computation.

的披露将基本重复向证券持有人提供的最近一期年报或最近一期经审计的财务报表所披露的信息,如关于重大会计政策和惯例的声明、自最近结束的一个会计年度年末以来账户金额或组成成分未发生重大变化的账户的详情,以及本《管理办法》《4-08规则》要求披露的详细信息,则可免于通过该等脚注进行信息披露。但是,如果在最近结束的一个会计年度年末之后发生了对注册人具有重大影响的事件,则应进行相关信息披露。披露信息应包括但不限于自最近结束的一个会计年度年末以来,以下项目发生的重大变动:会计原则和惯例;编制财务报表所用的会计估计;长期合同的状态;资本状况,包括新发生的重大借贷或现有融资安排的重大修改;以及因业务合并或处置而产生的报告实体。尽管有上述规定,但如果存在重大或有事项,即使自上一会计年度年末以来未发生重大变动,亦应披露上述信息。

(6)编制中期财务报表时,可免于提供本《管理办法》规定的详细附表。

(7)除了本节第(a)(2)款、第(a)(3)款和第(a)(4)款规定的财务报表外,处于发展阶段的注册人还应提供累积财务报表(简明程度以本款规定为准),以及《财务会计准则公告第7号——发展阶段企业的会计及报告》规定的信息披露,截止日期为最近一期资产负债表提交日。

(b)关于报表内容的其他要求。编制中期财务报表时,应适用如下额外要求:

(1)对于按规定须单独提交年度报表的每一或每组非并表子公司或50%或以下股权被控主体,应分别提供上述每一或每组子公司或主体的摘要损益表信息。但是,假使任何上述非并表子公司或主体自行以注册人身份行事时并不必按《13a-13规则》或《15d-13规则》向证券交易委员会提交季度财务信息,则也不必提交上述摘要信息。

(2)在适用情形下,损益表应列明普通股的每股盈利和每股宣布股息。在说明计算每股盈利使用的股数时,应同时说明计算每股盈利的基础。此外,请参见《S-K管理办法》第601(b)(11)条[《联邦规章汇编》第十七编第229.601(b)(11)节]的规定。

In addition, see Item 601(b)(11) of Regulation S-K, (17 CFR 229.601(b)(11)).

(3) If, during the most recent interim period presented, the registrant or any of its consolidated subsidiaries entered into a combination between entities under common control, the interim financial statements for both the current year and the preceding year shall reflect the combined results of the combined businesses. Supplemental disclosure of the separate results of the combined entities for periods prior to the combination shall be given, with appropriate explanations.

(4) Where a material business combination has occurred during the current fiscal year, pro forma disclosure shall be made of the results of operations for the current year up to the date of the most recent interim balance sheet provided (and for the corresponding period in the preceding year) as though the companies had combined at the beginning of the period being reported on. This pro forma information shall, at a minimum, show revenue, income before extraordinary items and the cumulative effect of accounting changes, including such income on a per share basis, net income, net income attributable to the registrant, and net income per share.

(5) Where the registrant has disposed of any significant segment of its business (as defined in paragraph 13 of Accounting Principles Board Opinion No. 30) during any of the periods covered by the interim financial statements, the effect thereof on revenues and net income—total and per share—for all periods shall be disclosed.

(6) In addition to meeting the reporting requirements specified by existing standards for accounting changes, the registrant shall state the date of any material accounting change and the reasons for making it. In addition, for filings on Form 10-Q, a letter from the registrant's independent accountant shall be filed as an exhibit (in accordance with the provisions of Item 601 of Regulation S-K, 17 CFR 229.601) in the first Form 10-Q after the date of an accounting change indicating whether or not the change is to an alternative principle which, in the accountant's judgment, is preferable under the circumstances; except that no letter from the accountant need be filed when the change is made in response to a standard adopted by the Financial Accounting Standards Board that requires such change.

(7) Any material retroactive prior period adjustment made during any period convered by the interim financial statements shall be disclosed, together with the effect thereof upon net income—total and per share—of any prior period included and upon the balance of retained earnings. If results of operations for any period presented have been adjusted retroactively by such an item subsequent to the initial reporting of such period, similar disclosure of the effect of the change shall be made.

(8) Any unaudited interim financial statements furnished shall reflect all adjustments which are, in the opinion of management, necessary to a fair statement of the

(3)如果在提交信息所对应的最近一期中期报告期,注册人或其任何并表子公司进行合并,且注册人或其并表子公司与合并对象受同一控制,则当年及上一年的中期财务报表均应反映该等业务合并后的合并成果。此外,对于合并前各报告期,应对合并实体各自的成果进行补充披露,并加以适当解释。

(4)如果在当前会计年度发生重大业务合并,应就当年直至最近一期中期资产负债表日(以及上一年度同期)的经营成果进行备考披露,将业务合并视为在报告期初已经发生。该备考信息至少应列明收入、计算非经常项目以及会计变更累积影响数之前的收益,包括每股收益、净收益、归属于注册人的净收益以及每股净收益。

(5)如果在中期财务报表覆盖的任何报告期内,注册人对其任何重大业务分部(定义见《会计原则委员会第30号意见》第13段)进行了处置,则应披露在中期财务报表覆盖的任何报告期内,该处置对收入和净收益的影响数(包括总体影响数和对每股的影响数)。

(6)除了满足现行标准针对会计变更规定的报告要求外,注册人还应说明任何重大会计变更的日期和原因。此外,对于提交《10-Q表格》的注册人,该注册人的独立会计师应按照《S-K管理办法》第601条的规定(见《联邦规章汇编》第十七编第229.601节),在每次会计变更发生后提交一封信函,附于会计变更日后提交的第一份《10-Q表格》之后,说明该会计师的意见,判断在该情形下该变更是否更为可取;但是,注册人按照财务会计准则委员会制定的标准要求作出相应会计变更的,不必提交会计师出具的上述信函。

(7)中期财务报表覆盖的任何报告期内,对之前的报告期作出任何重大追溯调整的,均应予以披露,同时亦应披露该追溯调整对之前的任何相关报告期的财务报表净收益(包括总收益和每股收益)产生的影响数以及对留存盈利余额的影响数。如果报表覆盖的任何报告期的成果在该期间的初步报告提交之后进行了追溯调整,也应针对变更的影响数进行类似披露。

(8)注册人提供的任何未审计中期财务报表应作出管理层认为必要的一切调整,以公允反映相应的中期成果,并应在上述财务报表中作出相应声明。举例而言,该等

results for the interim periods presented. A statement to that effect shall be included. Such adjustments shall include, for example, appropriate estimated provisions for bonus and profit sharing arrangements normally determined or settled at year-end. If all such adjustments are of a normal recurring nature, a statement to that effect shall be made; otherwise, there shall be furnished information describing in appropriate detail the nature and amount of any adjustments other than normal recurring adjustments entering into the determination of the results shown.

(c) *Periods to be covered.* The periods for which interim financial statements are to be provided in registration statements are prescribed elsewhere in this Regulation (see §§210.3-01 and 3-02). For filings on Form 10-Q, financial statements shall be provided as set forth in this paragraph (c):

(1) An interim balance sheet as of the end of the most recent fiscal quarter and a balance sheet as of the end of the preceding fiscal year shall be provided. The balance sheet as of the end of the preceding fiscal year may be condensed to the same degree as the interim balance sheet provided. An interim balance sheet as of the end of the corresponding fiscal quarter of the preceding fiscal year need not be provided unless necessary for an understanding of the impact of seasonal fluctuations on the registrant's financial condition.

(2) Interim statements of income shall be provided for the most recent fiscal quarter, for the period between the end of the preceding fiscal year and the end of the most recent fiscal quarter, and for the corresponding periods of the preceding fiscal year. Such statements may also be presented for the cumulative twelve month period ended during the most recent fiscal quarter and for the corresponding preceding period.

(3) Interim statements of cash flows shall be provided for the period between the end of the preceding fiscal year and the end of the most recent fiscal quarter, and for the corresponding period of the preceding fiscal year. Such statements may also be presented for the cumulative twelve month period ended during the most recent fiscal quarter and for the corresponding preceding period.

(4) Registrants engaged in seasonal production and sale of a single-crop agricultural commodity may provide interim statements of income and cash flows for the twelve month period ended during the most recent fiscal quarter and for the corresponding preceding period in lieu of the year-to-date statements specified in (2) and (3) above.

(d) *Interim review by independent public accountant.* Prior to filing, interim financial statements included in quarterly reports on Form 10-Q (17 CFR 249.308(a)) must be reviewed by an independent public accountant using professional standards and procedures for conducting such reviews, as established by generally accepted auditing standards, as may be modified or supplemented by the Commission. If, in any filing, the

调整应当包括通常在年末决定或结算的适当的预估奖金拨备和利润分享安排。如果所有调整均属正常的经常性调整,应作出相应声明;否则,应就确定报告成果时所作的正常经常性调整之外的调整,提供适当、详细的信息,说明任何调整的性质和金额。

(c)报表覆盖期间。本《管理办法》其他条款(见第210.3-01节和第210.3-02节)规定了应在注册声明中提供中期财务报表的期间。提交《10-Q表格》的注册人,则应按照本款下列规定提交财务报表:

(1)应提供截至最近一个财务季度季末的中期资产负债表和截至上一会计年度年末的资产负债表。截至上一会计年度年末的资产负债表的简明程度可与中期资产负债表相当。截至上一会计年度同期财务季度末的中期资产负债表可免予提供,但该等中期资产负债表对于理解季度性波动对注册人财务状况的影响不可或缺的情形除外。

(2)应提供覆盖下述期间的中期损益表:最近一财务季度、上一会计年度年末至最近一财务季度季末,以及上一会计年度的同期期间。该中期损益表覆盖的期间也可以是截至最近一个财务季度内的累计12个月的期间,以及上一个同期期间。

(3)应提供覆盖下述期间的中期现金流量表:上一会计年度年末到最近一个财务季度季末,以及上一会计年度的同期报告期。该中期现金流量表覆盖的期间也可以是截至最近一个财务季度内的累计12个月的期间,以及上一个同期期间。

(4)从事单一作物农业商品的季节性生产和销售的注册人可以提供覆盖下述期间的中期损益表及现金流量表:截至最近一个会计年度内的累计12个月的期间,以及上一个同期期间,而不必提供上文第(2)项和第(3)项规定的年初至今的报表。

(d)独立公共会计师的中期审查。按照《10-Q表格》[《联邦规章汇编》第十七编第249.308(a)节]提交的季度报告内的中期财务报表,提交前必须由一名独立公共会计师依据专业标准和程序进行审查,且该等专业标准和程序必须按照业内公认审计标准(证券交易委员会可对此进行修改或补充)制定。如果在任何提交的文件中,公司声明其中期财务报表已经由一名独立公共会计师进行过审查,则该会计师的审查报告

company states that interim financial statements have been reviewed by an independent public accountant, a report of the accountant on the review must be filed with the interim financial statements.

(e) *Filing of other interim financial information in certain cases.* The Commission may, upon the informal written request of the registrant, and where consistent with the protection of investors, permit the omission of any of the interim financial information herein required or the filing in substitution thereof of appropriate information of comparable character. The Commission may also by informal written notice require the filing of other information in addition to, or in substitution for, the interim information herein required in any case where such information is necessary or appropriate for an adequate presentation of the financial condition of any person for which interim financial information is required, or whose financial information is otherwise necessary for the protection of investors.

[46 FR 12489, Feb. 17, 1981, as amended at 50 FR 25215, June 18, 1985; 50 FR 49533, Dec. 3, 1985; 57 FR 45293, Oct. 1, 1992; 64 FR 73401, Dec. 30, 1999; 73 FR 956, Jan. 4, 2008; 74 FR 18616, Apr. 23, 2009]

Pro Forma Financial Information

Source: Sections 210.11–01 through 210.11–03 appear at 47 FR 29837, July 9, 1982, unless otherwise noted.

§210.11–01 Presentation requirements.

(a) Pro forma financial information shall be furnished when any of the following conditions exist:

(1) During the most recent fiscal year or subsequent interim period for which a balance sheet is required by §210.3–01, a significant business combination has occurred (for purposes of these rules, this encompasses the acquisition of an interest in a business accounted for by the equity method);

(2) After the date of the most recent balance sheet filed pursuant to §210.3–01, consummation of a significant business combination or a combination of entities under common control has occurred or is probable;

(3) Securities being registered by the registrant are to be offered to the security holders of a significant business to be acquired or the proceeds from the offered securities will be applied directly or indirectly to the purchase of a specific significant business;

(4) The disposition of a significant portion of a business either by sale, abandonment or distribution to shareholders by means of a spin–off, split–up or split–off has occurred

必须与中期财务报表一并提交。

(e)特定情形下其他中期财务信息的提交。注册人提出非正式书面请求的,证券交易委员会可以在符合投资者保护原则的前提下,允许注册人不提交上文规定的任何中期财务信息,或允许其提交性质相似的其他适当信息作为替代。如果为了充分说明按规定提交中期财务信息的主体的财务状况,或为了保护投资者,应提供其他必要或适当的信息,则证券交易委员会可以签发非正式书面通知,要求任何相关主体提交上文规定的中期信息之外的补充信息或替代信息。

[《联邦公报》第46卷第12489页,1981年2月17日,修正索引:《联邦公报》第50卷第25215页,1985年6月18日;《联邦公报》第50卷第49533页,1985年12月3日;《联邦公报》第57卷第45293页,1992年10月1日;《联邦公报》第64卷第73401页,1999年12月30日;《联邦公报》第73卷第956页,2008年1月4日;《联邦公报》第74卷第18616页,2009年4月23日。]

备考财务信息

行政规则来源:第210.11-01~210.11-03节,见《联邦公报》第47卷第29837页,1982年7月9日,除非另有说明。

第210.11-01节　列报要求

(a)满足以下任一条件的,即应提供任何备考财务信息:

(1)在最近一个会计年度或按照第210.3-01节规定应提交资产负债表的期后中期报告期,发生重大业务合并(就本规则而言,包括购买按权益法核算的企业权益);

(2)在按照第210.3-01节提交的最近一期资产负债表日之后,发生或很可能发生重大业务合并或受同一控制的实体的合并;

(3)注册人正在申请注册的证券的发售对象是作为目标收购对象的重要企业的证券持有人,或者,证券发售募集资金将直接或间接用于收购具体的重要企业。

(4)已经或很可能以剥离、分拆或分立的方式,通过出售、弃置或向股东进行分配,完成对企业重大部分的处置,且该等处置并未在所提交的注册人财务报表中予以

or is probable and such disposition is not fully reflected in the financial statements of the registrant included in the filing;

(5) During the most recent fiscal year or subsequent interim period for which a balance sheet is required by §210.3-01, the registrant has acquired one or more real estate operations or properties which in the aggregate are significant, or since the date of the most recent balance sheet filed pursuant to that section the registrant has acquired or proposes to acquire one or more operations or properties which in the aggregate are significant.

(6) Pro forma financial information required by §229.914 is required to be provided in connection with a roll-up transaction as defined in §229.901(c).

(7) The registrant previously was a part of another entity and such presentation is necessary to reflect operations and financial position of the registrant as an autonomous entity; or

(8) Consummation of other events or transactions has occurred or is probable for which disclosure of pro forma financial information would be material to investors.

(b) A business combination or disposition of a business shall be considered significant if:

(1) A comparison of the most recent annual financial statements of the business acquired or to be acquired and the registrant's most recent annual consolidated financial statements filed at or prior to the date of acquisition indicates that the business would be a significant subsidiary pursuant to the conditions specified in §210.1-02(w), substituting 20 percent for 10 percent each place it appears therein; or

(2) The business to be disposed of meets the conditions of a significant subsidiary in §210.1-02(w).

(c) The pro forma effects of a business combination need not be presented pursuant to this section if separate financial statements of the acquired business are not included in the filing.

(d) For purposes of this rule, the term business should be evaluated in light of the facts and circumstances involved and whether there is sufficient continuity of the acquired entity's operations prior to and after the transactions so that disclosure of prior financial information is material to an understanding of future operations. A presumption exists that a separate entity, a subsidiary, or a division is a business. However, a lesser component of an entity may also constitute a business. Among the facts and circumstances which should be considered in evaluating whether an acquisition of a lesser component of an entity constitutes a business are the following:

(1) Whether the nature of the revenue-producing activity of the component will remain generally the same as before the transaction; or

充分体现;

(5)在最近一个会计年度或按照第210.3-01节规定应提交资产负债表的期后中期报告期,注册人购置了一项房地产经营业务或一处物业或合计金额较高的多项房地产经营业务或多处物业,或者,在按照第210.3-01节提交的最近一期资产负债表日后,注册人购置了或计划购置一项房地产经营业务或一处物业或合计金额较高的多项房地产经营业务或多处物业。

(6)对于第229.901(c)节定义的并购重组交易,必须提交第229.914节规定的备考财务信息。

(7)该注册人曾是另一个实体的一部分,且该等列报对于反映该注册人作为一个独立实体的运营和财务状况而言不可或缺;或者

(8)已经发生或很可能发生其他事件或交易,且对于该等事件或交易而言,备考财务信息的披露对投资者而言具有重大意义。

(b)在以下情形下,业务合并或处置将视为重大合并或处置:

(1)把已收购企业或目标收购企业最近一个年度的财务报表和注册人在收购时或收购前提交的最近一个年度的合并财务报表相比较,比较结果显示根据第210.1-02(w)节规定的标准,该企业构成重要子公司,但比较时,每处出现的10%的标准均应替换为20%;或者

(2)待处置的企业符合第210.1-02(w)节规定的重要子公司的条件。

(c)如果提交文件中不包括被收购企业的单独财务报表,则企业合并的备考影响数不必按本节规定列报。

(d)就本规则而言,在界定"企业"之时应考虑相关事实和情况,并考虑该被收购实体在收购前后的经营是否有足够高的连续性,使披露之前的财务信息对于了解未来经营具有重大意义。在界定"企业"之时,均假定单独的实体、子公司或部门均构成一个"企业"。但是,实体中更微细的组成部分也可能构成"企业"。在判断对实体中更微细的组成部分进行的收购是否构成对企业的收购时,应考虑如下事实和情况:

(1)该实体组成部分创收活动的性质在交易后是否将保持大体一致;或者

(2) Whether any of the following attributes remain with the component after the transaction:

(i) Physical facilities,

(ii) Employee base,

(iii) Market distribution system,

(iv) Sales force,

(v) Customer base,

(vi) Operating rights,

(vii) Production techniques, or

(viii) Trade names.

(e) This rule does not apply to transactions between a parent company and its totally held subsidiary.

[47 FR 29837, July 9, 1982, as amended at 50 FR 49533, Dec. 3, 1985; 56 FR 57247, Nov. 8, 1991; 61 FR 54514, Oct. 18, 1996; 74 FR 18616, Apr. 23, 2009]

§210.11-02 Preparation requirements.

(a) *Objective.* Pro forma financial information should provide investors with information about the continuing impact of a particular transaction by showing how it might have affected historical financial statements if the transaction had been consummated at an earlier time. Such statements should assist investors in analyzing the future prospects of the registrant because they illustrate the possible scope of the change in the registrant's historical financial position and results of operations caused by the transaction.

(b) *Form and content.* (1) Pro forma financial information shall consist of a pro forma condensed balance sheet, pro forma condensed statements of income, and accompanying explanatory notes. In certain circumstances (*i.e.*, where a limited number of pro forma adjustments are required and those adjustments are easily understood), a narrative description of the pro forma effects of the transaction may be furnished in lieu of the statements described herein.

(2) The pro forma financial information shall be accompanied by an introductory paragraph which briefly sets forth a description of (i) the transaction, (ii) the entities involved, and (iii) the periods for which the pro forma information is presented. In addition, an explanation of what the pro forma presentation shows shall be set forth.

(3) The pro forma condensed financial information need only include major captions (*i.e.*, the numbered captions) prescribed by the applicable sections of this Regulation. Where any major balance sheet caption is less than 10 percent of total assets, the caption may be combined with others. When any major income statement caption is less than 15

(2)合并交易之后,该组成部分的以下任何方面是否将继续保持不变:

(i)实体设施;
(ii)员工基础;
(iii)市场分销体系;
(iv)销售队伍;
(v)客户基础;
(vi)经营权利;
(vii)生产技术;或者
(viii)商号。
(e)本规则不适用于母公司与其全资子公司之间的交易。

[《联邦公报》第47卷第29837页,1982年7月9日,修正索引:《联邦公报》第50卷第49533页,1985年12月3日;《联邦公报》第56卷第57247页,1991年11月8日;《联邦公报》第61卷第54514页,1996年10月18日;《联邦公报》第74卷第18616页,2009年4月23日。]

第210.11-02节　编制要求

(a)目标。备考财务信息应当表明如果交易在更早的时间完成可能对历史财务报表产生的影响,从而帮助投资者了解特定交易的持续影响。该等财务报表应当阐明交易可能造成注册人历史财务状况和经营成果发生变化的范围,以便帮助投资者分析注册人的前景。

(b)形式和内容。(1)备考财务信息应包含备考简要资产负债表、备考简要损益表以及说明性质的附注。在特定情形下(即只需作出少数几项备考调整且该等调整很容易理解时),可以仅提交一份关于交易模拟影响数的文字说明,而不必提供上文所述报表。

(2)备考财务信息前应附带一段引言,对下列内容进行简要说明:(i)交易;(ii)交易所涉实体;以及(iii)备考财务信息报告期。此外,还应附上一份关于备考信息内容的说明。

(3)备考简要财务信息仅需包含本《管理办法》相关条款规定的主要会计科目(即带有编号的科目)。金额小于总资产10%的资产负债表任何主要科目,可与其他科目归并。金额小于最近3个会计年度可归属于注册人的平均净收益15%的损益表任何主要科目,可与其他科目归并。计算可归属于注册人的平均净收益之时,应将亏损年度排

percent of average net income attributable to the registrant for the most recent three fiscal years, the caption may be combined with others. In calculating average net income attributable to the registrant, loss years should be excluded unless losses were incurred in each of the most recent three years, in which case the average loss shall be used for purposes of this test. Notwithstanding these tests, *de minimis* amounts need not be shown separately.

(4) Pro forma statements shall ordinarily be in columnar form showing condensed historical statements, pro forma adjustments, and the pro forma results.

(5) The pro forma condensed income statement shall disclose income (loss) from continuing operations before nonrecurring charges or credits directly attributable to the transaction. Material nonrecurring charges or credits and related tax effects which result directly from the transaction and which will be included in the income of the registrant within the 12 months succeeding the transaction shall be disclosed separately. It should be clearly indicated that such charges or credits were not considered in the pro forma condensed income statement. If the transaction for which pro forma financial information is presented relates to the disposition of a business, the pro forma results should give effect to the disposition and be presented under an appropriate caption.

(6) Pro forma adjustments related to the pro forma condensed income statement shall be computed assuming the transaction was consummated at the beginning of the fiscal year presented and shall include adjustments which give effect to events that are (i) directly attributable to the transaction; (ii) expected to have a continuing impact on the registrant; and (iii) factually supportable. Pro forma adjustments related to the pro forma condensed balance sheet shall be computed assuming the transaction was consummated at the end of the most recent period for which a balance sheet is required by §210.3-01 and shall include adjustments which give effect to events that are directly attributable to the transaction and factually supportable regardless of whether they have a continuing impact or are nonrecurring. All adjustments should be referenced to notes which clearly explain the assumptions involved.

(7) Historical primary and fully diluted per share data based on continuing operations (or net income if the registrant does not report either discontinued operations, extraordinary items, or the cumulative effects of accounting changes) for the registrant, and primary and fully diluted pro forma per share data based on continuing operations before nonrecurring charges or credits directly attributable to the transaction shall be presented on the face of the pro forma condensed income statement together with the number of shares used to compute such per share data. For transactions involving the issuance of securities, the number of shares used in the calculation of the pro forma per share data should be based on the weighted average number of shares outstanding during

除。如果最近3年每一年都发生亏损,则在进行测试,以判断是否符合上述标准时,应使用平均亏损数值。尽管有上述测试标准,金额较低,不具重大性的科目,不必单列。

(4)备考财务报表通常应当用多栏式表格列明简要历史报表、备考调整以及备考成果。

(5)备考简要损益表应当列明扣除可直接归属于交易的非经常性费用或贷方金额之前的持续经营损益。应当单独披露将计入注册人交易后12个月内的收益的,且直接由交易所导致的重大非经常性费用或贷方金额以及相关的课税影响数。应清楚说明备考简要损益表并未体现该等费用或贷方金额。如果备考财务信息涉及的交易关系到对某个企业的处置,备考成果应当体现此项处置交易,并通过适当的会计科目列示。

(6)与备考简要损益表相关的备考调整应当基于"交易在报告会计年度年初完成"此一假定进行计算,并应按照符合下列条件的事件进行调整:(i)可直接归属于交易项下;(ii)预期将对注册人产生持续影响;并且(iii)有事实根据。与备考简要资产负债表相关的备考调整应当基于"交易在按第210.3-01节要求提供资产负债表的最近一期报告期末完成"此一假定进行计算,并应体现可直接归属于交易项下、有事实根据的事件,无论其是否有持续影响或属于非经常性事件。所有调整均应当在附注中说明,对涉及的假设作出清楚的解释。

(7)在备考简要损益表正文中,应当列明在持续经营基础上计算的注册人原始和完全摊薄的历史每股数据(如果注册人未报告已终止经营的业务、非经常项目或会计原则变更的累积影响数,则应当列明净收益数据),以及在持续经营基础上计算的原始和完全摊薄的备考每股数据(该数据应为扣除可直接归属于交易项下的非经常性费用或贷方金额之前的数据),同时附上计算每股数据时使用的股数。对于涉及证券发行的交易,计算备考每股数据时使用的股数应当基于调整期间发行在外股份的加权平均数确定,体现期后发行的股份或"假设特定交易或事件在报告期初发生"时的假定发行股份。如果在交易中发行可转换证券,应当考虑备考每股数据可能发生的摊薄。

the period adjusted to give effect to shares subsequently issued or assumed to be issued had the particular transaction or event taken place at the beginning of the period presented. If a convertible security is being issued in the transaction, consideration should be given to the possible dilution of the pro forma per share data.

(8) If the transaction is structured in such a manner that significantly different results may occur, additional pro forma presentations shall be made which give effect to the range of possible results.

Instructions: 1. The historical statement of income used in the pro forma financial information shall not report operations of a segment that has been discontinued, extraordinary items, or the cumulative effects of accounting changes. If the historical statement of income includes such items, only the portion of the income statement through "income from continuing operations" (or the appropriate modification thereof) should be used in preparing pro forma results.

2. For a business combination, pro forma adjustments for the income statement shall include amortization, depreciation and other adjustments based on the allocated purchase price of net assets acquired. In some transactions, such as in financial institution acquisitions, the purchase adjustments may include significant discounts of the historical cost of the acquired assets to their fair value at the acquisition date. When such adjustments will result in a significant effect on earnings (losses) in periods immediately subsequent to the acquisition which will be progressively eliminated over a relatively short period, the effect of the purchase adjustments on reported results of operations for each of the next five years should be disclosed in a note.

3. For a disposition transaction, the pro forma financial information shall begin with the historical financial statements of the existing entity and show the deletion of the business to be divested along with the pro forma adjustments necessary to arrive at the remainder of the existing entity. For example, pro forma adjustments would include adjustments of interest expense arising from revised debt structures and expenses which will be or have been incurred on behalf of the business to be divested such as advertising costs, executive salaries and other costs.

4. For entities which were previously a component of another entity, pro forma adjustments should include adjustments similar in nature to those referred to in Instruction 3 above. Adjustments may also be necessary when charges for corporate overhead, interest, or income taxes have been allocated to the entity on a basis other than one deemed reasonable by management.

5. Adjustments to reflect the acquisition of real estate operations or properties for the pro forma income statement shall include a depreciation charge based on the new accounting basis for the assets, interest financing on any additional or refinanced debt,

（8）如果交易架构可能导致结果出现重大偏差，应针对该等可能出现的不同结果提供相关补充备考报告。

说明：1.在备考财务信息中使用的历史损益表不应报告已终止经营的业务分部、非经常项目或会计变更的累积影响数。如果历史损益表包含该等项目，在编制备考成果时只应使用损益表中“持续经营业务收益”部分的信息（或其适当修改后的信息）。

2.发生业务合并时，备考损益表调整应当包含基于被收购净资产的分摊收购价格计算的摊销、折旧和其他调整。在诸如金融机构收购等交易中，收购调整可能包括按收购当日被收购资产的公允价值大幅对被收购资产的历史成本进行的大幅调低。如果该等调整将对紧接收购之后的数个报告期的损益产生重大影响，且该等影响将在一个较短的期间内逐步消除，则应在附注中披露收购调整对未来5年每年报告的经营成果的影响数。

3.对于企业处置交易，备考财务信息应当首先以现有实体的历史财务报表为基础，删除将被剥离的企业，并列明为计算出现有实体剩余财务信息而作出的必要备考调整。例如，备考调整应当包含因债务结构调整而作出的利息费用调整以及被剥离企业已经或将要发生的相关成本（如广告费、管理人员薪资和其他成本）。

4.对于曾经属于另一实体一部分的实体，备考调整应包括性质与上文第3项说明中提及的调整类似的调整。如果公司总部费用、利息或所得税费用已分摊至该实体，且管理层认为分摊依据并不合理，也可能有必要进行调整。

5.涉及房地产经营业务或物业收购的备考损益表调整应包括在所涉资产的新会计基准上的折旧费用、任何补充或再融资债务的利息融资以及有事实依据的其他适当调整。请同时参见上文第4项说明。

and other appropriate adjustments that can be factually supported. See also Instruction 4 above.

6. When consummation of more than one transaction has occurred or is probable during a fiscal year, the pro forma financial information may be presented on a combined basis; however, in some circumstances (e.g., depending upon the combination of probable and consummated transactions, and the nature of the filing) it may be more useful to present the pro forma financial information on a disaggregated basis even though some or all of the transactions would not meet the tests of significance individually. For combined presentations, a note should explain the various transactions and disclose the maximum variances in the pro forma financial information which would occur for any of the possible combinations. If the pro forma financial information is presented in a proxy or information statement for purposes of obtaining shareholder approval of one of the transactions, the effects of that transaction must be clearly set forth.

7. Tax effects, if any, of pro forma adjustments normally should be calculated at the statutory rate in effect during the periods for which pro forma condensed income statements are presented and should be reflected as a separate pro forma adjustment.

(c) *Periods to be presented.* (1) A pro forma condensed balance sheet as of the end of the most recent period for which a consolidated balance sheet of the registrant is required by §210.3-01 shall be filed unless the transaction is already reflected in such balance sheet.

(2)(i) Pro forma condensed statements of income shall be filed for only the most recent fiscal year and for the period from the most recent fiscal year end to the most recent interim date for which a balance sheet is required. A pro forma condensed statement of income may be filed for the corresponding interim period of the preceding fiscal year. A pro forma condensed statement of income shall not be filed when the historical income statement reflects the transaction for the entire period.

(ii) For a business combination accounted for as a pooling of interests, the pro forma income statements (which are in effect a restatement of the historical income statements as if the combination had been consummated) shall be filed for all periods for which historical income statements of the registrant are required.

(3) Pro forma condensed statements of income shall be presented using the registrant's fiscal year end. If the most recent fiscal year end of any other entity involved in the transaction differs from the registrant's most recent fiscal year end by more than 93 days, the other entity's income statement shall be brought up to within 93 days of the registrant's most recent fiscal year end, if practicable. This updating could be accomplished by adding subsequent interim period results to the most recent fiscal year-end information and deducting the comparable preceding year interim period results.

6.如果在某个会计年度实际完成或可能完成一项以上的交易,可提供汇总备考财务信息;但是,在某些情形下(如根据可能或已经完成的交易的汇总情况,以及提交文件的性质),即使某些或所有交易单独而言不够成重要交易,但是针对各项交易分别提供备考财务信息仍可能能够更好地反映企业情况。提交汇总信息的,应在附注中对各项交易作出说明,并披露任何可能发生的合并将导致备考财务信息发生的最大变动值。如果为了获得股东对其中一项交易的批准而在征集投票权报告或信息说明书中提交该等备考财务信息,必须清楚载明该交易的影响数。

7.一般而言,备考调整的课税影响数(如有)应当按照备考简要损益表各报告期内有效的法定税率计算,并应作为单独的备考调整项在备考信息中予以反映。

(c)报告期。(1)应提交截至注册人按第210.3-01节的要求提交合并资产负债表的最近一个报告期期末的备考简要资产负债表,但相关交易已在该资产负债表中予以反映的除外。

(2)(i)仅需针对以下报告期提交备考简要损益表:最近一个会计年度,以及最近一个会计年度年末到应提交资产负债表的最近一个中期日的期间。可提交上一会计年度同期的中期报告期的备考简要损益表。如果历史损益表已反映整个期间的交易,则不必提交备考简要损益表。

(ii)对于以权益集合法核算的业务合并,应就注册人按规定应提交历史损益表的所有期间提交备考损益表(实际是在假设合并已经完成的条件下对历史损益表进行重述)。

(3)备考简要损益表的截止日期应当采用注册人会计年度的截止日期。如果交易涉及的任何其他实体最近一个会计年度的截止日期与注册人最近一会计年度的截止日期相差超过93日,在可行的条件下,该实体的损益表日应相应提前,使二者差距短于93日。此项更新可通过在截至最近一会计年度年末的信息基础上加上期后中期报告期成果,并减去上一年度可比中期报告期成果来实现。应当说明简要备考损益表中合并的报告期以及被排除或被重复计入的任何期间(如既作为该会计年度一部分,又作为期后中期报告期纳入的中期期间)的销售额、收入和收益。对于受制于第210.6-

Disclosure shall be made of the periods combined and of the sales or revenues and income for any periods which were excluded from or included more than once in the condensed pro forma income statements (e.g., an interim period that is included both as part of the fiscal year and the subsequent interim period). For investment companies subject to §§210.6–01 to 210.6–10, the periods covered by the pro forma statements must be the same.

(4) Whenever unusual events enter into the determination of the results shown for the most recently completed fiscal year, the effect of such unusual events should be disclosed and consideration should be given to presenting a pro forma condensed income statement for the most recent twelve-month period in addition to those required in paragraph (c)(2)(i) above if the most recent twelve-month period is more representative of normal operations.

[47 FR 29837, July 9, 1982, as amended at 50 FR 49533, Dec. 3, 1985; 74 FR 18616, Apr. 23, 2009]

§210.11–03 Presentation of financial forecast.

(a) A financial forecast may be filed in lieu of the pro forma condensed statements of income required by §210.11–02(b)(1).

(1) The financial forecast shall cover a period of at least 12 months from the latest of (i) the most recent balance sheet included in the filing or (ii) the consummation date or estimated consummation date of the transaction.

(2) The forecasted statement of income shall be presented in the same degree of detail as the pro forma condensed statement of income required by §210.11–02(b)(3).

(3) Assumptions particularly relevant to the transaction and effects thereof should be clearly set forth.

(4) Historical condensed financial information of the registrant and the business acquired or to be acquired, if any, shall be presented for at least a recent 12 month period in parallel columns with the financial forecast.

(b) Such financial forecast shall be presented in accordance with the guidelines established by the American Institute of Certified Public Accountants.

(c) Forecasted earnings per share data shall be substituted for pro forma per share data.

(d) This rule does not permit the filing of a financial forecast in lieu of pro forma information required by generally accepted accounting principles.

Form and Content of Schedules

general

§210.12–01 Application of §§210.12–01 to 210.12–29.

These sections prescribe the form and content of the schedules required by §§210.5–

01~210.6-10节的投资公司,备考报表的报告期必须相同。

(4)如果在确定最近结束的一个会计年度的成果时受到异常事件的影响,应当披露该等异常事件的影响数,同时,如最近的12个月期间能更好地反映正常经营状况,还应考虑在上文第(c)(2)(i)款规定的备考简要损益表之外再提交最近12个月期间的备考简要损益表。

[《联邦公报》第47卷第29837页,1982年7月9日,修正索引:《联邦公报》第50卷第49533页,1985年12月3日;《联邦公报》第74卷第18616页,2009年4月23日。]

第210.11-03节　财务预测列报

(a)可提交财务预测,用以替代第210.11-02(b)(1)节规定的备考简要损益表。

(1)财务预测报告期至少应为12个月,从下列日期起算(以较晚者为准):(i)提交文件中包含的最近一期资产负债表日,或者(ii)交易完成日期或预计完成日期。

(2)预测损益表列报的详细程度应当与第210.11-02(b)(3)节规定的备考简要损益表相同。

(3)应当明确说明与交易及其影响数直接相关的假设。

(4)应当在与财务预测并列的栏目中,提供注册人以及已收购企业或目标收购企业的历史简要财务信息(如有),且该等简要财务信息的覆盖期间至少应为最近12个月。

(b)财务预测应当按照美国注册会计师协会制定的指引列报。

(c)应以预测每股盈利数据替代备考每股数据。

(d)本规则不得解释为允许注册人提交财务预测,用以替代公认会计原则要求提供的备考信息。

附表的格式和内容

一般规定

第210.12-01节　第210.12-01~210.12-29节的适用范围

下列各节规定了第210.5-04节、第210.6-10节、第210.6A-05节和第210.7-05节要

04, 210.6-10, 210.6A-05, and 210.7-05.

[59 FR 65637, Dec. 20, 1994]

§§210.12-02—210.12-03 [Reserved]

§210.12-04 Condensed financial information of registrant.

(a) Provide condensed financial information as to financial position, cash flows and results of operations of the registrant as of the same dates and for the same periods for which audited consolidated financial statements are required. The financial information required need not be presented in greater detail than is required for condensed statements by §210.10-01(a)(2), (3) and (4). Detailed footnote disclosure which would normally be included with complete financial statements may be omitted with the exception of disclosures regarding material contingencies, long-term obligations and guarantees. Descriptions of significant provisions of the registrant's long-term obligations, mandatory dividend or redemption requirements of redeemable stocks, and guarantees of the registrant shall be provided along with a five-year schedule of maturities of debt. If the material contingencies, long-term obligations, redeemable stock requirements and guarantees of the registrant have been separately disclosed in the consolidated statements, they need not be repeated in this schedule.

(b) Disclose separately the amounts of cash dividends paid to the registrant for each of the last three fiscal years by consolidated subsidiaries, unconsolidated subsidiaries and 50 percent or less owned persons accounted for by the equity method, respectively.

[46 FR 56180, Nov. 16, 1981, as amended at 57 FR 45293, Oct. 1, 1992]

§210.12-05—210.12-08 [Reserved]

§210.12-09 Valuation and qualifying accounts.

Column A—Description[1]	Column B—Balance at beginning of period	Column C—Additions		Column D—Deductions—describe	Column E—Balance at end of period
		(1)—Charged to costs and expenses	(2)—Charged to other accounts—describe		

[1] List, by major classes, all valuation and qualifying accounts and reserves not included in specific schedules. Identify each class of valuation and qualifying accounts and reserves by descriptive title. Group (a) those valuation and qualifying accounts which are deducted in the balance sheet from the assets to which they apply and (b) those reserves which support the

求提供的附表的格式和内容。

[《联邦公报》第59卷第65637页,1994年12月20日。]

第210.12-02~210.12-03节 [保留]

第210.12-04节 注册人的简要财务信息

(a)按照应提交的经审计的合并财务报表的报告期和截止日期,提供关于注册人财务状况、现金流量和经营成果的简要财务信息。该等财务信息详细程度不必超过第210.10-01(a)(2)节、第210.10-01(a)(3)节和第210.10-01(a)(4)节关于简要报表的规定。完整财务报表中通常包含的详细脚注披露信息,在简要财务信息中可以省略,但是与重大或有事项、长期债务和担保有关的除外。关于注册人长期债务、可赎回股份的强制性股息或赎回要求以及注册人担保的重大条款,应当与5年间债务到期日列表一同提供。如果重大或有事项、长期债务、可赎回股份要求以及注册人担保已经在合并报表中进行过单独披露,不必在附表中重复。

(b)单独披露过去3个会计年度内每一年并表子公司以及按权益法核算的非并表子公司和50%或以下股权被控主体分别向注册人分配的现金股息的数额。

[《联邦公报》第46卷第56180页,1981年11月16日,修正索引:《联邦公报》第57卷第45293页,1992年10月1日。]

第210.12-05~210.12-08节 [保留]

第210.12-09节 估值和合格账户

A栏——名称[1]	B栏——期初余额	C栏——增加额		D栏——减少额—请予以说明	E栏——期末余额
		(1)——记入成本和费用借方	(2)记入其他账户借方——请予以说明		

1 按照主要类别列出未列入具体附表的所有估值和合格账户以及准备金。为每类估值和合格账户以及准备金提供一个描述性的名称。将(a)从资产负债表相关资产中扣除的估值和合格账户,以及(b)资产负债表科目"准备金"项下的准备金分组列出。单独而言对于增加额、减少额和余额不具重要性的估值和合格账户以及准备金,可以合为一组,仅列明

balance sheet caption, Reserves. Valuation and qualifying accounts and reserves as to which the additions, deductions, and balances were not individually significant may be grouped in one total and in such case the information called for under columns C and D need not be given.

[37 FR 14602, July 21, 1972. Redesignated and amended at 45 FR 63679, Sept. 25, 1980]

§§210.12–10—210.12–11 [Reserved]

for management investment companies

§210.12–12 Investments in securities of unaffiliated issuers.

Col. A	Col. B	Col. C
Name of issuer and title of issue[1,2]	Balance held at close of period. Number of shares—principal amount of bonds and notes[5]	Value of each item at close of period.[3,4,6,7,8]

[1] Each issue shall be listed separately: *Provided*, however, that an amount not exceeding five percent of the total of Column C may be listed in one amount as "Miscellaneous securities," provided the securities so listed are not restricted, have been held for not more than one year prior to the date of the related balance sheet, and have not previously been reported by name to the shareholders of the person for which the schedule is filed or to any exchange, or set forth in any registration statement, application, or annual report or otherwise made available to the public. If any securities are listed as "Miscellaneous securities," briefly explain in a footnote what the term represents.

[2] Categorize the schedule by (i) the type of investment (such as common stocks, preferred stocks, convertible securities, fixed income securities, government securities, options purchased, warrants, loan participations and assignments, commercial paper, bankers' acceptances, certificates of deposit, short-term securities, repurchase agreements, other investment companies, and so forth); and (ii) the related industry, country, or geographic region of the investment. Short-term debt instruments (*i.e.*, debt instruments whose maturities or expiration dates at the time of acquisition are one year or less) of the same issuer may be aggregated, in which case the range of interest rates and maturity dates shall be indicated. For issuers of periodic payment plan certificates and unit investment trusts, list separately: (i) Trust shares in trusts created or serviced by the depositor or sponsor of this trust; (ii) trust shares in other trusts; and (iii) securities of other investment companies. Restricted securities shall not be combined with unrestricted securities of the same issuer. Repurchase agreements shall be stated separately showing for each the name of the party or parties to the agreement, the date of the agreement, the total amount to be received upon repurchase, the repurchase date and description of securities subject to the repurchase agreements.

总数,并且可以不必提供C栏和D栏要求提供的信息。

[《联邦公报》第37卷第14602页,1972年7月21日,重新公布索引和修正索引:《联邦公报》第45卷第63679页,1980年9月25日。]

第210.12-10~210.12-11节 [保留]

适用于管理型投资公司

第210.12-12节 对非控制性关联发行人的证券投资

A栏	B栏	C栏
发行人名称以及证券发行的名称[1,2]	期末持有余额。股数—债券和票据本金金额[5]	每项期末价值[3,4,6,7,8]

1 每项发行均应单列:但是,金额不超过C栏总额5%的发行可在"杂项证券"项下加总列出,前提是此类证券不属于受限证券,在相关资产负债日之前持有期不超过一年,并且未曾按其发行名称向所提交附表代表的会计主体的股东或向任何交易所报告,或者在任何注册说明书、申请或年度报告中列明或以其他方式公开。"杂项证券"项下列有任何证券的,应在脚注中简要说明该术语的含义。

2 上表应按照以下标准进行分类:(i)投资类型(如普通股、优先股、可转换证券、固定收益证券、政府证券、已购买的期权、权证、联合贷款和贷款转让、商业票据、银行承兑票据、存款凭证、短期证券、回购协议、其他投资公司等);以及(ii)投资涉及的行业、国家或地理区域。同一发行人的短期债务票据[即购买时将在一年(含)内到期或期满的债务工具]可以合并为一类,在此情形下应当列明利率范围和票据到期日时间范围。对于定期缴款计划凭证和单位投资信托的发行人而言,应单独列出:(i)信托的交托人或发起人所设立或服务的信托的信托股份;(ii)其他信托的信托股份;以及(iii)其他投资公司的证券。同一发行人的受限证券不得与非受限证券合并为一类。每份回购协议均应单列,指明协议各方的名称、协议日期、回购时将收到的款项总额、回购日期和回购协议所涉证券的名称。

[3] The subtotals for each category of investments, subdivided by business grouping or instrument type, shall be shown together with their percentage value compared to net assets (§§210.6-04.19 or 210.6-05.4).

[4] Column C shall be totaled. The total of column C shall agree with the correlative amounts shown on the related balance sheet.

[5] Indicate by an appropriate symbol each issue of securities which is non-income producing. Evidences of indebtedness and preferred shares may be deemed to be income producing if, on the respective last interest payment date or date for the declaration of dividends prior to the date of the related balance sheet, there was only a partial payment of interest or a declaration of only a partial amount of the dividends payable; in such case, however, each such issue shall be indicated by an appropriate symbol referring to a note to the effect that, on the last interest or dividend date, only partial interest was paid or partial dividends declared. If, on such respective last interest or dividend date, no interest was paid or no cash or in kind dividends declared, the issue shall not be deemed to be income producing. Common shares shall not be deemed to be income producing unless, during the last year preceding the date of the related balance sheet, there was at least one dividend paid upon such common shares.

[6] Indicate by an appropriate symbol each issue of restricted securities. State the following in a footnote: (a) As to each such issue: (1) Acquisition date; (2) carrying value per unit of investment at date of related balance sheet, e.g., a percentage of current market value of unrestricted securities of the same issuer, etc.; and (3) the cost of such securities. (b) as to each issue acquired during the year preceding the date of the related balance sheet, the carrying value per unit of investment of unrestricted securities of the same issuer at: (1) The day the purchase price was agreed to; and (2) the day on which an enforceable right to acquire such securities was obtained. and (c) the aggregate value of all restricted securities and the percentage which the aggregate value bears to net assets.

[7] Indicate by an appropriate symbol each issue of securities held in connection with open put or call option contracts or loans for short sales.

[8] State in a footnote the following amounts based on cost for Federal income tax purposes: (a) Aggregate gross unrealized appreciation for all securities in which there is an excess of value over tax cost; (b) the aggregate gross unrealized depreciation for all securities in which there is an excess of tax cost over value; (c) the net unrealized appreciation or depreciation; and (d) the aggregate cost of securities for Federal income tax purposes.

[47 FR 56843, Dec. 21, 1982, as amended at 69 FR 11262, Mar. 9, 2004]

3 每类投资(按照业务分类或工具类型细分)的小计数额,应当与其在净资产中所占百分比共同列出(第210.6-04.19节或第210.6-05.4节)。

4 C栏的各项数额应予加总。C栏的总额应与相关资产负债表上列示的相关数额相符。

5 通过适当符号注明不产生收益的每项证券发行。如在相关资产负债表日前相关的最后利息支付日或股息宣布日,仅支付了部分利息或仅宣布了部分应付股息,债务凭证和优先股仍可视为已产生收益。但是,在上述情形下,应用适当的符号对每项发行作出标注,并通过相应的附注说明在最后的利息支付日或股息宣布日,仅支付了部分利息或仅宣布了部分股息。如果在上述最后利息支付日或股息宣布日,未支付利息或未宣布现金或实物股息,此项发行不得视为产生收益的证券发行。除非在相关资产负债表日前一年期间内至少支付了一次股息,否则普通股不得视为产生收益的证券。

6 通过适当符号注明每项受限证券的发行。应在脚注中说明:(a)与每项发行相关的下述信息:(1)收购日期;(2)在相关资产负债表日每投资单位的账面价值,例如同一发行人非受限证券当期市值的百分比等;和(3)该等证券的成本。(b)对于在相关资产负债日前一年内购买的每项证券发行,同一发行人非受限证券每投资单位在下列日期的账面价值:(1)就买价达成约定的日期;和(2)获得收购此证券的可强制执行权利的日期。以及(c)所有受限证券的总值以及该等总值占净资产的百分比。

7 通过适当符号注明与看跌或看涨期权合约中未平仓的合约或卖空交易贷款相关的每项证券发行。

8 通过脚注列明下列金额(基于计征联邦所得税时适用的成本计算):(a)价值高于税务成本的所有证券的未实现增值合计金额;(b)税务成本高于价值的所有证券的未实现贬值合计金额;(c)未实现增值或贬值净额,以及(d)计征联邦所得税时适用的证券合计成本。

[《联邦公报》第47卷第56843页,1982年12月21日,修正索引:《联邦公报》第69卷第11262页,2004年3月9日。]

§210.12–12A Investments—securities sold short.

[For management investment companies only]

Col. A	Col. B	Col. C
Name of issuer and title of issue[1]	Balance of short position at close of period. (number of shares)	Value of each open short position[2]

[1] Each issue shall be listed separately.

[2] Column C shall be totaled. The total of column C shall agree with the correlative amounts shown on the related balance sheet.

[47 FR 56844, Dec. 21, 1982]

§210.12–12B Open option contracts written.

[For management investment companies only]

Col. A	Col. B	Col. C	Col. D	Col. E
Name of issuer[1,2]	Number of contracts[3]	Exercise price	Expiration date	Value.[4]

[1] Information as to put options shall be shown separately from information as to call options.

[2] Options of an issuer where exercise prices or expiration dates differ shall be listed separately.

[3] If the number of shares subject to option is substituted for number of contracts, the column name shall reflect that change.

[4] Column E shall be totaled and shall agree with the correlative amount shown on the related balance sheet.

[47 FR 56844, Dec. 21, 1982]

§210.12–12C Summary schedule of investments in securities of unaffiliated issuers.

Column A	Column B	Column C	Column D
Name of issuer and title of issue[1,3,4,5,6]	Balance held at close of period. Number of shares—principal amount of bonds and notes[8]	Value of each item at close of period[2,7,9,10,11]	Percentage value compared to net assets.

第210.12-12A节　投资——卖空证券

[仅适用于管理型投资公司]

A栏	B栏	C栏
发行人名称和证券发行的名称[1]	期末空头持仓余额(股数)	每一未平仓空头持仓的价值[2]

1 应单列每项证券发行。

2 C栏的各项数额应予加总。C栏的总额应与相关资产负债表上列示的相关数额相符。

[《联邦公报》第47卷第56844页,1982年12月21日。]

第210.12-12B节　卖出的期权合约中未平仓的合约

[仅适用于管理型投资公司]

A栏	B栏	C栏	D栏	E栏
发行人名称[1,2]	合约数量[3]	行权价格	到期日	价值[4]

1 看跌期权和看涨期权的信息应分别列示。

2 同一发行人的不同期权,行权价格或到期日有差异的,应当分别列出。

3 如果用期权基础股票的股数替代合约数量,栏目名称应相应改变。

4 E栏的各项数额应予加总,总额应与相关资产负债表上列示的相关数额相符。

[《联邦公报》第47卷第56844页,1982年12月21日。]

第210.12-12C节　非控制性关联发行人证券投资摘要列表

A栏	B栏	C栏	D栏
发行人姓名和证券发行名称[1,3,4,5,6]	期末持有余额—股数—债券和票据本金数额[8]	每项期末价值[2,7,9,10,11]	占净资产的百分比

[1] Categorize the schedule by (a) the type of investment (such as common stocks, preferred stocks, convertible securities, fixed income securities, government securities, options purchased, warrants, loan participations and assignments, commercial paper, bankers' acceptances, certificates of deposit, short-term securities, repurchase agreements, other investment companies, and so forth); and (b) the related industry, country, or geographic region of the investment.

[2] The subtotals for each category of investments, subdivided by industry, country, or geographic region, shall be shown together with their percentage value compared to net assets.

[3] Except as provided in note 5, list separately the 50 largest issues and any other issue the value of which exceeded one percent of net asset value of the registrant as of the close of the period. For purposes of the list (including, in the case of short-term debt instruments, the first sentence of note 4), aggregate and treat as a single issue, respectively, (a) short-term debt instruments (*i.e.*, debt instruments whose maturities or expiration dates at the time of acquisition are one year or less) of the same issuer (indicating the range of interest rates and maturity dates); and (b) fully collateralized repurchase agreements (indicate in a footnote the range of dates of the repurchase agreements, the total purchase price of the securities, the total amount to be received upon repurchase, the range of repurchase dates, and description of securities subject to the repurchase agreements). Restricted and unrestricted securities of the same issue should be aggregated for purposes of determining whether the issue is among the 50 largest issues, but should not be combined in the schedule. For purposes of determining whether the value of an issue exceeds one percent of net asset value, aggregate and treat as a single issue all securities of any one issuer, except that all fully collateralized repurchase agreements shall be aggregated and treated as a single issue. The U.S. Treasury and each agency, instrumentality, or corporation, including each government-sponsored entity, that issues U.S. government securities is a separate issuer.

[4] If multiple securities of an issuer aggregate to greater than one percent of net asset value, list each issue of the issuer separately (including separate listing of restricted and unrestricted securities of the same issue) except that the following may be aggregated and listed as a single issue: (a) Fixed-income securities of the same issuer which are not among the 50 largest issues and whose value does not exceed one percent of net asset value of the registrant as of the close of the period (indicating the range of interest rates and maturity dates); and (b) U.S. government securities of a single agency, instrumentality, or corporation, which are not among the 50 largest issues and whose value does not exceed one percent of net asset value of the registrant as of the close of the period (indicating the range of interest rates and maturity dates). For each category identified pursuant to note 1, group all issues that are neither separately listed nor included in a group of securities that is listed in the aggregate as a single issue in a sub-category labeled "Other securities," and provide the information for Columns C and D.

1 上表应按照以下标准进行分类:(a)投资类型(如普通股、优先股、可转换证券、固定收益证券、政府证券、已购买的期权、权证、联合贷款和贷款转让、商业票据、银行承兑票据、存款凭证、短期证券、回购协议、其他投资公司等);以及(b)投资所涉的行业、国家或地理区域。

2 每类投资(按照行业、国家或地理区域细分)的小计数额应当与其在净资产中所占百分比共同列出。

3 除注释5另有规定外,应单独列出截至期末规模最大的50项证券发行以及价值超过注册人资产净值1%的所有证券发行。就上述清单而言(对于短期债务票据,包括注释4的第一句),应将下列各类发行全部合并为一项证券发行:(a)同一发行人的短期债务票据(即收购时将在一年内到期或期满的票据)(注明利率范围和到期日时间范围);以及(b)得到全额担保的回购协议(在脚注中说明各回购协议日期的范围、证券回购总价、回购时应收账款总额、回购日期的范围以及回购协议所涉证券的说明)。在确定证券发行是否属于前50项规模最大的证券发行之时,同一项证券发行中的受限和非受限证券应当予以合并计算,但在摘要列表中不应合并。在确定某项发行的价值是否超过资产净值的1%时,同一名发行人的所有证券也应合并,视为同一项发行,然而,发行人不同但均获得了全额担保的回购协议也应合并为一项发行。美国财政部以及发行美国政府证券的每一政府机关、职能部门或公司(包括政府发起的实体)均应视为独立的发行人。

4 如果某一发行人的多项证券合计金额超过净资产净值的1%,则应分别列出该发行人的每项证券发行(包括应当分列同一项发行中的受限证券和非受限证券),但是下列证券可以合并为一项发行:(a)同一发行人符合下述条件的固定收益证券:截至期末不属于规模最大的50项证券,价值也不超过注册人资产净值的1%(注明利率范围和到期日时间范围);以及(b)某一政府机关、职能部门或公司发行的符合下述条件的美国政府证券:截至期末该等证券不属于前50项规模最大的证券发行,价值也不超过注册人净资产净值的1%(注明利率范围和到期日时间范围)。对于注释1确定的每一类证券,凡是既未单列、也未在“其他证券”子类中合并为一项发行的,均应并为一组,提供C栏和D栏要求的信息。

[5] Any securities that would be required to be listed separately or included in a group of securities that is listed in the aggregate as a single issue may be listed in one amount as "Miscellaneous securities," provided the securities so listed are eligible to be, and are, categorized as "Miscellaneous securities" in the registrant's Schedule of Investments in Securities of Unaffiliated Issuers required under §210.12–12. However, if any security that is included in "Miscellaneous securities" would otherwise be required to be included in a group of securities that is listed in the aggregate as a single issue, the remaining securities of that group must nonetheless be listed as required by notes 3 and 4 even if the remaining securities alone would not otherwise be required to be listed in this manner (e.g., because the combined value of the security listed in "Miscellaneous securities" and the remaining securities of the same issuer exceeds one percent of net asset value, but the value of the remaining securities alone does not exceed one percent of net asset value).

[6] If any securities are listed as "Miscellaneous securities" pursuant to note 5 or "Other securities" pursuant to note 4, briefly explain in a footnote what those terms represent.

[7] Total Column C. The total of column C should equal the total shown on the related balance sheet for investments in securities of unaffiliated issuers.

[8] Indicate by an appropriate symbol each issue of securities which is non–income producing. Evidences of indebtedness and preferred shares may be deemed to be income producing if, on the respective last interest payment date or date for the declaration of dividends prior to the date of the related balance sheet, there was only a partial payment of interest or a declaration of only a partial amount of the dividends payable; in such case, however, each such issue shall be indicated by an appropriate symbol referring to a note to the effect that, on the last interest or dividend date, only partial interest was paid or partial dividends declared. If, on such respective last interest or dividend date, no interest was paid or no cash or in kind dividends declared, the issue shall not be deemed to be income producing. Common shares shall not be deemed to be income producing unless, during the last year preceding the date of the related balance sheet, there was at least one dividend paid upon such common shares.

[9] Indicate by an appropriate symbol each issue of restricted securities. State the following in a footnote: (a) as to each such issue: (1) Acquisition date; (2) carrying value per unit of investment at date of related balance sheet, e.g., a percentage of current market value of unrestricted securities of the same issuer, etc.; and (3) the cost of such securities. (b) as to each issue acquired during the year preceding the date of the related balance sheet, the carrying value per unit of investment of unrestricted securities of the same issuer at: (1) The day the purchase price was agreed to; and (2) the day on which an enforceable right to acquire such securities was obtained. and (c) the aggregate value of all restricted securities and the percentage which the aggregate value bears to net assets.

5 对于按规定应单列的证券或者应合并为一项发行的任何一组证券中所含的单只证券,可在“杂项证券”项下统一计入一个数额,前提是统一计入该等数额的所有证券均应有资格作为并且实际上已被并入第210.12-12节项下注册人《对非控制性关联发行人的证券投资列表》中的“杂项证券”。但是,包含在“杂项证券”中的任一证券,如果依照其他规定将与其他证券组成一组证券并合并为一项发行的,则该组所含其余证券仍应按注释3和注释4的要求列报,即使该等其余证券在未合并的情况下本身并不会被要求按注释3和注释4进行列报(如列入“杂项证券”的所涉证券与同一发行人其余证券的合计价值超过资产净值的1%,但是其余证券本身价值并未超过资产净值的1%)。

6 如果任何证券按照注释5被列为“杂项证券”或者按照注释4被列为“其他证券”,请在脚注中简要说明该等术语的含义。

7 C栏的各项数额应予加总, 总额应与相关资产负债表中对非控制性关联发行人的证券投资的总额相符。

8 通过适当符号注明不产生收益的每项证券发行。如在相关资产负债表日前相关的最后利息支付日或股息宣布日,仅支付了部分利息或仅宣布了部分应付股息,债务凭证和优先股仍可视为已产生收益。但是,在上述情形下,应用适当的符号对每项发行作出标注,并通过相应的附注说明在最后的利息支付日或股息宣布日,仅支付了部分利息或仅宣布了部分股息。如果在上述最后利息支付日或股息宣布日,未支付利息或未宣布现金或实物股息,此项发行不得视为产生收益的证券发行。除非在相关资产负债表日前一年期间内至少支付了一次股息,否则普通股不得视为产生收益的证券。

9 通过适当符号注明每项受限证券的发行。应在脚注中说明:(a)与每项发行相关的下述信息:(1)收购日期;(2)在相关资产负债表日每投资单位的账面价值,如同一发行人非受限证券的当期市值的百分比等;和(3)该等证券的成本。(b)对于在相关资产负债日前一年内购买的每项证券发行,同一发行人非受限证券每投资单位在下列日期的账面价值:(1)就买价达成约定的日期;和(2)获得收购此证券的可强制执行权利的日期。以及(c)所有受限证券的总值以及该等总值占净资产的百分比。

[10]Indicate by an appropriate symbol each issue of securities held in connection with open put or call option contracts or loans for short sales.

[11]State in a footnote the following amounts based on cost for Federal income tax purposes: (a) Aggregate gross unrealized appreciation for all securities in which there is an excess of value over tax cost; (b) the aggregate gross unrealized depreciation for all securities in which there is an excess of tax cost over value; (c) the net unrealized appreciation or depreciation; and (d) the aggregate cost of securities for Federal income tax purposes.

[69 FR 11262, Mar. 9, 2004]

§210.12-13 Investments other than securities.

[For management investment companies only]

Col. A	Col. B	Col. C
Description[1]	Balance held at close of period — quantity[2,3,5]	Value of each item at close of period[4,6,7]

[1]List each major category of investments by descriptive title.

[2]If practicable, indicate the quantity or measure in appropriate units.

[3]Indicate by an appropriate symbol each investment which is non-income producing.

[4]Indicate by an appropriate symbol each investment not readily marketable. The term "investment not readily marketable" shall include investments for which there is no independent publicly quoted market and investments which cannot be sold because of restrictions or conditions applicable to the investment or the company.

[5]Indicate by an appropriate symbol each investment subject to option. State in a footnote: (a) The quantity subject to option, (b) nature of option contract, (c) option price, and (d) dates within which options may be exercised.

[6]Column C shall be totaled and shall agree with the correlative amount shown on the related balance sheet.

[7]Sate in a footnote the following amounts based on cost for Federal income tax purposes: (a) Aggregate gross unrealized appreciation for all investments in which there is an excess of value over tax cost; (b) the aggregate gross unrealized depreciation for all investments in which there is an excess of tax cost over value; (c) the net unrealized appreciation or depreciation; and (d) the aggregate cost of investments for Federal income tax purposes.

10 通过适当符号注明与看跌或看涨期权合约中未平仓的合约或卖空交易贷款相关的每项证券发行。

11 通过脚注列明下列金额(基于计征联邦所得税时适用的成本计算):(a)价值高于税务成本的所有证券的未实现的增值合计金额;(b)税务成本高于价值的所有证券的未实现贬值合计金额;(c)未实现增值或贬值净额;以及(d)计征联邦所得税时适用的证券合计成本。

[《联邦公报》第69卷第11262页,2004年3月9日。]

第210.12-13节　证券以外的投资

[仅适用于管理型投资公司]

A栏	B栏	C栏
投资名称[1]	期末持有余额——数量[2,3,5]	每项投资的期末价值[4,6,7]

1 用描述性名称逐项列明主要投资类别。

2 如果可行,用适当单位说明数量或计量方法。

3 通过适当符号注明每项不产生收益的投资。

4 通过适当符号注明每项无法随时变现的投资。"无法随时变现的投资"包括不存独立公开报价市场的投资以及由于投资或相关公司受到限制或条件制约而不能出售的投资。

5 通过适当符号注明受到期权限制的每项投资。通过脚注说明:(a)受到期权限制的投资数量;(b)期权合约的性质;(c)期权价格;以及(d)期权行权的期限。

6 C栏的各项数额应予加总,总额应与相关资产负债表上列示的相关数额相符。

7 通过脚注列明下列金额(基于计征联邦所得税时适用的成本计算):(a)价值高于税务成本的所有投资的未实现的增值合计金额;(b)税务成本高于价值的所有投资的未实现贬值合计金额;(c)未实现增值或贬值净额;以及(d)计征联邦所得税时适用的投资合计成本。

§210.12–14 Investments in and advances to affiliates.

[For management investment companies only]

Col. A	Col. B	Col. C	Col. D	Col. E
Name of issuer and title of issue or nature of indebtedness[1]	Number of shares—principal amount of bonds, notes and other indebtedness held at close of period	Amount of equity in net profit and loss for the period[2,6]	Amount of dividends or interest[2,5]	Value of each item at close of period[2,3,4,5]
			(1) Credited to income	
			(2) Other	

[1](a) List each issue separately and group (1) Investments in majority–owned subsidiaries, segregating subsidiaries consolidated; (2) other controlled companies; and (3) other affiliates. (b) If during the period there has been any increase or decrease in the amount of investment in and advance to any affiliate, state in a footnote (or if there have been changes to numerous affiliates, in a supplementary schedule) (1) name of each issuer and title of issue or nature of indebtedness; (2) balance at beginning of period; (3) gross additions; (4) gross reductions; (5) balance at close of period as shown in Column E. Include in the footnote or schedule comparable information as to affiliates in which there was an investment at any time during the period even though there was no investment at the close of the period of report.

[2]Give totals for each group. If operations of any controlled companies are different in character from those of the company, group such affiliates (1) within divisions and (2) by type of activities.

[3]Columns C, D and E shall be totaled. The totals of Column E shall agree with the correlative amount shown on the related balance sheet.

[4](a) indicate by an appropriate symbol each issue of restricted securities. The information required by instruction 5 of §210.12–12 shall be given in a footnote. (b) Indicate by an appropriate symbol each issue of securities subject to option. The information required by instruction 5 of §210.12–13 shall be given in a footnote.

[5](a) include in Column D (1) as to each issue held at the close of the period, the dividends or interest included in caption 1 of the statement of operations. In addition, show as the final item in column D (1) the aggregate of dividends and interest included in the statement of operations in respect of investments in affiliates not held at the close of the period. The total of this column shall agree with the correlative amount shown on the related statement of operations.

(b) Include in Column D (2) all other dividends and interest. Explain in an appropriate

第210.12-14节 对控制性关联方的投资和垫款

[仅适用于管理型投资公司]

A栏	B栏	C栏	D栏	E栏
发行人名称以及证券发行名称或负债性质[1]	股数——期末持有的债券、票据和其他债务的本金数额	对期间内净损益享有的权益数额[2,6]	股息或利息数额[2,5]	每项发行的期末价值[2,3,4,5]
			(1)记入收益贷方	
			(2)其他	

1 (a)单独列出每项发行,并将投资分为以下几组:(1)对控股子公司的投资(并表子公司单列);(2)对其他受控公司的投资;以及(3)对其他控制性关联方的投资。(b)如果在报告期内对任何控制性关联方的投资或垫款数额有所增减,应在脚注中说明如下信息(如果发生变化的控制性关联方数量众多,应通过补充附表说明):(1)每名发行人名称以及证券发行的名称或债务性质;(2)期初余额;(3)总增加额;(4)总减少额;(5)E栏所示的期末余额。如在该期间内任何时间公司对某一控制性关联方进行过投资,即使在报告期末时并不持有该等投资,也应在脚注或附表中说明关于该等控制性关联方的可比信息。

2 提供每个组别的总额。如果任何受控公司的经营业务与注册人不同,均应在上述分组的基础上再按照业务活动类型,对该等控制性关联方进行进一步分组。

3 C栏、D栏和E栏的各项数额应予加总,E栏的总额应与相关资产负债表上列示的相关数额相符。

4 (a)通过适当符号注明每项受限证券的发行。应当通过脚注提供第210.12-12节的说明5要求提供的信息。(b)通过适当符号注明每项受期权限制的证券发行。应当通过脚注提供第210.12-13节的说明5要求提供的信息。

5 (a)在D(1)栏中,针对期末持有的每项发行,列示经营报表第一个科目中包含的股息或利息。此外,应将经营报表中与未在期末持有的对控制性关联方的投资相关的股息和利息总额作为D(1)栏的最后一项列明。本栏的总额应与相关经营报表中列示的相关数额相符。

(b)在D(2)栏中说明所有其他股息和利息。通过适当脚注说明对每个项目的处理

footnote the treatment accorded each item.

(c) Indicate by an appropriate symbol all non-cash dividends and explain the circumstances in a footnote.

(d) Indicate by an appropriate symbol each issue of securities which is non-income producing.

[6] The information required by column C shall be furnished only as to controlled companies.

[47 FR 56844, Dec. 21, 1982]

§210.12-15 Summary of investments—other than investments in related parties.

[For Insurance Companies]

Column A	Column B	Column C	Column D
Type of investment	Cost[1]	Value	Amount at which shown in the balance sheet[2]
Fixed maturities:			
Bonds:			
United States Government and government agencies and authorities			
States, municipalities and political subdivisions			
Foreign governments			
Public utilities			
Convertibles and bonds with warrants attached[3]			
All other corporate bonds			
Type of investment	Cost[1]	Value	Amount at which shown in the balance sheet[2]
Certificates of deposit			
Redeemable preferred stock			
Total fixed maturities			
Equity securities:			
Common stocks:			
Public utilities			

方法。

(c)通过适当符号注明所有非现金股息,并在脚注中说明具体情形。

(d)通过适当符号注明每项不产生收益的证券发行。

6 C栏要求提供的信息应限于与受控公司相关的信息。

[《联邦公报》第47卷第56844页,1982年12月21日。]

第210.12-15节 投资摘要——对关联方投资以外的投资

[适用于保险公司]

A栏	B栏	C栏	D栏
投资类型	成本[1]	价值	资产负债表列示数额[2]
固定期限类投资:			
债券:			
美国政府及政府机关和部门			
州、市和行政区域			
外国政府			
公用事业公司			
可转换债券以及附认股权证的债券[3]			
所有其他公司债券			
投资类型	成本[1]	价值	资产负债表列示数额[2]
存款凭证			
可赎回优先股			
固定期限类投资总计			
权益类证券:			
普通股:			
公用事业公司			

Column A	Column B	Column C	Column D
Banks, trust and insurance companies			
DG12.577mmIndustrial, miscellaneous and all other			
Nonredeemable preferred stocks			
DG12.577mmTotal equity securities			
Mortgage loans on real estate			
Real estate[4]			
Policy loans			
Other long-term investments			
Short-term investments			
Total investments			

[1] Original cost of equity securities and, as to fixed maturities, original cost reduced by repayments and adjusted for amortization of premiums or accrual of discounts.

[2] If the amount at which shown in the balance sheet is different from the amount shown in either column B or C, state the reason for such difference. The total of this column should agree with the balance sheet.

[3] All convertibles and bonds with warrants shall be included in this caption, regardless of issuer.

[4] State separately any real estate acquired in satisfaction of debt.

[46 FR 54337, Nov. 2, 1981]

§210.12–16 Supplementary insurance information.

[For insurance companies]

Column A	Column B	Column C	Column D	Column E	Column F	Column G	Column H	Column I	Column J	Column K
Segment[1]	Deferred policy acquisition cost (caption 7)	Future policy benefits, losses, claims and loss expenses (caption 13-a-1)	Unearned premiums (caption 13-a-2)	Other policy claims and benefits payable (caption 13-a-3)	Premium revenue (caption 1)	Net investment income (caption 2)[3]	Benefits, claims, losses, and settlement expenses (caption 5)	Amortization of deferred policy acquisition costs[4]	Other operating expenses[3,4]	Premiums written[2]
Total[5]										

续表

A 栏	B 栏	C 栏	D 栏
银行、信托和保险公司			
工业、杂项和所有其他			
不可赎回优先股			
权益类证券总计			
房地产抵押贷款			
房地产[4]			
保单贷款			
其他长期投资			
短期投资			
投资总计			

1 权益类证券的原始成本，以及固定期限类投资的扣除还款额并基于溢价或应计贴现摊销作出调整后的原始成本。

2 如果资产负债表列示的数额与B栏或C栏列示的数额不同，应说明存在该等差异的理由。本栏的总额应与资产负债表列示的相关数额相符。

3 本科目应包含所有可转换债券和附认股权证的债券，而不论债券发行人的身份为何。

4 单独列示在债务清偿过程中取得的任何房地产。

[《联邦公报》第46卷第54337页，1981年11月2日。]

第210.12-16节　补充保险信息

[适用于保险公司]

A 栏	B 栏	C 栏	D 栏	E 栏	F 栏	G 栏	H 栏	I 栏	J 栏	K 栏
节段[1]	递延保单取得成本（第7科目）	未来保单利益、损失、索赔和损失费用（第13－a－1科目）	预收保费（第13－a－2科目）	其他保单索赔和应付保单利益（第13－a－3科目）	保费收入（第1科目）	投资净收入（第2科目）[3]	利益、索赔、损失与理赔费用（第5科目）	递延保单取得成本摊销[4]	其他营业费用[3,4]	承保保费[2]
总计[5]										

[1] Segments shown should be the same as those presented in the footnote disclosures called for by generally accepted accounting principles.

[2] Does not apply to life insurance or title insurance. This amount should include premiums from reinsurance assumed, and be net of premiums on reinsurance ceded.

[3] State the basis for allocation of net investment income and, where applicable, other operating expenses.

[4] The total of columns I and J should agree with the amount shown for income statement caption 7.

[5] Totals should agree with the indicated balance sheet and income statement caption amounts, where a caption number is shown.

[46 FR 54338, Nov. 2, 1981, as amended at 57 FR 45293, Oct. 1, 1992; 64 FR 1734, Jan. 12, 1999]

§210.12–17 Reinsurance.

[For insurance companies]

Column A	Column B	Column C	Column D	Column E	Column F
	Gross amount	Ceded to other companies[1]	Assumed from other companies	Net amount[2]	Percentage of amount assumed to net[3]
Life insurance in force					
Premiums:					
Life insurance					
Accident and health insurance					
Property and liability insurance					
Title insurance					
Total premiums					

[1] Indicate in a note any amounts of reinsurance or coinsurance income netted against premiums ceded.

[2] This Column represents the total of column B less column C plus column D. The total premiums in this column should represent the amount of premium revenue on the income statement.

[3] Calculated as the amount in column D divided by amount in column E.

[46 FR 54338, Nov. 2, 1981]

1 应与公认会计原则要求在脚注中列明的节段相同。

2 不适用于寿险或产权保险。此数额应包含从分入再保险中获得的保费,并扣除分出再保险的保费。

3 说明投资净收入的分配依据,以及其他营业费用(如适用)。

4 I栏和J栏之和应与损益表第7科目的数额相符。

5 总额应与资产负债表和损益表相关科目列报的相关数额相符。

[《联邦公报》第46卷第54338页,1981年11月2日,修正索引:《联邦公报》第57卷第45293页,1992年10月1日;《联邦公报》第64卷第1734页,1999年1月12日。]

第210.12–17节 再保险

[适用于保险公司]

A栏	B栏	C栏	D栏	E栏	F栏
	总额	向其他公司分出的数额[1]	从其他公司分入的数额	净额[2]	分入数额占净额的百分比[3]
有效的寿险					
保费:					
寿险					
意外事故和健康保险					
财产和责任险					
产权保险					
保费总计					

1 通过注释说明任何再保险或共同保险收益扣除分保保费之后的数额。

2 此栏为B栏减去C栏加上D栏的计算结果。本栏中的保费总额应相当于损益表中的保费收入总额。

3 D栏的数额除以E栏数额。

[《联邦公报》第46卷第54338页,1981年11月2日。]

§210.12-18 Supplemental information (for property-casualty insurance underwriters).[1]

Affiliation with registrant	Deferred policy acquisition costs	Reserves for unpaid claims and claim adjustment expenses	Discount, if any, deducted in column C[4]	Unearned premiums	Earned premiums	Net investment income	Claims and claim adjustment expenses incurred related to		Amortization of deferred policy acquisition costs	Paid claims and claim adjustment expenses	Premiums written
							(1) Current year	(2) Prior years			
Column A	Column B	Column C	Column D	Column E	Column F	Column G		Column H	Column I	Column J	Column K
(a) Consolidated property-casualty entities[2]											
(b) Unconsolidated property-casualty subsidiaries[2,3]											
(c) Proportionate share of registrant and its subsidiaries' 50%-or-less-owned property-casualty equity investees[2,3]											

[1] Information included in audited financial statements, including other schedules, need not be repeated in this schedule. Columns B, C, D, and E are as of the balance sheet dates, columns F, G, H, I, J, and K are for the same periods for which income statements are presented in the registrant's audited consolidated financial statements.

[2] Present combined or consolidated amounts, as appropriate for each category, after intercompany eliminations.

[3] Information is not required here for 50%-or-less-owned equity investees that file similar information with th Commission as registrants in their own right, if that fact and the name of the affiliated registrant is stated. If ending reserves in any category (a), (b), or (c) above is less than 5% of the total reserves otherwise required to be reported in this schedule, that category may be omitted and that fact so noted. If the amount of the reserves attributable to 50%-or-less-owned equity investors that file this information as registrants in their own right

第210.12-18节　补充信息(适用于财险承保人)[1]

与注册人的控制性关联关系	递延保单取得成本	未付赔款和赔款调整费用准备金	C栏中扣除的任何折扣[4]	预收保费	满期保费	投资净收入	与下列期间相关的赔款和赔款调整费用准备金		递延保单取得成本摊销	已付赔款和赔款调整费用	承保保费
							(1)当年	(2)之前年度			
A栏	B栏	C栏	D栏	E栏	F栏	G栏		H栏	I栏	J栏	K栏
(a)并表财险实体[2]											
(b)非并表财险子公司[2,3]											
(c)注册人及其子公司持有50%或以下财险权益的投资对象按比例承担的份额[2,3]											

1 经审计的财务报表(包括其他附表)中已包含的信息,不必在本表中重复。B栏、C栏、D栏和E栏的信息的截止日期为资产负债表日,F栏、G栏、H栏、I栏、J栏和K栏的信息的报告期应以注册人经审计的合并财务报表中的损益表报告期为准。

2 列报进行公司间抵销之后每类实体或公司的汇总或合并数额(视具体情况而定)。

3 对于50%或以下股权被控,且本身作为注册人向证券交易委员会提交类似信息的投资对象,此处不要求提供与其相关的信息,前提是上述事实和该控制性关联注册人的名称已经列明。如果上文第(a)类、第(b)类或第(c)类中任何一类实体或公司的期末准备金低于按规定本表应报告的准备金总额的5%,该类别可予省略,并通过附注予以说明。如果50%或以下股权被控,且本身作为注册人提交该等信息的投资对象[1]的准备金数额超过

1　英文为“Investor”,但据上下文似应为“Investee”,译文已按后者处理。——译者注

exceeds 95% of the total category (c) reserves, information for the other 50%-or-less-owned equity investees need not be provided.

[4]Disclose in a footnote to this schedule the rate, or range of rates, estimated if necessary, at which the discount was computed for each category.

[49 FR 47599, Dec. 6, 1984]

for face-amount certificate investment companies

Source: Sections 210.12-21 to 210.12-41 appear at 16 FR 348, Jan. 13, 1951, unless otherwise noted. Redesignated at 45 FR 63679, Sept. 25, 1980.

§210.12-21 Investments in securities of unaffiliated issuers.

Column A—Name of issuer and title of issue[1]	Column B—Balance held at close of period. Number of shares—principal amount of bonds and notes[2]	Column C—Cost of each item[3,4]	Column D—Value of each item at close of period[3,5]

[1](a) The required information is to be given as to all securities held as of the close of the period of report. Each issue shall be listed separately.

(b) Indicate by an appropriate symbol those securities which are non-income-producing securities. Evidences of indebtedness and preferred shares may be deemed to be income-producing if, on the respective last interest payment date or dates for the declaration of dividends prior to the date of the related balance sheet, there was only a partial payment of interest or a declaration of only a partial amount of the dividends payable; in such case, however, each such issue shall be indicated by an appropriate symbol referring to a note to the effect that, on the last interest or dividend date, only partial interest was paid or partial dividends declared. If, on such respective last interest or dividend date, no interest was paid or no dividends declared, the issue shall not be deemed to be income-producing. Common shares shall not be deemed to be income-producing unless, during the last year preceding the date of the related balance sheet, there was at least one dividend paid upon such common shares. List separately (1) bonds; (2) preferred shares; (3) common shares. Within each of these subdivisions classify according to type of business, insofar as practicable: e.g., investment companies, railroads, utilities, banks, insurance companies, or industrials. Give totals for each group, subdivision, and class.

[2]Indicate any securities subject to option at the end of the most recent period and state in a note the amount subject to option, the option prices, and the dates within which such options

(c)类准备金总额的95%,则不必提供其他50%或以下股权被控的投资对象信息。

4 在本表中通过一个脚注中披露每类折扣的折扣率或折扣率范围(如有必要,可提供估计数字或范围)。

[《联邦公报》第49卷第47599页,1984年12月6日。]

适用于面额证券投资公司

行政规则来源:第210.12-21~210.12-41节,见《联邦公报》第16卷第348页,1951年1月13日,除非另有说明。重新公布索引:《联邦公报》第45卷第63679页,1980年9月25日。

第210.12-21节　对非控制性关联发行人的证券投资

A栏——发行人名称和证券发行名称[1]	B栏——期末持有余额。股数—债券和票据本金金额[2]	C栏——每项发行成本[3,4]	D栏——每项发行期末价值[3,5]

1 (a)应按规定提供报告期末持有的所有证券的相关信息。每项证券发行均应单列。

(b)通过适当符号注明不产生收益的证券。如在相关资产负债表日前相关的最后利息支付日或股息宣布日,仅支付了部分利息或仅宣布了部分应付股息,债务凭证和优先股仍可视为已产生收益。但是,在上述情形下,应用适当的符号对每项发行作出标注,并通过相应的附注说明在最后的利息支付日或股息宣布日,仅支付了部分利息或仅宣布了部分股息。如果在上述最后利息支付日或股息宣布日,未支付利息或未宣布股息,此项发行不得视为产生收益的证券发行。除非在相关资产负债表日前一年期间内至少支付了一次股息,否则普通股不得视为产生收益的证券。请分别列明:(1)债券;(2)优先股;(3)普通股。对于上述每一子类,应在可行范围内按照业务类型进行进一步划分:如投资公司、铁路、公用事业公司、银行、保险公司或工业公司。列出每个组别、子类和类别的总数。

2 列出截至最近期间期末仍受期权限制的任何证券,并在注释中说明受期权限制的数额、期权价格和期权行权期限。

may be exercised.

[3]Columns C and D shall be totaled. The totals of columns C and D should agree with the correlative amounts required to be shown by the related balance sheet captions. State in a footnote to column C the aggregate cost for Federal income tax purposes.

[4]If any investments have been written down or reserved against by such companies pursuant to §210.6-21(f), indicate each such item by means of an appropriate symbol and explain in a footnote.

[5]Where value is determined on any other basis than closing prices reported on any national securities exchange, explain such other basis in a footnote.

[47 FR 56844, Dec. 21, 1982]

§210.12-22 Investments in and advances to affiliates and income thereon.

Column A—Name of issuer and title of issue or amount of indebtedness[1]	Column B—Balance held at close of period—Number of shares—principal amount of bonds, notes and other indebtedness[2]	Column C—Cost of each item[3,4]	Column D—Amount at which carried at close of period[4,5]	Column E—Amount of dividends or interest[4,6]		Column F—Amount of equity in net profit and loss for the period[7]
				(1)—Credited to income	(2)—Other	

[1](a) The required information is to be given as to all investments in affiliates as of the close of the period. See captions 10, 13 and 20 of §210.6-22. List each issue and group separately (1) investments in majority-owned subsidiaries, segregating subsidiaries consolidated; (2) other controlled companies; and (3) other affiliates. Give totals for each group. If operations of any controlled companies are different in character from those of the registrant, group such affiliates within divisions (1) and (2) by type of activities.

(b) *Changes during the period.* If during the period there has been any increase or decrease in the amount of investment in any affiliate, state in a footnote (or if there have been changes as to numerous affiliates, in a supplementary schedule) (1) name of each issuer and title of issue; (2) balance at beginning of period; (3) gross purchases and additions; (4) gross sales and reductions; (5) balance at close of period as shown in column C. Include in such footnote or schedule comparable information as to affiliates in which there was an investment at any time during the period even though there was no investment in such affiliate as of the close of such period.

[2]Indicate any securities subject to option at the end of the most recent period and state in a footnote the amount subject to option, the option prices, and the dates within which such

3 C栏和D栏的各项数额应予加总。C栏和D栏的总数应与相关资产负债表列报的相关数额相符。在C栏脚注中说明在计征联邦所得税时适用的合计成本。

4 如果该等公司已按照第210.6-21(f)节减记投资或为投资提取准备金,应通过适当符号注明此类项目并在脚注中进行说明。

5 如果确定价值时的依据不是任何全国性证券交易所报告的收盘价格，应在脚注中说明确定该等价值的任何依据。

[《联邦公报》第47卷第56844页,1982年12月21日。]

第210.12-22节　对控制性关联方的投资和垫款以及由此产生的收益

A栏——发行人名称及证券发行名称或债务金额[1]	B栏——期末持有余额——股数——债券、票据和其他债务的本金金额[2]	C栏——每项成本[3,4]	D栏——期末持有数额[4,5]	E栏——股息或利息金额[4,6]		F栏——在期间净利润或损失中享有的权益数额[7]
				(1)——记入收益贷方	(2)——其他	

1 (a)应就报告期末持有的对所有控制性关联方的投资提供相关信息。见第210.6-22节第10项、第13项和第20项。请分别列出每项证券发行,并将投资分成下列几组:(1)对控股子公司的投资(并表子公司单列);(2)对其他受控公司的投资,以及(3)对其他控制性关联方的投资。列出每个组别的总数。如果任何受控公司的业务性质与注册人不同,应在上述第(1)组和第(2)组的基础上再按照业务活动类型,对该等控制性关联方进行进一步分组。

(b)报告期内发生的变更。如果报告期内对任何控制性关联方的投资额有所增减,应在脚注中说明如下信息(如果发生变化的控制性关联方数量众多,应通过补充附表说明):(1)每名发行人名称以及证券发行的名称;(2)期初余额;(3)购买和增加总额;(4)出售和减少总额;(5)C栏所示的期末余额。如在该期间内任何时间公司对某一控制性关联方进行过投资,即使在报告期末时并不持有该等投资,也应在脚注或附表中说明关于该等控制性关联方的可比信息。

2 注明在最近期间内受期权限制的任何证券，并在脚注中说明受期权限制的证券数额、期权价格以及期权行权期限。

options may be exercised.

[3] If the cost in column C represents other than cash expenditure, explain.

[4] (a) Columns C, D and E shall be totaled. The totals of columns C and D should agree with correlative amounts required to be shown by the related balance sheet captions. State in a footnote the aggregate cost for Federal income tax purposes.

(b) If any investments have been written down or reserved against by such companies pursuant to §210.6-21(f), indicate each such item by means of an appropriate symbol and explain in a footnote.

[5] State the basis of determining the amounts shown in column D.

[6] Show in column E(1) as to each issue held at close of period, the dividends or interest included in caption 1 of the profit and loss or income statement. In addition, show as the final item in column E(1) the aggregate dividends and interest included in the profit and loss or income statement in respect of investments in affiliates not held at the close of the period. The total of this column should agree with the amounts shown under such caption. Include in column E(2) all other dividends and interest. Explain briefly in an appropriate footnote the treatment accorded each item. Identify by an appropriate symbol all non-cash dividends and explain the circumstances in a footnote. See §§210.6-22(b) and 210.6-23(a).

[7] The information required by column F need be furnished only as to controlled companies. The equity in the net profit and loss of each person required to be listed separately shall be computed on an individual basis. In addition, there may be submitted the information required as computed on the basis of the statements of each such person and its subsidiaries consolidated.

§210.12-23 Mortgage loans on real estate and interest earned on mortgages.[1]

Part 1—Mortgage loans on real estate at close of period					Part 2—Interest earned on mortgages		
Column A—List by classification indicated below[2,3,7]	Column B—Prior liens[2]	Column C—Carrying amount of mortgage[8,9,10,11]	Column D—Amount of principal unpaid at close of period		Column E—Amount of mortgage being foreclosed	Column F—Interest due and accrued at end of period[6]	Column G—Interest income earned applicable to period[5]
			(1)—Total	(2)—Subject to delinquent interest[4]			
Liens on:							
Farms (total)							
Residential (total)							
Apartments and business (total)							
Unimproved (total)							
Total[12]							

3 如果C栏列示的成本不属于现金开支,应予说明。

4 (a)C栏、D栏和E栏的各项数额应予加总。C栏和D栏列出的总额应当与相关资产负债表科目中要求列示的相关数额相符。在脚注中说明计征联邦税收时适用的合计成本。

(b)如果该等公司已按照第210.6-21(f)节减记投资或为投资提取准备金,应通过适当符号注明此类项目并在脚注中作出说明。

5 说明确定D栏数额的依据。

6 在E(1)栏中,针对期末持有的每项发行,列示损益表第一个科目中包含的股息或利息。此外,将损益表中与未在期末持有的对控制性关联方投资相关的股息和利息总额作为E(1)栏的最后一项列明。本栏的总额应与该项目下列示的数额相符。在E(2)栏中计入其他股息和利息。通过适当的脚注简要说明对每个科目的处理方法。通过适当符号注明所有非现金股息,并在脚注中说明具体情形。参见第210.6-22(b)节和第210.6-23(a)节。

7 F栏要求提供的信息仅适用于受控公司。每个按规定应单独列报的主体在净利润和损失中享有的权益数额均应单独计算。此外,按规定应提交的信息可基于每一该等主体及其并表子公司的报表计算。

第210.12-23节　房地产抵押贷款以及从抵押中赚取的利息[1]

第1部分—期末房地产抵押贷款					第2部分—从抵押中赚取的利息		
A栏——基于下述分类的列表[2,3,7]	B栏——第一顺位留置权[2]	C栏——抵押品账面金额[8,9,10,11]	D栏——期末未付本金数额		E栏——被止赎的抵押品数额	F栏——期末到期和应计利息[6]	G栏——计入报告期的利息收益[5]
			(1)总计	(2)需支付拖欠利息的部分[4]			
下列各项上设置的留置权:							
农场(总数)							
住宅(总数)							
公寓和企业(总数)							
未利用的土地(总数)							
总计[12]							

[1] All money columns shall be totaled.

[2] If mortgages represent other than first liens, list separately in a schedule in a like manner, indicating briefly the nature of the lien. Information need not be furnished as to such liens which are fully insured or wholly guaranteed by an agency of the United States Government.

[3] In a separate schedule classify by states in which the mortgaged property is located the total amounts in support of columns B, C, D and E.

[4] (a) Interest in arrears for less than 3 months may be disregarded in computing the total amount of principal subject to delinquent interest.

(b) Of the total principal amount, state the amount acquired from controlled and other affiliates.

[5] In order to reconcile the total of column G with the amount shown in the profit and loss or income statement, interest income earned applicable to period from mortgages sold or canceled during period should be added to the total of this column.

[6] If the information required by columns F and G is not reasonably available because the obtaining thereof would involve unreasonable effort or expense, such information may be omitted if the registrant shall include a statement showing that unreasonable effort or expense would be involved. In such an event, state in column G for each of the above classes of mortgage loans the average gross rate of interest on mortgage loans held at the end of the fiscal period.

[7] Each mortgage loan included in column C in an amount in excess of $500,000 shall be listed separately. Loans from $100,000 to $500,000 shall be grouped by $50,000 groups, indicating the number of loans in each group.

[8] In a footnote to this schedule, furnish a reconciliation, in the following form, of the carrying amount of mortgage loans at the beginning of the period with the total amount shown in column C:

Balance at beginning of period		$	
Additions during period:			
New mortgage loans		$	
Other (describe)			
Deductions during period:			
Collections of principal		$	
Foreclosures			
Cost of mortgages sold			
Amortization of premium			
Other (describe)			
Balance at close of period		$	

1 所有涉及钱款的栏目均应列出总数。

2 如果抵押权不属于第一顺位留置权,应以类似方式通过附表单独列出,简要说明该留置权的性质。对于已提供完全保险或获得美国政府机关全额担保的留置权,不必提供相关信息。

3 通过一个单独附表,将B栏、C栏、D栏和E栏的总数额按照被抵押的房地产所在的州进行分类。

4 (a)在计算应付拖欠利息的本金部分时,可忽略欠付期限短于3个月的利息。

(b)在本金总额中,注明从受控的控制性关联方和其他控制性关联方取得的数额。

5 为使G栏的总数与损益表列示的数额相符,在此栏总数中应当加入因报告期内出售或撤销的抵押赚取的利息收益。

6 如果获取F栏和G栏要求的信息需要耗费过高的精力或费用,可免予提供该等信息,但是注册人应就此作出声明。在此情形下,应在G栏中说明在会计期间期末持有的上述各类别抵押贷款的平均总利率。

7 C栏中包含的数额超过50万美元的抵押贷款应当单独列示。10万美元~50万美元之间的贷款应当以5万美元为一单位进行分组,并注明每一组的贷款数量。

8 在本表的脚注中,提供期初抵押贷款的账面金额与C栏总数的对账调整表,格式如下:

期初余额		$	
本期增加额:			
新增抵押贷款		$	
其他(请说明)			
本期减少额:			
本金回收		$	
止赎数额			
已出售的抵押品之成本			
溢价摊销			
其他(请说明)			
期末余额		$	

If additions represent other than cash expenditures, explain. If any of the changes during the period result from transactions, directly or indirectly with affiliates, explain the bases of such transactions, and amounts involved. State the aggregate amount of mortgages (a) renewed and (b) extended. If the carrying amount of the new mortgages is in excess of the unpaid amount (not including interest) of prior mortgages, explain.

[9] If any item of mortgage loans on real estate investments has been written down or reserved against pursuant to §210.6–21 describe the item and explain the basis for the write–down or reserve.

[10] State in a footnote to column C the aggregate cost for Federal income tax purposes.

[11] If the total amount shown in column C includes intercompany profits, state the bases of the transactions resulting in such profits and, if practicable, state the amounts thereof.

[12] Summarize the aggregate amounts for each column applicable to captions 6(b), 6(c) and 12 of §210.6–22.

[16 FR 348, Jan. 13, 1951, as amended at 16 FR 2655, Mar. 24, 1951]

§210.12–24 Real estate owned and rental income.[1]

Part 1—Real estate owned at end of period							Part 2—Rental income		
Column A—List classification of property as indicated below[2,3]	Column B—Amount of incombrances	Column C—Initial cost to company	Column D—Cost of improvements, etc.	Column E—Amount at which carried at close of period[4,5,6,7]	Column F—Reserve for depreciation	Column G—Rents due and accrued at end of period	Column H—Total rental income applicable to period	Column I—Expended for interest, taxes, repairs and expenses	Column J—Net income applicable to period
Farms									
Residential									
Apartments and business									
Unimproved									
Total[8]									
Rent from properties sold during period									
Total									

[1] All money columns shall be totaled.

[2] Each item of property included in column E in an amount in excess of $100,000 shall be listed separately.

如果增加额不属于现金支出,应予说明。如果报告期内的变更由与控制性关联方开展的直接或间接交易所导致,应说明该等交易的基础以及所涉金额。列明(a)续展抵押,以及(b)延期抵押的总额。如果新增抵押的账面金额高于之前抵押的未付数额(不含利息),应予说明。

9 如果任何已按照第210.6-21节减记房地产投资抵押贷款项目或为之提取准备金,应对该等项目作出说明,并说明减记和提取准备金的依据。

10 在C栏的脚注中注明计征联邦所得税时适用的合计成本。

11 如果C栏列示的总数包括公司间利润,注明产生该等利润的交易基础以及(如可行)交易金额。

12 将适用第210.6-22节第6(b)科目、第6(c)科目和第12科目的每一栏目的总数进行汇总。

[《联邦公报》第16卷第348页,1951年1月13日,修正索引:《联邦公报》第16卷第2655页,1951年3月24日。]

第210.12-24节　自有房地产和租金收入[1]

第1部分—期末自有房地产							第2部分—租金收入		
A栏——基于下述分类的房地产列表[2,3]	B栏——权利负担数额	C栏——公司的初始成本	D栏——改建工程等的成本	E栏——期末结存数额[4,5,6,7]	F栏——折旧准备金	G栏——期末到期和应计租金	H栏——报告期内租金总收入	I栏——已支出的利息、税金、维修和费用	J栏——报告期内净收益
农场									
住宅									
公寓和企业									
未利用的土地									
总数[8]									
报告期内出售物业的租金									
总计									

1 所有涉及款项的栏目均应进行加总。

2 E栏中价值超过10万美元的房地产应当单独列示。

[3] In a separate schedule classify by states in which the real estate owned is located the total amounts in support of columns E and F.

[4] In a footnote to this schedule, furnish a reconciliation, in the following form, of the total amount at which real estate was carried at the beginning of the period with the total amount shown in column E:

If additions, except acquisitions through foreclosure, represent other than cash expenditures, explain. If any of the changes during the period result from transactions, directly or indirectly, with affiliates, explain and state the amount of any intercompany gain or loss.

Balance at beginning of period		$	
Additions during period:			
Acquisitions through foreclosure	$		
Other acquisitions			
Improvements, etc.			
Other (describe)			
Deductions during period:			
Cost of real estate sold	$		
Other (describe)			
Balance at close of period		$	

[5] If any item of real estate investments has been written down or reserved against pursuant to §210.6-21(f), describe the item and explain the basis for the write-down or reserve.

[6] State in a footnote to column E the aggregate cost for Federal income tax purposes.

[7] The amount of all intercompany profits included in the total of column E shall be stated if material.

[8] Summarize the aggregate amounts for each column applicable to captions 7 and 12 of §210.6-22.

[16 FR 348, Jan. 13, 1951, as amended at 16 FR 2655, Mar. 24, 1951. Redesignated at 45 FR 63679, Sept. 25, 1980]

§210.12-25 Supplementary profit and loss information.

[1] Amounts resulting from transactions with affiliates shall be stated separately.

[2] State separately each category of expense representing more than 5 percent of the total expense shown under this item.

3 通过一个单独附表,将E栏和F栏的总数按照自有房地产所在州进行分类。

4 通过本表的一个脚注,提供期初房地产结存总额与E栏总数的对账调整表,格式如下:

如果增加额(通过止赎取得的数额除外)不属于现金支出,应予说明。如果该期间的任何变更由与控制性关联方之间的直接或间接交易所导致,应予说明,并注明公司间任何损益的数额。

期初余额		$	
本期增加额:			
通过止赎取得的数额	$		
通过其他方式取得的数额			
改建工程等			
其他(请说明)			
本期减少额:			
已出售房地产的成本	$		
其他(请说明)			
期末余额		$	

5 如果任何已按照第210.6-21(f)节减记房地产投资项目或为之提供准备金,应对该等项目作出说明,并说明减记或准备金的依据。

6 在E栏的附注中说明计征联邦所得税时适用的合计成本。

7 列出E栏总数中包含的所有大额公司间利润。

8 将适用第210.6-22节第7项和第12项的每一栏目的总数汇总。

[《联邦公报》第16卷第348页,1951年1月13日,修正索引:《联邦公报》第16卷第2655页,1951年3月24日。重新公布索引:《联邦公报》第45卷第63679页,1980年9月25日。]

第210.12-25节　补充利润或损失信息

1 由与控制性关联方进行交易产生的数额应当单独列示。

2 占本科目总费用5%以上的每类费用均应单独列示。

Column A—Item[1]	Column B—Charged to investment expense	Column C—Charged to other accounts		Column D—Total
		(1)—Account	(2)—Amount	
1. Legal expenses (including those in connection with any matter, measure or proceeding before legislative bodies, officers or government departments)				
2. Advertising and publicity				
3. Sales promotion[2]				
4. Payments directly and indirectly to trade associations and service organizations, and contributions to other organizations				

§210.12–26 Certificate reserves.

Column A—Description[1]	Column B—Balance at beginning of period			Column C—Additions			Column D—Deductions			Column E—Balance at close of period		
	(1)—Number of accounts with security bidders	(2)—Amount of maturity value	(3)—Amount of reserved[2]	(1)—Charged to profit and loss or income	(2)—Reserve payments by certificate holders	(3)—Charged to other accounts describe	(1)—Maturities	(2)—Cash surenders prior to maturity	(3)—Other—describe	(1)—Number of accounts with security holders	(2)—Amount of maturity value	(3)—Amount of reserves[2]

[1] (a) Each series of certificates shall be stated separately. The description shall include the yield to maturity on an annual payment basis.

(b) For certificates of the installment type, information required by columns B, D (2) and (3) and E shall be given by age groupings, according to the number of months paid by security holders, grouped to show those upon which 1–12 monthly payments have been made, 13–24 payments, etc..

[2] (a) If the total of the reserves shown in these columns differs from the total of the reserves per the accounts, there should be stated (i) the aggregate difference and (ii) the difference on a $1,000 face–amount certificate basis.

(b) There shall be shown by footnote or by supplemental schedule (i) the amounts periodically credited to each class of security holders' accounts from installment payments and (ii) such other amounts periodically credited to accumulate the maturity amount of the certificate. Such information shall be stated on a $1,000 face–amount certificate basis for the

A栏——项目[1]	B栏——记入投资费用借方	C栏——记入其他账目借方		D栏——总数
		(1)账目	(2)数额	
1. 法律费用(包括与立法机构、官员或政府部门处理的任何问题、采取的措施或开展的程序有关的费用)				
2. 广告和宣传费				
3. 促销费用[2]				
4. 对行业协会和服务组织的直接和间接付款,以及向其他组织缴存的款项				

第210.12-26节 证券准备金

A栏——说明[1]	B栏——期初余额			C栏——增加额			D栏——减少额			E栏——期末余额		
	(1)证券竞买人账户数量	(2)到期值数额	(3)已计提准备金的数额[2]	(1)记入利润和损失或收益借方	(2)面额证券持有人准备金缴款	(3)记入其他账户借方(请说明)	(1)到期日	(2)到期日前交回的现金	(3)其他——请说明	(1)证券持有人账户数量	(2)到期值数额	(3)准备金数额[2]

1 (a)应单独列示每一系列的证券。项目说明应当包含年付到期收益率。

(b)对于分期付款型的证券,B栏、D(2)栏、D(3)栏以及E栏要求提供的信息应当根据证券持有人已付款的月数分组,将已支付1~12个月款项的和已支付13~24个月款项的证券等予以区分。

2 (a)如果该等栏目中列示的准备金总数与账户中列示的总数不同,应当说明:(i)总差额,以及(ii)以1000美元面额证券为单位表示的差额。

(b)通过脚注或补充附表说明:(i)定期记入每类证券持有人账户贷方的分期付款数额;以及(ii)定期累计记入面额证券到期价值贷方的其他数额。上述信息应当为整个面额证券有效期内的,以1000美元面额证券为单位表示的信息。

term of the certificate.

§210.12–27 Qualified assets on deposit.[1]

Column A—Name of depositary[2]	Column B—Cash	Column C—Investments in securities	Column D—First mortgages and other first liens on real estate	Column E—Other	Column F—Total[3]

[1] All money columns shall be totaled.

[2] Classify names of individual depositaries under group headings, such as banks and states.

[3] Total of column F shall agree with note required by caption 11 of §210.6–22 as to total amount of qualified Assets on Deposit.

for certain real estate companies

§210.12–28 Real estate and accumulated depreciation.[1]

[For Certain Real Estate Companies]

Column A—Description[2]	Column B—Encumbrances	Column C—Initial cost to company		Column D—Cost capitalized subsequent to acquisition		Column E—Gross amount of which carried at close of period[3,4,5,6,7]			Column F—Accumulated depreciation	Column G—Date of construction	Column H—Date acquired	Column I—Life on which depreciation in latest income statements is computed
		Land	Buildings and improvements	Improvements	Carrying costs	Land	Buildings and improvements	Total				

[1] All money columns shall be totaled.

[2] The description for each property should include type of property (e.g., unimproved land, shopping center, garden apartments, etc.) and the geographical location.

[3] The required information is to be given as to each individual investment included in column E except that an amount not exceeding 5 percent of the total of column E may be listed in one amount as "miscellaneous investments."

[4] In a note to this schedule, furnish a reconciliation, in the following form, of the total amount at which real estate was carried at the beginning of each period for which income statements are required, with the total amount shown in column E:

第210.12-27节　合格存管资产[1]

A栏——存管机构名称[2]	B栏——现金	C栏——证券投资	D栏——第一抵押权和其他房地产第一顺位留置权	E栏——其他	F栏——总计[3]

1 所有涉及款项的栏目均应予加总。

2 将各存管机构按照“银行”、“州”等组别分组。

3 F栏总数应当与第210.6-22节第11项要求提供的注释中所列合格存管资产的总数一致。

适用于特定房地产公司

第210.12-28节　房地产和累计折旧[1]

［适用于特定房地产公司］

A栏——说明[2]	B栏——权利负担	C栏——公司的初始成本		D栏——取得之后资本化的成本		E栏——期末结存总额[3,4,5,6,7]			F栏——累计折旧	G栏——施工日期	H栏——取得日期	I栏——最近一期损益表计算折旧时采用的使用寿命
		土地	建筑物和改建工程	改建工程	持有成本	土地	建筑物和改建工程	总计				

1 所有涉及款项的栏目均应予加总。

2 每项房地产的说明均应包含房地产类型(如未利用土地、购物中心、花园公寓等)以及地理位置信息。

3 应当针对E栏包含的每项单独投资分别提供信息，对于数额不超过E栏总数5%的投资,可以在“杂项投资”下合并为一个数额提供。

4 通过本表的一个附注,针对应提交损益表的每个报告期的期初房地产结存总额与E栏总数提供一份对账调整表,格式如下:

Balance at beginning of period		$						
Additions during period:								
Acquisitions through foreclosure	$							
Other acquisitions								
Improvements, etc.								
Other (describe)		$						
Deductions during period:								
Cost of real estate sold	$							
Other (describe)								
Balance at close of period		$						

If additions, except acquisitions through foreclosure, represent other than cash expenditures, explain. If any of the changes during the period result from transactions, directly or indirectly with affiliates, explain the bases of such transactions and state the amounts involved.

A similar reconciliation shall be furnished for the accumulated depreciation.

[5] If any item of real estate investments has been written down or reserved against, describe the item and explain the basis for the write-down or reserve.

[6] State in a note to column E the aggregate cost for Federal income tax purposes.

[7] The amount of all intercompany profits included in the total of column E shall be stated if material.

[38 FR 6068, Mar. 6, 1983. Redesignated at 45 FR 63630, Sept. 25, 1980]

§210.12-29 Mortgage loans on real estate.[1]

[For Certain Real Estate Companies]

Column A—Description[2,3,4]	Column B—Interest rate	Column C—Final maturity date	Column D—Periodic payment terms[5]	Column E—Prior liens	Column F—Face amount of mortgages	Column G—Carrying amount of mortgages[3,6,7,8,9]	Column H—Principal amount of loans subject to delinquent principal or interest[10]

[1] All money columns shall be totaled.

[2] The required information is to be given for each individual mortgage loan which exceeds three percent of the total of column G.

期初余额		$						
本期增加额:								
通过止赎取得的数额	$							
通过其他方式取得的数额								
改建工程等								
其他(请说明)		$						
本期减少额:								
已出售房地产的成本	$							
其他(请说明)								
期末余额		$						

如果增加额(通过止赎取得的数额除外)不属于现金支出,应予说明。如果该期间的任何变更由与控制性关联方开展的直接或间接交易所导致,请说明该等交易的基础以及交易所涉金额。

对于累计折旧,应提供一份类似的对账调整表。

5 如果任何已减记房地产投资项目或已为之提供准备金，应对该等项目作出说明，并说明减记和准备金的依据。

6 在E栏的附注中说明计征联邦所得税时适用的合计成本。

7 列出E栏总数中包含的所有大额公司间利润。

[《联邦公报》第38卷第6068页,1983年3月6日,重新公布索引:《联邦公报》第45卷第63630页,1980年9月25日。]

第210.12-29节　房地产抵押贷款[1]

[适用于特定房地产公司]

A栏——项目说明[2,3,4]	B栏——利率	C栏——最后到期日	D栏——定期付款条件[5]	E栏——优先留置权	F栏——抵押品面值	G栏——抵押品账面金额[3,6,7,8,9]	H栏——存在拖欠本金或利息的贷款的本金数额[10]

1 所有涉及款项栏目均应予加总。

2 对于数额超过G栏总数3%的每项抵押贷款,均应分别按规定提供相关信息。

[3] If the portfolio includes large numbers of mortgages most of which are less than three percent of column G, the mortgages not required to be reported separately should be grouped by classifications that will indicate the dispersion of the portfolio, *i.e.*, for a portfolio of mortgages on single family residential housing. The description should also include number of loans by original loan amounts (e.g., over $100,000, $50,000–$99,999, $20,000–$49,000, under $20,000) and type loan (e.g., VA, FHA, Conventional). Interest rates and maturity dates may be stated in terms of ranges. Data required by columns D, E and F may be omitted for mortgages not required to be reported individually.

[4] Loans should be grouped by categories, e.g., first mortgage, second mortgage, construction loans, etc., and for each loan the type of property, e.g., shopping center, high rise apartments, etc., and its geographic location should be stated.

[5] State whether principal and interest is payable at level amount over life to maturity or at varying amounts over life to maturity. State amount of balloon payment at maturity, if any. Also state prepayment penalty terms, if any.

[6] In a note to this schedule, furnish a reconciliation, in the following form, of the carrying amount of mortgage loans at the beginning of each period for which income statements are required, with the total amount shown in column G:

Balance at beginning of period		$	
Additions during period:			
New mortgage loans	$		
Other (describe)		$	
Deductions during period:			
Collections of principal	$		
Foreclosures			
Cost of mortgages sold			
Amortization of premium			
Other (describe)			
Balance at close of period		$	

If additions represent other than cash expenditures, explain. If any of the changes during the period result from transactions, directly or indirectly with affiliates, explain the bases of such transactions, and state the amounts involved. State the aggregate mortgages (a) renewed and (b) extended. If the carrying amount of new mortgages is in excess of the unpaid amount of the extended mortgages, explain.

[7] If any item of mortgage loans on real estate investments has been written down or reserved against, describe the item and explain the basis for the write–down or reserve.

[8] State in a note to column G the aggregate cost for Federal income tax purposes.

3 如果贷款组合中包含大量抵押贷款,且其中大部分数额均低于G栏总额的3%,则不必单独报告的抵押贷款应当按照类别进行分组,以表明贷款组合的分布状况,例如,对于独户住宅抵押贷款组合,该项说明还应包括不同本金数额(如超过10万美元、5万~9.9999万美元、2万~4.9万美元和2万美元以下)和类型(联邦住房管理局贷款、退伍军人贷款和传统贷款)的贷款数量。利率和到期日可以用一个范围来表示。不必单独报告的抵押贷款可免予提供D栏、E栏和F栏要求提供的信息。

4 贷款应当按照类型分组,例如第一抵押权贷款、第二抵押权贷款、施工贷款等,并且每项贷款均应注明房地产类型(如购物中心、高层公寓等)以及地理区域。

5 说明在贷款期间内本金和利息的偿还方式是等额分期偿还,还是不等额分期偿还。如贷款到期时存在大额尾付款的,应予说明。同时说明提前还款的违约金条款(如有)。

6 通过本表的一个附注,针对应提交损益表的每个期间期初抵押贷款结存总额与G栏总数提供一份对账调整表,格式如下:

期初余额		$	
本期增加额:			
新增抵押贷款	$		
其他(请说明)		$	
本期减少额:			
收回的本金	$		
止赎的数额			
出售的抵押品的成本			
溢价摊销			
其他(请说明)			
期末余额		$	

如果增加额不属于现金支出,应予说明。如果期间内的任何变更由与控制性关联方开展的直接或间接交易所导致,请说明该等交易的基础以及交易所涉金额。注明(a)已续展抵押,以及(b)已延期抵押的总数额。如果新抵押贷款的账面金额超过延期抵押贷款的未付数额,说明原因。

7 如果已减记房地产投资抵押贷款或已为之提供准备金,应对该等项目作出说明,并说明减记和准备金的依据。

8 在G栏的附注中说明计征联邦所得税时适用的合计成本。

[9] The amount of all intercompany profits in the total of column G shall be stated, if material.

[10] (a) Interest in arrears for less than 3 months may be disregarded in computing the total amount of principal subject to delinquent interest.

(b) Of the total principal amount, state the amount acquired from controlled and other affiliates.

[38 FR 6069, Mar. 6, 1973; 38 FR 7323, Mar. 20, 1973. Redesignated at 45 FR 63680, Sept. 25, 1980]

9 列出G栏总数中包含的所有大额公司间利润。

10 (a)在计算存在拖欠利息的本金总数时滞纳时间不超过3个月的迟付利息可忽略不计。

(b)在本金总额中,注明从受控公司和其他控制性关联方取得的数额。

[《联邦公报》第38卷第6069页,1973年3月6日;《联邦公报》第38卷第7323页,1973年3月20日。重新公布索引:《联邦公报》第45卷第63680页,1980年9月25日。]

PART 211—INTERPRETATIONS RELATING TO FINANCIAL REPORTING MATTERS

Subpart A Financial Reporting Releases

Subject	Release No.	Date	Fed. Reg. Vol. and page
Codification of financial reporting policies	1	Apr. 15, 1982	47 FR 21030
Disclosure considerations relating to foreign operations and foreign currency translation effects	6	Nov. 18, 1982	47 FR 53330
Accounting for extinguishment of debt	15	Dec. 22, 1983	49 FR 54
Certification of financial statements	16	Feb. 15, 1984	49 FR 6707
Independence of accountants	291	Apr. 10, 1981	46 FR 22569
Last-In, First-Out method of accounting for inventories	889	July 2, 1981	46 FR 36127
Significance of oral guarantees to the financial reporting process	22	Dec. 19, 1985	50 FR 51671
Disclosure of the effects of the Tax Reform Act of 1986	26	Oct. 30, 1986	51 FR 39652
Accounting for loan losses by registrants engaged in lending activities	28	Dec. 1, 1986	51 FR 44446
Statement of the Commission Regarding Disclosure Obligations of Companies Affected by the Government's Defense Contract Procurement Inquiry and Related Issues	32	Aug. 1, 1988	53 FR 29226
Management's Discussion and Analysis of Financial Condition and Results of Operations; Certain Investment Company Disclosures	36	May 18, 1989	54 FR 22427

第211部分——关于财务报告事项的解释

第A子部分 财务报告公告

主题	公告编号	日期	《联邦公报》卷数和页码
《财务报告政策汇编》	1	1982年4月15日	《联邦公报》第47卷第21030页
与外国经营和外国货币折算影响有关的披露考量因素	6	1982年11月18日	《联邦公报》第47卷第53330页
债务清偿会计	15	1983年12月22日	《联邦公报》第49卷第54页
财务报表证明	16	1984年2月15日	《联邦公报》第49卷第6707页
会计师独立性	291	1981年4月10日	《联邦公报》第46卷第22569页
后进先出存货会计法	889	1981年7月2日	《联邦公报》第46卷第36127页
财务报告流程中口头保证的重要性	22	1985年12月19日	《联邦公报》第50卷第51671页
《1986年税收改革法》影响的披露	26	1986年10月30日	《联邦公报》第51卷第39652页
从事贷款业务的注册人的贷款损失会计	28	1986年12月1日	《联邦公报》第51卷第44446页
《证券交易委员会关于受政府国防合同采购询价影响的公司披露义务及相关事宜的说明》	32	1988年8月1日	《联邦公报》第53卷第29226页
《管理层关于财务状况和经营成果的讨论与分析》;《特定投资公司的披露》	36	1989年5月18日	《联邦公报》第54卷第22427页

Subject	Release No.	Date	Fed. Reg. Vol. and page
Acceptability in financial statements of an accounting standard permitting the return of a nonaccrual loan to accrual status after a partial charge-off	37	July 29, 1991	56 FR 37000
Statement of the Commission Regarding Disclosure Obligations of Municipal Securities Issuers and Others	42	Mar. 9, 1994	59 FR 12758
Interpretation Regarding Substantive Repossession of Collateral	28A	May 12, 1994	59 FR 26109
Financial Statements and Periodic Reports For Related Issuers and Guarantors, Appendices A, B and C	55	Aug. 4, 2000	65 FR 51710
Bookkeeping Services Provided by Auditors to Audit Clients in Emergency or Other Unusual Situations	57	Sept. 14, 2001	66 FR 48336
Calculation of Average Weekly Trading Volume	58A	Sept. 27, 2001	66 FR 49274
Management's Discussion and Analysis of Financial Condition and Results of Operations	72	Dec. 19, 2003	68 FR 75065
Commission Guidance Regarding the Public Company Accounting Oversight Board's Auditing and Related Professional Practice Standard No. 1	73	May 20, 2004	69 FR 29066
Modernization of Oil and Gas Reporting	78	Dec. 31, 2008	74 FR 2192
Technical Amendments to Rules, Forms, Schedules and Codification of Financial Reporting Policies	79	Apr. 15, 2009	74 FR 18617
Commission Guidance Regarding the Financial Accounting Standards Board's Accounting Standards Codification	80A	Aug. 18, 2009	74 FR 42773
Commission Guidance Regarding Disclosure Related to Climate Change	82	Feb. 2, 2010	75 FR 6297
Commission Guidance on Presentation of Liquidity and Capital Resources Disclosures in Management's Discussion and Analysis	83	Sept. 17, 2010	75 FR 59896

续表

主题	公告编告	日期	《联邦公报》卷数和页码
财务报表中使用允许在对坏账进行部分冲销后将停息贷款转变为计息状态的会计准则的可接受性	37	1991 年 7 月 29 日	《联邦公报》第 56 卷第 37000 页
《证券交易委员会关于市政证券发行人及其他人的披露义务的说明》	42	1994 年 3 月 9 日	《联邦公报》第 59 卷第 12758 页
《关于实质重新占有担保品的解释》	28A	1994 年 5 月 12 日	《联邦公报》第 59 卷第 26109 页
《相关发行人和担保人的财务报表和定期报告》、附件 A、附件 B 和附件 C	55	2000 年 8 月 4 日	《联邦公报》第 65 卷第 51710 页
《在紧急情况或其他非常规情况下审计师为审计客户提供的簿记服务》	57	2001 年 9 月 14 日	《联邦公报》第 66 卷第 48336 页
《周均交易量的计算》	58A	2001 年 9 月 27 日	《联邦公报》第 66 卷第 49274 页
《管理层关于财务状况和经营成果的讨论与分析》	72	2003 年 12 月 19 日	《联邦公报》第 68 卷第 75065 页
《证券交易委员会关于公众公司会计监督委员会的审计及相关专业做法标准的第 1 号指导意见》	73	2004 年 5 月 20 日	《联邦公报》第 69 卷第 29066 页
《石油和天然气报告的现代化》	78	2008 年 12 月 31 日	《联邦公报》第 74 卷第 2192 页
《对规则、表格、附表和〈财务报告政策汇编〉的技术性修正》	79	2009 年 4 月 15 日	《联邦公报》第 74 卷第 18617 页
《证券交易委员会关于财务会计准则委员会的会计准则汇编的指导意见》	80A	2009 年 8 月 18 日	《联邦公报》第 74 卷第 42773 页
《证券交易委员会关于气候变化相关披露的指导意见》	82	2010 年 2 月 2 日	《联邦公报》第 75 卷第 6297 页
《证券交易委员会关于在管理层讨论与分析中列报流动性和资本来源披露的指导意见》	83	2010 年 9 月 17 日	《联邦公报》第 75 卷第 59896 页

Subpart B Staff Accounting Bulletins

Subject	Release No.	Date	Fed. Reg. Vol. and page
Publication of Staff Accounting Bulletin No. 39	SAB - 39	Oct. 15, 1980	45 FR 68388
Publication of Staff Accounting Bulletin No. 40	SAB - 40	Feb. 9, 1981	46 FR 11513
Publication of Staff Accounting Bulletin No. 41	SAB - 41	Feb. 18, 1981	46 FR 12698
Publication of Staff Accounting Bulletin No. 42	SAB - 42	Dec. 23, 1981	46 FR 63252
Publication of Staff Accounting Bulletin No. 43	SAB - 43	Jan. 5, 1982	47 FR 1266
Publication of Staff Accounting Bulletin No. 44	SAB - 44	Mar. 3, 1982	47 FR 10789
Publication of Staff Accounting Bulletin No. 45	SAB - 45	May 20, 1982	47 FR 23915
Publication of Staff Accounting Bulletin No. 46	SAB - 46	May 20, 1982	47 FR 23916
Publication of Staff Accounting Bulletin No. 47	SAB - 47	Sept. 16, 1982	47 FR 41727
Publication of Staff Accounting Bulletin No. 48	SAB - 48	Sept. 27, 1982	47 FR 43673
Publication of Staff Accounting Bulletin No. 47A	SAB - 47A	Sept. 29, 1982	47 FR 44722
Publication of Staff Accounting Bulletin No. 49	SAB - 49	Oct. 26, 1982	47 FR 49628
Publication of Staff Accounting Bulletin No. 49A	SAB - 49A	Jan. 18, 1983	48 FR 3585
Publication of Staff Accounting Bulletin No. 50	SAB - 50	Mar. 3, 1983	48 FR 10043
Publication of Staff Accounting Bulletin No. 51	SAB - 51	Mar. 29, 1983	48 FR 14595

第B子部分　工作人员会计公告

主题	公告编号	日期	《联邦公报》卷数和页码
《工作人员会计公告第39号》	SAB-39	1980年10月15日	《联邦公报》第45卷第68388页
《工作人员会计公告第40号》	SAB-40	1981年2月9日	《联邦公报》第46卷第11513页
《工作人员会计公告第41号》	SAB-41	1981年2月18日	《联邦公报》第46卷第12698页
《工作人员会计公告第42号》	SAB-42	1981年12月23日	《联邦公报》第46卷第63252页
《工作人员会计公告第43号》	SAB-43	1982年1月5日	《联邦公报》第47卷第1266页
《工作人员会计公告第44号》	SAB-44	1982年3月3日	《联邦公报》第47卷第10789页
《工作人员会计公告第45号》	SAB-45	1982年5月20日	《联邦公报》第47卷第23915页
《工作人员会计公告第46号》	SAB-46	1982年5月20日	《联邦公报》第47卷第23916页
《工作人员会计公告第47号》	SAB-47	1982年9月16日	《联邦公报》第47卷第41727页
《工作人员会计公告第48号》	SAB-48	1982年9月27日	《联邦公报》第47卷第43673页
《工作人员会计公告第47A号》	SAB-47A	1982年9月29日	《联邦公报》第47卷第44722页
《工作人员会计公告第49号》	SAB-49	1982年10月26日	《联邦公报》第47卷第49628页
《工作人员会计公告第49A号》	SAB-49A	1983年1月18日	《联邦公报》第48卷第3585页
《工作人员会计公告第50号》	SAB-50	1983年3月3日	《联邦公报》第48卷第10043页
《工作人员会计公告第51号》	SAB-51	1983年3月29日	《联邦公报》第48卷第14595页

Subject	Release No.	Date	Fed. Reg. Vol. and page
Publication of Staff Accounting Bulletin No. 52	SAB – 52	May 16, 1983	48 FR 23173
Publication of Staff Accounting Bulletin No. 53 [Reserved]			
Publication of Staff Accounting Bulletin No. 54	SAB – 54	Nov. 3, 1983	48 FR 51769
Publication of Staff Accounting Bulletin No. 55	SAB – 55	Nov. 30, 1983	48 FR 54811
Publication of Staff Accounting Bulletin No. 56	SAB – 56	Jan. 1, 1984	49 FR 4936
Publication of Staff Accounting Bulletin No. 58	SAB – 58	Mar. 19, 1985	50 FR 11657
Publication of Staff Accounting Bulletin No. 59	SAB – 59	Sept. 13, 1985	50 FR 37346
Publication of Staff Accounting Bulletin No. 60	SAB – 60	Dec. 27, 1985	50 FR 52916
Publication of Staff Accounting Bulletin No. 42A	SAB – 42A	Jan. 8, 1986	51 FR 739
Publication of Staff Accounting Bulletin No. 61	SAB – 61	May 6, 1986	51 FR 17331
Publication of Staff Accounting Bulletin No. 62	SAB – 62	July 7, 1986	51 FR 25194
Publication of Staff Accounting Bulletin No. 63	SAB – 63	Sept. 24, 1986	51 FR 33886
Publication of Staff Accounting Bulletin No. 64	SAB – 64	Oct. 8, 1986	51 FR 36007
Publication of Staff Accounting Bulletin No. 65	SAB – 65	Nov. 13, 1986	51 FR 41080
Publication of Staff Accounting Bulletin No. 66	SAB – 66	Nov. 25, 1986	51 FR 43594

续表

主题	公告编号	日期	《联邦公报》卷数和页码
《工作人员会计公告第52号》	SAB-52	1983年5月16日	《联邦公报》第48卷第23173页
《工作人员会计公告第53号[保留]》			
《工作人员会计公告第54号》	SAB-54	1983年11月3日	《联邦公报》第48卷第51769页
《工作人员会计公告第55号》	SAB-55	1983年11月30日	《联邦公报》第48卷第54811页
《工作人员会计公告第56号》	SAB-56	1984年1月1日	《联邦公报》第49卷第4936页
《工作人员会计公告第58号》	SAB-58	1985年3月19日	《联邦公报》第50卷第11657页
《工作人员会计公告第59号》	SAB-59	1985年9月13日	《联邦公报》第50卷第37346页
《工作人员会计公告第60号》	SAB-60	1985年12月27日	《联邦公报》第50卷第52916页
《工作人员会计公告第42A号》	SAB-42A	1986年1月8日	《联邦公报》第51卷第739页
《工作人员会计公告第61号》	SAB-61	1986年5月6日	《联邦公报》第51卷第17331页
《工作人员会计公告第62号》	SAB-62	1986年7月7日	《联邦公报》第51卷第25194页
《工作人员会计公告第63号》	SAB-63	1986年9月24日	《联邦公报》第51卷第33886页
《工作人员会计公告第64号》	SAB-64	1986年10月8日	《联邦公报》第51卷第36007页
《工作人员会计公告第65号》	SAB-65	1986年11月13日	《联邦公报》第51卷第41080页
《工作人员会计公告第66号》	SAB-66	1986年11月25日	《联邦公报》第51卷第43594页

Subject	Release No.	Date	Fed. Reg. Vol. and page
Publication of Staff Accounting Bulletin No. 67	SAB – 67	Dec. 8, 1986	51 FR 45314
Publication of Staff Accounting Bulletin No. 68	SAB – 68	May 4, 1987	52 FR 17396
Publication of Staff Accounting Bulletin No. 69	SAB – 69	May 8, 1987	52 FR 18200
Publication of Staff Accounting Bulletin No. 70	SAB – 70	June 5, 1987	52 FR 21933
Publication of Staff Accounting Bulletin No. 71	SAB – 71	Aug. 12, 1987	52 FR 31027
Publication of Staff Accounting Bulletin No. 72	SAB – 72	Nov. 10, 1987	52 FR 46454
Publication of Staff Accounting Bulletin No. 71A	SAB – 71A	Dec. 15, 1987	52 FR 48193
Publication of Staff Accounting Bulletin No. 73	SAB – 73	Dec. 30, 1987	53 FR 109
Publication of Staff Accounting Bulletin No. 74	SAB – 74	Dec. 30, 1987	53 FR 110
Publication of Staff Accounting Bulletin No. 75	SAB – 75	Jan. 4, 1988	53 FR 865
Publication of Staff Accounting Bulletin No. 76	SAB – 76	Jan. 12, 1988	53 FR 1341
Publication of Staff Accounting Bulletin No. 77	SAB – 77	Mar. 4, 1988	53 FR 7892
Publication of Staff Accounting Bulletin No. 78	SAB – 78	Aug. 25, 1988	53 FR 33454
Publication of Staff Accounting Bulletin No. 79	SAB – 79	Sept. 2, 1988	53 FR 34715
Publication of Staff Accounting Bulletin No. 80	SAB – 80	Nov. 21, 1988	53 FR 47801

续表

主题	公告编号	日期	《联邦公报》卷数和页码
《工作人员会计公告第67号》	SAB－67	1986年12月8日	《联邦公报》第51卷第45314页
《工作人员会计公告第68号》	SAB－68	1987年5月4日	《联邦公报》第52卷第17396页
《工作人员会计公告第69号》	SAB－69	1987年5月8日	《联邦公报》第52卷第18200页
《工作人员会计公告第70号》	SAB－70	1987年6月5日	《联邦公报》第52卷第21933页
《工作人员会计公告第71号》	SAB－71	1987年8月12日	《联邦公报》第52卷第31027页
《工作人员会计公告第72号》	SAB－72	1987年11月10日	《联邦公报》第52卷第46454页
《工作人员会计公告第71A号》	SAB－71A	1987年12月15日	《联邦公报》第52卷第48193页
《工作人员会计公告第73号》	SAB－73	1987年12月30日	《联邦公报》第53卷第109页
《工作人员会计公告第74号》	SAB－74	1987年12月30日	《联邦公报》第53卷第110页
《工作人员会计公告第75号》	SAB－75	1988年1月4日	《联邦公报》第53卷第865页
《工作人员会计公告第76号》	SAB－76	1988年1月12日	《联邦公报》第53卷第1341页
《工作人员会计公告第77号》	SAB－77	1988年3月4日	《联邦公报》第53卷第7892页
《工作人员会计公告第78号》	SAB－78	1988年8月25日	《联邦公报》第53卷第33454页
《工作人员会计公告第79号》	SAB－79	1988年9月2日	《联邦公报》第53卷第34715页
《工作人员会计公告第80号》	SAB－80	1988年11月21日	《联邦公报》第53卷第47801页

Subject	Release No.	Date	Fed. Reg. Vol. and page
Publication of Staff Accounting Bulletin No. 81	SAB – 81	Apr. 4, 1989	54 FR 14073
Publication of Staff Accounting Bulletin No. 82	SAB – 82	July 5, 1989	54 FR 29333
Publication of Staff Accounting Bulletin No. 83	SAB – 83	July 31, 1989	54 FR 32333
Publication of Staff Accounting Bulletin No. 84	SAB – 84	July 31, 1989	54 FR 32334
Publication of Staff Accounting Bulletin No. 85	SAB – 85	Sept. 18, 1989	54 FR 39351
Publication of Staff Accounting Bulletin No. 86	SAB – 86	Sept. 28, 1989	54 FR 41084
Publication of Staff Accounting Bulletin No. 87	SAB – 87	Dec. 12, 1989	54 FR 51880
Publication of Staff Accounting Bulletin No. 88	SAB – 88	Aug. 10, 1990	55 FR 33284
Publication of Staff Accounting Bulletin No. 89	SAB – 89	Jan. 7, 1991	56 FR 951
Publication of Staff Accounting Bulletin No. 90	SAB – 90	Jan. 31, 1991	56 FR 4939
Publication of Staff Accounting Bulletin No. 91	SAB – 91	July 17, 1991	56 FR 33376
Publication of Staff Accounting Bulletin No. 92	SAB – 92	June 14, 1993	58 FR 32843
Publication of Staff Accounting Bulletin No. 93	SAB – 93	Nov. 9, 1993	58 FR 59361
Publication of Staff Accounting Bulletin No. 94	SAB – 94	Apr. 24, 1995	60 FR 20022
Publication of Staff Accounting Bulletin No. 95	SAB – 95	Dec. 21, 1995	60 FR 66072

续表

主题	公告编号	日期	《联邦公报》卷数和页码
《工作人员会计公告第 81 号》	SAB－81	1989 年 4 月 4 日	《联邦公报》第 54 卷第 14073 页
《工作人员会计公告第 82 号》	SAB－82	1989 年 7 月 5 日	《联邦公报》第 54 卷第 29333 页
《工作人员会计公告第 83 号》	SAB－83	1989 年 7 月 31 日	《联邦公报》第 54 卷第 32333 页
《工作人员会计公告第 84 号》	SAB－84	1989 年 7 月 31 日	《联邦公报》第 54 卷第 32334 页
《工作人员会计公告第 85 号》	SAB－85	1989 年 9 月 18 日	《联邦公报》第 54 卷第 39351 页
《工作人员会计公告第 86 号》	SAB－86	1989 年 9 月 28 日	《联邦公报》第 54 卷第 41084 页
《工作人员会计公告第 87 号》	SAB－87	1989 年 12 月 12 日	《联邦公报》第 54 卷第 51880 页
《工作人员会计公告第 88 号》	SAB－88	1990 年 8 月 10 日	《联邦公报》第 55 卷第 33284 页
《工作人员会计公告第 89 号》	SAB－89	1991 年 1 月 7 日	《联邦公报》第 56 卷第 951 页
《工作人员会计公告第 90 号》	SAB－90	1991 年 1 月 31 日	《联邦公报》第 56 卷第 4939 页
《工作人员会计公告第 91 号》	SAB－91	1991 年 7 月 17 日	《联邦公报》第 56 卷第 33376 页
《工作人员会计公告第 92 号》	SAB－92	1993 年 6 月 14 日	《联邦公报》第 58 卷第 32843 页
《工作人员会计公告第 93 号》	SAB－93	1993 年 11 月 9 日	《联邦公报》第 58 卷第 59361 页
《工作人员会计公告第 94 号》	SAB－94	1995 年 4 月 24 日	《联邦公报》第 60 卷第 20022 页
《工作人员会计公告第 95 号》	SAB－95	1995 年 12 月 21 日	《联邦公报》第 60 卷第 66072 页

Subject	Release No.	Date	Fed. Reg. Vol. and page
Publication of Staff Accounting Bulletin No. 96	SAB – 96	Mar. 25, 1996	61 FR 12020
Publication of Staff Accounting Bulletin No. 97	SAB – 97	Aug. 6, 1996	61 FR 40721
Publication of Staff Accounting Bulletin No. 98	SAB – 98	Feb. 9, 1998	63 FR 6474
Publication of Staff Accounting Bulletin No. 99	SAB – 99	Aug. 19, 1999	64 FR 45150
Publication of Staff Accounting Bulletin No. 100	SAB – 100	Dec. 1, 1999	64 FR 67154
Publication of Staff Accounting Bulletin No. 101	SAB – 101	Dec. 9, 1999	64 FR 68936
Publication of Staff Accounting Bulletin No. 102	SAB – 102	July 6, 2001	66 FR 36457
Publication of Staff Accounting Bulletin No. 103	SAB – 103	May 16, 2003	68 FR 26840
Publication of Staff Accounting Bulletin No. 104	SAB – 104	Dec. 23, 2003	68 FR 74436
Publication of Staff Accounting Bulletin No. 105	SAB – 105	Mar. 15, 2004	69 FR 12067
Publication of Staff Accounting Bulletin No. 106	SAB – 106	Oct. 4, 2004	69 FR 59130
Publication of Staff Accounting Bulletin No. 107	SAB – 107	Apr. 1, 2005	70 FR 16694
Publication of Staff Accounting Bulletin No. 108	SAB – 108	Sept. 18, 2006	71 FR 54580
Publication of Staff Accounting Bulletin No. 109	SAB – 109	Nov. 9, 2007	72 FR 63484
Publication of Staff Accounting Bulletin No. 110	SAB – 110	Dec. 31, 2007	72 FR 74168

续表

主题	公告编号	日期	《联邦公报》卷数和页码
《工作人员会计公告第96号》	SAB－96	1996年3月25日	《联邦公报》第61卷第12020页
《工作人员会计公告第97号》	SAB－97	1996年8月6日	《联邦公报》第61卷第40721页
《工作人员会计公告第98号》	SAB－98	1998年2月9日	《联邦公报》第63卷第6474页
《工作人员会计公告第99号》	SAB－99	1999年8月19日	《联邦公报》第64卷第45150页
《工作人员会计公告第100号》	SAB－100	1999年12月1日	《联邦公报》第64卷第67154页
《工作人员会计公告第101号》	SAB－101	1999年12月9日	《联邦公报》第64卷第68936页
《工作人员会计公告第102号》	SAB－102	2001年7月6日	《联邦公报》第66卷第36457页
《工作人员会计公告第103号》	SAB－103	2003年5月16日	《联邦公报》第68卷第26840页
《工作人员会计公告第104号》	SAB－104	2003年12月23日	《联邦公报》第68卷第74436页
《工作人员会计公告第105号》	SAB－105	2004年3月15日	《联邦公报》第69卷第12067页
《工作人员会计公告第106号》	SAB－106	2004年10月4日	《联邦公报》第69卷第59130页
《工作人员会计公告第107号》	SAB－107	2005年4月1日	《联邦公报》第70卷第16694页
《工作人员会计公告第108号》	SAB－108	2006年9月18日	《联邦公报》第71卷第54580页
《工作人员会计公告第109号》	SAB－109	2007年11月9日	《联邦公报》第72卷第63484页
《工作人员会计公告第110号》	SAB－110	2007年12月31日	《联邦公报》第72卷第74168页

Subject	Release No.	Date	Fed. Reg. Vol. and page
Publication of Staff Accounting Bulletin No. 111	SAB – 111	Apr. 17, 2009	74 FR 17769
Publication of Staff Accounting Bulletin No. 112	SAB – 112	June 10, 2009	74 FR 27427
Publication of Staff Accounting Bulletin No. 113	SAB – 113	Nov. 4, 2009	74 FR 57063

Subpart C Accounting and Auditing Enforcement Releases

Subject	Release No.	Date	Fed. Reg. Vol. and page
Index of Accounting and Auditing Enforcement Releases	1	Apr. 15,1982	47 FR 21030

续表

主题	公告编号	日期	《联邦公报》卷数和页码
《工作人员会计公告第 111 号》	SAB－111	2009 年 4 月 17 日	《联邦公报》第 74 卷第 17769 页
《工作人员会计公告第 112 号》	SAB－112	2009 年 6 月 10 日	《联邦公报》第 74 卷第 27427 页
《工作人员会计公告第 113 号》	SAB－113	2009 年 11 月 4 日	《联邦公报》第 74 卷第 57063 页

第 C 子部分　会计审计实施公告

主题	公告编号	日期	《联邦公报》卷数和页码
《会计审计实施公告》索引	1	1982 年 4 月 15 日	《联邦公报》第 47 卷第 21030 页

PART 229 — STANDARD INSTRUCTIONS FOR FILING FORMS UNDER SECURITIES ACT OF 1933, SECURITIES EXCHANGE ACT OF 1934 AND ENERGY POLICY AND CONSERVATION ACT OF 1975 — REGULATION S-K

Authority: 15 U.S.C. 77e, 77f, 77g, 77h, 77j, 77k, 77s, 77z-2, 77z-3, 77aa(25), 77aa(26), 77ddd, 77eee, 77ggg, 77hhh, 77iii, 77jjj, 77nnn, 77sss, 78c, 78i, 78j, 78*l*, 78m, 78n, 78o, 78u-5, 78w, 78*ll*, 78mm, 80a-8, 80a-9, 80a-20, 80a-29, 80a-30, 80a-31(c), 80a-37, 80a-38(a), 80a-39, 80b-11, and 7201 *et seq.*; and 18 U.S.C. 1350, unless otherwise noted.

Link to an amendment published at 76 FR 6042, February 2, 2011.

Section 229.303 is also issued under secs. 3(a) and 401(a), Pub. L. No. 107-204, 116 Stat. 745.

Section 229.307 is also issued under secs. 3(a) and 302, Pub.L.No. 107-204, 116 Stat. 745.

Section 229.401 is also issued under secs. 3(a) and 407, Pub. L. 107-204, 116 Stat. 745.

Section 229.406 is also issued under secs. 3(a) and 406, Pub. L. 107-204, 116 Stat. 745.

Section 229.601 is also issued under secs. 3(a) and 406, Pub. L. 107-204, 116 Stat. 745.

Source: 47 FR 11401, Mar. 16, 1982, unless otherwise noted.

ATTENTION ELECTRONIC FILERS

THIS REGULATION SHOULD BE READ IN CONJUNCTION WITH REGULATION

第229部分——关于根据《1933年证券法》、《1934年证券交易法》和《1975年能源政策与保护法》提交表格的标准说明——《S-K管理办法》

法律依据:《美国法典》第十五编第77e节、第77f节、第77g节、第77h节、第77j节、第77k节、第77s节、第77z-2节、第77z-3节、第77aa(25)节、第77aa(26)节、第77ddd节、第77eee节、第77ggg节、第77hhh节、第77iii节、第77jjj节、第77nnn节、第77sss节、第78c节、第78i节、第78j节、第78*l*节、第78m节、第78n节、第78o节、第78u-5节、第78w节、第78*ll*节、第78mm节、第80a-8节、第80a-9节、第80a-20节、第80a-29节、第80a-30节、第80a-31(c)节、第80a-37节、第80a-38(a)节、第80a-39节、第80b-11节和第7201节及其后条文;以及《美国法典》第十八编第1350节,除非另有说明。

链接至《联邦公报》第76卷第6042页发布的修正(2011年2月2日)。

第229.303节同时见:第3(a)条和第401(a)条,第107-204号公法,《美国制定法汇编》第116卷第745页。

第229.307节同时见:第3(a)条和第302条,第107-204号公法,《美国制定法汇编》第116卷第745页。

第229.401节同时见:第3(a)条和第407条,第107-204号公法,《美国制定法汇编》第116卷第745页。

第229.406节同时见:第3(a)条和第406条,第107-204号公法,《美国制定法汇编》第116卷第745页。

第229.601节同时见:第3(a)条和第406条,第107-204号公法,《美国制定法汇编》第116卷第745页。

行政规则来源:《联邦公报》第47卷第11401页,1982年3月16日,除非另有说明。

以电子形式提交文件的人请注意

在阅读本《管理办法》时应同时参阅规范以电子格式编制和呈报文件的《S-T管理

S-T (PART 232 OF THIS CHAPTER), WHICH GOVERNS THE PREPARATION AND SUBMISSION OF DOCUMENTS IN ELECTRONIC FORMAT. MANY PROVISIONS RELATING TO THE PREPARATION AND SUBMISSION OF DOCUMENTS IN PAPER FORMAT CONTAINED IN THIS REGULATION ARE SUPERSEDED BY THE PROVISIONS OF REGULATION S-T FOR DOCUMENTS REQUIRED TO BE FILED IN ELECTRONIC FORMAT.

Subpart 229.1—General

§229.10(Item 10) General

(a) *Application of Regulation S-K.* This part(together with the General Rules and Regulations under the Securities Act of 1933, 15 U.S.C. 77a *et seq.*, as amended (*Securities Act*), and the Securities Exchange Act of 1934, 15 U.S.C. 78a *et seq.*, as amended(*Exchange Act*) (parts 230 and 240 of this chapter), the Interpretative Releases under these Acts (parts 231 and 241 of this chapter) and the forms under these Acts (parts 239 and 249 of this chapter)) states the requirements applicable to the content of the non-financial statement portions of:

(1) Registration statements under the Securities Act(part 239 of this chapter) to the extent provided in the forms to be used for registration under such Act; and

(2) Registration statements under section 12 (subpart C of part 249 of this chapter), annual or other reports under sections 13 and 15(d)(subparts D and E of part 249 of this chapter), going-private transaction statements under section 13(part 240 of this chapter), tender offer statements under sections 13 and 14(part 240 of this chapter), annual reports to security holders and proxy and information statements under section 14(part 240 of this chapter), and any other documents required to be filed under the Exchange Act, to the extent provided in the forms and rules under that Act.

(b) *Commission policy on projections.* The Commission encourages the use in documents specified in Rule 175 under the Securities Act (§230.175 of this chapter) and Rule 3b-6 under the Exchange Act (§240.3b-6 of this chapter) of management's projections of future economic performance that have a reasonable basis and are presented in an appropriate format. The guidelines set forth herein represent the Commission's views on important factors to be considered in formulating and disclosing such projections.

(1) *Basis for projections.* The Commission believes that management must have the option to present in Commission filings its good faith assessment of a registrant's future performance. Management, however, must have a reasonable basis for such an assessment.

办法》(本章第232部分)。对于应以电子格式提交的文件,本《管理办法》中关于纸质文件编制和呈报的规定均应替以《S-T管理办法》中的相应规定。

第229.1子部分—— 一 般 规 定

第229.10节(第10条) 一般规定

(a)《S-K管理办法》的适用范围。本部分(以及依据《1933年证券法》修正版(《美国法典》第十五编第77a节及其后条文,下称《证券法》)发布的《一般规则和规章》、《1934年证券交易法》修正版(《美国法典》第十五编第78a节及其后条文,下称《交易法》)(本章第230部分和第240部分)、关于该等法律的解释(本章第231部分和第241部分)以及该等法律涉及的表格(本章第239部分和第249部分)对以下文件中非财务报表的内容作出了相应规定:

(1)《证券法》(本章第239部分)下按照《证券法》规定的注册表格提交的注册说明书;和

(2)《交易法》第12条(本章第249部分第C子部分)中的注册说明书、第13条和第15(d)条(本章第249部分第D子部分和第E子部分)中的年度报告或其他报告、第13条(本章第240部分)中的退市交易声明、第13条和第14条(本章第240部分)中的股权收购要约声明、第14条(本章第240部分)下向证券持有人发布的年度报告、征集投票权报告和信息说明书,以及《交易法》要求提交的任何其他文件,但条件是上述所有文件均系按照《交易法》规定的表格和规则提交。

(b)证券交易委员会的预测政策。对于《证券法》的《175规则》(本章第230.175节)以及《交易法》的《3b-6规则》(本章第240.3b-6节)规定的文件,证券交易委员会鼓励在该等文件中使用具有合理依据,并以适当的格式列报的管理层关于未来经济绩效的预测。此处规定的指导方针反映了证券交易委员会认为在制定和披露上述预测时应予考虑的重要因素。

(1)预测依据。证券交易委员会认为,是否在向证券交易委员会提交的文件中对注册人的未来绩效作出善意评估,必须由管理层自行选择决定。但是,管理层进行上述评估时,必须具有合理依据。尽管过往的经营历史或预测经验可以作为管理层评估

Although a history of operations or experience in projecting may be among the factors providing a basis for management's assessment, the Commission does not believe that a registrant always must have had such a history or experience in order to formulate projections with a reasonable basis. An outside review of management's projections may furnish additional support for having a reasonable basis for a projection. If management decides to include a report of such a review in a Commission filing, there also should be disclosure of the qualifications of the reviewer, the extent of the review, the relationship between the reviewer and the registrant, and other material factors concerning the process by which any outside review was sought or obtained. Moreover, in the case of a registration statement under the Securities Act, the reviewer would be deemed an expert and an appropriate consent must be filed with the registration statement.

(2) *Format for projections.* In determining the appropriate format for projections included in Commission filings, consideration must be given to, among other things, the financial items to be projected, the period to be covered, and the manner of presentation to be used. Although traditionally projections have been given for three financial items generally considered to be of primary importance to investors (revenues, net income(loss) and earnings(loss) per share), projection information need not necessarily be limited to these three items. However, management should take care to assure that the choice of items projected is not susceptible of misleading inferences through selective projection of only favorable items. Revenues, net income(loss) and earnings(loss) per share usually are presented together in order to avoid any misleading inferences that may arise when the individual items reflect contradictory trends. There may be instances, however, when it is appropriate to present earnings (loss) from continuing operations, or income (loss) before extraordinary items in addition to or in lieu of net income(loss). It generally would be misleading to present sales or revenue projections without one of the foregoing measures of income. The period that appropriately may be covered by a projection depends to a large extent on the particular circumstances of the company involved. For certain companies in certain industries, a projection covering a two or three year period may be entirely reasonable. Other companies may not have a reasonable basis for projections beyond the current year. Accordingly, management should select the period most appropriate in the circumstances. In addition, management, in making a projection, should disclose what, in its opinion, is the most probable specific amount or the most reasonable range for each financial item projected based on the selected assumptions. Ranges, however, should not be so wide as to make the disclosures meaningless. Moreover, several projections based on varying assumptions may be judged by management to be more meaningful than a single number or range and would be permitted.

(3) *Investor understanding.* (i) When management chooses to include its projections

的依据之一,但证券交易委员会认为,注册人在作出具有合理依据的预测时,并不必然以拥有该等历史或经验为前提。由外部人员对管理层预测进行审查可以为预测依据的合理性提供进一步支持。若管理层决定在向证券交易委员会提交的文件中纳入该等外部审查报告,还应该披露审查人的资质、审查的范围、审查人和注册人之间的关系,以及与寻求或获得任何外部审查的程序相关的其他重大因素。此外,在根据《证券法》的规定提交注册说明书之时,审查人可视为专家,且在提交注册说明书时应一并提交一份适当的专家同意书。

(2)预测的格式。对于向证券交易委员会提交的文件中所包含的预测,在确定该等预测应采用的适当格式时,所考虑的因素至少应包括:需要预测的财务项目、预测应覆盖的期间、将采用的列报方式。尽管传统上,对于投资者而言,最为重要的预测是如下3个财务项目的预测:收入、净损益以及每股盈利(亏损),但预测的内容不必局限于此。但在选择预测项目时,管理层应注意,不得仅挑选有利的预测项目,以避免读者得出误导性的推论。由于各项目反映的趋势之间可能存在矛盾,为了避免产生任何误导性的推论,在预测中通常应同时列报收入、净损益以及每股盈利(亏损)3个财务项目。但是,在某些情况下,可能除了净损益外,还应当列报持续经营盈利(亏损)或扣除特别项目前的损益,或者只需列报持续经营收益(亏损)或扣除特别项目前的损益,而不必列报净损益。一般而言,在未提供上述任一收入测量指标的情况下作出的销售或收入预测很可能具有误导性。预测应当覆盖的期间在很大程度上取决于相关公司的具体情况。对于特定行业的特定公司而言,2年或3年的预测期间可能完全合理,而其他一些公司则可能无法为超出当年的预测提供合理依据。因此,管理层应根据具体情况选择最为适当的期间。此外,管理层在进行预测时,应基于选定的假设,对预测的每一财务项目,披露其认为最有可能实现的具体数额或最为合理的范围。但上述范围不得过大,以免披露丧失意义。此外,管理层可能认为基于不同的多种假设作出多种不同的预测比提供单一的数字或范围更有意义,在该种情况下,应允许作出多种不同的预测。

(3)投资者的理解。(i)若管理层选择在向证券交易委员会提交的文件中纳入其作

in a Commission filing, the disclosures accompanying the projections should facilitate investor understanding of the basis for and limitations of projections. In this regard investors should be cautioned against attributing undue certainty to management's assessment, and the Commission believes that investors would be aided by a statement indicating management's intention regarding the furnishing of updated projections. The Commission also believes that investor understanding would be enhanced by disclosure of the assumptions which in management's opinion are most significant to the projections or are the key factors upon which the financial results of the enterprise depend and encourages disclosure of assumptions in a manner that will provide a framework for analysis of the projection.

(ii) Management also should consider whether disclosure of the accuracy or inaccuracy of previous projections would provide investors with important insights into the limitations of projections. In this regard, consideration should be given to presenting the projections in a format that will facilitate subsequent analysis of the reasons for differences between actual and forecast results. An important benefit may arise from the systematic analysis of variances between projected and actual results on a continuing basis, since such disclosure may highlight for investors the most significant risk and profit-sensitive areas in a business operation.

(iii) With respect to previously issued projections, registrants are reminded of their responsibility to make full and prompt disclosure of material facts, both favorable and unfavorable, regarding their financial condition. This responsibility may extend to situations where management knows or has reason to know that its previously disclosed projections no longer have a reasonable basis.

(iv) Since a registrant's ability to make projections with relative confidence may vary with all the facts and circumstances, the responsibility for determining whether to discontinue or to resume making projections is best left to management. However, the Commission encourages registrants not to discontinue or to resume projections in Commission filings without a reasonable basis.

(c) *Commission policy on security ratings.* In view of the importance of security ratings (*ratings*) to investors and the marketplace, the Commission permits registrants to disclose, on a voluntary basis, ratings assigned by rating organizations to classes of debt securities, convertible debt securities and preferred stock in registration statements and periodic reports. In addition, the Commission permits, pursuant to Rule 134 (a) (14) under the Securities Act (§230.134 (a) (14) of this chapter), voluntary disclosure of ratings assigned by any nationally recognized statistical rating organizations (*NRSROs*) in certain communications deemed not to be a prospectus (*tombstone advertisements*). Set forth herein are the Commission's views on important matters to be considered in

出的预测,应在预测后附上相关披露,帮助投资者理解预测的依据和局限性。为此,应当告诫投资者不应过分高估管理层评估的确定性,同时,证券交易委员会认为,提供一份声明,说明管理层有意提供更新版的预测,可能会对投资者有所帮助。此外,证券交易委员会相信,披露管理层认为对预测而言意义最重大的假设或企业财务结果所基于的关键假设,可能有助于加强投资者对预测的理解;且证券交易委员会鼓励在披露假设时,为投资者提供一个对预测进行分析的框架。

(ii)管理层还应考虑是否应披露之前披露过的预测的准确度或误差情况,以帮助投资者意识到预测的局限性。为此,管理层应当考虑预测的列报格式,以便对实际结果和预测结果之间存在差异的原因进行后续分析。对预测和实际结果之间的差异进行连续性的系统分析,可突出业务经营中最重大的风险和利润敏感领域,为投资者提供重要帮助。

(iii)对于之前发布的预测,注册人有责任全面和及时地披露与其财务状况相关的、有利及不利的所有重大事实。管理层明知或应知其之前披露的预测不再具有合理依据时,亦应履行上述责任。

(iv)由于实际状况和情形不同,每个注册人作出具有相对把握的预测的能力也不尽相同,因此是否应停止或恢复预测最好交由管理层决定。但是,证券交易委员会鼓励注册人在没有合理依据的情况下不要停止或恢复向证券交易委员会提交文件中所作的预测。

(c)证券交易委员会的证券评级政策。考虑到证券评级("评级")对投资者和市场的重要性,证券交易委员会允许注册人在自愿的基础上,在注册说明书和定期报告中披露评级组织对其各类别的债务证券、可转换债务证券以及优先股作出的评级。此外,证券交易委员会允许,依据《证券法》的《134(a)(14)规则》[本章第230.134(a)(14)节],在某些被视为不属于招募说明书的资料中(证券发行非要约性公告)自愿披露任何国家认可的统计评级机构(NRSRO)授予的评级。对证券评级披露中应予注意的重要事项,证券交易委员会的观点如下。

disclosing security ratings.

(1) *Securities Act filings.* (i) If a registrant includes in a registration statement filed under the Securities Act any rating(s) assigned to a class of securities, it should consider including: (A) Any other rating intended for public dissemination assigned to such class by a NRSRO (*additional NRSRO rating*) that is available on the date of the initial filing of the document and that is materially different from any rating disclosed; and (B) the name of each rating organization whose rating is disclosed; each such rating organization's definition or description of the category in which it rated the class of securities; the relative rank of each rating within the assigning rating organization's overall classification system; and a statement informing investors that a security rating is not a recommendation to buy, sell or hold securities, that it may be subject to revision or withdrawal at any time by the assigning rating organization, and that each rating should be evaluated independently of any other rating. The registrant also should include the written consent of any rating organization that is not a NRSRO whose rating is included. With respect to the written consent of any NRSRO whose rating is included, see Rule 436(g) under the Securities Act (§230.436(g) of this chapter). When the registrant has filed a registration statement on Form F-9 (§239.39 of this chapter), see Rule 436(g) (§230.436(g) of this chapter) under the Securities Act with respect to the written consent of any rating organization specified in the Instruction to paragraph (a)(2) of General Instruction I of Form F-9.

(ii) If a change in a rating already included is available subsequent to the filing of the registration statement, but prior to its effectiveness, the registrant should consider including such rating change in the final prospectus. If the rating change is material or if a materially different rating from any disclosed becomes available during this period, the registrant should consider amending the registration statement to include the rating change or additional rating and recirculating the preliminary prospectus.

(iii) If a materially different additional NRSRO rating or a material change in a rating already included becomes available during any period in which offers or sales are being made, the registrant should consider disclosing such additional rating or rating change by means of post-effective amendment or sticker to the prospectus pursuant to Rule 424(b) under the Securities Act (§230.424(b) of this chapter), unless, in the case of a registration statement on Form S-3(§239.13 of this chapter), it has been disclosed in a document incorporated by reference into the registration statement subsequent to its effectiveness and prior to the termination of the offering.

(2) *Exchange Act filings.* (i) If a registrant includes in a registration statement or periodic report filed under the Exchange Act any rating(s) assigned to a class of securities, it should consider including the information specified in paragraphs (c)(1)(i)(A) and (B) of this section.

(1)根据《证券法》提交的文件。(i)若注册人在根据《证券法》提交注册说明书时纳入了对某一类别证券作出的评级,则该注册人应考虑同时提供:(A)在首次提交文件之日可获得的,且与任何已披露的评级存在重大差异的某一NRSRO对同类别证券做出的任何其他公开评级("其他NRSRO评级");和(B)作出所披露的评级的每个评级组织的名称、每个评级组织对其评定的证券所属类别的界定或说明、每个评级在评级组织的整体分类体系中的相对级别;同时,应向投资者作出包含以下内容的说明:证券评级并非对买入、卖出或持有证券提出的建议,评级组织可随时修订或撤销相关的评级,且每一评级均应独立于任何其他评级。若注册人披露的评级包括由某一家非NRSRO的评级组织作出的评级,则注册人还应提供该等评级组织出具的书面同意函。若注册人披露的评级包括由任何一家NRSRO作出的评级,请参见《证券法》的《436(g)规则》[本章第230.436(g)节]关于该等评级机构出具的书面同意函的规定。若注册人按照《F-9表格》(本章第239.39节)提交注册说明书,则对于《F-9表格》总体说明I第(a)(2)款规定的任何评级组织所出具的书面同意函,请参见《证券法》的《436(g)规则》[本章第230.436(g)节]的规定。

(ii)若在注册说明书提交之后、生效之前的期间内,注册说明书披露的评级发生了变更,注册人应考虑在最终招募说明书中披露评级发生的变更。若在上述期间内,评级发生了重大变更,或出现与任何已披露的评级存在重大差异的评级,注册人应考虑修改注册说明书,纳入该等变更或其他评级的信息,并重新发布初步招募说明书。

(iii)若在要约或出售的任何期间,其他NRSRO作出了具有重大差异的评级,或已披露的评级发生了重大变更,注册人应考虑根据《证券法》的《424(b)规则》[本章第230.424(b)节],对已生效的招募说明书进行修正,或者在其后附加增补页的方式,对该等其他评级或评级变更作出披露,除非注册人按照《S-3表格》(本章第239.13节)提交注册说明书,且该等变更已在注册说明书生效之后和发行终止之前的期间内,通过注册说明书引用纳入的某一文件进行披露。

(2)根据《交易法》提交的文件。(i)若某一注册人在根据《交易法》提交的注册说明书或定期报告中包含了某一类别证券的任何评级,则该注册人应考虑同时提供本节第(c)(1)(i)(A)款和第(c)(1)(i)(B)款规定的信息。

(ii) If there is a material change in the rating(s) assigned by any NRSRO(s) to any outstanding class(es) of securities of a registrant subject to the reporting requirements of section 13(a) or 15(d) of the Exchange Act, the registrant should consider filing a report on Form 8-K (§249.308 of this chapter) or other appropriate report under the Exchange Act disclosing such rating change.

(d) *Incorporation by Reference.* Where rules, regulations, or instructions to forms of the Commission permit incorporation by reference, a document may be so incorporated by reference to the specific document and to the prior filing or submission in which such document was physically filed or submitted. Except where a registrant or issuer is expressly required to incorporate a document or documents by reference (or for purposses of Item 1100(c) of Regulation AB (§229.1100(c)) with respect to an asset-backed issuer, as that term is defined in Item 1101 of Regulation AB(§229.1101)), reference may not be made to any document which incorporates another document by reference if the pertinent portion of the doucment containing the information or financial statements to be incorporated by reference includes an incorporation by reference to another document. No document on file with the Commission for more than five years may be incorporated by reference except:

(1) Documents contained in registration statements, which may be incorporated by reference as long as the registrant has a reporting requirement with the Commission; or

(2) Documents that the registrant specifically identifies by physical location by SEC file number reference, provided such materials have not been disposed of by the Commission pursuant to its Records Control Schedule (17 CFR 200.80f).

(e) *Use of non-GAAP financial measures in Commission filings.* (1) Whenever one or more non-GAAP financial measures are included in a filing with the Commission:

(i) The registrant must include the following in the filing:

(A) A presentation, with equal or greater prominence, of the most directly comparable financial measure or measures calculated and presented in accordance with Generally Accepted Accounting Principles (GAAP);

(B) A reconciliation(by schedule or other clearly understandable method), which shall be quantitative for historical non-GAAP measures presented, and quantitative, to the extent available without unreasonable efforts, for forward-looking information, of the differences between the non-GAAP financial measure disclosed or released with the most directly comparable financial measure or measures calculated and presented in accordance with GAAP identified in paragraph (e)(1)(i)(A) of this section;

(C) A statement disclosing the reasons why the registrant's management believes that presentation of the non-GAAP financial measure provides useful information to investors

(ii)若任何NRSRO对某一注册人的任何发行在外的证券类别作出的评级发生重大变更,且该等证券应根据《交易法》第13(a)条或第15(d)条进行报告,注册人应考虑按照《8-K表格》(本章第249.308节)提交报告,或根据《交易法》的规定提交其他适当报告,对该等评级变更进行披露。

(d)引用纳入。若证券交易委员会的规则、规章或关于表格的说明允许引用纳入,则可采用引用某一文件以及包含该文件的在先提交材料或呈报材料的方式纳入该特定文件。但在注册人或发行人被明确要求以引用方式纳入文件的情况下{或就《AB管理办法》第1100(c)条[第229.1100(c)节]关于资产支持证券发行人的规定而言,"资产支持证券发行人"定义见《AB管理办法》第1101条(第229.1101节)},若某一文件中涉及某些信息或财务报表的部分对另一文件进行了引用纳入,则不得对该等包含二次引用的文件进行引用。对于向证券交易委员会提交的时间超过5年的文件,不得以引用方式纳入,但以下文件除外:

(1)注册说明书中包含的文件,只要注册人有义务向证券交易委员会提交报告,该等文件即可通过引用方式纳入;或

(2)注册人通过证券交易委员会文档编号,具体指明其物理位置的文件,但前提是证券交易委员会尚未按照其《记录控制计划》(《联邦规章汇编》第十七编第200.80f节)处置该等资料。

(e)在向证券交易委员会提交的文件中使用非公认会计原则财务指标("非GAAP财务指标")。(1)无论何时,只要在向证券交易委员会提交的文件中使用了一项或数项非GAAP财务指标:

(i)注册人必须在提交的文件中:

(A)以同等或更加显著的方式,说明按照公认会计原则(GAAP)计算和列报的最具直接可比性的财务指标;

(B)通过附表或其他清晰易懂的方式,提供注册人披露或发布的非GAAP财务指标与本节第(e)(1)(i)(A)款所述的按照GAAP计算和列报的最具直接可比性的财务指标之间的调节表,调节表中应当对列报的非GAAP历史财务指标予以量化,并在可行且不必作出不合理努力的范围内,对前瞻性信息予以量化;

(C)说明注册人管理层认为非GAAP财务指标可为投资者提供有关注册人财务状况和经营成果的有用信息的理由;和

regarding the registrant's financial condition and results of operations; and

(D) To the extent material, a statement disclosing the additional purposes, if any, for which the registrant's management uses the non-GAAP financial measure that are not disclosed pursuant to paragraph (e)(1)(i)(C) of this section; and

(ii) A registrant must not:

(A) Exclude charges or liabilities that required, or will require, cash settlement, or would have required cash settlement absent an ability to settle in another manner, from non-GAAP liquidity measures, other than the measures earnings before interest and taxes (EBIT) and earnings before interest, taxes, depreciation, and amortization (EBITDA);

(B) Adjust a non-GAAP performance measure to eliminate or smooth items identified as non-recurring, infrequent or unusual, when the nature of the charge or gain is such that it is reasonably likely to recur within two years or there was a similar charge or gain within the prior two years;

(C) Present non-GAAP financial measures on the face of the registrant's financial statements prepared in accordance with GAAP or in the accompanying notes;

(D) Present non-GAAP financial measures on the face of any *pro forma* financial information required to be disclosed by Article 11 of Regulation S-X (17 CFR 210.11-01 through 210.11-03); or

(E) Use titles or descriptions of non-GAAP financial measures that are the same as, or confusingly similar to, titles or descriptions used for GAAP financial measures; and

(iii) If the filing is not an annual report on Form 10-K or Form 20-F (17 CFR 249.220f), a registrant need not include the information required by paragraphs (e)(1)(i)(C) and (e)(1)(i)(D) of this section if that information was included in its most recent annual report on Form 10-K or Form 20-F or a more recent filing, provided that the required information is updated to the extent necessary to meet the requirements of paragraphs (e)(1)(i)(C) and (e)(1)(i)(D) of this section at the time of the registrant's current filing.

(2) For purposes of this paragraph (e), a non-GAAP financial measure is a numerical measure of a registrant's historical or future financial performance, financial position or cash flows that:

(i) Excludes amounts, or is subject to adjustments that have the effect of excluding amounts, that are included in the most directly comparable measure calculated and presented in accordance with GAAP in the statement of income, balance sheet or statement of cash flows (or equivalent statements) of the issuer; or

(ii) Includes amounts, or is subject to adjustments that have the effect of including amounts, that are excluded from the most directly comparable measure so calculated and presented.

（D）说明未按照本节第（e）（1）（i）（C）款披露的注册人管理层使用非GAAP财务指标的其他重大目的（如有）；且

（ii）注册人不得：

（A）从非GAAP流动性指标中排除要求或将要求现金结算的费用或债务，或在无法以其他方式结算时要求现金结算的费用或债务，但息税前收益（EBIT）和息税折旧及摊销前收益（EBITDA）指标除外；

（B）在根据某一费用或收益性质，可合理预期两年内该等费用或收益可能重复发生的情况下，或在此前的两年内曾经发生过类似的费用或收益的情况下，对某一项非GAAP财务指标作出调整，以消除被认定为非经常性、偶然或临时性的项目或对该等项目的影响进行平稳化；

（C）在注册人根据GAAP编制的财务报表正文或其附注中列报非GAAP财务指标；

（D）在《S-X管理办法》第11条（《联邦规章汇编》第17编第210.11-01~210.11-03节）要求披露的任何备考财务信息正文中列报非GAAP财务指标；或

（E）对非GAAP财务指标使用与GAAP财务指标相同的名称或说明，或混淆性的类似名称或说明；

（iii）如提交的文件不属于按照《10-K表格》或《20-F表格》（《联邦规章汇编》第十七编第249.220f节）提交的年度报告，且在采用《10-K表格》或《20-F表格》的最近一期年度报告中或在更新的提交文件中已经包含了本节第（e）（1）（i）（C）款和第（e）（1）（i）（D）款要求提供的信息，则注册人不必在本次提交的文件中纳入该等信息，但是注册人应对要求提供的信息进行必要更新，使之在本次提交文件之时符合本节第（e）（1）（i）（C）款和第（e）（1）（i）（D）款的要求。

（2）就本第（e）款而言，非GAAP财务指标系指将产生如下效果的，关于注册人的历史或未来财务绩效、财务状况或现金流的数字指标：

（i）在发行人损益表、资产负债表或现金流量表（或同等报表）中，将按照GAAP计算和列报的最具直接可比性的财务指标中所包含的款项排除在外，或者可能需要进行具有排除该等款项效果的调整；或

（ii）纳入从按上述规定计算和列报的最具直接可比性的财务指标中排除的款项，或者可能需要进行具有纳入该等款项效果的调整。

(3) For purposes of this paragraph (e), GAAP refers to generally accepted accounting principles in the United States, except that:

(i) In the case of foreign private issuers whose primary financial statements are prepared in accordance with non-U.S. generally accepted accounting principles, GAAP refers to the principles under which those primary financial statements are prepared; and

(ii) In the case of foreign private issuers that include a non-GAAP financial measure derived from or based on a measure calculated in accordance with U.S. generally accepted accounting principles, GAAP refers to U.S. generally accepted accounting principles for purposes of the application of the requirements of this paragraph (e) to the disclosure of that measure.

(4) For purposes of this paragraph (e), non-GAAP financial measures exclude:

(i) Operating and other statistical measures; and

(ii) Ratios or statistical measures calculated using exclusively one or both of:

(A) Financial measures calculated in accordance with GAAP; and

(B) Operating measures or other measures that are not non-GAAP financial measures.

(5) For purposes of this paragraph (e), non-GAAP financial measures exclude financial measures required to be disclosed by GAAP, Commission rules, or a system of regulation of a government or governmental authority or self-regulatory organization that is applicable to the registrant. However, the financial measure should be presented outside of the financial statements unless the financial measure is required or expressly permitted by the standard-setter that is responsible for establishing the GAAP used in such financial statements.

(6) The requirements of paragraph (e) of this section shall not apply to a non-GAAP financial measure included in disclosure relating to a proposed business combination, the entity resulting therefrom or an entity that is a party thereto, if the disclosure is contained in a communication that is subject to §230.425 of this chapter, §240.14a-12 or §240.14d-2(b)(2) of this chapter or §229.1015 of this chapter.

(7) The requirements of paragraph (e) of this section shall not apply to investment companies registered under section 8 of the Investment Company Act of 1940 (15 U.S.C. 80a-8).

Note to paragraph (e). A non-GAAP financial measure that would otherwise be prohibited by paragraph (e)(1)(ii) of this section is permitted in a filing of a foreign private issuer if:

1. The non-GAAP financial measure relates to the GAAP used in the registrant's primary financial statements included in its filing with the Commission;

2. The non-GAAP financial measure is required or expressly permitted by the standard-setter that is responsible for establishing the GAAP used in such financial

(3)就本第(e)款而言,"GAAP"指美国公认会计原则,但是:

(i)在外国私募发行人根据非美国公认会计原则编制其主要财务报表的情况下,GAAP系指编制该等主要财务报表时所遵循的原则;及

(ii)在外国私募发行人使用的某项非GAAP财务指标系派生于或基于根据美国公认会计原则计算的指标的情况下,在将本第(e)款的规定适用于该等指标的披露之时,GAAP系指美国公认会计原则。

(4)就本第(e)款而言,非GAAP财务指标不包括:

(i)运营指标和其他统计指标;和

(ii)仅采用以下一项或两项指标计算的比值或统计指标:

(A)根据GAAP计算的财务指标;和

(B)不属于非GAAP财务指标的运营指标或其他指标。

(5)就本第(e)款而言,非GAAP财务指标不包括GAAP、证券交易委员会规则及适用于注册人的政府或政府部门或自律组织的监管体系要求披露的财务指标。但是,非GAAP财务指标均应在财务报表之外列报,但该等财务报表中使用的GAAP的标准制定者另行要求或明确允许在财务报表之内进行列报的除外。

(6)若按照本章第230.425节、第240.14a-12节或第240.14d-2(b)(2)节或第229.1015节规定发布的文件内已经包含相关披露,则在就提议的业务合并、合并后实体或作为合并一方的实体进行相关披露时,本节第(e)款的规定不适用于该等披露中包含的非GAAP财务指标。

(7)本节第(e)款的规定不适用于根据《1940年投资公司法》第8条(《美国法典》第十五编第80a-8节)注册的投资公司。

关于第(e)款的注释。在以下情况下,外国私募发行人可在其提交的文件中使用本条第(e)(1)(ii)款禁止使用的非GAAP财务指标:

1.非GAAP财务指标与注册人向证券交易委员会提交的文件中包含的主要财务报表所使用的GAAP相关;

2. 该等财务报表中使用的GAAP的标准制定者要求或明确允许使用该等非GAAP财务指标;及

statements; and

3. The non-GAAP financial measure is included in the annual report prepared by the registrant for use in the jurisdiction in which it is domiciled, incorporated or organized or for distribution to its security holders.

(f) *Smaller reporting companies.* The requirements of this part apply to smaller reporting companies. A smaller reporting company may comply with either the requirements applicable to smaller reporting companies or the requirements applicable to other companies for each item, unless the requirements for smaller reporting companies specify that smaller reporting companies must comply with the smaller reporting company requirements. The following items of this part set forth requirements for smaller reporting companies that are different from requirements applicable to other companies:

Index of Scaled Disclosure Available to Smaller Reporting Companies

Item 101	Description of business.
Item 201	Market price of and dividends on registrant's common equity and related stockholder matters.
Item 301	Selected financial data.
Item 302	Supplementary financial information.
Item 303	Management's discussion and analysis of financial condition and results of operations.
Item 305	Quantitative and qualitative disclosures about market risk.
Item 402	Executive compensation.
Item 404	Transactions with related persons, promoters and certain control persons.
Item 407	Corporate governance.
Item 503	Prospectus summary, risk factors, and ratio of earnings to fixed charges.
Item 504	Use of proceeds.
Item 601	Exhibits.

(1) *Definition of smaller reporting company.* As used in this part, the term *smaller reporting company* means an issuer that is not an investment company, an asset-backed issuer (as defined in §229.1101), or a majority-owned subsidiary of a parent that is not a smaller reporting company and that:

(i) Had a public float of less than $75 million as of the last business day of its most recently completed second fiscal quarter, computed by multiplying the aggregate worldwide number of shares of its voting and non-voting common equity held by non-

3.注册人为在其住所地、设立地或组建地使用或为向其证券持有人分发之目而编制的年度报告中包含该等非GAAP财务指标。

(f)小型报告公司。本部分的规定适用于小型报告公司。除非适用于小型报告公司的某项规定明确要求小型报告公司必须遵守该规定,否则对于每项规定,小型报告公司既可遵循适用于小型报告公司的规定,也可遵循适用于其他公司的规定。本部分以下各项列小型报告公司所适用的、与其他公司适用的规定存在差异的规定:

可供小型报告公司使用的简化披露索引

第 101 条	业务说明
第 201 条	注册人普通股权的市场价格、股息以及相关股东事项
第 301 条	择要列示的财务数据
第 302 条	补充财务信息
第 303 条	管理层关于财务状况和经营成果的论述和分析
第 305 条	市场风险的定量和定性披露
第 402 条	高管报酬
第 404 条	与关联人、发起人和特定控制人之间的交易
第 407 条	公司治理
第 503 条	招募说明书摘要、风险因素以及盈利对固定费用的比率
第 504 条	募集资金的使用
第 601 条	附录

(1)“小型报告公司”的定义。就本部分而言,“小型报告公司”一词系指除投资公司、资产支持证券发行人(定义见第229.1101节)或由一家非小型报告公司的母公司控制多数股权的子公司以外的发行人,且:

(i)该发行人在最近结束的倒数第二个财务季度的最后一个营业日的公众持股量低于7500万美元;此处的公众持股量应按如下方法计算:非关联方持有的具有表决权和不具有表决权的普通股的全球总数,乘以普通股主要市场上最近的普通股出售价

affiliates by the price at which the common equity was last sold, or the average of the bid and asked prices of common equity, in the principal market for the common equity; or

(ii) In the case of an initial registration statement under the Securities Act or Exchange Act for shares of its common equity, had a public float of less than $75 million as of a date within 30 days of the date of the filing of the registration statement, computed by multiplying the aggregate worldwide number of such shares held by non-affiliates before the registration plus, in the case of a Securities Act registration statement, the number of such shares included in the registration statement by the estimated public offering price of the shares; or

(iii) In the case of an issuer whose public float as calculated under paragraph (i) or (ii) of this definition was zero, had annual revenues of less than $50 million during the most recently completed fiscal year for which audited financial statements are available.

(2) *Determination:* Whether or not an issuer is a smaller reporting company is determined on an annual basis.

(i) For issuers that are required to file reports under section 13(a) or 15(d) of the Exchange Act, the determination is based on whether the issuer came within the definition of smaller reporting company, using the amounts specified in paragraph (f)(2)(iii) of this Item, as of the last business day of the second fiscal quarter of the issuer's previous fiscal year. An issuer in this category must reflect this determination in the information it provides in its quarterly report on Form 10-Q for the first fiscal quarter of the next year, indicating on the cover page of that filing, and in subsequent filings for that fiscal year, whether or not it is a smaller reporting company, except that, if a determination based on public float indicates that the issuer is newly eligible to be a smaller reporting company, the issuer may choose to reflect this determination beginning with its first quarterly report on Form 10-Q following the determination, rather than waiting until the first fiscal quarter of the next year.

(ii) For determinations based on an initial Securities Act or Exchange Act registration statement under paragraph (f)(1)(ii) of this Item, the issuer must reflect the determination in the information it provides in the registration statement and must appropriately indicate on the cover page of the filing, and subsequent filings for the fiscal year in which the filing is made, whether or not it is a smaller reporting company. The issuer must redetermine its status at the end of its second fiscal quarter and then reflect any change in status as provided in paragraph (f)(2)(i) of this Item. In the case of a determination based on an initial Securities Act registration statement, an issuer that was not determined to be a smaller reporting company has the option to redetermine its status at the conclusion of the offering covered by the registration statement based on the actual offering price and number of shares sold.

格或普通股买卖报价的平均值;或

(ii)在根据《证券法》或《交易法》首次提交普通股注册说明书的情况下,该发行人在注册说明书提交日后30日内的公众持股量低于7500万美元; 此处的公众持股量应按如下方法计算:非关联方在注册前持有的该等股份的全球总数加上注册说明书中包括的股份数量(如系根据《证券法》提交注册说明书),乘以该等股份的预期公开发行价格;或

(iii)在按照本定义第(i)款或第(ii)款计算得出的某一发行人的公众持股量为零的情况下,该发行人在最近结束的会计年度的年收入低于5000万美元,且发行人能够提供已审计财务报表。

(2)认定:每年均应对某一发行人是否属于小型报告公司作出认定。

(i)对于应按照《交易法》第13(a)条或第15(d)条的规定提交报告的发行人,在认定发行人是否符合小型报告公司的定义时,应使用本条第(f)(2)(iii)款规定的、发行人截至上一会计年度第二个财务季度的最后一个营业日的相关数字。该类别的发行人在按照《10-Q表格》编制下一年第一个财务季度的季度报告时,必须说明上述认定,在提交文件的封面并在同一会计年度的后续提交文件中说明其是否属于小型报告公司,但是如根据公众持股量认定该发行人新近获得了小型报告公司的资格,发行人可选择在作出上述认定后采用《10-Q表格》编制的第一份季度报告中说明上述认定,而不必等到下一年的第一个财务季度。

(ii)在以本条第(f)(1)(ii)款所述的根据《证券法》或《交易法》提交的首次注册说明书作为认定依据的情况下,发行人必须在注册说明书中提供反映上述认定的信息,且必须在该份提交文件的封面以及之后就同一会计年度提交的其他文件中以适当的方式说明其是否属于小型报告公司。发行人必须在第二个财务季度结束时对其身份重新进行认定,并按照本条第(f)(2)(i)款的规定提供反映其身份变更的信息。在以根据《证券法》提交的首次注册说明书作为认定依据的情况下,若某一发行人未被认定为具备小型报告公司身份,其可选择在相关注册说明书所涉及的发行结束时,以实际发行价格和出售的股份数量为依据对其身份进行重新认定。

(iii) Once an issuer fails to qualify for smaller reporting company status, it will remain unqualified unless it determines that its public float, as calculated in accordance with paragraph (f)(1) of this Item, was less than $50 million as of the last business day of its second fiscal quarter or, if that calculation results in zero because the issuer had no public equity outstanding or no market price for its equity existed, if the issuers had annual revenues of less than $40 million during its previous fiscal year.

[47 FR 11401, Mar. 16, 1982, as amended at 52 FR 21260, June 5, 1987; 58 FR 14665, Mar. 18, 1993; 58 FR 62029, Nov. 23, 1993; 60 FR 32824, June 23, 1995; 64 FR 61443, Nov. 10, 1999; 68 FR 4831, Jan. 30, 2003; 70 FR 1593, Jan. 7, 2005; 73 FR 956, Jan. 4, 2008]

Subpart 229.100—Business

§229.101(Item 101) Description of business.

(a) *General development of business.* Describe the general development of the business of the registrant, its subsidiaries and any predecessor(s) during the past five years, or such shorter period as the registrant may have been engaged in business. Information shall be disclosed for earlier periods if material to an understanding of the general development of the business.

(1) In describing developments, information shall be given as to matters such as the following: the year in which the registrant was organized and its form of organization; the nature and results of any bankruptcy, receivership or similar proceedings with respect to the registrant or any of its significant subsidiaries; the nature and results of any other material reclassification, merger or consolidation of the registrant or any of its significant subsidiaries; the acquisition or disposition of any material amount of assets otherwise than in the ordinary course of business; and any material changes in the mode of conducting the business.

(2) Registrants:

(i) Filing a registration statement on Form S-1 (§239.11 of this chapter) under the Securities Act or on Form 10 (§249.210 of this chapter) under the Exchange Act;

(ii) Not subject to the reporting requirements of section 13(a) or 15(d) of the Exchange Act immediately before the filing of such registration statement; and

(iii) That (including predecessors) have not received revenue from operations during each of the three fiscal years immediately before the filing of such registration

(iii)一旦发行人未获得小型报告公司资格,则除非出现以下情形,发行人将继续保持非小型报告公司的身份:该发行人按照本条第(f)(1)款计算确定的公众持股量在第二个财务季度的最后一个营业日低于5000万美元;或由于该发行人不存在发行在外的公众股权,或其现有股权没有相关市场价格,上述计算的结果为零,且该发行人在上一会计年度的年收入低于4000万美元。

[《联邦公报》第47卷第11404页,1982年3月16日,修正索引:《联邦公报》第52卷第21260页,1987年6月5日;《联邦公报》第58卷第14665页,1993年3月18日;《联邦公报》第58卷第62029页,1993年11月23日;《联邦公报》第60卷第32824页,1995年6月23日;《联邦公报》第64卷第61443页,1999年11月10日;《联邦公报》第68卷第4831页,2003年1月30日;《联邦公报》第70卷第1593页,2005年1月7日;《联邦公报》第73卷第956页,2008年1月4日。]

第229.100子部分——业　　务

第229.101节(第101条)　业务说明

(a)业务总体发展情况。说明过去5年内或自注册人开展业务以来(如注册人开展业务期间不足5年),注册人及其子公司和任何前身公司的业务总体发展情况。如对于理解总体业务发展情况有重要意义,还应披露之前期间的相关信息。

(1)在说明发展情况时,应当提供以下事项的相关信息:注册人的组建年份以及组织形式;注册人或其任何重要子公司的任何破产、接管或类似程序的性质及其后果;注册人或其任何重要子公司的任何其他重大资本结构重组、吸收合并或新设合并的性质及其后果;在正常业务运作外对任何重大资产的收购或处置;以及业务开展模式的任何重大变更。

(2)符合下述条件的注册人:

(i)按照《证券法》下的《S-1表格》(本章第239.11节)或《交易法》下的《10表格》(本章第249.210节)提交注册说明书;

(ii)在紧接着提交该等注册说明书之前不受制于《交易法》第13(a)条或第15(d)条规定的报告义务;且

(iii)在紧接提交该等注册说明书之前的3个会计年度中的任何一年均未取得任何经营收入(包括其前身亦未取得任何经营收入),应按如下规定提供信息:

statement, shall provide the following information:

(A) If the registration statement is filed prior to the end of the registrant's second fiscal quarter, a description of the registrant's plan of operation for the remainder of the fiscal year; or

(B) If the registration statement is filed subsequent to the end of the registrant's second fiscal quarter, a descripition of the registrant's plan of operation for the remainder of the fiscal year and for the first six months of the next fiscal year. If such information is not available, the reasons for its not being available shall be stated. Disclosure relating to any plan shall include such matters as:

(1) In the case of a registration statement on Form S-1, a statement in narrative form indicating the registrant's opinion as to the period of time that the proceeds from the offering will satisfy cash requirements and whether in the next six months it will be necessary to raise additional funds to meet the expenditures required for operating the business of the registrant; the specific reasons for such opinion shall be set forth and categories of expenditures and sources of cash resources shall be identified; however, amounts of expenditures and cash resources need not be provided; in addition, if the narrative statement is based on a cash budget, such budget shall be furnished to the Commission as supplemental information, but not as part of the registration statement;

(2) An explanation of material product research and development to be performed during the period covered in the plan;

(3) Any anticipated material acquisition of plant and equipment and the capacity thereof;

(4) Any anticipated material changes in number of employees in the various departments such as research and development, production, sales or administration; and

(5) Other material areas which may be peculiar to the registrant's business.

(b) *Financial information about segments.* Report for each segment, as defined by generally accepted accounting principles, revenues from external customers, a measure of profit or loss and total assets. A registrant must report this information for each of the last three fiscal years or for as long as it has been in business, whichever period is shorter. If the information provided in response to this paragraph (b) conforms with generally accepted accounting principles, a registrant may include in its financial statements a cross reference to this data in lieu of presenting duplicative information in the financial statements; conversely, a registrant may cross reference to the financial statements.

(1) If a registrant changes the structure of its internal organization in a manner that causes the composition of its reportable segments to change, the registrant must restate the corresponding information for earlier periods, including interim periods, unless it is impracticable to do so. Following a change in the composition of its reportable segments, a

（A）若注册人在其第二个财务季度结束之前提交注册说明书，应对该会计年度剩余期间的经营计划作出说明；或

（B）若注册人在其第二个财务季度结束之后提交注册说明书，应对该会计年度剩余期间以及下一个会计年度前6个月的经营计划作出说明。若无法提供该等信息，应说明无法提供的原因。与任何经营计划相关的披露均应包括如下信息：

（1）在按《S-1表格》提交注册说明书的情况下，注册人应通过一份文字说明阐明其对以下问题的看法：发行所募集的资金可在多长时间内满足其现金需求；在未来6个月内，注册人是否有必要筹集补充资金以满足其业务经营所需的支出。注册人应说明其得出该等看法的具体原因以及支出类别和现金准备的来源，但不必说明支出的金额和现金准备的需求量。此外，若上述文字说明以现金预算为依据，应将该等预算作为补充信息而非注册说明书的一部分提交给证券交易委员会。

（2）一份关于将在经营计划覆盖期间内开展的重大产品研发工作的说明；

（3）任何预期采购的重大厂房和设备以及该等厂房和设备的产能；

（4）各个部门（如研发、生产、销售或行政管理部门）雇员人数预期发生的任何重大变更；和

（5）根据注册人的业务而应特别提供的其他重大信息。

（b）关于业务分部的财务信息。就每个业务分部（定义见公认会计原则）提供关于来自外部客户的收入、损益指标和总资产的报告。注册人必须分别对最近3个会计年度或自其开展业务以来（如其业务开展期间不足3年）每一年的上述信息作出报告。如果按照本第（b）款规定提供的信息与公认会计原则相符，注册人可在其财务报表中对该等数据进行交叉引用，而不必在财务报表中重复列报该等信息；反之，注册人也可在业务分部的财务信息中对财务报表进行交叉引用。

（1）若因注册人改变其内部组织结构，导致其应报告业务分部的组成发生变更，只要可行，注册人即必须对之前期间（包括中期期间）的相关信息进行重述。继其应报告业务分部的组成发生变更后，注册人应披露其是否就之前期间的业务分部信息的相关内容作出了重述。若未作出重述，注册人应在变更发生当年分别在原有和现有的

registrant shall disclose whether it has restated the corresponding items of segment information for earlier periods. If it has not restated the items from earlier periods, the registrant shall disclose in the year in which the change occurs segment information for the current period under both the old basis and the new basis of segmentation, unless it is impracticable to do so.

(2) If the registrant includes, or is required by Article 3 of Regulation S-X (17 CFR 210) to include, interim financial statements, discuss any facts relating to the performance of any of the segments during the period which, in the opinion of management, indicate that the three year segment financial data may not be indicative of current or future operations of the segment. Comparative financial information shall be included to the extent necessary to the discussion.

(c) *Narrative description of business.* (1) Describe the business done and intended to be done by the registrant and its subsidiaries, focusing upon the registrant's dominant segment or each reportable segment about which financial information is presented in the financial statements. To the extent material to an understanding of the registrant's business taken as a whole, the description of each such segment shall include the information specified in paragraphs (c)(1)(i) through (x) of this section. The matters specified in paragraphs (c)(1)(xi) through (xiii) of this section shall be discussed with respect to the registrant's business in general; where material, the segments to which these matters are significant shall be identified.

(i) The principal products produced and services rendered by the registrant in the segment and the principal markets for, and methods of distribution of, the segment's principal products and services. In addition, state for each of the last three fiscal years the amount or percentage of total revenue contributed by any class of similar products or services which accounted for 10 percent or more of consolidated revenue in any of the last three fiscal years or 15 percent or more of consolidated revenue, if total revenue did not exceed $50,000,000 during any of such fiscal years.

(ii) A description of the status of a product or segment (e.g. whether in the planning stage, whether prototypes exist, the degree to which product design has progressed or whether further engineering is necessary), if there has been a public announcement of, or if the registrant otherwise has made public information about, a new product or segment that would require the investment of a material amount of the assets of the registrant or that otherwise is material. This paragraph is not intended to require disclosure of otherwise nonpublic corporate information the disclosure of which would affect adversely the registrant's competitive position.

(iii) The sources and availability of raw materials.

(iv) The importance to the segment and the duration and effect of all patents,

业务分部划分基础上对当期的分部信息作出披露，但不具可行性的情况除外。

（2）若注册人提供了，或《S-X管理办法》第3条（《联邦规章汇编》第十七编第210部分）要求其提供中期财务报表，论述相关期间内与任何业务分部绩效相关的任何事实，且管理层认为，根据该等事实，根据上文规定提供的3年期的业务分部财务数据包含的信息并不能反映分部目前或将来的运营，则注册人应提供论述所必要的比较财务信息。

（c）业务的文字说明。（1）说明注册人及其子公司开展和计划开展的业务，重点介绍注册人的主要业务分部或财务报表中提供了相关财务信息的每一应报告业务分部。为了全面了解注册人的业务，关于每一业务分部的说明均应包括本节第（c）（1）（i）款至第（c）（1）（x）款规定的对理解该等业务具有重要意义的信息。在论述注册人的整体业务时，应论述本节第（c）（1）（xi）款至第（c）（1）（xiii）款规定的事宜；在必要时，应说明该等事项对哪些业务分部意义重大。

（i）注册人在业务分部生产的主要产品和提供的主要服务以及该等产品和服务的主要市场及分销方式。此外，如果在最近3个会计年度的任何一年内任何一类相似产品或服务产生的收入达到注册人并表收入的10%（含）以上，或者在上述任何年度的年度总收入未超过5000万美元的情况下，达到并表收入的15%（含）以上，应说明在最近3个会计年度中该类产品或服务每一年的总收入金额或所占比例。

（ii）对于可能需要注册人作出重大资产投资或具有其他实质重要性的某一新产品或业务分部，如注册人已就该等产品或业务分部发布了公告，或通过其他方式发布了关于该等产品或业务的信息，则应对该等产品或业务分部的现状作出说明（如是否处于规划阶段，是否存在产品原型，产品设计的进度或是否需要进一步的工程设计）。对于披露之后将对注册人的竞争地位造成不利影响的非公开公司信息，本款无意要求予以披露。

（iii）原材料的来源和供应情况。

（iv）注册人持有的所有专利、商标、许可、特许经营权和特许权对业务分部的重要

trademarks, licenses, franchises and concessions held.

(v) The extent to which the business of the segment is or may be seasonal.

(vi) The practices of the registrant and the industry (respective industries) relating to working capital items (e.g., where the registrant is required to carry significant amounts of inventory to meet rapid delivery requirements of customers or to assure itself of a continuous allotment of goods from suppliers; where the registrant provides rights to return merchandise; or where the registrant has provided extended payment terms to customers).

(vii) The dependence of the segment upon a single customer, or a few customers, the loss of any one or more of which would have a material adverse effect on the segment. The name of any customer and its relationship, if any, with the registrant or its subsidiaries shall be disclosed if sales to the customer by one or more segments are made in an aggregate amount equal to 10 percent or more of the registrant's consolidated revenues and the loss of such customer would have a material adverse effect on the registrant and its subsidiaries taken as a whole. The names of other customers may be included, unless in the particular case the effect of including the names would be misleading. For purposes of this paragraph, a group of customers under common control or customers that are affiliates of each other shall be regarded as a single customer.

(viii) The dollar amount of backlog orders believed to be firm, as of a recent date and as of a comparable date in the preceding fiscal year, together with an indication of the portion thereof not reasonably expected to be filled within the current fiscal year, and seasonal or other material aspects of the backlog. (There may be included as firm orders government orders that are firm but not yet funded and contracts awarded but not yet signed, provided an appropriate statement is added to explain the nature of such orders and the amount thereof. The portion of orders already included in sales or operating revenues on the basis of percentage of completion or program accounting shall be excluded.)

(ix) A description of any material portion of the business that may be subject to renegotiation of profits or termination of contracts or subcontracts at the election of the Government.

(x) Competitive conditions in the business involved including, where material, the identity of the particular markets in which the registrant competes, an estimate of the number of competitors and the registrant's competitive position, if known or reasonably available to the registrant. Separate consideration shall be given to the principal products or services or classes of products or services of the segment, if any. Generally, the names of competitors need not be disclosed. The registrant may include such names, unless in the particular case the effect of including the names would be misleading. Where, however, the registrant knows or has reason to know that one or a small number of

性、有效期及影响。

(v)分部的业务是否或可能具有季节性、季节性的程度如何。

(vi)注册人及其各自的行业关于流动资本项目的惯例做法(如在下述情况下采取的惯例做法:注册人须拥有大量存货,以满足客户的快速交货要求或保证其自身可从供应商处获得持续的商品供应分配;注册人提供退货权利;或者注册人已向客户提供延期付款条件)。

(vii)说明业务分部对一个或少数几个客户的依赖性(任何一个丧失之后可能对业务分部造成重大不利影响的客户)。如果一个或多个业务分部对某一客户的销售总额达到或超过注册人并表收入的10%,且丧失该等客户将对注册人及其子公司整体上造成重大不利影响,则应当披露任何该等客户的名称及其与注册人或其子公司的关系(如有)。披露中也可说明其他客户的名称,但根据具体情形,说明该等名称可能造成误导的除外。就本款而言,受同一第三方控制的一组客户或相互具有关联关系的客户应视为单一客户。

(viii)截至最近的某一日期以及上一会计年度的某一可比日期,积压订单的金额(限于注册人认为已确认的订单),同时应说明据合理预期在当前会计年度无法满足的部分、积压的季节性因素或其他重大信息(确定订单包括已确定但尚未拨付资金的政府订单、已授予但尚未签署的合同;应提供一份适当的补充声明,说明该等订单的性质和金额。按照完成百分比或项目核算法已经纳入销售额或经营收入的订单部分不计入确定订单)。

(ix)可能需要对利润进行重新谈判,或者政府可选择终止承包或分包的任何重大业务部分的说明。

(x)注册人掌握或可合理获得的其所涉业务的竞争状况,包括如下具有重大性的信息:注册人参与竞争的特定市场、竞争对手数量预估以及注册人所处竞争地位。应按照业务分部的主要产品或服务、或产品或服务的类别(若有)分别作出说明。一般情况下,不必披露竞争对手的姓名。注册人也可说明竞争对手的名称,但在具体情形下,说明该等名称可能造成误导的除外。但是,如果注册人知道或应该知道某个或少数几个竞争对手占据了行业的主导地位,则应提供该等竞争对手的身份信息。在注册人知道或可合理了解的范围内,说明主要的竞争方式(如价格、服务、保证或产品性能),以及注册人竞争地位的积极和消极因素(若有)。

competitors is dominant in the industry it shall be identified. The principal methods of competition (e.g., price, service, warranty or product performance) shall be identified, and positive and negative factors pertaining to the competitive position of the registrant, to the extent that they exist, shall be explained if known or reasonably available to the registrant.

(xi) If material, the estimated amount spent during each of the last three fiscal years on company-sponsored research and development activities determined in accordance with generally accepted accounting principles. In addition, state, if material, the estimated dollar amount spent during each of such years on customer-sponsored research activities relating to the development of new products, services or techniques or the improvement of existing products, services or techniques.

(xii) Appropriate disclosure also shall be made as to the material effects that compliance with Federal, State and local provisions which have been enacted or adopted regulating the discharge of materials into the environment, or otherwise relating to the protection of the environment, may have upon the capital expenditures, earnings and competitive position of the registrant and its subsidiaries. The registrant shall disclose any material estimated capital expenditures for environmental control facilities for the remainder of its current fiscal year and its succeeding fiscal year and for such further periods as the registrant may deem materials.

(xiii) The number of persons employed by the registrant.

(d) *Financial information about geographic areas.* (1) State for each of the registrant's last three fiscal years, or for each fiscal year the registrant has been engaged in business, whichever period is shorter:

(i) Revenues from external customers attributed to:

(A) The registrant's country of domicile;

(B) All foreign countries, in total, from which the registrant derives revenues; and

(C) Any individual foreign country, if material. Disclose the basis for attributing revenues from external customers to individual countries.

(ii) Long-lived assets, other than financial instruments, long-term customer relationships of a financial institution, mortgage and other servicing rights, deferred policy acquisition costs, and deferred tax assets, located in:

(A) The registrant's country of domicile;

(B) All foreign countries, in total, in which the registrant holds assets; and

(C) Any individual foreign country, if material.

(2) A registrant shall report the amounts based on the financial information that it uses to produce the general-purpose financial statements. If providing the geographic information is impracticable, the registrant shall disclose that fact. A registrant may wish to provide, in addition to the information required by paragraph (d)(1) of this section, subtotals of

(xi)如具有重要意义,应提供按照公认会计原则确定的过去3个会计年度中每一年为公司发起的研发活动所支出金额的预估金额。此外,如具有重要意义,应提供在过去3个会计年度中每一年为客户发起的涉及新产品、服务或技术开发或现有产品、服务或技术改良的研发活动所支出金额的预估金额。

(xii)适当披露履行联邦、州和地方制定或通过的关于环境排放物质监管或其他涉及环境保护的法律法规可能对注册人及其子公司的资本性支出、盈利和竞争地位造成的重大影响。注册人应当披露本会计年度剩余期间、下一会计年度以及注册人认为重要的其他期间,预期将为环境监控设施提供的任何重大资本性支出。

(xiii)注册人聘用的人员数。

(d)各地理区域的财务信息。(1)说明注册人在过去3个会计年度中或自其开展业务以来(如其业务开展期间不足3年)每一年的下述财务信息:

(i)从外部客户取得的可归属于以下国家的收入:

(A)注册人住所地所在国;

(B)所有其他注册人收入来源国;和

(C)任何具有重要性的其他国家,同时应披露将从外部客户取得的收入归属于该等国家的依据。

(ii)位于以下地点的长期资产(金融工具、与某一金融机构的长期客户关系、抵押和其他服务权、递延保单取得成本和递延所得税资产除外):

(A)注册人住所地所在国;

(B)注册人持有资产的所有国家;和

(C)任何具有重要性的其他国家。

(2)注册人应基于其编制一般用途的财务报表时所使用的财务信息提供数据报告。若无法提供地域信息,注册人应如实披露。除本节第(d)(1)款要求提供的信息外,注册人还可提供多组国家地域信息的合计数据。若披露的信息符合公认会计原则,注册人可在其财务报表中对该等数据进行交叉引用,而不必在财务报表中重复列报该

geographic information about groups of countries. To the extent that the disclosed information conforms with generally accepted accounting principles, the registrant may include in its financial statements a cross reference to this data in lieu of presenting duplicative data in its financial statements; conversely, a registrant may cross-reference to the financial statements.

(3) A registrant shall describe any risks attendant to the foreign operations and any dependence on one or more of the registrant's segments upon such foreign operations, unless it would be more appropriate to discuss this information in connection with the description of one or more of the registrant's segments under paragraph (c) of this item.

(4) If the registrant includes, or is required by Article 3 of Regulation S-X(17 CFR 210), to include, interim financial statements, discuss any facts relating to the information furnished under this paragraph (d) that, in the opinion of management, indicate that the three year financial data for geographic areas may not be indicative of current or future operations. To the extent necessary to the discussion, include comparative information.

(e) *Available information.* Disclose the information in paragraphs (e)(1), (e)(2) and (e)(3) of this section in any registration statement you file under the Securities Act (15 U.S.C. 77a *et seq.*), and disclose the information in paragraphs (e)(3) and (e)(4) of this section if you are an accelerated filer or a large accelerated filer (as defined in §240.12b-2 of this chapter) filing an annual report on Form 10-K (§249.310 of this chapter):

(1) Whether you file reports with the Securities and Exchange Commission. If you are a reporting company, identify the reports and other information you file with the SEC.

(2) That the public may read and copy any materials you file with the SEC at the SEC's Public Reference Room at 100 F Street, NE., Washington, D.C. 20549. State that the public may obtain information on the operation of the Public Reference Room by calling the SEC at 1-800-SEC-0330. If you are an electronic filer, state that the SEC maintains an Internet site that contains reports, proxy and information statements, and other information regarding issuers that file electronically with the SEC and state the address of that site (*http://www.sec.gov*).

(3) You are encouraged to give your Internet address, if available, except that if you are an accelerated filer or a large accelerated filer filing your annual report on Form 10-K, you must disclose your Internet address, if you have one.

(4)(i) Whether you make available free of charge on or through your Internet website, if you have one, your annual report on Form 10-K, quarterly reports on Form 10-Q (§249.308a of this chapter), current reports on Form 8-K (§249.308 of this chapter), and amendments to those reports filed or furnished pursuant to Section 13(a) or 15(d) of

等信息;反之,注册人也可在各地理区域的财务信息中对财务报表进行交叉引用。

(3)注册人应说明国外经营活动可能伴随的任何风险以及注册人的一个或数个业务分部对该等国外经营活动的任何依赖性,但在根据本条第(c)款说明注册人的一个或数个业务分部时论述该等信息更为适宜的除外。

(4)若注册人提供了,或《S-X管理办法》第3条(《联邦规章汇编》第十七编第210部分)要求其提供中期财务报表,论述与本第(d)款下提供的信息相关的任何事实,且管理层认为,根据该等事实,就相关地理区域提供3年期的财务数据包含的信息并不能反映其当前或将来的运营,则注册人应提供该等论述所必要的比较信息。

(e)信息提供。在根据《证券法》(《美国法典》第十五编第77a节及其后条文)提交的任何注册说明书中披露本节第(e)(1)款、第(e)(2)款和第(e)(3)款规定的信息;按照《10-K表格》(本章第249.310节)提交年度报告的加速报告公司或大型加速报告公司(定义见本章第240.12b-2节)应披露本节第(e)(3)款和第(e)(4)款规定的信息:

(1)是否负有向证券交易委员会提交报告的义务。如属于报告公司,应说明向证券交易委员会提交的报告和其他信息。

(2)公众可在证券交易委员会华盛顿公共资料室(地址:华盛顿哥伦比亚特区东北分区100F大街,邮编:D.C. 20549)查阅和复制向证券交易委员会提供的任何资料。说明公众可通过致电证券交易委员会(1-800-SEC-0330)获取关于公共资料室服务的信息。电子文件提交人应说明可通过证券交易委员会的互联网查询发行人以电子形式提交的与其相关的报告、征集投票权报告和信息说明书以及其他信息,同时应提供网站地址(http://www.sec.gov)。

(3)证券交易委员会鼓励发行人提供其互联网地址(若有),但是,按照《10-K表格》提交年度报告的加速报告公司或大型加速报告公司必须提供互联网地址(若有)。

(4)(i)对于按照《10-K表格》提交的年度报告、按照《10-Q表格》(本章第249.308a节)提交的季度报告、按照《8-K表格》(本章第249.308节)提交的当期报告以及根据《交易法》第13(a)条或第15(d)条[《美国法典》第十五编第78m(a)节或第78o(d)节]提交或提供的上述报告的修正,是否将在以电子形式向证券交易委员会提交或提供该等

the Exchange Act (15 U.S.C. 78m(a) or 78o(d)) as soon as reasonably practicable after you electronically file such material with, or furnish it to, the SEC;

(ii) If you do not make your filings available in this manner, the reasons you do not do so (including, where applicable, that you do not have an Internet website); and

(iii) If you do not make your filings available in this manner, whether you voluntarily will provide electronic or paper copies of your filings free of charge upon request.

(f) *Reports to security holders.*Disclose the following information in any registration statement you file under the Securities Act:

(1) If the SEC's proxy rules or regulations, or stock exchange requirements, do not require you to send an annual report to security holders or to holders of American depository receipts, describe briefly the nature and frequency of reports that you will give to security holders. Specify whether the reports that you give will contain financial information that has been examined and reported on, with an opinion expressed "by" an independent public or certified public accountant.

(2) For a foreign private issuer, if the report will not contain financial information prepared in accordance with U.S. generally accepted accounting principles, you must state whether the report will include a reconciliation of this information with U.S. generally accepted accounting principles.

(g) *Enforceability of civil liabilities against foreign persons.* Disclose the following if you are a foreign private issuer filing a registration statement under the Securities Act:

(1) Whether or not investors may bring actions under the civil liability provisions of the U.S. Federal securities laws against the foreign private issuer, any of its officers and directors who are residents of a foreign country, any underwriters or experts named in the registration statement that are residents of a foreign country, and whether investors may enforce these civil liability provisions when the assets of the issuer or these other persons are located outside of the United States. The disclosure must address the following matters:

(i) The investor's ability to effect service of process within the United States on the foreign private issuer or any person;

(ii) The investor's ability to enforce judgments obtained in U.S. courts against foreign persons based upon the civil liability provisions of the U.S. Federal securities laws;

(iii) The investor's ability to enforce, in an appropriate foreign court, judgments of U.S. courts based upon the civil liability provisions of the U.S. Federal securities laws; and

(iv) The investor's ability to bring an original action in an appropriate foreign court

文件后合理可行的时间内尽快在互联网站上或通过互联网站(若有)免费向公众提供该等信息。

(ii)若不以上述方式向公众提供提交的文件,请说明原因[包括未开设互联网站的原因(若适用)];和

(iii)若不以上述方式向公众提供提交的文件,是否愿意在公众提出要求之时,免费提供所提交文件的电子或纸质版本。

(f)向证券持有人提供的报告。请在根据《证券法》提交的任何注册说明书中披露以下信息:

(1)若证券交易委员会的投票代理规则或规章,或证券交易所的规定并不要求向证券持有人或美国存托凭证的持有人发送年度报告,请简要说明将向证券持有人提供的报告性质以及提供频率。请说明提供的报告中是否将包含经过核查和报告并由一名独立公共会计师或注册公共会计师出具过意见的财务信息。

(2)对于外国私募发行人,若报告中不包括根据美国公认会计原则编制的财务信息,必须说明报告中是否将包含根据美国公认会计原则对相关信息作出的调节。

(g)外国主体民事责任的可执行性。根据《证券法》提交注册说明书的外国私募发行人应披露以下信息:

(1)投资者是否可以根据美国联邦证券法律中关于民事责任的条款,针对任何外国私募发行人、外国居民管理人员和董事、注册说明书中指明的任何外国居民承销商或专家提起诉讼;在发行人或上述其他主体的资产位于美国境外的情况下,投资者是否可以要求执行前述民事责任条款。披露必须涉及以下事项:

(i)投资者在美国境内对外国私募发行人或任何主体实施送达的能力;

(ii)投资者执行美国法院依据美国联邦证券法律中的民事责任条款针对外国主体作出的判决的能力;

(iii)投资者在相应外国法院申请执行美国法院依据美国联邦证券法律中的民事责任条款作出的判决的能力;和

(iv)投资者依据美国联邦证券法律中的民事责任条款在相应外国法院直接提起

to enforce liabilities against the foreign private issuer or any person based upon the U.S. Federal securities laws.

(2) If you provide this disclosure based on an opinion of counsel, name counsel in the prospectus and file as an exhibit to the registration statement a signed consent of counsel to the use of its name and opinion.

(h) *Smaller reporting companies.* A smaller reporting company, as defined by §229.10(f)(1), may satisfy its obligations under this Item by describing the development of its business during the last three years. If the smaller reporting company has not been in business for three years, give the same information for predecessor(s) of the smaller reporting company if there are any. This business development description should include:

(1) Form and year of organization;

(2) Any bankruptcy, receivership or similar proceeding; and

(3) Any material reclassification, merger, consolidation, or purchase or sale of a significant amount of assets not in the ordinary course of business.

(4) *Business of the smaller reporting company.* Briefly describe the business and include, to the extent material to an understanding of the smaller reporting company:

(i) Principal products or services and their markets;

(ii) Distribution methods of the products or services;

(iii) Status of any publicly announced new product or service;

(iv) Competitive business conditions and the smaller reporting company's competitive position in the industry and methods of competition;

(v) Sources and availability of raw materials and the names of principal suppliers;

(vi) Dependence on one or a few major customers;

(vii) Patents, trademarks, licenses, franchises, concessions, royalty agreements or labor contracts, including duration;

(viii) Need for any government approval of principal products or services. If government approval is necessary and the smaller reporting company has not yet received that approval, discuss the status of the approval within the government approval process;

(ix) Effect of existing or probable governmental regulations on the business;

(x) Estimate of the amount spent during each of the last two fiscal years on research and development activities, and if applicable, the extent to which the cost of such activities is borne directly by customers;

(xi) Costs and effects of compliance with environmental laws (federal, state and local); and

(xii) Number of total employees and number of full-time employees.

(5) *Reports to security holders.* Disclose the following in any registration statement you file under the Securities Act of 1933:

诉讼,要求强制执行外国私募发行人或任何主体的责任的能力。

(2)在基于律师意见作出本披露的情况下,请在招募说明书中指明律师的姓名,并以注册说明书附录的形式提交一份律师签署的同意使用其姓名和意见的同意函。

(h)小型报告公司。第229.10(f)(1)节定义的小型报告公司可通过对过去3年的业务发展情况作出说明,履行本条规定的义务。若小型报告公司开展业务的时间不足3年,应提供其前身公司(若有)的同等业务信息。业务发展说明应包括:

(1)组织形式和组建年份;

(2)任何破产、接管或类似程序;和

(3)任何重大资本结构重组、吸收合并、新设合并或并非在正常业务运作中发生的金额重大的资产购买或出售。

(4)小型报告公司的业务。简要说明小型报告公司的业务,并且应包括对理解小型报告公司具有重要意义的如下信息:

(i)主要产品或服务及其市场;

(ii)产品或服务的分销方式;

(iii)任何已对外公布的新产品或服务的现状;

(iv)业务竞争状况和小型报告公司在行业中的竞争地位和竞争方式;

(v)原材料的来源、供应情况以及主要供应商的名称;

(vi)对一个或少数几个主要客户的依赖性;

(vii)专利、商标、许可、特许经营、特许权、使用费协议或劳动合同,包括该等协议或合同的期限;

(viii)主要产品或服务是否需要取得任何政府批准。若须获得政府批准,但小型报告公司尚未获得该等批准,应说明政府批准程序的进展状况;

(ix)现行或可能颁布的政府规章对业务的影响;

(x)过去两个会计年度内每年研发活动开支的预估金额,且在适用的情况下,应说明客户直接承担的份额;

(xi)遵守(联邦、州或地方)环境法律的成本及效应;和

(xii)全体雇员人数和全职雇员人数。

(5)向证券持有人提供的报告。在根据《1933年证券法》提交的任何注册说明书中披露以下信息:

(i) If you are not required to deliver an annual report to security holders, whether you will voluntarily send an annual report and whether the report will include audited financial statements;

(ii) Whether you file reports with the Securities and Exchange Commission. If you are a reporting company, identify the reports and other information you file with the Commission; and

(iii) That the public may read and copy any materials you file with the Commission at the SEC's Public Reference Room at 100 F Street, NE., Washington, D.C. 20549, on official business days during the hours of 10 a.m. to 3 p.m. State that the public may obtain information on the operation of the Public Reference Room by calling the Commission at 1-800-SEC-0330. State that the Commission maintains an Internet site that contains reports, proxy and information statements, and other information regarding issuers that file electronically with the Commission and state the address of that site (*http://www.sec.gov*). You are encouraged to give your Internet address, if available.

(6) *Foreign issuers*. Provide the information required by Item 101(g) of Regulation S-K (§229.101(g)).

Instructions to Item 101:1. In determining what information about the segments is material to an understanding of the registrant's business taken as a whole and therefore required to be disclosed, pursuant to paragraph (c) of this Item, the registrant should take into account both quantitative and qualitative factors such as the significance of the matter to the registrant(e.g., whether a matter with a relatively minor impact on the registrant's business is represented by management to be important to its future profitability), the pervasiveness of the matter(e.g., whether it affects or may affect numerous items in the segment information), and the impact of the matter(e.g., whether it distorts the trends reflected in the segment information). Situations may arise when information should be disclosed about a segment, although the information in quantitative terms may not appear significant to the registrant's business taken as a whole.

2. Base the determination of whether information about segments is required for a particular year upon an evaluation of interperiod comparability. For instance, interperiod comparability would require a registrant to report segment information in the current period even if not material under the criteria for reportability of SFAS No. 131 if a segment has been significant in the immediately preceding period and the registrant expects it to be significant in the future.

3. The Commission, upon written request of the registrant and where consistent with the protection of investors, may permit the omission of any of the information required by this Item or the furnishing in substitution thereof of appropriate information of comparable character.

(i)如没有义务向证券持有人交付年度报告,是否会自愿发送年度报告以及报告中是否将包含已审计财务报表;

(ii)是否负有向证券交易委员会提交报告的义务。如属于报告公司,应说明向证券交易委员会提交的报告和其他信息;及

(iii)在官方工作日的上午10时至下午3时,公众可在证券交易委员会华盛顿公共资料室(地址:华盛顿哥伦比亚特区东北分区100F大街,邮编:D.C. 20549)查阅和复制向证券交易委员会提供的任何资料。说明公众可通过致电证券交易委员会(1-800-SEC-0330)获取关于公共资料室服务的信息。电子文件提交人应说明可通过证券交易委员会的互联网查询发行人以电子形式提交的与其相关的报告、征集投票权报告和信息说明书以及其他信息,同时应提供网站地址(http://www.sec.gov)。证券交易委员会建议提供互联网址(若有)。

(6)外国发行人。提供《S-K管理办法》第101(g)条[本章第229.101(g)节]规定的信息。

关于第101条的说明:1.根据本条第(c)款,在确定哪些业务分部的信息对理解注册人整体业务具有重要性并据此确定应披露的信息时,注册人应同时考虑定量和定性因素,如相关事项对注册人的重要性(如对注册人业务影响相对较小的事项,管理层是否认为该事项对其未来的盈利能力具有重要意义)、事项的广泛性(如该事项是否对业务分部信息中多项内容具有或可能具有影响),以及相关事项产生的影响(如该事项是否会歪曲业务分部信息中反映的趋势)。可能发生此类情形:虽然从数量角度而言,某信息对注册人的整体业务可能并不具有重要性,但在披露业务分部的相关信息时仍应进行披露。

2.在判断是否需要就某一特定年度提供业务分部信息时,应以对不同期间的可比性的评估为基础。例如,如果某一业务分部在上一个期间具有重要意义,且注册人预期其在未来仍将具有重要意义,即使该等分部信息按照《财务会计准则公告第131号》规定的报告标准并不具有重要性,但出于不同期间的可比性,注册人可能仍需要在当期报告中对相关分部信息进行报告。

3.经注册人书面请求且在符合保护投资者原则的情形下,证券交易委员会可允许注册人省略本条规定的任何项信息,或允许其提供具有可比特征的适当信息作为替代。

[47 FR 11401, Mar. 16, 1982, as amended at 63 FR 6381, Feb. 6, 1998; 64 FR 1734, Jan. 12, 1999; 67 FR 58504, Sept. 16, 2002; 70 FR 76641, Dec. 27, 2005; 73 FR 957, Jan. 4, 2008]

§229.102(Item 102) Description of property.

State briefly the location and general character of the principal plants, mines and other materially important physical properties of the registrant and its subsidiaries. In addition, identify the segment(s), as reported in the financial statements, that use the properties described. If any such property is not held in fee or is held subject to any major encumbrance, so state and describe briefly how held.

Instructions to Item 102: 1. What is required is such information as reasonably will inform investors as to the suitability, adequacy, productive capacity and extent of utilization of the facilities by the registrant. Detailed descriptions of the physical characteristics of individual properties or legal descriptions by metes and bounds are not required and shall not be given.

2. In determining whether properties should be described, the registrant should take into account both quantitative and qualitative factors. See Instruction 1 to Item 101 of Regulation S-K (§229.101).

3. In the case of an extractive enterprise, not involved in oil and gas producing activities, material information shall be given as to production, reserves, locations, development, and the nature of the registrant's interest. If individual properties are of major significance to an industry segment:

A. More detailed information concerning these matters shall be furnished; and

B. Appropriate maps shall be used to disclose location data of significant properties except in cases for which numerous maps would be required.

4. A registrant engaged in oil and gas producing activities shall provide the information required by Subpart 1200 of Regulation S-K.

5. In the case of extractive reserves other than oil and gas reserves, estimates other than proven or probable reserves (and any estimated values of such reserves) shall not be disclosed in any document publicly filed with the Commission, unless such information is required to be disclosed in the document by foreign or state law; provided, however, that where such estimates previously have been provided to a person (or any of its affiliates) that is offering to acquire, merge, or consolidate with the registrant, or otherwise to acquire the registrant's securities, such estimates may be included in documents relating to such acquisition.

6. The definitions in §210.4-10(a) of Regulation S-X [17 CFR 210] shall apply to this Item with respect to oil and gas operations.

[《联邦公报》第47卷第11401页,1982年3月16日,修正索引:《联邦公报》第63卷第6381页,1998年2月6日;《联邦公报》第64卷第1734页,1999年1月12日;《联邦公报》第67卷第58504页,2002年9月16日;《联邦公报》第70卷第76641页,2005年12月27日;《联邦公报》第73卷第957页,2008年1月4日。]

第229.102节(第102条) 财产说明

简要说明注册人及其子公司的主要厂房、矿产以及其他具有实质重要性的实物财产的位置和一般特征。此外,应根据财务报表的报告,指明使用该等财产的业务分部。如果注册人及其子公司拥有的任何该等财产不属于可自由继承的财产,或该等财产上存在任何重大权利负担,应对所有权状况和权利负担进行简要说明。

关于第102条的说明:1. 要求提供该等信息的目的是使投资者合理了解注册人设施的适当性、充分性、产能和利用程度。注册人不必且不应对各项财产的物理特征作出具体的说明或提供以地界表示的法定说明。

2.在判断是否应提供财产说明时,注册人应同时考虑定量和定性因素。参见关于《S-K管理办法》第101条的说明1(本章第229.101节)。

3.对于不从事油气生产活动的采掘企业,应当提供有关生产、储量、位置、开发和注册人权益性质等方面的重大信息。如单项资产对某一产业分部具有重要意义,应:

A.就该等事宜提供更为具体的信息;并

B.通过适当的地图披露该等重要资产的地理位置信息,但需要提供大量地图的情况除外。

4.从事油气生产活动的注册人应当提供《S-K管理办法》第1200子部分规定的信息。

5.若采掘业务涉及的资源为油气资源以外的其他资源储备,除证实储量或概算储量外,任何预估数据以及关于该等资源的任何预估价值,均不得在公开提交给证券交易委员会的任何文件中披露,但外国法律或州法律要求在文件中披露该等信息的除外;但是,如果该等预估之前已提供给向注册人提出控股合并、吸收合并或新设合并要约或其他形式的证券收购要约的某主体(或其任何关联方),则该等预估可以纳入与该等收购相关的文件之中。

6.就油气经营活动而言,《S-X管理办法》第210.4-10(a)条[《联邦规章汇编》第十七编第210部分]的定义应适用于本条规定。

7. The attention of issuers engaged in significant mining operations is directed to the information called for in Guide 7 (§229.801(g) and §229.802(g)).

8. The attention of certain issuers engaged in oil and gas producing activities is directed to the information called for in Securities Act Industry Guide 4 (referred to in §229.801(d)).

9. The attention of issuers engaged in real estate activities is directed to the information called for in Guide 5 (§229.801(e) of this chapter).

[47 FR 11401, Mar. 16, 1982, as amended at 64 FR 1735, Jan. 12, 1999; 73 FR 957, Jan. 4, 2008; 74 FR 2193, Jan. 14, 2009]

§229.103(Item 103) Legal proceedings.

Describe briefly any material pending legal proceedings, other than ordinary routine litigation incidental to the business, to which the registrant or any of its subsidiaries is a party or of which any of their property is the subject. Include the name of the court or agency in which the proceedings are pending, the date instituted, the principal parties thereto, a description of the factual basis alleged to underlie the proceeding and the relief sought. Include similar information as to any such proceedings known to be contemplated by governmental authorities.

Instructions to Item 103: 1. If the business ordinarily results in actions for negligence or other claims, no such action or claim need be described unless it departs from the normal kind of such actions.

2. No information need be given with respect to any proceeding that involves primarily a claim for damages if the amount involved, exclusive of interest and costs, does not exceed 10 percent of the current assets of the registrant and its subsidiaries on a consolidated basis. However, if any proceeding presents in large degree the same legal and factual issues as other proceedings pending or known to be contemplated, the amount involved in such other proceedings shall be included in computing such percentage.

3. Notwithstanding Instructions 1 and 2, any material bankruptcy, receivership, or similar proceeding with respect to the registrant or any of its significant subsidiaries shall be described.

4. Any material proceedings to which any director, officer or affiliate of the registrant, any owner of record or beneficially of more than five percent of any class of voting securities of the registrant, or any associate of any such director, officer, affiliate of the registrant, or security holder is a party adverse to the registrant or any of its subsidiaries or has a material interest adverse to the registrant or any of its subsidiaries also shall be described.

5. Notwithstanding the foregoing, an administrative or judicial proceeding (including,

7.从事大规模采矿经营活动的发行人应遵照《指引7》[第229.801(g)节和第229.802(g)节]提供规定的信息。

8.从事油气生产活动的特定发行人应遵照《证券法产业指引4》[见第229.801(d)节]提供规定的信息。

9.从事房地产业务的发行人应遵照《指引5》[本章第229.801(e)节]提供规定的信息。

[《联邦公报》第47卷第11401页,1982年3月16日,修正索引:《联邦公报》第64卷第1735页,1999年1月12日;《联邦公报》第73卷第957页,2008年1月4日;《联邦公报》第74卷第2193页,2009年1月14日。]

第229.103节(第103条) 法律程序

简要说明以注册人或其任何子公司为当事人或其任何财产为诉讼标的的任何重大未决法律程序,但因其业务性质产生的常见诉讼除外。说明审理该等法律程序的法院或机构的名称、起诉日期、主要当事人,同时应说明当事人在程序中主张的事实基础以及寻求的救济。注册人知道政府机构正在考虑提起任何该等法律程序的,亦应提供类似信息。

关于第103条的说明:1.如果注册人因其业务性质经常会引发过失诉讼或其他索赔,只有该等诉讼或索赔属于非常规诉讼索赔时才需要作出说明。

2.对于主要涉及赔偿金索赔的任何程序,且所涉金额(不计利息和费用)不超过注册人及其子公司流动资产合计金额10%的,不必提供相关信息。但是,在计算上述百分比时,如果任何程序所涉的法律和事实问题与其他未决程序或已知有提起之虞的程序大体相同,则该等程序所涉金额应合并计算。

3.无论说明1和说明2如何规定,与注册人或其任何重要子公司有关的任何重大破产、接管或类似程序均应如实说明。

4.注册人的任何董事、管理人员或关联方,持有注册人任何类别的有表决权证券5%以上的任何登记所有人或受益所有人,上述任何董事、管理人员、关联方或证券持有人的任何业务相关人作为当事人,针对注册人或其任何子公司提起任何重大程序,或在任何重大程序中拥有与注册人或其任何子公司相反的重大利益的,应对该等重大程序作出说明。

5.无论上文如何规定,按照已经颁布或通过的旨在监管环境排放物质或主旨在于

for purposes of A and B of this Instruction, proceedings which present in large degree the same issues) arising under any Federal, State or local provisions that have been enacted or adopted regulating the discharge of materials into the environment or primary for the purpose of protecting the environment shall not be deemed "ordinary routine litigation incidental to the business" and shall be described if:

A. Such proceeding is material to the business or financial condition of the registrant;

B. Such proceeding involves primarily a claim for damages, or involves potential monetary sanctions, capital expenditures, deferred charges or charges to income and the amount involved, exclusive of interest and costs, exceeds 10 percent of the current assets of the registrant and its subsidiaries on a consolidated basis; or

C. A governmental authority is a party to such proceeding and such proceeding involves potential monetary sanctions, unless the registrant reasonably believes that such proceeding will result in no monetary sanctions, or in monetary sanctions, exclusive of interest and costs, of less than $100,000; provided, however, that such proceedings which are similar in nature may be grouped and described generically.

Subpart 229.200 — Securities of the Registrant

§229.201 (Item 201) Market price of and dividends on the registrant's common equity and related stockholder matters.

(a) *Market information.* (1)(i) Identify the principal United States market or markets in which each class of the registrant's common equity is being traded. Where there is no established public trading market for a class of common equity, furnish a statement to that effect. For purposes of this Item the existence of limited or sporadic quotations should not of itself be deemed to constitute an "established public trading market." In the case of foreign registrants, also identify the principal established foreign public trading market, if any, for each class of the registrant's common equity.

(ii) If the principal United States market for such common equity is an exchange, state the high and low sales prices for the equity for each full quarterly period within the two most recent fiscal years and any subsequent interim period for which financial statements are included, or are required to be included by Article 3-01 through 3-04 of Regulation S-X(§210.3-01 through 3-04 of this chapter), or Article 8-02 through 8-03 of Regulation S-X (§210.8-02 through 8-03 of this chapter) in the case of smaller reporting companies, as reported in the consolidated transaction reporting system or, if not so reported, as reported on the principal exchange market for such equity.

保护环境的任何联邦、州或地方法律法规提起的行政或司法程序(就本说明A项和B项而言,包括涉及大体类似问题的程序)不应视为"因其业务性质产生的常见诉讼",且在满足下列任一条件的情况下,应对该等程序作出说明:

A.该等程序对注册人的业务或财务状况具有重大影响;

B.该等程序主要涉及赔偿金索赔或可能涉及罚款、资本性支出、递延费用、所得抵扣,且所涉金额(不计利息和费用)超过流动资产合计金额的10%;或

C.政府机构作为当事人参与了该等程序,且该等程序可能涉及罚款,除非注册人合理相信该等程序不会造成罚款,或即使造成罚款,其金额(不含利息和费用)也将低于10万美元;但是,性质类似的程序可以合并,并予以一般性的说明。

第229.200子部分——注册人的证券

第229.201节(第201条) 注册人普通股的市场价格和股息以及股东相关事项

(a)市场信息。(1)(i)指明注册人每一类别普通股在美国的主要交易市场(可以为一个或数个)。对于不存在稳定公开交易市场的任何类别的普通股,注册人应对此进行说明。就本条而言,有限或零星的报价本身不得视为构成"稳定公开交易市场"。对于外国注册人,还应注明每一类别普通股在外国的主要的稳定公开交易市场(如有)。

(ii)如果该等普通股在美国的主要交易市场为一家交易所,应说明下述期间内该等普通股的最高和最低卖出价:最近两个会计年度每一个完整的季度期间,以及提交财务报表的任何期后中期期间,或(对于小型报告公司而言)按照《S-X管理办法》第3-01~3-04条(本章第210.3-01~210.3-04节)或《S-X管理办法》第8-02~8-03条(本章第210.8-02~2108-03节)规定应提交财务报表的期后中期期间。该等卖价应为在合并交易报告系统中报告的价格,如果上述系统中不存在相关报告,则为在主要交易市场报告的卖价。

(iii) If the principal United States market for such common equity is not an exchange, state the range of high and low bid information for the equity for each full quarterly period within the two most recent fiscal years and any subsequent interim period for which financial statements are included, or are required to be included by Article 3 of Regulation S–X, as regularly quoted in the automated quotation system of a registered securities association, or where the equity is not quoted in such a system, the range of reported high and low bid quotations, indicating the source of such quotations. Indicate, as applicable, that such over–the–counter market quotations reflect inter–dealer prices, without retail mark–up, mark–down or commission and may not necessarily represent actual transactions. Where there is an absence of an established public trading market, reference to quotations shall be qualified by appropriate explanation.

(iv) Where a foreign registrant has identified a principal established foreign trading market for its common equity pursuant to paragraph (a)(1) of this Item, also provide market price information comparable, to the extent practicable, to that required for the principal United States market, including the source of such information. Such prices shall be stated in the currency in which they are quoted. The registrant may translate such prices into United States currency at the currency exchange rate in effect on the date the price disclosed was reported on the foreign exchange. If the primary United States market for the registrant's common equity trades using American Depositary Receipts, the United States prices disclosed shall be on that basis.

(v) If the information called for by this Item is being presented in a registration statement filed pursuant to the Securities Act or a proxy or information statement filed pursuant to the Exchange Act, the document also shall include price information as of the latest practicable date, and, in the case of securities to be issued in connection with an acquisition, business combination or other reorganization, as of the date immediately prior to the public announcement of such transaction.

(2) If the information called for by this paragraph (a) is being presented in a registration statement on Form S–1(§239.11 of this chapter) under the Securities Act or on Form 10(§249.210 of this chapter) under the Exchange Act relating to a class of common equity for which at the time of filing there is no established United States public trading market, indicate the amount(s) of common equity:

(i) That is subject to outstanding options or warrants to purchase, or securities convertible into, common equity of the registrant;

(ii) That could be sold pursuant to §230.144 of this chapter or that the registrant has agreed to register under the Securities Act for sale by security holders; or

(iii) That is being, or has been publicly proposed to be, publicly offered by the registrant(unless such common equity is being offered pursuant to an employee benefit

(iii)如果该等普通股在美国的主要交易市场并非一家交易所,应说明下述期间内该等普通股的最高和最低买入报价波动范围的信息:最近两个会计年度每一个完整的季度期间,以及提交财务报表的任何期后中期期间,或按照《S-X管理办法》第3条规定应提交财务报表的任何期后中期期间。该等信息应基于在某一注册证券业协会的自动报价系统中有经常性报价的买入报价信息,如果相关普通股不在上述系统中报价,则为所报告的最高和最低买入报价范围,同时应说明该等报价的来源。在适当情况下,应说明该等场外交易市场的报价反映的是不含零售加成、减成或佣金的交易商之间的价格,可能并不能反映真实交易。如不存在稳定公开交易市场,引用报价时应通过适当的说明予以界定。

(iv)如外国注册人已经按照本条第(a)(1)款的规定指明其普通股在国外的主要稳定交易市场,还应在可行范围内,参照对美国市场的相关规定,提供具有可比性的市场价格信息,包括提供该等信息的来源。该等价格应以股票的报价货币表示。注册人可以将该等价格换算为美国货币,换算时应采用该等披露价格于外国交易所报告当日的有效汇率。如果注册人的普通股的主要美国交易市场使用美国存托凭证交易,应在该等基础上披露股票的美国市场价格。

(v)如果本条要求提供的信息,在按照《证券法》提交的注册说明书或按照《交易法》提交的征集投票权报告或信息说明书中也会提供,文件中还应包括截至最近可行日期的价格信息;对于因收购、业务合并或其他重组发行的证券,则应包括截至该等交易公开宣布前一天的价格信息。

(2)如果本第(a)款要求提供的信息也会通过注册说明书作出说明,且该等注册说明书系按照《证券法》下的《S-1表格》(本章第239.11节)或《交易法》下的《10表格》(本章第249.210节)提交,同时在注册说明书提交之时尚不存在稳定的美国公开交易市场,应说明:

(i)可根据发行在外的认购期权或权证购买的注册人普通股数量,或可转换证券可转换的注册人普通股数量;

(ii)可以按照本章第230.144节卖出的普通股数量,或注册人已经同意根据《证券法》注册供证券持有人出售的普通股数量;

(iii)注册人正在公开发售或已经公开提议公开发售的普通股数量(根据员工福利计划或股息再投资计划发行的普通股除外),条件是该等发售将对注册人普通股的市

plan or dividend reinvestment plan), the offering of which could have a material effect on the market price of the registrant's common equity.

(b) *Holders.* (1) Set forth the approximate number of holders of each class of common equity of the registrant as of the latest practicable date.

(2) If the information called for by this paragraph (b) is being presented in a registration statement filed pursuant to the Securities Act or a proxy statement or information statement filed pursuant to the Exchange Act that relates to an acquisition, business combination or other reorganization, indicate the effect of such transaction on the amount and percentage of present holdings of the registrant's common equity owned beneficially by (i) any person (including any group as that term is used in section 13(d)(3) of the Exchange Act) who is known to the registrant to be the beneficial owner of more than five percent of any class of the registrant's common equity and (ii) each director and nominee and (iii) all directors and officers as a group, and the registrant's present commitments to such persons with respect to the issuance of shares of any class of its common equity.

(c) *Dividends.* (1) State the frequency and amount of any cash dividends declared on each class of its common equity by the registrant for the two most recent fiscal years and any subsequent interim period for which financial statements are required to be presented by §210.3 of Regulation S-X. Where there are restrictions (including, where appropriate, restrictions on the ability of registrant's subsidiaries to transfer funds to the registrant in the form of cash dividends, loans or advances) that currently materially limit the registrant's ability to pay such dividends or that the registrant reasonably believes are likely to limit materially the future payment of dividends on the common equity so state and either (i) describe briefly (where appropriate quantify) such restrictions, or (ii) cross reference to the specific discussion of such restrictions in the Management's Discussion and Analysis of financial condition and operating results prescribed by Item 303 of Regulation S-K (§229.303) and the description of such restrictions required by Regulation S-X in the registrant's financial statements.

(2) Where registrants have a record of paying no cash dividends although earnings indicate an ability to do so, they are encouraged to consider the question of their intention to pay cash dividends in the foreseeable future and, if no such intention exists, to make a statement of that fact in the filing. Registrants which have a history of paying cash dividends also are encouraged to indicate whether they currently expect that comparable cash dividends will continue to be paid in the future and, if not, the nature of the change in the amount or rate of cash dividend payments.

(d) *Securities authorized for issuance under equity compensation plans.* (1) In the following tabular format, provide the information specified in paragraph (d)(2) of this

场价格造成重大影响。

(b)持有人。(1)载明截至最近的一个可行日期,注册人每一类别普通股持有人的大致人数。

(2)如果本第(b)款要求提供的信息也会在并购、业务合并或其他重组发生时按照《证券法》提交的注册说明书或按照《交易法》提交的征集投票权报告或信息说明书中作出说明,则应说明该等交易对注册人的如下受益所有人当前持有的普通股数量和比例的影响:(i)注册人已知的持有注册人任何类别普通股5%以上的受益所有人[包括任何团体,"团体"一词的定义见《交易法》第13(d)(3)条];和(ii)每一位董事和提名董事;以及(iii)作为一个群体的注册人全体董事和管理人员。同时应说明注册人就其任何类别的普通股份发行向上述人员作出的承诺。

(c)股息。(1)说明注册人在下述期间就每一类别普通股宣布所有现金股息的频率和金额:最近两个会计年度,以及按照《S-X管理办法》第210.3条要求提交财务报表的任何期后中期期间。如果由于注册人的子公司以支付现金股息、贷款或垫付资金的形式向注册人转移资金的能力存在限制等适当情形,导致注册人现金股息支付能力当前存在重大限制,或注册人合理相信将来将产生该等重大限制,应作出相应说明,同时应(i)简要说明该等限制(适当情况下,应予量化);或(ii)交叉引用《S-K管理办法》第303条(第229.303节)规定的《管理层论述与分析》中关于财务状况和经营成果的讨论,以及《S-X管理办法》要求注册人在财务报表中提供的对该等限制的说明。

(2)如果注册人存在如下行为记录:虽然其盈利表明其有能力支付现金股息,但是实际并未支付,则鼓励注册人考虑其在可预见的未来支付现金股息的意愿问题,如果注册人并不存在该等意愿,应在提交文件中作出说明。同时,也鼓励拥有支付现金股息记录的注册人说明其是否预期未来仍将继续支付具有可比性的现金股息,如果答案是否定的,应说明现金股息支付的金额或费率的变化性质。

(d)股权报酬计划下获准发行的证券。(1)按下表格式根据本条第(d)(2)款的具体规定,就下述获准发行股权证券的报酬计划(包括个人报酬安排)提供截至最近结

Item as of the end of the most recently completed fiscal year with respect to compensation plans (including individual compensation arrangements) under which equity securities of the registrant are authorized for issuance, aggregated as follows:

(i) All compensation plans previously approved by security holders; and

(ii) All compensation plans not previously approved by security holders.

Equity Compensation Plan Information

Plan category	Number of securities to be issued upon exercise of outstanding options, warrants and rights	Weighted-average exercise price of outstanding options, warrants and rights	Number of securities remaining available for future issuance under equity compensation plans (excluding securities reflected in column (a))
	(a)	(b)	(c)
Equity compensation plans approved by security holders			
Equity compensation plans not approved by security holders			
Total			

(2) The table shall include the following information as of the end of the most recently completed fiscal year for each category of equity compensation plan described in paragraph (d)(1) of this Item:

(i) The number of securities to be issued upon the exercise of outstanding options, warrants and rights (column (a));

(ii) The weighted-average exercise price of the outstanding options, warrants and rights disclosed pursuant to paragraph (d)(2)(i) of this Item (column (b)); and

(iii) Other than securities to be issued upon the exercise of the outstanding options, warrants and rights disclosed in paragraph (d)(2)(i) of this Item, the number of securities remaining available for future issuance under the plan (column (c)).

(3) For each compensation plan under which equity securities of the registrant are authorized for issuance that was adopted without the approval of security holders, describe briefly, in narrative form, the material features of the plan.

Instructions to paragraph (d). 1. Disclosure shall be provided with respect to any compensation plan and individual compensation arrangement of the registrant (or parent,

束的会计年度年末的累计信息:

(i)证券持有人之前批准的所有报酬计划;及
(ii)证券持有人之前未批准的所有报酬计划。

股权报酬计划信息

计划类别	发行在外期权、权证和购股权行权时将发行的证券数量	发行在外期权、权证和购股权的加权平均行权价	股权报酬计划下仍然可以用于未来发行的证券数量(不含(a)栏中填写的证券)
	(a)	(b)	(c)
证券持有人批准的股权报酬计划			
证券持有人未批准的股权报酬计划			
合计			

(2)本表应包括本条第(d)(1)款所述每一类别股权报酬计划截至最近结束的会计年度年末的如下信息:

(i)发行在外期权、权证和购股权行权时将发行的证券数量[(a)栏];

(ii)根据本条第(d)(2)(i)款披露的发行在外期权、权证和购股权的加权平均行权价[(b)栏];及

(iii)扣除本条第(d)(2)(i)款披露的发行在外期权、权证和权利行权后将发行的证券之后,股权报酬计划下仍然可以用于未来发行的证券数量[不含(a)栏中填写的证券][(c)栏]。

(3)对于未获得证券持有人批准,但有权发行注册人股权证券的每一报酬计划,应对计划的主要特点进行简要的文字说明。

关于第(d)款的说明。1.披露应涵盖注册人(或注册人的母公司、子公司或关联方)符合下列条件的任何报酬计划和个人报酬安排:注册人在该等报酬计划和报酬安排

subsidiary or affiliate of the registrant) under which equity securities of the registrant are authorized for issuance to employees or non-employees (such as directors, consultants, advisors, vendors, customers, suppliers or lenders) in exchange for consideration in the form of goods or services as described in Statement of Financial Accounting Standards No. 123, *Accounting for Stock-Based Compensation*, or any successor standard. No disclosure is required with respect to:

a. Any plan, contract or arrangement for the issuance of warrants or rights to all security holders of the registrant as such on a pro rata basis (such as a stock rights offering); or

b. Any employee benefit plan that is intended to meet the qualification requirements of Section 401(a) of the Internal Revenue Code (26 U.S.C. 401(a)).

2. For purposes of this paragraph, an "individual compensation arrangement" includes, but is not limited to, the following: a written compensation contract within the meaning of "employee benefit plan" under §230.405 of this chapter and a plan (whether or not set forth in any formal document) applicable to one person as provided under Item 402(a)(6)(ii) of Regulation S-K (§229.402(a)(6)(ii)).

3. If more than one class of equity security is issued under its equity compensation plans, a registrant should aggregate plan information for each class of security.

4. A registrant may aggregate information regarding individual compensation arrangements with the plan information required under paragraph (d)(1)(i) and (ii) of this Item, as applicable.

5. A registrant may aggregate information regarding a compensation plan assumed in connection with a merger, consolidation or other acquisition transaction pursuant to which the registrant may make subsequent grants or awards of its equity securities with the plan information required under paragraph (d)(1)(i) and (ii) of this Item, as applicable. A registrant shall disclose on an aggregated basis in a footnote to the table the information required under paragraph (d)(2)(i) and (ii) of this Item with respect to any individual options, warrants or rights assumed in connection with a merger, consolidation or other acquisition transaction.

6. To the extent that the number of securities remaining available for future issuance disclosed in column (c) includes securities available for future issuance under any compensation plan or individual compensation arrangement other than upon the exercise of an option, warrant or right, disclose the number of securities and type of plan separately for each such plan in a footnote to the table.

7. If the description of an equity compensation plan set forth in a registrant's financial statements contains the disclosure required by paragraph (d)(3) of this Item, a cross-reference to such description will satisfy the requirements of paragraph (d)(3) of

下获准向雇员或非雇员(如董事、咨询师、顾问、卖方、客户、供应商和贷款人)发行股权证券,发行对价采用的形式为《财务会计准则公告第123号——基于股票的报酬的会计处理》或其任何后续标准中规定的货物或服务。但是,对于如下计划、合约或安排,不必进行披露:

a.为向注册人的全体证券持有人按比例发行权证或购股权(如配股)而设立的任何计划、合约或安排;或

b.按照《国内税收法典》第401(a)条[《美国法典》第二十六编第401(a)节]的资格要求设计的任何雇员福利计划。

2.就本款而言,“个人报酬安排”包括但不限于:属于本章第230.405节定义的“雇员福利计划”的书面报酬合同,以及适用于《S-K管理办法》第402(a)(6)(ii)条[第229.402(a)(6)(ii)节]规定的主体的报酬计划(无论是否载于任何正式文件之中)。

3.如果发行人在股票报酬计划下发行的股权证券的类别超过一个,应就每一类别证券提供各计划的汇总信息。

4.注册人可以将个人报酬安排信息和本条第(d)(1)(i)款和第(d)(1)(ii)款要求提供的计划信息汇总(如适用)。

5.注册人因吸收合并、新设合并或其他收购交易而继承报酬计划,且注册人可以根据该等计划对股权证券进行后续授予或奖励的,注册人可以将与该等计划相关的信息与在本条第(d)(1)(i)款和第(d)(1)(ii)款要求提供的计划信息进行汇总(如适用)。对于注册人因吸收合并、新设合并或其他收购交易而继承任何个人期权、权证或购股权的,注册人应通过表格的脚注,集中披露本条第(d)(2)(i)款和第(d)(2)(ii)款要求提供的信息。

6.如(c)栏披露的仍可用于未来发行的证券数量包括任何报酬计划或个人报酬安排下仍可用于未来发行的证券(期权、权证或购股权行权后将发行的证券除外),应在表格脚注中就每一该等计划分别披露对应的证券数量和计划类型。

7.如果注册人在财务报表中对股票报酬计划进行说明时,包含了本条第(d)(3)款要求披露的内容,交叉引用该等说明即视为履行本条第(d)(3)款的规定。

this Item.

8. If an equity compensation plan contains a formula for calculating the number of securities available for issuance under the plan, including, without limitation, a formula that automatically increases the number of securities available for issuance by a percentage of the number of outstanding securities of the registrant, a description of this formula shall be disclosed in a footnote to the table.

9. Except where it is part of a document that is incorporated by reference into a prospectus, the information required by this paragraph need not be provided in any registration statement filed under the Securities Act.

(e) *Performance graph.* (1) Provide a line graph comparing the yearly percentage change in the registrant's cumulative total shareholder return on a class of common stock registered under section 12 of the Exchange Act (as measured by dividing the sum of the cumulative amount of dividends for the measurement period, assuming dividend reinvestment, and the difference between the registrant's share price at the end and the beginning of the measurement period; by the share price at the beginning of the measurement period) with:

(i) The cumulative total return of a broad equity market index assuming reinvestment of dividends, that includes companies whose equity securities are traded on the same exchange or are of comparable market capitalization;*provided, however,*that if the registrant is a company within the Standard & Poor's 500 Stock Index, the registrant must use that index; and

(ii) The cumulative total return, assuming reinvestment of dividends, of:

(A) A published industry or line-of-business index;

(B) Peer issuer(s) selected in good faith. If the registrant does not select its peer issuer (s) on an industry or line-of-business basis, the registrant shall disclose the basis for its selection; or

(C) Issuer(s) with similar market capitalization(s), but only if the registrant does not use a published industry or line-of-business index and does not believe it can reasonably identify a peer group. If the registrant uses this alternative, the graph shall be accompanied by a statement of the reasons for this selection.

(2) For purposes of paragraph (e)(1) of this Item, the term "measurement period" shall be the period beginning at the "measurement point" established by the market close on the last trading day before the beginning of the registrant's fifth preceding fiscal year, through and including the end of the registrant's last completed fiscal year. If the class of securities has been registered under section 12 of the Exchange Act (15 U.S.C. 78*l*) for a shorter period of time, the period covered by the comparison may correspond to that time period.

8.如果一项股票报酬计划中设定有计算该计划下可用于发行的证券数量的公式,包括但不限于按照注册人发行在外证券数量的百分比自动提高可用于发行的证券数量的计算公式,应在表格脚注中披露对这一公式的说明。

9.本款要求提供的信息不必在根据《证券法》提交的任何注册说明书中披露,但是经引用而被纳入招募说明书的文件所含的信息除外。

(e)业绩图。(1)提供一份曲线图,将注册人根据《交易法》第12条注册的一类普通股的股东累计总回报的年度百分比变化情况与如下数据进行对比(上述百分比变化情况应通过如下方式计算:计量期间的累计股息额(指假设股息再投资基础上的数额)加上注册人在计量期间期末与期初的股价差额之和,除以计量期间期初的股价):

(i)在假设股息再投资的基础上计算的宽基股权市场指数的累计总回报,计算该等指数时应包括在同一个交易所交易股权证券的公司或市值具有可比性的公司;但是,如果注册人是一家股票被列入标准普尔500指数的公司,注册人必须使用该指数;及

(ii)假设股息再投资的基础上,下述各者的累计总回报:

(A)公开发布的行业或业务线指数;

(B)善意选定的参照发行人。如果注册人未基于行业或业务线选定参照发行人,注册人应披露其选定参照发行人的基础;或

(C)具有类似市值的发行人,但该种情况下,注册人必须不使用公开发布的行业或业务线指数,且认为其无法合理选定参照发行人。注册人选择本款规定的方式的,应在曲线图后附上一份说明,解释作出这一选择的理由。

(2)就本条第(e)(1)款而言,“计量期间”一词系指始于“计量起点”(即注册人之前第5个会计年度开始前的最后一个交易日收市之时),并止于注册人上一个完整会计年度年末(含)的期间。如果该类别证券已经根据《交易法》第12条(《美国法典》第十五编第78*l*节)进行注册,且注册期限短于上述期间,在进行对比时可采用注册期限。

(3) For purposes of paragraph (e)(1)(ii)(A) of this Item, the term "published industry or line-of-business index" means any index that is prepared by a party other than the registrant or an affiliate and is accessible to the registrant's security holders; *provided, however,* that registrants may use an index prepared by the registrant or affiliate if such index is widely recognized and used.

(4) If the registrant selects a different index from an index used for the immediately preceding fiscal year, explain the reason(s) for this change and also compare the registrant's total return with that of both the newly selected index and the index used in the immediately preceding fiscal year.

Instructions to Item 201(e): 1. In preparing the required graphic comparisons, the registrant should:

a. Use, to the extent feasible, comparable methods of presentation and assumptions for the total return calculations required by paragraph (e)(1) of this Item; *provided, however,* that if the registrant constructs its own peer group index under paragraph (e)(1)(ii)(B), the same methodology must be used in calculating both the registrant's total return and that on the peer group index; and

b. Assume the reinvestment of dividends into additional shares of the same class of equity securities at the frequency with which dividends are paid on such securities during the applicable fiscal year.

2. In constructing the graph:

a. The closing price at the measurement point must be converted into a fixed investment, stated in dollars, in the registrant's stock (or in the stocks represented by a given index) with cumulative returns for each subsequent fiscal year measured as a change from that investment; and

b. Each fiscal year should be plotted with points showing the cumulative total return as of that point. The value of the investment as of each point plotted on a given return line is the number of shares held at that point multiplied by the then-prevailing share price.

3. The registrant is required to present information for the registrant's last five fiscal years, and may choose to graph a longer period; but the measurement point, however, shall remain the same.

4. Registrants may include comparisons using performance measures in addition to total return, such as return on average common shareholders' equity.

5. If the registrant uses a peer issuer(s) comparison or comparison with issuer(s) with similar market capitalizations, the identity of those issuers must be disclosed and the returns of each component issuer of the group must be weighted according to the respective issuer's stock market capitalization at the beginning of each period for which a

(3)就本条第(e)(1)(ii)(A)款而言,“公开发布的行业或业务线指数”指由注册人或其关联方以外的当事方制定的,并且注册人证券持有人可以获得的任何指数;但是,如果注册人或其关联方制定的指数被广泛承认和使用,注册人也可以使用该等指数。

(4)如果注册人选择的指数与上一会计年度使用的指数不同,应解释作出这一变更的理由,并将新选择的指数与上一会计年度使用的指数所对应的注册人总回报进行对比。

关于第201(e)条的说明:1.在按照上文规定编制对比图时,注册人应:

a.在可行范围内,使用具有可比性的列示方法,和具有可比性的本条第(e)(1)款规定的总回报的计算假设;但是,如果注册人根据第(e)(1)(ii)(B)款创建了自身的参照集团指数,则在计算注册人总回报以及参照集团指数总回报时应使用相同的计算方法。

b.假设股息将用于再投资购买同一类别的股权证券,且股息再投资的频率与适用会计年度就该等证券支付股息的频率相同。

2.在构建图表时:

a.在计量起点的收盘价须换算成对注册人的股票(或对以某一给定指数表示的股票)的固定投资,并以美元表示;之后计量每一会计年度的累计回报时,应以该等投资产生的变化为准。

b.每一会计年度均应列示相应的点表示截至该点的累计回报。给定回报线上列示的每一点的投资价值为在该点持有的股份数目乘以当时的股价之积。

3.注册人按规定应列报前5个会计年度的信息,但也可以选择更长的绘图期间;但计量起点应保持不变。

4.除总回报以外,注册人还可以提供通过业绩指标进行的比较,如普通股股东权益的平均回报。

5.如果注册人使用一个或多个参照发行人进行比较,或使用与具有类似市值的发行人进行的比较,必须披露该等发行人的身份信息,且其中每一发行人的回报必须属于权重回报,权重比例根据各发行人在回报对应期间期初的股票市值计算。

return is indicated.

6. *Smaller reporting companies.* A registrant that qualifies as a smaller reporting company, as defined by §229.10 (f) (1), is not required to provide the information required by paragraph (e) of this Item.

7. The information required by paragraph (e) of this Item need not be provided in any filings other than an annual report to security holders required by Exchange Act Rule 14a-3 (17 CFR 240.14a-3) or Exchange Act Rule 14c-3 (17 CFR 240.14c-3) that precedes or accompanies a registrant's proxy or information statement relating to an annual meeting of security holders at which directors are to be elected (or special meeting or written consents in lieu of such meeting). Such information will not be deemed to be incorporated by reference into any filing under the Securities Act or the Exchange Act, except to the extent that the registrant specifically incorporates it by reference.

8. The information required by paragraph (e) of this Item shall not be deemed to be "soliciting material" or to be "filed" with the Commission or subject to Regulation 14A or 14C (17 CFR 240.14a-1-240.14a-104 or 240.14c-1-240.14c-101), other than as provided in this item, or to the liabilities of section 18 of the Exchange Act (15 U.S.C. 78r), except to the extent that the registrant specifically requests that such information be treated as soliciting material or specifically incorporates it by reference into a filing under the Securities Act or the Exchange Act.

Instructions to Item 201: 1. Registrants, the common equity of which is listed for trading on more than one securities exchange registered under the Exchange Act, are required to indicate each such exchange pursuant to paragraph (a)(1)(i) of this Item; such registrants, however, need only report one set of price quotations pursuant to paragraph (a)(1)(ii) of this Item; where available, these shall be the prices as reported in the consolidated transaction reporting system and, where the prices are not so reported, the prices on the most significant (in terms of volume) securities exchange for such shares.

2. Market prices and dividends reported pursuant to this Item shall be adjusted to give retroactive effect to material changes resulting from stock dividends, stock splits and reverse stock splits.

3. The computation of the approximate number of holders of registrant's common equity may be based upon the number of record holders or also may include individual participants in security position listings. See Rule 17Ad-8 under the Exchange Act. The method of computation that is chosen shall be indicated.

4. If the registrant is a foreign issuer, describe briefly:

A. Any governmental laws, decrees or regulations in the country in which the registrant is organized that restrict the export or import of capital, including, but not

6.小型报告公司。符合小型报告公司[定义见第229.10(f)(1)节]资格的注册人不必按照本条第(e)款的规定提供相关信息。

7.除以下文件之外,任何其他文件均不必按照本条第(e)款的规定提供相关信息:按照《交易法》的《14a-3规则》(《联邦规章汇编》第十七编第240.14a-3节)或《交易法》的《14c-3规则》(《联邦规章汇编》第十七编第240.14c-3节)要求,在与证券持有人选举董事的年度会议(或替代性的特别会议或书面同意)有关的征集投票权报告或信息说明书之前或一并向证券持有人提供的年度报告。该等信息不得视为通过引用纳入依据《证券法》或《交易法》提交的任何文件,但注册人特意通过引用将其纳入年度报告之中的除外。

8.本条第(e)款要求披露的信息不得视为"招揽资料",亦不得视为应向证券交易委员会"提交"的材料,或者受制于《14A管理办法》或《14C管理办法》(《联邦规章汇编》第十七编第240.14a-1~240.14a-104节,或第240.14c-1~240.14c-101节)的材料(本条另有规定除外),或者受制于《交易法》第18条(《美国法典》第十五编第78r节)规定的责任的材料,但注册人特别要求将该等信息视为招揽材料,或特别通过引用方式将该等信息纳入根据《证券法》或《交易法》提交的文件之中的除外。

关于第201条的说明:1.如注册人的普通股在根据《交易法》注册的一个以上的证券交易所上市交易,应按照本条第(a)(1)(i)款的规定说明交易其普通股的每一家交易所;但是该等注册人仅须按照本条第(a)(1)(ii)款的规定报告一套报价;报价应首选合并交易报价系统中报告的价格,如果无法获得该等价格,应以最重要的证券交易所(以交易量为标准)的报价为准。

2.按照本条报告的市场价格和股息应进行调整,以溯及性地反映因股票股息、分拆和反向分拆产生的重大变更。

3.在计算注册人普通股持有人的大致数量时,可以基于登记持股人的数量计算,也可以计入证券持仓清单中的个人参与者。参见《交易法》的《17Ad-8规则》。注册人应对其采用的计算方式作出说明。

4.如果注册人为外国发行人,应简要说明:

A.注册人组建地所在国限制资本进出口(包括但不限于外汇管制)的任何政府法律、法令或规章,或对向持有注册人普通股的非该国居民股东汇付股息或进行其他付

limited to, foreign exchange controls, or that affect the remittance of dividends or other payments to nonresident holders of the registrant's common equity; and

B. All taxes, including withholding provisions, to which United States common equity holders are subject under existing laws and regulations of the foreign country in which the registrant is organized. Include a brief description of pertinent provisions of any reciprocal tax treaty between such foreign country and the United States regarding withholding. If there is no such treaty, so state.

5. If the registrant is a foreign private issuer whose common equity of the class being registered is wholly or partially in bearer form, the response to this Item shall so indicate together with as much information as the registrant is able to provide with respect to security holdings in the United States. If the securities being registered trade in the United States in the form of American Depositary Receipts or similar certificates, the response to this Item shall so indicate together with the name of the depositary issuing such receipts and the number of shares or other units of the underlying security representing the trading units in such receipts.

[47 FR 11401, Mar. 16, 1982, as amended at 47 FR 25127, June 10, 1982; 47 FR 54768, Dec. 6, 1982; 67 FR 246, Jan. 2, 2002; 71 FR 53240, Sept. 8, 2006; 73 FR 957, Jan. 4, 2008]

§229.202(Item 202) Description of registrant's securities.

Note: If the securities being described have been accepted for listing on an exchange, the exchange may be identified. The document should not however, convey the impression that the registrant may apply successfully for listing of the securities on an exchange or that, in the case of an underwritten offering, the underwriters may request the registrant to apply for such listing, unless there is reasonable assurance that the securities to be offered will be acceptable to a securities exchange for listing.

(a) *Capital stock.* If capital stock is to be registered, state the title of the class and describe such of the matters listed in paragraphs (a)(1) through (5) as are relevant. A complete legal description of the securities need not be given.

(1) Outline briefly: (i) dividend rights; (ii) terms of conversion; (iii) sinking fund provisions; (iv) redemption provisions; (v) voting rights, including any provisions specifying the vote required by security holders to take action; (vi) any classification of the Board of Directors, and the impact of such classification where cumulative voting is permitted or required; (vii) liquidation rights; (viii) preemption rights; and (ix) liability to further calls or to assessment by the registrant and for liabilities of the registrant imposed on its stockholders under state statutes (e.g., to laborers, servants or employees of the registrant), unless such disclosure would be immaterial because the financial

款存在影响的任何政府法律、法令或规章。

B.持有普通股的美国股东按照注册人组建地所在外国国家的现行法律法规需要缴纳的所有税金(包括预提条款)。同时应简要说明该外国与美国签订的任何税务互惠协定中与预提税相关的条款。如果不存在该等协定,应如实说明。

5.注册人为外国私募发行人且其申请注册的普通股类别全部或部分属于不记名证券的,在按照本条规定提供信息时应如实说明,并在注册人能力范围内提供与其在美国持有证券相关的所有信息。申请注册的证券在美国以美国存托凭证或类似形式交易的,在按照本条规定提供信息时应提供发行该等凭证的存托人的名称,以及代表该等凭证的交易单位的标的证券数量或其他单位数量。

[《联邦公报》第47卷第11401页,1982年3月16日,修正索引:《联邦公报》第47卷第25127页,1982年6月10日;《联邦公报》第47卷第54768页,1982年12月6日;《联邦公报》第67卷第246页,2002年1月2日;《联邦公报》第71卷第53240页,2006年9月8日;《联邦公报》第73卷第957页,2008年1月4日。]

第229.202节(第202条) 注册人证券的说明

注:如果所说明的证券已获准在交易所上市,可以指明该交易所的名称。但是,文件不得使读者误认为注册人一定可以成功申请在某一交易所上市证券,或者,对于承销发行而言,使读者误认为承销商可以要求注册人申请上市,但有合理理由确信发行证券将获准在证券交易所上市的除外。

(a)资本股。如申请注册的是资本股,应说明该类资本股的名称,并说明下文第(a)(1)款至第(a)(5)款所列相关内容。不必对证券进行完整的法律说明。

(1)简要说明:(i)股息分配权;(ii)转换条款;(iii)偿债资金条款;(iv)回赎条款;(v)表决权,包括规定证券持有人采取行动时所需票数的任何条款;(vi)董事会作出的任何分类,以及在允许或要求采用累积投票制时,该等分类的影响;(vii)清算权;(viii)优先购买权;(ix)进一步买入证券的责任或者按注册人的要求没收款项的责任,以及注册人根据州法律要求对其股东施加的责任(如对注册人劳工、雇工或雇员承担的责任),但注册人的财务状况或其他因素使得州法律不太可能规定该责任,从而使披露丧失重要性的除外;(x)申请注册的证券的可转让性存在的任何限制;以及(xi)基于任何现有或未来的证券持有人持有大量证券而对之进行区别对待的任何条款。

resources of the registrant or other factors make it improbable that liability under such state statues would be imposed; (x) any restriction on alienability of the securities to be registered; and (xi) any provision discriminating against any existing or prospective holder of such securities as a result of such security holder owning a substantial amount of securities.

(2) If the rights of holders of such stock may be modified otherwise than by a vote of a majority or more of the shares outstanding, voting as a class, so state and explain briefly.

(3) If preferred stock is to be registered, describe briefly any restriction on the repurchase or redemption of shares by the registrant while there is any arrearage in the payment of dividends or sinking fund installments. If there is no such restriction, so state.

(4) If the rights evidenced by, or amounts payable with respect to, the shares to be registered are, or may be, materially limited or qualified by the rights of any other authorized class of securities, include the information regarding such other securities as will enable investors to understand such limitations or qualifications. No information need be given, however, as to any class of securities all of which will be retired, provided appropriate steps to ensure such retirement will be completed prior to or upon delivery by the registrant of the shares.

(5) Describe briefly or cross-reference to a description in another part of the document, any provision of the registrant's charter or by-laws that would have an effect of delaying, deferring or preventing a change in control of the registrant and that would operate only with respect to an extraordinary corporate transaction involving the registrant (or any of its subsidiaries), such as a merger, reorganization, tender offer, sale or transfer of substantially all of its assets, or liquidation. Provisions and arrangements required by law or imposed by governmental or judicial authority need not be described or discussed pursuant to this paragraph (a)(5). Provisions or arrangements adopted by the registrant to effect, or further, compliance with laws or governmental or judicial mandate are not subject to the immediately preceding sentence where such compliance did not require the specific provisions or arrangements adopted.

(b) *Debt securities.* If debt securities are to be registered, state the title of such securities, the principal amount being offered, and, if a series, the total amount authorized and the total amount outstanding as of the most recent practicable date; and describe such of the matter listed in paragraphs (b)(1) through (10) as are relevant. A complete legal description of the securities need not be given. For purposes solely of this Item, debt securities that differ from one another only as to the interest rate or maturity shall be regarded as securities of the same class. Outline briefly:

(1) Provisions with respect to maturity, interest, conversion, redemption,

(2)如果除通过发行在外股份简单多数或以上的票数表决通过以外(且该等表决是以发行在外股份作为一个类别证券进行的),股票持有人的权利还可以通过其他方式进行修改,应如实说明并简要解释原因。

(3)如果申请注册的是优先股,且如果股息或偿债资金分期付款尚存在任何逾期未付款项,则应简要说明注册人回购或回赎股份所面临的任何限制。如果不存在任何此类限制,应如实说明。

(4)如果申请注册的股份所代表的权利或者该股份上存在的应付款项受到或可能受到任何其他核定证券类型的权利的严重限制或约束,应披露该等其他证券的信息,以便投资者理解该等限制或约束。但是,如果产生限制或约束的任何证券类型将会全部收回,并且如果将采取适当的措施确保该等证券将会在注册人发行股份之时或之前被全部收回,则不必提供该等证券的信息。

(5)如果注册人章程或章程细则的任何条款具有推迟、递延或阻止注册人控制权变更的效力,而且如果该条款只有在注册人(或其任何子公司)参与非常规公司交易时才会适用(此类非常规公司交易包括吸收合并、重组、股权收购要约、公司绝大部分资产的出售或转让、清算等),应简要说明该等条款,或者,如果在文件内其他章节已对此进行说明,则应提供该等章节的交叉索引。法律或政府或司法机构强制要求作出的规定或安排不必按照本第(a)(5)款进行说明或论述。但是,如果注册人为了实现或促进对法律或政府或司法机构命令的合规而作出相应条款或安排,但法律或政府或司法机构本身并未要求作出该具体条款或安排,则不适用上一句的规定。

(b)债务证券。如果申请注册的是债务证券,应说明该证券的名称、发行本金额以及(如果以系列形式发行)核定发行的总金额以及截至最近可行日期发行在外的总金额;并说明下文第(b)(1)款至第(b)(10)款所列相关内容。不必对证券进行完整的法律说明。仅就本条而言,如果债务证券之间的差异仅限于利率或到期日,应视为同一类别的证券。简要说明:

(1)关于到期日、利息、转换、回赎、摊还、偿债资金或证券收回的条款;

amortization, sinking fund, or retirement;

(2) Provisions with respect to the kind and priority of any lien securing the securities, together with a brief identification of the principal properties subject to such lien;

(3) Provisions with respect to the subordination of the rights of holders of the securities to other security holders or creditors of the registrant; where debt securities are designated as subordinated in accordance with Instruction 1 to this Item, set forth the aggregate amount of outstanding indebtedness as of the most recent practicable date that by the terms of such debt securities would be senior to such subordinated debt and describe briefly any limitation on the issuance of such additional senior indebtedness or state that there is no such limitation;

(4) Provisions restricting the declaration of dividends or requiring the maintenance of any asset ratio or the creation or maintenance of reserves;

(5) Provisions restricting the incurrence of additional debt or the issuance of additional securities; in the case of secured debt, whether the securities being registered are to be issued on the basis of unbonded bondable property, the deposit of cash or otherwise; as of the most recent practicable date, the approximate amount of unbonded bondable property available as a basis for the issuance of bonds; provisions permitting the withdrawal of cash deposited as a basis for the issuance of bonds; and provisions permitting the release or substitution of assets securing the issue; *Provided, however,* That provisions permitting the release of assets upon the deposit of equivalent funds or the pledge of equivalent property, the release of property no longer required in the business, obsolete property, or property taken by eminent domain or the application of insurance moneys, and other similar provisions need not be described;

(6) The general type of event that constitutes a default and whether or not any periodic evidence is required to be furnished as to the absence of default or as to compliance with the terms of the indenture;

(7) Provisions relating to modification of the terms of the security or the rights of security holders;

(8) If the rights evidenced by the securities to be registered are, or may be, materially limited or qualified by the rights of any other authorized class of securities, the information regarding such other securities as will enable investors to understand the rights evidenced by the securities; to the extent not otherwise disclosed pursuant to this Item; no information need be given, however, as to any class of securities all of which will be retired, provided appropriate steps to ensure such retirement will be completed prior to or upon delivery by the registrant of the securities;

(2)关于为证券提供担保的任何质押的类型和顺位的条款,并简要说明该质押所涉主要财产;

(3)关于证券持有人权利从属于其他证券持有人或注册人债权人的条款;如果债务证券按照关于本条的说明1被指定为次级债券,则应说明截至最近可行日期根据该次级债务证券条款而享有优先偿还待遇的未清偿债务总额,并简要说明增发此类优先债务存在的任何限制或说明其不存在任何限制;

(4)关于限制宣布股息的条款、要求维持一定资产比例的条款或要求建立或维持准备金的条款;

(5)限制产生新债务或限制增发证券的条款;对于有担保的债务而言,应说明申请注册的证券的发行基础是可以发行债券但并未发行债券的财产、现金存款或是其他基础;截至最近可行日期,用做债券发行基础的可发行债券但并未发行债券的财产的大致总量;允许提取作为债券发行基础的现金存款的条款;以及允许解除或替换证券发行的担保资产的条款;但是,不必说明以下条款:允许在存入等额资金时或提供等值财产质押时解除担保资产的条款,允许解除业务中不再需要的财产担保、陈旧财产担保、国家征用财产担保或由于使用保险金而解除财产担保的条款以及其他类似条款;

(6)说明违约事件的一般类型,并说明是否需要定期提供证据证明不存在违约或证明对债券条款的遵守;

(7)关于修改担保或证券持有人权利条款的条款;

(8)如果申请注册的证券所代表的权利受到或可能受到任何其他核定证券类型的权利的重大限制或制约,应披露该等其他证券的信息,以便投资者理解该证券代表的权利。但是,如果产生限制或制约的任何证券类型将会全部收回,并且,如果将采取适当的措施确保该证券将会在注册人发行股份之时或之前全部收回,且本条其他规定并未要求进行披露,则不必提供关于该等证券的信息;

(9) If debt securities are to be offered at a price such that they will be deemed to be offered at an "original issue discount" as defined in paragraph (a) of section 1273 of the Internal Revenue Code (26 U.S.C. 1273), or if a debt security is sold in a package with another security and the allocation of the offering price between the two securities may have the effect of offering the debt security at such an original issue discount, the tax effects thereof pursuant to sections 1271–1278;

(10) The name of the trustee(s) and the nature of any material relationship with the registrant or with any of its affiliates; the percentage of securities of the class necessary to require the trustee to take action; and what indemnification the trustee may require before proceeding to enforce the lien.

(c) *Warrants and rights.* If the securities described are to be offered pursuant to warrants or rights state:

(1) The amount of securities called for by such warrants or rights;

(2) The period during which and the price at which the warrants or rights are exercisable;

(3) The amount of warrants or rights outstanding;

(4) Provisions for changes to or adjustments in the exercise price; and

(5) Any other material terms of such rights on warrants.

(d) *Other securities.* If securities other than capital stock, debt, warrants or rights are to be registered, include a brief description (comparable to that required in paragraphs (a), (b) and (c) of Item 202) of the rights evidenced thereby.

(e) *Market information for securities other than common equity.* If securities other than common equity are to be registered and there is an established public trading market for such securities (as that term is used in Item 201 of Regulation S–K (§229.201 of this chapter)) provide market information with respect to such securities comparable to that required by paragraph (a) of Item 201 of Regulation S–K (§229.201).

(f) *American Depositary Receipts.* If Depositary Shares represented by American Depositary Receipts are being registered, furnish the following information:

(1) The name of the depositary and the address of its principal executive office.

(2) State the title of the American Depositary Receipts and identify the deposited security. Describe briefly the terms of deposit, including the provisions, if any, with respect to:

(i) The amount of deposited securities represented by one unit of American Depositary Receipts;

(ii) The procedure for voting, if any, the deposited securities;

(9)如果申请发行的债务证券的价格水平导致该债务证券被视为按照《国内税收法典》第1273条第(a)款(《美国法典》第二十六编第1273节)定义的“原始发行折价”发行,或者如果债务证券和其他证券打包出售且两只证券之间分配发行价格的方式产生的效果相当于以原始发行折价来发行该债务证券,则应按照《国内税收法典》第1271条至第1278条说明相关的税收影响;

(10)应说明信托受托人的姓名及其与注册人或注册人的任何关联方存在的任何重大关系的性质;说明需要信托受托人采取行动的证券类别所占比例;以及在开始强制执行质押之前信托受托人可以要求获得的赔偿。

(c)权证和购股权。如果所说明的证券将根据权证或购股权发行,应说明:

(1)该等权证或购股权行权时需要发行的证券总量;
(2)该权证或购股权的可行权期间以及行权价;

(3)发行在外的权证或购股权总量;
(4)关于行权价变更或调整的条款;及
(5)关于该等权证或购股权的任何其他重大条款。[1]
(d)其他证券。如果申请注册的是资本股、债务、权证或购股权以外的证券,应参照第202条第(a)款、第(b)款和第(c)款的规定简要说明该证券代表的权利。

(e)普通股以外的证券的市场信息。如果申请注册的是普通股以外的证券且该证券存在稳定的公开交易市场[定义见《S-K管理办法》第201条(本章第229.201节)],则应参照《S-K管理办法》第201条(本章第229.201节)第(a)款的要求提供该证券的市场信息。

(f)美国存托凭证。如果申请注册的是美国存托凭证代表的存托股份,应提供如下信息:
(1)存托人的姓名以及其主要办事机构的地址。
(2)说明该美国存托凭证的名称以及存托担保。简要说明存托条款,包括以下条款(如适用):

(i)每一单位美国存托凭证所代表的存托证券数量;

(ii)该存托证券的表决程序(如有);

1 原文为“rights on warrants”,似应为“rights or warrants”,译文已按后者处理。——译者注

(iii) The collection and distribution of dividends;

(iv) The transmission of notices, reports and proxy soliciting material;

(v) The sale or exercise of rights;

(vi) The deposit or sale of securities resulting from dividends, splits or plans of reorganization;

(vii) Amendment, extension or termination of the deposit;

(viii) Rights of holders of receipts to inspect the transfer books of the depositary and the list of holders of receipts;

(ix) Restrictions upon the right to deposit or withdraw the underlying securities;

(x) Limitation upon the liability of the depositary.

(3) Describe all fees and charges which may be imposed directly or indirectly against the holder of the American Depositary Receipts, indicating the type of service, the amount of fee or charges and to whom paid.

Instructions to Item 202: 1. Wherever the title of securities is required to be stated, there shall be given such information as will indicate the type and general character of the securities, including the following:

A. In the case of shares, the par or stated value, if any; the rate of dividends, if fixed, and whether cumulative or non–cumulative; a brief indication of the preference, if any; and if convertible or redeemable, a statement to that effect;

B. In the case of debt, the rate of interest; the date of maturity or, if the issue matures serially, a brief indication of the serial maturities, such as "maturing serially from 1955 to 1960"; if the payment of principal or interest is contingent, an appropriate indication of such contingency; a brief indication of the priority of the issue; and, if convertible or callable, a statement to that effect; or

C. In the case of any other kind of security, appropriate information of comparable character.

2. If the registrant is a foreign registrant, include (to the extent not disclosed in the document pursuant to Item 201 of Regulation S–K (§229.201) or otherwise) in the description of the securities:

A. A brief description of any limitations on the right of nonresident or foreign owners to hold or vote such securities imposed by foreign law or by the charter or other constituent document of the registrant, or if no such limitations are applicable, so state;

B. A brief description of any governmental laws, decrees or regulations in the country in which the registrant is organized affecting the remittance of dividends, interest and other payments to nonresident holders of the securities being registered;

C. A brief outline of all taxes, including withholding provisions, to which United States security holders are subject under existing laws and regulations of the foreign

(iii)股息的收取及分发;

(iv)通知、报告和征集股东投票代理权材料的发送;

(v)权利的出售或行使;

(vi)因股息、分拆或重组计划而造成的证券存托或出售;

(vii)存托的修正、延期或终止;

(viii)凭证持有人查阅存托人转让账本以及凭证持有人名单的权利;

(ix)存托或提取标的证券的权利存在的限制;

(x)存托人的责任限制。

(3)说明可直接或间接向美国存托凭证持有人收取的所有费用和收费,包括服务类型、费用或收费金额以及收款人。

关于第202条的说明:1.需要说明证券名称的,应提供相关信息,说明证券的类型和一般特征,包括:

A.对于股份而言,应说明其票面价值(如有)、股息率(如息率属于固定息率),并说明股息是否累积;简要说明其优先性(如适用);如果股份属于可转换或可回赎股份,亦应如实说明;

B.对于债务而言,应说明利率、到期日;债务分期到期的,应提供相应的简要说明,如"1955年至1960年之间分期到期";如果本金或利息的支付取决于某些或有条件,应适当说明其或有性;简要说明债务发行的优先性;如果债务属于可转换或可回赎债务,亦应如实说明;或者

C.对于任何其他类型的证券而言,应提供具有可比性的适当信息。

2.如果注册人是外国注册人,应在证券说明中纳入如下信息(前提是该等信息并未按照《S-K管理办法》第201条(第229.201节)或其他规定在文件中进行披露):

A.如果外国法律或注册人的章程或其他章程性文件对非美国居民或非美国所有人持有该证券或根据该证券进行表决设有任何限制的,应对该等限制进行简要说明,如果并无此类限制,应如实说明;

B.对于向申请注册的证券的非美国居民持有人支付的股息、利息或其他款项,如果注册人组建地所在国家的任何政府法律、法令或条例对汇付该等股息、利息或其他款项存在影响,亦应简要说明;

C.简要列明按照注册人组建地所在国家的现行法律法规,美国证券持有人必须缴纳的所有税收(包括预提税规定);及

country in which the registrant is organized; and

D. A brief description of pertinent provisions of any reciprocal tax treaty between such foreign country and the United States regarding withholding or, if there is no such treaty, so state.

3. Section 305(a)(2) of the Trust Indenture Act of 1939, 15 U.S.C. 77aaa *et seq.*,as amended ("Trust Indenture Act"), shall not be deemed to require the inclusion in a registration statement or in a prospectus of any information not required by this Item.

4. Where convertible securities or stock purchase warrants are being registered that are subject to redemption or call, the description of the conversion terms of the securities or material terms of the warrants shall disclose:

A. Whether the right to convert or purchase the securities will be forfeited unless it is exercised before the date specified in a notice of the redemption or call;

B. The expiration or termination date of the warrants;

C. The kinds, frequency and timing of notice of the redemption or call, including the cities or newspapers in which notice will be published (where the securities provide for a class of newspapers or group of cities in which the publication may be made at the discretion of the registrant, the registrant should describe such provision); and

D. In the case of bearer securities, that investors are responsible for making arrangements to prevent loss of the right to convert or purchase in the event of redemption of call, for example, by reading the newspapers in which the notice of redemption or call may be published.

5. The response to paragraph (f) shall include information with respect to fees and charges in connection with (A) the deposit or substitution of the underlying securities; (B) receipt and distribution of dividends; (C) the sale or exercise of rights; (D) the withdrawal of the underlying security; and (E) the transferring, splitting or grouping of receipts. Information with respect to the right to collect the fees and charges against dividends received and deposited securities shall be included in response to this item.

6. For asset-backed securities, see also Item 1113 of Regulation AB (§229.1113).

[47 FR 11401, Mar. 16, 1982, as amended at 47 FR 54768, Dec. 6, 1982; 51 FR 42056, Nov. 20, 1986; 70 FR 1593, Jan. 7, 2005]

D.简要说明该外国政府与美国签订的任何互惠税收条约内的关于预提税的相关条款,如果并无此类条约,应如实说明。

3.《1939年信托契约法》(《美国法典》第十五编第77aaa节及其后条文)(修正版,下称《信托契约法》)第305(a)(2)条不得理解为要求在注册说明书或招募说明书中提供本条并不要求提供的任何信息。

4.如果申请注册的可转换证券或购股权证可回赎或受制于买入选择权,则在说明证券的转换条款或权证的重大条款时应披露如下内容:

A.转换或购买证券的权利是否应在回赎或买入通知规定的日期之前行使,否则将逾期作废;

B.权证的到期或终止日期;

C.回赎或买入通知的类型、频率和时间,包括将要发布通知的城市或报纸(如果证券规定,注册人可依其自由裁量权在某一类别的报纸和某一系列的城市中选择具体发布通知的报纸或城市,注册人应说明相关条款);及

D.对于不记名证券,投资者有责任作出相应安排,譬如阅读可能发布回赎或回购通知的报纸,从而防止在回赎或买入时丧失转换或购买的权利。

5.在按照第(f)款规定进行披露时,应提供与以下内容相关的费用和收费信息:(A)标的证券的存托或替换;(B)股息的收取和分配;(C)权利的出售或行使;(D)标的证券的提取;以及(E)凭证的转让、分拆或组合。对于针对股息收取和证券存托而收取费用的权利,应在按照本条规定进行的披露中予以说明。

6.对于资产支持证券,请同时参见《AB管理办法》第1113条(本章第229.1113节)的规定。

[《联邦公报》第47卷第11401页,1982年3月16日,修正索引:《联邦公报》第47卷第54768页,1982年12月6日;《联邦公报》第51卷第42056页,1986年11月20日;《联邦公报》第70卷第1593页,2005年1月7日。]

Subpart 229.300 — Financial Information

§229.301(Item 301) Selected financial data.

Furnish in comparative columnar form the selected financial data for the registrant referred to below, for

(a) Each of the last five fiscal years of the registrant (or for the life of the registrant and its predecessors, if less), and

(b) Any additional fiscal years necessary to keep the information from being misleading.

(c) *Smaller reporting companies.* A registrant that qualifies as a smaller reporting company, as defined by §229.10 (f) (1), is not required to provide the information required by this Item.

Instructions to Item 301:1. The purpose of the selected financial data shall be to supply in a convenient and readable format selected financial data which highlight certain significant trends in the registrant's financial condition and results of operations.

2. Subject to appropriate variation to conform to the nature of the registrant's business, the following items shall be included in the table of financial data: net sales or operating revenues; income(loss) from continuing operations; income(loss) from continuing operations per common share; total assets; long-term obligations and redeemable preferred stock(including long-term debt, capital leases, and redeemable preferred stock as defined in §210.5-02.27(a) of Regulation S-X [17 CFR 210]; and cash dividends declared per common share. Registrants may include additional items which they believe would enhance an understanding of and would highlight other trends in their financial condition and results of operations.

Briefly describe, or cross-reference to a discussion thereof, factors such as accounting changes, business combinations or dispositions of business operations, that materially affect the comparability of the information reflected in selected financial data. Discussion of, or reference to, any material uncertainties should also be included where such matters might cause the data reflected herein not to be indicative of the registrant's future financial condition or results of operations.

3. All references to the registrant in the table of selected financial data and in this Item shall mean the registrant and its subsidiaries consolidated.

4. If interim period financial statements are included, or are required to be included, by Article 3 of Regulation S-X, registrants should consider whether any or all of the

第229.300子部分 —— 财 务 信 息

第229.301节(第301条) 择要列示的财务数据

以栏目对照的表格形式择要提供注册人在下述期间的财务数据:

(a)注册人过去5个会计年度内每一年(如果注册人及其前身存续期间不足5年,则为其存续期间内的每一年),以及

(b)为确保信息不致产生误导性而有必要提供相关数据的任何其他会计年度。

(c)小型报告公司。符合第229.10(f)(1)节定义的小型报告公司资格的注册人不必按照本条规定提供信息。

关于第301条的说明:1.择要列示财务数据的目的是以简明易读的格式提供择要列示的财务数据,重点突出注册人财务状况和经营成果中的某些重要趋势。

2.财务数据表中应提供以下数据(可根据注册人的业务性质进行适当的变动):净销售额或经营收入;持续经营损益;持续经营每股普通股损益;总资产;长期债务和可回赎优先股[包括长期债务、资本租赁以及《S-X管理办法》第210.5-02.27(a)条(《联邦规章汇编》第十七编第210部分)定义的可回赎优先股];以及每股普通股派发的现金股息。如果注册人认为其他信息有助于理解并重点突出其财务状况和经营成果中的其他趋势,亦可予以说明。

简要说明将对择要列示的财务数据信息的可比性产生重大影响的因素,如会计变更、业务合并或业务运营部门的处置等;如他处已有说明,则应提供交叉索引。如果某些重大不确定性可能导致择要列示的财务数据包含的信息并不能反映注册人未来的财务状况或经营成果,则应对此进行论述或提供索引。

3.择要列示的财务数据表及本条中所述"注册人",均指注册人及其并表子公司。

4.如果该表格包含中期财务报表,或者如果《S-X管理办法》第3条要求包含中期财务报表,注册人应考虑是否应针对该中期阶段更新全部或部分择要列示的财务数据,

selected financial data need to be updated for such interim periods to reflect a material change in the trends indicated; where such updating information is necessary, registrants shall provide the information on a comparative basis unless not necessary to an understanding of such updating information.

5. A foreign private issuer shall disclose also the following information in all filings containing financial statements:

A. In the forepart of the document and as of the latest practicable date, the exchange rate into U.S. currency of the foreign currency in which the financial statements are denominated;

B. A history of exchange rates for the five most recent years and any subsequent interim period for which financial statements are presented setting forth the rates for period end, the average rates, and the range of high and low rates for each year; and

C. If equity securities are being registered, a five year summary of dividends per share stated in both the currency in which the financial statements are denominated and United States currency based on the exchange rates at each respective payment date.

6. A foreign private issuer shall present the selected financial data in the same currency as its financial statements. The issuer may present the selected financial data on the basis of the accounting principles used in its primary financial statements but in such case shall present this data also on the basis of any reconciliations of such data to United States generally accepted accounting principles and Regulation S-X made pursuant to Rule 4-01 of Regulation S-X (§210.4-01 of this chapter).

7. For purposes of this rule, the rate of exchange means the noon buying rate in New York City for cable transfers in foreign currencies as certified for customs purposes by the Federal Reserve Bank of New York. The average rate means the average of the exchange rates on the last day of each month during a year.

[47 FR 11401, Mar. 16, 1982, as amended at 47 FR 54768, Dec. 6, 1982; 52 FR 30919, Aug. 18, 1987; 73 FR 958, Jan. 4, 2008; 74 FR 18617, Apr. 23, 2009]

§229.302(Item 302) Supplementary financial information.

(a) Selected quarterly financial data. Registrants specified in paragraph (a)(5) of this Item shall provide the information specified below.

(1) Disclosure shall be made of net sales, gross profit (net sales less costs and expenses associated directly with or allocated to products sold or services rendered), income (loss) before extraordinary items and cumulative effect of a change in accounting, per share data based upon such income (loss), net income (loss) and net income (loss) attributable to the registrant, for each full quarter within the two most recent fiscal years and any subsequent interim period for which financial statements are included or are

从而反映数据所揭露的趋势的重要变化;如果有必要作出数据更新,注册人应以对照的方式提供信息,但此种方式对于理解更新信息并无必要的除外。

5.外国私募发行人还应在包含财务报表的所有提交文件中披露以下信息:

A.文件开篇应说明截至最近可行日期该财务报表采用的外国货币对美元的兑换比率;

B.提供过去5年以及提交财务报表的任何中期阶段的汇率走势,说明每一年的期末汇率、平均汇率及每年的最高和最低汇率;及

C.如果申请注册的是股权证券,则应提供每股股息的5年期摘要,并同时以该财务报表采用的货币单位以及按照各支付日期当天的汇率来计算的美元进行说明。

6.外国私募发行人应以其财务报表采用的货币提供择要列示的财务数据。发行人在择要列报财务数据之时,可选择其主要财务报表所遵循的会计原则,但在此情况下,该发行人还应根据《S-X管理办法》的《4-01规则》(本章第210.4-01节)按照美国公认会计原则以及《S-X管理办法》对择要列示的财务数据进行调节。

7.就本规则而言,汇率指美联储纽约银行核准的适用于海关的外汇电汇纽约市中午买入价。平均汇率指一年中每月最后一天汇率的平均值。

[《联邦公报》第47卷第11401页,1982年3月16日,修正索引:《联邦公报》第47卷第54768页,1982年12月6日;《联邦公报》第52卷第30919页,1987年8月18日;《联邦公报》第73卷第958页,2008年1月4日;《联邦公报》第74卷第18617页,2009年4月23日。]

第229.302节(第302条) 补充财务信息

(a)择要列示的季度财务数据。本条第(a)(5)款所述注册人应提供以下信息。

(1)应针对过去两个会计年度的每一完整季度,披露净销售额、毛利润(净销售额减去直接关乎或分摊至出售的产品或提供的服务的成本和费用)、计算非常规事项前的损益以及会计变更的累积影响、上述损益的每股数值、净损益和归属于注册人的净损益;如果表格包含任何中期财务报表,或者,如果《S-X管理办法》第3条(本章第210部分)要求表格包含任何中期财务报表,则还应针对该中期阶段披露上述信息。

required to be included by Article 3 of Regulation S-X (part 210 of this chapter).

(2) When the data supplied pursuant to paragraph (a) of this section vary from the amounts previously reported on the Form 10-Q (§249.308a of this chapter) filed for any quarter, such as would be the case when a combination between entities under common control occurs or where an error is corrected, reconcile the amounts given with those previously reported and describe the reason for the difference.

(3) Describe the effect of any disposals of segments of a business, and extraordinary, unusual or infrequently occurring items recognized in each full quarter within the two most recent fiscal years and any subsequent interim period for which financial statements are included or are required to be included by Article 3 of Regulation S-X, as well as the aggregate effect and the nature of year-end or other adjustments which are material to the results of that quarter.

(4) If the financial statements to which this information relates have been reported on by an accountant, appropriate professional standards and procedures, as enumerated in the Statements of Auditing Standards issued by the Auditing Standards Board of the American Institute of Certified Public Accountants, shall be followed by the reporting accountant with regard to the data required by this paragraph (a).

(5) This paragraph (a) applies to any registrant, except a foreign private issuer, that has securities registered pursuant to sections 12(b)(15 U.S.C. §78*l*(b))(other than mutual life insurance companies) or 12(g) of the Exchange Act (15 U.S.C. §78*l*(g)).

(b) *Information about oil and gas producing activities.* Registrants engaged in oil and gas producing activities shall present the information about oil and gas producing activities (as those activities are defined in Regulation S-X, §210.4-10(a)) specified in paragraphs 9-34 of Statement of Financial Accounting Standards ("SFAS") No. 69, "Disclosures about Oil and Gas Producing Activities." If such oil and gas producing activities are regarded as significant under one or more of the tests set forth in paragraph 8 of SFAS No. 69.

Instructions to paragraph (b):

1. (a) SFAS No. 69 disclosures that relate to annual periods shall be presented for each annual period for which an income statement is required. (b) SFAS No. 69 disclosures required as of the end of an annual period shall be presented as of the date of each audited balance sheet required, and (c) SFAS No. 69 disclosures required as of the beginning of an annual period shall be presented as of the beginning of each annual period for which an income statement is required.

2. This paragraph, together with §210.4-10 of Regulation S-X, prescribes financial reporting standards for the preparation of accounts by persons engaged, in whole or in part, in the production of crude oil or natural gas in the United States, pursuant to Section

(2)如果由于受同一第三方控制的实体的合并或者由于对以往错误的修订,导致按照本条第(a)款提供的数据与以往任一季度按照《10-Q表格》(本章第249.308a节)提交的数据存在差异,应对前后存在差异的数据进行调节,并说明产生差异的原因。

(3)应针对最近两个会计年度的每一完整季度,披露因任何业务分部处置而产生的影响,以及期间内被确认的特殊、非常规或偶发事件产生的影响,如果表格包含任何中期财务报表,或者,如果《S-X管理办法》第3条要求表格包含任何中期财务报表,还应针对每个中期阶段披露上述信息。同时应说明对该季度经营成果存在重大影响的年末调整或其他调整的整体影响和性质。

(4)如果上述信息所涉财务报表已由会计师进行报告,则该会计师在报告第(a)款规定的数据时应遵守美国注册会计师协会审计标准委员会发布的《审计标准公告》内所列的适当专业标准和程序。

(5)第(a)款适用于所有注册人,但按照《交易法》第12(b)条[《美国法典》第十五编第78l(b)节]或第12(g)条[《美国法典》第十五编第78l(g)节]注册证券的外国私募发行人(不包括互助人寿保险公司)除外。

(b)石油天然气生产活动信息。如果注册人从事石油和天然气生产活动,且如果该石油和天然气生产活动根据《第69号财务会计标准公告》第8款所列的一条或多条标准被视为重大活动,则注册人应说明《第69号财务会计标准公告》第9款至第34款列明的石油和天然气生产活动[定义见《S-X管理办法》,本章第210.4-10(a)条]的相关信息。

关于第(b)款的说明:

1.(a)按照《第69号财务会计标准公告》进行年度期间披露时应针对每一个按规定应提交损益表的年度期间进行披露;(b)《第69号财务会计标准公告》要求作出的截至某一年度期间期末的披露,其截止日期应为按规定应提交的每一份已审计资产负债表的日期;且(c)《第69号财务会计标准公告》要求作出的截至某一年度期间期初的披露,其截止日期应为按规定应提交的每一份损益表的日期。

2.根据《1975年能源政策与保护法》(《美国法典》第四十二编第8383节)(EPCA)第503条和《1974年能源供应和环境协调法》(《美国法典》第十五编第796节)(ESECA)第11(c)条(《1975年能源政策与保护法》第506条对此进行了修正),对于在美国完全从事

503 of the Energy Policy and Conservation Act of 1975 (42 U.S.C. 8383)("EPCA") and Section 11(c) of the Energy Supply and Environmental Coordination Act of 1974(15 U.S.C. 796)("ESECA") as amended by Section 506 of EPCA. The application of the paragraph to those oil and gas producing operations of companies regulated for ratemaking purposes on an individual-company-cost-of-service basis may, however, give appropriate recognition to differences arising because of the effect of the ratemaking process.

3. Any person exempted by the Department of Energy from any record-keeping or reporting requirements pursuant to Section 11(c) of ESECA, as amended, is similarly exempted from the related provisions of this paragraph in the preparation of accounts pursuant to EPCA. This exemption does not affect the applicability of this paragraph to filings pursuant to the federal securities laws.

(c) *Smaller reporting companies.* A registrant that qualifies as a smaller reporting company, as defined by §229.10 (f)(1), is not required to provide the information required by this Item.

[47 FR 11401, Mar. 16, 1982, as amended at 47 FR 57914, Dec. 29, 1982; 52 FR 30919, Aug. 18, 1987; 56 FR 30053, July 1, 1991; 64 FR 73402, Dec. 30, 1999; 73 FR 958, Jan. 4, 2008; 74 FR 18617, Apr. 23, 2009]

§229.303(Item 303) Management's discussion and analysis of financial condition and results of operations.

(a) *Full fiscal years.* Discuss registrant's financial condition, changes in financial condition and results of operations. The discussion shall provide information as specified in paragraphs(a)(1) through(5) of this Item and also shall provide such other information that the registrant believes to be necessary to an understanding of its financial condition, changes in financial condition and results of operations. Discussions of liquidity and capital resources may be combined whenever the two topics are interrelated. Where in the registrant's judgment a discussion of segment information or of other subdivisions of the registrant's business would be appropriate to an understanding of such business, the discussion shall focus on each relevant, reportable segment or other subdivision of the business and on the registrant as a whole.

(1) *Liquidity.* Identify any known trends or any known demands, commitments, events or uncertainties that will result in or that are reasonably likely to result in the registrant's liquidity increasing or decreasing in any material way. If a material deficiency is identified, indicate the course of action that the registrant has taken or proposes to take to remedy the deficiency. Also identify and separately describe internal and external sources of liquidity, and briefly discuss any material unused sources of liquid assets.

或兼营原油或天然气生产业务的主体而言,本款与《S-X管理办法》第210.4-10节共同构成其账目编制的财务报告标准。某些油气生产公司在制定费率方面将基于其具体的公司服务成本接受监管,对于此类公司,在适用本款规定时,可适当考虑因费率制定流程导致的差异。

3.任何主体获得能源部的豁免,不必遵守ESECA第11(c)条(修正版)关于任何记录保存或报告要求的,亦应同时豁免于本款关于按照《1975年能源政策与保护法》编制账目的相关规定。尽管有上述规定,但是,在按照联邦证券法律提交文件时,本款仍应照常适用。

(c)小型报告公司。符合第229.10(f)(1)节定义的小型报告公司资格的注册人不必按照本条规定提供信息。

[《联邦公报》第47卷第11401页,1982年3月16日,修正索引:《联邦公报》第47卷第57914页,1982年12月29日;《联邦公报》第52卷第30919页,1987年8月18日;《联邦公报》第56卷第30053页,1991年7月1日;《联邦公报》第64卷第73402页,1999年12月30日;《联邦公报》第73卷第958页,2008年1月4日;《联邦公报》第74卷第18617页,2009年4月23日。]

第229.303节(第303条) 管理层关于财务状况和经营成果的论述和分析

(a)完整会计年度。对注册人的财务状况、财务状况的变化和经营成果进行论述。该论述应提供本条第(a)(1)款至第(a)(5)款规定的信息,如果注册人认为其他信息对于理解其财务状况、财务状况的变化和经营成果具有必要性,也应提供该等额外信息。如流动性和资本资源之间存在相互联系,可予以合并论述。如果注册人认为,为了理解注册人某一业务,应适当论述该业务下的业务分部或其他部门,则除了对注册人进行整体论述之外,也应把论述重点放在每一相关的、应报告的业务分部或部门上。

(1)流动性。说明任何会或根据合理预期可能会造成注册人流动性大幅增减的任何已知趋势或任何已知需求、承诺、事件或不确定性。如果已发现存在重大的流动性不足问题,则应说明注册人已经或计划采取的应对行动。同时应指明并分别说明流动性的内部和外部来源,并简要论述任何未使用的重大流动资产来源。

(2) *Capital resources.* (i) Describe the registrant's material commitments for capital expenditures as of the end of the latest fiscal period, and indicate the general purpose of such commitments and the anticipated source of funds needed to fulfill such commitments.

(ii) Describe any known material trends, favorable or unfavorable, in the registrant's capital resources. Indicate any expected material changes in the mix and relative cost of such resources. The discussion shall consider changes between equity, debt and any off-balance sheet financing arrangements.

(3) *Results of operations.* (i) Describe any unusual or infrequent events or transactions or any significant economic changes that materially affected the amount of reported income from continuing operations and, in each case, indicate the extent to which income was so affected. In addition, describe any other significant components of revenues or expenses that, in the registrant's judgment, should be described in order to understand the registrant's results of operations.

(ii) Describe any known trends or uncertainties that have had or that the registrant reasonably expects will have a material favorable or unfavorable impact on net sales or revenues or income from continuing operations. If the registrant knows of events that will cause a material change in the relationship between costs and revenues (such as known future increases in costs of labor or materials or price increases or inventory adjustments), the change in the relationship shall be disclosed.

(iii) To the extent that the financial statements disclose material increases in net sales or revenues, provide a narrative discussion of the extent to which such increases are attributable to increases in prices or to increases in the volume or amount of goods or services being sold or to the introduction of new products or services.

(iv) For the three most recent fiscal years of the registrant or for those fiscal years in which the registrant has been engaged in business, whichever period is shortest, discuss the impact of inflation and changing prices on the registrant's net sales and revenues and on income from continuing operations.

(4) *Off-balance sheet arrangements.* (i) In a separately-captioned section, discuss the registrant's off-balance sheet arrangements that have or are reasonably likely to have a current or future effect on the registrant's financial condition, changes in financial condition, revenues or expenses, results of operations, liquidity, capital expenditures or capital resources that is material to investors. The disclosure shall include the items specified in paragraphs (a)(4)(i)(A), (B), (C) and (D) of this Item to the extent necessary to an understanding of such arrangements and effect and shall also include such other information that the registrant believes is necessary for such an understanding.

(A) The nature and business purpose to the registrant of such off-balance sheet arrangements;

（2）资本资源。（i）说明截至最近一个会计期间期末注册人作出的重大资本性支出承诺，并说明该资本性支出承诺的一般目的，以及注册人预期通过何种资金来源来履行该资本性支出承诺。

（ii）说明注册人资本资源中任何已知的重大有利或不利趋势。说明该等资源的组成以及相对成本预期发生的任何重大变化。进行论述时应考虑股本、债务和任何资产负债表外融资安排之间的变化。

（3）经营成果。（i）说明对由持续经营产生的已报告收益存在重大影响的任何非常规或偶发事件、交易或任何重大经济变化，并说明每宗事件、交易或每项变化对收益的影响程度。此外，如果注册人认为，为了理解注册人的经营成果而有必要说明收入或开支的任何其他重大组成部分，也应作出相应的说明。

（ii）说明已经或注册人合理预期将对净销售额、收入或持续经营盈利造成重大有利或不利影响的任何已知趋势或不确定性。如果注册人知道某些事件将导致成本和收入的关系产生重大变化（如劳动力或原材料成本的已知上涨趋势或价格上涨、存货调整），应披露该等关系的变化。

（iii）如果根据财务报表的披露，净销售额或收入发生了显著提高，则应提供相应的文字论述，说明该等提高在何等程度上是由价格上涨、出售的货物或服务数量增加或推出新产品或服务而导致的。

（iv）针对注册人过去3个会计年度或者注册人开展业务以来的会计年度（如注册人开展业务的期间不足3年），论述通胀和价格变动对注册人净销售额和收入以及对持续经营收入的影响。

（4）资产负债表外安排。（i）单列一节，论述注册人对或根据合理预期可能对下述各项产生对投资者而言意义重大的影响的相关资产负债表外安排：注册人的财务状况、财务状况变化、收入或支出、经营成果、流动性、资本性支出或资本资源。进行上述披露时，应纳入本条第（a）（4）（i）（A）款、第（a）（4）（i）（B）款、第（a）（4）（i）（C）款和第（a）（4）（i）（D）款规定的内容，前提是该等内容对理解上述安排及其影响是必要的；同时应纳入注册人认为对于理解上述安排及其影响具有必要性的其他信息。

（A）上述资产负债表外安排的性质及其对注册人具有的商业意义；

(B) The importance to the registrant of such off-balance sheet arrangements in respect of its liquidity, capital resources, market risk support, credit risk support or other benefits;

(C) The amounts of revenues, expenses and cash flows of the registrant arising from such arrangements; the nature and amounts of any interests retained, securities issued and other indebtedness incurred by the registrant in connection with such arrangements; and the nature and amounts of any other obligations or liabilities (including contingent obligations or liabilities) of the registrant arising from such arrangements that are or are reasonably likely to become material and the triggering events or circumstances that could cause them to arise; and

(D) Any known event, demand, commitment, trend or uncertainty that will result in or is reasonably likely to result in the termination, or material reduction in availability to the registrant, of its off-balance sheet arrangements that provide material benefits to it, and the course of action that the registrant has taken or proposes to take in response to any such circumstances.

(ii) As used in this paragraph (a)(4), the term *off-balance sheet arrangement* means any transaction, agreement or other contractual arrangement to which an entity unconsolidated with the registrant is a party, under which the registrant has:

(A) Any obligation under a guarantee contract that has any of the characteristics identified in paragraph 3 of FASB Interpretation No. 45, *Guarantor's Accounting and Disclosure Requirements for Guarantees, Including Indirect Guarantees of Indebtedness of Others* (November 2002) ("FIN 45"), as may be modified or supplemented, and that is not excluded from the initial recognition and measurement provisions of FIN 45 pursuant to paragraphs 6 or 7 of that Interpretation;

(B) A retained or contingent interest in assets transferred to an unconsolidated entity or similar arrangement that serves as credit, liquidity or market risk support to such entity for such assets;

(C) Any obligation, including a contingent obligation, under a contract that would be accounted for as a derivative instrument, except that it is both indexed to the registrant's own stock and classified in stockholders' equity in the registrant's statement of financial position, and therefore excluded from the scope of FASB Statement of Financial Accounting Standards No.133, *Accounting for Derivative Instruments and Hedging Activities* (June 1998), pursuant to paragraph 11(a) of that Statement, as may be modified or supplemented; or

(D) Any obligation, including a contingent obligation, arising out of a variable interest (as referenced in FASB Interpretation No. 46, *Consolidation of Variable Interest Entities* (January 2003), as may be modified or supplemented) in an unconsolidated entity

(B)上述资产负债表外安排对注册人的流动性、资本资源、市场风险支持、信用风险支持或其他利益方面具有的重要意义;

(C)注册人因上述安排产生的收入、费用和现金流的总量;注册人因上述安排而保留的任何权益、发行的证券以及由此产生的其他负债的性质和金额;注册人因上述安排而产生的其他重大义务或责任,或根据合理预期可能会发展为重大义务或责任的任何义务或责任(包括或有义务或责任)的性质和金额,并应说明将导致此类义务或责任产生的触发事件或情况;及

(D)任何会或根据合理预期可能会中断或大幅减少为注册人提供重大利益的资产负债表外安排的资金来源的已知事件、需求、承诺、趋势或不确定性,并应说明注册人已经或计划采取的应对行动。

(ii)就第(a)(4)款而言,"资产负债表外安排"一词系指以非注册人并表实体为一方的任何交易、协议或其他合约安排,且根据该交易、协议或合约安排:

(A)注册人在担保合同下承担任何义务,且该担保合同具有《财务会计准则委员会第45号解释——担保人关于担保的会计和披露要求(包括他人债务的间接担保)》(2002年11月)(FIN 45)(以不时修改或补充的版本为准)第3款所列的任一特征,且该合同并未被根据该解释第6款或第7款所作的FIN 45的初始确认和计量规定排除在外;

(B)注册人在转让给非并表实体的资产中具有保留权益或或有权益,或者在为该等非并表实体的此类资产提供信用、流动性或市场风险支持的类似安排中具有保留权益或或有权益;

(C)注册人在将被视为衍生工具的合约下承担任何义务(包括或有义务),但是,以下情况除外:该衍生工具与注册人自身的股票挂钩,且在注册人的财务状况声明中被归入股东权益,因此根据财务会计准则委员会的《财务会计准则公告第133号——衍生工具和套期保值活动的会计》(1998年6月)第11(a)款(以不时修改或补充的版本为准),而被排除在该公告的适用范围之外;或者

(D)注册人因对非并表实体持有可变权益[定义见《财务会计准则委员会第46号解释——可变权益实体的并表》(2003年1月),以不时修改或补充版本为准]而承担任何义务(包括或有义务),且该等权益对注册人具有重要意义,同时,该实体为注册人

that is held by, and material to, the registrant, where such entity provides financing, liquidity, market risk or credit risk support to, or engages in leasing, hedging or research and development services with, the registrant.

(5) *Tabular disclosure of contractual obligations.* (i) In a tabular format, provide the information specified in this paragraph (a)(5) as of the latest fiscal year end balance sheet date with respect to the registrant's known contractual obligations specified in the table that follows this paragraph (a) (5) (i). The registrant shall provide amounts, aggregated by type of contractual obligation. The registrant may disaggregate the specified categories of contractual obligations using other categories suitable to its business, but the presentation must include all of the obligations of the registrant that fall within the specified categories. A presentation covering at least the periods specified shall be included. The tabular presentation may be accompanied by footnotes to describe provisions that create, increase or accelerate obligations, or other pertinent data to the extent necessary for an understanding of the timing and amount of the registrant's specified contractual obligations.

Contractual obligations	Payments due by period			3-5 years	More than 5 years
	Total	Less than 1 year	1-3 years		
[Long - Term Debt Obligations]					
[Capital Lease Obligations]					
[Operating Lease Obligations]					
[Purchase Obligations]					
[Other Long - Term Liabilities Reflected on the Registrant's Balance Sheet under GAAP]					
Total					

(ii) *Definitions:* The following definitions apply to this paragraph (a)(5):

(A) *Long-term debt obligation* means a payment obligation under long-term borrowings referenced in FASB Statement of Financial Accounting Standards No. 47 *Disclosure of Long-Term Obligations* (March 1981), as may be modified or supplemented.

(B) *Capital lease obligation* means a payment obligation under a lease classified as a capital lease pursuant to FASB Statement of Financial Accounting Standards No. 13 *Accounting for Leases* (November 1976), as may be modified or supplemented.

(C) *Operating lease obligation* means a payment obligation under a lease classified

提供融资、流动性、市场风险或信用风险支持,或为注册人提供租赁、套期保值或研发服务。

(5)以表格形式披露合同义务。(i)以表格形式,针对本第(a)(5)(i)款后的表格内列明的注册人已知合同责任,提供截至最近一个会计年度年末的资产负债表之日的本第(a)(5)款规定的信息。注册人应按照合同义务类型提供合计信息。注册人也可基于其业务特征,使用其他分类方法对其合同义务进行分类说明,但是不论如何分类,提供的信息必须包括注册人在所有规定类别下承担的义务。所提供的信息至少应覆盖表格中规定的期间。可在表格内容中提供脚注,阐述创设、增加或加速义务履行的条款,或说明理解注册人所列合同义务的时间和金额所需的任何其他必要和相关的数据。

合同义务	按到期期限分列的付款			3~5年	5年以上
	总计	1年以内	1~3年		
(长期债务义务)					
(资本租赁义务)					
(经营租赁义务)					
(购买义务)					
(根据GAAP反映在注册人资产负债表内的其他长期债务)					
总计					

(ii)定义:以下定义适用于本第(a)(5)款:

(A)"长期债务义务"系指财务会计准则委员会的《财务会计准则公告第47号——长期义务披露》(1981年3月)(以不时修改或补充的版本为准)所指的长期贷款中的付款义务。

(B)"资本租赁义务"系指财务会计准则委员会的《财务会计准则公告第13号——租赁会计》(1976年11月)(以不时修改或补充的版本为准)内被归入资本租赁的租赁合约下的付款义务。

(C)"经营租赁义务"系指财务会计准则委员会的《财务会计准则公告第13号——租

as an operating lease and disclosed pursuant to FASB Statement of Financial Accounting Standards No. 13 *Accounting for Leases* (November 1976), as may be modified or supplemented.

(D) *Purchase obligation* means an agreement to purchase goods or services that is enforceable and legally binding on the registrant that specifies all significant terms, including: fixed or minimum quantities to be purchased; fixed, minimum or variable price provisions; and the approximate timing of the transaction.

Instructions to paragraph 303(a):

1. The registrant's discussion and analysis shall be of the financial statements and other statistical data that the registrant believes will enhance a reader's understanding of its financial condition, changes in financial condition and results of operations. Generally, the discussion shall cover the three-year period covered by the financial statements and shall use year-to-year comparisons or any other formats that in the registrant's judgment enhance a reader's understanding. However, where trend information is relevant, reference to the five-year selected financial data appearing pursuant to Item 301 of Regulation S-K (§229.301) may be necessary. A smaller reporting company's discussion shall cover the two-year period required in Article 8 of Regulation S-X and shall use year-to-year comparisons or any other formats that in the registrant's judgment enhance a reader's understanding.

2. The purpose of the discussion and analysis shall be to provide to investors and other users information relevant to an assessment of the financial condition and results of operations of the registrant as determined by evaluating the amounts and certainty of cash flows from operations and from outside sources.

3. The discussion and analysis shall focus specifically on material events and uncertainties known to management that would cause reported financial information not to be necessarily indicative of future operating results or of future financial condition. This would include descriptions and amounts of (A) matters that would have an impact on future operations and have not had an impact in the past, and (B) matters that have had an impact on reported operations and are not expected to have an impact upon future operations.

4. Where the consolidated financial statements reveal material changes from year to year in one or more line items, the causes for the changes shall be described to the extent necesary to an understanding of the registrant's businesses as a whole; *Provided, however,* That if the causes for a change in one line item also relate to other line items, no repetition is required and a line-by-line analysis of the financial statements as a whole is not required or generally appropriate. Registrants need not recite the amounts of changes from year to year which are readily computable from the financial statements. The

赁会计》(1976年11月)(以不时修改或补充的版本为准)内被归入经营租赁并根据该公告披露的租赁合约下的付款义务。

(D)"购买义务"系指具有可强制执行力且对注册人具有法律约束力的并规定了所有重大条款的货物或服务购买协议,该等重大条款包括:固定或最低购买数量;固定、最低或可变价格条款;交易的大致时间。

关于第303(a)款的说明:

1.注册人的论述和分析应针对财务报表以及注册人认为有助于读者理解其财务状况、财务状况的变化和经营成果的其他数据。一般而言,该论述应覆盖该财务报表所覆盖的3年期的期间,并应采取逐年对照的格式或者注册人认为有助于读者理解的任何其他格式。但是,如果趋势性的信息有参考价值,则可能有必要引用按照《S-K管理办法》第301条(本章第229.301节)所列明的5年期择要列示的财务数据。小型报告公司提供的论述应涵盖《S-X管理办法》第8条要求提供的2年期数据,并应采取逐年对照的格式或者注册人认为有助于读者理解的任何其他格式。

2.论述和分析旨在向投资者和其他使用者提供相关信息,使其能够借由评估运营或其他外部来源产生的现金流的金额和确定性,评估注册人的财务状况和经营成果。

3.论述和分析的重点应特别放在可能导致已报告的财务信息无法准确反映未来经营成果和财务状况且已为管理层所知的重大事件和不确定性之上,包括以下各项的说明及数量:(A)将对未来经营产生影响但未对既往经营产生影响的事项,以及(B)已经对已报告的经营数据产生影响但预期不会对未来经营产生影响的事项。

4.如果合并财务报表显示一个或多个行项目在不同年份之间存在重大变化,则应在理解注册人整体业务所必要的范围内,说明造成该变化的原因。但是,如果导致一个行项目变化的原因也是导致另外一个行项目变化的原因,则不必重复说明;注册人不必且一般情况下亦不宜对财务报表整体进行逐行分析。如果逐年的数量变化可直接依据报表计算得出,注册人不必予以赘述。论述不得仅仅重复合并财务报表内所列的量化数据。

discussion shall not merely repeat numerical data contained in the consolidated financial statements.

5. The term "liquidity" as used in this Item refers to the ability of an enterprise to generate adequate amounts of cash to meet the enterprise's needs for cash. Except where it is otherwise clear from the discussion, the registrant shall indicate those balance sheet conditions or income or cash flow items which the registrant believes may be indicators of its liquidity condition. Liquidity generally shall be discussed on both a long-term and short-term basis. The issue of liquidity shall be discussed in the context of the registrant's own business or businesses. For example a discussion of working capital may be appropriate for certain manufacturing, industrial or related operations but might be inappropriate for a bank or public utility.

6. Where financial statements presented or incorporated by reference in the registration statement are required by §210.4-08 (e)(3) of Regulation S-X [17 CFR part 210] to include disclosure of restrictions on the ability of both consolidated and unconsolidated subsidiaries to transfer funds to the registrant in the form of cash dividends, loans or advances, the discussion of liquidity shall include a discussion of the nature and extent of such restrictions and the impact such restrictions have had and are expected to have on the ability of the parent company to meet its cash obligations.

7. Any forward-looking information supplied is expressly covered by the safe harbor rule for projections. See Rule 175 under the Securities Act[17 CFR 230.175], Rule 3b-6 under the Exchange Act [17 CFR 240.3b-6] and Securities Act Release No. 6084 (June 25, 1979) (44 FR 38810).

8. Registrants are only required to discuss the effects of inflation and other changes in prices when considered material. This discussion may be made in whatever manner appears appropriate under the circumstances. All that is required is a brief textual presentation of management's views. No specific numerical financial data need be presented except as Rule3-20(c) of Regulation S-X(§210.3-20(c) of this chapter) otherwise requires. However, registrants may elect to voluntarily disclose supplemental information on the effects of changing prices as provided for in Statement of Financial Accounting Standards No. 89, "Financial Reporting and Changing Prices" or through other supplemental disclosures. The Commission encourages experimentation with these disclosures in order to provide the most meaningful presentation of the impact of price changes on the registrant's financial statements.

9. Registrants that elect to disclose supplementary information on the effects of changing prices as specified by SFAS No. 89, "Financial Reporting and Changing Prices," may combine such explanations with the discussion and analysis required pursuant to this Item or may supply such information separately with appropriate cross reference.

5.本条所用的“流动性”一词系指企业获得充足的现金满足其现金需求的能力。除非从论述本身已可得出清楚结论,否则,如果注册人认为某些资产负债表条件、收益或现金流项目能反映其流动性状况,亦应予指明。一般而言,关于流动性的论述应涉及短期和长期两方面,并在注册人自身业务的背景和范围内开展,如对于某些制造业、工业或相关运营而言,论述运营资本是适当的,但对于银行或公用事业企业来说则并非如此。

6.如果根据《S-X管理办法》第210.4-08(e)(3)节(《联邦规章汇编》第十七编第210部分)的规定,注册说明书中包含或引用纳入的财务报表必须披露并表和非并表子公司以现金股息、贷款或垫款的形式向注册人转移资金时所面临的限制,则论述流动性时还应论述上述限制的性质和程度,以及该限制已经或预期将对该母公司履行现金义务产生的影响。

7.所提供的任何前瞻性信息均明确适用数据预测的安全港规则。参见《证券法》的《175规则》(《联邦规章汇编》第十七编第230.175节)、《交易法》的《3b-6规则》(《联邦规章汇编》第十七编第240.3b-6节)以及《证券法第6084号公告》(1979年6月25日)(《联邦公报》第44卷第38810页)。

8.通胀和其他价格变动只有构成重大影响时,才须予以论述。论述形式不拘,根据具体情况而定,以适宜为准,但必须就管理层的观点提供简要的文字说明。不必说明具体的量化财务数据,但《S-X管理办法》的《3-20(c)规则》[本章第210.3-20(c)节]另有规定的除外。但是,注册人可选择按照《财务会计准则公告第89号——财务报告和价格变动》自愿披露补充信息或者通过其他补充披露说明价格变动产生的影响。证券交易委员会鼓励注册人尝试进行此类自愿披露,以便充分说明价格变动对注册人财务报表的影响。

9.如果注册人选择按照《财务会计准则公告第89号——财务报告和价格变动》的规定披露补充信息说明价格变动的影响,可将该等补充解释与按照本条要求提供的论述和分析结合起来,或者另行提供适当的交叉索引提供该等信息。

10. All references to the registrant in the discussion and in this Item shall mean the registrant and its subsidiaries consolidated.

11. Foreign private registrants also shall discuss briefly any pertinent governmental economic, fiscal, monetary, or political policies or factors that have materially affected or could materially affect, directly or indirectly, their operations or investments by United States nationals.

12. If the registrant is a foreign private issuer, the discussion shall focus on the primary financial statements presented in the registration statement or report. There shall be a reference to the reconciliation to United States generally accepted accounting principles, and a discussion of any aspects of the difference between foreign and United States generally accepted accounting principles, not discussed in the reconciliation, that the registrant believes is necessary for an understanding of the financial statements as a whole.

13. The attention of bank holding companies is directed to the information called for in Guide 3 (§229.801(c) and §229.802(c)).

14. The attention of property–casualty insurance companies is directed to the information called for in Guide 6 (§229.801(f)).

Instructions to paragraph 303(a)(4): 1. No obligation to make disclosure under paragraph (a)(4) of this Item shall arise in respect of an off–balance sheet arrangement until a definitive agreement that is unconditionally binding or subject only to customary closing conditions exists or, if there is no such agreement, when settlement of the transaction occurs.

2. Registrants should aggregate off–balance sheet arrangements in groups or categories that provide material information in an efficient and understandable manner and should avoid repetition and disclosure of immaterial information. Effects that are common or similar with respect to a number of off–balance sheet arrangements must be analyzed in the aggregate to the extent the aggregation increases understanding. Distinctions in arrangements and their effects must be discussed to the extent the information is material, but the discussion should avoid repetition and disclosure of immaterial information.

3. For purposes of paragraph (a)(4) of this Item only, contingent liabilities arising out of litigation, arbitration or regulatory actions are not considered to be off–balance sheet arrangements.

4. Generally, the disclosure required by paragraph (a)(4) shall cover the most recent fiscal year. However, the discussion should address changes from the previous year where such discussion is necessary to an understanding of the disclosure.

5. In satisfying the requirements of paragraph (a)(4) of this Item, the discussion of

10.论述中以及本条中所述的“注册人”均指注册人及其并表子公司。

11.外国私募注册人也应简要论述已经或可能直接或间接对其经营或美国国籍人士的投资产生重大影响的任何相关政府的经济、财政、货币或政治政策。

12.如果注册人是外国私募发行人,论述重点应放在注册说明书或报告中提交的主要财务报表之上。同时应说明根据美国公认会计原则进行的调节,并论述外国公认会计原则与美国公认会计原则之间存在的所有差异,条件是这些差异并未在与调节有关的章节中进行论述,但注册人认为论述该差异对于理解财务报表整体而言具有必要性。

13.银行控股公司应特别注意“第三号指引”[本章第229.801(c)节和第229.802(c)节]要求提供的信息。

14.财产及意外保险公司应特别注意“第六号指引”[本章第229.801(f)节]要求提供的信息。

关于第303(a)(4)款的说明:1.只有在无条件地具有约束力或者仅受限于常规交割条件的最终协议签订之时,或者交易最终成交之时(如果并未签订最终协议),注册人才有义务承担本条第(a)(4)款下关于资产负债表外安排的披露义务。

2.注册人应将资产负债表外安排分门别类地整合,以有效而易懂的方式提供重大信息,并应避免非重大信息的重复和披露。如果一系列资产负债表外安排具有共同或类似影响,在有助于理解的情况下必须对这一系列资产负债表外安排进行整体分析。论述这些安排之间的差异和影响时应确保论述的信息具有重要意义,同时避免非重大信息的重复和披露。

3.仅就本条第(a)(4)款而言,因诉讼、仲裁或监管行动产生的或有债务不应视为资产负债表外安排。

4.一般而言,第(a)(4)款要求提供的披露应覆盖最近一个会计年度。但是,如为理解披露信息所必要,亦应对涉及与上一年相比产生的变化进行论述。

5.在按照本条第(a)(4)款的规定论述资产负债表外安排时,不必重复财务报表脚

off-balance sheet arrangements need not repeat information provided in the footnotes to the financial statements, provided that such discussion clearly cross-references to specific information in the relevant footnotes and integrates the substance of the footnotes into such discussion in a manner designed to inform readers of the significance of the information that is not included within the body of such discussion.

(b) *Interim periods.* If interim period financial statements are included or are required to be included by Article 3 of Regulation S-X(17 CFR 210), a management's discussion and analysis of the financial condition and results of operations shall be provided so as to enable the reader to assess material changes in financial condition and results of operations between the periods specified in paragraphs (b)(1) and (2) of this Item. The discussion and analysis shall include a discussion of material changes in those items specifically listed in paragraph (a) of this Item, except that the impact of inflation and changing prices on operations for interim periods need not be addressed.

(1) *Material changes in financial condition.* Discuss any material changes in financial condition from the end of the preceding fiscal year to the date of the most recent interim balance sheet provided. If the interim financial statements include an interim balance sheet as of the corresponding interim date of the preceding fiscal year, any material changes in financial condition from that date to the date of the most recent interim balance sheet provided also shall be discussed. If discussions of changes from both the end and the corresponding interim date of the preceding fiscal year are required, the discussions may be combined at the discretion of the registrant.

(2) *Material changes in results of operations.*Discuss any material changes in the registrant's results of operations with respect to the most recent fiscal year-to-date period for which an income statement is provided and the corresponding year-to-date period of the preceding fiscal year. If the registrant is required to or has elected to provide an income statement for the most recent fiscal quarter, such discussion also shall cover material changes with respect to that fiscal quarter and the corresponding fiscal quarter in the preceding fiscal year. In addition, if the registrant has elected to provide an income statement for the twelve-month period ended as of the date of the most recent interim balance sheet provided, the discussion also shall cover material changes with respect to that twelve-month period and the twelve-month period ended as of the corresponding interim balance sheet date of the preceding fiscal year. Notwithstanding the above, if for purposes of a registration statement a registrant subject to paragraph (b) of §210.3-03 of Regulation S-X provides a statement of income for the twelve-month period ended as of the date of the most recent interim balance sheet provided in lieu of the interim income statements otherwise required, the discussion of material changes in that twelve-month period will be in respect to the preceding fiscal year rather than the corresponding

注中已经提供的信息,前提是该等论述已为相关脚注中的具体信息提供明确的交叉索引,并将脚注内容纳入论述之中,帮助读者理解该等并未包括在论述正文之中的信息的重要性。

(b)中期期间。如果注册人提供了中期财务报表,或者《S-X管理办法》第3条[《联邦规章汇编》第十七编第210部分]要求注册人提供中期财务报表,则应提供管理层关于财务状况和经营成果的论述和分析,以便读者评估在本条第(b)(1)款和第(b)(2)款规定的时期之间财务状况和经营成果的重大变化。该论述和分析应包括对本条第(a)款具体列明事项的重大变化的论述,但是不必论述中期期间通胀和价格变动对经营产生的影响。

(1)财务状况的重大变化。论述自上一会计年度年末至最近一期中期资产负债表日期之间财务状况发生的任何重大变化。如果该中期财务报表包括一份截至上一会计年度对应中期日期的中期资产负债表,则还应论述自该日期至所提供的最近一期中期资产负债表日期之间财务状况发生的任何重大变化。如果注册人必须论述上一个会计年度年末以来的变化和自上一个会计年度对应中期日期以来的变化,则注册人可依其自由裁量权决定是否将两个期间的变化合并论述。

(2)经营成果的重大变化。对于注册人的经营成果,应论述损益表覆盖的最近一会计年度年初至今的期间发生的任何重大变化,也应论述此前一会计年度对应期间的重大变化。如果注册人有义务或者选择提供最近一个财务季度的损益表,则还应论述该财务季度的重大变化以及此前一会计年度对应财务季度的重大变化。此外,如果注册人选择针对截至最近一期中期资产负债表日期的12个月的期间提交损益表,则还应论述该12个月内发生的重大变化以及此前一会计年度截至中期资产负债表日期的12个月内的重大变化。无论上文如何规定,就注册说明书而言,如果受制于《S-X管理办法》第210.3-03条第(b)款的注册人就截至最近一期中期资产负债表日期的12个月的期间提供了一份损益表,用以替代其他本应提交的中期损益表,在此情况下,应论述此前一会计年度的12个月期间的重大变化,而并非对应的上一个期间的重大变化。

preceding period.

Instructions to paragraph (b) of Item 303:

1. If interim financial statements are presented together with financial statements for full fiscal years, the discussion of the interim financial information shall be prepared pursuant to this paragraph (b) and the discussion of the full fiscal year's information shall be prepared pursuant to paragraph (a) of this Item. Such discussions may be combined.

2. In preparing the discussion and analysis required by this paragraph (b), the registrant may presume that users of the interim financial information have read or have access to the discussion and analysis required by paragraph (a) for the preceding fiscal year.

3. The discussion and analysis required by this paragraph (b) is required to focus only on material changes. Where the interim financial statements reveal material changes from period to period in one or more significant line items, the causes for the changes shall be described if they have not already been disclosed: *Provided, however,* That if the causes for a change in one line item also relate to other line items, no repetition is required. Registrants need not recite the amounts of changes from period to period which are readily computable from the financial statements. The discussion shall not merely repeat numerical data contained in the financial statements. The information provided shall include that which is available to the registrant without undue effort or expense and which does not clearly appear in the registrant's condensed interim financial statements.

4. The registrant's discussion of material changes in results of operations shall identify any significant elements of the registrant's income or loss from continuing operations which do not arise from or are not necessarily representative of the registrant's ongoing business.

5. The registrant shall discuss any seasonal aspects of its business which have had a material effect upon its financial condition or results of operation.

6. Any forward-looking information supplied is expressly covered by the safe harbor rule for projections. See Rule 175 under the Securities Act [17 CFR 230. 175], Rule 3b-6 under the Exchange Act [17 CFR 249.3b-6] and Securities Act Release No. 6084 (June 25, 1979) (44 FR 38810).

7. The registrant is not required to include the table required by paragraph (a)(5) of this Item for interim periods. Instead, the registrant should disclose material changes outside the ordinary course of the registrant's business in the specified contractual obligations during the interim period.

(c) *Safe harbor.* (1) The safe harbor provided in section 27A of the Securities Act of 1933 (15 U.S.C. 77z-2) and section 21E of the Securities Exchange Act of 1934 (15

关于第303条第(b)款的说明:

1.如果中期财务报表与完整会计年度的财务报表一并提交,则关于中期财务信息的论述应遵照本条第(b)款的规定编制,关于完整会计年度财务信息的论述应遵照本条第(a)款的规定编制。上述论述可以合并。

2.在按照本第(b)款编制论述和分析时,注册人可以推定中期财务信息的使用者已经阅读或者可以获得第(a)款要求提供的关于前一会计年度的论述和分析。

3.第(b)款规定的论述和分析必须将重点仅放在重大变化之上。如果该中期财务报表显示一项或多项重大报表行项目在不同期间发生了重大变化,而变化原因尚未披露,则应进行相应说明。但是,如果导致一个行项目变化的原因也是导致另外一个项目变化的原因,则不必重复说明;如果不同期间的数量变化可直接依据报表计算得出,注册人不必赘述。论述不得仅仅重复合并财务报表内所列的量化数据。提供的信息应为注册人不必花费不合理的努力或开支即可以获得,且注册人提交的简明中期财务报表未予清楚直观说明的信息。

4.注册人在论述经营成果的重大变化时,应指出持续经营损益中并非来自注册人继续经营的任何重要组成部分,或不一定能体现注册人继续经营的重要组成部分。

5.注册人应论述对其财务状况或经营成果已经造成重大影响的任何业务季节性特征。

6.所提供的任何前瞻性信息均明确适用数据预测的安全港规则。参见《证券法》的《175规则》(《联邦规章汇编》第十七编第230.175节)、《交易法》的《3b-6规则》(《联邦规章汇编》第十七编第240.3b-6节)以及《证券法第6084号公告》(1979年6月25日)(《联邦公报》第44卷第38810页)。

7.对于中期期间,注册人不必提供本条第(a)(5)款要求提供的表格。相反,注册人应针对该中期期间内表格中规定的注册人的合同义务在非正常业务过程中发生的重大变化进行披露。

(c)安全港。(1)《1933年证券法》第27A条(《美国法典》第十五编第77z-2节)和《1934年证券交易法》第21E条(《美国法典》第十五编第78u-5节)规定的安全港(下称

U.S.C. 78u–5)("statutory safe harbors") shall apply to forward–looking information provided pursuant to paragraphs (a)(4) and (5) of this Item, provided that the disclosure is made by: an issuer; a person acting on behalf of the issuer; an outside reviewer retained by the issuer making a statement on behalf of the issuer; or an underwriter, with respect to information provided by the issuer or information derived from information provided by the issuer.

(2) For purposes of paragraph (c) of this Item only:

(i) All information required by paragraphs (a)(4) and (5) of this Item is deemed to be a *forward looking statement* as that term is defined in the statutory safe harbors, except for historical facts.

(ii) With respect to paragraph (a)(4) of this Item, the meaningful cautionary statements element of the statutory safe harbors will be satisfied if a registrant satisfies all requirements of that same paragraph (a)(4) of this Item.

(d)*Smaller reporting companies.* A smaller reporting company, as defined by §229.10(f)(1), may provide the information required in paragraph (a)(3)(iv) of this Item for the last two most recent fiscal years of the registrant if it provides financial information on net sales and revenues and on income from continuing operations for only two years. A smaller reporting company is not required to provide the information required by paragraph (a)(5) of this Item.

[47 FR 11401, Mar. 16, 1982, as amended at 47 FR 29839, July 9, 1982; 47 FR 54768, Dec. 6, 1982; 52 FR 30919, Aug. 18, 1987; 68 FR 5999, Feb. 5, 2003; 73 FR 958, Jan. 4, 2008]

§229.304 (Item 304) Changes in and disagreements with accountants on accounting and financial disclosure.

(a)(1) If during the registrant's two most recent fiscal years or any subsequent interim period, an independent accountant who was previously engaged as the principal accountant to audit the registrant's financial statements, or an independent accountant who was previously engaged to audit a significant subsidiary and on whom the principal accountant expressed reliance in its report, has resigned (or indicated it has declined to stand for re–election after the completion of the current audit) or was dismissed, then the registrant shall:

(i) State whether the former accountant resigned, declined to stand for re–election or was dismissed and the date thereof.

(ii) State whether the principal accountant's report on the financial statements for either of the past two years contained an adverse opinion or a disclaimer of opinion, or was qualified or modified as to uncertainty, audit scope, or accounting principles; and also

法定安全港)应适用于根据本条第(a)(4)款和第(a)(5)款提供的前瞻性信息,但是,对于发行人提供的信息或者由发行人提供的信息所衍生的信息,由以下人进行披露:发行人;发行人代表;发行人聘请的代表发行人作出声明的外部审核人员;承销商。

(2)仅就本条第(c)款而言:

(i)本条第(a)(4)款和第(a)(5)款要求提供的所有信息均应视为"前瞻性声明"(定义见"法定安全港"),但是历史事实不在此限。

(ii)对于本条第(a)(4)款而言,如果注册人满足本条第(a)(4)款的所有要求,即视为已满足法定安全港关于有效警示性声明的要素要求。

(d)小型报告公司。小型报告公司[定义见第229.10(f)(1)节]如果仅提供2年的关于净销售额、收入以及持续经营盈利的财务信息,则该小型报告公司可按照本条第(a)(3)(iv)款的规定提供最近2个会计年度的信息。小型报告公司不必提供本条第(a)(5)款规定的信息。

[《联邦公报》第47卷第11401页,1982年3月16日,修正索引:《联邦公报》第47卷第29839页,1982年7月9日;《联邦公报》第47卷第54768页,1982年12月6日;《联邦公报》第52卷第30919页,1987年8月18日;《联邦公报》第68卷第5999页,2003年2月5日;《联邦公报》第73卷第958页,2008年1月4日。]

第229.304节(第304条)　会计师的变更以及会计师在会计和财务披露上的分歧

(a)(1)如果在注册人最近2个会计年度内或其后的任一中期期间,曾作为主会计师审计注册人财务报表的独立会计师或曾参与审计重要子公司且主会计师曾表达采信其审计报告的独立会计师辞职(或在当前审计结束后表示拒绝参与后续审计)或被辞退,注册人应:

(i)说明该前任会计师是辞职、拒绝参与后续审计还是被辞退,同时应说明相应日期;

(ii)说明主会计师在过去两年内任一年就财务报表出具的报告是否包含否定意见或是否曾拒绝发表意见,或者是否曾因不确定性因素、审计范围或会计原则而在出具意见时作出了保留或修改;同时,应说明每一份上述否定意见、拒绝发表意见、保留

describe the nature of each such adverse opinion, disclaimer of opinion, modification, or qualification.

(iii) State whether the decision to change accountants was recommended or approved by:

(A) Any audit or similar committee of the board of directors, if the issuer has such a committee; or

(B) The board of directors, if the issuer has no such committee.

(iv) State whether during the registrant's two most recent fiscal years and any subsequent interim period preceding such resignation, declination or dismissal there were any disagreements with the former accountant on any matter of accounting principles or practices, financial statement disclosure, or auditing scope or procedure, which disagreement(s), if not resolved to the satisfaction of the former accountant, would have caused it to make reference to the subject matter of the disagreement(s) in connection with its report. Also, (A) describe each such disagreement; (B) state whether any audit or similar committee of the board of directors, or the board of directors, discussed the subject matter of each of such disagreements with the former accountant; and (C) state whether the registrant has authorized the former accountant to respond fully to the inquiries of the successor accountant concerning the subject matter of each of such disagreements and, if not, describe the nature of any limitation thereon and the reason therefore. The disagreements required to be reported in response to this Item include both those resolved to the former accountant's satisfaction and those not resolved to the former accountant's satisfaction. Disagreements contemplated by this Item are those that occur at the decision-making level, *i.e.*, between personnel of the registrant responsible for presentation of its financial statements and personnel of the accounting firm responsible for rendering its report.

(v) Provide the information required by paragraph (a)(1)(iv) of this Item for each of the kinds of events (even though the registrant and the former accountant did not express a difference of opinion regarding the event) listed in paragraphs (a)(1)(v)(A) through (D) of this section, that occurred within the registrant's two most recent fiscal years and any subsequent interim period preceding the former accountant's resignation, declination to stand for re-election, or dismissal ("reportable events"). If the event led to a disagreement or difference of opinion, then the event should be reported as a disagreement under paragraph (a) (1) (iv) and need not be repeated under this paragraph.

(A) The accountant's having advised the registrant that the internal controls necessary for the registrant to develop reliable financial statements do not exist;

(B) The accountant's having advised the registrant that information has come to the

或修改的性质。

(iii)说明更换会计师的决定是否由以下实体所建议或批准:

(A)董事会下属的任何审计委员会或类似委员会(如果发行人设有该等委员会);或者

(B)董事会(如果发行人未设该等委员会)。

(iv)说明在注册人最近2个会计年度内以及上述辞职、拒绝参与后续审计或辞退事件发生前的任何一个中期期间,是否与该前任会计师在会计原则或实践、财务报表披露或审计范围或程序等任一事项上产生过任何分歧,且如果该等分歧未获得令该前任会计师满意的解决,将导致该会计师在其报告中述及产生分歧的内容。同时,应:(A)描述所有此类分歧;(B)说明董事会下属的任何审计委员会或类似委员会或董事会本身是否与该前任会计师就每一分歧事项开展过论述;并且(C)说明注册人是否授权前任会计师充分回应继任会计师关于该等分歧事项的询问,如未授权,说明其任何限制的性质和其中的原因。本条要求报告的分歧既包括已获得令该前任会计师满意的解决的分歧,也包括未获得令该前任会计师满意的解决的分歧。本条所述的分歧指在决策层面产生的分歧,即注册人负责列报财务报表的人员和会计师事务所负责提交报告的人员之间的分歧。

(v)如果在注册人最近2个会计年度内以及上述辞职、拒绝参与后续审计或辞退事件发生前的任何一个中期期间发生了本节第(a)(1)(v)(A)款至第(a)(1)(v)(D)款所列的任一类型的事件(即使注册人和该前任会计师并未就此事件发表过不同意见)(下称应报告事件),即应提供本条第(a)(1)(iv)款要求提供的信息。如果该事件导致分歧或意见不统一,则应根据第(a)(1)(iv)款将该事件作为分歧进行报告,而不必根据本款进行重复报告。

(A)会计师曾向注册人提供意见,称注册人缺乏编制可靠财务报表所需的内部控制;

(B)会计师曾向注册人提供意见,称该会计师注意到某些信息,使其无法再采信

accountant's attention that has led it to no longer be able to rely on management's representations, or that has made it unwilling to be associated with the financial statements prepared by management;

(C)(*1*) The accountant's having advised the registrant of the need to expand significantly the scope of its audit, or that information has come to the accountant's attention during the time period covered by Item 304 (a)(1)(iv), that if further investigated may:

(*i*) Materially impact the fairness or reliability of either: a previously issued audit report or the underlying financial statements; or the financial statements issued or to be issued covering the fiscal period(s) subsequent to the date of the most recent financial statements covered by an audit report (including information that may prevent it from rendering an unqualified audit report on those financial statements), or

(*ii*) Cause it to be unwilling to rely on management's representations or be associated with the registrant's financial statements, and

(*2*) Due to the accountant's resignation (due to audit scope limitations or otherwise) or dismissal, or for any other reason, the accountant did not so expand the scope of its audit or conduct such further investigation; or

(D)(*1*) The accountant's having advised the registrant that information has come to the accountant's attention that it has concluded materially impacts the fairness or reliability of either (*i*) a previously issued audit report or the underlying financial statements, or(*ii*) the financial statements issued or to be issued covering the fiscal period (s) subsequent to the date of the most recent financial statements covered by an audit report(including information that, unless resolved to the accountant's satisfaction, would prevent it from rendering an unqualified audit report on those financial statements), and

(*2*) Due to the accountant's resignation, dismissal or declination to stand for reelection, or for any other reason, the issue has not been resolved to the accountant's satisfaction prior to its resignation, dismissal or declination to stand for re-election.

(2) If during the registrant's two most recent fiscal years or any subsequent interim period, a new independent accountant has been engaged as either the principal accountant to audit the registrant's financial statements, or as an independent accountant to audit a significant subsidiary and on whom the principal accountant is expected to express reliance in its report, then the registrant shall identify the newly engaged accountant and indicate the date of such accountant's engagement. In addition, if during the registrant's two most recent fiscal years, and any subsequent interim period prior to engaging that accountant, the registrant(or someone on its behalf) consulted the newly engaged accountant regarding:

管理层的陈述,或者使其不愿意参与和管理层编制的财务报表有关的工作;

(C)(1)该会计师曾向注册人提供意见,称需要大幅扩大审计范围,或者,该会计师在第304(a)(1)(iv)项覆盖的期间内注意到某些信息,而对该信息的进一步调查可能会:

(*i*)严重影响以下任一报告或报表的公允性或可靠性:之前发布的审计报告或与审计报告的相关财务报表;或者,审计报告所覆盖的最新财务报表日期之后的会计期间内已发布或将发布的财务报表(包括有可能导致该会计师无法就上述财务报表提供无保留意见审计报告的信息),或者

(*ii*)导致该会计师不愿采信管理层的陈述或不愿参与和注册人的财务报表有关的工作;且

(2)由于该前任会计师的辞职(出于审计范围受限或其他原因)、被辞退或者其他任何原因,该会计师并未扩大审计范围亦未进行进一步的调查;或者

(D)(1)该会计师曾向注册人提供意见,称该会计师留意到某些信息,并得出结论认定该信息对以下任一报告或报表的公允性或可靠性存在严重影响:(*i*)之前发布的审计报告或与审计报告的相关财务报表;或者(*ii*)审计报告所覆盖的最新财务报表日期之后的会计期间内已发布或将发布的财务报表(包括如未获得令会计师满意的解决,会计师即无法就上述财务报表提供无保留意见审计报告的信息),并且

(2)由于该会计师的辞职、被辞退、拒绝参与后续审计或任何其他原因,该问题在该会计师辞职、被辞退或拒绝参与后续审计之前未能得到令该会计师满意的解决。

(2)如果在注册人最近2个会计年度内或其后的任何一个中期报告期间,一名新任独立会计师被聘为主会计师负责审计注册人的财务报表,或者被聘为独立会计师审计注册人的一个重要子公司且注册人的主会计师预期将对其报告表示采信,则注册人应提供该新任会计师的身份信息,并说明聘请该会计师的日期。此外,如果在注册人最近2个会计年度内以及聘请新会计师之前的任一个中期报告期间,注册人(或其代表)针对以下事项向该名新会计师进行了询问:

(i) Either: The application of accounting principles to a specified transaction, either completed or proposed; or the type of audit opinion that might be rendered on the registrant's financial statements, and either a written report was provided to the registrant or oral advice was provided that the new accountant concluded was an important factor considered by the registrant in reaching a decision as to the accounting, auditing or financial reporting issue; or

(ii) Any matter that was either the subject of a disagreement (as defined in paragraph 304(a)(1)(iv) and the related instructions to this item) or a reportable event (as described in paragraph 304(a)(1)(v)), then the registrant shall:

(A) So state and identify the issues that were the subjects of those consultations;

(B) Briefly describe the views of the newly engaged accountant as expressed orally or in writing to the registrant on each such issue and, if written views were received by the registrant, file them as an exhibit to the report or registration statement requiring compliance with this Item 304(a);

(C) State whether the former accountant was consulted by the registrant regarding any such issues, and if so, provide a summary of the former accountant's views; and

(D) Request the newly engaged accountant to review the disclosure required by this Item 304(a) before it is filed with the Commission and provide the new accountant the opportunity to furnish the registrant with a letter addressed to the Commission containing any new information, clarification of the registrant's expression of its views, or the respects in which it does not agree with the statements made by the registrant in response to Item 304(a). The registrant shall file any such letter as an exhibit to the report or registration statement containing the disclosure required by this Item.

(3) The registrant shall provide the former accountant with a copy of the disclosures it is making in response to this Item 304(a) that the former accountant shall receive no later than the day that the disclosures are filed with the Commission. The registrant shall request the former accountant to furnish the registrant with a letter addressed to the Commission stating whether it agrees with the statements made by the registrant in response to this Item 304(a) and, if not, stating the respects in which it does not agree. The registrant shall file the former accountant's letter as an exhibit to the report on registration statement containing this disclosure. If the former accountant's letter is unavailable at the time of filing such report or registration statement, then the registrant shall request the former accountant to provide the letter as promptly as possible so that the registrant can file the letter with the Commission within ten business days after the filing of the report or registration statement. Notwithstanding the ten business day period, the registrant shall file the letter by amendment within two business days of receipt; if the letter is received on a Saturday, Sunday or holiday on which the Commission is not open

(i)会计原则对某一项特定交易(不论是已完成交易还是拟开展的交易)的适用,或者可能就注册人财务报表提供的审计意见的类型,并且该新会计师向注册人提供了书面报告或口头意见,且注册人在该等报告或意见中作出的结论是注册人在就会计、审计或财务报告事宜作出决策时考虑的重要因素之一;或者

(ii)任何产生分歧的事项[定义见第304(a)(1)(iv)款和关于本条的相关说明]或者应报告事件[如第304(a)(1)(v)款所述],则注册人应:

(A)进行相应说明,并说明注册人向该新会计师询问的具体事项;

(B)简要说明该新会计师针对每一上述事项向注册人以口头或书面形式表达的观点,并且,如果注册人收到书面观点,则应将该书面观点作为附录附于按照本第304(a)条提交的报告或注册说明书之后;

(C)说明注册人是否针对以上任何事项向前任会计师作出过询问,如有,则应提供一份前任会计师观点的摘要;且

(D)在向证券交易委员会提交按照本第304(a)条的规定作出的披露之前,请求新任会计师审查该披露内容,并给予该新任会计师机会,使其能够向注册人提供一封致证券交易委员会的信件,信内应包含所有新信息、关于注册人观点的澄清或者该新任会计师与注册人就按照第304(a)条所作的声明存在分歧的内容。注册人应将此任何信件作为附录附于按照本条规定披露的报告或注册说明书之后。

(3)注册人应向该前任会计师提供一份其按照本第304(a)条规定作出的披露复本,并确保该前任会计师收到该等披露的日期不晚于注册人向证券交易委员会提交该等披露之日。注册人应请求该前任会计师向其提供一封致证券交易委员会的信件,信内应说明该前任会计师是否同意注册人按照本第304(a)条的要求所作的声明;如果该前任会计师对此存在分歧,应说明存在分歧的具体内容。注册人应将上述信件作为附录附于包含该披露信息的报告或注册说明书之后。如果在提交该报告或注册说明书之时尚未获得该前任会计师信件,则注册人应请求该前任会计师尽快提供信件,以便注册人能够在向证券交易委员会提交该报告或注册说明书后10个工作日之内提交该信件。尽管有上述10个工作日的期限规定,但是注册人应在收到信件后2个工作日内以修正稿的形式提交该信件;如果信件的收悉时间为证券交易委员会暂停工作的周六、周日或节假日,则上述2个工作日的期限应相应递延,从紧接其后的第一个工作日起算(含)。该前任会计师可向注册人提供一份中期信件,着重说明特定关切领域,并说明将于上述的10个工作日的期间内另行发送一份更详细的信件。如果确实存在中期信件,而在递交包含第304(a)条注册人披露信息的报告或注册说明书之时并未同

for business, then the two business day period shall begin to run on and shall include the first business day thereafter. The former accountant may provide the registrant with an interim letter highlighting specific areas of concern and indicating that a more detailed letter will be forthcoming within the ten business day period noted above. If not filed with the report or registration statement containing the registrant's disclosure under this Item 304(a), then the interim letter, if any, shall be filed by the registrant by amendment within two business days of receipt.

(b) If: (1) In connection with a change in accountants subject to paragraph (a) of this Item 304, there was any disagreement of the type described in paragraph (a)(1)(iv) or any reportable event as described in paragraph (a)(1)(v) of this Item;

(2) During the fiscal year in which the change in accountants took place or during the subsequent fiscal year, there have been any transactions or events similar to those which involved such disagreement or reportable event; and

(3) Such transactions or events were material and were accounted for or disclosed in a manner different from that which the former accountants apparently would have concluded was required, the registrant shall state the existence and nature of the disagreement or reportable event and also state the effect on the financial statements if the method had been followed which the former accountants apparently would have concluded was required.

These disclosures need not be made if the method asserted by the former accountants ceases to be generally accepted because of authoritative standards or interpretations subsequently issued.

Instructions to Item 304: 1. The disclosure called for by paragraph (a) of this Item need not be provided if it has been previously reported as that term is defined in Rule 12b-2 under the Exchange Act (§240.12b-2 of this chapter); the disclosure called for by paragraph (a) must be provided, however, notwithstanding prior disclosure, if required pursuant to Item 9 of Schedule 14A(§240.14a-101 of this chapter). The disclosure called for by paragraph (b) of this section must be furnished, where required, notwithstanding any prior disclosure about accountant changes or disagreements.

2. When disclosure is required by paragraph (a) of this section in an annual report to security holders pursuant to Rule 14a-3(§240.14a-3 of this chapter) or Rule 14c-3 (§240.14c-3 of this chapter), or in a proxy or information statement filed pursuant to the requirements of Schedule 14A or 14C(§240.14a-101 or §240.14c-101 of this chapter), in lieu of a letter pursuant to paragraph (a)(2)(D) or (a)(3), prior to filing such materials with or furnishing such materials to the Commission, the registrant shall furnish the disclosure required by paragraph (a) of this section to any former accountant engaged by the registrant during the period set forth in paragraph (a) of this section and to the

时递交该中期信件,则注册人应在收到该中期信件后2个工作日之内以修正稿的形式进行提交。

(b)如果:(1)就第304条第(a)款所述的会计师变更而言,存在第(a)(1)(iv)款所述类型的任何分歧,或者存在本条第(a)(1)(v)款所述的任何应报告事件;

(2)在会计师变更发生的会计年度或其后一会计年度,曾经发生过与涉及该等分歧或应报告事件的交易或事件类似的任何交易或事件;且

(3)该等交易或事件具有重要意义,且其会计和披露方式有别于该前任会计师应该会采取的必要处理方式,则注册人应说明该分歧或应报告事件的存在和性质,以及如果采用该前任会计师应该会采取的必要处理方式对财务报表会产生何等影响。

如果随后发布了权威标准或解释,从而导致该前任会计师所主张的方法不再具有公认性,则不必作出上述披露。

关于第304条的说明:1.如果本节第(a)款要求作出的披露已经按照《交易法》的《12b-2规则》(本章第240.12b-2节)进行了披露,则不必重复披露。但是,如果《附表14A》第9条(本章第240.14a-101节)要求作出相关披露,则尽管之前已进行过披露,亦必须再次披露第(a)款要求提供的信息。不论之前是否曾作出有关会计师变更或分歧的任何披露,均须按规定提供本条第(b)款要求的披露。

2.如果本条第(a)款要求在按照《14a-3规则》(本章第240.14a-3节)或《14c-3规则》(本章第240.14c-3节)向证券持有人提供的年度报告中作出披露,或者在按照《附表14A》或《附表14C》(本章第240.14a-101节或第240.14c-101节)的要求提交的征集投票权说明书或信息说明书中作出披露,以之替代第(a)(2)(D)款或第(a)(3)款要求规定的信件,则在向证券交易委员会提交或提供该等材料之前,注册人应向其在本节第(a)款规定的期间内聘用过的所有前任会计师作出本节第(a)款规定的披露,并向所有新任会计师作出相应的披露。如果任何会计师认为按照本条第(a)款所作的声明不准确或不完整,该会计师可简要说明其观点(篇幅一般不超过200字),并将该说明纳入年

newly engaged accountant. If any such accountant believes that the statements made in response to paragraph (a) of this section are incorrect or incomplete, it may present its views in a brief statement, ordinarily expected not to exceed 200 words, to be included in the annual report or proxy or information statement. This statement shall be submitted to the registrant within ten business days of the date the accountant receives the registrant's disclosure. Further, unless the written views of the newly engaged accountant required to be filed as an exhibit by paragraph (a)(2)(B) of this Item 304 have been previously filed with the Commission the registrant shall file a Form 8-K concurrently with the annual report or proxy or information statement for the purpose of filing the written views as exhibits thereto.

3. The information required by Item 304(a) need not be provided for a company being acquired by the registrant that is not subject to the filing requirements of either section 13(a) or 15(d) of the Exchange Act, or, because of section 12(i) of the Exchange Act, has not furnished an annual report to security holders pursuant to Rule 14a-3 or Rule 14c-3 for its latest fiscal year.

4. The term "disagreements" as used in this Item shall be interpreted broadly, to include any difference of opinion concerning any matter of accounting principles or practices, financial statement disclosure, or auditing scope or procedure which (if not resolved to the satisfaction of the former accountant) would have caused it to make reference to the subject matter of the disagreement in connection with its report. It is not necessary for there to have been an argument to have had a disagreement, merely a difference of opinion. For purposes of this Item, however, the term disagreements does not include initial differences of opinion based on incomplete facts or preliminary information that were later resolved to the former accountant's satisfaction by, and providing the registrant and the accountant do not continue to have a difference of opinion upon, obtaining additional relevant facts or information.

5. In determining whether any disagreement or reportable event has occurred, an oral communication from the engagement partner or another person responsible for rendering the accounting firm's opinion (or their designee) will generally suffice as the accountant advising the registrant of a reportable event or as a statement of a disagreement at the "decision-making level" within the accounting firm and require disclosure under this Item.

[53 FR 12929, Apr. 20, 1988, as amended at 54 FR 9774, Mar. 8, 1989]

§229.305 (Item 305) Quantitative and qualitative disclosures about market risk.

(a) *Quantitative information about market risk.* (1) Registrants shall provide, in their

度报告或征集投票权报告或信息说明书之中。上述说明应在会计师收到注册人的披露后10个工作日内提交给注册人。此外,除非本第304条第(a)(2)(B)款要求新任会计师以附录形式提交的书面观点此前已经提交给证券交易委员会,否则注册人应在提交年度报告或征集投票权说明书或信息说明书时一并提交《8-K表格》,以期通过附录形式提交该等书面观点。

3.如果注册人正在收购一家公司,而该公司并不受制于《交易法》第13(a)条或第15(d)条的文件提交要求,又或者由于适用《交易法》第12(i)条的规定,该公司并未按照《14a-3规则》或《14c-3规则》向证券持有人提交最近一个会计年度的年度报告,则注册人不必按照第304(a)条的规定就该公司提供相关信息。

4.本条使用的"分歧"一词应进行广义解释,包括关于会计原则或实践、财务报表披露或审计范围或程序的任何事宜的任何不同意见,且如果这些不同意见未能得到令前任会计师满意的解决,则会使该前任会计师在其报告中述及相关事项。分歧可以仅仅是意见的不同,不一定要发生过辩论。但是,就本条而言,如果意见的不同来自于对不完整事实或初步信息的初步判断,且在获取更充分的相关事实和信息后已获得令前任会计师满意的解决,注册人和会计师之后已就此达成统一意见的,则此类不同意见不属于本条所述的"分歧"。

5.一般而言,在判定是否曾发生过任何分歧或应报告事件时,被聘用的会计师事务所的合伙人或其他负责提供会计意见的人士(或其指定人)就应报告事件向注册人提出口头沟通的,即足以认定该会计师就应报告事件向注册人提出了有关意见,或者足以构成关于该会计师事务所内部"决策层面"分歧的声明,并应按照本条规定进行披露。

[《联邦公报》第53卷第12929页,1988年4月20日,修正索引:《联邦公报》第54卷第9774页,1989年3月8日。]

第229.305节(第305条) 市场风险定量与定性披露

(a)市场风险定量信息。(1)注册人应按下列三种备选披露方式之一,以报表货币

reporting currency, quantitative information about market risk as of the end of the latest fiscal year, in accordance with one of the following three disclosure alternatives. In preparing this quantitative information, registrants shall categorize market risk sensitive instruments into instruments entered into for trading purposes and instruments entered into for purposes other than trading purposes. Within both the trading and other than trading portfolios, separate quantitative information shall be presented, to the extent material, for each market risk exposure category(*i.e.*, interest rate risk, foreign currency exchange rate risk, commodity price risk, and other relevant market risks, such as equity price risk). A registrant may use one of the three alternatives set forth in this section for all of the required quantitative disclosures about market risk. A registrant also may choose, from among the three alternatives, one disclosure alternative for market risk sensitive instruments entered into for trading purposes and another disclosure alternative for market risk sensitive instruments entered into for other than trading purposes. Alternatively, a registrant may choose any disclosure alternative, from among the three alternatives, for each risk exposure category within the trading and other than trading portfolios. The three disclosure alternatives are:

(i) (A) (*1*) Tabular presentation of information related to market risk sensitive instruments; such information shall include fair values of the market risk sensitive instruments and contract terms sufficient to determine future cash flows from those instruments, categorized by expected maturity dates.

(*2*) Tabular information relating to contract terms shall allow readers of the table to determine expected cash flows from the market risk sensitive instruments for each of the next five years. Comparable tabular information for any remaining years shall be displayed as an aggregate amount.

(*3*) Within each risk exposure category, the market risk sensitive instruments shall be grouped based on common characteristics. Within the foreign currency exchange rate risk category, the market risk sensitive instruments shall be grouped by functional currency and within the commodity price risk category, the market risk sensitive instruments shall be grouped by type of commodity.

(*4*) See the Appendix to this Item for a suggested format for presentation of this information; and

(B) Registrants shall provide a description of the contents of the table and any related assumptions necessary to understand the disclosures required under paragraph (a)(1)(i)(A) of this Item 305; or

(ii) (A) Sensitivity analysis disclosures that express the potential loss in future earnings, fair values, or cash flows of market risk sensitive instruments resulting from one or more selected hypothetical changes in interest rates, foreign currency exchange rates,

提供截至最近一个会计年度年末的市场风险定量信息。在编制该定量信息时,注册人应将市场风险敏感工具划分为交易类工具和非交易类工具。在交易类和非交易类资产组合中,应就每一市场风险敞口类别(即利率风险、外币汇率风险、商品价格风险以及权益价格风险等其他相关市场风险)分别提交重大定量信息。注册人可选择本节规定的三种备选方式之一,按规定进行全部市场风险定量披露;也可以从三种备选方式中选择一种用于交易类市场风险敏感工具,另一种用于非交易类市场风险敏感工具;或者,注册人还可以从三种备选方式中选择任何备选披露方式,并将之适用于交易类和非交易类资产组合的每一种风险敞口类别。三种备选披露方式分别是:

(i)(A)(1)以表格形式列报与市场风险敏感工具相关的信息;上述信息应包括市场风险敏感工具的公允价值以及足以确定该等工具未来现金流的合约条款;市场风险敏感工具应按预期到期日进行分类。

(2)以表格形式列报的与合约条款相关的信息应使读者能够确定市场风险敏感工具在未来5年每一年的预期现金流。任何其余年度的可比性列表信息应通过一个总金额列明。

(3)在每一种风险敞口类别内,市场风险敏感工具应基于共同特点进行分组。在外币汇率风险类别内,市场风险敏感工具应按职能货币分组。在商品价格风险类别内,市场风险敏感工具应按商品类型分组。

(4)上述信息的建议提交格式,见本条之附件;且

(B)注册人应提供表格内容说明,并按本第305条第(a)(1)(i)(A)款的规定,提供理解披露内容所必需的所有相关假设;或

(ii)(A)提供敏感性分析披露,说明市场风险敏感工具的未来盈利、公允价值或现金流在选定期间内因利率、外币汇率、商品价格和其他相关市场利率或价格的一项或多项选定假设变更而引起的潜在损失。利率或价格选定假设的变更的重要性在市场

commodity prices, and other relevant market rates or prices over a selected period of time. The magnitude of selected hypothetical changes in rates or prices may differ among and within market risk exposure categories; and

(B) Registrants shall provide a description of the model, assumptions, and parameters, which are necessary to understand the disclosures required under paragraph (a)(1)(ii)(A) of this Item 305; or

(iii)(A) Value at risk disclosures that express the potential loss in future earnings, fair values, or cash flows of market risk sensitive instruments over a selected period of time, with a selected likelihood of occurrence, from changes in interest rates, foreign currency exchange rates, commodity prices, and other relevant market rates or prices;

(B)(*1*) For each category for which value at risk disclosures are required under paragraph (a)(1)(iii)(A) of this Item 305, provide either:

(*i*) The average, high and low amounts, or the distribution of the value at risk amounts for the reporting period; or

(*ii*) The average, high and low amounts, or the distribution of actual changes in fair values, earnings, or cash flows from the market risk sensitive instruments occurring during the reporting period; or

(*iii*) The percentage or number of times the actual changes in fair values, earnings, or cash flows from the market risk sensitive instruments exceeded the value at risk amounts during the reporting period;

(*2*) Information required under paragraph (a)(1)(iii)(B)(1) of this Item 305 is not required for the first fiscal year end in which a registrant must present Item 305 information; and

(C) Registrants shall provide a description of the model, assumptions, and parameters, which are necessary to understand the disclosures required under paragraphs (a)(1)(iii)(A) and (B) of this Item 305.

(2) Registrants shall discuss material limitations that cause the information required under paragraph (a)(1) of this Item 305 not to reflect fully the net market risk exposures of the entity. This discussion shall include summarized descriptions of instruments, positions, and transactions omitted from the quantitative market risk disclosure information or the features of instruments, positions, and transactions that are included, but not reflected fully in the quantitative market risk disclosure information.

(3) Registrants shall present summarized market risk information for the preceding fiscal year. In addition, registrants shall discuss the reasons for material quantitative changes in market risk exposures between the current and preceding fiscal years. Information required by this paragraph (a)(3), however, is not required if disclosure is not required under paragraph (a)(1) of this Item305 for the current fiscal year. Information

风险敞口类别之间可以各有不同;且

(B)注册人应按照本第305条第(a)(1)(ii)(A)款的规定,提供理解披露内容所需的模型、任何假设和参数介绍;或

(iii)(A)提供风险值披露,说明市场风险敏感工具的未来盈利、公允价值或现金流在选定期间内因利率、外币汇率、商品价格和其他相关市场利率或价格的变更引起的潜在损失,以及选定的事件发生可能性;

(B)(1)就需要根据本第305条第(a)(1)(iii)(A)款进行风险值披露的每一类别的市场风险敏感工具,提供下列类别信息之一:

(i)报告期间风险值的平均值、最高值和最低值,或风险值的分布;或

(ii)报告期间市场风险敏感工具的公允价值、盈利或现金流实际变动的平均值、最高值和最低值,或实际变动的分布;或

(iii)报告期间市场风险敏感工具公允价值、盈利或现金流的实际变动超过风险值的比例或次数;

(2)注册人在首个会计年度年末必须按本第305条的规定提交信息的,不必提交本第305条第(a)(1)(iii)(B)(1)款要求提交的信息;及

(C)注册人应按本第305条第(a)(1)(iii)(A)款和第(a)(1)(iii)(B)款的要求,提交理解披露内容所需的模型、假设和参数介绍。

(2)如果存在实质性限制,导致本第305条第(a)(1)款所要求提供的信息无法全面反映该实体的净市场风险敞口,注册人应对该等限制进行论述。该等论述应对定量市场风险披露信息所遗漏的工具、持仓和交易,或者定量市场风险披露信息已涵盖但并未充分反映的工具、持仓和交易的特点进行摘要介绍。

(3)注册人应提交上一会计年度的摘要性市场风险信息。此外,本会计年度和上一会计年度之间市场风险敞口量发生重大变动的,注册人应论述该等变动发生的原因。但是,如果本第305条第(a)(1)款不要求就本会计年度提供信息披露,则不必按本第(a)(3)款的规定提交信息。注册人在首个会计年度年末必须按第305条的规定提交信息的,不必提交本第(a)(3)款要求提交的信息。

required by this paragraph (a)(3) is not required for the first fiscal year end in which a registrant must present Item 305 information.

(4) If registrants change disclosure alternatives or key model characteristics, assumptions, and parameters used in providing quantitative information about market risk (e.g., changing from tabular presentation to value at risk, changing the scope of instruments included in the model, or changing the definition of loss from fair values to earnings), and if the effects of any such change is material, the registrant shall:

(i) Explain the reasons for the change; and

(ii) Either provide summarized comparable information, under the new disclosure method, for the year preceding the current year or, in addition to providing disclosure for the current year under the new method, provide disclosures for the current year and preceding fiscal year under the method used in the preceding year.

Instructions to paragraph 305(a): 1. Under paragraph 305(a)(1):

A. For each market risk exposure category within the trading and other than trading portfolios, registrants may report the average, high, and low sensitivity analysis or value at risk amounts for the reporting period, as an alternative to reporting year-end amounts.

B. In determining the average, high, and low amounts for the fiscal year under instruction 1.A. of the Instructions to Paragraph 305(a), registrants should use sensitivity analysis or value at risk amounts relating to at least four equal time periods throughout the reporting period(e.g., four quarter-end amounts, 12 month-end amounts, or 52 week-end amounts).

C. Functional currency means functional currency as defined by generally accepted accounting principles(see, e.g., FASB, *Statement of Financial Accounting Standards No. 52, "Foreign Currency Translation"*, ("FAS 52") paragraph 20 (December 1981)).

D. Registrants using the sensitivity analysis and value at risk disclosure alternatives are encouraged, but not required, to provide quantitative amounts that reflect the aggregate market risk inherent in the trading and other than trading portfolios.

2. Under paragraph 305(a)(1)(i):

A. Examples of contract terms sufficient to determine future cash flows from market risk sensitive instruments include, but are not limited to:

i. Debt instruments — principal amounts and weighted average effective interest rates;

ii. Forwards and futures — contract amounts and weighted average settlement prices;

iii. Options — contract amounts and weighted average strike prices;

iv. Swaps — notional amounts, weighted average pay rates or prices, and weighted average receive rates or prices; and

v. Complex instruments — likely to be a combination of the contract terms presented in 2.A.i. through iv. of this Instruction;

(4)如果注册人变更披露方式,或变更提供市场风险定量信息时所采用的主要模型的特点、假设和参数(如将以表格形式列报的披露方式变更为风险值披露方式,变更模型所涵盖的市场风险敏感工具范围,或将损失的界定标准从公允价值变更为盈利),且如果任何该等变更构成重大变更,则注册人应:

(i)解释变更的原因;并

(ii)提供采用新披露方法时得出的前一年度的摘要性可比信息,或者除采用新方法进行当前年度的披露外,另行提供采用上一年度的方法时得出的当前年度及上一年度的披露内容。

关于第305(a)款的说明:1.在第305(a)(1)款下:

A.对于每一交易类和非交易类资产组合市场风险敞口类别,注册人可以就报告期间内的敏感分析或风险值的平均值、最高值和最低值提供报告,以此代替年终数额的报告。

B.在根据关于第305(a)款的说明第1.A.条确定某会计年度的平均值、最高值和最低值时,注册人应采用报告期间内至少4段等长期间的敏感性分析或风险值(如4个季末值、12个月末值或52个周末值)。

C.职能货币是指公认会计原则定义的职能货币[如参见财务会计准则委员会:《第52号财务会计准则公报——"外币换算"》(FAS 52)第20款(1981年12月)]。

D.对于采用敏感性分析和风险值披露方式的注册人,鼓励但不要求其提供反映交易类与非交易类资产组合中市场风险总值的量化数值。

2.在第305(a)(1)(i)款下:

A.足以确定市场风险敏感工具未来现金流的合约条款举例如下:

i.债务工具——本金额与加权平均有效利率;

ii.远期和期货——合约金额与加权平均结算(交割)价格;

iii.期权——合约金额与加权平均行权价;

iv.互换——名义金额、加权平均支付利率或支付价格,以及加权平均接收利率或接收价格;及

v.复合工具——有可能为本说明第2.A.i项至第2.A.iv项所列举合约条款的组合;

B. When grouping based on common characteristics, instruments should be categorized, at a minimum, by the following characteristics, when material:

i. Fixed rate or variable rate assets or liabilities;

ii. Long or short forwards and futures;

iii. Written or purchased put or call options with similar strike prices;

iv. Receive fixed and pay variable swaps, receive variable and pay fixed swaps, and receive variable and pay variable swaps;

v. The currency in which the instruments′ cash flows are denominated;

vi. Financial instruments for which foreign currency transaction gains and losses are reported in the same manner as translation adjustments under generally accepted accounting principles (see, e.g., FAS 52 paragraph 20 (December 1981)); and

vii. Derivatives used to manage risks inherent in anticipated transactions;

C. Registrants may aggregate information regarding functional currencies that are economically related, managed together for internal risk management purposes, and have statistical correlations of greater than 75% over each of the past three years;

D. Market risk sensitive instruments that are exposed to rate or price changes in more than one market risk exposure category should be presented within the tabular information for each of the risk exposure categories to which those instruments are exposed;

E. If a currency swap (see, e.g., FAS 52 Appendix E for a definition of currency swap) eliminates all foreign currency exposures in the cash flows of a foreign currency denominated debt instrument, neither the currency swap nor the foreign currency denominated debt instrument are required to be disclosed in the foreign currency risk exposure category. However, both the currency swap and the foreign currency denominated debt instrument should be disclosed in the interest rate risk exposure category; and

F. The contents of the table and related assumptions that should be described include, but are not limited to:

i. The different amounts reported in the table for various categories of the market risk sensitive instruments (e.g., principal amounts for debt, notional amounts for swaps, and contract amounts for options and futures);

ii. The different types of reported market rates or prices (e.g., contractual rates or prices, spot rates or prices, forward rates or prices); and

iii. Key prepayment or reinvestment assumptions relating to the timing of reported amounts.

3. Under paragraph 305(a)(1)(ii):

A. Registrants should select hypothetical changes in market rates or prices that are

B.当根据市场风险敏感工具的共同特征进行分组时,至少应按下列具有实质性的特征对工具进行分类:

i.固定利率或浮动利率资产或负债;

ii.长期或短期远期和期货;

iii.行权价类似的已签出或已购买的买入或卖出期权;

iv.接受固定和支付浮动互换,接受浮动和支付固定互换,以及接受浮动和支付浮动互换;

v.工具现金流的计价货币;

vi.报告外币交易收益及损失,且报告方式与按公认会计原则进行换算调整的方式相同的金融工具[如参见FAS 52第20款(1981年12月)];及

vii.用于管理预期交易固有风险的衍生工具;

C.注册人可以汇总具有经济关联性、出于内部风险管理目的统一管理并且在过去3年中统计关联度高于75%的职能货币的相关信息;

D.如果市场风险敏感工具存在一个以上市场风险敞口类别的利率或价格变动风险,则应在以表格形式提供的信息内按该等工具所暴露的风险敞口类别对该等工具进行列报;

E.如果货币互换(关于货币互换定义,参见FAS 52附件E)消除了外币计价债务工具的现金流存在的全部外币风险敞口,则该货币互换和外币计价债务工具均不必在外币风险敞口类别中予以披露。但是,货币互换和外币计价债务工具均应在利率风险敞口类别中予以披露;及

F.应予说明的表格内容及相关假设包括但不限于:

i.表格中报告的不同类别市场风险敏感工具的不同数值(如债务本金额、互换名义金额、期权与期货合约金额);

ii.报告的市场利率或价格的不同类型(如合约利率或价格、即期利率或价格、远期利率或价格);及

iii.与报告金额的时间相关的主要提前还款或再投资假设。

3.在第305(a)(1)(ii)款下:

A.注册人应选取预期能够反映利率和价格近期合理可能变动的市场利率或价格

expected to reflect reasonably possible near-term changes in those rates and prices. In this regard, absent economic justification for the selection of a different amount, registrants should use changes that are not less than 10 percent of end of period market rates or prices;

B. For purposes of instruction 3.A. of the Instructions to Paragraph 305(a), the term *reasonably possible* has the same meaning as defined by generally accepted accounting principles (see, e.g., FASB, *Statement of Financial Accounting Standards No. 5, "Accounting for Contingencies,"* ("FAS 5") paragraph 3 (March 1975));

C. For purposes of instruction 3.A. of the Instructions to Paragraph 305(a), the term *near term* means a period of time going forward up to one year from the date of the financial statements (see generally AICPA, Statement of Position 94-6, "*Disclosure of Certain Significant Risks and Uncertainties,*" ("SOP 94-6") at paragraph 7 (December 30, 1994));

D. Market risk sensitive instruments that are exposed to rate or price changes in more than one market risk exposure category should be included in the sensitivity analysis disclosures for each market risk category to which those instruments are exposed;

E. Registrants with multiple foreign currency exchange rate exposures should prepare foreign currency sensitivity analysis disclosures that measure the aggregate sensitivity to changes in all foreign currency exchange rate exposures, including the effects of changes in both transactional currency/functional currency exchange rate exposures and functional currency/reporting currency exchange rate exposures. For example, assume a French division of a registrant presenting its financial statements in U.S. dollars ($US) invests in a deutschmark (DM)-denominated debt security. In these circumstances, the $US is the reporting currency and the DM is the transactional currency. In addition, assume this division determines that the French franc (FF) is its functional currency according to FAS 52. In preparing the foreign currency sensitivity analysis disclosures, this registrant should report the aggregate potential loss from hypothetical changes in both the DM/FF exchange rate exposure and the FF/$US exchange rate exposure; and

F. Model, assumptions, and parameters that should be described include, but are not limited to, how *loss* is defined by the model (e.g., loss in earnings, fair values, or cash flows), a general description of the modeling technique (e.g., duration modeling, modeling that measures the change in net present values arising from selected hypothetical changes in market rates or prices, and a description as to how optionality is addressed by the model), the types of instruments covered by the model (e.g., derivative financial instruments, other financial instruments, derivative commodity instruments, and whether other instruments are included voluntarily, such as certain commodity instruments and positions, cash flows from anticipated transactions, and certain financial instruments excluded under instruction

假设变更。为此,除非注册人能够证明选取其他数值具有经济合理性,否则应采用不低于期末市场利率或价格10%的变动值;

B.就关于第305(a)款的说明第3.A.条而言,“合理可能”一词的含义以公认会计原则的定义为准[如参见财务会计准则委员会:《第5号财务会计准则公报——“或有事项会计”》,(FAS 5)第3款(1975年3月)];

C.就关于第305(a)款的说明第3.A.条而言,“近期”一词指不超过财务报表日前一年的期间[参见美国注册会计师协会:《第94-6号立场公报——“特定重大风险和不确定性的披露”》(SOP 94-6)第7款(1994年12月30日)];

D.暴露于多个市场风险敞口类别的利率或价格变动的市场风险敏感工具应被纳入该等工具所暴露的每一市场风险类别的敏感性分析披露;

E.面临多重外币汇率风险敞口的注册人应编制可以衡量全部外币汇率变动风险敞口总敏感度的外币敏感性分析披露,包括交易货币/职能货币汇率风险敞口变动的影响,以及职能货币/报表货币汇率风险敞口变动的影响。例如,假设某注册人的法国部门以美元提交财务报表,而该部门同时投资以德国马克计价的债务证券。在该种情况下,美元为报表货币,而德国马克为交易货币。此外,假设该部门根据FAS 52确定法国法郎为其职能货币,则在编制外币敏感性分析披露时,注册人应报告德国马克/法国法郎汇率风险敞口假设变更引起的潜在损失总额,以及法国法郎/美元汇率风险敞口假设变更引起的潜在损失总额;及

F.应予说明的模型、假设和参数包括但不限于:模型如何定义“损失”(如盈利损失、公允价值损失或现金流损失),对建模技术的总体介绍(如时长建模、衡量因市场利率或价格的选定假设变更引起的净现值变动的建模以及对模型如何解决期权性风险的介绍),模型所涵盖的工具类型(如衍生金融工具、其他金融工具、衍生商品工具以及是否包含其他自选工具,如某些商品工具和持仓、预期交易现金流以及关于第305(a)款和第305(b)款的总体说明第3.C.ii.条所排除的某些金融工具),以及有关模型假设和参数的其他信息(如所采用市场利率或价格的选定假设变动的范围和时间、贴现率的确定方法以及主要提前还款或再投资假设)。

3.C.ii. of the General Instructions to Paragraphs 305 (a) and 305 (b)), and other relevant information about the model's assumptions and parameters, (e.g., the magnitude and timing of selected hypothetical changes in market rates or prices used, the method by which discount rates are determined, and key prepayment or reinvestment assumptions).

4. Under paragraph 305(a)(1)(iii):

A. The confidence intervals selected should reflect reasonably possible near-term changes in market rates and prices. In this regard, absent economic justification for the selection of different confidence intervals, registrants should use intervals that are 95 percent or higher;

B. For purposes of instruction 4.A. of the Instructions to Paragraph 305(a), the term *reasonably possible* has the same meaning as defined by generally accepted accounting principles (see, e.g., FAS 5, paragraph 3 (March 1975));

C. For purposes of instruction 4.A. of the Instructions to Paragraphs 305(a), the term *near term* means a period of time going forward up to one year from the date of the financial statements (see generally SOP 94-6, at paragraph 7 (December 30, 1994));

D. Registrants with multiple foreign currency exchange rate exposures should prepare foreign currency value at risk analysis disclosures that measure the aggregate sensitivity to changes in all foreign currency exchange rate exposures, including the aggregate effects of changes in both transactional currency/functional currency exchange rate exposures and functional currency/reporting currency exchange rate exposures. For example, assume a French division of a registrant presenting its financial statements in U.S. dollars ($US) invests in a deutschmark (DM)-denominated debt security. In these circumstances, the $US is the reporting currency and the DM is the transactional currency. In addition, assume this division determines that the French franc (FF) is its functional currency according to FAS 52. In preparing the foreign currency value at risk disclosures, this registrant should report the aggregate potential loss from hypothetical changes in both the DM/FF exchange rate exposure and the FF/$US exchange rate exposure; and

E. Model, assumptions, and parameters that should be described include, but are not limited to, how *loss* is defined by the model (e.g., loss in earnings, fair values, or cash flows), the type of model used (e.g., variance/covariance, historical simulation, or Monte Carlo simulation and a description as to how optionality is addressed by the model), the types of instruments covered by the model (e.g., derivative financial instruments, other financial instruments, derivative commodity instruments, and whether other instruments are included voluntarily, such as certain commodity instruments and positions, cash flows from anticipated transactions, and certain financial instruments excluded under instruction 3.C.ii. of the General Instructions to Paragraphs 305(a) and 305(b)), and other relevant

4.在第305(a)(1)(iii)款下:

A.所选置信区间应反映合理可能的市场利率和价格的近期变动。为此,除非注册人能够证明选择其他置信区间具有经济合理性,否则应采用不低于95%的区间;

B.就关于第305(a)款的说明第4.A.条而言,“合理可能”一词的含义以公认会计原则的定义为准[如参见《第5号财务会计准则公报》(FAS 5)第3款(1975年3月)];

C.就关于第305(a)款的说明第4.A.条而言,“近期”一词系指不超过财务报表日前一年的期间[参见美国注册会计师协会:《第94-6号立场公报》(SOP 94-6)第7款(1994年12月30日)];

D.有着多重外币汇率风险敞口的注册人应编制可以衡量全部外币汇率变动风险敞口总敏感度的外币敏感性分析披露, 包括交易货币/职能货币汇率风险敞口变动的影响,以及职能货币/报表货币汇率风险敞口变动的影响。例如,假设某注册人的法国部门以美元提交财务报表,而该部门同时投资以德国马克计价的债务证券。在该种情况下,美元为报表货币,而德国马克为交易货币。此外,假设该部门根据FAS 52确定法国法郎为其职能货币,则在编制外币敏感性分析披露时,注册人应报告德国马克/法国法郎汇率风险敞口假设变更引起的潜在损失总额,以及法国法郎/美元汇率风险敞口假设变更引起的潜在损失总额;及

E.应予说明的模型、假设和参数包括但不限于:模型如何定义“损失”(如盈利损失、公允价值损失或现金流损失),所采用模型的类型(如方差/协方差、历史模拟或蒙特卡洛模拟以及对模型如何解决期权性风险的介绍),模型所涵盖的工具类型[如衍生金融工具、其他金融工具、衍生商品工具以及是否包含其他自选工具,如某些商品工具和持仓、预期交易现金流以及关于第305(a)款和第305(b)款的总体说明第3.C.ii.条所排除的某些金融工具],以及有关模型假设和参数的其他相关信息(如持有时期、置信区间,同时在适当情况下,应说明不同市场风险敞口类别的风险值合并方法,如通过假设两者之间存在完全正相关性、独立性或实际观测的相关性进行累计)。

information about the model's assumptions and parameters, (e.g., holding periods, confidence intervals, and, when appropriate, the methods used for aggregating value at risk amounts across market risk exposure categories, such as by assuming perfect positive correlation, independence, or actual observed correlation).

5. Under paragraph 305(a)(2), limitations that should be considered include, but are not limited to:

A. The exclusion of certain market risk sensitive instruments, positions, and transactions from the disclosures required under paragraph 305(a)(1)(e.g., derivative commodity instruments not permitted by contract or business custom to be settled in cash or with another financial instrument, commodity positions, cash flows from anticipated transactions, and certain financial instruments excluded under instruction 3.C.ii. of the General Instructions to Paragraphs 305 (a) and 305 (b)). Failure to include such instruments, positions, and transactions in preparing the disclosures under paragraph 305(a)(1) may be a limitation because the resulting disclosures may not fully reflect the net market risk of a registrant; and

B. The ability of disclosures required under paragraph 305(a)(1) to reflect fully the market risk that may be inherent in instruments with leverage, option, or prepayment features (e.g., options, including written options, structured notes, collateralized mortgage obligations, leveraged swaps, and options embedded in swaps).

(b) *Qualitative information about market risk.* (1) To the extent material, describe:

(i) The registrant's primary market risk exposures;

(ii) How those exposures are managed. Such descriptions shall include, but not be limited to, a discussion of the objectives, general strategies, and instruments, if any, used to manage those exposures; and

(iii) Changes in either the registrant's primary market risk exposures or how those exposures are managed, when compared to what was in effect during the most recently completed fiscal year and what is known or expected to be in effect in future reporting periods.

(2) Qualitative information about market risk shall be presented separately for market risk sensitive instruments entered into for trading purposes and those entered into for purposes other than trading.

Instructions to paragraph 305(b): 1. For purposes of disclosure under paragraph 305(b), *primary market risk exposures* means:

A. The following categories of market risk: interest rate risk, foreign currency exchange rate risk, commodity price risk, and other relevant market rate or price risks (e.g., equity price risk); and

B. Within each of these categories, the particular markets that present the primary

5.在第305(a)(2)款下,应予考虑的限制包括但不限于:

A.从第305(a)(1)款要求提供的披露内容中排除某些市场风险敏感工具、持仓和交易[如合约或业务习惯不允许以现金或与其他金融工具交割的衍生商品工具、商品持仓、预期交易现金流,以及关于第305(a)款和第305(b)款的总体说明第3.C.ii.条所排除的某些金融工具]。如果在根据第305(a)(1)款编制的披露中未能涵盖上述工具、持仓和交易,则可能导致披露不能充分反映注册人的市场风险净值,从而构成一项限制;及

B.对于带有杠杆、期权或提前还款特性的市场风险工具(如期权,包括已签发期权、结构型票据、担保抵押债务、利用杠杆的互换及互换的内嵌期权)的固有市场风险,第305(a)(1)款要求提供的披露内容充分反映上述风险的能力。

(b)市场风险定性信息。(1)提供下列实质性信息:

(i)注册人的一级市场风险敞口;

(ii)该等风险敞口的管理方式。对管理方式的说明应包括但不限于对上述风险敞口的管理目标、总体战略和管理工具(如有)进行论述;及

(iii)与最近结束的会计年度内有效存在的风险敞口以及未来报告期间内已知或预期将有效存在的风险敞口相比,注册人的一级市场风险敞口的变动或该等风险敞口管理方式的变动。

(2)对于交易类和非交易类市场风险敏感工具,应分别提交市场风险定性信息。

关于第305(b)款的说明:1.就第305(b)款中的披露而言,"一级市场风险敞口"系指:

A.以下类别的市场风险:利率风险、外币汇率风险、商品价格风险以及其他相关市场费率或价格风险(如权益价格风险);及

B.在上述每一类别内,注册人存在一级风险损失的特定市场。例如,如果注册人面

risk of loss to the registrant. For example, if a registrant has a material exposure to foreign currency exchange rate risk and, within this category of market risk, is most vulnerable to changes in dollar/yen, dollar/pound, and dollar/peso exchange rates, the registrant should disclose those exposures. Similarly, if a registrant has a material exposure to interest rate risk and, within this category of market risk, is most vulnerable to changes in short-term U.S. prime interest rates, it should disclose the existence of that exposure.

2. For purposes of disclosure under paragraph 305(b), registrants should describe primary market risk exposures that exist as of the end of the latest fiscal year, and how those exposures are managed.

General Instructions to paragraphs 305(a) and 305(b): 1. The disclosures called for by paragraphs 305(a) and 305(b) are intended to clarify the registrant's exposures to market risk associated with activities in derivative financial instruments, other financial instruments, and derivative commodity instruments.

2. In preparing the disclosures under paragraphs 305(a) and 305(b), registrants are required to include derivative financial instruments, other financial instruments, and derivative commodity instruments.

3. For purposes of paragraphs 305(a) and 305(b), derivative financial instruments, other financial instruments, and derivative commodity instruments (collectively referred to as "market risk sensitive instruments") are defined as follows:

A. *Derivative financial instruments* has the same meaning as defined by generally accepted accounting principles (see, e.g., FASB, *Statement of Financial Accounting Standards No. 119, "Disclosure about Derivative Financial Instruments and Fair Value of Financial Instruments,"* ("FAS 119") paragraphs 5-7(October 1994)), and includes futures, forwards, swaps, options, and other financial instruments with similar characteristics;

B. *Other financial instruments* means all financial instruments as defined by generally accepted accounting principles for which fair value disclosures are required (see, e.g., FASB, *Statement of Financial Accounting Standards No. 107, "Disclosures about Fair Value of Financial Instruments,"* ("FAS 107") paragraphs 3 and 8 (December 1991)), except for derivative financial instruments, as defined above;

C. i. Other financial instruments include, but are not limited to, trade accounts receivable, investments, loans, structured notes, mortgage-backed securities, trade accounts payable, indexed debt instruments, interest-only and principal-only obligations, deposits, and other debt obligations;

ii. Other financial instruments exclude employers' and plans' obligations for pension and other post-retirement benefits, substantively extinguished debt, insurance contracts, lease contracts, warranty obligations and rights, unconditional purchase obligations,

临实质性的外币汇率风险敞口,且在该市场风险类别内,最可能遭受美元/日元、美元/英镑和美元/比索的汇率风险,则应披露上述风险敞口。与之类似,如果注册人面临实质性的利率风险,且在该市场风险类别内,最可能遭受美国短期最优惠利率变化的影响,则其应披露该等风险敞口的存在。

2.就第305(b)款中的披露而言,注册人应说明截至最近一会计年度年末的一级市场风险敞口,以及该等风险敞口的管理方式。

关于第305(a)款和第305(b)款的总体说明:1.第305(a)款和第305(b)款所要求提供的披露内容,其目的在于明确注册人与衍生金融工具、其他金融工具和衍生商品工具活动相关的市场风险敞口。

2.在根据第305(a)款和第305(b)款编制披露内容的过程中,注册人应将衍生金融工具、其他金融工具和衍生商品工具纳入其中。

3.就第305(a)款和第305(b)款而言,衍生金融工具、其他金融工具以及衍生商品工具(统称为"市场风险敏感工具")的定义如下:

A."衍生金融工具"之定义以公认会计原则为准(如参见财务会计准则委员会:《第119号财务会计准则公报——"衍生金融工具和金融工具公允价值披露"》[FAS 119)第5-7款(1994年10月)],包括期货、远期、互换、期权以及具有类似特点的其他金融工具;

B."其他金融工具"系指公认会计原则定义的应披露公允价值的全部金融工具[如参见财务会计准则委员会:《第107号财务会计准则公报——"金融工具公允价值披露"》(FAS 107)第3款和第8款(1991年12月)],但不包括上文所定义的衍生金融工具;

C.i."其他金融工具"包括但不限于购销应收账款、投资、贷款、结构型票据、抵押担保证券、购销应付账款、指数型债务工具、唯利率型或唯本金型义务、储蓄和其他债务凭证;

ii."其他金融工具"不包括员工和计划承担的退休金义务和其他退休后福利义务、已实质清偿的债务、保险合同、租赁合同、保义务与权利、无条件购买义务、以权益法核算的投资、对并表企业拥有的非控制权益以及注册人发行并归入财务状况报表股

investments accounted for under the equity method, noncontrolling interests in consolidated enterprises, and equity instruments issued by the registrant and classified in stockholders' equity in the statement of financial position(see, e.g., FAS 107, paragraph 8 (December 1991)). For purposes of this item, trade accounts receivable and trade accounts payable need not be considered other financial instruments when their carrying amounts approximate fair value; and

D.*Derivative commodity instruments* include, to the extent such instruments are not derivative financial instruments, commodity futures, commodity forwards, commodity swaps, commodity options, and other commodity instruments with similar characteristics that are permitted by contract or business custom to be settled in cash or with another financial instrument. For purposes of this paragraph, settlement in cash includes settlement in cash of the net change in value of the derivative commodity instrument (e.g., net cash settlement based on changes in the price of the underlying commodity).

4.A. In addition to providing required disclosures for the market risk sensitive instruments defined in instruction 2. of the General Instructions to Paragraphs 305(a) and 305 (b), registrants are encouraged to include other market risk sensitive instruments, positions, and transactions within the disclosures required under paragraphs 305(a) and 305(b). Such instruments, positions, and transactions might include commodity positions, derivative commodity instruments that are not permitted by contract or business custom to be settled in cash or with another financial instrument, cash flows from anticipated transactions, and certain financial instruments excluded under instruction 3.C.ii. of the General Instructions to Paragraphs 305(a) and 305(b).

B. Registrants that voluntarily include other market risk sensitive instruments, positions and transactions within their quantitative disclosures about market risk under the sensitivity analysis or value at risk disclosure alternatives are not required to provide separate market risk disclosures for any voluntarily selected instruments, positions, or transactions. Instead, registrants selecting the sensitivity analysis and value at risk disclosure alternatives are permitted to present comprehensive market risk disclosures, which reflect the combined market risk exposures inherent in both the required and any voluntarily selected instruments, position, or transactions. Registrants that choose the tabular presentation disclosure alternative should present voluntarily selected instruments, positions, or transactions in a manner consistent with the requirements in Item 305(a) for market risk sensitive instruments.

C. If a registrant elects to include voluntarily a particular type of instrument, position, or transaction in their quantitative disclosures about market risk, that registrant should include all, rather than some, of those instruments, positions, or transactions within those disclosures. For example, if a registrant holds in inventory a particular type of

东权益的股权工具［如参见FAS 107第8款（1991年12月）］。就本条规定而言，购销应收账款和购销应付账款的账面价值与公允价值相差不大时，不必被视为其他金融工具；及

D.“衍生商品工具”包括商品期货、商品远期、商品互换、商品期权以及合约或业务习惯允许以现金或其他金融工具结算的，具有类似特征的其他商品工具（前提是上述工具不属于衍生金融工具）。就本款而言，现金结算包括对衍生商品工具价值净变化的现金结算（如基于基础商品价格变化的净现金结算）。

4.A.除按规定提供关于第305（a）款和第305（b）款的总体说明第2条定义的市场风险敏感工具的披露信息外，鼓励注册人在第305（a）款和第305（b）款要求提供的披露内容中纳入其他市场风险敏感工具、持仓和交易。该等工具、持仓和交易可以包括商品持仓、合约或业务习惯不允许以现金或其他金融工具结算的衍生商品工具、预期交易现金流以及被第305（a）款和第305（b）款总体说明第3.C.ii.条排除的某些金融工具。

B.如果注册人选择敏感性分析或风险值披露方式，并自愿将其他市场风险敏感工具、持仓和交易纳入其市场风险定量披露，则该注册人不必就任何自愿选定的工具、持仓或交易另外进行市场风险披露。相反，选择该敏感性分析和风险值披露方式的注册人可以提交综合性市场风险披露，以反映必选和自选工具、持仓或交易中固有的合并市场风险敞口。选择表格列报的披露方式的注册人应按照第305（a）条对市场风险敏感工具的要求，以符合该等要求的方式对其任何自愿选定的工具、持仓或交易进行列报。

C.如果注册人自愿决定在其市场风险定量披露中纳入某一特定类型的工具、持仓或交易，该注册人应在该等披露内容中将上述工具、持仓或交易的全部而非部分纳入其中。例如，如果注册人在持有的工具、持仓或交易中有某一类型的商品持仓并决定在其市场风险披露中纳入该商品持仓，则该注册人应在市场风险定量披露中纳入全

commodity position and elects to include that commodity position within their market risk disclosures, the registrant should include the entire commodity position, rather than only a portion thereof, in their quantitative disclosures about market risk.

5.A. Under paragraphs 305(a) and 305(b), a materiality assessment should be made for each market risk exposure category within the trading and other than trading portfolios.

B. For purposes of making the materiality assessment under instruction 5.A. of the General Instructions to Paragraphs 305(a) and 305(b), registrants should evaluate both:

i. The materiality of the fair values of derivative financial instruments, other financial instruments, and derivative commodity instruments outstanding as of the end of the latest fiscal year; and

ii. The materiality of potential, near–term losses in future earnings, fair values, and/or cash flows from reasonably possible near–term changes in market rates or prices.

iii. If either paragraphs B.i. or B.ii. in this instruction of the General Instructions to Paragraphs 305(a) and 305(b) are material, the registrant should disclose quantitative and qualitative information about market risk, if such market risk for the particular market risk exposure category is material.

C. For purposes of instruction 5.B.i. of the General Instructions to Paragraphs 305(a) and 305(b), registrants generally should not net fair values, except to the extent allowed under generally accepted accounting principles (see, e.g., *FASB Interpretation No. 39, "Offsetting of Amounts Related to Certain Contracts"* (March 1992)). For example, under this instruction, the fair value of assets generally should not be netted with the fair value of liabilities.

D. For purposes of instruction 5.B.ii. of the General Instructions to Paragraphs 305(a) and 305(b), registrants should consider, among other things, the magnitude of:

i. Past market movements;

ii. Reasonably possible, near–term market movements; and

iii. Potential losses that may arise from leverage, option, and multiplier features.

E. For purposes of instructions 5.B.ii and 5.D.ii of the General Instructions to Paragraphs 305(a) and 305(b), the term *near term*means a period of time going forward up to one year from the date of the financial statements (see generally SOP 94–6, at paragraph 7 (December 30, 1994)).

F. For the purpose of instructions 5.B.ii. and 5.D.ii. of the General Instructions to Paragraphs 305(a) and 305(b), the term *reasonably possible* has the same meaning as defined by generally accepted accounting principles(see, e.g., FAS 5, paragraph 3 (March 1975)).

6. For purposes of paragraphs 305(a) and 305(b), registrants should present the information outside of, and not incorporate the information into, the financial statements

部商品持仓,而非仅仅是其中的一部分。

5.A.在第305(a)款和第305(b)款下:应对交易和非交易资产组合中每一市场风险敞口类别是否构成实质性风险进行评估。

B.在根据第305(a)款和第305(b)款总体说明第5A条进行实质性评估时,注册人应同时评估:

i.最近一会计年度年末尚未清偿的衍生金融工具、其他金融工具和衍生商品工具的公允价值的重大性;及

ii.市场利率或价格近期合理可能变动所产生的未来盈利、公允价值和/或现金流的潜在近期损失的重大性。

iii.如果根据关于第305(a)款和第305(b)款的总体说明第B.i.条或第B.ii.条进行的评估结果具有重大性,且具体市场风险敞口类别中的市场风险具有重大性,则注册人应披露该市场风险的定量或定性信息。

C.就关于第305(a)款和第305(b)款的总体说明第5.B.i.条而言,除非为公认会计原则所允许[如参见财务会计准则委员会第39号解释——"特定合约相关金额之抵消"(1992年3月)],注册人通常不得抵消公允价值。例如,根据本说明,资产公允价值一般不得与负债公允价值相抵消。

D.就关于第305(a)款和第305(b)款的总体说明第5.B.ii.条而言,注册人应考虑如下列事项的重要性:

i.过往市场动态;

ii.近期合理可能的市场动态;及

iii.因杠杆、期权和乘数效应可能产生的潜在损失。

E.就关于第305(a)款和第305(b)款的总体说明第5.B.ii.条和第5.D.ii.条而言,"近期"一词系指不超过财务报表日前一年的期间[参见美国注册会计师协会:《第94-6号立场公报》(SOP 94-6)第7款(1994年12月30日)]。

F.在关于第305(a)款和第305(b)款的总体说明第5.B.ii.条和第5.D.ii.条而言,"合理可能"一词的含义以公认会计原则的定义为准[如参见《第5号财务会计准则公报》(FAS 5)第3款(1975年3月)]。

6.就第305(a)款和第305(b)款而言,注册人应在财务报表以外提交信息,不得将该信息并入财务报表(包括财务报表的脚注)。此外,鼓励注册人在同一地点提供规定

(including the footnotes to the financial statements). In addition, registrants are encouraged to provide the required information in one location. However, alternative presentation, such as inclusion of all or part of the information in Management's Discussion and Analysis, may be used at the discretion of the registrant. If information is disclosed in more than one location, registrants should provide cross-references to the locations of the related disclosures.

7. For purposes of the instructions to paragraphs 305 (a) and 305 (b), *trading purposes* has the same meaning as defined by generally accepted accounting principles (see, e.g., FAS 119, paragraph 9a (October 1994)). In addition, *anticipated transactions* means transactions (other than transactions involving existing assets or liabilities or transactions necessitated by existing firm commitments) an enterprise expects, but is not obligated, to carry out in the normal course of business (see, e.g., *FASB, Statement of Financial Accounting Standards No. 80, "Accounting for Futures Contracts,"* paragraph 9, (August 1984)).

(c) *Interim periods.* If interim period financial statements are included or are required to be included by Article 3 of Regulation S-X(17 CFR 210), discussion and analysis shall be provided so as to enable the reader to assess the sources and effects of material changes in information that would be provided under Item 305 of Regulation S-K from the end of the preceding fiscal year to the date of the most recent interim balance sheet.

Instructions to paragraph 305 (c): 1. Information required under paragraph (c) of this Item 305 is not required until after the first fiscal year end in which this Item 305 is applicable.

(d) *Safe harbor.* (1) The safe harbor provided in Section 27A of the Securities Act of 1933 (15 U.S.C. 77z-2) and Section 21E of the Securities Exchange Act of 1934 (15 U.S.C. 78u-5)("statutory safe harbors") shall apply, with respect to all types of issuers and transactions, to information provided pursuant to paragraphs (a), (b), and (c) of this Item 305, provided that the disclosure is made by: an issuer; a person acting on behalf of the issuer; an outside reviewer retained by the issuer making a statement on behalf of the issuer; or an underwriter, with respect to information provided by the issuer or information derived from information provided by the issuer.

(2) For purposes of paragraph (d) of this Item 305 only:

(i) All information required by paragraphs (a), (b)(1)(i), (b)(1)(iii), and (c) of this Item 305 is considered *forward looking statements* for purposes of the statutory safe harbors, except for historical facts such as the terms of particular contracts and the number of market risk sensitive instruments held during or at the end of the reporting period; and

的信息。但是,注册人可依其自由裁量权决定采用其他列报方式,如注册人可选择纳入《管理层论述与分析》中的全部或部分信息。注册人在一处以上地点披露信息的,应提供与相关披露地点的交叉索引。

7.就关于第305(a)款和第305(b)款的说明而言,“交易类”一词的含义以公认会计原则的定义为准[如参见FAS 119第9a款(1994年10月)]。此外,“预期交易”系指某企业在正常业务运作中预期但无义务开展的交易(涉及现有资产或负债的交易或因现有确定承诺而必须开展的交易除外)[如参见财务会计准则委员会:《第80号财务会计准则公报——“期权合约核算”》第9款(1984年8月)]。

(c)中期期间。如果在披露内容中纳入中期财务报表,或《S-X管理办法》第3条[《联邦规章汇编》第十七编第210部分]要求纳入该等财务报表,则应提供相应的论述与分析,以便读者对根据《S-K管理办法》第305条提交的从上一会计年度年末至最近一期中期资产负债表之日的信息发生的实质性变化之来源与影响进行评估。

关于第305(c)款的说明:1.适用本第305条的首个会计年度年末之后,才需要按本第305条(c)款的规定提供相关信息。

(d)安全港。(1)就所有类型的发行人和交易而言,根据本第305条第(a)款、第(b)款和第(c)款提交的信息均应适用《1933年证券法》第27A条(《美国法典》第十五编第77z-2节)以及《1934年证券交易法》第21E条(《美国法典》第十五编第78u-5节)的安全港条款(“法定安全港”),但前提是披露主体为:发行人、发行人代表、发行人聘请的代表其作出声明的外部审核人;或承销商(就发行人所提供的信息或其衍生信息而言)。

(2)仅就本第305条第(d)款而言:

(i)就法定安全港而言,本第305条第(a)款、第(b)(1)(i)款、第(b)(1)(iii)款和第(c)款要求提供的所有信息均应视为前瞻性声明,但历史事实(如具体合约的条款以及在报告期间或报告期间末持有的市场风险敏感工具的数量)不在此限;及

(ii) With respect to paragraph (a) of this Item 305, the *meaningful cautionary statements* prong of the statutory safe harbors will be satisfied if a registrant satisfies all requirements of that same paragraph (a) of this Item 305.

(e) *Smaller reporting companies.* A smaller reporting company, as defined by §229.10(f)(1), is not required to provide the information required by this Item.

General Instructions to Paragraphs 305(a), 305(b), 305(c), 305(d), and 305(e): 1. Bank registrants, thrift registrants, and non-bank and non-thrift registrants with market capitalizations on January 28, 1997 in excess of $2.5 billion should provide Item 305 disclosures in filings with the Commission that include annual financial statements for fiscal years ending after June 15, 1997. Non-bank and non-thrift registrants with market capitalizations on January 28, 1997 of $2.5 billion or less should provide Item 305 disclosures in filings with the Commission that include financial statements for fiscal years ending after June 15, 1998.

2.A. For purposes of instruction 1. of the General Instructions to Paragraphs 305(a), 305(b), 305(c), 305(d), and 305(e),*bank registrants and thrift registrants* include any registrant which has control over a depository institution.

B. For purposes of instruction 2.A. of the General Instructions to Paragraphs 305(a), 305 (b), 305 (c), 305 (d), and 305 (e), a registrant has control over a depository institution if:

i. The registrant directly or indirectly or acting through one or more other persons owns, controls, or has power to vote 25% or more of any class of voting securities of the depository institution;

ii. The registrant controls in any manner the election of a majority of the directors or trustees of the depository institution; or

iii. The Federal Reserve Board or Office of Thrift Supervision determines, after notice and opportunity for hearing, that the registrant directly or indirectly exercises a controlling influence over the management or policies of the depository institution.

C. For purposes of instruction 2.B. of the General Instructions to Paragraphs 305(a), 305(b), 305(c), 305(d), and 305(e), a depository institution means any of the following:

i. An insured depository institution as defined in section 3(c)(2) of the Federal Deposit Insurance Act (12 U.S.C.A. Sec. 1813 (c));

ii. An institution organized under the laws of the United States, any State of the United States, the District of Columbia, any territory of the United States, Puerto Rico, Guam, American Somoa, or the Virgin Islands, which both accepts demand deposits or deposits that the depositor may withdraw by check or similar means for payment to third parties or others and is engaged in the business of making commercial loans.

D. For purposes of instruction 1. of the General Instructions to Paragraphs 305(a),

(ii)就本第305条第(a)款而言,如果注册人满足本第305条第(a)款的全部要求,即视为已满足法定安全港的“有效警示性声明”的要求。

(e)小型报告公司。第229.10(f)(1)节定义的小型报告公司不必提交本条规定的信息。

关于第305(a)款、第305(b)款、第305(c)款、第305(d)款和第305(e)款的总体说明:1.银行注册人、储蓄注册人和于1997年1月28日市值超过25亿美元的非银行和非储蓄注册人在向证券交易委员会进行报告时应按第305条的规定进行披露,包括提交在1997年6月15日之后结束的会计年度的年度财务报表。截至1997年1月28日市值不高于25亿美元的非银行和非储蓄注册人在向证券交易委员会进行报告时应按第305条的规定进行披露,包括提交在1998年6月15日之后结束的会计年度的财务报表。

2.A.就关于第305(a)款、第305(b)款、第305(c)款、第305(d)款和第305(e)款的总体说明第1条而言,“银行注册人”和“储蓄注册人”包括对存款机构拥有控制权的任何注册人。

B.就关于第305(a)款、第305(b)款、第305(c)款、第305(d)款和第305(e)款的总体说明第2.A.条而言,在下列情形下,注册人应认定为对某存款机构拥有控制权:

i.注册人直接或间接,或通过一名或多名其他主体拥有、控制存款机构,或拥有存款机构任何类别有表决权证券不低于25%的表决权;

ii.注册人能够以任何方式控制存款机构多数董事或理事的选举;或

iii.联邦储备委员会或储蓄机构监理局在发出通知和给予听证机会后认定注册人对存款机构的管理或政策直接或间接实施控制性影响。

C.就关于第305(a)款、第305(b)款、第305(c)款、第305(d)款和第305(e)款的总体说明第2.B.条而言,存款机构是指下列任何机构之一:

i.《联邦存款保险法》第3(c)(2)条[《美国法典注释》第十二编第1813(c)节]定义的受保存款机构;

ii.依据美国、美国任何一州、哥伦比亚特区、美国任何准州、波多黎各、关岛、美属萨摩亚或维京群岛法律组建的,接受活期存款或存款人可通过支票或类似的向第三方或其他人付款的手段提取的各种存款,并从事商业贷款业务的机构。

D.就关于第305(a)款、第305(b)款、第305(c)款、第305(d)款和第305(e)款的总体

305 (b), 305 (c), 305 (d) and 305 (e),*market capitalization* is the aggregate market value of common equity as set forth in General Instruction I.B.1. of Form S-3; provided however, that common equity held by affiliates is included in the calculation of market capitalization; and provided further that instead of using the 60 day period prior to filing referenced in General Instruction I.B.1. of Form S-3, the measurement date is January 28, 1997.

Appendix to Item 305 —Tabular Disclosures

The tables set forth below are illustrative of the format that might be used when a egistrant elects to present the information required by paragraph (a)(1)(i)(A) of Item 305 regarding terms and information about derivative financial instruments, other financial instruments, and derivative commodity instruments. These examples are for illustrative purposes only. Registrants are not required to display the information in the specific format illustrated below. Alternative methods of display are permissible as long as the disclosure requirements of the section are satisfied. Furthermore, these examples were designed primarily to illustrate possible formats for presentation of the information required by the disclosure item and do not purport to illustrate the broad range of derivative financial instruments, other financial instruments, and derivative commodity instruments utilized by registrants.

Interest Rate Sensitivity

The table below provides information about the Company's derivative financial instruments and other financial instruments that are sensitive to changes in interest rates, including interest rate swaps and debt obligations. For debt obligations, the table presents principal cash flows and related weighted average interest rates by expected maturity dates. For interest rate swaps, the table presents notional amounts and weighted average interest rates by expected (contractual) maturity dates. Notional amounts are used to calculate the contractual payments to be exchanged under the contract. Weighted average variable rates are based on implied forward rates in the yield curve at the reporting date. The information is presented in U.S. dollar equivalents, which is the Company's reporting currency. The instrument's actual cash flows are denominated in both U.S. dollars ($US) and German deutschmarks (DM), as indicated in parentheses.

说明第1条而言,"市值"是《S-3表格》第I.B.1.条总体说明中规定的普通股权总市值;但是,关联方持有的普通股权亦应计入市值,且计算基准日应为1997年1月28日,而非《S-3表格》第I.B.1.条总体说明中所述报告前60日的期间。

第305条 附件——列表披露

注册人决定按第305条第(a)(1)(i)(A)款要求提交相关信息,说明有关衍生金融工具、其他金融工具和衍生商品工具的条款与信息时,可参考下列作为格式示例的表格。这些示例仅供说明之用。注册人不必完全按下列具体格式列示信息。只要该条的披露要求得以满足,注册人即可采用其他列示方法。此外,这些示例的主要目的是说明按规定提交披露信息时可能采用的格式,并无意说明注册人所使用的衍生金融工具、其他金融工具和衍生商品工具极为宽广的范围。

利率敏感性

下表所示信息为与公司对利率变动敏感的衍生金融工具和其他金融工具(包括利率互换和债务凭证)相关的信息。就债务凭证而言,该表按预期到期日列报本金现金流和相关加权平均利率。就利率互换而言,该表按预期(合约)到期日列报名义本金和加权平均利率。名义金额用于计算将在合约下交换的合约支付款项。加权平均浮动利率系基于报表日收益率曲线代表的远期利率。上述信息按美元的等值货币,即公司的报表货币列报。如括号内所示,该工具的实际现金流以美元($US)和德国马克(DM)计价。

December 31, 19×1

	Expected maturity date							
	19X2	19X3	19X4	19X5	19X6	Thereafter	Total	Fair value
Liabilities	(US$ Equivalent in millions)							
Long - term Debt:								
Fixed Rate ($US)	$XXX	$XXX	$XXX	$XXX	$XXX	$XXX	$XXX	$XXX
Average interest rate	X. X%	X. X%	X. X%	X. X%	X. X%	X. X%	X. X%	
Fixed Rate (DM)	XXX	XXX	XXX	XXX	XXX	XXX	XXX	XXX
Average interest rate	X. X%	X. X%	X. X%	X. X%	X. X%	X. X%	X. X%	
Variable Rate ($US)	XXX	XXX	XXX	XXX	XXX	XXX	XXX	XXX
Average interest rate	X. X%	X. X%	X. X%	X. X%	X. X%	X. X%	X. X%	
Interest Rate Derivatives	(In millions)							
Interest Rate Swaps:								
Variable to Fixed ($US)	$XXX	$XXX	$XXX	$XXX	$XXX	$XXX	$XXX	$XXX
Average pay rate	X. X%	X. X%	X. X%	X. X%	X. X%	X. X%	X. X%	
Average receive rate	X. X%	X. X%	X. X%	X. X%	X. X%	X. X%	X. X%	
Fixed to Variable ($US)	XXX	XXX	XXX	XXX	XXX	XXX	XXX	XXX
Average pay rate	X. X%	X. X%	X. X%	X. X%	X. X%	X. X%	X. X%	
Average receive rate	X. X%	X. X%	X. X%	X. X%	X. X%	X. X%	X. X%	

Exchange Rate Sensitivity

The table below provides information about the Company's derivative financial instruments, other financial instruments, and firmly committed sales transactions by functional currency and presents such information in U.S. dollar equivalents.[1] The table summarizes information on instruments and transactions that are sensitive to foreign currency exchange rates, including foreign currency forward exchange agreements, deutschmark(DM)-denominated debt obligations, and firmly committed DM sales transactions. For debt obligations, the table presents principal cash flows and related weighted average interest rates by expected maturity dates. For firmly committed DM-sales transactions, sales amounts are presented by the expected transaction date, which are not expected to exceed two years. For foreign currency forward exchange agreements, the table presents

19×1年12月31日

	预期到期日							
	19X2	19X3	19X4	19X5	19X6	后续年份	总计	公允价值
负债	(单位:百万等值美元)							
长期债务:								
固定利率(美元 US)	美元 XXX	美元 XXX	美元 XXX	美元 XXX	美元 XXX	美元 XXX	美元 XXX	美元 XXX
平均利率	X. X%	X. X%	X. X%	X. X%	X. X%	X. X%	X. X%	
固定利率(DM)	XXX	XXX	XXX	XXX	XXX	XXX	XXX	XXX
平均利率	X. X%	X. X%	X. X%	X. X%	X. X%	X. X%	X. X%	
浮动利率(美元 US)	XXX	XXX	XXX	XXX	XXX	XXX	XXX	XXX
平均利率	X. X%	X. X%	X. X%	X. X%	X. X%	X. X%	X. X%	
利率衍生品	(单位:百万美元)							
利率互换:								
浮动与固定之比(美元 US)	美元 XXX	美元 XXX	美元 XXX	美元 XXX	美元 XXX	美元 XXX	美元 XXX	美元 XXX
平均支付利率	X. X%	X. X%	X. X%	X. X%	X. X%	X. X%	X. X%	
平均接收利率	X. X%	X. X%	X. X%	X. X%	X. X%	X. X%	X. X%	
浮动与固定之比(美元 US)	XXX	XXX	XXX	XXX	XXX	XXX	XXX	XXX
平均支付利率	X. X%	X. X%	X. X%	X. X%	X. X%	X. X%	X. X%	
平均接收利率	X. X%	X. X%	X. X%	X. X%	X. X%	X. X%	X. X%	

汇率敏感性

下表以职能货币提供关于公司衍生金融工具、其他金融工具和包销交易相关的信息，并以美元等值货币列报该等信息。[1]该表系外币汇率敏感工具和交易的信息总结,包括外币远期外汇协议、德国马克(DM)计价的债务凭证以及德国马克包销交易。对于债务凭证,下表按预期到期日列报本金现金流和相关加权平均利率。对于德国马克包销协议,销售金额按预期交易日列报,该期限预期不超过两年。对于外币远期外汇协议,下表按预期(合约)到期日列报名义金额和加权平均汇率。该等名义金额通常用于计算将在合约下交换的合约支付款项。

the notional amounts and weighted average exchange rates by expected (contractual) maturity dates. These notional amounts generally are used to calculate the contractual payments to be exchanged under the contract.

December 31, 19×1

1 The information is presented in U.S. dollars because that is the registrant's reporting currency.

	Expected maturity date							
	19X2	19X3	19X4	19X5	19X6	Thereafter	Total	Fair value
On – Balance Sheet Financial Instruments	(US$ Equivalent in millions)							
$ US Functional Currency[2]:								
Liabilities								
Long – Term Debt:								
Fixed Rate (DM)	$ XXX	$ XXX	$ XXX	$ XXX	$ XXX	$ XXX	$ XXX	$ XXX
Average interest rate	X. X	X. X	X. X	X. X	X. X	X. X	X. X	
	Expected maturity or transaction date							
Anticipated Transactions and Related Derivatives[3]	(US$ Equivalent in millions)							
$ US Functional Currency:								
Firmly committed Sales Contracts (DM)	$ XXX	$ XXX					$ XXX	$ XXX
Forward Exchange Agreements								
(Receive $ US/Pay DM):								
Contract Amount	XXX	XXX					XXX	XXX
Average Contractual Exchange Rate	X. X	X. X					X. X	

Commodity Price Sensitivity

The table below provides information about the Company's corn inventory and

2 Similar tabular information would be provided for other functional currencies.

3 Pursuant to General Instruction 4. to Items 305(a) and 305(b) of Regulation S-K, registrants may include cash flows from anticipated transactions and operating cash flows resulting from non-financial and non-commodity instruments.

19×1年12月31日

1 由于注册人的报表货币为美元,因此以美元列报上述信息。

	预期到期日							
	19X2	19X3	19X4	19X5	19X6	后续年份	总计	公允价值
资产负债表内金融工具	(单位:百万等值美元)							
美元职能货币:[2]								
负债								
长期债务:								
固定利率(DM)	美元 XXX	美元 XXX	美元 XXX	美元 XXX	美元 XXX	美元 XXX	美元 XXX	美元 XXX
平均利率	X. X	X. X	X. X	X. X	X. X	X. X	X. X	
	预期到期日或交易日							
预期交易和相关衍生品[3]	(单位:百万等值美元)							
美元职能货币:								
包销合约(DM)	美元 XXX	美元 XXX					美元 XXX	美元 XXX
远期外汇协议								
(接收美元/支付德国马克):								
合约金额	XXX	XXX					XXX	XXX
平均合约汇率	X. X	X. X					X. X	

商品价格敏感性

下表所示信息为与公司对商品价格变动(尤其是玉米价格变动)敏感的玉米存货

2 对于其他职能货币,应提供类似列表信息。

3 根据关于《S-K管理办法》第305(a)条和第305(b)条的总体说明4,注册人可以列入预期交易现金流以及非金融和非商品工具产生的经营现金流。

futures contracts that are sensitive to changes in commodity prices, specifically corn prices. For inventory, the table presents the carrying amount and fair value at December 31, 19×1. For the futures contracts the table presents the notional amounts in bushels, the weighted average contract prices, and the total dollar contract amount by expected maturity dates, the latest of which occurs one year from the reporting date. Contract amounts are used to calculate the contractual payments and quantity of corn to be exchanged under the futures contracts.

December 31, 19×1

	Carrying amount	Fair value
	(In millions)	
On Balance Sheet Commodity Position and Related Derivatives		
Corn Inventory[1]	$ XXX	$ XXX
	Expected	
	maturity	Fair
	1992	value
Related Derivatives		
Futures Contracts (Short):		
Contract Volumes (100,000 bushels)	XXX	
Weighted Average Price (Per 100,000 bushels)	$ X. XX	
Contract Amount ($ US in millions)	$ XXX	$ XXX

1 Pursuant to General Instruction 4. to Items 305(a) and 305(b) of Regulation S-K, registrants may include information on commodity positions, such as corn inventory.

[62 FR 6064, Feb. 10, 1997, as amended at 73 FR 958, Jan. 4, 2008; 74 FR 18617, Apr. 23, 2009]

§ 229.306 [Reserved]

§ 229.307(Item 307) Disclosure controls and procedures.

Disclose the conclusions of the registrant's principal executive and principal financial officers, or persons performing similar functions, regarding the effectiveness of the registrant's disclosure controls and procedures (as defined in §240.13a-15(e) or 240.15d-15(e) of this chapter) as of the end of the period covered by the report, based on the evaluation of these controls and procedures required by paragraph (b) of §240.13a-15 or 240.15d-15 of this chapter.

[68 FR 36663, June 18, 2003]

和期货合约相关的信息。对于存货,该表列报的为截至19×1年12月31日的账面金额和公允价值。对于期货合约,该表按预期到期日列报以蒲式耳计算的名义金额、加权平均合约价格以及美元合约总金额,预期到期日最晚为报表日后一年。合约金额用于计算期货合约下交换的合约支付款项和玉米数量。

19×1年12月31日

	账面金额	公允价值
	(单位:百万美元)	
资产负债表内商品持仓和相关衍生品		
玉米存货[1]	美元 XXX	美元 XXX
	预期	
	到期	公允
	1992	价值
相关衍生品		
期货合约(短期):		
合约数量(10 万蒲式耳)	XXX	
加权平均价格(10 万蒲式耳)	美元 X. XX	
合约金额(单位:百万美元)	美元 XXX	美元 XXX

1 根据关于《S-K管理办法》第305(a)条和第305(b)条的总体说明4.,注册人可以列入商品持仓信息,如玉米存货。

[《联邦公报》第62卷第6064页,1997年2月10日,修正索引:《联邦公报》第73卷第958页,2008年1月4日;《联邦公报》第74卷第18617页,2009年4月23日。]

第229.306节 [保留]

第229.307节(第307条) 披露控制和程序

披露注册人主要高管和主要财务官或者履行类似职责的人在按照本章第240.13a-15节第(b)款或第240.15d-15节对披露控制和程序进行评价的基础上,得出的关于截至报告期期末注册人的披露控制和程序[定义见本章第240.13a-15(e)节或第240.15d-15(e)节]的有效性的结论。

[《联邦公报》第68卷第36663页,2003年6月18日。]

§229.308(Item 308) Internal control over financial reporting.

(a) *Management's annual report on internal control over financial reporting.* Provide a report of management on the registrant's internal control over financial reporting (as defined in §240.13a-15(f) or 240.15d-15(f) of this chapter) that contains:

(1) A statement of management's responsibility for establishing and maintaining adequate internal control over financial reporting for the registrant;

(2) A statement identifying the framework used by management to evaluate the effectiveness of the registrant's internal control over financial reporting as required by paragraph (c) of §240.13a-15 or 240.15d-15 of this chapter;

(3) Management's assessment of the effectiveness of the registrant's internal control over financial reporting as of the end of the registrant's most recent fiscal year, including a statement as to whether or not internal control over financial reporting is effective. This discussion must include disclosure of any material weakness in the registrant's internal control over financial reporting identified by management. Management is not permitted to conclude that the registrant's internal control over financial reporting is effective if there are one or more material weaknesses in the registrant's internal control over financial reporting; and

(4) If the registrant is an accelerated filer or a large accelerated filer (as defined in §240.12b-2 of this chapter), or otherwise includes in its annual report a registered public accounting firm's attestation report on internal control over financial reporting, a statement that the registered public accounting firm that audited the financial statements included in the annual report containing the disclosure required by this Item has issued an attestation report on the registrant's internal control over financial reporting.

(b) *Attestation report of the registered public accounting firm.* If the registrant is an accelerated filer or a large accelerated filer(as defined in §240.12b-2 of this chapter), provide the registered public accounting firm's attestation report on the registrant's internal control over financial reporting in the registrant's annual report containing the disclosure required by this Item.

(c) *Changes in internal control over financial reporting.* Disclose any change in the registrant's internal control over financial reporting identified in connection with the evaluation required by paragraph (d) of §240.13a-15 or 240.15d-15 of this chapter that occurred during the registrant's last fiscal quarter (the registrant's fourth fiscal quarter in the case of an annual report) that has materially affected, or is reasonably likely to materially affect, the registrant's internal control over financial reporting.

Instructions to Item 308:1. A registrant need not comply with paragraphs(a) and (b) of this Item until it either had been required to file an annual report pursuant to section 13(a) or 15(d) of the Exchange Act (15 U.S.C. 78m or 78o(d)) for the prior fiscal year

第229.308节(第308条) 财务报告内部控制

(a)管理层关于财务报告内部控制的年度报告。提供管理层关于注册人财务报告内部控制[定义见本章第240.13a-15(f)节或第240.15d-15(f)节]的报告;报告应包含如下内容:

(1)关于管理层有责任为注册人建立和维持充分财务报告内部控制的声明;

(2)关于管理层在按照本章第240.13a-15节第(c)款或第240.15d-15节的要求评价注册人财务报告内部控制的有效性时使用的框架的声明;

(3)管理层对注册人截至最近一会计年度年末财务报告内部控制有效性的评估,包括关于财务报告内部控制是否有效的声明。此项分析必须披露管理层在注册人财务报告内部控制中发现的任何重大缺陷。如果在注册人的财务报告内部控制中发现一项或数项重大缺陷,管理层不得就注册人财务报告内部控制的有效性作出肯定性结论;且

(4)如果注册人属于加速报告公司或者大型加速报告公司(定义见本章第240.12b-2节),或者其年度报告中包含注册公共会计师事务所针对其财务报告内部控制作出的鉴证报告,应提供一份声明,说明对含有本条规定应披露材料的年度报告中的财务报表进行审计的注册公共会计师事务所已经就注册人的财务报告内部控制出具了鉴证报告。

(b)注册公共会计师事务所的鉴证报告。如果注册人属于加速报告公司或大型加速报告公司(定义见本章第240.12b-2节),应提供注册公共会计师事务所针对注册人含有本条规定应披露材料的年度报告中的财务报告内部控制作出的鉴证报告。

(c)财务报告内部控制变更。披露注册人财务报告内部控制的下列任何变更:按照本章第240.13a-15节第(d)款或第240.15d-15节规定进行评价时认定的在注册人上一财务季度(对于年度报告而言,指注册人第四财务季度)期间发生的,对注册人财务报告内部控制产生重大影响或者根据合理预期可能产生重大影响的任何变更。

关于第308条的说明:1.在注册人有义务按照《交易法》第13(a)条或第15(d)条[《美国法典》第十五编第78m节或第78o(d)节]提交上一会计年度年度报告或者实际向证券交易委员会提交上一会计年度年度报告之前,注册人不必遵循本条第(a)款和

or had filed an annual report with the Commission for the prior fiscal year. A registrant that does not comply shall include a statement in the first annual report that it files in substantially the following form: "This annual report does not include a report of management's assessment regarding internal control over financial reporting or an attestation report of the company's registered public accounting firm due to a transition period established by rules of the Securities and Exchange Commission for newly public companies."

2. The registrant must maintain evidential matter, including documentation, to provide reasonable support for management's assessment of the effectiveness of the registrant's internal control over financial reporting.

[68 FR 36663, June 18, 2003, as amended at 70 FR 1594, Jan. 7, 2005; 71 FR 76595, Dec. 21, 2006; 72 FR 35321, June 27, 2007; 75 FR 57387, Sept. 21, 2010]

Subpart 229.400 — Management and Certain Security Holders

§229.401 (Item 401) Directors, executive officers, promoters and control persons.

(a) *Identification of directors.* List the names and ages of all directors of the registrant and all persons nominated or chosen to become directors; indicate all positions and offices with the registrant held by each such person; state his term of office as director and any period(s) during which he has served as such; describe briefly any arrangement or understanding between him and any other person(s) (naming such person(s)) pursuant to which he was or is to be selected as a director or nominee.

Instructions to paragraph (a) of Item 401: 1. Do not include arrangements or understandings with directors or officers of the registrant acting solely in their capacities as such.

2. No nominee or person chosen to become a director who has not consented to act as such shall be named in response to this Item. In this regard, with respect to proxy statements, see Rule 14a-4(d) under the Exchange Act (§240.14a-4(d) of this chapter).

3. If the information called for by this paragraph (a) is being presented in a proxy or information statement, no information need be given respecting any director whose term of office as a director will not continue after the meeting to which the statement relates.

4. With regard to proxy statements in connection with action to be taken concerning

第(b)款的规定。不遵循上述规定的注册人应在提交的首份年度报告中参照如下格式提供一份大体类似的声明:“鉴于证券交易委员会规则为新公众公司设立了过渡期,本年度报告不包含管理层的财务报告内部控制评估报告,也不包括公司注册公共会计师事务所的鉴证报告。”

2.注册人必须保留相关证据材料(包括文件),以期在对注册人财务报告内部控制有效性进行评估的过程中为管理层提供合理支持。

[《联邦公报》第68卷第36663页,2003年6月18日,修正索引:《联邦公报》第70卷第1594页,2005年1月7日;《联邦公报》第71卷第76595页,2006年12月21日;《联邦公报》第72卷第35321页,2007年6月27日;《联邦公报》第75卷第57387页,2010年9月21日。]

第229.400子部分——管理层和特定证券持有人

第229.401节(第401条) 董事、高管、发起人和控制人

(a)列明董事身份信息。列明注册人所有董事以及被提名或选任为董事的所有人士的姓名和年龄,指明上述每个人在注册人内担任的所有职位和职务;说明其董事任期以及曾担任董事的任何期间,简要说明其与任何其他人之间就其过去或目前被选任或提名为董事一事所达成的任何安排或谅解,并列出任何该等其他人的姓名。

关于第401条第(a)款的说明:1.对于仅以注册人董事或管理人员身份行事的人,与其达成的安排或谅解不必提供。

2.被提名或者选任为董事,但是其本人并未同意担任该等职务的人不必按照本条要求列明。对此,请参见《交易法》的《14a-4(d)规则》[本章第240.14a-4(d)节]关于征集投票权报告的规定。

3.如果本第(a)款要求提供的信息已在征集投票权报告或信息说明书中提交,则对于在上述文件所涉会议结束之后不再继续担任任何董事的人,不必提供相关信息。

4.对于与董事选举行动相关的征集投票权报告,如果被提名的候选人的数量少于

the election of directors, if fewer nominees are named than the number fixed by or pursuant to the governing instruments, state the reasons for this procedure and that the proxies cannot be voted for a greater number of persons than the number of nominees named.

5. With regard to proxy statements in connection with action to be taken concerning the election of directors, if the solicitation is made by persons other than management, information shall be given as to nominees of the persons making the solicitation. In all other instances, information shall be given as to directors and persons nominated for election or chosen by management to become directors.

(b) *Identification of executive officers.* List the names and ages of all executive officers of the registrant and all persons chosen to become executive officers; indicate all positions and offices with the registrant held by each such person; state his term of office as officer and the period during which he has served as such and describe briefly any arrangement or understanding between him and any other person(s)(naming such person) pursuant to which he was or is to be selected as an officer.

Instructions to paragraph (b) of Item 401: 1. Do not include arrangements or understandings with directors or officers of the registrant acting solely in their capacities as such.

2. No person chosen to become anexecutive officer who has not consented to act as such shall be named in response to this Item.

3. The information regardingexecutive officers called for by this Item need not be furnished in proxy or information statements prepared in accordance with Schedule 14A under the Exchange Act (§240.14a-101 of this chapter) by registrants relying on General Instruction G of Form 10-K under the Exchange Act(§249.310 of this chapter); *Provided*, that such information is furnished in a separate item captioned "executive officers of the registrant" and included in Part I of the registrant's annual report on Form 10-K.

(c) *Identification of certain significant employees.* Where the registrant employs persons such as production managers, sales managers, or research scientists who are not executive officers but who make or are expected to make significant contributions to the business of the registrant, such persons shall be identified and their background disclosed to the same extent as in the case of executive officers. Such disclosure need not be made if the registrant was subject to section 13(a) or 15(d) of the Exchange Act or was exempt from section 13(a) by section 12(g)(2)(G) of such Act immediately prior to the filing of the registration statement, report, or statement to which this Item is applicable.

(d) *Family relationships.* State the nature of any family relationship between any director, executive officer, or person nominated or chosen by the registrant to become a

章程性文件中规定的数量或者依据该等文件确定的数量,应说明采取该等程序的理由,并说明所征集的投票权所能选举的人数不得超过提名候选人人数。

5.对于与董事选举行动相关的征集投票权报告,如果征集人不属于管理层,应当就征集人提名的候选人提供相关信息。在所有其他情形之下,应就各董事以及为管理层选举或选任董事而提名的候选人提供相关信息。

(b)列明高管信息。应列明注册人所有高管以及被选任为高管的所有人士的姓名和年龄,指明上述每个人在注册人内担任的所有职位和职务;说明其高管任期以及曾担任高管的任何期间,简要说明其与任何其他人之间就其过去或目前被选任或提名为高管一事所达成的任何安排或谅解,并列出任何该等其他人的姓名。

关于第401条第(b)款的说明:1.对于仅以注册人董事或管理人员身份行事的人,与其达成的安排或谅解不必提供。

2.被选任为高管,但是其本人并未同意担任该等职务的人不必按照本条要求列明。

3.本条要求提供的高管信息不必在注册人按照《交易法》的《附表14A》(本章第240.14a-101节)并援引《交易法》下《10-K表格》的总体说明G(本章第249.310节)编制的征集投票权报告或信息说明书中提供;但是,该等信息应在"注册人高管"的科目中单独列报,并包含在注册人按照《10-K表格》提交的年度报告的第一部分之中。

(c)列明特定重要雇员的信息。如果注册人雇用了生产经理、销售经理或科研人员等虽然不属于高管,但是对注册人业务作出了或预期将做出重大贡献的人,应列明该等人员,并披露他们的背景资料,披露范围与高管适用的程序相同。如果在紧接提交适用本条规定的注册说明书、报告或声明之前注册人受制于《交易法》第13(a)条或第15(d)条或者因该法的第12(g)(2)(G)条而豁免于第13(a)条的规定,则不必作出上述披露。

(d)亲属关系。说明任何董事、高管或被注册人提名或选任为董事或高管的人之间的任何亲属关系。

director or executive officer.

Instruction to paragraph 401(d): The term "family relationship" means anyrelationship by blood, marriage, or adoption, not more remote than first cousin.

(e) *Business experience* — (1) *Background.* Briefly describe the business experience during the past five years of each director, executive officer, person nominated or chosen to become a director or executive officer, and each person named in answer to paragraph (c) of Item 401, including: each person's principal occupations and employment during the past five years; the name and principal business of any corporation or other organization in which such occupations and employment were carried on; and whether such corporation or organization is a parent, subsidiary or other affiliate of the registrant. In addition, for each director or person nominated or chosen to become a director, briefly discuss the specific experience, qualifications, attributes or skills that led to the conclusion that the person should serve as a director for the registrant at the time that the disclosure is made, in light of the registrant's business and structure. If material, this disclosure should cover more than the past five years, including information about the person's particular areas of expertise or other relevant qualifications. When an executive officer or person named in response to paragraph (c) of Item 401 has been employed by the registrant or a subsidiary of the registrant for less than five years, a brief explanation shall be included as to the nature of the responsibility undertaken by the individual in prior positions to provide adequate disclosure of his or her prior business experience. What is required is information relating to the level of his or her professional competence, which may include, depending upon the circumstances, such specific information as the size of the operation supervised.

(2) *Directorships.* Indicate any other directorships held, including any other directorships held during the past five years, held by each director or person nominated or chosen to become a director in any company with a class of securities registered pursuant to section 12 of the Exchange Act or subject to the requirements of section 15(d) of such Act or any company registered as an investment company under the Investment Company Act of 1940, 15 U.S.C. 80a–1, *et seq.*, as amended, naming such company.

Instruction to Paragraph (e) of Item 401 : For the purposes of paragraph (e)(2), where the other directorships of each director or person nominated or chosen to become a director include directorships of two or more registered investment companies that are part of a "fund complex" as that term is defined in Item 22(a) of Schedule 14A under the Exchange Act (§240.14a–101 of this chapter), the registrant may, rather than listing each such investment company, identify the fund complex and provide the number of investment company directorships held by the director or nominee in such fund complex.

(f) *Involvement in certain legal proceedings.* Describe any of the following events

关于第401（d）款的说明。“亲属关系”一词系指因血缘、婚姻或领养而形成的任何关系，最远为嫡表（堂）兄弟姐妹关系。

（e）工作经历——（1）背景。简要说明每名董事、高管、被提名或选任为董事或高管的人以及按照第401条第（c）款的规定列明的每个人在过去5年的工作经历，包括：每个人在过去5年间的主要职业和受雇情况，与该等职业或受雇相关的任何公司或其他组织的名称和主要业务，以及该等公司或组织是否为注册人的母公司、子公司或其他关联方。另外，对于每名董事以及每个被提名或选任为董事的人，应在考虑注册人的业务和架构的基础上，简要分析在作出披露之时得出该等人员能胜任注册人董事一职的结论的理由，即该等人员所具备的具体经验、资质、特性或技能。如果5年之前的经历（包括关于此人的具体特长领域或其他相关资质的信息）具有重要意义，亦应纳入披露范围之内。如果按照第401条第（c）款的规定列明的高管或个人在注册人或其子公司的任职期限短于5年，应简要说明其在此之前承担的职责的性质，以便充分披露此前的工作经历。所提供的信息应针对该等人员的专业能力水准，根据具体情况，可能包括与其所负责的业务的规模有关的具体信息。

（2）董事职务。说明由每名董事或被提名或选任为董事的人在依据《交易法》第12条注册其某一类别证券的任何公司、受到该法第15（d）条规定约束的任何公司或者根据《1940年投资公司法》（修正版）（《美国法典》第十五编第80a-1节及其后条文）注册的投资公司兼任的任何董事职务（包括在过去5年期间兼任的任何董事职务），同时列明该等公司的名称。

关于第401条第（e）款的说明。就第（e）（2）款而言，当每名董事或被提名或选任为董事的人兼任董事职务的公司包括《交易法》的《附表14A》第22（a）条（本章第240.14a-101节）定义的“基金集合体”包含的两家（含）以上注册投资公司，注册人列明该基金集合体即可，不必一一列明每家投资公司，同时应提供董事或提名董事在该等基金集合体中兼任的投资公司董事职务的数量。

（f）对某些法律程序的参与。说明过去10年内发生的，对评估注册人任何董事、被

that occurred during the past ten years and that are material to an evaluation of the ability or integrity of any director, person nominated to become a director or executive officer of the registrant:

(1) A petition under the Federal bankruptcy laws or any state insolvency law was filed by or against, or a receiver, fiscal agent or similar officer was appointed by a court for the business or property of such person, or any partnership in which he was a general partner at or within two years before the time of such filing, or any corporation or business association of which he was anexecutive officer at or within two years before the time of such filing;

(2) Such person was convicted in a criminal proceeding or is a named subject of a pending criminal proceeding (excluding traffic violations and other minor offenses);

(3) Such person was the subject of any order, judgment, or decree, not subsequently reversed, suspended or vacated, of any court of competent jurisdiction, permanently or temporarily enjoining him from, or otherwise limiting, the following activities:

(i) Acting as a futures commission merchant, introducing broker, commodity trading advisor, commodity pool operator, floor broker, leverage transaction merchant, any other person regulated by the Commodity Futures Trading Commission, or an associated person of any of the foregoing, or as an investment adviser, underwriter, broker or dealer in securities, or as an affiliated person, director or employee of any investment company, bank, savings and loan association or insurance company, or engaging in or continuing any conduct or practice in connection with such activity;

(ii) Engaging in any type of business practice; or

(iii) Engaging in any activity in connection with the purchase or sale of any security or commodity or in connection with any violation of Federal or State securities laws or Federal commodities laws;

(4) Such person was the subject of any order, judgment or decree, not subsequently reversed, suspended or vacated, of any Federal or State authority barring, suspending or otherwise limiting for more than 60 days the right of such person to engage in any activity described in paragraph (f)(3)(i) of this section, or to be associated with persons engaged in any such activity;

(5) Such person was found by a court of competent jurisdiction in a civil action or by the Commission to have violated any Federal or State securities law, and the judgment in such civil action or finding by the Commission has not been subsequently reversed, suspended, or vacated;

(6) Such person was found by a court of competent jurisdiction in a civil action or by the Commodity Futures Trading Commission to have violated any Federal commodities law, and the judgment in such civil action or finding by the Commodity Futures Trading

提名担任董事或高管的人的能力或诚信具有重要意义的任何下列事件：

(1)在提交文件前2年内(含2年)，该人其担任普通合伙人的合伙或担任高管的任何公司或商业协会，根据联邦破产法或任何州的破产法主动提交破产请求书，或被提出破产请求，或者法院为该人/该等合伙的业务或财产指定了接管人、财务代理人或类似管理人；或者

(2)该人已在刑事程序中被定罪或者属于未决刑事程序中明确指明的犯罪嫌疑人(不包括交通违章或者其他轻罪)；

(3)该人被任何有管辖权的法院的任何命令、判决或裁定永久或临时性地禁止或限制其从事下列活动，且该等命令、判决或裁定之后未被推翻、中止或撤销：

(i)担任期货经纪商、介绍经纪人、商品交易顾问、商品基金管理人、场内经纪人、杠杆交易商、受商品期货交易委员会监管的任何其他主体或上述各方的业务相关人，或担任投资顾问、证券承销商、经纪人或自营商，或担任任何投资公司、银行、储蓄及贷款协会或保险公司的关联人、董事或雇员，或从事或持续从事与该等活动相关的任何行为或业务活动；

(ii)从事任何类型的商务活动；或者

(iii)从事与任何证券或商品的买卖有关的任何活动，或者涉嫌违反联邦或州证券法或联邦商品交易法的任何活动；

(4)该人被任何联邦或州政府部门的任何命令、判决或裁定禁止、中止从事本节第(f)(3)(i)款的任何活动或者充当从事任何该等活动的人的业务关联人，或受到其他方式的限制，且禁止、中止或限制时间达60日以上，且该等命令、判决或裁定之后未被推翻、中止或撤销；

(5)该人在民事诉讼中被有管辖权的法院认定或者被证券交易委员会认定违反了任何联邦或州证券法，并且该等民事诉讼的判决或者证券交易委员会的认定之后未被推翻、中止或撤销；

(6)该人在民事诉讼中被有管辖权的法院认定或者被商品期货交易委员会认定违反了任何联邦商品法律，并且该等民事诉讼的判决或者商品期货交易委员会的认定之后未被推翻、中止或撤销；

Commission has not been subsequently reversed, suspended or vacated;

(7) Such person was the subject of, or a party to, any Federal or State judicial or administrative order, judgment, decree, or finding, not subsequently reversed, suspended or vacated, relating to an alleged violation of:

(i) Any Federal or State securities or commodities law or regulation; or

(ii) Any law or regulation respecting financial institutions or insurance companies including, but not limited to, a temporary or permanent injunction, order of disgorgement or restitution, civil money penalty or temporary or permanent cease-and-desist order, or removal or prohibition order; or

(iii) Any law or regulation prohibiting mail or wire fraud or fraud in connection with any business entity; or

(8) Such person was the subject of, or a party to, any sanction or order, not subsequently reversed, suspended or vacated, of any self-regulatory organization (as defined in Section 3(a)(26) of the Exchange Act (15 U.S.C. 78c(a)(26))), any registered entity (as defined in Section 1(a)(29) of the Commodity Exchange Act (7 U.S.C. 1(a)(29))), or any equivalent exchange, association, entity or organization that has disciplinary authority over its members or persons associated with a member.

Instructions to paragraph (f) of Item 401 : 1. For purposes of computing the ten-year period referred to in this paragraph, the date of a reportable event shall be deemed the date on which the final order, judgment or decree was entered, or the date on which any rights of appeal from preliminary orders, judgments, or decrees have lapsed. With respect to bankruptcy petitions, the computation date shall be the date of filing for uncontested petitions or the date upon which approval of a contested petition became final.

2. If any event specified in this paragraph (f) has occurred and information in regard thereto is omitted on the grounds that it is not material, the registrant may furnish to the Commission, at time of filing (or at the time preliminary materials are filed, or ten days before definitive materials are filed in preliminary filing is not required, pursuant to Rule 14a-6 or 14c-5 under the Exchange Act(§§240.14a-6 and 240-14c-5 of this chapter)), as supplemental information and not as part of the registration statement, report, or proxy or information statement, materials to which the omission relates, a description of the event and a statement of the reasons for the omission of information in regard thereto.

3. The registrant is permitted to explain any mitigating circumstances associated with events reported pursuant to this paragraph.

4. If the information called for by this paragraph (f) is being presented in a proxy or information statement, no information need be given respecting any director whose term of office as a director will not continue after the meeting to which the statement relates.

（7）该人因涉嫌违反下列法律法规而成为任何联邦或州的司法或行政命令、判决、裁定或裁决的对象或当事方，且该等司法或行政命令、判决、裁定或裁决之后未被推翻、中止或撤销：

（i）任何联邦或州的证券或商品法律法规；或者

（ii）关于金融机构或保险公司的任何法律法规，包括但不限于临时或永久禁令、没收非法所得令或恢复原状令、民事罚款令、临时或永久的制止令或者免职令、禁制令；或者

（iii）禁止邮件或电报欺诈或者禁止与任何商业实体有关的欺诈的任何法律法规；或者

（8）该人为任何自律组织{定义见《交易法》第3(a)(26)条[《美国法典》第十五编第78c(a)(26)节]}、任何注册实体{定义见《商品交易法》第1(a)(29)条[《美国法典》第七编第1(a)(29)节]}，或者对其会员或会员的业务相关人有纪律处分权限的任何同等的交易所、协会、实体或组织的任何制裁或命令的对象或一方当事人，且该等制裁或命令未被后续推翻、中止或撤销；

关于第401条第(f)款的说明：1.在计算本款提及的10年期限时，应报告事件的日期应当视为作出最终命令、判决或判令的日期，或者就初步命令、判决或判令提起上诉的任何权利失效的日期。对于破产请求，计算日期应当为无争议请求的提交日或者有争议请求获得最终批准之日。

2.如果发生本第(f)款规定的任何事件，但是因其不具重要性而未提供相关信息，注册人可在提交文件时[或者在提交初步材料时；如不必提交初步材料，则在依据《交易法》的《14a-6规则》或《14c-5规则》（本章第240.14a-6节和第240-14c-5节）提交正式材料前10日]向证券交易委员会提交与被省略的信息有关的材料、对事件的说明以及关于省略相关信息的理由的声明，该等信息应作为补充信息，而非注册人说明书、报告或者征集投票权报告或信息说明书的一部分提交。

3.注册人在依据本款报告事件时，可说明任何相关的从轻情节。

4.如果本第(f)款要求提供的信息已在征集投票权报告或信息说明书中提交，则对于在上述文件所涉会议结束之后不再继续担任任何董事的人，不必提供相关信息。

5. This paragraph (f)(7) shall not apply to any settlement of a civil proceeding among private litigants.

(g) *Promoters and control persons.* (1) Registrants, which have not been subject to the reporting requirements of section 13(a) or 15(d) of the Exchange Act (15 U.S.C. 78m(a) or 78 *o*(d)) for the twelve months immediately prior to the filing of the registration statement, report, or statement to which this Item is applicable, and which had a promoter at any time during the past five fiscal years, shall describe with respect to any promoter, any of the events enumerated in paragraphs(f)(1) through(f)(6) of this Item that occurred during the past five years and that are material to a voting or investment decision.

(2) Registrants, which have not been subject to the reporting requirements of section 13(a) or 15(d) of the Exchange Act for the twelve months immediately prior to the filing of the registration statement, report, or statement to which this Item is applicable, shall describe with respect to any control person, any of the events enumerated in paragraphs (f)(1) through (f)(6) of this section that occurred during the past five years and that are material to a voting or investment decision.

Instructions to paragraph (g) of Item 401 : 1. Instructions 1. through 3. to paragraph (f) shall apply to this paragraph (g).

2. Paragraph (g) shall not apply to any subsidiary of a registrant which has been reporting pursuant to Section 13(a) or 15(d) of the Exchange Act for the twelve months immediately prior to the filing of the registration statement, report or statement.

[47 FR 11401, Mar. 16, 1982, as amended at 47 FR 55665, Dec. 13, 1982; 48 FR 19874, May 3, 1983; 49 FR 32763, Aug. 16, 1984; 52 FR 48982, Dec. 29, 1987; 59 FR 52695, Oct. 19, 1994; 70 FR 1594, Jan. 7, 2005; 71 FR 53241, Sept. 8, 2006; 73 FR 958, Jan. 4, 2008; 74 FR 68362, Dec. 23, 2009]

§229.402(Item 402) Executive compensation.

Link to an amendment published at 76 FR 6043, February 2, 2011.

(a) *General* — (1) *Treatment of foreign private issuers.* A foreign private issuer will be deemed to comply with this Item if it provides the information required by Items 6.B and 6.E.2 of Form 20-F(17 CFR 249.220f), with more detailed information provided if otherwise made publicly available or required to be disclosed by the issuer's home jurisdiction or a market in which its securities are listed or traded.

(2) *All compensation covered.* This Item requires clear, concise and understandable disclosure of all plan and non-plan compensation awarded to, earned by, or paid to the named executive officers designated under paragraph (a)(3) of this Item, and directors

5.本第(f)(7)款不适用于民事诉讼程序中私人当事人之间进行的任何和解。

(g)发起人和控制人。(1)在紧接提交适用本条的注册说明书、报告或声明之前12个月内不受制于《交易法》第13(a)条或第15(d)条[《美国法典》第十五编第78m(a)节或第78*o*(d)节]规定的报告义务的注册人,并且在过去5个会计年度内的任何时间下属任一子公司有发起人身份的,应当说明发起人在过去5年内发生的本条第(f)(1)款至第(f)(6)款列举的,且对表决或投资决策具有重要意义的任何事件。

(2)在紧接提交适用本条的注册说明书、报告或声明之前的12个月内不受制于《交易法》第13(a)条或第15(d)条规定的报告义务的注册人,应当说明任何控制人在过去5年期间内发生的本节第(f)(1)款至第(f)(6)款列举的,且对表决或投资决策具有重要意义的任何事件。

关于第401条第(g)款的说明:1.第(f)款的说明1至说明3应适用于本第(g)款。

2.对于在紧接提交注册说明书、报告或声明前12个月内依据《交易法》第13(a)条或第15(d)条提交报告的注册人,第(g)款不适用于其任何子公司。

[《联邦公报》第47卷第11401页,1982年3月16日,修正索引:《联邦公报》第47卷第55665页,1982年12月13日;《联邦公报》第48卷第19874页,1983年5月3日;《联邦公报》第49卷第32763页,1984年8月16日;《联邦公报》第52卷第48982页,1987年12月29日;《联邦公报》第59卷第52695页,1994年10月19日;《联邦公报》第70卷第1594页,2005年1月7日;《联邦公报》第71卷第53241页,2006年9月8日;《联邦公报》第73卷第958页,2008年1月4日;《联邦公报》第74卷第68362页,2009年12月23日。]

第229.402节(第402条) 高管报酬

链接至《联邦公报》第76卷第6043页(2011年2月2日)的修正。

(a)一般规定——(1)外国私募发行人的待遇。外国私募发行人提供《20-F表格》(《联邦规章汇编》第十七编第249.220f节)第6.B条和第6.E.2条规定的信息,同时提供其所在司法辖区或其证券上市或交易市场以其他方式公开或要求披露的更详细的信息的,即视为已符合本条规定。

(2)应予披露的报酬。根据本条规定,本条第(a)(3)款所指定的高级管理人员及本条第(k)款所指定的董事以及以任何身份向注册人及其子公司提供服务的任何人,因此获得、赚取或获付计划和非计划报酬的,必须以清晰、简洁、易懂的方式予以披露,

covered by paragraph (k) of this Item, by any person for all services rendered in all capacities to the registrant and its subsidiaries, unless otherwise specifically excluded from disclosure in this Item. All such compensation shall be reported pursuant to this Item, even if also called for by another requirement, including transactions between the registrant and a third party where a purpose of the transaction is to furnish compensation to any such named executive officer or director. No amount reported as compensation for one fiscal year need be reported in the same manner as compensation for a subsequent fiscal year; amounts reported as compensation for one fiscal year may be required to be reported in a different manner pursuant to this Item.

(3) *Persons covered.* Disclosure shall be provided pursuant to this Item for each of the following (the "named executive officers"):

(i) All individuals serving as the registrant's principalexecutive officer or acting in a similar capacity during the last completed fiscal year("PEO"), regardless of compensation level;

(ii) All individuals serving as the registrant's principal financial officer or acting in a similar capacity during the last completed fiscal year("PFO"), regardless of compensation level;

(iii) The registrant's three most highly compensatedexecutive officers other than the PEO and PFO who were serving as executive officers at the end of the last completed fiscal year; and

(iv) Up to two additional individuals for whom disclosure would have been provided pursuant to paragraph (a)(3)(iii) of this Item but for the fact that the individual was not serving as an executive officer of the registrant at the end of the last completed fiscal year.

Instructions to Item 402 (a) (3): 1. *Determination of most highly compensated executive officers.* The determination as to which executive officers are most highly compensated shall be made by reference to total compensation for the last completed fiscal year (as required to be disclosed pursuant to paragraph (c)(2)(x) of this Item) reduced by the amount required to be disclosed pursuant to paragraph (c)(2)(viii) of this Item, *provided, however,* that no disclosure need be provided for any executive officer, other than the PEO and PFO, whose total compensation, as so reduced, does not exceed $100,000.

2. *Inclusion of executive officer of subsidiary.* It may be appropriate for a registrant to include as named executive officers one or more executive officers or other employees of subsidiaries in the disclosure required by this Item. See Rule 3b-7 under the Exchange Act (17 CFR 240.3b-7).

3. *Exclusion of executive officer due to overseas compensation.* It may be appropriate

但本条明确规定不必披露的除外。所有该等报酬均应按照本条规定报告，不论其他规定是否同样要求对此进行报告；注册人与第三方之间开展交易，且交易目的之一是向任何该等具名高管或董事提供报酬的，该等交易亦应纳入报告范围。在某一会计年度作为报酬报告的金额不必再在下一会计年度以同样方式进行报告，但可能须按照本条规定以其他方式进行报告。

（3）适用人员。下列每一人员（“具名高管”）均须按本条规定进行相应披露：

（i）所有在上一完整会计年度担任注册人的主要高管或者以类似身份行事的个人（“主要高管”，PEO），不论报酬水平高低；

（ii）所有在上一完整会计年度担任注册人的主要财务官或者以类似身份行事的个人（“主要财务官”，PFO），不论报酬水平高低；

（iii）除主要高管和主要财务官以外，在上一完整会计年度年末担任注册人高管的三位报酬最高的高管；及

（iv）按照本条第（a）（3）（iii）款规定本应披露其相关信息，但在上一完整会计年度年末不再担任注册人高管的个人（不超过2名）。

关于第402（a）（3）项的说明：1.三位报酬最高高管的确定。确定报酬最高的高管之时，应将上一完整会计年度的报酬总额[该等报酬总额应按本条第（c）（2）（x）款规定予以披露]减去本条第（c）（2）（viii）款要求披露的金额，但是按照上述规定进行扣减后所得报酬总额不超过10万美元的任何高管（主要高管和主要财务官除外）不必披露。

2.纳入子公司高管。在适当情况下，注册人可以将其子公司的一名或数名高管或其他职员作为具名高管纳入本条规定的披露名单。参见《交易法》的《3b-7规则》（《联邦规章汇编》第十七编第240.3b-7节）。

3.排除获取海外报酬的高管。在有限和适当的情况下，对于主要因境外工作获取

in limited circumstances for a registrant not to include in the disclosure required by this Item an individual, other than its PEO or PFO, who is one of the registrant's most highly compensated executive officers due to the payment of amounts of cash compensation relating to overseas assignments attributed predominantly to such assignments.

(4) *Information for full fiscal year.* If the PEO or PFO served in that capacity during any part of a fiscal year with respect to which information is required, information should be provided as to all of his or her compensation for the full fiscal year. If a named executive officer (other than the PEO or PFO) served as an executive officer of the registrant (whether or not in the same position) during any part of the fiscal year with respect to which information is required, information shall be provided as to all compensation of that individual for the full fiscal year.

(5) *Omission of table or column.* A table or column may be omitted if there has been no compensation awarded to, earned by, or paid to any of the named executive officers or directors required to be reported in that table or column in any fiscal year covered by that table.

(6) *Definitions.* For purposes of this Item:

(i) The term *stock* means instruments such as common stock, restricted stock, restricted stock units, phantom stock, phantom stock units, common stock equivalent units or any similar instruments that do not have option-like features, and the term *option* means instruments such as stock options, stock appreciation rights and similar instruments with option-like features. The term *stock appreciation rights* ("*SARs*") refers to SARs payable in cash or stock, including SARs payable in cash or stock at the election of the registrant or a named executive officer. The term *equity* is used to refer generally to stock and/or options.

(ii) The term *plan* includes, but is not limited to, the following: Any plan, contract, authorization or arrangement, whether or not set forth in any formal document, pursuant to which cash, securities, similar instruments, or any other property may be received. A plan may be applicable to one person. Registrants may omit information regarding group life, health, hospitalization, or medical reimbursement plans that do not discriminate in scope, terms or operation, in favor of executive officers or directors of the registrant and that are available generally to all salaried employees.

(iii) The term *incentive plan* means any plan providing compensation intended to serve as incentive for performance to occur over a specified period, whether such performance is measured by reference to financial performance of the registrant or an affiliate, the registrant's stock price, or any other performance measure. An *equity incentive plan* is an incentive plan or portion of an incentive plan under which awards are granted that fall within the scope of Financial Accounting Standards Board Statement of

的相关现金报酬而成为注册人报酬最高高管之一的个人(主要高管或主要财务官除外),注册人可以不将其纳入本条规定的披露名单。

(4)完整会计年度的信息。对于某一会计年度内应按规定进行信息披露的任何期间,主要高管或者主要财务官只要曾在该期间内任职,即应就其在该完整会计年度的全部报酬提供相关信息。如果在某一会计年度内应按规定进行信息披露的任何期间,某具名高管(主要高管或主要财务官除外)曾担任注册人的高管(不论职位是否相同),即应就其在该完整会计年度的全部报酬提供相关信息。

(5)省略表格或者栏目。如果某表格或某栏要求具名高管或者董事进行报告,但任何该等具名高管或董事在该表所覆盖的任何会计年度未获得、赚取或者获付任何报酬,则该表格或栏目可予省略。

(6)定义。就本条而言:

(i)“股票”系指普通股、受限股票、受限股票单位、虚拟股票、虚拟股票单位、普通股等价单位或者不具有期权特性的任何类似票据;“期权”系指股票期权、股票增值权等票据及具有期权特性的类似票据。“股票增值权”(SAR)系指可用现金或股票支付的股票增值权,包括可由注册人或具名高管选择以现金或股票支付的股票增值权。“股权”统指股票和/或期权。

(ii)“计划”包括但不限于任何计划、合同、授权或安排,只要凭借任何该等计划、合同、授权或安排可以接收现金、证券、类似工具或者任何其他财产,而不论其是否载于任何正式文件之中。一项计划的适用对象可以仅限于单独一个主体。在计划范围、期限或运行方面对于注册人高管或者董事不给予任何优惠,且普遍适用于所有受薪职员的集体人寿、健康、住院或医疗报销计划,注册人可以免予提供相关信息。

(iii)“激励计划”系指旨在就特定期间提供绩效激励的任何计划,而不论该绩效的衡量标准是注册人或关联人的财务绩效、注册人的股价或者任何其他绩效衡量标准。“股权激励计划”系指《财务会计准则公告第123号(2004年修订版)——基于股份的支付》(以修改和补充版为准)(FAS 123R)规定范围内的向计划参与人授予奖励的激励计划或该计划的一部分。“非股权激励计划”系指不属于股权激励计划的激励计划或该计划的一部分。“激励计划奖励”系指依据激励计划授予的奖励。

Financial Accounting Standards No. 123(revised 2004), *Share-Based Payment*, as modified or supplemented("FAS 123R"). A *non-equity incentive plan* is an incentive plan or portion of an incentive plan that is not an equity incentive plan. The term *incentive plan award* means an award provided under an incentive plan.

(iv) The terms *date of grant* or *grant date* refer to the grant date determined for financial statement reporting purposes pursuant to FAS 123R.

(v) *Closing market price* is defined as the price at which the registrant's security was last sold in the principal United States market for such security as of the date for which the closing market price is determined.

(b) *Compensation discussion and analysis.*(1) Discuss the compensation awarded to, earned by, or paid to the named executive officers. The discussion shall explain all material elements of the registrant's compensation of the named executive officers. The discussion shall describe the following:

(i) The objectives of the registrant's compensation programs;

(ii) What the compensation program is designed to reward;

(iii) Each element of compensation;

(iv) Why the registrant chooses to pay each element;

(v) How the registrant determines the amount(and, where applicable, the formula) for each element to pay; and

(vi) How each compensation element and the registrant's decisions regarding that element fit into the registrant's overall compensation objectives and affect decisions regarding other elements.

(2) While the material information to be disclosed under Compensation Discussion and Analysis will vary depending upon the facts and circumstances, examples of such information may include, in a given case, among other things, the following:

(i) The policies for allocating between long-term and currently paid out compensation;

(ii) The policies for allocating between cash and non-cash compensation, and among different forms of non-cash compensation;

(iii) For long-term compensation, the basis for allocating compensation to each different form of award (such as relationship of the award to the achievement of the registrant's long-term goals, management's exposure to downside equity performance risk, correlation between cost to registrant and expected benefits to the registrant);

(iv) How the determination is made as to when awards are granted, including awards of equity-based compensation such as options;

(v) What specific items of corporate performance are taken into account in setting compensation policies and making compensation decisions;

(iv)“授予日”系指为财务报表报告之目的而按照FAS 123R确定的授予日期。

(v)“收盘市价”系指截至收盘市价确定之日,注册人的证券在该种证券的主要美国市场的最后出售价格。

(b)报酬论述与分析。(1)论述具名高管获得、赚取或获付的报酬。该等论述应对具名高管从注册人处获得的报酬的所有重大要素作出解释。论述应说明下列各项内容:

(i)注册人报酬计划的目标;
(ii)该报酬计划所奖励的绩效;
(iii)报酬要素;
(iv)注册人选择支付各报酬要素的原因;
(v)注册人确定各报酬要素应付金额的方式以及确定该等金额的公式(如适用);和
(vi)各报酬要素和注册人关于该要素的决定对注册人整体报酬目标的合适性以及对其他要素之决定的影响。

(2)视事实和情况不同,应通过《报酬论述与分析》披露的重大信息也会存在差异,如该等信息可能包括但不限于:

(i)长期报酬与当期报酬之间的分配政策;

(ii)现金报酬与非现金报酬之间的分配政策,以及不同形式的非现金报酬之间的分配政策;
(iii)长期报酬在各种不同形式的奖励之间的分配依据(如该奖励与注册人长期目标的实现之间的关系、管理层的股权业绩下跌风险、注册人成本与注册人预期收益之间的相互关系);

(iv)确定奖励授予时间的方式(包括基于股权的报酬奖励,例如期权);

(v)制定报酬政策及作出报酬决定时应考虑的具体公司业绩项;

(vi) How specific forms of compensation are structured and implemented to reflect these items of the registrant's performance, including whether discretion can be or has been exercised(either to award compensation absent attainment of the relevant performance goal(s) or to reduce or increase the size of any award or payout), identifying any particular exercise of discretion, and stating whether it applied to one or more specified namedexecutive officers or to all compensation subject to the relevant performance goal(s);

(vii) How specific forms of compensation are structured and implemented to reflect the namedexecutive officer's individual performance and/or individual contribution to these items of the registrant's performance, describing the elements of individual performance and/or contribution that are taken into account;

(viii) Registrant policies and decisions regarding the adjustment or recovery of awards or payments if the relevant registrant performance measures upon which they are based are restated or otherwise adjusted in a manner that would reduce the size of an award or payment;

(ix) The factors considered in decisions to increase or decrease compensation materially;

(x) How compensation or amounts realizable from prior compensation are considered in setting other elements of compensation (e.g., how gains from prior option or stock awards are considered in setting retirement benefits);

(xi) With respect to any contract, agreement, plan or arrangement, whether written or unwritten, that provides for payment(s) at, following, or in connection with any termination or change-in-control, the basis for selecting particular events as triggering payment (e.g., the rationale for providing a single trigger for payment in the event of a change-in-control);

(xii) The impact of the accounting and tax treatments of the particular form of compensation;

(xiii) The registrant's equity or other security ownership requirements or guidelines (specifying applicable amounts and forms of ownership), and any registrant policies regarding hedging the economic risk of such ownership;

(xiv) Whether the registrant engaged in any benchmarking of total compensation, or any material element of compensation, identifying the benchmark and, if applicable, its components (including component companies); and

(xv) The role ofexecutive officers in determining executive compensation.

Instructions to Item 402(b) : 1. The purpose of the Compensation Discussion and Analysis is to provide to investors material information that is necessary to an understanding of the registrant's compensation policies and decisions regarding the named

(vi)具体形式的报酬是如何架构和执行,以反映注册人的上述业绩项的,包括是否能够或者已经行使了自由裁量权(在未实现相关业绩目标的情况下授予报酬或者减少或增加任何奖励或分红的数额);说明每次裁量权的行使,并注明任何该等裁量权的行使仅适用于特定的一位或多位具名高管,或是适用于与该业绩目标挂钩的一切报酬;

(vii)具体形式的报酬是如何架构并执行,以反映具名高管的个人业绩和/或个人对注册人上述业绩项的贡献的;同时应说明个人业绩的组成部分和/或所考虑的贡献;

(viii)在注册人相关业绩衡量标准进行重订或者调整,导致奖励或付款金额被调低的情况下,注册人关于调整或收回奖励或付款的政策及决定;

(ix)决定实质性提高或降低报酬时所考虑的因素;

(x)在设定其他报酬要素时,对于可从以往报酬中实现的报酬或金额的考虑(如在设定退休福利时,是如何考虑之前的期权收益或股票奖励的);

(xi)对于任何书面或非书面合同、协议、计划或安排,如其规定相关实体发生任何终止或控制权变更之时、之后应进行付款或者应就任何该等终止或控制权变更支付相关款项,应说明选定该等触发付款之特定事件的依据(如针对发生控制权变更的情况,仅规定单一的触发付款事件的理由);

(xii)特定形式报酬的会计及税务处理的影响;

(xiii)注册人关于股权或其他证券所有权的规定或方针(具体说明所有权的相关数额和形式),以及任何注册人关于该所有权经济风险的套期保值政策;

(xiv)对于报酬总额或其任何重大要素,注册人是否进行了任何标杆调查,同时应注明所采用的标杆及其构成(如适用包括标杆调查的对象公司);及

(xv)高管在决定高管报酬中的角色。

关于第402(b)条的说明:1.《报酬论述与分析》的目的在于向投资者提供必要的重大信息,以帮助投资者理解注册人关于具名高管报酬的政策及决定。

executive officers.

2. The Compensation Discussion and Analysis should be of the information contained in the tables and otherwise disclosed pursuant to this Item. The Compensation Discussion and Analysis should also cover actions regarding executive compensation that were taken after the registrant's last fiscal year's end. Actions that should be addressed might include, as examples only, the adoption or implementation of new or modified programs and policies or specific decisions that were made or steps that were taken that could affect a fair understanding of the namedexecutive officer's compensation for the last fiscal year. Moreover, in some situations it may be necessary to discuss prior years in order to give context to the disclosure provided.

3. The Compensation Discussion and Analysis should focus on the material principles underlying the registrant's executive compensation policies and decisions and the most important factors relevant to analysis of those policies and decisions. The Compensation Discussion and Analysis shall reflect the individual circumstances of the registrant and shall avoid boilerplate language and repetition of the more detailed information set forth in the tables and narrative disclosures that follow.

4. Registrants are not required to disclose target levels with respect to specific quantitative or qualitative performance-related factors considered by the compensation committee or the board of directors, or any other factors or criteria involving confidential trade secrets or confidential commercial or financial information, the disclosure of which would result in competitive harm for the registrant. The standard to use when determining whether disclosure would cause competitive harm for the registrant is the same standard that would apply when a registrant requests confidential treatment of confidential trade secrets or confidential commercial or financial information pursuant to Securities Act Rule 406(17 CFR 230.406) and Exchange Act Rule 24b-2(17 CFR 240.24b-2), each of which incorporates the criteria for non-disclosure when relying upon Exemption 4 of the Freedom of Information Act (5 U.S.C. 552(b)(4)) and Rule 80(b)(4) (17 CFR 200.80 (b)(4)) thereunder. A registrant is not required to seek confidential treatment under the procedures in Securities Act Rule 406 and Exchange Act Rule 24b-2 if it determines that the disclosure would cause competitive harm in reliance on this instruction; however, in that case, the registrant must discuss how difficult it will be for the executive or how likely it will be for the registrant to achieve the undisclosed target levels or other factors.

5. Disclosure of target levels that are non-GAAP financial measures will not be subject to Regulation G(17 CFR 244.100—102) and Item 10(e) (§229.10(e)); however, disclosure must be provided as to how the number is calculated from the registrant's audited financial statements.

(c) *Summary compensation table* — (1) *General.* Provide the information specified in

2.《报酬论述与分析》应当提供本条规定的表格中包含的信息及本条另行要求披露的其他信息。《报酬论述与分析》还应当涵盖注册人上一会计年度结束之后针对高管报酬采取的行动。举例而言,应予论述分析的行动可能包括新计划和新政策的通过或执行,或修改后的计划和政策的通过或执行,或具体决定或措施之决定或采取,只要该等计划、政策、决定或措施能够影响对具名高管上一会计年度报酬的公允解读。此外,在某些情况下,为提供披露的相关背景,可能有必要对之前的年度进行论述。

3.《报酬论述与分析》的重点应为注册人关于高管报酬的政策和决定的重大原则,以及对该等政策和决定进行分析时所应关注的最重大的因素。《报酬论述与分析》应反映注册人的具体情况,且应避免使用套辞,并避免重复表格及其后的文字披露中所载的详细信息。

4. 对于报酬委员会或董事会考虑范围内的为业绩评估而设定的具体定量或定性因素目标水平,或者涉及商业秘密或机密性商业或财务信息的任何其他因素或标准,如果披露该等信息会令注册人遭受竞争性损害,则注册人不必披露。确定披露是否会令注册人遭受竞争性损害时所适用的标准,应与下列标准保持一致:注册人根据《证券法》的《406规则》(《联邦规章汇编》第十七编第230.406节)和《交易法》的《24b-2规则》(《联邦规章汇编》第十七编第240.24b-2节)申请对商业秘密或机密商业或财务信息采取保密措施时所适用的标准——上述此两条规则均采纳了申请适用《信息自由法》第4条豁免规定[《美国法典》第五编第552(b)(4)节]及依其颁发的《80(b)(4)规则》[《联邦规章汇编》第十七编第200.80(b)(4)节]时应遵守的保密标准。如果注册人认为遵守本说明进行披露会导致竞争性损害,则不必根据《证券法》的《406规则》和《交易法》的《24b-2规则》规定的程序申请采取保密措施;但是,在上述情况下,注册人必须论述高管实现未披露的目标水平或其他因素的困难度或可能性。

5.对非GAAP财务指标的目标水平进行披露,不必遵守《G管理办法》(《联邦规章汇编》第十七编第244.100-102节)和第10(e)条[第229.10(e)节]的规定;但是,必须披露注册人的已审计财务报表中计算该数字的方式。

(c)报酬简表——(1)一般规定。按下列《报酬简表》的格式,提供本条第(c)(2)款

paragraph (c)(2) of this Item, concerning the compensation of the named executive officers for each of the registrant's last three completed fiscal years, in a Summary Compensation Table in the tabular format specified below.

Summary Compensation Table

Name and principal position	Year	Salary ($)	Bonus ($)	Stock awards ($)	Option awards ($)	Non-equity incentive plan compensation ($)	Change in pension value and non-qualified deferred compensation earnings($)	All other compensation ($)	Total ($)
(a)	(b)	(c)	(d)	(e)	(f)	(g)	(h)	(i)	(j)
PEO									
PFO									
A									
B									
C									

(2) The Table shall include:

(i) The name and principal position of the namedexecutive officer (column (a));

(ii) The fiscal year covered (column (b));

(iii) The dollar value of base salary(cash and non-cash) earned by the namedexecutive officer during the fiscal year covered (column (c));

(iv) The dollar value of bonus (cash and non-cash) earned by the namedexecutive officer during the fiscal year covered (column (d));

Instructions to Item 402(c)(2)(iii) and(iv).1. If the amount of salary or bonus earned in a given fiscal year is not calculable through the latest practicable date, a

规定的关于具名高管在注册人过去3个完整会计年度中的每一会计年度的报酬信息。

报酬简表

姓名和主要职务	年份	工资（美元）	奖金（美元）	股票奖励（美元）	期权奖励（美元）	非股权激励计划报酬（美元）	退休金价值变动及无税收优惠资格的递延报酬收入（美元）	所有其他报酬（美元）	总计（美元）
(a)	(b)	(c)	(d)	(e)	(f)	(g)	(h)	(i)	(j)
主要高管									
主要财务官									
A									
B									
C									

(2)简表内容应包括：

(i)具名高管的姓名和主要职务[(a)栏]；

(ii)所涉会计年度[(b)栏]；

(iii)具名高管在该会计年度以美元计算的基本工资（包括现金和非现金工资）[(c)栏]；

(iv)具名高管在该会计年度以美元计算的奖金（包括现金和非现金奖金）[(d)栏]；

关于第402(c)(2)(iii)条和第402(c)(2)(iv)条的说明。1.如果某既定会计年度赚取的工资或奖金数额截至可行的最迟日期仍无法统计，应通过脚注如实说明，并提供

footnote shall be included disclosing that the amount of salary or bonus is not calculable through the latest practicable date and providing the date that the amount of salary or bonus is expected to be determined, and such amount must then be disclosed in a filing under Item 5.02(f) of Form 8-K (17 CFR 249.308).

2. Registrants shall include in the salary column (column (c)) or bonus column (column(d)) any amount of salary or bonus forgone at the election of a namedexecutive officer under which stock, equity-based or other forms of non-cash compensation instead have been received by the named executive officer. However, the receipt of any such form of non-cash compensation instead of salary or bonus must be disclosed in a footnote added to the salary or bonus column and, where applicable, referring to the Grants of Plan-Based Awards Table (required by paragraph (d) of this Item) where thestock, option or non-equity incentive plan award elected by the named executive officer is reported.

(v) For awards of stock, the aggregate grant date fair value computed in accordance with FASB ASC Topic 718 (column (e));

(vi) For awards of options, with or without tandem SARs (including awards that subsequently have been transferred), the aggregate grant date fair value computed in accordance with FASB ASC Topic 718 (column (f));

Instruction 1 to Item 402 (c)(2)(v) and (vi).For awards reported in columns (e) and (f), include a footnote disclosing all assumptions made in the valuation by reference to a discussion of those assumptions in the registrant's financial statements, footnotes to the financial statements, or discussion in the Management's Discussion and Analysis. The sections so referenced are deemed part of the disclosure provided pursuant to this Item.

Instruction 2 to Item 402 (c) (2) (v) and (vi).If at any time during the last completed fiscal year, the registrant has adjusted or amended the exercise price of options or SARs previously awarded to a named executive officer, whether through amendment, cancellation or replacement grants, or any other means ("repriced"), or otherwise has materially modified such awards, the registrant shall include, as awards required to be reported in column (f), the incremental fair value, computed as of the repricing or modification date in accordance with FASB ASC Topic 718, with respect to that repriced or modified award.

Instruction 3 to Item 402(c)(2)(v) and(vi). For any awards that are subject to performance conditions, report the value at the grant date based upon the probable outcome of such conditions. This amount should be consistent with the estimate of aggregate compensation cost to be recognized over the service period determined as of the grant date under FASB ASC Topic 718, excluding the effect of estimated forfeitures. In a footnote to the table, disclose the value of the award at the grant date assuming that the

预计可以确定该等工资或奖金数额的日期，届时必须按照《8-K表格》的第5.02(f)条(《联邦规章汇编》第十七编第249.308节)提交文件披露该等数额。

2.具名高管选择放弃工资或奖金，并因此收到股票、基于股权的报酬或其他形式的非现金报酬的，注册人应在工资栏[(c)栏]或奖金栏[(d)栏]填写该等被放弃的任何工资或奖金。但是，作为工资或奖金之替代而收到的任何此类形式的非现金报酬必须在工资或奖金栏的脚注中予以披露，同时，如适用在对具名高管选择的股票、期权或非股权激励奖励进行报告时，应按照本条第(d)款规定引用相关的《计划奖励授予表》。

(v)对于股票奖励，应按照《财务会计准则委员会会计准则汇编第718号专题》计算授予日的公允价值总额[(e)栏]；

(vi)对于期权奖励(包括后续转让的奖励)，无论是否附带并行的股票增值权，均应按照《财务会计准则委员会会计准则汇编第718号专题》计算授予日的公允价值总额[(f)栏]；

关于第402(c)(2)(v)条和第402(c)(2)(vi)条的说明1。对于在(e)栏和(f)栏报告的奖励，应插入一项脚注，借由引用注册人财务报表及其脚注中对假设条件的相关论述或者《管理层论述与分析》中的相关论述，披露估值中所采用的全部假设。所引用的条款应视为按照本条规定提供的披露内容的一部分。

关于第402(c)(2)(v)条和第402(c)(2)(vi)条的说明2。如果上一完整会计年度内的任何时候，注册人通过修正、撤销或者替换奖励授予的方式或任何其他方式，对之前授予具名高管的期权或股票增值权的行权价进行了调整或修正(“重新定价”)，或对奖励作出了其他重大修改，则注册人应在(f)栏的奖励中加入该等奖励在重新定价日或修改日的公允价值增值(按照《财务会计准则委员会会计准则汇编第718号专题》计算)。

关于第402(c)(2)(v)条和第402(c)(2)(vi)条的说明3。对于受业绩条件限制的任何奖励，应基于业绩条件可能实现的结果报告该奖励在授予日的价值。这一数额应与授予日按照《财务会计准则委员会会计准则汇编第718号专题》计算的应在任职期限内确认的报酬总成本估值(不考虑预计没收的影响)保持一致。如果表格中所报告的数额低于最高值，应在表格的脚注中披露假如业绩达到最高标准之时，奖励在授予日的价值。

highest level of performance conditions will be achieved if an amount less than the maximum was included in the table.

(vii) The dollar value of all earnings for services performed during the fiscal year pursuant to awards under non-equity incentive plans as defined in paragraph (a)(6)(iii) of this Item, and all earnings on any outstanding awards (column (g));

Instructions to Item 402(c)(2)(vii): 1. If the relevant performance measure is satisfied during the fiscal year (including for a single year in a plan with a multi-year performance measure), the earnings are reportable for that fiscal year, even if not payable until a later date, and are not reportable again in the fiscal year when amounts are paid to the named executive officer.

2. All earnings on non-equity incentive plan compensation must be identified and quantified in a footnote to column(g), whether the earnings were paid during the fiscal year, payable during the period but deferred at the election of the namedexecutive officer, or payable by their terms at a later date.

(viii) The sum of the amounts specified in paragraphs (c)(2)(viii)(A) and (B) of this Item (column (h)) as follows:

(A) The aggregate change in the actuarial present value of the namedexecutive officer's accumulated benefit under all defined benefit and actuarial pension plans (including supplemental plans) from the pension plan measurement date used for financial statement reporting purposes with respect to the registrant's audited financial statements for the prior completed fiscal year to the pension plan measurement date used for financial statement reporting purposes with respect to the registrant's audited financial statements for the covered fiscal year; and

(B) Above-market or preferential earnings on compensation that is deferred on a basis that is not tax-qualified, including such earnings on nonqualified defined contribution plans;

Instructions to Item 402(c)(2)(viii): 1. The disclosure required pursuant to paragraph (c)(2)(viii)(A) of this Item applies to each plan that provides for the payment of retirement benefits, or benefits that will be paid primarily following retirement, including but not limited to tax-qualified defined benefit plans and supplemental executive retirement plans, but excluding tax-qualified defined contribution plans and nonqualified defined contribution plans. For purposes of this disclosure, the registrant should use the same amounts required to be disclosed pursuant to paragraph (h)(2)(iv) of this Item for the covered fiscal year and the amounts that were or would have been required to be reported for the executive officer pursuant to paragraph (h)(2)(iv) of this Item for the prior completed fiscal year.

2. Regarding paragraph (c)(2)(viii)(B) of this Item, interest on deferred compensation

(vii)依据本条第(a)(6)(iii)款定义的非股权激励计划项下之奖励,在该会计年度内履行的服务的所有收益,以及任何未兑现奖励的所有收益的美元价值[(g)栏];

关于第402(c)(2)(vii)条的说明:1.如果某一会计年度内实现了相关业绩指标(包括在采用跨年业绩指标的计划内实现某一年的指标),则应对该会计年度的收益进行报告,即使该收益的应付日期在该会计年度之后,而在实际向具名高管支付的会计年度,不必再对该等数额进行报告。

2.基于非股权激励计划报酬获得的所有收益必须在(g)栏的脚注中注明,并予以量化,不论该等收益是在该会计年度支付,还是本应在该会计年度支付但具名高管选择递延支付,或者按其条款应在较晚日期支付。

(viii)本条第(c)(2)(viii)(A)款和第(c)(2)(viii)(B)款规定的下述金额之总计[(h)栏]:

(A)所有固定收益养老金和精算退休金计划(包括补充计划)项下具名高管的累计收益的精算现值在下述期间的变动总值:自注册人报告上一完整会计年度已审计财务报表时使用的退休金计划计量日,直至注册人报告所涉会计年度已审计财务报表时使用的退休金计划计量日;和

(B)在无税收优惠基础上递延支付的,高于市场水平或者优惠性的收益,包括从不能享受税收优惠的固定缴款养老金计划中获得的收益[(h)栏];

关于第402(c)(2)(viii)条的说明:1.本条第(c)(2)(viii)(A)款规定的披露适用于所有提供下述福利的计划:退休金或者主要在退休后发放的福利,包括但不限于符合税收优惠条件的固定收益养老金计划和补充高管退休金计划,但是不包括符合税收优惠条件的固定缴款养老金计划和不符合税收优惠条件的固定缴款养老金计划。就本款规定的披露而言,注册人使用的数额应为本条第(h)(2)(iv)款规定应就所涉会计年度披露的数额,以及根据本条第(h)(2)(iv)款规定就上一完整会计年度针对高管报告的数额,或本应就上一完整会计年度针对高管报告的数额。

2.就本条第(c)(2)(viii)(B)款而言,只有递延报酬的利率进行复利计算后超过相

is above-market only if the rate of interest exceeds 120% of the applicable federal long-term rate, with compounding (as prescribed under section 1274 (d) of the Internal Revenue Code, (26 U.S.C. 1274(d))) at the rate that corresponds most closely to the rate under the registrant's plan at the time the interest rate or formula is set. In the event of a discretionary reset of the interest rate, the requisite calculation must be made on the basis of the interest rate at the time of such reset, rather than when originally established. Only the above-market portion of the interest must be included. If the applicable interest rates vary depending upon conditions such as a minimum period of continued service, the reported amount should be calculated assuming satisfaction of all conditions to receiving interest at the highest rate. Dividends (and dividend equivalents) on deferred compensation denominated in the registrant's stock ("deferred stock") are preferential only if earned at a rate higher than dividends on the registrant's common stock. Only the preferential portion of the dividends or equivalents must be included. Footnote or narrative disclosure may be provided explaining the registrant's criteria for determining any portion considered to be above-market.

3. The registrant shall identify and quantify by footnote the separate amounts attributable to each of paragraphs (c)(2)(viii)(A) and (B) of this Item. Where such amount pursuant to paragraph (c)(2)(viii)(A) is negative, it should be disclosed by footnote but should not be reflected in the sum reported in column (h).

(ix) All other compensation for the covered fiscal year that the registrant could not properly report in any other column of the Summary Compensation Table (column (i)). Each compensation item that is not properly reportable in columns (c)-(h), regardless of the amount of the compensation item, must be included in column (i). Such compensation must include, but is not limited to:

(A) Perquisites and other personal benefits, or property, unless the aggregate amount of such compensation is less than $10,000;

(B) All "gross-ups" or other amounts reimbursed during the fiscal year for the payment of taxes;

(C) For any security of the registrant or its subsidiaries purchased from the registrant or its subsidiaries (through deferral of salary or bonus, or otherwise) at a discount from the market price of such security at the date of purchase, unless that discount is available generally, either to all security holders or to all salaried employees of the registrant, the compensation cost, if any, computed in accordance with FAS 123R;

(D) The amount paid or accrued to any namedexecutive officer pursuant to a plan or arrangement in connection with:

(1) Any termination, including without limitation through retirement, resignation, severance or constructive termination (including a change in responsibilities) of such

关联邦长期利率120%时,递延报酬的利息才能被认定为高于市场水平,复利计算以《国内税收法典》第1274(d)条[《美国法典》第二十六编第1274(d)节)]的规定为准,计算复利所采用的利率应为设定利率或公式时与注册人计划项中的利率最接近的利率。如遇自主调息,必须采用调息时的利率而非最初设定的利率。只有高于市场水平的利息才须纳入报告范围。如果相关利率因最短持续服务期限等条件有所不同,则在计算应报告数额时,应假定收取按最高利率计算之利息所需的条件均已满足。高管获得的以注册人股票("递延股票")表示的递延报酬的股息(及股息等价物),只有在其股息率高于注册人普通股股息率的情况下,才能被认定为优惠性的收益。股息或股息等价物只有具优惠性的部分须要纳入报告范围。脚注或文字披露可被用做解释注册人确定"高于市场水平"时适用的标准。

3.注册人应以脚注分别注明本条第(c)(2)(viii)(A)款和第(c)(2)(viii)(B)款中的金额,并予以量化。如果第(c)(2)(viii)(A)款中的金额为负数,应通过脚注予以披露,但是不应反映在(h)栏所报告的数额总和中。

(ix)注册人无法在《报酬简表》的任何其他栏目予以适当报告的所涉会计年度的所有其他报酬[(i)栏]。无法在(c)-(h)栏予以适当报告的报酬项目(不论报酬数额多少),均必须在(i)栏列出。该等报酬必须包括但不限于以下各项:

(A)特殊津贴及其他个人福利或财产,但总金额低于1万美元的除外;

(B)该会计年度为缴税而提供的所有"税款补足"或其他补偿数额;

(C)对于按低于购买日股票市价的价格,通过工资或奖金递延支付或其他方式从注册人或其子公司折价购买的注册人或其子公司的任何证券而言,其按照《美国财务会计准则公告第123号》(FAS 123R)计算的报酬成本(如有),但所有证券持有人或注册人的所有受薪雇员均可享受该折扣的除外;

(D)按照与下列事项有关的计划或安排而已向或应向任何具名高管支付的数额:

(1)任何该等高管与注册人及其子公司雇佣关系的终止,包括但不限于退休、辞职、辞退或推定解除雇佣关系(包括职责变更);或者

executive officer's employment with the registrant and its subsidiaries; or

(2) A change in control of the registrant;

(E) Registrant contributions or other allocations to vested and unvested defined contribution plans;

(F) The dollar value of any insurance premiums paid by, or on behalf of, the registrant during the covered fiscal year with respect to life insurance for the benefit of a named executive officer; and

(G) The dollar value of any dividends or other earnings paid on stock or option awards, when those amounts were not factored into the grant date fair value required to be reported for the stock or option award in column (e) or (f); and

Instructions to Item 402 (c) (2) (ix): 1. Non-equity incentive plan awards and earnings and earnings on stock and options, except as specified in paragraph (c)(2)(ix)(G) of this Item, are required to be reported elsewhere as provided in this Item and are not reportable as All Other Compensation in column (i).

2. Benefits paid pursuant to defined benefit and actuarial plans are not reportable as All Other Compensation in column (i) unless accelerated pursuant to a change in control; information concerning these plans is reportable pursuant to paragraphs(c)(2)(viii)(A) and (h) of this Item.

3. Any item reported for a namedexecutive officer pursuant to paragraph (c)(2)(ix) of this Item that is not a perquisite or personal benefit and whose value exceeds $10,000 must be identified and quantified in a footnote to column(i). This requirement applies only to compensation for the last fiscal year. All items of compensation are required to be included in the Summary Compensation Table without regard to whether such items are required to be identified other than as specifically noted in this Item.

4. Perquisites and personal benefits may be excluded as long as the total value of all perquisites and personal benefits for a namedexecutive officer is less than $10,000. If the total value of all perquisites and personal benefits is $10,000 or more for any named executive officer, then each perquisite or personal benefit, regardless of its amount, must be identified by type. If perquisites and personal benefits are required to be reported for a named executive officer pursuant to this rule, then each perquisite or personal benefit that exceeds the greater of $25,000 or 10% of the total amount of perquisites and personal benefits for that officer must be quantified and disclosed in a footnote. The requirements for identification and quantification apply only to compensation for the last fiscal year. Perquisites and other personal benefits shall be valued on the basis of the aggregate incremental cost to the registrant. With respect to the perquisite or other personal benefit for which footnote quantification is required, the registrant shall describe in the footnote its methodology for computing the aggregate incremental cost. Reimbursements of taxes

(2)注册人发生控制权变更;

(E)注册人对已归属及未归属的固定缴款养老金计划的供款或其他拨款;

(F)注册人或其代表在所涉会计年度为具名高管之利益缴纳的任何人寿保险保费的美元价值;和

(G)在计算(e)栏或(f)栏要求报告的股票或期权奖励在授予日的公允价值时,未予考虑的股票或期权奖励的任何股息或其他收益的美元价值;和

关于第402(c)(2)(ix)条的说明:1.非股权激励计划奖励和收益及股票和期权收益,除本条第(c)(2)(ix)(G)款另有明确规定外,须按本条规定通过其他栏目报告,不必在(i)栏作为“所有其他报酬”披露。

2.依据固定收益养老金计划和精算计划支付的福利,除非因控制权变更提前转归,否则不必作为“所有其他报酬”在(i)栏项下报告;关于该等计划的信息应按照本条第(c)(2)(viii)(A)款和第(h)款予以报告。

3.按本条第(c)(2)(ix)款针对具名高管报告的价值超过1万美元,但不属于津贴或个人福利的任何项目必须在(i)栏脚注中注明,并予以量化。这一要求仅适用于上一会计年度的报酬。所有报酬项目均必须在《报酬简表》中列明,不论除本条明确规定以外,是否有其他规定要求列明这些项目。

4.具名高管的全部津贴和个人福利的总价值低于1万美元的,可不设列津贴和个人福利项目。如果任何一名具名高管的全部津贴和个人福利的总价值为1万美元(含)以上,则每项津贴或个人福利均应分类列明,不论其金额多少。如果按照本规则规定需要报告某名具名高管的津贴和个人福利,则每项超过2.5万美元或者该高管津贴和个人福利总额10%(以较高者为准)的津贴或个人福利必须在脚注中予以量化和披露。注明和量化规定仅适用于上一会计年度的报酬。津贴和其他个人福利应以注册人的总增量成本为基础进行估值。对于须要在脚注中予以量化的津贴或其他个人福利,注册人应在脚注中阐明其计算总增量成本所使用的方法。与津贴或其他个人福利相关的退税必须列入(i)栏,并作为退税单独予以量化和注明[本条第(c)(2)(ix)(B)款],即使根据上文的规定,具名高管个人的全部津贴或个人福利因其总额低于1万美元而不必列明,或者要求注明但不要求单独量化。

owed with respect to perquisites or other personal benefits must be included in column (i) and are subject to separate quantification and identification as tax reimbursements (paragraph (c)(2)(ix)(B) of this Item) even if the associated perquisites or other personal benefits are not required to be included because the total amount of all perquisites or personal benefits for an individual named executive officer is less than $10,000 or are required to be identified but are not required to be separately quantified.

5. For purposes of paragraph (c)(2)(ix)(D) of this Item, an accrued amount is an amount for which payment has become due.

(x) The dollar value of total compensation for the covered fiscal year (column (j)). With respect to each namedexecutive officer, disclose the sum of all amounts reported in columns (c) through (i).

Instructions to Item 402(c): 1. Information with respect to fiscal years prior to the last completed fiscal year will not be required if the registrant was not a reporting company pursuant to section 13(a) or 15(d) of the Exchange Act (15 U.S.C. 78m(a) or 78o(d)) at any time during that year, except that the registrant will be required to provide information for any such year if that information previously was required to be provided in response to a Commission filing requirement.

2. All compensation values reported in the Summary Compensation Table must be reported in dollars and rounded to the nearest dollar. Reported compensation values must be reported numerically, providing a single numerical value for each grid in the table. Where compensation was paid to or received by a namedexecutive officer in a different currency, a footnote must be provided to identify that currency and describe the rate and methodology used to convert the payment amounts to dollars.

3. If a named executive officer is also a director who receives compensation for his or her services as a director, reflect that compensation in the Summary Compensation Table and provide a footnote identifying and itemizing such compensation and amounts. Use the categories in the Director Compensation Table required pursuant to paragraph (k) of this Item.

4. Any amounts deferred, whether pursuant to a plan established under section 401(k) of the Internal Revenue Code (26 U.S.C. 401(k)), or otherwise, shall be included in the appropriate column for the fiscal year in which earned.

(d) *Grants of plan-based awards table*. (1) Provide the information specified in paragraph (d)(2) of this Item, concerning each grant of an award made to a named executive officer in the last completed fiscal year under any plan, including awards that subsequently have been transferred, in the following tabular format:

5.就本条第(c)(2)(ix)(D)款而言,应计金额为到期应付金额。

(x)所涉会计年度总报酬的美元价值[(j)栏]。对于每名具名高管,披露在(c)栏至(i)栏报告的全部金额的总和。

关于第402(c)条的说明:1.如果注册人在上一完整会计年度之前的会计年度的任何时间不属于《交易法》第13(a)条或第15(d)条[《美国法典》第十五编第78m(a)节或第78o(d)节]规定的报告公司,则不必披露关于该会计年度的信息,但是如果按照证券交易委员会的文件提交规定应提供任何该等年度信息,则注册人应予提供。

2.在《报酬简表》中报告的所有报酬均应以美元为单位,并四舍五入取整。所报告的报酬价值必须采用数字形式,表格的每个单元格中仅提供一个数值。如果具名高管的报酬是以其他货币收付的,则必须通过脚注注明所使用的币种,并载明将所付金额转换成美元时采用的汇率和方法。

3.如果某位具名高管同时兼任受薪董事,应在《报酬简表》中反映其担任董事所获得的报酬,并通过脚注注明该报酬及金额项目明细。在进行上述报告时,应采用本条第(k)款规定的《董事报酬表》中划定的类别。

4.根据《国内税收法典》第401(k)条[(《美国法典》第二十六编第401(k)节]下设立的计划或因其他原因而递延支付的任何金额,应在赚取该金额的会计年度的相关栏目内列报。

(d)计划奖励授予表。(1)通过以下表格,就上一完整会计年度依据任何计划授予某位具名高管的每项奖励(包括后续转让的奖励)提供本条第(d)(2)款规定的信息:

Grants of Plan–Based Awards

Name	Grant date	Estimated future payouts under non – equity incentive plan awards			Estimated future payouts under equity incentive plan awards			All other stock awards: Number of shares of stock or units (#)	All other option awards: Number of securities underlying options (#)	Exercise or base price of option awards ($/Sh)	Grant date fair value of stock and option awards
		Threshold ($)	Target ($)	Maximum ($)	Threshold (#)	Target (#)	Maximum (#)				
(a)	(b)	(c)	(d)	(e)	(f)	(g)	(h)	(i)	(j)	(k)	(l)
PEO											
PFO											
A											
B											
C											

(2) The Table shall include:

(i) The name of the namedexecutive officer (column (a));

(ii) The grant date for equity–based awards reported in the table (column (b)). If such grant date is different than the date on which the compensation committee (or a committee of the board of directors performing a similar function or the full board of directors) takes action or is deemed to take action to grant such awards, a separate, adjoining column shall be added between columns (b) and (c) showing such date;

(iii) The dollar value of the estimated future payout upon satisfaction of the conditions in question under non–equity incentive plan awards granted in the fiscal year, or the applicable range of estimated payouts denominated in dollars (threshold, target and maximum amount) (columns (c) through (e));

(iv) The number of shares of stock, or the number of shares underlying options to be paid out or vested upon satisfaction of the conditions in question under equity incentive plan awards granted in the fiscal year, or the applicable range of estimated payouts denominated in the number of shares of stock, or the number of shares underlying options under the award (threshold, target and maximum amount) (columns (f) through (h));

(v) The number of shares of stock granted in the fiscal year that are not required to be disclosed in columns (f) through (h) (column (i));

计划奖励授予表

姓名	授予日期	非股权激励计划奖励的预计支付额			股权激励计划奖励的预计支付额			所有其他股票奖励：股票或单位数量(#)	所有其他期权奖励：期权标的证券数目(#)	期权奖励行权价或底价（美元/Sh）	股票和期权奖励在授予日的公允价值
		基准数额（美元）	目标额（美元）	最高额（美元）	基准数额（#）	目标额（#）	最高额（#）				
(a)	(b)	(c)	(d)	(e)	(f)	(g)	(h)	(i)	(j)	(k)	(l)
主要高管											
主要财务官											
A											
B											
C											

(2)计划奖励授予表应包括：

(i)具名高管姓名[(a)栏]；

(ii)表中报告的基于股权的奖励的授予日期[(b)栏]。如果该授予日期与报酬委员会(或者董事会或履行类似职责的董事会下属委员会)采取奖励授予行动或者视为采取奖励授予行动的日期不同,应在(b)栏和(c)栏之间增列一栏,注明采取上述行动的日期;

(iii)在相关条件满足之时,该会计年度授予的非股权激励计划奖励的预计支付的美元价值,或者以美元表示的预计支付额的范围(基准数额、目标额及最高额)[(c)栏至(e)栏];

(iv)在相关条件满足之时,根据该会计年度授予的股权激励计划奖励将予以支付或归属的股票数量、期权标的股份数量,或者该等数量的预计范围(基准数额、目标额及最高额)[(f)栏至(h)栏];

(v)会计年度内授予的不必通过(f)栏至(h)栏披露的股份数量[(i)栏];

(vi) The number of securities underlying options granted in the fiscal year that are not required to be disclosed in columns (f) through (h) (column (j));

(vii) The per-share exercise or base price of the options granted in the fiscal year (column(k)). If such exercise or base price is less than the closing market price of the underlying security on the date of the grant, a separate, adjoining column showing the closing market price on the date of the grant shall be added after column (k); and

(viii) The grant date fair value of each equity award computed in accordance with FAS 123R(column(*l*)). If at any time during the last completed fiscal year, the registrant has adjusted or amended the exercise or base price of options, SARs or similar option-like instruments previously awarded to a named executive officer, whether through amendment, cancellation or replacement grants, or any other means ("repriced"), or otherwise has materially modified such awards, the incremental fair value, computed as of the repricing or modification date in accordance with FAS 123R, with respect to that repriced or modified award, shall be reported.

Instructions to Item 402(d): 1. Disclosure on a separate line shall be provided in the Table for each grant of an award made to a named executive officer during the fiscal year. If grants of awards were made to a named executive officer during the fiscal year under more than one plan, identify the particular plan under which each such grant was made.

2. For grants of incentive plan awards, provide the information called for by columns (c), (d) and (e), or (f), (g) and (h), as applicable. For columns (c) and (f), *threshold* refers to the minimum amount payable for a certain level of performance under the plan. For columns (d) and (g), *target* refers to the amount payable if the specified performance target(s) are reached. For columns (e) and (h), *maximum* refers to the maximum payout possible under the plan. If the award provides only for a single estimated payout, that amount must be reported as the *target* in columns (d) and (g). In columns (d) and (g), registrants must provide a representative amount based on the previous fiscal year's performance if the target amount is not determinable.

3. In determining if the exercise or base price of an option is less than the closing market price of the underlying security on the date of the grant, the registrant may use either the closing market price as specified in paragraph (a)(6)(v) of this Item, or if no market exists, any other formula prescribed for the security. Whenever the exercise or base price reported in column (k) is not the closing market price, describe the methodology for determining the exercise or base price either by a footnote or accompanying textual narrative.

4. A tandem grant of two instruments, only one of which is granted under an incentive plan, such as an option granted in tandem with a performance share, need be reported only in column(i) or(j), as applicable. For example, an option granted in tandem

(vi)会计年度内授予的不必通过(f)栏至(h)栏披露的期权项下的标的证券的数量[(j)栏];

(vii)会计年度内授予的期权的每股行权价或底价[(k)栏]。该等行权价或底价低于标的证券在授予日的市场收盘价的,应紧接(k)栏之后增设一栏,列报授予日的市场收盘价;及

(viii)按照《财务会计准则公告第123R号》(FAS123R)计算的每一份基于股权的奖励在授予日的公允价值[(*l*)栏]。如果注册人在上一会计年度的任何时候通过修正、撤销或替代性授予或任何其他方式对此前授予具名高管的期权、股票增值权或其他与期权类似的工具的行权价或底价进行了调整或修正("重新定价"),或以其他方式对上述奖励进行了实质修改,应按照《财务会计准则公告第123R号》计算该等奖励截至"重新定价"日或修改日的公允价值增值,并进行报告。

关于第402(d)条的说明:1.表格中应以单独一行披露会计年度内向具名高管授予的每项奖励。在会计年度内依据一项以上的计划向具名高管授予奖励的,应明确指明每项授予根据的是哪一项计划。

2.就激励计划项下的奖励授予而言,应根据具体情况,按(c)栏、(d)栏和(e)栏,或(f)栏、(g)栏和(h)栏的要求提供相关信息。(c)栏和(f)栏中的"基准数额"系指:实现计划项下特定的业绩水平时应予支付的最低数额。(d)栏和(g)栏中的"目标额"系指:达到规定的业绩目标时应予支付的数额。(e)栏和(h)栏中的"最高额"系指:计划中规定的可能的最高支付数额。如果奖励仅提供了一个预估支付数额,该数额必须在(d)栏和(g)栏作为"目标额"报告。如果目标额无法确定,注册人必须基于上一会计年度的业绩,在(d)栏和(g)栏中提供一个代表性的数额。

3.注册人在判断某项期权的行权价或底价是否低于授予日标的证券的市场收盘价时,可使用本条第(a)(6)(v)款明确规定的市场收盘价,如果不存在相关市场,则可使用针对证券规定的任何其他计算公式。如果(k)栏中报告的行权价或底价不是市场收盘价,请通过脚注或随附的文字说明确定行权价或底价的方法。

4.并行授予两种工具,且仅其中一种工具系根据激励计划授予的(如在授予一份期权的同时并行授予一份业绩股),该授予只须视具体情况在(i)栏或(j)栏中报告。例如,在授予一份期权的同时并行授予一份业绩股的,仅须在(j)栏中作为期权授予报

with a performance share would be reported only as an option grant in column(j), with the tandem feature noted either by a footnote or accompanying textual narrative.

5. Disclose the dollar amount of consideration, if any, paid by theexecutive officer for the award in a footnote to the appropriate column.

6. If non-equity incentive plan awards are denominated in units or other rights, a separate, adjoining column between columns (b) and (c) shall be added quantifying the units or other rights awarded.

7. Options, SARs and similar option-like instruments granted in connection with a repricing transaction or other material modification shall be reported in this Table. However, the disclosure required by this Table does not apply to any repricing that occurs through a pre-existing formula or mechanism in the plan or award that results in the periodic adjustment of the option or SAR exercise or base price, an antidilution provision in a plan or award, or a recapitalization or similar transaction equally affecting all holders of the class of securities underlying the options or SARs.

8. For any equity awards that are subject to performance conditions, report in column (l) the value at the grant date based upon the probable outcome of such conditions. This amount should be consistent with the estimate of aggregate compensation cost to be recognized over the service period determined as of the grant date under FASB ASC Topic 718, excluding the effect of estimated forfeitures.

(e) *Narrative disclosure to summary compensation table and grants of plan-based awards table.* (1) Provide a narrative description of any material factors necessary to an understanding of the information disclosed in the tables required by paragraphs(c) and (d) of this Item. Examples of such factors may include, in given cases, among other things:

(i) The material terms of each namedexecutive officer's employment agreement or arrangement, whether written or unwritten;

(ii) If at any time during the last fiscal year, any outstanding option or other equity-based award was repriced or otherwise materially modified(such as by extension of exercise periods, the change of vesting or forfeiture conditions, the change or elimination of applicable performance criteria, or the change of the bases upon which returns are determined), a description of each such repricing or other material modification;

(iii) The material terms of any award reported in response to paragraph (d) of this Item, including a general description of the formula or criteria to be applied in determining the amounts payable, and the vesting schedule. For example, state where applicable that dividends will be paid on stock, and if so, the applicable dividend rate and whether that rate is preferential. Describe any performance-based conditions, and any other material conditions, that are applicable to the award. For purposes of the Table

告,并通过脚注或随附的文字说明其并行授予的性质。

5.高级管理人员就奖励支付任何对价的,应在适当栏目的脚注中披露对价的金额。

6.非根据股权激励计划授予的奖励以单位或其他权利表示其面值的,应在(b)栏和(c)栏之间增列一栏对上述授予的单位或权利进行量化说明。

7.因开展重新定价交易或进行其他重大修改而授予的期权、股票增值权及其他与期权类似的工具应在本表中报告。但是,计划或奖励中事先设定了公式或机制,对期权或股票增值权的行权价或底价进行定期调整,由此导致的任何重新定价均不适用本表的披露要求;此外,激励计划或奖励中的反稀释条款,或对期权或股票增值权项下同一类别标的证券的全部持有者产生同等影响的资本重组或类似交易,亦不适用本表的披露要求。

8.基于股权的奖励受制于业绩条件的,应基于该等条件可能实现的结果在(l)栏中报告奖励在授予日的价值。这一数额应与授予日按照《财务会计准则委员会会计准则汇编第718号专题》计算的应在任职期限内确认的报酬总成本估计数额(不考虑预计没收的影响)保持一致。

(e)对《报酬简表》和激励计划奖励授予表的文字披露。(1)对于本条第(c)款和第(d)款要求在上述表格中披露的信息,应就理解该等信息所必要的任何重大因素提供文字说明。例如,视具体情况,此类因素可包括但不限于:

(i)每一具名高管书面或非书面的雇佣协议或安排中的重大条款;

(ii)对每一项重新定价或重大修改的说明,前提是在上一会计年度内任何时间对任何未兑现的期权或其他基于股权的奖励进行了重新定价或其他重大修改(如行权期限被延长、归属或丧失条件发生变更、适用业绩标准被变更或取消,或者确定回报的基准发生变更);

(iii)本条第(d)款要求报告的任何奖励的重大条款,包括对确定应付数额的公式或标准和归属时间表的总体说明。例如,说明将就股票支付股息(如适用),此时,应说明适用的股息率,同时如股息率具有优先性,亦应予注明。对适用于任何奖励的业绩条件及任何其他重大条件进行说明。就本条第(d)款规定的表格和本条第(e)款规定的文字披露而言,业绩条件包括《财务会计准则公告第123R号》中定义的业绩条件和市场条件;及

required by paragraph (d) of this Item and the narrative disclosure required by paragraph (e) of this Item, performance-based conditions include both performance conditions and market conditions, as those terms are defined in FAS 123R; and

(iv) An explanation of the amount of salary and bonus in proportion to total compensation.

Instructions to Item 402(e)(1). 1. The disclosure required by paragraph (e)(1)(ii) of this Item would not apply to any repricing that occurs through a pre-existing formula or mechanism in the plan or award that results in the periodic adjustment of the option or SAR exercise or base price, an antidilution provision in a plan or award, or a recapitalization or similar transaction equally affecting all holders of the class of securities underlying the options or SARs.

2. Instructions 4 and 5 to Item 402(b) apply regarding disclosure pursuant to paragraph (e)(1) of this Item of target levels with respect to specific quantitative or qualitative performance-related factors considered by the compensation committee or the board of directors, or any other factors or criteria involving confidential trade secrets or confidential commercial or financial information, the disclosure of which would result in competitive harm for the registrant.

(2) [Reserved]

(f) *Outstanding equity awards at fiscal year-end table.* (1) Provide the information specified in paragraph (f)(2) of this Item, concerning unexercised options; stock that has not vested; and equity incentive plan awards for each named executive officer outstanding as of the end of the registrant's last completed fiscal year in the following tabular format:

Outstanding Equity Awards at Fiscal Year-End

	Option awards					Stock awards			
Name	Number of securities underlying unexercised options (#) exercisable	Number of securities underlying unexercised options (#) unexercisable	Equity incentive plan awards: number of securities underlying unexercised unearned options (#)	Option exercise price ($)	Option expiration date	Number of shares or units of stock that have not vested (#)	Market value of shares or units of stock that have not vested (#)	Equity incentive plan awards: number of unearned shares, units or other rights that have not vested (#)	Equity incentive plan awards: market or payout value of unearned shares, units or other rights that have not vested ($)

(iv)工资和奖金在总报酬中所占比例的说明。

关于第402(e)(1)条的说明。1.计划或奖励中事先设定了公式或机制,对期权或股票增值权的行权价或底价进行定期调整,由此导致的任何重新定价均不适用本条第(e)(1)(ii)款的披露要求;此外,激励计划或奖励中的反稀释条款,或对期权或股票增值权项下同类别标的证券的全部持有者产生同等影响的资本重组或类似交易,亦不适用本条第(e)(1)(ii)款的披露要求。

2.第402条(b)条的说明4和说明5适用于根据本条第(e)(1)款对如下事项进行的披露:报酬委员会或董事会考虑范围内的与绩效有关的具体定量或定性因素目标水平,或涉及商业秘密或机密性商业或财务信息,且披露之后会令注册人遭受竞争性损害的任何其他因素或标准。

(2)[保留]

(f)会计年度年末未兑现的股权奖励表。(1)在下列表格中提供本条第(f)(2)款规定的与如下各项相关的信息:截至注册人上一会计年度年末每一具名高管未行使的期权、尚未归属的股票以及未兑现的股权激励计划奖励。

会计年度年末未兑现的股权奖励

姓名	期权奖励					股票奖励			
	可行使但未行使的期权项下的标的证券数量(#)	不可行使且未行使的期权项下的标的证券数量(#)	股权激励计划奖励:未行使且尚未赚取的期权项下的标的证券数量(#)	期权行权价(美元)	期权到期日	尚未归属的股份或股票单位数量(#)	尚未归属的股份或股票单位的市值(#)	股权激励计划奖励:尚未赚取的或尚未归属的股份、单位或其他权利数量(#)	股权激励计划奖励:尚未赚取的或尚未归属的股份、单位或其他权利的市或支付价值(美元)

(a)	(b)	(c)	(d)	(e)	(f)	(g)	(h)	(i)	(j)
PEO									
PFO									
A									
B									
C									

(2) The Table shall include:

(i) The name of the namedexecutive officer (column (a));

(ii) On an award-by-award basis, the number of securities underlying unexercised options, including awards that have been transferred other than for value, that are exercisable and that are not reported in column (d) (column (b));

(iii) On an award-by-award basis, the number of securities underlying unexercised options, including awards that have been transferred other than for value, that are unexercisable and that are not reported in column (d) (column (c));

(iv) On an award-by-award basis, the total number of shares underlying unexercised options awarded under any equity incentive plan that have not been earned (column (d));

(v) For each instrument reported in columns (b), (c) and (d), as applicable, the exercise or base price (column (e));

(vi) For each instrument reported in columns (b), (c) and (d), as applicable, the expiration date (column (f));

(vii) The total number of shares of stock that have not vested and that are not reported in column (i) (column (g));

(viii) The aggregate market value of shares of stock that have not vested and that are not reported in column (j) (column (h));

(ix) The total number of shares of stock, units or other rights awarded under any equity incentive plan that have not vested and that have not been earned, and, if applicable the number of shares underlying any such unit or right (column (i)); and

(x) The aggregate market or payout value of shares of stock, units or other rights

续表

(a)	(b)	(c)	(d)	(e)	(f)	(g)	(h)	(i)	(j)
主要高管									
主要财务官									
A									
B									
C									

(2)表格中应包括:

(i)具名高管姓名[(a)栏];

(ii)按奖励逐一列明可行使且未在(d)栏报告的尚未行使的期权(包括已无偿转让的奖励)项下的标的证券数量[(b)栏];

(iii)按奖励逐一列明不可行使的且未在(d)栏报告的尚未行使的期权(包括已无偿转让的奖励)项下的标的证券数量[(c)栏];

(iv)按奖励逐一列明根据任何股权激励计划授予的尚未赚取且尚未行使的期权项下的标的股份的总数[(d)栏];

(v)(b)栏、(c)栏和(d)栏中(视具体情况而定)报告的每一工具的行权价或底价[(e)栏];

(vi)如适用,(b)栏、(c)栏和(d)栏中(视具体情况而定)报告的每一工具的到期日[(f)栏];

(vii)未在(i)栏报告的且尚未归属的股份总数[(g)栏];

(viii)未在(j)栏报告的且尚未归属的股份的总市值[(h)栏]。

(ix)任何股权激励计划下授予但尚未归属和尚未赚取的股份、单位或其他权利的总数,和(如适用)上述任何单位或权利项下的标的股份的数量[(i)栏];及

(x)任何股权激励计划下授予但尚未归属和尚未赚取的股份、单位或其他权利的

awarded under any equity incentive plan that have not vested and that have not been earned (column (j)).

Instructions to Item 402 (f)(2): 1. Identify by footnote any award that has been transferred other than for value, disclosing the nature of the transfer.

2. The vesting dates of options, shares of stock and equity incentive plan awards held at fiscal-year end must be disclosed by footnote to the applicable column where the outstanding award is reported.

3. Compute the market value of stock reported in column (h) and equity incentive plan awards of stock reported in column (j) by multiplying the closing market price of the registrant's stock at the end of the last completed fiscal year by the number of shares or units of stock or the amount of equity incentive plan awards, respectively. The number of shares or units reported in columns (d) or (i), and the payout value reported in column (j), shall be based on achieving threshold performance goals, except that if the previous fiscal year's performance has exceeded the threshold, the disclosure shall be based on the next higher performance measure (target or maximum) that exceeds the previous fiscal year's performance. If the award provides only for a single estimated payout, that amount should be reported. If the target amount is not determinable, registrants must provide a representative amount based on the previous fiscal year's performance.

4. Multiple awards may be aggregated where the expiration date and the exercise and/or base price of the instruments is identical. A single award consisting of a combination of options, SARs and/or similar option-like instruments shall be reported as separate awards with respect to each tranche with a different exercise and/or base price or expiration date.

5. Options or stock awarded under an equity incentive plan are reported in columns (d) or (i) and (j), respectively, until the relevant performance condition has been satisfied. Once the relevant performance condition has been satisfied, even if the option or stock award is subject to forfeiture conditions, options are reported in column (b) or (c), as appropriate, until they are exercised or expire, or stock is reported in columns (g) and (h) until it vests.

(g) *Option exercises and stock vested table*. (1) Provide the information specified in paragraph (g)(2) of this Item, concerning each exercise of stock options, SARs and similar instruments, and each vesting of stock, including restricted stock, restricted stock units and similar instruments, during the last completed fiscal year for each of the named executive officers on an aggregated basis in the following tabular format:

总市值或支付价值[(j)栏]。

关于第402(f)(2)条的说明:1.通过脚注说明任何已经无偿转让的奖励,并披露转让的性质。

2.截至会计年度年末尚未兑现的期权、股份和股权激励计划奖励的归属日期,必须在报告相关奖励的栏目添加脚注予以披露。

3.(h)栏中报告的股票市值和(j)栏中报告的股权激励计划奖励的市值应分别通过如下方式计算:注册人截至上一会计年度年末的股票市场收盘价乘以股份或股票单位数量,或乘以股权激励计划奖励的数量。(d)栏或(i)栏中报告的股份或单位数量,以及(j)栏中报告的支付价值,应基于所实现的业绩基准目标计算;但是上一会计年度业绩表现超出上述基准的,上述份额或单位数量应基于超出上一会计年度业绩的更高一级的业绩指标(目标额或最高额)进行披露。如果奖励仅提供了一个预估支付数额,应报告该支付数额。如果目标额无法确定,注册人必须基于上一会计年度的业绩,提供一个代表性的数额。

4.如不同工具的到期日和行权价及/或底价相同,可将多项奖励予以合计。由期权、股票升值权及/或与期权类似的工具混合构成的单一奖励,如各构成部分的行权价及/或底价或到期日不同,应作为不同的奖励分别报告。

5.在相关业绩条件满足之前,根据股权激励计划授予的期权或股票应分别通过(d)栏或(i)栏和(j)栏报告。一旦相关业绩条件得到满足之后,即使期权或股票奖励仍受制于丧失条件,在期权行使或到期前,期权仍应视适当情况通过(b)栏或(c)栏报告,在归属之前,股票仍应通过(g)栏和(h)栏报告。

(g)期权行使和股票归属表。(1)在下列表格中提供本条第(g)(2)款规定的与以下各项相关的信息:上一完整会计年度中每一具名高管行使的股票期权、股票增值权及类似工具的合计总额,以及获得归属的股票(包括受限股票、受限股票单位和类似工具)的合计总额:

Option Exercises and Stock Vested

Name	Option awards		Stock awards	
	Number of shares acquired on exercise (#)	Value realized on exercise($)	Number of shares acquired on vesting (#)	Value realized on vesting ($)
(a)	(b)	(c)	(d)	(e)
PEO				
PFO				
A				
B				
C				

(2) The Table shall include:

(i) The name of theexecutive officer (column (a));

(ii) The number of securities for which the options were exercised (column (b));

(iii) The aggregate dollar value realized upon exercise of options, or upon the transfer of an award for value (column (c));

(iv) The number of shares of stock that have vested (column (d)); and

(v) The aggregate dollar value realized upon vesting of stock, or upon the transfer of an award for value (column (e)).

Instruction to Item 402(g)(2). Report in column(c) the aggregate dollar amount realized by the named executive officer upon exercise of the options or upon the transfer of such instruments for value. Compute the dollar amount realized upon exercise by determining the difference between the market price of the underlying securities at exercise and the exercise or base price of the options. Do not include the value of any related payment or other consideration provided (or to be provided) by the registrant to or on behalf of a named executive officer, whether in payment of the exercise price or related taxes. (Any such payment or other consideration provided by the registrant is required to be disclosed in accordance with paragraph (c)(2)(ix) of this Item.) Report in column (e) the aggregate dollar amount realized by the named executive officer upon the vesting

期权行使和股票归属

姓名	期权奖励		股票奖励	
	行使期权获得的股份数量(#)	行使期权实现的价值(美元)	股票归属时获得的股份数量(#)	股票归属时实现的价值(美元)
(a)	(b)	(c)	(d)	(e)
主要高管				
主要财务官				
A				
B				
C				

(2)表格中应包括:

(i)高管姓名[(a)栏];

(ii)已行使期权项下的证券数量[(b)栏];

(iii)行使期权时或有偿转让某项奖励时实现的美元总价值[(c)栏];

(iv)已归属股票的股数[(d)栏];及

(v)股票归属时或有偿转让某项奖励时实现的美元总价值[(e)栏]。

关于第402(g)(2)条的说明。在(c)栏报告具名高管行使期权或有偿转让该等工具时实现的总额。行权时实现的总额应通过确定下述差额计算:行权时标的证券的市场价格与期权行权价或底价之间的差额。计算时不应考虑注册人向具名高管或代具名高管进行的任何相关支付或提供的(或将提供的)其他对价(不论是行权价或相关税金)的价值[注册人进行的上述任何支付或提供的其他对价均应按照本条第(c)(2)(ix)款的要求披露]。在(e)栏中报告具名高管在股票归属或有偿转让该等工具时实现的总额。归属时实现的总额应通过如下方式计算:股份或单位的数量乘以归属日标的股份的市值。行权或归属时实现的任何金额,如收款时出现递延,应在脚注中说明该金额总数,并披露该项递延的条件。

of stock or the transfer of such instruments for value. Compute the aggregate dollar amount realized upon vesting by multiplying the number of shares of stock or units by the market value of the underlying shares on the vesting date. For any amount realized upon exercise or vesting for which receipt has been deferred, provide a footnote quantifying the amount and disclosing the terms of the deferral.

(h)*Pension benefits*. (1) Provide the information specified in paragraph (h)(2) of this Item with respect to each plan that provides for payments or other benefits at, following, or in connection with retirement, in the following tabular format:

Pension Benefits

Name	Plan name	Number of years credited service(#)	Present value of accumulated benefit($)	Payments during last fiscal year($)
(a)	(b)	(c)	(d)	(e)
PEO				
PFO				
A				
B				
C				

(2) The Table shall include:

(i) The name of theexecutive officer (column (a));

(ii) The name of the plan (column (b));

(iii) The number of years of service credited to the namedexecutive officer under the plan, computed as of the same pension plan measurement date used for financial statement reporting purposes with respect to the registrant's audited financial statements for the last completed fiscal year (column (c));

(iv) The actuarial present value of the namedexecutive officer's accumulated benefit under the plan, computed as of the same pension plan measurement date used for financial statement reporting purposes with respect to the registrant's audited financial statements for the last completed fiscal year (column (d)); and

(v) The dollar amount of any payments and benefits paid to the namedexecutive officer during the registrant's last completed fiscal year (column (e)).

(h)养老金福利。(1)在下列表格中提供本条(h)(2)款规定关于下列每项计划的信息:规定应于退休时、退休后或针对退休进行支付或提供其他福利的计划:

养老金福利

姓名	计划名称	名义任职年限(#)	累计收益现值(美元)	上一会计年度的支付额(美元)
(a)	(b)	(c)	(d)	(e)
主要高管				
主要财务官				
A				
B				
C				

(2)表格中应包括:

(i)高管姓名[(a)栏];

(ii)计划的名称[(b)栏];

(iii)计划项下具名高管的名义任职年限,年限计算应截至同一退休金计划的计量日,即注册人上一完整会计年度已审计财务报表进行报告时使用的日期[(c)栏];

(iv)计划项下具名高管累计收益的当前精算价值,该价值的计算应截至同一退休金计划的计量日,即注册人上一完整会计年度已审计财务报表进行报告时使用的日期[(d)栏];

(v)注册人上一完整会计年度内向具名高管支付的任何付款及福利的总额[(e)栏];

Instructions to Item 402(h)(2): 1. The disclosure required pursuant to this Table applies to each plan that provides for specified retirement payments and benefits, or payments and benefits that will be provided primarily following retirement, including but not limited to tax-qualified defined benefit plans and supplemental executive retirement plans, but excluding tax-qualified defined contribution plans and nonqualified defined contribution plans. Provide a separate row for each such plan in which the named executive officer participates.

2. For purposes of the amount(s) reported in column (d), the registrant must use the same assumptions used for financial reporting purposes under generally accepted accounting principles, except that retirement age shall be assumed to be the normal retirement age as defined in the plan, or if not so defined, the earliest time at which a participant may retire under the plan without any benefit reduction due to age. The registrant must disclose in the accompanying textual narrative the valuation method and all material assumptions applied in quantifying the present value of the current accrued benefit. A benefit specified in the plan document or the executive's contract itself is not an assumption. Registrants may satisfy all or part of this disclosure by reference to a discussion of those assumptions in the registrant's financial statements, footnotes to the financial statements, or discussion in the Management's Discussion and Analysis. The sections so referenced are deemed part of the disclosure provided pursuant to this Item.

3. For purposes of allocating the current accrued benefit between tax qualified defined benefit plans and related supplemental plans, apply the limitations applicable to tax qualified defined benefit plans established by the Internal Revenue Code and the regulations thereunder that applied as of the pension plan measurement date.

4. If a namedexecutive officer's number of years of credited service with respect to any plan is different from the named executive officer's number of actual years of service with the registrant, provide footnote disclosure quantifying the difference and any resulting benefit augmentation.

(3) Provide a succinct narrative description of any material factors necessary to an understanding of each plan covered by the tabular disclosure required by this paragraph. While material factors will vary depending upon the facts, examples of such factors may include, in given cases, among other things:

(i) The material terms and conditions of payments and benefits available under the plan, including the plan's normal retirement payment and benefit formula and eligibility standards, and the effect of the form of benefit elected on the amount of annual benefits. For this purpose, normal retirement means retirement at the normal retirement age as defined in the plan, or if not so defined, the earliest time at which a participant may retire under the plan without any benefit reduction due to age;

关于第402(h)(2)条的说明:1.提供规定类型的退休付款和福利(或主要将在退休后支付的付款和福利)的每项计划,均应适用本表规定的披露,上述计划包括但不限于有税收优惠资格的固定收益养老金计划、高管补充退休计划,但不包括有税收优惠资格或者无税收优惠资格的固定缴款养老金计划。对于具名高管参与的每项上述计划,均应在表格中单列一行予以说明。

2.在计算(d)栏中报告的金额时,注册人必须使用公认会计原则规定财务报告应使用的相关假设,但退休年龄可假设为计划定义的正常退休年龄,如计划中未对此进行定义,可假设为在福利不因年龄因素降减的情况下,参与人根据计划可享受的最早退休时间。注册人必须在随附的文字说明中披露在对当期累计收益现值进行量化计算时使用的估值方法和所有重大假设。计划文件或高管的合同本身所规定的任何福利均不得作为假设。注册人可引用注册人财务报表、财务报表脚注中对上述假设的论述或者《管理层论述与分析》中的论述来完全或部分完成上述披露。上述引用内容应视为构成根据本条要求进行的披露的一部分。

3.在有税收优惠资格的固定收益养老金计划与相关的补充计划之间分配当期累计收益时,应适用《国内税收法典》及截至退休金计划计量日仍然有效的依《国内税收法典》颁发的规章针对有税收优惠资格的固定收益养老金计划设定的限制条件。

4.任何计划中具名高管的名义任职年限与其在注册人处的实际任职年限不同的,应通过脚注披露的形式对该等年限的差额以及任何相应增加的福利进行量化说明。

(3)对于本款规定的表格披露所涉的每项计划,应就理解该等计划所必要的任何重大因素提供简洁的文字说明。视实际情况,上述重大因素会有不同,如该等因素可包括但不限于:

(i)计划下提供的付款及福利的重大条款和条件,包括计划的正常退休付款和福利的计算公式及资格标准,以及所选择的福利形式对年度福利金额的影响。就上述规定而言,正常退休指按计划中定义的正常退休年龄退休,如计划中未对此进行定义,则指在福利不因年龄因素降减的情况下,按参与人根据计划可享受的最早退休时间退休;

(ii) If any namedexecutive officer is currently eligible for early retirement under any plan, identify that named executive officer and the plan, and describe the plan's early retirement payment and benefit formula and eligibility standards. For this purpose, early retirement means retirement at the early retirement age as defined in the plan, or otherwise available to the executive under the plan;

(iii) The specific elements of compensation (e.g., salary, bonus, etc.) included in applying the payment and benefit formula, identifying each such element;

(iv) With respect to namedexecutive officers' participation in multiple plans, the different purposes for each plan; and

(v) Registrant policies with regard to such matters as granting extra years of credited service.

(i) *Nonqualified defined contribution and other nonqualified deferred compensation plans.* (1) Provide the information specified in paragraph (i)(2) of this Item with respect to each defined contribution or other plan that provides for the deferral of compensation on a basis that is not tax-qualified in the following tabular format:

Nonqualified Deferred Compensation

Name	Executive contributions in last FY ($)	Registrant contributions in last FY ($)	Aggregate earnings in last FY ($)	Aggregate withdrawals/distributions ($)	Aggregate balance at last FYE ($)
(a)	(b)	(c)	(d)	(e)	(f)
PEO					
PFO					
A					
B					
C					

(2) The Table shall include:

(i) The name of theexecutive officer (column (a));

(ii) The dollar amount of aggregate executive contributions during the registrant's last fiscal year (column (b));

(iii) The dollar amount of aggregate registrant contributions during the registrant's

(ii)如果根据任何计划,任何具名高管当前享有提前退休的资格,应列明上述高管的姓名和计划的名称,并说明该计划中的提前退休付款和福利的计算公式及资格标准。就上述规定而言,提前退休指按计划中定义的提前退休年龄退休,或按计划另行规定的高管可享受的提前退休时间退休;

(iii)逐一列明适用付款和福利的计算公式时包括的具体报酬要素(如工资、奖金等);

(iv)具名高管参与不同计划的,说明每项计划的不同目的;及

(v)注册人给予额外名义任职年限等事项相关的政策。

(i)无税收优惠资格的固定缴款养老金计划及其他无税收优惠资格的递延报酬计划。(1)在下表中提供本条第(i)(2)款规定的与下列每项计划相关的信息:固定缴款养老金计划或其他无税收优惠资格的含有递延报酬安排的计划:

无税收优惠资格的递延报酬

姓名	上一会计年度高管的缴费(美元)	上一会计年度注册人的缴费(美元)	上一会计年度的总收益(美元)	提领/分配总额(美元)	上一会计年度年末结余总额(美元)
(a)	(b)	(c)	(d)	(e)	(f)
主要高管					
主要财务官					
A					
B					
C					

(2)表格中应包括:

(i)高管姓名[(a)栏];

(ii)注册人上一会计年度内高管缴费的总额[(b)栏];

(iii)注册人上一会计年度内注册人缴费的总额[(c)栏];

last fiscal year (column (c));

(iv) The dollar amount of aggregate interest or other earnings accrued during the registrant's last fiscal year (column (d));

(v) The aggregate dollar amount of all withdrawals by and distributions to the executive during the registrant's last fiscal year (column (e)); and

(vi) The dollar amount of total balance of the executive's account as of the end of the registrant's last fiscal year (column (f)).

Instruction to Item 402(i)(2). Provide a footnote quantifying the extent to which amounts reported in the contributions and earnings columns are reported as compensation in the last completed fiscal year in the registrant's Summary Compensation Table and amounts reported in the aggregate balance at last fiscal year end (column (f)) previously were reported as compensation to the named executive officer in the registrant's Summary Compensation Table for previous years.

(3) Provide a succinct narrative description of any material factors necessary to an understanding of each plan covered by tabular disclosure required by this paragraph. While material factors will vary depending upon the facts, examples of such factors may include, in given cases, among other things:

(i) The type(s) of compensation permitted to be deferred, and any limitations (by percentage of compensation or otherwise) on the extent to which deferral is permitted;

(ii) The measures for calculating interest or other plan earnings (including whether such measure(s) are selected by the executive or the registrant and the frequency and manner in which selections may be changed), quantifying interest rates and other earnings measures applicable during the registrant's last fiscal year; and

(iii) Material terms with respect to payouts, withdrawals and other distributions.

(j) *Potential payments upon termination or change-in-control.* Regarding each contract, agreement, plan or arrangement, whether written or unwritten, that provides for payment(s) to a named executive officer at, following, or in connection with any termination, including without limitation resignation, severance, retirement or a constructive termination of a named executive officer, or a change in control of the registrant or a change in the named executive officer's responsibilities, with respect to each named executive officer:

(1) Describe and explain the specific circumstances that would trigger payment(s) or the provision of other benefits, including perquisites and health care benefits;

(2) Describe and quantify the estimated payments and benefits that would be provided in each covered circumstance, whether they would or could be lump sum, or annual, disclosing the duration, and by whom they would be provided;

(3) Describe and explain how the appropriate payment and benefit levels are

(iv)注册人上一会计年度内应计利息或其他收益的总额[(d)栏];

(v)注册人上一会计年度内高管的提领及获得的分配的总额[(e)栏];及

(vi)截至注册人上一会计年度年末高管账户的结余总额[(f)栏]。

关于第402(i)(2)条的说明。在脚注中量化说明:缴费栏和收益栏报告的金额中已经作为上一完整会计年度的报酬在注册人的《报酬简表》中予以报告的额度,以及在截至上一会计年度年末总结余栏[(f)栏]报告的金额中已经作为向具名高管支付的报酬在注册人之前年度的《报酬简表》中予以报告的额度。

(3)对于本款规定的通过表格做出的披露所涉每项计划,应就理解该等计划所必要的任何重大因素提供简洁的文字说明。视实际情况,上述重大因素会有不同,如该等因素可包括但不限于:

(i)允许递延的报酬类型,及允许递延的任何程度限制(依报酬百分比或其他方式设定);

(ii)计算利息或其他计划收益的指标(包括如下说明:该等指标是否由高管或注册人选定,及选定指标可能发生变更的频率和方式),同时应对注册人上一会计年度适用的利率及其他收益指标进行量化说明;及

(iii)与支付、提领及其他分配相关的重大条款。

(j)终止或控制权变更时可能发生的支付。就任一书面或非书面的合同、协议、计划或安排而言,只要其规定应于终止时、终止后或就终止事项向具名高管进行相关支付(任何终止包括但不限于高管辞职、被辞退、退休或雇佣关系的推定终止,或注册人控制权的变更或具名高管职责的变更),即应针对上述具名高管:

(1)说明并解释将触发向具名高管提供付款或其他福利(包括特殊津贴和医疗保健福利)的特定情形;

(2)说明并量化在上述每一情形下预计将提供的付款及福利金额,该等付款及福利是否将或者是否可能一次性提供,或是逐年提供,同时应披露相应的提供期间以及提供主体;

(3)说明并解释在触发付款或提供福利的不同情形下,将如何确定恰当的支付和

determined under the various circumstances that trigger payments or provision of benefits;

(4) Describe and explain any material conditions or obligations applicable to the receipt of payments or benefits, including but not limited to non–compete, non–solicitation, non–disparagement or confidentiality agreements, including the duration of such agreements and provisions regarding waiver of breach of such agreements; and

(5) Describe any other material factors regarding each such contract, agreement, plan or arrangement.

Instructions to Item 402(j):1. The registrant must provide quantitative disclosure under these requirements, applying the assumptions that the triggering event took place on the last business day of the registrant's last completed fiscal year, and the price per share of the registrant's securities is the closing market price as of that date. In the event that uncertainties exist as to the provision of payments and benefits or the amounts involved, the registrant is required to make a reasonable estimate (or a reasonable estimated range of amounts) applicable to the payment or benefit and disclose material assumptions underlying such estimates or estimated ranges in its disclosure. In such event, the disclosure would require forward–looking information as appropriate.

2. Perquisites and other personal benefits or property may be excluded only if the aggregate amount of such compensation will be less than $10,000. Individual perquisites and personal benefits shall be identified and quantified as required by Instruction 4 to paragraph (c)(2)(ix) of this Item. For purposes of quantifying health care benefits, the registrant must use the assumptions used for financial reporting purposes under generally accepted accounting principles.

3. To the extent that the form and amount of any payment or benefit that would be provided in connection with any triggering event is fully disclosed pursuant to paragraph (h) or (i) of this Item, reference may be made to that disclosure. However, to the extent that the form or amount of any such payment or benefit would be enhanced or its vesting or other provisions accelerated in connection with any triggering event, such enhancement or acceleration must be disclosed pursuant to this paragraph.

4. Where a triggering event has actually occurred for a namedexecutive officer and that individual was not serving as a named executive officer of the registrant at the end of the last completed fiscal year, the disclosure required by this paragraph for that named executive officer shall apply only to that triggering event.

5. The registrant need not provide information with respect to contracts, agreements, plans or arrangements to the extent they do not discriminate in scope, terms or operation, in favor ofexecutive officers of the registrant and that are available generally to all salaried employees.

(k) *Compensation of directors.* (1) Provide the information specified in paragraph

福利水平;

(4)说明并解释接收付款或福利时应适用的任何重大条件或义务,包括但不限于:不竞争协议、不招揽协议、不损害名誉协议或保密协议,包括上述协议的期限及对违反上述协议放弃主张权利的条款;及

(5)说明与上述各合同、协议、计划或安排相关的任何其他重大因素。

关于第402(j)条的说明:1.注册人在按照上述规定进行量化披露时,应采用如下假设:触发付款或提供福利的事件在注册人上一完整会计年度的最后一个营业日发生,且注册人证券的每股价格为截至上述日期的市场收盘价。付款和福利或所涉及的金额存在不确定性的,注册人应对付款或福利进行合理预估(或提供一个合理预估的金额范围),并披露支持上述预估或预估范围的合理假设。出现上述情况的,须要提供适当的前瞻性信息进行披露。

2.特殊津贴和其他个人福利或财产,只有总额不超过1万美元时,才可免予披露。应按本条第(c)(2)(ix)款的说明4注明并量化个人的特殊津贴和福利。在量化医疗保健福利时,注册人必须使用公认会计原则规定财务报告应使用的相关假设。

3.因任何触发事件而提供的任何付款或福利之形式及金额已根据本条第(h)款或第(i)款予以充分披露的,可以引用该等披露。但是,因任何触发事件导致任何上述付款或福利的形式得到升级,或金额得到提高,或其归属或其他安排被提前的,该等升级、提高或提前必须根据本款予以披露。

4.如某一具名高管已实际发生触发事件,且该高管在上一会计年度年末时并未担任具名高管职位,则仅须就上述特定的触发事件按照本款规定对具名高管进行披露。

5.在计划范围、期限或运行方面不给予注册人高管或者董事任何优惠,且所有受薪雇员普遍享受的合同、协议、计划或安排,注册人可以免予提供相关信息。

(k)董事报酬。(1)在下表中提供本条第(k)(2)款规定的与注册人董事在上一完

(k)(2) of this Item, concerning the compensation of the directors for the registrant's last completed fiscal year, in the following tabular format:

Director Compensation

Name	Fees earned or paid in cash($)	Stock awards ($)	Option awards ($)	Non－equity incentive plan compensation($)	Change in pension value and nonqualified deferred compensation earnings	All other compensation($)	Total ($)
(a)	(b)	(c)	(d)	(e)	(f)	(g)	(h)
A							
B							
C							
D							
E							

(2) The Table shall include:

(i) The name of each director unless such director is also a namedexecutive officer under paragraph (a) of this Item and his or her compensation for service as a director is fully reflected in the Summary Compensation Table pursuant to paragraph (c) of this Item and otherwise as required pursuant to paragraphs (d) through (j) of this Item (column (a));

(ii) The aggregate dollar amount of all fees earned or paid in cash for services as a director, including annual retainer fees, committee and/or chairmanship fees, and meeting fees (column (b));

(iii) For awards of stock, the aggregate grant date fair value computed in accordance with FASB ASC Topic 718 (column (c));

(iv) For awards of options, with or without tandem SARs (including awards that subsequently have been transferred), the aggregate grant date fair value computed in accordance with FASB ASC Topic 718 (column (d));

*Instruction to Item 402(k)(2)(iii) and(iv).*For each director, disclose by footnote to the appropriate column: the grant date fair value of each equity award computed in accordance with FAS 123R; for each option, SAR or similar option like instrument for

整会计年度的报酬相关的信息:

董事报酬

姓名	已赚取的或已经以现金支付的费用(美元)	股票奖励(美元)	期权奖励(美元)	非股权激励计划报酬(美元)	养老金价值变动及无税收优惠资格的递延报酬收益	所有其他报酬(美元)	总计(美元)
(a)	(b)	(c)	(d)	(e)	(f)	(g)	(h)
A							
B							
C							
D							
E							

(2)表格中应包括:

(i)每名董事的姓名,但同时兼任本条第(a)款中的具名高管,并且其担任董事获得的报酬已通过本条第(c)款规定的《报酬简表》或按照本条第(d)款至第(j)款的规定予以完全列报的董事除外[(a)栏];

(ii)作为董事赚取或获付的所有现金费用的总额,包括年度聘用费、委员会和/或主席费用以及会议出席费[(b)栏];

(iii)对于股票奖励,应按照《财务会计准则委员会会计准则汇编第718号专题》计算授予日的公允价值总额[(c)栏];

(iv)对于期权奖励(包括后续转让的奖励),无论是否附带并行的股票增值权,均应按照《财务会计准则委员会会计准则汇编第718号专题》计算授予日的公允价值总额[(d)栏];

关于第402(k)(2)(iii)条和第402(k)(2)(iv)条的说明。对于每名董事,均应通过适当栏目的脚注披露如下信息:按照《财务会计准则公告第123R号》计算的每项基于股权的奖励在授予日的公允价值;注册人在上一会计年度的任何时候通过修正、撤销

which the registrant has adjusted or amended the exercise or base price during the last completed fiscal year, whether through amendment, cancellation or replacement grants, or any other means ("repriced"), or otherwise has materially modified such awards, the incremental fair value, computed as of the repricing or modification date in accordance with FAS 123R; and the aggregate number of stock awards and the aggregate number of option awards outstanding at fiscal year end. However, the disclosure required by this Instruction does not apply to any repricing that occurs through a pre-existing formula or mechanism in the plan or award that results in the periodic adjustment of the option or SAR exercise or base price, an antidilution provision in a plan or award, or a recapitalization or similar transaction equally affecting all holders of the class of securities underlying the options or SARs.

(v) The dollar value of all earnings for services performed during the fiscal year pursuant to non-equity incentive plans as defined in paragraph (a)(6)(iii) of this Item, and all earnings on any outstanding awards (column (e));

(vi) The sum of the amounts specified in paragraphs (k)(2)(vi)(A) and (B) of this Item (column (f)) as follows:

(A) The aggregate change in the actuarial present value of the director's accumulated benefit under all defined benefit and actuarial pension plans (including supplemental plans) from the pension plan measurement date used for financial statement reporting purposes with respect to the registrant's audited financial statements for the prior completed fiscal year to the pension plan measurement date used for financial statement reporting purposes with respect to the registrant's audited financial statements for the covered fiscal year; and

(B) Above-market or preferential earnings on compensation that is deferred on a basis that is not tax-qualified, including such earnings on nonqualified defined contribution plans;

(vii) All other compensation for the covered fiscal year that the registrant could not properly report in any other column of the Director Compensation Table (column (g)). Each compensation item that is not properly reportable in columns (b)-(f), regardless of the amount of the compensation item, must be included in column(g). Such compensation must include, but is not limited to:

(A) Perquisites and other personal benefits, or property, unless the aggregate amount of such compensation is less than $10,000;

(B) All "gross-ups" or other amounts reimbursed during the fiscal year for the payment of taxes;

(C) For any security of the registrant or its subsidiaries purchased from the registrant or its subsidiaries (through deferral of salary or bonus, or otherwise) at a

或替代性授予或任何其他方式对任何期权、股票增值权或其他与期权类似的工具的行权价或底价进行了调整或修正(“重新定价”),或以其他方式对上述奖励进行了实质修改的,应按照《财务会计准则公告第123R号》计算该等奖励截至重新定价或调整日的公允价值增值,以及截至会计年度年末未兑现的股票奖励的总数量和期权奖励的总数量。但是,计划或奖励中事先设定了公式或机制,对期权或股票增值权的行权价或底价进行定期调整,由此导致的任何重新定价均不适用本表格的披露要求;此外,激励计划或奖励中的反稀释条款,或对期权或股票增值权项下同一类别标的证券的全部持有者产生同等影响的资本重组或类似交易,亦不适用本表格的披露要求。

(v)依据本条第(a)(6)(iii)款定义的非股权激励计划在该会计年度内履行服务获得的所有收益,以及任何未兑现奖励的所有收益的美元价值[(e)栏];

(vi)本条第(k)(2)(vi)(A)款和第(k)(2)(vi)(B)款规定的下述金额之总计[(f)栏]:

(A)所有固定收益养老金和精算退休金计划(包括补充计划)项下董事的累计收益的精算现值在下述期间的变动总值:自注册人报告上一完整会计年度已审计财务报表时使用的退休金计划计量日,直至注册人报告所涉会计年度已审计财务报表时使用的退休金计划计量日;和

(B)在无税收优惠基础上递延支付的,高于市场水平或者优惠性的收益,包括从不能享受税收优惠的固定缴款养老金计划中获得的收益;

(vii)注册人无法在《董事报酬表》的任何其他栏目予以适当报告的所涉会计年度的所有其他报酬[(g)栏]。无法在(b)~(f)栏予以适当报告的报酬项目(不论报酬数额多少),均必须在(g)栏列出。该等报酬必须包括但不限于以下各项:

(A)特殊津贴及其他个人福利或财产,但总金额低于1万美元的除外;

(B)该会计年度为缴税而提供的所有“税款补足”或其他补偿数额。

(C)对于按低于购买日股票市价的价格,通过工资或奖金递延支付或其他方式从注册人或其子公司折价购买的注册人或其子公司的任何证券而言,其按照《美国财务

discount from the market price of such security at the date of purchase, unless that discount is available generally, either to all security holders or to all salaried employees of the registrant, the compensation cost, if any, computed in accordance with FAS 123R;

(D) The amount paid or accrued to any director pursuant to a plan or arrangement in connection with:

(1) The resignation, retirement or any other termination of such director; or

(2) A change in control of the registrant;

(E) Registrant contributions or other allocations to vested and unvested defined contribution plans;

(F) Consulting fees earned from, or paid or payable by the registrant and/or its subsidiaries (including joint ventures);

(G) The annual costs of payments and promises of payments pursuant to director legacy programs and similar charitable award programs;

(H) The dollar value of any insurance premiums paid by, or on behalf of, the registrant during the covered fiscal year with respect to life insurance for the benefit of a director; and

(I) The dollar value of any dividends or other earnings paid on stock or option awards, when those amounts were not factored into the grant date fair value required to be reported for the stock or option award in column (c) or (d); and

Instructions to Item 402(k)(2)(vii): 1. Programs in which registrants agree to make donations to one or more charitable institutions in a director's name, payable by the registrant currently or upon a designated event, such as the retirement or death of the director, are charitable awards programs or director legacy programs for purposes of the disclosure required by paragraph (k)(2)(vii)(G) of this Item. Provide footnote disclosure of the total dollar amount payable under the program and other material terms of each such program for which tabular disclosure is provided.

2. Any item reported for a director pursuant to paragraph (k)(2)(vii) of this Item that is not a perquisite or personal benefit and whose value exceeds $10,000 must be identified and quantified in a footnote to column (g). All items of compensation are required to be included in the Director Compensation Table without regard to whether such items are required to be identified other than as specifically noted in this Item.

3. Perquisites and personal benefits may be excluded as long as the total value of all perquisites and personal benefits for a director is less than $10,000. If the total value of all perquisites and personal benefits is $10,000 or more for any director, then each perquisite or personal benefit, regardless of its amount, must be identified by type. If perquisites and personal benefits are required to be reported for a director pursuant to this rule, then each perquisite or personal benefit that exceeds the greater of $25,000 or 10%

会计准则公告第123号》(FAS123R)计算的报酬成本(如有),但所有证券持有人或注册人的所有受薪雇员均可享受该折扣的除外;

(D)依照与下列事项有关的计划或安排而已向或应向任何具名高管支付的数额:

(1)上述董事辞职、退休或以其他任何形式终止与注册人的雇佣关系;或
(2)注册人发生控制权变更;
(E)注册人对已归属及未归属的固定缴款养老金计划的供款或其他拨款;

(F)从注册人及/或其子公司(包括合营企业)赚取的,或者该等公司支付或应付的咨询费;
(G)董事遗赠计划和类似慈善奖励计划项下付款和承诺付款的年度成本;

(H)注册人或其代表在所涉会计年度为董事之利益缴纳的任何寿险保险费的美元价值;和

(I)在计算(c)栏或(d)栏要求报告的股票或期权奖励在授予日的公允价值时,未予考虑的股票或期权奖励的任何股息或其他收益的美元价值;及

关于第402(k)(2)(vii)条的说明:1. 注册人同意以董事的名义向一家或数家慈善机构做出捐赠的计划[无论捐赠款是当期应付款项或是指定事件发生后(如董事的退休或死亡)应付的款项],属于本条第(k)(2)(vii)(G)款要求披露的慈善奖励计划或董事遗赠计划。应通过脚注披露计划项下的应付款项的总额,以及表格中要求披露的每一计划的其他重大条款。

2.按本条第(k)(2)(vii)款针对董事报告的价值超过1万美元,但不属于特殊津贴或个人福利的任何项目,必须在(g)栏的脚注中注明并予以量化。所有报酬项均应纳入“董事报酬表”,不论除本条明确规定以外,是否有其他规定要求列明这些项目。

3.具名高管的全部津贴和个人福利的总价值低于1万美元的,可不设列津贴和个人福利项目。如果任何一名具名高管的全部津贴和个人福利的总价值为1万美元以上,则每项津贴或个人福利均应分类列明,不论其金额多少。如果按照本规则规定须要报告某名具名高管的津贴和个人福利,则每项超过2.5万美元或者该高管津贴和个人福利总额10%(以较高者为准)的津贴或个人福利必须在脚注中予以量化和披露。津贴和其他个人福利应以注册人的总增量成本为基础进行估值。对于需要在脚注中予

of the total amount of perquisites and personal benefits for that director must be quantified and disclosed in a footnote. Perquisites and other personal benefits shall be valued on the basis of the aggregate incremental cost to the registrant. With respect to the perquisite or other personal benefit for which footnote quantification is required, the registrant shall describe in the footnote its methodology for computing the aggregate incremental cost. Reimbursements of taxes owed with respect to perquisites or other personal benefits must be included in column (g) and are subject to separate quantification and identification as tax reimbursements (paragraph (k)(2)(vii)(B) of this Item) even if the associated perquisites or other personal benefits are not required to be included because the total amount of all perquisites or personal benefits for an individual director is less than $10,000 or are required to be identified but are not required to be separately quantified.

(viii) The dollar value of total compensation for the covered fiscal year (column (h)). With respect to each director, disclose the sum of all amounts reported in columns (b) through (g).

Instruction to Item 402(k)(2). Two or more directors may be grouped in a single row in the Table if all elements of their compensation are identical. The names of the directors for whom disclosure is presented on a group basis should be clear from the Table.

(3) *Narrative to director compensation table.* Provide a narrative description of any material factors necessary to an understanding of the director compensation disclosed in this Table. While material factors will vary depending upon the facts, examples of such factors may include, in given cases, among other things:

(i) A description of standard compensation arrangements (such as fees for retainer, committee service, service as chairman of the board or a committee, and meeting attendance); and

(ii) Whether any director has a different compensation arrangement, identifying that director and describing the terms of that arrangement.

Instruction to Item 402(k). In addition to the Instruction to paragraphs(k)(2)(iii) and (iv) and the Instructions to paragraph (k)(2)(vii) of this Item, the following apply equally to paragraph (k) of this Item: Instructions 2 and 4 to paragraph (c) of this Item; Instructions to paragraphs(c)(2)(iii) and(iv) of this Item; Instructions to paragraphs (c)(2)(v) and (vi) of this Item; Instructions to paragraph (c)(2)(vii) of this Item; Instructions to paragraph (c)(2)(viii) of this Item; and Instructions 1 and 5 to paragraph (c)(2)(ix) of this Item. These Instructions apply to the columns in the Director Compensation Table that are analogous to the columns in the Summary Compensation Table to which they refer and to disclosures under paragraph (k) of this Item that correspond to analogous disclosures provided for in paragraph (c) of this Item to which

以量化的津贴或其他个人福利,注册人应在脚注中阐明其计算总增量成本所使用的方法。与津贴或其他个人福利相关的退税必须列入(g)栏,并作为退税单独予以量化和注明[本条第(k)(2)(vii)(B)款],即使根据上文的规定,具名高管个人的全部津贴或个人福利因其总额低于1万美元而不必列明,或者要求注明但不要求单独量化。

(viii)所涉会计年度总报酬的美元价值[(h)栏]。应针对每名具名高管,披露在(b)栏至(g)栏报告的所有数额的总和。

关于第402(k)(2)条的说明。如果两名(含)以上董事报酬的各项要素均相同,可以合并为一行报告。合并披露的董事的姓名应在表格中明确列示。

(3)《董事报酬表》的文字说明。应针对理解表格内披露的董事报酬所必需的任何重大因素提供文字说明。视实际情况,上述重大因素会有不同,如该等因素可能包括但不限于:

(i)标准报酬安排的说明(如聘任费、委员会任职费、董事长或委员会主席酬金以及会议出席费);和

(ii)任何董事是否存在不同的报酬安排,如有,应指明该董事并说明相关安排条款。

关于第402(k)条的说明。除关于本条第(k)(2)(iii)款、第(k)(2)(iv)款及第(k)(2)(vii)款的说明外,下列说明同样适用于本条第(k)款:关于本条第(c)款的说明2和说明4;关于本条第(c)(2)(iii)款和第(c)(2)(iv)款的说明;关于本条第(c)(2)(v)款和第(c)(2)(vi)款的说明;关于本条第(c)(2)(vii)款的说明;关于本条第(c)(2)(viii)款的说明;以及关于本条第(c)(2)(ix)款的说明1和说明5。上述说明适用于《董事报酬表》中与《报酬简表》中类似的相关栏目,以及本条第(k)款下与本条第(c)款中的披露类似的相关披露。

they refer.

(l) *Smaller reporting companies.* A registrant that qualifies as a "smaller reporting company," as defined by Item 10(f) (§229.10(f)(1)), may provide the scaled disclosure in paragraphs (m) through (r) instead of paragraphs (a) through (k) and (s) of this Item.

(m) *Smaller reporting companies —General —* (1) *All compensation covered.* This Item requires clear, concise and understandable disclosure of all plan and non-plan compensation awarded to, earned by, or paid to the named executive officers designated under paragraph (m)(2) of this Item, and directors covered by paragraph (r) of this Item, by any person for all services rendered in all capacities to the smaller reporting company and its subsidiaries, unless otherwise specifically excluded from disclosure in this Item. All such compensation shall be reported pursuant to this Item, even if also called for by another requirement, including transactions between the smaller reporting company and a third party where a purpose of the transaction is to furnish compensation to any such named executive officer or director. No amount reported as compensation for one fiscal year need be reported in the same manner as compensation for a subsequent fiscal year; amounts reported as compensation for one fiscal year may be required to be reported in a different manner pursuant to this Item.

(2) *Persons covered.* Disclosure shall be provided pursuant to this Item for each of the following (the "named executive officers"):

(i) All individuals serving as the smaller reporting company's principalexecutive officer or acting in a similar capacity during the last completed fiscal year ("PEO"), regardless of compensation level;

(ii) The smaller reporting company's two most highly compensatedexecutive officers other than the PEO who were serving as executive officers at the end of the last completed fiscal year; and

(iii) Up to two additional individuals for whom disclosure would have been provided pursuant to paragraph (m)(2)(ii) of this Item but for the fact that the individual was not serving as anexecutive officer of the smaller reporting company at the end of the last completed fiscal year.

Instructions to Item 402(m)(2): 1. *Determination of most highly compensated executive officers.* The determination as to which executive officers are most highly compensated shall be made by reference to total compensation for the last completed fiscal year (as required to be disclosed pursuant to paragraph (n)(2)(x) of this Item) reduced by the amount required to be disclosed pursuant to paragraph (n)(2)(viii) of this Item, *provided, however* , that no disclosure need be provided for any executive officer, other than the PEO, whose total compensation, as so reduced, does not exceed

(l)小型报告公司。某一注册人符合第10(f)条[第229.10(f)(1)条]定义的“小型报告公司”标准的,可按照本条第(m)款至第(r)款的规定进行简化披露,而不必按照第(a)款至第(k)款和第(s)款的规定进行披露。

(m)小型报告公司——一般规定——(1)所有应予披露的报酬。任何人根据本条第(m)(2)款指定的具名高管,以及任何人指定的本条第(r)款所涉董事,以任何身份向注册人及其子公司提供服务因此获得、赚取或获付计划和非计划报酬的,必须以清晰、简洁、易懂的方式披露该等报酬,但本条明确规定不必披露的除外。所有该等报酬均应按照本条规定报告,不论其他规定是否同样要求对此进行报告;注册人与第三方之间开展交易,且交易目的之一是向任何该等具名高管或董事提供报酬的,该等交易亦应纳入报告范围。在某一会计年度作为报酬报告的金额不必再在下一会计年度以同样方式进行报告,但可能须按照本条规定以其他方式进行报告。

(2)适用人员。下列每一人员(“具名高管”)均须按本条规定进行相应披露:

(i)所有在上一完整会计年度担任注册人的主要高管或者以类似身份行事的个人(“主要高管”),不论报酬水平高低;

(ii)除主要高管以外,在上一完整会计年度年末担任小型报告公司高管的两位报酬最高的高管;

(iii)按照本条第(m)(2)(ii)款规定本应披露相关信息,但在上一完整会计年度年末不再担任注册人高管的个人(不超过2名)。

关于第402(m)(2)条的说明:1.报酬最高高管的确定。确定报酬最高的高管之时,应将上一完整会计年度的报酬总额[该等报酬总额应按本条第(n)(2)(x)款规定予以披露]减去本条第(n)(2)(viii)款要求披露的金额,但是按照上述规定进行扣减后所得报酬总额不超过10万美元的任何高管(主要高管除外)不必披露。

$100,000.

2. *Inclusion of executive officer of a subsidiary.* It may be appropriate for a smaller reporting company to include as named executive officers one or more executive officers or other employees of subsidiaries in the disclosure required by this Item. See Rule 3b–7 under the Exchange Act (17 CFR 240.3b–7).

3. *Exclusion of executive officer due to overseas compensation.* It may be appropriate in limited circumstances for a smaller reporting company not to include in the disclosure required by this Item an individual, other than its PEO, who is one of the smaller reporting company's most highly compensated executive officers due to the payment of amounts of cash compensation relating to overseas assignments attributed predominantly to such assignments.

(3) *Information for full fiscal year.* If the PEO served in that capacity during any part of a fiscal year with respect to which information is required, information should be provided as to all of his or her compensation for the full fiscal year. If a named executive officer (other than the PEO) served as an executive officer of the smaller reporting company (whether or not in the same position) during any part of the fiscal year with respect to which information is required, information shall be provided as to all compensation of that individual for the full fiscal year.

(4) *Omission of table or column.* A table or column may be omitted if there has been no compensation awarded to, earned by, or paid to any of the named executive officers or directors required to be reported in that table or column in any fiscal year covered by that table.

(5) *Definitions.* For purposes of this Item:

(i) The term *stock* means instruments such as common stock, restricted stock, restricted stock units, phantom stock, phantom stock units, common stock equivalent units or any similar instruments that do not have option–like features, and the term *option* means instruments such as stock options, stock appreciation rights and similar instruments with option–like features. The term *stock appreciation rights* ("*SARs*") refers to SARs payable in cash or stock, including SARs payable in cash or stock at the election of the smaller reporting company or a named executive officer. The term *equity* is used to refer generally to stock and/or options.

(ii) The term *plan* includes, but is not limited to, the following: Any plan, contract, authorization or arrangement, whether or not set forth in any formal document, pursuant to which cash, securities, similar instruments, or any other property may be received. A plan may be applicable to one person. Smaller reporting companies may omit information regarding group life, health, hospitalization, or medical reimbursement plans that do not discriminate in scope, terms or operation, in favor of executive officers or directors of the

2.纳入子公司高管。在适当情况下,小型报告公司可以将其子公司的一名或数名高管或其他职员作为具名高管纳入本条规定的披露名单。参见《交易法》的《3b-7规则》(《联邦规章汇编》第十七编第240.3b-7节)。

3.排除获取海外报酬的高管。在有限和适当的情况下,对于主要因境外工作获取的相关现金报酬而成为小型报告公司报酬最高高管之一的个人(主要高管除外),小型报告公司可以不将其纳入本条规定的披露名单。

(3)完整会计年度的信息。对于某一会计年度内应按规定进行信息披露的任何期间,主要高管只要曾在该期间内任职,即应就其在该完整会计年度的全部报酬提供相关信息。如果在某一会计年度内应按规定进行信息披露的任何期间,某具名高管(主要高管除外)曾担任小型报告公司的高管(不论职位是否相同),即应就其在该完整会计年度的全部报酬提供相关信息。

(4)省略表格或栏。如果要求任何具名高管或者董事以某表格或某栏进行报告,但该等具名高管或董事在该表所覆盖的任何会计年度未获得、赚取或者获付任何报酬,则该表格或栏目可以省略。

(5)定义。就本条而言:

(i)"股票"系指普通股、受限股票、受限股票单位、虚拟股票、虚拟股票单位、普通股等价单位或者不具有期权特性的任何类似票据;"期权"指股票期权、股票增值权等工具及具有期权特性的类似票据。"股票增值权"("SARs")系指可用现金或股票支付的股票增值权,包括可由小型报告公司或具名高管选择以现金或股票支付的股票增值权。"股权"统指股票和/或期权。

(ii)"计划"包括但不限于任何计划、合同、授权或安排,只要凭借该等计划、合同、授权或安排可以收取现金、证券、类似工具或者任何其他财产,而不论其是否载于任何正式文件之中。一项计划的适用对象可以仅限于一个主体。在计划范围、期限或运行方面对于小型报告公司高管或者董事不给予任何优惠,且普遍适用于所有受薪职员的集体人寿、健康、住院或医疗报销计划,小型报告公司可以免予提供相关信息。

smaller reporting company and that are available generally to all salaried employees.

(iii) The term *incentive plan* means any plan providing compensation intended to serve as incentive for performance to occur over a specified period, whether such performance is measured by reference to financial performance of the smaller reporting company or an affiliate, the smaller reporting company's stock price, or any other performance measure. An equity incentive plan is an incentive plan or portion of an incentive plan under which awards are granted that fall within the scope of Financial Accounting Standards Board Statement of Financial Accounting Standards No. 123 (revised 2004), *Share-Based Payment* , as modified or supplemented ("FAS 123R"). A *non-equity incentive plan* is an incentive plan or portion of an incentive plan that is not an equity incentive plan. The term *incentive plan award* means an award provided under an incentive plan.

(iv) The terms *date of grant* or *grant date* refer to the grant date determined for financial statement reporting purposes pursuant to FAS 123R.

(v) *Closing market price* is defined as the price at which the smaller reporting company's security was last sold in the principal United States market for such security as of the date for which the closing market price is determined.

(n) *Smaller reporting companies* — *Summary compensation table* — (1) *General.* Provide the information specified in paragraph (n)(2) of this Item, concerning the compensation of the named executive officers for each of the smaller reporting company's last two completed fiscal years, in a Summary Compensation Table in the tabular format specified below.

Summary Compensation Table

Name and principal position	Year	Salary ($)	Bonus ($)	Stock awards ($)	Option awards ($)	Nonequity incentive plan compensation ($)	Nonqualified deferred compensation earnings($)	All other compensation($)	Total ($)
(a)	(b)	(c)	(d)	(e)	(f)	(g)	(h)	(i)	(j)
PEO									
A									
B									

(2) The Table shall include:

(i) The name and principal position of the namedexecutive officer (column (a));

(ii) The fiscal year covered (column (b));

(iii) The dollar value of base salary (cash and non-cash) earned by the named

(iii)“激励计划”系指旨在就特定期间提供绩效激励的任何计划,而不论该绩效的衡量标准是小型报告公司或关联人的财务绩效、小型报告公司的股价或者任何其他绩效衡量标准。“股权激励计划”系指《财务会计准则公告第123号(2004年修订版)——基于股份的支付》及其修改和补充(“FAS123R”)规定范围内的向计划参与人授予奖励的激励计划或该计划的一部分。“非股权激励计划”系指不属于股权激励计划的激励计划或该计划的一部分。“激励计划奖励”系指依据激励计划授予的奖励。

(iv)“授予日”系指为财务报表报告之目的而按照FAS123R确定的授予日期。

(v)“收盘市价”系指截至收盘市价确定之日,小型报告公司的证券在该种证券的主要美国市场的最后出售价格。

(n)小型报告公司——报酬简表——(1)一般规定。按下列报酬简表的格式,提供本条第(n)(2)款所规定的关于具名高管在小型报告公司过去两个完整会计年度每一会计年度的报酬信息。

报酬简表

姓名和主要职务	年份	工资(美元)	奖金(美元)	股票奖励(美元)	期权奖励(美元)	非股权激励计划报酬(美元)	无税收优惠资格的递延报酬收入(美元)	所有其他报酬(美元)	总计(美元)
(a)	(b)	(c)	(d)	(e)	(f)	(g)	(h)	(i)	(j)
主要高管									
A									
B									

(2)简表内容应包括:

(i)具名高管的姓名和主要职务[(a)栏];

(ii)所涉会计年度[(b)栏];

(iii)具名高管在该会计年度以美元计算的基本工资(包括现金和非现金工资)

executive officer during the fiscal year covered (column (c));

(iv) The dollar value of bonus (cash and non-cash) earned by the namedexecutive officer during the fiscal year covered (column (d));

Instructions to Item 402 (n)(2)(iii) and (iv): 1. If the amount of salary or bonus earned in a given fiscal year is not calculable through the latest practicable date, a footnote shall be included disclosing that the amount of salary or bonus is not calculable through the latest practicable date and providing the date that the amount of salary or bonus is expected to be determined, and such amount must then be disclosed in a filing under Item 5.02(f) of Form 8-K (17 CFR 249.308).

2. Smaller reporting companies shall include in the salary column (column (c)) or bonus column (column (d)) any amount of salary or bonus forgone at the election of a namedexecutive officer under which stock, equity-based or other forms of non-cash compensation instead have been received by the named executive officer. However, the receipt of any such form of non-cash compensation instead of salary or bonus must be disclosed in a footnote added to the salary or bonus column and, where applicable, referring to the narrative disclosure to the Summary Compensation Table (required by paragraph (o) of this Item) where the material terms of the stock, option or non-equity incentive plan award elected by the named executive officer are reported.

(v) For awards of stock, the aggregate grant date fair value computed in accordance with FASB ASC Topic 718 (column (e));

(vi) For awards of options, with or without tandem SARs (including awards that subsequently have been transferred), the aggregate grant date fair value computed in accordance with FASB ASC Topic 718 (column (f));

Instruction 1 to Item 402(n)(2)(v) and (n)(2)(vi).For awards reported in columns (e) and (f), include a footnote disclosing all assumptions made in the valuation by reference to a discussion of those assumptions in the smaller reporting company's financial statements, footnotes to the financial statements, or discussion in the Management's Discussion and Analysis. The sections so referenced are deemed part of the disclosure provided pursuant to this Item.

Instruction 2 to Item 402(n)(2)(v) and (n)(2)(vi).If at any time during the last completed fiscal year, the smaller reporting company has adjusted or amended the exercise price of options or SARs previously awarded to a named executive officer, whether through amendment, cancellation or replacement grants, or any other means ("repriced"), or otherwise has materially modified such awards, the smaller reporting company shall include, as awards required to be reported in column (f), the incremental fair value, computed as of the repricing or modification date in accordance with FASB ASC Topic 718, with respect to that repriced or modified award.

[(c)栏];

(iv)具名高管在该会计年度以美元计算的奖金(包括现金和非现金奖金)[(d)栏];

关于第402(n)(2)(iii)条和第402(n)(2)(iv)条的说明。1.如果在某既定会计年度赚取的工资或奖金数额截至最迟可行日期仍无法统计,应通过脚注如实说明,并提供预计可以确定工资或奖金数额的日期,届时必须按照《8-K表格》的第5.02(f)条(《联邦规章汇编》第十七编第249.308节)提交文件披露该等数额。

2.具名高管选择放弃任何工资或奖金,并因此收到股票、基于股权的报酬或其他形式的非现金报酬的,小型报告公司应在工资栏[(c)栏]或奖金栏[(d)栏]填写该等被放弃的工资或奖金。但是,作为工资或奖金之替代而收到的任何此类形式的非现金报酬必须在工资或奖金栏的脚注中予以披露,同时,如适用,在对具名高管选择的股票、期权或非股权激励计划奖励的重大条款进行报告时,应按照本条第(o)款的规定引用《报酬简表》的文字披露。

(v)对于股票奖励,应按照《财务会计准则委员会会计准则汇编第718号专题》计算授予日的公允价值总额[(e)栏];

(vi)对于期权奖励(包括后续转让的奖励),无论是否附带并行的股票增值权,均应按照《财务会计准则委员会会计准则汇编第718号专题》计算授予日的公允价值总额[(f)栏];

关于第402(n)(2)(v)条和第402(n)(2)(vi)条的说明1 。对于在(e)栏和(f)栏报告的奖励,应插入一项脚注,借由引用小型报告公司财务报表及其脚注中对假设条件的相关论述或者《管理层论述与分析》中的相关论述,披露估值中所采用的全部假设。所引用的条款应视为按照本条规定提供的披露内容的一部分。

关于第402(n)(2)(v)条和第402(n)(2)(vi)条的说明2。如果上一完整会计年度内的任何时候,小型报告公司通过修正、撤销或者替换奖励授予的方式或任何其他方式,对之前授予具名高管的期权或股票增值权的行权价进行了调整或修正("重新定价"),或对奖励作出了其他重大修改,则小型报告公司应在(f)栏的奖励中加入该等奖励在重新定价日或修改日的公允价值增值(按照《财务会计准则委员会会计准则汇编第718号专题》计算)。

Instruction 3 to Item 402(n)(2)(v) and (vi).For any awards that are subject to performance conditions, report the value at the grant date based upon the probable outcome of such conditions. This amount should be consistent with the estimate of aggregate compensation cost to be recognized over the service period determined as of the grant date under FASB ASC Topic 718, excluding the effect of estimated forfeitures. In a footnote to the table, disclose the value of the award at the grant date assuming that the highest level of performance conditions will be achieved if an amount less than the maximum was included in the table.

(vii) The dollar value of all earnings for services performed during the fiscal year pursuant to awards under non-equity incentive plans as defined in paragraph (m)(5)(iii) of this Item, and all earnings on any outstanding awards (column (g));

Instructions to Item 402 (n) (2) (vii).1. If the relevant performance measure is satisfied during the fiscal year (including for a single year in a plan with a multi-year performance measure), the earnings are reportable for that fiscal year, even if not payable until a later date, and are not reportable again in the fiscal year when amounts are paid to the named executive officer.

2. All earnings on non-equity incentive plan compensation must be identified and quantified in a footnote to column (g), whether the earnings were paid during the fiscal year, payable during the period but deferred at the election of the named executive officer, or payable by their terms at a later date.

(viii) Above-market or preferential earnings on compensation that is deferred on a basis that is not tax-qualified, including such earnings on nonqualified defined contribution plans (column (h));

Instruction to Item 402(n)(2)(viii).Interest on deferred compensation is above-market only if the rate of interest exceeds 120% of the applicable federal long-term rate, with compounding (as prescribed under section 1274(d) of the Internal Revenue Code, (26 U.S.C. 1274(d))) at the rate that corresponds most closely to the rate under the smaller reporting company's plan at the time the interest rate or formula is set. In the event of a discretionary reset of the interest rate, the requisite calculation must be made on the basis of the interest rate at the time of such reset, rather than when originally established. Only the above-market portion of the interest must be included. If the applicable interest rates vary depending upon conditions such as a minimum period of continued service, the reported amount should be calculated assuming satisfaction of all conditions to receiving interest at the highest rate. Dividends (and dividend equivalents) on deferred compensation denominated in the smaller reporting company's stock ("deferred stock") are preferential only if earned at a rate higher than dividends on the smaller reporting company's common stock. Only the preferential portion of the dividends

关于第402(n)(2)(v)条和第402(n)(2)(vi)条的说明3。对于受业绩条件限制的任何奖励,应基于业绩条件可能实现的结果报告该奖励在授予日的价值。这一数额应与授予日按照《财务会计准则委员会会计准则汇编第718号专题》计算的应在任职期限内确认的报酬总成本估值(不考虑预计没收的影响)保持一致。如果表格中所报告的数额低于最高值,应在表格的脚注中披露假如业绩达到最高标准之时,奖励在授予日的价值。

(vii)依据本条第(m)(5)(iii)款定义的非股权激励计划项下之奖励,在该会计年度内履行服务获得的所有收益,以及任何未兑现奖励的所有收益的美元价值[(g)栏]。

关于第402(n)(2)(vii)条的说明。1.如果某一会计年度内实现了相关业绩指标(包括在采用跨年业绩指标的计划内实现某一年的指标),则应对该会计年度的收益进行报告,即使该收益的应付日期在该会计年度之后,而在实际向具名高管支付的会计年度,不必再对该等数额进行报告。

2.基于非股权激励计划报酬获得的所有收益必须在(g)栏的脚注中注明,并予以量化,不论该等收益是在该会计年度支付,还是本应在该会计年度支付但具名高管选择递延支付,或者按其条款应在较晚日期支付。

(viii)在无税收优惠基础上递延支付的,高于市场水平或者优惠性的收益,包括从不能享受税收优惠的固定缴款养老金计划中获得的收益[(h)栏]。

关于第402(n)(2)(viii)条的说明。只有递延报酬的利率进行复利计算后超过相关联邦长期利率120%时,递延报酬的利息才能被认定为高于市场水平,复利计算以《国内税收法典》第1274(d)条[《美国法典》第26卷第1274(d)条)]的规定为准,计算复利所采用的利率应为设定利率或公式时, 与小型报告公司计划项下的利率最接近的利率。如遇自主调息,必须采用调息时的利率而非最初设定的利率。只有高于市场水平的利息才须纳入报告范围。如果相关利率因最短持续服务期限等条件有所不同,则在计算应报告数额时,应假定收取按最高利率计算之利息所需的条件均已满足。高管获得的以小型报告公司股票("递延股票")表示的递延报酬的股息(及股息等价物),只有在其股息率高于小型报告公司普通股股息率的情况下, 才能被认定为优惠性的收益。股息或股息等价物只有具优惠性的部分须要纳入报告范围。脚注或文字披露可被用作解释小型报告公司确定"高于市场水平"时适用的标准。

or equivalents must be included. Footnote or narrative disclosure may be provided explaining the smaller reporting company's criteria for determining any portion considered to be above-market.

(ix) All other compensation for the covered fiscal year that the smaller reporting company could not properly report in any other column of the Summary Compensation Table (column (i)). Each compensation item that is not properly reportable in columns (c) through (h), regardless of the amount of the compensation item, must be included in column (i). Such compensation must include, but is not limited to:

(A) Perquisites and other personal benefits, or property, unless the aggregate amount of such compensation is less than $10,000;

(B) All "gross-ups" or other amounts reimbursed during the fiscal year for the payment of taxes;

(C) For any security of the smaller reporting company or its subsidiaries purchased from the smaller reporting company or its subsidiaries (through deferral of salary or bonus, or otherwise) at a discount from the market price of such security at the date of purchase, unless that discount is available generally, either to all security holders or to all salaried employees of the smaller reporting company, the compensation cost, if any, computed in accordance with FAS 123R;

(D) The amount paid or accrued to any namedexecutive officer pursuant to a plan or arrangement in connection with:

(1) Any termination, including without limitation through retirement, resignation, severance or constructive termination (including a change in responsibilities) of such executive officer's employment with the smaller reporting company and its subsidiaries; or

(2) A change in control of the smaller reporting company;

(E) Smaller reporting company contributions or other allocations to vested and unvested defined contribution plans;

(F) The dollar value of any insurance premiums paid by, or on behalf of, the smaller reporting company during the covered fiscal year with respect to life insurance for the benefit of a namedexecutive officer; and

(G) The dollar value of any dividends or other earnings paid on stock or option awards, when those amounts were not factored into the grant date fair value required to be reported for the stock or option award in column (e) or (f); and

Instructions to Item 402(n)(2)(ix).

1. Non-equity incentive plan awards and earnings and earnings on stock or options, except as specified in paragraph (n)(2)(ix)(G) of this Item, are required to be reported elsewhere as provided in this Item and are not reportable as All Other Compensation in column (i).

(ix)小型报告公司无法在《报酬简表》的任何其他栏目予以适当报告的所涉会计年度的所有其他报酬[(i)栏]。无法在(c)~(h)栏予以适当报告的报酬项目(不论报酬数额多少),均必须在(i)栏列出。该等报酬必须包括但不限于以下各项:

(A)特殊津贴及其他个人福利或财产,但总金额低于1万美元的除外;

(B)该会计年度为缴税而提供的所有“税款补足”或其他补偿数额;

(C)对于按低于购买日股票市价的价格,通过工资或奖金递延支付或其他方式从小型报告公司或其子公司折价购买的小型报告公司或其子公司的任何证券而言,其按照《美国财务会计准则公告第123号》(FAS123R)计算的报酬成本(如有),但所有证券持有人或小型报告公司的所有受薪雇员均可享受该折扣的除外;

(D)依照与下列事项有关的计划或安排而已向或应向任何具名高管支付的数额:

(1)任何该等高管与小型报告公司及其子公司雇佣关系的终止,包括但不限于退休、辞职、辞退或推定解除雇佣关系(包括职责变更);或者

(2)小型报告公司发生控制权变更。

(E)小型报告公司对已归属及未归属的固定缴款养老金计划的供款或其他拨款;

(F)小型报告公司或其代表在所涉会计年度为具名高管之利益缴纳的任何人寿保险保费的美元价值;及

(G)在计算(e)栏或(f)栏要求报告的股票或期权奖励在授予日的公允价值时,未予考虑的股票或期权奖励的任何股息或其他收益的美元价值;和

关于第402(n)(2)(ix)条的说明。

1.非股权激励计划奖励和收益及股票和期权收益,除本条第(n)(2)(ix)(G)款另有明确规定外,须按本条规定通过其他栏目报告,不必在(i)栏作为“所有其他报酬”披露。

2. Benefits paid pursuant to defined benefit and actuarial plans are not reportable as All Other Compensation in column (i) unless accelerated pursuant to a change in control; information concerning these plans is reportable pursuant to paragraph (q)(1) of this Item.

3. Reimbursements of taxes owed with respect to perquisites or other personal benefits must be included in the columns as tax reimbursements (paragraph (n)(2)(ix)(B) of this Item) even if the associated perquisites or other personal benefits are not required to be included because the aggregate amount of such compensation is less than $10,000.

4. Perquisites and other personal benefits shall be valued on the basis of the aggregate incremental cost to the smaller reporting company.

5. For purposes of paragraph (n)(2)(ix)(D) of this Item, an accrued amount is an amount for which payment has become due.

(x) The dollar value of total compensation for the covered fiscal year (column (j)). With respect to each namedexecutive officer, disclose the sum of all amounts reported in columns (c) through (i).

Instructions to Item 402(n).

1. Information with respect to the fiscal year prior to the last completed fiscal year will not be required if the smaller reporting company was not a reporting company pursuant to section 13(a) or 15(d) of the Exchange Act (15 U.S.C. 78m(a) or 78o(d)) at any time during that year, except that the smaller reporting company will be required to provide information for any such year if that information previously was required to be provided in response to a Commission filing requirement.

2. All compensation values reported in the Summary Compensation Table must be reported in dollars and rounded to the nearest dollar. Reported compensation values must be reported numerically, providing a single numerical value for each grid in the table. Where compensation was paid to or received by a namedexecutive officer in a different currency, a footnote must be provided to identify that currency and describe the rate and methodology used to convert the payment amounts to dollars.

3. If a namedexecutive officer is also a director who receives compensation for his or her services as a director, reflect that compensation in the Summary Compensation Table and provide a footnote identifying and itemizing such compensation and amounts. Use the categories in the Director Compensation Table required pursuant to paragraph (r) of this Item.

4. Any amounts deferred, whether pursuant to a plan established under section 401(k) of the Internal Revenue Code (26 U.S.C. 401(k)), or otherwise, shall be included in the appropriate column for the fiscal year in which earned.

2.依据固定收益养老金计划和精算计划支付的福利,除非因控制权变更提前转归,否则不必作为“所有其他报酬”在(i)栏项下报告;关于该等计划的信息应按照本条第(q)(1)款予以报告。

3.即使相关特殊津贴或其他个人福利因总额低于1万美元而不必填写,因特殊津贴或其他个人福利产生的退税也必须作为退税在各栏中填写[本条第(n)(2)(ix)(B)款]。

4.特殊津贴和其他个人福利应基于小型报告公司的增量成本总额进行估值。

5.就本条第(n)(2)(ix)(D)款而言,应计金额指到期应付的金额。

(x)所涉会计年度总报酬的美元价值[(j)栏]。对于每名具名高管,披露(c)栏至(i)栏报告的全部金额的总和。

关于第402(n)条的说明。

1.如果小型报告公司在上一完整会计年度之前的会计年度的任何时间不属于《交易法》第13(a)条或第15(d)条[《美国法典》第十五编第78m(a)节或第78o(d)节]规定的小型报告公司,则不必披露关于该会计年度的信息,但是如果按照证券交易委员会的文件提交规定应提供任何该等年度信息,则小型报告公司应予提供。

2.在《报酬简表》中报告的所有报酬均应以美元为单位,并四舍五入取整。所报告的报酬价值必须采用数字形式,表格的每个单元格中仅提供一个数值。如果具名高管的报酬是以其他货币收付的,则必须通过脚注注明所使用的币种,并载明将所付金额转换成美元时采用的汇率和方法。

3.如果某位具名高管同时兼任受薪董事,应在《报酬简表》中反映其担任董事所获得的报酬,并通过脚注注明该报酬及金额项目明细。在进行上述报告时,应采用本条第(r)款规定的《董事报酬表》中划定的类别。

4.根据《国内税收法典》第401(k)条[《美国法典》第二十六编第401(k)节]下设立的计划或因其他原因而递延支付的任何金额,应在赚取该金额的会计年度的相关栏目内列报。

(o) *Smaller reporting companies — Narrative disclosure to summary compensation table*. Provide a narrative description of any material factors necessary to an understanding of the information disclosed in the Table required by paragraph (n) of this Item. Examples of such factors may include, in given cases, among other things:

(1) The material terms of each namedexecutive officer's employment agreement or arrangement, whether written or unwritten;

(2) If at any time during the last fiscal year, any outstanding option or other equity-based award was repriced or otherwise materially modified (such as by extension of exercise periods, the change of vesting or forfeiture conditions, the change or elimination of applicable performance criteria, or the change of the bases upon which returns are determined), a description of each such repricing or other material modification;

(3) The waiver or modification of any specified performance target, goal or condition to payout with respect to any amount included in non-stock incentive plan compensation or payouts reported in column (g) to the Summary Compensation Table required by paragraph (n) of this Item, stating whether the waiver or modification applied to one or more specified namedexecutive officers or to all compensation subject to the target, goal or condition;

(4) The material terms of each grant, including but not limited to the date of exercisability, any conditions to exercisability, any tandem feature, any reload feature, any tax-reimbursement feature, and any provision that could cause the exercise price to be lowered;

(5) The material terms of any non-equity incentive plan award made to a namedexecutive officer during the last completed fiscal year, including a general description of the formula or criteria to be applied in determining the amounts payable and vesting schedule;

(6) The method of calculating earnings on nonqualified deferred compensation plans including nonqualified defined contribution plans; and

(7) An identification to the extent material of any item included under All Other Compensation(column(i)) in the Summary Compensation Table. Identification of an item shall not be considered material if it does not exceed the greater of $25,000 or 10% of all items included in the specified category in question set forth in paragraph (n)(2)(ix) of this Item. All items of compensation are required to be included in the Summary Compensation Table without regard to whether such items are required to be identified.

Instruction to Item 402(o). The disclosure required by paragraph (o)(2) of this Item would not apply to any repricing that occurs through a pre-existing formula or mechanism in the plan or award that results in the periodic adjustment of the option or SAR exercise or base price, an antidilution provision in a plan or award, or a recapitalization or similar

(o)小型报告公司——对《报酬简表》的文字披露。对于本条第(n)款要求在上述表格中披露的信息,应就理解该等信息所必要的任何重大因素提供文字说明。例如,视具体情况,此类因素可包括但不限于:

(1)每一具名高管书面或非书面的雇佣协议或安排中的重大条款;

(2)对每一项重新定价或重大修改的说明,前提是在上一会计年度内任何时间对任何未兑现的期权或其他基于股权的奖励进行了重新定价或其他重大修改(如行权期限被延长、归属或丧失条件发生变更、适用业绩标准被变更或取消,或者确定回报的基准发生变更)。

(3)就本条第(n)款规定的《报酬简表》(g)栏内报告的非股票激励计划报酬或付款而言,与其任何数额有关的任何既定业绩指标、目标或付款条件的豁免或变更,同时说明豁免或变更是仅适用于一名或数名既定的具名高管,或是适用于受该等指标、目标或条件限制的所有报酬。

(4)每项授予的重大条款,包括但不限于行权起始日期、行权的任何条件、任何并行特性、任何重新授予特性、任何退税特性以及任何可能导致行权价降低的规定。

(5)在上一完整会计年度内授予具名高管的任何非股权激励计划奖励的重大条款,包括关于确定应付数额和归属时间表的公式或标准的总体说明。

(6)无税收优惠资格的递延报酬计划(包括无税收优惠资格的固定缴款养老金计划)的收益计算方法;和

(7)列明在“所有其他报酬”[《报酬简表》(i)栏]中包含的任何重大项目。如数额不超过2.5万美元或者在本条第(n)(2)(ix)款列明的相关类别中包含的所有项目总额10%(以数额较高者为准),不视为重大项目。所有报酬项目均应纳入《报酬简表》之中,无论该等项目是否被要求一一列明。

关于第402(o)条的说明。计划或奖励中事先设定了公式或机制,对期权或股票增值权的行权价或底价进行定期调整,由此导致的任何重新定价均不适用本条第(o)(2)款的披露要求;此外,激励计划或奖励中的反稀释条款,或对期权或股票增值权项下同一类别标的证券的全部持有者产生同等影响的资本重组或类似交易,亦不适用本

transaction equally affecting all holders of the class of securities underlying the options or SARs.

(p) *Smaller reporting companies — Outstanding equity awards at fiscal year-end table.* (1) Provide the information specified in paragraph (p)(2) of this Item, concerning unexercised options; stock that has not vested; and equity incentive plan awards for each named executive officer outstanding as of the end of the smaller reporting company's last completed fiscal year in the following tabular format:

Outstanding Equity Awards at Fiscal Year-End

Name	Option awards					Stock awards			
	Number of securities underlying unexercised options (#) exercisable	Number of securities underlying unexercised options (#) unexercisable	Equity incentive plan awards: Number of securities underlying unexercised unearned options (#)	Option exercise price ($)	Option expiration date	Number of shares or units of stock that have not vested (#)	Market value of shares of units of stock that have not vested ($)	Equity incentive plan awards: Number of unearned shares, units or other rights that have not vested (#)	Equity incentive plan awards: Market or payout value of unearned shares, units or other rights that have not vested ($)
(a)	(b)	(c)	(d)	(e)	(f)	(g)	(h)	(i)	(j)
PEO									
A									
B									

(2) The Table shall include:

(i) The name of the namedexecutive officer (column (a));

(ii) On an award-by-award basis, the number of securities underlying unexercised options, including awards that have been transferred other than for value, that are exercisable and that are not reported in column (d) (column (b));

(iii) On an award-by-award basis, the number of securities underlying unexercised options, including awards that have been transferred other than for value, that are unexercisable and that are not reported in column (d) (column (c));

(iv) On an award-by-award basis, the total number of shares underlying unexercised options awarded under any equity incentive plan that have not been earned (column (d));

条第(o)(2)款的披露要求。

(p)小型报告公司——会计年度年末未兑现的股权奖励表。(1)在下列表格中提供本条第(p)(2)款规定的与如下各项相关的信息:截至小型报告公司上一会计年度年末每一具名高管未行使的期权、尚未归属的股票以及未兑现的股权激励计划奖励:

截至会计年度年末未兑现的股权奖励

姓名	期权奖励					股票奖励			
	可行使但未行使的期权项下的标的证券数量(#)	不可行使且未行使的期权项下的标的证券数量(#)	股权激励计划奖励:未行使且尚未赚取的期权项下的标的证券数量(#)	期权行权价(美元)	期权到期日	尚未归属的股份或股票单位数量(#)	尚未归属的股份或股票单位的市值(美元)	股权激励计划:尚未赚取的或尚未归属的股份、单位或其他权利的数量(#)	股权激励计划奖励:尚未赚取的或尚未归属的股份、单位或其他权利的市值或支付价值(美元)
(a)	(b)	(c)	(d)	(e)	(f)	(g)	(h)	(i)	(j)
主要高管									
A									
B									

(2)表格中应包括:

(i)具名高管姓名[(a)栏];

(ii)按奖励逐一列明可行使且未在(d)栏报告的尚未行使的期权(包括已无偿转让的奖励)项下的标的证券数量[(b)栏];

(iii)按奖励逐一列明不可行使的且未在(d)栏报告的尚未行使的期权(包括已无偿转让的奖励)项下的标的证券数量[(c)栏];

(iv)按奖励逐一列明根据任何股权激励计划授予的尚未赚取且尚未行使的期权项下的标的股份的总数[(d)栏];

(v) For each instrument reported in columns (b), (c) and (d), as applicable, the exercise or base price (column (e));

(vi) For each instrument reported in columns (b), (c) and (d), as applicable, the expiration date (column (f));

(vii) The total number of shares of stock that have not vested and that are not reported in column (i) (column (g));

(viii) The aggregate market value of shares of stock that have not vested and that are not reported in column (j) (column (h));

(ix) The total number of shares of stock, units or other rights awarded under any equity incentive plan that have not vested and that have not been earned, and, if applicable the number of shares underlying any such unit or right (column (i)); and

(x) The aggregate market or payout value of shares of stock, units or other rights awarded under any equity incentive plan that have not vested and that have not been earned (column (j)).

Instructions to Item 402(p)(2).

1. Identify by footnote any award that has been transferred other than for value, disclosing the nature of the transfer.

2. The vesting dates of options, shares of stock and equity incentive plan awards held at fiscal-year end must be disclosed by footnote to the applicable column where the outstanding award is reported.

3. Compute the market value of stock reported in column (h) and equity incentive plan awards of stock reported in column (j) by multiplying the closing market price of the smaller reporting company's stock at the end of the last completed fiscal year by the number of shares or units of stock or the amount of equity incentive plan awards, respectively. The number of shares or units reported in column (d) or (i), and the payout value reported in column (j), shall be based on achieving threshold performance goals, except that if the previous fiscal year's performance has exceeded the threshold, the disclosure shall be based on the next higher performance measure (target or maximum) that exceeds the previous fiscal year's performance. If the award provides only for a single estimated payout, that amount should be reported. If the target amount is not determinable, smaller reporting companies must provide a representative amount based on the previous fiscal year's performance.

4. Multiple awards may be aggregated where the expiration date and the exercise and/or base price of the instruments is identical. A single award consisting of a combination of options, SARs and/or similar option-like instruments shall be reported as separate awards with respect to each tranche with a different exercise and/or base price or expiration date.

(v)(b)栏、(c)栏和(d)栏中(视具体情况而定)报告的每一工具的行权价或底价[(e)栏];

(vi)如适用,(b)栏、(c)栏和(d)栏中(视具体情况而定)报告的每一工具的到期日[(f)栏];

(vii)未在(i)栏报告的且尚未归属的股份总数[(g)栏];

(viii)未在(j)栏报告的且尚未归属的股份的市价总额[(h)栏];

(ix)任何股权激励计划下授予但尚未归属和尚未赚取的股份、单位或其他权利的总数,和(如适用)上述任何单位或权利项下的标的股份的数量[(i)栏];和

(x)任何股权激励计划下授予但尚未归属和尚未赚取的股份、单位或其他权利的市价或支付价值总额[(j)栏]。

关于第402(p)(2)条的说明。

1.通过脚注说明任何已经无偿转让的奖励,并披露转让的性质。

2.截至会计年度年末尚未兑现的期权、股份和股权激励计划奖励的归属日期,必须在报告相关奖励的栏目添加脚注予以披露。

3.(h)栏中报告的股票市值和(j)栏中报告的股权激励计划奖励的市值应分别通过如下方式计算:小型报告公司截至上一会计年度年末的股票市场收盘价乘以股份或股票单位数量,或乘以股权激励计划奖励的数量。(d)栏或(i)栏中报告的份额或单位数量,以及(j)栏中报告的支付价值,应基于所实现的业绩基准目标计算;但是,上一会计年度业绩表现超出上述基准的,上述份额或单位数量应基于超出上一会计年度业绩的更高一级的业绩指标(目标额或最高额)进行披露。如果奖励仅提供了一个预估支付数额,应报告该支付数额。如果目标额无法确定,小型报告公司必须基于上一会计年度的业绩,提供一个代表性的数额。

4.如不同工具的到期日和行权价及/或底价相同,可将多项奖励予以合计。由期权、股票升值权及/或与期权类似的工具混合构成的单一奖励,如各构成部分的行权价及/或底价或到期日不同,应作为不同的奖励分别报告。

5. Options or stock awarded under an equity incentive plan are reported in columns (d) or (i) and (j), respectively, until the relevant performance condition has been satisfied. Once the relevant performance condition has been satisfied, even if the option or stock award is subject to forfeiture conditions, options are reported in column (b) or (c), as appropriate, until they are exercised or expire, or stock is reported in columns (g) and (h) until it vests.

(q) *Smaller reporting companies — Additional narrative disclosure.* Provide a narrative description of the following to the extent material:

(1) The material terms of each plan that provides for the payment of retirement benefits, or benefits that will be paid primarily following retirement, including but not limited to tax-qualified defined benefit plans, supplemental executive retirement plans, tax-qualified defined contribution plans and nonqualified defined contribution plans.

(2) The material terms of each contract, agreement, plan or arrangement, whether written or unwritten, that provides for payment (s) to a namedexecutive officer at, following, or in connection with the resignation, retirement or other termination of a named executive officer, or a change in control of the smaller reporting company or a change in the named executive officer's responsibilities following a change in control, with respect to each named executive officer.

(r) *Smaller reporting companies — Compensation of directors.* (1) Provide the information specified in paragraph (r)(2) of this Item, concerning the compensation of the directors for the smaller reporting company's last completed fiscal year, in the following tabular format:

Director Compensation

Name	Fees earned or paid in cash ($)	Stock awards ($)	Option awards ($)	Non-equity incentive plan compensation ($)	Nonqualified deferred compensation earnings($)	All other compensation ($)	Total ($)
(a)	(b)	(c)	(d)	(e)	(f)	(g)	(h)
A							
B							
C							
D							
E							

(2) The Table shall include:

(i) The name of each director unless such director is also a namedexecutive officer under paragraph (m) of this Item and his or her compensation for service as a director is

5.在相关业绩条件满足之前,根据股权激励计划授予的期权或股票应分别通过(d)栏或(i)栏和(j)栏报告。一旦相关业绩条件得到满足之后,即使期权或股票奖励仍受制于丧失条件,在期权行使或到期前,期权仍应视适当情况通过(b)栏或(c)栏报告,在归属之前,股票仍应通过(g)栏和(h)栏报告。

(q)小型报告公司——补充文字披露。如具有重要意义,应提供下列各项的文字说明:

(1)规定支付退休金或者主要在退休后支付的福利的每项计划的重大条款,包括但不限于有税收优惠资格的固定收益养老金计划、高管补充退休计划、有税收优惠资格或者无税收优惠资格的固定缴款养老金计划。

(2)作出如下规定的每项书面或非书面合同、协议、计划或安排的重大条款:在具名高管辞职、退休或者因其他原因终止与公司的雇佣关系之时、之后应向该等高管提供付款或者应就该等情形提供相关付款;或者在小型报告公司发生控制权变更之时、之后应向具名高管提供付款或者应就该等变更提供相关付款;或者在控制权变更后,具名高管的职责在发生变更之时、之后应向该等高管提供付款或者应就该等情形提供相关付款。

(r)小型报告公司——董事报酬。(1)在下表中提供本条第(r)(2)款规定的与小型报告公司董事在上一完整会计年度的报酬相关的信息:

董事报酬

姓名	已赚取的或已经以现金支付的费用(美元)	股票奖励(美元)	期权奖励(美元)	非股权激励计划报酬(美元)	无税收优惠资格的递延报酬收益(美元)	所有其他报酬(美元)	总计(美元)
(a)	(b)	(c)	(d)	(e)	(f)	(g)	(h)
A							
B							
C							
D							
E							

(2)表格中应包括:

(i)每名董事的姓名,但同时兼任本条第(m)款中的具名高管,并且其担任董事获得的报酬已通过本条第(n)款规定的《报酬简表》或按照本条第(o)款至第(q)款的规定

fully reflected in the Summary Compensation Table pursuant to paragraph (n) of this Item and otherwise as required pursuant to paragraphs (o) through (q) of this Item (column (a));

(ii) The aggregate dollar amount of all fees earned or paid in cash for services as a director, including annual retainer fees, committee and/or chairmanship fees, and meeting fees (column (b));

(iii) For awards of stock, the aggregate grant date fair value computed in accordance with FASB ASC Topic 718 (column (c));

(iv) For awards of options, with or without tandem SARs (including awards that subsequently have been transferred), the aggregate grant date fair value computed in accordance with FASB ASC Topic 718 (column (d));

Instruction to Item 402(r)(2)(iii) and (iv). For each director, disclose by footnote to the appropriate column, the aggregate number of stock awards and the aggregate number of option awards outstanding at fiscal year end.

(v) The dollar value of all earnings for services performed during the fiscal year pursuant to non-equity incentive plans as defined in paragraph (m)(5)(iii) of this Item, and all earnings on any outstanding awards (column (e));

(vi) Above-market or preferential earnings on compensation that is deferred on a basis that is not tax-qualified, including such earnings on nonqualified defined contribution plans (column (f));

(vii) All other compensation for the covered fiscal year that the smaller reporting company could not properly report in any other column of the Director Compensation Table (column (g)). Each compensation item that is not properly reportable in columns (b) through (f), regardless of the amount of the compensation item, must be included in column (g) and must be identified and quantified in a footnote if it is deemed material in accordance with paragraph (o)(7) of this Item. Such compensation must include, but is not limited to:

(A) Perquisites and other personal benefits, or property, unless the aggregate amount of such compensation is less than $10,000;

(B) All "gross-ups" or other amounts reimbursed during the fiscal year for the payment of taxes;

(C) For any security of the smaller reporting company or its subsidiaries purchased from the smaller reporting company or its subsidiaries (through deferral of salary or bonus, or otherwise) at a discount from the market price of such security at the date of purchase, unless that discount is available generally, either to all security holders or to all salaried employees of the smaller reporting company, the compensation cost, if any, computed in accordance with FAS 123R;

予以完全列报的董事除外[(a)栏];

(ii)作为董事赚取或获付的所有现金费用的总额,包括年度聘用费、委员会和/或主席费用以及会议出席费[(b)栏];

(iii)对于股票奖励,应按照《财务会计准则委员会会计准则汇编第718号专题》计算授予日的公允价值总额[(c)栏];

(iv)对于期权奖励(包括后续转让的奖励),无论是否附带并行的股票增值权,均应按照《财务会计准则委员会会计准则汇编第718号专题》计算授予日的公允价值总额[(d)栏];

关于第402(r)(2)(iii)条和第402(r)(2)(iv)条的说明。对于每名董事,均应通过适当栏目的脚注披露截至会计年度年末尚未兑现的股票奖励总数和期权奖励总数。

(v)依据本条第(m)(5)(iii)款定义的非股权激励计划在该会计年度内履行服务获得的所有收益,以及任何未兑现奖励的所有收益的美元价值[(e)栏];

(vi)在无税收优惠基础上递延支付的,高于市场水平或者优惠性的收益,包括从不能享受税收优惠的固定缴款养老金计划中获得的收益[(f)栏];

(vii)小型报告公司无法在《董事报酬表》的任何其他栏目予以适当报告的所涉会计年度的所有其他报酬[(g)栏]。无法在(b)~(f)栏予以适当报告的报酬项目(不论报酬数额多少),如果根据本条第(o)(7)款视为具有重大意义,则必须在(g)栏列出并予以量化。该等报酬必须包括但不限于以下各项:

(A)特殊津贴及其他个人福利或财产,但总金额低于1万美元的除外;

(B)该会计年度为缴税而提供的所有“税款补足”或其他补偿数额。

(C)对于按低于购买日股票市价的价格,通过工资或奖金递延支付或其他方式从小型报告公司或其子公司折价购买的小型报告公司或其子公司的任何证券而言,其按照《美国财务会计准则公告第123号》(FAS123R)计算的报酬成本(如有),但所有证券持有人或小型报告公司的所有受薪雇员均可享受该折扣的除外;

(D) The amount paid or accrued to any director pursuant to a plan or arrangement in connection with:

(1) The resignation, retirement or any other termination of such director; or

(2) A change in control of the smaller reporting company;

(E) Smaller reporting company contributions or other allocations to vested and unvested defined contribution plans;

(F) Consulting fees earned from, or paid or payable by the smaller reporting company and/or its subsidiaries (including joint ventures);

(G) The annual costs of payments and promises of payments pursuant to director legacy programs and similar charitable award programs;

(H) The dollar value of any insurance premiums paid by, or on behalf of, the smaller reporting company during the covered fiscal year with respect to life insurance for the benefit of a director; and

(I) The dollar value of any dividends or other earnings paid on stock or option awards, when those amounts were not factored into the grant date fair value required to be reported for the stock or option award in column (c) or (d); and

Instruction to Item 402(r)(2)(vii). Programs in which smaller reporting companies agree to make donations to one or more charitable institutions in a director's name, payable by the smaller reporting company currently or upon a designated event, such as the retirement or death of the director, are charitable awards programs or director legacy programs for purposes of the disclosure required by paragraph (r)(2)(vii)(G) of this Item. Provide footnote disclosure of the total dollar amount payable under the program and other material terms of each such program for which tabular disclosure is provided.

(viii) The dollar value of total compensation for the covered fiscal year (column (h)). With respect to each director, disclose the sum of all amounts reported in columns (b) through (g).

Instruction to Item 402(r)(2). Two or more directors may be grouped in a single row in the Table if all elements of their compensation are identical. The names of the directors for whom disclosure is presented on a group basis should be clear from the Table.

(3) *Narrative to director compensation table.* Provide a narrative description of any material factors necessary to an understanding of the director compensation disclosed in this Table. While material factors will vary depending upon the facts, examples of such factors may include, in given cases, among other things:

(i) A description of standard compensation arrangements (such as fees for retainer, committee service, service as chairman of the board or a committee, and meeting attendance); and

(ii) Whether any director has a different compensation arrangement, identifying that

(D)依照与下列事项有关的计划或安排而已向或应向任何董事支付的数额:

(1)该等董事辞职、退休或以任何其他方式终止与公司的雇佣关系;或者
(2)小型报告公司发生控制权变更。
(E)小型报告公司报告期间已归属及未归属的固定缴款养老金计划的供款或其他拨款;
(F)从小型报告公司和/或其子公司(包括合营企业)赚取的,或者该等公司支付或应付的咨询费;
(G)董事遗赠计划和类似慈善奖励计划项下付款和承诺付款的年度成本;

(H)小型报告公司或其代表在所涉会计年度为董事之利益缴纳的任何寿险保险费的美元价值;和

(I)在计算(c)栏或(d)栏要求报告的股票或期权奖励在授予日的公允价值时,未予考虑的股票或期权奖励的任何股息或其他收益的美元价值;和

关于第402(r)(2)(vii)条的说明。小型报告公司同意以董事的名义向一家或数家慈善机构做出捐赠的计划[无论捐赠款是当期应付款项或是指定事件发生后(如董事的退休或死亡)应付的款项],属于本条第(r)(2)(vii)(G)款要求披露的慈善奖励计划或董事遗赠计划。应通过脚注披露计划项下的应付款项的总额,以及表格中要求披露的每一计划的其他重大条款。

(viii)所涉会计年度总报酬的美元价值[(h)栏]。应针对每名董事,披露在(b)栏至(g)栏报告的所有数额的总和。

关于第402(r)(2)条的说明。如果2名(含)以上董事报酬的各项因素均相同,可以合并为一行报告。合并披露的董事的姓名应在表格中明确列示。

(3)《董事报酬表》的文字说明。应针对理解表格内披露的董事报酬所必需的任何重大因素提供文字说明。视实际情况,上述重大因素会有不同,如该等因素可能包括但不限于:

(i)标准报酬安排的说明(如聘任费、委员会任职费、董事长或者委员会主席酬金以及会议出席费);和

(ii)任何董事是否存在不同的报酬安排,如有,应指明该董事并说明相关安排

director and describing the terms of that arrangement.

Instruction to Item 402(r). In addition to the Instruction to paragraph (r)(2)(vii) of this Item, the following apply equally to paragraph (r) of this Item: Instructions 2 and 4 to paragraph (n) of this Item; the Instructions to paragraphs (n)(2)(iii) and (iv) of this Item; the Instructions to paragraphs (n)(2)(v) and (vi) of this Item; the Instructions to paragraph (n)(2)(vii) of this Item; the Instruction to paragraph (n)(2)(viii) of this Item; the Instructions to paragraph (n)(2)(ix) of this Item; and paragraph (o)(7) of this Item. These Instructions apply to the columns in the Director Compensation Table that are analogous to the columns in the Summary Compensation Table to which they refer and to disclosures under paragraph (r) of this Item that correspond to analogous disclosures provided for in paragraph (n) of this Item to which they refer.

(s) *Narrative disclosure of the registrant's compensation policies and practices as they relate to the registrant's risk management.* To the extent that risks arising from the registrant's compensation policies and practices for its employees are reasonably likely to have a material adverse effect on the registrant, discuss the registrant's policies and practices of compensating its employees, including non-executive officers, as they relate to risk management practices and risk-taking incentives. While the situations requiring disclosure will vary depending on the particular registrant and compensation policies and practices, situations that may trigger disclosure include, among others, compensation policies and practices: at a business unit of the company that carries a significant portion of the registrant's risk profile; at a business unit with compensation structured significantly differently than other units within the registrant; at a business unit that is significantly more profitable than others within the registrant; at a business unit where compensation expense is a significant percentage of the unit's revenues; and that vary significantly from the overall risk and reward structure of the registrant, such as when bonuses are awarded upon accomplishment of a task, while the income and risk to the registrant from the task extend over a significantly longer period of time. The purpose of this paragraph (s) is to provide investors material information concerning how the registrant compensates and incentivizes its employees that may create risks that are reasonably likely to have a material adverse effect on the registrant. While the information to be disclosed pursuant to this paragraph (s) will vary depending upon the nature of the registrant's business and the compensation approach, the following are examples of the issues that the registrant may need to address for the business units or employees discussed:

条款。

关于第402(r)条的说明。除关于本条第(r)(2)(vii)款的说明之外,下列说明或条款同样适用于本条第(r)款:关于本条第(n)款的说明2和说明4;关于本条第(n)(2)(iii)款和第(n)(2)(iv)款的说明;关于本条第(n)(2)(v)款和第(n)(2)(vi)款的说明;关于本条第(n)(2)(vii)款的说明;关于本条第(n)(2)(viii)款的说明;关于本条第(n)(2)(ix)款的说明;以及关于本条第(o)(7)款的说明。[1] 上述说明适用于《董事报酬表》中与《报酬简表》中类似的相关栏目,以及本条第(r)款下与本条第(n)款下的披露类似的相关披露。

(s)注册人与风险管理相关的报酬政策和实践的文字披露。如果根据合理预期,注册人的雇员报酬政策和实践产生的风险可能对注册人产生重大不利影响,应在与注册人的风险管理实践和涉险激励相关的情况下,论述有关雇员(包括不属于高管的管理人员)的报酬政策和实践。须要披露的情形因具体注册人以及报酬政策和实践而异,举例而言,可能须要披露相关报酬政策和实践的情形包括但不限于:公司某一业务部门承担注册人大部分风险;某一业务部门的报酬结构与注册人其他部门显著不同;某一业务部门的盈利能力显著高于注册人其他部门;某一业务部门的报酬费用占部门收入较大比例;以及某一业务部门与注册人整体的风险和回报结构存在很大不同(如奖金的授予须基于某项任务的完成,而该任务给注册人带来的收入和风险分布在一个明显更长的期限内)。本款的目的是向投资者提供重大信息,说明根据合理预期,可能带来风险并给注册人造成重大不利影响的注册人对员工发放报酬和激励员工的方式。依据本款披露的信息可能因注册人的业务性质和报酬方法而异,作为示例,下文列举了注册人可能须要说明的关涉上述业务部门和雇员的某些问题:

1 按上下文,原文"and paragraph (o)(7) of this Item"疑误,似应为"and the Instructions to paragraph (o)(7) of this Item",译文已按后者处理。——译者注

(1) The general design philosophy of the registrant's compensation policies and practices for employees whose behavior would be most affected by the incentives established by the policies and practices, as such policies and practices relate to or affect risk taking by employees on behalf of the registrant, and the manner of their implementation;

(2) The registrant's risk assessment or incentive considerations, if any, in structuring its compensation policies and practices or in awarding and paying compensation;

(3) How the registrant's compensation policies and practices relate to the realization of risks resulting from the actions of employees in both the short term and the long term, such as through policies requiring claw backs or imposing holding periods;

(4) The registrant's policies regarding adjustments to its compensation policies and practices to address changes in its risk profile;

(5) Material adjustments the registrant has made to its compensation policies and practices as a result of changes in its risk profile; and

(6) The extent to which the registrant monitors its compensation policies and practices to determine whether its risk management objectives are being met with respect to incentivizing its employees.

*Instruction to Item 402.*Specify the applicable fiscal year in the title to each table required under this Item which calls for disclosure as of or for a completed fiscal year.

[71 FR 53241, Sept. 8, 2006; 71 FR 56225, Sept. 26, 2006, as amended at 71 FR 78350, Dec. 29, 2006; 73 FR 958, Jan. 4, 2008; 74 FR 68362, Dec. 23, 2009]

§229.403 (Item 403) Security ownership of certain beneficial owners and management.

(a) *Security ownership of certain beneficial owners.* Furnish the following information, as of the most recent practicable date, substantially in the tabular form indicated, with respect to any person (including any "group" as that term is used in section 13(d)(3) of the Exchange Act) who is known to the registrant to be the beneficial owner of more than five percent of any class of the registrant's voting securities. The address given in column (2) may be a business, mailing or residence address. Show in column (3) the total number of shares beneficially owned and in column (4) the percentage of class so owned. Of the number of shares shown in column (3), indicate by footnote or otherwise the amount known to be shares with respect to which such listed beneficial owner has the right to acquire beneficial ownership, as specified in Rule 13d-3(d)(1) under the Exchange Act (§240.13d-3(d)(1) of this chapter).

(1)对于其行为受报酬政策和实践下的激励措施影响最大的雇员,注册人报酬政策和实践的总体设计理念(条件是该等政策和实践与雇员代表注册人承受的风险相关或者对其有影响),以及该等政策和实践的执行方式;

(2)在构建报酬政策和实践过程中以及在授予和支付报酬过程中注册人的风险评估或激励考量(如有);

(3)从短期和长期来看,注册人的报酬政策和实践是否可能因雇员行动而引发风险,如该等政策和实践是否要求雇员在特定情况下退还报酬或对雇员施加持有期限制,从而可能导致相关风险。

(4)注册人关于根据风险特性变化而调整报酬政策和实践的政策;

(5)注册人因风险特性变化而对其报酬政策和实践所作的重大调整;和

(6)注册人为判定在激励员工同时风险管理目标是否得到实现,而对该政策和实践进行监控的程度。

关于第402条的说明。对于本条规定的提供截至某一会计年度的信息或提供某一完整会计年度信息的每个表格,应在表格标题中指明相关的会计年度年份。

[《联邦公报》第71卷第53241页,2006年9月8日;《联邦公报》第71卷第56225页,2006年9月26日,修正索引:《联邦公报》第71卷第78350页,2006年12月29日;《联邦公报》第73卷第958页,2008年1月4日;《联邦公报》第74卷第68362页,2009年12月23日。]

第229.403节(第403条) 特定受益所有人及管理层的证券所有权

(a)特定受益所有人的证券所有权。参照以下表格形式,提供截至最近可行日期的关于任何下述主体的信息:注册人所知的持有该注册人有表决权证券任一类别证券5%以上的受益所有人[包括《交易法》第13(d)(3)条所述的任何“团体”]。第(2)栏填写的地址可以是企业地址、邮递地址或住宅地址。在第(3)栏填写受益所有人持有的股份总数,在第(4)栏填写该等股份在相应股份类别中所占比例。在第(3)栏填写的股份数量中,以脚注或其他形式注明已明确知悉所列受益所有人根据《交易法》的《13d-3(d)(1)规则》[本章第240.13d-3(d)(1)节]有权获得受益所有权的股份数量。

(1) Title of class	(2) Name and address of beneficial owner	(3) Amount and nature of beneficial ownership	(4) Percent of class

(b) *Security ownership of management.* Furnish the following information, as of the most recent practicable date, in substantially the tabular form indicated, as to each class of equity securities of the registrant or any of its parents or subsidiaries, including directors' qualifying shares, beneficially owned by all directors and nominees, naming them, each of the named executive officers as defined in Item 402(a)(3) (§229.402(a)(3)), and directors and executive officers of the registrant as a group, without naming them. Show in column (3) the total number of shares beneficially owned and in column (4) the percent of the class so owned. Of the number of shares shown in column (3), indicate, by footnote or otherwise, the amount of shares that are pledged as security and the amount of shares with respect to which such persons have the right to acquire beneficial ownership as specified in §240.13d–3(d)(1) of this chapter.

(1) Title of class	(2) Name of beneficial owner	(3) Amount and nature of beneficial ownership	(4) Percent of class

(c) *Changes in control.* Describe any arrangements, known to the registrant, including any pledge by any person of securities of the registrant or any of its parents, the operation of which may at a subsequent date result in a change in control of the registrant.

Instructions to Item 403:1. The percentages are to be calculated on the basis of the amount of outstanding securities, excluding securities held by or for the account of the registrant or its subsidiaries, plus securities deemed outstanding pursuant to Rule 13d–3 (d)(1) under the Exchange Act 17(CFR 240.13d–3(d)(1)). For purposes of paragraph (b), if the percentage of shares beneficially owned by any director or nominee, or by all directors and officers of the registrant as a group, does not exceed one percent of the class so owned, the registrant may, in lieu of furnishing a precise percentage, indicate this fact by means of an asterisk and explanatory footnote or other similar means.

2. For the purposes of this Item, beneficial ownership shall be determined in accordance with Rule 13d–3 under the Exchange Act (§240.13d–3 of this chapter). Include such additional subcolumns or other appropriate explanation of column (3) necessary to reflect amounts as to which the beneficial owner has (A) sole voting power, (B) shared voting power, (C) sole investment power, or (D) shared investment power.

3. The registrant shall be deemed to know the contents of any statements filed with the Commission pursuant to section 13 (d) or 13 (g) of the Exchange Act. When

(1)证券类别名称	(2)受益所有人的姓名和地址	(3)受益所有权的数量和性质	(4)在相应股份类别内所占比例

(b)管理层的证券所有权。参照以下表格形式，提供截至最近可行日期的关于下述证券的信息：所有董事及提名董事、第402(a)(3)条[第229.402(a)(3)节]定义的每一具名高管，以及注册人的全体董事和高管作为受益所有人拥有的注册人或其任何母公司或子公司的每一类别的权益证券(包括董事的资格股)；董事及提名董事的姓名均应予注明，注册人的全体董事和高管则可统一予以说明，不必一一注明姓名。在第(3)栏填写受益所有人持有的股份总数，在第(4)栏填写该股份在相应股份类别内所占比例。在第(3)栏填写的股份数量中，以脚注或其他形式注明作为担保物质押的股份数量，以及该人有权获得本章第240.13d-3(d)(1)节规定的受益所有权的股份数量。

(1)证券类别名称	(2)受益所有人的姓名和地址	(3)受益所有权的数量和性质	(4)在相应股份类别内所占比例

(c)控制权变更。说明注册人所知的将来有可能导致注册人发生控制权变更的任何安排，包括任何主体对注册人或其任何母公司的证券所作的任何质押。

关于第403条的说明：1.百分比的计算基数应采用发行在外证券的数量(但不包括由注册人或其子公司的账户或为该等账户持有的证券)，加上被《交易法》的《13d-3(d)(1)规则》[《联邦规章汇编》第十七编第240.13d-3(d)(1)节]视为发行在外的证券。就第(b)款而言，如果任何董事或提名董事作为受益所有人持有的股份(或该注册人的全体董事和管理人员整体持有的股份)比例不超过该类别股份的1%，则该注册人可用星号、脚注或其他类似方式说明这一事实，而不必提供准确的百分比数字。

2.就本条的目的而言，应按照《交易法》的《13d-3规则》(即本章第240.13d-3节)确定受益所有权。如果为了反映受益所有人拥有的(A)独立表决权、(B)共享表决权、(C)独立投资权或(D)共享投资权的数量，可在第(3)栏增加必要的分栏或通过其他适当形式予以说明。

3.对于按照《交易法》第13(d)条或第13(g)条向证券交易委员会提交的任何说明书，注册人应视为已了解该等说明书的内容。在适用之时，注册人可采信该等说明书

applicable, a registrant may rely upon information set forth in such statements unless the registrant knows or has reason to believe that such information is not complete or accurate or that a statement or amendment should have been filed and was not.

4. For purposes of furnishing information pursuant to paragraph (a) of this Item, the registrant may indicate the source and date of such information.

5. Where more than one beneficial owner is known to be listed for the same securities, appropriate disclosure should be made to avoid confusion. For purposes of paragraph (b), in computing the aggregate number of shares owned by directors and officers of the registrant as a group, the same shares shall not be counted more than once.

6. Paragraph (c) of this Item does not require a description of ordinary default provisions contained in the charter, trust indentures or other governing instruments relating to securities of the registrant.

7. Where the holder(s) of voting securities reported pursuant to paragraph (a) hold more than five percent of any class of voting securities of the registrant pursuant to any voting trust or similar agreement, state the title of such securities, the amount held or to be held pursuant to the trust or agreement (if not clear from the table) and the duration of the agreement. Give the names and addresses of the voting trustees and outline briefly their voting rights and other powers under the trust or agreement.

[47 FR 11401, Mar. 16, 1982, as amended at 47 FR 55665, Dec. 13, 1982; 51 FR 42056, Nov. 20, 1986; 57 FR 48158, Oct. 21, 1992; 71 FR 53252, Sept. 8, 2006]

§229.404 (Item 404) Transactions with related persons, promoters and certain control persons.

(a) *Transactions with related persons.* Describe any transaction, since the beginning of the registrant's last fiscal year, or any currently proposed transaction, in which the registrant was or is to be a participant and the amount involved exceeds $120,000, and in which any related person had or will have a direct or indirect material interest. Disclose the following information regarding the transaction:

(1) The name of the related person and the basis on which the person is a related person.

(2) The related person's interest in the transaction with the registrant, including the related person's position(s) or relationship(s) with, or ownership in, a firm, corporation, or other entity that is a party to, or has an interest in, the transaction.

(3) The approximate dollar value of the amount involved in the transaction.

(4) The approximate dollar value of the amount of the related person's interest in the transaction, which shall be computed without regard to the amount of profit or loss.

(5) In the case of indebtedness, disclosure of the amount involved in the transaction

中提供的信息,但注册人明知或应知该信息并不完整、准确,或者存在应提交但实际未提交的声明或修正的除外。

4.在按照本条第(a)款提供信息之时,注册人可说明该信息的来源和日期。

5.如果已知同一证券存在一个以上的受益所有人,应进行适当的披露以避免混淆。就第(b)款而言,在计算注册人的董事和管理人员集体拥有的股份总数时,相同的股份不应重复计算。

6.本条第(c)款并不要求说明章程、信托契约或其他章程性文件中与注册人证券相关的一般性违约条款。

7.对于按照第(a)款报告的有表决权证券,如果证券持有人按照任何表决信托或类似协议持有该注册人任一类别的有表决权证券的5%以上,应说明该等证券的名称、根据信托或协议持有或将要持有的股份数量(如果表格提供的信息未明确列示)以及该协议的有效期。说明表决的信托受托人的姓名和地址,并简要说明该信托或协议向其赋予的表决权和其他权力。

[《联邦公报》第47卷第11401页,1982年3月16日,修正索引:《联邦公报》第47卷第55665页,1982年12月13日;《联邦公报》第51卷第42056页,1986年11月20日;《联邦公报》第57卷第48158页,1992年10月21日;《联邦公报》第71卷第53252页,2006年9月8日。]

第229.404节(第404条)　与关联人、发起人及特定控制人进行的交易

(a)与关联人进行的交易。对于该注册人已经或将要参与的自该注册人上一会计年度年初以来的所有交易或当前拟议开展的所有交易,如所涉金额超过12万美元,且在上述交易中任何关联人拥有或将拥有直接或间接重大利益的,应对此类交易予以说明。应针对上述交易披露如下信息:

(1)该关联人的姓名以及关联关系产生的基础。

(2)该关联人在与注册人进行的交易中所具有的利益,包括该关联人在作为交易方,或在对交易拥有利害关系的事务所、公司或其他实体中所担任的职位、存在的关系或拥有的所有权。

(3)交易所涉金额的大致美元价值。

(4)该关联人在交易中所具有的利益的大致美元价值,计算时不应考虑利润或亏损。

(5)披露交易所涉债务金额时,应包括披露期内尚未清偿的最大本金总额、截至

shall include the largest aggregate amount of principal outstanding during the period for which disclosure is provided, the amount thereof outstanding as of the latest practicable date, the amount of principal paid during the periods for which disclosure is provided, the amount of interest paid during the period for which disclosure is provided, and the rate or amount of interest payable on the indebtedness.

(6) Any other information regarding the transaction or the related person in the context of the transaction that is material to investors in light of the circumstances of the particular transaction.

Instructions to Item 404(a). 1. For the purposes of paragraph (a) of this Item, the term related person means:

a. Any person who was in any of the following categories at any time during the specified period for which disclosure under paragraph (a) of this Item is required:

i. Any director orexecutive officer of the registrant;

ii. Any nominee for director, when the information called for by paragraph (a) of this Item is being presented in a proxy or information statement relating to the election of that nominee for director; or

iii. Any immediate family member of a director or executive officer of the registrant, or of any nominee for director when the information called for by paragraph (a) of this Item is being presented in a proxy or information statement relating to the election of that nominee for director, which means any child, stepchild, parent, stepparent, spouse, sibling, mother-in-law, father-in-law, son-in-law, daughter-in-law, brother-in-law, or sister-in-law of such director, executive officer or nominee for director, and any person (other than a tenant or employee) sharing the household of such director, executive officer or nominee for director; and

b. Any person who was in any of the following categories when a transaction in which such person had a direct or indirect material interest occurred or existed:

i. A security holder covered by Item 403(a) (§229.403(a)); or

ii. Any immediate family member of any such security holder, which means any child, stepchild, parent, stepparent, spouse, sibling, mother-in-law, father-in-law, son-in-law, daughter-in-law, brother-in-law, or sister-in-law of such security holder, and any person (other than a tenant or employee) sharing the household of such security holder.

2. For purposes of paragraph (a) of this Item, a transaction includes, but is not limited to, any financial transaction, arrangement or relationship (including any indebtedness or guarantee of indebtedness) or any series of similar transactions, arrangements or relationships.

3. The amount involved in the transaction shall be computed by determining the

最近可行日期的未清偿总额、披露期偿还的本金数额、披露期偿还的利息总额以及该债务的利率或应付利息总额。

(6)根据交易的具体情形,与交易或关联人相关的任何对投资者具有重要意义的其他交易信息。

关于第404(a)条的说明。1.就本条第(a)款而言,"关联人"一词系指:

a.在本条第(a)款规定的披露的期间内的任何时候属于以下任一类别的任何人:

i.注册人的任何董事或高管;

ii.任何提名董事,此时本条第(a)款要求提供的信息将通过与该提名董事选举有关的征集投票权报告或信息说明书予以提供;或者

iii.注册人董事或高管的任何直系亲属,或任何提名董事的直系亲属(此时本条第(a)款要求提供的信息将通过与该提名董事选举有关的征集投票权或信息说明书予以提供);直系亲属指该董事、高管或提名董事的任何子女、继子女、父母、继父母、配偶、兄弟姐妹、配偶的父母、子女的配偶及兄弟姐妹的配偶,并包括与该董事、高管或提名董事共同生活的任何人(但不包括租客或雇员);及

b.该人拥有直接或间接重大利益的交易发生或存在时属于以下任一类别的任何人:

i.第403(a)条[第229.403(a)节]所涉的证券持有人;或者

ii.任何该等证券持有人的直系亲属;直系亲属指证券持有人的任何子女、继子女、父母、继父母、配偶、兄弟姐妹、配偶的父母、子女的配偶及兄弟姐妹的配偶,并包括与该证券持有人共同生活的任何人(但不包括租客或雇员);

2.就本条第(a)款的目的而言,交易包括但不限于任何金融交易、安排或关系(包括任何债务或债务担保)或任何系列的类似交易、安排或关系。

3.交易所涉金额的计算应以交易所涉金额的美元价值为准,同时:

dollar value of the amount involved in the transaction in question, which shall include:

a. In the case of any lease or other transaction providing for periodic payments or installments, the aggregate amount of all periodic payments or installments due on or after the beginning of the registrant's last fiscal year, including any required or optional payments due during or at the conclusion of the lease or other transaction providing for periodic payments or installments; and

b. In the case of indebtedness, the largest aggregate amount of all indebtedness outstanding at any time since the beginning of the registrant's last fiscal year and all amounts of interest payable on it during the last fiscal year.

4. In the case of a transaction involving indebtedness:

a. The following items of indebtedness may be excluded from the calculation of the amount of indebtedness and need not be disclosed: Amounts due from the related person for purchases of goods and services subject to usual trade terms, for ordinary business travel and expense payments and for other transactions in the ordinary course of business;

b. Disclosure need not be provided of any indebtedness transaction for the related persons specified in Instruction 1.b. to paragraph (a) of this Item; and

c. If the lender is a bank, savings and loan association, or broker–dealer extending credit under Federal Reserve Regulation T (12 CFR part 220) and the loans are not disclosed as nonaccrual, past due, restructured or potential problems (see Item III.C.1. and 2. of Industry Guide 3, Statistical Disclosure by Bank Holding Companies (17 CFR 229.802(c))), disclosure under paragraph (a) of this Item may consist of a statement, if such is the case, that the loans to such persons:

i. Were made in the ordinary course of business;

ii. Were made on substantially the same terms, including interest rates and collateral, as those prevailing at the time for comparable loans with persons not related to the lender; and

iii. Did not involve more than the normal risk of collectibility or present other unfavorable features.

5.a. Disclosure of an employment relationship or transaction involving an executive officer and any related compensation solely resulting from that employment relationship or transaction need not be provided pursuant to paragraph (a) of this Item if:

i. The compensation arising from the relationship or transaction is reported pursuant to Item 402 (§229.402); or

ii. Theexecutive officer is not an immediate family member (as specified in Instruction 1 to paragraph (a) of this Item) and such compensation would have been reported under Item 402 (§229.402) as compensation earned for services to the registrant if the executive officer was a named executive officer as that term is defined in Item 402

a.对于任何租赁或其他提供定期或分期付款的交易而言,应包括在该注册人最近一个会计年度年初之时或之后到期应付的所有定期或分期付款总额,包括在任何租赁期间或结束之时,或在其他提供定期或分期付款的交易期间或结束之时必须支付或者可以选择支付的任何金额;及

b.对于债务而言,应包括该注册人最近一个会计年度年初以来任何时候尚未清偿的所有债务的最大总额,以及在上一个会计年度应就该债务支付的所有利息金额。

4.对于涉及债务的交易而言:

a.以下债务可不纳入债务金额的计算,且不必披露:关联人根据一般交易条款购买货物或服务时应支付的金额、应就常规差旅和费用支付的金额以及在正常业务运作中应就其他交易支付的金额。

b.对于本条第(a)款的说明1.b.中规定的关联人而言,任何负债交易均不必披露;且

c.如果贷款人为银行、储蓄及贷款协会或者根据《联邦储备T管理规定》(《联邦规章汇编》第十二编第220部分)提供贷款的经纪自营商,并且,如果贷款并未作为停息、过期、重组或潜在问题予以披露(详见《银行控股公司的统计数据披露——行业指引之三》的第III.C.1条和第III.C.2条[《联邦规章汇编》第十七编第229.802(c)节],则按照本条第(a)款所作的披露可包括一份声明,说明向该等人借出的贷款的如下事实:

i.是在正常业务运作中提供的;

ii.与同期借给非关联方的具有可比性的贷款相比,其贷款条款大致相当,包括利率和担保条件等;和

iii.不涉及异常的收款风险或存在其他不利特征。

5.a.如果符合以下条件,则不必按照本条第(a)款披露涉及高管的雇佣关系或交易,且不必披露完全由该雇佣关系或交易产生的任何相关报酬:

i.因上述关系或交易产生的报酬已按照第402条(第229.402节)进行报告;或

ii.该高管并不属于直系亲属[详见本条第(a)款的说明1],且假设该高管为具名高管[定义见第402(a)(3)条(第229.402(a)(3)节)],则该报酬将按照第402条(第229.402节)作为为注册人提供服务而收取的报酬进行报告,并且注册人董事会已经批准该报酬,或者董事会的报酬委员会(或者履行类似职能的独立董事组成的团体)已经建议

(a)(3) (§229.402(a)(3)), and such compensation had been approved, or recommended to the board of directors of the registrant for approval, by the compensation committee of the board of directors (or group of independent directors performing a similar function) of the registrant.

b. Disclosure of compensation to a director need not be provided pursuant to paragraph (a) of this Item if the compensation is reported pursuant to Item 402(k) (§229.402(k)).

6. A person who has a position or relationship with a firm, corporation, or other entity that engages in a transaction with the registrant shall not be deemed to have an indirect material interest within the meaning of paragraph (a) of this Item where:

a. The interest arises only:

i. From such person's position as a director of another corporation or organization that is a party to the transaction; or

ii. From the direct or indirect ownership by such person and all other persons specified in Instruction 1 to paragraph (a) of this Item, in the aggregate, of less than a ten percent equity interest in another person (other than a partnership) which is a party to the transaction; or

iii. From both such position and ownership; or

b. The interest arises only from such person's position as a limited partner in a partnership in which the person and all other persons specified in Instruction 1 to paragraph (a) of this Item, have an interest of less than ten percent, and the person is not a general partner of and does not hold another position in the partnership.

7. Disclosure need not be provided pursuant to paragraph (a) of this Item if:

a. The transaction is one where the rates or charges involved in the transaction are determined by competitive bids, or the transaction involves the rendering of services as a common or contract carrier, or public utility, at rates or charges fixed in conformity with law or governmental authority;

b. The transaction involves services as a bank depositary of funds, transfer agent, registrar, trustee under a trust indenture, or similar services; or

c. The interest of the related person arises solely from the ownership of a class of equity securities of the registrant and all holders of that class of equity securities of the registrant received the same benefit on a pro rata basis.

(b) *Review, approval or ratification of transactions with related persons.* (1) Describe the registrant's policies and procedures for the review, approval, or ratification of any transaction required to be reported under paragraph (a) of this Item. While the material features of such policies and procedures will vary depending on the particular circumstances, examples of such features may include, in given cases, among other things:

注册人董事会批准该报酬。

b.如果相关报酬已经按照第402(k)条[第229.402(k)节]进行报告,则不必按照本条第(a)款披露董事的报酬。

6.某人如果在与注册人进行交易的事务所、公司或其他实体中担任职务或与之存在关系,则在符合以下条件之时,不应视为拥有本条第(a)款所指的间接重大利益:

a.该利益完全因以下原因产生:

i.该人在另一个交易方公司或组织中担任董事;

ii.该人及本条第(a)款说明1规定的所有其他人直接或间接合计持有另一个交易方(合伙除外)少于10%的股权权益;或

iii.由上述职位或持股共同产生;或

b.该利益完全由于该人在合伙中担任有限合伙人而产生,而该人以及本条第(a)款说明1中规定的所有其他人在该合伙中拥有少于10%的权益,并且,该人并非普通合伙人,也不在合伙中担任其他职位。

7.在符合以下条件之时,不必按照本条第(a)款进行披露:

a.交易的费率或收费通过竞争性投标确定,或者,交易涉及提供公共运输或承包运输服务或公用事业,且费率或收费符合法律或政府监管部门的规定;

b.交易涉及诸如银行存款、过户代理、注册、按照信托协议提供的信托服务或其他服务;或

c.该关联人拥有的利益完全因其拥有该注册人某一类别的股权证券而产生,且该注册人发行的该类别股权证券的所有持有人均按比例获得同样的利益。

(b)对与关联人进行的交易所作的审查、批准或确认。(1)对于本条第(a)款要求报告的任何交易,均应说明注册人的审查、批准或确认任何该等交易的政策和程序。该等政策和程序的主要特征视具体情况可能会有差异,举例而言,此类主要特征可包括但不限于:

(i) The types of transactions that are covered by such policies and procedures;

(ii) The standards to be applied pursuant to such policies and procedures;

(iii) The persons or groups of persons on the board of directors or otherwise who are responsible for applying such policies and procedures; and

(iv) A statement of whether such policies and procedures are in writing and, if not, how such policies and procedures are evidenced.

(2) Identify any transaction required to be reported under paragraph (a) of this Item since the beginning of the registrant's last fiscal year where such policies and procedures did not require review, approval or ratification or where such policies and procedures were not followed.

Instruction to Item 404 (b). Disclosure need not be provided pursuant to this paragraph regarding any transaction that occurred at a time before the related person became one of the enumerated persons in Instruction 1.a.i., ii., or iii. to Item 404 (a) if such transaction did not continue after the related person became one of the enumerated persons in Instruction 1.a.i., ii., or iii. to Item 404(a).

(c) *Promoters and certain control persons.* (1) Registrants that are filing a registration statement on Form S-1 under the Securities Act (§239.11 of this chapter) or on Form 10 under the Exchange Act (§249.210 of this chapter) and that had a promoter at any time during the past five fiscal years shall:

(i) State the names of the promoter(s), the nature and amount of anything of value (including money, property, contracts, options or rights of any kind) received or to be received by each promoter, directly or indirectly, from the registrant and the nature and amount of any assets, services or other consideration therefore received or to be received by the registrant; and

(ii) As to any assets acquired or to be acquired by the registrant from a promoter, state the amount at which the assets were acquired or are to be acquired and the principle followed or to be followed in determining such amount, and identify the persons making the determination and their relationship, if any, with the registrant or any promoter. If the assets were acquired by the promoter within two years prior to their transfer to the registrant, also state the cost thereof to the promoter.

(2) Registrants shall provide the disclosure required by paragraphs (c)(1)(i) and (c)(1)(ii) of this Item as to any person who acquired control of a registrant that is a shell company, or any person that is part of a group, consisting of two or more persons that agree to act together for the purpose of acquiring, holding, voting or disposing of equity securities of a registrant, that acquired control of a registrant that is a shell company. For purposes of this Item, *shell company* has the same meaning as in Rule 405 under the Securities Act (17 CFR 230.405) and Rule 12b-2 under the Exchange Act

(i)该等政策和程序所涉及的交易类型;

(ii)根据该等政策和程序应予适用的标准;

(iii)董事会或负责执行该等政策和程序的人士或团体;及

(iv)一份关于该等政策和程序是否为书面政策和程序的声明,如果政策和程序并无书面版本,应说明如何证明该等政策和程序。

(2)如果该等政策和程序不要求审查、批准或确认,或者该等政策和程序并未得到遵守,应具体说明自该注册人上一个会计年度年初以来,按照本条第(a)款应予报告的任何交易。

关于第404(b)条的说明。如果在关联人成为第404(a)条的说明1.a.i.、说明1.a.ii.或说明1.a.iii.内列举的人之后,交易不再继续开展,则不必按照本款规定就此前的任何交易进行披露。

(c)发起人和特定控制人。(1)注册人如果按照《证券法》(本章第239.11节)下的《S-1表格》或《交易法》(本章第249.210节)下的《10表格》提交注册说明书,并且,如果注册人在过去5个会计年度内的任何时间曾下属任一子公司有发起人身份的,应:

(i)说明发起人的姓名/名称,并说明每一发起人从注册人处直接或间接收到或将收到的任何有价物品(包括现金、财产、合同、期权或任何类型的权利)的性质和金额,并应说明该注册人因而收到或将收到的任何资产、服务或其他对价的性质和金额;且

(ii)对于注册人从发起人处收到或将收到的任何资产,应说明其金额以及确定该等金额时遵循或将遵循的原则,并应说明确定该等金额的人及其与注册人或任何发起人的关系(如有)。如果发起人获得资产的时间距离将资产转让给注册人的时间不足两年,还应说明发起人当时获得该等资产的成本。

(2)如果任何主体获得注册人的控制权,且注册人属于上市壳公司,或者,如果任何主体所在团体由两个(含)以上主体组成,该团体成员同意共同获得、持有、表决或处置注册人的股权证券,并获得注册人的控制权,且注册人属于上市壳公司,则注册人应按照本条第(c)(1)(i)款和第(c)(1)(ii)款的规定披露上述主体。对于本条而言,"上市壳公司"的定义见《证券法》的《405规则》(《联邦规章汇编》第十七编第230.405节)和《交易法》的《12b-2规则》(《联邦规章汇编》第十七编第240.12b-2节)。

(17 CFR 240.12b-2).

(d) *Smaller reporting companies.* A registrant that qualifies as a "smaller reporting company," as defined by §229.10(f)(1), must provide the following information in order to comply with this Item:

(1) The information required by paragraph (a) of this Item for the period specified there for a transaction in which the amount involved exceeds the lesser of $120,000 or one percent of the average of the smaller reporting company's total assets at year end for the last two completed fiscal years;

(2) The information required by paragraph (c) of this Item; and

(3) A list of all parents of the smaller reporting company showing the basis of control and as to each parent, the percentage of voting securities owned or other basis of control by its immediate parent, if any.

Instruction to Item 404(d).

1. Include information for any material underwriting discounts and commissions upon the sale of securities by the smaller reporting company where any of the persons specified in paragraph (a) of this Item was or is to be a principal underwriter or is a controlling person or member of a firm that was or is to be a principal underwriter.

2. For smaller reporting companies information shall be given for the period specified in paragraph (a) of this Item and, in addition, for the fiscal year preceding the small reporting company's last fiscal year.

Instructions to Item 404. 1. If the information called for by this Item is being presented in a registration statement filed pursuant to the Securities Act or the Exchange Act, information shall be given for the periods specified in the Item and, in addition, for the two fiscal years preceding the registrant's last fiscal year, unless the information is being incorporated by reference into a registration statement on Form S-4 (17 CFR 239.25), in which case, information shall be given for the periods specified in the Item.

2. A foreign private issuer will be deemed to comply with this Item if it provides the information required by Item 7.B. of Form 20-F (17 CFR 249.220f) with more detailed information provided if otherwise made publicly available or required to be disclosed by the issuer's home jurisdiction or a market in which its securities are listed or traded.

[71 FR 53252, Sept. 8, 2006, as amended at 73 FR 964, Jan. 4, 2008]

§ 229.405(Item 405) Compliance with section 16(a) of the Exchange Act.

Every registrant having a class of equity securities registered pursuant to section 12 of the Exchange Act (15 U.S.C. 78*l*), every closed-end investment company registered under the Investment Company Act of 1940 (15 U.S.C. 80a-1 *et seq.*), and every

(d)小型报告公司。注册人如果符合“小型报告公司”的条件[定义见第229.10(f)(1)节],则必须提供以下信息以遵守本条规定:

(1)按照本条第(a)款规定的期间,就下述交易提供该款要求提供的信息:所涉金额超过12万美元或超过该小型报告公司截至过去2个会计年度年底的总资产平均值的1%(以较低者为准)的交易;

(2)本条第(c)款要求提供的信息;及

(3)该小型报告公司所有母公司的列表,说明每一母公司的控制基础,并说明其直接母公司持有的有表决权证券的比例或其他控制基础(如有)。

关于第404(d)条的说明。

1.如果本条第(a)款规定的任何人曾经或将担任主承销商,或属于曾经或将担任主承销商的公司的控制人或成员,应提供关于该小型报告公司销售证券时的任何重大承销贴现和佣金的信息。

2.对于小型报告公司,提供的信息应覆盖本条第(a)款规定的期间,此外,还应覆盖该小型报告公司上一个会计年度之前的会计年度。

关于第404条的说明。1.如果注册人通过根据《证券法》或《交易法》提交的注册说明书列报本条要求提供的信息,则除本条规定的期间外,该等信息还应覆盖该注册人上一个会计年度之前的两个会计年度;但是,该等信息通过引用方式被纳入按照《S-4表格》(《联邦规章汇编》第十七编第239.25节)提交的注册说明书之中的,覆盖本条规定的期间即可。

2.如果外国私募发行人按照《20-F表格》第7.B.条(《联邦规章汇编》第十七编第249.220f节)的要求提供相关信息时,提供其母国或挂牌交易证券市场要求予以公开或披露的更为翔实的信息,在此情况下,该外国私募发行人将被视为已履行本条规定。

[《联邦公报》第71卷第53252页,2006年9月8日,修正索引:《联邦公报》第73卷第964页,2008年1月4日。]

第229.405节(第405条)　对《交易法》第16(a)条的合规

按照《交易法》第12条(《美国法典》第十五编第78l节)注册某一类别股权证券的每名注册人,根据《1940年投资公司法》(《美国法典》第十五编第80a-1节及其后条文)注册的每一家封闭式投资公司及按照《1935年公用事业控股公司法》(《美国法典》第十

holding company registered pursuant to the Public Utility Holding Company Act of 1935 (15 U.S.C. 79a *et seq.*) shall:

(a) Based solely upon a review of Forms 3 and 4 (17 CFR 249.103 and 249.104) and amendments thereto furnished to the registrant under 17 CFR 240.16a-3(e) during its most recent fiscal year and Forms 5 and amendments thereto (17 CFR 249.105) furnished to the registrant with respect to its most recent fiscal year, and any written representation referred to in paragraph (b)(1) of this section.

(1) Under the caption "Section 16(a) Beneficial Ownership Reporting Compliance," identify each person who, at any time during the fiscal year, was a director, officer, beneficial owner of more than ten percent of any class of equity securities of the registrant registered pursuant to section 12 of the Exchange Act, or any other person subject to section 16 of the Exchange Act with respect to the registrant because of the requirements of section 30 of the Investment Company Act or section 17 of the Public Utility Holding Company Act ("reporting person") that failed to file on a timely basis, as disclosed in the above Forms, reports required by section 16(a) of the Exchange Act during the most recent fiscal year or prior fiscal years.

(2) For each such person, set forth the number of late reports, the number of transactions that were not reported on a timely basis, and any known failure to file a required Form. A known failure to file would include, but not be limited to, a failure to file a Form 3, which is required of all reporting persons, and a failure to file a Form 5 in the absence of the written representation referred to in paragraph (b)(1) of this section, unless the registrant otherwise knows that no Form 5 is required.

Note: The disclosure requirement is based on a review of the forms submitted to the registrant during and with respect to its most recent fiscal year, as specified above. Accordingly, a failure to file timely need only be disclosed once. For example, if in the most recently concluded fiscal year a reporting person filed a Form 4 disclosing a transaction that took place in the prior fiscal year, and should have been reported in that year, the registrant should disclose that late filing and transaction pursuant to this Item 405 with respect to the most recently concluded fiscal year, but not in material filed with respect to subsequent years.

(b) With respect to the disclosure required by paragraph (a) of this section, if the registrant:

(1) Receives a written representation from the reporting person that no Form 5 is required; and

(2) Maintains the representation for two years, making a copy available to the Commission or its staff upon request, the registrant need not identify such reporting person pursuant to paragraph (a) of this section as having failed to file a Form 5 with

五编第79a节及其后条文)注册的每一家控股公司,均应:

(a)仅基于对如下材料的审查:按《联邦规章汇编》第十七编第240.16a-3(e)节提供给注册人的其最近一会计年度的《3表格》、《4表格》(《联邦规章汇编》第十七编第249.103和第249.104节)及其修正;以及提供给注册人的其最近一会计年度的《5表格》及其修正和本条第(b)(1)款所述的任何书面声明:

(1)在"第16(a)条受益所有权报告合规"一栏之下,逐一指明下述主体:在该会计年度的任何时间曾担任注册人董事、管理人员的人,或持有注册人按照《交易法》第12条注册的任一类别股权证券10%以上的受益所有人;或因《投资公司法》第30条或《公用事业控股公司法》第17条的规定,而必须就注册人遵守《交易法》第16条的任何其他人("报告人"),前提是该等报告人没有在最近一会计年度或之前的会计年度及时按《交易法》第16(a)条的规定提交如上述表格所披露的相关报告。

(2)针对每一上述主体,列明迟交报告的数量、未能及时报告的交易数量,以及任何已知的未能按规定提交表格的行为。已知悉的未能提交报告之行为包括但不限于:未能提交所有报告人均须提交的《3表格》,以及在未收到本条第b(1)款所述书面声明的情况下未能提交《5表格》,但注册人通过其他方式知悉不必提交《5表格》的除外。

注:如上所述,披露要求系基于对最近一会计年度呈交给注册人的与该年度相关的表格之审查。因此,未及时提交文件的行为仅须披露一次。例如,在最近结束的会计年度,某报告人提交的《4表格》披露了在前一会计年度进行且本应在该年度报告的某次交易,注册人应根据本第405条的规定,在就最近结束的会计年度提交的文件中披露该交易及迟交报告事宜,但不应在就之后的年度提交的文件中进行披露。

(b)就本条(a)款的披露要求而言,若:

(1)注册人收到报告人作出的不必提交《5表格》的书面声明;且

(2)注册人在两年内保存该书面声明,并在证券交易委员会或其工作人员提出要求时向其提供声明复件,则注册人不必按照本条(a)款的要求逐一指明未就该会计年度提交《5表格》的报告人。

respect to that fiscal year.

[56 FR 7265, Feb. 21, 1991, as amended at 61 FR 30391, June 14, 1996; 70 FR 46088, Aug. 9, 2005]

§229.406(Item 406) Code of ethics.

(a) Disclose whether the registrant has adopted a code of ethics that applies to the registrant's principalexecutive officer, principal financial officer, principal accounting officer or controller, or persons performing similar functions. If the registrant has not adopted such a code of ethics, explain why it has not done so.

(b) For purposes of this Item 406, the term *code of ethics* means written standards that are reasonably designed to deter wrongdoing and to promote:

(1) Honest and ethical conduct, including the ethical handling of actual or apparent conflicts of interest between personal and professional relationships;

(2) Full, fair, accurate, timely, and understandable disclosure in reports and documents that a registrant files with, or submits to, the Commission and in other public communications made by the registrant;

(3) Compliance with applicable governmental laws, rules and regulations;

(4) The prompt internal reporting of violations of the code to an appropriate person or persons identified in the code; and

(5) Accountability for adherence to the code.

(c) The registrant must:

(1) File with the Commission a copy of its code of ethics that applies to the registrant's principalexecutive officer, principal financial officer, principal accounting officer or controller, or persons performing similar functions, as an exhibit to its annual report;

(2) Post the text of such code of ethics on its Internet website and disclose, in its annual report, its Internet address and the fact that it has posted such code of ethics on its Internet Web site; or

(3) Undertake in its annual report filed with the Commission to provide to any person without charge, upon request, a copy of such code of ethics and explain the manner in which such request may be made.

(d) If the registrant intends to satisfy the disclosure requirement under Item 10 of Form 8-K regarding an amendment to, or a waiver from, a provision of its code of ethics that applies to the registrant's principalexecutive officer, principal financial officer, principal accounting officer or controller, or persons performing similar functions and that relates to any element of the code of ethics definition enumerated in paragraph (b) of this Item by posting such information on its Internet website, disclose the registrant's Internet address and such intention.

[《联邦公报》第56卷第7265页,1991年2月21日,修正索引:《联邦公报》第61卷第30391页,1996年6月14日;《联邦公报》第70卷第46088页,2005年8月9日。]

第229.406节(第406条) 职业道德规范

(a)披露注册人是否制定了适用于其主要高管、主要财务官、主要会计官或控制官,或履行类似职能的人员的职业道德规范。如注册人未制定该等规范,应说明原因。

(b)就第406条而言,"职业道德规范"系指设计合理的书面标准,旨在威慑不当行为并提倡及促进:

(1)诚实及道德的行为,包括以合乎职业道德的方式处理个人及职业关系中存在的实际或表面利益冲突;

(2)在注册人提交或呈交给证券交易委员会的报告和文件以及注册人的其他公开文件中作出完整、公平、准确、及时、易懂的披露;

(3)对适用的政府法律、规则及规章的合规;

(4)违反职业道德规范的行为向规范中指明的相关主体及时作出内部报告;及

(5)对职业道德规范的遵守实施问责。

(c)注册人必须:

(1)以年度报告的附录的形式,向证券交易委员会提交适用于其主要高管、主要财务官、主要会计官或控制官,或履行类似职能的人员的职业道德规范;

(2)在其网站上公布职业道德规范文本,并在其年度报告中披露相关网址,并披露该等职业道德规范已通过其网站予以公布的事实;或

(3)在向证券交易委员会提交的年度报告中,承诺在接到任何人提出的请求时,免费向之提供该职业道德规范的复件,并说明提出请求的具体方式。

(d)对于适用于其主要高管、主要财务官、主要会计官或控制官或履行类似职能的人员的职业道德规范之修正或豁免,若该等修正或豁免与本条第(b)款列举的职业道德规范定义的任何要素相关,则如注册人希望通过在网站上公布该等信息的方式履行《8-K表格》第10条的披露要求,应披露注册人的网址和通过上述方式进行披露的意向。

Instructions to Item 406. 1. A registrant may have separate codes of ethics for different types of officers. Furthermore, a *code of ethics* within the meaning of paragraph (b) of this Item may be a portion of a broader document that addresses additional topics or that applies to more persons than those specified in paragraph (a). In satisfying the requirements of paragraph (c), a registrant need only file, post or provide the portions of a broader document that constitutes a *code of ethics* as defined in paragraph (b) and that apply to the persons specified in paragraph (a).

[68 FR 5127, Jan. 31, 2003, as amended at 70 FR 1594, Jan. 7, 2005]

§229.407(Item 407) Corporate governance.

(a) *Director independence.* Identify each director and, when the disclosure called for by this paragraph is being presented in a proxy or information statement relating to the election of directors, each nominee for director, that is independent under the independence standards applicable to the registrant under paragraph (a)(1) of this Item. In addition, if such independence standards contain independence requirements for committees of the board of directors, identify each director that is a member of the compensation, nominating or audit committee that is not independent under such committee independence standards. If the registrant does not have a separately designated audit, nominating or compensation committee or committee performing similar functions, the registrant must provide the disclosure of directors that are not independent with respect to all members of the board of directors applying such committee independence standards.

(1) In determining whether or not the director or nominee for director is independent for the purposes of paragraph (a) of this Item, the registrant shall use the applicable definition of independence, as follows:

(i) If the registrant is a listed issuer whose securities are listed on a national securities exchange or in an inter-dealer quotation system which has requirements that a majority of the board of directors be independent, the registrant's definition of independence that it uses for determining if a majority of the board of directors is independent in compliance with the listing standards applicable to the registrant. When determining whether the members of a committee of the board of directors are independent, the registrant's definition of independence that it uses for determining if the members of that specific committee are independent in compliance with the independence standards applicable for the members of the specific committee in the listing standards of the national securities exchange or inter-dealer quotation system that the registrant uses for determining if a majority of the board of directors are independent. If the registrant does not have independence standards for a committee, the independence standards for that specific committee in the listing standards of the national securities exchange or

关于第406条的说明1.对于不同类型的管理人员,注册人可分别制定不同的职业道德规范。此外,本条第(b)款定义的“职业道德规范”不一定是一份独立文件,而可以是某一份文件的一部分,后者涵盖的内容可以更广,适用的主体也可以比第(a)款的规定更广。在履行第(c)款的规定之时,注册人仅须提交、发布或提供该文件中构成第(b)款定义的“职业道德规范”并适用于第(a)款指明的主体的部分。

[《联邦公报》第68卷第5127页,2003年1月31日,修正索引:《联邦公报》第70卷第1594页,2005年1月7日。]

第229.407节(第407条) 公司治理

(a)董事独立性。指明符合本条第(a)(1)款规定的适用于注册人的独立标准的每名董事;同时,在董事选举中按照本款规定在征集投票权报告或信息说明书中进行披露时,还应指明根据上述标准具备独立性的每名提名董事。此外,如该独立标准包含对董事会各委员会的独立性要求,则须按各委员会的独立标准指明报酬委员会、提名委员会或审计委员会中不具备独立性的董事。若注册人没有在董事会之外另设审计委员会、提名委员会、报酬委员会或履行类似职能的其他委员会,则注册人必须采用上述标准中包含的委员会独立标准,披露董事会所有成员中不具备独立性的董事。

(1)在判断董事或提名董事是否符合本条第(a)款的独立标准时,注册人应采用如下关于“独立”的适用定义:

(i)如注册人属于上市发行人,且其证券上市的全国性证券交易所或交易商报价系统要求过半数的董事具备独立性,则采用的定义应为注册人按照适用上市标准,判断是否过半数董事具备独立性时采用的“独立”的定义。在判断董事会下属委员会成员是否具备独立性时采用的定义应为:注册人用以判断过半数董事会成员是否具备独立性时所采用的该交易所或系统的上市标准中适用于具体的董事会下属委员会成员的独立性标准。若注册人没有针对委员会的独立标准,采用的定义应为注册人用以判断过半数董事会成员是否具备独立性时所采用的该交易所或系统的上市标准中适用于该具体委员会的独立性标准。

inter–dealer quotation system that the registrant uses for determining if a majority of the board of directors are independent.

(ii) If the registrant is not a listed issuer, a definition of independence of a national securities exchange or of an inter–dealer quotation system which has requirements that a majority of the board of directors be independent, and state which definition is used. Whatever such definition the registrant chooses, it must use the same definition with respect to all directors and nominees for director. When determining whether the members of a specific committee of the board of directors are independent, if the national securities exchange or national securities association whose standards are used has independence standards for the members of a specific committee, use those committee specific standards.

(iii) If the information called for by paragraph (a) of this Item is being presented in a registration statement on Form S–1 (§239.11 of this chapter) under the Securities Act or on a Form 10 (§249.210 of this chapter) under the Exchange Act where the registrant has applied for listing with a national securities exchange or in an inter–dealer quotation system that has requirements that a majority of the board of directors be independent, the definition of independence that the registrant uses for determining if a majority of the board of directors is independent, and the definition of independence that the registrant uses for determining if members of the specific committee of the board of directors are independent, that is in compliance with the independence listing standards of the national securities exchange or inter–dealer quotation system on which it has applied for listing, or if the registrant has not adopted such definitions, the independence standards for determining if the majority of the board of directors is independent and if members of the committee of the board of directors are independent of that national securities exchange or inter–dealer quotation system.

2. If a registrant elects to satisfy paragraph (c) of this Item by posting its code of ethics on its website pursuant to paragraph (c)(2), the code of ethics must remain accessible on its Web site for as long as the registrant remains subject to the requirements of this Item and chooses to comply with this Item by posting its code on its Web site pursuant to paragraph (c)(2).

(2) If the registrant uses its own definitions for determining whether its directors and nominees for director, and members of specific committees of the board of directors, are independent, disclose whether these definitions are available to security holders on the registrant's Web site. If so, provide the registrant's Web site address. If not, include a copy of these policies in an appendix to the registrant's proxy statement or information statement that is provided to security holders at least once every three fiscal years or if the policies have been materially amended since the beginning of the registrant's last fiscal year. If a current copy of the policies is not available to security holders on the

(ii)如注册人不属于上市发行人,则应采用要求过半数董事具备独立性的全国性证券交易所或报价系统关于"独立"的定义,并指明所选用的定义。无论选择何种定义,注册人均应将该定义统一适用于全体董事及提名董事统。在判断董事会具体委员会成员是否具备独立性时,如其标准被注册人采用的全国性证券交易所或全国性证券协会拥有针对具体委员会成员的独立性标准,则应采用该等委员会具体的标准。

(iii)如注册人申请在全国性证券交易所或报价系统申请上市,且该等交易所或报价系统要求过半数董事会成员具备独立性,同时,若按照《证券法》下的《S-1表格》(本章第239.11节)或《交易法》下的《10表格》(本章第249.210节)提交的注册说明书中载有本条第(a)款要求提供的信息,则应采用注册人用于判断过半数董事会成员是否具备独立性时所采用的"独立"定义,以及注册人用于判断董事会具体委员会成员是否具备独立性时采用的"独立"定义,且该等定义应与前述全国性证券交易所或报价系统申请上市时的独立性标准相符。若注册人没有采取上述定义,则应采用该证券交易所或报价系统用于判断过半数董事会成员及董事会具体委员会成员是否具备独立性时采用的独立标准。

2.若注册人选择按照第(c)(2)款的规定,通过在其网站上发布职业道德规范来履行本条第(c)款的要求,则在注册人受本条规定约束并选择按第(c)(2)款通过在网站上发布职业道德规范来履行本条规定的期间,注册人必须保证可以通过其网站访问该等职业道德规范。

(2)如果注册人采用自己的定义判断其董事、提名董事及董事会具体委员会成员是否具备独立性,则须披露证券持有人是否能通过注册人网站获得该定义;如可以,应提供公司网址;若不能,应在注册人征集投票权报告或信息说明书中以附件形式附上上述政策。上述征集投票权报告或信息说明书至少应每三个会计年度向证券持有人人提供一次;注册人在上一个会计年度年初之后对政策作出重大修正的,也应向证券持有人提供。若上述政策的最新版本并未通过注册人网站向证券持有人提供,并且也未作为附件附于注册人征集投票权报告或信息说明书之后,则应指明将该政策作为附件附于征集投票权报告或信息说明书之后的最近会计年度。

registrant's Web site, and is not included as an appendix to the registrant's proxy statement or information statement, identify the most recent fiscal year in which the policies were so included in satisfaction of this requirement.

(3) For each director and nominee for director that is identified as independent, describe, by specific category or type, any transactions, relationships or arrangements not disclosed pursuant to Item 404(a) (§229.404(a)), or for investment companies, Item 22(b) of Schedule 14A (§240.14a-101 of this chapter), that were considered by the board of directors under the applicable independence definitions in determining that the director is independent.

Instructions to Item 407(a). 1. If the registrant is a listed issuer whose securities are listed on a national securities exchange or in an inter-dealer quotation system which has requirements that a majority of the board of directors be independent, and also has exemptions to those requirements (for independence of a majority of the board of directors or committee member independence) upon which the registrant relied, disclose the exemption relied upon and explain the basis for the registrant's conclusion that such exemption is applicable. The same disclosure should be provided if the registrant is not a listed issuer and the national securities exchange or inter-dealer quotation system selected by the registrant has exemptions that are applicable to the registrant. Any national securities exchange or inter-dealer quotation system which has requirements that at least 50 percent of the members of a small business issuer's board of directors must be independent shall be considered a national securities exchange or inter-dealer quotation system which has requirements that a majority of the board of directors be independent for the purposes of the disclosure required by paragraph (a) of this Item.

2. Registrants shall provide the disclosure required by paragraph (a) of this Item for any person who served as a director during any part of the last completed fiscal year, except that no information called for by paragraph (a) of this Item need be given in a registration statement filed at a time when the registrant is not subject to the reporting requirements of section 13(a) or 15(d) of the Exchange Act (15 U.S.C. 78m(a) or 78*o* (d)) respecting any director who is no longer a director at the time of effectiveness of the registration statement.

3. The description of the specific categories or types of transactions, relationships or arrangements required by paragraph (a)(3) of this Item must be provided in such detail as is necessary to fully describe the nature of the transactions, relationships or arrangements.

(b) *Board meetings and committees; annual meeting attendance.* (1) State the total number of meetings of the board of directors (including regularly scheduled and special meetings) which were held during the last full fiscal year. Name each incumbent director

(3)对每位被指明的独立董事和独立提名董事,应根据具体类别或类型,说明未按照第404(a)条[第229.404(a)节]予以披露的任何交易、关系或安排;对于投资公司,应说明未按照《附表14A》第22(b)条(本章第240.142-101节)予以披露的董事会为判断董事是否具备独立性而适用"独立"定义时所考虑的交易、关系或安排。

关于第407(a)条的说明。1.如果注册人属于在全国性证券交易所或交易商报价系统上市的发行人,且该交易所或交易商报价系统要求董事会过半数成员具备独立性,但同时规定了该等要求的豁免(针对过半数董事会成员或委员会成员具备独立性要求的豁免),则援引该等豁免的注册人须披露豁免的内容,并阐释注册人认为应适用该豁免的依据。如注册人不属于上市发行人,且其选择的全国性证券交易所或交易商报价系统同样拥有适用于注册人的豁免,亦应按上述规定进行披露。任何全国性证券交易所或交易商报价系统,如要求一家小型发行人董事会至少50%的成员具备独立性,即应视为本条第(a)款披露规定所涉的要求过半数董事会成员具备独立性的全国性证券交易所或交易商报价系统。

2.注册人应为在上一完整会计年度的任何时期担任董事的任何人提供本条第(a)款规定的披露信息,但是,如注册人在某一期间内不必遵守《交易法》第13(a)条或第15(d)条[《美国法典》第十五编第78m(a)节或第78o(d)节]规定的报告义务,则在该期间内提交的注册说明书中,不必就在注册说明书生效期间已不再担任董事的任何人提供本条第(a)款要求提供的信息。

3.在按照本条第(a)(3)款规定对具体类别或类型的交易、关系或安排进行说明时,其详细程度必须足以完整说明该等交易、关系或安排的性质。

(b)董事会会议及委员会;年度大会的出席率。(1)阐明上一完整会计年度中董事会议召开的总次数(包括定期会议及特别会议)。同时,应指明上一完整会计年度出席率低于如下标准的每一位董事:

who during the last full fiscal year attended fewer than 75 percent of the aggregate of:

(i) The total number of meetings of the board of directors (held during the period for which he has been a director); and

(ii) The total number of meetings held by all committees of the board on which he served (during the periods that he served).

(2) Describe the registrant's policy, if any, with regard to board members' attendance at annual meetings of security holders and state the number of board members who attended the prior year's annual meeting.

Instruction to Item 407(b)(2). In lieu of providing the information required by paragraph (b)(2) of this Item in the proxy statement, the registrant may instead provide the registrant's Web site address where such information appears.

(3) State whether or not the registrant has standing audit, nominating and compensation committees of the board of directors, or committees performing similar functions. If the registrant has such committees, however designated, identify each committee member, state the number of committee meetings held by each such committee during the last fiscal year and describe briefly the functions performed by each such committee. Such disclosure need not be provided to the extent it is duplicative of disclosure provided in accordance with paragraph (c), (d) or (e) of this Item.

(c) *Nominating committee.* (1) If the registrant does not have a standing nominating committee or committee performing similar functions, state the basis for the view of the board of directors that it is appropriate for the registrant not to have such a committee and identify each director who participates in the consideration of director nominees.

(2) Provide the following information regarding the registrant's director nomination process:

(i) State whether or not the nominating committee has a charter. If the nominating committee has a charter, provide the disclosure required by Instruction 2 to this Item regarding the nominating committee charter;

(ii) If the nominating committee has a policy with regard to the consideration of any director candidates recommended by security holders, provide a description of the material elements of that policy, which shall include, but need not be limited to, a statement as to whether the committee will consider director candidates recommended by security holders;

(iii) If the nominating committee does not have a policy with regard to the consideration of any director candidates recommended by security holders, state that fact and state the basis for the view of the board of directors that it is appropriate for the registrant not to have such a policy;

(iv) If the nominating committee will consider candidates recommended by security holders, describe the procedures to be followed by security holders in submitting such

(i)在其担任董事期间举行的董事会议的75%;及

(ii)在其担任成员的所有董事会委员会举行的会议的75%。

(2)如注册人制定有关于董事会成员出席证券持有人年会的政策,应对该等政策进行说明,并阐明出席上一年度年会的董事会成员人数。

关于第407(b)(2)条的说明:注册人可以选择不在征集投票权报告中提供本条第(b)(2)款规定的信息,而提供可以访问上述信息的网址作为替代。

(3)说明注册人董事会之下是否设有常务审计委员会、提名及报酬委员会或其他履行类似职能的委员会。如注册人设有上述委员会,无论其名称如何,均应指明每名委员会成员、上一会计年度各委员会召开的委员会会议次数,并简要说明各委员会的职能。如在本条第(c)款、第(d)款或第(e)款里已对此作出相应披露,则不必重复披露。

(c)提名委员会。(1)如注册人没有设立常务提名委员会或履行类似职能的其他委员会,应阐明董事会认为不设立该等委员会并无不当的依据,并指明参与董事提名审议的每名董事。

(2)关于注册人的董事提名程序,应提供如下信息:

(i)说明提名委员会是否拥有章程,如有,应按照本条说明2的要求对提名委员会的章程作出披露。

(ii)如果提名委员会就证券持有人推荐的任何董事候选人的审议制度有相关政策,应对该政策的重大要素进行说明,该等说明应包括但不限于关于提名委员会是否会对证券持有人推荐的提名董事进行审议之声明;

(iii)如果提名委员会并未就证券持有人推荐的任何提名董事之审议制定任何政策,应如实说明,并说明董事会认为注册人不制定该等政策并无不当的依据;

(iv)如果提名委员会将对证券持有人推荐的董事候选人进行审议,应说明证券持有人推荐该等候选人时应遵循的程序;

recommendations;

(v) Describe any specific minimum qualifications that the nominating committee believes must be met by a nominating committee-recommended nominee for a position on the registrant's board of directors, and describe any specific qualities or skills that the nominating committee believes are necessary for one or more of the registrant's directors to possess;

(vi) Describe the nominating committee's process for identifying and evaluating nominees for director, including nominees recommended by security holders, and any differences in the manner in which the nominating committee evaluates nominees for director based on whether the nominee is recommended by a security holder, and whether, and if so how, the nominating committee (or the board) considers diversity in identifying nominees for director. If the nominating committee (or the board) has a policy with regard to the consideration of diversity in identifying director nominees, describe how this policy is implemented, as well as how the nominating committee (or the board) assesses the effectiveness of its policy;

(vii) With regard to each nominee approved by the nominating committee for inclusion on the registrant's proxy card (other than nominees who are executive officers or who are directors standing for re-election), state which one or more of the following categories of persons or entities recommended that nominee: Security holder, non-management director, chief executive officer, other executive officer, third-party search firm, or other specified source. With regard to each such nominee approved by a nominating committee of an investment company, state which one or more of the following additional categories of persons or entities recommended that nominee: Security holder, director, chief executive officer, other executive officer, or employee of the investment company's investment adviser, principal underwriter, or any affiliated person of the investment adviser or principal underwriter;

(viii) If the registrant pays a fee to any third party or parties to identify or evaluate or assist in identifying or evaluating potential nominees, disclose the function performed by each such third party; and

(ix) If the registrant's nominating committee received, by a date not later than the 120th calendar day before the date of the registrant's proxy statement released to security holders in connection with the previous year's annual meeting, a recommended nominee from a security holder that beneficially owned more than 5% of the registrant's voting common stock for at least one year as of the date the recommendation was made, or from a group of security holders that beneficially owned, in the aggregate, more than 5% of the registrant's voting common stock, with each of the securities used to calculate that ownership held for at least one year as of the date the recommendation was made, identify

(v)说明提名委员会认为其推荐的提名董事应具备的任何具体最低资质,并说明提名委员会认为注册人的董事必须具备的任何具体素质或技能;

(vi)说明提名委员会确定并评估提名董事(包括由证券持有人推荐的提名董事)的程序,包括提名委员会的评估方式是否会基于提名董事是否由证券持有人推荐而存在任何差别,如确实存在差别,应说明提名委员会(或董事会)在确定提名董事人选时对代表广泛性的考虑,如有所考虑,应说明方式。如果提名委员会(或董事会)对代表的广泛性制定有相关政策,应说明政策的落实方式,以及提名委员会(或董事会)评估该政策有效性的方式。

(vii)对于经提名委员会批准载入注册人投票卡的每位被提名人(被提名人同时担任高管或属于参与连任选举的董事的除外),应阐明该被提名人系由以下哪一类人员或实体推荐:证券持有人、不兼任管理职务的董事、首席执行官、其他高管、第三方猎头公司或其他具体来源。关于每位获得投资公司提名委员会批准的被提名人,应阐明该被提名人系由以下哪一类人员或实体推荐:证券持有人、董事、首席执行官、其他高管或该投资公司投资顾问的职员、主承销商或投资顾问或主承销商的任何关联人;

(viii)若注册人付费聘请任何第三方确定或评估潜在被提名人,或聘请其提供协助,应对每一该等第三方履行的职能进行披露;且

(ix)如注册人的提名委员会,在不晚于注册人向证券持有人发布的关于上一年度年会的征集投票权报告的日期前120个日历日的时间,收到受益拥有注册人超过5%的表决普通股且截至推荐日持股时间不短于一年的证券持有人作出的被提名人推荐,或总计受益拥有注册人超过5%的表决普通股且其中每名持有人截至推荐日持股时间均不短于一年的一组证券持有人作出的被提名人推荐,则应指明该候选人以及推荐候选人的证券持有人或一组证券持有人,并披露提名委员会是否会选择对该候选人进行提名,但是,未同时获得上述证券持有人和候选人书面同意的,不必进行上述指明和披露。

the candidate and the security holder or security holder group that recommended the candidate and disclose whether the nominating committee chose to nominate the candidate,*provided, however,* that no such identification or disclosure is required without the written consent of both the security holder or security holder group and the candidate to be so identified.

Instructions to Item 407(c)(2)(ix). 1. For purposes of paragraph (c)(2)(ix) of this Item, the percentage of securities held by a nominating security holder may be determined using information set forth in the registrant's most recent quarterly or annual report, and any current report subsequent thereto, filed with the Commission pursuant to the Exchange Act (or, in the case of a registrant that is an investment company registered under the Investment Company Act of 1940, the registrant's most recent report on Form N-CSR (§§249.331 and 274.128 of this chapter)), unless the party relying on such report knows or has reason to believe that the information contained therein is inaccurate.

2. For purposes of the registrant's obligation to provide the disclosure specified in paragraph (c)(2)(ix) of this Item, where the date of the annual meeting has been changed by more than 30 days from the date of the previous year's meeting, the obligation under that Item will arise where the registrant receives the security holder recommendation a reasonable time before the registrant begins to print and mail its proxy materials.

3. For purposes of paragraph (c)(2)(ix) of this Item, the percentage of securities held by a recommending security holder, as well as the holding period of those securities, may be determined by the registrant if the security holder is the registered holder of the securities. If the security holder is not the registered owner of the securities, he or she can submit one of the following to the registrant to evidence the required ownership percentage and holding period:

a. A written statement from the "record" holder of the securities (usually a broker or bank) verifying that, at the time the security holder made the recommendation, he or she had held the required securities for at least one year; or

b. If the security holder has filed a Schedule 13D (§240.13d-101 of this chapter), Schedule 13G (§240.13d-102 of this chapter), Form 3 (§249.103 of this chapter), Form 4 (§249.104 of this chapter), and/or Form 5 (§249.105 of this chapter), or amendments to those documents or updated forms, reflecting ownership of the securities as of or before the date of the recommendation, a copy of the schedule and/or form, and any subsequent amendments reporting a change in ownership level, as well as a written statement that the security holder continuously held the securities for the one-year period as of the date of the recommendation.

4. For purposes of the registrant's obligation to provide the disclosure specified in

关于第407(c)(2)(ix)条的说明。1.就本条第(c)(2)(ix)款而言,行使提名权的证券持有人持有的证券所占的百分比可通过如下信息确定:注册人按照《交易法》向证券交易委员会提交的最近的季度报告或年度报告以及后续提交的任何最新报告中所载的信息(如注册人属于按照《1940年投资公司法》注册的投资公司时,则可基于注册人按照《N-CSR表格》(本章第249.331节及第274.128节)提交的最近的报告中所载信息进行确定),但援引上述报告的相关方明知或有理由相信上述报告所载信息不准确的除外。

2.对于注册人按照本条第(c)(2)(ix)款的规定进行披露的义务而言,当年会日期与上一年年会日期相距超过30日时,注册人在印刷和寄送代理委托材料之前的合理时间收到证券持有人建议的,注册人即产生本条第(c)(2)(ix)款规定的披露义务。

3.就本条第(c)(2)(ix)款而言,如证券持有人系为注册证券所有人,则进行推荐的证券持有人持有的证券百分比以及持有证券的期间可由注册人确定。如证券持有人并非注册证券所有人,其可向注册人提交下列材料之一,以证明其符合持股百分比及持有期间的要求:

a.由证券的"记录"持有人(通常为经纪商或银行)提供的书面声明,证实该证券持有人作出推荐之时,其持有证券的期间不短于一年;或

b.若证券持有人已提交《附表13D》(本章第240.13d-101节)、《附表13G》(本章第240.13d-102节)、《3表格》(本章第249.103节)、《4表格》(本章第249.104节)和/或《5表格》(本章第249.105节)或上述文件或表格的修正或更新,以反映截至推荐日或推荐日之前的证券所有权信息,则应提交上述附表和/或表格之复本,并提交报告所有权变更的任何后续修正文件之复本,同时还应提交一份书面声明,证实截至推荐日,证券持有人已不间断地持股满一年时间。

4.对于注册人按照本条第(c)(2)(ix)款的规定进行披露的义务而言,在推荐之时,

paragraph (c)(2)(ix) of this Item, the security holder or group must have provided to the registrant, at the time of the recommendation, the written consent of all parties to be identified and, where the security holder or group members are not registered holders, proof that the security holder or group satisfied the required ownership percentage and holding period as of the date of the recommendation.

Instruction to Item 407(c)(2). For purposes of paragraph (c)(2) of this Item, the term *nominating committee* refers not only to nominating committees and committees performing similar functions, but also to groups of directors fulfilling the role of a nominating committee, including the entire board of directors.

(3) Describe any material changes to the procedures by which security holders may recommend nominees to the registrant's board of directors, where those changes were implemented after the registrant last provided disclosure in response to the requirements of paragraph (c)(2)(iv) of this Item, or paragraph (c)(3) of this Item.

Instructions to Item 407(c)(3). 1. The disclosure required in paragraph (c)(3) of this Item need only be provided in a registrant's quarterly or annual reports.

2. For purposes of paragraph (c)(3) of this Item, adoption of procedures by which security holders may recommend nominees to the registrant's board of directors, where the registrant's most recent disclosure in response to the requirements of paragraph (c)(2)(iv) of this Item, or paragraph (c)(3) of this Item, indicated that the registrant did not have in place such procedures, will constitute a material change.

(d) *Audit committee.* (1) State whether or not the audit committee has a charter. If the audit committee has a charter, provide the disclosure required by Instruction 2 to this Item regarding the audit committee charter.

(2) If a listed issuer's board of directors determines, in accordance with the listing standards applicable to the issuer, to appoint a director to the audit committee who is not independent (apart from the requirements in §240.10A–3 of this chapter), including as a result of exceptional or limited or similar circumstances, disclose the nature of the relationship that makes that individual not independent and the reasons for the board of directors' determination.

(3)(i) The audit committee must state whether:

(A) The audit committee has reviewed and discussed the audited financial statements with management;

(B) The audit committee has discussed with the independent auditors the matters required to be discussed by the statement on Auditing Standards No. 61, as amended

证券持有人或所涉的一组证券持有人必须已经向注册人提供被提名人的书面同意;如证券持有人或所涉的一组证券持有人成员并非注册持有人,须提供相关证据证明证券持有人或所涉的一组证券持有人截至推荐日满足持股百分比和持股期间的要求。

关于第407(c)(2)条的说明。就本条第(c)(2)款而言,“提名委员会”一词不仅指代提名委员会及履行类似职能的委员会,同时也指代发挥提名委员会作用的董事群体,包括整个董事会。

(3)证券持有人向注册人董事会推荐提名人的程序出现任何重大变动,且该等变动在注册人上一次按照本条第(c)(2)(iv)款或第(c)(3)款的规定进行披露后实施的,应如实说明。

关于第407(c)(3)条的说明。1.本条第(c)(3)款中要求进行的披露仅须通过注册人的季度或年度报告提供。

2.就本条第(c)(3)款而言,如果注册人按照本条第(c)(2)(iv)款或本条第(c)(3)款的要求作出的最近披露显示,所制定的证券持有人向注册人董事会推荐提名人的程序没有得到落实,即应视为构成重大变动。

(d)审计委员会。(1)说明审计委员会是否拥有章程,如有,则应按照本条说明2的规定对审计委员会的章程进行披露。

(2)如果出于特殊、例外情况或类似原因,上市发行人的董事会按照适用于发行人的上市标准,决定委派一名不具备独立性的董事在审计委员会任职(本章第240.10A-3节规定除外),应披露导致该董事不具备独立性的关系之性质,以及董事作出该等决定的理由。

(3)(i)审计委员会必须说明:

(A)审计委员会是否已经对已审计财务报表进行审查并与管理层进行过讨论;

(B)审计委员会是否已与独立审计师讨论过公众公司会计监督委员会在《3200T规则》中采用的《第61号审计标准公告》(修正版,AICPA,《职业标准》,AU第一卷第380

(AICPA, *Professional Standards*, Vol. 1. AU section 380),[1] as adopted by the Public Company Accounting Oversight Board in Rule 3200T;

(C) The audit committee has received the written disclosures and the letter from the independent accountant required by applicable requirements of the Public Company Accounting Oversight Board regarding the independent accountant's communications with the audit committee concerning independence, and has discussed with the independent accountant the independent accountant's independence; and

(D) Based on the review and discussions referred to in paragraphs (d)(3)(i)(A) through (d)(3)(i)(C) of this Item, the audit committee recommended to the board of directors that the audited financial statements be included in the company's annual report on Form 10-K (17 CFR 249.310) (or, for closed-end investment companies registered under the Investment Company Act of 1940 (15 U.S.C. 80a-1 *et seq.*), the annual report to shareholders required by section 30(e) of the Investment Company Act of 1940 (15 U.S.C. 80a-29(e)) and Rule 30d-1 (17 CFR 270.30d-1) thereunder) for the last fiscal year for filing with the Commission.

(ii) The name of each member of the company's audit committee (or, in the absence of an audit committee, the board committee performing equivalent functions or the entire board of directors) must appear below the disclosure required by paragraph (d)(3)(i) of this Item.

(4)(i) If the registrant meets the following requirements, provide the disclosure in paragraph (d)(4)(ii) of this Item:

(A) The registrant is a listed issuer, as defined in §240.10A-3 of this chapter;

(B) The registrant is filing an annual report on Form 10-K (§249.310 of this chapter) or a proxy statement or information statement pursuant to the Exchange Act (15 U.S.C. 78a *et seq.*) if action is to be taken with respect to the election of directors; and

(C) The registrant is neither:

(1) A subsidiary of another listed issuer that is relying on the exemption in §240.10A-3(c)(2) of this chapter; nor

(2) Relying on any of the exemptions in §240.10A-3(c)(4) through (c)(7) of this chapter.

(ii) (A) State whether or not the registrant has a separately-designated standing audit committee established in accordance with section 3(a)(58)(A) of the Exchange Act (15 U.S.C. 78c(a)(58)(A)), or a committee performing similar functions. If the registrant has such a committee, however designated, identify each committee member. If

1 Available at http://www.pcaobus.org/standars/interim_standards/auditing_standards/index_au.asp? series=300&section=300.

节[1])中要求论述的事宜;

(C)审计委员会是否已经根据公众公司会计监督委员会关于独立会计师与审计委员会之间就独立性进行沟通的适用规定,收到独立会计师出具的书面披露及信函,并已与独立会计师就独立会计师的独立性进行讨论;及

(D)审计委员会是否已经基于本条第(d)(3)(i)(A)款至第(d)(3)(i)(C)款中提及的审查和论述,向董事会建议将已审计财务报表纳入上一会计年度向证券交易委员会提交的如下文件之中:按照《10-K表格》(《联邦规章汇编》第十七编第249.310节)提交的公司年度报告{或,对于依据《1940年投资公司法》(《美国法典》第十五编第80a-1节及其后条文)注册的封闭式投资公司而言,纳入按《1940年投资公司法》第30(e)条[《美国法典》第十五编第80a-29(e)节]及《1940年投资公司法》下的《30d-1规则》[《联邦规章汇编》第十七编第270.30d-1节]规定向股东提交的年度报告}。

(ii)在本条第(d)(3)(i)款要求提供的披露中必须包含公司审计委员会每一成员的姓名(如未设立审计委员会,应包含履行同等职能的董事会下属委员会或整个董事会的成员名单)。

(4)(i)如果注册人满足以下要求,则应按照本条第(d)(4)(ii)款的规定进行披露:

(A)注册人是本章第240.10A-3节定义的上市发行人;

(B)对于注册人即将针对董事选举采取行动的情况而言,注册人有义务按照《10-K表格》(本章第249.310节)提交年度报告或按照《交易法》(《美国法典》第十五编第78a节及其后条文)提交征集投票权报告或信息说明书;

(C)同时,注册人:

(1)是援引本章第240.10A-3(c)(2)节豁免条款的另一上市发行人的子公司;且

(2)并未援引本章第240.10A-3(c)(4)~240.10A-3(c)(7)节的任何豁免条款。

(ii)(A)阐明注册人是否根据《交易法》的第3(a)(58)(A)条[《美国法典》第十五编第78c(a)(58)(A)节]单独设立了常务审计委员会,或单独设立了履行类似职能的委员会。如果注册人设有该等委员会,则无论其名称如何,均应指明委员会的每一名成员。若《交易法》第3(a)(58)(B)条[《美国法典》第十五编第78c(a)(58)(B)节]规定的

1 载 http://www.pcaobus.org/standards/interim_standards/auditing_standards/index_au.asp?series=300&section=300。

the entire board of directors is acting as the registrant's audit committee as specified in section 3(a)(58)(B) of the Exchange Act (15 U.S.C. 78c(a)(58)(B)), so state.

(B) If applicable, provide the disclosure required by §240.10A–3(d) of this chapter regarding an exemption from the listing standards for audit committees.

(5) *Audit committee financial expert.* (i)(A) Disclose that the registrant's board of directors has determined that the registrant either:

(1)Has at least one audit committee financial expert serving on its audit committee; or

(2) Does not have an audit committee financial expert serving on its audit committee.

(B) If the registrant provides the disclosure required by paragraph (d)(5)(i)(A)(1) of this Item, it must disclose the name of the audit committee financial expert and whether that person is independent, as *independence* for audit committee members is defined in the listing standards applicable to the listed issuer.

(C) If the registrant provides the disclosure required by paragraph (d)(5)(i)(A)(2) of this Item, it must explain why it does not have an audit committee financial expert.

Instruction to Item 407(d)(5)(i). If the registrant's board of directors has determined that the registrant has more than one audit committee financial expert serving on its audit committee, the registrant may, but is not required to, disclose the names of those additional persons. A registrant choosing to identify such persons must indicate whether they are independent pursuant to paragraph (d)(5)(i)(B) of this Item.

(ii) For purposes of this Item, an *audit committee financial expert* means a person who has the following attributes:

(A) An understanding of generally accepted accounting principles and financial statements;

(B) The ability to assess the general application of such principles in connection with the accounting for estimates, accruals and reserves;

(C) Experience preparing, auditing, analyzing or evaluating financial statements that present a breadth and level of complexity of accounting issues that are generally comparable to the breadth and complexity of issues that can reasonably be expected to be raised by the registrant's financial statements, or experience actively supervising one or more persons engaged in such activities;

(D) An understanding of internal control over financial reporting; and

(E) An understanding of audit committee functions.

(iii) A person shall have acquired such attributes through:

(A) Education and experience as a principal financial officer, principal accounting officer, controller, public accountant or auditor or experience in one or more positions that involve the performance of similar functions;

(B) Experience actively supervising a principal financial officer, principal

审计委员会的职能由整个董事会行使,应如实说明。

(B)在适用情况下,应按照本章第240.10A-3(d)节的规定对审计委员会上市标准的豁免进行披露。

(5)审计委员会财务专家。(i)(A)披露注册人董事会作出的如下决定:

(1)注册人的审计委员会至少包含一位审计委员会财务专家;或

(2)注册人的审计委员会不包含任何审计委员会财务专家。

(B)注册人按照本条第(d)(5)(i)(A)(1)款的规定进行披露的,必须披露审计委员会财务专家的姓名以及该专家是否具备独立性——审计委员会成员的"独立性"应采用适用于上市发行人的上市标准中的相关定义。

(C)注册人按照本条第(d)(5)(i)(A)(2)款的规定进行披露的,必须说明审计委员会中不包含财务专家的原因。

关于第407(d)(5)(i)条的说明。如果注册人董事会已决定注册人的审计委员会拥有一名以上的审计委员会财务专家,注册人可以,但没有义务披露其他专家的姓名。注册人选择披露其他专家的,必须说明根据本条第(d)(5)(i)(B)款该等专家是否具备独立性。

(ii)就本条而言,"审计委员会财务专家"指有以下特质的人:

(A)了解公认会计原则及财务报表;

(B)能够评估上述原则对预估数额、权责发生额及准备之会计的总体适用;

(C)有编制、审计、分析或评估如下财务报表的经验,即所涉会计事宜的范围和复杂程度,与注册人财务报表合理预期将发生的会计适宜总体类似的财务报表;或者,有积极监督从事上述编制、审计、分析或评估活动的主体的经验;

(D)了解对财务报告的内部控制;及

(E)了解审计委员会的职能。

(iii)财务专家应具备如下经历,始得认定为具有上述特质:

(A)作为主要财务官、主要会计官、控制官、公共会计师、审计师的教育背景和经历,或履行类似职能的一个或多个职位的经历;

(B)积极监督主要财务官、主要会计官、控制官、公共会计师、审计师或其他职能

accounting officer, controller, public accountant, auditor or person performing similar functions;

(C) Experience overseeing or assessing the performance of companies or public accountants with respect to the preparation, auditing or evaluation of financial statements; or

(D) Other relevant experience.

(iv) *Safe harbor.* (A) A person who is determined to be an audit committee financial expert will not be deemed an *expert* for any purpose, including without limitation for purposes of section 11 of the Securities Act (15 U.S.C. 77k), as a result of being designated or identified as an audit committee financial expert pursuant to this Item 407.

(B) The designation or identification of a person as an audit committee financial expert pursuant to this Item 407 does not impose on such person any duties, obligations or liability that are greater than the duties, obligations and liability imposed on such person as a member of the audit committee and board of directors in the absence of such designation or identification.

(C) The designation or identification of a person as an audit committee financial expert pursuant to this Item does not affect the duties, obligations or liability of any other member of the audit committee or board of directors.

Instructions to Item 407(d)(5). 1. The disclosure under paragraph (d)(5) of this Item is required only in a registrant's annual report. The registrant need not provide the disclosure required by paragraph (d)(5) of this Item in a proxy or information statement unless that registrant is electing to incorporate this information by reference from the proxy or information statement into its annual report pursuant to General Instruction G(3) to Form 10–K (17 CFR 249.310).

2. If a person qualifies as an audit committee financial expert by means of having held a position described in paragraph (d)(5)(iii)(D) of this Item, the registrant shall provide a brief listing of that person's relevant experience. Such disclosure may be made by reference to disclosures required under Item 401(e) (§229.401(e)).

3. In the case of a foreign private issuer with a two–tier board of directors, for purposes of paragraph (d)(5) of this Item, the term *board of directors* means the supervisory or non–management board. In the case of a foreign private issuer meeting the requirements of §240.10A–3(c)(3) of this chapter, for purposes of paragraph (d)(5) of this Item, the term *board of directors* means the issuer's board of auditors (or similar body) or statutory auditors, as applicable. Also, in the case of a foreign private issuer, the term *generally accepted accounting principles* in paragraph (d)(5)(ii)(A) of this Item means the body of generally accepted accounting principles used by that issuer in its primary financial statements filed with the Commission.

类似的人之经历;

(C)监督或评估公司绩效或公共会计师在财务报表的编制、审计或评价方面的表现之经历;或

(D)其他相关经历。

(iv)安全港。(A)被判定为审计委员会财务专家的人不得因为根据本第407条被指定或指明为审计委员会财务专家而被视为任何意义上的"专家",包括但不限于《证券法》第11条(《美国法典》第十五编第77k节)中的"专家"。

(B)任何个人根据本第407条被指定或指明为审计委员会财务专家的,仅承担作为董事会及审计委员会的成员本应承担的职责、义务或责任,除此之外,无任何其他职责、义务或责任。

(C)按照本条将任何人指定或指明为审计委员会财务专家的,董事会或审计委员会任何其他成员的职责、义务或责任不受影响。

关于第407(d)(5)条的说明。1.只有注册人的年度报告才须按照本条第(d)(5)款的规定进行披露。注册人不必在征集投票权报告或信息说明书中按照本条第(d)(5)款的规定进行披露,除非注册人按照《10-K表格》(《联邦规章汇编》第十七编第249.310节)的总体说明G(3)选择通过引用征集投票权报告或信息说明书的方式将该等信息纳入年度报告之中。

2.如果某人曾经担任本条第(d)(5)(iii)(D)款所述职位,并因此而拥有作为审计委员会财务专家的资格,注册人应当简要列明该人的相关经历。注册人可以引用按第401(e)条[第229.401(e)节]规定作出的披露,以履行上述披露规定。

3.就本条第(d)(5)款而言,如果注册人为外国私募发行人,且设有两级董事会,"董事会"一词指监事会或非管理董事会。如果外国私募发行人满足本章第240.10A-3(c)(3)节的要求,则本条第(d)(5)款中的"董事会"一词应根据具体情况,指发行人的审计委员会(或类似组织)或法定审计师。同时,如果注册人为外国私募发行人,则本条第(d)(5)(ii)(A)款中的"公认会计原则"指发行人向证券交易委员会提交的主要财务报表中使用的"公认会计原则"。

4. A registrant that is an Asset-Backed Issuer (as defined in §229.1101) is not required to disclose the information required by paragraph (d)(5) of this Item.

Instructions to Item 407(d). 1. The information required by paragraphs (d)(1)-(3) of this Item shall not be deemed to be "soliciting material," or to be "filed" with the Commission or subject to Regulation 14A or 14C (17 CFR 240.14a-1 through 240.14b-2 or 240.14c-1 through 240.14c-101), other than as provided in this Item, or to the liabilities of section 18 of the Exchange Act (15 U.S.C. 78r), except to the extent that the registrant specifically requests that the information be treated as soliciting material or specifically incorporates it by reference into a document filed under the Securities Act or the Exchange Act. Such information will not be deemed to be incorporated by reference into any filing under the Securities Act or the Exchange Act, except to the extent that the registrant specifically incorporates it by reference.

2. The disclosure required by paragraphs (d)(1)-(3) of this Item need only be provided one time during any fiscal year.

3. The disclosure required by paragraph (d)(3) of this Item need not be provided in any filings other than a registrant's proxy or information statement relating to an annual meeting of security holders at which directors are to be elected (or special meeting or written consents in lieu of such meeting).

(e) *Compensation committee.* (1) If the registrant does not have a standing compensation committee or committee performing similar functions, state the basis for the view of the board of directors that it is appropriate for the registrant not to have such a committee and identify each director who participates in the consideration of executive officer and director compensation.

(2) State whether or not the compensation committee has a charter. If the compensation committee has a charter, provide the disclosure required by Instruction 2 to this Item regarding the compensation committee charter.

(3) Provide a narrative description of the registrant's processes and procedures for the consideration and determination of executive and director compensation, including:

(i)(A) The scope of authority of the compensation committee (or persons performing the equivalent functions); and

(B) The extent to which the compensation committee (or persons performing the equivalent functions) may delegate any authority described in paragraph (e)(3)(i)(A) of this Item to other persons, specifying what authority may be so delegated and to whom;

(ii) Any role ofexecutive officers in determining or recommending the amount or form of executive and director compensation; and

(iii) Any role of compensation consultants in determining or recommending the amount or form of executive and director compensation (other than any role *limited* to

4.如注册人属于资产支持证券发行人(定义见第229.1101节),则不必按照本条第(d)(5)款的规定进行信息披露。

关于第407(d)条的说明。1.本条第(d)(1)款至第(d)(3)款要求披露的信息不得视为"招揽资料",亦不得视为应向证券交易委员会"提交"的材料,或者受制于《14A管理办法》或《14C管理办法》(《联邦规章汇编》第十七编第240.14a-1~240.14b-2节,或第240.14c-1~240.14c-101节)的材料(本条另有规定除外),或者受制于《交易法》第18条(《美国法典》第十五编第78r节)的责任的材料,除非注册人特别要求将该等信息视为招揽材料,或特别通过引用方式将该等信息纳入根据《证券法》或《交易法》提交的文件之中。该等信息不应视为通过引用而被纳入根据《证券法》或《交易法》提交的任何文件,但注册人特别通过引用纳入的除外。

2.在任何会计年度中,只需按照本条第(d)(1)款至第(d)(3)款的规定进行一次披露。

3.本条第(d)(3)款规定的披露只需在注册人举行选举董事的证券持有者年度大会时(或举行选举董事的特别会议或作出选举同事的书面同意时)提交的任何征集投票权报告或信息说明书中提供。

(e)报酬委员会。(1)如注册人没有设立常务报酬委员会或其他履行类似职能的委员会,则应说明董事会认为不设立该等委员会并无不当的依据,并指明参与审议高管及董事报酬的每名董事。

(2)说明报酬委员会是否拥有章程,如有,则应按照本条说明2的规定对报酬委员会的章程进行披露。

(3)就注册人关于审议及决定管理人员及董事报酬的程序和制度提供文字说明,包括:

(i)(A)报酬委员会(或履行同等职能的人)的权限范围;以及

(B)报酬委员会(或履行同等职能的人)转授本条第(e)(3)(i)(A)款所述的任何权限的限度,并明确说明可以转授的权限及对象;

(ii)在决定或建议高管及董事报酬的金额或形式的过程中,高管所起到的任何作用;及

(iii)在注册人的上一完整会计年度,在决定或建议高管及董事报酬的金额或形式的过程中,报酬顾问所起到的任何作用(但仅起下述作用的除外:针对在计划范围、期

consulting on any broad-based plan that does not discriminate in scope, terms, or operation, in favor of executive officers or directors of the registrant, and that is available generally to all salaried employees; or providing information that either is not customized for a particular registrant or that is customized based on parameters that are not developed by the compensation consultant, and about which the compensation consultant does not provide advice) during the registrant's last completed fiscal year, identifying such consultants, stating whether such consultants were engaged directly by the compensation committee (or persons performing the equivalent functions) or any other person, describing the nature and scope of their assignment, and the material elements of the instructions or directions given to the consultants with respect to the performance of their duties under the engagement:

(A) If such compensation consultant was engaged by the compensation committee (or persons performing the equivalent functions) to provide advice or recommendations on the amount or form of executive and director compensation (other than any role *limited* to consulting on any broad-based plan that does not discriminate in scope, terms, or operation, in favor of executive officers or directors of the registrant, and that is available generally to all salaried employees; or providing information that either is not customized for a particular registrant or that is customized based on parameters that are not developed by the compensation consultant, and about which the compensation consultant does not provide advice) and the compensation consultant or its affiliates also provided additional services to the registrant or its affiliates in an amount in excess of $120,000 during the registrant's last completed fiscal year, then disclose the aggregate fees for determining or recommending the amount or form of executive and director compensation and the aggregate fees for such additional services. Disclose whether the decision to engage the compensation consultant or its affiliates for these other services was made, or recommended, by management, and whether the compensation committee or the board approved such other services of the compensation consultant or its affiliates.

(B) If the compensation committee (or persons performing the equivalent functions) has not engaged a compensation consultant, but management has engaged a compensation consultant to provide advice or recommendations on the amount or form of executive and director compensation (other than any role *limited* to consulting on any broad-based plan that does not discriminate in scope, terms, or operation, in favor of executive officers or directors of the registrant, and that is available generally to all salaried employees; or providing information that either is not customized for a particular registrant or that is customized based on parameters that are not developed by the compensation consultant, and about which the compensation consultant does not provide advice) and such compensation consultant or its affiliates has provided additional services to the registrant

限或运行方面对于注册人高管或者董事不给予任何优惠且普遍适用于所有受薪职员的任何普适性计划提供咨询;提供非为特定注册人定制的信息;或提供为注册人定制的信息,但定制所基于的参数并非由报酬顾问制定,且报酬顾问未就此提供建议),同时应注明相关报酬顾问的身份信息,说明该报酬顾问是否直接受聘于报酬委员会(或履行同等职能的人)或任何其他主体(说明其工作任务的性质及范围),并说明报酬顾问接受的与履行其受聘任务相关的指示或指令中的重大要素:

(A)如上述报酬顾问接受报酬委员会(或履行同等职能的人)的聘请,就高管或董事报酬的金额或形式提出意见或建议(但仅起下述作用的服务除外:针对在计划范围、期限或运行方面对于注册人高管或者董事不给予任何优惠且普遍适用于所有受薪职员的任何普适性计划提供咨询;提供非为特定注册人定制的信息;或提供为注册人定制的信息,但定制所基于的参数并非由报酬顾问制定,且报酬顾问未就此提供建议),且该报酬顾问或其关联方在注册人上一完整会计年度还向注册人或其关联方提供了金额超过12万美元的其他服务,则应披露报酬顾问就决定或建议高管及董事报酬的金额或形式所获得的费用总额,以及就上述其他服务获得的费用总额。同时应披露提供该等其他服务的报酬顾问或其关联方是否由管理层决定或建议聘请,以及该等其他服务之提供是否已获得报酬委员会或董事会批准。

(B)如报酬委员会(或履行同等职能的人)没有聘请报酬顾问,但管理层聘请了报酬顾问就高管或董事报酬的金额或形式提出建议或意见(但下述服务除外:注册人高管或者董事在计划范围、期限或运行方面对于注册人高管或者董事不给予任何优惠,且普遍适用于所有受薪职员的任何普适性计划所提供的咨询;提供非为特定注册人定制的信息;或提供为注册人定制的信息,但定制所基于的参数并非由报酬顾问制定,且报酬顾问未就此提供建议),且该报酬顾问或其关联方在注册人上一完整会计年度还向注册人或其关联方提供金额超过12万美元的其他服务,则应披露报酬顾问就决定或建议高管及董事报酬的金额或形式所获得的费用总额,以及就上述其他服务获得的费用总额。

in an amount in excess of $120,000 during the registrant's last completed fiscal year, then disclose the aggregate fees for determining or recommending the amount cr form of executive and director compensation and the aggregate fees for any additional services provided by the compensation consultant or its affiliates.

(4) Under the caption "Compensation Committee Interlocks and Insider Participation":

(i) Identify each person who served as a member of the compensation committee of the registrant's board of directors (or board committee performing equivalent functions) during the last completed fiscal year, indicating each committee member who:

(A) Was, during the fiscal year, an officer or employee of the registrant;

(B) Was formerly an officer of the registrant; or

(C) Had any relationship requiring disclosure by the registrant under any paragraph of Item 404 (§229.404). In this event, the disclosure required by Item 404 (§229.404) shall accompany such identification.

(ii) If the registrant has no compensation committee (or other board committee performing equivalent functions), the registrant shall identify each officer and employee of the registrant, and any former officer of the registrant, who, during the last completed fiscal year, participated in deliberations of the registrant's board of directors concerningexecutive officer compensation.

(iii) Describe any of the following relationships that existed during the last completed fiscal year:

(A) Anexecutive officer of the registrant served as a member of the compensation committee (or other board committee performing equivalent functions or, in the absence of any such committee, the entire board of directors) of another entity, one of whose executive officers served on the compensation committee (or other board committee performing equivalent functions or, in the absence of any such committee, the entire board of directors) of the registrant;

(B) An executive officer of the registrant served as a director of another entity, one of whose executive officers served on the compensation committee (or other board committee performing equivalent functions or, in the absence of any such committee, the entire board of directors) of the registrant; and

(C) Anexecutive officer of the registrant served as a member of the compensation committee (or other board committee performing equivalent functions or, in the absence of any such committee, the entire board of directors) of another entity, one of whose executive officers served as a director of the registrant.

(iv) Disclosure required under paragraph (e)(4)(iii) of this Item regarding a compensation committee member or other director of the registrant who also served as

(4)在"报酬委员会的相互关系及内部人员参与"一栏之下:

(i)指明在上一完整会计年度担任注册人董事会下属报酬委员会(或履行同等职能的董事会下属委员会)成员的每一个人,并指明具有以下特征的委员会成员:

(A)在该会计年度中属于注册人的管理人员或职员;

(B)曾经担任注册人的管理人员;或

(C)曾经存在按照第404条(第229.404节)任何一款规定须要注册人予以披露的关系。在该等情况下,在指明上述成员的同时,应按照第404条(第229.404节)的规定披露相关信息。

(ii)如注册人没有设立报酬委员会(或其他履行同等职能的董事会下属委员会),注册人应指明所有在上一完整会计年度参与审议高管报酬的董事会审议过程的每名管理人员及职员以及任何前任管理人员。

(iii)对上一完整会计年度中存在的下列任何关系进行说明:

(A)注册人的高管担任另一实体的报酬委员会成员(或其他履行同等职能的董事会下属委员会成员;如未设立任何上述委员会,则为董事会成员),而该实体的高管之一则担任注册人的报酬委员会成员(或其他履行同等职能的董事会下属委员会成员;如未设立任何上述委员会,则为董事会成员);

(B)注册人的高管担任另一实体的董事,而该实体的高管之一则担任注册人的报酬委员会成员(或其他履行同等职能的董事会下属委员会成员;如未设立任何上述委员会,则为董事会成员);及

(C)注册人的高管担任另一实体的报酬委员会成员(或其他履行同等职能的董事会下属委员会成员;如未设立任何上述委员会,则为董事会成员),而该实体的高管之一则担任注册人的董事。

(iv)在按照本条第(e)(4)(iii)款的规定对注册人的报酬委员会成员或董事同时兼任另一实体高管之事宜进行披露的同时,应按照第404条的规定对该人进行相

anexecutive officer of another entity shall be accompanied by the disclosure called for by Item 404 with respect to that person.

*Instruction to Item 407(e)(4).*For purposes of paragraph (e)(4) of this Item, the term *entity* shall not include an entity exempt from tax under section 501 (c)(3) of the Internal Revenue Code (26 U.S.C. 501(c)(3)).

(5) Under the caption "Compensation Committee Report":

(i) The compensation committee (or other board committee performing equivalent functions or, in the absence of any such committee, the entire board of directors) must state whether:

(A) The compensation committee has reviewed and discussed the Compensation Discussion and Analysis required by Item 402(b) (§229.402(b)) with management; and

(B) Based on the review and discussions referred to in paragraph (e)(5)(i)(A) of this Item, the compensation committee recommended to the board of directors that the Compensation Discussion and Analysis be included in the registrant's annual report on Form 10-K (§249.310 of this chapter), proxy statement on Schedule 14A (§240.14a-101 of this chapter) or information statement on Schedule 14C (§240.14c-101 of this chapter).

(ii) The name of each member of the registrant's compensation committee (or other board committee performing equivalent functions or, in the absence of any such committee, the entire board of directors) must appear below the disclosure required by paragraph (e)(5)(i) of this Item.

Instructions to Item 407(e)(5). 1. The information required by paragraph (e)(5) of this Item shall not be deemed to be "soliciting material," or to be "filed" with the Commission or subject to Regulation 14A or 14C (17 CFR 240.14a-1 through 240.14b-2 or 240.14c-1 through 240.14c-101), other than as provided in this Item, or to the liabilities of section 18 of the Exchange Act (15 U.S.C. 78r), except to the extent that the registrant specifically requests that the information be treated as soliciting material or specifically incorporates it by reference into a document filed under the Securities Act or the Exchange Act.

2. The disclosure required by paragraph (e)(5) of this Item need not be provided in any filings other than an annual report on Form 10-K (§249.310 of this chapter), a proxy statement on Schedule 14A (§240.14a-101 of this chapter) or an information statement on Schedule 14C (§240.14c-101 of this chapter). Such information will not be deemed to be incorporated by reference into any filing under the Securities Act or the Exchange Act, except to the extent that the registrant specifically incorporates it by reference. If the registrant elects to incorporate this information by reference from the proxy or information statement into its annual report on Form 10-K pursuant to General Instruction G(3) to

关披露。

关于第407(e)(4)条的说明。就本条第(e)(4)款而言,“实体”一词不得包括按照《国内税收法典》第501(c)(3)条[《美国法典》第二十六编第501(c)(3)节]获得税务豁免的实体。

(5)在“报酬委员会报告”一栏之下:

(i)报酬委员会(或其他履行同等职能的董事会下属委员会;如未设立任何上述委员会,则为董事会)必须阐明:

(A)报酬委员会是否审查了第402(b)节[第229.402(b)节]要求提供的报酬论述及分析,并与管理层进行讨论;及

(B)报酬委员会是否已经基于本条第(e)(5)(i)(A)款中提及的审查和论述,向董事会推荐将报酬论述与分析纳入如下文件之中:按照《10-K表格》(本章第249.310节)提交的注册人年度报告;按照《附表14A》提交的征集代理权说明书(本章第240.14a-101节)或按照《附表14C》提交的信息说明书(本章第240.14c-101节)。

(ii)注册人报酬委员会的全体成员名单(或其他履行同等职能的董事会下属委员会的全体成员名单;如未设立任何上述委员会,则为董事会全体成员名单)必须按照本条第(e)(5)(i)款的规定进行披露。

关于第407(e)(5)条的说明。1.本条第(e)(5)款要求披露的信息不得视为“招揽资料”,亦不得视为应向证券交易委员会“提交”的材料,或者受制于《14A管理办法》或《14C管理办法》(《联邦规章汇编》第十七编第240.14a-1~240.14b-2节,或第240.14c-1~240.14c-101节)的材料(本条另有规定除外),或者受制于《交易法》第18条(《美国法典》第十五编第78r节)的责任的材料,除非注册人特别要求将该等信息视为招揽材料,或特别通过引用方式将该等信息纳入根据《证券法》或《交易法》提交的文件之中。

2.除以下文件外,任何其他提交文件不必按照本条第(e)(5)款的规定披露相关信息:按照《10-K表格》(本章第249.310节)提交的年度报告,按照《附表14A》(本章第240.14a-101节)提交的征集投票权报告或者按照《附表14C》(本章第240.14c-101节)提交的信息说明书。该等信息不得视为因引用而被纳入任何根据《证券法》或《交易法》提交的文件,但注册人特别通过引用方式将该等信息纳入提交文件的除外。如果注册人选择按照《10-K表格》的总体说明G(3)通过引用征集投票权报告或信息说明书将上述信息纳入其按照《10-K表格》提交的年度报告之中,则按照本条第(e)(5)款提供的披露信息将视为在按照《10-K表格》提交的年度报告中提供,而不得视为通过引

Form 10-K, the disclosure required by paragraph (e)(5) of this Item will be deemed furnished in the annual report on Form 10-K and will not be deemed incorporated by reference into any filing under the Securities Act or the Exchange Act as a result as a result of furnishing the disclosure in this manner.

3. The disclosure required by paragraph (e)(5) of this Item need only be provided one time during any fiscal year.

(f) *Shareholder communications.* (1) State whether or not the registrant's board of directors provides a process for security holders to send communications to the board of directors and, if the registrant does not have such a process for security holders to send communications to the board of directors, state the basis for the view of the board of directors that it is appropriate for the registrant not to have such a process.

(2) If the registrant has a process for security holders to send communications to the board of directors:

(i) Describe the manner in which security holders can send communications to the board and, if applicable, to specified individual directors; and

(ii) If all security holder communications are not sent directly to board members, describe the registrant's process for determining which communications will be relayed to board members.

Instructions to Item 407(f). 1. In lieu of providing the information required by paragraph (f)(2) of this Item in the proxy statement, the registrant may instead provide the registrant's Web site address where such information appears.

2. For purposes of the disclosure required by paragraph (f)(2)(ii) of this Item, a registrant's process for collecting and organizing security holder communications, as well as similar or related activities, need not be disclosed provided that the registrant's process is approved by a majority of the independent directors or, in the case of a registrant that is an investment company, a majority of the directors who are not "interested persons" of the investment company as defined in section 2(a)(19) of the Investment Company Act of 1940 (15 U.S.C. 80a-2(a)(19)).

3. For purposes of this paragraph, communications from an officer or director of the registrant will not be viewed as "security holder communications". Communications from an employee or agent of the registrant will be viewed as "security holder communications" for purposes of this paragraph only if those communications are made solely in such employee's or agent's capacity as a security holder.

4. For purposes of this paragraph, security holder proposals submitted pursuant to §240.14a-8 of this chapter, and communications made in connection with such proposals, will not be viewed as "security holder communications".

(g) *Smaller reporting companies.* A registrant that qualifies as a "smaller reporting

用披露的方式纳入按《证券法》或《交易法》提交的任何文件。

3.在任何会计年度中,只需按照本条第(e)(5)款的规定进行一次披露。

(f)股东通信。(1)说明注册人董事会是否制定了证券持有人向董事会发送通信的程序,如果未制定,应说明董事会认为注册人不制定该等程序并无不当的依据。

(2)如果注册人就证券持有人向董事会发送通信制定了相关程序:

(i)应说明证券持有人向董事会发送通信的方式,如适用,还应说明向具体董事发送通信的方式;且

(ii)如并非证券持有人发出的所有通信均被直接发送至董事会成员,应说明注册人在判断须转发给董事会成员的通信时所采用的程序。

关于第407(f)条的说明。1.注册人可以不通过征集投票权报告提供本条第(f)(2)款要求提供的信息,而提供可以访问该等信息的公司网址作为替代。

2.就本条第(f)(2)(ii)款要求披露的信息而言,如果注册人收集及组织证券持有人通信及相似或相关活动的程序已经获得过半数独立董事批准,或者,注册人是投资公司的,如果已获得过半数不属于《1940年投资公司法》第2(a)(19)条[《美国法典》第十五编第80a-2(a)19节]定义的"利害关系人"的董事批准,则不必披露该等程序。

3.就本款而言,注册人管理人员或董事的通信不视为"证券持有人通信"。注册人雇员或代理人发出的通信,只有在其以证券持有人身份发送时,始得视为本款所述的"证券持有人通信"。

4.就本款而言,按照本章第240.14a-8节提交的证券持有人提案以及与该等提案相关的通信,不视为"证券持有人通信"。

(g)小型报告公司。属于第229.10(f)(1)节定义的"小型报告公司"的注册人不必:

company", as defined by §229.10(f)(1), is not required to provide:

(1) The disclosure required in paragraph (d)(5) of this Item in its first annual report filed pursuant to section 13(a) or 15(d) of the Exchange Act (15 U.S.C. 78m(a) or 78o(d)) following the effective date of its first registration statement filed under the Securities Act (15 U.S.C. 77a *et seq.*) or Exchange Act (15 U.S.C. 78a *et seq.*); and

(2) Need not provide the disclosures required by paragraphs (e)(4) and (e)(5) of this Item.

(h)*Board leadership structure and role in risk oversight.* Briefly describe the leadership structure of the registrant's board, such as whether the same person serves as both principal executive officer and chairman of the board, or whether two individuals serve in those positions, and, in the case of a registrant that is an investment company, whether the chairman of the board is an "interested person" of the registrant as defined in section 2(a)(19) of the Investment Company Act (15 U.S.C. 80a-2(a)(19)). If one person serves as both principal executive officer and chairman of the board, or if the chairman of the board of a registrant that is an investment company is an "interested person" of the registrant, disclose whether the registrant has a lead independent director and what specific role the lead independent director plays in the leadership of the board. This disclosure should indicate why the registrant has determined that its leadership structure is appropriate given the specific characteristics or circumstances of the registrant. In addition, disclose the extent of the board's role in the risk oversight of the registrant, such as how the board administers its oversight function, and the effect that this has on the board's leadership structure.

*Instructions to Item 407.*1. For purposes of this Item:

a. *Listed issuer* means a listed issuer as defined in §240.10A-3 of this chapter;

b. *National securities exchange* means a national securities exchange registered pursuant to section 6(a) of the Exchange Act (15 U.S.C. 78f(a));

c. *Inter-dealer quotation system* means an automated inter-dealer quotation system of a national securities association registered pursuant to section 15A(a) of the Exchange Act (15 U.S.C. 78o-3(a)); and

d. *National securities association* means a national securities association registered pursuant to section 15A(a) of the Exchange Act(15 U.S.C. 78o-3(a)) that has been approved by the Commission (as that definition may be modified or supplemented).

2. With respect to paragraphs (c)(2)(i), (d)(1) and (e)(2) of this Item, disclose whether a current copy of the applicable committee charter is available to security holders on the registrant's Web site, and if so, provide the registrant's Web site address. If a current copy of the charter is not available to security holders on the registrant's Web site, include a copy of the charter in an appendix to the registrant's proxy or information

（1）在注册人按照《证券法》（《美国法典》第十五编第77a节及其后条文）或《交易法》（《美国法典》第十五编第78a节及其后条文）提交的第一份注册说明书的生效日期之后，在按《交易法》第13（a）条或第15（d）条[《美国法典》第十五编第78m（a）节或第78o（d）节]提交的第一份年度报告中提供本条第（d）（5）款要求披露的信息；及

（2）提供本条第（e）（4）款及第（e）（5）款要求披露的信息。

（h）董事会领导结构及在风险监督方面的作用。简要说明注册人董事会的领导结构，如主要高管及董事会主席由同一人兼任或是由两人分别担任；注册人为投资公司时，董事会主席是否属于《投资公司法》第2（a）（19）条[《美国法典》第十五编第80a-2（a）（19）节]定义的注册人的“利害关系人”。如果主要高管及董事会主席由同一人兼任，或者在注册人属于投资公司的情形下，董事会主席属于注册人的“利害关系人”，则应披露注册人是否有一名主导的独立董事及其在董事会领导中起到的特定作用。进行上述披露时，应指明注册人判定其领导结构符合其自身特点或情况的依据。此外，应披露董事会在注册人的风险监督方面所起作用的程度，如董事会如何执行其监督功能，以及该等执行方式对于董事会领导结构的影响。

关于第407条的说明。1.就本条而言：

a.“上市发行人”指本章第240.10A-3节定义的上市发行人；

b.“全国性证券交易所”指按照《交易法》第6（a）条[《美国法典》第十五编第78f（a）节]注册的全国性证券交易所；

c.“交易商报价系统”指按照《交易法》第15A（a）条[《美国法典》第十五编第78o-3（a）节]注册的全国性证券协会的交易商自动报价系统；且

d.“全国性证券协会”指按照《交易法》第15A（a）条[《美国法典》第十五编第78o-3（a）节]注册并获得证券交易委员会批准的全国性证券协会（该定义被修改或补充的，以修改或补充后的定义为准）。

2.就本条第（c）（2）（i）款、第（d）（1）款及第（e）（2）款而言，应披露证券持有人是否可通过注册人网站获得适用的最新版本的委员会章程，如果可以，应提供注册人的网站地址。如果证券持有人无法通过网站获得该等章程，则至少应每三个会计年度向证券持有人提供一次，作为附录附于注册人征集投票权报告或信息说明书之后，注册人在上一个会计年度年初之后对章程作出重大修正的，也应向证券持有人提供。若上述

statement that is provided to security holders at least once every three fiscal years, or if the charter has been materially amended since the beginning of the registrant's last fiscal year. If a current copy of the charter is not available to security holders on the registrant's Web site, and is not included as an appendix to the registrant's proxy or information statement, identify in which of the prior fiscal years the charter was so included in satisfaction of this requirement.

[71 FR 53254, Sept. 8, 2006, as amended at 73 FR 964, Jan. 4, 2008; 73 FR 57238, Oct. 2, 2008; 74 FR 68364, Dec. 23, 2009]

Subpart 229.500—Registration Statement and Prospectus Provisions

§229.501 (Item 501) Forepart of Registration Statement and Outside Front Cover Page of Prospectus.

The registrant must furnish the following information in plain English. See §230.421(d) of Regulation C of this chapter.

(a) *Front cover page of the registration statement.* Where appropriate, include the delaying amendment legend from §230.473 of Regulation C of this chapter.

(b) *Outside front cover page of the prospectus.* Limit the outside cover page to one page. If the following information applies to your offering, disclose it on the outside cover page of the prospectus.

(1) *Name.* The registrant's name. A foreign registrant must give the English translation of its name.

Instruction to paragraph 501(b)(1): If your name is the same as that of a company that is well known, include information to eliminate any possible confusion with the other company. If your name indicates a line of business in which you are not engaged or you are engaged only to a limited extent, include information to eliminate any misleading inference as to your business. In some circumstances, disclosure may not be sufficient and you may be required to change your name. You will not be required to change your name if you are an established company, the character of your business has changed, and the investing public is generally aware of the change and the character of your current business.

(2) *Title and amount of securities.* The title and amount of securities offered. Separately state the amount of securities offered by selling security holders, if any. If the underwriter has any arrangement with the issuer, such as an over-allotment option, under which the

章程的最新版本并未通过注册人网站向证券持有人提供,并且也未作为附件附于注册人征集投票权报告或信息说明书之后,则应指明将该章程作为附件附于征集投票权报告或信息说明书之后的最近会计年度,以履行本款规定。

[《联邦公报》第71卷第53254页,2006年9月8日,修正索引:《联邦公报》第73卷第964页,2008年1月4日;《联邦公报》第73卷第57238页,2008年10月2日;《联邦公报》第74卷第68364页,2009年12月23日。]

第229.500子部分——关于注册说明书和招募说明书的规定

第229.501节(第501条) 注册说明书的开篇部分和招募说明书的封首

注册人须以简明的英语提供下述信息。参见本章《C管理办法》第230.421(d)条的规定。

(a)注册说明书的封面。适当时,应插入依据本章《C管理办法》第230.473条规定作出的迟延生效修正标题。

(b)招募说明书的封首。招募说明书的封首不得超过一页。如适用于注册人的发行,下述信息应在招募说明书的封首中予以披露。

(1)名称。即注册人的名称,其中,外国注册人必须提供英译名称。

关于第501(b)(1)款的说明:如注册人的名称与著名公司的名称相同,应提供相关信息,以消除任何可能造成的混淆。如注册人名称中含有任一业务线的信息,而注册人实际上并未经营该业务线或仅在有限范围内开展该业务线的经营,则应提供相关信息,以消除任何可能产生的关于注册人业务的误导性推论。在某些情况下,按上述规定进行披露可能仍不足以消除混淆或误导,此时注册人可能需要变更其名称。如果注册人为一家已设立公司,其业务性质发生变更之时,只要公众投资者普遍知悉此项变更及其当前业务的性质,注册人即不需要变更其公司名称。

(2)证券名称及发行数量。即所发行证券的名称及其发行的数量。承诺出售的证券持有人所要约的证券数量(如有),应单独注明。如承销商与发行人已经就超额配售选择权等事项达成任何安排,且根据该等安排承销商可以在本次发行中额外购买股

underwriter may purchase additional shares in connection with the offering, indicate that this arrangement exists and state the amount of additional shares that the underwriter may purchase under the arrangement. Give a brief description of the securities except where the information is clear from the title of the security. For example, you are not required to describe common stock that has full voting, dividend and liquidation rights usually associated with common stock.

(3) *Offering price of the securities.* Where you offer securities for cash, the price to the public of the securities, the underwriter's discounts and commissions, the net proceeds you receive, and any selling shareholder's net proceeds. Show this information on both a per share or unit basis and for the total amount of the offering. If you make the offering on a minimum/maximum basis, show this information based on the total minimum and total maximum amount of the offering. You may present the information in a table, term sheet format, or other clear presentation. You may present the information in any format that fits the design of the cover page so long as the information can be easily read and is not misleading:

Instructions to paragraph 501(b)(3):1. If a preliminary prospectus is circulated and you are not subject to the reporting requirements of Section 13(a) or 15(d) of the Exchange Act, provide, as applicable:

(A) A bona fide estimate of the range of the maximum offering price and the maximum number of securities offered; or

(B) A bona fide estimate of the principal amount of the debt securities offered.

2. If it is impracticable to state the price to the public, explain the method by which the price is to be determined. If the securities are to be offered at the market price, or if the offering price is to be determined by a formula related to the market price, indicate the market and market price of the securities as of the latest practicable date.

3. If you file a registration statement on Form S-8, you are not required to comply with this paragraph (b)(3).

(4) *Market for the securities.* Whether any national securities exchange or the Nasdaq Stock Market lists the securities offered, naming the particular market(s), and identifying the trading symbol(s) for those securities;

(5) *Risk factors.* A cross-reference to the risk factors section, including the page number where it appears in the prospectus. Highlight this cross-reference by prominent type or in another manner;

(6) *State legend.* Any legend or statement required by the law of any state in which the securities are to be offered. You may combine this with any legend required by the SEC, if appropriate;

份,应注明此项安排存在的事实,并列明承销商依据此项安排可以额外购买的股份数量。请提供证券的简要说明,但从该证券的名称即已显而易见的信息除外。例如,对于普通股通常享有的完整表决权、分红权和参与清算的权利,注册人不必特别说明。

(3)证券发行价格。如以现金为对价发行证券,则应分别列明向公众发行证券的价格、向承销商提供的折扣和佣金、注册人收到的净募集资金以及任何出售证券的股东所得的净资金。上述数据应包括每股或每份额单位数据,以及以发行总额为基础计算的总计数据。如注册人发行证券时设定了最小或最大发行量,应列明其发行证券的最小数量和最大数量信息。上述信息可通过表格、条款清单或其他能够清晰呈现该信息的形式予以呈现。只要所呈现的信息清晰易读且不具误导性,则可以通过与封面设计相符的任何格式呈现该信息。

关于第501(b)(3)条的说明:1. 如果注册人分发的是初步招募说明书,且注册人不需要遵守《证券交易法》第13(a)条或第15(d)条的报告义务,则应视具体情况,提供下述相关信息:

(A)基于善意评估得出的发行证券的最高发行价格范围及其最高发行量的范围;或

(B)基于善意评估得出的发行债务证券的本金金额的范围。

2.如无法注明向公众发行的价格,应说明确定该等价格的方法。如证券按市场价格发行,或其发行价格将通过与其市场价格相关的公式确定,应注明截至最迟可行日期该证券的发行市场及其市场价格。

3.如按照《S-8表格》提交注册说明书,则不必遵守本第(b)(3)款的规定。

(4)证券市场。无论证券是在任何全国性证券交易所还是在纳斯达克证券交易所上市发行,均须指明该具体的发行市场并注明该等证券的交易代码。

(5)风险因素。应就与风险因素相关的章节提供交叉索引,包括该等章节在招募说明书中的页码。同时应以突出字体或其他形式对交叉索引进行突出强调。

(6)标注州法律规定的陈述或声明。注册人应按照拟发行证券的任何州的法律要求标注任何声明或陈述;在适当情形下,注册人可以将任何该等声明或陈述与按照证券交易委员会的要求作出的声明相结合。

(7) *Commission legend.* A legend that indicates that neither the Securities and Exchange Commission nor any state securities commission has approved or disapproved of the securities or passed upon the accuracy or adequacy of the disclosures in the prospectus and that any contrary representation is a criminal offense. You may use one of the following or other clear, plain language:

Example A: Neither the Securities and Exchange Commission nor any state securities commission has approved or disapproved of these securities or passed upon the adequacy or accuracy of this prospectus. Any representation to the contrary is a criminal offense.

Example B: Neither the Securities and Exchange Commission nor any state securities commission has approved or disapproved of these securities or determined if this prospectus is truthful or complete. Any representation to the contrary is a criminal offense.

(8) *Underwriting.* (i) Name(s) of the lead or managing underwriter(s) and an identification of the nature of the underwriting arrangements;

(ii) If the offering is not made on a firm commitment basis, a brief description of the underwriting arrangements. You may use any clear, concise, and accurate description of the underwriting arrangements. You may use the following descriptions of underwriting arrangements where appropriate:

Example A: Best efforts offering. The underwriters are not required to sell any specific number or dollar amount of securities but will use their best efforts to sell the securities offered.

Example B: Best efforts, minimum–maximum offering. The underwriters must sell the minimum number of securities offered(*insert number*) if any are sold. The underwriters are required to use only their best efforts to sell the maximum number of securities offered (*insert number*).

(iii) If you offer the securities on a best efforts or best efforts minimum/maximum basis, the date the offering will end, any minimum purchase requirements, and any arrangements to place the funds in an escrow, trust, or similar account. If you have not made any of these arrangements, state this fact and describe the effect on investors;

(9) *Date of prospectus.* The date of the prospectus;

(10) *Prospectus "Subject to Completion" legend.* If you use the prospectus before the effective date of the registration statement, a prominent statement that:

(i) The information in the prospectus will be amended or completed;

(ii) A registration statement relating to these securities has been filed with the Securities and Exchange Commission;

(iii) The securities may not be sold until the registration statement becomes effective; and

(iv) The prospectus is not an offer to sell the securities and it is not soliciting an

(7)标注与证券交易委员会有关的声明。注册人应标注如下声明:证券交易委员会或任何州的证券交易委员会均未批准或否决该证券，亦未就本招募说明书中披露内容的准确性、适当性发表意见;任何与上述声明相反的陈述均构成刑事犯罪。注册人可使用下述范例,或使用其他清楚简明的语言作出上述声明:

范例A:证券交易委员会或任何州的证券交易委员会均未批准或否决本证券,亦未就本招募说明书的适当性、准确性发表意见。与上述声明相反的任何陈述均构成刑事犯罪。

范例B:证券交易委员会或任何州的证券交易委员会均未批准或否决本证券,亦未认定本招募说明书是否真实、完整。与上述声明相反的任何陈述均构成刑事犯罪。

(8)承销。(i)应指明牵头承销商或主承销商的名称,并明确承销安排的性质。

(ii)如果以包销的方式发行证券,应对该项承销安排进行简要说明。注册人可以使用任何清楚、简明、准确的语言进行说明,在适当情况下,也可使用下述范例对该项承销安排进行说明:

范例A:尽最大努力进行代销。承销商没有义务出售任何具体数量或金额的证券,但承销商会尽其最大努力出售已发行的证券。

范例B:尽最大努力且规定最小—最大承销量的代销。承销商只要售出了任何发行证券,即必须保证售出的证券数量最少应达到最小发行量(请填写最小发行量)。对于最大发行证券售出量(请填写最大发行量),承销商仅须尽其最大努力即可。

(iii)如通过尽最大努力的代销或者通过尽最大努力且规定最小—最大承销量的代销方式发行证券,应指明发行结束的日期、任何最小购买量要求(如有)以及以托管、信托或存入类似账户的形式存放资金的任何安排。如未设置任何此类安排,应注明此项事实,并说明该情况对投资者的影响。

(9)招募说明书的日期,即招募说明书出具的日期。

(10)招募说明书中关于“有待完善”的标注。如在注册说明生效日之前使用招募说明书,应在显著的位置作出如下声明:

(i)本招募说明书中的信息有待修订或补充完善;

(ii)与招募说明书所涉证券有关的注册说明书已向证券交易委员会提交;

(iii)证券在注册说明书生效之前,不得出售;且

(iv)招募说明书并非证券出售要约,亦不构成在不允许发行或出售该等证券的任

offer to buy the securities in any state where offers or sales are not permitted. The legend may be in the following or other clear, plain language:

The information in this prospectus is not complete and may be changed. We may not sell these securities until the registration statement filed with the Securities and Exchange Commission is effective. This prospectus is not an offer to sell these securities and it is not soliciting an offer to buy these securities in any state where the offer or sale is not permitted.

(11) If you use §230.430A of this chapter to omit pricing information and the prospectus is used before you determine the public offering price, the information and legend in paragraph (b)(10) of this section.

*Instruction to Item 501:*For asset-backed securities, see also Item 1102 of Regulation AB (§229.1102).

[63 FR 6381, Feb. 6, 1998, as amended at 70 FR 1594, Jan. 7, 2005]

§229.502 (Item 502) Inside front and outside back cover pages of prospectus.

The registrant must furnish this information in plain English. See §230.421(d) of Regulation C of this chapter.

(a) *Table of contents.* On either the inside front or outside back cover page of the prospectus, provide a reasonably detailed table of contents. It must show the page number of the various sections or subdivisions of the prospectus. Include a specific listing of the risk factors section required by Item 503 of this Regulation S-K (17 CFR 229.503). You must include the table of contents immediately following the cover page in any prospectus you deliver electronically.

(b) *Dealer prospectus delivery obligation.* On the outside back cover page of the prospectus, advise dealers of their prospectus delivery obligation, including the expiration date specified by Section 4(3) of the Securities Act (15 U.S.C. 77d(3)) and §230.174 of this chapter. If you do not know the expiration date on the effective date of the registration statement, include the expiration date in the copy of the prospectus you file under §230.424(b) of this chapter. You do not have to include this information if dealers are not required to deliver a prospectus under §230.174 of this chapter or Section 24(d) of the Investment Company Act(15 U.S.C. 80a-24). You may use the following or other clear, plain language:

Dealer Prospectus Delivery Obligation

Until (*insert date*), all dealers that effect transactions in these securities, whether or not participating in this offering, may be required to deliver a prospectus. This is in addition to the dealers' obligation to deliver a prospectus when acting as underwriters and

何州就购买该等证券的要约招揽。注册人也可作出下述声明或者以其他清楚、简明的语言作出类似声明:

本招募说明书中的信息并不完整,且可能会发生变更。在向证券交易委员会提交的注册说明书生效之前,我们不得出售本招募说明书中所涉的证券。本招募说明书并非证券出售要约,亦不构成在不允许发行或出售该等证券的任何州就购买该等证券发出的要约招揽。

(11)如注册人援引本章第230.430A节的规定省略发行证券的定价信息,且在其确定公开发行价格之前使用招募说明书,则应提供本条第(b)(10)款规定的信息和声明。

关于第501条的说明:对于资产支持证券,请参见《AB管理办法》第1102条(第229.1102节)的规定。

[《联邦公报》第63卷第6381页,1998年2月6日,修正索引:《联邦公报》第70卷第1594页,2005年1月7日。]

第229.502节(第502条) 招募说明书的封二和封底

注册人须以简明的英语提供下述信息。参见本章《C管理办法》第230.421(d)节的规定。

(a)目录。注册人应在招募说明书的封二或封底提供合理详细的目录。目录必须列明招募说明书各章节或部分的页码,且应按照《S-K管理办法》第503条[《联邦规章汇编》第十七编第229.503节]的要求提供关于风险因素章节的具体清单。注册人在交付任何电子版本的招募说明书时,必须将目录插入招募说明书的封面之后。

(b)自营商交付招募说明书的义务。注册人应在招募说明书的封底向自营商告知其应承担的交付招募说明书的义务,包括《证券法》第4(3)条[《美国法典》第十五编第77d(3)节]以及本章第230.174节规定的到期日。如注册人无法根据注册说明书的生效日计算得出到期日,则应提供根据本章第230.424(b)节提交的招募说明书的到期日。如自营商没有义务根据本章第230.174节或《投资公司法》第24(d)条(《美国法典》第十五编第80a-24节)的规定交付招募说明书,则不必提供上述信息。注册人可以使用下述范例或其他清楚简明的语言向自营商告知上述义务:

自营商交付招募说明书的义务

在(请插入日期)之前,所有参与本招募说明书所涉证券之交易的自营商,无论其是否参与证券发行工作,均可能承担交付招募说明书的义务。本项义务是自营商在担任承销商时就未售出份额或认购证券交付招募说明书的义务之外另外负有的义务。

with respect to their unsold allotments or subscriptions.

[63 FR 6383, Feb. 6, 1998]

§229.503(Item 503) Prospectus summary, risk factors, and ratio of earnings to fixed charges.

The registrant must furnish this information in plain English. See §230.421 (d) of Regulation C of this chapter.

(a) *Prospectus summary.* Provide a summary of the information in the prospectus where the length or complexity of the prospectus makes a summary useful. The summary should be brief. The summary should not contain, and is not required to contain, all of the detailed information in the prospectus. If you provide summary business or financial information, even if you do not caption it as a summary, you still must provide that information in plain English.

Instruction to paragraph 503(a): The summary should not merely repeat the text of the prospectus but should provide a brief overview of the key aspects of the offering. Carefully consider and identify those aspects of the offering that are the most significant and determine how best to highlight those points in clear, plain language.

(b) *Address and telephone number.* Include, either on the cover page or in the summary section of the prospectus, the complete mailing address and telephone number of your principal executive offices.

(c) *Risk factors.* Where appropriate, provide under the caption "Risk Factors" a discussion of the most significant factors that make the offering speculative or risky. This discussion must be concise and organized logically. Do not present risks that could apply to any issuer or any offering. Explain how the risk affects the issuer or the securities being offered. Set forth each risk factor under a subcaption that adequately describes the risk. The risk factor discussion must immediately follow the summary section. If you do not include a summary section, the risk factor section must immediately follow the cover page of the prospectus or the pricing information section that immediately follows the cover page. Pricing information means price and price-related information that you may omit from the prospectus in an effective registration statement based on §230.430A (a) of this chapter. The risk factors may include, among other things, the following:

(1) Your lack of an operating history;

(2) Your lack of profitable operations in recent periods;

(3) Your financial position;

(4) Your business or proposed business; or

(5) The lack of a market for your common equity securities or securities convertible into or exercisable for common equity securities.

(d) *Ratio of earnings to fixed charges.* If you register debt securities, show a ratio of

[《联邦公报》第63卷第6383页,1998年2月6日。]

第229.503节(第503条) 招募说明书的摘要、风险因素和盈利对固定费用比率

注册人须以简明英语提供下述信息。参见本章《C管理办法》第230.421(d)条的规定。

(a)招募说明书的摘要。如招募说明书冗长复杂,注册人应提供必要的信息摘要。摘要应简明扼要,且不应也不必提供招募说明书中的所有详细信息。如果内容性质属于业务或财务信息的摘要,即使未冠以"摘要"的标题,仍须以简明的英语提供相关信息。

关于第503(a)条的说明:摘要不应仅为关于招募说明书的简单复述,而应对发行的主要方面作出概要总结。注册人应仔细考虑和指明对发行最为重要的方面的内容,再确定如何通过清楚、简明的语言最有效地突出强调该等内容。

(b)地址和电话。招募说明书的封面或摘要部分应注明注册人主要办事机构的完整邮寄地址和电话号码。

(c)风险因素。在适当情况下,注册人应在"风险因素"这一章节中就导致本次发行的投机性或风险性的最重大的因素进行论述。论述必须简明扼要且条理清晰,不应涉及任何发行人或任何发行均可能面临的风险。注册人应说明该等风险是如何对发行人或正在发行的证券产生影响的,同时应在子标题下对每项风险因素予以充分的说明。关于风险因素的论述必须紧接在摘要之后。如招募说明书中未提供摘要,关于风险因素的论述则必须紧接在招募说明书的封面之后,或者位于紧接招募说明书封面的定价信息章节之后。定价信息指价格以及与价格相关的信息,注册人可基于本章第230.430A(a)节的规定在有效注册说明书所包含的招募说明书中省略该等信息。风险因素包括但不限于以下几种情形:

(1)缺乏经营历史;
(2)近期的经营活动未盈利;
(3)注册人的财务状况;
(4)注册人的业务或拟开展的业务;或
(5)注册人的普通股权证券、可转换为普通股权证券或行权后可获得普通股权证券的证券不存在相应的市场。

(d)盈利对固定费用的比率。申请注册债务证券的,应列明盈利对固定费用的比

earnings to fixed charges. If you register preference equity securities, show the ratio of combined fixed charges and preference dividends to earnings. Present the ratio for each of the last five fiscal years and the latest interim period for which financial statements are presented in the document. If you will use the proceeds from the sale of debt or preference securities to repay any of your outstanding debt or to retire other securities and the change in the ratio would be ten percent or greater, you must include a ratio showing the application of the proceeds, commonly referred to as the pro forma ratio.

Instructions to paragraph 503(d):1. *Definitions*. In calculating the ratio of earnings to fixed charges, you must use the following definitions:

(A) *Fixed charges*. The term "fixed charges" means the sum of the following: (a) interest expensed and capitalized, (b) amortized premiums, discounts and capitalized expenses related to indebtedness, (c) an estimate of the interest within rental expense, and (d) preference security dividend requirements of consolidated subsidiaries.

(B) *Preference security dividend*. The term "preference security dividend" is the amount of pre–tax earnings that is required to pay the dividends on outstanding preference securities. The dividend requirement must be computed as the amount of the dividend divided by (1 minus the effective income tax rate applicable to continuing operations).

(C) *Earnings*. The term "earnings" is the amount resulting from adding and subtracting the following items. Add the following: (a) pre–tax income from continuing operations before adjustment for income or loss from equity investees; (b) fixed charges; (c) amortization of capitalized interest; (d) distributed income of equity investees; and (e) your share of pre–tax losses of equity investees for which charges arising from guarantees are included in fixed charges. From the total of the added items, subtract the following: (a) interest capitalized; (b) preference security dividend requirements of consolidated subsidiaries; and (c) the noncontrolling interest in pre–tax income of subsidiaries that have not incurred fixed charges. Equity investees are investments that you account for using the equity method of accounting. Public utilities following SFAS 71 should not add amortization of capitalized interest in determining earnings, nor reduce fixed charges by any allowance for funds used during construction.

2. *Disclosure*. Disclose the following information when showing the ratio of earnings to fixed charges:

(A) *Deficiency*. If a ratio indicates less than one–to–one coverage, disclose the dollar amount of the deficiency.

(B) *Pro forma ratio*. You may show the pro forma ratio only for the most recent fiscal year and the latest interim period. Use the net change in interest or dividends from the refinancing to calculate the pro forma ratio.

率。申请注册优先股权证券的，应列明固定费用和优先股股息之和对盈利的比率。注册人应列明下述期间的该等比率：最近5个会计年度中每一会计年度，以及所列报的最近一期中期财务报表所覆盖的期间。如注册人将出售债务证券或优先股权证券所募集的资金用于偿还其任何未清偿的债务或用于收回其他证券，且该等情况将导致上述比率变动幅度达10%（含）以上，则注册人必须提供上述募集资金的使用比率，即通常所称的"备考比率"。

关于第503（d）条的说明：1.定义。在计算盈利对固定费用的比率时，必须使用如下定义：

（A）"固定费用"。"固定费用"一词系指下述各项费用之和：（a）利息支出和资本化的利息，（b）与负债相关的摊销溢价、折扣和资本化费用，（c）租赁费用中的利息估计，和（d）应向并表子公司支付的优先证券股息。

（B）"优先证券股息"。"优先证券股息"一词系指税前盈利金额中应作为发行在外的优先证券的股息支付的部分。上述股息必须按照以下公式计算：股息金额÷（1– 持续经营所适用的有效所得税税率）。

（C）"盈利"。"盈利"一词系指对下述各项进行加减运算后所得的金额，即下述各项之和：（a）股权投资对象进行损益调整之前的税前持续经营盈利，（b）固定费用，（c）资本化利息摊销，（d）股权投资对象的已分配收益，和（e）注册人承担的权益投资对象的税前亏损份额（条件是因担保产生的费用已计入固定费用项下）；减去下述各项费用：（a）资本化的利息，（b）应向并表子公司支付的优先证券股息，和（c）对未产生固定费用的子公司税前所得拥有的非控制性权益。股权投资对象是指注册人通过权益核算法进行会计处理的投资。在确定上述盈利时，遵守《财务会计准则公告第71号》的公用设施不应在盈利中加入摊销的资本化利息，也不得通过为工程施工提供任何资金补助而减少固定费用。

2.披露。注册人在列明盈利对固定费用的比率时，应披露如下信息：

（A）亏损。如相关比率显示保障倍数低于1:1，应披露亏损的金额。

（B）备考比率。注册人可以仅列明最近一个会计年度和最近的中期期间的备考比率。在计算备考比率时，应使用再融资的利息或股息的净变动值。

(C) *Foreign private issuers.* A foreign private issuer must show the ratio based on the figures in the primary financial statement. A foreign private issuer must show the ratio based on the figures resulting from the reconciliation to U.S. generally accepted accounting principles if this ratio is materially different.

(D) *Summary Section.* If you provide a summary or similar section in the prospectus, show the ratios in that section.

3. *Exhibit.* File an exhibit to the registration statement to show the figures used to calculate the ratios. See paragraph (b)(12) of Item 601 of Regulation S-K (17 CFR 229.601(b)(12)).

(e) *Smaller reporting companies.* A registrant that qualifies as a smaller reporting company, as defined by §229.10(f), need not comply with paragraph (d) of this Item.

Instruction to Item 503: For asset-backed securities, see also Item 1103 of Regulation AB (§229.1103).

[63 FR 6383, Feb. 6, 1998, as amended at 70 FR 1594, Jan. 7, 2005; 73 FR 964, Jan. 4, 2008; 74 FR 18617, Apr. 23, 2009]

§229.504(Item 504) Use of proceeds.

State the principal purposes for which the net proceeds to the registrant from the securities to be offered are intended to be used and the approximate amount intended to be used for each such purpose. Where registrant has no current specific plan for the proceeds, or a significant portion thereof, the registrant shall so state and discuss the principal reasons for the offering.

Instructions to Item 504: 1. Where less than all the securities to be offered may be sold and more than one use is listed for the proceeds, indicate the order of priority of such purposes and discuss the registrant's plans if substantially less than the maximum proceeds are obtained. Such discussion need not be included if underwriting arrangements with respect to such securities are such that, if any securities are sold to the public, it reasonably can be expected that the actual proceeds will not be substantially less than the aggregate proceeds to the registrant shown pursuant to Item 501 of Regulation S-K (§229.501).

2. Details of proposed expenditures need not be given; for example, there need be furnished only a brief outline of any program of construction or addition of equipment. Consideration should be given as to the need to include a discussion of certain matters addressed in the discussion and analysis of registrant's financial condition and results of operations, such as liquidity and capital expenditures.

3. If any material amounts of other funds are necessary to accomplish the specified purposes for which the proceeds are to be obtained, state the amounts and sources of such

(C)外国私募发行人。外国私募发行人必须基于其主要财务报表中的数据列明盈利对固定费用的比率。如果该比率与基于美国公认会计原则进行调整后计算得出的盈利对固定费用比率有显著差异,该发行人还应列明基于美国公认会计原则进行调整后的数据计算得出的比率。

(D)摘要章节。如注册人在招募说明书提供了摘要或类似章节,应在该章节中列明各项比率。

3.附录。注册人应通过提交注册说明书的附录,列明用于计算各项比率的数据。参见《S-K管理办法》第601条第(b)(12)款[《联邦规章汇编》第十七编第229.601(b)(12)节]。

(e)小型报告公司。具有第229.10(f)节定义的小型报告公司资格的注册人,无须遵守本条第(d)款的规定。

关于第503条的说明:对于资产支持证券,请同时参见《AB管理办法》第1103条(第229.1103节)的规定。

[《联邦公报》第63卷第6383页,1998年2月6日,修正索引:《联邦公报》第70卷第1594页,2005年1月7日;《联邦公报》第73卷第964页,2008年1月4日;《联邦公报》第74卷第18617页,2009年4月23日。]

第229.504节(第504条) 募集资金的用途

注册人应说明其拟定的发行证券所募集净资金的主要用途,以及每一用途拟使用的大致金额。如注册人当前未制定具体的募集资金使用计划或者该计划仍存在尚未确定的重大内容,应如实说明,并且就发行的主要原因进行论述。

关于第504条的说明:1.如拟发行的证券不会全部出售且募集资金的用途不止一个,应注明各项用途的优先顺序;如计划使用的资金远低于注册人可募集的最高资金额,则应就注册人的计划进行论述。如关于该等证券的承销安排符合如下条件,则不必进行上述论述:根据合理预期,只要向公众出售任何证券,实际募集的资金即不会远低于根据《S-K管理办法》第501条(第229.501节)规定列明的注册人募集资金总额。

2.注册人不必披露其计划支出的详细情况,如注册人拟开展任何施工计划或添购设备的,仅须提供相关概述即可。但是,如关于注册人的财务状况和运营结果的论述和分析中提及了某些事项,如流动性和资本性支出等,则须考虑是否有必要提供关于该等事项的论述。

3.如为实现募集资金的特定目的,有必要使用任何其他大额资金,注册人应说明需要用于该特定目的的其他资金的具体金额、资金来源以及进行此项安排的依据。

other funds needed for each such specified purpose and the sources thereof.

4. If any material part of the proceeds is to be used to discharge indebtedness, set forth the interest rate and maturity of such indebtedness. If the indebtedness to be discharged was incurred within one year, describe the use of the proceeds of such indebtedness other than short–term borrowings used for working capital.

5. If any material amount of the proceeds is to be used to acquire assets, otherwise than in the ordinary course of business, describe briefly and state the cost of the assets and, where such assets are to be acquired from affiliates of the registrant or their associates, give the names of the persons from whom they are to be acquired and set forth the principle followed in determining the cost to the registrant.

6. Where the registrant indicates that the proceeds may, or will, be used to finance acquisitions of other businesses, the identity of such businesses, if known, or, if not known, the nature of the businesses to be sought, the status of any negotiations with respect to the acquisition, and a brief description of such business shall be included. Where, however, pro forma financial statements reflecting such acquisition are not required by Regulation S–X (17 CFR 210.01 through 210.12–29), including Rule 8–05 for smaller reporting companies, to be included in the registration statement, the possible terms of any transaction, the identification of the parties thereto or the nature of the business sought need not be disclosed, to the extent that the registrant reasonably determines that public disclosure of such information would jeopardize the acquisition. Where Regulation S–X, including Rule 8–04 for smaller reporting companies, as applicable, would require financial statements of the business to be acquired to be included, the description of the business to be acquired shall be more detailed.

7. The registrant may reserve the right to change the use of proceeds, provided that such reservation is due to certain contingencies that are discussed specifically and the alternatives to such use in that event are indicated.

[47 FR 11401, Mar. 16, 1982, as amended at 73 FR 964, Jan. 4, 2008]

§229.505(Item 505) Determination of offering price.

(a) *Common equity.* Where common equity is being registered for which there is no established public trading market for purposes of paragraph (a) of Item 201 of Regulation S–K (§229.201(a)) or where there is a material disparity between the offering price of the common equity being registered and the market price of outstanding shares of the same class, describe the various factors considered in determining such offering price.

(b) *Warrants, rights and convertible securities.* Where warrants, rights or convertible securities exercisable for common equity for which there is no established public trading market for purposes of paragraph (a) of Item 201 of Regulation S–K (§229.201(a)) are

4.如募集资金的任何重大部分将用于清偿债务，注册人应载明该项债务的利率和期限。如拟清偿的债务是在一年之内发生的，则应说明通过该等债务（运营资本所需的短期借款除外）募集的资金的使用。

5.如募集资金的任何重大部分将用于购买正常业务运作以外的资产，注册人应简要描述和说明该等资产的购买成本；从注册人的关联方或业务相关人手中购买资产的，还应披露卖方的名称以及确定注册人购买该资产所需成本时所遵循的原则。

6.如注册人表明其募集的资金可能用于或将用于收购其他企业，应在注册说明书中提供被收购企业身份信息（如已知具体收购对象），或者（若收购对象尚不明）提供其所寻找的被收购企业的性质、收购的任何谈判进展状况以及对该等企业的简要说明。但是，如果《S-X管理办法》（《联邦规章汇编》第十七编第210.01~210.12-29节），包括适用于小型报告公司的《8-05规则》，并未要求在注册说明书中提供反映此项收购的备考财务报表，且如果注册人合理判定公开披露将危害此项收购，则注册人不必披露下述信息：可能适用的任何交易条款、交易双方的身份以及注册人拟收购的企业之性质。如果《S-X管理办法》，包括适用于小型报告公司的《8-04规则》（如适用），要求在注册说明书中提供关于目标收购企业的财务报表，注册人应对目标收购企业进行更加详细的说明。

7.注册人可以保留变更募集资金的用途的权利，前提是作出此项保留的原因是为经过特别论述的或有事件作准备，且在出现或有情形时该等资金的备选用途也已注明。

［《联邦公报》第47卷第11401页，1982年3月16日，修正索引：《联邦公报》第73卷第964页，2008年1月4日。］

第229.505节（第505条） 发行价格的确定

（a）普通股。如果申请注册的普通股不具备《S-K管理办法》第201条第（a）款［第229.201（a）节］规定的稳定的公开交易市场，或者其发行价格与同类发行在外股份的市场价格之间存在重大差距，应说明确定该等发行价格时考虑的各项因素。

（b）认股权证、购股权和可转换证券。如果申请注册权证、购股权或可转换证券，且该等权证、购股权或可转换证券行权后将转换为不具备《S-K管理办法》第201条第（a）款［第229.201（a）节］规定的稳定的公开交易市场的普通股，应说明在确定其行权

being registered, describe the various factors considered in determining their exercise or conversion price.

§229.506(Item 506) Dilution.

Where common equity securities are being registered and there is substantial disparity between the public offering price and the effective cash cost to officers, directors, promoters and affiliated persons of common equity acquired by them in transactions during the past five years, or which they have the right to acquire, and the registrant is not subject to the reporting requirements of section 13(a) or 15(d) of the Exchange Act immediately prior to filing of the registration statement, there shall be included a comparison of the public contribution under the proposed public offering and the effective cash contribution of such persons. In such cases, and in other instances where common equity securities are being registered by a registrant that has had losses in each of its last three fiscal years and there is a material dilution of the purchasers' equity interest, the following shall be disclosed:

(a) The net tangible book value per share before and after the distribution;

(b) The amount of the increase in such net tangible book value per share attributable to the cash payments made by purchasers of the shares being offered; and

(c) The amount of the immediate dilution from the public offering price which will be absorbed by such purchasers.

§229.507(Item 507) Selling security holders.

If any of the securities to be registered are to be offered for the account of security holders, name each such security holder, indicate the nature of any position, office, or other material relationship which the selling security holder has had within the past three years with the registrant or any of its predecessors or affiliates, and state the amount of securities of the class owned by such security holder prior to the offering, the amount to be offered for the security holder's account, the amount and (if one percent or more) the percentage of the class to be owned by such security holder after completion of the offering.

§229.508(Item 508) Plan of distribution.

(a) *Underwriters and underwriting obligation.* If the securities are to be offered through underwriters, name the principal underwriters, and state the respective amounts underwritten. Identify each such underwriter having a material relationship with the registrant and state the nature of the relationship. State briefly the nature of the obligation of the underwriter(s) to take the securities.

Instruction to paragraph 508 (a): All that is required as to the nature of the underwriters' obligation is whether the underwriters are or will be committed to take and to pay for all of the securities if any are taken, or whether it is merely an agency or the

价或转换价格时考虑的各项因素。

第229.506节（第506条） 稀释

如果注册人申请注册普通股证券，且该等证券的公开发行价格与管理人员、董事、发起人和关联人在最近5年内的交易中购买的或其有权购买的普通股的实际现金成本之间存在实质差距，且注册人在提交注册说明书之前，不受《证券交易法》第13(a)条或第15(d)条的规定的报告义务之约束，则注册人应当提供以下两者的对比信息：拟议公开发行项下的公众出资与该等人的实际现金出资。在上述情况下，以及普通股证券注册人最近3年连续亏损且购买人的股权权益发生重大稀释的其他情况下，应披露以下各项信息：

(a)稀释前及稀释后的每股有形账面净值；

(b)该等每股有形账面净值因购买人以现金付款购买发行股份而增长的金额；及

(c)由公开发行价格导致的并由该等购买人吸收的直接稀释金额。

第229.507节（第507条） 献售证券持有人

如果注册的任何证券将由注册人代证券持有人要约，应列明该等证券持有人的姓名或名称，说明献售证券持有人最近3年内在注册人或其任何前身或关联方所担任的任何职位、职务的性质，或与注册人或其任何前身或关联方之间存在的其他重大关系的性质，并说明该等证券持有人在发行前拥有的该类别证券的数量，注册人计划代证券持有人发行的证券数量，以及发行完成后该等证券持有人拥有的该类别证券的数量和比例[如果比例超过1%（含）]。

第229.508节（第508条） 分销计划

(a)承销商及承销义务。通过承销商发行证券的，应列明主承销商并分别说明其承销量。列明与注册人存在重大关系的各承销商及该等关系的性质。简要说明承销商承购证券义务的性质。

关于第508(a)款的说明：说明承销商义务之性质时，仅须指明如下信息：承销商是否承诺或将承诺承购全部证券，以及是否将为承购的全部证券付款；或者承销商是否仅根据代理安排或“尽最大努力”类型的安排开展工作，仅有义务承购并支付其可以

type of *best efforts* arrangement under which the underwriters are required to take and to pay for only such securities as they may sell to the public. Conditions precedent to the underwriters' taking the securities, including *market-outs*, need not be described except in the case of an agency or *best efforts* arrangement.

(b) *New underwriters*. Where securities being registered are those of a registrant that has not previously been required to file reports pursuant to section 13(a) or 15(d) of the Exchange Act, or where a prospectus is required to include reference on its cover page to material risks pursuant to Item 501 of Regulation S-K (§229.501), and any one or more of the managing underwriter(s) (or where there are no managing underwriters, a majority of the principal underwriters) has been organized, reactivated, or first registered as a broker-dealer within the past three years, these facts concerning such underwriter(s) shall be disclosed in the prospectus together with, where applicable, the disclosures that the principal business function of such underwriter(s) will be to sell the securities to be registered, or that the promoters of the registrant have a material relationship with such underwriter (s). Sufficient details shall be given to allow full appreciation of such underwriter(s) experience and its relationship with the registrant, promoters and their controlling persons.

(c) *Other distributions*. Outline briefly the plan of distribution of any securities to be registered that are to be offered otherwise than through underwriters.

(1) If any securities are to be offered pursuant to a dividend or interest reinvestment plan the terms of which provide for the purchase of some securities on the market, state whether the registrant or the participant pays fees, commissions, and expenses incurred in connection with the plan. If the participant will pay such fees, commissions and expenses, state the anticipated cost to participants by transaction or other convenient reference.

(2) If the securities are to be offered through the selling efforts of brokers or dealers, describe the plan of distribution and the terms of any agreement, arrangement, or understanding entered into with broker(s) or dealer(s) prior to the effective date of the registration statement, including volume limitations on sales, parties to the agreement and the conditions under which the agreement may be terminated. If known, identify the broker(s) or dealer(s) which will participate in the offering and state the amount to be offered through each.

(3) If any of the securities being registered are to be offered otherwise than for cash, state briefly the general purposes of the distribution, the basis upon which the securities are to be offered, the amount of compensation and other expenses of distribution, and by whom they are to be borne. If the distribution is to be made pursuant to a plan of acquisition, reorganization, readjustment or succession, describe briefly the general effect of the plan and state when it became or is to become operative. As to any material amount

向公众出售的证券。除非承销商根据代理安排或“尽最大努力”安排开展工作,否则不必说明承销商承购证券的先决条件(包括“因市场情形退出承销”条款)。

(b)新承销商。如果申请注册的证券为之前不受《交易法》第13(a)条或第15(b)条的报告义务约束的注册人的证券,或者按照规定招募说明书应根据《S-K管理办法》第501条(第229.501节)在封面页上对重大风险作出说明,且任何一家或一家以上主承销商(或如无主承销商,则为大多数的主要承销商)是在最近3年内成立或首次注册为经纪自营商,或恢复经纪自营商资格的,应当在招募说明书中披露关于该等承销商的上述事实;如适用,应同时披露该等承销商的主要业务功能是销售申请注册的证券,或披露注册人的发起人与该等承销商存在重大关系。应当提供充分详细的信息,以便充分判断该等承包商的经验及其与注册人、发起人及其控制人之间的关系。

(c)其他分销方式。简要列举非通过承销商发行的任何注册证券的分销计划。

(1)如果任何证券系根据股息或利息再投资计划发行,且该等计划的条款对市场上某些证券的购买作出了规定,应说明注册人或计划参与人是否负责支付该计划产生的相关费用、佣金及开支。如果计划参与人负责支付该等费用、佣金及开支,应按交易或其他适宜的基准列明计划参与人预期支出的成本。

(2)如果证券发行采用经纪商或自营商销售的方式,应说明分销计划,并说明在注册说明书生效日之前与经纪商或自营商签订的任何协议、安排或谅解的条款,包括销售量限制、协议各方及决定协议终止的条件。如注册人已经知悉参与发行的经纪商或自营商及其各自的发行量,应如实说明。

(3)如果任何注册证券的发行不以现金作为对价,应简要说明:分销的总体目的、证券的发行基础、分销的报酬及其他分销的费用,以及该等费用的承担方。根据收购、重组、重整或继承计划进行分销的,应简要说明计划纲要及其实施或预计实施时间。对于根据计划收购的任何重大资产,应按照《S-K管理办法》第504条(第229.504节)的说明5提供相应信息。

of assets to be acquired under the plan, furnish information corresponding to that required by Instruction 5 of Item 504 of Regulation S-K(§229.504).

(d) *Offerings on exchange.* If the securities are to be offered on an exchange, indicate the exchange. If the registered securities are to be offered in connection with the writing of exchange-traded call options, describe briefly such transactions.

(e) *Underwriter's compensation.* Provide a table that sets out the nature of the compensation and the amount of discounts and commissions to be paid to the underwriter for each security and in total. The table must show the separate amounts to be paid by the company and the selling shareholders. In addition, include in the table all other items considered by the National Association of Securities Dealers to be underwriting compensation for purposes of that Association's Rules of Fair Practice.

Instructions to paragraph 508(e): 1. The term "commissions" is defined in paragraph (17) of Schedule A of the Securities Act. Show separately in the table the cash commissions paid by the registrant and selling security holders. Also show in the table commissions paid by other persons. Disclose any finder's fee or similar payments in the table.

2. Disclose the offering expenses specified in Item 511 of Regulation S-K (17 CFR 229.511).

3. If the underwriter has any arrangement with the issuer, such as an over-allotment option, under which the underwriter may purchase additional shares in connection with the offering, indicate that this arrangement exists and state the amount of additional shares that the underwriter may purchase under the arrangement. Where the underwriter has such an arrangement, present maximum-minimum information in a separate column to the table, based on the purchase of all or none of the shares subject to the arrangement. Describe the key terms of the arrangement in the narrative.

(f) *Underwriter's representative on board of directors.* Describe any arrangement whereby the underwriter has the right to designate or nominate a member or members of the board of directors of the registrant. The registrant shall disclose the identity of any director so designated or nominated, and indicate whether or not a person so designated or nominated, or allowed to be designated or nominated by the underwriter is or may be a director, officer, partner, employee or affiliate of the underwriter.

(g) *Indemnification of underwriters.* If the underwriting agreement provides for indemnification by the registrant of the underwriters or their controlling persons against any liability arising under the Securities Act, furnish a brief description of such indemnification provisions.

(h) *Dealers' compensation.* State briefly the discounts and commissions to be allowed or paid to dealers, including all cash, securities, contracts or other considerations to be

(d)场内发行。如果证券通过证券交易所发行,应指明证券交易所的名称。如果注册证券的发行与交易所交易的看涨期权的出售相关,应简要说明该等交易。

(e)承销商的报酬。在表格中列明报酬性质、就每只证券向承销商支付的折扣和佣金金额以及就所有证券支付的折扣和佣金总额。表格必须分别列明将由公司和献售股东支付的付款金额。此外,表格还应包含全国证券交易商协会据其《公平作业规则》视为承销报酬的所有其他项目。

关于第508(e)款的说明:1."佣金"一词的含义以《证券法》的《附表A》第(17)款之定义为准。应在表格内分别说明注册人和献售证券持有人以现金支付的佣金。表格还应包含其他人支付的佣金,并披露所有中介费或其他类似付款。

2.披露《S-K管理办法》第511条(《联邦规章汇编》第十七编第229.511节)规定的发行费用。

3.如果承销商与发行人之间订有任何安排,如承销商可根据超额配售选择权额外购买发行股份,应说明该安排的存在情况并说明承销商根据安排可额外购买的股份数量。如果承销商订有任何该等安排,应基于根据安排购买所有股份或完全不购买股份的情况,在表格内单列一栏填写最大值—最小值信息。对安排的主要条款提供文字说明。

(f)承销商在董事会的代表。如果承销商根据任何安排有权委任或提名注册人董事会成员,应说明该等安排。注册人应披露任何该等承销商委任或提名的董事的身份,并说明承销商委任、提名或有权委任、提名的人是否同时担任或是否可以担任承销商的董事、管理人员、合伙人、职员或关联方。

(g)对承销商的赔偿。如果承销协议规定注册人应就《证券法》下产生的任何责任向承销商或其控制人提供赔偿,简要说明该等赔偿规定。

(h)自营商的报酬。简要说明批准向自营商支付的或实际向交易商支付的折扣及佣金,包括所有现金、证券、合同或自营商将就证券出售收到的其他对价。如果任何交

received by any dealer in connection with the sale of the securities. If any dealers are to act in the capacity of sub-underwriters and are to be allowed or paid any additional discounts or commissions for acting in such capacity, a general statement to that effect will suffice without giving the additional amounts to be sold.

(i) *Finders.* Identify any finder and, if applicable, describe the nature of any material relationship between such finder and the registrant, its officers, directors, principal stockholders, finders or promoters or the principal underwriter(s), or if there is a managing underwriter(s), the managing underwriter(s), (including, in each case, affiliates or associates thereof).

(j) *Discretionary accounts.* If the registrant was not, immediately prior to the filing of the registration statement, subject to the requirements of section 13(a) or 15(d) of the Exchange Act, identify any principal underwriter that intends to sell to any accounts over which it exercises discretionary authority and include an estimate of the amount of securities so intended to be sold. The response to this paragraph shall be contained in a pre-effective amendment which shall be circulated if the information is not available when the registration statement is filed.

(k) *Passive market making.* If the underwriters or any selling group members intend to engage in passive market making transactions as permitted by Rule 103 of Regulation M (§242.103 of this chapter), indicate such intention and briefly describe passive market making.

(l) *Stabilization and other transactions.* (1) Briefly describe any transaction that the underwriter intends to conduct during the offering that stabilizes, maintains, or otherwise affects the market price of the offered securities. Include information on stabilizing transactions, syndicate short covering transactions, penalty bids, or any other transaction that affects the offered security's price. Describe the nature of the transactions clearly and explain how the transactions affect the offered security's price. Identify the exchange or other market on which these transactions may occur. If true, disclose that the underwriter may discontinue these transactions at any time;

(2) If the stabilizing began before the effective date of the registration statement, disclose the amount of securities bought, the prices at which they were bought and the period within which they were bought. If you use §230.430A of this chapter, the prospectus you file under §230.424(b) of this chapter or include in a post-effective amendment must contain information on the stabilizing transactions that took place before the determination of the public offering price; and

(3) If you are making a warrants or rights offering of securities to existing security holders and any securities not purchased by existing security holders are to be reoffered to the public, disclose in a supplement to the prospectus or in the prospectus used in

易商以次级承销商身份行事,且因此被批准享受或实际获得任何额外的折扣或佣金,应对此作出一般性声明,但不必额外说明出售数量。

(i)中介。列明所有中介,且如适用,应说明该等中介与注册人及其管理人员、董事、主要股东、中介或发起人、主要的承销商或主承销商(如有)(包括上述所有各者的关联方或业务相关人)之间存在的重大关系的性质。

(j)全权委托账户。如果注册人在提交注册说明书前不必遵守《交易法》第13(a)条或第15(d)条规定的义务,应列明有意向其任何全权委托账户出售证券的任何主要的承销商,同时对计划向该账户出售的证券数量进行预估。如注册说明书提交之时,无法获得本款要求提供的信息,则应在注册说明书生效前通过发布修正稿提供该等信息。

(k)消极做市。如果承销商或任何销售团队成员希望从事《M管理办法》的《103规则》(本章第242.103节)允许的消极做市交易,应说明该等意向,并简要说明消极做市交易。

(l)稳定操作及其他交易。(1)简要说明承销商计划在发行期间进行的,旨在稳定、维持或以其他方式影响已发行证券市场价格的任何交易,同时纳入关于如下交易的信息:稳定交易、辛迪加空头补进交易、惩罚性出价或影响已发行证券价格的任何其他交易。明确说明交易的性质,并解释交易是如何影响已发行证券价格的。列明可以进行该等交易的交易所或其他市场。如承销商确实可以随时中断该等交易,应如实披露;

(2)如果稳定操作交易在注册说明书生效日之前开始,应披露所购买证券的数量、购买价格及购买期限。如适用本章第230.430A节的规定,必须在根据本章第230.424(b)节提交的招募说明书或在生效后修正稿中包含的招募说明书中,提供确定公开发行价格之前进行的稳定操作交易信息;及

(3)如果面向现有的证券持有人发行权证或购股权,且未被现有证券持有人购买的任何证券将重新向公众发行,则应在招募说明书的补充材料中,或重新发行使用的招募说明书中披露以下信息:

connection with the reoffering:

(i) The amount of securities bought in stabilization activities during the offering period and the price or range of prices at which the securities were bought;

(ii) The amount of the offered securities subscribed for during the offering period;

(iii) The amount of the offered securities subscribed for by the underwriter during the offering period;

(iv) The amount of the offered securities sold during the offering period by the underwriter and the price or price ranges at which the securities were sold; and

(v) The amount of the offered securities that will be reoffered to the public and the public offering price.

[47 FR 11401, Mar. 16, 1982, as amended at 58 FR 19606, Apr. 15, 1993; 62 FR 543, Jan. 3, 1997; 62 FR 11323, Mar. 12, 1997; 63 FR 6384, Feb. 6, 1998]

§229.509(Item 509) Interests of named experts and counsel.

If (a) any expert named in the registration statement as having prepared or certified any part thereof (or is named as having prepared or certified a report or valuation for use in connection with the registration statement), or (b) counsel for the registrant, underwriters or selling security holders named in the prospectus as having given an opinion upon the validity of the securities being registered or upon other legal matters in connection with the registration or offering of such securities, was employed for such purpose on a contingent basis, or at the time of such preparation, certification or opinion or at any time thereafter, through the date of effectiveness of the registration statement or that part of the registration statement to which such preparation, certification or opinion relates, had, or is to receive in connection with the offering, a substantial interest, direct or indirect, in the registrant or any of its parents or subsidiaries or was connected with the registrant or any of its parents or subsidiaries as a promoter, managing underwriter (or any principal underwriter, if there are no managing underwriters) voting trustee, director, officer, or employee, furnish a brief statement of the nature of such contingent basis, interest, or connection.

Instructions to Item 509: 1. The interest of an expert (other than an accountant) or counsel will not be deemed substantial and need not be disclosed if the interest, including the fair market value of all securities of the registrant owned, received and to be received, or subject to options, warrants or rights received or to be received by the expert or counsel does not exceed $50,000. For the purpose of this Instruction, the term *expert* or counsel includes the firm, corporation, partnership or other entity, if any, by which such expert or counsel is employed or of which he is a member or of counsel to and all attorneys in the case of counsel, and all nonclerical personnel in the case of named

(i)发行期内通过稳定交易活动购买的证券数量,以及证券的购买价格或价格范围;

(ii)发行期内被认购的已发行证券的数量;

(iii)承销商在发行期内认购的已发行证券的数量;

(iv)承销商在发行期内出售的已发行证券的数量,以及证券的出售价格或价格范围;及

(v)重新向公众发行的已发行证券的数量及公开发行价格。

[《联邦公报》第47卷第11401页,1982年3月16日,修正索引:《联邦公报》第58卷第19606页,1993年4月15日;《联邦公报》第62卷第543页,1997年1月3日;《联邦公报》第62卷第11323页,1997年3月12日;《联邦公报》第63卷第6384页,1998年2月6日。]

第229.509节(第509条) 具名专家和顾问的权益

如果(a)注册说明书中指明的任何曾参与下述活动的专家:编制或认证注册说明书任何部分的内容(或编制或认证与注册说明书相关的报告或估价),或(b)招募说明书中指明的就注册证券有效性或证券注册或发行的其他法律事项为注册人、承销商或献售证券持有人提供意见的顾问:是在风险收费的基础上聘用的,或者,从参与该等编制、认证或提供意见之时或之后的任何时间开始直至与该等工作相关的注册说明书或相关部分内容生效之日为止,对注册人或其任何母公司或子公司直接或间接拥有重大权益,或将因发行获得该等权益,或作为发起人、主承销商(如无主承销商,则作为任何主要的承销商)、表决的信托受托人、董事、管理人员或职员与注册人或其任何母公司或子公司存在关系,应简要陈述该等风险收费安排、权益或关系的性质。

关于第509条的说明:1.如果专家(会计师除外)或顾问的权益,包括该专家或顾问已拥有的、接收的或即将接收的证券,或该专家或顾问接收的或即将接收的期权、权证或购股权项下的证券的公允市场价值不超过5万美元,则该专家或顾问的权益不视为重大权益,且不必披露。就本说明而言,“专家”或“顾问”一词包括该等专家或顾问就职的或担任其成员或顾问的事务所、公司、合伙或其他实体(如有);并且,对于顾问而言,包括代表该等事务所、公司、合伙或实体参与该等事项的所有律师,对于具名专家而言,包括代表该等事务所、公司、合伙或实体参与该等事项的所有非文员人员。

experts, participating in such matter on behalf of such firm, corporation, partnership or entity.

2. Accountants, providing a report on the financial statements, presented or incorporated by reference in the registration statement, should note §210.2–01 of Regulation S–X (17 CFR 210) for the Commission's requirements regarding "Qualification of Accountants" which discusses disqualifying interests.

§229.510(Item 510) Disclosure of Commission position on indemnification for Securities Act liabilities.

In addition to the disclosure prescribed by Item 702 of Regulation S–K (§229.702), if the undertaking required by paragraph (h) of Item 512 of Regulation S–K (§229.512) is not required to be included in the registration statement because acceleration of the effective date of the registration statement is not being requested, and if waivers have not been obtained comparable to those specified in paragraph (h), a brief description of the indemnification provisions relating to directors, officers and controlling persons of the registrant against liability arising under the Securities Act (including any provision of the underwriting agreement which relates to indemnification of the underwriter or its controlling persons by the registrant against such liabilities where a director, officer or controlling person of the registrant is such an underwriter or controlling person thereof or a member of any firm which is such an underwriter) shall be included in the prospectus, together with a statement in substantially the following form:

Insofar as indemnification for liabilities arising under the Securities Act of 1933 may be permitted to directors, officers or persons controlling the registrant pursuant to the foregoing provisions, the registrant has been informed that in the opinion of the Securities and Exchange Commission such indemnification is against public policy as expressed in the Act and is therefore unenforceable.

[47 FR 11401, Mar. 16, 1982, as amended at 56 FR 48103, Sept. 24, 1991]

§229.511(Item 511) Other expenses of issuance and distribution.

Furnish a reasonably itemized statement of all expenses in connection with the issuance and distribution of the securities to be registered, other than underwriting discounts and commissions. If any of the securities to be registered are to be offered for the account of security holders, indicate the portion of such expenses to be borne by such security holder.

Instruction to Item 511: Insofar as practicable, registration fees, Federal taxes, States taxes and fees, trustees' and transfer agents' fees, costs of printing and engraving, and legal, accounting, and engineering fees shall be itemized separately. Include as a separate item any premium paid by the registrant or any selling security holder on any policy

2.就注册说明书内列报或引用纳入的财务报表出具报告的会计师应当了解并遵守《S-X管理办法》第210.2-01条(《联邦规章汇编》第十七编第210节)中证券交易委员会关于"会计师资格"的规定,该条对会计师因其具有的利害关系而丧失资格的情形进行了论述。

第229.510节(第510条) 关于证券交易委员会对《证券法》责任的赔偿意见之披露

除《S-K管理办法》第702条(第229.702节)规定的披露外,如果由于注册说明书的生效日期不必提前,而不要求注册人在注册说明书内作出《S-K管理办法》第512条第(h)款(第229.512节)规定的承诺,且如果未获得与第(h)款规定的豁免具有可比性的豁免,则应在招募说明书中简要说明关于就《证券法》下产生的责任向注册人的董事、管理人员及控制人提供赔偿的条款(包括承销协议中关于在下述情况下,注册人就该等责任向承销商或其控制人提供赔偿的任何规定:注册人的董事、管理人员或控制人由该等承销商、承销商的控制人担任,或是承销商公司的成员担任),并参照如下基本格式,提供一份声明:

如前述规定允许就《1993年证券法》下产生的责任向注册人的董事、管理人员或控制人提供赔偿,注册人已明确知悉,证券交易委员会认为该等赔偿不符合《证券法》中的公共政策,因此不具强制执行力。

[《联邦公报》第47卷第11401页,1982年3月16日,修正索引:《联邦公报》第56卷第48103页,1991年9月24日。]

第229.511节(第511条) 其他发行及分销费用

注册人应就注册证券之发行和分销相关费用(不包括承销折扣和佣金)提供一份合理分项的明细报表。注册人申请注册的证券将由注册人代证券持有人发行的,说明应由该等证券持有人承担的费用比例。

关于第511条的说明:在可行的情况下,注册费、联邦税项、州税费、信托及过户代理费、打印刻字费以及法律、会计及工程费应逐项单列。注册人或任何献售证券持有人为注册证券发行及出售获取保单,从而为董事或管理人员可能产生的、与该等证券的注册、发行或出售相关的任何责任投保或获得赔偿的,因此支出的保费亦应单项列

obtained in connection with the offering and sale of the securities being registered which insures or indemnifies directors or officers against any liabilities they may incur in connection with the registration, offering, or sale of such securities. The information may be given as subject to future contingencies. If the amounts of any items are not known, estimates, identified as such, shall be given.

§229.512(Item 512) Undertakings.

Include each of the following undertakings that is applicable to the offering being registered.

(a) *Rule 415 Offering.*[1] Include the following if the securities are registered pursuant to Rule 415 under the Securities Act (§230.415 of this chapter):

The undersigned registrant hereby undertakes:

(1) To file, during any period in which offers or sales are being made, a post-effective amendment to this registration statement:

(i) To include any propectus required by section 10(a)(3) of the Securities Act of 1933;

(ii) To reflect in the prospectus any facts or events arising after the effective date of the registration statement (or the most recent post-effective amendment thereof) which, individually or in the aggregate, represent a fundamental change in the information set forth in the registration statement. Notwithstanding the foregoing, any increase or decrease in volume of securities offered (if the total dollar value of securities offered would not exceed that which was registered) and any deviation from the low or high end of the estimated maximum offering range may be reflected in the form of prospectus filed with the Commission pursuant to Rule 424(b)(§230.424(b) of this chapter) if, in the aggregate, the changes in volume and price represent no more than 20% change in the maximum aggregate offering price set forth in the "Calculation of Registration Fee" table in the effective registration statement.

(iii) To include any material information with respect to the plan of distribution not previously disclosed in the registration statement or any material change to such information in the registration statement;

Provided, however, That:

(A) Paragraphs (a)(1)(i) and (a)(1)(ii) of this section do not apply if the registration statement is on Form S-8 (§239.16b of this chapter), and the information required to be included in a post-effective amendment by those paragraphs is contained in reports filed with or furnished to the Commission by the registrant pursuant to section

1 Paragraph (a) reflects proposals made in Securities Act Release No. 6334 (Aug. 6, 1981).

明。信息可以根据未来的或有情况而具有不确定性。任何项目金额不确定的，应提供其估算金额，并说明该等金额的估算性质。

第229.512节（第512条） 承诺

应就申请注册的证券发行提供以下每一项适用承诺：

(a)《415规则》发行。[1]如证券将根据《证券法》的《415规则》（本章第230.415节）注册，应纳入如下内容：

下文签字注册人特此承诺：

(1)在任何发行或出售期间提交注册说明书的生效后修正稿，以：

(i)纳入《1993年证券法》第10(a)(3)条规定的任何招募说明书；

(ii)通过招募说明书反映注册说明书（或其最新的生效后修正稿）生效日后发生的、单独或从整体上构成注册说明书所列信息之根本变动的任何事实或事件。无论上文如何规定，如果证券的发行量出现任何增减（但发行证券的美元总值不超过注册的金额），或预估最大发行数额范围的最高值或最低值出现任何偏差，则该等增减及偏差可通过根据《424(b)规则》[本章第230.424(b)节]向证券交易委员会提交的招募说明书予以反映，前提是相关证券发行量及价格的变动总值不超过已生效注册说明书中“注册费计算”表所列的最高发行总价的20%。

(iii)纳入注册说明书之前未予披露的关于分销计划的任何重大信息，或注册说明书中关于分销计划的信息的任何重大变更；

但是：

(A)如果注册说明书系按照《S-8表格》（本章第239.16b节）提交，且本节第(a)(1)(i)款及第(a)(1)(ii)款要求在生效后修正稿中包含的信息已纳入注册人根据《1934年证券交易法》第13条或第15(d)条[《美国法典》第十五编第78m节或第78o(d)节]向证券交易委员会提交或提供的报告，且该等报告已通过引用方式纳入注册说明书之中，

1 第(a)款反映了《第6334号证券法公告》（1981年8月6日）中的提议。

13 or section 15(d) of the Securities Exchange Act of 1934 (15 U.S.C. 78m or 78o(d)) that are incorporated by reference in the registration statement; and

(B) Paragraphs (a)(1)(i), (a)(1)(ii) and (a)(1)(iii) of this section do not apply if the registration statement is on Form S-3 (§239.13 of this chapter) or Form F-3 (§239.33 of this chapter) and the information required to be included in a post-effective amendment by those paragraphs is contained in reports filed with or furnished to the Commission by the registrant pursuant to section 13 or section 15 (d) of the Securities Exchange Act of 1934 that are incorporated by reference in the registration statement, or is contained in a form of prospectus filed pursuant to Rule 424(b) (§230.424(b) of this chapter) that is part of the registration statement.

(C) *Provided further, however*, that paragraphs (a)(1)(i) and (a)(1)(ii) do not apply if the registration statement is for an offering of asset-backed securities on Form S-1 (§239.11 of this chapter) or Form S-3 (§239.13 of this chapter), and the information required to be included in a post-effective amendment is provided pursuant to Item 1100(c) of Regulation AB (§229.1100(c)).

(2) That, for the purpose of determining any liability under the Securities Act of 1933, each such post-effective amendment shall be deemed to be a new registration statement relating to the securities offered therein, and the offering of such securities at that time shall be deemed to be the initial bona fide offering thereof.

(3) To remove from registration by means of a post-effective amendment any of the securities being registered which remain unsold at the termination of the offering.

(4) If the registrant is a foreign private issuer, to file a post-effective amendment to the registration statement to include any financial statements required by "Item 8.A. of Form 20-F(17 CFR 249.220f)" at the start of any delayed offering or throughout a continuous offering. Financial statements and information otherwise required by Section 10(a)(3) of the Act need not be furnished, *provided* that the registrant includes in the prospectus, by means of a post-effective amendment, financial statements required pursuant to this paragraph (a)(4) and other information necessary to ensure that all other information in the prospectus is at least as current as the date of those financial statements. Notwithstanding the foregoing, with respect to registration statements on Form F-3 (§239.33 of this chapter), a post-effective amendment need not be filed to include financial statements and information required by Section 10(a)(3) of the Act or §210.3-19 of this chapter if such financial statements and information are contained in periodic reports filed with or furnished to the Commission by the registrant pursuant to section 13 or section 15(d) of the Securities Exchange Act of 1934 that are incorporated by reference in the Form F-3.

(5) That, for the purpose of determining liability under the Securities Act of 1933 to

则不适用本条第(a)(1)(i)款及第(a)(1)(ii)款的规定;且

(B)如果注册说明书系按照《S-3表格》(本章第239.13节)或《F-3表格》(本章第239.33节)提交,且本节第(a)(1)(i)款、第(a)(1)(ii)款及第(a)(1)(iii)款要求在生效后修正稿中包含的信息已纳入注册人根据《1934年证券交易法》第13条或第15(d)条向证券交易委员会提交的报告,且该等报告已通过引用方式纳入注册说明书之中,或者已纳入根据《424(b)规则》[本章第230.424(b)节]提交的招募说明书格式,且该等招募说明书构成注册说明书的一部分,则不适用本条第(a)(1)(i)款、第(a)(1)(ii)款及第(a)(1)(iii)款的规定。

(C)此外,如果注册说明书系按照《S-1表格》(本章第239.11节)或《S-3表格》(本章第239.13节)提交,且发行证券属于资产支持证券,且按规定应纳入生效后修正稿的信息已经按照《AB管理办法》第1100(c)条[第229.1100(c)节]的规定提供,则不适用第(a)(1)(i)款及第(a)(1)(ii)款的规定。

(2)在确定《1933年证券法》下的任何责任之时,该等生效后修正稿均应视为相关发行证券的新注册说明书,且届时该等证券发行应视为首次善意发行。

(3)对于发行终止时仍未售出的任何注册证券,以生效后修正稿形式撤销注册。

(4)如果注册人是外国私募发行人,应在任何延迟发行开始时或在持续发行期间提交注册说明书的生效后修正稿,以纳入"《20-F表格》第8.A.条(《联邦规章汇编》第十七编第249.220f节)"要求的任何财务报表。不必提供《1933年证券法》第10(a)(3)条另行要求提供的财务报表及信息,但是,注册人应通过生效后修正稿将本第(a)(4)款要求提供的财务报表及其他必要信息纳入招募说明书之中,以确保招募说明书中的所有其他信息至少应为截至财务报表日的最新信息。无论上文如何规定,就按照《F-3表格》(本章第239.33节)提交的注册说明书而言,如果《1933年证券法》第10(a)(3)条或本章第210.3-19节要求提供的财务报表及信息已纳入注册人根据《1934年证券法》第13条或第15(d)条向证券交易委员会提交的定期报告之中,且该等定期报告已通过引用方式纳入《F-3表格》,则不必通过提交生效后修正稿的方式纳入该等财务报表及信息。

(5)在确定《1933年证券法》下对任何购买人承担的责任之时:

any purchaser:

(i) If the registrant is relying on Rule 430B (§230.430B of this chapter):

(A) Each prospectus filed by the registrant pursuant to Rule 424(b)(3) (§230.424 (b)(3) of this chapter) shall be deemed to be part of the registration statement as of the date the filed prospectus was deemed part of and included in the registration statement; and

(B) Each prospectus required to be filed pursuant to Rule 424(b)(2), (b)(5), or (b)(7)(§230.424 (b)(2), (b)(5), or (b)(7) of this chapter) as part of a registration statement in reliance on Rule 430B relating to an offering made pursuant to Rule 415(a)(1)(i), (vii), or (x) (§230.415(a)(1)(i), (vii), or (x) of this chapter) for the purpose of providing the information required by section 10(a) of the Securities Act of 1933 shall be deemed to be part of and included in the registration statement as of the earlier of the date such form of prospectus is first used after effectiveness or the date of the first contract of sale of securities in the offering described in the prospectus. As provided in Rule 430B, for liability purposes of the issuer and any person that is at that date an underwriter, such date shall be deemed to be a new effective date of the registration statement relating to the securities in the registration statement to which that prospectus relates, and the offering of such securities at that time shall be deemed to be the initial *bona fide* offering thereof. *Provided, however,* that no statement made in a registration statement or prospectus that is part of the registration statement or made in a document incorporated or deemed incorporated by reference into the registration statement or prospectus that is part of the registration statement will, as to a purchaser with a time of contract of sale prior to such effective date, supersede or modify any statement that was made in the registration statement or prospectus that was part of the registration statement or made in any such document immediately prior to such effective date; or

(ii) If the registrant is subject to Rule 430C (§230.430C of this chapter), each prospectus filed pursuant to Rule 424(b) as part of a registration statement relating to an offering, other than registration statements relying on Rule 430B or other than prospectuses filed in reliance on Rule 430A (§230.430A of this chapter), shall be deemed to be part of and included in the registration statement as of the date it is first used after effectiveness.*Provided, however,* that no statement made in a registration statement or prospectus that is part of the registration statement or made in a document incorporated or deemed incorporated by reference into the registration statement or prospectus that is part of the registration statement will, as to a purchaser with a time of contract of sale prior to such first use, supersede or modify any statement that was made in the registration statement or prospectus that was part of the registration statement or made in any such document immediately prior to such date of first use.

(i)如果注册人援引《430B规则》(本章第230.430B节)的规定:

(A)注册人根据《424(b)(3)规则》[本章第230.424(b)(3)节]提交的各份招募说明书自视为构成注册说明书一部分并纳入注册说明书中之日起,应视为构成注册说明书的一部分;及

(B)注册人为按照《1933年证券法》第10(a)条的规定提供信息之目的,援引《430B规则》,并根据《424(b)(2)规则》、《424(b)(5)规则》或《424(b)(7)规则》[本章第230.424(b)(2)节、第230.424(b)(5)节或第230.424(b)(7)节]作为注册说明书的一部分,就根据《415(a)(1)(i)规则》、《415(a)(1)(i)(vii)规则》或《415(a)(1)(i)(x)规则》[本章第230.415(a)(1)(i)节、第230.415(a)(1)(vii)节或第230.415(a)(1)(x)节]进行的发行提交的各项招募说明书,应于该等招募说明书格式在生效后首次使用之日或招募说明书所述的发行证券销售合同生效或签署之日(以较早者为准)视为注册说明书的一部分并纳入注册说明书之中。根据《430B规则》的规定,就发行人及在该日担任承销商的任何主体的责任而言,该等日期应视为该招募说明书中相关证券的注册说明书的新的生效日,且届时该等证券的发行应视为首次善意发行。但是,对于在该等生效日期之前签署销售合同的购买人而言,注册说明书或作为注册说明书一部分的招募说明书中的任何声明,或通过引用方式纳入或视为纳入该等注册说明书或招募说明书的文件中的任何声明,均不得取代或修改置于该等生效日期之前在注册说明书或作为注册说明书一部分的招募说明书中做出的任何声明,或上述通过引用纳入的文件中作出的任何声明;或

(ii)如果注册人受制于《430C规则》(本章第230.430C节)的规定,则根据《424(b)规则》作为发行注册说明书之一部分提交的各份招募说明书[援引《430B规则》的注册说明书或援引《430A规则》提交的招募说明书(本章第230.430A节)除外]在生效后第一次使用之日应视为注册说明书的一部分并视为纳入注册说明书之中。但是,对于在该等首次使用之前签署销售合同的购买人而言,注册说明书或作为注册说明书一部分的招募说明书中的任何声明,或通过引用方式纳入或视为纳入该等注册说明书或招募说明书的文件中的任何声明,均不得取代或修改在该等首次使用日期之前在注册说明书或作为注册说明书一部分的招募说明书中作出的任何声明,或上述通过引用纳入的文件中作出的任何声明;

(6) That, for the purpose of determining liability of the registrant under the Securities Act of 1933 to any purchaser in the initial distribution of the securities:

The undersigned registrant undertakes that in a primary offering of securities of the undersigned registrant pursuant to this registration statement, regardless of the underwriting method used to sell the securities to the purchaser, if the securities are offered or sold to such purchaser by means of any of the following communications, the undersigned registrant will be a seller to the purchaser and will be considered to offer or sell such securities to such purchaser:

(i) Any preliminary prospectus or prospectus of the undersigned registrant relating to the offering required to be filed pursuant to Rule 424 (§230.424 of this chapter);

(ii) Any free writing prospectus relating to the offering prepared by or on behalf of the undersigned registrant or used or referred to by the undersigned registrant;

(iii) The portion of any other free writing prospectus relating to the offering containing material information about the undersigned registrant or its securities provided by or on behalf of the undersigned registrant; and

(iv) Any other communication that is an offer in the offering made by the undersigned registrant to the purchaser.

(b) *Filings incorporating subsequent Exchange Act documents by reference.* Include the following if the registration statement incorporates by reference any Exchange Act document filed subsequent to the effective date of the registration statement:

The undersigned registrant hereby undertakes that, for purposes of determining any liability under the Securities Act of 1933, each filing of the registrant's annual report pursuant to section 13(a) or section 15(d) of the Securities Exchange Act of 1934 (and, where applicable, each filing of an employee benefit plan's annual report pursuant to section 15(d) of the Securities Exchange Act of 1934) that is incorporated by reference in the registration statement shall be deemed to be a new registration statement relating to the securities offered therein, and the offering of such securities at that time shall be deemed to be the initial bona fide offering thereof.

(c) *Warrants and rights offerings.* Include the following, with appropriate modifications to suit the particular case, if the securities to be registered are to be offered to existing security holders pursuant to warrants or rights and any securities not taken by security holders are to be reoffered to the public:

The undersigned registrant hereby undertakes to supplement the prospectus, after the expiration of the subscription period, to set forth the results of the subscription offer, the transactions by the underwriters during the subscription period, the amount of unsubscribed securities to be purchased by the underwriters, and the terms of any subsequent reoffering thereof. If any public offering by the underwriters is to be made on

(6)在确定首次证券分销期间注册人在《1933年证券法》下对任何购买人承担的责任之时:

下文签名注册人承诺,在其根据本注册说明书进行首次证券发行期间,不论其采取什么承销方法向购买人出售证券,如果通过以下任何文件向该等购买人发行或出售证券,下文签名注册人将作为与购买人相对的出售人,并视为向该等购买人发行或出售该等证券:

(i)《424规则》(本章第230.424节)要求下文签名注册人就发行提交的初步招募说明书或招募说明书;

(ii)下文签名注册人或其代表就发行编制的,或下文签名注册人使用或引用的任何非正式书面招募说明书;

(iii)与发行相关的任何其他非正式书面招募说明书中包含下文签名注册人或其代表提供的关于该等注册人或其证券的重大信息的部分内容;及

(iv)构成下文签名注册人在发行中向购买人作出的要约的任何其他发布的文件。

(b)通过引用纳入后续《交易法》文件的提交文件。如果在注册说明书生效日期之后提交的任何《交易法》文件以引用方式被纳入注册说明书,应提供如下承诺:

下文签名注册人特此承诺,在确定《1933年证券法》下的任何责任之时,以引用方式纳入注册说明书的根据《1934年证券交易法》第13(a)条或第15(d)条提交的注册人年度报告[以及,如适用,根据《1934年证券交易法》第15(d)条提交的员工福利计划年度报告]应视为发行证券的新注册说明书,且该等证券的发行届时应视为首次善意发行。

(c)权证及购股权的发行。如果申请注册的证券将根据权证或购股权向现有证券持有人发行,且未被现有证券持有人购买的任何证券将重新向公众发行,则应提供如下承诺,并根据特殊情形进行适当的修改:

下文签名注册人特此承诺,在认购期届满后对招募说明书作出补充,列明认购要约的结果、承销商在认购期内达成的交易、承销商计划购买的未认购证券的数量以及任何后续重新发行的条款。如果承销商进行任何公开发行所依据的条款与招募说明书封面页所列条款不同,则应提交一份生效后修正稿,列明该等发行的条款。

terms differing from those set forth on the cover page of the prospectus, a post-effective amendment will be filed to set forth the terms of such offering.

(d) *Competitive bids.* Include the following, with appropriate modifications to suit the particular case, if the securities to be registered are to be offered at competitive bidding:

The undersigned registrant hereby undertakes (1) to use its best efforts to distribute prior to the opening of bids, to prospective bidders, underwriters, and dealers, a reasonable number of copies of a prospectus which at that time meets the requirements of section 10(a) of the Act, and relating to the securities offered at competitive bidding, as contained in the registration statement, together with any supplements thereto, and (2) to file an amendment to the registration statement reflecting the results of bidding, the terms of the reoffering and related matters to the extent required by the applicable form, not later than the first use, authorized by the issuer after the opening of bids, of a prospectus relating to the securities offered at competitive bidding, unless no further public offering of such securities by the issuer and no reoffering of such securities by the purchasers is proposed to be made.

(e) *Incorporated annual and quarterly reports.* Include the following if the registration statement specifically incorporates by reference (other than by indirect incorporation by reference through a Form 10-K(§249.310 of this chapter) report) in the prospectus all or any part of the annual report to security holders meeting the requirements of Rule 14a-3 or Rule 14c-3 under the Exchange Act (§240.14a-3 or §240.14c-3 of this chapter):

The undersigned registrant hereby undertakes to deliver or cause to be delivered with the prospectus, to each person to whom the prospectus is sent or given, the latest annual report to security holders that is incorporated by reference in the prospectus and furnished pursuant to and meeting the requirements of Rule 14a-3 or Rule 14c-3 under the Securities Exchange Act of 1934; and, where interim financial information required to be presented by Article 3 of Regulation S-X are not set forth in the prospectus, to deliver, or cause to be delivered to each person to whom the prospectus is sent or given, the latest quarterly report that is specifically incorporated by reference in the prospectus to provide such interim financial information.

(f) *Equity offerings of nonreporting registrants.* Include the following if equity securities of a registrant that prior to the offering had no obligation to file reports with the Commission pursuant to section 13(a) or 15(d) of the Exchange Act are being registered for sale in an underwritten offering:

The undersigned registrant hereby undertakes to provide to the underwriter at the closing specified in the underwriting agreements certificates in such denominations and registered in such names as required by the underwriter to permit prompt delivery to each purchaser.

(d)竞标。如果申请注册的证券将通过竞标方式发行,应提供如下承诺,并根据特殊情形作适当的修改:

下文签名注册人特此承诺:(1)尽其最大努力在开标之前,针对以竞标方式发行的证券向潜在投标人、承销商及自营商分发合理数量的招募说明书及其任何补充,该招募说明书届时按其包含在注册说明书中的内容应符合《1933年证券法》第10(a)条的要求;以及(2)在开标后经发行人授权首次使用以竞标方式发行的证券的招募说明书之前,提交注册说明书的修正稿,说明招标结果、重新发行条款及适用表格要求的相关事项,除非发行人不再公开发行该等证券且购买人未计划重新发行该等证券。

(e)通过引用纳入的年度报告及季度报告。如果注册说明书特别通过引用方式在招募说明书中纳入向证券持有人提供的、符合《交易法》的《14a-3规则》或《14c-3规则》(本章第240.14a-3节或第240.14c-3节)要求的全部或任何部分的年度报告[通过按照《10-K表格》(本章第249.310节)提交的报告间接引用纳入的除外],应提供如下承诺:

下文签名注册人特此承诺,将《1934年证券交易法》的《14a-3规则》或《14c-3规则》要求提供给证券持有人并以引用方式纳入招募说明书的最新年度报告连同招募说明书,交付或通过第三方交付给招募说明书的所有接收人;同时,如果招募说明书未列明《S-X管理办法》第3条要求提供的中期财务信息,应将特别以引用方式纳入招募说明书的最新季度报告交付或通过第三方交付给招募说明书的所有接收人,以提供该等中期财务信息。

(f)无报告义务的注册人的股本发行。如果注册人在发行前不必根据《交易法》第13(a)条或第15(d)条的规定承担向证券交易委员会提交报告的义务,且申请注册的证券属于注册人将通过承销发行出售的股本证券,应提供如下承诺:

下文签名注册人特此承诺,在承销协议规定的交割之时按承销商要求的面额及注册名称,向承销商提供相应的股权证明,以便承销商及时向各购买方进行交付。

(g) *Registration on Form S–4 or F–4 of securities offered for resale.* Include the following if the securities are being registered on Form S–4 or F–4 (§239.25, or 34 of this chapter) in connection with a transaction specified in paragraph (a) of Rule 145 (§230.145 of this chapter).

(1) The undersigned registrant hereby undertakes as follows: That prior to any public reoffering of the securities registered hereunder through use of a prospectus which is a part of this registration statement, by any person or party who is deemed to be an underwriter within the meaning of Rule 145(c), the issuer undertakes that such reoffering prospectus will contain the information called for by the applicable registration form with respect to reofferings by persons who may be deemed underwriters, in addition to the information called for by the other Items of the applicable form.

(2) The registrant undertakes that every prospectus (i) that is filed pursuant to paragraph (h)(1) immediately preceding, or (ii) that purports to meet the requirements of section 10 (a)(3) of the Act and is used in connection with an offering of securities subject to Rule 415 (§230.415 of this chapter), will be filed as a part of an amendment to the registration statement and will not be used until such amendment is effective, and that, for purposes of determining any liability under the Securities Act of 1933, each such post–effective amendment shall be deemed to be a new registration statement relating to the securities offered therein, and the offering of such securities at that time shall be deemed to be the initial bona fide offering thereof.

(h) *Request for acceleration of effective date or filing of registration statement becoming effective upon filing.* Include the following if acceleration is requested of the effective date of the registration statement pursuant to Rule 461 under the Securities Act (§230.461 of this chapter), if a Form S–3 or Form F–3 will become effective upon filing with the Commission pursuant to Rule 462(e) or (f) under the Securities Act (§230.462 (e) or (f) of this chapter), or if the registration statement is filed on Form S–8, and:

(1) Any provision or arrangement exists whereby the registrant may indemnify a director, officer or controlling person of the registrant against liabilities arising under the Securities Act, or

(2) The underwriting agreement contains a provision whereby the registrant indemnifies the underwriter or controlling persons of the underwriter against such liabilities and a director, officer or controlling person of the registrant is such an underwriter or controlling person thereof or a member of any firm which is such an underwriter, and

(3) The benefits of such indemnification are not waived by such persons:

Insofar as indemnification for liabilities arising under the Securities Act of 1933 may be permitted to directors, officers and controlling persons of the registrant pursuant to the

(g)为转售之目的按照《S-4表格》或《F-4表格》注册的证券发行。如果按照《S-4表格》或《F-4表格》(本章第239.25节或第239.34节)注册证券,且该等证券与《145规则》第(a)款(本章第230.145节)规定的交易相关,应提供如下承诺:

(1)下文签名注册人特此做出如下承诺:在被视为《145(c)规则》所定义的承销商的任何主体或任何一方利用构成本注册说明书一部分的招募说明书重新公开发行本注册说明书项下的注册证券之前,发行人承诺,除适用表格的其他项目要求提供的信息外,该等重新发行招募说明书还应包含可被视为承销商的主体根据适用注册表格的要求提供的重新发行信息。

(2)注册人承诺所有下述招募说明书均应作为注册说明书修正稿的一部分提交,且直至该等修正稿生效之时方可使用:(i)根据上文第(h)(1)款提交的招募说明书,或(ii)旨在满足《1933年证券法》第10(a)(3)条的要求并用于根据《415规则》(本章第230.415节)进行的证券发行的招募说明书。注册人进一步承诺,在确定《1933年证券法》下的任何责任之时,所有该等生效后的修正稿均应视为发行证券的新注册说明书,且该等证券的发行届时应视为其首次善意发行。

(h)要求注册说明书提前生效或于提交之时即时生效的请求。如果注册人根据《证券法》的《461规则》(本章第230.461节)要求将注册说明书的生效日期提前,或如果《S-3表格》或《F-3表格》将按照《证券法》的《462(e)规则》或《462(f)规则》[本章第230.462(e)节或第230.462(f)节]于提交给证券交易委员会之时立即生效,或者注册人按照《S-8表格》提交注册说明书,同时:

(1)根据现存的任何规定或安排,注册人可就《证券法》下产生的责任向董事、管理人员或控制人提供赔偿,或

(2)根据承销协议的规定,注册人应就该等责任向承销商或承销商的控制人提供赔偿,且该等承销商、承销商的控制人或承销商公司的任何成员由注册人的董事、管理人员或控制人担任;且

(3)该等人未放弃该等赔偿权益,

则应提供如下声明:

注册人已明确知悉,即使前述规定或其他规定允许就《1933年证券法》下产生的

foregoing provisions, or otherwise, the registrant has been advised that in the opinion of the Securities and Exchange Commission such indemnification is against public policy as expressed in the Act and is, therefore, unenforceable. In the event that a claim for indemnification against such liabilities (other than the payment by the registrant of expenses incurred or paid by a director, officer or controlling person of the registrant in the successful defense of any action, suit or proceeding) is asserted by such director, officer or controlling person in connection with the securities being registered, the registrant will, unless in the opinion of its counsel the matter has been settled by controlling precedent, submit to a court of appropriate jurisdiction the question whether such indemnification by it is against public policy as expressed in the Act and will be governed by the final adjudication of such issue.

(i) Include the following in a registration statement permitted by Rule 430A under the Securities Act of 1933 (§230.430A of this chapter):

The undersigned registrant hereby undertakes that:

(1) For purposes of determining any liability under the Securities Act of 1933, the information omitted from the form of prospectus filed as part of this registration statement in reliance upon Rule 430A and contained in a form of prospectus filed by the registrant pursuant to Rule 424(b) (1) or (4) or 497(h) under the Securities Act shall be deemed to be part of this registration statement as of the time it was declared effective.

(2) For the purpose of determining any liability under the Securities Act of 1933, each post-effective amendment that contains a form of prospectus shall be deemed to be a new registration statement relating to the securities offered therein, and the offering of such securities at that time shall be deemed to be the initial bona fide offering thereof.

(j) *Qualification of trust indentures under the Trust Indenture Act of 1939 for delayed offerings.* Include the following if the registrant intends to rely on section 305(b)(2) of the Trust Indenture Act of 1939 for determining the eligibility of the trustee under indentures for securities to be issued, offered, or sold on a delayed basis by or on behalf of the registrant:

The undersigned registrant hereby undertakes to file an application for the purpose of determining the eligibility of the trustee to act under subsection (a) of section 310 of the Trust Indenture Act ("Act") in accordance with the rules and regulations prescribed by the Commission under section 305(b)(2) of the Act.

(k) *Filings regarding asset-backed securities incorporating by reference subsequent Exchange Act documents by third parties.* Include the following if the registration statement incorporates by reference any Exchange Act document filed subsequent to the effective date of the registration statement pursuant to Item 1100(c) of Regulation AB (§229.1100(c)):

责任向注册人的董事、管理人员及控制人提供赔偿,证券交易委员会仍认为该等赔偿违反《1933年证券法》中的公共政策,不具强制执行力。如果该等董事、管理人员或控制人就注册证券提出上述责任索赔(在注册人的董事、管理人员或控制人在任何诉讼、案件或程序中获得胜诉的情况下,注册人向该等董事、管理人员或控制人支付其产生或招致的费用的除外),除非注册人的顾问认为该事项已在具有约束力的判例中获得解决,否则对于注册人做出该等赔偿是否违反《1933年证券法》中的公共政策这一问题,注册人应提交具有适当管辖权的法院并接受该等法院作出的最终裁决。

(i)注册说明书应包含《1933年证券法》的《430A规则》(本章第230.430A节)允许的下述承诺:

下文签名注册人特此承诺:

(1)在确定《1933年证券法》下的任何责任之时,在依据《430A规则》在作为本注册说明书之一部分提交的招募说明书中予以省略、但在依据《证券法》的《424(b)(1)规则》、《424(b)(4)规则》或《497(h)规则》提交的招募说明书中予以纳入的信息自宣布生效之时起应视为本注册说明书的一部分。

(2)在确定《1933年证券法》下的任何责任之时,所有生效后修正稿,只要包含招募说明书表格,即应视为发行证券的新注册说明书,且该等证券的发行届时应视为首次善意发行。

(j)延迟发行时《1939年信托契约法》下信托契约的资格。注册人或注册人代表延迟发行、要约或出售证券之时,如果注册人希望援引《1939年信托契约法》第305(b)(2)条的规定确定契约下信托受托人的资格,应提供如下承诺:

下文签名注册人特此承诺,其将为确定信托受托人在《信托契约法》第310条第(a)子条中的资格之目的,根据证券交易委员会依照该法第305(b)(2)条制定的规则及规章提交一份申请。

(k)通过引用方式将后续第三方《交易法》文件纳入关于资产支持证券的提交文件。如果在注册说明书生效日期后提交的任何《交易法》文件根据《AB管理办法》第1100(c)条[第229.1100(c)节]通过引用方式被纳入注册说明书,应提供如下承诺:

The undersigned registrant hereby undertakes that, for purposes of determining any liability under the Securities Act of 1933, each filing of the annual report pursuant to section 13(a) or section 15(d) of the Securities Exchange Act of 1934 of a third party that is incorporated by reference in the registration statement in accordance with Item 1100(c)(1) of Regulation AB (17 CFR 229.1100(c)(1)) shall be deemed to be a new registration statement relating to the securities offered therein, and the offering of such securities at that time shall be deemed to be the initial bona fide offering thereof.

(l) *Filings regarding asset-backed securities that provide certain information through an Internet Web site.* Include the following if the registration statement is to provide information required by Item 1105 of Regulation AB (§229.1105) through an Internet Web site in accordance with Rule 312 of Regulation S-T (§232.312 of this chapter):

The undersigned registrant hereby undertakes that, except as otherwise provided by Item 1105 of Regulation AB (17 CFR 229.1105), information provided in response to that Item pursuant to Rule 312 of Regulation S-T (17 CFR 232.312) through the specified Internet address in the prospectus is deemed to be a part of the prospectus included in the registration statement. In addition, the undersigned registrant hereby undertakes to provide to any person without charge, upon request, a copy of the information provided in response to Item 1105 of Regulation AB pursuant to Rule 312 of Regulation S-T through the specified Internet address as of the date of the prospectus included in the registration statement if a subsequent update or change is made to the information.

[47 FR 11401, Mar. 16, 1982]

Editorial Note: ForFederal Registercitations affecting §229.512, see the List of CFR Sections Affected, which appears in the Finding Aids section of the printed volume and at www.fdsys.gov.

Subpart 229.600—Exhibits

§229.601(Item 601) Exhibits.

(a) *Exhibits and index required.* (1) Subject to Rule 411(c) (§230.411(c) of this chapter) under the Securities Act and Rule 12b-32 (§240.12b-32 of this chapter) under the Exchange Act regarding incorporation of exhibits by reference, the exhibits required in the exhibit table shall be filed as indicated, as part of the registration statement or report.

(2) Each registration statement or report shall contain an exhibit index, which shall precede immediately the exhibits filed with such registration statement. For convenient

下文签名注册人特此承诺，在确定《1933年证券法》下的任何责任之时，第三方根据《1934年证券交易法》第13(a)条或第15(d)条提交的、并根据《AB管理办法》第1100(c)(1)条[《联邦规章汇编》第十七编第229.1100(c)(1)节]以引用方式纳入注册说明书的任何年度报告均应视为相关发行证券的新注册说明书，且该等证券的发行届时应视为其首次善意发行。

(l)通过互联网网站提供特定信息的关于资产支持证券的提交文件。如果注册说明书根据《S-T管理办法》的《312规则》(本章第232.312节)通过互联网网站提供《AB管理办法》第1105条(第229.1105节)规定的信息，应提供如下承诺：

下文签名注册人特此承诺，除《AB管理办法》第1105条(《联邦规章汇编》第十七编第229.1105节)另有规定的情形外，根据《S-T管理办法》的《312规则》(《联邦规章汇编》第十七编第232.312节)在招募说明书中指定的互联网网站上按第1105条要求提供的信息应视为注册说明书内含的招募说明书的一部分。此外，下文签名注册人特此承诺，对于根据《S-T管理办法》的《312规则》在指定互联网网站上按照《AB管理办法》第1105条的要求提供的截至注册说明书内含的招募说明书之日的信息，如果有任何后续更新或变更，注册人将根据申请人的要求免费向其提供该等信息的复印件。

[《联邦公报》第47卷第11401页，1982年3月16日。]

编者按：对第229.512节有影响的《联邦公报》索引，参见《受影响的联邦规章汇编条文列表》(见印刷版本的《检索协助》章节和www.fdsys.gov)。

第229.600子部分——附　　录

第229.601节(第601条)　附录

(a)须提供的附录和索引。(1)在不违反《证券法》的《411(c)规则》(本章第230.411(c)节)和《交易法》的《12b-32规则》(本章第240.12b-32节)关于以引用方式纳入附录的规定的前提下，附录一览表中规定的附录应按表格中注明的要求作为注册说明书或报告的一部分提交。

(2)每份注册说明书或报告均应包含一份附录索引，置于随注册说明书提交的附录之前。为引用方便起见，附录索引中每份附录的编号均应采用附录一览表中分配的

reference, each exhibit shall be listed in the exhibit index according to the number assigned to it in the exhibit table. The exhibit index shall indicate, by handwritten, typed, printed, or other legible form of notation in the manually signed original registration statement or report, the page number in the sequential numbering system where such exhibit can be found. Where exhibits are incorporated by reference, this fact shall be noted in the exhibit index referred to in the preceding sentence. Further, the first page of the manually signed registration statement shall list the page in the filing where the exhibit index is located. For a description of each of the exhibits included in the exhibit table, see paragraph (b) of this section.

(3) This Item applies only to the forms specified in the exhibit table. With regard to forms not listed in that table, reference shall be made to the appropriate form for the specific exhibit filing requirements applicable thereto.

(4) If a material contract or plan of acquisition, reorganization, arrangement, liquidation or succession is executed or becomes effective during the reporting period reflected by a Form 10–Q or Form 10–K, it shall be filed as an exhibit to the Form 10–Q or Form 10–K filed for the corresponding period. Any amendment or modification to a previously filed exhibit to a Form 10, 10–K or 10–Q document shall be filed as an exhibit to a Form 10–Q and Form 10–K. Such amendment or modification need not be filed where such previously filed exhibit would not be currently required.

*Instructions to Item 601:*1. If an exhibit to a registration statement (other than an opinion or consent), filed in preliminary form, has been changed only (A) to insert information as to interest, dividend or conversion rates, redemption or conversion prices, purchase or offering prices, underwriters' or dealers' commissions, names, addresses or participation of underwriters or similar matters, which information appears elsewhere in an amendment to the registration statement or a prospectus filed pursuant to Rule 424(b) under the Securities Act (§230.424(b) of this chapter), or (B) to correct typographical errors, insert signatures or make other similar immaterial changes, then, notwithstanding any contrary requirement of any rule or form, the registrant need not refile such exhibit as so amended. Any such incomplete exhibit may not, however, be incorporated by reference in any subsequent filing under any Act administered by the Commission.

2. In any case where two or more indentures, contracts, franchises, or other documents required to be filed as exhibits are substantially identical in all material respects except as to the parties thereto, the dates of execution, or other details, the registrant need file a copy of only one of such documents, with a schedule identifying the other documents omitted and setting forth the material details in which such documents differ from the document a copy of which is filed. The Commission may at any time in its discretion require filing of copies of any documents so omitted.

编号。附录索引应通过手写、打字、打印或其他可辨认的方式在手签的注册说明书或报告的原件上注明该附录所在的页码（页码编号应采用顺序编码系统）。通过引用方式纳入的附录，应于上一句所述的附录索引中注明。同时，应在手签的注册说明书的第一页注明附录索引在提交文件中的页码。对附录一览表中每份附录的说明，参见本节第（b）款。

（3）本条仅适用于附录一览表中规定的表格。未在附录一览表中列明的，应引用相关表格中适用于具体附录的文件提交要求。

（4）在《10-Q表格》或《10-K表格》反映的报告期间内签署或生效的所有重大合同或收购、重组、和解、清算、继承计划，均应作为相应期间提交的《10-Q表格》或《10-K表格》的附录提交。对之前提交的《10表格》、《10-Q表格》或《10-K表格》的附录的任何修正或修改均应作为《10-Q表格》或《10-K表格》的附录提交。如果暂时不必提供前述附录，则相应的修正或修改也不必提交。

关于第601条的说明：1.如果注册说明书的附录（不包括意见书或同意函）在预提交后发生了更改，且该等更改仅限于：（A）增加关于利率、股息率或转换率、回赎或转换价格、购买或发售价格、承销商或交易商佣金、名称/姓名、地址、承销商的参与或类似事项的信息，且这些信息已在注册说明书的修正稿或根据《证券法》的《424（b）规则》[本章第230.424（b）节]提交的招募说明书中进行了说明；或（B）改正字误、增加签名或类似的非实质更改，则无论任何规则或表格中是否存在相反规定，注册人都不必重新提交修正后的附录。但是，在根据证券交易委员会负责实施的法律提交任何后续文件之时，不得以引用方式纳入任何该等不完整附录。

2.如果要求以附录形式提交的信托契约、合同、特许或其他文件存在两份（含）以上，且在各重大方面基本一致，仅存在签约方、生效日期或其他细节上的差异，则注册人仅须提交一份文件，并提供一份附表注明略去的文件清单，详细说明这些文件和提交文件的重要差异。证券交易委员会可以依其自由裁量权在任何时间要求注册人提交按上述规定省略的文件。

3. Only copies, rather than originals, need be filed of each exhibit required except as otherwise specifically noted.

4. *Electronic filings*. Whenever an exhibit is filed in paper pursuant to a hardship exemption (§§232.201 and 232.202 of this chapter), the letter "P" (paper) shall be placed next to the exhibit in the list of exhibits required by Item 601(a)(2) of this Rule. Whenever an electronic confirming copy of an exhibit is filed pursuant to a hardship exemption (§232.201 or §232.202(d) of this chapter), the exhibit index should specify where the confirming electronic copy can be located; in addition, the designation "CE" (confirming electronic) should be placed next to the listed exhibit in the exhibit index.

Exhibit Table

Instructions to the Exhibit Table.

1. The exhibit table indicates those documents that must be filed as exhibits to the respective forms listed.

2. The "X" designation indicates the documents which are required to be filed with each form even if filed previously with another document, *Provided, However,*that such previously filed documents may be incorporated by reference to satisfy the filing requirements.

3. The number used in the far left column of the table refers to the appropriate subsection in paragraph (b) where a description of the exhibit can be found. Whenever necessary, alphabetical or numerical subparts may be used.

Exhibit Table

	Securities Act forms								Exchange Act forms				
	S–1	S–3	S–4[1]	S–8	S–11	F–1	F–3	F–4[1]	10	8–K[2]	10–D	10–Q	10–K
(1) Underwriting agreement	X	X	X		X	X	X	X		X			
(2) Plan of acquisition, reorganization, arrangement, liquidation or succession	X	X	X		X	X	X	X	X	X		X	X
(3)(i) Articles of incorporation	X		X		X	X		X	X	X	X	X	X
(ii) Bylaws	X		X		X	X		X	X	X	X	X	X
(4) Instruments defining the rights of security holders, including indentures	X	X	X	X	X	X	X	X	X	X	X	X	X
(5) Opinion re legality	X	X	X	X	X	X	X	X					
(6) [Reserved]	N/A	N/A	N/A	N/A	N/A	N/A	N/A	N/A	N/A	N/A	N/A	N/A	N/A

3.除非另有明确说明,每份附录仅须提交复印件,而不必提交原件。

4.电子提交。对于根据经济困境豁免(本章第232.201节和第232.202节)以纸质形式提交的附录,应在本规则第601(a)(2)条规定的附录列表中,在该附录旁注明字母“P”[英文单词“Paper”(纸质)的首字母]。对于根据经济困境豁免[本章第232.201节或第232.202(d)节]以电子确认形式提交的附录,应在附录索引中注明可获取该电子文件的方式,并在附录列报的附录索引中注明“CE”字样[英文词组“Confirming Electronic”(电子确认)的首字母缩写]。

附录一览表

关于附录一览表的说明。

1.附录一览表的作用在于列明必须作为所列表格之附录提交的文件。

2.符号“X”表示提交每份表格时必须随附的文件,不论该文件之前是否曾和其他文件一起提交过。但是,对于该等之前已经提交过的文件,可以通过引用纳入的方式履行提交要求。

3.下表最左栏中的数字指的是第(b)款中的对应的子条编号,可借以查找对附录的说明。如有必要,可按字母或数字对各子部分进行排序。

附录一览表

	《证券法》表格								《交易法》表格				
	S-1	S-3	S-4[1]	S-8	S-11	F-1	F-3	F-4[1]	10	8-K[2]	10-D	10-Q	10-K
(1)承销协议	X	X	X		X	X	X	X		X			
(2)收购、重组、和解、清算或继承计划	X	X	X		X	X	X	X	X	X		X	X
(3)(i)公司章程	X		X		X	X		X	X	X	X	X	X
(ii)内部章程	X		X		X	X		X	X	X	X	X	X
(4)界定证券持有人权利的文件,包括信托契约	X	X	X	X	X	X	X	X	X	X	X	X	X
(5)法律意见书	X	X	X	X	X	X	X	X					
(6)[保留]	N/A	N/A	N/A	N/A	N/A	N/A	N/A	N/A	N/A	N/A	N/A	N/A	N/A

	Securities Act forms								Exchange Act forms				
	S-1	S-3	S-4	S-8	S-11	F-1	F-3	F-4	10	8-K	10-D	10-Q	10-K
(7) Correspondence from an independent accountant regarding non-reliance on a previously issued audit report or completed interim review										X			
(8) Opinion re tax matters	X	X	X		X	X	X	X					
(9) Voting trust agreement	X		X		X	X		X	X				X
(10) Material contracts	X		X		X	X		X	X		X	X	X
(11) Statement re computation of per share earnings	X		X		X	X		X	X			X	X
(12) Statements re computation of ratios	X	X	X		X	X		X	X				X
(13) Annual report to security holders, Form 10-Q or quarterly report to security holders[3]			X										X
(14) Code of Ethics										X			X
(15) Letter re unaudited interim financial information	X	X	X	X	X	X	X	X				X	
(16) Letter re change in certifying accountant[4]	X		X		X				X	X			X
(17) Correspondence on departure of director										X			
(18) Letter re change in accounting principles												X	X
(19) Report furnished to security holders												X	
(20) Other documents or statements to security holders										X			
(21) Subsidiaries of the registrant	X		X		X	X		X	X				X
(22) Published report regarding matters submitted to vote of security holders											X	X	X

续表

	《证券法》表格								《交易法》表格				
	S－1	S－3	S－4	S－8	S－11	F－1	F－3	F－4	10	8－K	10－D	10－Q	10－K
(7)独立会计师关于不采信之前出具的审计报告或已完成的中期审查的通信。										X			
(8)税务意见书	X	X	X		X	X	X	X					
(9)表决权信托协议	X		X		X	X		X	X				X
(10)重大合同	X		X		X	X		X	X		X	X	X
(11)每股盈利的计算说明	X		X		X	X		X	X			X	X
(12)比率的计算说明	X	X	X		X	X		X	X				X
(13)向证券持有人提供的年度报告、《10－Q表格》或向证券持有人提供的季度报告[3]			X										X
(14)道德准则										X			X
(15)关于未审计的中期财务信息的信函	X	X	X	X	X	X	X	X				X	
(16)关于核证会计师变更的信函[4]	X		X		X				X	X			X
(17)关于董事离任的通信										X			
(18)关于会计原则变更的信函												X	X
(19)向证券持有人提供的报告												X	
(20)向证券持有人提供的其他文件或报表										X			
(21)注册人的子公司	X		X		X	X		X	X				X
(22)关于提交证券持有人表决的事务的公开报告											X	X	X

	Securities Act forms								Exchange Act forms				
	S－1	S－3	S－4	S－8	S－11	F－1	F－3	F－4	10	8－K	10－D	10－Q	10－K
(23) Consents of experts and counsel	X	X	X	X	X	X	X	X		X[5]	X[5]	X[5]	X[5]
(24) Power of attorney	X	X	X	X	X	X	X	X	X	X		X	X
(25) Statement of eligibility of trustee	X	X	X			X	X	X					
(26) Invitation for competitive bids	X	X	X			X	X	X					
(27) through (30) [Reserved]													
(31) (i) Rule 13a－14(a)/15d－14(a)													
Certifications (ii) Rule 13a－14/15d－14 Certifications												X	X
													X
(32) Section 1350 Certifications[6]												X	X
(33) Report on assessment of compliance with servicing criteria for asset-backed issuers													X
(34) Attestation report on assessment of compliance with servicing criteria for asset-backed securities													X
(35) Servicer compliance statement													X
(36) through (98) [Reserved]	N/A	N/A	N/A	N/A	N/A	N/A	N/A	N/A	N/A	N/A	N/A	N/A	N/A
(99) Additional exhibits	X	X	X	X	X	X	X	X	X	X	X	X	X
(100) XBRL-Related Documents									X	X		X	X
(101) Interactive Data File	X	X	X		X	X	X	X		X		X	X

1 An exhibit need not be provided about a company if: (1) With respect to such company an election has been made under Form S-4 or F-4 to provide information about such company

续表

	《证券法》表格								《交易法》表格				
	S－1	S－3	S－4	S－8	S－11	F－1	F－3	F－4	10	8－K	10－D	10－Q	10－K
(23)专家和律师同意书	X	X	X	X	X	X	X	X		X[5]	X[5]	X[5]	X[5]
(24)授权委托书	X	X	X	X	X	X	X	X	X	X		X	X
(25)信托受托人适格性声明	X	X	X			X	X	X					
(26)竞标邀请	X	X	X			X	X	X					
(27)至(30)[保留]													
(31)(i)《13a－14(a)规则》/《15d－14(a)规则》中的证明													
(ii)《13a－14规则》/《15d－14规则》中的证明												X	X
													X
(32)第1350条中的证明[6]												X	X
(33)关于资产支持证券发行人服务标准合规性的评估报告													X
(34)关于资产支持证券服务标准合规性评估的鉴证报告													X
(35)服务机构合规声明													X
(36)至(98)[保留]	N/A	N/A	N/A	N/A	N/A	N/A	N/A	N/A	N/A	N/A	N/A	N/A	N/A
(99)其他附录	X	X	X	X	X	X	X	X	X	X	X	X	X
(100)XBRL相关文件									X	X		X	X
(101)交互式数据文档	X	X	X		X	X	X	X		X		X	X

1 满足下述条件之时，不必提供该附录：(1)已根据《S-4表格》或《F-4表格》做出公司的选择，按照《S-3表格》或《F-3表格》规定的级别提供公司信息；且(2)如公司注册为首次

at a level prescribed by Form S-3 or F-3; and (2) the form, the level of which has been elected under Form S-4 or F-4, would not require such company to provide such exhibit if it were registering a primary offering.

2 A Form 8-K exhibit is required only if relevant to the subject matter reported on the Form 8-K report. For example, if the Form 8-K pertains to the departure of a director, only the exhibit described in paragraph (b)(17) of this section need be filed. A required exhibit may be incorporated by reference from a previous filing.

3 Where incorporated by reference into the text of the prospectus and delivered to security holders along with the prospectus as permitted by the registration statement; or, in the case of the Form 10-K, where the annual report to security holders is incorporated by reference into the text of the Form 10-K.

4 If required pursuant to Item 304 of Regulation S-K.

5 Where the opinion of the expert or counsel has been incorporated by reference into a previously filed Securities Act registration statement.

6 Pursuant to §§240.13a-13(b)(3) and 240.15d-13(b)(3) of this chapter, asset-backed issuers are not required to file reports on Form 10-Q.

(b) *Description of exhibits.* Set forth below is a description of each document listed in the exhibit tables.

(1) *Underwriting agreement.* Each underwriting contract or agreement with a principal underwriter pursuant to which the securities being registered are to be distributed; if the terms of such documents have not been determined, the proposed forms thereof. Such agreement may be filed as an exhibit to a report on Form 8-K (§249.308 of this chapter) which is incorporated by reference into a registration statement subsequent to its effectiveness.

(2) *Plan of acquisition, reorganization, arrangement, liquidation or succession.* Any material plan of acquisition, disposition, reorganization, readjustment, succession, liquidation or arrangement and any amendments thereto described in the statement or report. Schedules (or similar attachments) to these exhibits shall not be filed unless such schedules contain information which is material to an investment decision and which is not otherwise disclosed in the agreement or the disclosure document. The plan filed shall contain a list briefly identifying the contents of all omitted schedules, together with an agreement to furnish supplementally a copy of any omitted schedule to the Commission upon request.

(3) (i)*Articles of incorporation.* The articles of incorporation of the registrant or instruments corresponding thereto as currently in effect and any amendments thereto. Whenever the registrant files an amendment to its articles of incorporation, it must file a complete copy of the articles as amended. However, if such amendment is being reported

公开发行,该表格(其级别已根据《S-4表格》或《F-4表格》选定)不要求公司提供该附录。

2 只有和《8-K表格》报告的主题相关时,才须提供《8-K表格》的附录。例如,如果《8-K表格》所涉主题为董事离任,则仅须提交本节第(b)(17)款规定的附录。可以通过引用之前提交的文件的方式履行附录提交要求。

3 如已根据注册说明书以引用的方式纳入招募说明书,并与招募说明书一并送交证券持有人;或,在使用《10-K表格》的情况下,向证券持有人提交的年度报告已通过引用方式被纳入《10-K表格》。

4 如《S-K管理办法》第304条要求提交。

5 如专家或律师意见已通过引用方式被纳入之前根据《证券法》提交的注册说明书。

6 根据本章第240.13a-13(b)(3)节和第240.15d-13(b)(3)节,资产支持证券的发行人不必按照《10-Q表格》提交报告。

(b)附录说明。下文为对附录一览表所列每项文件的说明。

(1)承销协议。与每名负责分销申请注册的证券的主要承销商签订的承销合同或协议;如果合同或协议条款尚未最终确定,应提交合同或协议草案。该协议可作为《8-K表格》(本章第249.308节)报告的附录提交,并通过引用纳入注册说明书之中。

(2)收购、重组、和解、清算或继承计划。涉及收购、资产处置、重组、重整、继承、清算或和解的任何重大计划,以及在注册说明书或报告中说明的任何相关修正。这些附录的附表(或类似附属文件)不必提交,但附表中含有对投资决策具有重要意义,且未在协议或披露文件中予以披露的信息除外。所提交的计划应包含一份清单,简要注明各项被省略的附表的内容,并包括一份同意书,同意在证券交易委员会提出要求之时提供任何被省略的相关附表。

(3)(i)公司章程。注册人当前有效的公司章程或相当文件及其所有修正。注册人提交公司章程修正内容的,必须同时提交一份完整的修正后的公司章程。但是,如该修正已按照《8-K表格》(本章第249.308节)进行报告,则注册人只需以《8-K表格》的附录的形式提交修正内容文本。在上述情况下,注册人必须在下次根据《证券法》按本附

on Form 8–K (§249.308 of this chapter), the registrant is required to file only the text of the amendment as a Form 8–K exhibit. In such case, a complete copy of the articles of incorporation as amended must be filed as an exhibit to the next Securities Act registration statement or periodic report filed by the registrant to which this exhibit requirement applies. Where it is impracticable for the registrant to file a charter amendment authorizing new securities with the appropriate state authority prior to the effective date of the registration statement registering such securities, the registrant may file as an exhibit to the registration statement the form of amendment to be filed with the state authority. In such a case, if material changes are made after the copy is filed, the registrant must also file the changed copy.

(ii) *Bylaws.* The bylaws of the registrant or instruments corresponding thereto as currently in effect and any amendments thereto. Whenever the registrant files an amendment to the bylaws, it must file a complete copy of the amended bylaws. However, if such amendment is being reported on Form 8–K (§249.308 of this chapter), the registrant is required to file only the text of the amendment as a Form 8–K exhibit. In such case, a complete copy of the bylaws as amended must be filed as an exhibit to the next Securities Act registration statement or periodic report filed by the registrant to which this exhibit requirement applies.

(4) *Instruments defining the rights of security holders, including identures.* (i) All instruments defining the rights of holders of the equity or debt securities being registered including, where applicable, the relevant portion of the articles of incorporation or by–laws of the registrant.

(ii) Except as set forth in paragraph (b)(4)(iii) of this Item for filings on Forms S–1, S–4, S–11, N–14, and F–4 under the Securities Act (§§239.11, 239.25, 239.18, 239.23 and 239.34 of this chapter) and Forms 10 and 10–K under the Exchange Act (§§249.210 and 249.310 of this chapter) all instruments defining the rights of holders of long–term debt of the registrant and its consolidated subsidiaries and for any of its unconsolidated subsidiaries for which financial statements are required to be filed.

(iii) Where the instrument defines the rights of holders of long–term debt of the registrant and its consolidated subsidiaries and for any of its unconsolidated subsidiaries for which financial statements are required to be filed, there need not be filed:

(A) Any instrument with respect to long–term debt not being registered if the total amount of securities authorized thereunder does not exceed 10 percent of the total assets of the registrant and its subsidiaries on a consolidated basis and if there is filed an agreement to furnish a copy of such agreement to the Commission upon request;

(B) Any instrument with respect to any class of securities if appropriate steps to assure the redemption or retirement of such class will be taken prior to or upon delivery

录要求提交注册说明书或定期报告时，以附录形式提交完整的修正后的公司章程。如果注册人无法在注册说明书生效前向相应州政府机构提交批准发行新证券的章程修正内容，注册人可以注册说明书附录的形式提交该等修正的内容。在上述情况下，如果在提交后发生了重大变更，注册人必须提交变更后的文本。

（ii）内部章程。注册人当前有效的内部章程或相当文件及其所有修正内容。注册人提交内部章程修正内容的，必须同时提交一份完整的修正后的内部章程。但是，如该修正已按照《8-K表格》（本章第249.308节）进行报告，则注册人只需以《8-K表格》的附录的形式提交修正内容文本。在该种情况下，注册人必须在下次根据《证券法》按本附录要求提交注册说明书或定期报告时，以附录形式提交完整的修正后的内部章程。

（4）界定证券持有人权利的文件，包括信托契约。（i）界定申请注册的股权或债务证券持有人权利的所有文件，包括注册人公司章程和内部章程中的相关内容（如适用）。

（ii）除本条第（b）（4）（iii）款就根据《证券法》下的《S-1表格》、《S-4表格》、《S-11表格》、《N-14表格》和《F-4表格》（本章第239.11节、第239.25节、第239.18节、第239.23节和第239.34节）和根据《交易法》下的《10表格》和《10-K表格》（本章第249.210节和第249.310节）提交的文件另有规定外，界定下述主体的权利的所有文件均应提交：注册人、注册人的并表子公司以及注册人应提交财务报表的非并表子公司的长期债务的债权人。

（iii）有关文件界定了注册人以及注册人的并表子公司的长期债务之债权人权利的，以及注册人应提交非并表子公司财务报表的：

（A）若长期债务并非申请注册的长期债务，且其下核定发行的证券总额不超过注册人及其子公司总资产的10%，同时注册人曾提交一份同意书，同意在证券交易委员会提出要求之时提供该等协议的复本，则不必提交与该等长期债务相关的任何文件；

（B）对于任何类别的证券，若注册人已采取适当措施确保其将在注册人交付申请注册的证券之时或之前回赎或收回该等证券，则不必提交与该类型证券相关的任何

by the registrant of the securities being registered; or

(C) Copies of instruments evidencing scrip certificates for fractions of shares.

(iv) If any of the securities being registered are, or will be, issued under an indenture to be qualified under the Trust Indenture Act, the copy of such indenture which is filed as an exhibit shall include or be accompanied by:

(A) A reasonably itemized and informative table of contents; and

(B) A cross-reference sheet showing the location in the indenture of the provisions inserted pursuant to sections 310 through 318(a) inclusive of the Trust Indenture Act of 1939.

(v) With respect to Forms 8-K and 10-Q under the Exchange Act that are filed and that disclose, in the text of the Form 10-Q, the interim financial statements, or the footnotes thereto the creation of a new class of securities or indebtedness or the modification of existing rights of security holders, file all instruments defining the rights of holders of these securities or indebtedness. However, there need not be filed any instrument with respect to long-term debt not being registered which meets the exclusion set forth in paragraph (b)(4)(iii)(A) of this Item.

Instruction 1 to paragraph (b)(4): There need not be filed any instrument which defines the rights of participants (not as security holders) pursuant to an employee benefit plan.

Instruction 2 to paragraph (b)(4) (for electronic filings): If the instrument defining the rights of security holders is in the form of a certificate, the text appearing on the certificate shall be reproduced in an electronic filing together with a description of any other graphic and image material appearing on the certificate, as provided in Rule 304 of Regulation S-T (§232.304 of this chapter).

(5) *Opinion re legality.* (i) An opinion of counsel as to the legality of the securities being registered, indicating whether they will, when sold, be legally issued, fully paid and non-assessable, and, if debt securities, whether they will be binding obligations of the registrant.

(ii) If the securities being registered are issued under a plan and the plan is subject to the requirements of ERISA furnish either:

(A) An opinion of counsel which confirms compliance of the provisions of the written documents constituting the plan with the requirements of ERISA pertaining to such provisions; or

(B) A copy of the Internal Revenue Service determination letter that the plan is qualified under section 401 of the Internal Revenue Code; or

(iii) If the securities being registered are issued under a plan which is subject to the requirements of ERISA and the plan has been amended subsequent to the filing of

文件;且

(C)零股证书的证明文件复本不必提交。

(iv)如果申请注册的任何证券在或将在符合《信托契约法》规定的信托契约下发行,则在以附录形式提交该信托契约复本时,应同时提交:

(A)一份合理细分、信息翔实的目录;和

(B)一份交叉索引表,显示根据《1939年信托契约法》第310条至第318(a)条(含)插入的条款在该信托契约中的位置。

(v)根据《交易法》提交《8-K表格》和《10-Q表格》,且在《10-Q表格》正文中披露中期财务报表,或在其脚注中披露新类别证券或债务的创设或对证券持有人现有权利的变更的,应提交界定证券持有人或债权人权利的所有文件。但是,对于并未申请注册且符合本条第(b)(4)(iii)(A)款中的除外规定的长期债务,不必提交任何文件。

关于第(b)(4)款的说明1:对于雇员福利计划参与人的权利(而非作为证券持有人享有的权利)进行界定的文件,不必提交。

关于第(b)(4)款的说明2(适用于电子提交):如果界定证券持有人权利的文件是证书,则应在电子提交文件中复述证书上的文字,并根据《S-T管理办法》的《304规则》(本章第232.304节)的规定,对证书上的任何其他图形和图像资料进行说明。

(5)法律意见书。(i)就申请注册证券的合法性出具的律师意见,应说明证券在出售时是否将属于合法发行、款项全额缴清不必增缴的证券。如果是债务证券,应说明该债务证券是否构成对注册人具有约束力的义务。

(ii)如果申请注册的证券将在某一计划下发行,且该计划受制于《员工退休收入保障法》的规定,则须提交下列文件之一:

(A)律师意见书,确认该计划的书面文件条款符合《员工退休收入保障法》的相关规定;或

(B)美国国家税务局的信函复本,认定该计划符合《国内税收法典》第401条的规定;或

(iii)如果申请注册的证券将在某一计划下发行,且该计划受制于《员工退休收入保障法》的规定,同时在按照上文第(b)(5)(ii)(A)款或第(b)(5)(ii)(B)款的规定进行

paragraph (b)(5)(ii)(A) or (B) above, furnish either:

(A) An opinion of counsel which confirms compliance of the amended provisions of the plan with the requirements of ERISA pertaining to such provisions; or

(B) A copy of the Internal Revenue Service determination letter that the amended plan is qualified under section 401 of the Internal Revenue Code.

Note: Attention is directed to Item 8 of Form S-8 for exemptions to this exhibit requirement applicable to that Form.

(6) [Reserved]

(7) *Correspondence from an independent accountant regarding non-reliance on a previously issued audit report or completed interim review.* Any written notice from the registrant's current or previously engaged independent accountant that the independent accountant is withdrawing a previously issued audit report or that a previously issued audit report or completed interim review, covering one or more years or interim periods for which the registrant is required to provide financial statements under Regulation S-X (part 210 of this chapter), should no longer be relied upon. In addition, any letter, pursuant to Item 4.02(c) of Form 8-K(§249.308 of this chapter), from the independent accountant to the Commission stating whether the independent accountant agrees with the statements made by the registrant describing the events giving rise to the notice.

(8) *Opinion re tax matters.* For filings on Form S-11 under the Securities Act (§239.18) or those to which Securities Act Industry Guide 5 applies, an opinion of counsel or of an independent public or certified public accountant or, in lieu thereof, a revenue ruling from the Internal Revenue Service, supporting the tax matters and consequences to the shareholders as described in the filing when such tax matters are material to the transaction for which the registration statement is being filed. This exhibit otherwise need only be filed with the other applicable registration forms where the tax consequences are material to an investor and a representation as to tax consequences is set forth in the filing. If a tax opinion is set forth in full in the filing, an indication that such is the case may be made in lieu of filing the otherwise required exhibit. Such tax opinions may be conditioned or may be qualified, so long as such conditions and qualifications are adequately described in the filing.

(9) *Voting trust agreement.* Any voting trust agreements and amendments thereto.

(10) *Material contracts.* (i) Every contract not made in the ordinary course of business which is material to the registrant and is to be performed in whole or in part at or after the filing of the registration statement or report or was entered into not more than two years before such filing. Only contracts need be filed as to which the registrant or subsidiary of the registrant is a party or has succeeded to a party by assumption or

文件提交后对该计划进行了修正,则须提交下列文件之一:

(A)律师意见书,确认该计划书面文件的修正条款符合《员工退休收入保障法》的相关规定;或

(B)美国国家税务局的信函复本,认定该修正后的计划符合《国内税收法典》第401条的规定。

注意:请注意《S-8表格》第8条对适用于该表格的豁免提交附录的规定。

(6)[保留]

(7)独立会计师关于不采信之前出具的审计报告或已完成的中期审查的通信。注册人现任或前任独立会计师为了要撤销之前已出具的审计报告,或认为之前出具的审计报告或已完成的中期审查(无论是一年、多年或一个、多个中期期间,只要注册人根据《S-X管理办法》(本章第210部分)有提供财务报表的义务)不得再被采信,而出具的任何书面通知。包括独立会计师根据《8-K表格》(本章第249.308节)第4.02(c)条向证券交易委员会出具的关于该独立会计师是否同意注册人对触发该通知的事件所作解释的任何说明函。

(8)税务意见书。对于根据《证券法》下的《S-11表格》(第239.18节)提交的文件,或适用《证券法产业指引5》的文件,应提交律师、独立公共会计师或注册公共会计师出具的意见,或替以美国国家税务局的税收裁定,以期在注册人提交文件中所述的税务事项对注册人提交的注册说明书所涉交易存在重大税收影响之时,证明注册人提交文件中所述的税务事项及其对股东的影响。在其他情况下,只有当税收影响对投资者具有重要意义,且提交文件中对税收影响进行了声明之时,才须和其他注册表格一并提交该附录。如果提交文件中包含税务意见书,可以对此进行说明,进行说明之后即不必提交该附录。税务意见书可以限定条件或做出保留,只要这些条件和保留在提交文件中给予了充分说明。

(9)表决权信托协议。系指任何的表决权信托协议及其修正。

(10)重大合同。(i)系指并非在正常业务运作中签订,对注册人有重要意义且将在注册说明书或报告提交之时或之后全部或部分履行,或在提交注册说明书或报告前2年内签订的合同。只有注册人或其子公司作为缔约方,或因继承、转让而成为缔约方,或具有受益人权益的合同,才须向证券交易委员会提交。

assignment or in which the registrant or such subsidiary has a beneficial interest.

(ii) If the contract is such as ordinarily accompanies the kind of business conducted by the registrant and its subsidiaries, it will be deemed to have been made in the ordinary course of business and need not be filed unless it falls within one or more of the following categories, in which case it shall be filed except where immaterial in amount or significance:

(A) Any contract to which directors, officers, promoters, voting trustees, security holders named in the registration statement or report, or underwriters are parties other than contracts involving only the purchase or sale of current assets having a determinable market price, at such market price;

(B) Any contract upon which the registrant's business is substantially dependent, as in the case of continuing contracts to sell the major part of registrant's products or services or to purchase the major part of registrant's requirements of goods, services or raw materials or any franchise or license or other agreement to use a patent, formula, trade secret, process or trade name upon which registrant's business depends to a material extent;

(C) Any contract calling for the acquisition or sale of any property, plant or equipment for a consideration exceeding 15 percent of such fixed assets of the registrant on a consolidated basis; or

(D) Any material lease under which a part of the property described in the registration statement or report is held by the registrant.

(iii)(A) Any management contract or any compensatory plan, contract or arrangement, including but not limited to plans relating to options, warrants or rights, pension, retirement or deferred compensation or bonus, incentive or profit sharing (or if not set forth in any formal document, a written description thereof) in which any director or any of the namedexecutive officers of the registrant, as defined by Item 402(a)(3) (§229.402(a)(3)), participates shall be deemed material and shall be filed; and any other management contract or any other compensatory plan, contract, or arrangement in which any other executive officer of the registrant participates shall be filed unless immaterial in amount or significance.

(B) Any compensatory plan, contract or arrangement adopted without the approval of security holders pursuant to which equity may be awarded, including, but not limited to, options, warrants or rights (or if not set forth in any formal document, a written description thereof), in which any employee (whether or not anexecutive officer of the registrant) participates shall be filed unless immaterial in amount or significance. A compensation plan assumed by a registrant in connection with a merger, consolidation or other acquisition transaction pursuant to which the registrant may make further grants or awards

(ii)注册人及其子公司在其所经营类型的业务中惯用的合同将视为在日常经营中签订的合同,一般不必提交,但如属于以下一个或多个类别的合同,除非其金额或重要性不高,否则均应提交:

(A)承销商或注册说明书或报告中指明的董事、管理人员、发起人、表决的信托受托人或证券持有人作为一方当事人签订的任何合同,除非该合同仅涉及流动资产的买卖,且该资产买卖具有可确定的市场价格,且买卖按该市场价格执行;

(B)支撑注册人开展业务的任何基础性合同,如出售注册人主要一部分的商品或服务或购买注册人所需的主要一部分的货物、服务或原材料的常年合同,或在很大程度上支撑注册人业务开展的授权使用专利、配方、商业秘密、流程或商号的任何许可、特许协议或其他协议;

(C)任何资产、厂房或设备的购买或出售合同,且对价超过注册人并表固定资产的15%;或

(D)任何重大租约,且该租约中的、注册说明书或报告中所述部分房产由注册人拥有;

(iii)(A)任何管理层合同或报酬计划、合同或安排,包括但不限于与期权、权证或购股权、养老金、退休/递延报酬、奖金、激励或利润分享相关的计划(如未载入任何正式书面文件,可以是书面说明),只要有注册人的董事或第402(a)(3)条[第229.402(a)(3)节]定义的具名高管参与,即应视为重大计划、合同或安排,并应向证券交易委员会提交;注册人其他高管参与的任何其他管理层合同或任何报酬计划、合同、安排也应提交,但金额或重要性不高的除外。

(B)未经证券持有人批准通过的且可据以授予股权的任何报酬计划、合同、安排,包括但不限于期权、权证或购股权(如未载入任何正式书面文件,可以是书面说明),只要有注册人雇员(无论是否为注册人的高管)参与,均应向证券交易委员会提交,但金额或重要性不高的除外。就上一句规定而言,注册人因吸收合并、新设合并或其他收购交易而承继的报酬计划,如可能导致注册人进一步授予或奖励股权,即应视为注册人的报酬计划。

of its equity securities shall be considered a compensation plan of the registrant for purposes of the preceding sentence.

(C) Notwithstanding paragraph (b)(10)(iii)(A) above, the following management contracts or compensatory plans, contracts or arrangements need not be filed:

(1) Ordinary purchase and sales agency agreements.

(2) Agreements with managers of stores in a chain organization or similar organization.

(3) Contracts providing for labor or salesmen's bonuses or payments to a class of security holders, as such.

(4) Any compensatory plan, contract or arrangement which pursuant to its terms is available to employees, officers or directors generally and which in operation provides for the same method of allocation of benefits between management and nonmanagement participants.

(5) Any compensatory plan, contract or arrangement if the registrant is a foreign private issuer that furnishes compensatory information under Item 402(a)(1) (§229.402(a)(1)) and the public filing of the plan, contract or arrangement, or portion thereof, is not required in the registrant's home country and is not otherwise publicly disclosed by the registrant.

(6) Any compensatory plan, contract, or arrangement if the registrant is a wholly owned subsidiary of a company that has a class of securities registered pursuant to section 12 or files reports pursuant to section 15(d) of the Exchange Act and is filing a report on Form 10-K or registering debt instruments or preferred stock that are not voting securities on Form S-1.

Instruction 1 to paragraph (b)(10): With the exception of management contracts, in order to comply with paragraph (iii) above, registrants need only file copies of the various compensatory plans and need not file each individual director's or executive officer's personal agreement under the plans unless there are particular provisions in such personal agreements whose disclosure in an exhibit is necessary to an investor's understanding of that individual's compensation under the plan.

Instruction 2 to paragraph (b)(10): If a material contract is executed or becomes effective during the reporting period reflected by a Form 10-Q or Form 10-K, it shall be filed as an exhibit to the Form 10-Q or Form 10-K filed for the corresponding period.*See* paragraph (a)(4) of this Item. With respect to quarterly reports on Form 10-Q, only those contracts executed or becoming effective during the most recent period reflected in the report shall be filed.

(11) *Statement re computation of per share earnings*. A statement setting forth in reasonable detail the computation of per share earnings, unless the computation can be

(C)无论上文第(b)(10)(iii)(A)款如何规定,下列管理层合同或报酬计划、合同、安排均不必提交:

(1)普通的购买和销售代理合同;

(2)与连锁机构或类似机构的商店经理签订的协议;

(3)为工人、销售员提供奖金的合同,或向某类别证券持有人进行付款的合同等;

(4)普遍适用于职员、管理人员或董事,且在实施过程中对管理层和非管理层采用同等分配方式的任何报酬计划、合同或安排;

(5)根据第402(a)(1)条[第229.402(a)(1)节]披露报酬信息的注册人的任何报酬计划、合同、安排,条件是注册人的母国并不要求公开提交,且注册人也未另行公开披露该等报酬计划、合同、安排或其中的部分内容;

(6)作为某一公司的全资子公司的注册人的任何报酬计划、合同、安排,且该母公司拥有根据《交易法》第12条注册的某一类别证券,或根据《交易法》第15(d)条负有提交报告的义务,并且正在提交《10-K表格》报告,或正在申请注册《S-1表格》规定的表决权证券以外的债务工具或优先股。

关于第(b)(10)款的说明1:除管理层合同外,在履行上文第(iii)款的规定之时,注册人仅需提交各类报酬计划的复本,不必提交与各具体董事或高管之间根据计划签订的个人协议,除非该等个人协议中存在为使投资者理解该个人的计划报酬而有必要以附录形式向投资者披露的特殊条款。

关于第(b)(10)款的说明2:如果任何重大合同在《10-Q表格》和《10-K表格》所反映的报告期内签署或生效,则应以相关期间提交的《10-Q表格》和《10-K表格》的附录的形式提交该等重大合同。参见本条第(a)(4)款的规定。就按照《10-Q表格》提交的季度报告而言,只有在报告所反映的最近一个期间内签署或生效的合同才须提交。

(11)每股盈利的计算说明。应提交一份关于每股盈利的计算的合理详细的说明,但可以通过注册说明书或报告所包含的资料直接、清楚地进行该等计算的,不必另行

clearly determined from the material contained in the registration statement or report. The information with respect to the computation of per share earnings on both primary and fully diluted basis, presented by exhibit or otherwise, must be furnished even though the amounts of per share earnings on the fully diluted bases are not required to be presented in the income statement under the provisions of Accounting Principles Board Opinion No. 15. That Opinion provides that any reduction of less than 3% need not be considered as dilution (see footnote to paragraph 14 of the Opinion) and that a computation on the fully diluted basis which results in improvement of earnings per share not be taken into account (see paragraph 40 of the Opinion).

(12) *Statements re computation of ratios.* A statement setting forth in reasonable detail the computation of any ratio of earnings to fixed charges, any ratio of earnings to combined fixed charges and preferred stock dividends or any other ratios which appear in the registration statement or report. See Item 503(d) of Regulation S-K (§229.503(d)).

(13) *Annual report to security holders, Form 10-Q or quarterly report to security holders.* (i) The registrant's annual report to security holders for its last fiscal year, its Form 10-Q(if specifically incorporated by reference in the prospectus) or its quarterly report to security holders, if all or a portion thereof is incorporated by reference in the filing. Such report, except for those portions thereof that are expressly incorporated by reference in the filing, is to be furnished for the information of the Commission and is not to be deemed "filed" as part of the filing. If the financial statements in the report have been incorporated by reference in the filing, the accountant's certificate shall be manually signed in one copy. *See* Rule 411(b) (§230.411(b) of this chapter).

(ii) Electronic filings. If all, or any portion, of the annual or quarterly report to security holders is incorporated by reference into any electronic filing, all, or such portion of the annual or quarterly report to security holders so incorporated, shall be filed in electronic format as an exhibit to the filing.

(14) *Code of ethics.* Any code of ethics, or amendment thereto, that is the subject of the disclosure required by Item 406 of Regulation S-K (§229.406) or Item 10 of Form 8-K(§249.308 of this chapter), to the extent that the registrant intends to satisfy the Item 406 or Item 10 requirements through filing of an exhibit.

(15) *Letter re unaudited interim financial information.* A letter, where applicable, from the independent accountant that acknowledges awareness of the use in a registration statement of a report on unaudited interim financial information that pursuant to Rule 436(c) under the Securities Act (§230.436(c) of this chapter) is not considered a part of a registration statement prepared or certified by an accountant or a report prepared or certified by an accountant within the meaning of sections 7 and 11 of that Act. Such letter may be filed with the registration statement, an amendment thereto, or a report on Form

提供计算说明。每股盈利的计算信息应包括每股基本盈利和完全稀释的每股盈利,并必须通过附录或其他方式提交,即使《会计原则委员会第15号意见》不要求在损益表中提供完全稀释的每股盈利。根据上述意见,幅度低于3%的任何减少不必视为稀释(参见该意见第14款脚注),且如果以完全稀释为基础进行计算将导致每股盈利提高,则不应予以考虑(参见该意见第40款)。

(12)比率的计算说明。一份关于下述比率的详细、合理的说明:盈利对固定费用比率,盈利对合计固定费用和优先股股息的比率,以及注册说明书或报告中出现的任何其他比率。参见《S-K管理办法》第503(d)条[第229.503(d)节]。

(13)向证券持有人提供的年度报告、《10-Q表格》或向证券持有人提供的季度报告。(i)注册人向证券持有人提供的上一会计年度的年度报告、《10-Q表格》(如果已特别通过引用方式纳入招募说明书之中),或向证券持有人提供的季度报告,条件是该等报告或文件已通过引用方式全文或部分纳入提交文件之中。该等报告,除已明确通过引用方式纳入提交文件的部分外,应向证券交易委员会提交备案,不得视为作为提交文件的一部分"提交"。如果报告中的财务报表已通过引用方式纳入提交文件,会计师应手签一份证明。参见《411(b)规则》[本章第230.411(b)节]。

(ii)电子提交。如果向证券持有人提供的年度报告或季度报告全文或其中任何一部分已通过引用方式纳入任何电子提交文件之中,则该等年度报告或季度报告全文或部分应作为提交文件的附录以电子形式进行提交。

(14)道德准则。针对《S-K管理办法》第406条(第229.406节)或《8-K表格》(本章第249.308节)第10条要求披露的任何道德准则及其修正,注册人必须以附录形式提交该等准则及其修正,以满足第406条或第10条的要求。

(15)关于未审计的中期财务信息的信函。独立会计师出具的信函,承认其已注意到注册说明书中使用了未审计的中期财务信息报告,且根据《证券法》的《436(c)规则》[本章第230.436(c)节],该等信息不得视为会计师编制或核证的注册说明书或根据《证券法》第7条和第11条编制或认证的报告的一部分。该信函可以与注册说明书及其修正内容,或通过引用纳入注册说明书的《10-Q表格》报告一并提交。

10-Q which is incorporated by reference into the registration statement.

(16) *Letter re change in certifying accountant.* A letter from the registrant's former independent accountant regarding its concurrence or disagreement with the statements made by the registrant in the current report concerning the resignation or dismissal as the registrant's principal accountant.

(17) *Correspondence on departure of director.* Any written correspondence from a former director concerning the circumstances surrounding the former director's retirement, resignation, refusal to stand for re-election or removal, including any letter from the former director to the registrant stating whether the former director agrees with statements made by the registrant describing the former director's departure.

(18) *Letter re change in accounting principles.* Unless previously filed, a letter from the registrant's independent accountant indicating whether any change in accounting principles or practices followed by the registrant, or any change in the method of applying any such accounting principles or practices, which affected the financial statements being filed with the Commission in the report or which is reasonably certain to affect the financial statements of future fiscal years is to an alternative principle which in his judgment is preferable under the circumstances. No such letter need be filed when such change is made in response to a standard adopted by the Financial Accounting Standards Board that creates a new accounting principle, that expresses a preference for an accounting principle, or that rejects a specific accounting principle.

(19) *Report furnished to security holders.* If the registrant makes available to its security holders or otherwise publishes, within the period prescribed for filing the report, a document or statement containing information meeting some or all of the requirements of Part I of Form 10-Q, the information called for may be incorporated by reference to such published document or statement, provided copies thereof are included as an exhibit to the registration statement or to Part I of the Form 10-Q report.

(20) *Other documents or statements to security holders.* If the registrant makes available to its stockholders or otherwise publishes, within the period prescribed for filing the report, a document or statement containing information meeting some or all of the requirements of this form the information called for may be incorporated by reference to such published document or statement provided copies thereof are filed as an exhibit to the report on this form.

(21) *Subsidiaries of the registrant.* (i) List all subsidiaries of the registrant, the state or other jurisdiction of incorporation or organization of each, and the names under which such subsidiaries do business. This list may be incorporated by reference from a document which includes a complete and accurate list.

(ii) The names of particular subsidiaries may be omitted if the unnamed

(16)关于核证会计师变更的信函。注册人前任独立会计师出具的信函,说明其是否同意注册人在当期报告中提供的关于其作为注册人的主会计师辞职或解聘的声明。

(17)关于董事离任的通信。来自前任董事的任何书面通信,说明关于其退休、辞职、拒绝参选连任或免职的原因,包括前任董事向注册人出具的任何信函,说明其是否同意注册人提供的关于前任董事离任的声明。

(18)关于会计原则变更的信函。除非之前已经提交过该信函,否则注册人的独立会计师应出具一份信函,说明注册人所遵循的会计原则或惯例或其应用方法是否存在任何变化,从而影响到当期报告中向证券交易委员会提交的财务报表,或据合理预期,必然会影响之后会计年度的财务报表;同时应说明根据会计师基于具体情形的作出判断,被改变的原则是否为更适当的原则。但如果上述变化是因为财务会计准则委员会采用或明确推荐一项新的会计原则,或否定某项会计原则而作出的,则不必提交该信函。

(19)向证券持有人提供的报告。如果注册人在规定的报告提交期限内,向证券持有人提供或以其他方式公开了含有符合《10-Q表格》第I部分的部分或全部要求的信息的文件或报表,则可通过引用该等公开文件或报表的方式提供该等信息,但是该等公开文件或报表的复本应作为注册说明书的附录或《10-Q表格》第I部分的附录提交。

(20)向证券持有人提供的其他文件或说明。如果注册人在规定的报告提交期限内,向股票持有人提供或以其他方式公开了含有符合本表格部分或全部要求的信息的文件或报表,则可通过引用该等公开文件或报表的方式提供该等信息,但是该等公开文件或报表的复本应作为本表格的附录提交。

(21)注册人的子公司。(i)列出注册人的所有子公司,其设立或组建地所在州或其他司法辖区,以及该等子公司开展业务所使用的名称。如果子公司的完整、准确列表已存在于某文件之中,可通过引用该文件的方式提供该列表。

(ii)对于在本报告年度结束时,多个子公司作为一个整体考虑时认定其不构成一

subsidiaries, considered in the aggregate as a single subsidiary, would not constitute a significant subsidiary as of the end of the year covered by this report. (See the definition of "significant subsidiary" in Rule 1-02(w) (17 CFR 210.1-02(w)) of Regulation S-X.) The names of consolidated wholly-owned multiple subsidiaries carrying on the same line of business, such as chain stores or small loan companies, may be omitted, provided the name of the immediate parent, the line of business, the number of omitted subsidiaries operating in the United States and the number operating in foreign countries are given. This instruction shall not apply, however, to banks, insurance companies, savings and loan associations or to any subsidiary subject to regulation by another Federal agency.

(22) *Published report regarding matters submitted to vote of security holders.* Published reports containing all of the information called for by Item 4 of Part II of Form 10-Q or Item 4 of Part I of Form 10-K that is referred to therein in lieu of providing disclosure in Form 10-Q or 10-K, that are required to be filed as exhibits by Rule 12b-23(a)(3) under the Exchange Act (§240.12b-23(a)(3) of this chapter).

(23) *Consents of experts and counsel* — (i) *Securities Act filings.* All written consents required to be filed shall be dated and manually signed. Where the consent of an expert or counsel is contained in his report or opinion or elsewhere in the registration statement or document filed therewith, a reference shall be made in the index to the report, the part of the registration statement or document or opinion, containing the consent.

(ii) *Exchange Act reports.* Where the filing of a written consent is required with respect to material incorporated by reference in a previously filed registration statement under the Securities Act, such consent may be filed as exhibit to the material incorporated by reference. Such consents shall be dated and manually signed.

(24) *Power of attorney.* If any name is signed to the registration statement or report pursuant to a power of attorney, manually signed copies of such power of attorney shall be filed. Where the power of attorney is contained elsewhere in the registration statement or documents filed therewith a reference shall be made in the index to the part of the registration statement or document containing such power of attorney. In addition, if the name of any officer signing on behalf of the registrant is signed pursuant to a power of attorney, certified copies of a resolution of the registrant's board of directors authorizing such signature shall also be filed. A power of attorney that is filed with the Commission shall relate to a specific filing or an amendment thereto, provided, however, that a power of attorney relating to a registration statement under the Securities Act or an amendment thereto also may relate to any registration statement for the same offering that is to be effective upon filing pursuant to Rule 462(b) under the Securities Act (§230.462(b) of this chapter). A power of attorney that confers general authority shall not be filed with the

个重要子公司的,其名称可以省略。{“重要子公司”的定义见《S-X管理办法》的《1-02(w)规则》[《联邦规章汇编》第十七编第210.1-02(w)节]}。多个并表全资子公司,如果从事同一业务线,比如连锁店或小型贷款公司,其名称也可省略,仅须提供其直接母公司的名称、经营的业务线,对于省略名称的在美国和外国开展经营的子公司,说明其数目即可。但是,该规定不得适用于银行、保险公司、储蓄及贷款协会或须受制于其他联邦机构监管的子公司。

(22)关于提交证券持有人表决的事务的公开报告。该公开报告应包含《10-Q表格》第II部分第4条或《10-K表格》第I部分第4条要求提供的所有信息,并用以取代《交易法》的《12b-23(a)(3)规则》[本章第240.12b-23(a)(3)节]规定以附录形式提交的根据《10-Q表格》或《10-K表格》作出的披露。

(23)专家和律师同意书——(i)《证券法》下的文件提交。所有应按规定提交的书面同意均须注明日期并进行手签。如果专家或律师在其提供的报告、意见或注册说明书的其他章节或附随文件中作出同意,应在索引中引用包含该等同意的报告、注册说明书章节、附随文件或意见。

(ii)《证券法》报告。[1] 如果应针对之前根据《证券法》提交的注册说明书中引用纳入的某些材料提供书面同意,则该同意书可作为上述材料的附录提交,同时应注明日期并进行手签。

(24)授权委托书。如果注册说明书或报告上的任何签名系根据授权委托书签署,则应提交该等授权委托书的手签版本。如果授权委托书包含在注册说明书的其他章节或附随文件之中,应在索引中引用包含该等授权委托书的注册说明书章节或其他文件。并且,如果作为注册人代表的任何管理人员的签名系根据授权委托书签署,应同时提交经认证的注册人董事会批准进行该等签署的决议之复本。向证券交易委员会提交的授权委托书应注明其适用的具体提交文件或其修正,但是适用于根据《证券法》提交的某一注册说明书或其修正的授权委托书,同时也可适用于根据《证券法》的《462(b)规则》[本章第230.462(b)节]将于提交之时生效的、同一次发行的任何相关注册说明书。进行一般授权的授权委托书不必向证券交易委员会提交。

1 标题“*Exchange Act reports*”疑误,似应为“*Securities Act reports*”以保持与内容的一致,译文已按后者处理。——译者注

Commission.

(25) *Statement of eligibility of trustee.* (i) A statement of eligibility and qualification of each person designated to act as trustee under an indenture to be qualified under the Trust Indenture Act of 1939. Such statement of eligibility shall be bound separately from the other exhibits.

(ii) *Electronic filings.* The requirement to bind separately the statement of eligibility and qualification of each person designated to act as a trustee under the Trust Indenture Act of 1939 from other exhibits shall not apply to statements submitted in electronic format. Rather, such statements must be submitted as exhibits in the same electronic submission as the registration statement to which they relate, or in an amendment thereto, except that electronic filers that rely on Trust Indenture Act Section 305(b)(2) for determining the eligibility of the trustee under indentures for securities to be issued, offered or sold on a delayed basis by or on behalf of the registrant shall file such statements separately in the manner prescribed by §260.5b-1 through §260.5b-3 of this chapter and by the EDGAR Filer Manual.

(26) *Invitations for competitive bids.* If the registration statement covers securities to be offered at competitive bidding, any form of communication which is an invitation for competitive bid which will be sent or given to any person shall be filed.

(27)-(30) [Reserved]

(31)(i) *Rule 13a-14(a)/15d-14(a) Certifications.* The certifications required by Rule 13a-14(a) (17 CFR 240.13a-14(a)) or Rule 15d-14(a) (17 CFR 240.15d-14(a)) exactly as set forth below:

Certifications *I, [identify the certifying individual], certify that:

1. I have reviewed this [specify report] of [identify registrant];

2. Based on my knowledge, this report does not contain any untrue statement of a material fact or omit to state a material fact necessary to make the statements made, in light of the circumstances under which such statements were made, not misleading with respect to the period covered by this report;

3. Based on my knowledge, the financial statements, and other financial information included in this report, fairly present in all material respects the financial condition, results of operations and cash flows of the registrant as of, and for, the periods presented in this report;

4. The registrant's other certifying officer(s) and I are responsible for establishing and maintaining disclosure controls and procedures (as defined in Exchange Act Rules 13a-15(e) and 15d-15(e)) and internal control over financial reporting (as defined in Exchange Act Rules 13a-15(f) and 15d-15(f)) for the registrant and have:

(a) Designed such disclosure controls and procedures, or caused such disclosure

(25)信托受托人适格性声明。(i)关于被指定担任《1939年信托契约法》下的信托契约受托人的每一主体的适格性和资质声明。该等适格性声明应独立于其他附录单独提交。

(ii)电子提交。关于被指定担任《1939年信托契约法》下的信托契约受托人的每一主体的适格性和资质声明,如果是以电子形式提交的,则不必受到上述单独装订提交的限制。相反,该等声明必须作为相关的注册说明书或其修正内容的附录在同一批电子呈报文件中提交;但是在证券延期发行、发售或出售的情况下,电子文件提交人援引《信托契约法》第305(b)(2)条的规定代表注册人判断信托契约下受托人适格性的,电子提交人应按照本章第260.5b-1~260.5b-3节和《EDGAR提交人手册》规定的方式单独提交该等声明。

(26)竞标邀请。如果注册说明书中涉及以竞标方式发售的证券,应提交已经或将要向任何主体发出的构成竞标邀请的任何形式的通信。

(27)~(30)[保留]

(31)(i)《13a-14(a)规则》/《15d-14(a)规则》中的证明。《13a-14(a)规则》[《联邦规章汇编》第十七编第240.13a-14(a)节]或《15d-14(a)规则》[《联邦规章汇编》第十七编第240.15d-14(a)节]要求提供的证明格式具体如下:

证明*本人,[插入证明人姓名],兹证明:

1.本人已阅读[插入注册人身份信息]的本[指明报告名称];

2.据本人所知,本报告不包含任何对重大事实的不实陈述,此外,鉴于作出陈述的具体情况,亦未遗漏确保报告期间的陈述不具误导性所必要的任何重大事实;

3.据本人所知,本报告中的财务报表及其他财务信息,公正地反映了注册人截至报告期以及在报告期间内所有重要方面的财务状况、经营成果和现金流;

4.本人以及注册人其他作出证明的管理人员负责为注册人制定和维护披露控制措施和流程[定义见《交易法》的《13a-15(e)规则》和《15d-15(e)规则》]以及财务报告的内部控制措施[定义见《交易法》的《13a-15(f)规则》和《15d-15(f)规则》],并且已经:

(a)设计了披露控制措施和流程,或监督完成了披露控制措施和流程的设计,以确

controls and procedures to be designed under our supervision, to ensure that material information relating to the registrant, including its consolidated subsidiaries, is made known to us by others within those entities, particularly during the period in which this report is being prepared;

(b) Designed such internal control over financial reporting, or caused such internal control over financial reporting to be designed under our supervision, to provide reasonable assurance regarding the reliability of financial reporting and the preparation of financial statements for external purposes in accordance with generally accepted accounting principles;

(c) Evaluated the effectiveness of the registrant's disclosure controls and procedures and presented in this report our conclusions about the effectiveness of the disclosure controls and procedures, as of the end of the period covered by this report based on such evaluation; and

(d) Disclosed in this report any change in the registrant's internal control over financial reporting that occurred during the registrant's most recent fiscal quarter (the registrant's fourth fiscal quarter in the case of an annual report) that has materially affected, or is reasonably likely to materially affect, the registrant's internal control over financial reporting; and

5. The registrant's other certifying officer(s) and I have disclosed, based on our most recent evaluation of internal control over financial reporting, to the registrant's auditors and the audit committee of the registrant's board of directors (or persons performing the equivalent functions):

(a) All significant deficiencies and material weaknesses in the design or operation of internal control over financial reporting which are reasonably likely to adversely affect the registrant's ability to record, process, summarize and report financial information; and

(b) Any fraud, whether or not material, that involves management or other employees who have a significant role in the registrant's internal control over financial reporting.

Date:

____

____

____

*Provide a separate certification for each principalexecutive officer and principal financial officer of the registrant. See Rules 13a–14(a) and 15d–14(a).

(ii) *Rule 13a–14(d)/15d–14(d) Certifications.* If an asset-backed issuer (as defined in §229.1101), the certifications required by Rule 13a–14(d) (17 CFR 240.13a–14(d)) or Rule 15d–14(d) (17 CFR 240.15d–14(d)) exactly as set forth below:

保我们可以获知由注册人(包括其并表子公司)内部人员编制的与该等实体有关的重大信息(尤其是在本报告编制期间);

(b)设计了财务报告的内部控制措施,或监督完成了财务报告内部控制措施的设计,以合理确保财务报告的可信度,并确保可根据公认会计原则编制用于外部目的的财务报表;

(c)评估了注册人披露控制措施和流程的有效性,并在本报告中汇报了截至本报告期间期末我们基于该等评估所得出的结论;且

(d)在本报告中披露了注册人最近一个财务季度(就年度报告而言,则指注册人的第四个财务季度)发生的,已经或根据合理预期可能对注册人财务报告内部控制产生重大影响的注册人财务报告内部控制措施的任何变化;且

5.基于我们对注册人财务报告内部控制的最新评估,本人和注册人其他作出证明的管理人员已向注册人的审计师和董事会下属的审计委员会(或履行同等职能的人)披露了以下情况:

(a)财务报告内部控制设计或实施过程中存在的,根据合理预期可能对注册人记录、处理、总结、报告财务信息的能力产生不利影响的所有明显缺陷和重大弱点;及

(b)在注册人财务报告内部控制中起重要作用的管理层或其他雇员的任何欺诈行为(无论是否重大)。

日期:

____

______________________________[签名]

______________________________[职务]

*应就注册人的每名主要高管和主要财务官分别提交证明。参见《13a-14(a)规则》和《15d-14(a)规则》。

(ii)《13a-14规则》/《15d-14规则》中的证明。对于资产支持证券发行人(定义见第229.1101节),《13a-14(d)规则》[《联邦规章汇编》第十七编第240.13a-14(d)节]或《15d-14(d)规则》[《联邦规章汇编》第十七编第240.15d-14(d)节]要求提供的证明如下:

Certifications[1] I, [identify the certifying individual], certify that:

1. I have reviewed this report on Form 10–K and all reports on Form 10–D required to be filed in respect of the period covered by this report on Form 10–K of [identify the issuing entity] (the "Exchange Act periodic reports");

2. Based on my knowledge, the Exchange Act periodic reports, taken as a whole, do not contain any untrue statement of a material fact or omit to state a material fact necessary to make the statements made, in light of the circumstances under which such statements were made, not misleading with respect to the period covered by this report;

3. Based on my knowledge, all of the distribution, servicing and other information required to be provided under Form 10–D for the period covered by this report is included in the Exchange Act periodic reports;

4. [I am responsible for reviewing the activities performed by the servicer(s) and based on my knowledge and the compliance review(s) conducted in preparing the servicer compliance statement(s) required in this report under Item 1123 of Regulation AB, and except as disclosed in the Exchange Act periodic reports, the servicer(s) [has/have] fulfilled [its/their] obligations under the servicing agreement(s) in all material respects; and]

[fulfilled [its/their] obligations under the servicing agreement(s) in all material respects; and][2]

5. All of the reports on assessment of compliance with servicing criteria for asset–backed securities and their related attestation reports on assessment of compliance with servicing criteria for asset–backed securities required to be included in this report in accordance with Item 1122 of Regulation AB and Exchange Act Rules 13a–18 and 15d–18 have been included as an exhibit to this report, except as otherwise disclosed in this report. Any material instances of noncompliance described in such reports have been

1 With respect to asset–backed issuers, the certification must be signed by either: (1) The senior officer in charge of securitization of the depositor if the depositor is signing the report on Form 10–K; or (2) The senior officer in charge of the servicing function of the servicer if the servicer is signing the report on Form 10–K on behalf of the issuing entity. See Rules 13a–14(e) and 15d–14(e) (§§240.13a–14(e) and 240.15d–14(e)). If multiple servicers are involved in servicing the pool assets, the senior officer in charge of the servicing function of the master servicer (or entity performing the equivalent function) must sign if a representative of the servicer is to sign the certification. If there is a master servicer and one or more underlying servicers, the references in the certification relate to the master servicer. A natural person must sign the certification in his or her individual capacity, although the title of that person in the organization of which he or she is an officer may be included under the signature.

2 The first version of paragraph 4 is to be used when the servicer is signing the report on behalf of the issuing entity. The second version of paragraph 4 is to be used when the depositor is signing the report.

证明[1]本人,[注明证明人姓名],兹证明:

1.本人已阅读本《10-K表格》报告及[插入签发实体身份信息]在《10-K表格》报告期间应提交的所有《10-D表格》报告(下称《交易法》定期报告);

2.据本人所知,整个《交易法》定期报告均不包含任何对重大事实的不实陈述,此外,鉴于作出陈述的具体情况,亦未遗漏确保报告期间的陈述不具误导性所必要的任何重大事实;

3.据本人所知,《10-D表格》要求提供的本报告期间的所有分销、服务和其他信息均已纳入《交易法》定期报告之中;

4.[本人负责对服务机构的履约行为进行审查,根据本人了解的信息及遵照《AB管理办法》第1123条的规定为编制本报告所要求的服务机构合规声明而进行的合规审查,除已在《交易法》定期报告中予以披露的部分外,服务机构已履行其在服务协议中的所有重大义务;且]

(根据本人了解的信息和《AB管理办法》第1123条要求在本报告中提供的服务机构合规声明,除已在《交易法》定期报告中予以披露的部分外,服务机构已履行其在服务协议中的所有重大义务;且)[2]

5.根据《AB管理办法》第1122条和《交易法》的《13a-18规则》和《15d-18规则》,关于资产支持证券发行人服务标准合规性的评估报告及相关的鉴证报告均已作为本报告附录提交,但本报告另行作出了相反披露的除外。该等报告所述的所有重大不合规

1 就资产支持证券发行人而言,该证明必须由下列人员之一签署:(1)交存人负责证券化的高级管理人员(如果交存人签署《10-K表格》报告);或(2)服务机构负责提供服务的高级管理人员(如果服务机构代表发行实体签署《10-K表格》报告)。参见《13a-14(e)规则》和《15d-14(e)规则》[第240.13a-14(e)条和第240.15d-14(e)条]。多家服务机构参与为池内资产提供服务的,如需服务机构代表签署证明,则应由主服务机构(或履行同等职能的实体)负责提供服务的高级管理人员签署。存在一家主服务机构和一家或多家其他相关服务机构的,证明中所指为主服务机构。自然人必须以其个人身份签署证明,虽然在签名的下方可附上其在某一组织中担任的管理人员职务。

2 服务机构代表发行实体签署报告的,应采用第4款的第一个版本。交存人签署报告的,应采用第4款的第二个版本。

disclosed in this report on Form 10-K.[1]

[In giving the certifications above, I have reasonably relied on information provided to me by the following unaffiliated parties (name of servicer, sub-servicer, co-servicer, depositor or trustee).][2]

Date:

____

____

____

(32) *Section 1350 Certifications.* (i) The certifications required by Rule 13a-14(b) (17 CFR 240.13a-14(b)) or Rule 15d-14(b) (17 CFR 240.15d-14(b)) and Section 1350 of Chapter 63 of Title 18 of the United States Code (18 U.S.C. 1350).

(ii) A certification furnished pursuant to this item will not be deemed "filed" for purposes of Section 18 of the Exchange Act (15 U.S.C. 78r), or otherwise subject to the liability of that section. Such certification will not be deemed to be incorporated by reference into any filing under the Securities Act or the Exchange Act, except to the extent that the registrant specifically incorporates it by reference.

(33) *Report on assessment of compliance with servicing criteria for asset-backed securities.* Each report on assessment of compliance with servicing criteria required by §229.1122(a).

(34) *Attestation report on assessment of compliance with servicing criteria for asset-backed securities.* Each attestation report on assessment of compliance with servicing criteria for asset-backed securities required by §229.1122(b).

(35) *Servicer compliance statement.* Each servicer compliance statement required by §229.1123.

(36) through (98) [Reserved]

(99) *Additional exhibits.* (i) Any additional exhibits which the registrant may wish to file shall be so marked as to indicate clearly the subject matters to which they refer.

(ii) Any document (except for an exhibit) or part thereof which is incorporated by

1 The certification refers to the reports prepared by parties participating in the servicing function that are required to be included as an exhibit to the Form 10-K. See Item 1122 of Regulation AB (§229.1122) and Rules 13a-18 and 15d-18 (§§240.13a-18 and 240.15d-18 of this chapter). If a report that is otherwise required to be included is not attached, disclosure that the report is not included and an associated explanation must be provided in the Form 10-K report.

2 Because the signer of the certification must rely in certain circumstances on information provided by unaffiliated parties outside of the signer's control, this paragraph must be included if the signer is reasonably relying on information that unaffiliated trustees, depositors, servicers, sub-servicers or co-servicers have provided.

情况均已在本《10-K表格》报告中披露。[1]

[在作出上述证明时,本人合理采信了下列非关联方(服务机构、次级服务机构、联合服务机构、交存人或信托受托人名称)提供的信息][2]

日期:

____

______________________________[签名]

______________________________[职务]

(32)第1350条中的证明。(i)《13a-14(b)规则》[《联邦规章汇编》第十七编第240.13a-14(b)节]或《15d-14(b)规则》[《联邦规章汇编》第十七编第240.15d-14(b)节]和《美国法典》第十八编第63章第1350节(《美国法典》第十八编第1350节)要求提交的证明。

(ii)根据本条提供的证明不视为为《交易法》第18条(《美国法典》第十五编第78r节)之目的"提交"的证明,也不受该节责任的约束。除非注册人特别引用纳入,否则该证明不得视为通过引用而被纳入《证券法》或《交易法》下提交的文件。

(33)关于资产支持证券发行人服务标准合规性的评估报告。第229.1122(a)节规定的关于服务标准合规性的每份评估报告。

(34)关于资产支持证券服务标准合规性评估的鉴证报告。第229.1122(b)节规定的关于资产支持证券服务标准合规性评估的鉴证报告。

(35)服务机构合规声明。第229.1123节规定的每个服务机构的合规声明。

(36)~(98)[保留]

(99)其他附录。(i)注册人希望提交的任何其他附录,均应清楚地注明该附录的主题。

(ii)通过引用纳入提交文件的任何文件(附录除外)或其部分,且该等文件或其相

---

1 本证明针对的是参与提供服务的各方编制并应作为《10-K表格》的附录提交的各项报告。参见《AB管理办法》第1122条(第229.1122节)和《13a-18规则》、《15d-18规则》(本章第240.13a-18节和第240.15d-18节)。如果本应纳入的报告并未提交,则必须在《10-K表格》报告中披露该报告未提交的事实,并给出相关解释。

2 因为证明签署人在某些情况下必须采信不受其控制的非关联方提供的信息,所以如果签署人需要合理采信非关联信托受托人、交存人、服务机构、次级服务机构或联合服务机构提供的信息,本款必须包括在内。

reference in the filing and is not otherwise required to be filed by this Item or is not a Commission filed document incorporated by reference in a Securities Act registration statement.

(iii) If pursuant to Section 11(a) of the Securities Act (15 U.S.C. 77k(a)) an issuer makes generally available to its security holders an earnings statement covering a period of at least 12 months beginning after the effective date of the registration statement, and if such earnings statement is made available by "other methods" than those specified in paragraphs (a) or (b) of §230.158 of this chapter, it must be filed as an exhibit to the Form 10-Q or the Form 10-K, as appropriate, covering the period in which the earnings statement was released.

(100) *XBRL-Related Documents.* Only an electronic filer that prepares its financial statements in accordance with Article 6 of Regulation S-X (17 CFR 210.6-01 *et seq.*) is permitted to participate in the voluntary XBRL (eXtensible Business Reporting Language) program and, as a result, may submit XBRL-Related Documents (§232.11 of this chapter) in electronic format as an exhibit to: the filing to which they relate; an amendment to such filing; or a Form 8-K (§249.308 of this chapter) that references such filing, if the Form 8-K is submitted no earlier than the date of filing. Rule 401 of Regulation S-T (§232.401 of this chapter) sets forth further details regarding eligibility to participate in the voluntary XBRL program.

(101) *Interactive Data File.* An Interactive Data File (§232.11 of this chapter) is:

(i) *Required to be submitted and posted.* Required to be submitted to the Commission and posted on the registrant's corporate Web site, if any, in the manner provided by Rule 405 of Regulation S-T (§232.405 of this chapter) if the registrant does not prepare its financial statements in accordance with Article 6 of Regulation S-X (17 CFR 210.6-01 *et seq.*) and is described in paragraph (b)(101)(i)(A), (B) or (C) of this Item, except that an Interactive Data File: first is required for a periodic report on Form 10-Q (§249.308a of this chapter), Form 20-F (§249.220f of this chapter) or Form 40-F (§249.240f of this chapter), as applicable; is required for a registration statement under the Securities Act only if the registration statement contains a price or price range; and is required for a Form 8-K (§249.308 of this chapter) only when the Form 8-K contains audited annual financial statements that are a revised version of financial statements that previously were filed with the Commission that have been revised pursuant to applicable accounting standards to reflect the effects of certain subsequent events, including a discontinued operation, a change in reportable segments or a change in accounting principle, and, in such case, the Interactive Data File would be required only as to such revised financial statements regardless whether the Form 8-K contains other financial statements:

关部分并不属于本条要求提交的文件,也不属于通过引用纳入《证券法》注册说明书的向证券交易委员会提交的文件。

(iii)如果根据《证券法》第11(a)条[《美国法典》第十五编第77k(a)节],发行人向其证券持有人公开盈利表,且盈利表的覆盖期间自注册说明书生效日期之后起算,不短于12个月,同时该盈利表是以本章第230.158节第(a)款或第(b)款规定的方法以外的"其他方法"公开的,则必须视适当情况,将该盈利表作为覆盖相应期间的《10-Q表格》或《10-K表格》的附录提交。

(100)XBRL相关文件。只有根据《S-X管理办法》第6条(《联邦规章汇编》第十七编第210.6-01节及其后条文)的规定编制财务报表的电子文件提交人才被允许自愿选择参与XBRL(可扩展商业报告语言)计划,并以电子形式提交XBRL文件(本章第232.11节),并将其附于下述文件之后:相关的提交文件;提交文件的修正,或引用该等提交文件的《8-K表格》(本章第249.308节)(如果《8-K表格》的呈报日期不早于文件提交日)。《S-T管理办法》的《401规则》(本章第232.401节)对自愿选择参与XBRL计划的资格作了详细规定。

(101)交互式数据文档。交互式数据文档(本章第232.11节):

(i)需要呈报并公布。如果注册人没有根据《S-X管理办法》第6条(《联邦规章汇编》第十七编第210.6-01节及其后条文)编制财务报表,并且存在本条下文第(b)(101)(i)(A)款、第(b)(101)(i)(B)款或第(b)(101)(i)(C)款所述情形,则须向证券交易委员会呈报并按照《S-T管理办法》的《405规则》(本章第232.405节)规定的方式通过注册人的公司网站(如有)公示交互式数据文档,但是,以下报告或文件必须使用交互式数据文档:按照《10-Q表格》(本章第249.308a节)、《20-F表格》(本章第249.220f节)或《40-F表格》(本章第249.240f节)(以适用者为准)提交的定期报告;《证券法》中的注册说明书(仅限于注册说明书含有价格或价格范围之时);以及《8-K表格》(本章第249.308节),对于《8-K表格》,满足下述条件方须使用交互式数据文档:《8-K表格》中含有修订后的已审计财务报表——之前已向证券交易委员会提交过财务报表,但为了反映提交后发生的事件(比如经营中断、应报告分部的变化或会计原则的变化)而根据适用的会计原则对原财务报表进行了修订,在该种情况下,无论《8-K表格》是否含有其他财务报表,只有该等修订后的财务报表才需要使用交互式数据文档:

(A) A large accelerated filer (§240.12b-2 of this chapter) that had an aggregate worldwide market value of the voting and non-voting common equity held by non-affiliates of more than $5 billion as of the last business day of the second fiscal quarter of its most recently completed fiscal year that prepares its financial statements in accordance with generally accepted accounting principles as used in the United States and the filing contains financial statements of the registrant for a fiscal period that ends on or after June 15, 2009;

(B) A large accelerated filer not specified in paragraph (b)(101)(i)(A) of this Item that prepares its financial statements in accordance with generally accepted accounting principles as used in the United States and the filing contains financial statements of the registrant for a fiscal period that ends on or after June 15, 2010; or

(C) A filer not specified in paragraph (b)(101)(i)(A) or (B) of this Item that prepares its financial statements in accordance with either generally accepted accounting principles as used in the United States or International Financial Reporting Standards as issued by the International Accounting Standards Board, and the filing contains financial statements of the registrant for a fiscal period that ends on or after June 15, 2011.

(ii) *Permitted to be submitted.* Permitted to be submitted to the Commission in the manner provided by Rule 405 of Regulation S-T (§232.405 of this chapter) if the:

(A) Registrant prepares its financial statements:

(1) In accordance with either:

(*i*) Generally accepted accounting principles as used in the United States; or

(*ii*) International Financial Reporting Standards as issued by the International Accounting Standards Board; and

(2) Not in accordance with Article 6 of Regulation S-X (17 CFR 210.6-01 *et seq.*); and

(B) Interactive Data File is not required to be submitted to the Commission under paragraph (b)(101)(i) of this Item.

(iii) *Not permitted to be submitted.* Not permitted to be submitted to the Commission if the registrant prepares its financial statements in accordance with Article 6 of Regulation S-X (17 CFR 210.6-01 *et seq.*).

(C) *Smaller reporting companies.* A smaller reporting company need not provide the disclosure required in paragraph (b)(12) of this Item, Statements re computation of ratios.

[47 FR 11401, Mar. 16, 1982]

Editorial Note: ForFederal Registercitations affecting §229.601, see the List of CFR Sections Affected, which appears in the Finding Aids section of the printed volume and at www.fdsys.gov.

(A)在截至注册人最近结束的会计年度第二个财务季度的最后一个工作日,其非关联方持有的具有和不具有表决权的普通股在全世界的市值超过50亿美元,并且注册人系根据美国公认会计原则编制其财务报表的大型加速报告公司(本章第240.12b-2节),且提交文件中包括注册人截至2009年6月15日或其后某一日期的一个会计期间的财务报表;

(B)注册人系本条第(b)(101)(i)(A)款规定之外的根据美国公认会计原则编制财务报表的大型加速报告公司,且提交文件中包括注册人截至2010年6月15日或其后某一日期的一个会计期间的财务报表;或

(C)注册人系本条第(b)(101)(i)(A)款和第(b)(101)(i)(B)款规定之外的,根据美国公认会计原则或是国际会计准则委员会颁发的国际财务报告准则编制财务报表的提交人,且提交文件中包括注册人截至2011年6月15日或其后某一日期的一个会计期间的财务报表。

(ii)可以呈报。如果满足以下条件,则可以根据《S-T管理办法》的《405规则》(本章第232.405节)规定的方式向证券交易委员会呈报交互式数据文档:

(A)注册人编制财务报表时:

(1)遵循如下标准之一:

(*i*)美国公认会计原则;或

(*ii*)国际会计准则委员会颁发的国际财务报告准则;且

(2)非根据《S-X管理办法》第6条(《联邦规章汇编》第十七编第210.6-01节及其后条文)进行编制;且

(B)注册人不必根据本条第(b)(101)(i)款向证券交易委员会呈报交互式数据文档。

(iii)不允许呈报。注册人根据《S-X管理办法》第6条(《联邦规章汇编》第十七编第210.6-01节及其后条文)编制财务报表的,不得向证券交易委员会呈报交互式数据文档。

(C)小型报告公司。小型报告公司不必根据本条第(b)(12)款的要求披露比率计算说明。

[《联邦公报》第47卷第11401页,1982年3月16日。]

编者按:对第229.601节有影响的《联邦公报》索引,参见《受影响的联邦规章汇编条文列表》(见印刷版本的《检索协助》章节和www.fdsys.gov。

Subpart 229.700—Miscellaneous

§229.701(Item 701) Recent sales of unregistered securities; use of proceeds from registered securities.

Furnish the following information as to all securities of the registrant sold by the registrant within the past three years which were not registered under the Securities Act. Include sales of reacquired securities, as well as new issues, securities issued in exchange for property, services, or other securities, and new securities resulting from the modification of outstanding securities.

(a) *Securities sold.* Give the date of sale and the title and amount of securities sold.

(b) *Underwriters and other purchasers.* Give the names of the principal underwriters, if any. As to any such securities not publicly offered, name the persons or identify the class of persons to whom the securities were sold.

(c) *Consideration.* As to securities sold for cash, state the aggregate offering price and the aggregate underwriting discounts or commissions. As to any securities sold otherwise than for cash, state the nature of the transaction and the nature and aggregate amount of consideration received by the registrant.

(d) *Exemption from registration claimed.* Indicate the section of the Securities Act or the rule of the Commission under which exemption from registration was claimed and state briefly the facts relied upon to make the exemption available.

(e) *Terms of conversion or exercise.* If the information called for by this paragraph (e) is being presented on Form 8-K, Form 10-Q, Form 10-K, or Form 10-D under the Exchange Act (§249.308, §249.308(a), §240.310 or §249.312) of this chapter, and where the securities sold by the registrant are convertible or exchangeable into equity securities, or are warrants or options representing equity securities, disclose the terms of conversion or exercise of the securities.

(f) *Use of proceeds.* As required by §230.463 of this chapter, following the effective date of the first registration statement filed under the Securities Act by an issuer, the issuer or successor issuer shall report the use of proceeds on its first periodic report filed pursuant to sections 13(a) and 15(d) of the Exchange Act (15 U.S.C. 78m(a) and 78o(d)) after effectiveness of its Securities Act registration statement, and thereafter on each of its subsequent periodic reports filed pursuant to sections 13(a) and 15(d) of the Exchange Act through the later of disclosure of the application of all the offering proceeds, or disclosure of the termination of the offering. If a report of the use of proceeds is required

第229.700子部分——其　　他

第229.701节(第701条)　未注册证券的近期出售;注册证券募集资金的用途

按下文规定,针对注册人在过去3年内卖出的所有未在《证券法》下注册的证券提供相关信息。在该等信息中,应包括重新获得的证券的出售;新证券发行;为交换财产、服务或其他证券而发行的证券;以及因对发行在外证券进行变更而产生的新证券。

(a)已卖出证券。提供已卖出证券的卖出日期、名称和金额。

(b)承销商和其他买入方。提供主要的承销商的名称(如有)。对于未公开要约的所有证券,均应提供证券买入人的姓名/名称或类别。

(c)对价。对于以现金为对价卖出的证券,说明要约总价和承销折扣或佣金总额。对于以非现金对价卖出的任何证券,说明交易的性质和注册人收到的对价总额。

(d)豁免注册主张。注册人主张豁免注册的,应指明所依据的《证券法》条款或证券交易委员会规则,并简要说明支持注册豁免的事实。

(e)转换或行权条款。如果注册人已经按《交易法》下的《8-K表格》、《10-Q表格》、《10-K表格》或《10-D表格》[本章第249.308节、第249.308(a)节、第240.310节或第249.312节]提供本(e)款要求提供的信息,且注册人卖出的证券可转换为或可交换为股权证券,或属于代表股权证券的权证或期权,应披露证券转换或行权的条款。

(f)募集资金的使用。根据本章第230.463节的要求,在发行人根据《证券法》提交的首份注册说明书的生效日期之后,发行人或继任发行人应在按照《交易法》第13(a)条和第15(d)条[《美国法典》第十五编第78m(a)节和第78o(d)节]于其《证券法注册说明书》生效后提交的首次定期报告及每一份后续定期报告中报告募集资金的使用情况,直至所有募集资金的使用情况均已获得完全披露,或已作出证券发售终止的披露(以较迟者为准)。如果按规定应就前身发行人的首份生效的注册说明书提供募集资金的使用报告,该等报告应由继任发行人提供。对于本条第(f)(2)款至第(f)(4)款规定的信息,注册人仅须在《证券法》下提交的注册说明书生效后,在按照《交易法》第13

with respect to the first effective registration statement of the predecessor issuer, the successor issuer shall provide such a report. The information provided pursuant to paragraphs (f)(2) through (f)(4) of this Item need only be provided with respect to the first periodic report filed pursuant to sections 13(a) and 15(d) of the Exchange Act after effectiveness of the registration statement filed under the Securities Act. Subsequent periodic reports filed pursuant to sections 13(a) and 15(d) of the Exchange Act need only provide the information required in paragraphs (f)(2) through (f)(4) of this Item if any of such required information has changed since the last periodic report filed. In disclosing the use of proceeds in the first periodic report filed pursuant to the Exchange Act, the issuer or successor issuer should include the following information:

(1) The effective date of the Securities Act registration statement for which the use of proceeds information is being disclosed and the Commission file number assigned to the registration statement;

(2) If the offering has commenced, the offering date, and if the offering has not commenced, an explanation why it has not;

(3) If the offering terminated before any securities were sold, an explanation for such termination; and

(4) If the offering did not terminate before any securities were sold, disclose:

(i) Whether the offering has terminated and, if so, whether it terminated before the sale of all securities registered;

(ii) The name(s) of the managing underwriter(s), if any;

(iii) The title of each class of securities registered and, where a class of convertible securities is being registered, the title of any class of securities into which such securities may be converted;

(iv) For each class of securities (other than a class of securities into which a class of convertible securities registered may be converted without additional payment to the issuer) the following information, provided for both the account of the issuer and the account(s) of any selling security holder(s): the amount registered, the aggregate price of the offering amount registered, the amount sold and the aggregate offering price of the amount sold to date;

(v) From the effective date of the Securities Act registration statement to the ending date of the reporting period, the amount of expenses incurred for the issuer's account in connection with the issuance and distribution of the securities registered for underwriting discounts and commissions, finders'fees, expenses paid to or for underwriters, other expenses and total expenses. Indicate if a reasonable estimate for the amount of expenses incurred is provided instead of the actual amount of expense. Indicate whether such payments were:

(a)条和第15(d)条提交的定期报告中予以提供。如果本条第(f)(2)款至第(f)(4)款规定的任何信息在最后一次定期报告提交后发生了变更,在注册人按照《交易法》第13(a)条和第15(d)条提交的后续定期报告中,发行人仅须按照上述条款提供该等信息。在按照《交易法》提交首份定期报告,披露募集资金的使用情况时,发行人或继任发行人应纳入如下信息:

(1)披露募集资金使用信息的《证券法》注册说明书的生效日期,以及证券交易委员会向该注册说明书分配的文件编号。

(2)证券发售日期(如证券已经开始发售),或尚未开始发售的原因(如证券尚未开始发售);

(3)如果发售在任何证券被卖出之前即已终止,解释该等终止的原因;及

(4)如果发售并未在任何证券被卖出之前终止,应披露:

(i)发售是否已经终止,如果是,是否在全部注册证券被卖出之前终止;

(ii)牵头承销商的名称(如有);

(iii)每一类注册证券的名称;如果所注册的证券为可转换证券,该可转换证券可以转换的任何类别证券的名称;

(iv)对每一类别的证券(不必向发行人支付额外费用,可转换证券即可转换成的证券类别除外),应就发行人的账户和任何献售证券持有人的账户提供如下信息:注册金额、注册要约证券金额总价、卖出金额和截至报告当期卖出证券金额的要约总价;

(v)从《证券法》注册说明书生效日期至报告期间截止日期,发行人账户发生的与注册证券发行和分销相关的如下费用金额:承销折扣和佣金、中介费、付给承销商或为承销商支付的费用、其他费用和总费用。如果所提供的费用为合理预估金额,而非实际发生的费用金额,应如实说明。说明该等付款是否为:

(A) Direct or indirect payments to directors, officers, general partners of the issuer or their associates; to persons owning ten (10) percent or more of any class of equity securities of the issuer; and to affiliates of the issuer; or

(B) Direct or indirect payments to others;

(vi) The net offering proceeds to the issuer after deducting the total expenses described in paragraph (f)(4)(v) of this Item;

(vii) From the effective date of the Securities Act registration statement to the ending date of the reporting period, the amount of net offering proceeds to the issuer used for construction of plant, building and facilities; purchase and installation of machinery and equipment; purchases of real estate; acquisition of other business(es); repayment of indebtedness; working capital; temporary investments (which should be specified); and any other purposes for which at least five (5) percent of the issuer's total offering proceeds or $100,000 (whichever is less) has been used (which should be specified). Indicate if a reasonable estimate for the amount of net offering proceeds applied is provided instead of the actual amount of net offering proceeds used. Indicate whether such payments were:

(A) Direct or indirect payments to directors, officers, general partners of the issuer or their associates; to persons owning ten (10) percent or more of any class of equity securities of the issuer; and to affiliates of the issuer; or

(B) Direct or indirect payments to others; and

(viii) If the use of proceeds in paragraph (f)(4)(vii) of this Item represents a material change in the use of proceeds described in the prospectus, the issuer should describe briefly the material change.

Instructions. 1. Information required by this Item 701 need not be set forth as to notes, drafts, bills of exchange, or bankers′ acceptances which mature not later than one year from the date of issuance.

2. If the sales were made in a series of transactions, the information may be given by such totals and periods as will reasonably convey the information required.

[47 FR 11401, Mar. 16, 1982, as amended at 61 FR 54508, Oct. 18, 1996; 62 FR 39762, July 24, 1997; 70 FR 1597, Jan. 7, 2005; 73 FR 967, Jan. 4, 2008]

§229.702(Item 702) Indemnification of directors and officers.

State the general effect of any statute, charter provisions, by-laws, contract or other arrangements under which any controlling persons, director or officer of the registrant is insured or indemnified in any manner against liability which he may incur in his capacity as such.

(A)向下列人的直接或间接付款:发行人的董事、管理人员、普通合伙人或该等人员的业务相关人;持有发行人任何类别股权证券10%(含)以上的主体;发行人的关联方;或者

(B)向其他人的直接或间接付款;

(vi)扣除本条第(f)(4)(v)款列明的总费用后,支付给发行人的发售募集款项净额;

(vii)从《证券法》注册说明书生效日期至报告期间截止日期,发行人用于如下用途的发行募集资金净额:工厂、建筑和设施建设;购买和安装机器设备;购买不动产;收购其他业务;偿还债务;流动资本;临时投资(应具体说明);以及发行人至少投入了募集资金总额的5%或10万美元(以较少者为准)的任何其他目的(应具体说明)。如果所提供的金额为对发行募集资金净额使用的合理预估,而非实际使用金额,应如实说明。说明该等付款是否为:

(A)向下列人的直接或间接付款:发行人的董事、管理人员、普通合伙人或该等人员的业务相关人;持有发行人任何类别股权证券10%(含)以上的人;以及发行人的关联方;或者

(B)向其他人的直接或间接付款;

(viii)如果本条第(f)(4)(vii)款中募集资金的使用构成对招募说明书规定的募集资金使用的实质变更,发行人应对实质变更作出简要说明。

说明。1.对于发行日后一年内到期应付的票据、汇票、银行承兑汇票,不必提供本第701条要求提供的信息。

2.对于通过系列交易完成的证券出售,可提供总数和期间等信息,只要可以合理传递按规定应提供的信息即可。

[《联邦公报》第47卷第11401页,1982年3月16日,修正索引:《联邦公报》第61卷第54508页,1996年10月18日;《联邦公报》第62卷第39762页,1997年7月24日;《联邦公报》第70卷第1597页,2005年1月7日;《联邦公报》第73卷第967页,2008年1月4日。]

第229.702节(第702条) 董事和管理人员的赔偿

注册人的任何控制人、董事或管理人员根据任何制定法、章程条款、内部章程、合同或其他安排而获得任何形式的职务责任保险或赔偿的,应说明该等制定法、章程条款、内部章程、合同或其他安排的大致内容。

§229.703 Purchases of equity securities by the issuer and affiliated purchasers.

(a) In the following tabular format, provide the information specified in paragraph (b) of this Item with respect to any purchase made by or on behalf of the issuer or any "affiliated purchaser", as defined in §240.10b-18(a)(3) of this chapter, of shares or other units of any class of the issuer's equity securities that is registered by the issuer pursuant to section 12 of the Exchange Act (15 U.S.C. 781).

Issuer Purchases of Equity Securities

Period	(a) Total number of shares (or units) purchased	(b) Average price paid per share (or unit)	(c) Total number of shares (or units) purchased as part of publicly announced plans or programs	(d) Maximum number (or approximate dollar value) of shares (or units) that may yet be purchased under the plans or programs
Month #1 (identify beginning and ending dates)				
Month #2 (identify beginning and ending dates)				
Month #3 (identify beginning and ending dates)				
Total				

(b) The table shall include the following information for each class or series of securities for each month included in the period covered by the report:

(1) The total number of shares (or units) purchased (column (a));

Instruction to paragraph (b)(1) of Item 703: Include in this column all issuer repurchases, including those made pursuant to publicly announced plans or programs and those not made pursuant to publicly announced plans or programs. Briefly disclose, by footnote to the table, the number of shares purchased other than through a publicly announced plan or program and the nature of the transaction (e.g., whether the purchases were made in open-market transactions, tender offers, in satisfaction of the company's obligations upon exercise of outstanding put options issued by the company, or other transactions).

第229.703节 发行人和关联买方对股权证券的购买

(a)发行人或任何“关联买方”[如本章第240.10b-18(a)(3)节定义]或其代表买入发行人按照《交易法》第12条(《美国法典》第十五编第78l节)注册的股份或其他单位的任何类别的股权证券,应按照如下表格格式,提供本条第(b)款规定的信息。

发行人买入股权证券

期间	(a)买入股份(或单位)总数	(b)每股(或每单位)平均买入价格	(c)通过公开宣布的计划或项目买入的股份(或单位)总数	(d)根据计划或项目未来将买入的股份(或单位)的最大数量(或大致美元价值)
第1个月(标明该月的起始日期和结束日期)				
第2个月(标明该月的起始日期和结束日期)				
第3个月(标明该月的起始日期和结束日期)				
总计				

(b)本表格应就每一类别或系列证券提供报告期内每一月度的下列信息:

(1)买入股份(或单位)总数[(a)栏]

关于第703条第(b)(1)款的说明:在本栏纳入发行人开展的所有回购,包括按照和非按照公开宣布的计划或项目开展的回购。在表格脚注中简要披露非通过公开宣布的计划或项目买入的股数和交易性质(如是否通过公开市场交易、股权收购要约买入证券,或者在期权持有人行使公司发行的看跌期权时为履行公司义务而买入证券,或通过其他交易买入证券)。

(2) The average price paid per share (or unit) (column (b));

(3) The total number of shares (or units) purchased as part of publicly announced repurchase plans or programs (column (c)); and

(4) The maximum number (or approximate dollar value) of shares (or units) that may yet be purchased under the plans or programs (column (d)).

*Instructions to paragraphs (b)(3) and (b)(4) of Item 703:*1. In the table, disclose this information in the aggregate for all plans or programs publicly announced.

2. By footnote to the table, indicate:

a. The date each plan or program was announced;

b. The dollar amount (or share or unit amount) approved;

c. The expiration date (if any) of each plan or program;

d. Each plan or program that has expired during the period covered by the table; and

e. Each plan or program the issuer has determined to terminate prior to expiration, or under which the issuer does not intend to make further purchases.

*Instruction to Item 703:*Disclose all purchases covered by this Item, including purchases that do not satisfy the conditions of the safe harbor of §240.10b-18 of this chapter.

[68 FR 64969, Nov. 17, 2003]

Subpart 229.800—List of Industry Guides

§229.801 Securities Act industry guides.

(a)-(b) [Reserved]

(c) *Guide 3.* Statistical disclosure by bank holding companies.

(d) *Guide 4.* Prospectuses relating to interests in oil and gas programs.

(e) *Guide 5.* Preparation of registration statements relating to interests in real estate limited partnerships.

(f) *Guide 6. Disclosures concerning unpaid claims and claim adjustment expenses of property-casualty insurance underwriters.*

(g) *Guide 7.* Description of Property by Issuers Engaged or To Be Engaged in Significant Mining Operations.

[47 FR 11401, Mar. 16, 1982, and 49 FR 47600, Dec. 6, 1984, as amended at 57 FR 36466, Aug. 13, 1992; 61 FR 30401, June 14, 1996; 74 FR 2193, Jan. 14, 2009]

(2)每股(或每单位)平均买入价格[(b)栏];

(3)作为公开宣布的回购计划或项目的一部分而买入的股份(或单位)总数[(c)栏];及

(4)根据该计划或项目未来将买入的最大数量(或大致美元价值)[(d)栏]。

关于第703条第(b)(3)款和第(b)(4)款的说明:1.在本表中披露所有公开宣布的计划或项目的合计信息。

2.在表格脚注中注明:

a.每一计划或项目的宣布日期;

b.获批的金额(或股份或单位金额);

c.每一计划或项目的到期日(如有);

d. 本表格覆盖期间内到期的每一计划或项目;及

e.发行人已经决定提前终止的每一计划或项目,或发行人无意继续买入证券的计划或项目。

关于第703条的说明:披露本条规定涉及的所有买入,包括不满足本章第240.10b-18节安全港条件的买入。

[《联邦公报》第68卷第64969页,2003年11月17日。]

第229.800子部分——行业指引清单

第229.801节 《证券法》行业指引

(a)~(b)[保留]

(c)指引3。银行控股公司的统计数据披露。

(d)指引4。与石油和天然气项目权益相关的招募说明书。

(e)指引5。与房地产有限合伙权益相关的注册说明书之编制。

(f)指引6。与财险承保人未付理赔和理赔费用准备金有关的披露。

(g)指引7。从事或将从事重大采矿业务的发行人的财产说明。

[《联邦公报》第47卷第11401页,1982年3月16日,及《联邦公报》第49卷第47600页,1984年12月6日,修正索引:《联邦公报》第57卷第36466页,1992年8月13日;《联邦公报》第61卷第30401页,1996年6月14日;《联邦公报》第74卷第2193页,2009年1月14日。]

§ 229.802 Exchange Act industry guides.

(a)-(b) [Reserved]

(c) *Guide 3.* Statistical disclosure by bank holding companies.

(d) *Guide 4.* Disclosures concerning unpaid claims and claim adjustment expenses of property-casualty underwriters.

(e)-(f) [Reserved]

(g) *Guide 7.* Description of Property by Issuers Engaged or To Be Engaged in Significant Mining Operations.

[47 FR 11401, Mar. 16, 1982, as amended at 49 FR 47600, Dec. 6, 1984; 57 FR 36468, Aug. 13, 1992; 61 FR 30401, June 14, 1996; 74 FR 2193, Jan. 14, 2009]

Subpart 229.900—Roll-Up Transactions

Source: 56 FR 57247, Nov. 8, 1991, unless otherwise noted.

§229.901(Item 901) Definitions.

For the purposes of this subpart 229.900:

(a) *General partner* means the person or persons responsible under state law for managing or directing the management of the business and affairs of a partnership that is the subject of a roll-up transaction including, but not limited to, the general partner(s), board of directors, board of trustees, or other person(s) having a fiduciary duty to such partnership.

(b)(1) *Partnership* means any:

(i) Finite-life limited partnership; or

(ii) Other finite-life entity.

(2)(i) Except as provided in paragraph (b)(2)(ii) of this Item (§229.901(b)(2)(ii)), a limited partnership or other entity is "finite-life" if:

(A) It operates as a conduit vehicle for investors to participate in the ownership of assets for a limited period of time; and

(B) It has as a policy or purpose distributing to investors proceeds from the sale, financing or refinancing of assets or cash from operations, rather than reinvesting such proceeds or cash in the business (whether for the term of the entity or after an initial period of time following commencement of operations).

(ii) A real estate investment trust as defined in I.R.C. section 856 is not *finite-life* solely because of the distribution to investors of net income as provided by the I.R.C. if its

第229.802节　《交易法》行业指引

(a)~(b)[保留]

(c)指引3。银行控股公司的统计数据披露。

(d)指引4。与财险承保人未付理赔和理赔费用准备金有关的披露。

(e)~(f)[保留]

(g)指引7。从事或将从事重大采矿业务的发行人的财产说明。

[联邦公报》第47卷第11401页,1982年3月16日,修正索引:《联邦公报》第49卷第47600页,1984年12月6日;《联邦公报》第57卷第36468页,1992年8月13日;《联邦公报》第61卷第30401页,1996年6月14日;《联邦公报》第74卷第2193页,2009年1月14日。]

第229.900子部分——并购重组交易

行政规则来源:《联邦公报》第56卷第57247页,1991年11月8日,除非另有说明。

第229.901节(第901条)　定义

就本第229.900子部分而言:

(a)"普通合伙人"系指依据州法律,负责管理作为并购重组交易主体的合伙的业务和事务的人,或负责指导该等管理的人,包括但不限于普通合伙人、董事会、理事会或其他对合伙承担受信义务的人。

(b)(1)"合伙"系指以下任何一种企业:

(i)固定经营期限的有限合伙;或

(ii)其他固定经营期限的实体。

(2)(i)除本条第(b)(2)(ii)款[第229.901(b)(2)(ii)节]规定的情形外,满足以下条件的有限合伙或其他实体可认定为"固定经营期限"的实体:

(A)该实体只在有限的期间内充当投资工具,使投资者能够分享对资产的所有权;及

(B)根据该实体的政策或目的,在实体存续期间或在经营启动的初始期间届满之后,资产出售、融资、再融资所获得的收益或营业现金收入将用于向投资者进行分配,而不是用于对企业的再投资。

(ii)对于《国内税收法典》第856条定义的房地产投资信托,如果其未订立上述政策或目的——即将资产出售、融资、再融资所获得的收益或营业现金收入用于向投资

policies or purposes do not include the distribution to investors of proceeds from the sale, financing or refinancing of assets, rather than the reinvestment of such proceeds in the business.

(3) *Partnership* does not include any entity registered under the Investment Company Act of 1940 (15 U.S.C. 80a–1 *et seq.*) or any Business Development Company as defined in section 2(a)(48) of that Act (15 U.S.C. 80a–2(a)(48)).

(c)(1) Except as provided in paragraph (c)(2) or (c)(3) of this Item, (§229.901 (c)(2) or (c)(3)) *roll–up transaction* means a transaction involving the combination or reorganization of one or more partnerships, directly or indirectly, in which some or all of the investors in any of such partnerships will receive new securities, or securities in another entity.

(2) Notwithstanding paragraph (c)(1) of this Item, (§229.901 (c)(1)) *roll –up transaction* shall not include:

(i) A transaction wherein the interests of all of the investors in each of the partnerships are repurchased, recalled, or exchanged in accordance with the terms of the preexisting partnership agreement for securities in an operating company specifically identified at the time of the formation of the original partnership;

(ii) A transaction in which the securities to be issued or exchanged are not required to be and are not registered under the Securities Act of 1933 (15 U.S.C. 77a *et seq.*);

(iii) A transaction that involves only issuers that are not required to register or report under Section 12 of the Securities Exchange Act of 1934 (15 U.S.C. 78 *l*), both before and after the transaction;

(iv) A transaction that involves the combination or reorganization of one or more partnerships in which a non–affiliated party succeeds to the interests of a general partner or sponsor, if:

(A) Such action is approved by not less than 662/3% of the outstanding units of each of the participating partnerships; and

(B) As a result of the transaction, the existing general partners will receive only compensation to which they are entitled as expressly provided for in the preexisting partnership agreements;

(v) A transaction in which the securities offered to investors are securities of another entity that are reported under a transaction reporting plan declared effective before December 17, 1993 by the Commission under Section 11A of the Securities Exchange Act of 1934 (15 U.S.C. 78k–1), if:

(A) Such other entity was formed, and such class of securities was reported and regularly traded, not less than 12 months before the date on which soliciting material is mailed to investors; and

者进行分配,而不是用于对企业的再投资,则不得仅因为其需要按照《国内税收法典》的规定向投资者分配净收益而被认定为“固定经营期限”的实体。

(3)“合伙”不包括依据《1940年投资公司法》(《美国法典》第十五编第80a-1节及其后条文)注册的任何实体或该法第2(a)(48)条[《美国法典》第十五编第80a-2(a)(48)节]定义的任何“企业发展支持公司”。

(c)(1)除本条第(c)(2)款或第(c)(3)款[第229.901(c)(2)节或第229.901(c)(3)条]规定的情形外,“并购重组交易”指直接或间接涉及一家或一家以上合伙合并或重组的交易,并且在交易中,任何一家合伙的部分或全部投资者将获得新发行证券或另一个实体的证券。

(2)无论本节第(c)(1)款[第229.901(c)(1)节]如何规定,“并购重组交易”均不应包括下述情形下的交易:

(i)根据已经订立的合伙协议,投资者对合伙的所有权益均将被回购、撤销或交换,从而获得原合伙成立之时明确指定的一家经营公司的证券;

(ii)交易中发行或交换的证券不必且并未按照《1933年证券法》(《美国法典》第十五编第77a节及其后条文)进行注册;

(iii)交易中涉及的所有发行人均无义务根据《1934年证券交易法》第12条(《美国法典》第十五编第78*l*节)的规定进行注册或报告;

(iv)交易涉及一家或多家合伙的合并或重组,并且非关联方将通过交易继受普通合伙人或发起人的权益,且:

(A)该交易已获得每一参加交易的合伙持有不少于2/3(66%)发行在外的权益单位的合伙人批准;

(B)交易完成后,现有普通合伙人只能获得原合伙协议中已明确约定的补偿;

(v)交易中向投资者提供的证券属于另一个实体的证券,且该等证券已按照证券交易委员会根据《1934年证券交易法》的第11A条(《美国法典》第十五编第78k-1节)在1993年12月17日之前宣布有效的交易报告计划进行了报告,且:

(A)在招揽材料邮寄给投资者之前,上述另一实体成立的时间以及该类别证券的报告和正常交易时间不少于12个月;

(B) The securities of that entity issued to investors in the transaction do not exceed 20% of the total outstanding securities of the entity, exclusive of any securities of such class held by or for the account of the entity or a subsidiary of the entity; and

(C) For purposes of paragraph (c)(2)(v) of this Item (§229.901(c)(2)(v)), a *regularly traded* security means any security with a minimum closing price of $2.00 or more for a majority of the business days during the preceding three-month period and a six-month minimum average daily trading volume of 1,000 shares;

(vi) A transaction in which all of the investors' partnership securities are reported under a transaction reporting plan declared effective before December 17, 1993 by the Commission under Section 11A of the Securities Exchange Act of 1934 (15 U.S.C. 78k-1) and such investors receive new securities or securities in another entity that are reported under a transaction reporting plan declared effective before December 17, 1993 by the Commission under Section 11A of the Securities Exchange Act of 1934 (15 U.S.C. 78k-1), except that, for purposes of this paragraph, securities that are reported under a transaction reporting plan declared effective before December 17, 1993 by the Commission under Section 11A of the Securities Exchange Act of 1934 shall not include securities listed on the American Stock Exchange's Emerging Company Marketplace;

(vii) A transaction in which the investors in any of the partnerships involved in the transaction are not subject to a significant adverse change with respect to voting rights, the terms of existence of the entity, management compensation or investment objectives; or

(viii) A transaction in which all investors are provided an option to receive or retain a security under substantially the same terms and conditions as the original issue.

(3) The Commission, upon written request or upon its own motion, may exempt by rule or order any security or class of securities, any transaction or class of transactions, or any person or class of persons, in whole or in part, conditionally or unconditionally, from the definition of roll-up transaction or the requirements imposed on roll-up transactions by Items 902-915 of Regulation S-K (§§229.902-229.915), if it finds such action to be consistent with the public interest and the protection of investors.

(d) *Sponsor* means the person proposing the roll-up transaction.

(e) *Successor* means the surviving entity after completion of the roll-up transaction or the entity whose securities are being offered or sold to, or acquired by, limited partners of the partnerships or the limited partnerships to be combined or reorganized.

Instruction to Item 901. If a transaction is a roll-up transaction as defined in Item 901(c) of this subpart (§229.901(c)), the requirements of this subpart apply to each entity proposed to be included in the roll-up transaction, whether or not the entity is a "partnership" as defined in Item 901(b) of this subpart (§229.901(b)).

[56 FR 57247, Nov. 8, 1991, as amended at 59 FR 63682, Dec. 8, 1994]

(B)在交易中向投资者发行的该实体的证券,不超过该实体所有发行在外的证券(不包括该实体或其子公司自己持有的或为其账户下持有的证券)的20%;且

(C)就本条第(c)(2)(v)款[第229.901(c)(2)(v)节]而言,“正常交易”的证券系指之前3个月中的大部分营业日,最低收盘价不低于2美元且之前6个月的日均成交量不低于1000股的所有证券;

(vi)交易中所有投资者的合伙证券均已按照证券交易委员会根据《1934年证券交易法》第11A条(《美国法典》第十五编第78k-1节)在1993年12月17日之前宣布有效的交易报告计划进行了报告;而且上述投资者在交易中获得的新发行证券或另一个实体的证券已按照证券交易委员会根据《1934年证券交易法》第11A条(《美国法典》第十五编第78k-1节)在1993年12月17日之前宣布有效的交易报告计划进行了报告;但是,就本款而言,按照证券交易委员会根据《1934年证券交易法》第11A条(《美国法典》第十五编第78k-1节)在1993年12月17日之前宣布有效的交易报告计划进行报告的证券不包括在美国证券交易所新兴公司市场板块上市的证券;

(vii)交易中所涉及的任何一家合伙的投资者均不会在表决权、实体存续期限、管理层报酬或投资目标方面遭受重大不利变更;或者

(viii)交易中的所有投资者都获得了相应期权,可以按照与原发行大体相同的条款和条件获得或保留证券。

(3)证券交易委员会认定豁免符合公共利益和投资者保护原则的行为,可以主动或按照相关人提出的书面请求,发布规则或命令,有条件或无条件地,全部或部分地将任何证券、交易或主体或任何类别的证券、交易或主体豁免于并购重组交易的定义或《S-K管理办法》的第902~915条(第229.902~229.915节)就并购重组交易施加的要求。

(d)“发起人”系指提议开展并购重组交易的主体。

(e)“存续实体”系指并购重组交易完成后仍然存续的实体,或向参与合并或重组的合伙或有限合伙的有限合伙人要约、出售或提供证券的实体。

关于第901条的说明。如果某一交易属于本子部分第901(c)条[第229.901(c)节]所定义的并购重组交易,则本子部分的要求应适用于拟加入并购重组交易的每一实体,无论该实体是否为本子部分第901(b)条[第229.901(b)节]所定义的“合伙”。

[《联邦公报》第56卷第57247页,1991年11月8日,修正索引:《联邦公报》第59卷第

§229.902(Item 902) Individual partnership supplements.

(a) If two or more entities are proposed to be included in the roll-up transaction, provide the information specified in this Item (§229.902) in a separate supplement to the disclosure document for each entity.

(b) The separate supplement required by paragraph (a) of this Item (§229.902) shall be filed as part of the registration statement, shall be delivered with the prospectus to investors in the partnership covered thereby, and shall include:

(1) A statement in the forepart of the supplement to the effect that:

(i) Supplements have been prepared for each partnership;

(ii) The effects of the roll-up transaction may be different for investors in the various partnerships; and

(iii) Upon receipt of a written request by an investor or his representative who has been so designated in writing, a copy of any supplement will be transmitted promptly, without charge, by the general partner or sponsor.

This statement must include the name and address of the person to whom investors should make their request.

(2) A brief description of each material risk and effect of the roll-up transaction, including, but not limited to, federal income tax consequences, for investors in the partnership, with appropriate cross references to the discussions of the risks, effects and tax consequences of the roll-up transaction required in the principal disclosure document pursuant to Items 904 and 915 of this subpart (§229.904 and §229.915). Such discussion shall address the effect of the roll-up transaction on the partnership's financial condition and results of operations.

(3) A statement concerning whether the general partner reasonably believes that the roll-up transaction is fair or unfair to investors in the partnership, together with a brief discussion of the bases for such belief, with appropriate cross references to the discussion of the fairness of the roll-up transaction required in the principal disclosure document pursuant to Item 910 of this subpart (§229.910). If there are material differences between the fairness analysis for the partnership and for the other partnerships, such differences shall be described briefly in the supplement.

(4) A brief, narrative description of the method of calculating the value of the partnership and allocating interests in the successor to the partnership, and a table showing such calculation and allocation. Such table shall include the following information (or other information of a comparable character necessary to a thorough understanding of the calculation and allocation):

(i) The appraised value of each separately appraised significant asset (as defined in

63682页，1994年12月8日。］

第229.902节（第902条） 具体合伙的补充材料

（a）如果两个（含）以上的实体拟加入并购重组交易，应在每个实体的披露文件之外，通过单独的补充材料提供本条（第229.902节）明确规定的信息。

（b）本条（第229.902节）第（a）款要求提供的单独补充材料应作为注册说明书的一部分提交，并与向相关合伙投资者发出的招募说明书一同交付，并应包括：

（1）一份声明，安排在补充材料的开篇部分，说明如下内容：

（i）已针对每家合伙编制了相应的补充材料；

（ii）对不同合伙的投资者，并购重组交易的影响可能不同；且

（iii）在收到投资者或其书面指定的代表递交的书面请求后，普通合伙人或发起人将及时、免费向其发送任何补充材料的复本。

声明中必须列明接收投资者请求之主体的姓名/名称和地址。

（2）一份关于并购重组交易对合伙投资者具有的每一项重大风险和影响的简要说明（包括但不限于联邦所得税的影响），同时应适当引用根据本子部分第904条和第915条（第229.904节和第229.915节）应于主要披露文件中提供的关于并购重组交易的风险、后果及税收影响的论述。该等论述应阐述并购重组交易对合伙财务状况和经营成果的影响。

（3）一份关于普通合伙人合理地认为并购重组交易对合伙投资者是否公平的陈述，以及普通合伙人作出该等判断的基础的简短讨论，同时应适当地交叉引用根据本子部分第910条（第229.910节）应于主要披露文件中提供的关于并购重组交易公允性的论述。如果对某家合伙和其他合伙的公允性分析结果存在重大差异，应于补充材料中简要说明。

（4）一份关于计算合伙价值的方法以及向合伙分配存续实体权益的方法的简短文字说明，以及一份列明该等计算结果和分配结果的表格。上述表格中应包含下列信息（或透彻理解计算和分配所需的具有可比特征的其他信息）：

（i）合伙持有的每项单独估价的重大资产｛定义见本子部分第911（c）（5）条［第

Item 911(c)(5) of this subpart (§229.911(c)(5)) held by the partnership, or, if appraisals have not been obtained for each significant asset, the value assigned for purposes of the valuation of the partnership to each significant asset for which an appraisal has not been obtained;

(ii) The dollar amount of any mortgages or other similar liabilities to which each of such assets is subject;

(iii) Cash and cash equivalent assets held by the partnership;

(iv) Other assets held by the partnership;

(v) Other liabilities of the partnership;

(vi) The value assigned to the partnership;

(vii) The value assigned to the partnership per interest held by investors in the partnership (on an equivalent interest basis, such as per $1,000 original investment);

(viii) The aggregate number of interests in the successor to be allocated to the partnership and the percentage of the total interests of the successor;

(ix) The number of interests in the successor to be allocated to investors in the partnership for each interest held by such investors (on an equivalent interest basis, such as per $1,000 original investment); and

(x) The value assigned to the general partner's interest in the partnership, and the number of interests in the successor or other consideration to be allocated in the roll-up transaction to the general partner for such general partnership interest or otherwise as compensation or reimbursement for claims against or interests in the partnership, such as foregone fees, unearned fees and for fees to be earned on the sale or refinancing of an asset.

(5) The amounts of compensation paid, and cash distributions made, to the general partner and its affiliates by the partnership for the last three fiscal years and the most recently completed interim period and the amounts that would have been paid if the compensation and distributions structure to be in effect after the roll-up transaction had been in effect during such period. If any proposed change(s) in the business or operations of the successor after the roll-up transaction would change materially the compensation and distributions that would have been paid by the successor (e.g., if properties will be sold or purchased after the roll-up transaction and no properties were sold or purchased during the period covered by the table), describe such changes and the effects thereof on the compensation and distributions to be paid by the successor.

(6) Cash distributions made to investors during each of the last five fiscal years and most recently completed interim period, identifying any such distributions which represent a return of capital.

(7) An appropriate cross reference to selected financial information concerning the

229.911（c）（5）节］｝的评估价值，如未对每一项重大资产进行评估，则应提供对合伙进行估值时未评估的每项重大资产指定的价值；

（ii）上述每项资产上设定的任何抵押或其他类似责任的金额；

（iii）合伙所持有的现金和现金等价资产；

（iv）合伙持有的其他资产；

（v）合伙的其他负债；

（vi）合伙的指定价值；

（vii）合伙投资者持有的每一份权益的指定价值（以同等的权益单位为基础进行指定，如以每1000美元的原始投资为基础进行指定）；

（viii）分配给合伙的存续实体权益的总数及其占存续实体总权益的百分比；

（ix）合伙投资者基于其持有的每项权益获得分配的存续实体权益的数量（以相等的权益单位为基础进行分配，如以每1000美元的原始投资为基础进行分配）；及

（x）普通合伙人在合伙中持有的权益的指定价值，以及并购重组交易中为了获取普通合伙人的合伙权益，或者为了赔偿或补偿针对合伙提出的权利主张或对合伙拥有的权益（如放弃的费用、预收费用以及资产出售或再融资将获得的费用），而应在交易中分配给普通合伙人的存续实体权益的数量或其他对价。

（5）合伙在过去3个会计年度和最近结束的中期期间向普通合伙人及其关联方支付的报酬金额和提供的现金分配，以及假设并购重组交易在上述期间之前生效的情形下，按交易生效后的报酬和分配结构在上述期间内应向普通合伙人及其关联方支付的金额。如果拟在并购重组交易发生后对存续实体的业务或经营进行变动，且该等变动将对存续实体本应支付的报酬和进行的分配造成重大影响（如并购重组交易后将出售或购买资产，而在表格所覆盖的期间内没有出售或购买任何资产），应说明该等变动及其对存续实体将支付的报酬和进行的分配的影响。

（6）过去5个会计年度内每一会计年度以及最近结束的中期期间分配给投资者的现金，并应明确指出所有属于资本回报的分配项。

（7）适当交叉引用根据本子部分第914（b）（2）条［第229.914（b）（2）节］的相关要

partnership and the pro forma financial statements included in the principal disclosure document in response to Item 914(b)(2) of this subpart (§229.914(b)(2)).

§229.903(Item 903) Summary

(a) Provide in the forepart of the disclosure document a clear, concise and comprehensible summary of the roll-up transaction.

(b) The summary required by paragraph (a) of this Item (§229.903) shall include a summary description of each of the following items, as well as any other material terms or consequences of the roll-up transaction necessary to an understanding of such transaction:

(1) Each material risk and effect on investors, including, but not limited to:

(i) Changes in the business plan, voting rights, cash distribution policies, form of ownership interest or management compensation;

(ii) The general partner's conflicts of interest in connection with the roll-up transaction and in connection with the successor's future operations; and

(iii) The likelihood that securities received by investors in the roll-up transaction will trade at prices substantially below the value assigned to such securities in the roll-up transaction and/or the value of the successor's assets;

(2) The material terms of the roll-up transaction, including the valuation method used to allocate securities in the successor to investors in the partnerships;

(3) Whether the general partner reasonably believes that the roll-up transaction is fair or unfair to investors in each partnership, including a brief discussion of the bases for such belief;

(4) Any opinion from an outside party concerning the fairness of the roll-up transaction, including whether the opinion addresses the fairness of all possible combinations of partnerships or portions of partnerships, and contacts with any outside party concerning fairness opinions, valuations or reports in connection with the roll-up transaction required to be disclosed pursuant to Item 911 (a) (5) of this subpart (§229.911(a)(5));

(5) The background of and reasons for the roll-up transaction, as well as alternatives to the roll-up transaction described in response to Item 908 (b) of this subpart (§229.908 (b));

(6) Rights of investors to exercise dissenters' or appraisal rights or similar rights and to obtain a list of investors in the partnership in which the investor holds an interest; and

(7) If any affiliates of the general partner or the sponsor may participate in the business of the successor or receive compensation from the successor, an organizational chart showing the relationships between the general partner, the sponsor and their affiliates.

Instruction to Item 903. The description of the material risks and effects of the roll-

求,应于主要披露文件中披露的与合伙相关的择要列示的财务信息以及备考财务报表。

第229.903节(第903条) 摘要

(a)在披露文件的开篇,清晰、简洁、全面地提供并购重组交易的摘要信息。

(b)在本条(第229.903节)第(a)款要求提供的摘要中,应对下述每一项进行摘要说明,并简要说明理解并购重组交易所需的任何其他重大交易条款或后果:

(1)投资者所面临的每项重大风险及影响,包括但不限于:

(i)商业计划、表决权、现金分配政策、所有权形式或管理层报酬的变化;

(ii)普通合伙人存在的与并购重组交易和与存续实体未来经营相关的利益冲突;及

(iii)并购重组交易中投资者获得的证券之交易价格明显低于并购重组交易中该等证券的指定价值和/或存续实体的资产价值的可能;

(2)并购重组交易的重大条款,包括将存续实体证券分配给合伙投资者时使用的估值方法;

(3)普通合伙人是否合理地认为并购重组交易对每家合伙的投资者都是公平的,包括对普通合伙人作出该种判断的依据进行简要论述;

(4)外部当事方关于并购重组交易公允性的所有意见,包括这些意见是否涵盖了合伙或部分合伙可能的全部组合、与公允意见相关的任何外部当事方的联系信息,以及根据本子部分第911(a)(5)条[第229.911(a)(5)节]应予披露的与并购重组交易相关的估值和报告;

(5)并购重组交易的背景和原因,以及按照本子部分第908(b)条[第229.908(b)节]的要求对并购重组交易作出的替代方案;

(6)投资者行使异议权、评估权或者类似权利的权利,以及获得持有合伙权益的投资者名单的权利;及

(7)显示普通合伙人、发起人及其任何关联方之间关系的组织结构图,条件是普通合伙人或发起人的任何关联方可能参与存续实体的业务或接受存续实体提供的报酬。

关于第903条的说明。关于本条(第229.903节)第(b)(1)款要求提供的关于并购重

up transaction required by paragraph (b)(1) of this Item (§229.903) must be presented prominently in the forepart of the summary.

§229.904(Item 904) Risk factors and other considerations.

(a) Immediately following the summary required by Item 903 of this subpart (§229.903), describe in reasonable detail each material risk and effect of the roll-up transaction on investors in each partnership, including, but not limited to:

(1) The potential risks, adverse effects and benefits of the roll-up transaction for investors and for the general partner, including those which result from each matter described in response to Item 905 of this subpart (§229.905), with appropriate cross references to the comparative information required by Item 905;

(2) The material risks arising from an investment in the successor; and

(3) The likelihood that securities of the successor received by investors in the roll-up transaction will trade in the securities markets at a price substantially below the value assigned to such securities in the roll-up transaction and/or the value of the assets of the successor, and the effects on investors of such a trading market discount.

(b) Quantify each risk or effect to the extent practicable.

(c) State whether any of such risks or effects may be different for investors in any partnership and, if so, identify such partnership(s) and describe such difference(s).

Instruction to Item 904. The requirement to quantify the effects of the roll-up transaction shall include, but not be limited to:

(i) If cost savings resulting from combined administration of the partnerships is identified as a potential benefit of the roll-up transaction, the amount of cost savings and a comparison of such amount to the costs of the roll-up transaction; and

(ii) If there may be a material conflict of interest of the sponsor or general partner arising from its receipt of payments or other consideration as a result of the roll-up transaction, the amount of such payments and other consideration to be obtained in the roll-up transaction and a comparison of such amounts to the amounts to which the sponsor or general partner would be entitled without the roll-up transaction.

§229.905(Item 905) Comparative information.

(a)(1) Describe the voting and other rights of investors in the successor under the successor's governing instruments and under applicable law. Compare such rights to the voting and other rights of investors in each partnership subject to the transaction under the partnerships' governing instruments and under applicable law. Describe the effects of the change(s) in such rights.

(2) Describe the duties owed by the general partner of the successor to investors in the successor under the successor's governing instruments and under applicable law. Compare such duties to the duties owed by the general partner of each partnership to

组交易重大风险和影响的说明,必须在摘要的开篇以显著方式列明。

第229.904节(第904条) 风险因素和其他考量因素

(a)紧接本子部分第903条(第229.903节)要求提供的摘要之后,以合理详细的程度说明并购重组交易为每家合伙的投资者带来的每一项重大风险和影响,包括但不限于:

(1)并购重组交易中投资者和普通合伙人可能面临或获得的潜在风险、负面影响以及收益,包括本子部分第905条(第229.905节)规定的每一事项产生的潜在风险、负面影响及收益,同时应适当交叉引用第905条要求提供的比较信息;

(2)对存续实体进行投资产生的重大风险;及

(3)并购重组交易中投资者获得的证券之交易价格将明显低于并购重组交易中该等证券的指定价值和/或存续实体的资产价值的可能性,以及该等交易市场折价对投资者的影响。

(b)在可行范围内对每一风险和影响进行量化。

(c)说明并购重组交易是否会对任何一家合伙的投资者产生不同的风险和影响,如果产生不同的风险和影响,应指明该等合伙并说明不同之处。

关于第904条的说明。量化并购重组交易影响的要求包括但不限于:

(i)如果合伙的合并管理带来的成本节约被认为是并购重组交易潜在的利益之一,应说明成本节约的金额以及该等金额与并购重组交易成本之比较结果;及

(ii)如果发起人或普通合伙人因并购重组交易而接收的付款或对价可能引发重大利益冲突,应说明其将从并购重组交易中获得的该等付款或其他对价的金额,以及该等金额与发起人或普通合伙人在未发生并购重组交易的情况下本有权获得的金额之比较结果。

第229.905节(第905条) 比较信息

(a)(1)说明根据存续实体的章程性文件和适用法,存续实体投资者所拥有的表决权和其他权利。将该等权利与参与并购重组交易的每家合伙的投资者根据相应合伙的章程性文件和适用法所拥有的表决权和其他权利进行对比。说明该等权利变化的影响。

(2)说明根据存续实体的章程性文件和适用法,存续实体的普通合伙人对存续实体投资者承担的责任。将该等责任与每家合伙的普通合伙人根据相应合伙的章程性文件和适用法对合伙投资者承担的责任进行对比。说明该等责任变化的影响。

investors in the partnership under the partnership's governing instruments and under applicable law. Describe the effects of the change(s) in such duties.

(b)(1) Describe each item of compensation (including reimbursement of expenses) payable by the successor after the roll-up transaction to the general partner and its affiliates or to any affiliate of the successor. Compare such compensation to the compensation currently payable to the general partner and its affiliates by each partnership. Describe the effects of the change(s) in compensation arrangements.

(2) Describe each instance in which cash or other distributions may be made by the successor to the general partner and its affiliates or to any affiliate of the successor. Compare such distributions to the distributions currently paid or payable to the general partner and its affiliates by each partnership. Describe the effects of the change(s) in distribution arrangements. If distributions similar to those currently paid or payable by any partnership to the general partner or its affiliates will not be made by the successor, state whether or not other compensation arrangements with the successor described in response to paragraph (b)(1) of this Item (§229.905) (e.g., incentive fees payable upon sale of a property) will, in effect, replace such distributions.

(3) Provide a table demonstrating the changes in such compensation and distributions setting forth among other things:

(i) The actual amounts of compensation and distributions, separately identified, paid by the partnerships on a combined basis to the general partner and its affiliates for the partnerships' last three fiscal years and most recently ended interim periods; and

(ii) The amounts of compensation and distributions that would have been paid if the compensation and distributions structure to be in effect after the roll-up transaction had been in effect during such period.

(4) If any proposed change(s) in the business or operations of the successor after the roll-up transaction would change materially the compensation and distributions that would have been paid by the successor from that shown in the table provided in response to paragraph (b)(3)(ii) of this Item (§229.905) (e.g., if properties will be sold or purchased after the roll-up transaction and no properties were sold or purchased during the period covered by the table), describe such changes and the effects thereof on the compensation and distributions to be paid by the successor.

(5) Describe the material conflicts that may arise between the interests of the sponsor or general partner and the interests of investors in the successor as a result of the compensation and distribution arrangements described in response to paragraphs (b)(1) and (2) of this Item (§229.905) and describe any steps that will be taken to resolve any such conflicts.

(c) Describe any provisions in the governing instruments of the successor and any

(b)(1)说明并购重组交易完成后,存续实体应向普通合伙人及其关联方或向存续实体的任何关联方支付的每一项报酬(包括费用报销)。将该等报酬与当前每家合伙应向普通合伙人及其关联方支付的报酬进行对比。说明该等报酬安排变化的影响。

(2)说明存续实体可以向普通合伙人及其关联方或向存续实体的任何关联方进行现金分配或其他分配的每一种情况。将该等分配情况与当前每家合伙向普通合伙人及其关联方已进行或应进行分配的情况进行对比。说明该等分配安排变化的影响。如果存续实体不会按照合伙当前向或应向普通合伙人或其关联方支付的分配进行类似分配,说明存续实体是否会按照本条(第229.905节)第(b)(1)款的要求实施其他补偿计划(如在出售资产时支付激励费),作为此类分配之替代。

(3)提供一份表格,列明该等报酬和分配的变化,包括但不限于:

(i)分别说明各合伙在过去3个会计年度以及最近结束的中期期间内向普通合伙人及其关联方支付的报酬和分配的实际总数额;及

(ii)假设并购重组交易在上述期间之前生效的情形下,按交易生效后的报酬和分配结构在上述期间内应支付的报酬和分配数额。

(4)如果拟在并购重组交易发生后对存续实体的业务或经营进行任何变动,且该等变动将对本条(第229.905节)第(b)(3)(ii)款所述的表格中列明的存续实体本应支付的报酬和进行的分配造成重大影响(如并购重组交易后将出售或购买资产,而在表格所覆盖的期间内没有出售或购买任何资产),应说明该等变动及其对存续实体将支付的报酬和进行的分配的影响。

(5)说明本条(第229.905节)第(b)(1)款和第(b)(2)款所述的报酬和分配计划可能会引发的发起人或普通合伙人与存续实体投资者之间的重大利益冲突,并说明解决这类冲突需要采取的任何措施。

(c)说明存续实体章程性文件中与如下分配相关的任何规定以及存续实体普通合

policies of the general partner of the successor relating to distributions to investors of cash from operations, proceeds from the sale, financing or refinancing of assets, and any other distributions. Compare such provisions and policies to those of each of the partnerships. Describe the effects of any change(s) in such provisions or policies.

(d)(1) Describe each material investment policy of the successor, including, without limitation, policies with respect to borrowings by the successor. Compare such investment policies to the investment policies of each of the partnerships. Describe the effects of any change(s) in such policies.

(2) Describe any plans of the general partner, sponsor or of any person who will be an affiliate of the successor with respect to:

(i) A sale of any material assets of the partnerships;

(ii) A purchase of any material assets; and

(iii) Borrowings.

(3)(i) State whether or not specific assets have been identified for sale, financing, refinancing or purchase following the roll-up transaction.

(ii) If specific assets have been so identified, describe the assets and the proposed transaction.

(e) Describe any other similar terms or policies of the successor that are material to an investment in the successor. Compare any such terms or policies to those of each of the partnerships. Describe the effects of any change(s) in any such terms or policies.

Instructions to Item 905: (1) The information provided in response to this Item (§229.905) should be illustrated in tables or other readily understandable formats, which should be included together with the disclosures required by this Item.

(2) The information required by this Item (§229.905) shall be set forth in appropriate separate sections of the principal disclosure document.

§229.906(Item 906) Allocation of roll-up consideration.

(a) Describe in reasonable detail the method used to allocate interests in the successor to investors in the partnerships and the reasons why such method was used.

(b) Provide a table showing the calculation of the valuation of each partnership and the allocation of interests in the successor to investors. Such table shall include for each partnership the following information (or other information of a comparable character necessary to an understanding of the calculation and allocation):

(1) The value assigned to each significant category of assets of the partnership and the total value assigned to the partnership;

(2) The total value assigned to all partnerships;

(3) The aggregate amount of interests in the successor to be allocated to each partnership and the percentage of the total amount of all such interests represented

伙人与如下分配相关的任何政策:向投资者分配营业现金收入、资产出售收益、资产融资或再融资以及任何其他分配。将该等规定和政策与各合伙的相应规定和政策进行对比。说明任何该等规定或政策变化的影响。

(d)(1)说明存续实体的每一项重大投资政策,包括但不限于与存续实体借贷相关的政策。将该等投资政策与各合伙的投资政策进行对比。说明任何该等政策变化的影响。

(2)说明存续实体的普通合伙人、发起人或任何将构成存续实体关联方的主体与下列事项相关的所有计划:

(i)合伙任何重大资产的出售;

(ii)任何重大资产的购买;及

(iii)借贷。

(3)(i)说明是否已经确定在并购重组交易后进行出售、融资、再融资或购买的资产。

(ii)如果已经确定上述具体资产,对该资产以及拟开展的交易进行说明。

(e)说明对存续实体的投资具有重要意义的任何其他类似条款或政策。将该等条款或政策与各合伙的相应条款和政策进行对比。说明任何该等条款或政策变化的影响。

关于第905条的说明:(1)本条(第229.905节)规定的信息应以表格或其他明了易懂的方式提供,并纳入本条规定的披露内容之中。

(2)本条(第229.905节)规定的信息应在主要披露文件中通过适当的独立条款予以说明。

第229.906节(第906条) 并购重组交易对价的分配

(a)以合理详细程度说明向合伙投资者分配存续实体权益所使用的方法以及采用该方法的理由。

(b)提供一份表格,显示每家合伙的估值计算结果以及向存续企业投资者分配权益的结果。上述表格中应包含关于每家合伙的下列信息(或理解计算和分配所需的具有可比特征的其他信息):

(1)合伙每一类重大资产的指定价值以及合伙的总指定价值;

(2)所有合伙的总指定价值;

(3)分配给每家合伙的存续实体的权益总数及其分别占存续实体总权益的百分比;

thereby; and

(4) The amount of interests of the successor to be issued to investors per interest held in each partnership (on an equivalent interest basis, such as per $1,000 invested).

(c) If interests in the successor will be allocated to the general partner in exchange for its general partner interest or otherwise or if the general partner will receive other consideration in connection with the roll-up transaction:

(1) Describe in reasonable detail the method used to allocate interests in the successor to the general partner or to determine the amount of consideration payable to the general partner and the reasons such method(s) was used; and

(2) Identify the consideration paid by the general partner for interests in the partnerships that will be exchanged in the roll-up transaction.

§229.907(Item 907) Background of the roll-up transaction.

(a)(1) Furnish a summary of the background of the transaction. Such summary shall include, but not be limited to, a description of any contacts, negotiations or transactions concerning any of the following matters:

(i) A merger, consolidation, or combination of any of the partnerships;

(ii) An acquisition of any of the partnerships or a material amount of any of their assets;

(iii) A tender offer for or other acquisition of securities of any class issued by any of the partnerships; or

(iv) A change in control of any of the partnerships.

(2) The summary required by paragraph (a)(1) of this Item shall:

(i) Cover the period beginning with each partnership's second full fiscal year preceding the date of the filing of the roll-up transaction;

(ii) Include contacts, negotiations or transactions between the general partner or its affiliates and any person who would have a direct interest in the matters listed in paragraphs (a)(1)(i)-(iv) of this Item; and

(iii) Identify the person who initiated such contacts, negotiations or transactions.

(b) Briefly describe the background of each partnership, including, but not limited to:

(1) The amount of capital raised from investors, the extent to which net proceeds from the original offering of interests have been invested, the extent to which funds have been invested as planned and the amount not yet invested; and

(2) The partnership's investment objectives and the extent to which the partnership has achieved its investment objectives.

(c) Discuss whether the general partner (including any affiliated person materially dependent on the general partner's compensation arrangement with the partnership) or

(4)存续实体将按照投资者在每家合伙中所持有的权益数向投资者发行的权益额(以相等的权益单位为基础计算,如以每1000美元的原始投资为基础计算)。

(c)如果在并购重组交易中,作为与其持有的普通合伙人权益或其他权益的交换,普通合伙人将分得存续实体的权益,或者获得其他对价:

(1)应以合理的详细程度说明将存续实体权益分配给普通合伙人所使用的方法,或用以确定应向普通合伙人支付的对价数额的方法,以及采用这些方法的理由;及

(2)注明普通合伙人针对该等将在并购重组交易中交换的合伙权益所支付的对价。

第229.907节(第907条) 并购重组交易的背景

(a)(1)提供交易背景摘要。背景摘要中至少应说明与以下任何事项相关的接洽、谈判或交易:

(i)任何合伙的吸收合并、新设合并或业务合并;

(ii)对任何合伙或其任何重大资产的收购;

(iii)对任何合伙发行的任何类别证券提出的证券收购要约或其他收购要约;或

(iv)任何合伙发生的控制权变更。

(2)本条第(a)(1)款要求提供的摘要:

(i)所覆盖的期间应始于各合伙在并购重组交易报告日之前的倒数第二个完整会计年度;

(ii)应涵盖普通合伙人或其关联方与本条第(a)(1)(i)款至第(a)(1)(iv)款所列事项有直接利害关系的任何主体之间开展的接洽、谈判或交易;及

(iii)指明发起此类接洽、谈判和交易的主体的身份。

(b)简要介绍每家合伙的背景,包括但不限于:

(1)从投资者处募集的资本数额、原权益发行所募集的净资金的投资额度,以及该等资金按计划进行投资的额度和尚未投资的数额;及

(2)合伙的投资目标以及合伙对投资目标的实现程度。

(c)论述普通合伙人(包括严重依赖普通合伙人在合伙的报酬安排的所有关联人)或任何合伙自最近结束的会计年度开始以来是否出现了或有可能出现重大不利的财

any partnership has experienced since the commencement of the most recently completed fiscal year or is likely to experience any material adverse financial developments. If so, describe such developments and the effect of the transaction on such matters.

§229.908(Item 908) Reasons for and alternatives to the roll-up transaction.

(a) Describe the reason(s) for the roll-up transaction.

(b)(1) If the general partner or sponsor considered alternatives to the roll-up transaction being proposed, describe such alternative(s) and state the reason(s) for their rejection.

(2) Whether or not described in response to paragraph (b)(1) of this Item (§229.908), describe in reasonable detail the potential alternative of continuation of the partnerships in accordance with their existing business plans, including the effects of such continuation and the material risks and benefits that likely would arise in connection therewith, and, if applicable, the general partner's reasons for not considering such alternative.

(3) Whether or not described in response to paragraph (b)(1) of this Item (§229.908), describe in reasonable detail the potential alternative of liquidation of the partnerships, the procedures required to accomplish liquidation, the effects of liquidation, the material risks and benefits that likely would arise in connection with liquidation, and, if applicable, the general partner's reasons for not considering such alternative.

(c) State the reasons for the structure of the roll-up transaction and for undertaking such transaction at this time.

(d) State whether the general partner initiated the roll-up transaction and, if not, whether the general partner participated in the structuring of the transaction.

(e) State whether the general partner recommends the roll-up transaction and briefly describe the reasons for such recommendation.

§229.909(Item 909) Conflicts of interest.

(a) Briefly describe the general partner's fiduciary duties to each partnership subject to the roll-up transaction and each actual or potential material conflict of interest between the general partner and the investors relating to the roll-up transaction.

(b)(1) State whether or not the general partner has retained an unaffiliated representative to act on behalf of investors for purposes of negotiating the terms of the roll-up transaction. If no such representative has been retained, describe the reasons therefor and the risks arising from the absence of separate representation.

(2) If an unaffiliated representative has been retained to represent investors:

(i) Identify such unaffiliated representative;

(ii) Briefly describe the representative's qualifications, including a brief description of any other transaction similar to the roll-up transaction in which the representative has

务动态。如果已经出现或可能出现重大不利财务动态,应如实说明,并说明交易对该等事项的影响。

第229.908节(第908条) 并购重组交易的原因及替代方案

(a)说明进行并购重组交易的原因。

(b)(1)对于当前提议的并购重组交易,如果普通合伙人或发起人曾考虑替代方案,应说明该替代方案并说明替代方案被拒绝的原因。

(2)无论是否按照本条(第229.908节)第(b)(1)款的要求作出了说明,均应以合理详细的程度说明按照其现有的商业计划继续维持合伙这一可能的替代方案,包括继续维持合伙的影响、替代方案可能带来的重大风险和收益,如果适用,还应说明普通合伙人未考虑该替代方案的原因。

(3)无论是否按照本条(第229.908节)第(b)(1)款的要求作出了说明,均应以合理详细的程度说明对合伙进行清算这一可能的替代方案,并说明完成清算所需的程序、清算的影响、清算可能带来的重大风险和收益,如果适用,还应说明普通合伙人未考虑该替代方案的原因。

(c)说明选定并购重组交易结构的理由以及选择在此时开展并购重组交易的理由。

(d)说明并购重组交易是否由普通合伙人发起,如果不是,普通合伙人是否参与了交易结构的设定。

(e)说明普通合伙人是否建议实施并购重组交易,并简要说明建议的理由。

第229.909节(第909条) 利益冲突

(a)简要说明普通合伙人对涉及并购重组交易的每家合伙承担的受信义务,以及普通合伙人与投资者之间就并购重组交易实际存在或可能发生的每一项重大利益冲突。

(b)(1)说明普通合伙人是否聘请了非关联代表来代表投资者就并购重组交易条款开展谈判。如果没有聘请此等非关联代表,说明理由以及可能引发的风险。

(2)如果已经聘请了非关联方担任投资者代表,应:

(i)指明该非关联代表的身份;

(ii)简要介绍该代表的资格,包括该代表在过去5年内曾以类似身份提供过服务的、与并购重组交易相似的所有其他交易的简要介绍;

served in a similar capacity within the past five years;

(iii) Describe the method of selection of such representative, including a statement as to whether or not any investors were consulted in the selection of the representative and, if so, the names of such investors;

(iv) Describe the scope and terms of the engagement of the representative, including, but not limited to, what party will be responsible for paying the representative's fees and whether such fees are contingent upon the outcome of the roll-up transaction;

(v) Describe any material relationship between the representative or its affiliates and:

(A) The general partner, sponsor, any affiliate of the general partner or sponsor; or

(B) Any other person having a material interest in the roll-up transaction, which existed during the past two years or is mutually understood to be contemplated and any compensation received or to be received as a result of such relationship;

(vi) Describe in reasonable detail the actions taken by the representative on behalf of investors; and

(vii) Describe the fiduciary duties or other legal obligations of the representative to investors in each of the partnerships.

§229.910(Item 910) Fairness of the transaction.

(a) State whether the general partner reasonably believes that the roll-up transaction is fair or unfair to investors and the reasons for such belief. Such discussion must address the fairness of the roll-up transaction to investors in each of the partnerships and as a whole. If the roll-up transaction may be completed with a combination of partnerships consisting of less than all partnerships, or with portions of partnerships, the belief stated must address each possible combination.

(b) Discuss in reasonable detail the material factors upon which the belief stated in paragraph (a) of this Item (§229.910) is based and, to the extent practicable, the weight assigned to each such factor. Such discussion should include an analysis of the extent, if any, to which such belief is based on the factors set forth in Instructions (2) and (3) to this Item (§229.910), paragraph (b)(1) of Item 909 of this subpart (§229.909(b)(1)) and Item 911 of this subpart (§229.911). This discussion also must:

(1) Compare the value of the consideration to be received in the roll-up transaction to the value of the consideration that would be received pursuant to each of the alternatives discussed in response to Item 908(b) of this subpart (§229.908(b)); and

(2) Describe any material differences among the partnerships (e.g., different types of assets or different investment objectives) relating to the fairness of the transaction.

(c) If any offer of the type described in Instruction (2)(viii) to this Item

(iii)说明选任代表的方法,包括一份声明,说明在选择过程中是否咨询了任何投资者的意见,如果是,列明这些投资者的姓名/名称;

(iv)说明委聘代表的范围和协议条款,包括但不限于,将由哪一方负责支付代表的费用以及该等费用是否将取决于合并重组交易的结果;

(v)说明代表或其关联方与下列各方在过去两年内存在或已达成共识的任何重大关系:

(A)普通合伙人、发起人、普通合伙人或发起人的任何关联方;或者

(B)在过去两年内与并购重组交易存在重大利益关联的所有其他主体;同时应说明双方因该等关系而收到或将收到的任何报酬;

(vi)以合理的详细程度说明代表在代表投资者时采取的行动;并

(vii)说明代表对每家合伙的投资者所承担的受信义务或其他法律义务。

第229.910节(第910条) 交易的公允性

(a)说明普通合伙人是否合理地认为并购重组交易对投资者是公平的,以及作出该种判断的理由。关于上述问题的论述必须阐述并购重组交易对每家合伙投资者的公允性以及对全体投资者的公允性。如果可以在不牵涉所有合伙,或只牵涉一部分合伙的情况下完成并购重组交易,必须在普通合伙人的上述判断中阐明合并可能采取的所有形式。

(b)以合理详细程度说明做出本条(第229.910节)第(a)款所述判断所基的主要因素,以及在可行的范围内,说明每项因素所占的权重。应在关于上述问题的论述中,说明上述判断对下述因素的依赖程度(如有):本条(第229.910节)的说明(2)和说明(3)、本子部分第909条第(b)(1)款[第229.909(b)(1)节]和本子部分第911条(第229.911节)所述的各种因素。该等论述必须:

(1)对比下述两者的价值:并购重组交易中将获得的对价价值,以及执行本子部分第908(b)条(第229.908(b)节)所述的每一替代方案时将获得的对价价值;及

(2)说明合伙之间存在的与交易公允性有关的任何重大差别(如不同的资产类型或不同的投资目标)。

(c)如果曾收到本条(第229.910节)第(2)(viii)条说明中所述的任何要约,应说明

(§229.910) has been received, describe such offer and state the reason(s) for its rejection.

(d) Describe any factors known to the general partner that may affect materially the value of the consideration to be received by investors in the roll-up transaction, the values assigned to the partnerships for purposes of the comparisons to alternatives required by paragraph (b) of this Item (§229.910) and the fairness of the transaction to investors.

(e) State whether the general partner's statements in response to paragraphs (a) and (b) of this Item (§229.910) are based, in whole or in part, on any report, opinion or appraisal described in response to Item 911 of this subpart (§229.911). If so, describe any material uncertainties known to the general partner that relate to the conclusions in any such report, opinion or appraisal including, but not limited to, developments or trends that have affected or are reasonably likely to affect materially such conclusions.

Instructions to Item 910: (1) A statement that the general partner has no reasonable belief as to the fairness of the roll-up transaction to investors will not be considered sufficient disclosure in response to paragraph (a) of this Item (§229.910(a)).

(2) The factors which are important in determining the fairness of a roll-up transaction to investors and the weight, if any, which should be given to them in a particular context will vary. Normally such factors will include, among others, those referred to in paragraph (b)(1) of Item 909 (§229.909(b)(1)) and whether the consideration offered to investors constitutes fair value in relation to:

(i) Current market prices, if any;

(ii) Historic market prices, if any;

(iii) Net book value;

(iv) Going concern value;

(v) Liquidation value;

(vi) Purchases of limited partnership interests by the general partner or sponsor or their affiliates since the commencement of the partnership's second full fiscal year preceding the date of filing of the disclosure document for the roll-up transaction;

(vii) Any report, opinion, or appraisal described in Item 911 of this subpart (§229.911); and

(viii) Offers of which the general partner or sponsor is aware made during the preceding eighteen months for a merger, consolidation, or combination of any of the partnerships; an acquisition of any of the partnerships or a material amount of their assets; a tender offer for or other acquisition of securities of any class issued by any of the partnerships; or a change in control of any of the partnerships.

(3) The discussion concerning fairness should specifically address material terms of

该等要约以及要约被拒的理由。

(d)说明普通合伙人已经知悉的,可能对投资者在并购重组交易中获得的对价价值产生重大影响的任何因素,同时说明为比较本条(第229.910节)第(b)款规定的替代方案而为合伙指定的价值,以及交易对投资者的公允性。

(e)说明本条(第229.910节)第(a)款和第(b)款所述之普通合伙人声明是否全部或部分以本子部分第911条(第229.911节)所述的任何报告、意见或评估结果为基础。如果是,说明普通合伙人已经知悉的,与此等报告、意见或评估结果中的结论相关的重大不确定性,包括但不限于已经或根据合理预期可能对结论产生影响的发展情况或态势。

关于第910条的说明:(1)仅仅声明普通合伙人无法就并购重组交易是否对投资者具有公允性形成合理结论,不构成本条第(a)款[(第229.910(a)节]要求的充分披露。

(2)在判断并购重组交易对投资者的公允性时起重要作用的因素及其相应的分量,在不同的情况下会有所不同。在一般情况下,这些因素应包括但不限于第909条第(b)(1)款[第229.909(b)(1)节]所指的因素,并且还应基于如下参数考虑向投资者要约的对价是否构成公允价值:

(i)现行市场价格(如有);
(ii)历史市场价格(如有);
(iii)账面净值;
(iv)持续经营价值;
(v)清算价值;
(vi)自提交并购重组交易披露文件之前的倒数第二个完整会计年度开始后,普通合伙人或发起人或其关联方对有限合伙权益的收购;

(vii)本子部分第911条(第229.911节)所述的任何报告、意见或评估结果;及

(viii)普通合伙人或发起人知悉的,18个月内任何一家合伙被提出的吸收合并、新设合并或要约;对任何一家合伙或其大额资产的收购;对任何一家合伙发行的任何类别的证券提出的股权收购要约或进行的其他收购;或任何一家合伙的控制权变更。

(3)关于公允性的论述应具体论述交易的重大条款,并且还应基于如下参数考虑

the transaction including whether the consideration offered to investors constitutes fair value in relation to:

(i) The form and amount of consideration to be received by investors and the sponsor in the roll-up transaction;

(ii) The methods used to determine such consideration; and

(iii) The compensation to be paid to the sponsor in the future.

(4) Conclusory statements, such as "The roll-up transaction is fair to investors in relation to net book value, going concern value, liquidation value and future prospects of the partnership," will not be considered sufficient disclosure in response to paragraph (b) of this Item (§229.910(b)).

(5) Consideration should be given to presenting the comparative numerical data as to the value of the consideration being received by investors, liquidation value and other values in a tabular format. Financial and other information concerning the partnerships should be prepared based upon the most recent available information, such as, in the case of financial information, the periods covered by interim selected financial information included in the prospectus in accordance with Item 914 of this subpart (§229.914).

§229.911(Item 911) Reports, opinions and appraisals.

(a)(1) *All material reports, opinions or appraisals.* State whether or not the general partner or sponsor has received any report, opinion (other than an opinion of counsel) or appraisal from an outside party which is materially related to the roll-up transaction including, but not limited to, any such report, opinion or appraisal relating to the consideration or the fairness of the consideration to be offered to investors in connection with the roll-up transaction or the fairness of such transaction to the general partner or investors.

(2) With respect to any report, opinion or appraisal described in paragraph (a)(1) of this Item (§229.911);

(i) Identify such outside party;

(ii) Briefly describe the qualifications of such outside party;

(iii) Describe the method of selection of such outside party;

(iv) Describe any material relationship between:

(A) The outside party or its affiliates; and

(B) The general partner, sponsor, the successor or any of their affiliates,which existed during the past two years or is mutually understood to be contemplated and any compensation received or to be received as a result of such relationship;

(v) If such report, opinion or appraisal relates to the fairness of the consideration, state whether the general partner, sponsor or affiliate determined the amount of

向投资者提供的对价是否构成公允价值:

(i)投资者和发起人在并购重组交易中将获得的对价形式和数额;

(ii)确定该等对价时使用的方法;及

(iii)将来需要向发起人支付的报酬。

(4)仅提供结论性声明,如"考虑到账面净值、持续经营价值、清算价值以及合伙的前景,本宗并购重组交易对投资者是公平的",不构成本条第(b)款[(第229.910(b)节]要求的充分披露。

(5)应考虑采用表格的形式列报投资者将获得的对价价值、清算价值和其他价值等比较数据。关于合伙的财务信息和其他信息应基于可获得的最新信息编制,如就财务信息而言,应基于按照本子部分第914条(第229.914节)编制的招募说明书中所包含的择要列示的中期财务信息编制。

第229.911节(第911条) 报告、意见和评估

(a)(1)所有重大报告、意见和评估。说明普通合伙人或发起人是否曾收到外部当事方出具的任何与并购重组交易存在重大关系的报告、意见(非律师意见)或评估,包括但不限于关于任何下列事项的报告、意见或评估结果:并购重组交易中将向投资者提供的对价或者该等对价的公允性;或者此类交易对普通合伙人或投资者而言是否公平。

(2)就本条(第229.911节)第(a)(1)款所述的任何报告、意见或评估结果而言,应:

(i)指明该外部当事方的身份;

(ii)简要介绍该外部当事方的资格;

(iii)说明选择该外部当事方时使用的方法;

(iv)说明以下各方之间过去两年内存在的,或者双方已达成共识的任何重大关系:

(A)外部当事方或其关联方;及

(B)普通合伙人、发起人、存续实体或其任何关联方;同时应说明双方因该等关系而收到或已达成共识将收到的任何报酬;

(v)如果该等报告、意见或评估结果涉及对价的公允性,说明需要支付的对价数额系由普通合伙人、发起人或其关联方确定,或系由外部当事方所建议。

consideration to be paid or whether the outside party recommended the amount of consideration to be paid.

(vi) Furnish a summary concerning such report, opinion or appraisal which shall include, but not be limited to, the procedures followed; the findings and recommendations; the bases for and methods of arriving at such findings and recommendations; instructions received from the general partner, sponsor or its affiliates; and any limitation imposed by the general partner, sponsor or affiliate on the scope of the investigation. If any limitation was imposed by the general partner, sponsor or affiliate on the scope of the investigation, including, but not limited to, access to its personnel, premises, and relevant books and records, state the reasons therefor.

(vii) State whether any compensation paid to such outside party is contingent on the approval or completion of the roll-up transaction and, if so, the reasons for compensating such parties on a contingent basis.

(3) Furnish a statement to the effect that upon written request by an investor or his representative who has been so designated in writing, a copy of any such report, opinion or appraisal shall be transmitted promptly, without charge, by the general partner or sponsor. The statement also must include the name and address of the person to whom investors or their representatives should make their request.

(4) All reports, opinions or appraisals referred to in paragraph (a)(1) of this Item (§229.911) shall be filed as exhibits to the registration statement.

(5)(i) Describe any contacts in connection with the roll-up transaction between the sponsor or the general partner and any outside party with respect to the preparation by such party of an opinion concerning the fairness of the roll-up transaction, a valuation of a partnership or its assets, or any other report with respect to the roll-up transaction. No description is required, however, of contacts with respect to reports, opinions or appraisals filed as exhibits pursuant to paragraph (a)(4) of this Item (§229.911).

(ii) The description of contacts with any outside party required by paragraph (a)(5)(i) of this Item (§229.911) shall include the following:

(A) The identity of each such party;

(B) The nature of the contact;

(C) The actions taken by such party;

(D) Any views, preliminary or final, expressed on the proposed subject matter of the report, opinion or appraisal; and

(E) Any reasons such party did not provide a report, opinion or appraisal.

(b) *Fairness opinions:* (1) If any report, opinion or appraisal relates to the fairness of the roll-up transaction to investors in the partnerships, state whether or not the report, opinion or appraisal addresses the fairness of:

(vi)提供一份关于该等报告、意见或评估结果的摘要,摘要应包括但不限于以下内容:应遵循的程序;认定结果及相关建议;得出该等认定和建议所依据的基础和适用的方法;普通合伙人、发起人或其关联方发出的指示;以及普通合伙人、发起人或关联方对调查范围所施加的任何限制。如果普通合伙人、发起人或关联方对调查范围施加了任何限制,包括但不限于对其人员的接触、设施的访问或相关账册和记录的查阅施加了任何限制,应说明原因。

(vii)说明向该外部当事方支付报酬的先决条件是否为并购重组交易获得批准或成交,如果是,说明采用该种先决条件的理由。

(3)提供一份声明,指出在收到投资者或其书面指定的代表提交的书面请求后,普通合伙人或发起人将及时免费发送任何该等报告、意见或评估结果的一份复本。此声明中还必须列出负责接收投资者或其代表提出的请求之主体姓名/名称和地址。

(4)本条(第229.911节)第(a)(1)款所指的全部报告、意见或评估结果均应作为注册说明书的附录提交。

(5)(i)说明发起人或普通合伙人与任一外部当事方就下述内容进行的接洽:关于并购重组交易公允性的意见之编制、合伙或其资产的评估准备或与并购重组交易相关的任何其他报告之编制。但是,对于根据本条(第229.911节)第(a)(4)款作为附录提交的报告、意见或评估结果,不必就相关接洽提供任何说明。

(ii)本条(第229.911节)第(a)(5)(i)款要求就与任何外部当事方作出之接洽提供的相关说明应包括以下各项:

(A)每一该等外部当事方的身份;

(B)接洽的性质;

(C)该等当事方所采取的行动;

(D)对报告、意见和评估的拟议主题所发表的所有初步或最终观点;及

(E)该外部当事方未提供报告、意见或评估结果的任何原因。

(b)公允性意见:(1)如果任何报告、意见或评估结果涉及并购重组交易对合伙投资者所具有的公允性,说明该等报告、意见或评估结果是否阐述了:

(i) The roll-up transaction as a whole and to investors in each partnership; and

(ii) All possible combinations of partnerships in the roll-up transaction (including portions of partnerships if the transaction is structured to permit portions of partnerships to participate). If all possible combinations are not addressed:

(A) Identify the combinations that are addressed;

(B) Identify the person(s) that determined which combinations would be addressed and state the reasons for the selection of the combinations; and

(C) State that if the roll-up transaction is completed with a combination of partnerships not addressed, no report, opinion or appraisal concerning the fairness of the roll-up transaction will have been obtained.

(2) If the sponsor or the general partner has not obtained any opinion on the fairness of the proposed roll-up transaction to investors in each of the affected partnerships, state the sponsor's or general partner's reasons for concluding that such an opinion is not necessary in order to permit the limited partners or shareholders to make an informed decision on the proposed transaction.

(c) *Appraisals.* If the report, opinion or appraisal consists of an appraisal of the assets of the partnerships:

(1) Describe the purpose(s) for which the appraisals were obtained and their use in connection with the roll-up transaction;

(2) Describe which assets are covered by the appraisals and state the aggregate appraised value of the assets covered by the appraisals (including such value net of associated indebtedness). Provide a description of, and valuation of, any assets subject to any material qualifications by the appraiser and a summary of such qualifications;

(3) Identify the date as of which the appraisals were prepared. State whether and in what circumstances the appraisals will be updated. State whether any events have occurred or conditions have changed since the date of the appraisals that may have caused a material change in the value of the assets;

(4) Include as an appendix to the prospectus one or more tables setting forth the following information:

(i) The appraised value of any separately appraised asset that is significant to the partnership holding such asset;

(ii) If the appraiser considered different valuation approaches in preparing the appraisals of the assets identified in response to paragraph (c)(4)(i) of this Item (§229.911(c)(4)(i)), the value of each such asset under each valuation approach considered by the appraiser, identifying the valuation approach used by the appraiser in determining the appraised value and the reason such approach was chosen; and

(iii) All material assumptions used by the appraiser in appraising the assets

(i)整个并购重组交易的公允性以及对每家合伙的投资者的公允性;及

(ii)并购重组交易中合伙(包括合伙的一部分,条件是交易结构允许合伙的一部分参与交易)所有可能的合并形式。如果没有对所有可能的合并形式进行阐述,则应:

(A)指明进行了阐述合并形式;

(B)指明所阐述的合并是由谁确定的,以及选择这些合并的理由;且

(C)声明如果采用未阐述的合并方式完成并购重组交易,则不会获得关于并购重组交易公允性的报告、意见或评估结果。

(2)如果对于任何拟议的并购重组交易,发起人或普通合伙人没有获得关于该等交易对每家受影响的合伙投资者的公允性的意见,应说明发起人或普通合伙人认为没有该等意见有限合伙人或股东也能对拟议的交易作出知情决定的理由。

(c)评估。如果报告、意见或评估结果为对合伙资产的评估:

(1)说明进行该等评估的目的,以及就并购重组交易而言,该等评估的作用;

(2)说明评估涉及的资产,并注明该等评估所涉资产的估值总额(包括扣除相关负债之后的净值)。对于估价师作出重大保留的任何资产,均应提供相应说明及其估值,以及关于该等保留意见的摘要;

(3)注明评估的制作日期。说明是否需要对评估进行更新以及在何种情况下应进行更新。说明自评估日之后,是否发生了任何可能导致资产价值发生重大变化的事件或情形变更;

(4)在招募说明书后附上一个或多个表格作为附件,列报下列信息:

(i)单独评估的、对持有该等资产的合伙具有重要意义的资产之估值;

(ii)如果在准备对本条第(c)(4)(i)款[(第229.911(c)(4)(i)节]所述的资产进行评估时,估价师考虑采用不同的估值方法,应说明使用估价师考虑的每一种评估方法之时,每项资产将得出的估值;并应注明估价师在确定估值时采用的方法以及选择该种方法的理由;及

(iii)估价师在评估本条第(c)(4)(i)款[第229.911(c)(4)(i)节]所述的资产时所

identified in response to paragraph (c)(4)(i) of this Item (§229.911(c)(4)(i)), and, if the appraiser used different assumptions for any of such assets, the reasons the different assumptions were chosen.

(5) For purposes of this Item and Item 902 of this subpart (§229.902), an asset is "significant" to a partnership if it represents more than 10% of the value of the partnership's assets as of the end of the most recently-completed fiscal year or recently-completed interim period or if 10% or more of the partnership's cash flow or net income for the most recently-completed fiscal year or most recently-completed subsequent interim period was derived from such asset.

Instructions to Item 911: (1) The reports, opinions and appraisals required to be identified in response to paragraph (a) of this Item (§229.911) include any reports, opinions and appraisals which materially relate to the roll-up transaction whether or not relied upon, such as reports or opinions regarding alternatives to the roll-up transaction whether or not the alternatives were rejected.

(2) The information called for by paragraph (a)(2) of this Item (§229.911) should be given with respect to the firm which provides the report, opinion or appraisal rather than the employees of such firm who prepared it.

(3) With respect to appraisals, a summary prepared by the appraisers should not be included in lieu of the description of the appraisals required by paragraph (c) of this Item (§229.911). A clear and concise summary description of the appraisals is required.

[56 FR 57247, Nov. 8, 1991, as amended at 59 FR 63683, Dec. 8, 1994]

§229.912 (Item 912) Source and amount of funds and transactional expenses.

(a) State the source and total amount of funds or other consideration to be used in the roll-up transaction.

(b)(1) Furnish a reasonably itemized statement of all expenses incurred or estimated to be incurred in connection with the roll-up transaction including, but not limited to, filing fees, legal, financial advisory, accounting and appraisal fees, solicitation expenses and printing costs. Identify the persons responsible for paying any or all of such expenses.

(2) State whether or not any partnership subject to the roll-up transaction will be, directly or indirectly, responsible for any or all of the expenses of the transaction. If any partnership will be so responsible, state the amount to be provided by each partnership and the sources of capital to finance such amount.

(c) If all or any part of the consideration to be used by the sponsor or successor in the roll-up transaction is expected to be, directly or indirectly, provided by any partnership,

采用的全部重大假设,并且,如果估价师对上述资产中的任何资产采用了不同假设,应说明采用不同假设的原因。

(5)就本条与本子部分第902条(第229.902节)而言,对合伙"有重要意义的"资产是指,截至最近结束的会计年度年末或最近结束的中期期间期末,该项资产在合伙资产中所占的价值比例超过10%,或者,在最近结束的会计年度或即将结束的中期期间,合伙10%(含)以上的现金流或净收入来自该项资产。

关于第911条的说明:(1)本条(第229.911节)第(a)款要求提供的任何报告、意见和评估结果应包括与并购重组交易存在重大关系的报告、意见和评估结果,无论并购重组交易最终是否基于该等报告、意见或评估结果而开展,如无论替代方案是否被拒绝,均应提供关于替代方案的报告或意见。

(2)本条(第229.911节)第(a)(2)款要求提供的信息指提供该等报告、意见或评估结果的机构的信息,而非该等机构编制该等报告、意见或评估结果的具体员工的信息。

(3)关于评估结果,估价师编制的摘要,不得作为本条(第229.911条)第(c)款要求提供的评估说明之替代。评估结果摘要应清晰、简洁。

[《联邦公报》第56卷第57247页,1991年11月8日,修正索引:《联邦公报》第59卷第63683页,1994年12月8日。]

第229.912节(第912条) 资金来源、数额以及交易费用

(a)说明并购重组交易的资金或其他对价的来源及总额。

(b)(1)提供一份合理详细的费用明细报表,逐条列出并购重组交易期间已经发生或预期发生的相关费用,包括但不限于文件提交费、法律和金融咨询费、会计和评估费用、同意函征集费用及印刷成本。注明负责支付上述任何一项费用或全部费用的人。

(2)说明并购重组交易的部分或全部费用是否将直接或间接由参与交易的任何一家合伙负责承担。如果某一合伙将承担该等费用,说明每家合伙将提供的资金数额以及募集该等资金的来源。

(c)如果发起人或存续实体将就并购重组交易支付的全部或部分对价预期将由任一合伙直接或间接提供,应说明每家合伙将提供的金额以及筹募该等资金的来源。

state the amount to be provided by each partnership and the sources of capital to finance such amount.

(d) If all or any part of the funds or other consideration is, or is expected to be, directly or indirectly borrowed by the sponsor or successor for the purpose of the roll-up transaction:

(1) Provide a summary of each such loan agreement containing the identity of the parties, the term, the collateral, the stated and effective interest rates, and other material terms or conditions; and

(2) Briefly describe any plans or arrangements to finance or repay such borrowing, or, if no plans or arrangements have been made, make a statement to that effect.

(e) If the source of all or any part of the funds to be used in the roll-up transaction is a loan made in the ordinary course of business by a bank as defined by section 3(a)(6) of the Exchange Act and section 13(d) or 14(d) is applicable to such transaction, the name of such bank shall not be made available to the public if the person filing the statement so requests in writing and files such request, naming such bank, with the Secretary of the Commission.

§229.913(Item 913) Other provisions of the transaction.

(a) State whether or not appraisal rights are provided under applicable state law, under the partnership's governing instruments or will be voluntarily accorded by the successor, the general partner or the sponsor (or any of their affiliates) in connection with the roll-up transaction. If so, summarize such appraisal rights. If appraisal rights will not be available to investors who object to the transaction, briefly outline the rights which may be available to such investors under such law.

(b) If any provision has been made to allow investors to obtain access to the books and records of the partnership or to obtain counsel or appraisal services at the expense of the successor, the general partner, the partnership, the sponsor (or any of their affiliates), describe such provision.

(c) Discuss the investors' rights under federal and state law to obtain a partnership's list of investors.

§229.914(Item 914) Proforma financial statements: selected financial data.

(a) In addition to the information required by Item 301 of Regulation S-K, Selected Financial Data (§229.301), and Item 302 of Regulation S-K, Supplementary Financial Information (§229.302), for each partnership proposed to be included in a roll-up transaction provide: Ratio of earnings to fixed charges, cash and cash equivalents, total assets at book value, total assets at the value assigned for purposes of the roll-up transaction (if applicable), total liabilities, general and limited partners' equity, net increase (decrease) in cash and cash equivalents, net cash provided by operating

(d)如果为达成并购重组交易,发起人或存续实体通过或预期将通过直接或间接借贷的方式,募集全部或部分该等资金或其他对价,则应:

(1)提供每一份贷款协议的摘要,指明协议各当事方的身份、协议期限、担保品、设定利率、实际利率以及其他重大条款和条件;且

(2)简要说明针对此等借贷的融资或偿还计划或安排;如果没有制定此种计划或安排,应如实说明。

(e)如果并购重组交易所用的全部或部分资金来源为在正常业务运作中从《交易法》第3(a)(6)条所定义的银行获得的贷款,且该法第13(d)条或第14(d)条适用于该等交易,则如提交人提出书面保密要求,并已向证券交易委员会秘书提交了该等要求并指明请求保密的银行名称时,不得向公众公布银行名称。

第229.913节(第913条) 其他交易规定

(a)说明适用的州法律、合伙的章程性文件中是否规定了与并购重组交易相关的评估权利,或存续实体、普通合伙人或发起人(或其任一关联方)是否将自愿选择向投资者授予评估权。如果是,简要介绍该等评估权。如果反对交易的投资者没有权利进行评估,简要说明相关法律可能赋予这些投资者的权利。

(b)如果有任何规定允许投资者查阅合伙的账册或记录,或规定投资者应获得律师或评估服务,且费用由存续实体、普通合伙人、合伙、发起人(或其任一关联方)承担,应说明该等规定。

(c)论述根据联邦法律或州法律,投资者获得合伙投资者名单的权利。

第229.914节(第914条) 备考财务报表:择要列示的财务数据

(a)除了《S-K管理办法》第301条“择要列示的财务数据”(第229.301节)和《S-K管理办法》第302条“补充财务信息”(第229.302节)要求提供的信息外,对于拟纳入并购重组交易的每家合伙,还应提供如下信息:盈利对固定费用的比率、现金和现金等价物、总资产的账面价值、总资产在并购重组交易中的指定价值(如适用)、总负债、普通合伙人和有限合伙人的权益、现金和现金等价物的净增长(减少)、经营活动产生的净现金、分配;以及下述信息的单位数据:净损益、账面价值、并购重组交易的指定价值(如适用)以及分配(对于属于资本回报的分配,应单独注明)。上述信息覆盖的期间应

activities, distributions; and per unit data for net income(loss), book value, value assigned for purposes of the roll-up transaction (if applicable), and distributions (separately identifying distributions that represent a return of capital). This information should be provided for the same period(s) for which Selected Financial Data and Supplementary Financial Information are required to be provided. Additional or other information should be provided if material to an understanding of each partnership proposed to be included in a roll-up transaction.

(b) Provide pro forma financial information (including oil and gas reserves and cash flow disclosure, if appropriate), assuming:

(1) All partnerships participate in the roll-up transaction; and

(2) Participation in a roll-up transaction of those partnerships that on a combined basis have the lowest combined net cash provided by operating activities for the last fiscal year of such partnerships, *provided* participation by such partnerships satisfies all conditions to consummation of the roll-up transaction. If the combination of all partnerships proposed to be included in a roll-up transaction results in such lowest combined net cash provided by operating activities, this shall be noted and no separate pro forma financial statements are required.

(c) The pro forma financial statements required by paragraph (b) of this Item (§229.914) shall disclose the effect of the roll-up transaction on the successor's:

(1) Balance sheet as of the later of the end of the most recent fiscal year or the latest interim period;

(2) Statement of income (with separate line items to reflect income (loss) excluding and including the roll-up expenses and payments), earnings per share amounts, and ratio of earnings to fixed charges for the most recent fiscal year and the latest interim period;

(3) Statement of cash flows for the most recent fiscal year and the latest interim period; and

(4) Book value per share as of the later of the end of the most recent fiscal year or the latest interim period.

Instructions to Item 914: (1) Notwithstanding the provisions of this Item (§229.914), any or all of the information required by paragraphs (b) and (c) of this Item (§229.914) that is not material for the exercise of prudent judgment in regard to the matter to be acted upon, may be omitted.

(2) If the roll-up transaction is structured to permit participation by portions of partnerships, consideration should be given to the effect of such participation in preparing the pro forma financial statements reflecting a partial roll-up.

§229.915(Item 915) Federal income tax consequences.

(a) Provide a brief, clear and understandable summary of the material Federal

与“择要列示的财务数据”和“补充财务信息”要求覆盖的期间保持一致。对于拟纳入并购重组交易的每家合伙,还应提供对于了解该企业具有重要意义的附加信息或其他信息。

(b)提供备考财务信息(如果合适,应包括石油和天然气储备以及现金流披露),备考财务信息应基于如下假设:

(1)所有合伙均参与并购重组交易;且

(2)实际参与并购重组交易的各家合伙组合是上一个会计年度经营活动汇总现金流数额最低的组合,但是该等参与交易的合伙应满足并购重组交易的所有成交条件。如果拟纳入并购重组交易的所有各家合伙,合并后经营活动产生的净现金流数额为上述汇总现金流最低的组合,应予以注明,并且不必提供单独的备考财务报表。

(c)本条(第229.914节)第(b)款要求提供的备考财务报表应披露并购重组交易对存续实体下述报表或数据的影响:

(1)最近结束的会计年度或最近的中期期间的资产负债表,以较近者为准;

(2)损益表(通过单独的行项目列出扣除和未扣除重组交易费用和支出的损益)、每股盈利以及最近一个会计年度和中期期间的盈利对固定费用的比率;

(3)最近一个会计年度和上一个中期期间的现金流量表;

(4)最近结束的会计年度年末或最近的中期期末的每股账面价值,以较近者为准;

关于第914条的说明:(1)无论本条(第229.914节)如何规定,本条(第229.914节)第(b)款和第(c)款要求提供的任何或全部信息,如果对于应予采取行动的事宜的审慎判断并无重大助益,可予以省略。

(2)如果并购重组交易的结构允许合伙的一部分参与交易,在编制反映此等并购重组的备考财务报表时,应考虑该等部分参与的影响。

第229.915节(第915条) 联邦所得税的影响

(a)提供一份简明清晰易懂的摘要,说明并购重组交易和对存续实体进行投资产

income tax consequences of the roll-up transaction and an investment in the successor. Where a tax opinion has been provided, briefly summarize the substance of such opinion, including identification of the material consequences upon which counsel has not been asked, or is unable, to opine. If any of the material Federal income tax consequences are not expected to be the same for investors in all partnerships, the differences shall be described.

(b) State whether or not the opinion of counsel is included as an appendix to the prospectus. If filed as an exhibit to the registration statement and not included as an appendix to the prospectus, include a statement to the effect that, upon receipt of a written request by an investor or his representative who has been so designated in writing, a copy of the opinion of counsel will be transmitted promptly, without charge, by the general partner or sponsor. The statement should include the name and address of the person to whom investors should make their request.

Subpart 229.1000—Mergers and Acquisitions (Regulation M-A)

Source: 64 FR 61443, Nov. 10, 1999, unless otherwise noted.

§229.1000(Item 1000) Definitions.

The following definitions apply to the terms used in Regulation M-A (§§229.1000 through 229.1016), unless specified otherwise:

(a) *Associate* has the same meaning as in §240.12b-2 of this chapter;

(b) *Instruction C* means General Instruction C to Schedule 13E-3 (§240.13e-100 of this chapter) and General Instruction C to Schedule TO (§240.14d-100 of this chapter);

(c) *Issuer tender offer* has the same meaning as in §240.13e-4(a)(2) of this chapter;

(d) *Offeror* means any person who makes a tender offer or on whose behalf a tender offer is made;

(e) *Rule 13e-3 transaction* has the same meaning as in §240.13e-3(a)(3) of this chapter;

(f) *Subject company* means the company or entity whose securities are sought to be acquired in the transaction (e.g., the target), or that is otherwise the subject of the transaction;

(g) *Subject securities* means the securities or class of securities that are sought to be acquired in the transaction or that are otherwise the subject of the transaction; and

(h) *Third-party tender offer* means a tender offer that is not an issuer tender offer.

生的重大联邦所得税影响。如果已经获得税务意见,应提供简单的内容概要,并注明未征求或无法征求意见的重大联邦所得税影响。如果各合伙的各个投资者可能遭受不同的联邦所得税的任何重大影响,应说明其中的差异。

(b)说明律师意见是否已作为附件附于招募说明书之后。如果该等律师意见已作为注册说明书的附件提交,而没有作为附件纳入招募说明书,应说明如下内容:在收到投资者或其书面指定的代表发送的书面请求后,普通合伙人或发起人将及时、免费向其发送律师意见的复本。说明中应列明负责接收投资者请求之主体的姓名/名称和地址。

第229.1000子部分——并购(《M-A管理办法》)

行政规则来源:《联邦公报》第64卷第61443页,1999年11月10日,除非另有说明。

第229.1000节(第1000条) 定义

除非另有明确规定,《M-A管理办法》(第229.1000~229.1016节)中使用的术语应适用如下定义:

(a)“业务相关人”一词的含义以本章第240.12b-2节的规定为准;

(b)“说明C”指《附表13E-3》(本章第240.13e-100节)的总体说明C和《附表TO》(本章第240.14d-100节)的总体说明C;

(c)“发行人股权收购要约”一词的含义以本章第240.13e-4(a)(2)节的规定为准;

(d)“要约人”指发出股权收购要约的任何主体,或要约发出人所代表的任何主体;

(e)“《13e-3规则》交易”一词的含义以本章第240.13e-3(a)(3)节的规定为准;

(f)“标的公司”系指其证券将在交易中被收购的公司或实体(即目标公司或实体),或因其他原因构成交易标的的公司或实体;

(g)“标的证券”系指将在交易中被收购的证券或某一类别证券,或者因其他原因构成交易标的的证券或某一类别证券;及

(h)“第三方股权收购要约”系指发行人股权收购要约之外的股权收购要约。

§229.1001(Item 1001) Summary term sheet.

Summary term sheet. Provide security holders with a summary term sheet that is written in plain English. The summary term sheet must briefly describe in bullet point format the most material terms of the proposed transaction. The summary term sheet must provide security holders with sufficient information to understand the essential features and significance of the proposed transaction. The bullet points must cross-reference a more detailed discussion contained in the disclosure document that is disseminated to security holders.

Instructions to Item 1001: 1. The summary term sheet must not recite all information contained in the disclosure document that will be provided to security holders. The summary term sheet is intended to serve as an overview of all material matters that are presented in the accompanying documents provided to security holders.

2. The summary term sheet must begin on the first or second page of the disclosure document provided to security holders.

3. Refer to Rule 421(b) and (d) of Regulation C of the Securities Act (§230.421 of this chapter) for a description of plain English disclosure.

§229.1002(Item 1002) Subject company information.

(a) *Name and address.* State the name of the subject company (or the issuer in the case of an issuer tender offer), and the address and telephone number of its principal executive offices.

(b) *Securities.* State the exact title and number of shares outstanding of the subject class of equity securities as of the most recent practicable date. This may be based upon information in the most recently available filing with the Commission by the subject company unless the filing person has more current information.

(c) *Trading market and price.* Identify the principal market in which the subject securities are traded and state the high and low sales prices for the subject securities in the principal market (or, if there is no principal market, the range of high and low bid quotations and the source of the quotations) for each quarter during the past two years. If there is no established trading market for the securities (except for limited or sporadic quotations), so state.

(d) *Dividends.* State the frequency and amount of any dividends paid during the past two years with respect to the subject securities. Briefly describe any restriction on the subject company's current or future ability to pay dividends. If the filing person is not the subject company, furnish this information to the extent known after making reasonable inquiry.

(e) *Prior public offerings.* If the filing person has made an underwritten public offering of the subject securities for cash during the past three years that was registered

第229.1001节(第1001条) 条款清单摘要

条款清单摘要。向证券持有人提供用简明英语书写的条款清单摘要。条款清单摘要必须以要点列举的形式列报拟议交易的大部分重大条款。条款清单摘要必须向证券持有人提供充分的信息,使证券持有人足以理解拟议交易的基本特征和重大性。以要点形式列举重大条款时,必须交叉引用向证券持有人分发的披露文件中所包含的更详细的论述。

关于第1001条的说明:1.条款清单摘要不得完全复述将提供给证券持有人的披露文件中的信息。条款清单摘要的目的是对向证券持有人提供的附随文件中所述的所有重大事项作出概述。

2.条款清单摘要必须安插在向证券持有人提供的披露文件的第1页或第2页。

3.关于以简明英语进行披露之说明,请参见《证券法》的《C管理办法》的《421(b)规则》和《421(d)规则》(本章第230.421条)。

第229.1002节(第1002条) 标的公司信息

(a)名称和地址。说明标的公司的名称(就发行人股权收购要约而言,应说明发行人的名称),以及该公司主要高管的地址和电话号码。

(b)证券。说明截至最近的可行日期,作为标的股权证券类别中发行在外股份的具体名称和股数。作出上述说明时,可以基于现存最新的提交给证券交易委员会的目标公司文件,但文件提交人拥有更新的信息的除外。

(c)交易市场和价格。指明标的证券的主要交易市场,并说明标的证券在过去两年内每个季度在主要市场中的最高和最低卖出价(如果没有主要市场,应指明标的证券的最高和最低买入报价以及该等报价的来源)。如果除有限或零散的报价外,证券不存在稳定交易市场,应如实说明。

(d)股息。说明在过去2年内针对标的证券支付股息的频率和数额。简要介绍标的公司目前或将来支付股息的能力所存在的任何限制。如果文件提交人不是标的公司,应在进行合理的询问后,在所知范围内提供相关信息。

(e)之前的公开发行。如果文件提交人在过去3年内通过承销方式,对标的证券进行了以现金为对价的公开发行,且该等证券属于根据《1933年证券法》进行注册的证

under the Securities Act of 1933 or exempt from registration under Regulation A (§230.251 through §230.263 of this chapter), state the date of the offering, the amount of securities offered, the offering price per share (adjusted for stock splits, stock dividends, etc. as appropriate) and the aggregate proceeds received by the filing person.

(f) *Prior stock purchases.* If the filing person purchased any subject securities during the past two years, state the amount of the securities purchased, the range of prices paid and the average purchase price for each quarter during that period. Affiliates need not give information for purchases made before becoming an affiliate.

§229.1003(Item 1003) Identity and background of filing person.

(a) *Name and address.* State the name, business address and business telephone number of each filing person. Also state the name and address of each person specified in Instruction C to the schedule (except for Schedule 14D-9 (§240.14d-101 of this chapter)). If the filing person is an affiliate of the subject company, state the nature of the affiliation. If the filing person is the subject company, so state.

(b) *Business and background of entities.* If any filing person (other than the subject company) or any person specified in Instruction C to the schedule is not a natural person, state the person's principal business, state or other place of organization, and the information required by paragraphs (c)(3) and (c)(4) of this section for each person.

(c) *Business and background of natural persons.* If any filing person or any person specified in Instruction C to the schedule is a natural person, provide the following information for each person:

(1) Current principal occupation or employment and the name,principal business and address of any corporation or other organization in which the employment or occupation is conducted;

(2) Material occupations, positions, offices or employment during the past five years, giving the starting and ending dates of each and the name, principal business and address of any corporation or other organization in which the occupation, position, office or employment was carried on;

(3) A statement whether or not the person was convicted in a criminal proceeding during the past five years (excluding traffic violations or similar misdemeanors). If the person was convicted, describe the criminal proceeding, including the dates, nature of conviction, name and location of court, and penalty imposed or other disposition of the case;

(4) A statement whether or not the person was a party to any judicial or administrative proceeding during the past five years (except for matters that were dismissed without sanction or settlement) that resulted in a judgment, decree or final order enjoining the person from future violations of, or prohibiting activities subject to,

券,或根据《A管理办法》(本章第230.251~230.263节)获得了注册豁免,应说明发行的日期、发行的证券数量、每股发行价格(根据适当情况,基于股票分割、股票股息等原因进行调整后的价格)以及文件提交人获得的募集资金总额。

(f)之前的股票购买。如果文件提交人在过去2年之内曾购买任何标的证券,应说明已购证券数量、支付价格范围以及上述期间内每个季度的平均购买价。对于关联方在成为关联方之前购买的证券,不必提供相关信息。

第229.1003节(第1003条) 文件提交人的身份和背景

(a)名称和地址。列明每个文件提交人的名称、营业地址和公司电话号码。另请说明附表[《附表14D-9》(本章第240.14d-101节)除外]"说明C"中规定的每一主体的名称和地址。如果文件提交人是标的公司的关联方,说明该等关联关系的性质。如果文件提交人是标的公司,应如实说明。

(b)实体的业务和背景。如果任何文件提交人(标的公司除外)或附表的"说明C"中规定的任何主体不是自然人,应针对该等主体逐一说明其主要业务、所在的州或其组织机构的其他地点,以及本节第(c)(3)款和第(c)(4)款规定的信息。

(c)自然人的业务和背景。如果任何文件提交人或附表的"说明C"中规定的任何主体是自然人,应就该等主体逐一提供下列信息:

(1)目前的主要职业或职务以及该人从事该职业或职务的任何公司或其他组织的名称、主要业务和地址;

(2)在过去5年内所从事或担任过的主要职业、职位、官职或工作,并列明每次任职的起始和结束日期,以及所就职的任何公司或其他组织的主要业务和地址;

(3)关于如下事项的声明:在过去5年内,该人是否曾在刑事诉讼中被判有罪(交通违章或类似的轻罪除外)。如果该人曾被定罪,应说明该等刑事诉讼的情况,包括犯罪的日期、性质、法庭名称和地点以及案件的判罚或其他处置;

(4)关于如下事项的声明:在过去5年内,该人是否曾作为当事人参与任何司法或行政程序(未加处罚而被驳回或和解的案件除外),且司法或行政机构通过判决、裁定或最终命令责成该人将来不得再次违反联邦或州证券法,或从事联邦或州证券法禁止的行为,或司法或行政机构认定其曾从事任何违反联邦或州证券法的行为。说明该

federal or state securities laws, or a finding of any violation of federal or state securities laws. Describe the proceeding, including a summary of the terms of the judgment, decree or final order; and

(5) Country of citizenship.

(d) *Tender offer.* Identify the tender offer and the class of securities to which the offer relates, the name of the offeror and its address (which may be based on the offeror's Schedule TO (§240.14d-100 of this chapter) filed with the Commission).

Instruction to Item 1003. If the filing person is making information relating to the transaction available on the Internet, state the address where the information can be found.

§229.1004(Item 1004) Terms of the transaction.

(a) *Material terms.* State the material terms of the transaction.

(1) *Tender offers.* In the case of a tender offer, the information must include:

(i) The total number and class of securities sought in the offer;

(ii) The type and amount of consideration offered to security holders;

(iii) The scheduled expiration date;

(iv) Whether a subsequent offering period will be available, if the transaction is a third-party tender offer;

(v) Whether the offer may be extended, and if so, how it could be extended;

(vi) The dates before and after which security holders may withdraw securities tendered in the offer;

(vii) The procedures for tendering and withdrawing securities;

(viii) The manner in which securities will be accepted for payment;

(ix) If the offer is for less than all securities of a class, the periods for accepting securities on a pro rata basis and the offeror's present intentions in the event that the offer is oversubscribed;

(x) An explanation of any material differences in the rights of security holders as a result of the transaction, if material;

(xi) A brief statement as to the accounting treatment of the transaction, if material; and

(xii) The federal income tax consequences of the transaction, if material.

(2) *Mergers or similar transactions.* In the case of a merger or similar transaction, the information must include:

(i) A brief description of the transaction;

(ii) The consideration offered to security holders;

(iii) The reasons for engaging in the transaction;

(iv) The vote required for approval of the transaction;

等程序的情况,包括判决、裁定或最终命令的条款摘要;及

(5)国籍所在国。

(d)股权收购要约。指明股权收购要约、与该要约相关的证券类别、要约人的名称及其地址[该等信息可基于要约人向证券交易委员会提交的《TO附表》(本章第240.14d-100节)提供]。

关于第1003条的说明。如果文件提交人准备通过互联网公布与并购重组交易相关的信息,应说明相应网址。

第229.1004节(第1004条) 交易条款

(a)重大条款。说明交易的重大条款。

(1)股权收购要约。就股权收购要约而言,所提供的信息必须包括:

(i)要约所针对的证券总数和类型;

(ii)提供给证券持有人的对价类型和金额;

(iii)预定的要约到期日;

(iv)如果交易为第三方股权收购要约,是否将提供后续要约期间;

(v)要约是否可延期,如果可以,如何延期;

(vi)证券持有人禁止撤回出售证券期间的起始日期和结束日期;

(vii)出售和撤回证券的程序;

(viii)有偿收购证券的方式;

(ix)如果要约的对象只是某一类别证券的一部分,应说明按比例收购证券的期间,以及如果证券被超额认购,要约人当前的处理意向;

(x)如果交易完成后,证券持有人的权利出现任何重大差异,应如实说明;

(xi)关于交易中重大会计处理的简要说明;以及

(xii)交易的重大联邦所得税影响。

(2)吸收合并或类似交易。就吸收合并或类似交易而言,所提供的信息必须包括:

(i)交易的简要说明;

(ii)提供给证券持有人的对价;

(iii)参与交易的理由;

(iv)批准交易所需要的表决票数;

(v) An explanation of any material differences in the rights of security holders as a result of the transaction, if material;

(vi) A brief statement as to the accounting treatment of the transaction, if material; and

(vii) The federal income tax consequences of the transaction, if material.

Instruction to Item 1004(a): If the consideration offered includes securities exempt from registration under the Securities Act of 1933, provide a description of the securities that complies with Item 202 of Regulation S–K (§229.202). This description is not required if the issuer of the securities meets the requirements of General Instructions I.A, I.B.1 or I.B.2, as applicable, or I.C. of Form S–3 (§239.13 of this chapter) and elects to furnish information by incorporation by reference; only capital stock is to be issued; and securities of the same class are registered under section 12 of the Exchange Act and either are listed for trading or admitted to unlisted trading privileges on a national securities exchange; or are securities for which bid and offer quotations are reported in an automated quotations system operated by a national securities association.

(b) *Purchases.* State whether any securities are to be purchased from any officer, director or affiliate of the subject company and provide the details of each transaction.

(c) *Different terms.* Describe any term or arrangement in the Rule 13e–3 transaction that treats any subject security holders differently from other subject security holders.

(d) *Appraisal rights.* State whether or not dissenting security holders are entitled to any appraisal rights. If so, summarize the appraisal rights. If there are no appraisal rights available under state law for security holders who object to the transaction, briefly outline any other rights that may be available to security holders under the law.

(e) *Provisions for unaffiliated security holders.* Describe any provision made by the filing person in connection with the transaction to grant unaffiliated security holders access to the corporate files of the filing person or to obtain counsel or appraisal services at the expense of the filing person. If none, so state.

(f) *Eligibility for listing or trading.* If the transaction involves the offer of securities of the filing person in exchange for equity securities held by unaffiliated security holders of the subject company, describe whether or not the filing person will take steps to assure that the securities offered are or will be eligible for trading on an automated quotations system operated by a national securities association.

§229.1005 (Item 1005) Past contacts, transactions, negotiations and agreements.

(a) *Transactions.* Briefly state the nature and approximate dollar amount of any transaction, other than those described in paragraphs (b) or (c) of this section, that occurred during the past two years, between the filing person (including any person

(v)如果交易完成后,证券持有人的权利出现任何重大差异,应如实说明;

(vi)关于交易中重大会计处理的简要说明;以及

(vii)交易的重大联邦所得税影响。

关于第1004(a)条的说明:如果提供的对价中包括根据《1933年证券法》豁免登记的证券,对于符合《S-K管理办法》第202条(第229.202节)规定的证券,应提供相应的说明。以下情况可以不必提供此项说明:证券发行人满足《S-3表格》(本章第239.13节)的总体说明I.A、总体说明I.B.1或总体说明I.B.2(以适用者为准),或总体说明I. C.的要求,并且证券发行人选择以引用纳入的方式提供信息;发行仅限于资本股;且同类别证券已根据《交易法》第12条的规定进行了注册,或已上市交易,或已在全国性证券交易所获得非上市交易权;或者证券的买入/卖出报价在全国性证券协会运行的交易商自动报价系统中报告。

(b)购买。说明是否需要从标的公司的任何管理人员、董事或关联方手中购买任何证券以及每宗交易的详细信息。

(c)不同条款。说明《13e-3规则》中区别对待标的证券持有人的任何条款或安排。

(d)评估权。说明持不同意见的证券持有人是否享有任何评估权。如果是,对该等评估权进行概述。如果根据州法律,反对交易的证券持有人不享有评估权,简要概述证券持有人根据相关的州法律所享有的任何其他权利。

(e)关于非关联证券持有人的规定。文件提交人作出与交易相关的规定,允许非关联证券持有人查阅文件提交人的公司文档,或允许证券持有人获得文件提交人付费的律师或评估服务的,应如实说明。如果没有此类规定,亦应如实说明。

(f)上市或交易的资格。如果在交易中,文件提交人发出的要约是以其自身证券交换非关联证券持有人所持有的标的公司股权证券,应说明文件提交人是否将采取措施确保其要约的证券具有或将具有通过全国性证券协会运行的交易商自动报价系统交易的资格。

第229.1005节(第1005条) 既往接洽、交易、谈判和协议

(a)交易。简要说明过去两年中文件提交人(包括附表"说明C"中指定的任何主体)与下列各方进行的交易之性质以及交易的大致金额[不包括本节第(b)款和第(c)款所述交易];

specified in Instruction C of the schedule) and;

(1) The subject company or any of its affiliates that are not natural persons if the aggregate value of the transactions is more than one percent of the subject company's consolidated revenues for:

(i) The fiscal year when the transaction occurred; or

(ii) The past portion of the current fiscal year, if the transaction occurred in the current year; and

Instruction to Item 1005(a)(1): The information required by this Item may be based on information in the subject company's most recent filing with the Commission, unless the filing person has reason to believe the information is not accurate.

(2) Anyexecutive officer, director or affiliate of the subject company that is a natural person if the aggregate value of the transaction or series of similar transactions with that person exceeds $60,000.

(b) *Significant corporate events.* Describe any negotiations, transactions or material contacts during the past two years between the filing person (including subsidiaries of the filing person and any person specified in Instruction C of the schedule) and the subject company or its affiliates concerning any:

(1) Merger;

(2) Consolidation;

(3) Acquisition;

(4) Tender offer for or other acquisition of any class of the subject company's securities;

(5) Election of the subject company's directors; or

(6) Sale or other transfer of a material amount of assets of the subject company.

(c) *Negotiations or contacts.* Describe any negotiations or material contacts concerning the matters referred to in paragraph (b) of this section during the past two years between:

(1) Any affiliates of the subject company; or

(2) The subject company or any of its affiliates and any person not affiliated with the subject company who would have a direct interest in such matters.

Instruction to paragraphs (b) and (c) of Item 1005: Identify the person who initiated the contacts or negotiations.

(d) *Conflicts of interest.* If material, describe any agreement, arrangement or understanding and any actual or potential conflict of interest between the filing person or its affiliates and:

(1) The subject company, itsexecutive officers, directors or affiliates; or

(2) The offeror, itsexecutive officers, directors or affiliates.

（1）标的公司或其不属于自然人的任意关联方，条件是交易的总价值超过标的公司在以下期间的并表收入的1%：

（i）交易发生的会计年度；或

（ii）当前会计年度已经过的部分（如果交易发生在当前会计年度）；及

关于第1005（a）（1）条的说明：本条规定的信息可基于标的公司最近提交给证券交易委员会的信息提供，但文件提交人有理由认为该等信息不准确的除外。

（2）标的公司的自然人高管、董事或关联方，条件是与该等人进行的交易总价值或一系列类似交易的总价值超过6万美元。

（b）重大公司事件。说明过去两年内文件提交人（包括文件提交人的子公司以及附表“说明C”中指定的任何主体）与标的公司或其关联方就下列任一事项达成的所有谈判、交易或重大接洽：

（1）吸收合并；

（2）新设合并；

（3）收购；

（4）针对标的公司任一类别证券提出的收购要约或进行的其他收购；

（5）标的公司董事的选任；或

（6）标的公司大额资产的销售或其他转让。

（c）谈判或接洽。说明在过去两年内就本节第（b）款所述事项，与下列各方进行的所有谈判或重大接洽：

（1）标的公司的任一关联方；或

（2）标的公司或其任一关联方，以及与标的公司不存在关联关系，但可能与上述事项存在直接利害关系的任何人。

关于第1005条第（b）款和第（c）款的说明：指明发起接洽或谈判的主体的身份。

（d）利益冲突。说明文件提交人或其关联方与下列各方达成的所有重大协议、安排或谅解以及任何实际或潜在的重大利益冲突：

（1）标的公司及其高管、董事或关联方；或者

（2）要约人及其高管、董事或关联方。

Instruction to Item 1005(d): If the filing person is the subject company, no disclosure called for by this paragraph is required in the document disseminated to security holders, so long as substantially the same information was filed with the Commission previously and disclosed in a proxy statement, report or other communication sent to security holders by the subject company in the past year. The document disseminated to security holders, however, must refer specifically to the discussion in the proxy statement, report or other communication that was sent to security holders previously. The information also must be filed as an exhibit to the schedule.

(e) *Agreements involving the subject company's securities.* Describe any agreement, arrangement, or understanding, whether or not legally enforceable, between the filing person (including any person specified in Instruction C of the schedule) and any other person with respect to any securities of the subject company. Name all persons that are a party to the agreements, arrangements, or understandings and describe all material provisions.

Instructions to Item 1005(e): 1. The information required by this Item includes: the transfer or voting of securities, joint ventures, loan or option arrangements, puts or calls, guarantees of loans, guarantees against loss, or the giving or withholding of proxies, consents or authorizations.

2. Include information for any securities that are pledged or otherwise subject to a contingency, the occurrence of which would give another person the power to direct the voting or disposition of the subject securities. No disclosure, however, is required about standard default and similar provisions contained in loan agreements.

§229.1006(Item 1006) Purposes of the transaction and plans or proposals.

(a) *Purposes.* State the purposes of the transaction.

(b) *Use of securities acquired.* Indicate whether the securities acquired in the transaction will be retained, retired, held in treasury, or otherwise disposed of.

(c) *Plans.* Describe any plans, proposals or negotiations that relate to or would result in:

(1) Any extraordinary transaction, such as a merger, reorganization or liquidation, involving the subject company or any of its subsidiaries;

(2) Any purchase, sale or transfer of a material amount of assets of the subject company or any of its subsidiaries;

(3) Any material change in the present dividend rate or policy, or indebtedness or capitalization of the subject company;

(4) Any change in the present board of directors or management of the subject company, including, but not limited to, any plans or proposals to change the number or the term of directors or to fill any existing vacancies on the board or to change any

关于第1005(d)条的说明:如果文件提交人是标的公司,本款要求披露的信息不必在向证券持有人分发的文件中提供,条件是该等信息与之前提交给证券交易委员会的信息基本相同,并曾通过标的公司在过去一年内发送给证券持有人的征集投票权报告、报告或其他通信予以披露。但是,向证券持有人分发的文件必须具体引用之前发送给证券持有人的征集投票权报告、报告或其他通信中包含的论述。该等信息还必须作为附表的附录提交。

(e)涉及标的公司证券的协议。说明文件提交人(包括附表"说明C"中指定的任何主体)与任何其他人就标的公司任何证券达成的所有协议、安排或谅解(无论是否具有法律强制效力)。列明作为协议、安排或谅解当事方的所有主体,并说明其中的所有重大条款。

关于第1005(e)条的说明:1.本条要求提供的信息包括:证券的转让或表决;合资、贷款或期权安排;看涨期权或看跌期权;贷款担保;损失担保;代理委托书、同意或核准的提供或不予提供。

2.应纳入关于下述证券的信息:质押的证券,或存在其他或有情形的证券(前提是此等情形的发生将使其他人能够主导标的证券的表决或处置)。但是,不必披露贷款协议中的标准默认条款和类似条款。

第229.1006节(第1006条) 交易目的以及交易计划或建议书

(a)目的。说明交易目的。

(b)已收购证券的用途。说明交易中收购的证券是否将予以保留、注销、以库存证券方式持有或通过其他方式处置。

(c)计划。说明与下列事项相关或可能导致下列事项的任何计划、建议书或谈判:

(1)标的公司或其任何子公司的任何特大交易,如吸收合并、重组或清算;

(2)对标的公司或其任何子公司大额资产的任何收购、出售或转让;

(3)标的公司当前股息率或股息政策、负债或市值的任何重大变化;

(4)标的公司现任董事会或管理层的任何变化,包括但不限于任何以下计划或提议:变更董事人数或任期、填补董事会任何现有空缺或变更任何高管雇佣合同的任何重大条款;

material term of the employment contract of anyexecutive officer;

(5) Any other material change in the subject company's corporate structure or business, including, if the subject company is a registered closed-end investment company, any plans or proposals to make any changes in its investment policy for which a vote would be required by Section 13 of the Investment Company Act of 1940 (15 U.S.C. 80a-13);

(6) Any class of equity securities of the subject company to be delisted from a national securities exchange or cease to be authorized to be quoted in an automated quotations system operated by a national securities association;

(7) Any class of equity securities of the subject company becoming eligible for termination of registration under section 12(g)(4) of the Act (15 U.S.C. 78 *l*);

(8) The suspension of the subject company's obligation to file reports under Section 15(d) of the Act (15 U.S.C. 78o);

(9) The acquisition by any person of additional securities of the subject company, or the disposition of securities of the subject company; or

(10) Any changes in the subject company's charter, bylaws or other governing instruments or other actions that could impede the acquisition of control of the subject company.

(d) *Subject company negotiations.* If the filing person is the subject company:

(1) State whether or not that person is undertaking or engaged in any negotiations in response to the tender offer that relate to:

(i) A tender offer or other acquisition of the subject company's securities by the filing person, any of its subsidiaries, or any other person; or

(ii) Any of the matters referred to in paragraphs (c)(1) through (c)(3) of this section; and

(2) Describe any transaction, board resolution, agreement in principle, or signed contract that is entered into in response to the tender offer that relates to one or more of the matters referred to in paragraph (d)(1) of this section.

Instruction to Item 1006(d)(1): If an agreement in principle has not been reached at the time of filing, no disclosure under paragraph (d)(1) of this section is required of the possible terms of or the parties to the transaction if in the opinion of the board of directors of the subject company disclosure would jeopardize continuation of the negotiations. In that case, disclosure indicating that negotiations are being undertaken or are underway and are in the preliminary stages is sufficient.

§229.1007(Item 1007) Source and amount of funds or other consideration.

(a) *Source of funds.* State the specific sources and total amount of funds or other consideration to be used in the transaction. If the transaction involves a tender offer,

(5)标的公司在公司组织结构或业务方面的任何其他重大变化,对于注册封闭式投资公司而言,包括《1940年投资公司法》第13条规定应进行表决的投资政策的任何变更计划或提议(《美国法典》第十五编第80a-13节);

(6)即将从全国性证券交易所退市或被取消在全国性证券协会运行的交易商自动报价系统报价权的标的公司的任何类别的股权证券;

(7)根据《交易法》第12(g)(4)条(《美国法典》第十五编第78l节)符合注册终止条件的标的公司的任何类别的股权证券;

(8)标的公司暂停承担根据《交易法》第15(d)条(《美国法典》第十五编第78o节)提交报告的义务;

(9)任何主体收购标的公司证券,或处置标的公司证券;或

(10)标的公司章程、内部章程或其他章程性文件的任何变更,或可能妨碍收购标的公司控制权的其他行动。

(d)标的公司谈判。如果文件提交人系标的公司,应:

(1)说明该主体是否收到关于下列事项的收购要约,并正在据此开展或参与任何谈判:

(i)文件提交人、其任何子公司或任何其他主体对标的公司证券的收购要约或其他收购;或

(ii)本节第(c)(1)款至第(c)(3)款所述任何事项;并

(2)说明根据与本条第(d)(1)款所述一项或多项事项相关的收购要约而达成、通过或订立的任何交易、董事会决议、原则协议或已签署合同。

关于第1006(d)(1)条的说明:如果在提交文件时尚未达成原则协议,且标的公司董事会认为披露将损害谈判的持续开展,则不必按照本节第(d)(1)款披露交易可能达成的条款或当事方。在该种情况下,仅须披露谈判正在进行中,且仍处于初步阶段。

第229.1007节(第1007条)　资金或其他对价的来源及金额

(a)资金来源。说明交易将使用的资金或其他对价的具体来源及总额。如果交易涉及收购要约,应披露购买要约项下最大数量证券所需的资金或其他对价的金额。

disclose the amount of funds or other consideration required to purchase the maximum amount of securities sought in the offer.

(b) *Conditions*. State any material conditions to the financing discussed in response to paragraph (a) of this section. Disclose any alternative financing arrangements or alternative financing plans in the event the primary financing plans fall through. If none, so state.

(c) *Expenses*. Furnish a reasonably itemized statement of all expenses incurred or estimated to be incurred in connection with the transaction including, but not limited to, filing, legal, accounting and appraisal fees, solicitation expenses and printing costs and state whether or not the subject company has paid or will be responsible for paying any or all expenses.

(d) *Borrowed funds*. If all or any part of the funds or other consideration required is, or is expected, to be borrowed, directly or indirectly, for the purpose of the transaction:

(1) Provide a summary of each loan agreement or arrangement containing the identity of the parties, the term, the collateral, the stated and effective interest rates, and any other material terms or conditions of the loan; and

(2) Briefly describe any plans or arrangements to finance or repay the loan, or, if no plans or arrangements have been made, so state.

Instruction to Item 1007(d): If the transaction is a third–party tender offer and the source of all or any part of the funds used in the transaction is to come from a loan made in the ordinary course of business by a bank as defined by section 3(a)(6) of the Act (15 U.S.C. 78c), the name of the bank will not be made available to the public if the filing person so requests in writing and files the request, naming the bank, with the Secretary of the Commission.

§229.1008(Item 1008) Interest in securities of the subject company.

(a) *Securities ownership*. State the aggregate number and percentage of subject securities that are beneficially owned by each person named in response to Item 1003 of Regulation M–A (§229.1003) and by each associate and majority–owned subsidiary of those persons. Give the name and address of any associate or subsidiary.

Instructions to Item 1008(a): 1. For purposes of this section, beneficial ownership is determined in accordance with Rule 13d–3 (§240.13d–3 of this chapter) under the Exchange Act. Identify the shares that the person has a right to acquire.

2. The information required by this section may be based on the number of outstanding securities disclosed in the subject company's most recently available filing with the Commission, unless the filing person has more current information.

3. The information required by this section with respect to officers, directors and associates of the subject company must be given to the extent known after making

(b)条件。在按照本节第(a)款对融资进行论述时,应说明该等融资的任何重大条件。如果原始融资计划失败,应披露任何备选融资安排或备选融资计划。如不存在上述融资计划,亦应如实说明。

(c)费用。就因交易而产生或预计产生的全部费用,包括但不限于文件提交费、法律、会计和评估费、同意函征集费用和打印成本,提供合理详细的明细报表,并说明标的公司是否已经支付或将负责支付任何或全部该等费用。

(d)借入资金。如果出于交易,所需资金或其他对价的全部或任何部分将通过或预期将通过直接或间接借贷的方式筹集,应:

(1)提交每一贷款协议或安排的概要,包括当事方身份、期限、担保品、名义及实际利率以及贷款的任何其他重大条款或条件;并

(2)简要介绍贷款融资或偿还的任何计划或安排;如无该等计划或安排,亦应如实说明。

关于第1007(d)条的说明:如果该交易系第三方收购要约且交易中使用的全部或任何部分资金将来自《交易法》第3(a)(6)条(《美国法典》第十五编第78c节)定义的银行在正常业务运作中提供的贷款,则不必公开该银行名称,前提是文件提交人以书面形式向证券交易委员会秘书提出该等要求,并注明银行名称。

第229.1008节(第1008条) 标的公司证券权益

(a)证券所有权。说明按照《M-A管理办法》第1003条(第229.1003节)指明的主体受益拥有的,以及该等主体的每一业务相关人和其控股子公司受益拥有的标的证券的总数及百分比。列出所有业务相关人或子公司的名称和地址。

关于第1008(a)条的说明:1.就本节而言,是否属于受益所有权应根据《交易法》的《13d-3规则》(本章第240.13d-3节)判定。相关主体有权获得的股份均应注明。

2.本节要求提供的信息可基于标的公司最近一次向证券交易委员会提交的文件中披露的发行在外证券数量,但文件提交人拥有更新的信息的除外。

3.本节要求提供的关于标的公司管理人员、董事和业务相关人的信息必须为经过合理调查后获知的信息。

reasonable inquiry.

(b) *Securities transactions.* Describe any transaction in the subject securities during the past 60 days. The description of transactions required must include, but not necessarily be limited to:

(1) The identity of the persons specified in the Instruction to this section who effected the transaction;

(2) The date of the transaction;

(3) The amount of securities involved;

(4) The price per share; and

(5) Where and how the transaction was effected.

Instructions to Item 1008(b): 1. Provide the required transaction information for the following persons:

(a) The filing person (for all schedules);

(b) Any person named in Instruction C of the schedule and any associate or majority–owned subsidiary of the issuer or filing person (for all schedules except Schedule 14D–9 (§240.14d–101 of this chapter));

(c) Anyexecutive officer, director, affiliate or subsidiary of the filing person (for Schedule 14D–9 (§240.14d–101 of this chapter));

(d) The issuer and anyexecutive officer or director of any subsidiary of the issuer or filing person (for an issuer tender offer on Schedule TO (§240.14d–100 of this chapter)); and

(e) The issuer and any pension, profit–sharing or similar plan of the issuer or affiliate filing the schedule (for a going–private transaction on Schedule 13E–3 (§240.13e–100 of this chapter)).

2. Provide the information required by this Item if it is available to the filing person at the time the statement is initially filed with the Commission. If the information is not initially available, it must be obtained and filed with the Commission promptly, but in no event later than three business days after the date of the initial filing, and if material, disclosed in a manner reasonably designed to inform security holders. The procedure specified by this instruction is provided to maintain the confidentiality of information in order to avoid possible misuse of inside information.

§229.1009(Item 1009) Persons/assets, retained, employed, compensated or used.

(a) *Solicitations or recommendations.* Identify all persons and classes of persons that are directly or indirectly employed, retained, or to be compensated to make solicitations or recommendations in connection with the transaction. Provide a summary of all material terms of employment, retainer or other arrangement for compensation.

(b)证券交易。说明标的证券在过去60日中的任何交易。交易说明必须包括,但不限于:

(1)本节说明中规定的实施交易的主体之身份信息;

(2)交易日期;
(3)所涉证券数量;
(4)每股价格;及
(5)交易生效地点及方式。
关于第1008(b)条的说明:1.针对下列主体提供规定的交易信息:

(a)文件提交人(适用于全部附表);
(b)附表的说明C中所列任何主体,以及发行人或文件提交人的任何业务相关人或控股子公司[适用于《附表14D-9》(本章第240.14d-101节)以外的全部附表];

(c)文件提交人的任何高管、董事、关联方或子公司[适用于《附表14D-9》(本章第240.14d-101节)];
(d)发行人及发行人或文件提交人的任何子公司的任何高管或董事[适用于按照《附表TO》(本章第240.14d-100节)报告的发行人收购要约];及

(e)发行人和提交附表的发行人或关联方的任何养老金计划、利润分享计划或类似计划[适用于按照《附表13E-3》(本章第240.13e-100节)申报的下市交易]。

2.如果文件提交人在最初向证券交易委员会提交报表时已获得本条要求提供的信息,应提交该等信息;如果最初并未获得该等信息,则必须及时获得并向证券交易委员会提交该等信息,但在任何情况下均不得迟于初始提交日后3个营业日。如果信息属于重大信息,则应按照合理设计的方式予以披露以告知证券持有人。本条说明规定的程序系出于保密目的,以避免出现对内幕信息的不当利用。

第229.1009节(第1009条) 被聘用、雇佣、获付报酬或被使用的人员/资产

(a)招揽或推荐。列明为交易招揽或推荐之目的而被直接或间接雇佣、聘用或获付报酬的全部人员及其类别。提供雇佣、聘任或其他报酬安排的全部重大条款摘要。

(b) *Employees and corporate assets.* Identify any officer, class of employees or corporate assets of the subject company that has been or will be employed or used by the filing person in connection with the transaction. Describe the purpose for their employment or use.

Instruction to Item 1009(b): Provide all information required by this Item except for the information required by paragraph (a) of this section and Item 1007 of Regulation M–A (§229.1007).

§229.1010(Item 1010) Financial statements.

(a) *Financial information.* Furnish the following financial information:

(1) Audited financial statements for the two fiscal years required to be filed with the company's most recent annual report under sections 13 and 15(d) of the Exchange Act (15 U.S.C. 78m; 15 U.S.C. 78o);

(2) Unaudited balance sheets, comparative year–to–date income statements and related earnings per share data, statements of cash flows, and comprehensive income required to be included in the company's most recent quarterly report filed under the Exchange Act;

(3) Ratio of earnings to fixed charges, computed in a manner consistent with Item 503(d) of Regulation S–K (§229.503(d)), for the two most recent fiscal years and the interim periods provided under paragraph (a)(2) of this section; and

(4) Book value per share as of the date of the most recent balance sheet presented.

(b) *Pro forma information.* If material, furnish pro forma information disclosing the effect of the transaction on:

(1) The company's balance sheet as of the date of the most recent balance sheet presented under paragraph (a) of this section;

(2) The company's statement of income, earnings per share, and ratio of earnings to fixed charges for the most recent fiscal year and the latest interim period provided under paragraph (a)(2) of this section; and

(3) The company's book value per share as of the date of the most recent balance sheet presented under paragraph (a) of this section.

(c) *Summary information.* Furnish a fair and adequate summary of the information specified in paragraphs (a) and (b) of this section for the same periods specified. A fair and adequate summary includes:

(1) The summarized financial information specified in §210.1–02(bb)(1) of this chapter;

(2) Income per common share from continuing operations (basic and diluted, if applicable);

(3) Net income per common share (basic and diluted, if applicable);

(b)员工和公司资产。列明被文件提交人为交易之目的已经或将要雇佣或使用的标的公司的任何管理人员、任何类别职员或公司资产。说明雇佣上述人员或使用上述资产的目的。

关于第1009(b)条的说明:提供本条要求提供的全部信息,但不包括本节第(a)款以及《M-A管理办法》第1007条(第229.1007节)要求提供的信息。

第229.1010节(第1010条) 财务报表

(a)财务信息。应提供下列财务信息:

(1)根据《交易法》第13条和第15(d)条(《美国法典》第十五编第78m节和第78o节)应与公司最近一期年度报告一并提交的两会计年度的已审计财务报表;

(2)根据《交易法》应列入公司最近一期季度报告的未审计资产负债表、年初至今的比较损益表和相关每股盈利数据、现金流量表以及综合收益;

(3)按照与《S-K管理办法》第503(d)条[第229.503(d)节]相符的方式计算得出的最近2个会计年度及本节第(a)(2)款规定的中期期间的盈利对固定费用比率;及

(4)截至最近提交的一期资产负债表之日的每股账面价值。

(b)备考信息。提供重大备考信息,披露交易对下列事项产生的影响:

(1)截至根据本节第(a)款提交的最近一期资产负债表之日的公司资产负债表;

(2)公司在最近会计年度及本节第(a)(2)款规定的中期期间的损益表、每股收益以及盈利对固定费用比率;及

(3)截至根据本节第(a)款提交的最近一期资产负债表之日的公司每股账面价值;

(c)摘要信息。提供本节第(a)款和第(b)款规定的信息在同款规定的期间的公允和充分摘要。公允和充分摘要包括:

(1)本章第210.1-02(bb)(1)节规定的财务信息摘要;

(2)来自持续经营的普通股每股收益(基本收益和稀释后的收益,如适用);

(3)普通股每股净收益(基本收益和稀释后的收益,如适用);

(4) Ratio of earnings to fixed charges, computed in a manner consistent with Item 503(d) of Regulation S-K (§229.503(d));

(5) Book value per share as of the date of the most recent balance sheet; and

(6) If material, pro forma data for the summarized financial information specified in paragraphs (c)(1) through (c)(5) of this section disclosing the effect of the transaction.

§229.1011(Item 1011) Additional information.

Link to an amendment published at 76 FR 6044, February 2, 2011.

(a) *Agreements, regulatory requirements and legal proceedings.* If material to a security holder's decision whether to sell, tender or hold the securities sought in the tender offer, furnish the following information:

(1) Any present or proposed material agreement, arrangement, understanding or relationship between the offeror or any of its executive officers, directors, controlling persons or subsidiaries and the subject company or any of its executive officers, directors, controlling persons or subsidiaries (other than any agreement, arrangement or understanding disclosed under any other sections of Regulation M-A (§§229.1000 through 229.1016));

Instruction to paragraph (a)(1): In an issuer tender offer disclose any material agreement, arrangement, understanding or relationship between the offeror and any of its executive officers, directors, controlling persons or subsidiaries.

(2) To the extent known by the offeror after reasonable investigation, the applicable regulatory requirements which must be complied with or approvals which must be obtained in connection with the tender offer;

(3) The applicability of any anti-trust laws;

(4) The applicability of margin requirements under section 7 of the Act (15 U.S.C. 78g) and the applicable regulations; and

(5) Any material pending legal proceedings relating to the tender offer, including the name and location of the court or agency in which the proceedings are pending, the date instituted, the principal parties, and a brief summary of the proceedings and the relief sought.

Instruction to Item 1011 (a)(5): A copy of any document relating to a major development (such as pleadings, an answer, complaint, temporary restraining order, injunction, opinion, judgment or order) in a material pending legal proceeding must be furnished promptly to the Commission staff on a supplemental basis.

(b) *Other material information.* Furnish such additional material information, if any, as may be necessary to make the required statements, in light of the circumstances under which they are made, not materially misleading.

(4)按照与《S-K管理办法》第503(d)条[第229.503(d)节]相符的方式计算得出的盈利对固定费用比率;

(5)截至最近提交的一期资产负债表之日的每股账面价值;及

(6)本节第(c)(1)款至第(c)(5)款所规定财务摘要信息的重大备考数据,以披露交易影响。

第229.1011节(第1011条) 其他信息

链接至《联邦公报》第76卷第6044页(2011年2月2日)的修正。

(a)协议、监管要求和法律程序。提供对证券持有人决定是否出售、承诺出售或持有收购要约中的证券具有重大影响的下列信息:

(1)要约人或其任何高管、董事、控制人或子公司与标的公司或其任何高管、董事、控制人或子公司之间既有或拟议签订的任何重大协议、安排、谅解或关系[不包括根据《M-A管理办法》任何其他条款(第229.1000~229.1016节)披露的任何协议、安排或谅解];

对第(a)(1)款的说明:在发行人的股权收购要约中披露要约人与其任何高管、董事、控制人或子公司之间的任何重大协议、安排、谅解或关系。

(2)在要约人合理调查后所知悉的范围内,与收购要约相关的必须得到遵守的适用监管规定或必须获得的批准;

(3)反垄断法律的适用性;

(4)《交易法》第7条(《美国法典》第十五编第78g节)以及适用法规的保证金要求的适用性;及

(5)关于收购要约的任何重大未决法律程序,包括正在开展程序的法院或机构的名称和地点、程序启动日期、主要当事人以及程序和所寻求救济的摘要。

关于第1011(a)(5)条的说明:如重大未决法律程序出现重大进展,则必须及时向证券交易委员会工作人员补充提交与该等变化相关的任何文件(如诉辩状、答辩、起诉书、临时限制令、禁令、意见、判决或命令)的复件一份。

(b)其他重大信息。结合报表编制情况,提供使规定报表不致产生严重误导的其他重大信息(如有)。

§229.1012(Item 1012) The solicitation or recommendation.

(a) *Solicitation or recommendation.* State the nature of the solicitation or the recommendation. If this statement relates to a recommendation, state whether the filing person is advising holders of the subject securities to accept or reject the tender offer or to take other action with respect to the tender offer and, if so, describe the other action recommended. If the filing person is the subject company and is not making a recommendation, state whether the subject company is expressing no opinion and is remaining neutral toward the tender offer or is unable to take a position with respect to the tender offer.

(b) *Reasons.* State the reasons for the position (including the inability to take a position) stated in paragraph (a) of this section. Conclusory statements such as "The tender offer is in the best interests of shareholders" are not considered sufficient disclosure.

(c) *Intent to tender.* To the extent known by the filing person after making reasonable inquiry, state whether the filing person or any executive officer, director, affiliate or subsidiary of the filing person currently intends to tender, sell or hold the subject securities that are held of record or beneficially owned by that person.

(d) *Intent to tender or vote in a going-private transaction.* To the extent known by the filing person after making reasonable inquiry, state whether or not any executive officer, director or affiliate of the issuer (or any person specified in Instruction C to the schedule) currently intends to tender or sell subject securities owned or held by that person and/or how each person currently intends to vote subject securities, including any securities the person has proxy authority for. State the reasons for the intended action.

Instruction to Item 1012(d): Provide the information required by this section if it is available to the filing person at the time the statement is initially filed with the Commission. If the information is not available, it must be filed with the Commission promptly, but in no event later than three business days after the date of the initial filing, and if material, disclosed in a manner reasonably designed to inform security holders.

(e) *Recommendations of others.* To the extent known by the filing person after making reasonable inquiry, state whether or not any person specified in paragraph (d) of this section has made a recommendation either in support of or opposed to the transaction and the reasons for the recommendation.

§229.1013(Item 1013) Purposes, alternatives, reasons and effects in a going-private transaction.

(a) *Purposes.* State the purposes for the Rule 13e-3 transaction.

(b) *Alternatives.* If the subject company or affiliate considered alternative means to accomplish the stated purposes, briefly describe the alternatives and state the reasons for

第229.1012节(第1012条) 征集投票权或建议

(a)征集投票权或建议。说明征集投票权或建议的性质。说明建议的性质时,应说明文件提交人是否建议目标证券持有人接受或拒绝股权收购要约或建议就收购要约采取其他行动。如果文件提交人建议持有人采取其他行动,应说明其建议采取的行动。若文件提交人是目标公司且未提出建议,说明目标公司是否未就此作出任何表态,并将对收购要约保持中立态度,或者无法就收购要约作出表态。

(b)理由。说明采取本节第(a)款所述目标公司采取的态度(包括无法表态)的理由。"收购要约符合股东的最佳利益"等结论性陈述不构成充分披露。

(c)承诺出售意向。在文件提交人进行合理的询问后知悉的范围内,说明文件提交人或其任何高管、董事、关联方或子公司当前是否有意承诺出售、出售或持有其作为登记股东或受益所有人持有的目标证券。

(d)在下市交易中承诺出售或表决的意向。在文件提交人进行合理询问后知悉的范围内,说明发行人的任何高管、董事或关联方(或附表的说明C中规定的任何主体)当前是否有意承诺出售或出售其拥有或持有的目标证券及/或当前每个主体基于目标证券表决时将采取的表决态度,上述目标证券包括其拥有代理权的任何证券。说明采取上述行动的理由。

关于第1012(d)条的说明:若文件提交人在首次向证券交易委员会提交声明时可以获得本节要求提供的信息,应提供该等信息;反之,文件提交人须及时向证券交易委员会提交该等信息,但在任何情况下,提交时间均不得迟于首次提交声明之日后3个营业日。如果属于重大信息,须以合理设计的披露方式向证券持有人提供信息。

(e)其他人的建议。在文件提交人进行合理询问后知悉的范围内,说明本节第(d)款中规定的任何主体是否提出了支持或反对交易的建议,并说明建议的理由。

第229.1013节(第1013条) 下市交易的目的、备选方式、理由及影响

(a)目的。说明《13e-3规则》交易的目的。

(b)备选方式。如果目标公司或其关联方曾考虑以其他方式达成上述目的,简要说明该等备选方式并说明未予采纳的理由。

their rejection.

(c) *Reasons.* State the reasons for the structure of the Rule 13e–3 transaction and for undertaking the transaction at this time.

(d) *Effects.* Describe the effects of the Rule 13e–3 transaction on the subject company, its affiliates and unaffiliated security holders, including the federal tax consequences of the transaction.

Instructions to Item 1013: 1. Conclusory statements will not be considered sufficient disclosure in response to this section.

2. The description required by paragraph (d) of this section must include a reasonably detailed discussion of both the benefits and detriments of the Rule 13e–3 transaction to the subject company, its affiliates and unaffiliated security holders. The benefits and detriments of the Rule 13e–3 transaction must be quantified to the extent practicable.

3. If this statement is filed by an affiliate of the subject company, the description required by paragraph (d) of this section must include, but not be limited to, the effect of the Rule 13e–3 transaction on the affiliate's interest in the net book value and net earnings of the subject company in terms of both dollar amounts and percentages.

§229.1014(Item 1014) Fairness of the going-private transaction.

(a) *Fairness.* State whether the subject company or affiliate filing the statement reasonably believes that the Rule 13e–3 transaction is fair or unfair to unaffiliated security holders. If any director dissented to or abstained from voting on the Rule 13e–3 transaction, identify the director, and indicate, if known, after making reasonable inquiry, the reasons for the dissent or abstention.

(b) *Factors considered in determining fairness.* Discuss in reasonable detail the material factors upon which the belief stated in paragraph (a) of this section is based and, to the extent practicable, the weight assigned to each factor. The discussion must include an analysis of the extent, if any, to which the filing person's beliefs are based on the factors described in Instruction 2 of this section, paragraphs (c), (d) and (e) of this section and Item 1015 of Regulation M–A (§229.1015).

(c) *Approval of security holders.* State whether or not the transaction is structured so that approval of at least a majority of unaffiliated security holders is required.

(d) *Unaffiliated representative.* State whether or not a majority of directors who are not employees of the subject company has retained an unaffiliated representative to act solely on behalf of unaffiliated security holders for purposes of negotiating the terms of the Rule 13e–3 transaction and/or preparing a report concerning the fairness of the transaction.

(e) *Approval of directors.* State whether or not the Rule 13e–3 transaction was

(c)理由。说明设定《13e-3规则》交易结构的理由及在此时开展交易的理由。

(d)影响。说明《13e-3规则》交易对目标公司、目标公司关联方及非关联证券持有人的影响,包括交易在联邦税务方面产生的影响。

关于第1013条的说明:1.结论性陈述不视为满足本节规定的充分披露。

2.本节第(d)款要求提供的说明必须以合理详细程度论述《13e-3规则》交易对目标公司、目标公司关联方及非关联证券持有人的有利及不利影响。在可行的范围内,该等有利或不利影响应予以量化。

3.如声明系由目标公司的关联方提交,则按照本节第(d)款提供的说明须包括但不限于《13e-3规则》交易对该关联方享有的目标公司账面净值及净盈利所享有的权益的影响,影响应包括金额及比例两方面。

第229.1014节(第1014条) 下市交易的公允性

(a)公允性。说明目标公司或其关联方在提交声明时是否合理地认为《13e-3规则》交易对非关联证券持有人具有公允性。若任何董事对《13e-3规则》交易持有异议或放弃表决权,应注明该等董事,且如果进行合理询问后知悉该等董事提出异议或弃权的理由,应如实说明。

(b)判断公允性时考虑的因素。以合理详细的程度论述本节第(a)款所述观点所依据的重大因素,并在可行的范围内,说明各项因素所占的权重。如文件提交人得出的结论系基于关于本节的说明2、本节第(c)款、第(d)款和第(e)款以及《MA管理办法》第1015条(第229.1015节)所述因素,上述论述还应对该等因素与文件提交人的结论之间的联系的紧密性进行分析。

(c)证券持有人的批准。说明根据交易的架构,交易是否至少需要获得过半数非关联证券持有人的批准。

(d)非关联代表。说明是否目标公司的过半数非雇员董事已聘请非关联代表,由其全权代表非关联证券持有人谈判《13e-3规则》交易的条款及/或编制交易公允性报告。

(e)董事的批准。说明《13e-3规则》交易是否已获得目标公司过半数非雇员董

approved by a majority of the directors of the subject company who are not employees of the subject company.

(f) *Other offers.* If any offer of the type described in paragraph (viii) of Instruction 2 to this section has been received, describe the offer and state the reasons for its rejection.

Instructions to Item 1014 : 1. A statement that the issuer or affiliate has no reasonable belief as to the fairness of the Rule 13e–3 transaction to unaffiliated security holders will not be considered sufficient disclosure in response to paragraph (a) of this section.

2. The factors that are important in determining the fairness of a transaction to unaffiliated security holders and the weight, if any, that should be given to them in a particular context will vary. Normally such factors will include, among others, those referred to in paragraphs (c), (d) and (e) of this section and whether the consideration offered to unaffiliated security holders constitutes fair value in relation to:

(i) Current market prices;

(ii) Historical market prices;

(iii) Net book value;

(iv) Going concern value;

(v) Liquidation value;

(vi) Purchase prices paid in previous purchases disclosed in response to Item 1002(f) of Regulation M–A (§229.1002(f));

(vii) Any report, opinion, or appraisal described in Item 1015 of Regulation M–A (§229.1015); and

(viii) Firm offers of which the subject company or affiliate is aware made by any unaffiliated person, other than the filing persons, during the past two years for:

(A) The merger or consolidation of the subject company with or into another company, or *vice versa;*

(B) The sale or other transfer of all or any substantial part of the assets of the subject company; or

(C) A purchase of the subject company's securities that would enable the holder to exercise control of the subject company.

3. Conclusory statements, such as "The Rule 13e–3 transaction is fair to unaffiliated security holders in relation to net book value, going concern value and future prospects of the issuer" will not be considered sufficient disclosure in response to paragraph (b) of this section.

§229.1015(Item 1015) Reports, opinions, appraisals and negotiations.

(a) *Report, opinion or appraisal.* State whether or not the subject company or affiliate has received any report, opinion (other than an opinion of counsel) or appraisal

事批准。

(f)其他要约。若收到本节说明2第(viii)款所述其他类型的要约,应描述该要约并说明拒绝该要约的理由。

关于第1014条的说明:1.仅仅声明"发行人或关联方没有合理理由相信《13e-3规则》交易对非关联证券持有人具有公允性"不构成满足本节第(a)款规定的充分披露。

2.对于判断交易对非关联证券持有人的公允性具有重要意义的因素及其在特定背景下应占的分量(如有)会有所不同。通常,除本节第(c)款、第(d)款和第(e)款所述因素之外,还应基于如下参数考虑向非关联证券持有人提供的对价是否构成公允价值:

(i)现行市场价格;

(ii)历史市场价格;

(iii)账面净值;

(iv)持续经营价值;

(v)清算价值;

(vi)根据《M-A管理办法》第1002(f)条[第229.1002(f)条]披露的在之前的购买中支付的购买价格;

(vii)《M-A管理办法》第1015条(第229.1015节)所述任何报告、意见或评估结果;及

(viii)目标公司或关联方知悉的在过去两年内由任何非关联人(文件提交人除外)就下列各项所提出的确定性要约:

(A)对目标公司的吸收合并或新设合并,或目标公司对其他公司的吸收合并或新设合并;

(B)出售或以其他方式转让目标公司的所有或任何实质资产;或

(C)购买目标公司的证券,且购买后将导致持有人拥有目标公司的控制权。

3."《13e-3规则》交易在账面净值、持续经营价值及发行人的发展前景方面对非关联证券持有人是公平的"等结论性陈述不视为满足本节第(b)款规定的充分披露。

第229.1015节(第1015条) 报告、意见、评估结果及谈判

(a)报告、意见或评估结果。说明目标公司或关联方是否曾收到来自外部当事方的并与《13e-3规则》交易有重大关系的任何报告、意见(律师意见除外)或评估结果,包

from an outside party that is materially related to the Rule 13e-3 transaction, including, but not limited to: Any report, opinion or appraisal relating to the consideration or the fairness of the consideration to be offered to security holders or the fairness of the transaction to the issuer or affiliate or to security holders who are not affiliates.

(b) *Preparer and summary of the report, opinion or appraisal.* For each report, opinion or appraisal described in response to paragraph (a) of this section or any negotiation or report described in response to Item 1014(d) of Regulation M-A (§229.1014) or Item 14(b)(6) of Schedule 14A (§240.14a-101 of this chapter) concerning the terms of the transaction:

(1) Identify the outside party and/or unaffiliated representative;

(2) Briefly describe the qualifications of the outside party and/or unaffiliated representative;

(3) Describe the method of selection of the outside party and/or unaffiliated representative;

(4) Describe any material relationship that existed during the past two years or is mutually understood to be contemplated and any compensation received or to be received as a result of the relationship between:

(i) The outside party, its affiliates, and/or unaffiliated representative; and

(ii) The subject company or its affiliates;

(5) If the report, opinion or appraisal relates to the fairness of the consideration, state whether the subject company or affiliate determined the amount of consideration to be paid or whether the outside party recommended the amount of consideration to be paid; and

(6) Furnish a summary concerning the negotiation, report, opinion or appraisal. The summary must include, but need not be limited to, the procedures followed; the findings and recommendations; the bases for and methods of arriving at such findings and recommendations; instructions received from the subject company or affiliate; and any limitation imposed by the subject company or affiliate on the scope of the investigation.

Instruction to Item 1015(b): The information called for by paragraphs (b)(1), (2) and (3) of this section must be given with respect to the firm that provides the report, opinion or appraisal rather than the employees of the firm that prepared the report.

(c) *Availability of documents.* Furnish a statement to the effect that the report, opinion or appraisal will be made available for inspection and copying at the principal executive offices of the subject company or affiliate during its regular business hours by any interested equity security holder of the subject company or representative who has been so designated in writing. This statement also may provide that a copy of the report, opinion or appraisal will be transmitted by the subject company or affiliate to any

括但不限于:关于向证券持有人要约的对价或该等对价的公允性或关于该交易对发行人、发行人的关联方或非关联证券持有人的公允性的任何报告、意见或评估结果。

(b)报告、意见或评估结果的编制人及摘要。对于本节第(a)款所述的各项报告、意见或评估结果,或《M-A管理办法》第1014(d)条(第229.1014节)或《附表14A》第14(b)(6)条(本章第240.14a-101节)所述的关于交易条款的任何谈判或报告,应:

(1)说明该外部当事方及/或非关联代表的身份;

(2)简要说明该外部当事方及/或非关联代表的资质;

(3)说明选择该外部当事方及/或非关联代表时所使用的方法;

(4)说明下列各方在过去2年中存在的任何重大关系或双方已达成共识的任何重大关系,以及因该等关系而收到或预期收到的任何报酬:

(i)上述外部当事方及其关联方及/或非关联代表;与

(ii)目标公司或其关联方;

(5)说明对价金额是由目标公司或关联方决定的还是由外部当事方建议的(若报告、意见或评估结果涉及对价的公允性);并

(6)提供一份谈判、报告、意见或评估结果的摘要。摘要必须包括但不必局限于如下内容:采取的程序;结论及建议;得出该等结论及建议的依据及方法;目标公司或关联方作出的指示;以及目标公司或关联方对调查范围设定的任何限制。

关于第1015(b)条的说明:本节第(b)(1)款、第(b)(2)款及第(b)(3)款要求提供的信息指提供该等报告、意见或评估结果的机构的信息,而非该等机构编制该等报告、意见或评估结果的具体员工的信息。

(c)文件的提供。目标公司或关联方应作出如下声明:目标公司或关联方将在其在主要管理人员办公室提供上述报告、意见或评估结果,供目标公司的任何利益相关的股权证券持有人或其书面指定的代表在正常办公时间内查阅及复印。声明中还可规定,经任何利益相关的股权证券持有人提出要求,目标公司或关联方应向该证券持有人或其书面委托的代表提供一份该等报告、意见或评估结果的复本,相关费用由证券持有人承担。

interested equity security holder of the subject company or representative who has been so designated in writing upon written request and at the expense of the requesting security holder.

§229.1016(Item 1016) Exhibits.

File as an exhibit to the schedule:

(a) Any disclosure materials furnished to security holders by or on behalf of the filing person, including:

(1) Tender offer materials (including transmittal letter);

(2) Solicitation or recommendation (including those referred to in Item 1012 of Regulation M-A (§229.1012));

(3) Going-private disclosure document;

(4) Prospectus used in connection with an exchange offer where securities are registered under the Securities Act of 1933; and

(5) Any other disclosure materials;

(b) Any loan agreement referred to in response to Item 1007(d) of Regulation M-A (§229.1007(d));

Instruction to Item 1016(b): If the filing relates to a third-party tender offer and a request is made under Item 1007(d) of Regulation M-A (§229.1007(d)), the identity of the bank providing financing may be omitted from the loan agreement filed as an exhibit.

(c) Any report, opinion or appraisal referred to in response to Item 1014(d) or Item 1015 of Regulation M-A (§229.1014(d) or §229.1015);

(d) Any document setting forth the terms of any agreement, arrangement, understanding or relationship referred to in response to Item 1005(e) or Item 1011(a)(1) of Regulation M-A (§229.1005(e) or §229.1011(a)(1));

(e) Any agreement, arrangement or understanding referred to in response to §229.1005 (d), or the pertinent portions of any proxy statement, report or other communication containing the disclosure required by Item 1005(d) of Regulation M-A (§229.1005(d));

(f) A detailed statement describing security holders' appraisal rights and the procedures for exercising those appraisal rights referred to in response to Item 1004(d) of Regulation M-A (§229.1004(d));

(g) Any written instruction, form or other material that is furnished to persons making an oral solicitation or recommendation by or on behalf of the filing person for their use directly or indirectly in connection with the transaction; and

(h) Any written opinion prepared by legal counsel at the filing person's request and communicated to the filing person pertaining to the tax consequences of the transaction.

第229.1016节(第1016条) 附录

将如下材料作为附表的附录提交:

(a)文件提交人或其代表向证券持有人提供的任何披露材料,包括:

(1)收购要约材料(包括附函);

(2)征集投票权或建议(包括《M-A管理办法》第1012条(第229.1012节)所述邀请或建议);

(3)下市披露文件;

(4)对根据《1933年证券法》注册的证券提出交换要约时使用的招募说明书;及

(5)任何其他披露材料;

(b)根据《M-A管理办法》第1007(d)条[第229.1007(d)节]的规定披露的任何贷款协议;

关于第1016(b)条的说明:若提交文件涉及第三方收购要约,且文件提交人根据《M-A管理办法》第1007(d)条[第229.1007(d)节]提出了请求,作为附录提交的贷款协议可略去提供融资的银行的信息。

(c)根据《M-A管理办法》第1014(d)节或第1015条[第229.1014(d)节或第229.1015节]披露的任何报告、意见或评估结果;

(d)载明根据《M-A管理办法》第1005(e)条或第1011(a)(1)节[第229.1005(e)节或第229.1011(a)(1)节]披露的任何协议、安排、谅解或关系的条款的任何文件;

(e)根据第229.1005(d)节的规定披露的任何协议、安排或谅解,或任何代理委托书、报告或其他通信中包含《M-A管理办法》第1005(d)条[第229.1005(d)节]规定的披露的相关部分内容;

(f)关于根据《M-A管理办法》第1004(d)条[第229.1004(d)节]披露的证券持有人评估权和该等评估权行使程序的详细说明;

(g)文件提交人或其代表向口头征集投票权或提出建议的人提供其使用的与交易直接或间接相关的任何书面指示、表格或其他资料;及

(h)法律顾问经文件提交人要求编制并向文件提交人发送的关于交易的税收影响的任何书面意见。

Exhibit Table to Item 1016 of Regulation M–A

	13E –3	TO	14D –9
Disclosure Material	X	X	X
Loan Agreement	X	X	
Report, Opinion or Appraisal	X		
Contracts, Arrangements or Understandings	X	X	X
Statement re: Appraisal Rights	X		
Oral Solicitation Materials	X	X	X
Tax Opinion		X	

Subpart 229.1100—Asset–Backed Securities (Regulation AB)

Source: 70 FR 1597, Jan. 7, 2005, unless otherwise noted.

§229.1100(Item 1100) General

(a) *Application of Regulation AB.* Regulation AB (§§229.1100 through 229.1123) is the source of various disclosure items and requirements for "asset–backed securities" filings under the Securities Act of 1933 (15 U.S.C. 77a *et seq.*) (the "Securities Act") and the Securities Exchange Act of 1934 (the "Exchange Act") (15 U.S.C. 78a *et seq.*). Unless otherwise specified, definitions to be used in this Regulation AB, including the definition of "asset–backed security," are set forth in Item 1101.

(b) *Presentation of historical delinquency and loss information.* Several Items in Regulation AB call for the presentation of historical information and data on delinquencies and loss information. In providing such information:

(1) Present delinquency experience in 30 or 31 day increments, as applicable, beginning at least with assets that are 30 or 31 days delinquent, as applicable, through the point that assets are written off or charged off as uncollectable. At a minimum, present such information by number of accounts and dollar amount. Present statistical information in a tabular or graphical format, if such presentation will aid understanding.

(2) Disclose the total amount of delinquent assets as a percentage of the aggregate asset pool.

(3) Present loss and cumulative loss information, as applicable, regarding charge–offs, charge–off rate, gross losses, recoveries and net losses (with a description of how these terms are defined), the number and amount of assets experiencing a loss and the number and amount of assets with a recovery, the ratio of aggregate net losses to average

《M-A管理办法》第1016条附录一览表

	13E－3	TO	14D－9
披露材料	X	X	X
贷款协议	X	X	
报告、意见或评估结果	X		
合约、安排或谅解	X	X	X
关于评估权的说明	X		
口头征集投票权材料	X	X	X
税务意见		X	

第229.1100子部分——资产支持证券(《AB管理办法》)

行政规则来源:《联邦公报》第70卷第1597页,2005年1月7日,除非另有说明。

第229.1100节(第1100条) 一般规定

(a)《AB管理办法》申请。《AB管理办法》(第229.1100~229.1123节)是《1933年证券法》(《美国法典》第十五编第77a节及其后条文,下称《证券法》)和《1934年证券交易法》(《美国法典》第十五编第78节及其后条文,下称《交易法》)中关于"资产支持证券"提交文件的各种披露项目及提交要求的行政规则来源。除非另有规定,《AB管理办法》中使用的术语(包括"资产支持证券")之定义应以第1101条的规定为准。

(b)列报历史拖欠及损失信息。《AB管理办法》的多款规定均要求列报历史拖欠及损失信息和数据。在提供该等信息时,应:

(1)列报拖欠达30日或31日(以适用者为准)的情形,列报期间至少始于资产拖欠满30日或31日之时(以适用者为准),截至资产被当作呆账冲销或核销之时。至少应列报该等情况的账户数目及金额信息。若表格或图形有助于理解,应以表格或图形形式提供统计信息。

(2)披露拖欠资产总额占资产池总额的百分比。

(3)列报核销、核销率、损失总额、收回额及损失净额(并说明该等术语是如何界定的)的损失及累积损失信息(以使用者为准)、损失资产的数量及金额和收回资产的数量及金额、净损失总额占平均资产余额的比率以及遭受净损失的所有资产的平均净损失。

portfolio balance and the average of net loss on all assets that have experienced a net loss.

(4) Categorize all delinquency and loss information by pool asset type.

(5) In a registration statement under the Securities Act or the Exchange Act or in a prospectus to be filed pursuant to §230.424, describe how delinquencies, charge-offs and uncollectable accounts are defined or determined, addressing the effect of any grace period, re-aging, restructure, partial payments considered current or other practices on delinquency and loss experience.

(6) Describe any other material information regarding delinquencies and losses particular to the pool asset type(s), such as repossession information, foreclosure information and real estate owned (REO) or similar information.

(c) *Presentation of certain third party financial information.* If financial information of a third party is required in a filing by Item 1112(b) of this Regulation AB (Information regarding significant obligors) or Items 1114(b)(2) or 1115(b) of this Regulation AB (Information regarding significant provider of enhancement or other support), such information, in lieu of including such information, may be provided as follows:

(1) *Incorporation by reference.* If the following conditions are met, you may incorporate by reference (by means of a statement to that effect) the reports filed by the third party (or the entity that consolidates the third party) pursuant to section 13 (a) or 15(d) of the Exchange Act (15 U.S.C. 78m(a) or 78o(d)):

(i) Such third party or the entity that consolidates the third party is required to file reports with the Commission pursuant to section 13(a) or 15(d) of the Exchange Act.

(ii) Such third party or the entity that consolidates the third party has filed all reports and other materials required to be filed by such requirements during the preceding 12 months (or such shorter period that such party was required to file such reports and materials).

(iii) The reports filed by such third party, or entity that consolidates the third party, include (or properly incorporate by reference) the financial statements of such third party.

(iv) If incorporated by reference into a prospectus or registration statement, the prospectus also states that all documents subsequently filed by such third party, or the entity that consolidates the third party, pursuant to section 13 (a) or 15 (d) of the Exchange Act prior to the termination of the offering also shall be deemed to be incorporated by reference into the prospectus.

Instructions to Item 1100(c)(1): 1. In addition to the conditions in paragraph (c)(1) of this section, any information incorporated by reference must comply with all applicable Commission rules pertaining to incorporation by reference, such as Item 10 (d) of Regulation S-K (§229.10(d)), Rule 303 of Regulation S-T (§232.303 of this chapter),

(4)根据资产池内资产的类型划分所有拖欠及损失信息。

(5)在依照《证券法》或《交易法》提交的注册说明书中或根据第230.424节提交的招募说明书中,应说明拖欠、核销及呆账是如何界定或确定的,并说明任何宽限期、重新计期、重组、视为流动资产的分批付款或其他关于拖欠及损失的做法的影响。

(6)说明关于资产池内各类型资产拖欠及损失的任何其他重大信息,如收回、止赎和银行回收房产(REO)或类似信息。

(c)列报特定第三方财务信息。若本《AB管理办法》第1112(b)条(重大债务人信息)、第1114(b)(2)条或第1115(b)条(重大信用增级提供方或其他支持提供方信息)要求在相应的提交文件中包含第三方财务信息,该等信息可通过以下方式(而非直接纳入的方式)提供:

(1)以引用方式纳入提交文件。在满足下列条件的前提下,可通过引用方式将第三方或合并该第三方的实体根据《交易法》第13(a)条或第15(d)条[《美国法典》第十五编第78m(a)节或第78o(d)节]提交的报告纳入提交文件(并进行相应声明):

(i)《交易法》第13(a)条或第15(d)条要求该等第三方或合并该第三方的实体向证券交易委员会提交报告。

(ii)该等第三方或合并该第三方的实体在过去12个月内(或其他规定的更短期限内)按上述规定提交了所有报告及其他材料。

(iii)该等第三方或合并该第三方的实体提交的报告包含(或以引用方式适当纳入了)该等第三方的财务报表。

(iv)若以引用方式纳入招募说明书或注册说明书,则招募说明书还应包含以下声明:该等第三方或合并该等第三方的实体在发行终止以前根据《交易法》第13(a)条或第15(d)条后续提交的所有文件同样应视为以引用方式纳入招募说明书。

关于第1100(c)(1)条的说明:1.除本节第(c)(1)款规定的条件外,以引用方式纳入的所有信息均应符合证券交易委员会关于引用纳入的所有适用规则,如《S-K管理办法》第10(d)条[第229.10(d)条]、《S-T管理办法》的《303规则》(本章第232.303节)、《C管理办法》的《411规则》(本章第230.411节)及《交易法》的《12b-23规则》及《12b-32

Rule 411 of Regulation C (§230.411 of this chapter), and Rules 12b-23 and 12b-32 under the Exchange Act (§§240.12b-23 and 240.12b-32 of this chapter).

2. In addition, any applicable requirements under the Securities Act or the rules and regulations of the Commission regarding the filing of a written consent for the use of incorporated material apply to the material incorporated by reference.*See* , for example, §230.439 of this chapter.

3. Any undertakings set forth in Item 512 of Regulation S-K (§229.512) apply to any material incorporated by reference in a registration statement or prospectus.

4. If neither the third party nor any of its affiliates has had a direct or indirect agreement, arrangement, relationship or understanding, written or otherwise, relating to the ABS transaction, and neither the third party nor any of its affiliates is an affiliate of the sponsor, depositor, issuing entity or underwriter of the ABS transaction, then paragraph (c)(1)(ii) of this section is qualified by the knowledge of the registrant.

5. If you are relying on paragraph (c)(1) of this section to provide information required by Item 1112 of this Regulation AB regarding a significant obligor that is an asset-backed issuer and the pool assets relating to such significant obligor are asset-backed securities, then for purposes of paragraph (c)(1)(iii) of this section, the term "financial statements" means the information required by Instruction 3 of Item 1112 of this Regulation AB. Such information required by Instruction 3.a. of Item 1112 of this Regulation AB may be incorporated by reference from a prospectus that contains such information and is included in an effective Securities Act registration statement or filed pursuant to §230.424 of this chapter.

(2) *Reference information for significant obligors.* If the third party information relates to a significant obligor and the following conditions are met, you may include a reference to the third party's periodic reports (or the third party's parent with respect to paragraph (c)(2)(ii)(C) of this section) under section 13(a) or 15(d) of the Exchange Act (15 U.S.C. 78m(a) or 78o(d)) that are on file with the Commission (or otherwise publicly available with respect to paragraph (c)(2)(ii)(F) of this section), along with a statement of how those reports may be accessed, including the third party's name and Commission file number, if applicable (See, e.g., Item 1118 of this Regulation AB):

(i) Neither the third party nor any of its affiliates has had a direct or indirect agreement, arrangement, relationship or understanding, written or otherwise, relating to the asset-backed securities transaction, and neither the third party nor any of its affiliates is an affiliate of the sponsor, depositor, issuing entity or underwriter of the asset-backed securities transaction.

(ii) To the knowledge of the registrant, any of the following is true:

(A) The third party is eligible to use Form S-3 or F-3 (§239.13 or 239.33 of this

规则》(本章第240.12b-23节及第240.12b-32节)。

2.此外,《证券法》中的任何适用规定,或者证券交易委员会针对使用引用纳入之材料的同意书的提交所制定的规则及规章均适用于以引用方式纳入的材料。例如,参见本章第230.439节。

3.《S-K管理办法》第512条(第229.512节)规定的所有承诺均适用于以引用方式纳入注册说明书或招募说明书的任何材料。

4.若第三方及其任何关联方均不存在关于资产支持证券交易的书面或其他形式的直接或间接协议、安排、关系或谅解,且该等第三方或其任何关联方均非资产支持证券交易的发起人、交存人、发行实体或承销商的关联方,则本节第(c)(1)(ii)款的适用应以注册人明知的情况为限。

5.如注册人援引本节第(c)(1)款的规定提供《AB管理办法》第1112条要求提供的重大债务人信息,且该债务人属于资产支持证券发行人,同时与该等债务人相关的池内资产属于资产支持证券,则就本节第(c)(1)(iii)款而言,"财务报表"一词系指《AB管理办法》第1112条的说明3要求提供的信息。《AB管理办法》第1112条的说明3.a.要求提供的信息可通过引用下述文件的方式纳入:包含该等信息的《证券法》下有效的注册说明书所包含的招募说明书,或包含该等信息的根据本章第230.424节提交的招募说明书。

(2)引用重大债务人信息。若第三方信息与重大债务人相关且满足下列条件,注册人可引用在证券交易委员会备案的[或根据本节第(c)(2)(ii)(F)款以其他方式公开的]根据《交易法》第13(a)条或第15(d)条[《美国法典》第十五编第78m(a)节或第78o(d)节]提交的第三方定期报告[或本节第(c)(2)(ii)(C)款要求提交的第三方母公司报告],同时说明获取该等报告[包括第三方的名称及在证券交易委员会的备案号(若适用)]的方式(如请参见《AB管理办法》第1118条):

(i)第三方及其关联方均不存在关于资产支持证券交易的书面或其他形式的直接或间接协议、安排、关系或谅解,且该第三方或其任何关联方均非资产支持证券交易的发起人、交存人、发行实体或承销商的关联方。

(ii)据注册人所知,下列任何一项所述情形是真实的:

(A)第三方有资格根据《S-3表格》或《F-3表格》(本章第239.13节或第239.33节)的

chapter) for a primary offering of non-investment grade securities pursuant to General Instruction I.B.1 of such forms.

(B) The third party meets the requirements of General Instruction I.A. of Form S-3 or General Instructions 1.A.1, 2, 3, 4 and 6 of Form F-3 and the pool assets relating to such third party are non-convertible investment grade securities, as described in General Instruction 1.B.2 of Form S-3 or Form F-3.

(C) If the third party does not meet the conditions of paragraph (c)(2)(ii)(A) or (c)(2)(ii)(B) of this section and the pool assets relating to the third party are fully and unconditionally guaranteed by a direct or indirect parent of the third party, General Instruction I.C.3 of Form S-3 or General Instruction I.A.5 (iii) of Form F-3 is met with respect to the pool assets relating to such third party and the requirements of Rule 3-10 of Regulation S-X (§210.3-10 of this chapter) are satisfied regarding the information in the reports to be referenced.

(D) If the pool assets relating to the third party are guaranteed by a wholly owned subsidiary of the third party and the subsidiary does not meet the conditions of paragraph (c)(2)(ii)(A) or (c)(2)(ii)(B) of this section, the criteria in either paragraph (c)(2)(ii)(A) or paragraph (c)(2)(ii)(B) of this section are met with respect to the third party and the requirements of Rule 3-10 of Regulation S-X (§210.3-10 of this chapter) are satisfied regarding the information in the reports to be referenced.

(E) The pool assets relating to such third party are asset-backed securities and the third party is filing reports pursuant to section 12 or 15(d) of the Exchange Act(15 U.S.C. 78l or 78o(d)) and has filed all the material that would be required to be filed pursuant to section 13, 14 or 15(d) of the Exchange Act (15 U.S.C. 78m, 78n or 78o(d)) for a period of at least twelve calendar months and any portion of a month immediately preceding the filing referencing the third party's reports (or such shorter period that such third party was required to file such materials).

(F) The third party is a U.S. government-sponsored enterprise, has outstanding securities held by non-affiliates with an aggregate market value of $75 million or more, and makes information publicly available on an annual and quarterly basis, including audited financial statements prepared in accordance with generally accepted accounting principles covering the same periods that would be required for audited financial statements under Regulation S-X(§§210.1-01 through 210.12-29 of this chapter) and non-financial information consistent with that required by Regulation S-K (§§229.10 through 229.1123).

Instruction to Item 1100 (c)(2): If you are relying on paragraph (c)(2)(ii)(E) of this section because the pool assets relating to such third party are asset-backed securities, then for purposes of a registration statement under the Securities Act or the

总体说明I.B.1在非投资级证券的初次发行中使用该等表格。

(B)第三方符合《S-3表格》的总体说明I.A.的要求或《F-3表格》的总体说明1.A.1、1.A.2、1.A.3、1.A.4及1.A.6的要求,且与该第三方相关的池内资产为《S-3表格》的总体说明I.B.2或《F-3表格》所述的不可转换的投资级证券。

(C)第三方不满足本节第(c)(2)(ii)(A)款或第(c)(2)(ii)(B)款的条件,但第三方的直接或间接母公司为与第三方相关的池内资产提供充分、无条件的担保,与第三方相关的池内资产符合《S-3表格》的总体说明I.C.3的要求或《F-3表格》的总体说明I.A.5(iii)的要求,且所引用报告中的信息符合《S-X管理办法》的《3-10规则》(本章第210.3-10节)的要求。

(D)第三方的全资子公司为第三方的池内资产提供担保,且该子公司不符合本节第(c)(2)(ii)(A)款或第(c)(2)(ii)(B)款规定的条件,但是,该第三方符合本节第(c)(2)(ii)(A)款或第(c)(2)(ii)(B)款的标准,且所引用报告中的信息符合《S-X管理办法》的《3-10规则》(本章第210.3-10节)的要求。

(E)与该等第三方相关的池内资产属于资产支持证券,且该等第三方负有根据《交易法》第12条或第15(d)条[《美国法典》第十五编第78*l*节或第78o(d)节]提交报告的义务,并已根据《交易法》第13条、第14条或第15(d)条[《美国法典》第十五编第78m节、第78n节或第78o(d)节]的规定,至少就提交引用第三方报告的文件之前12个月(任何不满1个月的部分也应计算在内)的期间(或其他规定的较短期间)提交了所有要求提交的材料。

(F)第三方为美国政府发起企业,非关联方持有的发行在外的证券总市值达7500万美元(含)以上,并按年和按季公布信息,包括按照公认会计原则编制的已审计财务报表(覆盖期间为《S-X管理办法》(本章第210.1-01~210.12-29节)规定的已审计财务报表应覆盖的期间)及《S-K管理办法》(本章第229.10~229.1123节)要求提交的非财务信息等。

关于第1100(c)(2)条的说明:若注册人基于第三方的池内资产属于资产支持证券而援引本节第(c)(2)(ii)(E)款的规定,则就《证券法》或《交易法》中的注册说明书或根据第230.424节提交的招募说明书而言,还须引用以下第三方资产支持证券招募说

Exchange Act or a prospectus to be filed pursuant to §230.424 for your securities, you also must include a reference (including Commission reporting number and filing date) to the prospectus for the third party asset-backed securities that:

(a) Is either included in an effective Securities Act registration statement or filed pursuant to §230.424 of this chapter; and

(b) Contains the information required by Instruction 3.a. of Item 1112 of this Regulation AB.

(d) *Other participants to the transaction and pool assets representing interests in certain other asset pools.* (1) If the asset-backed securities transaction involves additional or intermediate parties not specifically identified in this Regulation AB, the disclosure required by this Regulation AB includes information to the extent material regarding any such party and its role, function and experience in relation to the asset-backed securities and the asset pool. Describe the material terms of any agreement with such party regarding the transaction, and file such agreement as an exhibit.

(2) If the asset pool backing the asset-backed securities includes one or more pool assets representing an interest in or the right to the payments or cash flows of another asset pool, then for purposes of this Regulation AB and §§240.13a-18 and 240.15d-18 of this chapter, references to the asset pool and the pool assets of the issuing entity also include the other asset pool and its pool assets if the following conditions are met:

(i) Both the issuing entity for the asset-backed securities and the entity issuing the pool asset to be included in the issuing entity's asset pool were established under the direction of the same sponsor or depositor.

(ii) The pool asset was created solely to satisfy legal requirements or otherwise facilitate the structuring of the asset-backed securities transaction.

*Instruction to Item 1100(d)(2).*Reference to the underlying asset pool includes, without limitation, compliance with applicable servicing criteria referenced in §§240.13a-18 and 240.15d-18 of this chapter and the servicer compliance statement required by Item 1123 of this Regulation AB. In addition, provide clear and concise disclosure, including by flow chart or other illustration, of the transaction and the various parties involved.

(e) *Foreign asset-backed securities.* If the asset-backed securities are issued by a foreign issuer (as defined in §230.405 of this chapter), backed by pool assets that are foreign assets, or affected by enhancement or support contemplated by Items 1114 or 1115 of this Regulation AB provided by a foreign entity, then in providing the disclosure required by this Regulation AB (including, but not limited to, Items 1104 and 1110 of this Regulation AB regarding origination and securitization practices, Item 1107 of this Regulation AB regarding the sale or transfer of the pool assets, bankruptcy remoteness

明书(包括证券交易委员会的报告编号及提交日期):

(a)包含在已生效的《证券法》注册说明书中的招募说明书或根据本章第230.424节提交的招募说明书;及

(b)包含《AB管理办法》第1112条的说明3.a.要求提交的信息的招募说明书。

(d)其他交易参与人以及代表其他特定资产池权益的池内资产。(1)如果资产支持证券交易涉及本《AB管理办法》中未具体指明的其他方或中间方,按本《AB管理办法》规定进行披露时应提供关于该等其他方或中间方及其在资产支持证券和资产池方面的作用、功能及经验的重大信息,同时应说明与该等其他方或中间方就交易达成的所有协议的重大条款,并将该等协议作为附录提交。

(2)如果支持资产支持证券的资产池所包含的一项或一项以上的池内资产代表了其他资产池款项或现金流的权益或权利,则就本《AB管理办法》及本章第240.13a-18节和第240.15d-18节而言,如果满足以下条件,则指称发行实体的资产池和池内资产时,应包括上述其他资产池及其池内资产:

(i)资产支持证券的发行实体,以及该等被纳入的其他池内资产的发行实体,均按照同一发起人或交存人的指示而设立。

(ii)池内资产仅为满足法律要求或以其他方式促进资产支持证券交易的架构的目的而设立。

关于第1100(d)(2)条的说明。提及基础资产池时,应加入包括但不限于如下内容:提供关于本章第240.13a-18节和第240.15d-18节规定的相关服务标准的合规声明以及本《AB管理办法》第1123条要求的服务合规声明的情形。此外,应通过流程图或其他方式对交易以及所涉各方进行清晰、简明的披露。

(e)外国资产支持证券。如果资产支持证券由外国发行人(定义见本章第230.405节)发行,由作为外国资产的池内资产支持,或者外国实体为之提供本《AB管理办法》第1114条或第1115条规定的信用增级或支持措施,则在进行本《AB管理办法》要求的披露时[包括但不限于下述条款要求的披露:本《AB管理办法》第1104条和第1110条(关于发起和证券化惯例的规定)、本《AB管理办法》第1107条(关于池内资产出售或转让、破产隔离及担保品保护的规定)、本《AB管理办法》第1108条(关于服务的规定)、本《AB管理办法》第1109条(关于信托受托人权利、职责及责任的规定)、本《AB管理办

and collateral protection, Item 1108 of this Regulation AB regarding servicing, Item 1109 of this Regulation AB regarding the rights, duties and responsibilities of the trustee, Item 1111 of this Regulation AB regarding the terms, nature and treatment of the pool assets and Items 1114 or 1115 of this Regulation AB, as applicable, regarding the enhancement provider), the filing must describe any pertinent governmental, legal or regulatory or administrative matters and any pertinent tax matters, exchange controls, currency restrictions or other economic, fiscal, monetary or potential factors in the applicable home jurisdiction that could materially affect payments on, the performance of, or other matters relating to, the assets contained in the pool or the asset-backed securities. See also Instruction 2 to Item 202 of Regulation S-K (§229.202). In addition, in a registration statement under the Securities Act, provide the information required by Item 101(g) of Regulation S-K (§229.101(g)). Disclosure also is required in Forms 10-D (§249.312 of this chapter) and 10-K (§249.310 of this chapter) with respect to the asset-backed securities regarding any material impact caused by foreign legal and regulatory developments during the period covered by the report which have not been previously described in a Form 10-D, 10-K or 8-K (§249.308 of this chapter) filed under the Exchange Act.

(f) *Filing of required exhibits.* Where agreements or other documents in this Regulation AB are specified to be filed as exhibits to a Securities Act registration statement, such final agreements or other documents, if applicable, may be incorporated by reference as an exhibit to the registration statement, such as by filing a Form 8-K in the case of offerings registered on Form S-3 (§239.13 of this chapter).

[70 FR 1597, Jan. 7, 2005, as amended at 70 FR 72373, Dec. 5, 2005]

§229.1101(Item 1101) Definitions.

The following definitions apply to the terms used in Regulation AB (§§229.1100 through 229.1123), unless specified otherwise:

(a) *ABS informational and computational material* means a written communication consisting solely of one or some combination of the following:

(1) Factual information regarding the asset-backed securities being offered and the structure and basic parameters of the securities, such as the number of classes, seniority, payment priorities, terms of payment, the tax, Employment Retirement Income Security Act of 1974, as amended, (29 U.S.C. 1001 *et seq.*) ("ERISA") or other legal conclusions of counsel, and descriptive information relating to each class (e.g., principal amount, coupon, minimum denomination, anticipated price, yield, weighted average life, credit enhancements, anticipated ratings, and other similar information relating to the proposed structure of the offering);

法》第1111条(关于池内资产条款、性质和处理的规定)以及,如适用,本《AB管理办法》第1114条或第1115条(关于信用增级措施提供方的规定)],提交文件中必须说明可能严重影响池内资产或资产支持证券中资产的支付、绩效或其他相关事项的母国任何政府、法律或监管或行政管理事项,以及任何税务、外汇管制、货币限制或者其他经济、财政、货币或相关潜在因素。同时可参见关于《S-K管理办法》第202条(第229.202节)的说明2。此外,应在依据《证券法》提交的注册说明书中按照《S-K管理办法》第101(g)条[第229.101(g)节]的要求提供相关信息。同时,对于报告期内外国法律及监管动态对资产支持证券造成的任何重大影响,如之前未根据《交易法》提交的《10-D表格》、《10-K表格》或《8-K表格》(本章第249.308节)中作出说明,应通过《10-D表格》(本章第249.312节)和《10-K表格》(本章第249.310节)予以披露。

(f)提交规定的附录。如果本《AB管理办法》规定将协议或其他文件作为《证券法》注册说明书的附录提交,可通过引用方式将该等最终协议或其他文件(如适用)纳入为注册说明书的附录,例如根据《S-3表格》(本章第239.13节)注册发行时提交《8-K表格》。

[《联邦公报》第70卷第1597页,2005年1月7日,修正索引:《联邦公报》第70卷第72373页,2005年12月5日。]

第229.1101节(第1101条) 定义

除非另有规定,《AB管理办法》(第229.1100~229.1123节)中使用的术语应适用如下定义:

(a)资产支持证券(ABS)信息和计算材料指完全由下列一项或若干项内容构成的书面通信:

(1)关于正在发行的资产支持证券以及证券结构和基本参数的事实性信息,如类别编号、优先性、优先求偿权、付款条件、税款、《1974年员工退休收入保障法》(修正版)(《美国法典》第二十九编第1001节及其后条文)(ERISA)或律师的其他法律结论以及关于每一类别证券的说明性信息(如本金金额、息票、最低面额、预期价格、收益、加权平均寿命、信用增级、预期评级以及与发行拟定结构相关的其他类似信息);

(2) Factual information regarding the pool assets underlying the asset-backed securities, including origination, acquisition and pool selection criteria, information regarding any prefunding or revolving period applicable to the offering, information regarding significant obligors, data regarding the contractual and related characteristics of the underlying pool assets (e.g., weighted average coupon, weighted average maturity, delinquency and loss information and geographic distribution) and other factual information concerning the parameters of the asset pool appropriate to the nature of the underlying assets, such as the type of assets comprising the pool and the programs under which the loans were originated;

(3) Identification of key parties to the transaction, such as servicers, trustees, depositors, sponsors, originators and providers of credit enhancement or other support, including a brief description of each such party's roles, responsibilities, background and experience;

(4) Static pool data, as referenced in Item 1105 of this Regulation AB, such as for the sponsor's and/or servicer's portfolio, prior transactions or the asset pool itself;

(5) Statistical information displaying for a particular class of asset-backed securities the yield, average life, expected maturity, interest rate sensitivity, cash flow characteristics, total rate of return, option adjusted spread or other financial or statistical information relating to the class or classes under specified prepayment, interest rate, loss or other hypothetical scenarios. Examples of such information under the definition include:

(i) Statistical results of interest rate sensitivity analyses regarding the impact on yield or other financial characteristics of a class of securities from changes in interest rates at one or more assumed prepayment speeds;

(ii) Statistical information showing the cash flows that would be associated with a particular class of asset-backed securities at a specified prepayment speed; and

(iii) Statistical information reflecting the financial impact of losses based on a variety of loss or default experience, prepayment, interest rate and related assumptions.

(6) The names of underwriters participating in the offering of the securities, and their additional roles, if any, within the underwriting syndicate;

(7) The anticipated schedule for the offering (including the approximate date upon which the proposed sale to the public will begin) and a description of marketing events (including the dates, times, locations, and procedures for attending or otherwise accessing them); and

(8) A description of the procedures by which the underwriters will conduct the offering and the procedures for transactions in connection with the offering with an underwriter or participating dealer (including procedures regarding account-opening and submitting indications of interest and conditional offers to buy).

(2)资产支持证券的基础池内资产的相关事实性信息，包括发起、收购及资产池选择标准、发行适用的任何预先融资期或循环期的信息、重大债务人信息、基础池内资产的合同及相关特征数据（如加权平均息票、加权平均到期日、历史拖欠和损失信息以及地理分布），以及根据基础资产的性质而应予提供的资产池参数方面的其他事实性信息，如构成资产池的资产类型及据以发起贷款的计划；

(3)交易主要当事方的身份信息，如服务机构、信托受托人、交存人、发起人、创建人及信用增级或其他支持提供方，包括关于该等各方的作用、责任、背景及经验的简要说明；

(4)本《AB管理办法》第1105条所述静态池数据，如与发起人和/或服务机构投资组合、之前的交易或资产池本身相关的数据；

(5)显示特定类别资产支持证券收益、平均寿命、预计到期日、利率敏感性、现金流特性、总回报率、期权调整利差的统计信息，或者在设定具体的提前偿还、利率、损失或其他假设的情况下关于该类别证券的其他财务或统计信息。举例而言，属于上述定义范围内的信息包括：

(i)关于在一种或多种假定提前偿还速度下利率改变对某类别证券收益或其他财务特性影响的利率敏感性分析统计结果；

(ii)显示某具体提前偿还速度下与特定类别资产支持证券相关联的现金流的统计信息；及

(iii)反映不同损失或违约记录、提前偿还、利率及相关假定条件下损失的财务影响的统计信息。

(6)参与证券发行的承销商的名称及其在承销团中的其他作用（如有）；

(7)发行预期的时间安排（包括拟定公开出售的大致起始日期）以及营销活动说明（包括日期、次数、地点及出席或其他参与程序）；及

(8)关于承销商的发行程序以及发行中与承销商或参与自营商开展交易的程序（包括开户程序以及提交兴趣表示和附条件认购要约的程序）的说明。

(b) *Asset-backed issuer* means an issuer whose reporting obligation results from either the registration of an offering of asset-backed securities under the Securities Act, or the registration of a class of asset-backed securities under section 12 of the Exchange Act (15 U.S.C. 78*l*).

(c)(1)*Asset-backed security* means a security that is primarily serviced by the cash flows of a discrete pool of receivables or other financial assets, either fixed or revolving, that by their terms convert into cash within a finite time period, plus any rights or other assets designed to assure the servicing or timely distributions of proceeds to the security holders; provided that in the case of financial assets that are leases, those assets may convert to cash partially by the cash proceeds from the disposition of the physical property underlying such leases.

(2) The following additional conditions apply in order to be considered an *asset-backed security:*

(i) Neither the depositor nor the issuing entity is an investment company under the Investment Company Act of 1940 (15 U.S.C. 80a-1 *et seq.*) nor will become an investment company as a result of the asset-backed securities transaction.

(ii) The activities of the issuing entity for the asset-backed securities are limited to passively owning or holding the pool of assets, issuing the asset-backed securities supported or serviced by those assets, and other activities reasonably incidental thereto.

(iii) No non-performing assets are part of the asset pool as of the measurement date.

(iv) Delinquent assets do not constitute 50% or more, as measured by dollar volume, of the asset pool as of the measurement date.

(v) With respect to securities that are backed by leases, the portion of the securitized pool balance attributable to the residual value of the physical property underlying the leases, as determined in accordance with the transaction agreements for the securities, does not constitute:

(A) For motor vehicle leases, 65% or more, as measured by dollar volume, of the securitized pool balance as of the measurement date.

(B) For all other leases, 50% or more, as measured by dollar volume, of the securitized pool balance as of the measurement date.

(3) Notwithstanding the requirement in paragraph (c)(1) of this section that the asset pool be a discrete pool of assets, the following are considered to be a discrete pool of assets for purposes of being considered an *asset-backed security:*

(i) *Master trusts.* The offering related to the securities contemplates adding additional assets to the pool that backs such securities in connection with future issuances of asset-backed securities backed by such pool. The offering related to the securities also may contemplate additions to the asset pool, to the extent consistent with paragraphs (c)(3)

(b)资产支持证券发行人系指因根据《证券法》注册资产支持证券发行或根据《交易法》(《美国法典》第十五编第78l节)第12条注册某类资产支持证券而承担报告义务的发行人。

(c)(1)资产支持证券系指主要通过独立应收账款池或其他金融资产的现金流提供服务的证券；上述金融资产包括在一定期间内根据其条款转换为现金的固定或循环金融资产,加上旨在保证向证券持有人提供服务或及时分配收益的任何权利或其他资产;但如金融资产属于租赁,该等资产可通过处置租赁标的实物财产获得现金收益的方式部分转换为现金。

(2)被视为构成资产支持证券的证券应满足下列附加条件:

(i)交存人或发行实体均不得属于依据《1940年投资公司法》(《美国法典》第十五编第80a-1节及其后条文)注册成立的投资公司,也不会因资产支持证券交易而成为投资公司。

(ii)资产支持证券发行实体的活动仅限于消极拥有或持有资产池、发行该等资产支持或服务的资产支持证券及其他合理的辅助性活动。

(iii)截至计量日,资产池中不得含有任何不良资产。

(iv)截至计量日,按照美元价值计量,拖欠资产不得达到资产池的50%(含)以上。

(v)对于租赁支持的证券而言,按照证券交易协议确定的、可归属于租赁标的实物财产的残值的证券化资产池余额部分不得达到:

(A)对于汽车租赁而言,截至计量日按照金额计量的证券化资产池余额的65%(含)以上。

(B)对于其他租赁而言,截至计量日按照金额计量的证券化资产池余额的50%(含)以上。

(3)尽管本节第(c)(1)款要求资产池必须为独立资产池,但以下内容在被认定为"资产支持证券"时均应被视为独立资产池:

(i)主信托。证券发行拟从事如下操作:未来发行由该资产池支持的资产支持证券时,向该等资产池中增加其他资产。对于具有循环期或其循环账户产生应收账款或其他金融资产的主信托而言,证券发行时也可计划从事如下操作:在符合本节第(c)(3)(ii)款和第(c)(3)(iii)款规定的范围内,在根据主信托的交易协议维持最低资产池余

(ii) and (c)(3)(iii) of this section, in connection with maintaining minimum pool balances in accordance with the transaction agreements for master trusts with revolving periods or receivables or other financial assets that arise under revolving accounts.

(ii) *Prefunding periods.* The offering related to the securities contemplates a prefunding account where a portion of the proceeds of that offering is to be used for the future acquisition of additional pool assets, if the duration of the prefunding period does not extend for more than one year from the date of issuance of the securities and the portion of the proceeds for such prefunding account does not involve in excess of:

(A) For master trusts, 50% of the aggregate principal balance of the total asset pool whose cash flows support the securities; and

(B) For other offerings, 50% of the proceeds of the offering.

(iii) *Revolving periods.* The offering related to the securities contemplates a revolving period where cash flows from the pool assets may be used to acquire additional pool assets, provided, that, for securities backed by receivables or other financial assets that do not arise under revolving accounts, the revolving period does not extend for more than three years from the date of issuance of the securities and the additional pool assets are of the same general character as the original pool assets.

Instructions to Item 1101(c). 1. For purposes of determining non-performing, delinquency and residual value thresholds, the "measurement date" means either:

a. The designated cut-off date for the transaction (*i.e.*, the date on and after which collections on the pool assets accrue for the benefit of asset-backed security holders), if applicable; or

b. In the case of master trusts, the date as of which delinquency and loss information or securitized pool balance information, as applicable, is presented in the prospectus for the asset-backed securities to be filed pursuant to §230.424(b) of this chapter.

2. Non-performing and delinquent assets that are not funded or purchased by proceeds from the securities and that are not considered in cash flow calculations for the securities need not be considered as part of the asset pool for purposes of determining non-performing and delinquency thresholds.

3. For purposes of determining non-performing, delinquency and residual value thresholds for master trusts, calculations are to be measured against the total asset pool whose cash flows support the securities.

4. For purposes of determining residual value thresholds, residual values need not be included in measuring against the thresholds to the extent a separate party is obligated for such amounts (e.g., through a residual value guarantee, residual value insurance or where the lessee is obligated to cover any residual losses).

(d) *Delinquent* , for purposes of determining if a pool asset is delinquent, means if a

额时,向资产池中增加资产。

(ii)预先融资期。证券发行拟设预先融资账户,将发行的部分募集资金用于将来收购其他池内资产,条件是预先融资期限自证券发行之日起不超过一年并且该等预先融资账户募集的资金部分不超过:

(A)对于主信托而言,以其现金流支持证券的总资产池本金总余额的50%;及

(B)对于其他发行而言,发行募集资金的50%。

(iii)循环期。证券发行拟设循环期,将源于池内资产的现金流用于收购其他池内资产,但对于应收账款支持的证券以及非因循环账户产生的其他金融资产,循环期限自证券发行之日起不超过3年并且增加的池内资产具有与原始池内资产相同的一般性质。

关于第1101(c)条的说明。1.在确定不良、拖欠及残值的临界值之时,“计量日”系指:

a.交易的指定截止日期(即池内资回款记入资产支持证券持有人权益之日或之后),如适用;或

b.在主信托的情况下,在根据本章第230.424(b)节提交的资产支持证券招募说明书中列报拖欠及损失信息或证券化资产池余额信息(如适用)之日。

2.在确定不良及拖欠临界值之时,非以证券募集资金融资或购买并且不计入证券现金流的不良及拖欠资产,不必视为资产池的一部分。

3.在确定主信托不良、拖欠及残值临界值之时,应基于以其现金流支持证券的资产池总额进行计算和计量。

4.在确定残值临界值之时,如有其他独立方对该等金额负责(如已提供残值担保、残值保险或者承租人负责补偿任何剩余损失),则在计量临界值之时,不必计入该等他方承担责任的残值。

(d)在确定池内资产是否存在拖欠之时,“拖欠”系指池内资产自约定到期日起逾

pool asset is more than 30 or 31 days or a single payment cycle, as applicable, past due from the contractual due date, as determined in accordance with any of the following:

(1) The transaction agreements for the asset-backed securities;

(2) The delinquency recognition policies of the sponsor, any affiliate of the sponsor that originated the pool asset or the servicer of the pool asset; or

(3) The delinquency recognition policies applicable to such pool asset established by the primary safety and soundness regulator of any entity listed in paragraph (d)(2) of this section or the program or regulatory entity that oversees the program under which the pool asset was originated.

(e) *Depositor* means the depositor who receives or purchases and transfers or sells the pool assets to the issuing entity. For asset-backed securities transactions where there is not an intermediate transfer of the assets from the sponsor to the issuing entity, the term depositor refers to the sponsor. For asset-backed securities transactions where the person transferring or selling the pool assets is itself a trust, the depositor of the issuing entity is the *depositor* of that trust.

(f) *Issuing entity* means the trust or other entity created at the direction of the sponsor or depositor that owns or holds the pool assets and in whose name the asset-backed securities supported or serviced by the pool assets are issued.

(g) *Non-performing* , for purposes of determining if a pool asset is non-performing, means a pool asset if any of the following is true:

(1) The pool asset would be treated as wholly or partially charged-off under the requirements in the transaction agreements for the asset-backed securities;

(2) The pool asset would be treated as wholly or partially charged-off under the charge-off policies of the sponsor, an affiliate of the sponsor that originates the pool asset or a servicer that services the pool asset; or

(3) The pool asset would be treated as wholly or partially charged-off under the charge-off policies applicable to such pool asset established by the primary safety and soundness regulator of any entity listed in paragraph (g)(2) of this section or the program or regulatory entity that oversees the program under which the pool asset was originated.

(h) *NRSRO* has the same meaning as the term "nationally recognized statistical rating organization" as used in §240.15c3-1(c)(2)(vi)(F) of this chapter.

(i) *Obligor* means any person who is directly or indirectly committed by contract or other arrangement to make payments on all or part of the obligations on a pool asset.

(j) *Servicer* means any person responsible for the management or collection of the pool assets or making allocations or distributions to holders of the asset-backed securities. The term *servicer* does not include a trustee for the issuing entity or the asset-backed securities that makes allocations or distributions to holders of the asset-backed securities

期30日或31日或者逾期一个付款周期(如适用)以上之情形,逾期应以如下任一标准判定:

(1)资产支持证券的交易协议;

(2)发起人、创建池内资产之发起人的任何关联方或池内资产服务机构的拖欠认定政策;或

(3)以下主体制定的适用于该等池内资产的拖欠认定政策:本节第(d)(2)款所列实体的主要安全及稳健性监管者,或者创建池内资产的项目,或负责监督该等项目的实体。

(e)交存人系指获取或购买池内资产并向发行实体转让或出售的交存人。对于发起人不通过中间方向发行实体转让资产的资产支持证券交易而言,交存人即指发起人。对于池内资产的转让人或出售人本身即为信托的资产支持证券交易而言,发行实体的交存人即为该信托的"交存人"。

(f)发行实体系指按照拥有或持有池内资产的发起人或交存人指示而设立,并以其自身名义发行池内资产支持或服务的资产支持证券的信托或其他实体。

(g)在判断池内资产是否属于不良资产之时,不良资产系指存在以下任一情形的池内资产:

(1)根据资产支持证券交易协议的要求,池内资产被视为全部或部分核销;

(2)根据发起人、创建池内资产的发起人的任何关联方或池内资产服务机构的核销政策,池内资产被视为全部或部分核销;或

(3)根据本节第(g)(2)款所列实体的主要安全及稳健性监管者制定的,或者创建池内资产的项目制定的,或负责监督该项目的实体制定的适用于该等池内资产的核销政策,池内资产被视为全部或部分核销。

(h)NRSRO之含义以本章第240.15c3-1(c)(2)(vi)(F)节所述"国家认可的统计评级机构"为准。

(i)债务人系指根据合同或其他安排就支付池内资产全部或部分债务负有直接或间接责任的主体。

(j)服务机构系指负责池内资产管理或收款,或向资产支持证券持有人进行分派或分配的主体。"服务机构"不包括向资产支持证券持有人进行分派或分配的发行实体或资产支持证券的信托受托人,前提是该信托受托人从服务机构处获取该等分派或分配而不以其他方式履行服务机构的功能。

if the trustee receives such allocations or distributions from a servicer and the trustee does not otherwise perform the functions of a servicer.

(k) *Significant obligor* means any of the following:

(1) An obligor or a group of affiliated obligors on any pool asset or group of pool assets if such pool asset or group of pool assets represents 10% or more of the asset pool.

(2) A single property or group of related properties securing a pool asset or a group of pool assets if such pool asset or group of pool assets represents 10% or more of the asset pool.

(3) A lessee or group of affiliated lessees if the related lease or group of leases represents 10% or more of the asset pool.

Instructions to Item 1101(k):1. Regarding paragraph (k)(3) of this section, the calculation must focus on the leases whose cash flow supports the asset–backed securities directly or indirectly (including the residual value of the physical property underlying the leases if a portion of the securitized pool balance is attributable to the residual value of such property), regardless of whether the asset pool contains the leases themselves, mortgages on properties that are the subject of the leases or other assets related to the leases.

2. If separate pool assets, or properties underlying pool assets, are cross–defaulted and/or cross–collateralized, such pool assets are to be aggregated and considered together in determining concentration levels.

3. If the pool asset is a mortgage or lease relating to real estate, the pool asset is non–recourse to the obligor, and the obligor does not manage the property or does not own other assets and has no other operations, then the obligor need not be considered a separate significant obligor from the real estate. Otherwise, the obligor is a separate significant obligor.

4. The determination of significant obligors is to be made as of the designated cut–off date for the transaction (*i.e.*, the date on and after which collections on the pool assets accrue for the benefit of asset–backed security holders), provided, that, in the case of master trusts, the determination is to be made as of the cut–off date (or issuance date if there is not a cut–off date) for each issuance of asset–backed securities backed by the same asset pool. In addition, if disclosure is required pursuant to either Item 6.05 of Form 8–K(17 CFR 249.308) or in a Form 10–D (17 CFR 249.312) pursuant to Item 1121(b) of this Regulation AB, the determination of significant obligors is to be made against the asset pool described in such report. However, if the percentage concentration regarding an obligor falls below 10% subsequent to the determination dates discussed in this Instruction, the obligor no longer need be considered a significant obligor.

(l) *Sponsor* means the person who organizes and initiates an asset–backed securities

(k)重大债务人系指以下任何主体:

(1)池内资产或池内资产组合的债务人或关联债务人群体,前提是该等池内资产或池内资产组合代表了资产池的10%(含)以上。

(2)担保池内资产或池内资产组合的单项财产或关联财产组合,前提是该等池内资产或池内资产组合代表了资产池的10%(含)以上。

(3)承租人或关联承租人群体,前提是相关租赁或关联租赁群体代表了资产池的10%(含)以上。

关于第1101(k)条的说明:1.对于本节第(k)(3)款,计算重点必须为以其现金流直接或间接支持资产支持证券的租赁(包括租赁标的实物资产的残值,如果证券化资产池余额部分可归属于该等财产的残值),而无论资产池是否包含租赁本身、租赁标的财产上的抵押或者与租赁相关的其他资产。

2.如果独立的池内资产或池内资产的基础财产发生交叉违约和/或交叉担保,该等池内资产应予合计并在确定集中水平时一并考虑。

3.如果池内资产为相关房地产的抵押或租赁,且债务人对池内资产没有追索权,同时也不管理财产,或不拥有其他资产并且没有其他运营业务,则不必将债务人视为该房地产的独立重大债务人。反之,债务人则构成独立的重大债务人。

4.重大债务人应在指定交易截止日期(即池内资产产生的回款记入资产支持证券持有人权益之日或之后)之前予以确定,但在主信托的情况下,则应在同一资产池支持的资产支持证券每次发行的截止日期(或发行日期,如果没有截止日期)之前确定。此外,如果《8-K表格》(《联邦规章汇编》第十七编第249.308节)第6.05条要求进行披露,或者本《AB管理办法》第1121(b)条要求通过《10-D表格》(《联邦规章汇编》第十七编第249.312节)进行披露,应基于该等报告所述的资产池确定重大债务人。但是,如果债务人的集中比率在本说明所述确定日期之后降至10%以下,则债务人不必继续被视为重大债务人。

(l)发起人系指通过直接或间接(包括通过关联方)向发行实体出售或转让资产以

transaction by selling or transferring assets, either directly or indirectly, including through an affiliate, to the issuing entity.

§229.1102(Item 1102) Forepart of registration statement and outside cover page of the prospectus.

In addition to the information required by Item 501 of Regulation S-K (§229.501), provide the following information on the outside front cover page of the prospectus. Present information regarding multiple classes in tables if doing so will aid understanding. If information regarding multiple classes cannot appear on the cover page due to space limitations, include the information in the summary or in an immediately preceding separate table.

(a) Identify the sponsor, the depositor and the issuing entity (if known).

(b) In identifying the title of the securities, include the series number, if applicable. If there is more than one class of securities offered, state the class designations of the securities offered.

(c) Identify the asset type(s) being securitized.

(d) Include a statement, if applicable and appropriately modified to the transaction, that the securities represent the obligations of the issuing entity only and do not represent the obligations of or interest in the sponsor, depositor or any of their affiliates.

(e) Identify the aggregate principal amount of all securities offered and the principal amount, if any, of each class of securities offered. If a class has no principal amount, disclose that fact, and, if applicable, state the notional amount, clearly identifying that the amount is a notional one. If the amounts are approximate, disclose that fact.

(f) Indicate the interest rate or specified rate of return of each class of security offered. If a class of securities does not bear interest or a specified return, disclose that fact. If the rate is based on a formula or is calculated in reference to a generally recognized interest rate index, such as a U.S. Treasury securities index, either provide the formula on the cover, or indicate that the rate is variable, indicate the index upon which the rate is based and indicate that further disclosure of how the rate is determined is included in the transaction summary.

(g) Identify the distribution frequency, by class or series where applicable, and the first expected distribution date for the asset-backed securities.

(h) Briefly describe any credit enhancement or other support for the transaction and identify any enhancement or support provider referenced in Items 1114(b) or 1115 of this Regulation AB.

Instruction to Item 1102: Also see Item 1113(f)(2) of this Regulation AB regarding the title of any class of securities with an optional redemption or termination feature that may be exercised when 25% or more of the original principal balance of the pool assets

组织和发起资产支持证券交易的主体。

第229.1102节(第1102条)　注册说明书开篇以及招募说明书的封首

除《S-K管理办法》第501条(第229.501节)要求提供的信息外,请在招募说明书封首提供以下信息。如果有助于理解,请以表格形式分类列报信息。如果因空间有限无法在封面显示多类信息,可以在摘要或摘要前紧接的表格中提供。

(a)注明发起人、交存人和发行实体(如已知)。

(b)注明证券名称时应包括序列号(如适用)。如果发行多个类别的证券,应提供发行证券的类别名称。

(c)注明被证券化的资产类型。

(d)提交一份根据交易进行适当调整后的声明(如适用),说明证券仅代表发行实体的义务而不代表发起人、交存人或其任何关联方的义务或权益。

(e)注明发行的所有证券的本金总额以及发行的各类别证券的本金金额(如有)。如果某类别证券没有本金金额,应如实披露,并说明名义金额(如适用),同时明确注明该金额仅为名义金额。如果金额为近似值,应如实披露。

(f)注明发行的各类别证券的利率或设定的回报率。如果某类别证券不计算利息或不设定具体回报,应如实披露。如果上述比率基于公式得出或者参照公认的利率指数(如美国财政部证券指数)计算,可在封面中提供该公式,或者注明比率具有可变动性,并提供比率所基的指数,说明比率的确定方式在交易摘要中作出进一步披露。

(g)按类别或系列(如适用)注明分配频率以及资产支持证券的首个预期分配日。

(h)概述交易的任何信用增级措施或其他支持,并注明本《AB管理办法》第1114(b)条或第1115条所述的所有信用增级或支持提供方。

关于第1102条的说明:请同时参见本《AB管理办法》第1113(f)(2)条关于如下证券的名称的规定:当池内资产原始本金余额的25%(含)以上仍未缴付时,可以行使具有回赎或终止选择权的任何类别证券。

are still outstanding.

§229.1103(Item 1103) Transaction summary and risk factors.

(a) *Prospectus summary.* In providing the information required by Item 503(a) of Regulation S-K(§229.503(a)), provide the following information in the prospectus summary, as applicable. Present information regarding multiple classes in tables if doing so will aid understanding. Consider using diagrams to illustrate the relationships among the parties, the structure of the securities offered (including, for example, the flow of funds or any subordination features) and any other material features of the transaction.

(1) Identify the participants in the transaction, including the sponsor, depositor, issuing entity, trustee and servicers contemplated by Item 1108(a)(2) of this Regulation AB, and their respective roles. Describe the roles briefly if they are not apparent from the title of the role. Identify any originator contemplated by Item 1110 of this Regulation AB and any significant obligor.

(2) Briefly identify the pool assets and summarize briefly the size and material characteristics of the asset pool. Identify the cut-off date or similar date for establishing the composition of the asset pool, if applicable.

(3) State briefly the basic terms of each class of securities offered. In particular:

(i) Identify the classes offered by the prospectus and any classes issued in the same transaction or residual or equity interests in the transaction that are not being offered by the prospectus.

(ii) State the interest rate or rate of return on each class of securities offered, to the extent that the rates on any class of securities were not disclosed in full on the prospectus cover page.

(iii) State the expected final and final scheduled maturity or principal distribution dates, if applicable, of each class of securities offered.

(iv) Identify the denominations in which the securities may be issued.

(v) Identify the distribution frequency on the securities.

(vi) Summarize the flow of funds, payment priorities and allocations among the classes of securities offered, the classes of securities that are not offered, and fees and expenses, to the extent necessary to understand the payment characteristics of the classes that are offered by the prospectus.

(vii) Identify any events in the transaction agreements that can trigger liquidation or amortization of the asset pool or other performance triggers that would alter the transaction structure or the flow of funds.

(viii) Identify any optional or mandatory redemption or termination features.

(ix) Identify any credit enhancement or other support for the transaction, as referenced in Items 1114(a) and 1115 of this Regulation AB, and briefly describe what

第229.1103节(第1103条) 交易摘要和风险因素

(a)招募说明书摘要。在提供《S-K管理办法》第503(a)条[第229.503(a)节]规定的信息时,应在招募说明书摘要中提供以下适用信息。如果表格有助于理解,应将多个类别的信息以表格形式列报。考虑使用图表来说明各当事方之间的关系、已要约的证券之结构(包括资金流或任何次级特征)以及交易的所有其他重大特征。

(1)指明参与并购重组交易的各当事方,包括发起人、交存人、发行实体、信托受托人和本《AB管理办法》第1108(a)(2)条规定的服务机构,以及他们各自的角色。如果各当事方的角色无法从称谓直接判断,应对其承担的角色予以简要说明。指明本《AB管理办法》第1110条规定的任何创建人和任何重要债务人。

(2)简要说明池内资产并简要概述该资产池的规模和重要特征。指明确定资产池组成的截止日期或类似日期(如适用)。

(3)简要介绍要约所针对的每一类别证券的基本条款。尤其应:

(i)指明招募说明书中要约的证券类别以及在同一交易中发行的证券类别,或招募说明书中未要约的交易的残值权益或股权权益。

(ii)说明未在招募说明书封面完全披露的任一类已要约证券的利率或回报率。

(iii)说明每一类已要约证券的预期和既定的最终到期日或本金分配日期(如有)。

(iv)指明可能发行的证券之面额。

(v)指明证券的分配频率。

(vi)以能够了解招募说明书中所述各类别证券的付款特征的披露程度,概述已要约的各类别证券、未要约的各类别证券、酬金和费用的资金流、支付优先顺序及分配情况。

(vii)指明交易协议中规定的能够导致资产池清算或摊还的全部事件,或其他能够导致交易结构或资金流发生变更的绩效因素。

(viii)指明任何选择性或强制性的提前回赎或终止特征。

(ix)指明如本《AB管理办法》第1114(a)条和第1115条所述、针对交易而设的信用增级措施或其他支持措施,并简述增级措施提供的保护和支持。指明本《AB管理办法》

protection or support is provided by the enhancement. Identify any enhancement provider referenced in Items 1114(b) and 1115 of this Regulation AB. Summarize how losses not covered by credit enhancement or support will be allocated to the securities.

(4) Identify any outstanding series or classes of securities that are backed by the same asset pool or otherwise have claims on the pool assets. In addition, state if additional series or classes of securities may be issued that are backed by the same asset pool and briefly identify the circumstances under which those additional securities may be issued. Specify if security holder approval is necessary for such issuances and if security holders will receive notice of such issuances.

(5) If the transaction will include prefunding or revolving periods, indicate:

(i) The term or duration of the prefunding or revolving period.

(ii) For prefunding periods, the amount of proceeds to be deposited in the prefunding account.

(iii) For revolving periods, the maximum amount of additional assets that may be acquired during the revolving period, if applicable.

(iv) The percentage of the asset pool and any class or series of the asset-backed securities represented by the prefunding account or the revolving period, if applicable.

(v) Any limitation on the ability to add pool assets.

(vi) The requirements for assets that may be added to the pool.

(6) If pool assets can otherwise be added, removed or substituted (for example, in the event of a breach in representations or warranties regarding pool assets), summarize briefly the circumstances under which such actions can occur.

(7) Summarize the amount or formula for calculating the fee that the servicer will receive for performing its duties, and identify from what source those fees will be paid and the distribution priority of those fees.

(8) Summarize the federal income tax issues material to investors of each class of securities offered.

(9) Indicate whether the issuance or sale of any class of offered securities is conditioned on the assignment of a rating by one or more rating agencies. If so, identify each rating agency and the minimum rating that must be assigned.

(b) *Risk factors.* In providing the information required by Item 503(c) of Regulation S-K [§229.503 (c)], identify any risks that may be different for investors in any offered class of asset-backed securities, and if so, identify such classes and describe such difference(s).

§229.1104(Item 1104) Sponsors.

Link to an amendment published at 76 FR 4511, January 26, 2011.

Provide the following information about the sponsor:

第1114(b)条和第1115条所指的所有信用增级提供方。概述信用增级或支持措施没有弥补的损失将如何向证券分摊。

(4)指明由同一资产池支持,或对池内资产享有其他权利主张的所有系列或类别的发行在外证券。另外,说明是否可以在同一资产池的支持下发行其他系列或类别的证券,并简要说明在何等情形可以发行此等其他证券。明确指明该等发行是否需要获得证券持有人的同意,以及证券持有人是否会收到关于该等证券发行的通知。

(5)如果交易将含有预先融资期或循环期,应指明以下事项:

(i)预先融资或循环的期限或持续时间。

(ii)对于预先融资期,应指明将存入预先融资账户的募集资金数额。

(iii)对于循环期,应指明在该等期限内可收购的额外资产的最大数额(如适用)。

(iv)资产池的结构百分比,以及预先融资账户下或循环期内的任一类别或系列的资产支持证券(如适用)。

(v)在池内加入其他资产的任何能力限制。

(vi)对于可加入资产池的资产的要求。

(6)如果能够在其他情况下(如在池内资产声明和保证遭到违反的情况下)增加、移除或替换池内资产,简要概述能够采取此类行动的情形。

(7)概述服务机构因为履行其职责而应得的费用数额或计算该等费用的公式,并指明支付该等费用的来源以及这些费用的分配优先顺序。

(8)概述每一类已要约证券的投资者面临的重大联邦所得税问题。

(9)指出已要约的任一类别证券的发行或销售是否取决于一个或多个评级机构的评级结果。如果是,注明所涉每一评级机构以及必须获得的最低评级。

(b)风险因素。在提供《S-K管理办法》第503(c)条[第229.503(c)节]规定的信息时,指明持有已要约的某一类资产支持证券是否可能会给投资者带来任何不同风险,如果是,指明该等类别的证券并说明该等不同风险。

第229.1104节(第1104条) 发起人

链接至《联邦公报》第76卷第4511页(2011年1月26日)发布的修正。

关于发起人,应提供下列信息:

(a) State the sponsor's name and describe the sponsor's form of organization.

(b) Describe the general character of the sponsor's business.

(c) Describe the sponsor's securitization program and state how long the sponsor has been engaged in the securitization of assets. The description must include, to the extent material, a general discussion of the sponsor's experience in securitizing assets of any type as well as a more detailed discussion of the sponsor's experience in and overall procedures for originating or acquiring and securitizing assets of the type included in the current transaction. Include to the extent material information regarding the size, composition and growth of the sponsor's portfolio of assets of the type to be securitized and information or factors related to the sponsor that may be material to an analysis of the origination or performance of the pool assets, such as whether any prior securitizations organized by the sponsor have defaulted or experienced an early amortization triggering event.

(d) Describe the sponsor's material roles and responsibilities in its securitization program, including whether the sponsor or an affiliate is responsible for originating, acquiring, pooling or servicing the pool assets, and the sponsor's participation in structuring the transaction.

§229.1105(Item 1105) Static pool information.

(a) For amortizing asset pools, unless the registrant determines that such information is not material:

(1) Provide static pool information, to the extent material, regarding delinquencies, cumulative losses and prepayments for prior securitized pools of the sponsor for that asset type.

(2) If the sponsor has less than three years of experience securitizing assets of the type to be included in the offered asset pool, consider providing instead static pool information, to the extent material, regarding delinquencies, cumulative losses and prepayments by vintage origination years regarding originations or purchases by the sponsor, as applicable, for that asset type. A vintage origination year represents assets originated during the same year.

(3) In providing the information required by paragraphs (a)(1) and (a)(2) of this section:

(i) Provide the requested information for prior pools or vintage origination years, as applicable, relating to the following time period, to the extent material:

(A) Five years, or

(B) For so long as the sponsor has been either securitizing assets of the same asset type (in the case of paragraph (a)(1) of this section) or making originations or purchases of assets of the same asset type(in the case of paragraph (a)(2) of this section) if less

(a)说明发起人的名称并介绍发起人的组织形式。

(b)说明发起人业务的一般特征。

(c)说明发起人的证券化计划以及从事资产证券化业务的年限。如具有重要意义，此等说明必须包括关于发起人在从事任何类型资产的证券化业务方面的经验的一般性论述，以及关于如下事项的详细论述：就当前交易所涉及的资产类别而言，发起人在资产创建、收购和证券化方面的经验以及总体操作程序。应纳入关于以下事项的重大信息：发起人将予以证券化的类型的资产之组合的规模、组成和增长情况；对分析资产池的创建或绩效有重大作用、且与发起人相关的信息或因素，如发起人之前组织的任何证券化是否出现过违约或发生了提前摊还触发事件。

(d)说明发起人在其证券化计划中的重要角色和职责，包括将由发起人还是其关联方负责池内资产的创建、收购、入池或为池内资产提供服务，以及发起人在确定交易结构过程中的参与度。

第229.1105节(第1105条)　静态池信息

(a)对于摊还型的资产池，注册人应提供如下信息(但注册人判定此等信息不属于重大信息的除外)：

(1)提供静态池关于以下事项的重大信息：发起人之前对该类资产进行证券化的资产池的拖欠、累计损失和提前还款情况。

(2)对于将包括在已要约的资产池中的资产类型，如果发起人证券化经验不足3年，应考虑提供替代性的关于以下事项的重大静态池信息：针对发起人创建或购买(以适用者为准)资产的各个创建年份，每一年份的拖欠、累计亏损和提前还款情况。创建年份意指：同一年创建的各项资产不尽相同，但都属于同一年份的概念。

(3)在提供本节第(a)(1)款和第(a)(2)款规定的信息时，应：

(i)提供关于之前的资产池或创建年份(以适用者为准)在下列时期内规定的重大信息：

(A)5年，或

(B)发起人从事同类资产证券化的期间[就本节第(a)(1)款而言]，或者创建或购买同类资产的期间[就本节第(a)(2)款而言](如上述期间不足5年)。

than five years.

(ii) Present delinquency, cumulative loss and prepayment data for each prior securitized pool or vintage origination year, as applicable, in periodic increments (e.g., monthly or quarterly), to the extent material, over the life of the prior securitized pool or vintage origination year. The most recent periodic increment for the data must be as of a date no later than 135 days of the date of first use of the prospectus.

(iii) Provide summary information for the original characteristics of the prior securitized pools or vintage origination years, as applicable and material. While the material summary characteristics may vary, these characteristics may include, among other things, the following: number of pool assets; original pool balance; weighted average initial loan balance; weighted average interest or note rate; weighted average original term; weighted average remaining term; weighted average and minimum and maximum standardized credit score or other applicable measure of obligor credit quality; product type; loan purpose; loan-to-value information; distribution of assets by loan or note rate; and geographic distribution information.

(b) For revolving asset master trusts, unless the registrant determines that such information is not material, provide, to the extent material, data regarding delinquencies, cumulative losses, prepayments, payment rate, yield and standardized credit scores or other applicable measure of obligor credit quality in separate increments based on the date of origination of the pool assets. While the material increments may vary, consider presenting such data at a minimum in 12-month increments through the first five years of the account's life (e.g., 0-12 months, 13-24 months, 25-36 months, 37-48 months, 49-60 months and 61 months or more).

(c) If the information that would otherwise be required by paragraph (a)(1), (a)(2) or (b) of this section is not material, but alternative static pool information would provide material disclosure, provide such alternative information instead. Similarly, information contemplated by paragraph (a)(1), (a)(2) or(b) of this section regarding a party or parties other than the sponsor may be provided in addition to or in lieu of such information regarding the sponsor if appropriate to provide material disclosure. In addition, other explanatory disclosure, including disclosure explaining the absence of any static pool information, may be provided.

(d) The following information provided in response to this section shall not be deemed to be a prospectus or part of a prospectus for the asset-backed securities nor shall such information be deemed to be part of the registration statement for the asset-backed securities:

(1) With respect to information regarding prior securitized pools of the sponsor that do not include the currently offered pool, information regarding prior securitized pools that

(ii)列报之前证券化的每一资产池或每个创建年份(以适用者为准)的拖欠、累计亏损和提前还款的重大数据(按每期增量形式列报,如月度或季度增量数据)。此等数据最近一期的增量信息的截止日期不得晚于首次使用招募说明书之日后第135日。

(iii)概述之前所有证券化资产池或创建年份(以适用者为准)的重大原始特征。这些重要的概要特征可以不同,包括但不限于:池内资产的数量;原始池内余额;初始贷款余额的加权平均值;加权平均利率或票面利率;加权平均原始期限;加权平均剩余期限;加权平均、最低及最高标准化信用分数或衡量债务人信用质量的其他适用指标;产品类型;贷款目的;贷款对估值比率;每项贷款或票面利率的资产分配;以及地理分布信息。

(b)就循环资产主信托而言,注册人应提供以下重大数据(但注册人判定该等信息不重要的除外):从资产池创建之日起拖欠、累计亏损、提前还款、支付利率、收益率和标准化的信用分数或衡量债务人信用质量的其他适用指标各自的增量。尽管这些重要增量可能会有所不同,注册人应考虑最少以12个月为单位来列报账户寿命内最初5年的增量(如第0~12个月、第13~24个月、第25~36个月、第37~48个月、第49~60个月以及第61个月以后的数据)。

(c)如果本节第(a)(1)款、第(a)(2)款或第(b)款要求提供的信息不属于重大信息,而采用静态池信息却能提供重大披露,则应提供该等替代性的静态池信息。同理,在适当情况下,如果按照本节第(a)(1)款、第(a)(2)款或第(b)款的规定另行提供其他当事方的信息,作为发起人相关信息的替代或补充,可以提供更重要的披露,则应提供该等其他当事方的信息作为补充或替代。另外,可以提供其他解释性的披露,包括对缺少任何静态池信息的原因进行解释等。

(d)根据本节相关要求提供的下列信息不得视为资产支持证券的招募说明书或招募说明书的一部分,也不得视为资产支持证券的注册说明书的一部分:

(1)发起人在2006年1月1日之前创建的先前的证券化资产池(不包括当前要约的资产池)的相关信息;及

were established before January 1, 2006; and

(2) With respect to information regarding the currently offered pool, information about the pool for periods before January 1, 2006.

(e) For prospectuses to be filed pursuant to §230.424 of this chapter that include information specified in paragraph (d)(1) or (d)(2) of this section, the prospectus shall disclose that such information is not deemed to be part of that prospectus or the registration statement for the asset-backed securities.

(f) If any of the information identified in paragraph (d)(1) or (d)(2) of this section that is to be provided in response to this section is unknown and not available to the registrant without unreasonable effort or expense, such information may be omitted, provided the registrant provides the information on the subject it possesses or can acquire without unreasonable effort or expense, and the registrant includes a statement in the prospectus showing that unreasonable effort or expense would be involved in obtaining the omitted information.

[70 FR 1597, Jan. 7, 2005, as amended at 70 FR 72373, Dec. 5, 2005]

§229.1106(Item 1106) Depositors.

If the depositor is not the same entity as the sponsor, provide separately the information regarding the depositor called for by paragraphs (a) and (b) of Item 1104 of this Regulation AB, and, to the extent the information would be material and materially different from the sponsor, paragraphs (c) and (d) of Item 1104 of this Regulation AB. In addition, provide the following information:

(a) The ownership structure of the depositor.

(b) The general character of any activities the depositor is engaged in other than securitizing assets and the time period during which it has been so engaged.

(c) Any continuing duties of the depositor after issuance of the asset-backed securities being registered regarding the asset-backed securities or the pool assets.

§229.1107(Item 1107) Issuing entities.

Provide the following information about the issuing entity:

(a) State the issuing entity's name and describe the issuing entity's form of organization, including the State or other jurisdiction under whose laws the issuing entity is organized. File the issuing entity's governing documents as an exhibit.

(b) Describe the permissible activities and restrictions on the activities of the issuing entity under its governing documents, including any restrictions on the ability to issue or invest in additional securities, to borrow money or to make loans to other persons. Describe any provisions in the issuing entity's governing documents allowing for modification of the issuing entity's governing documents, including its permissible

(2)当前要约的资产池在2006年1月1日之前的相关信息。

(e)对于将依据本章第230.424节提交,且含有本节第(d)(1)款或第(d)(2)款规定信息的招募说明书,该招募说明书应披露上述信息不得视为资产支持证券之招募说明书或注册说明书的一部分。

(f)如果注册人经过合理的努力或花费后仍然无法获知或获得本节第(d)(1)款或第(d)(2)款规定的任何信息,则可免予提供此等信息,但是注册人应提供其已经掌握或者经过合理的努力及花费后可以获得的关于该主题的信息,并且注册人须在招募说明书中附带一份声明,说明要获得省略的信息需要付出不合理的努力或花费。

[《联邦公报》第70卷第1597页,2005年1月7日,修正索引:《联邦公报》第70卷第72373页,2005年12月5日。]

第229.1106节(第1106条)　交存人

如果交存人和发起人不是同一个实体,应单独提供本《AB管理办法》第1104条第(a)款和第(b)款所规定的交存人信息,条件是该等信息具有重要性,并且与本《AB管理办法》第1104条第(c)款和第(d)款所述的发起人信息明显不同。另外,应提供下列信息:

(a)交存人的所有权结构。

(b)除证券化资产以外,交存人所从事的任何活动的一般特征以及交存人从事该等活动的期间。

(c)资产支持证券发行后,交存人仍应就资产支持证券或池内资产承担的任何职责。

第229.1107节(第1107条)　发行实体

提供关于发行实体的下列信息:

(a)说明发行实体的名称和组织形式,包括发行实体组建所依据的法律所属的州或其他司法辖区。将发行实体的章程性文件作为附录提交。

(b)说明根据发行实体的章程性文件,发行实体可以开展的活动及活动限制,包括对发行或投资其他证券、借款或向其他人发放贷款的能力的任何限制。说明发行实体的章程性文件中关于允许修改该等章程性文件(包括允许其开展的活动)的任何相关规定。

activities.

(c) Describe any specific discretionary activities with regard to the administration of the asset pool or the asset–backed securities, and identify the person or persons authorized to exercise such discretion.

(d) Describe any assets owned or to be owned by the issuing entity, apart from the pool assets, as well as any liabilities of the issuing entity, apart from the asset–backed securities. Disclose the fiscal year end of the issuing entity.

(e) If the issuing entity hasexecutive officers, a board of directors or persons performing similar functions, provide the information required by Items 401, 402, 403 404 and 407(a), (c)(3), (d)(4), (d)(5) and (e)(4) of Regulation S–K (§§229.401, 229.402, 229.403, 229.404 and 229.407(a), (c)(3), (d)(4), (d)(5) and (e)(4)) for the issuing entity.

(f) Describe the terms of any management or administration agreement regarding the issuing entity. File any such agreement as an exhibit.

(g) Describe the capitalization of the issuing entity and the amount or nature of any equity contribution to the issuing entity by the sponsor, depositor or other party.

(h) Describe the sale or transfer of the pool assets to the issuing entity as well as the creation (and perfection and priority status) of any security interest in favor of the issuing entity, the trustee, the asset–backed security holders or others, including the material terms of any agreement providing for such sale, transfer or creation of a security interest. File any such agreements as an exhibit. In addition to an appropriate narrative description, also provide this information graphically or in a flow chart if it will aid understanding.

(i) If the pool assets are securities, as defined under the Securities Act, state the market price of the securities and the basis on which the market price was determined.

(j) If expenses incurred in connection with the selection and acquisition of the pool assets are to be payable from offering proceeds, disclose the amount of such expenses. If such expenses are to be paid to the sponsor, servicer contemplated by Item 1108(a)(2) of this Regulation AB, depositor, issuing entity, originator contemplated by Item 1110 of this Regulation AB, underwriter, or any affiliate of the foregoing, separately identify the type and amount of expenses paid to each such party.

(k) Describe to the extent material any provisions or arrangements included to address any one or more of the following issues:

(1) Whether any security interests granted in connection with the transaction are perfected, maintained and enforced.

(2) Whether declaration of bankruptcy, receivership or similar proceeding with respect to the issuing entity can occur.

(c)说明与资产池或资产支持证券管理相关的任何具体的全权委托活动，并指明被授权行使该等权限的主体。

(d)说明除资产池外，发行实体拥有或即将拥有的任何资产，以及除资产支持证券外，发行实体的任何负债。披露发行实体的会计年度结束时间。

(e)如果发行实体拥有高管、董事会或履行类似职能的人，应提供《S-K管理办法》第401条、第402条、第403条、第404条以及第407(a)条、第407(c)(3)条、第407(d)(4)条、第407(d)(5)条及第407(e)(4)条[第229.401节、第229.402节、第229.403节、第229.404节和第229.407(a)节、第229.407(c)(3)节、第229.407(d)(4)节、第229.407(d)(5)节及第229.407(e)(4)节]中规定的关于发行实体的信息。

(f)说明与发行实体相关的任何管理协议之条款。将任何此等协议作为附录提交。

(g)说明发行实体的资本化情况以及发起人、交存人或其他当事方向发行实体的股权出资之数额或性质。

(h)说明向发行实体出售或转让池内资产的情况，以及任何以发行实体、信托受托人、资产支持证券持有人或其他人为受益人的担保物权之创设(及担保物权的完善和优先状态)，包括针对该等出售、转让或担保物权的创设所签订的任何协议中的重大条款。将任何此类协议作为附录提交。除了适当的文字说明，如果图表形式或流程图有助于理解，还应以图表或流程图提供信息。

(i)如果池内资产属于《证券法》所定义的证券，说明证券的市场价格以及确定该等市场价格的依据。

(j)如果与选择或收购池内资产相关的费用将通过发行募集的资金支付，披露该等费用的金额。如果该等费用将支付给发起人、本《AB管理办法》第1108(a)(2)条规定的服务机构、交存人、发行实体、本《AB管理办法》第1110条规定的创建人、承销人或上述任何一方的任一关联方，应分别指明将支付给每一上述各方的费用类型和金额。

(k)说明涉及以下一个或多个问题的任何重大规定或安排：

(1)与并购重组交易相关的任何担保物权是否获得了完善、维持和实施。

(2)发行实体是否可能发生宣告破产、接管或类似程序。

(3) Whether in the event of a bankruptcy, receivership or similar proceeding with respect to the sponsor, originator, depositor or other seller of the pool assets, the issuing entity's assets will become part of the bankruptcy estate or subject to the bankruptcy control of a third party.

(4) Whether in the event of a bankruptcy, receivership or similar proceeding with respect to the issuing entity, the issuing entity's assets will become subject to the bankruptcy control of a third party.

(l) If applicable law prohibits the issuing entity from holding the pool assets directly (for example, an "eligible lender" trustee must hold student loans originated under the Federal Family Education Loan Program of the Higher Education Act of 1965 (20 U.S.C. 1001 *et seq.*)), describe the arrangements instituted to hold the pool assets on behalf of the issuing entity. Include disclosure regarding the arrangements taken, as applicable, regarding the items in paragraph (k) of this section with respect to any such additional entity that holds such assets on behalf of the issuing entity.

[70 FR 1597, Jan. 7, 2005, as amended at 71 FR 53259, Sept. 8, 2006]

§229.1108(Item 1108) Servicers.

Provide the following information for the servicer.

(a) *Multiple servicers.* Where servicing of the pool assets utilizes multiple servicers (e.g., master servicers that oversee the actions of other servicers, primary servicers that have primary contact with the obligor, or special servicers for specific servicing functions):

(1) Provide a clear introductory description of the roles, responsibilities and oversight requirements of the entire servicing structure and the parties involved. In addition to an appropriate narrative discussion of the allocation of servicing responsibilities, also consider presenting the information graphically if doing so will aid understanding.

(2) Identify:

(i) Each master servicer;

(ii) Each affiliated servicer;

(iii) Each unaffiliated servicer that services 10% or more of the pool assets; and

(iv) Any other material servicer responsible for calculating or making distributions to holders of the asset-backed securities, performing work-outs or foreclosures, or other aspect of the servicing of the pool assets or the asset-backed securities upon which the performance of the pool assets or the asset-backed securities is materially dependent.

(3) Provide the information in paragraphs (b), (c) and (d) of this section, as applicable depending on the servicer's role, for each servicer identified in paragraphs (a)(2)(i),

(3)如果发起人、创建人、交存人或池内资产的其他出售人发生破产、接管或类似程序,发行实体的资产是否会成为破产财产的一部分或受限于第三方的破产管理。

(4)如果发行实体发生破产、破产管理或类似程序,发行实体的资产是否会受限于第三方的破产管理。

(l)如果适用法禁止发行实体直接持有池内资产[如“适格贷方”的信托受托人必须持有根据《1965年高等教育法》(《美国法典》第二十编第1001节及其后条文)下的美国联邦家庭教育贷款计划发起的学生贷款],应说明代表发行实体持有该等池内资产的安排。应根据具体情况,针对代表发行实体持有此等资产的任何此类其他实体披露已经实施的关于本节第(k)款各项的安排。

[《联邦公报》第70卷第1597页,2005年1月7日,修正索引:《联邦公报》第71卷第53259页,2006年9月8日。]

第229.1108节(第1108条) 服务机构

提供关于服务机构的下列信息:

(a)多个服务机构。如果管理池内资产使用了多个服务机构(如管理其他服务机构行为的总服务机构、主要负责联系债务人的主服务机构或执行特殊服务职能的特殊服务机构),则应:

(1)提供简明的介绍性说明,说明整个服务结构以及牵涉的各个当事方的角色、职责和管理要求。关于服务责任的分配,如果图表有助于理解,除了适当的文字说明,应另考虑提供图表形式的信息。

(2)指明:

(i)每一总服务机构;

(ii)每一关联服务机构;

(iii)对池内资产提供10%(含)以上服务的每一非关联服务机构;及

(iv)负责提供以下服务的任何其他重要服务机构:计算、对资产支持证券持有人进行分配、执行贷款调整或止赎服务,或池内资产或资产支持证券的其他方面的服务(池内资产或者资产支持证券的绩效对其存在重大依赖性的服务)。

(3)对于本节第(a)(2)(i)款、第(a)(2)(ii)款和第(a)(2)(iv)款中指明的每一服务机构,以及本节第(a)(2)(iii)款中指明的每一非关联服务机构,如其为20%(含)以上

(ii) and (iv) of this section and each unaffiliated servicer identified in paragraph (a)(2)(iii) of this section that services 20% or more of the pool assets

(b) *Identifying information and experience.* (1) State the servicer's name and describe the servicer's form of organization.

(2) State how long the servicer has been servicing assets. Provide, to the extent material, a general discussion of the servicer's experience in servicing assets of any type as well as a more detailed discussion of the servicer's experience in, and procedures for the servicing function it will perform in the current transaction for assets of the type included in the current transaction. Include to the extent material information regarding the size, composition and growth of the servicer's portfolio of serviced assets of the type included in the current transaction and information on factors related to the servicer that may be material to an analysis of the servicing of the assets or the asset-backed securities, as applicable.

(3) Describe any material changes to the servicer's policies or procedures in the servicing function it will perform in the current transaction for assets of the same type included in the current transaction during the past three years.

(4) Provide information regarding the servicer's financial condition to the extent that there is a material risk that the effect on one or more aspects of servicing resulting from such financial condition could have a material impact on pool performance or performance of the asset-backed securities.

(c) *Servicing agreements and servicing practices.* (1) Describe the material terms of the servicing agreement and the servicer's duties regarding the asset-backed securities transaction. File the servicing agreement as an exhibit.

(2) Describe to the extent material the manner in which collections on the assets will be maintained, such as through a segregated collection account, and the extent of commingling of funds that occurs or may occur from the assets with other funds, serviced assets or other assets of the servicer.

(3) Describe to the extent material any special or unique factors involved in servicing the particular type of assets included in the current transaction, such as subprime assets, and the servicer's processes and procedures designed to address such factors.

(4) Describe to the extent material the terms of any arrangements whereby the servicer is required or permitted to provide advances of funds regarding collections, cash flows or distributions, including interest or other fees charged for such advances and terms of recovery by the servicer of such advances. To the extent material, provide statistical information regarding servicer advances on the pool assets and the servicer's overall servicing portfolio for the past three years.

的池内资产提供服务,则应根据服务机构的角色,提供本节第(b)款、第(c)款和第(d)款规定的信息(以适用者为准)。

(b)身份信息和经验。(1)说明服务机构的名称以及服务机构的组织形式。

(2)说明服务机构从事资产服务的年限。如具有重要意义,应提供关于如下内容的一般性论述:服务机构在服务任何一类资产方面的经验;同时应提供一份更加详细的论述,介绍服务机构对当前交易所涉类型资产的服务经验以及在当前交易中履行服务职能的程序。提供关于以下内容的重大信息:对于当前交易涉及的资产类型,服务机构所服务的资产组合之规模、组成和增长,以及与服务机构相关、且对分析资产或资产支持证券(以适用者为准)之服务有重要意义的信息。

(3)说明过去3年中针对当前交易所涉及的同一类资产类型,服务机构的政策或在履行服务职能的程序方面所发生的任何重大变化。

(4)如服务机构的财务状况存在重大风险,可能影响服务的一个或多个方面,进而对资产池的绩效或资产支持证券的绩效产生重大影响,应提供关于该等财务状况的信息。

(c)服务协议和服务惯例。(1)说明服务协议中的重大条款,以及服务机构关于资产支持证券交易的责任。将服务协议作为附录提交。

(2)如具有重要意义,应说明维持资产产生的回款的方式(如通过独立的回款账户)以及含有其他资金的资产、接受服务的资产或服务机构的其他资产已发生或可能发生的资金混合程度。

(3)如具有重要意义,应说明在为当前交易包含的具体类型的资产提供服务时,所涉及的任何特殊或独特的因素(如次级资产),以及服务机构针对该等因素制定的程序。

(4)如具有重要意义,应说明规定或允许服务机构为回款、现金流或分配而垫付资金的任何安排的条款,包括服务机构就该等垫付资金收取的利息或其他费用,以及服务机构收回该等垫付资金的条款。提供关于如下内容的重大统计信息:服务机构为池内资产垫付的资金以及服务机构在过去3年内提供服务的整体资产组合。

(5) Describe to the extent material the servicer's process for handling delinquencies, losses, bankruptcies and recoveries, such as through liquidation of the underlying collateral, note sale by a special servicer or borrower negotiation or workouts.

(6) Describe to the extent material any ability of the servicer to waive or modify any terms, fees, penalties or payments on the assets and the effect of any such ability, if material, on the potential cash flows from the assets.

(7) If the servicer has custodial responsibility for the assets, describe material arrangements regarding the safekeeping and preservation of the assets, such as the physical promissory notes, and procedures to reflect the segregation of the assets from other serviced assets. If no servicer has custodial responsibility for the assets, disclose that fact, identify the party that has such responsibility and provide the information called for by this paragraph for such party.

(8) Describe any limitations on the servicer's liability under the transaction agreements regarding the asset-backed securities transaction.

(d) *Back-up servicing.* Describe the material terms regarding the servicer's removal, replacement, resignation or transfer, including:

(1) Provisions for selection of a successor servicer and financial or other requirements that must be met by a successor servicer.

(2) The process for transferring servicing to a successor servicer.

(3) Provisions for payment of expenses associated with a servicing transfer and any additional fees charged by a successor servicer. Specify the amount of any funds set aside for a servicing transfer.

(4) Arrangements, if any, regarding a back-up servicer for the assets and the identity of any such back-up servicer.

§229.1109 (Item 1109) Trustees.

Provide the following information for each trustee:

(a) State the trustee's name and describe the trustee's form of organization.

(b) Describe to what extent the trustee has had prior experience serving as a trustee for asset-backed securities transactions involving similar pool assets, if applicable.

(c) Describe the trustee's duties and responsibilities regarding the asset-backed securities under the governing documents and under applicable law. In addition, describe any actions required by the trustee, including whether notices are required to investors, rating agencies or other third parties, upon an event of default, potential event of default (and how defined) or other breach of a transaction covenant and any required percentage of a class or classes of asset-backed securities that is needed to require the trustee to take action.

(d) Describe any limitations on the trustee's liability under the transaction

(5)如具有重要意义,应说明服务机构在处理拖欠、损失、破产和没收款项方面的流程,如对相关担保品执行清算、通过特殊服务机构出售票据、与借款人谈判或资产保全措施。

(6)如具有重要意义,应说明服务机构放弃或修改资产的任意条款、费用、罚金或付款的能力,以及该等能力可能对资产潜在现金流产生的重大影响。

(7)如果服务机构对当前交易包含的具体类型的资产负有存管责任,说明关于保存和保护该等资产(如实体本票)的重大安排以及将该等资产与其他接受服务的资产分离的程序。如果所有服务机构均不对该等资产负有存管责任,应如实披露,指明对该等资产承担存管责任的当事方并按照本款规定披露关于该等当事方的信息。

(8)说明资产支持证券的交易协议对服务机构规定的任何责任限制。

(d)备用服务。说明关于服务机构的解聘、更换、重新指定或转让相关的重大条款,包括:

(1)选择继任服务机构的相关规定,以及继任服务机构必须满足的财务要求或其他要求。

(2)将服务转让给继任服务机构的流程。

(3)与服务转让相关的费用支付规定,以及由继任服务机构收取的所有其他费用的支付规定。指明为服务转让而留存的所有资金的数额。

(4)关于资产备用服务机构的安排(如有),以及该等备用服务机构的身份信息。

第229.1109节(第1109条) 信托受托人

提供关于每个信托受托人的下列信息:

(a)说明信托受托人的名称和组织形式。

(b)说明信托受托人之前在涉及类似池内资产的交易中作为资产支持证券信托受托人具有的经验程度(如有)。

(c)说明根据章程性文件和适用法,信托受托人对资产支持证券承担的责任和职责。另外,说明信托受托人有义务采取的任何行动,包括发生违约或潜在违约(说明相关定义)或者其他违反交易约定的情况下是否应向投资者、评级机构或其他第三方发送通知,以及证券在某一类别或多类别资产支持证券所占比例达到何等数额时要求信托受托人采取行动。

(d)说明资产支持证券交易协议对信托受托人规定的任何责任限制。

agreements regarding the asset-backed securities transaction.

(e) Describe any indemnification provisions that entitle the trustee to be indemnified from the cash flow that otherwise would be used to pay the asset-backed securities.

(f) Describe any contractual provisions or understandings regarding the trustee's removal, replacement or resignation, as well as how the expenses associated with changing from one trustee to another trustee will be paid.

Instruction to Item 1109. If multiple trustees are involved in the transaction, provide a description of the roles and responsibilities of each trustee.

§229.1110(Item 1110) Originators.

(a) Identify any originator or group of affiliated originators, apart from the sponsor or its affiliates, that originated, or is expected to originate, 10% or more of the pool assets.

(b) Provide the following information for any originator or group of affiliated originators, apart from the sponsor or its affiliates, that originated, or is expected to originate, 20% or more of the pool assets:

(1) The originator's form of organization.

(2) To the extent material, a description of the originator's origination program and how long the originator has been engaged in originating assets. The description must include a discussion of the originator's experience in originating assets of the type included in the current transaction. In providing the description, include, if material, information regarding the size and composition of the originator's origination portfolio as well as information material to an analysis of the performance of the pool assets, such as the originator's credit-granting or underwriting criteria for the asset types being securitized.

§229.1111(Item 1111) Pool assets.

Link to an amendment published at 76 FR 4243, January 25, 2011.

Describe the pool assets, including the information required by this Item 1111. Present statistical information in tabular or graphical format, if such presentation will aid understanding. Present statistical information in appropriate distributional groups or incremental ranges in addition to presenting appropriate overall pool totals, averages and weighted averages, if such presentation will aid in the understanding of the data. In addition to presenting the number, amount and percentage of pool assets by distributional group or range, also provide statistical information for each group or range by variables, to the extent material, such as, average balance, weighted average coupon, average age and remaining term, average loan-to-value or similar ratio and weighted average standardized credit score or other applicable measure of obligor credit quality. These variables are just examples and should be tailored to the particular asset class backing the asset-backed securities. Consider providing minimums and maximums when presenting averages on an

(e)如果任何补偿规定使信托受托人有权通过本应用于支付资产支持证券的现金流获得补偿,应对该等补偿规定予以说明。

(f)说明关于解聘、更换或重新指定信托受托人的任何合同条款或谅解,以及与变更信托受托人相关的费用的支付方式。

关于第1109条的说明。如果交易涉及多个信托受托人,应说明每个信托受托人的角色及职责。

第229.1110节(第1110条) 创建人

(a)指明发起人或其关联方之外、已创建或预期将创建10%(含)以上池内资产的创建人或一组关联创建人。

(b)针对发起人或其关联方之外、已创建或预期将要创建20%(含)以上池内资产的创建人或一组关联的创建人,提供如下信息:

(1)创建人的组织形式。

(2)如具有重要意义,说明创建人的创建计划,以及创建人从事资产创建的年限。该等说明中必须论及创建人对当前交易所涉资产类型的创建经验。在提供该等说明时,说明创建人所创建的资产组合之规模和组成,以及分析池内资产绩效所需的重大信息,如创建人对与当前证券化资产同一类型的资产的授信或承销标准。

第229.1111节(第1111条) 池内资产

链接至《联邦公报》第76卷第4243页(2011年1月25日)发布的修正。

对池内资产进行说明,包括提供本第1111条规定的信息。如果表格或图表有助于理解,则应以表格或图表形式列报相关统计信息。如除列报适当的资产池整体总计数值、平均值和加权平均值之外,提供适当的分配组或增量范围图有助于理解数据的含义,应通过的分配组或增量范围提供统计信息。除了通过分配组或范围列报资产池的数量、金额及百分比外,还应通过变量提供关于每个分配组或范围的重大统计信息,如平均余额、息票的加权平均值、平均存在年限和剩余期限、平均贷款价值比或其他类似比率,以及标准信用分数的加权平均值或衡量债务人信用质量的其他适用指标。上述变量列举仅属于示例性质,实际变量应根据资产支持证券的具体资产类别设定。在汇总列报每个分配组或范围的平均值时,可考虑提供相应的最大值和最小值。另外,可视具体情况,提供关于池内资产在一定期间内[如3年或该等资产存在的年限(以较低者为准)]的历史数据,以便对资产池数据进行关键评估。无论何时,对资产池整体余额的任何计算均应忽略所有为预先融资账户预留的资金。

aggregate basis and within each group or range. In addition, provide historical data on the pool assets as appropriate (e.g., the lesser of three years or the time such assets have existed) to allow material evaluation of the pool data. In making any calculations regarding overall pool balances, disregard any funds set aside for a prefunding account.

(a) *General information regarding pool asset types and selection criteria.* Provide the following information:

(1) A brief description of the type or types of pool assets to be securitized.

(2) A general description of the material terms of the pool assets.

(3) A description of the solicitation, credit-granting or underwriting criteria used to originate or purchase the pool assets, including, to the extent known, any changes in such criteria and the extent to which such policies and criteria are or could be overridden.

(4) The method and criteria by which the pool assets were selected for the transaction.

(5) The cut-off date or similar date for establishing the composition of the asset pool, if applicable.

(6) If legal or regulatory provisions (such as bankruptcy, consumer protection, predatory lending, privacy, property rights or foreclosure laws or regulations) may materially affect pool asset performance or payments or expected payments on the asset-backed securities, briefly identify these provisions and their effects on such items.

Instruction to Item 1111(a)(6): Unless a material concentration of assets exists, it is not necessary to provide details of the laws in each jurisdiction. Even in that case, a legalistic description or recitation of the laws or regulations in a particular jurisdiction is not required.

(b) *Pool characteristics.* Describe the material characteristics of the asset pool. Provide appropriate introductory and explanatory information to introduce the characteristics, the methodology used in determining or calculating the characteristics and any terms or abbreviations used. While the material characteristics will vary depending on the nature of the pool assets, such characteristics may include, among other things:

(1) Number of each type of pool assets.

(2) Asset size, such as original balance and outstanding balance as of a designated cut-off date.

(3) Interest rate or rate of return, including type of interest rate if the pool includes different types, such as fixed and floating rates.

(4) Capitalized or uncapitalized accrued interest.

(5) Age, maturity, remaining term, average life (based on different prepayment assumptions), current payment/prepayment speeds and pool factors, as applicable.

(6) Servicer distribution, if different servicers service different pool assets.

(a)关于池内资产类型和选择标准的一般信息。提供以下信息：

(1)将被证券化的一类或多类池内资产的简要说明。

(2)关于池内资产重大条款的总体说明。

(3)关于用以创建或购买池内资产的投票权征集、授信或承销标准的说明，包括说明此等标准的任何已知变更，以及在何等范围内，此等政策或标准已经或可能被推翻。

(4)为交易目的选择池内资产的方法和标准。

(5)确定资产池组成成分的截止日期或类似日期(如有)。

(6)如果法律或法规的规定(如关于破产、消费者保护、掠夺性贷款、隐私、财产权或止赎的法律或规章)可能会严重影响池内资产的绩效或资产支持证券的付款或预期付款，简要指明该等规定及其对以上各项的影响。

关于第1111(a)(6)条的说明：除非存在重大资产集中，否则不必提供每个司法辖区内的详细法律规定。即使存在重大的资产集中，也不必提供具体司法辖区的立法说明或复数该等法律法规。

(b)资产池特征。说明资产池的重大特征。适当介绍、解释资产池的特征、用以确定或计算该等特征的方法以及所采用的任何术语和缩写。然而，根据池内资产的性质，重大特征可以有所不同。该等特征可能包括但不限于以下各项：

(1)每类池内资产的数量。

(2)资产规模，如截至指定截止日期的原始余额和未结余额。

(3)利率或回报率；如果资产池包括不同的利率类型(如固定利率和浮动利率)，还应说明利率类型。

(4)已资本化或未资本化的应计利息。

(5)存在年限、到期日、剩余期限、基于不同提前付款假设的平均寿命、当前付款/提前还款速度以及资产池因素，以适用者为准。

(6)如果有不同的服务机构为不同的池内资产提供服务，应说明服务机构的

(7) If a loan or similar receivable:

(i) Amortization period.

(ii) Loan purpose (e.g., whether a purchase or refinance) and status, if applicable (e.g., repayment or deferment).

(iii) Loan-to-value (LTV) ratios and debt service coverage ratios (DSCR), as applicable.

(iv) Type and/or use of underlying property, product or collateral (e.g., occupancy type for residential mortgages or industry sector for commercial mortgages).

(8) If a receivable or other financial asset that arises under a revolving account, such as a credit card receivable:

(i) Monthly payment rate.

(ii) Maximum credit lines.

(iii) Average account balance.

(iv) Yield percentages.

(v) Type of asset.

(vi) Finance charges, fees and other income earned.

(vii) Balance reductions granted for refunds, returns, fraudulent charges or other reasons.

(viii) Percentage of full-balance and minimum payments made.

(9) If the asset pool includes commercial mortgages, the following information, to the extent material:

(i) For all commercial mortgages:

(A) The location and present use of each mortgaged property.

(B) Net operating income and net cash flow information, as well as the components of net operating income and net cash flow, for each mortgaged property.

(C) Current occupancy rates for each mortgaged property.

(D) The identity, square feet occupied by and lease expiration dates for the three largest tenants at each mortgaged property.

(E) The nature and amount of all other material mortgages, liens or encumbrances against such properties and their priority.

(ii) For each commercial mortgage that represents, by dollar value, 10% or more of the asset pool, as measured as of the cut-off date:

(A) Any proposed program for the renovation, improvement or development of such properties, including the estimated cost thereof and the method of financing to be used.

(B) The general competitive conditions to which such properties are or may be subject.

分布。

(7)对于贷款或类似的应收账款,应说明:

(i)摊还期间。

(ii)贷款目的(如购买或再融资),如适用,还应说明贷款状态(如还款中或延期中)。

(iii)贷款价值比(LTV)和偿债保障比率(DSCR),以适用者为准。

(iv)基础财产、产品或担保品的类型和/或用途(如对于住宅抵押品,应说明其入住类型,对于商业抵押品,应说明其所属行业类别)。

(8)如果循环账户产生了应收款项或其他金融资产(如信用卡应收款项),应说明其:

(i)每月付款率。

(ii)最高信用限额。

(iii)平均账户余额。

(iv)收益率百分比。

(v)资产类型。

(vi)财务费用、手续费和其他赚取的所得。

(vii)由于退款、退货、欺诈性收费或其他原因导致的余额降低。

(viii)占全部余额的百分比及已偿还的最低还款额。

(9)如果资产池中包含商业抵押品,应提供关于以下方面的重大信息:

(i)对于所有商业抵押品,应提供:

(A)每一已抵押房产的地址及当前用途。

(B)每一已抵押房产的净营业所得和净现金流信息,以及净营业所得和净现金流的组成。

(C)每一已抵押房产的当前入住率。

(D)每一已抵押房产的最大三个租户的身份信息、所租面积(平方英尺)以及租约到期日。

(E)该等房产上的所有其他重大抵押、留置权或产权负担的性质、金额及其优先顺序。

(ii)对于价值占资产池10%(含)以上的商业抵押品(截至截止日,以美元计价),应提供:

(A)该等房产的所有修缮、改良或开发计划草案,包括相关的预估费用和将采用的融资方法。

(B)该等房产面临或可能面临的一般竞争条件。

(C) Management of such properties.

(D) Occupancy rate expressed as a percentage for each of the last five years.

(E) Principal business, occupations and professions carried on in, or from the properties.

(F) Number of tenants occupying 10% or more of the total rentable square footage of such properties and principal nature of business of such tenant, and the principal provisions of the leases with those tenants including, but not limited to: rental per annum, expiration date, and renewal options.

(G) The average effective annual rental per square foot or unit for each of the last three years prior to the date of filing.

(H) Schedule of the lease expirations for each of the ten years starting with the year in which the registration statement is filed (or the year in which the prospectus supplement is dated, as applicable), stating:

(*1*) The number of tenants whose leases will expire.

(*2*) The total area in square feet covered by such leases.

(*3*) The annual rental represented by such leases.

(*4*) The percentage of gross annual rental represented by such leases.

Instruction to Item 1111(b)(9): What is required is information material to an investor's understanding of the asset-backed securities. Detailed descriptions of the physical characteristics of individual properties or legal descriptions by metes and bounds are not required.

(10) Whether the pool asset is secured or unsecured, and if secured, the type(s) of collateral.

(11) Standardized credit scores of obligors and other information regarding obligor credit quality.

(12) Billing and payment procedures, including frequency of payment, payment options, fees, charges and origination or payment incentives.

(13) Information about the origination channel and origination process for the pool assets, such as originator information (and how acquired) and the level of origination documentation required, as applicable.

(14) Geographic distribution, such as by state or other material geographic region. If 10% or more of the pool assets are or will be located in any one state or other geographic region, describe any economic or other factors specific to such state or region that may materially impact the pool assets or pool asset cash flows.

Instruction to Item 1111(b)(14): For most assets, such as credit card accounts, motor vehicle leases, trade receivables and student loans, the location of the asset is the underlying obligor's billing address. For assets involving real estate, such as mortgages,

(C)该等房产的管理。

(D)过去5年内每年的入住率(以百分比表示)。

(E)在该等房产中开展的主营业务、工作和专业业务。

(F)租用该等房产10%(含)以上可租面积的租户数、该等租户业务的主要性质以及与该等租户签订的主要租约条款,包括但不限于年租金、到期日以及续租选择权。

(G)文件提交之日前3年,每平方英尺或单位的平均有效年租金。

(H)从注册说明书提交当年(或招募说明书补充材料的年份,以适用者为准)开始计算的10年内每一年的租约到期表,列明:

(1)租约将到期的租户数。

(2)该等租约所覆盖的总面积(以平方英尺表示)。

(3)该等租约产生的年租金。

(4)该等租约产出的年租金占年度总租金的百分比。

关于第1111(b)(9)条的说明:要求提供的信息均属于对投资者理解资产支持证券具有重要意义的信息。不必提供各单独房产物理特征的详细说明或以地界表示的法定说明。

(10)池内资产是否具有担保,如有,应说明担保品的类型。

(11)债务人的标准信用分数和能够体现债务人信用质量的其他信息。

(12)收款和付款程序,包括付款频率、可选付款方式、费用、收费及创建或付款激励等。

(13)关于池内资产创建渠道和创建流程的信息,如创建人信息(包括该等信息是如何获得的)以及应就创建开展的文件编制的级别,以适用者为准。

(14)地理分布信息,如按州或其他重要地理区域划分的分布信息。如果有10%(含)以上的池内资产位于或将位于某一个州或其他地理区域,应说明该州或该地理区域可能对池内资产或池内资产现金流产生重大影响的任何特有经济因素或其他因素。

关于第1111(b)(14)条的说明:对于大多数资产而言,如信用卡账户、汽车租赁、购销应收账款和学生贷款等,资产所在位置的地址即为相关债务人的账单地址。对于涉及房地产的资产,例如抵押房产,相关房产所在的物理位置即为资产的位置。

the location of the asset is where the physical property underlying the asset is located.

(15) Other concentrations material to the asset type (e.g., school type for student loans). If material, provide information required by paragraph (b)(14) of this section regarding such concentrations, as applicable.

(c) *Delinquency and loss information.* Provide delinquency and loss information for the asset pool, including statistical information regarding delinquencies and losses.

(d) *Sources of pool cash flow.* If the cash flows from the pool assets that are to be used to support the asset-backed securities are to come from more than one source (such as separate cash flows from lease payments and from the sale of the residual asset at the termination of the lease), provide the following information:

(1) Disclose the specific sources of funds that will be used to make the payments and distributions on the asset-backed securities, and, if applicable, provide information on the relative amount and percentage of funds that are to be derived from each source, including a description of any assumptions, data, models and methodology used to derive such amounts. If payments on different classes or different categories of payments on or related to the asset-backed securities (e.g., principal, interest or expenses) are to come from different or segregated cash flows from the pool assets or other sources, disclose the source of funds that will be used for such payments.

(2) *Residual value information.* If the asset pool includes leases or other assets where a portion of the securitized pool balance is attributable to the residual value of the underlying physical property underlying the leases, disclose the following:

(i) How the residual values used to structure the transaction were estimated, including an explanation of any material discount rates, models or assumptions used and who selected such rates, models or assumptions.

(ii) Any material procedures or requirements incorporated to preserve residual values during the term of the lease, such as lessee responsibilities, prohibitions on subletting, indemnification or required insurance or guarantees.

(iii) The procedures by which the residual values will be realized and by whom those procedures will be carried out, including information on the experience of such party, any affiliations with a party described in Item 1119(a) of this Regulation AB and the compensation arrangements with such party.

(iv) Whether the pool assets are open-end leases (e.g., where the lessee is required to cover the shortfall between the residual value of the leased property and the sale proceeds) or closed-end leases (e.g., where the lessor is responsible for such shortfalls), and where both types of leases are included in the asset pool, the percentage of each.

(v) To the extent material, any lessor obligations that are required under the leases, and the effect or potential effect on the asset-backed securities from failure by the lessor

(15)对该类资产具有重要意义的其他集中(如学生贷款所涉学校类型)。如果具有重要意义,应按本节第(b)(14)款的规定提供关于该等集中的信息,以适用者为准。

(c)拖欠和损失信息。提供关于资产池的拖欠和损失信息,包括关于拖欠和损失的统计信息。

(d)资产池现金流的来源。如果池内资产产生的现金流将用于支持资产支持证券,且该等现金流将从一个以上的来源获得(如分别从租金付款和租约终止后剩余资产的出售获得现金流),应提供如下信息:

(1)披露用于资产支持证券的付款和分配的资金的具体来源,并且,如果适用,应说明每一资金来源将提供的资金数额及其所占的百分比,包括得出该等金额所采用的所有假设、数据、模型和方法。如果针对不同类型的资产支持证券的付款,或与资产支持证券相关的不同种类的付款(如本金、利息或支出)将通过资产池的不同现金流或彼此独立的现金流或其他资金来源支付,应披露将用于此等付款的资金来源。

(2)残值信息。如果资产池包括租赁资产或其他资产,且其中部分证券化的池内资产余额归属于租赁实体房产的残值,应披露如下信息:

(i)用于构建交易结构的残值是如何估算的,同时应解释所使用的任何重大折扣率、模型或假设,并说明该等折扣率、模型或假设是由哪一方选择的。

(ii)在租赁期间为保存残值而采用的所有重要程序或要求,如承租人责任、禁止转租规定、赔偿或保险或担保规定。

(iii)残值变现的程序以及执行该等程序的当事方,包括该当事方的经验、与本《AB管理办法》第1119(a)条所述之当事方之间的关联关系(如有)以及与该当事方签订的报酬安排。

(iv)池内资产属于开放式租赁财产(如所租房产残值与销售所得之间的差额应由承租人承担)或非开放式租赁财产(如该等差额应由出租人承担),如果资产池中包括上述两种财产,应说明两者各占的百分比。

(v)如具有重要意义,应说明出租人在租约下承担的所有义务,以及如果出租人不履行义务时将给资产支持证券带来的影响或潜在影响。

to perform its obligations.

(vi) Statistical information regarding estimated residual values for the pool assets.

(vii) Summary historical statistics on turn-in rates, if applicable, and residual value realization rates by the party responsible for such process over the past three years, or such longer period as is material to an evaluation of the pool assets.

(viii) The effect on security holders if not enough cash flow is received from the realization of the residual values, whether there are any provisions to address this contingency, and how any cash flow greater than that necessary to pay security holders will be allocated.

(e) *Representations and warranties and repurchase obligations regarding pool assets.* Summarize any representations and warranties made concerning the pool assets by the sponsor, transferor, originator or other party to the transaction, and describe briefly the remedies available if those representations and warranties are breached, such as repurchase obligations.

(f) *Claims on pool assets.* Describe any material direct or contingent claim that parties other than the holders of the asset-backed securities have on any pool assets. Also, describe any material cross-collateralization or cross-default provisions relating to the pool assets.

(g) *Revolving periods, prefunding accounts and other changes to the asset pool.* If the transaction contemplates a prefunding or revolving period, provide the following information, as applicable. Provide similar information regarding any other circumstances where pool assets may be added, substituted or removed from the asset pool, such as in the event of additional issuances of asset-backed securities in a master trust or a breach of a pool asset representation or warranty:

(1) The term or duration of any prefunding or revolving period.

(2) For prefunding periods, the amount of proceeds to be deposited in the prefunding account.

(3) For revolving periods, the maximum amount of additional assets that may be acquired during the revolving period, if applicable.

(4) The percentage of the asset pool and any class or series of the asset-backed securities represented by the prefunding account or the revolving account, if applicable.

(5) Triggers or events that would trigger limits on or terminate the prefunding or revolving period and the effects of such triggers. In particular for a revolving period, describe the operation of the revolving period and the amortization period.

(6) When and how new pool assets may be acquired during the prefunding or revolving period, and if, when and how pool assets can be removed or substituted. Describe any limits on the amount, type or speed with which pool assets may be acquired,

(vi)关于池内资产预估残值的统计信息。

(vii)过去3年内或对于评估池内资产具有重要意义的较长期间内,关于到期退还率的历史统计数据摘要(如有),以及负责执行变现的当事方对残值变现的比率。

(viii)如残值变现未获得足够的现金流将对证券持有人产生的影响;是否有任何准备金将用于应对此种意外;以及如果获得的现金流超过需要向证券持有人支付的金额,超出部分将如何分配。

(e)关于池内资产的声明、保证和回购义务。简要总结发起人、转让人、创建人或其他交易方对池内资产作出的任何声明和保证,并简要说明该等声明和保证被违反时可以获得的救济,如回购义务。

(f)对池内资产的权利主张。说明除资产支持证券持有人之外的其他当事方对任何池内资产直接或可能拥有的任何重大权利主张。另外,还应说明与池内资产相关的任何交叉担保和交叉违约规定。

(g)资产池的循环期、预先融资账户和其他变更。如果交易规定有预先融资期或循环期,应根据实际情况,提供下列信息。对于可以增加、替换或剔除池内资产的任何其他情形,如在主信托中额外发行资产支持证券,或者池内资产的声明或保证被违反之时,应提供类似信息:

(1)任何预先融资期或循环期的期限或持续时间。

(2)对于预先融资期,应指明将存入预先融资账户的募集资金数额。

(3)对于循环期,应指明在该等期限内可收购的额外资产的最大数额(如适用)。

(4)预先融资账户下或循环账户在资产池以及任一类别或系列的资产支持证券中所占的百分比(以适用者为准)。

(5)能够导致预先融资期或循环期受到限制或导致其终止的触发条件或事件,以及该等触发条件或事件的影响。尤其对于循环期,应说明循环期和摊还期内的运营。

(6)在预先融资或循环期内,可以在何等时间以及通过何等方式收购新的池内资产,以及是否、可以在什么时候以及通过何等方式来剔除或替换池内资产。说明收购、替换或剔除池内资产在金额、类型或速度方面的任何限制。

substituted or removed.

(7) The acquisition or underwriting criteria for additional pool assets to be acquired during the prefunding or revolving period, including a description of any differences from the criteria used to select the current asset pool.

(8) Which party has the authority to add, remove or substitute assets from the asset pool or determine if such pool assets meet the acquisition or underwriting criteria for additional pool assets. In addition, disclose whether or not there will be any independent verification of such person's exercise of authority or determinations.

(9) Any requirements to add or remove minimum amounts of pool assets and any effects of not meeting those requirements.

(10) If applicable, the procedures and standards for the temporary investment of funds in a prefunding or revolving account pending use (including the disposition of gains and losses on pending funds) and a description of the financial products or instruments eligible for such accounts.

(11) The circumstances under which funds in a prefunding or revolving account will be returned to investors or otherwise disposed of.

(12) A statement of whether, and if so, how, investors will be notified of changes to the asset pool.

§229.1112(Item 1112) Significant obligors of pool assets.

(a) *Descriptive information.* Provide the following information for each significant obligor:

(1) The name of the obligor.

(2) The organizational form and general character of the business of the obligor.

(3) The nature of the concentration of the pool assets with the obligor.

(4) The material terms of the pool assets and the agreements with the obligor involving the pool assets.

(b) *Financial information.* (1) If the pool assets relating to a significant obligor represent 10% or more, but less than 20%, of the asset pool, provide selected financial data required by Item 301 of Regulation S-K (§229.301) for the significant obligor, provided, however, that for a significant obligor under Item 1101(k)(2) of this Regulation AB, only net operating income for the most recent fiscal year and interim period is required.

(2) If pool assets relating to a significant obligor represent 20% or more of the asset pool, provide financial statements meeting the requirements of Regulation S-X (§§210.1-01 through 210.12-29 of this chapter), except §210.3-05 of this chapter and Article 11 of Regulation S-X (§§210.11-01 through 210.11-03 of this chapter), of the significant obligor. Financial statements of such obligor and its subsidiaries consolidated (as required

（7）将在预先融资或循环期内额外收购的池内资产的收购或承销标准，同时应说明该等标准与选择当前资产池的标准之任何差异。

（8）哪一方有权添加、剔除或替换资产池中的资产或者认定该等池内资产达到了新增池内资产的收购或承销标准。另外应披露，该方行使上述权限或进行上述认定时，是否将受到任何独立审核的限制。

（9）添加或剔除池内资产的任何最低数量要求，以及未达到该等要求的任何后果。

（10）如适用，应说明对预先融资或循环账户中暂未使用的资金进行临时投资的程序和标准（包括对暂未使用的资金的收益和损失的处理），以及有资格得到该等账户投资的金融产品或金融工具。

（11）在何等情形下预先融资或循环账户中的资金将返还给投资者或另行处置。

（12）说明资产池发生变更时，投资者是否会得到通知，如果是，将以何种方式获得通知。

第229.1112节（第1112条） 池内资产的重大债务人

（a）说明性信息。就每个重大债务人提供下列信息：

（1）债务人的名称/姓名。

（2）债务人的组织形式及一般业务特征。

（3）池内资产与债务人存在的集中关系的性质。

（4）关于池内资产的重大条款，以及与债务人签订的关于池内资产的协议的重大条款。

（b）财务信息。（1）如果与重大债务人相关的池内资产达到资产池的10%（含）以上，但不足20%，应按《S-K管理办法》第301条（第229.301节）的规定提供关于重大债务人的择要列示的财务数据，但是，对于本《AB管理办法》第1101（k）（2）条所述的重大债务人，只须提供最近一个会计年度和中期的净营业收入。

（2）如果与重大债务人相关的池内资产达到资产池的20%（含）以上，除本章第210.3-05节和《S-X管理办法》的第11条（本章第210.11-01~210.11-03节）规定的信息外，还应提供该等重大债务人的财务报表，且该等财务报表应符合《S-X管理办法》［本章第210.1-01~210.12-29节］的要求。该等债务人及其并表子公司的财务报表［如本章第240.14a-3（b）节所规定］应按照本条规定提交。

by §240.14a-3(b) of this chapter) shall be filed under this item.

Instructions to Item 1112 (b): 1. No information need be provided pursuant to paragraph (b) of this section if the obligations of the significant obligor as they relate to the pool assets are backed by the full faith and credit of the United States.

2. No information need be provided pursuant to paragraph (b) of this section if the obligations of the significant obligor as they relate to the pool assets are backed by the full faith and credit of a foreign government (as defined in §240.3b-4(a) of this chapter) if the pool assets are investment grade securities as defined in Item I.B.2 of Form S-3 (§239.13 of this chapter). If the pool assets are not investment grade securities, information required by paragraph (5) of Schedule B of the Securities Act (15 U.S.C. 77aa) regarding the foreign government may be incorporated by reference from a Commission filing in lieu of providing the financial information required pursuant to paragraph (b) of this section.

3. If the significant obligor is an asset-backed issuer and the pool assets relating to the significant obligor are asset-backed securities, provide the following information in lieu of the information required by paragraph (b) of this section:

a. For a registration statement under the Securities Act or the Exchange Act or a prospectus to be filed pursuant to §230.424 of this chapter, the information required by Items 1104 through 1115, 1117 and 1119 of this Regulation AB regarding such asset-backed securities; and

b. For an Exchange Act report on Form 10-K or Form 10-D (§249.310 or 249.312 of this chapter), the information required by General Instruction J. of Form 10-K regarding such asset-backed securities for the period for which the last Form 10-K of the asset-backed securities was due (or would have been due if such asset-backed securities are not required to file reports with the Commission pursuant to section 13(a) or 15(d) of the Exchange Act (15 U.S.C. 78m(a) or 78o(d)).

4. If the significant obligor is a foreign business (as defined §210.1-02 of this chapter):

a. Paragraph (b)(1) of this section may be complied with by providing the information required by Item 3.A. of Form 20-F (§249.220f of this chapter). If a reconciliation to U.S. generally accepted accounting principles called for by Instruction 2. to Item 3.A. of Form 20-F is unavailable or not obtainable without unreasonable cost or expense, at a minimum provide a narrative description of all material variations in accounting principles, practices and methods used in preparing the non-U.S. GAAP financial statements used as a basis for the selected financial data from those accepted in the U.S.

b. Paragraph (b)(2) of this section may be complied with by providing financial

关于第1112(b)条的说明:1.如果重大债务人关于池内资产的义务获得美国政府的充分认可和信用支持,则不必提供本条第(b)款规定的信息。

2.如果重大债务人关于池内资产的义务获得外国政府的充分认可和信用支持[定义见本章第240.3b-4(a)节],并且池内资产属于《S-3表格》第I.B.2条(本章第239.13节)所定义的投资级证券,则不必提供本节第(b)款规定的信息。如果池内资产不属于投资级证券,可以通过引用向证券交易委员会提交的文件来提供《证券法》《附表B》第(5)款(《美国法典》第十五编第77aa节)规定的关于外国政府的信息,以替代本节第(b)款所规定的财务信息。

3.如果重大债务人是资产支持证券的发行人并且和重大债务人相关的池内资产属于资产支持证券,则应提供以下信息替代本节第(b)款规定的信息:

a.对于《1933年证券法》或《1934年证券交易法》规定的注册说明书或根据本章第230.424节将要提交的招募说明书,应提供本《AB管理办法》第1104条至第1115条、第1117条和第1119条要求提供的关于该等资产支持证券的信息;及

b.对于按照《10-K表格》或《10-D表格》(本章第249.310节或第249.312节)提交的《交易法》报告,应提供《10-K表格》总体说明J要求提供的与资产支持证券相关的信息,信息所对应的期间应为就资产支持证券提交上一份《10-K表格》的期间(或者,如果资产支持证券不需要按照《交易法》第13(a)条或第15(d)条[《美国法典》第十五编第78m(a)节或第78o(d)节]的规定向证券交易委员会提交报告,则为假设须提供《10-K表格》时,上一份《10-K表格》所对应的期间)。

4.如果重大债务人为一家外国企业(定义见本章第210.1-02节):

a.提供《20-F表格》第3.A.条(本章第249.220f节)规定的信息即视为已履行本节第(b)(1)款的规定。如果《20-F表格》第3.A.条的说明2要求进行调节以符合美国公认会计原则,但实际无法进行该等调节或者调节需要支付不合理的成本或费用,至少应就编制非美国GAAP财务报表择要列示的财务数据时所使用的会计原则、实践和方法与美国公认会计原则、实践和方法的所有重大差别提供文字说明。

b.提供符合《20-F表格》第17条要求的财务报表(覆盖期间为《20-F表格》第8.A.条

statements meeting the requirements of Item 17 of Form 20–F for the periods specified by Item 8.A. of Form 20–F.

§229.1113(Item 1113) Structure of the transaction.

(a) *Description of the securities and transaction structure.* In providing the information required by Item 202 of Regulation S–K(§229.202), address the following specific factors relating to the asset–backed securities, as applicable:

(1) The types or categories of securities that may be offered, such as interest–weighted or principal–weighted classes (including IO (interest only) or PO (principal only) securities), planned amortization or companion classes or residual or subordinated interests.

(2) The flow of funds for the transaction, including the payment allocations, rights and distribution priorities among all classes of the issuing entity's securities, and within each class, with respect to cash flows, credit enhancement or other support and any other structural features designed to enhance credit, facilitate the timely payment of monies due on the pool assets or owing to security holders, adjust the rate of return on the asset–backed securities, or preserve monies that will or might be distributed to security holders. In addition to an appropriate narrative discussion of the allocation and priority structure of pool cash flows, present the flow of funds graphically if doing so will aid understanding. In the flow of funds discussion, provide information regarding any requirements directing cash flows from the pool assets (such as to reserve accounts, cash collateral accounts or expenses) and the purpose and operation of such requirements.

(3) In describing the interest rate or rate of return on the asset–backed securities and how such amounts are payable, explain how the rate is determined and how frequently it will be determined. If the rate to be paid can be a combination of two or more rates (such as the lesser of a variable rate or the actual weighted average net coupon on the pool assets), provide clear information regarding each rate and when each rate applies.

(4) How principal, if any, will be paid on the asset–backed securities, including maturity dates, amortization or principal distribution schedules, principal distribution dates, formulas for calculating principal distributions from the cash flows and other factors that will affect the timing or amount of principal payments for each class of securities.

(5) The denominations in which the asset–backed securities may be issued.

(6) Any specified changes to the transaction structure that would be triggered upon a default or event of default (such as a change in distribution priority among classes).

(7) Any liquidation, amortization, performance or similar triggers or events, and the rights of investors or changes to the transaction structure or flow of funds if such events were to occur.

中指定的期间)即视为已满足本条第(b)(2)款的要求。

第229.1113节(第1113条) 交易结构

(a)证券及交易结构的说明。在提供《S-K管理办法》第202条(第229.202节)规定的信息时,应阐述下列与资产支持证券相关的特定因素,以适用者为准:

(1)可供要约发售的证券类型或种类,如利率权重类或本金权重类[包括IO(仅付利息)证券或PO(仅付本金)证券]、计划摊还或附随证券类,或残留权益或次级权益类。

(2)交易的资金流,包括在发行实体所有类别的证券之间的付款分配及其享有的权利和分配优先级,以及每一类别证券内的现金流、信用增级或其他支持措施,以及为下述目的而设计的任何其他结构性特征:增强信用、促进池内资产的应付款项或欠付证券持有人的应付款项的及时还款、调整资产支持证券的回报率或储备将要或可能分配给证券持有人的现金。如果图表有助于理解,则除适当的文字说明之外,还应使用图表来说明资产池现金流的分配和优先级结构。在关于资金流的论述中,应提供关于池内资产现金流的导向要求的任何信息(如准备金账户、现金担保账户或费用),同时说明该等要求的目的和实际适用。

(3)在说明资产支持证券的利率或回报率以及该等款项在何等情况下成为应付时,说明确定利率的方式和频率。如果支付利率可以是两种(含)以上利率的组合(例如,池内资产可变利率或实际加权平均净票面利率中的较低者),应提供关于每项利率的明确信息,并说明将于何时采用哪种利率。

(4)资产支持证券的本金(如有)将如何支付,同时应说明资产支持证券的到期日、摊还或本金分配方案、本金分配日期、计算现金流的本金分配时所使用的公式,以及会影响每一类别证券本金支付的时间安排或数额的其他因素。

(5)可以发行的资产支持证券的面额。

(6)由违约或违约事件触发的交易结构的任何具体变更(如各类别证券的分配优先顺序的变更)。

(7)任何清算、摊还、履行或类似的触发事件,以及该等事件发生时,投资者将享有的权利或交易结构或资金流将发生的变更。

(8) Whether the servicer or other party is required to provide periodic evidence of the absence of a default or of compliance with the terms of the transaction agreements.

(9) If applicable, the extent, expressed as a percentage, the transaction is overcollateralized or undercollateralized as measured by comparing the principal balance of the asset-backed securities to the asset pool.

(10) Any provisions contained in other securities that could result in a cross-default or cross-collateralization.

(11) Any minimum standards, restrictions or suitability requirements regarding potential investors in purchasing the securities or any restrictions on ownership or transfer of the securities.

(12) Security holder vote required to amend the transaction documents and allocation of voting rights among security holders.

(b) *Distribution frequency and cash maintenance.* (1) Disclose the frequency of distribution dates for the asset-backed securities and the collection periods for the pool assets.

(2) Describe how cash held pending distribution or other uses is held and invested. Also describe the length of time cash will be held pending distributions to security holders. Identify the party or parties with access to cash balances and the authority to invest cash balances. Specify who determines any decisions regarding the deposit, transfer or disbursement of pool asset cash flows and whether there will be any independent verification of the transaction accounts or account activity.

(c) *Fees and expenses.* Provide in a separate table an itemized list of all fees and expenses to be paid or payable out of the cash flows from the pool assets. In itemizing the fees and expenses, also indicate their general purpose, the party receiving such fees or expenses, the source of funds for such fees or expenses (if different from other fees or expenses or if such fees or expenses are to be paid from a specified portion of the cash flows) and the distribution priority of such expenses. If the amount of such fees or expenses is not fixed, provide the formula used to determine such fees or expenses. The tabular presentation should be accompanied by footnotes or other accompanying narrative disclosure to the extent necessary for an understanding of the timing or amount of such fees or expenses, such as any restrictions or limits on fees or whether the estimate may change in certain instances, such as in an event of default (and how the fees would change in such an instance or the factors that would affect the change). In addition, through footnote or other accompanying narrative disclosure, describe if any, and if so how, such fees or expenses can be changed without notice to, or approval by, security holders and any restrictions on the ability to change a fee or expense amount, such as due to a change in transaction party.

(8)服务机构或者其他机构是否有义务定期提交证据,证明其不存在违约情形或证明其遵守了交易协议的条款。

(9)通过对比资产支持证券的本金余额和资产池,以百分数表示交易超额担保或担保不足的额度(如有)。

(10)可能造成交叉违约或交叉担保的其他证券中的任何规定。

(11)关于购买证券的潜在投资者的任何最低标准、限制或适当性要求,或者关于证券所有权或转让的限制。

(12)修正交易文件所需的证券持有人的表决票数以及表决权在证券投资者之间的分配。

(b)分配频率和现金的维持。(1)披露资产支持证券的分配频率以及池内资产的收款期限。

(2)说明为分配或其他用途而预留的现金的预留和投资程序。另外应说明用于向证券持有人分配的现金将预留多长时间。指明有权提取现金余额的当事方,以及将现金余额用于投资的权限。指明谁将负责作出关于池内资产现金流存款、转账或支出的决定,以及交易账户或账户行为是否接受任何独立审核。

(c)费用和支出。在一份单独的表格中逐条列报将通过或应通过池内资产现金流进行支付的所有费用和支出。在逐项列报费用和支出时,还应指明各项费用和支出的一般用途、接收该等费用和支出的当事方、该等费用和支出的资金来源(如果不同于其他费用或支出的资金来源,或者该等费用或支出将通过特定部分的现金流支付)以及分配优先顺序。如果该等费用或支出不是固定的,应提供用于计算该等费用或支出的公式。以表格形式进行列报时,应附带脚注或其他必要的文字披露,以帮助理解该等费用或支出的时间或数额,如任何费用限制或限额,或者在特定的情况下(如出现违约之时)该等预估值是否可能发生变动,以及出现该等情况时该等费用将如何发生变动或可能影响此等变动的因素。另外,应通过脚注或其他附带的文字披露说明:该等费用或开支是否可以在任何情形下(如交易当事方发生变动),在不通知或未经证券持有人批准的情况下变动,如果可以,将如何进行变动,以及更改该等费用或开支金额的任何能力限制。

(d) *Excess cash flow.* (1) Describe the disposition of residual or excess cash flows. Identify who owns any residual or retained interests to the cash flows if such person is affiliated with the sponsor, depositor, issuing entity or any entity identified in Item 1119(a) of this Regulation AB or if such person has rights that may alter the transaction structure beyond receipt of residual or excess cash flows. Describe such rights, as material.

(2) Disclose any requirements in the transaction agreements to maintain a minimum amount of excess cash flow or spread from, or retained interest in, the transaction and any actions that would be required or changes to the transaction structure that would occur if such requirements were not met.

(3) To the extent material to an understanding of the asset-backed securities, disclose any features or arrangements to facilitate a securitization of the excess cash flow or retained interest from the transaction, including whether any material changes to the transaction structure may be made without the consent of asset-backed security holders in connection with these securitizations.

(e) *Master trusts.* If one or more additional series or classes have been or may be issued that are backed by the same asset pool, provide information regarding the additional securities to the extent material to an understanding of their effect on the securities being offered, including the following:

(1) Relative priority of such additional securities to the securities being offered and rights to the underlying pool assets and their cash flows.

(2) Allocation of cash flow from the asset pool and any expenses or losses among the various series or classes.

(3) Terms under which such additional series or classes may be issued and pool assets increased or changed.

(4) The terms of any security holder approval or notification of such additional securities.

(5) Which party has the authority to determine whether such additional securities may be issued. In addition, if there are conditions to such additional issuance, disclose whether or not there will be an independent verification of such person's exercise of authority or determinations.

(f) *Optional or mandatory redemption or termination.* (1) If any class of the asset-backed securities includes an optional or mandatory redemption or termination feature, provide the following information:

(i) Terms for triggering the redemption or termination.

(ii) The identity of the party that holds the redemption or termination option or obligation, as well as whether such party is an affiliate of the sponsor, depositor, issuing

(d)超额现金流。(1)说明如何处置剩余现金流量或超额现金流量。指明拥有现金流剩余权益或保留权益的人,该等主体是否与发起人、交存人、发行实体或本《AB管理办法》第1119(a)条指明的任何实体存在关联关系,或者该等人除收取剩余现金流或超额现金流之外是否有权更改交易结构。如果具有重要意义,应说明该等权利。

(2)披露交易协议中关于就交易维持最低数额的超额现金流、利差或保留权益的任何规定,或者关于应采取的行动的规定,或者如果没达到这些要求之时,交易结构将发生何等变化。

(3)如对于理解资产支持证券具有重要意义,应披露为促进交易超额现金流或保留权益之证券化而设计的所有特征或作出的安排,包括是否不经过与证券化相关的资产支持证券持有人同意即可对交易结构作出重大变更。

(e)主信托。如果依托同一资产池的其他一个或多个系列或类别的证券已经发行或即将发行,应提供下列信息,条件是该等信息对于理解该等发行对当前要约发行的证券之影响具有重要意义:

(1)该等其他证券与当前要约证券相比具有的优先性,以及对相关池内资产及其现金流享有的权利。

(2)资产池现金流的分配,以及任何费用或损失在不同系列或类别证券之间的分配。

(3)该等其他系列或类别的证券应遵守的发行条款以及增加或变动池内资产应遵循的条款。

(4)关于任何证券持有人批准该等其他证券或获得相关通知的条款。

(5)哪一方有权决定该等其他证券是否可以发行。另外,如果关于该等其他发行存在相关条件,应披露上述主体行使上述权限或作出上述决定时是否将接受任何独立审核。

(f)选择性或强制性回赎或终止。(1)如果任何类别的资产支持证券具有选择性或强制性回赎或终止特征,应提供下列信息:

(i)触发回赎或终止的条款。

(ii)拥有回赎或终止选择权或承担回赎或终止义务的当事方身份,以及该等当事方是否与发起人、交存人、发行实体或本《AB管理办法》第1119(a)条中指明的任何实

entity or any entity identified in Item 1119(a) of this Regulation AB.

(iii) The amount of the redemption or repurchase price or formula for determining such amount.

(iv) The procedures for redemption or termination, including any notices to security holders.

(v) If the amount allocated to security holders is reduced by losses, the policy regarding any amounts recovered after redemption or termination.

(2) The title of any class of securities with an optional redemption or termination feature that may be exercised when 25% or more of the original principal balance of the pool assets is still outstanding must include the word "callable," *provided, however*, that in the case of a master trust, a title of a class of securities must include the word "callable" when an optional redemption or termination feature may be exercised when 25% or more of the original principal balance of the particular series in which the class was issued is still outstanding.

(g) *Prepayment, maturity and yield considerations.* (1) Describe any models, including the related material assumptions and limitations, used as a means to identify cash flow patterns with respect to the pool assets.

(2) Describe to the extent material the degree to which each class of securities is sensitive to changes in the rate of payment on the pool assets (e.g., prepayment or interest rate sensitivity), and describe the consequences of such changing rate of payment. Provide statistical information of such effects, such as the effect of prepayments on yield and weighted average life.

(3) Describe any special allocations of prepayment risks among the classes of securities, and whether any class protects other classes from the effects of the uncertain timing of cash flow.

§229.1114(Item 1114) Credit enhancement and other support, except for certain derivatives instruments.

(a) *Descriptive information.* To the extent material, describe the following, including a clear discussion of the manner in which each potential item is designed to affect or ensure timely payment of the asset-backed securities:

(1) Any external credit enhancement designed to ensure that the asset-backed securities or pool assets will pay in accordance with their terms, such as bond insurance, letters of credit or guarantees.

(2) Any mechanisms to ensure that payments on the asset-backed securities are timely, such as liquidity facilities, lending facilities, guaranteed investment contracts and minimum principal payment agreements.

(3) Any derivatives whose primary purpose is to provide credit enhancement related

体存在关联关系。

(iii)回赎或回购价格的数额或确定该等数额的公式。

(iv)回赎或终止程序,包括向证券持有人发送任何通知的程序。

(v)如果分配给证券持有人的数额因为亏损而有所减少,应说明回赎或终止后回收任何金额的相关政策。

(2)具有选择性回赎或终止特征,且可以在池内资产25%(含)以上的原始本金仍未缴付时行使该等回赎或终止选择权的证券类别,必须在其名称内包含“可提前回赎”字样;但是,在主信托的情况下,具有选择性回赎或终止特征,且可以在其所属的具体证券系列25%(含)以上的原始本金仍未缴付时行使该等回赎或终止选择权的证券类别,必须在其名称内包含“可提前回赎”字样。

(g)提前还款、到期日和收益考量因素。(1)说明识别池内资产的现金流模式所使用的任何模型,包括相关的重大假设和限制。

(2)如具有重要意义,应说明各类别证券对池内资产的付款率的敏感度(即提前还款或利率敏感性),并说明该等付款率变化的影响。提供关于该等影响的统计信息,例如,提前还款对收益以及加权平均寿命值的影响。

(3)说明在各类别证券之间对提前还款风险的特殊分配,以及是否有任一类别证券可以保护其他类别证券免受现金流时间不确定性的影响。

第229.1114节(第1114条) 特定衍生工具之外的信用增级和其他支持

(a)说明性信息。如具有重要意义,应说明下列事项,包括对为影响或确保资产支持证券的及时付款而设计每一个潜在项目的方式进行明确论述:

(1)为确保资产支持证券或池内资产能按照相应的条款进行付款的所有外部信用增级措施,如债券保险、信用证或担保。

(2)为确保资产支持证券能及时付款的所有机制,如流动性便利、贷款便利、担保投资合同和最低本金付款协议。

(3)主要目的是为池内资产或资产支持证券提供信用增级的任何衍生工具。

to pool assets or the asset-backed securities.

(4) Any internal credit enhancement as a result of the structure of the transaction that increases the likelihood that payments will be made on one or more classes of the asset-backed securities in accordance with their terms, such as subordination provisions, overcollateralization, reserve accounts, cash collateral accounts or spread accounts.

Instructions to Item 1114(a): 1. Include a description of the material terms of any enhancement or support described, including any limits on the timing or amount of the enhancement or support or any conditions that must be met before the enhancement or support can be accessed. The enhancement or support agreement is to be filed as an exhibit. Also describe any provisions regarding the substitution of enhancement or support.

2. This Item should not be construed as allowing anything other than an asset-backed security whose payment is based primarily by reference to the performance of the receivables or other financial assets in the asset pool.

(b) *Information regarding significant enhancement providers* — (1) *Descriptive information.* If an entity or group of affiliated entities providing enhancement or other support described in paragraph (a) of this section is liable or contingently liable to provide payments representing 10% or more of the cash flow supporting any offered class of asset-backed securities, provide the following information:

(i) The name of such enhancement provider.

(ii) The organizational form of enhancement provider.

(iii) The general character of the business of such enhancement provider.

(2) *Financial information.* (i) If any entity or group of affiliated entities providing enhancement or other support described in paragraph (a) of this section is liable or contingently liable to provide payments representing 10% or more, but less than 20%, of the cash flow supporting any offered class of the asset-backed securities, provide financial data required by Item 301 of Regulation S-K (§229.301) for each such entity or group of affiliated entities.

(ii) If any entity or group of affiliated entities providing enhancement or other support described in paragraph (a) of this section is liable or contingently liable to provide payments representing 20% or more of the cash flow supporting any offered class of the asset-backed securities, provide financial statements meeting the requirements of Regulation S-X (§§210.1-01 through 210.12-29 of this chapter), except §210.3-05 of this chapter and Article 11 of Regulation S-X (§§210.11-01 through 210.11-03 of this chapter), of such entity or group of affiliated entities. Financial statements of such enhancement provider and its subsidiaries consolidated (as required by §240.14a-3(b) of this chapter) shall be filed under this item.

(4)因交易结构而产生、能够提高某一类别或多类别资产支持证券按照相应条款进行付款的可能性的所有内部信用增级措施,如次级效力条款、超额担保、准备金账户、现金担保账户或利差账户。

关于第1114(a)条的说明:1.对于所述的任何信用增级或支持措施,均应提供关于重大条款的说明,包括任何增级或支持措施的时间或金额限制,或获取增级或支持措施前必须满足的任何条件。增级或支持协议应作为附录提交。此外,如增级或支持措施可通过其他方式替代,应说明相关规定。

2.除资产支持证券之外,本条不应理解为允许主要基于资产池中的应收账款或其他金融资产的绩效进行付款。

(b)关于重要信用增级机构的信息——(1)说明性信息。如果本节第(a)款所述的、提供信用增级或其他支持措施的某个实体或某一组关联实体负责提供或可能负责提供的付款达到支持任何一类已要约发售的资产支持证券的现金流的10%(含)以上,则应提供以下信息:

(i)该等信用增级机构的名称。

(ii)信用增级机构的组织形式。

(iii)该等信用增级机构业务的一般特征。

(2)财务信息。(i)如果本节第(a)款所述的、提供信用增级或其他支持措施的任何实体或任何一组关联实体负责提供或可能负责提供的付款达到支持任何一类已要约资产支持证券的现金流的10%(含)以上20%以下,则应提供《S-K管理办法》第301条(第229.301节)规定的关于每一该等实体或每组关联实体的财务信息。

(ii)如果本节第(a)款所述的、提供信用增级或其他支持措施的任何实体或任何一组关联实体负责提供或可能负责提供的付款达到支持任何一类已要约资产支持证券的现金流的20%(含)以上,则应提供关于每一该等实体或每组关联实体的财务报表,这些财务报表应符合《S-X管理办法》(本章第210.1-01~210.12-29节)的规定[本章第210.3-05节和《S-X管理办法》第11条的规定(本章第210.11-01~210.11-03节)除外]。该等信用增级机构及其并表子公司的财务报表[如本章第240.14a-3(b)节所规定]应按照本条的规定提交。

Instructions to Item 1114: 1. The requirements in paragraph (b) of this section apply to all providers of external credit enhancement or other support, other than those described in Item 1115 of this Regulation AB. Enhancement may support payment on the pool assets or payments on the asset–backed securities themselves.

2. No information need be provided pursuant to paragraph (b)(2) of this section if the obligations of the enhancement provider are backed by the full faith and credit of the United States.

3. No information need be provided pursuant to paragraph (b)(2) of this section if the obligations of the enhancement provider are backed by the full faith and credit of a foreign government (as defined in §240.3b–4(a) of this chapter) if the enhancement provider has an investment grade credit rating, as the term investment grade is used in Item I.B.2 of Form S–3 (§239.13 of this chapter). If the enhancement provider does not have an investment grade credit rating, information required by paragraph (5) of Schedule B of the Securities Act (15 U.S.C. 77aa) regarding the foreign government may be incorporated by reference from a Commission filing in lieu of providing the financial information required pursuant to paragraph (b)(2) of this section.

4. If the pool assets are student loans originated under the Federal Family Education Loan Program of the Higher Education Act of 1965 (20 U.S.C. 1001 *et seq.*) and the enhancement provider for the pool assets is a guarantee agency as defined under the Higher Education Act, then the following information may be provided in lieu of providing financial information required pursuant to paragraph (b)(2) of this section:

a. The number of pool assets and aggregate outstanding principal balance of pool assets guaranteed by the guarantee agency (both by number and percentage of the asset pool as of the cut–off date or other applicable date).

b. Disclosure of the following with respect to the guarantee agency, as applicable, including a brief description regarding the method of calculation, covering at least five federal fiscal years:

i. Aggregate principal amount of all student loans guaranteed.

ii. Reserve ratio.

iii. Recovery rate.

iv. Loss rate.

v. Claims rate.

5. If the enhancement provider is a foreign business (as defined §210.1–02 of this chapter):

a. Paragraph (b)(2)(i) of this section may be complied with by providing the information required by Item 3.A. of Form 20–F (§249.220f of this chapter). If a reconciliation to U.S. generally accepted accounting principles called for by Instruction 2.

关于第1114条的说明：1.本节第（b）款的规定适用于所有提供外部信用增级或其他支持措施的机构，不包括本《AB管理办法》第1115条所述的其他机构。增级措施可以为池内资产的付款或对资产支持证券本身的付款提供支持。

2.如果重要信用增级机构获得美国政府的充分认可和信用支持，则不必提供本节第（b）（2）款规定的信息。

3.如果信用增级机构获得外国政府的充分认可和信用支持［定义见本章第240.3b-4（a）节］，并且该等信用增级机构具有《S-3表格》第I.B.2条（本章第239.13节）所规定的投资级评级，则不必提供本节第（b）（2）款规定的信息。如果信用增级机构不具有投资级信用级别，可以通过引用向证券交易委员会提交的文件来提供《证券法》《附表B》第（5）款（《美国法典》第十五编第77aa节）所规定的关于外国政府的信息，以替代节条第（b）（2）款所规定的财务信息。

4.如果池内资产为根据《1965年高等教育法》（《美国法典》第二十编第1001节及其后条文）之美国联邦家庭教育贷款计划发起的学生贷款，并且池内资产的信用增级机构为《高等教育法》所定义的担保机构，则可以提供以下信息来替代本节第（b）（2）款规定的信息：

a.池内资产的数量以及有担保机构担保的池内资产的未缴付本金总余额（两者均需要以截至截止日或其他适用的日期的数字和占池内资产的百分比列报）。

b.披露关于担保机构的下列信息（以适用者为准），包括对计算方法的简述，所覆盖的期间至少为5个联邦会计年度：

i.所担保的全部学生贷款本金总额。
ii.准备金比率。
iii.偿还率。
iv.损失率。
v.索赔率。

5.如果重要信用增级机构是一家外国企业（定义见本章第210.1-02节）：

a.提供《20-F表格》第3.A.条（本章第249.220f节）规定的信息即视为已履行本节第（b）（2）（i）款的规定。如果《20-F表格》第3.A.条的说明2要求进行调节以符合美国公认会计原则，但实际无法进行该等调节或者调节需要支付不合理的成本或费用，至少应

to Item 3.A. of Form 20–F is unavailable or not obtainable without unreasonable cost or expense, at a minimum provide a narrative description of all material variations in accounting principles, practices and methods used in preparing the non–U.S. GAAP financial statements used as a basis for the selected financial data from those accepted in the U.S.

b. Paragraph (b)(2)(ii) of this section may be complied with by providing financial statements meeting the requirements of Item 17 of Form 20–F for the periods specified by Item 8.A. of Form 20–F.

§229.1115(Item 1115) Certain derivatives instruments.

This item relates to derivative instruments, such as interest rate and currency swap agreements, that are used to alter the payment characteristics of the cashflows from the issuing entity and whose primary purpose is not to provide credit enhancement related to the pool assets or the asset–backed securities. For purposes of this section, the "significance estimate" of the derivative instrument is to be determined based on a reasonable good–faith estimate of maximum probable exposure, made in substantially the same manner as that used in the sponsor's internal risk management process in respect of similar instruments. The "significance percentage" is the percentage that the amount of the significance estimate represents of the aggregate principal balance of the pool assets, provided, that if the derivative instrument relates only to one or more classes of the asset–backed securities, the "significance percentage" is the percentage that the amount of the significance estimate represents of the aggregate principal balance of such classes.

(a) *Descriptive information.* (1) Describe the following regarding the external counterparty:

(i) The name of the derivative counterparty.

(ii) The organizational form of the derivative counterparty.

(iii) The general character of the business of the derivative counterparty.

(2) Describe the operation and material terms of the derivative instrument, including any limits on the timing or amount of payments or any conditions to payments.

(3) Describe any material provisions regarding substitution of the derivative instrument.

(4) At a minimum, disclose whether the significance percentage, as calculated in accordance with this section, is less than 10%, at least 10% but less than 20%, or 20% or more.

(5) File the agreement relating to the derivative instrument as an exhibit.

(b) *Financial information.* (1) If the aggregate significance percentage related to any entity or group of affiliated entities providing derivative instruments contemplated by this section is 10% or more, but less than 20%, provide financial data required by Item 301 of

就编制作为择要列示的财务数据之基础的非美国GAAP财务报表时使用的会计原则、实践和方法与美国公认会计原则、实践和方法的所有重大差别提供文字说明。

b.提供符合《20-F表格》第17条要求的财务报表(覆盖期间为《20-F表格》第8.A.条规定的期间)即视为已履行本节第(b)(2)(ii)款的规定。

第229.1115节(第1115条) 特定衍生工具

本条规定涉及用于改变发行实体现金流的支付特征,并且其主要目的并不是为池内资产或资产支持证券提供相关信用增级的衍生工具,如利率与货币互换协议。就本条而言,衍生工具的"重要性预估值"将根据可能的最大风险敞口的合理善意预估来确定,作出上述合理善意预估的方式应与发起人类似工具的内部风险管理流程所采用的方式大体相同。"重要性百分比"系指重要性预估值占池内资产本金总余额的百分数,但是,如果衍生工具仅涉及一个或多个类别的资产支持证券,则"重要性百分比"系指重要性预估值占相应类别资产本金总余额的百分数。

(a)说明性信息。(1)说明关于外部交易对手方的下列信息:

(i)衍生交易对手方的名称。

(ii)衍生交易对手的组织形式。

(iii)衍生交易对手方业务的一般特征。

(2)说明衍生工具的运营和重大条款,包括对付款时间或金额的任何限制以及任何付款条件。

(3)如衍生工具可以替换,应说明关于该等替换的任何重大规定。

(4)至少应披露按照节条规定计算的重要性百分比是否为低于10%、10%(含)到20%(不含)之间,或20%(含)以上。

(5)将与衍生工具相关的协议作为附录提交。

(b)财务信息。(1)如果提供本节规定的衍生工具之任何实体或任何一组关联实体的相关重要性百分比总和达到10%(含)以上,但不足20%,则应按照《S-K管理办法》第301条(第229.301节)的规定提供关于该等实体或一组关联实体的财务信息。

Regulation S–K (§229.301) for such entity or group of affiliated entities.

(2) If the aggregate significance percentage related to any entity or group of affiliated entities providing derivative instruments contemplated by this section is 20% or more, provide financial statements meeting the requirements of Regulation S–X (§§210.1–01 through 210.12–29 of this chapter), except §210.3–05 of this chapter and Article 11 of Regulation S–X (§§210.11–01 through 210.11–03 of this chapter), of such entity or group of affiliated entities. Financial statements of such entity and its subsidiaries consolidated (as required by §240.14a–3(b) of this chapter) shall be filed under this item.

Instructions to Item 1115: 1. Instructions 2, 3 and 5 to Item 1114 of this Regulation AB apply to the information contemplated by paragraph (b) of this item.

2. This Item should not be construed as allowing anything other than an asset–backed security whose payment is based primarily by reference to the performance of the receivables or other financial assets in the asset pool.

§229.1116(Item 1116) Tax matters.

Provide a brief, clear and understandable summary of:

(a) The tax treatment of the asset–backed securities transaction under federal income tax laws.

(b) The material federal income tax consequences of purchasing, owning and selling the asset–backed securities. If any of the material federal income tax consequences are not expected to be the same for investors in all classes offered by the registration statement, describe the material differences.

(c) The substance of counsel's tax opinion, including identification of the material consequences upon which counsel has not been asked, or is unable, to opine.

§229.1117(Item 1117) Legal proceedings.

Describe briefly any legal proceedings pending against the sponsor, depositor, trustee, issuing entity, servicer contemplated by Item 1108(a)(3) of this Regulation AB, originator contemplated by Item 1110(b) of this Regulation AB, or other party contemplated by Item 1100(d)(1) of this Regulation AB, or of which any property of the foregoing is the subject, that is material to security holders. Include similar information as to any such proceedings known to be contemplated by governmental authorities.

§229.1118(Item 1118) Reports and additional information.

(a) *Reports required under the transaction documents.* Describe the reports or other documents provided to security holders required under the transaction agreements, including information included, schedule and manner of distribution or other availability, and the entity or entities that will prepare and provide the reports.

(b) *Reports to be filed with the Commission.* (1) Specify the names, and if available, the Commission file numbers of the entity or entities under which reports about

(2)如果提供本节规定的衍生工具之实体或一组关联实体的相关重要性百分比总和达到20%(含)以上,则应提供该等实体或该组关联实体符合《S-X管理办法》(本章第210.1-01~210.12-29节)要求的财务报表[本章第210.3-05节和《S-X管理办法》第11条(本章第210.11-01~210.11-03节)的规定除外]。该等实体及其并表子公司的财务报表[如本章第240.14a-3(b)节所规定]应按照本节的规定提交。

关于第1115条的说明:1.《AB管理办法》第1114条的说明2、说明3和说明5适用于本条第(b)款规定的信息。

2.除资产支持证券之外,本条不应理解为允许主要基于资产池中的应收账款或其他金融资产的绩效进行付款。

第229.1116节(第1116条) 税务事项

提供一份简明、易懂的摘要,说明以下事项:

(a)联邦所得税法对资产支持证券交易的税收处理。

(b)购买、拥有和出售资产支持证券的重大联邦所得税影响。如果预期注册说明书中已要约的各类别的证券投资者将遭受任何有所差异的联邦所得税重大影响,应说明其中的重大差异。

(c)律师税务意见的实质内容,并注明未征求或无法征求税务意见的重大联邦所得税影响。

第229.1117节(第1117条) 法律程序

简要说明针对发起人、交存人、信托受托人、发行实体、本《AB管理办法》第1108(a)(3)条规定的服务机构、本《AB管理办法》第1110(b)条规定的创建人或本《AB管理办法》第1100(d)(1)条规定的其他当事方提起的,或以上述各者财产为标的的对证券持有人意义重大的任何未决法律程序。注册人已知政府相关主管部门正在考虑提起任何该等程序的,亦应提供类似信息。

第229.1118节(第1118条) 报告和其他信息

(a)交易文件中要求提供的报告。说明交易协议要求向证券持有人提供的报告或其他文件,包括其中包含的信息、分配计划和方式或其他可派发利益的分配计划和方式,以及将负责编制并提供该等报告的实体。

(b)应向证券交易委员会提交的报告。(1)具体指明该等实体将向证券交易委员会提交的关于资产支持证券的报告的名称和档案编号(如果可以获得编号)。指明向

the asset-backed securities will be filed with the Securities and Exchange Commission. Identify the reports and other information filed with the Commission.

(2) State that the public may read and copy any materials filed with the Commission at the Commission's Public Reference Room at 100 F Street, NE., Washington, D.C. 20549, on official business days between the hours of 10 a.m. and 3 p.m. State that the public may obtain information on the operation of the Public Reference Room by calling the Securities and Exchange Commission at 1-800-SEC-0330. State that the Commission maintains an Internet site that contains reports, proxy and information statements, and other information regarding issuers that file electronically with the Commission and state the address of that site (*http://www.sec.gov*).

(c) *Web site access to reports.* (1) State whether the issuing entity's annual reports on Form 10-K (§249.310 of this chapter), distribution reports on Form 10-D (§249.312 of this chapter), current reports on Form 8-K (§249.308 of this chapter), and amendments to those reports filed or furnished pursuant to section 13(a) or 15(d) of the Exchange Act (15 U.S.C. 78m(a) or 78o(d)) will be made available on the Web site of a specified transaction party(e.g., the sponsor, depositor, servicer, issuing entity or trustee) as soon as reasonably practicable after such material is electronically filed with, or furnished to, the Commission.

(2) Disclose whether other reports to security holders or information about the asset-backed securities will be made available in this manner.

(3) If filings and other reports will be made available in this manner, disclose the Web site address where such filings may be found.

(4) If filings and other reports will not be made available in this manner, describe the reasons why they will not and whether an identified transaction party voluntarily will provide electronic or paper copies of those filings and other reports free of charge upon request.

[70 FR 1597, Jan. 7, 2005, as amended at 73 FR 967, Jan. 4, 2008]

§229.1119 (Item 1119) Affiliations and certain relationships and related transactions.

(a) Describe if so, and how, the sponsor, depositor or issuing entity is an affiliate (as defined in §230.405 of this chapter) of any of the following parties as well as, to the extent known and material, if so, and how, any of the following parties are affiliates of any of the other following parties:

(1) Servicer contemplated by Item 1108(a)(3) of this Regulation AB.

(2) Trustee.

(3) Originator contemplated by Item 1110 of this Regulation AB.

证券交易委员会提交的报告和其他信息。

(2)说明公众可以在上午10时至下午3时的正常办公时间前往位于华盛顿州哥伦比亚特区东北分区100F大街(邮编:D.C. 20549)的证券交易委员会公共资料室查阅并复印向证券交易委员会提交的任何资料。说明公众可以拨打1-800-SEC-0330致电证券交易委员会的公共资料室并借助其服务获取信息。说明证券交易委员会维护的网站上可以获得以电子方式提交给证券交易委员会的报告、征集投票权报告和其他信息说明书,以及关于发行人的其他信息,并说明该网站的网址(http://www.sec.gov)。

(c)通过网站查阅报告。(1)说明发行实体按照《10-K表格》(本章第249.310节)提交的年度报告、按照《10-D表格》(本章第249.312节)提交的分配报告、按照《8-K表格》(本章第249.308节)提交的现状报告以及按照《交易法》第13(a)条或第15(d)条[《美国法典》第十五编第78m(a)节或第78o(d)节]以电子方式向证券交易委员会提交或提供的上述报告之修正稿,是否将在向证券交易委员会提交或提供之后合理可行的时间通过指定交易当事方(如发起人、交存人、服务机构、发行实体或信托受托人)的网站予以提供。

(2)披露提供给证券持有人的其他报告或关于资产支持证券的其他信息是否将通过上述方式提供。

(3)如果提交的文件和其他报告将通过上述方式提供,应披露可以访问该等文件的网址。

(4)如果提交的文件和其他报告不会通过上述方式提供,说明其原因,并说明是否有任何交易方将自愿在收到请求后免费提供该等文件的电子或纸质版本。

[《联邦公报》第70卷第1597页,2005年1月7日,修正索引:《联邦公报》第73卷第967页,2008年1月4日。]

第229.1119节(第1119条) 关联、特定关系和关联交易

(a)说明发起人、交存人或发行实体是否属于下列任何当事方的关联方(定义见本章第230.405节),如果是,还应说明关联关系是如何形成的,并在已知和具有重要意义的情况下,说明下列当事方之间是否存在关联关系,如果是,还应说明关联关系是如何形成的:

(1)本《AB管理办法》第1108(a)(3)条规定的服务机构。

(2)信托受托人。

(3)本《AB管理办法》第1110条规定的创建人。

(4) Significant obligor contemplated by Item 1112 of this Regulation AB.

(5) Enhancement or support provider contemplated by Items 1114 or 1115 of this Regulation AB.

(6) Any other material parties related to the asset-backed securities contemplated by Item 1100(d)(1) of this Regulation AB.

(b) Describe whether there is, and if so the general character of, any business relationship, agreement, arrangement, transaction or understanding that is entered into outside the ordinary course of business or is on terms other than would be obtained in an arm's length transaction with an unrelated third party, apart from the asset-backed securities transaction, between the sponsor, depositor or issuing entity and any of the parties in paragraphs (a)(1) through (a)(6) of this section, or any affiliates of such parties, that currently exists or that existed during the past two years and that is material to an investor's understanding of the asset-backed securities.

Instruction to Item 1119(b): What is required is information material to an investor's understanding of the asset-backed securities. A detailed description or itemized listing of all commercial relationships among the parties is not required. Instead, the disclosure should indicate whether any relationships outside of the asset-backed securities transaction do exist that are outside the normal course and the general character of those relationships.

(c) Notwithstanding paragraph (b) of this section, describe, to the extent material, any specific relationships involving or relating to the asset-backed securities transaction or the pool assets, including the material terms and approximate dollar amount involved, between the sponsor, depositor or issuing entity and any of the parties in paragraphs (a)(1) through(a)(6) of this section, or any affiliates of such parties, that currently exists or that existed during the past two years.

Instruction to Item 1119: With respect to disclosure in an annual report on Form 10-K, information required by this Item 1119 may be omitted to the extent that substantially the same information had been provided previously in an annual report on Form 10-K (§249.310) for the asset-backed securities or in an effective registration statement under the Securities Act or a prospectus timely filed pursuant to §230.424 of this chapter under the same Central Index Key (CIK) code as the current annual report on Form 10-K.

§229.1120(Item 1120) Ratings.

Disclose whether the issuance or sale of any class of offered securities is conditioned on the assignment of a rating by one or more rating agencies, whether or not NRSROs. If so, identify each rating agency and the minimum rating that must be assigned. Describe any arrangements to have such rating monitored while the asset-backed securities are

(4)本《AB管理办法》第1112条规定的重大债务人。

(5)本《AB管理办法》第1114条或第1115条规定的信用增级或支持机构。

(6)与本《AB管理办法》第1100(d)(1)条规定的与资产支持证券相关的任何其他重要当事方。

(b)说明当前或过去2年内,发起人、交存人或发行实体与本条第(a)(1)款至第(a)(6)款所述的任一当事方或该等当事方的任何关联方之间,除了资产支持证券交易,是否达成了任何对投资者理解资产支持证券具有重要意义的任何如下业务关系、协议、安排、交易或谅解:在正常业务运作之外达成的,或者条款与非关联第三方达成的公平交易条款不同的业务关系、协议、安排、交易或谅解。如果有,应说明该等业务关系、协议、安排、交易或谅解的一般特征。

关于第1119(b)条的说明:本条要求提供的任何信息是对投资者理解资产支持证券具有重要意义的信息。不必就各当事方之间的商业关系提供详细说明及分项清单。相反,进行披露时仅须指明在资产支持证券交易之外是否存在任何非通过正常程序达成的关系以及该等关系的一般特征。

(c)无论本节第(b)款如何规定,如具有重要意义,应说明当前或过去2年内发起人、交存人或发行实体与本节第(a)(1)款至第(a)(6)款所述的任何当事方或其任何关联方之间存在的涉及资产支持证券或池内资产或与该等证券或资产相关的任何特定关系,包括重大条款和所涉的大致金额。

关于第1119条的说明:就按照《10-K表格》提交的年度报告进行的披露而言,第1119条要求提供的信息如与下述信息基本一致,可予省略:之前按照《10-K表格》(第249.310节)就资产支持证券提交的年度报告中的相关信息,或者按照《证券法》提交的有效的注册说明书中的信息,或按照本章第230.424节要求使用与按照《10-K表格》提交的当年年度报告同样的CIK代码及时提交的招募说明书中的信息。

第229.1120节(第1120条) 评级

披露已要约的任何类别证券的发行或出售是否取决于一个或多个评级机构提供的评级结果,无论该机构是否为NRSRO。如果是,指明各个评级机构的名称以及必须获得的最低评级。说明资产支持证券发行在外期间对该等评级结果的任何监控安排。

outstanding.

§229.1121(Item 1121) Distribution and pool performance information.

Link to an amendment published at 76 FR 4511, January 26, 2011.

(a) Describe the distribution for the related distribution period and the performance of the asset pool during the distribution period. Provide appropriate introductory and explanatory information to introduce any material terms, parties or abbreviations used (or a cross-reference to a Commission filing where such information may be found). Present statistical information in tabular or graphical format, if such presentation will aid understanding. While the material information regarding the related distribution and pool performance will vary depending on the nature of the transaction, such information may include, among other things:

(1) Any applicable record dates, accrual dates, determination dates for calculating distributions and actual distribution dates for the distribution period.

(2) Cash flows received and the sources thereof for distributions, fees and expenses (including portfolio yield, if applicable).

(3) Calculated amounts and distribution of the flow of funds for the period itemized by type and priority of payment, including:

(i) Fees or expenses accrued and paid, with an identification of the general purpose of such fees and the party receiving such fees or expenses.

(ii) Payments accrued or paid with respect to enhancement or other support identified in Item 1114 of this Regulation AB (such as insurance premiums or other enhancement maintenance fees), with an identification of the general purpose of such payments and the party receiving such payments.

(iii) Principal, interest and other distributions accrued and paid on the asset-backed securities by type and by class or series and any principal or interest shortfalls or carryovers.

(iv) The amount of excess cash flow or excess spread and the disposition of excess cash flow.

(4) Beginning and ending principal balances of the asset-backed securities.

(5) Interest rates applicable to the pool assets and the asset-backed securities, as applicable. Consider providing interest rate information for pool assets in appropriate distributional groups or incremental ranges.

(6) Beginning and ending balances of transaction accounts, such as reserve accounts, and material account activity during the period.

(7) Any amounts drawn on any credit enhancement or other support identified in Item 1114 of this Regulation AB, as applicable, and the amount of coverage remaining under any such enhancement, if known and applicable.

第229.1121节(第1121条)　分配和资产池绩效信息

链接至《联邦公报》第76卷第4511页(2011年1月26日)发布的修正。

(a)说明在相关分配期内的分配以及在该等分配期内资产池的绩效。提供适当的介绍性或解释性说明,介绍任何相关的重大条款、各当事方以及所使用的缩写(或者提供包含该等信息的向证券交易委员会提交的文件的交叉索引)。如果表格和图表有助于理解,应以表格或图表列报统计信息。与分配和资产池绩效相关的重大信息可能根据交易的性质而有所不同,举例而言,该等信息可能包括但不限于:

(1)分配期内的任何登记日期、应计日期、计算分配时采用的确定日期以及实际分配日期。

(2)收到的现金流以及分配、费用和支出的资金来源(包括资产组合收益,如适用)。

(3)该段期间内计算的资金流的金额和分配,按付款类型和付款优先顺序分项列明,包括:

(i)应计和实付费用或支出,指明该等费用的一般目的以及接收该等费用或支出的当事方。

(ii)与本《AB管理办法》第1114条中指明的信用增级或其他支持措施相关的应计或实付款项(如保险费或其他增级维护费),同时应指明该等付款的一般目的及接收该等付款的当事方。

(iii)按类型、类别或系列区分的资产支持证券的应计和实付本金、利息和其他分配,以及任何亏空或结转的本金和利息。

(iv)超额现金流的金额或者对超额现金流的处置。

(4)资产支持证券的期初和期末本金余额。

(5)池内资产和资产支持证券适用的利率(如适用)。应考虑通过适当的分配组或增量范围提供池内资产的利率信息。

(6)交易账户(如准备金账户)的期初和期末余额,以及该等期间内重大的账户活动。

(7)根据本《AB管理办法》第1114条中指明的任何信用增级或其他支持措施(以适用者为准)提取的任何款额,以及该等增级措施下的任何剩余保险金额(如果为注册人所知且适用)。

(8) Number and amount of pool assets at the beginning and ending of each period, and updated pool composition information, such as weighted average coupon, weighted average life, weighted average remaining term, pool factors and prepayment amounts. For asset–backed securities backed by leases where a portion of the securitized pool balance is attributable to residual values of the physical property underlying the leases, this information also would include turn–in rates and residual value realization rates.

(9) Delinquency and loss information for the period. In addition, describe any material changes to the information specified in Item 1100(b)(5) of this Regulation AB regarding the pool assets.

(10) Information on the amount, terms and general purpose of any advances made or reimbursed during the period, including the general use of funds advanced and the general source of funds for reimbursements.

(11) Any material modifications, extensions or waivers to pool asset terms, fees, penalties or payments during the distribution period or that have cumulatively become material over time.

(12) Material breaches of pool asset representations or warranties or transaction covenants.

(13) Information on ratio, coverage or other tests used for determining any early amortization, liquidation or other performance trigger and whether the trigger was met.

(14) Information regarding any new issuance of asset–backed securities backed by the same asset pool, any pool asset changes (other than in connection with a pool asset converting into cash in accordance with its terms), such as additions or removals in connection with a prefunding or revolving period and pool asset substitutions and repurchases (and purchase rates, if applicable), and cash flows available for future purchases, such as the balances of any prefunding or revolving accounts, if applicable. Disclose any material changes in the solicitation, credit–granting, underwriting, origination, acquisition or pool selection criteria or procedures, as applicable, used to originate, acquire or select the new pool assets.

(b) During a prefunding or revolving period, or if there has been a new issuance of asset–backed securities backed by the same pool under a master trust during the fiscal year of the issuing entity, provide the information required by Items 1110, 1111 and 1112 of this Regulation AB applied taking the revised pool composition into account in the Form 10–D report (§249.312 of this chapter) for the last required distribution of the fiscal year of the issuing entity. In addition, provide such updated information in the first Form 10–D report for the period in which the prefunding or revolving period ends (if applicable). However, no disclosure need be provided by this paragraph if the information has not materially changed from that previously provided in an Exchange Act report

(8)每个期间期初和期末池内资产的数量和金额,以及更新的资产池组成成分信息,如息票的加权平均值、剩余寿命的加权平均值、剩余期限的加权平均值、资产池系数和提前还款额。对于依托租赁的资产支持证券,如其中一部分证券化的资产池余额归属于租赁标的实体房产的残值,按上述规定提供信息时还应包括到期退还率和残值变现率。

(9)期间内的拖欠和损失信息。另外,应说明本《AB管理办法》第1100(b)(5)条中列明的池内资产信息的任何重大变更。

(10)期间内任何垫付或报销资金的数额、条款和一般目的,包括垫付资金的一般用途和报销费用的一般资金来源。

(11)在相关的分配期间池内资产条款、费用、罚金或付款的任何重大修改、延期或弃权,或随时间推移因累积而具有重大性的任何修改、延期或弃权。

(12)对池内资产声明或保证或交易约定的实质违反。

(13)用于确定任何提前摊还、清算或其他绩效触发事件以及在判断是否达到了触发标准时使用的比率、覆盖范围或其他测试。

(14)关于以下任何内容的信息:依托同一资产池的资产支持证券的任何新发行;任何池内资产的变动(不包括池内资产按其条款转换为现金的情况),如与预先融资期或循环期相关的资产添加或剔除以及池内资产的替换和回购(如适用,还应提供购买率);以及供将来购买之用的现金流,如所有任何预先融资账户或循环账户的余额(如适用)。披露创建、收购或选择新的池内资产时使用的招揽、授信、承销、创建、收购或资产池选择标准或程序的任何重大变更,以适用者为准。

(b)应就预先融资期或循环期,或就发行实体的会计年度(如在主信托下发行了新的依托同一资产池的资产支持证券),提供本《AB管理办法》第1110条、第1111条和第1112条要求提供的信息,同时应考虑关于发行实体会计年度内按规定进行的上一次分配的《10-D表格》报告(本章第249.312节)中关于资产池组成成分的修改。此外,应在第一份《10-D表格》报告中提供覆盖预先融资期和循环期截止日所在期间的更新信息(如有)。但是,如本款要求披露的信息与下述信息相比并未发生重大变动,则不必予以披露:之前提交的《交易法》报告中关于资产支持证券之信息,或者与按照《证券法》提交的有效的注册说明书中的信息,或按照本章第230.424节要求就依托包含本款所述的池内资产之资产池且使用同一CIK代码的资产支持证券的后续发行及时提交

relating to the asset-backed securities or in an effective registration statement under the Securities Act or a prospectus timely filed pursuant to §230.424 of this chapter under the same Central Index Key (CIK) code regarding a subsequent issuance of asset-backed securities backed by a pool of assets that includes the pool assets that are the subject of this paragraph.

§229.1122(Item 1122) Compliance with applicable servicing criteria.

(a) *Reports on assessment of compliance with servicing criteria for asset-backed securities.* As required by paragraph (b) of §240.13a-18 or 240.15d-18 of this chapter, provide as an exhibit from each party participating in the servicing function a report on an assessment of compliance with the servicing criteria set forth in paragraph (d) of this section that contains the following:

(1) A statement of the party's responsibility for assessing compliance with the servicing criteria applicable to it;

(2) A statement that the party used the criteria in paragraph (d) of this section to assess compliance with the applicable servicing criteria;

(3) The party's assessment of compliance with the applicable servicing criteria as of and for the period ending the end of the fiscal year covered by the Form 10-K report (§249.310 of this chapter). This discussion must include disclosure of any material instance of noncompliance identified by the party; and

(4) A statement that a registered public accounting firm has issued an attestation report on the party's assessment of compliance with the applicable servicing criteria as of and for the period ending the end of the fiscal year covered by the Form 10-K report.

(b) *Registered public accounting firm attestation reports.* Provide the registered public accounting firm's attestation report required by paragraph (c) of §240.13a-18 or 240.15d-18 of this chapter on the party's assessment of compliance with the applicable servicing criteria as an exhibit.

(c) *Additional disclosure for the Form 10-K report.* (1) If any party's report on assessment of compliance with servicing criteria required by paragraph (a) of this section, or related registered public accounting firm attestation report required by paragraph (b) of this section, identifies any material instance of noncompliance with the servicing criteria, identify the material instance of noncompliance in the report on Form 10-K.

(2) If any party's report on assessment of compliance with servicing criteria required by paragraph (a) of this section, or related registered public accounting firm attestation report required by paragraph (b) of this section, is not included as an exhibit to the Form 10-K report, disclosure that the report is not included and an associated explanation must be provided in the report on Form 10-K.

(d) *Servicing criteria* — (1) *General servicing considerations.* (i) Policies and

的招募说明书中包含的信息。

第229.1122节(第1122条) 适用服务标准合规

(a)关于资产支持证券是否达到相关服务标准的评估报告。按照本章第240.13a-18节第(b)款或第240.15d-18节的规定,以附录形式提供每一参与服务职能的当事方对服务是否达到本节第(d)款所述服务标准的评估报告,该报告中应包括:

(1)关于该方有责任评估是否达到适用服务标准的声明;

(2)关于该方采用了本节第(d)款所述标准评估是否达到适用服务标准的声明;

(3)该方的评估结果,说明截至《10-K表格》报告(本章第249.310节)所覆盖的会计年度年末之时以及于该会计年度年末结束的期间是否达到了相应服务标准。上述论述中必须披露该方认定的未达标情况的任何重大例证;及

(4)一份如下内容的声明:对于该方说明截至《10-K表格》报告所覆盖的会计年度年末之时以及于该会计年度年末结束的期间是否达到了相应服务标准的评估结果,注册公共会计事务所已出具了鉴证报告。

(b)注册公共会计师事务所的鉴证报告。按照本章第240.13a-18节第(c)款或第240.15d-18节的规定,以附录形式就当事方关于是否达到相应服务标准的评估结果提供注册公共会计师事务所鉴证报告。

(c)《10-K表格》报告的其他披露。(1)如果本节第(a)款要求提供的当事方关于服务是否达到标准的任何评估报告,或本节第(b)款要求提供的相关注册公共会计师事务所出具的鉴证报告认定存在未达服务标准的任何重大例证,应在《10-k表格》报告中指出未达标的重大例证。

(2)如果本节第(a)款要求提供的当事方关于服务是否达到标准的任何评估报告,或本节第(b)款要求提供的相关注册公共会计师事务所出具的鉴证报告未作为《10-K表格》报告的附录提供,应对此如实披露,并且必须在《10-K表格》报告中提供相关的解释。

(d)服务标准——(1)一般服务考量因素。(i)已按照交易协议制定用以监控任何

procedures are instituted to monitor any performance or other triggers and events of default in accordance with the transaction agreements.

(ii) If any material servicing activities are outsourced to third parties, policies and procedures are instituted to monitor the third party's performance and compliance with such servicing activities.

(iii) Any requirements in the transaction agreements to maintain a back-up servicer for the pool assets are maintained.

(iv) A fidelity bond and errors and omissions policy is in effect on the party participating in the servicing function throughout the reporting period in the amount of coverage required by and otherwise in accordance with the terms of the transaction agreements.

(2) *Cash collection and administration.* (i) Payments on pool assets are deposited into the appropriate custodial bank accounts and related bank clearing accounts no more than two business days of receipt, or such other number of days specified in the transaction agreements.

(ii) Disbursements made via wire transfer on behalf of an obligor or to an investor are made only by authorized personnel.

(iii) Advances of funds or guarantees regarding collections, cash flows or distributions, and any interest or other fees charged for such advances, are made, reviewed and approved as specified in the transaction agreements.

(iv) The related accounts for the transaction, such as cash reserve accounts or accounts established as a form of overcollateralization, are separately maintained (e.g., with respect to commingling of cash) as set forth in the transaction agreements.

(v) Each custodial account is maintained at a federally insured depository institution as set forth in the transaction agreements. For purposes of this criterion, "federally insured depository institution" with respect to a foreign financial institution means a foreign financial institution that meets the requirements of §240.13k-1(b)(1) of this chapter.

(vi) Unissued checks are safeguarded so as to prevent unauthorized access.

(vii) Reconciliations are prepared on a monthly basis for all asset-backed securities related bank accounts, including custodial accounts and related bank clearing accounts. These reconciliations:

(A) Are mathematically accurate;

(B) Are prepared within 30 calendar days after the bank statement cutoff date, or such other number of days specified in the transaction agreements;

(C) Are reviewed and approved by someone other than the person who prepared the reconciliation; and

(D) Contain explanations for reconciling items. These reconciling items are resolved

绩效或其他触发因素和违约事件的政策与程序。

(ii)在将任何重大服务活动外包给第三方的情况下,已制定用以监控第三方绩效及其是否达到服务标准的政策与程序。

(iii)交易协议中关于就池内资产维持备用服务机构的任何规定得到了维持。

(iv)在整个报告期间内,按照交易协议规定的保险金额以及其他条款,为参与服务职能的当事方提供了有效的忠诚保证保险以及错误和疏忽保单。

(2)现金收取和管理。(i)池内资产付款应在收悉之日后不超过2个工作日内,或在交易协议指定的天数内存入相应的存管银行账户及相关的银行清算账户。

(ii)只有获得授权的人员才能通过电汇代表债务人付款,或向投资者付款。

(iii)关于收款、现金流或分配的垫付资金或保证,以及任何针对该等垫付资金所收取的利息或其他费用均按照交易协议的规定进行支付、审查和批准。

(iv)相关交易账户(如现金准备账户或以超额担保形式设立的账户)均按照交易协议的规定维持独立(如与现金混合的情形)。

(v)每一存管账户均在交易协议中规定的联邦受保存款机构开立维护。就本条标准而言,在指称外国金融机构时,"联邦受保存款机构"系指符合本章第240.13k-1(b)(1)节要求的外国金融机构。

(vi)未开出的支票进行了妥善保管,以防擅自取用。

(vii)所有与资产支持证券证券相关的银行账户均每月进行调节,包括存管账户和相关的银行清算账户。且:

(A)该等调节具备数学意义上的精准性;

(B)该等调节在银行对账单截止日后30个日历日内或交易协议中规定的天数内作出;

(C)审核与批准该等调节的人与作出该等调节的人不同;且

(D)提供了关于调节项目的解释。这些调节项目在最初被确认后90个日历日内或

within 90 calendar days of their original identification, or such other number of days specified in the transaction agreements.

(3) *Investor remittances and reporting.* (i) Reports to investors, including those to be filed with the Commission, are maintained in accordance with the transaction agreements and applicable Commission requirements. Specifically, such reports:

(A) Are prepared in accordance with timeframes and other terms set forth in the transaction agreements;

(B) Provide information calculated in accordance with the terms specified in the transaction agreements;

(C) Are filed with the Commission as required by its rules and regulations; and

(D) Agree with investors' or the trustee's records as to the total unpaid principal balance and number of pool assets serviced by the servicer.

(ii) Amounts due to investors are allocated and remitted in accordance with timeframes, distribution priority and other terms set forth in the transaction agreements.

(iii) Disbursements made to an investor are posted within two business days to the servicer's investor records, or such other number of days specified in the transaction agreements.

(iv) Amounts remitted to investors per the investor reports agree with cancelled checks, or other form of payment, or custodial bank statements.

(4) *Pool asset administration.* (i) Collateral or security on pool assets is maintained as required by the transaction agreements or related pool asset documents.

(ii) Pool assets and related documents are safeguarded as required by the transaction agreements.

(iii) Any additions, removals or substitutions to the asset pool are made, reviewed and approved in accordance with any conditions or requirements in the transaction agreements.

(iv) Payments on pool assets, including any payoffs, made in accordance with the related pool asset documents are posted to the applicable servicer's obligor records maintained no more than two business days after receipt, or such other number of days specified in the transaction agreements, and allocated to principal, interest or other items (e.g., escrow) in accordance with the related pool asset documents.

(v) The servicer's records regarding the pool assets agree with the servicer's records with respect to an obligor's unpaid principal balance.

(vi) Changes with respect to the terms or status of an obligor's pool asset (e.g., loan modifications or re-agings) are made, reviewed and approved by authorized personnel in accordance with the transaction agreements and related pool asset documents.

(vii) Loss mitigation or recovery actions (e.g., forbearance plans, modifications and

交易协议规定的天数内得到了解决。

(3)向投资者提供的汇款与报告。(i)向投资者提供的报告,包括将提交给证券交易委员会的报告,均按照交易协议和适用的证券交易委员会要求得到了维护。具体而言,该等报告:

(A)在交易协议规定的时间框架内编制完成,并遵循交易协议中的其他条款;

(B)提供了根据交易协议条款计算得出的数据;

(C)系按照证券交易委员会的规则和规章向证券交易委员会提交。

(D)关于未付本金总余额与服务机构所服务的池内资产的数量,应与投资者和信托受托人的记录保持一致。

(ii)应向投资者支付的数额系按照交易协议中规定的时间框架、分配顺序和其他条款划拨并汇付给投资者。

(iii)向投资者提供的付款在两个工作日内或交易协议规定的其他期限内通过服务机构的投资者记录予以公布。

(iv)按照投资者报告汇付给投资者的款项与已注销的支票或其他形式的付款或存管银行对账单保持一致。

(4)池内资产管理。(i)池内资产的担保品或担保按照交易协议或相关池内资产文件进行维护。

(ii)池内资产和相关文件按照交易协议的规定妥善保管。

(iii)池内资产的添加、剔除或替换按照交易协议中设定的条件或要求进行操作、审查和批准。

(iv)按照相关的池内资产文件支付的池内资产付款,包括任何偿付,均在收到之日后两个工作日内或交易协议规定的其他天数内通过相关服务机构维护的债务人记录予以公布,并根据相关池内资产文件划拨到本金、利息或其他项目之中(如托管账户)。

(v)服务机构关于池内资产的记录与服务机构关于债务人未付本金余额的记录保持一致。

(vi)对债务人的池内资产的条款和状态的变更(如贷款修改或重定年限)按照交易协议和相关的池内资产文件由获得授权的人员进行操作、审查与批准。

(vii)缓解或弥补损失的行动(如作为止赎之替代的延期计划、修改和契约;止赎;

deeds in lieu of foreclosure, foreclosures and repossessions, as applicable) are initiated, conducted and concluded in accordance with the timeframes or other requirements established by the transaction agreements.

(viii) Records documenting collection efforts are maintained during the period a pool asset is delinquent in accordance with the transaction agreements. Such records are maintained on at least a monthly basis, or such other period specified in the transaction agreements, and describe the entity's activities in monitoring delinquent pool assets including, for example, phone calls, letters and payment rescheduling plans in cases where delinquency is deemed temporary (e.g., illness or unemployment).

(ix) Adjustments to interest rates or rates of return for pool assets with variable rates are computed based on the related pool asset documents.

(x) Regarding any funds held in trust for an obligor (such as escrow accounts):

(A) Such funds are analyzed, in accordance with the obligor's pool asset documents, on at least an annual basis, or such other period specified in the transaction agreements;

(B) Interest on such funds is paid, or credited, to obligors in accordance with applicable pool asset documents and state laws; and

(C) Such funds are returned to the obligor within 30 calendar days of full repayment of the related pool asset, or such other number of days specified in the transaction agreements.

(xi) Payments made on behalf of an obligor (such as tax or insurance payments) are made on or before the related penalty or expiration dates, as indicated on the appropriate bills or notices for such payments, provided that such support has been received by the servicer at least 30 calendar days prior to these dates, or such other number of days specified in the transaction agreements.

(xii) Any late payment penalties in connection with any payment to be made on behalf of an obligor are paid from the servicer's funds and not charged to the obligor, unless the late payment was due to the obligor's error or omission.

(xiii) Disbursements made on behalf of an obligor are posted within two business days to the obligor's records maintained by the servicer, or such other number of days specified in the transaction agreements.

(xiv) Delinquencies, charge-offs and uncollectable accounts are recognized and recorded in accordance with the transaction agreements.

(xv) Any external enhancement or other support, identified in Item 1114(a)(1) through(3) or Item 1115 of this Regulation AB, is maintained as set forth in the transaction agreements.

Instructions to Item 1122: 1. If certain servicing criteria are not applicable to the asserting party based on the activities it performs with respect to asset-backed securities

重新占有,以适用者为准)按照交易协议规定的时间框架或其他要求启动、开展和结束。

(viii)在池内资产过期的期间内按照交易协议的相关规定维护了催收行为记录。该等记录至少按月或交易协议规定的其他期间进行了维护,并说明了实体监控拖欠池内资产的行动,包括但不限于在拖欠被视为临时事件时(如生病或失业)进行的电话催收、信函催收与重新制定付款计划。

(ix)对采用可变利率的池内资产的利率或回报率的调整系根据相关的池内资产文件计算。

(x)对于为债务人信托持有的任何资金(如托管账户):

(A)该等资金至少每年或按交易协议中指定的其他期间,按照债务人的池内资产文件进行了分析;

(B)该等资金的利息已按照适用的池内资产文件和州法律付给债务人或计入其贷方;且

(C)该等资金已在相关池内资产获得全额付款后30个日历日内或交易协议规定的天数内退还给债务人。

(xi)代表债务人支付的款项(如税金或保险费)已在该等付款的相应账单或通知单所载相关罚款起征日或到期日当日或之前支付,条件是服务机构至少已在上述日期之前30个日历日或交易协议中指定的其他天数之前,获得上述相关支持。

(xii)代表债务人支付、与付款相关的任何滞纳金均通过服务机构的资金支付,并且未向债务人收取,但该等滞纳金是由于债务人的错误或疏忽造成的除外。

(xiii)代表债务人向投资者支付的款项在服务机构付款后两个工作日内或交易协议规定的其他天数内通过服务机构维护的债务人记录进行了公布。

(xiv)拖欠、核销和坏账账户已按照交易协议进行了确认和记录。

(xv)本《AB管理办法》第1114(a)(1)条至第1114(a)(1)(3)条或第1115条所述的任何外部信用增级或其他支持措施均按照交易协议得到了维持。

关于第1122条的说明:1.如果某一方基于其开展的与资产支持证券交易相关的整体活动(该等活动牵涉其自身并且依托的资产类型与资产支持证券依托的资产类型

transactions taken as a whole involving such party and that are backed by the same asset type backing the class of asset-backed securities, the inapplicability of the criteria must be disclosed in that asserting party's and the related registered public accounting firm's reports.

2. If multiple parties are participating in the servicing function, a separate assessment report and attestation report must be included for each party participating in the servicing function. A party participating in the servicing function means any entity (e.g., master servicer, primary servicers, trustees) that is performing activities that address the criteria in paragraph (d) of this section, unless such entity's activities relate only to 5% or less of the pool assets.

3. If the asset pool backing the asset-backed securities includes a pool asset representing an interest in or the right to the payments or cash flows of another asset pool and both the issuing entity for the asset-backed securities and the entity issuing the asset to be included in the issuing entity's asset pool were established under the direction of the same sponsor and depositor, see also Item 1100(d)(2) of this Regulation AB.

§229.1123(Item 1123) Srvicer compliance statement.

Provide as an exhibit a statement of compliance from the servicer, signed by an authorized officer of such servicer, to the effect that:

(a) A review of the servicer's activities during the reporting period and of its performance under the applicable servicing agreement has been made under such officer's supervision.

(b) To the best of such officer's knowledge, based on such review, the servicer has fulfilled all of its obligations under the agreement in all material respects throughout the reporting period or, if there has been a failure to fulfill any such obligation in any material respect, specifying each such failure known to such officer and the nature and status thereof.

Instruction to Item 1123: If multiple servicers are involved in servicing the pool assets, a separate servicer compliance statement is required from each servicer that meets the criteria in Item 1108(a)(2)(i) through (iii) of this Regulation AB.

相同),而主张其不应适用特定的服务标准,则必须在该方及相关注册公共会计师事务所的报告中对此进行披露。

2.多个当事方参与提供服务的,必须就每一参与服务职能的当事方分别提供评估报告和鉴证报告。参与服务的当事方指按照本节第(d)款所述标准开展活动的任何实体(如总服务机构、主服务机构和信托受托人),但该等实体的活动所涉及的资产不高于池内资产5%的除外。

3.如果资产支持证券依托的资产池包括属于另一个资产池的付款或现金流的权益的池内资产,并且资产支持证券的发行实体和将纳入发行实体资产池内的资产的发行实体均系根据同一发起人和交存人的指示组建,应同时参见本《AB管理办法》的第1100(d)(2)条的规定。

第229.1123节(第1123条) 服务机构合规性声明

提供一份服务机构提供的合规性声明作为附录,该声明应由服务机构的授权管理人员签署,说明下列事项:

(a)报告期间内服务机构根据相应的服务协议从事的活动及绩效已在该等管理人员的监督下进行了审查。

(b)尽该等管理人员所知,根据上述审查,服务机构在整个报告期间内,在各个重大方面均已完全履行了其在服务协议中的任何义务;如果服务机构在任何重大方面没有履行该等义务,应在该等管理人员所知的范围内指出每一项该等失败的性质及其情形。

关于第1123条的说明:如果多个服务机构介入资产池服务的,每个服务机构均应按照本《AB管理办法》第1108(a)(2)(i)条至第1108(a)(2)(iii)条规定的标准提供合规性声明。

Subpart 229.1200—Disclosure by Registrants Engaged in Oil and Gas Producing Activities

Source: 74 FR 2193, Jan. 14, 2009, unless otherwise noted.

§229.1201(Item 1201) General instructions to oil and gas industry-specific disclosures.

(a) If oil and gas producing activities are material to the registrant's or its subsidiaries' business operations or financial position, the disclosure specified in this Subpart 229.1200 should be included under appropriate captions (with cross references, where applicable, to related information disclosed in financial statements). However, limited partnerships and joint ventures that conduct, operate, manage, or report upon oil and gas drilling or income programs, that acquire properties either for drilling and production, or for production of oil, gas, or geothermal steam or water, need not include such disclosure.

(b) To the extent that Items 1202 through 1208 (§§229.1202-229.1208) call for disclosures in tabular format, as specified in the particular Item, a registrant may modify such format for ease of presentation, to add information or to combine two or more required tables.

(c) The definitions in Rule 4-10(a) of Regulation S-X(17 CFR 210.4-10(a)) shall apply for purposes of this Subpart 229.1200.

(d) For purposes of this Subpart 229.1200, the term *by geographic area* means, as appropriate for meaningful disclosure in the circumstances:

(1) By individual country;

(2) By groups of countries within a continent; or

(3) By continent.

§ 229.1202(Item 1202) Disclosure of reserves.

(a) *Summary of oil and gas reserves at fiscal year end.* (1) Provide the information specified in paragraph (a)(2) of this Item in tabular format as provided below:

第229.1200子部分——从事石油和天然气生产活动的注册人的披露事项

行政规则来源:《联邦公报》第74卷第2193页,2009年1月14日,除非另有说明。

第229.1201节(第1201条) 关于特别适用于石油和天然气行业披露的总体说明

(a)如果石油和天然气生产活动对注册人或其子公司的业务运营或财务状况具有重要意义,第229.1200子部分要求提供的信息应在适当的标题下披露(如适用,可以交叉引用财务报表中披露的信息)。但是,根据石油和天然气钻探或收益计划开展业务、经营、管理或进行报告的有限合伙与合资企业收购矿地用于钻探、生产(或仅生产)石油、天然气或地热蒸汽或地热水的,则不需要进行上述披露。

(b)如第1202条至第1208条(第229.1202~229.1208节)要求以表格形式披露信息,注册人可以为实现简明列报之目的修改该等格式以添加信息或合并两个(含)以上的要求提供的表格。

(c)本第229.1200子部分适用《S-X管理办法》的《4-10(a)规则》[《联邦规章汇编》第17编第210.4-10(a)节]中的定义。

(d)就本第229.1200子部分而言,在披露时,"按地理区域"根据具体情形指:

(1)按具体国家;

(2)按同一大洲内的一组国家;或

(3)按洲。

第229.1202节(第1202条) 储量披露

(a)截至会计年度年末石油和天然气储量概况。(1)以表格形式提供本条第(a)(2)款规定的信息,如下所示:

Summary of Oil and Gas Reserves as of Fiscal–Year End Based on Average Fiscal–Year Prices

Reserves category	Reserves				
	Oil (mbbls)	Natural gas (mmcf)	Synthetic oil (mbbls)	Synthetic gas (mmcf)	Product A (measure)
PROVED					
Developed:					
Continent A					
Continent B					
Country A					
Country B					
Other Countries in Continent B					
Undeveloped:					
Continent A					
Continent B					
Country A					
Country B					
Other Countries in Continent B					
TOTAL PROVED					
PROBABLE					
Developed					
Undeveloped					
POSSIBLE					
Developed					
Undeveloped					

(2) Disclose, in the aggregate and by geographic area and for each country containing 15% or more of the registrant's proved reserves, expressed on an oil–equivalent–barrels basis, reserves estimated using prices and costs under existing economic conditions, for the product types listed in paragraph (a)(4) of this Item, in the following categories:

(i) Proved developed reserves;

(ii) Proved undeveloped reserves;

(iii) Total proved reserves;

(iv) Probable developed reserves (optional);

基于会计年度平均价格的会计年度年末石油和天然气的储量概况

储量类别	储量				
	石油(千桶)	天然气(百万立方英尺)	合成油(千桶)	合成气(百万立方英尺)	A产品(计量单位)
证实储量					
已开发储量:					
A洲					
B洲					
A国					
B国					
B洲的其他国家					
未开发储量:					
A洲					
B洲					
A国					
B国					
B洲的其他国家					
总证实储量					
概算储量					
已开发储量					
未开发储量					
可能储量					
已开发储量					
未开发储量					

(2)披露根据现有经济条件下的价格和成本估算出的本条第(a)(4)款所列的每种产品的储量(以桶油当量为单位),包括总储量、按地理区域划分的储量以及占注册人证实储量15%(含)以上的每个国家的储量;储量应包括以下列类别:

(i)已开发证实储量;

(ii)未开发证实储量;

(iii)总证实储量;

(iv)已开发概算储量(可选);

(v) Probable undeveloped reserves (optional);

(vi) Possible developed reserves (optional); and

(vii) Possible undeveloped reserves (optional).

Instruction 1 to paragraph (a)(2): Disclose updated reserves tables as of the close of each fiscal year.

Instruction 2 to paragraph (a)(2): The registrant is permitted, but not required, to disclose probable or possible reserves pursuant to paragraphs (a)(2)(iv) through (a)(2)(vii) of this Item.

Instruction 3 to paragraph (a)(2): If the registrant discloses amounts of a product in barrels of oil equivalent, disclose the basis for such equivalency.

Instruction 4 to paragraph (a)(2): A registrant need not provide disclosure of the reserves in a country containing 15% or more of the registrant's proved reserves if that country's government prohibits disclosure of reserves in that country. In addition, a registrant need not provide disclosure of the reserves in a country containing 15% or more of the registrant's proved reserves if that country's government prohibits disclosure in a particular field and disclosure of reserves in that country would have the effect of disclosing reserves in particular fields.

(3) Reported total reserves shall be simple arithmetic sums of all estimates for individual properties or fields within each reserves category. When probabilistic methods are used, reserves should not be aggregated probabilistically beyond the field or property level; instead, they should be aggregated by simple arithmetic summation.

(4) Disclose separately material reserves of the following product types:

(i) Oil;

(ii) Natural gas;

(iii) Synthetic oil;

(iv) Synthetic gas; and

(v) Sales products of other non-renewable natural resources that are intended to be upgraded into synthetic oil and gas.

(5) If the registrant discloses probable or possible reserves, discuss the uncertainty related to such reserves estimates.

(6) If the registrant has not previously disclosed reserves estimates in a filing with the Commission or is disclosing material additions to its reserves estimates, the registrant shall provide a general discussion of the technologies used to establish the appropriate level of certainty for reserves estimates from material properties included in the total reserves disclosed. The particular properties do not need to be identified.

(7) *Preparation of reserves estimates or reserves audit.* Disclose and describe the internal controls the registrant uses in its reserves estimation effort. In addition, disclose

(v)未开发概算储量(可选);

(vi)已开发可能储量(可选);及

(vii)未开发可能储量(可选)。

关于第(a)(2)款的说明1:披露截至每一会计年度年末的更新储量表。

关于第(a)(2)款的说明2:注册人可以但非必须按照本条第(a)(2)(iv)款至第(a)(2)(vii)款的要求披露概算储量或可能储量。

关于第(a)(2)款的说明3:如果注册人以桶油当量为单位披露产量,还应披露计算该等当量的依据。

关于第(a)(2)款的说明4:对于占注册人证实储量15%(含)以上的国家,如果该国政府禁止披露关于该国储量的信息,则注册人可以不披露关于该国的储量信息。另外,对于占注册人证实储量15%(含)以上的国家,如果该国政府禁止披露关于某个特定油田的储量,而披露该国全国储量可能会导致披露特定油田的储量,则注册人可以不披露关于该国的储量信息。

(3)报告总储量应当为每一类别储量中各项资产或油田估值的简单运算加总。使用概率统计法时,储量不应为超出各项油田或矿地储量水平的概率值加总,而应为简单运算加总。

(4)分别披露下述产品类型的重大储量:

(i)石油;

(ii)天然气;

(iii)合成油;

(iv)合成气,以及

(v)以其他不可再生自然资源为原料升级到合成油或合成气的销售产品。

(5)如果注册人披露了概算储量或可能储量,应论述与此类储量估值相关的不确定性。

(6)如果注册人之前未在向证券交易委员会提交的文件中披露储量估值,或正在大幅增加其披露的储量估值,则对于披露的总储量中所包含的重大矿地储量估值,注册人应就判断该等估值的确定性的技术提供一般性论述,不需要指明具体矿地。

(7)储量估值或储量审计的编制。披露并说明注册人在计算储量估值过程中采用的内部控制措施。此外,披露管理该等储量估值编制的主要负责技术人员的资质,并

the qualifications of the technical person primarily responsible for overseeing the preparation of the reserves estimates and, if the registrant represents that a third party conducted a reserves audit, disclose the qualifications of the technical person primarily responsible for overseeing such reserves audit.

(8) *Third party reports*. If the registrant represents that a third party prepared, or conducted a reserves audit of, the registrant's reserves estimates, or any estimated valuation thereof, or conducted a process review, the registrant shall file a report of the third party as an exhibit to the relevant registration statement or other Commission filing. If the report relates to the preparation of, or a reserves audit of, the registrant's reserves estimates, it must include the following disclosure, if applicable to the type of filing:

(i) The purpose for which the report was prepared and for whom it was prepared;

(ii) The effective date of the report and the date on which the report was completed;

(iii) The proportion of the registrant's total reserves covered by the report and the geographic area in which the covered reserves are located;

(iv) The assumptions, data, methods, and procedures used, including the percentage of the registrant's total reserves reviewed in connection with the preparation of the report, and a statement that such assumptions, data, methods, and procedures are appropriate for the purpose served by the report;

(v) A discussion of primary economic assumptions;

(vi) A discussion of the possible effects of regulation on the ability of the registrant to recover the estimated reserves;

(vii) A discussion regarding the inherent uncertainties of reserves estimates;

(viii) A statement that the third party has used all methods and procedures as it considered necessary under the circumstances to prepare the report;

(ix) A brief summary of the third party's conclusions with respect to the reserves estimates; and

(x) The signature of the third party.

(9) For purposes of this Item 1202, the term *reserves audit* means the process of reviewing certain of the pertinent facts interpreted and assumptions underlying a reserves estimate prepared by another party and the rendering of an opinion about the appropriateness of the methodologies employed, the adequacy and quality of the data relied upon, the depth and thoroughness of the reserves estimation process, the classification of reserves appropriate to the relevant definitions used, and the reasonableness of the estimated reserves quantities.

(b) *Reserves sensitivity analysis (optional)*. (1) The registrant may, but is not required to, provide the information specified in paragraph (b)(2) of this Item in tabular format as provided below:

且,如果注册人声称储量审计系由第三方开展,则应披露管理该等储量审计的主要负责技术人员的资质。

(8)第三方报告。如果注册人声称储量估值或其预测价值由第三方编制,或储量审计由第三方执行,或者第三方提供或开展了流程审查,则注册人应将该等第三方的报告作为相关注册说明书的附录或提交给证券交易委员会的其他文件的附录提交。如果报告涉及注册人储量估值的编制或储量审计,应根据提交文件的类型纳入如下披露信息:

(i)报告的编制目的以及为谁而编制;

(ii)报告的生效日期以及完成日期;

(iii)报告所述储量占注册人总储量的比例以及报告所述储量分布的地理区域;

(iv)所使用的假设、数据、方法和程序,包括编制报告时已审核的注册人总储量的百分比,以及一份声明,说明为实现报告目的,所采用的假设、数据、方法和程序是适当的;

(v)关于主要经济假设的论述;

(vi)关于对注册人开采预估储量能力的监管可能产生的影响之论述;

(vii)关于储量估值固有不确定性的论述;

(viii)一份声明,说明第三方已经根据编制报告的具体情形使用了该等第三方认为必要的所有方法和程序;

(ix)简要说明第三方关于储量估值的结论;及

(x)第三方的签名。

(9)就本第1202条而言,"储量审计"一词系指审查另一方计算储量估值时依据的特定事实诠释和假设,并就下述各项提供意见的过程:所采用方法的适当性、基础数据的充分性和质量、储量估值程序的深度和彻底性、储量分类对于所用相关定义是否适当以及预估储量的合理性。

(b)储量敏感性分析(可选)。(1)注册人可以但并非必须采用下述表格形式提供本条第(b)(2)款规定的信息:

Sensitivity of Reserves to Prices by Principal Product Type and Price Scenario

Price case	Proved reserves					Probable reserves					Possible reserves				
	Oil	Gas	Syn. oil	Syn. gas	Product A	Oil	Gas	Syn. oil	Syn. gas	Product A	Oil	Gas	Syn. oil	Syn. gas	Product A
Scenario 1	mbbls	mmcf	mbbls	mmcf	measure	mbbls	mmcf	mbbls	mmcf	measure	mbbls	mmcf	mbbls	mmcf	measure
Scenario 2															

(2) The registrant may, but is not required to, disclose, in the aggregate, an estimate of reserves estimated for each product type based on different price and cost criteria, such as a range of prices and costs that may reasonably be achieved, including standardized futures prices or management's own forecasts.

(3) If the registrant provides disclosure under this paragraph (b), disclose the price and cost schedules and assumptions on which the disclosed values are based.

Instruction to Item 1202: Estimates of oil or gas resources other than reserves, and any estimated values of such resources, shall not be disclosed in any document publicly filed with the Commission, unless such information is required to be disclosed in the document by foreign or state law; provided, however, that where such estimates previously have been provided to a person (or any of its affiliates) that is offering to acquire, merge, or consolidate with the registrant or otherwise to acquire the registrant's securities, such estimate may be included in documents related to such acquisition.

§229.1203(Item 1203) Proved undeveloped reserves.

(a) Disclose the total quantity of proved undeveloped reserves at year end.

(b) Disclose material changes in proved undeveloped reserves that occurred during the year, including proved undeveloped reserves converted into proved developed reserves.

(c) Discuss investments and progress made during the year to convert proved undeveloped reserves to proved developed reserves, including, but not limited to, capital expenditures.

(d) Explain the reasons why material amounts of proved undeveloped reserves in individual fields or countries remain undeveloped for five years or more after disclosure as proved undeveloped reserves.

§229.1204 (Item 1204) Oil and gas production, production prices and production costs.

(a) For each of the last three fiscal years disclose production, by final product sold,

按主要产品类型和价格场景作出的储量敏感性分析

价格情形	证实储量					概算储量					可能储量				
	石油	天然气	合成油	合成气	产品A	石油	天然气	合成油	合成气	产品A	石油	天然气	合成油	合成气	产品A
场景1	千桶	百万立方英尺	千桶	百万立方英尺	计量单位	千桶	百万立方英尺	千桶	百万立方英尺	计量单位	千桶	百万立方英尺	千桶	百万立方英尺	计量单位
场景2															

(2)注册人可以但非必须基于不同的价格和成本标准(如可合理实现的价格和成本范围,包括标准化期货价格或管理层自身的预测)披露每一种产品类型的预估储量总值。

(3)注册人按照本条第(b)款进行披露的,应说明披露价值所基的价格和成本一览表以及假设条件。

关于第1202条的说明:除储量之外的石油或天然气预估,以及关于该等资源的任何预估价值,均不得在公开提交给证券交易委员会的任何文件中披露,但外国法律或州法律要求在文件中披露该等信息的除外;但是,如果在此之前,该等预估已经提供给向注册人提出控股合并、吸收合并或新设合并要约或其他形式的证券收购要约的某一主体(或其任何控制性关联方),则该等预估可以纳入与该等收购相关的文件之中。

第229.1203节(第1203条) 未开发证实储量

(a)披露截至年底的未开发证实储量总量。

(b)披露当年未开发证实储量总量发生的重大变化,包括已转换为已开发证实储量的未开发证实储量。

(c)披露当年内为将未开发证实储量转化为已开发证实储量而进行的投资和取得的进展,包括但不限于资本性支出。

(d) 解释某个油田或国家大量未开发证实储量在披露之后保持未开发状态长达5年(含)以上的原因。

第229.1204节(第1204条) 石油和天然气产量、生产价格和生产成本

(a)按照售出的最终产品,披露过去3个会计年度每一年的石油、天然气和其他产

of oil, gas, and other products. Disclosure shall be made by geographical area and for each country and field that contains 15% or more of the registrant's total proved reserves expressed on an oil-equivalent-barrels basis unless prohibited by the country in which the reserves are located.

(b) For each of the last three fiscal years disclose, by geographical area:

(1) The average sales price (including transfers) per unit of oil, gas and other products produced; and

(2) The average production cost, not including ad valorem and severance taxes, per unit of production.

Instruction 1 to Item 1204: Generally, net production should include only production that is owned by the registrant and produced to its interest, less royalties and production due others. However, in special situations (e.g., foreign production) net production before any royalties may be provided, if more appropriate. If "net before royalty" production figures are furnished, the change from the usage of "net production" should be noted.

Instruction 2 to Item 1204: Production of natural gas should include only marketable production of natural gas on an "as sold" basis. Production will include dry, residue, and wet gas, depending on whether liquids have been extracted before the registrant transfers title. Flared gas, injected gas, and gas consumed in operations should be omitted. Recovered gas-lift gas and reproduced gas should not be included until sold. Synthetic gas, when marketed as such, should be included in natural gas sales.

Instruction 3 to Item 1204: If any product, such as bitumen, is sold or custody is transferred prior to conversion to synthetic oil or gas, the product's production, transfer prices, and production costs should be disclosed separately from all other products.

Instruction 4 to Item 1204: The transfer price of oil and gas (natural and synthetic) produced should be determined in accordance with SFAS 69.

Instruction 5 to Item 1204: The average production cost, not including ad valorem and severance taxes, per unit of production should be computed using production costs disclosed pursuant to SFAS 69. Units of production should be expressed in common units of production with oil, gas, and other products converted to a common unit of measure on the basis used in computing amortization.

§229.1205 (Item 1205) Drilling and other exploratory and development activities.

(a) For each of the last three fiscal years, by geographical area, disclose:

(1) The number of net productive and dry exploratory wells drilled; and

(2) The number of net productive and dry development wells drilled.

(b) *Definitions*. For purposes of this Item 1205, the following terms shall be defined as follows:

品的产量。应披露占注册人总证实储量15%或以上的每个国家和油田的信息,但储量所在国家禁止披露该等信息的除外,披露应以桶油当量为单位,按地理区域进行。

(b)对于过去3个会计年度的每一年,按地理区域披露:

(1)石油、天然气和其他产品的单位销售价格(包括转让价格);及

(2)平均生产成本,不包括单位生产的从价税和开采税。

关于第1204条的说明1:一般而言,净产量应为注册人所拥有以及为注册人利益而产出的产量扣除矿区使用费和其他生产费用后的净值。但是,如果在特殊情况下(如国外生产)不扣除矿区使用费更为恰当,则可以提供未扣除该等使用费的净产量。如果提供的产量数字为"未扣除矿区使用费的净产量",应注明"净产量"一词含义的变化。

关于第1204条的说明2:天然气产量仅得包括"实际售出"的可出售天然气。根据液化天然气是否在注册人转让矿权之前开采,产量包括干气、残渣气和湿气。火炬气、注入气和运营中消耗的气量均不应计算在内。开采的气举气和再生气,只有售出后才能计入产量。合成气只有作为合成气销售时,才应包含在天然气的销售额中。

关于第1204条的说明3:如果任何产品(如沥青),在转换为合成油或合成气之前被售出或保管人发生改变,则该等产品应区别于所有其他产品,单独披露其产量、转让价格和生产成本。

关于第1204条的说明4:所生产的石油和天然气(包括天然气和合成气)的转让价格应根据《财务会计准则公告第69号》确定。

关于第1204条的说明5:不含从价税和开采税的单位产品平均生产成本,应使用根据《财务会计准则公告第69号》披露的生产成本进行计算。石油、天然气和其他产品的产量单位应采用计算摊销时通常采用的计量单位。

第229.1205节(第1205条) 钻探和其他勘探与开发活动

(a)对于过去3个会计年度中的每一年,应按地理区域披露:

(1)钻探的净生产井数与勘探干井数;及

(2)钻探的净生产井数与开发干井数。

(b)定义。就本第1205条而言,下列术语应具有如下定义:

(1) A *dry well* is an exploratory, development, or extension well that proves to be incapable of producing either oil or gas in sufficient quantities to justify completion as an oil or gas well.

(2) A *productive well* is an exploratory, development, or extension well that is not a dry well.

(3) *Completion* refers to installation of permanent equipment for production of oil or gas, or, in the case of a dry well, to reporting to the appropriate authority that the well has been abandoned.

(4) The *number of wells drilled* refers to the number of wells completed at any time during the fiscal year, regardless of when drilling was initiated.

(c) Disclose, by geographic area, for each of the last three years, any other exploratory or development activities conducted, including implementation of mining methods for purposes of oil and gas producing activities.

§229.1206(Item 1206) Present activities.

(a) Disclose, by geographical area, the registrant's present activities, such as the number of wells in the process of being drilled (including wells temporarily suspended), waterfloods in process of being installed, pressure maintenance operations, and any other related activities of material importance.

(b) Provide the description of present activities as of a date at the end of the most recent fiscal year or as close to the date that the registrant files the document as reasonably possible.

(c) Include only those wells in the process of being drilled at the "as of" date and express them in terms of both gross and net wells.

(d) Do not include wells that the registrant plans to drill, but has not commenced drilling unless there are factors that make such information material.

§229.1207(Item 1207) Delivery commitments.

(a) If the registrant is committed to provide a fixed and determinable quantity of oil or gas in the near future under existing contracts or agreements, disclose material information concerning the estimated availability of oil and gas from any principal sources, including the following:

(1) The principal sources of oil and gas that the registrant will rely upon and the total amounts that the registrant expects to receive from each principal source and from all sources combined;

(2) The total quantities of oil and gas that are subject to delivery commitments; and

(3) The steps that the registrant has taken to ensure that available reserves and supplies are sufficient to meet such commitments for the next one to three years.

(b) Disclose the information required by this Item:

(1)“干井”系指已证明无法产出足量的石油或天然气,导致其无法作为石油或天然气井而完井,从而丧失意义的勘探井、开发井或扩边井。

(2)“生产井”系指不属于干井的勘探井、开发井或扩边井。

(3)“完井”系指安装永久性的石油或天然气生产设备,或者对于干井,则指向相关机构报告该等干井已被放弃。

(4)“钻探井数”系指在会计年度的任何时间完井的井数,而不论其开钻时间是否位于该会计年度。

(c)按照地理区域披露在过去3个会计年度中的每一年所开展的任何其他勘探或开发行动,包括石油、天然气生产活动中实施的采矿方法。

第229.1206节(第1206条) 当前活动

(a)按照地理区域披露注册人的当前活动,如钻探之中的井数(包括临时中止的井)、安装过程中的注水、压力维持操作以及任何其他相关的重要活动。

(b)提供截至最近一个会计年度年末或合理地尽可能接近注册人提交文件之日的日期关于当前活动的说明。

(c)披露时仅得包括截至截止日期时仍在钻探的井,并提供总井数和净井数。

(d)不得包括注册人计划钻探但尚未开始钻探的井,但存在相关因素使该等信息构成重大信息的除外。

第229.1207节(第1207条) 交付承诺

(a)如果注册人承诺将根据现有合约或协议在近期内交付石油或天然气,且该等石油或天然气的数量属于固定数量或可以确定的数量,应披露所有主要石油和天然气任何供应源的预计供应量,包括:

(1)注册人所倚赖的主要石油和天然气供应源,以及注册人预期从每个主要供应源获得的总产量以及预期从所有供应源获得的总产量;

(2)承诺交付的石油和天然气总量;及

(3)注册人已经采取的用以确保该等储量和供给充足,能满足下1~3年的交付承诺的措施。

(b)按照本条规定进行信息披露时,应:

(1) In a form understandable to investors; and

(2) Based upon the facts and circumstances of the particular situation, including, but not limited to:

(i) Disclosure by geographic area;

(ii) Significant supplies dedicated or contracted to the registrant;

(iii) Any significant reserves or supplies subject to priorities or curtailments which may affect quantities delivered to certain classes of customers, such as customers receiving services under low priority and interruptible contracts;

(iv) Any priority allocations or price limitations imposed by Federal or State regulatory agencies, as well as other factors beyond the registrant's control that may affect the registrant's ability to meet its contractual obligations (the registrant need not provide detailed discussions of price regulation);

(v) Any other factors beyond the registrant's control, such as other parties having control over drilling new wells, competition for the acquisition of reserves and supplies, and the availability of foreign reserves and supplies, which may affect the registrant's ability to acquire additional reserves and supplies or to maintain or increase the availability of reserves and supplies; and

(vi) Any impact on the registrant's earnings and financing needs resulting from its inability to meet short-term or long-term contractual obligations. (See Items 303 and 1209 of Regulation S-K (§§229.303 and 229.1209).)

(c) If the registrant has been unable to meet any significant delivery commitments in the last three years, describe the circumstances concerning such events and their impact on the registrant.

(d) For purposes of this Item, *available reserves* are estimates of the amounts of oil and gas which the registrant can produce from current proved developed reserves using presently installed equipment under existing economic and operating conditions and an estimate of amounts that others can deliver to the registrant under long-term contracts or agreements on a per-day, per-month, or per-year basis.

§229.1208(Item 1208) Oil and gas properties, wells, operations, and acreage.

(a) Disclose, as of a reasonably current date or as of the end of the fiscal year, the total gross and net productive wells, expressed separately for oil and gas (including synthetic oil and gas produced through wells) and the total gross and net developed acreage (*i.e.*, acreage assignable to productive wells) by geographic area.

(b) Disclose, as of a reasonably current date or as of the end of the fiscal year, the amount of undeveloped acreage, both leases and concessions, if any, expressed in both gross and net acres by geographic area, together with an indication of acreage concentrations, and, if material, the minimum remaining terms of leases and concessions.

(1)采用投资者能够理解的形式;并

(2)以具体情形下的事实和情况为基础,包括但不限于:

(i)按照地理区域披露;

(ii)注册人专属或已签约的重要供应源;

(iii)任何在供应上存在优先次序或可能存在限产情形的重要储量或供应源,条件是该等供应优先次序或限产可能影响对特定类别客户的交付,如所接受的服务优先级别较低且可中断合约的客户;

(iv)联邦或州监管机构规定的任何优先权分配或价格限制,以及超出注册人控制范围且可能影响注册人履行合同义务的能力的其他因素(注册人不必提供关于价格监管的详细论述);

(v)超出注册人控制范围,并可能影响注册人收购其他储量和供应源或者维持或增加储量和供应源的可获得性的任何其他因素,如对钻探新井拥有控制权的其他当事方、储量或供应源收购中面临的竞争以及国外储量和供应源的可获得性;及

(vi)无法履行合同短期义务或长期义务对注册人盈利和财务需求造成的任何影响[参见《S-K管理办法》的第303条和第1209条(第229.303节和第229.1209节)]。

(c)如果注册人在过去3年曾出现无法履行重大交付承诺的任何情形,说明关于该等事件的具体情况及其对注册人的影响。

(d)就本条而言,可用储量系指注册人通过当前已安装设备,在现有的经济和运营条件下可以从现有的已开发证实储量中生产的石油和天然气预估产量,以及其他方根据长期合约或协议每日、每月或每年可以向注册人交付的预估产量。

第229.1208节(第1208条) 石油和天然气矿地、井、运营和面积

(a)披露截至合理的当前日期或会计年度年末生产井的总井数和净井数,按石油和天然气(包括通过生产井产出的合成油与合成气)区分,并按照地理区域披露总开发面积和净开发面积(即归属于生产井的面积)。

(b)披露截至合理的当前日期或会计年度年末,租用及有特许权的未开发面积(如有),按照地理区域以总面积和净面积(英亩)表示,同时提供面积集中度,并且,如果具有重要意义,还应提供租约和特许权的最短剩余期限。

(c) *Definitions.* For purposes of this Item 1208, the following terms shall be defined as indicated:

(1) A *gross well or acre* is a well or acre in which the registrant owns a working interest. The number of gross wells is the total number of wells in which the registrant owns a working interest. Count one or more completions in the same bore hole as one well. In a footnote, disclose the number of wells with multiple completions. If one of the multiple completions in a well is an oil completion, classify the well as an oil well.

(2) A *net well or acre* is deemed to exist when the sum of fractional ownership working interests in gross wells or acres equals one. The number of net wells or acres is the sum of the fractional working interests owned in gross wells or acres expressed as whole numbers and fractions of whole numbers.

(3) *Productive wells* include producing wells and wells mechanically capable of production.

(4) *Undeveloped acreage* encompasses those leased acres on which wells have not been drilled or completed to a point that would permit the production of economic quantities of oil or gas regardless of whether such acreage contains proved reserves. Do not confuse undeveloped acreage with undrilled acreage held by production under the terms of the lease.

(c)定义。就本第1208条而言,下列术语应适用如下定义:

(1)“总井数或总面积”系指注册人拥有有效权益的井或面积。总井数是权益人拥有有效权益的井的总数。同一个钻孔内的一次或多次完井计为一口井。应在脚注中披露存在多次完井的井数。如果一口井的一次或多次完井为石油完井,应将该井划为油井。

(2)“净井数或净面积”,只有在总井或总面积中拥有的非完整有效权益之和构成一个整数时,才能认定存在净井数或净面积。净井数或净面积是在总井数或总面积中拥有的非完整有效权益之和,以整数和分数表示。

(3)“生产井”包括已投入生产的井和已经安装好机械设备可以随时投入生产的井。

(4)“未开发面积”系指钻井或完井工作尚未实现可以产出经济数量的石油或天然气的租赁面积,而无论该块面积中是否包含证实储量。切勿将未开发面积与租约条款中的为生产预留的未钻井面积相混淆。

Glossary 词汇表

"Annualizing" data	"年化"数据
Accelerated filer	加速报告人
Accounting for stock-based compensation	《股份薪酬的会计处理》
Accrual or settlement accounting	权责发生制或结算制
Accruals	应计项目
Accumulated depreciation and amortization	累计折旧和摊销
Actuarial pension plan	精算退休金计划
Additional paid-in capital	资本溢价
Age of financial statements	财务报表表龄
American depositary receipts	美国存托凭证
Arm's length transaction	公平交易
Asset-backed issuer	资产支持证券发行人
Attestation report	鉴证报告
Auditing Standards Board of the American Institute of Certified Public Accountants	美国注册会计师协会审计标准委员会
Bank holding company	银行控股公司
Bank Holding Company Act	《银行控股公司法》
Bearer securities	不记名证券
Bottom hole contributions	井底成本分摊
Broad equity market index	宽基股权市场指数
Brokerage commissions	经纪佣金
Capital gain	资本利得
Capitalized leases	资本化租赁
Carrying amount	账面金额
Cash deposits	现金存款
Cash dividends	现金股息
Centipoise	厘泊
Certified public accountant	注册公共会计师
Claim adjustment expenses	理赔费用准备金
Classified balance sheets	分类资产负债表
Code of the District of Columbia	《哥伦比亚特区法典》

续表

Codification of Financial Reporting Policies	《财务报告政策汇编》
Commission merchant	期货经纪商
Commodity pool operator	商品基金管理人
Commodity trading advisor	商品交易顾问
Concurring partner	复核合伙人
Condensate	凝析油
Condensed consolidating financial information	简要并表财务信息
Consolidated revenue	并表收入
Contingency reserves	应急准备金
Control person	控制人
Convertible debt securities	可转换债务证券
Coordinating audit partner	协理审计合伙人
Coupon	息票
Credit enhancement	信用增级
Daily trading volume	日均成交量
Dealer markups	经纪商加成
Debtor-creditor relationship	债权债务关系
Deferred compensation	递延报酬
Discretionary accounts	全权委托账户
Dividend equivalents	股息等价物
Dry hole contributions	干井成本分摊
EBIT	息税前收益
EBITDA	息税折旧及摊销前收益
Energy Policy and Conservation Act of 1975	《1975 年能源政策与保护法》
Energy Supply and Environmental Coordination Act of 1974	《1974 年能源供应与环境协调法》
Equity compensation plan	股权报酬计划
Equity method of accounting	权益核算法
ERISA	《员工退休收入保障法》
Exchange offer	交换要约
Excise taxes	消费税
Ex-dividend date	除息日
Exercise price	行权价

续表

Exploratory-type stratigraphic test wells	勘探型地层试井
Extension well	探边井
Extraction equipment	萃取设备
Extraordinary items	非经常项目
Face-amount certificate	面额证券
Federal Deposit Insurance Act	《联邦存款保险法》
Federal deposit insurance corporation	联邦存款保险公司
Field	油田
Fiscal period	会计期间
Fiscal year	会计年度
Floor broker	场内经纪人
Foreclosure	止赎
Full cost method	完全成本法
GAAP	公认会计原则
General partner	普通合伙人
Going-private transaction	下市交易
Governing document	章程性文件
Grandfathering	不溯及既往
IFRS	《国际财务报告准则》
Income from continuing operations	持续经营收益
Income recognition	所得确认
Income tax effects	所得税影响数
Information statements	信息说明书
Injunction	禁令
Insurance ceded	分出保险
Insurance commissions, fees and premiums	保险佣金、费用和保费
Insurance holding company	保险控股公司
Interim period	中期期间
Internal control	内部控制
Internal Revenue Code	《国内税收法典》
Introducing broker	介绍经纪人
Investees	投资对象
Investment company	投资公司

续表

Issuer	发行人
Large accelerated filer	大型加速报告人
Lead partner	主查合伙人
Lease financing	租赁融资
Leverage transaction merchant	杠杆交易商
LIFO inventory	后进先出库存法
List of CFR Sections Affected	《受影响的联邦规章汇编条文列表》
Majority-owned subsidiary	控股子公司
Management's Discussion and Analysis	《管理层论述与分析》
Managing underwiter	主承销商
Master trust	主信托
Net income (loss)	净损益
Net tangible book	有形账面净值
Non-GAAP financial measures	非 GAAP 财务指标
NRSRO	国家认可的统计评级机构
Oil-equivalent-barrels	桶油当量
Open-market transactions	公开市场交易
Operating lease	经营租赁
Opinion re tax matters	税务意见书
Option	期权
Option adjusted spread	期权调整利差
Originator	创建人
Ownership Interest	所有者权益
Par value	票面价值
Passive market making	消极做市
Peer issuer	参照发行人
Penalty bid	惩罚性出价
Pension plan	养老金计划
Pleadings	诉辩状
Pool asset	池内资产
Possible reserves	可能储量
Power of attorney	授权委托书

续表

Preferred stocks subject to mandatory redemption requirements	可强制回赎的优先股
Prefunding period	预先融资期
Prepayment	提前还款
Principal amount	本金金额
Principal underwirter	主要的承销商
Pro forma financial statements	备考财务报表
Probable reserves	概算储量
Profit-sharing plan	利润分享计划
Promoter	创始人
Property-casualty insurance	财险
Prospectus	招募说明书
Proved reserves	证实储量
Provision for doubtful accounts and notes	呆账备抵
Proxy statement	征集投票权报告
Public accountant	公共会计师
Public company accounting oversight board	美国公众公司会计监督委员会
Public float	公众持股量
Public utility company	公用事业公司
Public Utility Holding Company Act	《公用事业控股公司法》
Qualifications of accountants	会计师资格
Qualitative disclosures	定性披露
Quantitative disclosures	定量披露
Ratio of earnings to fixed charges	盈利对固定费用比率
Real Estate Investment Trusts	房地产投资信托
Redemption	回赎
Registrant	注册人
Registration statement	注册说明书
Related parties	关联方
Replacement cost	重置成本
Reporting currency	报表货币
Results of operations	经营成果
Retail mark-up, mark-down or commission	零售加成、减成或佣金

续表

Revolving period	循环期
Risk exposure	风险敞口
Rules of Fair Practice	《公平作业规则》
Safe harbor rule	安全港规则
Schedule of Investments in Securities of Unaffiliated Issuers	《对非控制性关联发行人的证券投资列表》
Security rating	证券评级
Service well	辅助井
Significant obligor	重大债务人
Significant subsidiary	重要子公司
Sinking fund	偿债基金
Smaller reporting companies	小型报告公司
Sponsor	发起人
Spousal equivalent	事实配偶
Standard & Poor's 500 Stock Index	标准普尔 500 指数
Statement of cash flows	现金流量表
Statement of financial accounting standards	财务会计准则公告
Statement of income	损益表
Statements of Auditing Standards	《审计标准公告》
Statements of operations	经营报表
Successful efforts method	成功成本法
Suitability	适当性
Summary Compensation Table	《报酬简表》
Temporary restraining order	临时限制令
Trust Indenture Act of 1939	《1939 年信托契约法》
U. S. Generally Accepted Accounting Principles	《美国公认会计原则》
Uncollectable account	呆帐
Underwriter	承销商
Undistributed earnings	未分配盈利
Unearned income	消极所得
Unearned premiums	预收保费
Unmatured drafts and bills of exchange	未到期票据和汇票
Unrealized intercompany profits and losses	未实现公司间损益

续表

Valuation allowances	估价备抵
Weighted average interest rate	加权平均利率
Weighted average maturity	加权平均期限
Wholly owned subsidiary	全资子公司

Postscript

China's capital market was established and has developed on the basis of the experience of major foreign capital markets. As a result China constantly is faced with issues for which it needs to acquire knowledge of, learn from and refer to examples set by foreign capital market systems. However, the current Chinese translations of foreign securities and futures legislations are not sufficiently systematic, professional, authoritative and are often inaccurate. The acquisition of a comprehensive and precise knowledge of the operating systems and regulatory rules of major foreign capital markets is essential for China to benefit from the experience developed and lessons drawn by these markets and thus is objectively necessary for China to further improve the Chinese capital market system construction, promote a stable and healthy development of said system and enhance the participation of Chinese market entities in international competition. For the aforementioned purposes, the China Securities Regulatory Commission (CSRC) has herby initiate the project to translate the most important foreign capital market legislations published as the Digest of Legislation Related to Foreign Capital Markets (hereinafter referred to as the "Digest"). The Digest is composed of such translations after editing, creating an authoritative platform through which the most significant foreign capital markets laws and regulations are to be introduced to China. The Shanghai Stock Exchange (SSE) has undertaken to organize the translation of selected laws and regulations governing the operation of the securities markets in the United States.

To facilitate the implementation of the project, accordance to the overall arrangement of the CSRC, we established a mechanism which consisted of entrusting the translation to a translation team through a bidding process and the translation review to relevant experts to ensure the quality of the translation. In the bidding process, the translation team was selected based on its competences in legal translation and the quality of its trial translation. On the other hand, the translation draft was reviewed and validated by individuals from relevant units and departments of the CSRC and prestigious universities deemed to be experts in the concerned foreign languages and the Chinese language, well versed in Chinese and relevant foreign laws and having an in-depth knowledge of both Chinese and foreign capital markets. In addition, we have designated those experts, whose work experience and educational background are the most relevant to the subject matters dealt with in the translation works, to revise the same. All translation works have gone through

后　　记

中国资本市场是在学习、借鉴境外主要资本市场经验的基础上建立并发展起来的。在此过程中,仍不断遇到需要了解、借鉴、参考境外市场制度的问题。但是,现有的境外证券期货法律的中文译本,存在系统性、专业性、权威性、准确性不足等问题。全面、准确掌握境外主要资本市场运行制度、监管规则的信息,是科学借鉴发达市场经验教训的必要基础,是进一步完善市场制度建设、推进市场稳定健康发展、推动市场主体参与国际竞争的客观要求。为此,中国证监会启动了打造介绍境外市场法律制度权威平台的项目,即组织翻译主要资本市场重要法律规则,并将翻译成果编辑成《境外资本市场重要法律文献译丛》(以下简称《译丛》)公开出版发行。在本次项目中,上海证券交易所承担了美国证券市场重要法律文献翻译出版的有关工作。

为了做好此项工作,我们根据中国证监会的统一要求,建立了"竞标择优确定翻译人员、专家评审保证翻译质量"的工作机制:一方面,以法律文献翻译实力和试译稿质量为标准,采用竞标择优方式选定翻译单位;另一方面,从证监会系统相关单位、部门和知名高校院所等推荐的"三通"专家(即精通中外语言、精通中外法律、精通中外资本市场)中,抽选工作学习经历与具体项目最相关的专家对翻译稿进行多轮审校,并在同翻译人员进行充分沟通的基础上定稿。

several rounds of examination and review by the assigned experts and are finalized as a joint effort of the reviewing experts and the translation team.

As the SEC Rules and Regulations, which is a part of the Digest, is about to come to the press, we would like to express our earnest and profound gratitude to many organizations and individuals as follows. First of all, we would like to thank the Department of Legal Affairs of the CSRC and its members involved in the book. As the organizer of the project, they made the careful arrangement for the project and gave us valuable guidance, and set a good example with the EU Directive for Markets in Financial Instruments published earlier as a part of the Digest. Secondly, our thanks are due to the translation team from Ubica Translation Center Beijing led by Ms. Chu Naiming and Prof. Guo Li and Mr. Liu Zhuang, our reviewing experts; together they completed the translation and the review work conscientiously and rigorously. In particular, our thanks go to Prof. Wu Zhipan from Peking University, who amid his heavy schedule took up the overall and final review of the work and contributed a preface for this book. Thirdly, we owe our gratitude to relevant other departments and units of the CSRC and the SSE, as well as Peking University Law School and its scholars, for the valuable support they gave to our endeavor. Finally, we thank the staff at Law Press · China, especially Ms. Shen Xiaoying and Ms. Wang Jinjing, who contributed enormously to the editing and publication of the book. Again, we addressed our most sincere thanks to all those who mentioned above!

Due to time constraints pertaining to the translation and editing work, errors and inaccuracies in the book will be inevitable. Your comments, critic and corrections will be welcome.

Shanghai Stock Exchange

December 2012

在《译丛》之《美国证券交易委员会自身组织与通用规章》即将付梓之际,作为本书翻译出版的承办单位,我们有许多发自肺腑的感谢之辞:首先,感谢中国证监会法律部及其相关工作人员,作为《译丛》的组织者,他们为本书的翻译和出版做了全面且细致的统筹和指导,其组织完成的《译丛》之《欧盟金融工具市场指令》为本书树立了榜样;其次,感谢瞿乃明女士带领的北京优笔客翻译中心的翻译团队,郭雳教授、刘庄先生等评审专家,他们以认真负责的态度和严谨务实的作风,完成了翻译和审校工作,其中特别要感谢北京大学吴志攀教授在百忙之中拨冗亲自承担总译校工作,并为本书作序;再次,感谢中国证监会其他相关会内部门及其工作人员,上海证券交易所相关部门及其工作人员,北京大学法学院及有关专家学者,对我们工作的支持;最后,感谢法律出版社及其相关工作人员,尤其是沈小英女士、王津京女士,为本书的编辑、出版做了大量工作。我们在此一并致以诚挚的谢意!

由于编译时间有限,书中难免有疏漏、不足之处,欢迎读者批评指正。

上海证券交易所

2012 年 12 月

图书在版编目(CIP)数据

美国证券交易委员会自身组织与通用规章:全2册/中国证券监督管理委员会组织编译.—北京:法律出版社,2013.2
(境外资本市场重要法律文献译丛)
ISBN 978-7-5118-4542-9

Ⅰ.①美… Ⅱ.①中… Ⅲ.①证券法—研究—美国
Ⅳ.①D971.222.8

中国版本图书馆CIP数据核字(2013)第018423号

责任编辑/王津京　　**装帧设计**/贾丹丹

出版/法律出版社　　**编辑统筹**/财税出版分社
总发行/中国法律图书有限公司　　**经销**/新华书店
印刷/北京中科印刷有限公司　　**责任印制**/吕亚莉

开本/787毫米×1092毫米　1/16　　**印张**/59　　**字数**/1170千
版本/2013年4月第1版　　**印次**/2013年4月第1次印刷

法律出版社/北京市丰台区莲花池西里7号(100073)
电子邮件/info@lawpress.com.cn　　**销售热线**/010-63939792/9779
网址/www.lawpress.com.cn　　**咨询电话**/010-63939796

中国法律图书有限公司/北京市丰台区莲花池西里7号(100073)
全国各地中法图分、子公司电话:
第一法律书店/010-63939781/9782　**西安分公司**/029-85388843　**重庆公司**/023-65382816/2908
上海公司/021-62071010/1636　**北京分公司**/010-62534456　**深圳公司**/0755-83072995

书号:ISBN 978-7-5118-4542-9　　**定价(上、下册):**560.00元

(如有缺页或倒装,中国法律图书有限公司负责退换)